The New York State Directory

2016–2017

The New York State Directory

Grey House Publishing
AMENIA, NY 12501

PUBLISHER: Leslie Mackenzie
EDITOR: Richard Gottlieb
EDITORIAL DIRECTOR: Laura Mars
EDITORIAL RESEARCH: Jennifer Bossert; Jael Bridgemahon; Kathlyn Del Castillo

PRODUCTION MANAGER: Kristen Thatcher
MARKETING DIRECTOR: Jessica Moody

Grey House Publishing, Inc.
4919 Route 22
Amenia, NY 12501
518.789.8700
FAX 518.789.0545
www.greyhouse.com
e-mail: books @greyhouse.com

The New York State directory. — [1st ed.] (1983)-

Annual
ISSN: 0737-1314

1. New York (State)—Officials and employees—Directories. 2. Government executives—New York (State)—Directories. 3. Legislators—New York (State)—Directories.

JK3430 .N52
353.9747002

New York State Directory **ISBN: 978-1-61925-917-1**
2 Volume Set (*New York State Directory* and *Profiles of New York State*) ISBN: 978-1-61925-918-8

Printed in Canada

TABLE OF CONTENTS

Introduction . . . vii
Organization of Data . . . ix
Acronyms . . . xi

SECTION 1: New York State Branches of Government
Executive Branch . . . 3
Legislative Branch . . . 15
Senate, Membership & Committees . . . 15
Assembly, Membership & Committees . . . 27
Judicial Branch . . . 45

SECTION 2: Policy Areas
Agriculture . . . 69
Banking & Finance . . . 78
Commerce, Industry & Economic Development . . . 83
Corporations, Authorities & Commissions . . . 95
Crime & Corrections . . . 108
Education . . . 119
Elections . . . 130
Energy, Utility & Communication Services . . . 140
Environment & Natural Resources . . . 147
Government Operations . . . 160
Health . . . 173
Housing & Community Development . . . 187
Human Rights . . . 194
Insurance . . . 200
Judicial & Legal Systems . . . 206
Labor & Employment Practices . . . 219
Mental Hygiene . . . 227
Municipal & Local Governments . . . 234
Public Employees . . . 240
Real Property . . . 245
Social Services . . . 250
Taxation & Revenue . . . 263
Tourism, Arts & Sports . . . 270
Transportation . . . 283
Veterans & Military . . . 293

SECTION 3: State & Local Government Public Information
Public Information Offices . . . 303
US Congress, Membership & Committees . . . 311
County Government . . . 325
Municipal Government . . . 341

SECTION 4: Political Parties & Related Organizations
Political Parties . . . 371
Lobbyists . . . 377
Political Action Committees . . . 479

SECTION 5: Business
Chambers of Commerce and Economic & Industrial Development Organizations . . . 501

SECTION 6: News Media
Newspapers, News Services, Magazines, Radio & Television . . . 523

SECTION 7: Education
Colleges & Universities . . . 543
Public School Districts . . . 567

SECTION 8: Biographies
Executive Branch . . . 605
New York State Senate . . . 608
New York State Assembly . . . 620
US Senate: New York Delegation . . . 646
US House of Representatives: New York Delegation . . . 647

APPENDICES
Financial Plan Overview
Cash Disbursements by Function—All Government Funds . . . 653
Indexes
Name Index . . . 657
Organization Index . . . 739
Geographic Index . . . 805
Demographic & Reference Maps
Populated Places, Transportation & Physical Features . . . 861
Congressional Districts . . . 862
Federal Lands & Indian Reservations . . . 877
Hazard Events and Losses, 1960-2012 . . . 878
Population . . . 879
Percent White . . . 880
Percent Black . . . 881
Percent Asian . . . 882
Percent Hispanic . . . 883
Median Age . . . 884
Median Household Income . . . 885
Median Home Value . . . 886
Percent High School Graduates . . . 887
Percent College Graduates . . . 888
Percent of Population who Voted for Barack Obama in 2012 . . . 889

INTRODUCTION

This 2016/2017 edition of *The New York State Directory* is a comprehensive guide to public officials and private sector organizations and individuals who influence public policy in the state of New York. Fully updated with current addresses and office holders, this edition includes dozens of four-color maps—Demographic and Congressional Maps that show population, race, employment, home value, education, income, voter distribution, and break outs of New York's congressional districts.

Arrangement

The New York State Directory includes 45 chapters, arranged in eight sections, plus Appendices. A list of detailed sources appears in the Organization of Data that follows this introduction.

Section One includes three chapters: Executive Branch, Legislative Branch, and the Judicial Branch of New York State government. This section profiles the public officials in the state's executive departments, administrative agencies, and court system. Detailed listings of departments and agencies appear in Section Two.

Section Two includes 25 chapters covering the most significant public policy issue areas from Agriculture to Veterans & Military. Arranged in alphabetical order, each Policy Area chapter identifies the state, local, and federal agencies and officials that formulate or implement policy. Each chapter ends with a list of Private Sector experts and advocates who influence the policy process.

Section Three is comprised of four chapters with state and local government information: Public Information Offices; U.S. Congress Membership & Committees; County Government; and Municipal Government.

Section Four includes three chapters—Political Parties, Lobbyists, and Political Action Committees—all with comprehensive contact information.

Section Five has two Business chapters—Chambers of Commerce and Economic & Industrial Development Organizations. All listings have valuable contact information and key executives.

Section Six is News Media—detailed listings for Newspapers, News Services, News Magazines, News Radio and News Television stations that serve New York State. Listings include current contact information, plus valuable key executives.

Section Seven covers Education in two chapters—New York State Colleges & Universities, and Public School Districts in the state.

Section Eight includes 245 current, comprehensive Biographies of all New York state lawmakers: Executive; New York Senate; New York Assembly; U.S. Senate; and U.S. House of Representatives. All profiles include office addresses with phone numbers, fax numbers and email addresses, making it easy to contact these influential individuals.

Appendices

- **Financial Plan Overview:** Cash Disbursements by Department, projected to FY 2020.
- **Three Indexes:** Name Index; Organization Index; and Geographic Index.
- **Demographic & Reference Maps:** four-color maps that show political districts, physical features, racial breakdown, age, income, education, congressional districts, and more.

Every reasonable effort has been made to ensure that information in *The New York State Directory* is as accessible and accurate as possible. Organizational, agency, and key official updates and verification were made as late as May 2016. Continuing assistance and cooperation from state, regional, county, municipal, and federal officials and staff have helped make *The New York State Directory* a unique and valuable resource. We are grateful to these individuals and the private sector sources listed for their generous contributions of time and insight.

In addition to this latest edition of the *Directory,* Grey House offers a companion volume, *Profiles of New York State.* This comprehensive volume provides demographic, economic, religious, geographic, and historical details on the more than 2,500 places that make up New York state—counties, cities, towns, and villages. In addition, *Profiles of New York State* includes chapters on Education, Ancestry, Hispanic & Asian Populations, Climate, plus four-color maps, comparative statistics and rankings.

ORGANIZATION OF DATA

Section 1: New York State Branches of Government

Executive Branch. Outlines key staff in the Governor's and Lieutenant Governor's offices and senior officials in New York state executive departments and agencies. Biographies for the senior executive branch officials appear in the Biographies section at the back of the book.

Legislative Branch. Covers the state Senate and Assembly leadership, membership, administrative staff, and standing committees and subcommittees. Committee listings include the Chairperson, Ranking Minority Member, Majority and Minority committee members, committee staff, and key Senate or Assembly Majority and Minority staff assignments. Biographies with district office information for Senators and Assembly members appear in the Biographies section at the back of the book.

Judicial Branch. Identifies the state courts, judges who currently sit on these courts, and the clerk of each court. Includes the Court of Appeals, Appellate Division courts, Supreme Court, Court of Claims, New York City courts, county courts, district courts and city courts outside New York City. The county judge section identifies the specific court with which the judge is associated.

Section 2: Policy Areas

This section classifies New York state government activity into 25 major policy areas. Each policy area lists key individuals in the New York state government, federal government, and the private sector who have expertise in the area of government activity. All entries show organization name, individual name, title, address, telephone number, and fax number. Internet and e-mail addresses are included where available.

Each policy area includes the following information:

New York State

Governor's Office. Identifies the Governor's legal and program staff assigned to the policy area.

Executive Department & Related Agencies. Provides a complete organizational description of the primary state departments and agencies responsible for the policy area. Also includes those state departments and agencies whose activities relate to the policy area.

Corporations, Authorities & Commissions. Covers independent public and quasi-private sector agencies in the state, as well as intrastate bodies to which New York sends a representative.

Legislative Standing Committees. Lists committees and subcommittees which oversee governmental activities in that policy area, their respective chairpersons, and ranking minority members.

U.S. Government

Executive Departments & Related Agencies. Identifies federal departments and agencies located in or assigned to the New York region.

U.S. Congress. Lists congressional committees which oversee federal activities in that policy area, their respective chairpersons, ranking minority members, and NY delegation members.

Private Sector Sources

Includes an alphabetized list of public interest groups, trade and professional associations, corporations, and academia, with the associated individuals who have expertise in the policy area.

Section 3: State & Local Government Public Information

Public Information Offices. Lists key contacts in state government public information offices and libraries.

U.S. Congress. Lists all New York State delegates to the Senate and the House of Representatives with their Washington, DC office, phone and fax numbers, and e-mail addresses. Biographies with district office information for each New York Senator and Representative appear in the *Biographies* section at the back of the book. Provides a comprehensive list of all Senate and House standing, select, and special committees and subcommittees. Each committee and subcommittee entry includes the chairperson, ranking minority member, and assigned members from the New York delegation.

County Government. Identifies senior government officials in all New York counties.

Municipal Government. Identifies senior public officials for cities, towns, and villages in New York with populations greater than 20,000. All New York City departments are included in the city listing.

Section 4: Political Parties & Related Organizations

Political Parties. Lists statewide party officials and county chairpersons for the Conservative, Democratic, Independence and Republican parties.

Lobbyists. Identifies registered lobbyists and clients.

Political Action Committees. Lists registered political action committees and their treasurers.

Section 5: Business

Chambers of Commerce. Lists contact information for chambers of commerce, and economic and industrial development organizations and their primary officials.

Section 6: News Media

Identifies daily and weekly newspapers in New York, major news services with reporters assigned to cover state government, radio stations with a news format, and television stations with independent news staff. Newspapers are categorized by the primary city they serve. Staff listings include managing, news, and editorial page editors, and political reporters. News service entries include bureau chiefs and reporters. Radio and television entries include the news director.

Section 7: Education

SUNY and Other Universities and Colleges. Includes the board of trustees, system administration, the four University Centers, and all colleges and community colleges in the SUNY system; the central administration and all colleges in the CUNY system; and independent colleges and universities. Each college includes the name of its top official, usually the president or dean, as well as address, telephone number and Internet address.

Public School Administrators. Lists school district administrators by county and school district. The New York City School's subsection includes officials in the Chancellor's office. Following are BOCES District Superintendents by supervisory district and the education administrators of schools operated by the state or other public agencies.

Section 8: Biographies

Includes political biographies of all individuals representing New York state's Executive Branch, New York state Assembly members, New York state Senate members, US Senators from New York, and US Representatives from New York

Appendices

Financial Plan Overview
Cash Disbursements By Function—All Government Funds. Provides information excerpted from the New York State FY 2017 Enacted Budget Financial Plan.

Indexes

Name Index. Includes every official and executive name listed in *The New York State Directory*.

Organizations Index. Includes the names of the top three organization levels in all New York state executive departments and agencies, as well as public corporations, authorities, and commissions. In addition, this index includes all organizations listed in the Private Sector section of each policy chapter, as well as lobbyist organizations and political action committees, chambers of commerce, newspapers, news services, radio and television stations, SUNY and CUNY locations, and private colleges.

Geographic Index. Includes the organizations listed in the *Government and Private Sector Organizations Index* (see above) arranged by the city location.

Demographic & Reference Maps
Populated Places, Transportation & Physical Features
Congressional Districts
Federal Lands & Indian Reservations
Core Based Statistical Areas, Counties, and Independent Cities
Hazard Events and Losses
Population
Percent White
Percent Black
Percent Asian
Percent Hispanic
Median Age
Median Household Income
Median Home Value
Percent High School Graduates
Percent College Graduates
Percent of Population who Voted for Barack Obama in 2012

ACRONYMS

AAA	Automobile Association of America
AAAA	Army Aviation Association of America
AARP	American Association of Retired Persons
AFA	Air Force Association
AFL-CIO	American Federation of Labor/Congress of Industrial Organizations
AFSA	Air Force Sergeants Association
AFSCME	American Federation of State, County & Municipal Employees
AFWOA	Air Force Women Officers Association
AHRC	Association for the Help of Retarded Children
AIA	American Institute of Architects
AIVF	Association of Independent Video & Filmmakers
AMAC	Association for Metroarea Autistic Children
AMSUS	Association of Military Surgeons of the US
ASPCA	American Society for the Prevention of Cruelty to Animals
AUSA	Association of the US Army
BAC	Bricklayers & Allied Craftsmen
BIANYS	Brain Injury Association of NYS
BLS	Bureau of Labor Statistics
BOCES	Board of Cooperative Educational Services
CASES	Center for Alternative Sentencing & Employment Services
CBVH	Commission for the Blind & Visually Handicapped
CGR	Center for Governmental Research
CHIP	Community Housing Improvement Program
CIO	Chief Information Office
COA	Commissioned Officers Association
COMPA	Committee of Methadone Program Administrators
COPE	Committee on Political Education
CPB	Customs & Border Protection
CPR	Institute for Conflict Prevention and Resolution
CSD	Central School District
CUNY	City University of New York
DHS	Department of Homeland Security
FEGS	Federation Employment & Guidance Service
FEMA	Federal Emergency Management Agency
FRA	Fleet Reserve Association
FRIA	Friends & Relatives of Institutionalized Aged
HANNYS	Hunger Action Network of New York State
HFA	Housing Finance Agency
IBPAT	International Brotherhood of Painters & Allied Trades
IBT	International Brotherhood of Teamsters
ILGWU	International Ladies' Garment Workers' Union
IOLA	Interest on Lawyers Account
IUE	International Union of Electrical, Radio & Machine Workers
IUOE	International Union of Operating Engineers
MADD	Mothers Against Drunk Driving
MBBA	Municipal Bond Bank Agency
MCA	Military Chaplains Association
MCL	Marine Corps League
MOAA	Military Officers Association of America
MOPH	Military Order of the Purple Heart
MTA	Metropolitan Transportation Authority

NAIFA	North American Insurance & Finance Association
NERA	National Enlisted Reserve Association
NGAUS	National Guard Association of the US
NLN	National League for Nursing
NLUS	Navy League of the US
NMFA	National Military Family Association
NOFA	Northeast Organization Farming Association
NOW	National Organization for Women
NRA	National Reserve Association
NYC	New York City
NYANA	New York Association for New Americans
NYAPRS	New York Association of Psychiatric Rehabilitation Services
NYATEP	New York Association of Training & Employment Professionals
NYCCT	New York Community College Trustees
NYS	New York State
NYSARC	New York State Association for Retarded Citizens
NYSANA	New York State Association of Nurse Anesthetists
NYSHESC	New York State Higher Education Services Corp
NYSIR	New York State Insurance Reciprocal
NYSID	New York State Industries for the Disabled
NYSSMA	New York State School Music Association
NYSEG	New York State Electric & Gas Corporation
NYSTEC	New York State Technology Enterprise Corporation
NYSTEA	New York State Transportation Engineering Alliance
NYU	New York University
OOA	Office of Administration
PAC	Political Action Committee
PACE	Political Action for Candidates' Election
PAF	Political Action Fund
PAT	Political Action Team
PBA	Patrolmen's Benevolent Association
PCNY	Police Conference of New York
PEF	Political Education Fund - and - Public Employees Federation
PRLDEF	Puerto Rican Legal Defense and Education Fund
PSRC	Professional Standards Review Council
RCIL	Resource Center for Independent Living
RID	Rid Intoxicated Drivers
RIOC	Roosevelt Island Operating Corporation
ROA	Reserve Officers Association
SCAA	Schuyler Center for Analysis & Advocacy
SEMO	State Emergency Management Office
SENSES	Statewide Emergency Network for Social & Economic Security
SIFMA	Securities Industry and Financial Markets Association
SONYMA	State of New York Mortgage Agency
SUNY	State University of New York
UNYAN	United New York Ambulance Network
USWA	United Steel Workers of America
VESID	Vocational & Educational Services for Individuals with Disabilities Office
VFW	Veterans of Foreign Wars
VISN	Veterans Integrated Service Network
VWIN	Veterans Widows International Network
WHEDCO	Women's Housing & Economic Development Corporation

Section 1:
BRANCHES OF GOVERNMENT

EXECUTIVE BRANCH

This chapter provides a summary of officials in the Executive Branch. For a more detailed listing of specific executive and administrative departments and agencies, refer to the appropriate policy area in Section 2 or to the Organizations Index. Biographies for the senior Executive Branch officials appear in a separate section in the back of the book.

NEW YORK STATE

Governor (also see Governor's Office):
Andrew M Cuomo 518-474-8390
Lieutenant Governor:
Kathleen C Hochul 518-402-2292
Chief Information Officer & Director, Office of Information Technology Services (also see CIO Office & Office of Information Technology Services):
Maggie Miller 518-408-2140
Comptroller (also see State Comptroller, Office of the):
Thomas P DiNapoli . . . . 518-474-4044 or 212-681-4491
Attorney General (also see Law Department):
Eric T Schneiderman . . . . 518-776-2000 or 212-416-8050
Acting Secretary of State (also see State Department):
Rossana Rosado 518-474-0050

Governor's Office

Executive Chamber
State Capitol
Albany, NY 12224
518-474-8390 Fax: 518-474-1513
Web site: www.governor.ny.gov; www.ny.gov

Governor:
Andrew M Cuomo 518-474-8390
Secretary to the Governor:
William Mulrow 518-474-4246
Counsel to the Governor:
Alphonso David 518-474-8343
Chief of Staff:
Melissa DeRosa . . . . 518-474-8418 or 212-681-4640
Director, Communications:
James Allen. . . . . 518-474-8418 or 212-681-4640

Office of the Secretary

Secretary to the Governor:
William Mulrow 518-474-4246
Director, State Operations:
James Malatras 518-486-9871
Counselor to the Governor:
Linda Lacewell 518-474-4623
Special Counsel to the Governor:
Rick Cotton. 518-474-8434
Special Advisor to the Governor:
Rodney Capel 212-681-4580
Deputy Director of State Operations:
Rosemary Powers 518-473-9958
Deputy Director of State Operations:
Andrew Kennedy 518-474-3478
Deputy Director of State Operations:
Matthew Millea. 518-474-9883
Deputy Secretary for Executive Operations:
Jill DesRosiers 518-402-2403
Deputy Secretary for Civil Rights:
Norma Ramos 212-681-4584
Chairman of Energy & Finance for New York:
Richard Kauffman. 518-681-4580
Deputy Secretary, Education:
Jere Hochman 518-474-9883
Deputy Secretary, Environment:
Venetia Lannon. 518-408-2552
Deputy Secretary, Food & Agriculture:
Patrick Hooker 518-486-3960
Deputy Secretary for General Government Financial Services:
Brandan Fitzgerald 518-474-5442
Deputy Secretary, Health & Human Services:
Paul Francis. 518-408-2500
Deputy Secretary for Labor:
Elizabeth de Leon Bhargava. 212-681-4584
Deputy Secretary, Transportation:
Ron Thaniel. 518-408-2555
Deputy Secretary, Public Safety:
Rachel Small 518-474-3522
Director of Policy:
John Maggiore 518-408-2576

Communications

Director, Communications:
James Allen. 518-474-8418

Counsel

Counsel to the Governor:
Alphonso David 518-474-8343
First Assistant Counsel:
Sandi Toll 518-474-8434

New York City Office

633 Third Ave, 38th Fl, New York, NY 10017
212-681-4580
Governor:
Andrew M Cuomo 212-681-4580

Washington Office of the Governor

444 N Capitol St NW, Washington, DC 20001
202-434-7100
Director:
Alexander Cochran 202-434-7100

Lieutenant Governor's Office

Executive Chamber
State Capitol
Albany, NY 12224
518-402-2292 Fax: 518-474-1513

633 Third Ave
New York, NY 10017
212-681-4575

Lieutenant Governor:
Kathleen C Hochul . . . . 518-402-2292 or 212-681-4575
Chief of Staff:
Jeffrey Pearlman 518-402-2292
Deputy Chief of Staff:
Melissa Bochenski 518-402-2292
Press Secretary:
Chris White. 518-402-2292
Director, External Affairs:
Jeffrey Lewis. 212-681-4571
Director, Constituent Services:
Jelanie DeShong 212-681-4571

EXECUTIVE DEPARTMENTS AND RELATED AGENCIES

Aging, Office for the

2 Empire State Plaza
Albany, NY 12223

Offices and agencies generally appear in alphabetical order, except when specific order is requested by listee.

518-474-4425 or 800-342-9871 Fax: 518-474-0608
e-mail: nysofa@aging.ny.gov
Web site: www.aging.ny.gov

Director:
Corinda Crossdale . . . 518-474-4425
Executive Deputy Director:
Greg Olsen . . . 518-474-7012
Counsel:
Jennifer Washington . . . 518-474-0388
Deputy Director, Agency Operations:
John Cochran . . . 518-486-3661
Deputy Director, Division of Aging Network Operations:
John J Lynch . . . 518-473-4808
Deputy Director, Division of Policy, Planning, Program & Outcomes:
Laurie Pferr . . . 518-474-7012
Public Information Officer:
Reza Mizbani . . . 518-474-7181
e-mail: reza.mizbani@aging.ny.gov
Director of Aging Projects:
Kelly Mateja . . . 518-473-7424
Federal Relations/FOIL Officer, Staff Liaison:
Stephen Syzdek . . . 518-474-5041

Agriculture & Markets Department

10B Airline Dr
Albany, NY 12235
518-457-3880 or 800-554-4501 Fax: 518-457-3087
e-mail: info@agriculture.ny.gov
Web site: www.agriculture.ny.gov

Commissioner:
Richard Ball . . . 518-457-8876
First Deputy Commissioner:
Jen McCormick . . . 518-457-2771
e-mail: jen.mccormick@agriculture.ny.gov
Deputy Commissioner:
Maria Knirk . . . 518-457-2771
e-mail: maria.knirk@agriculture.ny.gov
Deputy Commissioner:
Jackie Moody-Czub . . . 518-485-7728
e-mail: jackie.moody-czub@agriculture.ny.gov
Counsel:
Scott Wyner . . . 518-457-1059
e-mail: scott.wyner@agriculture.ny.gov
Public Information Officer:
Jola Szubielski . . . 518-485-7728/fax: 518-457-3087
e-mail: jola.szubielski@agriculture.ny.gov

New York State Liquor Authority (Division of Alcoholic Beverage Control)

317 Lenox Ave
New York, NY 10027
212-961-8300 Fax: 212-961-8299
Web site: www.sla.ny.gov

80 S Swan St
Ste 900
Albany, NY 12210-8002
518-474-3114
Fax: 518-402-4015

535 Washington Street
Buffalo, NY 14203
Fax:

Chair:
Vincent Bradley . . . 212-961-8300 or 518-473-6559
Commissioner:
Kevin Kim . . . 518-474-3114 or 212-961-8300
Director, Information Technology:
Michael Drake . . . 518-474-3114/fax: 518-402-4015
CEO:
Kerri O'Brien . . . 518-474-3114
Director, Enforcement:
Noel Colon . . . 518-474-3114
Counsel:
Jacqueline Flug . . . 518-474-3114/fax: 518-402-2304
e-mail: legal@sla.ny.gov
Director, Public Affairs:
William Crowley . . . 518-474-3114 or 518-474-4875
fax: 518-473-9565
e-mail: press.office@sla.ny.gov

Alcoholism & Substance Abuse Services, Office of

1450 Western Ave
Albany, NY 12203
518-473-3460 Fax: 518-457-5474
e-mail: communications@oasas.ny.gov
Web site: www.oasas.ny.gov

501 7th Ave
8th Fl
New York, NY 10018
646-728-4533

Commissioner:
Arlene Gonzalez-Sanchez . . . 518-457-2061
Executive Deputy Commissioner:
Sean M. Byrne . . . 518-485-2337
Office of the Medical Director (Acting):
Charles W Morgan MD . . . 845-359-8500
Chief Counsel, Office of Counsel & Internal Controls:
Robert Kent . . . 518-485-2312
Acting Assoc Cmsr, Division of Prevention & Housing:
Mary Ann DiChristopher . . . 518-485-6022
Associate Commissioner, Fiscal Administration Division:
P David Sawicki . . . 518-457-5312
Associate Commissioner, Treatment & Practice Innovation Division:
Steve Hanson . . . 518-457-7077 or 585-461-0410
Associate Commissioner, Quality Assurance & Performance Improvement Division:
Charles W Monson . . . 518-485-2257
Director, Governmental Affairs, Grants Management:
Patricia Zuber-Wilson . . . 518-485-1484
Associate Commissioner, Outcome Management & System Information Division:
William F. Hogan . . . 518-485-2322
Director, Public Information & Communications:
Susan A Craig, MPH . . . 518-457-8299/fax: 518-485-6014

Financial Services Department

One State Street
New York, NY 10004-1511
212-709-3500 or 877-226-5697
e-mail: public-affairs@dfs.ny.gov
Web site: www.dfs.ny.gov

Acting Superintendent:
Maria T Vullo . . . 212-709-3501 or 518-474-4567
fax: 212-709-3520
Deputy Superintendent & General Counsel:
Marjorie Gross . . . 212-709-1640/fax: 212-480-5256
Deputy Superintendent, Community Regional Banks:
Martin Cofsky . . . 212-709-1610
Deputy Superintendent, Property/Casual Markets:
Michael Moriarty . . . 212-480-5127

Offices and agencies generally appear in alphabetical order, except when specific order is requested by listee.

Director, Criminal Investigations Bureau:
Ricardo Velez 212-709-3554
Chief Information Officer:
William Rachmiel 212-709-5420
Director, Frauds:
Frank Orlando 212-480-5770
Acting Director, Capital Markets Division:
Matti Peltonen 212-480-5071/fax: 212-480-6085
Director, Public Affairs:
Andrew Mais 212-480-5257/fax: 212-480-6077

Budget, Division of the

State Capitol
Albany, NY 12224
518-473-3885 Fax: 518-474-9041
Web site: www.budget.ny.gov

Director:
Robert F Mujica 518-474-2300
Deputy Director:
Sandra Beattie 518-474-6497
Deputy Director:
David Lara 518-402-4246
Budget Services Head:
Vacant 518-474-6300
Public Protection Head:
Robert Barbato 518-474-4313
Press Officer:
Morris Peters 518-473-3885/fax: 518-474-9041
e-mail: dob.sm.press@budget.ny.gov

CIO & Office of Information Technology Services (ITS)

State Capitol
Empire State Plaza
PO Box 2062
Albany, NY 12220-0062
518-402-2537 or 866-789-4638 Fax: 518-474-1196
e-mail: customer.relations@its.ny.gov
Web site: www.its.ny.gov

Chief Information Officer/Director of ITS:
Maggie Miller 518-408-2140
Executive Deputy Chief Information Officer:
Mahesh Nattanmai 518-408-2140
Chief Technology Officer:
Rajiv Rao 518-486-9200
Counsel & Legal Services:
Shoshanah Bewlay 518-408-2484
Director, Administration:
Terri Papa 518-408-2484
Chief Data Officer:
Barbara Cohn 518-473-9450
Director, Enterprise Information Security Office:
Vacant 518-242-5200
e-mail: eiso@its.ny.gov
Director, Public Information:
Vacant 518-408-3899

Children & Family Services, Office of

52 Washington St
Rensselaer, NY 12144
518-473-7793 Fax: 518-486-7550
Web site: www.ocfs.ny.gov

Acting Commissioner:
Sheila Poole 518-402-3108
Executive Deputy Commissioner:
Sheila Poole 518-402-3108
Assisant Commissioner, Communications:
Jennifer Givner . . . . . . 518-402-3130 or 518-473-7793
fax: 518-486-7550
e-mail: info@ocfs.state.ny.us
Acting Deputy Commissioner, Legal Affairs & General Counsel:
Lee Prochera 518-473-8418
Associate Commissioner, Administration/Human Resources:
James Barron 518-486-6942
Deputy Commissioner, Child Welfare & Community Service:
Laura Velez 518-474-3377
Deputy Commissioner, Juvenile Justice & Opportunity for Youth:
Ines Neives 518-473-1786
CIO:
Rick Ryan 518-402-3194
Associate Commissioner, Blind & Visually Handicapped Commission:
Brian S Daniels 518-474-7812

Council on Children & Families . . . . . . fax: 518-473-2570

52 Washington Street, West Bldg, Ste 99, Rensselaer, NY 12144
518-473-3652 Fax: 518-473-2570
e-mail: council@ccf.ny.gov
Web site: www.ccf.ny.gov

Executive Director:
Deborah Benson 518-473-3652/fax: 518-473-2570
e-mail: debbie.benson@ccf.ny.gov
Deputy Director & Counsel:
Elana Marton 518-473-3652
e-mail: elena.marton@ccf.ny.gov
Project Director, Head Start Collaboration:
Patricia Persell 518-474-9352
e-mail: patricia.persell@ccf.ny.gov
Project Director, Kids Count:
Mary DeMasi 518-473-3652
e-mail: mary.demasi@ccf.ny.gov

Civil Service Department

Alfred E Smith State Ofc Bldg
Albany, NY 12239
518-457-2487 or 877-697-5627
Web site: www.cs.ny.gov

President:
Vacant 518-457-3701
Executive Deputy Commissioner:
Lola Brabham 518-473-5698
Deputy Commissioner, Operations:
Vacant 518-473-5711
Deputy Commissioner, Administration:
Deirdre Taylor 518-473-5694
Deputy Commissioner/General Counsel:
Ilene Lees 518-473-2624
Director, Workforce & Occupational Planning:
Vacant 518-473-6411
Director, Financial Administration:
Vacant 518-473-2269
Director, Employee Benefits:
Robert Dubois 518-473-1977/fax: 518-473-3292
Human Resources & Administrative Planning:
Valerie Morrison 518-473-4306
Public Information Officer:
Ed Walsh 518-457-9375/fax: 518-473-2372
e-mail: pio@cs.state.ny.us

Civil Service Commission

President:
Vacant 518-457-3701
Commissioner:
Caroline Ahl 518-473-6326
Commissioner:
Jeanique Greene 518-473-6326

Offices and agencies generally appear in alphabetical order, except when specific order is requested by listee.

Consumer Protection, Division of
One Commerce Plaza
99 Washington Ave
Albany, NY 12231
518-474-8583 or 800-697-1220 Fax: 518-473-9055
Web site: www.dos.ny.gov/consumerprotection/

Executive Deputy Director, Consumer Protection:
Aiesha Battle . . . 518-474-2363

Corrections & Community Supervision Department
1220 Washington Ave
Bldg 2 State Campus
Albany, NY 12226-2050
518-457-8126 Fax: 518-457-7252
Web site: www.doccs.ny.gov

Acting Commissioner:
Anthony Annucci . . . 518-457-8134
Assistant Commissioner & Executive Assistant:
Diane L Van Buren . . . 518-457-1281
Special Assistant to Commissioner:
Terri Pratt . . . 518-457-8134
Executive Deputy Commissioner:
Anthony Annucci . . . 518-457-1748 or 518-485-9613
Deputy Commissioner, Administrative Services:
Daniel F. Martuscello III . . . 518-457-8188
Deputy Commissioner, Correctional Facility Operations:
Joseph Bellnier . . . 518-457-8138
Deputy Commissioner, Health Services Division/Chief Medical Officer:
Carl Koenigsmann . . . 518-457-7073
Assistant Commissioner, Program Services:
Catherine Jacobsen . . . 518-408-5825
Director, Public Information:
Linda Foglia . . . 518-457-8182/fax: 518-457-7070

Council on the Arts
300 Park Avenue South
10th Floor
New York, NY 10010
212-459-8800 or 800-510-0021
e-mail: info@arts.ny.gov
Web site: www.nysca.org

Chair:
Dr Barbaralee Diamonstein-Spielvogel . . . 212-459-8800
Interim Executive Director:
Jackie Snyder . . . 212-459-8808
e-mail: executive.director@arts.ny.gov
Deputy Executive Director, Programs:
Megan White . . . 212-459-8806
e-mail: megan.white@arts.ny.gov
Director, Agency Operations:
Brenda Brown . . . 212-459-8827
e-mail: brenda.brown@arts.ny.gov
Manager, Information Technology:
Lenn Ditman . . . 212-459-8810
e-mail: lenn.ditman@arts.ny.gov
Director, Administrative Services:
Tracy Hamilton-Thompson . . . 212-459-8822
e-mail: tracy.hamilton@arts.ny.gov

Victim Services, Office of
55 Hanson Place
10th Fl
Brooklyn, NY 11217-1523
718-923-4325 or 800-247-8035 Fax: 718-923-4347
Web site: www.ovs.ny.gov

80 S Swan Street
2nd Floor
Albany, NY 12210
518-457-8727
Fax: 518-457-8658

Director:
Elizabeth Cronin Esq . . . 518-485-5719
General Counsel/Legal Unit:
John Watson . . . 518-457-8066/fax: 518-457-8658
Deputy Director for Administration:
Virginia Miller . . . 518-457-8003
Granst & Victim Assistance Programs:
Emma Graham . . . 518-485-0943
Director, Public Information:
Janine Kava . . . 518-457-8828
Deputy Director, Claims:
Maureen Fahy . . . 518-457-8050

Criminal Justice Services, Division of
80 South Swan Street
Albany, NY 12210
518-457-5837 or 800-262-3257 Fax: 518-457-3089
e-mail: info@dcjs.ny.gov
Web site: www.criminaljustice.ny.gov

Executive Deputy Commissioner:
Michael C Green . . . 518-457-1260
Deputy Commissioner, Program Development & Funding:
Jeffrey Bender . . . 518-457-8462
First Deputy Commissioner:
Mark Bonacquist . . . 518-457-1260
Deputy Commissioner & Counsel:
John Czajka . . . 518-457-4181
Deputy Commissioner, Public Safety:
Michael Wood . . . 518-485-7620
Deputy Commissioner, Criminal Justice Operations:
Joe Morrissey . . . 518-485-2995
Director, Human Resources Management:
Karen Davis . . . 518-485-1704
Director, Finance:
Mary Ann Rossi . . . 518-457-6105
Deputy Commissioner, Justice Research & Performance:
Terry Salo . . . 518-457-7301
Deputy Director, Public Information:
Janine Kava . . . 518-457-8906/fax: 518-485-7715
e-mail: janine.kava@dcjs.ny.gov

Developmental Disabilities Planning Council
One Commerce Plaza
Ste 1230
Albany, NY 12210
518-486-7505 or 800-395-3372 Fax: 518-402-3505
e-mail: ddpc@ddpc.ny.gov
Web site: www.ddpc.ny.gov

Chairperson:
James Traylor . . . 518-486-7505
Vice Chairperson:
Thomas Burke . . . 518-486-7505
Executive Director:
Sheila M Carey . . . 518-486-7505
e-mail: sheila.carey@ddpc.ny.gov
Deputy Director-Program Development Specialist:
Anna Lobosco . . . 518-486-7505
e-mail: anna.lobosco@ddpc.ny.gov
Public Information Officer:
Thomas F Lee . . . 518-486-7505/fax: 518-486-3505
e-mail: thomas.lee@ddpc.ny.gov

Offices and agencies generally appear in alphabetical order, except when specific order is requested by listee.

Education Department
State Education Bldg
89 Washington Ave
Albany, NY 12234
518-474-3852 Fax: 518-486-5631
Web site: www.nysed.gov

Commissioner & University President:
MaryEllen Elia 518-474-5844
Executive Deputy Commissioner:
Elizabeth Berlin 518-473-8381
General Counsel:
Richard Trautwein 518-474-6400
e-mail: legal@nysed.gov
Deputy Commissioner, Higher Education:
John D'Agati. 518-486-3633
Deputy Commissioner, Cultural Education Office:
Vacant 518-474-5976/fax: 518-486-4850
Deputy Commissioner, Office of the Professions:
Douglas Lentivech. . . . . 518-486-1765 or 518-474-3817 x440
Sr Deputy Commissioner, Office of P-12 Education Policy:
Jhone Ebert 518-474-3862
e-mail: nysedp12@nysed.gov
Deputy Commissioner, Adult Career & Continuing Ed Svcs (ACCES):
Kevin Smith 518-474-2714
e-mail: accesdeputy@nysed.gov
Deputy Commissioner, Research & Collections:
Sharon Cates-Williams 518-473-4706
Chief, External Affairs (Communications):
Dennis Tompkins. 518-474-1201/fax: 518-473-2977

Elections, State Board of
40 N Pearl Street
Suite 5
Albany, NY 12207
518-474-6220 or TTY: 800-367-8683 Fax: 518-486-4068
e-mail: info@elections.ny.gov
Web site: www.elections.ny.gov

Co-Chair:
Peter S Kosinski 518-474-8100
Co-Chair:
Douglas A Kellner 518-474-8100
Commissioner:
Andrew J Spano 518-474-8100
Commissioner:
Gregory P Peterson. 518-474-8100
Co-Executive Director:
Todd Valentine 518-474-6336/fax: 518-474-1008
Co-Executive Director:
Robert A Brehm 518-474-6336/fax: 518-474-1008
Special Counsel:
Kimberly Galvin 518-474-6367
Administrative Officer:
Thomas A Jarose. 518-474-6336
Director, Election Operations:
Anne E Svizzero 518-473-5086/fax: 518-486-4546
Director, Public Information:
John W Conklin. 518-474-1953/fax: 518-473-8315
Counsel/Enforcement:
Risa Sugarman 518-486-7858
e-mail: enforcement@elections.ny.gov

Homeland Security & Emergency Services, Division of
1220 Washington Ave
Bldg. 7A
Suite 710
Albany, NY 12242
518-242-5000 Fax: 518-322-4978
Web site: www.dhses.ny.gov

633 Third Ave
32nd Fl
New York, NY 10017
212-867-7060

Commissioner:
John P Melville. 518-292-2301
Assistant Director, Office of Counterterrorism:
David Sheppard. 518-242-5121
Director, Fire Prevention Bureau & State Fire Administrator:
Bryant Stevens 518-474-6746
e-mail: fire@dhses.ny.gov
Director, Upstate Intergovernmental Affairs:
Brian Shea. 518-292-2301
Assistant Director, OEM Training:
Richard French 518-292-2357
Executive Assistant to the Commissioner:
Norma Soodsma 518-242-5085
Director, Office of Interoperable & Emergency Communications:
Robert Barbato 518-292-4913
e-mail: dhsesoiec@dhses.ny.gov
Public Information Officer:
Kristin Devoe. 518-242-5153/fax: 518-322-4978

Empire State Development Corporation
633 Third Ave
New York, NY 10017
212-803-3100 Fax: 212-803-3131
e-mail: esd@esd.ny.gov
Web site: www.esd.ny.gov

625 Broadway
Albany, NY 12207
518-292-5200

95 Perry Street
Ste 500
Buffalo, NY 14203
716-846-8200
Fax: 716-846-8260

President & CEO:
Howard Zemsky . . . . . 212-803-3700 or 518-292-5100
Public Affairs:
Kay Sarlin Wright. 800-260-7313
e-mail: esdpressoffice@esd.ny.gov
Chief of Staff & COO:
Mehul Patel . . . . . 212-803-3700 or 518-292-5100
Business Attraction & Expansion:
John Gilstrap 212-803-3700
General Counsel:
Liz Fine 212-803-3100

Employee Relations, Governor's Office of
Two Empire State Plz
Ste 1201
Albany, NY 12223
518-473-8766 Fax: 518-473-6795
e-mail: info@goer.ny.gov
Web site: www.goer.ny.gov

Interim Director:
Michael N Volforte 518-474-6988/fax: 518-486-7304
Deputy Director, Contract Negotiations & Administration:
Vacant 518-473-3130/fax: 518-486-7304

Offices and agencies generally appear in alphabetical order, except when specific order is requested by listee.

Associate General Counsel:
Amy Petragnani 518-473-4596/fax: 518-486-7303
Director, Administration:
Mary Hines 518-473-3467/fax: 518-473-6725
CIO/Information Technology Division:
Moses M Kamya PhD 518-486-1305/fax: 518-473-6294

Environmental Conservation Department
625 Broadway
Albany, NY 12233-0001
518-402-8545 Fax: 518-402-9016
Web site: www.dec.ny.gov

Acting Commissioner:
Basil Seggos 518-402-8545/fax: 518-402-8541
Executive Deputy Commissioner:
Kenneth Lynch 518-402-8560
General Counsel:
Tom Berkman 518-402-9185/fax: 518-402-9018
Assistant Commissioner, Hearings & Mediation:
Louis Alexander 518-402-8537
Assistant Commissioner, Natural Resources:
Kathy Moser 518-402-8533/fax: 518-402-9016
Deputy Commissioner, Administration:
Jeffrey Stefanko 518-402-9401
Assistant Commissioner, Public Protection:
Christian Ballantyne 518-402-8549/fax: 518-402-9016
Deputy Commissioner, Remediation & Materials Management:
Gene Leff 518-402-2794/fax: 518-402-8541
Assistant Commissioner, Air Resources, Climate Change & Energy:
Jared Snyder 518-402-8549
Assistant Commissioner, Water Resources Office:
James Tierney 518-402-2794
Director, Public Affairs:
Emily DeSantis 518-402-8560
e-mail: pressoffice@dec.ny.gov

General Services, Office of
Corning Tower, 41st Fl
Empire State Plaza
Albany, NY 12242
518-474-3899 Fax: 518-474-1546
Web site: www.ogs.ny.gov

Commissioner:
RoAnn Destito 518-474-5991/fax: 518-486-9179
Executive Deputy Commissioner:
Karen B Tyler 518-473-6953
Deputy Commissioner, Administration:
Gail Hammond 518-474-3199
Deputy Commissioner, Design & Construction:
Margaret Larkin 518-474-0337/fax: 518-486-9135
Deputy Commissioner, Information Technology & Procurement Services:
Vacant 518-473-3933/fax: 518-486-9166
Deputy Commissioner, Legal Services & Counsel:
Bradley Allen 518-474-5988/fax: 518-473-4973
Director, Real Estate Planning & Development Group:
James Sproat 518-474-4944
Director, Communications:
Heather Groll 518-474-5987/fax: 518-402-5146
e-mail: heather.groll@ogs.ny.gov

Health Department
Corning Tower
Empire State Plaza
Albany, NY 12237
518-474-2011
Web site: www.health.ny.gov

Commissioner:
Howard Zucker, MD, JD 518-474-2011
Executive Deputy Commissioner:
Sally Dreslin, MS, RN 518-474-2011
Assistant Commissioner, Governmental & External Affairs:
Amy Nickson 518-473-1124/fax: 518-473-9674
Health Cluster CIO:
John P McInnes 518-474-8373/fax: 518-474-2288
Deputy Commissioner & State Medicaid Director:
Jason A Helgerson 518-474-3018/fax: 518-486-1346
General Counsel:
Richard J Zahnleuter 518-474-7553/fax: 518-473-2802
Deputy Commissioner, Public Health:
Brad Hutton, MPH 518-473-0771
Director, Health Emergency Preparedness:
Michael J Primeau 518-474-2893
Director, AIDS Institute:
Dan O'Connell . . . . . 518-474-6399 or 212-417-5500
Director, Center for Community Health:
Vacant 518-473-4371
Director, Family Health:
Lauren Tobias 518-474-6968/fax: 518-474-7054
Deputy Commissioner, Primary Care & Health Systems Management:
Daniel B Sheppard 518-474-1686
Director, The Wadsworth Center:
Jill Taylor, PhD 518-474-3157/fax: 518-474-3439
Director, Public Affairs:
James C Plastiras 518-474-7354 x1
Deputy Director, Public Affairs:
Marci Natale 518-474-7354 x1

Housing & Community Renewal
Hampton Plaza
38-40 State St
Albany, NY 12207
866-275-3427 or 518-473-2526
Web site: www.nyshcr.org

641 Lexington Ave
New York, NY 10022
866-275-3427

Commissioner/CEO:
James S Rubin 518-486-3370
Acting President, Office of Community Renewal:
Chris Leo 212-480-6707
President, Office of Finance & Development:
Marian Zucker . . . . . 518-486-3370 or 212-480-6772
fax: 518-473-9462
Director, Fair & Equitable Housing:
Wanda Graham 518-474-2057/fax: 518-474-5247
Chief Public Information Officer:
Charni Sochet 212-872-0681

Hudson River Valley Greenway
625 Broadway, 4th Fl
Albany, NY 12207
518-473-3835 Fax: 518-473-4518
e-mail: hrvg@hudsongreenway.ny.gov
Web site: www.hudsongreenway.ny.gov

Greenway Conservancy for the Hudson River Valley
Acting Chair:
Sara Griffen 518-473-3835
Executive Director (Acting):
Mark Castiglione 518-473-3835

Offices and agencies generally appear in alphabetical order, except when specific order is requested by listee.

Hudson River Valley Greenway Communities Council
Board Chair:
Barnabas McHenry Esq. 518-473-3835/fax: 212-681-4552
Executive Director (Acting):
Mark Castiglione. 518-473-3835

Human Rights, State Division of
1 Fordham Plaza, 4th Fl
Bronx, NY 10458
718-741-8400 or 888-392-3644 Fax: 718-741-8279
e-mail: infobronx@dhr.ny.gov
Web site: www.dhr.ny.gov

Commissioner:
Helen Diane Foster 718-741-8326
First Deputy Commissioner:
Valerie P. Dent 718-741-8330
PR & Communications:
Leticia Theodore-Greene 718-741-3223
e-mail: lgreene@dhr.ny.gov
Deputy Commissioner, Regional Affairs & Federal Programs:
Gina N Martinez 718-741-8440
Deputy Commissioner, Enforcement:
Melissa Franco 718-741-8400
Director, Housing Investigations Unit:
William Lamot 718-741-8435
General Counsel:
Caroline Downey 718-741-8398
Public Information Officer:
Lourdes Centeno 718-741-3223
e-mail: lcenteno@dhr.ny.gov

Inspector General (NYS), Office of the
Empire State Plaza
Bldg 2, 16th Fl
Albany, NY 12223
518-474-1010 or 800-367-4448 Fax: 518-486-3745
e-mail: igpress@ig.ny.gov
Web site: www.ig.ny.gov

61 Broadway
12th Floor
New York, NY 10006
212-635-3150
Fax: 212-809-6287

State Inspector General:
Catherine Leahy Scott . . . . . 212-635-3150 or 518-474-1010
e-mail: inspector.general@ig.ny.gov
Executive Inspector General:
Spencer Freeman. 212-635-3150
Deputy Inspector General - Investigations:
Bernard Cosenza. 212-635-3150
Director, Communications:
William P. Reynolds. 518-474-1010

Insurance Fund (NYS)
One Watervliet Ave Ext
Albany, NY 12206
518-437-6400
Web site: www.nysif.com

199 Church St
New York, NY 10007
212-587-9000

Executive Director & CEO:
Eric Madoff. . . . . 212-312-7004 or 518-437-5220
Deputy Executive Director:
Dorothy Carey. 212-312-9933
Deputy Executive Director:
Colleen Gardner 212-587-9000
Deputy Executive Director:
Shirley Stark 212-312-9917
Chief Fiscal Officer:
Susan D Sharp. 518-437-6168
Public Information Officer:
Robert Lawson. 518-437-3504/fax: 518-437-1849
General Attorney:
Gregory Allen 518-437-5220
Director, Administration:
Joseph Mullen 518-437-5220

Insurance Fund Board of Commissioners
Chair:
Kenneth R Theobalds 518-437-5220
Vice Chair:
Barry Swidler 518-437-5220
Secretary to the Board:
Michael Miliano 212-312-7408

Labor Department
Building 12, Room 500
Harriman State Office Campus
Albany, NY 12240
518-457-9000 Fax: 518-457-6908
e-mail: nysdol@labor.ny.gov
Web site: www.labor.ny.gov

Commissioner:
Roberta Reardon 518-457-9000
Executive Deputy Commissioner:
Mario Musolino 518-457-4318
Acting Counsel:
Pico Ben-Amotz 518-457-3665
Director, Special Investigations:
John Dormin 518-457-7012
Acting Deputy Commissioner, Employment Security:
Mary Batch 518-457-5124
Acting Deputy Commissioner, Workforce Development:
Karen Coleman 518-457-4317
Director, Safety & Health:
Eileen Franko 518-457-3518
Director, Communications:
Leo Rosales 518-457-5519/fax: 518-485-1126
e-mail: leo.rosales@labor.ny.gov
Director, Personnel:
Carol Owsiany 518-457-1020

Law Department
120 Broadway
New York, NY 10271-0332
212-416-8000 or 800-771-7755
Web site: www.ag.ny.gov

State Capitol
Albany, NY 12224-0341
518-776-2000
Fax: 518-650-9401

Attorney General:
Eric T Schneiderman . . . . . 212-416-8050 or 518-776-2000
Chief Deputy Attorney General & Counsel:
Jason Brown 212-416-8050
Chief Deputy Attorney General & Counsel:
Janet Sabel 212-416-8050

Solicitor General:
Barbara D Underwood . . . . 212-416-8016 or 518-776-2002
Executive Deputy Attorney General, Criminal Justice:
Kelly Donovan 212-416-8050
Executive Deputy Attorney General, Economic Justice:
Manisha Sheth 212-416-8050
Executive Deputy Attorney General, Social Justice:
Alvin L Bragg, Jr. 212-416-8450/fax: 212-416-8942
Executive Deputy Attorney General, Regional Affairs:
Martin J Mack 716-853-8451
Press Secretary:
Matt Mittenthal 212-416-8060/fax: 212-416-6005

New York State Gaming Commission

One Broadway Center
PO Box 7500
Schenectady, NY 12301-7500
518-388-3300 Fax: 518-388-3423
e-mail: info@gaming.ny.gov
Web site: www.gaming.ny.gov

Executive Director:
Robert Williams 518-388-3400
General Counsel:
Edmund Burns 518-388-3408
Director, Lottery Division:
Gardner Gurney 518-388-3406
Director, Communications & Public Information Officer:
Christy Calicchia 518-388-3415/fax: 518-388-3423
Director, Marketing:
Daniel J Martin 518-388-3491
Public Information Officer:
Lee Park 518-395-5400/fax: 518-453-8867
e-mail: lee.park@racing.ny.gov

Mental Health, Office of

44 Holland Ave
Albany, NY 12229
518-474-4403 or 800-597-8481 Fax: 518-474-2149
Web site: www.omh.ny.gov

Commissioner:
Ann Marie T Sullivan MD 518-474-4403
Executive Deputy Commissioner:
Martha Schaefer 518-474-7056/fax: 518-473-4690
Deputy Commissioner & Counsel:
Joshua Pepper 518-474-1331/fax: 518-473-7863
Medical Director:
Lloyd I Sederer, MD . . . . 212-330-1650 x. 360
Chief Financial Officer:
Emil Slane 518-474-3631
Director, Center for Human Resource Management:
J. Lynn Heath 518-474-0171
Director, Public Affairs:
Benjamin Rosen 518-474-6540/fax: 518-473-3456

NYS Office for People with Developmental Disabilities

44 Holland Avenue
Albany, NY 12229
866-946-9733 or TTY: 866-933-4889 Fax: 518-474-1335
Web site: www.opwdd.ny.gov

Acting Commissioner:
Kerry Delaney 518-473-1997
Acting Executive Deputy Commissioner:
Helene DeSanto 518-473-1997
General Counsel:
Roger Bearden 518-473-1873
Director of Internal Audit:
James Nellegar 518-474-4376
Director, Advocacy Services:
Deborah Franchini 518-473-1997
Director, Communications & Public Affairs:
Jennifer O'Sullivan 518-474-6601
e-mail: communications.office@opwdd.ny.gov

Military & Naval Affairs, Division of

330 Old Niskayuna Rd
Latham, NY 12110
518-786-4786 or 518-489-6188 Fax: 518-786-4649
Web site: www.dmna.ny.gov

Adjutant General:
Major Gen Anthony P German 518-786-4502
e-mail: pat.murphy@us.army.mil
Adjutant General - Air:
Anthony P. German 518-786-4317
Executive Officer:
Donald McKnight 518-786-4388
e-mail: bob.epp@us.army.mil
Legal Counsel:
Robert G Conway, Jr 518-786-4541
Joint Chief of Staff:
Col. Raymond L. Shields 518-786-4417
e-mail: renwick.payne@us.army.mil
Director, Governmental Community Affairs:
James M Huelle 518-786-4580
Director, Public Affairs:
Col David Warager 518-786-4581/fax: 518-786-4649
e-mail: david.warager@dmna.nyg.ny.gov
Director, Budget & Finance:
Robert A Martin 518-786-4514

Motor Vehicles Department

6 Empire State Plaza
Albany, NY 12228
Web site: www.dmv.ny.gov

Executive Deputy Commissioner:
Theresa L Egan 518-474-0846/fax: 518-474-0712
Deputy Commissioner, Administration:
Gregory J Kline 518-474-6876/fax: 518-474-0712
Deputy Commissioner, Legal Affairs:
Neal Schoen 518-473-1965/fax: 518-474-0712
Deputy Commissioner, Operations & Customer Service:
Timothy Blennon 518-474-0846
Deputy Commissioner, Safety, Consumer Protection & Clean Air:
Heriberto Barbot 518-402-4860/fax: 518-474-0712
Director, Agency Program Services:
Ann Scott 518-474-8328
Director, Driver Safety Programs:
Gerald Clark 518-473-7197
Assistant Commissioner, Communications:
Joseph Morrissey 518-473-7000/fax: 518-473-1930

NYSTAR - Division of Science, Technology & Innovation

30 South Pearl St
11th Fl
Albany, NY 12207
518-292-5700 Fax: 518-292-5798
e-mail: nystarsupport@esd.ny.gov
Web site: www.csd.ny.gov/nystar

Director:
Edward Reinfurt 518-292-5700
Deputy Director:
Edward J Hamilton 518-292-5700

Offices and agencies generally appear in alphabetical order, except when specific order is requested by listee.

Director, Communications/Government Affairs:
Jannette Rondo 518-292-5700/fax: 518-292-5798
Director, Regional Technology Development:
Matthew Watson 518-292-5700
Counsel:
Paul Jesep 518-292-5700

Parks, Recreation & Historic Preservation, NYS Office of

Empire State Plaza, Bldg 1
625 Broadway, 12207
Albany, NY 12238
518-486-0456 Fax: 518-486-2924
Web site: www.nysparks.com

Commissioner:
Rose Harvey 518-474-0443
Executive Deputy Commissioner:
Andrew Beers 518-474-0020/fax: 518-474-4492
Deputy Commissioner, Finance & Administration:
Melinda Scott 518-474-0414
Director, Operations & Programs:
Marc Talluto 518-474-0440
Deputy Commissioner, Historic Preservation:
Ruth Pierpont 518-237-8643 x3269
Secretary:
Virginia Davis 518-474-0443
General Counsel:
Paul Laudato 518-474-0414
Park Police/Director, Law Enforcement:
Chief Jay Kirschner 518-474-4029/fax: 518-408-1032
Deputy Public Information Officer:
Dan Keefe 518-486-1868

Parole Board, The

Corrections & Community Supervision
97 Central Ave
Albany, NY 12206
518-473-9548 Fax: 518-473-6037
Web site: www.parole.ny.gov; doccs.ny.gov

Acting Commissioner:
Anthony J Annucci 518-473-9548
Chief Counsel:
Terrence X Tracy 518-473-5671/fax: 518-473-9760
Public Information Offficer:
Vacant 518-486-4631/fax: 518-473-6037
Director, Administrative Services:
Jeffrey Nesich 518-473-3901/fax: 518-486-5858
Deputy Commissioner, Community Supervision:
Angela Jiminez . . . . . 518-473-9672 or 212-239-5730
Director, Internal Operations:
Timothy O'Brien 518-408-3473

Prevention of Domestic Violence, Office for the

80 South Swan Street
11th Fl Rm 1157
Albany, NY 12210
518-457-5800 Fax: 518-457-5810
e-mail: opdvpublicinfo@opdv.ny.gov
Web site: www.opdv.ny.gov

90 Church St, 13th Fl
New York, NY 10007
212-417-4477
Fax: 212-417-4972

Executive Director:
Gwen Wright 518-457-5800
Director, NYC Program:
Sujata Warrier 212-417-4477
Counsel:
Johanna Sullivan 518-457-5800
Director, Prevention & Human Services:
Gwen Wright 518-457-5916
Fiscal Officer:
Linda Cassidy 518-457-7995
Public Information Officer:
Suzanne Cecala 518-457-5744
e-mail: suzanne.cecala@opdv.ny.gov

Public Employment Relations Board

PO Box 2074
Empire State Plaza
Agency Bldg 2, 18/20 Fl
Albany, NY 12220
518-457-2578 Fax: 518-457-2664
e-mail: perbinfo@perb.ny.gov
Web site: www.perb.ny.gov

Chair:
Seth H Agata 518-457-2578
Member:
Allen DeMarco 518-457-2578
Member:
Robert Hite 518-457-2578
Executive Director:
Anthony Zumbolo 518-457-2676
Counsel:
David P Quinn 518-457-2678
Secretary to the Board:
Sheila Talavera 518-457-2578
Director, Conciliation Office:
Kevin B. Flanigan 518-457-2690
Director, Employment Practices & Representation:
Monte Klein 518-457-5973

Public Service Commission

NYS Dept of Public Service
3 Empire State Plaza
Albany, NY 12223-1350
518-474-7080 Fax: 518-474-0421
Web site: www.dps.ny.gov

Chairman:
Audrey Zibelman 518-474-2532/fax: 518-473-2838
Commissioner:
Diane X Burman . . . . . 518-474-2503 or 212-417-3168
fax: 518-473-2838
Commissioner:
Gregg C. Sayre . . . . . 518-474-2503 or 212-417-3168
fax: 518-473-2838
Commissioner:
Patricia L Acampora . . . . . 518-474-2503 or 212-417-3168
fax: 518-473-2838
Chief of Staff:
Thomas Congdon 518-408-1978
Secretary to the Commission:
Kathleen H Burgess 518-474-6530/fax: 518-474-9842
e-mail: secretary@dps.ny.gov
Executive Deputy:
Judith Lee 518-408-1978/fax: 518-473-2838
General Counsel:
Kimberly Harriman 518-474-2510/fax: 518-486-5710
Director, Consumer Services Office:
Michael Corso 518-474-4686
e-mail: csd@dps.ny.gov

Offices and agencies generally appear in alphabetical order, except when specific order is requested by listee.

Utility Rates & Services:
Rajendra Addepalli 518-474-8986
Director, Office of Administration:
Sorelle Brauth 518-474-2508/fax: 518-474-0413
Director, Telecommunications:
Karen Geduldig 518-474-1668/fax: 518-474-5616
Director, Accounting & Finance:
Doris Stout . . . . 518-474-4508 or 212-417-2136
Director, Public Affairs:
James Denn 518-474-7080/fax: 518-474-0421
e-mail: james.denn@dps.ny.gov

Real Property Tax Services, Office of

NYS Dept of Tax & Finance
WA Harriman State Campus
Bldg 8A
Albany, NY 12227
518-457-7377 or 518-591-5232
Web site: www.tax.ny.gov/about/orpts

Acting Secretary of Board & Assistant Deputy Commissioner:
Susan Savage 518-474-3793
State Board Member:
John M Bacheller 518-474-3793
State Board Member (Chair):
Matthew Rand. 518-474-3793
State Board Member:
Edgar A King 518-474-3793
Assistant to the Board:
Darlene Maloney
e-mail: darlene.maloney@tax.ny.gov

State Comptroller, Office of the

110 State St, 15th Fl
Albany, NY 12236-0001
518-474-4044 Fax: 518-473-3004
e-mail: contactus@osc.state.ny.us
Web site: www.osc.state.ny.us

59 Maiden Lane
New York, NY 10038
212-383-1600

State Comptroller:
Thomas P DiNapoli . . . . 518-474-4040 or 212-681-4491
First Deputy Comptroller:
Pete Grannis . . . . 518-474-2909 or 212-681-4469
Chief of Staff:
Shawn Thompson 518-474-4044
Deputy Comptroller & Chief Information Officer:
Robert Loomis 518-486-4349
Information Enterprise Applications & IT Business Management:
Mary Anne Barry 518-474-8089
Director, Communications:
Jennifer Freeman . . . . 518-474-4015 or 212-681-4840
Assistant Comptroller, Business Communications:
Ellen Evans. . . . . 518-474-4040 or 212-681-4489
Deputy Comptroller, Human Resources & Administration:
Angela Dixon 518-474-5512
Inspector General - Internal Audit:
Stephen Hamilton 518-408-4906
General Counsel:
Nancy Groenwegen. 518-474-3444
Executive Deputy Comptroller, Operations:
John Traylor 518-402-4103
Deputy Comptroller, City of New York:
Ken Bleiwas 212-383-3900
e-mail: osdc@osc.state.ny.us
Deputy Comptroller, Budget & Policy Analysis:
Robert Ward 518-473-4333
Deputy Comptroller, Intergovernmental Relations:
Vacant 518-402-3234

State Department

One Commerce Plaza
99 Washington Avenue
Albany, NY 12231-0001
518-474-4750 Fax: 518-474-4597
e-mail: info@dos.ny.gov
Web site: www.dos.ny.gov

123 William Street
New York, NY 10038-3804
212-417-5800
Fax: 212-417-2383

Acting Secretary of State:
Rossana Rosado 518-474-0050
First Deputy Secretary of State:
Daniel Shapiro 518-474-4750
Principal Attorney:
William Sharp 518-474-6740/fax: 518-473-9211
Deputy Secretary, Licensing:
Marcos Vigil 518-4743-2728
Deputy Secretary of State, Local Government Services:
Dierdre Scozzafava 518-473-3355/fax: 518-474-6572
Deputy Secretary, Communications & Community Affairs:
Vacant 518-486-9846/fax: 518-474-4765
e-mail: info@dos.state.ny.us

State Police, Division of

Bldg 22, State Campus
1220 Washington Ave
Albany, NY 12226-2252
518-457-2180
e-mail: nyspmail@troopers.ny.gov
Web site: www.troopers.ny.gov

Superintendent:
Joseph A D'Amico 518-457-6721
First Deputy Superintendent:
Kevin T Gagan 518-457-6711/fax: 518-485-7505
Counsel:
Vacant 518-457-6137/fax: 518-485-1164
Assistant Deputy Superintendent, Administration:
Terence P O'Mara 518-457-6622/fax: 518-485-5051
Deputy Superintendent, Employee Relations:
Francis P Christensen 518-457-3572/fax: 518-485-7505
Deputy Superintendent, Technology & Communications:
Steven F Cumoletti 518-457-6621
Deputy Superintendent, Internal Affairs:
Anthony G Ellis 518-485-6018
Director, Public Information:
Darcy Wells 518-457-2180/fax: 518-485-7818
e-mail: pio@troopers.ny.gov

Tax Appeals, Division of

Agency Building 1
Empire State Plaza
Albany, NY 12223
518-266-3000 Fax: 518-271-0886
e-mail: nysdota@dta.ny.gov
Web site: www.dta.ny.gov

Offices and agencies generally appear in alphabetical order, except when specific order is requested by listee.

Tax Appeals Tribunal
President & Commissioner:
Roberta Moseley 518-266-3050
Commissioner:
Charles H Nesbitt 518-266-3050
Commissioner:
James H Tully Jr 518-266-3050
Counsel:
Timothy J Alston. 518-266-3052
Secretary to the Tribunal:
Jean A McDonnell 518-266-3036

Administrative Law Judges & Officers
Supervising Administrative Law Judge:
Daniel J Ranalli 518-266-3000
Presiding Officer:
Alexander F Chu-Fong 518-266-3000

Taxation & Finance Department
State Campus
Bldg 9, Rm 227
Albany, NY 12227
518-457-4242 Fax: 518-457-2486
Web site: www.tax.ny.gov

Commissioner:
Jerry Boone 518-457-2244
Executive Deputy Commissioner:
Nonie Manion 518-457-7358
Deputy Commissioner & Counsel:
Amanda Hiller 518-457-3746/fax: 518-457-8247
Deputy Commissioner & Treasurer:
Aida M Brewer 518-474-4250/fax: 518-402-4118
Deputy Commissioner, Criminal Enforcement:
Letizia Tagliaferro . . . . 518-457-9692 or 800-225-5829
Deputy Commissioner, Tax Policy Analysis:
Robert D Plattner 518-457-4337
Deputy Commissioner, Processing & Taxpayer Svcs:
Edward Chaszczewski 518-457-1000
Chief Financial Officer & Budget/Management Analysis:
Eric Mostert 518-485-5080
Director, Public Information:
Geoffrey Gloak 518-457-7377

Temporary & Disability Assistance, Office of
40 N Pearl St
Albany, NY 12243
518-473-1090 or 518-474-9516 Fax: 518-486-6255
e-mail: nyspio@otda.ny.gov
Web site: www.otda.ny.gov

Commissioner:
Samuel D Roberts 518-474-4152/fax: 518-486-6255
Deputy Commissioner, Center for Child Well-Being:
Eileen Stack 518-474-1078
Deputy Commissioner, Center for Specialized Services:
Linda L Glassman 518-486-4151
Director, Budget, Finance & Data Management:
Nancy Maney 518-474-0183
Deputy Commissioner, Operations & Program Support:
Wilma Brown Phillips 518-473-3912
Acting CIO, Information Technology:
Rick Ryan 518-486-1012
Deputy Commissioner, Center for Employment & Economic Supports:
Phyllis Morris 518-474-9222/fax: 518-474-5281
General Counsel:
Krista Rock 518-474-9502
Acting Director, Intergovernmental Affairs Office:
Ryan Richard 518-486-1012
Director, Public Information:
Kristi L. Berner 518-474-9516/fax: 518-486-6935
e-mail: nyspio@otda.ny.gov

Transportation Department
50 Wolf Road
Albany, NY 12232
518-457-5100 or 518-457-6195 Fax: 518-457-5583
Web site: www.dot.ny.gov

Commissioner:
Matthew J Driscoll 518-457-4422
Operations & Asset Management Division:
Roderic Sechrist 518-485-0887
Director, Legal Affairs Division:
David Cherubin 518-457-2411
CFO/Finance Office:
Ron Epstein 518-457-2320
Director, Administrative Services Division:
Vacant 518-457-6300
Acting Director, Policy & Planning Division:
Ron Epstein 518-457-2320
Director, Audit:
John Samaniuk 518-485-8262
Chief Engineer/Engineering Division:
Phillip Eng 518-457-4430
Acting Director, Communications Office:
Jennifer Post 518-457-6400/fax: 518-457-6506

Veterans' Affairs, Division of
2 Empire State Plaza
17th Fl
Albany, NY 12223-1551
518-474-6114 or 888-838-7697 Fax: 518-473-0379
e-mail: dvainfo@veterans.ny.gov
Web site: www.veterans.ny.gov

Acting Director:
William A Kraus 518-474-6114
Executive Deputy Director:
Vacant 518-474-6114
Secretary to the Director:
Mary Quay 518-474-6114
e-mail: m.quay@veterans.ny.gov
Deputy Director, Administration & Budget:
Michelle LaRock 518-474-6114
e-mail: mlarock@veterans.state.ny.us
Deputy Director, Programs, Operations & Training:
Christine Tarnowski 518-474-6784
e-mail: ctarnowski@veterans.state.ny.us
Counsel:
Samuel Spitzberg 518-474-6114
e-mail: sspitzberg@veterans.ny.gov
Assistant Director, Communications:
Casey Lumbra 518-486-5251
e-mail: clumbra@veterans.state.ny.us
Deputy Director, Eastern Region:
Andrew Roberts 718-722-2584
Deputy Director, Western Region:
Vacant 716-847-3414/fax: 716-847-3410

Welfare Inspector General, Office of NYS
Empire State Plaza
Agency Bldg 2
16th Floor
Albany, NY 12223
518-474-1010 or 800-682-4530 Fax: 518-486-3745
e-mail: inspector.general@ig.ny.gov
Web site: www.owig.ny.gov

Offices and agencies generally appear in alphabetical order, except when specific order is requested by listee.

Acting Welfare Inspector General:
Catherine Leahy Scott . . . . 212-635-3150 or 518-474-1010
Chief Investigator:
Joseph Bucci 718-923-4290
Confidential Assistant/Office Manager:
Joy Quiles 718-923-4290/fax: 718-923-4310
e-mail: joy.quiles@owig.ny.gov

Workers' Compensation Board
328 State Street
Schenectady, NY 12305
518-462-8880 or 877-632-4996 Fax: 518-473-1415
e-mail: publicinfo@wcb.ny.gov
Web site: www.wcb.ny.gov

Executive Director:
MaryBeth Woods 518-408-0469
Chair, Board of Commissioners:
Robert E Beloten 518-408-0469/fax: 518-473-1415
Vice Chair:
Ken Munnelly 518-408-0469/fax: 518-473-1415
Secretary to the Board:
Sandra M Olson 518-402-6070
Chief, Security:
Sylvio Mantello 518-402-0172/fax: 518-402-6100
General Counsel:
Vacant 518-486-9564/fax: 518-402-0113
Director, Public Information:
Rachel McEneny 518-408-5592/fax: 518-473-1415
e-mail: publicinfo@wcb.ny.gov
Advocate for Injured Workers:
Edwin Ruff . . . . 800-580-6665 or 518-474-8182
fax: 518-486-7510

Offices and agencies generally appear in alphabetical order, except when specific order is requested by listee.

LEGISLATIVE BRANCH SENATE

Members of the Senate welcome e-mail correspondence from the public. They may reply by e-mail, or by mail when more extensive follow-up is necessary. Please include both an e-mail and mailing address in all correspondence. Biographies of Senate Members appear in a separate section in the back of the book.

STATE SENATE LEADERSHIP

State Capitol
Albany, NY 12247
Web site: www.nysenate.gov

ADMINISTRATION

Francis W Patience 518-455-2051/fax: 518-455-3332
Title: Secretary of the Senate

Kathy Pendergast 518-455-2201/fax: 518-455-6742
Title: Director, Appointments Office

General Information 800-342-9860
Title: Bill Status Hotline

Christopher J Cook 518-455-2246/fax: 518-426-6842
Title: Director, Chamber Operations

Mary Carey 518-455-2245/fax: 518-426-6842
Title: Journal Clerk

Douglas J Breakell 518-455-2521/fax: 518-426-6743
Title: Director, Legislative Services

James Giliberto 518-455-2468/fax: 518-426-6901
Title: Legislative Librarian, Legislative Library

George Federoff 518-455-2338/fax: 518-455-3332
Title: Sergeant-at-Arms

Nicholas Parrella 518-455-7150/fax: 518-426-6827
Title: Director, Student Programs Office

Tracy Starr 518-455-3145/fax: 518-426-6831
Title: District Office Coordinator

Dawn Harrington 518-455-3376/fax: 518-426-6927
Title: Personnel Officer

James Bell 518-455-2313/fax: 518-455-7339
Title: Director, Technology Services

REPUBLICAN CONFERENCE LEADERSHIP

John J Flanagan (R) 518-455-2071
e-mail: flanagan@nysenate.gov
Title: Temporary President of the Senate & Majority Leader

Catharine M Young (R) 518-455-3563
e-mail: cyoung@nysenate.gov
Title: Chair of Senate Finance Committee

John A DeFrancisco (R) 518-455-3511
e-mail: jdefranc@nysenate.gov
Title: Deputy Majority Leader, Legislative Operations

Joseph Griffo (R) 518-455-2015
e-mail: griffo@nysenate.gov
Title: Assistant Senate Majority Whip

James L Seward (R) 518-455-3131
e-mail: seward@nysenate.gov
Title: Chairman, Majority Program Development Committee

Kemp Hannon (R) 518-455-2200
e-mail: hannon@nysenate.gov
Title: Assistant Majority Leader, Operations

Kenneth P LaValle (R) 518-455-3121
e-mail: lavalle@nysenate.gov
Title: Chair, Senate Majority Conference

Hugh T Farley (R) 518-455-2181
e-mail: farley@nysenate.gov
Title: Vice President Pro Tempore

William J Larkin Jr (R) 518-455-2770
e-mail: larkin@nysenate.gov
Title: Assistant Majority Leader for House Operations

Andrew Lanza (R) 518-455-3215
e-mail: lanza@nysenate.gov
Title: Deputy Majority Leader for Government Oversight & Accountability

Michael F Nozzolio (R) 518-455-2366
e-mail: nozzolio@nysenate.gov
Title: Majority Whip of the Senate

Carl L Marcellino (R) 518-455-2390
e-mail: marcelli@nysenate.gov
Title: Vice Chair, Senate Majority Conference

Michael Ranzenhofer (R) 518-455-3161
e-mail: ranz@nysenate.gov
Title: Deputy Majority Leader for Economic Development

Patrick M Gallivan (R) 518-455-3471
e-mail: gallivan@nysenate.gov
Title: Liaison to the Executive Branch

Martin J Golden (R) 518-455-2730
e-mail: golden@nysenate.gov
Title: Secretary of the Senate Majority Conference

Elizabeth O'C Little (R) 518-455-2811
e-mail: little@nysenate.gov
Title: Deputy Majority Whip for the Senate

Joseph Robach (R) 518-455-2909
e-mail: robach@nysenate.gov
Title: Chairman, Majority Steering Committee

Patricia Ritchie (R) 518-455-3438
e-mail: ritchie@nysenate.gov
Title: Deputy Majority Leader for Senate/Assembly Relations

John J Bonancic (R) 518-455-3181
e-mail: bonacic@nysenate.gov
Title: Deputy Majority Leader, State/Federal Relations

REPUBLICAN CONFERENCE STAFF

Diane Burman 518-455-2675/fax: 518-426-6830
Title: Counsel to the Republican Conference

Irene Villacci 518-455-2533/fax: 518-426-6974
Title: Counsel to the Majority Leader

Thomas Dunham 518-455-2381/fax: 518-426-6818
Title: Director of Majority Operations

Joseph Sorbero 518-455-3171/fax: 518-426-6950
Title: Special Advisor to Republican Conference Leader

Offices and agencies generally appear in alphabetical order, except when specific order is requested by listee.

Janet L Reilly 518-455-2589/fax: 518-426-6965
Title: Majority Calendar Clerk

Robert Mujica 518-455-2675/fax: 518-426-6830
Title: Secretary to the Finance Committee & Senior Advisor for Policy

Kelly Cummings 518-455-2264/fax: 518-455-2260
Title: Director, Republican Conference

Eileen Miller 518-455-3545/fax: 518-426-6917
Title: Director, Media Services

Douglas Breakell 518-455-2550/fax: 518-426-6743
Title: Director, Legislative Services

INDEPENDENT DEMOCRATIC CONFERENCE LEADERSHIP

Jeffrey D. Klein (D-R-W-I) 518-455-3595
e-mail: jdklein@nysenate.gov
Title: Independent Democratic Conference Leader

David J. Valesky (D-W-I) 518-455-2838
e-mail: valesky@nysenate.gov
Title: Independent Democratic Conference Leader for Legislative Operations

David Carlucci (D-W-I) 518-455-2991
e-mail: carlucci@nysenate.gov
Title: Independent Democratic Conference Whip

Diane J. Savino (D-W-I) 518-455-2437
e-mail: savino@nysenate.gov
Title: Independent Democratic Conference Liason to the Executive Branch

Tony Avella (D-W-I) 518-455-2210
e-mail: savino@nysenate.gov
Title: Assistant Conference Leader, Policy & Administration of Independent Democratic Conference

DEMOCRATIC CONFERENCE LEADERSHIP

Andrea Stewart-Cousins (D) 518-455-2585
e-mail: scousins@nysenate.gov
Title: Democratic Leader

Michael Gianaris (D) 518-455-3486
e-mail: gianaris@nysenate.gov
Title: Deputy Democratic Leader

Toby Ann Stavisky (D) 518-455-3461
e-mail: stavisky@nysenate.gov
Title: Assistant Democratic Leader for Conference Operations

Martin M Dilan (D) 518-455-2177
e-mail: dilan@nysenate.gov
Title: Assistant Democratic Leader for Policy & Administration

Jose M. Serrano (D) 518-455-2795
e-mail: serrano@nysenate.gov
Title: Chair of Democratic Conference

Ruth Hassell-Thompson (D) 518-455-2061
e-mail: hasselt@nysenate.gov
Title: Vice Chair of Democratic Conference

Kevin S. Parker (D) 518-455-2580
e-mail: parker@nysenate.gov
Title: Assistant Democratic Leader, Intergovernmental Affairs

Jose Peralta (D) 518-455-2529
e-mail: jperalta@nysenate.gov
Title: Democratic Conference Whip

Timothy Kennedy (D) 518-455-2426
e-mail: kennedy@nysenate.gov
Title: Assistant Democratic Conference Whip

Bill Perkins (D) 518-455-2441
e-mail: perkins@nysenate.gov
Title: Deputy Democratic Conference Whip

Liz Krueger (D) 518-455-2297
e-mail: lkrueger@nysenate.gov
Title: Ranking Democratic Member of the Senate Finance Committee

Velmanette Montgomery (D) 518-455-3451
e-mail: montgome@nysenate.gov
Title: Secretary of the Senate Democratic Conference

Neil D. Breslin (D) 518-455-2225
e-mail: breslin@nysenate.gov
Title: Assistant Democratic Leader, Floor Operations

Daniel Squadron (D) 518-455-2625
e-mail: squadron@nysenate.gov
Title: Deputy Democratic Conference Floor Leader

Gustavo Rivera (D) 518-455-3395
e-mail: grivera@nysenate.gov
Title: Chair, Democratic Program Development

DEMOCRATIC CONFERENCE STAFF

John Tomlin 518-455-2800
Title: Chief of Staff to the Democratic Leader

Celeste Knight 518-455-3401/fax: 518-455-2816
Title: Special Assistant

Keith St John 518-455-2711/fax: 518-426-6955
Title: Deputy Counsel

Mary K Berger 518-455-2636/fax: 518-455-2816
Title: Director, Minority Operations

Joseph Pennisi 518-455-2217/fax: 518-426-6839
Title: Comptroller, Senate Minority

Tracey Pierce-Smith 518-455-2501/fax: 518-426-6930
Title: Director, Minority Conference Services

Vacant 518-455-2415/fax: 518-426-6933
Title: Press Secretary to the Minority Leader

STATE SENATE ROSTER

Multiple party abbreviations following the names of legislators indicate that those legislators ran as the Senate candidate for each identified party. Source: NYS Board of Elections. Party abbreviations: Conservative (C), Democrat (D), Green (G), Independent (I), Liberal (L), Republican (R), Working Families (WF)

Joseph P Addabbo Jr (D) 518-455-2322/fax: 518-426-6875
District: 15 *Room:* 613 LOB *e-mail:* addabbo@nysenate.gov
Committees: Aging; Civil Service & Pensions; Education; Labor; Racing, Gaming & Wagering (Ranking Member); Veterans, Homeland Security & Military Affairs (Ranking Member)
Senior Staff: Patricia McCabe

Frederick J Akshar, II (R) 518-455-2677/fax: 518-426-6720
District: 52 *Room:* 805 LOB *e-mail:* akshar@nysenate.gov
Committees: Banks; Cities; Codes; Elections (Chair); Labor; Consumer Protection; Crime

George Amedore, Jr (R) 518-455-2350/fax: 518-426-6751
District: 46 *Room:* 802 LOB *e-mail:* amedore@nysenate.gov
Committees: Alcoholism & Drug Abuse (Chair); banks; Consumer Protection; Elections; Judiciary; Social Services; Veterans' Affairs
Senior Staff: Douglas Breakell

Tony Avella (D-WF) 518-455-2210/fax: 518-426-6736
District: 11 *Room:* 902 LOB *e-mail:* avella@nysenate.gov
Title: Assistant Conference Leader, Policy & Administration of Independent Democratic Conference
Committees: Banks; Cultural Affairs, Tourism, Parks & Recreation;, Education; Elections; Environmental Conservation; Ethics (Chair); Housing, Construction & Community Development; Insurance; Judiciary; Transportation
Senior Staff: Seth Urbinder

John J Bonacic (R). 518-455-3181/fax: 518-426-6948
District: 42 *Room:* 509 LOB *e-mail:* bonacic@nysenate.gov
Title: Deputy Majority Leader, State/Federal Relations
Committees: Alcoholism & Drug Abuse; Banks; Children & Families; Finance; Housing, Construction & Community Dvlpmnt; Judiciary (Chair); Racing, Gaming & Wagering (Chair); Rules; Cultural Affrs Tourism, Parks & Recreation
Senior Staff: Andrew Winchell

Philip M. Boyle (R) 518-455-3411/fax: 518-426-6973
District: 4 *Room:* 814 LOB *e-mail:* pboyle@nysenate.gov
Committees: Codes; Consumer Protection; Commerce, Economic Development & Small Business (Chair); Housing, Construction & Community Development; Local Government; Racing, Gaming & Wagering
Senior Staff: Tom Connolly

Neil D Breslin (D). 518-455-2225/fax: 518-426-6807
District: 44 *Room:* 414 CAP *e-mail:* breslin@nysenate.gov
Title: Assistant Democratic Leader, Floor Operations
Committees: Banks; Education; Finance; Higher Education; Insurance (Ranking Member); Judiciary; Rules
Senior Staff: Maureen Cetrino

David Carlucci (D-W-I) 518-455-2991/fax: 518-426-6737
District: 38 *Room:* 815 LOB *e-mail:* carlucci@nysenate.gov
Title: Independent Democratic Conference Whip
Committees: Alchlsm & Drg Abuse; Enrgy & Telecomm.; Infrstrctre & Cptl Invstmnt; Insrnce; Invstgtns & Gov't Ops., Mntl Hlth & Dvlpmntl Dsblts; Social Services (Chair); Racing, Gaming & Wgring; Rules; Vtrn's Affrs; Hmlnd Scrty & Mltry Affrs
Senior Staff: Jay Martin

Leroy Comrie (D). 518-455-2701/fax: 518-455-2816
District: 14 *Room:* 617 LOB *e-mail:* comrie@nysenate.gov
Committees: Agriculture; Civil Service & Pensions; Consumer Protection; Elections; Infrastructure & Capital Investments; Judiciary; Racing & Wagering; Veterans, Homeland Security & Military Affairs
Senior Staff: Derrick Davis

Thomas D Croci (R) 518-455-3570/fax: 518-426-6745
District: 3 *Room:* 306 LOB *e-mail:* croci@nysenate.gov
Committees: Alcoholism & Drug Abuse; Civil Service & Pensions; Energy & Telecommunications; Higher Education; Infrastructure & Capital Investments; Veterans, Homeland Security & Military Affairs (Chair)
Senior Staff: Christopher Molluso

John A DeFrancisco (R) 518-455-3511/fax: 518-426-6952
District: 50 *Room:* 416 CAP *e-mail:* jdefranc@nysenate.gov
Title: Deputy Majority Leader, Legislative Operations
Committees: Banks; Cities; Codes; Crime Victims, Crime & Correction; Finance (Chair); Judiciary; Labor
Senior Staff: Dorothy Pohlid

Ruben Diaz Sr (D) 518-455-2511/fax: 518-426-6945
District: 32 *Room:* 606 LOB *e-mail:* diaz@nysenate.gov
Committees: Aging (Ranking Member); Banks; Finance; Investigations & Government Operations; Judiciary; Transportation
Senior Staff: Helen Jacome

Martin M Dilan (D) 518-455-2177/fax: 518-426-6947
District: 18 *Room:* 711B LOB *e-mail:* dilan@nysenate.gov
Title: Asst Democratic Leader, Policy & Administration
Committees: Civil Service & Pensions; Elections; Energy & Telecommunications; Finance; Infrastructure & Capital Investments; Judiciary; Labor; Rules; Transportation (Ranking Member)
Senior Staff: Heath Heimroth

Adriano Espaillat (D) 518-455-2041/fax: 518-426-6847
District: 31 *Room:* 513 LOB *e-mail:* espailla@nysenate.gov
Committees: Codes; Finance; Higher Education; Housing, Construction & Community Development (Ranking Member); Insurance; Judiciary; Rules
Senior Staff: Aneiry Batista

Hugh T Farley (R-C-I) 518-455-2181/fax: 518-455-2271
District: 49 *Room:* 711 LOB *e-mail:* farley@nysenate.gov
Title: Vice President Pro Tempore
Committees: Banks (Vice Chair); Education; Ethics; Finance; Health; Rules; Social Services
Senior Staff: Patricia Pietrusza

Simcha Felder (D) 518-455-2754/fax: 518-426-6931
District: 17 *Room:* 944 LOB *e-mail:* felder@nysenate.gov
Committees: Aging; Children & Families (Chair); Commerce, Economic Development & Small Business; Health; Infrastructure & Capital Investments; Mental Health & Developmental Disabilities
Senior Staff: Cirel Neumann

John J Flanagan (R-I-C). 518-455-2071/fax: 518-426-6904
District: 2 *Room:* 330 CAP *e-mail:* flanagan@nysenate.gov
Title: Temporary President of the Senate & Majority Leader
Committees: Rules (Chair)
Senior Staff: Raymond Bennardo

Rich Funke (R-C-I) 518-455-2215/fax: 518-426-6745
District: 55 *Room:* 905 LOB *e-mail:* funke@nysenate.gov
Committees: Aging; Agriculture; Cities; Commerce, Economic Development & Small Business; Consumer Protection; Elections (Chair); Environmental Conservation; Higher Education
Senior Staff: Matt Nelligan

Patrick M. Gallivan (R) 518-455-3471/fax: 518-426-6949
District: 59 *Room:* 947 LOB *e-mail:* gallivan@nysenate.gov
Title: Liaison to the Executive Branch
Committees: Agriculture; Codes; Commerce, Econ Development & Small Business; Crime Victims, Crime & Correction (Chair); Elections; Finance; Higher Education; Housing Construction & Community Development; Infrastructure & Capital Investment; Labor; Transportation
Senior Staff: A.J. Baynes

Michael N Gianaris (D). 518-455-3486/fax: 518-426-6929
District: 12 *Room:* 413 CAP *e-mail:* gianaris@nysenate.gov
Title: Deputy Democratic Leader
Committees: Ethics; Finance
Senior Staff: Michael Sais

Martin J. Golden (R-C) 518-455-2730/fax: 518-426-6910
District: 22 *Room:* 409 LOB *e-mail:* golden@nysenate.gov
Title: Secretary of the Senate Majority Conference
Committees: Aging; Civil Service & Pensions (Chair); Banks; Codes; Finance; Health; Insurance; Investigations & Government Operations; Veterans, Homeland Security & Military Affairs
Senior Staff: Gerard Kassar

Joseph A Griffo (R-C)............... 518-455-3334/fax: 518-426-6921
District: 47 *Room:* 612 LOB *e-mail:* griffo@nysenate.gov
Title: Assistant Senate Majority Whip
Committees: Codes; Cmmrce, Ecnmc Dvlpmnt & Smll Bsness; Crime Vctms,Crime& Crrctn; Cltrl Affrs, Tourism, Prks & Rec.; Enrgy & Telecomm (Chair); Finance; Hgher Ed; Rcing, Gming & Wgrnig; Vtrns', Hmlnd Scrty & Mltry Affrs
Senior Staff: Dwight Evans

Jesse Hamilton (D).................. 518-455-2431/fax: 518-426-6856
District: 20 *Room:* 608 LOB *e-mail:* hamilton@nysenate.gov
Committees: Agriculture; Banks; Codes; Commerce, Economic Development & Small Business; Education; Energy & Telecommunications; Mental Health & Developmental Disabilities
Senior Staff: Jarvis Houston

Kemp Hannon (R-I-C)............... 518-455-2200/fax: 518-426-6954
District: 6 *Room:* 420 CAP *e-mail:* hannon@nysenate.gov
Title: Assistant Majority Leader, Operations
Committees: Finance; Health (Chair); Judiciary; Labor; Mental Health & Developmental Disabilities; Rules
Senior Staff: Phil Hecken

Ruth Hassell-Thompson (D-WF)..... 518-455-2061/fax: 518-426-6998
District: 36 *Room:* 707 LOB *e-mail:* hasselt@nysenate.gov
Title: Vice Chair, Democratic Conference
Committees: Alcoholism & Drug Abuse; Commerce, Economic Development & Small Business; Crime Victims, Crime & Correction (Ranking Member); Finance; Health; Rules
Senior Staff: Gerard Savage

Brad Hoylman (D).................... 518-455-2451/fax: 518-426-6846
District: 27 *Room:* 413 LOB *e-mail:* hoylman@nysenate.gov
Committees: Aging; Crime Victim, Crime & Correction; Environmental Conservation (Ranking Member); Health; Investigations & Government Operations (Ranking Member); Judiciary; Local Governments; Cultural Affairs; Tourism, Parks & Recreation
Senior Staff: Peter Ajemian

Todd Kaminsky (D).................. 518-455-3401/fax: 518-426-6914
District: 9 *Room:* 311 LOB *e-mail:* kaminsky@nysenate.gov
Committees: Local Government (RM); Alcoholism & Drug Abuse; Codes; Environmental Conservation; Finance; Health; Transportation; Veterans, Homeland Security & Military Affairs

Timothy Kennedy (D).............. 518-455-2426/fax: 518-426-6851
District: 63 *Room:* 506 LOB *e-mail:* kennedy@nysenate.gov
Title: Assistant Democratic Conference Whip
Committees: Banks; Commerce, Economic Development & Small Business (Ranking Member); Cultural Affairs, Tourism, Parks & Recreation; Energy & Telecommunications; Finance; Insurance; Infrastructure & Capital Investment; Transportation
Senior Staff: Lauren Rivett

Jeffrey D Klein (D) 518-455-3595/fax: 518-426-6887
District: 34 *Room:* 913 LOB *e-mail:* jdklein@nysenate.gov
Title: Independent Democratic Conference Leader
Committees:
Senior Staff: John Emrick

Liz Krueger (D-WF) 518-455-2297/fax: 518-426-6874
District: 28 *Room:* 808 LOB *e-mail:* lkrueger@nysenate.gov
Committees: Codes; Elections; Finance (Ranking Member); Higher Education; Housing, Construction & Community Development; Mental Health & Developmental Disabilities; Rules
Senior Staff: Brad Usher

Kenneth P LaValle (R-I-C)........... 518-455-3121/fax: 518-426-6826
District: 1 *Room:* 806 LOB *e-mail:* lavalle@nysenate.gov
Title: Chair, Senate Majority Conference
Committees: Aging; Education; Environmental Conservation; Finance; Higher Education (Chair); Insurance; Judiciary; Rules; Social Services
Senior Staff: Joann Scalia

Andrew J Lanza (R-I)............... 518-455-3215/fax: 518-426-6852
District: 24 *Room:* 708 LOB *e-mail:* lanza@nysenate.gov
Title: Deputy Majority Leader for Government Oversight & Accountability
Committees: Cities (Chair); Civil Service & Pensions; Codes; Education; Ethics; Finance; Insurance; Judiciary
Senior Staff: John Turoski

William J Larkin Jr (R-C)........... 518-455-2770/fax: 518-426-6923
District: 39 *Room:* 502 CAP *e-mail:* larkin@nysenate.gov
Title: Assistant Majority Leader for House Operations
Committees: Corporations, Authorities & Commissions; Finance; Health; Insurance; Rules; Transportation; Veterans, Homeland Security & Military Affairs
Senior Staff: Jennifer Downs

George S. Latimer (D)............... 518-455-2031/fax: 518-455-6860
District: 37 *Room:* 615 LOB *e-mail:* latimer@nysenate.gov
Committees: Banks; Consumer Protection; Education (Ranking Member); Environmental Conservation; Insurance; Local Government; Racing, Gaming & Wagering
Senior Staff: Victor Mallison

Elizabeth O'C Little (R-I-C)........ 518-455-2811/fax: 518-426-6873
District: 45 *Room:* 310 LOB *e-mail:* little@nysenate.gov
Title: Deputy Majority Whip for the Senate
Committees: Energy & Telecommunications; Consumer Protection; Crime Victims, Crime & Correction; Cultural Affairs, Tourism, Parks & Recreation (Chair); Education; Environmental Conservation; Health; Finance; Rules
Senior Staff: Daniel MacEntee

Carl L Marcellino (R)............... 518-455-2390/fax: 518-426-6975
District: 5 *Room:* 811 LOB *e-mail:* marcelli@nysenate.gov
Title: Vice Chair, Senate Majority Conference
Committees: Investigations & Government Operations (Chair); Banks; Cultural Affairs, Tourism, Parks & Recreation; Education; Environmental Conservation; Finance; Labor; Rules; Infrastructure & Capital Investment (Chair); Transportation (Vice Chair)
Senior Staff: Kirk Ives

Kathleen A. Marchione (R-C)........ 518-455-2381/fax: 518-426-6985
District: 43 *Room:* 918 LOB *e-mail:* marchione@nysenate.gov
Committees: Consumer Protection; Cultural Affairs; Tourism, Parks & Recreation; Elections; Labor; Local Government (Chair); Racing, Gaming & Wagering; Aging; Banks
Senior Staff: Joshua Fitzpatrick

Jack Martins (R) 518-455-3265/fax: 518-426-6739
District: 7 *Room:* 915 LOB *e-mail:* martins@nysenate.gov
Committees: Banks; Civil Service & Pensions; Corporations, Authorities & Commissions; Finance; Health; Insurance; Labor (Chair); Social Services
Senior Staff: Paul Ehrlich

Velmanette Montgomery (D)......... 518-455-3451/fax: 518-426-6854
District: 25 *Room:* 903 LOB *e-mail:* montgome@nysenate.gov
Title: Secretary of the Senate Democratic Conference
Committees: Agriculture; Children & Families (Ranking Member); Crime Victims, Crime & Correction; Education; Finance; Health; Rules
Senior Staff: Susan Leung

Terrence Murphy (R) 518-455-3111/fax: 518-426-6977
District: 40 *Room:* 817 LOB *e-mail:* murphy@nysenate.gov
Committees: Banks; Ethics; Health; Investigations & Government Operations; Labor; Local Governments; Mental Health & Developmental Disabilities
Senior Staff: Matthew Slater

Michael F Nozzolio (R-C)............ 518-455-2366/fax: 518-426-6953
District: 54 *Room:* 503 CAP *e-mail:* nozzolio@nysenate.gov
Title: Majority Whip of the Senate
Committees: Codes (Chair); Elections; Crime Victims, Crime & Correction; Finance; Housing, Construction & Community Development; Investigations

& Government Operations; Judiciary; Racing, Gaming & Wagering; Rules; Transportation
Senior Staff: Joan Grela

Thomas F O'Mara (R) 518-455-2091/fax: 518-426-6976
District: 58 *Room:* 848 LOB *e-mail:* omara@nysenate.gov
Committees: Agriculture; Banks; Codes; Energy & Telecommunications; Environmental Conservation (Chair); Finance; Insurance; Investigations & Government Operations; Judiciary; Transportation
Senior Staff: Pierson Ellis

Robert G Ortt (R) 518-455-2024/fax: 518-426-6987
District: 62 *Room:* 815 LOB *e-mail:* ortt@nysenate.gov
Committees: Cities; Civil Service & Pensions; Corporations, Authorities & Commissions; Environmental Conservation; Local Government; Mental Health & Developmental Disabilities (Chair); Veterans, Homeland Security & Military Affairs
Senior Staff: Scott Kiedrowski

Marc Panepinto (D).................518-455-2760/fax: 518-426-6760
District: 60 *Room:* 302 LOB *e-mail:* panepinto@nysenate.gov
Committees: Agriculture (Ranking Member); Codes; Health; Housing, Construction & Community Development; Insurance; Local Government (Ranking Member); Transportation; Veterans, Homeland Security & Military Affairs
Senior Staff: Danny Corum

Kevin S Parker (D-WF) 518-455-2580/fax: 518-426-6843
District: 21 *Room:* 604 LOB *e-mail:* parker@nysenate.gov
Title: Assistant Democratic Leader, Intergovernmental Affairs
Committees: Alcoholism & Drug Abuse (Ranking Member); Banks; Cultural Affairs, Tourism, Parks & Recreation; Energy & Telecommunications (Ranking Member); Finance; Higher Education; Insurance; Rules
Senior Staff: Vaughn Mayers

Jose Peralta (D) 518-455-2529/fax: 518-455-6909
District: 13 *Room:* 415 LOB *e-mail:* jperalta@nysenate.gov
Title: Democratic Conference Whip
Committees: Cities, Consumer Protection; Crime Victims, Crime & Correction; Education; Finance; Higher Education; Labor (Ranking Member)
Senior Staff: Nancy Conde

Bill Perkins (D-WF)................518-455-2441/fax: 518-426-6809
District: 30 *Room:* 517 LOB *e-mail:* perkins@nysenate.gov
Title: Deputy Democratic Conference Whip
Committees: Crime Victims, Crime & Correction; Codes; Corporations, Authorities & Commissions (Ranking Member); Finance; Judiciary; Labor; Rules; Transportation
Senior Staff: Cordell Cleare

Roxanne Persaud (D) 518-455-2788
District: 19 *Room:* 504 LOB *e-mail:* persaud@nysenate.gov
Committees: Children & Families; Cities; Civil Service & Pensions; Health; Commerce, Economic Development & Small Business; Cult Affrs, Tourism, Parks & Recreation; Social Services
Senior Staff: Lateef Turral

Michael H Ranzenhofer (R-I-C)......518-455-3161/fax: 518-426-6963
District: 61 *Room:* 609 LOB *e-mail:* ranz@nysenate.gov
Title: Deputy Majority Leader, Economic Development
Committees: Agriculture; Corporations, Authorities & Commissions (Chair); Education; Finance; Judiciary; Racing, Gaming & Wagering; Transportation
Senior Staff: Kathy Donner

Patricia Ritchie (R) 518-455-3438/fax: 518-426-6740
District: 48 *Room:* 412 LOB *e-mail:* ritchie@nysenate.gov
Title: Deputy Majority Leader for Senate/Assembly Relations
Committees: Agriculture (Chair); Alcoholism & Drug Abuse; Civil Service & Pensions; Crime Victims, Crime & Corrections; Cultural Affairs, Tourism, Parks & Recreation; Energy & Telecommunications; Finance; Higher Education; Local Government; Transportation
Senior Staff: Sarah Compo

J Gustavo Rivera (D)...............518-455-3395/fax: 518-426-6858
District: 33 *Room:* 408 LOB *e-mail:* grivera@nysenate.gov
Title: Chair of Democratic Conference Program Development
Committees: Crime Victims, Crime & Corrections; Ethics; Finance; Health (Ranking Member); Higher Education; Labor; Mental Health & Developmental Disabilities
Senior Staff: Katrina Asante

Joseph E Robach (R-I-C)............518-455-2909/fax: 518-426-6938
District: 56 *Room:* 803 LOB *e-mail:* robach@nysenate.gov
Title: Chairman, Majority Steering Committee
Committees: Commerce, Economic Development & Small Business; Consumer Protection; Education; Finance; Higher Education; Infrastructure & Capital Investment; Labor; Transportation (Chair)
Senior Staff: Kate Munzinger

James Sanders (D).................518-455-3531/fax: 518-426-6859
District: 10 *Room:* 508 LOB *e-mail:* sanders@nysenate.gov
Committees: Banks; Civil Service & Pensions (RM); Commerce, Economic Development & Small Business; Cultural Affairs, Tourism, Parks & Recreation; Insurance; Labor; Racing, Gaming & Wagering; Veterans, Homeland Security & Military Affairs
Senior Staff: Clyde Vaneo

Diane J Savino (D).................518-455-2437/fax: 518-426-6943
District: 23 *Room:* 315 LOB *e-mail:* savino@nysenate.gov
Title: Independent Democratic Conference Liaison to the Executive Branch
Committees: Banks (Chair); Children & Families; Cities; Codes; Civil Service & Pensions; Consumer Protection; Crime Victims, Crime & Correction; Finance; Judiciary; Labor
Senior Staff: Robert Cataldo

Sue Serino (R)......................518-455-2945/fax: 518-426-6770
District: 41 *Room:* 812 LOB *e-mail:* serino@nysenate.gov
Committees: Aging (Chair; Children & Families; Cultural Affairs, Tourism, Parks & Recreation; Education; Higher Education; Judiciary; Mental Health & Developmental Disabilities
Senior Staff: Caroline Chauvin

Jose M Serrano (D) 518-455-2795/fax: 518-426-6886
District: 29 *Room:* 406 LOB *e-mail:* serrano@nysenate.gov
Title: Chair of Democratic Conference
Committees: Aging; Agriculture; Children & Families; Consumer Protection; Cultural Affairs, Tourism, Parks & Recreation (Ranking Member); Environmental Conservation; Mental Health & Developmental Disabilities; Veterans, Homeland Security & Military Affairs
Senior Staff: Gregory Meyer, Esq.

James L Seward (R-I-C)............518-455-3131/fax: 518-455-3123
District: 51 *Room:* 430 CAP *e-mail:* seward@nysenate.gov
Title: Chairman, Majority Program Development Committee
Committees: Agriculture; Education; Finance; Health; Higher Education; Insurance (Chair); Mental Health & Developmental Disabilities; Rules
Senior Staff: Duncan S Davie

Daniel Squadron (D-WF)............518-455-2625/fax: 518-426-6956
District: 26 *Room:* 515 LOB *e-mail:* squadron@nysenate.gov
Title: Deputy Democratic Conference Floor Leader
Committees: Cities; Codes (Ranking Member); Corporations, Authorities & Commissions; Finance; Investigations & Government Operations; Social Services; Transportation
Senior Staff: Adrian Gonzalez

Toby Ann Stavisky (D-WF)..........518-455-3461/fax: 518-426-6857
District: 16 *Room:* 706 LOB *e-mail:* stavisky@nysenate.gov
Title: Assistant Democratic Leader for Conference Operations
Committees: Education; Finance; Health; Higher Education (Ranking Member); Judiciary; Transportation
Senior Staff: Michael Favilla

Offices and agencies generally appear in alphabetical order, except when specific order is requested by listee.

Andrea Stewart-Cousins (D) 518-455-2585/fax: 518-426-6811
District: 35 *Room:* 907 LOB *e-mail:* scousins@nysenate.gov
Title: Democratic Leader
Committees: Rules (Ranking Member)
Senior Staff: Jeffery Pearlman

David J Valesky (D) 518-455-2838/fax: 518-426-6885
District: 53 *Room:* 512 LOB *e-mail:* valesky@nysenate.gov
Title: Independent Democratic Conference Leader, Legislative Operations
Committees: Aging; Agriculture; Commerce, Economic Development & Small Business; Education; Health; Higher Education; Finance; Local Government; Rules; Transportation
Senior Staff: Jessica DeCerce

Michael Venditto (R) 518-455-3341/fax: 518-426-6823
District: 8 *Room:* 946 LOB *e-mail:* venditto@nysenate.gov
Committees: Consumer Protection (Chair); Crime Victims, Crime & Correction; Insurance; Judiciary; Labor;
Senior Staff: John Banville

Catharine M Young (R-C-I) 518-455-3563/fax: 518-426-6905
District: 57 *Room:* 428 CAP *e-mail:* cyoung@nysenate.gov
Title: Chair of Senate Finance Committee
Committees: Agriculture; Children & Families; Environmental Conservation; Finance; Health; Housing, Construction & Community Development (Chair); Insurance; Rules; Transportation
Senior Staff: Jessica Jeune

STATE SENATE STANDING COMMITTEES

Aging
Chair:
Sue Serino (R). 518-455-2945
Ranking Minority Member:
Ruben Diaz Sr (D) 518-455-2511

Committee Staff
Committee Director:
Caroline Chauvin 518-455-2945
Republican Assistant Counsel:
Barbara McRedmond 518-455-2484

Membership

Majority
Kathleen A. Marchione
Martin J Golden
Kenneth P LaValle
Rich Funke

Minority
Simcha Felder
Brad Hoylman
Joseph P Addabbo Jr
Jose Serrano
David Valesky

Agriculture
Chair:
Patricia Ritchie (R). 518-455-3438
Ranking Minority Member:
Marc Panepinto (D) 518-455-2760

Committee Staff
Committee Director:
Todd Kusnierz. 518-455-3438

Key Senate Staff Assignments
Republican Assistant Counsel:
Paul Midey 518-455-2599

Membership

Majority
Patrick Gallivan
Thomas O'Mara
Michael Ranzenhofer
Rich Funke
James L Seward
Catharine Young

Minority
Jose Serrano
David Valesky
Jesse Hamilton
Leroy Comrie
Velmanette Montgomery

Alcoholism & Drug Abuse
Chair:
George Amedore Jr (R). 518-455-2350
Ranking Minority Member:
Kevin Parker (D). 518-455-2580

Membership

Majority
Thomas Croci
Patricia Ritchie
John J Bonacic

Minority
David Carlucci
Todd Kaminsky

Banks
Chair:
Diane J Savino (D) 518-455-2437
Ranking Minority Member:
Jesse Hamilton (D) 518-455-2431

Committee Staff

Key Senate Staff Assignments
Republican Senior Counsel:
Robert Farley 518-455-3127
Democratic Associate Counsel:
Richard Jacobson

Membership

Majority
Kathleen Marchione
George A Amedore Jr
Hugh T Farley
Jack Martins
John J Bonacic
Frederick J Akshar, II
Martin Golden
Carl L Marcellino
Thomas O'Mara
Terrence Murphy

Minority
George Latimer
Kevin S. Parker
James Sanders, Jr.
Tony Avella
Neil D Breslin
Ruben Diaz Sr
Timothy M Kennedy

Children & Families
Chair:
Tony Avella (D) 518-455-2210
Ranking Minority Member:
Velmanette Montgomery (D) .518-455-3451

Membership

Majority
John J. Bonacic
Catharine M Young
Sue Serino

Minority
Diane Savino
Roxanne Persaud

Cities
Chair:
Simcha Felder (D). 518-455-2754
Ranking Minority Member:
Daniel Squadron (D). 518-455-2625

Committee Staff
Clerk:
Nancy Probst. 518-455-3215

Offices and agencies generally appear in alphabetical order, except when specific order is requested by listee.

Key Senate Staff Assignments
Republican Assistant Counsel:
Skip Piscitelli 518-455-2595

Membership

Majority
Frederick J Akshar, II
Robert G Ortt
Rich Funke

Minority
Jose Peralta
Roxanne Persaud
Diane J Savino

Civil Service & Pensions
Chair:
Martin J Golden (R) 518-455-2730
Ranking Minority Member:
James Sanders, Jr. (D). 518-455-3531

Committee Staff
Clerk:
Meg Brown 518-455-2730

Key Senate Staff Assignments
Republican Senior Counsel:
Lisa Harris 518-455-2751

Membership

Majority
Patricia Ritchie
Andrew Lanza
Thomas Croci
Robert G Ortt
Jack Martins

Minority
Joseph Addabbo Jr.
Leroy Comrie
James Sanders, Jr.
Roxanne Persaud
Diane J Savino

Codes
Chair:
Michael F. Nozzolio (R) 518-455-2366
Ranking Minority Member:
Daniel L. Squadron (D) 518-455-2625

Committee Staff
Clerk:
Meg Fitzgerald 518-455-2366

Key Senate Staff Assignments
Republican Senior Counsel:
NancyLynn Thiel 518-455-2576
Democratic Associate Counsel:
Alejandra Paulino 518-455-2628

Membership

Majority
Philip Boyle
Michael Venditto
Martin Golden
Thomas O'Mara
Frederick J Akshar, II
Patrick Gallivan
Joseph A Griffo

Minority
Diane J Savino
Liz Krueger
Bill Perkins
Jesse Hamilton
Adriano Espaillat
Todd Kaminsky

Commerce, Economic Development & Small Business
Chair:
Philip Boyle (R) 518-455-3411
Ranking Minority Member:
Timothy Kennedy (D). 518-455-2426

Committee Staff
Clerk:
Deanna Schneider 518-455-3411

Key Senate Staff Assignments
Republican Senior Counsel:
Ryan McAllister 518-455-2483
Democratic Budget Analyst:
Paul Alexander 518-455-2695

Membership

Majority
Patrick M. Gallivan
Rich Funke
Joseph A Griffo
Joseph E Robach

Minority
Roxanne Persaud
David J Valesky
James Sanders, Jr.
Simcha Felder
Ruth Hassell-Thompson

Consumer Protection
Chair:
Michael Venditto (R) 518-455-3341
Ranking Minority Member:
Leroy Comrie (D) 518-455-2701

Committee Staff

Key Senate Staff Assignments
Republican Senior Counsel:
Lisa Harris 518-455-2751
Democratic Associate Counsel:
Richard Jacobson 518-455-2711

Membership

Majority
Frederick J Akshar, II
Rich Funke
George Amedore Jr
Philip Boyle
Joseph E Robach

Minority
Diane Savino
Jose Peralta
George Latimer
Jose M. Serrano

Corporations, Authorities & Commissions
Chair:
Michael Ranzenhofer (R) 518-455-3161
Ranking Minority Member:
Bill Perkins (D). 518-455-2441

Committee Staff
Committee Director:
Jessica Pollack 518-455-3161

Key Senate Staff Assignments
Repulican Assistant Counsel:
James Curran 518-455-2486
Democratic Associate Counsel:
Dan Ranellone 518-455-2852

Membership

Majority
Robert G Ortt
George A Amedore, Jr
Jack Martins
William L. Larkin, Jr.

Minority
Daniel L. Squadron

Crime Victims, Crime & Correction
Chair:
Patrick M. Gallivan (R) 518-455-3471

Offices and agencies generally appear in alphabetical order, except when specific order is requested by listee.

Ranking Minority Member:
Ruth Hassell-Thompson (D)............................518-455-2061

Committee Staff
Clerk:
Zach Primeau..518-455-3471

Key Senate Staff Assignments
Republican Assistant Counsel:
Kenneth Connolly......................................518-455-2342

Membership

Majority
Elizabeth O'C. Little
Frederick J Akshar, II
Joseph Griffo
Patricia Ritchie
Michael Venditto
Michael Nozzolio

Minority
Velmanette Montgomery
Jose Peralta
J Gustavo Rivera
Bill Perkins
Diane J Savino

Cultural Affairs, Tourism, Parks & Recreation
Chair:
Rich Funke (R)..518-455-2215
Ranking Minority Member:
Jose Serrano (D)......................................518-455-2795

Committee Staff
Clerk:
Mary Pat McDonald.....................................518-455-2811

Key Senate Staff Assignments
Republican Assistant Counsel:
Skip Piscitelli.......................................518-455-2595
Policy Analyst:
Andrew Postiglione....................................518-455-2977

Membership

Majority
Kathleen Marchione
Carl L. Marcellino
Patricia Ritchie
Elizabeth O'C Little
Sue Serino
Joseph A. Griffo

Minority
Tony Avella
Brad Hoylman
Timothy Kennedy
James Sanders Jr
Roxanne Persaud

Education
Chair:
Carl L Marcellino (R).................................518-455-2390
Ranking Minority Member:
George Latimer (D)....................................518-455-2031

Committee Staff
Committee Clerk:
Robin Mueller...518-455-2631

Key Senate Staff Assignments
Republican Assistant Counsel:
James Curran..518-455-2486
Director, Budget Studies:
Felix Muniz...518-455-2641

Membership

Majority
Elizabeth O'C. Little
Kenneth P. LaValle
Andrew Lanza
Sue Serino
James L Seward
Hugh T Farley
Thomas Croci
Michael H Ranzenhofer
Joseph E Robach

Minority
Tony Avella
Velmanette Montgomery
Jose Peralta
Toby Ann Stavisky
Joseph P Addabbo Jr
Neil D Breslin
Jesse Hamilton
David Valesky

Elections
Chair:
Frederick J Akshar, II (R)............................518-455-2677
Ranking Minority Member:
Leroy Comrie (D)......................................518-455-2701

Committee Staff
Clerk:
Lisa Sams...518-455-2215

Key Senate Staff Assignments
Republican Senior Counsel:
John Ciampoli...518-455-2565
Democratic Senior Counsel:
Christopher Higgins...................................518-455-3447

Membership

Majority
George Amedore Jr
Patrick Gallivan
Kathleen Marchione
Michael Nozzolio

Minority
Tony Avella
Liz Krueger
Martin Malave Dilan

Energy & Telecommunications
Chair:
Joseph A Griffo (R)...................................518-455-3334
Ranking Minority Member:
Kevin Parker (D)......................................518-455-2580

Committee Staff
Clerk:
Regina Boyd...518-455-2024
Chief of Staff:
Dwight Evans..518-455-3334

Key Senate Staff Assignments
Repulican Senior Counsel:
Emma Maceko...518-455-2908
Democratic Budget Analyst:
Paul Alexander

Membership

Majority
Thomas Croci
Jack Martins
Thomas O'Mara
Patricia Ritchie
Elizabeth O'C Little

Minority
David Carlucci
Jesse Hamilton
Timothy Kennedy
Martin Malave Dilan

Environmental Conservation
Chair:
Thomas O'Mara (R).....................................518-455-2091
Ranking Minority Member:
Brad Hoylman (D)......................................518-455-2451

Committee Staff
Chief of Staff:
Pierson Ellis...518-455-2091

Key Senate Staff Assignments
Republican Assistant Counsel:
Paul Midey 518-455-2599

Membership

Majority

Elizabeth O'C Little
Catharine M Young
Robert G Ortt
Carl Marcellino
Kenneth P LaValle
Rich Funke

Minority

Joseph Adabbo
Todd Kaminsky
George Latimer
Tony Avella
Adriano Espaillat

Ethics

Chair:
Thomas Croci (R) 518-455-3570
Ranking Minority Member:
Michael Gianaris (D) 518-455-3486

Key Senate Staff Assignments

Democratic Deputy Counsel:
Keith St John. 518-455-2711
Republican Assistant Counsel:
Adam Richardson 518-455-2506

Membership

Majority

Andrew Lanza
Hugh T Farley
Terrence Murphy

Minority

Gustavo Rivera

Finance

Chair:
Catharine M Young (R) 518-455-3563
Ranking Minority Member:
Liz Krueger (D). 518-455-2297

Committee Staff

Secretary to the Committee & Chief of Staff:
Robert Mujica 518-455-2880

Key Senate Staff Assignments
Director of Budget Studies:
Felix Muniz 518-455-2642
Democratic Secretary to Finance:
Louie Tobias 518-455-2641

Membership

Majority

Philip Boyle
Carl L Marcellino
Joseph E Robach
Thomas O'Mara
Kemp Hannon
Michael N. Ranzenhofer
Patrick Gallivan
John J Bonacic
Andrew J Lanza
Catharine M Young
Kenneth P LaValle
Kathleen Marchione
Joseph A Griffo
James L Seward
William J Larkin Jr
Patricia Ritchie
Jack Martins
Martin J Golden
Elizabeth O'C Little

Minority

Neil D Breslin
Velmanette Montgomery
Jose Peralta
Ruben Diaz Sr
Diane Savino
Ruth Hassell-Thompson
Martin Malave Dilan
Kevin S Parker
Adriano Espaillat
David Valesky
Todd Kaminsky
Toby Ann Stavisky
Timothy Kennedy
J Gustavo Rivera
Daniel L Squadron

Health

Chair:
Kemp Hannon (R). 518-455-2200
Ranking Minority Member:
J. Gustavo Rivera (D) 518-455-3395

Committee Staff

Committee Director:
Kristin Sinclair 518-455-2200

Key Senate Staff Assignments
Republican Program Director:
J Thomas Wickham Jr 518-455-2675
Republican Assistant Counsel:
David Previte 518-455-2604

Membership

Majority

Terrence Murphy
James L Seward
William J Larkin Jr
Elizabeth O'C Little
Martin J Golden
Hugh T Farley
Catharine M Young
Jack Martins

Minority

Brad Hoylman
Ruth Hassell-Thompson
David J Valesky
Toby Ann Stavisky
Velmanette Montgomery
Roxanne Persaud
Todd Kaminsky
Simcha Felder

Higher Education

Chair:
Kenneth P LaValle (R) 518-455-3121
Ranking Minority Member:
Toby Ann Stavisky (D). 518-455-3461

Committee Staff

Committee Director:
Kristin Sinclair 518-455-2200

Key Senate Staff Assignments
Republican Program Director:
Tom Wickham 518-455-2068
Democratic Associate Counsel:
Dan Leinung 518-455-2821

Membership

Majority

Patrick Gallivan
Rich Funke
Robert G Ortt
Michael Venditto
Thomas Croci
Joseph A Griffo
James L Seward
Joseph E Robach
Sue Serino
Patricia Ritchie

Minority

Adriano Espaillat
J Gustavo Rivera
Jose Peralta
Neil D Breslin
David Valesky
Kevin S Parker
Liz Krueger

Housing, Construction & Community Development

Chair:
Elizabeth O'C. Little (R) 518-455-2811
Ranking Minority Member:
Adriano Espaillat (D) 518-455-2041

Committee Staff

Clerk:
Chelsey Watroba. 518-455-3563

Offices and agencies generally appear in alphabetical order, except when specific order is requested by listee.

Key Senate Staff Assignments
Republican Senior Counsel:
Robert Gibbon 518-455-2876
Democratic Special Counsel:
John Allen..518-455-5545

Membership

Majority
Philip Boyle
Patrick Gallivan
John J. Bonacic
Catharine M Young

Minority
Liz Krueger
Marc Panepinto
Tony Avella

Infrastructure & Capital Investment
Chair:
Andrew J Lanza (R) 518-455-3215
Ranking Member:
Timothy Kennedy (D)...............................518-455-2426

Committee Staff
Committee Director:
Deborah Peck Kelleher.............................518-455-2390
Republican Senior Counsel:
Adam Richardson 518-455-2406

Membership

Majority
Patrick Gallivan
Joseph Robach
Thomas Croci

Minority
David Carlucci
Martin Malave Dilan
Simcha Felder
Leroy Comrie

Insurance
Chair:
James L Seward (R) 518-455-3131
Ranking Minority Member:
Neil D Breslin (D)................................518-455-2225

Committee Staff
Committee Director:
Natalie Bernardi 518-455-3131

Key Senate Staff Assignments
Republican Senior Counsel:
Robert Farley 518-455-3127
Republican Assistant Counsel:
Frank Alleva......................................518-455-2488
Democratic Associate Counsel:
Richard Jacobson

Membership

Majority
William J Larkin Jr
Martin J Golden
Michael Venditto
Sue Serino
Thomas O'Mara
Terrance Murphy
Kenneth P LaValle
Jack Martins
Andrew J Lanza

Minority
Timothy Kennedy
Jesse Hamilton
James Sanders Jr
Kevin S Parker
Marc Panepinto
David Carlucci
George Latimer
Tony Avella

Investigations & Government Operations
Chair:
Andrew J Lanza (R) 518-455-3215
Ranking Minority Member:
Brad Hoylman (D) 518-455-2451

Committee Staff
-lerk:
Deborah Peck Kelleher

Key Senate Staff Assignments
Republican Senior Counsel:
Ryan McAllister...................................518-455-2914
Democratic Senior Counsel:
Christopher Higgins

Membership

Majority
Martin J Golden
Terrence Murphy
Michael F Nozzolio
Thomas O'Mara

Minority
David Carlucci
Ruben Diaz Sr
Daniel Squadron

Judiciary
Chair:
John J Bonancic (R) 518-455-3181
Ranking Minority Member:
Ruth Hassell-Thompson (D).........................518-455-2061

Committee Staff
Legislative Assistant:
Conor Gillis......................................518-455-3181

Membership

Majority
Michael Venditto
Michael H Ranzenhofer
Kenneth P LaValle
Kemp Hannon
George Amedore Jr
Sue Serino
Andrew J Lanza
Thomas Croci
Michael F Nozzolio
Philip Boyle
Thomas O'Mara

Minority
Tony Avella
Neil D Breslin
Diane Savino
Toby Ann Stavisky
Leroy Comrie
Bill Perkins
Martin Malave Dilan
Adriano Espaillat
Ruben Diaz Sr
Brad Hoylman

Labor
Chair:
Jack Martins (R) 518-455-3265
Ranking Minority Member:
Jose R Peralta (D)................................518-455-2529

Committee Staff
Legislative Director:
Peter Faherty.....................................518-455-3265

Key Senate Staff Assignments

Membership

Majority
Terrence Murphy
Frederick J Akshar, II
Michael Venditto
Patrick Gallivan
Kemp Hannon
Carl L Marcellino
Robert G Ortt
Joseph Robach

Minority
Joseph P Addabbo Jr
Bill Perkins
James Sanders, Jr.
Martin Malave Dilan
Diane J Savino
J Gustavo Rivera

Offices and agencies generally appear in alphabetical order, except when specific order is requested by listee.

Local Government
Chair:
Kathleen Marchione (R) 518-455-2381
Ranking Minority Member:
Todd Kaminsky (D) 518-455-3401

Committee Staff
Legislative Director:
Daphne Jordan 518-455-2381

Key Senate Staff Assignments
Republican Assistant Counsel:
Robert Gibbon 518-455-2876
Democratic Budget Analyst:
Teria Cooper 518-455-2793

Membership
Majority
Terrence Murphy
Patricia Ritchie
Philip Boyle
Robert G Ortt

Minority
Brad Hoylman
David Valesky
George Latimer

Mental Health & Developmental Disabilities
Chair:
Robert G Ortt (R) 518-455-2024
Ranking Minority Member:
Jesse Hamilton (D) 518-455-2431

Committee Staff
Legislative Director:
Joe Erdman 518-455-2024

Key Senate Staff Assignments
Republican Assistant Counsel:
Carmen Barber 518-455-2480

Membership
Majority
Terrence Murphy
Kemp Hannon
Sue Serino
James Seward

Minority
J Gustavo Rivera
Jose Serrano
Simcha Felder
Liz Krueger
David Carlucci

Racing, Gaming & Wagering
Chair:
John J Bonacic (R) 518-455-3181
Ranking Minority Member:
Joseph Addabbo Jr. (D) 518-455-2322

Committee Staff
Legislative Assistant:
Conor Gillis 518-455-3181

Membership
Majority
Kathleen Marchione
Joseph Griffo
Michael F Nozzolio
Michael Ranzenhofer
Philip Boyle

Minority
David Carlucci
Leroy Comrie
George Latimer
James Sanders, Jr.

Rules
Chair:
John J Flanagan (R) 518-455-2071
Ranking Minority Member:
Andrea Stewart-Cousins (D) 518-455-2585

Membership
Majority
Hugh T Farley
Andrew J Lanza
John A DeFrancisco
James L Seward
Michael F Nozzolio
Kemp Hannon
William J Larkin Jr
Joseph Robach
Kenneth P LaValle
Carl L Marcellino
John Bonacic
Elizabeth O'C. Little

Minority
Neil D Breslin
David Carlucci
Velmanette Montgomery
Liz Krueger
Adriano Espaillat
David Valesky
Bill Perkins
Martin Malave Dilan
Kevin S Parker
Ruth Hassell-Thompson
Michael Gianaris

Social Services
Chair:
David Carlucci (D) 518-455-2991

Committee Staff
Committee Director:
Evan Sullivan 518-455-2991

Key Senate Staff Assignments
Republican Program Associate:
Niko Ladopoulos 518-455-2482
Democratic Budget Analyst:
Cheryl Halter

Membership
Majority
George Amedore Jr
Kenneth P LaValle
Jack Martins
Hugh T Farley

Minority
Daniel L Squadron
Roxanne Persaud

Transportation
Chair:
Joseph E Robach (R) 518-455-2909
Ranking Minority Member:
Martin Malave Dilan (D) 518-455-2177

Committee Staff
Committee Clerk:
Michelle Cameron

Key Senate Staff Assignments
Republican Senior Counsel:
Lisa Harris 518-455-2751
Democratic Associate Counsel:
Dan Ranellone 518-455-2852

Membership
Majority
Patrick Gallivan
Michael F Nozzolio
Patricia Ritchie
Thomas O'Mara
William J Larkin Jr
Catharine M Young
Jack Martins
Michael H Ranzenhofer

Minority
Todd Kaminsky
Timothy Kennedy
Bill Perkins
David J Valesky

Ruben Diaz Sr
Tony Avella
Daniel L Squadron
Toby Ann Stavisky

Veterans, Homeland Security & Military Affairs
Chair:
Thomas Croci (R) 518-455-3570
Ranking Minority Member:
Joseph P Addabbo Jr (D) 518-455-2322

Committee Staff
Legislative Director:
Jennifer Slagen 518-455-4265

Key Senate Staff Assignments
Democratic Associate Counsel:
Nic Rangel 518-455-7925
Republican Senior Counsel:
Bob Farley 518-455-3111

Membership

Majority
Martin J Golden
Kathleen Marchione
George Amedore Jr
William J Larkin Jr
Robert G Ortt

Minority
Simcha Felder
David Carlucci
Leroy Comrie
Jose Serrano
Todd Kaminsky
James Sanders, Jr.

SENATE SELECT & SPECIAL COMMITTEES & SPECIAL TASK FORCES

Libraries, Select Committee on
Chair:
Hugh T Farley (R) 518-455-2181/fax: 518-455-2271

Science, Technology, Incubation & Entrepreneurship, Select Committee on
Chair:
Martin J Golden (R) 518-455-2730

JOINT LEGISLATIVE COMMISSIONS

Administrative Regulations Review, Legislative Commission on
Senate Co-Chair:
Terrence Murphy (R) 518-455-3111
Assembly Co-Chair:
Kenneth Zebrowski (D) 518-455-5735
Assembly Program Manager:
Rich Murphy 518-455-5091/fax: 518-455-4175

Demographic Research & Reapportionment, Legislative Task Force on
Senate Co-Chair:
Michael F Nozzolio (R) 518-455-2366
Assembly Co-Chair:
Marcos A Crespo (D) 518-455-5514
Co-Executive Director:
Frank Tassone 212-618-1100/fax: 212-618-1135
Co-Executive Director:
Karen Blatt. 212-618-1100/fax: 212-618-1135

Ethics Committee, Legislative
Senate Co-Chair:
Andrew Lanza (R) 518-455-3215
Assembly Co-Chair:
Charles D Lavine (D) 518-455-4546
Executive Director/Counsel:
Lisa P Reid 518-432-7837
e-mail: lreid@nysenate.gov

Government Administration, Legislative Commission on
Senate Vice-Chair:
Vacant 518-455-0000
Assembly Chair:
Brian Kavanagh (D) 518-455-5506

Rural Resources, Legislative Commission on
Senate Chair:
Patricia Ritchie (R) 518-455-3438
e-mail: ruralres@nysenate.gov
Assembly Chair:
Frank Skartados (D) 518-455-5762
Republican Counsel:
Barbara McRedmond. 518-455-2069/fax: 518-486-6919

LEGISLATIVE BRANCH ASSEMBLY

STATE ASSEMBLY LEADERSHIP

Members of the Assembly welcome e-mail correspondence from the public. They may reply by e-mail, or by mail when more extensive follow-up is necessary. Please include both an e-mail and mailing address in all correspondence. Biographies of Assembly Members appears in a separate section in the back of the book.

State Capitol
Albany, NY 12248
Web site: www.assembly.state.ny.us

ADMINISTRATION

Laurene R Kretzler 518-455-4242/fax: 518-455-4935
Title: Clerk of the Assembly

Wayne P Jackson 518-455-3797/fax: 518-455-4445
Title: Sergeant-at-Arms, Chamber

Michael Kane 518-455-5767/fax: 518-455-4963
Title: Director, Communication Information Services (CIS)

Vicki Chase 518-455-5767/fax: 518-455-4963
Title: Director, Information Services

John P Wellspeak 518-455-4411/fax: 518-455-4298
Title: Director, Administration

Kathleen McCarty 518-455-4704/fax: 518-455-4705
Title: Director, Internship Program

Mike Gaffney 518-455-5165/fax: 518-455-4741
Title: Director, Document Room

Robin Marilla 518-455-4218/fax: 518-455-5175
Title: Public Information Officer

Vacant 518-455-2468/fax: 518-426-6901
Title: Reference Librarian, Legislative Library

Jim Devine 518-455-5190/fax: 518-455-4517
Title: Director, Operations

MAJORITY LEADERSHIP

Carl E Heastie (D) 518-455-3791
e-mail: speaker@assembly.state.ny.us
Title: Speaker

Joseph Morelle 518-455-5373
e-mail: morellej@assembly.state.ny.us
Title: Majority Leader

Herman D Farrell, Jr (D) 518-455-5491
e-mail: farrelh@assembly.state.ny.us
Title: Chair, Ways & Means Committee

Earlene Hooper (D) 518-455-5861
e-mail: hoopere@assembly.state.ny.us
Title: Deputy Speaker

Jeffrion L. Aubrey (D) 518-455-4561
e-mail: aubryj@assembly.state.ny.us
Title: Speaker Pro Tempore

N Nick Perry (D) 518-455-4166
e-mail: perryn@assembly.state.ny.us
Title: Assistant Speaker Pro Tempore

Felix Ortiz (D) 518-455-3821
e-mail: ortizf@assembly.state.ny.us
Title: Assistant Speaker

Vivian E Cook (D) 518-455-4203
e-mail: cookv@assembly.state.ny.us
Title: Chair, Committee on Standing Committees

Phil Ramos (D) 518-455-5185
e-mail: ramosp@assembly.state.ny.us
Title: Deputy Majority Leader

Dov Hikind (D) 518-455-5721
e-mail: hikindd@assembly.state.ny.us
Title: Assistant Majority Leader

William Colton (D) 518-455-5828
e-mail: coltonw@assembly.state.ny.us
Title: Majority Whip

Jose Rivera (D) 518-455-5414
e-mail: riveraj@assembly.state.ny.us
Title: Deputy Majority Whip

Al Stirpe (D) 518-455-4505
e-mail: stirpea@assembly.state.ny.us
Title: Assistant Majority Whip

Michelle Schimel (D) 518-455-5192
e-mail: schimelm@assembly.state.ny.us
Title: Chair, Majority Conference

Aravella Simotas (D) 518-455-5014
e-mail: simotasa@assembly.state.ny.us
Title: Vice Chair, Majority Conference

David I Weprin (D) 518-455-5806
e-mail: weprind@assembly.state.ny.us
Title: Secretary, Majority Conference

Barbara Lifton (D) 518-455-5444
e-mail: liftonb@assembly.state.ny.us
Title: Chair, Majority Steering

Vacant (D) 518-455-0000
Title: Vice Chair, Majority Steering

Carmen Arroyo (D) 518-455-5402
e-mail: arroyoc@assembly.state.ny.us
Title: Chair, Majority Program

Michael Miller (D) 518-455-4621
e-mail: millermg@ssembly.state.ny.us
Title: Chair, Majority House Operations

MAJORITY STAFF

Vacant . . . .
Title: Chief of Staff to the Speaker

Michael Whyland 518-455-3888/fax: 518-455-3858
Title: Press Secretary to the Speaker

Neil Fisher 518-455-4736/fax: 518-455-5428
Title: Director, Index Services

John Hudder 518-455-4386/fax: 518-455-5573
Title: Executive Director, Program Development

Bill Collins 518-455-4191/fax: 518-455-4103
Title: Counsel to the Majority

Matthew Howard 518-455-3786/fax: 518-455-4445
Title: Secretary to the Committee on Ways & Means

Offices and agencies generally appear in alphabetical order, except when specific order is requested by listee.

MINORITY LEADERSHIP

Brian M Kolb (R) 518-455-3751
e-mail: kolbb@assembly.state.ny.us
Title: Minority Leader

Jane Corwin (R) 518-455-4601
e-mail: corwinj@assembly.state.ny.us
Title: Minority Leader Pro Tempore

Tom McKevitt (R).................................518-455-5341
e-mail: mckevit@assembly.state.ny.us
Title: Assistant Minority Leader Pro Tempore

Marc Butler (R).................................518-455-5393
e-mail: butlerm@assembly.state.ny.us
Title: Ranking Minority Member, Committee on Standing Committees

William Barclay (R) 518-455-5841
e-mail: barclaW@assembly.state.ny.us
Title: Deputy Minority Leader

Gary Finch (R).................................518-455-5878
e-mail: finchG@assembly.state.ny.us
Title: Assistant Minority Leader

Stephen Hawley (R) 518-455-5811
e-mail: hawleys@assembly.state.ny.us
Title: Assistant Minority Leader

James Tedisco (R).................................518-455-5772
e-mail: tediscj@assembly.state.ny.us
Title: Minority Whip

Andrew Raia (R) 518-455-5952
e-mail: raiaA@assembly.state.ny.us
Title: Deputy Minority Whip

Michael Montesano (R).................................518-455-4684
e-mail: montesanom@assembly.state.ny.us
Title: Assistant Minority Whip

Clifford W Crouch (R).................................518-455-5741
e-mail: crouchc@assembly.state.ny.us
Title: Chair, Minority Conference

Peter Lopez (R) 518-455-5363
e-mail: lopezp@assembly.state.ny.us
Title: Vice Chair, Minority Conference

Philip Palmesano (R 518-455-5791
e-mail: palmesanop@asembly.state.ny.us
Title: Secretary, Minority Conference

Michael Fitzpatrick (R) 518-455-5021
e-mail: fitzpatrickm@assembly.state.ny.us
Title: Chair, Minority Joint Conference Committee

David McDonough (R).................................518-455-4633
e-mail: mcdonoughd@assembly.state.ny.us
Title: Vice Chair, Minority Joint Conference Committee

Joseph Giglio (R).................................518-455-5241
e-mail: giglioj@assembly.state.ny.us
Title: Chair, Minority Steering Committee

Edward Ra (R).................................518-455-4627
e-mail: rae@assembly.state.ny.us
Title: Vice Chair, Minority Steering Committee

Joseph Saladino (R) 518-455-5305
e-mail: saladij@assembly.state.ny.us
Title: Chair, Minority Program Committee

Janet Duprey (R).................................518-455-5943
e-mail: palmesanop@assembly.state.ny.us
Title: Vice Chair, Program Committee

Vacant (R).................................518-455-0000
Title: Chair, Minority House Operations

Robert Oaks (R).................................518-455-5655
e-mail: oaksR@assembly.state.ny.us
Title: Ranking Minority Member, Ways & Means

MINORITY STAFF

Doug Finch 518-455-3751/fax: 518-455-3750
e-mail: finchd@assembly.state.ny.us
Title: Chief of Staff

Judy Skype 518-455-4211/fax: 518-455-3758
Title: Deputy Chief of Staff

Michael Fraser.......................518-455-3751/fax: 518-455-3750
e-mail: fraserm@assembly.state.ny.us
Title: Director, Minority Communications

Harry MacAvoy.......................518-455-5002/fax: 518-455-5829
Title: Director, Minority Research & Program Development

Rebecca D'Agati.......................518-455-5161/fax: 518-455-4550
Title: Director, Minority Ways & Means Staff

STATE ASSEMBLY ROSTER

Multiple party abbreviations following the names of legislators indicate that those legislators ran as the Assembly candidate for each identified party. Source: NYS Board of Elections. Party abbreviations: Conservative (C), Democrat (D), Green (G), Independent (I), Liberal (L), Republican (R), Right to Life (RL), Veterans (VE), Working Families (WF)

Peter J Abbate, Jr (D)..............518-455-3053/fax: 518-455-5524
District: 49 *Room:* 839 LOB *e-mail:* abbatep@assembly.state.ny.us
Committees: Aging; Banks; Consumer Affairs & Protection; Governmental Employees (Chair); Labor

Thomas Abinanti (D)..............518-455-5753/fax: 518-455-5920
District: 92 *Room:* 744 LOB *e-mail:* abinantit@assembly.state.ny.us
Committees: Codes; Corporations, Authorities & Commissions; Election Law; Environmental Conservation; Health; Libraries & Education Technology (Chair)
Senior Staff: Joanne Sold

Carmen E Arroyo (D)..............518-455-5402/fax: 518-455-4681
District: 84 *Room:* 734 LOB *e-mail:* arroyoc@assembly.state.ny.us
Title: Chair, Majority Program
Committees: Aging; Alcoholism & Drug Abuse; Children & Families; Education
Senior Staff: Isamar Rodriguez

Jeffrion L Aubry (D)..............518-455-4561/fax: 518-455-4565
District: 35 *Room:* 646 LOB *e-mail:* aubryj@assembly.state.ny.us
Title: Speaker Pro Tempore
Committees: Governmental Employees; Rules; Social Services; Ways & Means
Senior Staff: Mary C Nicholson

William A Barclay (R-I-C)..........518-455-5841/fax: 518-455-5362
District: 120 *Room:* 521 LOB *e-mail:* barclaw@assembly.state.ny.us
Title: Deputy Minority Leader
Committees: Energy; Insurance (Ranking Minority Member); Judiciary; Rules; Ways & Means
Senior Staff: Jennifer Cook

Didi Barrett (D) 518-455-5177/fax: 518-455-5418
District: 106 *Room:* 553 LOB *e-mail:* barrettd@assembly.state.ny.us
Committees: Aging; Agriculture; Economic Development, Job Creation; Commerce & Industry; Mental Health; Tourism, Parks, Arts & Sports Development; Veterans' Affairs
Senior Staff: Nick Melson

Charles Barron (D) 518-455-5912
District: 60 *Room:* 532 LOB *e-mail:* barronc@assembly.state.ny.us
Committees: Aging; Alcoholism & Drug Abuse; Economic Development, Job Creation, Commerce & Industry; Energy; Small Business; Social Services
Senior Staff: Viola Plummer

Michael R Benedetto (D) 518-455-5296/fax: 518-455-4641
District: 82 *Room:* 842 LOB *e-mail:* benedettom@assembly.state.ny.us
Committees: Agriculture; Cities (Chair); Education; Governmental Operations; Labor; Ways & Means
Senior Staff: Ben Randazzo

Rodneyse Bichotte (D) 518-455-5385
District: 42 *Room:* 833 LOB *e-mail:* bichotter@assembly.state.ny.us
Committees: Banks; Economic Development, Job Creation, Commerce & Industry; Governmental Ops; Housing; Small Business; Social Services
Senior Staff: Rona Taylor

Michael Blake (D) 518-455-5272
District: 79 *Room:* 919 LOB *e-mail:* blakem@assembly.state.ny.us
Committees: Banks; Correction; Election Law; Governmental Ops; Housing; Veterans' Affairs
Senior Staff: Aaron Carr

Kenneth Blankenbush (R) 518-455-5797/fax: 518-455-5289
District: 117 *Room:* 322 LOB *e-mail:* blankenbushk@assembly.state.ny.us
Committees: Agriculture (Ranking Member); Corporations, Authorities & Commissions; Insurance; Tourism, Parks, Arts & Sports Development
Senior Staff: Brian Peck

Karl Brabenec (R) 518-455-5991/fax: 518-455-5929
District: 98 *Room:* 523 LOB *e-mail:* brabeneck@assembly.state.ny.us
Committees: Aging; Cities; Election Law; Labor; Local Governments
Senior Staff: Joseph Colcman

Edward C. Braunstein (D) 518-455-5425/fax: 518-455-4648
District: 26 *Room:* 557 LOB *e-mail:* braunsteine@assembly.state.ny.us
Committees: Aging; Cities; Health; Insurance; Judiciary; Small Business
Senior Staff: David Fischer

James F Brennan (D) 518-455-5377/fax: 518-455-5592
District: 44 *Room:* 422 LOB *e-mail:* brennanj@assembly.state.ny.us
Committees: Codes; Corporations, Authorities & Commissions (Chair); Education; Real Property Taxation
Senior Staff: Melanie Hirsch Riback

Anthony J Brindisi (D) 518-455-5454/fax: 518-455-5928
District: 119 *Room:* 538 LOB *e-mail:* brindisia@assembly.state.ny.us
Committees: Aging; Economic Development, Job Creation, Commerce & Industry; Energy; Higher Education; Transporation; Veterans' Affairs
Senior Staff: Caitlin Calogero

Harry Bronson (D) 518-455-4527/fax: 518-455-5342
District: 138 *Room:* 502 LOB *e-mail:* bronsonh@assembly.state.ny.us
Committees: Agriculture; Economic Development, Job Creation, Commerce & Industry; Labor; Local Governments; Transportation
Senior Staff: Jen Skoog-Harvey

David Buchwald (D) 518-455-5397/fax: 518-455-5041
District: 93 *Room:* 331 LOB *e-mail:* buchwaldd@assembly.state.ny.us
Committees: Consumer Affairs & Protection; Corporations, Authorities & Commissions; Election Law; Governmental Operations; Judiciary; Local Governments
Senior Staff: Daniel Weisfield

Marc W Butler (R-I-C) 518-455-5393/fax: 518-455-5889
District: 118 *Room:* 525 LOB *e-mail:* butlerm@assembly.state.ny.us
Title: Ranking Minority Member, Committee on Standing Committees
Committees: Agriculture; Economic Development, Job Creation, Commerce & Industry; Environmental Conservation; Higher Education; Insurance; Rules
Senior Staff: Deborah Dempsey Scialdo

Kevin A Cahill (D) 518-455-4436/fax: 518-455-5576
District: 103 *Room:* 716 LOB *e-mail:* cahillk@assembly.state.ny.us
Committees: Ethics & Guidance; Economic Development, Job Creation, Commerce & Industry; Health; Higher Education; Insurance (Chair); Ways & Means
Senior Staff: Evan Gallo

Alice Cancel (D) 518-455-3640
District: 65 *Room:* 548 LOB *e-mail:* cancelA@assembly.state.ny.us
Committees: Banks; Cities; Housing; Social Services

Ron Castorina, Jr (R) 518-455-4495/fax: 518-455-4501
District: 62 *Room:* 428 LOB *e-mail:*
Committees:

John D Ceretto (R) 518-455-5284/fax: 518-455-5694
District: 145 *Room:* 320 LOB *e-mail:* cerettoj@assembly.state.ny.us
Committees: Cities; Education; Energy; Labor; Tourism, Parks, Arts & Sports (Ranking Member)
Senior Staff: William Angus

William Colton (D-WF) 518-455-5828/fax: 518-455-5706
District: 47 *Room:* 733 LOB *e-mail:* coltonw@assembly.state.ny.us
Title: Majority Whip
Committees: Correction; Environmental Conservation; Governmental Employees; Labor; Rules; Ways & Means
Senior Staff: Susan Zhuang

Vivian E Cook (D) 518-455-4203/fax: 518-455-3606
District: 32 *Room:* 939 LOB *e-mail:* cookv@assembly.state.ny.us
Title: Chair, Committee on Standing Committees
Committees: Codes; Corporations, Authorities & Commissions; Housing; Insurance; Rules; Ways & Means
Senior Staff: Joyce Corker

Jane L Corwin (R) 518-455-4601/fax: 518-455-5257
District: 144 *Room:* 446 LOB *e-mail:* corwinj@assembly.state.ny.us
Title: Minority Leader Pro Tempore
Committees: Corporations, Authorities & Commissions (Ranking Member); Education; Environmental Conservation; Mental Health; Ways & Means
Senior Staff: Kim Laurie

Marcos Crespo (D) 518-455-5514/fax: 518-455-5827
District: 85 *Room:* 454 LOB *e-mail:* crespoM@assembly.state.ny.us
Committees: Alcoholism & Drug Abuse; Cities; Energy; Environmental Conservation; Insurance; Transportation
Senior Staff: Matthew Shuffler

Clifford W Crouch (R) 518-455-5741/fax: 518-455-5864
District: 122 *Room:* 450 LOB *e-mail:* crouchc@assembly.state.ny.us
Title: Chair, Minority Conference
Committees: Agriculture; Economic Development, Job Creation, Commerce & Industry; Labor; Rules; Ways & Means
Senior Staff: Kathleen Mami-Moore

Brian Curran (R) 518-455-4656/fax: 518-455-4643
District: 21 *Room:* 318 LOB *e-mail:* curranb@assembly.state.ny.us
Committees: Banks; Ethics & Guidance (Ranking Member); Insurance; Labor; Veterans Affairs
Senior Staff: Leslie Rothschild

Michael J Cusick (D) 518-455-5526/fax: 518-455-4760
District: 63 *Room:* 724 LOB *e-mail:* cusickm@assembly.state.ny.us
Committees: Election Law (Chair); Governmental Employees; Higher Education; Mental Health; Transportation; Veterans' Affairs; Ways & Means
Senior Staff: Sharon L Grobe

Offices and agencies generally appear in alphabetical order, except when specific order is requested by listee.

Steven H Cymbrowitz (D) 518-455-5214/fax: (518) 455-5738
District: 45 *Room:* 824 LOB *e-mail:* cymbros@assembly.state.ny.us
Committees: Aging; Codes; Environmental Conservation; Health; Insurance
Senior Staff: Adrienne Knoll

Maritza Davila (D). 518-455-5537/fax: 518-455-5789
District: 53 *Room:* 631 LOB *e-mail:* davilaM@assembly.state.ny.us
Committees: Alcoholism & Drug Abuse; Children & Families; Correction; Economic Development, Job Creation, Commerce & Industry; Housing; Social Services
Senior Staff: Rachel Fuentes

Michael G DenDekker (D) 518-455-4545/fax: 518-455-4547
District: 34 *Room:* 841 LOB *e-mail:* dendekkerm@assembly.state.ny.us
Committees: Aging; Alcoholism & Drug Abuse; Governmental Employees; Labor; Transportation; Veterans' Affairs (Chair)
Senior Staff: Maureen Allen

Erik M Dilan (D) 518-455-5821
District: 54 *Room:* 921 LOB *e-mail:* dilane@assembly.state.ny.us
Committees: Cities; Consumer Affairs & Protection; Corporations, Authorities & Commissions; Governmental Operations; Housing; Insurance
Senior Staff: Videsh Persaud

Jeffrey Dinowitz (D-WF) 518-455-5965/fax: 518-455-4437
District: 81 *Room:* 941 LOB *e-mail:* dinowij@assembly.state.ny.us
Committees: Consumer Affairs & Protection (Chair); Election Law; Health; Judiciary; Rules
Senior Staff: Randi Martos

David DiPietro (R-C). 518-455-5314/fax: 518-455-5761
District: 147 *Room:* 543 LOB *e-mail:* dipietrod@assembly.state.ny.us
Committees: Alcoholism & Drug Abuse; Economic Development, Job Creation, Commerce & Industry; Labor; Small Business (Ranking Member); Transportation
Senior Staff: Loren Gierlinger

Janet L Duprey (R) 518-455-5943/fax: 518-455-5761
District: 115 *Room:* 635 LOB *e-mail:* dupreyj@assembly.state.ny.us
Title: Vice Chair, Program Committee
Committees: Correction; Governmental Operations (Ranking Minority Member); Higher Education; Rules; Ways & Means
Senior Staff: Jill Abdallah

Steven C Englebright (D) 518-455-4804/fax: 518-455-5795
District: 4 *Room:* 621 LOB *e-mail:* engles@assembly.state.ny.us
Committees: Environmental Conservation (Chair); Education; Energy; Higher Education; Rules
Senior Staff: Maria Hoffman

Patricia Fahy (D). 518-455-4178
District: 109 *Room:* 452 LOB *e-mail:* fahyp@assembly.state.ny.us
Committees: Banks; Children and Families; Environmental Conservation; Higher Education; Tourism, Parks, Arts & Sports Development
Senior Staff: Catherine Fahey

Herman D Farrell, Jr (D). 518-455-5491/fax: 518-455-5776
District: 71 *Room:* 923 LOB *e-mail:* farrelh@assembly.state.ny.us
Title: Chair, Ways & Means Committee
Committees: Rules; Ways & Means (Chair)
Senior Staff: Marcia Coleman

Gary D Finch (R-C). 518-455-5878/fax: 518-455-3895
District: 126 *Room:* 448 LOB *e-mail:* finchg@assembly.state.ny.us
Title: Assistant Minority Leader
Committees: Agriculture; Banks; Correction; Insurance; Rules
Senior Staff: Suzanne Redmond

Michael J Fitzpatrick (R-C). 518-455-5021/fax: 518-455-4394
District: 8 *Room:* 458 LOB *e-mail:* fitzpatrickm@assembly.state.ny.us
Title: Chair, Minority Joint Conference Committee
Committees: Higher Education; Housing (Ranking Minority Member); Labor; Ways & Means
Senior Staff: Kathy Albrecht

Christopher Friend (R). 518-455-4538/fax: 518-455-5922
District: 124 *Room:* 938 LOB *e-mail:* friendc@assembly.state.ny.us
Committees: Aging; Children & Families (Ranking Member); Corporations Authorities & Commissions; Housing; Local Governments (Ranking Member)
Senior Staff: Scott Esty

Sandra R Galef (D-I). 518-455-5348/fax: 518-455-5728
District: 95 *Room:* 641 LOB *e-mail:* galefs@assembly.state.ny.us
Committees: Corporations Authorities & Commissions; Election Law; Governmental Operations; Health; Real Property Taxation (Chair)
Senior Staff: Dana Levenberg

David F Gantt (D) 518-455-5606/fax: 518-455-5419
District: 137 *Room:* 830 LOB *e-mail:* ganttd@assembly.state.ny.us
Committees: Economic Development, Job Creation, Commerce & Industry; Local Governments; Rules; Transportation (Chair); Ways & Means
Senior Staff: Nick Thony

Andrew R Garbarino (R-I-C). 518-455-4611
District: 7 *Room:* 529 LOB *e-mail:* garbarinoa@assembly.state.ny.us
Committees: Banks; Health; Environmental Conservation; Higher Education; Racing & Wagering
Senior Staff: Josh Ringel

Joe Giglio (R-I-C). 518-455-5241/fax: 518-455-5869
District: 148 *Room:* 439 LOB *e-mail:* giglioj@assembly.state.ny.us
Title: Chair, Minority Steering Committee
Committees: Aging; Children & Families; Codes; Correction (Ranking Minority Member); Ethics & Guidance
Senior Staff: Michael Brisky

Mark Gjonaj (D) 518-455-8444/fax: 518-455-4649
District: 80 *Room:* 633 LOB *e-mail:* gjonajm@assembly.state.ny.us
Committees: Banks; Local Government; Real Property Taxation; Small Business; Tourism, Parks, Arts & Sports Development
Senior Staff: Renee Montminy

Deborah J Glick (D) 518-455-4841/fax: 518-455-4649
District: 66 *Room:* 717 LOB *e-mail:* glickd@assembly.state.ny.us
Committees: Environmental Conservation; Governmental Operations; Higher Education (Chair); Rules; Ways & Means
Senior Staff: Sarah Sanchala

Phillip Goldfeder (D). 518-455-4292/fax: 518-455-4723
District: 23 *Room:* 542 LOB *e-mail:* goldfederp@ assembly.state.ny.us
Committees: Aging; Corporations, Authorities & Commissions; Governmental Employees; Insurance; Mental Health; Racing & Wagering
Senior Staff: Angela Katz

Andrew Goodell (R) 518-455-4511/fax: 518-455-4328
District: 150 *Room:* 545 LOB *e-mail:* goodella@assembly.state.ny.us
Committees: Governmental Operations; Health; Judiciary; Social Services
Senior Staff: Michele Krege

Richard N Gottfried (D-WF). 518-455-4941/fax: 518-455-5939
District: 75 *Room:* 822 LOB *e-mail:* gottfriedr@assembly.state.ny.us
Committees: Health (Chair); Higher Education; Rules
Senior Staff: Richard Conti

Alfred C Graf (R). 518-455-5937/fax: 518-455-4784
District: 5 *Room:* 433 LOB *e-mail:* grafa@assembly.state.ny.us
Committees: Codes; Housing (Ranking Member); Education; Judiciary
Senior Staff: Angela Ventrice

Aileen M Gunther (D-C). 518-455-5355/fax: 518-455-5239
District: 100 *Room:* 826 LOB *e-mail:* gunthea@assemby.state.ny.us
Committees: Agriculture; Environmental Conservation; Health; Mental Health (Chair); Racing & Wagering; Real Property Taxation
Senior Staff: Allison Horan

Stephen Hawley (R) 518-455-5811/fax: 518-455-5558
District: 139 *Room:* 329 LOB *e-mail:* hawleys@assembly.state.ny.us
Title: Assistant Minority Leader
Committees: Agriculture; Insurance; Veterans' Affairs; Ways & Means
Senior Staff: Eileen Banker

Carl E Heastie (D) 518-455-3791/fax: 518-455-4812
District: 83 *Room:* 932 LOB *e-mail:* speaker@assembly.state.ny.us
Title: Speaker
Committees: Rules
Senior Staff: Jevonni Brooks

Andrew Hevesi (D) 518-455-4926/fax: 518-455-5173
District: 28 *Room:* 844 LOB *e-mail:* hevesia@assembly.state.ny.us
Committees: Energy; Health; Insurance; Labor; Social Services (Chair)
Senior Staff: Christopher Kaznowski

Dov Hikind (D) 518-455-5721/fax: 518-455-5948
District: 48 *Room:* 551 LOB *e-mail:* hikindd@assembly.state.ny.us
Title: Assistant Majority Leader
Committees:
Senior Staff: Marc B Kronenberg

Earlene Hooper (D-I) 518-455-5861/fax: 518-455-4329
District: 18 *Room:* 739 LOB *e-mail:* hoopere@assembly.state.ny.us
Title: Deputy Speaker
Committees: Education; Rules; Ways & Means
Senior Staff: Arndreia M Goodbee

Pamela Hunter (D) 518-455-5383
District: 128 *Room:* 432 LOB *e-mail:* hunterp@assembly.state.ny.us
Title: Deputy Speaker
Committees: Insurance; Social Services; Transportation; Veterans' Affairs

Alicia Hyndman (D) 518-455-4451
District: 29 *Room:* 820 LOB *e-mail:*
Committees: Aging; Economic Development, Job Creation, Commerce & Industry; Small Business; Transportation

Ellen Jaffee (D) 518-455-5118/fax: 518-455-5119
District: 97 *Room:* 650 LOB *e-mail:* jaffeee@assembly.state.ny.us
Committees: Children & Families; Economic Development, Job Creation, Commerce & Industry; Environmental Conservation; Health; Higher Education; Mental Health; Oversight, Analysis & Investigation (Chair)
Senior Staff: Tiffany Card

Kimberly Jean-Pierre (D) 518-455-5787/fax: 518-455-3976
District: 11 *Room:* 530 LOB *e-mail:* jeanpierrek@assembly.state.ny.us
Committees: Banks; Economic Development, Job Creation, Commerce & Industry; Mental Health; Transportation
Senior Staff: Bilal Malik

Mark Johns (R) 518-455-5784/fax: 518-455-4639
District: 135 *Room:* 549 LOB *e-mail:* johnsm@assembly.state.ny.us
Committees: Aging; Alcoholism & Drug Abuse; Governmental Employees; Governmental Operations; Housing
Senior Staff: Sean Delehanty

Latoya Joyner (D) 518-455-5671/fax: 518-455-5461
District: 77 *Room:* 427 LOB *e-mail:* joynerl@assembly.state.ny.us
Committees: Aging; Consumer Affairs; Housing; Insurance; Judiciary; Social Services
Senior Staff: Jamie Gilkey

Steve Katz (R) 518-455-5783/fax: 518-455-5543
District: 94 *Room:* 718 LOB *e-mail:* katzs@assembly.state.ny.us
Committees: Aging; Alcoholism & Drug Abuse; Economic Development, Job Creation, Commerce & Industry; Housing; Mental Health
Senior Staff: Tara Keegan

Brian P Kavanagh (D) 518-455-5506/fax: 518-455-4801
District: 74 *Room:* 419 LOB *e-mail:* kavanaghb@assembly.state.ny.us
Committees: Cities; Corporations, Authorities & Commissions; Election Law; Environmental Conservation; Housing; Labor
Senior Staff: Anna Pycior

Michael P Kearns (D) 518-455-4691
District: 142 *Room:* 431 LOB *e-mail:* kearnsm@assembly.state.ny.us
Committees: Banks; Cities; Housing; Oversight, Analysis & Investigation
Senior Staff: Kelly Krug

Ron Kim (D) 518-455-5411/fax: 518-455-4650
District: 40 *Room:* 429 LOB *e-mail:* kimr@assembly.state.ny.us
Committees: Children & Families; Corporations, Authorities & Commissions; Education; Governmental Operations; Housing; Social Services
Senior Staff: Yuh-Line Niou

Brian M Kolb (R-I-C) 518-455-3751/fax: 518-455-4650
District: 131 *Room:* 933 LOB *e-mail:* kolbb@assembly.state.ny.us
Title: Minority Leader
Committees: Rules (Ranking Member)
Senior Staff: Judy Skype

Kieran Michael Lalor (R-I-C) 518-455-5725/fax: 518-455-5729
District: 105 *Room:* 531 LOB *e-mail:* lalork@assembly.state.ny.us
Committees: Banks; Governmental Operations; Real Property Taxation (Ranking Member); Small Business; Veterans' Affairs
Senior Staff: Chris Covucci

Charles D Lavine (D) 518-455-5456/fax: 518-455-5467
District: 13 *Room:* 441 LOB *e-mail:* lavinec@assembly.state.ny.us
Committees: Codes; Ethics & Guidance (Chair); Health; Higher Education; Insurance; Judiciary
Senior Staff: Tara Butler-Sahai

Peter Lawrence (R) 518-455-4664/fax: 518-455-3093
District: 134 *Room:* 722 LOB *e-mail:* lawrencep@assembly.state.ny.us
Committees: Ethics & Guidance; Higher Education; Oversight, Analysis & Investigation; Racing & Wagering; Small Business
Senior Staff: Aaron Baker

Joseph R Lentol (D) 518-455-4477/fax: 518-455-4599
District: 50 *Room:* 632 LOB *e-mail:* lentolj@assembly.state.ny.us
Committees: Codes (Chair); Election Law; Rules; Ways & Means
Senior Staff: Catherine E Peake

Barbara S Lifton (D) 518-455-5444/fax: 518-455-4640
District: 125 *Room:* 555 LOB *e-mail:* liftonb@assembly.state.ny.us
Title: Chair, Majority Steering
Committees: Agriculture; Education; Election Law; Environmental Conservation; Higher Education; Rural Resources
Senior Staff: Linda Smith

Guillermo Linares (D) 518-455-5807
District: 72 *Room:* 534 LOB *e-mail:* linaresg@assembly.state.ny.us
Committees: Aging; Banks; Cities; Housing; Mental Health
Senior Staff: Herminio Martinez

Peter D Lopez (R) 518-455-5363/fax: 518-455-5856
District: 102 *Room:* 402 LOB *e-mail:* lopezp@assembly.state.ny.us
Title: Vice Chair Minority Conference
Committees: Agriculture; Alcoholism & Drug Abuse; Corporations, Authorities & Commissions; Education; Environmental Conservation
Senior Staff: Hannah Roberti

Donna A Lupardo (D) 518-455-5431/fax: 518-455-5693
District: 123 *Room:* 626 LOB *e-mail:* lupardod@assembly.state.ny.us
Committees: Children & Families (Chair); Economic Development, Job Creation, Commerce & Industry; Environmental Conservation; Higher Education; Transportation
Senior Staff: Joan Marcy

Chad A Lupinacci (R-C-I-WF) 518-455-5732/fax: 518-455-5553
District: 10 *Room:* 937 LOB *e-mail:* lupinaccic@assembly.state.ny.us
Committees: Election Law; Higher Education; Judiciary; Tourism, Parks, Arts & Sports Development; Transportation
Senior Staff: Frances Spatafora

William Magee (D-I) 518-455-4807/fax: 518-455-5237
District: 121 *Room:* 828 LOB *e-mail:* mageew@assembly.state.ny.us
Committees: Aging; Agriculture (Chair); Banks; Higher Education; Local Governments
Senior Staff: Laura Martino

William B Magnarelli (D-WF-VE) 518-455-4826/fax: 518-455-5498
District: 129 *Room:* 837 LOB *e-mail:* magnarw@assembly.state.ny.us
Committees: Economic Development, Job Creation, Commerce & Industry; Education; Oversight, Analysis & Investigation; Local Governments (Chair); Rules
Senior Staff: Christine H Slocum

Nicole Malliotakis (R-C) 518-455-5716/fax: 518-455-5970
District: 64 *Room:* 725 LOB *e-mail:* malliotakisn@assembly.state.ny.us
Committees: Banks; Corporations, Authorities & Commissions; Government Employees (Ranking Member); Transportation; Ways & Means
Senior Staff: Paul Marrone

Margaret M Markey (D) 518-455-4755/fax: 518-455-5032
District: 30 *Room:* 712 LOB *e-mail:* markeym@assembly.state.ny.us
Committees: Labor; Racing & Wagering; Tourism, Parks, Arts & Sports Development (Chair); Rules; Ways & Means
Senior Staff: Eileen Boland

Shelly Mayer (D) 518-455-3662/fax: 518-455-5499
District: 90 *Room:* 327 LOB *e-mail:* mayers@assembly.state.ny.us
Committees: Children & Families; Cities; Health; Education; Labor; Social Services
Senior Staff: Rachel A. Estroff

John T McDonald III (D) 518-455-4474/fax: 518-455-4727
District: 108 *Room:* 417 LOB *e-mail:* mcdonaldj@assembly.state.ny.us
Committees: Aging; Alcoholism & Drug Abuse; Cities; Mental Health; Real Property Taxation; Insurance
Senior Staff: Emily Shover

David G McDonough (R-C-I) 518-455-4633/fax: 518-455-5559
District: 14 *Room:* 443 LOB *e-mail:* mcdonod@assembly.state.ny.us
Title: Vice Chair, Minority Joint Conference Committee
Committees: Consumer Affairs & Protection; Education; Health; Transportation (Ranking Minority Member); Veterans' Affairs
Senior Staff: Lynette Liverani

Tom McKevitt (R) 518-455-5341/fax: 518-455-4346
District: 17 *Room:* 546 LOB *e-mail:* mckevit@assembly.state.ny.us
Title: Assistant Minority Leader Pro Tempore
Committees: Codes; Consumer Affairs & Protection; Election Law; Local Governments
Senior Staff: Lynn Schaefering

Steve McLaughlin (R) 518-455-5777/fax: 518-455-5923
District: 107 *Room:* 533 LOB *e-mail:* mclaughlins@assembly.state.ny.us
Committees: Children & Families; Economic Development, Job Creation, Commerce and Industry (RM); Education; Social Services
Senior Staff: Jennifer Polaro

Michael Miller (D) 518-455-4621/fax: 518-455-5361
District: 38 *Room:* 542 LOB *e-mail:* millermg@assembly.state.ny.us
Title: Chair, House Operations
Committees: Aging; Banks; Education; House Operations (Chair); Labor; Racing & Wagering; Veterans' Affairs
Senior Staff: Angel Vazquez

Michael Montesano (R-I-C) 518-455-4684/fax: 518-455-5477
District: 15 *Room:* 437 LOB *e-mail:* montesanom@assembly.state.ny.us
Title: Assistant Minority Whip
Committees: Codes; Corporations, Authorities & Commissions; Ethics & Guidance; Judiciary (Ranking Member); Oversight, Analysis & Investigation (Ranking Member)
Senior Staff: Ida McQuair

Joseph D Morelle (D) 518-455-5373/fax: 518-455-5647
District: 136 *Room:* 926 LOB *e-mail:* morellej@assembly.state.ny.us
Title: Majority Leader
Committees:
Senior Staff: Kristin Anderson

Walter T Mosley (D) 518-455-5325/fax: 518-455-3684
District: 57 *Room:* 528 LOB *e-mail:* mosleyw@assembly.state.ny.us
Committees: Banks; Codes; Correction; Education; Housing
Senior Staff: Gigi Elliott-Davis

Francisco Moya (D) 518-455-4567/fax: 518-455-5375
District: 39 *Room:* 727 LOB *e-mail:* moyaf@assembly.state.ny.us
Committees: Corporations, Authorities & Commissions; Energy; Housing; Insurance; Labor; Ways & Means
Senior Staff: Meghan Tadio

Dean Murray (R) 518-455-4901/fax: 518-455-5908
District: 3 *Room:* 430 LOB *e-mail:* murrayd@assembly.state.ny.us
Committees: Aging; Education; Small Business; Tourism, Parks, Arts & Sports Development; Transportation
Senior Staff: Ed Flood

Bill Nojay (R-I) 518-455-5662/fax: 518-455-5918
District: 133 *Room:* 527 LOB *e-mail:* nojayw@assembly.state.ny.us
Committees: Consumer Affairs & Proteection; Election Law (Ranking Member); Mental Health; Transportation
Senior Staff: Barbara Collins

Catherine T Nolan (D) 518-455-4851/fax: 518-455-3847
District: 37 *Room:* 836 LOB *e-mail:* nolanc@assembly.state.ny.us
Committees: Corporations, Authorities & Commissions; Education (Chair); Rules; Veterans' Affairs; Ways & Means
Senior Staff: Kathleen Whynot

Daniel J O'Donnell (D) 518-455-5603/fax: 518-455-3812
District: 69 *Room:* 526 LOB *e-mail:* odonnelld@assembly.state.ny.us
Committees: Codes; Correction (Chair); Education; Environmental Conservation; Judiciary; Tourism, Parks, Arts & Sports
Senior Staff: Nicholas O'Neill

Robert C Oaks (R-C) 518-455-5655/fax: 518-455-5407
District: 130 *Room:* 444 CAP *e-mail:* oaksr@assembly.state.ny.us
Title: Ranking Minority Member, Ways & Means
Committees: Rules; Ways & Means (Ranking Member)
Senior Staff: Myra Brown

Felix W Ortiz (D) 518-455-3821/fax: 518-455-3828
District: 51 *Room:* 731 LOB *e-mail:* ortizf@assembly.state.ny.us
Title: Assistant Speaker
Committees: Correction; Labor; Rules; Ways & Means
Senior Staff: Jeffrey Wice

Steven Otis (D) 518-455-4897/fax: 518-455-4861
District: 91 *Room:* 325 LOB *e-mail:* otiss@assembly.state.ny.us
Committees: Agriculture; Corporations Authorities & Commissions; Environmental Conservation; Libraries & Education Technology; Local Governments; Tourism, Parks, Arts & Sports Development
Senior Staff: Debra Lagapa

Offices and agencies generally appear in alphabetical order, except when specific order is requested by listee.

Philip Palmesano (R). 518-455-5791/fax: 518-455-4644
District: 132 *Room:* 723 LOB *e-mail:* palmesanop@assembly.state.ny.us
Title: Secretary, Minority Conference
Committees: Corporations, Authorities & Commissions; Energy (Ranking Member); Libraries & Education Technology; Real Property Taxation; Tourism, Parks, Art & Sports Development
Senior Staff: Sperry Navone

Anthony H Palumbo (R). 518-455-5294/fax: 518-455-4740
District: 2 *Room:* 719 LOB *e-mail:* palumba@assembly.state.ny.us
Committees: Consumer Affairs & Protection (Ranking Member); Environmental Conservation; Governmental Employees; Judiciary; Social Services
Senior Staff: Jennine Kubik

Amy R Paulin (D). 518-455-5585/fax: 518-455-5409
District: 88 *Room:* 713 LOB *e-mail:* paulina@assembly.state.ny.us
Committees: Energy (Chair); Education; Health; Higher Education
Senior Staff: Nancy Fisher

Crystal D Peoples-Stokes (D). 518-455-5005/fax: 518-455-5471
District: 141 *Room:* 625 LOB *e-mail:* peoplec@assembly.state.ny.us
Committees: Alcoholism & Drug Abuse; Environmental Conservation; Governmental Operations (Chair); Health; Higher Education; Insurance
Senior Staff: Mark Boyd

N Nick Perry (D) 518-455-4166/fax: 518-455-5478
District: 58 *Room:* 736 LOB *e-mail:* perryn@assembly.state.ny.us
Title: Assistant Speaker Pro Tempore
Committees: Banks; Codes; Labor; Rules; Transportation; Ways & Means
Senior Staff: Joyce Elie

Victor Pichardo (D). 518-455-5511/fax: 518-455-5449
District: 86 *Room:* 920 LOB *e-mail:* pichardov@assembly.state.ny.us
Committees: Cities; Higher Education; Housing; Real Property Taxation; Small Business; Social Services
Senior Staff: Nicole Lauterbach

James Gary Pretlow (D). 518-455-5291/fax: 518-455-5447
District: 89 *Room:* 845 LOB *e-mail:* pretloj@assembly.state.ny.us
Committees: Codes; Insurance; Racing & Wagering (Chair); Rules; Ways & Means
Senior Staff: Janet E Edwards

Dan Quart (D). 518-455-4794/fax: 518-455-4629
District: 73 *Room:* 741 LOB *e-mail:* quartd@assembly.state.ny.us
Committees: Alcoholism & Drug Abuse; Consumer Affairs & Protection; Corporations, Authorities & Commissions; Insurance; Judiciary; Tourism, Parks, Arts & Sports Development
Senior Staff: Amanda Wallwin

Edward Ra (R). 518-455-4627/fax: 518-455-4643
District: 19 *Room:* 544 LOB *e-mail:* rae@assembly.state.ny.us
Title: Vice Chair, Minority Steering Committee
Committees: Codes; Education (Ranking Member); Health; Higher Education; Transportation
Senior Staff: Vacant

Andrew P Raia (R-C-I). 518-455-5952/fax: 518-455-5804
District: 12 *Room:* 629 LOB *e-mail:* raiaa@assembly.state.ny.us
Title: Deputy Minority Whip
Committees: Banks; Environmental Conservation; Health; Housing; Rules
Senior Staff: Judy VanAmburgh

Philip R Ramos (D-I-WF) 518-455-5185/fax: 518-455-5236
District: 6 *Room:* 648 LOB *e-mail:* ramosp@assembly.state.ny.us
Title: Deputy Majority Leader
Committees: Aging; Education; Local Governments; Ways & Means
Senior Staff: Erik Vasquez

Diana C Richardson (WF). 518-455-5262
District: 43 *Room:* 834 LOB *e-mail:* richardsond@assembly.state.ny.us
Committees: Banks; Corporations, Authorities & Commissions; Economic Development, Job Creation, Commerce & Industry; Mental Health; Small Business
Senior Staff: Vacant

Jose Rivera (D). 518-455-5414/fax: 518-455-5322
District: 78 *Room:* 536 LOB *e-mail:* riveraj@assembly.state.ny.us
Title: Deputy Majority Whip
Committees: Aging; Agriculture; Insurance; Small Business
Senior Staff: Jasmin Clavasquin

Annette Robinson (D). 518-455-5474/fax: 518-455-5857
District: 56 *Room:* 424 LOB *e-mail:* robinsona@assembly.state.ny.us
Committees: Aging; Banks (Chair); Children & Families; Housing; Oversight, Analysis & Investigation; Real Property Taxation; Small Business
Senior Staff: Adrienne Johnson

Robert J Rodriguez (D) 518-455-4781/fax: 518-455-3893
District: 68 *Room:* 729 LOB *e-mail:* rodriguezrj@assembly.state.ny.us
Committees: Banks; Corporations, Authorities & Commissions; Housing; Labor; Mental Health; Ways & Means
Senior Staff: Maggie McDermott

Linda B Rosenthal (D-WF) 518-455-5802/fax: 518-455-5015
District: 67 *Room:* 627 LOB *e-mail:* rosentl@assembly.state.ny.us
Committees: Agriculture; Alcoholism & Drug Abuse (Chair); Education; Energy; Health; Housing; Tourism, Parks, Arts & Sports Development
Senior Staff: Lauren Schuster

Nily Rozic (D-WF). 518-455-5172/fax: 518-455-5479
District: 25 *Room:* 820 LOB *e-mail:* rozicn@assembly.state.ny.us
Committees: Children & Families; Corporations, Authorities & Commissions; Correction; Environmental Conservation; Labor
Senior Staff: Erin Rogers

Addie J Russell (D-WF) 518-455-5545/fax: 518-455-5751
District: 116 *Room:* 456 LOB *e-mail:* russella@assembly.state.ny.us
Committees: Agriculture; Corporations, Authorities & Commissions; Economic Development, Job Creation, Commerce & Industry; Energy; Local Governments; Veterans' Affairs
Senior Staff: Mark Pacilio

Sean Ryan (D). 518-455-4886/fax: 518-455-4890
District: 149 *Room:* 540 LOB *e-mail:* ryans@assembly.state.ny.us
Committees: Banks; Education; Energy; Environmental Conservation; Local Governments; Veterans' Affairs
Senior Staff: Joshua Pennel

Joseph S Saladino (R). 518-455-5305/fax: 518-455-5024
District: 9 *Room:* 720 LOB *e-mail:* saladij@assembly.state.ny.us
Title: Chair, Minority Program Committee
Committees: Environmental Conservation; Governmental Employees; Labor; Libraries & Education Technology (Ranking Member); Ways & Means
Senior Staff: Victoria Ventura

Angelo Santabarbara (D). 518-455-5197/fax: 518-455-5024
District: 111 *Room:* 654 LOB *e-mail:* santabarbaraa@assembly.state.ny.us
Committees: Agriculture; Energy; Governmental Employees; Racing & Wagering; Small Business; Veterans' Affairs
Senior Staff: Gerard Parisi

Michelle Schimel (D). 518-455-5192/fax: 518-455-4921
District: 16 *Room:* 702 LOB *e-mail:* schimelm@assembly.state.ny.us
Title: Chair, Majority Conference
Committees: Environmental Conservation; Governmental Operations; Local Governments; Transportation; Veterans' Affairs
Senior Staff: Nicole Duckham

Robin L Schimminger (D-I-C) 518-455-4767/fax: 518-455-4724
District: 140 *Room:* 847 LOB *e-mail:* schimmr@assembly.state.ny.us
Committees: Codes; Economic Development, Job Creation, Commerce & Industry (Chair); Health; Ways & Means
Senior Staff: Kenneth L Berlinski

Rebecca Seawright (D) 518-455-5676
District: 76 *Room:* 818 LOB *e-mail:* seawrightr@assembly.state.ny.us
Committees: Banks; Consumer Affairs & Protection; Corporations, Authorities & Commissions; Judiciary; Tourism, Parks, Arts & Sports Development
Senior Staff: Cali Madia

Luis R Sepulveda (D) 518-455-5102/fax: 518-455-5459
District: 87 *Room:* 432 LOB *e-mail:* sepulvedal@assembly.state.ny.us
Committees: Aging; Agriculture; Banks; Correction; Housing
Senior Staff: Thomas Musich

Michael Simanowitz (D) 518-455-4404
District: 27 *Room:* 742 LOB *e-mail:* simanowitzm@assembly.state.ny.us
Committees: Aging; Agriculture; Consumer Affairs & Protection; Economic Development, Job Creation, Commerce & Industry; Higher Education; Small Business
Senior Staff: Scott Wolff

Jo Anne Simon (D) 518-455-5426
District: 52 *Room:* 326 LOB *e-mail:* simonj@assembly.state.ny.us
Committees: Consumer Affairs & Protection; Higher Education; Judiciary; Labor; Transportation
Senior Staff: Ptahra Jeppe

Aravella Simotas (D) 518-455-5014/fax: 518-455-4044
District: 36 *Room:* 652 LOB *e-mail:* simotasa@assembly.state.ny.us
Title: Vice Chair, Majority Conference
Committees: Banks; Consumer Affairs & Protection; Corporations, Authorities & Commissions; Energy
Senior Staff: Samantha Darche

Frank Skartados (D) 518-455-5762/fax: 518-455-5593
District: 104 *Room:* 435 LOB *e-mail:* skartadosf@assembly.state.ny.us
Committees: Agriculture; Economic Development; Local Governments; Small Business; Tourism, Parks, Arts & Sports Development; Transportation
Senior Staff: Steve Gold

James Skoufis (D) 518-455-5441/fax: 518-455-5884
District: 99 *Room:* 821 LOB *e-mail:* skoufisj@assembly.state.ny.us
Committees: Agriculture; Local Governments; Insurance; Labor; Transportation; Veterans' Affairs
Senior Staff: Laurie Tautel

Michaelle C Solages (D) 518-455-4465/fax: 518-455-5560
District: 22 *Room:* 619 LOB *e-mail:* solagesm@assembly.state.ny.us
Committees: Consumer Affairs & Protection; Governmental Employess; Libraries & Education Technology; Racing & Wagering; Social Services
Senior Staff: Marthe Desdunes

Dan Stec (R-I-C) 518-455-5565/fax: 518-455-7710
District: 114 *Room:* 940 LOB *e-mail:* stecd@assembly.state.ny.us
Committees: Banks, Environmental Conservation (Ranking Member); Local Governments; Social Services; Tourism, Parks, Arts & Sports Development
Senior Staff: Debbie Capezzuti

Phil Steck (D) 518-455-5931/fax: 518-455-5840
District: 110 *Room:* 819 LOB *e-mail:* steckp@assembly.state.ny.us
Committees: Children & Families; Health; Insurance; Judiciary; Transportation
Senior Staff: Thad Rutherford

Al Stirpe (D) 518-455-4505/fax: 518-455-5593
District: 127 *Room:* 656 LOB *e-mail:* stirpea@assembly.state.ny.us
Title: Assistant Majority Whip
Committees: Agriculture; Alcoholism & Drug Abuse; Economic Development, Job Creation, Commerce & Industry; Higher Education; Tourism, Parks, Arts & Sports Development
Senior Staff: Dorothy Money

James N Tedisco (R-I-C) 518-455-5772/fax: 518-455-3750
District: 112 *Room:* 404 LOB *e-mail:* tediscj@assembly.state.ny.us
Title: Minority Whip
Committees: Banks; Economic Development, Job Creation, Commerce & Industry; Racing & Wagering; Rules
Senior Staff: Adam Kramer

Claudia Tenney (R) 518-455-5334/fax: 518-455-5391
District: 101 *Room:* 426 LOB *e-mail:* tenneyc@assembly.state.ny.us
Committees: Banks (Ranking Member); Codes; Education; Social Services; Veterans' Affairs
Senior Staff: Karen Newton

Fred W Thiele, Jr (D) 518-455-5997/fax: 518-455-5963
District: 1 *Room:* 746 LOB *e-mail:* thielef@assembly.state.ny.us
Committees: Education; Environmental Conservation; Small Business (Chair); Oversight, Analysis & Investigation; Transportation; Ways & Means
Senior Staff: Lisa Lombardo

Matthew Titone (D-WF) 518-455-4677/fax: 518-455-5946
District: 61 *Room:* 643 LOB *e-mail:* titonem@assembly.state.ny.us
Committees: Education; Environmental Conservation; Health; Judiciary; Social Services; Tourism, Parks, Arts & Sports Development
Senior Staff: Chris Bauer

Michele R Titus (D) 518-455-5668/fax: 518-455-3892
District: 31 *Room:* 522 LOB *e-mail:* titusm@assembly.state.ny.us
Committees: Children & Families; Codes; Education; Ethics & Guidance; Labor (Chair); Judiciary
Senior Staff: A Richard McKoy

Latrice Walker (D) 518-455-4466
District: 55 *Room:* 628 LOB *e-mail:* walkerl@assembly.state.ny.us
Committees: Correction; Economic Development, Job Creation, Commerce & Industry; Election Law; Energy; Housing
Senior Staff: Alicha Ampry-Samuel

Raymond Walter (R) 518-455-4618/fax: 518-455-5023
District: 146 *Room:* 550 LOB *e-mail:* walterr@assembly.state.ny.us
Committees: Economic Development, Job Creation, Commerce & Industry; Health; Housing; Insurance; Ways & Means
Senior Staff: Erin Baker

Helene E Weinstein (D) 518-455-5462/fax: 518-455-5752
District: 41 *Room:* 831 LOB *e-mail:* weinsth@assembly.state.ny.us
Committees: Aging; Codes; Judiciary (Chair); Rules; Ways & Means
Senior Staff: Yehuda Schupper

David I Weprin (D) 518-455-5806/fax: 518-455-5977
District: 24 *Room:* 602 LOB *e-mail:* weprind@assembly.state.ny.us
Title: Secretary, Majority Conference
Committees: Banks; Cities; Codes; Election Law; Judiciary; Ways & Means
Senior Staff: Janna Davis

Jaime R Williams (D) 518-455-5211
District: 59 *Room:* 324 LOB *e-mail:*
Committees: Children & Familes; Environmental Conservation; Tourism, Parks, Arts & Sports Development; Transportation

Carrie Woerner (D) 518-455-5404/fax: 518-455-3727
District: 113 *Room:* 323 LOB *e-mail:* woernerc@assembly.state.ny.us
Committees: Agriculture; Local Governments; Racing & Wagering; Small Business; Tourism, Parks, Arts & Sports Development
Senior Staff: Mark Luciano

Offices and agencies generally appear in alphabetical order, except when specific order is requested by listee.

Angela M Wozniak (C) 518-455-5921/fax: 518-455-3962
District: 143 *Room:* 721 LOB *e-mail:* wozniaka@assembly.state.ny.us
Committees: Aging; Children & Families; Cities; Labor; Local Governments
Senior Staff: Beth Bochiechio

Keith L T Wright (D) 518-455-4793/fax: 518-455-3890
District: 70 *Room:* 943 LOB *e-mail:* wrightk@assembly.state.ny.us
Committees: Codes; Correction; Housing (Chair); Rules; Ways & Means
Senior Staff: Jeanine Johnson

Kenneth Zebrowski (D-I-C-WF) 518-455-5735/fax: 518-455-5561
District: 96 *Room:* 637 LOB *e-mail:* zebrowskik@assembly.state.ny.us
Committees: Codes; Environmental Conservation; Ethics & Guidance; Government Employees; Judiciary; Labor
Senior Staff: Chris Bresnan

STATE ASSEMBLY STANDING COMMITTEES

Aging

Chair:
Steven Cymbrowitz (D) 518-455-5214
Ranking Minority Member:
Angela M Wozniak (C) 518-455-5921

Committee Staff
Clerk:
Lena DeThomasis 518-455-5965

Key Assembly Staff Assignments
Majority Program Analyst:
Erin Cunningham 518-455-4355

Membership

Majority
Peter Abbate, Jr.
Edward Braunstein
John McDonald III
Michael DenDekker
Didi Barrett
William Magee
Annette Robinson
Phil Ramos
Charles Barron
Guillermo Linares
Michael Simanowitz
Carmen Arroyo
Anthony Brindisi
Helene Weinstein
Phillip Goldfeder
Pamela Harris
Michael Miller
Jose Rivera
Alicia Hyndman
Latoya Joyner
Luis Sepulveda

Minority
Christopher Friend
Dean Murray
Steve Katz
Joseph Giglio
Mark Johns
Karl Brabenec

Agriculture

Chair:
William Magee (D) 518-455-4807
Ranking Minority Member:
Kenneth Blankenbush (R) 518-455-5797

Committee Staff
Clerk:
Connie Groves 518-455-4807

Key Assembly Staff Assignments
Majority Program & Legislative Analyst:
Robert Stern 518-455-4928
Minority Analyst/Counsel:
Nicholas Forst 518-455-4515
Majority Associate Counsel:
Felicia Reid 518-455-4285

Membership

Majority
Didi Barrett
Michael Benedetto
Barbara Lifton
Linda Rosenthal
Addie Russell
Luis Sepulveda
Frank Skartados
Carrie Woerner
Harry Bronson
Aileen Gunther
Steven Otis
Jose Rivera
Angelo Santabarbara
Michael Simanowitz
James Skoufis
Al Stirpe

Minority
Marc Butler
Gary Finch
Peter Lopez
Clifford Crouch
Stephen Hawley

Alcoholism & Drug Abuse

Chair:
Linda Rosenthal (D) 518-455-5802
Ranking Minority Member:
Mark Johns (R) 518-455-5784

Committee Staff
Clerk:
Holly Francisco 518-455-5802

Key Assembly Staff Assignments
Majority Program Analyst:
Alexis Conti 518-455-4371
Majority Associate Counsel:
Jennifer Sacco
Minority Analyst/Counsel:
Sarah Shearer 518-455-4285

Membership

Majority
Carmen Arroyo
Pamela Harris
Charles Barron
Crystal D Peoples-Stokes
Al Stirpe
Maritza Davila
Michael G DenDekker
John McDonald III
Dan Quart

Minority
David DiPietro
Peter Lopez
Steven Katz

Banks

Chair:
Annette Robinson (D) 518-455-5474
Ranking Minority Member:
Claudia Tenney (R) 518-455-5334

Committee Staff
Clerk:
Virginia Rawlins 518-455-5474

Key Assembly Staff Assignments
Majority Principal Analyst:
Peter Hoffman 518-455-4928
Majority Associate Counsel:
Teri Kleinmann 518-455-4928
Minority Analyst/Counsel:
Michelle Pellegri-Buono 518-455-5230

Membership

Majority
Peter J Abbate, Jr
Patricia Fahy
Michael Kearns
William Magee
Walter Mosley
Rodneyse Bichotte
Mark Gjonaj
Michael Blake
Michael Miller
N. Nick Perry

Offices and agencies generally appear in alphabetical order, except when specific order is requested by listee.

Robert Rodriguez
Sean Ryan
Luis Sepulveda
Alice Cancel
David Weprin
Kimberly Jean-Pierre
Rebecca Seawright
Aravella Simotas
Guillermo Linares

Minority
Gary Finch
Andrew Garbarino
Dan Stec
James Tedisco
Keiran Michael Lalor
Brian Curran
Nicole Malliotakis
Diana Richardson
Andrew Raia

Children & Families

Chair:
Donna Lupardo (D) 518-455-5431
Ranking Minority Member:
Steven McLaughlin (R) 518-455-5777

Committee Staff

Clerk:
Jeff Quain 518-455-4451
Majority Assistant Secretary:
Rebecca Mudie 518-455-4881

Key Assembly Staff Assignments
Majority Program & Counsel Legislative Analyst:
Naomi Schultz 518-455-4371

Membership

Majority
Carmen Arroyo
Patricia Fahy
Ellen Jaffee
Shelley Mayer
Nily Rozic
Michele R Titus
Pamela Harris
Maritza Davila
Jaime Williams
Annette M. Robinson
Phil Steck

Minority
Joe Giglio
Christopher Friend
Angela M Wozniak

Cities

Chair:
Michael Benedetto (D) 518-455-5296
Ranking Minority Member:
Vacant (R) 518-455-0000

Committee Staff

Clerk:
Judith Talar 518-455-5296

Key Assembly Staff Assignments
Majority Assistant Secretary:
Julia Mallalieu
Minority Analyst/Counsel:
Edmund V Wick 518-455-4262

Membership

Majority
Alice Cancel
Marcos Crespo
Brian P. Kavanagh
Erik Dilan
John McDonald III
David Weprin
Edward Braunstein
Victor Pichardo
Michael Kearns
Shelley Mayer
Guillermo Linares

Minority
Andrew Goodell
Angela M Wozniak
Karl Brabenec

Codes

Chair:
Joseph R Lentol (D) 518-455-4477
Ranking Minority Member:
Al Graf (R) 518-455-5937

Committee Staff

Clerk:
Wilda Lang 518-455-4477

Key Assembly Staff Assignments
Senior Team Counsel:
Marty Rosenbaum 518-455-4313
Counsel:
Jonathan Bailey 518-455-4313
Majority Program Analyst:
Nathaniel Jenkins
Minority Analyst/Counsel:
Lori Smith

Membership

Majority
Thomas Abinanti
Vivian E Cook
Charles D Lavine
Daniel J. O'Donnell
James Gary Pretlow
Michele R. Titus
David Weprin
Kenneth Zebrowski
James F. Brennan
Steven Cymbrowitz
Walter Mosley
N Nick Perry
Robin L. Schimminger
Helene Weinstein
Keith L. Wright

Minority
Joseph Giglio
Tom McKevitt
Edward Ra
Claudia Tenney
Michael Montesano

Consumer Affairs & Protection

Chair:
Jeffrey Dinowitz (D) 518-455-5965
Ranking Minority Member:
Anthony Palumbo (R) 518-455-5294

Committee Staff

Clerk:
William Schwartz 518-455-5965

Key Assembly Staff Assignments
Majority Legislative Analyst:
Michael Szydlo 518-455-4355
Minority Analyst/Counsel:
Edmund V Wick 518-455-4262

Membership

Majority
Peter J Abbate, Jr
Erik Dilan
Dan Quart
Jo Anne Simon
Rebecca Seawright
David Buchwald
Latoya Joyner
Michael Simanowitz
Aravella Simotas
Michaelle Solages

Minority
Tom McKevitt
David McDonough
Bill Nojay

Corporations, Authorities & Commissions

Chair:
James F Brennan (D) 518-455-5377
Ranking Minority Member:
Jane Corwin (R) 518-455-4601

Offices and agencies generally appear in alphabetical order, except when specific order is requested by listee.

Committee Staff
Clerk:
Lisa Forkas 518-455-5753

Key Assembly Staff Assignments
Majority Assistant Secretary:
Christian Malagna 518-455-4881
Majority Associate Counsel:
Gregory Berck 518-455-4881

Membership

Majority
Thomas Abinanti
Sandra R Galef
Philip Goldfeder
Brian P. Kavanagh
Francisco Moya
Steven Otis
Robert Rodriguez
Rebecca Seawright
Addie J. Russell
Vivian E Cook
David Buchwald
Erik Dilan
Ron Kim
Catherine T. Nolan
Dan Quart
Aravella Simotas
Nily Rozic

Minority
Ken Blankenbush
Nicole Malliotakis
Philip Palmesano
Peter Lopez
Christopher Friend
Michael Montesano
Diana Richardson

Correction
Chair:
Daniel O'Donnell (D) 518-455-5603
Ranking Minority Member:
Joseph Giglio (R) 518-455-5241

Committee Staff
Clerk:
Cheryl Myers 518-455-4548

Key Assembly Staff Assignments
Majority Counsel:
Dianna Goodwin 518-455-4313
Minority Analsyt/Counsel:
Lori Smith 518-455-5002

Membership

Majority
William Colton
Felix W Ortiz
Nily Rozic
Walter Mosley
Keith L. T. Wright
Maritza Davila
Michael Blake
Luis Sepulveda
Latrice Walker

Minority
Janet L Duprey
Gary Finch

Economic Development, Job Creation, Commerce & Industry
Chair:
Robin L Schimminger (D) 518-455-4767
Ranking Minority Member:
Raymond Walter (R) 518-455-4618

Committee Staff
Clerk:
Patrice Mago 518-455-4767

Key Assembly Staff Assignments
Majority Program Analyst:
Lekeya Martin 518-455-4928
Minority Analyst/Counsel:
Michelle Pellegri-Buono

Membership

Majority
Didi Barrett
Anthony Brindisi
Kevin A Cahill
Frank Skartados
Al Stirpe
Donna Lupardo
Michael Simanowitz
Alicia Hyndman
Addie J Russell
Maritza Davila
Harry Bronson
David F Gantt
William B Magnarelli
Charles Barron
Rodneyse Bichotte
Latrice Walker
Kimberly Jean-Pierre
Ellen Jaffee

Minority
Marc Butler
Diana Richardson (WF)
Steven McLaughlin
James Tedisco
Clifford W Crouch
David DiPietro
Steve Katz

Education
Chair:
Catherine Nolan (D) 518-455-4851
Ranking Minority Member:
Edward Ra (R) 518-455-4627

Committee Staff
Committee Clerk:
Kimberly Shannon

Key Assembly Staff Assignments
Majority Program Analyst:
Diane Girourard
Minority Analyst/Counsel:
Kristin Frank 518-455-4258

Membership

Majority
Carmen E Arroyo
James F Brennan
Anthony Brindisi
Linda Rosenthal
Barbara Lifton
Ron Kim
Michael Miller
Daniel J O'Donnell
Steven Otis
Fred W Thiele, Jr
Michele Titus
Michael Benedetto
Walter Mosley
Steven C Englebright
Earlene Hooper
William B Magnarelli
Shelley Mayer
Sean Ryan
Amy R Paulin
Philip R Ramos
Matthew Titone

Minority
Jane L Corwin
Peter Lopez
Steven McLaughlin
Claudia Tenney
Al Graf
David McDonough
Dean Murray

Election Law
Chair:
Michael Cusick (D) 518-455-5526
Ranking Minority Member:
Bill Nojay (R) 518-455-5662

Committee Staff
Legislative Director:
Sharon Grobe 518-455-4313

Key Assembly Staff Assignments
Majority Program Analyst:
Matthew Aumand 518-455-4313
Majority Assistant Secretary:
Daniel Salvin
Majority Counsel:
Jessica Norgrove

Offices and agencies generally appear in alphabetical order, except when specific order is requested by listee.

Minority Analyst/Counsel:
James Walsh

Membership

Majority

Thomas Abinanti
Michael Blake
Sandra R. Galef
Joseph R Lentol
Latrice Walker
David Buchwald
Jeffrey Dinowitz
Brian P. Kavanagh
Barbara Lifton
David Weprin

Minority

Karl Brabenec
Tom McKevitt
Chad Lupinacci

Energy

Chair:
Amy Paulin (D) . . . 518-455-5585
Ranking Minority Member:
Philip Palmesano (R) . . . 518-455-5791

Committee Staff

Clerk:
Andrew Buder . . . 518-455-3786

Key Assembly Staff Assignments

Majority Associate Consel:
Nairobi Vives
Minority Analyst/Counsel:
Jennifer Grasso

Membership

Majority

Marcos Crespo
Charles Barron
Francisco Moya
Addie Russell
Aravella Simotas
Latrice Walker
Steven C. Englebright
Andrew Hevesi
Linda Rosenthal
Sean Ryan
Angelo Santabarbara

Minority

William Barclay
John Ceretto
Andrew Garbarino
Steven McLaughlin

Environmental Conservation

Chair:
Steven Englebright (D) . . . 518-455-4804
Ranking Minority Member:
Dan Stec (R) . . . 518-455-5565

Committee Staff

Clerk:
Ryan Vineyard . . . 518-455-2091

Key Assembly Staff Assignments

Majority Program Analyst:
Michelle Milot
Minority Analyst/Counsel:
Nicholas Forst . . . 518-455-4515

Membership

Majority

William Colton
Deborah J Glick
Ellen Jaffee
Thomas Abinanti
Sean Ryan
Barbara S Lifton
Nily Rozic
Daniel J O'Donnell
Crystal D Peoples-Stokes
Steven Cymbrowitz
Aileen M Gunther
Brian P Kavanagh
Marcos Crespo
Patricia Fahy
Donna Lupardo
Steven Otis
Fred W Thiele, Jr
Michelle Schimel
Matthew Titone
Kenneth Zebrowski
Jaime Williams

Minority

Marc Butler
Andrew Raia
Peter D. Lopez
Anthony Palumbo
Jane Corwin
Andrew Garbarino
Joseph S. Saladino

Ethics & Guidance

Chair:
Charles Lavine (D) . . . 518-455-5456
Ranking Minority Member:
Brian Curran (R) . . . 518-455-4656

Membership

Majority

Aravella Simotas
Kenneth Zebrowski
Michele R. Titus

Minority

Peter Lawrence
Michael Montesano
Jospeh Giglio

Governmental Employees

Chair:
Peter J Abbate, Jr (D) . . . 518-455-3053
Ranking Minority Member:
Nicole Malliotakis (R) . . . 518-455-5716

Committee Staff

Clerk:
Christine Eppelmann . . . 518-455-3053

Key Assembly Staff Assignments

Majority Assistant Secretary:
Jennifer Best . . . 518-455-4311
Minority Analyst/Counsel:
Douglas Goldman . . . 518-455-4637

Membership

Majority

Jeffrion L Aubry
William Colton
Michael G DenDekker
Michaelle Solages
Kenneth Zebrowski
Alec Brook-Krasny
Michael J Cusick
Philip Goldfeder
Angelo Santabarbara

Minority

Anthony Palumbo
John Ceretto
Mark Johns
Joseph Saladino

Governmental Operations

Chair:
Crystal Peoples-Stokes (D) . . . 518-455-5005
Ranking Minority Member:
Janet L Duprey (R) . . . 518-455-5943

Committee Staff

Clerk:
Leah Halton-Pope . . . 518-455-5436

Key Assembly Staff Assignments

Majority Assistant Secretary:
Aaron Suggs
Majority Associate Counsel:
Kerryanne Burke . . . 518-455-4355
Minority Analyst/Counsel:
Logan Smith . . . 518-455-4626

Offices and agencies generally appear in alphabetical order, except when specific order is requested by listee.

Membership

Majority

Michael Benedetto
Sandra R Galef
Michelle Schimel
ErikM Dilan
David Buchwald
Michael Blake
Deborah Glick
Ron Kim
Rodneyse Bichotte

Minority

Kieran Michael Lalor
Mark Johns
Andrew Goodell

Health

Chair:
Richard N Gottfried (D) 518-455-4941
Ranking Minority Member:
Andrew Raia (R) 518-455-4495

Committee Staff

Clerk:
Helen Dong 518-455-4941

Key Assembly Staff Assignments

Majority Assistant Secretary:
Rebecca Mudie 518-455-4311
Majority Program Analyst:
Michelle Newman
Minority Analyst/Counsel:
Sarah Shearer

Membership

Majority

Ellen Jaffee
Steven Cymbrowitz
Sandra R Galef
Andrew Hevesi
Charles D Lavine
Shelley Mayer
Amy R Paulin
Edward Braunstein
Robin L Schimminger
Kevin A Cahill
Jeffrey Dinowitz
Aileen M Gunther
Thomas Abinanti
Matthew Titone
Ron Kim
Crystal D Peoples-Stokes
Linda B Rosenthal
Phil Steck

Minority

Janet Duprey
Edward Ra
Raymond Walter
Andrew Goodell
David G McDonough
Andrew Garbarino

Higher Education

Chair:
Deborah J Glick (D) 518-455-4841
Ranking Minority Member:
Chad Lupinacci (R) 518-455-5732

Committee Staff

Clerk:
Charles LuDuc 518-455-4841
Legislative Director:
Teresa Swidorski 518-455-4841

Key Assembly Staff Assignments

Majority Associate Counsel:
Gregory Berck
Minority Analyst/Counsel:
Kristin Frank 518-455-4258

Membership

Majority

Pamela Harris
Patricia Fahy
Steven C Englebright
Ellen Jaffee
Barbara S Lifton
William Magee
Al Stirpe
Victor Pichardo
Crystal D Peoples-Stokes
Kevin A Cahill
Michael J Cusick
Richard N Gottfried
Charles D Lavine
Donna Lupardo
Jo Anne Simon
Michael Simanowitz
Amy R Paulin
Anthony Brindisi

Minority

Marc W Butler
Peter Lawrence
Michael J Fitzpatrick
Andrew Garbarino
Edward Ra
Janet Duprey

Housing

Chair:
Keith L.T. Wright (D) 518-455-4793
Ranking Minority Member:
Michael J Fitzpatrick (R) 518-455-5021

Committee Staff

Clerk:
Francisco Polanco 518-455-5537

Key Assembly Staff Assignments

Majority Program Analyst:
Anthony Kergaravat 518-455-4355
Majority Associate Counsel:
Felicia Reid 518-455-4355
Minority Analyst/Counsel:
Edmund V Wick 518-455-4262

Membership

Majority

Rodneyse Bichotte
Michael Blake
Vivian E Cook
Michael Kearns
Ron Kim
Brian P Kavanagh
Linda B Rosenthal
Maritza Davila
Latrice Walker
Luis Sepulveda
Victor Pichardo
Alice Cancel
Erik Dilan
Latoya Joyner
Francisco Moya
Robert Rodriguez
Walter Mosley
Guillermo Linares
Annette M Robinson

Minority

Al Graf
Mark Johns
Raymond Walter
Andrew P Raia
Steve Katz
Christopher Friend

Insurance

Chair:
Kevin Cahill (D) 518-455-4436
Ranking Minority Member:
William A Barclay (R) 518-455-5841

Committee Staff

Clerk:
Vincent Rossetti 518-455-4436

Key Assembly Staff Assignments

Majority Assistant Secretary:
Jennifer Best 518-455-4311
Majority Program Analyst:
Dallas Trombley
Minority Analyst/Counsel:
Douglas Goldman 518-455-4637

Membership

Majority

Erik Dilan
Steven H Cymbrowitz
Marcos Crespo
Crystal D Peoples-Stokes
Vivian E Cook
Philip Goldfeder
Charles D Lavine
Latoya Joyner

Offices and agencies generally appear in alphabetical order, except when specific order is requested by listee.

James Gary Pretlow
James Skoufis
Jose Rivera
Phil Steck
Pamela Harris
Francisco Moya
John McDonald III
Andrew Hevesi

Minority

Marc W Butler
Stephen Hawley
Raymond Walter
Brian Curran
Gary Finch
Ken Blankenbush

Judiciary

Chair:
Helene E. Weinstein (D). 518-455-5462
Ranking Minority Member:
Michael Montesano (R) 518-455-4684

Committee Staff

Clerk:
Sarah Beaver. 518-455-5462

Key Assembly Staff Assignments

Counsel:
Richard Ancowitz. 518-455-4313
Team Counsel:
Clayton Rivet 518-455-4313
Associate Counsel:
Amy Naggs. 518-455-4313
Minority Analyst:
Nicholas Forst. 518-455-4515

Membership

Majority

Edward Braunstein
David Buchwald
Charles D Lavine
Phil Steck
Dan Quart
Jo Anne Simon
Michele R Titus
Jeffrey Dinowitz
Latoya Joyner
Aravella Simotas
Matthew Titone
Rebecca Seawright
David Weprin
Kenneth Zebrowski

Minority

William A Barclay
Chad Lupinacci
Anthony Palumbo
Al Graf
Andrew Goodell

Labor

Chair:
Michele Titus (D) 518-455-5668
Ranking Minority Member:
Karl Brabenec (R). 518-455-5991

Committee Staff

Clerk:
Claude Nelson. 518-455-5668

Key Assembly Staff Assignments

Majority Assistant Secretary:
Jennifer Best 518-455-4311
Minority Analyst/Counsel:
Douglas Goldman. 518-455-4637

Membership

Majority

Peter J Abbate, Jr
Guillermo Linares
Michael DenDekker
Brian P Kavanagh
Francisco Moya
Nily Rozic
Jo Anne Simon
Harry Bronson
Michael Benedetto
William Colton
Andrew Hevesi
Shelley Mayer
Margaret M Markey
James Skoufis
Felix W Ortiz
Michael Miller
Robert Rodriguez
Kenneth Zebrowski
N Nick Perry

Minority

David DiPietro
Michael Fitzpatrick
Joseph Saladino
Brian Curran
Angela M Wozniak
Clifford W Crouch

Libraries & Education Technology

Chair:
Thomas Abinanti (D) 518-455-5753
Ranking Minority Member:
Joseph Saladino (R) 518-455-5305

Committee Staff

Clerk:
Doug Rosenthal. 518-455-5585

Key Assembly Staff Assignments

Majority Program Analyst:
Steve McCutcheon 518-455-3786
Minority Analyst/Counsel:
Kristin Frank. 518-455-4258

Membership

Majority

Michaelle Solages
Steven Otis

Minority

John Ceretto
Philip Palmesano

Local Governments

Chair:
William B Magnarelli (D). 518-455-4826
Ranking Minority Member:
Christopher Friend (R) 518-455-4583

Committee Staff

Committee Director:
Craig Swiecki 518-455-4826

Key Assembly Staff Assignments

Majority Assistant Secretary:
Julia Mallalieu 518-455-4363
Majority Program Analyst:
Alice Baumgartner
Minority Analyst/Counsel:
Logan Smith 518-455-4626

Membership

Majority

Harry Bronson
David F Gantt
Mark Gjonaj
William Magee
Carrie Woerner
Addie J Russell
Sean Ryan
Kimberly Jean-Pierre
Steven Otis
David Buchwald
James Skoufis
Philip R Ramos
Michelle Schimel
Frank Skartados

Minority

Karl Brabenec
Dan Stec
Tom McKevitt
Angela M Wozniak

Mental Health

Chair:
Aileen Gunther (D) 518-455-5355
Ranking Minority Member:
Steve Katz (R). 518-455-5783

Committee Staff

Clerk:
Tom Gatto 518-455-5102

Offices and agencies generally appear in alphabetical order, except when specific order is requested by listee.

Key Assembly Staff Assignments
Majority Program Analyst:
Willie Sanchez 518-455-3786
Minority Analyst/Counsel:
Sarah Shearer 518-455-4285

Membership

Majority
Luis Sepulveda
Kimberly Jean-Pierre
John McDonald III
Ellen Jaffee
Michael J Cusick
Didi Barrett
Angelo Santabarbara
Robert Rodriguez

Minority
Jane L Corwin
Bill Nojay
Diana Richardson

Oversight, Analysis & Investigation

Chair:
Ellen Jaffee (D). 518-455-5118
Ranking Minority Member:
Peter Lawrence (R). 518-455-4664

Membership

Majority
William B Magnarelli
Fred W. Thiele, Jr.
Michael Kearns

Minority
Michael Montesano

Racing & Wagering

Chair:
James Gary Pretlow (D) 518-455-5291
Ranking Minority Member:
Andrew Garbarino (R) 518-455-4611

Committee Staff

Clerk:
Kaitesi Munroe

Key Assembly Staff Assignments
Majority Assistant Secretary:
Jennifer Best. 518-455-4311
Minority Analyst/Counsel:
Edmund V Wick. 518-455-4262

Membership

Majority
Aileen Gunther
Michaelle Solages
Angelo Santabarbara
Michael Miller
Margaret M Markey
Philip Goldfeder
Carrie Woerner

Minority
James Tedisco
Peter Lawrence

Real Property Taxation

Chair:
Sandra R Galef (D). 518-455-5348
Ranking Minority Member:
Kieran Michael Lalor (R). 518-455-5725

Committee Staff

Clerk:
Rebecca Southard-Kreiger 518-455-5348

Key Assembly Staff Assignments
Majority Program Analyst:
Lauren Denison 518-455-4363
Minority Analyst/Counsel:
Logan Smith 518-455-4265

Membership

Majority
James F Brennan
Aileen M Gunther
Mark Gjonaj
John McDonald III
Victor Pichardo
Annette M Robinson

Minority
Philip Palmesano

Rules

Chair:
Carl Heastie (D) 518-455-3791
Ranking Minority Member:
Brian M Kolb (R) 518-455-3751

Membership

Majority
Jeffrion L Aubry
Herman D Farrell, Jr
Deborah J Glick
Earlene Hooper
Joseph R Lentol
Joseph D Morelle
William Magnarelli
Keith L T Wright
James Gary Pretlow
Steve Englebright
Vivian E Cook
David F Gantt
Richard N Gottfried
Margaret Markey
William Colton
Catherine T Nolan
Jeffrey Dinowitz
Felix W Ortiz
N Nick Perry
Helene E Weinstein

Minority
Clifford W Crouch
Marc Butler
Gary Finch
James Tedisco
William Barclay
Janet Duprey
Andrew Raia
Robert C Oaks

Small Business

Chair:
Fred Thiele, Jr (D). 518-455-5997
Ranking Minority Member:
David DiPietro (R) 518-455-5314

Committee Staff

Clerk:
Lisa Lombardo 518-455-5997

Key Assembly Staff Assignments
Majority Associate Counsel:
Victoria Choi 518-455-4928

Membership

Majority
Charles Barron
Jose Rivera
Victor Pichardo
Alicia Hyndman
Michael Simanowitz
Angelo Santabarbara
Rodneyse Bichotte
Annette M Robinson
Mark Gjonaj
Frank Skartados
Carrie Woerner

Minority
Peter Lawrence
Dean Murray
Diane Richardson
Kieran Michael Lalor

Social Services

Chair:
Andrew Hevesi (D). 518-455-4926
Ranking Minority Member:
Andrew Goodell (R) 518-455-4511

Offices and agencies generally appear in alphabetical order, except when specific order is requested by listee.

Committee Staff
Clerk:
Rebecca Rasmussen 518-455-4926

Key Assembly Staff Assignments
Majority Assistant Secretary:
Rebecca Mudie 518-455-4371
Majority Associate Counsel:
Jennifer Sacco
Minority Analyst/Counsel:
Lori Smith 518-455-4265

Membership

Majority
Maritza Davila
Jeffrion Aubry
Ron Kim
Victor Pichardo
Pamela Harris
Michaelle Solages
Shelley Mayer
Alice Cancel
Charles Barron
Rodneyse Bichotte
Latoya Joyner
Matthew Titone

Minority
Steven McLaughlin
Claudia Tenney
Anthony Palumbo
Dan Stec

Tourism, Parks, Arts & Sports Development
Chair:
Margaret Markey (D) 518-455-4755
Ranking Minority Member:
John Ceretto (R) 518-455-5284

Committee Staff
Clerk:
Alyssa McCoy 518-455-5373

Key Assembly Staff Assignments
Majority Assistant Secretary:
Aaron Suggs 518-455-4355
Majority Program Analyst:
Yolanda Bostic 518-455-4928

Membership

Majority
Al Stirpe
Rebecca Seawright
Dan Quart
Frank Skartados
Daniel J O'Donnell
Carrie Woerner
Linda Rosenthal
Didi Barrett
Mark Gjonaj
Jaime Williams
Patricia Fahy
Steven Otis
Matthew Titone

Minority
Ken Blankenbush
Dean Murray
Dan Stec
Chad Lupinacci
Philip Palmesano

Transportation
Chair:
David F Gantt (D) 518-455-5606
Ranking Minority Member:
David G McDonough (R) 518-455-4633

Committee Staff
Clerk:
Kathryn F Curren 518-455-5606

Key Assembly Staff Assignments
Majority Principal Analyst:
Julie Barney 518-455-4881
Majority Associate Counsel:
Michael Hernandez 518-455-4881
Minority Analyst/Counsel:
Jennifer Grasso 518-455-4264

Membership

Majority
Kimberly Jean-Pierre
Michael Cusick
Jo Anne Simon
Pamela Hunter
Michelle Schimel
Harry Bronson
Frank Skartados
Fred W Thiele, Jr.
Phil Steck
Michael G DenDekker
Anthony Brindisi
Donna Lupardo
N Nick Perry
Alicia Hyndman
Marcos Crespo
Jaime Williams
James Skoufis

Minority
Chad Lupinacci
Nicole Malliotakis
David DiPietro
Bill Nojay
Edward Ra
Dean Murray

Veterans' Affairs
Chair:
Michael DenDekker (D) 518-455-4545
Ranking Minority Member:
Stephen Hawley (R) 518-455-5811

Committee Staff
Clerk:
Kenny Mendoza 518-455-4545

Key Assembly Staff Assignments
Majority Program Analyst:
Joanne Martin 518-455-4355
Minority Analyst/Counsel:
Logan Smith 518-455-4626

Membership

Majority
Michael J Cusick
Pamela Hunter
Catherine T Nolan
Addie J Russell
Sean Ryan
Michelle Schimel
Michael Blake
Angelo Santabarbara
Didi Barrett
Michael Miller
Anthony Brindisi
James Skoufis

Minority
Brian Curran
David McDonough
Kieran Michael Lalor
Claudia Tenney

Ways & Means
Chair:
Herman D Farrell, Jr (D) 518-455-5491
Ranking Minority Member:
Bob Oaks (R) 518-455-5655

Committee Staff
Clerk:
Debra Devine 518-455-3786

Key Assembly Staff Assignments
Director of Economic Studies:
Audra Nowosielski 518-455-4006
Secretary:
Blake G Washington 518-455-4054

Membership

Majority
Jeffrion L Aubry
William Colton
Michael Benedetto
Deborah J Glick
Kevin A Cahill
Vivian E Cook
David F Gantt
Earlene Hooper

Michael Cusick
Felix Ortiz
Phil Ramos
Robert Rodriguez
Catherine T Nolan
James Gary Pretlow
Robin L Schimminger
Fred W Thiele, Jr.
Edward Braunstein
Keith L T Wright
Joseph R Lentol
Francisco Moya
N Nick Perry
David Weprin
Margaret Markey
Helene E Weinstein

Minority

William A Barclay
Nicole Malliotakis
Raymond Walter
Michael Fitzpatrick
Joseph Saladino
Janet Duprey
Clifford W Crouch
Jane Corwin
Stephen Hawley

ASSEMBLY TASK FORCES & CAUCUS

Food, Farm & Nutrition, Task Force on

Chair:
Addie Russell (D) 518-455-5545
Program Manager:
Robert Stern 518-455-5203

People with Disabilities Task Force

Chair:
David Weprin (D) 518-455-5806

Puerto Rican/Hispanic Task Force

Chair:
Marcos Crespo (D) 518-455-5514
Legislative Director:
Guillermo Martinez 518-455-3608

Skills Development & Career Education, Legislative Commission on

Assembly Chair:
Harry Bronson (D) 518-455-4527
Program Manager:
Brenda Carter 518-455-4865/fax: 518-455-4175

State-Federal Relations, Legislative Task Force on

Assembly Chair:
Matthew Titone (D) 518-455-4677
Program Manager:
Robert Stern 518-455-3632

University-Industry Cooperation, Task Force on

Chair:
Vacant 518-455-0000
Coordinator:
Maureen Schoolman 518-455-3632/fax: 518-455-4175

Women's Issues, Task Force on

Chair:
Aravella Simotas (D) 518-455-5014
Coordinator:
Christina Williams 518-455-3632/fax: 518-455-4574

JOINT LEGISLATIVE COMMISSIONS

Administrative Regulations Review, Legislative Commission on

Assembly Co-Chair:
Kenneth Zebrowski (D) 518-455-5735
Senate Co-Chair:
Terrence Murphy (R) 518-455-3111
Assembly Program Manager:
Rich Murphy 518-455-5091/fax: 518-455-4175

Demographic Research & Reapportionment, Legislative Task Force on

Assembly Co-Chair:
Marcos A Crespo (D) 518-455-5514
Senate Co-Chair:
Michael F Nozzolio (D) 518-455-2366
Co-Executive Director:
Karen Blatt 212-618-1100/fax: 212-618-1135
Co-Executive Director:
Frank Tassone 212-618-1100/fax: 212-618-1135

Ethics Committee, Legislative

Assembly Co-Chair:
Charles D. Lavine (D) 518-455-4546
Senate Co-Chair:
Andrew Lanza (R) 518-455-3215
Director/Counsel:
Lisa P Reid 518-432-7837
e-mail: lreid@nysenate.gov

Government Administration, Legislative Commission on

Assembly Chair:
Brian Kavanagh (D) 518-455-5506
Senior Program Manager:
Philip Johnson 518-455-3632/fax: 518-455-4574

Rural Resources, Legislative Commission on

Assembly Chair:
Frank Skartados (D) 518-455-5762
Senate Chair:
Patricia Ritchie (R) 518-455-3438
Republican Counsel:
Barbara McRedmond 518-455-2069

Science & Technology, Legislative Commission on

Assembly Chair:
Francisco Moya (D) 518-455-4567
Senior Program Manager:
Philip Johnson 518-455-5081/fax: 518-455-4859

JUDICIAL BRANCH

COURT OF APPEALS

The Court of Appeals is the highest court in New York State, hearing both civil and criminal appeals. This court consists of the Chief Judge and six Associate Judges. Judges are appointed by the Governor for fourteen-year terms or until age seventy, whichever comes first. The Court of Appeals receives direct appeal on matters where the only question relates to the constitutionality of a State or Federal statute. The Court also establishes policy for administration of the New York State Unified Court System.

Court of Appeals
20 Eagle Street
Albany, NY 12207-1095
518-455-7700
Web site: www.nycourts.gov/ctapps/

Clerk of the Court/Legal Counsel:
John P Asiello 518-455-7700
e-mail: coa@courts.state.ny.us
Deputy:
John P Asiello 518-455-7700
Public Information Officer:
Gary Spencer 518-455-7711
e-mail: gspencer@courts.state.ny.us
Chief Judge:
Janet DiFiore

Associate Judges
Jenny Rivera
Sheila Abdus-Salaam
Michael J Garcia
Leslie E Stein
Eugene F Pigott
Eugene M Fahey

APPELLATE DIVISIONS

The Appellate Divisions of the Supreme Court exist for each of New York State's four Judicial Departments. Each Judicial Department is comprised of one or more of the State's twelve judicial districts and has Governor appointed Presiding and Associate Justices. The Presiding Justice serves the duration of his/her term as a Supreme Court Justice. Associate Justices serve for the shorter of a five-year term or the balance of their term. Supreme Court Justices are required to retire at age seventy, unless they become "Certificated" by the Administrative Board of the Courts. Justices may serve after age seventy under Certification for two-year terms, until age seventy-six. The Appellate Divisions review appeals from the Superior Court decisions in civil and criminal cases, and from Appellate Terms and County Courts in civil cases.

1st Department
Judicial Districts 1, 12
Courthouse
27 Madison Ave
New York, NY 10010
212-340-0400 Fax: 212-889-4412

Clerk of the Court:
Suzanna Molina Rojas 212-340-0400
Acting Presiding Justice:
Peter Tom

Associate Justices
Rolando T Acosta
Barbara R Kapnick
Ellen Gesmer
Angela M Mazzarelli
Dianne T Renwick
Richard T Andrias
Marcy L Kahn
David Friedman
Karla Moskowitz
Rosalyn H Richter
David B Saxe
Peter Tom
Paul G. Feinman
Troy K. Webber
John W Sweeny Jr
Sallie Manzanet-Daniels
Judith J. Gische

2nd Department
Judicial Districts 2, 9, 10, 11, 13
45 Monroe Pl
Brooklyn, NY 11201
718-875-1300

Clerk of the Court:
Aprilanne Agostino . . . . 718-722-6324 or 718-722-6307
fax: 212-419-8457
e-mail: ad2-clerksoffice@courts.state.ny.us
Justice:
Randall T. Eng

Associate Justices
Colleen Duffy
Hector D LaSalle
Cheryl E Chambers
Mark C Dillon
John M Leventhal
Sheri S Roman
L. Priscilla Hall
Leonard B. Austin
Valerie Brathwaite Nelson
William F. Mastro
Ruth C Balkin
Joseph J Maltese
Thomas A Dickerson
Robert J Miller
Reinaldo E Rivera
Francesca E. Connolly
Sylvia C. Hinds-Radix
Jeffrey A. Cohen
Sandra L. Sgroi

3rd Department
Judicial Districts 3, 4, 6
Capitol Station
PO Box 7288
Albany, NY 12224-0288
518-471-4777

Clerk of the Court:
Robert D Mayberger 518-471-4777/fax: 518-471-4750
e-mail: ad3clerksoffice@nycourts.gov
Presiding Justice:
Karen K Peters

Associate Justices
John A Lahtinen
Robert C Mulvay
Michael C. Lynch
Christine M. Clark
Elizabeth A. Garry
William E McCarthy
Eugene P. Devine
Sharon A. M. Aarons
John C Egan Jr.

4th Department
Judicial Districts 5, 7, 8
50 East Ave
Rochester, NY 14604-2214
585-530-3100 Fax: 585-530-3247

Clerk of the Court:
Frances E Cafarell 585-530-3100
Presiding Justice:
Gerald J. Whalen

Associate Justices
Edward D. Carni
Brian F. DeJoseph
John V Centra
Stephen K. Lindley
Shirley Troutman
John M Curran
Nancy E Smith
Erin M Peradotto
Henry J. Scudder
Patrick H. NeMoyer

Offices and agencies generally appear in alphabetical order, except when specific order is requested by listee.

SUPREME COURT

The Supreme Court consists of twelve Judicial Districts, which are comprised of County Courts within NYS (See County Court information in related section). Justices are elected by their Judicial Districts for fourteen-year terms, unless they reach age seventy before term expiration. Justices may serve beyond age seventy if Certificated (see Apellate Divisions for definition). The Supreme Court generally hears cases outside the jurisdiction of other courts, such as: civil matters with monetary limits exceeding that of the lower courts; divorce, separation and annulment proceedings; equity suits; and criminal prosecutions of felonies.

1st Judicial District

New York County

Administrative Judge, Civil:
Peter H. Moulton
Administrative Judge, Criminal:
Michael Obus
Chief Clerk, Civil Branch:
Norman Goodman. 646-386-5955
Chief Clerk, Criminal Branch:
Barry Clarke, Esquire 646-386-3900/fax: 212-374-3177
e-mail: amurphy@courts.state.ny.us

Judges

Kathryn E. Freed
Ellen M. Coin
Nancy M. Bannon
Arlene Bluth
Eileen Bransten
Matthew Cooper
Laura E. Drager
Fern Fisher
Ira Gammerman
Ellen Gesmer
Douglas E. Hoffman
Alexander Hunter
Deborah Kaplan
Barbara R. Kapnick
Cynthia Kern
Jeffrey K. Oing
Raymond Guzman (Cert)
Kelly O'Neill Levy
Joan B. Lobis
Lawrence Marks
Michael Stallman
Peter Moulton
Paul Wooten
Rena Uviller (Cert)
Lois B. York
Margaret Chan
Carol R Edmead
Lucy Billings
Sherry Klein Heitler
Richard Brown
Tandra Dawson
Arthur F. Engoron
Marcy S. Friedman
Phyllis Gangel-Jacob
Shlomo S. Hagler
Carol E. Huff
Barbara Jaffe
Debra A. James
Tanya Kennedy
Shirley Kornreich
Martin Shulman
Joan Kenny
Doris Ling-Cohan
Joan A. Madden
Milton A. Tingling
George Silver
Manuel Mendez
Geoffrey D.S. Wright
Ronald A. Zweibel (Cert)

2nd Judicial District

Kings County

Administrative Judge, Criminal:
Matthew J. D'Emic
Administrative Judge, Civil:
Lawrence Knipel
Chief Clerk, Criminal Division:
Daniel M. Alessandrino
Chief Clerk, Civil Division:
Charles A. Small, Esq.

Judges

Rachel A. Adams
Jack Battaglia
Noach Dear
Laura Lee Jacobson
Larry Martin
Karen B. Rosenberg
David Schmidt
Sylvia Ash
Gloria Dabiri
Carolyn DeMarest
Joseph J. Maltese
Ann Pfau
Karen Rothenberg
Kenneth Sherman
Debra Silber
Jeffrey Sunshine
Delores Thomas
Mark I Partnow
Michael L Pesce
Francois A Rivera
Wayne P Saitta
Martin M Solomon
David B Vaughan
Ellen Spodek
Peter Sweeney
Carl J. Landicino
Michelle Weston
Eric I Prus
Leon Ruchelsman
Arthur M Schack
James P Sullivan

3rd Judicial District

Albany, Columbia, Greene, Rensselaer, Schoharie, Sullivan & Ulster Counties

Administrative Judge:
Thomas A. Breslin
District Executive:
Beth Diebel 518-285-8300/fax: 518-285-6169
e-mail: 3rdjdadministration@nycourts.gov

Judges

Christopher E Cahill
Lisa M. Fisher
Christine Ryba
Patrick J McGrath
Joseph C Teresi
Richard Mott
George B Ceresia Jr
Raymond Elliott
Richard J McNally Jr
Stephan G. Schick
James Gilpatric

4th Judicial District

Counties: Clint, Essex, Frankln, Fultn, Hamiltn, Montg, St Lawr, Saratga, Schenectady, Warren & Wash

Administrative Judge:
Vito C Caruso
District Executive:
Joanne B. Haelen, Esq. 518-285-5099/fax: 518-453-8988

Judges

Richard T Aulisi
David R Demarest
Stephen A Ferradino
Robert J Muller
Vincent J Reilly, Jr.
Ann C. Crowell
Thomas Buchanan
David B. Krogmann
Stan Pritzker
John Ellis
Joseph Sise
Thomas D Nolan, Jr.
Robert J. Chauvin
Christine M. Clark
Barry D. Kramer

5th Judicial District

Herkimer, Jefferson, Lewis, Oneida, Onondaga & Oswego Counties

Administrative Judge:
James C Tormey III
District Executive:
Michael A Klein 315-671-2111/fax: 315-671-1175
e-mail: 5thjdadministration@nycourts.gov

Judges

Bernadette T. Clark
Hugh A Gilbert
Deborah H Karalunas
Patrick F MacRae
James P Murphy
Anthony J Paris
James McCarthy
Charles C. Merrell
Erin P. Gall
Brian F DeJoseph
Donald A Greenwood
Samuel D Hester
Kevin G Young
David A. Murad
Norman W Seiter Jr
James P. McClusky
Norman I. Siegel

6th Judicial District

Broome, Chemung, Chenango, Cortland, Delaware, Madison, Otsego, Schuyler, Tioga & Tompkins Counties

Administrative Judge:
Michael V. Coccoma

District Executive:
Gregory A. Gates 607-240-5350/fax: 212-295-4927
e-mail: 6jd-res@nycourts.gov

Judges

Kevin M Dowd
Donald F. Cerio, Jr.
Judith F O'Shea
Jeffrey A Tait
Robert C. Mulvey
Ferris D Lebous
Eugene D. Faughnan
Phillip R Rumsey
Molly Fitzgerald

7th Judicial District

Cayuga, Livingston, Monroe, Ontario, Seneca, Steuben, Wayne & Yates Counties

Administrative Judge:
Craig J. Doran
District Executive:
Ronald Pawelczak. 585-371-3266

Judges

Francis A Affronti
Kenneth R Fisher
John Owens
Matthew A Rosenbaum
Ann Marie Taddeo
Daniel Doyle
J. Scott Odorisi
Richard Dollinger
John J. Ark
Evelyn Frazee
William P Polito
Thomas A Stander
Elma A. Bellini
Thomas Moran
Alex R. Renzi
Joanne Winslow

8th Judicial District

Allegany, Cattaraugus, Chautauqua, Erie, Genesee, Niagara, Orleans & Wyoming Counties

Administrative Judge:
Paula L. Feroleto
District Executive:
Andrew B Isenberg 716-845-2506/fax: 716-845-7500
e-mail: aisenber@nycourts.gov

Judges

Tracey A Bannister
Ralph A Boniello, III
Russell Buscaglia
Mark J. Grisanti
James Dillon
Timothy Drury
Joseph R Glownia
Richard C Kloch Sr
John A Michalek
John F O'Donnell
Sharon S. Townsend
John L. Michalski
Timothy Walker
Penny Wolfgang
Paul B. Wojtaszek
M William Boller
Christopher J Burns
Frank Caruso
Diane Y Devlin
J. David Sampson
Jeremy J. Moriarty, III
Deborah A Haendiges
Frederick J Marshall
Emilio Colaiacovo
Deborah A. Chimes
Mark A. Montour
Donna M Siwek
Henry Nowak
Catherine Nugent-Panepinto

9th Judicial District

Dutchess, Orange, Putnam, Rockland & Westchester Counties

Administrative Judge:
Alan B Sheinkman
District Executive:
Nancy M. Mangold 914-824-5100/fax: 914-995-4946
e-mail: 9thjdadministration@nycourts.gov
Chief Clerk:
Michael Thompson 845-431-1710/fax: 845-431-1743

Judges

Lester B Adler
Victor J. Alfieri
James V Brands
Robert H Freehill
Catherine M. Bartlett
Orazio Bellantoni
Linda Christopher
Margaret Garvey
William J Giacomo
William A Kelly
John Colangelo
Victor Grossman
Lewis Lubell
Lawrence H. Ecker
Paul I. Marx
James D. Pagones
Robert A. Onofry
Sandra Sciortino
Mary H Smith
Bruce E Tolbert
Sam Walker
Linda S Jamieson
Robert M. Berliner
Robert M. Dibella
Joan B Lefkowitz
Francesca Connolly
Gerald Loehr
J Emmett Murphy
Francis A. Nicolai
Maria G. Rosa
Elaine Slobod
Christine A Sproat
Maria S. Vazquez-Doles
Charles D. Wood

10th Judicial District

Nassau & Suffolk Counties

Administrative Judge, Nassau:
Thomas A. Adams
Administrative Judge, Suffolk:
C. Randall Hinrichs
District Executive:
Warren G Clark 631-853-7742/fax: 631-853-7741
Chief Clerk, Nassau:
Kathryn Driscoll Hopkins, Esq. 516-493-3400
Chief Clerk, Suffolk:
Michael Scardino 631-852-2334

Judges

W. Gerard Asher
Paul J Baisley, Jr
Jeffrey S. Brown
Robert A. Bruno
Julianne Capetola
William J. Condon
Robert B Cozzens, Jr.
Timothy S. Driscoll
Antonio Brandveen
Elizabeth H Emerson
Thomas Feinman
John Michael Galasso
Jeffrey A. Goodstein
Randy S. Marber
Jack L Libert
Norman Janowitz
H. Patrick Leis III
Anthony Marano
John J. Leo
Carol MacKenzie
Peter H. Mayer
Anthony L Parga
George Peck
William B Rebolini
Daniel Palmieri
Howard E Sturim
David Reilly
A. Gail Prudenti
Joseph A. Santorelli
Thomas F Whelan
F Dana Winslow
Richard Ambro
Stacy D. Bennett
Anna Anzalone
Stephen A Bucaria
John B. Collins
Andrew A. Crecca
Vito M. DeStefano
Arthur M Diamond
Martin I. Efman
Jerry Garguilo
William G Ford
Angela G Iannacci
Sharon Gianelli
Howard Heckman
William J Kent
Gary F. Knobel
Roy S Mahon
Hector D. LaSalle
Edward A. Maron
Karen Murphy
James McCormack
Francis Ricigliano
Arthur G Pitts
Jerome Murphy
Sondra K. Pardes
Joseph C. Pastoressa
Robert F Quinlan
Denise Sher
Leonard Steinman
Hope Zimmerman
Michele M Woodard

11th Judicial District

Queens County

Administrative Judge, Civil:
Jeremy S. Weinstein
Administrative Judge, Criminal:
Joseph Zayas
Chief Clerk, Civil:
Tracy Catapano-Fox 718-298-1000
Chief Clerk, Criminal:
Maureen D'Aquila 718-298-1408

Offices and agencies generally appear in alphabetical order, except when specific order is requested by listee.

Judges
Augustus C Agate
Pam Jackman Brown
Denis J. Butler
Arthur J Cooperman (Cert)
Timothy Duffiey
David Elliot
William M Erlbaum
Phyllis Orlikoff Flug
Stephen Knopf
Howard G Lane
Ronald D Hollie
Lee A. Mayersohn
Robert C Kohm
Robert Nahman
Daniel Lewis
Leslie J. Purificacion
Steven W. Paynter
Jaime Antonio Rios
Martin E Ritholtz
Frederick D R Sampson
Sidney F Strauss
Jeremy S Weinstein
Michael B Aloise
Valerie Brathwaite Nelson
Richard Lance Buchter
Anna Culley
Darrell L. Gavin
Rudolph Greco
Kevin Kerrigan
James J Golia
Marguerite A Grays
Duane A Hart
Jeffrey D. Lebowitz
Orin R Kitzes
Gregory L Lasak
Diccia Pineda-Kirwan
Robert J McDonald
Peter O'Donoghue
Thomas Raffaele
Bernice D. Siegal
Roger N Rosengarten
Martin J Schulman
Janice A Taylor
Allan B Weiss

12th Judicial District
Bronx County
Chief Administrative Judge, Civil:
Douglas E. McKeon
Administrative Judge, Criminal:
Robert Torres
Chief Clerk, Criminal Division:
Steven B Clark. 718-618-3000/fax: 718-618-3585
Chief Clerk, Civil Division:
Tracy Pardo 718-618-1400

Judges
John A Barone
Wilma Guzman
Dominic R. Massaro (Cert)
Larry Schachner
Yvonne Gonzalez
Howard H. Sherman
La Tia W Martin
Richard L Price (Cert)
Robert A Sackett (Cert)
Kenneth Thompson, Jr
Alison Y Tuitt
Sharon Aarons
Mary Briganti-Hughes
Laura G Douglas
Mark Friedlander
Alexander W Hunter
George Villegas
Douglas E McKeon
Norma Ruiz
Barry Salman
Robert E Torres

13th Judicial District
Richmond County
Administrative Judge:
Judith N. McMahon
Chief Clerk:
Joseph Como 718-675-8700

Judges
Thomas P. Aliotta
Catherine M. DiDomenico
Joseph J. Maltese
Barbara I. Panepinto
Stephen J. Rooney
Robert J. Collini
John A. Fusco
Philip G. Minardo
Leonard P. Rienzi
Charles Troia

COURT OF CLAIMS

*The Court of Claims is a special trial court that hears and determines only claims against the State of New York. Court of Claims judges are appointed by the Governor for nine-year terms. Certain judges of this court, as designated herein by an *, also serve as acting Supreme Court Justices for the assigned judicial district.*

Court of Claims
Robert Abrams Justice Bldg
Capitol Station
PO Box 7344
Albany, NY 12224
518-432-3441 Fax: 518-432-3483

Clerk of the Court:
Robert T DeCataldo. 518-432-3411/fax: 518-432-3483
e-mail: rdecatal@nycourts.gov
Presiding Judge:
Richard E Sise 518-432-3435/fax: 518-432-3428

Judges
W. Brooks De Bow
John J Brunetti*
Russell P Buscaglia
Thomas J Carroll
Robert J Collini*
James H. Ferreira
Vincent M Del Guidice*
Stephen J. Lynch
Judith A Hard
Michael E Hudson
Richard C Kloch
Christopher McCarthy
Martin Marcus*
Daniel Martin*
Thomas J McNamara*
Stephen J Mignano
Richard Molea*
Michael F Mullen*
Richard Platkin
Stephen J Rooney*
Terry J Ruderman
Thomas H Scuccimarra
Richard E Sise
Gina Lopez-Summa
David A. Weinstein
Antonio I Brandveen*
Glen T. Bruening
Gregory Carro*
Margaret L Clancy*
Francis T Collins
Matthew J D'Emic*
Diane L Fitzpatrick
Philip M Grella*
Alan L Honorof*
John G Ingram*
Albert Lorenzo*
Guy J Mangano, Jr*
Alan C Marin
Frank P. Milano
Nicholas V Midey Jr
Renee Forgensi Minarik
Jeremiah J Moriarity III
Juanita B Newton
Philip J Patti
Catherine C. Schaewe
Melvin Schweitzer
Norman I Siegel*
Faviola Soto
O. Peter Sherwood
Maxwell T Wiley*

NEW YORK CITY COURTS

*New York City has its own Civil, Criminal and Family courts, separate from the County Court system. The NYC Civil Court hears civil cases involving amounts up to $25,000, and its judges are elected for ten-year terms. The NYC Criminal Court conducts trials of misdemeanors and violations. Criminal Court judges act as magistrates for all criminal offenses and are appointed by the City's Mayor for ten-year terms. The NYC Family Court hears matters involving children and families, such as: child protection, delinquency, domestic violence, guardianship, parental rights and spousal and child support. Family Court judges are appointed by the City's Mayor for ten-year terms. Certain judges of the Civil Court, as designated herein by an *, are also assigned to serve in other courts.*

Civil Court, NYC
Deputy Chief Administrative Judge:
Fern A Fisher
Chief Clerk:
Carol Alt 646-386-5409/fax: 212-374-5709

Bronx County
851 Grand Concourse, Bronx, NY 10451
Clerk of the County:
Eddy Valdez 718-618-2500

Kings County
141 Livingston St, Brooklyn, NY 11201
Clerk of the County:
Lydia Grima 347-404-9133

Offices and agencies generally appear in alphabetical order, except when specific order is requested by listee.

New York County
111 Centre St, New York, NY 10013
Clerk of the County:
Serena Spingle 646-386-5730

Queens County
89-17 Sutphin Blvd, Jamaica, NY 11435
Clerk of the County:
Maurien Giddens

Richmond County
927 Castleton Ave, Staten Island, NY 10310
Clerk of the County:
Deborah Torforice 718-675-8458

Judges

Rachel Amy Adams*
Frederick Arriaga*
Ben R. Barbato
Loren Baily-Schiffman*
Arthur Birnbaum
Reginald A. Boddie
Joseph Capella*
Joseph Capella
David P. Cohen
Noach Dear
Mary K. Dollard
Raymond L. Bruce*
Raul Cruz
Dena E. Douglas*
Timothy J. Dufficy
Genine D. Edwards
Saralee Evans*
Paul G. Feinman*
Fern A. Fisher
Marcy S. Friedman*
Michael Gerstein*
Doris Gonzalez*
Stephen S. Gottlieb
Rudolph E. Greco
Stanley Green*
Maureen Healy
Dawn M. Jimenez-Salta
Barbara Jaffe*
Ingrid Joseph*
Deborah A. Kaplan*
Robert Kalish*
Kathy J. King*
Sarah L. Krauss*
Richard Latin
Katherine A. Levine
Diana A. Lebedeff*
Andrea Masley
Ira H. Margulis*
Orlando Marrazzo, Jr.
Donald A. Miles
Peter K. Moulton
Kelly O'Neill*
Lisa S. Ottley
Jodi Orlow
Barbara I. Panepinto*
Mary O'Donoghue*
Linda Poust-Lopez*
Robert R. Reed
Julia I. Rodriguez*
Laura Safer-Espinoza*
Saliann Scarpulla*
Barry Schwartz
Jennifer Schecter*
Debra Silber*
Shawndaya L. Simpson*
Harold Adler*
Francis M Alessandro
Nancy Bannon
Johnny Lee Baynes
Arlene P Bluth
Cheree A. Buggs
Margaret A. Chan
Devin P. Cohen
Mitchell Danziger
Laura G. Douglas*
Dorothy K. Chin Brandt*
Matthew F. Cooper*
Marilyn G. Diamond*
James E. D'Auguste*
Arthur F. Engoron
Joseph J. Esposito*
Carol Feinman*
Pamela Fisher
Kathryn E. Freed
Robin S. Garson
Ellen Frances Gesmer*
Lisbeth Gonzalez
Bernard J. Graham*
Desmond A. Green*
Liana Gruebel*
Shlomo S. Haggler*
Pam Jackman-Brown*
Debra A. James*
Tanya Kennedy
Joan M. Kenney*
Michael Katz*
Lynn R. Kotier*
Dennis Lebwhol*
Evelyn J. LaPorte*
Gerald Lebovitz*
Charles Lopresto
Nelinda Malave-Gonzalez
Shari Michels*
Rita Mella*
Manuel J. Mendez*
Frank Nervo*
Ann E. O'Shea*
Terrence O'Connor
Jose A. Padilla
Kibbie F. Payne*
Geraldine Pickett*
Leslie J. Purificacion
Eileen A. Rakower*
Leticia Ramirez*
Debrarose Samuels
Larry S. Schachner*
Robin K. Sheares
Kenneth Sherman
George J. Silver*
Anil C. Singh*
Karen Smith*
Michael D. Stallman*
Peter Paul Sweeney*
Elizabeth Taylor
Analisa Torres*
Carmen R. Velasquez
William A. Viscovich
Jacqueline Williams
John H. Wilson*
Charles Solomon*
Philip S. Straniere
Fernando Tapiat*
Harriet Thompson
Wavny Toussaint*
Carolyn E. Wade
Edgar G. Walker
Betty J. Williams*

Housing Court Judges

Paul L. Alpert
Gilbert Badillo
Hannah Cohen
Timmie E. Elsner
Marc Finkelstein
Cheryl Gonzalez
Sheldon J. Halprin
David J. Kaplan
Jerald R. Kline
Joel Kullas
John S. Lansden
Andrew Lehrer
Jaya Madhavan
Rubin Martino
Kevin McClanahan
Kimberly Moser
Eleanora Ofshtein
Eardell J. Rashford
Jose Rogriguez
Phyllis Saxe
Jean T. Schneider
Marcia Sikowitz
John Stanley
Louis J. Villella
Steven A. Weissman
Elizabeth J. Yalin Tao
Susan Avery
Ronni D Birnbaum
Marian C. Doherty
Anthony J. Fiorella
Thomas M. Fitzpatrick
Arlene H. Hahn
Inez Hoyos
Anne Katz
Sabrina B. Kraus
Lydia C. Lai
Laurie L. Lau
Ulysses B. Leveret
Laurie Marin
Gary Marton
Maria Milin
Marina Mundy
Michael J. Pinckney
Maria Ressos
Verna Saunders
Bruce E. Scheckowitz
Michelle D. Schreiber
Brenda S. Spears
Jack Stoller
Deighton S. Waithe
Peter Wendt

Criminal Court, NYC

Administrative Judge:
Barry Kamins
Chief Clerk:
Justin Barry 646-386-4600/fax: 212-374-4835

Bronx County
215 E 161st St., Bronx, NY 10451
Chief Clerk:
William Kalish 718-618-2460/fax: 718-537-5164

Kings County
120 Schermerhorn St, Brooklyn, NY 11201
Borough Chief Clerk:
Antonio Diaz 347-404-9400/fax: 718-643-5234

New York County
100 Centre St, New York, NY 10013
Borough Chief Clerk:
Donald Vasti 646-386-4511/fax: 212-374-5293

Queens County
125-01 Queens Blvd, Kew Gardens, NY 11415
Borough Chief Clerk:
Carey Wone. 718-298-0792/fax: 718-520-4712

Richmond County
67 Targee St, Staten Island, NY 10304
Borough Chief Clerk:
Ada Molina 718-675-8558/fax: 718-390-8405

Judges

Bruce Allen
A. Kirke Bartley
Efrain L. Alvarado
Lewis Bartstone

Peter J. Benitez
Joel L. Blumenfeld
James M. Burke
Gregory Carro
John Cataldo
Ellen M. Coin
Daniel Conviser
Joseph J. Dawson
Laura E. Drager
Thomas A. Farber
Anthony J. Ferrara
Daniel P. Fitzgerald
Lenora Gerald
Joel M. Goldberg
James P. Griffin
Josephe Gubbay
Roger S. Hayes
Douglas E. Hoffman
Melissa C. Jackson
Diane R. Kiesel
Barry Kron
Judith S. Lieb
Juan Marchan
Alan D. Marrus
Daniel McCullough
Edward McLaughlin
Suzanne J. Melendez
Salvatore J. Modica
Suzanne M. Mondo
Cassandra Mullen
Barbara F. Newman
Mary O'Donoghue
Eugene Oliver
Ann Pfau
Leonard P. Rienzi
Jennifer Schecter
Charles H. Solomon
Larry R. Stephen
Megan Tallmer
Renak Uviller
Richard M. Weinberg
Maxwell Wiley
Bonnie G. Wittner
Alvin M. Yearwood
Ronald Zweibel
Miriam Best
Denis J. Boylet
Alexander Calabrese
Richard D. Carruthers
Danny K. Chun
John P. Collins
Myriam Cyrulnik
Tandra Dawson
Ralph A. Fabrizio
Joann Ferdinand
Neil Jon Firetog
William E. Garnett
Arlene D. Goldberg
Ethan Greenberg
Michael A. Gross
William S. Harrington
Patricia E. Henry
Nicholas Iacovetta
Marcy L. Kahn
Jill Konviser
John B. Latella
Gene R. Lopez
Lawrence Marks
Seth L. Marvin
William L. McGuire, Jr.
Alan J. Meyer
William Miller
William I. Mogulescu
John S. Moore
Pauline Mullings
Patricia M. Nunez
Michael J. Obus
Eduardo Padro
Ruth Pickholz
Neil E. Ross
Matthew Sciarrino, Jr.
Michael R. Sonberg
Robert M. Stolz
Analisa Torres
Laura A. Ward
Renee A. White
Patricia Anne Williams
Douglas S. Wong
Joseph A. Zayas

Family Court, NYC

Administrative Judge:
Edwina G. Richardson-Mendelson
Chief Clerk:
George Cafasso....................646-386-5170 or 212-374-3700
fax: 212-374-3257

Bronx County
900 Sheridan Ave, Bronx, NY 10451
e-mail: bronxfamilycourt@nycourts.gov
Clerk of Court:
Michael J. Williams 718-618-2098/fax: 718-590-7875

Kings County
330 Jay St, Brooklyn, NY 11201
e-mail: kingsfamilycourt@nycourts.gov
Clerk of Court:
Robert Ratanski..................347-401-9600/fax: 347-401-9609

New York County
60 Lafayette St, New York, NY 10013
e-mail: manhattanfamilycourt@nycourts.gov
Clerk of Court:
Evelyn Hasanoeddin 646-386-5200/fax: 212-748-5272

Queens County
151-20 Jamaica Ave, Jamaica, NY 11432
e-mail: queensfamilycourt@nycourts.gov
Clerk of Court:
Vaunda L. Harris-Shrachan 718-298-0197/fax: 718-297-2826

Richmond County
100 Richmond Terrace, Staten Island, NY 10301
e-mail: richmondfamilycourt@nycourts.gov
Clerk of Court:
William J Quirk..................718-675-8800/fax: 718-390-5247

Judges
Michael A Ambrosio
Stephen J Bogacz
Guy P. DePhillips
Sidney Gribetz
John M. Hunt
Arnold Lim
Ruben A. Martino
Emily M. Olshansky
Jeanette Reitz
Edwina G. Richardson-Mendelson
Gayle P. Roberts
Barbara Salinitro
Carol Ann Stokinger
Stewart H. Weinstein
Mary E Bednar
Tandra L. Dawson
Monica Drinane (Supervising)
Douglas Hoffman
Susan R. Larabee
Fran L. Lubow
Martin P. Murphy
Jane Pearl
Clark V. Richardson
Marybeth S. Richroath
Helene Sacco
Gloria Sosa-Lintner
Daniel Turbow

COUNTY COURTS

NYS has three types of courts designated at a county level: County Court, Family Court and Surrogate's Court. The County Court is authorized to handle criminal prosecutions of offenses committed within the county and hears civil cases involving amounts up to $25,000. County Court judges are elected for ten-year terms. The Family Court hears matters involving children and families (for types of court matters see NYC Courts). Family Court judges are elected for ten-year terms. The Surrogate's Court hears cases involving the affairs of decedents, including the probate of wills, and administration of estates and adoptions. Surrogates are elected for ten-year terms. This section also includes Supreme Court clerks and their addresses. Additional information and a list of judges for the NYS Supreme Court is provided in the related Section.

Albany County

Judges
County:
Peter Lynch
Surrogate:
Stacy Pettit
Family:
Susan Kushner
County:
Stephen W Herrick
Family:
Richard Rivera
Family:
Gerard E Maney
Family:
Margaret T Walsh

County Court
Albany County Judicial Center, 6 Lodge Street, Albany, NY 12207
Chief Clerk:
Charles E Diamond................518-285-8777/fax: 518-436-3986

Family
30 Clinton Ave, Albany, NY 12207
Chief Clerk:
Cynthia Robinson.................518-285-8600/fax: 518-462-4248

Deputy Chief Clerk-Surrogate:
Deborah Kearns. 518-285-8585/fax: 518-462-0194

Supreme Court & Surrogate
Courthouse, Room 102, 16 Eagle St, Albany, NY 12207
Chief Clerk-Supreme/County:
Charles E Diamond 518-285-8989/fax: 518-487-5020

Allegany County

Judges
Multi-Bench:
Thomas Paul Brown
Multi-Bench:
Terrence M. Parker

Supreme, County, Family & Surrogate's Courts. fax: 585-268-7090
7 Court St, Belmont, NY 14813-1084
585-268-5800 Fax: 585-268-7090
Chief Clerk-County/Supreme:
Laura Gabler. 585-268-5941
e-mail: lgabler@nycourts.gov
Chief Clerk-Family:
Kelly Buckley. 585-268-9667
e-mail: kbuckley@nycourts.gov
Chief Clerk-Surrogate's:
Dorine Jacobs 585-268-5815
e-mail: dgjacobs@nycourts.gov

Bronx County

Judges
Surrogate:
Nelinda Malave-Gonzalez

COUNTY & FAMILY COURTS: See New York City Courts

Supreme & Surrogate's Courts
851 Grand Concourse, Bronx, NY 10451
Clerk-Civil Division:
Eddy Valdez 718-618-2500
Chief Clerk-Surrogate:
Michael P. Hausler 718-618-2300

Broome County

Judges
Family:
Richard H Miller II
Family (Supervising):
Rita Connerton
County:
Joseph Cawley
Surrogate:
David H. Guy
Family:
Spero Pines
Family:
Mark H Young
County:
Kevin P Dooley

County, Family
65 Hawley St, Binghamton, NY 13902
Chief Clerk-Family:
Debbi D Singer 607-240-5799/fax: 607-240-5904
Deputy Chief Clerk-County/Supreme:
Christine Martin 607-240-5800/fax: 607-240-5940

Surrogate & Supreme Court
92 Court St, Binghamton, NY 13901
607-840-5789
Chief Clerk-Surrogate:
Rebecca A Malmquist. 607-240-5789/fax: 607-778-2308

Cattaraugus County

Judges
Multi-Bench:
Ronald D Ploetz
Multi-Bench:
Michael L Nenno

Supreme & Family Court
One Leo Moss Dr, Olean, NY 14760
Chief Clerk-Family:
Denise Filjones 716-373-8035/fax: 716-373-0449
e-mail: dfiljone@nycourts.gov

Supreme, County & Surrogate's Courts
Courthouse, 303 Court St, Little Valley, NY 14755
Chief Clerk-Surrogate:
Christine Wrona 716-938-2327
e-mail: cwrona@nycourts.gov
Chief Clerk-Supreme:
Verna Dry 716-938-2388/fax: 716-938-6413
e-mail: vdry@nycourts.gov

Cayuga County

Judges
Multi-Bench (Acting):
Mark H Fandrich
County/Family:
Thomas G Leone

Family Court
152 Genesee St, Auburn, NY 13021
e-mail: cayugafamilycourt@courts.state.ny.us
Chief Clerk:
L.D. Serafino . . . . 315-237-6450 or 315-237-6400
fax: 315-237-6451

Chautauqua County

Judges
Surrogate:
Stephen W Cass
Family:
Jeffrey Piazza
Family:
Judith S Claire
County:
John T Ward

Family Court
2 Academy Street, Ste 5, Mayville, NY 14757
Chief Clerk-Family:
Frank Baggiano 716-753-4351/fax: 716-753-4350
e-mail: fbaggian@nycourts.gov

Supreme & County Courts
County Courthouse, 3 North Erie Street, PO Box 292, Mayville, NY 14757-0292
Chief Clerk:
Kathleen Krauza 716-753-4266/fax: 716-753-4993
e-mail: kkrauza@nycourts.gov

Surrogate Court
Gerace Bldg, Courthouse, PO Box C, Mayville, NY 14757
Chief Clerk:
Curt N Meeder. 716-753-4339/fax: 716-753-4600

Offices and agencies generally appear in alphabetical order, except when specific order is requested by listee.

Chemung County

Judges
Family:
Mary M Tarantelli
Surrogate:
Richard W Rich Jr
County:
Richard W Rich
County/Surrogate:
James T Hayden

Family Court
203-209 William St, PO Box 588, Elmira, NY 14902-0558
e-mail: chemungfamilycourt@nycourts.gov
Chief Clerk:
Rebecca Walp 607-873-9500/fax: 212-884-8950

Supreme & County Courts
Courthouse, 224 Lake St, PO Box 588, Elmira, NY 14902-0588
Chief Clerk-County/Supreme:
Nancy Kreisler 607-873-9450/fax: 646-963-6605

Surrogate Court
203-205 Lake St, PO Box 588, Elmira, NY 14902-0588
e-mail: 6jdchmsurr@courts.state.ny.us
Chief Clerk-Surrogate:
Laurie Hubbard 607-837-9440/fax: 646-963-6606

Chenango County

Judges
Multi-Bench:
Frank B. Revoir

Supreme, County, Family & Surrogate's Courts
West Park Place, Norwich, NY 13815
Chief Clerk-Surrogate:
Linda Wiley . . . . 607-337-1827 or 607-337-1822
fax: 607-963-6603
Deputy Chief Clerk-Family:
Karen L Mealey 607-337-1824/fax: 607-240-5848
Chief Clerk-County/Supreme:
Catherine A Schell 607-337-1457/fax: 917-522-3477
e-mail: cschell@courts.state.ny.us

Clinton County

Judges
Family:
Timothy J Lawliss
County:
Patrick R McGill
Surrogate:
Kevin K. Ryan

Supreme, County, Family & Surrogate's Courts
137 Margaret St, Plattsburgh, NY 12901
e-mail: clintonsupremeco@nycourts.gov
Chief Clerk-Family:
Cathy Williams 518-536-3820
e-mail: clintonfamily@nycourts.gov
Chief Clerk-County/Supreme:
Jan M Lavigne 518-536-3840/fax: 518-536-3830
e-mail: clintonsupremeco@nycourts.gov
Chief Clerk-Surrogate:
Lise Johnson 518-536-3830
e-mail: clintonsurrogate@nycourts.gov

Columbia County

Judges
Multi-Bench:
Richard Koweek
Multi-Bench:
Jonathan D Nichols

Supreme, County, Family & Surrogate's Courts. fax: 518-267-3126
401 Union Street, Hudson, NY 12534
518-267-3150 Fax: 518-267-3126
Chief Clerk-Multi:
David Cardona 518-267-3150
Chief Clerk-Surrogate:
Teresa Slemp 518-267-3150

Cortland County

Judges
Multi-Bench:
William F Ames
Multi-Bench:
Julie A Campbell

Supreme, County, Family & Surrogate's Courts
Courthouse, 46 Greenbush St, Ste 301, Cortland, NY 13045-2725
Chief Clerk-Family:
Laurie L Case 607-218-3325/fax: 646-963-6452
e-mail: cortlandfamily@courts.state.ny.us
Chief Clerk-County/Supreme:
Karen Jordan 607-218-3320/fax: 646-963-6452
e-mail: kjordan@nycourts.gov
Chief Clerk-Surrogate:
Lynne Day 607-218-3335/fax: 212-457-2661
e-mail: cortlandsurrogate@courts.state.ny.us

Delaware County

Judges
Multi-Bench:
Richard D Northrup Jr
County:
John F Lambert (Acting)
County:
Brian O Burns (Acting)
Family:
Gary A Rosa

Supreme, County, Family & Surrogate's Courts
Courthouse, 3 Court St, Delhi, NY 13753
Chief Clerk-County/Supreme:
Kelly Sanfilippo 607-746-2131/fax: 646-963-6402
Chief Clerk-Surrogate:
Lisa Hulse 607-746-2126/fax: 646-963-6403
Chief Clerk-Family:
Lori Metzko 607-746-2298/fax: 646-963-6400

Dutchess County

Judges
County:
Peter M. Forman
Family:
Denise M. Watson
Family:
Tracy MacKenzie
County:
Craig Stephen Brown
Surrogate:
James D Pagones
Family:
Joan Posner

Offices and agencies generally appear in alphabetical order, except when specific order is requested by listee.

Family:
Joseph Egitto

Family Court
50 Market St, Poughkeepsie, NY 12601
Chief Clerk-Family:
Peter A Palladino 845-431-1850/fax: 845-486-2510

Supreme, County & Surrogate's Courts
Courthouse, 10 Market St, Poughkeepsie, NY 12601
Chief Clerk-Surrogate:
Erica DeTraglia, Esq. 845-431-1770/fax: 845-476-3659
Chief Clerk-County/Supreme:
Michael Thompson 845-431-1710/fax: 845-431-1743

Erie County

Judges
Family:
Brenda Freedman
Family:
Mary G Carney
Family:
Kevin M Carter
County:
James F Bargnesi
Family:
Sharon LoVallo
County:
Sheila DiTullio
Family:
Lisa Bloch Rodwin
Family:
Deanne Tripi
Surrogate:
Barbara Howe
County:
T P Franczyk
County:
Michael F Pietruszka
Family:
Margaret O Szczur
County:
Kenneth Case

Family Court
One Niagara Plz, Buffalo, NY 14202
Chief Clerk:
Frank J Boccio 716-845-7444/fax: 716-845-7546
e-mail: fboccio@nycourts.gov

Surrogate's Court . . . . fax: 716-845-7566
Erie County Hall, 92 Franklin St, Buffalo, NY 14202
716-845-2560 Fax: 716-845-7566
Chief Clerk-Surrogate (Temporary):
Joseph Shifflett 716-845-9454/fax: 716-845-7565
e-mail: jshiffle@courts.state.ny.us

Supreme & County Court
25 Delaware Ave, Buffalo, NY 14202
Chief Clerk-County/Supreme:
Ellis W. Bozzolo 716-845-9301/fax: 716-851-3293
e-mail: ebozzolo@nycourts.gov

Essex County

Judges
Multi-Bench:
Richard D Meyer

Supreme, County, Family & Surrogate's Courts
Courthouse, 7559 Court St, PO Box 217, Elizabethtown, NY 12932
Chief Clerk-Surrogate:
Mary Ann Badger 518-873-3384/fax: 518-873-3626
Chief Clerk-Family (Acting):
Mary Ann Badger 518-873-3320/fax: 518-451-8739
Chief Clerk-Supreme/County:
Terry A Mitchell 518-873-3370/fax: 518-451-8738

Franklin County

Judges
Multi-Bench:
Robert G Main, Jr
Family:
Derek P Champagne

Supreme, County, Family & Surrogate's Courts
Courthouse, 355 W Main St, Malone, NY 12953
Chief Clerk-Surrogate:
Martha A LaBarge. 518-353-7350/fax: 518-285-6175
Chief Clerk-Family:
Janice F Mock 518-353-7360/fax: 518-481-5453
Chief Clerk-Supreme/County:
Jodi L. Wood. 518-353-7340/fax: 518-481-5456

Fulton County

Judges
County/Surrogate:
Louise K Sira
County/Surrogate:
Polly A Hoye
Family:
Edward F. Skoda

Supreme, County, Family & Surrogate's Courts
223 W Main St, Johnstown, NY 12095
Chief Clerk-County/Supreme:
Nancy Garavelli 518-736-5662/fax: 518-762-5078
Chief Clerk-Surrogate:
Rachel M Finnegan 518-736-5697/fax: 518-762-6372
Chief Clerk-Family:
Lisa Tricozzi 518-762-3840/fax: 518-451-8745

Genesee County

Judges
Family:
Eric R Adams
Multi-Bench:
Robert C Noonan

Supreme, County, Family & Surrogate's Courts
County Courts Facility, 1 W Main St, Batavia, NY 14020
Chief Clerk-Family:
Laurie Johnston 585-344-2230/fax: 585-344-8520
e-mail: ljohnsto@nycourts.gov
Chief Clerk-County/Supreme:
Mary Lou Strathearn 585-344-2550 x2239/fax: 585-344-8517
e-mail: mstrathe@nycourts.gov
Chief Clerk-Surrogate:
Michele Westfall-Owens 585-344-2550 x2240/fax: 585-344-8517
e-mail: mawestfa@nycourts.gov

Greene County

Judges
Multi-Bench:
Charles M. Tailleur
Multi-Bench:
Terry J. Wilhelm

Offices and agencies generally appear in alphabetical order, except when specific order is requested by listee.

Supreme, County, Family & Surrogate's Courts
Courthouse, 320 Main St, Catskill, NY 12414
Chief Clerk-County/Supreme:
Ellen Brower. . . . 518-625-3160
Chief Clerk-Surrogate:
Eric Maurer. . . . 518-625-3150
Chief Clerk-Family:
Brenda VanDermark. . . . 518-625-3180

Hamilton County

Judges
Multi-Bench:
S Peter Feldstein

County, Family & Surrogate's Courts
139 White Birch Lane, PO Box 780, Indian Lake, NY 12842
Chief Clerk:
Araina Eldridge 518-648-5411/fax: 518-453-8687

Herkimer County

Judges
County/Surrogate:
John H. Crandall
Family:
John J. Brennan

Family Court
County Office & Court Facility, 301 N Washington St, Suite 2501, Herkimer, NY 13350
Chief Clerk:
Lynn M Kohl. . . . 315-867-1139/fax: 315-867-1369

Supreme, County & Surrogate's Courts
County Office & Court Facility, 301 N Washington St, Herkimer, NY 13350
Chief Clerk - Supreme:
Paul B. Heintz. . . . 315-867-1346/fax: 315-866-1802
Chief Clerk:
Mary T. Grogan. . . . 315-867-1367/fax: 315-866-1722

Jefferson County

Judges
Family:
Richard V Hunt
County:
Kim H Martusewicz
Surrogate:
Peter A Schwerzmann

County, Family & Surrogate's Courts
163 Arsenal St, Watertown, NY 13601
Chief Clerk-Family:
Valerie Boyle 315-785-3001/fax: 315-266-4776
Chief Clerk-Surrogate:
Benjamin Cobb 315-785-3019/fax: 315-785-5194

Supreme Court
State Office Bldg, 317 Washington St, Watertown, NY 13601
Chief Clerk-County/Supreme:
Deanna L. Morse. . . . 315-785-7906/fax: 315-266-4779

Kings County

Judges
Surrogate:
Margarita Lopez Torres
Surrogate:
Diana A. Johnson

COUNTY & FAMILY COURTS: See New York City Courts

Supreme Court
Civil: 360 Adams St, Criminal: 320 Jay St, Brooklyn, NY 11201
Chief Clerk-Criminal:
Daniel M. Allessandrino. . . . 347-396-1100
Chief Clerk-Civil:
Charles A. Small, Esq. 718-675-7699

Surrogate's Court
2 Johnson St, Brooklyn, NY 11201
Chief Clerk-Surrogate:
Doreen Quinn. . . . 718-643-7098 or 347-404-9700

Lewis County

Judges
Multi-Bench:
Daniel R. King

Supreme, County, Family & Surrogate's Courts
Courthouse, 7660 N State St, Lowville, NY 13367
Chief Clerk-Family:
Lori Pfendler 315-376-5345/fax: 315-376-5189
Chief Clerk-Surrogate:
Lori Pfendler 315-376-5344/fax: 315-376-1647
Chief Clerk-County/Supreme:
Bart R Pleskach . . . . 315-376-5366 or 315-376-5347
fax: 315-376-4198

Livingston County

Judges
Family:
Thomas Moran
County:
Dennis S Cohen
County:
Robert B Wiggins

Supreme, County, Family & Surrogate's Courts
Courthouse, 2 Court St, Geneseo, NY 14454-1030
e-mail: livingstonfamilycourt@nycourts.gov
Chief Clerk - Family:
Nanette Galvin 585-371-3919/fax: 585-371-3933
Chief Clerk - Supreme/County:
Jose Cruzado 585-371-3920/fax: 585-371-3935
Chief Clerk - Family:
Robert M. Lewis 585-371-3919/fax: 585-371-3933

Madison County

Judges
County:
Patrick J O'Sullivan
Multi-Bench:
Dennis K McDermott

Supreme, County, Family & Surrogate's Courts
Courthouse, 138 N Court St, Wampsville, NY 13163-0545
Chief Clerk-Family:
Karen McKie. . . . 315-231-5310/fax: 646-963-6589
e-mail: madisonfamilycourt@courts.state.ny.us
Chief Clerk-County/Supreme:
Tracy Damchieco 315-231-5301/fax: 646-963-6588
Chief Clerk-Surrogate:
Deborah Samoyedny. . . . 315-231-5321/fax: 646-963-6594
e-mail: dsamoyed@nycourts.gov

Monroe County

Judges

Multi-Bench:
James E Walsh
Multi-Bench:
James A Vazzana
Multi-Bench:
Patricia Gallaher
County:
Victoria M Argento
County:
Christopher Ciacco
County:
John L DeMarco
Multi-Bench:
Joan S. Kohout
County:
Gail A. Donofrio
County:
Vincent M Dinolfo
County:
Douglas A Randall
Multi-Bench:
Joseph G. Nesser
Multi-Bench:
John Gallagher
Multi-Bench:
Dandrea L. Ruhlmann
Surrogate:
John M Owens

Supreme, County, Family & Surrogate's Courts. fax: 585-371-3313
Hall of Justice, 99 Exchange Blvd, Rochester, NY 14614
585-371-3310 Fax: 585-371-3313
Chief Clerk-Surrogate:
Mark L. Annunziata 585-371-3289
e-mail: mannunzi@nycourts.gov
Chief Clerk-County:
Lisa Preston . . . . 585-428-2020 or 585-428-2331
fax: 585-428-2190
e-mail: monroe_superior@courts.state.ny.us
Chief Clerk-Family:
Loreen Nash 585-371-3544/fax: 585-371-3585
e-mail: monroefamilycourt@nycourts.gov

Montgomery County

Judges

County:
Felix J Catena
Family:
Philip V Cortese
Surrogate:
Guy P Tomlinson

Supreme, County, Family & Surrogate's Courts
Courthouse, 58 Broadway, PO Box 1500, Fonda, NY 12068-1500
Chief Clerk-Surrogate:
Alison Thomas-Oravsky, Esq. 518-853-8108/fax: 518-853-8230
Chief Clerk-Family:
Laurie Furnare. 518-853-8133/fax: 518-238-4370
Chief Clerk-County/Supreme:
Timothy J Riley. 518-853-4516/fax: 518-853-3596

Nassau County

Judges

County:
David J Ayres
County:
Meryl J Berkowitz
County:
Angelo A. Delligatti
County:
Joseph Calabrese
County:
Jerald S Carter
Family:
Julianne S Eisman
Family:
Teresa K. Corrigan
County:
Robert H. Spergel
County:
Steven M Jaeger
County:
John M. Galasso
Family:
Edmund M. Dane
Family:
Ellen R. Greenberg
Family:
Robin M. Kent
County:
James P McCormack
Family:
Merik A. Aaron
County:
George R Peck
Surrogate:
Edward W. McCarthy, III
County:
Tammy S Robbins
County:
David P Sullivan
Family:
Conrad D. Singer

County & Surrogate's Courts
262 Old Country Rd, Mineola, NY 11501
516-493-3800 or 516-493-3710
Chief Clerk-County:
Donald F. Vetter. 516-493-3710
Chief Clerk-Surrogate:
Michael Murphy 516-493-3805

Family Court
1200 Old Country Rd, Westbury, NY 11590
516-493-4000
Chief Clerk:
Rosalie Fitzgerald. 516-493-4000

Supreme Court
Supreme Court Bldg, 100 Supreme Court Dr, Mineola, NY 11501
Chief Clerk:
Kathryn D Hopkins 516-493-3400

New York County

Judges

Surrogate:
Nora S. Anderson

COUNTY & FAMILY COURTS: See New York City Courts

SUPREME COURT, Civil Term
60 Centre St, New York, NY 10007
Clerk:
Norman Goodman 646-386-5955

Offices and agencies generally appear in alphabetical order, except when specific order is requested by listee.

SUPREME COURT, Criminal Term
100 Centre St, New York, NY 10013
Clerk:
Barry Clarke 646-386-3900/fax: 212-748-5129

Surrogate's Court
31 Chambers St, New York, NY 10007
Chief Clerk:
Diana Sanabria 646-386-5000

Niagara County

Judges
Family:
Kathleen Wojtaszek-Gariano
County/Surrogate:
Matthew J Murphy
Family:
John F. Batt
County/Surrogate:
Sara Sheldon Farkas

County, Family & Surrogate's Courts
Courthouse, 175 Hawley St, Lockport, NY 14094
Chief Clerk-Family:
William F McCarthy 716-278-1880/fax: 716-278-1877
e-mail: wmccarth@nycourts.gov
Chief Clerk-County/Supreme:
Michael C. Veruto, Esq. 716-278-1800/fax: 716-278-1809
e-mail: mveruto@nycourts.gov
Chief Clerk-Surrogate:
Angela Stamm-Philipps, Esq. 716-439-7130/fax: 716-439-7157

County, Supreme & Family Courts
Delsignore Civic Bldg, 775 Third St, Niagara Falls, NY 14301

Oneida County

Judges
Family:
Randall B Caldwell
County (Supervising):
Barry M Donalty
County:
Michael L Dwyer
Surrogate:
Louis P. Gigliotti
Family:
James R Griffith
Family (Rome):
Joan E. Shkane

Supreme, County & Family Courts
Courthouse, 200 Elizabeth St, Utica, NY 13501
Chief Clerk-Supreme/County:
Kathleen Aiello 315-266-4200/fax: 315-798-6047
Chief Clerk-Family:
Barbara A Porta.................. 315-266-4444/fax: 315-798-6404

Surrogate's Court
County Office Bldg, 800 Park Ave, 8th Fl, Utica, NY 13501
Chief Clerk:
Kristine K Pecheone 315-266-4550/fax: 315-797-9237

Onondaga County

Judges
County:
Anthony F Aloi
County:
Joseph E Fahey
Family:
Michael Hanuszczak
Family:
Julie A. Cecile
Family:
Michele Pirro Bailey
Family:
Martha E Mulroy
Surrogate:
Ava S Raphael
County:
Thomas J. Miller
Family (Supervisory):
Martha Walsh Hood

Supreme, County, Family & Surrogate's Courts
Courthouse, 401 Montgomery St, Syracuse, NY 13202
Chief Clerk-Family:
David Primo, Esq. 315-671-2000/fax: 315-671-1163
Chief Clerk-Supreme/County:
Patricia J Noll.................... 315-671-1030 or 315-671-1020
fax: 315-671-1176
Chief Clerk-Surrogate:
Ellen S Weinstein Esq. 315-671-2100/fax: 315-671-1162

Ontario County

Judges
Multi-Bench:
Williamk F Kocher
Multi-Bench:
Frederick G Reed
Family (Acting):
Stephen D. Aronson

Supreme, County, Family & Surrogate's Courts
Courthouse, 27 N Main St, Canandaigua, NY 14424-1459
Chief Clerk-Supreme/County:
Marcilyn Morrisey 585-412-5300/fax: 585-412-5327
Chief Clerk-Surrogate's:
Elizabeth Simpson. 585-412-5301/fax: 585-412-5331
Chief Clerk - Family:
Robin Russell 585-412-5299/fax: 585-412-5327
e-mail: ontariofamilycourt@nycourts.gov

Orange County

Judges
County:
Jeffrey G Berry
Family:
Andrew P Bivona
County:
Nicholas DeRosa
Family:
Debra Kiedaisch
Family:
Carol S Klein
County:
Robert H. Freehill
Surrogate:
Robert A Onofry
Family:
Lori Currier Woods

Supreme, County & Family Courts
285 Main St, Goshen, NY 10924
Chief Clerk-County/Supreme:
Lynn McKelvey 845-476-3500
Chief Clerk-Family:
Elizabeth Holbrook...............................845-476-3520

Offices and agencies generally appear in alphabetical order, except when specific order is requested by listee.

Surrogate's Court
Courthouse, 30 Park Pl, Goshen, NY 10924
Chief Clerk:
Jeanne Smith 845-476-3655/fax: 845-291-2196

Orleans County

Judges
Multi-Bench:
James P Punch

Supreme, County, Family & Surrogate's Courts
Courthouse Square, 1 S. Main Street, Suite 3, Albion, NY 14411-1497
Chief Clerk-Surrogate:
Deborah Berry 585-589-4457/fax: 585-589-0632
e-mail: dberry@nycourts.gov
Chief Clerk-Family:
Laurie A Bower 585-589-4457/fax: 585-589-0632
e-mail: lbower@nycourts.gov
Chief Clerk-County/Supreme:
Kristin Nicholson 585-589-5458/fax: 585-589-0632
e-mail: knichols@nycourts.gov

Oswego County

Judges
Surrogate:
Spencer Ludington
County:
Walter W Hafner, Jr
County:
Donald E. Todd
Family:
Kimberly M. Seager

Family Court
Public Safety Ctr, 39 Churchill Rd, Oswego, NY 13126
Chief Clerk-Family:
Kathleen L. Halstead 315-349-3350/fax: 315-349-3457

Supreme, County & Surrogate's Courts
Courthouse, 25 E Oneida St, Oswego, NY 13126
Chief Clerk-Surrogate:
Cheryl Blake 315-349-3295/fax: 315-349-8514
Chief Clerk-County/Supreme:
Sonya Malone 315-349-3277/fax: 315-266-4519

Otsego County

Judges
Multi-Bench:
Brian D Burns
Multi-Bench:
John F Lambert

Supreme, County, & Surrogate's Courts
197 Main St, Cooperstown, NY 13326
Chief Clerk-County/Supreme:
Michael McGovern 607-547-4364/fax: 646-963-6663
e-mail: mmcgove1@nycourts.gov
Chief Clerk-Family:
Karen A Nichols 607-547-4264/fax: 212-457-2956
e-mail: otsegofamilycourt@courts.state.ny.us
Chief Clerk-Surrogate:
Lisa Weite 607-547-4213/fax: 607-240-5966
e-mail: lweite@nycourts.gov

Family Court
County Annex Building, 32 Chestnut Street, Cooperstown, NY 13326
Chief Clerk-Family:
Karen A Nichols 607-547-4264/fax: 212-457-2956
e-mail: otsegofamilycourt@nycourts.gov

Putnam County

Judges
Multi-Bench:
James F Reitz
Multi-Bench:
James T Rooney

Supreme, County & Family Courts
20 County Center, Carmel, NY 10512

Surrogate's Court
44 Gleneida Ave, Carmel, NY 10512
Chief Clerk-Family:
Karen O'Connor 845-208-7805/fax: 845-228-9614
Chief Clerk-County/Supreme:
Karen O'Connor 845-208-7830/fax: 845-208-7869
Chief Clerk-Surrogate:
Linda M Schwark 845-208-7860/fax: 845-228-5761

Queens County

Judges
Surrogate:
Peter Kelly

COUNTY & FAMILY COURTS: See New York City Courts

Supreme & Surrogate's Courts
88-11 Sutphin Blvd, Jamaica, NY 11435
Chief Clerk:
Margaret Gribbon. . . . . 718-298-0400 or 718-298-0500

Rensselaer County

Judges
Family:
Catherine Cholakis
Family:
Elizabeth Marie Walsh
County - Part Time:
Henry F. Zwack
Surrogate:
Paul V. Morgan Jr.
County:
Debra J Young
County:
Andrew G. Ceresia
County - Part Time:
Michael Melkonian

Family Court
1504 Fifth Ave, Troy, NY 12180
Chief Clerk:
Barbara Cottrell. 518-435-5515/fax: 518-272-6573

Supreme, County & Surrogate's Courts . . . . . fax: 518-285-5077
Courthouse, 80 Second Street, Troy, NY 12180
Chief Clerk-Surrogate:
Susan Wilson. 518-285-6100/fax: 518-272-5452
Chief Clerk-County/Supreme:
Richard F Reilly, Jr. 518-285-5025/fax: 518-270-3714

Richmond County

Judges
Surrogate:
Robert J. Gigante

COUNTY & FAMILY COURTS: See New York City Courts

Supreme & Surrogate's Courts
County Courthouse, 18 Richmond Terrace, Staten Island, NY 10301

Offices and agencies generally appear in alphabetical order, except when specific order is requested by listee.

Chief Clerk-Surrogate:
Ronald M Cerrachio 718-675-8500
Chief Clerk-Supreme:
Joseph Como 718-675-8700

Rockland County

Judges
County:
Charles A Apotheker
Family:
Sherri L. Eisenpress
County:
William K Nelson
Surrogate:
Thomas E Walsh, II
Family:
William P Warren

Supreme, County, Family & Surrogate's Courts
Courthouse, 1 S Main St, New City, NY 10956
Chief Clerk-Family:
Anna Kosovych. 845-483-8210/fax: 845-638-5319
Chief Clerk-County/Supreme:
John F Hussey 845-483-8310/fax: 845-638-5312
Chief Clerk-Surrogate:
Virginia Athens 845-483-8260/fax: 845-638-5632

Saratoga County

Judges
Family:
Courtenay W Hall
Family:
Jennifer Jensen Bergan
County:
James A Murphy III
Surrogate:
Richard Kupferman

Family Court
35 W High St, Ballston Spa, NY 12020
Chief Clerk:
Dennis Bruce. 518-451-8888/fax: 518-453-5942

Supreme, County & Surrogate's Courts
30 McMaster St, Bldg 3, Ballston Spa, NY 12020
Chief Clerk-Surrogate:
Catharine Ruggles 518-451-8830/fax: 518-453-8693
Chief Clerk-County/Supreme:
Carianne Brimhall 518-451-8840/fax: 518-453-5937

Schenectady County

Judges
County:
Matthew J Sypniewski
Surrogate:
Vincent W. Versaci
Family:
Jill S Polk
Family:
Mark L Powers
Family:
Kevin A. Burke

Family Court
County Office Bldg, 620 State St, Schenectady, NY 12305
Chief Clerk:
Denise Riggi 518-285-8435/fax: 518-393-1565

Supreme, County & Surrogate's Courts
Courthouse, 612 State St, Schenectady, NY 12305
Chief Clerk-Surrogate:
Paula Miller. 518-285-8455/fax: 518-451-8732
Chief Clerk-County/Supreme:
Mary Adams 518-285-8401/fax: 518-451-8731

Schoharie County

Judges
Multi-Bench:
George R Bartlett, III

Supreme, County, Family & Surrogate's Courts
Courthouse, 290 Main St, PO Box 669, Schoharie, NY 12157-0669
Chief Clerk-Surrogate/Family/County/Supreme:
F Christian Spies. 518-453-6998

Schuyler County

Judges
Multi-Bench:
Dennis J. Morris

Supreme, County, Family & Surrogate's Courts
Courthouse, 105 9th St, Unit 35, Watkins Glen, NY 14891
Chief Clerk-Family:
Amanda Riley 607-535-7143/fax: 646-963-6590
e-mail: alriley@courts.state.ny.us
Chief Clerk-County/Supreme:
Rita S Decker 607-535-7760/fax: 646-963-6590
e-mail: rdecker@nycourts.gov
Chief Clerk-Surrogate:
Michele Ormsbee 607-535-7144/fax: 646-963-6590

Seneca County

Judges
Multi-Bench:
W. Patrick Falvey
Multi-Bench:
Dennis F Bender

Supreme, County, Family & Surrogate's Courts
Courthouse, 48 W Williams St, Waterloo, NY 13165
Chief Clerk-Family:
Conchetta M Brown 315-835-6231/fax: 315-835-6234
e-mail: senecafamilycourt@nycourts.gov
Chief Clerk-Supreme/County:
Susan Maleski 315-835-6229/fax: 315-835-6234
Chief Clerk-Surrogate:
Jane Lawson 315-835-6232/fax: 315-835-6234

St Lawrence County

Judges
Family:
Cecily L. Morris
County:
Jerome J Richards
Surrogate:
John F Richey

Supreme, County, Family & Surrogate's Courts
Courthouse, 48 Court St, Canton, NY 13617-1194
Chief Clerk-County/Supreme:
Mary B Curran 315-379-2219/fax: 315-379-2423
e-mail: mcurran@courts.state.ny.us
Chief Clerk-Family:
Rhonda Poupore 315-379-2410/fax: 315-386-3197
Chief Clerk-Surrogate:
Debra Dow 315-379-2217/fax: 315-379-2372

Steuben County

Judges

Multi-Bench:
Peter C Bradstreet
Multi-Bench:
Marianne Furfure
Multi-Bench:
Joseph W Latham

Supreme, County, Family & Surrogate's Courts

Courthouse, 3 E Pulteney Sq, Bath, NY 14810
Chief Clerk - Family:
April L Din 607-622-8218/fax: 607-622-8239
e-mail: steubenfamilycourt@nycourts.gov
Chief Clerk - Surrogate's:
Sara A Barefoot. 607-622-8221/fax: 607-622-8243
Chief Clerk - Supreme/County:
Betty Gerych 607-622-8219/fax: 607-622-8244

Suffolk County

Judges

County/Acting Surrogate Judge:
Stephen L Braslow
Family:
Marlene Budd
County:
Stephen M. Behar
Surrogate:
John M Czygier, Jr
County:
Joseph Farnetti
Family:
David Freundlich
County:
Ralph T Gazzillo
Family:
Denise F. Molia
Family:
Richard Hoffman
County:
James C Hudson
County:
Barbara Kahn
Family:
John Kelly
Family:
Martha L Luft
Family:
Caren Loguercio
County:
Jeffrey Arlen Spinner
Family:
Bernard Cheng
Family:
Andrew G Tarantino Jr
County:
John Iliou
Family:
Theresa Whelan
County:
James F. Quinn

County Court

210 Center Dr, Riverhead, NY 11901
Chief Clerk:
Frank L. Tropea. 631-852-2120/fax: 631-852-2568

Family Court

Courthouse, 400 Carleton Ave, Central Islip, NY 11722
Chief Clerk:
Terry Matyszczyk. 631-853-4289

Supreme Court

235 Griffing Ave, Riverhead, NY 11901
Chief Clerk:
Michael Scardino 631-852-2334

Surrogate's Court

320 Center Dr, Riverhead, NY 11901
Chief Clerk:
Michael Cipollino. 631-852-1746

Sullivan County

Judges

County:
Frank J LaBuda
Surrogate:
Michael McGuire
Family:
Mark M Meddaugh

Surrogate's & Family Courts

Government Ctr, 100 North St, Monticello, NY 12701
Chief Clerk-Surrogate:
Rita Guarnaccia. 845-791-3500/fax: 845-481-9337
Chief Clerk-Family:
Christina Benson. 845-791-3505/fax: 845-476-3620

Supreme & County Court

Courthouse, 414 Broadway, Monticello, NY 12701
Chief Clerk-Supreme/County:
Sarah Katzman 845-791-3540/fax: 845-791-6170

Tioga County

Judges

Multi-Bench:
Gerald Keene

Supreme County, Family & Surrogate's Courts

Court Annex, 20 Court St, PO Box 10, Owego, NY 13827
Chief Clerk-Family:
Denise Marsili. 607-689-6077/fax: 646-963-6399
Chief Clerk-Surrogate:
Deborah Stone. 607-689-6099/fax: 646-963-6398
Chief Clerk-Supreme/County:
Janean Cook 607-689-6102/fax: 212-401-5970

Tompkins County

Judges

Multi-Bench:
John C Rowley
Multi-Bench:
Joseph R. Cassidy

Supreme, County, Family & Surrogate's Courts

Courthouse, 320 N Tioga St, Ithaca, NY 14850
Chief Clerk-Surrogate:
Lori S Decker 607-216-6655/fax: 212-457-2952
Chief Clerk-County/Supreme:
Mary C Hodges . . . . 607-216-6630 or 607-216-6610
fax: 212-401-9071
Chief Clerk-Family:
Cheryl Lidell Obenauer. 607-216-6640/fax: 212-457-2951
e-mail: tpkfamily@nycourts.gov

Offices and agencies generally appear in alphabetical order, except when specific order is requested by listee.

Ulster County

Judges
County:
Donald Williams
Family:
Marianne O Mizel
Family:
Keri Savona
Surrogate:
Mary MacMaster Work
Family:
Anthony McGinty

Family Court
16 Lucas Ave, Kingston, NY 12401
Chief Clerk:
Kathy Lasko 845-481-9430/fax: 845-483-8114
e-mail: ulsterfamilycourt@nycourts.gov

Supreme & County Courts
Courthouse, 285 Wall St, Kingston, NY 12401
Chief Clerk:
Claudia Jones 845-481-9375/fax: 845-476-3619

Surrogate's Court
240 Fair St, Kingston, NY 12401
Chief Clerk:
Linda McCluskey 845-481-9338/fax: 845-483-8427
e-mail: ulstersurrogatecourt@nycourts.gov

Warren County

Judges
Family:
Paulette M Kershko
County/Surrogate:
John S Hall Jr

Supreme, County, Family & Surrogate's Courts
Municipal Ctr, 1340 State Rte 9, Lake George, NY 12845
Chief Clerk-Family:
Donna Hamell 518-761-6500/fax: 518-761-6230
Chief Clerk-Surrogate:
Deborah Ricci 518-761-6514/fax: 518-761-7698
Chief Clerk-County/Supreme:
Joanne Mann 518-761-6431/fax: 518-761-6253

Washington County

Judges
Multi-Bench:
Adam Michelini
Multi-Bench:
Kelly S McKeighan

Supreme, County, Family & Surrogate's Courts
Courthouse, 383 Broadway, Fort Edward, NY 12828-1015
Chief Clerk-County/Supreme:
Tricia Robarge. 518-746-2521/fax: 518-746-2519
Chief Clerk-Family:
Josephine Doll. 518-746-2501/fax: 518-746-2503
Chief Clerk-Surrogate:
Barbara Smith 518-746-2545/fax: 518-746-2547

Wayne County

Judges
Multi-Bench:
Dennis M Kehoe
Multi-Bench:
John B Nesbitt
Multi-Bench:
Daniel G. Barrett

Supreme, County, Family & Surrogate's Courts
Hall of Justice, 54 Broad St, Rm 106, Lyons, NY 14489-1199
Chief Clerk-Surrogate's:
Christina Herman 315-665-8119/fax: 315-665-8106
Chief Clerk-Family:
Vacant 315-665-8115/fax: 315-665-8106
e-mail: waynefamilycourt@courts.state.ny.us
Chief Clerk-Supreme/County:
Julie Brooks. 315-665-8117/fax: 315-665-8106

Westchester County

Judges
County:
Susan M Capeci
County:
David F. Everett
County:
Susan Cacace
County:
Barry Warhit
County:
David S. Zuckerman
Surrogate:
Brandon R. Sall
County:
James W Hubert
County:
Barbara G Zambelli

Supreme, County & Family Courts
111 Dr Martin Luther King Jr Blvd, White Plains, NY 10601
Chief Clerk-Family:
James McAllister. 914-824-5500/fax: 914-995-8650
Chief Clerk-County/Supreme:
Nancy J. Barry, Esq. 914-824-5873

Surrogate's Court
111 Dr Martin Luther King Jr Blvd, 19th Fl, White Plains, NY 10601
Chief Clerk:
Joseph Accetta. 914-824-5656/fax: 914-995-3728

Wyoming County

Judges
Multi-Bench:
Michael Mohun
Multi-Bench:
Michael F Griffith

Supreme, County, Family & Surrogate's Courts
Courthouse, 147 N Main St, Warsaw, NY 14569
Chief Clerk-Surrogate:
William D Beyer 585-786-3148/fax: 585-786-3800
e-mail: wbeyer@nycourts.gov
Chief Clerk-Family:
Jacqueline DiAngelo 585-786-3148/fax: 585-786-3800
e-mail: jdiangel@nycourts.gov
Chief Clerk-County/Supreme:
Rebecca Miller . . . . 585-786-3148 or 585-786-2253
fax: 585-786-2818
e-mail: rmmiller@nycourts.gov

Yates County

Judges
Multi-Bench:
W Patrick Falvey

Offices and agencies generally appear in alphabetical order, except when specific order is requested by listee.

Supreme, County, Family & Surrogate's Courts
Courthouse, 415 Liberty St, Penn Yan, NY 14527-1191
Chief Clerk-Spreme/County:
Carol B. Winslow 315-536-5126/fax: 315-536-5190
e-mail: yatesfamilycourt@courts.state.ny.us

DISTRICT COURTS

District Courts exist in Nassau County and in five western towns of Suffolk County. District Courts have civil jurisdiction up to $15,000, and criminal jurisdiction for misdemeanors, violations and lesser offenses. Judges are elected for six-year terms by their judicial districts.

Nassau County

Chief Clerk:
Eileen Bianchi 516-493-4162

1st, 2nd & 4th District Courts
99 Main St, Hempstead, NY 11550
516-493-4200
Deputy Chief Clerk, 4th:
Michael Beganskas 516-572-2355
Deputy Chief Clerk, 1st & 2nd:
Kenneth Roll 516-572-2355

3rd District Court
435 Middle Neck Rd, Great Neck, NY 11023
District Executive:
Paul Lamanna, Esq. 516-493-3000/fax: 516-493-3390

Judges
Valerie Alexander
Joseph Girardi
Andrew M. Engel
Rhonda E. Fischer
David Goodsell
William Hohauser
Robert E. Pipia
Scott H. Siller
Terence P. Murphy
Anthony W Paradiso
Erica L Prager
Andrea Phoenix
David P. Sullivan
(Supervising):
Norman St George
Joy M. Watson
James M. Darcy
Eric Bjorneby
Tricia M. Ferrell
Scott Fairgrieve
Darlene D. Harris
Susan T. Kluewer
Douglas J. Lerose
Martin J Massell
William J O'Brien
Colin F. O'Donnell
Anthony W. Paradiso
Francis Ricigliano
Helen Voutsinas

Suffolk County

Chief Clerk:
Michael Paparatto 631-853-4530

1ST DISTRICT COURT, Civil Term . . . . fax: 631-854-9681
3105 Veterans Memorial Hwy, Ronkonkoma, NY 11779
631-854-9676 Fax: 631-854-9681

1ST DISTRICT COURT, Criminal Term . . . . fax: 631-853-4505
Courthouse, 400 Carleton Ave, Central Islip, NY 11722
631-853-7500 Fax: 631-853-4505

2nd District Court . . . . fax: 631-854-1127
30 East Hoffman Avenue, Lindenhurst, NY 11757
631-854-1121 Fax: 631-854-1127

3rd District Court . . . . fax: 631-854-4549
1850 New York Ave, Huntington Station, NY 11746
631-854-4545 Fax: 631-854-4549

4th District Court . . . . fax: 631-853-5951
Veterans' Memorial Highway, North County Cplx Bldg C158, Hauppauge, NY 11787
631-853-5400 Fax: 631-853-5951

5th District Court . . . . fax: 631-854-9681
3105 Veterans Memorial Hwy, Ronkonkoma, NY 11779
631-854-9676 Fax: 631-854-9681

6th District Court . . . . fax: 631-854-1444
150 W Main St, Patchogue, NY 11772
631-854-1440 Fax: 631-854-1444

Judges
Robert L Cicale
Janine A. Barbera-Dalli
Chris Ann Kelley
(Supervising):
Karen Kerr
Richard T. Dunne
Patricia Grant Flynn
James P Flanagan
James F Matthews
Derrick Robinson
Karen M Wilutis
John P Schettino
Anthony Senft
Stephen L. Ukeiley
Pierce F Cohalan
Toni A Bean
James McDonough
Carl Copertino
Linda J Kevins
C Stephen Hackeling
Jennifer A. Henry
Gaetan B Lozito
Vincent J. Martorana
David A. Morris
Marion Rose Tinari

CITY COURTS OUTSIDE NEW YORK CITY

City Courts outside New York City have civil jurisdiction up to $15,000 and criminal jurisdiction over misdemeanors or lesser offenses. City Court judges are either elected or appointed for terms of ten years for full-time judges and six years for part-time judges.

Albany

Judges
Criminal:
William A Carter
Traffic/Civil:
Helena Heath
Criminal:
Thomas K Keefe
Criminal:
Rachel L Kretser
Traffic/Civil:
Gary F Stiglmeier

Civil Court
Albany City Hall, Room 209, 24 Eagle Street, Albany, NY 12207
Chief Clerk:
Anthony Mancino 518-453-4640/fax: 518-453-8679
e-mail: albanycivilcourt@nycourts.gov

Criminal Court
Public Safety Bldg, 1 Morton Ave, Albany, NY 12202
Chief Clerk:
Anthony Mancino 518-453-5520/fax: 518-453-8990
e-mail: albanycriminalcourt@nycourts.gov

Traffic Court
Albany City Hall Basement, 24 Eagle St, Albany, NY 12207
Chief Clerk:
Anthony Mancino 518-453-4630/fax: 518-453-8699
e-mail: albanytrafficcourt@nycourts.gov

Amsterdam

Judges
William J Mycek
Lisa W Lorman

Civil & Criminal Courts
Public Safety Bldg, Rm 208, 1 Guy Park Ave Ext, Amsterdam, NY 12010
Chief Clerk:
Melanie Hartman. 518-842-9510/fax: 518-453-8646

Auburn

Judges
Michael F McKeon
David B Thurston

Civil & Criminal Courts
157 Genesee St, Auburn, NY 13021
315-237-6420
Chief Clerk:
Deborah L Robillard 315-237-6420/fax: 315-237-6421

Batavia

Judges
Robert J Balbick
Durin B Rogers

Civil & Criminal Courts . . . . fax: 585-344-8556
Facility Bldg, 1 W Main St, Batavia, NY 14020
585-344-2550 x2417 Fax: 585-344-8556
Chief Clerk:
Paula DaBella 585-344-2550 x2426
e-mail: pdabella@nycourts.gov

Beacon

Judges
Rebecca S Mensch
Timothy G Pagones

Civil & Criminal Courts
1 Municipal Plz, Ste 2, Beacon, NY 12508
Chief Clerk:
Debra Antonelli. 845-431-1900/fax: 845-838-5041

Binghamton

Judges
Carol A Cocchiola
Daniel L Seiden
William C Pelella

Civil & Criminal Courts
City Hall, Governmental Plz, 38 Hawley St, 5th Fl, Binghamton, NY 13901
Chief Clerk:
Sherry L Baker 607-772-7006/fax: 607-772-7041
e-mail: sbaker@nycourts.gov

Buffalo

Judges
(Chief):
Thomas P Amodeo
Patrick M Carney
Betty Calvo-Torres
Craig D Hannah
Susan Eagan
JaHarr Pridgen
Barbara Johnson-Lee
Amy C Martoche
Joseph A Fiorella
Debra L Givens
Kevin J Keane
James A McLeod
Diane Wray
Robert T Russell Jr

Civil & Criminal Courts . . . . fax: 716-847-8257
50 Delaware Ave, Buffalo, NY 14202
716-845-2600 Fax: 716-847-8257
Chief Clerk:
Erika Webb. 716-845-2654
e-mail: ewebb@nycourts.gov

Canandaigua

Judges
Stephen D Aronson
John A Schuppenhauer

Civil & Criminal Courts
City Hall, 2 N Main St, Canandaigua, NY 14424
585-412-5170
Chief Clerk:
Lisa R Gardner 585-412-5170/fax: 585-412-5172

Cohoes

Judges
Andra Ackerman
Thomas Marcelle

Civil, Criminal & Traffic Courts
City Hall, 97 Mohawk St, PO Box 678, Cohoes, NY 12047
Chief Clerk:
Margaret A Siciliano. 518-453-5501/fax: 518-233-8202
e-mail: cohoescitycourt@nycourts.gov

Corning

Judges
George J Welch, Jr
Mathew Kelly McCarthy

Civil & Criminal Courts
500 Nasser Civic Ctr Plaza, Ste 101, Corning, NY 14830
e-mail: corningcity@nycourts.gov
Chief Clerk:
Colleen A Flanagan. 607-654-6033/fax: 607-654-6030

Cortland

Judges
Lawrence J Knickerbocker
Elizabeth A Burns

Civil & Criminal Courts
City Hall, 25 Court St, Cortland, NY 13045
Chief Clerk:
Diana L Davis 607-218-3300/fax: 607-218-3299

Dunkirk

Judges
Walter F Drag
John M Kuzdale (Acting)

Civil & Criminal Courts
City Hall, 342 Central Ave, Dunkirk, NY 14048-2122
Chief Clerk:
Jean Dill 716-366-2055/fax: 716-366-3622
e-mail: jdill@nycourts.gov

Elmira

Judges
Steven W Forrest
Ottavio Campanella

Civil & Criminal Courts
317 E Church St, Elmira, NY 14901
e-mail: elmiracitycourt@courts.state.ny.us
Deputy Chief Clerk:
Casey Johnson. 607-837-9520/fax: 212-401-9240

Fulton

Judges
David H Hawthorne
Jerome A Mirabito

Civil & Criminal Courts
Municipal Bldg, 141 S First St, Fulton, NY 13069
e-mail: fulton_city@courts.state.ny.us

Chief Clerk:
Maureen Ball....................315-593-8400/fax: 315-266-4753
e-mail: mball@courts.state.ny.us

Geneva

Judges
Timothy J Buckley
Elisabeth A Toole
David L Foster

Civil & Criminal Courts
255 Exchange St, Geneva, NY 14456
315-237-6575
Chief Clerk:
Josephine Guard..................315-789-6575/fax: 315-237-6415

Glen Cove

Judges
Joseph D McCann
Richard J McCord

Civil & Criminal Courts
13 Glen St, Glen Cove, NY 11542
Chief Clerk:
Stacey Gallo.....................516-403-2441/fax: 516-676-1570

Glens Falls

Judges
Gary C Hobbs
Nikki J Moreschi

Civil & Criminal Courts
City Hall, 42 Ridge St, 3rd Fl, Glens Falls, NY 12801
Chief Clerk:
Lisa Ghenoiu.....................518-798-4714/fax: 518-453-8623

Gloversville

Judges
Traci Di Mezza
Cory Dalmata

Civil & Criminal Courts
City Hall, 3 Frontage Rd, Gloversville, NY 12078
Chief Clerk:
Rebecca Rose...................518-773-4527/fax: 518-773-4599

Hornell

Judges
Joseph E Damrath
David E Coddington

Civil & Criminal Courts
PO Box 627, 82 Main St, Hornell, NY 14843
e-mail: hornellcity@nycourts.gov
Chief Clerk:
Love Griffin....................607-590-3314/fax: 607-590-3316

Hudson

Judges
John Connor, Jr.
Mark Portin

City Court
429 Warren St, Hudson, NY 12534
Chief Clerk:
Jamie Empire....................518-267-3082/fax: 212-457-2682
e-mail: hudsoncitycourt@nycourts.gov

Ithaca

Judges
Scott A. Miller
Richard M Wallace

Civil & Criminal Courts
118 E Clinton St, Ithaca, NY 14850
e-mail: ithacacitycourt@nycourts.gov
Chief Clerk:
Ronna J Collins..................607-216-6660/fax: 607-240-5821

Jamestown

Judges
John L LaMancuso
Frederick A Larson

Civil & Criminal Courts
Municipal Bldg, 200 E 3rd St, Jamestown, NY 14701
Chief Clerk:
Lisa Meacham....................716-483-7561/fax: 716-483-7519
e-mail: lmeacham@nycourts.gov

Johnstown

Judges
Michael C Viscosi
Brett A Preston

Civil & Criminal Courts
City Hall, 33-41 E Main St, Ste 105, Johnstown, NY 12095
Chief Clerk:
Stephen Russo...................518-762-0007/fax: 578-453-8651

Kingston

Judges
Lawrence E Ball
Philip W. Kirschner

City Court
Kingston City Court, 1 Garraghan Dr, Kingston, NY 12401
Chief Clerk:
Nicole Murphy...................845-481-9350/fax: 845-483-8113
e-mail: kingstoncitycourt@nycourts.gov

Lackawanna

Judges
(Chief):
Frederic J Marrano
Norman LeBlanc Jr (Associate)

Civil & Criminal Courts..................fax: 716-845-7599
City Hall, 714 Ridge Rd, Lackawanna, NY 14218
716-845-7220 Fax: 716-845-7599
Chief Clerk:
Vacant.............................716-845-7220

Little Falls

Judges
Joy Malone
Mark Rose

Civil & Criminal Courts
City Hall, 659 E Main St, Little Falls, NY 13365
Chief Clerk:
Patrice M Gleim.................315-619-3408/fax: 315-266-4711

Lockport

Judges
William J Watson
Thomas M DiMillo

Civil & Criminal Courts
1 Locks Plz, Lockport, NY 14094
716-280-6205
Chief Clerk:
Colleen Wagner...................716-280-6207/fax: 716-439-6684
e-mail: cjwagner@nycourts.gov

Offices and agencies generally appear in alphabetical order, except when specific order is requested by listee.

Long Beach

Judges
Frank Dikranis
Corey E Klein

Civil & Criminal Courts
1 W Chester St, Long Beach, NY 11561
516-442-8544
Chief Clerk:
Robert Davis 516-442-8555/fax: 516-889-3511

Mechanicville

Judges
John H Ciulla Jr
Joseph W Sheehan

Civil & Criminal Courts
City Hall, 36 N Main St, Mechanicville, NY 12118
Chief Clerk:
Francine Baker 518-453-5959/fax: 518-453-8678

Middletown

Judges
Steven Brockett
Robert Moson

Civil & Criminal Courts
2 James St, Middletown, NY 10940
Chief Clerk:
Linda Padden. 845-476-3630/fax: 845-343-5737

Mount Vernon

Judges
William Edwards
Adrian N Armstrong
Adam Seiden
Nichelle A Johnson

Civil & Criminal Courts
2 Roosevelt Square N, 2nd Floor, Mount Vernon, NY 10550
Chief Clerk:
Lawrence Darden 914-831-6440/fax: 914-824-5511

New Rochelle

Judges
Susan I Kettner
Anthony A. Carbone

Civil & Criminal Courts
475 North Ave, New Rochelle, NY 10801
Chief Clerk:
James Generoso. 914-358-8000/fax: 914-654-0344

Newburgh

Judges
Peter M Kulkin
Paul D Trachte
E. Loren Williams

Civil & Criminal Courts
300 Broadway, Newburgh, NY 12550
Chief Clerk:
Jasmin Reyes-Finch 845-483-8100/fax: 845-565-0230

Niagara Falls

Judges
Danielle Restaino
Robert Merino
Mark A Violante (Chief)
Diane Vitello

Civil & Criminal Courts . . . . fax: 716-278-9809
1925 Main Street, Niagara Falls, NY 14305
716-371-4100 Fax: 716-278-9809
Chief Clerk:
Maureen Hourihan 716-371-4110/fax: 716-278-9869
e-mail: mhourina@nycourts.gov

North Tonawanda

Judges
Shawn P Nickerson
William R Lewis

Civil & Criminal Courts
City Hall, 216 Payne Ave, North Tonawanda, NY 14120
Chief Clerk:
Jennifer Steele. 716-845-7240/fax: 716-743-1754
e-mail: jasteele@nycourts.gov

Norwich

Judges
James G. Cushman
James Downey

Civil & Criminal Courts
1 Court Plz, Norwich, NY 13815
Chief Clerk:
Irene Williams. 607-334-1224/fax: 646-963-6432

Ogdensburg

Judges
Gary R Alford
William Small

Civil & Criminal Courts
330 Ford St, Ogdensburg, NY 13669
Chief Clerk:
Lisa Marie Meyer 315-393-3941/fax: 315-393-6839

Olean

Judges
William J Gabler
Daniel R Palumbo

Civil & Criminal Courts
101 E State St, PO Box 631, Olean, NY 14760
Acting Chief Clerk:
Verna Dry 716-376-5620/fax: 716-376-5623
e-mail: vdry@nycourts.gov

Oneida

Judges
Anthony P Eppolito
Michael J Misiaszek

Civil & Criminal Courts
Municipal Bldg, 108 Main St, Oneida, NY 13421
e-mail: oneidacitycourt@courts.state.ny.us
Chief Clerk:
Lynne Mondrick 315-266-4740/fax: 646-963-6435

Oneonta

Judges
Lucy P Bernier
Richard W. McVinney

Civil & Criminal Courts
Public Safety Bldg, 81 Main St, Oneonta, NY 13820
Chief Clerk:
Catherine J Tisenchek 607-432-4480/fax: 646-963-6433

Oswego

Judges
James M Metcalf
David J Roman

Offices and agencies generally appear in alphabetical order, except when specific order is requested by listee.

Civil & Criminal Courts
Conway Municipal Ctr, 20 W Oneida St, Oswego, NY 13126
e-mail: osw_city_ct@courts.state.ny.us
Chief Clerk:
Cassie Kinney 315-343-0415/fax: 315-266-4752

Peekskill

Judges
Thomas R Langan
Reginald Johnson

Civil & Criminal Courts
2 Nelson Ave, Peekskill, NY 10566
Chief Clerk:
Concetta (Tina) Cardinale. 914-831-6480/fax: 914-736-1889

Plattsburgh

Judges
John F. Niles
Mark J Rogers

Civil & Criminal Courts
24 US Oval, Plattsburgh, NY 12903
Chief Clerk:
Kimberly Crow. 518-536-3870

Port Jervis

Judges
James M Hendry III
Matthew D. Witherow

Civil & Criminal Courts
20 Hammond St, Port Jervis, NY 12771
Chief Clerk:
Catherine Quinn 845-476-3700/fax: 845-476-3691

Poughkeepsie

Judges
Frank M. Mora
Thomas J O'Neill

Civil & Criminal Courts
62 Civic Ctr Plaza, Poughkeepsie, NY 12601
Chief Clerk:
Jean Jicha 845-483-8200/fax: 845-483-8127

Rensselaer

Judges
Kathleen L Robichaud
Carmelo Laquidara

Civil & Criminal Courts
City Hall, 62 Washington Street, Rensselaer, NY 12144
e-mail: rensselaercitycourt@nycourts.gov
Chief Clerk:
Barbara Agans. 518-453-4680/fax: 518-453-8996

Rochester

Judges
Melchor E Castro
Maija C Dixon
Jack Elliott
Stephen T Miller
Caroline Morrison
Charles F Crimi Jr
Leticia D Astacio
Teresa D Johnson
Thomas R Morse
Ellen Yacknin

Civil Court . . . . fax: 585-371-3427
99 Exchange Boulevard, 6 Hall of Justice, Rochester, NY 14614
585-371-3412 Fax: 585-371-3427
Chief Clerk:
Eugene Crimi 585-428-3527

Criminal Court . . . . fax: 585-371-3430
123 Public Safety Bldg, Rochester, NY 14614
585-371-3413 Fax: 585-371-3430
Chief Clerk:
Eugene Crimi 585-371-3413

Rome

Judges
John C Gannon
Gregory J. Amoroso

Civil & Criminal Courts
100 W Court St, Rome, NY 13440
Chief Clerk:
Matthew Brown. 315-266-4700/fax: 315-266-4705

Rye

Judges
Joseph L. Latwin
Robert S. Cypher

Civil & Criminal Courts
21 McCullough Pl, Rye, NY 10580
Chief Clerk:
Antoinette Cipriano. 914-831-6400/fax: 914-831-6546

Salamanca

Judges
William J Gabler
Alan L Spears

Civil & Criminal Courts
225 Wildwood Ave, Salamanca, NY 14779
Chief Clerk:
Stella Johnston 716-945-4153/fax: 716-945-2362
e-mail: ssjohnst@courts.state.ny.us

Saratoga Springs

Judges
James E Doern
Jeffrey D. Wait

Civil & Criminal Courts
City Hall, 474 Broadway, Ste 3, Saratoga Springs, NY 12866
Chief Clerk:
Casey Scatena 518-451-8780/fax: 518-453-8686

Schenectady

Judges
Mark W. Blanchfield
Mark J Caruso
Guido A Loyola
Robert W Hoffman

Civil Court
City Hall, 105 Jay St, Schenectady, NY 12305
Chief Clerk:
Robin Farmer 518-453-6989/fax: 518-285-8984

Criminal Court
531 Liberty St, Schenectady, NY 12305
Chief Clerk:
Robin Farmer 518-453-6989/fax: 518-453-8983

Sherrill

Judges
James W Betro

Civil & Criminal Courts
373 Sherrill Rd, Sherrill, NY 13461
Chief Clerk:
Carol A Shea 315-266-4411/fax: 315-266-4344

Syracuse

Judges
Vanessa E Bogan
Stephen J Dougherty
Theodore H. Limpert
Kate Rosenthal
Karen M Uplinger
James H Cecile
Rory A. McMahon
Mary Anne Doherty
Ross P Andrews

Civil & Criminal Courts
505 S State St, Syracuse, NY 13202
Chief Clerk:
Lucia Sander .315-671-2700/fax: 315-671-2741

Tonawanda

Judges
Chief:
Mark Saltarelli
Dean Lilac

Civil & Criminal Courts . . . . .fax: 716-845-7590
200 Niagara St, Tonawanda, NY 14150
716-845-2160 Fax: 716-845-7590
Chief Clerk:
Mary Strobel. 716-845-2164
e-mail: mstrobel@nycourts.gov

Troy

Judges
Christopher T Maier
Matthew J Turner
Jill Kehn

Civil & Criminal Court
51 State St, 2nd & 3rd Floors, Troy, NY 12180
Chief Clerk:
Karen DeBenedetto. 518-453-5900/fax: 518-274-2816
e-mail: troycitycourt@nycourts.gov

Utica

Judges
F Christopher Giruzzi
Gerald J Popeo
Ralph J Eannace

Civil & Criminal Courts
411 Oriskany St W, Utica, NY 13502
315-266-4600
Chief Clerk:
Steven R Pecheone 315-266-4606/fax: 315-792-8038

Watertown

Judges
Catherine J. Palermo
Eugene R Renzi

Civil & Criminal Courts
Municipal Bldg, 245 Washington St, Watertown, NY 13601
Chief Clerk:
Benjamin Cobb 315-785-7785/fax: 315-266-4783

Watervliet

Judges
Thomas Lamb
Susan B Reinfurt

Civil & Criminal Courts
2 - 15th St, Watervliet, NY 12189
Chief Clerk:
Robin Robillard. 518-453-5550/fax: 518-453-8995
e-mail: watervlietcitycourt@nycourts.gov

White Plains

Judges
JoAnn Friia
Barbara A Leak
Brian Hansbury
Eric P Press

Civil & Criminal Courts
77 S Lexington Ave, White Plains, NY 10601
Chief Clerk:
Eileen Byrne 914-824-5675/fax: 914-824-5858

Yonkers

Judges
Thomas Quinones
Arthur J Doran, III
Evan Inlaw
Thomas R Daly
Edward J. Gaffney
Michael A Martinelli

Civil & Criminal Courts
100 S Broadway, Yonkers, NY 10701
Chief Clerk:
Marisa Garcia 914-831-6450/fax: 914-377-6395

Offices and agencies generally appear in alphabetical order, except when specific order is requested by listee.

Section 2:
POLICY AREAS

AGRICULTURE

NEW YORK STATE

GOVERNOR'S OFFICE

Governor's Office
Executive Chamber
State Capitol
Albany, NY 12224
518-474-8390 Fax: 518-474-1513
Web site: www.ny.gov

Governor:
Andrew M Cuomo 518-474-8390
Secretary to the Governor:
William Mulrow 518-474-4246
Counsel to the Governor:
Alphonso David 518-474-8343
Chief of Staff:
Melissa DeRosa . . . . 518-474-8418 or 212-681-4640
Director, Communications:
James Allen. . . . . 518-474-8418 or 212-681-4640
Deputy Secretary, Food & Agriculture:
Patrick Hooker 518-486-3960
Chairman of Energy & Finance for New York:
Richard Kauffman. 518-681-4580

EXECUTIVE DEPARTMENTS AND RELATED AGENCIES

Agriculture & Markets Department
10B Airline Dr
Albany, NY 12235
518-457-3880 or 800-554-4501 Fax: 518-457-3087
e-mail: info@agriculture.ny.gov
Web site: www.agriculture.ny.gov

Commissioner:
Richard Ball 518-457-8876
First Deputy Commissioner:
Jen McCormick. 518-457-2771
e-mail: jen.mccormick@agriculture.ny.gov
Deputy Commissioner, Administration:
Phil Giltner 518-457-2771
e-mail: phil.giltner@agriculture.ny.gov
Deputy Commissioner:
Maria Knirk. 518-485-7728
e-mail: maria.knirk@agriculture.ny.gov
Deputy Commissioner:
Jackie Moody-Czub 518-485-7728
e-mail: jackie.moody-czub@agriculture.ny.gov
Director, Internal Audit:
Joe Morrissey 518-457-2771
e-mail: joe.morrissey@agriculture.ny.gov
Director, Internal Audit:
Joe Morrissey 518-485-2771
e-mail: joe.morrissey@agriculture.ny.gov
Agency Emergency Management Coordinator:
Kelly Nilsson 518-457-2771
e-mail: kelly.nilsson@agriculture.ny.gov
Director, Intergovernmental Affairs:
Geoff Palmer. 518-457-2771
e-mail: geoff.palmer@agriculture.ny.gov
Special Assistant:
Frank Rooney 518-485-7728
e-mail: frank.rooney@agriculture.ny.gov
Public Information Officer:
Jola Szubielski. 518-485-7728/fax: 518-457-3087
e-mail: jola.szubielski@agriculture.ny.gov

Agricultural Development Division
Director, Agricultural Development:
Kevin King 518-457-7076/fax: 518-457-2716
e-mail: kevin.king@agriculture.ny.gov
Access To Healthy Foods:
Jonathan Thomson 518-485-8902
e-mail: jonathan.thomson@agriculture.ny.gov
Marketing & Promotion:
Sue Santamarina 518-457-7229
e-mail: sue.santamarina@agriculture.ny.gov
Business Development:
Steve McGrattan 518-457-7836
e-mail: steve.mcgrattan@agriculture.ny.gov
Special Projects:
Tim Pezzolesi 518-457-8883
e-mail: tim.pezzolesi@agriculture.ny.gov

Agricultural Districts
Manager:
Bob Somers. 518-457-3738
e-mail: bob.somers@agriculture.ny.gov

Animal Industry . . . . fax: 518-485-7773
Director:
Dr. David Smith 518-457-3502
e-mail: david.smith@agriculture.ny.gov

Counsel's Office . . . . fax: 518-457-8842
Counsel:
Scott Wyner 518-457-1059
e-mail: scott.wyner@agriculture.ny.gov

Fiscal Management . . . . fax: 518-485-7750
Director:
Lucy Roberson 518-457-2080
e-mail: lucy.roberson@agriculture.ny.gov

Food Laboratory . . . . fax: 518-485-8097
Director:
Dr. Maria Ishida 518-457-4477
e-mail: maria.ishida@agriculture.ny.gov
Assistant Director:
Debra Oglesby 518-485-5012
Associate Food Chemist:
Robert Sheridan 518-457-8885
e-mail: robert.sheridan@agriculture.ny.gov
Associate Food Chemist:
Virginia Greene. 518-485-8098

Food Safety & Inspection . . . . fax: 518 485-8986
Director:
Stephen Stich 518-457-4492
e-mail: stephen.stich@agriculture.ny.gov
Assistant Director:
John Luker 518-457-5382
e-mail: john.luker@agriculture.ny.gov
Director, Field Operations:
Erin Sawyer. 518-457-5380
e-mail: erin.sawyer@agriculture.ny.gov

Field Operations
Brooklyn . . . . fax: 718-722-2510
55 Hanson Place, Rm 378, Brooklyn, NY 11217-1583
Chief Inspector:
Richard Olson 718-722-2876
Buffalo . . . . fax: 716-847-3155
535 Washington Ave, Ste 203, Buffalo, NY 14203
Supervising Inspector:
Dan Gump 716-847-3185

Offices and agencies generally appear in alphabetical order, except when specific order is requested by listee.

Hauppauge
Suffolk State Ofc Bldg, Veterans' Memorial Hwy, Happauge, NY 11787
631-952-3079
Vacant

Rochester . . . . fax: 716-424-1248
1530 Jefferson Rd, Rochester, NY 14623
585-427-2273 Fax: 716-424-1248
Supervising Food Inspector:
Evelyn Miles 585-427-0200

Syracuse . . . . fax: 315-487-1064
Art & Home Center, New York State Fairgrounds, Syracuse, NY 13209
Supervising Food Regional Supervisor:
Vacant 315-487-0852

Human Resources . . . . fax: 518-457-8852
Director:
Mark Vanderpoel 518-457-3216
e-mail: mark.vanderpoel@agriculture.ny.gov

Information Systems . . . . fax: 518-457-7815
Director:
Carm Turpin 518-457-7368

Kosher Law Enforcement
Director:
Rabbi Aaron Metzger 718-722-2852
e-mail: kosher@agriculture.ny.gov

Milk Control & Dairy Services . . . . fax: 518-485-8730
Director, Milk Control:
Casey McCue 518-457-1772
e-mail: casey.mccue@agriculture.ny.gov
Director, Dairy Services:
Dan McCarthy 518-457-1772
e-mail: dan.mccarthy@agriculture.ny.gov
Director, Dairy Services:
Dan McCarthy 518-457-1772
Market Research Information & Reporting:
David Del Cogliano 518-457-1772
e-mail: david.delcogliano@agriculture.ny.gov

New York City Office . . . . fax: 718-722-2510
55 Hanson Place, Brooklyn, NY 11217-1583
Chief, Food Safety & Inspection:
Richard Olson 718-722-2876

Plant Industry . . . . fax: 518-457-1204
Director:
Christopher Logue 518-457-2087
e-mail: christopher.logue@agriculture.ny.gov

Soil & Water Conservation Committee . . . . fax: 518-457-3412
10B Airline Drive, Albany, NY 12235
518-457-3738 Fax: 518-457-3412
Web site: www.nys-soilandwater.org
Chair:
Dale Stein 518-457-3738
Executive Director:
Michael Latham 518-457-3738
e-mail: michael.latham@agriculture.ny.gov
Coordinator, Agricultural Environmental Management Program:
Greg Albrecht 607-330-1242
e-mail: greg.albrecht@agriculture.ny.gov

State Fair . . . . fax: 315-487-9260
581 State Fair Blvd, Syracuse, NY 13209
315-487-7711 Fax: 315-487-9260
Web site: www.nysfair.org
Acting Director:
Troy Waffner 315-487-7711 x1200

Statistics . . . . fax: 518-453-6564
Fax: 518-453-6564
Web site: www.nass.usda.gov
State Statistician:
Blair Smith 518-487-5570
e-mail: blair.smith@nass.usda.gov

Weights & Measures . . . . fax: 518-457-5693
4 Burnett Blvd, Rm 216, Poughkeepsie, NY 12603
Director:
Michael Sikula 518-457-3146
e-mail: mike.sikula@agriculture.ny.gov

NEW YORK STATE LEGISLATURE

See Legislative Branch in Section 1 for additional Standing Committee and Subcommittee information.

Assembly Standing Committees

Agriculture
Chair:
William Magee (D) 518-455-4807
Ranking Minority Member:
Kenneth Blankenbush (R) 518-455-5797

Assembly Task Force

Food, Farm & Nutrition, Task Force on
Chair:
Addie Russell (D) 518-455-5545
Ranking Minority Member:
Peter Lopez 518-455-5363

Senate Standing Committees

Agriculture
Chair:
Patricia Ritchie (R) 518-455-3438
Ranking Minority Member:
Marc Panepinto (D) 518-455-2350

Senate/Assembly Legislative Commissions

Rural Resources, Legislative Commission on
Senate Chair:
Patricia Ritche (R) 518-455-3438
Assembly Chair:
Frank Skartados (D) 518-455-5762
Member:
Barbara Lifton 518-455-5444

U.S. GOVERNMENT

EXECUTIVE DEPARTMENTS AND RELATED AGENCIES

Commodity Futures Trading Commission
Three Lafayette Centre
1155 21st Street Northwest
Washington, DC 20581
202-418-5000 Fax: 202-418-5521
e-mail: questions@cftc.gov
Web site: www.cftc.gov

Eastern Region
140 Broadway, New York, NY 10005
646-746-9700

Regional Counsel:
Lenel Hickson Jr.

US Commerce Department

1401 Constitution Avenue NW
Washington, DC 20230
202-482-2000
Web site: www.commerce.gov

National Oceanic & Atmospheric Administration

1401 Constitution Avenue NW, Room 5128, Washington, DC 20230

National Weather Service, Eastern Region
630 Johnson Avenue, Suite 202, Bohemia, NY 11716
631-244-0100
e-mail: erhwebmaster@noaa.gov
Web site: www.weather.gov/erh/
Director, Eastern Region:
Jason Tuell, Ph.D. 631-244-0101
e-mail: jason.tuell@noaa.gov
Regional Program Manager:
John Koch. 631-244-0104
e-mail: john.koch@noaa.gov
Regional Program Manager:
Jeff Waldstreicher. 631-244-0131
e-mail: jeff.waldstreicher@noaa.gov
Chief, Meteorological Services Division:
John Guiney 631-244-0121
e-mail: john.guiney@noaa.gov
Chief, Hydrologic Services Division:
Vacant. 631-244-0111
Chief, Scientific Services Division:
Kenneth Johnson 631-244-0136
e-mail: kenneth.johnson@noaa.gov

US Department of Agriculture

1400 Independence Avenue SW
Washington, DC 20250
202-720-2791
Web site: www.usda.gov

Agricultural Marketing Service

1445 Federal Drive, Montgomery, AL 36107
334-223-7488
e-mail: amsadministratoroffice@ams.usda.gov

Dairy Programs
Web site: www.ams.usda.gov/about-ams/programs-offices/dairy-program
Northeast Marketing Area
302A Washington Avenue Extension, Albany, NY 12203-7303
e-mail: maalbany@fedmilk1.com
Web site: www.fmmone.com
Market Administrator:
Erik F Rasmussen 518-452-4410

Specialty Crops Program
SC Inspection Division—Jamaica Office . . . . fax: 718-558-8628
158-15 Liberty Avenue, Room 4022, Jamaica, NY 11433
718-558-8632 Fax: 718-558-8628
Officer-in-Charge:
Jagarnauth Persaud 718-558-8632
SC Inspection Division—Bronx Office . . . . fax: 718-589-5108
275B New York City Terminal Market, Bronx, NY 10474-7351
718-991-7665 Fax: 718-589-5108
Officer-in-Charge:
Anthony Georgiana 718-991-7665

USDA-AMS Poultry Grading Branch
Gastonia Region—New York Office . . . . fax: 518-459-5163
21 Aviation Road, Albany, NY 12205
Coordinator:
James Wagoner 518-457-2090

Agricultural Research Service

Northeast Area
Ithaca NY Research Units
Robert W Holley Center for Agriculture & Health
583 Tower Road, Ithaca, NY 14853
607-255-5480
Center Director & Research Leader:
Leon V. Kochian 607-255-5480
e-mail: leon.kochian@ars.usda.gov
Geneva NY Research Units
Plant Genetic Resources & Grape Genetic Research Units . . . . fax: 315-787-2483
Grape Genetics Research Unit, USDA, ARS, 630 West North Street, Geneva, NY 14456
315-787-2340 Fax: 315-787-2483
Research Leader:
Gan-Yuan Zhong 315-787-2482/fax: 315-787-2483
e-mail: ganyuan.zhong@ars.usda.gov

Animal & Plant Health Inspection Service

Web site: www.aphis.usda.gov

Plant Protection Quarantine (PPQ) Programs-Eastern Region. . . . fax: 919-855-7611
920 Main Campus Drive, Suite 150, Raleigh, NC 27606-5202
919-855-7600 Fax: 919-855-7611
Plant Health Director:
Deb Stewart
Avoca Work Unit
8237 Kanona Road, Avoca, NY 14809-9729
607-566-2212
Director:
Daniel J Kepich 607-566-2212
e-mail: daniel.j.kepich@aphis.usda.gov
Buffalo Work Station
1 Peace Bridge Plaza, Suite 314, Buffalo, NY 14213
Identifier:
Stephen Young. 607-329-6351
e-mail: stephen.t.young@aphis.usda.gov
Canandaigua Work Station
3037 County Road 10, Canandaigua, NY 14424
Senior PPQ Officer:
Cynthia Estey 585-394-0525 x5
e-mail: cynthia.a.estey@aphis.usda.gov
Champlain Work Station . . . . fax: 585-394-8367
217 West Service Road, Champlain, NY 12919
PPQ Officer:
Thomas Colarusso 518-298-5529
e-mail: thomas.w.colarusso@aphis.usda.gov
Ellicottville Work Station
8 Martha Street, Ellicottville, NY 14731
PPQ Officer:
Jacqueline Klahn 716-699-8954
e-mail: jacquelineklahn@aphis.usda.gov
JFK International Airport Inspection Station
230-59 International Airport Center Blvd, Suite 100, Jamaica, NY 11413
718-553-3500
Supervisory PPQ Officer:
Joanne Alba-Foster 718-553-3503
New York State Office
500 New Karner Road, Suite 2, Albany, NY 12205-3857
State Plant Health Director:
Diana Hoffman 518-218-7510
e-mail: diana.l.hoffman@aphis.usda.gov
Oneida Work Station
248 Main Street, 1st Floor, Oneida, NY 13421

Policy Areas

Senior PPQ Officer:
Paul F Wrege 315-361-4281
e-mail: paul.f.wrege@usda.gov

Westhampton Beach Work Station .... fax: 631-288-6021
4 Stewart Avenue, Westhampton Beach, NY 11978-1103
PPQ Officer:
William Hsiang 631-288-4191
e-mail: william.w.hsiang@aphis.usda.gov

Veterinary Services

NY Animal Import Center .... fax: 718-553-3572
200 Drury Lane, Rock Tavern, NY 12575
718-553-3570 Fax: 718-553-3572
Web site: www.aphis.usda.gov/animal-health/
Director:
Renee Oleck 845-838-5500
e-mail: vspsnic@aphis.usda.gov

New York Area Office
500 New Karner Road, 2nd Floor, Albany, NY 12205
Center Director, Veterinary Services:
Dr Roxanne C Mullaney 518-218-7540/fax: 518-218-7545
e-mail: vspsny@aphis.usda.gov

Cornell Cooperative Extension Service
Cornell University, Roberts Hall, Room 365, Ithaca, NY 14853

Farm Service Agency, New York State Office ... fax: 315-477-6323
441 South Salina Street, Suite 536, Syracuse, NY 13202
State Executive Director:
James Barber............................... 315-477-6300
e-mail: james.barber@ny.usda.gov

Food & Nutrition Service
Web site: www.fns.usda.gov

Northeast Regional Office
10 Causeway Street, Room 501, Boston, MA 02222-1069
617-565-6370
Acting Regional Administrator:
Kurt Messner 617-565-6370

New York City Field Office
201 Varick Street, Room 609, New York, NY 10014
212-620-6307
Section Chief:
Denise Thomas............................... 212-620-6338

Food Safety & Inspection Service
Web site: www.fsis.usda.gov

National Agricultural Statistics Service-NY Field Office ..... fax: 800-591-3834
10B Airline Drive, Albany, NY 12235
800-821-1276 or 518-457-5570 Fax: 800-591-3834
Web site: www.nass.usda.gov
State Statistician:
Blair Smith 518-457-5570
e-mail: blair.smith@nass.usda.gov

Office of the Inspector General, Northeast Region .... fax: 212-264-8416
26 Federal Plaza, Room 1409, New York, NY 10278-0004
Special Agent-in-Charge:
William Squires 212-264-8400

Rural Development
Web site: www.rd.usda.gov/ny

New York State Regional Office .... fax: 315-477-6438
441 South Salina Street, Suite 357, Syracuse, NY 13202-2541
315-477-6400 or TTY:315-477-6447 Fax: 315-477-6438
Acting State Director:
Scott Collins 315-477-6437/fax: 855-477-8540

Eastern Region Area Director:
Ronda Falkena............................... 845-343-1872 x4
Northern Region Area Director:
Brian Murray............................... 315-386-2401 x4
Western Region Area Director:
Jim Walfrand............................... 585-343-9167 x4

USDA/GIPSA, Packers & Stockyards Programs Eastern Regional Office .... fax: 404-562-5848
75 Ted Turner Drive SW, Suite 230, Atlanta, GA 30303
404-562-5840 Fax: 404-562-5848
Regional Director:
Elkin Parker 404-562-5840
e-mail: elkin.w.parker@usda.gov

US Department of Homeland Security (DHS)
Web site: www.dhs.gov

Customs & Border Protection (CBP)
877-227-5511
Web site: www.cbp.gov

Agricultural Inspections (AI)

Albany, Port of .... fax: 518-431-0203
445 Broadway, Room 216, Albany, NY 12207
518-431-0200 Fax: 518-431-0203
Port Director:
Andrew Wescott............ 518-431-0200/fax: 518-431-0203

Alexandria Bay .... fax: 315-482-5304
46735 Interstate Route 81, Alexandria Bay, NY 13607
315-482-2065 Fax: 315-482-5304
Supervisory CBP Officer:
Darren Erwin 315-482-2681
e-mail: darren.r.erwin@cbp.dhs.gov

Binghamton Airport .... fax: 607-763-4292
2534 Airport Road, Box 4, Johnson City, NY 13790
607-763-4294 Fax: 607-763-4292
Port Director:
Vacant

Buffalo, Port of
726 Exchange Street, Suite 400, Buffalo, NY 14210
Supervisory CBP Officer:
Gary Friedman

Champlain, Port of .... fax: 518-298-8395
237 West Service Road, Champlain, NY 12919
518-298-8311 Fax: 518-298-8395
Port Director:
Paul Mongillo 518-298-8311

JFK International Airport Area Office .... fax: 718-487-5191
John F. Kennedy International Airport, Building #77, Jamaica, NY 11430
718-487-5164 Fax: 718-487-5191
Public Affairs Officer:
Anthony Bucci............................... 646-733-3275
e-mail: anthony.bucci@cbp.dhs.gov

Massena, Port of
30M Seaway International Bridge, PO Box 207, Rooseveltown, NY 13683
315-769-3091
Tribal Liaison Officer:
Tracey S. Casey............................... 315-769-3091

Ogdensburg, Port of
Ogdensburg Bridge Plaza, 104 Bridge Approach Road, Ogdensburg, NY 13669
315-393-1390
Port Director:
Wade Davis 313-393-1390

Rochester, Port of .... fax: 585-263-5828
1200 Brooks Avenue, Rochester, NY 14624
585-263-6293 Fax: 585-263-5828

Offices and agencies generally appear in alphabetical order, except when specific order is requested by listee.

Port Director:
Ronald Menz 585-263-6293

Syracuse, Port of
152 Air Cargo Road, Suite 201, North Syracuse, NY 13212
315-455-8446
Port Director:
David Harris. 315-455-8446

Trout River, Port of . . . . fax: 518-483-3717
17013 State Route 30, Constable, NY 12926
518-483-0821 Fax: 518-483-3717
Public Affairs Liaison:
Richard Misztal 716-626-0400

U.S. CONGRESS

See U.S. Congress Chapter for additional Standing Committee and Subcommittee information.

House of Representatives Standing Committees

Agriculture
Committee Chair:
K. Michael Conaway (R-TX-11)
Ranking Member:
Collin C. Peterson (D-MN-07)

Appropriations
Chair:
Harold Rogers (R-KY)
Ranking Minority Member:
Nita Lowey (D-NY)
New York Delegate:
Steve Israel (D)
New York Delegate:
Jose E Serrano (D)

Subcommittee
Agriculture, Rural Development, FDA & Related Agencies
Chair:
Robert Aderholt (R-AL) 202-225-2638
Ranking Member:
Sam Farr (D-CA)

Senate Standing Committees

Agriculture, Nutrition & Forestry
Chair:
Pat Roberts (R-KS)
Ranking Member:
Debbie Stabenow (D-MI)

Appropriations
Chair:
Thad Cochran (R-MS) 202-224-5054
Vice Chair:
Barbara A. Mikulski (D-MD)

Subcommittee
Agriculture, Rural Development, FDA & Related Agencies
Chair:
Jerry Moran (R-KS). 202-224-6521
Ranking Member:
Jeff Merkley (D-OR)

PRIVATE SECTOR

Agricultural Affiliates
3568 Snders Settlement Road, Sanborn, NY 14132
562-522-1736
Advise & inform agriculture industry on labor issues & related public policy
Paul Baker, Executive Director

American Farmland Trust, New York Office
112 Spring Street, Suite 207, Saratoga Springs, NY 12866
518-581-0078 Fax: 518-581-0079
Web site: www.farmland.org/newyork
Advocacy & education to protect farmland & promote environmentally sound farming practices
David Haight, New York State Director
Tammey Holtby, Operations Coordinator

American Society for the Prevention of Cruelty to Animals (ASPCA)
424 East 92nd Street, New York, NY 10128-6804
212-876-7700 or 888-666-2279
e-mail: publicinformation@aspca.org
Web site: www.aspca.org
Promoting humane treatment of animals, education & advocacy programs & conducting statewide anti-cruelty investigation & enforcement
Matthew Bershadker, President & Chief Executive Officer

Associated New York State State Food Processors Inc
150 State Street, Rochester, NY 14614
585-256-4614
Web site: www.nyfoodprocessors.org
Jeffrey Hartline, President

Birds Eye Foods Inc
399 Jefferson Road, Parsippany, NJ 07054
800-432-3102
Web site: www.birdseye.com
Produces & markets processed food products
Mike Barkley, Executive Vice President

Christmas Tree Farmers Association of New York Inc
PO Box 705, Salem, NY 12865
518-854-7386 Fax: 518-854-7387
e-mail: info@ctfany.org
Web site: www.christmastreesny.org
Producer of fresh Christmas trees & evergreen wreaths
Mary Jeanne Packer, Executive Director

Consumers Union
101 Truman Avenue, Yonkers, NY 10703-1057
914-378-2000 Fax: 914-378-2900
Web site: www.consumerreports.org; www.consumersunion.org
Advocacy and policy to improve consumer products and address food safety issues, including genetically engineered food, microbial safety of food, toxic chemical issues, pesticides, integrated pest management, sustainable agriculture
Jean Halloran, Director, Food Policy Initiatives

Community & Regional Development Institute (CaRDI)
275 Warren Hall, Cornell University, Ithaca, NY 14853
607-255-9510 Fax: 607-255-2231
e-mail: cardi@cornell.edu
Web site: www.cardi.cals.cornell.edu
Provides research, training, education & policy analysis on community & regional development issues
Jennifer Jensen, Communications & Outreach Coordinator

Cornell Cooperative Extension, Pesticide Management Education Program
5142 Comstock Hall, Cornell University, Ithaca, NY 14853-0901
607-255-1866 Fax: 607-255-3075
e-mail: rdg5@cornell.edu
Web site: pmep.cce.cornell.edu
Provides training materials, outreach & information on pesticides and pests
Ronald D Gardner, Program Coordinator

Policy Areas

Cornell Cooperative Extension, Agriculture & Food Systems Program
272 Morrison, Cornell University, New York, NY 14853
607-255-2878
e-mail: tro2@cornell.edu
Web site: www.cce.cornell.edu
Research to enhance the food systems and agricultural resources of New York
Tom Overton, Associate Director, Agriculture & Life Sciences

Cornell University, Department of Applied Economics & Management
Warren Hall, Ithaca, NY 14853
607-255-4576
Web site: www.dyson.cornell.edu
Agricultural economics
William Lesser, Interim Director
Andrew Novakovic, Associate Director for Engagement

Cornell University, FarmNet Program
Dept of Applied Economics & Management, 415 Warren Hall, Ithaca, NY 14853-7801
607-255-4121 or 800-547-3276 Fax: 607-254-7435
e-mail: nyfarmnet@cornell.edu
Web site: www.nyfarmnet.org
Farm family resource library; financial & family consultations; workshops for agricultural services professionals & farmers
Ed Staehr, Executive Director

Cornell University, PRO-DAIRY Program
College of Agriculture & Life Sciences, 272 Morrison Hall, Ithaca, NY 14853
607-255-2878 Fax: 607-255-1335
e-mail: tro2@cornell.edu
Web site: www.prodairy.cals.cornell.edu
Applied research and extension education program for dairy farmers in New York
Tom Overton, Program Director

Dairy Farmers of America Northeast
5001 Brittonfield Parkway, Syracuse, NY 13057
315-431-1352 or 816-801-6455
Web site: www.dfamilk.com
Markets, sells & processes milk and dairy products
Brad Keating, Senior Vice President & Chief Operating Officer

Empire State Honey Producers Association
437 Hurley Road, Brasher Falls, NY 13613
315-769-2566
Web site: www.eshpa.org
Association for beekeepers in New York State serving to protect & promote the honey bee and honey production
Mark Berninghausen, President

Empire State Potato Growers Inc
PO Box 566, Stanley, NY 14561-0566
585-526-5356 or 877-697-7837 Fax: 585-526-6576
e-mail: mwickham@hypotatoes.org
Web site: www.empirepotatogrowers.com
To foster the potato industry in NYS
Melanie Wickham, Executive Director

Farm Sanctuary
3100 Aikens Road, PO Box 150, Watkins Glen, NY 14891
607-583-2225 Fax: 607-583-2041
e-mail: info@farmsanctuary.org
Web site: www.farmsanctuary.org
Farm animal rescue & protection; public information programs & advocacy for the humane treatment of animals
Gene Baur, President

Farmedic Training Program
20 Church Street, PO Box 5670, Cortland, NY 13045
800-822-3747
e-mail: farmedic@mcneilandcompany.com
Web site: www.farmedic.com
Training programs for emergency providers & agricultural workers to reduce mortality, injury & property loss from agricultural emergencies
Dave Denniston, Executive Director

Farmers' Market Federation of NY
117 Highbridge Street, Fayetteville, NY 13066
315-400-1447 Fax: 844-300-6809
Web site: www.nyfarmersmarket.com
Education & services for New York farmers' market managers, farmers & sponsors.
Diane Eggert, Director

Food Industry Alliance of New York State Inc
130 Washington Avenue, Albany, NY 12210
518-434-1900 Fax: 518-434-9962
Web site: www.fiany.com
Association of retail grocery, cooperative, wholesale & supplier/manufacturer food companies
Michael Rosen, President & CEO

Fund for Animals (The)
200 West 57th Street, New York, NY 10019
212-757-3425 or 888-405-3863 Fax: 212-246-2633
e-mail: info@fundforanimals.org
Web site: www.fundforanimals.org
Animal protection through education, advocacy programs & hands-on veterinary care
Marian Probst, Chair

Garden Gate Greenhouse
11649 West Perrysburg Road, Perrysburg, NY 14129
716-532-6282
Greenhouse plant production
Gary Patterson, President

Global Gardens Program, New York Botanical Garden (The)
2900 Southern Blvd, Bronx, NY 10458-5126
718-817-8700 Fax: 718-220-6504
Web site: www.nybg.org
Promoting understanding of ethnic diversity & the interconnectedness of cultures through gardening
Gregory Long, Chief Executive Officer

GreenThumb
100 Gold Street, Suite 3100, New York, NY 10038
212-602-5300 Fax: 212-602-5334
e-mail: greenthumbinfo@parks.nyc.gov
Web site: www.greenthumbnyc.org
Development & preservation of community gardens; workshops addressing a variety of topics including gardening, farming & community organizing
Bill LoSasso, Director

Greenmarket/Council on the Environment of NYC
100 Gold Street, Suite 3300, New York, NY 10038
212-788-7900 Fax: 212-788-7913
Web site: www.grownyc.org
Promotes regional sustainable agriculture & improves access to locally grown agricultural products
Marcel Van Ooyen, Executive Director

Hill, Gosdeck & McGraw LLC
99 Washington Avenue, Suite 400, Albany, NY 12210
518-463-5449 Fax: 518-463-0947
e-mail: jeffhill@hgmlobby.com
Workers compensation, group self insurance and food industry regulation
Jeffrey L Hill, Partner

Humane Society of the United States, New York State
200 West 57th Street, Suite 705, New York, NY 10019
917-331-7187
Web site: www.humanesociety.org
Promotes humane treatment of animals; abuse & violence prevention; animal rescue & disaster preparedness
Brian Shapiro, State Director

Long Island Farm Bureau
104 Edwards Avenue, Suite 3, Calverton, NY 11933
631-727-3777 Fax: 631-727-3721
e-mail: askus@lifb.com
Web site: www.lifb.com
Seeks to provide protection for the agricultural industries in Long Island and New York State
Karen Rivara, President

Long Island Nursery & Landscape Association Inc
136 Everett Road, Albany, NY 12205
518-694-5540 or 516-249-0545 Fax: 518-427-9495
e-mail: info@linla.org
Web site: www.linla.org
Non-profit organization representing Long Island's horticulture industry
Carol Saporito, President

National Potato Board
McCormick Farms Inc
4189 Route 78, Bliss, NY 14024
585-322-7274 Fax: 585-322-7495
Crop farm
Jim McCormick, President & CEO

My-T Acres Inc
8127 Lewiston Road, Batavia, NY 14020
585-343-1026 Fax: 585-343-2051
Vegetable crops & grain
Peter Call, Co-Owner

NOFA-NY Certified Organic LLC
840 Upper Front Street, Binghamton, NY 13905-1542
607-724-9851 Fax: 607-724-9853
e-mail: certifiedorganic@nofany.org
Web site: www.nofany.org
Organic farming certification
Lori Kenyon, Certification Director

NY Farms!
125 Williams Road, Candor, NY 13743
607-659-3710 Fax: 607-659-3710
Web site: www.nyfarms.info
Aims to promote farming, protect farmland & improve food systems in New York State
Mary Jeanne Packer, Executive Director

NYS Agricultural Society
1818 Linwood Road, Linwood, NY 14486
315-727-5449
e-mail: ann@nysagsociety.org
Web site: www.nysagsociety.org
Provides education, leadership & recognition programs to develop, promote & enhance the agriculture industry of New York State
Ann Shephard, Executive Secretary

NYS Arborists
136 Everett Road, Albany, NY 12205
518-694-5507 Fax: 518-935-9436
e-mail: info@nysarborists.com
Web site: www.nysarborists.com
Association representing arborists & educators; promotes education & research about trees & conservation
Trevor Hall, President

NYS Association for Food Protection
Cornell University, Dept of Food Science, 116 Stocking Hall, Ithaca, NY 14853
607-255-2892 Fax: 607-255-7619
e-mail: jgg3@cornell.edu
Web site: www.nysafp.com
Association serving to enable exchange of information on food supply protection
Janene Lucia, Executive Secretary

NYS Association of Veterinary Technicians Inc
PO Box 760, Glenmont, NY 12077
518-779-0775
Web site: www.nysavt.org
Association supporting the veterinary technician profession
Donna Meier, President

NYS Berry Growers Association
3568 Saunders Settlement Road, Sanborn, NY 14132
716-807-6827
e-mail: nysbga@gmail.com
Web site: www.hort.cornell.edu
Provides education about berries & promotes the interests of berry growers
Paul Baker, Executive Secretary

NYS Cheese Manufacturers Association, Department of Food Science
Cornell University, 116 Stocking Hall, Ithaca, NY 14853
607-255-2892 Fax: 607-255-7619
e-mail: jgg3@cornell.edu
Web site: www.nyscheesemakers.com
Cheese manufacturing education & product promotion
Janene Lucia, Secretary

NYS Grange
100 Grange Place, Cortland, NY 13045
607-756-7553 Fax: 607-756-7757
e-mail: nysgrange@nysgrange.org
Web site: www.nysgrange.org
Advocacy, education & services for farm, rural & suburban families
Kathy E Miller, Director

NYS Horticultural Society
630 West North Street, Geneva, NY 14456
315-787-2404 Fax: 315-787-2216
e-mail: nyshs@hotmail.com
Web site: www.nyshs.org
Advocacy, education & member services for the New York State fruit industry
Paul Baker, Executive Director

NYS Nursery/Landscape Association
136 Everett Road, Albany, NY 12205
518-694-4430 Fax: 518-694-4431
e-mail: info@nysnla.com
Web site: www.nysnla.com
Trade association representing the nursery & landscape business professionals of New York State
Holly Cargill-Cramer, Executive Director

NYS Turfgrass Association
PO Box 612, Latham, NY 12110
518-783-1229 or 800-873-8873 Fax: 518-783-1258
e-mail: nysta@nysta.org
Web site: www.nysta.org
Provides education & research for individuals in the turfgrass & grounds industry
Elizabeth Seme, Executive Director

Offices and agencies generally appear in alphabetical order, except when specific order is requested by listee.

NYS Vegetable Growers Association Inc
8351 Lewiston Road, Batavia, NY 14020
585-993-0775
e-mail: nysvegetablegrowers@gmail.com
Web site: www.nysvga.org
Produce industry education & product promotion
Brian Reeves, President

NYS Weights & Measures Association
7660 State Street, Lowville, NY 13367
315-377-2069 Fax: 315-376-5874
e-mail: barbcooper@lewiscounty.ny.org
Web site: www.nyswma.com
Promote uniformity in measure accuracy, enforcement standards & legal requirements
Barbara J Cooper, Director

National Coffee Association
45 Broadway, Suite 1140, New York, NY 10006
212-766-4007 Fax: 212-766-5815
Web site: www.ncausa.org
Represents & supports the nation's coffee industry
William Murray, President & Chief Executive Officer

National Grape Cooperative-Welch Foods Inc
300 Baker Avenue, Suite 101, Concord, MA 01742
978-371-1000 or 800-340-6870 Fax: 978-371-3879
Web site: www.welchs.com
Manufacturer of juices, jams & jellies.
Bradley Irwin, President & Chief Executive Officer

New York Agriculture in the Classroom
Cornell University, Dept of Horticulture, 134 Plant Science Building, Ithaca, NY 14853
518-480-1978
e-mail: nyaitc@cornell.edu
Web site: www.agclassroom.org
Program serving to improve agricultural literacy by collaborating with community educators & farmers to raise awareness about agricultural production & food systems
Katie Bigness, Coordinator

New York Apple Association Inc
7645 Main Street, PO Box 350, Fishers, NY 14453-0350
585-924-2171 Fax: 585-924-1629
Web site: www.nyapplecountry.com
Promotes NYS apples & apple products
James Allen, President & CEO

New York Beef Industry Council Inc
PO Box 250, Westmoreland, NY 13490
315-339-6922 Fax: 315-339-6931
e-mail: cgillis@nybeef.org
Web site: www.nybeef.org
Non-profit organization conducting beef promotion & enhancing opportunities for cattle producers in NYS
Carol Gillis, Executive Director

New York Center for Agricultural Medicine & Health, Bassett Healthcare
1 Atwell Road, Cooperstown, NY 13326
800-343-7527 or 607-547-6023 Fax: 607-547-6087
e-mail: info@nycamh.com
Web site: www.nycamh.com
Occupational health & medicine in agriculture
John May, MD, Deputy Director

New York Farm Bureau
159 Wolf Road, PO Box 5330, Albany, NY 12205-0330
518-436-8495 or 800-342-4143 Fax: 518-431-5656
e-mail: info@nyfb.org
Web site: www.nyfb.org
Resources, education, advocacy, services & programs for the agricultural industry & community
Jeff Kirby, Executive Director

New York Corn & Soybean Growers Association
PO Box 133, Silver Springs, NY 14550
585-689-2321
Web site: www.nycornsoy.org
Grassroots organization focused on advancing the interests of corn & soybean producers
Steve Van Voorhis, President

New York Holstein Association
957 Mitchell Street, Ithaca, NY 14850
607-273-7591 or 800-834-4644 Fax: 607-273-7612
e-mail: pgifford@nyholsteins.com
Web site: www.nyholsteins.com
Dairy breed association serving to promote & develop Holstein breed cattle
Patricia G Gifford, Executive Manager

New York Pork Producers Coop
5146 Transit Road, Depew, NY 14043
716-697-3031
Web site: www.newyorkpork.org
Education & promotion of pork industry in NY
Krista Jaskier, Executive Secretary/State Contact

New York Seed Improvement Project, Cornell University, Plant Breeding Department
Cornell University, 240 Emerson Hall, Ithaca, NY 14853
607-255-9869 Fax: 607-255-9048
e-mail: pma3@cornell.edu
Web site: www.plbrgen.cals.cornell.edu
Provides seed certification for the state of NY & develops seed stocks for certified seed growers
Phil Atkins, Manager

New York State Association of Agricultural Fairs Inc
67 Verbeck Avenue, Schaghticoke, NY 12154
518-753-4956 Fax: 518-753-0208
e-mail: carousels4@aol.com
Web site: www.nyfairs.org
Utilizes fairs to promote agricultural development in NYS
Norma W Hamilton, Executive Secretary

New York State Maple Producers Association Inc
301 Myron Road, Syracuse, NY 13219
315-877-5795 Fax: 315-488-0459
e-mail: office@nysmaple.com
Web site: www.nysmaple.com
Promoting quality maple products through education & research
Helen Thomas, Executive Director

New York State Veterinary Medical Society
100 Great Oaks Blvd, Suite 127, Albany, NY 12203
518-869-7867 or 800-876-9867
e-mail: staff@nysvms.org
Web site: www.nysvms.org
Association for veterinarians in NYS
Jennifer Mauer, Executive Director

New York Thoroughbred Breeders Inc
57 Phila Street, Saratoga Springs, NY 12866
518-587-0777 Fax: 518-587-1551
e-mail: info@nytbreeders.org
Web site: www.nytbreeders.org
Jeffrey Cannizzo, Executive Director

New York Wine & Grape Foundation
800 South Main Street, Suite 200, Canandaigua, NY 14424
585-394-3620 Fax: 585-394-3649
e-mail: info@newyorkwines.org
Web site: www.newyorkwines.org
Promotion of winery products & tours; research for wine & grape related products
James Trezise, President

Northeast Dairy Foods Association Inc
427 South Main Street, North Syracuse, NY 13212
315-452-6455 Fax: 315-452-1643
Web site: www.nedairyfoods.org
Full service trade association representing the dairy processing, manufacturing & distribution industry of New York & surrounding states
Bruce W Krupke, Executive Vice President

Northeast Organic Farming Association of New York
1423 Hathaway Drive, Farmington, NY 14425
585-271-1979 Fax: 585-271-7166
e-mail: info@nofany.org
Web site: www.nofany.org
Association of farmers, gardeners & consumers promoting a sustainable food system in NYS through education, advocacy & organic food production
Nancy Apolito, Interim Executive Director

Community & Economic Development PathStone Corporation
400 East Avenue, Rochester, NY 14607
585-340-3300 or 800-888-6770
e-mail: smitchell@pathstone.org
Web site: www.pathstone.org
Provides services, advocacy & assistance for farmworker, rural & urban communities
Stuart J. Mitchell, President & CEO

Public Markets Partners/Baum Forum
5454 Palisade Avenue, Bronx, NY 10471
718-884-5716
e-mail: events@baumforum.org
Web site: www.baumforum.org
Organizes educational programs & events designed to address farming issues, promote regional agriculture & encourage healthy food systems
Hilary Baum, President

Regional Farm & Food Project
PO Box 621, Saratoga Springs, NY 12866
518-858-6866
Web site: www.farmandfood.org
Non-profit organization focused on building supply & demand for local food products and providing resources for farmers & consumers in the greater Hudson-Mohawk Valley region
Suzanne Carreker-Voigt, Chair

Seneca Foods Corporation
3736 South Main Street, Marion, NY 14505
315-926-8100 Fax: 315-926-8300
e-mail: webmaster@senecafoods.com
Web site: www.senecafoods.com
Fruit & vegetable food products
Kraig H Kayser, President & CEO

NYS Bar Association
Special Committee on Animals & the Law
1 Elk Street, Albany, NY 12207
518-463-3200 Fax: 518-463-5993
Web site: www.nysba.org
Provides resources & programs about animal law & related issues
Natalie A Carraway, Chair

Tea Association of the USA Inc
362 5th Avenue, Suite 801, New York, NY 10001
212-986-9415 Fax: 212-697-8658
e-mail: info@teausa.com
Web site: www.teausa.com
Trade association for the tea industry
Peter Goggi, President

United Dairy Cooperative Services Inc
12 North Park Street, Seneca Falls, NY 13148
315-568-2750 Fax: 315-568-2752
Management, accounting & payroll services to agriculture industry
Robert Nichols, President

Upstate Niagara Cooperative Inc
25 Anderson Road, Buffalo, NY 14225
716-892-3156 Fax: 716-892-3157
e-mail: emailus@upstateniagara.com
Web site: www.upstateniagara.com
Markets milk & dairy products
Lawrence Webster, Chief Executive Officer

Policy Areas

Offices and agencies generally appear in alphabetical order, except when specific order is requested by listee.

BANKING AND FINANCE

NEW YORK STATE

GOVERNOR'S OFFICE

Governor's Office
Executive Chamber
State Capitol
Albany, NY 12224
518-474-8390 Fax: 518-474-1513
Web site: www.ny.gov

Governor:
Andrew M Cuomo 518-474-8390
Secretary to the Governor:
William Mulrow 518-474-4246
Counsel to the Governor:
Alphonso David 518-474-8343
Chief of Staff:
Melissa DeRosa . . . . 518-474-8418 or 212-681-4640
Deputy Secretary for General Government Financial Services:
Brandan Fitzgerald 518-474-5442
Director, Communications:
James Allen. . . . . 518-474-8418 or 212-681-4640

EXECUTIVE DEPARTMENTS AND RELATED AGENCIES

Financial Services Department
One State Street
New York, NY 10004-1511
212-480-6400 or 800-342-3736
e-mail: public-affairs@dfs.ny.gov
Web site: www.dfs.ny.gov

Acting Superintendent:
Maria T Vullo 212-709-3501/fax: 212-709-3520
Acting Chief of Staff:
Dan Burstein 212-709-1651
e-mail: daniel.burstein@dfs.ny.gov
Director, Administration & Operations:
Chad Loshbaugh 518-473-0365
General Counsel:
Celeste Koeleveld 212-356-2300
Executive Deputy Superintendent, Enforcement:
Matthew L. Levine
Executive Deputy Superintendent, Communications & Strategy:
Richard A. Loconte
Special Assistant to the Superintendent:
Jennifer L. Smith
Senior Public Information Specialist:
Ronald Klug 212-709-1691
Consumer Representative, State Charter Advisory Board:
Vacant 212-709-3500

Banking Division
Deputy Superintendent:
Vacant 212-709-1690

Insurance Division
Deputy Superintendent, Property & Casual Markets:
Michael Moriarty. 212-480-5127/fax: 212-480-2310
Chief, Life Insurance Bureau:
Gail Keren 212-480-5030/fax: 212-480-5329
Chief, Health Insurance Bureau:
Vacant 518-486-2970
Chief Insurance Examiner 3:
Michael Maffei 212-480-5023

Financial Frauds & Consumer Protection Division
Director, Frauds:
Frank Orlando 212-480-5770/fax: 212-480-6066
Assistant Director, Frauds:
Angelo Carbone 212-480-5688

Capital Markets Division
Acting Director, Capital Markets:
Matti Peltonen 212-480-5071/fax: 212-480-6085

Real Estate Finance Division
Deputy Superintendent, Mortgage Banking:
Rhonda Ricketts 212-709-5540

Law Department
120 Broadway
New York, NY 10271-0332
212-416-8000 or 800-771-7755
Web site: www.ag.ny.gov

State Capitol
Albany, NY 12224-0341
518-776-2000
Fax: 518-650-9401

Attorney General:
Eric T Schneiderman . . . . 212-416-8050 or 518-776-2000
Director, Public Information:
Shawn Morris 518-776-2357/fax: 518-650-9401
Press Secretary:
Matt Mittenthal 212-416-8060/fax: 212-416-6005

Economic Justice
Executive Deputy Attorney General:
Manisha Sheth. 212-416-8050

Antitrust Bureau
Bureau Chief:
Eric J Stock 212-416-8262/fax: 212-416-6015
e-mail: eric.stock@ag.ny.gov

Consumer Frauds & Protection Bureau
Bureau Chief:
Jane Azia. 212-416-8300/fax: 212-416-8003

Internet Bureau
Bureau Chief:
Kathleen McGee 212-416-8433/fax: 212-416-8369
e-mail: ifraud@ag.ny.gov

Investor Protection Bureau
Bureau Chief:
Chad Johnson 212-416-8225/fax: 212-416-8816

Real Estate Finance Bureau
Bureau Chief:
Marissa Piesman 212-416-8102/fax: 212-416-8136

CORPORATIONS, AUTHORITIES AND COMMISSIONS

New York State Homes & Community Renewal
641 Lexington Ave
New York, NY 10022
866-275-3427
e-mail: hcrinfo@nyshcr.org
Web site: www.nyshcr.org

Offices and agencies generally appear in alphabetical order, except when specific order is requested by listee.

Hampton Plaza
38-40 State Street
Albany, NY 12207
518-473-2526

Commissioner & CEO:
James S Rubin 212-480-6705
Executive Deputy Commissioner/COO:
Betsy Mallow 212-480-6700
Executive Deputy Commissioner, Housing Development:
RuthAnne Visnauskas 212-480-6700
General Counsel:
Adam Schuman 212-480-6700
Chief of Staff:
Meredith Levine 212-480-6700
Director, Fair Housing & Equal Opportunity:
Wanda Graham 212-480-6700

NEW YORK STATE LEGISLATURE

See Legislative Branch in Section 1 for additional Standing Committee and Subcommittee information.

Assembly Standing Committees

Banks
Chair:
Annette Robinson (D) 518-455-5474
Ranking Minority Member:
Claudia Tenney (R) 518-455-5334

Senate Standing Committees

Banks
Chair:
Diane J Savino (D) 518-455-2437
Ranking Minority Member:
Jesse Hamilton (D) 518-455-2431

U.S. GOVERNMENT

EXECUTIVE DEPARTMENTS AND RELATED AGENCIES

Export Import Bank of the United States
Web site: www.exim.gov

Northeast Regional Office . . . . fax: 212-809-2687
Ted Weiss Federal Building, 290 Broadway, 13th Floor, New York, NY 10007
212-809-2650 Fax: 212-809-2687
Regional Director:
Gregory Smith 212-809-2652
e-mail: gregory.smith@exim.gov

Federal Deposit Insurance Corporation
877-275-3342
Web site: www.fdic.gov

Division of Depositor and Consumer Protection
350 Fifth Avenue, Suite 1200, New York, NY 10118-0110
800-334-9593 or 917-320-2500
Regional Director:
John Vogel
Deputy Regional Director:
John P Conneely

Federal Reserve System

Federal Reserve Bank of New York
33 Liberty Street, New York, NY 10045
212-720-5000
e-mail: general.info@ny.frb.org
Web site: www.newyorkfed.org
President:
William C Dudley
First Vice President:
Michael Strine
Chair:
Emily K Rafferty

National Credit Union Administration
Web site: www.ncua.gov

Albany Region
9 Washington Square, Washington Avenue Extension, Albany, NY 12205
518-862-7400
e-mail: region1@ncua.gov
Regional Director:
L J Blankenberger 518-862-7400/fax: 518-862-7420

US Treasury Department
Web site: www.treasury.gov

Comptroller of the Currency
Web site: www.occ.treas.gov

Northeastern District Office . . . . fax: 212-790-4058
340 Madison Avenue, 5th Floor, New York, NY 10173-0002
212-790-4000 Fax: 212-790-4058
Deputy Comptroller:
Kristin Kiefer 212-790-4001/fax: 212-790-4058
Associate Deputy Comptroller:
Maureen Whalen 212-790-4061
District Counsel:
Jonathan Rushdoony 212-790-4010

US Mint
Web site: www.usmint.gov
Plant Manager:
Ellen McCullom 845-446-6200

U.S. CONGRESS

See U.S. Congress Chapter for additional Standing Committee and Subcommittee information.

House of Representatives Standing Committees

Financial Services
Chair:
Jeb Hensarling (R-TX)
Ranking Member:
Maxine Waters (D-CA)
New York Delegate:
Peter T. King (R)
New York Delegate:
Carolyn B. Maloney (D)
New York Delegate:
Nydia M. Velazquez (D)
New York Delegate:
Gregory W. Meeks (D)

Policy Areas

Offices and agencies generally appear in alphabetical order, except when specific order is requested by listee.

Senate Standing Committees

Banking, Housing & Urban Affairs
Chair:
Richard Shelby (R-AL) 202-224-5744/fax: 202-224-3416
Ranking Member:
Sherrod Brown (D-OH)
New York Delegate:
Charles E Schumer (D) 202-224-6542

PRIVATE SECTOR

American Express Company
200 Vesey Street, New York, NY 10285-3106
212-640-2000 Fax: 212-640-0404
Web site: www.americanexpress.com
Consumer lending, travel services, proprietary database marketing, insurance underwriting & investment services
Stephen Lemson, Vice President, State & Government Affairs

American International Group Inc
175 Water Street, New York, NY 10038
212-770-7000
Web site: www.aig.com
International business, insurance & financial services
Phil Fasano, Chief Information Officer

Antalek & Moore Insurance Agency
340 Main Street, Beacon, NY 12508
845-245-6216 or 800-860-7176 Fax: 845-831-5631
Web site: www.antalek-moore.com
Provides insurance & risk management services
Patrick C Moore, Partner

Apple Bank for Savings
122 East 42nd Street, 9th Fl, New York, NY 10168
914-902-2775
Web site: www.applebank.com
Personal & business banking services
Steven C Bush, President & Chief Executive Officer

Astoria Bank
1 Astoria Bank Plaza, Lake Success, NY 11042-1085
516-327-3000 Fax: 516-327-7860
Web site: www.astoriabank.com
Alan P Eggleston, Senior Executive Vice President

Bank of Akron
46 Main Street, Akron, NY 14001
716-542-5401 or 877-542-5401 Fax: 716-542-5510
Web site: www.bankofakron.com
Director - Independent Bankers Association of New York State (IBANYS); personal & business banking; financial services
E Peter Forrestel, II, President & Chief Executive Officer

Brown Brothers Harriman & Co
140 Broadway, New York, NY 10005-1101
212-483-1818
Web site: www.bbh.com
Provides private banking & investment management services
Andrew P Hofer, Managing Director/Head of Taxable Portfolio Management

Canandaigua National Bank & Trust Co
72 South Main Street, Canandaigua, NY 14424
585-394-4260 or 800-724-2621 Fax: 585-396-1355
e-mail: ghamlin@cnbank.com
Web site: www.cnbank.com
Full service banking
George W Hamlin, Chairman, Trust Officer & Senior Policy Advisor
Frank H Hamlin, President & Chief Executive Officer

Capital One Bank
275 Broadhollow Road, Melville, NY 11747
631-844-1376
Web site: www.capitalone.com
Heidi Joseph, Regional Executive

Citigroup Inc
388 Greenwich Street, New York, NY 10013
212-559-1000 or 800-285-3000
Web site: www.citigroup.com
Commercial & retail banking
Michael L Corbat, Chief Executive Officer

The Clearing House Association, LLC
1114 Avenue of the Americas, 17th Floor, New York, NY 10036
212-613-0100 Fax: 212-612-9253
e-mail: tchinfo@theclearinghouse.org
Web site: www.theclearinghouse.org
Electronic funds transfer
James Aramanda, President & Chief Executive Officer

Community Bank N.A.
5790 Wildewaters Parkway, Suite 170, Syracuse, NY 13214
315-445-2282 or 800-388-4679
Web site: www.communitybankna.com
Personal & business banking
Mark Tryniski, President & Chief Executive Officer

Cornell University, Economics Department
404 Uris Hall, Ithaca, NY 14853
607-255-4254 Fax: 607-255-2818
e-mail: lb19@cornell.edu
Web site: www.economics.cornell.edu
Economic research; microeconomic theory & financial economics
Lawerence Blume, Chair

Deutsche Bank
60 Wall Street, New York, NY 10005
212-250-2500
Web site: www.db.com
Investment, private & commercial banking; wealth & asset management
Dr. Marcus Schenck, Chief Financial Officer

Federal Home Loan Bank of New York
101 Park Avenue, New York, NY 10178-0599
212-681-6000 Fax: 212-441-6890
Web site: www.fhlbny.com
Provides credit products, correspondent services & community lending programs for members
Jose R. Gonzalez, President & Chief Executive Officer

Financial Services Forum
601 Thirteenth Street NW, Suite 750 South, Washington, DC 20005
202-457-8765 Fax: 202-457-8769
Web site: www.financialservicesforum.org
Organization consisting of CEOs of sixteen of the largest financial institutions in the US
Brian T Moynihan, Chair

Goldman Sachs & Co
200 West Street, 29th Floor, New York, NY 10282
202-902-1000
Web site: www.goldmansachs.com
Investment banking & management
Lloyd C Blankfein, Chairman & Chief Executive Officer

HSBC USA Inc
452 Fifth Avenue, New York, NY 10018
212-525-5000
Web site: www.us.hsbc.com
Commercial & retail banking
Mark Zaeske, Chief Financial Officer

Offices and agencies generally appear in alphabetical order, except when specific order is requested by listee.

IRX Therapeutics Inc
140 West 57th St, Ste 3D, New York, NY 10019
212-582-1199 Fax: 212-582-3659
e-mail: jhwang@irxtherapeutics.com
Web site: www.irxtherapeutics.com
Jeffrey Hwang, President/Chief Operating Officer

Independent Bankers Association of NYS
19 Dove Street, Suite 101, Albany, NY 12210
518-436-4646 Fax: 518-436-4648
e-mail: johnw@ibanys.net
Web site: www.ibanys.net
Represents New York's independent community banks
John J Witkowski, President & Chief Executive Officer

JPMorgan Chase & Co
270 Park Avenue, New York, NY 10017-2070
212-464-1909
Web site: www.jpmorganchase.com
Financial services, investment banking & asset management
Jamie Dimon, Chairman & Chief Executive Officer

KeyBank
65 Dutch Hill Road, Orangeburg, NY 10962
845-398-2280 or 845-365-5890 Fax: 845-365-5890
Web site: www.key.com
Retail & commercial banking; investment management
Ruth Mahoney, Market President

Kudlow & Company LLC
301 Tahmore Drive, Fairfield, CT 06825
203-228-5050 Fax: 203-228-5040
e-mail: svarga@kudlow.com
Web site: www.kudlow.com
Economic research & consulting services

Lake Shore Savings
128 East Fourth Street, Dunkirk, NY 14048
716-366-4070 Fax: 716-366-2965
e-mail: dave.mancuso@lakeshoresavings.com
Web site: www.lakeshoresavings.com
Personal & business banking with focus on mortgage, real estate, commercial & consumer loans
Daniel Reininga, President & Chief Executive Officer

M&T Bank Corporation
One M&T Plaza, 345 Main Street, Buffalo, NY 14203-2399
716-842-4470 Fax: 716-842-5839
e-mail: rwilmers@mtb.com
Web site: www.mtb.com
Commercial, savings & mortgage banking services
Robert G Wilmers, Chairman & Chief Executive Officer

MBIA Insurance Corporation
1 Manhattanville Road, Suite 301, Purchase, NY 10577
914-273-4545
Web site: www.mbia.com
Municipal bond insurance & specialized financial services
Jay Brown, Chief Executive Officer

Mallory Factor Inc
555 Madison Avenue, New York, NY 10022
212-350-0000 Fax: 212-350-0001
Consulting & financial services
Mallory Factor, President

Merrill Lynch & Co Inc
4 World Financial Center, 250 Vesey Street, New York, NY 10080
800-637-7455
Web site: www.ml.com
Securities, capital markets & financial services
Andy M Sieg, Managing Director

Morgan Stanley
1585 Broadway Avenue, New York, NY 10036
212-761-4000 Fax: 212-762-7994
Web site: www.morganstanley.com
Investment banking, asset management & financial services
James Gorman, Chairman & Chief Executive Officer

Municipal Credit Union
22 Cortlandt Street, New York, NY 10007-3107
212-238-3512
Web site: www.nymcu.org
Credit union serving members in New York
Kam Wong, President & Chief Executive Officer

NBT Bancorp Inc.
PO Box 351, Norwich, NY 13815
607-337-2265 or 800-628-2265
e-mail: customerservice@nbtbank.com
Web site: www.nbtbank.com
Commercial banking
Martin A Dietrich, President & Chief Executive Officer

National Federation of Community Development Credit Unions
39 Broadway, Suite 2140, New York, NY 10006-3063
212-809-1850 Fax: 212-809-3274
e-mail: info@cdcu.coop
Web site: www.cdcu.coop
Association of credit unions serving lower-income people & communities
Cathie Mahon, President & Chief Executive Officer

Navicore Solutions
200 US Highway 9, Manalapan, NJ 07726
800-992-4557
Web site: www.navicoresolutions.org
Credit counseling & debt management services
Diane Gray, Vice President of Counseling & Education

New York Bankers Association
99 Park Avenue, 4th Floor, New York, NY 10016-1502
212-297-1600 Fax: 212-297-1658
e-mail: msmith@nyba.com
Web site: www.nyba.com
Association providing education, advocacy & services for the banking industry of New York State
Michael P Smith, President & Chief Executive Officer

New York Community Bank
615 Merrick Avenue, Westbury, NY 11590
877-786-6560
Web site: www.mynycb.com
Joseph R. Ficalora, President & Chief Executive Officer

New York Credit Union Association
1021 Watervliet-Shaker Road, PO Box 15118, Albany, NY 12212-5118
518-437-8100 or 800-342-9835 Fax: 518-437-8284
e-mail: info@nycua.org
Web site: www.nycua.org
Supports & advocates for credit unions throughout NYS
William J Mellin, President & Chief Executive Officer

New York Stock Exchange
11 Wall Street, New York, NY 10005
212-656-3000
Web site: www.nyse.com
Anthony J Albanese, Chief Regulatory Officer

Norddeutsche Landesbank Girozentrale
1114 Avenue of the Americas, 20th Floor, New York, NY 10036
212-398-7300 Fax: 212-812-6860
Web site: www.nordlb.com
Christian Jagenberg, Executive Vice President & General Manager

Offices and agencies generally appear in alphabetical order, except when specific order is requested by listee.

North Country Savings Bank
127 Main Street, Canton, NY 13617
315-386-4533 Fax: 315-386-3739
e-mail: voakes@northcountrysavings.com
Web site: www.northcountrysavings.com
Victoria A Oakes, Assistant Vice President

Pioneer Savings Bank
21 Second Street, Troy, NY 12180
518-687-5400 Fax: 518-274-1060
Web site: www.pioneerbanking.com
Thomas L. Amell, President & Chief Executive Officer

Securities Industry & Financial Markets Association (SIFMA)
120 Broadway, 35th Floor, New York, NY 10271
212-313-1200 Fax: 212-313-1301
e-mail: inquiry@sifma.org
Web site: www.sifma.org
Association representing the securities industry of the United States
Kenneth E Bentsen Jr., President & Chief Executive Officer

Sullivan & Cromwell
125 Broad Street, New York, NY 10004-2498
212-558-4000 Fax: 212-558-3588
Web site: www.sullcrom.com
Bank regulation & acquisition law
H Rodgin Cohen, Partner & Senior Chairman
Joseph Shenker, Partner & Chairman

TD Bank N.A.
1 Old Loudon Road, Latham, NY 12110
518-785-8628
Web site: www.tdbank.com
Commercial, retail & investment banking
Gail Jefferson, Assistant Vice President

Tompkins Financial Corporation
110 North Tioga Street, PO Box 460, Ithaca, NY 14851
607-273-3210 Fax: 607-273-0063
e-mail: sromaine@tompkinstrust.com
Web site: www.tompkinsfinancial.com
$5.5 Billion financial services holding company headquartered in Ithaca, NY. Parent company to Tompkins Trust Company, The Bank of Castile and Mahopac National Bank, as well as Tompkins Insurance Services & Tompkins Financial.
Stephen S Romaine, President & Chief Executive Officer

Ulster Savings Bank
180 Schwank Drive, Kingston, NY 12401
845-338-6322 or 866-440-0391 Fax: 845-339-9008
Web site: www.ulstersavings.com
Banking services including consumer loans, commercial mortgages & online banking
Glenn Sutherland, Interim President & Chief Executive Officer

Valley National Bank
1455 Valley Road, Wayne, NJ 07470
973-686-5034 or 800-522-4100 Fax: 973-694-2261
e-mail: rfraser@valleynationalbank.com
Web site: www.valleynationalbank.com
Full-service banking, cash management, municipal leasing & public finance
Ronald Fraser, First Vice President, Municipal & Government

White & Case LLP
1155 Avenue of the Americas, New York, NY 10036-2787
212-819-8200 Fax: 212-354-8113
e-mail: dwall@whitecase.com
Web site: www.whitecase.com
Advises domestic & foreign banks on the nature & structure of their operations & activities in the US & abroad
Duane D Wall, Partner of Counsel

COMMERCE, INDUSTRY & ECONOMIC DEVELOPMENT

NEW YORK STATE

GOVERNOR'S OFFICE

Governor's Office
Executive Chamber
State Capitol
Albany, NY 12224
518-474-8390 Fax: 518-474-1513
Web site: www.ny.gov

Governor:
Andrew M Cuomo 518-474-8390
Secretary to the Governor:
William Mulrow 518-474-4246
Counsel to the Governor:
Alphonso David 518-474-8343
Deputy Secretary for General Government Financial Services:
Brandan Fitzgerald 518-474-5442
First Assistant Counsel:
Sandi Toll 518-474-8434
Chief of Staff:
Melissa DeRosa . . . . . 518-474-8418 or 212-681-4640
Director, Communications:
James Allen . . . . . 518-474-8418 or 212-681-4640

EXECUTIVE DEPARTMENTS AND RELATED AGENCIES

New York State Liquor Authority (Division of Alcoholic Beverage Control)
80 S Swan St
Ste 900
Albany, NY 12210-8002
518-474-3114 Fax: 518-402-4015
Web site: www.sla.ny.gov

317 Lenox Ave
New York, NY 10027
212-961-8300
Fax: 212-961-8299

Chair:
Vincent Bradley . . . . . 212-961-8300 or 518-473-6559
Commissioner:
Jeanique Greene . . . . . 212-961-8300 or 518-474-3114
Commissioner:
Kevin Kim . . . . . 212-961-8300 or 518-474-3114
Director, Enforcement:
Noel Colon 518-474-3114
Counsel:
Jacqueline Flug 518-474-3114/fax: 518-402-2304

Administration
Secretary to the Authority (Acting):
Jacqueline Held 518-473-6559
Deputy Commissioner, Administration:
Chad Loshbaugh 518-473-0365
Director, Public Affairs:
William Crowley . . . . . 518-474-3114 or 518-474-4875
fax: 518-473-9565
e-mail: press.office@sla.ny.gov

Licensing & Enforcement

Albany (Zone II)
80 S Swan St, Ste 900, Albany, NY 12210-8002
CEO:
Kerri O'Brien 518-474-3114/fax: 518-402-2304
Deputy Counsel:
Lisa Bonacci 518-474-3114
Director, Information Technology:
Michael Drake 518-474-3114

Buffalo (Zone III)
Iskalo Electric Tower, 535 Washington St, Ste 303, Buffalo, NY 14203
Deputy Commissioner, Licensing:
David L Edmunds Jr. 716-847-3001
Supervising Beverage Control Investigator:
Gary Bartikofsky 716-847-3035

New York City (Zone I)
317 Lenox Avenue, New York, NY 10027
Deputy Chief Executive Officer:
Michael Jones 212-961-8300
Supervising Beverage Control Investigator:
Franklin Englander 212-961-8376

Budget, Division of the
State Capitol
Albany, NY 12224
518-473-0580 or 518-473-3885 Fax: 518-474-9041
Web site: www.budget.ny.gov

Director:
Robert F Mujica 518-474-2300
Deputy Director:
Sandra Beattie 518-474-6497
Deputy Director:
David Lara 518-402-4246
Budget Services Head:
Vacant 518-474-6300
Public Protection Head:
Robert Barbato 518-474-4313
Press Officer:
Morris Peters 518-473-3885/fax: 518-474-9041
e-mail: dob.sm.press@budget.ny.gov

Consumer Protection, Division of
One Commerce Plaza
99 Washington Ave
Albany, NY 12231
518-474-8583 or 800-697-1220 Fax: 518-473-9055
Web site: www.dos.ny.gov/consumerprotection/

Executive Deputy Director, Consumer Protection:
Aiesha Battle 518-474-2363

Empire State Development Corporation
633 Third Ave
New York, NY 10017
212-803-3100 Fax: 212-803-3131
e-mail: esd@esd.ny.gov
Web site: www.esd.ny.gov

625 Broadway
Albany, NY 12207
518-292-5100

95 Perry Street
Ste 500
Buffalo, NY 14203

Offices and agencies generally appear in alphabetical order, except when specific order is requested by listee.

716-846-8200
Fax: 716-846-8260

President & CEO:
Howard Zemsky 212-803-3700
e-mail: president@esd.ny.gov
Business Attraction & Expansion:
John Gilstrap . . . . 212-803-3700 or 518-292-5100
Chief of Staff & COO:
Mehul J. Patel 212-803-3700
Public Affairs:
Kay Sarlin Wright 800-260-7313
e-mail: esdpressoffice@esd.ny.gov

Law Department
120 Broadway
New York, NY 10271-0332
212-416-8000 or 800-771-7755
Web site: www.ag.ny.gov

State Capitol
Albany, NY 12224-0341
518-776-2000
Fax: 518-650-9401

Attorney General:
Eric T Schneiderman . . . . 212-416-8050 or 518-776-2000
Chief of Staff:
Brian Mahanna 212-416-8050
COO:
Jeanette Moy 518-776-2500/fax: 518-915-7753
Press Secretary:
Matt Mittenthal 212-416-8060/fax: 212-416-6005
Solicitor General:
Barbara D Underwood . . . . 212-416-8016 or 518-402-2074

Economic Justice
Executive Deputy Attorney General:
Manisha Sheth 212-416-8050

Antitrust Bureau
Bureau Chief:
Eric J Stock 212-416-8282/fax: 212-416-6015
e-mail: eric.stock@ag.ny.gov

Consumer Frauds Bureau
Bureau Chief:
Jane Azia . . . . 212-416-8300 or 518-776-2307
fax: 212-416-6003

Internet Bureau
Bureau Chief:
Kathleen McGee 212-416-8433/fax: 212-416-8369

Investor Protection Bureau
Bureau Chief:
Chad Johnson 212-416-8225/fax: 212-416-8816

State Counsel
Chief Deputy Attorney General & Counsel:
Janet Sabel 212-416-8050
Chief Deputy Attorney General & Counsel:
Jason Brown 212-416-8050

Claims Bureau
Bureau Chief:
Katharine Brooks . . . . 518-776-2300 or 212-416-8500

NYSTAR - Division of Science, Technology & Innovation
30 South Pearl St
11th Fl
Albany, NY 12207
518-292-5700 Fax: 518-292-5798
Web site: www.esd.ny.gov/nystar

Director:
Edward Reinfurt 518-292-5700
Deputy Director:
Edward J Hamilton 518-292-5700
Director, Communications/Government Affairs:
Jannette Rondo 518-292-5700/fax: 518-292-5798
Regional Technology Development:
Matthew Watson 518-292-5700
Counsel:
Paul Jesep 518-292-5700

Centers for Advanced Technology

Center for Advanced Ceramic Technology at Alfred University
2 Pine Street, Alfred, NY 14802-1296
e-mail: cactinfo@alfred.edu
Web site: cact.alfred.edu
Director:
Dr Matthew M Hall 607-871-2486/fax: 607-871-3469
e-mail: hallmm@alfred.edu

Center for Advanced Materials Processing at Clarkson Univ
CAMP, Box 5665, Potsdam, NY 13699-5665
Web site: www.clarkson.edu/camp
Director:
S V Babu 315-268-2336/fax: 315-268-7615
e-mail: babu@clarkson.edu

Center for Advanced Tech in Biomedical & Bioengineering
University at Buffalo, 701 Ellicott St, Buffalo, NY 14203
Web site: www.bioinformatics.buffalo.edu/cat
Co-Director:
Alexander N. Cartwright PhD 716-645-0312
Co-Director:
Marnie LaVigne PhD 716-645-0312
e-mail: lavigne2@buffalo.edu

Sensor CAT-Diagnostic Tools & Sensor Systems
SUNY Stony Brook, Suffolk Hall, Room 115B, Stony Brook, NY 11794-3717
e-mail: sensor@ece.sunysb.edu
Web site: sensorcat.sunysb.edu
Director:
Serge Luryi . . . . 631-632-1368 or 631-632-8420
fax: 631-632-8529

Center for Emerging & Innovative Sciences
Univ of Rochester, Taylor Hall, 260 Hutchinson Rd, Rochester, NY 14627-0194
Web site: www.ceis.rochester.edu
Director:
Mark Bocko 585-275-0547
e-mail: mark.bocko@seas.rochester.edu

Center for Advanced Information Management
Columbia University, 630 W 168th St, Bldg 130, New York, NY 10032
Web site: www.cat.columbia.edu
Director:
George Hripcsak 212-305-2944/fax: 212-305-0196

Center for Advanced Technology in Life Science Enterprise
Cornell University, 130 Biotechnology Bldg, Ithaca, NY 14853-2703
Web site: www.biotech.cornell.edu/cat
Director:
George Grills 607-255-9693
e-mail: biotech@cornell.edu

Center for Advanced Technology in Photonics Applications
CUNY, Steinman Hall T606, 160 Convent Avenue, New York, NY 10031
Web site: www.cunycat.org
Director:
David T. Crouse, PhD 212-650-5330/fax: 212-650-7760
e-mail: crouse@cunycat.org

Ctr for Advanced Tech in Telecommunications at Polytech Univ
5 MetroTech Center, 9th Floor, Brooklyn, NY 11201
Web site: catt.poly.edu
Director:
Shivendra S Panwar . . . . 718-260-3050 or 718-260-3740
fax: 718-260-8687
e-mail: panwar@catt.poly.edu

Center for Automation Technologies & Systems at Rensselaer
CII 8011, 110 8th Street, Troy, NY 12180
e-mail: cats-info@rpi.edu
Web site: www.cats.rpi.edu
Director:
John Wen. 518-276-8744/fax: 518-276-4897

Center for Advanced Medical Biotechnology
Biotechnology Building, 2nd Floor, Stony Brook, NY 11790
Web site: www.biotech.sunysb.edu
Director:
Clinton T Rubin PhD 631-632-8521/fax: 631-632-8577

Center for Computer Applications & Software Engineering
Syracuse University, 2-212 Ctr for Science & Tech, Syracuse, NY 13244
Web site: www.case.syr.edu
Director:
Pramod Varshney 315-443-1060/fax: 315-443-4745
e-mail: varshney@syr.edu

Center in Nanomaterials and Nanoelectronics
251 Fuller Road, Albany, NY 12203
Director:
Michael Fancher 518-437-8686/fax: 518-437-8687

Future Energy Systems CAT at Rensselaer Polytechnic Inst
110 8th Street, Troy, NY 12180
e-mail: cfes@rpi.edu
Web site: www.rpi.edu/cfes
Director:
Dr. Jian Sun. 518-276-8297/fax: 518-276-6844
e-mail: jsun@ecse.rpi.edu

Integrated Electronics Engineering Center at Binghamton
IEEC, Vestal Pkwy East, PO Box 6000, Binghamton, NY 13902-6000
e-mail: ieec@binghamton.edu
Web site: www.binghamton.edu/ieec/
Director:
Daryl Santos 607-777-4769/fax: 607-777-4683

Regional Technology Development Centers

Alliance for Manufacturing & Technology
59 Court St, 6th Fl, State St Entrance, Binghamton, NY 13901
e-mail: info@amt-mep.org
Web site: www.amt-mep.org
Executive Director:
Edward Gaetano. 607-774-0022 x304/fax: 607-774-0026

Center for Economic Growth
30 Pearl Street, Ste 100, Albany, NY 12207
e-mail: ceg@ceg.org
Web site: www.ceg.org
President/CEO:
F Michael Tucker 518-465-8975/fax: 518-465-6681
e-mail: miket@ceg.org

Central New York Technology Development Organization
445 Electronics Pkwy, Ste 206, Liverpool, NY 13088
Web site: www.tdo.org
President/CEO:
Robert I Trachtenberg 315-425-5144/fax: 315-233-1259
e-mail: rtrachtenberg@tdo.org

Council for Interntl Trade, Tech, Education & Communication
Peyton Hall, Box 8561, Main St, Clarkson University, Potsdam, NY 13669
Web site: www.citec.org
Executive Director:
William P. Murray 315-268-3778 x29/fax: 315-268-4432
e-mail: murray@citec.org

High Technology of Rochester
150 Lucius Gordon Drive, Suite 100, West Henrietta, NY 14586
Web site: www.htr.org
President:
Jim Sendall 585-214-2400
e-mail: info@htr.org

Hudson Valley Technology Development Center
1450 Route 300, Building 1, Newburgh, NY 12550
Web site: www.hvtdc.org
Executive Director:
Thomas G Phillips, Sr 845-391-8214 x3006/fax: 845-845-8218
e-mail: tom.phillips@hvtdc.org

Industrial & Technology Assistance Corp
39 Broadway, Suite 100, New York, NY 10006
Web site: www.itac.org
President:
Sara Garretson. 212-809-3900/fax: 646-588-5156
e-mail: sgarretson@itac.org

Long Island Forum for Technology
510 Grumman Road West, Bay Shore, NY 11706
e-mail: info@lift.org
Web site: www.lift.org
Executive Director:
William Wahlig. 631-969-3700/fax: 631-846-2789
e-mail: bwahlig@lift.org

Mohawk Valley Applied Technology Corp
207 Genesee St, Ste 405, Utica, NY 13501
Web site: www.mvatc.com
President:
Paul MacEnroe 315-793-8050/fax: 315-793-8057
e-mail: paulm@mvatc.com

INSYTE Consulting (Western NY Technology Development Ctr)
726 Exchange St, Ste 812, Buffalo, NY 14210
Web site: www.insyte-consulting.com
President:
Benjamin Rand 716-636-3626/fax: 716-845-6418
e-mail: brand@insyte-consulting.com

State Department

One Commerce Plaza
99 Washington Avenue
Albany, NY 12231
518-474-4750 Fax: 518-474-4765
Web site: www.dos.ny.gov

123 William St
New York, NY 10038
212-417-5801
Fax: 212-417-5805

Acting Secretary of State:
Rossana Rosado 518-474-0050
First Deputy Secretary of State:
Daniel Shapiro 518-474-4750

Offices and agencies generally appear in alphabetical order, except when specific order is requested by listee.

Deputy Secretary of State, Public Affairs:
Vacant 212-417-5800
Assistant Secretary of State, Communications:
Vacant 518-474-4752/fax: 518-474-4597
e-mail: info@dos.state.ny.us
Principal Attorney:
William Sharp 518-474-6740/fax: 518-473-9211
Deputy Secretary of State, Local Government & Community Services:
Robert Elliott 518-486-9888/fax: 518-474-6572

Licensing Services Division
Deputy Secretary of State:
Marcos Vigil 518-473-2728/fax: 518-473-2730
e-mail: licensing@dos.state.ny.us

Administrative Rules Division
Manger, Publications:
Maribeth St. Germain 518-474-6957/fax: 518-473-9055
e-mail: adminrules@dos.state.ny.us

Cemeteries Division
Director:
Richard D Fishman . . . . . 518-474-6226 or 212-417-5713
fax: 518-473-0876
e-mail: cemeteries@dos.state.ny.us

Corporations, State Records & UCC Division
Director:
Sandra J. Tallman 518-473-2492/fax: 518-474-1418
e-mail: corporations@dos.ny.gov

Taxation & Finance Department
State Campus
Bldg 9, Rm 227
Albany, NY 12227
518-457-4242 Fax: 518-457-2486
Web site: www.tax.ny.gov

Commissioner:
Jerry Boone 518-457-2244
Executive Deputy Commissioner:
Nonie Manion 518-457-7358
Deputy Commissioner & Counsel:
Amanda Hiller 518-457-3746/fax: 518-457-8247
Director, Conciliation & Mediation Services:
Kevin Law 518-485-8063
Director, Executive Correspondence & Legislative Affairs:
Maryann Tucker 518-457-2398
Director, Public Information:
Geoffrey Gloak 518-457-7377

Office of Processing & Taxpayer Services (OPTS)
Deputy Commissioner:
Edward Chaszczewski 518-457-1000

Human Resources Management
Director:
Gina Lysyczyn 518-457-2786

Operations Support Bureau
Director:
Lisa Negus 518-457-4250

Office of Budget & Management Analysis
Chief Financial Officer:
Eric Mostert 518-485-5080

Planning & Management Analysis Bureau
Director:
Mary Ellen Nagengast 518-457-8660

Office of Information Technology Services
Chief Information Officer:
Daniel Chan 518-292-7808

Office of Processing & Taxpayer Services
Director:
Helen Pelersi 518-591-1944

Office of State Treasury
Deputy Commissioner & Treasurer:
Aida Brewer 518-474-4250/fax: 518-402-4118

Office of Criminal Enforcement
Deputy Commissioner:
Letizia Tagliaferro 518-457-9692

Audit Division
Director, Tax Audits:
Joe Carzo 518-451-8910

Collections & Civil Enforcement
Director:
Patricia Coneys 518-457-1138

Office of Tax Policy Analysis
Deputy Commissioner:
Robert D Plattner 518-457-4357

CORPORATIONS, AUTHORITIES AND COMMISSIONS

Central New York Regional Market Authority
2100 Park St
Syracuse, NY 13208
315-422-8647 Fax: 315-422-6897
Web site: cnyrma.com

Acting Commissioner of Agricultural Markets:
Richard A Ball 315-422-8647
Commissioner's Representative:
Troy Waffner 315-422-8647

Development Authority of the North Country
317 Washington Street
Watertown, NY 13601
315-661-3200
e-mail: info@danc.org
Web site: www.danc.org

Chair:
Gary Turck 315-661-3200
Executive Director:
James Wright 315-661-3200
Deputy Executive Director:
Thomas R Sauter 315-661-3200
e-mail: tsauter@danc.org
Director, Engineering:
Carrie Tuttle 315-661-3210/fax: 315-786-2971
Telecom Division Manager:
David Wolf 315-661-3200
e-mail: oatn@danc.org
Landfill Superintendent:
Steve McElwain 315-661-3230
Director, Regional Development:
Michelle Capone 315-661-3200

Great Lakes Commission
2805 S Industrial Hwy
Ste 100
Ann Arbor, MI 48104-6791

Offices and agencies generally appear in alphabetical order, except when specific order is requested by listee.

734-971-9135 Fax: 734-971-9150
e-mail: teder@glc.org
Web site: www.glc.org

Chairman:
Jon W Allan 517-284-5035
e-mail: allanj@michigan.gov
Vice Chair:
Jon W Allan 517-284-5035
e-mail: allanj@michigan.gov
Acting New York State Commissioner:
Basil Seggos 518-402-8540
e-mail: joseph.martens@dec.ny.gov
Executive Director:
Tim A Eder 734-971-9135
e-mail: teder@glc.org
Deputy Director:
Thomas R Crane 734-971-9135
e-mail: tcrane@glc.org
CIO:
Stephen J Cole 734-971-9135
e-mail: scole@glc.org
Program Director:
Victoria Pebbles 734-971-9135
e-mail: vpebbles@glc.org
Communications Director:
Beth Wanamaker. 734-971-9135
e-mail: beth@glc.org
Policy Director:
Matthew Doss 734-971-9135
e-mail: mdoss@glc.org

United Nations Development Corporation
Two United Nations Plaza, 27th Fl
New York, NY 10017
212-888-1618 Fax: 212-588-0758
e-mail: info@undc.org
Web site: www.undc.org

Chair, Board of Directors:
George Klein. 212-888-1618
Sr VP & General Counsel/Secretary:
Robert Cole. 212-888-1618
Vice President:
Kenneth Coopersmith 212-888-1618
Controller/Treasurer:
Jorge Ortiz. 212-888-1618

NEW YORK STATE LEGISLATURE

See Legislative Branch in Section 1 for additional Standing Committee and Subcommitee information.

Assembly Standing Committees

Cities
Chair:
Michael Benedetto (D) 518-455-5296
Ranking Minority Member:
Vacant (R). 518-455-0000

Consumer Affairs & Protection
Chair:
Jeffrey Dinowitz (D). 518-455-5965
Ranking Minority Member:
Anthony Palumbo (R). 518-455-5294

Corporations, Authorities & Commissions
Chair:
James F Brennan (D) 518-455-5377
Ranking Minority Member:
Jane Corwin (R) 518-455-4601

Economic Development, Job Creation, Commerce & Industry
Chair:
Robin L Schimminger (D) 518-455-4767
Ranking Minority Member:
Raymond Walter (R). 518-455-4618

Small Business
Chair:
Fred Thiele, Jr (D). 518-455-5997
Ranking Minority Member:
David DiPietro (R) 518-455-5314

Assembly Task Forces

University-Industry Cooperation, Task Force on
Chair:
Vacant (D). 518-455-0000
Coordinator:
Maureen Schoolman 518-455-3632/fax: 518-455-4175

Senate Standing Committees

Cities
Chair:
Simcha Felder (D). 518-455-2754
Ranking Minority Member:
Daniel Squadron (D). 518-455-2625

Commerce, Economic Development & Small Business
Chair:
Philip Boyle (R) 518-455-3411
Ranking Minority Member:
Timothy Kennedy (D). 518-455-2426

Consumer Protection
Chair:
Michael Venditto (R) 518-455-3341
Ranking Minority Member:
Leroy Comrie (D) 518-455-2701

Corporations, Authorities & Commissions
Chair:
Michael Ranzenhofer (R) 518-455-3161
Ranking Minority Member:
Bill Perkins (D). 518-455-2441

Senate/Assembly Legislative Commissions

Rural Resources, Legislative Commission on
Senate Chair:
Patricia Ritchie (R) 518-455-3438
Assembly Vice Chair:
Frank Skartados (D) 518-455-5762
Counsel:
Barbara McRedmond 518-455-2069

U.S. GOVERNMENT

EXECUTIVE DEPARTMENTS AND RELATED AGENCIES

Commodity Futures Trading Commission
Web site: www.cftc.gov

Offices and agencies generally appear in alphabetical order, except when specific order is requested by listee.

Eastern Region
140 Broadway, New York, NY 10005
646-746-9700
Regional Counsel:
Lenel Hickson Jr. 646-746-9700/fax: 646-746-9938

Consumer Product Safety Commission
301-504-7923 or 800-504-0124 Fax: 301-504-0124
Web site: www.cpsc.gov

Eastern Regional Center
201 Varick Street, Room 903, New York, NY 10014
212-620-4120
Acting Director:
Vacant

Export Import Bank of the United States
Web site: www.exim.gov

Northeast Regional Office . . . . fax: 212-809-2687
Ted Weiss Federal Building, 290 Broadway, 13th Floor, New York, NY 10007
212-809-2650 Fax: 212-809-2687
Regional Director:
Gregory Smith 212-809-2652/fax: 212-809-2687
e-mail: gregory.smith@exim.gov

Federal Trade Commission
212-607-2829 Fax: 212-607-2822
Web site: www.ftc.gov

Northeast Regional Office . . . . fax: 212-607-2822
1 Bowling Green, New York, NY 10004
877-382-4357 Fax: 212-607-2822
Regional Director:
William H. Efron 212-607-2829

Small Business Administration
Web site: www.sba.gov

Region II New York . . . . fax: 212-264-4963
26 Federal Plaza, Suite 3108, New York, NY 10278
212-264-1450 Fax: 212-264-4963
Regional Administrator:
Kellie LeDet
Regional Communications Director:
Rita Chappelle

District Offices

Buffalo . . . . fax: 716-551-4418
130 South Elmwood Avenue, Suite 540, Buffalo, NY 14202
716-551-4301 Fax: 716-551-4418
District Director:
Franklin J Sciortino 716-551-4305/fax: 716-481-1974
e-mail: franklin.sciortino@sba.gov

New Jersey . . . . fax: 973-645-6265
2 Gateway Center, Suite 1501, Newark, NJ 07102
973-645-2434 Fax: 973-645-6265
District Director:
Alfred Titone 973-645-3680/fax: 202-481-6560
e-mail: alfred.titone@sba.gov

New York City . . . . fax: 212-264-4963
26 Federal Plaza, Suite 3100, New York, NY 10278
212-264-4354 Fax: 212-264-4963
District Director:
Beth Goldberg

Syracuse . . . . fax: 315-471-9288
224 Harrison Street, Suite 506, Syracuse, NY 13202
315-471-9393 Fax: 315-471-9288
District Director:
Bernard J Paprocki
e-mail: bernard.paprocki@sba.gov

New York Small Business Development Center
State University of New York, 10 North Pearl Street, Albany, NY 12246
800-732-7232 or 518-944-2840
Chair:
Brad Rosenstein

US Commerce Department
Web site: www.commerce.gov

Census Bureau
Web site: www.census.gov

New York Region
32 Old Slip, 9th Floor, New York, NY 10005
212-584-3400 or 800-991-2520
e-mail: new.york.regional.office@census.gov
Regional Director:
Jeff T. Behler. 212-584-3400/fax: 212-584-3402

Economic Development Administration
Web site: www.eda.gov

Philadelphia Region (includes New York)
The Curtis Center, 601 Walnut Street, Suite 140 South, Philadelphia, PA 19106
Regional Director:
Linda Cruz-Carnall 215-597-4603/fax: 215-597-1063
e-mail: lcruz-carnall@eda.gov

Minority Business Development Agency
Web site: www.mbda.gov

New York Region
26 Federal Plaza, New York, NY 10278
212-264-3262

New York Business Center
535 Fifth Avenue, 16th Floor, New York, NY 10017
646-821-4008
Project Director:
Paul Sawyer

South Bronx Business Center
555 Bergen Avenue, 3rd Floor, Bronx, NY 10455
718-732-7540
Project Director:
Sharon Higgins

Williamsburg Business Center
12 Heyward Street, 2nd Floor, Brooklyn, NY 11211
718-522-5620
Contact:
Yehuda Turner

National Oceanic & Atmospheric Administration

National Weather Service, Eastern Region
630 Johnson Avenue, Suite 202, Bohemia, NY 11716
Web site: www.weather.gov/erh/
Director:
Jason Tuell
e-mail: jason.tuell@noaa.gov
Deputy Director:
Mickey J Brown 631-244-0100
Regional Program Manager:
John Koch. 631-244-0104
e-mail: john.koch@noaa.gov
Regional Program Manager:
Jeff Waldstreicher. 631-244-0131
e-mail: jeff.waldstreicher@noaa.gov

Offices and agencies generally appear in alphabetical order, except when specific order is requested by listee.

Scientific Services Division Chief:
Kenneth Johnson
e-mail: kenneth.johnson@noaa.gov
Meteorological Services Division Chief:
John Guiney 631-244-0121
e-mail: john.guiney@noaa.gov

National Weather Service
Center for Environmental Science & Tech, 251 Fuller Road, Suite B-300, Albany, NY 12203-3640
Science & Operations Officer:
Warren Snyder 518-435-9580

US Commercial Service - International Trade Administration
Web site: www.trade.gov

Buffalo US Export Assistance Center
130 South Elmwood Avenue, Suite 530, Buffalo, NY 14202
e-mail: office.buffalo@trade.gov
Web site: www.export.gov/newyork/bflorochsyr
Director:
Rosanna Masucci 716-551-4191/fax: 716-551-5290
e-mail: rosanna.masucci@trade.gov

Harlem US Export Assistance Center . . . . fax: 212-860-6203
163 West 125th Street, Suite 901, New York, NY 10027
212-860-6200 Fax: 212-860-6203
e-mail: office.harlem@trade.gov
Web site: www.export.gov/newyork/harlem
USEAC Director:
K L Fredericks. 212-860-6200/fax: 212-860-6203
e-mail: kl.fredericks@trade.gov

Long Island US Export Assistance Center
Commercial Service Long Island, PO Box 423, Old Westbury, NY 11568-0210
e-mail: officelongislandny@trade.gov
Web site: www.export.gov/newyork/longisland
Director:
Susan Sadocha 516-427-9117
e-mail: susan.sadocha@trade.gov

New York US Export Assistance Center
Ted Weiss Federal Building, 290 Broadway, Suite 1312, New York, NY 10007
USEAC Director:
Carmela Mammas 212-809-2676/fax: 212-809-2687
e-mail: carmela.mammas@trade.gov

US Department of Agriculture

Rural Development
Web site: www.rd.usda.gov

New York State Office. . . . . fax: 315-477-6438
441 South Salina Street, Suite 357, Syracuse, NY 13202-2541
315-477-6400 Fax: 315-477-6438
Acting New York State Director:
Scott Collins 315-477-6437
Special Projects Coordinator:
Christopher Stewart

US Justice Department
Web site: www.justice.gov

Antitrust Division-New York Field Office . . . . fax: 212-335-8021
26 Federal Plaza, Room 3630, New York, NY 10278-0004
212-335-8000 Fax: 212-335-8021
e-mail: newyork.atr@usdoj.gov
Chief:
Jeffrey Martino
Assistant Chief:
Stephen J. McCahey

Civil Division-Commercial Litigation Branch
950 Pennsylvania Avenue NW, Washington, DC 20530-0001
202-514-2000
e-mail: civil.feedback@usdoj.gov
Principal Deputy Assistant Attorney General:
Benjamin C Mizer

Community Relations Service
600 East Street NW, Suite 6000, Washington, DC 20530
202-305-2935
e-mail: askcrs@usdoj.gov
Acting Director:
Paul Monteiro

Community Relations Service-Northeast & Caribbean Region
26 Federal Plaza, Suite 36-118, New York, NY 10278
CRS Conciliator:
Linda Ortiz

US Securities & Exchange Commission
Web site: www.sec.gov

New York Regional Office
200 Vesey Street, Suite 400, New York, NY 10281-1022
212-336-1100
e-mail: newyork@sec.gov
Regional Director:
Andrew Calamari 212-336-1100

Enforcement Division
Director:
Andrew Ceresney 202-551-4500

Investment Management
Director:
David Grim 202-551-6720

U.S. CONGRESS

See U.S. Congress Chapter for additional Standing Committee and Subcommittee information.

House of Representatives Standing Committees

Energy & Commerce
Chair:
Fred Upton (R-MI)
Ranking Member:
Frank Pallone (D-NJ)
New York Delegate:
Eliot L. Engel (D) 202-225-2464
New York Delegate:
Paul Tonko (D)
New York Delegate:
Yvette Clarke (D)
New York Delegate:
Chris Collins (R)

Foreign Affairs
Chair:
Edward R. Royce (R-CA)
Ranking Member:
Eliot L. Engel (D-NY)
New York Delegate:
Gregory W. Meeks (D)
New York Delegate:
Brian Higgins (D)
New York Delegate:
Grace Meng (D)

Offices and agencies generally appear in alphabetical order, except when specific order is requested by listee.

Policy Areas

New York Delegate:
Lee M. Zeldin (R)
New York Delegate:
Daniel Donovan (R)

Small Business
Chair:
Steve Chabot (R-OH)
Ranking Member:
Nydia Velazquez (D-NY)
New York Delegate:
Richard Hanna (R)
New York Delegate:
Chris Gibson (R)
New York Delegate:
Grace Meng (D)
New York Delegate:
Yvette Clarke (D)

Joint Senate & House Standing Committees

Economic Committee, Joint
Chair:
Daniel Coats (R-IN)
Vice Chair:
Pat Tiberi (R-OH)
Ranking Member:
Carolyn Maloney (D-NY)

Senate Standing Committees

Commerce, Science & Transportation
Chair:
John Thune (R-SD) 202-224-2321
Ranking Member:
Bill Nelson (D-FL)

Finance
Chair:
Orrin G. Hatch (R-UT) 202-224-5251
Ranking Member:
Ron Wyden (D-OR)

Foreign Relations
Chair:
Bob Corker (R-TN) 202-224-3344
Ranking Member:
Ben Cardin (D-MD)

Small Business & Entrepreneurship
Chair:
David Vitter (R-LA) 202-224-4623
Ranking Member:
Jeanne Shaheen (D-NH)

PRIVATE SECTOR

Altria Client Services
677 Broadway, Suite 1207, Albany, NY 12207
518-431-8090
Web site: www.altria.com
Manufacturing & marketing of foods, tobacco, alcoholic beverages
Martin J Barrington, Chairman & Chief Executive Officer

American Chemistry Council
One Commerce Plaza, 99 Washington Avenue, Suite 701, Albany, NY 12210
518-432-7835 Fax: 518-426-2276
e-mail: steve_rosario@americanchemistry.com
Web site: www.americanchemistry.com
Stephen Rosario, Director, Northeast Region

American Council of Engineering Companies of NY (ACEC New York)
6 Airline Drive, Albany, NY 12205
518-452-8611 Fax: 518-452-1710
e-mail: acecny@acecny.org
Web site: www.acecny.org
Business association for consulting engineering firms
Jay J Simson, President

American Institute of Architects (AIA) New York State Inc
50 State Street, 5th Floor, Albany, NY 12207
518-449-3334 Fax: 518-426-8176
e-mail: aianys@aianys.org
Web site: www.aianys.org
Architectural regulations, state policy, smart growth & affordable housing
Georgi Ann Bailey, Executive Director

American Management Association International
1601 Broadway, New York, NY 10019
212-586-8100 or 877-566-9441 Fax: 212-891-0368
Web site: www.amanet.org
Business education & management training programs for individuals & organizations
Edward T Reilly, President & Chief Executive Officer

Associated Builders & Contractors, Empire State Chapter
6369 Collamer Road East, Syracuse, NY 13057
315-463-7539 or 800-477-7743 Fax: 315-463-7621
e-mail: empire@abcnys.org
Web site: www.abcnys.org
Merit shop construction trade association
Brian Sampson, President

Associated General Contractors of America, NYS Chapter
10 Airline Drive, Suite 203, Albany, NY 12205-1025
518-456-1134 Fax: 518-456-1198
e-mail: agcadmin@agcnys.org
Web site: www.agcnys.org
Represents contractors & companies in the construction industry
Michael J Elmendorf II, President & Chief Executive Officer

Association Development Group Inc
136 Everett Road, Albany, NY 12205
518-465-7085 Fax: 518-427-9495
e-mail: info@adgcommunications.com
Web site: www.adgcommunications.com
Association management, communications, education & training, strategic planning, leadership & membership support, advocacy, database design
Kathleen A Van De Loo, President & Chief Executive Officer

Association for a Better New York
355 Lexington Avenue, 8th Floor, New York, NY 10017
212-370-5800 Fax: 212-661-5877
Web site: www.abny.org
Networking & advocacy for the development of businesses & communities in New York
Angela Pinsky, Executive Director

Better Business Bureau of Metropolitan New York
30 East 33rd Street, 12th Floor, New York, NY 10016
212-533-6200 Fax: 212-477-4912
e-mail: inquiry@newyork.bbb.org
Web site: www.bbb.org/new-york-city
Membership organization promoting ethical business practices
Claire Rosenzweig, President & Chief Executive Officer

Brown & Kelly, LLP
800 Main Place Tower, 350 Main Street, Buffalo, NY 14202
716-854-2620 Fax: 716-854-0082
e-mail: mail@brownkelly.com
Kenneth A. Krajewski, Managing Partner

Building Contractors Association
451 Park Avenue South, 4th Floor, New York, NY 10016
212-683-8080 Fax: 212-683-0404
e-mail: johare@ny-bca.com
Web site: www.ny-bca.com
Association representing construction organizations in New York
John O'Hare, Assistant Managing Director

Building Industry Association of NYC Inc
3130 Amboy Road, Staten Island, NY 10306
718-720-3070 Fax: 718-720-3088
e-mail: jessica@webuildnyc.com
Web site: www.webuildnyc.com
Jessica Fortino, Executive Officer

Business Council for International Understanding
1501 Broadway, Suite 2300, New York, NY 10018
212-490-0460 Fax: 212-697-8526
Web site: www.bciu.org
Promotes relationships between business & government leaders & provides services to develop international commerce & trade
Peter J Tichansky, President & Chief Executive Officer

Business Council of New York State Inc
152 Washington Avenue, Albany, NY 12210
518-465-7511 or 800-358-1202 Fax: 518-465-4389
e-mail: heather.briccetti@bcnys.org
Web site: www.bcnys.org
Business organization representing the interests of firms in New York State
Heather C. Briccetti, President & Chief Executive Officer

Center for Economic Growth Inc
39 North Pearl Street, Suite 100, Albany, NY 12207
518-465-8975 Fax: 518-465-6681
e-mail: ceg@ceg.org
Web site: www.ceg.org
Business membership non-profit promoting economic & business development in the Capital Region and Tech Valley
Michael J. Hickey, Interim President & Chief Executive Officer

Columbia University, Technology Ventures
80 Claremont Avenue, 4th Floor, New York, NY 10027
212-854-8444 Fax: 212-854-8463
e-mail: techventures@columbia.edu
Web site: www.techventures.columbia.edu
Identifies & patents new products & transfers inventions from academic research to industry organizations
Orin Herskowitz, Executive Director

Conference Board (The)
845 Third Avenue, New York, NY 10022-6600
212-759-0900 or 212-339-0345
e-mail: matteo.tonello@conferenceboard.org
Web site: www.conference-board.org
Research for business
Matteo Tonello, Vice President & Managing Director

Construction Contractors Association of the Hudson Valley Inc
330 Meadow Avenue, Newburgh, NY 12550
845-562-4280 Fax: 845-562-1448
e-mail: info@ccahv.com
Web site: www.ccahv.com
Association representing commercial & industrial building contractors in Hudson Valley
A. Alan Seidman, Executive Director

Consumers Union
101 Truman Avenue, Yonkers, NY 10703-1057
914-378-2000 Fax: 914-378-2900
Web site: www.consumerreports.org; www.consumersunion.org
Publisher of Consumer Reports magazine; independent, nonprofit organization serving consumers through marketplace testing & research
Marta Tellado, President & Chief Executive Officer

Cornell University, Economics Department
404 Uris Hall, Ithaca, NY 14853
607-255-4254 Fax: 607-255-2818
e-mail: lb19@cornell.edu
Web site: www.economics.cornell.edu
Economic research; microeconomic theory & financial economics
Lawerence Blume, Chair

Dale Carnegie & Associates Inc
780 Third Avenue, New York, NY 10017
212-750-4455 or 800-231-5800
Web site: www.dalecarnegie.com
Executive leadership training
Joseph K. Hart, President & Chief Executive Officer

Davis Polk & Wardwell
450 Lexington Avenue, New York, NY 10017
212-450-4000 Fax: 212-701-5800
e-mail: gencoun@davispolk.com
Web site: www.davispolk.com
Securities litigation & antitrust law
Charles S. Duggan, General Counsel

Development Counsellors International
215 Park Avenue South, 14th Floor, New York, NY 10003
212-725-0707 Fax: 212-725-2254
Web site: www.aboutdci.com
Marketing services for economic development & tourism
Andrew T Levine, President & Chief Creative Officer

EVCI Career Colleges Holding Corp
1 Van Der Donck Street, Yonkers, NY 10701-7049
914-623-0700 Fax: 914-964-8222
Owns & operates accredited career & college centers in NY & PA emphasizing business, technology & allied health programs
Vacant, President & Chief Executive Officer

Eastern Contractors Association Inc
6 Airline Drive, Albany, NY 12205-1095
518-869-0961 Fax: 518-869-2378
e-mail: info@ecainc.org
Web site: www.ecainc.org
Commercial development & construction
Todd G Helfrich, President & Chief Executive Officer

Eastman Kodak Company
343 State Street, Rochester, NY 14650
585-724-4000 or 866-563-2533
Web site: www.kodak.com
Manufactures & markets imaging systems & related services
Terry Taber, Senior Vice President & Chief Technical Officer

Empire Center for New York State Policy
100 State Street, Suite 600, Albany, NY 12207
518-434-3100 Fax: 518-434-3130
e-mail: info@empirecenter.org
Web site: www.empirecenter.org
An independent non-profit organization working to foster economic growth & freedom in New York State through research & education
Edmund J McMahon, President

Empire State Restaurant & Tavern Association Inc
12 Sheridan Avenue, Albany, NY 12207
518-436-8121 Fax: 518-436-7287
e-mail: esrta@verizon.net
Web site: www.esrta.org
Grassroots organization promoting the interests of on-premise beverage alcohol licensees
Scott Wexler, Executive Director

Policy Areas

Offices and agencies generally appear in alphabetical order, except when specific order is requested by listee.

Empire State Society of Association Executives Inc
120 Defreest Drive, Suite 1, Troy, NY 12180
518-463-1755 Fax: 518-463-5257
e-mail: vanessa@essae.org
Web site: www.essae.org
Education, information, research & networking for professional staff of trade, business & professional associations
Vanessa E. LaClair, Executive Director

Eric Mower & Associates
211 West Jefferson Street, Syracuse, NY 13202
315-466-1000 Fax: 315-466-2000
e-mail: csteenstra@mower.com
Web site: www.mower.com
Marketing communications & issues management
Chris Steenstra, Managing Partner

NYS Bar Assn, Antitrust Law Section
Federal Trade Commission
1 Bowling Green, Suite 318, New York, NY 10004
212-607-2829
Edith Ramirez, Chair

Food Industry Alliance of New York State Inc
130 Washington Avenue, Albany, NY 12210
518-434-1900 Fax: 518-434-9962
e-mail: michael@fiany.com
Web site: www.fiany.com
Association of retail grocery, cooperative, wholesale & supplier/manufacturer food companies
Michael Rosen, President & Chief Executive Officer

General Contractors Association of NY
60 East 42nd Street, Suite 3510, New York, NY 10165-3598
212-687-3131 Fax: 212-808-5267
e-mail: info@gcany.net
Web site: www.gcany.com
Heavy construction, transportation
Denise M. Richardson, Executive Director

Gilbert Tweed Associates Inc
415 Madison Avenue, 20th Floor, New York, NY 10017
212-758-3000 Fax: 212-832-1040
e-mail: spinson@gilberttweed.com
Web site: www.gilberttweed.com
Executive searches in public transit, transportation, energy, utilities, communication & insurance
Stephanie L Pinson, President

NYS Bar Assn, Intellectual Property Law Section
Hartman & Winnicki, PC
West 115 Century Road, Suite 120, Paramus, NJ 07652
201-967-8040 Fax: 201-967-0590
e-mail: rick@ravin.com
Web site: www.hartmanwinnicki.com
Richard L. Ravin, Member

IBM Corporation
1 New Orchard Road, Armonk, NY 10504-1722
914-499-1900
Web site: www.ibm.com
Technology & business consulting company
Virginia M. Rometty, President & Chief Executive Officer

International Flavors & Fragrances Inc
521 West 57th Street, New York, NY 10019-2960
212-765-5500 Fax: 212-708-7132
Web site: www.iff.com
Creates & manufactures flavors & fragrances for consumer products
Andreas Fibig, Chairman & Chief Executive Officer

Macy's Inc
151 West 34th Street, New York, NY 10001
212-494-3000
Retail department/specialty stores
Edward Jay Goldberg, Senior Vice President Government & Consumer Affairs

Manhattan Institute for Policy Research
52 Vanderbilt Avenue, 2nd Floor, New York, NY 10017
212-599-7000 Fax: 212-599-3494
e-mail: communications@manhattan-institute.org
Web site: www.manhattan-institute.org
Produces & promotes research on taxes, welfare, education & other public policy issues
Lawrence J. Mone, President

Manufacturers Association of Central New York
5788 Wildewaters Parkway, Suite 5, Syracuse, NY 13214
315-474-4201 Fax: 315-474-0524
e-mail: kburns@macny.org
Web site: www.macny.org
Association of manufacturers providing training, networking opportunities, advocacy, purchasing solutions, resources & services for members
Karyn Burns, Vice President, Communications & Government Relations

NYS Bar Assn, Business Law Section
Menaker & Herrmann LLP
10 East 40th Street, New York, NY 10016
212-545-1900 Fax: 212-545-1656
e-mail: info@mhjur.com
Web site: www.mhjur.com
Offers counsel in Antitrust, Corporate/Commercial Transactions, Commercial Litigation, Commodities, Futures & Derivatives
Samuel F. Abernethy, Partner

Mid-Hudson Pattern for Progress
3 Washington Center, Newburgh, NY 12550
845-565-4900 Fax: 845-565-4918
e-mail: rdegroat@pfprogress.org
Web site: www.pattern-for-progress.org
Regional planning, research & policy development
Jonathan Drapkin, President & Chief Executive Officer

NY Society of Association Executives Inc (NYSAE)
322 Eighth Avenue, Suite 702, New York, NY 10001-8001
212-206-8230 Fax: 212-645-1147
e-mail: info@nysaenet.org
Web site: www.nysaenet.org
Association dedicated to advancing the interests of members of not-for-profit organizations in metropolitan NY
Joel A. Dolci, President & Chief Executive Officer

NYS Association of Electrical Contractors
PO Box 807, Latham, NY 12110
518-852-0154 or 800-724-1904 Fax: 518-713-2627
e-mail: jfm@nysaec.org
Web site: www.nysaec.org
Represents the interests of electrical contractors
Jay Mangione, Executive Director

NYS Builders Association Inc
152 Washington Avenue, Albany, NY 12210
518-465-2492 Fax: 518-465-0635
e-mail: info@nysba.com
Web site: www.nysba.com
Advocates for the advancement of the building & housing industry; provides programs, research & education for members
Lewis Dubuque, Executive Vice President

Offices and agencies generally appear in alphabetical order, except when specific order is requested by listee.

NYS Building & Construction Trades Council
50 State Street, 3rd Floor, Albany, NY 12207
518-435-9108 Fax: 518-435-9204
e-mail: nybuildingtrades@me.com
Web site: www.nybuildingtrades.com
Represents the interests & protects the rights of unionized construction workers in New York
James Cahill, President

NYS Clinical Laboratory Association Inc
394 Waverly Avenue, Brooklyn, NY 11238
718-857-0414 Fax: 718-857-5628
e-mail: info@nyscla.com
Web site: www.nyscla.com
Not-for-profit trade association dedicated to advancing the business interests of New York State's clinical laboratory industry
Thomas Rafalsky, President

NYS Economic Development Council
111 Washington Avenue, 6th Floor, Albany, NY 12210
518-426-4058 Fax: 518-426-4059
e-mail: mcmahon@nysedc.org
Web site: www.nysedc.org
Economic development professionals membership organization
Brian T. McMahon, Executive Director

NYS Society of Certified Public Accountants
14 Wall Street, 19th Floor, New York, NY 10005
800-537-3635 Fax: 866-495-1354
e-mail: jbarry@nysscpa.org
Web site: www.nysscpa.org
Advocacy & information for the certified public accountants of New York State
Joanne S. Barry, Executive Director

NYS Trade Adjustment Assistance Center
81 State Street, Suite 4, Binghamton, NY 13901
607-771-0875 or 844-279-0705 Fax: 607-724-2404
e-mail: info@nystaac.org
Web site: www.nystaac.org
Offers aid to New York manufacturers & service companies that are competing with foreign imports
Louis G. McKeage, Director

National Association of Black Accountants, NY Chapter
PO Box 2791, Grand Central Station, New York, NY 10163
212-969-0560 Fax: 646-349-9620
e-mail: info@nabany.org
Web site: www.nabany.org
Represents the interests of African Americans & other minorities in the fields of accounting, auditing, business, consulting, finance & information technology
Rosalind P. Danner, President

National Federation of Independent Business
100 State Street, Suite 440, Albany, NY 12207
518-434-1262 or 609-989-8777 Fax: 518-426-8799
e-mail: mike.durant@nfib.org
Web site: www.nfib.com/new-york/
Small business advocacy; supporting pro-small business candidates at the state & federal levels
Michael P. Durant, State Director

New York Association of Convenience Stores
130 Washington Avenue, Suite 300, Albany, NY 12210-2219
518-432-1400 Fax: 518-432-7400
e-mail: info@nyacs.org
Web site: www.nyacs.org
Serves New York State's convenience store industry
Jim Calvin, President

New York Biotechnology Association (The)
205 East 42nd Street, 14th Floor, New York, NY 10017
212-433-2623 Fax: 212-433-0779
e-mail: info@nyba.org
Web site: www.newyorkbio.org
Promotes the development & growth of NYS-based biotechnology and life science research organizations through the provision of services & information
Nathan P. Tinker, PhD, Executive Director

New York Building Congress
44 West 28th Street, 12th Floor, New York, NY 10001-4212
212-481-9230 Fax: 212-447-6037
e-mail: info@buildingcongress.com
Web site: www.buildingcongress.com
Membership association dedicated to advancing New York City's construction industry
Richard T. Anderson, President

New York Business Development Corporation
50 Beaver Street, Suite 500, Albany, NY 12207
518-463-2268 Fax: 518-463-0240
e-mail: mackrell@nybdc.com
Web site: www.nybdc.com
Small business lending; loan programs
Patrick J. MacKrell, President & Chief Executive Officer

New York Mercantile Exchange Inc
1 North End Avenue, New York, NY 10282-1101
212-299-2000 Fax: 212-301-4568
Web site: www.cmegroup.com
Commodity trading
Terrence A. Duffy, Executive Chairman & President

New York State Auto Dealers Association
37 Elk Street, Albany, NY 12207
518-463-1148 Fax: 518-432-1309
Web site: www.nysada.com
Association representing vehicle dealers in New York State
Robert Vancavage, President

New York State Restaurant Association
409 New Karner Road, Suite 202, Albany, NY 12205
518-452-4222 or 800-452-5212 Fax: 518-452-4497
e-mail: info@nysra.org
Web site: www.nysra.org
Promotes and protects the food service industry in New York State
Melissa Autilio Fleischut, President & Chief Executive Officer

New York Technology Council
307 West 38th Street, 13th Floor, New York, NY 10018
646-435-1088
e-mail: info@nytech.org
Web site: www.nytech.org
Promotes New York City's technology industry
Erik Grimmelmann, President & Chief Executive Officer

New York University Stern School of Business, Berkley Center for Entrepreneurship & Innovation
40 West Fourth Street, Suite 400, New York, NY 10012
212-998-0070
Web site: www.stern.nyu.edu
Programs & services designed to provide venture development assistance to NYU students, researchers & entrepreneurs
Luke Williams, Executive Director

Policy Areas

Offices and agencies generally appear in alphabetical order, except when specific order is requested by listee.

Northeast Equipment Dealers Association Inc
128 Metropolitan Park Drive, Liverpool, NY 13088
315-457-0314 or 800-932-0607 Fax: 315-451-3548
e-mail: rgaiss@ne-equip.com
Web site: www.ne-equip.org
Association of agricultural, industrial & outdoor power equipment dealers in the Northeast region of the US
Ralph Gaiss, Executive VP & CEO

Partnership for New York City
One Battery Park Plaza, 5th Floor, New York, NY 10004-1479
212-493-7400 or 212-493-7548 Fax: 212-344-3344
Web site: www.pfnyc.org
Business organization working in partnership with government, labor & the nonprofit sectors to develop New York City's economy
Kathryn S. Wylde, President & Chief Executive Officer

Pepsi Co
700 Anderson Hill Road, MD 3/1-311, Purchase, NY 10577
914-253-2000 Fax: 914-253-2070
Web site: www.pepsi.com
Manufactures, sells & distributes soft drinks, concentrates, syrups, snack foods & beverages
Indra K. Nooyi, Chairman & Chief Executive Officer

Perry Davis Associates
25 West 45th Street, Suite 1405, New York, NY 10036
212-840-1166 Fax: 212-840-1514
e-mail: perry@perrydavis.com
Web site: www.perrydavis.com
Economic development, training, fundraising & management consulting for nonprofit organizations
Perry Davis, President

Printing Industries Alliance
636 North French Road, Suite 1, Amherst, NY 14228
716-691-3211 or 800-777-4742 Fax: 716-691-4249
e-mail: tfreeman@pialliance.org
Web site: www.pialliance.org
Trade association providing services & support for the graphic communications industry of NY, Northern NJ & Northwestern PA
Timothy Freeman, President

NYS Bar Assn, Multi-jurisdictional Practice Cmte
Proskauer Rose LLP
11 Times Square, New York, NY 10036
212-969-3000 Fax: 212-969-2900
e-mail: info@proskauer.com
Web site: www.proskauer.com
Klaus Eppler, Partner

Public Policy Institute of NYS Inc
152 Washington Avenue, Albany, NY 12210
518-465-7511 Fax: 518-432-4537
Web site: www.ppinys.org
Conducts & publishes research on NYS economic development issues
Heather C. Briccetti, President & Chief Executive Officer

Regional Plan Association
4 Irving Place, 7th Floor, New York, NY 10003
212-253-2727 Fax: 212-253-5666
e-mail: twright@rpa.org
Web site: www.rpa.org
Association seeking to enhance economic development & quality of life in the New York metropolitan region through advocacy & research
Thomas K. Wright, President

Retail Council of New York State
258 State Street, Albany, NY 12210
518-465-3586 or 800-442-3589 Fax: 518-465-7960
e-mail: info@retailcouncilnys.com
Web site: www.retailcouncilnys.com
Serves retailers, merchants & other goods & services providers based in New York State
Ted Potrikus, President & Chief Executive Officer

Software & Information Industry Association
1090 Vermont Avenue NW, 6th Floor, Washington, DC 20005-4095
202-289-7442 Fax: 202-289-7097
Web site: www.siia.net
Issues affecting the software & information industry, in particular electronic commerce & the digital marketplace
Ken Wasch, President

Support Services Alliance Inc
165 Main Street, Oneida, NY 13421
315-363-6584
Payroll services for businesses
Steven Cole, Chief Executive Officer

The New York State Society of Professional Engineers Inc (NYSSPE)
6 Airline Drive, Suite 114, Albany, NY 12205
518-283-7490 Fax: 518-283-7495
Web site: www.nysspe.org
Represents professional engineers in NYS & promotes the ethical practice of engineering
Anthony Fasano, Executive Director

UHY Advisors
4 Tower Place, Executive Park, 7th Floor, Albany, NY 12203
518-449-3171 Fax: 518-449-5832
e-mail: hfoote@uhy-us.com
Web site: www.uhy-us.com
Professional financial, tax, business & tax advisory services for mid-sized to larger companies
Howard Foote, Managing Director & Chief Financial Officer

Wegmans Food Markets Inc
1500 Brooks Avenue, PO Box 30844, Rochester, NY 14603-0844
585-464-4760 or 800-934-6267 Fax: 585-464-4669
Web site: www.wegmans.com
Mary Ellen Burris, Senior Vice President, Consumer Affairs

Women's Business Center of New York State
200 Genesee Street, Utica, NY 13502
315-733-9848 or 877-844-9848 Fax: 315-733-0247
e-mail: nywbc@aol.com
Web site: www.nywbc.org
Dedicated to helping women reach their entrepreneurial goals & aspirations through assistance & training
Donna L. Rebisz, Project Director

Women's Venture Fund Inc
220 Fifth Avenue, 9th Floor, New York, NY 10001
212-563-0499
e-mail: info@wvf-ny.org
Web site: www.womensventurefund.org
Provides support for women entrepreneurs through training, advisory services, loans & technical assistance
Maria Otero, President & Founder

Zogby Analytics
901 Broad Street, Utica, NY 13501
315-624-9642
Web site: www.zogbyanalytics.com
Polling, surveys, focus groups, market research studies & data analysis for businesses & communities
Jonathan Zogby, Chief Executive Officer

CORPORATIONS, AUTHORITIES & COMMISSIONS

NEW YORK STATE

Adirondack Park Agency
1133 NYS Route 86
PO Box 99
Ray Brook, NY 12977
518-891-4050 Fax: 518-891-3938
Web site: www.apa.ny.gov

Chair:
Leilani Ulrich 518-891-4050
Executive Director:
Terry Martino 518-891-4050
Counsel:
James Townsend 518-891-4050
Public Relations:
Keith McKeever 518-891-4050
e-mail: keith.mckeever@apa.y.gov

Agriculture & NYS Horse Breeding Development Fund
1 Broadway Center
Suite 602
Schenectady, NY 12305
518-388-0178 Fax: 518-347-1483
e-mail: info@nysirestakes.com
Web site: www.nysirestakes.com

Acting Executive Director:
Ron Ochrym 518-388-0178
Counsel:
Mark Stuart 518-388-0178

Albany County Airport Authority
Albany International Airport
Administration Building
2nd Floor
Albany, NY 12211
518-242-2222 x1 Fax: 518-242-2641
e-mail: info@albanyairport.com
Web site: www.albanyairport.com/airport-authority.php

Chief Executive Officer:
John A O'Donnell PE 518-242-2222 x1
Chief Financial Officer:
William O'Reilly 518-242-2222 x1
Director, Public Affairs:
Douglas I. Myers 518-242-2222 x1
Counsel:
Peter F Stuto. 518-242-2222 x1
Airport Planner:
Stephen A Iachetta 518-242-2222 x1
Administrative Services:
Liz Charland 518-242-2222 x1

Albany Port District Commission
106 Smith Blvd, Admin Bldg
Port of Albany
Albany, NY 12202
518-463-8763 Fax: 518-463-8767
e-mail: portofalbany@portofalbany.us
Web site: www.portofalbany.us

Chair:
Georgette Steffens. 518-463-8763
General Manager:
Richard Hendrick 518-463-8763
e-mail: rhendrick@portofalbany.us
Counsel:
Thomas Owens 518-694-0910

Atlantic States Marine Fisheries Commission
1050 N. Highland Street
Ste 200 A-N
Arlington, VA 22201
703-842-0740 Fax: 703-842-0741
e-mail: info@asmfc.org
Web site: www.asmfc.org

Chair (NH):
Douglas E Grout 603-868-1095
e-mail: douglas.grout@wildlife.nh.gov
Vice Chair (NY):
James Gilmore. 631-444-0433
Governor's Appointee, New York:
Emerson C Hasbrouck, Jr 631-928-1524
Executive Director:
Robert E Beal 703-842-0740
e-mail: rbeal@asmfc.org
Director Communications:
Tina Berger 703-842-0740
e-mail: tberger@asmfc.org

Battery Park City Authority (Hugh L Carey)
One World Financial Center, 24th Fl
200 Liberty Street
New York, NY 10281
212-417-2000 Fax: 212-417-2001
e-mail: info.bpc@bpca.ny.gov
Web site: www.bpca.ny.gov

Chairman & CEO:
Dennis Mehiel. 212-417-2000
President & Chief Operating Officer:
Shari Hyman 212-417-4205/fax: 212-417-4153
Vice Chair:
Donald Cappocia. 212-417-2000
Member:
Hector Batista 212-417-2000
Member:
Lester Petracca 212-417-2000
Member:
Martha J Gallo. 212-417-2000
VP External Relations:
Robin Forst 212-417-2276/fax: 212-417-2279
e-mail: robin.forst@bpca.ny.gov

Brooklyn Navy Yard Development Corporation
63 Flushing Ave, Unit #300
Bldg 292, 3rd Fl
Brooklyn, NY 11205
718-907-5900 Fax: 718-643-9296
e-mail: info@brooklynnavyyard.org
Web site: www.brooklynnavyyard.org

Chair:
Henry Gutman. 718-907-5900
President & Chief Executive Officer:
David Ehrenberg. 718-907-5900
Executive Vice President/Chief Operating Officer:
Elliot S. Matz 718-907-5900

Offices and agencies generally appear in alphabetical order, except when specific order is requested by listee.

Policy Areas

General Counsel:
Paul Kelly 718-907-5900
EVP/Chief of Staff:
Clare Newman 718-907-5900
Senior Vice President, External Affairs:
Richard Drucker 718-907-5900

Buffalo & Fort Erie Public Bridge Authority (Peace Bridge Authority)
One Peace Bridge Plaza
Buffalo, NY 14213-2494
716-884-6744 Fax: 716-884-2089
Web site: www.peacebridge.com

Chair (US):
William Hoyt 716-884-6744/fax: 716-883-7246
Vice Chair (Canada):
Anthony M Annunziata 716-884-6744/fax: 716-883-7246
General Manager:
Ron Rienas 716-884-6744

Capital District Regional Off-Track Betting Corporation
510 Smith St
Schenectady, NY 12305
518-344-5266 or 800-292-2387 Fax: 518-370-5460
e-mail: customerservice@capitalotb.com
Web site: www.capitalotb.com

Chair:
Marcel Webb.. 518-344-5225
Board Secretary & Director:
F James Mumpton.. 518-344-5225
President & Chief Executive Officer:
John F Signor 518-344-5225
VP, Corporate Operations:
Tod Grenci 518-344-5408
VP, Legal Affairs/General Counsel:
Robert Hemsworth 518-344-5298
VP, Finance/Comptroller:
Nancy Priputen-Madrian 518-344-5233
VP, Human Resources:
Robert Dantz.. 518-344-5301

Capital District Regional Planning Commission
One Park Place
Suite 102
Albany, NY 12205
518-453-0850 Fax: 518-453-0856
e-mail: cdrpc@cdrpc.org
Web site: www.cdrpc.org

Executive Director:
Rocco A Ferraro 518-453-0850
e-mail: rocky@cdrpc.org
Financial Officer:
Tim Canty 518-453-0850

Capital District Transportation Authority
110 Watervliet Ave
Albany, NY 12206
518-437-8300 or 518-482-8822 Fax: 518-437-8318
Web site: www.cdta.org

Chair:
David M Stackrow 518-437-8311
Vice Chair:
Georgeanna Nugent Lussier 518-437-8311
CEO:
Carm Basile 518-437-6840/fax: 518-437-8349
e-mail: carmb@cdta.org
General Counsel:
Amanda A Avery........................ 518-437-8315/fax: 518-437-8318
e-mail: amandaa@cdta.org
VP, Finance & Administration:
Michael P Collins 518-437-8330/fax: 518-437-8347
e-mail: mikec@cdta.org
Director of Transportation:
Frederick C Gilliam........................ 518-437-8372/fax: 518-437-8328
e-mail: fredg@cdta.org
VP, Planning & Infrastructure:
Christopher G Desany 518-437-8320/fax: 518-437-8328
e-mail: chrisd@cdta.org

Catskill Off-Track Betting Corporation
Park Place
Box 3000
Pomona, NY 10970
845-362-0407 Fax: 845-362-0419
e-mail: otb@interbets.com; customerservice@interbets.com
Web site: www.interbets.com

President:
Donald J Groth 845-362-0400

Central New York Regional Market Authority
2100 Park St
Syracuse, NY 13208
315-422-8647 Fax: 315-422-6897
Web site: cnyrma.com

Acting Commissioner of Agricultural Markets:
Richard A Ball 315-422-8647
Commissioner's Representative:
Troy Waffner 315-422-8647

Central New York Regional Transportation Authority
200 Cortland Ave
PO Box 820
Syracuse, NY 13205-0820
315-442-3400 Fax: 315-442-3337
Web site: www.centro.org

Chair, Board of Directors:
Brian M Schultz 315-442-3300
CEO:
Richard Lee.. 315-442-3360
VP, Finance:
Christine LoCurto 315-442-3355
Counsel:
Barry Shulman 315-442-3400

Central Pine Barrens Joint Planning & Policy Commission
624 Old Riverhead Road
Westhampton Beach, NY 11978
631-288-1079 Fax: 631-288-1367
e-mail: info@pb.state.ny.us
Web site: www.pb.state.ny.us

Chair & Governor's Appointee & Region 1 Director DEC:
Peter A Scully.. 631-288-1079
Member & Suffolk County Executive:
Steve Bellone 631-288-1079
Member & Brookhaven Town Supervisor:
Edward P. Romaine 631-288-1079

Offices and agencies generally appear in alphabetical order, except when specific order is requested by listee.

Member & Riverhead Town Supervisor:
Sean M Walter 631-288-1079
Member & Southampton Town Supervisor:
Anna E Throne-Holst 631-288-1079

City University Construction Fund
555 W 57th St, 10th Fl
New York, NY 10019
212-541-0171 Fax: 212-541-0175

Interim Executive Director:
Judith Bergtraum....................................646-664-2605
e-mail: iris.weinshall@mail.cuny.edu
Counsel:
Frederick Schaffer....................................646-664-9210
e-mail: frederick.schaffer@mail-cuny.edu

Delaware River Basin Commission
25 State Police Drive
PO Box 7360
West Trenton, NJ 08628-0360
609-883-9500 Fax: 609-883-9522
Web site: www.nj.gov/drbc

New York Member/Chair:
Andrew M Cuomo 518-474-8390
Executive Director:
Steve Tambini 609-883-9500 x200
e-mail: steve.tambini@drbc.nj.gov
Commission Secretary & Assistant General Counsel:
Pamela Bush 609-883-9500 x203
e-mail: pamela.bush@drbc.nj.gov
General Counsel:
Kenneth J Warren 484-383-4834
e-mail: kwarren@warrenenvcounsel.com
Communications Manager:
Clarke Rupert....................................609-883-9500 x260
e-mail: clarke.rupert@drbc.nj.gov

Development Authority of the North Country
317 Washington Street
Watertown, NY 13601
315-661-3200
e-mail: info@danc.org
Web site: www.danc.org

Chair:
Gary Turck 315-661-3200
Executive Director:
James Wright 315-661-3200
Deputy Executive Director:
Thomas R Sauter....................................315-661-3200
e-mail: tsauter@danc.org
Director, Engineering:
Carrie Tuttle 315-661-3210
Telecom Division Manager:
David Wolf 315-661-3200
e-mail: oatn@danc.org
Landfill Superintendent:
Steve McElwain 315-661-3230
Director, Regional Development:
Michelle Capone....................................315-661-3200

Empire State Development Corporation
633 Third Avenue
New York, NY 10017
212-803-3100
e-mail: capitaldist@esd.ny.gov
Web site: www.esd.ny.gov

625 Broadway
Albany, NY 12207
518-292-5200

95 Perry Street
Ste 500
Buffalo, NY 14203
716-846-8200
Fax: 716-846-8260

President & CEO:
Howard Zemsky 212-803-3700
e-mail: president@esd.ny.gov
Business Attraction & Expansion:
John Gilstrap....................................212-803-3700
Public Affairs:
Kay Sarlin Wright....................................800-260-7313
e-mail: esdpressoffice@esd.ny.gov
Chief of Staff & COO:
Mehul J. Patel 212-803-3700

Great Lakes Commission
2805 S Industrial Hwy
Ste 100
Ann Arbor, MI 48104-6791
734-971-9135 Fax: 734-971-9150
e-mail: teder@glc.org
Web site: www.glc.org

Chairman:
Jon W Allan 517-284-5035
e-mail: allanj@michigan.gov
Acting New York State Commissioner:
Basil Seggos 518-402-8540/fax: 518-402-8541
e-mail: joseph.martens@dec.ny.gov
Executive Director:
Tim A Eder 734-971-9135
e-mail: teder@glc.org
Deputy Director:
Thomas R Crane....................................734-971-9135
e-mail: tcrane@glc.org
CIO:
Stephen J Cole 734-971-9135
e-mail: scole@glc.org
Program Director:
Victoria Pebbles 734-971-9135
e-mail: vpebbles@glc.org
Communications Director:
Beth Wanamaker....................................734-971-9135
e-mail: beth@glc.org
Policy Director:
Matthew Doss....................................734-971-9135
e-mail: mdoss@glc.org

Hudson River-Black River Regulating District
Hudson River Area Office
350 Northern Blvd, Ste 304
Albany, NY 12204
518-465-3491 Fax: 518-432-2485
e-mail: hrao@hrbrrd.com
Web site: www.hrbrrd.com

Chair:
Mark M Finkle 518-465-3491
Executive Director (Acting):
Richard J Ferrara....................................518-465-3491
Chief Engineer:
Robert S Foltan....................................518-465-3491

Offices and agencies generally appear in alphabetical order, except when specific order is requested by listee.

Chief Fiscal Officer:
Richard J Ferrara 518-465-3491
General Counsel:
Robert P Leslie 518-465-3491

Interest on Lawyer Account (IOLA) Fund of the State of NY

11 East 44th St
Ste 1406
New York, NY 10017
646-865-1541 or 800-222-4652 Fax: 646-865-1545
e-mail: iolaf@iola.org
Web site: www.iola.org

Chair:
Mary Rothwell Davis 646-865-1541
Executive Director:
Christopher O'Malley 646-865-1541
General Counsel:
Christine M Fecko 646-865-1541
Director of Administration:
Michele D Agard 646-865-1541

Interstate Environmental Commission

2800 Victory Blvd
6S-106
Staten Island, NY 10314
718-982-3792 Fax: 718-698-8472
e-mail: iecmail@iec-nynjct.org
Web site: www.iec-nynjct.org

Chair (CT):
Patricia Sesto 212-967-1414
Vice Chair (NY):
Judith L Baron 212-967-1414
Vice Chair (NJ):
John M Scagnelli 212-967-1414
Senior Manager:
Evelyn R Powers 212-967-1414

Interstate Oil & Gas Compact Commission

PO Box 53127
900 NE 23rd St
Oklahoma City, OK 73152-3127
405-525-3556 Fax: 405-525-3592
e-mail: iogcc@iogcc.state.ok.us
Web site: www.iogcc.ok.gov

Chair:
Governor Mary Fallin (OK) 405-525-3556
Vice Chair:
David Porter 405-525-3556
Executive Director:
Mike Smith 405-525-3556
New York State Official Representative:
Bradley J Field 518-402-8076
Communications Manager:
Carol Booth 405-525-3556

Lake George Park Commission

75 Fort George Rd
PO Box 749
Lake George, NY 12845
518-668-9347 Fax: 518-668-5001
e-mail: info@lgpc.state.ny.us
Web site: www.lgpc.state.ny.us

Chair:
Bruce E Young 518-668-9347
Executive Director:
David Wick 518-668-9347
e-mail: dave@lgpc.state.ny.us
Counsel:
Eileen Haynes 518-668-9347
Director of Law Enforcement:
F. Joe Johns 518-668-9347
e-mail: jjohns@lgpc.state.ny.us
Director, Operations:
Keith Fish 518-668-9347
e-mail: keith@lgpc.state.ny.us

Lawyers' Fund for Client Protection

119 Washington Ave
Albany, NY 12210
518-434-1935 or 800-442-FUND Fax: 518-434-5641
e-mail: info@nylawfund.org
Web site: www.nylawfund.org

Chair:
Eric A Seiff 518-434-1935
Vice Chair:
Nancy Burner 518-434-1935
Executive Director & Counsel:
Timothy O'Sullivan 518-434-1935

Legislative Bill Drafting Commission

Capitol, Rm 308
Albany, NY 12224
518-455-7500 Fax: 518-455-7598

Commissioner:
Randall G Bluth 518-455-7506
e-mail: bluth@lbdc.state.ny.us

Legislative Retrieval System . . . . fax: 518-455-7679
1450 Western Ave, Albany, NY 12203
800-356-6566 Fax: 518-455-7679
Director:
Burleigh McCutcheon 518-455-7672
e-mail: mccutcheon@lbdc.state.ny.us

MTA (Metropolitan Transportation Authority)

347 Madison Ave
New York, NY 10017
212-878-7000 Fax: 212-878-7264
Web site: www.mta.info

Chairman/CEO:
Thomas F. Prendergast 212-878-7200
Director of Security:
Raymond Diaz 212-878-7155
Director, Government & Community Affairs:
Justin Bernbach 212-878-7160
Senior Director, Human Resources/Retirement:
Margaret M. Connor
CAO/Employee Relations:
Anita Miller 212-878-7438
Auditor General:
Michael J Fucilli 212-878-7000
Director, Special Project Development & Planning:
William Wheeler 212-878-7278
Chief Financial Officer:
Robert E. Foran
General Counsel:
Jerome F Page 212-878-7313/fax: 212-878-7050
Chief of Staff:
Donna Evans 212-878-7206

Offices and agencies generally appear in alphabetical order, except when specific order is requested by listee.

Director, External Communications:
Adam Lisberg 212-878-7440

MTA Bridges & Tunnels
2 Broadway
22nd Floor
New York, NY 10004-2801
646-252-7000 Fax: 646-252-7408
Web site: www.mta.info/bandt

Chairman/CEO:
Thomas F. Prendergast 212-878-7200
President:
Donald Spero 212-360-3100
Chief Engineer:
Joseph Keane 212-878-7200
Vice President, Administration:
Sharon Gallo-Kotcher 212-360-3015
Vice President, Operations:
Patrick Parisi 212-878-7200
Chief Procurement Officer:
Gavin Masterson 646-252-7084
Vice President, Staff Services & Chief of Staff:
Albert Rivera 646-252-7421
Chief Financial Officer (Acting):
Mildred Chua 646-252-7132
General Counsel:
M. Margaret Terry 212-878-7200
Manager, Public Affairs:
Judith Glave 646-252-7276

MTA Bus Company
2 Broadway
New York, NY 10004
212-878-7174 Fax: 212-878-0205
Web site: www.mta.info/busco

Chairman/CEO:
Thomas F. Prendergast 212-878-7200
President:
Darryl Irick 212-878-7174

MTA Capital Construction Program
2 Broadway
8th Floor
New York, NY 10002
646-252-4575
Web site: www.mta.info/capital

Chairman/CEO:
Thomas F. Prendergast 212-878-7200
President:
Dr Michael Horodniceanu 646-252-4277
Chief of Staff:
Ayala Malinovitz 646-252-4011
Senior Director, Government & Community Affairs:
Richard Mulieri 646-252-4197
Executive Vice President:
William Goldstein 646-252-4277
Senior Vice President & General Counsel:
Evan Eisland 646-252-4274
Senior Director/Chief Procurement Officer:
David Cannon 646-252-2321
Vice President/Chief Engineer:
Mike Kyriacou 646-252-4500
Senior Vice President & Program Executive, East Side Access:
Alan Paskoff 212-967-0118
Senior Vice President & Program Executive, 2nd Ave Subway:
William Goodrich 212-510-2661
VP & Program Executive, #7 Subway Line Extension:
Mark Schiffman 646-252-3723
Director, System Safety & Security:
Eric Osnes 646-252-4556
Vice President, Program Controls & Quality Safety:
Raymond Schaeffer 646-252-5393
Vice President, Planning, Development & External Relations:
Joseph Petrocelli 646-252-3813

MTA Long Island Rail Road
Jamaica Station
Jamaica, NY 11435
718-558-7400 Fax: 718-558-8212
Web site: www.mta.info/lirr

Chairman/CEO:
Thomas F. Prendergast 212-878-7200
President:
Patrick A Nowakowski 718-558-8252
Executive Vice President:
Albert Cosenza 718-558-7993
e-mail: accosen@lirr.org
Chief Information Officer:
Scott Dieterich 718-588-8166
Vice President, General Counsel & Secretary:
Richard Gans 718-558-8264
Vice President, Labor Relations:
Michael Chirillo 718-558-7405
Vice President, Market Development & Public Affairs:
Joseph Calderone 718-558-7301
Vice President, ESA/Special Projects:
John Coulter 718-558-7363
e-mail: jwcoult@lirr.org
Director, System Safety:
Frank Lo Presti 718-558-7711
General Manager, Public Affairs:
Susan McGowan 718-558-7400

MTA Metro-North Railroad
347 Madison Ave
New York, NY 10017
212-340-2677 Fax: 212-340-4995
Web site: www.mta.info/mnr

Chairman/CEO:
Thomas F. Prendergast 212-878-7200
President:
Joseph Giulietti 212-340-2677
General Counsel:
Seth Cummins 212-340-4933
VP, Finance & Informational Systems:
D. Kim Porcelain 212-340-2636
Senior VP, Operations:
Robert Lieblong 212-499-4300
Senior Director, Capital Planning & Program:
John Kennard 212-340-2500
Chief of Staff & Operations:
David Treasure 212-340-2677
Chief Safety & Security Officer:
Anne Kirsch 212-340-4913
Senior Director, Capital Programs:
Timothy McCartney 212-340-4913
Vice President, Business Operations:
Thomas Tendy 212-672-1251
Senior Director, Corporate & Public Affairs:
Mark Mannix 212-340-2142

MTA New York City Transit
2 Broadway
New York, NY 10004

Offices and agencies generally appear in alphabetical order, except when specific order is requested by listee.

Policy Areas

718-330-3000 Fax: 718-596-2146
Web site: www.mta.info/nyct

Chairman/CEO:
Thomas F. Prendergast 212-878-7200
President:
Veronique Hakim 646-252-5800
Chief Transportation Officer:
Herbert Lambert 718-330-3000
Vice President, Labor Relations:
Christopher Johnson 718-330-3000
Vice President, Corporate Communications:
Paul Fleuranges 646-252-5873
Vice President, Technology & Information Services:
Signey Gellineau 718-330-3000
Vice President & General Counsel:
Martin Schnabel 718-694-3900
Director, Labor Relations:
Andrew Paul 646-252-5880

MTA Office of the Inspector General

2 Penn Paza, 5th Fl
New York, NY 10121
212-878-0000 or 800-682-4448 Fax: 212-878-0003
e-mail: complaints@mtaig.org
Web site: www.mtaig.state.ny.us

Inspector General:
Barry L Kluger 212-878-0000

Nassau Regional Off-Track Betting Corporation

139 Liberty Ave
Mineola, NY 11501
516-572-2800 Fax: 516-572-2840
e-mail: webmaster@nassauotb.com
Web site: www.nassauotb.com

President:
Joseph G. Cairo, Jr. 516-572-2800
Director, Facilities Development:
John J Sparacio 516-572-2800

New England Interstate Water Pollution Control Commission

Wannalancit Mills
650 Suffolk Street
Suite 410
Lowell, MA 01854
978-323-7929 Fax: 978-323-7919
e-mail: mail@neiwpcc.org
Web site: www.neiwpcc.org

Chair (ME):
Michael Kuhns 978-323-7929
Vice Chair (MA):
Douglas Fine 978-323-7929
Commissioner, New York State:
Basil Seggos 518-485-8940
Executive Director:
Ronald F Poltak 978-323-7929
e-mail: rpoltak@neiwpcc.org
Deputy Director:
Susan Sullivan 978-323-7929
e-mail: ssullivan@neiwpcc.org

New York City Housing Development Corporation

110 William St
10th Fl
New York, NY 10038
212-227-5500 Fax: 212-227-6865
e-mail: info@nychdc.com
Web site: www.nychdc.com

Chairperson:
Vicki Been 212-863-6100
President:
Gary D Rodney 212-227-3600
Executive VP/COO & General Counsel:
Richard Froehlich 212-227-7435
Executive VP, Real Estate:
Paula R Carethers 212-227-6846
Senior Vice President, Portfolio Management:
Teresa Gigliello 212-227-9133
Vice President, Loan Servicing:
Karen Santiago 212-227-7494
Chief Credit Officer:
Mary Horn 212-227-9724
Communications/Press Office:
Vacant 212-227-2644

New York City Residential Mortgage Insurance Corporation

Chair:
Vicki Been 212-863-6100
President:
Gary D Rodney 212-227-3600

New York City School Construction Authority

30-30 Thomson Ave
Long Island City, NY 11101-3045
718-472-8000 Fax: 718-472-8840
Web site: www.nycsca.org

Chair/Chancellor:
Carmen Farina 718-472-8000
President & Chief Executive Officer:
Lorraine Grillo 718-472-8001
Executive Vice President & General Counsel:
Ross J Holden 718-472-8220
VP, Finance:
Marianne Egri 718-472-8012
VP, Construction Management:
Vacant 718-472-8359
VP, Architecture & Engineering:
E Bruce Barrett, RA 718-472-8710
VP, Administration:
Rebecca Fraley-Corrado 718-472-8149

New York Convention Center Operating Corporation

655 W 34th St
New York, NY 10001-1188
212-216-2000 Fax: 212-216-2588
e-mail: moreinfo@javitscenter.com
Web site: www.javitscenter.com

Chair:
Henry Silverman 212-216-2130
President/CEO:
Alan Steel 212-216-2000
SVP/Chief Financial Officer:
John Menapace 212-216-2369
SVP/General Counsel:
Bradley Siciliano 212-216-2125
SVP, Sales & Marketing:
Doreen Guerin 212-216-2335

Offices and agencies generally appear in alphabetical order, except when specific order is requested by listee.

New York Metropolitan Transportation Council
25 Beaver St
Ste 201
New York, NY 10004
212-383-7200 Fax: 212-383-2418
e-mail: nymtc-web@dot.ny.gov
Web site: www.nymtc.org

Interim Executive Director:
Lisa Daglian 212-383-7200
Acting Director, Administration:
Nina Del Senno 212-383-2402
e-mail: nina.delsenno@dot.ny.gov
Director, Planning:
Gerard J Bogacz 212-383-7260
e-mail: gerry.bogacz@dot.ny.gov
PIO:
Stacy Graham-Hunt 212-383-7203
e-mail: stacy.graham-hunt@dot.ny.gov

New York Power Authority
123 Main Street
Mailstop 10-H
White Plains, NY 10601-3170
914-681-6200 Fax: 914-390-8190
e-mail: info@nypa.gov
Web site: www.nypa.gov

Chairman:
John R. Koelmel 914-287-3636
President & Chief Executive Officer:
Gil C Quiniones 914-287-3501
SVP, Corporate Affairs:
Rocco Iannarelli 518-433-6700
Chief Operating Officer:
Edward A Welz 518-433-6700
EVP & General Counsel:
Justin E Driscoll 914-681-6200

New York State Assn of Fire Districts
PO Box 1419
Massapequa, NY 11758
631-947-2079 or 800-520-9594 Fax: 631-207-1655
Web site: www.firedistnys.com

President:
Anthony J Gallino 631-831-6875
e-mail: president@afdsny.org
First Vice President:
Thomas Rinaldi 518-664-6538
e-mail: 1vp.president@afdsny.org
Second Vice President:
Frederick Senti Jr 516-486-3023
e-mail: 2vp.president@afdsny.org
Secretary & Treasurer:
Joseph P DeStefano 631-947-2079
e-mail: dacomish@aol.com
Counsel:
William N Young . . . . 800-349-2904 or 518-456-6767
fax: 518-456-4644
e-mail: byoung@yfkblaw.com

New York State Athletic Commission
123 William St
2nd Floor
New York, NY 10038
212-417-5700 Fax: 212-417-4987
e-mail: info@dos.ny.gov
Web site: www.dos.ny.gov/athletic

Chair:
Tom Hoover 212-417-5700

New York State Board of Law Examiners
Corporate Plaza Bldg 3
254 Washington Ave Ext
Albany, NY 12203-5195
518-453-5990 Fax: 518-452-5729
Web site: www.nybarexam.org

Chair:
Diane F Bosse 518-453-5990
Executive Director:
John J McAlary 518-453-5990

New York State Bridge Authority
Mid-Hudson Bridge Plaza
PO Box 1010
Highland, NY 12528
845-691-7245 Fax: 845-691-3560
e-mail: info@nysba.ny.gov
Web site: www.nysba.ny.gov

Chair:
Richard A. Gerentine 845-691-7245
Vice Chair:
Joseph Ramaglia 845-691-7245
Executive Director:
Joseph Ruggiero 845-691-7245
Director, IT:
Gregory J Herd 518-828-4107
Director, Toll Collections & Operations:
Wayne V Ferguson 845-691-7245

New York State Commission of Correction
80 South Swan St
12th Fl
Albany, NY 12210
518-485-2346 Fax: 518-485-2467
e-mail: infoscoc@scoc.ny.gov
Web site: www.scoc.ny.gov

Chairman:
Thomas A Beilein 518-485-2330
Commissioner:
Phyllis Harrison-Ross M.D.
Commissioner:
Thomas Loughren 518-485-2436
Assistant to Chair:
Patricia Amati 518-485-2330
Counsel:
Brian Callahan 518-485-2346
Chair, Citizens' Policy & Complaint Review Council:
Thomas Loughren 518-485-2346
Chair, Medical Review Board:
Phyllis Harrison-Ross 518-485-2346
Director, Operations:
James Lawrence 518-485-2346
Deputy Director, Operations:
Richard Kinney 518-457-6110
Deputy Director, Public Information:
Walter McClure 518-485-2346

New York State Commission on Judicial Nomination

c/o Greenberg Traurig LLP
54 State Street
Albany, NY 12207
518-689-1400 Fax: 518-689-1499
Web site: www.nysegov.com/cjn/

Chair:
Vacant 212-735-3680
Counsel:
Henry Greenberg. 518-689-1400
e-mail: greenbergh@gtlaw.com

New York State Commission on the Restoration of the Capitol

Corning Tower, 31st Fl
Empire State Plaza
Albany, NY 12242
518-473-0341 Fax: 518-486-5720

Executive Director:
Andrea J Lazarski 518-473-0341
e-mail: andrea.lazarski@ogs.ny.gov

New York State Disaster Preparedness Commission

Building 22, Suite 101
1220 Washington Ave
Albany, NY 12226-2251
518-292-2301 or 518-292-2200 Fax: 518-322-4978
Web site: www.dhses.ny.gov/oem/disaster-prep/

Chairman/Director:
Jerome M Hauer 518-292-2301

New York State Dormitory Authority

515 Broadway
Albany, NY 12207-2964
518-257-3000 Fax: 518-257-3100
e-mail: dabonds@dasny.org
Web site: www.dasny.org

One Penn Plaza
52nd Fl
New York, NY 10119-0098
212-273-5000
Fax: 212-273-5121

539 Franklin St
Buffalo, NY 14202-1109
716-884-9780
Fax: 716-884-9787

Chair:
Alfonso L Carney Jr 518-257-3000/fax: 518-257-3100
President/CEO:
Paul T Williams Jr. 518-257-3180/fax: 518-257-3183
Vice President:
Michael T Corrigan 518-257-3192/fax: 518-257-3183
Acting Chief Financial Officer:
Linda H Button 518-257-3562/fax: 518-257-3100
General Counsel:
Michael Cusack 518-257-3120/fax: 518-257-3101
Managing Director, Construction:
Stephen D Curro, PE 518-257-3271/fax: 518-257-3100
e-mail: scurro@dasny.org
Managing Director, Public Finance & Portfolio Monitoring:
Portia Lee. 518-257-3362/fax: 518-257-3100
e-mail: plee@dasny.org
Public Information Officer:
John Chirlin. 518-257-3380
e-mail: jchirlin@dasny.org

New York State Energy Research & Development Authority

17 Columbia Circle
Albany, NY 12203-6399
518-862-1090 Fax: 518-862-1091
e-mail: info@nyserda.ny.gov
Web site: www.nyserda.ny.gov

Chairman:
Richard L Kauffman 518-862-1090
President & CEO:
John B Rhodes 518-862-1090 x3278
General Counsel:
Noah C Shaw 518-862-1090 x3280
Program Manager, Economic Development & Community Outreach:
Kelly Tyler . . . . 716-842-1522 x 3005
e-mail: kelly.tyler@nyserda.ny.gov
Director, Communications:
Kate Muller. 518-862-1090 x3582/fax: 518-862-1091
e-mail: kate.muller@nyserda.ny.gov

New York State Environmental Facilities Corp

625 Broadway
Albany, NY 12207-2997
518-402-6924 or 800-882-9721 Fax: 518-486-9323
e-mail: press@efc.ny.gov
Web site: www.nysefc.org

President/CEO:
Sabrina M Ty 518-402-6951
Legal Division/General Counsel:
James R Levine. 518-402-6969
Director, Engineering & Program Management:
Timothy P Burns. 518-402-7396
Director, Technical Advisory Services:
Vacant 518-402-7461
Director, PIO:
Jon Sorensen 518-402-6924
e-mail: press@efc.ny.gov; jon.sorensen@efc.ny.gov
Controller & Director, Corporate Operations:
Michael Malinoski 518-486-9267

New York State Gaming Commission

PO Box 7500
Schenectady, NY 12301-7500
518-388-3300 or 518-388-3415 Fax: 518-388-3423
e-mail: info@gaming.ny.gov
Web site: www.gaming.ny.gov

Member:
Peter Moschetti 518-388-3300
Member:
Todd R Snyder 518-388-3300
Member:
Barry C Sample. 518-388-3300
Member:
John A Crotty 518-395-5400
Member:
John J Poklemba 518-388-3300
Executive Director:
Robert Williams 518-388-3300

Offices and agencies generally appear in alphabetical order, except when specific order is requested by listee.

Public Information Officer:
Christy Calicchia. 518-388-3415
e-mail: lee.park@gaming.ny.gov

Joint Commission on Public Ethics (JCOPE)
540 Broadway
Albany, NY 12207
518-408-3976 Fax: 518-408-3975
e-mail: jcope@jcope.ny.gov
Web site: www.jcope.ny.gov

Executive Director:
Seth Agata. 518-408-3976
Chair:
Daniel J Horwitz. 518-408-3976
General Counsel:
Monica Stamm 518-408-3976
Chief of Staff:
Kevin T Gagan .518-408-3976/fax: 518-408-3975

New York State Financial Control Board
123 William St
23rd Fl
New York, NY 10038-3804
212-417-5046 Fax: 212-417-5055
e-mail: nysfcb@fcb.state.ny.us
Web site: www.fcb.state.ny.us

Acting Executive Director:
Jeffrey Sommer. 212-417-5066
Deputy Director, Expenditure & Covered Organization Analysis:
Dennis DeLisle 212-417-5069
Deputy Director, Finance & Capital Analysis:
Jewel A Douglas. 212-417-5067
Acting Deputy Director, Economic & Revenue Analysis:
Martin Fischman. 212-417-5068
Associate Director, Administration:
Mattie W Taylor 212-417-5053

New York State Higher Education Services Corp (NYSHESC)
99 Washington Ave
Albany, NY 12255
888-697-4372
Web site: www.hesc.ny.gov

Executive Vice President & Acting President:
Elsa Magee 518-474-5592/fax: 518-474-5593
e-mail: elsa.magee@hesc.ny.gov
Director, Training & Information Services:
Teresa Gehrer .518-402-6429/fax: 518-474-2839
Director, Federal Relations:
Frank Ballmann. 202-721-1186
e-mail: frank.ballmann@hesc.ny.gov
Director, Audit:
Matt Downey. 518-473-2287/fax: 518-486-6515
e-mail: matt.downey@hesc.ny.gov
General Counsel:
Thomas Brennan 518-473-1585/fax: 518-486-6515
e-mail: thomas.brennan@hesc.ny.gov
Communications/PIO:
Vacant. . . . . .518-474-5592 or 518-474-5775
fax: 518-474-5593
Director, Federal Operations:
Victor Stucchi .518-486-5885/fax: 518-402-3276
e-mail: victor.stucchi@hesc.ny.gov
Administrative Officer & CFO:
Warren Wallin .518-486-5885/fax: 518-474-4301
e-mail: warren.wall@hesc.ny.gov

New York State Homes & Community Renewal
641 Lexington Ave
New York, NY 10022
866-275-3427
e-mail: hcrinfo@nyshcr.org
Web site: www.nyshcr.org

Hampton Plaza
38-40 State Street
Albany, NY 12207
518-473-2526

Commissioner & CEO:
James S Rubin. 212-480-6705
Executive Deputy Commissioner/COO:
Betsy Mallow 212-480-6700
Executive Deputy Commissioner, Housing Development:
RuthAnne Visnauskas. 212-480-6700
General Counsel:
Adam Schuman. 212-480-6700
Chief of Staff:
Meredith Levine 212-480-6700
Director, Fair Housing & Equal Opportunity:
Wanda Graham 212-480-6700
Public Information:
. 212-872-0338

New York State Judicial Conduct Commission
61 Broadway
12th Floor
New York, NY 10006
646-386-4800 Fax: 646-458-0037
e-mail: cjc@cjc.ny.gov
Web site: www.cjc.ny.gov

Corning Tower
Suite 2301
Empire State Plaza
Albany, NY 12223
518-453-4600
Fax: 518-486-1850

Chair:
Joseph W Belluck 646-386-4800
Vice Chair:
Paul B Harding 646-386-4800
Administrator & Counsel:
Robert H Tembeckjian 646-386-4800
Deputy Administrator in Charge, Albany Office:
Cathleen Cenci 518-453-4600
Deputy Administrator in Charge, Rochester Office:
John J Postel 585-232-5756
Deputy Administrator in Charge, New York City Office:
Mark Levine 646-386-4800
Deputy Administrator, Litigation:
Edward Lindner 518-474-5617
Clerk:
Jean M Savanyu, Esq 646-386-4800

New York State Law Reporting Bureau
17 Lodge Street
Albany, NY 12207
518-453-6900 Fax: 518-426-1640
Web site: www.courts.state.ny.us/reporter

State Reporter:
William J Hooks 518-453-6900

Policy Areas

Deputy State Reporter:
Katherine D LaBoda, Esq. 518-453-6900
e-mail: Reporter@courts.state.ny.us
Assistant State Reporter:
Cara J Broussea, Esq. 518-453-6900
e-mail: Reporter@courts.state.ny.us

New York State Law Revision Commission
80 New Scotland Ave
Albany, NY 12208
518-472-5858 Fax: 518-445-2303
e-mail: nylrc@albanylaw.edu
Web site: www.lawrevision.state.ny.us

Chairman:
Peter J Kiernan 518-472-5858
Executive Director:
Rose Mary Bailly 518-472-5858

New York State Liquor Authority
80 S Swan St, Ste 900
9th Floor
Albany, NY 12210
518-474-3114
Web site: www.sla.ny.gov

Chairman:
Vincent Bradley . . . . 518-473-6559 or 212-961-8300
Commissioner:
Kevin Kim . . . . 518-474-3114 or 212-961-8300
Counsel:
Jacqueline Flug 518-474-3114/fax: 518-402-2304
e-mail: legal@sla.ny.gov
CEO:
Kerri O'Brien 518-474-3114
e-mail: licensing.information@sla.ny.gov
Director, Public Affairs:
William Crowley . . . . 518-474-3114 or 518-474-4875
fax: 518-473-9565
e-mail: press.office@sla.ny.gov

New York State Olympic Regional Development Authority
Olympic Center
2634 Main Street
Lake Placid, NY 12946
518-523-1655 Fax: 518-523-9275
e-mail: info@orda.org
Web site: www.orda.org/corporate

President & CEO:
Ted Blazer 518-523-1655 x201
e-mail: blazer@orda.org
Vice President:
Jeffrey Byrne 518-523-1655 x203
e-mail: byrne@orda.org
Olympic Center Manager:
Dennis Allen 518-523-1655 x222
e-mail: allen@orda.org
Director, Corporate Development:
Jeff Potter 518-523-1655
e-mail: jpotter@orda.org
Director, Events:
Katie Million 518-523-1655 x212
e-mail: kmillion@orda.org
Director, Finance:
Padraig Power 518-523-1655 x217
e-mail: ppower@orda.org
Communications Manager:
Jon Lundin 518-523-1655
e-mail: jlundin@orda.org

New York State Teachers' Retirement System
10 Corporate Woods Dr
Albany, NY 12211-2395
518-447-2900 or 800-348-7298 Fax: 518-447-2695
e-mail: media@nystrs.org
Web site: www.nystrs.org

Executive Director:
Thomas K Lee. 518-447-2726
General Counsel:
Joseph J. Indelicato, Jr. 518-447-2722
Actuary:
Richard Young 518-447-2692
Managing Director Operations:
Kevin Schaefer 518-447-2730
Director, Member Relations:
Sheila Gardella 518-447-2684
Manager, Public Information:
John Cardillo 518-447-4743/fax: 518-447-2875
e-mail: john.cardillo@nystrs.org
Managing Director, Real Estate:
David C. Gillian 518-447-2751

New York State Thoroughbred Breeding & Development Fund Corporation
One Broadway Center
Suite 601
Schenectady, NY 12305
518-388-0174 Fax: 518-344-1235
e-mail: nybreds@nybreds.com
Web site: www.nybreds.com

Executive Director:
Tracy Egan 518-388-0174

New York State Thruway Authority
200 Southern Blvd
PO Box 189
Albany, NY 12201
518-436-2700 Fax: 518-436-2899
Web site: www.thruway.ny.gov

Chair:
Joanne M Mahoney. 518-436-3000
Interim Executive Director:
Maria Lehman. 518-436-2900
General Counsel:
Gordon Cuffy 518-436-2840
CFO:
Matt Howard 518-436-2840
Director, Media Relations & Communications:
Jennifer Givner 518-471-5300

New York State Canal Corporation
Web site: www.canals.ny.gov
Interim Executive Director:
Maria Lehman 518-436-3055/fax: 518-471-5023
Director of Canals:
Brian U. Stratton 518-436-3055

New York State Tug Hill Commission
Dulles State Office Bldg
317 Washington St
Watertown, NY 13601

Offices and agencies generally appear in alphabetical order, except when specific order is requested by listee.

315-785-2380 Fax: 315-785-2574
e-mail: tughill@tughill.org
Web site: www.tughill.org

Chair:
Jan Bogdanowicz 315-785-2380
Executive Director:
Katie Malinowski 315-785-2570
e-mail: katie@tughill.org

Niagara Falls Bridge Commission

5365 Military Rd
Lewiston, NY 14092
716-285-6322 or 905-354-5641 Fax: 716-282-3292
e-mail: general_inquiries@niagarafallsbridges.com
Web site: www.niagarafallsbridges.com

Chair:
Linda L McAusland 716-285-6322
Vice Chair:
Russell G Quarantello 716-285-6322
Treasurer:
Harry R Palladino 716-285-6322
Secretary:
John Lopinski 716-285-6322

Niagara Frontier Transportation Authority

181 Ellicott St
Buffalo, NY 14203
716-855-7300 or 800-622-1220 Fax: 716-855-6655
e-mail: info@nfta.com
Web site: www.nfta.com

Chair:
Howard Zemsky 716-855-7232
Executive Director:
Kimberley A Minkel 716-855-7470
Chief Financial Officer:
John Cox 716-855-7300
General Counsel:
David J State 716-855-7686
Director, Aviation:
William Vanecek 716-630-6030
Director, Human Resources:
Karen Novo 716-855-7343
Director, Public Transit:
Thomas George 716-855-7390
Director, Engineering:
Michael Bykowski 716-855-7389
Director, Public Affairs:
C Douglas Hartmayer 716-855-7420
Chief, NFTA Police:
George W. Gast 716-855-7666

Northeastern Forest Fire Protection Commission

21 Parmenter Terrace
PO Box 6192
China Village, ME 04926
207-968-3782 Fax: 207-968-3782
e-mail: info@nffpc.org
Web site: www.nffpc.org

Executive Committee Chair:
Steven Sinclair 802-241-3680
e-mail: ssinclair@vermont.gov
Executive Director/Center Manager:
Thomas G Parent 207-968-3782
e-mail: necompact@fairpoint.net
Operations Committee, Chair:
Rick Vollick 413-770-1235
e-mail: rvollick@gmail.com
New York Fire Prevention & Education:
Andrew Jacob 518-402-8840
e-mail: atjacob@gw.dec.state.ny.us

Ogdensburg Bridge & Port Authority

One Bridge Plaza
Ogdensburg, NY 13669
315-393-4080 Fax: 315-393-7068
e-mail: obpa@ogdensport.com
Web site: www.ogdensport.com

Chair:
Samuel J LaMacchia 315-393-4080
Executive Director:
Wade A Davis 315-393-4080
e-mail: wadavis@ogdensport.com

Ohio River Valley Water Sanitation Commission

5735 Kellogg Ave
Cincinnati, OH 45230
513-231-7719 Fax: 513-231-7761
e-mail: info@orsanco.org
Web site: www.orsanco.org

New York State Commissioner:
Douglas E Conroe 513-231-7719
New York State Commissioner:
Michael P Wilson 513-231-7719
New York State Commissioner:
Basil Seggos 513-231-7719
Executive Director:
Richard Harrison . . . . 513-231-7719 ext 105
e-mail: rharrison@orsanco.org
Source Water Protection/Emergency Response/External Relations:
Jerry Schulte . . . . 513-231-7719 ext 104
e-mail: jschulte@orsanco.org
Communications Coordinator:
Lisa Cochran . . . . 513-231-7719 ext 102
e-mail: lcochran@orsanco.org

Port Authority of New York & New Jersey

4 World Trade Center
150 Greenwich Street
New York, NY 10007
212-435-7000 Fax: 212-435-4032
Web site: www.panynj.gov

Chair, New Jersey:
John J Degnan 212-435-7000
Vice Chair, New York:
Scott H Rechler 212-435-7000
Executive Director:
Patrick Foye 212-435-7271
Director World Trade Center Operations:
Hugh P McCann 212-435-7887
Director, Government & Community Affairs - NY (Acting):
Ian R Van Praagh 212-435-6903
Assistant General Counsel:
Carlene V McIntyre 212-435-3515
Chief Financial Officer:
Elizabeth McCarthy 212-435-7738
Director Media Relations:
Ron Marsico 212-435-7777/fax: 212-435-4032
Director, Public Safety/Superintendent of Police:
Michael A Fedorko 212-435-7000

Offices and agencies generally appear in alphabetical order, except when specific order is requested by listee.

Policy Areas

Chief Engineer:
James A Starace 212-435-7449
Office of Secretary:
Karen E Eastman....212-435-6528

Port of Oswego Authority
1 East Second St
Oswego, NY 13126
315-343-4503 Fax: 315-343-5498
e-mail: shipping@portoswego.com
Web site: www.portoswego.com

Chairman:
Terrence Hammill....315-343-4503
e-mail: chairman@portoswego.com
Executive Director & CEO:
Zelko N. Kirincich....315-343-4503 x111
e-mail: zkirincich@portoswego.com
Manager, Administrative Services/Facility Security Officer:
William Scriber 315-343-4503 x108
e-mail: wscriber@portoswego.com
Supervisor of Marina Operations:
Bernie Bacon....315-343-1967
e-mail: oswegomarina@yahoo.com

Rochester-Genesee Regional Transportation Authority-RTS
1372 E Main St
PO Box 90629
Rochester, NY 14609
585-654-0200 or 585-288-1700 Fax: 585-654-0224
Web site: www.myrts.com

Chief Executive Officer:
Bill Carpenter 585-654-0200
Chief Operating Officer:
Miguel A Velazquez....585-654-0200
Chief Financial Officer:
Scott Adair 585-654-0200
General Counsel/CAO:
Daniel DeLaus 585-654-0200
Public Information Officer:
Tom Brede....585-654-0730

Roosevelt Island Operating Corporation (RIOC)
591 Main St
Roosevelt Island, NY 10044
212-832-4540 Fax: 212-832-4582
e-mail: information@rioc.ny.gov
Web site: www.rioc.ny.gov

President/CEO:
Charlene M Indelicato....212-832-4540 x319
Director Island Operations:
Cyril Opperman 212-832-4583
e-mail: cyril.opperman@rioc.ny.gov
VP/General Counsel:
Donald D. Lewis 212-832-4540 x311
e-mail: donald.lewis@rioc.ny.gov
VP/Chief Financial Officer:
Frances Walton 212-832-4540 x350
Director Public Safety:
Captain Estrella Suarez....212-832-4545
e-mail: keith.guerra@rioc.ny.gov

State University Construction Fund
353 Broadway
Albany, NY 12246
518-320-3200 Fax: 518-443-1008
Web site: www.sucf.suny.edu

General Manager:
Robert M Haelen....518-320-1502
Associate Counsel:
Terese Meagher....518-320-1746

Suffolk Regional Off-Track Betting Corporation
425 Oser Ave
Ste 2
Hauppauge, NY 11788
631-853-1000 Fax: 631-853-1086
e-mail: customerservice@suffolkotb.com
Web site: www.suffolkotb.com

President/CEO:
Philip C. Nolan 631-853-1000
Vice President:
Anthony Pancella 631-853-1000
General Counsel:
James McManmon 631-853-1000
Director Governmental & Public Affairs:
Debbie Pfeiffer 631-853-1000

Thousand Islands Bridge Authority
PO Box 428, Collins Landing
43530 Interstate 81
Alexandria Bay, NY 13607
315-482-2501 or 315-658-2281 Fax: 315-482-5925
e-mail: info@tibridge.com
Web site: www.tibridge.com

Chair:
Robert Barnard 315-482-2501
Executive Director:
Robert G Horr, III....315-482-2501
e-mail: roberthorr@tibridge.com
Legal Counsel:
Dennis Whelpley....315-482-2501

Uniform State Laws Commission
c/o Coughlin & Gerhart LLP
99 Corporate Drive
PO Box 2059
Binghamton, NY 13902-2039
607-723-9511 Fax: 607-723-1530

Chair:
Richard B Long....607-821-2202
e-mail: rlong@cglawoffices.com
Member:
Sandra Stern 212-207-8150
Member:
Norman L. Greene 212-661-5030
Member:
Justin L. Vigdor....585-232-5300 ext 228
Member:
Mark F Glaser....518-689-1413

United Nations Development Corporation
Two United Nations Plaza, 27th Fl
New York, NY 10017
212-888-1618 Fax: 212-588-0758
e-mail: info@undc.org
Web site: www.undc.org

Offices and agencies generally appear in alphabetical order, except when specific order is requested by listee.

Chair, Board of Directors:
George Klein 212-888-1618
Sr VP & General Counsel/Secretary:
Robert Cole 212-888-1618
Controller/Treasurer:
Jorge Ortiz 212-888-1618
Vice President:
Kenneth Coopersmith 212-888-1618

Waterfront Commission of New York Harbor

39 Broadway, 4th Fl
New York, NY 10006
212-742-9280 Fax: 212-480-0587
Web site: www.wcnyh.org

Commissioner, New York:
Ronald Goldstock 212-742-9280
Commissioner, New Jersey:
Michael Murphy 212-742-9280
Executive Director:
Walter M Arsenault 212-905-9201
General Counsel:
Phoebe S Sorial 212-742-8965

Western Regional Off-Track Betting Corp

8315 Park Road
Batavia, NY 14020
585-343-3750 Fax: 585-343-6873
e-mail: info@westernotb.com
Web site: www.westernotb.com

Chair:
Richard D Bianchi 585-343-3750
President & Chief Executive Officer:
Michael D Kane 585-343-3750
VP-Administration:
William R White 585-343-3750
General Counsel:
Henry Wojtaszek 585-343-3750
Director, Video Gaming:
Mark Wolf 585-343-3750
Communications/Mutuels Manager:
James Haas 585-343-3750
Manager, Branch Operations:
Edward Merriman 585-343-3750

Policy Areas

Offices and agencies generally appear in alphabetical order, except when specific order is requested by listee.

CRIME & CORRECTIONS

NEW YORK STATE

GOVERNOR'S OFFICE

Governor's Office
Executive Chamber
State Capitol
Albany, NY 12224
518-474-8390 Fax: 518-474-1513
Web site: www.ny.gov

Governor:
Andrew M Cuomo 518-474-8390
Secretary to the Governor:
William Mulrow 518-474-4246
Counsel to the Governor:
Alphonso David 518-474-8343
First Assistant Counsel:
Sandi Toll 518-474-8434
Chief of Staff:
Melissa DeRosa . . . . 518-474-8418 or 212-681-4640
Director, Communications:
James Allen. . . . . 518-474-8418 or 212-681-4640

EXECUTIVE DEPARTMENTS AND RELATED AGENCIES

Corrections & Community Supervision Department
1220 Washington Ave
Bldg 2 State Campus
Albany, NY 12226-2050
518-457-8126 Fax: 518-457-7252
Web site: www.doccs.ny.gov

Acting Commissioner:
Anthony Annucci 518-457-8134
Executive Deputy Commissioner:
Anthony Annucci . . . . 518-457-1748 or 518-485-9613
Deputy Commissioner & Counsel:
Maureen Boll 518-485-9613
Assistant Commissioner & Executive Assistant:
Diane L Van Buren. 518-457-1281
Special Assistant to Commissioner:
Terri Pratt 518-457-8134
Health Services Deputy Commissioner/Chief Medical Officer:
Carl Koenigsmann MD. 518-457-7073
Deputy Commissioner, Program Services:
Jeffrey McKoy 518-457-5555
Asst Commissioner, Program Services:
Catherine Jacobsen 518-408-5825
Director, Public Information:
Linda Foglia. 518-457-8182/fax: 518-457-7070

Administrative Services
Deputy Commissioner:
Daniel F. Martuscello III 518-457-8188
Assistant Commissioner:
Thomas Corcoran 518-457-7135

Budget & Finance Division
Director:
Sandy Downey 518-457-5562

Diversity Management
Director:
Deborah E. Nazon 518-485-5806

Human Resources Management Division
Director, Personnel:
Darren Ayotte 518-457-9887
Support Operations
550 Broadway, Menands, NY 12204
Director:
Nannette Ferri. 518-436-7886 x3015

Inmate Grievance
Director:
Karen Bellamy 518-457-1885
Deputy Commissioner, Correctional Industries & Accreditation:
Osbourne A McKay 518-485-2858

Internal Controls
Director:
Peter Berezny 518-485-1394
Special Assistant for Labor Relations:
John Shipley 518-457-7291

Training Academy
1134 New Scotland Rd, Albany, NY 12208
Director:
Joseph Tewksbury 518-489-9072

Correctional Facility Operations
Deputy Commissioner:
Joseph Bellnier 518-457-8138
Assistant Commissioner:
Patricia Le Coney 518-457-5902
Chief of Investigations & Inspector General:
Vernon Fonda 518-457-2653
Associate Commissioner, Population Management:
Ann Marie McGrath 518-457-7261

Correctional Industries Division . . . . fax: 518-436-6007
Corcraft Products, 550 Broadway, Albany, NY 12204
Fax: 518-436-6007
Web site: www.corcraft.org
Director:
Michael Hurt 518-436-6321 x2305

Facilities
Adirondack Correctional Facility
196 Ray Brook Rd, Box 110, Route 86, Ray Brook, NY 12977-0110
Superintendent:
Jeffrey Tedford 518-891-1343
Albion Correctional Facility
3595 State School Rd, Albion, NY 14411
Superintendent:
William Powers 585-589-5511
Altona Correctional Facility
555 Devils Den Rd, Altona, NY 12910
Superintendent:
John Demars. 518-236-7841
Attica Correctional Facility
639 Exchange Street, Attica, NY 14011-0149
Superintendent:
Mark Bradt. 585-591-2000
Auburn Correctional Facility
135 State St, Auburn, NY 13024
Superintendent:
Harold Graham. 315-253-8401
Bare Hill Correctional Facility
Caller Box #20 181 Brand Rd, Malone, NY 12953
Superintendent:
Bruce Yelich 518-483-8411
Bayview Correctional Facility
550 West 20th St, New York, NY 10011
Superintendent:
Vacant 212-255-7590
Beacon Correctional Facility
50 Camp Beacon Rd, PO Box 780, Beacon, NY 12508-0780

Superintendent:
Gail Thomas....................................845-831-4200

Bedford Hills Correctional Facility
247 Harris Rd, Bedford Hills, NY 10507
Superintendent:
Sabina Kaplan..................................914-241-3100

Butler Correctional Facility
PO Box 388, 14001 Westbury Cutoff Rd, Red Creek, NY 13143
Superintendent:
Sheryl Zenzen..................................315-754-8001

Cape Vincent Correctional Facility
36560 Route 12E, Box 599, Cape Vincent, NY 13618
Superintendent:
Patricia LeConey...............................315-654-4100

Cayuga Correctional Facility
PO Box 1150, 2202 Route 38A, Moravia, NY 13119-1150
Superintendent:
David Stallone.................................315-497-1110

Chateaugay Correctional Facility
PO Box 320, 7874 Route 11, Chateaugay, NY 12920
Superintendent:
Michael Lira...................................518-497-3300

Clinton Correctional Facility
PO Box 2000, 1156 Route 374, Cook St, Dannemora, NY 12929
Superintendent:
Thomas LaValley.......................518-492-2511 x2099

Collins Correctional Facility
PO Box 490, Middle Rd, Collins, NY 14034-0490
Superintendent:
Michael Graziano...............................716-532-4588

Coxsackie Correctional Facility
11260 Route 9W, Box 200, West Coxsackie, NY 12051-0200
Superintendent:
Daniel Martuscello.............................518-731-2781

Downstate Correctional Facility
121 Red Schoolhouse Rd, PO Box 445, Fishkill, NY 12524-0445
Superintendent:
Ada Perez......................................845-831-6600

Eastern NY Correctional Facility
30 Institution Rd, Box 338, Napanoch, NY 12458-0338
Superintendent:
Thomas Griffin.................................845-647-7400

Edgecombe Correctional Facility
611 Edgecombe Ave, New York, NY 10032-4398
Superintendent:
Shelda Washington..............................212-923-2575

Elmira Correctional Facility
1879 Davis St, PO Box 500, Elmira, NY 14902-0500
Superintendent:
Paul Chappius..................................607-734-3901

Fishkill Correctional Facility
18 Strack Dr, PO Box 307, Prospect Street, Beacon, NY 12508
Superintendent:
William Connolly...............................845-831-0400

Five Points Correctional Facility
Caller Box 400, 6000 State Rte 96, Romulus, NY 14541
Superintendent:
Michael Sheahan................................607-869-5111

Franklin Correctional Facility
62 Bare Hill Rd, PO Box 10, Malone, NY 12953
Superintendent:
Darwin LaClair.................................518-483-6040

Gouverneur Correctional Facility
112 Scotch Settlement Rd, PO Box 370, Gouverneur, NY 13642-0370
Superintendent:
Elizabeth O'Meara..............................315-287-7351

Gowanda Correctional Facility
PO Box 350, South Rd, Gowanda, NY 14070-0350
Superintendent:
John Lempke....................................716-532-0177

Great Meadow Correctional Facility
11739 State Rte 22, Box 51, Comstock, NY 12821
Superintendent:
Steve Racette..................................518-639-5516

Green Haven Correctional Facility
594 Rte 216, Stormville, NY 12582
Superintendent:
William Lee....................................845-221-2711

Greene Correctional Facility
PO Box 8, 165 Plank Rd, Coxsackie, NY 12051-0008
Superintendent:
Brandon Smith..................................518-731-2741

Groveland Correctional Facility
7000 Sonyea Rd, PO Box 50, Sonyea, NY 14556
Superintendent:
Sandra Amoia-Kowalczyk.........................585-658-2871

Hale Creek ASACTC
279 Maloney Rd, Johnstown, NY 12095
Superintendent:
David Hallenbeck...............................518-736-2094

Hudson Correctional Facility
Box 576, 56 East Court St, Hudson, NY 12534-0576
Superintendent:
Donna Lewin....................................518-828-4311

Lakeview Shock Incarceration Correctional Facility
9300 Lake Ave, PO Box T, Brocton, NY 14716
Superintendent:
Malcolm Cully..................................716-792-7100

Lincoln Correctional Facility
31-33 West 110th St, New York, NY 10026-4398
Superintendent:
Wendy Featherstone.............................212-860-9400

Livingston Correctional Facility
7005 Sonyea Rd, PO Box 49, Sonyea, NY 14556-0049
Superintendent:
Michelle Artus.................................585-658-3710

Marcy Correctional Facility
PO Box 5000, 9000 Old River Rd, Marcy, NY 13403
Superintendent:
Charles Kelly..................................315-768-1400

Mid-State Correctional Facility
PO Box 216, 9005 Old River Rd, Marcy, NY 13403-0216
Superintendent:
John Colvin....................................315-768-8581

Mohawk Correctional Facility
6100 School Road, PO Box 8451, Rome, NY 13440
Superintendent:
Paul Gonyea....................................315-339-5232

Monterey Shock Incarceration Correctional Facility
2150 Evergreen Hill Rd, RD #1, Beaver Dams, NY 14812-9718
Superintendent:
Leroy Fields...................................607-962-3184

Moriah Shock Incarceration Correctional Facility
PO Box 999, Mineville, NY 12956-0999
Superintendent:
Bruce McCormick................................518-942-7561

Mt McGregor Correctional Facility
1000 Mt McGregor Rd, Box 2071, Wilton, NY 12831-5071
Superintendent:
William Haggett................................518-587-3960

Ogdensburg Correctional Facility
One Correction Way, Ogdensburg, NY 13669-2288
Superintendent:
Larry Frank....................................315-393-0281

Orleans Correctional Facility
3595 Gaines Basin Rd, Albion, NY 14411
Superintendent:
Sandra Dolce...................................585-589-6820

Otisville Correctional Facility
57 Sanitorium Rd, Box 8, Otisville, NY 10963-0008

Offices and agencies generally appear in alphabetical order, except when specific order is requested by listee.

Policy Areas

Superintendent:
Kathleen Gerbing 845-386-1490

Queensboro Correctional Facility
47-04 Van Dam St, Long Island City, NY 11101-3081
Superintendent:
Dennis Breslin 718-361-8920

Riverview Correctional Facility
PO Box 158, 1110 Tibbits Dr, Ogdensburg, NY 13669
Superintendent:
Calvin Rabsatt 315-393-8400

Rochester Correctional Facility
470 Ford St, Rochester, NY 14608-2499
Superintendent:
Sheryl Zenzen 585-454-2280

Shawangunk Correctional Facility
200 Quick Rd, PO Box 750, Wallkill, NY 12589-0750
Superintendent:
Joseph Smith 845-895-2081

Sing Sing Correctional Facility
354 Hunter St, Ossining, NY 10562
Superintendent:
Michael Capra 914-941-0108

Southport Correctional Facility
236 Bob Masia Dr, PO Box 2000, Pine City, NY 14871
Superintendent:
Stephen Wenderlich 607-737-0850

Sullivan Correctional Facility
Box 116, 325 Riverside Dr, Fallsburg, NY 12733-0116
Superintendent:
Patrick Griffin 845-434-2080

Taconic Correctional Facility
250 Harris Rd, Bedford Hills, NY 10507-2498
Superintendent:
Patty Nelson 914-241-3010

Ulster Correctional Facility
750 Berme Rd, PO Box 800, Napanoch, NY 12458
Superintendent:
Jerome Nicolato 845-647-1670

Upstate Correctional Facility
PO Box 2000, 309 Bare Hill Rd, Malone, NY 12953
Superintendent:
David Rock 518-483-6997

Wallkill Correctional Facility
50 McKenderick Rd, PO Box G, Wallkill, NY 12589-0286
Superintendent:
Timothy Laffin Sr 845-895-2021

Washington Correctional Facility
72 Lock 11 Lane, Box 180, Comstock, NY 12821-0180
Superintendent:
Tim Sheehan 518-639-4486

Watertown Correctional Facility
23147 Swan Rd, Watertown, NY 13601-9340
Superintendent:
Barry McArdle 315-782-7490

Wende Correctional Facility
3040 Wende Rd, PO Box 1187, Alden, NY 14004-1187
Superintendent:
Dale Artus 716-937-4000

Willard Drug Treatment Center
7116 County Route 132, PO Box 303, Willard, NY 14588
Superintendent:
Ricky Bartlett 607-869-5500

Woodbourne Correctional Facility
99 Prison Rd, PO Box 1000, Woodbourne, NY 12788
Superintendent:
Robert Cunningham 845-434-7730

Wyoming Correctional Facility
3203 Dunbar Rd, PO Box 501, Attica, NY 14011
Superintendent:
David Unger 585-591-1010

Security Staffing Unit
Director:
Philip Battiste 518-485-5407

Special Operations
Director, Corrections Emergency Response Team (Cert):
Col. Dennis Bradford 518-457-2006
Director, CIU:
James O'Gorman 518-457-2006
Director, Special Housing/Inmate Disciplinary Program:
Albert Prack 518-457-2337

Health Services Division

Deputy Commissioner/Chief Medical Officer:
Carl Koenigsmann MD 518-457-7072
Assistant Commissioner, Health Services:
Elizabeth Ritter 518-445-6176

Correctional Health Services
Director:
Nancy Lyng 518-445-6176

Dental Services
Director:
Mary D'Silva DDS 518-445-6176

Mental Health
Director:
Doris Ramirez-Romero 518-445-6071

Population Management

Chief of Investigations:
Vernon Fonda . . . . 518-457-2653 or 518-457-2653

Management Information Services
Director/CIO:
Thomas Herzog 518-457-2540

Program Planning, Research & Evaluation
Director:
Paul Korotkin 518-408-0424

Program Services

Deputy Commissioner:
Jeffrey McKoy 518-457-5555
Assistant Commissioner:
Catherine Jacobsen 518-408-5825

Education
Director:
Linda Hollmen 518-402-0092

Guidance & Counseling
Director:
Joanne Nigro 518-402-1789

Library Services
Supervising Librarian:
Barbara Ost 518-485-7109

Ministerial, Family & Volunteer Services
Director:
Cheryl V Morris 518-402-1700

Substance Abuse Treatment Services
Director:
Rachael Young 518-402-1745

Victim Services, Office of

80 S Swan Street
2nd Fl
Albany, NY 12210
518-457-8727 or 800-247-8035 Fax: 518-457-8658
Web site: www.ovs.ny.gov

Offices and agencies generally appear in alphabetical order, except when specific order is requested by listee.

55 Hanson Place
10th Fl
Brooklyn, NY 11217-1523
718-923-4325
Fax: 718-923-4347

Director:
Elizabeth Cronin Esq 518-485-5719
Deputy Director for Administration:
Virginia A Miller 518-457-8003
Crime Victim Compensation Investigations (Brooklyn):
Claudette Christian Bullock 718-923-4348
Crime Victim Compensation Investigations (Albany):
Karen Senez 518-457-8060
General Counsel/Legal Unit:
John Watson 518-457-8066/fax: 518-457-8658
Director, Public Information:
Janine Kava 518-457-8828

Criminal Justice Services, Division of

80 S. Swan St
Albany, NY 12210
518-457-5837 or 800-262-3257 Fax: 518-457-3089
e-mail: info@dcjs.ny.gov
Web site: www.criminaljustice.ny.gov

Executive Deputy Commissioner:
Michael C Green 518-457-1260
Executive Deputy Commissioner:
Michael C Green 518-457-6091
Affirmative Action Officer:
Wanda Trouche 518-485-7962
Director, Public Information:
Janine Kava 518-457-8906/fax: 518-485-7715
e-mail: janine.kava@dcjs.ny.gov

Administration Office

First Deputy Commissioner:
Mark Bonacquist 518-457-1260

Administrative Services

Director:
Vacant 518-457-4168

Human Resources Management

Director:
Karen Davis 518-485-1704

State Finance & Budget

Director, Finance:
Mary Ann Rossi 518-457-6105
Director, Internal Audit & Compliance:
Bob Wright 518-485-5823

Advisory Groups

Juvenile Justice Advisory Group

Chair:
Vacant 518-457-3670

NYS Motor Vehicle & Insurance Fraud Prevention Board

Chair:
Vacant 518-485-8462

Legal Services

Deputy Commissioner & Counsel:
John Czajka 518-457-4181

Missing & Exploited Children Clearinghouse

Director:
Kenneth R Buniak 518-485-7641

Commission on Forensic Science

Office of Forensic Services

Director:
Vacant 518-457-4181

Office of Criminal Justice Operations

Director, Criminal Justice Operations:
Joe Morrissey 518-485-2995

Office of Operations

Assistant Director:
Vacant 518-457-6050
Chief, Operations:
Dona Call 518-485-7688
Manager, State Identification:
Ann Sammons 518-457-3700

Office of Justice Information Services

Deputy Commissioner:
Anne Roest 518-485-7176

Information Technology Development Group

Director:
Connie Snyder 518-485-7154

Information Technology Services Group

Assistant Director:
Alex Roberts 518-457-3743

Office of Sex Offender Management

Director:
Risa Sugarman 518-457-6985

Office of Justice Statistics & Performance

Director:
Terry Salo 518-457-7301
Chief, Crimestat Unit:
Paula K Lockhart 518-485-7122
Chief, Crime Reporting & Statistical Services Unit:
Adam Dean 518-457-8381

Office of Public Safety

Law Enforcement Accreditation Council

Municipal Police Training Council

State Committee for Coordination of Police Services for Elderly (TRIAD)

Statewide Law Enforcement Telecommunications Committee

Deputy Commissioner:
Michael Wood 518-485-7620
Supervisor, Program Services:
John R Digman 518-485-1411
Supervisor, Administrative Services & Security Guard Advisory Council:
Debra Bourque 518-485-1416

Office of Strategic Planning

Justice Systems Analysis Unit

Chief:
David vanAlstyne 518-457-7301

Funding & Program Assistance Office

Deputy Commissioner:
Jeffrey Bender 518-457-8462
Assistant Director:
Ron Dickens 518-457-8406

Operation IMPACT Coordinator

Director:
Julie Pasquini 518-485-7923

Inspector General (NYS), Office of the

Empire State Plaza
Bldg 2, 16th Fl
Albany, NY 12223
518-474-1010 or 800-367-4448 Fax: 518-486-3745
Web site: www.ig.ny.gov

61 Broadway
12th Fl
New York, NY 10006
212-635-3150
Fax: 212-809-6287

State Inspector General:
Catherine Leahy Scott . . . . 212-635-3150 or 518-474-1010
e-mail: inspector.general@ig.ny.gov
Executive Deputy Inspector General:
Spencer Freedman. 212-635-3150
Chief Investigator:
William Hebert 212-635-3150
Director, Public Information:
Kate Gurnett 518-474-1010

Law Department

120 Broadway
New York, NY 10271-0332
212-416-8000 or 800-771-7755
Web site: www.ag.ny.gov

State Capitol
Albany, NY 12224-0341
518-776-2000
Fax: 518-650-9401

Attorney General:
Eric T Schneiderman . . . . 212-416-8050 or 518-776-2000
COO:
Jeanette Moy. . . . . 212-416-8050 or 518-473-7900
Press Secretary:
Matt Mittenthal 212-416-8060/fax: 212-416-6005

Appeals & Opinions

Solicitor General:
Barbara D Underwood . . . . 212-416-8016 or 518-402-2074
Deputy Solicitor General, Criminal Appeals:
Nikki Kowalski 212-416-8370
Deputy Solicitor General:
Anisha Dasgupta 212-416-8921
Deputy Solicitor General:
Steven Wu 212-416-6312/fax: 212-416-8962

Law Library

Chief, Library Services:
Patricia Partello 518-776-2566/fax: 518-915-7737
Legal Support Analyst:
Vacant 212-416-8012/fax: 212-416-6130

Criminal Justice

Executive Deputy Attorney General:
Kelly Donovan 212-416-8050

Criminal Enforcement & Financial Crimes Bureau

Bureau Chief:
Gary Fishman . . . . 212-416-8750 or 518-776-2370

Medicaid Fraud Control Unit

120 Broadway, 13th Fl, New York, NY 10271-0007
Deputy Attorney General:
Amy Held 212-417-5250/fax: 212-417-4284

Guns, Gangs & Drugs Initiative

Special Deputy Attorney General:
Carl J Boykin 315-793-2502

Economic Justice

Executive Deputy Attorney General:
Manisha Sheth. 212-416-8050
Deputy Attorney General:
Virginia Chavez Romano 212-416-8389

Antitrust Bureau

Bureau Chief:
Eric J Stock 212-416-8282/fax: 212-416-6015
e-mail: eric.stock@ag.ny.gov

Consumer Frauds Bureau

Bureau Chief:
Jane Azia 212-416-6067/fax: 212-416-6003

Social Justice

Executive Deputy Attorney General:
Alvin L Bragg, Jr. 212-416-8075/fax: 212-416-8942

Civil Rights Bureau

Bureau Chief:
Lourdes Rosado. 212-416-8250/fax: 212-416-8074

Investigations

Chief, Investigations:
Dominick Zarrella. 212-416-6328 or 518-486-4540
fax: 212-416-8773

State Counsel

Chief Deputy Attorney General & Counsel:
Janet Sabel 212-416-8050
Chief Deputy Attorney General & Counsel:
Jason Brown 212-416-8050

Civil Recoveries Bureau

Bureau Chief:
John Cremo 518-776-2173/fax: 518-915-7731

Claims Bureau

Bureau Chief:
Katharine Brooks . . . . 518-776-2300 or 212-416-8500

Litigation Bureau

Bureau Chief:
Jeffrey Dvorin . . . . 518-776-2300 or 212-416-8610

Real Property Bureau

Bureau Chief:
Alison Crocker 518-776-2700

Parole Board, The

Corrections & Community Supervision
97 Central Ave
Albany, NY 12206
518-473-9400 Fax: 518-473-6037
Web site: www.parole.ny.gov; doccs.ny.gov

Executive Office

Acting Commissioner:
Anthony J Annucci 518-473-9548
Secretary to the Chair:
Rachael Seguin 518-473-9548
Public Information Officer:
Vacant 518-486-4631/fax: 518-473-6037
Administrative Assistant:
Lorraine Morse 518-473-5424/fax: 518-473-6037

Administrative Services

Director:
Jeffrey Nesich 518-473-3901/fax: 518-486-5858

Offices and agencies generally appear in alphabetical order, except when specific order is requested by listee.

Director, Human Resource Management:
Barbara Farley 518-473-3901
Labor Relations Representative:
Vacant 518-474-5612

Clemency Unit
97 Central Ave, Albany, NY 12206
Director:
Frank Herman 518-485-8953

Information Services
Director:
John Armitage 518-445-7558/fax: 518-445-7553

Office of Counsel
Chief Counsel:
Terrence X Tracy 518-473-5671/fax: 518-473-9760

Parole Operations Unit
Deputy Commissioner, Community Supervision:
Angela Jiminez 212-239-5730
Director, Internal Operations:
Timothy O'Brien 518-408-3473
Deputy Director, Sex Offenders Mgmt Unit:
Mary Osborne 518-473-5572
Regional Dir-Region I:
Michael Falk 212-736-9880
Regional Dir-Region II:
Milton Brown 718-558-5227
Regional Dir-Region III:
Steven Claudio 914-654-8690
Regional Dir-Region IV:
Michael Burdi 518-459-7469
Regional Dir-Region V:
Eugenio Russi 585-232-6927

Policy Analysis
Director:
Michael R Buckman 518-445-6071

Victim Impact Unit . . . . fax: 518-493-9659
Parole Officer:
Barbara Tobin 518-486-4400
Parole Officer:
Christine Robinson 518-486-4400

Prevention of Domestic Violence, Office for the
80 South Swan Street
11th Fl Rm 1157
Albany, NY 12210
518-457-5800 Fax: 518-457-5810
e-mail: opdvpublicinfo@opdv.ny.gov
Web site: www.opdv.ny.gov

90 Church St, 13th Fl
New York, NY 10007
212-417-4477
Fax: 212-417-4972

Executive Director:
Gwen Wright 518-457-5800
Fiscal Officer:
Linda Cassidy 518-457-7995
Public Information Officer:
Suzanne Cecala 518-457-5744
e-mail: suzanne.cecala@opdv.ny.gov

State Police, Division of
Building 22, State Campus
1220 Washington Ave
Albany, NY 12226-2252
518-457-2180
e-mail: nyspmail@troopers.ny.gov
Web site: www.troopers.ny.gov

Superintendent:
Joseph A D'Amico 518-457-6721
First Deputy Superintendent:
Kevin T Gagan 518-457-6711/fax: 518-485-7505
Counsel:
Glenn Valle 518-457-6137/fax: 518-485-1164

Administration
Director:
Terence P O'Mara 518-457-6622/fax: 518-485-5051

Forensic Investigation Center
Director, Staff Inspector:
Gerald M Zeosky 518-457-2466/fax: 518-457-2477

Public Information
Director, Technical Lieutenant:
Glenn R Miner 518-457-2180/fax: 518-485-7818
e-mail: nyspmail@troopers.ny.gov

Employee Relations
Deputy Superintendent:
Francis P Christensen 518-457-3572/fax: 518-485-7505

Human Resources
Deputy Superintendent:
Bryon Christman 518-485-5044/fax: 518-485-2293

State Police Academy
Director:
Major Ellwood A Sloat, Jr 518-457-7254/fax: 518-485-1454

Field Command
Deputy Superintendent:
Vacant 518-457-6554/fax: 518-457-4779

Internal Affairs
Deputy Superintendent:
Anthony G Ellis 518-485-6018

CORPORATIONS, AUTHORITIES AND COMMISSIONS

New York State Commission of Correction
80 South Swan St
12th Fl
Albany, NY 12210
518-485-2346 Fax: 518-485-2467
e-mail: infoscoc@scoc.ny.gov
Web site: www.scoc.ny.gov

Chairman:
Thomas A Beilein 518-485-2330
Assistant to Chair:
Patricia Amati 518-485-2330
Counsel:
Brian Callahan 518-485-2346
Chair, Citizens' Policy & Complaint Review Council:
Thomas Loughren 518-485-2346
Chair, Medical Review Board:
Phyllis Harrison-Ross 518-485-2346
Deputy Director, Operations:
Richard Kinney 518-457-6110

Offices and agencies generally appear in alphabetical order, except when specific order is requested by listee.

Policy Areas

Director, Operations:
James Lawrence 518-485-2346
Deputy Director Public Information:
Walter McClure 518-485-2346

NEW YORK STATE LEGISLATURE

See Legislative Branch in Section 1 for additional Standing Committee and Subcommittee information.

Assembly Standing Committees

Alcoholism & Drug Abuse
Chair:
Linda Rosenthal (D) 518-455-5802
Ranking Minority Member:
Mark Johns (R) 518-455-5784

Codes
Chair:
Joseph R Lentol (D) 518-455-4477
Ranking Minority Member:
Al Graf (R) 518-455-5937

Correction
Chair:
Daniel O'Donnell (D) 518-455-5603
Ranking Minority Member:
Joe Giglio (R) 518-455-5241

Senate Standing Committees

Codes
Chair:
Michael F Nozzolio (R) 518-455-2366
Ranking Minority Member:
Daniel Squadron (D) 518-455-2625

Crime Victims, Crime & Correction
Chair:
Patrick M Gallivan (R) 518-455-3471
Ranking Minority Member:
Ruth Hassell-Thompson (D) 518-455-2061

U.S. GOVERNMENT

EXECUTIVE DEPARTMENTS AND RELATED AGENCIES

US Justice Department
Web site: www.justice.gov

Bureau of Alcohol, Tobacco, Firearms & Explosives
Web site: www.atf.gov

New York Field Division . . . . fax: 646-335-9061
Financial Square, 32 Old Slip, Suite 3500, New York, NY 10005
646-335-9060 Fax: 646-335-9061
e-mail: nydiv@atf.gov
Special Agent-in-Charge:
Delano Reid
Public Information Officer:
Charles Mulham

Drug Enforcement Administration - New York Task Force
99 10th Avenue, New York, NY 10011
212-337-3900
Web site: www.dea.gov
Special Agent-in-Charge:
James J. Hunt
Associate Special Agent-in-Charge:
Wilbert L Plummer 212-337-2901
Public Information Officer:
Erin Mulvey 212-337-2906

Federal Bureau of Investigation - New York Field Offices
Web site: www.fbi.gov

Albany . . . . fax: 518-431-7463
200 McCarty Avenue, Albany, NY 12209
518-465-7551 Fax: 518-431-7463
Web site: www.fbi.gov/albany
Special Agent-in-Charge:
Andrew Vale 518-465-7551

Buffalo . . . . fax: 716-843-5288
One FBI Plaza, Buffalo, NY 14202-2698
716-856-7800 Fax: 716-843-5288
Web site: www.fbi.gov/buffalo
Special Agent-in-Charge:
Adam S. Cohen 716-856-7800

New York City
26 Federal Plaza, 23rd Floor, New York, NY 10278-0004
212-384-1000 or 212-384-2100
Assistant Director-in-Charge:
Diego Rodriguez 212-384-1000

Federal Bureau of Prisons
Web site: www.bop.gov

Brooklyn Metropolitan Detention Center . . . . fax: 718-840-5005
80 29th Street, Brooklyn, NY 11232
718-840-4200 Fax: 718-840-5005
Warden:
Frank Strada 718-840-4200/fax: 718-840-5005

CCM New York . . . . fax: 718-840-4207
100 29th Street, Brooklyn, NY 11232
718-840-4219 Fax: 718-840-4207

Federal Correctional Institution at Otisville . . . . fax: 845-386-6727
Two Mile Drive, PO Box 600, Otisville, NY 10963
845-386-6700 Fax: 845-386-6727
Warden:
Monica Recktenwald

Metropolitan Correctional Center . . . . fax: 646-836-7751
150 Park Row, New York, NY 10007
646-836-6300 Fax: 646-836-7751
Warden:
Maureen Baird

Ray Brook Federal Correctional Institution
128 Ray Brook Road, Ray Brook, NY 12977
Warden:
Donald Hudson 518-897-4000/fax: 518-897-4216

Secret Service - New York Field Offices

Albany
7 Southwoods Blvd, Suite 305-A, Albany, NY 12211
Resident Agent-in-Charge:
William Leege 518-427-0400

Buffalo
598 Main Street, Suite 300, Buffalo, NY 14202
Special Agent-in-Charge:
Tracy Gast 716-551-4401

JFK/LGA
230-59 Rockaway Blvd, Suite 265, Springfield Gardens, NY 11413
718-553-0911
Resident Agent-in-Charge:
John McQuade 718-553-0911

Melville
145 Pinelawn Road, Suite 200N, Melville, NY 11747
631-293-4028
Resident Agent-in-Charge:
Farrell Dolan 631-293-4028

New York City
335 Adams Street, 32nd Floor, Brooklyn, NY 11201
718-840-1000
Special Agent-in-Charge:
Robert J. Sica 718-840-1000

Rochester
100 Chestnut Street, Suite 1820, Rochester, NY 14604
585-232-4160
Special Agent:
Joel Blackerby 585-232-4160

Syracuse . . . . fax: 315-448-0302
100 South Clinton Street, Suite 1371, Syracuse, NY 13261
315-448-0304 Fax: 315-448-0302
Resident Agent-in-Charge:
Timothy Kirk 315-448-0304

White Plains
140 Grand Street, Suite 801, White Plains, NY 10601
914-682-6300
Resident Agent-in-Charge:
Jeff Wood 914-682-6300

US Attorney's Office - New York

Eastern District . . . . fax: 718-254-7508
271 Cadman Plaza East, Brooklyn, NY 11201
718-254-7000 Fax: 718-254-7508
US Attorney:
Robert L. Capers 718-254-7000/fax: 718-254-7508
Assistant United States Attorney:
James R. Cho 718-254-6519/fax: 718-254-7508
Assistant United States Attorney:
Joseph Anthony Marutollo 718-254-6288/fax: 718-254-7508
Assistant United States Attorney:
Elliot M. Schachner 718-254-6053/fax: 718-254-7508
Executive Assistant United States Attorney:
William J. Muller 718-254-7000/fax: 718-254-7508
Assistant United States Attorney, Criminal Division:
Zainab Ahmad
Deputy Chief, Civil Division:
Gail Matthews
Chief of Affirmative Civil Enforcement, Civil Division:
John Vagelatos

Northern District . . . . fax: 315-448-0689
315-448-0672 Fax: 315-448-0689

Albany
445 Broadway, Room 218, Albany, NY 12207-2924
Assistant United States Attorney:
Thomas Spina Jr.

Binghamton . . . . fax: 607-773-2901
319 Federal Building, 15 Henry Street, Binghamton, NY 13901
607-773-2887 Fax: 607-773-2901
Assistant United States Attorney:
Miro Lovric

Plattsburgh . . . . fax: 518-314-7811
14 Durkee Street, Suite 340, Plattsburgh, NY 12901
518-314-7800 Fax: 518-314-7811
Assistant United States Attorney:
Elizabeth Horsman

Syracuse . . . . fax: 315-448-0689
100 South Clinton Street, PO Box 7198, Syracuse, NY 13261-7198
315-448-0672 Fax: 315-448-0689
United States Attorney:
Richard S. Hartunian 315-448-0672
Assistant United States Attorney:
Tamara B. Thomson 315-448-0672
Assistant United States Attorney, Chief Civil Division:
Thomas Spina Jr.
Assistant United States Attorney, Chief Criminal Division:
Elizabeth C. Coombe
Administrative Officer:
Martha Stratton 315-448-0672/fax: 315-448-0689

Southern District . . . . fax: 212-637-2685
1 St. Andrew's Plaza, New York, NY 10007
212-637-2200 Fax: 212-637-2685

New York City
United States Attorney:
Preet Bharara
Deputy United States Attorney:
Joon H. Kim 212-637-2200
Chief, Criminal Division:
Daniel Stein 212-637-2200
Chief, Civil Division:
Sara L. Shudofsky 212-637-2800
Deputy Chief, Criminal Division:
Andrew Dember 212-637-2200
Assistant United States Attorney, Civil Division:
Rebecca Martin 212-637-2800

White Plains
300 Quarropas Street, White Plains, NY 10601-4150
914-993-1900 or 914-993-1916
Assistant United States Attorney, White Plains Co-Chief:
Perry Carbone 914-993-1900

Western District

Buffalo . . . . fax: 716-551-3052
138 Delaware Avenue, Buffalo, NY 14202
716-843-5700 Fax: 716-551-3052
United States Attorney:
William J. Hochul, Jr.
Assistant United States Attorney, Appellate Division Chief:
Joseph J. Karaszewski
Assistant United States Attorney, Civil Division Chief:
Mary Pat Fleming 716-843-5867
Assistant United States Attorney, Criminal Division Chief:
Joseph M. Guerra, III 716-843-5824
Assistant United States Attorney, National Security Coordinator:
Anthony M. Bruce 716-843-5886
Assistant United States Attorney, General Crimes Section Chief:
Michael DiGiacomo
Administrative Officer:
Amy L. Smith 716-843-5700

Rochester . . . . fax: 585-263-6226
100 State Street, Suite 500, Rochester, NY 14614
585-263-6760 Fax: 585-263-6226
Assistant United States Attorney-in-Charge:
Richard A. Resnick 585-263-6760

US Marshals' Service - New York

Eastern District

Brooklyn
US Courthouse, 225 Cadman Plaza, Brooklyn, NY 11201
718-260-0440
United States Marshal:
Charles Dunne

Central Islip
100 Federal Plaza, Central Islip, NY 11722
631-712-6000
United States Marshal:
Charles Dunne

Northern District

Albany
James T. Foley Courthouse, 445 Broadway, Albany, NY 12201

Policy Areas

518-472-5401
United States Marshal:
David McNulty

Binghamton
US Courthouse & Federal Building, 15 Henry Street, Binghamton, NY 13902
607-773-2723
United States Marshal:
David McNulty

Syracuse
100 South Clinton Street, Syracuse, NY 13261
315-473-7601
United States Marshal:
David McNulty

Utica
Alexander Pirnie Federal Building, 10 Broad Street, Room 213, Utica, NY 13501
315-793-8109
United States Marshal:
David McNulty

Southern District
500 Pearl Street, New York, NY 10007
United States Marshal:
Michael Greco 212-331-7200/fax: 212-637-6130

Western District
Buffalo
2 Niagara Street, Buffalo, NY 14202
716-348-5300
United States Marshal:
Charles Salina

Rochester
US Courthouse, 100 State Street, Room 2240, Rochester, NY 14614
585-263-5787
United States Marshal:
Charles Salina

US Parole Commission
90 K Street NE, 3rd Floor, Washington, DC 20530
Chairman:
J. Patricia Wilson Smoot 202-346-7000

U.S. CONGRESS

See U.S. Congress Chapter for additional Standing Committee and Subcommittee information.

House of Representatives Standing Committees

Judiciary
Chair:
Bob Goodlatte (R-VA)
Ranking Member:
John Conyers, Jr. (D-MI)
New York Delegate:
Hakeem Jeffries (D)
New York Delegate:
Jerrold Nadler (D) 202-225-5635

Subcommittee
Crime, Terrorism, Homeland Security & Investigations
Chair:
Jim Sensenbrenner, Jr. (R-WI)
Ranking Member:
Sheila Jackson Lee (D-TX) 202-225-3816

Senate Standing Committees

Judiciary
Chair:
Chuck Grassley (R-IA) 202-224-3744
Ranking Member:
Patrick Leahy (D-VT)
New York Delegate:
Charles Schumer (D) 202-224-6542

PRIVATE SECTOR

American Society for the Prevention of Cruelty to Animals (ASPCA)
424 East 92nd Street, New York, NY 10128-6804
212-876-7700 or 888-666-2279
e-mail: publicinformation@aspca.org
Web site: www.aspca.org
Promoting humane treatment of animals, education & advocacy programs & conducting statewide anti-cruelty investigation & enforcement
Matthew Bershadker, President & Chief Executive Officer

Associated Licensed Detectives of New York State
PO Box 13684, Albany, NY 12212
518-621-4517 or 800-417-0710 Fax: 518-621-4516
e-mail: info@aldonys.org
Web site: www.aldonys.org
Membership association representing the interests of the NYS private investigation industry
Gil Alba, President

Ballard Spahr LLP New York
919 Third Avenue, 37th Floor, New York, NY 10022
212-223-0200 Fax: 212-223-1942
e-mail: stillmanc@ballardspahr.com
Web site: www.ballardspahr.com
White collar criminal law
Charles A. Stillman, Partner

Berkshire Farm Center & Services for Youth
13640 State Route 22, Canaan, NY 12029
518-781-4567 Fax: 518-781-0507
e-mail: info@berkshirefarm.org
Web site: www.berkshirefarm.org
Child welfare agency for troubled youth & families
Timothy Giacchetta, President & Chief Executive Officer

CUNY John Jay College of Criminal Justice
899 10th Avenue, New York, NY 10019
212-237-8600 Fax: 212-237-8607
e-mail: jtravis@jjay.cuny.edu
Web site: www.jjay.cuny.edu
Criminal justice, police & fire science, forensic science & psychology, international criminal justice, public administration
Jeremy Travis, President

Center for Alternative Sentencing & Employment Services (CASES)
151 Lawrence Street, 3rd Floor, Brooklyn, NY 11201
212-553-6300 Fax: 718-596-3872
e-mail: info@cases.org
Web site: www.cases.org
Advocacy for the use of community sanctions designed to improve behavioral health & public safety
Joel Copperman, President & Chief Executive Officer

Center for Law & Justice
Pine West Plaza, Building 2, Washington Ave. Exit, Albany, NY 12205
518-427-8361 Fax: 518-427-8362
e-mail: cflj@verizon.net
Web site: www.cflj.org
Advocacy for fair treatment of disadvantaged & low-income NY communities in the legal & criminal justice systems; referrals, workshops, outreach & education
Dr. Alice P. Green, Executive Director

Coalition Against Domestic Violence, NYS
119 Washington Avenue, Albany, NY 12210
518-482-5465 Fax: 518-482-3807
e-mail: vasquez@nyscadv.org
Web site: www.nyscadv.org
Domestic violence prevention; training, technical assistance, events & publications
Tammy Van Epps, President

Coalition Against Sexual Assault (NYS)
28 Essex Street, Albany, NY 12206
518-482-4222 Fax: 518-482-4248
e-mail: jzannoni@nyscasa.org
Web site: www.nyscasa.org
Advocacy, public education, technical assistance & training
Joanne Zannoni, Executive Director

Correctional Association of New York
2090 Adam Clayton Powell Blvd, Suite 200, New York, NY 10027
212-254-5700 Fax: 212-473-2807
e-mail: selijah@correctionalassociation.org
Web site: www.correctionalassociation.org
Advocates for improved prison conditions & a fair criminal justice system
Soffiyah Elijah, Executive Director

NYS Bar Assn, Public Trust & Confidence in the Legal System
Debevoise & Plimpton LLP
919 Third Avenue, New York, NY 10022
212-909-6000 Fax: 212-909-6836
e-mail: torewyler@debevoise.com
Web site: www.debevoise.com
Tom Orewyler, Head of Communications

Education & Assistance Corporation Inc
50 Clinton Street, Suite 107, Hempstead, NY 11550
516-539-0150 Fax: 516-539-0160
e-mail: lelder@eacinc.org
Web site: www.eacinc.org
Advocacy, education & counseling programs & services for youth, seniors, families & communities in need
Lance W. Elder, President & Chief Executive Officer

Fortune Society (The)
29-76 Northern Blvd, Long Island City, NY 11101
212-691-7554 Fax: 212-255-4948
e-mail: jpage@fortunesociety.org
Web site: www.fortunesociety.org
Promotes alternatives to incarceration & provides services for ex-offenders, including education, counseling, HIV/AIDS services, substance abuse & mental health treatment, referrals, employment skills training & transitional housing programs
JoAnne Page, President & Chief Executive Officer

Hofstra University, School of Law
121 Hofstra University, Hempstead, NY 11549-1210
516-463-5858
e-mail: hofstralaw@hofstra.edu
Web site: www.law.hofstra.edu
Antitrust, criminal law, evidence
Eric Lane, Dean

Law Offices of Stanley N Lupkin
98 Cutter Mill Road, Suite 227N, Great Neck, NY 11021
516-482-1223
e-mail: slupkin@gnlaw.com
Corporate, criminal & financial investigations, integrity monitorships
Stanley N. Lupkin, Partner

Legal Action Center
225 Varick Street, 4th Floor, New York, NY 10014
212-243-1313 or 800-223-4044 Fax: 212-675-0286
e-mail: lacinfo@lac.org
Web site: www.lac.org
Promotes alternatives to incarceration & advocates for policies that address issues relating to alcohol/drug abuse, HIV/AIDS & criminal justice
Paul N. Samuels, President & Director

Legal Aid Society
199 Water Street, New York, NY 10038
212-557-3300 Fax: 212-509-8761
Web site: www.legal-aid.org
Criminal defense & appeals
Seymour W. James, Jr., Attorney-in-Chief

NYS Bar Assn, Criminal Justice Section
Michael T Kelly, Esq
207 Admirals Walk, Buffalo, NY 14202
716-361-5828 Fax: 866-574-0725
Sean Patrick Kelly, Attorney

Mothers Against Drunk Driving (MADD) of NYS
33 Walt Whitman Road, Suite 307, Huntington Station, NY 11746
631-547-6233 Fax: 631-547-6235
e-mail: ny.state@madd.org
Web site: www.madd.org
Advocacy, public education & victim support
Rich Mallow, Executive Director

NYS Association of Chiefs of Police Inc
2697 Hamburg Street, Schenectady, NY 12303
518-355-3371 Fax: 518-356-5767
e-mail: nysacop@nycap.rr.com
Web site: www.nychiefs.org
Association of police chiefs dedicated to maintaining law & order in NYS
Margaret Ryan, Executive Director

NYS Correctional Officers & Police Benevolent Association Inc
102 Hackett Blvd, Albany, NY 12209
518-427-1551 or 888-484-7279 Fax: 518-426-1635
e-mail: nyscopba@nyscopba.org
Web site: www.nyscopba.org
Promotes the interests of New York State's correctional officers
Michael B. Powers, President

NYS Council of Probation Administrators
PO Box 2, 272 Broadway, Albany, NY 12203
518-487-5200 Fax: 518-487-5204
e-mail: info@nyscopa.com
Web site: www.nyscopa.com
Works to advance the interests of probation administrators in NYS, provide information on probation & develop strategies for crime prevention
Joy Bennett, President

NYS Defenders Association
194 Washington Avenue, Suite 500, Albany, NY 12210-2314
518-465-3524 Fax: 518-465-3249
Web site: www.nysda.org
Criminal defense
Jonathan E. Gradess, Executive Director

Offices and agencies generally appear in alphabetical order, except when specific order is requested by listee.

NYS Deputies Association Inc
61 Laredo Drive, Rochester, NY 14624
585-247-9322 Fax: 585-247-6661
e-mail: executivedirector@nysdeputy.org
Web site: www.nysdeputy.org
Thomas H. Ross, Executive Director

NYS Law Enforcement Officers Union, Council 82, AFSCME, AFL-CIO
Hollis V Chase Building, 63 Colvin Avenue, Albany, NY 12206
518-489-8424 or 800-724-0482 Fax: 518-435-1523
e-mail: c82@council82.org
Web site: www.council82.org
Union representing New York State's law enforcement officers & professionals; provides advocacy, support & research assistance for its members
James Lyman, Executive Director

NYS Sheriffs' Association
27 Elk Street, Albany, NY 12207
518-434-9091 Fax: 518-434-9093
e-mail: pkehoe@nysheriffs.org
Web site: www.nysheriffs.org
Not-for-profit corporation dedicated to providing support for sheriffs in NYS
Peter R. Kehoe, Executive Director

New York State Law Enforcement Council
One Hogan Place, New York, NY 10013
212-335-8927 Fax: 212-335-3808
Advocates for NY's law enforcement community & works to enhance the quality of justice & safety in NY
Kate Hogan, Chair

Osborne Association
809 Westchester Avenue, Bronx, NY 10455
718-707-2600 Fax: 718-707-3102
e-mail: info@osborneny.org
Web site: www.osborneny.org
Career/educational counseling, job referrals & training for recently released prisoners, substance abuse treatment, case management, HIV/AIDS counseling, family services, parenting education, re-entry services, housing placement assistance
Elizabeth A. Gaynes, President & Chief Executive Officer

Pace University, School of Law, John Jay Legal Services Inc
78 North Broadway, White Plains, NY 10603
914-422-4333 Fax: 914-422-4391
e-mail: gflint@law.pace.edu
Web site: www.law.pace.edu/john-jay-legal-services
Law school client representation clinical program specializing in the areas of criminal trial advocacy, disability rights litigation/transactional representation, immigration & investor rights/securities arbitrations
Margaret M. Flint, Executive Director

Patrolmen's Benevolent Association
125 Broad Street, 11th Floor, New York, NY 10004-2400
212-298-9100 or 212-349-7560
e-mail: rzink@nycpba.org
Web site: www.nycpba.org
NYC patrolmen's union
Patrick J. Lynch, President

Police Conference of NY Inc (PCNY)
112 State Street, Suite 1120, Albany, NY 12207
518-463-3283 Fax: 518-463-2488
e-mail: pcnyinfo@pcny.org
Web site: www.pcny.org
Advocacy for law enforcement officers
Richard Wells, President

Prisoners' Legal Services of New York
41 State Street, Suite M112, Albany, NY 12207
518-445-6050
Protects the rights of prisoners & advocates for humane prison conditions
Karen L. Murtagh, Executive Director

Remove Intoxicated Drivers (RID-USA Inc)
1013 Nott Street, PO Box 520, Schenectady, NY 12301
518-372-0034 or 888-283-5144 Fax: 518-370-4917
Web site: www.rid-usa.org
Victims' rights, alcohol policy & public awareness
Doris Aiken, President

Rochester Interfaith Jail Ministry Inc
2 Riverside Street, Rochester, NY 14613
585-458-5423
Support services for ex-offenders, the incarcerated & their families
Robert Crystal, Director

Services for the UnderServed (SUS)
305 Seventh Avenue, 10th Floor, New York, NY 10001
212-633-6900
e-mail: info@sus.org
Web site: www.sus.org
Disabilities services & support, substance abuse treatment & counseling, shelters & homelessness prevention services, low-income & supported housing
Donna Colonna, Chief Executive Officer

Stony Brook Drinking Driver Program LLC
PO Box 263, Holtsville, NY 11742
631-716-2001 Fax: 631-716-4439
e-mail: classes@stonybrookddp.com
Web site: www.stonybrookddp.com
Drinking & driving education & prevention
Judith Forde, Director

Trooper Foundation-State of New York Inc
3 Airport Park Blvd, Latham, NY 12110-1441
518-785-1002 Fax: 518-785-1003
e-mail: rmincher@nystf.org
Web site: www.nystrooperfoundation.org
Provides training, education, programs & services for NYS Police
Rachael L. Mincher, President

Vera Institute of Justice
233 Broadway, 12th Floor, New York, NY 10279-1299
212-334-1300 Fax: 212-941-9407
e-mail: contactvera@vera.org
Web site: www.vera.org
Works to ensure fair & equitable systems of justice & safety through research, technical assistance & demonstration projects
Nicholas Turner, President & Director

Women's Prison Association & Home Inc
110 Second Avenue, New York, NY 10003
646-292-7740 or 646-292-7748 Fax: 646-292-7763
e-mail: info@wpaonline.org
Web site: www.wpaonline.org
Community corrections & family preservation programs
Georgia Lerner, Executive Director

EDUCATION

NEW YORK STATE

GOVERNOR'S OFFICE

Governor's Office
Executive Chamber
State Capitol
Albany, NY 12224
518-474-8390 Fax: 518-474-1513
Web site: www.ny.gov

Governor:
Andrew M Cuomo 518-474-8390
Secretary to the Governor:
William Mulrow 518-474-4246
Counsel to the Governor:
Alphonso David 518-474-8343
Director of Policy:
John Maggiore 518-408-2576
Deputy Secretary, Education:
Jere Hochman 518-474-9883
Chief of Staff:
Melissa DeRosa . . . . .518-474-8418 or 212-681-4640
Director, Communications:
James Allen. . . . . .518-474-8418 or 212-681-4640

EXECUTIVE DEPARTMENTS AND RELATED AGENCIES

Board of Regents
89 Washington Ave
EB, Rm 110
Albany, NY 12234
518-474-5889 Fax: 518-486-2405
e-mail: regentsoffice@nysed.gov
Web site: www.regents.nysed.gov

Chancellor:
Betty A Rosa (2018) 518-474-5889
e-mail: Regent.Rosa@nysed.gov
Vice Chancellor:
T. Andrew Brown (2017) 585-454-3667
e-mail: Regent.Brown@nysed.gov
Education Commissioner, USNY President:
MaryEllen Elia 518-474-5844
Secretary to the Board:
Anthony Lofrumento 518-474-5889
Member:
James E Cottrell (2019) 718-270-2331
e-mail: regent.cottrell@nysed.gov
Member:
Luis O Reyes (2021). 518-474-5889
e-mail: Regent.Reyes@nysed.gov
Member:
Josephine Finn (2019). 518-474-5889
e-mail: regentFinn@nysed.gov
Member:
Kathleen M Cashin (2020) 518-474-5889
e-mail: regent.cashin@nysed.gov
Member:
Elizabeth S. Hakanson 518-474-5889
e-mail: Regent.Hakanson@nysed.gov
Member:
Judith Johnson (2020). 518-474-5889
e-mail: regentchapey@nysed.gov
Member:
Wade S Norwood (2019) 585-436-2944
e-mail: regent.norwood@nysed.gov
Member:
Catherine Collins (2020). 518-474-5889
e-mail: regent.collins@nysed.gov
Member:
Judith Chin (2018) 518-474-5889
e-mail: regent.chin@nysed.gov
Member:
Christine D Cea (2019). 718-494-5306
e-mail: regent.Cea@nysed.gov
Member:
Nan Eileen Mead 518-474-5889
e-mail: Regent.Mead@nysed.gov
Member:
Beverly Ourderkirk (2020). 315-375-8596
e-mail: regent.ouderkirk@nysed.gov
Member:
James R Tallon, Jr (2017). 212-494-0777
e-mail: regent.tallon@nysed.gov
Member:
Roger B Tilles (2020) 516-364-2533
e-mail: regent.tilles@nysed.gov
Member:
Lester W Young, Jr (2020) 718-722-2796
e-mail: regent.young@nysed.gov

Children & Family Services, Office of
52 Washington St
Rensselaer, NY 12144
518-473-7793 Fax: 518-486-7550
Web site: www.ocfs.state.ny.us

Acting Commissioner:
Sheila Poole 518-402-3108
Executive Secretary:
Nancy Degree 518-402-3108
Executive Deputy Commissioner:
Sheila Poole 518-402-3108
Assistant Commissioner, Communications:
Jennifer Givner 518-402-3130
e-mail: cfspio@dfa.state.ny.us
Bureau of Policy Analysis:
Rayana Gonzales. 518-473-1776
Deputy Commissioner, Juvenile Justice & Opportunity for Youth:
Ines Neives 518-473-1786
Deputy Commissioner, Child Welfare & Community Service:
Laura Velez. 518-474-3377
Director of Regional Operations:
Jim Hart. 518-473-1790

Regional Operations
Deputy Commissioner, Childcare Services:
Janice Molnar 518-486-6247
Acting Associate Commissioner, Youth Programs & Services:
Joseph Tomassone 518-486-6766

Education Department
State Education Bldg
89 Washington Ave
Albany, NY 12234
518-474-3852 Fax: 518-486-5631
Web site: www.nysed.gov

Commissioner & University President:
MaryEllen Elia 518-474-5844
Chief, External Affairs (Communications):
Dennis Tompkins 518-474-1201

Policy Areas

Offices and agencies generally appear in alphabetical order, except when specific order is requested by listee.

Executive Deputy Commissioner:
Elizabeth Berlin 518-473-8381
General Counsel:
Robert Trautwein 518-474-6400
e-mail: legal@nysed.gov
Chief of Staff:
James N Baldwin 518-474-5844
Associate Commissioner, Special Education:
Rebecca Cort. 518-473-4818

Cultural Education Office
10A 33 Cultural Education Center, Madison Avenue, Albany, NY 12230
Web site: www.oce.nysed.gov
Deputy Commissioner:
Vacant 518-474-5976

Educational Television & Public Broadcasting
Acting Director:
Thomas Ruller 518-474-5862
e-mail: tom.ruller@nysed.gov

State Archives
e-mail: archinfo@mail.nysed.gov
Assistant Commissioner & State Archivist:
Thomas Ruller 518-474-6926
e-mail: tom.ruller@nysed.gov
Coordinator, Training & Publications:
Rich Sloma 518-474-6926
e-mail: archtrain@nysed.gov
Archival Services:
Maria Holden 518-474-6276
Reference & Research Services:
James Folts 518-474-8955
e-mail: archref@nysed.gov
State Records Center Services:
Maggi Gonsalves . . . . . 518-457-4801 or 518-457-1040
e-mail: records@nysed.gov
Government Records Services:
David Lowry. 518-474-6926
e-mail: david.lowry@nysed.gov
Administrative & Technical Services:
Michelle Arpey. 518-474-6926
e-mail: michelle.arpey@nysed.gov
Educational Programs:
Julie Daniels 518-473-8495
e-mail: archedu@nysed.gov

State Library
222 Madison Ave, Cultural Education Center, Albany, NY 12230
Web site: www.nysl.nysed.gov
Assistant Commissioner & State Librarian:
Bernard Margolis 518-474-5930
e-mail: bernard.margolis@nysed.gov
Acting Director, Research Library:
Bernard Margolis 518-473-1189
Technical Services & Systems:
Liza Duncan 518-474-5946
e-mail: liza.duncan@nysed.gov
Coordinator Statewide Library Services:
Carol Ann Desch 518-474-7196
e-mail: carol.desch@nysed.gov
Talking Book & Braille Library (Acting):
Bernard Margolis 518-474-5935

State Museum Office
www.nysm.nysed.gov,
Director:
Mark A Schaming. 518-474-5812
e-mail: mark.schaming@nysed.gov
Coordinator, Public Programs:
Nicole LaFountain 518-474-0575
e-mail: nicole.lafountain@nysed.gov

State Historian:
Vacant. 518-473-1299

Research and Collections
Director:
Dr. John P. Hart 518-474-5816
e-mail: john.hart@nysed.gov
Assistant Director:
Robert Daniels 518-473-8121
e-mail: rdaniels@mail.nysed.gov
Collections Database Manager:
Ellen Stevens 518-474-5816
State Archaeologist:
Christina B Reith 518-402-5975

Office of Performance Improvement & Management Services/CFO
Web site: www.oms.nysed.gov
Deputy Commissioner:
Sharon Cates-Williams 518-473-4706
Chief Financial Officer:
Donald Juron. 518-474-7751
Diversity, Ethics & Access:
Steven Earle 518-474-1265
Facilities & Business Services:
Vacant 518-474-7770
Human Resources Management:
Annette Franchini 518-474-5883
Grant Finance:
Sarah Martin 518-474-4875
Audit Services:
Thalia Melendez 518-473-4516
Budget Coordination & Financial Administration:
Andrew Klippel 518-486-1708
Education Finance Director:
Brian Cechnicki 518-486-2422
State Review:
Justyn Bates 518-485-9373
Rate Setting Unit:
Suzanne Bolling 518-474-3227
STAC (Systems to Track & Account for Children):
Edgar Waaler 518-474-7116

Information Technology Services
Chief Information Officer:
Vacant. 518-474-4660
Information Technology Services (ITS) Director:
Vacant. 518-474-4640

Office of P-12 Education Policy
89 Washington Ave, EB West 2nd Fl Mezzanine, Albany, NY 12234
Web site: www.p12.nysed.gov
Sr Deputy Commissioner:
Jhone Ebert 518-474-3862/fax: 518-473-2056
e-mail: nysedp12@nysed.gov
Basic Educational Data System (BEDS):
Rose LeRoy. 518-474-7965
Office of Early Learning:
Elizabeth Morcom-Kenney. 518-474-5807
e-mail: oel@nysed.gov
Title 1 School & Community Service:
Maxine Meadows Shuford 518-473-0295
Office of Innovation & School Reform:
Cheryl Atkinson 518-473-8852
Native American Education:
Clarissa Jacobs-Roraback. 518-474-0537

P-12 School Services
Deputy Commissioner:
Vacant. 518-474-2238

Offices and agencies generally appear in alphabetical order, except when specific order is requested by listee.

Child Nutrition Program Administration
Lead Contact:
Paula Tyner-Doyle 518-473-8781
Educational Management Services
Lead Contact:
Christina Coughlin 518-474-6541
Facilities & Planning
Lead Contact:
Carl Thurnau 518-474-3906
Grants Management
Lead Contact:
Maureen Lavare 518-474-3936
Lead Contact:
David Frank 518-474-1762
Assistant Commissioner:
Renee Rider 518-474-4817
Lead Contact:
Eric Suhr 518-486-1547

Office of Higher Education
89 Washington Ave, Room 977 EB Annex, Albany, NY 12234
e-mail: hedepcom@nysed.gov
Web site: www.highered.nysed.gov
Deputy Commissioner:
John D'Agati 518-486-3633

Office of K-16 Initiatives & Access Programs
Executive Director:
Stanley S Hansen, Jr 518-474-3719/fax: 518-474-7468
e-mail: kiap@nysed.gov
College & University Evaluation
Coordinator:
Leslie Templeman 518-474-2593/fax: 518-486-2779
e-mail: ocueinfo@nysed.gov
Research & Information Systems
Coordinator:
Glenwood Rowse 518-474-5091
e-mail: growse@mail.nysed.gov

Office of Teaching Initiatives
Teacher Certification, Teacher Policy & School Personnel Review
Assistant Director:
Ann Jasinski 518-474-4661
e-mail: tcert@nysed.gov
Director, Office of School Personnel Review:
Vacant 518-473-2998
e-mail: ospra@nysed.gov

Office of the Professions . . . . fax: 518-474-3863
89 Washington Ave, EB, 2nd Fl, West Wing, Albany, NY 12234
Fax: 518-474-3863
Web site: www.op.nysed.gov
Deputy Commissioner:
Douglas Lentivech . . . . 518-486-1765 or 518-474-3817 x440

Office of Professional Responsibility
Professional Examinations
475 Park Ave South, New York, NY 10016
Director:
Harrison Fisher 518-474-3817
Director, Investigations:
Donald Dawson 212-951-6444
Director, Legal Services:
Andrew Tolkoff 212-951-6550
Director, Prosecutions:
George Ding 212-951-6410
Director, Professional Education:
William Murphy 518-474-3817 x300
Assistant Director, Comparative Education:
Dennis Mbuyi 518-474-3817 x300

Professional Education Program Review
Assistant Director:
Mei Zhou 518-474-3817 x360
e-mail: opprogs@nysed.gov

Professional Licensing Services
Director:
Susan Naccarato 518-474-3817 x340
e-mail: opdpls@nysed.gov

Office of Adult Career & Continuing Education Services (ACCES) . . . . fax: 518-474-8802
89 Washington Ave, 5th Fl, EBA, Albany, NY 12234
Fax: 518-474-8802
Web site: www.acces.nysed.gov
Deputy Commissioner:
Kevin Smith 518-474-2714
e-mail: accesdeputy@nysed.gov
Assistant Commissioner:
Debora Brown-Johnson 518-402-3955/fax: 518-473-6073
e-mail: accesadm@nysed.gov
Director, Proprietary School Supervision:
Vacant 518-474-3969/fax: 518-473-3644
e-mail: BPSS@nysed.gov
Director, Adult Education Program & Policy:
Mark Leinung 518-474-8892/fax: 518-474-0319
e-mail: AEPP@nysed.gov
Director, Operations:
Harold Matott 518-474-2714/fax: 518-474-8802
e-mail: accesdeputy@nysed.gov

Fiscal & Administrative Services
Coordinator:
Rosemary Johnson 518-486-4038

Vocational Rehabilitation Administration
Coordinator:
Frank Coco 518-473-1626/fax: 518-486-6252
e-mail: accesadm@nysed.gov
Manager, Independent Living Centers:
Robert Gumson 518-474-2925
e-mail: rgumson@mail.nysed.gov
Albany District Office
80 Wolf Road, Ste 200, Albany, NY 12205
Manager:
Barbara Arisohn 518-473-8097/fax: 518-457-4562
Bronx District Office
1215 Zerega Ave, Bronx, NY 10462
Manager:
Judith Pina 718-931-3500/fax: 718-931-4299
Brooklyn District Office
55 Hanson Pl, 2nd Fl, Brooklyn, NY 11217-1578
Manager:
Mark Weinstein 718-722-6700/fax: 718-722-6714
Buffalo District Office
508 Main St, Buffalo, NY 14202
Manager:
Christine Luly 716-848-8001/fax: 716-848-8103
Hauppauge District Office
State Office Bldg, 250 Veterans Memorial Hwy, Room 3A-12, Hauppauge, NY 11788
Manager:
Sandy Silver 631-952-6357/fax: 631-952-5826
Garden City District Office
711 Stewart Ave, Ste 4, Garden City, NY 11530
Regional Coordinator:
Veronica Rose-Craig 516-227-6800/fax: 516-227-6834
Malone District Office
209 W Main St, Ste 3, Malone, NY 12953
Manager:
Pamela Dority 518-483-3530/fax: 518-483-3552

Manhattan District Office
116 West 32nd St, 6th Fl, New York, NY 10001
Regional Coordinator:
JoAnne Schwartz 212-630-2300/fax: 212-630-2365

Mid-Hudson District Office
Manchester Mill Ctr, 301 Manchester Rd, Ste 200, Poughkeepsie, NY 12603
Regional Coordinator:
Daniel O'Shea 845-452-5325/fax: 845-452-5336

Queens District Office
11-15 47th Ave, Long Island City, NY 11101
Manager:
Magaly Lovell 347-510-3100/fax: 718-784-3702

Rochester District Office
109 S Union St, 2nd Fl, Rochester, NY 14607
Regional Coordinator:
Danielle Maloy. 585-238-2900/fax: 585-325-2001

Southern Tier District Office
44 Hawley St, 7th Fl, Rm 705, Binghamton, NY 13901
Regional Coordinator:
Jack Lance 607-721-8400/fax: 607-721-8390

Syracuse District Office
State Ofc Bldg 333 E Washington St, 2nd Fl, Rm 230, Syracuse, NY 13202-1428
Manager:
Patrick Sheppard. 315-428-4179/fax: 315-428-4280

Utica District Office
207 Genesee St, State Ofc Bldg, Utica, NY 13501-2812
Manager:
Judith Petroski 315-793-2536/fax: 315-793-2724

White Plains District Office
75 South Broadway, 2nd Fl, White Plains, NY 10601
Manager:
Linda Schramm. 914-946-1313/fax: 914-946-1726

NYSTAR - Division of Science, Technology & Innovation

30 South Pearl St
11th Fl
Albany, NY 12207
518-292-5700 Fax: 518-292-5798
Web site: www.esd.ny.gov/nystar

Director:
Edward Reinfurt 518-292-5700
Deputy Director:
Edward J Hamilton 518-292-5700
Director, Communications/Government Affairs:
Jannette Rondo 518-292-5700/fax: 518-292-5798
Regional Technology Development:
Matthew Watson 518-292-5700
Counsel:
Paul Jesep 518-292-5700

Centers for Advanced Technology

Center for Advanced Ceramic Technology at Alfred University
2 Pine Street, Alfred, NY 14802-1296
e-mail: cactinfo@alfred.edu
Web site: cact.alfred.edu
Director:
Dr Matthew M Hall. 607-871-2486/fax: 607-871-3469

Center for Advanced Materials Processing at Clarkson Univ
CAMP, Box 5665, Potsdam, NY 13699-5665
Web site: www.clarkson.edu/camp
Director:
S V Babu 315-268-2336/fax: 315-268-7615
e-mail: babu@clarkson.edu

Center for Advanced Tech in Biomedical & Bioengineering
Univeristy at Buffalo, 701 Ellicott Street, Buffalo, NY 14203
Web site: www.bioinformatics.buffalo.edu/
Co-Director:
Alexander N. Cartwright PhD 716-645-0312
Co-Director:
Marnie LaVigne PhD 716-645-0312
e-mail: lavigne2@buffalo.edu

Sensor CAT-Diagnostic Tools & Sensor Systems
SUNY at Stony Brook, Suffolk Hall, Room 115B, Stony Brook, NY 11794-3717
e-mail: sensor@ece.sunysb.edu
Web site: sensorcat.sunysb.edu
Director:
Serge Luryi. . . . . 631-632-1368 or 631-632-8420
fax: 631-632-8529

Center for Emerging & Innovative Sciences
Univ of Rochester, 2 Taylor Hall, 260 Hutchison Rd, Rochester, NY 14627
Web site: www.ceis.rochester.edu
Director:
Mark Bocko 585-275-0547
e-mail: mark.bocko@seas.rochester.edu

Center for Advanced Information Management
Columbia University, 630 W 168th St, Bldg 30, New York, NY 10032
Web site: www.cat.columbia.edu
Director:
George Hripcsak 212-305-2944/fax: 212-305-0196

Center for Advanced Technology in Life Science Enterprise
Cornell University, 130 Biotechnology Bldg, Ithaca, NY 14853-2703
Web site: www.biotech.cornell.edu/cat
Director:
George Grills 607-255-9693
e-mail: biotech@cornell.edu

Center for Advanced Technology in Photonics Applications
CUNY, Steinman Hall T606, 16D Convent Avenue, New York, NY 10031
Web site: www.cunycat.org
Director:
David T. Crouse, PhD 212-650-5330
e-mail: crouse@cunycat.org

Center for Automation Technologies & Systems at Rensselaer
CII 8011, 110 8th Street, Troy, NY 12180
e-mail: cats-info@rpi.edu
Web site: www.cats.rpi.edu
Director:
John Wen. 518-276-8744/fax: 518-276-4897

Center for Advanced Medical Biotechnology
Biotechnology Building, 2nd Floor, Stony Brook, NY 11790
Web site: www.biotech.sunysb.edu
Director:
Clinton T Rubin PhD 631-632-8521/fax: 631-632-8577

Center for Computer Applications & Software Engineering
Syracuse University, 2-212 Ctr for Science & Tech, Syracuse, NY 13244
Web site: www.case.syr.edu
Director:
Pramod Varshney 315-443-1060/fax: 315-443-4745
e-mail: varshney@syr.edu

Center in Nanomaterials and Nanoelectronics
251 Fuller Road, Albany, NY 12203
Web site: csne.albany.edu
Director:
Michael Fancher 518-437-8686/fax: 518-437-8687

Ctr for Advanced Tech in Telecommunications at Polytech Univ
5 MetroTech Center, 9th Floor, Brooklyn, NY 11201
Web site: catt.poly.edu

Offices and agencies generally appear in alphabetical order, except when specific order is requested by listee.

Director:
Shivendra S Panwar . . . . 718-260-3050 or 718-260-3740
fax: 718-260-3074
e-mail: panwar@catt.poly.edu

Future Energy Systems CAT at Rensselaer Polytechnic Inst
110 8th Street, Troy, NY 12180
e-mail: cfes@rpi.edu
Web site: www.rpi.edu/cfes
Director:
Dr. Jian Sun 518-276-8294/fax: 518-276-6844
e-mail: jsun@ecse.rpi.edu

Integrated Electronics Engineering Center at Binghamton
IEEC, Vestal Pkwy East, PO Box 6000, Binghamton, NY 13902-6000
e-mail: ieec@binghamton.edu
Web site: www.binghamton.edu/ieec/
Director:
Daryl Santos 607-777-4769/fax: 607-777-4683

Regional Technology Development Centers

Alliance for Manufacturing & Technology
69 Court St, 6th Fl, State St Entrance, Binghamton, NY 13901
e-mail: info@amt-mep.org
Web site: www.amt-mep.org
Executive Director:
Edward Gaetano. 607-774-0022 x304/fax: 607-774-0026

Center for Economic Growth
30 Pearl St, Ste 100, Albany, NY 12207
e-mail: ceg@ceg.org
Web site: www.ceg.org
President/CEO:
F Michael Tucker 518-465-8975/fax: 518-465-6681
e-mail: miket@ceg.org

Central New York Technology Development Organization
445 Electronics Pkwy, Ste 206, Liverpool, NY 13088
e-mail: mail@tdo.org
Web site: www.tdo.org
President/CEO:
Robert I Trachtenberg. 315-425-5144/fax: 315-233-1259
e-mail: rtrachtenberg@tdo.org

Council for Interntl Trade, Tech, Education & Communication
Peyton Hall, Box 8561, Main St, Clarkson University, Potsdam, NY 13669
Web site: www.citec.org
Executive Director:
William P. Murray 315-268-3778 x29/fax: 315-268-4432
e-mail: murray@citec.org

High Technology of Rochester
150 Lucius Gordon Dr, Suite 100, West Henrietta, NY 14586
Web site: www.htr.org
President:
Jim Sendall 585-214-2400
e-mail: info@htr.org

Hudson Valley Technology Development Center
1450 Route 300, Building 1, Newburgh, NY 12550
e-mail: info@hvtdc.org
Web site: www.hvtdc.org
Executive Director:
Thomas G Phillips, Sr 845-391-8214 x3006/fax: 845-845-8218
e-mail: tom.phillips@hvtdc.org

Industrial & Technology Assistance Corp
39 Broadway, Suite 1110, New York, NY 10006
Web site: www.itac.org
President:
Sara Garretson. 212-809-3900/fax: 646-588-5156
e-mail: sgarretson@itac.org

Long Island Forum for Technology
510 Grumman Road West, Bethpage, NY 11714
e-mail: info@lift.org
Web site: www.lift.org
Executive Director:
William Wahlig. 631-969-3700/fax: 631-846-2789
e-mail: bwahlig@lift.org

Mohawk Valley Applied Technology Corp
207 Genesee St, Ste 405, Utica, NY 13501
Web site: www.mvatc.com
President:
Paul MacEnroe 315-793-8050/fax: 315-793-8057
e-mail: paulm@mvatc.com

INSYTE Consulting (Western NY Technology Development Ctr)
726 Exchange St, Ste 812, Buffalo, NY 14210
Web site: www.insyte-consulting.com
President:
Benjamin Rand 716-636-3626/fax: 716-845-6418
e-mail: brand@insyte.org

CORPORATIONS, AUTHORITIES AND COMMISSIONS

City University Construction Fund
555 W 57th St
11th Fl
New York, NY 10019
212-541-0171 Fax: 212-541-1014

Interim Executive Director:
Judith Bergtraum. 646-664-2605
e-mail: iris.weinshall@mail.cuny.edu
Counsel:
Frederick Schaffer. 646-664-9210
e-mail: frederick.schaffer@mail.cuny.edu

New York City School Construction Authority
30-30 Thomson Ave
Long Island City, NY 11101-3045
718-472-8000 Fax: 718-472-8840
Web site: www.nycsca.org

Chair/Chancellor:
Carmen Farina. 718-472-8000
President & Chief Executive Officer:
Lorraine Grillo 718-472-8001
Executive Vice President & General Counsel:
Ross J Holden 718-472-8220
VP, Finance:
Marianne Egri 718-472-8012
VP, Construction Management:
Vacant 718-472-8359
VP, Architecture & Engineering:
E Bruce Barrett, RA 718-472-8710
VP, Administration:
Rebecca Fraley-Corrado 718-472-8149

New York State Dormitory Authority
515 Broadway
Albany, NY 12207-2964
518-257-3000 Fax: 518-257-3100
e-mail: dabonds@dasny.org
Web site: www.dasny.org

One Penn Plaza
52nd Fl
New York, NY 10119-0098

Offices and agencies generally appear in alphabetical order, except when specific order is requested by listee.

212-273-5000
Fax: 212-273-5121

539 Franklin St
Buffalo, NY 14202-1109
716-884-9780
Fax: 716-884-9787

Chair:
Alfonso L Carney Jr 518-257-3000/fax: 518-257-3100
President/CEO:
Paul T Williams Jr. 518-257-3180/fax: 518-257-3183
Vice President:
Michael T Corrigan 518-257-3192/fax: 518-257-3183
Acting Chief Financial Officer:
Linda H Button 518-257-3562/fax: 518-257-3100
General Counsel:
Michael Cusack 518-257-3120/fax: 518-257-3101
Managing Director, Construction:
Stephen D Curro, PE 518-257-3271/fax: 518-257-3100
e-mail: scurro@dasny.org
Managing Director, Public Finance & Portfolio Monitoring:
Portia Lee. 518-257-3362/fax: 518-257-3100
e-mail: plee@dasny.org
Public Information Officer:
John Chirlin. 518-257-3380
e-mail: jchirlin@dasny.org

New York State Higher Education Services Corp (NYSHESC)

99 Washington Ave
Albany, NY 12255
888-697-4372
Web site: www.hesc.ny.gov

Executive Vice President & Acting President:
Elsa Magee 518-474-5592/fax: 518-474-5593
e-mail: elsa.magee@hesc.ny.gov
Director, Federal Relations:
Frank Ballmann. 202-721-1186
e-mail: frank.ballmann@hesc.ny.gov
Director, Audit:
Matt Downey. 518-473-2287/fax: 518-486-6515
e-mail: matt.downey@hesc.ny.gov
General Counsel:
Thomas Brennan 518-473-1585/fax: 518-486-6515
e-mail: thomas.brennan@hesc.ny.gov
Communications/PIO:
Vacant. . . . . 518-474-5775 or 518-474-5592
fax: 518-474-5593
Director, Federal Operations:
Victor Stucchi 518-486-5885/fax: 518-402-3276
e-mail: victor.stucchi@hesc.ny.gov
Administrative Officer & CFO:
Warren Wallin 518-474-7505/fax: 518-474-4301
e-mail: victor.stucchi@hesc.ny.gov
Director, Training & Information Services:
Teresa Gehrer 518-402-6429/fax: 518-474-2839

New York State Teachers' Retirement System

10 Corporate Woods Dr
Albany, NY 12211-2395
518-447-2900 or 800-348-7298 Fax: 518-447-2695
e-mail: media@nystrs.org
Web site: www.nystrs.org

Executive Director:
Thomas K Lee. 518-447-2726
General Counsel:
Joseph J. Indelicato, Jr. 518-447-2722
Actuary:
Richard Young 518-447-2692
Managing Director Operations:
Kevin Schaefer 518-447-2730
Director, Member Relations:
Sheila Gardella 518-447-2684
Manager, Public Information:
John Cardillo 518-447-4743/fax: 518-447-2875
e-mail: john.caradillo@nystrs.org
Managing Director, Real Estate:
David C. Gillian 518-447-2751
Managing Director, Private Equity:
John W. Virtanen 518-447-2751

State University Construction Fund

353 Broadway
Albany, NY 12246
518-320-3200 Fax: 518-443-1008
Web site: www.sucf.suny.edu

General Manager:
Robert M Haelen. 518-320-1502
Associate Counsel:
Terese Meagher. 518-320-1746

NEW YORK STATE LEGISLATURE

See Legislative Branch in Section 1 for additional Standing Committee and Subcommittee information.

Assembly Standing Committees

Education
Chair:
Catherine T Nolan (D) 518-455-4851
Ranking Minority Member:
Edward Ra (R) 518-455-4627

Higher Education
Chair:
Deborah J Glick (D) 518-455-4841
Ranking Minority Member:
Chad Lupinacci (R). 518-455-5732

Libraries & Education Technology
Chair:
Thomas Abinanti (D) 518-455-5753
Ranking Minority Member:
Joseph Saladino. 518-455-5305

Assembly Task Forces

Skills Development & Career Education, Legislative Commission on
Assembly Chair:
Harry Bronson (D) 518-455-4527
Program Manager:
Brenda Carter. 518-455-4865/fax: 518-455-4175

University-Industry Cooperation, Legislative Task Force on
Chair:
Vacant (D). 518-455-0000
Coordinator:
Maureen Schoolman 518-455-3632/fax: 518-455-4175

Offices and agencies generally appear in alphabetical order, except when specific order is requested by listee.

Senate Standing Committees

Education
Chair:
Carl L Marcellino (R) 518-455-2390
Ranking Minority Member:
George Latimer (D). 518-455-2031

Higher Education
Chair:
Kenneth P LaValle (R) 518-455-3121
Ranking Minority Member:
Toby Ann Stavisky (D). 518-455-3461

U.S. GOVERNMENT

EXECUTIVE DEPARTMENTS AND RELATED AGENCIES

National Archives & Records Administration

Franklin D Roosevelt Presidential Library & Museum
4079 Albany Post Road, Hyde Park, NY 12538
846-486-7770
Web site: www.fdrlibrary.marist.edu
Director:
Paul M. Sparrow 845-486-7741
e-mail: paul.sparrow@nara.gov

US Defense Department
e-mail: www.defense.gov

US Military Academy
622 Swift Road, West Point, NY 10996
845-938-4011
Web site: www.usma.edu
Superintendent:
Lt. Gen. Robert L. Caslen, Jr.
Public Affairs:
Staff Sgt. Vito Bryant

US Education Department
Web site: www.ed.gov

Region 2 - NY, NJ, PR, Vi . . . . . . fax: 646-428-3904
32 Old Slip, 25th Floor, New York, NY 10005
646-428-3906 Fax: 646-428-3904
e-mail: ocr.newyork@ed.gov
Communications Director:
Jacquelyn Pitta 646-428-3906
Education Program Specialist:
Taylor Owen Ramsey 646-428-3906

Civil Rights
Regional Director:
Timothy Blanchard 646-428-3805
Chief Civil Rights Attorney:
Rachel Pomerantz. 646-428-3835

Federal Student Aid
Director:
Robin R. Shinn 646-428-3770
e-mail: robin.shinn@ed.gov
Team Leader:
Susan Ferraiole 646-428-3771
e-mail: susan.ferraiole@ed.gov

Office of Inspector General
Regional Inspector General, Audit:
Daniel P. Schultz 646-428-3888
e-mail: daniel.schultz@ed.gov
Special Agent-in-Charge:
Brian Hickey. 646-428-3874

Office of Management
Human Resources Specialist:
Vacant

US Transportation Department
Web site: www.transportation.gov

US Merchant Marine Academy . . . . . . fax: 516-773-5774
300 Steamboat Road, Kings Point, NY 11024
516-773-5800 Fax: 516-773-5774
Web site: www.usmma.edu
Superintendent:
Rear Admiral James A. Helis

U.S. CONGRESS

See U.S. Congress Chapter for additional Standing Committee and Subcommittee information.

House of Representatives Standing Committees

Education & the Workforce
Chair:
John Kline (R-MN). 202-225-2271
Ranking Member:
Robert C. Scott (D-VA) 202-225-8351
New York Delegate:
Hakeem S. Jeffries (D) 202-225-5936
New York Delegate:
Elise Stefanik (R) 202-225-4611

Senate Standing Committees

Health, Education, Labor & Pensions
Chair:
Lamar Alexander (R-TN). 202-224-4944
Ranking Member:
Patty Murray (D-WA). 202-224-2621

PRIVATE SECTOR

ASPIRA of New York Inc
630 9th Avenue, Suite 302, New York, NY 10036
212-564-6880 Fax: 212-564-7152
e-mail: mgonzalez@nyaspira.org
Web site: www.aspirany.org
Works towards the social advancement of youth in the Puerto Rican & Latino communities through the provision of educational programs & services
Dr. Mark Gonzalez, Chief Executive Officer

Advocates for Children of New York Inc
151 West 30th Street, 5th Floor, New York, NY 10001
212-947-9779 Fax: 212-947-9790
e-mail: info@advocatesforchildren.org
Web site: www.advocatesforchildren.org
Advocacy for public education for all NYS children
Kim Sweet, Executive Director

Africa-America Institute (The)
420 Lexington Avenue, Suite 1706, New York, NY 10170-0002
212-949-5666 Fax: 212-682-6174
e-mail: aainy@aaionline.org
Web site: www.aaionline.org
Organization committed to fostering development in Africa through advanced education & professional training
Amini Kajunju, President & Chief Executive Officer

Agudath Israel of America
42 Broadway, 14th Floor, New York, NY 10004
212-797-9000 Fax: 646-254-1600
e-mail: news@agudathisrael.org
Religious school education; Orthodox Judaism
Dovid Zwiebel, Executive Vice President

American Higher Education Development Corporation
116 Village Blvd, Suite 200, Princeton, NJ 08540
646-569-5681
e-mail: stave@ahed.com
Web site: www.ahed.com
Acquisition of & investment in post-secondary education institutions
Stephen Tave, President & Chief Executive Officer

Associated Medical Schools of New York
1270 Avenue of the Americas, Suite 606, New York, NY 10020
212-218-4610 Fax: 212-218-4278
e-mail: info@amsny.org
Web site: www.amsny.org
A consortium of the sixteen medical schools in New York State; advocacy, resources & educational development programs
Jo Wiederhorn, President & Chief Executive Officer

Association of Proprietary Colleges
121 State Street, Albany, NY 12207
518-437-1867 Fax: 518-436-4751
e-mail: apc@apc-colleges.org
Web site: www.apc-colleges.org
Association representing the proprietary colleges of New York State
Donna S. Gurnett, Executive Director

Catholic School Administrators Association of NYS
525 4th Avenue, Troy, NY 12182
518-273-1205 Fax: 518-273-1206
e-mail: csaanysoffice@nycap.rr.com
Web site: www.csaanys.org
Carol Geddis, Executive Director

Center for Educational Innovation - Public Education Association
28 West 44th Street, Suite 801, New York, NY 10036
212-302-8800 Fax: 212-302-0088
e-mail: info@the-cei.org
Web site: www.the-cei.org
Advocacy & public information for NYC public education
Seymour Fliegel, President

Cerebral Palsy Associations of New York State
330 West 34th Street, 15th Floor, New York, NY 10001-2488
212-947-5770 Fax: 212-594-4538
e-mail: information@cpofnys.org
Web site: www.cpofnys.org
Serves individuals with cerebral palsy & other significant disabilities as well as their families through advocacy, technical assistance, publications & networking events
Susan Constantino, President & Chief Executive Officer

Coalition of New York State Career Schools (The)
437 Old Albany Post Road, Garrison, NY 10524
845-788-5070 Fax: 845-788-5071
Web site: www.cnyscs.com
Licensed trade & business schools in NYS
Terence M. Zaleski, Executive Director & Counsel

Commission on Independent Colleges & Universities
17 Elk Street, PO Box 7289, Albany, NY 12224
518-436-4781 Fax: 518-436-0417
Web site: www.cicu.org
Association dedicated to promoting the public policy interests of New York State's independent colleges & universities; advocacy, research, publications & programs
Laura L. Anglin, President

Conference of Big 5 School Districts
74 Chapel Street, Albany, NY 12207
518-465-4274 Fax: 518-465-0638
e-mail: big5@big5schools.org
Web site: www.big5schools.org
Georgia M. Asciutto, Executive Director

Cornell University
314 Day Hall, Ithaca, NY 14853
607-254-4636 Fax: 607-254-6225
e-mail: info@cornell.edu
Web site: www.cornell.edu
Joel Malina, Vice President for University Relations

Cornell University, Rural Schools Association of NYS
Warren Hall 275 Flex, Cornell University, Ithaca, NY 14853
607-255-8709 or 518-250-5710 Fax: 607-254-2896
e-mail: dal295@cornell.edu
Web site: www.cardi.cals.cornell.edu/programs/rsa
Advocacy for small & rural school districts throughout New York
David A. Little, Executive Director

Cornell University, School of Industrial & Labor Relations
309 Ives Hall, Ithaca, NY 14853
607-255-2762 or 607-255-3276 Fax: 607-255-2185
e-mail: hallock@cornell.edu
Web site: www.ilr.cornell.edu
Education, workforce preparedness; student peer culture, employee training, recruitment & selection practices
Kevin Hallock, Dean

Council of School Supervisors & Administrators
40 Rector Street, 12th Floor, New York, NY 10006
212-823-2020 Fax: 212-962-6130
e-mail: ernest@csa-nyc.org
Web site: www.csa-nyc.org
Ernest Logan, President

ExpandED Schools
1440 Broadway, 16th Floor, New York, NY 10018
646-943-8700
e-mail: info@expandedschools.org
Web site: www.expandedschools.org
Non-profit organization dedicated to ensuring that all children in NYS have access to quality in-school, after-school & summer programs
Lucy N. Friedman, President

Council on the Environment of NYC, Environmental Education
100 Gold Street, Suite 3300, New York, NY 10038
212-788-7900 Fax: 212-788-7913
Web site: www.grownyc.org
Environmental education & action training programs for students
Marcel Van Ooyen, Executive Director

Fordham University
441 East Fordham Road, Bronx, NY 10458
718-817-1000
e-mail: president@fordham.edu
Web site: www.fordham.edu
Joseph M. McShane, President

Jewish Education Project (The)
520 Eighth Avenue, 15th Floor, New York, NY 10018
646-472-5300 Fax: 646-472-5421
e-mail: info@jewishedproject.org
Web site: www.jewishedproject.org
Advancing & enhancing Jewish education
Tara Slone-Goldstein, President

Learning Leaders
75 Maiden Lane, Room 801, New York, NY 10038
212-213-3370 Fax: 212-213-0787
e-mail: info@learningleaders.org
Web site: www.learningleaders.org
Provides volunteers & parents with resources & training workshops designed to help New York City's public school students develop study, organizational & other school-based skills
Jane Heaphy, Executive Director

Library Trustees Association of NYS
PO Box 11048, Albany, NY 12211
518-445-9505
Web site: www.librarytrustees.org
Patricia Fontanella, President

MDRC
16 East 34th Street, 19th Floor, New York, NY 10016-4326
212-532-3200 Fax: 212-684-0832
e-mail: information@mdrc.org
Web site: www.mdrc.org
Nonprofit research & field testing of education & employment programs for disadvantaged adults & youth
Gordon Berlin, President

Museum Association of New York
265 River Street, Troy, NY 12180
518-273-3400 Fax: 518-273-3416
e-mail: info@manyonline.org
Web site: www.manyonline.org
An information & advocacy resource for the state's museum community
Devin Lander, Executive Director

New York Community Colleges Association of Presidents
c/o Onondaga Community College, 4585 West Seneca Turnpike, Syracuse, NY 13215-4585
315-498-2214 Fax: 315-469-4475
Kevin Dunn, President

NYC Board of Education Employees, Local 372/AFSCME, AFL-CIO
125 Barclay Street, 6th Floor, New York, NY 10007
212-815-1372 Fax: 212-815-1347
Web site: www.local372.org
Shaun D. Francois, President

NYS Alliance for Arts Education
PO Box 2217, Albany, NY 12220-0217
518-473-0823 Fax: 518-486-7329
e-mail: info@nysaae.org
Web site: www.nysaae.org
State & local advocacy, professional development, technical assistance & information for educators, organizations, artists, parents & policymakers
Carol Brown, President

NYS Association for Health, Physical Education, Recreation & Dance
77 North Ann Street, Little Falls, NY 13365
315-823-1015 Fax: 315-823-1012
Web site: www.nysahperd.org
Promoting, educating & creating opportunites for physical education, health, recreation & dance professionals
James Rose, President

NYS Association for the Education of Young Children
230 Washington Avenue Ext, Albany, NY 12203-5390
518-867-3517 Fax: 518-867-3520
e-mail: contactus@nysaeyc.org
Web site: www.nysaeyc.org
Advocacy, education & support for individuals working in the early care & education profession in NYS
Kristen Kerr, Executive Director

NYS Association of School Business Officials
453 New Karner Road, Albany, NY 12205
518-434-2281 Fax: 518-434-1303
e-mail: asbomail@nysasbo.org
Web site: www.nysasbo.org
Leadership in the practice of school business management
Michael J. Borges, Executive Director

NYS Association of Small City School Districts
c/o Biggerstaff Law Firm, 1280 New Scotland Road, Slingerlands, NY 12159
518-475-9500 Fax: 518-475-7677
e-mail: reb@biggerstaff-firm.com
Web site: scsd.neric.org
Advocacy for small city school districts
Robert Biggerstaff, Executive Director

NYS Head Start Association
230 Washington Avenue Ext, Albany, NY 12203
518-452-0897 Fax: 518-452-0898
e-mail: nyshsa@gmail.com
Web site: www.nysheadstart.org
Educational program designed to meet the needs of low-income children & their families
Ouida Foster Toutebon, Executive Director

NYS Public High School Athletic Association
8 Airport Park Blvd, Latham, NY 12110
518-690-0771 Fax: 518-690-0775
Web site: www.nysphsaa.org
Promotes fair & safe interschool athletic competition & activities among secondary schools in NYS
Robert Zayas, Executive Director

NYS Reading Association
PO Box 874, Albany, NY 12201-0874
518-741-0032 Fax: 518-741-0032
Web site: www.nyreading.org
Literacy education advocacy & professional development programs for educators
Eileen LaSpaluto, President

Nelson A Rockefeller Inst of Govt, Higher Education Program
411 State Street, Albany, NY 12203-1003
518-443-5522 or 518-443-5837 Fax: 518-443-5788
e-mail: info@rockinst.suny.edu
Web site: www.rockinst.org
Accountability & autonomy in public higher education; system governance; performance funding, budgeting, reporting & assessment
Thomas L. Gais, Director

New York Community College Trustees (NYCCT)
State University Plaza, S-123, Albany, NY 12246
518-320-1302 or 518-320-1100 Fax: 518-320-1543
e-mail: cynthia.demarest@suny.edu
Web site: www.suny.edu/nycct
Education, advocacy & communication for the trustees of NYS community colleges
Cynthia Demarest, President & Chief Executive Officer

New York Library Association (The)
6021 State Farm Road, Guilderland, NY 12084
518-432-6952 Fax: 518-427-1697
e-mail: info@nyla.org
Web site: www.nyla.org
Advocacy on behalf of public, college & school libraries on funding & legislation
Jeremy Johannesen, Executive Director

Policy Areas

Offices and agencies generally appear in alphabetical order, except when specific order is requested by listee.

New York State Association of Independent Schools
17 Elk Street, 1st Floor, Albany, NY 12207
518-694-5500 Fax: 518-694-5501
e-mail: mark@nysais.org
Web site: www.nysais.org
Accreditation & evaluation of member schools, professional development programs, advocacy, information & statistics
Mark W. Lauria, Executive Director

New York State Catholic Conference
465 State Street, Albany, NY 12203-1004
518-434-6195 Fax: 518-434-9796
e-mail: info@nyscatholic.org
Web site: www.nyscatholic.org
Represents the public policy interests of NYS Bishops in the areas of health, education, welfare & human/civil rights with the objective of achieving justice for all individuals
Richard E. Barnes, Executive Director

New York State Congress of Parents & Teachers Inc
One Wembley Court, Albany, NY 12205-3830
518-452-8808 or 877-569-7782 Fax: 518-452-8105
e-mail: pta.office@nyspta.org
Web site: www.nyspta.org
Advocates for & promotes education, health & welfare for all children
Bonnie Russell, President

New York State Council of School Superintendents
7 Elk Street, 3rd Floor, Albany, NY 12207-1002
518-449-1063 Fax: 518-426-2229
Web site: www.nyscoss.org
Robert J. Reidy, Jr., Executive Director

New York State School Boards Association
24 Century Hill Drive, Suite 200, Latham, NY 12110-2125
518-783-0200 Fax: 518-783-0211
e-mail: info@nyssba.org
Web site: www.nyssba.org
Public school leadership advocates
Timothy G. Kremer, Executive Director

New York State School Music Association (NYSSMA)
718 The Plain Road, Westbury, NY 11590-5931
516-997-7200 Fax: 516-997-1700
e-mail: executive@nyssma.org
Web site: www.nyssma.org
Advocacy for quality music education for all students in member school programs
Steven E. Schopp, Executive Director

New York State United Teachers/AFT, NEA, AFL-CIO
800 Troy-Schenectady Road, Latham, NY 12110-2455
518-213-6000 or 800-342-9810 Fax: 518-213-6415
Web site: www.nysut.org
Represents employees & retirees of NY's public schools, colleges & healthcare facilities
Karen E. Magee, President

New York University
25 West 4th Street, 5th Floor, New York, NY 10012
212-998-6840 Fax: 212-995-4021
e-mail: jhb5@nyu.edu
Web site: www.nyu.edu
Office of Public Affairs
John Beckman, Vice President

Niagara University
Alumni Hall, Niagara University, NY 14109-2014
716-286-8352 Fax: 716-286-8349
e-mail: downs@niagara.edu
Web site: www.niagara.edu
Timothy M. Downs, Chief Academic Officer

ProLiteracy Worldwide
104 Marcellus Street, Syracuse, NY 13204
315-422-9121 or 888-528-2224 Fax: 315-422-6369
e-mail: info@proliteracy.org
Web site: www.proliteracy.org
Promotes educational programs & services designed to help adults & families gain literacy skills
Kevin Morgan, President & Chief Executive Officer

Rensselaer Polytechnic Institute
110 8th Street, Troy, NY 12180
518-276-2750 Fax: 518-276-3715
e-mail: media@rpi.edu
Web site: www.rpi.edu
Strategic Communications & External Relations
Allison Newman, Associate Vice President, External Relations & Administration

Research Foundation of SUNY
PO Box 9, Albany, NY 12201-0009
518-434-7000 Fax: 518-434-9108
e-mail: cathy.kaszluga@rfsuny.org
Web site: www.rfsuny.org
Facilitates research, education & public service at SUNY campuses
Catherine Kaszluga, Vice President for Strategy & Planning

Rochester School for the Deaf
1545 St Paul Street, Rochester, NY 14621
585-544-1240 Fax: 585-544-0383
e-mail: info@rsdeaf.org
Web site: www.rsdeaf.org
Complete educational program for deaf, blind & physically disabled students in NYS
Antony A.L. McLetchie, Superintendent & Chief Executive Officer

Schuyler Center for Analysis & Advocacy (SCAA)
540 Broadway, Albany, NY 12207
518-463-1896 Fax: 518-463-3364
e-mail: kbreslin@scaany.org
Web site: www.scaany.org
Advocacy & policy analysis on education, child welfare, health, economic security, mental health, revenue & taxation issues
Kate Breslin, President & Chief Executive Officer

School Administrators Association of NYS
8 Airport Park Blvd, Latham, NY 12110
518-782-0600 Fax: 518-782-9552
e-mail: kcasey@saanys.org
Web site: www.saanys.org
Advocacy & services for New York State's public school leaders
Kevin S. Casey, Executive Director

Sports & Arts in Schools Foundation
58-12 Queens Blvd, Suite 1, Woodside, NY 11377
718-786-7110 Fax: 718-205-1098
e-mail: info@sasfny.org
Web site: www.sasfny.org
Organizes activities to help underachieving NYC students build their skills & improve wellness
James R. O'Neill, Chief Executive Officer

Syracuse University, Maxwell School of Citizenship & Public Affairs
200 Eggers Hall, Syracuse, NY 13244-1020
315-443-2252
e-mail: info@maxwell.syr.edu
Web site: www.maxwell.syr.edu
Education, healthcare, entrepreneurship policies, social welfare, income distribution & comparative social policies
James B. Steinberg, Dean

Offices and agencies generally appear in alphabetical order, except when specific order is requested by listee.

Syracuse University, Office of Government & Community Relations
Room 2-212, Center for Science & Technology, Syracuse, NY 13244-4100
315-443-3919 Fax: 315-443-3676
e-mail: gcr@syr.edu
Web site: gcr.syr.edu
Eric Persons, Associate Vice President

Teachers College, Columbia University
525 West 120th Street, New York, NY 10027
212-678-3000 Fax: 212-678-3682
e-mail: fuhrman@tc.columbia.edu
Web site: www.tc.columbia.edu
Education policy
Susan H. Fuhrman, President

Teaching Matters Inc
475 Riverside Drive, Suite 1270, New York, NY 10115-0122
212-870-3505 Fax: 212-870-3516
e-mail: inquiry@teachingmatters.org
Web site: www.teachingmatters.org
Technology planning & professional development for NYC public schools
Lynette Guastaferro, Executive Director

United Federation of Teachers
52 Broadway, New York, NY 10004
212-777-7500
e-mail: mmulgrew@uft.org
Web site: www.uft.org
Advocacy for education & healthcare professionals
Michael Mulgrew, President

United University Professions
800 Troy-Schenectady Road, Latham, NY 12110-2424
800-342-4206 Fax: 866-812-9446
e-mail: fkowal@uupmail.org
Web site: www.uupinfo.org
SUNY labor union of academic & other professional faculty
Frederick E. Kowal, President

Western New York Library Resources Council
Airport Commerce Park East, 4950 Genesee Street, Suite 170, Cheektowaga, NY 14225
716-633-0705 Fax: 716-288-9400
e-mail: sknab@wnylrc.org
Web site: www.wnylrc.org
Consortium of Western NY libraries dedicated to improving access to information & promoting resource sharing & library interests
Sheryl Knab, Executive Director

ELECTIONS

NEW YORK STATE

GOVERNOR'S OFFICE

Governor's Office
Executive Chamber
State Capitol
Albany, NY 12224
518-474-8390 Fax: 518-474-1513
Web site: www.ny.gov

Governor:
Andrew M Cuomo 518-474-8390
Secretary to the Governor:
William Mulrow 518-474-4246
Counsel to the Governor:
Alphonso David 518-474-8343
Chief of Staff:
Melissa DeRosa . . . . 518-474-8418 or 212-681-4640
Director, Communications:
James Allen . . . . 518-474-8418 or 212-681-4640
Deputy Secretary for Civil Rights:
Norma Ramos 212-681-4584
First Assistant Counsel:
Sandi Toll 518-474-8434

EXECUTIVE DEPARTMENTS AND RELATED AGENCIES

Elections, State Board of
40 N Pearl Street
Suite 5
Albany, NY 12207-2729
518-474-6220 Fax: 518-486-4068
e-mail: info@elections.ny.gov
Web site: www.elections.ny.gov

Co-Chair:
Peter S Kosinski 518-474-8100
Co-Chair:
Douglas A Kellner 518-474-8100
Commissioner:
Andrew J Spano 518-474-8100
Commissioner:
Gregory P Peterson 518-474-8100
Co-Executive Director:
Todd Valentine 518-474-6336/fax: 518-474-1008
Co-Executive Director:
Robert A Brehm 518-474-6336/fax: 518-474-1008
Director, Public Information:
John W Conklin 518-474-1953/fax: 518-473-8315

Administrative Services
Administrative Officer:
Thomas A Jarose 518-474-6336/fax: 518-474-1008

Campaign Finance
Campaign Finance:
Campaign Finance/ Compliance Call Center 518-474-8200/fax: 518-486-6627
e-mail: cfinfo@elections.ny.gov

Counsel/Enforcement
Counsel:
Risa Sugarman 518-486-7858
e-mail: enforcement@elections.ny.gov
Co-Counsel:
Kimberly Galvin 518-474-6367/fax: 518-486-4068
Co-Counsel:
Brian M Quail 518-474-6367
Deputy Counsel:
William McCann 518-474-2063

County Boards of Elections

Albany . . . . fax: 518-487-5077
32 N Russell Rd, Albany, NY 12206
Fax: 518-487-5077
e-mail: boardofelections@albanycounty.com
Web site: www.albanycounty.com
Commissioner:
Matthew Clyne (D) 518-487-5060
Commissioner:
Rachel L Bledi (R) 518-487-5060
Deputy Commissioner:
Kathleen A Donovan (D) 518-487-5060
Deputy Commissioner:
Ellen Graziano (R) 518-487-5060

Allegany . . . . fax: 585-268-9406
6 Schuyler Street, Belmont, NY 14813
Fax: 585-268-9406
e-mail: acboe@alleganyco.com
Web site: www.alleganyco.com
Commissioner:
Michael J McCormick (D) 585-268-9295
e-mail: mccormm@alleganyco.com
Commissioner:
Richard Hollis (R) 585-268-9294
e-mail: hollisrg@alleganyco.com
Deputy Commissioner:
Barbara Broughton (D) 585-268-9295
e-mail: broughB@aleganyco.com
Deputy Commissioner:
Marcy Crawford (R) 585-268-9294
e-mail: crawfoMJ@alleganyco.com

Broome . . . . fax: 607-778-2174
Gov't Plaza, 60 Hawley St, PO Box 1766, Binghamton, NY 13902
Fax: 607-778-2174
e-mail: bcboe@co.broome.ny.us
Commissioner:
John Perticone (D) 607-778-2172
Commissioner:
Vacant (R) 607-778-2172
Deputy Commissioner:
Christina Dutko (D) 607-778-2172
Deputy Commissioner:
Karen A Davis (R) 607-778-2172

Cattaraugus . . . . fax: 716-938-2775
207 Rock City St, Ste 100, Little Valley, NY 14755
Fax: 716-938-2775
e-mail: boe-support@cattco.org
Web site: www.cattco.org
Commissioner:
Kevin Burleson (D) 716-938-2404
e-mail: KCBurleson@cattco.org
Commissioner:
Michael M Brisky (R) 716-938-2405
Deputy Commissioner:
Laura Howard (D) 716-938-2403
Deputy Commissioner:
Krenda Hale (R) 716-938-2401

Cayuga . . . . fax: 315-253-1289
157 Genesee Street (Basement), Auburn, NY 13021

Fax: 315-253-1289
e-mail: election@cayugacounty.us
Web site: www.co.cayuga.ny.us/election
Commissioner:
Katie Lacey (D) 315-253-1285
e-mail: klacey@cayugacounty.us
Commissioner:
Cherl Heary (R) 315-253-1285
e-mail: cheary@cayugacounty.us
Deputy Commissioner:
Deborah Calarco (D) 315-253-1285
e-mail: dcalarco@cayugacounty.us
Deputy Commissioner:
Roberta Massarini (R) 315-253-1285

Chautauqua . . . . fax: 716-753-4111
7 North Erie St, Mayville, NY 14757
716-753-4580 Fax: 716-753-4111
e-mail: vote@co.chautauqua.ny.us
Web site: www.co.chautauqua.ny.us
Commissioner:
Norman P Green (D). 716-753-4580
e-mail: GreenN@co.chautauqua.ny.us
Commissioner:
Brian C Abram (R). 716-753-4580
e-mail: AbramB@co.chautauqua.ny.us
Commissioner:
Doris Parment (D) 716-753-4580
Commissioner:
Nacole Ellis (R) 716-753-4580

Chemung . . . . fax: 607-737-5499
378 S Main Street, PO Box 588, Elmira, NY 14902-0588
607-737-5475 Fax: 607-737-5499
e-mail: votechemung@co.chemung.ny.us
Web site: www.chemungcounty.com
Commissioner:
Cindy Emmer (D). 607-737-5475
Commissioner:
Robert D Siglin (R) 607-737-5475
e-mail: rsiglin@co.chemung.ny.us
Deputy Commissioner:
Mary Collins (D) 607-737-5475
e-mail: marycollins@co.chemung.ny.us
Deputy Commissioner:
Linda A Forrest (R) 607-737-5475
e-mail: lforrest@co.chemung.ny.us

Chenango . . . . fax: 607-337-1766
5 Court Street, Norwich, NY 13815
607-337-1760 Fax: 607-337-1766
e-mail: boe@co.chenango.ny.us
Web site: www.co.chenango.ny.us
Commissioner:
Carol A Franklin (D) 607-337-1765
e-mail: carolf@co.chenango.ny.us
Commissioner:
Mary Lou A Monahan (R) 607-337-1764
Deputy Commissioner:
Carly J Hendricks (D). 607-337-1764
Deputy Commissioner:
Jamie Anderson (R) 607-337-1764

Clinton . . . . fax: 518-565-4508
County Gov't Center, 137 Margaret St, Ste 104, Plattsburgh, NY 12901
Fax: 518-565-4508
e-mail: boe@co.clinton.ny.us
Web site: www.clintoncountygov.com
Commissioner:
Mary R Dyer (D) 518-565-4740
Commissioner:
Gregory Campbell (R) 518-565-4740
Deputy Commissioner:
Susan R Castine (D) 518-565-4740
Deputy Commissioner:
Kara McBrayer (R). 518-565-4740

Columbia . . . . fax: 518-828-2624
401 State St, Hudson, NY 12534
Fax: 518-828-2624
e-mail: elections@columbiacountyny.com
Web site: www.columbiacountyny.com
Commissioner:
Virginia Martin (D) 518-828-3115
Commissioner:
Jason Nastke (R). 518-828-3115
Deputy Commissioner:
Hilary Hillman (D) 518-828-3115
e-mail: hilary.hillman@columbiacountyny.com
Deputy Commissioner:
Kathy L Harter (R) 518-828-3115
e-mail: kathy.harter@columbiacountyny.com

Cortland . . . . fax: 607-758-5513
112 River Street, Ste 1, Cortland, NY 13045
607-758-5032 Fax: 607-758-5513
e-mail: elections@cortland-co.org
Web site: www.cortland-co.org
Commissioner:
Thomas Henry Brown (D) 607-753-5033
e-mail: tbrown@cortland-co.org
Commissioner:
Robert C Howe (R). 607-753-5031
e-mail: rhowe@cortland-co.org

Delaware . . . . fax: 607-746-6516
3 Gallant Ave, Delhi, NY 13753
607-832-5321 Fax: 607-746-6516
e-mail: boe.move@co.delaware.ny.us
Web site: www.co.delaware.ny.us
Commissioner:
Judith Garrison (D). 607-832-5321
Commissioner:
William J Campbell (R) 607-832-5321
Deputy Commissioner:
Paula Schermerhorn (D). 607-832-5321
Deputy Commissioner:
Robin L Alger (R) 607-832-5321

Dutchess . . . . fax: 845-486-2483
47 Cannon St, Poughkeepsie, NY 12601
Fax: 845-486-2483
e-mail: dutchesselections@dutchessny.gov
Web site: www.dutchesselections.com
Commissioner:
Marco Caviglia (D). 845-486-2473
e-mail: mcaviglia@dutchessny.gov
Commissioner:
Erik Haight (R) 845-486-2473
e-mail: ehaight@dutchessny.gov
Deputy Commissioner:
Daniel Miller (D) 845-486-2477
e-mail: dmiller@dutchessny.gov
Deputy Commissioner:
Erin Reverri (R) 845-486-2475
e-mail: ereverri@dutchessny.gov

Erie . . . . fax: 716-858-8282
134 West Eagle St, Buffalo, NY 14202
Fax: 716-858-8282
Web site: elections.erie.gov
Commissioner:
Leonard Lenihan (D) 716-858-7787

Commissioner:
Ralph M Mohr (R) 716-858-7786
Deputy Commissioner:
Arthur O Eve Jr (D) 716-858-8891
Deputy Commissioner:
Robin Sion (R) 716-858-8891

Essex . . . . fax: 518-873-3479
7551 Court Street, PO Box 217, Elizabethtown, NY 12932
518-873-3474 Fax: 518-873-3479
e-mail: essexelections@co.essex.ny.us
Web site: www.co.essex.ny.us/elect.asp
Commissioner:
Mark C. Whitney (D) 518-873-3475
e-mail: mwhitney@co.essex.ny.us
Commissioner:
Allison McGahay (R) 518-873-3478
e-mail: amcgahay@co.essex.ny.us
Deputy Commissioner:
Holly Rollins (D) 518-873-3477
e-mail: hrollins@co.essex.ny.us
Deputy Commissioner:
Shona Doyle (R) 518-873-3476
e-mail: sdoyle@co.essex.ny.us

Franklin . . . . fax: 518-481-6018
335 West Main St, Ste 161, Malone, NY 12953-1823
518-481-1663 Fax: 518-481-6018
e-mail: boe@co.franklin.ny.us
Web site: franklincony.org
Commissioner:
Kelly Cox (D) 518-481-1662
e-mail: kcox@co.franklin.ny.us
Commissioner:
Tracy Sparks (R) 518-481-1661
e-mail: tsparks@co.franklin.ny.us
Deputy Commissioner:
Linda S. Maneely (D) 518-481-1663
Deputy Commissioner:
Erin Brockway (R) 518-481-1663
e-mail: ebrockway@co.franklin.ny.us

Fulton . . . . fax: 518-736-1612
2714 State Highway 29, Ste 1, Johnstown, NY 12095-9946
Fax: 518-736-1612
e-mail: boe@co.fulton.ny.us
Web site: www.fultoncountyny.org
Commissioner:
Lynne Rubscha (D) 518-736-5526
Commissioner:
Lee A Hollenbeck (R) 518-736-5526
Deputy Commissioner:
Michele Miller (D) 518-736-5526
Deputy Commissioner:
Theresa E Dugan (R) 518-736-5526

Genesee . . . . fax: 585-344-8562
County Bldg One, 15 Main St, PO Box 284, Batavia, NY 14021
Fax: 585-344-8562
e-mail: election@co.genesee.ny.us
Web site: www.co.genesee.ny.us
Commissioner:
Lorie J Longhany (D) 585-344-2550
Commissioner:
Richard Siebert (R) 585-344-2550
Deputy Commissioner:
Karen S Gannon (D) 585-344-2250
Deputy Commissioner:
Melissa L Gaebler (R) 585-344-2250

Greene . . . . fax: 518-719-3784
411 Main Street, Ste 437, Catskill, NY 12414
Fax: 518-719-3784
e-mail: elections@discovergreene.com
Web site: greenegovernment.com
Commissioner:
Marie Metzler (D) 518-719-3550
e-mail: mmetzler@discovergreene.com
Commissioner:
Brent Bogardus (R) 518-719-3550
e-mail: bbogardus@discovergreene.com
Deputy Commissioner:
Casey McCarthy (D) 518-719-3550
Deputy Commissioner (Acting):
Carol Engelmann (R) 518-719-3550

Hamilton . . . . fax: 518-548-6345
Route 8, PO Box 175, Lake Pleasant, NY 12108
Fax: 518-548-6345
e-mail: elections@hamiltoncountyny.gov
Web site: www.hamiltoncounty.com
Commissioner:
Cathleen E Rogers (D) 518-548-4684
Commissioner:
Marie Buanno (R) 518-548-4684
Deputy Commissioner:
Jaime Parslow (D) 518-548-4684
Deputy Commissioner:
Virginia E Morris (R) 518-548-4684

Herkimer . . . . fax: 315-867-1106
109 Mary Street, Suite 1306, Herkimer, NY 13350
315-867-1102 Fax: 315-867-1106
e-mail: boeinfo@herkimercounty.org
Web site: herkimercounty.org
Commissioner:
Connie L Shepherd (D) 315-867-1103
Commissioner:
Louis Patrick Christie (R) 315-867-1104
Deputy Commissioner:
Robert Drumm (D) 315-867-1102
Deputy Commissioner:
Jennifer Williams (R) 315-867-1102

Jefferson . . . . fax: 315-785-5197
175 Arsenal St, 4th Floor, Watertown, NY 13601
Fax: 315-785-5197
Web site: www.co.jefferson.ny.us
Commissioner:
Babette M. Hall (D) 315-785-3027
e-mail: babetteh@co.jefferson.ny.us
Commissioner:
Jude Seymour (R) 315-785-3027
Deputy Commissioner:
Michelle LaFave (D) 315-785-3027
Deputy Commissioner:
Trina L Kampnich (R) 315-785-3027

Lewis . . . . fax: 315-376-2860
7660 N. State St, Lowville, NY 13367
Fax: 315-376-2860
e-mail: elections@lewiscountyny.org
Web site: www.lewiscountyny.org
Commissioner:
Lindsay Burriss (D) 315-376-5329
e-mail: lindsayburriss@lewiscounty.ny.gov
Commissioner:
Ann M Nortz (R) 315-376-5329
e-mail: annortz@lewiscounty.ny.gov
Deputy Commissioner:
Nicole Demo (D)
Deputy Commissioner:
Angela Peters (R)

Offices and agencies generally appear in alphabetical order, except when specific order is requested by listee.

Livingston . . . . fax: 585-243-7015
County Government Ctr, 6 Court St, Rm 104, Geneseo, NY 14454-1043
Fax: 585-243-7015
e-mail: elections@co.livingston.ny.us
Commissioner:
David DiPasquale (D) 585-243-7090
Commissioner:
Nancy L Leven (R) 585-243-7090
e-mail: nleven@co.livingston.ny.us
Deputy Commissioner:
Laura Schoonover (D) 585-243-7090
e-mail: lschoonover@co.livingston.ny.us
Deputy Commissioner:
Diana Farrell (R) 585-243-7090

Madison . . . . fax: 315-366-2532
North Court St, County Office Bldg, PO Box 666, Wampsville, NY 13163
Fax: 315-366-2532
e-mail: boecommissioners@madisoncounty.ny.gov
Web site: www.madisoncounty.org
Commissioner:
Laura P Costello (D) 315-366-2231
Commissioner:
Kelley S Hood (R) 315-366-2231
Deputy Commissioner:
Ann L Jones (D) 315-366-2231
Deputy Commissioner:
Mary Egger (R) 315-366-2231

Monroe . . . . fax: 585-324-1612
39 Main St West, Rochester, NY 14614
585-753-1550 Fax: 585-324-1612
e-mail: mcboe@monroecounty.gov
Web site: www.monroecounty.gov
Commissioner:
Thomas F Ferrarese (D) 585-753-1550/fax: 585-753-1531
e-mail: tFerrarese@monroecounty.gov
Commissioner:
David Van Varick (R) 585-753-1550/fax: 585-753-1521
Deputy Commissioner:
Colleen Anderson (D) 585-753-1550/fax: 585-753-1531
Deputy Commissioner:
Douglas E French (R) 585-753-1550/fax: 585-753-1521

Montgomery . . . . fax: 518-853-8392
Old Court House, 9 Park St, PO Box 1500, Fonda, NY 12068-1500
518-853-8180 Fax: 518-853-8392
e-mail: boe@co.montgomery.ny.us
Commissioner:
Jamie M Duchessi (D) 518-853-8181
Commissioner:
Terrance J Smith (R) 518-853-8182
Deputy Commissioner:
Caroline Swartz (D) 518-853-8183
Deputy Commissioner:
Wendy D. Shaver (R) 518-853-8183

Nassau . . . . fax: 516-571-2058
240 Old Country Rd, 5th Fl, Mineola, NY 11501
Fax: 516-571-2058
e-mail: fedmil@nassaucountyny.gov
Web site: www.nassaucountyny.gov
Commissioner:
David J Gugerty (D) 516-571-2411
Commissioner:
Louis G Savinetti (R) 516-571-2411
Deputy Commissioner:
Michael Santeramo (D) 516-571-2411
Deputy Commissioner:
Carol Demauro Busketta (R) 516-571-2411

New York City . . . . fax: 212-487-5349
32 Broadway, 7th Fl, New York, NY 10004
Fax: 212-487-5349
e-mail: electioninfo@boe.nyc.ny.us
Web site: www.vote.nyc.ny.us
Executive Director:
Michael J Ryan (D) 212-487-5300
Deputy Executive Director:
Dawn Sandow (R) 212-487-5300
Administrative Manager:
Pamela Green Perkins (D) 212-487-5300
Operations Manager:
Georgea Kontzamanis (R) 212-487-5300

Bronx . . . . fax: 718-299-2140
1780 Grand Concourse, 5th Fl, Bronx, NY 10457
Fax: 718-299-2140
e-mail: voterreg@boe.nyc.ny.us
Commissioner:
Bianca Perez (D) 718-299-9017
Commissioner:
Michael A Rendino (R) 718-299-9017
Deputy Chief Clerk:
Marricka Scott-McFadden (D) 718-299-9017
Deputy Chief Clerk:
Anthony J Ribustello (R) 718-299-9017

Kings . . . . fax: 718-246-5958
345 Adams St, 4th Fl, Brooklyn, NY 11201
Commissioner:
John Flateau (D) 718-797-8800
Commissioner:
Simon Shamoun (R) 718-797-8800
Deputy Chief Clerk:
BettyAnn Canizio (D) 718-797-8800
Chief Clerk:
Diane Haslett Rudiano (R) 718-797-8800

New York . . . . fax: 646-638-2047
200 Varick St, 10th Fl, New York, NY 10014
Commissioner:
Alan Schulkin (D) 212-886-2100
Commissioner:
Frederic M Umane (R) 212-886-2100
e-mail: fumane@boe.nyc.ny.us
Chief Clerk:
Greg Lehman (R) 212-886-2100
Deputy Chief Clerk:
William A Allen (D) 212-886-2100

Queens . . . . fax: 718-459-3384
118-35 Queens Blvd, Forest Hills, NY 11375
Commissioner:
Jose M Araujo (D) 718-730-6730
Commissioner:
Michael Michel (R) 718-730-6730
Chief Clerk:
Barbara Conacchio (D) 718-730-6730
Deputy Chief Clerk:
Bart Haggerty (R) 718-730-6730

Richmond . . . . fax: 718-876-0912
1 Edgewater Plaza, Staten Island, NY 10305
Fax: 718-876-0912
e-mail: voterreg@boe.nyc.ny.us
Commissioner:
Maria R Guastella (D) 718-876-0079
Commissioner:
Ronald Castorina, Jr (R) 718-876-0079
Chief Clerk:
Sheila Del Giorno (D) 718-876-0079
Deputy Chief Clerk:
Anthony Andruili (R) 718-876-0079

Niagara . . . . fax: 716-438-4054
111 Main Street, Ste 100, Lockport, NY 14094

Policy Areas

Offices and agencies generally appear in alphabetical order, except when specific order is requested by listee.

716-438-4040 Fax: 716-438-4054
e-mail: ncboe@niagaracounty.com
Web site: www.elections.niagara.ny.us
Commissioner:
Lora A. Allen (D) 716-438-4041
e-mail: lora.allen@niagaracounty.com
Commissioner:
Jennifer Fronczak (R) 716-438-4040
e-mail: jennifer.fronczak@niagaracounty.org
Deputy Commissioner:
Darryl DiNoto (D) 716-438-4041
Deputy Commissioner:
Michael Carney (R) 716-438-4040

Oneida . . . . fax: 315-798-6412
Union Station, 321 Main St, 3rd Fl, Utica, NY 13501
Fax: 315-798-6412
e-mail: boardofelections@ocgov.net
Web site: www.ocgov.net
Commissioner:
Jordan S Karp (D) 315-798-5761
Commissioner:
Rose Grimaldi (R) 315-798-5763
e-mail: rgrimaldi@ocgov.net
Deputy Commissioner:
Carolann N. Cardone (D) 315-798-5765
Deputy Commissioner:
Catherine A Dumka (R) 315-798-5765

Onondaga . . . . fax: 315-435-8451
1000 Erie Boulevard West, Syracuse, NY 13204
Fax: 315-435-8451
e-mail: elections@ongov.net
Web site: www.ongov.net
Commissioner:
Dustin M. Czarny (D) 315-435-3312
Commissioner:
Helen M Kiggins-Walsh (R) 315-435-3312

Ontario . . . . fax: 585-393-2941
74 Ontario St, Canandaigua, NY 14424
Fax: 585-393-2941
e-mail: boe@co.ontario.ny.us
Web site: www.co.ontario.ny.us/elections
Commissioner:
Mary Q Salotti (D) 585-396-4005
e-mail: mary.salotti@co.ontario.ny.us
Commissioner:
Michael J Northrup (R) 585-396-4005
e-mail: michael.northrup@co.ontario.ny.us
Clerk to Commissioner:
Karen Reed (D) 585-396-4005
Clerk to Commissioner:
Karen Bodine (R) 585-396-4005

Orange . . . . fax: 845-291-2437
75 Webster Ave, PO Box 30, Goshen, NY 10924
845-360-6500 Fax: 845-291-2437
e-mail: elections@orangecountygov.com
Web site: www.orangecountygov.com
Commissioner:
Susan Bahren (D) 845-360-6500
Commissioner:
David C Green (R) 845-360-6500
Deputy Commissioner:
Louise Vandemark (D) 845-360-6500
Deputy Commissioner:
Courtney Canfield Greene (R) 845-360-6500

Orleans . . . . fax: 585-589-2771
14012 State Rte 31, Albion, NY 14411
Fax: 585-589-2771
Web site: www.orleansny.com
Commissioner:
Janice E Grabowski (D) 585-589-3274
e-mail: janice.grabowski@orleansny.com
Commissioner:
Sylvia Shoemaker (R) 585-589-3274
Deputy Commissioner:
Eileen Aina (D) 585-589-3274
Deputy Commissioner:
Dorothy Morgan (R) 585-589-3274

Oswego . . . . fax: 315-349-8357
185 E Seneca St, Box 9, Oswego, NY 13126
Fax: 315-349-8357
Web site: www.co.oswego.ny.us/boe/index.html
Commissioner:
Richard Atkins (D) 315-349-8350
Commissioner:
Peggy Bickford (R) 315-349-8350
Deputy Commissioner:
Teresa Munger (D) 315-349-8350
Deputy Commissioner:
Marianne B. Ingerson (R) 315-349-8350

Otsego . . . . fax: 607-547-4248
140 County Hwy 33W, Ste 2, Cooperstown, NY 13326
Fax: 607-547-4248
e-mail: boe@otsegocounty.com
Web site: www.otsegocounty.com/depts/boe
Commissioner:
Michael Henrici (D) 607-547-4325
e-mail: henricim@otsegocounty.com
Commissioner:
Lori L Lehenbauer (R) 607-547-4247
e-mail: lehenbauerl@otsegocounty.com
Deputy Commissioner:
Victoria A Curtis (D) 607-547-4325
Deputy Commissioner:
Christina A Morrison (R) 607-547-4247

Putnam . . . . fax: 845-808-1920
25 Old Rte 6, Carmel, NY 10512
Fax: 845-808-1920
e-mail: putnamcountyelections@putnamcountyny.gov
Web site: www.putnamcountyny.com/boe/index.htm
Commissioner:
Catherine Croft (D) 845-808-1300
Commissioner:
Anthony G Scannapieco, Jr (R) 845-808-1300
Deputy Commissioner:
Andrea Basli (D) 845-808-1300
Deputy Commissioner:
Kelly K Primavera (R) 845-808-1300

Rensselaer . . . . fax: 518-270-2909
Ned Pattison Govt Ctr, 1600 Seventh Ave, Troy, NY 12180
Fax: 518-270-2909
e-mail: renscoboe@rensco.com
Commissioner:
Edward G McDonough (D) 518-270-2990
Commissioner:
Larry A Bugbee (R) 518-270-2990

Rockland . . . . fax: 845-638-5196
11 New Hempstead Rd, New City, NY 10956
Fax: 845-638-5196
e-mail: rcmove@co.rockland.ny.us
Commissioner:
Kristen Zebrowski (D) 845-638-5172
Commissioner:
Louis C Babcock (R) 845-638-5172

Deputy Commissioner:
Kathleen Pietanza (D). 845-638-5172
Deputy Commissioner:
Gerard Rogers (R) 845-638-5172

Saint Lawrence . . . . fax: 315-386-2737
80 State Hwy 310, Canton, NY 13617
Fax: 315-386-2737
Web site: www.co.st-lawrence.ny.us
Commissioner:
Jennie H Bacon (D) 315-379-2202
e-mail: jbacon@stlawco.org
Commissioner:
Thomas A Nichols (R) 315-379-2202
e-mail: tnichols@stlawco.org
Deputy Commissioner:
Seth Belt (D). 315-379-2202
e-mail: sbelt@stlawco.org
Deputy Commissioner:
Thomas O Hardiman (R) 315-379-2202

Saratoga . . . . fax: 518-884-4751
50 W High St, Ballston Spa, NY 12020
Fax: 518-884-4751
e-mail: elections@saratogacountyny.gov
Web site: www.saratogacountyny.gov
Commissioner:
William Fruci (D). 518-885-2249
Commissioner:
Roger J Schiera (R) 518-885-2249
Deputy Commissioner:
Carol Turney (D) 518-885-2249
Deputy Commissioner:
John Marcellus (R). 518-885-2249

Schenectady . . . . fax: 518-377-2716
388 Broadway, Ste E, Schenectady, NY 12305-2520
Fax: 518-377-2716
e-mail: boe@schenectadycounty.com
Web site: www.schenectadycounty.com
Commissioner:
Amy M Hild (D). 518-377-2469
Commissioner:
Darlene D Harris (R) 518-377-2469
Deputy Commissioner:
Laura Fronk (D) 518-377-2469
Deputy Commissioner:
Philip Aydinian (R) 518-377-2469

Schoharie . . . . fax: 518-295-8419
County Office Bldg, 284 Main St, PO Box 99, Schoharie, NY 12157
Fax: 518-295-8419
e-mail: boe@co.schoharie.ny.us
Commissioner:
Clifford C Hay (D). 518-295-8388
Commissioner:
Lewis L Wilson (R) 518-295-8388
Deputy Commissioner:
Richard Shultes (D) 518-295-8388
e-mail: rich.shultes@co.schoharie.ny.us
Deputy Commissioner:
Sara Davies-Griffin (R) 518-295-8388
e-mail: griffins@co.schoharie.ny.us

Schuyler . . . . fax: 607-535-8364
County Ofc Bldg, 105 Ninth St, Unit 13, Watkins Glen, NY 14891-9972
Fax: 607-535-8364
e-mail: elections@co.schuyler.ny.us
Commissioner:
John L Vona (D). 607-535-8195
Commissioner:
Joseph Fazzary (R). 607-535-8195
Deputy Commissioner:
Carolyn Elkins (D) 607-535-8195
Deputy Commissioner:
Cindy L Cady (R) 607-535-8195

Seneca . . . . fax: 315-539-3710
1 DiPronio Dr, Waterloo, NY 13165
Fax: 315-539-3710
e-mail: boe@co.seneca.ny.us
Web site: www.co.seneca.ny.us/boe
Commissioner:
Ruth V Same (D) 315-539-1760
e-mail: rsame@co.seneca.ny.us
Commissioner:
Tiffany Folk (R) 315-539-1760
Deputy Commissioner:
Carl J Same (D) 315-539-1760
e-mail: csame@co.seneca.ny.us
Deputy Commissioner:
Sherrill A O'Brien (R) 315-539-1760

Steuben . . . . fax: 607-664-2376
3 E Pulteney Square, Bath, NY 14810
607-664-2260 Fax: 607-664-2376
e-mail: elections@co.steuben.ny.us
Web site: www.steubencony.org
Commissioner:
Kelly J Penziul (D). 607-664-2260
Commissioner:
Veronica Olin (R). 607-664-2260
e-mail: veronica@co.steuben.ny.us
Deputy Commissioner:
Colleen A Hauryski (D) 607-664-2260
Deputy Commissioner:
Angelia M Cornish (R). 607-664-2260

Suffolk. . . . . fax: 631-852-4590
Yaphank Ave, PO Box 700, Yaphank, NY 11980
Commissioner:
Anita S Katz (D). 631-852-4500
Commissioner:
Nick LaLota (R) 631-852-4500
Deputy Commissioner:
Jeanne O'Rourke (D) 631-852-4500
Deputy Commissioner:
Betty Manzella (R). 631-852-4500

Sullivan . . . . fax: 845-807-0410
Government Ctr, 100 North St, PO Box 5012, Monticello, NY 12701-5192
Commissioner:
Ann Prusinski (D). 845-807-0400
Commissioner:
Lori Benjamin (R) 845-807-0400
Deputy Commissioner:
Honora Wohl (D) 845-807-0400
Deputy Commissioner:
Pam Murran (R) 845-807-0400

Tioga . . . . fax: 607-687-6348
1062 State Rte 38, PO Box 306, Owego, NY 13827
607-687-8261 Fax: 607-687-6348
e-mail: votetioga@co.tioga.ny.us
Web site: www.tiogacountyny.com
Commissioner:
John J Langan (D) 607-687-8261
e-mail: langanj@co.tioga.ny.us
Commissioner:
Bernadette M Toombs (R) 607-687-8261
e-mail: toombsb@co.tioga.ny.us
Deputy Commissioner:
Sandra Saddlemire (D). 607-687-8261
e-mail: saddlemires@co.tioga.ny.us

Offices and agencies generally appear in alphabetical order, except when specific order is requested by listee.

Policy Areas

Deputy Commissioner:
Lin Layman (R) 607-687-8261
e-mail: laymanl@co.tioga.ny.us

Tompkins . . . . .fax: 607-274-5533
Court House Annex, 128 E Buffalo St, Ithaca, NY 14850
Fax: 607-274-5533
e-mail: movehelp@tompskins-co.org
Web site: www.tompkins-co.org/boe
Commissioner:
Stephen M DeWitt (D) 607-274-5522
e-mail: sdewitt@tompkins-co.org
Commissioner:
Elizabeth W Cree (R) 607-274-5522
e-mail: ecree@tompkins-co.org
Deputy Commissioner:
Laura Norman (D) 607-274-5522
Deputy Commissioner:
Kari L Stamm (R) 607-274-5522

Ulster . . . . .fax: 845-334-5434
284 Wall Street, Kingston, NY 12401
Fax: 845-334-5434
e-mail: elections@co.ulster.ny.us
Web site: www.co.ulster.ny.us/elections/
Commissioner:
C Victor Work (D) 845-334-5470
Commissioner:
Thomas F Turco (R) 845-334-5470
Deputy Commissioner:
Ashley Dittus (D) 845-334-5470
Deputy Commissioner:
Patty Jacobsen (R) 845-334-5470

Warren . . . . .fax: 518-761-6480
County Municipal Center, 1340 State Rte 9, 3rd Fl, Lake George, NY 12845
518-761-6456 Fax: 518-761-6480
e-mail: boe@warrencountyny.gov
Web site: www.warrencountyny.gov/boe
Commissioner:
Elizabeth J McLaughlin (D). 518-761-6459
Commissioner:
Mary Beth Casey (R) 518-761-6458
Deputy Commissioner:
Kimberly Ross (D) 518-761-6456
Deputy Commissioner:
Emily Kladis (R). 518-761-6457

Washington. . . . . .fax: 518-746-2179
383 Broadway, Fort Edward, NY 12828
518-746-2180 Fax: 518-746-2179
e-mail: boardofelections@co.washington.ny.us
Commissioner:
Jeffrey J Curtis (D) 518-746-2180
Commissioner:
Leslie Allen (R) 518-746-2180
Deputy Commissioner:
Melinda Suprenant (D). 518-746-2180
Deputy Commissioner:
Thomas Rogers (R). 518-746-2180

Wayne . . . . .fax: 315-946-7409
7376 State Route 31, PO Box 636, Lyons, NY 14489
Fax: 315-946-7409
e-mail: elections@co.wayne.ny.us
Web site: www.co.wayne.ny.us
Commissioner:
Mark H Alquist (D) 315-946-7400
Commissioner:
Marjorie M Bridson (R) 315-946-7400
Deputy Commissioner:
Joyce A Krebbeks (D) 315-946-7400
e-mail: jkrebbeks@co.wayne.ny.us
Deputy Commissioner:
Kelley M Borrelli (R) 315-946-7400

Westchester . . . . .fax: 914-995-3190
25 Quarropas Street, White Plains, NY 10601
Fax: 914-995-3190
e-mail: boe-west@westchestergov.com
Commissioner:
Reginald A LaFayette (D). 914-995-5700/fax: 914-995-7753
Commissioner:
Douglas A Colety (R) 914-995-5700
Deputy Commissioner:
Jeannie L Palazola (D) 914-995-5700
Deputy Commissioner:
Dotty DiPalo (R). 914-995-5700

Wyoming. . . . . .fax: 585-786-8843
4 Perry Avenue, Warsaw, NY 14569-1329
Fax: 585-786-8843
e-mail: boewyoming@wyomingco.net
Web site: www.wyomingco.net
Commissioner:
Anna Mae Balmas (D) 585-786-8931
Commissioner:
James E Schlick (R) 585-786-8931
Deputy Commissioner:
Jeanne M Williams (D) 585-786-8931
e-mail: jewilliams@frontiernet.net
Deputy Commissioner:
Wendy Simpson (R) 585-786-8931
e-mail: wlsimpson@frontiernet.net

Yates . . . . .fax: 315-536-5523
417 Liberty St, Ste 1124, Penn Yan, NY 14527
Fax: 315-536-5523
e-mail: boardofelections@yatescounty.org
Commissioner:
Robert Brechko (D) 315-536-5135
Commissioner:
Amy J Daines (R) 315-536-5135
Deputy Commissioner:
Sandra P McKay (D) 315-536-5135
Deputy Commissioner:
Helen J Scarpechi (R). 315-536-5135

Election Operations

Director Election Operations:
Anna E Svizzero 518-473-5086/fax: 518-486-4546
Deputy Director Election Operations:
Brendon Lovullo 518-473-5086/fax: 518-486-4546

General Information

Director, Public Information:
John W Conklin 518-474-1953
Deputy Director, Public Information:
Thomas E Connolly
e-mail: info@elections.ny.gov

Information Technology Unit

Manager, Data Processing/CTO:
Mark Goldhaber 518-473-4803

CORPORATIONS, AUTHORITIES AND COMMISSIONS

Joint Commission on Public Ethics (JCOPE)

540 Broadway
Albany, NY 12207

518-408-3976 Fax: 518-408-3975
e-mail: jcope@jcope.ny.gov
Web site: www.jcope.ny.gov

Executive Director:
Seth Agata....518-408-3976
Chair:
Daniel J Horwitz....518-408-3976
General Counsel:
Monica Stamm....518-408-3976
Chief of Staff:
Kevin T Gagan....518-408-3976/fax: 518-408-3975

NEW YORK STATE LEGISLATURE

See Legislative Branch in Section 1 for additional Standing Committee and Subcommittee information.

Assembly Standing Committees

Election Law
Chair:
Michael Cusick (D)....518-455-5526
Ranking Minority Member:
Bill Nojay (R)....518-455-5662

Senate Standing Committees

Elections
Chair:
Frederick J Akshar, II (R)....518-455-2677
Ranking Minority Member:
Leroy Comrie (D)....518-455-2701

Senate/Assembly Legislative Commissions

Demographic Research & Reapportionment, Legislative Task Force on
Senate Co-Chair:
Michael F Nozzolio (R)....518-455-2366
Assembly Co-Chair:
Marcos A Crespo (D)....518-455-5514
Assembly Program Manager:
Karen Blatt....212-618-1100/fax: 212-618-1135
Executive Director:
Frank Tassone....212-618-1110/fax: 212-618-1135

U.S. GOVERNMENT

EXECUTIVE DEPARTMENTS AND RELATED AGENCIES

Federal Election Commission
999 E Street NW
Washington, DC 20463
202-694-1000 or 800-424-9530
e-mail: info@fec.gov
Web site: www.fec.gov

Chair:
Matthew S. Petersen
e-mail: commissionerpetersen@fec.gov
Vice Chair:
Steven T. Walther
e-mail: swalther@fec.gov
Commissioner:
Caroline C. Hunter
e-mail: commissionerhunter@fec.gov
Commissioner:
Ann M. Ravel
e-mail: commissionerravel@fec.gov
Commissioner:
Ellen L. Weintraub
e-mail: commissionerweintraub@fec.gov

US Commission on Civil Rights
Web site: www.usccr.gov

EASTERN REGION (includes New York State)
624 9th Street NW, Suite 500, Washington, DC 20425
Regional Director:
Ivy L. Davis....202-376-7533 or TTY: 202-376-8116

U.S. CONGRESS

See U.S. Congress Chapter for additional Standing Committee and Subcommittee information.

House of Representatives Standing Committees

Oversight & Government Reform
Chair:
Jason Chaffetz (R-UT)....202-225-7751
Ranking Member:
Elijah Cummings (D-MD)....202-225-4741
New York Delegate:
Carolyn B. Maloney (D)....202-225-7944

Subcommittee
Government Operations
Chair:
Mark Meadows (R-NC)....202-225-6401
Ranking Member:
Gerald Connolly (D-VA)....202-225-1492

Ethics
Chair:
Charles W. Dent (R-PA)....202-225-6411
Ranking Member:
Linda T. Sanchez (D-CA)....202-225-6676

Senate Standing Committees

Ethics, Select Committee on
Chair:
Johnny Isakson (R-GA)....202-224-3643
Vice Chair:
Barbara Boxer (D-CA)....202-224-3553

Homeland Security & Governmental Affairs
Chair:
Ron Johnson (R-WI)....202-224-5323
Ranking Member:
Thomas R. Carper (D-DE)....202-224-2441

PRIVATE SECTOR

Arthur J Finkelstein & Associates Inc
16 North Astor, Irvington, NY 10533
914-591-8142
Election polling & consulting
Arthur J. Finkelstein, President

Branford Communications
611 Broadway, New York, NY 10012
212-260-9905 Fax: 212-260-9908
Media consulting; print production & advertising

Ernest Lendler, President

Bynum, Thompson, Ryer
2120 L Street NW, Suite 305, Washington, DC 20037
202-263-4383
e-mail: thompson@btrsc.com
Web site: www.btrsc.com
Campaign communication, strategy & media production
Jim Thompson, Owner

CUNY Graduate School, Center for Urban Research
365 5th Avenue, New York, NY 10016-4309
212-817-2030 Fax: 212-817-1575
e-mail: cur@gc.cuny.edu
Web site: www.gc.cuny.edu
Political participation, voting behavior, NYC politics & urban economic & demographic change
John Mollenkopf, Director

Century Foundation (The)
1 Whitehall Street, 15th Floor, New York, NY 10004
212-452-7700 Fax: 212-535-7534
e-mail: info@tcf.org
Web site: www.tcf.org
Research & analysis of domestic & foreign policy issues, including matters relating to education, the workforce, health care, human rights & election reform
Lucy Muirhead, Vice President, Communications

Citizen Action of New York
94 Central Avenue, Albany, NY 12206
518-465-4600 Fax: 518-465-2890
e-mail: info@citizenactionny.org
Web site: www.citizenactionny.org
Campaign finance reform; health care advocacy & consumer protection; education
Karen Scharff, Executive Director

Columbia Law School, Legislative Drafting Research Fund
435 West 116th Street, New York, NY 10027-7297
212-854-2640 or 212-854-5633 Fax: 212-854-7946
e-mail: rb34@columbia.edu
Web site: www.law.columbia.edu
State & local government law, property law & election law
Richard Briffault, Director & Professor of Legislation

Common Cause/NY
80 Broad Street, New York, NY 10004
212-691-6421 Fax: 212-807-1809
e-mail: nyoffice@commoncause.org
Web site: www.commoncause.org/states/new-york/
Campaign finance reform, ballot access, political gift disclosure & public interest lobbying
Susan Lerner, Executive Director

Conservative Party of NYS
325 Parkview Drive, Schenectady, NY 12303
518-356-7882 Fax: 518-356-3773
e-mail: cpnys@nybiz.rr.com
Web site: www.cpnys.org
Campaign consulting services & funding for Conservative Party political candidates
Shaun Marie Levine, Executive Director

Cookfair Media Inc
536 Buckingham Avenue, Syracuse, NY 13210
315-478-3359 Fax: 315-478-5236
Campaign media production, print production & advertising
John R. Cookfair, III, President

Democratic Congressional Campaign Committee
430 South Capitol Street SE, Washington, DC 20003
202-863-1500 Fax: 202-485-3436
Web site: www.dccc.org
Funding for Democratic congressional candidates; campaign strategy
Ben Ray Lujan, Chair

Election Computer Services Inc
197 County Route 7, Pine Plains, NY 12567
518-398-8844 or 212-750-8844
Computer services, voter lists & direct mail
Marguerite Terwilliger, Principal

EMILY's List
1800 M Street NW, Suite 375N, Washington, DC 20036
202-326-1400 Fax: 202-326-1415
Web site: www.emilyslist.org
Political network for pro-choice Democratic women political candidates
Jessica O'Connell, Executive Director

Harris Poll (The)
155 Corporate Woods, Rochester, NY 14623
585-272-8400 or 877-919-4765
Web site: www.theharrispoll.com
Polls on a range of topics, including politics, the economy, health & sports
Kathy Steinberg, Director

League of Women Voters of New York State
62 Grand Street, Albany, NY 12207-2712
518-465-4162 Fax: 518-465-0812
e-mail: laura@lwvny.org
Web site: www.lwvny.org
Public policy issues forum; good government advocacy
Laura Ladd Bierman, Executive Director

Marist Institute for Public Opinion
Marist College, 3399 North Road, Poughkeepsie, NY 12601
845-575-5050 Fax: 845-575-5111
e-mail: lee.miringoff@marist.edu
Web site: www.maristpoll.marist.edu
Develops & conducts nonpartisan public opinion polls on elections & issues
Lee M. Miringoff, Director

NY League of Conservation Voters/NY Conservation Education Fund
30 Broad Street, 30th Floor, New York, NY 10004
212-361-6350 Fax: 212-361-6363
e-mail: info@nylcvef.org
Web site: www.nylcvef.org
Endorsement of pro-environmental candidates; environmental advocacy & education statewide
Marcia Bystryn, President

NYC Campaign Finance Board
100 Church Street, 12th Floor, New York, NY 10007
212-409-1800 Fax: 212-409-1705
Web site: www.nyccfb.info
Public funding of candidates for NYC elective offices
Amy M. Loprest, Executive Director

NYS Right to Life Committee
41 State Street, Suite M-100, Albany, NY 12207
518-434-1293 Fax: 518-426-1200
e-mail: admin@nysrighttolife.org
Web site: www.nysrighttolife.org
Lori Kehoe, Executive Director

National Organization for Women, NYS
150 West 28th Street, Suite 304, New York, NY 10001
212-627-9895 Fax: 212-627-9861
e-mail: nownewyorkstate@gmail.com
Web site: www.nownys.org
Campaign assistance & funding for political candidates who support women's equality; legislative lobbying on women's issues
Sonia Ossorio, President

New School for Social Research, Department of Politics
6 East 16th Street, Room 711A, New York, NY 10003
212-229-5747 x3090 Fax: 212-229-5473
e-mail: kalyvasa@newschool.edu
Web site: www.newschool.edu
Political issues & analysis
Andreas Kalyvas, Chair

New York Republican State Committee
315 State Street, Albany, NY 12210
518-462-2601 Fax: 518-449-7443
Web site: www.newyork.gop
Jason Weingartner, Executive Director

New York State Democratic Committee
750 Third Avenue, 31st Floor, New York, NY 10017
212-725-8825 Fax: 212-725-8867
Web site: www.nydems.org
Sheila Comar, Executive Commitee Chair

New York University, Departmentt of Politics
19 West 4th Street, 2nd Floor, New York, NY 10012-9580
212-998-8500 Fax: 212-995-4184
e-mail: russell.hardin@nyu.edu
Web site: www.politics.as.nyu.edu
Collective action & social movements; nationalism & ethnic conflict; constitutionalism
Russell Hardin, Professor of Politics

New York University, Graduate School of Journalism
20 Cooper Square, 6th Floor, New York, NY 10003
212-998-7980 Fax: 212-995-4148
e-mail: perri.klass@nyu.edu
Web site: www.journalism.nyu.edu
Public information & knowledge
Perri Klass, Director

New York Wired for Education LLC
251 Fuller Road, Room B150, Albany, NY 12203
518-462-1780
Web site: www.metrixlearning.com
Brian S. Lee, Chief Executive Officer

Nostradamus Advertising
884 West End Avenue, Suite 2, New York, NY 10025
212-581-1362
e-mail: nos@nostradamus.net
Web site: www.nostradamus.net
Print production, media consulting, direct mail development
Barry N. Sher, President

Public Agenda
6 East 39th Street, 9th Floor, New York, NY 10016
212-686-6610 Fax: 212-889-3461
e-mail: info@publicagenda.org
Web site: www.publicagenda.org
Nonpartisan, nonprofit organization dedicated to conducting unbiased public opinion research & producing fair-minded citizen education materials
Will Friedman, President

SUNY at Albany, Nelson A Rockefeller College
135 Western Avenue, Albany, NY 12222
518-442-5244 Fax: 518-442-5298
e-mail: hildreth@albany.edu
Web site: www.albany.edu/rockefeller
Intergovernmental relations; NY state & local government; ethics in government; election systems & voting
Anne Hildreth, Associate Professor

SUNY at New Paltz, College of Liberal Arts & Sciences
1 Hawk Drive, New Paltz, NY 12561-2499
845-257-7869 or 877-696-7411
e-mail: millerj@newpaltz.edu
Web site: www.newpaltz.edu
Local & state government process & structure; regionalism; politics & election law
Jeff Miller, Political Science Chair & Associate Professor

Sheinkopf Communications
152 Madison Avenue, Suite 1603, New York, NY 10016
212-725-2378 Fax: 212-725-6896
Strategic message counseling for corporate & political clients
Hank Sheinkopf, President

US Term Limits Foundation
1250 Connecticut Avenue NW, Suite 200, Washington, DC 20036
202-261-3532
Web site: www.termlimits.org
Works to combat government malpractice
Howard Rich, Chairman

Women's Campaign Fund
718 7th Street NW, 2nd Floor, Washington, DC 20001
202-796-8259
e-mail: info@wcfonline.org
Web site: www.wcfonline.org
Support for women political candidates & advocacy for more women in government & elected office
Betsy Mullins, President & Chief Executive Officer

Women's City Club of New York
110 West 40th Street, Suite 1002, New York, NY 10018
212-353-8070 Fax: 212-228-4665
e-mail: info@wccny.org
Web site: www.wccny.org
Nonpartisan, nonprofit activist organization whose mission is to inform public policy & enhance the quality of life for all New Yorkers through education, advocacy & issue analysis
Jacqueline M. Ebanks, Executive Director

Working Families Party
1 Metrotech Center North, 11th Floor, Brooklyn, NY 11217
718-222-3796 Fax: 718-246-3718
e-mail: wfp@workingfamiliesparty.org
Web site: www.workingfamilies.org
Bill Lipton, State Director

Zogby Analytics
901 Broad Street, Utica, NY 13501
315-624-9642
Web site: www.zogbyanalytics.com
Polling, surveys, focus groups, market research studies & data analysis for businesses & communities
Jonathan Zogby, Chief Executive Officer

Policy Areas

ENERGY, UTILITY & COMMUNICATION SERVICES

NEW YORK STATE

GOVERNOR'S OFFICE

Governor's Office
Executive Chamber
State Capitol
Albany, NY 12224
518-474-8390 Fax: 518-474-1513
Web site: www.ny.gov

Governor:
Andrew M Cuomo 518-474-8390
Secretary to the Governor:
William Mulrow 518-474-4246
Counsel to the Governor:
Alphonso David 518-474-8343
Chairman of Energy & Finance for New York:
Richard Kauffman. 518-408-2552
Chief of Staff:
Melissa DeRosa . . . . 518-474-8418 or 212-681-4640
Director, Communications:
James Allen. . . . . 518-474-8418 or 212-681-4640

EXECUTIVE DEPARTMENTS AND RELATED AGENCIES

CIO & Office of Information Technology Services (ITS)
State Capitol, ESP
PO Box 2062
Albany, NY 12220-0062
518-402-2537 or 866-789-4638 Fax: 518-474-1196
e-mail: customer.relations@its.ny.gov
Web site: www.its.ny.gov

Chief Information Officer & Director:
Maggie Miller. 518-408-2140
Executive Deputy CIO:
Mahesh Nattanmai 518-408-2140
Counsel & Legal Services:
Shoshanah Bewlay 518-486-9200
Director, Public Information:
Vacant 518-408-3899

Administration
Chief Operating Officer:
Ray Rose 518-402-7000
Director, Administration:
Terri Papa 518-408-2484
Chief Technology Officer:
Rajiv Rao 518-486-9200
Chief Data Officer:
Barbara Cohn. 518-474-3019/fax: 518-486-7923
Director, Enterprise Information Security Office:
Vacant 518-242-5200
e-mail: eiso@its.ny.gov
Chief Portfolio Officer:
Nancy Mulholland 518-473-9450

Consumer Protection, Division of
One Commerce Plaza
99 Washington Avenue
Albany, NY 12231
518-474-8583 or 800-697-1220 Fax: 518-473-9055
Web site: www.dos.ny.gov/consumerprotection/

Executive Deputy Director:
Aiesha Battle. 518-474-2363

Law Department
120 Broadway
New York, NY 10271-0332
212-416-8000 or 800-771-7755
Web site: www.ag.ny.gov

State Capitol
Albany, NY 12224-0341
518-776-2000
Fax: 518-650-9401

Attorney General:
Eric T Schneiderman . . . . 212-416-8050 or 518-776-2000
Chief of Staff:
Brian Mahanna 212-416-8050
Director, Public Information:
Shawn Morris 518-776-2357/fax: 518-650-9401
Press Secretary:
Matt Mittenthal 212-416-8060/fax: 212-416-6005

Economic Justice
Executive Deputy Attorney General:
Manisha Sheth. 212-416-8050

Internet Bureau
Bureau Chief:
Kathleen McGee 212-416-8433/fax: 212-416-8369

Public Service Commission
NYS Dept of Public Service
3 Empire State Plaza
Albany, NY 12223-1350
518-474-7080 Fax: 518-474-0421
Web site: www.dps.ny.gov

Chairman:
Audrey Zibelman. 518-474-2532/fax: 518-473-2838
Executive Deputy:
Judith Lee 518-408-1978/fax: 518-473-2838
General Counsel:
Kimberly Harriman 518-408-1978/fax: 518-473-2838
Manager of Utility Rates & Services:
William Bouteiller. 518-402-5674/fax: 518-473-2838
General Counsel:
Peter McGowan 518-474-2510
Secretary to the Commission:
Kathleen H Burgess. 518-474-6530/fax: 518-474-9842
e-mail: secretary@dps.ny.gov
Director, Public Affairs:
James Denn 518-474-7080/fax: 518-473-2838
e-mail: james.denn@dps.ny.gov

Accounting & Finance Office
Director:
Doris Stout . . . . 518-474-4508 or 212-417-2136

Consumer Policy Office
Director:
Douglas Elfner. 518-402-5786/fax: 518-473-5685

Consumer Services Office
Director:
Sandra Sloane 518-474-3280
e-mail: csd@dps.ny.gov

Offices and agencies generally appear in alphabetical order, except when specific order is requested by listee.

Consumer Complaints 1-800-342-3377
e-mail: csd@dps.ny.gov

Energy Efficiency & the Environment
Acting Director:
Colleen Gerwitz 518-474-2350
Deputy Director:
James Austin 518-473-4635/fax: 518-473-5026
Chief, Renewable Energy:
Christina Palmero 518-474-1612/fax: 518-474-5026
Chief, Analysis & Modeling:
Steven Keller 518-486-2430/fax: 518-473-1498

Electric, Gas & Water Office
Managing Executive Director, Utility Rates & Services:
Rajendra Addepalli 518-473-8986/fax: 518-473-2420
Deputy Director, Gas, Water & Steam:
Michael Scott 518-474-1372/fax: 518-473-4992
Chief, Electric Rates & Tariffs:
Bruce Alch 518-486-2400/fax: 518-473-5204
Chief, Distribution Systems:
Michael Worden 518-486-2498/fax: 518-473-2420
Chief, Bulk Electric Systems:
Tammy Mitchell 518-486-2462/fax: 518-473-2420
Chief, Policy Coordination:
William Heinrich 518-473-3402/fax: 518-473-2420
Chief, Gas Rates & Tariffs:
Thomas Coonan 518-473-6694/fax: 518-473-4992
Chief, Gas Policy & Supply:
Cynthia McCarran 518-474-1396/fax: 518-473-4992
Chief, Water:
James Evensen 212-417-2321/fax: 212-417-2324
Chief, Safety, Electric, Gas & Steam:
Gavin S Nicoletta 518-486-2496/fax: 518-473-1498
Chief, Utility Security:
John Sennett 518-402-5445/fax: 518-473-5685

Hearings & Alternative Dispute Resolution Office
Chief Administrative Law Judge:
Elizabeth Liebschutz 518-474-4520/fax: 518-473-3263

Industry & Governmental Relations Office
Managing Director:
Michael Corso 518-474-4686

Office of Administration
Director:
Sorelle Brauth 518-474-2508/fax: 518-474-0413
Adminstrative Management:
Judy Regan 518-474-1990/fax: 518-474-0413
Finance & Budget:
Carole Gnacik 518-474-2516/fax: 518-473-9990
Human Resources:
Janice Nissen 518-486-2626/fax: 518-473-9990
Information Services Director:
Carmela Turpin 518-486-4960/fax: 518-473-7815
Internal Audit:
Theresa Schillaci 518-473-2079/fax: 518-486-6081

Regulatory Economics Office
Director:
Mark Reeder 518-474-1721

Office of Telecommunications
Director:
Karen Geduldig 518-474-1668/fax: 518-474-5616

CORPORATIONS, AUTHORITIES AND COMMISSIONS

Interstate Oil & Gas Compact Commission
PO Box 53127
900 NE 23rd St
Oklahoma City, OK 73152-3127
405-525-3556 Fax: 405-525-3592
e-mail: iogcc@iogcc.state.ok.us
Web site: www.iogcc.ok.gov

Chair:
Governor Mary Fallin (OK) 405-525-3556
Vice Chair:
David Porter 405-525-3556
Executive Director:
Mike Smith 405-525-3556
New York State Official Representative:
Bradley J Field 518-402-8076
Communications Manager:
Carol Booth 405-525-3556

New York Power Authority
123 Main Street
Mailstop 10-H
White Plains, NY 10601-3170
914-681-6200 Fax: 914-390-8190
e-mail: info@nypa.gov
Web site: www.nypa.gov

Chairman:
John R. Koelmel 914-287-3636
President & Chief Executive Officer:
Gil C Quiniones 914-287-3501
SVP, Corporate Affairs:
Rocco Iannarelli 518-433-6700
Chief Operating Officer:
Edward A Welz 518-433-6700
EVP & General Counsel:
Justin E Driscoll 914-681-6200

New York State Energy Research & Development Authority
17 Columbia Circle
Albany, NY 12203-6399
518-862-1090 Fax: 518-862-1091
e-mail: info@nyserda.ny.gov
Web site: www.nyserda.ny.gov
Chairman:
Richard L Kauffman 518-862-1090
President & CEO:
John B Rhodes 518-862-1090 x3278
General Counsel:
Noah C Shaw 518-862-1090 x3280
Program Manager, Economic Development & Community Outreach:
Kelly Tyler . . . . 716-842-1522 x. 3005
e-mail: kelly.tyler@nyserda.ny.gov
Director, Communications:
Kate Muller 518-862-1090 x3582/fax: 518-862-1091
e-mail: kate.muller@nyserda.ny.gov

NEW YORK STATE LEGISLATURE

See Legislative Branch in Section 1 for additional Standing Committee and Subcommittee information.

Policy Areas

Assembly Standing Committees

Energy
Chair:
Amy Paulin (D)....518-455-5585
Ranking Minority Member:
Philip Palmesano (R)....518-455-5791

Senate Standing Committees

Energy & Telecommunications
Chair:
Joseph A Griffo (R)....518-455-3334
Ranking Minority Member:
Kevin Parker (D)....518-455-2580

U.S. GOVERNMENT

EXECUTIVE DEPARTMENTS AND RELATED AGENCIES

Federal Communications Commission
e-mail: fccinfo@fcc.gov
Web site: www.fcc.gov

Office of Media Relations....fax: 866-418-0232
445 12th Street SW, Room CY-C314, Washington, DC 20554
888-225-5322 Fax: 866-418-0232
Director:
Shannon Gilson

Nuclear Regulatory Commission
Web site: www.nrc.gov

REGION I (includes New York State)
2100 Renaissance Blvd, Suite 100, King of Prussia, PA 19406-2713
Regional Administrator:
Daniel Dorman
Deputy Regional Administrator:
David Lew
Senior Public Affairs Officer:
Diane Screnci

US Department of Agriculture
Web site: www.usda.gov

Rural Development
Web site: www.rd.usda.gov/ny

New York State Office....fax: 315-477-6438
The Galleries of Syracuse, 441 South Salina Street, Suite 357, Syracuse, NY 13202-2541
TTY: 315-477-6447 or 315-477-6400 Fax: 315-477-6438
Acting State Director:
Scott Collins....315-477-6437
Special Projects Coordinator:
Christopher Stewart

Eastern New York Office....fax: 855-889-1632
255 Dolson Avenue, Suite 104, Middletown, NY 10940
845-343-1872 x4 Fax: 855-889-1632
Director:
Ronda Falkena....845-343-1872 x4

Western New York Office....fax: 607-753-3190
1 North Main Street, 2nd Floor, Cortland, NY 13045
607-753-0851 Fax: 607-753-3190
Director:
Jim Walfrand....585-343-9167 x4

US Department of Energy
Web site: www.energy.gov

Federal Energy Regulatory Commission

New York Regional Office
19 West 34th Street, Suite 400, New York, NY 10001-3006
Regional Engineer:
John Spain

Office of External Affairs
888 First Street NE, Washington, DC 20426
866-208-3372
Director:
Leonard Tao....202-502-8004/fax: 202-208-2106

Laboratories

Brookhaven National Laboratory
External Affairs & Stakeholder Relations
PO Box 5000, Upton, NY 11973-5000
Director, Stakeholder & Community Relations Office:
David Manning
Office of the Director
2 Center Street, Upton, NY 11973
Director:
Doon Gibbs

Knolls Atomic Power Laboratory- KAPL Inc
2401 River Road, Niskayuna, NY 12309

U.S. CONGRESS

See U.S. Congress Chapter for additional Standing Committee and Subcommittee information.

House of Representatives Standing Committees

Appropriations
Chair:
Harold Rogers (R-KY)....202-225-4601
Ranking Member:
Nita M. Lowey (D-NY)....202-225-6506
New York Delegate:
Steve Israel (D)....202-225-3335
New York Delegate:
Jose E. Serrano (D)....202-225-4361
Subcommittee
Energy & Water Development
Chair:
Mike Simpson (R-ID)....202-225-5531
Ranking Member:
Marcy Kaptur (D-OH)....202-225-4146

Energy & Commerce
Chair:
Fred Upton (R-MI)....202-225-3761
Ranking Member:
Frank Pallone (D-NJ)....202-225-4671
New York Delegate:
Eliot L. Engel (D)....202-225-2464
New York Delegate:
Paul Tonko (D)....202-225-5076
New York Delegate:
Yvette Clarke (D)....202-225-6231
New York Delegate:
Chris Collins (R)....202-225-5265

Offices and agencies generally appear in alphabetical order, except when specific order is requested by listee.

Subcommittee
Energy & Power
Chair:
Ed Whitfield (R-KY) 202-225-3115
Ranking Member:
Bobby L. Rush (D-IL) 202-225-4372
New York Delegate:
Eliot L. Engel (D) 202-225-2464
New York Delegate:
Paul Tonko (D) 202-225-5076

Natural Resources
Chair:
Rob Bishop (R-UT) 202-225-0453
Ranking Member:
Raul M. Grijalva (D-AZ) 202-225-2435

Subcommittees
Energy & Mineral Resources
Chair:
Doug Lamborn (R-CO) 202-225-4422
Ranking Member:
Alan Lowenthal (D-CA) 202-225-7924
Water, Power & Oceans
Chair:
John Fleming (R-LA). 202-225-2777
Ranking Member:
Jared Huffman (D-CA) 202-225-5161

Science, Space & Technology
Chair:
Lamar Smith (R-TX). 202-225-4236
Ranking Member:
Eddie Bernice Johnson (D-TX) 202-225-8885

Subcommittee
Energy
Chair:
Randy Weber (R-TX) 202-225-2831
Ranking Member:
Alan Grayson (D-FL). 202-225-9889

Senate Standing Committees

Appropriations
Chair:
Thad Cochran (R-MS) 202-224-5054
Vice Chair:
Barbara A. Mikulski (D-MD). 202-224-4654

Subcommittee
Energy & Water Development
Chair:
Lamar Alexander (R-TN) 202-224-4944
Ranking Member:
Dianne Feinstein (D-CA). 202-224-3841

Commerce, Science & Transportation
Chair:
John Thune (R-SD). 202-224-2321
Ranking Member:
Bill Nelson (D-FL) 202-224-5274

Subcommittee
Aviation Operations, Safety & Security
Chair:
Kelly Ayotte (R-NH) 202-224-3324
Ranking Member:
Maria Cantwell (D-WA) 202-224-3441
Space, Science & Competitiveness
Chair:
Ted Cruz (R-TX) 202-224-5922

Ranking Member:
Gary Peters (D-MI) 202-224-6221

Energy & Natural Resources
Chair:
Lisa Murkowski (R-AK). 202-224-6665
Ranking Member:
Maria Cantwell (D-WA). 202-224-3441

PRIVATE SECTOR

AT&T Corporation
One AT&T Way, Bedminster, NJ 07921
908-234-6507
Web site: www.att.com
Telecommunications services & systems
Edward Amoroso, Senior Vice President & Chief Security Officer

Association of Public Broadcasting Stations of NY Inc
33 Elk Street, Suite 200, Albany, NY 12207
518-462-1590 Fax: 518-462-1390
Public television
Peter Repas, Executive Director

CBS Corporation
51 West 52nd Street, New York, NY 10019-6188
212-975-4321
Web site: www.cbscorporation.com
TV & radio broadcasting, news, entertainment
Leslie Moonves, Chairman, President & Chief Executive Officer

Cable Telecommunications Association of New York, Inc
54 State Street, Suite 800, Albany, NY 12207
518-463-6676 Fax: 518-463-0574
Advocates for & represents the interests of the cable television industry
James Reynolds, Director

Cablevision Systems Corporation
1111 Stewart Avenue, Bethpage, NY 11714-3581
866-200-7273
e-mail: lrosenbl@cablevision.com
Web site: www.cablevision.com
Owns & operates cable television systems & programming networks; provides telecommunications services
Lisa Rosenblum, Executive Vice President, Government & Public Affairs

Central Hudson Gas & Electric Corporation
284 South Avenue, Poughkeepsie, NY 12601
845-452-2700 Fax: 845-486-5658
Web site: www.centralhudson.com
Delivers natural gas & electricity to consumers
Michael L. Mosher, President & Chief Executive Officer

Consolidated Edison Energy
Cooper Station, PO Box 138, New York, NY 10276-0138
800-752-6633
Web site: www.coned.com
John H. Banks III, Vice President, Government & Community Relations

Constellation Energy
Metro-North Region, 810 7th Avenue, Suite 400, New York, NY 10019
212-885-6400 Fax: 212-883-5888
Web site: www.constellation.com
Energy services provider
Joseph Nigro, Chief Executive Officer

Crane & Parente, PLLC
48 Howard Street, Albany, NY 12207
518-432-8000
Governmental relations, banking & financial services, corporate law, construction law, energy, utilities, communications, land use, environmental & wireless telecommunications law

James B. Crane, II, Managing Member

Empire State Petroleum Association Inc
56 Clifton Country Road, Suite 108, Clifton Park, NY 12065
518-280-6645 Fax: 518-280-6670
Web site: www.eseany.org
Petroleum industry lobby & trade association
Thomas J. Peters, Chief Executive Officer

Energy Coalition New York
1 Commerce Plaza, Albany, NY 12260
518-487-7600
Electric & natural gas utility companies
William Y. Crowell III, Executive Director

Entek Power Services
11 Satterly Rd, East Setauket, NY 11733
631-751-9800 Fax: 631-980-3759
e-mail: info@entekpower.com
Web site: www.entekpower.com
Energy consulting
Harry Davitian, President

Entergy Nuclear Northeast
440 Hamilton Avenue, White Plains, NY 10601
914-272-3200 Fax: 914-272-3205
Web site: www.entergy.com
Operator of nuclear power plants across the US
John A. Ventosa, Chief Operating Officer, Northern Fleet

Exxon Mobil Corporation
1400 Old Country Road, Suite 203, Westbury, NY 11590
516-333-0171
Web site: www.exxonmobil.com
Donald L Clarke, Manager, Public Affairs Northeast

Frontier, A Citizens Communications Co
19 John Street, Middletown, NY 10940
845-344-9801 Fax: 845-343-3768
Web site: www.frontier.com
Full service telecommunications provider
Ellen Amarosa, Manager

Fund for the City of New York, Center for Internet Innovation
121 Avenue of the Americas, 6th Floor, New York, NY 10013-1590
212-925-6675 Fax: 212-925-5675
Web site: www.fcny.org
Developing technology systems & applications that help advance the operations & performance of NY government & nonprofit organizations
Mary McCormick, President

NYS Bar Assn, Electronic Communications Task Force
Heslin Rothenberg Farley & Mesiti PC
5 Columbia Cir, Albany, NY 12203
518-452-5600 Fax: 518-452-5579
e-mail: dpm@hrfmlaw.com
Web site: www.hrfmlaw.com
David P. Miranda, Partner

Hess Corporation
1185 Avenue of the Americas, 40th Floor, New York, NY 10036
212-997-8500 Fax: 212-536-8390
Web site: www.hess.com
Manufactures & markets petroleum products; operates gasoline outlets
John B. Hess, Chief Executive Officer

NYS Bar Assn, Media Law Committee
Hogan Lovells US LLP
875 Third Avenue, New York, NY 10022
212-918-3000 Fax: 212-918-3100
e-mail: warren.gorrell@hoganlovells.com
Web site: www.hoganlovells.com
J. Warren Gorrell, Jr., Partner

Independent Oil & Gas Association of New York
38 Lake Street, Hamburg, NY 14075
716-202-4688 Fax: 716-202-4689
e-mail: brgill@iogany.org
Web site: www.iogany.org
Trade association representing oil & natural gas producers, drillers & affiliated service companies
Bradley Gill, Executive Director

Independent Power Producers of NY Inc
194 Washington Avenue, Suite 315, Albany, NY 12210
518-436-3749 Fax: 518-436-0369
e-mail: gavin@ippny.org
Web site: www.ippny.org
Companies developing alternative, environmentally friendly electric generating facilities
Gavin J. Donohue, President & Chief Executive Officer

Komanoff Energy Associates
11 Hanover Square, 21st Floor, New York, NY 10005
212-260-5237
e-mail: kea@igc.org
Web site: www.carbontax.org
Energy, utilities & transportation consulting
Charles Komanoff, Director

Mechanical Technology Incorporated
325 Washington Avenue Ext., Albany, NY 12205
518-218-2550 Fax: 518-533-2201
Web site: www.mechtech.com
New energy technologies, precision measurement & testing instruments
Kevin G. Lynch, Chairman & Chief Executive Officer

Municipal Electric Utilities Association
6652 Hammersmith Drive, East Syracuse, NY 13057
315-453-7851 Fax: 315-453-7849
e-mail: info@meua.org
Web site: www.meua.org
Tony Modafferi, Executive Director

NY Oil Heating Association
183 Madison Avenue, Suite 1403, New York, NY 10016
212-695-1380 Fax: 212-594-6583
e-mail: info@nyoha.org
Web site: www.nyoha.org
Represents NYC's fuel industry
Rocco Lacertosa, President & Chief Executive Officer

NY Press Association
621 Columbia Street Ext., Suite 1, Cohoes, NY 12047
518-464-6483 Fax: 518-464-6489
e-mail: mkrea@nynewspapers.com
Web site: www.nynewspapers.com
Weekly community & ethnic newspaper publishers
Michelle K. Rea, Executive Director

NY Propane Gas Association
PO Box 760, Clifton Park, NY 12065
518-383-3823 Fax: 518-383-3824
Web site: www.nypropane.com
Promotes & represents the interests of New York's propane industry through education & networking
Rick Cummings, President

NYS Broadcasters Association
1805 Western Avenue, Albany, NY 12203
518-456-8888 Fax: 518-456-8943
e-mail: ddonovan@nysbroadcasters.org
Web site: www.nysbroadcasters.org
Trade association for NYS television & radio stations
David Donovan, President & Executive Director

Offices and agencies generally appear in alphabetical order, except when specific order is requested by listee.

NYS Forum Inc
24 Aviation Road, Albany, NY 12205
518-438-7414 Fax: 518-438-1416
e-mail: info@nysforum.org
Web site: www.nysforum.org
Information technology management; assists government officials & entities with knowledge transfer & exchange
Joan Sullivan, Executive Director

NYS Technology Enterprise Corporation (NYSTEC)
540 Broadway, 3rd Floor, Albany, NY 12207
888-969-7832 Fax: 518-431-7037
e-mail: nystec@nystec.com
Web site: www.nystec.com
Technology acquisition, technology management & engineering services to government clients & other institutions
Mike Walsh, President & Chief Executive Officer

National Economic Research Associates
1166 Avenue of the Americas, 29th Floor, New York, NY 10036
212-345-3000 Fax: 212-345-4650
Web site: www.nera.com
Utility & transportation regulation, deregulation & antitrust
Dr. Andrew Carron, Chairman

NYS Bar Assn, Public Utility Law Committee
National Fuel Gas Company
6363 Main Street, Williamsville, NY 14221
716-857-7000 or 716-686-6123
Web site: www.nationalfuel.com
Natural gas distribution, storage, production & marketing
Ronald J. Tanski, President & Chief Executive Officer

National Grid
300 Erie Blvd West, Syracuse, NY 13202
315-428-5430 or 800-642-4272
Web site: www.nationalgridus.com
Chris Murphy, Vice President

New York Independent System Operator - Not For Profit
10 Krey Blvd, Rensselaer, NY 12144
518-356-6000 or 518-356-7325 Fax: 518-356-7524
Web site: www.nyiso.com
Grid operator
Kevin Lanahan, Vice President, External Affairs

New York News Publishers Association
252 Hudson Avenue, Albany, NY 12210
518-449-1667 or 800-777-1667 Fax: 518-449-5053
e-mail: dianenynpa@aol.com
Web site: www.nynpa.com
Represents NY's daily, weekly & online newspapers; provides training, networking & support
Diane Kennedy, President

New York Press Photographers Association
Church St. Station, PO Box 3346, New York, NY 10008-3346
212-889-6633 Fax: 212-889-6634
e-mail: office@nyppa.org
Web site: www.nyppa.org
Bruce Cotler, President

Rochester Gas and Electric Corporation
New York State Electric & Gas Corporation (NYSEG)
18 Link Drive, PO Box 5224, Binghamton, NY 13902-5224
607-762-7200 or 800-572-1111
Web site: www.nyseg.com
Philip Thompson, Regional Operations Manager

New York State Petroleum Council
150 State Street, Albany, NY 12207
518-465-3563 Fax: 518-465-4022
Web site: www.api.org
Petroleum industry lobby
Karen Moreau, Executive Director

New York State Telecommunications Association Inc
4 Tower Place, 2nd Floor, Albany, NY 12203
518-443-2700 Fax: 518-443-2810
e-mail: info@nysta.com
Web site: www.nysta.com
Robert R. Puckett, President

New York Technology Council
307 West 38th Street, 13th Floor, New York, NY 10018
646-435-1088
e-mail: info@nytech.org
Web site: www.nytech.org
Promotes New York City's technology industry
Erik Grimmelmann, President & Chief Executive Officer

Northeast Gas Association
75 Second Avenue, Suite 510, Needham, MA 02494-2859
781-455-6800 Fax: 781-455-6828
Web site: www.northeastgas.org
Trade association serving the natural gas industry of the Northeast US through education, training, research, planning & development
Thomas M. Kiley, President & Chief Executive Officer

Oil Heat Institute of Long Island
200 Parkway Drive South, Suite 202, Hauppauge, NY 11788
631-360-0200 Fax: 631-360-0781
e-mail: info@ohili.org
Web site: www.ohili.org
Heating oil industry association
Kevin M. Rooney, Chief Executive Officer

Orange & Rockland Utilities Inc
One Blue Hill Plaza, Pearl River, NY 10965
845-352-6000 Fax: 845-577-6914
Web site: www.oru.com
Electric & gas utility
Timothy P. Cawley, President & Chief Executive Officer

Plug Power Inc
968 Albany Shaker Road, Latham, NY 12110
518-782-7700 Fax: 518-782-9060
Web site: www.plugpower.com
Fuel cell research & development for small stationary applications
Gerard L. Conway, Jr., Vice President of Government Affairs & General Counsel

Public Utility Law Project of New York Inc
90 State Street, Suite 601, Albany, NY 12207-1715
518-449-3375 or 800-255-7857 Fax: 518-449-1769
e-mail: info@pulp.tc
Web site: www.pulp.tc
Advocacy of universal service, affordability & customer protection for residential utility consumers
Richard Berkley, Executive Director

Rochester Gas & Electric Corporation
89 East Avenue, Rochester, NY 14649-0001
800-295-7323
Web site: www.rge.com
Dick Marion, Economic Development Specialist

Sithe Global
757 Third Avenue, 24th Floor, New York, NY 10017
212-351-0000 Fax: 212-351-0880
Web site: www.sitheglobal.com
Electric generation facility development
Martin B. Rosenberg, Chief Executive Officer

Soligent Distribution LLC - East Coast Distribution Center
3 Security Drive, Suite 303, Cranbury, NJ 08512
609-860-6444
Web site: www.soligent.net
Solar distribution; solar energy equipment & services
Jonathan Doochin, Chief Executive Officer

Spanish Broadcasting System Network Inc
26 West 56th Street, New York, NY 10019
212-541-9200 Fax: 212-541-9295
Web site: www.spanishbroadcasting.com
Spanish language FM radio stations
Eric Garcia, General Manager

Verizon Communications
140 West Street, New York, NY 10013
212-395-1000 or 800-837-4966
Web site: www.verizon.com
Telecommunications services for northeastern US
David Lamendola, Director of Government Affairs, NY & CT

Viacom Inc
1515 Broadway, New York, NY 10036
212-258-6000
Web site: www.viacom.com
International media, entertainment
Philippe Dauman, President & Chief Executive Officer

Wall Street Journal (The)
1211 Avenue of the Americas, New York, NY 10036
212-416-2000 or 800-568-7625 Fax: 212-416-2720
Web site: www.wsj.com
Gerard Baker, Editor in Chief

WNET New York Public Media
825 Eighth Avenue, New York, NY 10019
212-560-2000 or 212-560-1313 Fax: 212-560-2001
e-mail: programming@thirteen.org
Web site: www.wnet.org
Producer of arts, public affairs & educational programs; broadcast & online media
Neal Shapiro, President & Chief Executive Officer

ENVIRONMENT & NATURAL RESOURCES

NEW YORK STATE

GOVERNOR'S OFFICE

Governor's Office
Executive Chamber
State Capitol
Albany, NY 12224
518-474-8390 Fax: 518-474-1513
Web site: www.ny.gov

Governor:
Andrew M Cuomo 518-474-8390
Secretary to the Governor:
William Mulrow 518-474-4246
Counsel to the Governor:
Alphonso David 518-474-8343
Chairman of Energy & Finance for New York:
Richard Kauffman. 518-408-2552
Deputy Secretary, Environment:
Venetia Lannon. 518-408-2552
Chief of Staff:
Melissa DeRosa . . . . 518-474-8418 or 212-681-4640
Director, Communications:
James Allen. . . . . 518-474-8418 or 212-681-4640

EXECUTIVE DEPARTMENTS AND RELATED AGENCIES

Empire State Development Corporation
633 Third Ave
New York, NY 10017
212-803-3100 Fax: 212-803-3131
Web site: www.esd.ny.gov

625 Broadway
Albany, NY 12207
518-292-5200

95 Perry Street
Ste 500
Buffalo, NY 14203
716-846-8200
Fax: 716-846-8260

President & CEO:
Howard Zemsky 212-803 3700
Public Affairs:
Kay Sarlin Wright. 800-260-7313
e-mail: esdpressoffice@esd.ny.gov

Environmental Conservation Department
625 Broadway
Albany, NY 12233
518-402-8545 Fax: 518-402-9016
Web site: www.dec.ny.gov

Commissioner:
Joseph J Martens 518-402-8545/fax: 518-402-8541
Executive Deputy Commissioner:
Kenneth Lynch 518-402-8560
Public Affairs:
Emily DeSantis. 518-402-8560
Deputy Commissioner, Administration:
Jeffrey Stefanko 518-402-9401
Director, Internal Audit & Investigation:
Anne Lapinski. 518-402-8184
Secretary to the Commissioner:
Dawn Sherwin. 518-402-8545

Air Resources, Climate Change & Energy Office
Assistant Commissioner:
Jared Snyder 518-402-8549

Air Resources Division
Acting Director:
Steve Flint 518-402-8452/fax: 518-402-9035

Climate Change Office
Acting Director:
Lois New. 518-402-8448

Office of Remediation & Materials Management
Deputy Commissioner:
Gene Leff. 518-402-2794/fax: 518-402-8541

Environmental Remediation Division
Director:
Robert Schick 518-402-9706/fax: 518-402-9020

Mineral Resources Division
Director:
Catherine Dickert 518-402-8076/fax: 518-402-8060

Materials Management Division
Director:
David Vitale 518-402-8652/fax: 518-402-9024

General Counsel's Office
General Counsel:
Tom Berkman 518-402-9185/fax: 518-402-9018

Hearings & Mediation Services Office
Asst Commissioner:
Louis Alexander 518-402-8537

Natural Resources Office
Assistant Commissioner:
Kathy Moser 518-402-8533/fax: 518-402-9016

Fish, Wildlife & Marine Resources Division
Director:
Patricia Riexinger 518-402-8924/fax: 518-402-9027

Lands & Forests Division
Director:
Robert Davies 518-402-9405/fax: 518-402-9028
e-mail: lf.lands@dec.ny.gov

Water Resources Office
Assistant Commissioner:
James Tierney 518-402-2794

Water Division
Director:
Mark Klotz 518-402-8233/fax: 518-402-9029

Information Services Division
Director:
Leslie Brennan 518-402-9860/fax: 518-402-9031

Management & Budget Division
Director:
Nancy Lussier 518-402-9228/fax: 518-402-9023

Operations Division
Director:
Mark Malinoski. 518-402-9055/fax: 518-402-9053

Offices and agencies generally appear in alphabetical order, except when specific order is requested by listee.

Public Affairs & Education Division
Director:
Emily DeSantis 518-402-8560/fax: 518-402-9036
e-mail: pressoffice@dec.ny.gov

Office of Employee Relations
Director:
Mark Cadrette 518-402-9388/fax: 518-486-9957

Public Information
Press Operations:
Emily DeSantis 518-402-8560/fax: 518-402-9016

Public Protection Office
Assistant Commissioner:
Christian Ballantyne 518-402-8549/fax: 518-402-9016

Forest Protection & Fire Management Division
Acting Director:
Eric Lahr 518-402-8839/fax: 518-402-8840

Law Enforcement Division
Director:
Joe Schneider 518-402-8829/fax: 518-402-8830

Regional Offices

Region 1
SUNY - 50 Circle Rd, Stony Brook, NY 11790
Director:
Craig Meek Gallagher 631-444-0345/fax: 631-444-0349

Region 2
One Hunters Pt Plaza, 47-40 21st St, Long Island City, NY 11101-5407
Acting Director:
Steven Zahn 718-482-4949/fax: 718-482-4026

Region 3
21 S Putt Corners Rd, New Paltz, NY 12561-1696
Director:
Martin Brand 845-256-3000/fax: 845-255-3042

Region 4
1130 N Westcott Rd, Schenectady, NY 12306-2014
Director:
Keith Goertz 518-357-2068/fax: 518-357-2398

Region 5
1115 Rte 86, PO Box 296, Ray Brook, NY 12977
e-mail: r5info@gw.dec.state.ny.us
Director:
Robert Stegemann 518-897-1211/fax: 518-897-1394

Region 6
317 Washington St, Watertown, NY 13601-3787
Director:
Judy Drabicki 315-785-2239/fax: 315-785-2242

Region 7
615 Erie Blvd West, Syracuse, NY 13204-2400
Director:
Kenneth Lynch 315-426-7403/fax: 315-426-7408

Region 8
6274 E Avon-Lima Rd, Avon, NY 14414-9519
Director:
Paul D'Amato 585-226-5366/fax: 585-226-9485

Region 9
270 Michigan Ave, Buffalo, NY 14203
Director:
Abby Snyder 716-851-7200/fax: 716-851-7211

Special Programs

Great Lakes Program
Region 9 NYS DEC, 270 Michigan Ave, Buffalo, NY 14203
Coordinator:
Donald Zelazny 716-851-7220/fax: 716-851-7226

Hudson River Estuary Program
Region 3 NYS DEC, 21 S Putt Corners Rd, New Paltz, NY 12561
Special Asst:
Frances Dunwell 845-256-3016/fax: 845-255-3649
e-mail: hrep@gw.dec.state.ny.us

Health Department
Corning Tower
Empire State Plaza
Albany, NY 12237
518-474-2011
Web site: www.health.ny.gov

Commissioner:
Howard Zucker, MD, JD 518-474-2011
Executive Deputy Commissioner:
Sally Dreslin, MS, RN 518-474-2011
Deputy Commissioner, Administration:
Michael J. Nazarko 518-474-8565

Public Affairs
Director:
James C Plastiras 518-474-7354 x1
Deputy Director:
Marci Natale 518-474-7354 x1

Center for Environmental Health
547 River St, Troy, NY 12180
Director:
Dr. Nathan Graber 518-402-7500

Division of Environmental Health Assessment
Director:
Kevin Gleason 518-402-7511

Division of Environmental Health Investigation
Director:
Vacant 518-402-7510

Division of Environmental Health Protection
Director:
Michael Cambridge 518-402-7500

Wadsworth Center
Director:
Jill Taylor, PhD 518-474-3157/fax: 518-474-3439
Deputy Director:
Victoria Derbyshire 518-474-7592
Associate Director, Administration:
Carlene Van Patten 518-474-7592
Associate Director, Research & Technology:
Erasmus Schneider 518-473-4856
Associate Director, Medical Affairs:
Anne Walsh 518-474-7592

Environmental Health Sciences
Director:
Ken Aldous 518-474-7161/fax: 518-473-2895
Deputy Director:
Patrick Parsons 518-474-7161

Hudson River Valley Greenway
625 Broadway
4th Floor
Albany, NY 12207

Offices and agencies generally appear in alphabetical order, except when specific order is requested by listee.

518-473-3835 Fax: 518-473-4518
e-mail: hrvg@hudsongreenway.ny.gov
Web site: www.hudsongreenway.ny.gov

Greenway Conservancy for the Hudson River Valley
Acting Chair:
Sara Griffen. 518-473-3835
Executive Director (Acting):
Mark Castiglione. 518-473-3835

Hudson River Valley Greenway Communities Council
Board Chair:
Barnabas McHenry 518-473-3835
Executive Director (Acting):
Mark Castiglione. 518-473-3835

Law Department
120 Broadway
New York, NY 10271-0332
212-416-8000 or 800-771-7755
Web site: www.ag.ny.gov

State Capitol
Albany, NY 12224-0341
518-776-2000
Fax: 518-650-9401

Attorney General:
Eric T Schneiderman . . . . .212-416-8050 or 518-776-2000
Chief of Staff:
Brian Mahanna 212-416-8050
Press Secretary:
Matt Mittenthal .212-416-8060/fax: 212-416-6005
Bureau Chief, Litigation Bureau:
Jeffrey Dvorin. . . . . .518-776-2300 or 212-416-8610

Social Justice
Executive Deputy Attorney General:
Alvin L Bragg, Jr. 212-416-8450/fax: 212-416-8942

Environmental Protection Bureau
Bureau Chief:
Lemuel Srolovic . . . . .518-776-2400 or 212-416-8448
fax: 518-416-6007

Parks, Recreation & Historic Preservation, NYS Office of
Empire State Plaza, Bldg 1
625 Broadway, 12207
Albany, NY 12238
518-486-0456 Fax: 518-486-2924
Web site: www.nysparks.com

Commissioner:
Rose Harvey 518-474-0443
Executive Deputy Commissioner:
Andrew Beers 518-474-0020
Deputy Commissioner, Finance & Administration:
Melinda Scott 518-474-0414
Deputy Commissioner, Natural Resources:
Tom Alworth. 518-474-0414
Counsel:
Paul Laudato 518-474-0414
Public Information Officer:
Randy Simmons 518-486-1868
Chief Park Police/Director, Law Enforcement:
Jay Kirschner 518-474-4029/fax: 518-408-1032

Field Services
Peebles Island, PO Box 189, Waterford, NY 12118
Deputy Commissioner:
Ruth Pierpont 518-237-8643

Historic Sites Bureau
Peebles Island, Waterford, NY 12188
Acting Director:
Mark Peckham 518-237-8643

Marine & Recreational Vehicles
Director:
Brian Kempf 518-474-0445/fax: 518-408-1030

Environmental Management
Director:
Pamela Otis 518-474-0409/fax: 518-474-7013

State Comptroller, Office of the
110 State St, 15th Fl
Albany, NY 12236-0001
518-474-4044 Fax: 518-473-3004
Web site: www.osc.state.ny.us

59 Maiden Lane
New York, NY 10038
212-383-1600

State Comptroller:
Thomas DiNapoli . . . . .518-474-4040 or 212-681-4469

Executive Office
First Deputy Comptroller:
Pete Grannis . . . . .518-474-2909 or 212-681-4469
Chief of Staff:
Shawn Thompson 518-474-4044
General Counsel:
Nancy Groenwegen. 518-474-3444

Oil Spill Fund Office
Executive Director:
David J Hasso 518-474-6657/fax: 518-474-9979

State Department
123 William St
New York, NY 10038
212-417-5800 Fax: 212-417-2383
Web site: www.dos.ny.gov

One Commerce Plaza
99 Washington Avenue
Albany, NY 12231
518-474-4750
Fax: 518-474-4597

Acting Secretary of State:
Rossana Rosado 518-474-0050
First Deputy Secretary of State:
Daniel Shapiro 518-474-4750
Assistant Secretary of State, Communications:
Vacant 518-474-4752/fax: 518-474-4597
e-mail: info@dos.state.ny.us
Deputy Secretary of State, Public Affairs:
Vacant. 212-417-5800
Principal Attorney:
William Sharp 518-474-6740/fax: 518-473-9211

Local Government & Community Services
Deputy Secretary of State:
Dierdre Scozzafava. 518-473-3355

Offices and agencies generally appear in alphabetical order, except when specific order is requested by listee.

Coastal Resources & Waterfront Revitalization Division
Director:
George Stafford 518-474-6000/fax: 518-473-2464
e-mail: coastal@dos.state.ny.us

Community Services Division
Director:
Veronica Cruz 518-474-5741/fax: 518-486-4663
e-mail: commserv@dos.state.ny.us

CORPORATIONS, AUTHORITIES AND COMMISSIONS

Adirondack Park Agency
1133 NYS Route 86
PO Box 99
Ray Brook, NY 12977
518-891-4050 Fax: 518-891-3938
Web site: www.apa.ny.gov

Chair:
Leilani Ulrich 518-891-4050
Executive Director:
Terry Martino 518-891-4050
Counsel:
James Townsend 518-891-4050
Public Relations:
Keith McKeever 518-891-4050
e-mail: keith.mckeever@apa.ny.gov

Atlantic States Marine Fisheries Commission
1050 N Highland Street
Ste 200 A-N
Arlington, VA 22201
703-842-0740 Fax: 703-842-0741
e-mail: info@asmfc.org
Web site: www.asmfc.org

Chair (NH):
Douglas E Grout 603-868-1095
e-mail: douglas.grout@wildlife.nh.gov
Vice Chair (NY):
James Gilmore 516-444-0433
Governor's Appointee, New York:
Emerson C Hasbrouck, Jr 631-928-1524
Executive Director:
Robert E. Beal 703-842-0740
e-mail: rbeal@asmfc.org
Director Communications:
Tina Berger 703-842-0740
e-mail: tberger@asmfc.org

Central Pine Barrens Joint Planning & Policy Commission
624 Old Riverhead Road
Westhampton Beach, NY 11978
631-288-1079 Fax: 631-228-1367
e-mail: info@pb.state.ny.us
Web site: www.pb.state.ny.us

Chair & Governor's Appointee & Region 1 Director DEC:
Peter A Scully 631-288-1079
Member & Suffolk County Executive:
Steve Bellone 631-288-1079
Member & Brookhaven Town Supervisor:
Edward P. Romaine 631-288-1079
Member & Riverhead Town Supervisor:
Sean M Walter 631-288-1079
Member & Southampton Town Supervisor:
Anna E Throne-Holst 631-288-1079

Delaware River Basin Commission
25 State Police Dr
PO Box 7360
West Trenton, NJ 08628-0360
609-883-9500 Fax: 609-883-9522
Web site: www.nj.gov/drbc

New York Member/Chair:
Andrew M Cuomo 518-474-8390
Executive Director:
Steve Tambini 609-883-9500 x200
e-mail: steve.tambini@drbc.nj.gov
Commission Secretary & Assistant General Counsel:
Pamela Bush 609-883-9500 x203
e-mail: pamela.bush@drbc.nj.gov
General Counsel:
Kenneth J Warren 484-383-4834
e-mail: kwarren@warrenenvcounsel.com
Communications Manager:
Clarke Rupert 609-883-9500 x260
e-mail: clarke.rupert@drbc.nj.gov

Great Lakes Commission
2805 S Industrial Hwy
Ste 100
Ann Arbor, MI 48104-6791
734-971-9135 Fax: 734-971-9150
e-mail: teder@glc.org
Web site: www.glc.org

Chairman:
Jon W Allan 517-284-5035
e-mail: allanj@michigan.gov
New York State Commissioner:
Joseph Martens 518-402-8540
e-mail: joseph.martens@dec.ny.gov
Executive Director:
Tim A Eder 734-971-9135
e-mail: teder@glc.org
Deputy Director:
Thomas R Crane 734-971-9135
e-mail: tcrane@glc.org
CIO:
Stephen J Cole 734-971-9135
e-mail: scole@glc.org
Program Director:
Victoria Pebbles 734-971-9135
e-mail: vpebbles@glc.org
Communications Director:
Beth Wanamaker 734-971-9135
e-mail: beth@glc.org
Policy Director:
Matthew Doss 734-971-9135
e-mail: mdoss@glc.org

Hudson River-Black River Regulating District
Hudson River Area Office
350 Northern Blvd, Ste 304
Albany, NY 12204
518-465-3491 Fax: 518-432-2485
e-mail: hrao@hrbrrd.com
Web site: www.hrbrrd.com

Chair:
Mark M Finkle 518-465-3491
Executive Director (Acting):
Richard J Ferrara 518-465-3491
Chief Engineer:
Robert S Foltan 518-465-3491

Offices and agencies generally appear in alphabetical order, except when specific order is requested by listee.

Chief Fiscal Officer:
Robert J Ferrara ... 518-465-3491
General Counsel:
Robert P Leslie ... 518-465-3491

Interstate Environmental Commission
2800 Victory Blvd
6S-106
Staten Island, NY 10314
718-982-3792 Fax: 718-698-8472
e-mail: iecmail@iec-nynjct.org
Web site: www.iec-nynjct.org

Chair (CT):
Patricia Sesto ... 212-967-1414
Vice Chair (NY):
Judith L Baron ... 212-967-1414
Vice Chair (NJ):
John M Scagnelli ... 212-967-1414
Associate Director:
Evelyn R Powers ... 212-967-1414

Interstate Oil & Gas Compact Commission
PO Box 53127
900 NE 23rd St
Oklahoma City, OK 73152-3127
405-525-3556 Fax: 405-525-3592
e-mail: iogcc@iogcc.state.ok.us
Web site: www.iogcc.ok.gov

Chair:
Governor Mary Fallin (OK) ... 405-525-3556
Vice Chair:
David Porter ... 405-525-3556
Executive Director:
Mike Smith ... 405-525-3556
New York State Official Representative:
Bradley J Field ... 518-402-8076
Communications Manager:
Carol Booth ... 405-525-3556

Lake George Park Commission
75 Fort George Rd
PO Box 749
Lake George, NY 12845
518-668-9347 Fax: 518-668-5001
e-mail: info@lgpc.state.ny.us
Web site: www.lgpc.state.ny.us

Chair:
Bruce F Young ... 518-668-9347
Executive Director:
David Wick ... 518-668-9347
e-mail: dave@lgpc.state.ny.us
Counsel:
Eileen Haynes ... 518-668-9347
Director of Law Enforcement:
F. Joe Johns ... 518-668-9347
e-mail: jjohns@lgps.state.ny.us
Director, Operations:
Keith Fish ... 518-668-9347
e-mail: keith@lgpc.state.ny.us

New England Interstate Water Pollution Control Commission
Wannalacit Mills
650 Suffolk Street
Suite 410
Lowell, MA 01854
978-323-7929 Fax: 978-323-7919
e-mail: mail@neiwpcc.org
Web site: www.neiwpcc.org

Chair (ME):
Michael Kuhns ... 978-323-7929
Vice Chair (MA):
Douglas Fine ... 978-323-7929
Commissioner, New York State:
Basil Seggos ... 518-485-8940
Executive Director:
Ronald F Poltak ... 978-323-7929
e-mail: rpoltak@neiwpcc.org
Deputy Director:
Susan Sullivan ... 978-323-7929
e-mail: ssullivan@neiwpcc.org

New York State Energy Research & Development Authority
17 Columbia Circle
Albany, NY 12203-6399
518-862-1090 Fax: 518-862-1091
e-mail: info@nyserda.ny.gov
Web site: www.nyserda.ny.gov

Chairman:
Richard L Kauffman ... 518-862-1090
President & CEO:
John B Rhodes ... 518-862-1090 x3278
General Counsel:
Noah C Shaw ... 518-862-1090 x3280
Program Manager, Economic Development & Community Outreach:
Kelly Tyler ... 716 842 1522 x 3005
e-mail: kelly.tyler@nyserda.ny.gov
Director, Communications:
Kate Muller ... 518-862-1090 x3582/fax: 518-862-1091
e-mail: katc.muller@nyserda.ny.gov

New York State Environmental Facilities Corp
625 Broadway
Albany, NY 12207-2997
518-402-6924 or 800-882-9721 Fax: 518-486-9323
e-mail: press@efc.ny.gov
Web site: www.nysefc.org

President/CEO:
Sabrina M Ty ... 518-402-6951
Legal Division/General Counsel:
James R Levine ... 518-402-6969
Director, Engineering & Program Management:
Timothy P Burns ... 518-402-7396
Director, Technical Advisory Services:
Vacant ... 518-402-7461
Director, PIO:
Jon Sorensen ... 518-402-6924
e-mail: press@efc.ny.gov; jon.sorensen@efc.ny.gov
Controller & Director, Corporate Operations:
Michael Malinoski ... 518-486-9267

New York State Tug Hill Commission
Dulles State Office Bldg
317 Washington St
Watertown, NY 13601
315-785-2380 Fax: 315-785-2574
e mail: tughill@tughill.org
Web site: www.tughill.org

Offices and agencies generally appear in alphabetical order, except when specific order is requested by listee.

Chair:
Jan Bogdanowicz 315-785-2380
Executive Director:
Katie Malinowski 315-785-2570
e-mail: katie@tughill.org

Northeastern Forest Fire Protection Commission
21 Parmenter Terrace
PO Box 6192
China Village, ME 04926
207-968-3782 Fax: 207-968-3782
e-mail: info@nffpc.org
Web site: www.nffpc.org

Executive Committee Chair:
Steven Sinclair 802-241-3680
e-mail: ssinclair@vermont.gov
Executive Director/Center Manager:
Thomas G Parent. 207-968-3782
e-mail: necompact@fairpoint.net
Operations Committee, Chair:
Rick Vollick 413-770-1235
e-mail: rvollick@gmail.com
New York State Fire Prevention & Education:
Andrew Jacob 518-402-8840
e-mail: atjacob@gw.dec.state.ny.us

Ohio River Valley Water Sanitation Commission
5735 Kellogg Ave
Cincinnati, OH 45230
513-231-7719 Fax: 513-231-7761
e-mail: info@orsanco.org
Web site: www.orsanco.org

New York State Commissioner:
Douglas E Conroe. 513-231-7719
New York State Commissioner:
Michael P Wilson 513-231-7719
New York State Commissioner:
Basil Seggos 518-457-3446
Executive Director:
Richard Harrison . . . . .513-231-7719 ext 105
e-mail: rharrison@orsanco.org
Source Water Protection/Emergency Response/External Relations:
Jerry Schulte. . . . . .513-231-7719 ext 104
e-mail: jschulte@orsanco.org
Communications Coordinator:
Lisa Cochran . . . . .513-231-7719 ext 102
e-mail: lcochran@orsanco.org

NEW YORK STATE LEGISLATURE

See Legislative Branch in Section 1 for additional Standing Committee and Subcommittee information.

Assembly Standing Committees

Environmental Conservation
Chair:
Steven Englebright (D). 518-455-4804
Ranking Minority Member:
Dan Stec (R) 518-455-5565

Senate Standing Committees

Environmental Conservation
Chair:
Thomas O'Mara (R) 518-455-2091
Ranking Minority Member:
Brad Hoylman (D) 518-455-2451

Senate/Assembly Legislative Commissions

Rural Resources, Legislative Commission on
Senate Chair:
Patricia Ritchie (R) 518-455-3438
Assembly Vice Chair:
Frank Skartados (D) 518-455-5762
Counsel:
Barbara McRedmond 518-455-2069

U.S. GOVERNMENT

EXECUTIVE DEPARTMENTS AND RELATED AGENCIES

US Commerce Department
Web site: www.commerce.gov

National Oceanic & Atmospheric Administration

National Marine Fisheries Svc, Greater Atlantic Regional Office
55 Great Republic Drive, Gloucester, MA 01930
978-281-9300
Web site: www.greateratlantic.fisheries.noaa.gov
Regional Administrator:
John K. Bullard

National Weather Service, Eastern Region
630 Johnson Avenue, Suite 202, Bohemia, NY 11716
Web site: www.weather.gov/erh/
Director, Eastern Region:
Jason Tuell, Ph.D. 631-244-0101
e-mail: jason.tuell@noaa.gov
Deputy Director:
Mickey J Brown 631-244-0100
Meteorological Services Division Chief:
John Guiney 631-244-0121
e-mail: john.guiney@noaa.gov
Scientific Services Division Chief:
Kenneth Johnson 631-244-0136
e-mail: kenneth.johnson@noaa.gov

US Defense Department
e-mail: www.defense.gov

Army Corps of Engineers
Web site: www.usace.army.mil

Great Lakes & Ohio River Division (Western NYS)
550 Main Street, Room 10524, Cincinnati, OH 45202-3222
Commander:
BG Richard G. Kaiser. 513-684-3010
Buffalo District Office . . . . .fax: 716-879-4195
1776 Niagara Street, Buffalo, NY 14207
716-879-4104 or 800-833-6390 x3 Fax: 716-879-4195
District Commander:
LTC Karl D. Jansen
Deputy Commander:
MAJ Jared E. Runge

North Atlantic Division
302 General Lee Avenue, Brooklyn, NY 11252
Commander & Division Engineer:
BG William H. Graham
Deputy Commander:
Colonel Leon F. Parrott
Director of Programs:
David J. Leach

Director of Business:
Vincent E. Grewatz
Public Affairs Specialist:
Edward Loomis....................................347-370-4550
Program Directorate
Director of Programs:
David J. Leach....................................347-370-4550
Chief, Civil Works Integration Division:
Linda Monte
Chief, Military Integration Division:
Thomas Harnedy
Chief, Program Support Division:
Joseph Vietri....................................718-765-7080
Regional Business Directorate
Regional Director of Business:
Vincent E. Grewatz
Chief Financial Officer:
John Primavera
Chief, Business Management Division:
Lawrence Mazzola....................................718-765-7127
Business Technical Division:
Alan Huntley

US Department of Agriculture

Forest Service-Northeastern Area State & Private Forestry
11 Campus Blvd, Newtown Square, PA 19073
Area Director:
Tony L. Ferguson....................................610-557-4103
Deputy Area Director:
James S. Barresi....................................610-557-4103
Asst Director, Forest Health & Economics:
Ralph H. Crawford....................................610-557-4158
Fire Management Specialist:
James H. Furman....................................850-882-8399
Asst Director, Forest Management:
Mark P. Buccowich....................................610-557-4029
Deputy Director, WERC:
Edward T. Cesa....................................304-285-1530

Forest Service-Northern Research Station
11 Campus Blvd, Suite 200, Newtown Square, PA 19073
Acting Director:
Tony L. Ferguson....................................610-557-4017
Deputy Director:
Lon M. Yeary....................................608-231-9320

Forest Service-Region 9
Web site: www.fs.fed.us

Green Mountain & Finger Lakes....................................fax: 802-747-6766
231 North Main Street, Rutland, VT 05701
802-747-6700 Fax: 802-747-6766
Finger Lakes National Forest....................................fax: 607-546-4474
5218 State Route 414, Hector, NY 14841
District Ranger:
Jodie Vanselow

Natural Resources Conservation Service....................................fax: 315-477-6550
441 South Salina Street, Suite 354, Syracuse, NY 13202-2450
Fax: 315-477-6550
Web site: www.nrcs.usda.gov
State Conservationist:
Greg Kist

US Department of Homeland Security (DHS)

National Urban Security Technology Laboratory
201 Varick Street, 5th Floor, New York, NY 10014
Director:
Dr. Adam Hutter
e-mail: adam.hutter@dhs.gov

Administration
Director:
Alfred Crescenzi

Systems Division
Director:
Lawrence Ruth....................................212-620-3609
e-mail: lawrence.ruth@dhs.gov

Testbeds Division
Acting Director:
Lawrence Ruth

US Department of the Interior
Web site: www.doi.gov

Bureau of Land Management
e-mail: woinfo@blm.gov
Web site: www.blm.gov

Eastern States Office (includes New York State)....fax: 202-912-7710
20 M Street NE, Suite 950, Washington, DC 20003
202-912-7700 Fax: 202-912-7710
Acting State Director:
Ann DeBlasi

Fish & Wildlife Service....................................fax: 413-253-8308
413-253-8200 Fax: 413-253-8308
e-mail: northeast@fws.gov
Web site: www.fws.gov

Northeast Region (includes New York State).......fax: 413-253-8308
300 Westgate Center Drive, Hadley, MA 01035-9587
Regional Director:
Wendi Weber

Geological Survey
Web site: ny.usgs.gov

Water Resources Division - New York State District Office
425 Jordan Road, Troy, NY 12180-8349
Director:
Robert Breault....................................518-285-5661
Coram Sub-District Office....................................fax: 631-736-4283
2045 Route 112, Bldg 4, Coram, NY 11727
Sub-District Chief:
Stephen A. Terracciano....................................631-736-0783
Ithaca Sub-District Office....................................fax: 607-266-0217
30 Brown Road, Ithaca, NY 14850-1573
Sub-District Chief:
Edward F. Bugliosi....................................607-266-0217 x3005

National Park Service-Northeast Region
200 Chestnut Street, US Custom House, Philadelphia, PA 19106
Web site: www.nps.gov
Northeast Regional Director:
Mike Caldwell....................................215-597-7013/fax: 215-597-0815

Fire Island National Seashore....................................fax: 631-289-4898
120 Laurel Street, Patchogue, NY 11772-3596
631-687-4750 Fax: 631-289-4898
Superintendent:
K. Christopher Soller

Office of the Secretary, Environmental Policy & Compliance

Northeast Region (includes New York State)
15 State Street, Suite 400, Boston, MA 02109
Regional Environmental Officer:
Andrew L. Raddant..............617-223-8565/fax: 617-223-8569

Offices and agencies generally appear in alphabetical order, except when specific order is requested by listee.

Office of the Solicitor

Northeast Region (includes New York State) .... fax: 617-527-6848
One Gateway Center, Suite 612, Newton, MA 02458-2881
Attorney Advisor:
Peg Romanik 617-527-3400
Attorney Advisor:
Martha F. Ansty 617-527-3400
Attorney Advisor:
Mark D. Barash 617-527-3400
Attorney:
Brianna Kenny 617-527-3400
Attorney Advisor:
Andrew Tittler 617-527-3400

US Environmental Protection Agency

Web site: www.epa.gov

Region 2 - New York .... fax: 212-637-3526
290 Broadway, New York, NY 10007-1866
212-637-3660 Fax: 212-637-3526
Regional Administrator:
Judith A. Enck 212-637-5000
Deputy Regional Administrator:
Catherine McCabe

Caribbean Environmental Protection Division (CEPD)
Acting Director:
Jose Font

Clean Air & Sustainability Division (CASD)
Acting Director:
Ariel Iglesias 212-637-3315

Clean Water Division (CWD)
Director:
Joan Matthews 212-637-3724

Division of Enforcement & Compliance Assistance (DECA)
Director:
Dore LaPosta 212-637-4000

Division of Environmental Science & Assessment (DESA)
2890 Woodbridge Avenue, Edison, NJ 08837-3679
Director:
Anahita Williamson

Emergency & Remedial Response Division (ERRD)
Director:
Walter Mugdan

Policy & Management, Office of
Acting Asst Regional Administrator:
John Filippelli 212-637-3736

Public Affairs Division (PAD)
Director:
Andre Bowser

Regional Counsel, Office of (ORC)
Director:
Eric Schaaf 212-637-3107
e-mail: schaaf.eric@epa.gov

U.S. CONGRESS

See U.S. Congress Chapter for additional Standing Committee and Subcommittee information.

House of Representatives Standing Committees

Agriculture
Chair:
K. Michael Conaway (R-TX) 202-225-3605
Ranking Member:
Collin C. Peterson (D-MN) 202-225-2165

Subcommittees

Biotechnology, Horticulture & Research
Chair:
Rodney Davis (R-IL) 202-225-2371
Ranking Member:
Suzan DelBene (D-WA) 202-225-6311

Conservation & Forestry
Chair:
Glenn Thompson (R-PA) 202-225-5121
Ranking Member:
Michelle Lujan Grisham (D-NM) 202-225-6316

General Farm Commodities & Risk Management
Chair:
Rick Crawford (R-AR) 202-225-4076
Ranking Member:
Timothy J. Walz (D-MN) 202-225-2472

Livestock & Foreign Agriculture
Chair:
David Rouzer (R-NC) 202-225-2731
Ranking Member:
Jim Costa (D-CA) 202-225-3341

Nutrition
Chair:
Jackie Walorski (R-IN) 202-225-3915
Ranking Member:
Jim McGovern (D-MA) 202-225-6101

Energy & Commerce
Chair:
Fred Upton (R-MI) 202-225-3761
Ranking Member:
Frank Pallone (D-NJ) 202-225-4671
New York Delegate:
Eliot L. Engel (D) 202-225-2464
New York Delegate:
Paul Tonko (D) 202-225-5076
New York Delegate:
Yvette Clarke (D) 202-225-6231
New York Delegate:
Chris Collins (R) 202-225-5265

Subcommittees

Environment & the Economy
Chair:
John Shimkus (R-IL) 202-225-5271
Ranking Member:
Paul Tonko (D-NY) 202-225-5076

Natural Resources
Chair:
Rob Bishop (R-UT) 202-225-0453
Ranking Member:
Raul Grijalva (D-AZ) 202-225-2435

Science, Space & Technology
Chair:
Lamar Smith (R-TX) 202-225-4236
Ranking Member:
Eddie Bernice Johnson (D-TX) 202-225-8885
New York Delegate:
Paul Tonko (D) 202-225-5076

Subcommittee
Environment
Chair:
Jim Bridenstine (R-OK) 202-225-2211
Ranking Member:
Suzanne Bonamici (D-OR) 202-225-0855

Transportation & Infrastructure
Chair:
Bill Shuster (R-PA) 202-225-2431
Ranking Member:
Peter A. DeFazio (D-OR) 202-225-6416
New York Delegate:
Richard L. Hanna (R) 202-225-3665
New York Delegate:
John Katko (R) 202-225-3701
New York Delegate:
Sean Patrick Maloney (D) 202-225-5441
New York Delegate:
Jerrold Nadler (D) 202-225-5635

Subcommittee
Water Resources & Environment
Chair:
Bob Gibbs (R-OH) 202-225-6265
Ranking Member:
Grace F. Napolitano (D-CA) 202-225-5256
New York Delegate:
Sean Patrick Maloney (D) 202-225-5441
New York Delegate:
John Katko (R) 202-225-3701

Senate Standing Committees

Agriculture, Nutrition & Forestry
Chair:
Pat Roberts (R-KS) 202-224-4774
Ranking Member:
Debbie Stabenow (D-MI) 202-224-4822

Subcommittee
Conservation, Forestry & Natural Resources
Chair:
David Perdue (R-GA) 202-224-3521
Ranking Member:
Michael Bennet (D-CO) 202-224-5852

Commerce, Science & Transportation
Chair:
John Thune (R-SD) 202-224-2321
Ranking Member:
Bill Nelson (D-FL) 202-224-5274

Subcommittee
Oceans, Atmosphere, Fisheries and Coast Guard
Chair:
Marco Rubio (R-FL) 202-224-3041
Ranking Member:
Cory Booker (D-NJ) 202-224-3224

Energy & Natural Resources
Chair:
Lisa Murkowski (R-AK) 202-224-6665
Ranking Member:
Maria Cantwell (D-WA) 202-224-3441

Environment & Public Works
Chair:
James M. Inhofe (R-OK) 202-224-4721
Ranking Member:
Barbara Boxer (D-CA) 202-224-3553
New York Delegate:
Kirsten Gillibrand (D) 202-224-4451

PRIVATE SECTOR

Adirondack Council Inc (The)
103 Hand Avenue, Suite 3, PO Box D-2, Elizabethtown, NY 12932
518-873-2240 or 877-873-2240 Fax: 518-873-6675
e-mail: info@adirondackcouncil.org
Web site: www.adirondackcouncil.org
Seeks to promote & protect the environmental well-being of Adirondack Park through education, research & advocacy
William C. Janeway, Executive Director

AECOM Environmental Services
100 Park Avenue, New York, NY 10017
212-973-2999 Fax: 212-682-5287
e-mail: info@aecom.com
Web site: www.aecom.com
Environmental assessment, management, engineering, remediation & related services
Michael S. Burke, Chief Executive Officer

American Farmland Trust, New York Office
112 Spring Street, Suite 207, Saratoga Springs, NY 12866
518-581-0078 Fax: 518-581-0079
e-mail: newyork@farmland.org
Web site: www.farmland.org/newyork
Advocacy & education to protect farmland & promote environmentally sound farming practices
David Haight, New York State Director

American Museum of Natural History
Central Park West at 79th Street, New York, NY 10024-5192
212-769-5100 Fax: 212-769-5018
Web site: www.amnh.org
Education, exhibition & scientific research
Ellen V. Futter, President

Audubon New York
2 Third Street, Suite 480, Troy, NY 12180
518-869-9731 Fax: 518-869-0737
e-mail: ecrotty@audubon.org
Web site: ny.audubon.org
Protecting birds, other wildlife & their habitats
Erin Crotty, Executive Director

Audubon Society of NYS Inc (The) / Audubon International
120 Defreest Drive, Troy, NY 12180
518-767-9051 or 844-767-9051 Fax: 518-767-9076
e-mail: doug@auduboninternational.org
Web site: www.auduboninternational.org
Wildlife & water conservation; environmental education; sustainable land management
Doug Bechtel, Executive Director

Brooklyn Botanic Garden
1000 Washington Avenue, Brooklyn, NY 11225-1099
718-623-7200 Fax: 718-857-2430
Web site: www.bbg.org
Comprehensive study of plant biodiversity in metropolitan New York; home gardener's resource center
Scot Medbury, President

Business Council of New York State Inc
152 Washington Avenue, Albany, NY 12210
518-465-7511 or 800-358-1202 Fax: 518-465-4389
e-mail: heather.briccetti@bcnys.org
Web site: www.bcnys.org
Taxation, economic development, workers' compensation
Heather C. Briccetti, President & Chief Executive Officer

Policy Areas

Offices and agencies generally appear in alphabetical order, except when specific order is requested by listee.

CWM Chemical Services LLC
1550 Balmer Road, PO Box 200, Model City, NY 14107
716-286-1550
Hazardous waste treatment, storage & disposal
Michael Mahar, District Manager

Cary Institute of Ecosystem Studies
PO Box AB, Millbrook, NY 12545-0129
845-677-5343 Fax: 845-677-5976
Web site: www.caryinstitute.org
Ecosystem research; curriculum development & on-site ecology education
Dr. Joshua R. Ginsberg, President

Catskill Center for Conservation & Development, The
43355 State Highway, PO Box 504, Arkville, NY 12406-0504
845-586-2611 Fax: 845-586-3044
e-mail: cccd@catskillcenter.org
Web site: www.catskillcenter.org
Advocacy for environmental & economic health of the Catskill Mountain region
Jeff Senterman, Executive Director

Center for Environmental Information Inc
700 West Metro Park, Rochester, NY 14623
585-233-6086
Web site: www.geneseeriverwatch.org
Public information & education on environmental topics
George Thomas, Executive Director

Citizens' Environmental Coalition
33 Central Avenue, 3rd Floor, Albany, NY 12210
518-462-5527 Fax: 518-465-8349
e-mail: cectoxic@igc.org
Web site: www.cectoxic.org
Organizing & assistance for communities concerned about toxic waste, air & water contamination & pollution prevention
Barbara Warren, Executive Director

Colgate University, Department of Geology
13 Oak Drive, Hamilton, NY 13346
315-228-7201 Fax: 315-228-7187
e-mail: mswong@colgate.edu
Web site: departments.colgate.edu/geology
Metamorphic & igneous petrology, Isotope geochemistry
Martin Wong, Chair, Department of Geology

Columbia University, MPA in Environmental Science & Policy
420 West 118th Street, Room 1408, New York, NY 10027
212-854-4445 or 212-854-6216 Fax: 212-864-3748
e-mail: sc32@columbia.edu
Web site: mpaenvironment.ei.columbia.edu
Urban & environmental policy; public management
Steven Cohen, Program Director

Cornell Cooperative Extension, Environment & Natural Resources Initiative
365 Roberts Hall, Cornell University, Ithaca, NY 14853
607-255-2237 Fax: 607-255-0788
e-mail: cce-contact@cornell.edu
Web site: www.cce.cornell.edu/program/environment
Working to improve the quality & sustainability of human environments & natural resources
Deb Grantham, Assistant Director

Cornell University Atkinson Center for a Sustainable Future
200 Rice Hall, Cornell University, Ithaca, NY 14853-5601
607-255-7535 Fax: 607-255-6714
Web site: www.acsf.cornell.edu
Environmental research
Frank DiSalvo, Director

Dionondehowa Wildlife Sanctuary & School - Not For Profit
148 Stanton Road, Shushan, NY 12873
518-854-7764
e-mail: dionondehowa@yahoo.com
Web site: www.dionondehowa.org
Conservation & land use issues, conscious living, nature studies & healing & expressive arts
Bonnie Hoag, Co-Founder & Director

Ecology & Environment Inc
368 Pleasant View Drive, Lancaster, NY 14086-1397
716-684-8060 Fax: 716-684-0844
e-mail: info@ene.com
Web site: www.ene.com
Environmental scientific & engineering consulting
Gerard A. Gallagher III, President & Chief Executive Officer

Empire State Forest Products Association
47 Van Alstyne Drive, Rensselaer, NY 12144
518-463-1297 Fax: 518-426-9502
e-mail: esfpa@esfpa.org
Web site: www.esfpa.org
John Bartow, Executive Director

Environmental Advocates of New York
353 Hamilton Street, Albany, NY 12210
518-462-5526 Fax: 518-427-0381
e-mail: info@eany.org
Web site: www.eany.org
Works to protect the environment of NYS by supporting conservation efforts & promoting policies that safeguard natural resources & public health
Peter Iwanowicz, Executive Director

Environmental Business Association of NYS Inc
126 State Street, 3rd Floor, Albany, NY 12207-1637
518-432-6400 x227 Fax: 518-432-1383
e-mail: info@eba-nys.org
Web site: www.eba-nys.org
Supports businesses that provide products & services to prevent, monitor, control or remediate pollution or generate, conserve and/or recycle energy & resources
Suzanne Maloney, Executive Director

Environmental Defense Fund
257 Park Avenue South, New York, NY 10010
212-505-2100 Fax: 212-505-2375
Web site: www.edf.org
Fred Krupp, President

GreenThumb
100 Gold Street, Suite 3100, New York, NY 10038
212-602-5300 Fax: 212-602-5334
e-mail: greenthumbinfo@parks.nyc.gov
Web site: www.greenthumbnyc.org
Development & preservation of community gardens; workshops addressing a variety of topics including gardening, farming & community organizing
Bill LoSasso, Director

Greene County Soil & Water Conservation District
907 Greene County Office Building, Cairo, NY 12413
518-622-3620 Fax: 518-622-0344
e-mail: jeff@gcswcd.com
Web site: www.gcswcd.com
Natural resource conservation, agriculture & water quality programs, environmental education, stormwater management & wetland mitigation
Jeff Flack, Executive Director

Offices and agencies generally appear in alphabetical order, except when specific order is requested by listee.

Greenmarket/Grow NYC
100 Gold Street, Suite 3300, New York, NY 10038
212-788-7900 Fax: 212-788-7913
Web site: www.grownyc.org
Promotes regional sustainable agriculture & improves access to locally grown agricultural products; recycling initiatives & environmental programs
Marcel Van Ooyen, Executive Director

Hawk Creek Wildlife Center Inc
PO Box 662, East Aurora, NY 14052-0662
716-652-8646 Fax: 716-652-8646
Web site: www.hawkcreek.org
Non-profit organization focused on animal rehabilitation, conservation efforts, environmental education & research
Loretta C. Jones, President

Hofstra University, School of Law
121 Hofstra University, Hempstead, NY 11549
516-463-5858
e-mail: hofstralaw@hofstra.edu
Web site: www.law.hofstra.edu
Land use & environmental law
Eric Lane, Dean

Hudson River Environmental Society, Inc
PO Box 279, Marlboro, NY 12542
e-mail: hudsonriverenvironmental@gmail.com
Web site: www.hres.org
Facilitates & coordinates research in the physical & biological sciences, environmental engineering & resource management in the Hudson River region
Lucy Johnson, President

Hudson River Sloop Clearwater Inc
724 Wolcott Avenue, Beacon, NY 12508
845-265-8080 Fax: 845-831-2821
e-mail: office@clearwater.org
Web site: www.clearwater.org
Hudson River water quality, environmental education & advocacy
Dave Conover, Interim Executive Director

INFORM Inc
PO Box 320403, New York, NY 11232
212-361-2400 Fax: 212-361-2412
e-mail: ramsey@informinc.org
Web site: www.informinc.org
Produces educational films about the impact of human activity on natural resources & public health
Virginia Ramsey, Executive Producer

Land Trust Alliance Northeast Program
112 Spring Street, Suite 204, Saratoga Springs, NY 12866
518-587-0774 Fax: 518-587-9586
e-mail: northeast@lta.org
Web site: www.landtrustalliance.org
Promotes voluntary land conservation; provides leadership, information, skills & resources needed by land trusts
Kevin Case, Northeast Director

Messinger Woods Wildlife Care & Education Center Inc
PO Box 508, Orchard Park, NY 14127
716-345-4239
e-mail: info@messingerwoods.org
Web site: www.messingerwoods.org
Conservation & wildlife protection efforts through education, community awareness & promotion of quality wildlife rehabilitation & care
Judy Seiler, President

Modutank Inc
41-04 35th Avenue, Long Island City, NY 11101
718-392-1112 or 800-245-6964 Fax: 718-786-1008
e-mail: info@modutank.com
Web site: www.modutank.com
Manufactures modular storage tanks for potable water, wastewater & liquid chemicals
Reed Margulis, President

NY League of Conservation Voters/NY Conservation Education Fund
30 Broad Street, 30th Floor, New York, NY 10004
212-361-6350 Fax: 212-361-6363
e-mail: info@nylcv.org
Web site: www.nylcv.org
Endorsement of pro-environmental candidates; environmental advocacy & education statewide
Marcia Bystryn, President

NY Sea Grant
125 Nassau Hall, SUNY at Stony Brook, Stony Brook, NY 11794-5001
631-632-6905 Fax: 631-632-6917
e-mail: nyseagrant@stonybrook.edu
Web site: www.seagrant.sunysb.edu
Research, education & training related to ocean, coastal & Great Lakes resources
William Wise, Director

NYC Community Garden Coalition
232 East 11th Street, New York, NY 10003
347-699-6099
Web site: www.nyccgc.org
Works to preserve NYC's community gardens through education & advocacy
Aziz Dehkan, Executive Director

NYS Association for Solid Waste Management
346 East Road, St. Johnsville, NY 13452
518-568-2095
e-mail: jbnysaswm@gmail.com
Web site: www.nysaswm.org
Represents solid waste professionals in NYS & advocates for environmentally sound waste management practices
Jeff Bouchard, Executive Director

NYS Water Resources Institute of Cornell University
Cornell University, 230 Riley-Robb Hall, Ithaca, NY 14853-5701
607-254-7163 Fax: 607-255-4449
e-mail: nyswri@cornell.edu
Web site: wri.cals.cornell.edu
Education, research, investigation & technical assistance to agencies & communities concerned with water resources
M. Todd Walter, Director

National Wildlife Federation - Northeast Regional Center
149 State Street, Suite 1, Montpelier, VT 05602
802-229-0650 Fax: 802-229-4532
Web site: www.nwf.org/northeast
Conservation education, litigation & advocacy for policies to restore & protect habitat & wildlife
Curtis Fisher, Regional Executive Director

Natural Resources Defense Council
40 West 20th Street, 11th Floor, New York, NY 10011
212-727-2700 Fax: 212-727-1773
e-mail: nrdcinfo@nrdc.org
Web site: www.nrdc.org
Litigation, legislation advocacy & public education to preserve & protect the environment & public health
Rhea Suh, President

Policy Areas

Nature Conservancy (The)
195 New Karner Road, Suite 200, Albany, NY 12205
518-690-7850 Fax: 518-869-2332
e-mail: nys@tnc.org
Web site: www.nature.org
Works to preserve land & water, protect oceans & develop solutions to climate change & other environmental challenges
Bill Ulfelder, New York Executive Director

New York Forest Owners Association Inc
PO Box 541, Lima, NY 14485
800-836-3566
e-mail: president@nyfoa.org
Web site: www.nyfoa.org
Promote & nurture private woodland stewardship
Charles Stackhouse, President

New York Public Interest Research Group
9 Murray Street, Lower Level, New York, NY 10007
212-349-6460 Fax: 212-349-1366
Web site: www.nypirg.org
Environmental preservation, public health, consumer protection & government reform
Blair Horner, Executive Director

New York State Conservation Council
8 East Main Street, Ilion, NY 13357-1899
315-894-3302 Fax: 315-894-2893
e-mail: nyscc@nyscc.com
Web site: www.nyscc.com
Promotes conservation, wise use & management of natural resources
A. Charles Parker, President

New York State Woodsmen's Field Days Inc
PO Box 123, 120 Main Street, Boonville, NY 13309
315-942-4593 Fax: 315-942-4452
e-mail: fielddays@aol.com
Web site: www.starinfo.com/woodsmen/
Promoting the forest products industry
Phyllis White, Executive Coordinator

New York Water Environment Association Inc (NYWEA)
525 Plum Street, Suite 102, Syracuse, NY 13204
315-422-7811 or 877-556-9932 Fax: 315-422-3851
e-mail: pcr@nywea.org
Web site: www.nywea.org
Organization working to protect water resources through education, science & training
Patricia Cerro-Reehil, Executive Director

Northeastern Loggers' Association
3311 State Route 28, PO Box 69, Old Forge, NY 13420
315-369-3078 Fax: 315-369-3736
Web site: www.northernlogger.com
Joseph E. Phaneuf, Executive Director

Open Space Institute
1350 Broadway, Suite 201, New York, NY 10018-7799
212-290-8200 Fax: 212-244-3441
Web site: www.osiny.org
Preserves & protects farmland, forests, water & historic landscapes through land acquisition, research, conservation & environmental education
Christopher J. Elliman, President & Chief Executive Officer

Pace University, School of Law Center for Environmental Legal Studies
78 North Broadway, White Plains, NY 10603
914-422-4214 Fax: 914-422-4248
e-mail: nrobinson@law.pace.edu
Web site: www.law.pace.edu
US & international environmental law
Nicholas A. Robinson, Co-Director

Proskauer Rose LLP
Eleven Times Square, New York, NY 10036-8299
212-969-3000 Fax: 212-969-2900
e-mail: info@proskauer.com
Web site: www.proskauer.com
Joseph M. Leccese, Chairman

Radiac Environmental Services
261 Kent Avenue, Brooklyn, NY 11249
718-963-2233 Fax: 718-388-5107
e-mail: jtekin@radiacenv.com
Web site: www.radiacenv.com
Radioactive & chemical waste disposal, decontamination & remediation
John Tekin, Manager

Radon Testing Corp of America Inc
2 Hayes Street, Elmsford, NY 10523-2502
914-345-3380 or 800-457-2366 Fax: 914-345-8546
e-mail: info@rtca.com
Web site: www.rtca.com
Radon detection services for health departments, municipalities & homeowners
Nancy Bredhoff, President

Rensselaer Polytechnic Inst, Ecological Economics, Values & Policy Program
Dept of Science & Tech Studies, 110 Eighth Street, Troy, NY 12180
518-276-6000
Web site: www.rpi.edu/academics/interdisciplinary/eevp.html
Educating leaders for a sustainable future

Riverhead Foundation for Marine Research & Preservation (The)
467 East Main Street, Riverhead, NY 11901
631-369-9840 Fax: 631-369-9826
Web site: www.riverheadfoundation.org
Marine conservation through education, rehabilitation & research
Robert A. DiGiovanni, Jr., Executive Director & Senior Biologist

Riverkeeper Inc
20 Secor Road, Ossining, NY 10562
914-478-4501 or 800-217-4837 Fax: 914-478-4527
e-mail: info@riverkeeper.org
Web site: www.riverkeeper.org
Nonprofit member-supported environmental organization working to protect the Hudson River & its tributaries as well as safeguard NYC & Hudson Valley's drinking water supply
Paul Gallay, President & Hudson Riverkeeper

Rural Water Association
PO Box 487, Claverack, NY 12513-0487
518-828-3155 Fax: 518-828-0582
e-mail: nyrwa@nyruralwater.org
Web site: www.nyruralwater.org
Protects small water & wastewater systems through training & technical assistance
Patricia Scalera, Chief Executive Director

SCS Engineers PC
4 Executive Blvd, Suite 303, Suffern, NY 10901
845-357-1510 Fax: 845-357-1049
e-mail: gmccarron@scsengineers.com
Web site: www.scsengineers.com
Environmental consulting
Greg McCarron, Vice President

Offices and agencies generally appear in alphabetical order, except when specific order is requested by listee.

SUNY at Cortland, Center for Environmental & Outdoor Education
PO Box 2000, Cortland, NY 13045
607-753-5488 Fax: 607-753-5985
e-mail: robert.rubendall@cortland.edu
Web site: www.cortland.edu
Robert L. Rubendall, Director

NYS Bar Assn, Environmental Law Section
Sahn Ward Coschignano, PLLC
333 Earle Ovington Blvd, Suite 601, Uniondale, NY 11553
516-228-1300 Fax: 516-228-0038
e-mail: info@swc-law.com
Web site: www.swc-law.com
Miriam E. Villani, Partner

Scenic Hudson
1 Civic Center Plaza, Suite 200, Poughkeepsie, NY 12601
845-473-4440 Fax: 845-473-2648
e-mail: info@scenichudson.org
Web site: www.scenichudson.org
Environmental advocacy, air & water quality, riverfront protection, land/historic preservation, smart growth planning
Ned Sullivan, President

Sierra Club, Atlantic Chapter
353 Hamilton Street, Albany, NY 12210-1709
518-426-9144
e-mail: atlantic.chapter@sierraclub.org
Web site: www.atlantic2.sierraclub.org
Environmental protection advocacy & education; outdoor recreation
Roger Downs, Conservation Director

Spectra Environmental Group Inc
19 British American Blvd West, Latham, NY 12110
518-782-0882 Fax: 518-782-0973
e-mail: rlafleur@spectraenv.com
Web site: www.spectraenv.com
Environmental & infrastructure engineering, architecture, surveying, air quality, ground penetrating radar & power generation consulting & services
Robert C. LaFleur, President

St John's University, School of Law
8000 Utopia Pkwy, Queens, NY 11439
718-990-6600
Environmental law
Jack A. Raisner, Professor

Sustainable Management LLC
1370 Broadway, 5th Floor, New York, NY 10018
646-380-1940 Fax: 646-380-1220
Environmental planning & housing development consulting services
Ethan Eldon, President

Syracuse University Press
621 Skytop Road, Suite 110, Syracuse, NY 13244-5290
315-443-5534 Fax: 315-443-5545
e-mail: supress@syr.edu
Web site: www.syracuseuniversitypress.syr.edu
Adirondack & regional NYS studies series
Alice Randel Pfeiffer, Director

Syracuse University, Maxwell School of Citizenship & Public Affairs
200 Eggers Hall, Syracuse, NY 13244-1020
315-443-2252
e-mail: whlambri@maxwell.syr.edu
Web site: www.maxwell.syr.edu
Environment & energy; social & economic policy
W. Henry Lambright, Professor

Trees New York
100 Gold Street, Suite 3100, New York, NY 10038
212-227-1887 Fax: 212-732-5325
e-mail: info@treesny.org
Web site: www.treesny.org
Planting, preserving & protecting street trees; urban forestry resources, reference materials & programs in NYC
Nelson Villarrubia, Executive Director

University of Rochester School of Medicine
601 Elmwood Avenue, Box EHSC, Rochester, NY 14642
585-275-4203 Fax: 585-256-2591
Web site: www2.envmed.rochester.edu
Environmental health science & toxicology education & research
Thomas W. Clarkson, Professor, Department of Environmental Medicine

Upstate Freshwater Institute
PO Box 506, Syracuse, NY 13214
315-431-4962 Fax: 315-431-4969
e-mail: uficontact@upstatefreshwater.org
Web site: www.upstatefreshwater.org
Freshwater water quality research
Steven W. Effler, Chief Executive Officer & Director of Research

Waterkeeper Alliance
180 Maiden Lane, Suite 603, New York, NY 10038
212-747-0622
e-mail: info@waterkeeper.org
Web site: www.waterkeeper.org
Seeks to protect & restore the quality of the world's waterways
Marc Yaggi, Executive Director

Whiteman Osterman & Hanna LLP
One Commerce Plaza, Albany, NY 12260
518-487-7600 Fax: 518-487-7777
e-mail: druzow@woh.com
Web site: www.woh.com
Environmental & zoning law
Daniel A. Ruzow, Partner

Wildlife Conservation Society
2300 Southern Blvd, Bronx, NY 10460
718-220-5100
e-mail: jcalvelli@wcs.org
Web site: www.wcs.org
Biodiversity conservation & education
John F. Calvelli, Executive Vice President, Public Affairs

Policy Areas

GOVERNMENT OPERATIONS

NEW YORK STATE

GOVERNOR'S OFFICE

Governor's Office
Executive Chamber
State Capitol
Albany, NY 12224
518-474-8390 Fax: 518-474-1513
Web site: www.ny.gov

Governor:
Andrew M Cuomo 518-474-8390
Secretary to the Governor:
William Mulrow 518-474-4246
Counsel to the Governor:
Alphonso David 518-474-8343
Deputy Director of State Operations:
Rosemary Powers 518-473-9958
Deputy Secretary for Executive Operations:
Jill DesRosiers 518-402-2403
Director of Policy:
John Maggiore 518-408-2576
Deputy Secretary, Public Safety:
Rachel Small 518-474-3522
Chief of Staff:
Melissa DeRosa . . . . . 518-474-8418 or 212-681-4640
Director, Communications:
James Allen . . . . . 518-474-8418 or 212-681-4640

New York City Office
633 Third Ave, 38th Fl, New York, NY 10017

Washington Office of the Governor
444 N Capitol St NW, Washington, DC 20001
Director:
Alexander Cochran 202-434-7100

Lieutenant Governor's Office
Executive Chamber
State Capitol
Albany, NY 12224
518-402-2292 Fax: 518-474-1513

633 Third Ave
New York, NY 10017
212-681-4575

Lieutenant Governor:
Kathleen C Hochul . . . . . 518-402-2292 or 212-681-4575

EXECUTIVE DEPARTMENTS AND RELATED AGENCIES

Budget, Division of the
State Capitol
Albany, NY 12224
518-473-0580 Fax: 518-474-9041
Web site: www.budget.ny.gov

Director:
Robert F Mujica 518-474-2300
Deputy Director:
Sandra Beattie 518-474-6497
Deputy Director:
David Lara 518-402-4246
Budget Services Head:
Vacant 518-474-6300
Public Protection Head:
Robert Barbato 518-474-4313
Press Officer:
Morris Peters 518-473-3885
e-mail: dob.sm.press@nysemail.state.ny.us

CIO & Office of Information Technology Services (ITS)
State Capitol, ESP
PO Box 2062
Albany, NY 12220-0062
518-402-2537 or 866-789-4638 Fax: 518-474-1196
Web site: www.its.ny.gov

Chief Information Officer & Director:
Maggie Miller 518-408-2140
Executive Deputy CIO:
Mahesh Nattanmai 518-408-2140
Counsel & Legal Services:
Shoshanah Bewlay 518-408-2484
Director, Public Information:
Vacant 518-408-3899
Chief Portfolio Officer:
Nancy Mulholland 518-473-9450
COO:
Ray Rose 518-402-7000
Director, Administration:
Terri Papa 518-408-2484
Chief Technology Officer:
Rajiv Rao 518-408-2484
Chief Data Officer:
Barbara Cohn 518-474-3019

Homeland Security & Emergency Services, Division of
1220 Washington Ave
Bldg. 7A
Suite 710
Albany, NY 12242
518-242-5000 Fax: 518-322-4978
Web site: www.dhses.ny.gov

633 Third Ave
32nd Fl
New York, NY 10017
212-867-7060

Commissioner:
John P Melville 518-292-2301
Assistant Director, Office of Counterterrorism:
David Sheppard 518-242-5121
Director, Upstate Intergovernmental Affairs:
Brian Shea 518-292-2301
State Fire Administrator & Director, Fire Prevention:
Bryant Stevens 518-474-6746/fax: 518-474-3240
e-mail: fire@dhses.ny.gov
Director, Office of Interoperable & Emergency Communications:
Robert Barbato 518-292-4913
e-mail: dhsesoiec@dhses.ny.gov
Public Information Officer:
Kristin Devoe 518-242-5153

General Services, Office of
Corning Tower, 41st Fl
Empire State Plaza
Albany, NY 12242
518-474-3899 Fax: 518-474-1546
Web site: www.ogs.ny.gov

Offices and agencies generally appear in alphabetical order, except when specific order is requested by listee.

Commissioner:
RoAnn Destito 518-474-5991
Executive Deputy Commissioner:
Karen B Tyler 518-473-6953
Deputy Commissioner, Counsel:
Bradley Allen. 518-474-5988/fax: 518-473-4973
Director, Communications:
Heather Groll. 518-474-5987/fax: 518-402-5146
e-mail: heather.groll@ogs.ny.gov

Administration
Deputy Commissioner:
Gail Hammond 518-474-3199
CFO, Administration:
Brian C Matthews 518-474-4546/fax: 518-486-3651
Director, Financial Administration:
Robert Curtin 518-474-4546
Director, Human Resources Management:
Matthew Guinare. 518-474-5995/fax: 518-473-8610
Director, Personnel:
Christina Gavin. 518-474-5995
Director, Bureau of Risk, Insurance & Fleet Management:
Leighann Brown 518-474-4725

Support Services
Director, Support Services Operations:
Thomas Osterhout 518-402-5557
Printing & Mailing Services:
Annemarie Pingelski 518-457-6593
Assistant Director, State & Federal Surplus Property:
Michael Harris 518-457-6335
Director, Food Distribution & Warehousing:
Annemarie Garceau 518-474-5122
Director, Fleet Management:
Christian Jackstadt 518-457-1744
e-mail: nys.alt.fuel@cgs.ny.gov
Director, Mail & Freight Security Services:
Arthur Hasson. 518-474-6707

Design & Construction
Deputy Commissioner:
Margaret Larkin 518-474-0337
e-mail: design.construction@cgs.ny.gov
Director, Construction:
Marc Prendergest. 518-474-0331/fax: 518-474-8201
Director, Contract Administration:
John D Lewyckyj. 518-474-0201/fax: 518-473-5221
Director, Design:
Erik Deyoe, PE 518-474-0337

Information Technology & Procurement Services
Deputy Commissioner:
Vacant 518-473-3933/fax: 518-486-9166

Information Resource Management
Director, Technical Services:
Federico Polsinelli 518-402-5246
Asst Director, Technical Services:
Eliel Mamousette 518-473-4788

Procurement Services Group
Deputy Chief:
Susan Filburn 518-474-5294
Director:
Bruce Hallenbeck 518-408-1705
Director:
Kathleen McAuley 518-474-1994
Assistant Director:
Anne Samson 518-474-3855

Real Estate Planning & Development Group
Director, Real Estate Planning & Development:
James Sproat 518-474-4944
Asst Director, Real Estate Planning & Development:
Robert W Lazarou. 518-474-4944
Bureau Chief, Land Management:
Charles Scheifer 518-474-2195
Asst Director, Real Estate Planning - Upstate:
Leah Nicholson. 518-486-1484

Real Property Management Group
Deputy Commissioner:
Eric S. McShane 518-474-6057/fax: 518-474-1523
Director, Empire State Plaza & Downtown Buildings:
Carl Olsen 518-474-6148
Director, Downstate Regional Buildings:
Kevin Cahill. 718-923-4448/fax: 718-923-4451
Assistant Director, Empire State Plaza & Downtown Buildings:
Andy Papale 518-402-5753
Director, Upstate Harriman State Office Campus:
Louis Salerno. 518-457-2290/fax: 518-457-8297
Director, Utilities Management:
Robert Lobdell. .518-474-3249/fax: 518-402-5682

Empire State's Convention & Cultural Events Office
Director:
Susan Cleary. 518-474-0549
Manager, Convention Center:
Vacant 518-474-0558/fax: 518-473-2190
Director, Curatorial & Tour Services:
Barbara Maggio 518-473-7521
NYS Vietnam Memorial:
Information 518-474-2418

Inspector General (NYS), Office of the
Empire State Plaza
Bldg 2, 16th Fl
Albany, NY 12223
518-474-1010 or 800-367-4448 Fax: 518-486-3745
Web site: www.ig.ny.gov

State Inspector General:
Catharine Leahy Scott . . . . .212-635-3150 or 518-474-1010
e-mail: inspector.general@ig.ny.gov
Executive Deputy Inspector General:
Spencer Freedman. 212-635-3150
Deputy Inspector General, Investigations:
Bernard Cosenza. 212-635-3150
Director, Communications:
William P. Reynolds. 518-474-1010

Law Department
120 Broadway
New York, NY 10271-0332
212-416-8000 or 800-771-7755
Web site: www.ag.ny.gov

State Capitol
Albany, NY 12224-0341
518-776-2000
Fax: 518-650-9401

Attorney General:
Eric T Schneiderman . . . . .212-416-8050 or 518-776-2000
Chief Deputy Attorney General & Counsel:
Janet Sabel 212-416-8050
Chief Deputy Attorney General & Counsel:
Jason Brown 212-416-8050
COO:
Jeanette Moy. . . . . .212-416-8050 or 518-473-7900
fax: 518-474-0680
Executive Deputy Attorney General for Criminal Justice:
Kelly Donovan 212-416-8050

Offices and agencies generally appear in alphabetical order, except when specific order is requested by listee.

Policy Areas

State Comptroller, Office of the

110 State St, 15th Fl
Albany, NY 12236-0001
518-474-4044 Fax: 518-473-3004
e-mail: contactus@osc.state.ny.us
Web site: www.osc.state.ny.us

59 Maiden Lane
New York, NY 10038
212-383-1600

State Comptroller:
Thomas P DiNapoli . . . . . 518-474-4040 or 212-681-4469
Deputy Comptroller, Budget & Policy Analysis:
Robert Ward 518-473-4333
Assistant Comptroller, Labor Affairs:
Kathy McCormack 518-473-8409

Executive Office

First Deputy Comptroller:
Pete Grannis . . . . . 518-474-2909 or 212-681-4469
Chief of Staff:
Shawn Thompson 518-474-4044
Deputy Comptroller & Chief Information Officer:
Robert Loomis 518-486-4349
Enterprise Applications & IT Business Management:
Mary Anne Barry 518-474-8089
Director, Communications:
Jennifer Freeman . . . . . 518-474-4015 or 212-681-4840
Assistant Comptroller, Business Communications:
Ellen Evans . . . . . 518-474-4040 or 212-681-4489
Deputy Comptroller, Office of the State Deputy Comptroller for the City of New York:
Ken Bliewas 212-383-3905

Human Resources & Administration

Deputy Comptroller, Human Resources & Administration:
Angela Dixon 518-474-5512
Assistant Comptroller, Administration:
Larry Appel 518-402-3043
Director, Financial Administration:
Brian Matthews 518-474-2709
Assistant Director, Management Services:
Beth Bristol 518-486-7433

Inspector General

Inspector General - Internal Audit:
Stephen Hamilton 518-408-4906

Intergovernmental Affairs

Deputy Comptroller:
Vacant 518-402-3234

Legal Services

General Counsel:
Nancy Groenwegen 518-474-3444
Special Counsel for Ethics:
Barbara Smith 518-408-3855

Operations

Executive Deputy Comptroller:
John Traylor 518-402-4103
Deputy Comptroller, Contracts & Expenditures:
Margaret N. Becker 518-486-9544
Deputy Comptroller, Payroll, Accounting & Revenue Services (PARS):
Chris Gorka 518-408-4149

Pension Investment & Cash Management

Assistant Comptroller, Real Estate Investments:
Marjorie Tsang 212-681-2589

Retirement

Deputy Comptroller:
Kevin Murray 518-474-2600

Local Government & School Accountability

Deputy Comptroller:
Steve Hancox 518-474-4037

State Government Accountability

Executive Deputy Comptroller:
Andrew San Filippo 518-474-4593
Deputy Comptroller:
Elliot Pagliaccio 518-473-3596
Assistant Comptroller:
Jerry Barber 518-473-0334

State Department

One Commerce Plaza
99 Washington Ave
Albany, NY 12231
518-474-4750 Fax: 518-474-4765
Web site: www.dos.ny.gov

123 William St
New York, NY 10038
212-417-5801
Fax: 212-417-5805

Acting Secretary of State:
Rossana Rosado 518-474-0050
First Deputy Secretary of State:
Daniel Shapiro 518-474-4750
Deputy Secretary of State, Public Affairs:
Vacant 212-417-5800
Principal Attorney:
William Sharp 518-474-6740/fax: 518-473-9211
Assistant Secretary of State, Communications:
Vacant 518-474-4752/fax: 518-474-4597
e-mail: info@dos.state.ny.us

Licensing Services Division

Deputy Secretary of State:
Marcos Vigil 518-473-2728/fax: 518-473-2730
e-mail: licensing @dos.state.ny.us

Administrative Rules Division

Manager, Publications:
Maribeth St. Germain 518-474-6957/fax: 518-473-9055
e-mail: adminrules@dos.state.ny.us

Cemeteries Division

Director:
Richard D Fishman . . . . . 518-474-6226 or 212-417-5713
fax: 518-473-0876
e-mail: cemeteries@dos.state.ny.us

Corporations, State Records & UCC Division

Director:
Sandra J. Tallman 518-473-2492/fax: 518-474-1418
e-mail: corporations@dos.ny.gov

Local Government & Community Services

Deputy Secretary of State:
Dierdre Scozzafava 518-473-3355

Coastal Resources & Waterfront Revitalization Division

Director:
George Stafford 518-474-6000
e-mail: coastal@dos.state.ny.us

Offices and agencies generally appear in alphabetical order, except when specific order is requested by listee.

Code Enforcement & Administration Division
Director:
Ronald E Piester 518-474-4073/fax: 518-486-4487
e-mail: codes@dos.state.ny.us

Community Services Division
Director:
Veronica Cruz 518-474-5741/fax: 518-486-4663
e-mail: commserv@dos.state.ny.us

Local Government Services Division
Deputy Secretary of State:
Dierdre Scozzafava 518-473-3355/fax: 518-474-6572
e-mail: localgov@dos.ny.gov

Open Government Committee
Executive Director:
Robert J Freeman 518-474-2518/fax: 518-474-1927
e-mail: opengov@dos.state.ny.us

Operations
Director, Administration & Management:
Judith E Kenny 518-474-4751/fax: 518-474-4765

Administrative Support Services
Director:
Rebecca Sebesta 518-473-8221/fax: 518-473-7182

Affirmative Action . . . . . fax: 518-473-3294
Affirmative Action Officer:
Teneka Frost-Amusa 518-474-6740

Fiscal Management
Director:
George Lupe 518-474-2754/fax: 518-474-4777

Human Resources Management
Director:
Philip Kelly 518-474-2752/fax: 518-473-3294

Internal Audit
Acting Director:
Louis Canter 518-474-1859

Information Technology Management
Director:
Steven S Lovelett 518-474-8512/fax: 518-474-6239

Regional Services
Assistant Director:
Brian S. Tollisen 518-474-4073/fax: 518-474-5788

Regional Offices

Region 9 - Capital District Office . . . . . fax: 518-477-2369
One Commerce Plaza, 99 Washington Avenue, Albany, NY 12231
518-474-7497 Fax: 518-477-2369
Regional Representative:
Joseph McGrath 518-477-7497

Region 4 - Kingston Office . . . . . fax: 845-334-9373
One Albany Avenue, Suite G-%, Kingston, NY 12401
845-334-9768 Fax: 845-334-9373
Regional Representative:
Dan Nichols 845-334-9768/fax: 845-334-9373

Region 1 - Buffalo Office . . . . . fax: 716-847-7941
65 Court St, Room 208, Buffalo, NY 14202
716-847-7611 or 716-847-7612 Fax: 716-847-7941
Regional Representative:
Kumar Vijaykumar 716-847-7611
Regional Representative:
Andrew Hvisdak 716-847-7612

Region 12/13 - Long Island Office . . . . . fax: 631-952-4911
Suffolk State Office Bldg., 250 Veterans Memorial Highway, Hauppauge, NY 11788
631-952-4915 Fax: 631-952-4911
Regional Representative:
Courtney Nation 631-952-4915/fax: 631-952-4911
Regional Representative:
Richard Smith 631-952-4912

Region 10 - Northern New York Office
PO Box 341, Lake George, NY 12845
Regional Representative:
Whitney Russell 518-441-1895/fax: 518-668-5369

Region 2 - Peekskill Office
2 John Walsh Blvd., Suite 206, Peekskill, NY 10566
Regional Representative:
Erika Krieger 914-734-1347/fax: 914-734-1763

Region 5 - Syracuse Office
St Ofc Bldg, 333 E Washington St, Rm 514, Syracuse, NY 13202
Regional Representative:
James King 315-428-4434/fax: 578-428-4655

Region 6 - Utica Office
State Office Bldg, 207 Genesee St, Utica, NY 13501
Regional Representative:
Thomas Romanowski 315-793-2526/fax: 315-793-2569

Region 7/8 - Western New York Office
PO Box 141, Conesus, NY 14435
585-402-3017
Regional Representative:
Deborah Babbitt 585-402-3017

State Athletic Commission
123 William St, 2nd Fl, New York, NY 10038
Chair:
Tom Hoover 212-417-5700/fax: 212-417-4987
e-mail: athletic@dos.ny.gov

Welfare Inspector General, Office of NYS
Empire State Plaza
Agency Bldg 2
16th Floor
Albany, NY 12223
518-474-1010 or 800-682-4530 Fax: 518-486-3745
e-mail: inspector.general@ig.ny.gov
Web site: www.owig.state.ny.us

Acting Welfare Inspector General:
Catherine Leahy Scott . . . . . 518-474-1010 or 212-635-3150
Chief Investigator:
Joseph Bucci 718-923-4290
Confidential Assistant:
Joy Quiles 718-923-4290
e-mail: joy.quiles@owig.ny.gov

CORPORATIONS, AUTHORITIES AND COMMISSIONS

Legislative Bill Drafting Commission
Capitol, Rm 308
Albany, NY 12224
518-455-7500 Fax: 518-455-7598
Commissioner:
Randall G Bluth 518-455-7506
e-mail: bluth@lbdc.state.ny.us

Legislative Retrieval System . . . . . fax: 518-455-7679
1450 Western Ave, Albany, NY 12203
800-356-6566 Fax: 518-455-7679
Director:
Burleigh McCutcheon 518-455-7672
e-mail: mccutcheon@lbdc.state.ny.us

Offices and agencies generally appear in alphabetical order, except when specific order is requested by listee.

New York State Athletic Commission
123 William St
2nd Fl
New York, NY 10038
212-417-5700 Fax: 212-417-4987
e-mail: info@dos.ny.gov
Web site: www.dos.ny.gov/athletic

Chair:
Tom Hoover 212-417-5700

New York State Commission on the Restoration of the Capitol
Corning Tower, 31st Fl
Empire State Plaza
Albany, NY 12242
518-473-0341 Fax: 518-486-5720

Executive Director:
Andrea J Lazarski 518-473-0341
e-mail: andrea.lazarski@ogs.ny.gov

New York State Disaster Preparedness Commission
Building 22, Suite 101
1220 Washington Ave
Albany, NY 12226-2251
518-292-2301 or 518-292-2200 Fax: 518-322-4978
Web site: www.dhses.ny.gov/oem/disaster-prep/

Chairman/Director:
Jerome M Hauer 518-292-2301

New York State Dormitory Authority
515 Broadway
Albany, NY 12207-2964
518-257-3000 Fax: 518-257-3100
e-mail: dabonds@dasny.org
Web site: www.dasny.org

One Penn Plaza
52nd Fl
New York, NY 10119-0098
212-273-5000
Fax: 212-273-5121

539 Franklin St
Buffalo, NY 14202-1109
716-884-9780
Fax: 716-884-9787

Chair:
Alfonso L Carney Jr 518-257-3000/fax: 518-257-3100
President/CEO:
Paul T Williams Jr. 518-257-3180/fax: 518-257-3183
Vice President:
Michael T Corrigan 518-257-3192/fax: 518-257-3183
Chief Financial Officer:
Linda H Button 518-257-3562/fax: 518-257-3100
General Counsel:
Michael Cusack 518-257-3120/fax: 518-257-3101
Managing Director, Construction:
Stephen D Curro, PE 518-257-3271/fax: 518-257-3100
e-mail: scurro@dasny.org
Managing Director, Public Finance & Portfolio Monitoring:
Portia Lee. 518-257-3362/fax: 518-257-3100
e-mail: plee@dasny.org
Public Information Officer:
John Chirlin. 518-257-3380
e-mail: jchirlin@dasny.org

Joint Commission on Public Ethics (JCOPE)
540 Broadway
Albany, NY 12207
518-408-3976 Fax: 518-408-3975
e-mail: jcope@jcope.ny.gov
Web site: www.jcope.ny.gov

Executive Director:
Seth Agata. 518-408-3976
Chair:
Daniel J Horwitz 518-408-3976
General Counsel:
Monica Stamm 518-408-3976
Chief of Staff:
Kevin T Gagan 518-408-3976

New York State Financial Control Board
123 William St
23rd Fl
New York, NY 10038-3804
212-417-5046 Fax: 212-417-5055
e-mail: nysfcb@fcb.state.ny.us
Web site: www.fcb.state.ny.us

Acting Executive Director:
Jeffrey Sommer. 212-417-5066
Deputy Director, Expenditure & Covered Organization Analysis:
Dennis DeLisle 212-417-5069
Acting Deputy Director, Economic & Revenue Analysis:
Martin Fischman. 212-417-5068
Associate Director, Administration:
Mattie W Taylor 212-417-5053

New York State Law Reporting Bureau
17 Lodge Street
Albany, NY 12207
518-453-6900 Fax: 518-426-1640
Web site: www.courts.state.ny.us/reporter

State Reporter:
William J Hooks 518-453-6900
Deputy State Reporter:
Katherine D LaBoda, Esq. 518-453-6900
e-mail: Reporter@courts.state.ny.us
Assistant State Reporter:
Cara J Broussea, Esq. 518-453-6900
e-mail: Reporter@courts.state.ny.us

Uniform State Laws Commission
c/o Coughlin & Gerhart LLP,
99 Corporate Drive
PO Box 2089
Binghamton, NY 13902-2039
607-723-9511 Fax: 607-723-1530

Chair:
Richard B Long. 607-821-2202
e-mail: rlong@cglawoffices.com
Member:
Sandra Stern 212-207-8150
Member:
Norman L. Greene 212-661-5030
Member:
Justin L. Vigdor . . . . 585-232-5300 ext 228

Offices and agencies generally appear in alphabetical order, except when specific order is requested by listee.

Member:
Mark F Glaser 518-689-1413

United Nations Development Corporation

Two United Nations Plaza
27th Fl
New York, NY 10017
212-888-1618 Fax: 212-588-0758
e-mail: info@undc.org
Web site: www.undc.org

Chair, Board of Directors:
George Klein 212-888-1618
Sr VP & General Counsel/Secretary:
Robert Cole 212-888-1618
Controller/Treasurer:
Jorge Ortiz 212-888-1618
Vice President:
Kenneth Coopersmith 212-888-1618

NEW YORK STATE LEGISLATURE

See Legislative Branch in Section 1 for additional Standing Committee and Subcommittee information.

Assembly Standing Committees

Consumer Affairs & Protection
Chair:
Jeffrey Dinowitz (D) 518-455-5965
Ranking Minority Member:
Anthony Palumbo (R) 518-455-5294

Corporations, Authorities & Commissions
Chair:
James F Brennan (D) 518-455-5377
Ranking Minority Member:
Jane Corwin (R) 518-455-4601

Ethics & Guidance
Chair:
Charles Lavine (D) 518-455-5456
Ranking Minority Member:
Brian Curran (R) 518-455-4656

Governmental Operations
Chair:
Crystal Peoples-Stokes (D) 518-455-5005
Ranking Minority Member:
Janet Duprey (R) 518-455-5943

Oversight, Analysis & Investigation
Chair:
Ellen Jaffee (D) 518-455-5118
Ranking Minority Member:
Peter Lawrence (R) 518-455-4664

Rules
Chair:
Carl Heastie (D) 518-455-3791
Ranking Minority Member:
Brian M Kolb (R) 518-455-3751

Ways & Means
Chair:
Herman D Farrell, Jr (D) 518-455-5491
Ranking Minority Member:
Bob Oaks (R) 518-455-5655

Assembly Task Forces & Caucus

State-Federal Relations Task Force
Assembly Chair:
Matthew Titone (D) 518-455-4677
Program Manager:
Robert Stern 518-455-3632

Senate Standing Committees

Civil Service & Pensions
Chair:
Martin J Golden (R) 518-455-2730
Ranking Minority Member:
James Sanders, Jr. (D) 518-455-3531

Consumer Protection
Chair:
Michael Venditto (R) 518-455-3341
Ranking Minority Member:
Leroy Comrie (D) 518-455-2701

Corporations, Authorities & Commissions
Chair:
Michael Ranzenhofer (R) 518-455-3161
Ranking Minority Member:
Bill Perkins (D) 518-455-2441

Ethics
Chair:
Thomas Croci (R) 518-455-3570
Ranking Minority Member:
Michael Gianaris (D) 518-455-3486

Finance
Chair:
Catharine M Young (R) 518-455-3563
Ranking Minority Member:
Liz Krueger (D) 518-455-2297

Investigations & Government Operations
Chair:
Andrew J Lanza (R) 518-455-3215
Ranking Minority Member:
Brad Hoylman (D) 518-455-2451

Rules
Chair:
John J Flanagan (R) 518-455-2071
Ranking Minority Member:
Andrea Stewart-Cousins (D) 518-455-2585

Senate/Assembly Legislative Commissions

Ethics Committee, Legislative
Senate Co-Chair:
Andrew J Lanza (R) 518-455-3215
Assembly Co-Chair:
Charles Lavine (D) 518-455-4546
Director/Counsel:
Lisa P. Reid
e-mail: lreid@nysenate.gov

Government Administration, Legislative Commission on
Assembly Chair:
Brian Kavanaugh (D) 518-455-5506
Senate Vice Chair:
Vacant 518-455-0000

Policy Areas

AMERICAN INDIAN TRIBES

Cayuga Nation of New York
2540 SR-89
PO Box 803
Seneca Falls, NY 13148
315-568-0750 Fax: 315-568-0752
Web site: www.cayuganation-nsn.gov

Federal Representative:
Clint Halftown

Oneida Indian Nation
2037 Dream Catcher Plaza
Oneida, NY 13421
315-829-8900 or 800-685-6115 Fax: 315-829-8958
e-mail: info@oneida-nation.org
Web site: www.oneidaindiannation.com

Nation Repesentative:
Ray Halbritter

Onondaga Nation
3951 Route 11
Nedrow, NY 13120
315-492-1922 Fax: 315-469-4717
e-mail: admin@onondaganation.org
Web site: www.onondaganation.org

Chief:
Sidney Hill

Seneca Nation of Indians
William Seneca Building
12837 Route 438
Irving, NY 14081
716-532-4900
e-mail: sni@sni.org
Web site: www.sni.org

President:
Maurice A John, Sr

Shinnecock Indian Nation
PO Box 5006
Southampton, NY 11969-5006
631-283-6143 or 631-287-3752 Fax: 631-283-0751
e-mail: sination@optonline.net

Chairperson:
Daniel Collins, Sr.
Director of Communications:
Beverly Jensen
e-mail: nationsvoice@shinnecock.org

St Regis Mohawk Tribe
412 State Route 37
Akwesasne, NY 13655
518-358-2272 Fax: 518-358-3203
e-mail: communications@srmt-nsn.gov
Web site: www.srmt-nsn.gov

Tribal Clerk:
Betty Roundpoint 518-358-2272

Unkechaug Nation
Poospatuck Reservation
PO Box 86
Mastic, NY 11950
631-281-6464 or 631-281-4143 Fax: 631-281-2125
e-mail: hwal1@aol.com
Web site: http://unkechaug.wordpress.com/

Chief:
Harry Wallace

U.S. GOVERNMENT

EXECUTIVE DEPARTMENTS AND RELATED AGENCIES

New York Regional Office . . . . .fax: 212-352-5441
201 Varick Street, Suite 1025, New York, NY 10014
855-855-1961 or 212-352-5440 Fax: 212-352-5441
e-mail: nyinfo@peacecorps.gov
Web site: www.peacecorps.gov
Regional Recruitment Supervisor:
Anthony Trujillo 212-352-5440
Public Affairs Specialist:
Elizabeth Chamberlain 774-330-9200
e-mail: echamberlain@peacecorps.gov

US Department of Homeland Security (DHS)
Web site: www.dhs.gov

Bureau of Immigration & Customs Enforcement (ICE)
Web site: www.ice.gov

New York District Office . . . . .fax: 646-230-3255
601 West 26th Street, 7th Floor, New York, NY 10001
646-230-3200 Fax: 646-230-3255
Special Agent-in-Charge:
Raymond R. Parmer Jr.

Buffalo Office . . . . .fax: 716-565-9509
1780 Wehrle Drive, Suite D, Williamsville, NY 14221
716-565-2039 Fax: 716-565-9509
Special Agent-in-Charge:
James C. Spero

Customs & Border Protection (CBP)
202-325-8000 or 877-227-5511
Web site: www.cbp.gov

Agriculture Inspections (AI)

Buffalo, Port of
726 Exchange Street, Suite 400, Buffalo, NY 14210
Supervisory CBP Officer:
Gary Friedman 716-843-8300

Champlain, Port of . . . . .fax: 518-298-8395
237 West Service Road, Champlain, NY 12919
518-298-8311 Fax: 518-298-8395
Port Director:
Paul Mongillo 518-298-8311/fax: 518-298-8395

JFK International Airport Area Office . . . . .fax: 718-487-5191
JFK International Airport, Building 77, 2nd Floor, Jamaica, NY 11430
718-487-5164 Fax: 718-487-5191
Public Affairs Officer:
Anthony Bucci 646-733-3275

Buffalo Field Office
300 Airborne Parkway, Suite 300, Buffalo, NY 14225
716-626-0400
Acting Director:
Rose Hilmey 716-626-0400

Offices and agencies generally appear in alphabetical order, except when specific order is requested by listee.

Albany, Port of . . . . fax: 518-431-0203
445 Broadway, Room 216, Albany, NY 12207
518-431-0200 Fax: 518-431-0203
Port Director:
Andrew Wescott

Alexandria Bay, Port of . . . . fax: 315-482-5304
46735 Interstate Route 81, Alexandria Bay, NY 13607
315-482-2065 Fax: 315-482-5304
Supervisory CBP Officer:
Darren Erwin 315-482-2681

Binghamton, Port of
2534 Airport Road, Box 4, Johnson City, NY 13790
607-763-4294

Buffalo, Port of
726 Exchange Street, Suite 400, Buffalo, NY 14210
716-843-8300
Supervisory CBP Officer:
Gary Friedman 716-843-8300

Champlain, Port of . . . . fax: 518-298-8395
237 West Service Road, Champlain, NY 12919
518-298-8311 Fax: 518-298-8395
Area Port Director:
Paul Mongillo 518-298-8311

Massena, Port of
30M Seaway International Bridge, Rooseveltown, NY 13683
315-769-3091
Tribal Liaison Officer:
Tracey S. Casey 315-769-3091

Ogdensburg, Port of
104 Bridge Approach Road, Ogdensburg, NY 13669
Port Director:
Wade Davis 313-393-1390

Rochester, Port of . . . . fax: 585-263-5828
1200 Brooks Avenue, Rochester, NY 14624
585-263-6293 Fax: 585-263-5828
Port Director:
Ronald Menz 585-263-6293

Rome, Port of
650 Hanger Road, Rome, NY 13441
315-356-4731

Syracuse, Port of
152 Air Cargo Road, Suite 201, Syracuse, NY 13212
315-455-8446
Port Director:
David Harris. 315-455-8446

Trout River, Port of . . . . fax: 518-483-3717
17013 State Route 30, Constable, NY 12926
518-483-0821 Fax: 518-483-3717

New York Field Office. . . . . fax: 646-733-3245
1 World Trade Center, Suite 50.200, New York, NY 10007
646-733-3100 Fax: 646-733-3245
Director, Field Operations:
Robert E. Perez
Public Affairs Specialist:
Anthony Bucci 646-733-3275

Field Counsel - New York
Deputy Associate Chief Counsel:
Colleen Piccone

Laboratory Division
Director:
Laura W. Goldstein 973-368-1900

National Urban Security Technology Laboratory
201 Varick Street, 5th Floor, New York, NY 10014
Director:
Dr. Adam Hutter

Administration
Director:
Alfred Crescenzi

Systems Division
Director:
Lawrence Ruth 212-620-3609
e-mail: lawrence.ruth@dhs.gov

Testbeds Division
Acting Director:
Lawrence Ruth

Federal Emergency Management Agency (FEMA)
TTY: 800-462-7585 or 202-646-2500
Web site: www.fema.gov

New York Regional Office
26 Federal Plaza, New York, NY 10278-0002
212-680-3600
Regional Administrator:
Jerome Hatfield

Federal Protective Service (The)
26 Federal Plaza, Room 17-130, New York, NY 10278
Director:
L. Eric Patterson

Plum Island Animal Disease Center
PO Box 848, Greenport, NY 11944
Director:
Larry Barrett

Transportation Security Administration (TSA)
75-20 Astoria Blvd, Suite 300, East Elmhurst, NY 11370
718-426-1350
Regional Spokesperson:
Lisa Farbstein

US Citizenship & Immigration Services (USCIS)
TTY: 800-767-1833 or 800-375-5283
Web site: www.uscis.gov

Buffalo District Office. . . . . fax: 716-551-3131
Federal Center, 306 Delaware Avenue, Buffalo, NY 14202
District Director:
Edward A. Newman 716-843-7900

Albany Field Office
1086 Troy-Schenectady Road, Latham, NY 12110
Field Office Director:
Gwynne Dinolfo

CIS Asylum Offices

New York Asylum Office
1065 Stewart Avenue, Suite 200, Bethpage, NY 11714
516-261-0000
Director:
Patricia Menges 516-261-0000
Deputy Director:
Ashley Caudill-Mirillo

Newark Asylum Office-Including NYS not served by New York City
1200 Wall Street West, 4th Floor, Lyndhurst, NJ 07071
201-508-6100
Director:
Susan Raufer 201-531-0555
Deputy Director:
Sunil R. Varghese

New York City District Office
Jacob K. Javits Federal Building, 26 Federal Plaza, Room 3-120, New York, NY 10278
District Director:
Phyllis Coven

Long Island Field Office
30 Barretts Avenue, Holtsville, NY 11742
Field Office Director:
Elizabeth Miller

Policy Areas

Offices and agencies generally appear in alphabetical order, except when specific order is requested by listee.

Queens Field Office
26 Federal Plaza, Room 8-100, New York, NY 10278
Field Office Director:
Bryan P. Christian

US General Services Administration

Web site: www.gsa.gov

Region 2—New York
1 World Trade Center, 55th Floor, Room 55W09, New York, NY 10007-0089
212-264-3305
Regional Administrator:
Denise L. Pease 212-264-2600
e-mail: denise.pease@gsa.gov
Special Assistant to the Regional Administrator:
Dawne Troupe 212-264-2041
e-mail: dawne.troupe@gsa.gov
Human Resources Officer:
Maureen Gannon 215-446-4963
e-mail: maureen.gannon@gsa.gov
Regional Counsel:
Carol Latterman 212-264-8308
e-mail: carol.latterman@gsa.gov

Federal Acquisition Service
FAS Regional Commissioner:
Gregory Hammond 212-264-3590
e-mail: gregory.hammond@gsa.gov
Director, Supply & Acquisition Center:
Peter Han 212-264-6949
e-mail: peter.han@gsa.gov
Director, Fleet Management Services Division:
Brian Smith 212-264-3930
e-mail: brian.smith@gsa.gov
Director, Customer Accounts & Research Division:
Frank Mayer 212-264-1179
e-mail: frank.mayer@gsa.gov
Director, Personal Property Division:
Christina Shaw 215-446-5083
e-mail: christina.shaw@gsa.gov
Acting Director, Network Services Division:
Theresa Ramos 212-264-2690
e-mail: theresa.ramos@gsa.gov
Director, Assisted Acquisition Services Division:
Joann Lee 212-264-1885
e-mail: joann.lee@gsa.gov

Inspector General's Office
Regional Director, Audit:
Steve Jurysta 212-264-8620

Public Buildings Service
PBS Regional Commissioner:
Frank Santella 212-264-4282
e-mail: frank.santella@gsa.gov
Director, Project Management Division:
Ken Chin 212-264-0802
e-mail: ken.chin@gsa.gov
Director, Leasing Division:
Warren Hall 212-264-4241
e-mail: warren.hall@gsa.gov
Director, Facilities Management & Services Program Division:
David Segermeister 212-264-4273
e-mail: david.segermeister@gsa.gov
Director, Portfolio Management Division:
Vincent Scalcione 212-264-1547
e-mail: vincent.scalcione@gsa.gov

US Government Printing Office

e-mail: infonewyork@gpo.gov
Web site: www.gpo.gov

Region 2-I (New York)
Printing Procurement Office . . . . fax: 212-264-2413
26 Federal Plaza, Room 2930, New York, NY 10278
212-264-2252 Fax: 212-264-2413
Manager:
Debra Rozdzielski

US Postal Service

Web site: www.usps.com

NORTHEAST AREA (Includes part of New York State)
6 Griffin Road North, Windsor, CT 06006-7070
800-275-8777
Vice President, Delivery Operations:
Edward F. Phelan Jr.

US State Department

Web site: www.state.gov

Bureau of Educational & Cultural Affairs-NY Pgm Branch
666 Fifth Avenue, Suite 603, New York, NY 10103
212-399-5750
Web site: www.eca.state.gov
Director:
Donna F. Shirreffs 212-399-5750

US Mission to the United Nations
799 UN Plaza, New York, NY 10017
US Permanent Representative to the United Nations:
Samantha Power
US Deputy Permanent Representative to the United Nations:
Michele J. Sison
Alternate Representative for Special Political Affairs to the United Nations:
David Pressman
US Representative on the Economic & Social Council at the United Nations:
Sarah Mendelson
US Representative to the United Nations for UN Management & Reform:
Isobel Coleman

U.S. CONGRESS

See U.S. Congress Chapter for additional Standing Committee and Subcommittee information.

House of Representatives Standing Committees

Oversight & Government Reform
Chair:
Jason Chaffetz (R-UT) 202-225-7751
Ranking Member:
Elijah Cummings (D-MD) 202-225-4741
New York Delegate:
Carolyn B. Maloney (D) 202-225-7944

Homeland Security
Chair:
Michael McCaul (R-TX) 202-225-2401
Ranking Member:
Bennie G. Thompson (D-MS) 202-225-5876
New York Delegate:
Brian Higgins (D) 202-225-3306
New York Delegate:
Kathleen M. Rice (D) 202-225-5516
New York Delegate:
Peter T. King (R) 202-225-7896

New York Delegate:
John Katko (R) 202-225-3701
New York Delegate:
Dan Donovan (R) 202-225-3371

Subcommittees

Emergency Preparedness, Response and Communications

Chair:
Dan Donovan (R-NY) 202-225-3371
Ranking Member:
Donald M. Payne (D-NJ)...................... 202-225-3436

Cybersecurity, Infrastructure Protection, and Security Technologies

Chair:
John Ratcliffe (R-TX) 202-225-6673
Ranking Member:
Cedric L. Richmond (D-LA).................... 202-225-6636

Counterterrorism & Intelligence

Chair:
Peter T. King (R-NY) 202-225-7896
Ranking Member:
Brian Higgins (D-NY)........................... 202-225-3306

Oversight & Management Efficiency

Chair:
Scott Perry (R-PA).............................. 202-225-5836
Ranking Member:
Bonnie Watson Coleman (D-NJ)................ 202-225-5801

Transportation Security

Chair:
John Katko (R-NY) 202-225-3701
Ranking Member:
Kathleen M. Rice (D-NY)....................... 202-225-5516

Intelligence, Permanent Select Committee on

Chair:
Devin Nunes (R-CA) 202-225-2523
Ranking Member:
Adam Schiff (D-CA) 202-225-4176

Subcommittee

Emerging Threats

Chair:
Tom Rooney (R-FL) 202-225-5792
Ranking Member:
Mike Quigley (D-IL)............................. 202-225-4061

Ethics

Chair:
Charles W. Dent (R-PA).............................. 202-225-6411
Ranking Member:
Linda T. Sanchez (D-CA).............................. 202-225-6676

Senate Standing Committees

Ethics, Select Committee on

Chair:
Johnny Isakson (R-GA) 202-224-3643
Vice Chair:
Barbara Boxer (D-CA) 202-224-3553

Homeland Security & Governmental Affairs

Chair:
Ron Johnson (R-WI)................................... 202-224-5323
Ranking Member:
Thomas R. Carper (D-DE) 202-224-2441

Indian Affairs, Committee on

Chair:
John Barrasso (R-WY) 202-224-6441
Vice Chair:
Jon Tester (D-MT) 202-224-2644

Intelligence, Select Committee on

Chair:
Richard Burr (R-NC) 202-224-3154
Vice Chair:
Dianne Feinstein (D-CA) 202-224-3841

Judiciary

Chair:
Chuck Grassley (R-IA)................................ 202-224-3744
Ranking Member:
Patrick Leahy (D-VT)................................. 202-224-4242
New York Delegate:
Charles E. Schumer (D) 202-224-6542

Subcommittees

Crime & Terrorism

Chair:
Lindsey Graham (R-SC) 202-224-5972
Ranking Member:
Sheldon Whitehouse (D-RI) 202-224-2921

Immigration and The National Interest

Chair:
Jeff Sessions (R-AL) 202-224-4124
Ranking Member:
Charles E. Schumer (D-NY) 202-224-6542

PRIVATE SECTOR

Academy of Political Science

475 Riverside Drive, Suite 1274, New York, NY 10115-1274
212-870-2500 Fax: 212-870-2202
e-mail: aps@psqonline.org
Web site: www.psqonline.org
Analysis of government, economic & social issues
Demetrios James Caraley, President

Albany Law School, Government Law Center

80 New Scotland Avenue, Albany, NY 12208-3494
518-445-2311
e-mail: rbres@albanylaw.edu
Web site: www.albanylaw.edu
Legal aspects of public policy reform
Ray Brescia, Director, Government Law Center & Associate Professor of Law

Association of Government Accountants, NY Capital Chapter

PO Box 1923, Albany, NY 12201
Web site: www.aganycap.org
Education for the government financial management community
Jamie Cote, Chapter President

Center for Governmental Research Inc (CGR)

1 South Washington Street, Suite 400, Rochester, NY 14614-1135
585-325-6360 Fax: 888-388-8521
e-mail: info@cgr.org
Web site: www.cgr.org
Nonprofit institution devoted to providing policy analysis in the areas of government, education, economics, public finance, health & human services
Dr. Joseph Stefko, President & Chief Executive Officer

Center for Technology in Government, University at Albany, SUNY

187 Wolf Road, Suite 301, Albany, NY 12205-1138
518-442-3892 Fax: 518-442-3886
e-mail: info@ctg.albany.edu
Web site: www.ctg.albany.edu
Works to enhance the quality of government & public services through research, partnership projects & the development of innovative strategies in technology, policy & management
Theresa Pardo, Director

Policy Areas

Citizens Union of the City of New York
299 Broadway, Suite 700, New York, NY 10007-1978
212-227-0342 Fax: 212-227-0345
e-mail: citizens@citizensunion.org
Web site: www.citizensunion.org
Government watchdog organization; city & state public policy issues; political & government reform
Dick Dadey, Executive Director

Coalition of Fathers & Families NY, PAC
PO Box 252, Stillwater, NY 12170
518-288-6755
e-mail: info@fafny.org
Web site: www.fafny.org
Political action for fathers & families in New York
Jack Frost, President

Columbia University, Exec Graduate Pgm in Public Policy & Administration
420 West 118th Street, Room 1408, New York, NY 10027
212-854-4445 Fax: 212-864-3748
e-mail: sc32@columbia.edu
Web site: www.sipa.columbia.edu
Urban & environmental policy; public management
Steven Cohen, Director, Program in Environmental Science & Policy

Common Cause/NY
80 Broad Street, New York, NY 10004
212-691-6421 Fax: 212-807-1809
e-mail: nyoffice@commoncause.org
Web site: www.commoncause.org/states/new-york/
Campaign finance reform, ballot access, political gift disclosure & public interest lobbying
Susan Lerner, Executive Director

NYS Bar Assn, Task Force to Review Terrorism Legislation Cmte
Connors LLP
1000 Liberty Building, 424 Main Street, Buffalo, NY 14202-3510
716-852-5533 Fax: 716-852-5649
Web site: www.connorsllp.com
Vincent E. Doyle, III, Partner

Council of State Governments, Eastern Conference
22 Cortlandt Street, 22nd Floor, New York, NY 10007
212-482-2320 Fax: 212-482-2344
e-mail: info_erc@csg.org
Web site: www.csg-erc.org
Training, research & information sharing for state government officials
Wendell Hannaford, Regional Director

Crane & Parente, PLLC
48 Howard Street, Albany, NY 12207
518-432-8000
Governmental relations, banking & financial services, corporate law, construction law, energy, utilities, communications, land use, environmental & wireless telecommunications law
James B. Crane, II, Managing Member

DeGraff, Foy & Kunz, LLP
41 State Street, Albany, NY 12207
518-462-5300 Fax: 518-436-0210
e-mail: inquiry@dfklawfirm.com
Web site: www.degraff-foy.com
Government relations, administrative law & tax exempt/municipal financing, education, energy, transportation, public authorities & the environment
David F. Kunz, Managing Partner

Fiscal Policy Institute
1 Lear Jet Lane, Latham, NY 12110
518-786-3156 Fax: 518-786-3146
e-mail: deutsch@fiscalpolicy.org
Web site: www.fiscalpolicy.org
Nonpartisan research & education; tax, budget, economic & related public policy issues that affect quality of life & economic well-being
Ron Deutsch, Executive Director

Fordham University, Department of Political Science
441 East Fordham Road, Bronx, NY 10458
718-817-3964
e-mail: rhume@fordham.edu
Web site: www.fordham.edu
American politics & political theory; importance of gender in understanding modes of governance; campaign management
Dr. Robert J. Hume, Department Chair

Geto & de Milly Inc
276 Fifth Avenue, Suite 806, New York, NY 10001
212-686-4551 Fax: 212-213-6850
e-mail: pr@getodemilly.com
Web site: www.getodemilly.com
Public & government relations
Ethan Geto, President

NYS Bar Assn, Legislative Policy Cmte
Greenberg Traurig, LLP
54 State Street, 6th Floor, Albany, NY 12207
518-689-1400 Fax: 518-689-1499
e-mail: info@gtlaw.com
Web site: www.gtlaw.com
Henry M. Greenberg, Partner

Institute of Public Administration/NYU Wagner
295 Lafayette Street, 2nd Floor, New York, NY 10012-9604
212-998-7400
e-mail: wagner.officeofthedean@nyu.edu
Web site: www.wagner.nyu.edu
Public policy & public service research, consulting & educational institute
Sherry Glied, Dean & Professor of Public Service

KPMG LLP
515 Broadway, Albany, NY 12207-2974
518-427-4600 Fax: 518-689-4717
e-mail: us-mktwebmaster@kpmg.com
Web site: www.kpmg.com
State & local government audit & advisory service
Nancy Valley, Managing Partner

League of Women Voters of New York State
62 Grand Street, Albany, NY 12207-2712
518-465-4162 Fax: 518-465-0812
e-mail: laura@lwvny.org
Web site: www.lwvny.org
Public policy issues forum; good government advocacy
Laura Ladd Bierman, Executive Director

Manhattan Institute for Policy Research
52 Vanderbilt Avenue, 2nd Floor, New York, NY 10017
212-599-7000 Fax: 212-599-3494
e-mail: communications@manhattan-institute.org
Web site: www.manhattan-institute.org
Produces & promotes research on taxes, welfare, education & other public policy issues
Lawrence J. Mone, President

Offices and agencies generally appear in alphabetical order, except when specific order is requested by listee.

NYS Bar Assn, Court Structure & Judicial Selection Cmte
McMahon & Grow
301 North Washington Street, PO Box 4350, Rome, NY 13442-4350
315-336-4700 Fax: 315-336-5851
e-mail: rsimons@mgglaw.com
Web site: www.mgglaw.com
Retired Judge-NYS Court of Appeals
Hon Richard D. Simons, Chair

NYS Bar Assn, Federal Constitution & Legislation Cmte
Mulholland & Knapp, LLP
110 East 42nd Street, Suite 1302, New York, NY 10017
212-702-9027 Fax: 212-702-9092
e-mail: admin@mklex.com
Web site: www.mklex.com
Robert P. Knapp, III, Chair

NY Coalition of 100 Black Women - Not For Profit
PO Box 2555, Grand Central Station, New York, NY 10163
212-517-5700
Web site: www.cobwfounders.org
Leadership by example; advocates & agents for change; improving the quality of life by focusing resources in education, health & community services
Avalyn Simon, President

NY StateWatch Inc
126 State Street, 4th Floor, Albany, NY 12207
518-449-7425
e-mail: mikep@statewatch.com
Web site: www.nystatewatch.net
Legislative information service; bill tracking
Michael Poulopoulos, Director

NYS Association of Counties
540 Broadway, 5th Floor, Albany, NY 12207
518-465-1473 Fax: 518-465-0506
Web site: www.nysac.org
Lobbying, research & training services
Stephen J. Acquario, Executive Director

NYS Bar Assn, Mass Disaster Response Committee
NYS Grievance Committee
Renaissance Plaza, 335 Adams Street, Suite 2400, Brooklyn, NY 11201-3745
718-923-6300 Fax: 718-624-2978

NYS Bar Assn, Law Youth & Citizenship Committee
NYS Supreme Court
92 Franklin Street, 2nd Floor, Buffalo, NY 14202
716-845-9327 Fax: 716-851-5163
Oliver C. Young, Principal Court Attorney

Nelson A Rockefeller Institute of Government
411 State Street, Albany, NY 12203-1003
518-443-5522 Fax: 518-443-5788
e-mail: info@rockinst.suny.edu
Web site: www.rockinst.org
Management & finance, welfare, social services, health, education, homeland security & public safety at state & local levels of government
Thomas L. Gais, Director

New York Public Interest Research Group
9 Murray Street, Lower Level, New York, NY 10007
212-349-6460 Fax: 212-349-1366
Web site: www.nypirg.org
Environmental preservation, public health, consumer protection & government reform
Blair Horner, Executive Director

New York State Directory
4919 Route 22, PO Box 56, Amenia, NY 12501
518-789-8700 or 800-562-2139 Fax: 518-789-0556
e-mail: books@greyhouse.com
Web site: www.greyhouse.com
State government public policy directory
Leslie Mackenzie, Publisher

Pioneer Savings Bank
21 Second Street, Troy, NY 12180
518-687-5400 Fax: 518-274-1060
Web site: www.pioneerbanking.com
Thomas L. Amell, President & Chief Executive Officer

PricewaterhouseCoopers LLP
3600 HSBC Center, Buffalo, NY 14203-2879
716-856-4650 Fax: 716-856-1208
Web site: www.pwc.com
Mark Ross, Managing Partner

Spec Cmte on Collateral Consequence of Criminal Proceedings
Proskauer Rose LLP
11 Times Square, New York, NY 10036
212-969-3000 Fax: 212-969-2900
e-mail: info@proskauer.com
Web site: www.proskauer.com
Peter J.W. Sherwin, Partner

Public Agenda
6 East 39th Street, 9th Floor, New York, NY 10016
212-686-6610 Fax: 212-889-3461
e-mail: info@publicagenda.org
Web site: www.publicagenda.org
Nonpartisan, nonprofit organization dedicated to conducting unbiased public opinion research & producing fair-minded citizen education materials
Will Friedman, President

SUNY at Albany, Center for Women in Government & Civil Society
135 Western Avenue, Draper Hall, Room 302, Albany, NY 12222
518-442-3900 Fax: 518-442-3877
e-mail: cwgcs@albany.edu
Web site: www.cwig.albany.edu
Works to strengthen women's public policy leadership & advance equality in government, nonprofit & business sectors through education, research, leadership development & advocacy for equitable policies & practices
Dina Refki, Executive Director

SUNY at Albany, Rockefeller College
135 Western Avenue, Albany, NY 12222
518-442-5244 Fax: 518-442-5298
e-mail: hildreth@albany.edu
Web site: www.albany.edu/rockefeller
Intergovernmental relations; NY state & local government; ethics in government; election systems & voting
Anne Hildreth, Associate Professor

SUNY at New Paltz, College of Liberal Arts & Sciences
1 Hawk Drive, New Paltz, NY 12561-2499
845-257-7869 or 877-696-7411
e-mail: barrettl@newpaltz.edu
Web site: www.newpaltz.edu
Local & state government process & structure; regionalism; politics & election law
Laura Barrett, Dean

SUNY at New Paltz, Department of History
600 Hawk Drive, New Paltz, NY 12561-2440
845-257-3545 Fax: 845-257-2735
Web site: www.newpaltz.edu/history/
Historical studies of legal systems, economic & business institutions, technology, cultures & societies

Policy Areas

Andrew Evans, Chair

Syracuse University, Maxwell School of Citizenship & Public Affairs
200 Eggers Hall, Syracuse, NY 13244-1020
315-443-2252
e-mail: info@maxwell.syr.edu
Web site: www.maxwell.syr.edu
Education, healthcare, entrpreneurship policies, social welfare, income distribution & comparative social policies
James B. Steinberg, Dean

Offices and agencies generally appear in alphabetical order, except when specific order is requested by listee.

HEALTH

NEW YORK STATE

GOVERNOR'S OFFICE

Governor's Office
Executive Chamber
State Capitol
Albany, NY 12224
518-474-8390 Fax: 518-474-1513
Web site: www.ny.gov

Governor:
Andrew M Cuomo 518-474-8390
Secretary to the Governor:
William Mulrow 518-474-4246
Counsel to the Governor:
Alphonso David 518-474-8343
Deputy Secretary, Health & Human Services:
Paul Francis. 518-408-2500
Chief of Staff:
Melissa DeRosa . . . . 518-474-8418 or 212-681-4640
Director, Communications:
James Allen. . . . . 518-474-8418 or 212-681-4640

EXECUTIVE DEPARTMENTS AND RELATED AGENCIES

Alcoholism & Substance Abuse Services, Office of
1450 Western Ave
Albany, NY 12203
518-473-3460 Fax: 518-457-5474
e-mail: communications@oasas.ny.gov
Web site: www.oasas.ny.gov

501 7th Ave
8th Fl
New York, NY 10018
646-728-4533

Commissioner:
Arlene Gonzalez-Sanchez. 518-457-2061
Executive Deputy Commissioner:
Sean M. Byrne 518-485-2337

Bureau of Public Information & Communications
Director, Public Information & Communications:
Susan A Craig, MPH 518-457-8299

Office of Counsel & Internal Controls
Director:
Robert Kent. 518-485-2312
Office of Audit Services:
Steven Shrager 518-485-2053
Internal Control Unit:
Sandra Scleicher 518-485-1109

Office of Governmental Affairs & Grants Mgmt
Director:
Patricia Zuber-Wilson. 518-485-1484

Office of NYC Operations, Affirmative Action & Bureau of Recovery
COO:
Ramon Rodriguez 646-728-4720
Affirmative Action Unit Officer:
Loretta Poole. 646-728-4530
Recovery Initiatives:
Lureen McNeil 518-457-6750

Office of Medical Director
Medical Director:
Charles W Morgan, MD 845-359-8500
Director, Health Initiatives:
Peggy Bonneau 518-457-5989

Fiscal Administration Division
Associate Commissioner:
P David Sawicki 518-457-5312

Bureau of Budget Management
Director:
Tara Gabriel 518-485-2193

Bureau of Capital Management
Director:
Jeff Emad 518-457-2545

Bureau of Financial Management
Director:
Kevin Doherty 518-457-3562

Bureau of Health Care Financing & 3rd Party Reimbursement
Director:
Laurie Felter 518-457-5312

Outcome Management & System Information Division
Associate Commissioner:
William F. Hogan 518-485-2322

Bureau of State/Local Planning
Director:
Vacant. 518-485-2322

Bureau of Data Analysis, Data Quality & Evaluation
Director:
Vacant. 518-485-7189

Bureau of Research, Epidemiology & Practice Improvement
Director:
Vacant. 518-485-5989

Office of Statewide Field Operations
Director:
Sean Byrne 518-485-2337

Prevention, Housing & Management Services Division
Acting Associate Commissioner:
Mary Ann DiChristopher 518-485-6022

Bureau of Housing
Director:
Henri Williams 518-485-0496

Bureau of Prevention Services
Director:
Scott Brady 518-457-4384

Bureau of Management Services
Director:
Vacant. 518-485-6689

Information Technology Services
Director:
Laura Frost 518-485-2351

Quality Assurance & Performance Improvement Division
Associate Commissioner:
Charles W Monson 518-485-2257

Bureau of Certification & Systems Management
Director:
Janet Paloski 518-485-2250

Offices and agencies generally appear in alphabetical order, except when specific order is requested by listee.

Bureau of Standards Compliance
Director:
Vacant....................518-485-2255

Bureau of Talent Management & Credentializing
Director:
Julia Fesko....................518-485-2033

Treatment & Practice Innovation Division
Associate Commissioner:
Steve Hanson....................518-457-7077

Bureau of Addiction Treatment Centers
Assistant Director:
Paula Bradwell....................518-457-7077 or 585-461-0410

Education Department
State Education Bldg
89 Washington Ave
Albany, NY 12234
518-474-3852 Fax: 518-486-5631
Web site: www.nysed.gov

Commissione & University President:
MaryEllen Elia....................518-474-5844
Executive Deputy Commissioner:
Elizabeth Berlin....................518-473-8381
General Counsel:
Robert Trautwein....................518-474-6400
e-mail: legal@nysed.gov
Office of Innovation and School Reform:
Cheryl Atkinson....................518-473-8852

Office of the Professions....................fax: 518-474-1449
89 Washington Ave, EB, 2nd Fl, West Mezz, Albany, NY 12234
Fax: 518-474-1449
Web site: www.op.nysed.gov
Deputy Commissioner:
Douglas Lentivech....................518-486-1765 or 518-474-3817 x440

Office of Professional Responsibility
Director, Professional Examinations:
Harrison Fisher....................518-474-3817 x290

Professional Education Program Review
Assistant Director:
Mei Zhou....................518-474-3817 x360
e-mail: opprogs@nysed.gov

Professional Licensing Services
Director:
Susan Naccarato....................518-474-3817 x340

Health Department
Corning Tower
Empire State Plaza
Albany, NY 12237
518-474-2011
Web site: wwww.health.ny.gov

Office of the Commissioner
Commissioner:
Howard Zucker, MD, JD....................518-474-2011
Executive Deputy Commissioner:
Sally Dreslin, MS, RN....................518-474-2011

Division of Administration
Deputy Commissioner, Administration:
Michael J. Nazarko....................518-474-8565

AIDS Institute
Director:
Dan O'Connell....................212-417-5500 or 518-473-6399
Deputy Director, HIV Health Care, Surveillance & Data Systems:
Mona Scully....................518-474-8404
Deputy Director, Office Medicaid Policy & Programs:
Ira Feldman....................518-486-1383
Deputy Director, Surveillance, Prevention, Drug User Health & Administration:
Valerie White....................518-474-5577
Director, DEER:
James Tesoriero....................518-473-3379
Assistant Director, NYC Office:
Joan Edwards....................212-417-4508
Medical Director, Office of the Medical Director:
Bruce D Agins....................212-417-4536
Deputy Director, Office of the Medical Director:
Lyn Stevens....................518-473-8815

Center for Community Health
Director:
Vacant....................518-473-4371
Associate Director:
Adrienne Mazeau....................518-473-4371/fax: 518-473-8389

Chronic Disease Prevention & Adult Health Division
Director:
Barbara Wallace....................518-474-0512/fax: 518-474-5396
Associate Director:
Rachel Iverson....................518-474-0512/fax: 518-474-5396

Epidemiology Division
Director:
Debra Blog, M.D.....................518-473-4464/fax: 518-473-2301
Associate Director:
Stephanie Ostrowski....................518-473-4465/fax: 518-473-2301

Family Health Division
Director:
Lauren Tobias....................518-474-6968/fax: 518-474-7054
Associate Director:
Wendy Shaw....................518-474-6968
Medical Director:
Marilyn Kacica....................518-473-9883
Associate Medical Director:
Christopher A Kus....................518-473-9883

Information Technology & Project Management
Director:
Linh Le....................518-473-1809/fax: 518-486-1632
Assistant Director:
Audra McDonald....................518-408-1121

Minority Health
Director:
Yvonne Graham....................518-474-2180/fax: 518-474-4695

Nutrition Division
Director:
Loretta Santilli....................518-402-7090/fax: 518-402-1149
Associate Director:
Patricia Race....................518-402-7090/fax: 518-402-1149
Associate Director:
Jill Dunkel....................518-402-7090/fax: 518-402-1149

Center for Environmental Health
Director:
Dr. Nathan Graber....................518-402-7500

Division of Environmental Health Assessment
Director:
Kevin Gleason....................518-402-7511

Offices and agencies generally appear in alphabetical order, except when specific order is requested by listee.

Division of Environmental Health Investigation
Director:
Vacant 518-402-7510

Division of Environmental Health Protection
Director:
Michael Cambridge 518-402-7500

Office of Governmental & External Affairs
Assistant Commissioner:
Amy Nickson 518-473-1124/fax: 518-473-9674

Division of Council Operations
Deputy Director:
Kelly Seebald 518-474-8009

Division of External Affairs
Deputy Director:
Angie Corsi 518-473-8007

Division of Governmental Affairs
Deputy Director:
Esti Alonso 518-473-1124

Office of Health Insurance Programs
Deputy Commissioner & State Medicaid Director:
Jason A. Helgerson 518-474-3018/fax: 518-486-1346
Deputy Director:
Elizabeth Misa 518-474-8646/fax: 518-486-1346
Medical Director:
Alda Osinaga, MD 518-486-1042
Medical Director:
Douglas Fish, MD 518-473-0919
Director, Division of Eligibility & Marketplace Integration:
Judith Arnold 518-474-0180
Director, Division of OHIP Operations Systems:
Anton Venter 518-433-3453
Director, Division of OHIP Operations:
Jonathan Bick 518-474-8161
Director, Division of Health Plan Contracting & Oversight:
Vallencia Lloyd 518-474-5737
Director, Division of Program Development & Mngmnt:
Gregory Allen 518-473-0919
Director & CFO, Division of Finance & Rate Setting:
John Ulberg 518-474-6350
Director, Division of Long Term Care:
Mark Kissinger 518-402-5673
Director, Division of Employee & Program Support:
Ralph Bielefeldt 518-486-5386

Office of Quality & Patient Safety
Director:
Patrick Roohan 518-473-2941
Deputy Director:
Joseph Anarella 518-486-9012
Medical Director:
Foster Gesten, MD, FACP 518-486-6865

Office of Public Health
Deputy Commissioner:
Brad Hutton, MPH 518-473-0771
Deputy Director:
Ellen Anderson 518-473-0771
Director, Office of Public Health Practice:
Sylvia Pirani 518-473-4223
Director, Health Emergency Preparedness:
Michael Primeau 518-474-2893

School of Public Health, SUNY at Albany . . . . . fax: 518-402-0329
One University Place, Rensselaer, NY 12144
518-402-0283 Fax: 518-402-0329
Dean:
Philip C Nasca PhD 518-402-0281/fax: 518-402-0329
Assistant Dean, Administration:
Deb Oriola 518-402-0281

Health Facilities Management
Director:
David J Hernandez 518-474-2772/fax: 518-474-0611

Helen Hayes Hospital
Rte 9W, West Haverstraw, NY 10993-1195
845-786-4000
e-mail: info@helenhayeshospital.org
Web site: www.helenhayeshospital.org
CEO:
Edmund Coletti 845-786-4202/fax: 845-947-0036
COO:
Kathleen Martucci 845-786-4201

New York State Veterans' Home at Batavia
220 Richmond Ave, Batavia, NY 14020
585-345-2000
Web site: www.nysvets.org
Administrator:
Joanne I Hernick 585-345-2076/fax: 585-345-9030
Acting Medical Director:
Margaret Mitchell, MD 585-345-2042
Director, Nursing:
Stephanie Sulyma 585-345-2000 x2041

New York State Veterans' Home at Montrose . . . . . fax: 914-788-6100
2090 Albany Post Rd, Montrose, NY 10548
Fax: 914-788-6100
Web site: www.nysvets.org
Administrator:
Nancy Baa-Danso 914-788-6003
Acting Medical Director:
George Gorich, MD 914-788-6025
Director, Nursing:
Christene St Paul Joseph 914-788-6021

New York State Veterans' Home at Oxford
4211 State Highway 220, Oxford, NY 13830
607-843-3100
Web site: www.nysvets.org
Administrator:
James Wyzykowski 607-843-3129/fax: 607-843-3199
Medical Director:
Donna Hussman, MD 607-843-3140

New York State Veterans' Home at St Albans
178-50 Linden Blvd, Jamaica, NY 11434-1467
718-990-0300
Administrator:
Neville Goldson 718-990-0329
Medical Director:
Thomas Bizarro MD 718-990-0328
Director, Nursing:
Elmina Wilson-Hew 718-990-0316

Health Research Inc
Riverview Center, 150 Broadway, Ste 560, Menands, NY 12204-2719
Web site: www.healthresearch.org
Executive Director:
Cheryl Mattox 518-431-1204

Office of Primary Care & Health Systems Management
Deputy Commissioner:
Daniel B Sheppard 518-474-1686
Deputy Director & Director, Office of Professional Medical Conduct:
Keith W Servis 518-408-1828
Director, Planning & Performance Group (PPG):
Paul Ambrose 518-486-9177
Director, Administrative Mgmnt Services Group (AMS):
Karyn Andrade 518-486-9177
Director, Data Management, Analysis & Research Group (DAR):
Ying Wang 518-473-7019

Offices and agencies generally appear in alphabetical order, except when specific order is requested by listee.

Assistant Director, Center for Health Care Provider Services & Oversight (PSO):
Mark Hennessey 518-485-9914
Director, Division of Adult Care Facilities & Assisted Living Surveillance:
Valerie Deetz 518-408-1133
Deputy Director, Division of Adult Care Facilities & Assisted Living Surveillance:
Timothy Perry-Coon. 518-408-1133
Director, Bureau of Emergency Medical Services:
Lee Burns 518-402-0997
Deputy Director, Office of Professional Medical Conduct (OPMC):
Paula M Breen. 518-402-0855
Director, Division of Nursing Homes & Intermediate Care Facilities:
Shelly Glock 518-408-1267

Human Resources Management Group

Director:
Joyce M Neznek 518-473-3394/fax: 518-486-7374

Operations Management Group

Director:
John Reith 518-474-6936/fax: 518-474-8163

Office of Information Technology Services (ITS) Health Cluster

Health Cluster CIO:
John P McInnes 518-474-8373/fax: 518-474-2288
Acting Deputy CIO, Health Cluster:
Linh Le 518-474-8373/fax: 518-474-2288
Health Cluster Co-Deputy CIO:
Robert Pennacchia. 518-474-8373/fax: 518-474-2288
Health Cluster Co-Deputy CIO:
Linh Le . . . . . 518-473-1809 or 518-474-8373
fax: 518-474-2288

Legal Affairs

General Counsel:
Richard J Zahnleuter 518-474-7553/fax: 518-473-2802
Deputy General Counsel:
Elsie Chun 518-474-7553/fax: 518-473-2802
Director, Bureau of Adjudication:
James Horan 518-402-0748/fax: 518-402-0751
Director, Bureau of Administrative Hearings:
Mark Fleischer. 518-473-1707/fax: 518-486-1858
Director, Bureau of House Counsel:
Justin Pfeiffer 518-473-3233/fax: 518-473-2019
Director, Bureau of Litigation:
Michael Bass 518-473-4631/fax: 518-473-2802
Director, Bureau of Health Insurance Programs:
Daniel Tarantino 518-408-1495/fax: 518-486-4834
Director, Bureau of Health Facility Planning & Development:
Mark Furnish 518-473-3303/fax: 518-473-2019
Chief Counsel, Professional Medical Conduct Unit:
Henry Weintraub 518-474-8266/fax: 518-473-2430
Acting Records Access Officer:
Danielle Levine. 518-474-8734

Task Force On Life & The Law

90 Church St, New York, NY 10007
Executive Director:
Stuart C Sherman 212-417-5444

Public Affairs

Director:
James C Plastiras 518-474-7354 x1
Deputy Director:
Marci Natale. 518-474-7354 x1

Regional Offices

Central New York Regional Office

217 S Salina St, 3rd Fl, Syracuse, NY 13202
315-477-8100
Director:
David C. Brittain, MD 315-477-8100
Deputy Director:
Maria MacPherson 315-477-8100

Metropolitan Area/Regional Office

90 Church St, New York, NY 10007
Regional Director:
Celeste M Johnson 212-417-5550
Deputy Regional Director:
Ellen Poliski 212-417-5550

Western Regional Office

584 Delaware Ave, Buffalo, NY 14202-1295
716-847-4500
Acting Associate Commissioner:
Gregory Young. 716-847-4505

Roswell Park Cancer Institute Corporation

Elm & Carlton Streets, Buffalo, NY 14263-0999
716-845-2300
Web site: www.roswellpark.org
President/CEO:
Candace S Johnson, PhD. 716-845-5772/fax: 716-845-8261
Executive Director:
Vacant 716-845-3385
Chief Medical Officer:
Boris Kuvshinoff, MD 716-845-7724
Legal Counsel:
Michael Sexton 716-845-8717
VP, Government Affairs:
Lisa Damiani. 716-845-3079
e-mail: lisa.damiani@roswellpark.org

Wadsworth Center

Director:
Jill Taylor. 518-474-3157/fax: 518-474-3439
Deputy Director:
Vicky Derbyshire 518-474-7592
Associate Director, Administration:
Carlene Van Patten 518-474-7592
Associate Director, Research & Technology:
Erasmus Schneider 518-473-4856
Associate Director, Laboratory Operations:
Elizabeth Mahoney 518-474-1002
Associate Director, Medical Affairs:
Anne Walsh. 518-474-7592

Environmental Health Sciences

Director:
Ken Aldous 518-474-7161/fax: 518-473-2895
Deputy Director:
Patrick Parsons 518-474-7161

Genetics

Director:
Keith Derbyshire 518-473-6079
Deputy Director:
Michele Caggana 518-473-3854

Herbert W Dickerman Library . . . . . fax: 518-474-3933

518-474-6172 Fax: 518-474-3933

Infectious Disease

Director:
Ron Limberger 518-474-8660
Deputy Director:
Kathleen McDonough 518-486-4253

Laboratory Quality Certification

Director:
Michael Ryan 518-473-3424

Offices and agencies generally appear in alphabetical order, except when specific order is requested by listee.

Translational Medicine
Director:
Michael Koonce 518-486-1490
Deputy Director:
Rajendra Agrawal 518-486-5797

Financial Services Department

One State Street
New York, NY 10001
212-480-6500 or 518-474-6600
e-mail: public-affairs@dfs.ny.gov
Web site: www.dfs.ny.gov

Acting Superintendent:
Maria T Vullo 212-709-3501
Deputy Superintendent & General Counsel:
Marjorie Gross 212-709-1640
Chief Administrative Officer:
Cheryl Aini 518-473-6160
Director, Communications:
David Neustadt 212-480-5265/fax: 212-480-6077
Assistant Director, Administration & Operations:
Lori Fraser. 518-486-4737

Health Bureau

Chief:
Vacant 518-486-2970/fax: 518-474-3397

Life Bureau

Chief Examiner:
Gail Keren 212-480-5030/fax: 212-480-5329

Labor Department

Building 12, Room 500
Harriman State Office Campus
Albany, NY 12240
518-457-9000 Fax: 518-457-6908
e-mail: nysdol@labor.ny.gov
Web site: www.labor.ny.gov

Commissioner:
Roberta Reardon 518-457-9000
Director, Communications:
Leo Rosales 518-457-5519/fax: 518-485-1126
e-mail: leo.rosales@labor.ny.gov

Worker Protection

Deputy Commissioner, Workforce Protection, Standards & Licensing:
Pico Ben-Amotz 518-457-4317

Safety & Health Division
Director:
Eileen Franko 518-457-3518/fax: 518-457-1519

Asbestos Control Bureau
Program Manager:
Robert Perez 518-457-1255/fax: 518-485-8054

Industry Inspection Unit
Program Manager, License & Certification:
Martha Waldman 518-457-2375

On-Site Consultation Unit
Program Manager:
James Rush 518-457-2238/fax: 518-457-3454

Public Employees Safety & Health (PESH) Unit
Program Manager:
Normand Labbe 518-457-1263/fax: 518-457-5545

Law Department

120 Broadway
New York, NY 10271-0332
212-416-8000 or 800-771-7755
Web site: www.ag.ny.gov

State Capitol
Albany, NY 12224-0341
518-776-2000
Fax: 518-650-9401

Attorney General:
Eric T Schneiderman . . . . 212-416-8050 or 518-776-2000
Chief of Staff:
Brian Mahanna 212-416-8050
Director, Public Information:
Shawn Morris 518-776-2357/fax: 518-650-9401
Press Secretary:
Matt Mittenthal 212-416-8060/fax: 212-416-6005

Criminal Justice

Executive Deputy Attorney General:
Kelly Donovan 212-416-8050

Medicaid Fraud Control Unit
Deputy Attorney General in Charge & Director:
Amy Held 212-417-5250/fax: 212-417-4284
First Asst Attorney General, Legal Affrs:
Monica Hickey-Martin 212-417-5339/fax: 212-417-4284
First Asst Attorney General, Operations:
Florence L Finkle 212-417-5850
Deputy Regional Director, Buffalo:
Gary A Baldauf 716-853-8507/fax: 716-852-8525
Regional Director, Long Island:
Jane Turkin 631-952-6400/fax: 631-952-6382
Regional Director, Rochester:
Catherine Wagner 716-262-2860/fax: 716-262-2866
Regional Director, Syracuse:
Ralph Tortora, III 315-423-1104/fax. 315-423-1120
Deputy Regional Director, Pearl River:
Anne S Jardine 845-732-7525/fax: 845-732-7555

Social Justice

Executive Deputy Attorney General:
Alvin L Bragg, Jr. 212-416-8450/fax: 212-416-8942

Healthcare Bureau
Bureau Chief:
Lisa Landau . . . . 518-776-2477 or 212-416-6305
fax: 518-650-9365

State Counsel

Chief Deputy Attorney General & Counsel:
Jason Brown 212-416-8050
Chief Deputy Attorney General & Counsel:
Janet Sabel 212-416-8050

Claims Bureau
Bureau Chief:
Katharine Brooks . . . . 518-776-2300 or 212-416-8500

Litigation Bureau
Bureau Chief:
Jeffrey Dvorin . . . . 518-776-2300 or 212-416-8610

CORPORATIONS, AUTHORITIES AND COMMISSIONS

New York State Dormitory Authority

515 Broadway
Albany, NY 12207-2964
518-257-3000 Fax: 518-257-3100
e-mail: dabonds@dasny.org
Web site: www.dasny.org

Offices and agencies generally appear in alphabetical order, except when specific order is requested by listee.

Policy Areas

One Penn Plaza
52nd Fl
New York, NY 10119-0098
212-273-5000
Fax: 212-273-5121

539 Franklin St
Buffalo, NY 14202-1109
716-884-9780
Fax: 716-884-9787

Chair:
Alfonso L Carney Jr 518-257-3000/fax: 518-257-3100
President/CEO:
Paul T Williams Jr. 518-257-3180/fax: 518-257-3183
Vice President:
Michael T Corrigan 518-257-3192/fax: 518-257-3183
Chief Financial Officer:
Linda H Button 518-257-3562/fax: 518-257-3100
General Counsel:
Michael Cusack 518-257-3120/fax: 518-257-3101
Managing Director, Construction:
Stephen D Curro, PE 518-257-3271/fax: 518-257-3100
e-mail: scurro@dasny.org
Managing Director, Public Finance & Portfolio Monitoring:
Portia Lee. 518-257-3362/fax: 518-257-3100
e-mail: plee@dasny.org
Public Information Officer:
John Chirlin. 518-257-3380
e-mail: jchirlin@dasny.org

NEW YORK STATE LEGISLATURE

See Legislative Branch in Section 1 for additional Standing Committee and Subcommittee information.

Assembly Standing Committees

Aging
Chair:
Steven Cymbrowitz (D) 518-455-5214
Ranking Minority Member:
Angela M Wozniak (C). 518-455-5921

Alcoholism & Drug Abuse
Chair:
Linda Rosenthal (D) 518-455-5802
Ranking Minority Member:
Mark Johns (R) 518-455-5784

Children & Families
Chair:
Donna Lupardo (D). 518-455-5431
Ranking Minority Member:
Stevenr McLaughlin (R) 518-455-5777

Consumer Affairs & Protection
Chair:
Jeffrey Dinowitz (D). 518-455-5965
Ranking Minority Member:
Anthony Palumbo (R). 518-455-5294

Health
Chair:
Richard N Gottfried (D) 518-455-4941
Ranking Minority Member:
Andrew Raia (R). 518-455-5952

Senate Standing Committees

Aging
Chair:
Sue Serino (R). 518-455-2945
Ranking Minority Member:
Ruben Diaz Sr (D) 518-455-2511

Children & Families
Chair:
Tony Avella (D) 518-455-2210
Ranking Minority Member:
Velmanette Montgomery (D) 518-455-3451

Consumer Protection
Chair:
Michael Venditto (R) 518-455-3341
Ranking Minority Member:
Leroy Comrie (D) 518-455-2701

Health
Chair:
Kemp Hannon (R). 518-455-2200
Ranking Minority Member:
J. Gustavo Rivera (D) 518-455-3395

Social Services
Chair:
David Carlucci (D) 518-455-2991

U.S. GOVERNMENT

EXECUTIVE DEPARTMENTS AND RELATED AGENCIES

US Department of Agriculture
Web site: www.usda.gov

Food & Nutrition Service

Northeast Regional Office
10 Causeway Street, Room 501, Boston, MA 02222-1069
Acting Regional Administrator:
Kurt Messner

New York City Field Office
201 Varick Street, Room 609, New York, NY 10014
212-620-6307
Section Chief:
Denise Thomas 212-620-6338

Food Safety & Inspection Service
Web site: www.fsis.usda.gov

Field Operations-Philadelphia District Office (includes New York) fax: 215-597-4217
701 Market Street, Suite 4100A, Philadelphia, PA 19106
215-597-4219 Fax: 215-597-4217
District Manager:
Susan Scarcia 215-430-6302

US Department of Health & Human Services
Web site: www.hhs.gov

Administration for Children & Families . . . . fax: 212-264-4881
26 Federal Plaza, Room 4114, New York, NY 10278
212-264-2890 Fax: 212-264-4881
Web site: www.acf.hhs.gov
Regional Administrator:
Joyce A. Thomas

Administration on Aging . . . . fax: 212-264-0114
26 Federal Plaza, Room 38-102, New York, NY 10278
212-264-2976 Fax: 212-264-0114
Web site: www.aoa.gov
Regional Administrator:
Kathleen Otte
e-mail: kathleen.otte@acl.hhs.gov

Centers for Disease Control & Prevention
Web site: www.cdc.gov

Agency for Toxic Substances & Disease Registry-EPA Region 2
290 Broadway North, 20th Floor, New York, NY 10007
Web site: www.atsdr.cdc.gov
Regional Director:
Leah Graziano, RS 212-637-4306
e-mail: lge2@cdc.gov

New York Quarantine Station . . . . fax: 718-553-1524
JFK International Airport, Terminal 4, Room 219.016, 2nd Floor, East Concourse, Jamaica, NY 11430-1081
718-553-1685 Fax: 718-553-1524
Officer-in-Charge:
Donald Spatz

Centers for Medicare & Medicaid Services
26 Federal Plaza, Room 3811, New York, NY 10278-0063
Web site: www.cms.gov
Regional Administrator:
Raymond Hurd 617-565-1188
e-mail: robosora@cms.hhs.gov
Deputy Regional Administrator:
Dr. Gilbert Kunken 212-616-2205/fax: 212-264-6189
e-mail: gilbert.kunken@cms.hhs.gov

Medicaid and Children's Health Operations
Associate Regional Administrator:
Michael Melendez 212-616-2430
e-mail: ronydmch@cms.hhs.gov

Medicare Financial Management & Fee for Service Operations
Associate Regional Administrator:
Victoria Abril 212-616-2505

Medicare Quality Improvement and Survey & Certification Operations
Associate Regional Administrator:
William R. Taylor. 617-565-1323
e-mail: robosdqi@cms.hhs.gov

Food & Drug Administration
888-463-6332
Web site: www.fda.gov

Northeast Region
158-15 Liberty Avenue, Jamaica, NY 11433
Deputy Regional Director:
W. Charles Becoat

New York District Office
District Director:
Ronald Pace

Northeast Regional Laboratory
158-15 Liberty Avenue, Jamaica, NY 11433
Director:
Vacant

Health Resources & Svcs Admin-Region 2
26 Federal Plaza, Room 3337, New York, NY 10278
212-264-4498
Regional Administrator:
Ronald Moss 212-264-2664
e-mail: ronald.moss@hrsa.hhs.gov
Deputy Regional Administrator:
Cheryl Donald 212-264-4498
e-mail: cheryl.donald@hrsa.hhs.gov
Senior Public Health Analyst:
George Pourakis 212-264-4498
e-mail: george.pourakis@hrsa.hhs.gov

Indian Health Services-Area Office
5600 Fishers Lane, Rockville, MD 20857
301-443-3593
Principal Deputy Director:
Mary L. Smith 301-443-3593

Office of Assistant Secretary for Preparedness & Response
Web site: www.phe.gov

National Disaster Medical System
200 Independence Avenue SW, Room 638G, Washington, DC 20201
Acting Director:
Ron Miller

Office of Secretary's Regional Representative-Region 2-NY . . fax: 212-264-3620
26 Federal Plaza, Suite 3835, New York, NY 10278
212-264-4600 Fax: 212-264-3620
Regional Director:
Jackie Cornell-Bechelli

Office for Civil Rights . . . . fax: 202-619-3818
26 Federal Plaza, Suite 3312, New York, NY 10278
Fax: 202-619-3818
Web site: www.hhs.gov/ocr
Regional Manager:
Linda Colon 212-264-3313

Office of General Counsel
26 Federal Plaza, Room 3908, New York, NY 10278
Chief Counsel:
Joel Lerner 212-264-6373

Office of Inspector General
Regional Inspector General, Audit:
James P. Edert. 212-264-4620
Regional Special Agent in Charge of Investigations:
Scott J. Lampert
Regional Inspector General, Evaluations & Inspections:
Jodi Nudelman

Office of the Assistant Secretary for Health (ASH)
26 Federal Plaza, Suite 3835, New York, NY 10278
Regional Health Administrator:
Michelle S. Davis 212-264-2560
Regional Public Affairs Specialist:
Karina Aguilar 212-264-2535
e-mail: karina.aguilar@hhs.gov
Regional Family Planning Consultant:
Delores Stewart 212-264-3935
e-mail: delores.stewart@hhs.gov
Regional Minority Health Consultant:
Marline Vignier 212-264-2560
Regional Women's Health Coordinator:
Sandra Bennett-Pagan 212-264-4628

US Department of Homeland Security (DHS)
Web site: www.dhs.gov

Federal Emergency Management Agency (FEMA)
TTY: 800-462-7585 or 202-646-2500

New York Regional Office
26 Federal Plaza, New York, NY 10278-0002
212-680-3600

Offices and agencies generally appear in alphabetical order, except when specific order is requested by listee.

Regional Administrator:
Jerome Hatfield

US Labor Department

Web site: www.dol.gov

Occupational Safety & Health Adminstration (OSHA)....... fax: 212-337-2371

201 Varick Street, Room 670, New York, NY 10014
212-337-2378 Fax: 212-337-2371
Web site: www.osha.gov
Regional Administrator:
Robert D. Kulick

Albany Area Office
401 New Karner Road, Suite 300, Albany, NY 12205-3809
Area Director:
Kim Castillon 518-464-4338/fax: 518-464-4337

Buffalo Area Office
130 South Elmwood Avenue, Suite 500, Buffalo, NY 14202-2465
Area Director:
Michael Scime.................. 716-551-3053/fax: 716-551-3126

Long Island Area Office
1400 Old Country Road, Suite 208, Westbury, NY 11590
Area Director:
Anthony Ciuffo 516-334-3344/fax: 516-334-3326

Manhattan Area Office
201 Varick Street, Room 908, New York, NY 10014
Area Director:
Kay Gee.................. 212-620-3200/fax: 212-620-4121

Syracuse Area Office
3300 Vickery Road, North Syracuse, NY 13212
Area Director:
Christopher Adams 315-451-0808/fax: 315-451-1351

Tarrytown Area Office
660 White Plains Road, 4th Floor, Tarrytown, NY 10591-5107
Area Director:
Diana Cortez 914-524-7510/fax: 914-524-7515

U.S. CONGRESS

See U.S. Congress Chapter for additional Standing Committee and Subcommittee information.

House of Representatives Standing Committees

Agriculture

Chair:
K. Michael Conaway (R-TX) 202-225-3605
Ranking Member:
Collin C. Peterson (D-MN).................. 202-225-2165

Subcommittee
Nutrition
Chair:
Jackie Walorski (R-IN) 202-225-3915
Ranking Member:
Jim McGovern (D-MA).................. 202-225-6101

Energy & Commerce

Chair:
Fred Upton (R-MI) 202-225-3761
Ranking Member:
Frank Pallone (D-NJ) 202-225-4671
New York Delegate:
Eliot L. Engel (D) 202-225-2464
New York Delegate:
Paul Tonko (D) 202-225-5076
New York Delegate:
Yvette Clarke (D) 202-225-6231
New York Delegate:
Chris Collins (R).................. 202-225-5265

Subcommittee
Health
Chair:
Joseph Pitts (R-PA) 202-225-2411
Ranking Member:
Gene Green (D-TX).................. 202-225-1688
New York Delegate:
Eliot L. Engel (D) 202-225-2464

Ways & Means

Chair:
Kevin Brady (R-TX).................. 202-225-4901
Ranking Member:
Sander Levin (D-MI) 888-810-3880
New York Delegate:
Charles B. Rangel (D).................. 202-225-4365
New York Delegate:
Joseph Crowley (D) 202-225-3965
New York Delegate:
Tom Reed (R) 202-225-3161

Subcommittee
Health
Chair:
Pat Tiberi (R-OH) 202-225-5355
Ranking Member:
Jim McDermott (D-WA) 202-225-3106

Senate Standing Committees

Aging, Special Committee on

Chair:
Susan M. Collins (R-ME) 202-224-2523
Ranking Member:
Claire McCaskill (D-MO).................. 202-224-6154

Agriculture, Nutrition & Forestry

Chair:
Pat Roberts (R-KS).................. 202-224-4774
Ranking Member:
Debbie Stabenow (D-MI) 202-224-4822

Health, Education, Labor & Pensions

Chair:
Lamar Alexander (R-TN) 202-224-4944
Ranking Member:
Patty Murray (D-WA).................. 202-224-2621

Subcommittees
Primary Health & Retirement Security
Chair:
Michael B. Enzi (R-WY).................. 202-224-3424
Ranking Member:
Bernie Sanders (D-VT) 202-224-5141

PRIVATE SECTOR

Adelphi NY Statewide Breast Cancer Hotline & Support Program
Adelphi University, Social Work Building, 1 South Avenue, PO Box 701, Garden City, NY 11530-0701
800-877-8077 or 516-877-4320 Fax: 516-877-4336
e-mail: breastcancerhotline@adelphi.edu
Web site: breast-cancer.adelphi.edu
Breast cancer support, information & referral hotline for all of New York State; community education, support groups, counseling & advocacy
Hillary Rutter, Executive Director

Alliance for Positive Health
927 Broadway, Albany, NY 12207-1306
518-434-4686 or 800-201-2437 Fax: 518-427-8184
e-mail: info@alliancefph.org
Web site: www.allianceforpositivehealth.org
Provides HIV/AIDS education & testing to at-risk individuals; offers assistance & care coordination to persons with chronic diseases; advocacy for better access to quality health services
William F. Faragon, Executive Director

Alzheimer's Association, Northeastern NY
4 Pine West Plaza, Suite 405, Albany, NY 12205
518-867-4999 or 800-272-3900 Fax: 518-867-4997
e-mail: infoneny@alz.org
Web site: www.alz.org/northeasternny
Research & support for individuals affected by Alzheimer's disease
Elizabeth Smith Boivin, Executive Director & Chief Executive Officer

American Cancer Society-Capital NY Region
1 Penny Lane, Latham, NY 12110
518-220-6901 or 800-227-2345
Web site: www.cancer.org
Kathryn Ozimek, Director, Human Resources

American College of Nurse-Midwives, NYC Chapter
426 13th Street, Brooklyn, NY 11215
e-mail: gina@communitygyn.com
Web site: www.nycmidwives.org
Midwifery/women's health
Gina Eichenbaum-Pikser, Co-Chair

American College of Physicians, New York Chapter
744 Broadway, Albany, NY 12207
518-427-0366 Fax: 518-427-1991
e-mail: info@nyacp.org
Web site: www.nyacp.org
Develops & advocates for policies on health issues
Linda A. Lambert, Executive Director

American Congress of Obstetricians & Gynecologists/NYS
100 Great Oaks Blvd, Suite 109, Albany, NY 12203
518-436-3461 Fax: 518-426-4728
e-mail: info@ny.acog.org
Web site: www.acogny.org
Women's health care & physician education
Christa R. Christakis, Executive Director

American Heart Association Founders Affiliate
122 East 42nd Street, 18th Floor, New York, NY 10168
212-878-5900
Web site: www.heart.org
Research, education & community service to reduce disability & death from heart disease & stroke
Heather Kinder, Executive Vice President

American Liver Foundation, Greater NY Chapter
39 Broadway, Suite 2700, New York, NY 10006
212-943-1059 Fax: 212-943-1314
Web site: www.liverfoundation.org
Disease research, public education & patient support
Paul Bolter, Community Outreach & Education Manager

American Lung Association of NYS Inc
418 Broadway, 1st Floor, Albany, NY 12207
518-465-2013
e-mail: info@lungne.org
Web site: www.lung.org
Education, research & advocacy for lung health & lung disease prevention
Michael Seilback, Vice President, Public Policy & Communications

AMSUS-The Society of Federal Health Professionals
9320 Old Georgetown Road, Bethesda, MD 20814
301-897-8800 Fax: 301-530-5446
Web site: www.amsus.org
Works to improve federal healthcare service & represent military, federal & international health care professionals
VADM Mike Cowan, Executive Director

Associated Medical Schools of New York
1270 Avenue of the Americas, Suite 606, New York, NY 10020
212-218-4610 Fax: 212-218-4278
e-mail: info@amsny.org
Web site: www.amsny.org
A consortium of the sixteen medical schools in New York State; advocacy, resources & educational development programs
Jo Wiederhorn, President & Chief Executive Officer

Bausch & Lomb Inc
1400 North Goodman Street, Rochester, NY 14609
800-553-5340 Fax: 585-338-6896
Web site: www.bausch.com
Development, manufacture & marketing of contact lenses & lens care products, opthalmic surgical & pharmaceutical products
RJ Crawford, Procurement Manager

New York University School of Medicine Bellevue Hospital Center, Department of Emergency Medicine
462 First Avenue, Room A345, New York, NY 10016
212-562-6561 Fax: 212-562-3001
e-mail: robert.femia@nyumc.org
Web site: www.med.nyu.edu
Emergency medicine; medical toxicology
Robert J. Femia, Chair

Brain Injury Association of NYS (BIANYS)
10 Colvin Avenue, Albany, NY 12206
518-459-7911 or 800-228-8201 Fax: 518-482-5285
e-mail: info@bianys.org
Web site: www.bianys.org
Public education & advocacy for individuals & families affected by brain injuries
Eileen Reardon, Executive Director

Bristol-Myers Squibb Co
345 Park Avenue, New York, NY 10154
212-546-4000 or 800-332-2056
Web site: www.bms.com
Develops & markets pharmaceuticals
Giovanni Caforio, Chief Executive Officer

Bronx-Lebanon Hospital Center
1276 Fulton Avenue, Bronx, NY 10456
718-590-1800 or 718-326-4591 Fax: 718-299-5447
e-mail: ecsvp@erols.com
Web site: www.bronxcare.org
Dr. Sridhar Chilimuri, Chairman, Department of Medicine

Policy Areas

Offices and agencies generally appear in alphabetical order, except when specific order is requested by listee.

Center for Hearing and Communication
50 Broadway, 6th Floor, New York, NY 10004-1607
917-305-7700 or TTY: 917-305-7999 Fax: 917-305-7888
e-mail: postmaster@chchearing.org
Web site: www.chchearing.org
Rehabilitation & other services for deaf & hard of hearing individuals
Laurie Hanin, Executive Director

Cerebral Palsy Associations of New York State
330 West 34th Street, 15th Floor, New York, NY 10001-2488
212-947-5770 Fax: 212-594-4538
e-mail: information@cpofnys.org
Web site: www.cpofnys.org
Serves individuals with cerebral palsy & other significant disabilities as well as their families through advocacy, technical assistance, publications & networking events
Susan Constantino, President & Chief Executive Officer

Coalition of Fathers & Families NY
PO Box 252, Stillwater, NY 12170
518-288-6755
e-mail: info@fafny.org
Web site: www.fafny.org
Political action, education & advocacy for fathers & families in NY
Jack Frost, President

Columbia University, Mailman School of Public Health
722 West 168th Street, New York, NY 10032
212-305-3927 Fax: 212-305-9342
e-mail: lpfried@columbia.edu
Web site: www.mailman.columbia.edu
Theory, analysis & development of policy & programs supporting public health & human rights
Linda Fried, Dean

Commissioned Officers Assn of the US Public Health Svc Inc (COA)
8201 Corporate Drive, Suite 200, Landover, MD 20785
301-731-9080 Fax: 301-731-9084
e-mail: jcurrie@coausphs.org
Web site: www.coausphs.org
Committed to improving the public health of the US; supports the interests of corps officers & advocates through leadership, training, education & communication
Jim Currie, Executive Director

Committee of Methadone Program Administrators Inc of NYS (COMPA)
911 Central Avenue, Suite 322, Albany, NY 12206
e-mail: info@compa-ny.org
Web site: www.compa-ny.org
Substance abuse treatment through pharmacotherapy; advocacy, community education, standards & regulatory review & policy development
Allegra Schorr, President

Commonwealth Fund
1 East 75th Street, New York, NY 10021-2692
212-606-3800 Fax: 212-606-3500
e-mail: info@cmwf.org
Web site: www.commonwealthfund.org
Supports independent research on health access, coverage & quality issues affecting minorities, women, children, elderly & low-income individuals
David Blumenthal, President

Community Health Care Association of NYS
111 Broadway, Suite 1402, New York, NY 10006
212-279-9686 Fax: 212-279-3851
e-mail: info@chcanys.org
Web site: www.chcanys.org
Advocacy, education & services for the medically underserved throughout NYS
Elizabeth H. Swain, President & Chief Executive Officer

Community Healthcare Network
60 Madison Avenue, 5th Floor, New York, NY 10010
212-545-2400 or 866-246-8259
Web site: www.chnnyc.org
Health & social services for low-income, ethnically diverse, medically underserved neighborhoods of NYC
Robert Hayes, President & Chief Executive Officer

Outreach & Extension
Cornell Cooperative Extension, College of Human Ecology, Nutrition, Food Safety & Security
249 Martha Van Rensselaer Hall, Cornell University, Ithaca, NY 14853
607-254-6517 Fax: 607-255-4071
e-mail: kak33@cornell.edu
Web site: www.cce.cornell.edu
Promoting nutritional well-being; safe preparation & storage of food; reducing food insecurity; improving access to health services
Kim Kopko, Assistant Director, Human Ecology

County Nursing Facilities of New York Inc
c/o NYSAC, 540 Broadway, 5th Floor, Albany, NY 12207
518-465-1473 Fax: 518-465-0506
Web site: www.nysac.org
Edmond Marchi, President

Dental Hygienists' Association of the State of New York Inc
PO Box 16041, Albany, NY 12212
518-477-0343
e-mail: info@dhasny.org
Web site: www.dhasny.org
Professional association representing registered dental hygienists; working to improve the oral health of New Yorkers
Beth Krueger, Executive Director

Doctors Without Borders USA
333 7th Avenue, 2nd Floor, New York, NY 10001-5004
212-679-6800 Fax: 212-679-7016
Web site: www.doctorswithoutborders.org
International medical assistance for victims of natural or man-made disasters & armed conflict
Jason Cone, Executive Director

Empire Blue Cross & Blue Shield
1 Liberty Plaza, New York, NY 10006
212-476-1000 Fax: 212-476-1281
Web site: www.empireblue.com
Health insurance
Lawrence Schreiber, President

Empire State Association of Assisted Living
646 Plank Road, Suite 207, Clifton Park, NY 12065
518-371-2573 Fax: 518-371-3774
e-mail: lnewcomb@esaal.org
Web site: www.esaal.org
Trade association representing NYS assisted living providers
Lisa Newcomb, Executive Director

Epilepsy Coalition of New York State Inc
450 West Nyack Road, West Nyack, NY 10980
845-627-0627
e-mail: jgayepi@efsny.com
Web site: www.epilepsyny.org
Epilepsy awareness & advocacy for improved services for people with epilepsy
Janice W. Gay, President

Excellus BCBS
165 Court Street, Rochester, NY 14647
585-454-1700 Fax: 585-238-4233
Web site: www.excellusbcbs.com
Health insurance
Dorothy Coleman, Executive Vice President

Offices and agencies generally appear in alphabetical order, except when specific order is requested by listee.

Eye-Bank for Sight Restoration Inc (The)
120 Wall Street, New York, NY 10005-3902
212-742-9000 Fax: 212-269-3139
e-mail: info@ebsr.org
Web site: www.eyedonation.org
Cornea & scleral transplants, eye donations
Patricia Dahl, Executive Director & Chief Executive Officer

Family Planning Advocates of New York State
194 Washington Avenue, Suite 620, Albany, NY 12210
518-436-8408 Fax: 518-436-0004
e-mail: info@familyplanningadvocates.org
Web site: www.familyplanningadvocates.org
Reproductive rights
Kim Atkins, Chair

Generic Pharmaceutical Association
777 Sixth Street NW, Suite 510, Washington, DC 20001
202-249-7100 Fax: 202-249-7105
e-mail: media@gphaonline.org
Web site: www.gphaonline.org
Association for manufacturers & suppliers of prescription drugs & pharmaceuticals; works to improve access to affordable generic medicines
Chester Davis, President & Chief Executive Officer

Gertrude H Sergievsky Center (The)
630 West 168th Street, New York, NY 10032
212-305-2515 Fax: 212-305-2426
e-mail: rpm2@columbia.edu
Web site: www.cumc.columbia.edu
Neurological disease research correlating epidemiological techniques with genetic analysis & clinical investigation
Richard Mayeux, Director

Greater New York Hospital Association
555 West 57th Street, 15th Floor, New York, NY 10019
212-246-7100 Fax: 212-262-6350
e-mail: info@gnyha.org
Web site: www.gnyha.org
Trade association representing the interests of more than 160 hospitals & health systems
Kenneth E. Raske, President

Group Health Inc
PO Box 3000, New York, NY 10116-3000
212-501-4444 or 800-624-2414
Web site: www.emblemhealth.com
Health insurance

Healthcare Association of New York State
1 Empire Drive, Rensselaer, NY 12144
518-431-7600 Fax: 518-431-7915
Web site: www.hanys.org
Representing New York's not-for-profit & public hospitals, health systems & continuing care providers
Dennis Whalen, President

Home Care Association of New York State Inc
388 Broadway, 4th Floor, Albany, NY 12207
518-426-8764 Fax: 518-426-8788
e-mail: info@hcanys.org
Web site: www.hca-nys.org
Advocacy for home health care & related health services
Joanne Cunningham, President

Hospice & Palliative Care Association of NYS Inc
2 Computer Drive West, Suite 105, Albany, NY 12205
518-446-1483 Fax: 518-446-1484
e-mail: info@hpcanys.org
Web site: www.hpcanys.org
Hospice & palliative care information & referral service; educational programs; clinical, psychosocial & bereavement issues
Timothy D. Nichols, President & Chief Executive Officer

INFORM Inc
PO Box 320403, Brooklyn, NY 11232
212-361-2400 Fax: 212-361-2412
e-mail: ramsey@informinc.org
Web site: www.informinc.org
Produces educational films about the impact of human activity on natural resources & public health
Virginia Ramsey, Executive Producer

Institute for Family Health (The)
2006 Madison Avenue, New York, NY 10035
212-633-0800 Fax: 212-691-4610
Web site: www.institute.org
Family practice healthcare for NYC's underserved; health professions training; research & advocacy
Neil S. Calman, President & Chief Executive Officer

Iroquois Healthcare Alliance
15 Executive Park Drive, Clifton Park, NY 12065
518-383-5060 Fax: 518-383-2616
e-mail: gfitzgerald@iroquois.org
Web site: www.iroquois.org
Represents healthcare providers in upstate New York
Gary Fitzgerald, President

LeadingAge New York
13 British American Blvd, Suite 2, Latham, NY 12110-1431
518-867-8383 Fax: 518-867-8384
e-mail: info@leadingageny.org
Web site: www.leadingageny.org
Represents continuing care providers
James W. Clyne Jr., President

Lighthouse Guild
15 West 65th Street, New York, NY 10023
800-284-4422
Web site: www.lighthouseguild.org
Vision rehabilitation, research, education & awareness
Alan R. Morse, President & Chief Executive Officer

Marion S Whelan School of Practical Nursing
Geneva General Hospital, 196 North Street, Geneva, NY 14456
315-787-4005 Fax: 315-787-4770
Web site: www.flhealth.org
Health education; clinical training
Victoria Record, EdD, RN, CNE, Director

Medical Society of the State of NY, Governmental Affairs Division
1 Commerce Plaza, 99 Washington Avenue, Suite 408, Albany, NY 12210
518-465-8085 Fax: 518-465-0976
e-mail: mssny@mssny.org
Web site: www.mssny.org
Healthcare legislation & advocacy
Elizabeth Dears, Senior VP

Memorial Sloan-Kettering Cancer Center
1275 York Avenue, New York, NY 10065
212-639-2000 Fax: 212-639-3576
Web site: www.mskcc.org
National Cancer Institute designated comprehensive cancer center; research, education & patient care
Avice Meehan, Senior VP & Chief Communications Officer

Policy Areas

Offices and agencies generally appear in alphabetical order, except when specific order is requested by listee.

Montefiore Health System, Albert Einstein College of Medicine, OB/GYN & Women's Health
1300 Morris Park Avenue, Belfer Educational Center, Room 501, Bronx, NY 10461
718-430-2000 or 718-430-3581 Fax: 718-430-8739
e-mail: alance@montefiore.org
Web site: www.einstein.yu.edu
Avalon Lance, Unified Administrator

Mount Sinai Health System
One Gustave L. Levy Plaza, New York, NY 10029-6574
212-241-6500 or 212-590-3300
Web site: www.mountsinai.org
Kenneth L. Davis, MD, President & Chief Executive Officer

NY Health Information Management Association Inc
1450 Western Avenue, Suite 101, Albany, NY 12203
518-435-0422 Fax: 518-463-8656
e-mail: nyhima@caphill.com
Web site: www.nyhima.org
Michele B. Bohley, President & Chair

NY Physical Therapy Association
971 Albany Shaker Road, Latham, NY 12110
518-459-4499 Fax: 518-459-8953
e-mail: kgarceau@nypta.org
Web site: www.nypta.org
Kelly Garceau, Executive Director

NY State Society of Physician Assistants
100 North 20th Street, Suite 400, Philadelphia, PA 19103
877-769-7722 Fax: 215-564-2175
e-mail: info@nysspa.org
Web site: www.nysspa.org
Kyle Fernley, Executive Director

NYS Academy of Family Physicians
260 Osborne Road, Albany, NY 12211-1822
518-489-8945 or 800-822-0700 Fax: 518-489-8961
e-mail: fp@nysafp.org
Web site: www.nysafp.org
Vito F. Grasso, Executive Vice President

NYS Association of County Health Officials
One United Way, Pine West Plaza, Albany, NY 12205
518-456-7905 Fax: 518-452-5435
e-mail: linda@nysacho.org
Web site: www.nysacho.org
Linda Wagner, Executive Director

NYS Association of Health Care Providers
20 Corporate Woods Blvd, 2nd Floor, Albany, NY 12211
518-463-1118 Fax: 518-463-1606
e-mail: hcp@nyshcp.org
Web site: www.nyshcp.org
Home health care; health care services for the aging
Claudia Hammar, President

NYS Association of Nurse Anesthetists (NYSANA)
c/o McKenna Management, 6 Boston Road, Suite 202, Chelmsford, MA 01824
978-674-6214 Fax: 978-250-1117
e-mail: admin@nysana.com
Web site: www.nysana.com
Joanne Woersching, President

NYS Dental Association
20 Corporate Woods Blvd, Suite 602, Albany, NY 12211
518-465-0044 Fax: 518-465-3219
e-mail: info@nysdental.org
Web site: www.nysdental.org
Mark J. Feldman, D.M.D., Executive Director

NYS Federation of Physicians & Dentists
521 5th Avenue, Suite 1700, New York, NY 10175-0003
212-986-3859
Larry Nathan, Executive Director

NYS Optometric Association Inc
119 Washington Avenue, 2nd Floor, Albany, NY 12210
518-449-7300 or 800-342-9836 Fax: 518-432-5902
e-mail: nysoa2020@gmail.com
Web site: www.nysoa.org
Jan Dorman, Executive Director

NYS Public Health Association
PO Box 38127, Albany, NY 12203
518-427-5835
e-mail: info@nyspha.org
Web site: www.nyspha.org
Advocates for policies to protect public health & enhance health equity in NYS
Michael Seserman, President

National Amputation Foundation Inc
40 Church Street, Malverne, NY 11565
516-887-3600 Fax: 516-887-3667
e-mail: amps76@aol.com
Web site: www.nationalamputation.org
Provides services designed to help amputees, including AMP-to-AMP & medical giveaway programs, information, resources, hospital visits & support group & amputee organization referrals
Paul Bernacchio, President

National League for Nursing (NLN)
61 Broadway, New York, NY 10006
212-363-5555
Web site: www.nln.org
Promotes superior nursing education & the nursing profession; provides research grants, networking opportunities & professional development programs
Dr. Beverly Malone, Chief Executive Officer

National Marfan Foundation
22 Manhasset Avenue, Port Washington, NY 11050
516-883-8712 Fax: 516-883-8040
e-mail: staff@marfan.org
Web site: www.marfan.org
Marfan syndrome research, education & support
Michael Weamer, President & Chief Executive Officer

New Jewish Home (The)
120 West 106th Street, New York, NY 10025
212-870-5000 or 212-870-4715
e-mail: aweiner@jewishhome.org
Web site: www.jewishhome.org
Long term care & rehabilitation
Audrey Weiner, President & Chief Executive Officer

New School University, Milano School of International Affairs, Management & Urban Policy
72 Fifth Avenue, 3rd Floor, New York, NY 10011
212-229-5150 Fax: 212-627-2695
Web site: www.newschool.edu
Michelle J. DePass, Dean

New York AIDS Coalition
231 W 29th St, New York, NY 10001
212-629-3075 Fax: 212-629-8409
e-mail: jdarden@nyaidsc.org
Web site: www.nyaidscoalition.org
HIV/AIDS-related public policy & education
James Darden, Office Manager

New York Health Care Alliance
39 Broadway, Suite 1710, New York, NY 10006
212-425-5050 or 877-446-9422 Fax: 212-968-7710
e-mail: info@nyhca.com
Web site: www.nyhca.com
Nursing facilities affiliation focused on disseminating information, addressing health plans & facilities issues & providing patient placement services
Neil J. Heyman, Chief Executive Officer

New York Health Plan Association
90 State Street, Suite 825, Albany, NY 12207-1717
518-462-2293 Fax: 518-462-2150
e-mail: info@nyhpa.org
Web site: www.nyhpa.org
Promotes managed care & health service plans
Andrew Fogarty, Director, Government Affairs

New York Medical College
40 Sunshine Cottage Road, Valhalla, NY 10595
914-594-4000
e-mail: francis_belloni@nymc.edu
Web site: www.nymc.edu
Cardiovascular physiology, graduate education
Francis L. Belloni, Dean, Graduate School of Basic Medical Sciences

New York Medical College, Department of Medicine
19 Skyline, Valhalla, NY 10595
914-594-2080 Fax: 914-493-7506
e-mail: lerner@nymc.edu
Web site: www.nymc.edu
Research, education & clinical training
Robert G. Lerner, Professor of Medicine

New York Medical College, School of Health Sciences and Practice
School of Health Science & Practice Bldg, Valhalla, NY 10595
914-594-4510 or 914-594-4531 Fax: 914-594-4292
e-mail: shsp@nymc.edu
Web site: www.nymc.edu/school-of-health-sciences-and-practice-shsp
Public health education & research
Robert W. Amler, Dean

New York Presbyterian Hospital
525 East 68th Street, New York, NY 10065
212-746-5454
Web site: www.nyp.org; www.weill.cornell.edu
Steven J. Corwin, MD, President & Chief Executive Officer

New York State Association of Ambulatory Surgery Centers
C/N Group Inc., Center for Ambulatory Surgery, LLC, 550 Orchard Park Road, B101, West Seneca, NY 14224
716-997-9474 or 716-896-3815
e-mail: nysaasc@gmail.com
Web site: www.nysaasc.org
Promotes superior ambulatory surgical care in NYS
Thomas Faith, President

New York State Health Facilities Association Inc
33 Elk Street, Suite 300, Albany, NY 12207-1010
518-462-4800 Fax: 518-426-4051
e-mail: info@nyshfa.org
Web site: www.nyshfa.org
Association for long term care providers
Richard J. Herrick, President & Chief Executive Officer

New York State Nurses Association
131 West 33rd Street, 4th Floor, New York, NY 10001
212-785-0157
e-mail: info@nysna.org
Web site: www.nysna.org
Labor union & professional association for registered nurses
Jill Furillo, Executive Director

New York State Ophthalmological Society
408 Kenwood Avenue, Delmar, NY 12054
518-439-2020 Fax: 518-439-2040
e-mail: admin@nysos.com
Web site: www.nysos.com
Robin M. Pellegrino, Executive Director

New York State Osteopathic Medical Society
1855 Broadway, New York, NY 10023
212-261-1784 or 800-841-4131 Fax: 212-261-1786
e-mail: info@nysoms.org
Web site: www.nysoms.org
Represents the interests of osteopathic physicians through information dissemination, advocacy, continuing medical education programs & other membership services
Steven I. Sherman, President

New York State Podiatric Medical Association
555 Eighth Avenue, Suite 1902, New York, NY 10018
212-996-4400 Fax: 646-672-9344
e-mail: info@nyspma.org
Web site: www.nyspma.org
Association working to promote the interests of the podiatric community through advocacy, information & continuing medical education
Michael Borden, Executive Director

New York State Radiological Society Inc
585 Stewart Avenue, Suite 412, Garden City, NY 11530
516-222-1150 Fax: 516-222-1204
e-mail: nysrad@aol.com
Web site: www.nysrs.org
Richard A. Schiffer, Executive Director

New York University, Robert F Wagner Graduate School of Public Service
295 Lafayette Street, Room 3040A, New York, NY 10012-9604
212-998-7400 or 212-998-7455
e-mail: john.billings@nyu.edu
Web site: www.wagner.nyu.edu
Health policy & management education
John Billings, Director, Health Policy & Management Program

Next Wave Inc
24 Madison Avenue Extension, Albany, NY 12203
518-452-3351 Fax: 518-452-3358
Web site: www.nextwave.info
Health services research, evaluation & management consulting
John D. Shaw, President

Northeast Business Group on Health Inc
61 Broadway, Suite 2705, New York, NY 10006
212-252-7440 Fax: 212-252-7448
e-mail: laurel@nebgh.org
Web site: www.nebgh.org
Business employers addressing healthcare cost & quality; non-profit coalition of health systems & organizations
Laurel Pickering, President & Chief Executive Officer

Nurse Practitioner Association NYS (The)
12 Corporate Drive, Clifton Park, NY 12065
518-348-0719 Fax: 518-348-0720
e-mail: info@thenpa.org
Web site: www.thenpa.org
Representation, communication & advocacy
Stephen Ferrara, Executive Director

Policy Areas

Path2Parenthood
315 Madison Avenue, Suite 901, New York, NY 10017
888-917-3777
e-mail: info@path2parenthood.org
Web site: www.path2parenthood.org
Education, support, advocacy, resources & outreach programs centered on infertility, reproductive health & adoption
Ken Mosesian, Executive Director

Pharmacists Society of the State of New York
210 Washington Avenue Extension, Albany, NY 12203
518-869-6595 or 800-632-8822 Fax: 518-464-0618
e-mail: kathy.febraio@pssny.org
Web site: www.pssny.org
Continuing education, public information, health advocacy
Kathy Febraio, Executive Director

Premier Senior Living LLC
299 Park Avenue, 6th Floor, New York, NY 10171
800-380-8908
Web site: www.pslgroupllc.com
Assisted living, memory & personal care services
Robert P. Borsody, Co-Founder & Managing Member

Radon Testing Corp of America Inc
2 Hayes Street, Elmsford, NY 10523-2502
914-345-3380 or 800-457-2366 Fax: 914-345-8546
e-mail: info@rtca.com
Web site: www.rtca.com
Radon detection services for health departments, municipalities & homeowners
Nancy Bredhoff, President

Regeneron Pharmaceuticals Inc
777 Old Saw Mill River Road, Tarrytown, NY 10591-6707
914-847-7000
Web site: www.regeneron.com
Biopharmaceutical company focused on the development of therapeutic drugs for serious medical conditions, including rheumatoid arthritis, cancer, asthma & obesity
Leonard S. Schleifer, President & Chief Executive Officer

SUNY at Albany, School of Public Health, Center for Public Health Preparedness
One University Place, Rensselaer, NY 12144-3456
518-402-0344 Fax: 518-402-4656
e-mail: cphp@uamail.albany.edu
Web site: www.ualbanycphp.org
Edward Waltz, Director

The Bachmann-Strauss Dystonia & Parkinson Foundation Inc
PO Box 38016, Albany, NY 12203
212-509-0995 x331
Web site: www.dystonia-parkinsons.org
Funds research & creates public awareness of dystonia & Parkinson's disease
Bonnie Strauss, President & Founder

True, Walsh & Sokoni, LLP
950 Danby Road, Suite 310, Ithaca, NY 14850
607-273-2301 Fax: 607-272-1901
e-mail: info@truewalshlaw.com
Web site: www.truewalshlaw.com
Health care, corporate law & estate planning/administration
Sally T. True, Partner

United Hospital Fund of New York
1411 Broadway, 12th Floor, New York, NY 10018
212-494-0700 Fax: 212-494-0800
e-mail: jtallon@uhfnyc.org
Web site: www.uhfnyc.org
Health services research, public policy analysis & program development
James R. Tallon, Jr., President

United New York Ambulance Network (UNYAN)
1450 Western Avenue, Suite 101, Albany, NY 12203
518-694-4420
e-mail: info@unyan.net
Web site: www.unyan.net
Membership corporation for emergency medical transportation professionals
Lester Freemantle, Chair

We Move
204 W 84th St, New York, NY 10024
800-437-6682 Fax: 212-875-8389
e-mail: wemove@wemove.org
Web site: www.wemove.org
Education & information about movement disorders for both healthcare providers & patients
Susan B Bressman, President

NYS Bar Assn, Health Law Section
Wilson Elser Moskowitz Edelman & Dicker
677 Broadway, Albany, NY 12207
518-449-8893 Fax: 518-449-8927
e-mail: jonathan.bing@wilsonelser.com
Web site: www.wilsonelser.com
Jonathan L. Bing, Partner

Winthrop University Hospital
259 First Street, Mineola, NY 11501
516-663-0333 or 516-663-2200
Web site: www.winthrop.org
John F. Collins, President & Chief Executive Officer

HOUSING & COMMUNITY DEVELOPMENT

NEW YORK STATE

GOVERNOR'S OFFICE

Governor's Office
Executive Chamber
State Capitol
Albany, NY 12224
518-474-8390 Fax: 518-474-1513
Web site: www.ny.gov

Governor:
Andrew M Cuomo 518-474-8390
Secretary to the Governor:
William Mulrow 518-474-4246
Counsel to the Governor:
Alphonso David 518-474-8343
Chief of Staff:
Melissa DeRosa . . . . 518-474-8418 or 212-681-4640
Director, Communications:
James Allen. . . . . 518-474-8418 or 212-681-4640
Deputy Secretary for Civil Rights:
Norma Ramos 212-681-4584

EXECUTIVE DEPARTMENTS AND RELATED AGENCIES

Housing & Community Renewal, Division of
Hampton Plaza
38-40 State St
Albany, NY 12207
866-275-3427 or 518-473-2526
Web site: www.nyshcr.org

641 Lexington Ave
New York, NY 10022
866-275-3427

Commissioner:
James S Rubin. 518-486-3370
Executive Assistant:
Denise Flowers 518-473-0632
Public Information Officer:
Charni Sochet 212-872-0681

Administration
Deputy Commissioner:
Sharon Devine. 518-473-0632

Housing Information Systems
Director:
David Dietrich. 518-473-5681/fax: 518-486-5056

Office of Training & Professional Development
Director:
Katherine Champagne 518-473-6128

Support Services/Processing Services Unit
Director:
Theodore T Minissale 518-486-6166/fax: 518-486-3366

Community Development
Assistant Commissioner, Capital Finance:
Sean Fitzgerald 518-473-8732
Asst Commissioner, Underwriting & Design Services:
Ellen M Coyle 518-473-3890/fax: 518-473-7357
Community Development/Downstate:
Earnest Langhorne 212-480-7473

Community Service Bureau/Technical Assistance Unit
Director:
Pat Doyle. 518-473-3247/fax: 518-486-5186

Energy Rehabilitation Services
Director:
Thom Carey. 518-474-5700/fax: 518-474-9907

Environmental Analysis Unit
Director:
Barbara Wigzell 518-473-0457

Housing Trust Fund Program
Program Manager:
Thomas Koenig. 518-486-7682/fax: 518-486-3410

Regional Offices
Finger Lakes, Western NY, Southern Tier
535 Washington St, Buffalo, NY 14203
Regional Director:
Leonard Skrill 716-847-7955
New York City, Long Island, Hudson Valley
641 Lexington Ave, New York, NY 10022
Regional Director:
Greg Watson 212-688-4000

Fair Housing & Equal Opportunity
Director:
Wanda Graham 518-474-6157/fax: 518-473-3173

Housing Operations
Deputy Commissioner:
Vacant 212-480-6440/fax: 212-480-7169
Asst Commissioner, Section 8:
Alan Smith 518-480-7764
Asst Commissioner, Housing Operations:
Richmond McCurnin. 212-480-6444/fax: 212-480-7169

Manufactured Homes
Director:
Maralyne P Fleischman 518-474-9586

Housing Management Bureau
Director:
Robert D'Amico 212-480-6266
Mobile Home Unit
Director:
Dominic Cardillo. . . . . 800-432-4210 or 518-486-6267
fax: 518-486-3366
Subsidy Services
Director:
Blanca Cardona 212-480-6674

Legal Affairs
General Counsel:
Gary R Connor 212-480-6707
Deputy General Counsel:
Mark Colon. 212-480-6727

General Law
Managing Attorney:
Sheldon Melnitsky 212-480-6789/fax: 212-480-7416
Supervising Attorney:
Brian P McCartney. 518-486-6337

Policy & Intergovernmental Relations
Deputy Commissioner:
Lorrie Pizzola 518-474-9553/fax: 518-473-9462
Legislative Liaison:
Vacant 518-473-2519/fax: 518-474-5752

Offices and agencies generally appear in alphabetical order, except when specific order is requested by listee.

Rent Administration
Deputy Commissioner:
Woody Pascal 718-262-4822/fax: 718-262-4008

Luxury Decontrol/Overcharge
Acting Bureau Chief:
John Lance 718-262-4081

Property Management
Bureau Chief:
Paul Fuller 718-262-4768/fax: 718-262-7938

Rent Control/ETPA
Bureau Chief/Deputy Counsel:
Michael Rosenblatt 718-262-4713/fax: 718-262-4008

Rent Information Services
Bureau Chief:
Bruce Falbo 718-262-4914/fax: 718-262-4008

Law Department
120 Broadway
New York, NY 10271-0332
212-416-8000 or 800-771-7755
Web site: www.ag.ny.gov

State Capitol
Albany, NY 12224-0341
518-776-2000
Fax: 518-650-9401

Attorney General:
Eric T Schneiderman . . . . . 212-416-8050 or 518-776-2000
Chief of Staff:
Brian Mahanna 212-416-8050
Press Secretary:
Matt Mittenthal 212-416-8060/fax: 212-416-6005

Social Justice
Executive Deputy Attorney General:
Alvin L Bragg, Jr. 212-416-8075/fax: 212-416-8942

Civil Rights Bureau
Bureau Chief:
Lourdes Rosado 212-416-8250/fax: 212-416-8074

Economic Justice
Executive Deputy Attorney General:
Manisha Sheth 212-416-8050

Consumer Frauds & Protection Bureau
Bureau Chief:
Jane Azia 212-416-8300/fax: 212-416-6003

State Counsel
Chief Deputy Attorney General & Counsel:
Janet Sabel 212-416-8050
Chief Deputy Attorney General & Counsel:
Jason Brown 212-416-8050
Executive Deputy Attorney General, State Counsel:
Kent T. Stauffer 212-416-8252/fax: 212-416-6001

Litigation Bureau
Bureau Chief:
Jeffrey Dvorin . . . . . 518-776-2300 or 212-416-8610

Real Property Bureau
Bureau Chief:
Alison Crocker 518-776-2700/fax: 518-474-0862

CORPORATIONS, AUTHORITIES AND COMMISSIONS

Capital District Regional Planning Commission
One Park Place
Suite 102
Albany, NY 12205
518-453-0850 Fax: 518-453-0856
e-mail: cdrpc@cdrpc.org
Web site: www.cdrpc.org

Executive Director:
Rocco A Ferraro 518-453-0850
e-mail: rocky@cdrpc.org
Financial Officer:
Tim Canty 518-453-0850

Development Authority of the North Country
317 Washington Street
Watertown, NY 13601
315-661-3200
e-mail: info@danc.org
Web site: www.danc.org

Chair:
Gary Turck 315-661-3200
Executive Director:
James Wright 315-661-3200
Deputy Executive Director:
Thomas R Sauter 315-661-3200
e-mail: tsauter@danc.org
Director, Engineering:
Carrie Tuttle 315-661-3210
Telecom Division Manager:
David Wolf 315-661-3200
e-mail: oatn@danc.org
Landfill Superintendent:
Steve McElwain 315-661-3230
Director, Regional Development:
Michelle Capone 315-661-3200

Empire State Development Corporation
633 Third Ave
New York, NY 10017
212-803-3100 Fax: 212-803-3131
Web site: www.esd.ny.gov

625 Broadway
Albany, NY 12207
518-292-5100

95 Perry Street
Ste 500
Buffalo, NY 14203
716-846-8200
Fax: 716-846-8260

President & CEO:
Howard Zemsky 212-803-3700
e-mail: president@esd.ny.gov
Business Attraction & Expansion:
John Gilstrap 212-803-3700
Public Affairs:
Kay Sarlin Wright 800-260-7313
e-mail: esdpressoffice@esd.ny,gov
Chief of Staff & COO:
Mehul J. Patel . . . . . 212-803-3700 or 518-292-5100

Offices and agencies generally appear in alphabetical order, except when specific order is requested by listee.

New York City Housing Development Corporation
110 William St
10th Fl
New York, NY 10038
212-227-5500 Fax: 212-227-6865
e-mail: info@nychdc.com
Web site: www.nychdc.com

Chairman:
Vicki Been 212-863-6100
President:
Gary D Rodney 212-227-3600
Executive VP/COO & General Counsel:
Richard Froehlich 212-227-7435
Executive VP, Real Estate:
Paula R Carethers 212-227-6846
Senior Vice President, Portfolio Management:
Teresa Gigliello 212-227-9133
Vice President, Loan Servicing:
Karen Santiago 212-227-7494
Chief Credit Officer:
Mary Horn 212-227-9724
Communications/Press Office:
Vacant 212-227-2644

New York City Residential Mortgage Insurance Corporation
Chair:
Vicki Been 212-863-6100
President:
Gary D Rodney 212-227-3600

Roosevelt Island Operating Corporation (RIOC)
591 Main St
Roosevelt Island, NY 10044
212-832-4540 Fax: 212-832-4582
e-mail: information@rioc.ny.gov
Web site: www.rioc.ny.gov

President/CEO:
Charlene M Indelicato 212-832-4540 x319
Director Island Operations:
Cyril Opperman 212-832-4583
e-mail: cyril.opperman@rioc.ny.gov
VP/General Counsel:
Donald D. Lewis 212-832-4540 x319
e-mail: donald.lewis@rioc.ny.gov
VP/Chief Financial Officer:
Frances Walton 212-832-4540 x350
Director Public Safety:
Captain Estrella Suarez 212-832-4545
e-mail: keith.guerra@rioc.ny.gov

State of New York Mortgage Agency (SONYMA)
641 Lexington Ave
4th Floor
New York, NY 10022
212-688-4000 Fax: 212-872-0789
Web site: www.nyshcr.org

Commissioner & CEO:
Darryl C. Towns 212-688-4000
President, Finance & Development:
Marian Zucker 212-688-4000
Director, Fair Housing & Equal Opportunity:
Wanda Graham 212-688-4000
Director, Public Information:
Charni Sochet 212-872-0338

NEW YORK STATE LEGISLATURE

See Legislative Branch in Section 1 for additional Standing Committee and Subcommittee information.

Assembly Standing Committees

Housing
Chair:
Keith L.T. Wright (D) 518-455-4793
Ranking Minority Member:
Michael J Fitzpatrick (R) 518-455-5021

Local Government
Chair:
William B Magnarelli (D) 518-455-4826
Ranking Minority Member:
Christopher Friend (R) 518-455-4538

Senate Standing Committees

Housing, Construction & Community Development
Chair:
Elizabeth O'C. Little (R) 518-455-2811
Ranking Minority Member:
Adriano Espaillat (D) 518-455-2041

Local Government
Chair:
Kathleen Marchione (R) 518-455-2381
Ranking Minority Member:
Todd Kaminsky (D) 518-455-3401

U.S. GOVERNMENT

EXECUTIVE DEPARTMENTS AND RELATED AGENCIES

US Department of Agriculture

Rural Development
Web site: www.rd.usda.gov/ny

New York State Office . . . . fax: 315-477-8540
The Galleries of Syracuse, 441 South Salina Street, Suite 357, Syracuse, NY 13202
TTY: 315-477-6447 or 315-477-6400 Fax: 315-477-8540
Acting State Director:
Scott Collins 215-477-6400
Special Projects Coordinator:
Christopher Stewart
Eastern Region Area Director:
Ronda Falkena 845-343-1872 x4
Northern Region Area Director:
Brian Murray 315-386-2401 x4
Western Region Area Director:
Jim Walfrand 585-343-9167 x4

US Housing & Urban Development Department
Web site: www.hud.gov

New York State Office . . . . fax: 212-264-0246
26 Federal Plaza, Suite 3541, New York, NY 10278-0068
212-264-8000 Fax: 212-264-0246
Regional Administrator:
Holly M. Leicht 212-542-7109
e-mail: holly.m.leicht@hud.gov
Deputy Regional Administrator:
Mirza Orriols 212-542-7109
e-mail: mirza.orriols@hud.gov

Public Affairs Officer:
Charles McNally 212-542-7647
e-mail: charles.e.mcnally@hud.gov

Administration
Deputy Director, Field Support Services:
Lisa Surplus 212-542-7331

Community Planning & Development
Director:
Vincent Hom 212-542-7401
e-mail: vincent.hom@hud.gov

Fair Housing & Equal Opportunity Office
Regional Director:
Jay Golden 212-542-7507

Field Offices
Albany Area Office & Financial Operations Center fax: 518-464-4300
52 Corporate Circle, Albany, NY 12203-5121
518-862-2800 Fax: 518-464-4300
Field Office Director:
Jaime Forero
Buffalo Area Office . . . . fax: 716-551-5752
465 Main Street, Lafayette Court, 2nd Floor, Buffalo, NY 14203-1780
Field Office Director:
Joan Spilman 716-551-5755

General Counsel
Regional Counsel:
John Cahill 212-542-7200

Housing
Director, Oversight & Accountability Division:
Phyllis Ford 212-542-7171

Inspector General
Assistant Special Agent-in-Charge:
Heather Yannello
Assistant Regional Inspector General, Audit:
Karen A. Campbell

Public Housing
Director:
Luigi D'Ancona 212-542-7649

U.S. CONGRESS

See U.S. Congress Chapter for additional Standing Committee and Subcommittee information.

House of Representatives Standing Committees

Financial Services
Chair:
Jeb Hensarling (R-TX) 202-225-3484
Ranking Member:
Maxine Waters (D-CA) 202-225-2201
Vice Chairman:
Patrick T. McHenry (R-NC) 202-225-2576
New York Delegate:
Peter T. King (R) 202-225-7896
New York Delegate:
Carolyn B. Maloney (D) 202-225-7944
New York Delegate:
Gregory W. Meeks (D) 202-225-3461
New York Delegate:
Nydia M. Velazquez (D) 202-225-2361

Subcommittee
Housing & Insurance
Chair:
Blaine Luetkemeyer (R-MO) 202-225-2956
Ranking Member:
Emanuel Cleaver (D-MO) 202-225-4535
Vice Chairman:
Lynn A. Westmoreland (R-GA) 202-225-5901
New York Delegate:
Nydia M. Velazquez (D) 202-225-2361

Transportation & Infrastructure
Chair:
Bill Shuster (R-PA) 202-225-2431
Ranking Member:
Peter A. DeFazio (D-OR) 202-225-6416
New York Delegate:
Sean Patrick Maloney (D) 202-225-5441
New York Delegate:
Richard L. Hanna (R) 202-225-3665
New York Delegate:
John Katko (R) 202-225-3701
New York Delegate:
Jerrold Nadler (D) 202-225-5635

Subcommittee
Economic Development, Public Buildings & Emergency Management
Chair:
Lou Barletta (R-PA) 202-225-6511
Ranking Member:
Andre Carson (D-IN) 202-225-4011

Senate Standing Committees

Banking, Housing & Urban Affairs
Chair:
Richard Shelby (R-AL) 202-224-5744
Ranking Member:
Sherrod Brown (D-OH) 202-224-2315
New York Delegate:
Charles E. Schumer (D) 202-224-6542

PRIVATE SECTOR

Albany County Rural Housing Alliance Inc
PO Box 407, 24 Martin Road, Voorheesville, NY 12186
518-765-2425 Fax: 518-765-9014
e-mail: jeisgruber@acrha.org
Web site: www.acrha.org
Development & management of low income housing; home repair programs; housing counseling & education
Judith Eisgruber, Executive Director

American Institute of Architects (AIA) New York State Inc
50 State Street, 5th Floor, Albany, NY 12207
518-449-3334 Fax: 518-426-8176
e-mail: aianys@aianys.org
Web site: www.aianys.org
Architectural regulations, state policy, smart growth & affordable housing
Georgi Ann Bailey, Executive Director

Association for Community Living
28 Corporate Drive, Suite 102, Clifton Park, NY 12065
518-688-1682 Fax: 518-688-1686
e-mail: admin@aclnys.org
Web site: www.aclnys.org
Membership organization comprised of agencies that provide housing & rehabilitation services to individuals with mental illness
Antonia M. Lasicki, Executive Director

Association for Neighborhood & Housing Development
50 Broad Street, Suite 1402, New York, NY 10004-2699
212-747-1117 Fax: 212-747-1114
e-mail: benjamin.d@anhd.org
Web site: www.anhd.org
Umbrella organization providing assistance to NYC nonprofits advocating for affordable housing & neighborhood preservation
Benjamin Dulchin, Executive Director

Association for a Better New York
355 Lexington Avenue, 8th Floor, New York, NY 10017
212-370-5800 Fax: 212-661-5877
Web site: www.abny.org
Networking & advocacy for the development of businesses & communities in New York
Angela Pinsky, Executive Director

Brooklyn Housing & Family Services Inc
415 Albemarle Road, Brooklyn, NY 11218
718-435-7585 Fax: 718-435-7605
e-mail: ljayson@brooklynhousing.org
Web site: www.brooklynhousing.org
Homelessness prevention, landlord/tenant dispute resolution & advocacy, immigration services & assistance for victims of mortgage foreclosure
Larry Jayson, Executive Director

CUNY Hunter College, Urban Affairs & Planning Department
695 Park Avenue, West Building, Room 1611, New York, NY 10065
212-772-5518 Fax: 212-772-5593
e-mail: urban@hunter.cuny.edu
Web site: www.hunterurban.org
Urban planning & public policy education, theory & research
Stanley Moses, Chair

Center for an Urban Future
120 Wall Street, 20th Floor, New York, NY 10005
212-479-3344 Fax: 212-479-3338
e-mail: cuf@nycfuture.org
Web site: www.nycfuture.org
Policy institute dedicated to addressing the critical problems facing cities through research reports, forums & events
Jonathan Bowles, Executive Director

Citizens Housing & Planning Council of New York
42 Broadway, Suite 2010, New York, NY 10004
212-286-9211 Fax: 212-286-9214
e-mail: info@chpcny.org
Web site: www.chpcny.org
Jerilyn Perine, Executive Director

Community Housing Improvement Program (CHIP)
5 Hanover Square, Suite 1605, New York, NY 10004
212-838-7442 Fax: 212-838-7456
e-mail: info@chipnyc.org
Web site: www.chipnyc.org
Representing NYC apartment building owners
Patrick J. Siconolfi, Executive Director

Community Preservation Corporation (The)
28 East 28th Street, 9th Floor, New York, NY 10016-7943
212-869-5300 Fax: 212-683-0694
Web site: www.communityp.com
Multifamily housing rehabilitation financing for NYC & NJ neighborhoods
Rafael E. Cestero, President & Chief Executive Officer

Community Service Society of New York
633 Third Avenue, 10th Floor, New York, NY 10017
212-254-8900 or 212-614-5538
e-mail: info@cssny.org
Web site: www.cssny.org
Research & advocacy for public policies & programs that improve housing conditions & opportunities for low-income NYC residents & communities
David R. Jones, President & Chief Executive Officer

Cornell Cooperative Extension, Community & Economic Vitality Program
356 Roberts Hall, Cornell University, Ithaca, NY 14853
607-255-8546
Web site: www.cce.cornell.edu
Work with community leaders, extension educators & elected officials to strengthen the vitality of New York's communities
Christopher Watkins, Director, Cornell Cooperative Extension

Federal Home Loan Bank of New York
101 Park Avenue, New York, NY 10178-0599
212-681-6000 Fax: 212-441-6890
Web site: www.fhlbny.com
Jose R. Gonzalez, President & Chief Executive Officer

Grow NYC
100 Gold Street, Suite 3300, New York, NY 10038
212-788-7900 Fax: 212-788-7913
Web site: www.grownyc.org
Material & technical assistance for housing groups to create & maintain open community gardens & other public open spaces in NYC
Marcel Van Ooyen, Executive Director

Hofstra University, School of Law
121 Hofstra University, Hempstead, NY 11549
516-463-5858
e-mail: hofstralaw@hofstra.edu
Web site: www.law.hofstra.edu
Land use & environmental law
Eric Lane, Dean

Housing Action Council Inc - Not For Profit
55 South Broadway, 2nd Floor, Tarrytown, NY 10591
914-332-4144 Fax: 914-332-4147
e-mail: hac@affordablehomes.org
Web site: www.housingactioncouncil.org
Financial feasibility, land use & zoning & affordable housing
Rosemarie Noonan, Executive Director

Housing Works Inc
57 Willoughby Street, 2nd Floor, Brooklyn, NY 11201
347-473-7400 or TTY: 212-925-9560
e-mail: info@housingworks.org
Web site: www.housingworks.org
Housing, health care, advocacy, job training & support services for homeless NY residents with HIV/AIDS
Charles King, President & Chief Executive Officer

Hudson Valley Pattern for Progress
3 Washington Center, Newburgh, NY 12550
845-565-4900 Fax: 845-565-4918
e-mail: jdrapkin@pfprogress.org
Web site: www.pattern-for-progress.org
Regional planning, research & policy development
Jonathan Drapkin, President & Chief Executive Officer

Local Initiatives Support Corporation
501 Seventh Avenue, New York, NY 10018
212-455-9800 Fax: 212-682-5929
Web site: www.lisc.org
Supports the development of local leadership & the creation of affordable housing, commercial, industrial & community facilities, businesses & jobs
Michael Rubinger, President & Chief Executive Officer

NY Housing Association Inc
634 Watervliet Shaker Road, Latham, NY 12110
518-867-3242 or 800-721-4663
e-mail: info@nyhousing.org
Web site: www.nyhousing.org
Manufactured, factory built, modular & mobile housing

Policy Areas

Nancy P. Geer, Executive Director

Tenants & Neighbors
236 West 27th Street, 4th Floor, New York, NY 10001
212-608-4320 Fax: 212-619-7476
e-mail: info@tandn.org
Web site: www.tandn.org
Organizing support, training, technical assistance & advocacy around tenants' rights & the preservation of affordable housing
Katie Goldstein, Executive Director

National Trust for Historic Preservation
2600 Virginia Avenue NW, Suite 1100, Washington, DC 20037
202-588-6000 or 800-944-6847 Fax: 202-588-6038
e-mail: info@savingplaces.org
Web site: www.savingplaces.org
Provides leadership, education, advocacy & resources to preserve America's historic places & revitalize communities
Stephanie K. Meeks, President & Chief Executive Officer

Neighborhood Preservation Coalition of NYS Inc
100 State Street, Suite 710, Albany, NY 12207
518-432-6757 Fax: 518-432-6758
e-mail: p.gilbert@npcnys.org
Web site: www.npcnys.org
Community organizations united to preserve & revitalize neighborhoods
Paula Gilbert, Executive Director

Nelson A Rockefeller Inst of Govt, Urban & Metro Studies
411 State Street, Albany, NY 12203-1003
518-443-5522 Fax: 518-443-5788
e-mail: patricia.cadrette@rockinst.suny.edu
Web site: www.rockinst.org
Research on community capacity building, impacts of welfare reform on community development corporations, empowerment zone/enterprise communities & neighborhood preservation
Patricia Cadrette, Project Administrative Officer

New School University, Milano School of International Affairs, Management & Urban Policy
72 Fifth Avenue, 3rd Floor, New York, NY 10011
212-229-5150 Fax: 212-627-2695
Web site: www.newschool.edu
Research, policy analysis & evaluation on community development & urban poverty
Michelle DePass, Dean

New York Building Congress
44 West 28th Street, 12th Floor, New York, NY 10001-4212
212-481-9230 Fax: 212-447-6037
e-mail: info@buildingcongress.com
Web site: www.buildingcongress.com
Coalition of design, construction & real estate organizations
Richard T. Anderson, President

New York Community Bank
615 Merrick Avenue, Westbury, NY 11590
877-786-6560
Web site: www.mynycb.com
Joseph R. Ficalora, President & Chief Executive Officer

New York Landmarks Conservancy
1 Whitehall Street, New York, NY 10004
212-995-5260 Fax: 212-995-5268
e-mail: info@nylandmarks.org
Web site: www.nylandmarks.org
Technical & financial assistance for preservation & reuse of landmark buildings
Peg Breen, President

New York Lawyers for the Public Interest
151 West 30th Street, 11th Floor, New York, NY 10001-4017
212-244-4664 Fax: 212-244-4570
Web site: www.nylpi.org
Disability rights law; access to health care; environmental justice & community development; Pro Bono Clearinghouse services
McGregor Smyth, Executive Director

New York State Community Action Association
2 Charles Blvd, Guilderland, NY 12084
518-690-0491 Fax: 518-690-0498
Web site: www.nyscommunityaction.org
Assists with the growth of community action agencies dedicated to improving the quality of life for low-income New Yorkers through education, technical assistance, training & advocacy
Karla Digirolamo, Chief Executive Officer

New York State Rural Advocates
PO Box 104, Blue Mountain Lake, NY 12812
518-352-7787
Advocacy & education for affordable housing for rural New Yorkers
Nancy Berkowitz, Coordinator

New York State Rural Housing Coalition Inc
79 N Pearl Street, Albany, NY 12207
518-458-8696 Fax: 518-458-8896
e-mail: colin@ruralhousing.org
Web site: www.ruralhousing.org
Affordable rural & small city housing; community & economic development
Colin McKnight, Acting Deputy Director

New York University, Wagner Graduate School
295 Lafayette Street, 2nd Floor, New York, NY 10012
212-998-7400
e-mail: mitchell.moss@nyu.edu
Web site: www.wagner.nyu.edu
Urban planning research; urban challenges, economic growth, housing, environmental planning & community development
Mitchell L. Moss, Professor of Urban Policy & Planning

Park Resident Homeowners' Association Inc
PO Box 68, Ontario, NY 14519
315-524-6703 Fax: 315-524-6703
e-mail: info@prho.com
Web site: www.prho.com
Protecting the rights of homeowners living in mobile/manufactured park communities in NYS
George R Miles, President

Parodneck Foundation (The)
121 6th Avenue, Suite 501, New York, NY 10013
212-431-9700 Fax: 212-431-9783
e-mail: kwray@parodneckfoundation.org
Web site: www.parodneckfoundation.org
Resident-controlled housing; community development
Ken Wray, Executive Director

PathStone Corporation
400 East Avenue, Rochester, NY 14607-1910
585-340-3300 or 800-888-6770
e-mail: smitchell@pathstone.org
Web site: www.pathstone.org
Housing assistance & rehabilitation, property management, real estate development & community revitalization services
Stuart J. Mitchell, President & Chief Executive Officer

Pratt Center for Community Development
200 Willoughby Avenue, 3rd Floor East, Brooklyn, NY 11205
718-636-3486
e-mail: afriedman@prattcenter.net
Web site: www.prattcenter.net
Training, technical assistance & advocacy in community economic development & sustainability
Adam Friedman, Executive Director

Project for Public Spaces
419 Lafayette Street, 7th Floor, New York, NY 10003
212-620-5660 Fax: 212-620-3821
e-mail: info@pps.org
Web site: www.pps.org
Nonprofit organization providing community planning, design & development services
Fred Kent, President

Regional Plan Association
4 Irving Place, 7th Floor, New York, NY 10003
212-253-2727 Fax: 212-253-5666
e-mail: twright@rpa.org
Web site: www.rpa.org
Association seeking to enhance economic development & quality of life in the New York metropolitan region through advocacy & research
Thomas K. Wright, President

Rent Stabilization Assn of NYC Inc
123 William Street, 14th Floor, New York, NY 10038
212-214-9200 Fax: 212-732-7519
Web site: www.rsanyc.net
NYC property owners organization
Joseph Strasburg, President

Settlement Housing Fund Inc
247 West 37th Street, 4th Floor, New York, NY 10018
212-265-6530 Fax: 212-757-0571
Web site: www.settlementhousingfund.org
Low & moderate income housing development, leasing, community development
Alexa Sewell, President

Urban Homesteading Assistance Board
120 Wall Street, 20th Floor, New York, NY 10005
212-479-3300 Fax: 212-344-6457
e-mail: help@uhab.org
Web site: www.uhab.org
Training, technical assistance & services for development & preservation of low income cooperative housing
Andrew Reicher, Executive Director

Women's Housing & Economic Development Corporation (WHEDCO)
50 East 168th Street, Bronx, NY 10452
718-839-1100 Fax: 718-839-1170
e-mail: communications@whedco.org
Web site: www.whedco.org
Non-profit organization dedicated to the development of communities & affordable housing
Nancy Biberman, President

Policy Areas

Offices and agencies generally appear in alphabetical order, except when specific order is requested by listee.

HUMAN RIGHTS

NEW YORK STATE

GOVERNOR'S OFFICE

Governor's Office
Executive Chamber
State Capitol
Albany, NY 12224
518-474-8390 Fax: 518-474-1513
Web site: www.ny.gov

Governor:
Andrew M Cuomo 518-474-8390
Secretary to the Governor:
William Mulrow 518-474-4246
Counsel to the Governor:
Alphonso David 518-474-8343
Deputy Secretary for Civil Rights:
Norma Ramos 212-681-4584
Chief of Staff:
Melissa DeRosa . . . . 518-474-8418 or 212-681-4640
Director, Communications:
James Allen. . . . . 518-474-8418 or 212-681-4640

EXECUTIVE DEPARTMENTS AND RELATED AGENCIES

Civil Service Department
Alfred E Smith State Ofc Bldg
Albany, NY 12239
518-457-2487 or 877-697-5627
Web site: www.cs.ny.gov

Commissioner:
Vacant 518-457-3701
Executive Deputy Commissioner:
Lola Brabham 518-473-5698
Deputy Commissioner, Operations:
Vacant 518-473-5711
Deputy Commissioner, Administration:
Deirdre Taylor. 518-473-5694
Public Information Officer:
Ed Walsh 518-457-9375/fax: 518-473-2372
e-mail: pio@cs.state.ny.us

Classification & Compensation Division
Director:
Patricia A. Itite. 518-474-1011/fax: 518-474-0787

Developmental Disabilities Planning Council
One Commece Plaza
Ste 1230
Albany, NY 12210
518-486-7505 or 800-395-3372 Fax: 518-402-3505
e-mail: ddpc@ddpc.ny.gov
Web site: www.ddpc.ny.gov

Chairperson:
James Traylor 518-486-7505
Vice Chairperson:
Thomas Burke. 518-486-7505
Executive Director:
Sheila M Carey 518-486-7505
e-mail: sheila.carey@ddpc.ny.gov
Deputy Director-Program Development Specialist:
Anna Lobosco 518-486-7505
e-mail: anna.lobosco@ddpc.ny.gov
Public Information Officer:
Thomas F Lee 518-486-7505/fax: 518-486-3505
e-mail: thomas.lee@ddpc.ny.gov

Human Rights, State Division of
1 Fordham Plaza, 4th Fl
Bronx, NY 10458
718-741-8400 or 888-392-3644 Fax: 718-741-8279
e-mail: infobronx@dhr.ny.gov
Web site: www.dhr.ny.gov

Commissioner:
Helen Diane Foster 718-741-8326
First Deputy Commissioner:
Valerie P. Dent 718-741-8330
Deputy Commissioner, Regional Affairs:
Gina N Martinez 718-741-8324
Deputy Commissioner, Federal Programs:
Edward Watkins 718-741-8440
Deputy Commissioner, Enforcement:
Melissa Franco 718-741-8400
General Counsel:
Caroline Downey 718-741-8398
Equal Opportunity Officer:
Rockwell J Chin 718-741-8309
Director, Disability Rights:
John Herrion 718-741-8332
RIO:
Leticia Theodore-Greene 718-741-3223
e-mail: lgreene@dhr.ny.gov

Regional Offices

Albany
Empire State Plaza, Agency Bldg., 2nd Floor, Albany, NY 12220
Regional Director:
Victor DeAmelia 518-474-2705/fax: 518-473-3422
e-mail: infoalbany@dhr.ny.gov

Binghamton
44 Hawley St, Rm 603, Binghamton, NY 13901
Regional Director:
Victor DeAmelia 607-721-8467/fax: 607-721-8470
e-mail: infobinghamton@dhr.ny.gov

Brooklyn
55 Hanson Place, Rm 1084, Brooklyn, NY 11217
Regional Director:
William Lamot 718-722-2385/fax: 718-722-2869
e-mail: infobrooklyn@dhr.ny.gov

Buffalo
W J Mahoney State Ofc Bldg, 65 Court St, Ste 506, Buffalo, NY 14202
e-mail: infobuffalo@dhr.ny.gov
Regional Director:
Tasha Moore 716-847-7632/fax: 716-847-7625

Housing Investigations Unit
1 Fordham Plaza, 4th Fl, Bronx, NY 10458
Regional Director:
William Lamot . . . . 718-741-8435/fax: 718-741—8103

Manhattan (Upper)
State Ofc Bldg, 163 W 125th St, 4th Fl, New York, NY 10027
Regional Director:
David Powell. 212-961-8650/fax: 212-961-4425

Nassau County
175 Fulton Ave, Ste 404, Hempstead, NY 11550
e-mail: infolongisland@dhr.ny.gov

Offices and agencies generally appear in alphabetical order, except when specific order is requested by listee.

Regional Director:
Ronald Brinn 516-538-1360/fax: 516-483-6589

Peekskill
8 John Walsh Blvd, Ste 204, Peekskill, NY 10566
Regional Director:
Roberto Chavez 914-788-8050/fax: 914-788-8059
e-mail: infopeekskill@dhr.ny.gov

Rochester
One Monroe Sq, 259 Monroe Ave, Ste 308, Rochester, NY 14607
Regional Director:
Julia Day 585-238-8250/fax: 585-238-8259
e-mail: inforochester@dhr.ny.gov

Suffolk County
State Office Bldg., 250 Veterans Memorial Highway, Suite 2B-49, Hauppauge, NY 11788
Regional Director:
Ronald Brinn 631-952-6434/fax: 631-952-6436
e-mail: infolongisland@dhr.ny.gov

Syracuse
333 E Washington St, Rm 543, Syracuse, NY 13202
e-mail: infosyracuse@dhr.ny.gov
Regional Director:
Julia Day 315-428-4633/fax: 315-428-4638

Law Department
120 Broadway
New York, NY 10271-0332
212-416-8000 or 800-771-7755
Web site: www.ag.ny.gov

State Capitol
Albany, NY 12224-0341
518-776-2000
Fax: 518-650-9401

Attorney General:
Eric T Schneiderman . . . . 212-416-8050 or 518-776-2000
Chief of Staff:
Brian Mahanna 212-416-8050
Press Secretary:
Matt Mittenthal 212-416-8060/fax: 212-416-6005

Social Justice
Executive Deputy Attorney General:
Alvin L Bragg, Jr. 212-416-8450/fax: 212-416-8942

Civil Rights Bureau
Bureau Chief:
Lourdes Rosado 212-416-8250/fax: 212-416-8074

Temporary & Disability Assistance, Office of
40 N Pearl St
Albany, NY 12243
518-473-1090
e-mail: nyspio@otda.ny.gov
Web site: www.otda.ny.gov

Commissioner:
Samuel D Roberts 518-474-4152
State Legislative Coordinator:
Judi West 518-474-7420
Director, Public Information:
Kristi L. Berner 518-474-9516/fax: 518-486-6935
e-mail: nyspio@otda.ny.gov

Center for Employment & Economic Supports
Deputy Commissioner:
Phyllis Morris 518-474-9222/fax: 518-474-5281

Operations & Program Support
Deputy Commissioner:
Wilma Brown Phillips 518-473-3912

NEW YORK STATE LEGISLATURE

See Legislative Branch in Section 1 for additional Standing Committee and Subcommittee information.

Assembly Standing Committees

Aging
Chair:
Steven Cymbrowitz (D) 518-455-5214
Ranking Minority Member:
Angela M Wozniak (C) 518-455-5921

Correction
Chair:
Daniel O'Donnell (D) 518-455-5603
Ranking Minority Member:
Joe Giglio (R) 518-455-5241

Labor
Chair:
Michele Titus (D) 518-455-5668
Ranking Minority Member:
Karl Brabenec (R) 518-455-5991

Mental Health
Chair:
Aileen Gunther (D) 518-455-5355
Ranking Minority Member:
Steven Katz (R) 518-455-5783

Assembly Task Forces

Puerto Rican/Hispanic Task Force
Chair:
Marcos Crespo (D) 518-455-5514
Executive Director:
Guillermo Martinez 518-455-3608

Women's Issues, Task Force on
Chair:
Aravella Simotas (D) 518-455-5014
Coordinator:
Christina Williams (R) 518-455-3632/fax: 518-455-4574

Senate Standing Committees

Aging
Chair:
Sue Serino (R) 518-455-2945
Ranking Minority Member:
Ruben Diaz Sr (D) 518-455-2511

Crime Victims, Crime & Correction
Chair:
Patrick Gallivan (R) 518-455-3471
Ranking Minority Member:
Ruth Hassell-Thompson (D) 518-455-2061

Labor
Chair:
Jack Martins (R) 518-455-3265

Offices and agencies generally appear in alphabetical order, except when specific order is requested by listee.

Ranking Minority Member:
Jose R Peralta (D) 518-455-2529

Mental Health & Developmental Disabilities
Chair:
Robert G Ortt (R) 518-455-2024
Ranking Minority Member:
Jesse Hamilton (D) 518-455-2431

U.S. GOVERNMENT

EXECUTIVE DEPARTMENTS AND RELATED AGENCIES

Equal Employment Opportunity Commission
Web site: www.eeoc.gov

New York District . . . . fax: 212-336-3790
33 Whitehall Street, 5th Floor, New York, NY 10004
800-669-4000 or TTY: 800-669-6820 Fax: 212-336-3790
Director:
Kevin J. Berry. . . . . 800-669-4000 or TTY: 800-669-6820
fax: 212-336-3790

Buffalo Local . . . . fax: 716-551-4387
6 Fountain Plaza, Suite 350, Buffalo, NY 14202
800-669-4000 or TTY: 800-669-6820 Fax: 716-551-4387
Director:
John E. Thompson Jr. 800-669-4000/fax: 716-551-4387

US Commerce Department
Web site: www.commerce.gov

Minority Business Development Agency
Web site: www.mbda.gov

New York Region
26 Federal Plaza, New York, NY 10278
212-264-3262

New York Business Center
535 Fifth Avenue, 16th Floor, New York, NY 10017
648-821-4008
Project Director:
Paul Sawyer

South Bronx Business Center
555 Bergen Avenue, 3rd Floor, Bronx, NY 10455
718-732-7540
Project Director:
Sharon Higgins

Williamsburg Business Center
12 Heyward Street, 2nd Floor, Brooklyn, NY 11211
718-522-5620
Contact:
Yehuda Turner

US Commission on Civil Rights
Web site: www.usccr.gov

EASTERN REGION (includes New York State)
624 9th Street NW, Suite 500, Washington, DC 20425
Regional Director:
Ivy L. Davis 202-376-7533/fax: 202-376-7548

US Department of Health & Human Services
Web site: www.hhs.gov

Office of Secretary's Regional Representative-Region 2-NY . . fax: 212-264-3620
26 Federal Plaza, Suite 3835, New York, NY 10278
Regional Director:
Jackie Cornell-Bechelli. 212-264-4600

Office for Civil Rights . . . . fax: 202-619-3818
26 Federal Plaza, Suite 3312, New York, NY 10278
Fax: 202-619-3818
Web site: www.hhs.gov/ocr
Regional Manager:
Linda Colon 212-264-3313

US Department of Homeland Security (DHS)
Web site: www.dhs.gov

US Citizenship & Immigration Services (USCIS)
TTY: 800-767-1833 or 800-375-5283
Web site: www.uscis.gov

Buffalo District Office . . . . fax: 716-551-3131
306 Delaware Avenue, Buffalo, NY 14202
District Director:
Edward A. Newman 716-843-7900
Albany Sub Office
1086 Troy-Schenectady Road, Latham, NY 12110
Director:
Gwynne Dinolfo 518-786-3210

CIS Asylum Offices
New York Asylum Office
1065 Stewart Avenue, Suite 200, Bethpage, NY 11714
516-261-0000
Director:
Patricia Menges 516-261-0000
Deputy Director:
Ashley Caudill-Mirillo. 516-261-0000
Newark Asylum Office-Including NYS not served by New York City
1200 Wall Street West, 4th Floor, Lyndhurst, NJ 07071
201-508-6100
Director:
Susan Raufer 201-531-0555
Deputy Director:
Sunil R. Varghese

New York City District Office
26 Federal Plaza, 3rd Floor, Room 3-120, New York, NY 10278
District Director:
Phyllis Coven
Long Island Field Office
30 Barretts Avenue, Holtsville, NY 11742
Field Office Director:
Elizabeth Miller

U.S. CONGRESS

See U.S. Congress Chapter for additional Standing Committee and Subcommittee information.

House of Representatives Standing Committees

Education & the Workforce
Chair:
John Kline (R-MN). 202-225-2271
Ranking Member:
Robert C. Scott (D-VA) 202-225-8351
New York Delegate:
Hakeem S. Jeffries (D) 202-225-5936
New York Delegate:
Elise Stefanik (R) 202-225-4611

Foreign Affairs
Chair:
Edward R. Royce (R-CA). 202-225-4111

Ranking Member:
Eliot L. Engel (D-NY) 202-225-2464
New York Delegate:
Brian Higgins (D) 202-225-3306
New York Delegate:
Grace Meng (D) 202-225-2601
New York Delegate:
Gregory W. Meeks (D) 202-225-3461
New York Delegate:
Daniel Donovan (R) 202-225-3371
New York Delegate:
Lee M. Zeldin (R) 202-225-3826

Subcommittee
Terrorism, Nonproliferation and Trade
Chair:
Ted Poe (R-TX) 202-225-6565
Ranking Member:
William Keating (D-MA) 202-225-3111
New York Delegate:
Brian Higgins (D) 202-225-3306

Senate Standing Committees

Indian Affairs, Committee on

Chair:
John Barrasso (R-WY) 202-224-6441
Vice Chair:
Jon Tester (D-MT) 202-224-2644

PRIVATE SECTOR

American Jewish Committee
165 East 56th Street, New York, NY 10022-2709
212-751-4000 Fax: 212-891-1450
Web site: www.ajc.org
Promoting tolerance, mutual respect & understanding among diverse ethnic, racial & religious groups; advocacy, communications & global diplomacy
David Harris, Chief Executive Officer

Amnesty International USA
5 Penn Plaza, 16th Floor, New York, NY 10001
212-807-8400 Fax: 212-627-1451
e-mail: aimember@aiusa.org
Web site: www.amnestyusa.org
Worldwide campaigning movement working to promote internationally recognized human rights
Margaret Huang, Interim Executive Director

Anti-Defamation League
605 Third Avenue, New York, NY 10158
212-885-7700 or 866-386-3235
e-mail: adlmedia@adl.org
Web site: www.adl.org
Fighting anti-Semitism worldwide
Jonathan Greenblatt, National Director

Asian American Legal Defense and Education Fund
99 Hudson Street, 12th Floor, New York, NY 10013-2815
212-966-5932 or 800-966-5946 Fax: 212-966-4303
e-mail: info@aaldef.org
Web site: www.aaldef.org
Defends civil rights of Asian Americans through litigation, advocacy, education & community organizing
Margaret Fung, Executive Director

Bond Schoeneck & King PLLC
One Lincoln Center, 110 West Fayette Street, Syracuse, NY 13202-1355
315-218-8000 Fax: 315-218-8100
Web site: www.bsk.com
Serves clients across a range of practice areas, including energy, natural resources, health care & higher education
Kevin M. Bernstein, Chair, Management Committee

CIDNY - Queens
80-02 Kew Gardens Road, Suite 107, Kew Gardens, NY 11415
646-442-1520 or TTY: 718-886-0427 Fax: 347-561-4883
Web site: www.cidny.org
Rights & advocacy for disabled individuals
Susan Dooha, Executive Director
Cyrus Kazi, Director of Administration

Cardozo School of Law
55 Fifth Avenue, New York, NY 10003
212-790-0200 Fax: 212-790-0205
e-mail: mrosnfld@yu.edu
Web site: www.cardozo.yu.edu
Law & theory of human rights
Michel Rosenfeld, Justice Sidney L Robins Professor of Human Rights

Center for Constitutional Rights
666 Broadway, 7th Floor, New York, NY 10012
212-614-6464 Fax: 212-614-6499
e-mail: info@ccrjustice.org
Web site: www.ccrjustice.org
Dedicated to protecting human rights & driving social change through litigation, communications, education & advocacy
Vincent Warren, Executive Director

Center for Independence of the Disabled in NY (CIDNY)
841 Broadway, Suite 301, New York, NY 10003
212-674-2300 or TTY: 212-674-5619 Fax: 212-254-5953
Web site: www.cidny.org
Rights & advocacy for disabled individuals
Susan Dooha, Executive Director

Center for Migration Studies of New York Inc
307 East 60th Street, 4th Floor, New York, NY 10022
212-337-3080
e-mail: cms@cmsny.org
Web site: www.cmsny.org
Facilitates the study of international migration & promotes public policies that protect the rights of migrants & refugees
Donald M. Kerwin, Jr., Executive Director

Children's Rights Inc
330 Seventh Avenue, 4th Floor, New York, NY 10001
212-683-2210 or 888-283-2210 Fax: 212-683-4015
e-mail: info@childrensrights.org
Web site: www.childrensrights.org
Advocacy & litigation on behalf of abused & neglected children
Sandy Santana, Executive Director

Citizens' Committee for Children of New York Inc
14 Wall Street, Suite 4E, New York, NY 10005-2173
212-673-1800 Fax: 212-979-5063
e-mail: info@cccnewyork.org
Web site: www.cccnewyork.org
Public policy research, education & advocacy for children's rights & services
Jennifer March, Executive Director

Columbia University, Mailman School of Public Health
722 West 168th Street, New York, NY 10032
212-305-3927 Fax: 212-305-9342
e-mail: lpfried@columbia.edu
Web site: www.mailman.columbia.edu
Theory, analysis & development of policy & programs supporting public health & human rights
Linda Fried, Dean

Cornell University, School of Industrial & Labor Relations
309 Ives Hall, Cornell University, Ithaca, NY 14853
607-255-2762 Fax: 607-255-2185
e-mail: hallock@cornell.edu
Web site: www.ilr.cornell.edu
Inequality, discrimination, workplace ethics; occupational segregation
Kevin Hallock, Dean

Drum Major Institute for Public Policy - Not For Profit
3041 Broadway, 4th Floor, Auburn Hall, New York, NY 10027
212-203-9219
e-mail: info@drummajorinstitute.org
Web site: www.drummajorinst.org
Think tank dedicated to facilitating dialogue on social issues & promoting public policies to drive economic justice & social change
PJ Kim, Executive Director

NYS Bar Assn, Diversity and Inclusion Cmte
Epstein Becker & Green, PC
250 Park Avenue, New York, NY 10177
212-351-4500 Fax: 212-878-8600
e-mail: kstandard@ebglaw.com
Web site: www.ebglaw.com
Kenneth G. Standard, Co-Chair

Family Planning Advocates of New York State
194 Washington Avenue, Suite 620, Albany, NY 12210
518-436-8408 Fax: 518-436-0004
e-mail: info@familyplanningadvocates.org
Web site: www.familyplanningadvocates.org
Reproductive rights
Kim Atkins, Chair

Filipino American Human Services Inc (FAHSI)
18514 Hillside Avenue, Jamaica, NY 11432
718-883-1295 Fax: 718-523-9606
e-mail: fahsi@fahsi.org
Web site: www.fahsi.org
FAHSI is a community-based, non-profit organization committed to serving NYC's Filipino & Filipino-American communities through education, advocacy, referrals, counseling services & support programs
Zultan Bermudez, Chair

NYS Bar Assn, Disability Rights Cmte
Girvin & Ferlazzo, PC
20 Corporate Woods Blvd, Albany, NY 12211
518-462-0300 Fax: 518-462-5037
Tara Lynn Moffett, Chair

Human Rights First
75 Broad Street, 31st Floor, New York, NY 10004
212-845-5200 Fax: 212-845-5299
e-mail: feedback@humanrightsfirst.org
Web site: www.humanrightsfirst.org
Advocacy for the promotion & protection of fundamental human rights worldwide
Elisa Massimino, President & Chief Executive Officer

Human Rights Watch
350 Fifth Avenue, 34th Floor, New York, NY 10118-3299
212-290-4700 Fax: 212-736-1300
e-mail: hrwnyc@hrw.org
Web site: www.hrw.org
Working with victims & activists to prevent discrimination, defend human rights & uphold political freedom across the world through research, reporting & advocacy
Kenneth Roth, Executive Director

International Institute of Buffalo, NY, Inc
864 Delaware Avenue, Buffalo, NY 14209
716-883-1900 Fax: 716-883-9529
e-mail: iib@iibuff.org
Web site: www.iibuff.org
Assists newly arrived refugees & immigrants with critical needs, medical care & employment training/placement; legal immigration service, translation & interpretation services, school advocacy
Eva Hassett, Executive Director

Jewish Community Relations Council of NY Inc
225 West 34th Street, Suite 1607, New York, NY 10122
212-983-4800 Fax: 212-983-4084
Web site: www.jcrcny.org
Serves as coordinating body for more than 60 Jewish organizations in metropolitan NY; promotes & protects the rights of NY's Jewish community
Michael S. Miller, Executive Vice President & Chief Executive Officer

Lambda Legal
120 Wall Street, 19th Floor, New York, NY 10005-3919
212-809-8585 Fax: 212-809-0055
Web site: www.lambdalegal.org
Protects the rights of gay, lesbian, bisexual & transgender people as well as individuals with HIV
Kevin M. Cathcart, Executive Director

LatinoJustice PRLDEF
99 Hudson Street, 14th Floor, New York, NY 10013-2815
212-219-3360 or 800-328-2322 Fax: 212-431-4276
Web site: www.latinojustice.org
Secures, promotes & protects the civil & human rights of the Latino community through litigation, policy analysis, education & advocacy
Juan Cartagena, President & General Counsel

Lesbian, Gay, Bisexual & Transgender Community Center - Not For Profit
208 West 13th Street, New York, NY 10011-7702
212-620-7310 Fax: 212-924-2657
e-mail: info@gaycenter.org
Web site: www.gaycenter.org
Mental health counseling, substance abuse treatment & counseling, after-school youth services, HIV/AIDS services, advocacy, cultural programs, affordable meeting & conference services, community-building
Glennda Testone, Executive Director

National Council of Jewish Women
475 Riverside Drive, Suite 1901, New York, NY 10115
212-645-4048 Fax: 212-645-7466
e-mail: action@ncjw.org
Web site: www.ncjw.org
Human rights & social service advocacy & education
Nancy K. Kaufman, Chief Executive Officer

National Organization for Women, NYS
150 West 28th Street, Suite 304, New York, NY 10001
212-627-9895 Fax: 212-627-9861
e-mail: nownewyorkstate@gmail.com
Web site: www.nownys.org
Legislative lobbying on issues affecting women
Sonia Ossorio, President

Offices and agencies generally appear in alphabetical order, except when specific order is requested by listee.

New School for Social Research, Department of Politics
6 East 16th Street, Room 711A, New York, NY 10003
212-229-5747 x3090 Fax: 212-229-5473
e-mail: kalyvasa@newschool.edu
Web site: www.newschool.edu
Comparative politics, human rights, nationalism & ethnicity
Andreas Kalyvas, Chair

New School for Social Research, Zolberg Institute on Migration & Mobility
6 East 16th Street, 10th Floor, New York, NY 10003
e-mail: migration@newschool.edu
Web site: www.newschool.edu
International migrations, refugees
Alexandra Delano, Director

New York Civil Liberties Union
125 Broad Street, 19th Floor, New York, NY 10004
212-607-3300 Fax: 212-607-3318
Web site: www.nyclu.org
Civil rights & civil liberties
Donna Lieberman, Executive Director

New York Civil Rights Coalition
424 West 33rd Street, Suite 350, New York, NY 10001
212-563-5636 Fax: 212-563-9757
e-mail: contact@nycivilrights.org
Web site: www.nycivilrights.org
Advocacy of racial equality & multiracial cooperation in advancing social progress through the protection & enforcement of civil rights & the unlearning of stereotypes
Michael Meyers, President & Executive Director

New York Immigration Coalition (The)
131 West 33rd Street, Suite 610, New York, NY 10001
212-627-2227 Fax: 212-627-9314
Web site: www.thenyic.org
Nonprofit umbrella advocacy organization for groups assisting immigrants & refugees in NYS
Steven Choi, Executive Director

New York Lawyers for the Public Interest
151 West 30th Street, 11th Floor, New York, NY 10001-4017
212-244-4664 Fax: 212-244-4570
Web site: www.nylpi.org
Disability rights law; access to health care; environmental justice & community development; Pro Bono Clearinghouse services
McGregor Smyth, Executive Director

New York State Council of Churches
1580 Central Avenue, Albany, NY 12205
518-436-9319 Fax: 518-427-6705
e-mail: nyscoc@aol.com
Web site: www.nyscoc.org
Organization of Christian churches in NYS working to address social justice issues & protect Christian communities through education & worship
Rev. Peter M. Cook, Executive Director

Open Society Foundations
224 West 57th Street, New York, NY 10019
212-548-0600 Fax: 212-548-4600
Web site: www.opensocietyfoundations.org
Works to build inclusive societies through the promotion of equitable public policies & the development of initiatives for justice, education & public health advancement
Christopher Stone, President

Resource Center for Independent Living (RCIL)
409 Columbia Street, PO Box 210, Utica, NY 13503-0210
315-797-4642 or TTY: 315-797-5837 Fax: 315-797-4747
Web site: www.rcil.com
Services & advocacy for disabled people; public information, community education & awareness
Zvia McCormick, Chief Executive Officer

SUNY Buffalo Human Rights Center
SUNY Buffalo Law School, 710 O'Brian Hall, Buffalo, NY 14260
716-645-2257
e-mail: buffalohrc@gmail.com
Web site: www.law.buffalo.edu
Supports, promotes & fosters the study & practice of human rights law through student internships & human rights conferences & events
Tara J. Melish, Director & Associate Professor

Schuyler Center for Analysis & Advocacy (SCAA)
540 Broadway, Albany, NY 12207
518-463-1896 Fax: 518-463-3364
e-mail: kbreslin@scaany.org
Web site: www.scaany.org
Advocacy & policy analysis on education, child welfare, health, economic security, mental health, revenue & taxation issues
Kate Breslin, President & Chief Executive Officer

Self Advocacy Association of NYS
500 Balltown Road, Building 12, Schenectady, NY 12304
518-382-1454 Fax: 518-382-1594
e-mail: sholmes@sanys.org
Web site: www.sanys.org
Advocacy for & by persons with developmental disabilities to ensure civil rights & opportunities
Steve Holmes, Administrative Director

Simon Wiesenthal Center, Museum of Tolerance NY
226 East 42nd Street, New York, NY 10017
212-697-1180
e-mail: motny@wiesenthal.com
Web site: www.wiesenthal.com
Preserves the memory of the Holocaust & invites individuals to consider issues of prejudice & tolerance through workshops, exhibits, training programs & educational outreach
Stacey Eliuk, Program Manager

Tanenbaum Center for Interreligious Understanding
254 West 31st Street, 7th Floor, New York, NY 10001
212-967-7707 Fax: 212-967-9001
e-mail: info@tanenbaum.org
Web site: www.tanenbaum.org
Puts interreligious understanding into practice; reduces and prevents prejudice & violence done in the name of religion
Joyce S. Dubensky, Chief Executive Officer

The Legal Aid Society
199 Water Street, New York, NY 10038
212-577-3300 Fax: 212-509-8761
Web site: www.legal-aid.org
Seymour W. James, Jr., Attorney-in-Chief

Whiteman Osterman & Hanna LLP
One Commerce Plaza, Albany, NY 12260
518-487-7600 Fax: 518-487-7777
Web site: www.woh.com
William S. Nolan, Partner

Women's Refugee Commission
122 East 42nd Street, New York, NY 10168-1289
212-551-3115 Fax: 212-551-3180
e-mail: info@wrcommission.org
Web site: www.womensrefugeecommission.org
Advocacy on behalf of refugee women & children worldwide
Sarah Costa, Executive Director

INSURANCE

NEW YORK STATE

GOVERNOR'S OFFICE

Governor's Office
Executive Chamber
State Capitol
Albany, NY 12224
518-474-8390 Fax: 518-474-1513
Web site: www.ny.gov

Governor:
Andrew M Cuomo 518-474-8390
Secretary to the Governor:
William Mulrow 518-474-4246
Counsel to the Governor:
Alphonso David 518-474-8343
Chief of Staff:
Melissa DeRosa . . . . 518-474-8418 or 212-681-4640
Director, Communications:
James Allen. . . . . 518-474-8418 or 212-681-4640

EXECUTIVE DEPARTMENTS AND RELATED AGENCIES

Financial Services Department
One State Street
New York, NY 10001
212-480-6400 or 518-474-6600
e-mail: public-affairs@dfs.ny.gov
Web site: www.dfs.ny.gov

Acting Superintendent:
Maria T Vullo 212-709-3501
Assistant Director, Administration & Operations:
Lori Fraser. 518-486-4737
Deputy Superintendent & General Counsel:
Marjorie Gross 212-709-1640
Deputy Superintendent, Community Regional Banks:
Martin Cofsky 212-709-1610
Director, Criminal Investigations Bureau:
Ricardo Velez 212-709-3554
Chief Information Officer:
William Rachmiel 212-709-5420
Senior Public Information Specialist:
Ronald Klug. 212-480-2285/fax: 212-480-6077
Consumer Representative, State Charter Advisory Board:
Vacant 212-709-3500

Banking Division
Deputy Superintendent:
Vacant 212-709-1690

Insurance Division
Deputy Superintendent, Property & Casualty Markets:
Michael Moriarty. 212-480-5127/fax: 212-480-2310
Chief, Life Insurance Bureau:
Gail Keren. 212-480-5030
Chief, Health Insurance Bureau:
Vacant 518-486-2970/fax: 518-474-3397
Insurance Examiner 3:
Michael Maffei 212-480-5023

Financial Frauds & Consumer Protection Division
Director, Frauds:
Frank Orlando 212-480-5770/fax: 212-480-6066
Assistant Director, Frauds:
Angelo Carbone 212-480-5688

Capital Markets Division
Acting Director, Capital Markets:
Matti Peltonen 212-480-5071/fax: 212-480-6085
Deputy Superintendent, Mortgage Banking:
Rhonda Ricketts 212-480-5540

Insurance Fund (NYS)
One Watervliet Ave Ext
Albany, NY 12206
518-437-6400
Web site: www.nysif.com

199 Church St
New York, NY 10007
212-587-9000

Executive Director & CEO:
Eric Madoff. . . . . 212-312-7004 or 518-437-5220
Deputy Executive Director:
Dorothy Carey. 212-312-9933
Deputy Executive Director:
Shirley Stark 212-312-9917
Deputy Executive Director:
Colleen Gardner 212-587-9000
Chief Fiscal Officer:
Susan D Sharp. 518-437-6168
General Attorney:
Gregory Allen 518-437-5220
Public Information Officer:
Robert Lawson. 518-437-3504/fax: 518-437-1849

Administration
Director:
Joseph Mullen 518-437-5220

Claims & Medical Operations
Director:
Edward Hiller 212-312-7880

Confidential Investigations
Director:
George T Tidona. 631-756-4007

Field Services
Director:
Armin Holdorf 212-587-5225

Information Technology Service
Chief Information Officer:
Sean O'Brien. 518-437-4361
Director, ITS:
Laurie Endries. 518-437-3130

Insurance Fund Board of Commissioners
Chair:
Kenneth R Theobalds 518-437-5220
Vice Chair:
Barry Swidler 518-437-5220
Secretary to the Board:
Francine James 212-312-7408
Member (ex-officio)/Commissioner, NYS Dept of Labor:
Peter M. Rivera 518-437-5220
Member:
Eileen A Frank 518-437-5220
Member:
Joseph Canovas. 518-437-5220
Member:
David E Ourlicht. 518-437-5220

Offices and agencies generally appear in alphabetical order, except when specific order is requested by listee.

Investments
Director:
Miriam Martinez . . . 212-587-6550

NYSIF District Offices

Albany
1 Watervliet Ave Ext, Albany, NY 12206
Business Manager:
Augusto Bortoloni . . . 518-437-6401/fax: 518-437-8021

Buffalo
225 Oak St, Buffalo, NY 14203
Business Manager:
Ronald Reed . . . 716-851-2004/fax: 716-851-2131

Binghamton
Glendale Technology Park, 2001 E Perimeter Rd, Endicott, NY 13760
Business Manager:
Thomas Racko . . . 607-741-6023/fax: 607-741-5029

Nassau County, Long Island
8 Corporate Center Dr, 2nd Fl, Melville, NY 11747
Business Manager:
Cliff Meister . . . 631-756-4003/fax: 631-756-4030

Rochester
100 Chestnut St, Ste 1000, Rochester, NY 14604
Business Manager:
Lisa Ellsworth . . . 585-258-2100/fax: 585-258-2065

Suffolk County, Long Island
8 Corporate Center Dr, 3rd Fl, Melville, NY 11747
Business Manager:
Catherine Carillo . . . 631-756-4330/fax: 631-756-4260

Syracuse
1045 Seventh North St, Liverpool, NY 13088
Business Manager:
Patricia Albert . . . 315-453-8300/fax: 315-453-8313

White Plains
105 Corporate Park Dr, Ste 200, White Plains, NY 10604
Business Manager:
Carl Heitner . . . 914-701-6292/fax: 914-701-2181

Premium Audit
Director:
Glenn Cunningham . . . 212-587-7470

Underwriting
Director:
John Massetti . . . 212-312-7012

Labor Department
Building 12, Room 500
Harriman State Office Campus
Albany, NY 12240
518-457-9000 Fax: 518-457-6908
e-mail: nysdol@labor.ny.gov
Web site: www.labor.ny.gov

Commissioner:
Roberta Reardon . . . 518-457-9000
Executive Deputy Commissioner:
Mario Musolino . . . 518-457-4318
Director, Communications:
Leo Rosales . . . 518-457-5519/fax: 518-485-1126
e-mail: leo.rosales@labor.ny.gov

Hazard Abatement Board
Chair:
Katherine D. Schrier . . . 518-457-7629

Employment Relations Board
Chair:
Jerome Lefkowitz . . . 518-457-2664
e-mail: perbinfo@perb.ny.gov

Industrial Board of Appeals
Chair:
Anne P Stevason . . . 518-474-4785

Unemployment Insurance Appeal Board
Chair:
Leonard Polletta . . . 518-402-0205
Executive Director:
Susan Borenstein . . . 518-402-0205

State Workforce Investment Board
Chair:
Vacant . . . 518-457-8312/fax: 518-485-8604

Law Department
120 Broadway
New York, NY 10271-0332
212-416-8000 or 800-771-7755
Web site: www.ag.ny.gov

State Capitol
Albany, NY 12224-0341
518-776-2000
Fax: 518-650-9401

Attorney General:
Eric T Schneiderman . . . 212-416-8050 or 518-776-2000
Chief of Staff:
Brian Mahanna . . . 212-416-8050
Press Secretary:
Matt Mittenthal . . . 212-416-8060/fax: 212-416-6005

State Counsel
Chief Deputy Attorney General & Counsel:
Janet Sabel . . . 212-416-8050
Chief Deputy Attorney General & Counsel:
Jason Brown . . . 212-416-8050
Executive Deputy Attorney General, State Counsel:
Kent T. Stauffer . . . 212-416-8252/fax: 212-416-6001

Civil Recoveries Bureau
Bureau Chief:
John Cremo . . . 518-776-2173/fax: 518-915-7731

Claims Bureau
Bureau Chief:
Katharine Brooks . . . 518-776-2300 or 212-416-8500

Litigation Bureau
Bureau Chief:
Jeffrey Dvorin . . . 518-776-2300 or 212-416-8610
fax: 518-473-1572

Real Property Bureau
Bureau Chief:
Alison Crocker . . . 518-776-2700

Workers' Compensation Board
328 State Street
Schenectady, NY 12305
518-462-8880 or 877-632-4996 Fax: 518-473-1415
e-mail: publicinfo@wcb.ny.gov
Web site: www.wcb.ny.gov

Executive Director:
MaryBeth Woods . . . 518-408-0469

Policy Areas

Offices and agencies generally appear in alphabetical order, except when specific order is requested by listee.

Chair, Board of Commissioners:
Robert E Beloten 518-408-0469/fax: 518-473-1415
Vice Chair:
Ken Munnelly 518-408-0469/fax: 518-473-1415
General Counsel:
Vacant 518-486-9564/fax: 518-402-0113
Director, Public Information:
Rachel McEneny 518-408-5592/fax: 518-473-1415
e-mail: publicinfo@wcb.ny.gov
Fraud Inspector General:
Vacant . . . . 888-363-6001 or 518-473-4839
fax: 518-402-1059
Advocate for Business:
Neil Gilberg 518-486-3331
Advocate for Injured Workers:
Edwin Ruff . . . . 800-580-6665 or 518-471-8182
fax: 518-486-7510

Administration
Facilities Management:
Michael DeBarr. 518-486-9597
Chief, Security:
Sylvio Mantello 518-402-0172/fax: 518-402-6100
Director, Human Resources:
Gilda Hernandez 518-486-3348/fax: 518-486-6364
Affirmative Action Officer:
Jaime Benitez. 518-486-5128/fax: 518-486-6364

Information Management Systems
Director:
Vacant 518-474-6557/fax: 518-474-9367
Director, Continuous Improvement/MIS:
Thomas Wegener 518-486-5143

Operations
Director, Bureau of Compliance:
Vacant 518-474-9598/fax: 518-402-6201

District Offices

Albany
100 Broadway-Menands, Albany, NY 12241
District Manager:
Laurie Hart 866-750-5157/fax: 518-473-9166

Binghamton
State Office Bldg, 44 Hawley St, Binghamton, NY 13901
District Manager:
David Gardiner. 866-802-3604/fax: 607-721-8464

Brooklyn
111 Livingston St, 22nd Fl, Brooklyn, NY 11201
District Manager:
Tom Agostino. 800-877-1373/fax: 718-802-6642

Buffalo
Ellicott Sq Building, 295 Main Street Ste 400, Buffalo, NY 14203
District Manager:
Michelle Hirsch 866-211-0645/fax: 716-842-2171

Long Island
220 Rabro Drive, Ste 100, Hauppauge, NY 11788-4230
District Manager:
Bryan Pile. 866-681-5354/fax: 631-952-7966

Manhattan
215 W 125th St, New York, NY 10027
District Manager:
Sherri Cunningham. 800-877-1373/fax: 212-864-7204

Peekskill
41 N Division St, Peekskill, NY 10566
District Manager:
Vacant. 866-746-0552/fax: 914-788-5809

Queens
168-46 91st Ave, 3rd Fl, Jamaica, NY 11432
District Manager:
Bryan Pile. 800-877-1373

Rochester
130 Main St West, Rochester, NY 14614
District Manager:
Matthew Bligh 866-211-0644/fax: 585-238-8351

Syracuse
935 James Street, Syracuse, NY 13203
District Manager:
Marc Johnson 866-802-3730/fax: 315-423-2938

Workers' Compensation Board of Commissioners
Commissioner & Vice Chair:
Ken Munnelly 518-408-0469
Commissioner:
Richard A Bell 518-408-0469
Commissioner:
Mark D Higgins 518-408-0469
Commissioner:
Linda Hull. 518-408-0469
Commissioner:
Candace K Finnegan. 914-788-5890
Commissioner:
Samuel G Williams. 518-408-0469
Commissioner:
Freida Foster 518-408-0469
Commissioner:
Ellen O Paprocki. 315-423-1276
Commissioner:
Conrad W Lower 518-408-0469
Commissioner:
Loren Lobban 518-408-0469
Secretary to the Board:
Sandra M Olson 518-402-6070

NEW YORK STATE LEGISLATURE

See Legislative Branch in Section 1 for additional Standing Committee and Subcommittee information.

Assembly Standing Committees

Insurance
Chair:
Kevin Cahill (D) 518-455-4436
Ranking Minority Member:
William Barclay (R) 518-455-5841

Labor
Chair:
Michele Titus (D) 518-455-5668
Ranking Minority Member:
Karl Brabenec (R). 518-455-5991

Senate Standing Committees

Insurance
Chair:
James L Seward (R) 518-455-3131
Ranking Minority Member:
Neil D Breslin (D). 518-455-2225

Labor
Chair:
Jack Martins (R) 518-455-3265
Ranking Minority Member:
Jose R Peralta (D). 518-455-2529

U.S. GOVERNMENT

U.S. CONGRESS

See U.S. Congress Chapter for additional Standing Committee and Subcommittee information.

House of Representatives Standing Committees

Financial Services
Chair:
Jeb Hensarling (R-TX) 202-225-3484
Ranking Member:
Maxine Waters (D-CA) 202-225-2201
Vice Chairman:
Patrick T. McHenry (R-NC) 202-225-2576
New York Delegate:
Peter T. King (R) 202-225-7896
New York Delegate:
Carolyn B. Maloney (D) 202-225-7944
New York Delegate:
Gregory W. Meeks (D) 202-225-3461
New York Delegate:
Nydia M. Velazquez (D) 202-225-2361

Subcommittee
Capital Markets & Government Sponsored Enterprises
Chair:
Scott Garrett (R-NJ) 202-225-4465
Ranking Member:
Carolyn B. Maloney (D-NY) 202-225-7944
New York Delegate:
Gregory W. Meeks (D) 202-225-3461
New York Delegate:
Peter T. King (R) 202-225-7896

Senate Standing Committees

Finance
Chair:
Orrin G. Hatch (R-UT) 202-224-5251
Ranking Member:
Ron Wyden (D-OR) 202-224-5244

Subcommittees
Health Care
Chair:
Patrick J. Toomey (R-PA) 202-224-4254
Ranking Member:
Debbie Stabenow (D-MI) 202-224-4822
Social Security, Pensions and Family Policy
Chair:
Dean Heller (R-NV) 202-224-6244
Ranking Member:
Sherrod Brown (D-OH) 202-224-2315

PRIVATE SECTOR

American International Group Inc
175 Water Street, New York, NY 10038
212-770-7000
Web site: www.aig.com
International business, government & financial services
Victor Aviles, Director, Corporate Communications

Aon Service Corporation
199 Water St, 35th Fl, New York, NY 10038
212-441-1150 Fax: 212-441-1929
e-mail: ellen_perle@aon.com
Web site: www.aon.com
Regulatory Law Licensing
Ellen Perle, Chief General Counsel/Regulatory Law Licensing

Associated Risk Managers of New York Inc
4 Airline Drive, Suite 205, Albany, NY 12205
518-690-2072 or 800-735-5441 Fax: 518-690-2074
e-mail: arm@armnortheast.com
Web site: www.armnortheast.com
John McLaughlin, Executive Director

Connors & Corcoran PLLC
Times Square Bldg, 45 Exchange St, Ste 250, Rochester, NY 14614
585-232-5885 Fax: 585-546-3631
e-mail: ebuholtz@connorscorcoran.com
Web site: www.connorscorcoran.com
Eileen E Buholtz, Member

DeGraff, Foy, & Kunz, LLP
90 State Street, Albany, NY 12207
518-462-5300 Fax: 518-436-0210
e-mail: firm@degraff-foy.com
Web site: www.degraff-foy.com
Tax law & procedure, administrative law
David Kunz, Managing Partner

Dupee & Monroe, PC
211 Main Street, Box 470, Goshen, NY 10924
845-294-8900 Fax: 845-294-3619
e-mail: law@dupeelaw.com
Web site: www.dupeelaw.com
Litigation, personal injury law, medical malpractice, product liability, civil rights, discrimination, sexual harassment
James E Monroe, Managing Partner

Empire Blue Cross & Blue Shield
1 Liberty Plaza, New York, NY 10006
212-476-1000 Fax: 212-476-1281
Web site: www.empireblue.com
Health insurance
Lawrence Schreiber, President

Equitable Life Assurance Society of the US
1290 Ave of the Americas, New York, NY 10104
212-314-3828 Fax: 212-707-1890
e-mail: wendy.cooper@axa.financial.com
Web site: www.axa-financial.com
Life insurance regulation
Wendy E Cooper, Senior Vice President & Associate General Counsel, Government Relations

Excellus Health Plan Inc
165 Court Street, Rochester, NY 14647
585-327-7581 Fax: 585-327-7585
e-mail: stephen.sloan@excellus.com
Web site: www.excellus.com
Health insurance
Stephen R Sloan, Senior Vice President & Chief Administrative Officer, General Counsel

Excess Line Association of New York
One Exchange Plz, 55 Broadway, 29th Fl, New York, NY 10006
646-292-5555 Fax: 626-292-5505
e-mail: dmaher@elany.org
Web site: www.elany.org
Industry advisory association; facilitate & encourage compliance with the excess line law
Daniel F Maher, Executive Director

Offices and agencies generally appear in alphabetical order, except when specific order is requested by listee.

Group Health Inc
441 9th Ave, 8th Fl, New York, NY 10001
212-615-0891 Fax: 212-563-8561
e-mail: jgoodwin@ghi.com
Web site: www.ghi.com
Affordable, quality health insurance for working individuals & families
Jeffrey Goodwin, Director, Governmental Relations

Insurance Brokers' Association of the State of New York
119 Washington Avenue, Suite 300, Albany, NY 12210
518-694-5504
e-mail: info@ibany.org
Web site: www.ibany.org
Dianne Patterson, Executive Director

Life Insurance Council of New York, Inc
551 Fifth Ave, 29th Floor, New York, NY 10176
212-986-6181 Fax: 212-986-6549
e-mail: tworkman@licony.org
Web site: www.licony.org
Promote a legislative, regulatory & judicial environment that encourages members to conduct & grow their business
Thomas E Workman, President & Chief Executive Officer

Marsh & McLennan Companies
1166 6th Ave, New York, NY 10036-2774
212-345-5000
e-mail: barbara.perlmutter@mmc.com
Web site: www.mmc.com
Risk & insurance services; investment management; consulting
Barbara S Perlmutter, Senior Vice President, Public Affairs

Medical Society of the State of New York, Div of Socio-Medical Economics
856 Merrick Avenue, Westbury, NY 11590
516-488-6100
e-mail: rmcnally@mssny.org
Web site: www.mssny.org
Workers compensations; health insurance programs
Regina McNally, Vice President

MetLife
27-01 Queens Plaza North, Long Island City, NY 11101
212-578-3968 Fax: 212-578-8869
e-mail: jfdonnellan@metlife.com
Web site: www.metlife.com
MetLife, Inc is a leading provider of insurance and financial services.
James F Donnellan, Vice President Government & Industry Relations

NY Life Insurance Co
51 Madison Ave, Suite 1111, New York, NY 10010
212-576-7000 Fax: 212-576-4473
e-mail: gayle_yeomans@newyorklife.com
Web site: www.newyorklife.com
Insurance products & financial services
Gayle A Yeomans, Vice President Government Affairs

NY Property Insurance Underwriting Association
100 William St, New York, NY 10038
212-208-9700 Fax: 212-344-9676
Web site: www.nypiua.com
Joseph Calvo, President

NYMAGIC Inc
919 3rd Ave, 10th Fl, New York, NY 10022-3919
212-551-0600 Fax: 212-551-0724
e-mail: info@mmo.com
Web site: www.nymagic.com
Marine insurance & excess & surplus lines
A George Kallop, President & CEO

New York Insurance Association Inc
130 Washington Ave, Albany, NY 12210
518-432-4227 Fax: 518-432-4220
Web site: www.nyia.org
Property & casualty insurance
Ellen Melchionni, President

New York Long-Term Care Brokers Ltd
11 Halfmoon Executive Park, Clifton Park, NY 12065
518-371-5522 x116 Fax: 518-371-6131
e-mail: kjohnson@nyltcb.com
Web site: www.nyltcb.com
Long-term care, life & disability insurance; consulting & sales to individual consumers & financial service industry professionals
Kevin Johnson, President & CEO

New York Municipal Insurance Reciprocal (NYMIR)
150 State Street, Albany, NY 12207
518-465-7552 Fax: 518-465-0724
e-mail: jcrawford@kcnymir.org
Web site: www.nymir.org
Property and casualty insurance services for municipalities
Kevin Crawford, Executive Director

New York Schools Insurance Reciprocal (NYSIR)
333 Earle Ovington Blvd, Suite 1030, Uniondale, NY 11553
516-393-2329 or 800-476-9747 Fax: 516-227-2352
e-mail: jgoncalves@wrightrisk.com
Web site: www.nysir.org
Insurance & risk management services for public school districts
Joseph Goncalves, Executive Director

NAIFA - New York State
38 Sheridan Ave, Albany, NY 12210
518-462-5567 Fax: 518-462-5569
e-mail: naifanewyork@aol.com
Web site: www.naifanys.org
Association of individuals engaged in the sale of life, health & property/casualty insurance & related financial services
Mark L Yavornitzki, Executive Vice President & Chief Administrative Officer

Professional Insurance Agents of New York State
25 Chamberlain St, PO Box 997, Glenmont, NY 12077-0997
800-424-4244 Fax: 888-225-6935
e-mail: kenb@piaonline.org
Web site: www.piany.org
Ken Bessette, President/Chief Executive Officer

SBLI USA Mutual Life Insurance Company Inc
460 W 34th St, Suite 800, New York, NY 10001-2320
212-356-0327 Fax: 212-624-0700
e-mail: dklugman@sbliusa.com
Web site: www.sbliusa.com
Corporate insurance regulatory law & government affairs
Vikki Pryor, President & Chief Executive Officer

St John's University-Peter J Tobin College of Business, School of Risk Mgmt
8000 Utopia Pkwy, Queens, NY 11439
718-990-6800
Web site: www.stjohns.edu
Victoria Shoaf, Dean

Stroock & Stroock & Lavan LLP
180 Maiden Lane, New York, NY 10038-4982
212-806-5541 Fax: 212-806-2541
e-mail: dgabay@stroock.com
Insurance, reinsurance, corporate & regulatory law
Donald D Gabay, Attorney

Offices and agencies generally appear in alphabetical order, except when specific order is requested by listee.

Support Services Alliance Inc
107 Prospect St, PO Box 130, Schoharie, NY 12157
800-322-3920 or 518-295-7966 Fax: 518-295-8556
e-mail: info@ssamembers.com
Web site: www.smallbizgrowth.com
Small business support services & insurance
Steven Cole, President

Unity Mutual Life Insurance Co
507 Plum St, PO Box 5000, Syracuse, NY 13250-5000
315-448-7000 Fax: 315-448-7100
e-mail: jwason@unity-life.com
Web site: www.unity-life.com
Jay Wason, Jr, General Counsel

Utica Mutual Insurance Co
PO Box 530, Utica, NY 13503-0530
1-800-274-1914 Fax: 315-734-2662
Web site: www.uticanational.com
Property, casualty insurance
Richard Creedon, Executive Vice President, Claims & General Counsel

JUDICIAL & LEGAL SYSTEMS

NEW YORK STATE

GOVERNOR'S OFFICE

Governor's Office
Executive Chamber
State Capitol
Albany, NY 12224
518-474-8390 Fax: 518-474-1513
Web site: www.ny.gov

Governor:
Andrew M Cuomo 518-474-8390
Secretary to the Governor:
William Mulrow 518-474-4246
Counsel to the Governor:
Alphonso David 518-474-8343
Chief of Staff:
Melissa DeRosa . . . . 518-474-8418 or 212-681-4640
Director, Communications:
James Allen. . . . . 518-474-8418 or 212-681-4640
Director, State Operations:
James Malatras 518-486-9871
Deputy Director for State Operations:
Rosemary Powers 518-473-9958
First Assistant Counsel:
Sandi Toll 518-474-8434

EXECUTIVE DEPARTMENTS AND RELATED AGENCIES

Criminal Justice Services, Division of
80 South Swan Street
Albany, NY 12210
518-457-5837 or 800-262-3252 Fax: 518-457-3089
e-mail: infodcjsc@dcjs.ny.gov
Web site: www.criminaljustice.ny.gov

Executive Deputy Commissioner:
Michael C Green. 518-457-1260
Affirmative Action Officer:
Wanda Trouche. 518-485-7962
Deputy Director, Public Information:
Janine Kava 518-457-8906/fax: 518-485-7715
e-mail: janine.kava@dcjs.ny.gov
Deputy Director, Public Information:
Walt McClure 518-457-8828
e-mail: walter.mcclure@dcjs.ny.gov

Human Resources Management
Director:
Karen Davis 518-485-1704

State Finance & Budget
Director, Finance:
Mary Ann Rossi 518-457-6105

Legal Services
Deputy Commissioner & Counsel:
John Czajka. 518-457-4181

Commission on Forensic Science

Office of Forensic Services
Director:
Vacant. 518-457-4181

Office of Criminal Justice Operations
Director, Criminal Justice Operations:
Joe Morrissey 518-485-2995

Highway Safety & Technology Unit
518-485-7620

Office of Justice Information Systems
Deputy Commissioner:
Anne Roest 518-485-7176

Information Technology Development Group

Information Technology Services Group
Director:
Alex Roberts. 518-457-3743

Office of Sex Offender Registry
Director:
Michelle Mulligan 518-457-3121

Office of Justice Research & Performance
Deputy Commissioner:
Terry Salo 518-457-3724
Chief, Crimestat Unit:
Paula K Lockhart 518-485-7122
Chief, Crime Reporting & Statistical Services Unit:
Adam Dean 518-457-8381

Office of Public Safety

Law Enforcement Accreditation Program

Police & Peace Officer Registry & Training

Missing Persons Clearinghouse

Security Guard Program
Deputy Commissioner:
Michael Wood. 518-485-7620
Director:
Julie Pasquini 518-457-2666
e-mail: julie.pasquini@dcjs.ny.gov

Funding & Program Development Office
Deputy Commissioner:
Jeffrey Bender 518-457-8462

Operation IMPACT Coordinator
Director:
Julie Pasquini 518-485-7923

Law Department
120 Broadway
New York, NY 10271-0332
212-416-8000 or 800-771-7755
Web site: www.ag.ny.gov

State Capitol
Albany, NY 12224-0341
518-776-2000
Fax: 518-650-9401

Attorney General:
Eric T Schneiderman . . . . 212-416-8050 or 518-776-2000

Administration
Agency Bldg 4, Empire State Plaza, Albany, NY 12224-0341
COO:
Jeanette Moy 518-776-2500/fax: 518-915-7753

Budget & Fiscal Management
Director (Acting):
Peter O'Neil 518-776-2110/fax: 518-915-7751

Offices and agencies generally appear in alphabetical order, except when specific order is requested by listee.

Human Resources Management
Director:
Robert Pablo . . . 518-776-2500

Legal Recruitment
Asst Attorney General in Charge:
Sandra J Grannum . . . 212-416-8080/fax: 212-416-8264

Appeals & Opinions Division
Solicitor General:
Barbara D Underwood . . . 212-416-8016 or 518-776-2002
Deputy Counsel:
John Amodeo . . . 518-776-2000

Law Library
Chief, Library Services:
Patricia Partello . . . 518-776-2566/fax: 518-915-7737
Legal Support Analyst:
Vacant . . . 212-416-8012/fax: 212-416-6130

Criminal Justice
Executive Deputy Attorney General, Criminal Justice:
Kelly Donovan . . . 212-416-8050

Criminal Enforcement & Financial Crimes Bureau
Bureau Chief:
Gary Fishman . . . 518-776-2370 or 212-416-8750

Medicaid Fraud Control Unit
120 Broadway, 13th Fl, New York, NY 10271-0007
Deputy Attorney General in Charge & Director:
Amy Held . . . 212-417-5250/fax: 212-417-4284
Asst Deputy Attorney General:
Paul J Mahoney . . . 212-417-5254
Deputy Regional Director, Buffalo:
Gary A Baldauf . . . 716-853-8507/fax: 716-852-8525
Regional Director, Long Island:
Jane Turkin . . . 631-952-6400/fax: 631-952-6382
Regional Director, Albany:
Kathleen Boland . . . 518-533-6011/fax: 518-533-6012
Regional Director, Rochester:
Catherine Wagner . . . 585-262-2860/fax: 585-262-2866
Regional Director, Syracuse:
Ralph Tortora, III . . . 315-423-1104/fax: 315-423-1120
Deputy Regional Director, Pearl River:
Anne S Jardine . . . 845-732-7525/fax: 845-732-7555

Economic Justice
Executive Deputy Attorney General, Economic Justice:
Manisha Sheth . . . 212-416-8050

Antitrust Bureau
Bureau Chief:
Eric J Stock . . . 212-416-8282/fax: 212-416-6015
e-mail: eric.stock@ag.ny.gov

Consumer Frauds & Protection Bureau
Bureau Chief:
Jane Azia . . . 212-416-8300/fax: 212-416-6003

Internet Bureau
Bureau Chief:
Kathleen McGee . . . 212-416-8433/fax: 212-416-8369

Investor Protection Bureau
Bureau Chief:
Chad Johnson . . . 212-416-8225/fax: 212-416-8816

Intergovernmental Relations
Deputy Director, Intergovernmental Affairs:
Lilliam Perez . . . 212-416-6044
Director, Intergovernmental Affairs:
Michael Meade . . . 212-416-8985

Office of the Attorney General
Chief of Staff:
Brian Mahanna . . . 212-416-8050
Senior Advisor/Director, Operations:
Christina Harvey . . . 212-416-8095
Deputy Counsel:
John Amodeo . . . 518-776-2000
Legislative Policy Advisor:
Kate M Powers . . . 518-776-2444/fax: 518-650-9401
Press Secretary:
Matt Mittenthal . . . 212-416-8060/fax: 212-416-6005
Director, Correspondence:
Jennifer Ticknor . . . 518-776-2356
Director, Public Information:
Shawn Morris . . . 518-776-2357/fax: 518-650-9401

Investigations
Chief, Investigations:
Dominick Zarrella . . . 212-416-6328/fax: 212-416-8773
Assistant Chief Investigator - Downstate:
John McManus . . . 212-416-8786
First Deputy Chief Investigator:
John Reidy . . . 212-416-6394

Social Justice
Executive Deputy Attorney General, Social Justice:
Alvin L Bragg, Jr. . . . 212-416-8450/fax: 212-416-8942

Charities Bureau
Bureau Chief:
James G Sheehan . . . 212-416-8410/fax: 212-416-8393

Civil Rights Bureau
Bureau Chief:
Lourdes Rosado . . . 212-416-8250/fax: 212-416-8074

Environmental Protection Bureau
Bureau Chief:
Lemuel Srolovic . . . 518-776-2400 or 212-416-8448

Healthcare Bureau
Bureau Chief:
Lisa Landau . . . 518-776-2477 or 212-416-6305
fax: 518-650-9365

Regional Offices Division
Executive Deputy Attorney General, Regional Offices:
Martin J Mack . . . 716-853-8451

Binghamton
State Office Bldg, 44 Hawley St, 17th Fl, Binghamton, NY 13901-4433
Asst Attorney General in Charge:
James E. Shoemaker . . . 607-721-8771/fax: 607-721-8787

Brooklyn
55 Hanson Place, Ste 1080, Brooklyn, NY 11217
Asst Attorney General in Charge (Acting):
Matthew Eubank . . . 718-722-3949/fax: 718-722-3951

Buffalo
Main Place Tower, Ste 300A, 350 Main St, Buffalo, NY 14202
Asst Attorney General in Charge:
J. Michael Russo . . . 716-853-8400/fax: 716-853-8571

Harlem
163 West 125th St, Ste 1324, New York, NY 10027
Asst Attorney General in Charge:
Roberto Lebron . . . 212-364-6010/fax: 646-356-3000

Nassau
200 Old Country Rd, Ste 460, Mineola, NY 11501-4241
Asst Attorney General in Charge:
Valerie Singleton . . . 516-248-3302/fax: 516-747-6432

Offices and agencies generally appear in alphabetical order, except when specific order is requested by listee.

Policy Areas

Plattsburgh
43 Durkee St, Ste 700, Plattsburgh, NY 12901
Asst Attorney General in Charge:
Glen Michaels 518-562-3288/fax: 518-562-3293

Poughkeepsie
One Civic Ctr Plaza, Suite 401, Poughkeepsie, NY 12601
Asst Attorney General in Charge:
Jill Faber 845-485-3900/fax: 845-452-3303

Rochester
144 Exchange Blvd, 2nd Fl, Rochester, NY 14614-2176
Asst Attorney General in Charge:
Ted O'Brien 585-327-3220/fax: 585-546-7514

Suffolk
300 Motor Pkwy, Ste 230, Hauppauge, NY 11788
Asst Attorney General in Charge:
Kimberly Kinirons 631-231-2424/fax: 631-435-4757

Syracuse
615 Erie Blvd West, Suite 102, Syracuse, NY 13204
Asst Attorney General in Charge:
Ed Thompson 315-448-4800/fax: 315-448-4853

Utica
207 Genesee St, Room 508, Utica, NY 13501
Asst Attorney General in Charge:
James Williams 315-793-2225/fax: 315-793-2228

Watertown
Dulles St Ofc Bldg, 317 Washington St, Watertown, NY 13601
Asst Attorney General in Charge:
Deanna Nelson 315-785-2444/fax: 315-785-2294

Westchester
44 S Broadway, White Plains, NY 10601
Asst Attorney General in Charge:
Gary S Brown 914-422-8755/fax: 914-422-8706

State Counsel
Chief Deputy Attorney General & Counsel:
Janet Sabel 212-416-8050
Chief Deputy Attorney General & Counsel:
Jason Brown 212-416-8050
Executive Deputy Attorney General, State Counsel:
Kent T. Stauffer 212-416-8252/fax: 212-416-6001

Civil Recoveries Bureau
Bureau Chief:
John Cremo 518-776-2173/fax: 518-915-7731

Claims Bureau
Bureau Chief:
Katharine Brooks . . . . 518-776-2300 or 212-416-8500

Litigation Bureau
Bureau Chief:
Jeffrey Dvorin . . . . 518-776-2300 or 212-416-8610

Real Property Bureau
Bureau Chief:
Alison Crocker 518-776-2700

JUDICIAL SYSTEM AND RELATED AGENCIES

Attorney Grievance Committee

1st Judicial Dept, Judicial Dist 1, 12
61 Broadway, 2nd Fl, New York, NY 10006
Chief Counsel:
Jorge Dopico 212-401-0800/fax: 212-287-1045

2nd Judicial Dept, Judicial Dist 2, 9, 10, 11, 13

Judicial Dist 2, 11, 13
Renaissance Plz, 335 Adams St, Ste 2400, Brooklyn, NY 11201-3745
Chief Counsel:
Diana M Kearse 718-923-6300/fax: 718-624-2978

Judicial Dist 9
399 Knollwood Rd, Ste 200, White Plains, NY 10603
Chief Counsel:
Gary L Casella 914-824-5070/fax: 914-949-0997

Judicial Dist 10
150 Motor Pkwy, Ste 102, Hauppauge, NY 11788
Chief Counsel:
Robert A. Green 631-231-3775/fax: 516-364-7355

3rd Judicial Dept, Judicial Dist 3, 4, 6
Committee on Professional Standards, 286 Washington Ave Ext, Ste 200, Albany, NY 12203
518-285-8350
Web site: www.nycourts.gov/ad3/cops/index.html
Chief Counsel:
Monica A. Duffy 518-285-8350/fax: 518-453-4643
e-mail: AD3COPS@nycourts.gov
Deputy Chief Counsel:
Michael G Gaynor 518-285-8350/fax: 518-453-4643
e-mail: AD3COPS@nycourts.gov

4th Judicial Dept, Dist 5, 7, 8
Web site: www.nycourts.gov/courts/ad4/AG

Judicial Dist 5 . . . . fax: 315-401-3339
224 Harrison St, Ste 408, Syracuse, NY 13202-3066
Chief Counsel:
Gregory J Huether 315-401-3344
Principal Counsel:
Anthony J Gigliotti 315-401-3344

Judicial Dist 7 . . . . fax: 585-530-3191
50 East Ave, Ste 404, Rochester, NY 14604-2206
Chief Counsel:
Gregory J Huether 585-530-3180
Principal Counsel:
Daniel A Drake 585-530-3180

Judicial Dist 8 . . . . fax: 716-856-2701
438 Main St, Ste 800, Buffalo, NY 14202
Chief Counsel:
Gregory J Huether 716-845-3630
Principal Counsel:
Roderick Quebral 716-845-3630

Law Guardian Program

3rd Judicial Dept . . . . fax: 518-471-4757
PO Box 7288, Capital Station, Albany, NY 12224-0288
Fax: 518-471-4757
Web site: www.nycourts.gov/ad3/OAC/index.html
Director:
Betsy R Ruslander 518-471-4825
e-mail: ad3oac@nycourts.gov

4th Judicial Dept . . . . fax: 585-530-3175
50 East Ave, Ste 304, Rochester, NY 14604
Fax: 585-530-3175
Web site: www.nycourts.gov/courts/ad4/AFC
Director:
Tracy M Hamilton . . . . 585-530-3170 or 585-530-3176
e-mail: thamilto@nycourts.gov
Assistant Program Director:
Christine Constantine 585-530-3178
e-mail: cconstan@nycourts.gov

Offices and agencies generally appear in alphabetical order, except when specific order is requested by listee.

Mental Hygiene Legal Service

1st Judicial Dept
41 Madison Ave, 26th Fl, New York, NY 10010
Director:
Marvin Bernstein....................646-386-5891/fax: 212-779-7899
Deputy Director:
Stephen Harkavy....................................646-386-5891

2nd Judicial Dept
170 Old Country Rd, Rm 500, Mineola, NY 11501
Director:
Michael D Neville..................516-493-3976/fax: 646-963-6640
e-mail: mneville@nycourts.gov
Deputy Director:
Dennis Feld...516-493-3975
e-mail: mneville@nycourts.gov

3rd Judicial Dept
40 Steuben St, Ste 501, Albany, NY 12207
Web site: www.nycourts.gov/ad3/mhls/index.html
Director:
Sheila E Shea.......................518-451-8710/fax: 518-453-6915
Deputy Director:
Shannon Stockwell...................................518-451-8710

4th Judicial Dept
50 East Ave, Ste 402, Rochester, NY 14604
Web site: www.nycourts.gov/ad4
Director:
Emmett J Creahan....................................585-530-3050
Deputy Director:
Kevin Wilson.......................585-530-3050/fax: 585-530-3079

Unified Court System

25 Beaver St
Room 852
New York, NY 10004
212-428-2700 Fax: 212-428-2508
e-mail: questions@nycourts.gov
Web site: www.nycourts.gov

Agency Bldg 4, 20th Fl
Empire State Plaza
Albany, NY 12223
518-474-3828
Fax: 518-473-5514

Administrative Board of the Courts

Appellate Division

1st Judicial Department
Courthouse, 27 Madison Ave, New York, NY 10010
Presiding Justice:
Luis A. Gonzalez....................................212-340-0400

2nd Judicial Department
45 Monroe Place, Brooklyn, NY 11201
Presiding Justice:
Randall T. Eng......................................718-875-1300

3rd Judicial Department
Capitol Station, ESP, PO Box 7288, Albany, NY 12224
Presiding Justice:
Karen K. Peters.....................................518-471-4777

4th Judicial Department
50 East Ave, Rochester, NY 14604
Presiding Justice:
Henry Scudder.......................................585-530-3100

Court of Appeals
230 Park Ave, Suite 826, New York, NY 10169
Chief Judge:
Jonathan Lippman..................212-661-6787/fax: 212-682-2778

Court Administration

Chief Administrative Judge:
A. Gail Prudenti....................................212-428-2120
Administrative Director, Office of Court Admin:
Lawrence K Marks....................................212-428-2884
Deputy Chief Administrative Judge, Courts in NYC:
Fern A. Fisher......................................646-386-4200
Deputy Chief Administrative Judge, Courts outside NYC:
Michael V. Coccoma..................................518-474-3828
Chief, Policy & Planning:
Judy Harris Kluger..................................212-428-2130
Executive Assistant to Deputy Chief Admin Judge, Courts in NYC:
Maria Logus...646-386-4201
Executive Assistant to Deputy Chief Admin Judge, Courts outside NYC:
Peter J. Ryan.......................................518-474-3828
Chief of Staff:
Paul Lewis..212-428-2120
Executive Director:
Ron Younkins..212-428-2126

Administrative Judge to the Court of Claims (NYS). fax: 866-413-1069
Justice Bldg, Capitol Station, PO Box 7344, Albany, NY 12224
Presiding Judge:
Richard E Sise......................................518-432-3435

Administrative Judges to the Courts in New York City

1st Judicial District (Judicial Department 1)
Administrative Judge, Civil Term:
Sherry Klein-Heitler................................646-386-3211
Administrative Judge, Criminal Term:
Michael Obus..646-386-4051

2nd Judicial District (Judicial Department 2)
320 Jay St, Brooklyn, NY 11201
Administrative Judge:
Barry Kamins..347-296-1200

Civil Court
111 Centre St, New York, NY 10013
Administrative Judge:
Lawrence Knipel...................646 386 5400/fax: 212 374 5709

Criminal Court
100 Centre St, Rm 549A, New York, NY 10013
Administrative Judge:
Barry Kamins.......................646-386-4700 or 347-296-1000
fax: 212-374-3004

Family Court
60 Lafayette St, 11th Floor, New York, NY 10013
Administrative Judge:
Edwina Richardson-Mendelson . 646-386-5190/fax: 212-374-2127

Administrative Judges to the Courts outside New York City

3rd Judicial District (Judicial Department 3)
Courthouse, 80 Second St, Troy, NY 12180
Acting Administrative Judge:
Thomas Mercure.....................518-285-6152/fax: 518-270-3788

4th Judicial District (Judicial Department 3)
612 State St, Schenectady, NY 12305
Administrative Judge:
Vito Caruso........................518-285-8415/fax: 518-347-1972

5th Judicial District (Judicial Department 4)
Onondaga County Court House, 401 Montgomery St, Syracuse, NY 13202
Administrative Judge:
James C Tormey.....................315-671-2111/fax: 315-671-1183

6th Judicial District (Judicial Department 3)
320 North Tioga Street, Ithaca, NY 14850
Administrative Judge:
Robert Mulvey.......................................607-272-0466

Policy Areas

Offices and agencies generally appear in alphabetical order, except when specific order is requested by listee.

7th Judicial District (Judicial Department 4)
Hall of Justice, Civic Center Plz, 99 Exchange Blvd, Rochester, NY 14614
Administrative Judge:
Craig J. Doran 585-396-4239
8th Judicial District (Judicial Department 4)
Erie County Hall, 92 Franklin St, Buffalo, NY 14202
Administrative Judge:
Paula L. Feroleto 716-845-9438/fax: 716-855-1611
9th Judicial District (Judicial Department 2)
County Court House, 111 Dr Martin Luther King Blvd, White Plains, NY 10601
Administrative Judge:
Alan Scheinkman 914-824-5100/fax: 914-995-4111
10th Judicial District (Judicial Department 2)
Administrative Judge, Nassau County:
Thomas Adams 516-571-2684/fax: 516-571-3713
Administrative Judge, Suffolk County:
C.ÆRandall Hinrichs 631-853-5368/fax: 631-853-7741
11th Judicial District (Judicial Department 2)
88-11 Sutphin Blvd, Jamaica, NY 11435
Administrative Judge, Civil:
Jeremy Weinstein 718-298-1100/fax: 718-520-2499
Administrative Judge, Criminal:
Joseph Zayas
12th Judicial District (Judicial Department 1)
851 Grand Concourse, Bronx, NY 10451
Administrative Judge (Civil & Criminal):
Douglas E. McKeon 718-618-1441
Deputy Administrative Judge (Criminal):
Robert Torres 718-618-3700
13th Judicial District Administrative Judge:
Judith N. McMahon 718-618-3700

Counsel's Office
Counsel:
Vacant 212-428-2160/fax: 212-428-2155

Management Support
Administrative Services Office
Director:
Laura Weigley Ross 212-428-2860/fax: 212-428-2819
Deputy Director:
Vacant 212-428-2812/fax: 212-428-2819
Court Operations
Director:
Nancy M Mangold 212-428-2761/fax: 518-428-2768
Coordinator, Alternative Dispute Resolution Program:
Daniel M Weitz 212-428-2892/fax: 212-428-2696
e-mail: dweitz@nycourts.gov
Director, Court Research & Technology:
Chester Mount 212-428-2990/fax: 212-428-2987
Chief of Court Security Services:
Howard Metzdorff 212-428-2766/fax: 212-428-2768
e-mail: ops1@nycourts.gov
Director, Internal Controls Office:
Dennis Donnelly 518-238-4303/fax: 518-238-2086
Inspector General:
Sherrill Spatz .... 646-386-3500 or 212-514-7158
e-mail: sspatz@courts.state.ny.us
Deputy Inspector General:
Carol Hamm
e-mail: chamm@courts.state.ny.us
Chief Law Librarian, Legal Info & Records Mgmt:
Ellen Robinson 518-238-4373/fax: 518-238-2894
Managing Inspector General, Bias Matters:
Kay-Ann Porter Campbell 877-263-2427
e-mail: ieporter@courts.state.ny.us
Managing Inspector General, Fiduciary Appointments:
Elizabeth Candreva 646-386-3514
e-mail: ecandreva@courts.state.ny.us

Financial Management & Audit Services
Empire State Plaza, Bldg 4, Ste 2001, Albany, NY 12223-1450
Director:
Charles Hughes 518-473-5511
Workforce Diversity
Director:
S. Anthony Walters 212-428-2540/fax: 212-428-2545
e-mail: twalters@nycourts.gov
Management Analyst:
Michael J. Moore 212-428-2683/fax: 212-428-2545
e-mail: mmoore@nycourts.gov
Court Analyst:
Doretha L. Jackson 212-428-2540
e-mail: dljackson@nycourts.gov
Deputy Director, Staffing & Security Services:
Gregory J. Salerno 646-386-3400/fax: 212-295-4876
e-mail: gsalerno@courts.stae.ny.us
Chief of Training/Commanding Officer - NYS Court Officers Academy:
Chief Joseph Bacceilieri 646-386-5660/fax: 212-406-4533
Public Affairs Office
Director:
Gregory Murray 212-428-2116/fax: 212-428-2117
e-mail: opaoutreach@courts.state.ny.us
Director, Communications:
David Bookstaver 212-428-2500/fax: 212-428-2507
e-mail: dbooksta@courts.state.ny.us
Assistant Director, Communications Specialist:
Arlene Hackel 212-428-2116
e-mail: ahackel@courts.state.ny.us
Officer:
Gary Spencer 518-455-7711
e-mail: gspencer@courts.state.ny.us

CORPORATIONS, AUTHORITIES AND COMMISSIONS

Interest on Lawyer Account (IOLA) Fund of the State of NY
11 East 44th St
Ste 1406
New York, NY 10017
646-865-1541 or 800-222-4652 Fax: 646-865-1545
e-mail: iolaf@iola.org
Web site: www.iola.org

Chair:
Mary Rothwell Davis 646-865-1541
Executive Director:
Christopher O'Malley 646-865-1541
General Counsel:
Christine M Fecko 646-865-1541
Director of Administration:
Michele D Agard 646-865-1541

Lawyers' Fund for Client Protection
119 Washington Ave
Albany, NY 12210
518-434-1935 or 800-442-FUND Fax: 518-434-5641
e-mail: info@nylawfund.org
Web site: www.nylawfund.org

Chair:
Eric A Seiff 518-434-1935
Vice Chair:
Nancy Burner 518-434-1935
Executive Director & Counsel:
Timothy O'Sullivan 518-434-1935

Offices and agencies generally appear in alphabetical order, except when specific order is requested by listee.

New York State Board of Law Examiners
Corporate Plaza Bldg 3
254 Washington Ave Ext
Albany, NY 12203-5195
518-453-5990 Fax: 518-452-5729
Web site: www.nybarexam.org

Chair:
Diane F Bosse 518-453-5990
Executive Director:
John J McAlary 518-453-5990

New York State Commission on Judicial Nomination
c/o Greenberg Traurig LLP
54 State Street
Albany, NY 12207
518-689-1400 Fax: 518-689-1499
Web site: www.nysegov.com/cjn/

Chair:
Vacant
Counsel:
Henry Greenberg 518-689-1400
e-mail: greenbergh@gtlaw.com

New York State Judicial Conduct Commission
61 Broadway
12th Fl
New York, NY 10006
646-386-4800 Fax: 646-458-0037
e-mail: cjc@cjc.ny.gov
Web site: www.cjc.ny.gov

Corning Tower
Suite 2301
Empire State Plaza
Albany, NY 12223
518-453-4600
Fax: 518-486-1850

Chair:
Joseph W Belluck 646-386-4800
Vice Chair:
Paul B Harding 646-386-4800
Administrator & Counsel:
Robert H Tembeckjian 646-386-4800
Deputy Administrator in Charge, Albany Office:
Cathleen Cenci 518-453-4600
Deputy Administrator in Charge, Rochester Office:
John J Postel 585-232-5756
Deputy Administrator in Charge, New York City Office:
Mark Levine 646-386-4800
Deputy Administrator, Litigation:
Edward Lindner 518-474-5617
Clerk:
Jean M Savanyu, Esq 646-386-4800

New York State Law Reporting Bureau
17 Lodge Street
Albany, NY 12207
518-453-6900 Fax: 518-426-1640
Web site: www.courts.state.ny.us/reporter

State Reporter:
William J Hooks 518-453-6900
Deputy State Reporter:
Katherine D LaBoda 518-453-6900
e-mail: Reporter@courts.state.ny.us
Assistant State Reporter:
Cara J Broussea, Esq. 518-453-6900
e-mail: Reporter@courts.state.ny.us

New York State Law Revision Commission
80 New Scotland Ave
Albany, NY 12208
518-472-5858 Fax: 518-445-2303
e-mail: nylrc@albanylaw.edu
Web site: www.lawrevision.state.ny.us

Chairman:
Peter J Kiernan 518-472-5858
Executive Director:
Rose Mary Bailly 518-472-5858

Uniform State Laws Commission
c/o Coughlin & Gerhart LLP
99 Corporate Drive
PO Box 2039
Binghamton, NY 13902-2039
607-723-9511 Fax: 607-723-1530

Chair:
Richard B Long 607-821-2202
e-mail: rlong@cglawoffices.com
Member:
Sandra Stern 212-207-8150
Member:
Norman L. Greene 212-661-5030
Member:
Justin L. Vigdor . . . . 585-232-5300 ext 228
Member:
Mark F Glaser 518-689-1413

NEW YORK STATE LEGISLATURE

See Legislative Branch in Section 1 for additional Standing Committee and Subcommittee information.

Assembly Standing Committees

Codes
Chair:
Joseph R Lentol (D) 518-455-4477
Ranking Minority Member:
Al Graf (R) 518-455-5937

Judiciary
Chair:
Helene E Weinstein (D) 518-455-5462
Ranking Minority Member:
Michael Montesano (R) 518-455-4684

Senate Standing Committees

Codes
Chair:
Michael F. Nozzolio (R) 518-455-2366
Ranking Minority Member:
Daniel L. Squadron (D) 518-455-2625

Judiciary
Chair:
John J Bonacic (R) 518-455-3181

Offices and agencies generally appear in alphabetical order, except when specific order is requested by listee.

Ranking Minority Member:
Ruth Hassell-Thompson (D)........................518-455-2061

U.S. GOVERNMENT

EXECUTIVE DEPARTMENTS AND FEDERAL COURTS

US Federal Courts

US Bankruptcy Court - New York

Eastern District
271-C Cadman Plaza East, Suite 1595, Brooklyn, NY 11201-1800
347-394-1700
Web site: www.nyeb.uscourts.gov
Chief Judge:
Carla E. Craig........................347-394-1700
Clerk of the Court:
Robert A. Gavin Jr........................347-394-1700

Northern District
James T. Foley Courthouse, 445 Broadway, Suite 330, Albany, NY 12207
518-257-1661
Web site: www.nynb.uscourts.gov
Chief Bankruptcy Judge:
Margaret Cangilos-Ruiz........................518-257-1661
Clerk of the Court:
Kim F. Lefebvre........................518-257-1661

Southern District
1 Bowling Green, New York, NY 10004-1408
212-668-2870
Web site: www.nysb.uscourts.gov
Chief Judge:
Cecelia G. Morris........................212-668-2870
Clerk of the Court:
Vito Genna........................212-668-2870

Western District
300 Pearl Street, Suite 250, Buffalo, NY 14202
Web site: www.nywb.uscourts.gov
Chief Judge:
Carl L. Bucki........................716-362-3200
Clerk of the Court:
Lisa Bertino Beaser........................716-362-3281

US Court of Appeals for the Second Circuit
Thurgood Marshall U.S. Courthouse, 40 Foley Square, New York, NY 10007
212-857-8500
Web site: www.ca2.uscourts.gov
Circuit Executive:
Karen Greve Milton................212-857-8700/fax: 212-857-8680
Clerk of the Court:
Catherine O'Hagan Wolfe........................212-857-8500

US Court of International Trade ....fax: 212-264-1085
One Federal Plaza, New York, NY 10278-0001
212-264-2800 Fax: 212-264-1085
Web site: www.cit.uscourts.gov
Chief Judge:
Timothy C. Stanceu........................212-264-2923
Clerk of the Court:
Tina Potuto Kimble........................212-264-2814
e-mail: clerk@cit.uscourts.gov

US DISTRICT COURT - NEW YORK (part of the Second Circuit)
225 Cadman Plaza East, Brooklyn, NY 11201
Web site: www.nyed.uscourts.gov

Eastern District
718-613-2600
Chief District Judge:
Dora L. Irizarry
Clerk of the Court:
Douglas C. Palmer
Chief Magistrate Judge:
Roanne L. Mann
District Executive:
Eugene J. Corcoran
Chief Probation Officer:
Edward Kanaley

Northern District
100 South Clinton Street, PO Box 7367, Syracuse, NY 13261-7367
315-234-8500
Web site: www.nynd.uscourts.gov
Chief District Judge:
Glenn T. Suddaby
Chief Magistrate Judge:
David E. Peebles
Clerk of the Court:
Lawrence K. Baerman........................315-234-8500
Chief Probation Officer:
Matt Brown

Southern District
300 Quarropas Street, White Plains, NY 10601-4150
914-390-4100
Web site: www.nysd.uscourts.gov
Chief District Judge:
Loretta A. Preska........................212-805-0240
Chief Magistrate Judge:
Debra Freeman........................212-805-4250
District Executive:
Edward Friedland
Clerk of the Court:
Ruby J. Krajick
Deputy in Charge:
Robert Rogers

Western District
2 Niagara Square, Buffalo, NY 14202-3350
716-551-1700
Web site: www.nywd.uscourts.gov
Chief District Judge:
Frank P. Geraci, Jr.
Clerk of the Court:
Mary C. Loewenguth
Magistrate Judge:
Hugh B. Scott

US Tax Court
Web site: www.ustaxcourt.gov
Chief Judge:
Michael B. Thornton........................202-521-0777
Clerk of the Court:
Stephanie A. Servoss........................202-521-0700

US Justice Department
Web site: www.justice.gov

Antitrust Division—New York Field Office
26 Federal Plaza, Room 3630, New York, NY 10278-0004
Chief:
Jeffrey Martino................212-335-8019/fax: 212-335-8021
Assistant Chief:
Stephen J. McCahey........................212-335-8026

Civil Division - Commercial Litigation Branch
26 Federal Plaza, Room 346, New York, NY 10278

Offices and agencies generally appear in alphabetical order, except when specific order is requested by listee.

Attorney-in-Charge:
Barbara S. Williams 212-264-9240

Community Relations Service - Northeast & Caribbean Region

26 Federal Plaza, Suite 36-118, New York, NY 10278
Regional Director:
Reinaldo Rivera, Jr. 212-264-0700/fax: 212-264-2143

OFFICE OF INSPECTOR GENERAL (including New York State)

Audit Division
701 Market Street, Suite 201, Philadelphia, PA 19106
Regional Audit Manager:
Thomas O. Puerzer 215-580-2111/fax: 215-597-1348

Investigations Division
1 Battery Park Plaza, 29th Floor, New York, NY 10004
Special Agent-in-Charge:
Ronald G. Gardella

US Attorney's Office - New York

Eastern District . . . . fax: 718-254-7508
271 Cadman Plaza East, Brooklyn, NY 11201
718-254-7000 Fax: 718-254-7508
US Attorney:
Robert L. Capers 718-254-7000/fax: 718-254-7508
Assistant US Attorney:
James R. Cho. 718-254-6519/fax: 718-254-7508
Assistant US Attorney:
Joseph Anthony Marutollo 718-254-6288/fax: 718-254-7508
Assistant US Attorney:
Elliot M. Schachner. 718-254-6053/fax: 718-254-7508
Executive Assistant US Attorney:
William J. Muller 718-254-7000/fax: 718-254-7508
Assistant US Attorney, Criminal Division:
Zainab Ahmad
Deputy Chief, Civil Division:
Gail Matthews
Chief of Affirmative Civil Enforcement, Civil Division:
John Vagelatos

Northern District
Albany . . . . fax: 518-431-0249
445 Broadway, Room 218, Albany, NY 12207-2924
518-431-0247 Fax: 518-431-0249
Assistant US Attorney:
Thomas Spina Jr.
Binghamton . . . . fax: 607-773-2901
319 Federal Building, 15 Henry Street, Binghamton, NY 13901
607-773-2887 Fax: 607-773-2901
Assistant US Attorney:
Miro Lovric
Plattsburgh . . . . fax: 518-314-7811
14 Durkee Street, Suite 340, Plattsburgh, NY 12901
518-314-7800 Fax: 518-314-7811
Assistant US Attorney:
Elizabeth Horsman
Syracuse . . . . fax: 315-448-0689
100 South Clinton Street, PO Box 7198, Syracuse, NY 13261-7198
315-448-0672 Fax: 315-448-0689
US Attorney:
Richard S. Hartunian 315-448-0672
Assistant US Attorney:
Tamara B. Thomson. 315-448-0672
Assistant US Attorney, Chief Civil Division:
Thomas Spina Jr.
Assistant US Attorney, Chief Criminal Division:
Elizabeth C. Coombe

Southern District
New York City
1 Saint Andrews Plaza, New York, NY 10007
212-637-2200
US Attorney:
Preet Bharara
Deputy US Attorney:
Joon H. Kim. 212-637-2200
Chief, Criminal Division:
Daniel Stein
Chief, Civil Division:
Sara L. Shudofsky
White Plains
300 Quarropas Street, White Plains, NY 10601-4150
914-993-1900 or 914-993-1916
Assistant US Attorney, White Plains Co-Chief:
Perry Carbone 914-993-1900

Western District
Buffalo
138 Delaware Avenue, Buffalo, NY 14202
716-843-5700
US Attorney:
William J. Hochul, Jr.
Chief of Appellate Division:
Joseph J. Karaszewski
Assistant US Attorney, Civil Division Chief:
Mary Pat Fleming 716-843-5867
Chief, Criminal Division:
Joseph M. Guerra, III. 716-843-5824
Assistant US Attorney, National Security Coordinator:
Anthony M. Bruce
Chief, General Crimes Section:
Michael DiGiacomo
Administrative Officer:
Amy L. Smith
Rochester . . . . fax: 585-263-6226
100 State Street, Suite 500, Rochester, NY 14614
585-263-6760 Fax: 585-263-6226
Assistant US Attorney-in-Charge:
Richard A. Resnick 585-263-6760

US Marshals' Service - New York

Eastern District
Brooklyn
225 Cadman Plaza, Brooklyn, NY 11201
US Marshal:
Charles Dunne 718-260-0400
Central Islip
100 Federal Plaza, Central Islip, NY 11722
US Marshal:
Charles Dunne 631-712-6000

Northern District
Albany
James T. Foley Courthouse, 445 Broadway, Albany, NY 12201
US Marshal:
David McNulty 518-472-5401
Binghamton
US Courthouse & Federal Building, 15 Henry Street, Binghamton, NY 13902
US Marshal:
David McNulty 607-773-2723
Syracuse
US District Courthouse, 100 South Clinton Street, Syracuse, NY 13261
US Marshal:
David McNulty 315-473-7601
Utica
Alexander Pirnie Federal Building, 10 Broad Street, Room 213, Utica, NY 13501

Policy Areas

US Marshal:
David McNulty 315-793-8109

Southern District
500 Pearl Street, New York, NY 10007
US Marshal:
Michael Greco 212-331-7200/fax: 212-637-6130

Western District
Buffalo
2 Niagara Square, Buffalo, NY 14202
US Marshal:
Charles Salina 716-348-5300
Rochester
US Courthouse, 100 State Street, Room 2240, Rochester, NY 14614
US Marshal:
Charles Salina 585-263-5787

US Trustee - Bankruptcy, Region 2
201 Varick Street, Suite 1006, New York, NY 10014
US Trustee:
William K. Harrington. 212-510-0500/fax: 212-668-2256

U.S. CONGRESS

See U.S. Congress Chapter for additional Standing Committee and Subcommittee information.

House of Representatives Standing Committees

Judiciary
Chair:
Bob Goodlatte (R-VA) 202-225-5431
Ranking Member:
John Conyers, Jr. (D-MI) 202-225-5126
New York Delegate:
Hakeem Jeffries (D) 202-225-5936
New York Delegate:
Jerrold Nadler (D). 202-225-5635

Senate Standing Committees

Judiciary
Chair:
Chuck Grassley (R-IA). 202-224-3744
Ranking Member:
Patrick Leahy (D-VT). 202-224-4242
New York Delegate:
Charles E. Schumer (D) 202-224-6542

PRIVATE SECTOR

Maxwell S Pfeifer, Chair

NYS Bar Assn, International Law & Practice Section
Alston & Bird LLP
90 Park Ave, 15th Fl, New York, NY 10016-1387
212-210-9540 Fax: 212-210-9444
e-mail: pmfrank@alston.com
Jamie Hutchinson, Chair

NYS Bar Assn, Lawyer Referral Service Cmte
Amdursky Pelky Fennell & Wallen
26 E Oneida St, Oswego, NY 13126-2695
315-343-6363 Fax: 315-343-0134
e-mail: apfwlaw@twcny.rr.com
Web site: www.apfwlaw.com
Timothy J Fennell, Chair

Asian American Legal Defense and Education Fund
99 Hudson St, 12th Fl, New York, NY 10013-2815
212-966-5932 or 800-966-5946 Fax: 212-966-4303
e-mail: info@aaldef.org
Web site: www.aaldef.org
Defend civil rights of Asian Americans through litigation, legal advocacy & community education
Margaret Fung, Executive Director

Association of the Bar of the City of New York
42 W 44th St, New York, NY 10036-6689
212-382-6655 Fax: 212-768-8630
e-mail: jbigelsen@nycbar.org
Web site: www.nycbar.org
Jayne Bigelsen, Director, Communications/Legislative Affrs

NYS Bar Assn, Review the Code of Judicial Conduct Cmte
Securities Industry & Financial Markets Association (SIFMA)
360 Madison Ave, 18th Fl, New York, NY 10017-7111
646-637-9200 Fax: 646-637-9126
e-mail: mgross@bondmarkets.com
Web site: www.sifma.org
Herbert H McDade III, Chair

NYS Bar Assn, President's Cmte on Access to Justice
Boylan Brown
2400 Chase Sq, Rochester, NY 14604
585-232-5300 x256 Fax: 585-232-3528
e-mail: info@boylanbrown.com
Web site: www.boylanbrown.com
C Bruce Lawrence, Secretary New York State Bar Association

NYS Bar Assn, Tort System Cmte
Bracken Margolin Besunder LLP
1050 Old Nichols Road, Suite 200, Islandia, NY 11749
631-234-8585 Fax: 631-234-8702
e-mail: jbracken@bmlawllp.com
Web site: www.bmblawllp.com
John P Bracken, Judicial Screening

Brooklyn Law School
250 Joralemon St, Brooklyn, NY 11201
718-780-7900 Fax: 718-780-0393
e-mail: joan.wexler@brooklaw.edu
Web site: www.brooklaw.edu
18 legal clincs include immigration, new media, the arts, criminal defense and prosecution, bankruptcy, real estate, health, and securities arbitration.
Joan G Wexler, Dean

NYS Bar Assn, Cyberspace Law Cmte
Thelen Reid Brown Raysman & Steiner
875 Third Ave, New York, NY 10022
212-603-2196 Fax: 212-603-2001
e-mail: jneuburger@thelen.com
Web site: www.thelen.com
Jeffrey D Neuburger, Chair

CASA - Advocates for Children of NYS
32 Essex St, Albany, NY 12206
518-426-5354 Fax: 518-426-5348
e-mail: mail@casanys.org
Web site: www.casanys.org
Volunteer advocates appointed by family court judges to represent abused & neglected children in court
Penny Page, Executive Director

CPR, The International Institute for Conflict Prevention & Resolution
575 Lexington Ave, 21st Fl, New York, NY 10022
212-949-6490 Fax: 212-949-8859
e-mail: info@cpradr.org
Web site: www.cpradr.org
Alternative dispute resolution
Kathleen A Bryan, President & Chief Executive Officer

Center for Court Innovation
520 8th Ave, New York, NY 10018
212-397-3050 Fax: 212-397-0985
e-mail: info@courtinnovation.org
Web site: www.courtinnovation.org
Foster innovation within NYS courts addressing quality-of-life crime, substance abuse, child neglect, domestic violence & landlord-tenant disputes
Greg Berman, Director

Center for Judicial Accountability Inc (CJA)
283 Soundview Avenue, White Plains, NY 10606-3821
914-421-1200 Fax: 914-684-6554
e-mail: mail@judgewatch.org
Web site: www.judgewatch.org
National, nonpartisan, non-profit citizens' organization documentingthe politicization & corruption of the judicial selection & discipline processes
Doris L Sassower, President

Center for Law & Justice
Pine West Plaza, Bldg 2, Washington Ave Ext, Albany, NY 12205
518-427-8361 Fax: 518-427-8362
e-mail: cflj@verizon.net
Web site: www.timesunion.com/communities/cflj
Advocacy for fair treatment of poor people & communities of color by the justice system; referral, workshops, community lawyering & education
Alice P Green, Executive Director

Coalition of Fathers & Families NY, PAC
PO Box 782, Clifton Park, NY 12065
518-383-8202
e-mail: pac@fafny.org
Web site: www.fafny.org/fafnypac.htm
Political Action for fathers and families in New York
James Hays, Treasurer

NYS Bar Assn, Trial Lawyers Section
Connors & Connors, PC
766 Castleton Ave, Staten Island, NY 10310
718-442-1700 Fax: 718-442-1717
e-mail: jpc@connorslaw.com
Web site: www.connorslaw.com
John P Connors, Jr, Chair

NYS Bar Assn, Torts, Insurance & Compensation Law Section
Connors & Corcoran LLP
Times Square Bldg, 45 Exchange St, Ste 250, Rochester, NY 14614
585-232-5885 Fax: 585-546-3631
e-mail: law@connorscorcoran.com
Web site: www.connorscorcoran.com
Eileen E Buholtz, Partner

Cornell Law School, Legal Information Institute
Myron Taylor Hall, Ithaca, NY 14853
607-255-1221 Fax: 607-255-7193
e-mail: lii@lii.law.cornell.edu
Web site: www.law.cornell.edu
Distributes legal documents via the web & electronic mail
Thomas R Bruce, Director

NYS Bar Assn, Judicial Section
Court of Claims
140 Grand St, Ste 507, White Plains, NY 10601
914-289-2310 Fax: 914-289-2313
e-mail: truderma@courts.state.ny.us
Hon Terry Jane Ruderman, Judge

NYS Bar Assn, Federal Constitution & Legislation Cmte
Day Pitney LLP
7 Times Square, New York, NY 10036-7311
973-966-8180 Fax: 973-966-1015
e-mail: jmaloney@daypitney.com
Web site: www.daypitney.com
One Jefferson Road, Parsippany, New Jersey 07054
John C Maloney Jr, Partner

NYS Bar Assn, Trusts & Estates Law Section
Day Pitney LLP
7 Times Square, 41st & 42nd St, New York, NY 10036
212-297-5800 or 212-297-2468 Fax: 212-916-2940
e-mail: gwwhitaker@daypitney.com
Web site: www.daypitney.com
Domestic and international trusts and estates.
G Warren Whitaker,

NYS Bar Assn, Public Trust & Confidence in the Legal System
Debevoise & Plimpton LLP
919 Third Ave, New York, NY 10022
212-909-6000 Fax: 212-909-6836
e-mail: azgorgun@debevoise.com
Web site: www.debevoise.com
Ellen Lieberman,

NYS Bar Assn, Alternative Dispute Resolution Cmte
Elayne E Greenberg, MS, Esq
25 Potters Lane, Great Neck, NY 11024
516-829-5521 Fax: 516-466-8130
e-mail: elayneegreenberg@juno.com
Elayne E Greenberg, Chair

Empire Justice Center
119 Washington Ave, Albany, NY 12210
518-462-6831 Fax: 518-462-6687
e-mail: aerickson@empirejustice.org
Web site: www.empirejustice.org
Policy analysis and research in issues impacting civil legal matters for low-income residents
Anne Erickson, President & CEO

NYS Bar Assn, Review Judicial Nominations Cmte
Englert, Coffey, McHugh & Fantauzzi LLP
224 State St, PO Box 1092, Schenectady, NY 12305
518-370-4645 Fax: 518-374-5422
e-mail: pcoffey@ecmlaw.com
Web site: www.englertcoffeymchugh.com
Peter V Coffey, Chair

NYS Bar Assn, Cmte on the Jury System
FitzGerald Morris et al
One Broad St Plz, PO Box 2017, Glens Falls, NY 12801-4360
518-745-1400 Fax: 518-745-1576
e-mail: pdf@fmbf-law.com
Peter D FitzGerald, Chair

Fund for Modern Courts (The)
351 W 54th St, New York, NY 10019
212-541-6741 Fax: 212-541-7301
e-mail: justice@moderncourts.org
Web site: www.moderncourts.org
Improve the administration & quality of justice in NYS courts
Dennis R Hawkins, Executive Director

NYS Bar Assn, Court Operations Cmte
Getnick, Livingston, Atkinson, Gigliotti & Priore LLP
258 Genesee St, Ste 401, Utica, NY 13502-4642
315-797-9261 Fax: 315-732-0755
e-mail: mgetnick@glagplawfirm.com
Linda A Juteau, Office Manager

NYS Bar Assn, Labor & Employment Law Section
Goodman & Zuchlewski LLP
500 5th Ave, Ste 5100, New York, NY 10110-5197
212-869-4646 Fax: 212-869-4648
e-mail: pz@kzlaw.net
Pearl Zuchlewski, Chair

Harris Beach LLP
99 Garnsey Rd, Pittsford, NY 14534
585-419-8800 Fax: 585-419-8801
e-mail: vbuzard@harrisbeach.com

NYS Bar Assn, Intellectual Property Law Section
Hartman & Winnicki, PC
115 W Century Rd, Paramus, NJ 7654
201-967-8040 Fax: 201-967-0590
e-mail: rick@ravin.com
Web site: www.hartmanwinnicki.com
Internet and Computer Law, Intellectual Property Law, and Debtors & Creditors Rights.
Richard L Ravin, Chair

NYS Bar Assn, Fiduciary Appointments Cmte
Harvey B Besunder PC
One Suffolk Sq, Ste 315, Islandia, NY 11749
631-234-9240 Fax: 631-234-9278
e-mail: hbb@besunderlaw.com
Harvey Besunder, Owner

NYS Bar Assn, Procedures for Judicial Discipline Cmte
Hollyer Brady et al
380 Madison Avenue, 22nd Fl, New York, NY 10017
212-818-1110 Fax: 212-818-0494
e-mail: hollyer@butzel.com
A Rene Hollyer, Chair

JAMS
620 Eighth Ave, 34th Floor, New York, NY 10018
212-607-2763 Fax: 212-751-4099
e-mail: mshaw@jamsadr.com
Web site: www.jamsadr.com
Mediation of civil, commercial & employment disputes; training & systems design
Margaret L Shaw, Mediator & Arburator

NYS Bar Assn, Real Property Section
Law Office of Anne Reynolds Copps
126 State St, 6th Fl, Albany, NY 12207
518-436-4170 Fax: 518-436-1456
e-mail: arcopps@nycap.rr.com
Web site: arcopps.net
Anne Reynolds Copps, Partner/Owner

NYS Bar Assn, General Practice Section
Law Offices of Frank G. D'Angelo & Associates
901 Stewart Avenue, Suite 230, Garden City, NY 11530
516-742-7601 or 516-222-1122 Fax: 516-742-6070
e-mail: fgdangeloesq@aol.com
Queens Village Office- 224-44 Braddock Ave, Queens Village, NY 11428
Phone; 718-776-7475
Frank G D'Angelo, Elder Law Attorney

Legal Action Center
225 Varick Street, 4th Floor, New York, NY 10014
212-243-1313 Fax: 212-675-0286
e-mail: lacinfo@lac.org
Web site: www.lac.org
Legal & policy issues, alcohol/drug abuse, AIDS & criminal justice
Paul N Samuels, President & Director

Legal Aid Society
199 Water Street, New York, NY 10038
212-577-3277 Fax: 212-809-1574
Web site: www.legal-aid.org
Civil & criminal defense, appeals, juvenile rights, civil legal services
Steven Banks, Attorney-In-Chief

NYS Bar Assn, Legal Aid Cmte/Funding for Civil Legal Svcs Cmte
Legal Services of the Hudson Valley
90 Maple Avenue, White Plains, NY 10601
914-949-1305 x136 Fax: 914-949-6213
e-mail: bfinkelstein@lshv.org
Web site: www.lshv.org
Established to provide free legal representation in civil matters to low-income people. Legal assistance is provided in the following areas; Westchester, Putnam, Dutchess, Orange, Sullivan and Ulster Counties.
Barbara D Finkelstein, Executive Director

Levene, Gouldin & Thompson LLP
PO Box F-1706, 450 Plaza Drive, Binghamton, NY 13902
607-584-5706 Fax: 607-763-9212
e-mail: jpollock@binghamtonlaw.com
Web site: www.binghamtonlaw.com
Commercial and personal injury litigation
John J. Pollock, Managing Partner

NYS Bar Assn, Elder Law Section
Littman Krooks LLP
399 Knollwood Rd, White Plains, NY 10603
914-684-2100 Fax: 914-684-9865
e-mail: hkrooks@lkllp.com
Web site: www.lkrlaw.com
Harold S Krooks, Chair

NYS Bar Assn, Unlawful Practice of Law Cmte
Schlather, Geldenhuys, Stumbar & Salk
200 E Buffalo St, PO Box 353, Ithaca, NY 14851
607-273-2202 Fax: 607-273-4436
e-mail: mjs@lsss-law.com
Web site: www.ithacalaw.com
Mark J Solomon, Chair

NYS Bar Assn, Court Structure & Judicial Selection Cmte
McMahon & Grow
301 N Washington St, PO Box 4350, Rome, NY 13442-4350
315-336-4700 Fax: 315-336-5851
e-mail: mgglaw@dreamscape.com
Web site: www.mgglaw.com
Hon Richard D Simons,

NYS Bar Assn, Resolutions Committee
Meyer Suozzi English & Klein, PC
990Stewart Ave, Garden City, NY 11530-9194
516-592-5704 Fax: 516-741-6706
e-mail: atlevin@nysbar.com
A Thomas Levin, Chair

NYS Bar Assn, Commercial & Federal Litigation Section
Montclare & Wachtler
67 Wall St, 22nd Fl, New York, NY 10005
212-509-3900 Fax: 212-509-7239
e-mail: ljwachtler@montclarewachtler.com
Lauren J Wachtler, Chair

NY County Lawyers' Association
14 Vessey St, New York, NY 10007
212-267-6646 Fax: 212-406-9252
e-mail: mflood@nycla.org
Web site: www.nycla.org
Stewart D Aaron, President

NYS Association of Criminal Defense Lawyers
245 Fifth Ave, 19th Fl, New York, NY 10016
212-532-4434 Fax: 212-532-4668
e-mail: nysacdl@aol.com
Web site: www.nysacdl.org
Criminal law
Patricia Marcus, Executive Director

NYS Bar Assn, Cmte on Diversity & Leadership Development
1 Elk St, Albany, NY 12207
518-487-5555 or 212-351-4670 Fax: 212-878-8641
e-mail: kstandard@ebglaw.com
Kenneth G Standard, Co-Chair

NYS Council of Probation Administrators
Box 2 272 Broadway, Albany, NY 12204
518-434-9194 Fax: 518-434-0392
e-mail: president@nyscopa.org
Web site: www.nyscopa.org
Provide supervision & investigation services to courts
Patricia Aikens, President

NYS Court Clerks Association
170 Duane St, New York, NY 10013
212-941-5700 Fax: 212-941-5705
Kevin E Scanlon, Sr, President

NYS Defenders Association
194 Washington Ave, Ste 500, Albany, NY 12210-2314
518-465-3524 Fax: 518-465-3249
e-mail: info@nysda.org
Web site: www.nysda.org
Criminal defense
Jonathan E Gradess, Executive Director

NYS Dispute Resolution Association
255 River St, #4, Troy, NY 12180
518-687-2240 Fax: 518-687-2245
e-mail: nysdra@nysdra.org
Web site: www.nysdra.org
Dispute resolution-mediation, arbitration, facilitation
Lisa U Hicks, Executive Director

NYS Magistrates Association
750 Delaware Ave, Delmar, NY 12054-1124
518-439-1087 Fax: 518-439-1204
e-mail: nysma@juno.com
Web site: www.mysma.net
Association of town & village justices
Tanja Sirago, Executive Director

NYS Bar Assn, Civil Practice Law & Rules Committee
NYS Supreme Court
50 Delaware Ave, Buffalo, NY 14202
716-845-9478 Fax: 716-851-3265
e-mail: sgerstma@courts.state.ny.us
Sharon Stern Gerstman, Chair

National Academy of Forensic Engineers
174 Brady Ave, Hawthorne, NY 10532
914-741-0633 Fax: 914-747-2988
e-mail: nafe@nafe.org
Web site: www.nafe.org
Engineering consultants to legal professionals & expert witnesses in court, arbitration & administrative adjudication proceedings
Marvin M Specter, P.E., L.S, Executive Director

NYS Bar Assn, Public Utility Law Committee
National Fuel Gas Distribution
455 Main St, Buffalo, NY 14203
716-686-6123
Web site: www.natfuel.com
Michael W Reville, Chair

NYS Bar Assn, Municipal Law Section
New York State Court of Claims
500 Court Exchange Bldg, 144 Exchange Blvd, Rochester, NY 14614
585-987-4212 Fax: 585-262-3019
e-mail: rminarik@courts.state.ny.us
Web site: www.nyscourtofclaims.courts.state.ny.us/
Hon Renee Forgensi Minarik,

New York State Law Enforcement Council
One Hogan Place, New York, NY 10013
212-335-8927 Fax: 212-335-3808
Web site: www.nyslec.org
Founded in 1982 as a legislative advocate for NY's law enforcement community. The members represent leading law enforcement professionals throughout the state. An active voice and participant in improving the quality of justice and a safer NY.
Leroy Frazer, Jr, Coordinator

New York State Supreme Court Officers Association
299 Broadway, Suite 1100, New York, NY 10007-1921
212-406-4292 or 212-406-4276 Fax: 212-791-8420
e-mail: lbroderick@nysscoa.org
Web site: www.nysscoa.org
Supreme Court Officers Union
John P McKillop, President

New York State Trial Lawyers
132 Nassau St, 2nd Fl, New York, NY 10038-2486
212-349-5890 Fax: 212-608-2310
e-mail: info@nystla.org
Web site: www.nystla.org
Lawrence Park, Executive Director

New York University School of Law
40 Washington Square South, New York, NY 10012
212-998-6100
e-mail: trevor.morrison@nyu.edu
Web site: www.law.nyu.edu
Judicial education & research
Trevor W. Morrison, Dean

NYS Bar Assn, Media Law Committee
New Yorker
1 World Trade Center, New York, NY 10007
800-444-7570
e-mail: fabio.bertoni@newyorker.com
Web site: www.newyorker.com
Fabio Bertoni, Member

NYS Bar Assn, Courts of Appellate Jurisdiction Cmte
Norman A Olch, Esq
233 Broadway, Suite 705, New York, NY 10279
212-964-6171 Fax: 212-964-7634
e-mail: norman@nolch.com
Norman A Olch, Chair

NYS Bar Assn, Judicial Campaign Monitoring Cmte
Ostertag O'Leary & Barrett
17 Collegeview Ave, Poughkeepsie, NY 12603
845-486-4300 Fax: 845-486-4080
e-mail: r.ostertag@verizon.net
Robert L Ostertag, Chair

Pace University, School of Law, John Jay Legal Services Inc
80 N Broadway, White Plains, NY 10603-3711
914-422-4333 Fax: 914-422-4391
e-mail: jjls@law.pace.edu
Web site: www.law.pace.edu
Law school clinical program with programs in the areas of health law, poverty law, domestic violence, immigration, criminal justice, and investor rights.
Margaret M Flint, Executive Director

Prisoners' Legal Services of New York
114 Prospect St, Ithaca, NY 14850-5616
607-273-2283 Fax: 607-272-9122
e-mail: kmmonks@plsny.org
Susan Johnson, Executive Director

Pro Bono Net
151 West 30th St, 10th Fl, New York, NY 10001
212-760-2554 Fax: 212-760-2557
e-mail: info@probono.net
Web site: www.probono.net; www.lawhelp.org
Connects & organizes the public interest legal community in an online environment; a lawyer-to-lawyer network
Mark O'Brien, Executive Director

NYS Bar Assn, Multi-jurisdictional Practice Cmte
Proskauer Rose LLP
1585 Broadway, New York, NY 10036-8299
212-969-3000 Fax: 212-969-2900
e-mail: keppler@proskauer.com
Web site: www.proskauer.com
Business Law, Securities
Klaus Eppler, Partner

Puerto Rican Legal Defense & Education Fund Inc (PRLDEF)
99 Hudson St, 14th Fl, New York, NY 10013-2815
212-219-3360 or 800-328-2322 Fax: 212-431-4276
e-mail: info@prldef.org
Web site: www.prldef.org
Secure, promote & protect the civil & human rights of the Puerto Rican & wider Latino community through litigation, policy analysis & education
Cesar A Perales, President & General Counsel

NYS Bar Assn, Judicial Campaign Conduct Cmte
Supreme Court
401 Montgomery St, Rm 401, Syracuse, NY 13202-2127
315-671-1100 Fax: 315-671-1183
e-mail: maklein@courts.state.ny.us
Michael A Klein, Chair

Vera Institute of Justice
233 Broadway, 12th Fl, New York, NY 10279-1299
212-334-1300 Fax: 212-941-9407
e-mail: contactvera@vera.org
Web site: www.vera.org
Research, design & implementation of demonstration projects in criminal justice & social equity in partnership with government & nonprofit organizations. Involved in child-welfare, cost-benefit analysis, substance abuse and mental health.
Michael Jacobson, Director

NYS Bar Assn, Family Law Section
Vincent F Stempel, Jr Esq
1205 Franklin Ave, Ste 280, Garden City, NY 11530
516-742-8620 Fax: 516-742-6859
e-mail: vstempel@yahoo.com
Vincent F Stempel, Jr, Chair

Volunteers of Legal Service, Inc
281 Park Avenue South, New York, NY 10010
212-966-4400 Fax: 212-219-8943
e-mail: blienhard@volsprobono.org
Providing pro bono civil legal services to poor people in New York City.
Bill Lienhard, Executive Director

NYS Bar Assn, Diversity & Leadership Development Cmte
Whiteman Osterman & Hanna LLP
One Commerce Plaza, Albany, NY 12260
518-487-7600 Fax: 518-487-7777
e-mail: lptharp@woh.com
Web site: www.woh.com
Lorraine Power Tharp, Partner

NYS Bar Assn, Health Law Section
Wilson Elser Moskowitz Edelman & Dicker
677 Broadway, Albany, NY 12207
518-449-8893 Fax: 518-449-4292
e-mail: philip.rosenberg@wilsonelser.com
Philip Rosenberg,

Women's Bar Association of the State of New York
PO Box 936, Planetarium Station, New York, NY 10024-0546
212-362-4445 Fax: 212-721-1620
e-mail: info@wbasny.org
Web site: www.wbasny.org
Linda A Chiaverini, Executive Director

LABOR & EMPLOYMENT PRACTICES

NEW YORK STATE

GOVERNOR'S OFFICE

Governor's Office
Executive Chamber
State Capitol
Albany, NY 12224
518-474-8390 Fax: 518-474-1513
Web site: www.ny.gov

Governor:
Andrew M Cuomo 518-474-8390
Secretary to the Governor:
William Mulrow 518-474-4246
Counsel to the Governor:
Alphonso David 518-474-8343
Deputy Secrtary, Labor:
Elizabeth de Leon Bhargava 212-681-4584
Chief of Staff:
Melissa DeRosa . . . . 518-474-8418 or 212-681-4640
Director, Communications:
James Allen . . . . 518-474-8418 or 212-681-4640

EXECUTIVE DEPARTMENTS AND RELATED AGENCIES

Insurance Fund (NYS)
One Watervliet Ave Ext
Albany, NY 12206
518-437-6400
Web site: www.nysif.com

199 Church St
New York, NY 10007
212-587-9000

Executive Director & CEO:
Eric Madoff . . . . 212-312-7004 or 518-437-5220
Deputy Executive Director:
Dorothy Carey 212-312-9933
Deputy Executive Director:
Shirley Stark 212-312-9917
Chief Fiscal Officer:
Susan D Sharp 518-437-6168
General Attorney:
Gregory Allen 518 437 5220
Public Information Officer:
Robert Lawson 518-437-3504/fax: 518-437-1849
Deputy Executive Director:
Colleen Gardner 518-437-3504/fax: 518-437-1849

Administration
Director:
Joseph Mullen 518-437-5220

Claims & Medical Operations
Director:
Edward Hiller 212-312-7880

Confidential Investigations
Director:
George Tidona 631-756-4007

Field Services
Director:
Armin Holdorf 212-587-5225

Information Technology Service
Chief Information Officer:
Sean O'Brien 518-437-4361
Director, ITS:
Laurie Endries 518-437-3130

Insurance Fund Board of Commissioners
Chair:
Kenneth R Theobalds 518-437-5220
Vice Chair:
Barry Swidler 518-437-5220
Secretary to the Board:
Michael Miliano 212-312-7408
Member(ex-offico)/Commissioner, NYS Dept of Labor:
Peter M. Rivera 518-437-5220
Member:
Eileen A Frank 518-437-5220
Member:
Joseph Canovas 518-437-5220
Member:
David E Ourlicht 518-437-5220

Investments
Director:
Miriam Martinez 212-587-6550

NYSIF District Offices

Albany
1 Watervliet Ave Ext, Albany, NY 12206
Business Manager:
Augusto Bortoloni 518-437-6401/fax: 518-437-8021

Buffalo
225 Oak St, Buffalo, NY 14203
Business Manager:
Ronald Reed 716 851 2001/fax: 716 851 2131

Binghamton
Glendale Technology Park, 2001 E Perimeter Rd, Endicott, NY 13760
Business Manager:
Thomas Racko 607-741-6023/fax: 607-741-5029

Nassau County, Long Island
8 Corporate Center Dr, 2nd Fl, Melville, NY 11747
Business Manager:
Cliff Meister 631-756-4003/fax: 631-756-4030

Rochester
100 Chestnut St, Ste 1000, Rochester, NY 14604
Business Manager:
Lisa Ellsworth 585-258-2100/fax: 585-258-2065

Suffolk County, Long Island
8 Corporate Center Dr, 3rd Fl, Melville, NY 11747
Business Manager:
Catherine Carillo 631-756-4330/fax: 631-756-4260

Syracuse
1045 Seventh North St, Liverpool, NY 13088
Business Manager:
Patricia Albert 315-453-8300/fax: 315-453-8313

White Plains
105 Corporate Park Dr, Ste 200, White Plains, NY 10604
Business Manager:
Carl Heitner 914-701-6292/fax: 914-701-2181

Premium Audit
Director:
Glenn Cunningham 212-587-7470

Policy Areas

Offices and agencies generally appear in alphabetical order, except when specific order is requested by listee.

Underwriting
Director:
John Massetti 212-312-7012

Labor Department

Building 12, Room 500
Harriman State Office Campus
Albany, NY 12240
518-457-9000 Fax: 518-457-6908
e-mail: nysdol@labor.ny.gov
Web site: www.labor.ny.gov

Commissioner:
Roberta Reardon 518-457-9000
Executive Deputy Commissioner:
Mario Musolino 518-457-4318

Hazard Abatement Board
Chair:
Katherine D. Schrier 518-457-7629

Employment Relations Board
Chair:
Jerome Lefkowitz 518-457-2664
e-mail: perbinfo@perb.ny.gov

Industrial Board of Appeals
Chair:
Anne P Stevason 518-474-4785

Unemployment Insurance Appeal Board
Chair:
Leonard Polletta 518-402-0205
Executive Director:
Susan Borenstein....................................518-402-0205

Administration & Public Affairs
Director:
Roger Bailie 518-457-2647
Director, Communications:
Leo Rosales 518-457-5519/fax: 518-485-1126
e-mail: leo.rosales@labor.ny.gov
Director, Personnel:
Carol Owsiany 518-457-1020
Acting Director, Staff & Organization Development:
Sherry Edwards....................................518-457-7442
Director, Equal Opportunity Development:
Omoye Cooper 518-457-1984

Counsel's Office
Acting Counsel:
Pico Ben-Amotz 518-457-3665

Federal Programs
Deputy Commissioner, Federal Programs:
Bruce Herman....................................518-485-6410

Employment Services Division
Director:
Vacant....................................518-457-3584
Assistant Director:
Russell Oliver....................................518-457-3584

Unemployment Insurance Division
Director:
Richard Marino 518-457-2878/fax: 518-485-8604

Workforce Development & Training Division
Director:
Karen Coleman 518-457-0380/fax: 518-457-9526
Employability Development/Apprentice Training
Acting Director:
Yue Yee 518-457-6820

Labor Planning & Technology
Director, Enterprise Architecture:
David A. Palmisano 518-485-7395

Research & Statistics Division
Chief:
Bohdan Wynnyk....................................518-485-7990
Chief of Labor Market Information:
Norman Steele....................................518-457-6638
Statewide Labor Market Analyst:
Kevin Jack....................................518-457-2919
e-mail: kevin.jack@labor.ny.gov

Special Investigations
Director:
John Dormin 518-457-7012
Director, Internal Audit:
Timothy Burleski 518-457-7012

Veterans Services
Program Coordinator:
Vacant....................................518-457-1343

Employer Services
Director:
Vacant....................................518-457-6821
Rural Labor Services:
Valerie Sewell....................................518-485-8539

Regional Offices
Central/Mohawk Valley ....fax: 315-793-2342
207 Genesee St, Ste 712, Utica, NY 13501
Finger Lakes Region ....fax: 585-258-8859
276 Waring Road, Rochester, NY 14607
Greater Capital District ....fax: 518-462-2777
175 Central Ave, Albany, NY 12206-2902
Hudson Valley ....fax: 914-287-2058
120 Bloomingdale Rd, White Plains, NY 10605
Long Island Region ....fax: 516-934-8553
303 W Old County Rd, Hicksville, NY 11801
New York City....................fax: 212-621-0730
247 West 54th St, New York, NY 10019
Southern Tier ....fax: 607-741-4516
2001 Perimeter Rd East, Ste 3, Endicott, NY 13760
Western Region ....fax: 716-851-2792
284 Main St, Buffalo, NY 14202

Worker Protection
Deputy Commissioner, Workforce Development:
Karen A. Coleman 518-457-4317

Labor Standards Division
Director:
Carmine Ruberto 518-457-4256

Public Work Bureau
Director:
Chris Alund 518-485-5696

Safety & Health Division
Director:
Eileen Franko 518-457-3518/fax: 518-457-1519
Asbestos Control Bureau
Program Manager:
Robert Perez....................518-457-1255/fax: 518-485-8054
Industry Inspection Unit
Program Manage, License & Certification:
Martha Waldman....................................518-457-2735
On-site Consultation Unit
Program Manager:
James Rush....................518-457-2238/fax: 518-457-3454

Offices and agencies generally appear in alphabetical order, except when specific order is requested by listee.

Public Employees Safety & Health (PESH) Unit
Program Manager:
Normand Labbe 518-457-1263/fax: 518-457-5545

Law Department

120 Broadway
New York, NY 10271-0332
212-416-8000 or 800-771-7755
Web site: www.ag.ny.gov

State Capitol
Albany, NY 12224-0341
518-776-2000
Fax: 518-650-9401

Attorney General:
Eric T Schneiderman . . . . 212-416-8050 or 518-776-2000
Chief of Staff:
Brian Mahanna 212-416-8050
Press Secretary:
Matt Mittenthal 212-416-8060/fax: 212-416-6005

Social Justice

Executive Deputy Attorney General:
Alvin L Bragg, Jr 212-416-8450

Civil Rights Bureau
Bureau Chief:
Lourdes Rosado. 212-416-8250/fax: 212-416-8074

State Counsel

Chief Deputy Attorney General & Counsel:
Harlan Levy 212-416-8525
Executive Deputy Attorney General, State Counsel:
Kent T Stauffer . . . . 212-416-8252 or 518-473-8946
fax: 212-416-6001

Civil Recoveries Bureau
Bureau Chief:
John Cremo 518-776-2173/fax: 518-915-7731

Workers' Compensation Board

328 State Street
Schenectady, NY 12305
518-462-8880 or 877-632-4996 Fax: 518-473-1415
e-mail: publicinfo@wcb.ny.gov
Web site: www.wcb.ny.gov

Executive Director:
MaryBeth Woods 518-408-0469
Chair, Board of Commissioners:
Robert E Beloten 518-408-0469/fax: 518-473-1415
Vice Chair:
Ken Munnelly 518-408-0469/fax: 518-473-1415
General Counsel:
Vacant 518-486-9564/fax: 518-402-0113
Director, Public Information:
Rachel McEneny 518-408-5592/fax: 518-473-1415
e-mail: publicinfo@wcb.ny.gov
Fraud Inspector General:
Vacant 888-363-6001/fax: 518-402-1059
Advocate for Business:
Neil Gilberg 518-486-3331
Advocate for Injured Workers:
Edwin Ruff . . . . 800-580-6665 or 518-471-8182
fax: 518-486-7510

Administration

Director, Facilities Management:
Michael DeBarr. 518-486-9597
Chief, Security:
Sylvio Mantello 518-402-0172/fax: 518-402-6100
Director, Human Resources:
Gilda Hernandez 518-486-3348/fax: 518-486-6364
Affirmative Action Officer:
Jaime Benitez. 518-486-5128/fax: 518-486-6364

Information Management Systems

Director:
Vacant
Director, Continuous Improvement/MIS:
Thomas Wegener 518-486-5143

Operations

Director, Bureau of Compliance:
Vacant 518-474-9598/fax: 518-402-6201

District Offices

Albany
100 Broadway-Menands, Albany, NY 12241
District Manager:
Laurie Hart 866-750-5157/fax: 518-473-9166

Binghamton
State Office Bldg, 44 Hawley St, Binghamton, NY 13901
District Manager:
David Gardiner. 866-802-3604/fax: 607-721-8464

Brooklyn
111 Livingston St, 22nd Fl, Brooklyn, NY 11201
District Manager:
Tom Agostino 800-877-1373/fax: 718-802-6642

Buffalo
Ellicott Sq Building, 295 Main Street Ste 400, Buffalo, NY 14203
District Manager:
Michelle Hirsch 866-211-0645/fax: 716-842-2171

Long Island
220 Rabro Drive, Ste 100, Hauppauge, NY 11788-4230
District Manager:
Bryan Pile 866-681-5354/fax: 631-952-7966

Manhattan
215 W 125th St, New York, NY 10027
District Manager:
Sherri Cunningham. 800-877-1373/fax: 212-864-7204

Peekskill
41 N Division St, Peekskill, NY 10566
District Manager:
Luis A Torres 866-746-0552/fax: 914-788-5809

Queens
168-46 91st Ave, 3rd Fl, Jamaica, NY 11432
District Administrator:
Bryan Pile 800-877-1373/fax: 718-291-7248

Rochester
130 Main St West, Rochester, NY 14614
District Manager:
Matthew Bligh 866-211-0644/fax: 585-238-8351

Syracuse
935 James Street, Syracuse, NY 13203
District Manager:
Marc Johnson 866-802-3730/fax: 315-423-2938

Workers' Compensation Board of Commissioners

Commissioner & Vice Chair:
Ken Munnelly 518-408-0469
Commissioner:
Kenneth Munnelly 518-408-0469
Commissioner:
Mark D Higgins 518-408-0469
Commissioner:
Conrad W Lower 518-408-0469
Commissioner:
Loren Lobban 518-408-0469
Commissioner:
Linda Hull 518-408-0469

Commissioner:
Candace K Finnegan 914-788-5890
Commissioner:
Freida Foster 518-408-0469
Commissioner:
Samuel G Williams 518-408-0469
Commissioner:
Ellen O Paprocki 315-423-1276
Secretary to the Board:
Sandra M Olson 518-402-6070

CORPORATIONS, AUTHORITIES AND COMMISSIONS

Waterfront Commission of New York Harbor
39 Broadway
4th Fl
New York, NY 10006
212-742-9280 Fax: 212-480-0587
Web site: www.wcnyh.org

Commissioner, New York:
Ronald Goldstock 212-742-9280
Commissioner, New Jersey:
Michael Murphy 212-742-9280
Executive Director:
Walter M Arsenault 212-905-9201

NEW YORK STATE LEGISLATURE

See Legislative Branch in Section 1 for additional Standing Committee and Subcommittee information.

Assembly Standing Committees

Labor
Chair:
Michele Titus (D) 518-455-5668
Ranking Minority Member:
Karl Brabenec (R) 518-455-5991

Assembly Task Forces

Puerto Rican/Hispanic Task Force
Chair:
Marcos Crespo (D) 518-455-5514
Executive Director:
Guillermo Martinez 518-455-3608

Skills Development & Career Education, Legislative Commission on
Assembly Chair:
Harry Bronson (D) 518-455-4527
Program Manager:
Brenda Carter 518-455-4865

Women's Issues, Task Force on
Chair:
Aravella Simotas (D) 518-455-5014
Coordinator:
Christina Williams 518-455-3632/fax: 518-455-4574

Senate Standing Committees

Labor
Chair:
Jack Martins (R) 518-455-3265
Ranking Minority Member:
Jose R Peralta (D) 518-455-2529

U.S. GOVERNMENT

EXECUTIVE DEPARTMENTS AND RELATED AGENCIES

Equal Employment Opportunity Commission
Web site: www.eeoc.gov

New York District
33 Whitehall St, 5th Fl, New York, NY 10004
District Director:
Kevin J. Berry . . . . 800-669-4000 or 800-669-6820 tty
fax: 212-336-3790

Buffalo Local
6 Fountain Plaza, Ste 350, Buffalo, NY 14202
Director:
John E Thompson Jr . . . . 800-669-4000 or 800-669-3820 tty
fax: 716-551-4387

Federal Labor Relations Authority
Web site: www.flra.gov

Boston Regional Office . . . . fax: 617-565-6262
O'Neill Federal Bldg, 10 Causeway St, Ste 472, Boston, MA 02222
617-565-5100 Fax: 617-565-6262
Regional Director:
Phillip T. Roberts 617-424-5730/fax: 312-886-5997

Federal Mediation & Conciliation Service
Web site: www.fmcs.gov

Northeastern Region . . . . fax: 973-297-4860
1 Newark Center, 16th Floor, Newark, NJ 07102
732-726-3120 Fax: 973-297-4860
Regional Director:
Ken Kowalski 973-645-2000
Director, Mediation Services:
Jack Sweeny 973-645-2200
e-mail: jsweeny@fmcs.gov

National Labor Relations Board
Web site: www.nlrb.gov

Region 2 - New York City Metro Area . . . . fax: 212-264-2450
26 Federal Plaza, Rm 3614, New York, NY 10278-0104
212-264-0300 Fax: 212-264-2450
Regional Director:
Karen P. Fernbach 212-264-0300/fax: 212-264-2450

Region 29 - Brooklyn Area . . . . fax: 718-330-7579
Two MetroTech Center, 100 Myrtle Ave, 5th Fl, Brooklyn, NY 11201-4201
718-330-7713 Fax: 718-330-7579
Regional Director:
James G. Paulsen 718-330-7713/fax: 718-330-7579

Region 3 - Buffalo Area . . . . fax: 716-551-4972
Niagara Center Building, 130 South Elmowood Ave, Ste 630, Buffalo, NY 14202-2387
716-551-4931 Fax: 716-551-4972
Regional Director:
Rhonda P. Ley 716-551-4931/fax: 716-551-4972

Albany Resident Office . . . . fax: 518-431-4157
Leo W O'Brien Fed Bldg, Rm 342, Clinton Ave and N Pearl St, Albany, NY 12207-2350
518-431-4155 Fax: 518-431-4157
Resident Officer:
Jon Mackle 518-431-4155/fax: 518-431-4157

Offices and agencies generally appear in alphabetical order, except when specific order is requested by listee.

US Labor Department
Web site: www.dol.gov

Bureau of Labor Statistics (BLS)
201 Varick St, Rm 808, New York, NY 10014
Web site: www.bls.gov
Regional Commissioner (NY & Boston):
Deborah A. Brown 617-565-2331
Reg Comm (NY):
Vacant

Employee Benefits Security Administration (EBSA)
33 Whitehall St, Ste 1200, New York, NY 10004
Regional Director:
Jonathan Kay.......................212-607-8600/fax: 212-607-8681

Employment & Training Administration (ETA)
JFK Federal Bldg, Rm E/350, 25 New Sudbury Street, Boston, MA 02203
Regional Administrator:
Holly O'Brien 617-788-0170/fax: 617-788-0101

Employment Standards Administration

Federal Contract Compliance Programs Office (OFCCP)
26 Federal Plaza, Rm. 36-116, New York, NY 10278
Regional Director:
Eduardo Fountaine 646-264-3170/fax: 646-264-3009

Labor-Management Standards Office (OLMS)
Web site: www.olms.dol.gov

Buffalo District Office
130 South Elmwood Street, Suite 510, Buffalo, NY 14202
District Director:
Joseph Wasik 716-842-2900/fax: 716-842-2901

New York District Office
201 Varick St, Rm 878, New York, NY 10014
District Director:
Adrianna Vamuateas 646-264-3190/fax: 646-264-3191

Wage-Hour Division (WHD)-Northeast Regional Office
170 So Independence Mall, Ste 850 West, Philadelphia, PA 19106
Regional Admin:
Corlis L Sellers 215-861-5800/fax: 215-861-5840

Albany District Office
Leo W O'Brien Fed Bldg, Rm 822, Albany, NY 12207
District Director:
Jay Rosenblum...........................518-431-6460

Long Island District Office
1400 Old Country Rd, Ste 410, Westbury, NY 11590
District Director:
Irv Miljoner 516-338-1890/fax: 516-338-8901

New York City District Office
26 Federal Plz, Rm 3700, New York, NY 10278
District Director:
Maria Rosado 212-264-8185/fax: 212-264-9548

Workers' Compensation Programs (OWCP)
201 Varick St, Rm 740, New York, NY 10014
Regional Director:
Zev Sapir...212-868-0844

Inspector General

Inspector General's Office for Audit (OIG-A)
201 Varick St, Rm 871, New York, NY 10014
Audit Director:
Mark Schwartz 646-264-3511

Occupational Safety & Health Administration (OSHA)
201 Varick St, Rm 670, New York, NY 10014
212-337-2378
Web site: www.osha.gov
Regional Administrator:
Robert Kulick 212-337-2378

Albany Area Office
401 New Karner Rd, Ste 300, Albany, NY 12205-3809
Area Director:
Kimberly Castillion...............518-464-4338/fax: 518-464-4337

Buffalo Area Office
130 Elmwood Avenue, Suite 500, Buffalo, NY 14026
Area Director:
Arthur Dube 716-551-3053/fax: 716-551-3126

Manhattan Area Office
201 Varick St, Rm 908, New York, NY 10014
Area Director:
Richard Mendelson 212-620-3200/fax: 212-620-4121

Queens Area Office
45-17 Marathon Parkway, Little Neck, NY 11362
Assistant Area Director:
Kay Gee........................718-279-9060/fax: 718-279-9057

Syracuse Area Office
3300 Vickery Rd, North Syracuse, NY 13212
Area Director:
Christopher Adams 315-451-0808/fax: 315-451-1351

Tarrytown Area Office
660 White Plains Rd, 4th Floor, Tarrytown, NY 10591-5107
Area Director:
Diana Cortez 914-524-7510/fax: 914-524-7515

Office of Asst Secretary for Administration & Mgmt (OASAM)
201 Varick St, Rm 815, New York, NY 10014
Regional Administrator (NY & Boston):
Mark D. Falk..646-264-5018

Office of the Solicitor ....fax: 646-246-3660
201 Varick St, Rm 983, New York, NY 10014
646-264-3650 Fax: 646-246-3660
Reg Solicitor:
Patricia M Rodenhausen 212-337-2078/fax: 212-337-2112

Region 2 - New York Office of Secretary's Representative
201 Varick St, Rm 605-B, New York, NY 10014
Secretary's Regional Representative (SRR):
Angelica O Tang 212-337-2317/fax: 212-337-2586

Jobs Corps (JC)
JFK Fed Bldg, Room E350, Boston, NY 02203
Regional Director:
Joseph A Semansky 617-788-0197/fax: 617-788-0184

Office of Public Affairs (OPA) (serving New York State)
JFK Federal Bldg, Rm E120, Boston, MA 2203
Regional Director, Public Affairs:
John Chavez 617-565-2072/fax: 617-565-2076

Region 2 New York - Women's Bureau (WB) ... fax: 646-264-3794
201 Varick St, Rm 602, New York, NY 10014-4811
646-264-3789 Fax: 646-264-3794
Regional Administrator:
Grace Protos 646-264-3789
e-mail: protos.grace@dol.gov

US Merit Systems Protection Board
Web site: www.mspb.gov

New York Field Office
26 Federal Plaza, Room 3137A, New York, NY 10278
Chief Administrative Judge:
Arthur S. Joseph 212-264-9372/fax: 212-264-1417

Offices and agencies generally appear in alphabetical order, except when specific order is requested by listee.

US Office of Personnel Management

Web site: www.usajobs.opm.gov

PHILADELPHIA SERVICE CENTER (serving New York)
William J Green Fed Bldg, Rm 3256, 600 Arch St, Philadelphia, PA 19106
Director:
Joseph D Stix 215-861-3031/fax: 215-861-3030
e-mail: philadelphia@opm.gov

US Railroad Retirement Board

Web site: www.rrb.gov

New York District Offices

Albany . . . . fax: 518-431-4000
11A Clinton Avenue, Suite 264, Albany, NY 12207-2399
877-772-5772 Fax: 518-431-4000
District Manager:
Daniel M Layton, Jr 877-772-5772/fax: 518-431-4000
e-mail: albany@rrb.gov

Buffalo . . . . fax: 716-551-3802
186 Exchange Streeet, Suite 110, Buffalo, NY 14204-2085
877-772-5772 Fax: 716-551-3802
District Manager:
Philip C Dissek 877-772-5772/fax: 716-551-3802
e-mail: buffalo@rrb.gov

New York . . . . fax: 212-264-1687
26 Federal Plaza, Rm 3404, New York, NY 10278
877-772-5772 Fax: 212-264-1687
District Manager:
Rose I Jonas 877-772-5772/fax: 212-264-1687
e-mail: newyork@rrb.gov

Westbury . . . . fax: 516-334-4763
1400 Old Country Rd, Ste 202, Westbury, NY 11590
877-772-5772 or 716-835-7808 Fax: 516-334-4763
District Manager:
Marie Baran 877-772-5772/fax: 516-334-4763

U.S. CONGRESS

See U.S. Congress Chapter for additional Standing Committee and Subcommittee information.

House of Representatives Standing Committees

Education & Labor

Chair:
John Kline (R-MN) 202-225-2271
Ranking Member:
George Miller (D-CA) 202-225-2095
New York Delegate:
Timothy H Bishop (D) 202-225-3826
New York Delegate:
Carolyn McCarthy (D) 202-225-5516
New York Delegate:
Paul Tonko (D) 202-225-5076

Small Business

Chair:
Sam Graves (R-MO) 202-225-7041
Ranking Member:
Nydia Velazquez (D-NY) 202-225-2361
New York Delegate:
Grace Meng (D) 202-225-2601

Subcommittees

Contracting and Workforce
Chair:
Richard L. Hanna (R-NY) 202-225-3665
Ranking Member:
Grace Meng (D-NY) 202-225-2601
Chair:
David Schweikert (R-AZ) 202-225-2190
Ranking Member:
Yvette Clarke (D-NY) 202-225-6231

Senate Standing Committees

Health, Education, Labor & Pensions

Chair:
Tom Harkin (D-IA) 202-224-3254
Ranking Member:
Lamar Alexander (R-TN) 202-224-4944

Small Business & Entrepreneurship

Chair:
Mary L. Landrieu (D-LA) 202-224-5824
Ranking Member:
James E. Risch (R-ID) 202-224-2752

PRIVATE SECTOR

1199 SEIU United Healthcare Workers East
310 W 43rd St, New York, NY 10036
212-261-2222 Fax: 212-956-5140
Web site: www.1199seiuonline.org
Representing New York State healthcare workers
George Gresham, President

Abilities Inc, Abilities!
201 IU Willets Rd, Albertson, NY 11507-1599
516-465-1400 or 516-747-5355 (TTY) Fax: 516-465-3757
e-mail: jswiesky@abilitiesinc.org
Web site: www.abilitiesinc.org
Provides comprehensive services to help individuals with disabilities reach their employment goals; provides support services & technical assistance to employers who hire persons with disabilities
Alice Muterspaw, Consumer Services/Provider Relations Director

American Federation of Teachers
555 New Jersey Ave NW, Washington, DC 20001
800-238-1133 Fax: 202-393-7479
e-mail: emcelroy@aft.org
Web site: www.aft.org
Edward J McElroy, President

Associated Builders & Contractors, Construction Training Center of NYS
6369 Collamer Drive, East Syracuse, NY 13057-1115
315-463-7539 or 800-477-7743 Fax: 315-463-7621
e-mail: info@abc.org
Web site: www.abc.org/newyork
Merit shop construction trades apprenticeship program
Thomas Schlueter, Vice President of Education Programs

Blitman & King LLP
443 N Franklin St, Ste 300, Syracuse, NY 13204
315-422-7111 Fax: 315-471-2623
e-mail: btking@bklawyers.com
Web site: www.bklawyers.com
Labor & employee benefits
Bernard T King, Attorney/Senior Partner

Offices and agencies generally appear in alphabetical order, except when specific order is requested by listee.

Center for an Urban Future
120 Wall St, 20th Fl, New York, NY 10005
212-479-3319 Fax: 212-479-3338
e-mail: cuf@nycfuture.org
Web site: www.nycfuture.org
A New York City-based think tank that publishes studies about economic development, workforce development and other critical issues facing New York.
Jonathan Bowles, Director

Civil Service Employees Union (CSEA), Local 1000, AFSCME, AFL-CIO
143 Washington Ave, Capitol Station Box 7125, Albany, NY 12210-0125
518-257-1000 or 800-342-4146 Fax: 518-462-3639
Web site: www.csealocal1000.org
Public/private employees union
Danny Donohue, President

Communications Workers of America, District 1
80 Pine St, 37th Floor, New York, NY 10005
212-344-2515 Fax: 212-425-2947
Web site: www.cwa-union.org
Christopher Shelton, Vice President

Cornell University, Institute on Conflict Resolution
412 Dolgen Hall, Ithaca, NY 14853-3901
607-255-5378 Fax: 607-255-6974
e-mail: dbl4@cornell.edu
Web site: www.ilr.cornell.edu
Collective bargaining; dispute resolution, negotiation
David Lipsky, Director

Cornell University, Sch of Industr & Labor Relations Institute for Workplace Studies
16 E 34th Street, 4th Fl, New York, NY 10016
212-340-2850 Fax: 212-340-2893
e-mail: sb22@cornell.edu
Web site: www.ilr.cornell.edu/iws
Substance abuse in the workplace; power & bargaining in organizations
Samuel B Bacharach, McKelvey-Grant Professor & Director

Cornell University, School of Industrial & Labor Relations
Ives Hall, Ithaca, NY 14853-3901
607-255-4375 or 607-255-2223 Fax: 607-255-1836
e-mail: vmb2@cornell.edu
Web site: www.ilr.cornell.edu
Immigration policy; labor market trends & analysis
Vernon Briggs, Professor

Cullen & Dykman LLP
100 Quentin Roosevelt Blvd, Garden City Ctr, Garden City, NY 11530-4850
516-357-3703 Fax: 516-296-9155
e-mail: gfishberg@cullenanddykman.com
Web site: www.cullenanddykman.com
Municipal & labor law
Gerard Fishberg, Partner

Empire State Regional Council of Carpenters
1284 Central Avenue, Ste 1, Albany, NY 12205
518-459-7182 Fax: 518-459-7798
e-mail: jminer@empirestatecarpenters.org
Michael Conroy, Political Director

JAMS
620 Eighth Avenue, 34th Floor, New York, NY 10018
212-751-2700 Fax: 212-751-4099
Web site: www.jamsadr.com
Mediation of civil, commercial & employment disputes: training & systems design
Carol Wittenberg, Arbitrator/Mediator

Kaye Scholer LLP
250 West 55th Street, New York, NY 10019-9710
212-836-8000 Fax: 212-836-8689
e-mail: william.wallace@kayescholer.com
Web site: www.kayescholer.com
Chair, Labor & Employment Law Group (representing employers)
William E. Wallace, Jr., Partner

NYS Bar Assn, Labor & Employment Law Section
Kraus & Zuchlewski LLP
500 Fifth Ave, Ste 5100, New York, NY 10110
212-869-4646 Fax: 212-869-4648
e-mail: pz@kzlaw.net
Pearl Zuchlewski, Chair

Lancer Insurance Co/Lancer Compliance Services
370 West Park Ave, Long Beach, NY 11561-3245
516-432-5000 Fax: 516-431-0926
e-mail: bcrescenzo@lancer-ins.com
Substance abuse management & testing services for the transportation industry
Bob Crescenzo, Vice President

MDRC
16 East 34th St, 19th Floor, New York, NY 10016-5936
212-532-3200 Fax: 212-684-0832
e-mail: information@mdrc.org
Web site: www.mdrc.org
Nonprofit research & field testing of education & employment programs for disadvantaged adults & youth
Gordon Berlin, President

Manhattan-Bronx Minority Business Enterprise Center
225 W 34th St, Ste 2007, New York, NY 10122
212-947-5351 or 212-947-4900 Fax: 212-947-1506
e-mail: mbmbdc@manhattanmbec.com
Web site: www.manhattanmbec.com
Information & advocacy for local employment & business & contract opportunities
Lorraine Kelsey, Executive Director

NY Association of Training & Employment Professionals (NYATEP)
540 Broadway, 5th Floor, Albany, NY 12207
518-433-1200 Fax: 518-433-7424
e-mail: jtwomey@nyatep.org
Web site: www.nyatep.org
Represent local workforce development partnerships
John Twomey, Executive Director

NYS Building & Construction Trades Council
50 State Street, 3rd Floor, Albany, NY 12207
518-435-9108 Fax: 518-435-9204
e-mail: nybuildingtrades@me.com
Web site: www.nybuildingtrades.com
James Cahill, President

NYS Industries for the Disabled (NYSID) Inc
11 Columbia Circle Dr., Albany, NY 12203
518-463-9706 or 800-221-5994 Fax: 518-463-9708
e-mail: administrator@nysid.org
Web site: www.nysid.org
Business development through 'preferred source' purchasing to increase employment opportunities for people with disabilities
Lawrence L Barker, Jr, President & Chief Executive Officer

National Federation of Independent Business
100 State Street, Suite 440, Albany, NY 12207
518-434-1262 Fax: 518-426-8799
e-mail: mike.durant@nfib.org
Web site: www.nfib.com/new-york/
Small business advocacy; supporting pro-small business candidates at the state & federal levels
Michael P. Durant, State Director

National Writers Union
113 University Pl, 6th Fl, New York, NY 10003
212-254-0279 Fax: 212-254-0673
e-mail: nwu@nwu.org
Web site: www.nwu.org
Gerard Colby, President

New York Committee for Occupational Safety & Health
61 Broadway, Suite 1710, New York, NY 10006
212-227-6440 Fax: 212-227-9854
e-mail: nycosh@nycosh.org
Web site: www.nycosh.org
Provide occupational safety & health training & technical assistance
Joel Shufro, Executive Director

New York State Nurses Association
11 Cornell Rd, Latham, NY 12110
518-782-9400 x279 Fax: 518-783-5207
e-mail: executive@nysna.org
Web site: www.nysna.org
Labor union & professional association for registered nurses

New York University, Graduate School of Journalism
20 Cooper Square, 6th Floor, New York, NY 10003
212-998-7980 Fax: 212-995-4148
Web site: www.journalism.nyu.edu
Labor issues & reporting
Perri Klass, Director

Osborne Association
809 Westchester Avenue, Bronx, NY 10455
718-707-2600 Fax: 718-707-3102
e-mail: info@osborneny.org
Web site: www.osborneny.org
Career/educational counseling, job referrals & training for recently released prisoners, substance abuse treatment, case management, HIV/AIDS counseling & prevention, family services, parenting education, re-entry services, housing placement assistan
Tanya L Phillips, Director of Employment & Training

Public/Private Ventures
The Chanin Building, 122 East 42nd St, 42nd Fl, New York, NY 10168
212-822-2400 Fax: 212-949-0439
e-mail: kfaulhaber@ppv.org
Web site: www.ppv.org
A national nonprofit, nonpartisan organization that tackles critical challenges facing low-income communities by seeking out and designing innovative programs, rigorously testing them, and promoting the solutions proven to work.
Sheila Maguire, VP, Labor Market Initiatives

Realty Advisory Board on Labor Relations
292 Madison Ave, New York, NY 10017
212-889-4100 Fax: 212-889-4105
e-mail: jberg@rabolr.com
Web site: www.rabolr.com
Labor negotiations for realtors & realty firms
James Berg, President

Transport Workers Union of America, AFL-CIO
1700 Broadway, 2nd Fl, New York, NY 10019
212-259-4900 Fax: 212-265-5704
Web site: www.twu.com
Bus, train, railroad & airline workers' union
James C Little, International President

UNITE HERE
275 7th Ave, Fl 11, New York, NY 10001-6708
212-265-7000 Fax: 212-765-7751
e-mail: brayor@unitehere.org
Web site: www.uniteunion.org
Bruce Raynor, General President

United Food & Commercial Workers Local 1
5911 Airport Road, Oriskany, NY 13424
315-797-9600 or 800-697-8329 Fax: 315-793-1182
e-mail: organize@ufcwone.org
Web site: www.ufcwone.org
Frank C DeRiso, President

Vedder Price PC
1633 Broadway, New York, NY 10019
212-407-7750 or 917-214-6441 Fax: 212-407-7799
e-mail: akoral@vedderprice.com
Web site: www.vedderprice.com
Representing Management
Alan M Koral, Shareholder

Vladeck, Waldman, Elias & Engelhard PC
1501 Broadway, Suite 800, New York, NY 10036
212-403-7300 Fax: 212-221-3172
e-mail: jvladeck@vladeck.com
Employment law, including discrimination cases
Judith Vladeck, Senior Law Partner

MENTAL HYGIENE

NEW YORK STATE

GOVERNOR'S OFFICE

Governor's Office
Executive Chamber
State Capitol
Albany, NY 12224
518-474-8390 Fax: 518-474-1513
Web site: www.ny.gov

Governor:
Andrew M Cuomo 518-474-8390
Secretary to the Governor:
William Mulrow 518-474-4246
Counsel to the Governor:
Alphonso David 518-474-8343
Deputy Secretary, Health & Human Services:
Paul Francis. 518-408-2500
Chief of Staff:
Melissa DeRosa . . . . 518-474-8418 or 212-681-4640
Director, Communications:
James Allen. . . . . 518-474-8418 or 212-681-4640

EXECUTIVE DEPARTMENTS AND RELATED AGENCIES

Alcoholism & Substance Abuse Services, Office of
1450 Western Ave
Albany, NY 12203
518-473-3460 Fax: 518-457-5474
e-mail: communications@oasas.ny.gov
Web site: www.oasas.ny.gov

501 7th Ave
8th Fl
New York, NY 10018
646-728-4533

Commissioner:
Arlene Gonzalez-Sanchez. 518-457-2061
Executive Deputy Commissioner:
Sean M. Byrne 518-485-2337
Director, Public Information & Communications:
Susan A Craig, MPH. 518-457-8299/fax: 518-485-6014
Office & Wellness & Medical Direction (Acting):
Charles W Morgan, MD 845-359-8500
Director, Internal Audit:
Steven Shrager 518-485-2255
Affirmative Action Officer:
Loretta Poole. 646-728-4530
Director, Office of Statewide Field Operations:
Kathleen Caggiano-Siino 518-457-1758

Fiscal Administration Division
Associate Commissioner:
P David Sawicki 518-457-5312
Director, Facility Evaluation & Inspection Unit:
John Van Horn 518-485-2246
Director, Bureau of Capital Management:
Jeff Emad 518-457-2545
Director, Budget Management:
Tara Gabriel 518-485-2193
Director, Bureau of Health Care Financing & 3rd Party Reimbursement:
Laurie Felter 518-457-2545

Quality Assurance & Performance Improvement Division
Associate Commissioner:
Charles W Monson 518-485-2257
Director, Bureau of Standards Compliance:
William Lachanski 518-485-2255

Prevention, Housing, Technology & Management Services Division
Acting Associate Commissioner:
Mary Ann DiChristopher 518-485-6022
Director, Management Services:
Vacant 518-485-6689

Outcome Management & System Information Division
Associate Commissioner:
William F. Hogan 518-485-2322
Director, Bureau of State/Local Planning & Outcome Mgmt:
Vacant 518-485-2322
Director, Bureau of Research, Epidemiology & Practice Improvement:
Vacant 518-485-5989

Developmental Disabilities Planning Council
One Commerce Plaza
Ste 1230
Albany, NY 12210
518-486-7505 or 800-395-3372 Fax: 518-402-3505
e-mail: ddpc@ddpc.ny.gov
Web site: www.ddpc.ny.gov

Chairperson:
James Traylor 518-486-7505
Vice Chairperson:
Thomas Burke. 518-486-7505
Executive Director:
Sheila M Carey 518-486-7505
e-mail: sheila.carey@ddpc.ny.gov
Deputy Director-Program Development Specialist:
Anna Lobosco 518-486-7505
e-mail: anna.lobosco@ddpc.ny.gov
Public Information Officer:
Thomas F Lee 518-486-7505/fax: 518-486-3505
e-mail: thomas.lee@ddpc.ny.gov

Education Department
State Education Bldg
89 Washington Ave
Albany, NY 12234
518-474-3852 Fax: 518-486-5631
Web site: www.nysed.gov

Commissioner & University President:
MaryEllen Elia 518-474-5844
Executive Deputy Commissioner:
Elizabeth Berlin 518-473-8381
General Counsel:
Robert Trautwein 518-474-6400
e-mail: legal@nysed.gov
Office of Innovation and School Reform:
Cheryl Atkinson 518-473-8852

Office of the Professions. . . . . fax: 518-474-3863
89 Washington Ave, EB, 2nd Fl, West Mezz, Albany, NY 12234
Fax: 518-474-3863
Web site: www.op.nysed.gov
Deputy Commissioner:
Douglas Lentivech. . . . . 518-486-1765 or 518-474-3817 x440
e-mail: opopr@nysed.gov

Offices and agencies generally appear in alphabetical order, except when specific order is requested by listee.

Office of Professional Responsibility
Director, Professional Examinations:
Harrison Fisher 518-474-3817 x440

Professional Education Program Review
Assistant Director:
Mei Zhou 518-474-3817 x360
e-mail: opprogs@nysed.gov

Professional Licensing Services
Director:
Susan Naccarato 518-474-3817 x340
e-mail: opdpls@nysed.gov

Office of Adult Career & Continuing Education Services (ACCES) . . . . fax: 518-474-8802

89 Washington Ave, 5th Fl, EBA, Albany, NY 12234
Fax: 518-474-8802
Web site: www.acces.nysed.gov
Deputy Commissioner:
Kevin Smith 518-474-2714
e-mail: accesdeputy@nysed.gov
Assistant Commissioner:
Deborah Brown-Johnson 518-402-3955/fax: 518-473-6073
e-mail: accesadm@nysed.gov

Fiscal & Administrative Services
Coordinator:
Rosemary Johnson 518-486-4038
Director, Adult Education Program & Policy:
Mark Leinung 518-474-8892
e-mail: AEPP@nysed.gov
Coordinator:
Pat Geary 518-486-3220

Quality Assurance - Statewide Special Education
Statewide Coordinator:
James DeLorenzo 518-402-3353

State School for the Blind at Batavia
2A Richmond Ave, Batavia, NY 14020
Superintendent:
Erin Fairben 585-343-5384

Vocational Rehabilitation Operations
Assistant Commsioner:
Debora Brown-Jackson 518-402-3955
e-mail: dbrowngr@mail.nysed.gov

Mental Health, Office of

44 Holland Ave
Albany, NY 12229
518-474-4403 Fax: 518-474-2149
Web site: www.omh.ny.gov

Commissioner:
Ann Marie T Sullivan MD 518-474-4403
Executive Deputy Commissioner:
Martha Schaefer 518-474-7056/fax: 518-473-4690
Medical Director:
Lloyd I Sederer, MD . . . . 212-330-1650 x 360
Deputy Commissioner & Counsel:
Joshua Pepper 518-474-1331/fax: 518-473-7863

Division of Adult Services

Senior Deputy Commissioner & Division Director:
Robert Myers, PhD 518-486-4327/fax: 518-473-4690
State Operated Children's & Adult Svcs: Associate Commissioner/Deputy Director:
May Lum 518-474-0121/fax: 518-473-7926

Division of Integrated Community Services for Children & Families

Associate Commissioner:
Donna Bradbury 518-473-6328/fax: 518-473-4690

Center for Human Resource Management

Director:
J. Lynn Heath 518-474-0171/fax: 518-474-7536

Center for Information Technology

Deputy Commissioner & CIO:
John Norton 518-474-7359/fax: 518-473-2778

Division of Forensic Services

Associate Commissioner:
Donna Hall, PhD 518-549-5000/fax: 518-549-5090

Facilities

NYC Children's Center-Bronx Campus
1000 Waters Place, Bronx, NY 10461-2799
Acting Executive Director:
Anita Daniels 718-239-3600/fax: 718-862-3669

Bronx Psychiatric Center
1500 Waters Place, Bronx, NY 10461-2796
Executive Director:
Pamela Turner 718-862-3300/fax: 718-826-4858

Brooklyn Children's Center
1819 Bergen St, Brooklyn, NY 11233
Acting Executive Director:
Anita Daniels 718-613-3100/fax: 718-221-4500

Buffalo Psychiatric Center
400 Forest Ave, Buffalo, NY 14213-1298
Acting Executive Director:
Celia Spacone, PhD 716-816-2001/fax: 716-885-0710

Capital District Psychiatric Center
75 New Scotland Ave, Albany, NY 12208-3474
Executive Director:
William Dickson 518-549-6000/fax: 518-549-6804

Central New York Psychiatric Center
PO Box 300, Marcy, NY 13404-0300
Acting Director:
Peter Russell 315-765-3620/fax: 315-765-3629

Creedmoor Psychiatric Center
79-25 Winchester Blvd, Queens Village, NY 11427-2199
Executive Director:
Ann Marie Barbarotta 718-264-3600/fax: 718-264-3635

Elmira Psychiatric Center
100 Washington St, Elmira, NY 14902-1527
Executive Director:
Mark Stephany 607-737-4738/fax: 607-737-9080

Greater Binghamton Health Center
425 Robinson St, Binghamton, NY 13904-1775
Acting Executive Director:
Mark Stephany 607-773-4082/fax: 607-773-4387

Hutchings Psychiatric Center
620 Madison St, Syracuse, NY 13210-2319
Executive Director:
Mark Cattalani 315-426-3632/fax: 315-426-3603

Kingsboro Psychiatric Center
681 Clarkson Ave, Brooklyn, NY 11203-2199
Executive Director:
Deborah Parchment 718-221-7395/fax: 718-221-7206

Offices and agencies generally appear in alphabetical order, except when specific order is requested by listee.

Kirby Forensic Psychiatric Center
600 East 125th St, Wards Island, NY 10035
Executive Director:
Vinny Miccoli 646-672-5858/fax: 646-672-6446

Manhattan Psychiatric Center
600 East 125th St, Wards Island, NY 10035-6098
Executive Director:
Vinny Miccoli 646-672-5858/fax: 646-672-6446

Mid-Hudson Forensic Psychiatric Center
2834 Route 17-M, New Hampton, NY 10958
Executive Director:
Joseph Freebern. 845-374-8700/fax: 845-374-8861

Mohawk Valley Psychiatric Center
1400 Noyes St, Utica, NY 13502-3082
Acting Executive Director:
Mark Cattalani. 315-738-4404/fax: 315-738-4414

Nathan S Kline Institute for Psychiatric Research
140 Old Orangeburg Rd, Orangeburg, NY 10952-1197
Director:
Donald C. Goff, MD 845-398-5500/fax: 845-398-5510

New York Psychiatric Institute
1051 Riverside Dr, New York, NY 10032-2695
Director:
Jeffrey A Lieberman, MD. 212-543-5000/fax: 212-543-5200

Pilgrim Psychiatric Center
998 Crooked Hill Rd, West Brentwood, NY 11717-1087
Executive Director:
Kathy O'Keefe 631-761-2616/fax: 631-761-2194

Queens Children's Psychiatric Center
74-03 Commonwealth Blvd, Bellerose, NY 11426-1890
Acting Executive Director:
Anita Daniels. 718-264-4500/fax: 718-740-0968

Rochester Psychiatric Center
1111 Elmwood Ave, Rochester, NY 14620-3972
Executive Director:
Elizabeth Suhre 585-241-1594/fax: 585-241-1424

Rockland Children's Psychiatric Center
2 First Avenue, Orangeburg, NY 10962-1199
Acting Executive Director:
Christopher Tavella PhD. 845-359-7400/fax: 845-680-8900

Rockland Psychiatric Center
140 Old Orangeburg Rd, Orangeburg, NY 10962-1196
Executive Director:
Christopher Tavella, PhD 845-359-1000/fax: 845-680-5580

Sagamore Children's Psychiatric Center
197 Half Hollow Rd, Dix Hills, NY 11746
Acting Executive Director:
Kathy O'Keefe 631-370-1700/fax: 631-370-1714

South Beach Psychiatric Center
777 Seaview Ave, Staten Island, NY 10305-3499
Executive Director:
Roseanne Gaylor. 718-667-2709/fax: 718-667-2344

St Lawrence Psychiatric Center
1 Chimney Point Dr, Ogdensburg, NY 13669-2291
Executive Director:
Tim Farrell. 315-541-2112/fax: 315-541-2041

Western New York Children's Psychiatric Center
1010 East & West Rd, West Seneca, NY 14224-3699
Acting Executive Director:
David Privett, LCSW 716-677-7000/fax: 716-675-6455

Office of Consumer Affairs
Director:
John Allen 518-473-6579/fax: 518-474-8998

Office of Financial Management
Deputy Commissioner & Chief Financial Officer:
Emil Slane 518-474-3631/fax: 518-473-4690

Office of Public Affairs
Director:
Benjamin Rosen. 518-474-6540/fax: 518-473-3456

Office of Quality Management
Deputy Commissioner:
Marcia Fazio 518-474-6587

NYS Office for People with Developmental Disabilities

44 Holland Ave
Albany, NY 12229
866-946-9733 or TTY: 866-933-4889 Fax: 518-474-1335
Web site: www.opwdd.ny.gov

Acting Commissioner:
Kerry Delaney. 518-473-1997
Director, Advocacy Services:
Deborah Franchini 518-473-1997
General Counsel:
Roger Bearden 518-473-1873
Deputy Commissioner, Enterprise Solutions:
Kevin Valenchis 518-473-9697
Director, Legislative & Intergovernmental Affairs:
Greg Roberts 518-473-8084
Affirmative Action/Equal Opportunity:
Keith Gilmore 518-473-8084
Director, Internal Audit:
James Nellegar 518-474-4376

New York City Regional Office
75 Morton St, New York, NY 10014
Director:
Donna Limiti 212-229-3231/fax: 212-229-3234

Information Support Services
Balltown & Consaul Roads, Schenectady, NY 12304
Director:
Dianne Henk 518-473-1997

Developmental Disabilities Services Offices - State Operations

Bernard Fineson Developmental Disabilities Services Office

Hillside Complex Bldg 12, 80-45 Winchester Blvd, Queens Vlg, NY 11427
Director:
Jan Williamson 718-217-5890

Brooklyn Developmental Disabilities Services Office
888 Fountain Ave, Brooklyn, NY 11208
Director:
Sheryl Minter-Brooks 718-642-6000/fax: 718-642-6282

Broome Developmental Disabilities Services Office
249 Glenwood Rd, Binghamton, NY 13905
Director:
Jim Skrzeckowski 607-770-0211/fax: 607-770-8037

Capital District Developmental Disabilities Services Office

Offices and agencies generally appear in alphabetical order, except when specific order is requested by listee.

Balltown & Consaul Rds, Schenectady, NY 12304
Acting Director:
Stephanie Dunham 518-370-7331/fax: 518-370-7401

Central New York Developmental Disabilities Services Office

101 W Liberty St, Box 550, Rome, NY 13442
Deputy Director:
Lynette O'Brien . . . . 315-336-2300 or 315-473-2949
fax: 315-339-5456

Finger Lakes Developmental Disabilities Services Office

620 Westfall Rd, Rochester, NY 14620
Director:
Michael Feeney 585-461-8500/fax: 585-461-8764

Hudson Valley Developmental Disabilities Services Office

Admin Bldg, 2 Ridge Rd, PO Box 470, Thiells, NY 10984
Director:
Catherine Varano 845-947-6000/fax: 845-947-6004

Long Island Developmental Disabilities Services Officezz

45 Mall Dr, Ste 1, Commack, NY 11725
Deputy Director:
Barry Ockner 631-493-1701/fax: 631-493-1803

Metro New York Developmental Disabilities Services Office

75 Morton St, New York, NY 10014
Deputy Director:
Joyce White 646-766-3471

Staten Island Developmental Disabilities Services Office

1150 Forest Hill Rd, Staten Island, NY 10314
Director:
Sheryl Minter-Brooks 718-983-5321/fax: 718-983-9768

Sunmount Developmental Disabilities Services Office
2445 State Rte 30, Tupper Lake, NY 12986-2502
Acting Director:
Stephanie Dunham 518-359-3311/fax: 518-359-2276

Taconic Developmental Disabilities Services Office
26 Center Circle, Wassaic, NY 12592
Deputy Director:
Jackie DeVille 845-877-6821/fax: 845-877-9177

Western New York Developmental Disabilities Services Office
1200 East & West Rd, West Seneca, NY 14224
Director:
Kirk Maurer 716-674-6310/fax: 716-674-7488

Institute for Basic Research in Developmental Disabilities
1050 Forest Hill Rd, Staten Island, NY 10314
Director:
Donna Limiti 718-983-5233

JUDICIAL SYSTEM AND RELATED AGENCIES

Mental Hygiene Legal Service

1st Judicial Dept
41 Madison Ave, 26th Fl, New York, NY 10010
Director:
Marvin Bernstein 212-779-1734/fax: 212-779-7899

2nd Judicial Dept
170 Old Country Rd, Rm 500, Mineola, NY 11501
Director:
Michael D Neville 516-493-3976/fax: 646-963-6640

3rd Judicial Dept
40 Steuben St, Ste 501, Albany, NY 12207-2109
Web site: www.nycourts.gov/ad3/mhls/index.html
Director:
Sheila E Shea 518-451-8710/fax: 518-453-6915

4th Judicial Dept
50 East Ave, Ste 402, Rochester, NY 14604
Web site: www.courts.state.ny.us/ad4/mhls/
Director:
Emmett J Creahan 585-530-3050
Deputy Director:
Kevin Wilson 585-530-3050/fax: 585-530-3079

NEW YORK STATE LEGISLATURE

See Legislative Branch in Section 1 for additional Standing Committee and Subcommittee information.

Assembly Standing Committees

Alcoholism & Drug Abuse
Chair:
Linda Rosenthal (D) 518-455-5802
Ranking Minority Member:
Mark Johns (R) 518-455-5784

Mental Health
Chair:
Aileen Gunther (D) 518-455-5355
Ranking Minority Member:
Steven Katz (R) 518-455-5783

Senate Standing Committees

Mental Health & Developmental Disabilities
Chair:
Robert G Ortt (R) 518-455-2024
Ranking Minority Member:
Jesse Hamilton (D) 518-455-2431

PRIVATE SECTOR

AIM Services Inc
4227 Route 9, Saratoga Springs, NY 12866
518-587-3208 Fax: 518-587-7236
e-mail: aimservices@aimservicesinc.org
Web site: www.aimservicesinc.org
Residential & home-based services for individuals with developmental disabilities & traumatic brain injuries
June MacClelland, Executive Director

Albert Einstein College of Medicine - Division of Substance Abuse
260 E 161 Street, Track Level, Bronx, NY 10451
718-993-3397 Fax: 718-993-2460
e-mail: schurch@dosa.aecom.yu.edu
Web site: www.einsteinrecovery.org
Sarah Church, PhD, Director

AMAC, Association for Metroarea Autistic Children
25 W 17th St, New York, NY 10011
212-645-5005 Fax: 212-645-0170
e-mail: rica@amac.org
Web site: www.amac.org
Providing lifelong services to austistic & special needs children & adults; specializing in applied behavior analysis (ABA) methodology; serving ages 2 years to adults, schools, camps, group homes
Frederica Blausten, Executive Director

Association for Addiction Professionals of New York
PO Box 4053, Albany, NY 12204
877-862-2769 Fax: 585-394-1111
e-mail: info@appnycounselor.com
Web site: www.aapnycounselor.com
Alcohol & chemical dependency counselor organization; addiction treatment & prevention
Ford Haverly, President

Association for Community Living
28 Corporate Drive, Suite 102, Clifton Park, NY 12065
518-688-1682 Fax: 518-688-1686
e-mail: admin@aclnys.org
Web site: www.aclnys.org
Membership organization for agencies that provide housing & rehab services to individuals diagnosed with serious mental illness
Antonia Lasicki, Director

Association for Eating Disorders - Capital Region
PO Box 3123, Saratoga Springs, NY 12866
518-464-9043
e-mail: CRAEDOffice@GMail.com
Web site: www.craed.org
Support & referral services, wellness programs & education for recovering individuals, parents & health professionals
William Friske, Treasurer

AHRC New York City
83 Maiden Lane, New York, NY 10038
212-780-2500 or 212-780-2692 Fax: 212-780-2353
e-mail: webmaster@ahrcnyc.org
Web site: www.ahrcnyc.org
Also known as the NYS Chapter of NYSARC, Inc. Social services, education, medical services, advocacy & public information on developmental disabilities
Michael Goldfarb, Executive Director

Brain Injury Association of NYS (BIANYS)
10 Colvin Ave, Albany, NY 12206
518-459-7911 or 800-444-6443 Fax: 518-482-5285
e-mail: info@bianys.org
Web site: www.bianys.org
Public education & advocacy for persons with brain injury & their families
Judith I Avner, Executive Director

Cerebral Palsy Associations of New York State
330 West 34th Street, 15th Floor, New York, NY 10001-2488
212-947-5770 Fax: 212-594-4538
e-mail: information@cpofnys.org
Web site: www.cpofnys.org
Serves individuals with cerebral palsy & other significant disabilities as well as their families through advocacy, technical assistance, publications & networking events
Susan Constantino, President & Chief Executive Officer

Children's Village (The)
Echo Hills, Dobbs Ferry, NY 10522
914-693-0600 x1201 Fax: 914-674-9208
e-mail: jkohomban@childrensvillage.org
Web site: www.childrensvillage.org
Residential school, located 20 minutes outside of NYC. Treatment & prevention of behavioral problems for youth; residential & community-based services; mental health, education, employment & runaway shelter services
Jeremy Kohomban, PhD, President & Chief Executive Officer

Coalition of Behavioral Health Agencies, Inc (The)
90 Broad St, New York, NY 10004-2205
212-742-1600 x115 Fax: 212-742-2080
e-mail: mailbox@coalitionny.org
Web site: www.coalitionny.org
Advocacy organization representing over 100 nonprofit, community-based mental health and addictions services agencies in NYC.
Phillip A Saperia, Executive Director

Committee of Methadone Program Administrators Inc of NYS (COMPA)
1 Columbus Place, 4th Fl, Albany, NY 12207
518-689-0457 Fax: 518-426-1046
e-mail: compahb@hotmail.com
Web site: www.compa-ny.org
Methadone treatment & substance abuse coalition building; advocacy, community education, standards & regulatory review & policy development
Henry Bartlett, Executive Director

Families Together in NYS Inc
737 Madison Avenue, Albany, NY 12208
518-432-0333 x20 or 888-326-8644 (referr Fax: 518-434-6478
e-mail: info@ftnys.org
Web site: www.ftnys.org
Advocacy for families with children having special social, emotional & behavioral needs; working to improve services & support for children & families
Paige Pierce, Executive Director

Federation Employment & Guidance Service (FEGS) Inc
315 Hudson St, 9th Fl, New York, NY 10013
212-366-8400 Fax: 212-366-8441
e-mail: info@fegs.org
Web site: www.fegs.org
Diversified health & human services system to help individuals achieve their potential at work, at home, at school and in the community
Jonas Waizer, PhD, Chief Operating Officer

Federation of Organizations Inc
One Farmingdale Road, Route 109, West Babylon, NY 11704-6207
631-669-5355 Fax: 631-669-1114
e-mail: bfaron@fedoforg.org
Web site: www.fedoforg.org
Social welfare agency with programs in mental health & aging
Barbara Faron, CEO

Policy Areas

Offices and agencies generally appear in alphabetical order, except when specific order is requested by listee.

InterAgency Council of Mental Retardatn & Developmental Disabilities
150 W 30th Street, 15th Floor, New York, NY 10001
212-645-6360 or 917-750-1497 Fax: 212-627-8847
e-mail: mames@iacny.org
Web site: www.iacny.org
A membership association representing non-profit providers of services to individuals with developmental disabilities in the metropolitan NYC area.
Margery E Ames, Executive Director

Jewish Board of Family & Children's Services
120 W 57th St, New York, NY 10019
212-582-9100 or 888-523-2769 Fax: 212-956-5676
e-mail: asiskind@jbfcs.org
Web site: www.jbfcs.org
Mental health services/human services
Alan B Siskind, PhD, Executive Vice President & Chief Executive Officer

Lesbian, Gay, Bisexual & Transgender Community Ctr - Not For Profit
208 W 13th St, New York, NY 10011-7702
212-620-7310 Fax: 212-924-2657
e-mail: enealy@gaycenter.org
Web site: www.gaycenter.org
Mental health counseling, out-patient chemical dependency treatment center, after-school youth services, HIV/AIDS services, advocacy, cultutral programs, affordable meeting and conference services, and community-building.
Miriam Yeung, Director, Public Policy

Lifespire
1 Whitehall Street, 9th Floor, New York, NY 10004
212-741-0100 Fax: 212-463-9814
e-mail: info@lifespire.org
Web site: www.lifespire.org
Services for adults with developmental disabilites throughout the five boroughs of New York City
Mark van Voorst, President & Chief Executive Officer

Mental Health Association of NYC Inc
666 Broadway, Ste 200, New York, NY 10012
212-254-0333 x307 Fax: 212-529-1959
e-mail: helpdesk@mhaofnyc.org
Web site: www.mhaofnyc.org
Advocacy, public education, community-based services
Giselle Stolper, Executive Director

Mental Health Association of NYS Inc
194 Washington Ave, Ste 415, Albany, NY 12210
518-434-0439 Fax: 518-427-8676
e-mail: info@mhanys.org
Web site: www.mhanys.org
Technical assistance, advocacy, training & resource clearinghouse
Glen Liebman, Chief Executive Officer

NAMI-NYS
260 Washington Ave, Albany, NY 12210
518-462-2000 Fax: 518-462-3811
e-mail: info@naminys.org
Web site: www.naminys.org
Family and consumer advocates for those with mental illness.
Donald P Capone, Executive Director

NY Council on Problem Gambling
100 Great Oaks Boulevard, Suite 126, Albany, NY 12203
518-867-4084 Fax: 518-867-4087
e-mail: jmaney@nyproblemgambling.org
Web site: www.nyproblemgambling.org
Statewide helpline, public information, referral svcs, advocacy for treatment & support svcs, in-service training & workshops
James Maney, Executive Director

NY Counseling Association Inc
PO Box 12636, Albany, NY 12212-2636
518-235-2026 Fax: 518-235-0910
e-mail: nycaoffice@nycounseling.org
Web site: www.nycounseling.org
Counseling professionals in education, mental health, career, employment, rehabilitation & adult development
Donald Newell, Executive Manager

NYS Association of Community & Residential Agencies
99 Pine St, Ste C-110, Albany, NY 12207
518-449-7551 Fax: 518-449-1509
e-mail: nysacra@nysacra.org
Web site: www.nysacra.org
Advocating for agencies that serve individuals with developmental disabilities
Ann M Hardiman, Executive Director

NYS Conference of Local Mental Hygiene Directors
99 Pine Street, Ste C100, Albany, NY 12207
518-462-9422 Fax: 518-465-2695
e-mail: ds@clmhd.org
Web site: www.clmhd.org
Duane Spilde, LCSWR, ACSW, Executive Director

NYS Council for Community Behavioral Healthcare
911 Central Avenue, Suite 152, Albany, NY 12206-1350
518-461-8200
e-mail: nyscouncil@albany.twcbc.com
Web site: www.nyscouncil.org
Statewide membership organization representing community mental health centers
Lauri Cole, Executive Director

NYS Psychological Association
3 Pine West Plaza, Suite 308, Albany, NY 12205
518-437-1040 Fax: 518-437-0177
e-mail: nyspa@nyspa.org
Web site: www.nyspa.org
Promote & advance profession of psychology; referral service
Tom Cote, Executive Director

NYSARC Inc
393 Delaware Ave, Delmar, NY 12054
518-439-8311 Fax: 518-439-1893
e-mail: info@nysarc.org
Web site: www.nysarc.org
Developmental disabilities programs, services & advocacy
Marc N Brandt, Executive Director

New York Association of Psychiatric Rehabilitation Services (NYAPRS)
194 Washington Avenue, Suite 400, Albany, NY 12210
518-436-0008 Fax: 518-436-0044
e-mail: harveyr@nyaprs.org
Web site: www.nyaprs.org
Promoting the recovery, rehabilitation & rights of New Yorkers with psychiatric disabilities
Harvey Rosenthal, Executive Director

New York Presbyterian Hospital, Department of Psychiatry
180 Fort Washington Ave, Room 270, New York, NY 10032
212-305-9249 Fax: 212-305-4724
e-mail: hjs1@columbia.edu
Psychotherapy & public policy
Herbert J Schlesinger, PhD, Director, Clinical Psychology

New York State Rehabilitation Association
155 Washington Ave, Suite 410, Albany, NY 12210
518-449-2976 Fax: 518-426-4329
e-mail: nysra@nyrehab.org
Web site: www.nyrehab.org
Political advocacy, education, communications, networking & referral services for people with disabilities
Jeff Wise, JD, Vice President

Postgrad Center for Mental Health, Child, Adolescent & Family-Couples
138 E 26th St, Fl 4, New York, NY 10010-1843
212-576-4190 Fax: 212-576-4129
Psychotherapy & assessment services for children, adolescents & families
Diana Daimwood, Director

Postgraduate Center for Mental Health
344 W 36th St, New York, NY 10018
212-560-6757 Fax: 212-244-2034
e-mail: mholman@pgcmh.org
Web site: www.pgcmh.org
Community-based rehabilitation & employment services for adults with mental illness
Marcia Holman, CSW/Vice President, Clinical Services

Research Foundation for Mental Hygiene Inc
Riverview Center, 150 Broadway, Suite 301, Menands, NY 12204
518-474-5661 Fax: 518-474-6995
Not-for-profit responsible for administering grants & sponsored research contracts for the NYS Department of Mental Health & its agencies
Robert E Burke, Managing Director

SUNY at Albany, Professional Development Program, NE States Addiction
Rockefeller College, 1400 Washington Ave, Room 412A, Albany, NY 12222
518-956-7800 Fax: 518-956-7865
e-mail: lparsons@pdp.albany.edu
Web site: www.pdp.albany.edu
Dissemination of current research & best clinical practice information; coursework & programs for professionals in the field of addictions
Eugene J Monaco, Director

Samaritan Village Inc
138-02 Queens Blvd, Briarwood, NY 11435
718-206-2000 Fax: 718-657-6982
Web site: www.samaritanvillage.org
Substance abuse treatment; residential & outpatient therapeutic community
Ron Solarz, Executive Director

Schuyler Center for Analysis & Advocacy (SCAA)
540 Broadway, Albany, NY 12207
518-463-1896 Fax: 518-463-3364
e-mail: kbreslin@scaany.org
Web site: www.scaany.org
Advocacy, analysis & forums on mental health issues.
Kate Breslin, President & Chief Executive Officer

Self Advocacy Association of NYS
Capital District DSO, 500 Balltown Rd, Schenectady, NY 12304
518-382-1454 Fax: 518-382-1594
e-mail: sholmes@earthlink.net
Web site: www.sanys.org
Advocacy for & by persons with developmental disabilities to ensure civil rights & opportunities
Steve Holmes, Adminstrative Director

Springbrook
2705 State Hwy 28, Oneonta, NY 13820
607-286-7171 Fax: 607-286-7166
e-mail: kennedyp@springbrookny.org
Web site: www.springbrookny.org
Education/mental hygiene
Patricia E Kennedy, Executive Director

St Joseph's Rehabilitation Center Inc
PO Box 470, Saranac Lake, NY 12983
518-891-3950 or 518-891-3801 Fax: 518-891-3986
e-mail: stjoes@sjrcrehab.org
Web site: www.sjrcrehab.org
Inpatient & outpatient alcohol & substance abuse treatment
Robert A Ross, CEO

Statewide Black & Puerto Rican/Latino Substance Abuse Task Force
2730 Atlantic Ave, Brooklyn, NY 11207-2820
718-647-8275 Fax: 718-647-7889
e-mail: info@nytaskforce.org; nystaskforce@ad.com
Web site: www.nytaskforce.org
Substance abuse, HIV/AIDS & HepC prevention & treatment
Ralph Gonzalez, Executive Director

University at Buffalo, Research Institute on Addictions
1021 Main St, Buffalo, NY 14203-1016
716-887-2566 Fax: 716-887-2252
e-mail: connors@ria.buffalo.edu
Web site: www.ria.buffalo.edu
Alcohol & substance abuse prevention, treatment & policy research
Gerard Connors, Director

YAI/National Institute for People with Disabilities
460 W 34th St, New York, NY 10001-2382
212-273-6110 or 866-2-YAI-LINK Fax: 212-947-7524
e-mail: jmlcares@yai.org
Web site: www.yai.org
Programs, services & advocacy for people with autism, mental retardation & other developmental disabilities as well as learning disabilities of all ages & their families; special education & early learning programs
Joel M Levy, Chief Executive Officer

Yeshiva University, A Einstein Clg of Med, Div of Subs Abuse
1510 Waters Place, Bronx, NY 10461
718-409-9450 x312 Fax: 718-892-7115
e-mail: schurch@dosa.aecom.yu.edu
Web site: www.einsteinrecovery.org
Screening, assessment, diagnosis, treatment, support services, research & teaching & training related to chemical dependency & substance abuse
Sarah Church, PhD, Executive Director

Policy Areas

MUNICIPAL & LOCAL GOVERNMENTS

NEW YORK STATE

GOVERNOR'S OFFICE

Governor's Office
Executive Chamber
State Capitol
Albany, NY 12224
518-474-8390 Fax: 518-474-1513
Web site: www.ny.gov

Governor:
Andrew M Cuomo 518-474-8390
Secretary to the Governor:
William Mulrow 518-474-4246
Counsel to the Governor:
Alphonso David 518-474-8343
Chief of Staff:
Melissa DeRosa ....518-474-8418 or 212-681-4640
Director, Communications:
James Allen........................518-474-8418 or 212-681-4640
Director, State Operations:
James Malatras 518-486-9871

New York City Office
633 Third Ave, New York, NY 10017

EXECUTIVE DEPARTMENTS AND RELATED AGENCIES

Budget, Division of the
State Capitol
Albany, NY 12224
518-473-3885 Fax: 518-474-9041
Web site: www.budget.ny.gov

Director:
Robert F Mujica 518-474-2300
Deputy Director:
Sandra Beattie..518-474-6497
Deputy Director:
David Lara 518-402-4246
Budget Services Head:
Vacant..518-474-6300
Public Protection Head:
Robert Barbato 518-474-4313
Press Officer:
Morris Peters..518-473-3885
e-mail: dob.sm.press@budget.ny.gov

Civil Service Department
Alfred E Smith State Ofc Bldg
Albany, NY 12239
518-457-2487
Web site: www.cs.ny.gov

President:
Vacant..518-457-3701
Executive Deputy Commissioner:
Lola Brabham 518-473-5698
Deputy Commissioner, Operations:
Vacant..518-473-5711
Deputy Commissioner, Administration:
Deirdre Taylor..518-473-5694
Deputy Commissioner/General Counsel:
Ilene Lees 518-473-2624
Director, Workforce & Occupational Planning:
Vacant..518-473-6411
Director, Financial Administration:
Vacant..518-473-2269
Director, Human Resources & Administrative Planning:
Valerie Morrisson..518-473-4306
Public Information Officer:
Ed Walsh 518-457-9375/fax: 518-473-2372
e-mail: pio@cs.state.ny.us

Divisions

Classification & Compensation Division
Director:
Patricia A. Itite 518-474-1011/fax: 518-474-0787

Employee Benefits Division
Director:
Robert DuBois........................518-473-1977/fax: 518-473-3292
Director, Employee Insurance Programs:
Mary B Frye 518-457-1771/fax: 518-473-3292
Asst Director, Financial Management & Accounting:
David Boland 518-402-4264

Employee Health Services Division
Administrator, EHS:
Maria C Steinbach........................518-233-3112/fax: 518-233-3133
Director, Health Services Nursing:
Mary M McSweeney 518-233-3112

Information Resource Management
Director:
Frank Slade..518-473-7516
e-mail: frank.slade@cs.state.ny.us

Commission Operations & Municipal Assistance Division
Director:
Nancy B. Kiyonaga 518-473-5022
Local Examinations:
Will Martin 518-473-5055

Staffing Services Division
Director:
Blaine Ryan-Lynch..518-473-6437
Asst Director:
Richard Papa..518-473-6436

Testing Services Division
Director:
Marcia Dudden..518-474-2105
Assistant Director:
Debbi Parrington 518-486-4590

Civil Service Commission
President:
Vacant..518-457-3701
Commissioner:
Caroline Ahl 518-473-6598
Commissioner:
Jeanique Greene 518-473-6598

Criminal Justice Services, Division of
80 South Swan Street
Albany, NY 12210
518-457-5837 or 800-262-3252 Fax: 518-457-3089
e-mail: infobcjc@dcjs.ny.gov
Web site: www.criminaljustice.ny.gov

Acting Commissioner:
Sean M Byrne..518-457-1260
Executive Deputy Commissioner:
Michael C Green..518-457-1260

Offices and agencies generally appear in alphabetical order, except when specific order is requested by listee.

Affirmative Action Officer:
Wanda Trouche 518-485-7962
Deputy Director, Public Information:
Janine Kava 518-457-8906/fax: 518-485-7715
e-mail: janine.kava@dcjs.ny.gov

Human Resources Management
Director:
Karen Davis 518-485-1704

State Finance & Budget
Director, Finance:
Mary Ann Rossi 518-457-6105

Legal Services
Deputy Commissioner & Counsel:
John Czajka 518-457-4181

Office of Forensic Services
Director:
Vacant 518-457-4181

Office of Criminal Justice Operations
Director, Human Resources Management:
Joe Morrissey 518-485-2995

Office of Justice Information Systems
Deputy Commissioner:
Anne Roest 518-485-7176

Office of Public Safety

Law Enforcement Accreditation Program
Deputy Commissioner:
Michael Wood 518-485-7620
Director:
Debra Bourque 518-485-1416

Funding & Program Development Office
Deputy Commissioner:
Jeffrey Bender 518-457-8462

Homeland Security & Emergency Services, Division of
1220 Washington Ave
Bldg. 7A
Suite 710
Albany, NY 12242
518-242-5000
Web site: www.dhses.ny.gov

633 Third Ave
32nd Fl
New York, NY 10017
212-867-7060

Commissioner:
John P Melville 518-292-2301
Assistant Director, Office of Counterterrorism:
David Sheppard 518-242-5121
Director, Upstate Intergovernmental Affairs:
Brian Shea 518-292-2301
State Fire Administrator & Director, Fire Prevention:
Bryant Stevens 518-474-6746/fax: 518-474-3240
e-mail: fire@dhses.ny.gov
Director, Office of Interoperable & Emergency Communications:
Robert Barbato 518-292-4913
e-mail: dhsesoiec@dhses.ny.gov
Public Information Officer:
Kristin Devoe 518-242-5153/fax: 518-322-4978

Real Property Tax Services, Office of
WA Harriman State Campus
Bldg. 8A
Albany, NY 12227
518-4757-7377 or 518-591-5232
e-mail: nysorps@orps.state.ny.us
Web site: www.tax.ny.gov/about/orpts

Acting Secretary of the Board & Assistant Deputy Commissioner:
Susan Savage 518-474-6742
State Board Member (Chair):
Matthew Rand 518-474-3793
State Board Member:
John M. Bacheller 518-474-3793
State Board Member:
Edgar A King 518-474-3793
Assistant to the Board:
Darlene Maloney 518-474-3793
e-mail: darlene.maloney@tax.ny.gov

Albany (Northern Region)
WA Harriman State Campus, Bldg. 8A, Albany, NY 12227
Regional Director:
Robert Aiken 518-486-4403/fax: 518-435-8593
e-mail: orpts.northern@tax.ny.gov

Batavia (Western Region)
Genesee County Bldg 2, 3837 W Main Rd, Batavia, NY 14020
Regional Director:
Christine Bannister 585-343-4363/fax: 585-435-8598
e-mail: orpts.western@tax.ny.gov

Long Island Satellite Office
250 Veterans Memorial Hgwy, Rm 4A-6, Hauppauge, NY 11788
Manager:
Steve Hartnett 631-595-4071/fax: 518-435-8572
e-mail: orpts.southern@tax.ny.gov

South
44 S. Broadway, 6th Floor, White Plains, NY 10601
Regional Director:
John Wolham 914-215-6300/fax: 518-435-8498
e-mail: orpts.southern@tax.ny.gov

Ray Brook Satellite Office
884 NYS Rte 86, PO Box 309, Ray Brook, NY 12977
Regional Director:
Robert Aiken 518-891-1780/fax: 518-435-8593
e-mail: orpts.raybrook@tax.ny.gov

Syracuse (Central Region)
333 E. Washington St, Syracuse, NY 13202
Regional Director:
Teresa Frank 315-471-2347/fax: 315-435-8583
e-mail: orpts.central@tax.ny.gov

State Comptroller, Office of the
110 State St, 15th Fl
Albany, NY 12236
518-474-4044 Fax: 518-473-3004
Web site: www.osc.state.ny.us

59 Maiden Lane
New York, NY 10038
212-383-1600

State Comptroller:
Thomas P DiNapoli . . . . . . 518-474-4040 or 212-681-4469
Deputy Comptroller, Budget & Policy Analysis:
Robert Ward 518-473-4333

Policy Areas

Assistant Comptroller, Labor Affairs:
Kathy McCormack 518-473-8409

Executive Office
First Deputy Comptroller:
Pete Grannis . . . . 518-474-2909 or 212-681-4469
Chief of Staff:
Shawn Thompson 518-474-4044
Deputy Comptroller & Chief Information Officer:
Robert Loomis 518-486-4349
Director, Enterprise Applications & IT Business Management:
Mary Anne Barry . . . . 518-474-8089 or 212-681-4840
Director, Communications:
Jennifer Freeman . . . . 518-474-4015 or 518-473-8940
Assistant Comptroller, Business Communications:
Ellen Evans . . . . 518-474-4040 or 212-681-4489
Deputy Comptroller, Office of the State Deputy Comptroller for the City of New York:
Ken Bleiwas 212-383-3905

Human Resources & Administration
Deputy Comptroller, Human Resources & Administration:
Angela Dixon 518-474-5512
Assistant Comptroller, Administration:
Larry Appel 518-402-3043
Director, Financial Administration:
Brian Matthews 518-474-2709
Director, Management Services:
Beth Bristol 518-486-7433

Inspector General
Inspector General, Internal Audit:
Stephen Hamilton 518-549-2393

Intergovernmental Affairs
Deputy Comptroller:
Vacant 212-402-3234

Legal Services
General Counsel:
Nancy Groenwegen 518-474-3444
Special Counsel for Ethics:
Barbara Smith 518-408-3855

Operations
Executive Deputy Comptroller:
John Traylor 518-408-4103
Deputy Director, Payroll, Accounting and Revenue Services (PARS):
Chris Gorka 518-408-4149

Retirement
Deputy Comptroller:
Kevin Murray 518-474-2600

State Government Accountability
Executive Deputy Comptroller:
Andrew SanFilippo 518-474-4593
Deputy Comptroller:
Elliot Pagliaccio 518-473-3596
Assistant Comptroller:
Jerry Barber 518-473-0334

Local Government and School Accountability
Deputy Comptroller:
Steve Hancox 518-474-4037
Assistant Comptroller:
John Traylor 518-474-4037

State Department
One Commerce Plaza
99 Washington Avenue
Albany, NY 12231
518-474-4750 Fax: 518-474-4765
Web site: www.dos.ny.gov

123 William St
New York, NY 10038
212-417-5801
Fax: 212-417-5805

Acting Secretary of State:
Rossana Rosado 518-474-0050
First Deputy Secretary of State:
Daniel Shapiro 518-474-4750
Deputy Secretary of State, Public Affairs:
Vacant 212-417-5800
Principal Attorney:
William Sharp 518-474-6740/fax: 518-473-9211
Assistant Secretary of State, Communications:
Vacant 518-474-4752/fax: 518-474-4597
e-mail: info@dos.state.ny.us

Local Government & Community Services
Deputy Secretary of State:
Dierdre Scozzafava 518-473-3355

Coastal Resources & Waterfront Revitalization Division
Director:
George Stafford 518-474-6000
e-mail: coastal@dos.state.ny.us

Code Enforcement & Administration Division
Director:
Ronald E Piester 518-474-4073/fax: 518-486-4487
e-mail: codes@dos.state.ny.us

Community Services Division
Director:
Veronica Cruz 518-474-5741/fax: 518-486-4663
e-mail: commserv@dos.state.ny.us

Local Government Services Division
Deputy Secretary of State:
Dierdre Scozzafava 518-473-3355/fax: 518-474-6572
e-mail: localgov@dos.ny.gov

Open Government Committee
Executive Director:
Robert J Freeman 518-474-2518/fax: 518-474-1927
e-mail: opengov@dos.state.ny.us

CORPORATIONS, AUTHORITIES AND COMMISSIONS

New York State Assn of Fire Districts
PO Box 1419
Massapequa, NY 11758
631-947-2079 or 800-520-9594 Fax: 631-207-1655
Web site: www.firedistnys.com

President:
Anthony J Gallino 631-831-6875
e-mail: president@afdsny.org
First Vice President:
Thomas Rinaldi 518-664-6538
e-mail: 1vp.president@afdsny.org
Second Vice President:
Frederick Senti Jr 516-486-3023
e-mail: 2vp.president@afdsny.org
Secretary & Treasurer:
Joseph P DeStefano . . . . 631-947-2079 or 800-520-9594
fax: 516-799-2516
e-mail: dacomish@aol.com

Counsel:
William N Young . . . . 800-349-2904 or 518-456-6767
fax: 518-456-4644
e-mail: byoung@yfkblaw.com

New York State Disaster Preparedness Commission
Building 22, Suite 101
1220 Washington Ave
Albany, NY 12226-2251
518-292-2301 or 518-292-2200 Fax: 518-322-4978
Web site: www.dhses.ny.gov/oem/disaster-prep/

Chairman/Director:
Jerome M Hauer 518-292-2301

NEW YORK STATE LEGISLATURE

See Legislative Branch in Section 1 for additional Standing Committee and Subcommittee information.

Assembly Legislative Commissions

State Federal Relations, Task Force on
Assembly Chair:
Matthew Titone (D) 518-455-4677
Program Manager:
Robert Stern 518-455-3632

Assembly Standing Committees

Cities
Chair:
Michael Benedetto (D) 518-455-5296
Ranking Minority Member:
Vacant (R). 518-455-0000

Economic Development, Job Creation, Commerce & Industry
Chair:
Robin L Schimminger (D) 518-455-4767
Ranking Minority Member:
Raymond Walter (D). 518-455-4618

Housing
Chair:
Keith L.T. Wright (D). 518-455-4793
Ranking Minority Member:
Michael J Fitzpatrick (R) 518-455-5021

Local Government
Chair:
William B Magnarelli (D). 518-455-4826
Ranking Minority Member:
Christopher Friend (R) 518-455-4538

Transportation
Chair:
David F Gantt (D). 518-455-5606
Ranking Minority Member:
David G McDonough (R) 518-455-4633

Ways & Means
Chair:
Herman D Farrell, Jr (D). 518-455-5491
Ranking Minority Member:
Bob Oaks (R) 518-455-5655

Senate Standing Committees

Cities
Chair:
Simcha Felder (D). 518-455-2754
Ranking Minority Member:
Daniel Squadron (D). 518-455-2625

Commerce, Economic Development & Small Business
Chair:
Philip Boyle (R) 518-455-3411
Ranking Minority Member:
Timothy Kennedy (D). 518-455-2426

Finance
Chair:
Catharine M Young (R) 518-455-3563
Ranking Minority Member:
Liz Krueger (D). 518-455-2297

Housing, Construction & Community Development
Chair:
Elizabeth O'C. Little (R) 518-455-2811
Ranking Minority Member:
Adriano Espaillat (D) 518-455-2041

Local Government
Chair:
Kathleen Marchione (R). 518-455-2381
Ranking Minority Member:
Todd Kaminsky (D) 518-455-3401

Transportation
Chair:
Joseph E Robach (R) 518-455-2909
Ranking Minority Member:
Martin Malave Dilan (D) 518-455-2177

PRIVATE SECTOR

Association of Fire Districts of the State of NY Inc
948 North Bay Avenue, North Massapequa, NY 11758-2581
516-799-8575 or 800-520-9594 Fax: 516-799-2516
e-mail: FNOC@aol.com
Web site: www.firedistnys.com
Obtain greater economy in the administration of fire district affairs
Frank A Nocerino, Secretary-Treasurer

Association of Towns of the State of New York
150 State St, Albany, NY 12207
518-465-7933 Fax: 518-465-0724
e-mail: jhaber@nytowns.org
Web site: www.nytowns.org
Advocacy, education for local government
G Jeffrey Haber, Executive Director

Citizens Budget Commission
One Penn Plaza, Ste 640, New York, NY 10119
212-279-2605 Fax: 212-868-4745
e-mail: cmb2@ls2.nyu.edu
Web site: www.cbcny.org
Nonpartisan, nonprofit civic organization devoted to influencing constructive change in the finances and services of New York City and New York State government
Charles Brecher, Executive VP & Director, Research

Policy Areas

Citizens Union of the City of New York
299 Broadway, Rm 700, New York, NY 10007-1978
212-227-0342 Fax: 212-227-0345
e-mail: citizens@citizensunion.org
Web site: www.citizensunion.org
Government watchdog organization; city & state public policy issues; political and government reform
Dick Dadey, Executive Director

Columbia Law School, Legislative Drafting Research Fund
435 W 116th St, New York, NY 10027-7297
212-854-2640 or 212-854-2638 Fax: 212-854-7946
e-mail: rb34@columbia.edu
Web site: www.law.columbia.edu
State & local government law, property law & election law
Richard Briffault, Vice Dean & Executive Director

Council of State Governments, Eastern Conference
100 Wall St, 20th Fl, New York, NY 10005
212-482-2320 Fax: 212-482-2344
e-mail: alan@csgeast.org
Web site: www.csgeast.org
Training, research & information sharing for state government officials
Alan V Sokolow, Regional Director

Cullen & Dykman LLP
100 Quentin Roosevelt Blvd, Garden City Ctr, Garden City, NY 11530-4850
516-357-3703 Fax: 516-396-9155
e-mail: gfishberg@cullenanddykman.com
Web site: www.cullenanddykman.com
Municipal & labor law
Gerard Fishberg, Partner

Fordham University, Department of Political Science
441 East Fordham Road, Bronx, NY 10458
718-817-3960 Fax: 718-817-3972
e-mail: kantor@fordham.edu
Urban politics, urban economic development and the social condition of American cities.
Paul Kantor, Professor of Political Science

Fund for the City of New York
121 Ave of the Americas, 6th Fl, New York, NY 10013
212-925-6675 Fax: 212-925-5675
e-mail: mmccormick@fcny.org
Web site: www.fcny.org
Innovations in policy, programs, practice & technology to advance the functioning of government & nonprofit organizations in NYC & beyond
Mary McCormick, President

Genesee Transportation Council
50 West Main Street, Suite 8112, Rochester, NY 14614-1227
585-232-6240 Fax: 585-262-3106
e-mail: rperrin@gtcmpo.org
Web site: www.gtcmpo.org
Nine-county metropolitan planning organization
Richard Perrin, Executive Director

Hawkins Delafield & Wood LLP
One Chase Manhattan Plaza, 42nd Fl, New York, NY 10005
212-820-9300 Fax: 212-820-9391
e-mail: hzucker@hawkins.com
Web site: www.hawkins.com
Transportation, municipal & local government law
Howard Zucker, Partner

Housing Action Council Inc - Not For Profit
55 S Broadway, Tarrytown, NY 10591
914-332-4144 Fax: 914-332-4147
e-mail: rnoonan@affordablehomes.org
Financial feasibility, land use & zoning & affordable housing
Rosemarie Noonan, Executive Director

Institute of Public Administration/NYU Wagner
295 Lafayette St, 2nd Floor, New York, NY 10012-9604
212-998-7400
e-mail: wagner@nyu.edu
Web site: www.wagner.nyu.edu
Non-profit research, consulting & educational institute
David Mammen, President

KPMG LLP
345 Park Avenue, New York, NY 10154-0102
212-758-9700 Fax: 212-758-9819
Web site: www.kpmg.com
Accounting
Lynne Doughtie, Chairman & Chief Executive Officer

League of Women Voters of New York State
62 Grand St, Albany, NY 12207-2712
518-465-4162 Fax: 518-465-0812
e-mail: lwvny@lwvny.org
Web site: www.lwvny.org
Public policy issues forum; good government advocacy
Kristen Hansen, Executive Director

MBIA Insurance Corporation
113 King St, Armonk, NY 10504
914-273-4545 Fax: 914-765-3555
e-mail: ethel.geisinger@mbia.com
Web site: www.mbia.com
Insure municipal bonds & structured transactions
Ethel Z Geisinger, Vice President, Government Relations

Manhattan Institute, Center for Civic Innovation
52 Vanderbilt Ave, 2nd Fl, New York, NY 10017
212-599-7000 Fax: 212-599-3494
Web site: www.manhattan-institute.org
Urban policy, reinventing government, civil society
Lindsay Young, Executive Director, Communications

Moody's Investors Service, Public Finance Group
99 Church St, New York, NY 10007
212-553-7780 Fax: 212-298-7113
e-mail: dennis.farrell@moodys.com
Web site: www.moodys.com
Municipal debt ratings & analysis
Dennis M Farrell, Group Managing Director

NY State Association of Town Superintendents of Highways Inc
119 Washington Avenue, Suite 300, Albany, NY 12210
518-694-9313 Fax: 518-694-9314
e-mail: info@nystownhwys.org
Web site: www.nystownhwys.org
Michael K Thompson, Communications Director

NYS Association of Counties
540 Broadway, 5th Floor, Albany, NY 12207
518-465-1473 Fax: 518-465-0506
e-mail: info@NYSAC.org
Web site: www.nysac.org
Lobbying, research & training services
Stephen J Acquario, Executive Director

NYS Conference of Mayors & Municipal Officials
119 Washington Ave, Albany, NY 12210
518-463-1185 Fax: 518-463-1190
e-mail: info@nycom.org
Web site: www.nycom.org
Legislative advocacy for NYS cities & villages
Peter A Baynes, Executive Director

Offices and agencies generally appear in alphabetical order, except when specific order is requested by listee.

NYS Magistrates Association
750 Delaware Ave, Delmar, NY 12054-1124
518-439-1087 Fax: 518-439-1204
e-mail: nysma@juno.com
Web site: www.nysma.net
Association of town & village justices
Tanja Sirago, Executive Director

New York Municipal Insurance Reciprocal (NYMIR)
150 State Street, Albany, NY 12207
518-465-7552 Fax: 518-465-0724
e-mail: kcrawford@kcnymir.org
Web site: www.nymir.org
Property and casualty insurance services for municipalities
Kevin Crawford, Executive Director

New York State Government Finance Officers Association Inc
126 State St, 5th Fl, Albany, NY 12207
518-465-1512 Fax: 518-434-4640
e-mail: info@nysgfoa.org
Web site: www.nysgfoa.org
Membership organization dedicated to the professional management of governmental resources
Maura K Ryan, Executive Director

New York University, Wagner Graduate School
295 Lafayette Street, 2nd Floor, New York, NY 10012
212-998-7400
e-mail: mitchell.moss@nyu.edu
Web site: www.wagner.nyu.edu
Research on urban planning & development, with special emphasis on technology & the future of cities
Mitchell L. Moss, Professor of Urban Policy & Planning

Syracuse University, Maxwell School of Citizenship & Public Affairs
215 Eggers Hall, Syracuse, NY 13244-1090
315-443-4000 Fax: 315-443-9721
e-mail: sibretsc@maxwell.syr.edu
Capital financing & debt management; public employee pensions; financial management
Stuart Bretschneider, Associate Dean & Chair, Professor of Public Administration

Urbanomics
115 Fifth Ave, 3rd Fl, New York, NY 10003
212-353-7464 Fax: 212-353-7494
e-mail: r.armstrong@urbanomics.org
Web site: www.urbanomics.org
Economic development planning studies, market studies, tax policy analyses, program evaluations, economic & demographic forecasts
Regina B Armstrong, Principal

Whiteman Osterman & Hanna LLP
One Commerce Plaza, Albany, NY 12260
518-487-7600 Fax: 518-487-7777
e-mail: lptharp@woh.com
Web site: www.woh.com
Lorraine Power Tharp, Partner

PUBLIC EMPLOYEES

NEW YORK STATE

GOVERNOR'S OFFICE

Governor's Office
Executive Chamber
State Capitol
Albany, NY 12224
518-474-8390 Fax: 518-474-1513
Web site: www.ny.gov

Governor:
Andrew M Cuomo 518-474-8390
Secretary to the Governor:
William Mulrow 518-474-4246
Counsel to the Governor:
Alphonso David 518-474-8343
Deputy Secretary, Public Safety:
Rachel Small 518-474-3522
Chief of Staff:
Melissa DeRosa . . . . 518-474-8418 or 212-681-4640
Director, Communications:
James Allen . . . . 518-474-8418 or 212-681-4640
First Assistant Counsel:
Sandi Toll 518-474-8434

EXECUTIVE DEPARTMENTS AND RELATED AGENCIES

Civil Service Department
Alfred E Smith State Ofc Bldg
Albany, NY 12239
518-457-2487 or 877-697-5627
Web site: www.cs.state.ny.us

President:
Vacant 518-457-3701
Executive Deputy Commissioner:
Lola Brabham 518-473-5698
Deputy Commissioner, Operations:
Vacant 518-473-5711
Deputy Commissioner, Administration:
Deirdre Taylor 518-473-5694
Deputy Commissioner/General Counsel:
Ilene Lees 518-473-2624
Director, Workforce & Occupational Planning:
Vacant 518-473-6411
Director, Financial Administration:
Vacant 518-473-2269
Director, Human Resources Administrative Planning:
Valerie Morrison 518-473-4306
Public Information Officer:
Ed Walsh 518-457-9375/fax: 518-473-2372

Divisions

Classification & Compensation Division
Director:
Patricia A. Itite 518-474-1011/fax: 518-474-0787

Employee Benefits Division
Director:
Robert DuBois 518-473-1977/fax: 518-473-3292
Director, Employee Insurance Programs:
Mary B Frye 518-457-1771/fax: 518-473-3292
Asst Director, Financial Management & Accounting:
David Boland 518-402-4264

Employee Health Services Division
Administrator, EHS:
Maria C Steinbach 518-233-3112/fax: 518-233-3133
Director, Health Services Nursing:
Mary M McSweeney 518-233-3112

Information Resource Management
Director:
Frank Slade 518-473-7516
e-mail: frank.slade@cs.state.ny.us

Commission Operations & Municipal Assistance Division
Director:
Nancy B. Kiyonaya 518-473-5022
Local Examinations:
Will Martin 518-473-5055

Staffing Services Division
Director:
Blaine Ryan-Lynch 518-473-6437
Asst Director:
Richard Papa 518-473-6436

Testing Services Division
Director:
Marcia Dudden 518-474-2105
Director:
Debbi Parrington 518-486-4590

Civil Service Commission
President:
Vacant 518-457-3701
Commissioner:
Caroline Ahl 518-473-6598
Commissioner:
Caroline Ahl 518-473-6326
Commissioner:
Jeanique Greene 518-473-6598

Employee Relations, Governor's Office of
Two Empire State Plz
Ste 1201
Albany, NY 12223-1250
518-473-8766 Fax: 518-486-7304
e-mail: info@goer.ny.gov
Web site: www.goer.ny.gov

Interim Director:
Michael N Volforte 518-474-6988/fax: 518-486-7304
Deputy Director, Contract Negotiations & Administration:
Vacant 518-473-3130/fax: 518-486-7304
Associate General Counsel:
Amy Petragnani 518-473-4596/fax: 518-486-7303
Director, Administration:
Mary Hines 518-473-3467/fax: 518-473-6294
Acting Director, Employee Benefits Unit:
Darryl Decker 518-473-6211/fax: 518-473-6294
Information Security Officer:
Jeff Reilly 518-486-1305/fax: 518-473-6294
Payroll Benefits Administrator:
Kelly J. Catman 518-473-3466/fax: 518-486-5602
Director, Workforce & Organizational Development Unit:
Lori Zwicker 518-474-6772/fax: 518-474-8587
Management/Confidential Affairs:
Lynda Scalzo 518-473-8317

Labor/Management Committees

Family Benefits Committee
55 Elk St, Rm 301C, Albany, NY 12210-2331
Staff Director:
Deborah Long Miller 518-473-8091/fax: 518-473-3581

NYS/CSEA Discipline Unit . . . . fax: 518-486-9737
55 Elk St, Rm 301D, Albany, NY 12210-2333
Arbitration Panel Coordinator:
Linda Ronda 518-473-6070

NYS/CSEA Partnership for Education & Training . . fax: 518-473-9457
240 Washington Ave Extension, Ste 502, Albany, NY 12203
800-253-4332 or 518-486-7814 Fax: 518-473-9457
Co-Director:
Jeannine Morell 518-486-7814
Co-Director:
Peter Trolio 518-486-7814

NYS/SSU Joint Labor-Management Committee . . . . fax: 518-457-9445
55 Elk St, Rm 301-B, Albany, NY 12210
Employee Program Assistant:
Vacant 518-457-9420

NYS/UUP Labor-Management Committee . . . . fax: 518-457-9445
55 Elk St, Rm 301-C, Albany, NY 12210
Executive Director:
Phillip H. Smith 518-486-4666/fax: 518-486-4667
e-mail: nysuuplmc@goer.state.ny.us

Statewide Employee Assistance Programs . . . . fax: 518-486-9796
55 Elk St, Rm 301A, Albany, NY 12210-2316
800-822-0244 Fax: 518-486-9796
Asst Director:
Karen Dunn 518-486-9769

Public Employment Relations Board

Empire State Plaza
Agency Bldg 2, 18/20 Fl
PO Box 2074
Albany, NY 12220
518-457-2578 Fax: 518-457-2664
e-mail: perbinfo@perb.ny.gov
Web site: www.perb.ny.gov

Chair:
Seth H Agata 518-457-2578
Member:
Robert Hite 518-457-2578
Executive Director:
Anthony Zumbolo 518-457-2676
Counsel:
David P Quinn 518-457-2678
Secretary to the Board:
Sheila Talavera 518-457-2578

Administration Section
Administrative Officer:
Jonathan O'Rourke 518-457-2923

Conciliation Office
Director:
Kevin B. Flanigan 518-457-2690

District Offices

Buffalo
Electric Tower, 535 Washington St, Ste 302, Buffalo, NY 14203
Regional Director:
Gregory Poland 716-847-3449/fax: 716-847-3690

New York City
55 Hanson Pl, Ste 700, Brooklyn, NY 11217
Mediator:
Karen R. Kenney 718-722-4545/fax: 718-722-4550

Employment Practices & Representation Section
Director:
Monte Klein 518-457-5973
Asst Director:
Susan Comenzo 518-457-5973

Legal Section
Associate Counsel & Director, Litigation:
David P Quinn 518-457-2678

State Comptroller, Office of the

110 State St, 15th Fl
Albany, NY 12236-0001
518-474-4044 Fax: 518-473-3004
Web site: www.osc.state.ny.us

59 Maiden Lane
New York, NY 10038
212-383-1600

State Comptroller:
Thomas P DiNapoli . . . . 518-474-4040 or 212-681-4469

Operations
Executive Deputy Comptroller, Operations:
John Traylor 518-402-4103

Payroll & Revenue Services Division
Deputy Comptroller:
Daniel Berry 518-408-4149
Director, Unclaimed Funds:
Lawrence Schantz 518-473-6438
Director, State Payroll Services:
Robin R Rabii 518-474-3400

Executive Office
First Deputy Comptroller:
Pete Grannis 518-474-2909
Chief of Staff:
Shawn Thompson 518-474-4044
Deputy Comptroller & Chief Information Officer:
Robert Loomis 518-486-4003

Retirement Services
Deputy Comptroller:
Kevin Murray 518-474-2600
Asst Comptroller:
Nancy Burton 518-474-4600

Accounting Bureau
Director:
Michelle Camuglia 518-474-3670

Actuarial Bureau
Actuary:
Teri Landin 518-474-4537

Benefit Calculations & Disbursements
Director:
James Normile 518-474-5556

Disability Processing/Hearing Administration
Director:
Kathy Nowak 518-473-1347

Member & Employee Services
Director:
Ginger Dame 518-474-1101

Retirement Communications
Director:
Paul Kentoffio 518-474-7096

Policy Areas

CORPORATIONS, AUTHORITIES AND COMMISSIONS

New York State Teachers' Retirement System
10 Corporate Woods Dr
Albany, NY 12211-2395
518-447-2900 or 800-348-7298 Fax: 518-447-2695
e-mail: media@nystrs.state.ny.us
Web site: www.nystrs.org

Executive Director:
Thomas K Lee 518-447-2726
General Counsel:
Joseph J. Indelicato, Jr. 518-447-2722
Actuary:
Richard Young 518-447-2692
Managing Director Operations:
Kevin Schaefer 518-447-2730
Director, Member Relations:
Sheila Gardella 518-447-2684
Manager, Public Information:
John Cardillo 518-447-4743/fax: 518-447-2875
e-mail: john.caradillo@nystrs.org
Managing Director Real Estate:
David C. Gillian 518-447-2751
Managing Director, Private Equity:
John W. Virtanen

NEW YORK STATE LEGISLATURE

See Legislative Branch in Section 1 for additional Standing Committee and Subcommittee information.

Assembly Standing Committees

Governmental Employees
Chair:
Peter J Abbate, Jr (D) 518-455-3053
Ranking Minority Member:
Nicole Malliotakis (R) 518-455-5716

Labor
Chair:
Michele Titus (D) 518-455-5668
Ranking Minority Member:
Karl Brabenec (R) 518-455-5991

Senate Standing Committees

Civil Service & Pensions
Chair:
Martin J Golden (R) 518-455-2730
Ranking Minority Member:
James Sanders, Jr. (D) 518-455-3531

Labor
Chair:
Jack Martins (R) 518-455-3265
Ranking Minority Member:
Jose R Peralta (D) 518-455-2529

Senate/Assembly Legislative Commissions

Government Administration, Legislative Commission on
Assembly Chair:
Brian P. Kavanagh (D) 518-455-5506
Senate Vice Chair:
Vacant 518-455-0000

U.S. GOVERNMENT

EXECUTIVE DEPARTMENTS AND RELATED AGENCIES

US Merit Systems Protection Board
Web site: www.mspb.gov

New York Field Office
26 Federal Plaza, Room 3137A, New York, NY 10278-0022
Chief Administrative Judge:
Arthur S. Joseph 212-264-9372/fax: 212-264-1417

US Office of Personnel Management
Web site: www.usajobs.opm.gov

PHILADELPHIA SERVICE CENTER (serving New York)
William J Green Fed Bldg, Rm 3400, 600 Arch St, Philadelphia, PA 19106
Director:
Joseph D Stix 215-861-3031/fax: 215-861-3030
e-mail: philadelphia@opm.gov

U.S. CONGRESS

See U.S. Congress Chapter for additional Standing Committee and Subcommittee information.

House of Representatives Standing Committees

Oversight and Government Reform
Chair:
Darrell E. Issa (R-CA) 202-225-3906
Ranking Member:
Elijah Cummings (D-MD) 202-225-4741
New York Delegate:
Carolyn B Maloney (D) 202-225-7944

Subcommittee
Federal Workforce, Postal Service and the District of Columbia
Chair:
Blake Farenthold (R-TX) 202-225-7742
Ranking Member:
Stephen F. Lynch (D-MA) 202-225-8273

Senate Standing Committees

Homeland Security & Governmental Affairs
Chair:
Thomas R. Carper (D-DE) 202-224-2441
Ranking Member:
Tom Coburn (R-OK) 202-224-5754

PRIVATE SECTOR

AFSCME District Council 37
150 State St, Albany, NY 12207
518-436-0665 or 212-815-1550 Fax: 518-436-1066
NYC employees union
Wanda Williams, Director

American Federation of State, County and Municipal Employees (AFSCME)
212 Great Oaks Blvd, Albany, NY 12203
518-869-2245 Fax: 518-869-8649
e-mail: bmcdonnell@afscme.org
Web site: www.afscme.org
Union representing public service & healthcare workers; American Federation of State, County & Municipal Employees
Brian McDonnell, Legislative & Political Director

Civil Service Employees Assn of NY (CSEA), Local 1000, AFSCME, AFL-CIO
143 Washington Ave, Albany, NY 12210
518-257-1000 or 800-342-4146 Fax: 518-462-3639
Web site: www.csealocal1000.org
Public/private employees union
Danny Donohue, President

Cornell University, School of Industrial & Labor Relations
356 ILR Research Bldg, Ithaca, NY 14853-3901
607-255-7581 Fax: 607-255-0245
e-mail: klb23@cornell.edu
Web site: www.ilr.cornell.edu
Public sector organizations; leadership; temporary & contract workers; union organizing; & collective bargaining
Kate Bronfenbrenner, Director, Labor Education Research

District Council 37, AFSCME, AFL-CIO
125 Barclay St, New York, NY 10007
212-815-1000 Fax: 212-815-1402
e-mail: dsullivan@dc37.net
Web site: www.dc37.net
NYC employees union
Dennis Sullivan, Director, Research & Negotiations

NYC Board of Education Employees, Local 372/AFSCME, AFL-CIO
125 Barclay Street, 6th Floor, New York, NY 10007
212-815-1372 Fax: 212-815-1347
Web site: www.local372.com
Veronica Montgomery-Costa, President - District Council 37/372

NYS Association of Chiefs of Police Inc
2697 Hamburg Street, Schenectady, NY 12303-3783
518-355-3371 Fax: 518-356-5767
e-mail: nysacop@nycap.rr.com
Web site: www.nychiefs.org
Joseph S Dominelli, Executive Director

NYS Association of Fire Chiefs
1670 Columbia Turnpike, Box 328, East Schodack, NY 12063-0328
518-477-2631 Fax: 518-477-4430
e-mail: tlabelle@nysfirechiefs.com
Web site: www.nysfirechiefs.com
Thomas LaBelle, Executive Director

NYS Correctional Officers & Police Benevolent Association Inc
102 Hackett Blvd, Albany, NY 12209
518-427-1551 or 888-484-7279 Fax: 518-426-1635
e-mail: nyscopba@nyscopba.org
Web site: www.nyscopba.org
Mary Gulino,

NYS Court Clerks Association
170 Duane St, New York, NY 10013
212-941-5700 Fax: 212-941-5705
Kevin E Scanlon, Sr, President

NYS Deputies Association Inc
61 Laredo Dr, Rochester, NY 14624
585-247-9322 Fax: 585-247-6661
e-mail: tross1@rochester.rr.com
Web site: www.nysdeputy.org
Thomas H Ross, Executive Director

NYS Bar Assn, Attorneys in Public Service Cmte
NYS Health Department
Corning Tower, Empire State Plaza, Albany, NY 12237
518-474-2011
Web site: www.health.ny.gov
Advancing the interests of NY governmental & not-for-profit attorneys
Hon James F Horan, Administrative Law Judge

NYS Law Enforcement Officers Union, Council 82, AFSCME, AFL-CIO
Hollis V Chase Bldg, 63 Colvin Ave, Albany, NY 12206
518-489-8424 Fax: 518-489-8430
e-mail: c82@council82.org
Web site: www.council82.org
Daniel J Valente, Legislative Director

NYS Parole Officers Association
PO Box 5821, Albany, NY 12205-0821
518-393-6541 Fax: 518-393-6541
e-mail: hsj195@localnet.com
Professional association representing NYS parole officers
H Susan Jeffords, President

NYS Sheriffs' Association
27 Elk St, Albany, NY 12207
518-434-9091 Fax: 518-434-9093
e-mail: pkehoe@nysheriffs.org
Web site: www.nysheriffs.org
Peter R Kehoe, Executive Director

New York State Law Enforcement Council
One Hogan Place, New York, NY 10013
212-335-8927 Fax: 212-335-3808
Web site: www.nyslec.org
Founded in 1982 as a legislative advocate for NY's law enforcement community. The members represent leading law enforcement professionals throughout the state. An active voice and participant in improving the quality of justice and a safer NY.
Leroy Frazer, Jr, Coordinator

New York State Public Employees Federation (PEF)
1168-70 Troy-Schenectady Rd, PO Box 12414, Albany, NY 12212
518-785-1900 x211 Fax: 518-783-1117
e-mail: kbrynien@pef.org
Web site: www.nyspef.org
Professional, scientific & technical employees union
Kenneth D Brynien, President

New York State Supreme Court Officers Association
299 Broadway, Suite 1100, New York, NY 10007-1921
212-406-4292 or 212-406-4276 Fax: 212-791-8420
e-mail: lbroderick@nysscoa.org
Web site: www.nysscoa.org
Supreme Court Officers Union
John P McKillop, President

New York State United Teachers/AFT, AFL-CIO
800 Troy-Schenectady Road, Latham, NY 12110-2455
518-213-6000 or 800-342-9810
Web site: www.nysut.org
Richard Iannuzzi, President

Organization of NYS Management Confidential Employees
5 Pine West Plaza, Suite 513, Albany, NY 12205
518-456-5241 or 800-828-6623 Fax: 518-456-3838
e-mail: nysomce@gmail.com
Web site: www.nysomce.org
Professional organization of state management & confidential employees
Barbara Zaron, President

Patrolmen's Benevolent Association
40 Fulton St, 17th Fl, New York, NY 10038
212-233-5531 Fax: 212-233-3952
e-mail: union@nycpba.org
Web site: www.nycpba.org
NYC patrolmen's union
Patrick Lynch, President

Policy Areas

Police Conference of NY Inc (PCNY)
112 State St, Ste 1120, Albany, NY 12207
518-463-3283 Fax: 518-463-2488
e-mail: pcnyinfo@pcny.org
Web site: www.pcny.org
Advocacy for law enforcement officers
Richard Wells, President

Professional Fire Fighters Association Inc (NYS)
174 Washington Avenue, Albany, NY 12210
518-436-8827 Fax: 518-436-8830
e-mail: profire@nyspffa.org
Web site: www.nyspffa.org
Union representing city, village & town firefighters
Michael McManus, President

Retired Public Employees Association
435 New Karner Road, Albany, NY 12205-3833
518-869-2542 Fax: 518-869-0631
e-mail: mail@rpea.org
Web site: www.rpea.org
Advocacy for retired public employees & their families
Alan Dorn, Executive Director
Anthony Cantore, Legislative Representative

State Employees Federal Credit Union
1239 Washington Avenue, Albany, NY 12206-1067
518-452-8234 Fax: 518-464-5227
Web site: www.sefcu.com
John Gallagher, Director, Internal Audit

Syracuse University, Maxwell School of Citizenship & Public Affairs
215 Eggers Hall, Syracuse, NY 13244-1090
315-443-4000 Fax: 315-443-9721
e-mail: sibretsc@maxwell.syr.edu
Capital financing & debt management; public employee pensions; financial management
Stuart Bretschneider, Associate Dean & Chair, Professor of Public Administration

Trooper Foundation-State of New York Inc
3 Airport Park Blvd, Latham, NY 12110-1441
518-785-1002 Fax: 518-785-1003
e-mail: rmincher@nystf.org
Web site: www.nystrooperfoundation.org
Supports programs & services of the NYS Police
Rachael L Mincher, Foundation Administrator

Uniformed Fire Officers Association
225 Broadway, Suite 401, New York, NY 10007
212-293-9300 Fax: 212-292-1560
e-mail: administrator@ufoa.org
Web site: www.ufoa.org
NYC fire officers' union
John J McDonnell, President

United Transportation Union
35 Fuller Road, Suite 205, Albany, NY 12205
518-438-8403 Fax: 518-438-8404
e-mail: sjnasca@aol.com
Web site: www.utu.org
Federal government railroad, bus & airline employees; public employees
Samuel Nasca, Legislative Director

United University Professions
PO Box 15143, Albany, NY 12212-5143
518-640-6600 Fax: 518-640-6698
e-mail: feedback@uupmail.org
Web site: www.uupinfo.org
SUNY labor union of academic & other professional faculty
William E Scheuerman, President

Offices and agencies generally appear in alphabetical order, except when specific order is requested by listee.

REAL PROPERTY

NEW YORK STATE

GOVERNOR'S OFFICE

Governor's Office
Executive Chamber
State Capitol
Albany, NY 12224
518-474-8390 Fax: 518-474-1513
Web site: www.ny.gov

Governor:
Andrew M Cuomo 518-474-8390
Secretary to the Governor:
William Mulrow 518-474-4246
Counsel to the Governor:
Alphonso David 518-474-8343
Chief of Staff:
Melissa DeRosa .518-474-8418 or 212-681-4640
Director, Communications:
James Allen. . . . . .518-474-8418 or 212-681-4640
First Assistant Counsel:
Sandi Toll 518-474-8434

EXECUTIVE DEPARTMENTS AND RELATED AGENCIES

General Services, Office of
Corning Tower, 41st Fl
Empire State Plaza
Albany, NY 12242
518-474-3899 Fax: 518-474-1546
Web site: www.ogs.ny.gov

Commissioner:
RoAnn Destito 518-474-5991
First Deputy Commissioner:
Karen B Tyler 518-473-6953
Director, Communications:
Heather Groll. 518-474-5987/fax: 518-474-3187
e-mail: heather.groll@ogs.ny.gov

Real Estate Planning & Development Group
Director, Real Estate Planning & Development:
James Sproat 518-474-4944
Asst Director, Real Estate Planning & Development:
Robert W Lazarou. 518-486-7963
Bureau Chief, Land Management:
Charles Sheifer 518-474-2195
Asst Director, Real Estate Planning - Upstate:
Leah Nicholson 518-486-1484

Real Property Management Group
Deputy Commissioner:
Eric S McShane .518-474-6057/fax: 518-474-1523
Director, Downstate Regional Buildings:
Kevin Cahill. 718-923-4448/fax: 718-923-4451
Assistant Regional Director, Empire State Plaza & Downtown Buildings:
Andy Papale 518-402-5753
Director, Upstate Harriman State Office Campus:
Louis Salerno. 518-457-2290/fax: 518-457-8297
Director, Utilities Management:
Robert Lobdell. .518-474-3249/fax: 518-402-5682

Law Department
120 Broadway
New York, NY 10271-0332
212-416-8000 or 800-771-7755
Web site: www.ag.ny.gov

State Capitol
Albany, NY 12224-0341
518-776-2000
Fax: 518-650-9401

Attorney General:
Eric T Schneiderman . . . . .212-416-8050 or 518-776-2000

Social Justice
Executive Deputy Attorney General:
Alvin L Bragg, Jr. 212-416-8450/fax: 212-416-8942

Civil Rights Bureau
Bureau Chief:
Lourdes Rosado. 212-416-8250/fax: 212-416-8074

Investor Protection Bureau
Bureau Chief:
Chad Johnson .212-416-8225/fax: 212-416-8816

State Counsel
Chief Deputy Attorney General & Counsel:
Janet Sabel 212-416-8050
Chief Deputy Attorney General & Counsel:
Jason Brown 212-416-8050

Claims Bureau
Bureau Chief:
Katharine Brooks . . . . .518-776-2300 or 212-416-8500

Real Property Bureau
Bureau Chief:
Alison Crocker 518-776-2700

Real Property Tax Services, Office of
WA Harriman State Campus
Albany, NY 12227
518-457-7377 or 518-591-5232
e-mail: nysorps@orps.state.ny.us
Web site: www.tax.ny.gov/about/orpts/

Acting Secretary of Board & Assistant Deputy Commissioner:
Susan Savage 518-474-6742
State Board Member (Chair):
Matthew Rand. 518-474-3793
State Board Member:
John M. Bacheller. 518-474-3793
State Board Member:
Edgar A. King 518-474-3793
Assistant to Board:
Darlene Maloney. 518-474-3793
e-mail: darlene.maloney@tax.ny.gov

Research, Information & Policy Development
Director:
James Dunne 518-473-4532
e-mail: jim.dunne@orps.state.ny.us
Director:
David Williams 518-473-8743
e-mail: dave.williams@orps.state.ny.us

Albany (Northern Region)
WA Harriman State Campus, Bldg 8A, Albany, NY 12227

Policy Areas

Regional Director:
Robert Aiken 518-486-4403/fax: 518-435-8573
e-mail: orpts.northern@tax.ny.gov

Batavia (Western Region)
Genesee County Bldg 2, 3837 W Main Rd, Batavia, NY 14020
Regional Director:
Christine Bannister 585-343-4363/fax: 518-435-8598
e-mail: orpts.western@tax.ny.gov

Long Island Satellite Office
250 Veterans Memorial Hgwy, Rm 4A-6, Hauppauge, NY 11788
Manager:
Steve Hartnett 631-595-4071/fax: 518-435-8572
e-mail: orpts.southern@tax.ny.gov

Newburgh (South)
263 Route 17K, Ste 2001, Newburgh, NY 12550
Regional Director:
John Wolham 845-567-2648/fax: 518-435-8498
e-mail: orpts.southern@tax.ny.gov

Ray Brook Satellite Office
884 NYS Rte 86, PO Box 309, Ray Brook, NY 12977
Regional Director:
Robert Aiken 518-891-1780/fax: 518-435-8593
e-mail: orpts.raybrook@tax.ny.gov

Syracuse (Central Region) . . . . fax: 315-471-3634
401 South Salina St, 5th Floor, Syracuse, NY 13202
Regional Director:
Teresa Frank 315-471-2347/fax: 518-435-8583
e-mail: internet.central@orps.state.ny.us

Transportation Department
50 Wolf Road
Albany, NY 12232
518-457-5100 or 518-457-6195 Fax: 518-457-5583
Web site: www.dot.ny.gov

Commissioner:
Matthew J Driscoll 518-457-4422
Operations & Asset Management Division:
Roderic Sechrist 518-485-0887

Engineering Division
Chief Engineer:
Phillip Eng 518-457-4430
Office of Design:
Richard Lee. 518-457-6452
Office of Structures:
Richard Marchione 518-457-6827
Office of Environment:
Dan Hitt. 518-457-5672
Office of Major Projects:
Marie Corrado. 518-4585-5025
Office of Technical Services:
Robert Sack, PE 518-457-4445
Office of Construction:
Brian DeWald, PE. 518-457-6472
Office of Construction:
Jose Rivera, PE 518-457-6472

NEW YORK STATE LEGISLATURE

See Legislative Branch in Section 1 for additional Standing Committee and Subcommittee information.

Assembly Standing Committees

Economic Development, Job Creation, Commerce & Industry
Chair:
Robin L Schimminger (D) 518-455-4767
Ranking Minority Member:
Raymond Walter (R). 518-455-54618

Housing
Chair:
Keith L.T. Wright (D). 518-455-4793
Ranking Minority Member:
Michael J Fitzpatrick (R) 518-455-5021

Real Property Taxation
Chair:
Sandra R Galef (D) 518-455-5348
Ranking Minority Member:
Kieran Michael Lalor (R) 518-455-5125

Senate Standing Committees

Commerce, Economic Development & Small Business
Chair:
Philip Boyle (R) 518-455-3411
Ranking Minority Member:
Timothy Kennedy (D). 518-455-2426

Housing Construction & Community Development
Chair:
Elizabeth O'C. Little (R) 518-455-2811
Ranking Minority Member:
Adriano Espaillat (D) 518-455-2041

U.S. GOVERNMENT

EXECUTIVE DEPARTMENTS AND RELATED AGENCIES

US Department of Agriculture

Rural Development
Web site: www.rurdev.usda.gov/ny

New York State Office. . . . . fax: 315-477-6438
The Galleries of Syracuse, 441 S Salina St, Ste 357, Syracuse, NY 13202-2441
315-477-6400 Fax: 315-477-6438
State Director:
Stanley Telega 315-477-6437

US General Services Administration
Web site: www.gsa.gov

Region 2—New York
26 Federal Plaza, Rm 18-102, New York, NY 10278
212-264-9290
Regional Administrator:
Denise L. Pease. 212-264-2600
e-mail: denise.pease@gsa.gov
Special Assistant to the Regional Administrator:
Gita J. Stulberg 212-264-2600/fax: 212-264-3998
e-mail: guita.stulberg@gsa.gov

Administration
Director, Program Support & Human Resources:
Joseph J Giorgianni. 212-264-0780/fax: 212-264-6798
e-mail: joseph.giorgianni@gsa.gov

Federal Supply Service
Acting Asst Regional Administrator:
Charles B Weill. 212-264-3590/fax: 212-264-9759

Federal Technology Service
Asst Regional Administrator (Acting):
Steve Ruggiero 212-264-3590
e-mail: steve.ruggiero@gsa.gov

Inspector General's Office
Asst Regional Inspector, Investigations:
Daniel Walsh 212-264-7300/fax: 212-264-7154
Regional Director, Audit:
Joseph Mastropietro 212-264-8620

Public Buildings Service
Regional Commissioner:
Joanna Rosato 212-264-4282
e-mail: joanna.rosato@gsa.gov
Deputy Asst Regional Administrator:
Vacant 212-264-4285
Director, Property Management:
David Segermeister 212-264-4273/fax: 212-264-2746
Director, Realty Services:
Donald W Eigendorff 212-264-4210/fax: 212-264-9400

PRIVATE SECTOR

Appraisal Education Network School & Merrell Institute
1461 Lakeland Ave, Bohemia, NY 11716
631-563-7720 Fax: 631-563-7719
e-mail: bcm@doctor.com
Web site: www.merrellinstitute.com
Real estate sales, broker, appraiser, mortgage & property management education courses, paralegal, continuing education, home inspection
Bill C Merrell, Director

Brookfield Properties Corporation
Three World Financial Center, 200 Vesey Street, 11th Floor, New York, NY 10281
212-417-7000 Fax: 212-417-7214
e-mail: kkane@brookfieldproperties.com
Web site: www.brookfieldproperties.com
Commercial real estate
Kathleen G Kane, General Counsel

Building & Realty Institute
80 Business Park Dr, Armonk, NY 10504
914-273-0730 Fax: 914-273-7051
e-mail: aaaa@buildersinstitute.org
Web site: www.buildersinstitute.org
Building, realty & construction industry membership organization
Albert A Annunziata, Executive Director

NYS Bar Assn, Real Property Law Section
D H Ferguson, Attorney, PLLC
141 Sully's Trail, Suite 12, Pittsford, NY 14534
585-586-0459 or 585-586-0450 Fax: 585-586-2297
e-mail: dhferguson@frontiernet.net
Dorothy H Ferguson, Chair

DTZ/Cushman & Wakefield
277 Park Avenue, New York, NY 10172
212-758-0800 Fax: 212-758-6192
Web site: www.dtz.cassidyturley.com
Commercial real estate & property management services
Peter Hennessy, President, New York Tri-State Region

Ernst & Young
5 Times Square, New York, NY 10036-6350
212-773-4500 Fax: 212-773-4986
e-mail: dale.reiss@ey.com
Web site: www.ey.com
Dale Anne Reiss, Global & Americas Director Real Estate

FirstService Williams
380 Madison Ave, 3rd Floor, New York, NY 10017
212-716-3760 Fax: 212-716-3710
e-mail: jcaridi@fswre.com
Web site: www.fswre.com
Real estate brokerage, ownership, sales, leasing, management & consulting
Joseph J Caridi, Executive Managing Director

Fisher Brothers
299 Park Ave, New York, NY 10171
212-752-5000 Fax: 212-940-6879
Real estate investment & development
Arnold Fisher, Partner

Glenwood Management Corporation
1200 Union Turnpike, New Hyde Park, NY 11040
718-343-6400 Fax: 718-343-0009
Web site: www.glenwoodmanagement.com
Property management
Leonard Litwin, President

Greater Rochester Association of Realtors Inc
930 East Avenue, Rochester, NY 14607
585-292-5000 Fax: 585-292-5008
e-mail: karenw@grar.net
Web site: www.homesteadnet.com
Karen Wingender, Chief Executive Officer

Greater Syracuse Association of Realtors Inc
5958 East Taft Road, North Syracuse, NY 13212
315-457-5979 Fax: 315-457-5884
Web site: www.cnyrealtor.com
Lynnore Fetyko, Chief Executive Officer

H J Kalikow & Co LLC
101 Park Ave, 25th Fl, New York, NY 10178
212-808-7000 Fax: 212-573-6380
Web site: www.hjkalikow.com
Real estate development
Peter S Kalikow, President

J J Higgins Properties Inc
20 North Main St, Pittsford, NY 14534
585-381-6030 Fax: 585-381-0571
e-mail: jjhigginsproperties@frontiernet.net
Web site: www.jjhigginsproperties.com
Residental properties, relocation, commercial properties, home sales & listings, buyer agency
John J Higgins, President

Landauer Realty Group Inc
1177 Avenue of the Americas, New York, NY 10036
212-759-9700 or 212-326-4752 Fax: 212-326-4802
e-mail: david.arena@grubb-ellis.com
Web site: www.landauer.com
Commercial real estate appraisers, analysts & transaction consultants
David Arena, President

MJ Peterson Corporation
501 Audubon Pkwy, Amherst, NY 14228
716-688-1234 Fax: 716-688-5463
e-mail: 1peterson@mjpeterson.com
Web site: www.mjpeterson.com
Residential, commercial, property management, development and new homes
Victor L Peterson, Jr, President

Mancuso Business Development Group
56 Harvester Ave, Batavia, NY 14020
585-343-2800 Fax: 585-343-7096
e-mail: tom@mancusogroup.com
Web site: www.mancusogroup.com
Improve operating performances of multi tenant industrial and office and business incubator properties
Tom Mancuso, President

Metro/Colvin Realty Inc
2211 Sheridan Dr, Kenmore, NY 14223
716-874-0110 Fax: 716-874-9015
e-mail: metrocolvin1@aol.com
Residential & commercial property
John Riordan, President

Metro/Horohoe-Leimbach
3199 Delaware Ave, Kenmore, NY 14217
716-873-5404 Fax: 716-873-8901
e-mail: whorohoe@aol.com
Web site: metrohorohoe.com
Residential real estate
William Horohoe, President

NY Commercial Association of Realtors
130 Washington Ave, Albany, NY 12210
518-463-0300 Fax: 518-462-5474
e-mail: nyscar@att.net
Web site: www.nyscarxchange.com
Commercial real estate
Maureen D Wilson, President

NYS Association of Realtors
130 Washington Ave, Albany, NY 12210-2298
518-463-0300 Fax: 518-462-5474
e-mail: admin@nysar.com
Web site: www.nysar.com
Duncan R MacKenzie, Chief Executive Officer

NYS Land Title Association
2 Rector St, Ste 901, New York, NY 10006-1819
212-964-3701 Fax: 212-964-7185
e-mail: rgt@nyslta.org
Web site: www.nyslta.org
Trade association for title insurance industry
Robert Treuber, Executive Vice President

NYS Society of Real Estate Appraisers
130 Washington Ave, Albany, NY 12210-2298
518-463-0300 Fax: 518-462-5474
e-mail: nyssrea@nysar.com
Web site: www.nyrealestateappraisers.com
Real estate appraisal
Wayne Feinberg, President

Community Bankers Assn of NY State, Mortgages & Real Estate Cmte
New York Community Bank
615 Merrick Ave, Westbury, NY 11590
516-683-4100 Fax: 516-683-8344
Web site: www.mynycb.com
James O'Donovan, Chair

New York Landmarks Conservancy
1 Whitehall St, 21 Fl, New York, NY 10004
212-995-5260 Fax: 212-995-5268
e-mail: nylandmarks@nylandmarks.org
Web site: www.nylandmarks.org
Technical & financial assistance for preservation & reuse of landmark buildings
Peg Breen, President

New York State Assessors' Association
PO Box 888, Middletown, NY 10940
845-344-0292 Fax: 845-343-8238
e-mail: nysaa@nyassessor.com
Web site: www.nyassessor.com
Real property tax issues
Thomas Frey, Executive Director

Pomeroy Appraisal Associates Inc
Pomeroy Pl, 225 W Jefferson St, Syracuse, NY 13202
315-422-7106 Fax: 315-476-1011
e-mail: dfisher@pomeroyappraisal.com
Web site: www.pomeroyappraisal.com
Real estate appraisal & consultation
Donald A Fisher, MAI, ARA

R W Bronstein Corporation
3666 Main St, Buffalo, NY 14226
716-835-7400 or 800-642-2500 Fax: 716-835-7419
e-mail: value@bronstein.net
Web site: www.bronstein.net
Real estate, appraisals & auctions; valuation & marketing of all types of realty and chattels
Richard W Bronstein, President

Real Estate Board of New York Inc
570 Lexington Ave, New York, NY 10022
212-532-3120 Fax: 212-481-0122
e-mail: stevenspinola@rebny.com
Web site: www.rebny.com
Representing real estate professionals & firms in New York City
Steven Spinola, President

Realty Advisory Board on Labor Relations
292 Madison Ave, New York, NY 10017
212-889-4100 Fax: 212-889-4105
e-mail: jberg@rabolr.com
Web site: www.rabolr.com
Labor negotiations for realtors & realty firms
James Berg, President

Realty USA
6505 E Quaker Rd, Orchard Park, NY 14127
716-662-2000 Fax: 716-662-3385
e-mail: mwhitehead@realtyusa.com
Web site: www.realtyusa.com
Residential real estate
Merle Whitehead, President & Chief Executive Officer

Red Barn Properties
Six Schoen Pl, Pittsford, NY 14534
585-381-2222 x11 Fax: 585-381-1854
e-mail: estelle@redbarnproperties.com
Web site: www.redbarnproperties.com
Specializing in local, national & global residential relocation
Estelle O'Connell, Relocation Director

Related Companies LP
60 Columbus Circle, 19th Fl, New York, NY 10023
212-421-5333 Fax: 212-801-1036
e-mail: bbeal@related.com
Web site: www.related.com
Residential & commercial real estate
Bruce A Beal, Jr, Executive Vice President, NY Development Group

Robert Schalkenbach Foundation
90 John Street, Suite 501, New York, NY 10038
212-683-6424 Fax: 212-683-6454
e-mail: msullivan@schalkenbach.org
Web site: www.schalkenbach.org
Land value taxation, real property & economic publications
Mark A Sullivan, Administrative Director

Roohan Realty
519 Broadway, Saratoga Springs, NY 12866-2208
518-587-4500 Fax: 518-587-4509
e-mail: troohan@roohanrealty.com
Web site: www.roohanrealty.com
Commercial & residential property
J Thomas Roohan, President

Silverstein Properties Inc
7 World Trade Center, 250 Greenwich Street, 38th Floor, New York, NY 10036
212-490-0666 Fax: 212-687-0067
NYC commercial real estate
Larry A Silverstein, President, Chief Executive Officer

Sonnenblick-Goldman Company
712 Fifth Ave, New York, NY 10019
212-841-9200 Fax: 212-262-4224
e-mail: asonnenblick@sonngold.com
Web site: www.sonngold.com
Real estate investment banking
Arthur I Sonnenblick, Senior Managing Director

Tishman Speyer Properties
Rockefeller Center, 45 Rockefeller Plaza, New York, NY 10111
212-715-0300 Fax: 212-319-1745
e-mail: jspeyer@tishmanspeyer.com
Web site: www.tishmanspeyer.com
Owners/builders
Jerry I Speyer, President

UJA-Federation of New York
130 E 59th St, New York, NY 10022
212-980-1000 Fax: 212-836-1653
e-mail: flynnc@ujafedny.org
Web site: www.ujafedny.org
Real property portfolio management
John S Ruskay, Executive Vice President & Chief Executive Officer

SOCIAL SERVICES

NEW YORK STATE

GOVERNOR'S OFFICE

Governor's Office
Executive Chamber
State Capitol
Albany, NY 12224
518-474-8390 Fax: 518-474-1513
Web site: www.ny.gov

Governor:
Andrew M Cuomo 518-474-8390
Secretary to the Governor:
William Mulrow 518-474-4246
Counsel to the Governor:
Alphonso David 518-474-8343
Deputy Secretary, Health & Human Services:
Paul Francis. 518-408-2500
Chief of Staff:
Melissa DeRosa . . . . 518-474-8418 or 212-681-4640
Director, Communications:
James Allen. . . . . 518-474-8418 or 212-681-4640
Deputy Secretary for Executive Operations:
Jill DesRosiers 518-402-2403
Director, State Operations:
James Malatras 518-486-9871

EXECUTIVE DEPARTMENTS AND RELATED AGENCIES

Aging, Office for the
2 Empire State Plaza
Albany, NY 12223
518-474-4425 or 800-342-9871 Fax: 518-474-0608
e-mail: nysofa@aging.ny.gov
Web site: www.aging.ny.gov

Director:
Corinda Crossdale. 518-474-4425
Executive Deputy Director:
Greg Olsen 518-474-7012
Counsel:
Jennifer Washington 518-474-0388
Public Information Officer:
Reza Mizbani 518-474-7181
e-mail: reza.mizbani@aging.ny.gov
Deputy Director, Agency Operations:
John Cochran 518-486-3661
e-mail: reza.mizbani@aging.ny.gov
Deputy Director, Division of Policy, Planning, Program & Outcomes:
Laurie Pferr. 518-474-7012

Federal Relations
Staff Liaison:
Stephen Syzdek. 518-474-5041
Deputy Director:
John J Lynch 518-473-4808

Aging Projects
Director:
Kelly Mateja 518-473-7424

Agriculture & Markets Department
10B Airline Dr
Albany, NY 12235
518-457-3880 or 800-554-4501 Fax: 518-457-3087
e-mail: info@agriculture.ny.gov
Web site: www.agriculture.ny.gov

Commissioner:
Richard Ball 518-457-8876
First Deputy Commissioner:
Jen McCormick. 518-457-2771
e-mail: jen.mccormick@agriculture.ny.gov
Public Information Officer:
Jola Szubielski 518-485-7728/fax: 518-457-3087
e-mail: jola.szubielski@agriculture.ny.gov

Agricultural Development Division
Director:
Kevin King 518-457-7076
e-mail: kevin.king@agriculture.ny.gov

Alcoholism & Substance Abuse Services, Office of
1450 Western Ave
Albany, NY 12203
518-473-3460 Fax: 518-457-5474
e-mail: communications@oasas.ny.gov
Web site: www.oasas.ny.gov

501 7th Ave
8th Fl
New York, NY 10018
646-728-4533

Commissioner:
Arlene Gonzalez-Sanchez. 518-457-2061
Executive Deputy Commissioner:
Sean M. Byrne 518-485-2337
Wellness & Medical Direction Office (Acting):
Charles W Morgan, MD 845-359-8500
Director, Office of Counsel & Internal Controls:
Robert Kent. 518-485-2312
Director, Governmental Affairs, Grants Mgmt:
Patricia Zuber-Wilson. 518-485-1484
Director, Bureau of Statewide Field Operations/NYC Operations:
Manuel Mosquera 518-485-1758

Bureau of Public Information & Communications
Director:
Susan A Craig, MPH. 518-457-8299/fax: 518-485-6014

Fiscal Administration Division
Associate Commissioner:
P David Sawicki 518-457-5312
Director, Bureau of Budget Management:
Tara Gabriel 518-485-2193
Director, Bureau of Capital Management:
Jeff Emad 518-457-2545
Director, Bureau of Health Care Financing & Performance Improvement:
Laurie Felter 518-457-2545

Outcome Management & System Information Division
Associate Commissioner:
William F. Hogan 518-485-2322

Prevention, Housing & Management Services Division
Acting Associate Commissioner:
Mary Ann DiChristopher 518-485-6022
Director, Bureau of Housing & Employment:
Henri Williams 518-485-0498
Director, Bureau of Prevention Services:
Scott Brady 518-457-4384
Director, Management Services:
Vacant 518-485-6689

Director, Bureau of Recovery Services:
Susan Brandau 518-485-2107

Quality Assurance & Performance Improvement Division
Associate Commissioner:
Charles W Monson 518-485-2257
Director, Bureau of Certification:
Janet Paloski 518-485-2250
Director, Bureau of Standards Compliance:
William Lanchanski 518-485-2255
Director, Bureau of Workforce Developement & Fiscal Evaluation:
Douglas Rosenberry 518-485-2033

Treatment & Practice Innovation Division
Associate Commissioner:
Steve Hanson 518-457-7077
Assistant Director, Bureau of Addiction Treatment Centers:
Paula Bradwell . . . . . 518-457-7077 or 585-461-0410

Children & Family Services, Office of
52 Washington St
Rensselaer, NY 12144
518-473-7793 Fax: 518-486-7550
Web site: www.ocfs.ny.gov

Acting Commissioner:
Sheila Poole 518-402-3108
Ombudsman:
Viola I Abbitt 518-486-7082
Executive Deputy Commissioner:
Sheila Poole 518-402-3108
Executive Secretary:
Nancy Degree 518-402-3108

Administration, Division of
Associate Commissioner:
James Barron. 518-486-6942
Contract Management:
Richard DiMezza 518-486-7224

Financial Management, Office of
Associate Commissioner:
Derek Holtzclaw. 518-486-7218
Director, Budget Management Bureau:
Gabrielle Ares. 518-474-1361
Director, Financial Operations:
Susan A Costello 518-486-3848

Commission for the Blind & Visually Handicapped (CBVH)
Associate Commissioner:
Brian S Daniels. 518-474-7812
Director, Bureau of Program Evaluation,Support & Business Svcs:
Roger Gray 518-474-7812
Director, Bureau of Field Operations & Implementation:
Janice O'Connor 518-473-9685

Child Welfare and Community Services, Division of (CWCS)
Deputy Commissioner:
Laura Velez. 518-474-3377

Special Populations, Office of
Assistant Commissioner:
Lisa Ghartey Ogundimu 518-473-9447
State Central Registry
Director:
Linda A. Joyce. 518-474-9607
Native American Services
Affairs Specialist:
Vacant 716-847-3123

Prevention, Permanency & Program Support, Office of
Associate Commissioner:
Renee Hallock 518-402-3181
Adult Protective Services
Director:
Alan Lawitz 518-402-6782
Adoption Services
Director:
Brenda Rivers 518-473-1901

Child Care Services, Division of (DCCS)
Deputy Commissioner:
Janice Molnar 518-486-6247

Information Technology, Division of
40 N Pearl Street, Albany, NY 12243
Business Solutions Director:
John Birtwistle 518-408-3046
CIO:
Rick Ryan 518-402-3194

Legal Affairs, Division of
Acting Deputy Commissioner & General Counsel:
Lee Prochera 518-473-8418

Communications, Office of
Assistant Commissioner for Communications:
Jennifer Givner 518-402-3130

Juvenile Justice & Opportunities for Youth, Division of (DJJOY)
Deputy Commissioner:
Ines Neives 518-473-1786

Facility Management, Office of
Associate Commissioner:
Vacant. 518-473-4411
Facility Coordinator:
Wendy Phillips 212-961-4121
Facility Coordinator:
Dan Comins 607-538-1401
ACA Accreditation Coordinator:
Kurt Pfisterer. 518-408-3825
Supervisor, Facilities Fire Safety:
Scott Hecox. 518-473-5325
DOJ Settlement Coordinator:
Edgardo Lopez 315-479-8356
Director, Management & Program Supprot, Bureau of:
Merle Brandwene 518-486-7029

Community Partnerships, Office of
Associate Commissioner:
Tim Roche. 518-486-7170
Director, Upstate/Long Island:
Daniel Maxwell. 518-486-4018
Downstate Area Manager:
Robert Ellis 212-961-4112
Director, Technical Support, IT, Office of:
Jeff Evans 518-486-4335

Special Investigations Unit
Chief of Investigations:
Lisa Thorne. 518-474-9478

Strategic Planning & Policy Development, Office of
Director:
Vacant. 518-473-1776
Bureau of Policy Analysis:
Rayana Gonzales. 518-473-6237
Bureau of Research, Evaluation & Performance Analytics:
Rebecca Colman 518-474-9426
Director, Special Projects, Bureau of:
Greg Owens 518-473-3990

Offices and agencies generally appear in alphabetical order, except when specific order is requested by listee.

Native American Services .... fax: 716-847-3812
716-847-3123 Fax: 716-847-3812
Director:
Vacant 716-847-3123

Youth Development, Office of .... fax: 518-473-6692
52 Washington Avenue, Room 1155, Rensselaer, NY 12144
Director:
Matt Beck 518-402-3296

Council on Children & Families (CCF)
52 Washington St, West Bldg, Ste 99, Rensselaer, NY 12144
Web site: www.ccf.ny.gov
Executive Director:
Deborah Benson 518-473-3652/fax: 518-473-2570
e-mail: debbie.benson@ccf.ny.gov
Deputy Director & Counsel:
Elana Marton.................... 518-473-3652
e-mail: elana.marton@ccf.ny.gov

Bureau of Policy, Research & Planning
Project Director, Head Start Collaboration:
Patricia Persell 518-473-3652
e-mail: patricia.persell@ccf.ny.gov

Bureau of Interagency Coordination & Case Resolution
Project Director, Kids Count:
Mary DeMasi 518-474-3652
e-mail: mary.demasi@ccf.ny.gov

Victim Services, Office of
80 South Swan Street
2nd Floor
Albany, NY 12210
518-457-8727 or 800-247-8035 Fax: 518-457-8658
Web site: www.ovs.ny.gov

55 Hanson Place
10th Fl
Brooklyn, NY 11217
718-923-4325
Fax: 718-923-4347

Director:
Elizabeth Cronin Esq 518-485-5719
General Counsel/Legal Unit:
John Watson 518-457-8066/fax: 518-457-8658
Deputy Director for Administration:
Virginia Miller 518-457-8003
Deputy Director, Claims:
Maureen Fahy.................... 518-457-8050
Crime Victim Compensation Investigations (Brooklyn):
Claudette Christian Bullock 718-923-4348
Director of Compensation:
Noreen Fyvie.................... 518-457-8727

Developmental Disabilities Planning Council
One Commerce Plaza
Ste 1230
Albany, NY 12210
518-486-7505 or 800-395-3372 Fax: 518-402-3505
e-mail: ddpc@ddpc.ny.gov
Web site: www.ddpc.ny.gov

Chairperson:
James Traylor 518-486-7505
Vice Chairperson:
Thomas Burke.................... 518-486-7505
Executive Director:
Sheila M Carey 518-486-7505
e-mail: sheila.carey@ddpc.ny.gov
Deputy Director-Program Development Specialist:
Anna Lobosco.................... 518-486-7505
e-mail: anna.lobosco@ddpc.ny.gov
Public Information Officer:
Thomas F Lee 518-486-7505/fax: 518-486-3505
e-mail: thomas.lee@ddpc.ny.gov

Education Department
State Education Bldg
89 Washington Ave
Albany, NY 12234
518-474-3852 Fax: 518-486-5631
Web site: www.nysed.gov

Commissioner & University President:
MaryEllen Elia 518-474-5844
Executive Deputy Commissioner:
Elizabeth Berlin 518-474-8381
Chief, External Affairs (Communications):
Dennis Tompkins 518-474-1201

Office of the Professions.................... fax: 518-474-1449
89 Washington Ave, EB, 2nd Fl, West Mezz, Albany, NY 12234
Fax: 518-474-1449
Web site: www.op.nysed.gov
Deputy Commissioner:
Douglas Lentivech.................... 518-474-3817 x440
e-mail: opopr@nysed.gov

Special Education
Assistant Commissioner:
James P. DeLorenzo 518-474-3817 x440
e-mail: opexdir@mail.nysed.gov
Coordinator, Special Education Policy & Professional Development:
Patricia J. Geary.................... 518-474-3817 x360
Supervisor, Program Development & Support:
Noel Granger.................... 518-474-3817 x340

Office of Adult Career & Continuing Education Services (ACCES).................... fax: 518-474-8802
One Commerce Plaza, Rm 1606, Albany, NY 12234
Fax: 518-474-8802
Web site: www.vesid.nysed.gov
Deputy Commissioner:
Kevin Smith 518-474-2714
e-mail: accesdeputy@nysed.gov

State School for the Blind at Batavia
2A Richmond Ave, Batavia, NY 14020
Superintendent:
Dr. Mathis A. Calvin, III 585-343-5384
e-mail: mcalvin@mail.nysed.gov

Vocational Rehabilitation Operations
Coordinator:
Frank Coco 518-473-1626/fax: 518-486-6252
e-mail: accesadm@nysed.gov

Labor Department
Building 12, Room 500
Harriman State Office Campus
Albany, NY 12240
518-457-9000 Fax: 518-457-6908
e-mail: nysdol@labor.ny.gov
Web site: www.labor.ny.gov

Commissioner:
Roberta Reardon 518-457-9000

Offices and agencies generally appear in alphabetical order, except when specific order is requested by listee.

Executive Deputy Commissioner:
Mario Musolino 518-457-4318
Acting Counsel:
Pico Ben-Amotz 518-457-7069
Director, Special Investigations:
John Dormin 518-457-7012
Director, Communications:
Leo Rosales 518-457-5519/fax: 518-485-1126
e-mail: leo.rosales@labor.ny.gov

Federal Programs
Deputy Commissioner, Federal Programs:
Bruce Herman 518-485-6410

Employment Services Division
Director:
Vacant 518-457-3584

Unemployment Insurance Division
Director:
Richard Marino 518-457-2878/fax: 518-485-8604

Workforce Development & Training Division
Acting Director:
Karen Coleman 518-457-4317/fax: 518-457-9526

Veterans Services
Program Coordinator:
Vacant 518-457-1343

Worker Protection
Deputy Commissioner, Workforce Development:
Karen A. Coleman 518-457-4317

Labor Standards Division
Director:
Carmine Ruberto 518-457-4256

Safety & Health Division
Director:
Eileen Franko 518-457-3518/fax: 518-457-1519

Prevention of Domestic Violence, Office for the

80 South Swan Street
11th Fl Rm 1157
Albany, NY 12210
518-457-5800 or 800-942-6906 Fax: 518-457-5810
Web site: www.opdv.ny.gov

Executive Director:
Gwen Wright 518-457-5800
Director, NYC Program:
Sujata Warrier 212-417-4477
Counsel:
Johanna Sullivan 518-457-5800
Fiscal Officer:
Linda Cassidy 518-457-7995
Public Information Officer:
Suzanne Cecala 518-457-5744
e-mail: suzanne.cecala@opdv.ny.gov

Temporary & Disability Assistance, Office of

40 N Pearl St
Albany, NY 12243
518-473-1090
e-mail: nyspio@otda.ny.gov
Web site: www.otda.ny.gov

Commissioner:
Samuel D Roberts 518-474-4152

Budget, Finance & Data Management
Director:
Nancy Maney 518-474-0183

Center for Child Well-Being
Deputy Commissioner & Director:
Eileen Stack 518-474-1078

Disability Determinations Division
Deputy Commissioner:
Gloria S Toal 518-473-0070

Center for Employment & Economic Supports
Deputy Commissioner:
Phyllis Morris 518-474-9222/fax: 518-474-5281

Information Technology Services
Acting Director:
Rick Ryan 518-486-1012

Legal Affairs Division
General Counsel:
Krista Rock 518-474-9502

Operations & Program Support
Deputy Commissioner:
Wilma Brown Phillips 518-473-3912

Public Information
Director:
Kristi L. Berner 518-474-9516/fax: 518-486-6935
e-mail: nyspio@otda.ny.gov

Welfare Inspector General, Office of NYS

Chisholm State Office Building
55 Hanson Place
Room 650
Brooklyn, NY 11217
518-474-1010 or 800-682-4530 Fax: 518-486-3745
e-mail: owig@dfa.state.ny.us
Web site: www.owig.ny.gov

Acting Welfare Inspector General:
Catherine Leahy Scott . . . . 518-474-1010 or 212-635-3150
Chief Investigator:
Joseph Bucci 718-923-4290
Confidential Assitant to the Inspector General:
Joy Quiles 718-923-4290
e-mail: joy.quiles@owig.ny.gov

NEW YORK STATE LEGISLATURE

See Legislative Branch in Section 1 for additional Standing Committee and Subcommittee information.

Assembly Standing Committees

Aging
Chair:
Steven Cymbrowitz (D) 518-455-5214
Ranking Minority Member:
Angela M Wozniak (C) 518-455-5921

Alcoholism & Drug Abuse
Chair:
Linda Rosenthal (D) 518-455-5802
Ranking Minority Member:
Mark Johns (R) 518-455-5784

Offices and agencies generally appear in alphabetical order, except when specific order is requested by listee.

Children & Families
Chair:
Donna Lupardo (D) 518-455-5431
Ranking Minority Member:
Stevenr McLaughlin (R) 518-455-5777

Social Services
Chair:
Andrew Hevesi (D) 518-455-4926
Ranking Minority Member:
Andrew Goodell (R) 518-455-4511

Assembly Task Forces

Puerto Rican/Hispanic Task Force
Chair:
Marcos Crespo (D) 518-455-5514
Executive Director:
Guillermo Martinez 518-455-3608

Women's Issues, Task Force on
Chair:
Aravella Simotas (D) 518-455-5014
Coordinator:
Christina Williams 518-455-3632/fax: 518-455-4574

Senate Standing Committees

Aging
Chair:
Sue Serino (R)) 518-455-2945
Ranking Minority Member:
Ruben Diaz Sr (D) 518-455-2511

Children & Families
Chair:
Tony Avella (D) 518-455-2210
Ranking Minority Member:
Velmanette Montgomery (D) 518-455-3451

Social Services
Chair:
David Carlucci (D) 518-455-2991

U.S. GOVERNMENT

EXECUTIVE DEPARTMENTS AND RELATED AGENCIES

Corporation for National & Community Service
Web site: www.cns.gov

New York Program Office
52 Washington Street, Room 228, North Building, Rensselaer, NY 12144-2796
Executive Director:
Mark J. Walter 518-473-8882/fax: 518-402-3817
e-mail: mark.walter@newyorkersvolunteer.ny.gov

Social Security Administration
Web site: www.socialsecurity.gov

Region 2—New York . . . . fax: 212-264-6372
26 Federal Plz, Rm 3904, New York, NY 10278
Regional Commissioner:
Beatrice M Disman 212-264-3915
Deputy Regional Commissioner:
Paul M Doersam 212-264-3915
Employer Services Liaison Officer:
Tyrone S. Benefield 212-264-1117
Executive Officer:
Bernie Bowles 212-264-4007

Office of Hearings & Appeals
Regional Chief Administrative Law Judge:
G Stephen Wright 212-264-4036

Office of Quality Assurance
Director:
Susan Pike 212-264-2827

Office of the General Counsel
Chief Counsel:
Lewis Spivak 212-264-3650

Program Operations Center
Director:
Janet Mullarkey 212-264-4004

Public Affairs
Public Affairs Director:
John E Shallman 212-264-2500/fax: 212-264-1444

US Department of Health & Human Services
Web site: www.os.dhhs.gov; www.hhs.gov/region2/

Administration for Children & Families . . . . fax: 212-264-4881
26 Federal Plaza, Rm 4114, New York, NY 10278
212-264-2890 Fax: 212-264-4881
Web site: www.acf.hhs.gov
Regional Administrator:
Joyce A. Thomas 212-264-2890

Administration on Aging . . . . fax: 212-264-0114
26 Federal Plaza, Rm 38-102, New York, NY 10278
212-264-2976 Fax: 212-264-0114
Web site: www.aoa.gov
Regional Administrator:
Kathleen Otte 212-264-2976
e-mail: kathleen.otte@aoa.hhs.gov

Centers for Disease Control & Prevention
Web site: www.cdc.gov

Agency for Toxic Substances & Disease Registry-EPA Region 2
290 Broadway, 20th Fl, New York, NY 10007
Web site: www.atsdr.cdc.gov
Director:
Leah Graziano, RS 212-637-4306/fax: 212-637-3253

New York Quarantine Station . . . . fax: 718-553-1524
Terminal 4E, Rm 219 016, JFK Airport, 2nd Floor, East Concourse, Jamaica, NY 11430-1081
718-553-1685 Fax: 718-553-1524
Officer-in-Charge:
Margaret A Becker 718-553-1685/fax: 718-553-1524

Centers for Medicare & Medicaid Services
26 Federal Plaza, Rm 3811, New York, NY 10278
Web site: www.cms.hhs.gov
Consortium Administrator:
James T. Kerr 212-616-2205/fax: 212-264-6189
e-mail: james.kerr@cms.hhs.gov
Regional Administrator:
Jay Weisman, MD 212-616-2500

Medicaid and Children's Health (DMCH)
Associate Regional Administrator:
Michael Melendez

Medicare Financial Management (DMFM)
Associate Regional Administrator:
Vacant
e-mail: peter.reisman@cms.hhs.gov

Offices and agencies generally appear in alphabetical order, except when specific order is requested by listee.

Medicare Operations Division (DMO)
Associate Regional Administrator:
Reginald Slaten. 212-616-2300
e-mail: jose.mirabal@cms.hhs.gov

Food & Drug Administration
888-463-6332
Web site: www.fda.gov

Northeast Region
158-15 Liberty Ave, Jamaica, NY 11433
Regional Director:
Elizabeth O'Malley 718-340-7000/fax: 718-662-5434
New York District Office
District Director:
Ronald Pace 718-662-5447/fax: 718-662-5665
Northeast Regional Laboratory
158-15 Liberty Ave, Queens, NY 11433
Director:
Michael J Palmieri 718-662-5450/fax: 718-662-5439

Health Resources & Svcs Admin Office of Performance Review . . . . .fax: 212-264-2673
26 Federal Plaza, Rm 3337, New York, NY 10278
Regional Division Director:
Ron Moss 212-264-2664
e-mail: robert.moss@hrsa.hhs.gov
Operations Director:
Margaret Lee. 212-264-2571
e-mail: margaret.lee@hrsa.hhs.gov
Director, Ofc of Engineering Services:
Emilio Pucillo 212-264-3600
e-mail: emilio.pucillo@hrsa.hhs.gov

Indian Health Services-Area Office . . . . .fax: 615-467-1501
711 Stewarts Ferry Pike, Nashville, TN 37214-2634
Director:
Martha Ketcher, MBA/HCM 615-467-1500

Office of Secretary's Regional Representative-Region 2-NY . . fax: 212-264-3620
26 Federal Plaza, Rm 3835, New York, NY 10278
Regional Director:
Deborah Konopko. 212-264-4600
e-mail: deborah.konopko@hhs.gov
Sr Intergovernmental Affairs Specialist:
Dennis Gonzalez 212-264-4600
e-mail: dennis.gonzalez@hhs.gov
Intergovernmental Affairs Specialist:
Katherine Williams 212-264-4600
e-mail: katherine.williams@hhs.gov

Office for Civil Rights . . . . .fax: 212-264-3039
26 Federal Plaza, Rm 3312, New York, NY 10278
Fax: 212-264-3039
Web site: www.hhs.gov/ocr
Regional Manager:
Michael Carter. 212-264-3313/fax: 212-264-3039
Deputy Regional Manager:
Linda Colon 212-264-3313

Office of General Counsel
26 Federal Plaza, Rm 3908, New York, NY 10278
Chief Counsel:
Joel Lerner 212-264-6373

Office of Inspector General
Regional Inspector General, Audit:
James P Edert 212-264-4620
Regional Inspector General & Regional Coordinator, Investigations:
Gary Heuer 212-264-1691
Regional Inspector General, Evaluations & Inspections:
Jodi Nudelman 212-264-1998

Office of Public Health & Science
26 Federal Plaza, Rm 3835, New York, NY 10278
Acting Regional Health Administrator:
Robert Davidson 212-264-2560
e-mail: rdavidson@osophs.dhhs.gov
Deputy Regional Health Administrator:
Robert L Davidson 212-264-2560
e-mail: rdavidson@osophs.dhhs.gov
Regional Family Planning Consultant:
Robin Lane 212-264-3935
e-mail: rlane@osophs.hhs.gov
Regional Minority Health Consultant:
Claude Colimon 212-264-2560
Regional Women's Health Coordinator:
Sandra Estepa 212-264-2560

U.S. CONGRESS

See U.S. Congress Chapter for additional Standing Committee and Subcommittee information.

House of Representatives Standing Committees

Ways & Means
Chair:
Dave Kamp (R-MI). 202-225-3561
New York Delegate:
Charles B. Rangel (D). 202-225-4365
New York Delegate:
Joseph Crowley (D) 202-225-3965
New York Delegate:
Tom Reed (R) 202-225-3106

Subcommittee
Social Security
Chair:
Sam Johnson (R-TX). 202-225-4201
Ranking Member:
Xavier Becerra (D-CA) 202-225-6325

Senate Standing Committees

Health, Education, Labor & Pensions
Chair:
Tom Harkin (D-IA). 202-224-3254
Ranking Member:
Lamar Alexander (R-TN) 202-224-4944

Aging, Special Committee on
Chair:
Bill Nelson (D-FL) 202-224-5274
Ranking Member:
Susan Collins (R-ME). 202-224-2523

PRIVATE SECTOR

AARP
780 3rd Ave, Fl 33, New York, NY 10017-2024
866-227-7442 Fax: 212-644-6390
Web site: www.aarp.org
AARP
Lois Aronstein, NY State Director

Policy Areas

Offices and agencies generally appear in alphabetical order, except when specific order is requested by listee.

Abilities Inc, at Abilities!
201 IU Willets Rd, Albertson, NY 11507-1599
516-465-1490 or 516-747-5355 (TTY) Fax: 516-405-3757
e-mail: amuterspaw@abilitiesinc.org
Web site: www.abilitiesinc.org
Provides comprehensive services to help individuals with disabilities reach their employment goals; provides support services & technical assistance to employers who hire persons with disabilities.
Alice Muterspaw, Director of Consumer Services & Provider Relations

Action for a Better Community Inc
550 E Main St, Rochester, NY 14604
585-325-5116 or 585-295-1726 Fax: 585-325-9108
e-mail: fcaldwell@abcinfo.org
Web site: www.abcinfo.org
Advocacy for programs enabling the low-income to become self-sufficient; social services for the needy
Freddie Caldwell, Deputy Director

American Red Cross in NYS
33 Everett Rd, Albany, NY 12205-1437
518-458-8111 x5113 Fax: 518-459-8262
e-mail: elizabeth.briand@redcross.org
Elizabeth H Briand, Director, State Government Relations

Asian American Federation
120 Wall St, 9th Floor, New York, NY 10005
212-344-5878 Fax: 212-344-5636
e-mail: info@aafederation.org
Web site: www.aafederation.org
Nonprofit leadership organization for member health & human services agencies serving the Asian American community
Cao K. O, Executive Director

Asian Americans for Equality
108 Norfolk Street, New York, NY 10002
212-979-8381 Fax: 212-979-8386
e-mail: info@aafe.org
Web site: www.aafe.org
Equal opportunities for minorities; affordable housing development, homeownership counseling, immigration services, housing rights
Christopher Kui, Executive Director

Berkshire Farm Center & Services for Youth
13640 Route 22, Canaan, NY 12029
518-781-4567 ext2211 Fax: 518-781-4577
e-mail: dharrington@berkshirefarm.org
Web site: www.berkshirefarm.org
Multi-function agency for troubled youth & families
Harith Flagg, Chief Executive Officer

Big Brothers Big Sisters of NYC
223 East 30th St, New York, NY 10016
212-686-2042 Fax: 212-779-1221
e-mail: help@bigsnyc.org
Web site: www.bigsnyc.org
Providing disadvantaged youth with one-to-one, long-term relationships with a trained volunteer
Hector Batista, Executive Director

CIDNY - Queens
137-02A Northern Blvd, Flushing, NY 11354
646-442-1520 or TTY 718-886-0427 Fax: 718-886-0428
Web site: www.cidny.org
Rights & advocacy for the disabled
Susan Dooha, Executive Director

CASA - Advocates for Children of NYS
911 Central Avenue, Suite 117, Albany, NY 12206
518-426-5354 Fax: 518-426-5348
e-mail: mail@casanys.org
Web site: www.casanys.org
Volunteer advocates appointed by family court judges to represent abused & neglected children in court
Penny Page, Executive Director

Camp Venture Inc
25 Smith Street, Suite 510, Nanuet, NY 10954
845-624-3860 Fax: 845-624-7064
Web site: www.campventure.org
Services for the developmentally disabled
Daniel Lukens, Executive Director

Catholic Charities of Onondaga County
1654 W Onondaga St, Syracuse, NY 13204
315-424-1800 Fax: 315-424-8262
Web site: www.ccoc.us
Eleanor Carr, Director, Elder Abuse Prevention Program

Center for Anti-Violence Education Inc
327 7th St, 2nd Fl, Brooklyn, NY 11215
718-788-1775 Fax: 718-499-2284
e-mail: info@caeny.org
Web site: www.caeny.org
Self-defense & violence prevention education for children, youth, women & LGBT people
Tracy Hobson, Executive Director

Center for Family & Youth (The)
135 Ontario Street, PO Box 6240, Albany, NY 12206
518-462-4585 or 518-462-5366 Fax: 518-427-1465
e-mail: dbosworth@ctrfamyouth.com
Child welfare services, Project STRIVE
David A Bosworth, Executive Director

Center for Independence of the Disabled in NY (CIDNY)
841 Broadway, Ste 301, New York, NY 10003
212-674-2300 or TTY: 212-674-5619 Fax: 212-254-5953
Web site: www.cidny.org
Rights & advocacy for the disabled
Susan Dooha, Executive Director

Center for Urban Community Services
198 E 121st Street, New York, NY 10035
212-801-3300 Fax: 212-635-2191
e-mail: cucsinfo@cucs.org
Web site: www.cucs.org
Services to the homeless & low-income individuals, training & technical assistance to not-for-profit organizations
Anthony Hannigan, Executive Director

Center for Disability Services
314 S Manning Blvd, Albany, NY 12208
518-437-5700 Fax: 518-437-5705
Web site: www.cfdsny.org
Medical & dental services; education, adult & residential services & service coordination
Alan Krafchin, President & Chief Executive Officer

Cerebral Palsy Associations of New York State
330 West 34th Street, 15th Floor, New York, NY 10001-2488
212-947-5770 Fax: 212-594-4538
e-mail: information@cpofnys.org
Web site: www.cpofnys.org
Serves individuals with cerebral palsy & other significant disabilities as well as their families through advocacy, technical assistance, publications & networking events
Susan Constantino, President & Chief Executive Officer

Children's Aid Society (The)
105 E 22nd St, New York, NY 10010
212-949-4921 Fax: 212-460-5941
e-mail: pmoses@childrensaidsociety.org
Web site: www.childrensaidsociety.org
Child welfare, health, foster care/adoption, preventive services, community centers & public schools, camps
C Warren Moses, Chief Executive Officer

Children's Rights Inc
330 Seventh Ave, 4th Floor, New York, NY 10001
212-683-2210 Fax: 212-683-4015
e-mail: info@childrensrights.org
Web site: www.childrensrights.org
Advocacy & class action lawsuits on behalf of abused & neglected children
Marcia Robinson Lowry, Executive Director

Children's Village (The)
Echo Hills, Dobbs Ferry, NY 10522
914-693-0600 x1201 Fax: 914-674-9208
e-mail: jkohomban@childrensvillage.org
Web site: www.childrensvillage.org
Residential school, located 20 minutes outside of NYC. Treatment & prevention of behavioral problems for youth; residential & community-based services; mental health, education, employment & runaway shelter services
Jeremy Kohomban, PhD, President & Chief Executive Officer

Citizens' Committee for Children of New York Inc
14 Wall Street, Suite 4E, New York, NY 10005-2173
212-673-1800 Fax: 212-979-5063
e-mail: info@cccnewyork.org
Web site: www.cccnewyork.org
Public policy advocacy for children's rights & services; promoting improved quality of life for NYC children & families in need
Jennifer March, Executive Director

Coalition Against Domestic Violence, NYS
350 New Scotland Ave, Albany, NY 12208
518-482-5465 Fax: 518-482-3807
e-mail: vasquez@nyscadv.org
Web site: www.nyscadv.org
Jessica Vasquez, Executive Director

Coalition for Asian American Children & Families
50 Broad St, Rm 1701, New York, NY 10004
212-809-4675 Fax: 212-785-4601
e-mail: cacf@cacf.org
Web site: www.cacf.org
Advocacy for programs & policies supporting Asian American children & families; training & resources for service providers
Wayne H Ho, Executive Director

Coalition for the Homeless
129 Fulton St, 1st Flr, New York, NY 10038
212-776-2000 Fax: 212-964-1303
e-mail: info@cfthomeless.org
Web site: www.coalitionforthehomeless.org
Food, shelter, clothing assistance program, services for homeless New Yorkers
Mary Brosnahan Sullivan, Executive Director

Coalition of Animal Care Societies (The)
437 Old Albany Post Rd, Garrison, NY 10524
845-788-5070 Fax: 845-788-5071
e-mail: tzaleski@sprynet.com
Association of humane societies & animal welfare groups in NYS
Terence M Zaleski, Special Counsel

Coalition of Fathers & Families NY
PO Box 782, Clifton Park, NY 12065
518-383-8202
e-mail: fafny@fafny.org
Web site: www.fafny.org/fafnypac.htm
Working to keep fathers & families together
James Hays, President

Commission on Economic Opportunity for the Greater Capital Region
2331 Fifth Ave, Troy, NY 12180
518-272-6012 Fax: 518-272-0658
e-mail: kgordon@ceo-cap.org
Web site: www.ceo-cap.org
Preserve & advance the self-sufficiency, well-being & growth of individuals & families through education, guidance & resources
Karen E Gordon, Executive Director

Community Healthcare Network
79 Madison Avenue, Fl 6, New York, NY 10016-7802
212-366-4500 Fax: 212-463-8411
e-mail: cabate@chnnyc.org
Web site: www.chnnyc.org
Health & social services for low-income, ethnically diverse, medically underserved neighborhoods of NYC
Catherine Abate, President & Chief Executive Officer

Cornell Cooperative Extension, College of Human Ecology, Nutrition, Health
186 Martha Van Rensselaer Hall, Cornell University, Ithaca, NY 14853-4401
607-255-2247 Fax: 607-254-4403
e-mail: jas56@cornell.edu
Web site: www.cce.cornell.edu
Children, youth & family economic & social well-being
Josephine Swanson, Associate Director, Assistant Dean

Council of Community Services of NYS Inc
272 Broadway, Albany, NY 12204
518-434-9194 x103 Fax: 518-434-0392
e-mail: info@ccsnys.org
Web site: www.ccsnys.org
Build healthy, caring communities & human care delivery systems through a strong charitable nonprofit sector & quality community-based planning
Doug Sauer, Executive Director

Council of Family & Child Caring Agencies
254 West 31st Street, 5th Floor, New York, NY 10001
212-929-2626 Fax: 212-929-0870
e-mail: jpurcell@cofcca.org
Web site: www.cofcca.org
Child welfare services membership organization
Jim Purcell, Chief Executive Officer

EPIC-Every Person Influences Children Inc
1000 Main St, Buffalo, NY 14202
716-332-4100 Fax: 716-332-4101
Web site: www.epicforchildren.org
Uniting parents, teachers & community members to prevent child abuse & neglect, school dropout, juvenile crime, substance abuse & teenage pregnancy
Vito J Borrello, President

Early Care & Learning Council
230 Washington Ave Ext, Albany, NY 12203-5390
518-690-4217 Fax: 518-690-2887
e-mail: mbasloe@earlycareandlearning.org
Web site: www.earlycareandlearning.org
Advocacy & education for the development of accessible and affordable, quality child care services
Marsha Basloe, Executive Director

Offices and agencies generally appear in alphabetical order, except when specific order is requested by listee.

Education & Assistance Corp Inc
50 Clinton St, Ste 107, Hempstead, NY 11550
516-539-0150 Fax: 516-539-0160
e-mail: lelder@eacinc.org
Web site: www.eacinc.org
Rehabilitation for nonviolent offenders; advocacy, education & counseling programs for youth, elderly & families
Lance W Elder, President & Chief Executive Officer

Empire Justice Center
119 Washington Ave, Albany, NY 12210
518-462-6831 Fax: 518-462-6687
e-mail: nkrupski@empirejustice.org
Web site: www.empirejustice.org
Empire Justice protects and strengthens the legal rights of people in New York State who are poor, disabled or disenfranchised.
Anne Erickson, President & Chief Executive Officer

Family Planning Advocates of New York State
17 Elk St, Albany, NY 12207
518-436-8408 Fax: 518-436-0004
e-mail: info@fpaofnys.org
Web site: www.fpaofnys.org
Reproductive rights
JoAnn M Smith, President/Chief Executive Officer

Federation Employment & Guidance Service (FEGS) Inc
315 Hudson St, 9th Fl, New York, NY 10013
212-366-8400 Fax: 212-366-8441
e-mail: info@fegs.org
Web site: www.fegs.org
Diversified health & human services system to help individuals achieve their potential at work, at home, at school and in the community
Gail Magaliff, Chief Executive Officer

Federation of Protestant Welfare Agencies Inc
281 Park Ave South, New York, NY 10010
212-777-4800 x322 Fax: 212-673-4085
e-mail: fgoldman@fpwa.org
Web site: www.fpwa.org
Childcare & child welfare, HIV/AIDS, elderly, income security
Fatima Goldman, Executive Director

Filipino American Human Services Inc (FAHSI)
185-14 Hillside Ave, Jamaica, NY 11432
718-883-1295 Fax: 718-523-9606
e-mail: admin@fahsi.org
Web site: www.fahsi.org
FAHSI is a community-based, non-profit organization dedicated to serving the Filipino and Filipino American community of New York City, particularly, marginalized sections such as youth, women, recent immigrants, and the elderly.
Johanna Martinez LMSW, Executive Director

Fordham University, Graduate School of Social Service
113 West 60th Street, Lincoln Center, New York, NY 10023
212-636-6616 Fax: 212-636-7876
e-mail: vaughan@fordham.edu
Web site: www.fordham.edu
Social work education, clinical social work, administration, client centered management
Peter B Vaughan, Dean

Friends & Relatives of Institutionalized Aged Inc (FRIA)
18 John St, Suite 905, New York, NY 10038
212-732-5667 or 212-732-4455 Fax: 212-732-6945
e-mail: fria@fria.org
Web site: www.fria.org
Free bilingual telephone helpline for information assistance and complaints about nursing homes, assisted living and other long-term care issues.
Betti Weimersheimer, Executive Director

Green Chimneys School-Green Chimneys Children's Services Inc
400 Doansburg Rd, Box 719, Brewster, NY 10509
845-279-2995 x119 Fax: 845-279-3077
Web site: www.greenchimneys.org
Residential treatment programs for emotionally troubled children & youths; therapeutic/educational Farm & Wildlife Conservation Center programs; therapeutic day school program
Joseph A Whalen, Executive Director

Guide Dog Foundation for the Blind Inc
371 East Jericho Turnpike, Smithtown, NY 11787-2976
631-930-9000 or 800-548-4337 Fax: 631-930-9009
e-mail: info@guidedog.org
Web site: www.guidedog.org
Provide guide dogs without charge to sight-impaired persons seeking enhanced mobility & independence
Wells B Jones, Chief Executive Officer

HeartShare Human Services of New York, Roman Catholic Diocese of Brooklyn
12 MetroTech Center, 29th Floor, Brooklyn, NY 11201
718-422-HEART Fax: 718-522-4506
e-mail: info@heartshare.org
Web site: www.heartshare.org
Service for the developmentally disabled children & family services & programs for people with HIV/AIDS
William R Guarinello, President & Chief Executive Officer

Helen Keller Services for the Blind
57 Willoughby Street, Brooklyn, NY 11201
718-522-2122 Fax: 718-935-9463
e-mail: info@helenkeller.org
Web site: www.helenkeller.org
Preschool, rehabilitation, employment & senior services, low vision & braille library services
Deborah Rodriguez-Samuelson, Director of Communications & Development

Hispanic Federation
55 Exchange Place, 5th Floor, New York, NY 10005
212-233-8955 Fax: 212-233-8996
Web site: www.hispanicfederation.org
Technical assistance, capacity building, grantmaking & advocacy for Latino nonprofit service providers
Lillian Rodriguez Lopez, President

Hispanic Outreach Services
40 North Main Ave, 5th Floor, Albany, NY 12010
518-453-6655 Fax: 518-641-6830
e-mail: elaine.escobales@reda.org
Web site: www.hispanicoutreachservices.org
Social service, youth guidance, language translation & immigration assistance programs
Elaine Escobales, Executive Director

Hospice & Palliative Care Association of NYS Inc
2 Computer Drive West, Suite 105, Albany, NY 12205
518-446-1483 Fax: 518-446-1484
e-mail: info@hpcanys.org
Web site: www.hpcanys.org
Hospice & palliative care information & referral service; educational programs; clinical, psychosocial & bereavement issues
Kathy A McMahon, President & Chief Executive Officer

Housing Works Inc
57 Willoughby Street, Brooklyn, NY 11201
347-473-7400 Fax: 347-473-7464
Web site: www.housingworks.org
Housing, health care, advocacy, job training & support services for homeless NY residents with HIV or AIDS
Michael Kink, Statewide Advocacy Coordinator & Legislative Counsel

Humane Society of the United States, New York State
200 West 57th Street, Suite 705, New York, NY 10019
917-331-7187
Web site: www.humanesociety.org
Promotes humane treatment of animals; abuse & violence prevention; animal rescue & disaster preparedness
Brian Shapiro, State Director

Hunger Action Network of NYS (HANNYS)
275 State St, Albany, NY 12210
518-434-7371 Fax: 518-434-7390
e-mail: bhpham@hungeractionnys.org
Web site: www.hungeractionnys.org
Developing unified efforts to address the root causes of hunger & promote social justice
Bich Ha Pham, Executive Director

Hunter College, Brookdale Center for Healthy Aging and Longevity
425 E 25th St, New York, NY 10010
212-481-5420 or 212-481-4595 Fax: 212-481-3791
e-mail: mfahs@huntercuny.edu
Web site: www.brookdale.org
Policy research & development, training, publications & resources for institutions & community agencies
Marianne Fahs, Executive Director

Institute for Socio-Economic Studies
10 New King St, White Plains, NY 10604
914-686-7112 Fax: 914-686-0581
e-mail: info@socioeconomic.org
Web site: www.socioeconomic.org
Welfare reform, socioeconomic incentives, tax & healthcare reform
Leonard M Greene, President

Japanese American Social Services Inc
100 Gold St, Lower Level, New York, NY 10038
212-442-1541 Fax: 212-442-8627
e-mail: info@jassi.org
Web site: www.jassi.org
Bilingual/bicultural programs; assistance with government benefits, housing, immigration & legal rights
Margaret Fung, Executive Director

Korean Community Services of Metropolitan NY
149 West 24th St, 6th Fl, New York, NY 10011
212-463-9685 Fax: 212-463-8347
e-mail: kcskcsny.org
Web site: www.kcsny.org
Develop & deliver social services to support & assist members of the Korean & neighboring communities
Shin Son, Executive Director

NYS Bar Assn, Children & the Law Committee
Law Office of Anne Reynolds Copps
126 State St, 6th Fl, Albany, NY 12207
518-436-4170 Fax: 518-436-1456
e-mail: arcopps@nycap.rr.com
Anne Reynolds Copps, Chair

Lesbian, Gay, Bisexual & Transgender Community Ctr - Not For Profit
208 W 13th Street, New York, NY 10011-7702
212-620-7310 Fax: 212-924-2657
e-mail: info@gaycenter.org
Web site: www.gaycenter.org
Mental health counseling, out-patient chemical dependency treatment center, after-school youth services, HIV/AIDS services, advocacy, cultural programs, affordable meeting and conference services, and community-building.
Glennda Testone, Executive Director
Rob Wheeler, Director of Operations

Little Flower Children & Family Services
186 Joralemon St, Brooklyn, NY 11201-4326
718-875-3500 ext3650 or 631-929-6200 ext1123 Fax: 718-260-8863
e-mail: stupph@lfchild.org
Web site: www.littleflowerny.org
Foster care, adoption, child welfare, residential treatment services and residences for the developmentally disabled & day care; union free school district; corporate eldercare counseling services.
Hon. Herbert W. Stupp, Chief Executive Officer

Littman Krooks LLP
655 Third Ave, New York, NY 10017
212-490-2020 Fax: 212-490-2990
e-mail: bkrooks@littmankrooks.com
Web site: www.littmankrooks.com
Elder law and special needs planning
Bernard A Krooks, Partner

March of Dimes Birth Defects Foundation
1275 Mamaroneck Ave, White Plains, NY 10605
914-997-4641 Fax: 914-997-4662
e-mail: dstaples@marchofdimes.com
Web site: www.marchofdimes.com

New York Association for New Americans, Inc (NYANA)
2 Washington St, 9th Fl, New York, NY 10004-1102
212-425-2900 Fax: 212-344-1621
e-mail: jlazar@nyana.org
Web site: www.nyana.org
Social service referrals for immigrants
Joseph Lazar, CEO

NY Counseling Association Inc
PO Box 12636, Albany, NY 12212-2636
518-235-2026 Fax: 518-235-0910
e-mail: nycaoffice@nycounseling.org
Web site: www.nycounseling.org
Counseling professionals in education, mental health, career, employment, rehabilitation & adult development
Donald Newell, Executive Manager

NY Foundation for Senior Citizens Inc
11 Park Place, 14th Fl, New York, NY 10007-2801
212-962-7559 Fax: 212-227-2952
e-mail: nyfscinc@aol.com
Web site: www.nyfsc.org
Social services for seniors in New York City
Linda Hoffman, President

NYC Coalition Against Hunger
16 Beaver St, 3rd Fl, New York, NY 10004
212-825-0028 Fax: 212-825-0267
e-mail: jberg@nyccah.org
Web site: www.nyccah.org
Joel Berg, Executive Director

NYS Association of Area Agencies on Aging
272 Broadway, Albany, NY 12204-2717
518-449-7080 Fax: 518-449-7055
e-mail: office@nysaaaa.org
Web site: www.nysaaaa.org
Agencies working to enhance effectiveness of programs for older persons
Laura A Cameron, Executive Director

NYS Corps Collaboration
24 Century Hill Drive, Ste 200, Latham, NY 12110
518-470-4995 Fax: 518-783-3577
e-mail: info@nyscc.net
Web site: www.nyscc.net
Statewide youth service & conservation corps addressing society's unmet needs & buiding self-esteem, a sense of civic responsibility & leadership skills

Offices and agencies generally appear in alphabetical order, except when specific order is requested by listee.

Linda J Cohen, Executive Director

NYS Industries for the Disabled (NYSID) Inc
11 Columbia Circle Drive, Albany, NY 12203
518-463-9706 or 800-221-5994 Fax: 518-463-9708
e-mail: administrator@nysid.org
Web site: www.nysid.org
Business development through 'preferred source' purchasing to increase employment opportunities for people with disabilities
Ronald P Romano, President & Chief Executive Officer

National Association of Social Workers, NYS Chapter
188 Washington Ave, Albany, NY 12210-2304
518-463-4741 or 800-724-6279 Fax: 518-463-6446
e-mail: info@naswnys.org
Web site: www.naswnys.org
Professional development & specialized training for professional social workers; standards for social work practice; advocacy for policies, services & programs that promote social justice
Jacqueline Melecio, Assistant Executive Director

National Council of Jewish Women
53 W 23rd St, 6th Fl, New York, NY 10010
212-645-4048 Fax: 212-645-7466
e-mail: action@ncjw.org
Web site: www.ncjw.org
Human rights & social service advocacy & education
Phyllis Snyder, President

National Urban League Inc (The)
120 Wall St, New York, NY 10005
212-558-5300 Fax: 212-344-5332
e-mail: info@nul.org
Web site: www.nul.org
Community-based movement devoted to empowering African Americans to enter the economic & social mainstream
Michele M Moore, Senior Vice President Communications & Marketing

Nelson A Rockefeller Inst of Govt, Federalism Research Grp
411 State St, Albany, NY 12203-1003
518-443-5522 Fax: 518-443-5788
e-mail: gaist@rockinst.org
Web site: www.rockinst.org
State management systems for social service programs
Thomas L Gais, Co-Director

New York Association of Homes & Services for the Aging
150 State St, Ste 301, Albany, NY 12207-1698
518-449-2707 Fax: 518-455-8908
e-mail: cyoung@nyahsa.org
Web site: www.nyahsa.org
Long term care
Carl Young, President

New York Community Trust (The)
909 Third Avenue, 22nd Fl, New York, NY 10022
212-686-0010 Fax: 212-532-8528
e-mail: info@nycommunitytrust.org
Web site: www.nycommunitytrust.org
Administrators of philanthropic funds
Lorie A Slutsky, President/Director

New York Public Welfare Association
130 Washington Ave, Albany, NY 12210
518-465-9305 Fax: 518-465-5633
e-mail: nypwa@nycap.rr.com
Web site: www.nypwa.com
Partnership of local social services districts dedicated to improve the quality & effectiveness of social welfare policy
Sheila Harrigan, Executive Director

New York Society for the Deaf
161 William St, 11th Fl, New York, NY 10038
646-278-8172 or TTY: 646-278-8171 Fax: 212-777-5740
Web site: www.nysd.org
Ensure full & equal access to appropriate, comprehensive clinical, residential & support services for deaf & deaf-blind persons
Kathleen Cox, Executive Director

New York State Association of Family Service Agencies Inc
29 North Hamilton Street, Suite 112, Poughkeepsie, NY 12601
845-790-5900 Fax: 845-790-5922
e-mail: info@nysafsa.org
Web site: www.nysafsa.org
Provides a forum for the exchange of information on issues relevant to children and families.
Allan Thomas, Executive Director

New York State Catholic Conference
465 State St, Albany, NY 12203-1004
518-434-6195 Fax: 518-434-9796
e-mail: info@nyscatholic.org
Web site: www.nyscatholic.org
Identify, formulate & implement public policy objectives of the NYS Bishops in health, education, welfare, human & civil rights
Richard E Barnes, Executive Director

New York State Citizens' Coalition for Children Inc
410 East Upland Road, Ithaca, NY 14850-2551
607-272-0034 Fax: 607-272-0035
e-mail: office@nysccc.org
Web site: www.nysccc.org
Adoption & foster care advocacy
Judith Ashton, Executive Director

New York State Community Action Association
2 Charles Blvd, Guilderland, NY 12084
518-690-0491 Fax: 518-690-0498
e-mail: dan@nyscaaonline.org
Web site: www.nyscaaonline.org
Dedicated to the growth & education of community action agencies in NYS to sustain their efforts in advocating & improving the lives of low-income New Yorkers
Daniel Maskin, Chief Executive Officer

New York State Rehabilitation Association
155 Washington Ave, Suite 410, Albany, NY 12210
518-449-2976 Fax: 518-426-4329
e-mail: nysra@nyrehab.org
Web site: www.nyrehab.org
Political advocacy, education, communications, networking & referral services for people with disabilities
Jeff Wise, JD, President

New York Urban League
204 W 136th St, New York, NY 10030
212-926-8000 Fax: 212-283-2736
Web site: www.nyul.org
Social services, job training, education & advocacy
Darwin M Davis, President & Chief Executive Officer

Nonprofit Coordinating Committee of New York
1350 Broadway, Rm 1801, New York, NY 10018-7802
212-502-4191 Fax: 212-502-4189
e-mail: mclark@npccny.org
Web site: www.npccny.org
Advocacy & government activities monitoring for NYC nonprofits
Michael Clark, Executive Director/President

North Shore Animal League America
25 Lewyt Street, Port Washington, NY 11050
516-883-7900 x257 Fax: 516-944-5732
e-mail: webmaster@nsalamerica.org
Web site: www.nsalamerica.org
Rescue, care & adoption services for orphaned companion animals
Perry Fina, Director, Marketing

Planned Parenthood of NYC, Inc
26 Bleecker St, New York, NY 10012
212-274-7292 Fax: 212-274-7276
e-mail: carla.goldstein@ppnyc.org
Web site: www.ppnyc.org
Carla Goldstein, Vice President, Public Affairs

Prevent Child Abuse New York
33 Elk Street, 2nd Floor, Albany, NY 12207
518-445-1273 or 800-CHILDREN Fax: 518-436-5889
e-mail: info@preventchildabuseny.org
Web site: www.preventchildabuseny.org
Child abuse prevention advocacy, education, technical assistance
Christine Deyss, Executive Director

ProLiteracy Worldwide
1320 Jamesville Ave, Syracuse, NY 13210-4224
315-422-9121 Fax: 315-422-6369
e-mail: info@proliteracy.org
Web site: www.proliteracy.org
Sponsors educational programs & services to empower adults & families through the acquisition of literacy skills & practices
Rochelle A Cassella, Director, Corporate Communications

Public/Private Ventures
The Chanin Building, 122 East 42nd St, 42nd Fl, New York, NY 10168
212-822-2400 Fax: 212-949-0439
e-mail: kfaulhaber@ppv.org
Web site: www.ppv.org
A national nonprofit, nonpartisan organization that tackles critical challenges facing low-income communities by seeking out and designing innovatove programs, rigorously testing them, and promoting the solutions proven to work.
Sheila Maguire, VP, Labor Market Initiatives

Resource Center for Independent Living (RCIL)
401-409 Columbia St, PO Box 210, Utica, NY 13503-0210
315-797-4642 or TTY 315-797-5837 Fax: 315-797-4747
e-mail: burt.danovitz@rcil.com
Web site: www.rcil.com
Services & advocacy for the disabled; public information & community education and awareness.
Burt Danovitz, Executive Director

Roman Catholic Diocese of Albany, Catholic Charities
40 N Main Ave, Albany, NY 12203
518-453-6650 Fax: 518-453-6792
Web site: www.ccrcda.org
Social & human services assistance: housing, shelters, day care, counseling, transportation, health & emergency
Sister Maureen Joyce, Chief Executive Officer

Rural & Migrant Ministry Inc
PO Box 4757, Poughkeepsie, NY 12602
845-485-8627 Fax: 845-485-1963
e-mail: hope@ruralmigrantministry.org
Web site: www.ruralmigrantministry.org
Working to end poverty & increase self-determination, education & economic resources for migrant farmworkers & the rural poor
Richard Witt, Executive Director

PathStone Corporation
400 East Ave, Rochester, NY 14607
585-340-3365 Fax: 585-340-3357
e-mail: jlewis@pathstone.org
Web site: www.pathstone.org
Advance self-sufficiency of farm workers, low-income & other disenfranchised people & communities through advocacy & programs including training & employment, housing child development, health & safety, & home ownership
Jeffrey Lewis, Senior VP Planning & Research

Salvation Army, Empire State Division
PO Box 148, Syracuse, NY 13206-0148
315-434-1300 x310 Fax: 315-434-1399
Web site: www.salvationarmy.org
Donald Lance, Divisional Commander

Springbrook NY, Inc
2705 State Highway 28, Oneonta, NY 13820
607-286-7171 Fax: 607-286-7166
e-mail: kennedyp@springbrookny.org
Web site: www.springbrookny.org
Patricia E Kennedy, Executive Director

Center for Policy Research
Syracuse University, Maxwell School of Citizenship & Public Affairs
200 Eggers Hall, Syracuse, NY 13244-1020
315-443-3114 Fax: 315-443-1081
e-mail: ctrpol@syr.edu
Web site: www.maxwell.syr.edu
Education, healthcare, entrepreneurship policies, social welfare, income distribution & comparative social policies
Christine L Himes, Professor of Sociology, Director

United Jewish Appeal-Federation of Jewish Philanthropies of NY
130 East 59th Street, New York, NY 10022
212-980-1000 Fax: 518-463-1266
e-mail: contact@ujafedny.org
Web site: www.ujafedny.org
Cares for those in need, rescues those in harm's way, and renews and strengthens the Jewish people in New York, in Israel , and around the world.
Jerry Levin, President

United Neighborhood Houses - Not For Profit
70 W 36th St, 5th Fl, New York, NY 10018
212-967-0322 Fax: 212-967-0792
e-mail: nwackstein@unhny.org
Web site: www.unhny.org
Federation of NYC settlement houses that provides issue advocacy & management assistance for member agencies' social, educational & cultural programs
Nancy Wackstein, Executive Director

United Way of Central New York
518 James St, PO Box 2129, Syracuse, NY 13220-2227
315-428-2216
e-mail: ccollie@unitedway-cny.org
Web site: www.unitedway-cny.org
Fundraising & support to human & social services organizations
Craig E Collie, Vice President, Volunteer Resource Development

United Way of New York City
2 Park Ave, New York, NY 10016
212-251-2500 Fax: 212-696-1220
e-mail: lmandell@uwnyc.org
Web site: www.unitedwaynyc.org
Works with partners from all sectors to create, support, & execute strategic initiatives that seek to achieve measurable improvement in the lives of the city's most valuable residents and communities
Lawrence Mandell, President & Chief Executive Officer

Policy Areas

Upstate Homes for Children & Adults Inc
2705 State Hwy 28, Oneonta, NY 13820
607-286-7171 Fax: 607-286-7166
e-mail: kennedyp@upstatehome.org
Web site: www.upstatehome.org
Education/mental hygiene
Patricia E Kennedy, Executive Director

Welfare Research Inc
112 State St, Suite 1340, Albany, NY 12207
518-432-2563 Fax: 518-432-2564
e-mail: administration@welfareresearch.org
Web site: www.welfareresearch.org
Contract research in social service & related policy areas
Virginia Hayes Sibbison, Executive Director

World Hunger Year Inc
505 Eighth Ave, Suite 2100, New York, NY 10018-6582
212-629-8850 Fax: 212-465-9274
e-mail: why@worldhungeryear.org
Web site: www.worldhungeryear.org
Addresses root causes of hunger & poverty by promoting effective & innovative community-based solutions
Bill Ayres, Executive Director

YAI/National Institute for People with Disabilities
460 W 34th St, New York, NY 10001-2382
212-273-6110 or 866-2-YAI-LINK Fax: 212-947-7524
e-mail: jmlcares@yai.org
Web site: www.yai.org
Programs, services & advocacy for people with autism, mental retardation & other developmental disabilities of all ages, and their families; special education & early learning programs
Joel M Levy, Chief Executive Officer

Offices and agencies generally appear in alphabetical order, except when specific order is requested by listee.

TAXATION & REVENUE

NEW YORK STATE

GOVERNOR'S OFFICE

Governor's Office
Executive Chamber
State Capitol
Albany, NY 12224
518-474-8390 Fax: 518-474-1513
Web site: www.ny.gov

Governor:
Andrew M Cuomo 518-474-8390
Secretary to the Governor:
William Mulrow 518-474-4246
Counsel to the Governor:
Alphonso David 518-474-8343
Chief of Staff:
Melissa DeRosa . . . . 518-474-8418 or 212-681-4640
Director, Communications:
James Allen. . . . . 518-474-8418 or 212-681-4640

EXECUTIVE DEPARTMENTS AND RELATED AGENCIES

New York State Liquor Authority (Division of Alcoholic Beverage Control)
80 S Swan St
Ste 900
Albany, NY 12210-8002
518-474-3114 Fax: 518-402-4015
Web site: www.sla.ny.gov

317 Lenox Ave
New York, NY 10027
212-961-8300
Fax: 212-961-8299

Chair:
Vincent Bradley . . . . 212-961-8300 or 518-473-6559
Commissioner:
Kevin Kim . . . . 212-961-8300 or 518-473-6559
Counsel:
Jacqueline Flug 518-474-3114/fax: 518-402-2304

Administration
Secretary to the Authority (Acting):
Jacqueline Held. 518-473-6559
Deputy Commissioner, Administration:
Chad Loshbaugh 518-473-0365
Director, Public Affairs:
William Crowley . . . . 518-474-3114 or 518-474-4875
fax: 518-473-9565

Licensing & Enforcement

Albany (Zone II)
80 S Swan St, Ste 900, Albany, NY 12210-8002
CEO:
Kerri O'Brien 518-474-3114
Deputy Counsel:
Lisa Bonacci 518-474-3114
Director, Information Technology:
Michael Drake. 518-474-3114/fax: 518-473-7527

Buffalo (Zone III)
Iskalo Electric Tower, 535 Washington St, Ste 303, Buffalo, NY 14203
716-847-3035
Deputy Commissioner, Licensing:
David L Edmunds Jr. 716-847-3001
Supervising Beverage Control Investigator:
Gary Bartikofsky 716-847-3035

New York City (Zone I)
317 Lenox Avenue, New York, NY 10027
212-961-8385
Supervising Beverage Control Investigator:
Franklin Englander 212-961-8376
Deputy Chief Executive Officer:
Michael Jones 212-961-8300

Budget, Division of the
State Capitol
Albany, NY 12224
518-473-3885 Fax: 518-474-9041
Web site: www.budget.ny.gov

Director:
Robert F Mujica 518-474-2300
Deputy Director:
Sandra Beattie 518-474-6497
Deputy Director:
David Lara 518-402-4246
Budget Services Head:
Vacant 518-474-6300
Public Protection Head:
Robert Barbato 518-474-4313
Press Officer:
Morris Peters. 518-473-3885
e-mail: dob.sm.press@budget.ny.gov

Law Department
120 Broadway
New York, NY 10271-0332
212-416-8000 or 800-771-7755
Web site: www.ag.ny.gov

State Capitol
Albany, NY 12224-0341
518-776-2000
Fax: 518-650-9401

Attorney General:
Eric T Schneiderman . . . . 212-416-8050 or 518-776-2000

Social Justice
Executive Deputy Attorney General:
Alvin L Bragg, Jr. 212-416-8075/fax: 212-416-8942

Charities Bureau
Bureau Chief:
James G Sheehan 212-416-8410

Economic Justice
Executive Deputy Attorney General:
Manisha Sheth. 212-416-8050

Internet Bureau
Bureau Chief:
Kathleen McGee 212-416-8433/fax: 212-416-8369

Investor Protection Bureau
Bureau Chief:
Chad Johnson 212 416 8225/fax: 212-416-8816

State Counsel
Chief Deputy Attorney General & Counsel:
Janet Sabel 212-416-8050
Chief Deputy Attorney General & Counsel:
Jason Brown 212-416-8050

Civil Recoveries Bureau
Bureau Chief:
John Cremo 518-776-2173/fax: 518-915-7731

Litigation Bureau
Bureau Chief:
Jeffrey Dvorin ....518-776-2300 or 212-416-8610

New York State Gaming Commission
One Broadway Center
PO Box 7500
Schenectady, NY 12301-7500
518-388-3300 Fax: 518-388-3423
Web site: www.gaming.ny.gov

Director:
Robert Williams 518-388-3400
General Counsel:
Ed Burns 518-388-3408
Director, Lottery Division:
Gardner Gurney 518-388-3406
Director, Communications:
Christy Calicchia................518-388-3415/fax: 518-388-3423
Director, Marketing:
Daniel J Martin 518-388-3430/fax: 518-388-3433

Regional Offices

Eastern Region
One Broadway Center, Suite 700, Schenectady, NY 12301
Contact:
Fred Chick.......................518-388-3428/fax: 518-388-3437

Central/Finger Lakes Regions
Rochester Office
First Federal Plaza Bldg, 28 E Main St, Rochester, NY 14614
Contact:
Vacant.......................585-246-4200/fax: 585-246-4201
Syracuse Office
Deys Centennial Bldg, 401 S Salina St, Syracuse, NY 13202
Contact:
Robin Sywulski 315-448-4300/fax: 315-448-4313

Hudson Valley Region
18 Westage Drive, Ste 6, Fishkill, NY 12524
Contact:
Georgene Perlman...............845-897-2412/fax: 845-897-3528

Long Island Region
1000 Zeckendorf Blvd, Garden City, NY 11530
Contact:
Jim Benoit........................516-222-8260/fax: 516-222-8279

New York City Region
15 Beaver St, New York, NY 10004
Contact:
Thomas Breig 646-486-6100/fax: 646-486-6177

Western Region
165 Genesse St, Buffalo, NY 14203
Contact:
Doug Bautz 716-847-3469/fax: 716-847-3479

Gaming Commission
Executive Director:
Robert Williams 518-388-3400

Communications:
Christy Calicchia 518-388-3415

Real Property Tax Services, Office of
WA Harriman State Campus
Bldg. 8A
Albany, NY 12227
518-457-7377 or 518-591-5232
e-mail: nysorps@orps.state.ny.us
Web site: www.tax.ny.gov/about/orpts

Acting Secretary of the Board & Assistant Deputy Commissioner:
Susan Savage 518-474-6742
State Board Member:
Darlene Maloney.....................................518-474-3793
e-mail: darlene.maloney@tax.ny.gov
State Board Member (Chair):
Matthew Rand..518-474-3793
State Board Member:
John M. Bacheller....................................518-474-3793
e-mail: geoffrey.gloak@orps.state.ny.us
State Board Member:
Edgar A King 518-474-3793
e-mail: geoffrey.gloak@orps.state.ny.us

Albany (Northern Region)
WA Harriman State Campus, Bldg. 8A, Albany, NY 12227
Regional Director:
Robert Aiken....................518-486-4403/fax: 518-435-8593
e-mail: orpts.northern@tax.ny.gov

Batavia (Western Region)
Genesee County Bldg 2, 3837 W Main Rd, Batavia, NY 14020
Regional Director:
Christine Bannister 585-343-4363/fax: 585-435-8598
e-mail: orpts.western@tax.ny.gov

Long Island Satellite Office
250 Veterans Memorial Hgwy, Rm 4A-6, Hauppauge, NY 11788
Manager:
Steve Hartnett 631-595-4071/fax: 518-435-8572
e-mail: orpts.southern@tax.ny.gov

South
44 S. Broadway, 6th Floor, White Plains, NY 10601
Regional Director:
John Wolham 914-215-6300/fax: 518-435-8498
e-mail: orpts.southern@tax.ny.gov

Ray Brook Satellite Office
884 NYS Rte 86, PO Box 309, Ray Brook, NY 12977
Regional Director:
Robert Aiken....................518-891-1780/fax: 518-435-8593
e-mail: orpts.raybrook@tax.ny.gov

Syracuse (Central Region)
333 E. Washington ST, Syracuse, NY 13202
Regional Director:
Teresa Frank 315-471-2347/fax: 518-435-8583
e-mail: orpts.central@tax.ny.gov

Tax Appeals, Division of
Agency Building 1
Empire State Plaza
Albany, NY 12223
518-266-3000 Fax: 518-271-0886
e-mail: nysdota@dta.ny.gov
Web site: www.dta.ny.gov

Offices and agencies generally appear in alphabetical order, except when specific order is requested by listee.

Tax Appeals Tribunal
President & Commissioner:
Roberta Moseley 518-266-3050
Commissioner:
Charles H Nesbitt 518-266-3050
Commissioner:
James H Tully Jr 518-266-3050
Counsel:
Timothy J Alston 518-266-3052
Secretary to the Tribunal:
Jean A McDonnell 518-266-3036

Administrative Law Judges & Officers
Supervising Administrative Law Judge:
Daniel J Ranalli 518-266-3000
Presiding Officer:
Alexander F Chu-Fong 518-266-3000

Taxation & Finance Department
State Campus
Bldg 9, Rm 227
Albany, NY 12227
518-457-4242 Fax: 518-457-2486
Web site: www.tax.ny.gov

Commissioner:
Jerry Boone 518-457-2244
Executive Deputy Commissioner:
Nonie Manion 518-457-7358
Deputy Commissioner & Counsel:
Amanda Hiller 518-457-3746/fax: 518-457-8247
Director, Conciliation & Mediation Services:
Kevin Law 518-485-8063
Director, Executive Correspondence & Legislative Affairs:
Maryann Tucker 518-457-2398
Director, Public Information:
Geoffrey Gloak 518-457-7377

Office of Processing & Taxpayer Services (OPTS)
Deputy Commissioner:
Edward Chaszczewski 518-457-1000

Human Resources Management
Director:
Gina Lysyczyn 518-457-2786

Operations Support Bureau
Director:
Lisa Negus 518-457-4250

Office of Budget & Management Analysis
Chief Financial Officer:
Eric Mostert 518-485-5080
Director:
Eric Mostert 518-457-9559

Planning & Management Analysis Bureau
Director:
Mary Ellen Nagengast 518-457-8660

Office of Information Technology Services
Chief Information Officer:
Daniel Chan 518-292-7808

Office of Processing & Taxpayer Services
Director:
Helen Pelersi 518-591-1944

Office of State Treasury
Deputy Commissioner & Treasurer:
Aida Brewer 518-474-4250/fax: 518-402-4118

Office of Criminal Enforcement
Deputy Commissioner:
Letizia Tagliaferro 518-457-9692

Audit Division
Director, Tax Audits:
Joe Carzo 518-451-8910

Collections & Civil Enforcement
Director:
Patricia Coneys 518-591-1980

Office of Tax Policy Analysis
Deputy Commissioner:
Robert D Plattner 518-457-4357

CORPORATIONS, AUTHORITIES AND COMMISSIONS

New York State Financial Control Board
123 William St
23rd Fl
New York, NY 10038-3804
212-417-5046 Fax: 212-417-5055
e-mail: nysfcb@fcb.state.ny.us
Web site: www.fcb.state.ny.us

Acting Executive Director:
Jeffrey Sommer 212-417-5066
Deputy Director, Expenditure & Covered Organization Analysis:
Dennis DeLisle 212-417-5069
Deputy Director, Finance & Capital Analysis:
Jewel A. Douglas
Acting Deputy Director, Economic & Revenue Analysis:
Martin Fischman 212-417-5068
Associate Director, Administration:
Mattie W Taylor 212-417-5053

NEW YORK STATE LEGISLATURE

See Legislative Branch in Section 1 for additional Standing Committee and Subcommittee information.

Assembly Standing Committees

Racing & Wagering
Chair:
James Gary Pretlow (D) 518-455-5291
Ranking Minority Member:
Andrew Garbarino (R) 518-455-4611

Real Property Taxation
Chair:
Sandra R Galef (D) 518-455-5348
Ranking Minority Member:
Kieran Michael Lalor 518-455-5725

Ways & Means
Chair:
Herman D Farrell, Jr (D) 518-455-5491
Ranking Minority Member:
Bob Oaks (R) 518-455-5655

Senate Standing Committees

Finance
Chair:
Catharine M Young (R) 518-455-3563
Ranking Minority Member:
Liz Krueger (D) 518-455-2297

Offices and agencies generally appear in alphabetical order, except when specific order is requested by listee.

Racing, Gaming & Wagering
Chair:
John J Bonacic (R) 518-455-3181
Ranking Minority Member:
Joseph Addabbo, Jr. (D) 518-455-2322

U.S. GOVERNMENT

EXECUTIVE DEPARTMENTS AND RELATED AGENCIES

US Department of Homeland Security (DHS)
Web site: www.dhs.gov

Bureau of Immigration & Customs Enforcement (ICE)
Web site: www.ice.gov

New York District Office
601 W 26th St, Ste 700, New York, NY 10001
Special Agent-in-Charge:
Andrew M. McLees 646-230-3200
Albany Sub Office
1 Clinton Avenue, #746, Albany, NY 12207-2354
Group Supervisor:
LeRoy Tario 518-220-2100
Resident Agent-in-Charge:
Jack McQuade 518-220-2100

Customs & Border Protection (CBP)
202-354-1000
Web site: www.cbp.gov

Buffalo Field Office
300 Airborne Parkway, Suite 300, Buffalo, NY 14225
716-626-0400
Director:
James T. Engelman 716-626-0400 x201/fax: 716-626-9281
Albany, Port of
445 Broadway, Room 216, Albany, NY 12207
518-431-0200
Port Director:
Drew Wescott 518-431-0200/fax: 518-431-0203
Buffalo, Port of
Larkin at Exchange, 726 Exchange, Suite 400, Buffalo, NY 14210
716-843-8300
Area Port Director:
Joseph Wilson 716-843-8300
Champlain, Port of . . . . fax: 518-298-8395
237 W Service Rd, Champlain, NY 12919
518-298-8311 Fax: 518-298-8395
Area Port Director:
Christopher Perry 518-298-8347/fax: 518-298-8314
Ogdensburg, Port of
104 Bridge Approach Rd, Ogdensburg, NY 13669
Port Director:
William Mitchell 315-393-1390/fax: 315-393-7472

New York Field Office . . . . fax: 646-733-3245
1 Penn Plaza, 11th Fl, New York, NY 10119
646-733-3100 Fax: 646-733-3245
Director, Field Operations:
Susan T Mitchell 646-733-3100
Public Affairs Liaison:
John Saleh 646-733-3215
Field Counsel - New York
Director, New York Field Operations:
Robert Perez 646-733-3200
Laboratory Division
Director:
Tom Governo 973-368-1901

US Justice Department
Web site: www.usdoj.gov

Bureau of Alcohol, Tobacco, Firearms & Explosives
Web site: www.atf.gov

New York Field Division . . . . fax: 646-335-9061
Financial Square, 32 Old Slip, Suite 3500, New York, NY 10005
646-335-9060 Fax: 646-335-9061
Special Agent-in-Charge:
Delano Reid 646-335-9060
Public Information Officer:
Charles Mulham 646-335-9000

US Treasury Department
Web site: www.treasury.gov

Internal Revenue Service
Web site: www.irs.gov

Appeals Unit - Office of Directors
290 Broadway, 13th Fl, New York, NY 10007
Director, Appeals, Area 1 (Large Business & Specialty):
Richard Guevara 212-298-2270/fax: 212-298-2282
Director, Appeals, Area 1 (General):
Raymond Wolff 212-298-2400/fax: 212-298-2648

Criminal Investigation Unit - New York Field Office
Spec Agent-in-Chg:
Toni Weirauch

Large & Mid-Size Business Division (LMSB)
290 Broadway, 12th Fl, New York, NY 10007
Director, Financial Services:
Rosemary Sereti 212-298-2130/fax: 212-298-2124
Office of Chief Counsel LMSB Area 1 . . . . fax: 917-421-3937
33 Maiden Ln, 12th Fl, New York, NY 10038
Area Counsel:
Roland Barral 917-421-4667
Deputy Area Counsel:
Peter J Graziano 917-421-4632

Management Information Technology Services - Northeast Area
290 Broadway, 12th Fl, New York, NY 10007
Director, Information Technology:
Vacant 212-298-2050/fax: 212-298-2595

Office of Chief Counsel
33 Maiden Ln, 14th Fl, New York, NY 10038
Area Counsel for SBSE & W & I:
Frances Regan 917-421-4737/fax: 917-421-3944
Associate Area Counsel for SBSE & W & I:
Janet F Appel 516-688-1707

Small Business & Self-Employed Division (SBSE)
New York SBSE Compliance Services
290 Broadway, 14th Fl, New York, NY 10007
Program Manager, Compliance Centers Document Matching Programs:
Shirley Greene 212-298-2001/fax: 212-298-2062
SBSE-Compliance Area 2/New York
290 Broadway, 7th Fl, New York, NY 10007
Director, Compliance Area 2:
Michael Donovan 212-436-1886/fax: 212-436-1046
SBSE-Taxpayer Education & Communication (TEC)
10 Metro Tech Center, 625 Fulton St, 6th Fl, Brooklyn, NY 11201
Area Director:
Ellen Murphy 718-488-2000/fax: 718-488-2077

Tax Exempt & Government Entities Div (TEGE)-Northeast Area
10 Metro Tech Center, 625 Fulton St, PO Box 029162, Brooklyn, NY 11201

Area Manager, Employee Plans:
Robert Henn 718-488-2014

TEGE Area Counsel's Office
1600 Stewart Ave, Ste 601, Westbury, NY 11590
Area Counsel:
Laurence Ziegler. 516-688-1701/fax: 516-688-1750

Taxpayer Advocate Service (TAS)

Andover Campus Service Center
310 Lowell St, Stop 120, Andover, MA 1812
Taxpayer Advocate for Upstate NY:
Vicki L Coss. 973-474-5549/fax: 978-247-9034

Brookhaven Campus Service Center
1040 Waverly Ave, Stop 02, Holtsville, NY 11742
Taxpayer Advocate for Downstate NY:
Ed Safrey 631-654-6686/fax: 631-447-4879

Brooklyn Office
2 Metro Tech Center, 100 Myrtle Avenue, 7th Floor, Brooklyn, NY 11201
Taxpayer Advocate:
Anita Kitson 718-834-2200/fax: 718-834-6545

Manhattan Office
290 Broadway, 5th Fl, New York, NY 10007
Taxpayer Advocate:
Peter L Gorga, Jr. 212-436-1011/fax: 212-436-1900

Office of Director, Area 1 (New York State & New England)
290 Broadway, 14th Fl, New York, NY 10007
Area Director:
Mary Ann Silvaggio 212-298-2015/fax: 212-298-2016

Upstate New York Office
Leo O'Brien Federal Bldg, Rm 354, 1 Clinton Sq, Albany, NY 12207
Taxpayer Advocate:
Georgeann Smith 518-427-5413/fax: 518-427-5494

Western New York State Office
201 Como Park Blvd, Buffalo, NY 14227-1416
Taxpayer Advocate:
William Wirth. 716-686-4850/fax: 716-686-4851

Wage & Investmnt Div-Stakehldr Partnership Ed & Comm (SPEC)

Albany Territory
1 Clinton Ave, Rm 600, Albany, NY 12207
Territory Manager:
Amy Albee. 518-427-5424

Area 1 Director's Office
135 High St, Hartford, CT 06103
Area Director:
Robert Nadeau 860-756-4566

Buffalo Territory
201 Como Park Blvd, Cheektowaga, NY 14227
Territory Manager:
Rick Pearl. 716-961-5123

New York Territory
290 Broadway, 7th Fl, New York, NY 10007
Territory Mgr:
Susan Quackenbush 212-436-1517

US Mint . . . . fax: 845-446-6258
Rte 218, PO Box 37, West Point, NY 10996
Fax: 845-446-6258
Web site: www.usmint.gov
Plant Manager:
David Motl 800-872-6468

U.S. CONGRESS

See U.S. Congress Chapter for additional Standing Committee and Subcommittee information.

House of Representatives Standing Committees

Appropriations
Chair:
Harold Rogers (R-KY) 202-225-4601
Ranking Member:
Nita M. Lowey (D-NY) 202-225-6506
New York Delegate:
Bill Owens (D) 202-225-4611
New York Delegate:
Jose E Serrano (D) 202-225-4361

Budget
Chair:
Paul Ryan (R-WI). 202-225-4601
Ranking Member:
Chris Van Hollen (D-MD) 202-225-5341
New York Delegate:
Hakeem Jeffries (D) 202-225-5936

Ways & Means
Chair:
Dave Camp (R-MI). 202-225-3561
Ranking Member:
Sander Levin (D-MI) 202-225-3880
New York Delegate:
Joseph Crowley (D) 202-225-3965
New York Delegate:
Tom Reed (R) 202-225-3161
New York Delegate:
Charles B. Rangel (D). 202-225-4365

Joint Senate & House Standing Committees

Joint Committee on Taxation
Chair:
Dave Camp (R-MI). 202-224-3561
Vice Chair:
Max Baucus (D-MT) 202-225-2651

Senate Standing Committees

Appropriations
Chair:
Barbara A. Mikulski (D-MD). 202-224-4654
Vice Chair:
Richard C. Shelby (R-AL) 202-224-5744

Budget
Chair:
Patty Murray (D-WA). 202-224-2621
Ranking Member:
Jeff Sessions (R-AL). 202-224-4124

Finance
Chair:
Max Baucus (R-MT). 202-224-2651
Ranking Member:
Orrin G. Hatch (R-UT) 202-224-5251

Subcommittee

Taxation & IRS Oversight
Chair:
Michael F. Bennet (D-CO) 202-224-5852
Ranking Member:
Michael B. Enzi (R-WY). 202-224-3424

Homeland Security & Governmental Affairs
Chair:
Thomas R. Carper (D-DE) 202-224-2441
Ranking Member:
Tom Coburn (R-OK) 202-224-5754

Offices and agencies generally appear in alphabetical order, except when specific order is requested by listee.

PRIVATE SECTOR

NYS Bar Assn, Pension Simplification Cmte
Alvin D Lurie PC
13 Country Club Drive, Larchmont, NY 10538
914-834-6725 Fax: 914-834-6725
e-mail: allurie@optonline.net
First recipient of Lifetime Employee Benefits Achievement Award of American Bar Association's Employee Benefits Committee of the Tax Section. 1st appointee of Assistant Commissioner in the Internal Revenue Service.
Alvin D Lurie, President

Association of Towns of the State of New York
150 State St, Albany, NY 12207
518-465-7933 Fax: 518-465-0724
e-mail: jhaber@nytowns.org
Web site: www.nytowns.org
Advocacy, education for local government
G Jeffrey Haber, Executive Director

Citizens Budget Commission
Two Penn Plaza, Fifth Floor, New York, NY 10121
212-279-2605 Fax: 212-868-4745
e-mail: cmb2@nyu.edu
Web site: www.cbcny.org
Nonpartisan, nonprofit civic organization devoted to influencing constructive change in the finances and services of New York City and New York State government
Charles Brecher, Consulting Research Director

Council of State Governments, Eastern Conference
100 Wall St, 20th Fl, New York, NY 10005
212-482-2320 Fax: 212-482-2344
e-mail: alan@csgeast.org
Web site: www.csgeast.org
Economic & fiscal programs
Alan V Sokolow, Regional Director

NYS Bar Assn, Tax Section
Sullivan & Cromwell LLP
125 Broad Street, New York, NY 10004
212-558-4000 Fax: 212-558-3588
Web site: www.sullcrom.com
David P Hariton, Chair

NYS Bar Assn, Trusts & Estates Law Section
Day Pitney LLP
7 Times Square, 41st & 42nd St, New York, NY 10036
212-297-5800 or 212-297-2468 Fax: 212-916-2940
e-mail: gwwhitaker@daypitney.com
Web site: www.daypitney.com
Domestic and international trusts and estates.
G Warren Whitaker,

Fiscal Policy Institute
1 Lear Jet Lane, Latham, NY 12110
518-786-3156
e-mail: mauro@fiscalpolicy.org
Web site: www.fiscalpolicy.org
Nonpartisan research & education; tax, budget, economic & related public policy issues
Frank Mauro, Executive Director

Community Bankers Assn of NY State, Accounting & Taxation Cmte
North Fork Bank
275 Broadhollow Road, Melville, NY 11747
631-844-1004
Web site: www.greenpoint.com
Aurelie Campbell, Co-Chair

Hawkins Delafield & Wood LLP
One Chase Manhattan Plaza, 43rd Floor, New York, NY 10005
212-820-9434 Fax: 212-820-9666
e-mail: jprogers@hawkins.com
Web site: www.hawkins.com
Tax law; public finance & municipal contracts
Joseph P Rogers, Jr, Counsel

Manhattan Institute, Center for Civic Innovation
52 Vanderbilt Ave, 2nd Fl, New York, NY 10017
212-599-7000 Fax: 212-599-3494
Web site: www.manhattan-institute.org
NY city & state tax, fiscal policy
Lindsay Young, Executive Director, Communications

Moody's Investors Service, Public Finance Group
99 Church St, New York, NY 10007
212-553-7780 Fax: 212-298-7113
e-mail: dennis.farrell@moodys.com
Web site: www.moodys.com
Municipal debt ratings & analysis
Dennis M Farrell, Group Managing Director

NYS Conference of Mayors & Municipal Officials
119 Washington Ave, Albany, NY 12210
518-463-1185 Fax: 518-463-1190
e-mail: info@nycom.org
Web site: www.nycom.org
Legislative advocacy for NYS cities & villages
Peter A Baynes, Executive Director

National Federation of Independent Business
100 State Street, Suite 440, Albany, NY 12207
518-434-1262 Fax: 518-426-8799
e-mail: mike.durant@nfib.org
Web site: www.nfib.com/new-york/
Small business advocacy; supporting pro-small business candidates at the state & federal levels
Michael P. Durant, State Director

Nelson A Rockefeller Institute of Government
411 State St, Albany, NY 12203-1003
518-443-5522 Fax: 518-443-5788
e-mail: nathanr@rockinst.org
Web site: www.rockinst.org
Management & finance of welfare, health & employment of state & local governments nationally & especially in NY
Richard P Nathan, Director

New York State Assessors' Association
PO Box 888, Middletown, NY 10940
845-344-0292 Fax: 845-343-8238
e-mail: nysaa@nyassessor.com
Web site: www.nyassessor.com
Real property tax issues
Thomas Frey, Executive Secretary

New York State Government Finance Officers Association Inc
126 State St, 5th Fl, Albany, NY 12207
518-465-1512 Fax: 518-434-4640
e-mail: info@nysgfoa.org
Web site: www.nysgfoa.org
Membership organization dedicated to the professional management of governmental resources
Brian Roulin CPA, President

New York State Society of Certified Public Accountants
3 Park Avenue, 18th Floor, New York, NY 10016-5991
212-719-8418 Fax: 212-719-3364
e-mail: doleary@nysscpa.org
Web site: www.nysscpa.org
Dennis O'Leary, Director, Government Relations

New York State Society of Enrolled Agents
Office of David J Silverman
866 UN Plaza, #415, New York, NY 10017
212-752-6983 Fax: 212-758-5478
e-mail: taxproblm@aol.com
Web site: www.nyssea.org
David J Silverman, Chair, Legislative/Government Relations Committee

Robert Schalkenbach Foundation
90 John Street, Suite 501, New York, NY 10038
212-683-6424 Fax: 212-683-6454
e-mail: msullivan@schalkenbach.org
Web site: www.schalkenbach.org
Land value taxation, real property & economic publications
Mark A Sullivan, Administrative Director

Urbanomics
115 Fifth Ave, 3rd Fl, New York, NY 10003
212-353-7462 Fax: 212-353-7494
e-mail: r.armstrong@urbanomics.org
Web site: www.urbanomics.org
Economic development planning studies, market studies, tax policy analyses, program evaluations, economic & demographic forecasts
Regina B Armstrong, Principal

Wachtell, Lipton, Rosen & Katz
51 W 52nd St, New York, NY 10019
212-403-1241 Fax: 212-403-2241
e-mail: pccanellos@wlrk.com
Web site: www.wlrk.com
Tax law
Peter C Canellos, Office of Counsel

TOURISM, ARTS & SPORTS

NEW YORK STATE

GOVERNOR'S OFFICE

Governor's Office
Executive Chamber
State Capitol
Albany, NY 12224
518-474-8390 Fax: 518-474-1513
Web site: www.ny.gov

Governor:
Andrew M Cuomo 518-474-8390
Secretary to the Governor:
William Mulrow 518-474-4246
Counsel to the Governor:
Alphonso David 518-474-8343
Director of Policy:
John Maggiore 518-408-2576
Chief of Staff:
Melissa DeRosa . . . . 518-474-8418 or 212-681-4640
Director, Communications:
James Allen. . . . . 518-474-8418 or 212-681-4640
First Assistant Counsel:
Sandi Toll 518-474-8434

EXECUTIVE DEPARTMENTS AND RELATED AGENCIES

Council on the Arts
300 Park Avenue South
10th Floor
New York, NY 10010
212-459-8800 or 800-510-0021
e-mail: info@arts.ny.gov
Web site: www.nysca.org

Chair:
Dr Barbaralee Diamonstein-Spielvogel 212-459-8800
Interim Executive Director:
Jackie Snyder 212-459-8808
e-mail: executive.director@arts.ny.gov
Deputy Executive Director, Programs:
Megan White. 212-459-8806
e-mail: megan.white@arts.ny.gov
Director, Agency Operations:
Brenda Brown. 212-459-8827
e-mail: brenda.brown@arts.ny.gov

Administrative Services
Director:
Tracy Hamilton-Thompson. 212-459-8822
e-mail: tracy.hamilton@arts.ny.gov
Purchasing:
Judy Evans 212-459-8817
e-mail: judy.evans@arts.ny.gov

Fiscal Management
Associate Auditor:
Edward Leung. 212-459-8813
e-mail: edward.leung@arts.ny.gov

Information Technology
Manager:
Lenn Ditman 212-459-8810
e-mail: lenn.ditman@arts.ny.gov

Program Staff

Architecture & Design/Facilities/Museum
Director:
Kristen Herron 212-459-8825
e-mail: kristin.herron@arts.ny.gov

Arts Education/Literature
Director:
Kathleen Masterson 212-459-8826
e-mail: kathleen.masterson@arts.ny.gov

Dance/Theatre/Individual Artists
Director:
Deborah Lim. 212-459-8820
e-mail: deborah.lim@arts.ny.gov

Electronic Media & Film/Visual Arts
Director:
Karen Helmerson 212-459-8824
e-mail: karen.helmerson@arts.ny.gov

Folk Arts/Music
Director:
Robert Baron 212-459-8821
e-mail: robert.baron@arts.ny.gov

Special Arts Services/Regional Economic Development
Director:
Susan Peirez 212-459-8829
e-mail: susan.peirez@arts.ny.gov
Director:
Leanne Tintori Wells 212-459-8816
e-mail: leanne.wells@arts.ny.gov

Education Department
State Education Bldg
89 Washington Ave
Albany, NY 12234
518-474-3852 Fax: 518-486-5631
Web site: www.nysed.gov

Commissioner & University President:
MaryEllen Elia 518-474-5844
Executive Deputy Commissioner:
Elizabeth Berlin 518-473-8381
General Counsel:
Robert Trautwein 518-474-6400
e-mail: legal@nysed.gov
Chief of Staff & Deputy Commissioner, Innovation:
Allison Armour-Garb 518-486-1713

Cultural Education Office
10A 33 Cultural Education Center, Madison Ave, Albany, NY 12230
Web site: www.oce.nysed.gov
Deputy Commissioner:
Vacant 518-474-5976/fax: 518-486-4850

State Museum Office
Director:
Mark Schaming. 518-474-5812
e-mail: mark.schaming@nysed.gov
Coordinator, Public Programs:
Nicole LaFountain 518-474-0575
e-mail: nicole.lafountain@nysed.gov
State Historian:
Vacant. 518-473-1299

Research and Collections
Director:
Dr. John P. Hart 518-474-5816
e-mail: john.hart@nysed.gov

Offices and agencies generally appear in alphabetical order, except when specific order is requested by listee.

Assistant Director:
Robert Daniels 518-474-5816

Empire State Development Corporation

633 Third Ave
New York, NY 10017
212-803-3100 Fax: 212-803-3131
Web site: www.esd.ny.gov

625 Broadway
Albany, NY 12207
518-292-5200

95 Perry Street
Ste 500
Buffalo, NY 14203
716-846-8200
Fax: 716-846-8260

President & CEO:
Howard Zemsky 212-803-3700
Public Affairs:
Kay Sarlin Wright 800-260-7313
e-mail: esdpressoffice@esd.ny.gov

General Services, Office of

Corning Tower, 41st Fl
Empire State Plaza
Albany, NY 12242
518-474-3899 Fax: 518-474-1546
Web site: www.ogs.ny.gov

Commissioner:
RoAnn Destito 518-474-5991
First Deputy Commissioner:
Karen B Tyler 518-473-6953
Director, Communications:
Heather Groll. 518-474-5987/fax: 518-474-3187
e-mail: heather.groll@ogs.ny.gov

Empire State's Convention & Cultural Events Office

Director:
Susan Cleary 518-474-0549
Manager, Convention Center:
Vacant 518-474-0558/fax: 518-473-2190
Director, Marketing:
Michael J Snyder 518-474-0538
Director, Curatorial & Tour Services:
Barbara Maggio 518-473-7521

Hudson River Valley Greenway

625 Broadway
4th Floor
Albany, NY 12207
518-473-3835 Fax: 518-473-4518
e-mail: hrvg@hudsongreenway.ny.gov
Web site: www.hudsongreenway.ny.gov

Greenway Conservancy for the Hudson River Valley

Acting Chair:
Sara Griffen. 518-473-3835
Executive Director (Acting):
Mark Castiglione. 518-473-3835

Hudson River Valley Greenway Communities Council

Board Chair:
Barnabas McHenry 518-473-3835
Executive Director (Acting):
Mark Castiglione. 518-473-3835

Parks, Recreation & Historic Preservation, NYS Office of

Empire State Plaza, Bldg 1
625 Broadway, 12207
Albany, NY 12238
518-486-0456 Fax: 518-486-2924
Web site: www.nysparks.com

Commissioner:
Rose Harvey 518-474-0443
Executive Deputy Commissioner:
Andrew Beers 518-474-0020
Deputy Commissioner, Finance & Administration:
Melinda Scott 518-474-0414
Deputy Commissioner, Historic Preservation:
Ruth Pierpont. 518-237-8643 x3269
Secretary:
Virginia Davis. 518-474-0443
Counsel:
Paul Laudato 518-474-0414
Deputy Commissioner, Natural Resources:
Tom Alworth. 518-474-0414
Park Police/Director, Law Enforcement:
Jay Kirschner. 518-474-4029/fax: 518-408-1032
Deputy Public Information Officer:
Dan Keefe 518-486-1868
Chief Public Information Officer:
Randy Simon. 518-486-1868

Concession Management

Director:
Harold Hagemann 518-486-2932/fax: 518-486-2372

Historic Preservation

Field Services
Peebles Island, PO Box 189, Waterford, NY 12118
Deputy Commissioner:
Ruth Pierpont 518-237-8643

Historic Sites Bureau
Peebles Island, Waterford, NY 12188
Acting Director:
Mark Peckham 518-237-8643

Marine & Recreational Vehicles

Director:
Brian Kempf 518-474-0445/fax: 518-408-1030

Regional Offices

Director, Regional Programs & Services:
Debra Keville 518-474-8081

Central Region . . . . .fax: 315-492-3277
6105 E Seneca Turnpike, Jamesville, NY 13078-9516
315-492-1756 Fax: 315-492-3277
Regional Director:
Robert Hiltbrand. 315-492-1756

Finger Lakes Region . . . . .fax: 607-387-3390
2221 Taughannock Park Rd, Box 1055, Trumansburg, NY 14886
607-387-7041 Fax: 607-387-3390
Regional Director:
Tim Joseph 607-387-7041

Long Island Region . . . . .fax: 631-422-0638
625 Belmont Ave, Box 247, West Babylon, NY 11702-0247
631-669-1000 Fax: 631-422-0638
Acting Regional Director:
George Gorman 631-321-3403

Policy Areas

Offices and agencies generally appear in alphabetical order, except when specific order is requested by listee.

Palisades Region . . . . fax: 845-786-2776
Administration Headquarters, Bear Mountain, NY 10911
Executive Director:
Jim Hall. 845-786-2701

Saratoga/Capital District Region . . . . fax: 518-584-5694
19 Roosevelt Drive, Saratoga Springs, NY 12866
518-584-2000 Fax: 518-584-5694
Regional Director:
Alane Ball Chinian 518-584-2000

Thousand Islands Region . . . . fax: 315-482-9413
Keewaydin State Park, 45165 NYS Rte 12, Alexandria Bay, NY 13607
315-482-2593 Fax: 315-482-9413
:
Kevin Kieff. 315-482-2593

Regional Offices-Downstate District

New York City Region . . . . fax: 212-961-4382
A C Powell State Ofc Bldg, 163 W 125th St, New York, NY 10027
212-866-3100 Fax: 212-961-4382
Regional Director:
Karen Phillips. 212-866-3100

Taconic Region. . . . . fax: 845-889-8217
9 Old Post Road, PO Box 308, Staatsburg, NY 12580
845-889-4100 Fax: 845-889-8217
Regional Director:
Linda Cooper 845-889-4100

Regional Offices-Western District

Allegany Region. . . . . fax: 716-354-6725
2373 Allegany State Park, Suite 3, Salamanca, NY 14779
716-354-9101 Fax: 716-354-6725
Acting Regional Director:
Mark Whitecomb 716-354-9101

Genesee Region . . . . fax: 585-493-5272
One Letchworth State Park, Castile, NY 14427-1124
585-493-3600 Fax: 585-493-5272
Regional Director:
Richard Parker 585-493-3600

Niagara Region & Western District Office. . . . . fax: 716-278-1725
Niagara Frontier Park Region, Prospect P, PO Box 1132, Niagara Falls, NY 14303-0132
716-278-1770 Fax: 716-278-1725
:
Mark Thomas 716-278-1770

Environmental Management

Director:
Pamela Otis 518-474-0409/fax: 518-474-7013

New York State Gaming Commission

PO Box 7500
Schenectady, NY 12301-7500
518-388-3300 or 518-388-3400 Fax: 518-347-3423
e-mail: info@gaming.ny.gov
Web site: www.gaming.ny.gov

Member:
Peter Moschetti 518-388-3400
Member:
Todd R Snyder 518-388-3400
Member:
Barry C Sample. 518-388-3400
Member:
John Poklemba 518-388-3400
Member:
John A Crotty 518-388-3400
Executive Director:
Robert Williams 518-388-3400
Public Information Officer:
Christy Calicchia. 518-388-3415

CORPORATIONS, AUTHORITIES AND COMMISSIONS

Adirondack Park Agency

1133 NYS Route 86
PO Box 99
Ray Brook, NY 12977
518-891-4050 Fax: 518-891-3938
Web site: www.apa.ny.gov

Chair:
Leilani Ulrich 518-891-4050
Executive Director:
Terry Martino 518-891-4050
Counsel:
James Townsend. 518-891-4050
Public Relations:
Keith McKeever 518-891-4050
e-mail: keith.mckeever@apa.ny.gov

Agriculture & NYS Horse Breeding Development Fund

1 Broadway Center
Suite 602
Schenectady, NY 12305
518-388-0178 Fax: 518-347-1483
e-mail: info@nysirestakes.com
Web site: www.nysirestakes.com

Acting Executive Director:
Ron Ochrym 518-388-0178
Counsel:
Mark Stuart 518-388-0178

Battery Park City Authority (Hugh L Carey)

One World Financial Center, 24th Fl
200 Liberty Street
New York, NY 10281
212-417-2000 Fax: 212-417-2001
e-mail: info.bpc@bpca.ny.gov
Web site: www.bpca.ny.gov

Chair & Chief Operating Officer:
Dennis Mehiel. 212-417-2000
President & Chief Operating Officer:
Shari Hyman 212-417-4205/fax: 212-417-4153
Vice Chair:
Donald Cappocia. 212-417-2000
Member:
Hector Batista 212-417-2000
Member:
Lester Petracca 212-417-2000
Member:
Martha J Gallo. 212-417-2000
VP External Relations:
Robin Forst 212-417-2276/fax: 212-417-2279
e-mail: robin.forst@bpca.ny.gov

Capital District Regional Off-Track Betting Corporation

510 Smith St
Schenectady, NY 12305
518-344-5266 or 800-292-2387 Fax: 518-370-5460
e-mail: customerservice@capitalotb.com
Web site: www.capitalotb.com

Offices and agencies generally appear in alphabetical order, except when specific order is requested by listee.

Chair:
Marcel Webb 518-344-5225
Board Secretary & Director:
F James Mumpton 518-344-5225
President & Chief Executive Officer:
John F Signor 518-344-5225
VP, Corporate Operations:
Tod Grenci 518-344-5408
VP, Legal Affairs/General Counsel:
Robert Hemsworth 518-344-5298
VP, Finance/Comptroller:
Nancy Priputen-Madrian 518-344-5233
VP, Human Resources:
Robert Dantz 518-344-5301

Catskill Off-Track Betting Corporation

Park Place
Box 3000
Pomona, NY 10970
845-362-0407 Fax: 845-362-0419
e-mail: otb@interbets.com; customerservice@interbets.com
Web site: www.interbets.com

President:
Donald J Groth 845-362-0400

Nassau Regional Off-Track Betting Corporation

139 Liberty Ave
Mineola, NY 11501
516-572-2800 Fax: 516-572-2840
e-mail: webmaster@nassauotb.com
Web site: www.nassauotb.com

President:
Joseph G Cairo, Jr. 516-572-2800
Director, Facilities Development:
John J Sparacio 516-572-2800

New York Convention Center Operating Corporation

655 W 34th St
New York, NY 10001-1188
212-216-2000 Fax: 212-216-2588
e-mail: moreinfo@javitscenter.com
Web site: www.javitscenter.com

Chair:
Henry Silverman 212-216-2130
President & Chief Operating Officer:
Alan Steel 212-216-2000
Senior Vice President & Chief Financial Officer:
John Menapace 212-216-2369
Senior Vice President & General Counsel:
Bradley Siciliano 212-216-2125
Senior Vice President, Sales & Marketing:
Doreen Guerin 212-216-2335

New York State Athletic Commission

123 William St
2nd Fl
New York, NY 10038
212-417-5700 Fax: 212-417-4987
e-mail: info@dos.ny.gov
Web site: www.dos.ny.gov/athletic

Chair:
Tom Hoover 212-417-5700

New York State Commission on the Restoration of the Capitol

Corning Tower, 31st Fl
Empire State Plaza
Albany, NY 12242
518-473-0341 Fax: 518-486-5720

Executive Director:
Andrea J Lazarski 518-473-0341
e-mail: andrea.lazarski@ogs.ny.gov

New York State Olympic Regional Development Authority

Olympic Center
2634 Main St
Lake Placid, NY 12946
518-523-1655 Fax: 518-523-9275
e-mail: info@orda.org
Web site: www.orda.org/corporate

President & CEO:
Ted Blazer 518-523-1655 x201
e-mail: blazer@orda.org
Vice President:
Jeffrey Byrne 518-523-1655 x203
e-mail: byrne@orda.org
Olympic Center Manager:
Dennis Allen 518-523-1655 x222
e-mail: allen@orda.org
Director, Corporate Development:
Jeff Potter 518-523-1655
e-mail: jpotter@orda.org
Director, Events:
Katie Million 518-523-1655 x212
e-mail: kmillion@orda.org
Director, Finance:
Padraig Power 518-523-1655 x217
e-mail: ppower@orda.org
Communications Manager:
Jon Lundin 518-523-1655
e-mail: jlundin@orda.org

New York State Thoroughbred Breeding & Development Fund Corporation

One Broadway Center
Suite 601
Schenectady, NY 12305
518-388-0174 Fax: 518-344-1235
e-mail: nybreds@nybreds.com
Web site: www.nybreds.com

Executive Director:
Tracy Egan 518-388-0174

New York State Thruway Authority

200 Southern Blvd
PO Box 189
Albany, NY 12201
518-436-2700 Fax: 518-436-2899
Web site: www.thruway.ny.gov

Chair:
Joanne M Mahoney 518-436-3000
Interim Executive Director:
Maria Lehman 518-436-2900
General Counsel:
Gordon Cuffy 518-436-2840

Offices and agencies generally appear in alphabetical order, except when specific order is requested by listee.

Policy Areas

Director, Media Relations & Communications:
Jennifer Givner 518-471-5300
CFO:
Matt Howard 518-436-2840
Director, Administrative Services:
John F. Barr 518-436-2700

New York State Canal Corporation

Web site: www.canals.ny.gov
Interim Executive Director:
Maria Lehman 518-436-3055/fax: 518-471-5023

Roosevelt Island Operating Corporation (RIOC)

591 Main St
Roosevelt Island, NY 10044
212-832-4540 Fax: 212-832-4582
e-mail: information@rioc.ny.gov
Web site: www.rioc.ny.gov

President/CEO:
Charlene M Indelicato 212-832-4540 x319
Director Island Operations:
Cyril Opperman 212-832-4583
e-mail: cyril.opperman@rioc.ny.gov
VP/General Counsel:
Donald D. Lewis 212-832-4540 x311
e-mail: donald.lewis@rioc.ny.gov
VP/Chief Financial Officer:
Frances Walton 212-832-4540 x350
Interim Director Public Safety:
Captain Estrella Suarez 212-832-4545
e-mail: keith.guerra@rioc.ny.gov

Suffolk Regional Off-Track Betting Corporation

425 Oser Ave
Ste 2
Hauppauge, NY 11788
631-853-1000 Fax: 631-853-1086
e-mail: customerservice@suffolkotb.com
Web site: www.suffolkotb.com

President/CEO:
Philip C. Nolan 631-853-1000
Vice President:
Anthony Pancella 631-853-1000
General Counsel:
James McManmon 631-853-1000
Director Governmental & Public Affairs:
Debbie Pfeiffer 631-853-1000

Western Regional Off-Track Betting Corp

8315 Park Road
Batavia, NY 14020
585-343-3750 Fax: 585-343-6873
e-mail: info@westernotb.com
Web site: www.westernotb.com

Chair:
Richard D Bianchi 585-343-3750
President & Chief Executive Officer:
Michael D Kane 585-343-3750
General Counsel:
Henry Wojtaszek 585-343-3750
Director, Video Gaming:
Mark Wolf 585-343-3750
Communications/Mutuels Manager:
James Haas 585-343-3750
Manager, Branch Operations:
Edward Merriman 585-343-3750
VP-Administration:
William R White 585-343-3750

CONVENTION & VISITORS BUREAUS

Convention Centers & Visitors Bureaus

Albany County Convention & Visitors Bureau . . fax: 518-434-0887
25 Quackenbush Sq, Albany, NY 12207
800-258-3582 or 518-434-1217 Fax: 518-434-0887
Web site: www.albany.org
President & CEO:
Michele Vennard 518-434-1217 x300/fax: 518-434-0887
e-mail: mvennard@albany.org

Greater Binghamton New York Convention and Visitors Bureau
49 Court St, 2nd Floor, PO Box 995, Binghamton, NY 13902
800-836-6740 or 607-772-8860
Web site: www.binghamtoncvb.com; www.visitbinghamton.org
President:
Lou Santoni
e-mail: lou@visitbinghamton.org

Buffalo Niagara Convention & Visitors Bureau
617 Main St, Ste 200, Buffalo, NY 14203
800-283-3256
e-mail: info@visitbuffaloniagara.com
Web site: www.visitbuffaloniagara.com
President & CEO:
Patrick Kaler 716-961-0200
e-mail: kaler@visitbuffaloniagara.com

Chautauqua County Visitors Bureau
Chautauqua Main Gate, Route 394, PO Box 1441, Chautauqua, NY 14722
866-908-4569
e-mail: info@tourchautauqua.com
Web site: www.tourchautauqua.com
Executive Director:
Andrew Nixon 716-357-4569/fax: 716-357-2284
e-mail: nixon@tourchautauqua.com

Greater Rochester Visitors Association
Visit Rochester, 45 East Ave, Ste 400, Rochester, NY 14604-2294
800-677-7282
Web site: www.visitrochester.com
Director:
Michael Hardy 585-279-8303
e-mail: michaelh@visitrochester.com

Ithaca/Tompkins County Convention & Visitors Bureau
904 E Shore Dr, Ithaca, NY 14850
800-28-ITHACA
e-mail: info@visitithaca.com
Web site: www.visitithaca.com
Director:
Fred Bonn 607-272-1313/fax: 607-272-7617
e-mail: fred@visitithaca.com

Lake Placid/Essex County Convention & Visitors Bureau
2608 Main St, Lake Placid, NY 12946
800-447-5224
Web site: www.lakeplacid.com
CEO:
James McKenna 518-523-2445/fax: 518-523-2605
e-mail: james@lakeplacid.com

Long Island Convention & Visitors Bureau & Sports Commission
330 Motor Pkwy, Ste 203, Hauppauge, NY 11788
877-386-6654
e-mail: tourism@discoverlongisland.com
Web site: www.discoverlongisland.com

Offices and agencies generally appear in alphabetical order, except when specific order is requested by listee.

President:
R Moke McGowan 631-951-3900 x305/fax: 631-951-3439
e-mail: mmcgowan@discoverlongisland.com

NYC & Company/Convention & Visitors Bureau fax: 212-245-5943
810 Seventh Ave, 3 Fl, New York, NY 10019
212-484-1200 Fax: 212-245-5943
e-mail: visitorinfo@nycgo.com
Web site: www.nycgo.com
CEO:
George Fertitta 212-484-1265/fax: 212-245-5943

Oneida County Convention & Visitors Bureau
Oneida Cty Welcome Ctr, PO Box 551, dba: Oneida County Tourism, Utica, NY 13503-0551
800-426-3132 or 888-999-6560
Web site: www.oneidacountycvb.com
President:
Kelly Blazosky 315-724-7221/fax: 315-724-7335
e-mail: kelly@oneidacountytourism.com

Ontario County/Finger Lakes Visitors Connection
25 Gorham St, Canandaigua, NY 14424
877-386-4669
e-mail: info@visitfingerlakes.com
Web site: www.visitfingerlakes.com
President:
Valerie Knoblauch 585-394-3915/fax: 585-394-4067

Saratoga Convention & Tourism Bureau
60 Railroad Pl, Ste 100, Saratoga Springs, NY 12866
855-424-6073
Web site: www.discoversaratoga.org
President:
Todd Garofano 518-584-1531 x106/fax: 518-584-2969
e-mail: todd@discoversaratoga.org

Steuben County Conference & Visitors Bureau
1 West Market St, Corning, NY 14830
866-946-3386
e-mail: sccvb@corningfingerlakes.com
Web site: www.corningfingerlakes.com
President:
Peggy Coleman 607-936-6544/fax: 607-936-6575
e-mail: pcoleman@corningfingerlakes.com

Sullivan County Visitors Association
100 Sullivan Avenue, Suite 2, PO Box 248, Ferndale, NY 12734
800-882-2287
Web site: www.scva.net
President & CEO:
Roberta Byron Lockwood 845-747-4449/fax: 845-747-4468
e-mail: sctoursim@scva.net

Syracuse Convention & Vistors Bureau
572 S Salina St, Syracuse, NY 13202
800-234-4797
e-mail: info@visitsyracuse.org
Web site: www.visitsyracuse.org
President:
David Holder 315-470-1911/fax: 315-471-8545
e-mail: dholder@visitsyracuse.org

Tourism Bureau of the Thousand Islands Region
Box 400, Alexandria Bay, NY 13607
800-847-5263
Web site: www.visit1000islands.com
Director of Tourism:
Gary DeYoung 315-482-2520/fax: 315-482-5906
e-mail: gary@visit1000islands.com

Westchester County Tourism & Film
148 Martine Ave, Ste 104, White Plains, NY 10601
800-833-9282
e-mail: tourism@westchestergov.com
Web site: www.thewestchesterway.com
Director of Tourism:
Natasha Caputo 914-995-8502
e-mail: ncaputo@visitwestchesterny.com

NEW YORK STATE LEGISLATURE

See Legislative Branch in Section 1 for additional Standing Committee and Subcommittee information.

Assembly Standing Committees

Racing & Wagering
Chair:
James Gary Pretlow (D) 518-455-5291
Ranking Minority Member:
Andrew Garbarino (R) 518-455-4611

Tourism, Parks, Arts & Sports Development
Chair:
Margaret Markey (D) 518-455-4755
Ranking Minority Member:
John Ceretto (R) 518-455-5284

Senate Standing Committees

Cultural Affairs, Tourism, Parks & Recreation
Chair:
Rich Funke (R) 518-455-2215
Ranking Minority Member:
Jose Serrano (D) 518-455-2795

Racing, Gaming & Wagering
Chair:
John J Bonacic (R) 518-455-3181
Ranking Minority Member:
Joseph Addabbo, Jr (D) 518-455-2322

U.S. GOVERNMENT

EXECUTIVE DEPARTMENTS AND RELATED AGENCIES

National Archives & Records Administration

Franklin D Roosevelt Presidential Library & Museum
4079 Albany Post Rd, Hyde Park, NY 12538
845-486-7770
Web site: www.fdrlibrary.marist.edu
Director:
Lynn A. Bassanese 845-486-7741
e-mail: lynn.bassanese@nara.gov

Smithsonian Institution

Cooper-Hewitt National Design Museum
2 East 91st St, New York, NY 10128
212-849-8400
Web site: www.cooperhewitt.org
Director:
Caroline Bauman 212-849-8400

National Museum of the American Indian-George Gustav Heye Center
US Custom House, One Bowling Green, New York, NY 10004
212-514-3700
Web site: www.nmai.si.edu

Policy Areas

GGHC Director:
Kevin Gouer 212-514-3700

US Department of the Interior
202-208-3100
e-mail: webteam@ios.doi.gov
Web site: www.doi.gov

Fish & Wildlife Service-Northeast Region . . . . . fax: 413-253-8308
300 Westgate Center Dr, Hadley, MA 01035-9589
413-253-8200 Fax: 413-253-8308
e-mail: northeast@fws.gov
Regional Director:
Wendi Weber 413-253-8300

National Park Service-Northeast Region
200 Chestnut St, US Custom House, 5th Floor, Philadelphia, PA 19106
Web site: www.nps.gov
Northeast Regional Director:
Dennis R. Reidenbach 215-597-5823
National Heritage Area Program Director:
Peter Samuel
e-mail: peter samuel@nps.gov

Fire Island National Seashore . . . . . fax: 631-289-3010
120 Laurel St, Patchogue, NY 11772-3596
631-289-4750 Fax: 631-289-3010
Web site: www.nps.gov/fiis/
Superintendent:
Chris Soller 631-289-4750/fax: 631-289-3010

Fort Stanwix National Monument . . . . . fax: 315-334-5051
112 E Park St, Rome, NY 13440
315-338-7730 Fax: 315-334-5051
Web site: www.nps.gov/fost/
Superintendent:
Deborah Conway 315-338-7730/fax: 315-334-5051

Gateway National Recreation Area
210 New York Ave, Staten Island, NY 10305
Web site: www.nps.gov/gate
General Superintendent:
Linda Canzanelli 718-354-4606/fax: 718-354-4764
Jamaica Bay Unit
Coordinator:
Dave Taft 718-338-3379
Sandy Hook Unit
Coordinator:
Pete McCarthy 732-872-5970
Staten Island Unit
Coordinator:
Brian Feeney 718-354-6970

Manhattan Sites
26 Wall St, New York, NY 10005
212-668-5180
Web site: www.nps.gov/masi
Commissioner:
Maria Burtes 212-668-2322

Martin Van Buren National Historic Site . . . . . fax: 518-758-6986
1013 Old Post Rd, Kinderhook, NY 12106
518-758-9689 Fax: 518-758-6986
Web site: www.nps.gov/mava
Superintendent:
Daniel J Dattilio 518-758-9689/fax: 518-758-6986

Roosevelt-Vanderbilt National Historic Sites
4097 Albany Post Rd, Hyde Park, NY 12538
845-229-9115 x. 2010
Web site: www.nps.gov/hofr
Superintendent:
Sarah Olson 845-229-9115/fax: 845-229-0739

Sagamore Hill National Historic Site . . . . . fax: 516-922-4792
20 Sagamore Hill Road, Oyster Bay, NY 11771
516-922-4788 Fax: 516-922-4792
Web site: www.nps.gov/sahi
Superintendent:
Tom Ross 516-922-4788/fax: 516-922-4792

Saratoga National Historical Park . . . . . fax: 518-664-3349
648 Rt 32, Stillwater, NY 12170
518-664-9821 X224 Fax: 518-664-3349
Web site: www.nps.gov/sara
Superintendent:
Joe Finan . . . . . 518-664-9821 ext 224/fax: 518-664-3349

Statue of Liberty National Monument & Ellis Island
Liberty Island, New York, NY 10004
TTY: 212-363-3211 or 212-363-3200
Web site: www.nps.gov/stli/
Superintendent:
David Luchsinger 212-363-3200

Theodore Roosevelt Inaugural National Historic Site fax: 716-884-0330
641 Delaware Ave, Buffalo, NY 14202
716-884-0095 Fax: 716-884-0330
Web site: www.nps.gov/thri/
Superintendent:
Molly Quackenbush 716-884-0095/fax: 716-884-0330

Women's Rights National Historical Park . . . . . fax: 315-568-2141
136 Fall St, Seneca Falls, NY 13148
315-568-2991 Fax: 315-568-2141
Web site: www.nps.gov/wori
Superintendent:
Tammy Duchesne 315-568-2991/fax: 315-568-2141

U.S. CONGRESS

See U.S. Congress Chapter for additional Standing Committee and Subcommittee information.

House of Representatives Standing Committees

Natural Resources
Chair:
Doc Hastings (R-WA) 202-225-5816
Ranking Minority Member:
Edward J. Markey (D-MA) 202-225-2836

Subcommittee
Public Lands & Environmental Regulations
Chair:
Rob Bishop (R-UT) 202-225-0453
Ranking Minority Member:
Raul M. Grijalva (D-AZ) 202-225-2435

Senate Standing Committees

Energy & Natural Resources
Chair:
Ron Wyden (D-OR) 202-224-5244
Ranking Minority Member:
Lisa Murkowski (R-AK) 202-224-6665

Subcommittees
National Parks
Chair:
Mark Udall (D-CO) 202-224-4971
Public Lands, Forests & Mining
Chair:
Joe Manchin (D-WV) 202-224-3954

Ranking Minority Member:
John Barrasso (R-WY) 202-224-6441

PRIVATE SECTOR

AAA Northway
1626 Union St, Schenectady, NY 12309
518-374-4575 Fax: 518-374-3140
Web site: www.aaanorthway.com
Capital region membership, travel & touring sales & services
Eric Stigberg, Marketing, Public & Government Affairs Manager

AAA Western and Central NY
100 International Dr, Buffalo, NY 14221
716-626-3225 Fax: 716-631-5925
e-mail: wsmith@nyaaa.com
Web site: www.AAA.com
Wallace Smith, Vice President

Adirondack Lakes Center for the Arts
Rte 28, PO Box 205, Blue Mountain Lake, NY 12812-0205
518-352-7715 Fax: 518-352-7333
e-mail: alca@frontiernet.net
Web site: www.adk-arts.org
Multi/Arts Center
Stephen Svoboda, Executive Director

Adirondack/Pine Hill/NY Trailways
499 Hurley Ave, Hurley, NY 12443-5119
845-339-4230 Fax: 845-853-7035
e-mail: info@trailwaysny.com
Web site: www.trailwaysny.com
Tour & charter service
Eugene J Berardi, Jr, President

Alliance for the Arts
330 W 42nd St, Ste 1701, New York, NY 10036
212-947-6340 Fax: 212-947-6416
e-mail: info@allianceforarts.org
Web site: www.allianceforarts.org
Advocacy, promotion, research, information, referrals & publications
Randall Bourscheidt, President

Alliance of Resident Theatres/New York (ART/New York)
520 Eighth Ave, Ste 319, New York, NY 10018
212-244-6667 Fax: 212-714-1918
Web site: www.art-newyork.org
Services & advocacy for New York City's not-for-profit theatre community
Virginia P Louloudes, Executive Director

American Museum of Natural History
Central Park West at 79th St, New York, NY 10024-5192
212-769-5100 Fax: 212-769-5018
e-mail: info@amnh.org
Web site: www.amnh.org
Education, exhibition & scientific research
Ellen V Futter, President

Art & Science Collaborations Inc
130 East End Ave 1A, New York, NY 10028
505-988-2994
e-mail: asci@asci.org
Web site: www.asci.org
Raising public awareness of art & artists using science & technology to explore new forms of creative expression
Cynthia Pannucci, Director

ArtsConnection Inc (The)
520 8th Ave, #321, New York, NY 10018
212-302-7433 Fax: 212-302-1132
e-mail: artsconnection@artsconnection.org
Web site: www.artsconnection.org
Arts-in-education programming & training for children, teachers & artists
Steven Tennen, Executive Director

Associated Musicians of Greater New York, Local 802 AFM, AFL-CIO
322 West 48th St, 5th Fl, New York, NY 10036
212-245-4802 Fax: 212-245-6255
e-mail: pmolloy@local802afm.org
Web site: www.local802afm.org
Paul Molloy, Political/Public Relations Director

Association of Independent Video & Filmmakers (AIVF), (The)
304 Hudson St, 6th Fl, New York, NY 10013
212-807-1400 Fax: 212-463-8519
e-mail: info@aivf.org
Web site: www.aivf.org
Membership service organization for independent producers & filmmakers
Beni Matias, Executive Director

Automobile Club of New York
1415 Kellum Place, Garden City, NY 11530
516-873-2252 Fax: 516-873-2375
Web site: www.aaany.com
Dennis J Crossley, President

Brooklyn Botanic Garden
1000 Washington Ave, Brooklyn, NY 11225-1009
718-623-7200 Fax: 718-857-2430
Web site: www.bbg.org
Comprehensive study of plant biodiversity in metropolitan New York; home gardener's resource center
Scot Medbury, President & CEO

Brooklyn Museum of Art
200 Eastern Pkwy, Brooklyn, NY 11238
718-638-5000 Fax: 718-501-6136
Web site: www.brooklynmuseum.org
Schawannah Wright, Manager, Community Involvement

Buffalo Bills
One Bills Drive, Orchard Park, NY 14127
716-648-1800 x8701 Fax: 716-648-3202
Web site: www.buffalobills.com
Scott Berchtold, Vice President-Communications

Buffalo Sabres
One Seymour H Knox III Plz, Buffalo, NY 14203
716-855-4100 x526 Fax: 716-855-4110
e-mail: michael.gilbert@sabres.com
Web site: www.sabres.com
Michael Gilbert, Director Public Relations

Buffalo Trotting Association Inc
5600 McKinley Parkway, Hamburg, NY 14075
716-649-1280 Fax: 716-649-0033
e-mail: mangoj@buffaloraceway.com
Web site: www.buffaloraceway.com
Harness horse racing
James Mango, General Manager

CUNY New York City College of Technology, Hospitality Mgmt
300 Jay St, Room 220, Brooklyn, NY 11201-2983
718-260-5630 Fax: 718-260-5997
Web site: www.nyct.cuny.edu
Hospitality & food service management; tourism
Jerry Van Loon, Professor & Chair

Campground Owners of New York
1 Grove Street, Suite 200, Pittsford, NY 14534
585-586-4360 Fax: 585-586-4360
e-mail: cony@frontiernet.net
Web site: www.nycampgrounds.com
Donald G Bennett Jr, Executive Administrator

Coalition of Living Museums
1000 Washington Ave, Brooklyn, NY 11225
718-623-7225 or 718-623-7373 Fax: 718-857-2430
e-mail: loiscarswell@bbg.org
Web site: www.livingmuseums.org
Advocacy organization for living museums (zoos, botanical gardens, aquaria, arboreta & nature centers) in NYS
Lois Carswell, Chair, Steering Committee

Cold Spring Harbor Fish Hatchery & Aquarium
1660 Route 25A, Cold Spring Harbor, NY 11724
516-692-6768 Fax: 516-692-6769
e-mail: cshfha@optonline.net
Web site: www.cshfha.org
Largest living collection of NYS freshwater fish, amphibians & turtles
Norman Soule, Director

Columbia University, School of the Arts
305 Dodge Hall, 2960 Broadway, MC1808, New York, NY 10027
212-854-2134 Fax: 212-854-7733
e-mail: bwf3@columbia.edu
Web site: www.columbia.edu/cu/arts
Bruce W Ferguson, Dean

Culinary Institute of America
1946 Campus Drive, Hyde Park, NY 12538-1499
845-452-9600
e-mail: N_Harvin@culinary.edu
Web site: www.ciachef.edu
Four-year regionally accredited college offering Associate and Occupational Studies and Bachelor of Professional Studies in culinary and baking/pastry arts management. Campuses in Hyde Park, New York, and St Helena, California.
Victor A.L. Gielisse, Vice President for Advancement & Business Development

Darien Lake Theme Park Resort
9993 Allegheny Rd, PO Box 91, Darien Center, NY 14040
585-599-4641 Fax: 585-599-4053
e-mail: info@godarienlake.com
Web site: www.godarienlake.com
Darien Lake Theme Park Resort is New York State's largest theme park and resort, located between Buffalo and Rochester, NY and just a short drive from Niagara Falls.
Christopher Thorpe, Vice President & General Manager

Egg (The), Center for the Performing Arts
Empire State Plaza, PO Box 2065, Albany, NY 12220
518-473-1061 or 518-473-1845 Fax: 518-473-1848
e-mail: info@theegg.org
Web site: www.theegg.org
Dance, theatre, family entertainment, music, special events
Peter Lesser, Executive Director

NYS Bar Assn, Entertainment, Arts & Sports Law Section
Elissa D Hecker, Esq
90 Quail Close, Irvington, NY 10533
914-478-0457
e-mail: eheckeresq@yahoo.com
Elissa D Hecker, Chair

Empire State Restaurant & Tavern Association Inc
12 Sheridan Avenue, Albany, NY 12207
518-436-8121 Fax: 518-436-7287
e-mail: esrta@verizon.net
Web site: www.esrta.org
Scott Wexler, Executive Director

Entertainment Software Association
317 Madison Ave, 22nd Fl, New York, NY 10017
917-522-3250 Fax: 917-522-3258
Web site: www.theesa.com
Michael D Gallagher, President/CEO

Exhibition Alliance Inc (The)
Route 12B South, PO Box 345, Hamilton, NY 13346
315-824-2510 Fax: 315-824-1683
e-mail: donnao@exhibitionalliance.org
Web site: www.exhibitionalliance.org
Exhibit-related services for museums in NYS & the surrounding region
Donna Ostraszewski Anderson, Executive Director

Farmer's Museum (The)
PO Box 30, Cooperstown, NY 13326
607-547-1400 Fax: 607-547-1404
e-mail: m.bruce@nysha.org
Web site: www.farmersmuseum.org
Historical & cultural exhibition, preservation and education
D Stephen Elliott, President

Film/Video Arts
270 W 96th St, New York, NY 10025
212-941-8787
e-mail: mariopaoli@fva.com
Web site: www.fva.com
Low cost training, postproduction suites, fiscal sponsorship, mentorship, internships
Chloe Kurabi, Programs Director, Fiscal Sponsorship and Filmmaker

Finger Lakes Racing Association
PO Box 25250, Farmington, NY 14425
585-924-3232 Fax: 585-924-3239
Web site: www.fingerlakesracetrack.com
Horse racing & video lottery gaming
Christian Riegle, General Manager

Finger Lakes Tourism Alliance
309 Lake St, Penn Yan, NY 14527
315-536-7488 Fax: 315-536-1237
e-mail: info@fingerlakes.org
Web site: www.fingerlakes.org
Regional tourism promotion
Cynthia Kimble, President

Gertrude Stein Repertory Theatre (The)
15 West 26th St, 2nd Fl, New York, NY 10010
212-725-0436 Fax: 212-725-7267
e-mail: info@gerstein.org
Web site: www.gertstein.org
Avant garde theater emphasizing international collaboration in experimental works incorporating new technologies
Liz Dreyer, General Manager

Great Escape Theme Park LLC (The)
PO Box 511, Lake George, NY 12845
518-792-3500 Fax: 518-792-3404
Web site: www.thegreatescape.com
John Collins, General Manager

Offices and agencies generally appear in alphabetical order, except when specific order is requested by listee.

Harvestworks
596 Broadway, Suite 602, New York, NY 10012
212-431-1130 Fax: 212-431-8473
e-mail: info@harvestworks.org
Web site: www.harvestworks.org
Nonprofit arts organization providing computer education & production studios for the digital media arts
Carol Parkinson, Director

Historic Hudson Valley
150 White Plains Rd, Tarrytown, NY 10591
914-631-8200 Fax: 914-631-0089
e-mail: mail@hudsonvalley.org
Web site: www.hudsonvalley.org
Tourism promotion
Waddell Stillman, President

Hotel Association of New York City Inc
320 Park Ave, 22nd Fl, New York, NY 10022-6838
212-754-6700 Fax: 212-688-2838
e-mail: jspinnato@hanyc.org
Web site: www.hanyc.org
Joseph E Spinnato, President

Hudson River Cruises
Rondout Landing, 1 East Strand Street, Kingston, NY 12401-3605
845-340-4700 or 800-843-7472 Fax: 845-340-4702
e-mail: hudsonrivercruises@hvc.rr.com
Web site: www.hudsonrivercruises.com
Sightseeing, music & dinner cruises and Private Charters
Sandra Henne, President

Hunter Mountain Ski Bowl
PO Box 295, Hunter, NY 12442
888-486-8376 or 518-263-4223 Fax: 518-263-3704
e-mail: info@huntermtn.com
Web site: www.huntermtn.com
Skiing, snowshoeing, snowboarding & snowtubing; coaching & race camps; summer & fall festivals; Kaatskill Mountain Club/Hotel, Loftside Village Condominiums, and other Four Season Mountain Resort activities.
Orville A Slutzky, General Manager

Jewish Museum (The)
1109 Fifth Ave, New York, NY 10128-0117
212-423-3271 Fax: 212-423-3233
e-mail: ascher@thejm.org
Web site: www.thejewishmuseum.org
Museum of art and Jewish culture
Anne Scher, Director, Communications

Lincoln Center for the Performing Arts Inc
70 Lincoln Center Plaza, New York, NY 10023-6583
212-875-5319 Fax: 212-875-5456
e-mail: jberry@lincolncenter.org
Web site: www.lincolncenter.org
Guided tours of Lincoln Center; Meet-the-Artist programs
Jennifer Berry, Director, Visitor Services

Lower Manhattan Cultural Council
125 Maiden Lane, 2nd Floor, New York, NY 10038
212-219-9401 Fax: 212-219-2058
e-mail: info@lmcc.net
Web site: www.lmcc.net
Supporting Manhattan arts organizations through funding assistance, support for creation & presentation of work & audience development
Mark Vevle, Director, Marketing & Communications

Madison Square Garden Corp
Two Penn Plaza, Madison Square Garden, New York, NY 10121
212-465-6000 Fax: 212-465-4423
Web site: www.thegarden.com
NY Knicks, NY Rangers,NY Liberty concerts, special events
Barry Watkins, Senior Vice President, Communications

Major League Baseball
245 Park Ave, New York, NY 10167
212-931-7800 Fax: 212-949-5654
Web site: www.mlb.com
Rich Levin, Senior Vice President, Public Relations

Metropolitan Museum of Art (The)
1000 Fifth Ave, New York, NY 10028
212-535-7710 Fax: 212-650-2102
Web site: www.metmuseum.org
Philippe de Montebello, Director;, Harold Holzer, Senior Vice President for External Affairs

Monticello Gaming & Raceway
204 Rte 17-B, PO Box 5013, Monticello, NY 12701
845-794-4100 Fax: 845-791-1402
Web site: www.monticelloraceway.com
Horse racing and video gaming machines.
Clifford Ehrlich, Senior Vice President/General Manager

Museum Association of New York
265 River St, Troy, NY 12180
518-273-3400 Fax: 518-273-3416
e-mail: info@manyonline.org
Web site: www.manyonline.org
An information and advocacy resource for the state's museum community.
Anne Ackerson, Director

NY Film Academy
100 East 17th St, New York, NY 10003-2160
212-674-4300 Fax: 212-477-1414
e-mail: film@nyfa.com
Web site: www.nyfa.com
Film making and acting for film.
Jerry Sherlock, President & Founder

NY State Historical Association/Fenimore Art Museum
PO Box 800, Cooperstown, NY 13326-0800
607-547-1400 Fax: 607-547-1404
e-mail: m.bruce@nysha.org
Web site: www.nysha.org; www.farmersmuseum.org
Historical & cultural exhibition, preservation & education
Paul S D'Ambroso, PhD, President/Chief Executive Officer

NYC Arts Coalition
351 West 54th St, New York, NY 10019
212-246-3788 Fax: 212-246-3366
e-mail: info@nycityartscoalition.org
Web site: www.nycityartscoalition.org
Develops public policy analysis, provides reports on arts policy & funding issues & acts as an advocacy vehicle for a united voice for the nonprofit arts sector
Norma P Munn, Chair

NYS Alliance for Arts Education
PO Box 2217, Albany, NY 12220-0217
800-ARTS-N-ED or 518-473-0823 Fax: 518-486-7329
e-mail: info@nysaae.org
Web site: www.nysaae.org
Advocacy, professional development, technical assistance & information for educators, organizations, artists, parents, policymakers
Jeremy Johannesen, Executive Director

NYS Arts
PO Box 96, Mattituck, NY 11952-0096
631-298-1234 Fax: 631-298-1101
e-mail: jkweiner@NYSARTS.org
Web site: www.nysarts.org
Technical assistance, professional development & advocacy services
Angela Lipfert, Office Manager

Offices and agencies generally appear in alphabetical order, except when specific order is requested by listee.

Policy Areas

NYS Outdoor Guides Association
1936 Saranac Ave, Suite 2 PO Box 150, Lake Placid, NY 12946-1402
866-469-7642 or 518-359-8194 Fax: 518-359-8194
e-mail: info@nysoga.org
Web site: www.nysoga.org
Provides information about member guide services & the profession of guiding through distribution of printed/electronic material and educational programs. Provides NYS licensed guides with support services, representation and sense of community
Sonny Young, President

NYS Passenger Vessel Association
PO Box 98, Brightwaters, NY 11718
631-321-9005
e-mail: info@cruisenewyork.com
Web site: www.cruisenewyork.com
Promote cruises on NYS's waterways
Mike Eagan, Treasurer

NYS Theatre Institute
37 First St, 1218 O, Troy, NY 12180
518-274-3200 Fax: 518-274-3815
e-mail: nysti@capital.net
Web site: www.nysti.org
Professional theater productions for family and school audiences; training & education, internships, community/school outreach & cultural exchange programs
Patricia Di Benedetto Snyder, Producing Artistic Director

NYS Turfgrass Association
PO Box 612, Latham, NY 12110
518-783-1229 Fax: 518-783-1258
e-mail: nysta@nysta.org
Web site: www.nysta.org
Grow & manage turf for golf courses, ball fields & landscape
Beth Same, Executive Director

National Basketball Association
645 5th Ave, New York, NY 10022
212-407-8000 Fax: 212-826-0579
Web site: www.nba.com
Brian McIntyre, Senior Vice President, Communications

National Football League
280 Park Ave, New York, NY 10017
212-450-2000 Fax: 212-681-7599
e-mail: aiellog@nfl.com
Web site: www.nfl.com
Greg Aiello, Vice President, Public Relations

National Hockey League
15, 1185 Avenue of the Americas, New York, NY 10036
212-789-2000 Fax: 212-789-2020
e-mail: fbrown@nhl.com
Web site: www.nhl.com
Frank Brown, Vice President, Media Relations

National Women's Hall of Fame
PO Box 335, 76 Fall Street, Seneca Falls, NY 13148
315-568-8060 Fax: 315-568-2976
Web site: www.greatwomen.org
The hall celebrates outstanding American women & their achievements
Billie Luisi-Potts, Executive Director

New School University, Department of Sociology
65 Fifth Ave, New York, NY 10003
212-229-5782 or 212-229-5737 Fax: 212-229-5595
e-mail: zolbergv@newschool.edu
Web site: www.newschool/edu
Sociology of the arts; censorship; collective memory; outsider art
Vera Zolberg, Professor, Sociology & Liberal Studies

New York Academy of Art Inc
111 Franklin St, New York, NY 10013-2911
212-966-0300 Fax: 212-966-3217
e-mail: info@nyaa.edu
Web site: www.nyaa.edu
Wayne A Linker, Executive Director

New York Aquarium
Surf Ave at West 8th St, Brooklyn, NY 11224
718-265-3428 or 718-265-FISH Fax: 718-265-3400
e-mail: fhackett@wcs.org
Web site: www.nyaquarium.com
Conservation, education & research
Fran Hackett, Communications

New York Artists Equity Association Inc
498 Broome St, New York, NY 10013
212-941-0130 Fax: 212-941-0138
e-mail: reginas@tiac.net
Web site: www.anny.org
Web based advocacy for visual arts & cultural organizations; Call first to send fax
Regina Stewart, Executive Director

New York City Opera
20 Lincoln Center, New York, NY 10023
212-870-5600 Fax: 212-724-1120
Web site: www.nycopera.com
Susan Woelzl, Director, Press & Public Relations

New York Foundation for the Arts
155 Ave of the Americas, 14th Floor, New York, NY 10013-1507
212-366-6900 Fax: 212-366-1778
e-mail: nyfainfo@nyfa.org
Web site: www.nyfa.org
Advocacy, leadership, financial & resource support & collaborative relationships with those committed to the arts
Theodore S Berger, Executive Director

New York Giants
Giants Stadium, East Rutherford, NJ 07073
201-935-8111 Fax: 201-935-8493
Web site: www.giants.com
Pat Hanlon, Vice President, Communications

New York Hall of Science
4701 111th Street, Queens, NY 11368
718-699-0005 x323 Fax: 718-699-1341
e-mail: wbrez@nyscience.org
Web site: www.nysci.org
Hands-on science exhibits & education program
Mary Record, Director, Communications

New York Islanders
1535 Old Country Rd, Plainview, NY 11803
516-501-6700 Fax: 516-501-6762
e-mail: customerservice@newyorkislanders.com
Web site: www.newyorkislanders.com
Chris Botta, Vice President, Communications

New York Jets
1000 Fulton Ave, Hempstead, NY 11550
516-560-8100 Fax: 516-560-8197
e-mail: rcolangelo@jets.nfl.com
Web site: www.newyorkjets.com
Bruce Speight, Public Relations

Offices and agencies generally appear in alphabetical order, except when specific order is requested by listee.

New York Marine Trades Association
194 Park Ave, Suite B, Amityville, NY 11701
631-691-7050 Fax: 631-691-2724
e-mail: csqueri@aol.com
Web site: www.nymta.com
Promote & protect the marine & boating industry; own & operate two boat shows; monitor local, state & federal marine legislation
Christopher Squeri, Executive Director

New York Mets
Shea Stadium, 123-01 Roosevelt Ave, Flushing, NY 11368
718-507-6387 Fax: 718-639-3619
Web site: www.mets.com
Fred Wilpon, Chairman & Chief Executive Officer

New York Racing Association
PO Box 90, Jamaica, NY 11417
718-641-4700 Fax: 718-843-7673
e-mail: nyra@nyraing.com
Web site: www.nyra.com
Horse racing at Aqueduct, Belmont Park, and Saratoga.
Francis LaBelle, Jr, Director, Communications

New York State Hospitality & Tourism Association
80 Wolf Rd, Albany, NY 12205
800-642-5313 x13 or 518-465-2300 Fax: 518-465-4025
e-mail: dan@nyshta.org
Web site: www.nyshta.org
Hotels, motels, amusement parks & attractions
Daniel C Murphy, President

New York State Restaurant Association
409 New Karner Rd, Albany, NY 12205
518-452-4222 Fax: 518-452-4497
e-mail: ricks@nysra.org
Web site: www.nysra.org
Rick J Sampson, President & Chief Executive Officer

New York State School Music Association (NYSSMA)
718 The Plain Rd, Westbury, NY 11590-5931
516-997-7200 Fax: 516-997-1700
e-mail: executive@nyssma.org
Web site: www.nyssma.org
Advocacy for a quality school music education for every student
Steven Schopp, Executive Director

New York State Snowmobile Association
PO Box 612, Long Lake, NY 12847
518-624-3849 Fax: 518-624-2441
e-mail: jimjennings@nyssnowassoc.org
Web site: www.nyssnowassoc.org
Working to preserve & enhance snowmobiling & improve trails, facilities & services for participants
Jim Jennings, Executive Director

New York State Theatre Education Association
63 Hecla St, Buffalo, NY 14216
716-837-9434 Fax: 716-626-8207
e-mail: rogersouth@aol.com
Web site: www.nystea.org
Working to preserve & enhance drama & theater education & opportunities in NY schools & communities
Roger Paolini, President

New York State Travel & Vacation Association
PO Box 285, Akron, NY 14001
888-698-2970 or 716-542-1586 Fax: 716-542-1404
e-mail: info@nystva.org
Web site: www.nystva.org
The NYSTVA is the tourism industry's leader in communication, legislative awareness, professional development, and promotion.
Dawn L Borchert, Executive Director

New York University, Tisch School of the Arts
721 Broadway, New York, NY 10003
212-998-1800
Web site: www.tisch.nyu.edu
Allyson Green, Dean, Tisch School of the Arts

New York Wine & Grape Foundation
800 S Main St, Ste 200, Canandaigua, NY 14424
585-394-3620 Fax: 585-394-3649
e-mail: info@newyorkwines.org
Web site: www.newyorkwines.org
Promotion of wine & grape products of New York; research for wine & grape related products & issues
James Trezise, President

New York Yankees
800 Ruppert Place, Bronx, NY 10451
718-293-4300 Fax: 718-293-8431
Web site: www.yankees.com
Randy Levine, President

Resources for Artists with Disabilities Inc
77 7th Ave, Suite PHH, New York, NY 10011-6644
212-691-5490 Fax: 212-691-5490
Organizes & promotes exhibition opportunities for visual artists with physical disabilities
Dr Lois Kaggen, President & Founder

Saratoga Gaming & Raceway
PO Box 356, Saratoga Springs, NY 12866
518-584-2110 or 518-581-5748 Fax: 518-583-1269
e-mail: info@saratogaraceway.com
Web site: www.saratogaraceway.com
Horse racing
John R Matarazzo, Director of Racing Operations

Seaway Trail Inc
401 West Main Street, Ray & West Main Streets, PO Box 660, Sackets Harbor, NY 13685
315-646-1000 or 800-SEAWAY-T Fax: 315-646-1004
e-mail: info@seawaytrail.com
Web site: www.seawaytrail.com
Promotes coastal recreation, economic development, resource management & heritage, cultural, agricultural & culinary tourism along a 454 mile NYS highway system
Teresa Mitchell, President

Ski Areas of New York Inc
PO Box 928, Tupper Lake, NY 12986
518-796-3601 or 315-696-6550 Fax: 315-696-6567
e-mail: scottbrandi@iskiny.com
Web site: www.iskiny.com
Promote skiing in NYS
Scott Brandi, President

Solomon R Guggenheim Foundation
1071 5th Ave, New York, NY 10128
212-423-3680
e-mail: directorsoffice@guggenheim.org
Web site: www.guggenheim.org
Thomas Krens, Director

Special Olympics New York, Inc
504 Balltown Road, Schenectady, NY 12304-2290
518-388-0790 Fax: 518-388-0795
Web site: www.nyso.org
Not-for-profit organization provides year-round sports training & competition in Olympic-style sports for athletes with intellectual disabilities.
Neal J Johnson, President & Chief Executive Officer

Sports & Arts in Schools Foundation
58-12 Queens Blvd, Suite 1 - 59th Entrance, Woodside, NY 11377
718-786-7110 Fax: 718-786-7635
e-mail: info@sasfny.org
Web site: www.sasfny.org
After-school, summer camps & clinics, winter-break festival
James R O'Neill, Executive Director

Staten Island Zoo
614 Broadway, Staten Island, NY 10310
718-442-3101 Fax: 718-981-8711
e-mail: kmithcell@statenislandzoo.org
Web site: www.statenislandzoo.org
Kenneth C. Mitchell, Interim Executive Director

Tribeca Film Institute
32 Avenue of the Americas, 27 FL, New York, NY 10013
212-274-8080 Fax: 212-274-8081
Web site: www.tribecafilminstitute.org
Anna Ponder, Executive Director

USA Track & Field, Adirondack Association Inc
233 Fourth St, Troy, NY 12180
518-273-5552 Fax: 518-273-0647
e-mail: info@usatfadir.org
Web site: www.usatfadir.org
Leadership & opportunities for athletes pursuing excellence in running, race walking & track & field
George Regan, President

Vernon Downs/Gaming-Racing-Entertainment
4229 Stuhlman Rd, PO Box 1040, Vernon Downs, NY 13476
315-829-2201 Fax: 315-829-3787
e-mail: vernonevents@vernondowns.com
Web site: www.vernondowns.com
Horse racing, concerts, motorcross, motorcycle, craft fairs & other entertainment
Ursula Hardin, President

Willow Mixed Media Inc
PO Box 194, Glenford, NY 12433
845-657-2914
e-mail: video@hvc.rr.com
Web site: www.willowmixedmedia.org
Not-for-profit specializing in documentary video & arts projects addressing social concerns
Tobe Carey, President

Yonkers Raceway
810 Central Park Ave, Yonkers, NY 10704
914-968-4200 Fax: 914-968-4479
Web site: www.yonkersraceway.com
Horse racing and video gaming entertainment
Timothy Rooney, President

Offices and agencies generally appear in alphabetical order, except when specific order is requested by listee.

TRANSPORTATION

NEW YORK STATE

GOVERNOR'S OFFICE

Governor's Office
Executive Chamber
State Capitol
Albany, NY 12224
518-474-8390 Fax: 518-474-1513
Web site: www.ny.gov

Governor:
Andrew M Cuomo 518-474-8390
Secretary to the Governor:
William Mulrow 518-474-4246
Counsel to the Governor:
Alphonso David 518-474-8343
Chief of Staff:
Melissa DeRosa . . . . . . 518-474-8418 or 212-681-4640
Director, Communications:
James Allen. . . . . . 518-474-8418 or 212-681-4640
Deputy Secretary, Transportation:
Ron Thaniel. 518-408-2555
Deputy Secretary, Public Safety:
Rachel Small. 518-474-3522

EXECUTIVE DEPARTMENTS AND RELATED AGENCIES

Motor Vehicles Department
6 Empire State Plaza
Albany, NY 12228
Web site: www.dmv.ny.gov

Executive Deputy Commissioner:
Theresa L Egan 518-474-0846/fax: 518-474-0712
Assistant Commissioner, Communications:
Joseph Morrissey. 518-473-7000/fax: 518-473-1930

Administration, Office for
Deputy Commissioner:
Gregory J Kline. 518-474-6876/fax: 518-474-0712
Director, Audit Services:
Jannette Potera 518-474-0881
Director, Fiscal Management:
Paul Gauthier 518-474-7602
Director, Human Resources:
Vacant 518-474-7602
Director, Agency Program Services:
Ann Scott 518-474-8328
Labor Relations:
Nancy Spenziero. 518-474-2902
Director, Program Analysis:
Mary Bidell. 518-474-0623

Governor's Traffic Safety Committee
Web site: www.safeny.ny.gov
Assistant Commissioner:
Chuck DeWeese 518-474-0972
Director, Traffic Safety Committee:
Jim Allen. 518-474-5777

Legal Affairs, Office for
Deputy Commissioner, Legal Affairs:
Neal Schoen. 518-473-1965/fax: 518-474-0712
Director, Legal:
Ida Traschen 518-474-0871
Appeals Board:
Deborah Dugan. 518-474-0645

Operations & Customer Service, Office for
Deputy Commissioner:
Timothy Blennon 518-474-0846
Legislative Liaison:
Meg Murray 518-474-7726
Director, Field Operations:
Cheryl Wasley. 518-486-7400
Director, Operations:
Joseph Crisafulli 518-473-7254
Director, Central Office Operations:
Roseanne Kitchner 518-402-4746

Safety, Consumer Protection & Clean Air, Office for
Deputy Commissioner:
Heriberto Barbot 518-402-4860/fax: 518-474-0712
Director, Driver/Vehicle Safety:
Jean Rosenthal 518-473-3347
Director, Field Investigation:
Owen McShane. 518-474-8805
Director, Driver Safety Programs:
Gerald Clark 518-473-7197
Vehicle Safety & Clean Air:
Steve Cooper. 518-474-3785

Transportation Department
50 Wolf Road
Albany, NY 12232
518-457-5100 or 518-457-6195 Fax: 518-457-5583
Web site: www.dot.ny.gov

Commissioner:
Matthew J Driscoll 518-457-4422
Executive Deputy Commissioner:
Stanley Gee. 518-457-4422
CIO/Information Technology Division:
Nancy Mulholland 518-485-8853
Director, Legal Affairs Division:
David Cherubin. 518-457-2411
Operations & Asset Management Division:
Roderic Sechrist 518-485-0887
Acting Director, Policy & Planning Division:
Ron Epstein. 518-457-2320
Chief Engineer/Engineering Division:
Phillip Eng 518-457-4430
Director, Audit:
John Samaniuk 518-485-8262
Director, Communications Office (Acting):
Jennifer Post 518-457-6400

Administrative Services Division
Director:
Vacant. 518-457-6300
Director, Human Resources:
Raymond LaMarco 518-485-7043
Director, Contract Management Bureau:
Bill Howe 518-457-2600
Director, Communications Office (Acting):
Jennifer Post 518-457-6400/fax: 518-457-6506
Director, Facilities Management:
Mark Reuss 518-457-6445
Director, Purchase Unit:
Matthew Haas 518-457-4401

Engineering Division
Chief Engineer & Assistant Commissioner:
Phillip Eng 518-457-4430
Office of Design:
Richard Lee. 518-457-6452

Offices and agencies generally appear in alphabetical order, except when specific order is requested by listee.

Office of Structures:
Richard Marchione 518-457-6827
Office of Environment:
Dan Hitt. . . . 518-457-5672
Office of Major Projects:
Marie Corrado. . . . 518-485-5025
Office of Technical Services:
Robert Sack, PE 518-457-4445
Office of Construction:
Brian DeWald, PE. . . . 518-457-6472
Office of Construction:
Jose Rivera, PE 518-457-6472

Legal Affairs Division
Director, Legal Affairs Division:
David Cherubin. . . . 518-457-2411

Information Technology Division
CIO:
Patrick Bennison. . . . 518-457-2800
Business Solutions Bureau:
Gerry Ecker. . . . 518-457-7835
Project Management Office:
Michael Roberts 518-457-9101
Statewide Customer Support Bureau:
Pat Bennison. . . . 518-457-2800
Technical Services Bureau (Acting):
Perry Taglienti 518-457-2800

Operations & Asset Management Division
Director:
Roderic Sechrist 518-485-0887
Modal Safety & Security Office:
William Leonard. . . . 518-457-6512
Fleet Administration & Support Office:
Robert D Martz 518-457-2875
Emergency Transportation Operations:
Dawn Arnold. . . . 518-457-1673
Transportation Maintenance Office:
Bob Winans. . . . 518-457-6435
Traffic Safety & Mobility Office (Acting):
Todd B Westhuis 518-457-0271
Employee Health & Safety:
Brian Gibney. . . . 518-457-2420

Policy & Planning Division
Acting Deputy Commissioner:
Ron Epstein. . . . 518-457-2320
CFO/Finance Office:
Ron Epstein. . . . 518-457-2320
Policy, Planning & Performance Office:
Lynn Weiskopf 518-457-2320
Integrated Modal Services:
Diane Kenneally 518-457-2320
Regional Planning & Program Coordination:
Dave Rettig. . . . 518-457-2320

Audit & Civil Rights Division
Director, Audit:
John Samaniuk 518-485-8262
Office of Civil Rights:
Sondra Little 518-457-1129
Contract Audit Bureau:
Joseph Stuhlman. . . . 518-457-3180
Enterprise Risk Management (Acting):
Kimberly Doran 518-457-4685
Internal Audit Bureau:
Theresa Vottis. . . . 518-457-4671
Investigations Bureau:
Robert Keihm 518-457-6446

Office of Regional Affairs
Director:
Vacant. . . . 518-457-2470

Regional Offices

Region 1
50 Wolf Road, Albany, NY 12232
Director:
Sam Zhou. . . . 518-451-3522

Region 2
Utica State Ofc Bldg, 207 Genesee St, Utica, NY 13501
Director:
Barbara Mattice 315-793-2447

Region 3
State Ofc Bldg, 333 E Washington St, Syracuse, NY 13202
Director:
Carl F Ford 315-428-4351/fax: 315-428-4834

Region 4
1530 Jefferson Rd, Rochester, NY 14623
Director:
Kevin Bush 585-272-3310/fax: 585-427-8480

Region 5
100 Seneca Street, Buffalo, NY 14203
Director:
Darrell F Kaminski. . . . 716-847-3238/fax: 716-847-3961

Region 6
107 Broadway, Hornell, NY 14843
Director:
Brian Kelly 607-324-8404/fax: 607-324-0790

Region 7
Dulles State Ofc Bldg, 317 Washington St, Watertown, NY 13601
Director:
Steve Kokkoris. . . . 315-785-2333/fax: 315-785-2507

Region 8
Eleanor Roosevelt State Ofc Bldg, 4 Burnett Blvd, Poughkeepsie, NY 12603
Director:
William Gorton. . . . 845-431-5750/fax: 845-431-5703

Region 9
44 Hawley St, Binghamton, NY 13901
Director:
Jack Williams 607-721-8116/fax: 607-721-8119

Region 10
State Ofc Bldg, 250 Veterans Memorial Hwy, Hauppauge, NY 11788
Director:
Joseph Brown 631-952-6632/fax: 631-952-6311

Region 11
One Hunters Point Plaza, 47-40 21st St, Long Island City, NY 11101
Director:
Sonia Pichardo 718-482-4526/fax: 718-482-4525

CORPORATIONS, AUTHORITIES AND COMMISSIONS

Albany County Airport Authority
Albany International Airport
Administration Building
Second Floor
Albany, NY 12211
518-242-2222 x1 Fax: 518-242-2641
e-mail: info@albanyairport.com
Web site: www.albanyairport.com/airport-authority.php

Chief Executive Officer:
John A O'Donnell PE 518-242-2222 x1
Chief Financial Officer:
William O'Reilly 518-242-2222 x1
Director, Public Affairs:
Douglas I. Myers 518-242-2222 x1

Counsel:
Peter F Stuto 518-242-2222 x1
Airport Planner:
Stephen A Iachetta 518-242-2222 x1
Administrative Services:
Liz Charland 518-242-2222 x1

Albany Port District Commission
106 Smith Blvd, Admin Bldg
Port of Albany
Albany, NY 12202
518-463-8763 Fax: 518-463-8767
e-mail: portofalbany@portofalbany.us
Web site: www.portofalbany.us

Chair:
Georgette Steffens 518-463-8763
General Manager:
Richard Hendrick 518-463-8763
e-mail: rhendrick@portofalbany.us
Counsel:
Thomas Owens 518-694-0910

Buffalo & Fort Erie Public Bridge Authority (Peace Bridge Authority)
One Peace Bridge Plaza
Buffalo, NY 14213-2494
716-884-6744 Fax: 716-884-2089
Web site: www.peacebridge.com

Chair (US):
William Hoyt 716-884-6744/fax: 716-883-7246
Vice Chair (Canada):
Anthony M Annunziata 716-884-6744/fax: 716-883-7246
General Manager:
Ron Rienas 716-884-6744

Capital District Transportation Authority
110 Watervliet Ave
Albany, NY 12206
518-437-8300 or 518-482-8822 Fax: 518-437-8318
Web site: www.cdta.org

Chair:
David M Stackrow 518-437-8311
Vice Chair:
Georgeanna Nugent Lussier 518-437-8311
CEO:
Carm Basile 518-437-6840/fax: 518-437-8349
e-mail: carmb@cdta.org
General Counsel:
Amanda A Avery 518-437-8315/fax: 518-473-8318
e-mail: amandaa@cdta.org
VP, Finance & Administration:
Michael P Collins 518-437-8330/fax: 518-437-8347
e-mail: mikec@cdta.org
Director of Transportation:
Frederick C Gilliam 518-437-8372/fax: 518-437-8328
e-mail: fredg@cdta.org
VP, Planning & Infrastructure:
Christopher G Desany 518-437-8320/fax: 518-437-8328
e-mail: chrisd@cdta.org

Central New York Regional Transportation Authority
200 Cortland Ave
PO Box 820
Syracuse, NY 13205-0820
315-442-3400 Fax: 315-442-3337
Web site: www.centro.org

Chair, Board of Directors:
Brian M Schultz 315-442-3300
CEO:
Richard Lee 315-442-3360
VP, Finance:
Christine LoCurto 315-442-3355
Counsel:
Barry Shulman 315-442-3400

MTA Bridges & Tunnels
2 Broadway
22nd Floor
New York, NY 10004-2801
646-252-7000 Fax: 646-252-7408
Web site: www.mta.info/bandt

President:
Donald Spero 212-360-3100
Chief Engineer:
Joseph Keane 212-878-7200
Vice President, Administration:
Sharon Gallo-Kotcher 212-360-3015
Vice President, Operations:
Patrick Parisi 212-878-7200
Chief Procurement Officer:
Gavin Masterson 646-252-7084
Vice President, Staff Services & Chief of Staff:
Albert Rivera 646-252-7421
Chief Financial Officer (Acting):
Mildred Chua 646-252-7132
General Counsel:
M. Margaret Terry 212-878-7200
Manager, Public Affairs:
Judith Glave 646-252-7276

MTA Bus Company
2 Broadway
New York, NY 10004
212-878-7174 Fax: 2512-878-0205
Web site: www.mta.info/busco

President:
Daryl Irick 212-878-7174

MTA Capital Construction
2 Broadway
8th Fl
New York, NY 10002
646-252-4575
Web site: www.mta.info/capital

President:
Dr Michael Horodniceanu 646-252-4277
Chief of Staff:
Ayala Malinovitz 646-252-4011
Senior Director, Government & Community Affairs:
Richard Mulieri 646-252-4197
Executive Vice President:
William Goldstein 646-252-4277
Senior Vice President & General Counsel:
Evan Eisland 646-252-4274
Senior Director & Chief Procurement Officer:
David Cannon 646-252-2321
Vice President & Chief Engineer:
Mike Kyriacou 646-252-4500

Policy Areas

Senior Vice President & Program Executive, East Side Access:
Alan Paskoff 212-967-0118
Senior Vice President & Program Executive, 2nd Ave Subway:
William Goodrich 212-510-2661
VP & Program Executive, #7 Subway Line Extension:
Mark Schiffman 646-252-3723
Director, System Safety & Security:
Eric Osnes 646-252-4556
Vice President, Program Controls & Quality Safety:
Raymond Schaeffer 646-252-5393
Vice President, Planning, Development & External Relations:
Joseph Petrocelli 646-252-3813

MTA Long Island Rail Road

Jamaica Station
Jamaica, NY 11435
718-558-7400 Fax: 718-558-8212
Web site: www.mta.info/lirr

President:
Patrick A Nowakowski 718-558-8252
Executive Vice President:
Albert Cosenza 718-558-7993
e-mail: accosen@lirr.org
Chief Information Officer:
Scott Dieterich 718-588-8166
Vice President, General Counsel & Secretary:
Richard Gans 718-558-8264
Chief Engineer:
Kevin Tomlinson 718-558-7400
Vice President, Labor Relations:
Michael Chirillo 718-558-7405
Vice President, Market Development & Public Affairs:
Joseph Calderone 718-558-7301
Vice President, ESA/Special Projects:
John Coulter 718-558-7363
e-mail: jwcoult@lirr.org
Director, Safety System:
Frank Lo Presti 718-588-7711
General Manager, Public Affairs:
Susan McGowan 718-558-7400

MTA Metro-North Railroad

347 Madison Ave
New York, NY 10017
212-340-2677 Fax: 212-340-4995
Web site: www.mta.info/mnr

President:
Joseph Giulietti 212-340-2677
General Counsel:
Seth Cummins 212-340-4933
VP, Finanace & Informational Systems:
D. Kim Porcelain 212-340-2636
Senior VP, Operations:
Robert Lieblong 212-499-4300
Senior Director, Capital Planning & Program:
John Kennard 212-340-2500
Chief of Staff & Operations:
David Treasure 212-340-2677
Chief Safety & Security Officer:
Anne Kirsch 212-340-4913
Senior Director, Capital Programs:
Timothy McCartney 212-499-4403
Vice President, Business Operations:
Thomas Tendy 212-672-1251
Senior Director, Corporate & Public Affairs:
Mark Mannix 212-340-2142

MTA New York City Transit

2 Broadway
New York, NY 10004
718-330-3000 Fax: 718-596-2146
Web site: www.mta.info/nyct

President:
Veronique Hakim 646-252-5800
Chief Transportation Officer:
Herbert Lambert 718-330-3000
Vice President, Labor Relations:
Christopher Johnson 718-330-3000
Vice President, Corporate Communications:
Paul Fleuranges 646-252-5873
Vice President, Technology & Information Services:
Sidney Gellineau 718-330-3000
Vice President & General Counsel:
Martin Schnabel 718-694-3900
Director, Labor Relations:
Andrew Paul 646-252-5880
Chief Officer, Staten Island Railway:
John Gaul 718-876-8239

MTA (Metropolitan Transportation Authority)

347 Madison Ave
New York, NY 10017
212-878-7000 Fax: 212-878-7264
Web site: www.mta.info

Chairman/CEO:
Thomas F. Prendergast 212-878-7200
Director of Security:
Raymond Diaz 212-878-7155
Deputy Executive Director, Government & Community Affairs:
Justin Bernbach 212-878-7160
Senior Director, Human Resources/Retirement:
Margaret M. Connor
CAO/Employee Relations:
Anita Miller 212-878-7438
Auditor General:
Michael J Fucilli 212-878-7236
Chief Financial Officer:
Robert E Foran 212-878-7278
Chief Financial Officer:
Robert E. Foran
General Counsel:
Jerome F Page 212-878-7313/fax: 212-878-7050
Chief of Staff:
Donna Evans 212-878-1001
Director, External Communications:
Adam Lisberg 212-878-7440

MTA Office of the Inspector General

2 Penn Plaza, 5th Fl
New York, NY 10121
212-878-0000 or 800-682-4448 Fax: 212-878-0003
Web site: www.mtaig.state.ny.us

Inspector General:
Barry L Kluger 212-878-0000

New York Metropolitan Transportation Council

25 Beaver Street
Ste 201
New York, NY 10004
212-383-7200 Fax: 212-383-2418
e-mail: nymtc-web@dot.ny.gov
Web site: www.nymtc.org

Interim Executive Director:
Lisa Daglian 212-383-7200
Acting Director, Administration:
Nina Del Senno 212-383-2402
e-mail: nina.delsenno@dot.ny.gov
Director, Planning:
Gerard J Bogacz 212-383-7260
e-mail: gerry.bogacz@dot.ny.gov
PIO:
Stacy Graham-Hunt 212-383-7203
e-mail: stacy.graham-hunt@dot.ny.gov

New York State Bridge Authority
Mid-Hudson Bridge Plaza
PO Box 1010
Highland, NY 12528
845-691-7245 Fax: 845-691-3560
e-mail: info@nysba.ny.gov
Web site: www.nysba.ny.gov

Chair:
Richard A. Gerentine 845-691-7245
Vice Chair:
Joseph Ramaglia 845-691-7245
Executive Director:
Joseph Ruggiero 845-691-7245
Director, IT:
Gregory J Herd 518-828-4107
Director, Toll Collections & Operations:
Wayne V Ferguson 845-691-7245

New York State Thruway Authority
200 Southern Blvd
PO Box 189
Albany, NY 12201
518-436-2700 Fax: 518-436-2899
Web site: www.thruway.ny.gov

Chair:
Joanne M Mahoney 518-436-3000
Interim Executive Director:
Maria Lehman 518-436-2900
General Counsel:
Gordon Cuffy 518-436-2840
CFO:
Matt Howard 518-436-2840
Director, Media Relations & Communications:
Jennifer Givner 518-471-5300
e-mail: publicinfo@thruway.ny.gov
Director, Administrative Services:
John F. Barr
e-mail: publicinfo@thruway.ny.gov

New York State Canal Corporation
Web site: www.canals.ny.gov
Interim Executive Director:
Maria Lehman 518-436-3055/fax: 518-471-5023

Niagara Falls Bridge Commission
5365 Military Rd
Lewiston, NY 14092
716-285-6322 or 905-354-5641 Fax: 716-282-3292
e-mail: general_inquiries@niagarafallsbridges.com
Web site: www.niagarafallsbridges.com

Chair:
Linda L McAusland 716-285-6322
Vice Chair:
Russell G Quarantello 716-285-6322
Treasurer:
Harry R Palladino 716-285-6322
Secretary:
John Lopinski 716-285-6322

Niagara Frontier Transportation Authority
181 Ellicott St
Buffalo, NY 14203
716-855-7300 or 800-622-1220 Fax: 716-855-6655
e-mail: info@nfta.com
Web site: www.nfta.com

Chair:
Howard Zemsky 716-855-7232
Executive Director:
Kimberley A Minkel 716-855-7470
Chief Financial Officer:
John Cox 716-855-7300
General Counsel:
David J State 716-855-7686
Director, Aviation:
William Vanecek 716-630-6030
Director, Human Resources:
Karen Novo 716-855-7343
Director, Public Transit:
Thomas George 716-855-7390
Director, Engineering:
Michael Bykowski 716-855-7389
Director, Public Affairs:
C Douglas Hartmayer 716-855-7420
Chief, NFTA Police:
George W. Gast 716-855-7666

Ogdensburg Bridge & Port Authority
One Bridge Plaza
Ogdensburg, NY 13669
315-393-4080 Fax: 315-393-7068
e-mail: obpa@ogdensport.com
Web site: www.ogdensport.com

Chair:
Samuel J LaMacchia 315-393-4080
Deputy Executive Director:
Wade A Davis 315-393-4080
e-mail: wadavis@ogdensport.com

Port Authority of New York & New Jersey
4 World Trade Center
150 Greenwich Street
New York, NY 10007
212-435-7000 Fax: 212-435-4032
Web site: www.panynj.gov

Chair, New Jersey:
John J Degnan 212-435-7000
Vice Chair, New York:
Scott H Rechler 212-435-7000
Executive Director:
Patrick Foye 212-435-7271
Director World Trade Center Operations:
Hugh P McCann 212-435-7887
Director Government & Community Affairs - NY (Acting):
Ian R Van Praagh 212-435-6903
Assistant General Counsel:
Carlene V McIntyre 212-435-3515
Chief Financial Officer:
Elizabeth McCarthy 212-435-7738
Director Media Relations:
Ron Marsico 212-435-7777/fax: 212-435-4032

Offices and agencies generally appear in alphabetical order, except when specific order is requested by listee.

Director, Public Safety/Superintendent of Police:
Michael A Fedorko 212-435-7000
Chief Engineer:
James A Starace 212-435-7449

Port of Oswego Authority
1 East Second St
Oswego, NY 13126
315-343-4503 Fax: 315-343-5498
e-mail: shipping@portoswego.com
Web site: www.portoswego.com

Chair:
Terrence Hammill 315-343-4503
e-mail: chairman@portoswego.com
Executive Director & CEO:
Zelko N. Kirincich 315-343-4503 x111
e-mail: zkirincich@portoswego.com
Manager, Administrative Services/Facility Security Officer:
William Scriber 315-343-4503 x108
e-mail: wscriber@portoswego.com
Supervisor of Marina Operations:
Bernie Bacon 315-343-1967
e-mail: oswegomarina@yahoo.com

Rochester-Genesee Regional Transportation Authority-RTS
1372 E Main St
PO Box 90629
Rochester, NY 14609
585-654-0200 Fax: 585-654-0224
Web site: www.myrts.com

Chief Executive Officer:
Bill Carpenter 585-654-0200
Chief Operating Officer:
Miguel A Velazquez 585-654-0200
Chief Financial Officer:
Scott Adair 585-654-0200
General Counsel/CAO:
Daniel DeLaus 585-654-0200
Public Information Officer:
Tom Brede 585-654-0730

Thousand Islands Bridge Authority
PO Box 428, Collins Landing
43530 Interstate 81
Alexandria Bay, NY 13607
315-482-2501 or 315-658-2281 Fax: 315-482-5925
e-mail: info@tibridge.com
Web site: www.tibridge.com

Chair:
Robert Barnard 315-482-2501
Executive Director:
Robert G Horr, III 315-482-2501
e-mail: roberthorr@tibridge.com
Legal Counsel:
Dennis Whelpley 315-482-2501

Waterfront Commission of New York Harbor
39 Broadway
4th Fl
New York, NY 10006
212-742-9280 Fax: 212-480-0587
Web site: www.wcnyh.org

Commissioner, New York:
Ronald Goldstock 212-742-9280
Commissioner, New Jersey:
Michael Murphy 212-742-9280
Executive Director:
Walter M Arsenault 212-905-9201

NEW YORK STATE LEGISLATURE

See Legislative Branch in Section 1 for additional Standing Committee and Subcommittee information.

Assembly Standing Committees

Corporations, Authorities & Commissions
Chair:
James F Brennan (D) 518-455-5377
Ranking Minority Member:
Jane Corwin (R) 518-455-4601

Economic Development, Job Creation, Commerce & Industry
Chair:
Robin L Schimminger (D) 518-455-4767
Ranking Minority Member:
Raymond Walter (R) 518-455-4618

Transportation
Chair:
David F Gantt (D) 518-455-5606
Ranking Minority Member:
David G McDonough (R) 518-455-4633

Senate Standing Committees

Commerce, Economic Development & Small Business
Chair:
Philip Boyle (R) 518-455-3411
Ranking Minority Member:
Timothy Kennedy (D) 518-455-2426

Corporations, Authorities & Commissions
Chair:
Michael Ranzenhofer (R) 518-455-3161
Ranking Minority Member:
Bill Perkins (D) 518-455-2441

Transportation
Chair:
Joseph Robach (R) 518-455-2909
Ranking Minority Member:
Martin Malave Dilan (D) 518-455-2177

U.S. GOVERNMENT

EXECUTIVE DEPARTMENTS AND RELATED AGENCIES

Federal Maritime Commission
Web site: www.fmc.gov

New York Area Office
Bldg 75, Rm 205B, JFK Intl Airport, Jamaica, NY 11430
Area Rep:
Emanuel J Mingione 718-553-2228/fax: 718-553-2229

National Transportation Safety Board
Web site: www.ntsb.gov

Aviation Division, Northeast Regional Office
2001 Route 46, Ste 203, Parsippany, NJ 07054

Offices and agencies generally appear in alphabetical order, except when specific order is requested by listee.

Regional Director:
David Muzio

Office of Administrative Law Judges
490 L'Enfant Plaza, ESW, Washington, DC 20594
Chief Judge:
Alfonso J. Montano 202-314-6151/fax: 202-314-8758

US Department of Homeland Security (DHS)
Web site: www.dhs.gov

Transportation Security Administration (TSA)
201 Varick St, Rm 1101, New York, NY 10014
Regional Spokesperson:
Lisa Farbstein 212-620-3608

US Transportation Department
Web site: www.dot.gov

Federal Aviation Administration-Eastern Region
One Aviation Plaza, Jamaica, NY 11434-4809
718-553-3001
Web site: www.faa.gov
Regional Administrator:
Carmine Gallo 718-553-3001
Deputy Regional Administrator:
Diane Crean 718-553-3001

Accounting Division
Manager:
Fred Glassberg 718-553-4190

Aerospace Medicine Division
Regional Flight Surgeon:
Harriet Lester 718-553-3300

Air Traffic Division
Acting Area Director:
John G McCartney 718-553-4500

Airports Division
Manager:
Steve Urlass 516-227-3803

Aviation Information & Services Division
Manager:
Alan Siperstein 718-553-3358

Engineering Services
Manager:
Selin Haber 718-553-3400

Flight Standards Division
Manager:
John M. Krepp . . . . 516-228-8029 x. 200

Human Resource Management Division
Manager:
Gloria Quay 718-553-3132

Logistics Division
Manager:
Vacant 718-553-3050

Military Liaison Officers to the Federal Aviation Admin (NYS)
12 New England Executive Park, Burlington, MA 1803
Air Force Regional Representatives
Representative:
Vacant 781-238-7901/fax: 781-238-7903
Transportation Specialist:
Cheryl W Carpenter 781-238-7910
e-mail: cheryl.w.carpenter@faa.gov
Army Regional Representatives
Liaison Officer:
LTC Bill Walsh 781-238-7906
e-mail: bill.walsh@faa.gov
Liaison Officer:
MSGT Jason Williams 781-238-7905
e-mail: jason.williams@faa.gov
Navy Regional Representatives
Liaison Officer:
CDR Rick Perez 781-238-7907
e-mail: rick.perez@faa.gov
Liaison Officer:
ACCS Mark Moon 781-238-7908/fax: 781-238-7902
e-mail: mark.moon@faa.gov

Runway Safety Manager
Manager:
Bill DeGraaff 718-553-3326

Federal Highway Administration-New York Division . . . . fax: 518-431-4121
Leo W O'Brien Federal Bldg, Rm 719 Clinton Ave & N Pearl St, Albany, NY 12207
518-431-4125 Fax: 518-431-4121
Web site: www.fhwa.dot.gov
Division Administrator:
John M. McDade 518-431-8897
e-mail: john.mcdade@dot.gov
Acting Chief Operating Officer:
Robert Clark 518-431-8879
e-mail: robert.clark@dot.gov
NYC Federal Aid Liaison:
John Formosa 212-668-2205
e-mail: john.formosa@dot.gov
Engineer Coordinator:
Joan P. Walters 518-431-8868
e-mail: joan.walters@dot.gov

Federal Motor Carrier Safety Admin-New York Division . . . . fax: 518-431-4140
Leo O'Brien Federal Bldg, Rm 815, Clinton Avenue & North Pearl Street, Albany, NY 12207
518-431-4145 Fax: 518-431-4140
Web site: www.fmcsa.dot.gov
Division Administrator:
Brian Temperine 518-431-4145 x311
Field Office Supervisor, Upstate:
Pamela Noyes 518-431-4145 x316
State Program Specialist:
Vacant
Manager, Intelligent Transportation Systems Commercial Vehicle Operati:
Carolyn Temperine 518-431-4145 x270

Federal Railroad Administration-Field Offices
Web site: www.fra.dot.gov

Hazardous Material
1 Aviation Plaza, Jamaica, NY 11434-4089
Inspector:
Steven Joseph 718-553-2596
e-mail: steven.joseph@faa.gov

Highway-Rail Grade Crossing
PO Box 2144, Ballston Spa, NY 12020
Program Manager:
Randall L Dickinson 518-899-5372/fax: 518-899-5372

Federal Transit Administration, Region II-New York
One Bowling Green, Rm 429, New York, NY 10004-1415
Web site: www.fta.dot.gov
Regional Admin:
Marilyn G. Shazor 212-668-2170/fax: 212-668-2136

Offices and agencies generally appear in alphabetical order, except when specific order is requested by listee.

Maritime Administration
Web site: www.marad.dot.gov

Great Lakes Region (includes part of New York State)
500 West Madison Street, Suite 1110, Chicago, IL 60661
312-353-1032
Regional Director:
Floyd Miras 312-353-1032/fax: 312-353-1036
e-mail: floyd.miras@dot.gov

North Atlantic Region
One Bowling Green, Rm 418, New York, NY 10004
Regional Director:
Jeffrey Flumignan. 212-668-3330
e-mail: flumignan@dot.gov

US Merchant Marine Academy
300 Steamboat Rd, Kings Point, NY 11024-1699
516-726-5800
Web site: www.usmma.edu
Superintendent:
RADM James A. Helis. 516-726-5800

National Highway Traffic Safety Administration, Reg II-NY
222 Mamaroneck Ave, Suite 204, White Plains, NY 10605
Web site: www.nhtsa.dot.gov
Team Leader:
Richard Simon. .914-682-6162/fax: 914-682-6239
e-mail: region2@dot.gov

Office of Inspector General, Region II-New York
80 Madison Lane, New York, NY 10038
Web site: www.oig.dot.gov
Inspector General:
Debra Herlica. .212-825-2413/fax: 212-825-3238
e-mail: dherlica@doi.nyc.gov

Saint Lawrence Seaway Development Corporation
180 Andrews St, Massena, NY 13662
Web site: www.greatlakes-seaway.com
Assoc Administrator:
Salvatore Pisani 315-764-3209/fax: 315-764-3235
e-mail: sal.pisani@sls.dot.gov

U.S. CONGRESS

See U.S. Congress Chapter for additional Standing Committee and Subcommittee information.

House of Representatives Standing Committees

Transportation & Infrastructure
Chair:
Bill Shuster (R-PA). 202-225-2431
Ranking Minority Member:
Nick J. Rahall II (D-WV) 202-225-3452
New York Delegate:
Sean Patrick Maloney (D). 202-225-5441
New York Delegate:
Timothy H Bishop (D) 202-225-3826
New York Delegate:
Richard L. Hanna 202-225-3665
New York Delegate:
Jerrold Nadler (D). 202-225-5635

Senate Standing Committees

Commerce, Science & Transportation
Chair:
John D Rockefeller IV (D-WV) 202-224-6472
Vice Chair:
John Thune (R-SD). 202-224-2321

Environment & Public Works
Chair:
Barbara Boxer (D-CA) 202-224-8832
Ranking Minority Member:
David Vitter (R-LA) 202-224-4623
New York Delegate:
Kirsten Gillibrand (D). 202-224-4451

Subcommittee
Transportation & Infrastructure
Chair:
Max Baucus (D-MT) 202-224-2651
Ranking Minority Member:
John Barrasso (R-WY) 202-224-6441

PRIVATE SECTOR

ALSTOM Transportation Inc
1 Transit Dr, Hornell, NY 14843
607-281-2487 Fax: 607-324-2641
e-mail: chuck.wochele@transport.alstom.com
Web site: www.transport.alstom.com
High-speed trains, rapid transit vehicles, commuter cars, AC propulsion & signaling, passenger locomotives
Wallace Smith, Vice President
Chuck Wochele, Vice President Business Development

A&W Architects and Engineers
Ammann & Whitney Consulting Engineers
96 Morton St, New York, NY 10014
212-462-8500 Fax: 212-929-5356
e-mail: nivanoff@ammann-whitney.com; asandor@ammann-whitney.com
Web site: www.ammann-whitney.com
Planning, engineering & construction mgmt for airport, transit, gov't, recreation & commercial facilities; highways; bridges
Nick Ivanoff, President & Chief Executive Officer

Automobile Club of New York
1415 Kellum Place, Garden City, NY 11530
516-873-2259 Fax: 516-873-2355
Web site: www.aaany.com
John Corlett, Director Government Affairs

Automotive Technology & Energy Group of Western NY
2568 Walden Avenue, Suite 103, Cheektowaga, NY 14225
716-651-4645 Fax: 716-651-4662
Garage & service station owners
Robert Gliss, Executive Director

British Airways PLC
75-20 Astoria Blvd, Jackson Heights, NY 11370
347-418-4729 Fax: 347-418-4204
e-mail: john.lampl@ba.com
Web site: www.ba.com
John Lampl, Vice President, Corporate Communications-Americas

CP Rail System
200 Clifton Corporate Parkway, PO Box 8002, Clifton Park, NY 12065
518-383-7200 Fax: 518-383-7222
Freight transport
Brent Szafron, Service Area Manager

DKI Engineering & Consulting USA, PC, Corporate World Headquarters
632 Plank Rd, Ste 208, Clifton Park, NY 12065
518-373-4999 Fax: 518-373-8989
e-mail: dki123@aol.com
Web site: www.dkitechnologies.com
Design, engineering, planning, construction management & program management oversight for airports, bridges, highways, railroads, transit, tunnels, water & wastewater facilities
D K Gupta, President & Chief Executive Officer

Empire State Passengers Association
PO Box 434, Syracuse, NY 13209
716-741-6384 Fax: 716-632-3044
e-mail: bbecker@esparail.org
Web site: www.esparail.org
Advocacy for improvement of rail passenger service
Bruce Becker, President

Ethan C Eldon Associates Inc
1350 Broadway, Ste 612, New York, NY 10018
212-967-5400 Fax: 212-967-2747
e-mail: eceaethan@aol.com
Environmental, EIS, traffic, hazardous & solid waste consulting
Ethan C Eldon, President

Gandhi Engineering Inc
111 John St, 3rd Fl, New York, NY 10038-3002
212-349-2900 Fax: 212-285-0205
e-mail: gandhi@gandhieng.com
Web site: www.gandhieng.com
Consulting architects & engineers; infrastructure projects & transportation facilities
Kirti Gandhi, President

General Contractors Association of NY
60 East 42nd St, Rm 3510, New York, NY 10165
212-687-3131 Fax: 212-808-5267
e-mail: felice@gca.gcany.net
Heavy construction, transportation
Felice Farber, Director, External Affairs

Jacobs Engineering
260 Madison Ave, 12th Floor, Suite 1200, New York, NY 10016
212-268-1500 Fax: 212-481-9484
Web site: www.jacobs.com
Multi-modal surface transportation planning, design, engineering, construction & inspection services
Vincent Mangieri, Vice President

Komanoff Energy Associates
636 Broadway, Rm 602, New York, NY 10012-2623
212-260-5237
e-mail: kea@igc.org
Energy, utilities & transportation consulting
Charles Komanoff, Director

Konheim & Ketcham Inc
175 Pacific St, Brooklyn, NY 11201
718-330-0550 Fax: 718-330-0582
e-mail: csk@konheimketcham.com
Web site: www.konheimketcham.com
Environmental impact analysis, traffic engineering, transportation planning & technical assistance to community groups
Carolyn Konheim, President

Kriss, Kriss, Brignola & Persing, LLP
350 Northern Blvd, Ste 306, Albany, NY 12204
518-449-2037 Fax: 518-449-7875
e-mail: office@krisslaw.com
Web site: www.krisslawoffice.com
Advocates for highway & auto safety
Mark C Kriss, Partner

Long Island Rail Road Commuter's Council
347 Madison Ave, 8th Fl, New York, NY 10017
212-878-7087 Fax: 212-878-7461
e-mail: mail@lirrcc.org
Web site: www.lirrcc.org
Represent interest of LIRR riders
Mark Epstein, Chair

Metro-North Railroad Commuter Council
347 Madison Ave, New York, NY 10017
212-878-7077 or 212-878-7087 Fax: 212-878-7461
e-mail: mail@pcac.org
Web site: www.pcac.org
Represent interests of MNR riders
William Henderson, Chair

NY Airport Service
15 Second Ave, Brooklyn, NY 11215
718-875-8200 Fax: 718-875-7056
Web site: www.nyairportservice.com
Airport shuttle bus services
Mark Marmurstein, Vice President

NY State Association of Town Superintendents of Highways Inc
119 Washington Avenue, Suite 300, Albany, NY 12210
518-694-9313 Fax: 518-694-9314
e-mail: info@nystownhwys.org
Web site: www.nystownhwys.org
Michael K Thompson, Communications Director

NYS Association of Service Stations & Repair Shops
6 Walker Way, Albany, NY 12205-4946
518-452-4367 Fax: 518-452-1955
e-mail: nysassn@together.net
Web site: www.nysassrs.com
Protect the interests of independent service stations & repair shops & the motoring public
Ralph Bombardiere, Executive Director

NYS County Hwy Super Assn / NY Aviation Mgt Assn / NY Public Transit Assn
119 Washington Ave, Ste 100, Albany, NY 12210
518-465-1694 Fax: 518-465-1942
e-mail: info@countyhwys.org; info@nyama.com; nypta@atdial.net
Web site: www.countyhwys.org; www.nyama.com; www.nytransit.org
County highways & bridges in NYS; aviation industry in NYS; public transit industry in NYS
Kathleen A Van De Loo, Communications Director

National Economic Research Associates
308 N Cayuga St, Ithaca, NY 14850
607-277-3007 Fax: 607-277-1581
e-mail: alfred.kahn@nera.com
Web site: www.nera.com
Utility & transportation regulation, deregulation & antitrust
Alfred E Kahn, Professor Emeritus & Special Consultant

New England Steampship Agents Inc
730 Downing St, Niskayuna, NY 12309
518-463-5749 Fax: 518-463-5751
e-mail: nesa0025@aol.com
Domestic transportation, vessel agency/husbandry, customs brokerage & vessel brokerage
Diane Delory, President

Offices and agencies generally appear in alphabetical order, except when specific order is requested by listee.

Policy Areas

New York & Atlantic Railway (NYA)
68-01 Otto Rd, Glendale, NY 11385
7189497-3023 Fax: 718-497-3364
e-mail: pvictor@anacostia.com
Web site: www.anacostia.com
Freight transport
Paul Victor, President

New York Public Interest Research Group Straphangers Campaign
9 Murray Street, Lower Level, New York, NY 10007
212-349-6460 Fax: 212-349-1366
e-mail: grussian@nypirg.org
Web site: www.straphangers.org; www.nypirg.org
Mass transit & government reform
Gene Russianoff, Senior Staff Attorney

New York Roadway Improvement Coalition (NYRIC)
629 Old White Plains Road, Tarrytown, NY 10591
914-631-6070 Fax: 914-631-5172
e-mail: cicwhv@cicnys.org
Heavy highway & bridge construction
Ross Pepe, President

New York Shipping Association Inc
100 Wood Ave South, Ste 304, Iselin, NJ 08830-2716
732-452-7800 Fax: 732-452-6312
e-mail: jcobb@nysanet.org
Web site: www.nysanet.org
Maximizing the efficiency, cost competitiveness, safety & quality of marine cargo operations in the Port of New York & New Jersey
James H Cobb, Jr, Director, Governmental Affairs

New York State Auto Dealers Association
37 Elk St, Albany, NY 12207
518-463-1148 x204 Fax: 518-432-1309
e-mail: bob@nysada.com
Web site: www.nysada.com
Robert Vancavage, President

New York State Motor Truck Association
828 Washington Ave, Albany, NY 12203-1622
518-458-9696 Fax: 518-458-2525
e-mail: kadams@nytrucks.org
Web site: www.nytrucks.org
Safety & regulatory compliance
Kendra Adams, Executive Director

New York State Transportation Engineering Alliance (NYSTEA)
99 Pine St, Ste 207, Albany, NY 12207
518-436-0786 Fax: 518-427-0452
e-mail: sdm@fwc-law.com
Transportation & infrastructure
Stephen D Morgan, Secretary

New York, Susquehanna & Western Railway Corporation, The
1 Railroad Ave, Cooperstown, NY 13326-1110
607-547-2555 Fax: 607-547-9834
e-mail: nfenno@nysw.com
Web site: www.nysw.com
Subsidiaries operate freight railroad systems
Nathan R Fenno, President

Parsons Brinckerhoff
One Penn Plaza, New York, NY 10119
212-465-5000 Fax: 212-465-5096
e-mail: bennett@pbworld.com
Web site: www.pbworld.com
Engineering, planning, construction management & consulting for transit & transportation, power & telecom projects
Joel H Bennett, Senior Vice President

Regional Plan Association
4 Irving Place, 7th Fl, New York, NY 10003
212-253-2727 Fax: 212-253-5666
e-mail: jeff@rpa.org
Web site: www.rpa.org
Regional transportation planning & development issues
Jeffrey M Zupan, Senior Fellow, Transportation

Seneca Flight Operations
2262 Airport Dr, Penn Yan, NY 14527
315-536-4471 Fax: 315-536-4558
e-mail: rleppert@senecafoods.com
Web site: www.senecafoods.com
Executive air transportation
Richard Leppert, General Manager

Simmons-Boardman Publishing Corp
345 Hudson St, 12th Fl, New York, NY 10014-4590
212-620-7200 Fax: 212-633-1863
e-mail: sbrailgroup@sbpub.com
Web site: www.railwayage.com or www.rtands.com or www.railjournal.com
Publisher of: Railway Age, International Railway Journal & Rapid Transit Review, Railway Track & Structures
Robert DeMarco, Publisher

Systra Consulting Inc
470 Seventh Ave, 10th Floor, New York, NY 10018
212-494-9111 Fax: 212-494-9112
Web site: www.systraconsulting.com
Engineering consultants specializing in urban rail & transit systems, passenger & freight railroads & high speed rail
Peter Allibone, Executive Vice President

Transport Workers Union of America, AFL-CIO
1700 Broadway, 2nd Fl, New York, NY 10019
212-259-4900 Fax: 212-265-5704
Web site: www.twu.com
Bus, train, railroad & airline workers' union
James C Little, International President

Transportation Alternatives
111 John Street, Suite 260, New York, NY 10038
212-629-8080 Fax: 212-629-8334
e-mail: info@transalt.org
Web site: www.transalt.org
NYC commute alternatives, traffic calming, pedestrian safety issues, bicycling, public space
Paul Steely White, Executive Director

Tri-State Transportation Campaign
350 W 31st St, Room 802, New York, NY 10001-2726
212-268-7474 Fax: 212-268-7333
e-mail: tstc@tstc.org
Web site: www.tstc.org
Public interest, transit advocacy, planning & environmental organizations working to reform transportation policies
Kate Slevin, Executive Director

United Transportation Union
35 Fuller Road, Suite 205, Albany, NY 12205
518-438-8403 Fax: 518-438-8404
e-mail: sjnasca@aol.com
Web site: www.utu.org
Federal government railroad, bus & airline employees; public employees
Samuel Nasca, Legislative Director

Urbitran Group
71 West 23rd St, 11th Fl, New York, NY 10010
212-366-6200 Fax: 212-366-6214
e-mail: mhorodnicaenu@urbitran.com
Web site: www.urbitran.com
Engineering, architecture & planning
Michael Horodnicaenu, President & Chief Executive Officer

VETERANS AND MILITARY

NEW YORK STATE

GOVERNOR'S OFFICE

Governor's Office
Executive Chamber
State Capitol
Albany, NY 12224
518-474-8390 Fax: 518-474-1513
Web site: www.ny.gov

Governor:
Andrew M Cuomo 518-474-8390
Secretary to the Governor:
William Mulrow 518-474-4246
Counsel to the Governor:
Alphonso David 518-474-8343
Chief of Staff:
Melissa DeRosa . . . . 518-474-8418 or 212-681-4640
Director, Communications:
James Allen. . . . . 518-474-8418 or 212-681-4640

EXECUTIVE DEPARTMENTS AND RELATED AGENCIES

Health Department
Corning Tower
Empire State Plaza
Albany, NY 12237
518-474-2011
Web site: www.health.ny.gov

Health Facilities Management
Director:
David J Hernandez 518-474-2772/fax: 518-474-0611

Helen Hayes Hospital
Rte 9W, West Haverstraw, NY 10993-1195
845-786-4000
e-mail: info@helenhayeshospital.org
Web site: www.helenhayeshospital.org
CEO:
Edmund Coletti 845-786-4202/fax: 845-947-0036
Chief Operating Officer:
Kathleen Martucci 845-786-4201

New York State Veterans' Home at Batavia
220 Richmond Ave, Batavia, NY 14020
585-345-2000
Web site: www.nysvets.org
Administrator:
Joanne I Hernick 585-345-2076/fax: 585-345-9030
Acting Medical Director:
Margaret Mitchell, MD 585-345-2042
Director, Nursing:
Stephanie Sulyma 585-345-2000 x2041

New York State Veterans' Home at Montrose . . . . . . fax: 914-788-6100
2090 Albany Post Rd, Montrose, NY 10548
Fax: 914-788-6100
Web site: www.nysvets.org
Administrator:
Nancy Baa-Danso. 914-788-6003
Medical Director:
George Gorich, MD 914-788-6025
Director, Nursing:
Christene St Paul Joseph 914-788-6021

New York State Veterans' Home at Oxford
4211 State Highway 220, Oxford, NY 13830
607-843-3100
Web site: www.nysvets.org
Administrator:
James Wyzykowski. 607-843-3129/fax: 607-843-3199
Acting Medical Director:
Donna Hussman, MD 607-843-3140
Director, Nursing:
Linda Winston 607-843-3165

New York State Veterans' Home at St Albans
178-50 Linden Blvd, Jamaica, NY 11434-1467
718-990-0300
Web site: www.nysvets.org
Administrator:
Neville Goldson 718-990-0329
Medical Director:
Thomas Bizarro MD. 718-990-0328
Director, Nursing:
Elmina Wilson-Hew 718-990-0316

Labor Department
Building 12, Room 500
Harriman State Office Campus
Albany, NY 12240
518-457-9000 Fax: 518-457-6908
e-mail: nysdol@labor.ny.gov
Web site: www.labor.ny.gov

Commissioner:
Roberta Reardon 518-457-9000
Executive Deputy Commissioner:
Mario Musolino 518-457-4318

Federal Programs
Deputy Commissioner, Federal Programs:
Bruce Herman. 518-485-6410

Employment Services Division
Director:
Vacant. 518-457-3584
Assistant Director:
Russell Oliver. 518-457-3584

Veterans Services
Program Coordinator:
Vacant. 518-457-1343

Employer Services
Director:
Vacant. 518-457-6821
Rural Labor Services:
Valerie Sewell. 518-457-8539

Military & Naval Affairs, Division of
330 Old Niskayuna Rd
Latham, NY 12110
518-786-4786 or 518-489-6188 Fax: 518-786-4649
Web site: www.dmna.ny.gov

Adjutant General:
Major Gen Anthony P German. 518-786-4502
e-mail: pat.murphy@us.army.mil
Adjutant General - Air:
Anthony P. German 518-786-4317
Executive Officer:
Donald McKnight. 518-786-4388
Legal Counsel:
Robert G Conway, Jr 518-786-4541

Offices and agencies generally appear in alphabetical order, except when specific order is requested by listee.

Director, Budget & Finance:
Robert A Martin 518-786-4514
Director, Governmental & Community Affairs:
James M Huelle. 518-786-4580
Director, Public Affairs:
David Warager. 518-786-4581/fax: 518-786-4649
e-mail: david.warager@dmna.nyg.ny.gov

Veterans' Affairs, Division of

2 Empire State Plaza
17th Fl
Albany, NY 12223-1551
518-474-6114 or 888-838-7697 Fax: 518-473-0379
e-mail: dvainfo@veterans.ny.gov
Web site: www.veterans.ny.gov

Acting Director:
William A Kraus. 518-474-6114
Executive Deputy Director:
Vacant 518-474-6114
Secretary to the Director:
Mary Quay 518-474-6114
e-mail: m.quay@veterans.ny.gov
Deputy Director, Administration & Budget:
Michelle LaRock. 518-474-6114
e-mail: mlarock@veterans.state.ny,us
Counsel:
Samuel Spitzberg 518-474-6114
e-mail: sspitzberg@veterans.ny.gov
Deputy Director, Programs, Operations & Training:
Christine Tarnowski 518-474-6784
e-mail: ctarnowski@veterans.state.ny.us
Assistant Director, Communications:
Casey Lumbra. 518-486-5251
e-mail: clumbra@veterans.state.ny.us

Bureau of Veterans Education

Bureau Chief:
James Bombard. 518-474-5322
Supervisor:
Craig Farley 518-474-7606

Counseling & Claims Service

Web site: www.veterans.state.ny.us/ofcs.htm
State Veteran Counselor:
Sue Doan. 315-428-4046
State Veteran Counselor:
Lloyd Collins 315-428-4046
State Veteran Counselor:
Mark Tamkus 315-785-2468

Eastern Region
55 Hanson Place, Brooklyn, NY 11217
Deputy Director:
Andrew Roberts 718-722-2584

Western Region
65 Court St, ste 310, Buffalo, NY 14202-3406
Deputy Director:
Vacant 716-847-3414/fax: 716-847-3410

Veterans' Service Organizations

Albany Housing Coalition Inc . . . . fax: 518-465-6499
278 Clinton Ave, Albany, NY 12210
Fax: 518-465-6499
e-mail: admin@ahcvets.org
Web site: www.ahcvets.org
Executive Director:
Joseph Sluszka 518-465-5251
e-mail: jsluszka@ahcvets.org
Director, Veterans Svcs:
Lee Vartigan 518-465-5251
e-mail: l.vartigan@ahcvets.org

COPIN HOUSE (Homeless Veterans) . . . . fax: 716-283-5712
5622 Buffalo Ave, Niagara Falls, NY 14304
Executive Director:
Sharon McGrath 716-283-5622

Continuum of Care for Homeless Veterans in New York City

30th Street Shelter
400-430 East 30th St, New York, NY 10016
Director:
Yvonne Ballard. 212-481-4730

Project TORCH, Veterans Health Care Center
40 Flatbush Ave Ext, 8th Fl, Brooklyn, NY 11201
Program Coordinator:
Julie Irwin 718-439-4345/fax: 718-439-4356

Hicksville Counseling Center, Veterans' Resource Center . . . fax: 516-935-2717
385 West John St, Hicksville, NY 11801
Director, Substance Abuse Program & Veterans Resource Center:
Geryl Pecora 516-935-6858

Saratoga Cnty Rural Preservation Co (Homeless Veterans)
36 Church Ave, Ballston Spa, NY 12020
Web site: www.vethelpny.org
Executive Director:
Cheryl Hage-Perez. 518-885-0091/fax: 518-885-0998
e-mail: chp@saratogarpc.org

Suffolk County United Veterans Halfway House Project Inc
PO Box 598, Patchogue, NY 11772
Executive Director:
John Lynch 631-924-8088/fax: 631-924-0160

Veterans House (The) . . . . fax: 518-465-6499
180 First St, Albany, NY 12210
House Manager:
John Jacobie 518-449-8430

Veterans Outreach Center Inc. . . . . fax: 585-546-5234
447 South Ave, Rochester, NY 14620
Fax: 585-546-5234
Web site: www.veteransoutreachcenter.org
SSVF Program Manager:
Sean Sizer 585-295-7801
e-mail: info@veteransoutreachcenter.org

Veterans Services Center of the Southern Tier . . fax: 607-771-9395
174 Clinton St, Binghamton, NY 13905
Executive Director:
Patricia Gaven. 607-771-8387

Veterans' Coalition of the Hudson Valley . . . . fax: 845-471-6113
9 Vassar St, Poughkeepsie, NY 12601
845-471-6113 Fax: 845-471-6113
Administrator:
Marilyn Wickman. 845-471-6113
e-mail: vetcoal@aol.com

CORPORATIONS, AUTHORITIES AND COMMISSIONS

Brooklyn Navy Yard Development Corporation

63 Flushing Ave, Unit #300
Bldg 292, 3rd Fl
Brooklyn, NY 11205

718-907-5900 Fax: 718-643-9296
e-mail: info@brooklynnavyyard.org
Web site: www.brooklynnavyyard.org

Chair:
Henry Gutman 718-907-5900
President & Chief Executive Officer:
David Ehrenberg 718-907-5900
Executive Vice President & Chief Operating Officer:
Elliot S. Matz 718-907-5900
Senior Vice President, External Affairs:
Richard Drucker 718-907-5900
EVP/Chief of Staff:
Clare Newman 718-907-5900
General Counsel:
Paul Kelly 718-907-5900

NEW YORK STATE LEGISLATURE

See Legislative Branch in Section 1 for additional Standing Committee and Subcommittee information.

Assembly Standing Committees

Veterans Affairs
Chair:
Michael DenDekker (D) 518-455-4545
Ranking Minority Member:
Stephen Hawley (R) 518-455-5811

Senate Standing Committees

Veterans, Homeland Security & Military Affairs
Chair:
Thomas Croci (R) 518-455-3570
Ranking Minority Member:
Joseph P Addabbo, Jr (D) 518-455-2322

U.S. GOVERNMENT

EXECUTIVE DEPARTMENTS AND RELATED AGENCIES

US Defense Department
e-mail: www.defenselink.mil

AIR FORCE-National Media Outreach . . . . . fax: 212-784-0149
805 Third Ave, 9th Fl, New York, NY 10022
Director:
Angela Billings 212-784-0147
e-mail: big.saf@us.af.mil
Public Relations Director:
Wesley Preston Miller 212-784-0147
e-mail: jason.medina@afnews.af.mil

Air National Guard

Francis S Gabreski Airport, 106th Rescue Wing . . . . fax: 631-723-7179
150 Old Riverhead Rd, Westhampton Beach, NY 11978
Commander:
Col. Thomas J. Owens II 631-723-7400
Public Affairs Officer:
Tech Sgt. Eric Miller 631-723-7470

Hancock Field, 174th Fighter Wing
6001 E Molloy Rd, Syracuse, NY 13211
315-454-6146
Commander:
Col. Greg A. Semmel 315-454-6146

Army

Fort Drum . . . . . fax: 315-772-8295
10012 South Riva Ridge Loop, Fort Drum, NY 13602-5028
315-772-5461 Fax: 315-772-8295
Web site: www.drum.army.mil
Commander:
Maj. Stephen J. Townsend 315-772-8295
Community Relations Officer:
Lori Haney 315-772-8295

Fort Hamilton . . . . . fax: 718-630-4709
Fort Hamilton, New York, NY 11252
Commander:
Col. Eluyn Gines 718-630-4101

Watervliet Arsenal
1 Buffington Street, Watervliet, NY 12189-4050
518-266-5111
Commander:
Mark F. Migaleddi 518-266-5111
Public Affairs Officer:
John Snyder 518-266-5055

Marine Corps

1st Marine Corps District
605 Stewart Ave, Garden City, NY 11530
Commander:
Col. J.J. Dill 516-228-5661
Executive Officer:
Lt. Col. Mark T. Donar 516-228-5661

Public Affairs Office . . . . . fax: 212-784-0169
805 Third Ave, 9th Fl, New York, NY 10022
Director:
Lt. Col. Christopher Perrine 347-292-8762

Navy

Saratoga Springs Naval Support Unit
19 JF King Dr, Saratoga Springs, NY 12866-9267
Commander:
CDR Vince D. Garcia 518-886-0200/fax: 518-886-0120

US Department of Veterans Affairs
Web site: www.va.gov

National Cemetery Administration
Web site: www.cem.va.gov

Bath National Cemetery
San Juan Ave, Bath, NY 14810
Director:
Walter Baroody 607-664-4853/fax: 607-664-4761

Calverton National Cemetery
210 Princeton Blvd, Calverton, NY 11933-1031
Director:
Michael G Picerno 631-727-5410

Cypress Hills National Cemetery . . . . . fax: 631-694-5422
625 Jamaica Ave, Brooklyn, NY 11208
631-454-4949 Fax: 631-694-5422
Director:
Michael G Picerno 631-454-4949/fax: 631-694-5422

Gerald B.H. Solomon Saratoga National Cemetery
200 Duell Rd, Schuylerville, NY 12871-1721
Director:
Daniel Cassidy 518-581-9128/fax: 518-583-6975

Long Island National Cemetery . . . . . fax: 631-694-5422
2040 Wellwood Ave, Farmingdale, NY 11735
631-454-4949 Fax: 631-694-5422

Director:
Michael G Picerno 631-454-4949/fax: 631-694-5422

Woodlawn National Cemetery
1825 Davis St, Elmira, NY 14901
Director:
Walter Baroody 607-732-5411/fax: 607-742-1769

VA Regional Office of Public Affairs, Field Operations Svc
245 W Houston St, Ste 315B, New York, NY 10014
Regional Director:
Lawrence M Devine 212-807-3429/fax: 212-807-4030
Public Affairs Specialist:
James A Blue 212-807-3429
Public Affairs Specialist:
Leo Marinacci 212-807-3429

Veterans Benefits Administration

Buffalo Regional Office
130 South Elmwood Avenue, Buffalo, NY 14202-2478
800-827-1000
Regional Director:
Donna Ferrell 716-857-3020/fax: 716-551-3072
Assistant Director:
Lillie Jackson 800-827-1000
Veterans Service Center Manager:
James Rogers 800-827-1000
Regional Counsel:
Joseph Moreno 800-827-1000
Vocational Rehabilitation & Employment Division:
Joseph Senulis 800-827-1000
Chief, Education Division:
Robert Quall 800-827-1000

New York City Regional Office .... fax: 212-807-4024
245 West Houston St, New York, NY 10014-4085
Director:
Patricia Amberg-Blyskal 212-807-3055
Veterans Benefits & Services Officer:
Joseph Collorafi 212-807-3420
Vocational Rehabilitation & Counseling Division:
Bernard Finger 212-807-3030

Veterans Health Admin Integrated Svc Network (VISN)

VA Healthcare Network Upstate New York (VISN2)
113 Holland Ave, Bldg 7, Albany, NY 12208
Web site: www.va.gov/visns/visn02
Acting Network Director:
Michael Finegan 518-626-7317 x67317
Network Communications Manager:
Kathleen Hider 585-463-2642/fax: 585-463-2649

Albany VA Medical Center
113 Holland Ave, Albany, NY 12208
Director:
Lisa W. Weiss, MS 518-626-5000
Patient Advocate:
Bridgette Qualls 518-626-7125

Batavia VA Medical Center .... fax: 585-344-3305
222 Richmond Ave, Batavia, NY 14020
716-343-7500 Fax: 585-344-3305
Director:
Brian G. Stiller 716-862-8529
Patient Advocate:
Tom Bligh 585-297-1257

Bath VA Medical Center
76 Veterans Ave, Bath, NY 14810
Director:
Michael Swartz 607-664-4722
Patient Advocate:
Cheryl Mills

Buffalo VA Medical Center .... fax: 716-862-8759
3495 Bailey Ave, Buffalo, NY 14215
716-834-9200 Fax: 716-862-8759
Director:
Brian G. Stiller 716-862-8529
Public Affairs Officer:
Christine Krupski 716-862-8852

Canandaigua VA Medical Center
400 Fort Hill Ave, Canandaigua, NY 14424
Director:
Michael Swartz 585-394-2000
Patient Advocate:
Laurie Guererri 585-393-7612
e-mail: robert.babcock2@med.va.gov

Syracuse VA Medical Center & Clinics
800 Irving Ave, Syracuse, NY 13210
Director:
James Cody 315-425-4892
e-mail: james.cody@med.va.gov
Patient Advocate:
Colleen Lancette 315-425-4345

VA NY/NJ Veterans Healthcare Network (VISN3)
Bldg 16, 130 W Kingsbridge Rd, Bronx, NY 10468
Web site: www.va.gov/visns/visn03
Network Director:
Michael A. Sabo 718-741-4143/fax: 718-741-4141
Chief Medical Officer:
Joan McInerney, MD

James J. Peters VA Medical Center .... fax: 718-741-4269
130 W Kingsbridge Rd, Bronx, NY 10468
Director:
MaryAnn Musumeci 718-584-9000 x6512
Director of Government/Community Relations:
Jim Connell

Brooklyn Campus of the NY Harbor Healthcare System
800 Poly Pl, Brooklyn, NY 11209
718-836-6600
Director:
John J Donnellan, Jr 718-630-3521/fax: 718-630-2840
Associate Director:
Veronica J Foy 718-630-3524

Castle Point Campus of the VA Hudson Vly Healthcare System .. fax: 845-838-5193
PO Box 100, 100 Rte 9D, Castle Point, NY 12511
845-831-2000 Fax: 845-838-5193
Executive Director:
Michael A Sabo 845-737-4400 x2460

Montrose Campus of the VA Hudson Valley Healthcare System .. fax: 914-788-4244
2094 Albany Post Rd, Montrose, NY 10548
Director:
Michael A. Sabo 914-737-4400
Public Affairs:
Nancy A Winter 914-737-4400 x2255

New York Campus of the NY Harbor Healthcare System
423 East 23rd St, New York, NY 10010
212-686-7500
Executive Chief of Staff:
Michael S Simberkoff 212-951-3417
Associate Director:
Martina A Parauda 212-951-3240

Northport VA Medical Center .... fax: 631-754-7933
79 Middleville Rd, Northport, NY 11768
Director:
Robert Schuster 631-261-4400 x2747
Public Affairs Officer:
Joe Sledge

US Labor Department
Web site: www.dol.gov/vets/

Offices and agencies generally appear in alphabetical order, except when specific order is requested by listee.

Field Offices

New York State Field Offices

Albany . . . . fax: 518-435-0833

Harriman State Campus, Bldg 12, Rm 518, Albany, NY 12240-0099
518-457-7465 Fax: 518-435-0833

Director:
Barry Morgan 518-457-7465/fax: 518-435-0833

Veteran's Program Assistant:
Joan M Cramer. 518-457-7465
e-mail: cramer.joan@dol.gov

Brooklyn

9 Bond Street, Room 301/302, Brooklyn, NY 11201

Assistant Director:
Daniel A Friedman. 718-613-3676
e-mail: friedman.daniel@dol.gov

Veteran's Program Specialist:
Edward L. Diaz 718-613-3676
e-mail: diaz.edward.L@dol.gov

US State Department

Web site: www.state.gov

US Mission to the United Nations

799 United Nations Plaza, New York, NY 10017

Permanent US Representative to the United Nations:
Ambassador Susan E. Rice

Deputy Permanent US Representative to the United Nations:
Ambassador Rosemary A. DiCarlo

Alternate Representative for Special Political Affairs to the United Nations:
Ambassador Jeffrey DeLaurentis

U.S. CONGRESS

See U.S. Congress Chapter for additional Standing Committee and Subcommittee information.

House of Representatives Standing Committees

Armed Services

McKeon (R-CA):
Howard P. Buck'''' . . . . Chair or 202-225-1956

Ranking Minority Member:
Adam Smith (D-WA) 202-225-8901

New York Delegate:
Dan Maffei (D) 202-225-3701

New York Delegate:
Chris Gibson (R). 202-225-5614

Veterans' Affairs

Chair:
Jeff Miller (R-FL). 202-225-4136

Ranking Minority Member:
Michael H. Michaud (D-ME) 202-225-6306

Senate Standing Committees

Armed Services

Chair:
Carl Levin (D-MI). 202-224-6221

Ranking Minority Member:
James M. Inhofe (R-OK) 202-224-4721

Veterans' Affairs

Chair:
Bernard Sanders (D-VT). 202-224-5141

Ranking Minority Member:
Richard Burr (R-NC) 202-224-3154

PRIVATE SECTOR

369th Veterans Association Inc
PO Box 91, Lincolnton Station, New York, NY 10037
212-281-3308 Fax: 212-281-6308
e-mail: jamnat@earthlink.net
Web site: www.home.earthlink.net/~natlvets/
Assistance & referrals for all veterans
Nathaniel James, National President

Air Force Association (AFA)
1501 Lee Highway, Arlington, VA 22209-1198
703-247-5800 Fax: 703-247-5853
Web site: www.afa.org
Support & advance the interest & recognition of the US Air Force
Donald L Peterson, Executive Director

Air Force Sergeants Association (AFSA), Division 1
557 Sixth St, Dover, NH 3820
603-742-4844
e-mail: acaldwell557@comcast.net
Web site: www.afsahq.org
Protect rights & benefits of enlisted personnel-active, retired, National Guard, reserve & their families
Alfred B Caldwell, President Division 1

Air Force Women Officers Associated (AFWOA)
PO Box 780155, San Antonio, TX 78278
210-481-6383
e-mail: patriciamurphy@afwoa.com
Web site: www.afwoa.org
Represent interests of active duty, retired & former women officers of the Air Force; preserve the history & promote recognition of the role of military women
Col Patricia M Murphy, USAF Retired, President

Albany Housing Coalition Inc
278 Clinton Ave, Albany, NY 12210
518-465-5251 Fax: 518-465-6499
e-mail: admin@ahcvets.org
Web site: www.ahcvets.org
Providing a continuum of affordable housing for veterans & their families; rental housing referrals
Bryon Koshgarian, Phd, Director, Veterans Services

American Legion, Department of New York
112 State St, Suite 1300, Albany, NY 12207
518-463-2215 Fax: 518-427-8443
e-mail: info@nylegion.org
Web site: www.ny.legion.org
Advocate for veterans; entitlements for wartime veterans, their families & service to the community, children & youth of our nation
Richard M Pedro, New York State Adjutant

American Military Retirees Association Inc
5436 Peru St, Ste 1, Plattsburgh, NY 12901
800-424-2969 or 518-563-9479 Fax: 518-324-5204
e-mail: info@amra1973.org
Web site: www.amra1973.org
Works on behalf of military retirees aand their families to protect their rights and benefits under the law and to lobby on their behalf in Washington D.C. and elsewhere.
Peg Bergeron, Executive Director

Army Aviation Association of America (AAAA)
755 Main St, Ste 4D, Monroe, CT 06468-2830
203-268-2450 Fax: 203-268-5870
Advance the cause & recognition of US Army aviation; benefit all personnel, current, retired, families & survivors
William R Harris, Executive Director

Army Aviation Association of America (AAAA), Empire Chapter
3 Glendale Dr, Clifton Park, NY 12065
518-786-4397 Fax: 518-786-4393
e-mail: mark.f.burke@us.army.mil
Advance the cause & recognition of US Army aviation; benefit all Army aviation personnel, current, retired, families & survivors
COL Mark F Burke, Chapter President

Association of Military Surgeons of the US (AMSUS), NY Chapter
105 Franklin Ave, Malverne, NY 11565-1926
516-542-0025 Fax: 516-593-3114
e-mail: amsusny@aol.com
Improve federal healthcare service; support & represent military & other health care professionals
Col John J Hassett, USAR, President NY Chapter

Association of the US Army (AUSA)
2425 Wilson Blvd, Arlington, VA 22201
703-841-4300 x639 or 800-336-4570 Fax: 703-525-9039
e-mail: wloper@ausa.org
Web site: www.ausa.org
Champion the cause & objectives of the US Army by public relations, communications & legislative action
William Loper, Director Government Affairs

Black Veterans for Social Justice Inc
665 Willoughby Street, Brooklyn, NY 11221
718-852-6004 Fax: 718-852-4805
e-mail: admin@bvsj.org; cfo@bvsj.org
Web site: www.bvsj.org
Assist all veterans in obtaining benefits, entitlements, employment & housing
Job Mashariki, President & Chief Executive Officer

Blinded Veterans Association New York Inc
245 W Houston St, 2nd Fl, Rm 208, New York, NY 10014
212-807-3173 Fax: 212-807-4022
Web site: www.bva.org
Jack Shapiro, Director

Catholic War Veterans of the United States of America
346 Broadway, Suite 812, New York, NY 10013
212-962-0988 Fax: 212-894-0517
e-mail: nyscwv@aol.com
Web site: www.nycatholicwarvets.org
Veterans & auxiliary of the Roman Catholic faith; assisting all veterans & their families
Richard Dogal, MA, State Commander

Commissioned Officers Assn of the US Public Health Svc Inc (COA)
8201 Corporate Dr, Ste 200, Landover, MD 20785
301-731-9080 Fax: 301-731-9084
e-mail: gfarrell@coausphs.org
Web site: www.coausphs.org
Committed to improving the public health of the US; supports corps officers & advocates for their interests through leadership, education & communication
Jerry Farrell, Executive Director

Disabled American Veterans, Department of New York
162 Atlantic Ave, Lynbrook, NY 11563-3597
516-887-7100 Fax: 516-887-7175
e-mail: davny@optonline.net
Web site: www.davny.org
Service, support & enhance healthcare & benefits for wartime disabled veterans
Sidney Siller, Adjutant

Fleet Reserve Association (FRA)
125 North West St, Alexandria, VA 22314
703-683-1400 Fax: 703-549-6610
e-mail: news-fra@fra.org
Web site: www.fra.org
Serving the interests of active duty, retired & reserve enlisted members of the US Navy, Marine Corps & Coast Guard
Joseph L Barnes, National Executive Secretary & Chief Lobbyist

Fleet Reserve Association (FRA), NE Region (NJ, NY, PA)
1118 West Jefferson Street, Philadelphia, PA 19122-3442
215-235-7796 Fax: 215-765-2671
e-mail: charleserainey@post.com
Web site: www.fra.org
Serving the interests of active duty, retired & reserve enlisted members of the US Navy, Marine Corps & Coast Guard
Charles Rainey, Regional President

Gold Star Wives of America Inc
24 Clayton Blvd, Baldwin, NY 10505
914-305-2322
National nonprofit working to advance issues important to military service widows
Mary Dwyer, President

Jewish War Veterans of the USA
1811 R St NW, Washington, DC 20009
202-265-6280 Fax: 202-234-5662
e-mail: jwv@jwv.org
Web site: www.jwv.org
Honoring & supporting all Jewish war veterans, their benefits & rights; fight bigotry & discrimination; patriotic voice of American Jewry
Steve Zeitz, National Commander

Jewish War Veterans of the USA, State of NY
346 Broadway, Rm 817, New York, NY 10013
212-349-6640 Fax: 212-577-2575
e-mail: deptny.jwv@juno.com
Web site: www.jwv.org
Honoring & supporting Jewish war veterans
Saul Rosenberg, Department Commander

Korean War Veterans
54 Lyncrest Drive, Rochester, NY 14616-5238
518-865-0145
e-mail: kwvfn@aol.com
Web site: www.kwva.org
Ensuring that Korean war vets are remembered
Frank Nicalozzo, President

Marine Corps League
PO Box 505, White Plains, NY 10602
914-941-2118 Fax: 914-864-7129
e-mail: llc1@mclwestchester.com
Web site: www.mclwestchester.org
Marine Corps fraternal/veterans association
Lu Caldara, Coordinator

Marine Corps League (MCL)
PO Box 3070, Merrifield, VA 22116
703-207-9588 or 800-625-1775 Fax: 703-207-0047
e-mail: mcl@mcleague.org
Web site: www.mcleague.org
Support & promote the interests, history & tradition of the Marine Corps & all Marines
Michael Blum, Executive Director

Marine Corps League (MCL), Department of NY
46 Marine Corp Blvd, Staten Island, NY 10301
718-447-2306 Fax: 718-556-0590
Support & promote the interests, history & tradition of the Marine Corps & all Marines

Bob Powell, Commandant, Department of NY

Military Chaplains Association of the USA (MCA)
PO Box 7056, Arlington, VA 22207
703-533-5890
e-mail: chaplains@mca-usa.org
Web site: www.mca-usa-org
Promotes the recognition & interests of military, Civil Air Patrol & VA chaplains; develops & encourages candidates through national institutes, scholarships & outreach
David White, Executive Director

Military Officers Association of America
201 N Washington St, Alexandria, VA 22314-2539
703-549-2311 or 800-234-6622 Fax: 703-838-8173
Web site: www.moaa.org
Preserve earned entitlements of members of the uniformed services, their families & survivors; support of strong national defense; scholarship & support to members' families
Col Steve Strobridge, USAF Retired, Director Government Relations

Military Officers Association of America (MOAA), NYS Council
258 Randwood Dr, Williamsville, NY 14221
716-689-6295 Fax: 716-847-6405
e-mail: patc258@aol.com
Benefit members of uniformed services, active & retired, family & survivors; promote strong national defense
Col Patrick Cunningham, USA Retired, President, NYS Council of Chapters

Military Order of the Purple Heart
Syracuse Veterans Administration Medical, 800 Irving Ave, Room A176, Syracuse, NY 13210-2796
315-425-4685
e-mail: catherine.alexander@med.va.gov
Veterans' benefits & rehabilitation
Catherine Alexander, National Service Officer

Military Order of the Purple Heart (MOPH)
5413B Backlick Rd, Springfield, VA 22151
703-642-5360 Fax: 703-642-1841
e-mail: goberh@aol.com
Web site: www.purpleheart.org
Congressionally chartered organization representing the interests of America's combat-wounded veterans
Hershel Gober, National Legislative Director

Montford Point Marine Association
346 Broadway St, New York, NY 10013
212-267-3318 Fax: 212-566-4903
Web site: www.montfordpointmarines.com
James Maillard, Financial Secretary

National Amputation Foundation Inc
40 Church St, Malverne, NY 11565
516-887-3600 Fax: 516-887-3667
e-mail: amps76@aol.com
Web site: www.nationalamputation.org
Programs & services geared to help the amputee; donated medical equipment give-away program. Items must be picked up at the office-for anyone in need. Scholarship program for students with major limb amputation attending college full-time.
Paul Bernacchio, President

National Guard Association of the US (NGAUS)
One Massachusetts Ave NW, Washington, DC 20001
202-789-0031 Fax: 202-682-9358
e-mail: ngaus@ngaus.org
Web site: www.ngaus.org
Promote the interests of the Army National Guard through legislative action;
Bill Goss, Director, Legislative Affairs

National Military Family Association (NMFA)
2500 North Van Dorn St, Ste 102, Alexandria, VA 22302-1601
703-931-6632 or 800-260-0218 Fax: 703-931-4600
e-mail: families@nmfa.org
Web site: www.nmfa.org
Service to the families of active duty, retirees, reserve & National Guard uniformed personnel
Joyce Raezer, Director Government Relations

Naval Enlisted Reserve Association (NERA)
6703 Farragut Ave, Falls Church, VA 22042-2189
703-534-1329 or 800-776-9020
e-mail: members@nera.org
Web site: www.nera.org
Ensuring strong & well-trained Naval, Coast Guard & Marine Corps Reserves; improving reserve equipment, promotion, pay & retirement benefits through legislative action
Stephen R Sandy, Executive Director

Naval Reserve Association (NRA)
1619 King St, Alexandria, VA 22314-3647
703-548-5800 or 866-672-4968 Fax: 866-683-3647
e-mail: membership@navy-reserve.org
Web site: www.navy-reserve.org
Premier education & professional organization for Naval Reserve officers & the association voice of the Naval Reserve
Ike Puzon, USNR Retired, Director of Legislation

Navy League of the US (NLUS)
2300 Wilson Blvd, Arlington, VA 22201-3308
703-528-1775 or 800-356-5760 Fax: 703-528-2333
e-mail: jfleet@navyleague.org
Web site: www.navyleague.org
Citizens in support of the Sea Services
John Fleet, Director for Legislative Affairs

Navy League of the US (NLUS), New York Council
c/o US Coast Guard, Battery Park Bldg, 1 South St, Rm 318, New York, NY 10004
212-825-7333 Fax: 212-668-2138
e-mail: navyleaguenyc.aol.com
Web site: www.nynavyleague.org
Represent citizens in support of the Sea Services
J Robert Lunney, President

New Era Veterans, Inc
1150 Commonwealth Avenue, Bronx, NY 10472
718-904-7036 Fax: 718-904-7024
Housing and services for homeless veterans.
Jason Ortiz, Program Director

New York State Air Force Association
PO Box 539, Merrick, NY 11566-0539
516-623-5714
e-mail: brave3@aaahawk.com
Web site: www.nysafa.org
Support & advance the interest & recognition of the US Air Force
Robert Braverman, Vice President Government Relations

North Country Vietnam Veterans Association, Post 1
PO Box 1161, 27 Town Line Rd, Plattsburgh, NY 12901
518-563-3426
e-mail: kenhynes@charter.net; secretary@ncvva.org
Web site: www.ncvva.org
Peer counseling & referral
Ken Hynes, Contact

Reserve Officers Association (ROA)
One Constitution Ave, NE, Washington, DC 20002
202-479-2200 or 800-809-9448 Fax: 202-547-1641
Web site: www.roa.org
Advance the cause of reserve officers through legislative action; promote the interests & recognition of ROTC & military academy students
Susan Lukas, Legislative Director

Office of Chief, Army Reserves
3 Wildwood Rd, Congers, NY 10920
845-638-5215 or 845-596-3494 Fax: 845-638-5035
e-mail: robert.j.winzinger@us.army.mil
Advance the cause of reserve officers of the US Armed Forces; promote the interests & recognition of ROTC & military academy students
Robert Winzinger, Army Reserve Ambassador - New York

United Spinal Association
75-20 Astoria Blvd, Jackson Heights, NY 11370
718-803-3782 Fax: 718-803-0414
e-mail: info@unitedspinal.org
Web site: www.unitedspinal.org
Managed & long-term care, disability assistance & benefits, advocacy & legislation
Linda Gutmann, Advocacy

Veterans of Foreign Wars
1044 Broadway, Albany, NY 12204
518-463-7427 Fax: 518-426-8904
Web site: www.vfwny.com
Art Koch III, State Adjutant

Veterans of Foreign Wars (VFW)
200 Maryland Ave, NE, Washington, DC 20002
202-543-2239 Fax: 202-543-0961
e-mail: dcullinan@vfw.org
Web site: www.vfw.org
Legislative action, community service & volunteerism in support of the nation's veterans, their families & survivors
Dennis Cullinan, Director National Legislative Affairs

Veterans' Widows International Network Inc (VWIN)
3657 E South Laredo, Aurora, CO 80013
303-693-4745
e-mail: vwin95@aol.com
Web site: www.vetsurvivors.com
Outreach to American veterans' survivors; assist with obtaining benefits; provide local contacts & support

Vietnam Veterans of America, NYS Council
8 Queen Dian Lane, Queensbury, NY 12804
518-293-7801
e-mail: nedvva@adelphia.net
Ned D Foote, President

Women Marines Association
59 Sawyer Ave, Dorchester, MA 02125-2040
617-265-1572
e-mail: sgtkwm@aol.com
Web site: www.womenmarines.org
Catherine Carpenter, Area 1 Director

Offices and agencies generally appear in alphabetical order, except when specific order is requested by listee.

Section 3:
STATE & LOCAL GOVERNMENT PUBLIC INFORMATION

PUBLIC INFORMATION OFFICES

This chapter includes state public information contacts with telephone and fax numbers as well as e-mail and Web site addresses, if available. For additional information, please refer to the related policy area or the indexes.

NEW YORK STATE

GOVERNOR'S OFFICE

Governor's Office
Web site: www.governor.ny.gov; www.ny.gov

Director, Communications:
James Allen. . . . . 518-474-8418 or 212-681-4640

Washington Office of the Governor
Director:
Alexander Cochran 202-434-7100

Lieutenant Governor's Office
Chief of Staff:
Jeffrey Pearlman 518-402-2292

EXECUTIVE & ADMINISTRATIVE DEPARTMENTS & AGENCIES

Aging, Office for the
Web site: www.aging.ny.gov

Public Information Officer:
Reza Mizbani 518-474-7181
e-mail: reza.mizbani@aging.ny.gov

Agriculture & Markets Department
Web site: www.agriculture.ny.gov

Public Information Officer:
Jola Szubielski 518-485-7728/fax: 518-457-3087
e-mail: jola.szubielski@agriculture.ny.gov

New York State Liquor Authority (Division of Alcoholic Beverage Control)
Web site: www.sla.ny.gov

Director, Public Affairs:
William Crowley . . . . . 518-474-3114 or 518-474-4875
fax: 518-473-9565
e-mail: press.office@sla.ny.gov

Alcoholism & Substance Abuse Services, Office of
Web site: www.oasas.ny.gov
Director, Public Information Office:
Susan A Craig, MPH 518-457-8299

Financial Services Department
Web site: www.dfs.ny.gov

Director, Public Affairs:
Andrew Mais 212-480-5257/fax: 212-480-6077
e-mail: public-affairs@dfs.ny.gov
Senior Public Information Specialist:
Ronald Klug 212-480-2285

Budget, Division of the
Web site: www.budget.ny.gov

Press Officer:
Morris Peters 518-473-3885/fax: 518-474-9041
e-mail: dob.sm.press@nysemail.state.ny.us

CIO & Office of Information Technology Services (ITS)
518-402-2537 or 866-789-4638 Fax: 518-474-1196
Web site: www.its.ny.gov

Director, Public Information:
Vacant . . . . . 518-402-3899 or 518-473-9450

Children & Family Services, Office of
Web site: www.ocfs.ny.gov

Council on Children & Families
Web site: www.ccf.ny.gov
Executive Director:
Deborah Benson 518-473-3652/fax: 518-473-2570
e-mail: debbie.benson@ccf.ny.gov

Civil Service Department
e-mail: pio@cs.state.ny.us
Web site: www.cs.ny.gov

Public Information Officer:
Ed Walsh 518-457-9375/fax: 518-473-2372

Consumer Protection, Division of
Web site: www.dos.ny.gov/consumerprotection/

Executive Deputy Director:
Aiesha Battle 518-474-2363

Corrections & Community Supervision Department
Web site: www.doccs.ny.gov

Director, Public Information:
Linda Foglia 518-457-8182/fax: 518-457-7070

Council on the Arts
Web site: www.nysca.org

Manager, Information Technology:
Lenn Ditman 212-459-8810
e-mail: lenn.ditman@arts.ny.gov

Victim Services, Office of
Web site: www.ovs.ny.gov

Director, Public Information:
Janine Kava 518-457-8828/fax: 518-457-8658

Criminal Justice Services, Division of
Web site: www.criminaljustice.ny.gov

Deputy Director, Public Information:
Janine Kava 518-457-8906/fax: 518-485-7715
e-mail: janine.kava@dcjs.ny.gov

Developmental Disabilities Planning Council
Web site: www.ddpc.ny.gov

Public Information Officer:
Thomas F Lee 518-486-7505
e-mail: thomas.lee@ddpc.ny.gov

Education Department
Web site: www.nysed.gov

Chief, External Affairs:
Dennis Tompkins 518-474-1201/fax: 518-473-2977

State & Local Government Public Information

Offices and agencies generally appear in alphabetical order, except when specific order is requested by listee.

Secretary to the Board of Regents:
Anthony Lofrumento 518-474-5889

State Library
Web site: www.nysl.nysed.gov
Assistant Commissioner & State Librarian:
Bernard Margolis 518-474-5930
e-mail: bernard.margolis@nysed.gov

Elections, State Board of
e-mail: info@elections.ny.gov
Web site: www.elections.ny.gov

Director, Public Information:
John W Conklin 518-474-1953/fax: 518-473-8315

Homeland Security & Emergency Services, Division of
Web site: www.dhses.ny.gov

Public Information Officer:
Kristin Devoe. 518-242-5153/fax: 518-322-4978

Empire State Development Corporation
Web site: www.esd.ny.gov

Public Affairs:
Kay Sarlin Wright 800-260-7313
e-mail: esdpressoffice@esd.ny.gov

Employee Relations, Governor's Office of
Web site: www.goer.ny.gov

Management/Confidential Affairs:
Lynda Scalzo. 518-473-8317

Environmental Conservation Department
Web site: www.dec.ny.gov

Director, Public Information:
Emily DeSantis 518-402-8560
e-mail: pressoffice@dec.ny.gov
Director, Public Affairs & Education Division:
Laurel Remus. 518-402-8049/fax: 518-402-9036

General Services, Office of
Web site: www.ogs.ny.gov

Director, Communications:
Heather Groll. 518-474-5987/fax: 518-474-3187
e-mail: heather.groll@ogs.ny.gov

Health Department
Web site: www.health.ny.gov

Director, Public Affairs:
James C Plastiras 518-474-7354 x1
Deputy Director, Public Affairs:
Marci Natale. 518-474-7354 x1

Housing & Community Renewal, Division of
Web site: www.nyshcr.org

Director, Communications:
Charni Sochet 212-872-0681

Hudson River Valley Greenway
Web site: www.hudsongreenway.ny.gov

Acting Executive Director, Communities Council:
Mark Castiglione 518-473-3835/fax: 518-473-4518
Acting Executive Director, Greenway Conservancy:
Mark Castiglione 518-473-3835/fax: 518-473-4518

Human Rights, State Division of
Web site: www.dhr.ny.gov

Public Information Officer:
Lourdes Centeno 718-741-3223/fax: 718-741-3214
e-mail: lcenteno@dhr.ny.gov

Inspector General (NYS), Office of the
Web site: www.ig.ny.gov

Director, Communications:
William Reynolds 518-474-1010/fax: 518-486-3745

Insurance Fund (NYS)
Web site: www.nysif.com

Public Information Officer:
Robert Lawson. 518-437-3504/fax: 518-437-1849

Labor Department
Web site: www.labor.ny.gov

Director, Communications:
Leo Rosales 518-457-5519/fax: 518-485-1126
e-mail: leo.rosales@labor.ny.gov

Law Department
Web site: www.ag.ny.gov

Press Secretary:
Matt Mittenthal 212-416-8060/fax: 212-416-6005

New York State Gaming Commission
Web site: www.nylottery.ny.gov; www.gaming.ny.gov

Director, Communications:
Christy Calicchia 518-388-3415/fax: 518-388-3423
Public Information Officer:
Christy Calicchia 518-388-3415/fax: 518-388-3423

Mental Health, Office of
Web site: www.omh.ny.gov

Director, Public Affairs:
Benjamin Rosen. 518-474-6540/fax: 518-473-3456

NYS Office for People with Developmental Disabilities
e-mail: communications.office@opwdd.ny.gov
Web site: www.opwdd.ny.gov

Director, Communications & PA:
Jennifer O'Sullivan 518-474-6601/fax: 518-473-1271
Director Public Information:
Dianne Henk 518-473-1997

Military & Naval Affairs, Division of
Web site: www.dmna.ny.gov

Director, Public Affairs:
David Warager. 518-786-4581/fax: 518-786-4649
e-mail: david.warager@dmna.nyg.ny.gov

Motor Vehicles Department
Web site: www.dmv.ny.gov

Assistant Commissioner, Communications:
Joseph Morrissey. 518-473-7000/fax: 518-473-1930

NYSTAR - Division of Science, Technology & Innovation
Web site: www.esd.ny.gov/nystar

Director, Communications/Government Affairs:
Jannette Rondo 518-292-5700/fax: 518-292-5798
e-mail: nystarsupport@esd.ny.gov

Parks, Recreation & Historic Preservation, NYS Office of
Web site: www.nysparks.com

Deputy Public Information Officer:
Dan Keefe 518-486-1868/fax: 518-486-2924
Public Information Officer:
Randy Simons 518-486-1868

Parole Board, The
Web site: www.parole.ny.gov; doccs.ny.gov

Administrative Assistant:
Lorraine Morse 518-473-5424/fax: 518-473-6037

Prevention of Domestic Violence, Office for the
Web site: www.opdv.ny.gov

Public Information Officer:
Suzanne Cecala 518-457-5744/fax: 518-457-5810
e-mail: suzanne.cecala@opdv.ny.gov

Public Employment Relations Board
e-mail: perbinfo@perb.ny.gov
Web site: www.perb.ny.gov

Executive Director:
Anthony Zumbolo 518-457-2676/fax: 518-457-2664

Public Service Commission
Web site: www.dps.ny.gov

Director, Telecommunications:
Karen Geduldig 518-474-1668/fax: 518-474-5616
Director, Public Affairs:
James Denn 518-474-7080/fax: 518-473-2838
e-mail: james_denn@dps.ny.gov

Real Property Tax Services, Office of
Web site: www.tax.ny.gov/about/orpts

Director, Public Information:
Vacant 518-486-3418/fax: 518-474-9276

State Comptroller, Office of the
Web site: www.osc.state.ny.us

Director, Communications:
Jennifer Freeman . . . . 518-474-4015 or 212-681-4840
fax: 518-473-8940

State Department
Web site: www.dos.state.ny.us

Deputy Secretary, Public Affairs:
Vacant 518-474-4752/fax: 518-474-4597
e-mail: info@dos.state.ny.us

State Police, Division of
Web site: www.troopers.ny.gov

Director, Public Information:
Darcy Wells 518-457-2180/fax: 518-485-7818
e-mail: pio@troopers.ny.gov

Tax Appeals, Division of
Web site: www.dta.ny.gov

Secretary to the Tribunal:
Jean A McDonnell 518-266-3050

Taxation & Finance Department
Web site: www.tax.ny.gov

Director, Public Information:
Geoffrey Gloak . . . . 518-457-4242 or 518-457-7377
fax: 518-457-2486

Temporary & Disability Assistance, Office of
Web site: www.otda.ny.gov

Director, Public Information:
Kristi L. Berner 518-474-9516/fax: 518-486-6935
e-mail: nyspio@otda.ny.gov

Transportation Department
Web site: www.dot.ny.gov

Director, Communications Office (Acting):
Jennifer Post 518-457-6400/fax: 518-457-6506
Public Information Officer:
Jennifer Post 518-457-6400
e-mail: jennifer.post@dot.ny.gov

Veterans' Affairs, Division of
e-mail: dvainfo@veterans.ny.gov
Web site: www.veterans.ny.gov

Counsel:
Samuel Spitzberg 518-474-6114

Welfare Inspector General, Office of NYS
e-mail: owig@dfa.state.ny.us
Web site: www.owig.ny.gov

Executive Deputy Inspector General:
Spencer Freedman 212-417-2395/fax: 212-417-5849

Workers' Compensation Board
Web site: www.wcb.ny.gov

Director, Public Information:
Rachel McEneny 518-408-5592/fax: 518-473-1415
e-mail: publicinfo@wcb.ny.gov

JUDICIAL SYSTEM AND RELATED AGENCIES

Unified Court System
Web site: www.nycourts.gov

Director, Public Affairs:
Gregory Murray 212-428-2116/fax: 212-428-2117
Director, Communications:
David Bookstaver 212-428-2500/fax: 212-428-2507
e-mail: dbooksta@courts.state.ny.us
Chief Law Librarian:
Ellen Robinson 518-238-4373/fax: 518-238-2894

LEGISLATIVE BRANCH

Assembly
Press Secretary to the Speaker:
Michael Winyland 518-455-3888/fax: 518-455-3858

Offices and agencies generally appear in alphabetical order, except when specific order is requested by listee.

Director, Minority Communications:
Michael Fraser 518-455-3751/fax: 518-455-3750
e-mail: fraserm@assembly.state.ny.us
Public Information Officer:
Robin Marilla. 518-455-4218/fax: 518-455-5175
Director, Communications:
Michael Kane. 518-455-5767/fax: 518-455-4963
Director, Information Services:
Vicki Chase 518-455-5767/fax: 518-455-4963

Legislative Library

Legislative Librarian:
Ellen Breslin 518-455-2468/fax: 518-426-6901
Legislative Librarian:
James Giliberto 518-455-2468
Law Librarian:
Kate Balassie. 518-455-2468
Law Librarian:
Stephen Gersztoff 518-455-2468

Senate

Director, Majority Communications:
Kelly Cummings 518-455-2264/fax: 518-455-2260
Majority Press Secretary:
Kris Thompson 518-455-3191/fax: 518-455-2448
Director, Minority Communications:
Curtis Taylor 518-455-2415/fax: 518-426-6933
Minority Press Secretary:
Vacant 518-455-2415/fax: 518-426-6955
Director, Student Programs Office:
Krista Ketterer. 518-455-2611/fax: 518-432-5470

CORPORATIONS, AUTHORITIES AND COMMISSIONS

Adirondack Park Agency

Web site: www.apa.ny.gov

Public Relations:
Keith McKeever 518-891-4050/fax: 518-891-3938
e-mail: keith.mckeever@apa.ny.gov

Agriculture & NYS Horse Breeding Development Fund

Web site: www.nysirestakes.com

Acting Executive Director:
Ron Ochrym 518-388-0178/fax: 518-347-1483

Albany County Airport Authority

Web site: www.albanyairport.com/airport-authority.php

Director, Public Affairs:
Douglas I. Myers 518-242-2222 x1/fax: 518-242-2641
e-mail: info@albanyairport.com

Albany Port District Commission

Web site: www.portofalbany.us

General Manager:
Richard Hendrick 518-463-8763/fax: 518-463-8767
e-mail: rhendrick@portofalbany.us; portofalbany@portofalbany.us

Atlantic States Marine Fisheries Commission

Web site: www.asmfc.org

Director Communications:
Tina Berger 703-842-0740/fax: 703-842-0741
e-mail: tberger@asmfc.org

Battery Park City Authority (Hugh L Carey)

Web site: www.bpca.ny.gov

VP External Relations:
Robin Forst 212-417-2276/fax: 212-417-2279
e-mail: robin.forst@bpca.ny.gov

Brooklyn Navy Yard Development Corporation

e-mail: info@brooklynnavyyard.org
Web site: www.brooklynnavyyard.org

Senior Vice President, External Affairs:
Richard Drucker 718-907-5900/fax: 718-643-9296

Buffalo & Fort Erie Public Bridge Authority (Peace Bridge Authority)

Web site: www.peacebridge.com

General Manager:
Ron Rienas. 716-884-6744/fax: 716-884-2089

Capital District Regional Off-Track Betting Corporation

e-mail: customerservice@capitalotb.com
Web site: www.capitalotb.com

Secretary & Director:
F James Mumpton 518-344-5225/fax: 518-370-5460

Capital District Regional Planning Commission

e-mail: cdrpc@cdrpc.org
Web site: www.cdrpc.org

Financial Officer:
Tim Canty 518-453-0850/fax: 518-453-0856

Capital District Transportation Authority

Web site: www.cdta.org

VP, Planning & Infrastructure:
Christopher G Desany 518-437-8320/fax: 518-437-8328
e-mail: chrisd@cdta.org

Catskill Off-Track Betting Corporation

Web site: www.interbets.com

President:
Donald J Groth 845-362-0400/fax: 845-362-0419
e-mail: otb@interbets.com; customerservice@interbets.com

Central New York Regional Market Authority

Web site: cnyrma.com

Commissioner's Representative:
Troy Waffner. 315-422-8647/fax: 315-442-6897

Central New York Regional Transportation Authority

Web site: www.centro.org

CEO:
Richard Lee 315-442-3360/fax: 315-422-3337

Central Pine Barrens Joint Planning & Policy Commission

e-mail: info@pb.state.ny.us
Web site: www.pb.state.ny.us

Chair:
Peter A Scully 631-288-1079/fax: 631-288-1367

City University Construction Fund

Counsel:
Frederick Schaffer. 646-664-9210
e-mail: frederick.schaffer@mail.cuny.edu

Offices and agencies generally appear in alphabetical order, except when specific order is requested by listee.

Delaware River Basin Commission
Web site: www.nj.gov/drbc

Communications Manager:
Clarke Rupert 609-883-9500 x260/fax: 609-883-9522
e-mail: clarke.rupert@drbc.nj.gov

Development Authority of the North Country
Web site: www.danc.org

Executive Director:
James Wright 315-661-3200

Empire State Development Corporation
Web site: www.esd.ny.gov

Public Affairs:
Kay Sarlin Wright 800-260-7313
e-mail: esdpressoffice@esd.ny.gov

Great Lakes Commission
Web site: www.glc.org

Communications Director:
Beth Wanamaker 734-971-9135/fax: 734-971-9150
e-mail: beth@glc.org

Hudson River-Black River Regulating District
Web site: www.hrbrrd.com

Executive Director (Acting):
Richard J Ferrara 518-465-3491/fax: 518-432-2485
e-mail: hrao@hrbrrd.com

Interest on Lawyer Account (IOLA) Fund of the State of NY
Web site: www.iola.org

Executive Director:
Christopher O'Malley 646-865-1541/fax: 646-865-1545

Interstate Environmental Commission
Web site: www.iec-nynjct.org

Senior Manager:
Evelyn R Powers 212-967-1414/fax: 212-967-1430
e-mail: iecmail@iec-nynjct.org

Interstate Oil & Gas Compact Commission
Web site: www.iogcc.ok.gov

Communications Manager:
Carol Booth 405-525-3556/fax: 405-525-3592
e-mail: iogcc@iogcc.state.ok.us

Lake George Park Commission
Web site: www.lgpc.state.ny.us

Executive Director:
David Wick 518-668-9347/fax: 518-668-5001
e-mail: info@lgpc.state.ny.us

Lawyers' Fund for Client Protection
Web site: www.nylawfund.org

Executive Director & Counsel:
Timothy O'Sullivan 518-434-1935/fax: 518-434-5641
e-mail: info@nylawfund.org

Legislative Bill Drafting Commission
Commissioner:
Randall G Bluth 518-455-7506/fax: 518-455-7598

MTA (Metropolitan Transportation Authority)
Web site: www.mta.info

Director, External Communications:
Adam Lisberg 212-878-7440/fax: 212-878-7030

MTA Bridges & Tunnels
Web site: www.mta.info/handt

Manager, Public Affairs:
Judith Glave 646-252-7276

MTA Bus Company
Web site: www.mta.info/busco

Media Relations:
Adam Lisberg 212-878-7440/fax: 212-878-7030

MTA Capital Construction
Web site: www.mta.info/capconstr

Senior Director/Chief Procurement Officer:
David Cannon 646-252-2678

MTA Long Island Rail Road
Web site: www.mta.info/lirr

General Manager, Public Affairs:
Susan McGowan 718-558-7301/fax: 718-558-8212

MTA Metro-North Railroad
Web site: www.mta.info/mnr

Senior Director, Corporate & Public Affairs:
Mark Mannix 212-340-2142/fax: 212-340-3460
Vice President, Business Operations:
Thomas Tendy 212-672-1251

MTA New York City Transit
Web site: www.mta.info/nyct

Corporate Communications:
Paul Fleuranges 646-252-5873

MTA Office of the Inspector General
Web site: www.mtaig.state.ny.us

Inspector General:
Barry L Kluger 212-878-0000/fax: 212-878-0003

Nassau Regional Off-Track Betting Corporation
Web site: www.nassauotb.com

Director, Public Affairs:
Vacant 516-572-2800 x124/fax: 516-572-2840

New England Interstate Water Pollution Control Commission
Web site: www.neiwpcc.org

Director of Communications:
Adam Auster 978-349-2507
e-mail: aauster@neiwpcc.org

State & Local Government Public Information

Offices and agencies generally appear in alphabetical order, except when specific order is requested by listee.

New York City Housing Development Corporation
e-mail: info@nychdc.com
Web site: www.nychdc.com

Communications/Press Office:
Vacant 212-227-2644/fax: B12-227-8580

New York City School Construction Authority
Web site: www.nycsca.org

Executive Director & Chief of Staff:
Maria Mostajo 718-472-8149

New York Convention Center Operating Corporation
Web site: www.javitscenter.com

SVP/Chief Communications Officer:
Tony Sclafani 212-216-2325
e-mail: tsclafani@javitscenter.com

New York Metropolitan Transportation Council
Web site: www.nymtc.org

Public Information Officer:
Stacy Graham-Hunt 212-383-7203/fax: 212-383-2418
e-mail: stacy.graham-hunt@dot.ny.gov

New York Power Authority
Web site: www.nypa.gov

Public Information Officer:
Maura Balaban 914-390-8171
e-mail: maura.balaban@nypa.gov
Public Information Officer:
Paul DeMichele 914-390-8196
e-mail: paul.demichele@nypa.gov

New York State Assn of Fire Districts
Web site: www.firedistnys.com

Counsel:
William N Young . . . . 800-349-2904 or 518-456-6767
fax: 518-456-4644
e-mail: byoung@yfkblaw.com

New York State Athletic Commission
Web site: www.dos.ny.gov/athletic

Chair:
Tom Hoover 212-417-5700/fax: 212-417-4987
e-mail: info@dos.ny.gov

New York State Board of Law Examiners
Web site: www.nybarexam.org

Executive Director:
John J McAlary 518-453-5990/fax: 518-452-5729

New York State Bridge Authority
e-mail: info@nysba.ny.gov
Web site: www.nysba.ny.gov

Director, Toll Collections Operations:
Wayne V Ferguson 845-691-7245

New York State Commission of Correction
Web site: www.scoc.ny.gov

Deputy Director Public Information:
Walter McClure 518-485-2346/fax: 518-485-2467
e-mail: infoscoc@scoc.ny.gov

New York State Commission on Judicial Nomination
Web site: www.nysegov.com/cjn/

Counsel:
Henry Greenberg 518-689-1400/fax: 518-689-1499
e-mail: greenbergh@gtlaw.com

New York State Commission on the Restoration of the Capitol
Executive Director:
Andrea J Lazarski 518-473-0341/fax: 518-486-5720
e-mail: andrea.lazarski@ogs.ny.gov

New York State Disaster Preparedness Commission
Web site: www.dhses.ny.gov/oem/disaster-prep/

Chairman/Director:
Jerome M Hauer 518-292-2301/fax: 518-322-4978

New York State Dormitory Authority
Web site: www.dasny.org

Public Information Officer:
John Chirlin 518-257-3380/fax: 518-257-3387
e-mail: jchirlin@dasny.org

New York State Energy Research & Development Authority
e-mail: info@nyserda.ny.gov
Web site: www.nyserda.ny.gov
Director, Communications:
Kate Muller 518-862-1090 x3582/fax: 518-862-1091
e-mail: kate.muller@nyserda.ny.gov

New York State Environmental Facilities Corp
Web site: www.nysefc.org

Director, PIO:
Jon Sorensen 518-402-6924/fax: 518-486-9323
e-mail: press@efc.ny.gov; jon.sorensen@efc.ny.gov

Joint Commission on Public Ethics (JCOPE)
Web site: www.jcope.ny.gov
Director, External Affairs:
Walter J McClure 518-408-3976/fax: 518-408-3975
Chief of Staff:
Kevin T Gagan 518-408-3976/fax: 518-408-3975

New York State Financial Control Board
Web site: www.fcb.state.ny.us

Acting Executive Director:
Jeffrey Sommer 212-417-5066/fax: 212-417-5055

New York State Higher Education Services Corp (NYSHESC)
e-mail: hescpublicaffairsoffice@hesc.ny.gov
Web site: www.hesc.ny.gov

Communications Division:
Vacant . . . . 518-474-5592 or 518-474-5775
fax: 518-474-5593

New York State Judicial Conduct Commission
Web site: www.cjc.ny.gov

Offices and agencies generally appear in alphabetical order, except when specific order is requested by listee.

Administrator & Counsel:
Robert H Tembeckjian 646-386-4800
e-mail: cjc@cjc.ny.gov
Information Officer:
Amy Carpinello. 646-386-4800

New York State Law Reporting Bureau
Web site: www.courts.state.ny.us/reporter

State Reporter:
William J Hooks 518-453-6900
Deputy State Reporter:
Katherine D LaBoda 518-453-6900/fax: 518-426-1640
e-mail: Reporter@courts.state.ny.us

New York State Law Revision Commission
Web site: www.lawrevision.state.ny.us

Executive Director:
Rose Mary Bailly. 518-472-5858/fax: 518-445-2303

New York State Liquor Authority
Web site: www.sla.ny.gov

Director, Public Affairs:
William Crowley . . . . .518-474-3114 or 518-474-4875
fax: 518-473-9565
e-mail: press.office@sla.ny.gov

New York State Olympic Regional Development Authority
Web site: www.orda.org/corporate

Communications Manager:
Jon Lundin. 518-523-1655/fax: 518-523-9275
e-mail: jlundin@orda.org

New York State Teachers' Retirement System
Web site: www.nystrs.org

Manager, Public Information:
John Cardillo 518-447-4743/fax: 518-447-2875
e-mail: john.cardillo@nystrs.org

New York State Thoroughbred Breeding & Development Fund Corporation
Web site: www.nybreds.com

Executive Director:
Tracy Egan. 518-388-0174/fax: 518-344-1235

New York State Thruway Authority
Web site: www.thruway.ny.gov

Director, Media Relations & Communications:
Jennifer Givner 518-471-5300
e-mail: publicinfo@thruway.ny.gov

New York State Tug Hill Commission
Web site: www.tughill.org

Executive Director:
Katie Malinowski 315-785-2570/fax: 315-785-2574
e-mail: katie@tughill.org

Niagara Falls Bridge Commission
Web site: www.niagarafallsbridges.com

General Manager:
Lew Holloway. 716-285-6322 ext4151/fax: 716-282-3292

Niagara Frontier Transportation Authority
Web site: www.nfta.com

Director, Public Affairs:
C Douglas Hartmayer 716-855-7420/fax: 716-855-6655
e-mail: info@nfta.com

Northeastern Forest Fire Protection Commission
Web site: www.nffpc.org

Executive Director/Center Manager:
Thomas G Parent 207-968-3782/fax: 207-968-3782
e-mail: necompact@fairpoint.net

Ogdensburg Bridge & Port Authority
Web site: www.ogdensport.com

Executive Director:
Wade A Davis 315-393-4080/fax: 315-393-7068
e-mail: wadavis@ogdensport.com

Ohio River Valley Water Sanitation Commission
Web site: www.orsanco.org

Communications Coordinator:
Lisa Cochran. . . . . 513-231-7719 ext 102/fax: 513-231-7761
e-mail: lcochran@orsanco.org
Public Information:
Melissa Mann . . . . 513-231-7719 ext 101/fax: 513-231-7761
e-mail: mmann@orsanco.org

Port Authority of New York & New Jersey
Web site: www.panynj.gov

Director Media Relations:
Ron Marsico 212-435-7777/fax: 212-435-4032

Port of Oswego Authority
Web site: www.portoswego.com

Executive Director & CEO:
Zelko N. Kirincich 315-343-4503 x111/fax: 315-343-5498
e-mail: zkirincich@portoswego.com

Rochester-Genesee Regional Transportation Authority-RTS
Web site: www.myrts.com

Public Information Officer:
Tom Brede 585-654-0730/fax: 585-654-0224

Roosevelt Island Operating Corporation (RIOC)
Web site: www.rioc.ny.gov

Community Relations:
Erica Spencer-El. 212-832-4540 x349/fax: 212-832-4582
e-mail: erica.spencer-el@rioc.ny.gov

State University Construction Fund
Web site: www.sucf.suny.edu

Deputy General Manager:
W. Thomas Mannix. 518-320-1630/fax: 518-443-1008

State of New York Mortgage Agency (SONYMA)
Web site: www.nyshcr.org

Director, Public Information:
Charni Sochet 212-872-0338
e-mail: plentz@nyhomes.org

Offices and agencies generally appear in alphabetical order, except when specific order is requested by listee.

State & Local Government Public Information

State of New York Municipal Bond Bank Agency (MBBA)
e-mail: abergamo@nyhomes.org
Web site: www.nyhomes.org

Senior VP & Director of Communications:
Philip Lentz 212-872-0679/fax: 212-872-0789
e-mail: plentz@nyhomes.org

Suffolk Regional Off-Track Betting Corporation
Web site: www.suffolkotb.com

Director, Governmental & Public Affairs:
Debbie Pfieffer 631-853-1000/fax: 631-853-1086
e-mail: customerservice@suffolkotb.com

Thousand Islands Bridge Authority
Web site: www.tibridge.com

Executive Director:
Robert G Horr, III 315-482-2501/fax: 315-482-6064
e-mail: roberthorr@tibridge.com

Uniform State Laws Commission
Chair:
Richard B Long 607-821-2202/fax: 607-723-1530
e-mail: rlong@cglawoffices.com

United Nations Development Corporation
Web site: www.undc.org

Vice President:
Kenneth Coopersmith 212-888-1618/fax: 212-588-0758

Waterfront Commission of New York Harbor
Web site: www.wcnyh.org

Executive Director:
Walter M Arsenault. 212-905-9201/fax: 212-480-0587

Western Regional Off-Track Betting Corp
Web site: www.westernotb.com

Communications/Mutuels Manager:
James Haas 585-343-3750/fax: 585-344-6188

Offices and agencies generally appear in alphabetical order, except when specific order is requested by listee.

U.S. CONGRESS

U.S. SENATE: NEW YORK DELEGATION

Internet access, including e-mail addresses, is available at: www.senate.gov. Biographies of Senate Members appear in a separate section in the back of the book.

Kirsten E Gillibrand (D) ....(202) 224-4451/fax: 202-228-0282
478 Russell Senate Office Building, Washington, DC 20510
Committees: Foreign Relations;Agriculture; Environment and Public Works; Special Committee on Aging; Senate Armed Services

Charles E Schumer (D)..............202-224-6542/fax: 202-228-3027
313 Hart Senate Office Building, Washington, DC 20510
Committees: Senate Finance; Joint Economic; Judiciary; Rules and Administration; Banking, Housing, and Urban Affairs

U.S. HOUSE OF REPRESENTATIVES: NEW YORK DELEGATION

Internet access, including e-mail addresses, is available at: www.house.gov. Biographies of House Members appear in a separate section in the back of the book.

Gary L Ackerman (D)...............202-225-2601/fax: 202-225-1589
2243 Rayburn House Office Bldg, Washington, DC 20515
Congressional District: 5
Committees: Foreign Affairs; Financial Services

Timothy H Bishop (D)...............202-225-3826/fax: 202-225-3143
306 Canon House Office Building, Washington, DC 20515
Congressional District: 1
Committees: Education and Labor; Transportation and Infrastructure; Budget

Ann Marie Buerkle (D) 315-423-5657
1630 Longworth House Office Building, Washington, DC 20515
Congressional District: 25
Committees: Foreign Affairs; Oversight and Government Reform; Veterans Affairs

Yvette D Clarke (D)................202-225-6231/fax: 202-226-0112
1029 Longworth House Office Building, Washington, DC 20515
Congressional District: 11
Committees: Homeland Security; Small Business

Joseph Crowley (D).................................202-225-3965
2404 Rayburn House Office Building, Washington, DC 20515
Congressional District: 7
Committees: Ways and Means; Foreign Affairs

Eliot L Engel (D) 202-225-2464/fax: 202-225-5513
2161 Rayburn House Office Building, Washington, DC 20515
Congressional District: 17
Committees: Energy and Commerce; Foreign Affairs

Chris Gibson (R) 202-225-5614/fax: 202-225-1168
120 Cannon HOB, Washington, DC 20515
Congressional District: 20
Committees: Agriculture; Armed Services

Michael Grimm (R).................202-225-3371/fax: 202-226-1272
323 Cannon House Office Building, Washington, DC 20515
Congressional District: 13
Committees: Financial Services

Richard Hanna (R) 607-756-2470
127 Cannon House Office Building, Washington, DC 20515
Congressional District: 24
Committees: Transportation and Infrastructure; Education and the Workforce

Nan Hayworth (R)..................202-225-5441/fax: 202-225-3289
1217 Longworth House Office Building, Washington, DC 20515
Congressional District: 19
Committees: Financial Services

Brian Higgins (D)..................202-225-3306/fax: 202-226-0347
431 Cannon House Office Building, Washington, DC 20515
Congressional District: 27
Committees: Foreign Affairs; Homeland Security

Maurice D Hinchey (D).............202-225-6335/fax: 202-226-0774
2431 Rayburn House Office Building, Washington, DC 20515
Congressional District: 22
Committees: Appropriations

Steve Israel (D)...................202-225-3335/fax: 202-225-4669
2457 Rayburn House Office Building, Washington, DC 20515
Congressional District:
Committees: Appropriations

Pete King (R) 202-225-7896
339 Cannon House Office Building, Washington, DC 20515
Congressional District: 3
Committees: Homeland Security; Financial Services

Nita M Lowey (D) 202-225-6506/fax: 202-225-0546
2329 Rayburn House Office Building, Washington, DC 20515
Congressional District: 18
Committees: House Appropriations; Homeland Security

Carolyn B Maloney (D) 202-225-7944/fax: 202-225-4709
2332 Rayburn House Office Building, Washington, DC 20515
Congressional District: 14
Committees: Financial Services; Oversight and Government Reform

Carolyn McCarthy (D).............202-225-5516/fax: 202-225-5758
2346 Rayburn House Office Building, Washington, DC 20515
Congressional District: 4
Committees: Education and Labor; Financial Services

Gregory W Meeks (D)...............202-225-3461/fax: 202-226-4169
2342 Rayburn House Office Building, Washington, DC 20515
Congressional District: 6
Committees: Financial Services; Foreign Affairs

Jerrold Nadler (D)...................................202-225-5635
2334 Rayburn House Office Building, Washington, DC 20515
Congressional District: 8
Committees: Judiciary; Transportation and Infrastructure

Bill Owens (R).....................202-225-4611/fax: 202-226-0621
2366 Rayburn House Office Building, Washington, DC 20515-3223
Congressional District: 23
Committees: Agriculture; Armed Services; Small Business

Charles B Rangel (D) 202-225-4365/fax: 202-225-0816
2354 Rayburn House Office Building, Washington, DC 20515
Congressional District: 15
Committees: Ways and Means; Taxation

Tom Reed (R) 202-225-3161/fax: 202-226-6599
1208 Longworth House Office Building, Washington, DC 20515
Congressional District: 29
Committees: Rules

Jose E Serrano (D).................202-225-4361/fax: 202-225-6001
2227 Rayburn House Office Building, Washington, DC 20515
Congressional District: 16
Committees: Appropriations

Louise M Slaughter (D) 202-225-3615/fax: 202-225-7822
2469 Rayburn House Office Building, Washington, DC 20515
Congressional District: 28
Committees: Rules

Paul D Tonko (D) 202-225-5076/fax: 202-225-5077
128 Cannon House Office Building, Washington, DC 20515
Congressional District: 21
Committees: Budget; Science and Technology

Edolphus Towns (D) 202-225-5936/fax: 202-225-1018
2232 Rayburn House Office Building, Washington, DC 20515
Congressional District: 10
Committees: Energy and Commerce; Oversight and Government

Nydia M Velazquez (D). 202-225-2361/fax: 202-226-0327
2466 Rayburn House Office Building, Washington, DC 20515
Congressional District: 12
Committees: Small Business; Financial Services

Anthony D Weiner (D) 202-225-6616
2104 Rayburn House Office Building, Washington, DC 20515
Congressional District: 9
Committees: Homeland Security; Judiciary

U.S. SENATE STANDING COMMITTEES

Agriculture, Nutrition & Forestry

328A Senate Russell Office Building
Washington, DC 20510
202-224-2035
Web site: www.agriculture.senate.gov

Chair:
Tom Harkin (D-IA). 202-224-3254
Ranking Republican Member:
Saxby Chambliss (R-GA). 202-224-3521

Subcommittees

Domestic and Foreign Marketing, Inspection and Plant & Animal Health
Chair:
Max Baucus (D-MT) 202-224-2651
Ranking Member:
Vacant

Energy, Science and Technology
Chair:
Kent Conrad (D-ND) 202-224-2043
Ranking Member:
John Thune (R-SD) 202-224-2321

Nutrition & Food Assistance, Sustainable & Organic Agriculture & Gen Legis
Chair:
Patrick J Leahy (D-VT) 202-224-4242
Ranking Member:
Norm Coleman (R-MN) 202-224-5641

Production, Income Protection and Price Support
Chair:
Blanche L Lincoln (D-AR). 202-224-4843
Ranking Member:
Pat Roberts (R-KS). 202-224-4774

Rural Revitalization, Conservation, Forestry and Credit
Chair:
Debbie Stabenow (D-MI). 202-224-4822
Ranking Member:
Mike Crapo (R-ID). 202-224-6142

Appropriations

The Capitol
S-128
Washington, DC 20510
202-224-7363
Web site: www.appropriations.senate.gov

Chair:
Daniel K Inouye (D-HI) 202-224-3934
Vice Chair:
Thad Cochran (R-MS) 202-224-5054

Subcommittees

Agriculture, Rural Development, FDA, and Related Agencies
Chair:
Herb Kohl (D-WI) 202-224-5653
Ranking Member:
Sam Brownback (R-KS). 202-224-6521

Commerce, Justice, Science and Related Agencies
Chair:
Barbara Mikulski (D-MD) 202-224-4645
Ranking Member:
Richard Shelby (R-AL) 202-224-5744

Defense
Chair:
Daniel Inouye (D-HI). 202-224-3934
Ranking Member:
Thad Cochran (R-MS) 202-224-5054

Energy and Water Development
Chair:
Byron Dorgan (D-ND) 202-224-2551
Ranking Member:
Robert Bennett (R-UT). 202-224-5444

Financial Services and General Government
Chair:
Richard Durbin (D-IL) 202-224-2152
Ranking Member:
Susan M Collins (R-ME) 202-224-2523

Homeland Security
Chair:
Robert C Byrd (D-WV) 202-224-3954
Ranking Member:
George V Voinovich (R-OH). 202-224-3353

Interior, Environment and Related Agencies
Chair:
Dianne Feinstein (D-CA) 202-224-3841
Ranking Member:
Lamar Alexander (R-TN). 202-224-4944

Labor, Health and Human Services, Education and Related Agencies
Chair:
Tom Harkin (D-IA) 202-224-3254
Ranking Member:
Arlen Specter (R-PA) 202-224-4254

Legislative Branch
Chair:
Ben Nelson (D-NE) 202-224-6551
Ranking Member:
Barbara Mikulsi (R-MD) 202-224-4645

Military Construction, Veterans Affairs and Related Agencies
Chair:
Tim Johnson (D-SD) 202-224-5842
Ranking Member:
Kay Bailey Hutchison (R-TX) 202-224-5922

State, Foreign Operations and Related Programs
Chair:
Patrick Leahy (D-VT). 202-224-4242
Ranking Member:
Judd Gregg (D-NH) 202-224-3324

Offices and agencies generally appear in alphabetical order, except when specific order is requested by listee.

Transportation, Housing and Urban Development, and Related Agencies
Chair:
Patty Murray (D-WA) 202-224-2621
Ranking Member:
Christopher Bond (R-MO) 202-224-5721

Armed Services
Russell Senate Office Building
Room SR-228
Washington, DC 20510
202-224-3871
Web site: www.armed-services.senate.gov

Chair:
Carl Levin (D-MI) 202-224-6221
Ranking Member:
John McCain (R-AZ) 202-224-2235

Subcommittees

Airland
Chair:
Joseph I Liberman (D-CT) 202-224-4041
Ranking Member:
John Thune (R-SD) 202-224-2321

Emerging Threats & Capabilities
Chair:
Jack Reed (D-RI) 202-224-4642
Ranking Member:
Roger F Wicker (R-MS) 202-224-6253

Personnel
Chair:
Ben Nelson (D-FL) 202-224-5274
Ranking Member:
Lindsey O Graham (R-SC) 202-224-5972

Readiness & Management Support
Chair:
Evan Bayh (D-IN) 202-224-5623
Ranking Member:
Richard Burr (R-NC) 202-224-3154

SeaPower
Chair:
Edward M Kennedy (D-MA) 202-224-4543
Ranking Member:
Mel Martinez (R-FL) 202-224-3041

Strategic Forces
Chair:
Bill Nelson (D-FL) 202-224-5274
Ranking Member:
Jeff Sessions (R-AL) 202-224-4124

Banking, Housing & Urban Affairs
534 Dirksen Seanate Office Building
Washington, DC 20510
202-224-7391
Web site: www.banking.senate.gov

Chair:
Christopher J Dodd (D-CT) 202-224-2823
Ranking Member:
Richard C Shelby (R-AL) 202-224-5744

Subcommittees

Economic Policy
Chair:
Sherrod Brown (D-OH) 202-224-2315
Ranking Member:
Jim DeMint (R-SC) 202-224-6121

Financial Institutions
Chair:
Tim Johnson (D-SD) 202-224-5842
Ranking Member:
Mike Crapo (R-ID) 202-224-6142

Housing, Transportation and Community Development
Chair:
Robert Menendez (D-NJ) 202-224-4744
Ranking Member:
David Vitter (R-LA 202-224-4623

Securities, Insurance and Investment
Chair:
Jack Reed (D-RI) 202-224-4642
Ranking Member:
Jim Bunning (R-KY) 202-224-4343

Security and International Trade and Finance
Chair:
Evan Bayh (D-IN) 202-224-5623
Ranking Member:
Bob Corker (R-TN) 202-224-3344

Budget
624 Dirksen Senate Office Building
Washington, DC 20510
202-224-0642
Web site: www.budget.senate.gov

Chair:
Kent Conrad (D-ND) 202-224-0642
Ranking Member:
Judd Gregg (R-NH) 202-224-0642

Commerce, Science & Transportation
508 Dirksen Building
Washington, DC 20510
202-224-5115
Web site: www.commerce.senate.gov

Chair:
John D Rockefeller, IV (D-WV) 202-224-6472
Ranking Member:
Kay Bailey Hutchison (R-TX) 202-224-5922

Subcommittees

Aviation Operations, Safety & Security
Chair:
Byron L Dorgan (D-ND) 202-224-9000
Ranking Member:
Jim DeMint (R-SC) 202-224-5184

Communications, Technology, & the Internet
Chair:
John Kerry (D-MA) 202-224-0415
Ranking Member:
John Ensign (R-NV) 202-224-4852
Chair:
Amy Klobuchar (R-MN) 202-224-1270
Ranking Member:
Mel Martinez (R-FL) 202-224-5183

Consumer Protection, Product Safety, & Insurance
Chair:
Mark Pryor (D-AR) 202-224-1270
Ranking Member:
Roger F Wicker (R-MS) 202-224-5183

State & Local Government Public Information

Oceans, Atmosphere, Fisheries and Coast Guard
Chair:
Maria Cantwell (D-WA) 202-224-4912
Ranking Member:
Olympia J Snowe (R-ME) 202-224-8172

Science and Space
Chair:
Bill Nelson (D-FL) 202-224-0415
Ranking Member:
David Vitter (R-LA) 202-224-4852

Surface Transportation & Merchant Marine Infrastructure, Safety & Security
Chair:
Frank R Lautneberg (D-NJ) 202-224-9000
Ranking Member:
John Thune (R-SD) 202-224-4852

Energy & Natural Resources

304 Dirksen Senate Building
Washington, DC 20510
202-224-4971
Web site: energy.senate.gov

Chair:
Jeff Bingaman (D-NM) 202-224-5521
Ranking Member:
Lisa Murkowski (R-AK) 202-224-6665

Subcommittees

Energy
Chair:
Maria Cantwell (D-WA) 202-224-4971
Ranking Member:
James E Risch (R-ID) 202-224-0541

National Parks
Chair:
Mark Udall (D-CO) 202-224-4971
Ranking Member:
Richard Burr (R-NC) 202-224-0539

Public Lands & Forests
Chair:
Ron Wyden (D-OR) 202-224-4971
Ranking Member:
John Barrasso (R-WY) 202-224-7970

Water & Power
Chair:
Debbie Stabenow (D-MI) 202-224-4971
Ranking Member:
Sam Brownback (R-KS) 202-224-7970

Environment & Public Works

410 Dirksen Senate Building
Washington, DC 20510
202-224-8832
Web site: http://epw.senate.gov

Chair:
Barbara Boxer (D-CA) 202-224-8832
Ranking Minority Member:
James M Inhofe (R-OK) 202-224-6176
New York Delegate:
Kisrten Gillibrand (D) 202-224-4451

Subcommittees

Children's Health
Chair:
Amy Klobuchar (D-MN) 202-224-3244
Ranking Member:
Lamar Alexander (R-TN) 202-224-4944

Clean Air and Nuclear Safety
Chair:
Thomas R Carper (D-DE) 202-224-2441
Ranking Member:
David Vitter (R-LA) 202-224-4623

Green Jobs and the New Economy
Chair:
Bernard Sanders (D-VT) 202-224-5141
Ranking Member:
Christopher S Bond (R-MO) 202-224-5721

Oversight
Chair:
Sheldon Whitehouse (D-RI) 202-224-2921
Ranking Member:
John Barrasso (R-WY) 202-224-6441

Superfund, Toxics and Environmental Health
Chair:
Frank R Lautenberg (D-NJ) 202-224-3224
Ranking Member:
Arlen Specter (R-PA) 202-224-4254

Transportation & Infrastructure
Chair:
Max Baucus (D-MT) 202-224-2651
Ranking Member:
Johnny Isakson (R-GA) 202-224-3643

Water & Wildlife
Chair:
Benjamin L Cardin (D-MD) 202-224-4524
Ranking Member:
Mike Crapo (R-ID) 202-224-6142

Finance

219 Dirksen Senate Building
Washington, DC 20510
202-224-4515
Web site: www.finance.senate.gov

Chair:
Max Baucus (D-MT) 202-224-2651
Ranking Member:
Chuck Grassley (R-IA) 202-224-3744

Subcommittees

Energy, Natural Resources and Infrastructure
Chair:
Jeff Bingaman (D-NM) 202-224-5521
Ranking Member:
Jim Bunning (R-KY) 202-224-4343

Health Care
Chair:
John D Rockefeller, IV (D-WV) 202-224-6472
Ranking Member:
Orrin G Hatch (R-UT) 202-224-5251

International Trade, and Global Competitiveness
Chair:
Ron Wyden (D-OR) 202-224-5244
Ranking Member:
Mike Crapo (R-ID) 202-224-6142

Social Security, Pensions, and Family Policy
Chair:
Blanche L Lincoln (D-AR)........................202-224-1371
Ranking Member:
Pat Roberts (R-KS)........................202-224-4774

Taxation, IRS Oversight and Long-Term Growth
Chair:
Kent Conrad (D-ND)........................202-224-2043
Ranking Member:
Jon Kyl (R-AZ)........................202-224-4521

Foreign Relations
Dirksen Senate Building
Washington, DC 20510
202-224-4651
Web site: www.foreign.senate.gov

Chair:
John F Kerry (D-MA)........................202-224-2742
Ranking Member:
Richard G Lugar (R-IN)........................202-224-0360

Subcommittees

African Affairs
Chair:
Russell D Feingold (D-WI)........................202-224-5323
Ranking Minority Member:
Johnny Isakson (R-GA)........................202-224-3643

East Asian & Pacific Affairs
Chair:
Jim Webb (D-VA)........................202-224-4024
Ranking Member:
Republican Leader Designee

European Affairs
Chair:
Jeanne Shaheen (D-NH)........................202-224-2841
Ranking Member:
Jim DeMint (R-SC)........................202-224-6121

International Development, Foreign Assist, Economic Affairs & Environment
Chair:
Robert Menendez (D-NJ)........................202-224-4744
Ranking Member:
Bob Corker (R-TN)........................202-224-3344

International Ops & Orgs, Human Rights, Democracy & Global Women's Issues
Chair:
Barbara Boxer (D-CA)........................202-224-3553
Ranking Member:
Roger F Wicker (R-MS)........................202-224-6253

Near Eastern and South and Central Asian Affairs
Chair:
Robert P Casey, Jr (D-PA)........................202-224-6324
Ranking Member:
James E Risch (R-ID)........................202-224-2752

Western Hemisphere, Peace Corps & Narcotics Affairs
Chair:
Christopher J Dodd (D-CT)........................202-224-2823
Ranking Member:
John Barrasso (R-WY)........................202-224-6441

Health, Education, Labor, & Pensions
428 Dirksen Senate Building
Washington, DC 20510
Web site: www.help.senate.gov

Chair:
Edward M Kennedy (D-MA)........................202-224-4543
Ranking Member:
Michael B Enzi (R-WY)........................202-224-3424
New York Delegate:
Hillary Rodham Clinton (D)........................202-224-4451

Subcommittees

Children and Families
Chair:
Christopher J Dodd (D-CT)........................202-224-2823
Ranking Member:
Lamar Alexander (R-TN)........................202-224-4944

Employment & Workplace Safety
Chair:
Patty Murray (D-WA)........................202-224-2621
Ranking Member:
Johnny Isakson (R-GA)........................202-224-3643

Retirement and Aging
Chair:
Barbara Mikulski (D-MD)........................202-224-4654
Ranking Member:
Richard Burr (R-NC)........................202-224-3154
New York Delegate:
Hillary Rodham Clinton (D-NY)........................202-224-4451

Homeland Security & Governmental Affairs
340 Dirksen Senate Building
Washington, DC 20510
202-224-2627
Web site: www.hsgac.senate.gov

Chair:
Joseph I Lieberman (D-CT)........................202-224-4041
Ranking Member:
Susan Collins (R-ME)........................202-224-2523

Subcommittees

Disaster Recovery
Chair:
Mary L Landrieu (D-LA)........................202-224-5824
Ranking Member:
Lindsey O Graham (R-SC)........................202-224-4751

Federal Financial Mgt, Govt Info, Federal Svcs, & International Security
Chair:
Thomas R Carper (D-DE)........................202-224-2441
Ranking Member:
John Coburn (R-AZ)........................202-224-2235

Oversight of Government Management,Federal Workforce & District of Columbia
Chair:
Daniel K Akaka (D-HI)........................202-224-6361
Ranking Member:
George V Voinovich (R-OH)........................202-224-3353

Permanent Subcommittee on Investigations
Chair:
Carl Levin (D-MI)........................202-224-6221
Ranking Member:
Tom Coburn (R-OK)........................202-224-5754

State, Local, and Private Sector Preparedness and Integration
Chair:
Mark L Pryor (D-AR)........................202-224-2353
Ranking Member:
John Ensign (R-NV)........................202-224-6244

Judiciary
226 Dirksen Senate Building
Washington, DC 20510
Web site: www.judiciary.senate.gov

Chair:
Patrick J Leahy (D-VT) 202-224-4242
Ranking Member:
Arlen Specter (R-PA) 202-224-4254

Subcommittees

Administrative Oversight & the Courts
Chair:
Sheldon Whitehead (D-RI) 202-224-2921
Ranking Member:
Jeff Sessions (R-AL) 202-224-4124

Antitrust, Competition Policy & Consumer Rights
Chair:
Herb Kohl (D-WI) 202-224-5653
Ranking Member:
Orrin G Hatch (R-UT) 202-224-5251

Constitution, The
Chair:
Russell D Feingold (D-WI) 202-224-5323
Ranking Member:
Tom Coburn (R-OK) 202-224-5754

Crime & Drugs
Chair:
Richard J Durbin (D-IL) 202-224-2152
Ranking Member:
Lindsey O Graham (R-SC) 202-224-5972

Immigration, Refugees and Border Security
Chair:
Charles E Schumer (D-NY) 202-224-6542
Ranking Member:
John Cornyn (R-TX) 202-224-2934
Chair:
Benjamin L Cardin (D-MD) 202-224-4524
Ranking Member:
Jon Kyl (R-AZ) 202-224-4521

Rules & Administration
305 Russell Senate Building
Washington, DC 20510
202-224-6352
Web site: www.rules.senate.gov

Chair:
Charles E Schumer (D-NY) 202-224-6542
Ranking Member:
Bob Bennett (R-UT) 202-224-5444

Small Business & Entrepreneurship
428A Russell Senate Building
Washington, DC 20510
202-224-5175
Web site: www.sbc.senate.gov

Chair:
Mary L Landrieu (D-LA) 202-224-5824
Ranking Member:
Olympia J Snowe (R-ME) 202-224-5344

Veterans' Affairs
412 Russell Senate Building
Washington, DC 20510
202-224-9126
Web site: www.veterans.senate.gov

Chair:
Daniel Akaka (D-HI) 202-224-6361
Ranking Member:
Richard Burr (R-NC) 202-224-3154

OTHER, SELECT & SPECIAL COMMITTEES

Aging, Special Committee on
G31 Dirksen Senate Building
Washington, DC 20510
202-224-5364
Web site: www.aging.senate.gov

Chair:
Herb Kohl (D-WI) 202-224-5653
Vice Chair:
Gordon Smith (R-OR) 202-224-3753

Ethics, Select Committee on
220 Hart Building
Washington, DC 20510
202-224-2981
Web site: www.ethics.senate.gov

Chair:
Barbara Boxer (D-CA) 202-224-3553
Vice Chair:
Johnny Isakson (R-GA) 202-224-3643

Indian Affairs, Committee on
838 Hart Office Building
Washington, DC 20510
202-224-2251
Web site: indian.senate.gov

Chair:
Byron L Dorgan (D-ND) 202-224-2251
Vice Chair:
John Barrasso (R-WY) 202-224-6641

Intelligence, Select Committee on
211 Hart Senate Building
Washington, DC 20510
202-224-1700
Web site: www.intelligence.senate.gov

Chair:
Dianne Feinstein (D-CA) 202-224-3841
Vice Chair:
Christopher S Bond (R-MO) 202-224-5721

U.S. HOUSE OF REPRESENTATIVES STANDING COMMITTEES

Agriculture
1301 Longworth House Office Building
Washington, DC 20515
202-225-2171
Web site: agriculture.house.gov

Chair:
Collin C Peterson (D-MN) 202-225-2165
Ranking Member:
Frank D Lucas (R-OK) 202-225-5565

Offices and agencies generally appear in alphabetical order, except when specific order is requested by listee.

Subcommittees

Conservation, Credit, Energy, and Research
Chair:
Tim Holden (D-PA) 202-225-5546
Ranking Member:
Bob Goodlatte (D-VA) 202-225-5431

Department Operations, Oversight, Nutrition, & Forestry
Chair:
Joe Baca (D-CA) 202-225-6161
Ranking Member:
Jeff Fortenberry (R-NE 202-225-4806

General Farm Commodities & Risk Management
Chair:
Leonard L Boswell (D-IA) 202-225-3806
Ranking Member:
Jerry Moran (R-KS) 202-225-2715

Horticulture and Organic Agriculture
Chair:
Dennis A Cardoza (D-CA) 202-225-6131
Ranking Member:
Jean Schmidt (R-OH) 202-225-3164

Livestock, Dairy, and Poultry
Chair:
David Scott (D-GA) 202-225-2939
Ranking Member:
Randy Neugebauer (R-TX) 202-225-4005

Specialty Crops, Rural Development and Foreign Agriculture
Chair:
Mike McIntyre (D-NC) 202-225-2731
Ranking Member:
K Michael Conaway (R-TX) 202-225-3605

Appropriations
H-218 US Capitol
Washington, DC 20515
202-225-2771
Web site: appropriations.house.gov

Chair:
David R Obey (D-WI) 202-225-3365
Ranking Member:
Jerry Lewis (R-CA) 202-225-5861
New York Delegate:
Maurice D Hinchey (D) 202-225-6335
New York Delegate:
Steve Israel (D) 202-225-3335
New York Delegate:
Nita M Lowey (D) 202-225-6506
New York Delegate:
Jose E Serrano (D) 202-225-4361

Subcommittees

Agriculture, Rural Development, FDA & Related Agencies
Chair:
Rosa DeLauro (D-CT) 202-225-3661
Ranking Member:
Jack Kingston (R-GA) 202-225-5831

Commerce, Justice, Science and Related Agencies
Chair:
Alan B Mollohan (D-WV) 202-225-4172
Ranking Member:
Frank R Wolf (R-VA) 202-225-5136

Defense
Chair:
John P Murtha (D-PA) 202-225-2847
Ranking Member:
C W Bill Young (R-FL) 202-225-5961

Energy and Water Development
Chair:
Peter J Visclosky (D-IN) 202-225-2461
Ranking Member:
Rodney P Frelinhuysen (R-NJ) 202-225-5034

Financial Services and General Government
Chair:
Jose Serrano (D-NY) 202-225-4361
Ranking Member:
Jo Ann Emerson (R-MO) 202-225-4404

Homeland Security
Chair:
David E Price (D-NC) 202-225-1784
Ranking Member:
Harold Rogers (R-KY) 202-225-4601

Interior, Environment and Related Agencies
Chair:
Norman D Dicks (D-WA) 202-225-5916
Ranking Member:
Michael K Simpson (R-ID) 202-225-5531

Labor, Health & Human Services, Education and Related Agencies
Chair:
David R Obey (D-WI) 202-225-3365
Ranking Member:
Todd Tiahrt (R-KS) 202-225-6216

Legislative Branch
Chair:
Debbie Wasserman Schultz (D-FL) 202-225-7931
Ranking Member:
Robert B Aderholt (R-AL) 202-225-4876

Military Construction, Veterans Affairs and Related Agencies
Chair:
Chet Edwards (D-TX) 202-225-6105
Ranking Member:
Zach Wamp (R-TN) 202-225-3271

State, Foreign Operations and Related Programs
Chair:
Nita M Lowey (D-NY) 202-225-6506
Ranking Member:
Kay Granger (R-TX) 202-225-5071

Transportation, Housing and Urban Development, and Related Agencies
Chair:
John W Olver (D-MA) 202-225-5335
Ranking Member:
Tom Latham (R-IA) 202-225-5476

Armed Services
2120 Rayburn House Building
Washington, DC 20515
202-225-9077 Fax: 202-225-4151
Web site: www.house.gov/hasc/

Chair:
Ike Skelton (D-MO) 202-225-2876
Ranking Member:
John M McHugh (R-NY) 202-225-4611
New York Delegate:
Eric JJ Massa (D) 202-225-3161

New York Delegate:
Scott Murphy (D) 202-225-5614

Subcommittees

Air and Land Forces
Chair:
Neil Abercrombie (D-HI) 202-225-2726
Ranking Member:
Roscoe G Bartlett (R-MD) 202-225-2721

Military Personnel
Chair:
Susan A Davis (D-CA) 202-225-2040
Ranking Member:
Joe Wilson (R-SC) 202-225-2452

Oversight and Investigations
Chair:
Vic Snyder (D-AR) 202-225-2506
Ranking Member:
Rob Wittman (R-VA) 202-225-4261

Readiness
Chair:
Solomon P Ortiz (D-TX) 202-225-7742
Ranking Member:
J Randy Forbes (R-VA) 202-225-6365

Seapower and Expeditionary Forces
Chair:
Gene Taylor (D-MS) 202-225-5772
Ranking Member:
W Todd Akin (R-MO) 202-225-2561

Strategic Forces
Chair:
Ellen O Tauscher (D-CA) 202-225-1880
Ranking Member:
Michael Turner (R-OH) 202-225-6465

Terrorism, Unconventional Threats and Capabilities
Chair:
Adam Smith (D-WA) 202-225-8901
Ranking Member:
Jeff Miller (R-TX) 202-225-4136

Budget
207 Cannon House Building
Washington, DC 20515
202-226-7200 Fax: 202-225-9905
Web site: http://budget.house.gov

Chair:
John M Spratt, Jr (D-SC) 202-225-5501
Ranking Member:
Paul Ryan (R-WI) 202-225-3031
New York Delegate:
Tim Bishop (D) 202-225-3826

Education & Labor
2181 Rayburn House Building
Washington, DC 20515
202-225-3725
Web site: http://edworkforce.house.gov

Chair:
George Miller (D-CA) 202-225-2095
Ranking Member:
Howard P (Buck) McKeon (R-CA) 202-225-1956
New York Delegate:
Timothy H Bishop (D) 202-225-3826
New York Delegate:
Yvette Clarke (D) 202-225-6231
New York Delegate:
Carolyn McCarthy (D) 202-225-5516
New York Delegate:
Paul Tonko (D) 202-225-5076

Subcommittees

Early Childhood, Elementary and Secondary Education
Chair:
Dale E Kildee (D-MI) 202-225-3611
Ranking Member:
Michael N Castle (R-DE) 202-225-4165

Healthy Families and Communities
Chair:
Carolyn McCarthy (D-NY) 202-225-5516
Ranking Member:
Todd (Russell) Platts (R-PA) 202-225-5836

Higher Education, Lifelong Learning, and Competitiveness
Chair:
Rub,n Hinojosa (D-TX) 202-225-2531
Ranking Member:
Brett Guthrie (R-KY) 202-225-3501

Health, Employment, Labor and Pensions
Chair:
Robert Andrews (D-NJ) 202-225-6501
Ranking Member:
John Kline (R-MN) 202-225-2271

Workforce Protections
Chair:
Lynn C Woolsey (D-CA) 202-225-5161
Ranking Member:
Tom Price (R-GA) 202-225-4501

Energy & Commerce
2125 Rayburn House Building
Washington, DC 20515
202-225-2927
Web site: energycommerce.house.gov

Chair:
Henry A Waxman (D-CA) 202-225-3976
Ranking Member:
Joe Barton (R-TX) 202-225-2002
New York Delegate:
Eliot L Engel (D) 202-225-2464
New York Delegate:
Anthony D Weiner (D) 202-225-6616

Subcommittees

Commerce, Trade & Consumer Protection
Chair:
Bobby L Rush (D-IL) 202-225-4372
Ranking Member:
George Radanovich (R-CA) 202-225-4540

Communications, Technology & the Internet
Chair:
Rick Boucher (D-VA) 202-225-3861
Ranking Member:
Cliff Stearns (R-FL) 202-225-5744

Energy & the Environment
Chair:
Edward J Markey (D-MA) 202-225-2836
Ranking Member:
Fred Upton (R-MI) 202-225-3761

Health
Chair:
Frank J Pallone, Jr (D-NJ) 202-225-4671
Ranking Member:
Nathan Deal (R-GA) 202-225-5211

Oversight & Investigations
Chair:
Bart Stupak (D-MI) 202-225-4735
Ranking Member:
Greg Walden (R-OR) 202-225-6730

Financial Services
2129 Rayburn House Building
Washington, DC 20515
202-225-4247 Fax: 202-225-6952
Web site: http://financialservices.house.gov

Chair:
Barney Frank (D-MA) 202-225-5931
Ranking Member:
Spencer Bachus (R-AL) 202-225-4921
New York Delegate:
Gary L Ackerman (D) 202-225-2601
New York Delegate:
Peter T King (R) 202-225-7896
New York Delegate:
Christopher Lee (R) 202-225-5265
New York Delegate:
Dan Maffei (D) 202-225-3701
New York Delegate:
Carolyn B Maloney (D) 202-225-7944
New York Delegate:
Carolyn McCarthy (D) 202-225-5516
New York Delegate:
Gregory W Meeks (D) 202-225-3461
New York Delegate:
Nydia M Velazquez (D) 202-225-2361

Subcommittees

Capital Markets, Insurance & Government Sponsored Enterprises
Chair:
Paul E Kanjorski (D-PA) 202-225-6511
Ranking Member:
Scott Garrett (R-NJ) 202-225-4465
New York Delegate:
Gary L Ackerman (D) 202-225-2601
New York Delegate:
Peter T King (R) 202-225-7896
New York Delegate:
Carolyn McCarthy (D) 202-225-5516
New York Delegate:
Carolyn B Maloney (D) 202-225-7944
New York Delegate:
Nydia M Velazquez (D) 202-225-2361

Domestic Monetary Policy & Technology
Chair:
Melvin L Watt (D-NC) 202-225-1510
Ranking Member:
Ron Paul (R-TX) 202-225-2831
New York Delegate:
Carolyn B Maloney (D) 202-225-7944
New York Delegate:
Gregory W Meeks (D) 202-225-3461

Financial Institutions & Consumer Credit
Chair:
Luis V Gutierrez (D-IL) 202-225-8203
Ranking Member:
Jeb Hensarling (R-TX) 202-225-3484
New York Delegate:
Gary L Ackerman (D) 202-225-2601
New York Delegate:
Peter King (R) 202-225-7896
New York Delegate:
Christopher Lee (R) 202-225-5265
New York Delegate:
Carolyn B Maloney (D) 202-225-7944
New York Delegate:
Carolyn McCarthy (D) 202-225-5516
New York Delegate:
Gregory W Meeks (D) 202-225-3461

Housing & Community Opportunity
Chair:
Maxine Waters (D-CA) 202-225-2201
Ranking Member:
Shelley Moore Capito (R-WV) 202-225-2711
New York Delegate:
Dan Maffei (D) 202-225-3701
New York Delegate:
Nydia M Velazquez (D) 202-225-2361

International Monetary Policy & Trade
Chair:
Gregory W Meeks (D-NY) 202-225-3461
Ranking Member:
Gary Miller (R-CA) 202-225-3201
New York Delegate:
Dan Maffei (D) 202-225-3701

Oversight & Investigations
Chair:
Dennis Moore (D-KS) 202-225-2865
Ranking Member:
Judy Biggert (R-IL) 202-225-3515
New York Delegate:
Christopher Lee (R) 202-225-5265

Foreign Affairs
2170 Rayburn House Building
Washington, DC 20515
202-225-5021
Web site: foreignaffairs.house.gov

Chair:
Howard L Berman (D-CA) 202-225-3531
Ranking Member:
Ileana Ros- Lehtinen (R-FL) 202-225-3931
New York Delegate:
Gary Ackerman (D) 202-225-2601
New York Delegate:
Joseph Crowley (D) 202-225-3965
New York Delegate:
Eliot L Engel (D) 202-225-2464
New York Delegate:
Michael E McMahon (D) 202-225-3371
New York Delegate:
Gregory W Meeks (D) 202-225-3461

Subcommittees

Africa & Global Health
Chair:
Donald M Payne (D-NJ) 202-225-3436
Ranking Member:
Christopher H Smith (R-NJ) 202-225-3765
New York Delegate:
Gregory W Meeks (D) 202-225-3461

Offices and agencies generally appear in alphabetical order, except when specific order is requested by listee.

State & Local Government Public Information

Asia, the Pacific and the Global Environment
Chair:
Eni F H Faleomavaega (D-AS) 202-225-8577
Ranking Member:
Donald A Manzullo (R-IL). 202-225-5676
New York Delegate:
Gary L Ackerman (D). 202-225-2601
New York Delegate:
Eliot L Engel (D) 202-225-2464
New York Delegate:
Gregory W Meeks (D) 202-225-3461

Europe
Chair:
Robert Wexler (D-FL) 202-225-3001
Ranking Member:
Elton Gallegly (R-CA) 202-225-5811
New York Delegate:
Michael E McMahon (D) 202-225-3371

International Organizations, Human Rights and Oversight
Chair:
Bill Delahunt (D-MA) 202-225-3111
Ranking Member:
Dana Rohrabacher (R-CA). 202-225-2415

Middle East and South Asia
Chair:
Gary Ackerman (D-NY). 202-225-2601
Ranking Member:
Dan Burton (R-IN) 202-225-2276
New York Delegate:
Joseph Crowley (D) 202-225-3965
New York Delegate:
Eliot L Engel (D) 202-225-2464
New York Delegate:
Michael E McMahon (D) 202-225-3371

Terrorism, Nonproliferation and Trade
Chair:
Brad Sherman (D-CA) 202-225-5911
Ranking Member:
Edward R Royce (R-CA) 202-225-4111

Western Hemisphere
Chair:
Eliot Engel (D-NY) 202-225-2464
Ranking Member:
Connie Mack (R-FL) 202-225-2536
New York Delegate:
Joseph Crowley (D) 202-225-3965
New York Delegate:
Gregory W Meeks (D) 202-225-3461

Homeland Security
176 Ford House Building
Washington, DC 20515
202-226-2616 Fax: 202-226-4499
Web site: www.hsc.house.gov

Chair:
Bennie G Thompson (D-MS) 202-225-5876
Ranking Member:
Peter T King (R-NY) 202-225-7896
New York Delegate:
Yvette D Clarke (D) 202-225-6231
New York Delegate:
Eric JJ Massa (D) 202-225-3161

Subcommittees

Border, Maritime and Global Counterterrorism
Chair:
Loretta Sanchez (D-CA). 202-225-2965
Ranking Member:
Mark Souder (R-IN) 202-225-4436

Emergency Communications, Preparedness and Response
Chair:
Henry Cuellar (D-TX) 202-225-1640
Ranking Member:
Mark Rogers (R-AL) 202-225-3261

Emerging Threats, Cybersecurity and Science and Technology
Chair:
Yvette D Clark (D-NY) 202-225-6231
Ranking Member:
Dan Lundgren (R-CA) 202-225-5716

Intelligence, Information Sharing and Terrorism Risk Assessment
Chair:
Jane Harman (D-CA) 202-225-8220
Ranking Member:
Michael McCall (R-TX). 202-225-2401

Management, Investigations and Oversight
Chair:
Christopher P Carney (D-PA) 202-225-3731
Ranking Member:
Gus Bilirakis (R-FL). 202-225-5755

Transportation Security and Infrastructure Protection
Chair:
Sheila Jackson- Lee (D-TX). 202-225-3816
Ranking Member:
Charlie Dent (R-PA). 202-225-6411

House Administration
1309 Longworth Building
Washington, DC 20515
202-225-2061 Fax: 202-226-2774
Web site: http://cha.house.gov

Chair:
Robert A Brady (D-PA) 202-225-4731
Ranking Member:
Dan Lundgren (R-CA) 202-225-5671

Judiciary
2138 Rayburn House Building
Washington, DC 20515
Web site: www.judiciary.house.gov

Chair:
John Conyers, Jr (D-MI). 202-225-5126
Ranking Member:
Lamar S Smith (R-TX). 202-225-4236
New York Delegate:
Dan Maffei (D) 202-225-3701
New York Delegate:
Jerrold Nadler (D). 202-225-5635
New York Delegate:
Anthony D Weiner (D) 202-225-6616

Subcommittees

Commercial & Administrative Law
Chair:
Steve Cohen (D-TN). 202-225-3265
Ranking Member:
Trent Franks (R-AZ). 202-225-4576

Constitution, Civil Rights and Civil Liberties
Chair:
Jerrold Nadler (D-NY) 202-225-5635
Ranking Member:
F James Sensenbrenner, Jr (R-WI) 202-225-5101

Courts & Competition Policy
Chair:
Hank Johnson (D-GA) 202-225-1605
Ranking Member:
Howard Coble (R-NC) 202-225-3065

Crime, Terrorism and Homeland Security
Chair:
Robert C Scott (D-VA) 202-225-8351
Ranking Member:
Louie Gohmert (R-TX) 202-225-3035

Immigration, Citizenship, Refugees, Border Security and International Law
Chair:
Zoe Lofgren (D-CA) 202-225-3072
Ranking Member:
Steve King (R-IA) 202-225-4426

Natural Resources
1324 Longworth Building
Washington, DC 20515
202-225-6065 Fax: 202-225-1931
Web site: resourcescommittee.house.gov

New York Delegate:
Maurice D Hinchey (D) 202-225-6335
Chair:
Nick J Rahall, II (D-WV) 202-225-3452
Ranking Member:
Doc Hastings (R-WA) 202-225-5816

Office of Indian Affairs

Subcommittees

Energy & Mineral Resources
Chair:
Jim Costa (D-CA) 202-225-3341
Ranking Member:
Doug Lamborn (R-CO) 202-225-4422

Insular Affairs, Oceans & Wildlife
Chair:
Madelaine Z Bordallo (D-Guam) 202-225-1188
Ranking Member:
Henry E Brown, Jr (R-SC) 202-225-3176

National Parks, Forests and Public Lands
Chair:
Raul M Grijalva (R-AZ) 202-225-2435
Ranking Member:
Rob Bishop (R-UT) 202-225-0453

Water & Power
Chair:
Grace F Napolitano (D-CA) 202-225-5256
Ranking Member:
Cathy McMorris Rodgers (R-WA) 202-225-2006

Oversight and Government Reform
2157 Rayburn House Building
Washington, DC 20515
202-225-5051
Web site: oversight.house.gov

Chair:
Edolphus Towns (D-NY) 202-225-5936
Ranking Member:
Darrell E Issa (R-CA) 202-225-3906
New York Delegate:
Carolyn B Maloney (D) 202-225-7944
New York Delegate:
John M McHugh (R) 202-225-4611

Subcommittees

Domestic Policy
Chair:
Dennis J Kucinich (D-OH) 202-225-5871
Ranking Member:
Jim Jordan (R-OH) 202-225-2676

Federal Workforce, Postal Service and the District of Columbia
Chair:
Stephen F Lynch (D-MA) 202-225-8273
Ranking Member:
Jason Chaffetz (R-UT) 202-225-7751
New York Delegate:
Carolyn D Maloney (D) 202-225-7944

Government Management, Organization and Procurement
Chair:
Diane E Watson (D-CA) 202-225-7084
Ranking Member:
Brian Bilbray (R-CA) 202-225-0508

Information Policy, Census and National Archives
Chair:
William Lacy Clay (D-MO) 202-225-2406
Ranking Member:
Patrick McHenry (R-NC) 202-225-2576
New York Delegate:
Carolyn B Maloney (D) 202-225-7944

National Security and Foreign Affairs
Chair:
John F Tierney (D-MA) 202-225-8020
Ranking Member:
Jeff Flake (R-AZ) 202-225-2635
New York Delegate:
Carolyn B Maloney (D) 202-225-7944

Rules
H-312 The Capitol
Washington, DC 20515
202-225-9091
Web site: www.rules.house.gov

Chair:
Louise McIntosh Slaughter (D-NY) 202-225-3615
Ranking Member:
David Dreier (R-CA) 202-225-2305

Subcommittees

Legislative & Budget Process
Chair:
Alcee L Hastings (D-FL) 202-225-1313
Ranking Member:
Lincoln Diaz-Balart (R-FL) 202-225-4211

Rules & Organization of the House
Chair:
James F McGovern (D-MA) 202-225-6101
Ranking Member:
Pete Sessions (R-TX) 202-225-2231

Science & Technology
2321 Rayburn Building
Washington, DC 20515
202-225-6375 Fax: 202-225-3895
Web site: www.house.gov/science

Chair:
Bart Gordon (D-TN) 202-225-4231
Ranking Member:
Ralph M Hall (R-TX) 202-225-6673
New York Delegate:
Paul D Tonko (D) 202-225-5076

Subcommittees

Energy & Environment
Chair:
Brian Baird (D-WA) 202-225-3536
Ranking Member:
Bob Inglis (R-SC) 202-225-6030

Investigations and Oversights
Chair:
Brad Miller (D-NC) 202-225-3032
Ranking Member:
Paul C Brown (R-GA) 202-225-4101

Research and Science Education
Chair:
Daniel Lipinski (D-IL) 202-225-5701
Ranking Member:
Vernon J Ehlers (R-MI) 202-225-3831

Space and Aeronautics
Chair:
Gabrielle Giffords (D-AZ) 202-225-2542
Ranking Member:
Pete Olson (R-TX) 202-225-5951

Technology and Innovation
Chair:
David Wu (D-OR) 202-225-0855
Ranking Member:
Adrian Smith (R-NE) 202-225-6435

Small Business
2361 Rayburn House Building
Washington, DC 20515
202-225-4038 Fax: 202-226-5276
Web site: www.house.gov/smbiz

Chair:
Nydia Velazquez (D-NY) 202-225-2361
Ranking Member:
Sam Graves (R-MO) 202-225-7041
New York Delegate:
Yvette D Clark (D) 202-225-6231

Subcommittees

Contracting and Technology
Chair:
Glenn C Nye III (D-IA) 202-225-4215
Ranking Member:
Aaron Schock (R-IL) 202-225-6201

Finance and Tax
Chair:
Kurt Schrader (D-OR) 202-225-5711
Ranking Member:
Vern Buchanan (R-FL) 202-225-5015

Investigations and Oversight
Chair:
Jason Altmire (D-PA) 202-225-2565
Ranking Member:
Mary Fallin (R-OK) 202-225-2132

Regulations and Health Care
Chair:
Kathy Dahlkemper (D-PA) 202-225-5406
Ranking Member:
Lynn Westmoreland (R-GA) 202-225-5901

Rural and Urban Entrepreneurship
Chair:
Heath Shuler (D-NC) 202-225-6401
Ranking Member:
Blaine Luetkemeyer (R-MO) 202-225-2956

Standards of Official Conduct
HT-2, The Capitol
Washington, DC 20515
202-225-7103 Fax: 202-225-7392
Web site: ethics.house.gov

Chair:
Zoe Lofgren (D-CA) 202-225-3072
Ranking Member:
Jo Bonner (R-AL) 202-225-4931

Transportation & Infrastructure
2165 Rayburn House Building
Washington, DC 20515
202-225-4472 Fax: 202-226-1270
Web site: www.transportation.house.gov

Chair:
James L Oberstar (D-MN) 202-225-4472
Ranking Member:
John L Mica (R-FL) 202-225-4035
New York Delegate:
Michael A Arcuri (D) 202-225-3665
New York Delegate:
Timothy H Bishop (D) 202-225-3826
New York Delegate:
John J Hall (D) 202-225-5441
New York Delegate:
Michael E McMahon (D) 202-225-3371
New York Delegate:
Jerrold Nadler (D) 202-225-5635

Subcommittees

Aviation
Chair:
Jerry F Costello (D-IL) 202-225-5661
Ranking Member:
Thomas E Petri (R-WI) 202-225-2476
New York Delegate:
John J Hall (D) 202-225-5441
New York Delegate:
Michael E McMahon (D) 202-225-3371

Coast Guard & Maritime Transportation
Chair:
Elijah E Cummings (D-MD) 202-225-4741
Ranking Member:
Frank LoBiondo (R-NJ) 202-225-6572
New York Delegate:
Timothy H Bishop (D) 202-225-3826
New York Delegate:
Michael E McMahon (D) 202-225-3371

Economic Development, Public Buildings & Emergency Management
Chair:
Eleanor Holmes Norton (D-DC) 202-225-9961
Ranking Member:
Mario Diaz-Balart (R-FL) 202-225-4211
New York Delegate:
Michael A Arcuri (D) 202-225-3665

Highway and Transit
Chair:
Peter A DeFazio (D-OR) 202-225-9989
Ranking Minority Member:
John J Duncan, Jr (R-TN) 202-225-5435
New York Delegate:
Michael A Arcuri (D) 202-225-3665
New York Delegate:
Timothy H Bishop (D) 202-225-3826
New York Delegate:
John J Hall (D) 202-225-5441
New York Delegate:
Jerrold Nadler (D) 202-225-5635

Railroads, Pipelines and Hazardous Materials
Chair:
Corrine Brown (D-FL) 202-225-3274
Ranking Member:
Bill Schuster (PA) 202-225-2431
New York Delegate:
Michael A Arcuri (D) 202-225-3665
New York Delegate:
Michael E McMahon (D) 202-225-3371
New York Delegate:
Jerrold Nadler (D) 202-225-5635

Water Resources & Environment
Chair:
Eddie Bernice Johnson (D-TX) 202-225-0060
Ranking Member:
John Boozman (R-AR) 202-225-4301
New York Delegate:
Timothy H Bishop (D) 202-225-3826
New York Delegate:
John J Hall (D) 202-225-5441

Veterans' Affairs
335 Cannon House Building
Washington, DC 20515
202-225-9756
Web site: www.veterans.house.gov

Chair:
Bob Filner (D-CA) 202-225-8045
Ranking Member:
Steve Buyer (D-IN) 202-225-5037
New York Delegate:
John J Hall (D) 202-225-5441

Subcommittees

Disability Assistance & Memorial Affairs
Chair:
John Hall (D-NY) 202-225-5441
Ranking Member:
Doug Lamborn (R-CO) 202-225-4422

Economic Opportunity
Chair:
Stephanie Herseth Sandlin (D-SD) 202-225-2801
Ranking Member:
John Boozman (R-AR) 202-225-4301

Health
Chair:
Mike Michaud (D-ME) 202-225-6306
Ranking Member:
Henry E Brown, Jr (R-SC) 202-225-3176

Oversight & Investigations
Chair:
Harry E Mitchell (D-AZ) 202-225-2190
Ranking Member:
Phil Roe (R-TN) 202-225-6356

Ways & Means
1102 Longworth House Building
Washington, DC 20515
202-225-3625 Fax: 202-225-2610
Web site: waysandmeans.house.gov

Chair:
Charles B Rangel (D-NY) 202-225-4365
Ranking Member:
Dave Camp (R-MI) 202-225-3561
New York Delegate:
Joseph Crowley (D) 202-225-3965
New York Delegate:
Brian Higgins (D) 202-225-3306

Subcommittees

Health
Chair:
Fortney Pete Stark (D-CA) 202-225-5065
Ranking Member:
Wally Herger (D-CA) 202-225-3076

Income Security and Family Support
Chair:
Jim McDermott (D-WA) 202-225-3106
Ranking Member:
John Linder (R-GA) 202-225-

Oversight
Chair:
John Lewis (D-GA) 202-225-3801
Ranking Member:
Charles W Boustany, Jr (R-LA) 202-225-2031
New York Delegate:
Brian Higgins (D) 202-225-3306

Select Revenue Measures
Chair:
Richard E Neal (D-MA) 202-225-5601
Ranking Member:
Pat Tiberi (R-OH) 202-225-5355
New York Delegate:
Joseph Crowley (D) 202-225-3965

Social Security
Chair:
John S Tanner (D-TN) 202-225-4714
Ranking Member:
Sam Johnson (R-TX) 202-225-4201
New York Delegate:
Joseph Crowley (D) 202-225-3965

Trade
Chair:
Sander M Levin (MI) 202-225-4961
Ranking Member:
Kevin Brady (R-TX) 202-225-4901

OTHER, SELECT & SPECIAL COMMITTEES

Energy Independence & Global Warming, House Select Committee on
B243 Longworth House Building
Washington, DC 20515
202-225-4012 Fax: 202-225-4092
Web site: globalwarming.house.gov

Chair:
Ed Markey (D-MA) 202-225-2836
Ranking Member:
James F Sensenbrenner, Jr (R-WI) 202-225-5101

Intelligence, House Permanent Select Committee on
Web site: intelligence.house.gov

Chair:
Silvestre Reyes (D-TX) 202-225-4831
Ranking Member:
Peter Hoekstra (R-MI) 202-225-4401

Subcommittees

Intelligence Community Management
Chair:
Anna G Eshoo (D-CA) 202-225-8104
Ranking Member:
Sue Myrick (R-NC) 202-225-1976

Oversight and Investigations
Chair:
Jan Schakowsky (D-AL) 202-225-2111
Ranking Member:
Jeff Miller (R-FL) 202-225-4136

Technical and Tactical Intelligence
Chair:
C A Dutch Ruppersberger (D-MD) 202-225-3061
Ranking Member:
Mack Thornberry (R-TX) 202-225-3706

Terrorism/HUMIT, Analysis and Counterintelligence
Chair:
Mike Thompson (D-CA) 202-225-3311
Ranking Member:
Mike Rogers (R-MI) 202-225-4872

JOINT SENATE AND HOUSE COMMITTEES

Economic Committee, Joint
Web site: www.house.gov/jec

Chair, House:
Carolyn B Maloney (D-NY) 202-224-7944
Vice Chair, Senate:
Charles E Schumer (D-NY) 202-224-6542
Ranking Member, House:
Kevin Brady (R-TX) 202-225-4901
Ranking Member, Senate:
Sam Brownback (R-KS) 202-225-6521
New York Delegate:
Maurice D Hinchey (D) 202-224-6335

Library, Joint Committee on the
Chair:
Charles E Schumer (D-NY) 202-224-6542
Ranking Member:
Robert Bennett (R-UT) 202-224-5444

Printing, Joint Committee on
Web site: www.jcp.senate.gov

Chair:
Charles E Schumer (D-NY 202-224-6542
Vice Chair:
Robert F Bennett (R-UT) 202-224-5444

Taxation, Joint Committee on
1015 Longworth House Building
Washington, DC 20515
202-225-3621
Web site: www.house.gov/jct

Chair:
Charles B Rangel (D-NY) 202-225-4365
Vice Chair:
Max Baucus (D-MT) 202-224-2651

Offices and agencies generally appear in alphabetical order, except when specific order is requested by listee.

COUNTY GOVERNMENT

This section identifies senior government officials in all New York counties.

COUNTY GOVERNMENT

Albany County
112 State Street
Albany, NY 12207
518-447-7040 Fax: 518-447-5589
Web site: www.albanycounty.com

Chairman, County Legislature (D):
Shawn M. Morse 518-447-7168/fax: 518-447-5695
e-mail: shawn.morse@albanycounty.com
County Executive:
Daniel P. McCoy 518-447-7040/fax: 518-447-5589
e-mail: county_executive@albanycounty.com
County Clerk:
Thomas G Clingan. 518-487-5100/fax: 518-487-5099
e-mail: countyclerk@albanycounty.com
County Attorney:
Thomas Marcelle 518-447-7110/fax: 518-447-5564
District Attorney:
P David Soares 518-487-5460/fax: 518-487-5093
Sheriff:
Craig D. Apple, Sr. 518-487-5400/fax: 518-487-5037
Comptroller:
Michael F Conners, II 518-447-7130/fax: 518-433-1554
e-mail: mconners@albanycounty.com
General Services Commissioner:
John T. Evers 518-447-7210/fax: 518-447-7747
Commissioner, Management & Budget:
David Friedfel 518-447-5525/fax: 518-447-5589
e-mail: budget@albanycounty.com

Allegany County
County Office Bldg, 7 Court St
Belmont, NY 14813
585-268-9222 Fax: 585-268-9446
Web site: www.alleganyco.com

Chairman, Board of Legislators (R):
Curtis W Crandall 585-268-9222
Majority Leader (R):
Theodore L Hopkins 585-268-9222
Minority Leader (D):
Vacant 585-268-9222
Clerk, Board of Legislators:
Brenda A Rigby Riehle 585-268-9222/fax: 585-268-9446
e-mail: rigbyba@alleganyco.com
County Administrator:
John E Margeson 585-268-9217/fax: 585-268-9623
e-mail: margesj@alleganyco.com
County Clerk:
Robert L Christman 585-268-9270/fax: 585-268-9659
e-mail: christr@alleganyco.com
District Attorney (Acting):
Keith Slep 585-268-9225/fax: 585-268-9727
e-mail: slepka@alleganyco.com
Public Defender:
Barbara J Kelley 585-268-9246/fax: 585-268-5888
e-mail: kelleybj@alleganyco.com
Sheriff:
Rick Whitney 585-268-9200/fax: 585-268-9484
e-mail: whitneyrl@alleganyco.com
Treasurer:
Terri L Ross 585-268-9289/fax: 585-268-7506
e-mail: rosstl@alleganyco.com
County Attorney:
Thomas A Miner 585-268-9410/fax: 585-268-9651
e-mail: minerta@alleganyco.com
Director, Emergency Management & Fire:
Jeff Luckey 585-268-5290
e-mail: luckeyj@alleganyco.com
Superintendent, Public Works:
Guy James 585-268-9230/fax: 585-268-9648
e-mail: roeskeds@alleganyco.com
Fire Coordinator:
Paul W Gallmann 585-268-5290/fax: 585-268-9695
e-mail: gallmapw@alleganyco.com
County Historian:
Craig R Braack 585-268-9293
e-mail: historian@alleganyco.com

Bronx County (NYC Borough of the Bronx)
851 Grand Concourse
Room 118
Bronx, NY 10451
866-797-7214 Fax: 718-590-8122
Web site: www.bronxcountyclerksoffice.com

Borough President:
Ruben Diaz Jr 718-590-3557/fax: 718-590-3537
Deputy Borough President:
Aurelia Greene 718-590-4036
County Clerk:
Luis M. Diaz 866-797-7214/fax: 718-590-8122
e-mail: hdiaz@courts.state.ny.us
District Attorney:
Robert T Johnson 718-590-2000/fax: 718-590-2190

Broome County
County Office Bldg
60 Hawley St
PO Box 1766
Binghamton, NY 13902-1766
607-778-2109 Fax: 607-778-2044
e-mail: legclerk@co.broome.ny.us
Web site: www.gobroomecounty.com

Chairman, County Legislature (D):
Jerry F Marinich 607-778-2131/fax: 607-778-8869
e-mail: jmarinich@co.broome.ny.us
Majority Leader (D):
Wayne Howard 607-778-2131/fax: 607-778-8869
e-mail: whoward2@co.broome.ny.us
Minority Leader (R):
Mark R Whalen 607-778-2131/fax: 607-778-8869
e-mail: mwhalen2@co.broome.ny.us
County Executive:
Debra A. Preston 607-778-2109/fax: 607-778-2044
e-mail: bfiala@co.broome.ny.us
County Clerk:
Richard R Blythe 607-778-2255/fax: 607-778-2243
e-mail: clerkinfo@co.broome.ny.us
District Attorney:
Gerald F Mollen 607-778-2423/fax: 607-778-8870
e-mail: gmollen@co.broome.ny.us
Public Defender:
Jay L Wilber 607-778-2403/fax: 607-778-2432
e-mail: jwilber@co.broome.ny.us
Sheriff:
David E Harder 607-778-1911/fax: 607-778-2100
e-mail: bcsheriff@co.broome.ny.us

Offices and agencies generally appear in alphabetical order, except when specific order is requested by listee.

Director, Emergency Services:
Brett B Chellis....................607-778-2170/fax: 607-778-1150
e-mail: bchellis@co.broome.ny.us
Office of Management & Budget:
Marie F. Kalka....................607-778-2467/fax: 607-778-2044
e-mail: jknebel@co.broome.ny.us
County Historian:
Gerald R Smith....................607-778-2076/fax: 607-778-6249
e-mail: gsmith@co.broome.ny.us

Cattaraugus County
County Center
303 Court St
Little Valley, NY 14755
716-938-2577 Fax: 716-938-2760
Web site: www.cattco.org

Chair, County Legislature (R):
Norman L. Marsh....................716-938-6620/fax: 716-938-9698
Vice Chairman (R):
Michael T O'Brien....................716-938-9111 x2386
Majority Leader (R):
James J Snyder....................716-938-9111 x2333
Minority Leader (D):
Linda Witte....................716-938-9111 x2397
County Administrator & Clerk, Legislature:
Jack Searles....................716-938-9111 x2577/fax: 716-938-9306
e-mail: jrsearles@cattco.org
County Clerk:
James Griffith....................716-938-2297/fax: 716-938-6009
e-mail: jkgriffith@cattco.org
County Attorney:
Thomas C. Brady....................716-938-2931/fax: 716-938-2763
District Attorney:
Lori Pettit Rieman....................716-938-2220/fax: 716-938-2763
Sheriff:
Dennis B John....................716-938-9111 x2204/fax: 716-938-6420
e-mail: dbjohn@cattco.org
Treasurer:
Joseph Keller....................716-373-2290/fax: 716-938-2762
e-mail: jgkeller@cattco.org
Public Defender:
Mark S Williams....................716-373-0004 x11/fax: 716-373-3462
e-mail: mswilliams@cattco.org
County Historian:
Sharon Fellows....................716-353-8200 x4721
e-mail: scfellows@cattco.org

Cayuga County
160 Genesee St
Auburn, NY 13021
315-253-1525 Fax: 315-253-1586
Web site: www.cayugacounty.us

Chairman, County Legislature (R):
Peter A Tortorici....................315-253-1273
e-mail: chairman@co.cayuga.ny.us
Clerk, Legislature:
Sheila Smith....................315-253-1498
e-mail: lclerk@cayugacounty.us
County Manager:
Wayne D Allen....................315-253-1525
e-mail: wallen@cayugacounty.us
County Clerk:
Susan M Dwyer....................315-253-1271
e-mail: sdwyer@cayugacounty.us
County Attorney:
Fredrick Westphal....................315-253-1274
e-mail: coatty@cayugacounty.us
District Attorney:
Jon E Budelmann....................315-253-1391
e-mail: cayugada@cayugacounty.us
Director, Planning & Economic Development:
Steve Lynch....................315-253-1276
e-mail: planning@cayugacounty.us
Emergency Management Director:
Brian P Dahl....................315-255-1161
e-mail: ccoes@cayugacounty.us
Sheriff:
David S Gould....................315-253-1222
e-mail: sheriff@cayugacounty.us
Treasurer:
Jim H Orman....................315-253-1211
e-mail: treasurer@cayugacounty.us
County Historian:
Linda Frank....................315-253-1300
e-mail: historian@cayugacounty.us

Chautauqua County
3 N Erie St
Mayville, NY 14757-1007
716-753-4241 Fax: 716-753-4756
Web site: www.co.chautauqua.ny.us

Majority Leader (D):
Maria Kindberg....................716-753-4215
e-mail: chuckcornell@hotmail.com
Gould, III:
Frank Jay"" ....Chairman, City Legis or 716-753-4215
Clerk, Legislature:
Janet M. Jankowski....................716-753-4215
e-mail: cafliscj@co.chautauqua.ny.us
County Executive:
Gregory J Edwards....................716-753-4211
e-mail: edwardsg@co.chautauqua.ny.us
County Clerk:
Sandra K Sopak....................716-753-4331/fax: 716-753-4293
District Attorney:
David Foley....................716-753-4241
Public Defender:
Nathaniel L. Barone, II....................716-753-4376
Director, Emergency Services:
Julius Leone....................716-753-4341
Sheriff:
Joseph A Gerace....................716-753-2131
Finance Director:
Susan Marsh....................716-753-4223

Chemung County
John H Hazlett Bldg, 203 Lake St
PO Box 588
Elmira, NY 14902-0588
607-737-2912 Fax: 607-737-0351
e-mail: info@chemungcounty.com
Web site: www.chemungcounty.com

Chairman, County Legislature (R):
Donna Draxler....................607-737-2066/fax: 607-737-2851
e-mail: cmilliken@co.chemung.ny.us
Majority Leader (R):
Sidney S Graubard....................607-737-2066/fax: 607-737-2851
Minority Leader (D):
Theodore A Bennett....................607-737-2066/fax: 607-737-2851
e-mail: ted.benn@verizon.net
Clerk, Legislature:
Linda D Palmer....................607-737-2066/fax: 607-737-2851
e-mail: lpalmer@co.chemung.ny.us

Offices and agencies generally appear in alphabetical order, except when specific order is requested by listee.

County Executive:
Thomas J Santulli 607-737-2912/fax: 607-737-0351
e-mail: tsantulli@co.chemung.ny.us
County Clerk:
Catherine K Hughes 607-737-2920/fax: 607-737-2897
e-mail: chughes@co.chemung.ny.us
District Attorney:
Weeden A Wetmore 607-737-2944/fax: 607-737-2965
e-mail: wwetmore@co.chemung.ny.us
Public Defender:
Scott N Fierro 607-737-2969/fax: 607-737-2853
Sheriff:
Christopher J Moss 607-737-2987/fax: 607-737-2930
e-mail: cmoss@co.chemung.ny.us

Chenango County

County Office Bldg
5 Court St
Norwich, NY 13815
607-337-1700 Fax: 607-334-8768
Web site: www.co.chenango.ny.us

Chairman, Board of Supervisors (R):
Lawrence N Wilcox 607-337-1401
Clerk, Board of Supervisors:
R C Woodford 607-337-1430
County Clerk:
Mary C Weidman 607-337-1450
Sheriff:
Ernest R Cutting Jr 607-334-2000
Treasurer:
William E Evans 607-337-1414
Director, Public Works:
Shawn Fry P.E., L.S. 607-337-1710
County Historian:
Patricia E. Evans 607-337-1845

Clinton County

County Government Ctr
137 Margaret St, Ste 208
Plattsburgh, NY 12901
518-565-4600 Fax: 518-565-4616
e-mail: legislature@co.clinton.ny.us
Web site: www.clintoncountygov.com

Chairman (R):
James R Langley, Jr. 518-643-9052/fax: 518-643-6640
e-mail: langleyins@charter.net
Majority Leader (R):
Samuel J Trombley 518-597-7742/fax: 518-594-7742
e-mail: trombleyma@aol.com
Minority Leader (D):
Dr John Gallagher 518-561-0484
e-mail: vze3gnnn@verizon.net
Clerk, Board of Legislators & County Administrator:
Michael E Zurlo 518-565-4600/fax: 518-565-4616
e-mail: legislature@co.clinton.ny.us
County Clerk:
John H Zurlo 518-565-4700/fax: 518-565-4718
County Attorney:
William Favreau 518-561-4400/fax: 518-561-4848
District Attorney:
Andrew J Wylie 518-565-4770/fax: 518-565-4777
e-mail: da@co.clinton.ny.us
Director, Emergency Services:
Eric Day 518-565-4791/fax: 518-566-1202
e-mail: e911@co.clinton.ny.us
Sheriff:
David N Favro 518-565-4300/fax: 518-565-4333
e-mail: sheriff@co.clinton.ny.us
Treasurer:
Joseph W Giroux 518-565-4730/fax: 518-565-4516
e-mail: treasurer@co.clinton.ny.us

Columbia County

401 State St
Hudson, NY 12534
518-828-1527 Fax: 518-822-0684
e-mail: dicosmo@govt.co.columbia.ny.us
Web site: www.columbiacountyny.com

Chairman, Board of Supervisors (R):
Patrick M Gratton 518-828-1527/fax: 518-828-0684
e-mail: pat.gratton@govt.co.columbia.ny.us
County Clerk:
Holly C Tanner 518-828-3339/fax: 518-828-5299
e-mail: htanner@govt.co.columbia.ny.us
County Attorney:
Robert J Fitzsimmons 518-828-3303/fax: 518-828-9535
District Attorney:
Paul Czajka 518-828-3414
Public Defender:
Robert W. Linville 518-828-3410/fax: 518-828-4076
Sheriff:
David W Harrison Jr 518-828-0601/fax: 518-828-9088
Fire Coordinator:
John Howe 518-822-8610/fax: 518-828-1279
Director, Emergency Management:
William Black 518-828-1212/fax: 518-828-1279
Treasurer:
PJ Keeler 518-828-0513/fax: 518-822-1110
County Historian:
Mary Howell 518-828-3442/fax: 518-828-2969
e-mail: mhowell@govt.co.columbia.ny.us

Cortland County

County Office Bldg
60 Central Ave
Cortland, NY 13045
607-753-5048 Fax: 607-756-3492
Web site: www.cortland-co.org

Chairperson, County Legislature (D):
Mike Park 607-753-5048
e-mail: rjwilliams@cortland-co.org
Clerk, Legislature:
Jeremy Boylan 607-753-5049/fax: 607-756-3492
e-mail: jboylan@cortland-co.org
County Clerk:
Elizabeth P Larkin 607-753-5021
e-mail: clarkin@cortland-co.org
County Attorney:
Edward Purser 607-753-5095
e-mail: epurser@cortland-co.org
District Attorney:
Mark Suben 607-753-5008
Public Defender:
Edward Goehler 607-753-5046/fax: 607-753-0781
e-mail: publicdefender@cortland-co.org
Sheriff:
Lee A Price 607-753-5006
e-mail: lprice@cortland-co.org
Fire/Emergency Management Coordinator:
Scott Roman 607-753-5064/fax: 607-756-8457
e-mail: grduell@cortland-co.org
Treasurer:
Cynthia Monroe 607-753-5070/fax: 607-758-5512
e-mail: pomara@cortland-co.org

County Historian:
Jeremy Boylan 607-753-5360
e-mail: jboylan@cortland-co.org

Delaware County

County Office Bldg
111 Main St
Delhi, NY 13753
607-746-2603 Fax: 607-746-7012
Web site: www.co.delaware.ny.us

Chairman, Board of Supervisors (R):
James E Eisel, Sr. 607-652-4350
Vice Chairman, Board of Supervisors (R):
Tina Mole 607-832-4312
Clerk, Board of Supervisors:
Christa M Schafer 607-832-5110/fax: 607-832-5111
e-mail: cob@co.delaware.ny.us
County Clerk:
Sharon O'Dell 607-746-2123
County Attorney:
Richard B Spinney 607-652-3443/fax: 607-652-3334
District Attorney:
Richard D Northrup, Jr 607-746-3557/fax: 607-746-2297
Sheriff:
Thomas E Mills 607-746-2336/fax: 607-746-8151
County Treasurer:
Beverly J Shields 607-832-5070/fax: 607-832-5077
e-mail: treas@co.delaware.ny.us
Director, Emergency Services:
Richard Bell 607-746-9600
Commissioner, Public Works:
Wayne Reynolds 607-746-2128
County Historian:
Gabrielle Price 607-746-8660
e-mail: hist@co.delaware.ny.us

Dutchess County

County Office Bldg
22 Market St, 6th Fl
Poughkeepsie, NY 12601
845-486-2100 Fax: 845-486-2113
e-mail: internetsupport1@co.dutchess.ny.us
Web site: www.dutchessny.gov

Chairman, County Legislature (R):
Robert Rolison 845-486-2100/fax: 845-486-2113
Majority Leader (D):
Sandra Goldberg 845-297-76770
Minority Leader (R):
Gary Cooper 845-297-8757/fax: 845-486-2113
County Executive:
Marcus J. Molinaro 845-486-2000/fax: 845-486-2021
e-mail: countyexec@co.dutchess.ny.us
Clerk, Legislature:
Carolyn Morris 845-486-2100/fax: 845-486-2113
e-mail: countylegislature@co.dutchess.ny.us
County Clerk:
Bradford Kendall 845-486-2120/fax: 845-486-2138
County Attorney:
James M Fedorchak 845-486-2110/fax: 845-486-2002
e-mail: countyattorney@co.dutchess.ny.us
District Attorney:
William V Grady 845-486-2300/fax: 845-486-2324
Public Defender (Acting):
Thomas Angell 845-486-2280/fax: 845-486-2266
e-mail: publicdefender@co.dutchess.ny.us
Sheriff:
Adrian H Anderson 845-486-3800
e-mail: sheriff@co.dutchess.ny.us
Comptroller:
Jim Coughlan 845-486-2050/fax: 845-486-2055
e-mail: comptroller@co.dutchess.ny.us
Finance Commissioner:
Pamela Barrack 845-486-2025/fax: 845-486-2198
e-mail: rptaxfinance@co.dutchess.ny.us
Emergency Response Coordinator:
Dana Smith 845-486-2080/fax: 845-486-3998
e-mail: response911@co.dutchess.ny.us
County Historian:
William P. Tatum, III 845-486-2381
e-mail: dchistory@co.dutchess.ny.us

Erie County

County Office Bldg
95 Franklin St
16th Fl
Buffalo, NY 14202
716-858-7500 Fax: 716-858-8895
e-mail: public_feedback@erie.gov
Web site: www2.erie.gov

Chair, County Legislature (D):
Betty Jean Grant 716-894-0914/fax: 716-896-1463
e-mail: bjg@erie.gov
Majority Leader, County Legislature (D):
Thomas J. Mazur 716-893-4385/fax: 716-894-4539
e-mail: mazurt@erie.gov
Minority Leader, County Legislature (R):
John J Mills 716-858-8850/fax: 716-858-8818
e-mail: jmills13@erie.gov
Clerk, Legislature:
Robert M Graber 716-858-7500/fax: 716-858-8895
County Executive:
Mark C Poloncarz 716-858-8500
County Clerk:
Christopher L Jacobs 716-858-8785/fax: 716-858-6550
e-mail: eriecountyclerk@erie.gov
District Attorney:
Frank A Sedita III 716-858-2400/fax: 716-858-7425
Sheriff:
Timothy B Howard 716-585-7618
Civil Defense/Disaster Preparedness Deputy Commissioner:
Dean Messing 716-858-8477/fax: 716-858-7937
e-mail: messingd@erie.gov
Comptroller:
Stefan I. Mychajliw 716-858-8400/fax: 716-858-8507

Essex County

County Government Ctr
7551 Court St
PO Box 217
Elizabethtown, NY 12932
518-873-3350 Fax: 518-873-3356
Web site: www.co.essex.ny.us

Chairman, Board of Supervisors (D):
Randall T Douglas
Vice Chairman, Board of Supervisors (R):
Robert T Politi
e-mail: super@northelba.org
Clerk, Board of Supervisors:
Judith A. Garrison 518-873-3353/fax: 518-873-3356
e-mail: dpalmer@co.essex.ny.us
County Manager:
Daniel Palmer 518-873-3333/fax: 518-873-3339
e-mail: danp@co.essex.ny.us

Offices and agencies generally appear in alphabetical order, except when specific order is requested by listee.

County Clerk:
Joseph A Provoncha . . . 518-873-3601/fax: 518-873-3548
e-mail: jprovon@co.essex.ny.us
County Attorney:
Daniel Manning III . . . 518-873-3380/fax: 518-873-3894
e-mail: dmanning@co.essex.ny.us
District Attorney:
Kristy Sprague . . . 518-873-3335/fax: 518-873-3788
e-mail: ksprague@co.essex.ny.us
Public Defender:
Brandon E Boutelle . . . 518-873-3880/fax: 518-873-3888
Sheriff:
Richard C Cutting . . . 518-873-6902/fax: 518-873-6949
Director, Emergency Services:
Donald Jaquish . . . 518-873-3900/fax: 518-873-3963
e-mail: wwade@co.essex.ny.us
Treasurer:
Michael G Diskin . . . 518-873-3317/fax: 518-873-3318
e-mail: mdiskin@co.essex.ny.us

Franklin County

Courthouse
355 W Main St
Malone, NY 12953
518-481-1641 or 800-397-8686 Fax: 518-483-0141
Web site: www.franklincony.org

Chairman, County Legislature (D):
D. Billy Jones . . . 518-353-1204/fax: 518-481-1639
Vice Chairman, County Legislature (D):
Gordan Crossman . . . 518-483-5634/fax: 518-481-1639
Majority Leader, County Legislature (D):
Guy Smith . . . 518-358-2592/fax: 518-481-1639
Minority Leader, County Legislature (R):
Paul A Maroun . . . 518-359-3066/fax: 518-481-1639
e-mail: wawbeek@aol.com
Clerk, Legislature:
Gloria Valone . . . 518-481-1640/fax: 518-481-1639
County Manager:
Thomas Leitz . . . 518-481-1693
e-mail: jfeeley@co.franklin.ny.us
County Clerk:
Wanda D Murtagh . . . 518-481-1681/fax: 518-483-9143
e-mail: wmurtagh@co.franklin.ny.us
County Attorney:
Jonathan J Miller . . . 518-483-8400/fax: 518-483-2054
District Attorney:
Derek P Champagne . . . 518-481-1544/fax: 518-481-1545
e-mail: da@co.franklin.ny.us
Public Defender:
Thomas G Soucia . . . 518-481-1624
Sheriff:
Kevin Mulverhill . . . 518-483-3304
e-mail: jpelkey@co.franklin.ny.us
Director, Emergency Services:
Ricky Provost . . . 518-483-2580
e-mail: rprovost@co.franklin.ny.us
Treasurer:
Byron A Varin . . . 518-481-1513/fax: 518-483-2326
e-mail: bvarin@co.franklin.ny.us
Conflict Defender:
Lorellei Miller . . . 518-481-1593
Assigned Counsel Coordinator:
Jill Dyer . . . 518-481-1423

Fulton County

County Office Bldg
223 W Main St
Johnstown, NY 12095
518-736-5540 Fax: 518-762-0224
e-mail: fultbos@co.fulton.ny.us
Web site: www.fultoncountyny.gov

Chairman, Board of Supervisors:
WIlliam H. Waldron . . . 518-736-5540
County Clerk:
William E Eschler . . . 518-736-5555/fax: 518-762-9214
District Attorney:
Louise K. Sira . . . 518-736-5511/fax: 518-762-2042
Public Defender:
J Gerard McAuliffe, Jr. . . . 518-736-5820/fax: 518-762-0122
Sheriff:
Thomas J Lorey . . . 518-736-2100/fax: 518-736-2126
Treasurer:
Edgar T Blodgett . . . 518-736-5580/fax: 518-736-1794
Fire Coordinator & Director, Civil Defense:
Allan Polmateer . . . 518-736-5858/fax: 518-762-4938
County Historian:
Peter Betz . . . 518-736-5667

Genesee County

Old Courthouse, 7 Main Street
Batavia, NY 14020
585-344-2550 Fax: 585-344-8582
e-mail: legis@co.genesee.ny.us
Web site: www.co.genesee.ny.us

County Manager:
Jay Gsell . . . 585-344-2550 x2204/fax: 585-344-8582
e-mail: comanager@co.genesee.ny.us
District Attorney:
Lawrence Friedman . . . 585-344-2550 x2250/fax: 585-344-8544
Public Defender:
Gary Horton . . . 585-344-2550 x2280/fax: 716-344-8553
e-mail: publicdefender@co.genesee.ny.us
Sheriff:
Gary T Maha . . . 585-345-3000
e-mail: sheriff@co.genesee.ny.us
Treasurer:
Scott D German . . . 585-344-2550 x2210
e-mail: treas@co.genesee.ny.us
County Historian:
Susan L Conklin . . . 585-344-2550 x2613
e-mail: history@co.genesee.ny.us

Greene County

411 Main St, 4th Fl
PO Box 467
Catskill, NY 12414
518-719-3270 Fax: 518-719-3793
e-mail: countyadministrator@discovergreene.com
Web site: www.greenegovernment.com

Chairman, County Legislature (R):
Wayne Speenburgh . . . 518-929-1200/fax: 518-719-3793
e-mail: legislative@discovergreene.com
County Administrator (Acting):
Shaun S Groden . . . 518-719-3270/fax: 518-719-3793
e-mail: countyadministrator@discovergreene.com
County Clerk:
Michael Flynn . . . 518-719-3255/fax: 518-719-3284
e-mail: countyclerk@discovergreene.com
County Attorney:
Carol D Stevens . . . 518-719-3540/fax: 518-719-3790
e-mail: cstevens@discovergreene.com
District Attorney:
Terry J Wilhelm . . . 518-719-3590/fax: 518-719-3792
e-mail: twilhelm@discovergreene.com

Offices and agencies generally appear in alphabetical order, except when specific order is requested by listee.

Public Defender:
Angelo F. Scaturro 518-719-3220/fax: 518-719-3785
e-mail: publicdefender@discovergreene.com
Sheriff:
Gregory R Seeley 518-943-3300/fax: 518-943-6832
e-mail: sheriff@discovergreene.com
Director, Emergency Services:
John P Farrell Jr. 518-622-3643/fax: 518-622-0572
e-mail: emergency@discovergreene.com
Treasurer:
Peter Markov. 518-719-3530
e-mail: wvermilyea@discovergreene.com

Hamilton County

County Courthouse, Rte 8
PO Box 205
Lake Pleasant, NY 12108
518-548-6651 Fax: 518-548-7608
e-mail: hamcosup@klink.net
Web site: www.hamiltoncounty.com

Chairman, Board of Supervisors (R):
William G Farber 518-548-6385
e-mail: chairman@hamiltoncountyny.gov
Deputy Chairman, Board of Supervisors:
Brian Towers. 518-548-6385
e-mail: inletsupervisor@eagle-wireless.com
Clerk, Board of Supervisors:
Laura A Abrams 518-548-6651/fax: 518-548-7608
e-mail: clerkofboard@hamiltoncountyny.gov
County Clerk:
Jane S. Zarecki. 518-548-7111/fax: 518-548-9740
County Attorney:
Charles Getty Jr 315-336-3900/fax: 315-336-3902
e-mail: cgetty@gettylaw.com
District Attorney:
Marsha Purdue. 518-648-5113/fax: 518-648-5724
e-mail: districtattorney@hamiltoncountyny.gov
Sheriff:
Karl G Abrams. 518-548-3113/fax: 518-548-5704
e-mail: sheriff@hamiltoncountyny.gov
Treasurer:
Beth Hunt. 518-548-7911/fax: 518-548-4519
e-mail: treasurer@hamiltoncountyny.gov

Herkimer County

109 Mary St, Ste 1204
Herkimer, NY 13350
315-867-1108 Fax: 315-867-1109
e-mail: hclegislature@herkimercounty.org
Web site: herkimercounty.org

Chairman, County Legislature (R):
Vincent Bono. 315-867-1108/fax: 315-867-1109
Majority Leader (R):
Patrick E Russell 315-867-1108/fax: 315-867-1109
Minority Leader (D):
John L Brezinski 315-867-1108/fax: 315-867-1109
Clerk, Legislature:
Carole L LaLonde 315-867-1108/fax: 315-867-1109
County Administrator:
James W Wallace, Jr 315-867-1112/fax: 315-867-1109
County Clerk:
Sylvia M Rowan 315-867-1129
District Attorney:
John H Crandall. 315-867-1155/fax: 315-867-1348
Sheriff:
Christopher P Farber 315-867-1167/fax: 315-867-1354
Director, Emergency Management:
Robert Vandawalker 315-867-1212/fax: 315-867-5873
e-mail: rvandawalker@herkimercounty.org
Treasurer:
Kim Enea. 315-867-1145/fax: 315-867-1315
e-mail: kenea@herkimercounty.org

Jefferson County

County Office Bldg
175 Arsenal St
Watertown, NY 13601
315-785-3075 Fax: 315-785-5070
Web site: www.co.jefferson.ny.us

Chairwoman, Board of Legislators (R):
Carolyn D Fitzpatrick 315-785-3075
e-mail: carolynf@co.jefferson.ny.us
County Administrator/Budget Officer & Clerk, Board:
Robert F Hagemann, III. 315-785-3075/fax: 315-785-5070
Deputy County Administrator:
Michael E Kaskan 315-785-3075/fax: 315-785-5070
County Clerk:
Cheryl D Lane 315-785-3081/fax: 315-785-5145
County Attorney:
David J Paulsen 315-785-3088/fax: 315-785-5178
District Attorney:
Cindy Intschert 315-785-3053/fax: 315-785-3371
Public Defender:
Julie Hutchins 315-785-3152/fax: 315-785-5060
e-mail: joannem@co.jefferson.ny.us
Sheriff:
John P Burns
Director, Fire & Emergency Management (Acting):
Joseph D Plummer 315-786-2654
Treasurer:
Karen Christie 315-785-3055/fax: 315-785-7589

Kings County (NYC Borough of Brooklyn)

209 Joralemon St
Brooklyn, NY 11201
718-802-3700
Web site: www.brooklyn-usa.org

Borough President (D):
Marty Markowitz 718-802-3700
e-mail: askmarty@brooklynbp.nyc.gov
Deputy Borough President:
Sandra Chapman 718-802-3884
e-mail: ygraham@brooklynbp.nyc.gov
County Clerk:
Nancy T Sunshine. 347-404-9772
District Attorney:
Charles J Hynes 718-250-2000
e-mail: schmj@brroklynda.org

Lewis County

Courthouse
7660 N State St
Lowville, NY 13367
315-377-2000 Fax: 315-376-5445
e-mail: it@lewiscountyny.org
Web site: www.lewiscountyny.org

Clerk, Board of Legislature:
Terry Clark 315-376-5355/fax: 315-376-5445
e-mail: legislature@lewiscountyny.org
County Clerk:
Douglas P Hanno. 315-376-5333/fax: 315-376-3768
e-mail: clerk@lewiscountyny.org

County Attorney:
Richard Graham....................315-376-5282/fax: 315-376-3857
e-mail: rgraham@lewiscountyny.org
District Attorney:
Leanne Moser....................315-376-5390/fax: 315-376-5873
e-mail: lmoser@lewiscountyny.org
Public Defender:
Lewis Defenders PLLC..............315-376-7543/fax: 315-376-8766
Sheriff:
Michael Carpinelli.................315-376-3511/fax: 315-376-5232
e-mail: LCSD@lewiscountyny.org
Treasurer:
Patricia O'Brien...................315-376-5325/fax: 315-376-8552
e-mail: treasurer@lewiscountyny.org
County Manager:
David Pendergast..................315-376-5354/fax: 315-376-5445
e-mail: county.manager@lewiscountyny.org
Fire & Emergency Management:
James Martin......................315-376-5305/fax: 315-376-5293
County Historian:
Lewis County Historical Society.........................315-376-2825

Livingston County

Government Center
6 Court St, Rm 302
Geneseo, NY 14454
585-243-7030 Fax: 585-335-1701
e-mail: vamico@co.livingston.ny.us
Web site: www.co.livingston.state.ny.us

Chairman, Board of Supervisors (R):
James C Merrick.................................585-243-7030
Vice Chairman, Board of Supervisors (R):
Gary D Moore....................................585-243-7030
Clerk, Board of Supervisors:
Virginia O Amico................................585-243-7030
e-mail: vamico@co.livingston.ny.us
County Administrator:
Ian M Coyle.....................................585-243-7040
e-mail: icoyle@co.livingston.ny.us
County Clerk:
James A Culbertson..............................585-243-7010
e-mail: jculbertson@co.livingston.ny.us
County Attorney:
David J Morris..................................585-243-7033
e-mail: dmorris@co.livingston.ny.us
District Attorney:
Gregory J. McCaffrey............................585-243-7020
Public Defender:
Marcea Clark Tetamore.............585-243-7028/fax: 585-243-7193
e-mail: lcpd@co.livingston.ny.us
Emergency Management Services:
Kevin Niedermaier...............................585-243-7160
e-mail: kniedermaier@co.livingston.ny.us
Sheriff:
John M York.......................585-243-7120/fax: 585-243-7104
e-mail: lcso@co.livingston.ny.us
Treasurer:
Carolyn D Taylor..................585-243-7050/fax: 585-243-7597
e-mail: ctaylor@co.livingston.ny.us
Historian:
Amie Alden........................585-243-7955/fax: 585-243-7956
e-mail: historian@co.livingston.ny.us

Madison County

County Office Bldg
138 N Court St
PO Box 635
Wampsville, NY 13163
315-366-2201 Fax: 315-366-2502
e-mail: supervisors@co.madison.ny.us
Web site: www.madisoncounty.gov

Chairman, Board of Supervisors (R):
John M Becker.....................315-366-2201/fax: 315-366-2502
Clerk, Board of Supervisors:
Cindy Urtz........................315-366-2201/fax: 315-366-2502
County Clerk:
Kenneth J Kunkel Jr.............................315-366-2261
County Attorney:
S John Campanie...................315-366-2203/fax: 315-366-2502
District Attorney:
William G Gabor...................315-366-2236/fax: 315-366-2503
Public Defender Director:
Paul H Hadley.....................315-366-2585/fax: 315-366-2583
Fire Coordinator/Emergency Preparedness:
Joe DeFrancisco...................315-366-2258/fax: 315-366-2452
Sheriff:
Allen Riley.......................315-366-2318/fax: 315-366-2286
Treasurer:
Cindy Edick.......................315-366-2371/fax: 315-366-2705
Public Information Officer:
Sharon A Driscoll...............................315-366-2788

Monroe County

County Office Bldg
39 W Main St
Rochester, NY 14614
585-753-1950 Fax: 585-753-1932
Web site: www.monroecounty.gov

President, County Legislature (R):
Jeffrey R Adair...................585-753-1950/fax: 585-753-1932
Majority Leader (R):
William W. Napier.................585-753-1922/fax: 585-753-1960
Minority Leader (D):
Joe Rittler.......................585-753-1941/fax: 585-753-1946
Clerk, Legislature:
Cheryl Rozzi....................................585-753-1950
e-mail: crozzi@monroecounty.gov
County Executive:
Maggie Brooks.....................585-753-1000/fax: 585-753-1014
e-mail: countyexecutive@monroecounty.gov
County Clerk:
Cheryl Dinolfo....................585-753-1600/fax: 585-753-1624
e-mail: mcclerk@monroecounty.gov
District Attorney:
Sandra Doorley....................585-753-4500/fax: 585-753-4576
e-mail: districtattorney@monroecounty.gov
Sheriff:
Patrick M O'Flynn.................585-753-4178/fax: 585-753-4524
e-mail: sherriff@monroecountysheriff.info
Public Defender:
Tim Donaher.......................585-753-4210/fax: 585-753-4234
e-mail: mcpublicdefender@monroecounty.gov
Chief Financial Officer:
Robert Franklin...................585-753-1157/fax: 585-753-1133
e-mail: mcfinance@monroecounty.gov
Director, Communications:
Justin Feasel.....................585-753-1080/fax: 585-753-1068
e-mail: communications@monroecounty.gov
County Historian:
Carolyn Vacca.....................585-385-8244/fax: 585-428-8353

Montgomery County

County Annex Bldg
PO Box 1500
Fonda, NY 12068-1500

Offices and agencies generally appear in alphabetical order, except when specific order is requested by listee.

518-853-4304 Fax: 518-853-8220
Web site: www.co.montgomery.ny.us

Chairman, Board of Supervisors:
John W. Thayer 518-853-4304/fax: 518-853-8220
Clerk, Board of Supervisors:
Robin Loske 518-853-4304/fax: 518-853-8220
County Clerk:
Helen A Bartone 518-853-8111/fax: 518-853-8171
County Attorney:
Douglas E Landon 518-843-1300/fax: 518-842-5331
District Attorney:
James E Conboy 518-853-8250/fax: 518-853-8212
Public Defender:
William Martuscello 518-853-8305/fax: 518-853-8308
Sheriff:
Michael J Amato 518-853-5500/fax: 518-853-4096
Director, Emergency Management/Fire Coordinator:
Adam Schwabrow 518-853-4011/fax: 518-853-4714
Treasurer:
Shawn J Bowerman 518-853-8175/fax: 518-853-8344
County Historian:
Kelly A. Farquhar 518-853-8187/fax: 518-853-8392

Nassau County

1550 Franklin Avenue
Mineola, NY 11501
516-571-3000 or 516-571-6200 Fax: 516-739-2636
Web site: www.nassaucountyny.gov

Presiding Officer of the Legislature (D):
Peter J Schmitt 516-571-6212
Deputy Presiding Officer of the Legislature (R):
John J Ciotti 516-571-6203
Minority Leader (R):
Diane Yatauro 516-571-6218/fax: 516-571-6158
Clerk, Legislature:
William J Muller 516-571-4252
County Executive:
Edward P Mangano 516-571-3131
County Clerk:
Maureen O'Connell 516-571-2664
County Attorney:
John Ciampoli 516-571-3056
District Attorney:
Kathleen M Rice 516-571-3800
e-mail: nassauda@nassauda.org
Emergency Management Commissioner:
James J Callahan II 516-573-0636
Police Commissioner:
Thomas V. Dale 516-573-8800
Comptroller:
George Maragos 516-571-2386
e-mail: nccomptroller@nassaucountyny.gov
Treasurer:
John A Mastromarino 516-571-2090

New York County (NYC Borough of Manhattan)

Municipal Bldg
One Centre St, 19th Fl
New York, NY 10007
212-669-8300 Fax: 212-669-4305
Web site: www.mbpo.org

Borough President:
Scott M Stringer 212-669-8300
e-mail: bp@manhattanbp.org
County Clerk:
Norman Goodman 646-386-5955
District Attorney:
Cyrus Vance, Jr. 212-335-9000
Public Advocate:
Betsy Gotbaum 212-669-7200/fax: 212-669-4091

Niagara County

County Courthouse
175 Hawley Street
1st Floor
Lockport, NY 14094
716-439-7000 Fax: 716-439-7124
Web site: www.niagaracounty.com

Chairman, County Legislature (R):
William L Ross 716-731-5949
e-mail: william.ross@niagaracounty.com
Majority Leader (R):
Richard Updegrove 716-434-2140
e-mail: richard.updegrove@niagaracounty.com
Minority Leader (D):
Dennis F Virtuoso 716-284-1582
e-mail: dennis.virtuoso@niagaracounty.com
Clerk, Legislature:
Mary Jo Tamburlin 716-439-7177/fax: 716-439-7124
County Manager:
Jeffrey M Glatz 716-439-7006/fax: 716-439-7212
e-mail: jeff.glatz@niagaracounty.com
County Clerk:
Wayne F Jagow 716-439-7022/fax: 716-439-7035
e-mail: niagaracountyclerk@niagaracounty.com
County Attorney:
Claude A Joerg 716-439-7105/fax: 716-439-7114
e-mail: claude.joerg@niagaracounty.com
District Attorney:
Michael J Violante 716-439-7085/fax: 716-439-7102
e-mail: ncda@niagaracounty.com
Public Defender:
David J Farrugia 716-439-7071
Sheriff:
James R Voutour 716-438-3393/fax: 716-438-3357
Emergency Services, Acting Director:
John F Cecula III
fax: 716-438-3173
Treasurer:
Kyle R Andrews 716-439-7018/fax: 716-439-7021

Oneida County

County Office Bldg
800 Park Ave
Utica, NY 13501
315-798-5900 Fax: 315-798-5924
e-mail: bol@co.oneida.ny.us or bol@ocgov.net
Web site: www.co.oneida.ny.us or www.ocgov.net

Chairman, County Legislature (R):
Gerald J Fiorini 315-798-5900
e-mail: gfiorini@ocgov.net
Majority Leader (R):
David J Wood 315-337-1989
e-mail: dwood@ocgov.net
Minority Leader (D):
Patricia A Hudak 315-339-9960
e-mail: phudak@ocgov.net
County Executive:
Anthony J Picente Jr 315-798-5800/fax: 315-798-2390
e-mail: ce@ocgov.net
County Clerk:
Sandra J DePerno 315-798-5794
e-mail: countyclerk@ocgov.net

County Attorney:
Gregory J. Amoroso, Esq. 315-798-5910/fax: 315-798-5603
e-mail: countyattorney@ocgov.net
District Attorney:
Scott D McNamara 315-798-5766/fax: 315-798-5582
e-mail: smcnamara@ocgov.net
Public Defender-Criminal Division:
Frank J Nebush Jr 315-798-5870/fax: 315-734-0364
e-mail: pubdef@ocgov.net
Public Defender-Civil Division:
Frank J Furno. 315-266-6100/fax: 315-266-6105
e-mail: pdcivil@ocgov.net
Sheriff:
Rob M. Maciol. 315-738-7804/fax: 315-765-2205
Finance Commissioner:
Anthony R Carvelli 315-798-5750

Onondaga County

401 Montgomery Street
Room 407
Syracuse, NY 13202
315-435-2070 Fax: 315-435-8434
Web site: www.ongov.net

Chairman, County Legislature (R):
J. Ryan McMahon II 315-435-2070/fax: 315-435-8434
County Executive:
Joanne M Mahoney 315-435-3516/fax: 315-435-8582
Clerk, Legislature:
Deborah L Maturo 315-435-2070/fax: 315-435-8434
e-mail: debbiematuro@ongov.net
County Clerk:
Sandra A. Schepp 315-435-2227/fax: 315-435-2229
County Attorney:
Gordon J Cuffy
District Attorney:
William J Fitzpatrick. 315-435-2470
Emergency Management Director:
Peter P Alberti 315-435-2525/fax: 315-435-3309
e-mail: emweb01@ongov.net
Sheriff:
Kevin E Walsh 315-435-3044
Commissioner:
Kevin Wisely 315-435-3044
Comptroller:
Robert E Antonacci 315-435-2130/fax: 315-435-2250
e-mail: bobantonacci@ongov.net
Chief Fiscal Officer:
Steven Morgan. 315-435-2426/fax: 315-435-2421

Ontario County

Ontario Co Municipal Bldg
20 Ontario St
1st Fl Mezzanine
Canandaigua, NY 14424
585-396-4447 Fax: 585-396-8818
e-mail: bos@co.ontario.ny.us
Web site: www.co.ontario.ny.us

Chairman, Board of Supervisors (R):
Theodore Fafinski 585-396-4447/fax: 585-396-8818
Vice Chairman, Board of Supervisors (R):
Wayne F Houseman 585-396-4447
Clerk, Board of Supervisors:
Karen R DeMay. 585-396-4447/fax: 585-396-8818
e-mail: karen.demay@co.ontario.ny.us
County Administrator:
John E. Garvey 585-396-4400
e-mail: county.administrator@co.ontario.ny.us
County Clerk:
Matthew J. Hoose 585-396-4200
Human Resources Director:
Mary A. Krause . . . . 585-396-4465 or 315-719-0321
District Attorney:
R Michael Tantillo. 585-396-4010/fax: 585-396-4860
e-mail: michael.tantillo@co.ontario.ny.us
Emergency Management Director:
Jeffrey R Harloff 585-396-4310/fax: 585-396-4583
Public Works Commissioner:
Bill Wright. 585-396-4000/fax: 585-396-4283

Orange County

County Government Center
255 Main St
Goshen, NY 10924
845-291-4800
e-mail: legislature@co.orange.ny.us
Web site: www.co.orange.ny.us

Chairman, County Legislature (R):
Michael R Pillmeier 845-651-7415
Majority Leader (R):
Melissa Bonacic 845-858-2546
Minority Leader (D):
Jeffrey D Berkman 845-342-6813
County Executive:
Edward A Diana 845-291-2700/fax: 845-291-2724
County Clerk:
Donna L Benson 845-291-2690/fax: 845-291-2691
County Attorney:
David L Darwin 845-291-3150
District Attorney:
Francis D Phillips 845-291-2050
Emergency Services Commissioner:
Walter C Koury. 845-615-0400
Sheriff:
Carl E DuBois 845-291-4033/fax: 845-294-1590
Finance Commissioner:
Joel Kleiman 845-291-2485/fax: 845-291-2516
Historian:
Cornelia W. Bush 845-291-2388/fax: 845-291-2027

Orleans County

Courthouse Sq
3 South Main St
Albion, NY 14411-1495
585-589-7053 Fax: 585-589-1618
Web site: www.orleansny.com

Chairman, County Legislature (R):
David Callard 585-589-7053
Vice Chairman (R):
George Bower. 585-589-7053
Clerk, Legislature:
Nadine P Hanlon 585-589-7053/fax: 585-589-1618
e-mail: hanlonn@orleansny.com
Chief Administrative Officer:
Charles H Nesbitt Jr 585-589-7053/fax: 585-589-1618
e-mail: cnesbitt@orleansny.com
County Clerk:
Karen Lake-Maynard. 585-589-5334/fax: 585-589-0181
e-mail: lakemaynardk@orleansny.com
County Attorney:
David C Schubel 585-798-2250/fax: 585-798-0776
e-mail: occoa@orleansny.com
District Attorney:
Joseph V Cardone 585-590-4130/fax: 585-590-4129
e-mail: da@orleansny.com

State & Local Government Public Information

Offices and agencies generally appear in alphabetical order, except when specific order is requested by listee.

Public Defender:
Sanford A Church 585-589-7335/fax: 585-589-2592
Emergency Management Director:
Paul Wagner 585-589-4414/fax: 585-589-7671
e-mail: pwagner@orleansny.com
Sheriff:
Scott D Hess 585-590-4142/fax: 585-590-4178
e-mail: ocsher@orleansny.com
Treasurer:
Susan M Heard 585-589-5353/fax: 585-589-9220
e-mail: sheard@orleansny.com
County Historian:
C W Lattin. 585-589-4174

Oswego County

46 E Bridge St
Oswego, NY 13126
315-349-8230 Fax: 315-349-8237
Web site: www.co.oswego.ny.us

Chairman, County Legislature (R):
Fred Beardsley. 315-349-8230/fax: 315-349-8237
Majority Leader (R):
James Oldenburg 315-343-3744/fax: 315-668-3638
Minority Leader (D):
Michael Kunzwiler 315-343-8358
e-mail: mikekunzwiler@twcny.rr.com
Clerk, Legislature:
Wendy Falls. 315-349-8230/fax: 315-349-8237
e-mail: tjerrett@oswegocounty.com
County Administrator:
Philip R Church 315-349-8235/fax: 315-349-8237
e-mail: pchurch@oswegocounty.com
County Clerk:
Michael C. Backus 315-349-8621/fax: 315-349-8383
e-mail: williamsg@oswegocounty.com
County Attorney:
Richard C Mitchell 315-349-8296
e-mail: rich@oswegocounty.com
District Attorney/Coroner:
Gregory S. Oakes. 315-349-3200/fax: 315-349-3212
e-mail: doddd@oswegocounty.com
Treasurer:
Fred Beardsley. 315-349-8393/fax: 315-349-8255
e-mail: cwolford@oswegocounty.com
Sheriff:
Reuel A Todd 315-349-3302/fax: 315-349-3303
e-mail: mtodd@oswegocounty.com
Vice Chairman:
Kevin Gardner 315-349-8230/fax: 315-349-8237
e-mail: mtodd@oswegocounty.com

Otsego County

County Office Bldg
197 Main St
Cooperstown, NY 13326-1129
607-547-4202 Fax: 607-547-4260
e-mail: childl@otsegocounty.com
Web site: www.otsegocounty.com

Chairman, Board of Representatives (R):
Kathleen Clark 607-988-7844
e-mail: dubbenf@otsegocounty.com
Vice Chairman, Board of Representatives (R):
James V Johnson. 607-547-2095
e-mail: johnsonjv@otsegocounty.com
Clerk, Board of Representatives:
Carol McGovern 607-547-4202/fax: 607-547-4260
e-mail: mcgovern@otsegocounty.com
County Clerk:
Kathy Sinnott Gardner. 607-547-4276/fax: 607-547-7544
e-mail: gardnerk@otsegocounty.com
County Attorney:
Ellen Coccoma. 607-547-4208/fax: 607-547-7572
e-mail: coccomae@otsegocounty.com
District Attorney:
John M Muehl 607-547-4249/fax: 607-547-4373
e-mail: distatty@otsegocounty.com
Public Defender:
Richard A Rothermel 607-432-7410
Sheriff:
Richard Devlin Jr . . . . . 607-547-4271 or 607-547-4273
fax: 607-547-6413
e-mail: sheriff@otsegocounty.com
Coordinator, Emergency Services:
Kevin N. Ritton. 607-547-4227
e-mail: rittonk@otsegocounty.com
Treasurer:
Dan Crowell. 607-547-4235/fax: 607-547-7579
e-mail: crowelld@otsegocounty.com
County Historian:
Vacant 607-397-9705

Putnam County

40 Gleneida Avenue
Carmel, NY 10512
845-225-8690 Fax: 845-225-0715
e-mail: putcoleg@putnamcountyny.com
Web site: www.putnamcountyny.com

Chairman, County Legislature (R):
Richard T. Othmer, Jr.. . . . . 845-808-1020/fax: 845-225-0715
Deputy Chair, County Legislature (R):
Anthony DiCarlo 845-808-1020/fax: 845-225-0715
Clerk, Legislature:
Diane Schonfeld 845-808-1020/fax: 845-808-1933
Legislative Counsel:
Clement Van Ross 845-808-1020/fax: 845-808-1933
County Executive:
Mary Ellen Odell 845-808-1001/fax: 845-808-1901
County Clerk:
Dennis J Sant 845-808-1142
County Attorney:
Jennifer S Bumgarner 845-228-0480
District Attorney:
Adam Levy 845-808-1050
Emergency Services Bureau Commissioner:
Adam B. Stiebeling 845-808-4000/fax: 845-808-4010
e-mail: administration@pcbes.org
Sheriff:
Donald Blaine Smith 845-225-4300/fax: 845-225-4399
Finance Commissioner:
William J Carlin, Jr. . . . . . 845-808-1075 or 845-808-1910
fax: 845-225-8290
County Historian:
Vacant 845-808-1420/fax: 845-278-4865
e-mail: putpast@bestweb.net

Queens County (NYC Borough of Queens)

120-55 Queens Blvd
Kew Gardens, NY 11424
718-286-3000 Fax: 718-286-2876
e-mail: info@queensbp.org
Web site: www.queensbp.org

Borough President:
Helen M Marshall 718-286-3000/fax: 718-286-2876
Director of Community Boards:
Barry Grodenchik 718-286-2900

Offices and agencies generally appear in alphabetical order, except when specific order is requested by listee.

Public Information Officer/Press Office:
Daniel Andrews 718-286-2640
County Clerk:
Gloria D'Amico . . . . 718-298-0605 or 718-520-3137
District Attorney:
Richard A Brown 718-286-6000
Communications Director:
Kevin R Ryan
e-mail: krryan@queensda.org
Public Administrator:
Lois M Rosenblatt . . . . 718-526-5037 or 718-520-3710
fax: 718-526-5043
e-mail: mail@queenscountypa.com
Counsel:
Gerard J Sweeney 718-459-9000/fax: 718-459-3163

Rensselaer County

Ned Pattison Government Center
1600 Seventh Avenue
Troy, NY 12180
518-270-2880 Fax: 518-270-2983
Web site: www.rensco.com or www.rensselaercounty.org

Chairperson, County Legislature (R):
Martin T Reid 518-270-2880/fax: 518-270-2983
e-mail: mreid@rensco.com
Vice Chairman (R):
Stan Brownell 518-270-2880/fax: 518-270-2983
e-mail: sbrownell@rensco.com
Vice Chairman-Finance (R):
Philip Danaher 518-270-2880/fax: 518-270-2983
e-mail: pdanaher@rensco.com
Majority Leader (C):
Kenneth H Herrington 518-270-2880/fax: 518-270-2983
e-mail: kherrington@rensco.com
Minority Leader (D):
Peter Grimm 518-270-2890/fax: 518-270-2975
e-mail: pryand3troy@rensco.com
Clerk, Legislature:
JanŠt Marra
e-mail: jallard@rensco.com
County Executive:
Kathleen M Jimino 518-270-2900/fax: 518-270-2961
County Clerk:
Frank Merola 518-270-4080/fax: 518-271-7998
County Attorney:
Stephen A Pechenik 518-270-2950/fax: 518-270-2954
District Attorney:
Richard J McNally Jr 518-270-4040
Public Defender:
Jerome K Frost 518-270-4030
Sheriff:
Jack Mahar 518-266-1900/fax: 518-270-5447
Chief Fiscal Officer:
Michael J Slawson 518-270-2750/fax: 518-270-2728

Richmond County (NYC Borough of Staten Island)

Borough Hall
120 Borough Hall
Staten Island, NY 10301
718-816-2000 Fax: 718-876-2026
Web site: www.statenislandusa.com

Borough President:
James P Molinaro 718-816-2000
County Clerk:
Stephen J Fiala 718-675-7700
District Attorney:
Daniel M Donovan Jr 718-876-6300
e-mail: info@rcda.nyc.gov

Rockland County

County Office Bldg
11 New Hempstead Rd
New City, NY 10956
845-638-5100 Fax: 845-638-5675
Web site: rocklandgov.com

Chairwoman, County Legislature (D):
Harriet D Cornell 845-638-5269
e-mail: cornellh@co.rockland.ny.us
Majority Leader (D):
Jay Hood, Jr. 845-638-5751
Minority Leader (R):
Christopher J. Carey 845-638-5100
Clerk, Legislature:
Laurence O Toole 845-638-5100/fax: 845-638-5675
e-mail: toolel@co.rockland.ny.us
County Executive:
C Scott Vanderhoef 845-638-5122
County Clerk:
Paul Piperato 845-638-5070/fax: 845-638-5647
e-mail: rocklandcountyclerk@co.rockland.ny.us
Director Veterans Services:
Gerald Donnellan 845-638-5244/fax: 845-638-5730
e-mail: jerry@rockvets.com
District Attorney:
Thomas P Zugibe 845-638-5001/fax: 845-638-5298
Public Defender:
James D Licata 845-638-5660
e-mail: licataj@co.rockland.ny.us
Sheriff:
Louis Falco, III 845-638-5400/fax: 845-638-5035
Finance/Budget Commissioner:
Stephen F. DeGroat 845-638-5131
e-mail: kopfc@co.rockland.ny.us

Saratoga County

County Municipal Center
40 McMaster St
Ballston Spa, NY 12020
518-884-4742 Fax: 518-884-4723
Web site: www.saratogacountyny.gov

Chairman, Board of Supervisors (R):
Alan Grattidge
County Administrator:
Spencer P Hellwig 518-884-4742/fax: 518-884-4723
Clerk, Board of Supervisors:
Pamela A Hargrave 518-885-2240/fax: 518-884-4771
Deputy County Clerk:
Charles Foehser, II 518-885-2213/fax: 518-884-4726
County Attorney:
Stephen M Dorsey 518-884-4770/fax: 518-884-4720
e-mail: saracaty@govt.co.saratoga.ny.us
District Attorney:
James A Murphy, III 518-885-2263/fax: 518-884-8627
Public Defender:
John H Ciulla Jr 518-884-4795/fax: 518-884-4789
e-mail: sarpdinfo@govt.co.saratoga.ny.us
Veterans Services:
Felipe Moon 518-884-4115/fax: 518-884-4290
County Treasurer:
Sam Pitcheralle 518-884-4724/fax: 518-884-4775

Schenectady County

County Legislature
620 State St
Schenectady, NY 12305

State & Local Government Public Information

518-388-4280 Fax: 518-388-4591
Web site: www.schenectadycounty.com

Chairperson, County Legislature (D):
Judith Dagostino 518-388-4280/fax: 518-388-4591
Majority Leader (D):
Gary Hughes 518-388-4280/fax: 518-388-4591
Minority Leader (R):
James Buhrmaster 518-388-4280/fax: 518-388-4591
Clerk, Legislature:
Goeffrey T Hall 518-388-4280/fax: 518-388-4591
County Clerk:
John J Woodward 518-388-4220/fax: 518-388-4224
e-mail: john.woodward@schenectadycounty.com
District Attorney:
Robert M Carney 518-388-4364
e-mail: districtattorney@schenectadycounty.com
Public Defender:
Mark J Caruso 518-386-2266
Sheriff:
Dominic A. D'Agostino 518-388-4300/fax: 518-388-4593
Director, Emergency Management:
Mark LaViolette . . . . . 518-370-3113 ext. 1
Deputy Director, Emergency Management:
Kyle Rudolph . . . . . 518-370-3113 ext. 5

Schoharie County

Cty Office Bldg
284 Main Street, Rm 365
PO Box 429
Schoharie, NY 12157
518-295-8347 Fax: 518-295-8482
Web site: www.schohariecounty-ny.gov

Chairman, Board of Supervisors (R):
Philip Skowfoe, Jr. 518-827-4896/fax: 518-827-7972
Clerk, Board of Supervisors:
Sheryl Largeteau 518-295-8421/fax: 518-295-8482
e-mail: millerk@co.schoharie.ny.us
County Clerk:
M Indica Jaycox 518-295-8316/fax: 518-295-8338
County Attorney:
Michael West. 518-296-8844/fax: 518-296-8855
District Attorney:
James L Sacket 518-295-2272/fax: 518-295-2273
Sheriff:
Anthony F Desmond 518-295-2266/fax: 518-295-2267
Director, Emergency Management:
Kevin Neary. 518-295-2276/fax: 518-296-8632
Treasurer:
William E Cherry. 518-295-8386/fax: 518-295-8364
Administrator Legal Defense:
Raynor B Duncombe 518-295-7515/fax: 518-295-7519

Schuyler County

County Bldg
105 Ninth St, Unit 6
Watkins Glen, NY 14891
607-535-8100 Fax: 607-535-8109
e-mail: legislature@co.schuyler.ny.us
Web site: www.schuylercounty.us

Chairman, County Legislature (R):
Dennis A Fagan 607-535-8100
Clerk, Legislature:
Stacey B Husted 607-535-8100
County Clerk:
Linda M Compton 607-535-8133/fax: 607-535-8130
e-mail: lcompton@co.schuyler.ny.us
County Administrator:
Timothy M O'Hearn 607-535-8106/fax: 607-535-8108
e-mail: tohearn@co.schuyler.ny.us
District Attorney:
Joseph G Fazzary. 607-535-8383/fax: 607-535-8385
Public Defender:
Wesley A. Rose, Esq. 607-535-6400/fax: 607-535-6404
Sheriff:
William E Yessman Jr. 607-535-8222/fax: 607-535-8216
e-mail: wyessman@co.schuyler.ny.us
Treasurer:
Gary Whyman 607-535-8181/fax: 607-535-8187
County Historian:
Marion M. Boyce 607-535-4730

Seneca County

County Office Bldg
1 DiPronio Dr
Waterloo, NY 13165
315-539-1700 Fax: 315-539-0207
e-mail: supervisors@co.seneca.ny.us
Web site: www.co.seneca.ny.us

Chairman, Board of Supervisors (R):
Robert W Hayssen. 315-539-1700/fax: 315-539-0207
Majority Leader (R):
Robert Shipley 315-539-1700/fax: 315-539-0207
e-mail: rshipley@co.seneca.ny.us
Minority Leader (D):
Cindy Garlick Lorenzetti. 315-539-1700/fax: 315-539-0207
e-mail: cindyl@rochester.rr.com
Clerk, Board of Supervisors:
Margaret E Li. 315-539-1700/fax: 315-539-0207
County Clerk:
Christina L Lotz 315-539-1771
e-mail: clotz@co.seneca.ny.us
County Manager:
C. Mitchell Rowe. 315-539-1701/fax: 315-539-0207
e-mail: mrowe@co.seneca.ny.us
County Attorney:
Frank R Fisher 315-539-1989/fax: 315-539-1657
e-mail: ffisher@co.seneca.ny.us
District Attorney:
Barry Porsch 315-539-1300/fax: 315-539-0531
e-mail: da@co.seneca.ny.us
Sheriff:
Jack S Stenberg 315-220-3200/fax: 315-220-3478
Public Defender:
Michael J Mirras 315-568-4975
Treasurer:
Nicholas A Sciotti 315-539-1735/fax: 315-539-1731
e-mail: nsciotti@co.seneca.ny.us
County Historian:
Walter Gable 315-539-1785
e-mail: wgable@co.seneca.ny.us

St Lawrence County

County Courthouse
48 Court St
Canton, NY 13617
315-379-2276 Fax: 315-379-2463
Web site: www.co.st-lawrence.ny.us

Chair, Board of Legislators (D):
Jonathan S. Putney 315-379-2276/fax: 315-379-2463
e-mail: jputney@stlawco.org
Vice Chair, Board of Legislators (R):
Donald Peck. 315-379-2276/fax: 315-379-2463
e-mail: peck_donald@yahoo.com

County Administrator:
Karen St Hilaire 315-379-2276/fax: 315-379-2463
e-mail: ksth@co.st-lawrence.ny.us
County Clerk:
MaryLou Rupp 315-379-2237/fax: 315-379-2302
Dept Head, County Attorney:
Michael Crowe 315-379-2269/fax: 315-379-2254
District Attorney:
Nicole M Duve 315-379-2225/fax: 315-379-2301
Public Defender:
Stephen D. Button 315-379-2115/fax: 315-386-8241
Emergency Services, Dept Head:
Joseph M. Gilbert 315-379-2240/fax: 315-379-0681
e-mail: thowie@co.st-lawrence.ny.us
Sheriff (Department Head):
Kevin M Wells 315-379-2222/fax: 315-379-0335
e-mail: kwells@stlawco.org
Treasurer:
Kevin Felt 315-386-2234/fax: 315-379-5274
e-mail: kfelt@co.st-lawrence.ny.us

Steuben County

County Office Bldg
3 East Pulteney Square
Bath, NY 14810
607-776-9631 Fax: 607-776-6926
e-mail: scplanning@co.steuben.ny.us
Web site: www.steubencony.org

Chairman, County Legislature (R):
Joseph J Hauryski 607-664-2247
Vice Chair, County Legislature (R):
Patrick McAllister 607-664-2247
Clerk, County Legislature:
Brenda Mori 607-664-2247/fax: 607-664-2282
County Administrator:
Mark R Alger 607-664-2245/fax: 607-664-2282
County Clerk:
Judith M Hunter 607-664-2563
District Attorney:
Brooks Baker 607-664-2270
Public Defender:
Philip J. Roche, Esq. 607-664-2413/fax: 607-664-2410
Acting Director:
Timothy D. Marshall 607-664-2700
Sheriff:
David V. Cole . . . . . 607-622-3901 or 800-724-7777
Treasurer:
Patrick F Donnelly 607-664-2488/fax: 607-664-2188
e-mail: treasurer@co.steuben.ny.us
Historian:
Twila O'Dell 607-664-2199
e-mail: historian@co.steuben.ny.us

Suffolk County

William H Rogers Building
725 Veterans Memorial Hwy
North County Complex
Smithtown, NY 11787
631-853-4070 Fax: 631-853-4899
Web site: www.suffolkcountyny.gov

Presiding Officer, County Legislature (D):
DuWayne Gregory 631-854-1111/fax: 631-854-1114
e-mail: duwayne.gregory@suffolkcountyny.gov
Deputy Presiding Officer, County Legislature (D):
Rob Calarco 631-854-1400/fax: 631-854-1403
Majority Leader (D):
Kara Hahn 631-854-1650/fax: 631-854-1653
Minority Leader (R):
Kevin McCaffrey 631-854-1100/fax: 631-854-1103
e-mail: kevin.mccaffrey@suffolkcountyny.gov
Clerk, County Legislature:
Jason Richberg 631-853-4070/fax: 631-853-4899
e-mail: jason.richberg@suffolkcountyny.gov
County Executive:
Steven Bellone 631-853-4000
e-mail: county.executive@suffolkcountyny.gov
County Clerk:
Judith A Pascale 631-852-2000
e-mail: countyclerk@suffolkcountyny.gov
County Attorney:
Dennis M Brown 631-853-4049/fax: 631-853-5169
District Attorney:
Thomas J Spota 631-853-4161
e-mail: infoda@suffolkcountyny.gov
Director, Emergency Management:
Edward C Schneyer 631-852-4900/fax: 631-852-4922
e-mail: scdfres@suffolkcountyny.gov
Sheriff:
Vincent F DeMarco 631-852-2200
e-mail: suffolk_sheriff@suffolkcountyny.gov
Comptroller:
John M Kennedy Jr 631-853-5040
e-mail: comptroller@suffolkcountyny.gov
Treasurer:
Barry S Paul 631-852-1500/fax: 631-852-1507
e-mail: treasurer@suffolkcountyny.gov

Sullivan County

County Gov't Center
100 North St
PO Box 5012
Monticello, NY 12701
845-807-0435 Fax: 845-807-0447
e-mail: info@co.sullivan.ny.us
Web site: www.co.sullivan.ny.us

Chairman (D):
Scott B Samuelson 845-807-0443
e-mail: scott.samuelson@co.sullivan.ny.us
Vice-Chairman (D):
Eugene L. Benson 845-807-0439
e-mail: gene.benson@co.sullivan.ny.us
Majority Leader (D):
Kathleen LaBuda 845-807-0442
e-mail: kathy.labuda@co.sullivan.ny.us
Minority Leader (R):
Alan J. Sorenson 845-807-0444
e-mail: alan.sorensen@co.sullivan.ny.us
Acting County Manager:
Joshua Potosek 845-807-0450/fax: 845-807-0460
County Clerk:
Daniel Briggs 845-807-0411/fax: 845-807-0434
County Attorney:
Sam Yasgur 845-807-0560/fax: 845-807-0574
District Attorney:
James R Farrell 845-794-3344/fax: 845-794-3646
Public Safety Commissioner:
Richard A Martinkovic 845-807-0512
Sheriff:
Michael A Schiff 845-794-7100/fax: 845-794-7100
County Treasurer:
Ira J Cohen 845-807-0200/fax: 845-807-0220
e-mail: ira.cohen@co.sullivan.ny.us

State & Local Government Public Information

Tioga County
56 Main St
Owego, NY 13827
607-687-8200 or 607-687-8240 Fax: 607-687-8232
Web site: www.tiogacountyny.com

Chair, County Legislature (R):
Martha Sauerbrey 607-687-2911/fax: 607-687-8232
e-mail: sauerbreym@co.tioga.ny.us
Clerk, County Legislature:
Maureen L Dougherty 607-687-8235/fax: 607-687-8232
e-mail: doughertym@co.tioga.ny.us
County Clerk:
Andrea Klett 607-687-8660/fax: 607-687-8686
County Attorney:
Judith M Quigley 607-687-8253/fax: 607-223-7003
e-mail: quigleyj@co.tioga.ny.us
District Attorney:
Kirk Martin 607-687-8650
Public Defender:
George C Awad Jr. 607-687-1000
Director, Emergency Management:
Richard LeCount 607-687-2023
e-mail: tcemo@co.tioga.ny.us
Sheriff:
Gary W Howard 607-687-1010
Treasurer:
James P McFadden 607-687-8670/fax: 607-223-7035
e-mail: mcfaddenj@co.tioga.ny.us

Tompkins County
125 E Court St
Ithaca, NY 14850
607-274-5551 Fax: 607-274-5558
Web site: www.tompkins-co.org

Chairman, County Legislature (D):
Martha Robertson 607-274-5434/fax: 607-274-5430
e-mail: mrobertson@tompkins-co.org
County Administrator:
Joe Mareane 607-274-5551/fax: 607-274-5558
County Clerk:
Aurora R Valenti 607-274-5431/fax: 607-274-5445
e-mail: countyclerkmail@tompkins-co.org
County Attorney:
Jonathan Wood 607-274-5546/fax: 607-274-5547
e-mail: countyattorney@tompkins-co.org
District Attorney:
Gwen Wilkinson 607-274-5461/fax: 607-274-5429
Sheriff:
Kenneth W Lansing 607-257-1345/fax: 607-266-5436
Finance Director:
David Squires 607-274-5545
e-mail: finance@tompkins-co.org
Historian:
Vacant 607-274-5434
e-mail: historian@tompkins-co.org

Ulster County
County Office Bldg
244 Fair Street
6th Floor
Kingston, NY 12401
845-340-3800 Fax: 845-334-5724
e-mail: exec@co.ulster.ny.us
Web site: www.co.ulster.ny.us

Chairman, County Legislature (D):
Terry L Bernardo 845-340-3900/fax: 845-340-3651
Majority Leader (D):
Kenneth J. Ronk, Jr. 845-340-3900
Minority Leader (R):
David B. Donaldson 845-340-3900
Clerk of the County Legislature:
Victoria Fabella 845-340-3900/fax: 845-340-3651
County Executive:
Michael P Hein 845-340-3800/fax: 845-334-5724
e-mail: exec@co.ulster.ny.us
County Clerk:
Nina Postupack 845-340-3288/fax: 845-340-3299
e-mail: countyclerk@co.ulster.ny.us
County Attorney:
Beatrice Havranek 845-340-3685/fax: 845-340-3691
e-mail: bhav@co.ulster.ny.us
District Attorney:
D Holley Carnright 845-340-3280/fax: 845-340-3185
Public Defender:
Andrew Kossover 845-340-3232/fax: 845-340-3744
e-mail: akos@co.ulster.ny.us
Director, Emergency Management:
Arthur R Snyder 845-331-7000/fax: 845-331-1738
e-mail: asny@co.ulster.ny.us
Sheriff:
PJ Van Blarcum 845-338-3640/fax: 845-331-2810
e-mail: sheriff@co.ulster.ny.us
Commissioner of Finance:
Burt Gulnick, Jr. 845-340-3460/fax: 845-340-3430
e-mail: bgul@co.ulster.ny.us
Historian:
Anne M Gordon 845-331-7380
e-mail: pasaran@msn.com

Warren County
Municipal Center
1340 State Rte 9
Lake George, NY 12845
800-958-4748 x143 Fax: 518-761-6368
Web site: www.warrencountyny.gov

Chairman, Board of Supervisors (R):
Kevin B. Geraghty 518-761-6536
Clerk, Board of Supervisors:
Joan Sady 518-761-6563
Commissioner, Administrative & Fiscal Services:
JoAnn McKinstry 518-761-7655
County Clerk:
Pamela J Vogel 518-761-6427/fax: 518-761-6551
County Attorney:
Martin D. Auffredov 518-761-6463/fax: 518-761-6377
District Attorney:
Kathleen B Hogan 518-761-6405/fax: 518-761-6254
Public Defender:
John P M Wappett 518-761-6207/fax: 518-761-6208
Treasurer:
Michael R. Swan 518-761-6379/fax: 518-761-6470
Historian:
Ann McCann 518-761-6544/fax: 518-761-6551

Washington County
383 Broadway
Fort Edward, NY 12828
518-746-2100 Fax: 518-746-2108
Web site: www.co.washington.ny.us

Chairman, Board of Supervisors:
John A. Rymph 518-746-2210
Clerk, Board of Supervisors:
Debbie Prehoda 518-746-2210

Offices and agencies generally appear in alphabetical order, except when specific order is requested by listee.

County Administrator:
Kevin G Hayes 518-746-2590
County Clerk:
Dona Crandall 518-746-2170/fax: 518-746-2177
County Attorney:
Roger A Wickes 518-746-2216
District Attorney:
Kevin C Kortright 518-746-2525
Public Defender:
Vacant 518-747-2403
Sheriff:
Jeff Murphy 518-746-2475
Fire Coordinator:
Raymond Rathbun 518-746-2255
Treasurer:
Albert Nolette 518-746-2220

Wayne County

Wayne County Courthouse
26 Church St
Lyons, NY 14489
315-946-5400 Fax: 315-946-5407
Web site: www.co.wayne.ny.us

Chairman, Board of Supervisors (R):
James Hoffman 315-946-5400/fax: 315-946-5407
e-mail: jhoffman@co.wayne.ny.us
County Administrator:
James Marquette 315-946-5480/fax: 315-946-5407
County Clerk:
Michael Jankowski 315-946-7470/fax: 315-946-5978
e-mail: mjankowski@co.wayne.ny.us
County Attorney:
Daniel Connors 315-946-7442
District Attorney:
Richard Healy 315-946-5905/fax: 315-946-5911
Public Defender:
Ronald C Valentine 315-946-7472
Director, Emergency Management:
George Bastedo 315-946-5663/fax: 315-946-9721
Sheriff:
Barry Virts 315-946-9711/fax: 315-946-5811
Treasurer:
Thomas A Warnick 315-946-7441/fax: 315-946-5949
e-mail: warnicktreasurer@co.wayne.ny.us
County Historian:
Peter Evans 315-946-5470
e-mail: historian@co.wayne.ny.us

Westchester County
Board of Legislators

800 Michaelian Office Bldg
148 Martine Ave, 8th Fl
White Plains, NY 10601
914-995-2800 Fax: 914-995-3884
Web site: www.westchesterlegislators.com

Chair, Board of Legislators (D):
Kenneth W Jenkins 914-995-2829
e-mail: ryan@westchesterlegislators.com
Majority Leader (D):
Peter Harckham 914-995-2810
e-mail: rogowsky@westchesterlegislators.com
Minority Leader (R):
James Maisano 914-995-2826
Clerk, Board of Legislature & Chief of Staff:
Tina Seckerson 914-995-2823
e-mail: tinas@westchesterlegislators.com

Westchester County
Administration

900 Michaelian Office Building
148 Martine Ave
White Plains, NY 10601
914-995-2900
Web site: www3.westchestergov.com

County Executive:
Robert P. Astorino 914-995-2900
e-mail: ce@westchestergov.com
Deputy County Executive:
Kevin J. Plunkett 914-995-2909/fax: 914-995-3372
County Clerk:
Timothy C Idoni 914-995-3080/fax: 914-995-4030
County Attorney:
Robert Meehan 914-995-2690
e-mail: rfm5@westchestergov.com
District Attorney:
Janet Difiore 915-995-3414
Sheriff/Public Safety Commissioner:
George Longworth 914-864-7710
e-mail: gnl1@westchestergov.com
Finance Commissioner:
Ann Marie Berg 914-995-2757/fax: 914-995-3230
e-mail: ppp7@westchestergov.com
Public Works Acting Commissioner:
Jay T. Pisco 914-995-2546/fax: 914-995-4479
e-mail: jtp2@westchestergov.com
Emergency Management Office:
John M. Cullen 914-231-1851/fax: 914-231-1622
e-mail: jmc5@westchestergov.com

Wyoming County

Gov't Center, 143 N Main St
Warsaw, NY 14569
585-786-8800 Fax: 585-786-8802
e-mail: CKetchum@wyomingco.net
Web site: www.wyomingco.net

Chairman, Board of Supervisors (R):
A Berwanger 585-786-8800/fax: 585-786-8802
e-mail: abberwanger@wyomingco.net
Vice Chairman, Board of Supervisors (R):
Douglas Patti 585-786-8800
Clerk, Board of Supervisors:
Cheryl J Ketchum 585-786-8800/fax: 585-786-8802
e-mail: cketchum@wyomingco.net
County Clerk:
Rhonda Pierce 585-786-8810/fax: 585-786-3703
e-mail: county.clerk@wyomingco.net
County Attorney:
James Wvjcik 585-591-1724/fax: 585-591-1722
District Attorney:
Donald G O'Geen 585-786-8822/fax: 585-786-8842
e-mail: dogeen@wyomingco.net
Public Defender:
Norman P Effman 585-756-8450/fax: 585-786-8478
e-mail: attlegal@yahoo.com
Director, Fire & Emergency Management:
Anthony Santoro 585-786-8867/fax: 585-786-8961
e-mail: asantoro@wyomingco.net
Sheriff:
Farris H Heimann 585-786-2255/fax: 585-786-8961
e-mail: fheimann@wyomingco.net
Treasurer:
Cheryl Mayer 585-786-8812/fax: 585-786-0466
e-mail: cdmayer@wyomingco.net

County Historian:
Doris Bannister 585-786-8818

Yates County

417 Liberty St
Penn Yan, NY 14527
315-536-5150 Fax: 315-536-5166
Web site: www.yatescounty.org

Chairman, County Legislature (R):
H Taylor Fitch 315-536-5150/fax: 315-536-5166
e-mail: legislature@yatescounty.org
County Administrator:
Sarah Purdy 315-536-5509/fax: 315-536-5118
e-mail: ycadministrator@yatescounty.org
Clerk, County Legislature:
Connie C Hayes......................315-536-5150/fax: 315-536-5166
e-mail: legislature@yatescounty.org
County Clerk:
Julie D Betts 315-536-5120/fax: 315-536-5545
e-mail: countyclerk@yatescounty.org
County Attorney:
Scott P. Falvey......................315-531-3233/fax: 315-531-3234
District Attorney:
Jason Cook............................315-536-5550/fax: 315-536-5556
Public Defender:
Edward J Brockman ....585-374-6439 or 315-536-0352
Sheriff:
Ronald G Spike 315-536-4438/fax: 315-536-5191
e-mail: sheriff@yatescounty.org
Treasurer:
Winona B. Flynn..315-536-5192
e-mail: treasurer@yatescounty.org
Emergency Management Director:
Vacant 315-536-3000/fax: 315-536-5106
e-mail: emergencymanagement@yatescounty.org
Historian:
Frances Dumas 315-536-5147/fax: 315-531-3226
e-mail: history@yatescounty.org

Offices and agencies generally appear in alphabetical order, except when specific order is requested by listee.

MUNICIPAL GOVERNMENT

This section identifies senior public officials for cities, towns and villages in New York State with populations greater than 20,000. New York City departments are included in the city listing.

MUNICIPAL GOVERNMENT

Albany, City of
City Hall
24 Eagle St
Albany, NY 12207
518-434-5175
e-mail: webmaster@ci.albany.ny.us
Web site: www.albanyny.gov

Mayor:
Gerald D Jennings 518-434-5100/fax: 518-434-5013
e-mail: mayor@ci.albany.ny.us
Deputy Mayor:
Philip F Calderone 518-434-5077/fax: 518-434-5074
President, Common Council:
Carolyn McLaughlin 518-462-1458
e-mail: onlybelv@aol.com
City Clerk:
Nala Woodward 518-434-5090/fax: 518-434-5081
e-mail: cityclerk@ci.albany.ny.us
Corporation Counsel:
John Reilly 518-434-5050/fax: 518-434-5070
City Deputy Auditor:
Debra Perks 518-434-5023
City Treasurer:
Kathy Sheehan 518-434-5036/fax: 518-434-5041
e-mail: sheehank@ci.albanu.ny.us
Commissioner, General Services:
Nicolas J D'Antonio 518-432-1144/fax: 518-427-7499
e-mail: generalservices@ci.albany.ny.us
Commissioner, Assessment & Taxation:
Keith McDonald 518-434-5155/fax: 518-434-5013
e-mail: skrokoff@albany-ny.org
Police Chief:
Steven Krokoff 518-462-8013
e-mail: skrokoff@albany-ny.org
Fire Chief/Emergency Services:
Robert Forezzi Sr. 518-447-7877/fax: 518-434-8675
Director, Community Development:
Faye Andrews 518-434-5265
Director, Building & Codes:
Jeffrey Jamison 518-434-5165/fax: 518-434-6015

Amherst, Town of
5583 Main St
Williamsville, NY 14221
716-631-7000 Fax: 716-631-7146
e-mail: webmaster@amherst.ny.us
Web site: www.amherst.ny.us

Town Supervisor:
Barry A Weinstein 716-631-7032
e-mail: bweinstein@amherst.ny.us
Town Clerk:
Marjory Jaeger 716-631-7021 x7010/fax: 716-631-7152
e-mail: dbucki@amherst.ny.us
Town Attorney:
E Thomas Jones 716-631-7164
e-mail: tjones@amherst.ny.us
Comptroller:
Darlene Carroll 716-631-7008
e-mail: dcarroll@amherst.ny.us
Director Emergency Services & Safety:
James J Zymanek 716-839-6707
e-mail: jzymanek@amherst.ny.us
Police Chief:
John C Askey 716-689-1311/fax: 716-689-1310
e-mail: jmoslow@apdny.org

Auburn, City of
Memorial City Hall
24 South Street
Auburn, NY 13021
315-255-4104 Fax: 315-253-8345
Web site: auburnny.gov

Mayor:
Michael Quill 315-255-4104/fax: 315-253-8345
e-mail: mayorquill@ci.auburn.ny.us
City Manager:
Doug Selby 315-255-4146/fax: 315-255-4735
e-mail: citymanager@ci.auburn.ny.us
City Clerk:
Debra A McCormick 315-255-4100/fax: 315-255-4181
e-mail: dmccormick@ci.auburn.ny.us
Corporation Counsel:
John Rossi 315-255-4176/fax: 315-255-4735
e-mail: jrossi@ci.auburn.ny.us
Planning & Economic Development Director:
Jennifer Haines 315-255-4115/fax: 315-253-0282
e-mail: jhaines@ci.auburn.ny.us
Comptroller:
Lauren Poehlman 315-255-4138/fax: 315-255-4727
Treasurer:
Robert Gauthier 315-255-4143/fax: 315-255-4727
e-mail: rgauthier@ci.auburn.ny.us
Police Chief:
Brian Neagle 315-253-3235/fax: 315-255-2601
Fire Chief:
Jeff Dygert 315-253-4031/fax: 315-252-0318

Babylon, Town of
200 E Sunrise Highway
Lindenhurst, NY 11757-2598
631-957-3000 Fax: 631-957-7440
e-mail: info@townofbabylon.com
Web site: www.townofbabylon.com

Town Supervisor:
Rich Schaffer 631-957-3072/fax: 631-957-7440
Town Clerk:
Carol Quirk 631-957-4291
Town Attorney:
Joseph Wilson 631-957-3029
Comptroller:
Victoria Marotta 631-957-3179
Commissioner, Public Works:
Tom Stay 631-957-3161
Deputy Commissioner, Public Safety:
Patrick Farrell 631-422-7600/fax: 631-893-1031
Commissioner, General Services:
Theresa Sabatino 631-957-3025

Bethlehem, Town of
445 Delaware Ave
Delmar, NY 12054

State & Local Government Public Information

Offices and agencies generally appear in alphabetical order, except when specific order is requested by listee.

518-439-4955 Fax: 518-439-1699
e-mail: djacon@townofbethlehem.org
Web site: www.townofbethlehem.org

Town Supervisor:
John Clarkson 518-439-4955 x1164
e-mail: jclarkson@townofbethlehem.org
Town Clerk:
Nanci Moquin. 518-439-4955 x1183/fax: 518-439-1699
e-mail: nmoquin@townofbethlehem.org
Town Attorney:
James Potter 518-439-4955 x1164
e-mail: jpotter@townofbethlehem.org
Comptroller:
Michael E. Cohen 518-439-4955 x1123
e-mail: mcohen@townofbethlehem.org
Police Chief:
Louis G Corsi 518-439-9973/fax: 518-439-6965
Emergency Management Director:
John E Brennan 518-439-4955 x1166
e-mail: jbrennan@townofbethlehem.org
Historian:
Susan E Leath 518-439-4955 x1160
e-mail: sleath@townofbethlehem.org

Binghamton, City of

City Hall
38 Hawley St
Binghamton, NY 13901
607-772-7005 Fax: 607-772-0508
Web site: www.cityofbinghamton.com

Mayor:
Matthew T Ryan 607-772-7001/fax: 607-772-7079
e-mail: mayor@cityofbinghamton.com
Executive Assistant to the Mayor:
Andrew Block 607-772-7001/fax: 607-772-7079
e-mail: awblock@cityofbinghamton.com
City Clerk:
Angela Holmes 607-772-7005/fax: 607-772-7155
e-mail: clerk@cityofbinghamton.com
Corporation Counsel:
Kenneth Frank. 607-772-7013
City Treasurer:
Pauline Penrose 607-772-7027/fax: 607-772-7015
e-mail: treasurer@cityofbinghamton.com
City Assessor:
Scott Snyder. 607-772-7002/fax: 607-772-7106
e-mail: assessor@cityofbinghamton.com
Commissioner, Public Works:
Luke Day 607-772-7021/fax: 607-772-7023
e-mail: dpw@cityofbinghamton.com
Police Chief:
Joseph Zikuski. 607-772-7090/fax: 607-772-7996
e-mail: police@cityofbinghamton.com
Acting Administrator, Civil Service:
Judith Robb 607-772-7008/fax: 607-772-7066
e-mail: cs@cityofbinghamton.com
Acting Director, Finance/Comptroller:
Charles Pearsall 607-772-7011/fax: 607-772-7106
e-mail: finance@cityofbinghamton.com
Director, Planning/Housing/Community Development:
Tarik Abdelazim 607-772-7028/fax: 607-772-7063
e-mail: tabdelazim@cityofbinghamton.com
Director, Economic Development:
Merry Harris 607-772-7161/fax: 607-772-7244
e-mail: maharris@cityofbinghamton.com

Brighton, Town of

2300 Elmwood Ave
Rochester, NY 14618
585-784-5250 Fax: 585-784-5373
Web site: www.townofbrighton.org

Town Supervisor:
William W Moehle 585-784-5252
e-mail: sandra.frankel@townofbrighton.org
Town Clerk:
Dan Aman 585-784-5240/fax: 585-784-5374
Director, Finance:
Suzanne Zaso. 585-784-5210/fax: 585-784-5396
e-mail: suzanne.zaso@townofbrighton.org
Police Chief:
Mark Henderson 585-784-5150/fax: 585-784-5151
Fire Marshal:
Christopher Roth 585-784-5220/fax: 585-785-5207
e-mail: christopher.roth@townofbrighton.org
Town Attorney:
Kenneth W. Gordon 585-244-1070/fax: 585-244-1085
Commissioner, Public Works:
Tim Keef 585-784-5250/fax: 585-784-5223
e-mail: tim.keef@townofbrighton.org
Director, Communications:
Douglas Clapp. 585-784-5253
e-mail: doug.clapp@townofbrighton.org

Brookhaven, Town of

One Independence Hill
Farmingville, NY 11738
631-451-6655 Fax: 631-451-6677
Web site: www.brookhaven.org

Town Supervisor:
Edward P. Romaine 631-451-8696/fax: 631-451-6447
Town Clerk/Registrar:
Patricia Eddington 631-451-9101/fax: 631-451-9264
Commissioner of Finance:
Tamara Wright. 631-451-6680/fax: 631-451-6692
e-mail: finance@brookhaven.org
Commissioner, Public Safety:
Peter O'Leary 631-451-6291/fax: 631-451-6908

Buffalo, City of

City Hall
65 Niagara Square
Buffalo, NY 14202
716-851-4200 Fax: 716-851-4360
Web site: www.ci.buffalo.ny.us

Mayor:
Byron W Brown
e-mail: mayor@city-buffalo.com
Council President:
Richard A. Fontana 716-851-5151/fax: 716-851-5141
e-mail: rfontana@city-buffalo.com
City Clerk:
Gerald Chwalinski 716-851-5431/fax: 716-851-4845
e-mail: gchwalinski@city-buffalo.com
Comptroller:
Mark JF Schroeder 716-851-5255/fax: 716-851-4031
e-mail: mschroeder@city-buffalo.com
Commissioner, Administration, Finance & Urban Affairs:
Donna Estrich 716-851-5922
e-mail: destrich@city-buffalo.com
Police Commissioner:
Daniel Derenda . . . . 716-851-4444 or 716-851-4571

Fire Commissioner:
Garnell W Whitfield Jr 716-851-5333
e-mail: gwhitfield@bfdny.org
Director Emergency Management:
Garnell W. Whitfield, Jr. 716-851-5333/fax: 716-851-5341
e-mail: gwhitfield@city-buffalo.com

Camillus, Town of
4600 W Genesee Street
Syracuse, NY 13219
315-488-1335 Fax: 315-488-8768
Web site: www.townofcamillus.com

Town Supervisor:
Mary Ann Coogan 315-488-1335/fax: 315-488-8768
e-mail: macoogan@townofcamillus.com
Town Clerk:
Martha Dickson-McMahon 315-488-1234/fax: 315-488-8983
e-mail: mdickson@townofcamillus.com
Comptroller:
Catherine Albunio 315-488-2266/fax: 315-468-4179
e-mail: calbunio@townofcamillus.com
Police Chief:
Thomas Winn 315-487-0102/fax: 315-487-5572
e-mail: twinn@townofcamillus.com

Carmel, Town of
Town Hall
60 McAlpin Ave
Mahopac, NY 10541
845-628-1500 Fax: 845-628-7434
Web site: www.ci.carmel.ny.us

Town Supervisor:
Kenneth Schmitt 845-628-1500/fax: 845-628-6836
Town Clerk:
Ann Spofford 845-628-1500/fax: 845-628-7434
Town Counsel:
Gregory Folchetti 845-225-1900/fax: 845-228-4228
Police Chief:
Michael R Johnson 845-628-1300/fax: 845-628-2597

Cheektowaga, Town of
Town Hall
3301 Broadway
Cheektowaga, NY 14227
716-686-3400 Fax: 716-686-3515
Web site: www.tocny.org

Town Supervisor:
Mary F Holtz 716-686-3465/fax: 716-686-3551
Town Clerk:
Alice Magierski 716-686-3434/fax: 716-686-3515
e-mail: townclerkwebmail@tocny.org
Town Attorney:
Kevin Schenk 716-686-3457/fax: 716-686-3997
e-mail: lawweb@tocny.org
Emergency Services Manager:
Earl Loder 716-893-0847/fax: 716-893-0835
e-mail: eloder@tocny.org
Police Chief:
David Zack 716-686-3500/fax: 716-685-1239

Chili, Town of
3235 Chili Avenue
Rochester, NY 14624
585-889-3550 Fax: 585-889-8710
e-mail: info@townofchili.org
Web site: www.townofchili.org

Town Supervisor:
David Dunning 585-889-6111
Town Clerk:
Richard J Brongo 585-889-6122
e-mail: rbrongo@townofchili.org
Director of Finance:
Dianne O'Meara 585-889-6120
Town Historian:
Bonnie Moore 585-889-6123

Cicero, Town of
Town Hall
8236 S Main St
PO Box 1517
Cicero, NY 13039
315-699-1414 Fax: 315-699-0039
Web site: www.ciceronewyork.net

Town Supervisor:
Jim Corl 315-699-1414
e-mail: jcorl@ciceronewyork.net
Town Clerk:
Tracy M Cosilmon 315-699-8109/fax: 315-699-0039
e-mail: clerk@ciceronewyork.net
Comptroller:
Shirlie Stuart 315-699-2759/fax: 315-698-0851
e-mail: sstuart@ciceronewyork.net
Receiver of Taxes:
Sharon Edick 315-699-2756/fax: 315-699-9562
e-mail: sedick@ciceronewyork.net
Police Chief:
Joseph F Snell Jr 315-699-3677/fax: 315-699-8128

Clarence, Town of
1 Town Place
Clarence, NY 14031
716-741-8930 Fax: 716-741-4715
Web site: www.clarence.ny.us

Town Supervisor:
David C. Hartzell, Jr. 716-741-8930/fax: 716-741-4715
e-mail: dhartzell@clarence.ny.us
Town Clerk:
Nancy C Metzger 716-741-8938/fax: 716-407-2190
e-mail: nmetzger@clarence.ny.us
Town Attorney:
Lawrence M. Meckler 716-741-8935/fax: 716-741-4715
e-mail: lmeckler@clarence.ny.us
Chief Security Officer:
Joseph D Meacham 716-406-8928
e-mail: jmeacham@clarence.ny.us

Clarkstown, Town of
10 Maple Ave
New City, NY 10956
845-639-2050 Fax: 845-639-2008
Web site: www.town.clarkstown.ny.us

Town Supervisor:
Alexander J Gromack 845-639-2050/fax: 845-634-5456
e-mail: a.gromack@town.clarkstown.org
Deputy Supervisor:
Councilman Shirley Lasker 845-639-2050/fax: 845-634-5456
e-mail: slasker@clarkstown.org

State & Local Government Public Information

Town Clerk:
Justin Sweet....................845-639-2010/fax: 845-639-2008
e-mail: clerk@clarkstown.org
Town Attorney:
Amy Mele....................845-639-2060/fax: 845-639-2189
e-mail: legal@town.clarkstown.ny.us

Clay, Town of
4401 State Route 31
Clay, NY 13041
315-652-3800 Fax: 315-622-7259
Web site: www.townofclay.org

Town Supervisor:
Damian M Ulatowski..........315-652-3800 x114/fax: 315-622-7259
e-mail: supervisor@townofclay.org
Town Clerk:
Jill Hageman-Clark..........315-652-3800 ext 145/fax: 315-622-7259
e-mail: townclerk@townofclay.org
Town Attorney:
Robert M Germain..........315-652-3800 x151/fax: 315-622-7259
e-mail: legal@townofclay.org
Commissioner of Finance:
John Shehadi....................315-652-3800 x121
Commissioner, Public Safety:
Mark Territo....................315-622-7259
e-mail: planning@townofclay.org
Fire Chief:
Daniel L Ford....................315-625-4242

Clifton Park, Town of
1 Town Hall Plaza
Clifton Park, NY 12065
518-371-6651 Fax: 518-371-1136
e-mail: info@cliftonpark.org
Web site: www.cliftonpark.org

Town Supervisor:
Philip Barrett....................518-371-6651/fax: 518-371-1136
Town Administrator:
Michael Shahen....................518-371-6651 ext243
Town Clerk:
Patricia O'Donnell....................518-371-6681/fax: 518-383-5088
e-mail: townclerk@cliftonpark.org
Comptroller:
Mark Heggen....................518-371-6651/fax: 518-371-1136
Historian:
John Scherer....................518-371-2691/fax: 518-383-2668

Colonie, Town of
Memorial Town Hall
534 Loudon Rd
Newtonville, NY 12128
518-783-2700 Fax: 518-782-2360
e-mail: colonie@colonie.org
Web site: www.colonie.org

Town Supervisor:
Paula A Mahan....................518-783-2700
Town Clerk:
Elizabeth A DelTorto....................518-783-2734/fax: 518-783-3409
e-mail: deltortoe@colonie.org
Town Attorney:
Michael C Magguilli....................518-783-2704/fax: 518-786-7324
e-mail: attorney@colonie.org
Comptroller:
Craig Blair....................518-783-2708/fax: 518-783-2877
e-mail: blairc@colonie.org
Emergency Management & Planning:
Michael Rayball....................518-782-2609
e-mail: Rayballm@colonie.org
Police Chief:
Steven H Heider....................518-783-2744/fax: 518-786-7326
e-mail: heiders@colonie.org
Public Works Commissioner:
John H Cunningham....................518-783-6292/fax: 518-785-3529
e-mail: infodpw@colonie.org
Town Historian:
Kevin Franklin....................518-782-2601
e-mail: historian@colonie.org

Cortlandt, Town of
1 Heady St
Cortlandt Manor, NY 10567-1224
914-734-1002 Fax: 914-734-1025
e-mail: townhall@townofcortlandt.com
Web site: www.townofcortlandt.com

Town Supervisor:
Linda D Puglisi....................914-734-1002/fax: 914-734-1003
e-mail: lindap@townofcortlandt.com
Town Clerk:
Joann Dyckman....................914-734-1020/fax: 914-734-1102
Town Attorney:
Thomas F Wood....................914-736-0930/fax: 914-736-9082
Comptroller:
Glenn Cestaro....................914-734-1071/fax: 914-734-1077
e-mail: glennc@townofcortlandt.com
DES/Director:
Jeff Coleman....................914-737-0100/fax: 914-862-3376
e-mail: jefft@townofcortlandt.com
Homeland Security:
Linda Puglisi....................914-734-1001
e-mail: jefft@townofcortlandt.com

DeWitt, Town of
5400 Butternut Drive
East Syracuse, NY 13057-8509
315-446-3910 Fax: 315-449-2065
Web site: www.townofdewitt.com

Town Supervisor:
Edward M Michalenko..........315-446-3910 ext5/fax: 315-449-0620
e-mail: supervisor@townofdewitt.com
Town Clerk:
Barbara K Klim..........315-446-3910 ext 2/fax: 315-449-2065
e-mail: clerk@townofdewitt.com
Police Chief:
Eugene J Conway....................315-449-3640/fax: 315-449-3644
e-mail: police@townofdewitt.com
Comptroller:
Timothy Redmond..........315-446-3392 ext 6/fax: 315-449-2065
e-mail: comptroller@townofdewitt.com

East Fishkill, Town of
Town Hall
330 Route 376
Hopewell Junction, NY 12533
845-221-9191
Web site: www.eastfishkillny.org

Town Supervisor:
John L Hickman Jr....................845-221-4303
e-mail: hickmanj@eastfishkillny.org
Town Clerk:
Carol Hurray....................845-221-9191

Offices and agencies generally appear in alphabetical order, except when specific order is requested by listee.

Police Chief:
Brian C Nichols 845-221-2111
Fire Inspector:
William Stuart......................................845-221-0378

East Hampton, Town of

159 Pantigo Rd
East Hampton, NY 11937
631-324-4140 Fax: 631-324-2789
e-mail: info@town.east-hampton.ny.us
Web site: www.town.east-hampton.ny.us

Town Supervisor:
William J Wilkinson 631-324-4140/fax: 631-324-2789
Town Clerk:
Fred Overton 631-324-4142/fax: 631-324-4128
e-mail: Foverton@town.east-hampton.ny.us
Division of Finance/ Budget Officer:
Len Bernard.........................631-324-4141/fax: 631-324-2789
e-mail: lbernard@town.east-hampton.ny.us
Town Attorney:
John Jilnicki.........................631-324-8787/fax: 631-329-5371
e-mail: jjilnicki@town.east-hampton.ny.us
Police Chief:
Edward V Ecker Jr....................631-537-7575/fax: 631-537-6833
Emergency Services:
Bruce Bates...631-324-1736
Chief Fire Marshall:
David Browne 631-329-3473/fax: 631-329-9403
e-mail: dbrowne@town.east-hampton.ny.us

Eastchester, Town of

Town Hall
40 Mill Rd
Eastchester, NY 10709
914-771-3300 Fax: 914-771-3366
Web site: www.eastchester.org

Town Supervisor:
Anthony S Colavita 914-771-3301/fax: 914-793-2168
e-mail: supervisor@eastchester.org
Town Clerk:
Linda Doherty 914-771-3351/fax: 914-771-3366
e-mail: townclerk@eastchester.org
Town Attorney:
Louis J. Reda 914-771-3325/fax: 914-771-3367
e-mail: legal@eastchester.org
Comptroller:
Dawn T Donovan 914-771-3330/fax: 914-771-9409
e-mail: comptroller@eastchester.org

Elmira, City of

City Hall
317 E Church St
Elmira, NY 14901
607-737-5644 Fax: 607-737-5824
Web site: www.cityofelmira.net

Mayor:
Susan J. Skidmore...................................607-737-5644
City Manager:
John J Burin 607-737-5644
City Clerk:
Angela J Williams...................607-737-5672/fax: 607-737-5783
Chamberlain:
David Vandermark 607-737-5661/fax: 607-737-5783
Director, Public Works:
Brian Beasley 607-737-5679

Police Chief:
Michael Robertson 607-737-5811
Fire Chief:
Patrick Bermingham 607-737-5700

Fishkill, Town of

807 Route 52
Fishkill, NY 12524
845-831-7800 Fax: 845-831-6040
e-mail: tof@fishkill-ny.gov
Web site: www.fishkill-ny.gov

Town Supervisor:
Robert LaColla..............................845-831-7800 x. 3309
Town Clerk:
Darlene Bellis ....845-831-7800 x. 3329
e-mail: dbellis@fishkill-ny.gov
Comptroller:
Dawn H. Kertesz-Lee 845-831-7800 x3339
e-mail: rwheeling@fishkill-ny.gov

Freeport, Village of

46 North Ocean Ave
Freeport, NY 11520
516-377-2200 Fax: 516-377-2323
e-mail: freeportmail1@freeportny.gov
Web site: www.freeportny.com

Village Mayor:
Robert T. Kennedy 516-377-2252/fax: 516-377-2323
e-mail: mayor@freeportny.gov
Village Clerk:
Pamela Walsh Boening 516-377-2300/fax: 516-771-4127
Village Attorney:
Howard E Colton.....................516-377-2249/fax: 516-377-2366
e-mail: hcolton@freeportny.gov
Treasurer:
Ismaela Hernandez 516-377-2212/fax: 516-377-2255
e-mail: vmontes@freeportny.gov
Superintendent, Public Works:
Robert R. Fisenne, P.E..............................516-377-2289
e-mail: srichardson@freeportny.gov
Emergency Management Director:
Richard E Holdener 516-377-2188
e-mail: rholdener@freeportny.gov
Police Chief:
Miguel Bermudez 516-377-2411/fax: 516-377-2432
e-mail: mwoodword@freeportny.gov
Secretary to Fire Chief:
Raymond Maguire 516-377-2190
e-mail: rmaguire@freeportny.gov
Chief of the Fire Department:
Stanley Kistela 516-377-2190
e-mail: rmaguire@freeportny.gov

Garden City, Village of

351 Stewart Ave
Garden City, NY 11530
516-465-4000 Fax: 516-742-5223
Web site: www.gardencityny.net

Mayor:
John J. Watras......................................516-465-4051
e-mail: mayor@gardencityny.net
Administrator:
Robert L Schoelle, Jr 516-465-4051
e-mail: rschoelle@gardencityny.net

State & Local Government Public Information

Offices and agencies generally appear in alphabetical order, except when specific order is requested by listee.

Fire Chief:
William J Castoro 516-746-4130
e-mail: wcastoro@gardencityny.net
Director, Public Works:
Robert J Mangan 516-465-4004
e-mail: rmangan@gardencityny.net

Gates, Town of

1605 Buffalo Rd
Gates, NY 14624
585-247-6100 Fax: 585-247-0017
e-mail: admin@townofgates.org
Web site: www.townofgates.org

Town Supervisor:
Mark W Assini 585-247-6100
Town Clerk:
Richard A Warner 585-247-6100
e-mail: rwarner@townofgates.org
Finance Director:
Art Plewa 585-247-6100
Police Chief:
David R DiCaro 585-247-2262
Director, Building & Public Works:
John Lathrop 585-247-6100 x241
Town Historian:
Judy DeRooy........ 585-247-6100

Glen Cove, City of

9 Glen St
Glen Cove, NY 11542
516-676-2000 Fax: 516-676-0108
Web site: www.glencove-li.com

Mayor:
Ralph V Suozzi 516-676-2004/fax: 516-676-0108
e-mail: rsuozzi@cityofglencoveny.org
City Clerk:
Tina Pemberton........ 516-676-3345 or 516-676-3357
e-mail: tpemberton@cityofglencoveny.org
City Attorney:
Vincent Taranto 516-759-1111
e-mail: vtaranto@cityofglencoveny.org
Controller:
Sal Lombardi........ 516-676-2789
e-mail: slombardi@cityofglencoveny.org
Director, Public Works:
William Archambault........ 516-676-4402
e-mail: publicworks@cityofglencoveny.org
Police Chief:
William Whitton 516-676-1000
e-mail: wwhitton@cityofglencoveny.org

Glenville, Town of

18 Glenridge Rd
Glenville, NY 12302
518-688-1200 Fax: 518-384-0140
Web site: www.townofglenville.org

Town Supervisor:
Christopher A Koetzle........ 518-688-1202/fax: 518-384-0140
e-mail: ckoetzle@townofglenville.org
Town Clerk:
Linda Neals 518-688-1200x402/fax: 518-384-0140
e-mail: lneals@townofglenville.org
Town Attorney:
Michael R Cuevas 518-688-1200/fax: 518-384-0140
Town Planner:
Kevin Corcoran........ 518-688-1200x407/fax: 518-384-0140
e-mail: kcorcoran@townofglenville.org
Comptroller:
Jason Cuthbert........ 518-688-1200 ext306/fax: 518-384-0140
e-mail: gphillips@townofglenville.org
Highway Superintendent & Commissioner, Public Works:
Thomas Coppola 518-382-1406/fax: 518-382-3015
e-mail: tcoppola@townofglenville.org
Historian:
Joan Szablewski 518-982-0643/fax: 518-384-0140
Police Chief:
Michael Ranalli........ 518-384-3444/fax: 518-384-0141
e-mail: mranalli@townofglenville.org

Grand Island, Town of

Grand Island Town Hall
2255 Baseline Road
Grand Island, NY 14072
716-773-9618 Fax: 716-773-9618
e-mail: www.gigov.com

Town Supervisor:
Mary Cooke........ 716-773-9600/fax: 716-773-9618
e-mail: supervisor@grand-island.ny.us
Assistant/Deputy Supervisor:
Elizabeth Wilbert........ 716-773-9600/fax: 716-773-9618
e-mail: lwilbert@grand-island.ny.us
Town Clerk:
Pattie Frentzel 716-773-9600/fax: 716-773-9618
e-mail: pfrentzel@grand-island.ny.us
Town Attorney:
Peter Godfrey........ 716-773-9600/fax: 716-773-9618
e-mail: www.hodgsonruss.com
Town Accountant:
Pamela Barton 716-773-9600/fax: 716-773-9618
e-mail: pbarton@grand-island.ny.us
Town Assessor:
Judy M Tafelski........ 716-773-9600/fax: 716-773-9618
e-mail: assessor@grand-island.ny.us

Greece, Town of

1 Vince Tofany Blvd
Greece, NY 14612
585-225-2000 Fax: 585-225-1915
Web site: greeceny.gov

Town Supervisor:
John T Auberger 585-723-2311
Deputy Town Supervisor:
Jeffery McCann........ 585-723-2000
Director, Constituent Services:
Kathryn J Firkins 585-723-2000
Town Clerk:
Patricia Anthony 585-723-2341/fax: 585-723-2459
e-mail: panthony@townofgreece.ny.gov
Town Attorney:
Jeffery McCann........ 585-225-2000/fax: 585-225-1915
Director, Finance:
Rick Pellegrino 585-723-2335
Police Chief:
Todd Baxter 585-865-9200
Town Assessor:
Leo Carroll 585-723-2308

Greenburgh, Town of

177 Hillside Avenue
Greenburgh, NY 10607

Offices and agencies generally appear in alphabetical order, except when specific order is requested by listee.

914-993-1500 Fax: 914-993-1626
Web site: www.greenburghny.com

Town Supervisor:
Paul J Feiner 914-993-1540/fax: 914-993-1541
e-mail: pfeiner@greenburghny.com
Town Clerk:
Judith A Beville.......................914-993-1500/fax: 914-993-1626
e-mail: townclerk@greenburghny.com
Historian:
Frank Jazzo 914-993-1641/fax: 914-993-1626
Chief of Police:
Joseph DiCarlo 914-682-5300/fax: 914-683-5342

Guilderland, Town of

Town Hall
5209 Western Turnpike
PO Box 339
Guilderland, NY 12084
518-356-1980 Fax: 518-356-3955
Web site: www.townofguilderland.org

Town Supervisor:
Kenneth Runion 518-356-1980 x1022/fax: 518-356-5514
e-mail: runionk@townofguilderland.org
Town Clerk:
Rosemary Centi.......................518-356-1980/fax: 518-356-3955
Police Chief:
Carol Lawlor 518-356-1980/fax: 518-356-4668
e-mail: lawlorc@guilderlandpd.org
Town Historian:
Alice Begley.................518-356-1980 x1050/fax: 518-356-3955
e-mail: abegley27@aol.com

Hamburg, Town of

6100 South Park Ave
Hamburg, NY 14075
716-649-6111 Fax: 716-649-4087
Web site: www.townofhamburgny.com

Town Supervisor:
Steven J Walters 716-649-6111 x2381
e-mail: supervisor@townofhamburgny.com
Town Clerk:
Catherine A Rybczynski 716-649-6111 x2360/fax: 716-646-1384
e-mail: townclerk@townofhamburgny.com
Senior Public Safety Dispatcher:
Thomas E Taylor...............................716-649-6111 x2412
e-mail: e911@townofhamburgny.com
Town Historian:
James Baker...................................716-649-6111 x. 2400

Harrison, Town/Village of

11 Heineman Place
Harrison, NY 10528
914-670-3000 Fax: 914-835-8067
Web site: www.harrison-ny.gov

Supervisor/Mayor:
Ron Belmont 914-670-3005/fax: 914-835-8067
e-mail: jwalsh@harrison-ny.gov
Town Clerk:
Jacqueline Greer 914-670-3030/fax: 914-835-2009
e-mail: jgreer@harrison-ny.gov
Comptroller/Treasurer:
Maureen MacKenzie 914-670-3080/fax: 914-835-2759
e-mail: comptroller@harrison-ny.gov
Police Chief:
Anthony Marraccini 914-967-5110
Commissioner, Public Works:
Anthony P Robinson 914-670-3229/fax: 914-835-2387
e-mail: arobinson@harrison-ny.gov
Fire Marshal/Fire Prevention Dept:
Robert Fitzsimmons....................914-670-3051/fax: 914-670-3170

Haverstraw, Town of

1 Rosman Rd
Garnerville, NY 10923
845-429-2200 Fax: 845-429-4701
Web site: www.townofhaverstraw.us

Town Supervisor:
Howard T Phillips, Jr.................845-429-2200/fax: 845-429-4701
Town Clerk:
Karen L. Bulley ....845-942-3727 or 845-942-3728
fax: 845-942-4964
Town Attorney:
William Stein 845-429-2200
Finance Director:
Michael J Gamboli 845-429-2200

Hempstead, Town of

Town Hall Plaza
1 Washington St
Hempstead, NY 11550
516-489-5000 Fax: 516-538-2908
Web site: www.townofhempstead.org; www.toh.li

Town Supervisor:
Kate Murray...................................516-489-6000 x3260
Town Clerk:
Mark A Bonilla 516-489-5000 x3046
e-mail: markbon@hotmail.org

Hempstead, Village of

99 Nichols Court
Hempstead, NY 11550
516-489-3400 Fax: 516-489-4285
Web site: www.villageofhempstead.org

Mayor:
Wayne J Hall Sr 516-478-6200
Village Clerk:
Patricia Perez 516-478-6202
e-mail: clerksoffice@villageofhempsteadny.gov
Public Works Director:
Frank Germinaro 516-489-3400 x270
Chief of Police:
Michael McGown 516-483-6200

Henrietta, Town of

475 Calkins Rd
Henrietta, NY 14467
585-334-7700 Fax: 585-334-9667
Web site: www.henrietta.org

Town Supervisor:
Michael B Yudelson 585-359-7001/fax: 585-334-9667
e-mail: supervisor@townofhenrietta.org
Town Clerk:
Leann Case 585-334-7700/fax: 585-334-9667
Sewer, Drainage, & Sidewalks Foreman:
Michael Catalano......................585-444-2211/fax: 585-359-7029
e-mail: cmarshall@townofhenrietta.org

Huntington, Town of

100 Main St
Huntington, NY 11743

State & Local Government Public Information

631-351-3000 Fax: 631-424-7856
Web site: http://huntingtonny.gov

Town Supervisor:
Frank P Petrone 631-351-3030/fax: 631-424-7856
e-mail: fpetrone@town.huntington.ny.us
Town Clerk:
Jo-Ann Raia 631-351-3206/fax: 631-351-3205
e-mail: jraia@town.huntington.ny.us
Town Attorney:
Cindy Elan-Mangano 631-351-3042/fax: 631-351-3032
e-mail: townattorney@town.huntington.ny.us
Public Safety Director:
Vacant 631-351-3167/fax: 631-351-3169
e-mail: publicsafety@town.huntington.ny.us
Director, General Services:
Thomas J Boccard 631-351-3365/fax: 631-351-3337
e-mail: genservices@town.huntington.ny.us
Historian:
Robert C Hughes 631-351-3244/fax: 631-351-3245
e-mail: huntingtonhistorial@verizon.net

Hyde Park, Town of

4383 Albany Post Rd
Hyde Park, NY 12538
845-229-5111 Fax: 845-229-0831
Web site: www.hydeparkny.us

Town Supervisor:
Aileen Rohr 845-229-5111 x8/fax: 845-229-0831
e-mail: supervisor@hydeparkny.us
Town Clerk:
Donna McGrogan 845-229-5111 x5/fax: 845-229-7583
e-mail: tcc-1@hydeparkny.us
Police Chief:
Eric Paolilli 845-229-9340/fax: 845-229-6953
e-mail: police@hydeparkny.us
Town Historian:
Carey Rhinevault 845-229-8225

Irondequoit, Town of

Town Hall
1280 Titus Ave
Rochester, NY 14617
585-467-8840 Fax: 585-467-7294
e-mail: feedback@irondequoit.org
Web site: www.irondequoit.org

Town Supervisor:
Mary Joyce D'Aurizio 585-336-6034
e-mail: feedback@irondequoit.org
Town Clerk/Receiver of Taxes:
Barbara Genier 585-336-6045
e-mail: bgenier@irondequoit.org
Comptroller:
Annie C Sealy 585-336-6010
e-mail: asealy@irondequoit.org
Fire Marshal:
Greg Merrick 585-336-6097
e-mail: firemarshal@irondequoit.org
Town Historian:
Patricia Wayne 585-336-7269
e-mail: pwayne@irondequoit.org

Islip, Town of

Town Hall
655 Main St
Islip, NY 11751
631-224-5500 or 631-224-5691 Fax: 631-581-8424
Web site: www.townofislip-ny.gov

Town Supervisor:
Tom Croci 631-224-5500
e-mail: supervisorsoffice@townofislip-ny.gov
Town Clerk:
Olga H. Murray 631-224-5490/fax: 631-224-5574
e-mail: townclerk@townofislip-ny.gov
Town Attorney:
Robert L. Cicale 631-224-5550/fax: 631-224-5573
e-mail: townattorney@townofislip-ny.gov
Comptroller:
Joseph Ludwig 631-595-3840/fax: 631-224-5701
e-mail: comptroller@townofislip-ny.gov
Receiver of Taxes:
Alexis Weik 631-224-5580
e-mail: vallen@townofislip-ny.gov
Commissioner, Public Works:
Thomas Owens 631-224-5600
e-mail: commissioner-dpw@townofislip-ny.gov
Harbor Police Chief:
Robert Sgroi 631-224-5656
e-mail: harborpolice@townofislip-ny.gov

Ithaca, City of

City Hall
108 E Green St
Ithaca, NY 14850
607-274-6570 Fax: 307-274-6432
Web site: www.cityofithaca.org

Mayor:
Svante Myrick 607-274-6501/fax: 607-274-6526
e-mail: asherman@cityofithaca.org
City Clerk:
Julie Conley Holcomb 607-274-6570/fax: 607-274-6432
e-mail: julieh@cityofithaca.org
City Chamberlain:
Debra Parsons 607-274-6580/fax: 607-272-7348
e-mail: debrap@cityofithaca.org
City Attorney:
Aaron O. Lavine 607-274-6504/fax: 607-274-6507
e-mail: attorney@cityofithaca.org
Controller:
Steven P Thayer 607-274-6576/fax: 607-274-6415
e-mail: dredsicker@cityofithaca.org
Police Chief (Acting):
John R. Barber 607-272-9973
e-mail: edv@cityofithaca.org

Ithaca, Town of

Town Hall
215 North Tioga Street
Ithaca, NY 14850
607-273-1721
Web site: www.town.ithaca.ny.us

Town Supervisor:
Herb Engman 607-273-1721 x125
e-mail: Hengman@town.ithaca.ny.us
Town Clerk:
Paulette Terwilliger 607-273-1721 x110
e-mail: pterwilliger@town.ithaca.ny.us
Town Budget Officer:
Al Carvill 607-273-1721 x113
e-mail: acarvill@town.ithaca.ny.us
Town Historian:
Laura Johnson-Kelly
e-mail: lwjl@town.ithaca.ny.us

Jamestown, City of
Municipal Bldg
200 E Third St
Jamestown, NY 14701
716-483-7612 Fax: 716-483-7502
Web site: www.jamestownny.net

Mayor:
Samuel Teresi 716-483-7600/fax: 716-483-7591
City Clerk:
James Olson. 716-483-7612/fax: 716-483-7502
Corporation Counsel:
Marilyn Fiore-Lehman 716-483-7540/fax: 716-483-7591
Comptroller:
Joseph A Bellitto 716-483-7538/fax: 716-483-7771
Director Financial Services:
James Olson. 716-483-7512/fax: 716-483-7502
Police Chief/Director Public Safety:
Harry Snellings 716-483-7536/fax: 716-483-7722

Kingston, City of
420 Broadway
Kingston, NY 12401
845-331-0080 Fax: 845-334-3904
Web site: www.ci.kingston.ny.us

Mayor:
Shayne R Gallo 845-334-3902/fax: 845-334-3904
e-mail: mayor@kingston-ny.gov
City Clerk:
Carly Williams. 845-334-3915/fax: 845-334-3918
e-mail: cwilliams@kingston-ny.gov
Corporation Counsel:
Andrew Zweben 845-334-3947/fax: 845-334-3959
e-mail: corpcounsel@kingston-ny.gov
Comptroller:
John Tucy 845-334-3935/fax: 845-334-3944
e-mail: comptroller@kingston-ny.gov
Executive Director, Community Development:
Michael Murphy 845-334-3924/fax: 845-334-3932
e-mail: mmurphy@kingston-ny.gov
Chief of Police/Commissioner:
Egidio F. Tinti . . . . . 845-331-1671 or 845-943-5720
e-mail: gkeller@kingston-ny.gov
Fire Chief:
John Reinhardt. 845-331-1326/fax: 845-331-3252
e-mail: fire@kingston-ny.gov

Lancaster, Town of
21 Central Ave
Lancaster, NY 14086
716-683-1610 Fax: 716-683-0512
e-mail: lookatus@lancasterny.com
Web site: www.erie.gov/lancaster/depts

Town Supervisor:
Dino J Fudoli 716-683-1610/fax: 716-683-0512
Town Clerk:
Johanna M Coleman 716-683-9028/fax: 716-683-2094
e-mail: jcoleman@lancaster.ny.com
Town Attorney:
John M Dudziak 716-684-3342/fax: 716-681-7475
e-mail: jdudziak@lancasterny.com
Director, Administration & Finance:
David J Brown 716-683-1610
Police Chief:
Gerald Gill Jr 716-683-2800/fax: 716-681-2352
Emergency Management/Nat'l Disaster Coordinator:
Robert MacPeek 716-684-1232/fax: 716-684-1237
Town Assessor:
Christine Fusco. 716-683-1311 x112/fax: 716-681-7054
e-mail: assessor@lancasterny.com
Historian:
Edward Mikula 716-683-6529

LeRay, Town of
8650 LeRay Street
Evans Mill, NY 13637-3191
315-629-4052 Fax: 315-629-4393
Web site: www.townofleray.org

Town Supervisor:
Ronald C Taylor 315-629-5532/fax: 315-629-4393
e-mail: lerayadmin@nnymail.com
Town Clerk/Receiver/Registrar:
Mary C Smith 315-629-4052/fax: 315-629-4393
e-mail: lerayclerk@nnymail.com

Lindenhurst, Village of
430 S Wellwood Ave
Lindenhurst, NY 11757
631-957-7500 Fax: 631-957-4605
e-mail: info@villageoflindenhurst.com
Web site: www.villageoflindenhurst.com

Village Mayor:
Thomas A Brennan 631-957-7500
Deputy Mayor:
Kevin McCaffey 631-957-7500
Clerk/Treasurer:
Shawn Cullinane
Deputy Clerk:
Doug M Madlon
Fire Marshall:
Richard Lyman 631-957-7514

Lockport, City of
Lockport Municipal Building
One Locks Plaza
Lockport, NY 14094
716-439-6665 Fax: 716-439-6668
Web site: www.elockport.com

Mayor:
Michael W Tucker. 716-439-6665/fax: 716-439-6668
City Clerk:
Richelle J. Pasceri 716-439-6676/fax: 716-439-6650
Treasurer:
Michael White. 716-439-6744/fax: 716-439-6617
Police Chief:
Lawrence Eggert. 716-439-6689
Fire Department Chief:
Thomas J Passuite. 716-439-6724

Lockport, Town of
6560 Dysinger Rd
Lockport, NY 14094
716-439-9520 Fax: 716-439-0528
Web site: www.elockport.com

Town Supervisor:
Marc Smith 716-439-9520/fax: 716-439-0528
Town Clerk:
Nancy Brooks 716-439-9524/fax: 716-438-5465
Town Historian:
Laurence Haseley 716-438-2159

State & Local Government Public Information

Offices and agencies generally appear in alphabetical order, except when specific order is requested by listee.

Long Beach, City of
City Hall
1 West Chester St
Long Beach, NY 11561
516-431-1000 Fax: 516-431-1389
e-mail: info@longbeachny.org
Web site: www.longbeachny.org

City Manager:
Jack Schnirman 516-431-1001
e-mail: citymanager@longbeach.ny.org
City Clerk:
David W Fraser 516-431-1002/fax: 516-431-2717
Corporation Counsel:
Corey Klein 516-431-1003
Comptroller:
Jeff Nogid 516-431-1004
Police Commissioner:
Michael Tangney 516-431-1800
e-mail: lbpd@longbeachny.org

Lysander, Town of
Town Hall
8220 Loop Rd
Baldwinsville, NY 13027
315-638-4264 Fax: 315-635-1515
Web site: www.townoflysander.org

Town Supervisor:
John A Salisbury 315-857-0281/fax: 315-635-1515
e-mail: supervisor@townoflysander.org
Town Clerk:
Lisa Dell 315-638-0224/fax: 315-635-1515
e-mail: townclerk@townoflysander.org
Comptroller:
David J Rahrle 315-635-1443/fax: 315-635-1515
e-mail: comptroller@townoflysander.org
Town Historian:
Bonnie Kisselstein 315-638-0224/fax: 315-635-1515
e-mail: bkissels@twcny.rr.com

Mamaroneck, Town of
Town Center
740 W Boston Post Rd
Mamaroneck, NY 10543
914-381-7805 Fax: 914-381-7809
e-mail: townclerk@townofmamaroneck.org
Web site: www.townofmamaroneck.org

Town Supervisor:
Nancy Seligson
e-mail: supervisor@townofmamaroneck.org
Town Administrator:
Stephen Altieri 914-381-7810/fax: 914-381-7809
e-mail: townadministrator@townofmamaroneck.org
Town Clerk:
Christina Battalia 914-381-7870/fax: 914-381-7813
e-mail: townclerk@townofmamaroneck.org
Police Chief:
Richard Rivera 914-381-6100/fax: 914-381-7897
e-mail: policechief@townofmamaroneck.org
Emergency Management Coordinator:
Michael Liverzani 914-381-7838

Manlius, Town of
301 Brooklea Dr
Fayetteville, NY 13066
315-637-3521 Fax: 315-637-0713
Web site: www.townofmanlius.org

Town Supervisor:
Edmond J Theobald 315-637-3414/fax: 315-637-0713
e-mail: etheobald@townofmanlius.org
Town Clerk:
Allison A Edsall 315-637-3521/fax: 315-637-0713
Receiver of Taxes:
Laura Peschel 315-637-6481/fax: 315-637-0713
Police Chief:
Francis Marlowe 315-682-2212/fax: 315-682-4527

Middletown, City of
City Hall
16 James St
Middletown, NY 10940
845-346-4100 Fax: 845-343-7439
Web site: www.middletown-ny.com

Mayor:
Joseph M DeStefano 845-346-4100/fax: 845-343-7439
e-mail: mayor@middletown-ny.com
Common Council President:
J Miguel Rodrigues 845-742-8775
e-mail: mrodrigues@middletown-ny.com
Common Council Clerk/Registrar:
John Naumchik 845-346-4168/fax: 845-344-5428
City Attorney:
Alex Smith 845-346-4140/fax: 845-346-4146
Treasurer:
Donald Paris 845-346-4150/fax: 845-343-1101
Commissioner, Public Works:
Jacob Tawil 845-343-3169/fax: 845-343-4014
Chief of Police:
Ramon Bethencourt 845-343-3151/fax: 845-343-2660
e-mail: rbethencourt@middletown-ny.com
Fire Chief:
Tom Amodio 845-344-5003/fax: 845-344-5031
e-mail: info@middletownfiredept.com

Monroe, Town of
11 Stage Road
Monroe, NY 10950
845-783-1900 Fax: 845-782-5597
Web site: www.monroeny.org

Town Supervisor:
Sandy Leonard 845-783-1900 x227/fax: 845-782-5597
e-mail: cathy@monroeny.org
Town Clerk:
Mary Ellen Beams 845-783-1900 x221/fax: 845-782-5597
e-mail: maryellen@monroeny.org
Tax Collector:
Mary Ellen Beams 845-783-1990 x221/fax: 845-782-5597
Historian:
James Nelson 845-783-3406
e-mail: nelsonja@fastmail.fm

Montgomery, Town of
110 Bracken Rd
Montgomery, NY 12549
845-457-2660 Fax: 845-457-2613
Web site: www.townofmontgomery.com

Town Supervisor:
Michael Hayes 845-457-2600
Town Clerk:
Tara Stickles 845-457-2660/fax: 845-457-2613

Town Attorney:
Charles T Bazydlo 845-361-3668
Receiver of Taxes:
Janice A Cocks 845-457-2630/fax: 845-457-2613
e-mail: tomtax@frontiernet.net
Police Chief:
Arnold Amthor 845-457-9211
e-mail: TMPDChief@frontiernet.net
Town Historian:
Suzanne Isaksen 845-457-9098
e-mail: tomhistorian@frontiernet.net

Mount Pleasant, Town of

One Town Hall Plaza
Valhalla, NY 10595
914-742-2360 Fax: 914-769-3155
Web site: www.mtpleasantny.com

Town Supervisor:
Joan A Maybury 914-742-2301/fax: 914-769-3155
e-mail: jmaybury@mtpleasantny.com
Town Clerk:
Patricia June Scova 914-742-2312/fax: 914-747-6172
e-mail: pscova@mtpleasantny.com
Deputy Town Attorney:
Christopher W. McClure 914-742-2357/fax: 914-769-3155
Comptroller:
Tina Peretti 914-742-2360
Police Chief:
Louis Alagno 914-769-1941/fax: 914-769-7199
e-mail: lalagno@mtpleasantny.com

Mount Vernon, City of

City Hall
1 Roosevelt Square
Mount Vernon, NY 10550
914-665-2300 Fax: 914-665-2496
Web site: cmvny.com

Mayor:
Ernest D. Davis 914-665-2360
e-mail: mayor@cmvny.com
City Clerk/Registrar:
George Brown 914-665-2348
Comptroller:
Maureen Walker 914-665-2312
Police Commissioner:
John Roland 914-665-2500
Police Chief:
James Dumser 914-665-2500
Fire Chief:
Edward Stephenson 914-665-2626
Deputy Public Works Commissioner:
Curtis J Woods 914-665-2334

New Hartford, Town of

Butler Hall
48 Genesee Street
New Hartford, NY 13413
315-733-7500
Web site: www.newhartfordtown.com

Town Supervisor:
Patrick M Tyksinski 315-733-7500 x2332
e-mail: nhsupervisor@town.new-hartford.ny.us
Town Clerk:
Gail Wolanin Young 315-733-7500 x2322/fax: 315-797-9986
e-mail: gyoung@town.new-hartford.ny.us
Receiver of Taxes:
Gail Wolanin Young 315-733-7500 x2324/fax: 315-797-9986
e-mail: hilarie@town.new-hartford.ny.us
Police Chief:
Michael Inserra 315-724-7111/fax: 315-724-8618
e-mail: mis108@town.new-hartford.ny.us

New Rochelle, City of

City Hall
515 North Ave
New Rochelle, NY 10801
914-654-2000 Fax: 914-654-2174
Web site: www.newrochelleny.com

Mayor:
Noam Bramson 914-654-2150/fax: 914-654-2357
e-mail: nbramson@newrochelleny.com
City Manager:
Charles B Strome III 914-654-2140/fax: 914-654-2174
e-mail: cstrome@newrochelleny.com
City Clerk:
Bennie F Giles 914-654-2159/fax: 914-654-2158
e-mail: bgiles@newrochellenewyork.com
Corporation Counsel:
Kathleen Gill 914-654-2120/fax: 914-654-2345
Finance Commissioner:
Howard Rattner 914-654-2062/fax: 914-654-2344
Public Works Commissioner:
Alexander Tergis 914-654-2129/fax: 914-654-2195
e-mail: atergis@newrochelleny.com
Police Commissioner:
Patrick J Carroll 914-654-2228
Fire Chief:
Louis DeMeglio 914-654-2212/fax: 914-632-2907
e-mail: rkiernan@newrochelleny.com

New Windsor, Town of

555 Union Avenue
New Windsor, NY 12553
845-565-8800 Fax: 845-563-4693
e-mail: info@town.new-windsor.ny.us
Web site: http://town.new-windsor.ny.us

Town Supervisor/Chief Fiscal Officer:
George A Green 845-563-4610/fax: 845-563-4610
Town Clerk:
Deborah Green 845-563-4611/fax: 845-563-4611
e-mail: dgreen@town.new-windsor.ny.us
Town Attorney:
Michael Blythe 845-563-4630/fax: 845-563-4630
e-mail: mblythe@town.new-windsor.ny.us
Comptroller:
Jack Finnegan 845-563-4623/fax: 845-563-4623
Police Chief:
Michael C Biasotti 845-565-7000/fax: 845-563-4694
e-mail: pdadmin@town.new-windsor.ny.us
Fire Inspector & Department Head:
Jennifer Gallagher 845-563-4618/fax: 845-563-4618
Town Historian:
Glenn Marshall
e-mail: historynw@aol.com

New York City

City Hall
New York, NY 10007
212-788-3000 Fax: 212-788-3247
Web site: www.nyc.gov

State & Local Government Public Information

Mayor:
Michael R Bloomberg . . . . 212-788-3000 or 212-639-9675
fax: 212-312-0700
First Deputy Mayor:
Patricia E Harris 212-788-3000/fax: 212-312-0700
Deputy Mayor, Economic Development:
Robert K. Steel 212-788-3000/fax: 212-312-0700
Deputy Mayor, Government Affairs:
Howard Wolfson 212-788-3000/fax: 212-312-0700
Deputy Mayor, Legal Affairs:
Carol A Robles-Roman 212-788-3000/fax: 212-312-0700
Deputy Mayor, Operations:
Cas Holloway 212-788-3000/fax: 212-312-0700
Deputy Mayor, Education & Community Development:
Dennis M Walcott 212-788-3000/fax: 212-312-0700
Director, Communications:
James Anderson 212-788-3000
Senior Advisor to Mayor:
Shea Fink 212-788-3000/fax: 212-312-0700
Press Secretary:
Stu Loeser 212-788-3000/fax: 212-788-2460

Aging, Dept for the, NYC . . . . fax: 212-442-1095
2 Lafayette St, New York, NY 10007
212-442-1322 Fax: 212-442-1095
Web site: www.nyc.gov/aging
Commissioner:
Lilliam Barrios-Paoli
e-mail: emendez@aging.nyc.gov
First Deputy Commissioner:
Sally Renfro
e-mail: srenfro@aging.nyc.gov
General Counsel:
Steven Foo 212-442-3159
e-mail: mamurphy@aging.nyc.gov
Deputy Commissioner, External Affairs:
Caryn Resnick 212-442-1277
e-mail: cresnick@aging.nyc.gov
Executive Director, Aging in NY Fund:
Ali Hodin-Baier 212-442-1375
Director, Public Affairs:
Christopher Miller
e-mail: cmiller@aging.nyc.gov

Public Design Commission, NYC . . . . fax: 212-788-3086
City Hall, 3rd Fl, New York, NY 10007
212-788-3071 Fax: 212-788-3086
Web site: www.nyc.gov/artcommission
Executive Director:
Jackie Snyder. 212-788-3071/fax: 212-788-3086
e-mail: jsnyder@cityhall.nyc.gov
President:
Signe Nielsen. 212-788-3071/fax: 212-788-3086
Project Manager:
Rivka Weinstock 212-788-3071/fax: 212-788-3086
Special Projects Manager:
Julianna Monjeau 212-788-3071/fax: 212-788-3086
Sculptor:
Maria Elena-Gonzalez. 212-788-3071/fax: 212-788-3086
Painter:
Byron Kim. 212-788-3071/fax: 212-788-3086
Architect:
James Stewart Polshek 212-788-3071/fax: 212-788-3086
Director, Tour Programs:
Joan H Bright. 212-788-3071/fax: 212-788-3086

Buildings, Department of, NYC. . . . . fax: 212-566-3784
280 Broadway, 7th Fl, New York, NY 10007-1801
212-566-5000 or TTY: 212-566-4769 Fax: 212-566-3784
Web site: www.nyc.gov/buildings
Commissioner:
Robert D LiMandri 212-566-0011
First Deputy Cmsr, Operations:
Thomas Fariello, R.A.
Deputy Commissioner, Technology & Analysis:
Marilyn King-Festa 212-566-4225/fax: 212-566-3865
Deputy Commissioner, Technical Affairs:
Fatma Amer
General Counsel:
Mona Sehgal 212-566-3291/fax: 212-566-3843

Campaign Finance Board, NYC . . . . fax: 212-306-7143
40 Rector St, 7th Fl, New York, NY 10006
212-306-7100 Fax: 212-306-7143
e-mail: info@nyccfb.info
Web site: www.nyccfb.info
Chair:
Joseph P Parkes
Executive Director:
Amy M Loprest
Chief of Administrative Services:
Elizabeth Bauer
Director of External Affairs:
Eric Friedman

City Council, NYC. . . . . fax: 212-788-7093
250 Broadway, 18th Fl, New York, NY 10007
212-788-7084 Fax: 212-788-7093
Web site: council.nyc.gov
Speaker:
Christine C Quinn 212-788-7210
Minority Leader:
James S Oddo 718-980-1017/fax: 718-980-1051
e-mail: joddo@council.nyc.gov
Deputy Majority Leader:
Leroy G Comrie. 718-766-3700/fax: 718-766-3798

City Planning, Department of, NYC . . . . fax: 212-720-3219
22 Reade St, New York, NY 10007-1216
212-720-3300 Fax: 212-720-3219
Web site: www.nyc.gov
Chair:
Amanda M Burden
Executive Director:
Richard Barth
Director, Operations:
David J Zagor 212-720-3650
Director, Public Affairs:
Rachaele Raynoff 212-720-3471
General Counsel:
David Karnovsky 212-720-3400

Citywide Administrative Services, Department of, NYC . . . . . fax: 212-669-8992
One Centre St, 17th Fl S, New York, NY 10007
212-669-7000 Fax: 212-669-8992
Web site: www.nyc.gov/dcas
Commissioner:
Edna Wells Handy
Chief Communication Officer:
Julianne Cho 212-669-7140

Civil Service Commission, NYC
1 Centre Street, 2300 N, New York, NY 10007
212-669-2609
e-mail: commission@nyc.csc.nyc.gov
Web site: www.nyc.gov/html/csc
Chairwoman:
Nancy G. Chaffetz
Acting Director & General Counsel:
Norma I Lopez 212-669-2609

Offices and agencies generally appear in alphabetical order, except when specific order is requested by listee.

Office Manager:
Evelyn Horowitz 212-669-2608

Collective Bargaining, Office of, NYC . . . . . fax: 212-306-7167
40 Rector St, 7th Fl, New York, NY 10006
212-306-7160 Fax: 212-306-7167
e-mail: nyc-ocb@ocb.nyc.gov
Web site: www.ocb-nyc.org
Director:
Marlene A Gold
Deputy Chair, Dispute Resolution:
Susan Panepento
General Counsel:
Philip Maier

Comptroller, NYC . . . . . fax: 212-669-2707
Municipal Bldg, One Centre St, Rm 530, New York, NY 10007
212-669-3500 Fax: 212-669-2707
Web site: www.comptroller.nyc.gov
Comptroller:
John C Liu
First Deputy Comptroller:
Ricardo E. Morales
Deputy Comptroller/General Counsel:
Valerie Budzik
Deputy Comptroller, Public Finance:
Carol Kostik
Deputy Comptroller, Budget and Public Affairs:
Ari Hoffnung

Conflicts of Interest Board, NYC . . . . . fax: 212-442-1407
2 Lafayette St, Ste 1010, New York, NY 10007
212-442-1400 Fax: 212-442-1407
Web site: www.nyc.gov/ethics
Executive Director:
Mark Davies 212-442-1424
e-mail: davies@coib.nyc.gov
Deputy Exec Director/General Counsel:
Wayne G Hawley 212-442-1415
e-mail: hawley@coib.nyc.gov
Director, Enforcement:
Carolyn Lisa Miller 212-442-1419
e-mail: miller@coib.nyc.gov
Director, Administration:
Ute O'Malley 212-442-1427
e-mail: omalley@coib.nyc.gov
Director, Information Technology:
Derick Yu 212-442-1605
e-mail: yu@coib.nyc.gov
Director, Training/Education Unit:
Alexander Kipp 212-442-1421
e-mail: kipp@coib.nyc.gov
Director, Financial Disclosure/Special Counsel:
Felicia A. Mennin 212-442-1455
e-mail: mennin@coib.nyc.gov

Consumer Affairs, Department of, NYC . . . . . fax: 212-487-4221
42 Broadway, New York, NY 10004
212-487-4401 Fax: 212-487-4221
Web site: www.nyc.gov/html/dca
Commissioner:
Jonathan Mintz
Deputy Director, Communications:
Vacant 212-487-4283

Correction, Board of, NYC . . . . . fax: 212-788-7860
51 Chambers St, Room 923, New York, NY 10007
212-788-7840 Fax: 212-788-7860
Web site: www.nyc.gov/boc
Chair:
Gerald Harris
e-mail: nycboc@earthlink.net
Executive Director:
Cathy Porter
Director, Field Operations:
Felix Martinez

Correction, Department of, NYC . . . . . fax: 646-248-1219
60 Hudson St, 6th Fl, New York, NY 10013-4393
212-266-1500 Fax: 646-248-1219
Web site: www.nyc.gov/doc
Commissioner:
Dora B Schriro
Senior Dep Commissioner:
John J Antonelli

Cultural Affairs, Department of, NYC
31 Chambers St, New York, NY 10007
212-513-9300
Web site: www.nyc.gov/html/dcla
Commissioner:
Kate D Levin
Deputy Commissioner:
Margaret Morton
Chief of Staff:
Shirley Levy

Design & Construction, Dept of, NYC . . . . . fax: 718-391-1608
30-30 Thomson Avenue, Long Island City, NY 11101
718-391-1000 Fax: 718-391-1608
Web site: www.nyc.gov/html/ddc
Commissioner:
David J Burney 718-391-1000
Chief of Staff:
Ana Barrio 718-391-2300/fax: 718-391-1893
Public Information:
Joe Soldevere 718-391-1641/fax: 718-391-2600
Chief Contracting Officer:
Carol DiAgostino 718-391-1501/fax: 718-391-2600
General Counsel:
David Varoli 718-391-1721/fax: 718-391-2600

Disabilities, Mayor's Office, for People with . . . . . fax: 212-341-9843
100 Gold Street, 2nd Floor, New York, NY 10038
212-788-2830 or TTY 212-504-4115 Fax: 212-341-9843
Web site: www.nyc.gov/html/mopd
Commissioner:
Matthew P Sapolin 212-788-2830

Economic Development Corp, NYC
110 William Street, New York, NY 10038
212-619-5000 or 888-692-0100
Web site: www.nycedc.com
President:
Seth W Pinsky 212-312-3500
Senior VP, Budget:
Tom Jones 212-312-3877

Education, Dept of, NYC . . . . . fax: 212-374-5588
52 Chambers St, New York, NY 10007
718-935-2000 Fax: 212-374-5588
Web site: www.nycenet.edu
Chancellor:
Dennis M Walcott
Deputy Chancellor, Finance/Admin:
Photeine Anagnostopoulos
Deputy Chancellor, Teaching/Learning:
Eric Nadelstern
Director, Strategic Partnerships:
Stephanie Dua
General Counsel & Legal Services Office:
Courtenaye Jackson-Chase
Executive Director, Intergovernmental Affairs:
Lenny Speiller

Offices and agencies generally appear in alphabetical order, except when specific order is requested by listee.

State & Local Government Public Information

Communications & Media Relations:
David Cantor

Elections, Board of, NYC .... fax: 212-487-5349
32 Broadway, 7th Fl, New York, NY 10004-1609
212-487-5300 or TDD 212-487-5496 Fax: 212-487-5349
Web site: www.vote.nyc.ny.us
President, Commissioners:
Frederic M. Umane
e-mail: fumane@boe.nyc.ny.us
Executive Director:
Vacant
e-mail: webmail_ravitzj@boe.nyc.ny.us
Deputy Executive Director:
Dawn Sandow
e-mail: webmail_sandow@boe.nyc.ny.us
Administrative Manager:
Pamela Perkins
e-mail: webmail_perkinsp@boe.nyc.ny.us
Director, Public Affairs & Communications:
Valerie Vazquez
e-mail: webmail_vazquezv@boe.nyc.ny.us

Environmental Protection, Department of, NYC
59-17 Junction Blvd, 13th Fl, Flushing, NY 11373-5108
212-639-6975
Web site: www.nyc.gov/dep
Commissioner:
Carter Strickland 718-595-6565
e-mail: cward@dep.nyc.gov
First Dep Commissioner/Exec Dir Water Board:
Steven Lawitts 718-595-6576
Chief of Staff:
Kathryn Garcia
General Counsel:
Mark D Hoffer 718-595-6528
Director, Public & Intergovernmental Affairs:
Charles G Sturcken 718-595-6568

Equal Employment Practices Commission, NYC fax: 212-615-8931
253 Broadway, Suite 602, New York, NY 10007
212-615-8939 Fax: 212-615-8931
Web site: www1.nyc.gov/site/eepc/index.page
Executive Director:
Charise L. Terry 212-615-8933/fax: 212-615-8931
e-mail: cterry@eepc.nyc.gov
Deputy Director/Agency Counsel:
Judith Garcia Quinonez 212-615-8940
e-mail: jquinonez@eepc.nyc.gov
Agency Attorney/Director, Compliance:
Marie E Giraud 212-615-8942
e-mail: mgiraud@eepc.nyc.gov

Film, Theatre & Broadcasting, Mayor's Office of, NYC ..... fax: 212-307-6237
Ed Sullivan Theatre Bldg, 1697 Broadway, Ste 602, New York, NY 10019
212-489-6710 Fax: 212-307-6237
e-mail: info@film.nyc.gov
Web site: www.nyc.gov/film
Commissioner:
Katherine Oliver
Deputy Commissioner:
John Battista 212-489-6710
Director, Production:
Dean McCann 212-489-6710

Finance, Department of, NYC
One Centre Street, 22nd Floor, New York, NY 10007
212-639-9675
e-mail: starkm@finance.nyc.gov
Web site: www.nyc.gov/finance
Commissioner:
David M Frankel
First Deputy Commissioner:
Rochelle Patricof 212-669-2525
Assistant Commissioner, Communications/Government Affairs:
Sam Miller
Budget Director:
Pat Mattera-Russell
Treasury Deputy Commissioner:
Robert Lee

Fire Department, NYC .... fax: 718-999-2582
9 Metrotech Center, 8th Fl, Brooklyn, NY 11201
718-999-2000 Fax: 718-999-2582
Web site: www.nyc.gov/fdny
Commissioner:
Salvatore J Cassano
First Deputy Commissioner:
Daniel Shacknai
Chief of NYC Fire Department:
Edward Kilduff
Deputy Commissioner, Administration:
Douglas White
Deputy Commissioner, Technology & Support Services:
Joel Golub
Deputy Commissioner, Intergovernmental Affairs:
Daniel Shacknai 718-999-2013
Deputy Commissioner, Legal:
Mylan Denerstein 718-999-2016
Deputy Commissioner, Public Information:
Francis X Gribbon
Chief of Operations:
James Esposito

Health & Hospitals Corporation, NYC .... fax: 212-788-0040
125 Worth St, New York, NY 10013
212-788-3321 Fax: 212-788-0040
Web site: www.nyc.gov/hhc
Presdient/CEO:
Alan D Aviles
Senior VP, Corporate Planning/Community Health/Intergvt Relations:
LaRay Brown
Senior VP, Operations:
Frank J Cirillo
Senior VP/Chief Medical Officer, Medical & Professional Affairs:
Ross Wilson 212-788-3648
Senior VP, Finance/Capital/CFO:
Marlene Zurack 212-788-3494
General Counsel (Senior VP General Counsel):
Salvatore J Russo
Senior VP Corporate Communications & Marketing:
Ana Marengo

Health & Mental Hygiene, Dept of, NYC .... fax: 212-964-0472
125 Worth St, New York, NY 10013
212-788-5290 or 212-825-5400 Fax: 212-964-0472
Web site: www.nyc.gov/html/doh
Commissioner:
Thomas Farley 212-219-5261
Executive Deputy Commissioner, Mental Hygiene:
Adam Karpati
Chief of Staff:
Emiko Otsubo
Deputy Commissioner, Administration:
Julie Friesen
Deputy Commissioner, Disease Control:
Jay Varma
Deputy Commissioner, Health Care Access/Improvement:
Amanda Parsons
Deputy Commissioner, Epidemiology:
Carolyn Greene

Offices and agencies generally appear in alphabetical order, except when specific order is requested by listee.

Deputy Commissioner, Environmental Health:
Daniel Kass
Deputy Commissioner, Health Promotion/Disease Prevention:
Andrew Goodman
General Counsel:
Thomas Merrill 212-788-5290

Homeless Services, Department of, NYC . . . . fax: 212-361-7950
33 Beaver St, 17th Fl, New York, NY 10004
212-361-8000 Fax: 212-361-7950
Web site: www.nyc.gov/dhs
Commissioner:
Seth Diamond
EEO Officer:
Mark Neal
Deputy Commissioner, Communications/External Affairs:
Barbara Brancaccio
General Counsel:
Michele Ovesey
Deputy Commissioner, Prevention, Policy & Planning:
Ellen Howard-Cooper
Deputy Commissioner, Adult Services:
Douglas C. James
Executive Deputy Commissioner, Family Services:
Anne Heller
Deputy Commissioner, Facility Maint/Development:
Yianna Pavlakos

Housing Authority, NYC . . . . fax: 212-306-8888
250 Broadway, New York, NY 10007
212-306-3000 Fax: 212-306-8888
Web site: www.nyc.gov/nycha
Chairman:
John B Rhea
General Manager:
Cecil House
Acting Executive Vice President, Legal Affairs & General Counsel:
K. MacNeal
Chief of Staff:
H. Morillo
Chief Information Officer & Executive Vice President:
A. Riazi
Deputy General Mgr, Finance:
Felix Lam
Executive Vice President, Operations:
C. Laboy-Diaz
Executive Vice President & Chief, Administration:
N. Rivers
Executive Vice President, Community Programs:
S. Myrie

Housing Preservation & Development, Dept of, NYC . . . . fax: 212-863-6302
100 Gold St, 5th Fl, New York, NY 10038
212-863-6300 Fax: 212-863-6302
Web site: www.nyc.gov/hpd
Commissioner:
Mathew M Wambua
Firsy Deputy Commissioner:
Douglas Apple
Deputy Commissioner/Legal Affairs:
Matthew Shafit
Senior Counsel, State & Legislative Affairs:
Joseph Rosenberg
Assistant Commissioner, Housing Supervision:
J. Walpert
Assistant Commissioner, Preservation Services:
E. Enderlin 212-863-7001
Assistant Commissioner, Administration:
J. Cucchiaro

Deputy Commissioner, Community Partnerships:
Kimberly D Hardy 212-863-5128/fax: 212-863-8907

Human Resources Administration, Dept of, NYC fax: 212-331-8042
150 Greenwich St., 42nd Fl, New York, NY 10007
929-221-7315 Fax: 212-331-8042
e-mail: banksst@hra.nyc.gov
Web site: www.nyc.gov/html/hra
Commissioner:
Robert Doar. 212-331-6000
e-mail: egglestonv@hra.nyc.gov
First Deputy Commissioner:
Patricia M Smith 212-331-6230
Senior Exec Dep Commissioner:
Thomas DePippo. 212-331-6000
Exec Dep Commissioner, Medical Insur/Community Svcs Administration:
Mary Harper 212-273-0001
Executive Deputy Commissioner, Finance Office:
Jill Berry 212-331-3980
Agency Chief Contracting Officer:
Vincent Pullo 212-331-3434
Executive Deputy Commissioner, Family Independence Administration:
Matt Brune 212-331-6180
Deputy Commissioner, Data Reporting & Analysis:
Joe DeMartino. 212-331-6000
Executive Deputy Commissioner, Staff Resources:
Rachel Levine 212-331-3333
Executive Deputy Commissioner, Customized Assistance Services:
Frank R Lipton 212-495-2606
Deputy Commissioner, General Support Services:
Joseph Santino 212-274-5200
Deputy Commissioner, Constituency Services & Policy Improvement:
Jane Corbett
Executive Deputy Commissioner, Domestic Violence & Emergency Intervention Office:
Cecile Noel 212-331-4500
Chief Integrity Officer, Ingestigation, Revenue & Enforcement:
James Sheehan 212-274-4740
First Deputy General Counsel, Legal Affairs:
Maureen Walsh 212-331-6167
Chief of Staff:
Anne Heller. 212-331-6225
Deputy Commissioner, Communications & Marketing:
Connie Ress 212-331-6200

Human Rights Commission on, NYC . . . . fax: 212-306-7658
40 Rector St, 10th Fl, New York, NY 10006
212-306-5070 Fax: 212-306-7658
Web site: www.nyc.gov/cchr
Commissioner:
Patricia L Gatling 212-306-7560
Deputy Commissioner/General Counsel:
Cliff Mulqueen 212-306-7741
Executive Director, Law Enforcement:
Carlos Velez 212-306-7764
Deputy Commissioner, Public Affairs:
Dr Lee Hudson 212-306-7773
Director, Communications:
Betsy Herzog. 212-306-7530
Executive Director, Community Relations:
Alexander Korkhov 212-306-7423

Information Technology & Telecommunications, Dept of, NYC . . . . fax: 212-788-8130
75 Park Place, 9th Fl, New York, NY 10007
212-788-6600 Fax: 212-788-8130
Web site: www.nyc.gov/doitt
Commissioner:
Rahul N. Merchant 212-788-6633
EEO Officer:
Emily Johnson. 212-788-6624

Offices and agencies generally appear in alphabetical order, except when specific order is requested by listee.

Chief of Staff/Governance & External Affairs:
Evan Hines 718-403-8100
Executive Assistant, NYC 3-1-1:
Jessica Diaz 212-504-4421
General Counsel:
Charles Fraser 212-788-6640
Deputy Commissioner, Finance/Admin:
Brett Robinson 212-788-6616

Investigation, Department of, NYC . . . . fax: 212-825-2823
80 Maiden Lane, New York, NY 10038
212-825-5900 Fax: 212-825-2823
Web site: www.nyc.gov/html/doi
Commissioner:
Rose Gill Hearn 212-825-5913
e-mail: rghearn@doi.nyc.gov
Chief of Staff:
Michael Vitiello 212-825-2870
Deputy Commissioner, Investigations:
Kim Berger 212-825-5979
General Counsel:
Marjorie Landa 212-825-2404
Public Information Officer:
Diane Struzzi 212-825-3514

Juvenile Justice, Department of, NYC . . . . fax: 212-442-8546
110th William St., 14th Floor, New York, NY 10038
212-442-8000 or TTY/TDD:212-442-8578 Fax: 212-442-8546
e-mail: nycdjj@djj.nyc.gov
Web site: www.nyc.gov/html/acs
Commissioner:
Ronald E. Richter 212-442-7630
First Deputy Commissioner:
Judith Pincus 212-442-7510/fax: 212-442-8512
Deputy Commissioner, Operations & Detention:
Jerome Davis 212-442-7245/fax: 212-442-8508
Deputy Commissioner, Administration:
Donald Brosen 212-442-7840/fax: 212-442-8512
General Counsel:
Joseph Cardieri 212-442-7530/fax: 212-442-8517
Deputy Commissioner, Communications and Community Affairs:
Michael Fagan 212-442-7534/fax: 718-935-6454

Labor Relations, Office of, NYC . . . . fax: 212-306-7202
40 Rector St, 4th Fl, New York, NY 10006
212-306-7200 Fax: 212-306-7202
Web site: www.nyc.gov/html/olr
Commissioner:
James F Hanley 212-306-7200
Associate Commissioner:
Jean N Brewer
General Counsel:
Mayra Bell 212-306-7230/fax: 212-306-7223
Director, Employee Benefits Program:
Dorothy A Wolfe 212-306-7200

Landmarks Preservation Commission, NYC . . . . fax: 212-669-7960
One Centre Street, 9th Fl North, New York, NY 10007
212-669-7817 Fax: 212-669-7960
Web site: www.nyc.gov/html/lpc
Chair:
Robert B Tierney 212-669-7888
e-mail: rtierney@lpc.nyc.gov

Law, Department of, NYC . . . . fax: 212-788-0367
100 Church St, New York, NY 10007-2601
212-788-0303 Fax: 212-788-0367
Web site: www.nyc.gov/html/law
Corporation Counsel:
Michael A Cardozo 212-356-1000/fax: 212-356-1148
e-mail: mcardozo@law.nyc.gov
Managing Attorney:
G Foster Mills 212-356-2200/fax: 212-356-3585
e-mail: gmills@law.nyc.gov
Chief of Operations:
Kenneth J Majerus . . . . 212-356-4040 or 212-356-4049
e-mail: kmajerus@lawny.gov
Director, Legal Recruitment:
Stuart Smith 212-356-4070/fax: 212-227-6177
Inspector General:
Michael Siller . . . . 212-825-0646 or 212-825-2505
e-mail: cmorrick@doi.nyc.gov
Communications Director:
Kate Ahlers . . . . 212-356-4001 or 212-788-8716
fax: 212-788-8716
e-mail: kahlers@law.nyc.gov

Legislative Affairs Office, NYC Mayor's City . . . fax: 212-788-2647
253 Broadway, 14th Fl, New York, NY 10007
212-788-3678 Fax: 212-788-2647
e-mail: citylegislativeaffairs@cityhall.nyc.gov
Web site: www.nyc.gov/html/moiga
Director:
Patrick Wehle 212-788-3678/fax: 212-788-2647

Legislative Affairs Office, NYC Mayor's State . . fax: 518-462-5870
119 Washington Ave, 3rd Fl, Albany, NY 12210
518-447-5200 Fax: 518-462-5870
Director:
Joseph N. Garba 212-278-8820/fax: 212-278-1497

Library, Brooklyn Public . . . . fax: 718-398-6798
203 Arlington Avenue, Warwick St., Brooklyn, NY 11207
718-277-6105 Fax: 718-398-6798
Web site: www.bklynpubliclibrary.org
President & CEO:
Linda E Johnson 718-230-2403
Chair, BPL Foundation:
Anthony W Crowell 718-230-2158
Director, Public Affairs:
Antonia Yuille Williams 718-277-6105

Library, New York Public . . . . fax: 212-930-9299
5th Ave & 42nd St, New York, NY 10018
212-930-0800 or 212-340-0849 Fax: 212-930-9299
Web site: www.nypl.org
President & CEO:
Dr. Anthony W. Marx 212-930-0736
e-mail: president@nypl.org
Senior VP, External Affairs:
Vacant 212-930-0611
Chief Operating Officer:
David Offensend 212-930-0600
Vice President, Development:
Jennifer Zaslow 212-930-0692
e-mail: hlubov@nypl.org
Director, Budget & Planning:
Marjoel Montalbo 212-592-7400/fax: 212-592-7440
Vice President, Government & Community Affairs:
George D. Mihaltses 212-930-0051
VP, Communications & Marketing:
Ken Weine 212-592-7700

Library, Queens Borough Public . . . . fax: 718-291-8936
89-11 Merrick Blvd, Jamaica, NY 11432
718-990-0700 or TTY 718-990-0809 Fax: 718-291-8936
Web site: www.queenslibrary.org
President & CEO:
Thomas W Galante 718-990-0700
e-mail: thomas.w.galante@queenslibrary.org
Director, Government Affairs:
Jonathan Chung 718-990-0700

Offices and agencies generally appear in alphabetical order, except when specific order is requested by listee.

Director, Communications:
Joanne King 718-990-0704/fax: 718-291-2695
e-mail: joanne.king@queenslibrary.org

Loft Board, NYC . . . . fax: 212-788-7501
100 Gold St, 2nd Fl, New York, NY 10038
212-788-7610 Fax: 212-788-7501
Web site: www.nyc.gov/html/loft
Chairperson:
Robert D LiMandri 212-788-7610
Executive Director:
Lanny R Alexander 212-788-7619

Management & Budget, Office of, NYC . . . . fax: 212-788-6300
75 Park Place, 8th Fl, New York, NY 10007
212-788-5800 Fax: 212-788-6300
Web site: www.nyc.gov/omb
Director:
Mark Page 212-788-5900
First Deputy Director:
Stuart Klein 212-788-5904
Deputy Director/General Counsel:
Marjorie Henning 212-788-5880
Deputy Director:
P V Anatharam 212-788-5894
Deputy Director:
Michael Dardia 212-788-5891

Medical Examiner, Office of Chief, NYC . . . . fax: 212-447-2716
520 First Ave, New York, NY 10016
212-447-2030 Fax: 212-447-2716
Web site: www.nyc.gov/html/ocme
Acting Chief Medical Examiner:
Barbara A. Sampson 212-447-2034
First Deputy Commissioner:
Barbara Sampson 212-447-2335
Deputy Commissioner, Administration/Finance:
Janice English 212-447-5351
Director, Medicolegal Investigations:
Barbara Butcher 212-447-2036
Director, Public Affairs:
Ellen Borakove 212-447-2401/fax: 212-447-2755
General Counsel:
Jody Lipton 212-447-2046

Parks & Recreation, Department of, NYC . . . . fax: 212-360-1329
The Arsenal, Central Park, 830 Fifth Ave, New York, NY 10065
212-360-8111 Fax: 212-360-1329
e-mail: commissioner@parks.nyc.gov
Web site: www.nyc.govparks.org
Commissioner:
Veronica M. White 212-360-1305/fax: 202-360-1345
First Deputy Commissioner, Operations:
Liam Kavanagh 212-360-1307
Deputy Commissioner, Capital Projects:
Theresa Braddick 718-760-6602
Assistant Commissioner, Public Programs:
Annika Holder 212-360-1381
Deputy Commissioner, Management/Budget:
Robert L Garafola 212-360-1302
Director, Public Affairs:
Vicki Karp 212-360-1311

Police Department, NYC . . . . fax: 646-610-5865
One Police Plaza, New York, NY 10038
646-610-5000 Fax: 646-610-5865
Web site: www.nyc.gov/nypd
Police Commissioner:
Raymond W Kelly 646-610-5410
First Dep Commissioner:
Rafael Pineiro 646-610-5420
Deputy Commissioner, Strategic Initiatives:
Michael J Farrell 646-610-8534
Deputy Commissioner, Counter Terrorism:
Richard A Daddario 646-610-6169
Deputy Commissioner, Intelligence:
David Cohen 646-610-5403
Deputy Commissioner, Equal Employment Opportunity:
Neldra M Zeigler 646-610-5330
Deputy Commissioner, Labor Relations:
John P Beirne 646-610-5060
Deputy Commissioner, Trials:
Martin G Karopkin 646-610-5424
Deputy Commissioner, Training:
Dr. James O'Keefe 646-610-4675
Deputy Commissioner, Legal Matters:
Douglas B. Maynard 646-610-5336
Deputy Commissioner, Management & Budget:
Vincent Grippo 646-610-6670
Deputy Commissioner, Operations:
John Bilich 646-610-6100
Deputy Commissioner, Technological Development:
V James Onalfo 646-610-6873
Deputy Commissioner, Public Information:
Paul J Browne 646-610-6700

Probation, Department of, NYC . . . . fax: 212-361-0686
33 Beaver St, New York, NY 10004
212-361-8973 Fax: 212-361-0686
Web site: www.nyc.gov/html/prob
Commissioner:
Vincent N Schriraldi 212-361-8977/fax: 212-361-8985
e-mail: mhorn@probation.nyc.gov
Senior Policy Advisor to the Commissioner:
Mark Ferrante 212-361-8970
e-mail: mferrante@probation.nyc.gov
Director, Press & Public Information:
Ryan Dodge 212-232-0684
e-mail: rdodge@probation.nyc.gov
Chief of Staff:
Michael Ognibene 212-361-8973
General Counsel:
Wayne McKenzie 212-232-0700
Deputy Commissioner, Administration:
Michael Forte 212-361-8965
Deputy Commissioner, Family Court Services:
Patricia Brennan 212-232-0486
Deputy Commssioner, Adult Services:
Clinton Lacey 212-361-8982
Chief Information Officer:
Barry Abrams 212-232-0455

Public Advocate, Office of the . . . . fax: 212-669-4701
Municipal Bldg, One Centre St, 15th Fl North, New York, NY 10007
212-669-7200 Fax: 212-669-4701
Web site: www.pubadvocate.nyc.gov
Public Advocate:
Bill de Blasio 212-669-4102
e-mail: bgotbaum@pubadvocate.nyc.gov
General Counsel:
Steven Newmark 212-669-4719
e-mail: snewmark@pubadvocate.nyc.gov
Chief of Staff:
Dominick Williams 212-669-4743
e-mail: dwilliams@pubadvocate.nyc.gov
Director, Administration:
Elba Feliciano 212-669-2179
e-mail: elba@pubadvocate.nyc.gov
Director, Intergovernmental Affairs:
Warren Gardiner 212-669-4388
e-mail: wgardiner@pubadvocate.nyc.gov

State & Local Government Public Information

Offices and agencies generally appear in alphabetical order, except when specific order is requested by listee.

Executive Assistant:
Jane Schatz 212-669-4258
e-mail: jschatz@pubadvocate.nyc.gov

Records & Information Services, Dept of, NYC . fax: 212-788-8614
31 Chambers St, Rm 305, New York, NY 10007
212-639-9675 or TTY: 212-788-8615 Fax: 212-788-8614
Web site: www.nyc.gov/records
Deputy Commissioner:
Eileen M Flannelly 212-788-8607
e-mail: bgandersson@records.nyc.gov
Director, Administration:
Vickie Moore 212-788-8622
Director, Municipal Archives:
Leonora Gidlund 212-788-8585
Director, Municipal Records Management Division:
Pearl L Boatswain 212-788-8550
Director, City Hall Library:
Paul C Perkus 212-788-8596

Rent Guidelines Board, NYC . . . . fax: 212-385-2554
51 Chambers St, Ste 202, New York, NY 10007
212-385-2934 Fax: 212-385-2554
e-mail: ask@housingnyc.com
Web site: www.nycrgb.org
Chair:
Jonathan L Kimmel 212-385-2934
e-mail: chair@housingnyc.com
Executive Director:
Andrew McLaughlin
Public Information Officer:
Charmaine Superville
Senior Research Associate:
Brian Hoberman 212-385-2934

Sanitation, Department of, NYC
346 Broadway, 10th Floor, New York, NY 10013
e-mail: comroffc@dsny.nyc.gov
Web site: www.nyc.gov/html/dsny
Commissioner:
John J Doherty 646-885-5020
First Deputy Commissioner:
Bernard Sullivan 646-885-4727
Deputy Commissioner, of Public Info & Community Affairs:
Vito A Turso 646-885-5020/fax: 212-791-3386

Small Business Services, Department of, NYC . . . fax: 212-618-8991
110 William St, 7th Fl, New York, NY 10038
212-513-6300 Fax: 212-618-8991
Web site: www.nyc.gov/html/sbs
Commissioner:
Robert W Walsh 212-513-6350
First Deputy Commissioner, Financial Management/Administration:
Andrew Schwartz 212-513-6428
Assistant Commissioner, Business Development & Recruitment:
Katherine Janeski 212-618-6710
General Counsel:
Deborah Buyer 212-442-6432
Assistant Commissioner, Finance & Administration:
Shaazad Ali 212-618-8735
Chief of Staff:
Sarah Krauss 212-513-6300

Sports Commission, NYC . . . . fax: 212-788-7514
2 Washington Street, 15th Floor, New York, NY 10004
877-692-7767 Fax: 212-788-7514
Web site: www.nyc.gov/html/mail/html/mailsports.html
Commissioner:
Kenneth J Podziba 212-487-5676
e-mail: kpodziba@cityhall.nyc.gov

Standards & Appeals, Board of, NYC . . . . fax: 212-788-8769
40 Rector Street, 9th Floor, New York, NY 10006
212-788-8500 Fax: 212-788-8769
e-mail: ppacific@dcas.nyc.gov
Web site: www.nyc.gov/html/bsa
Chair:
Meenakshi Srinivasan 212-788-8547
Vice Chair:
Christopher Collins
Commissioner:
Susan M Hinkson
Executive Director:
Jeff Mulligan 212-788-8805

Tax Commission, NYC . . . . fax: 212-669-8636
Municipal Building, 1 Centre St, Rm 936, New York, NY 10007
212-669-4410 Fax: 212-669-8636
Web site: www.nyc.gov/html/taxcomm
President:
Glenn Newman 212-669-4401
Director, Operations:
Myrna Hall 212-669-4420/fax: 212-669-2003
Director, Information Technology:
Iftikhar Ahmad 212-669-2954
Director, Appraisal & Hearings:
Carlo Silvestri 212-669-4402
General Counsel:
Vacant 212-669-4407

Taxi & Limousine Commission, NYC . . . . fax: 212-676-1100
40 Rector St, New York, NY 10006
212-639-9675 Fax: 212-676-1100
Web site: www.nyc.gov/taxi
Commissioner/Chair/CEO:
David Yassky 212-676-1003
Chief of Staff:
Ira Goldstein 212-676-1017/fax: 212-676-2002
First Deputy Commissioner:
Andrew Salkin . . . . 212-676-1147 or 212-676-1148
Deputy Commissioner, Legal Affairs:
Charles Fraser 212-676-1117
Deputy Commissioner, Licensing:
Barbara Schechter . . . . 718-391-5667 or 718-391-5666
Deputy Commissioner, Public Affairs:
Allan J Fromberg 212-676-1013/fax: 212-676-1101
Deputy Commissioner of Financial Management & Administration:
Louis Tazzi 212-676-1035

Transportation, Department of, NYC
55 Water Street, 9th Floor, New York, NY 10041
212-639-9675 or TTY: 212-504-4115
Web site: www.nyc.gov/dot
Commissioner:
Janette Sadik-Khan 212-676-0868/fax: 212-442-7007
First Deputy Commissioner:
Lori Ardito 212-839-6403
Deputy Commissioner, External Affairs:
Seth Solomonow 212-839-4850
Deputy Commissioner, Sidewalks & Inspection Mgmt Division:
Leon W Heyward 212-839-4300

Veterans' Affairs, Mayor's Office of, NYC . . . . . . fax: 212-442-4170
346 Broadway, 8 W, New York, NY 10007
212-442-4171 Fax: 212-442-4170
Web site: www.nyc.gov/html/vets
Commissioner:
Terrance Holliday 212-442-4171
Deputy Commissioner:
Clarice Joynes 212-442-4171

Voter Assistance Commission (VAC), NYC . . . . fax: 212-788-2527
100 Gold Street, 2nd Floor, New York, NY 10038

212-788-8384 Fax: 212-788-2527
Web site: www.nyccfb.info
Chairman:
Joseph P. Parkes 212-306-7100/fax: 212-306-7143
Vice Chair:
Jane Kalmus 212-306-7100
Executive Director/Coordinator:
Amy M. Loprest 212-306-7100

Water Finance Authority, Municipal, NYC . . . . . fax: 212-788-9197
75 Park Place, 6th Fl, New York, NY 10007
212-788-5889 Fax: 212-788-9197
Web site: www.nyc.gov/html/nyw
Executive Director:
Thomas G Paolicelli 212-788-5889
e-mail: paolicellit@omb.nyc.gov
Comptroller:
Michele Mark Levine 212-788-5889
e-mail: levinem@omb.nyc.gov

Youth & Community Development, Department of, NYC . . . fax: 212-442-5998
156 William St, New York, NY 10038
212-442-5900 or 800-246-4646 Fax: 212-442-5998
Web site: www.nyc.gov/dycd
Commissioner:
Jeanne B Mullgrav. 212-442-6006/fax: 212-442-5998
e-mail: jmullgrav@dycd.nyc.gov
General Counsel:
Everett Hughes 212-442-5980
Chief of Staff:
Heriberto Barbot 212-442-5989
Deputy Commissioner, Administration:
Carlos Cortes. 212-442-8573
e-mail: ccortes@dycd.nyc.gov
Deputy Commissioner, Community Development:
Suzanne M Lynn. 212-442-6015

New York City Boroughs

Bronx (Bronx County) . . . . fax: 718-590-3537
Executive Division, 851 Grand Concourse, 3rd Floor, Bronx, NY 10451
718-590-3500 Fax: 718-590-3537
e-mail: webmail@bronxbp.nyc.gov
Web site: bronxboropres.nyc.gov
Borough President:
Rueben Diaz Jr 718-590-3557
Deputy Borough President:
Aurelia Greene 718-590-4036
Director, Communications:
John DeSio 718-590-3543
e-mail: jdesio@bronxbg.ny.gov
Counsel:
Al Rodriguez. 718-590-8555
e-mail: arodriguez@bronxbp.ny.gov
Press Secretary:
Liseth Perez-Almeida 718-590-2509
e-mail: lalmeida@bronxbp.nyc.gov

Brooklyn (Kings County). . . . . fax: 718-802-3805
Borough Hall, 209 Joralemon St, Brooklyn, NY 11201
718-802-3700 Fax: 718-802-3805
Web site: www.brooklyn-usa.org
Borough President:
Marty Markowitz 718-802-3700
e-mail: askmarty@brooklynbp.nyc.gov
Deputy Borough President:
Sandra Chapman. 718-802-3884
e-mail: ygraham@brooklynbp.nyc.gov

Manhattan (New York County). . . . . fax: 212-669-4305
Municipal Bldg, One Centre St, 19th Fl, New York, NY 10007
212-669-8300 Fax: 212-669-4305
Web site: www.mbpo.org
Borough President:
Scott M Stringer 212-669-8155
e-mail: bp@manhattanbp.org
Deputy Borough President:
Rose Pierre-Louis 212-669-8137
e-mail: rpierre-louis@manhattanbp.org
Chief of Staff:
Alaina Gilligo 212-669-2527
e-mail: agilligo@manhattanbp.org
General Counsel:
Jimmy Yan 212-669-8157
e-mail: jyan@manhattanbp.org
Director of Human Resources & Operations:
Lisa Kaufer 212-669-8300
e-mail: lkaufer@manhattanbp.org
Director, Policy & Research:
David Saltonstall. 212-669-8300
e-mail: dsaltonstall@manhattanbp.org
Director, Communications:
Josh Getlin 212-669-8139
e-mail: jgetlin@manhattanbp.org
Press Secretary:
Audrey Gelman 212-669-3882/fax: 212-669-3380
e-mail: agelman@manhattanbp.org

Queens (Queens County) . . . . fax: 718-286-2876
Executive Division, 120-55 Queens Blvd, Kew Gardens, NY 11424
718-286-3000 Fax: 718-286-2876
e-mail: info@queensbp.org
Web site: www.queensbp.org
Borough President:
Helen M Marshall 718-286-3000/fax: 718-286-2876
Deputy Borough President:
Barry Grodenchik 718-286-2900
Chief of Staff:
Alexandra Rosa. 718-286-3000
General Counsel:
Hugh Weinberg. 718-286-3000
Director, Management & Budget:
Carol Ricci 718-286-2660
Director, Planning & Development:
Irving Poy 718-286-2860
Immigrant/Intercultural Affairs:
Susie Tanenbaum 718-286-2741
Press Office:
Daniel Andrews 718-286-2640

Staten Island (Richmond County) . . . . fax: 718-816-2026
10 Richmond Terrace, Room 120, Staten Island, NY 10301
718-816-2000 Fax: 718-816-2026
Web site: www.statenislandusa.com
Borough President:
James P Molinaro 718-816-2200
Deputy Borough President:
Edward Burke 718-816-2231
Chief of Staff:
Joseph Sciortino 718-816-2058
Legal Counsel:
John Zaccone 718-816-2056
Borough Commissioner, DOT:
Thomas Cocola 718-816-2373

Newburgh, City of
83 Broadway
Newburgh, NY 12550
845-569-7300 Fax: 845-569-7370
e-mail: info@mail.cityofnewburgh-ny.gov
Web site: www.cityofnewburgh-ny.com

Mayor:
Judy Kennedy 845-569-7303
City Manager:
Richard F Herbeck 845-569-7301
Acting Director, Planning & Development:
Ian MacDougall 845-569-9400/fax: 845-569-9700
e-mail: elynch@cityofnewburgh-ny.gov
City Clerk:
Lorene Vitek 845-569-7311/fax: 845-569-7314
e-mail: lvitek@cityofnewburgh-ny.gov
Corporation Counsel:
Michelle Kelson 845-569-7335/fax: 845-569-7338
Chief:
Michael Ferrara 845-561-3131/fax: 845-565-5662
e-mail: nfdchief@cityofnewburgh-ny.gov
Fire Chief:
Michael Vatter 845-569-7415/fax: 845-569-7435
Historian:
Mary McTamaney 845-569-8090
e-mail: newburghhistory@usa.com

Newburgh, Town of

1496 Rte 300
Newburgh, NY 12550
845-564-4552 Fax: 845-566-9486
Web site: www.townofnewburgh.org

Town Supervisor:
Wayne C Booth 845-564-4552/fax: 845-566-9486
e-mail: townsupervisor@hvc.rr.com
Town Clerk:
Andrew J Zarutskie 845-564-4554/fax: 945-564-8589
e-mail: town-clerk@hvc.rr.com
Accountant:
Jacqueline Calarco 845-564-5220
e-mail: accountant@hvc.rr.com
Police Chief:
Michael Clancy 845-564-1100/fax: 845-564-1870
e-mail: jjmahoney@hvc.rr.com

Niagara Falls, City of

City Hall
745 Main St, PO Box 69
Niagara Falls, NY 14302-0069
716-286-4300 Fax: 716-286-4349
Web site: www.niagarafallsusa.org

Mayor:
Paul Dyster 716-286-4310/fax: 716-286-4349
City Administrator:
Donna D Owens 716-286-4320/fax: 716-286-4376
City Clerk:
Carol Antonucci 716-286-4393
e-mail: cantonucci@falls.niagara.ny.us
Corporate Counsel:
Craig H Johnson 716-286-4422/fax: 716-286-4424
Controller:
Maria C Brown 716-286-4340
Police Superintendent:
John Chella 716-286-4545
Director, Public Works & Parks:
David L Kinney 716-286-4940/fax: 716-286-4877

Niskayuna, Town of

One Niskayuna Circle
Niskayuna, NY 12309
518-386-4500 Fax: 518-386-4592
Web site: www.niskayuna.org

Town Supervisor:
Joe Landry 518-386-4503/fax: 518-386-4592
e-mail: supervisor@niskayuna.org
Deputy Town Clerk:
Barbara Nottke 518-386-4511/fax: 518-386-4509
e-mail: bnottke@niskayuna.org
Comptroller:
Paul Sebesta 518-386-4508/fax: 518-386-4592
e-mail: psebesta@niskayuna.com
Town Attorney:
Peter Scagnelli 518-386-4503/fax: 518-386-4592
Police Chief:
John Lubrant 518-386-4585/fax: 518-386-4594
e-mail: jlubrant@niskyuna.com

North Hempstead, Town of

220 Plandome Rd
Manhasset, NY 11030
516-869-6311 Fax: 516-627-4204
e-mail: feedback@northhempstead.com
Web site: www.northhempstead.com

Town Supervisor:
Jon Kaiman 516-869-6311
e-mail: kaimanj@northhempstead.com
Town Clerk:
Leslie Gross 516-869-6311
e-mail: grossl@northhempstead.com
Town Attorney:
Richard S Finkel 516-869-7600
e-mail: finkelr@northhempstead.com
Director, Public Safety:
Andrew DeMartin 516-869-6311
e-mail: demartin@northhempstead.com
Commissioner, Public Works:
Paul DiMaria 516-739-6710
e-mail: guineyj@northhempstead.com
Commissioner, Finance:
JoAnne Taormina 516-869-6311
e-mail: taorminaja@northhempstead.com
Comptroller:
Kathleen Mitterway 516-869-7766
e-mail: mitterwayk@northhempstead.com
Community Services:
Kimberly Corcoran 516-869-6311
e-mail: corcorank@northhempstead.com

North Tonawanda, City of

City Hall
216 Payne Ave
North Tonawanda, NY 14120
716-695-8555 Fax: 716-695-8557
Web site: www.northtonawanda.org

Mayor:
Robert G Ortt 716-695-8540/fax: 716-695-8541
e-mail: robertort@northtonawanda.org
Common Council President:
Richard L. Andres, Jr. 716-695-8555/fax: 716-695-8557
e-mail: catherinesch@northtonawanda.org
City Clerk:
Scott P Kiedrowski 716-695-8555/fax: 716-695-8557
e-mail: scottkie@northtonawanda.org
City Attorney:
Shawn P Nickerson 716-695-8590/fax: 716-695-8592
City Engineer:
Dale W Marshall 716-695-8565/fax: 716-695-8568
e-mail: dalemar@northtonawanda.org
Police Chief:
William R. Hall 716-692-4325/fax: 716-692-4321

Fire Chief:
Joseph L Krantz....................716-693-2201/fax: 716-693-2216

Onondaga, Town of
5020 Ball Road
Syracuse, NY 13215
315-469-3888 Fax: 315-498-6129
Web site: www.townofonondagany.com

Town Supervisor:
Thomas Andino....................315-469-3888/fax: 315-498-6129
Town Clerk:
Lisa Goodwin....................315-469-1583/fax: 315-469-3461
e-mail: lgoodwin@townofonondaga.com
Tax Receiver:
Michele Kresser....................315-469-0483/fax: 315-469-3461
Town Attorney:
Kevin Gilligan....................315-422-1152/fax: 315-422-1139
Town Historian:
Mary Nowyj....................315-214-2383

Orangetown, Town of
26 Orangeburg Rd
Orangeburg, NY 10962
845-359-5100 Fax: 845-359-2623
Web site: www.orangetown.com

Town Supervisor:
Andy Stewart....................845-359-5100 x2261
e-mail: supervisor@orangetown.com
Town Clerk:
Charlotte E Madigan..........845-359-5100 x5004/fax: 845-359-5126
e-mail: townclerk@orangetown.com
Town Attorney:
John S Edwards..............845-359-5100 x2215/fax: 845-359-2715
e-mail: townattorney@orangetown.com
Director, Finance:
Jeffrey W. Bencik....................845-359-5100 x2204
e-mail: jbencik@orangetown.com
Police Chief:
Kevin A Nulty....................845-359-3700
e-mail: orangetownpd@yahoo.com

Orchard Park, Town of
4295 S Buffalo Rd
Orchard Park, NY 14127
716-662-6400 Fax: 716-662-6479
e-mail: colarussoj@orchardparkny.org
Web site: www.orchardparkny.org

Town Supervisor:
Janis Colarusso....................716-662-6400
e-mail: opsupervisor@orchardparkny.org
Town Clerk:
Carol R Hutton....................716-662-6410
e-mail: optownclerk@orhardpark.ny.org
Receiver of Taxes:
Carol R. Hutton....................716-662-6405/fax: 716-662-6465
e-mail: optax@orchardparkny.org

Ossining, Town of
16 Croton Ave
Ossining, NY 10562
914-762-6000 Fax: 914-762-7710
Web site: www.townofossining.com

Town Supervisor:
Susanne Donnelly....................914-762-6001/fax: 914-762-0833
e-mail: sdonnelly@townofossining.com
Town Clerk:
MaryAnn Roberts....................914-762-8428/fax: 914-914-0627
e-mail: townclerk@townofossining.com
Receiver of Taxes:
Gloria Fried....................914-762-8790/fax: 914-762-0635
Police Chief:
Mark E Busche....................914-762-6007/fax: 914-762-6900
e-mail: topd@ossiningtownpolice.com

Ossining, Village of
16 Croton Ave
Ossining, NY 10562
914-941-3554
Web site: www.villageofossining.org

Mayor:
William R Hanauer....................914-941-3554
Village Manager:
Richard A Leins....................914-941-3554
Village Clerk:
Mary Ann Roberts....................914-762-8428/fax: 914-762-7710
Corporation Counsel:
Lori Lee Dickson....................914-941-3554/fax: 914-941-5940
Police Chief:
Joseph Burton Jr....................914-941-4099

Owego, Town of
2354 NYS Route 434
Apalachin, NY 13732
607-687-0123 Fax: 607-687-5191
Web site: www.townofowego.com

Town Supervisor:
Donald Castellucci Jr....................607-687-0123/fax: 607-687-5191
e-mail: dcastellucci@townofowego.com
Town Clerk/Receiver of Taxes:
Michael E Zimmer....................607-687-0123 or 607-687-6381
e-mail: owegotownclerk@gmail.com
Town Attorney:
Eric Gartenman....................607-687-0123
Director, Water/Sewer:
Michael Trivisonno....................607-625-2197
e-mail: mtrivisonno@townofowego.com
Town Historian:
Vacant....................607-687-1961

Oyster Bay, Town of
Town Hall East
54 Audrey Ave
Oyster Bay, NY 11771
516-624-6498 Fax: 516-624-6387
Web site: www.oysterbaytown.com

Town Supervisor:
John Venditto....................516-624-6350
Town Clerk:
Steven L Labriola....................516-624-6332
Attorney:
Gregory J Giammalvo....................516-624-6150
Comptroller:
Robert J McEvoy....................516-624-6440

Peekskill, City of
City Hall
840 Main Street
Peekskill, NY 10566
914-737-3400
Web site: www.cityofpeekskill.com

Offices and agencies generally appear in alphabetical order, except when specific order is requested by listee.

Mayor:
Mary F Foster . . . 914-734-4105
Acting City Manager:
Brian Havranek . . . 914-734-4246
e-mail: rfinn@cityofpeekskill.com
City Clerk:
Pamela Beach . . . 914-737-3400
e-mail: pbeach@cityofpeekskill.com
Comptroller:
Charles Emberger . . . 914-734-4118
e-mail: cemberger@cityofpeekskill.com
Police Chief:
Eric Johansen
e-mail: ejohansen@police.com

Penfield, Town of
3100 Atlantic Ave
Penfield, NY 14526
585-340-8600 Fax: 585-340-8667
Web site: www.penfield.org

Town Supervisor:
Tony LaFountain . . . 585-340-8630/fax: 585-340-8762
e-mail: supervisor@penfield.org
Town Clerk:
Amy Steklof . . . 585-340-8629/fax: 585-340-8752
e-mail: clerk@penfield.org
Fire Marshal:
Wayne Cichetti . . . 585-340-8643/fax: 585-340-8644
e-mail: firemarshal@penfield.org
Town Historian:
Kathy Kanauer . . . 585-340-8740/fax: 585-340-8748
e-mail: historian@penfield.org

Perinton, Town of
1350 Turk Hill Rd
Fairport, NY 14450
585-223-0770 Fax: 585-223-3629
Web site: www.perinton.org

Town Supervisor:
James E Smith . . . 585-223-0770
Town Clerk:
Jennifer West . . . 585-223-0770
Public Works:
Thomas C Beck . . . 585-223-5115
Director, Finance:
Kevin Spacher . . . 585-223-0770
Historian:
Bill Poray . . . 585-223-0770

Pittsford, Town of
11 S Main St
Pittsford, NY 14534
585-248-6200 Fax: 585-248-6247
Web site: www.townofpittsford.com

Town Supervisor:
Sandra F. Zutes . . . 585-248-6220/fax: 585-248-6247
e-mail: szutes@townofpittsford.org
Town Clerk:
Pat Chuhta . . . 585-248-6210/fax: 585-248-6440
e-mail: pchuhta@townofpittsford.org
Town Attorney:
Richard T Williams II . . . 585-248-6216
e-mail: rwilliams@townofpittsford.org
Director, Finance:
Gregory J Duane . . . 585-248-6225/fax: 585-248-6247
e-mail: gduane@townofpittsford.org
Town Historian:
Audrey M Johnson . . . 585-248-6245/fax: 585-248-6247
e-mail: ajohnson@townofpittsford.org

Port Chester, Village of
222 Grace Church St
Port Chester, NY 10573
914-939-5202 Fax: 914-937-3169
e-mail: krang@villageofportchester-ny.com
Web site: www.portchesterny.com

Mayor:
Neil J. Pagano . . . 914-939-5201
e-mail: dpilla@portchesterny.com
Village Manager:
Christopher Steers . . . 914-939-2200/fax: 914-937-3169
Treasurer:
Leonie Douglas . . . 914-939-5205/fax: 914-305-2570
Village Attorney:
Anthony Cerreto . . . 914-939-5208/fax: 914-937-3169
Public Works General Foreman:
Rocky Morabito . . . 914-939-5207
Police Chief:
Joseph Krzeminski . . . 914-939-1000/fax: 914-939-2303

Poughkeepsie, City of
62 Civic Center Plaza
Poughkeepsie, NY 12601
845-451-4072
e-mail: info@cityofpoughkeepsie.com
Web site: www.cityofpoughkeepsie.com

Mayor:
John C Tkazyik . . . 845-451-4073/fax: 845-451-4201
e-mail: jtkazyik@cityofpoughkeepsie.com
City Administrator:
Milo Bunyi . . . 845-451-4072/fax: 845-451-4013
e-mail: mbunyi@cityofpoughkeepsie.com
City Chamberlain/Clerk:
Deanne Flynn . . . 845-451-4276/fax: 845-451-4239
e-mail: dflynn@cityofpoughkeepsie.com
Acting Finance Commissioner:
Karen Sorrell . . . 845-451-4027/fax: 845-451-4028
e-mail: ksorrell@cityofpoughkeepsie.com
Police Chief:
Ronald Knapp . . . 845-451-4132

Poughkeepsie, Town of
One Overocker Rd
Poughkeepsie, NY 12603
845-485-3600 Fax: 845-485-3701
Web site: www.townofpoughkeepsie.com

Town Supervisor:
Todd Taneredi . . . 845-485-3607/fax: 845-485-3701
e-mail: ttancredi@townofpoughkeepsie-ny.gov
Town Clerk:
Susan Miller . . . 845-485-3620/fax: 845-485-8583
e-mail: smiller@townofpoughkeepsie-ny.gov
Comptroller:
Jim Wojtowicz . . . 845-485-3610/fax: 845-485-1130
e-mail: jwojtowicz@townofpoughkeepsie-ny.gov
Police Chief:
Thomas Mauro . . . 845-485-3666/fax: 845-485-3756
e-mail: townpolice@hotmail.com

Queensbury, Town of
742 Bay Road
Queensbury, NY 12804

518-761-8200 Fax: 518-798-8359
Web site: www.queensbury.net

Town Supervisor:
Dan Stec. 518-761-8229/fax: 518-798-8359
e-mail: supervisor@queensbury.net
Town Clerk/Receiver of Taxes:
Darleen Dougher. 518-761-8234
e-mail: townclerk@queensbury.net
Town Counsel, Legal Assistant:
Pamela Hunsinger 518-761-8251/fax: 518-745-4408
e-mail: towncounsel@queensbury.net
Fire Marshal:
Mike Palmer 518-761-8206/fax: 518-745-4437
e-mail: firemarshal@queensbury.net
Historian:
Dr Marilyn VanDyke 518-761-8252
e-mail: historian@queensbury.net

Ramapo, Town of

Town Hall, 237 Route 59
Suffern, NY 10901
845-357-5100 Fax: 845-357-3877
e-mail: supervisor@ramapo-ny.org
Web site: www.ramapo.org

Town Supervisor:
Christopher P St Lawrence 845-357-5100 x202
Town Clerk:
Christian G Sampson 845-357-5100 x263/fax: 845-357-8513
e-mail: townclerk@ramapo.org
Town Attorney:
Michael L Klein. 845-357-5100 x237
Director, Finance:
Nathan Oberman 845-357-5100 x247
Director, Public Works:
Ted Dzurinko. 845-357-0591 x112
Police Chief:
Peter Brower 845-357-2400

Riverhead, Town of

200 Howell Avenue
Riverhead, NY 11901
631-727-3200 Fax: 631-727-6712
e-mail: info@riverheadli.com
Web site: www.townofriverheadny.gov

Town Supervisor:
Sean Walter 631-727-3200 x251
e-mail: pjc@riverheadli.com
Town Clerk:
Diane M Wilhelm. 631-727-3200 x260/fax: 631-208-4034
e-mail: wilhelm@riverheadli.com
Fire Marshal:
Craig Zitek 631-727-3200 x209/fax: 631-727-3370
e-mail: zitek@riverheadli.com
Town Attorney:
Robert Kozakiewicz. 631-727-3200 x216/fax: 631-727-6712
e-mail: rfk@riverheadli.com

Rochester, City of

City Hall
30 Church St
Rochester, NY 14614
585-428-5990 Fax: 585-428-6059
e-mail: info@cityofrochester.gov
Web site: www.cityofrochester.gov

Mayor:
Thomas S Richards 585-428-7045
Deputy Mayor:
Leonard E. Redon 585-428-7163
Council President:
Lovely A Warren 585-428-7538
City Clerk:
Daniel B Karin 585-428-7421
e-mail: dan.karin@cityofrochester.gov
Corporation Counsel:
Robert Bergin 585-428-6990
e-mail: Richardt@cityofrochester.gov
City Treasurer:
Charles A Benincasa. 585-428-6705
e-mail: charles.benincasa@cityofrochester.gov
Commissioner, Environmental Services:
Paul Holahan. 585-428-6855
e-mail: paul.holahan@cityofrochester.gov
Police Chief:
James Sheppard. 585-428-7033
e-mail: shepparj@cityofrochester.gov
Fire Chief:
Salvatore Mitrano, III 585-428-7037
e-mail: john.caufield@cityofrochester.gov
Director, Emergency Communications:
John M Merklinger 585-528-2200
e-mail: john.merklinger@cityofrochester.gov
Director, Finance:
Brian L Roulin 585-428-7151
e-mail: brian.roulin@cityofrochester.gov

Rockville Centre, Village of

1 College Place
Rockville Centre, NY 11571
516-678-9300 Fax: 516-678-9225
Web site: www.rvcny.us

Village Mayor:
Francis X Murray 516-678-9260
Deputy Clerk Treasurer/Payroll:
Mary Schmeling 516-678-9263
Village Attorney:
Vacant 516-678-9206
Comptroller:
Michael Schussheim 516-678-9226
Police Commissioner:
Charles Gennario 516-766-1500
Superintendent, Public Works:
Harry Weed. 516-678-9293

Rome, City of

City Hall
Liberty Plaza
198 N Washington St
Rome, NY 13440
315-339-7677 Fax: 315-339-7667
Web site: www.romenewyork.com

Mayor:
Joseph R Fusco Jr 315-339-7677/fax: 315-339-7667
Common Council President:
John J Mazzaferro. 315-838-1731
City Clerk:
Louise Glasso 315-339-7658/fax: 315-838-1160
e-mail: jreid@romecitygov.com
Corporation Counsel:
Timothy Benedict 315-339-7668/fax: 315-838-1166
Treasurer:
David Nolan. 315-339-7690/fax: 315-838-1165

Public Safety Commissioner:
Mike Grande 315-339-7676/fax: 315-339-7667
Commissioner, Public Works:
Frank Tallarino 315-339-7625/fax: 315-339-1167

Rotterdam, Town of

John F Kirvin Government Center
1100 Sunrise Blvd
Rotterdam, NY 12306
518-355-7575 x393 Fax: 518-355-7837
Web site: www.rotterdamny.org

Town Supervisor:
Harry C Buffardi 518-355-7575 x393
e-mail: fdelgallo@rotterdamny.org
Town Clerk:
Diane M. Marco 518-355-7575 x318
e-mail: eesposito@rotterdamny.org
Town Attorney:
Kate McGuirl 518-355-7575
Comptroller:
Jackie Every 518-355-7575 x394
e-mail: paragosa@rotterdamny.org
Police Chief:
James Hamilton 518-355-7331
e-mail: jhamilton@rotterdamny.org
Public Works Coordiantor:
Vince Romano 518-355-7575 x395/fax: 518-355-2725
e-mail: vromano@rotterdamny.org

Rye, Town of

10 Pearl St
Port Chester, NY 10573
914-939-3075 Fax: 914-939-1465
e-mail: super@townofryeny.com
Web site: www.townofryeny.com

Town Supervisor:
Joseph Carvin 914-939-3075
Town Clerk:
Hope B Vespia 914-939-3570
Town Attorney:
Paul Noto 914-698-9331
Comptroller:
David Byrnes 914-934-8489
Commissioner, Public Safety:
Richard Greenberg 914-939-3098

Salina, Town of

201 School Rd
Liverpool, NY 13088
315-457-6661 Fax: 315-457-4317
Web site: salina.ny.us

Town Supervisor:
Mark A Nicotra 315-457-6661/fax: 315-457-4476
e-mail: supervisor@salina.ny.us
Town Clerk:
Jeannie Ventre 315-457-2710/fax: 315-457-4317
Town Attorney:
Timothy A. Frateschi 315-475-6661
Comptroller:
Greg Maxwell 315-451-4210

Saratoga Springs, City of

City Hall
474 Broadway
Saratoga Springs, NY 12866
518-587-3550 Fax: 518-587-1688
e-mail: email@saratoga-springs.org
Web site: www.saratoga-springs.org

Mayor:
Scott Johnson 518-587-3550 x2514
Accounts Commissioner:
John Franck 518-587-3550 x2543
Finance Commissioner:
Michele Madigan 518-587-3550 x2571
Public Safety Commissioner:
Christian Mathiesen 518-587-3550 x2627
Public Works Commissioner:
Anthony Scirocco 518-587-3550 x2561

Saugerties, Town of

4 High Street
Saugerties, NY 12477
845-246-2800 Fax: 845-246-0355
Web site: www.saugerties.ny.us

Town Supervisor:
Kelly Myers 845-246-2800 x345/fax: 845-247-0355
e-mail: kmyers@saugerties.ny.us
Town Clerk:
Lisa Stanley 845-246-2800 x343/fax: 845-246-0127
e-mail: lstanley@saugerties.ny.us
Accounting Office:
Deborah Martino 845-246-2800 x348
e-mail: dmartino@saugerties.ny.us

Schenectady, City of

City Hall
105 Jay St
Schenectady, NY 12305
518-382-5000 Fax: 518-382-5272
Web site: www.cityofschenectady.com

Mayor:
Gary McCarthy 518-382-5000/fax: 518-382-5272
e-mail: mayor@nycap.rr.com
City Council President:
Margaret King 518-370-1885
City Clerk:
Chuck Thorne 518-382-5199 x5303
e-mail: cityclk1@nycap.rr.com
Finance Commissioner:
Deborah W. DeGenova 518-382-5010
Public Safety Commissioner:
Wayne Bennett 518-382-5201/fax: 518-382-5299
e-mail: wbennett@schenectadypd.com
Historian:
Don Rittner 518-788-1255
Police Chief:
Brian Kilcullen 518-382-5201/fax: 518-382-5299

Smithtown, Town of

99 W Main St
PO Box 9090
Smithtown, NY 11787
631-360-7600 Fax: 631-360-7668
Web site: www.smithtownny.gov

Town Supervisor:
Patrick R Vecchio 631-360-7600/fax: 631-360-7668
Town Clerk:
Vincent Puleo 631-360-7620/fax: 631-360-7692
e-mail: vpuleo@tosgov.com

Town Attorney:
John B. Zollo 631-360-7570/fax: 631-360-7719
e-mail: townattorney@tosgov.com
Comptroller:
Louis A. Necroto 631-360-7530/fax: 631-360-7625
Director, Public Safety:
Chief John Valentine 631-360-7553/fax: 631-360-7677
e-mail: publicsafety@tosgov.com

Southampton, Town of
116 Hampton Rd
Southampton, NY 11968
631-283-6000 Fax: 631-283-5606
e-mail: webmaster@southamptontownny.gov
Web site: www.southamptontownny.gov

Town Supervisor:
Anna Throne-Holst 631-283-6055/fax: 631-287-5708
e-mail: athrone-holst@southamptontownny.gov
Town Clerk:
Hon Sundy A Schermeyer............631-287-5740/fax: 631-283-5606
e-mail: sschermeyer@southhamptontownny.gov
Town Attorney:
Michael C Sordi 631-287-3065
Comptroller:
Leonard J. Marchese 631-702-1887/fax: 631-287-5709
e-mail: lmarchese@southamptontownny.gov
Commissioner, Public Works/Highway Superintendent:
Alex D Gregor 631-728-3600/fax: 631-728-3605
e-mail: agregor@southamptontownny.gov
Police Chief:
Robert Pearce 631-728-5000
e-mail: rpearce@southamptontownny.gov
Town Historian:
Henry Moeller...631-287-5740

Southold, Town of
53095 Route 25
PO Box 1179
Southold, NY 11971
631-765-1800 Fax: 631-765-6145
Web site: southoldtown.ny.gov

Town Supervisor & Emergency Coordinator:
Scott A Russell 631-765-1889/fax: 631-765-1823
e-mail: supervisor@town.southold.ny.us
Town Clerk/Registrar:
Elizabeth A Neville................631-765-1800/fax: 631-765-6145
e-mail: e.neville@town.southold.ny.us
Comptroller:
John Cushman 631-765-4333/fax: 631-765-1366
e-mail: accounting@town.southold.ny.us
Town Attorney:
Martin Finnegan 631-765-1939/fax: 631-765-6639
e-mail: martin.finnegan@town.southold.ny.us
Police Chief:
Martin Flatley 631-765-2600/fax: 631-734-2315
Historian:
Antonia Booth 631-765-1981/fax: 631-765-1366
e-mail: antonia.booth@town.southold.ny.us

Spring Valley, Village of
200 North Main Street
Spring Valley, NY 10977
845-352-1100 Fax: 845-352-1164
Web site: www.villagespringvalley.org

Mayor:
Noramie Jasmin.......................................845-573-5864
Village Clerk:
Sherry M Scott......................................845-517-1128 x108
e-mail: sscott@villagespringvalley.org
Treasurer:
Kuruvilla Cherian 845-517-1121 x101
e-mail: kcherian@villagespringvalley.org
Superintendent:
Neil Vitiello 845-573-1198 x253/fax: 845-573-5802
Police Chief:
Paul J. Modica ....845-573-5833 or 845-356-7400
fax: 845-573-5859

Syracuse, City of
233 East Washington St
203 City Hall
Syracuse, NY 13202
315-448-8005 Fax: 315-448-8067
e-mail: cityhall@ci.syracuse.ny.us
Web site: www.syracuse.ny.us

Mayor:
Stephanie A Miner.................315-448-8005/fax: 315-448-8067
e-mail: cityhall@syrgov.net
Common Council President:
Hon Van B Robinson 315-448-8466/fax: 315-448-8423
City Clerk:
John P Copanas 315-448-8216/fax: 315-448-8489
Commissioner, Assessment:
David Clifford....................315-448-8280/fax: 315-448-8190
e-mail: assessment@syrgov.net
Commissioner, Neighborhood & Business Development:
Paul Driscoll 315-448-8100/fax: 315-488-8036
e-mail: cd@ci.syracuse.ny.us
Commissioner, Finance:
David DelVecchio 315-448-8279/fax: 315-448-8424
e-mail: finance@ci.syracuse.ny.us
Director, Administration & Budget Management:
Mary Vossler ....315-448-8252 or 315-448-8116
e-mail: budget@syrgov.net
Police Chief:
Frank L Fowler 315-442-5111/fax: 315-442-5198
Fire Chief:
Paul Linnertz 315-473-5525/fax: 315-422-7766

Tonawanda, Town of
2919 Delaware Ave
Kenmore, NY 14217
716-877-8800 Fax: 716-877-0578
Web site: www.tonawanda.ny.us

Town Supervisor:
Anthony F Caruana 716-877-8804/fax: 716-877-1261
e-mail: acaruana@tonawanda.ny.us
Town Clerk:
Marguerite Greco 716-877-8800 x810/fax: 716-877-0578
e-mail: mbrinson@tonawanda.ny.us
Town Attorney:
John J Flynn......................716-875-9947/fax: 716-875-9948
e-mail: jflynn@tonawanda.ny.us
Comptroller:
Edward D Mongold..................716-877-8810/fax: 716-877-8236
e-mail: emongold@tonawanda.ny.us
Police Chief:
Anthony J Palombo 716-876-6607/fax: 716-876-6644

Troy, City of
City Hall
1776 Sixth Avenue
Troy, NY 12180

State & Local Government Public Information

Offices and agencies generally appear in alphabetical order, except when specific order is requested by listee.

518-270-4401 Fax: 518-270-4609
Web site: www.troyny.gov

Mayor:
Lou Rosamilia....................518-279-7130/fax: 518-270-4609
e-mail: mayorsoffice@troyny.gov
President, City Council:
Lynn Kopka....................518-279-7317/fax: 518-270-4639
e-mail: citycouncil@troyny.gov
City Clerk:
William A McInerney....................518-279-7134
Chief of Police:
John Tedesco....................518-270-4421
Fire Chief:
Thomas O Garrett....................518-270-4471

Union, Town of

3111 E Main St
Endwell, NY 13760
607-786-2900 Fax: 607-786-2998
Web site: www.townofunion.com

Town Supervisor:
Rose Sotak....................607-786-2995/fax: 607-786-2998
e-mail: rsotak@townofunion.com
Town Clerk:
Gail L Springer....................607-786-2915/fax: 607-786-2913
e-mail: townclerk@townofunion.com
Town Attorney:
Alan J Pope....................607-786-2910
e-mail: attorney@townofunion.com
Comptroller/Finance:
Laura Lindsley....................607-786-2930/fax: 607-786-2998
e-mail: llindsley@townofunion.com
Historian:
Suzanne Meredith....................607-786-5786
e-mail: historian@townofunion.com

Utica, City of

City Hall
One Kennedy Plz
Utica, NY 13502
315-797-5847 Fax: 315-734-9250
Web site: www.cityofutica.com

Mayor:
Robert Palmieri....................315-792-0100
e-mail: mayor@cityofutica.com
Common Council President:
William C Morehouse....................315-792-0113/fax: 315-792-0220
City Clerk:
Joan M Brenon....................315-792-0113/fax: 315-792-0220
e-mail: jbrenon@cityofutica.com
First Assistant Corporation Counsel:
Charles N Brown....................315-792-0171/fax: 315-792-0175
e-mail: ulaw@cityofutica.com
Comptroller:
Michael T. Cerminaro....................315-792-0133/fax: 315-797-5847
e-mail: mcerminaro@cityofutica.com
City Assessor:
David H Williams....................315-792-0125/fax: 315-792-9028
e-mail: dwilliams@cityofutica.com
Commissioner, Parks & Public Works:
David Short....................315-738-0172
e-mail: dshort@cityofutica.com
Deputy City Engineer:
Goran Smiljic....................315-792-0152/fax: 315-792-0236
e-mail: engineering@cityofutica.com

Valley Stream, Village of

123 S Central Ave
Valley Stream, NY 11580
516-825-4200 Fax: 516-825-8316
Web site: www.vsvny.org

Mayor:
Edwin Fare....................516-825-4200
Village Clerk/Administrator:
Robert Barra....................516-825-4200
e-mail: vsclerk@valleystream.govoffice.com
Treasurer:
Michael J. Fox....................516-825-4200

Vestal, Town of

605 Vestal Parkway West
Vestal, NY 13850
607-748-1514 Fax: 607-786-3631
Web site: www.vestalny.com

Town Supervisor:
W. John Schaffer....................607-748-1514 x329
Town Clerk:
Emil Bielecki....................607-748-1514 ext321
e-mail: ebielecki@vestalny.com
Town Attorney:
David Berger....................607-748-1514 ext389
e-mail: dbergerattorney@stny.rr.com
Comptroller:
Laura McKane....................607-748-1514 ext324
e-mail: lmckane@vestalny.com
Police Chief:
John Butler....................607-754-2386 ext341
e-mail: jbutler@vestalny.com
Fire Chief:
Pat McPherson....................607-748-1514 x383
e-mail: pmcpherson_vfd@vestalny.com
Historian:
Margaret Hadsell....................607-754-4243
e-mail: mhadsell@vestalny.com

Wallkill, Town of

99 Tower Drive
Building A
Middletown, NY 10941
845-692-7800
Web site: www.townofwallkill.com

Town Supervisor:
Dan Depew....................845-692-7832/fax: 845-692-2546
e-mail: supervisor@townofwallkill.com
Town Clerk:
Louisa Ingrassia....................845-692-7826/fax: 845-692-6051
Chief of Police:
Robert Hertman....................845-692-7859/fax: 845-692-4166
e-mail: chiefofpolice@townofwallkill.com

Wappinger, Town of

20 Middlebush Road
Wappinger Falls, NY 12590
845-297-5771 Fax: 845-298-1478
Web site: www.townofwappinger.us

Town Supervisor:
Barbara Gutzler....................845-297-2744
Town Clerk:
Christine Fulton....................845-297-5771/fax: 845-298-1478
Receiver of Taxes:
Patricia Maupin....................845-297-4342/fax: 845-298-1478

Offices and agencies generally appear in alphabetical order, except when specific order is requested by listee.

Fire Inspector:
Mark Liebermann 845-297-1373
Historian:
Constance O Smith

Warwick, Town of
132 Kings Highway
Warwick, NY 10990
845-986-1124
e-mail: townhall@townofwarwick.org
Web site: www.townofwarwick.org

Town Supervisor:
Michael Sweeton 845-986-1120 x240
Deputy Supervisor:
James Gerstner................................845-986-1120 x241
Town Clerk:
Marjorie Quackenbush 845-986-1124 x246
Public Works Commissioner:
Jeffrey Feagles 845-986-3358
Police Chief:
Thomas McGovern Jr 845-986-3423

Watertown, City of
245 Washington St, Rm 302
Watertown, NY 13601
315-785-7730 Fax: 315-785-7796
Web site: www.watertown-ny.gov

Mayor:
Jeffrey E Graham...................315-785-7720/fax: 315-782-9014
e-mail: jgraham@watertown-ny.gov
City Manager:
Sharon Addison....................315-785-7730/fax: 315-782-9014
City Clerk:
Ann Saunders.......................315-785-7780/fax: 315-785-7796
Comptroller:
James Mills 315-785-7754/fax: 315-785-7826
e-mail: jmills@watertown-ny.gov
Fire Chief:
Dale Herman 315-785-7800/fax: 315-785-7821
e-mail: firechief@watertown-ny.gov

Webster, Town of
1000 Ridge Rd
Webster, NY 14580
585-872-1000 Fax: 585-872-1352
Web site: www.ci.webster.ny.us

Supervisor:
Ronald Nesbitt 585-872-1000
e-mail: supervisor@ci.webster.ny.us
Town Clerk:
Barbara Ottenschot 585-872-1000/fax: 585-872-7058
e-mail: townclerk@ci.webster.ny.us
Director, Finance:
Kathy Tanea.........................585-872-7067/fax: 585-872-7008
e-mail: finance@ci.webster.ny.us
Public Works:
Gary Kleist..........................585-872-7025/fax: 585-872-1352
Police:
Gerald Pickering...............585-872-1216 x240/fax: 585-872-7010
e-mail: police@ci.webster.ny.us
Historian:
Lynn Barton 585-265-3308

West Seneca, Town of
1250 Union Rd
West Seneca, NY 14224
716-674-5600 Fax: 716-677-4330
Web site: www.westseneca.net

Town Supervisor:
Sheila Meegan ....716-997-7200 or 716-558-3202
e-mail: smeegan@twsny.org
Town Clerk:
Jacqueline A. Felser 716-558-3215
e-mail: jfelser@twsny.org
Town Attorney:
Shawn P Martin 716-558-3240
e-mail: shawn.martin@twsny.org
Comptroller:
Robert J Bielecki...716-558-3205
e-mail: rbielecki@swccpas.com
Police Chief:
Daniel Denz 716-674-2280
e-mail: denz@wspolice.com

White Plains, City of
City Hall
255 Main St
White Plains, NY 10601
914-422-1200 Fax: 914-422-1395
e-mail: webpo@white-plains.ny.us
Web site: www.cityofwhiteplains.com

Mayor:
Thomas M Roach 914-422-1411
Common Council President:
Beth N. Smayda 914-419-6891
e-mail: bsmayda@bethsmayda.com
Commissioner, Public Works:
Joseph Nicoletti Jr...914-422-1206
Chief of Police:
James Bradley..914-422-6230

Yonkers, City of
City Hall
40 S Broadway
Yonkers, NY 10701-3700
914-377-6000 Fax: 914-377-6048
Web site: www.cityofyonkers.com

Mayor:
Mike Spano..914-377-6300
Chief of Staff:
Rachelle Richard...914-377-6300
President, City Council:
Chuck Lesnick 914-377-6060
e-mail: chuck.lesnick@yonkersny.gov
Acting City Clerk:
Vincent E. Spano 914-377-6020
Corporation Counsel:
MIchael V. Curti...914-377-6250
City Assessor:
Mark Russell..914-377-6200
Acting Commissioner, Affordable Housing:
William J. Schneider...914-377-6501
Commissioner, Finance & Mgmt Services:
James LaPerche..914-377-6100
Commissioner, Parks, Recreation & Conservation:
Yvette E. Hartsfield 914-377-6450
e-mail: yvette.hartsfield@yonkersny.gov
Commissioner, Public Works:
Thomas G. Meier 914-377-6270
Acting Commissioner, Planning & Development:
Wilson Kimball...914-377-6150
e-mail: wilson.kimball@yonkersny.gov

State & Local Government Public Information

Offices and agencies generally appear in alphabetical order, except when specific order is requested by listee.

Director, Public Affairs & Community Relations:
Richard Halevy 914-377-6053
Director Economic Development:
Louis C Kirven 914-377-6797/fax: 914-377-6003
e-mail: louis.kirven@yonkersny.gov
Emergency Management Director:
John Donaghy 914-377-7325/fax: 914-965-8430
Police Commissioner:
Charles Gardner 914-377-7900
Fire Commissioner:
Anthony Pagano 914-377-7500

Yorktown, Town of

363 Underhill Avenue
Yorktown Heights, NY 10598
914-962-5722 Fax: 914-962-1731
Web site: www.yorktownny.org

Town Supervisor:
Michael Grace 914-962-5722 x271/fax: 914-962-1004
e-mail: supervisor@yorktownny.org
Town Clerk:
Alice Roker. 914-962-5722 x209/fax: 914-962-6591
e-mail: townclerk@yorktownny.org
Comptroller:
Patricia Caporale 914-962-5722 x206/fax: 914-962-1004
Chief of Police:
Daniel McMahon. 914-962-4141/fax: 914-962-4458
e-mail: info@yorktownpd.org

Offices and agencies generally appear in alphabetical order, except when specific order is requested by listee.

Section 4:
POLITICAL PARTIES & RELATED ORGANIZATIONS

NEW YORK POLITICAL PARTIES

NEW YORK STATE CONSERVATIVE PARTY

New York State Conservative Party
486 78th St
Suite 2
Brooklyn, NY 11209
718-921-2158 Fax: 718-921-5268
e-mail: cpnys@nycap.rr.com
Web site: www.cpnys.org

Capital District Office
325 Parkview Dr
Schenectady, NY 12303
518-356-7882
Fax: 518-356-3773

Statewide Party Officials

State Chairman:
Michael R. Long 718-921-2158/fax: 718-921-5268
486 78th St, Brooklyn, NY 11209
Executive Committee Member:
Carol Birkholz. 518-623-9151
1 Pucker St, Warrenburg, NY 12885
State Vice Chairman:
Gerard Kassar 718-748-9010
7520 10th Avenue, Brooklyn, NY 11228
Executive Director:
Shaun Marie. 518-356-7882/fax: 518-356-3773
325 Parkview Dr, Schenectady, NY 12303
Regional Vice Chairman:
Ralph C. Lorigo 716-675-8611
75 Rolling Woods, West Seneca, NY 14224
Secretary:
Howard Lim, Jr. 914-939-7180
83 Valley Terrace, Rye Brook, NY 10573-2137
Treasurer:
Frances Vella-Marrone 718-748-1797
7317 12th Avenue, Brooklyn, NY 11228
State Vice Chairman:
Allen Roth. 516-766-2784
255 Raymond Street, Rockville Centre, NY 11570

County Chairs

Albany
Richard M. Stack 518-465-5715
53 Nicholas Dr, Albany, NY 12205

Bronx
William Newmark. 718-822-0504
3252 Phillip Ave, Bronx, NY 10465

Broome
James M. Thomas 607-343-8767
25 Woodlawn Road, Binghamton, NY 13901-4454

Cattaraugus
Leonard C Caros 716-676-3965
7072 Route 16S, Franklinville, NY 14737-0000

Cayuga
Gregory S. Rigby 315-253-0736
124 Owasco St, Auburn, NY 13021-0000

Chautauqua
Anna M. Wilcox 716-672-8595
3105 Cable Road, Freedonia, NY 14063-0000

Chemung
Louis F. DeCicco 607-796-5129
4905 Hillview Road, Millport, NY 14864

Columbia
Matthew G. Torrey 518-392-9610
91 Nelson Avenue, Ghent, NY 12075

Delaware
John Bjorkander 845-676-4604
Wolf Hollow Road, Andes, NY 13731

Dutchess
Maureen L. Natrella 845-242-3015
1906 Route 52, Suite H, Hopewell Junction, NY 12533

Erie
Esquire:
Ralph C. Lorigo 716-675-8611
75 Rolling Woods, West Seneca, NY 14224

Essex
William McGahay. 518-369-3700
33 Greenwood Street, Lake Placid, NY 12946

Franklin
Esquire:
Robert E. White 518-327-3714
559 County Route 60, Rainbow Lake, NY 12976-0000

Fulton
Wayne Brooks. 518-725-1270
95 E Fulton St, Gloversville, NY 12078-3217

Genesee
Arthur R. Munger 585-762-9323
2753 Pearl St Rd, Batavia, NY 14020

Greene
Nicholas J. Passero 518-622-9407
264 Sweetwater Lane, Round Top, NY 12473

Herkimer
Daniel Pollak. 315-717-2789
124 Folts Rd, Herkimer, NY 13350

Jefferson
Kenneth H. Parks 315-786-2012
19520 Ball Rd, Black River, NY 13612

Kings
Gerard Kassar 718-748-9010
7521 10th Ave, Brooklyn, NY 11228

Livingston
Jason J. McGuire. 585-734-2199
1851 Livingston Street, Lima, NY 14485

Madison
Christopher J. Kendall 315-684-7810
6 Cedar Street, Morrisville, NY 13408

Monroe
Esquire:
Thomas D. Cook. 585-381-1988
29 Washington Avenue, Pittsford, NY 14534

Montgomery
Robert Mead 518-842-4345
1 Northhampton Road, Amsterdam, NY 12010

Nassau
Daniel F. Donovan Jr. 516-433-8568
1 Sydney Street, Plainview, NY 11803

New York
Stuart J. Avrick 212-912-0022

Offices and agencies generally appear in alphabetical order, except when specific order is requested by listee.

375 S End Avenue, New York, NY 10280

Niagara
Daniel Weiss....................................716-531-5332
1028 87th Street, Niagara Falls, NY 14304

Oneida
M. Julie Miller....................................315-735-7367
466 Tryon Rd, Utica, NY 13502

Onondaga
Austin W. Olmsted....................................315-696-8417
6519 Route 80, Apulia Station, NY 13020

Ontario
Michael Kloppel....................................585-393-9575
179 West Avenue, Canandaigua, NY 14424

Orange
John P. DeLessio....................................845-562-4963
7 Hill Street, Newburgh, NY 12550

Orleans
Lofthouse Allen....................................585-659-8382
2191 Center Road, Kendall, NY 14476

Oswego
Ronald K. Greenleaf....................................315-564-6427
879 Cayuga Street, Hannibal, NY 13074

Otsego
Sheila Ross....................................607-547-4037
32 Walnut Street, Cooperstown, NY 13326-0000

Putnam
James M. Maxwell....................................845-628-7716
117 Vista Terrace South, Mahopac, NY 10541

Queens
Thomas M. Long....................................718-474-3826
6 Beach 219th St, Rockaway Point, NY 11697

Rensselaer
William T. Fiacco....................................518-892-9273
3 Ruffinen Drive, Wynatskill, NY 12198

Richmond
Harold J. Wagner....................................718-720-7364
31 Longview Road, Staten Island, NY 10304

Rockland
Edward J. Lettre....................................845-624-8494
34 Auner Road, West Nyack, NY 10994

Saratoga
Robert D. Zordon....................................518-233-0121
1 Robin Lane, Waterford, NY 12188

Schenectady
Randy M. Pascarella....................................518-355-8753
610 Becker Crossing, Schenectady, NY 12306

Schoharie
William A. Hanson....................................607-588-6107
801 State Route 990 V, Gilboa, NY 12076

Schuyler
Linda D. Moore....................................607-535-7591
2485 Irelandville Rd, Watkins Glen, NY 14891

Seneca
William R. White....................................315-539-2534
19 Brookside Dr, Waterloo, NY 13165

St Lawrence
Henry Ford....................................315-262-2824
113 Stowe Bay Rd, Colton, NY 13625

Steuben
Donald E. Gwinner....................................607-329-6765
5582 Sanford Rd, Savona, NY 14879

Suffolk
Edward M. Walsh, Jr....................................631-581-1781
211 Apex Lane, East Islip, NY 11730-3304

Sullivan
Steven J. Burke....................................845-434-2293
68 Cole Road, Hurleyville, NY 12747

Tioga
Bruce Ludwig....................................607-223-4173
652 Anderson Hill Road, Candor, NY 13743-2412

Ulster
Edward J. Gaddy....................................845-336-2020
176 Jocky Hill Rd, Kingston, NY 12401

Warren
Carol Birkholz....................................518-623-9151
1 Pucker St, Warrensburg, NY 12885

Washington
Beverly A. Jakway....................................518-260-3661
2092 County Road 43, Fort Ann, NY 12827

Wayne
James F. Quinn, Jr....................................315-483-2240
8239 Lake St Ext, Sodus Point, NY 14555

Westchester
Hugh Fox Jr....................................914-494-3306
262 Hoover Road, Yonkers, NY 10710

NEW YORK STATE DEMOCRATIC PARTY

New York State Democratic Committee
750 Third Avenue
31st Floor
New York, NY 10017
212-725-8825 Fax: 212-725-8867
Web site: www.nydems.org

Statewide Party Officials
State Chair:
Vacant
Executive Director:
Basil Smikle Jr
750 Third Avenue, New York, NY 10017
Young Democrats:
Glenn Oldhoff
60 Madison Avenue, Ste 1201, New York, NY 10010
Executive Committee Chair:
Sheila Comar
29 Depot Street, Middle Granville, NY 12849
Treasurer:
David A Alpert....................914-946-8300/fax: 914-946-8090
170 East Post Rd, White Plains, NY 10601

County Chairs

Albany
Matthew J. Clyne....................................518-438-8282
22 Colvin Ave, Albany, NY 12206

Allegany
Robert Christman

Bronx
Jeffrey Dinowitz....................718-679-9000/fax: 347-281-5984
1640 Eastchester Rd, Bronx, NY 10461

Offices and agencies generally appear in alphabetical order, except when specific order is requested by listee.

Broome
Jim Testani 607-773-8369
PO Box 854, Binghamton, NY 13902

Cattaraugus
Joyce Melfi

Cayuga
Kate Lacey
144 Genesee Street, Auburn, NY 13021

Chautauqua
Norman Green

Chemung
Susan Skidmore 607-737-8261
518 West Third Street, Elmira, NY 14901

Chenango
Patrick McNeil
110 Fuller Road, Norwich, NY 13815

Clinton
Martin Mannix Jr. 518-569-5615
80 Rand Hill Road, Morissonville, NY 12962

Columbia
Cyndy Hall 518-851-7980
PO Box 507, Ghent, NY 12075

Cortland
Sandy Price
129 Port Watson Street, Cortland, NY 13045

Delaware
Tom Schimmerling
PO Box 366, New Kingston, NY 12459

Dutchess
Elisa Sumner
488 Freedom Plains Rd., Poughkeepsie, NY 12603

Erie
Jeremy Zellner. 716-853-2511
295 Main Street, Buffalo, NY 14203

Essex
Bethany A. Kosmider 518-597-9760
340 Buck Mountain Road, Crown Point, NY 12928-2021

Franklin
Joseph Pickreign 518-891-1174/fax: 518-891-1174
PO Box 6, Saranac Lake, NY 12983

Fulton
Edmund C. Jasewicz 518-736-5526/fax: 518-736-1612
2714 State Highway 29, Johnstown, NY 12095-9946

Genesee
Lorie Longhany. 585-409-6373
8535 East Main Road, LeRoy, NY 14482

Greene
Doreen Davis 518-678-0317
PO Box 590, Palenville, NY 12463

Hamilton
Linda M Mitchell 518-648-5327
Tower Hill Rd, PO Box 163, Indian Lake, NY 12842

Herkimer
Richard Souza

Jefferson
Sean Hennessey 315-788-4590
95 Public Square, Watertown, NY 13601

Kings
Frank Seddio

Lewis
Ed Murphy 315-346-6473
PO Box 76, Beaver Falls, NY 13305

Livingston
Judith Hunter
39 South St, Geneseo, NY 14454

Madison
Marianne Simberg
433 Florence Ave, Oneida, NY 13421

Monroe
Joseph D Morelle. 585-232-2410/fax: 585-232-1223
1150 University Avenue, Rochester, NY 14607

Montgomery
Bethany Schumann 518-684-0236
286 Guy Park Avenue, Amsterdam, NY 12010

Nassau
Jay S. Jacobs 516-294-3366/fax: 516-873-0810
1 Old County Rd, Carle Place, NY 11514

New York
Keith L.T. Wright 212-687-6540/fax: 212-818-1723

Niagara
Nick J. Forster

Oneida
William Barry 315-736-3447

Onondaga
Mark English. 315-422-0345
615 West Genesee Street, Syracuse, NY 13204

Ontario
Judith Baker

Orange
Jonathan G Jacobson. 845-567-6778
843 Union Ave, New Windsor, NY 12553

Orleans
Jeanne Crane 585-682-3089
13087 Hanlon Rd, Albion, NY 14411

Oswego
Michael Kunzwiler 315-422-0345
615 West Genesee Street, Syracuse, NY 13204

Otsego
Richard D. Abbate 607-544-5039

Putnam
Victor Grossman
PO Box 639, Carmel, NY 10512

Queens
Joseph Crowley 718-268-5100/fax: 718-268-7363

Rensselaer
Thomas W. Wade 518-273-3367
PO Box 846, Troy, NY 12181

Richmond
John Gulino 718-983-5009/fax: 718-983-5541
35 New Dorp Plaza, Staten Island, NY 10306

Rockland
Kristen Zebrowski Stavisky 917-312-8939
106 Strawtown Road, West Nyack, NY 10994

Saratoga
Charley Brown
PO Box 124, Saratoga Springs, NY 12866

Schenectady
Brian Quail 518-388-9988

Schoharie
Cliff Hay 518-234-7165
337 Barnerville Rd., Cobleskill, NY 12043

Schuyler
Dale Walter

Seneca
Theodore H Young 315-539-9614/fax: 315-539-9614
PO Box 555, Seneca Falls, NY 13148

St Lawrence
Mark Bellardini....................315-265-4023
645 River Road, Norwood, NY 13668

Steuben
Shawn D. Hogan 607-324-7421/fax: 607-324-3150
12 Mays Avenue, Hornell, NY 14843

Suffolk
Richard H. Schaffer....................631-439-0400/fax: 631-439-0404
1461 Lakeland Avenue, Bohemia, NY 11716

Sullivan
Steve Wilkinson 845-665-6152
PO Box 502, Kiamesha Lake, NY 12751

Tioga
Patricia Bence
3543 Bornt Hill Road, Endicott, NY 13760

Tompkins
Irene W. Stein 607-266-7579/fax: 607-266-7571
PO Box 6798, Ithaca, NY 14851

Ulster
Frank Cardinale....................845-512-1630/fax: 845-512-1630
32 John St, Kingston, NY 12401

Warren
Lynne Boecher

Washington
Sheila Comar....................518-642-9566
29 Depot St, Middle Granville, NY 12849

Wayne
Mark H. Alquist 315-589-8864
4046 Wayne Street, Williamson, NY 14589

Westchester
Reginald A. LaFayette 914-995-5705
170 East Post Road, White Plains, NY 10601

Wyoming
Harold Bush Jr....................585-786-8113

Yates
Carolyn Schaffer....................315-536-0007
2997 Merritt Hill Rd, Penn Yan, NY 14527

NEW YORK STATE GREEN PARTY

New York State Green Party
365 Potomac Avenue
Buffalo, NY 14213
Web site: www.web.gpnys.com

Statewide Party Officials
Co-Chair:
Gloria Mattera....................917-886-4538
Co-Chair:
Michael O'Neil 917-825-3562
Secretary:
Peter LaVenia
Treasurer:
Eric Jones
365 Potomac Avenue, Buffalo, NY 14213

NEW YORK STATE INDEPENDENCE PARTY

New York State Independence Party
225 Broadway
#2010
New York, NY 10007
Web site: www.ipnyc.org

County Chairs

Bronx
Nardo Reyes

Kings
Robert Conroy....................718-415-0571
323 Putnam Avenue, Brooklyn, NY 11216

Manhattan
Cathy L. Stewart 212-962-1699
225 Broadway, New York, NY 10007

Queens
Nancy Hawkins

Richmond
Sarah D. Lyons 718-447-9689
36 Hamilton Ave, Staten Island, NY 10305

NEW YORK STATE REPUBLICAN PARTY

New York State Republican Party
315 State St
Albany, NY 12210
518-462-2601 Fax: 518-449-7443
e-mail: frontdesk@nygop.org
Web site: www.newyork.gop

Statewide Party Officials
Chairman:
Edward F Cox....................518-462-2601
315 State St, Albany, NY 12210
Executive Director:
Jason Weingartner
315 State St, Albany, NY 12210
Secretary:
Colleen Ryan....................518-462-2601
315 State St, Albany, NY 12210
Treasurer:
John Riedman 518-462-2601
315 State St, Albany, NY 12210
First Vice Chairman:
Bill Reilich....................518-462-2601/fax: 518-449-7443
315 State St, Albany, NY 12210
National Committeeman:
Charles P. Joyce
National Committeewoman:
Jennifer Saul Rich 518-462-2601/fax: 518-449-7443
315 State St, Albany, NY 12210

Offices and agencies generally appear in alphabetical order, except when specific order is requested by listee.

County Officials

Albany
Rachel Bledi
32 North Russell Road, Albany, NY 12206

Allegany
Mike Healy 585-268-5644
PO Box 23, Belmont, NY 14813

Bronx
Jay Savino 718-792-5800/fax: 718-863-2301
3029 Middletown Road, Bronx, NY 10461

Broome
Dave C. Hamlin 607-723-8201
59 Court Street, Binghamton, NY 13901

Cattaraugus
Paula Snyder 716-376-7569

Cayuga
Cherl Heary 315-255-1103/fax: 315-364-5164
PO Box 2, Auburn, NY 13021

Chautauqua
Allan Hendrickson 716-450-3813

Chemung
Mike Krusen 607-732-1245/fax: 607-739-4583
9 Longmeadow Dr, Elmira, NY 14905

Chenango
Thomas L Morrone 607-334-3234/fax: 607-334-4625
213 Randall Ave, Norwich, NY 13815-1613

Clinton
Don Lee. 518-569-9578
16 Ilene Drive, Morrisonville, NY 12962

Columbia
Greg Fingar. 518-329-1636
PO Box 1067, Hudson, NY 12534

Cortland
John Folmer 607-745-6207
PO Box 5522, Cortland, NY 13045

Delaware
Maria Kelso. 607-434-9483

Dutchess
Michael McCormack 914-475-5342
18 Beavers Edge Road, Rhinebeck, NY 12572

Erie
Nickolas Langworthy 716-856-8700/fax: 716-856-8703
715 Main Street, Buffalo, NY 14203

Essex
Ronald Jackson 518-963-7104

Franklin
Rolland Thomas 518-651-5225

Fulton
Susan McNeil 518-332-9722
2010 County Highway 107, Amsterdam, NY 12010

Genesee
Richard Siebert 585-343-5925/fax: 585-344-8521
8585 Seven Springs Rd, Batavia, NY 14020

Greene
Brent Bogardus 518-369-6098
7 Molly White Drive, Coxsackie, NY 12051

Hamilton
William Osborne. 518-775-3285

Herkimer
Sylvia Rowan 315-866-7884

Jefferson
Don Coon. 315-788-4120/fax: 315-786-1387
200 Washington Street, Watertown, NY 13601

Kings
Craig Eaton 718-332-7766/fax: 718-332-5898
1662 Sheepshead Bay Rd, Brooklyn, NY 11235

Lewis
Roscoe K. Fawcett Jr. 315-348-9991

Livingston
Lowell Conrad. 585-243-2665/fax: 585-243-2711
123 Main St, PO Box 123, Geneseo, NY 14454-1113

Madison
Ken Kunkel. 315-637-3663

Monroe
William Reilich 585-546-8040/fax: 585-546-8519
460 State Street, Rochester, NY 14608

Montgomery
Joe Emanuele 518-376-8084

Nassau
Joseph Mondello 516-334-5800/fax: 516-333-4406
164 Post Ave, Westbury, NY 11590

New York
Daniel Isaacs 212-517-8444
122 East 83rd Street, New York, NY 10028

Niagara
Michael Norris. 716-946-5576/fax: 716-433-0032
PO Box 1127, Lockport, NY 14095

Oneida
Peter Sobel 315-327-8152

Onondaga
Tom Dadey 315-471-2020/fax: 315-471-2033
375 West Onondaga St, Syracuse, NY 13202-3207

Ontario
Doug Finch 585-329-7278

Orange
William L DeProspo 845-294-6467/fax: 845-294-7928
75 Main St, Goshen, NY 10924

Orleans
Edward Morgan. 585-638-5352/fax: 585-638-6214
3132 Hurlburton Rd, Holley, NY 14470

Oswego
Michael Backus. 315-342-0840
102 West Utica Street, Oswego, NY 13126

Otsego
Sheila Ross 607-547-8390
PO Box 55, Fly Creek, NY 13337

Putnam
James Dibella 917-703-6975

Queens
Philip Ragusa. 718-690-3737/fax: 718-746-6356
24-55 Francis Lewis Blvd., Whitestone, NY 11357

Rensselaer
John Rustin 518-470-4791

Richmond
Robert Scamardella 718-442-9000

Rockland
Vincent Reda 845-634-7100/fax: 845-634-2423
172 S Main St, PO Box 201, New City, NY 10956

Saratoga
John Herrick 518-462-2601/fax: 518-581-0748
125 High Rock Avenue, Saratoga Springs, NY 12866

Schenectady
Jim Buhrmaster 518-365-4809

Schoharie
Lewis Wilson 518-234-2534

Schuyler
Philip Barnes 607-535-4600
203 Lakeview Avenue, Watkins Glen, NY 14891

Seneca
Sue Ann Fisher 315-651-0381

St Lawrence
Tom Jenison 518-462-2601
PO Box 775, Canton, NY 13617

Steuben
Rusty Smith 607-329-9508

Suffolk
John Jay LaValle 631-580-1482/fax: 631-580-1490
1150 Portion Road, Holtsville, NY 11742

Sullivan
Richard Coomb 845-701-3342
PO Box 747, Monticello, NY 12701

Tioga
Don Leonard 607-589-4501/fax: 607-723-3246
PO Box 361, Spencer, NY 14883

Tompkins
James Drader 607-227-4503

Ulster
Roger Rascoe 845-338-6245
159 Green St, Kingston, NY 12402

Warren
Michael Grasso .518-656-9093/fax: 518-783-8754
23 Rapaport Drive, Lake George, NY 12845

Washington
John Patterson 518-692-7920

Wayne
Daniel Olson 315-946-4937/fax: 315-946-4937
12 William St, PO Box 200, Lyons, NY 14489

Westchester
Douglas Colety .914-949-3020/fax: 914-949-2275
214 Mamaroneck Ave, White Plains, NY 10601

Wyoming
Gordon Brown 716-675-8620/fax: 716-675-1619
PO Box 191, Warsaw, NY 14569

Yates
Sandra King 585-703-4714
4419 Italy Valley Road, Penn Yan, NY 14527

NEW YORK STATE RIGHT TO LIFE PARTY

New York State Right to Life Party
41 State Street
Suite M-100
Albany, NY 12207
518-434-1293
e-mail: admin@nysrighttolife.org
Web site: www.nysrighttolife.org

NEW YORK STATE WORKING FAMILIES PARTY

New York State Working Families Party
1 Metrotech Center North
11th Floor
Brooklyn, NY 11217
718-222-3796 Fax: 718-246-3718
e-mail: wfp@workingfamiliesparty.org
Web site: www.workingfamiliesparty.org

Offices and agencies generally appear in alphabetical order, except when specific order is requested by listee.

LOBBYISTS

Each entry includes the name of the registered principal lobbyist, then lists names of additional lobbyists as well as all clients.

1199 SEIU United Healthcare Workers East (FKA 1199/SEIU New York's Health & Human Service Union)
330 West 42nd Street
7th Floor
New York, NY 10036
212-603-1735

Lobbyists:
Lillie Carino
Dick Farfaglia
Patrick Gaspard
George Gresham
Antonella Pechtel

1199/SEIU & GNYHA Healthcare Education Project
330 West 42nd Street
Room 739
New York, NY 10036
212-603-1741

Lobbyists:
Jessica Shearer

249 W 28th Street Properties, LLC
100 Washington Street
Newark, NJ 07102
973-643-7700

Lobbyists:
Jill Fink

92nd Street Young Men's and Young Women's Hebrew Association
1395 Lexington Avenue
New York, NY 10128
212-415-5470

Lobbyists:
Sol Adler

99 Solutions LLC
20 Jay Street
Suite 1006
Brooklyn, NY 11201

Clients:
American Racing and Entertainment, LLC
CSC Holdings, LLC (Cablevision)
Downtown Brooklyn Partnership, Inc.
L & M Development Partners, Inc.
Madison Realty Capital Advisors LLC (FKA Madison Realty Capital)
Putting New Yorkers to Work
Real Estate Board of New York
University (New York)
Urban Strategic Partners, LLC

Lobbyists:
Shevonn Howard
Jacquelyn Williams

Academy of Medicine (NY) (The)
1216 Fifth Avenue
New York, NY 10029
212-822-7222

Lobbyists:
Ruth Finkelstein
Ana Garcia
Simone-Marie Meeks

Accenture LLP
800 Coonecticut Ave NW
Ste 600
Washington, DC 20006
202-533-1140

Clients:
Accenture LLP

Lobbyists:
Ken Dircks
Steve Hurst
Sterling McCullough
Rick Webb

Ace Group - North America
436 Walnut St.
WA04P
Philadelphia, PA 19106
215-640-5741

Lobbyists:
Robert Diubaldo
Saraiya Kashyap

Acquard, Milissa
1170 Main St
Buffalo, NY 14209
716-882-1025

Clients:
Elizabeth Pierce Olmsted Medical Center for the Visually Impaired

Adams, Daniel J
47 Sweetbrier Dr
Ballston Lake, NY 12019
518-877-8225

Clients:
Brewers Association, Inc (NYS)
Illinois Tool Works Inc
Matt Brewing Co (The)

Adams, John
400 Calgon Carbon Drive
Pittsburgh, PA 15205
412-787-6662

Clients:
Calgon Carbon Corporation

Adirondack Council Inc (The)
PO Box D2
Elizabethtown, NY 12932
518-873-2240
e-mail: info@adirondackcouncil.org
Web site: www.adirondackcouncil.org

Political Parties, Lobbyists & PACs

Offices and agencies generally appear in alphabetical order, except when specific order is requested by listee.

Clients:
Adirondack Council Inc (The)

Lobbyists:
Kevin Chlad
Diana Fish
Scott Lorey

Adolf, Jay
305 Broadway
Suite 900
New York, NY 10007
212-897-5848

Clients:
Physician's Reciprocal Insurers

Advance Group Inc (The)
481 Eighth Avenue
Suite 1202
New York, NY 10001
212-239-7323

Clients:
Children's Health Fund
Communication Workers of America Local 1180
Hotel and Motel Trades Council AFL-CIO (NY)

Lobbyists:
Katie Franger
Laura Kavanagh
Scott Levenson
Lindsey Melfi
Jonathan Yedin

Advocates for Children of New York, Inc. (FKA Sweet, Kim)
151 West 30th Street
5th Floor
New York, NY 10001
212-947-9779

Lobbyists:
Randi Levine
Kim Madden
Christian Villenas

Aetna
151 Farmington Ave
Hartford, CT 06156
518-451-3125

Clients:
Aetna

Lobbyists:
Maggie Moree
Susan Tully Abdo

After-School Corporation (The) (FKA Ford, Barry)
1440 Broadway
16th Floor
New York, NY 10018
646-943-8756

Clients:
After-School Corporation (The)

Lobbyists:
Lucy Friedman
Rachel Sabella
Saskia Traill

Ahern, Barbara J
One Commerce Plaza, Ste 400
Albany, NY 12210
518-463-0723
e-mail: bjahern@albany.net

Clients:
Croplife America
First Data Corporation & Subsidiaries
Hearing Healthcare Alliance of NY Inc (HHCANY)
Responsible Industry for a Sound Environment (RISE)

AIA New York State, Inc. (FKNA Rodriguez, Barbara J.)
AIA New York State, Inc.
52 South Pearl Street
Third Floor
Albany, NY 12207
518-449-3334

Lobbyists:
Edward C Farrell

AJ Consulting Services LLC
175 Swift Road
Voorheesville, NY 12186
518-439-6265

Clients:
Mercy College

Lobbyists:
Abe Lackman

Akerman Senterfitt LLP (FKA Stadtmauer Bailkin LLP)
850 Third Avenue, 19th Floor
New York, NY 10022
212-751-8600

Clients:
Azimuth Development Group, LLC
Macy's Retail Holdings, Inc. (FKA Macys East a Division of Macy's Retail Holdings, Inc.)

Lobbyists:
Richard Bowers
Jessica Loeser
Lance Michaels
Steven Polivy
Steven Sinacori
Calvin Wong
Howard Zipser

Albany Law School of Union University
80 New Scotland Avenue
Albany, NY 12208
518-445-2380

Lobbyists:
Helen Adams-Keane
Thomas Guernsey
Patricia Salkin

Offices and agencies generally appear in alphabetical order, except when specific order is requested by listee.

Albany-Colonie Regional Chamber of Commerce
5 Computer Drive South
Albany, NY 12205-1608
518-413-1417

Lobbyists:
Mark Eagan
Nicholas Vaughn

Allegue, Raul R
The Travelers Companies Inc & Subsidiary
1 Tower Square - 8MS
Hartford, CT 06183
860-277-4738

Clients:
Travelers Indemnity Company (The)

Lobbyists:
John D Miletti

Alliance for Donation, Inc. (New York) (FKA Stark, Lynette)
185 Jordan Road
Troy, NY 12180
518-326-3237

Lobbyists:
Melanie Evans
Aisha Tator

Alliance for Downtown New York, Inc.
120 Broadway
Suite 3340
New York, NY 10271
212-566-6700

Lobbyists:
Elizabeth Berger

Alliance for Quality Education (FKA Easton, Regina N)
94 Central Ave
Albany, NY 12206
518-432-5315

Clients:
Alliance for Quality Education

Lobbyists:
William Easton
Zakiyah Shaakir

Allinger, Stephen (FKA Nelson, Debra)
United Teachers (NYS)
800 Troy-Schenectady Rd
Latham, NY 12110-2455
518-213-6000

Clients:
Professional Staff Congress (The)
United Teachers (NYS)

Lobbyists:
Heather Barmore
Christopher Black
John Costello
John Green
Richard Iannuzzi
Daniel Kinley
Patrick Lyons
Maria Neira
Andrew Pallotta
Jacqueline Paredes
Melinda Persons
Charles Santelli
Peter Savage

Allocco, Carol
13 Sky Hollow Dr
Menands, NY 12204
518-432-8636
e-mail: callocco@corus.jnj.com

Clients:
Johnson & Johnson Services

Altman, Frederick M
6 Walker Way
Albany, NY 12205-4946
518-690-2828

Clients:
Associated Licensed Detectives of NYS, Inc

Altman, Robert S.
Robert S Altman, Esq., PLLC
27 Whitehall St
New York, NY 10004
212-232-8713

Clients:
Building Industry Assn of NY Inc
Queens & Bronx Building Assn

Altria Client Services Inc. and its Affiliates
101 Constitution Avenue, NW
Suite 400W
Washington, DC 20002
202-354-1500

Clients:
Altria Client Services Inc. and its Affiliates

Lobbyists:
Sven Bergmann
David Fernandez
Mary Margaret Marrin
Molly Slingerland
Michael Thorne-Begland

Alzheimer's Association, New York City Chapter
360 Lexington Avenue
4th Floor
New York, NY 10017
646-744-2900

Lobbyists:
Gail Allen
Lou-Ellen Barkan
Hillary Caceres
Ed Cisek
Patricia Dibenedetto
Elizabeth Hodges
Karen Holland
Fai Lin Lau
Anastasiya Lee
Sharon Lee
Jed Levine

Political Parties, Lobbyists & PACs

Offices and agencies generally appear in alphabetical order, except when specific order is requested by listee.

Niurqui Maiano
Paula Rice
Elizabeth Santiago
Hillary Stuchin

Amanus Consulting Group
7 Sunrise Terrace
Clifton Park, NY 12065
518-424-4248

Clients:
Luther Forest Technology Campus Economic Development

Lobbyists:
Michael Relyea

AMDEC Foundation, Inc. (FKA AMDEC Policy Group, Inc.)
45 Rockefeller Plaza
Suite 1960
New York, NY 10111
212-218-5640
e-mail: info@amdec.org
Web site: www.amdec.org

Clients:
AMDEC Foundation

Lobbyists:
Maria K Mitchell

American Academy of Pediatrics District II (NYS)
1325 Franklin Avenue
Garden City, NY 11530
516-326-0310

Clients:
American Academy of Pediatrics District II (NYS)

Lobbyists:
Ellie Ward

American Beverage Association
1101 Sixteenth Street, NW
Washington, DC 20036
202-463-6732

Clients:
American Beverage Association

Lobbyists:
James McGreevy
Geena Gent
Sandra Grance

American Cancer Society Cancer Action Network
19 Dove St
Albany, NY 12210
518-449-5438

Clients:
American Cancer Society Cancer Action Network

Lobbyists:
Michele Bonan
Michael Burgess
Hillary Clark
Michael Davoli
Blair Horner
Theresa Tolokonsky

American Cancer Society, Inc.
One Penny Lane
Latham, NY 12110
518-454-4021

Clients:
American Cancer Society, Inc.

Lobbyists:
Don Boshart
Jan Chytilo
Peter Cittadino
Arianna De Felice
Danielle Heller
Nicole Larose
Susan Moranda
Michael Porpiglia
Martha Ryan
Carla Sterling
Joan Sterling
Jason Warchal

American Congress of Obstetricians & Gynecologists, Inc. District II
100 Great Oaks Blvd
Suite 109
Albany, NY 12203
518-436-3461
e-mail: info@ny.acog.org
Web site: www.acogny.org

Clients:
American Congress of Obstetricians & Gynecologists, Inc.

Lobbyists:
Christa R. Christakis
Kathryn Gordon
Norain Siddiqui

American Diabetes Association
10 Speen Street
2nd Floor
Framingham, MA 01701
617-482-4580

Clients:
American Diabetes Association

Lobbyists:
Stephen Habbe
Travis Heider

American Farmland Trust
112 Spring St
Suite 207
Saratoga Springs, NY 12866
518-581-0078

Clients:
Ameican Farmland Trust

Lobbyists:
David Haight
Diane Held
Laurie Ten Eyck

American Heart Assn/American Stroke Assn
440 New Karner Rd
Albany, NY 12205
518-869-4052
e-mail: paul.hartman@heart.org
Web site: www.americanheart.org; www.strokeassociation.org

Clients:
American Heart Assn/American Stroke Assn

Lobbyists:
Robert Collins
Jessica Dimeo
Maria Galarza
Julianne Hart
Mark Hurley
Brooks Lancaster
Zainab Magdon-Ismail
Katherine McCarthy
Jennifer Pratt
Kristy Smord
Carolyn Torella
Robin Vitale
Cathy Wilkins

American Institute of Architects New York Chapter
536 LaGuardia Place
New York, NY 10012
212-683-0023

Clients:
American Institute of Architects - New York Chapter

Lobbyists:
Fredric Bell
Jay Bond

American Insurance Assn
95 Columbia St
Albany, NY 12210-2707
518-462-1695
e-mail: ghenning@aiadc.org
Web site: www.aiadc.org

Clients:
American Insurance Assn

Lobbyists:
Gary Henning
John Murphy
Kenneth Stoller

AMGEN
601 13th Street, NW
12th Floor
Washington, DC 20005
202-585-9614

Lobbyists:
Lauren Novakowski

Anglin, Laura L.
17 Elk Street
PO Box 7289
Albany, NY 12224
518-436-4781

Clients:
Commission on Independent Colleges & Universities (CICU)

Lobbyists:
Susan Nesbitt Perez
Christopher Nolin
Sheila C Seery
Terri Standish-Kuon
Elizabeth Van Nest

ANHD, Inc.
50 Broad St, Ste 1125
New York, NY 10004
212-747-1117

Clients:
ANHD, Inc.

Lobbyists:
Benjamin Dulchin
Moses Gates
Bonnie Nesbitt
Ericka Stallings
Barika Williams

Anson, Joseph L.
10 Applewood Drive
Rexford, NY 12148-1601
518-371-0393

Clients:
Bayer Healthcare LLC

APAX Partners, LP
601 Lexington Ave
New York, NY 10022
212-753-6300

Clients:
APAX Partners, LP

Lobbyists:
Karla Garcia
David Kim

APICHA Community Health Center
400 Broadway
New York, NY 10013
212-334-7940

Clients:
Asian & Pacific Islander Coalition on HIV/AIDS, Inc.

Lobbyists:
David Boyd
Marcelito Custodio, M.D.
John Rafael Flores
Gertrudes Pajaron
Teresita Rodriguez

Apple Association, Inc. (NY)
7645 Main Street
PO Box 350
Fishers, NY 14453-0350
585-924-2171
e-mail: jimallen@nyapplecountry.com
Web site: www.nyapplecountry.com

Clients:
Apple Association, Inc. (NY)

Lobbyists:
James Allen

Apple Inc.
C/O 591 Redwood Highway
Bldg 4000
Mill Valley, CA 94941-3039
415-389-6800

Clients:
Apple Inc.

Lobbyists:
Scott Hughes
Jeffrey Lane
Fred Zeytoonjian

Arts Coalition (NYC)
809 West 181 Street
#1638
New York, NY 10033
212-246-3788

Clients:
Arts Coalition (NYC)

Lobbyists:
Norma Munn

Arvai, Joni
4 Westbrook Rd
West Hartford, CT 06107
860-206-9574

Clients:
Bristol-Meyers Squibb Company

Arzt, George Communications Inc
123 William Street
22nd Floor
New York, NY 10038
212-608-0333
e-mail: chief@arztcomm.com

Clients:
11 East 68th Street LLC
47th Street Business Improvement District
A.M Property Holding Corp.
Abax Incorporated
Age 680 Madison LLC
Blood Center (NY)
Broadway Trio
Concerned Physicians for Long Island College Hospital, Inc.
Cooper and 6th Property LLC
CPS Fee Company LLC
Crossroads Ventures, LLC
CRP/Extell Riverside LP
EXG 430W37 LLC
Extell 57th Tower LLC
Extell Development Company
Extell GT LLC
Generation 21 NY, Inc.
Gilbane Building Company
Glenwood POH LLC
Greater Jamaica Development Corporation
Henningson, Durham, & Richardson Architecture and Engineering, PC
Lend Lease (US) Construction LMB, Inc.
MP Liberty Development, LLC
New School (The)
PCV St Owner LP
RJM/EM 4 E 94th Street, LLC
SJP TS JV, LLC
Ska Marin
St. Barnabas Hospital
Structured Employment and Economic Development Corporation

Lobbyists:
George Arzt
Jane Crotty
Maya Gelfand
Fred Winters

Asciutto, Georgia M
74 Chapel Street
Albany, NY 12207
518-465-4274
e-mail: big5schools@mindspring.com

Clients:
Conference of Big 5 School Districts

Lobbyists:
Jennifer Pyle

Asian American Coalition for Children and Families, Inc.
50 Broad Street
18th Floor
New York, NY 10004
212-809-4675

Clients:
Asian American Coalition for Children and Families

Lobbyists:
Noilyn Abesamis-Mendoza
Wayne Ho
Elizabeth Lee
Vanessa Leung
Marissa Martin
Kim To
Mitchell Wu

Associated General Contractors of New York State, LLC
10 Airline Drive
Albany, NY 12205
518-452-1782

Lobbyists:
Michael Elmendorf
Joseph Hogan
Walter Pacholczak

Associated Medical Schools of New York
1270 Avenue of the Americas
Suite 606
New York, NY 10020
212-218-4610

Lobbyists:
Crystal Mainiero
Samuel Mott
Jo Wiederhorn

Assn for Community Living
28 Corporate Drive
Suite 102
Clifton Park, NY 12065
518-688-1682

Clients:
Assn for Community Living

Lobbyists:
Antonia M. Lasicki

Association of Chiefs of Police
2697 Hamburg St
Schenectady, NY 12303
518-355-3371

Clients:
Association of Chiefs of Police

Assn of Community & Residential Agencies (NYS)
99 Pine St, Ste C110
Albany, NY 12207
518-449-7551
Web site: www.nysacra.org

Clients:
Assn of Community & Residential Agencies (NYS)

Lobbyists:
Ann Hardiman
James Kosakoski
Kathleen Mayo

Assn of Counties & Its Affiliated Organizations (NYS)
540 Broadway 5th Floor
Albany, NY 12207
518-465-1473
Web site: www.nysac.org

Clients:
Assn of Counties & Its Affiliated Organizations (NYS)

Lobbyists:
Stephen Acquario
Patrick Cummings
Mark Lavigne
Dave Lucas
Melissa Tiberio
Kathryn Vescio

Association of County Health Officials (New York State)
One United Way
Pine West Plaza
Albany, NY 12205-5555
518-456-7905

Lobbyists:
Linda Wagner

Association of Legal Aid Attorneys UAW 2325 (AFL-CIO)
568 Broadway, 702A
New York, NY 10012-3225
212-343-0708

Lobbyists:
George Albro
Deborah Wright

Association of New York State Youth Bureaus
1653 Central Avenue
Albany, NY 12205
518-436-8712

Lobbyists:
Jacqueline Negri

Assn of PBAS, Inc (NYS)
111 Washington Ave
Albany, NY 11210-2207
518-465-1141

Clients:
Assn of PBAS, Inc (NYS)

Lobbyists:
James Carver
William Diebold
Lou Dini
Mickey Gilbride
James Hughes
Lou Matarazzo
Paul Nunziato
Michael Palladino
Peter B Paterson
Edward Perkins
William Plant
Vincent Provenzano
Fred Sales
Daniel Sisto
Gordon Warnock

Association of Realtors (New York State) (FKA-Mackenzie, Duncan)
Association of Realtors (NYS)
130 Washington Avenue
Albany, NY 12210-2220
518-463-0300

Lobbyists:
Blaise DiBernardo
Mackenzie Duncan
Anthony Gatto
Michael Kelly
Derick King

Association of Towns of the State of NY
150 State Street
Albany, NY 12207
518-465-7933

Lobbyists:
Chris Anderson
Sarah Brancatella
Gerry Geist
Mike Kenneally
Lori Mithen-Demasi

Association on Independent Living
99 Washington Avenue
Suite 806A
Albany, NY 12210
518-465-4650

Clients:
Association on Independent Living (NY)

Lobbyists:
Lindsey Miller
Melanie Shaw

Astellas Pharma US, Inc.
1 Astellas Way
Northbrook, IL 60062
224-205-8800

Clients:
Astellas Pharma

Lobbyists:
Paul Miller

AT&T Inc. and Its Affiliates (FKA Roos, David)
111 Washington Avenue
Suite 700
Albany, NY 12210-2213
518-463-3107
Web site: www.att.com

Lobbyists:
Anna Adams-Sarthou
Edward Bergstraesser
Deborah Bierbaum
Marry Burgess
Kevin Hanna
Amy Hines Kramer
Elizabeth Segal
Marissa Shorenstein

ATU NY State Legislative Conference Board
2115 Central Avenue
Box 15
Schenectady, NY 12304-4415
646-739-1121

Lobbyists:
Luis Alzate
Tom Carney
Daniel Cassella
Michael Cordiello
Vincent Crehan
Mark Guerling
James Hedge
Mark Henry
John Lyons
Ira Miller
Peter Schiraldi
Angelo Tanzi
Eric Wessell

Audubon New York
National Audubon Society
200 Trillium Lane
Albany, NY 12203
518-869-9731
Web site: www.ny.audubon.org

Lobbyists:
Albert Caccese
Graham Cox
Laura McCarthy

Automobile Dealers Assn (NYS)
37 Elk Street
PO Box 7347
Albany, NY 12224-0347
518-463-1148
Web site: www.nysada.com

Clients:
Automobile Dealers Assn (NYS)

Lobbyists:
Robert E Vancavage

AXA Real Estate Investment Managers US
1290 Avenue of the Americas
12th Floor
New York, NY 10104

Clients:
AXA Real Estate Investment Managers US

Lobbyists:
Charlene Behnke
Theo Dunoyer
Dennis Lopez
Isabelle Scemama

Baker & Hostetler LLP
1050 Connecticut Avenue
Suite 1100
Washington, DC 20036-5303

Clients:
Colgate-Palmolive Company

Lobbyists:
Nicole Jefferson
Tom McDonald

BALCONY-Business and Labor Coalition of New York
4 West 43rd Street
Suite 405
New York, NY 10036
212-219-7777

Lobbyists:
Louis Gordon

Bank of America Corporation and Subsidiaries
1 Bryant Park
NY1-100-12-01
New York, NY 10036
646-743-1359
Web site: www.bankofamerica.com

Lobbyists:
Holly Andreozzi
Maria Barry
Samuel Benigno
Mike Bowen
Karyn Brownell
Kathryn J. Busch
Peter Cunningham
Harry Curtis
Judi Cyr
Peter Forsgren
Craig Fowler
Allison Fresher
Todd Gomez
Brian Grip
Maragret Guarino
Eric Hanly
Matthew Harblin
Michael Hatfield
Matt Hoganbruen
Kyle Kincaid
Nicole Mancini

Pamela Opperman
Kelly Parden
David Petraglia
Debbie Phinney
Ed Powers
Eva Roldan
Joseph Santoro
Margaret Scopelianos
Sanjiv Shah
Daron Tubian
William Weir
Michele Wilson

Bankers Association, Inc.
C/O Bankers Association, Inc. (NY)
99 Park Avenue
4th Floor
New York, NY 10016-1502
212-297-1699

Lobbyists:
Karen Armstrong
Clare Cusack
Roberta Kotkin
Michael P. Smith

Banks, Steven
Legal Aid Society (The)
199 Water St
New York, NY 10038
212-577-3277
e-mail: sbanks@legal-aid.org

Clients:
Legal Aid Society (The)

Barclays Capital Inc.
745 Seventh Avenue
New York, NY 10019
212-526-4655

Lobbyists:
Jeff Anderson
Kym Arnone
William Bloom
Mohamed Elkordy
Jason Gans
Stephen Howard
Richard Rein
Johnny Wu

Barlette, Richard
10 Krey Boulevard
Rensselaer, NY 12144-9681
518-356-8883

Clients:
Independent System Operator, Inc. (New York)

Lobbyists:
Kimberly Ireland

Barnes, Richard E
C/O Catholic Conference (NYS)
465 State St
Albany, NY 12203-1004
518-434-6195
Web site: www.nyscatholic.org

Clients:
Catholic Conference (NYS)

Lobbyists:
James Cultrara
S Earl Eichelberger
Clayton Eichelberger
Kathleen M Gallagher
Dennis Poust

Barrett Associates
95 Columbia St
Albany, NY 12210-2707
518-465-5340

Clients:
Acadia Insurance Company
Ambrose Employer Group, LLC
America's Health Insurance Plans
Automobile Insurance Plan (NY)
Buckeye Partners, L.P
Capital One Financial Corporation
Care One Services, Inc. (National Strategies, LLC)
Central Mutual Fire Insurance Co. (NY)
Coventry
Ebay, Inc.
IAAC, Inc.
Independent Insurance Agents & Brokers of NY
Pitney Bowes, Inc.
Procter & Gamble
Property Insurance Underwriting Association
Travelers Indemnity Company (The)
United Services Automobile Association (USAA)

Lobbyists:
Michael V Barrett
Peter Carr
Jill Muratori

Bartimole, John E (FKA Western NY Healthcare Association) (FKA Larowe, Mary)
Western New York Healthcare Association
1876 Niagara Falls Blvd
Tonawanda, NY 14150-6439
716-695-0843

Lobbyists:
Paul Sweet

Bayview Asset Management
4425 Ponce De Leon Blvd
Coral Gables, FL 33146
305-341-3693

Lobbyists:
David Ertel
Howard Shoer

Beaudoin & Company (FKA Beaudoin, Heather)
275 7th Avenue, 18th Floor
New York, NY 10011
347-922-1074

Clients:
Building & Construction Trades Council of Greater New York
International Brotherhood of Teamsters Port Division
Joint Council #16, International Brotherhood of Teamsters
Major League Soccer

Lobbyists:
Heather Beaudoin
Rebecca Lynch

Bee Ready Fishbein Hatter & Donovan, LLP (FKA Bee, Peter A)
170 Old Country Road
Mineola, NY 11501
516-746-5599
Web site: www.beereadylaw.com

Clients:
Cablevision (CSC Holdings, Inc.)

Lobbyists:
Peter A Bee

Beha, Alyson
55 Broad St
23rd Floor
New York, NY 10004
212-838-9410

Clients:
New Yorkers for Parks

Lobbyists:
Alyson Beha
Jessica Feldman
Holly Leicht
Emily Walker
Edward Wallace
Robin Weinstein
James Yolles

Behan Communications, Inc.
83 Glen Street
PO Box 2077
Glens Falls, NY 12801
518-792-3856

Clients:
Catholic Conference Policy Group, Inc.
Finch Paper LLC

Lobbyists:
Mark Behan
John Brodt
William Callen
Patrick Dowd
Joan Gerhardt

Bender Cantone Consulting
1407 Broadway
Suite 1708
New York, NY 10018
347-328-1088

Clients:
Association of Car Wash Owners, Inc.
County of Suffolk Department of Economic Development and Planning
Genting NY
Lettire Construction Corp.
New York Yankees Partnership
Onexim Basketball, LLC
Virtu Financial LLC

Lobbyists:
Bruce Bender
Scott Cantone

Bennett Firm, Inc (The)
PO Box 38004
Albany, NY 12203
518-439-0077

Clients:
Coalition of Specialty Care Physicians
Society of Orthopaedic Surgeons (NYS)

Lobbyists:
Heather Bennett

Billig, Jacob
146 Rock Hill Dr
Rockhill, NY 12775
845-434-4780

Clients:
Trading Cove NY, LLC

Binghamton University
PO Box 6000
Binghamton, NY 13902-6000
607-777-5014

Lobbyists:
Terrence Kane
Mary Lou Sollis
Harvey Stenger

Blackstone Alternative Asset Management L.P
345 Park Avenue
New York, NY 10154
212-583-5000

Lobbyists:
J. Tomlinson Hill
John McCormick
Brian Schwartz

Bloom Energy Corporation
PO Box 1406
Princeton, NJ 08540
212-920-7151

Lobbyists:
Charles Fox

Boehringer Ingelheim Pharmaceuticals, Inc.
9660-138 Falls of Neuse Road
PO Box 188
Raleigh, NC 27615
919-556-6491

Lobbyists:
Gail Amato
Joseph Oros

Lobbyists:
Paul Fanikos

Bogdan Lasky & Frazier, LLC
111 Washington Avenue
Suite 750
Albany, NY 12210-2213

518-434-9000
e-mail: etricomi@blklobby.com
Web site: www.blklobby.com

Clients:
Alfred University
Anheuser-Busch Companies, Inc.
Association of Nurse Anesthetists, Inc. (NYS)
Astrazeneca Pharmaceuticals
Darden Restaurants, Inc.
Entertainment Software Association
International Council of Shopping Centers
International Game Technology
McLane Company, Inc.
Midland Credit Management, Inc.
Midtown Surgery Center, LLC
Motion Picture Association of America, Inc.
National Association of Theatre Owners of NYS
Providers Alliance
Sergeants Benevolent Association
Shell Energy North America
Society of New York Office Based Surgery Facilities
Sprint Nextel Corporation
Tecmar, LTD
Time Warner, Inc.
Toy Industry Association, Inc.
Wine Institute

Lobbyists:
Edward A Bogdan III
Kyle R. Christiansen
Diane E Frazier
Mary K Kopley
James A Lasky

Bolton St. Johns, Inc.
146 State St
Albany, NY 12207
518-462-4620
e-mail: mail@boltonstjohns.com
Web site: www.boltonstjohns.com

Clients:
1199 SEIU United Healthcare Workers East
AIDS Healthcare Foundation
AIRBNB, Inc.
Alliance of New York State YMCAs, Inc.
AMDEC Foundation, Inc.
American Council of Engineering Companies of NY (FKA Association of Consulting Engineers (NYS))
American Solar Partners
Amsterdam Nursing Home Corp.
Apple Valley Waste Conversions
Aquest South Park LLC
Baker Victory Services
Bluestone Gas Corporation of New York, Inc.
BMM Testlabs
Caesars Entertainment Operating Company, Inc.
Camp Dresser McKee & Smith
Care for the Homeless
City of Lackawanna
Clark Patterson Lee
Committee for Taxi Safety
Community Health Project, Inc.
Continuing Care Leadership Coalition
Corizon Health, Inc.
Correctional Officers and Police Benevolent Association, Inc. (NYS)
Elevator Industry Work Preservation Fund
Empire Education Corporation
Empire State Pride Agenda, Inc.
ENDO Pharmaceuticals, Inc.
Express Scripts, Inc.
Fashion Institute of Technology
Fifth Avenue Arcade, Inc.
Figure Skating in Harlem, Inc.
Financial Services Institute, Inc.
First Alert
Focused Technologies Imaging Services LLC
Gay & Lesbian Anti-Violence Project (NYC)
Gonzalez Saggio & Harlan LLP
Google, Inc.
Greater New York Hospital Association
Hailo Network USA, Inc.
Hartland Asset Management
Immigration Coalition, Inc.
Island Peer Review Organization, Inc. (IPRO)
IUOE Local 17
JPAY, Inc.
Kaleida Health
Keycorp & Subsidiaries
Kingsbrook Jewish Medical Center
Lackawanna School District
Lesbian & Gay Community Services Center, Inc.
Lifealike, LTD
Local 338 RWDSU
Long Island Federation of Labor, AFL-CIO
Major League Soccer, L.L.C.
Medical Answering Services, LLC
Medtronic, Inc.
Mehigan Bellone & Associates, Inc.
Mentoring Partnership Coalition
Metlife
Metropolitan Museum of Art (The)
MLOTTO, Inc.
Morphotrust USA, Inc.
NANOS Research
National Youth Recovery Foundation
New School (The)
Open View Consulting
Oracle America, Inc.
People, Inc.
Pfizer, Inc.
Phelps Dodge Refining Corporation (Subsidiary of Freeport-McMoran Corporation)
Pipe Trades Association
Pratt Holdings USA (FKA Visy Paper (NY))
RAI Services Company
Recording Industry Association of America, Inc.
Retail, Wholesale and Department Store Union (RWDSU)
Rocking the Boat, Inc.
Sacandaga Protection Company
Saratoga Hospital
Selective Staffing Solutions
Share Our Strength, Inc.
Shawanga Lodge, LLC
Siemens Industry, Inc.
St. Mary's Healthcare System For Children, Inc.
St. Regis Mohawk Tribe
Steamfitters Local 638 PAC
StoryCorps
Sysco Food Services of Albany, LLC
Transportation Alternatives, Inc.
Trustees of Columbia University in the City of NY (The)
Upstate New York Transplant Services
Verizon New York, Inc.
Vornado Realty L.P.
Western Union
WestField, LLC
Wholesale Beer Distributors Association (NYS)
Window Covering Manufacturers Association
Women's Housing & Economic Development Corporation

Offices and agencies generally appear in alphabetical order, except when specific order is requested by listee.

Yum! Brands, Inc.

Lobbyists:
Natasha Avanessians
Donald Baker
Brendan Baxter
David Beier
Tom Connolly
Georgio DeRosa
Edward Draves
Emily Giske
Michael Keogh
Julian Kline
Bill McCarthy
John McCarthy
John O'Donnell
Tweeps Phillips
Patricia Reilly

Boltz, John J Consulting
14 Linden Ct
Clifton Park, NY 12065
518-371-2790

Clients:
Altria Client Services, Inc.
First Data Corporation & its Subsidiaries (Barbara J. Ahern)
Kraft Foods Global, Inc,
Millercoors, LLC

Lobbyists:
Christina M. Bolton
John J Boltz

Bombardier Transit Corporation & Affiliates (FKA Bombardier Transit Corporation)
71 Wall Street
Plattsburgh, NY 12901
518-566-0150

Clients:
Bombardier Transit Corporation

Lobbyists:
Raymond Bachant
Robert E Furniss

Bombardiere, Ralph
C/O Assn of Svc. Stations & Repair Shops
6 Walker Way
Albany, NY 12205-4946
518-452-1979
e-mail: nysassn@together.net
Web site: www.nysassrs.com

Clients:
Assn of Service Stations & Repair Shops, Inc. (NYS)

Bonagura, David
5 Times Square
New York, NY 10036
212-773-7111

Clients:
Ernst & Young LLP

Lobbyists:
Mark Costello
Carmine Di Sibio
Michael Dings
Tom Griffith
Scott Halliday
Robert Jacobs
Samuel Johnson
Linda Lam
Peter Lease
Mark Manoff
Robert Marzziotti
David Milkosky
Kurt Neidhardt
Randy Nelson
Roger Savell

Bond, Schoeneck & King, PLLC
22 Corporate Woods Blvd
Suite 501
Albany, NY 12211-2503
518-533-3000

Clients:
Automobile Dealers Association (NYS)
Colgate University
Collectors Association, Inc. (NYS)
Financial Service Centers of New York, Inc.
Griffiss Local Development Corporation
Intuit, Inc.
Lowville Academy and Central School
Matt Brewing Company (The)
Ski Areas of NY, Inc.

Lobbyists:
Hermes Fernandez
Frank C. Mayer
Raymond Meier
Matthew A. Young

Bookman, Esq., Robert S
325 Broadway
Suite 501
New York, NY 10007
212-513-1988

Clients:
Hospitality Alliance, Inc.

Bopp, Linda
Nutrition Consortium of NYS, Inc.
14 Computer Drive East, 2nd Floor
Albany, NY 12205
518-436-8757

Clients:
Nutrition Consortium of NYS, Inc.

Lobbyists:
Gail Cooney
Casey Dinkin
Misha Marvel
Rachel Rupright
Rachel Rupright
Dawn Secor

Botanical Garden (The) (NY)
2900 Southern Boulevard
Bronx, NY 10458
718-817-8518

Clients:
Botanical Garden (NY) (The)

Lobbyists:
Aaron Bouska
J V Cossaboom
Elizabeth Figueroa
Todd Forrest
Carolyn Laney
Gregory Long
Michael Rivadeneyra

Bottlers Association (New York State)
99 Pine Street
Suite 207
Albany, NY 12207
518-436-0786

Lobbyists:
Tom Strahle
Phillip Swink
C. Thomas Tenney
Donald Thomas
Peter Wilcox
Bill Wilson

Boucher, Paul
1290 Avenue of the Americas
New York, NY 10104
212-314-3946

Clients:
AXA Equitable Life Insurance Company

Lobbyists:
Kermit Brooks

Brennan Center for Justice at New York
161 Avenue of the Americas
12th Floor
New York, NY 10013
646-292-8310

Lobbyists:
David Earley
Eliza Goitein
Mark Ladov
Larry Norden
Faiza Patel
Myrna Perez
Mike Price
Lee Rowland
Adam Skaggs
Ian Vandenwalker
Michael Waldman
Wendy Weiser
Kelly Williams

Brescia, Richard
321 Loudon Road
Loudonville, NY 12211
518-436-6733

Clients:
Propane Gas Association (NY)

Briand, Elizabeth H (FKA Striar, Gary)
American Red Cross-Greater NY
33 Everett Rd
Albany, NY 12205-1437
518-458-8111

Clients:
American Red Cross in Greater NY

Brickfield, Burchette, Ritts & Stone, P.C.
1025 Thomas Jefferson Street, NW
Suite 800
Washington, DC 20007-5201
202-342-0800

Clients:
Nucor Steel Auburn, Inc.

Lobbyists:
James Brew

Brighter Choice Foundation
395 Elk Street
3rd Floor
Albany, NY 12206
518-694-4115

Clients:
Brighter Choice Foundation

Lobbyists:
Daniel O'Connor

Broadcasters Association, Inc.
1805 Western Avenue
Albany, NY 12203
518-456-8888

Lobbyists:
David Donovan
Richard Novik

Bronx River Alliance, Inc.
One Bronx River Parkway
Bronx, NY 10462
718-430-4665

Lobbyists:
Linda Cox
Robin Kriesberg

Brookhaven Science Associates, LLC
Brookhaven National Laboratory
Building 400
Upton, NY 11973-5000
631-344-4747

Lobbyists:
Sam Aronson
Mike Bebon
Doon Gibbs
Marge Lynch
Mann Reinhold
Jim Misewich
Gerry Stokes

Brooklyn Museum
Terri Jackson
200 Eastern Parkway
Brooklyn, NY 11238
718-501-6332

Lobbyists:
Terri Jackson

Brooks, Helen M
590 Broadway
Menands, NY 12204
518-698-3422

Clients:
FedEx Corporation

Brown & Weinraub, PLLC
50 State Street
4th Floor
Albany, NY 12207
518-427-7350

Clients:
Accela, Inc.
Aeon Nexus Corporation
American International Group, Inc.
Applied Materials
Arnot-Ogden Medical Center
Association of Alcoholism & Substance Abuse Providers, Inc. (NY)
Astellas
Building & Construction Trades Council (NYS)
CAMBA (FKA Church Avenue Merchants Block Association, Inc.)
Catholic Health Services of Long Island
Catskill Regional Off-Track Betting Corporation
Center for Discovery
Charles T. Sitrin Network of Homes & Services, Inc.
Clearing House Association, LLC (The)
Community Health Care Association of New York State
DePaul
Ditmas Park Rehab Care Center
Dominion Voting Systems Inc.
Empire Generating Co., LLC
Entergy Nuclear Operations, Inc.
Extended Home Care
Finger Lakes Health Systems Agency
Government Employees Insurance Company (GEICO)
Hartland Asset Management
Hope Network
Hospitals Insurance Company, Inc.
Hudson Headwaters Health Network
Jewish Senior Life
KPMG, LLP
Living Essentials, LLC
LV Apartments LP
Merscorp, Inc.
MS Hospital
Nicholas Noyes Memorial Hospital
Novartis Pharmaceuticals Corporation
NTT Data, Inc.
NYU Langone Medical Center
ODA Primary Health Care Center
Oracle America, Inc.
Pacifica Ventures, LLC
Parsons Brinckerhoff, Inc.
Premium Finance Association
Proton Management, LLC
Psychotherapy & Counseling Center (New York)
Real Estate Tax Review Bar Association
Refuah Health Center
Richmond University Medical Center
Rochester Malls, LLC
Roswell Park Cancer Institute
Sibley Redevelopment Limited Partnership
Solar Energy Industries Association
Southampton Hospital
Stony Brook University Hospital
Sunrun, Inc.
Trading Cove New York, LLC
United Healthcare Services, Inc.
VNA of Albany, Inc.
Westmoreland Consulting, LLC
Whitney Capital LLC
William F. Ryan Health Center
Yahoo! Inc.
Young Adult Institute, Inc.
Zuffa LLC

Lobbyists:
Neil Benjamin
Michael Boxley
Patrick Brown
Jeffrey Buley
Justin Driscoll
John Harris
Carolyn Kerr
Ron Rock
David Weinraub

Brown, Arthur M.
PO Box 252
Speculator, NY 12164
518-635-0556

Clients:
Accenture, LTD.
Computer Aid, Inc.
Unique Comp, Inc.

Browne, Brian
St John's University-Manhattan Campus
101 Murray St
New York, NY 10007
212-284-7005
Web site: www.stjohns.edu

Clients:
St John's University

Bryan Cave, LLP
1290 Avenue of the Americas
New York, NY 10104
212-541-2389

Clients:
390 Tower Associates LLC
Gerard Avenue LLC
MTM Associates, LLC
University (New York)

Lobbyists:
Phyllis Arnold
Frank Chaney
Robert Davis
Judith Gallent
Philip Karmel
Margery Perlmutter
Ivan Schonfeld
Stanley Santos

Buffalo State College
665 Main Street
Suite 200
Buffalo, NY 14203
716-878-4324

Lobbyists:
William Benfanti

Offices and agencies generally appear in alphabetical order, except when specific order is requested by listee.

Builders Association (NYS)
One Commerce Plaza
Suite 704
Albany, NY 12210
518-465-2492

Clients:
Builders Association (NYS)

Lobbyists:
Lewis Dubuque

Building & Construction Trades Council (NYS)
50 State Street
3rd Floor
Albany, NY 12207
518-435-9108

Clients:
Building & Construction Trades Council (NYS)

Lobbyists:
James Cahill
Megan Pliscofsky

Building & Construction Trades Council of Greater NY
71 West 23rd Street
Suite 501-03
New York, NY 10010
212-647-0700

Clients:
Building & Construction Trades Council of Greater NY

Lobbyists:
Paul Fernandes
Gary Labarbera

Burgos, Tonio & Associates
Trinity Centre
115 Broadway, Ste 1504
New York, NY 10006
212-566-5600

Clients:
American Airlines
Ben Barnes Group LP
Beverage Works NY, Inc. (The)
Broadway 4D Theater NY, LLC
Daytop Village, Inc.
Deepwater Wind,LLC
EmblemHealth Services Company, LLC
Genon Bowline, LLC
Greater New York Hospital Association
Jones Lang Lasalle
National Grid USA
Pfizer, Inc.
Shipping Association, Inc.
Union Community Health Center
United Water New York, Inc.
Univision Communications, Inc.
Verizon Corporate Resources Group LLC (FKA Verizon NY)
Williams Companies (The)

Lobbyists:
Jemine Burgos
Tonio Burgos
John Charlson
Francisco Diaz Jr.
Christopher Hahn
Seth Kaye
Ninfa Segarra

Business Council of NYS, Inc.
152 Washington Ave
Albany, NY 12210-2289
518-465-7511

Clients:
Business Council of NYS, Inc. (The)

Lobbyists:
Heather Briccetti
Marcus Ferguson
Lev Ginsberg
Catherine Jimenez
Heather Jung
Kenneth Pokalsky

Byrne, Elizabeth
One Orange Way
C1N
Windsor, CT 06095
860-580-2799

Clients:
ING America Insurance Holdings

Byrne, Kevin
200 Seaport Blvd
Boston, MA 02210-0000
617-563-4162

Clients:
Fidelity Capital Markets, a Division of National Financial Services

Lobbyists:
Kevin Byrne
Elizabeth Hanify
Suresh Perera

Cacsars Entertainment Operating Company, Inc.
One Caesars Palace Drive
Las Vegas, NV 89109
702-407-6000

Lobbyists:
David Statz
Joseph Tyrrell
Thomas Minnick
Darren Suarez

Calvin, James S
C/O Assn of Convenience Stores (NY)
130 Washington Avenue
Suite 300
Albany, NY 12210
518-432-1400
e-mail: jim@nyacs.org
Web site: www.nyacs.org

Clients:
Assn of Convenience Stores (NY)

Camba, Inc. (FKA Church Avenue Merchants Block Association, Inc.)
1720 Church Avenue
Brooklyn, NY 11226

Offices and agencies generally appear in alphabetical order, except when specific order is requested by listee.

718-287-2600

Lobbyists:
Jeffrey Austin
Valerie Barton-Richardson
Tyesha Branch
Caitlyn Brazill
Kevin Coffey
Dany Cunningham
Sharon Daly-Browne
Thomas Dambakly
Kathy Dros
Kaida Edwards
Michael Erhard
Alison Goldberg
Claire Harding-Keefe
Stacy Ann Harris
Christie Hodgkins
Robin Landes
Mary Ann Lanzetta
Kathleen Masters
Janet Miller
Marjorie Momplaisir-Ellis
Joanne Oplustil
Jude Pierre
Patrick Pyronneau
Eileen Reilly
Rick Rodriguez
David Rowe
Matthew Schedler
Gary Sutnick
Frances Weinstock
David Zelamsky

Canisius College
2001 Main St
LY 209
Buffalo, NY 14208
716-888-2793

Lobbyists:
J. Patrick Greenwald
John J. Hurley
Debra Park
Patrick Richey
Melinda Sanderson

Cantore, Anthony S.
1073 Serafini Drive
Schenectady, NY 12303-5107
518-869-2542

Clients:
Retired Public Employees Association, Inc.

Capalino, James F & Associates Inc
233 Broadway
Suite 850
New York, NY 10279
212-616-5810
e-mail: james@capalino.com
Web site: www.capalino.com

Clients:
250 East 57th Street, LLC
328-36 West 53rd Street Redevelopment Company, LP
341-363 West 50th Street, LLC
3530 WPR LLC
39 West 23rd Street, LLC
414-24 West 48th Street Redevelopment Company, LP
444 Realty Company, LLC
Academy of Medicine (NY)
Acadia 161st Street, LLC
Albee Development, LLC
All Stars Project, Inc., The
American Institute of Architects - New York Chapter
American Youth Hostels, Inc.
Axis Group, Inc.
Axton Owner, LLC
Beth Israel Medical Center
BSDM Inc.
CBS Outdoor, Inc. (FKA Viacom Outdoor, Inc.)
Central United Talmudical Academy
Circle Entertainment, Inc.
Coach Farm Enterprises, Inc.
Computers for Youth
Douglaston Development LLC
Equality Charter School
Freeze Frame LLC
Gansevoort Market, Inc.
Healthcare Chaplaincy, The
HFZ Highline LLC
Hudson Eagle, LLC
Industry City Associates, LLC
Inwood House
ISJ Commercial Corp.
Jamestown Premier Chelsea Market, LP
Knic Partners LLC
Lands End Associates, LP
Langan Engineering & Environmental Services, Inc.
Leader House Associates, LP
Lower East Side District Management Association, Inc.
Madison Equities LLC
Manhattan by Sail Inc.
Manhattan School of Music
Media Metrica Ltd.
Metro Storage NY, LLC
Metropolitan Arts & Antiques Pavillion, LTD.
Midtown Trackage Ventures LLC
MPE Hotel I Tenant (Downtown NY) LLC
MTM Associates, LLC
National Media Services, Inc.
New Amsterdam Public Market Association, Inc.
Riverview Redevelopment Company LP
Rivington House- The Nicholas A. Rango Health Care Facility
Safe Space
Second Stage Theatre
Snowplow LLC
Solomon R. Guggenheim Museum
Stiles Properties, LLC
Sunnyside Community Services, Inc.
Trinity School
Two Bridges Associates, LP
Underground Development Foundation
Urban Muse LLC
Urban Space Holdings, Inc.
Wholeness of Life Center, Inc.
WW Acquisitions and Development LLC
Young Women's Leadership Network

Lobbyists:
James F Capalino
George Fontas
Ben Kleinbaum
Brooke Schafran
Travis Terry
Mark Thompson

Capital District Physicians' Health Plan Inc
500 Patroon Creek Blvd
Albany, NY 12206-1057
518-641-5211
Web site: www.cdphp.com

Clients:
Capital District Physicians' Health Plan Inc

Lobbyists:
John Bennett
Robert R Hinckley

Capital Public Affairs
111 Washington Ave, Rm 104
Albany, NY 12210
518-465-8760

Clients:
Pharmacists Society of the State of NY
Society of Oral and Maxillofacial Surgeons (NYS)

Lobbyists:
Elizabeth M Lasky
Roy E Lasky

Capitol Consultants Inc (NY)
33 Elk Street
Suite 210
Albany, NY 12207
518-449-3333

Clients:
BP America Inc

Lobbyists:
Siobhan McGrath

Capitol Group, LLC
111 Washington Ave
Albany, NY 12210
518-463-4841
e-mail: nick@capitolgroupllc.com; tim@capitolgroupllc.com
Web site: www.capitolgroupllc.com

Clients:
American Safety Institute, Inc.
Association of Plumbing, Heating & Cooling Contractors, Inc. (NYS)
Clarity Imaging Technologies, Inc.
Clorox Company (The)
Consumer Healthcare Products Assn
Drexel Hamilton
Empire State Marine Trades Association
Envisage Information Systems, LLC
Grocery Manufacturers Assn (FKA Grocery Manufacturers of America)
Independent Health Association, Inc.
Long Island Forum for Technology
Morgan Construction Enterprises, Inc.
National Association of Professional Employer Organizations
National Shooting Sports Foundation, Inc.
Physicians Reciprocal Insurers
Rent A Center (Stateside Associates)
Rite Aid Corporation
Snowmobile Association (NYS)
Systech International
Tobacconist Association of NYS
TWC Administration LLC
Waste Management
Yonkers Raceway

Lobbyists:
Nicholas Barrella
Kathryn Holman
Timothy Sheridan

Capitol Hill Management Services Inc
1450 Western Avenue
Suite 101
Albany, NY 12203
518-463-8644
e-mail: chms@caphill.com
Web site: www.caphill.com

Clients:
Advocates for Adult Day Services
American Massage Therapy Assoc. - NY Chapter
Arcadis-US
Automotive Recyclers Association
Battery and Energy Storage Technology Consortium, Inc.
Capital Region Building Owners and Managers Association
Chamber Alliance of New York State
Council of Senior Centers and Services
Crossbow Coalition,Inc.
Custom Crews, Inc.
Dig Safely New York, Inc.
Epilepsy Foundation of Northeastern New York, Inc.
Maternity & Early Childhood Foundation, Inc.
Outdoor Advertising Council of NY, Inc.
Public Adjusters Association
Society of Opticians, Inc. (NYS)

Lobbyists:
John A Graziano, Jr
Rebecca Marino

Capitol Public Strategies, LLC (FKA McCulley & Associates, Inc.)
121 State Street
3rd Floor
Albany, NY 12207
518-432-3300

Clients:
Monroe County

Lobbyists:
David Catalfamo
Kelly MacMillan
Jeffrey Lovell
James McCulley
William McGahay
Ryan Moore
Ryan Moses
Robert Bulman

Capitol Strategies Group, LLC
30 S Pearl St
PO Box 445
Albany, NY 12207
518-432-3676

Clients:
Carahsoft Technology Corporation
Colt Refining and Recycling
Daw Systems, Inc.
Gartner Inc.
Hitachi Data Systems Corporation
Lexmark International, Inc.
Novell

Quest Public Sector, Inc.
Windstream Corporation

Lobbyists:
Robert Burdick
Christopher Cotrona

Capvest Partners LLP
677 Broadway
9th Floor
Albany, NY 12207
518-449-8893

Clients:
Capvest Partners LLP

Lobbyists:

Carey Group LLC
100 Wall Street
23rd Floor
New York, NY 10005
212-912-3661
Web site: www.careyllc.com

Clients:
125 MEC Center LLC
195 Broadway LLC
Cambridge Petroleum Corporation
Equity One, Inc.
Oliveira Contracting, Inc.
Proton Management LLC
Salmar Properties LLC
Triangle Equities

Lobbyists:
Michael Carey
Regina Demilia
Stephen Hayes

Carl Andrews & Associates, Inc.
111 Washington Avenue
Suite 750
Albany, NY 12210
518-810-0222

Clients:
Glenwood Management Corp
TD Bank, N.A.

Lobbyists:
Carl Andrews
Jahmila Joseph

Carnevale Consulting, LLC
Po Box 21
Wynantskill, NY 12198
518-326-4582

Clients:
Arista Networks
Avaya
BMC
GCOM
Salesforce.com, Inc.
Time Warner Cable

Lobbyists:
Carmella Carnevale

Carpino, Peter
United Way of Greater Rochester
75 College Ave
Rochester, NY 14607-1009
585-242-6400

Clients:
United Way of Greater Rochester

Lobbyists:
Dawn Borgeest
Patricia Davis
Jennifer Higgins

Carson, Martin
105 Fiddlers Elbow Rd
Middle Falls, NY 12848
518-692-3162

Clients:
Lorillard, Inc.

Casey Strategic Relations
518-331-8837

Clients:
American College of Occupational and Environmental Medicine
MedBox

Lobbyists:
Glen Casey

Casey, Teresa M.
Mackin & Casey
139 Lancaster Street
Albany, NY 12210-1903
518-449-4698

Clients:
Association of Financial Guarantee Insurers

Casey, William R.
65 East 55th St
30th Floor
New York, NY 10022
212-812-3100

Clients:
King Street Capital Management, L.P.

Lobbyists:
Brian Higgins
John Purcell

Catholic Community Relations Council of New York, Inc.
1011 First Avenue
16th Floor
New York, NY 10022
212-371-1011

Clients:
Catholic Community Relations Council of New York, Inc.

Lobbyists:
Joseph Rosenburg

Catskill Center for Conservation and Development, Inc.
P.O. Box 504
Route 28
Arkville, NY 12406
845-586-2611

Clients:
Catskill Center for Conservation and Development, Inc.

Lobbyists:
Peter Manning
Alan White

Center for Charter School Excellence (NYC)
111 Broadway
Suite 604
New York, NY 10006
212-437-8300
Web site: www.nycchartercenter.org

Clients:
Center for Charter School Excellence (NYC)

Lobbyists:
Valerie Babb
David Golovner
James D. Merriman
Michael Reginer

Center for Children's Initiatives, Inc.
322 Eighth Avenue
New York, NY 10001
212-929-7686

Lobbyists:
Rhonda Carlos Smith
Betty Holcomb
Darius Charney

Center for Constitutional Rights (501C3 Organization With 501H Election)
666 Broadway
7th Floor
New York, NY 10012
212-614-6469

Clients:
Center for Constitutional Rights

Lobbyists:
Deborah Popowski
Annette Warren Dickerson
Qa'id Jacobs
Jennifer Nessel
Camilo Ramirez
Meejin Richart
Vincent Warren
An-Tuan Williams
Chauniqua Young
Nahal Zamani

Center for Disability Rights, Inc.
497 State Street
Rochester, NY 14608
585-546-7510

Clients:
Center for Disability Rights, Inc.

Lobbyists:
David Atias
Bruce Darling
Leah Farrell
Chris Hilderbrant
Lara Kassel

Center for Liver Transplantation
185 Jordan Rd
Troy, NY 12180
518-533-7877

Lobbyists:
Samantha Delair
Samantha Taylor

Centerstate Corporation for Economic Opportunity
572 S. Salina St
Syracuse, NY 13202
315-470-1800

Lobbyists:
Thomas Blanchard
David Holder
David Mankiewicz
Seth Mulligan
Mitchell Patterson
Dominic Robinson
Kevin Schwab
Robert Simpsons
Benjamin Sio
Deborah Warner

Central Hudson Gas & Electric Corporation (FKA Glusko, John)
C/O Central Hudson Gas & Electric Corp.
284 South Avenue
Poughkeepsie, NY 12601-4879
845-486-5201

Lobbyists:
Anthony Campagiorni
Steven Lant
James Laurito

Central New York School Boards Association
6390 Fly Road
East Syracuse, NY 13057
315-463-1904

Lobbyists:
Charles Borgognoni
Rick Timbs

Central Labor Council (NYC)
275 Seventh Avenue
New York, NY 10001
212-604-9552

Lobbyists:
Anthony Thomas

Cetrino, Thomas
90 State Street
Suite 1029
Albany, NY 12207
518-432-4003

Political Parties, Lobbyists & PACs

Clients:
Public Employees Federation

Lobbyists:
Wayne Bayer
Thomas Cetrino
Carlos Garcia
Susan Kent
Patricia Lavin
Christopher Leo
Musa Moore
John Murphy

Chadwick, Cindy
C/O Electric & Gas Corporation (NYS)
18 Link Dr, PO Box 5224
Binghamton, NY 13902-5224
607-762-7310
e-mail: ctchadwick@nyseg.com
Web site: www.nyseg.com

Clients:

Changaris, Steve
482 Southbridge St
Suite 373
Auburn, MA 01501
800-679-6263

Clients:
National Solid Wastes Management Association
Electric & Gas Corp (NYS)
Rochester Gas & Electric Corp

Chase Paymentech Solutions, LLC
14221 Dallas Parkway
Dallas, TX 75254-2942
614-865-3856

Lobbyists:
James P. Fleming
Dave Jimenez
Matthew P. Leman

Chesapeake Appalachia, LLC
6040 North Western Avenue
Oklahoma City, OK 73118
405-935-7888

Lobbyists:
Michael Atchie
Michael Brownell
William Freeman
Brian Grove
Paul Hartman
Jennifer Hoffman
Scott Rotruck
Matt Sheppard
David Spigelmyer

Chesterton, Jan Marie
1 Computer Drive S
Albany, NY 12205
518-465-2300

Clients:
Hospitality & Tourism NYS

Children's Aid Society (The)
105 East 22nd Street
New York, NY 10010
917-286-1554

Lobbyists:
Richard Buery
Adria Cruz
Katherine Eckstein
Lorena Jimenez
William Weisberg

Children's Health Fund (The)
215 West 125th Street
New York, NY 10027
212-535-9400

Lobbyists:
Deirdre Byrne
Dennis Johnson

Chin, Francis Y.
390 Greenwich Street
2nd Floor
New York, NY 10013
212-723-5576

Clients:
Citi Group Global Markets, Inc.

Lobbyists:
Douglas Auslander
Jay Bartlett
Matthew Bissonette
Daniel Cohen
Jennifer Conovitz
Benjamin Cooper
Paul Creedon
Robert DeMichiel
Andrew Ditton
Richard Gerwitz
Thomas Green
Steven Hall
Adam Halvorsen
Raymond High
Kristen Johanson
Michael Koessel
Barry Krinsky
Mike Leffler
David Livingstone
Bartley Livolsi
Ronald Marino
Shai Markowicz
Robert McMaster
Sandeep Satish
Matthew Tesseyman
Daniel Tomson
Miriam Wrobel
Tricia Yarger
William Yates

CitiGroup Management Corp.
1101 Pennsylvania Ave. NW
Suite 1000
Washington, DC 20004
202-879-6805

Lobbyists:
Mary Griffin

Offices and agencies generally appear in alphabetical order, except when specific order is requested by listee.

Citizens Campaign for the Environment
225A Main St
Farmingdale, NY 11735
516-390-7150
e-mail: ccefli@citizenscampaign.org
Web site: www.citizenscampaign.org

Clients:
Citizens Campaign for the Environment

Lobbyists:
William Cooke
Maureen Dolan
Sarah Eckle
Adrienne Esposito
Brian Smith

Citizens Committee for New York City
77 Water St
Suite 202
New York, NY 10005
212-989-0909

Lobbyists:
Peter Kostmayer

Citizens' Committee for Children of New York Inc
14 Wall Street
Suite 4E
New York, NY 10005-2173
212-673-1800
Web site: www.cccnewyork.org

Clients:
Citizens' Committee for Children of New York Inc

Lobbyists:
Stephanie Gendell
Alexis Henry
Lena Jayaram
Gregory Klemens
Jennifer March
Apurva Mehrota
Francisco Miguel Araiza
Julio Minaya
Elysia Murphy
Ariel Savransky

City Harvest
6 East 32nd Street
New York, NY 10016
917-351-8700

Lobbyists:
Kate Mackenzie

City University of New York (CUNY)
111 Washington Ave
Suite 605
Albany, NY 12210
518-463-2177
Web site: www.cuny.edu

Clients:
City University of New York (CUNY)

Lobbyists:
Anthony Achille
Susan Agin
Michelle Anderson
Dean Balsamini
Peter Barbatis
Herb Berman
William Boone
Stephen Brier
Diane Call
Claudia Chan
Vincent Clark
Valli Cook
Ben Corpus
Mario Dellapina
Danielle Dimitrov
Allan Dobrin
Staci Emanuel
Scott Evenbeck
Ricardo R. Fernandez
Arthur Flung
William Fritz
Kathleen Galvez
Donna Gerstle
Eileen Goldmann
Matthew Goldstein
Karen Gould
Sumil Gupta
Sue Henderson
Jay Hershenson
Russell Holtzer
Kenichi Iwama
Howard Johnson
Marcia Keizs
MaryKaye Kellogg
William Kelly
Hugo Kijne
John Kotowski
Alexandra Logue
Eric Lugo
Ernesto Malave, Jr.
Felix Matos-Rodgriguez
Lavita McMath-Turner
Gail Mellow
John Mogulescu
James Muyskens
Moses Newsome
Gbubemi Okotieuro
Antonio Perez
Ira Persky
Regina Peruggi
Alice Pisciotta
William Pollard
F. Quintanilla
Jennifer J. Raab
Ana Garcia Reyes
Augie Rivera
Joshua Rivera
Chris Rosa
Jeff Rosenstock
Angela Sales
Frank Sanchez
Matt Sapienza
Frederick Schaffer
Stephen Schechter
Marc Shaw
Stephen Shepard
Maureen Shields
Pamela Silverblatt
Earl Simon
Gilian Small
Lisa Stoiano-Coico
Stuart Suss
Jeremy Travis

Carmen Vazquez
Mitchell Wallerstein
Iris Weinshall
Carol White
Karen Witherspoon
Paulette Zalduondo-Henriquez
Rosemary Zins

Civil Service Employees Assn, Inc
143 Washington Ave
Albany, NY 12210
518-257-1319

Clients:
Civil Service Employees Assn, Inc

Lobbyists:
Denise Berkley
Lester Crockett
Danny Donohue
Kathy Garrison
Nicholas Lamorte
Joseph McMullen
Billy Riccaldo
Mary Sullivan
Florence Tripi
Colleen Wheaton

Clarkson University (FKA Wood Jr., Robert H.)
8 Clarkson Ave
Potsdam, NY 13699-5537
315-268-6474

Clients:

Clean and Healthy New York, Inc.
62 Grand St.
Albany, NY 12207
518-708-3875

Lobbyists:
Roberta Chase
Kathleen Curtis
Clarkson University

Lobbyists:
Anthony G Collins
Robert H Wood, Jr

Clearing House Payments Company L.L.C.
1001 Pennsylvania Avenue NW
Suite 720
North Tower
Washington, DC 20004
202-649-4600

Clients:
Clearing House Payments Company L.L.C.

Lobbyists:
Jill Hershey
Jeremy Newell
David Wagner

Cleary, Kevin Government Relations, LLC
111 Washington Avenue
7th Floor
Albany, NY 12210
518-210-2399

Clients:
Aetna
American Coatings Association, Inc.
Association on Independent Living, Inc. (NY)
Consumer Directed Personal Assistance Association of NYS
CVS Pharmacy, Inc.
Delta Dental of Pennsylvania
Fountain House
Institute for Community Living, Inc.
Magellan Health Services, Inc.
Reckitt Benckiser Pharmaceuticals, Inc.

Lobbyists:
Kevin J. Cleary

CNA
CNA Plaza
43rd Fl
Chicago, IL 60685
312-822-1740

Clients:
CNA

Lobbyists:
Heather Davis
Christine Hanlon
Jon Kantor
Seth Lamont
Mike Warnick

Coalition Against Domestic Violence (NYS)
350 New Scotland Avenue
Albany, NY 12208
518-482-5465

Lobbyists:
Elizabeth Bliss
Connie Neal

Coalition Against Hunger (NYC)
16 Beaver Street
3rd Floor
New York, NY 10004
212-825-0028

Lobbyists:
Joel Berg

Coalition Against Sexual Assault (NYS)
C/O Coalition Against Sexual Assault
28 Essex Street
Albany, NY 12206
518-482-4222
Web site: www.nyscasa.org

Lobbyists:
Wendi Bazan Pazik
Joanne Zannoni

Coalition for Auto Repair Equality (CARE)
105 Oronoco Street
Suite 115
Alexandria, VA 22314
703-519-7555

Lobbyists:
Sandy Bass-Cors
Ray Pohlman

Coalition for Children's Mental Health Services (NYS)
PO Box 7124
Albany, NY 12224-0124
518-436-8715

Clients:
Coalition for Children's Mental Health Services (NYS)

Lobbyists:
Jacqueline Negri
Andrea Smyth

Coalition for Economic Justice
237 Main St
Suite 1200
Buffalo, NY 14203
716-892-5877

Lobbyists:
Jennifer Diagostino
Andrew Reynolds
Micaela Shapiro-Shellaby

Coalition for Education Reform & Accountability
4 Chelsea Place
2nd Floor
Clifton Park, NY 12065
518-383-1342

Clients:
Coalition for Education Reform & Accountability

Lobbyists:
Brian D Backstrom

Lobbyists:
Peter Murphy

Coalition for the Homeless
146 Washington Avenue
Albany, NY 12210
518-436-5612

Lobbyists:
Mary Brosnahan Sullivan
Patrick Markee
Ann Nortz
Giselle Routhier

Coalition for the Last Store on Main Street
99 Pine Street
Albany, NY 12207
518-436-0786

Lobbyists:
Michael Corera
Bob Fink
Mitchell Herman
Stefan Kalogrichs
Burt Natanus
Jeff Saunders
John Semmeles
Ed Wassner

Coalition of Institutionalized Aged and Disabled (FKA Lieberman, Geoff)
Coalition of Institutionalized Aged & Disabled
425 East 25th Street
New York, NY 10010
212-481-7572
Web site: www.ciadny.org

Lobbyists:
Judith K. Canepa
Gary Levin
Geoff Lieberman

Cobb Jr, James H
New York Shipping Association, Inc
333 Thornall Street
Suite 3A
Edison, NJ 08837
732-452-7808

Clients:
Shipping Association, Inc (NY)

Coca-Cola Refreshments USA, Inc.
One Coca-Cola Plaza
Atlanta, GA 30313
203-341-0687

Clients:
Coca-Cola Refershments USA, Inc.

Lobbyists:
Antonio Anaya
Donna Cirolia
Gary McElyea
Maria Pignataro
Lillian Rodriguez Lopez
Harriet Tolve

COFCCA Inc
254 West 31st St, 5th Fl
New York, NY 10001
212-929-2626

Clients:
COFCCA Inc

Lobbyists:
Sophine Charles
Mary Jane Dessables
Dianne Heggie
Edith Holzer
Meredith Lafave
Diane Leske
Lee Lounsbury
James Purcell

Coffin, Brian M.
C/O Empire State Pride Agenda
126 State Street
4th Floor
Albany, NY 12207
518-472-3330

Lobbyists:
Jonathan Lang
Nathan Schaefer

Offices and agencies generally appear in alphabetical order, except when specific order is requested by listee.

Coller Capital Limited and it's Affiliate Coller Capital, Inc.
33 Cavendish Square
London, NY

Clients:
Coller Capital, Inc.

Lobbyists:
Jeremy Coller
Susan Flynn
Tim Jones
Frank Morgan

Columbian Mutual Life Insurance Company
Vestal Parkway East
PO Box 1381
Binghamton, NY 13901-1381
607-724-2472

Lobbyists:
Patrick A. Mannion
Thomas Rattmann

Colwell Colwell & Petroccione, LLP (FKA Colwell Ferrentino & Petroccione, LLP)
20 Corporate Woods Blvd.
Albany, NY 12211
518-462-4242

Clients:
Empire State Petroleum Association, Inc.
Industries for the Blind of NYS, Inc.
Small Customer Marketer Coalition

Lobbyists:
Emilio Petroccione

Community Health Care Association of New York State
535 Eighth Avenue
8th Floor
New York, NY 10018
212-279-9686

Lobbyists:
Beverly Grossman
Lisa Perry Hellerstein
Elizabeth Swain
Kameron Wells

Community Preservation Corporation (The)
28 East 28th Street
9th Floor
New York, NY 10016-7943
212-869-5300

Lobbyists:
Rafael Cestero
Richard Conley
Richard Kumro
Sadie McKeown
Alexa Sewell

Community Research Initiative on AIDS, Inc.
575 8th Avenue
Suite 502
New York, NY 10018
212-924-3934
Web site: www.acria.org

Lobbyists:
Benjamin Bashein

Comprehensive Health Management, Inc. (FKA Wellcare Health Plans, Inc.)
8735 Henderson Road
Ren 2
Tampa, FL 33634
813-206-1099

Lobbyists:
Elliott Shaw

Condon, Joseph M.
5 Hanover Square
Suite 1605
New York, NY 10004
212-838-7442

Clients:
Community Housing Improvement Program, Inc. (CHIP)

Conference of Local Mental Hygiene Directors (NYS)
41 State Street
Suite 505
Albany, NY 12207
518-462-9422
Web site: www.clmhd.org

Lobbyists:
Jeremy Darman
Kelly Hansen

Conference of Mayors & Municipal Officials (NYS)
119 Washington Ave
Albany, NY 12210
518-463-1185

Clients:
Conference of Mayors & Municipal Officials (NYS)

Lobbyists:
Peter Baynes
Wade Beltramo
John Mancini
Jennifer Purcell
Richard Sinnott
Jane Tsamardinos
Barbara Van Epps
Deanna Walker

Connelly Communications, Inc.
C/O Greenberg Traurig
54 State Street
6th Floor
Albany, NY 12207
518-689-1400

Clients:
Doctors Council

Lobbyists:
Maureen Connelly
Michael Woloz

Connelly McLaughlin & Woloz

C/O Greenberg Traurig
54 State Street, 6th Floor
Albany, NY 12207
518-689-1400

Clients:
Altria Client Services Inc. and its Affiliates
Balmar Parc LLC
Building Trades Employers Association
Chetrit Group (The)
CHIP-Community Housing Improvement Program, Inc
Clear Channel Outdoor
Creative Mobile Technology
Gansevoort Street Properties, LLC
Hunter College
International Code Council, Inc.
Metropolitan Parking Association, Inc.
Metropolitan Taxi Board of Trade
Museum of Modern Art (The)
Nightingale-Bamford School
Oil Heating Assn (NY)
One York Street Condominium
Park Avenue Armory
Toll Brothers, Inc.
Velodrome of New York City, Inc.
WB Stellar IP Owner LLC
William Gottlieb Management Co. LLC

Lobbyists:
Maureen Connelly
Kathy Cudahy
Martin McLaughlin
Michael Woloz

Consortium for Worker Education

275 Seventh Avenue
18th Floor
New York, NY 10001
212-647-1900
Web site: www.cwe.org

Lobbyists:
Heather Beaudoin

Consolidated Edison Company of New York, Inc.

4 Irving Place
Room 1650-S
New York, NY 10003
518-434-1193

Lobbyists:
John Banks
Karen Bourgeois
Thomas Brizzolara
Dan Brown
Kevin Burke
Kim Campbell
Larry Carbone
Rebecca Craft
Christine Cummings
Eric Dessen
David Gmach
Al Grillo
Philip Halliburton
Martin Heslin
Robert Hoglund
Stephen Ianello
Rolando Infante
Nick Inga
Mark Irving
Aseem Kapur
Kevin Lanahan
John Leo
William Longhi
John McMahon
Sandra Miller
Luke Mohaghan
John Mucci
Stuart Nachmias
Joseph Oates
Nelson Perez
Francis Peverly
Randolph Price
Jessica Reinhardt
Kenneth Reinhart
Frances Resheske
Marc Richter
Sara Schoenwetter
Steven Scotti
Joseph Segarra
William Slade
Colin Smart
Eric Soto
Greg Stephenson
Richard Struck
William Talbot
Joseph Tringali
Tom Tropea
Stephen Wemple
William White
Neil Winter

Constantinople & Vallone Consulting LLC (FKA Constantinople Consulting)

233 Broadway Suite 830
New York, NY 10279
212-393-6500
e-mail: constantinople@worldnet.att.net

Clients:
133 Greenwich Street Associates LLC
133 Greenwich Street Associates LLC
380 Development LLC
580 Park Avenue, Inc.
Applied Projects Company, Inc.
Bayonne Energy Center LLC
Bayrock Sapir Organization LLC
Bizzi & Partners Development LLC
Brooklyn Navy Yard Cogeneration Partners L.P.
Carmel Car and Limousine Service
Catapult Learning
Citizen Schools, Inc.
Coach USA Northeast, Inc.
College Board (The)
Dial 7 Car and Limousine Service, Inc.
Elmhurst Dairy, Inc.
Empire Office, Inc.
Forestdale, Inc.
H&M LLC
J.H. Reid, General Contractor
JC Penney Corporation, Inc.
Junior Tennis League, Inc.
McGrath Matter Associates, Inc.
Mega Contracting Group LLC
Premier Magnesia LLC
Prestige Properties and Development Co.
Prismatic Development Corporation
QSAC, Inc.

Quadlogic Controls Corporation
Shikibo LTD.
Solow Management Corp.
Sports and Arts in Schools Foundation
St. Michael's Cemetary
TA Ahern Contractors Corp.
TD Bank US Holding Company
Walgreen Co.
Waste Management of New York LLC
Yorkshire Towers
YYY 35th Street LLC

Lobbyists:
Robert Avaltroni
Francis Constantinople
Anthony Constantinople Jr.
Anthony Constantinople III
Irma Frier
Robert Kevin Jones
Keith Powers
Anthony Riccio
Melissa Rusinek
Paul Vallone
Perry Vallone
Peter Vallone Sr.

Consumers Union of US, Inc.
1535 Mission Street
San Francisco, CA 94103
415-431-6747

Lobbyists:
Chuck Bell
Elizabeth Foley
Norma Garcia
Jean Halloran
Michael Hansen
Michelle Jun
Suzanne Martindale
Elizabeth McGiffert
Chris Meyer
Kathy Mitchell
Minerva Novoa
Urvashi Rangan
Rob Schneider

Coppola, John
1 Columbia Place
Albany, NY 12207
518-426-3122
e-mail: jcoppola@asapnys.org
Web site: www.asapnys.org

Clients:
Assn of Alcoholism & Substance Abuse Providers Inc (NY)

Cordo & Company, LLC
100 State Street
Suite 400
Albany, NY 12207
518-445-2535

Clients:
1199 SEIU United Healthcare Workers East
1199 SEIU & GNYHA Healthcare Education Project
Amerigroup New York, LLC (DBA Amerigroup Community Care)
Beer Wholesalers Association, Inc. (NYS)
Camelot Global Services Limited
Cigar Association of America, Inc.
Commission on Independent Colleges & Universities (CICU)
CompPharma LLC
Consortium for Worker Education
Council for the Humanities (NY)
CVS Caremark Corporation
Elisa Seeger
Feld Entertainment, Inc.
Fig LLC
Genting New York LLC
Halmar International LLC
National Popular Vote, Inc.
New York English Schools Association (NYESA)
Oz Systems
Property Casualty Insurers Association of America (PCI)
Short Term Rental and Hospitality Association
Siemens Enterprise Communications, Inc.
Tracfone Wireless, Inc.
TripAdvisor Media Group
Visiting Nurse Service of NY

Lobbyists:
Michael Cinquanti
John Cordo
Kimberley Cutler
Steven Harris
Antoinette Heuber
Kristin Ruggles
Caley Taratus
Larisa Wick

Corlett, John A (FKA Marta Genovese)
1415 Kellum Place
Garden City, NY 11530-1690
516-873-2259

Clients:
AAA New York State, Inc.
Automobile Club of New York, Inc.

Lobbyists:
Jeffrey Frediani
Edward Welsh

Corning Place Consulting, LLC
121 State St
Albany, NY 12207-0693
518-689-7270

Clients:
4201 Schools Association
Association of Proprietary Colleges
Empire State Association of Assisted Living
Independent Oil and Gas Association of NY
LaSalle School
Literacy New York, Inc.
NYSCOP, Inc.
Police Benevolent Association of New York State
Professional Fire Fighters Association, Inc.
Unshackle Upstate (Rochester Business Alliance)
Viscardi Center, The

Lobbyists:
Deborah Fasser
Andrew Gregory
Paul Larrabee
James Smith

Correctional Officers & Police Benevolent Association, Inc. (NYS) (FKA Leo, Christopher)
102 Hackett Boulevard
Albany, NY 12209
518-427-1551

Lobbyists:
Chris Hickey
Donn Rowe
John Telisky
Daniel Valente

Couch White, LLP
540 Broadway
PO Box 22222
Albany, NY 12201
518-426-4600
e-mail: bbrenner@couchwhite.com
Web site: www.couchwhite.com

Clients:
Association of Realtors

Lobbyists:
Lawrence Malone
Leonard Singer
Michael Wallender

Council for Community Behavioral Healthcare
911 Central Avenue
Suite 152
Albany, NY 12206-1350
518-461-8200

Clients:
Council for Community Behavioral Healthcare

Lobbyists:
Lauri Cole

Council for the Humanities
150 Broadway
Suite 1700
New York, NY 10038-4401
212-233-1131

Lobbyists:
Sara Ogger

Council of Nonprofits, Inc.
272 Broadway
Albany, NY 12204
518-434-9194

Lobbyists:
Melissa Currado
Kelly Mathews
William Sauer
Amber Vanderwarker
Valerie Venezia
David Watson
Mike West

Council of Senior Centers & Services of NYC, Inc.
49 West 45th Street
7th Floor
New York, NY 10036
212-398-6565

Lobbyists:
Igal Jellinek
Bobbie Sackman

Council of the City of New York (The)
111 Washington Ave, Ste 410
Albany, NY 12210-2208
518-462-5461
Web site: www.council.nyc.ny.us

Clients:
Council of the City of New York (The)

Lobbyists:
Natasha Kerry

County Medical Society New York (FKA Malone, Cheryl)
New York County Medical Society
31 West 34th Street
Suite 7053
New York, NY 10001
212-684-4670

Clients:
County Medical Society (New York)

Lobbyists:
Sony Hilado
Lisa Joseph
Cheryl Malone
Susan Tucker

Covanta Energy Corporation
445 South St
Morristown, NJ 07960
862-435-5246
Web site: www.covantaholding.com

Lobbyists:
Bonny Betancourt
Ellie Booth
Michael Cavaliere
Daniel Dorlon
Paul Gilman
Scott Henderson
Rick Sandner
Paula Soos-Kobylski
Paul Stauder

Cozen O'Connor (FKA Wolfblock LLP)
277 Park Avenue
New York, NY 10172
212-297-2678

Clients:
Advocacy Association, Inc.
Air-Conditioning, Heating and Refridgeration Institute
American Council of Engineering Companies of New York
Greenpoint Industrial Center, Inc.
Houghton Mifflin Harcourt Publishing Company
ICONPLANS LLC
Rational Services Limited
Teacher's College, Columbia University

Lobbyists:
Kenneth Fisher
Vivien Krieger
Paul Proulx
Alan Rubin

Offices and agencies generally appear in alphabetical order, except when specific order is requested by listee.

Stuart Shorenstein

Clients:
Albany Information Technology Group, LLC
ARE-East River Science Park LLC
Cable Telecommunications Assn of NY, Inc (The)
Coastal Distribution, LLC
COMCAST
Delaware North Companies, Inc
Empire Racing Associates
Higher Education Initiative (New York State)
Institutional Life Markets Association, Inc
Judge Rotenberg Center
Library Association (NY)
Lift
Nestle Waters North America Inc.
Nucor Steel Aubrun, Inc.
Omni Childhood Center
PMSI
Roundabout Theatre Company
School Boards Association (NYS)
Stoneriver Pharmacy Solutions, Inc. (FKA Third Party Solutions)
Sunshine Development School, Inc.
United NY Ambulance Network
Zelle Hoffmann Voelbel & Mason LLP
Constance Crane
James B Crane
Andrea Debow
Christopher Duryea
George Penn
Steven Sanders

Crisis Program (The)
10 Airline Drive
Suite 203
Albany, NY 12205
518-456-1134

Lobbyists:
Michael Elmendorf II
Walter Pacholczak

Crosier, Barbara V
C/O United Cerebral Palsy Assn of NYS
90 State St, Ste 929
Albany, NY 12207
518-436-0178
e-mail: bcrosier@cerebralpalsynys.org
Web site: www.cerebralpalsynys.org

Clients:
United Cerebral Palsy Associations of NYS

Lobbyists:
Michael Alvaro
Susan Constantino

Curran, Brian F
C/O Public Employees Federation
100 State Street
Albany, NY 12207-1806
518-432-4003

Clients:
SEIU Local 200 United

Lobbyists:
Kenneth Brynien
Ryan Delgado
Musa Moore
John Murphy
Alan Schulkin

D'Ambrosio, John A
Orange County Chamber of Commerce
30 Scotts Corner Drive
Montgomery, NY 12549
845-457-9700

Clients:
Orange County Chamber of Commerce (The)

Lobbyists:
Carol Smith

D'Onofrio, Paul
67 Chestnut St
Albany, NY 12210
518-432-7393

Clients:
Assn of Electrical Workers (NYS)
Council of Sheet Metal Workers Int'l Assn (NYS)
Monticello Raceway Management Inc

Dadey, Dick (FKA Citizens Union of the City of New York)
Citizens Union of NYC
299 Broadway, Ste 700
New York, NY 10007
212-227-0342

Clients:
Citizens Union of the City of New York

Lobbyists:
Alex Camarda
Rachel Fauss

Dagnello, Vito
P.O. Box 706
St. James, NY 11780
631-208-1326

Clients:
United Correction Officers Coalition

Daiichi Sankyo, Inc.
1825 K Street NW
Suite 425
Washington, DC 20006
202-223-6575

Lobbyists:
Craig Nowacki

Dairylea Cooperative, Inc.
5001 Brittonfield Pkwy
P.O. Box 4844
Syracuse, NY 13221-4844
315-433-0100

Lobbyists:
William Beeman
Karen Cartier
Ed Gallagher
Leon Graves
John Siglow

Offices and agencies generally appear in alphabetical order, except when specific order is requested by listee.

Sanford Stauffer
Gregory Wickham

Dan Klores Communications, Inc. DBA DKC Government Affairs
111 Washington Avenue
Albany, NY 12210
518-813-4832

Clients:
A. Servidone, Inc.
Alliant Insurance Services
Atlantic Auto Mall
Birchez Associates, LLC
Cable Telecommunications Association of NY, Inc. (The)
Central Life Sciences (Fleishman-Hillard, Inc.)
Consolidated Edison Company of New York, Inc.
CSC Holdings, Inc. FKA Cablevision Systems Corporation
D&D Power, Inc.
Dack Consulting Services, Inc.
Delta Air Lines, Inc.
Empire Resorts, Inc.
Farmingdale State College
Fidelity Investments
Friends of the High Line
Frontier Healthcare Management Services, Inc.
Gaming Association, Inc.
Home Care Association of NYS
Homeward Bound Adirondacks
Hudson Valley Fois Gras (HVFG, LLC)
Independent System Operator, Inc.
JP Morgan Chase & Co.
Linium LLC
Madison Square Garden
Major League Soccer
Professional Insurance Agents of New York
PSCH, Inc.
Southern Wine & Spirits of America, Inc.
Transmission Developers, Inc.
Trial Lawyers Association
TWC Administration LLC
WNET.org

Lobbyists:
Daniel Cain
Allison Lee
Andrew Marocco
Marie Ternes
Michelle Tuchman
Paul Zuber

Darwak, Stephanie
3 Independence Row
Stillwater, NY 12170
518-664-5880

Clients:
State Osteopathic Medical Society (NY)

Davidoff, Hutcher & Citron LLP
150 State Street
Suite 502
Albany, NY 12207
518-465-8230

Clients:
114 Kenmare Associates, LLC
212 LaFayette Associates, LLC
Abbott Laboratories
ABBVIE, Inc.
Adelphi University
Akwesasne Convenience Store Association
All Shows LLC
Association of Water & Sewer Excavators, Inc
Carpet and Rug Institute (The)
Castagna Realty
Center for Educational Innovation - Public Education Association (CEI-PEA)
Community Bancorp, Inc.
Coney Island Holdings LLC
Council of School Supervisors & Administrators
Court Reporters Association, Inc. (NYS)
Creditors Bar Association
DriversEd.com
Easy Choice Health Plan of New York
Fairmont Capital LLC
Figli Di San Gennaro, Inc.
Gateway College AS
Helen Keller Services for the Blind
Hunts Point Terminal Produce Cooperative Association, Inc.
IDT Energy
Local Control for Local Progress, Inc.
Looks Great Services, Inc.
Master Plumbers Council of the City of New York, Inc.
Metropolitan Package Store Association
Nassau County Village Officials Assn
National Insurance Crime Bureau
Nestle Waters North America Holdings Inc
New York Alliance of Library Systems
New York Cosmos LLC
New York Institute of Energy and Water
Northeast Kidney Foundation
O'Connor Capital Partners
Oxford Nursing Home, Inc.
Palladia Inc (Formerly Project Return Foundation Inc)
Penzim Produce Corp
Plyndirio LLC
Queens Borough Public Library
RCN Telecom Services, Inc.
Redvision Systems, Inc.
Reed Elsevier, Inc.
Staffing Assn (NY)
Taxicab Service Assn
Touro College
Town Hall Foundation, Inc.
United Hebrew of New Rochelle
Verde Electric Corporation
Vision Rehabilitation Assn (NYVRA) (NY)
Young Adult Institute, Inc.

Lobbyists:
Leslie Barbara
Charles Capetanakis
Jeff Citron
Peter R Crouse
Sean Crowley
Sid Davidoff
Arthur Goldstein
Anna Lisa Greco
John B Kiernan
Stephen A Malito
Howard Weiss
Derek Wolman
Michael Zapson

DCI Group AZ, LLC (FKA DCI Group, LLC)
2340 E Beardsley Road
Suite 100
Phoenix, AZ 85024
602-387-8000
Web site: www.dcigroup.com

Offices and agencies generally appear in alphabetical order, except when specific order is requested by listee.

Political Parties, Lobbyists & PACs

Clients:
Altria Client Services Inc. and its Affiliates

Lobbyists:
Dan Combs
Charles Joslin IV

DDC Advocacy
174 Waterfront St
Suite 500
National Harbor, MD 20745
301-686-8000

Clients:
American Petroleum Institute

Lobbyists:
Bill Toye

Debevoise & Plimpton LLP
919 Third Avenue
New York, NY 10022
212-909-6000

Clients:
Columbian Mutual Life Insurance Comapny
Excess Line Association of NY

Lobbyists:
Eric R. Dinallo
Wolcott B. Dunham Jr.

Defenders Justice Fund, NYS
194 Washington Avenue
Suite 500
Albany, NY 12210
518-465-0519

Lobbyists:

Defoyd, Katherine
500 Summit Avenue
Maplewood, NJ 07040
973-650-5983

Clients:
Jonathan Gradess
Armory Foundation (The)
Mount Sanai Hospital (The)
Road Runners Foundation (NY)

Delbello Donnellan Weingarten Wise & Wiederkehr, LLP
One North Lexington Avenue
11th Floor
White Plains, NY 10601
914-681-0200

Clients:
Avalonbay Communities, Inc.
Cappelli Enterprises, Inc.
Fareri Associates
FC Yonkers Associates LLC
Forest City Residential Group, Inc.
Frontier Healthcare Management Services, Inc.
Wilder Balter Partners, Inc.

Lobbyists:
Ann Carson
Alfred Delbello
Alfred Donnellan
Janet Giris
Michael Schwarz
Mark Weingarten
Peter Wise

Deloitte & Touche LLP
30 Rockefeller Plaza
New York, NY 10112
973-602-4321

Lobbyists:
Doris Imperati
Henry Phillips
Gordon Sanit
Beth A. Schneider
Lisa Tracy Smith
Suzanne Whitworth

Deloitte Consulting
39 N. Pearl St.
3rd Floor
Albany, NY 12207
518-472-4990

Lobbyists:
Frank Pisciotta
Stewart Rog

Delta Air Lines, Inc.
112 West 34th Street
Suite 2104
New York, NY 10120
646-871-6985

Lobbyists:
Gail Grimmett

Desales Media Group, Inc.
1712 10th Ave
Brooklyn, NY 11215
718-499-9705

Lobbyists:
Vincent Levien

Destiny USA Management Company, LLC
4 Clinton Square
Syracuse, NY 13202
315-422-7000

Lobbyists:
David Aitken
Robert Congel
Bruce Kenan

Deutsch, Ronald
212 Great Oaks Blvd
Albany, NY 12203
518-452-2130

Clients:
New Yorkers for Fiscal Fairness

Deutsche Bank Trust Company
60 Wall Street
New York, NY 10005
212-250-2500

Offices and agencies generally appear in alphabetical order, except when specific order is requested by listee.

Lobbyists:
Willaim Baneky
Lucille Douglas
Elizabeth Zieglmeier

Dimaio, Mark
19 Longacre Court
Hockessin, DE 19707
302-437-4550

Clients:
Otsuka America Pharmaceutical, Inc.

Diageo
801 Main Avenue
Norwalk, CT 06851
203-229-4504

Clients:
Diageo, PLC

Lobbyists:
Dwayne Kratt

Diorio, L Todd
451 Little Britian Rd
Newburgh, NY 12550
845-565-2737

Clients:
Hudson Valley Building & Construction Trades Council
Laborers Int'l Union of North America AFL-CIO, Local 17

DirecTv
90 State Street
Suite 700
Albany, NY 122047
518-591-4639

Lobbyists:
Damon Stewart

Distilled Spirits Council of the US (FKA Wojnar, David E.)
C/O Distilled Spirits Council of the US
1250 I Street NW
Ste 400
Washington, DC 20005-3998
202-682-8836
Web site: www.discus.org

Lobbyists:
Jay Hibbard

Distinctive Public Affairs, LLC
2156 Cruger Avenue
Suite 45
Bronx, NY 10462
718-704-7039

Clients:
Coalition for Opportunity in Education, Inc.

Lobbyists:
Marysol Rodriguez

District Council 37, AFSCME
125 Barclay St
New York, NY 10007
212-815-1500
Web site: www.district37.net

Clients:
District Council 37, AFSCME

Lobbyists:
Oliver Gray
Ashton Matyi
Sybil McPherson
Wanda Williams

Dominion Resources
C/O Dominion Resources
701 E. Cary St.
21st Floor
Richmond, VA 23219
717-236-9261

Lobbyists:
Donald Houser

Donohue, Gavin J
Independent Power Prodeucers of NY, Inc.
194 Washington Ave2
Suite 315
Albany, NY 12210
518-436-3749
e-mail: gavin@ippny.org
Web site: www.ippny.org

Lobbyists:
Radmila Miletich

Drexelius, Jr., John R.
PO Box 141
Buffalo, NY 14223
716-316-7552

Clients:
Developmental Disability Alliance of Western New York

Driscoll Group, Inc.
45-23 47th Street
Sunnyside, NY 11377
347-808-8614

Clients:
176 Woodward Owner LLC
Business Outreach Center Network, Inc.
Cement League
Child Center of New York
Edgestone Group LLC
Everyone Reading, Inc.
JMED Holding LLC
Lifeline Center for Child Development (The)
Queens College (Research Foundation of the City University of New York)
Queens Economic Development Corporation
S.W. Anderson Sales Corporation

Drug Policy Alliance
131 West 33rd Street
15th Floor
New York, NY 10001

Political Parties, Lobbyists & PACs

212-613-8048

Lobbyists:
Kassandra Frederique
Evan Goldstein
Julie Netherland
Gabriel Sayegh

Dryfoos Group
45-02 Ditmars Blvd
Suite 1016
Astoria, NY 11105
347-642-5320

Clients:
Brooklyn Children's Museum
Community Works
Inside Broadway
Junior Tennis League (NY)
Literacy, Inc.
Midori and Friends
QSAC
Shareing & Careing Inc
Sports & Arts in School Foundation

Lobbyists:
Laura Jean Hawkins
Carol Swift

Duane Morris LLP
99 Washington Ave
Suite 803
Albany, NY 12210
518-598-1900

Clients:
Mortgage Insurance Companies of America
State Farm Insurance Companies

Lobbyists:
Edmond Valente

Duca, Anthony
5 Chelsea Court
Medford, NJ 08055
609-923-0577

Clients:
EISAI, Inc.

Duffy, Margaret
360 West 31st Street
5th Floor
New York, NY 10001
518-462-0787

Clients:
Amerigroup New York LLC

Dunne, John
225 Broadway
Suite 401
New York, NY 10007
212-293-9300

Clients:
Uniformed Fire Officers Association (NYC)

Lobbyists:
Marty Steadman

Durrani, Waqas
100 Motor Parkway
Suite 140
Hauppauge, NY 11788
634-233-6050

Clients:
Allstate Insurance Company

Lobbyists:
Vince Fusco
Bill Vainisi

Durst Development LLC
One Bryant Park
New York, NY 10036
212-257-6600

Lobbyists:
Jordan Barowitz

Durst Organization, Inc. (The)
One Bryant Park
New York, NY 10036
212-257-6600

Lobbyists:
Jordan Barowitz

E-3 Communications
551 Franklin Street
Buffalo, NY 14202
716-854-8182
Web site: www.e3communications.com

Clients:
Absolut Management Facilities, Inc.
Association of Ambulatory Surgery Centers
Beech-Nut Nutrition Corporation
Buffalo Police Benevolent Association, Inc.
Lawley Insurance
National Fuel Gas Company
Noco Energy Corporation
School Administrators Association of New York State
Vinyl Institute (The)

Lobbyists:
Kevin Banes
Earl Wells

Early Care and Learning Council
230 Washington Avenue Extension
Albany, NY 12203
518-690-4217

Lobbyists:
Marsha Basloe
Jessica Klos

Easter Seals New York
633 Third Avenue
6th Floor
New York, NY 10017
212-220-2290

Offices and agencies generally appear in alphabetical order, except when specific order is requested by listee.

Lobbyists:
Julie Bazan
Daniel Cooke
Kavan Desai
James DiBenedetto
Joseph Dichiara
Robin Doick
James Fahey
Kanti Gala
Neil Gala
Larry Gammon
John Hayes
Philip Laffey
Richard Lauricella
Mark Legaspi
John Mascialino
Gerald Mattimore
John McGrath
Heather Mills
Sylvia Ng
Aris Pavlides
Stanley Schlein
Sue Silsby
Neil Sullivan
Angela Torres
Elin Treanor
Dave Vanblarcom
Thomas Westle
Mick Wood

Eber, Lester
155 Paragon Drive
Rochester, NY 14624
585-317-1024

Clients:
Southern Wine & Spirits of America, Inc.

Economic Development Council Inc (NYS)
111 Washington Avenue 6th Floor
Albany, NY 12210
518-426-4058
e-mail: mcmahon@nysedc.org
Web site: www.nysedc.org

Clients:
Economic Development Council Inc (NYS)

Lobbyists:
Brian T McMahon

Edison Spring Street Company LLC
100 Washington St
Newark, NJ 07102
973-643-7700

Lobbyists:
Anthony Borelli

Education Reform Now Advocacy, Inc.
928 Broadway
New York, NY 10010
212-614-3213

Lobbyists:
Elisabeth Ling
Joe Williams

Education Reform Now, Inc.
928 Broadway
New York, NY 10010
212-614-3213

Lobbyists:
Elisabeth Ling
Joe Williams

Edward K. Flynn
520 Madison Avenue
8th Floor
New York, NY 10022
212-336-7029

Clients:
Jefferies LLC

Lobbyists:
Kojo Asiedu
Harold Bean
Roy Carlberg
Jeffrey Cohen
Neil Flanagan
Kenneth Gibbs
John Kearney
Joseph Nocerino
Shawn Sinel
William Torsiglieri

Egan, Paul (FKA Reiskin, Marvin)
C/O United Federation of Teachers
52 Broadway
New York, NY 10004
212-777-7500

Clients:
United Federation of Teachers

Lobbyists:
Jasaun Boone
Carol Gerstl
Jason Goldman
Jeremy Hoffman
Sandra March
Briget Rein

Eisland Strategies LLC
2600 Netherland Ave
Suite 811
Bronx, NY 10463
718-549-1950

Clients:
Marshall E. Bloomfield

Lobbyists:
June Eisland

Elk Street Group LLC
25 Elk Street
Albany, NY 12207
518-813-4383

Clients:
Beauty Schools Association
Catskill Off-Track Betting Corporation
Children's Institute
Exxon Mobil Corporation

Political Parties, Lobbyists & PACs

Offices and agencies generally appear in alphabetical order, except when specific order is requested by listee.

Innocence Project (The)
Law School Admission Council
Norfolk Southern Corporation
Osborne Association
Partnership of Upstate Legal Services
Patrick F. Adams, P.C.
Pfizer, Inc.
PMSI
Ramapo Organized for Sustainability and a Safe Aquifer
Reckitt Benckiser, Inc.
Reenergy Holdings LLC
Stoneriver Pharmacy Solutions, Inc.
U.S Communities
United New York Ambulance Network
Williams Companies, Inc.

Lobbyists:
Andrea Debow
Diana Georgia
Pablo Rivera
Edward Wassermann

Emblemhealth Services Company, LLC
55 Water Street
New York, NY 10041
646-447-7091

Lobbyists:
David Abernethy
Frank Branchini
Arthur Byrd
Mohamed Diab
Dan Finke
William Gillespie
Jeff Goodwin
Nick Kambolis
William Lamoreaux
Charlene Maher
Edward Mailander
Bill Mastro
Eliza Ng
Jay Schoenfeld
Wanda Wareham
Tony Watson

EMD Serono, Inc.
975 F. Street NW
Suite 330
Washington, DC 20004
202-626-2596

Lobbyists:
Ethel Knighton

Empire Advocates LLC
80 State Street
Albany, NY 12207
315-436-1352

Clients:
America's Natural Gas Alliance, Inc.

Lobbyists:
Paul B. Powers
Nancy Testani

Empire Consultants
580 Park Avenue
Suite 1B
New York, NY 10021
212-838-6600

Clients:
Dominican College
Empire City Labs
Rose Group Park Ave. LLC
Strike Force Protective Services, Inc.

Lobbyists:
Joseph Mirto

Empire Generating Co. LLC
100 Constitution Plaza
10th Floor
Hartford, CT 06095
860-656-0822

Lobbyists:
James Ginnetti

Empire Government Strategies
1425 RXR Plaza
East Tower - 15th Floor
Uniondale, NY 11556-1425
516-663-6688

Clients:
Bowling Proprietors Association
Caithness Long Island II LLC
Educational Houseing Servies, Inc.
Medical Staff Leadership Council
Plumbing Foundation City of New York, Inc.
USPLabs LLC

Lobbyists:
Anthony Figliola
Arthur Jerry Kremer

Empire Justice Center (FKA Greater Upstate Law Project)
1 West Main Street
Suite 200
Rochester, NY 14614
585-454-4060

Clients:
Empire Justice Center

Lobbyists:
Susan Antos
Linda Bennet-Rodriguez
Kristin Brown
Kate Callery
Robert Cisneros
Trilby Dejung
Anne Erickson
Rita Eygabroad Garretson
Don Friedman
Geoffrey Hale
Mike Hanley
Linda Hassberg
Bryan Hetherington
Kirsten Keefe
Cheryl Keshner
Ruhi Maker

Offices and agencies generally appear in alphabetical order, except when specific order is requested by listee.

Kevin Purcell
Reyna Remolete Hayashi
Cathy Roberts
Amy Schwartz
Lousie Tarantino
Barbara Van Kerkhove
Daniel Villena
Barbara Weiner
Tamara Wright

Empire State Association of Assisted Living (FKA Empire State Association of Adult Homes & Assisted)
646 Plank Road
Suite 207
Clifton Park, NY 12065
518-371-2573

Lobbyists:
James Kane
Lisa Newcomb

Empire State College, State University of NY
Empire State College
2 Union Avenue
Saratoga Springs, NY 12866-4931
518-587-2100
e-mail: marycaroline.powers@esc.edu
Web site: www.esc.edu

Clients:
Empire State College, State University of NY

Lobbyists:
Michael Mancini
Mary Powers

Empire State Forest Products Association
47 Van Alstyne Drive
Rensselaer, NY 12144
518-463-1297

Lobbyists:
Eric Carlson

Empire State Petroleum Association, Inc.
80 Wolf Rd
Suite 308
Albany, NY 12205
518-449-0702

Lobbyists:
Thomas Peters

Empire Strategic Planning, Inc.
111 Washington Avenue
Suite 103
Albany, NY 12210
518-701-2713

Clients:
ACS Home Care LLC
Bikepath Country
ECG Engineering P.C.
Glenwood Management Corporation
Grahel Associates LLC
Messenger & Courier Association
O'Connor Davies Munns & Dobbins LLP
Paraco Gas
Saint Joseph's Medical Center
Specialty Wine Retailers Association
Vista Developers Corp
Westchester County Correction Superior Officers Association
White Birch, LLC (FKA Camarda Realty Investments)
Zachy's Wine & Liquor Store, Inc.

Lobbyists:
James Cavanaugh
Maureen Kronau
John J. Spano

Employer Alliance for Affordable Health Care
PO Box 1412
Albany, NY 12201-1412
518-462-2296
Web site: employeralliance.com

Clients:
Employer Alliance for Affordable Health Care

Lobbyists:
Pamela Finch

Entergy Nuclear Operations, Inc
440 Hamilton Ave
White Plains, NY 10601
914-272-3350

Clients:
Entergy Nuclear Operations, Inc

Lobbyists:
Joanne Fernandez
Rick Smith
Kenneth Theobalds
Michael T. Twomey

Enterprise Holdings
1550 Route 23 North
Wayne, NJ 07470
973-709-2396

Clients:
Enterprise Holdings

Lobbyists:
Judson Church
Tomi Gerber
Todd Stockton
Dean Thompson

Entertainment Software Association
575 7th Street, NW
Suite 300
Washington, DC 20004
202-223-2400

Lobbyists:
Thomas Foulkes

Environmental Advocates of NY
353 Hamilton St
Albany, NY 12210
518-462-5526

Clients:
Environmental Advocates of NY

Offices and agencies generally appear in alphabetical order, except when specific order is requested by listee.

Lobbyists:
Melissa Andreychek
Saima Anjam
Ross Gould
Alison Jenkins
Robert J Moore
Katherine Nadeau
Travis Proulx
David Vanluven

Environmental Defense Fund
257 Park Avenue South
New York, NY 10010
212-505-2100

Lobbyists:
Mary Barber
Abbie Brown
Mark Brownstein
Andrew Darrell
Adam Peltz
Raya Salter
Isabelle Silverman
Elizabeth Stein
Jim Tripp

EPL/Environmental Advocates
353 Hamilton Street
Albany, NY 12210
518-462-5526

Lobbyists:
Melissa Andreychek
Saima Anjam
Ross Gould
Alison Jenkins
Robert J. Moore
Katherine Nadeau
Travis Proulx
David Vanluven

EQT Partners AB
677 Broadway
9th Floor
Albany, NY 12207
518-449-8893

Lobbyists:
Conni Jonsson
Jussi Saarinen
Jan Stahlberg
Marcus Wallinder

EQT Partner AS
677 Broadway
9th Floor
Albany, NY 12207
518-449-8893

Lobbyists:
Christian Sinding

EQT Partners Asia Limited
677 Broadway
9th Floor
Albany, NY 12207
518-449-8893

Lobbyists:
Wolfgang Gorny
Martin Mok

EQT Partners GMBH
677 Broadway
9th Floor
Albany, NY 12207
518-449-8893

Lobbyists:
Marcus Brennecke

EQT Partners, Inc.
1114 Avenue of the Americas
38th Floor
New York, NY 10036
917-281-0850

Lobbyists:
Erwin Thompson
James Wilson

EQT Partners UK Advisors LLP
677 Broadway
9th Floor
Albany, NY 12207
518-449-8893

Lobbyists:
Tequila Bone
Christian Broberg
Paul De Rome
Stephen Escudier
Paul Johnson
Cyril Konopelski
David Slade
Lloyd Thomas

Every Voice
1211 Connecticut Avenue NW
Suite 600
Washington, DC 20036
202-640-5600

Lobbyists:
David Donnelly
Rahna Epting
Jeff Robinson
Jennifer Linn
Johnny Papagiannis
Adam Smith

Excelsior Advocates, LLC
403 Livingston Avenue
Albany, NY 12206
518-441-1884

Clients:
Coalition of Neighborhood Centers
General Motors Corporation
Rochester Genesee Regional Transportation Authority

Lobbyists:
Robert Gaddy

Offices and agencies generally appear in alphabetical order, except when specific order is requested by listee.

Exelon Generation Company LLC
300 Exelon Way
Kennett Square, PA 19348
610-765-6920

Lobbyists:
Daniel Allegretti
Christopher Wentlent

Express Scripts Holding Co.
300 New Jersey Avenue NW
Suite 600
Washington, DC 20001
202-383-7983

Lobbyists:
Jonah Houts

Extell Development Company
805 Third Ave
7th Floor
New York, NY 10022
212-712-6000
Web site: www.extelldev.com

Lobbyists:
Gary Barnett
Donna Gargano
Lela Goren
Raizy Haas
Anthony Mannarino
Jeff Torkin

Faist Government Affairs Group, LLC
54 Willett Street
Albany, NY 12210-1104
518-432-0599
e-mail: tfaist@aol.com

Clients:
American International Group, Inc.
Chemical Alliance (NYS)
Council of Insurance Brokers of Greater NY, Inc
E.I. Du Pont De Nemours and Company
Fashion Jewelry Trade Association
FMC Corporation
Guardian Life Insurance Co of America
Halogenated Solvents Industry Alliance, Inc.
National Assn of Health Underwriters
Palliatech, Inc.
Wine & Grape Foundation (NY)

Lobbyists:
Thomas W Faist

Families Together in NYS, Inc.
737 Madison Avenue
Albany, NY 12208
518-432-0333

Lobbyists:
Paige Pierce

Family Planning Advocates of New York State
17 Elk Street
Albany, NY 12207
518-436-8408

Lobbyists:
Carol Blowers
Tracey M. Brooks
Carolyn Ehrlich
Georgana Hanson
Kelli Owens
Dianne Patterson
Ronora Pawelko

Farber, Felice
60 East 42 Street, Suite 3510
New York, NY 10165
212-687-3131

Clients:
General Contractors Association of NY, Inc.

Lobbyists:
Denise Richardson

Farm Bureau, Inc. (NY)
159 Wolf Road
PO Box 5530
Albany, NY 12205-0330
518-436-8495

Lobbyists:
Steven Ammerman
Bambi Baehrel
Richard Ball
Timothy Bigham
William Hamilton
Marilyn Howard
T. Mark James
Donald Jensen
Amanda Krenning
Catherine Mural
Dean Norton
Eric Ooms
Fred Perrin
Jaclyn Sears
Julie Suarez
John Wagner
Lindsay Wickham
Jeffrey Williams
Nicole Willis
Kelly Young

Farmers Insurance Group
PO Box 201
Saratoga Springs, NY 12866
518-867-9255

Lobbyists:
Nicholas Masi

Fassler, Michael S
C/O Beth Abraham Family of Health Svcs
612 Allerton Ave
Bronx, NY 10467-7404
718-519-4001

Clients:
Centerlight Health Systems

Lobbyists:
Joseph Healy
Jacqueline Kennedy-Sadler
Paul Rosenfeld

Faucher, Jennifer
2790 Bragg Street
Apt 511
Brooklyn, NY 11235
917-687-0261

Clients:
Public Employees Federation

Featherstonhaugh, Wiley & Clyne, LLP
99 Pine St
Albany, NY 12207
518-436-0786

Clients:
AAA New York State, Inc.
Altria Client Services, Inc.
Association of Cemeteries (NYS)
Bottlers Association (NYS)
Building Congress (NY) (The)
Construction Industry Council of Westchester & Hudson Valley, Inc.
CVS Pharmacy, Inc.
Empire Merchants North, LLC
Empire Merchants, LLC
Entergy Nuclear Operations, Inc.
Estate of Marilyn Monroe LLC
Experience Hendrix LLC
Financial Service Centers of New York
Forest Lawn Cemetery/Cremation Group (The)
Friends of Democracy New York
Gaming Association, Inc.
General Contractors Association of NY, Inc. (The)
Goldman Sachs Group, Inc. (The) & Its Subsidiaries & Affiliates
Green-Wood Cemetary (The)
GTech Corporation
Just Energy New York Corporation (FKA Energy Savings)
Kohl Partners
Long Island Contractors Association
McKissack Group, Inc. (The)
Metropolitan Life Insurance Company
Nutrition Association
Park Outdoor Advertising of NY, Inc.
Roadway Imporvement Coalition (NY)
Society of Physician Assistants (NYS)
Thoroughbred Horsemens Association, Inc. (NY)
Tracfone Wireless, Inc.
UNISYS Corporation
United Healthcare Services, Inc.
Woodlawn Cemetery (The)
Yaddo

Lobbyists:
Elizabeth Clyne
James Featherstonhaugh
David Fleming
Dan Hallenbeck
John Hardy
Frank Hoare
Jonathan McCardle
Stephen Morgan
John Olsen

Federation of Mental Health Services, Inc. (The)
104-70 Queens Blvd.
Forest Hills
New York, NY 11375
718-275-6010

Lobbyists:
John Rossland

Federation of School Administrators (NYS) (FKA Gibbons, Brian)
40 Rector Street
12th Floor
New York, NY 10006-1729
212-823-2020

Lobbyists:
Crystal Boling-Barton
Dee Dee Goidel
Ernest Logan
Peter McNally
Steve Murphy
Alithia Rodriguez-Rolon

Feld Entertainment
8607 Westwood Center Dr
Vienna, VA 22182
703-749-5570

Clients:
Feld Entertainment, Inc

Lobbyists:
Thomas Albert
Sarah Lashford

Ferramosca, Joseph
189 Montague St
Suite 400
Brooklyn, NY 11201
718-243-0222

Clients:
Assistant Deputy Warden - Deputy Warden's Association
Correct Captain's Association, Dept. of Corrections, City of New York

Ferris, William E
AARP
One Commerce Plaza, Ste 706
Albany, NY 12260
518-434-4194
e-mail: wferris@aarp.org
Web site: www.aarp.org/ny

Clients:
AARP

Lobbyists:
William Armbuster
Chaunda Ball
Christine Deska
Lindsey Etringer
Beth Finkel
David Irwin
Stacy Kratz
Kristin Legere
Yvette Martinez
David McNally
Erin Mitchell
Laura Palmer
Dionne Polite
Will Stoner
Christopher Widelo

Finch Paper LLC
One Glen Street
Glens Falls, NY 12801

518-793-2541

Lobbyists:
Rob Baron
Kyle Brock
Sandra LaBarren
Michael McLarty
Joseph Raccuia

Fisher Development Strategies
21 Choir Lane
Westbury, NY 11590
516-238-0186

Clients:
Chamber Players International
Nassau Community College
Nassau County Firefighters Museum & Education Ctr

Lobbyists:
Daniel Fisher Jr.

Fitzgerald, Gary J
Iroquois Healthcare Alliance
17 Executive Park Drive
Clifton Park, NY 12065
518-383-5060
e-mail: gfitzgerald@iroquois.org
Web site: www.iroquois.org

Clients:
Iroquois Healthcare Alliance

Lobbyists:
Stacy Connors
Allan Filler

Fitzgerald, Kevin
11921 Freedom Drive
Reston, VA 20190
212-816-3656

Clients:
CitiBank, N.A.

Lobbyists:
Ciara Imelda Deane
Joseph Imbro
Thomas C. Murphy
Gary Schneider

Fitzpatrick, Christine M
Adult Day Health Care Council
13 British American Blvd
Latham, NY 12110-1431
518-449-2707 x130
e-mail: cfitzpatrick@nyahsa.org
Web site: www.nyahsa.org

Clients:
Adult Day Health Care Council (ADHCC)

Lobbyists:
Anne Hille

FMR LLC
82 Devonshire Street, NSA
Boston, MA 02109
617-563-9891

Lobbyists:
Mark Gallagher
John Muggeridge
Maria Nieves

Focus Media Group, Inc.
10 Matthews Street
Goshen, NY 10924
845-294-3342

Clients:
Empire Resorts, Inc.

Lobbyists:
Joshua Cohen

Foley & Lardner LLP
90 Park Avenue
New York, NY 10016
212-338-3568

Clients:
Brookdale University Hospital and Medical Center
Jamaica Hospital Medical Center
Nassau Health Care Corporation

Lobbyists:
Jeffrey Thrope

Food & Water Watch
68 Jay St
Suite 713
Brooklyn, NY 11201
718-943-8068

Lobbyists:
Corinne Rosen
Eric Weltman

Food Bank for New York City
39 Broadway
10th Floor
New York, NY 10006
212-566-7855

Lobbyists:
Aine Duggan
Triada Stampas

Food Industry Alliance of NYS Inc
130 Washington Ave
Albany, NY 12210
518-434-1900

Clients:
New Yorkers for Real Recycling Reform (Food Industry Alliance of NYS Inc)

Lobbyists:
Jay Peltz
James T Rogers
Michael E Rosen

Forest City Ratner Companies
1 Metrotech Center North
11th Floor
Brooklyn, NY 11201
718-923-8429

Political Parties, Lobbyists & PACs

Lobbyists:
David Berliner
Ashley Cotton
Maryanne Gilmartin
Bruce Ratner
Katherine Welch

Forum Strategies & Communications
641 Lexington Avenue
14th Floor
New York, NY 10022
212-554-2155

Clients:
Altria Client Services, Inc.

Lobbyists:
Richard Frisch
David Laufer
Michele Mitola

Foundation for Opportunity in Education (The)
26 Century Hill Drive
Suite 203
Latham, NY 12110
518-640-8344

Lobbyists:
Thomas Carroll
Peter Murphy

Frack Action Fund, Inc.
c/o F&WW
68 Jay Street
Suite 713
Brooklyn, NY 11201
518-322-2978

Lobbyists:
John Armstrong
Julia Walsh

Fried Frank Harris Shriver & Jacobson, LLP
One New York Plaza
New York, NY 10004-1980
212-859-8473

Clients:
117th Street Equities LLC
Archdiocese of New York
Cornell University
Durst Organization (The)
Greenpoint Landing Associates LLC
Jamestown Premier Chelsea Market, L.P.
Major League Soccer LLC
Rector, Church-Wardens and Vestrymen of Trinity Church in the City of New York (The)
Related Companies, L.P. (The)
Rudin Management Company, Inc.
SL Green Realty Company
TF Cornerstone, Inc.

Lobbyists:
David Badain
Adrienne Bernard
Zachary Bernstein
Holly Chen
Michele Chirco
Ilana Ettinger
David Geist
Tal Golumb
Hanna Gustafsson
Stephen Lefkowitz
Richard Leland
Jonathan Mechanic
Melanie Meyers
Carol Rosenthal

Friedlander Group (The)
1 Seaport Plaza
199 Water Street
27th Floor
New York, NY 10038
212-233-5555

Clients:
Community First Party
NYSHA Inc.
Shema Kolainu-Hear Our Voices
XChange Telecom Corp.

Lobbyists:
Ezra Friedlander

Friedman, John P
United Services Automobile Association
325 Columbia Tpk
Florham Park, NJ 07932
973-377-6662
e-mail: john.friedman@usaa.com

Clients:
United Services Automobile Assn (USAA)

Friends of the High Line, Inc.
The Diller-von Furstenberg Building
820 Washington Street
New York, NY 10014
212-206-9922
Web site: www.thehighline.org

Lobbyists:
Joshua David
Gonzalo Casals
Robert Hammond
Julie Twitmyer

Frost, Robert D.
220 Fifth Avenue
19th Floor
New York, NY 10001
212-813-3575

Clients:
Industco Holdings, LLC

Lobbyists:
Alan Gifford Miller

Fund for the City of New York (FKA Employment & Training Coalition (NYC))
121 Avenue of the Americas
6th Floor
New York, NY 10013
212-925-6675

Offices and agencies generally appear in alphabetical order, except when specific order is requested by listee.

Lobbyists:
Anu Bhagwati
James Brodick
Haidee Cabusora
Michael Carey
Janet Carter
Samantha Clare
Michelle Del Guercio
Amy Ellenbogen
Carol Fisler
Mae Watson Grote
Richard Moses
Ambika Panday
Lindsay Pankok
John Raskin
Carolyn Ratcliffe
Susan Rodriguez
Gloria Searson
Alfred Siegel
DC Vito
Christopher Walter
Phillip Zielinski

Funeral Directors Association, Inc. (NYS)
1 South Family Drive
Albany, NY 12205
518-452-8230

Lobbyists:
Bonnie McCullough
Randy McCullough

Gallo, Richard J.
123 State Street
Albany, NY 12207-1622
518-465-3545

Clients:
Davita Inc.
Psychiatric Association, Inc. (NYS)

Gaming Association
99 Pine Street
Suite 210
Albany, NY 12207
518-436-1122

Lobbyists:
Matthew Cunningham
James Featherstonhaugh
Dan Sommer
Michael Wilton

Garfinkel, Neil
Abrams Garfinkel Margolis Bergson, LLP
1430 Broadway
17th Floor
New York, NY 10018
212-201-1170

Clients:
Real Estate Board of NY, Inc.

Gay Men's Health Crisis Inc
446 West 33rd Street
New York, NY 10001-2601
212-367-1000
e-mail: ronaldj@gmhc.org
Web site: www.gmhc.org

Clients:
Gay Men's Health Crisis Inc

Lobbyists:
Michael Czaczkes
Anthony Hayes

Geiger, Bruce W & Associates
111 Washington Ave, Ste 606A
Albany, NY 12210
518-432-1607

Clients:
28 New York Masters of Foxhounds
Alzheimer's Disease Resource Center
Associated Dog Clubs of New York State, Inc.
Aviation Management Association (NY) (Association of Counties (NY))
County Highway Superintendents Assn (NYS) (Association of Counties (NYS))
Empire State Marine Trades Association (Capitol Group, LLC)
Long Island Gasoline Retailers Association (William A. Schnell & Associates, Inc.)
Pinelawn Cemetery
Rural Electric Cooperative Association, Inc. (NYS)
Snowmobile Association (NYS) (Capitol Group, LLC)

Lobbyists:
Bruce W Geiger

General Electric Company (FKA Farrell, Pamela)
1299 Pennsylvania Avenue
Suite 900
Washington, DC 2004
202-637-4455

Clients:
General Electric Company

Lobbyists:
James McGaugh
Scott Roberti

General Motors Corporation
25 Massachusetts Avenue, NW
Suite 400
Washington, DC 20001
202-775-5056

Clients:
General Motors Corporation

Lobbyists:
John Blanchard
Brian Lee
Jeffrey Perry
Bryan Roosa

Genovese, John
1095 Avenue of the Americas
New York, NY 10036-6769
212-578-6499

Clients:
Metropolitan Life Insurance Company

Offices and agencies generally appear in alphabetical order, except when specific order is requested by listee.

Lobbyists:
Timothy Ring
Michael Zarcone

Genworth Financial
700 12th Street, NW
Suite 710
Washington, DC 20005
202-662-2568

Lobbyists:
Samuel Morgante
David Sloane
John Taggart

George J. Hochbrueckner & Associates, Inc.
PO Box 637
Laurel, NY 11948
518-456-3629

Clients:
Town of Riverhead
Vision Quest Lighting

Lobbyists:
George Hochbrueckner

Gergela III, Joseph
C/O Long Island Farm Bureau
104 Edwards Avenue
Suite 3
Calverton, NY 11933
631-727-3777

Clients:
Long Island Farm Bureau

Geto & De Milly Inc
276 Fifth Avenue
Suite 806
New York, NY 10001
212-686-4551
e-mail: pr@getodemilly.com
Web site: www.getodemilly.com

Clients:
Algin Management Co., LLC
Atlantic Realty Development Corporation
CAMBA, Inc.
Center Against Domestic Violence
Edwin Gould Services for Children & Families
FC Yonkers Associates LLC
Island Tennis LP D/B/A Sportime
Jewish Home & Hospital Lifecare System
Lightstone Bronx Venture LLC
Lightstone Real Estate Partners LLC
LM Legacy Group LLC
Local 802, American Federation of Musicians of Greater New York

Lobbyists:
Mark Benoit
Michele De Milly
Laura Dolan
Ethan Geto
Julie Hendricks-Atkins
Daniel White
Westchester County PBA

Gilbane Building Company
3150 Brunswick Pike
Suite 300
Lawrenceville, NJ 08648
609-671-4385

Clients:
Gilbane Building Company

Lobbyists:
Denis Boylan
Sean Cahill
Dennis Cornick
William DeCamp III
Jon Dibiase
William Gilbane, III
Neil Heyman
John Larow
Nadera Persaud
Judith Pullar
Matthew Simone
Lee Sokloski

Gilberti Stinziano Heintz & Smith, PC (FKA) Devorsetz Stinziano Gilberti Heintz & Smith, PC
555 E Genesee St
Syracuse, NY 13202-2159
518-476-2001

Clients:
Catskill Off-Track Betting Corporation
Young Men's Christian Association and Women's Community Center of Rome, New York, Inc.

Lobbyists:
Thomas Kelly
Tarky Lombardi Jr.
Andrew Maniglia

Clients:
Nat'l Assn of Energy Service Companies

Glazer, Robert
560 White Plains Road
Suite 500
Tarrytown, NY 10591
914-333-5809

Clients:
ENT and Allergy Associates, LLP

Lobbyists:
Andrew Franklin
Phyllis Schaffer-Cohen

Glenwood Poh
31 West 11th Street
New York, NY 10011
917-362-2200

Clients:
Glenwood Poh LLC

Lobbyists:
Ron Shemesh

Offices and agencies generally appear in alphabetical order, except when specific order is requested by listee.

Global Strategy Group
895 Broadway
5th Floor
New York, NY 10003
212-260-8813

Client:
Major League Soccer LLC

Lobbyists:
Justin Lapatine
Marcia Maxwell
Jon Silvan

Goens, Darin
11250 Waples Mill Road
Fairfax, VA 22030
703-267-1250

Clients:
National Rifle Association of America

Golden, Ben
NYSARC
393 Delaware Ave
Delmar, NY 12054-3094
518-439-8311

Clients:
Arc Inc (NYS)

Lobbyists:
Paul Kietzman
John Sherman

Golden Tree Asset Management LP
300 Park Avenue
21st Floor
New York, NY 10022
212-847-3500

Lobbyists:
Kevin McAdams
V. Theodore Roosevelt
Robert Zimardo

Goldman Harris LLC (FKA Law Offices of Howard Goldman, LLC)
475 Park Avenue South
28th Floor
New York, NY 10016
212-935-1622

Clients:
62 Wooster LLC
Metro Storage NY LLC
S.L. Green Realty Corporation

Lobbyists:
Howard Goldman
Caroline Harris
Keli Lin
Fred T. Milani
Ezra Moser
Eugene Travers

Goldman Sachs & Co.
200 West Street
29th Floor
New York, NY 10282
212-902-1000

Lobbyists:
Michael Borys
Gregory Carey
Willie DiBlasi
Edward Droesch
Chris Elmore
Nikki Faison-Miller
Marvin Markus
Arthur Miller
Joseph Natoli
Robert O'Connor
Sandy Pae
Jeffrey Scruggs
Stacy Sonnenberg
Jill Toporek
David Utz
Kevin Willens
Bervan Yeh

Golub, David
461 Nott Street
Schenectady, NY 12308
518-379-1421

Clients:
Golub Corporation (The)

Lobbyists:
Neil Golub
Jerel Golub
William Kenneally
Carrie Terraferma

Good Shepherd Services
305 Seventh Avenue
9th Floor
New York, NY 10001
212-243-7070

Lobbyists:
Amy Cohen
Sr. Paulette Lomonaco
Susan Singh
Michelle Yanche

Goode, Christian
110-00 Rockaway Blvd
Jamaica, NY 11420
718-215-2813

Clients:
Genting New York LLC

Google, Inc.
2350 Kerner Blvd
Suite 250
San Rafael, CA 94901
415-389-6800

Lobbyists:
William Floyd

Gordian Group, Inc. (The)
30 Patewood Drive
Suite 350
Greenville, SC 29615
800-874-2291

Lobbyists:
Thomas DiGangi
Paul Schreyer

Gotham Government Relations
1399 Franklin Avenue
Suite 200
Garden City, NY 11530
516-880-8170

Clients:
Allstate Insurance Company
Association of Wholesale Marketers and Distributors (NYS)
AU Foundation, Inc.
Brooklyn Bar Association Volunteer Lawyers Project
Cam-Held Enterprise, Inc. DBA Just Kids
Family Residences & Essential Enterprises
First Equity Abstract Corporation
Flair Beverage Corp.
Florida Compass Group/Premier Pawn & Jewelry in New York
Old Westbury College Foundation, Inc.
Ovation LLC
Red Apple Group
School for Language and Communication Development
Talon Air, Inc.

Lobbyists:
Diane Cahill
Bradley Gerstman
Robert J. Malito
David Schwartz

Gould, David (FKA Tallon Jr., James R.)
C/O United Hospital Fund
Empire State Building
350 5th Ave., 23rd Floor
New York, NY 10118-2399
212-494-0740

Clients:
United Hospital Fund

Governmental Insight LTD
379 Kenridge Rd
Lawrence, NY 11559
917-861-6776

Clients:
AFL-CIO
Injured Workers Alliance
Triad Group LLC
Union of Police Associations
Utility Workers of America Local 1-2

Lobbyists:
Arthur Wilcox

Grant Thornton LLP
2350 Kerner Blvd
Suite 250
San Rafael, CA 94901
415-389-6800

Lobbyists:
Tamara Anger
Anna Danegger
Terry Hastings
Douglas Lapham

Gray Media
1028 Boulevard
Suite 237
West Hartford, CT 06119
860-398-3916

Clients:
Pfizer Inc.

Lobbyists:
Jennifer Daly

Greater New York Health Care Facilities Association
519 8th Avenue
16th Floor
New York, NY 10018
212-643-2828

Lobbyists:
Michael A.L. Balboni

Greater NY Hospital Association, Subsidiaries & Affiliate (FKA Greater NY Hospital Association)
555 West 57th Street
Suite 1500
New York, NY 10019-2425
212-246-7100

Lobbyists:
Lloyd Bishop
Deborah Brown
Alison Burke
Karen Heller
Bridgett Ingraham-Roberts
Tim Johnson
Lee Perlman
Stewart Presser
Kenneth Raske
David Rich
Lorraine Ryan
Kathleen Shure
Zeynep Sumer
Susan Waltman
Elisabeth Wynn

Greenberg Traurig, LLP
54 State Street
6th Floor
Albany, NY 12207
518-689-1400
Web site: www.gtlaw.com

Clients:
13th Avenue Supermarket LLC
219-25 LLC
Ace Group- North America
Alliance for Children with Special Needs-School Age (NYS)
American Fair Credit Council
Argonaut Holdings LLC
Arker Diversified Companies
Association of Licensed Midwives
Association of School Psychologists
AT&T Services, Inc.

Offices and agencies generally appear in alphabetical order, except when specific order is requested by listee.

Auto Collision Technician's Association, Inc.
Bar Association
Barclays Capital, Inc.
Capital Region Council for Young Children with Special Needs
Certification Board for Nutrition Specialists
Child Resource Center, Inc.
Children's Day Treatment Coalition
Christie's
CNA
Coalition for Children With Special Needs
Coalition for Quality Assisted Living, Inc.
Coalition of Community Development Financial Institutions
Coalition of Ignition Interlock Manufacturers
Compliance Technologies Corporation, Inc.
Credit Union Association of New York
Daiichi Sankyo, Inc.
Direct Buy Holdings and it's Affiliates
Eastman Kodak Company
Empire State Water Well Drillers Association
Enterprise Holdings, Inc.
Forests Lots LLC
Geneva Worldwide, Inc.
GKC Industries, Inc.
Greater New York Health Care Facilities Association
H.W. Lochner, Inc.
Hartford Financial Services Group, Inc.
Health Plan Association
Healthplex, Inc.
Healthport Technologies, LLC
Honda North America, Inc.
Housing Association, Inc.
Hudson Alliance for Children with Special Needs
Hunts Point Cooperative Market, Inc.
IMS Health
Industco Holdings, LLC
International American University College of Medicine
Jewish Home Lifecare
Just Kids Diagnostic and Treatment Center
Just Kids Early Childhood Learning Center
Kaplan Higher Education
Lexington School for the Deaf/Center for the Deaf, Inc.
Liberty Mutual Group
Life Insurance Council of New York, Inc.
Logic Technology, Inc.
Long Island Coalition for Children with Special Needs
Maximus
Metropolitan Transportation Authority
MGM Resorts International
Microsoft Corporation
Momentive Performance Materials USA, Inc.
National Academy of Elder Law Attorneys New York Chapter
National Academy of Recording Arts & Sciences
National Conference of Commissioners in Uniform State Laws
News Corporation
North Shore Board of Education
NTT Data, Inc.
Nurse Practitioner Association NYS
NYSARC, Inc.
Partners Health Plan, Inc.
Phillips 66 Company
Podiatric Medical Association
Primerica Life Insurance Company
Prudential Financial, Inc.
Radar Associates, Inc.
Reed Elsevier, Inc.
Senior Care Pharmacy Alliance
Senior Whole Health
Servicemaster Company (The)
Sotheby's
Stop DWI Coordinators Association
Teva Pharmaceuticals USA, Inc.
Thrivent Financial for Lutherans
Tomra
Total Recall Corporation
Town of Huntington
Toys
Union College
Verax Biomedical Incorporated
Verifone, Inc.
Walter Kidde Portable Equipment, Inc.
Waterview at Greenpoint LLC
Wellcare of NY
Western Central Coalition for Children with Special Needs
Zurich

Lobbyists:
Michael Berlin
Lynelle Bosworth
Deidre Carson
Christopher Cernik
Diana Dellamere
James Dillon
Dan Egers
Mark Glaser
Robert Harding
Nick Hockens
Carla Hogan
Harold Iselin
Robert Ivanhoe
Warren Karp
Pamela Madeiros
John Mascialino
Michael Murphy
Joshua Oppenheimer
Jeffrey Pearlman
Jane Preston
Elizabeth Sacco
Jay Segal
Edward Wallace

Greenwich Village Society for Historic Preservation
232 East 11th St
New York, NY 10003
212-475-9585

Lobbyists:
Lloyd Andito
Amanda Davis
Andrew Durniak
Dana Schulz
Sheryl Woodruff

Greller, Matthew
75 Clinton Avenue
Millburn, NJ 07041
917-345-0005

Clients:
Liberty Natural Gas LLC
National Association of Theatre Owners, Inc.

Griffin Associates, LLC
600 Broadway
1st Floor - South
Albany, NY 12207
518-463-5949

Clients:
Explore Information Services, LLC
Millennium Pharmaceuticals, Inc.
Momentive Performance Materials (Plummer & Associates, LLC)

Lobbyists:
John Griffin

GSO Capital Partners LP
345 Park Avenue
31st Floor
New York, NY 10154
212-503-2157

Lobbyists:
John Cashwell
Beth Chartoff
Mary Lynn Eubanks
Doyle Queally
Matthew Quigley
Geoff Stockwell

Gtech Corporation
Gtech Center
8th Floor
10 Memorial Blvd
Providence, RI 02903
401-392-7459

Lobbyists:
Donald Sweitzer

Guardian Life Insurance Company
Seven Hanover Square
H23E
New York, NY 10004-2616
212-598-8956

Clients:
Guardian Life Insurance Company of America (The)

Lobbyists:
Ellie Jurado-Nieves
Ulysses Lee
Tracy Rich

Habitat for Humanity of New York State
911 E. Main Street
Endicott, NY 13760
607-748-4138

Lobbyists:
Judith Nelson

Hackensack University Medical Center
30 Prospect Avenue
Research Building, Room 240
Hackensack, NJ 07601

Lobbyists:
Erin Ihde

Hager, Susan
C/O United Way of NYS
155 Washington Ave
Albany, NY 12210
518-463-2522
e-mail: hagers@uwnys.org
Web site: www.uwnys.org

Clients:
United Way of NYS

Halpin Public Affairs
55 The Crescent
Babylon, NY 11702
516-848-0444

Clients:
Cablevision (CSC Holdings, Inc.)
Outlook Group, Inc.

Lobbyists:
Patrick Halpin

Hannan and O'Connell, Inc.
107 Washington Ave
Albany, NY 12210-2200
518-465-6550
e-mail: khannan401@aol.com
Web site: www.kthpa.com

Clients:
Campground Owners of New York, Inc.
Conpor Conference of Private Organizations (NYS)
Council of Professional Geologists NYS
Empire State Towing & Recovery Association
Firemen's Association of the State of NY
Hannaford Supermarkets
Millenium Laboratories
National Coalition of Pharmaceutical Distributors
Pest Management Coalition
VSweeps

Lobbyists:
Kirby T Hannan
Peter O'Connell

Hannesson, Paul (FKA McCormick, Lynde) (FKA Gaylord, Joan)
Christian Science Committee
340 Madison Avenue
Suite 429
New York, NY 10173
212-661-3838

Clients:
Chrsitian Science Committee on Publication for NY

Harlem United: Community AIDS Center, Inc.
306 Lenox Avenue
3rd Floor
New York, NY 10027
212-803-2850

Lobbyists:
Doug Berman
Soroya Elcock
Kimberleigh Smith

Harris, Steven W., LLC
119 Washington Avenue
Suite 2C
Albany, NY 12210
518-445-2535

Clients:
RAI Services Company

Lobbyists:
Steven Harris

Offices and agencies generally appear in alphabetical order, except when specific order is requested by listee.

Harter Secrest & Emery, LLP
1600 Bausch & Lomb Place
Rochester, NY 14604-2711
585-232-6500
e-mail: admin@hselaw.com
Web site: www.hartersecrest.com

Clients:
Alliance for Fine Wine Wholesalers, Ltd (NY)
Association of Safety Group Managers
ATU NY State Legislative Conference Board
Biotechnology Assn Inc (NY)
Buffalo & Pittsburgh Railroad Inc
Chiropractic Assn Inc (NYS)
Clinical Laboratory Assn Inc (NYS)
Cold Spring Harbor Laboratory
Empire State Petroleum Association, Inc.
Finger Lakes Horsemen's Benv & Protective Assn Inc
Genesee & Wyoming Railroad Company
Gershon & Company
GlaxoSmithKline, PLC
Hall of Science (NY)
Movers & Warehousemens Association Inc (NYS)
Municipal Electric Utilities Association
O-At-Ka Milk Products Cooperative, Inc.
Premier Exhibitions, Inc.
Roberts Wesleyan College
Rochester & Southern Railroad Inc
Rochester Technology & Manufacturing Association, Inc.
Rubber Manufacturers Association
South Buffalo Railway Company
Telecommunications Assn Inc (NYS)
Upstate Niagara Cooperative Inc (FKA Upstate Farms Cooperative Inc)

Lobbyists:
John Jennings
Amy Kellogg
Donald S Mazzulo
Richard E Scanlan

Hartford Financial Services Group, Inc. (The)
200 Hopmeadow Street
A4E-9
Simsbury, CT 06089
860-843-4587

Clients:
Hartford Financial Services Group, Inc. (The Hartford)

Lobbyists:
Thomas Bartell

Hawayek, Jonathan F
728 Main St
East Aurora, NY 14052
716-652-2038

Clients:
Allergan, Inc

Hawkins, Dennis (FKA Jockers, Ken)
351 West 54th Street
New York, NY 10019
212-541-6741

Clients:
Fund for Modern Courts

Lobbyists:
Dennis Hawkins

Denise Kronstadt

Health Facilities Association
33 Elk Stret
Suite 300
Albany, NY 12207-1010
518-462-4800

Lobbyists:
Gayle Farman
Stephen Hanes
Richard Herrick
Nancy Leveille
Karen Morris
Richard Patterson
Carl Pucci
Shelley Wagar Sabo

Health Plan Assn Inc (NY)
90 State Street
Suite 825
Albany, NY 12207-1717
518-462-2293
e-mail: info@nyhpa.org
Web site: www.nyhpa.org

Clients:
Health Plan Assn Inc (NY)

Lobbyists:
Rose Dunhan
Andrew Fogarty
Arlene Halpert
Paul F Macielak
Leslie S Moran
Sheila Nelson

Healthcare Association of New York State
One Empire Drive
Rensselear, NY 12144
518-431-7600

Clients:
Healthcare Association of New York State
Nassau-Suffolk Hospital Council, Inc.
Northern Metropolitan Hospital Association
Suburban Hospital Alliance of New York State

Lobbyists:
William Allison
Todd Ball
Sherry Chorost
Christa Christakis
Kathleen Ciccone
Eileen Clinton
Kevin Dahill
Wendy Darwell
Robin Frank
Christina Gahan
Sean Gemerek
Jeffrey Gold
Valerie Grey
Stephen Harwell
Frederick Heigel
Cara Henley
Nicholas Henley
Amy Jones
Steven Kroll
Nancy Landor
Debora LeBarron

Political Parties, Lobbyists & PACs

Offices and agencies generally appear in alphabetical order, except when specific order is requested by listee.

Jennifer Lee
Cindy Levernois
Janine Logan
Melissa Mansfield
Edward McGill
Robert McLeod
Christina Miller-Foster
Molly Poleto
Karen Roach
Sara Rosenberger
Jerry Salkowe
Daniel Sisto
Angela Skretta
Christopher Smith
Mary Therriault
William Vanslyke
Shelby Wafer
Sue Ellen Wagner
Dennis Whalen

Healthcare Tort Reform Coalition (NY)
C/O Combined Coordinating Council, Inc.
14 Penn Plaza, Ste 720
New York, NY 10122
212-643-8100

Clients:
Healthcare Tort Reform Coalition (NY)

Lobbyists:
Terence Kelleher
Lisa Kramer
Christopher Smith

Henderson Global Investors (North America) Inc.
1 Financial Plaza
19th Floor
Hartford, CT 06103
860-723-8609

Lobbyists:
Daniel McDonough
Mark Toomey

Herrick, Feinstein LLP
2 Park Avenue
New York, NY 10016
212-592-1428

Clients:
Nissan North America, Inc.

Lobbyists:
Kevin Fullington
Michael McMahon

Heyman, Neil
C/O Southern NY Association
39 Broadway, Ste 1710
New York, NY 10006
212-425-5050
e-mail: njheyman@snya.com
Web site: www.snya.org

Clients:
Southern NY Assn

Higgins Roberts Beyerl & Coan, PC
1430 Balltown Rd
Niskayuna, NY 12309
518-374-3399

Clients:
Society of Anesthesiologists, Inc (NYS)

Lobbyists:
Charles J Assini Jr

Hill & Gosdeck
One Commerce Plaza
99 Washington Ave, Ste 400
Albany, NY 12210
518-463-5449
e-mail: nylobbyists@aol.com

Clients:
Alliance of Automobile Manufacturers
American Cleaning Institute
AOL, LLC
Arise, Inc.
Association of Marraige and Family Therapy, Inc.
AT&T, Inc.
Builders Exchange, Inc.
Concentra Health Services, Inc.
Consumer Data Industry Association
Facebook, Inc.
International Business Machine Corporation
International Paper
Lexmark International, Inc.
MillerCoors LLC
Monsanto Company
New York State Higher Education Initiative
Newspaper Publishers Association
Proctors Theater
SCA Tissue North America LLC
USA Training Company, Inc.
Veterinary Medical Society
Walgreen Co.

Lobbyists:
Thomas J Gosdeck
Jeffrey L Hill
Denise Murphy McGraw
Frank Nemeth

Hillside Family of Agencies
1183 Monroe Ave
Rochester, NY 14620
312-856-4836

Lobbyists:
Clyde Comstock
Dennis Richardson

Hinman Straub Advisors, LLC
121 State St
Albany, NY 12207-1693
518-436-0751
e-mail: reception@hspm.com
Web site: www.hspm.com

Clients:
4201 Schools Association
Academic Dental Centers (NYS)
Albert Einstein College of Medicine
Alliance of Boys & Girls Clubs, Inc. (NYS)

Offices and agencies generally appear in alphabetical order, except when specific order is requested by listee.

American Forest & Paper Association (Multistate Associates Incorporated)
American Safety Council
Americans United for Life
Associated Medical Schools of NY
Association for Superintendents of School Buildings & Grounds (NYS)
Association of Proprietary Colleges
Bard College
Boces Educational Consortium (The)
Capital District Physician's Health Plan
Caterpillar, Inc.
Centers for Specialty Care Group
Children's Aid Society (The)
Cigna Companies
Coalition of 853 Schools, Inc.
Coalition of Special Acts School Districts
COFCCA, Inc.
Computer Sciences Corporation
Consolidated Edison Company of NY, Inc.
Consumer Electronics Association
Contemporary Services Corporation
Dietetic Association
Education & Research Network, Inc.
Elizabeth Seton Pediatric Center
Empire State Association of Assisted Living
Equinox, Inc.
Estee Lauder Companies, Inc.
Excellus Health Plan, Inc.
Federation of Mental Health Services, Inc.
Federation of School Administrators
First Lincoln Holdings LLC
Foundling
Free Community Papers of New York
Fresenius Medical Care North America
H.O. Penn Caterpillar
HealthFirst
Hillside Family of Agencies
Hofstra University
HSBC North America
Hudson Center for Health Equity & Quality
Independent Oil & Gas Association of NY
Institute for Special Education
International Bottled Water Association
Iroquois Pipeline Operating Company
Island Harvest LTD
Jewish Home of Rochester (The)
Johnstown Fire Fighters Association Local 779
Le Moyne College
LeadingAge New York
Life Insurance Council of New York, Inc.
Literacy New York, Inc.
McGraw-Hill Education
Medical College (NY)
Mental Health Counselors Association (NY)
National Health Care Associates, Inc.
National Pork Producers Council
NationWide Mutual Insurance Company
Ophthalmological Society
Organization of NYS Management/Confidential Employees, Inc.
Parker Jewish Institute for Health Care & Rehabilitation
Police Benevolent Association of New York State
Professional Fire Fighters Association, Inc.
Public Health Solutions
Rescare, Inc.
Selfhelp Community Services, Inc.
Seneca Nation of Indians
Southworth-Milton
St. Anns of Greater Rochester, Inc.
State University of New York at Stony Brook
Stonehenge Capital Corporation
Support Services Alliance, Inc.
Supreme Court Justices Association of the City of New York
Tech Valley School Foundation
Tectonic Engineering & Surveying Consultants P.C.
To Life
Toyota Motor North America, Inc.
Treated Wood Council, Inc.
UCB, Inc.
Unshackle Upstate
Verizon NY
Wellpoint, Inc.
Wing of the Civil Air Patrol
X-Ray Optical Systems, Inc.

Lobbyists:
John Black
James Carr
Bartley J Costello, III
Terri Crowley
Caron Crummey
Sean M Doolan
Joseph Dougherty
Heather Evans
Michael Fallon
John Federman
Mara Ginsberg
Vincent Graber
Tracy Lloyd
Matthew O'Connor
Donald Robbins
Kelly Ryan
John Saccocio
Janet Silver

Hiscock & Barclay, LLP
Hiscock & Barclay, LLP
300 South Street
Syracuse, NY 13202-2078
315-425-2873

Clients:
Superfund Coalition, Inc. (NYS)

Lobbyists:
Angela M. Barry
David Burch
Maureen O. Helmer
Kevin R. McAuliffe
Michael McNulty
Thomas F Walsh
Jerry Weiss

Hodes & Landy
284 State St
Albany, NY 12210
518-465-8303
e-mail: nhodcs@hodesassoc.org

Clients:
Assisted Living Federation of America (ALFA)
Benchmark Senior Living
Boehringer Ingelgheim Pharmaceuticals, Inc.
DentaQuest LLC
Dominican Village
Emeritus Senior Living
Insperity Services, L.P.
Lifetouch National School Studios, Inc.
Metropolitan College of New York
Public Consulting Group
Sony Pictures Entertainment
US BioLogic

Lobbyists:
Courtney David
Nancy L Hodes
Virginia Lynch-Landy
Michele O'Connor

Hofstra University
101 Hofstra University
Hempstead, NY 11549-1010
516-463-1800

Lobbyists:
Melissa Connolly
Dolores Fredrich
Stuart Rabinowitz

Holloway, Jr, Floyd
C/O State Farm Insurance Co
6 Hillman Drive
Suite 200
Chadds Ford, PA 19317-9039
610-361-4150
e-mail: floyd.holloway.clxm@statefarm.com

Clients:
State Farm Insurance Companies

Lobbyists:
Tim McFadden
Carolyn Schwadron
Joe Spicer

Home Care Assn of NYS Inc
388 Broadway
4th Floor
Albany, NY 12207
518-426-8764
e-mail: info@hcanys.org
Web site: www.hca-nys.org

Clients:
Home Care Assn of NYS Inc

Lobbyists:
Al Cardillo
Patrick Conole
Joanne Cunningham
Andrew Koski

Homeless Services United (FKA Council on Homeless Policies & Services)
446 West 33rd Street
6th Floor
New York, NY 10001-2601
212-367-1562

Lobbyists:
Eric Lee
Joan Montbach

Honeywell International, Inc.
101 Constitution Avenue NW
Suite 500 West
Washington, DC 20001
202-662-2612

Lobbyists:
Lawrence Kast

Horton, Dan J
C/O Nielsen, Merksamer, Et Al.
2350 Kerner Blvd., Suite 250
San Rafael, CA 94901
415-389-6800

Clients:
Exxon Mobil Corporation

Hotel & Motel Trades Council, AFL-CIO
707 Eighth Avenue
New York, NY 10036
212-492-2102

Lobbyists:
Josh Gold

Housing Conservation Coordinators
777 Tenth Ave
New York, NY 10019
212-541-5996

Clients:
Housing Conservation Coordinators

Lobbyists:
Bennett Baumer
Sarah Desmond
Rachel Jaffe
Robert Kalin
Matthew Klein

Howard Hughes Corporation (The)
13355 Noel Rd
22nd Floor
Dallas, TX 75240
214-741-7744

Lobbyists:
Christopher J. Curry
John DeWolf
Grant Herlitz
Adam Meister
David Weinreb

HR&A Advisors, Inc.
99 Hudson Street
3rd Floor
New York, NY 10013
212-977-5597

Clients:
Major League Soccer

Lobbyists:
John Alschuler
Cary Hirschstein

HSBC - North America Holdings, Inc.
452 Fifth Avenue
New York, NY 10018
212-525-5000

Lobbyists:
Kevin Fromer
Craig Lassen
Margaret McGovern
Faye Polayes
James Stiegel

Hudson Eagle LLC
435 Hudson St
Suite 402
New York, NY 10014
212-477-8008

Lobbyists:
Greg Carney

Hudson Valley Community College
80 Vandenburgh Avenue
Troy, NY 12180
518-629-8071

Lobbyists:
Joel Fatato
James Lagatta
Lucille Marion
Andrew Matonak
Kathryn Navarra Bradley
Karen Seward

Hunger Action Network of NYS
275 State Street
Albany, NY 12210
518-434-7371

Lobbyists:
Mark Dunlea

Hurley, Alicia D. (FKA Haberman, Michael)
70 Washington Square South
New York, NY 10012
212-998-6859

Clients:
University (NY)

Lobbyists:
Robert Berne
Kathleen Bernier
Lynne Brown
Gilda Ventresca Ecroyd
Robert Grossman
Steven Heuer
Sayar Lonial
Jennifer Pautz
John Sexton

Hutton & Solomon, LLP
232 Madison Avenue
Suite 700
New York, NY 10016
212-682-5702
Web site: www.hstax.com

Clients:
Eponymous Associates

Lobbyists:
Kenneth Moore
Stephen Solomon

Hynes, Daniel
200 E. Randolph Street
Chicago, IL 60601
312-726-0140

Clients:
Ariel Investments LLC

Ianno, Dominick
1 Walnut St.
Boston, MA 02108
617-201-9142

Clients:
Pfizer, Inc.

Immigration Coalition, Inc (NY)
137-139 W 25th St, 12th Fl
New York, NY 10001
212-627-2227

Clients:
Immigration Coalition, Inc (NY)

Lobbyists:
Jacqueline Esposito
Silvia Gonzales
Chung-Wha Hong
Karen Kaminsky
Melanie Reyes
Jacqueline Vimo
Jackie Wong

Independent Bankers Association of New York State
19 Dove Street
Albany, NY 12210
518-436-4646

Lobbyists:
Stephen Rice

Independent Health Association, Inc.
511 Farber Lakes Drive
Buffalo, NY 14221
716-635-3714

Lobbyists:
Scott Campbell
Michael Cropp
Don Gibson
Teresa Glanowski
David Naramore
Ann Pentkowski
Iris Schifeling
Julie St. Cyr
Dietra Steed
Jennifer Stoklosa
Robert Tracy

J Strategies, Inc.
8016 Bridgeport-Kirkville Road
Kirkville, NY 13082
315-382-6607

Clients:
Lilly USA
Pfizer, Inc.
Pharmaceutical Research and Manufacturers of America
Winn Companies

Lobbyists:
Jessica Johnson
Julie Miner
Jenna Peppenelli

Offices and agencies generally appear in alphabetical order, except when specific order is requested by listee.

Jaime Venditti

Institute of International Bankers
299 Park Avenue
17th Floor
New York, NY 10171
212-421-1611

Lobbyists:
Richard Coffman
Sarah Miller

Insurance Association, Inc. (NY)
130 Washington Avenue
Albany, NY 12210-2219
518-432-4227

Lobbyists:
Marc Craw
Ellen Melchionni

Inventiv Health, Inc.
C/O Nielsen Merksamer, Et Al.
2350 Kerner Blvd
Suite 250
San Rafael, CA 94901
415-389-6800

Clients:
Allergan, Inc.

Lobbyists:
Jack Quinn

Irving Place Capital Management L.P.
745 Fifth Avenue
7th Floor
New York, NY 10151
212-551-4520

Lobbyists:
Philip M. Carpenter III
Patricia Grad
John D. Howard
Robert Juneja
Douglas Korn
Eve Mongiardo
Richard L. Perkal

Island Peer Review Organization, Inc.
1979 Marcus Avenue
First Floor
Lake Success, NY 11042-1072
516-326-7767 or 516-326-6182 Fax: 516-328-2310
e-mail: bschwartz@ipro.org

Lobbyists:
Harry Feder
Jaz-Michael King
Dan Schweitzer
Patti Weinberg
Marilyn Zumbo

Island Public Affairs
277 Indian Head Rd
Kings Park, NY 11754
631-724-0017

Clients:
Adelante of Suffolk County, Inc
Hands Across Long Island Inc
National Foundation for Human Potential Inc

Lobbyists:
Steven Moll

J.P. Morgan Securities Inc.
270 Park Avenue
38th Floor
New York, NY 10017
212-270-2428

Lobbyists:
Michael Altman
Brian Gonor
Peter McCarthy
Brian Middlebrook
Kyle Pulling

Janney Montgomery Scott LLC
575 Lexington Ave
35th Floor
New York, NY 10022
646-840-4616

Lobbyists:
Vivian Altman
Joseph Bosch
Elizabeth Caputo
Daniel Froehlich
Steve Nelson

JEM Associates NY, Inc.
224 Euclid Avenue
Albany, NY 12208
518-281-3322

Clients:
7-Eleven, Inc.
American Chemistry Council, Inc.
Chinese-American Planning Council, Inc.
Court Officers Benevolent Association of Nassau County, Inc.
Dr Pepper Snapple Group
Feld Entertainment
Good Shepherd Services
New Square Community Planning and Development Corporation
Pratt Institute
RAI Services Company
Reach Out and Read of Greater New York
WNET

Lobbyists:
James McMahon

Jenkins, Joanne E
C/O NY Life Insurance
111 Washington Ave
Albany, NY 12210
518-463-6649

Clients:
Life Insurance Co (NY)

Lobbyists:
Scott L. Berlin
Sheila Davidson
Tom English
Theodore Mathas

Carol Mayer
Joseph Muratore
George Nichols
Michael Oleske
Joel Steinberg
Rebecca Strutton
Maria Sullivan
Michael J Tobin
Gil Valdes
Douglas A. Wheeler

Jennison Associates LLC
466 Lexington Avenue
New York, NY 10017
973-367-3135
Web site: www.jennison.com

Lobbyists:
Peter H. Reinemann

Jerome, Stephen
121 State Street
Albany, NY 12207
518-437-1867

Clients:
Association of Proprietary Colleges

Jewish Association for Services for the Aged (FKA Saiger, Molly)
247 West 37th Street
9th Floor
New York, NY 10018
212-273-5260
Web site: www.jasa.org

Lobbyists:
Jolene Boden
Amy Chalfy
Donna Dougherty
Leah Ferster
Molly Krakowski
Donald Manning
Danielle Palmisano
Alla Pliss
Martha Pollack
Elaine Rockoff

Jewish Home and Hospital for Aged (The)
120 West 106th Street
New York, NY 10025
212-870-4600

Lobbyists:
Patricia Beilman
Kay Boonshoft
Rachel Fredman
Bridget Gallagher
Thomas Gilmartin
Bruce Nathanson
Judith Nicholson
Laura Radensky
Cara Unowsky
Audrey Weiner

JGN Associates LLC
190 Lape Rd
Nassau, NY 12123
518-766-7136

Clients:
Mutualink, Inc.

Lobbyists:
James Natoli

JJMH Consulting
90 State Street
Suite 700
Albany, NY 12207
518-591-4660

Clients:
Are-East Rive Science Park, LLC
Friedman & Moses
Omni Childhood Center
Stuyvesant Town-Peter Cooper Village Tenants Association

Lobbyists:
Steven Sanders

JLO Consultant, Inc.
139 Shear Hill Road
Mahopac, NY 10541
646-522-7914

Clients:
LaGuardia Community College

Lobbyists:
Jose Orengo

Jobs with Justice (NY)
50 Broadway
16th Floor
New York, NY 10004
212-631-0886

Lobbyists:
Nathalic Alegre
Matt Ryan

Jockey Club (The)
40 East 52nd Street
New York, NY 10022
212-521-5309

Lobbyists:
James L. Gagliano
Matt F. Juliano

John Hancock Life Insurance
601 Congress Street
Boston, MA 02210
617-663-2486

Lobbyists:
James Gallagher
Linda Watters

Johnson & Johnson Health Care Systems, Inc.
175 Hilltop Drive
Churchville, PA 18966
215-357-0495

Lobbyists:
Nick Rebholz

Johnson, Russ
8246 Ashington Drive
Baldwinsville, NY 13027-8715
415-389-6800

Clients:
Pfizer, Inc.

Johnston, Christine
C/O Association of Health Care Providers
20 Corporate Woods Blvd
2nd Floor
Albany, NY 12211
518-463-1118

Clients:
Association of Health Care Providers, Inc.

Lobbyists:
Nancy Erodes
Christine Johnston
Megan Tangjerd
Catherine Tully

Joint Industry Board of the Electrical Industry
58-11 Harry Van Arsdale Jr. Avenue
Flushing, NY 11365
718-591-2000

Lobbyists:
Robert McCormick
Humberto Restrepo

Jones, Jeff
55 Brookline Avenue
Albany, NY 12203-1804
518-265-0719

Clients:
Healthy Schools Network, Inc.
Land Trust Alliance Northeast Program
Natural Resources Defense Council
New Partners for Community Revitalization, Inc.

JPMorgan Chase Bank, National Association
270 Park Avenue
37th Floor
New York, NY 10017
212-270-0530

Lobbyists:
Martha Beard
Douglas A. Bennett
Steve Bernstein
Gerard J. Buchko
Michelle L. Buonfiglio
Wayne Burrell
Charles Callahan
Robin Chappelle Golston
Michelle Cipriani
Leonard T. Colica
Louis A. Constantino
Thomas P. Daly
Sandra T. Davis
Susan M. Farrell
Elizabeth French
John P. Gardell, Jr.
Michael S. Gardner
Debra B. Gentile
Peter Gibson
Robert W. Gibson
Scott M. Grossman
Peter D. Johnsen
Robert J. Kane
Craig M. Kantor
Tim Kemp
Karen P. Keogh
Jan Konigsberg
Marjorie V. Lauri
Angela L. Lavis
Alexander B. Leonard
Chad M. Levy
Carol B. Mark
Shirley McCoy
Nancy K. McDonnell
Ruth McMahon
Louise R. Meyer
Timothy Minahan
Edward J. Muendell
Lori A. Nelson
Michael James Nevins
Timothy G. Noble
Katy A. O'Donnell
Patricia A. O'Donnell
Lester J. Owens
Manny Patino
Jennifer A. Pegg
Michael Pressman
Chris Redvers
Robert J. Rehm
Susan M. Ridler
Alphonso Robinson
Lucas M. Ruglis
Matthew B. Sarson
Jeff Schor
John Simeone
Debbi M. Tholl
Pamela T. Thomson
Lisa A. Valle
Christopher Vavrina
Frederick Vosburgh

Justice, Lawrence P.
111 Washington Ave
Suite 203
Albany, NY 12210
518-368-7539

Clients:
Hudson River Pilots' Association
Industry AD HOC Committee on Pilotage

Justin McCarthy Consulting Services, Inc.
677 Broadway
12th Floor
Albany, NY 12207
518-424-7347

Clients:
Arista Power, Inc.
Capital District Regional Off-Track Betting Corporation
CDS Monarch
Correction Officers' Benevolent Association, City of New York, Inc.
Flaum Management Company, Inc.
Genessee County Economic Development Center
Monroe County Water Authority
Passero Associates
Seneca County IDA

Offices and agencies generally appear in alphabetical order, except when specific order is requested by listee.

Lobbyists:
Justin McCarthy

Kalanz, Edward
C/O Bridge & Tunnel Officers Benevolent Association
1140 Bay Street, Suite A&B
Staten Island, NY 10305
718-727-7613

Kantor Davidoff Mandelker Twomey Gallanty & Kesten, PC
415 Madison Avenue
16th Floor
New York, NY 10017
212-682-8383

Clients:
Metropolitan Retail Assn, LLC (NY)
Sports & Arts in Schools Foundation

Lobbyists:
Lawrence A Mandelker

Kaplan, Alden B.
83 Maiden Lane
New York, NY 10038
917-716-7111

Clients:
AHRC-NYC

Kasirer Consulting
321 Broadway, Ste 201
New York, NY 10007
212-285-1800
e-mail: skasirer@kasirerconsulting.com

Clients:
145 Americas Condominium
384 Bridge Street LLC
390 Tower LLC
50 Varick LLC
American Cancer Society, Inc.
Arcadis U.S., Inc.
Area Property Partners
Astoria Generating Company LP
ATCO Properties & Management, Inc.
Atlantic Yards Development Company
BCMUSA
Big Brothers Big Sisters of NYC
Brookfield Financial Properties, Inc.
Brooklyn Botanic Garden Corporation
CEMUSA, Inc.
City Meals-On-Wheels
Cooper Union for Advancement of Science and Art (The)
Cornell University
CSC Holdings LLC
Cubic Transportation Systems, Inc.
Delta Air Lines, Inc.
Eastern Region Helicopter Council
ELAD US Holding, Inc.
FCC Construction, Inc.
For the Benefit of Red Hook 100 LLC, Red Hook 212 LLC, and Red Hook 300 LLC
Foundling Hospital
GE Transportation Systems Global Signaling LLC
General Electric Company
Global Aerospace, Inc. and United States Aviation Underwriters, Inc
GT Forge, Inc. DBA GET Taxi
Hewlett Packard Company
Historical Society
Host Hotels and Resorts L.P.
KM Associates of NY, Inc.
Legal Assistance Group
Lend Lease Construction LMB, Inc.
Lincoln Center for the Performing Arts, Inc.
Looks Great Services, Inc.
Macerich
Macerich
Madison Square Garden L.P.
Metropolitan Realty Group LLC
MGM Resorts International Operations, Inc.
Mission Society (NYC)
Motion Picture Association of America, Inc.
Mount Sinai Hospital
Naftali Group (The)
NBC Universal
New Planet Energy LLC
New Visions for Public Schools, Inc.
Nontraditional Employment for Women
Northside Center for Child Development, Inc.
Paco Realty, LLC
Plumbing Foundation City of New York, Inc.
Project Renewal
Rainbow Media Holdings LLC
Rescare, Inc.
Restoration Project
Safe Horizon, Inc.
SDS Great Jones LLC
Silverite Construction
SL Green Realty Company
South Street Seaport Limited Partnership
Stahl York Avenue LLC
Steinway Child and Family Services
T&T Scrap LLC
Underground Utilities, Inc.
United American Land LLC

Lobbyists:
Omar Alvarellos
Julie Greenberg
Sara Kasirer
Peter Krokondelas

Katz, Arthur H
542 3rd Avenue
Brooklyn, NY 11220
718-439-9011

Clients:
Assn of Wholesale Marketers & Distributors (NYS)

Kaysen, Mary
104 Valley Street
Beverly Farms, MA 01915
978-232-1147

Clients:
Bristol-Myers Squibb Company

Kehoe, Clare
St. Joseph's College
245 Clinton Avenue
Brooklyn, NY 11205
718-940-5579

Offices and agencies generally appear in alphabetical order, except when specific order is requested by listee.

Clients:
St. Joseph's College

Lobbyists:
Michael Banach
Nancy Connors
James Graham
Elizabeth Hill

Kennedy, Ronald F.
C/O Bar Association (NYS)
One Elk Street
Albany, NY 12207
518-487-5652

Clients:
Bar Association (NYS)

Lobbyists:
Patricia K. Bucklin
Seymour W. James, Jr.
Kevin M. Kerwin
Richard Rifkin
David M. Schraver

Ketzer, Bill
P.O. Box 310
Glenmont, NY 12077
646-315-1416

Clients:
American Society for the Prevention of Cruelty to Animals (ASPCA)

Lobbyists:
Debora Bresch
Bill Ketzer
Cori Menkin
Edwin Sayres
Michelle Villagomez
Stacy Wolf

Keycorp & Subsidiaries
127 Public Square
Cleveland, OH 44114
216-689-3420

Clients:
Keycorp & Subsidiaries

Lobbyists:
Bonnie Bale
Tracy Barney
Patricia C. Barrett
Lyman A. Buck III
Lori Capron
James Carriero
Derek Chauvette
Robin J. Commerford
Thomas Coverick
James G Criniti
Kristy David
Jeffrey Eades
Amanda Earnshaw
Joseph Eicheldinger
Susan Facciola
Jason Fenwick
Greg Fertel
David Folcomer
Linda Freeman
Jeffrey Freese
Mike Garibaldi
Andrew C. Goff
Ken Gruber
Edward J. Hackett
Jose R. Herrera
Matthew Hunt
Shane Kranov
Victor Kunakowsky
Patrick J Lillo
Mitchell W Miller
Kathy Mizener
George Mohan
Susan Mooradian
Mark Morrison
Michael Moss
Steven M. Pierce
Christopher J. Puliese
Gary Quenneville
Tawana Smith
Jeffrey Stone
Brenda L. Stout
David J Sylvan
Gerhard O Voggel
Anne Marie Warren

Kiernan-Pagani, Kathleen
101 Constitution Ave
Suite 700
Washington, DC 20001
202-624-2463

Clients:
American Council of Life Insurers

King, Barbara
555 W 57th St, 5th Fl
New York, NY 10019
212-523-5367
e-mail: bking@chpnet.org
Web site: www.wehealnewyork.org

Clients:
Beth Israel Medical Ctr
St Luke's-Roosevelt Hospital Ctrs

Lobbyists:
Bradley Korn

Kramer Levin Naftalis & Frankel, LLP
1177 Ave of Americas
New York, NY 10036
212-715-7835
Web site: www.kramerlevin.com

Clients:
525 West 52nd Street Development LLC
AMV Unitel LLC
Broadway Trio LLC
Charlton Soho LLC
Columbus Square Management LLC
Hebrew Home at Riverdale Foundation
Jujamcyn Theaters LLC
Lenox Terrace Development Associates
Midtown Trackage Ventures LLC
MSG Holdings L.P.
Nederlander Organization, Inc.
Shubert Organization, Inc. (The)
South Street Seaport L.P.
Strategic 34th Street LLC

Offices and agencies generally appear in alphabetical order, except when specific order is requested by listee.

Lobbyists:
Valerie Campbell
Robert E Flahive
Albert Fredericks
James Greilsheimer
Marcie Kesner
Robin Kramer
Elizabeth Larsen
Samuel H Lindenbaum
Cynthia Lovinger
James P Powers
Sheila Pozon
Paul D Selver
Michael T Sillerman
Patrick Sullivan
Gary R Tarnoff
Adam Taubman
Elise Wagner

Kramer, Jason
NYSHEI
22 Corporate Woods
3rd Floor
Albany, NY 12211
518-443-5444

Clients:
Higher Education Initiative

Kriss Kriss & Brignola, LLP
350 Northern Blvd.
Suite 306
Albany, NY 12204
518-449-2037

Clients:
Society of Professional Engineers, Inc.

Lobbyists:
Mark Kriss

Kwan, Patrick
200 West 57th Street
Suite 705
New York, NY 10019
917-331-7187

Clients:
Humane Society of the United States (The)

Lackman, Abraham M.
Praxis Insights, Inc.
580 Broadway
Suite 1001
New York, NY 10012
518-605-6103

Clients:
Stony Brook Foundation

Lobbyists:
Abraham M. Lackman

Lambert, Linda A
C/O Am. College of Physicians
744 Broadway
Albany, NY 12207-1817
518-427-0366

Clients:
American College of Physicians Services, Inc. (NY)

Lobbyists:
Gary Babette

Land Title Association, Inc.
2 Rector Street
Suite 901
New York, NY 10006-1819
212-964-3701

Lobbyists:
Robert Treuber

Land Trust Alliance Northeast Program
112 Spring Street
Suite 205
Saratoga Springs, NY 12866
518-587-0774

Lobbyists:
Kevin Case
Katrina Howey
Ethan Winter

Langdon, David
491 State Street
3A
Albany, NY 12203-1019
518-432-5440

Clients:
Aetna, Inc.
Brighter Choice Foundation (The)
Charter School Association
Coalition for Opportunity in Education, Inc.
Community Service Society

Lanotte, Michael A.
1021 Watervliet-Shaker Road
Suite 3
Albany, NY 12205
518-437-8236

Clients:
Credit Union Association

Lobbyists:
Ronald D. McLean
Henry Meier
William Mellin

Lasky, Roy
111 Washington Ave
Albany, NY 12210
518-573-8647

Clients:
Dental Association
Medical Liability Mutual Insurance Company

Law Office of Usher Fogel
557 Central Ave
Suite 4A
Cedarhurst, NY 11516
516-967-3242

Political Parties, Lobbyists & PACs

Clients:
Small Customer Marketer Coalition

Lobbyists:
Usher Fogel

LCI LLC
677 Broadway
Suite 1105
Albany, NY 12207
518-410-2024

Clients:
General Motors LLC

Lobbyists:
Christopher Grimaldi

League of Conservation Voters
30 Broad Street
30th Floor
New York, NY 10004
212-361-6350

Lobbyists:
Marcia Bystryn
Ricardo Gotla
Joshua Klainberg

League of Women Voters of New York State
62 Grand Street
Albany, NY 12207
518-465-4162

Clients:
League of Women Voters of New York State

Lobbyists:
Aimee Allaud
Janet Aram
Barbara Bartoletti
Laura Bierman
Ruth Bonn
Marian Bott
Ann Brandon
Lori Dawson
Georgia DeGregorio
Sally Dreslin
Cheryl Feldman
Gladys Gifford
Judie Gorenstein
Lois Haignere
Arlene Hinkemeyer
Anne Huberman
Ann Ingleman
Ellen Kotlow
Polly Kuhn
Carol Meller
Susan Multer
Suzanne Perry
Sarah Podber
Beth Radow
Sally Robinson
Helga Schroeter
Kay Sharp
Barbara Thomas
Therese Warden
Roberta Wiernak
Carly Wise

Lefebvre, Steve
6369 Collamer Drive
East Syracuse, NY 13057
315-463-7539

Clients:
Associated Builders and Contractors, Inc.

Lobbyists:
Marci Miller
Ruth Mulford
Joshua Reap

Legal Assistance Group (NY)
7 Hanover Square
18th Floor
New York, NY 10004
212-613-5000

Lobbyists:
Julie Brandfield
Phyllis Brochstein
Laura Davis
Antoinette Delruelle
Ann Dibble
Randal Jeffrey
Irina Matiychenko
Randye Retkin
Lisa Rivera
Alison Sclater
Jane Greengold Stevens
Kim Susser

Legal Information for Families Today (LIFT)
32 Court Street
Suite 1208
Brooklyn, NY 11201
646-613-9633

Lobbyists:
Liv Johanson Berg
Sharon A. Myrie

Legal Services NYC
40 Worth Street
Suite 606
New York, NY 10013
646-442-3654

Lobbyists:
M. Audrey Carr
Jennifer Ching
Saba Debesu
Peggy Earisman
Meghan Faux
Tara Foster
Nancy Goldhill
Justin Haines
Jacob Inwald
Tyler Johnson
Edward Josephson
Peter Kempner
Pavita Krishnaswany
Jennifer Levy
Nelson Mar
Anne Nacinovich
Jose Quesada
Raun Rasmussen
Jennifer Sinton

Betty Staton
Tanya Wong

Lehrer, Sander
41 Madison Ave
41st Floor
New York, NY 10010
212-763-4150

Clients:
United Nations Development Corporation

Lesbian and Gay Community Services Center, Inc.
208 West 13th Street
New York, NY 10011
212-620-7310

Lobbyists:
Carrie Davis
Jefffrey Klein
Jose Lugaro
Glennda Testone
Robert Wheeler
Robert Woodworth

Levin, Brenda
301 East 48th Street #8E
New York, NY 10017-1741
212-755-7996

Levin, David
P.O. Box 25
New Baltimore, NY 12124
518-269-6830

Clients:
Capital Region Norml NY

Levine, Paul
Jewish Board of Family & Children Svcs
120 W 57th St
New York, NY 10019
212-632-4614

Clients:
Jewish Board of Family & Children's Services Inc

Lobbyists:
Carmen Collado
Lenny Rodriguez

Levy Ratner P.C.
80 Eighth Avenue
8th Floor
New York, NY 10011
212-627-8100

Lobbyists:
Kevin Finnegan

Levy, Norman P.C.
575 Madison Avenue
New York, NY 10022
212-605-0313

Lobbyists:
Norman Levy
Henry Sheinkopf

Library Assn (NY)
C/O Library Association (NY)
6021 State Farm Road
Guilderland, NY 12084-1802
518-432-6952
e-mail: nyladirector@pobox.com
Web site: www.nyla.org

Clients:
Library Assn (NY)

Lobbyists:
Michael J Borges

Lieberman, Mark L
900 Merchants Concourse, Ste 314
Westbury, NY 11590
516-228-4226

Clients:
American Lawyer Media
Court Clerks Assn (NYS)
EAC Inc
Forestcitydaly Housing
Glenwood Management Corp
Nassau Regional Off-Track Betting Corporation
Lockwood, Kessler & Bartlett Inc
Sanitary District No 6
Town of Hempstead

Lobbyists:
Rosemarie Garipoli
Reynold Levy
Maureen McCormick
Scott Noppe-Brandon
Melissa Thornton

Lilly USA LLC
555 12th Street NW
Suite 650
Washington, DC 12210
518-434-8435

Lobbyists:
Tamara Atkins
John Ewashko
Anmari Hanrahan

Lincoln Center for the Performing Arts, Inc.
70 Lincoln Center Plaza
New York, NY 10023-6583
212-875-5000

Lobbyists:
Jennifer Berry
Russell Granet
Jessica Handrik
Hillary McAndrew-Plate
Tamar Podell
Levy Reynolds
Matthew Troy

LJM Rad, LLC
P.O. Box 38227
50 Beaver Street
Albany, NY 12203
518-677-2135

Offices and agencies generally appear in alphabetical order, except when specific order is requested by listee.

Lobbyists:
Michael McNulty
Louis R. Thompson
Jerry A. Weiss

Local 6, Hotel & Club Employees & Bartenders Union, AFL-CIO
709 Eighth Avenue
New York, NY 10036
212-492-2102

Lobbyists:
Jan Dunford
Neal Kwatra

LoCicero & Tan Inc
123 William St, 22nd Fl
New York, NY 10038
212-608-0888

Clients:
Bluestone Organization (The)
Covanta Energy Corp
Community Preservation Corporation (The)
Council of Senior Ctrs & Services of NYC Inc
Erie Basin Marine Associates (Kelly & Roth)
Fashion Institute of Technology
Flushing Commons
Forest City Ratner Companies
Gannett Fleming Engineers & Architects PC
Hospital for Special Surgery
Kingston Avenue Development LLC
Knickerbocker Plaza Associates
Millenium Partners
NYU School of Medicine
New York Botanical Garden (The)
Sequoia Community Initiatives (Consumer Info & Dispute Resolution)
SL Green Realty Corp
Snug Harbor Cultural Center
TDC Development & Construction Corp
TKGG LLC
Towers at Spring Creek
Village Care of NY Inc
Yonkers Contracting Co Inc
JBI International

Lobbyists:
John LoCicero
Eva Tan

Logan, Ernest
Council of School Supervs/Administrators
16 Court St
Brooklyn, NY 11241-1254
718-852-3000

Clients:
Council of School Supervisors & Administrators

Lobbyists:
Peter McNally
Rolon Alithia Rodriguez

Long Island Board of Realtors (FKA Kaplan, Randy L.)
Randy Kaplan C/O Long Island Board of Realtors
300 Sunrise Highway
West Babylon, NY 11704
631-661-4800

Lobbyists:
Philip Weiden

Long Island Contractors Association, Inc.
150 Motor Parkway
Suite 307
Hauppauge, NY 11788
631-231-5422

Lobbyists:
Marc Herbst

Long Term Care Community Coalition (FKA Nursing Home Community Coalition)
1 Penn Plaza
Suite 6252
New York, NY 10119
212-385-0355 Fax: 212-239-2801
e-mail: info@ltccc.org
Web site: www.ltccc.org

Clients:
Long Term Care Community Coalition (FKA Nursing Home Community Coalition)

Lobbyists:
Richard J. Mollot

Losquadro, Steven E.
649 Route 25A
Suite 4
Rocky Point, NY 11778
631-744-9070

Clients:
Caithness Long Island II, LLC

Louloudes, Virginia
520 Eighth Ave, Suite 319
New York, NY 10018-3011
212-244-6667
e-mail: questions@art-newyork.org
Web site: www.offbroadwayonline.com

Clients:
Alliance of Resident Theatres/New York

Luria, Robert S
12 Spruce Run
East Greenbush, NY 12061-9611
518-477-2581
e-mail: robert.s.luria@gsk.com

Clients:
GlaxoSmithKline, PLC

Lutheran Augustana Center for Extended Care and Rehabilitation
6434 2nd Avenue
Brooklyn, NY 11220
718-630-7335

Lobbyists:
David Rose

Offices and agencies generally appear in alphabetical order, except when specific order is requested by listee.

Lutheran Medical Center
150 55th Street
Brooklyn, NY 11220
718-630-7335

Lobbyists:
Claudia Caine
Wendy Goldstein
Richard Langfelder
Mary Quinones

Luthin Associates, Inc
535 Main Street
Allenhurst, NJ 07711
732-774-0005

Clients:
Consumer Power Advocates

Lobbyists:
Catherine Luthin

Lutz, Jr., Alexander
520 West 48th Street
New York, NY 10019
212-875-2396

Lobbyists:
Theresa Bischoff
Denise Bloise
Jackie Dragone
Bonnie Fletcher
Scott Graham
Rosemary Mackey
Sonia Martinez
Alice Rivera
Corwin Smith
Olivier Szlos
Enrique Vega

Lynch, Bill Associates, LLC
308 Lenox Avenue
4th Floor
New York, NY 10027
212-283-7515

Clients:
CSC Holdings Inc
Downtown Brooklyn Partnership (The)
Industrial Technology Assistance Corp
Thor 280 Richards Street LLC
Trustees of Columbia University in the City of NY (The)

Lobbyists:
William Lynch
William Lynch, Jr.
Norman McConney
Luther Smith
Arelis Tavares
Kevin Wardally

Lynch, Patricia Associates
677 Broadway, Suite 1105
Albany, NY 12207
518-432-9220
e-mail: plynch@plynchassociates.com

Clients:
88 Greenwich Owner LLC
AHRC New York City
Albany Port District Commission
Alliance for Downtown New York, Inc.
Alliantgroup
American Chemistry Council
American Traffic Solutions
Association of Legal Aid Attorneys UAW 2325
Avis Budget Car Rental LLC
Buffalo Niagara Medical Campus, Inc.
Buffalo State College
Cablevision
Caramoor
Cathedral of the Immaculate Conception Restoration Committee
Catholic Conference Policy Group, Inc.
Catholic Health System
Champion Learning Center LLC
City of Buffalo
City of Yonkers
Coalition for the Homeless, Inc.
Coca-Cola Refreshments USA, Inc.
Columbia Development Companies
ConnectEdu, Inc.
Delbello Donnellan Weingarten Wise & Wiederkehr LLP
Destiny USA
Devon Capital LLP
Drum Route 11
Dunkin' Brands, Inc.
Eastern Paramedics, Inc.
Economic Development Council
Educational Housing Services, Inc.
Empire State Passengers Association
Fluor Enterprises, Inc.
Ford Gum & Machine Company, Inc.
Gaia Plant Based Medicine
Gaming Association
Gar Associates, Inc.
General Motors LLC
Genting New York LLC
Greater New York Hospital Association
Harlem Children Society
Henningson Durham & Richardson Architecture and Engineering P.C.
Honeywell International, Inc.
Integrated Medical Professionals PLLC
Interior Designers for Legislation in New York
JMA
John Mezzalingua Associates D/B/A PPC
Kulanu
LCO Buildings LLC
Legal Aid Society (The)
Lifespan of Greater Rochester, Inc.
Lightstone Group LLC
Maid of the Mist Corporation
Maritime Association
McKissack and McKissack
Medical Answering Services
Menorah Campus, Inc.
Mohawk Ambulance Service
Motor Truck Association
MSG Holdings L.P.
National Grid
Niagara University
Noble Environmental Power LLC
Pharmaceutical Research and Manufacturers of America
Polytechnic University of New York University
Prime LLC
Pyramid Management Group LLC
Related Companies L.P.
Rochester Genesee Regional Transportation Authority
Shephardic Heritage Museum
SHFL Entertainment, Inc.
Sorrento Lactalis, Inc.

Offices and agencies generally appear in alphabetical order, except when specific order is requested by listee.

Political Parties, Lobbyists & PACs

Stony Brook Foundation, Inc.
Success Academy Charter Schools
Surf Manor Home for Adults
Suse and Peter Lowenstein
Tappan Zee Constructors, LLC
Taubman Company (The)
Technet
Transpro Consulting LLC
Trinet
US Digital Gaming, Inc.
Vornado Realty L.P.
Walt Disney Company (The)
Western Regional Off-Track Betting Corp.
Yeshiva University

Lobbyists:
Christopher Bombardier
Michelle Cummings
Danna Deblasio
Sam Gerrity
Christopher Grimaldi
Patricia Lynch
Patrick McCarthy
Mark Meyerhoffer
Jim Quent
Lisa Reid
Enrique Sosa
Paul Tokasz

M + R Strategic Services (FKA M & R Strategic Services)
80 Broad St.
17th Floor
New York, NY 10004
212-764-3878

Clients:
AIDS Service Center of NYC
Defenders Association (NYS)
Homeless Services United
Naral Pro-Choice NY
Pratt Center for Community Direct Marketing Association

Lobbyists:
Robert Liff
Ya-Ting Liu
Arthur Malkin
Kim Milbrath
Michael O'Loughlin
Rebecca Wallach

Madden, Susan (FKA Benson, Kathleen)
Museum of the City of New York
1220 Fifth Avenue
New York, NY 10029
917-492-3302

Lobbyists:
Martin McLaughlin
Ronay Menschel

Maher Jr., Daniel F.
C/O Excess Line Assn of NY
55 Broadway, 1 Exchange Plz, 29th Fl
New York, NY 10006-3728
646-292-5500
e-mail: dmaher@elany.org
Web site: www.elany.org

Clients:
Excess Line Assn of NY

Major League Soccer, LLC
420 Fifth Avenue
7th Floor
New York, NY 10018
212-450-1260

Lobbyists:
Mark Abbott
Don Garber
Brett Lashbrook

Malkin & Ross
80 State Street, 11th Floor
Albany, NY 12207-1801
518-449-3359
e-mail: amalkin@malkinross.com
Web site: www.malkinross.com

Clients:
Academy of Medicine (NY)
ALCOA, Inc.
Alliance for Clean Energy New York, Inc.
Alzheimer's Association, New York City Chapter
American Lung Association of New York
AmidaCare
Ascension Health
Assembly of the Association of Surgical Technologists
Association of Central Service Professionals
Barrier Free Living Family of Companies
Boyd Gaming
Brooklyn Botanic Garden
Brotherhood/Sister Sol
Business Outreach Center Network, Inc.
Camp Directors
Citizens Committee for Children of NY, Inc.
Coalition for the Homeless
Coalition of Behavioral Health Agencies, Inc.
Coalition of New York State Alzheimer's Association Chapters
Congregation of Yeshiva Machzikei Hadas
Court Appointed Special Advocates
Defenders Association
Direct Marketers and Publishers
Drug Policy Alliance
Elliott Management
Federation of Protestant Welfare Agencies
Food and Water Watch
Gay Men's Health Crisis, Inc.
Human Services Council
Judge Rotenberg Center
Learning Through an Expanded Arts Program
Legal Assistance Group
LI CSP-MSA Association
Lower Eastside Service Center, Inc.
Make the Road New York
Naral Pro-Choice New York
National Employment Lawyers Association
Nestle Waters North America Holdings, Inc.
New Yorkers for Fair Automobile Insurance Reform, Inc.
Nurses Association
Open Space Institute
Parent Child HOme Program, Inc.
Pharmacists Society
Police Benevolent Association of New York State
Regional Community Service Programs
Rehabilitation Association
Safe Horizon, Inc.

School Nutrition Association
Takeda Pharmaceuticals America
Therapeutic Communities Association of NY, Inc.
United Way of New York City
Village of Kiryas Joel
Visa, Inc.
Whitney M. Young Jr. Health Services
Yeled V'Yalda Early Childhood Center

Lobbyists:
Jay Adolf
Cynthia Dames
Laura Darman
Gene De Santis
Mary Ann Donnaruma
Arthur Malkin
Terry Pratt
Brendan Principato
Donald Ross
Jessica Schafroth
Christine Tramontano
Tracy Tress
Victoria Zwickel
Steven Sanders

Manatt, Phelps & Phillips, LLP
30 S Pearl Street
12th Fl
Albany, NY 12207
518-431-6700

Clients:
83-30 Austin Street LLC
Assn of Public Broadcasting Stations of NY
American Council of Life Insurers
Bayer Healthcare
Brain Trauma Foundation
Brooklyn Information & Culture
Callen-Lorde Coomunity Health Center
Coalition for Medically Fragile Children
Concepts of Independent Choices
Community Health Care Assoc of NYS
Corporation for Supportive Housing
Coalition of Voluntary Safety Net Hospitals (NYS)
Coalition of Prepaid Health Svcs Plans (NYS)
East Side Rezoning Alliance
El Paso Corporation
Federation of Protestant Welfare Agencies Inc
Glimmerglass Coalition
Group Health Incorporated
Health & Hospitals Corp (NYC)
Hewlett-Packard Company
Independent Care System (ICS)
Living Independently Inc
Memorial Sloan-Kettering Cancer Center
Montefiore Medical Ctr
NYS Council of Health-System Pharmacists
National Multiple Sclerosis Society, NY MS Coalition Action Netwo
Primary Care Development Corporation
Project Samaritan AIDS Services Inc
Ralph Lauren Center for Cancer Care & Prevention
Samaritan Village Inc
St Raymond Community Outreach
Structured Employment Economic Development Corp
Sephardic Bikur Holim
Structural Biology Center (NY)
Verizon Wireless
Visiting Nurse Service of NY

Lobbyists:
Robert Belfort
Karyn Bell
William Bernstein
Kalpana Bhandarkar
Patricia Boozang
Melinda Dutton
John Faso
Anthony Fiori
Paul Gangsei
Kerry Griffin
Susan Ingargiola
George Kalkines
Alice Lam
Emily Lee
David Oakley
Steve Polan
Helen Pfister
Jeremiah Sheehan
Joann Smith
Jeffrey Thrope
Mark Ustin
James Walsh
Vanessa Wisniewski
Marcia Alazraki
Melinda Dutton
Leah Griggs Pauly
Emily Lee
James Lytle
Elizabeth Mundinger
Helen Pfister

Manhattan Chamber of Commerce, Inc.
1375 Broadway
3rd Floor
New York, NY 10018
212-473-7875

Lobbyists:
Ronald Paltrowitz
Nancy Ploeger
Don Winter

Maniscalco, John D
14 Penn Plz, Ste 1102
New York, NY 10122
212-695-1380
e-mail: nyoilheating@nyoha.org
Web site: www.nyoha.org

Clients:
Oil Heating Assoc

Mannella, Peter F.
266 Hudson Ave
Albany, NY 12210
518-463-4937

Clients:
Association for Pupil Transportation (New York)

Manufacturers Assn of Central NY Inc
One Webster's Landing, 5th Fl
Syracuse, NY 13202-1044
315-474-4201

Clients:
Council of Industry of Southeastern NY
Manufacturers Assn of Central NY Inc

Political Parties, Lobbyists & PACs

Offices and agencies generally appear in alphabetical order, except when specific order is requested by listee.

Lobbyists:
Karyn Burns
Randall Wolken

March of Dimes Birth Defects Foundation New York Chapter
515 Madison Avenue
20th Floor
New York, NY 10022
212-353-8353

Lobbyists:
Nelson Andino
Caitlin Conner
Frank Demeo
Susan Rose
Dennis Schrader

Marcus Attorneys
13 Greene Avenue
Brooklyn, NY 11238
718-643-6555

Lobbyists:
Katrice Clermont
Philip Lavender
Jed S. Marcus
Amy Mayer
Jennifer Payne
Guillermo Santiago

Maritato, Anna Maria
284 State Street, 2nd Floor
Albany, NY 12210
518-463-9133

Clients:
Pfizer Inc

Markee, Lionel
111 Washington Ave
Suite 404
Albany, NY 12210-2210
518-465-6294

Clients:
Association of PBAS, Inc.
International Longshoremen's Association, AFL-CIO
Sanitation Officer's Association
Vietnam Veterans of America, New York State Council

Lobbyists:
Louis Matarazzo

Marsh, Wassermann & McHugh, LLC
677 Broadway
Albany, NY 12207
518-436-6000
e-mail: marshpc@attglobal.net

Clients:
Amerigroup New York LLC/Amerigroup Community Care (FKA Care Plus Health Plan)
Assn of Independent Schools (NYS)
ATM Industry Association
Atomic Learning Inc
Auxilia
Canadian National Railway
Cardtronics LP
Chief Executives Network for Manufacturing
Education & Work Consortium (The)
Eyemed Vision Care LLC
Greater NY Health Care Facilities Assoc
Greene International Golf Assn
LB Furniture Industries LLC
Medstat
Metropolitan College of NY
Morton Grove Pharmaceuticals
National Safety Commission Inc
SSP Companies
Tier Technologies
Town Clerks Assn Inc (NYS)
UST Public Affairs Inc
Western Union

Lobbyists:
J. Scott Bonacic
Blaise S. Dibernardo
Darcy L. Green
Kerry D. Marsh
Juan A. Martinez
Patrick J. McHugh
Edward H Wassermann
Diana P. Georgia
Ryan V. Horstmyer

Martin Begun D/B/A Martin S. Begun Consulting
400 East 67th Street
Unit 22A
New York, NY 10065
212-308-2114

Clients:
NYU School of Medicine
NYU Hospitals Center

Lobbyists:
Martin Begun

Martin J. McLaughlin Communications, Inc.
54 State St
6th Floor
Albany, NY 12207
518-689-1436

Clients:
Verizon NY

Lobbyists:
Cathy Cudahy
Martin McLaughlin
Michael Woloz

Masiello, Martucci, Calabrese and Associates (FKA Government Action Professionals, Inc.)
Cathedral Place
298 Main Street
Suite 300
Buffalo, NY 14202-4005
716-923-4156

Clients:
Allergan USA, Inc.
Arcadis U.S., Inc.
Brennan Center for Justice
Buffalo City Cemetary, Inc.
Buffalo Zoo
CCS Oncology

Offices and agencies generally appear in alphabetical order, except when specific order is requested by listee.

Clarence Building Materials and Supplies/Ray-Gar Construction
County of Niagara
Delta Sonic
Fair Committee
Hamister Group, Inc.
Health Transportation Network
Insight Associates
John W. Danforth Company
Kaleida Health
Kissling Interests (The)
Mensch Capital Partners, Inc.
Mikhail Strut, MD.
Niagara Frontier Transpotation Authority
Norstar Development USA, LP
Palladian Health
Phillips Lytle LLP
Shea's Buffalo Theatre
St. John Fruit Belt Development Corporation
Try-It Distributing Company
Wendel LLC

Lobbyists:
Carl Calabrese
Victor Martucci
Anthony Masiello
Patricia Paul
Matthew J. Plunkett

Massachusetts Mutual Life Insurance Company
Massachusetts Mutual Life Insurance Company
1295 State Street
Springfield, MA 01111
413-744-7204

Lobbyists:
Dennis Herchel

Master, Robert
C/O Communications Workers of America
80 Pine St, 37th Fl
New York, NY 10005
212-344-2515

Clients:
Communications Workers of America, District 1

Lobbyists:
Kenneth Peres
Peter Sikora

Matarazzo, Louis
36 Muirfield Rd
Rockville Centre, NY 11570
516-642-3900

Clients:
Captains Endowment Assn, NYC Police Department
Detectives Endowment Assn, Police Dept of NYC
Public Employee Conference (NYS)

Mathews, Dan
1123 Broadway, Suite 704
New York, NY 10010
212-226-8247

Lobbyists:
Karla Waples

Matusic, Karen
2350 Kerner Blvd
Suite 250
San Rafael, CA 94901
415-389-6800

Clients:
Exxon Mobil Corporation

MC Asset Management Americas, LTD.
655 Third Ave
2nd Floor
New York, NY 10017
212-644-1840

Clients:
MC Financial Services LTD.

Lobbyists:
John Dearing
Gregory Eudicone

McCormack, Jr., R. Christopher
111 Washington Avenue
Suite 200
Albany, NY 12210
518-436-4077

Clients:
Bank of America Corporation and Subsidiaries
RAI Services Company

McDonnell, Brian
212 Great Oaks Boulevard
Albany, NY 12203
518-869-2245

Lobbyists:
Jillian Matundan

McGrath Matter Associates
1500 Broadway
Suite 812
New York, NY 10036
212-354-5588
Web site: www.mcgrathmatter.com

Lobbyists:
Scott Matter
George McGrath

McGuire, Jason J.
P.O. Box 107
Spencerport, NY 14559-0107
585-225-2340

Clients:
New Yorkers for Constitutional Freedoms

Lobbyists:
Stephen Hayford, Esq.
Duane Motley

McGuire, Michael J
Mason Tenders Dist. Council of Grtr NY
266 W 37th St, 7th Fl
New York, NY 10018
212-452-9501

Political Parties, Lobbyists & PACs

Offices and agencies generally appear in alphabetical order, except when specific order is requested by listee.

Clients:
Mason Tenders District Council Greater NY & Long Island PAC

Lobbyists:
Kris Kohler
James Hegarty
Peter Zarcone

McKenna Long & Aldridge, LLP
111 Washington Avenue
Albany, NY 12210
518-462-1800

Clients:
ALS Association of Greater New York (The)
Bellefaire JCB
Bombardier Transit Corporation
Brookhaven Memorial Hospital Medical Center
CBS Outdoor
Devry Incorporated
Fire Island Association, Inc.
Gilbane Building Company
Gordian Group, Inc. (The)
HealthPass
HNTB Corporation
Institute for International Bankers
Koch Companies Public Sector, LLC and it's Affiliates
OTG Management
Safelite Group, Inc.
Suffolk Regional Off-Track Betting Corporation
Talisman Energy USA, Inc.

Lobbyists:
Charles E. Dorkey III
Chris Graham
Michael Klein
Kathleen O'Connor
Timothy Plunkett
Frank Rapoport
Amy Solomon

McLean, Mary Ann
459 Mayfair Drive
Poinciana, FL 34759
863-427-3491

Clients:
Athletic Trainers' Association New York State
Society of Clinical Social Work, Inc. (NYS)

McMahon, Kathy A.
21 Aviation Rd
Suite 9
Albany, NY 12205
518-446-1483

Clients:
Hospice and Palliative Care Association of NYS

McManus, Michael T.
119 Washington Ave
#306
Albany, NY 12210
518-436-8827

Clients:
Professional Fire Fighters Association, Inc.

Lobbyists:
Samuel Fresina

Meara Avella Dickinson
111 Washington Avenue, Suite 305
Albany, NY 12210
518-472-2288

Lobbyists:
Michael Avella
Christina Dickinson
Brian Meara

Meara, Brian R, Public Relations Inc
321 Broadway
New York, NY 10007
518-472-2288

Clients:
ABC Inc
Altria Corporate Services Inc (ALCS)
American Lawyer Media Co
Assurant Solutions
Black Car Assistance Corporation
Black Car Operators' Injury Compensation Fund (NY)
Bus Association of NYS Inc
CBS Corporation
Delaware North Companies Gaming & Entertainment Inc
Court Officers Assn (NYS)
EAC Inc
Empire State Assn of Adult Homes & Assist Living Facilities
Finger Lakes Racing Association
Glenwood Management Corporation
Insurance Premium Finance Assn Inc
Long Island Power Authority
Nassau Regional Off-Track Betting Corporation
NBC Universal
Jets LLC (NY)
NYU School of Medicine
Parker Jewish Inst for Health Care & Rehab
Physicians' Reciprocal Insurers
Reliant Resources Inc
Retailers Alliance (The)
Solow Management Company
Simon Weisenthal Ctr Museum of Tolerance
Shinnecock Nation Gaming Authority
Silvercup Studios
Southern Tier Acquisition, LLC
Suffolk County Court Employees
Transit Alliance
Uniformed Fire Officers Assn (NYC)
Vanguard Car Rental USA Inc
Verizon
Wilmorite Holdings, LP
Yankees Partnership (NY)
Educational Housing Services (Regional Programs Inc)
Empire Resorts Inc
Guardian Life Insurance Company of America (The)
Lincoln Center for the Performing Arts Inc
New York Medical Staff Leadership Council
NYC & Company
NYC 2012

Lobbyists:
Michael Avella
Christina Dickinson
Brian R Meara

Medical Society of the State of New York
One Commerce Plaza
Suite 408
Albany, NY 12210

Offices and agencies generally appear in alphabetical order, except when specific order is requested by listee.

518-465-8085

Lobbyists:
Morris Auster, Esq.
Patricia F. Clancy
Barbara K. Ellman
Robert J. Hughes
Andrew Y. Kleinman
Philip Schuh
Sam L. Unterricht

Medtronic, Inc. (FKA Dena Scearce)
710 Medtronic Parkway
LS380
Minneapolis, MN 55432-5604
763-505-2597

Lobbyists:
William Fehrenbach
Dena Scearce

Memorial Sloan-Kettering Cancer Center
1275 York Avenue
New York, NY 10065
646-227-2788

Lobbyists:
James Gillson
Cynthia McCollum
Katherine Mikk
Paul Nelson

Mental Health Association in NYS
194 Washington Ave, Ste 415
Albany, NY 12210
518-434-0439
e-mail: mhapres@mhanys.org
Web site: www.mhanys.org

Clients:
Mental Health Association of NYC Inc

Lobbyists:
Glenn Liebman
John Richter

Mental Health Association of New York
50 Broadway
19th Floor
New York, NY 10012
212-964-5253
Web site: www.mhaofnyc.org

Lobbyists:
Michael B. Friedman
Giselle Stolper
Kimberly Williams
Carol Altieri

Merck Sharp & Dohme Corp. (Affiliates: Schering Corp and Merck Schering-Plough Pharmaceuticals)
351 North Sumneytown Pike
UG3A-94
North Wales, PA 19454
267-305-2384

Lobbyists:
Matthew Badalucco
Bindi Patel

Mercury Public Affairs LLC
7 World Trade Center
250 Greenwich Street
36th Floor
New York, NY 10007
212-681-1380

Clients:
Addiction Treatment Providers Association
Advanced Biohealing a Shire Company
AT&T
AutoDesk, Inc.
Centerlight Health Systems
Children's Hospital of Philadelphia
CWA Local 1182
Dart Container Corporation
FJC Security Services, Inc.
IBM Corporation
Intergraph Corporation
OHEL Children's Home & Family Services
Premier Kids Care, Inc.
Sallie Mae, Inc.
Shinnecock Nation Gaming Authority
Source Corp.
St. Johns Riverside Hospital
Twin America
United Ambulette Coalition
Van Wagner Communications LLC

Lobbyists:
Thomas Doherty
Fernando Ferrer
Jonathan Greenspun
Michael McKeon

Merrill Lynch & Company, Inc.
222 Broadway
16th Floor
New York, NY 10038
212-670-2905

Lobbyists:
Maxine Awner
Robert Barber
William Bloom
James Calpin
Jeffrey Carey
Spencer Coker
Paul Critchlow
Mark Eidlin
Barbara Feldman
Christopher Fink
John Hallacy
Michael Jang
Susan Jun
John Keane
Richard Lasala
John Lawlor
Mark Liff
Brian Maier
David Notkin
James O'Connor
Rebecca Reape
Carol Rein
James Ryan
Garth Schulz
Chris Sebastian
David Stephens

Christopher Straub
Jeffrey Sula
Martha Wooding
Elvir Mujanovic

Metropolitan Jewish Health System (FKA Cross, Jeannie H.)
Metropolitan Jewish Health System
6323 Seventh Avenue
Brooklyn, NY 11220-4711
718-614-4183

Lobbyists:
Hany Abdelaal
Debra Boyce Martinez
Lurlene Buckley
Susan Caputo
Laurie Chichester
Jeannie Cross
Sandra Esner
Eli Feldman
Lydia Galeon
Diane Gallo
Barbara Hiney
Randall Klein
Shmuel Lefkowich
Joyce Little
Barbara Lyon
Ronald Milch
Derek Murray
David Nussbaum
Osarhiemen Okpeseyi
Tara Ragbir
Yeruchim Silber
Sandra Schau
Mary Wagner
Carol Altieri
Al Balko
Ron Chaffin
Gary Kleinberg
Robert Leamer
Emily Pring

Meyer Suozzi English & Klein, PC
One Commerce Plaza, Ste 1705
Albany, NY 12260
518-465-5551

Clients:
1199/SEIU New York's Health & Human Services Union
Actors Fund of America (The)
Brooklyn Public Library
City Works Foundation, (The)
Committee for Occupational Safety & Health (NY)
Committee for Workers' Compensation Reform
Conservation Service Group
Council for Unity
Consortium for Workers Education
Forest City Ratner Companies
Fractured Atlas
Friends of NY Racing Inc
Local 802, American Federation of Musicians of Greater NY
Int'l Brotherhood of Teamsters, AFL-CIO (Local 237)
Laborers' Political Action Committee (NYS)
Garment Industry Development Corporation
Local 1180, CWA, AFL-CIO
Mount Sinai Medical Center
Retail Wholesale Department Store Union
MFY Legal Services
Screen Actors Guild (National & Hollywood Offices)
Suffolk County Correction Officers Assn
Susquehanna & Western Railway Corp (NY)
Production Alliance (NY)
Unite Here
Utility Workers Union, Local 1-2, AFL-CIO
SEIU Local 200 United
Workers' Compensation Alliance
Working Today
SEIU, Local 300
Traffipax Inc

Lobbyists:
Deanne Braveman
Thomas Hartnett
Richard D Winsten

Michael Balboni, Esq.
50 Meritoria Drive
East Williston, NY 11596
516-567-0345

Clients:
1199 SEIU Greater New York Worker Participation Fund
Raytheon Company

Lobbyists:
Michael Balboni

Mid-Hudson Catskill Rural & Migrant Ministry Inc
360 Noxon Rd
PO Box 4757
Poughkeepsie, NY 12602
845-485-8627
e-mail: hope@ruralmigrantministry.org
Web site: www.ruralmigrantministry.org

Clients:
Mid-Hudson Catskill Rural & Migrant Ministry Inc

Lobbyists:
Jordan Wells
Richard Witt, Jr

Miller, Craig J.
137 Harrison St
Gloversville, NY 12078
518-773-7371

Clients:
Frontier Communications

Millman, Claude
7 World Trade Center
New York, NY 10007
212-808-8100

Clients:
Institute for Puerto Rican/Hispanic Elderly

Milroy, James
Erwin 218
SUNY Geneseo
Geneseo, NY 14454
585-245-5704

Clients:
SUNY Geneseo

Offices and agencies generally appear in alphabetical order, except when specific order is requested by listee.

Mirram Group, LLC (The)
895 Broadway, 5th Fl
New York, NY 10003
212-505-6633
e-mail: mirramgroup@aol.com

Clients:
Atlantic Development Co
Cable Telecommunications Association of NY
Coalition for the Homeless
First (NY)
Food Industry Alliance of NYS
Healthcare Education Project
Healthplex Inc
Monroe College
Morris Heights Health Center
New Visions for Public Schools
Protecting America.org
Transport Workers Union, Local 100
TVG Network
UBS Securities
Urban Health Plan Inc
World Trade Center Properties

Lobbyists:
Bernard Bryan
Luis A Miranda Jr
Gloria Mullen
Roberto Ramirez Sr
Kim Ramos
Catherine Torres

Mirrer, Louise
170 Central Park West
New York, NY 10024
212-873-3400

Clients:
Historical Society (NY)

Montalbano Initiatives Inc
64 Fulton St, Ste 603
New York, NY 10038
212-587-0587
Web site: www.nyclobbyist.com

Clients:
Covenant House NY
Teamsters Local 237
Trust for Public Land

Lobbyists:
Vincent Montalbano

Montefiore Medical Center
677 Broadway
Suite 1101
Albany, NY 12207
518-701-2713

Lobbyists:
Roberto Garcia
Deborah Konopko
Kate Rose

Moon Capital Management LP
499 Park Avenue
8th Floor
New York, NY 10022
212-652-4500

Lobbyists:
Ian Lindsay
Allyce O'Brien
Ramesh Parameswar
Veronica Wong

Mooney, William
1133 Westerchester Avenue
S-217
White Plains, NY 10604
914-948-6444

Lobbyists:
Amy Allen
Dorothy Forinca

Moreau, Karen
150 State St.
4th Floor
Albany, NY 12207-1675
518-465-3563

Clients:
American Petroleum Institute

Lobbyists:
Cathy Kenny
Maryann McCarthy

Morgan Stanley & Co. Incorporated
1585 Broadway
New York, NY 10036
212-761-4000
Web site: www.morganstanley.com

Lobbyists:
Randall Campbell
Michael Colton
Paula Dagen
Darryl Davis
Dennis Farrell
Grant Fraunfelder
David Hammer
Kent Hitchcock
Daniel Kelly
Melissa Labuda
Ben Langmead
Todd Lee
Richard McDermott
James McIntyre
Richard Molke
Edward Moulin
Lou Palladino
Geoff Proulx
Kevin Schwartz
Robert Shearer
R. Stratford Shields
Ira Smelkinson
Barbara Thomas
Charles Visconsi
Richard Weiss
Perry J. Offutt
Perry J. Offutt
David Rush

Morris, Mark
217 Great Oaks Blvd.
Albany, NY 12203-5964
518-862-0110

Clients:
Healthcare Professionals Insurance Company

Morse, Alan
Jewish Guild for the Blind (The)
15 W 65th St
New York, NY 10023
212-769-6215
e-mail: armorse@jgb.org
Web site: www.jgb.org

Clients:
Jewish Guild for the Blind (The)

Lobbyists:
Annemarie O'Hearn

Mosaic Federal Affairs LLC
One Park Place
300 South State Street
10th Floor
Syracuse, NY 13202
315-425-2839

Lobbyists:
Michael Brower

Motion Picture Association of America, Inc.
1600 Eye Street N.W.
Washington, DC 20006
202-293-1966
Web site: www.mpaa.org

Lobbyists:
Angela Miele
Vans Stevenson

Motorola, Inc.
1303 East Algonquin Road
7th Floor
Schaumburg, IL 60196
847-538-1955

Lobbyists:
Maureen Donovan

Mount Sinai Medical Center
One Gustave L Levy Pl
Box 1499
New York, NY 10029-6574
212-659-9011

Clients:
Mount Sinai Medical Center

Lobbyists:
Brad Beckstrom

Movement Group, LLC
1133 Broadway
Suite 416
New York, NY 10010
212-309-2863

Lobbyists:
Jan Feuerstadt
Charles King

MSG Holdings, L.P.
2 Penn Plaza
New York, NY 10121
212-465-6310

Lobbyists:
Irene Baker
Alex Diaz
Joel Fisher
Matthew Gorton
Annette Juriaco
Jeremiah O'Shea
Marc Schoenfeld
Hal Weidenfeld

Mueller, Tricia
91 Fieldcrest Avenue
Raritan Plaza II
2nd Floor
Edison, NJ 08837
914-592-0100

Clients:
Northeast Regional Council of Carpenters NY Political Education Committee

Lobbyists:
Tricia Brown

Muhs, Robert E.
c/o Avis Budget Group, Inc.
8 Sylvan Way
Parsippany, NY 07054
973-496-3532

Clients:
Avis Budget Group, Inc.

Municipal Art Society
457 Madison Ave
New York, NY 10022
212-935-3960

Clients:
Municipal Art Society

Lobbyists:
Melissa Baldock
Eve Baron
Micaela Birmingham
Vin Cipolla
Jasper Goldman
Vanessa Gruen
Lisa Kersavage
Frank Sanchis
David Schnakenberg
Lacey Tauber

Murray, Claire
1 Empire Drive
Rensselaer, NY 12144
518-273-1525

Offices and agencies generally appear in alphabetical order, except when specific order is requested by listee.

Clients:
New York Organization of Nurse Executives

MVP Health Insurance Co. and Its Affiliates (FKA MVP Service Corporation)
625 State Street
Schnectady, NY 12305
518-388-2235
Web site: www.mvphealthcare.com

Lobbyists:
Frank Fanshawe
David Oliker

MyWireless.org
MyWireless.org
1400 16th Street
NW Suite 600
Washington, DC 20036
202-736-3889
Web site: www.mywireless.org

Lobbyists:
Brian Johnston

NADAP
355 Lexington Avenue
New York, NY 10017
212-986-1170
Web site: www.nadap.org

Lobbyists:
John Darin
Elizabeth Madison
Sunita Manurekar
Karen Morton
Maria Pasceri
Lucy Redzeposki
Gary Stankowski

Nagel Law Office, PLLC
224 W 35th Street
Suite 508
New York, NY 10001
212-904-1139

Lobbyists:
William Nagel

NARAL Pro-Choice, New York
470 Park Ave S
7th Fl
New York, NY 10016
212-343-0114
e-mail: info@prochoiceny.org
Web site: www.prochoiceny.org

Clients:
NARAL Pro-Choice, New York

Lobbyists:
Emily Alexander
Myra Batchelder
Amy Boldesser
Mary Alice Carr
Kelli Conlin
Katherine Grainger
Angela Hooton
Lalena Howard
Debbie Johnson
Sabrina Shulman
Andrew Stern

Nasca, Samuel J
35 Fuller Road
Suite 205
Albany, NY 12205
518-438-8403
e-mail: sjnasca@aol.com

Clients:
United Transportation Union

Nassau Community College
One Education Drive
Garden City, NY 11530
516-572-7811
Web site: www.ncc.edu

Lobbyists:
Mary Adams
Frank (Chuck) Cutolo
John Durso
Carol Friedman
Alan Gurien
Joseph Muscarella
Reginald Tuggle
Donald Astrab
James Large
John LeBoutillier

National Assn of Chain Drug Stores
328 Still River Rd
Still River, MA 01467
978-456-9235
Web site: www.nacds.org

Clients:
National Assn of Chain Drug Stores

Lobbyists:
Anne Fellows

National Association of Mutual Insurance Companies (NAMIC)
3601 Vincennes Road
Indianapolis, IN 46268
317-875-5250

Lobbyists:
Paul Tetrault

National Assn of Social Workers (NYS Chapter) (FKA Paupini, Sara)
188 Washington Ave
Albany, NY 12210
518-463-4741

Clients:
National Assn of Social Workers (NYS Chapter)

Lobbyists:
Reinaldo Cardona
Kelley Martinson
Karin Moran

Political Parties, Lobbyists & PACs

Offices and agencies generally appear in alphabetical order, except when specific order is requested by listee.

National Association of Social Workers - New York City Chapter
50 Broadway
Suite 1001
New York, NY 10004
212-668-0050

Lobbyists:
Launa Kliever
Harriet Putterman
Robert Schachter

National Employment Law Project
75 Maiden Lane, Suite 601
New York, NY 10038
212-285-3025

Lobbyists:
Annette Bernhardt
Tsedeye Gebreselassie
Sarah Leberstein
Sarah Leberstein
Paul Sonn
Andrew Stettner

National Federation of Independent Business
100 State Street
Suite 440
Albany, NY 12207
518-434-1262

Lobbyists:
Michael P. Durant

National Fuel Gas Company
C/O National Fuel Gas Company
6363 Main Street
Williamsville, NY 14221-5887
716-857-7780

Lobbyists:
Edward J. Damico
Patrick Kelly

National Grid
111 Washington Avenue
Albany, NY 12210
518-417-3102

Lobbyists:
Timothy Brennan
Echo Cartwright
Eileen Cifone
Anthony Curcio
Bart Franey
Cosmo Iannicco
Kim Ireland
Ron Macklin
Belinda Pagdanganan
John Pettigrew
Marcy Reed
Dean Seavers
Victor Vientos

National Multiple Sclerosis Society, New York City Chapter
733 3rd Avenue, 3rd Floor
New York, NY 10017-3288
212-463-7787

Lobbyists:
Debby Bennett
Robin Einbinder
Pamela Weiner

National Railroad Passenger Corporation
60 Massachusetts Avenue NE
Washington, DC 20002
202-906-4088

Clients:
AMTRAK

Lobbyists:
Frances Bourne
Clifford Cole
Alfred Fazio
Andrew Galloway
Stephen Gardner
William Hollister
Danielle Hunter
Marilyn Jamison
Robert Lacroix
Joseph McHugh
Tom Moritz
Dana Schaeffer
Petra Todorovich Messick

National Strategies, Inc.
95 Columbia Street
Albany, NY 12210
518-432-0488
Web site: www.nationalstrategiesinc.com

Lobbyists:
Arthur Brown
Roy Cales
Agostino Cangemi
Alfred Gordon
Gino Menchini
Susan Pedo
Ruth Walters

Natural Resources Defense Council (FKA Goldstein, Eric)
40 West 20th Street
11th Floor
New York, NY 10011
212-727-2700
Web site: www.nrdc.org

Lobbyists:
Margaret Brown
Pierce Bull
Alison Chase Granshaw
Sarah Chassis
Donna DeCostanzo
Eric Goldstein
Nathanael Greene
Ashok Gupta
David Hawkins
Darby Hoover
Albert Huang
Mark Izeman
Peter Lehner
Lawrence Levine
Luis Martinez
Jackson Morris
Yerina Mugica

Daniel Raichel
Nathan Rosenburg
Richard Schrader
Brad Sewell
Katherine Sinding-Daly
Lisa Speer
Luke Tonacle
Julie Truax
Samantha Wilt

Nature Conservancy (The) (FKA Janeway, William C.)
195 New Karner Road
Suite 200
Albany, NY 12205
518-690-7873
Web site: www.nature.org

Lobbyists:
Colin Apse
Laura Bavaro
Marisa Biehl
Marci Bortman
Dirk Bryant
Michael Carr
Christopher Clapp
Sarah Clarkin
Katie Dolan
Neil Gifford
Wayne Grothe
Paul Hartman
Chris Hawver
David Higby
Kelly Hines
Jim Howe
Kara Jackson
Joseph Jannsen
Marilyn Jordan
Nancy Kelley
Meagan Kelly
Cara Lee
Stuart Lowrie
Nicole Maher
Patricia Manzi
Kevin McDonald
Patrick McGlew
Kathy Moser
Rita Murray
Zack Odell
Jessica Ottney Mahar
Alpa Pandya
Randy Parsons
Connie Prickett
Gregory Sargis
Michael Scheibel
George Schuler
Hilary Smith
Mark Smith
Timothy Tear
Bill Ulfelder
Troy Weldy
Alan White
Tony Wilkinson
Nathan Woiwode

NBCUniversal
30 Rockefeller Plaza
New York, NY 10112
212-664-2227

Lobbyists:
Brian O'Leary
Veronica Sullivan

Neidl, Michael
100 South Swan Street
Albany, NY 12210
518-436-8516

Clients:
AFL-CIO

Lobbyists:
Suzy Ballantyne
Joseph Canovas
Mario Cilento
Ryan Delgado
Michael Neidl

Neighborhood Family Services Coalition
120 Broadway
Suite 230
New York, NY 10271
212-619-1656

Lobbyists:
Kam Chi Li
Sierra Stoneman-Bell

Lobbyists:
Bernell Grier

New Yorkers Against Gun Violence
87 Lafayette Street
3rd Floor
New York, NY 10013
212-679-2345

Lobbyists:
Leah Gunn Barrett
Barbara Hohlt

Newspaper Publishers Assn (NY)
252 Hudson Avenue
Albany, NY 12210
518-449-1667

Clients:
Newspaper Publishers Assn (NY)

Lobbyists:
Diane Kennedy

Nicholas & Lence Communications LLC
28 West 44th Street
Suite 1217
New York, NY 10036
212-938-0001
Web site: www.nicholaslence.com

Lobbyists:
Jennifer Landis
George Lence
Cristyne Nicholas
Jennifer Landis
Jessica Proud
Evlyn Tsimis

Nicolson, Karen
237 Main Street
Buffalo, NY 14226
716-853-3087

Clients:
Legal Services for the Elderly, Disabled or Disadvantaged of Western New York, Inc.

Nissan North America, Inc.
One Nissan Way
Franklin, TN 37067
615-725-1000

Lobbyists:
Joe Castelli
Mike Hobson
Timothy Slattery
Tracy Woodard

Nixon Peabody, LLP
677 Broadway
10th Floor
Albany, NY 12207
518-427-2650

Clients:
Assn of Laser Hair Removal Specialists, Inc (NYS)
Bellevue Women's Medical Center, Inc

Lobbyists:
Peter Millock
Robert Burgdorf
Thomas Reynolds

Nolan & Heller, LLP
39 North Pearl St
3rd Fl
Albany, NY 12207
518-449-3300
e-mail: tburke@nolanandheller.com

Clients:
Empire State Subcontractors Assn

Lobbyists:
Terence Burke
Brennan Francis

Norfolk Southern Corporation
4600 Deer Path Road
Harrisburg, PA 17110
717-541-2250

Lobbyists:
Michael Fesen

North Shore Land Alliance
151 Post Rd.
Old Westbury, NY 11568
516-626-0908
Web site: www.northshorelandalliance.org

Lobbyists:
Judith Goldsborough
Barbara Hoover
Jane Jackson
Lisa Ott
Carol Schmiddlapp

North Star Fund
520 8th Avenue
New York, NY 10018
212-620-9110

Clients:
Communities United for Police Reform

Lobbyists:
Priscilla Gonzalez
Joo-Hyun Kang

Northeast Government Consulting LLC
501 St Davids Lane
Niskayuna, NY 12309
518-469-8795
Web site: www.ngclobby.com

Lobbyists:
David Carroll
Gregory G. Podbielski

Northern Manhattan Improvement Corporation
76 Wadsworth Avenue
New York, NY 10033
212-822-8300

Lobbyists:
Matthew Chachere
Maria Lizardo
Barbara Lowry
Kenneth Rosenfeld

Northern Metropolitan Hospital Assn
1383 Veterans Memorial Hwy
Suite 26
Hauppauge, NY 11788
631-435-3000

Clients:
Northern Metropolitan Hospital Assn

Lobbyists:
Kevin Dahill
Janine Logan

Novartis Pharmaceuticals Corporation
One Health Plaza
East Hanover, NJ 07936
862-778-8421

Lobbyists:
Sara David

NP Associates, LLC
704 N. McBride Street
Syracuse, NY 13208
315-422-5311

Lobbyists:
Nicholas Pirro

Nurses Association (NYS)
c/o Nurses Association (NYS)
11 Cornell Road
Latham, NY 12110-1499

Offices and agencies generally appear in alphabetical order, except when specific order is requested by listee.

518-782-9400

Lobbyists:
Kristin Abrams
Eileen Avery
John Berry
Ellen Brickman
Nicole Burckard
Michael Chacon
Elaine Charpentier
Jay Dwyer
Camille Edwards
Deborah Elliott
Shaun Flynn
Renee Gecsedi
Tina Gerardi
Michelle Hart
Michael Hertz
Roberta Murphy
Carol Pitman
Roxanne Romney
Crystal Shipp
Kevin Smith
Lucille Sollazzo
Therese Wittner

Nyprocoa, Inc.
Trinity Centre
115 Broadway
Ste 1504
New York, NY 10006
212-566-5600

Lobbyists:
Tonio Burgos
Francisco Diaz Jr.
Joseph Fiordaliso
Matthew Greller
Ninfa Segarra
Michael Klein
Manuel Mirabal

NYSPIA Political Committee, Inc.
11 North Pearl Street
Suite 1202
Albany, NY 12207
518-436-0120

Lobbyists:
Jeffrey Kayser

O'Brien & Gere Limited
5000 Brittonfield Parkway
East Syracuse, NY 13057
315-437-6100
Web site: www.obg.com

Lobbyists:
Stephen Anagnost
Michelle Baines
Timothy Barry
Robert Bowers
Terry Brown
Christopher Calkins
Christopher Campbell
Gary Cannerelli
Richard Cawley
Stephen Commesso
Douglas Crawford
Paul Curran
R. Leland Davis
Stephen Delano
Robert Delorenzo
Marc Dent
Ricky Duff
Thomas Dumm
Thomas Dussing
Steven Eckler
Brian Edwards
James Evans
Stephen Fisher
George Fleming
James Fox
Robert Ganley
Richard Gell
Peter Gibbons
Mark Greene
Peter Grevelding
Scott Grieco
Ronald Harting
James Heckathorne
Christian Hine
Wayne Hoagland
Kevin Ignaszak
Kenneth Jones
Lowell Kachalsky
Swiatoslav Kaczmar
Robert Keyser
Michael Kolceski
James Kyles
Clare Leary
Dwight Macarthur
Terrence Madden
Maureen Markert
Michelle Mcentire
David Meixell
Stephen Mooney
Ralph Morse
Sami Nasr
Robert Neimeier
Jamie Dirk Newtown
Holly Nicholas
Jennifer Olivo
Lynette Paduano
Ronald Panek
Mark Parrish
George Rest
Steven Roland
John Rooney
Darcy Sachs
Scott Scheidelman
Hubert Schlientz
John Shaheen
Stuart Spiegel
Alan Steinhauer
Karen Storne
Guy Swenson
Matthew Traister
Douglas Warneck
Ralph Whedon
David Wilson
Cherylann Wiseman
Deborah Wright

O'Connell and Aronowitz
54 State Street
9th Floor
Albany, NY 12207-2501
518-462-5601

Political Parties, Lobbyists & PACs

Offices and agencies generally appear in alphabetical order, except when specific order is requested by listee.

Lobbyists:
Peter Danzinger

O'Connell, Maurice J.
One Bell Crossing Road
Selkirk, NY 12158
518-767-6445

Lobbyists:
William Goetz

O'Malley, Michael
15 Mountain View Road
Warren, NJ 07059
908-903-7004

Clients:
Chubb & Son, a Division of Federal Insurance Company

Ohrenstein & Brown, LLP
1010 Franklin Ave, 2nd Fl
PO Box 9243
Garden City, NY 11530-9243
516-873-6334
Web site: www.oandb.com

Clients:
Jamaica Hospital Medical Center
Marsh USA Inc

Lobbyists:
Michael Brown
Manfred Ohrenstein

Open Space Institute
1350 Broadway
Suite 201
New York, NY 10018
212-629-3981

Lobbyists:
Christopher Ellman
Wes Gillingham
Jennifer Grossman
Joseph Martens

Ophthalmological Society (NYS)
408 Kenwood Avenue
Delmar, NY 12054
518-439-2020

Lobbyists:
Robin Pellegrino

Orange Regional Medical Center
Orange Regional Medical Center
707 East Main Street
Middletown, NY 10940
845-333-1000
Web site: www.ormc.org

Lobbyists:
Rosemary Frado

Organization of NYS Management/Confidential Employees Inc
3 Washington Square
Albany, NY 12205-5523
518-456-5241
e-mail: omce@aol.com
Web site: www.nysomce.org

Clients:
Org of NYS Mgmt/Confidential Employees, Inc

Lobbyists:
Joseph Sano
Barbara Zaron

Osteopathic Medical Society
1855 Broadway
New York, NY 10023
212-261-1784

Lobbyists:
Barbara Greenwald

Ostroff, Hiffa & Associates Inc
12 Sheridan Ave
Albany, NY 12207
518-436-6202
e-mail: ostroff_associates@msn.com
Web site: www.ostroff-hiffa.com

Clients:
380 Development LLC
Adirondack Pine Hill NY Trailways
Amerada Hess Corporation
Assn of Town Superintendents of Highways Inc (NYS)
CATS VLT, LLC (Canadian American Transportation Systems)
Catholic Family Center
Cemetery Employer Assn of Greater NY
Cephalon Inc
Courtroom Television Network
Creative Coalition (The)
Crisis Program (The)
Dreyfus Corporation (The)
Duke Energy Corporation
Empire State Restaurant & Tavern Assn
Fahs Construction Group (Fahs-Rolston Paving Corp)
FlexCare
Central NY Railroad
Greater NY Health Care Facilities Assn
Cross Harbor Railroad (NY)
Hubbell Galvanizing
International Imaging Technology Council (I-ITC)
Liquid Asphalt Distributors Assoc Inc of NY
Monument Builders Assn (NYS)
Mount St Mary's Hospital & Health Center
Cumberland Packing Corporation
Public Library (NY), Astor, Lenox & Tilden Foundations
Electric & Gas Corporation (NYS)
Eponymous Associates LLC (FKA Steiner Studios)
Pratt Institute
Riverside South Planning Corp
Rochester Gas & Electric Corp
Suit-Kote Corp
UST Public Affairs Inc
United Health Services
Washington Cemetery
Western NY Energy LLC

Offices and agencies generally appear in alphabetical order, except when specific order is requested by listee.

Lobbyists:
Megan Bailey
David Dudley
Frederick T Hiffa
Richard L Ostroff
Barbara Lee Steigerwald
Erin T Waterhouse
Scott Wexler
Lisa Wickens

P.S. 1 Contemporary Art Center
22-25 Jackson Avenue
Long Island City, NY 11101-5324
718-786-3098

Lobbyists:
Antoine Guerrero
Yun Joo Kang

Pace University
161 William Street
19th Floor
New York, NY 10038
212-346-1274

Lobbyists:
Jane Aoyama-Martin
Jessica Bacher
John Cronin
Stephen Friedman
Jeffrey Lejava
Franz Litz
Jackson Morris
Eric Morrissey
Jennie Nolon
John Nolon
Tiffany Zezula

Park Strategies, LLC
101 Park Ave, Ste 2506
New York, NY 10178
212-883-5608

Clients:
Aetna Inc
Concerned Home Care Providers
Cendant Car Rental Group Inc
Correction Officers & Police Benevolent Assn Inc
Covanta Energy Corp
Energy East Corporation
Health Care Subrogation Group
Canadian American Transportation Systems, LLC
Lilac Capital LLC
LS Power Associates LLC
Madison Square Garden LP
Manhattan Theatre Club
Magna Entertainment Corp
NYU Child Study Center
Sheriff Officers Assn
Subway Surface Supervisors Assn
Vector Group, Ltd

Lobbyists:
Anthony Cancellieri
Alfonse M D'Amato
Armand D'Amato
Christopher P D'Amato
Joel Giambra
Robert McBride
Melvin Miller
David Poleto
Gregory Serio
John Zagame
Peter Molinaro
Kraig Siracuse

Parks & Trails New York
29 Elk Street
Albany, NY 12207
518-434-1583

Lobbyists:
Martin Daley
Robin Dropkin
Wally Elton
Frances Gotcsik
Shawn McConnell

Parkside Group, LLC
132 Nassau St, Ste 400
New York, NY 10038
212-571-7717
Web site: www.theparksidegroup.com

Clients:
345 E 62nd Street Associate
AAFE Managment Co
AFSCME Local 2021
American Museum of the Moving Image Inc
Assn for the Advancement of Blind & Retarded Inc
Assn for Neurologically Impaired Brain Injured Children Inc
Brooklyn Public Library
Business Outreach Center Network Inc
Central Labor Council (NYC)
Coastal Communications Services Inc
Committee for Hispanic Children & Families
Communication Workers of America Local 1180
Community Bank (NY)
Council Management Inc
Communication Workers of America, Local 1182
Danaher Controls Inc
Flushing Commons LLC
Flushing Council on Culture & the Arts Inc
Fresh Direct, LLC
Gloria Wise Boys & Girls Club Inc
Hospital Medical Center of Queens (NY)
Jamaica Ctr for Arts & Learning Inc
Church Avenue Merchants Block Association Inc
Metropolitan Life Insurance Co
Mulvihill ICS Inc
New York Cares Inc
Plaza College
Queens Centers for Progress Inc
Queens Chamber of Commerce
Queens Child Guidance Center Inc
Queens Economic Development Corp
Queens Centers for Progress Inc
Queens Theatre in the Park
Queensborough Comm College Auxiliary Enterprise Assn Inc
Rockaway Development & Revitalization Corp
Service Employees International Union, Local 300
South Queens Boys & Girls Club Inc
Strive
Supershuttle NY Inc
Telebeam Telecommunications Corp
United Food & Commercial Workers Dist Cncl of NY & Northern NJ
Community Financial Services Association of America
Crystal Window & Door Systems, Ltd
Educational Assistance Corporation
Entergy Nuclear Operations Inc

Gaucho LLC
Gowanus Village 1 Inc
Jets (NY)
National Council to Prevent Delinquency Inc
Nextel Operations Inc
NYC & Company
Pratt Institute for Community & Environment Development
Queens College Foundation-Research of CUNY

Lobbyists:
William Driscoll
Jake Dilemani
Harry Giannoulis
Barry Grodenchik
Violet Moss
Tiffany Raspberry
Evan Stavisky
Damon Stewart
Cassandra Lovejoy

Partnership for NYC (FKA Mele, Don)
One Battery Park Plaza
New York, NY 10004-1479
212-493-7400
Web site: www.nycp.org

Lobbyists:
Maria Gotsch
Marysol Rodriguez
Michael Simas
Kathryn Wylde

Pastel & Rosen, LLP
130 Washington Ave
Albany, NY 12210
518-462-4715

Clients:
Carco Group Inc
Chubb & Son (Division of Federal Insurance Co)
Coalition for Mold Reform (State Farm Insurance Cos)
Fireman's Fund Insurance Co
Insurance Brokers' Association of the State of New York
Professional Insurance Wholesalers Assoc of NYS Inc
Progressive Insurance Companies

Lobbyists:
Robert S Pastel
Michael E Rosen

Patrolmen's Benevolent Association
40 Fulton Street
New York, NY 10038
212-298-9193

Lobbyists:
Frank Tramontano

Clients:
Bank Street College of Education
Trial Lawyers Association

Pepe, Ross J
CIC of Westchester
629 Old White Plains Rd
Tarrytown, NY 10591-5100
914-631-6070

Clients:
Construction Industry Cncl of Westchester & Hudson Valley Inc

Perry Capital LLC
767 Fifth Ave
19th Floor
New York, NY 10153
212-583-4000

Lobbyists:
Doreen Mochrie

Perry, Edmund F.
International Business Machines Corp.
1301 K Street N.W.
Suite 1200
Washington, DC 20005-3307
202-515-5039

Lobbyists:
Rodney Atkins
Michael Cadigan
Marianne Cooper
Kathleen Ginn
Ambuj Goyal
Phillip Guido
Bronwyn Guthrie
Robert E. Hanson, Jr.
John Kelly
David Lederbach
Tim Mann
Lisa Mativi
Steve Mills
Ed Perry
Linda Sanford
John Teltsch
Brian Whitfield

Perry, Robert
CLU-NY
125 Broad St, 19th Fl
New York, NY 10004
212-607-3323

Clients:
Civil Liberties Union (NY)

Lobbyists:
Linda Berns
Andrea Callan
Corinne Carey
John Curr
Gary Dudup
Christopher Dunn
Arthur Eisenberg
Matt Faiella
Barrie Gewanter
Angela Jones
Tara Keenan-Thomas
Donna Lieberman
Socheaita Meng
Johanna Miller
Udi Ofer
Fidelia Orozco
Ari Rosmarin
Ami Sanghvi
Rahul Saskena
Galen Sherwin
Melanie Trimble
Ed Wasserman
Katharine Brodoe
Erica Braudy

Lisa LaPlace
Adriana Pinon
Ariel Samach

Pershing Square Capital Management L.P.
888 7th Ave
42nd Floor
New York, NY 10019
212-813-3700

Lobbyists:
Steve Symonds

Persons, Eric
2-212 Center for Science and Technology
Syracuse, NY 13244-4100
315-443-3919

Clients:
Syracuse University

Lobbyists:
Joseph Alfieri
Eric Beattie
Doug Biklen
Edward Bogucz
Nancy Cantor
D. Chase Catalano
Thomas Dennison
Bradley Ellis
William Eppel
Theodore Hagelin
J. Michael Haynie
Marilyn Higgins
George Langford
Gina Lee-Glauser
Deborah Meyer
Michael Morris
Diana Napolitano
Mary Pagan
Eric Persons
Marsha Senior
Abbott Sherburne
James Spencer
Eric Spina
Michael Sponsler
Kevin Sweder
Timothy Sweet
Joey Tse
Mary Ann Tyszko
Laura Welch
Mark Weldon

PFM Asset Management, LLC
Two Logan Square
18th & Arch Streets
Philadelphia, PA 19103
215-567-6100

Lobbyists:
Stephen Faber
Sarah Underer

Phillips Lytle
437 Madison Ave
New York, NY 10022
212-508-0470

Clients:
Stealth Communications Services LLC

Lobbyists:
David Bronston

Phillips Nizer, LLP
666 Fifth Ave
New York, NY 10103-0084
212-977-9700

Clients:
CSC Holdings, Inc

Lobbyists:
Kevin McGrath

Pioneer Savings Bank
21 Second Street
Troy, NY 12180
518-284-4800

Lobbyists:
Eileen Bagnoli
James McGlynn
Frank C. Sarratori
John Scarchilli
Thomas Thouin
Fonza Wells

Pitta, Bishop, Del Giorno & Giblin, LLC
111 Washington Avenue
Albany, NY 12210
518-449-3320

Lobbyists:
Carlos Beato
Robert Bishop
Mickey Cekovic
Theresa Cosgrove
Jon Del Giorno
Gordon Forbes
Vincent Giblin
Matthew Mataraso
Vincent Pitta
Vito Pitta

Plummer & Wigger, LLC (FKA Griffin, Plummer & Associates)
111 Washington Avenue
Suite 602
Albany, NY 12210
518-463-5949
Web site: www.plummerwigger.com

Clients:
Direct Marketing Association
Delaware Engineering
Farm Credit East
General Electric Company
Genworth Financial
Greene County Coalition for Economic Equality, LLC
Hunter Mountain Ski Bowl
Schenectady Metroplex Development Authority
Momentive Performance Materials USA Inc.
Mutualink Inc.
Railroads of New York

Lobbyists:
Michael R. Doyle
Daniel Plummer
Scott Wigger

Podiatric Medical Association (NYS)
555 Eighth Avenue
Suite 1902
New York, NY 10018
212-996-4400

Lobbyists:
Michael Borden

Police Benevolent Association of New York State
11 North Pearl St
Suite 1200
Albany, NY 12207
518-433-5472

Lobbyists:
Peter Barry
Robert Cavanagh
Dan Defedericis
Gary Friedrich
Mike Mabee
Jim McCartney
Bernie Rivers
Thomas Smith
Manny Vilar

Police Benevolent Assn of the NYS Troopers Inc
120 State St
Albany, NY 12207
518-462-7448
e-mail: nystpba@capital.net
Web site: www.nystpba.org

Clients:
Police Benevolent Assn of the NYS Troopers Inc

Lobbyists:
Thomas Mungeer
Daniel Sisto
Gordon Warnock

Police Conference of NY, Inc.
112 State Street
Suite 1120
Albany, NY 12207
518-462-7448

Lobbyists:
Dixon Palmer
Richard Wells

Powers & Company
22 Clinton Avenue
3rd Floor
Albany, NY 12207
518-431-0720

Clients:
Auxilia
BearingPoint
Broadcasters Assn (NYS)
Capital Region Center for Arts in Education
Colony Liquor & Wine Distributors, LLC
Computer Associates
Data Industries
Delaware Engineering
Glenwood Management Corporation
Hodgson Russ LLP
Laborers PAC (NYS)
Law Enforcement Officers Union, Distr Cncl 82 (NYS)
Lincoln Center for the Performing Arts
Lucid Solutions Group Inc.
Motorola Inc.
Oneida Tribe of Wisconsin (Power Plant Entertainment NY)
Penn Credit Corporation
Pro Tech Monitoring Inc.
PSCH Inc.
Racing and Gaming Services Inc
Salient Corporation
Shaker Museum (The)
Siena College
Trustco Bank
Universal Dynamix LLC
Verizon
Wegmans Food Markets Inc.
Yankees Partnership (NY)

Lobbyists:
Don Clarey
Thomas J Murphy
James Natoli
Jose Paulino
Jason A Powers
Matthew Powers
William Powers

Powers Global Strategies, LLC
140 Broadway
46th Floor
New York, NY 10005
212-582-0833

Clients:
3M Company
ADT Security Services Inc.
Beth Israel Medical Center
Bureau Veritas North America Inc.
BearingPoint Inc.
Central Park Boathouse LLC
Conti of New York LLC
Educational Housing Services
Hess Corporation
Long Island College Hospital (The)
Ports America Inc.
St Luke's-Roosevelt Hospital Centers
Science Application International Corp.
Sea Crest Construction Corp.
TRC
United Parcel Service
Valeray Real Estate Co. Inc.
Varsity Bus Co. Inc.
Verizon Services Group

Lobbyists:
Sylvia Ng
Peter Powers

Praxiis Business Advisors
5266 Seneca Street
West Seneca, NY 14224
716-675-6001

Offices and agencies generally appear in alphabetical order, except when specific order is requested by listee.

Clients:
KCI Technologies Inc.

Presbyterian Hospital (NY)
C/O Milstein Hospital Building
177 Ft Washington Ave, MHB1-HS214
New York, NY 10032
212-305-4223

Clients:
Presbyterian Hospital (NY)

Lobbyists:
Julio Batista
Willa Brody
Mary Hanrahan
David Liss
Helen Morik
Violet Moss
Wayne Osten
Herbert Pardes, MD
William A Polf, PhD
Phillip Wilner, MD

Preservation League of NYS (FKA DiLorenzo, Jay)
44 Central Avenue
Albany, NY 12206
518-462-5658
Web site: www.preservenys.org

Lobbyists:
Jay Dilorenzo
Daniel Mackay

PriceWaterhouseCoopers LLP
677 Broadway
Albany, NY 12207
518-427-4552

Lobbyists:
Gerard Bielak
Adam Bowman
Stephen Cairns
Brian Castelli
Joseph Devita
Brendan Dougher
Patricia Duffy
Steven Elek
Ann Filiault
Steven Gurtman
David Lee
Worth MacMurray
David Mandelbaum
Stephen Mark Moore
John Mattie
Doug Mears
Christopher O'Brien
Patrick Pilch
Lisa Preddice
William Reidy
Raveen Roa
Gary Ryan
Michael Tosh
Christopher Turner
Robert Valletta
Andrew Ward
Tim Weld
Bradley Williams

Primary Care Development Corporation
45 Broadway
Suite 530
New York, NY 10006
212-437-3926

Lobbyists:
Anne Dyjak
Daniel Lowenstein
William O'Brien

Professional Agencies for Children's Therapy Services
90 State Street
Suite 700
Albany, NY 12207
518-591-4659

Lobbyists:
Steven Sanders

Promontory Interfinancial Network LLC
1515 North Courthouse Road
Suite 1200
Arlington, VA 22201
703-292-3400

Lobbyists:
Jason Blair
Don Daily
Pam Denson
Ed Dunkelberger
Steve Kinner
Doug Phillips

Property Casualty Insurers Association of America (PCI) (FKA O'Brien, Frank)
90 South Swan Street
Albany, NY 12210
518-443-2200

Lobbyists:
Paul Blume, Jr.
Frank O'Brien

Prospect Park Alliance
95 Prospect Park West
Brooklyn, NY 11215
718-965-8953

Lobbyists:
Eric Landau

Prudential Financial, Inc. (Formerly Michael F. McCann)
751 Broad Street
Newark, NJ 07102
973-367-3135
Web site: www.prudential.com

Lobbyists:
Maureen E. Adolf
Riva F. Kinstlick
Robert Montellione
Michael McCann
Barbara Rothermel
Lee F. Wood

Prudential Insurance Company of America (The) (Formerly John J. Kalamarides)
280 Trumbull Street
Hartford, CT 06103
973-367-3135
Web site: www.prudential.com

Lobbyists:
John Barrasso
Gabriel D'Ulisse
Mark Grier
Karen Hilenski
Robert Katz
Michael Knowling
Robert Luciani
Robert Moore
Frank Mursko
Jennifer Nichols
Glenn O'Brien
Marc Pester
Lisa Powell
Raymond Sweetland
Anton Tansil
Carl Wagner
William Walsh
Andrew Shainberg

Prudential Investment Management, Inc. (Formerly Bernard B. Winograd)
100 Mulberry Street
Gateway Center Three
Newark, NJ 07102
973-367-3135
Web site: www.prudential.com

Lobbyists:
Charles F. Lowrey
James T. Murphy
Kevin Myers
Miguel C. Thames
Cliff Axelson
Sara Bonesteel
Mark Hoffmeister
Miguel C. Thames
Allen Weaver

Public Financial Management, Inc.
40 Wall Street
49th Floor
New York, NY 10005
212-809-4212

Lobbyists:
Randall Bauer
Errol Brick
John Cape
Tim Carden
Steven Hass
Rian Irani
Tracey Keays
Damon Lee
Milly Lee
Michael Nadol
Robert Rich
Geoffrey Stewart
Scott Trommer
John F. White

Public Interest Research Group (NY)
9 Murray Street
Lower Level
New York, NY 10007
212-349-6460

Lobbyists:
Alicia Aimer
Cathleen Breen
Emily Boerner
Ryan Bullerdick
Brenden Colling
Benjamin Deangelis
Alicia Elmer
Alex Freundlich
Russ Haven
Blair Horner
Alexandra Jean
Roberto Lobianco
Melissa Lynch
Tishima Moore
James Munro
Michael O'Connor
Nicole Phister
Neal Rosenstein
Gene Russianoff
Tracy Shelton
Chia-Chia Song
Joseph Stelling
Daniel Tome
Corey Torreto

Public Interest Research Group Fund, Inc. (New York)
9 Murray Street
BSMT B1
New York, NY 10007
212-349-6460

Lobbyists:
Russ Haven
Blair Horner
Jeremiah Makarowski
Michael Romeo
Joe Stelling

Public Library, Astor, Lenox & Tilden Foundations (NY) (The)
5th Ave & 42nd St
New York, NY 10018-2788
212-930-0611

Clients:
Public Library, Astor, Lenox & Tilden Foundations (NY)

Lobbyists:
Catherine Dunn
Paul Leclerc

Public Welfare Assn (NY)
130 Washington Ave
Albany, NY 12210
518-465-9305
e-mail: nypwa@nycap.rr.com
Web site: www.nypwa.com

Clients:
Public Welfare Assn (NY)

Offices and agencies generally appear in alphabetical order, except when specific order is requested by listee.

Lobbyists:
Sheila Harrigan
Andrea Smyth

Pujolas, Elizabeth
9 Bellair Road
Boston, MA 02132
617-323-1175

Clients:
Medimmune, Inc.

Pullium, Daniel
75 Gerber Road East
South Windsor, CT 06074
860-644-4000

Clients:
TicketNetwork, Inc.

Lobbyists:
Natalie Carpenter

Purdue Pharma L.P.
One Stamford Forum
201 Tresser Blvd.
Stamford, CT 06901
203-588-8121

Lobbyists:
Mike McGlinn
Melissa Petro

Pyle & Associates, Inc.
PO Box 25001
Georgetown Station
Washington, DC 20027-8001
202-333-8190

Lobbyists:
Nicholas Pyle

Quantitative Management Associates LLC
100 Mulberry Street
Gateway Center Two
Newark, NJ 07102
973-367-3135

Lobbyists:
Bradford J. Allinson
Margaret S. Stumpp

Queens Chamber of Commerce
75-20 Astoria Blvd.
Suite 140
Jackson Heights, NY 11370
718-898-8500

Lobbyists:
Carol Conslato
Jack Friedman

Racing Association, Inc.
110-00 Rockaway Boulevard
New York, NY 11420
718-641-4700

Lobbyists:
Charles J. Kruzansky
David J. Skorton

RAI Services Company (FKA Reynolds American, Inc.)
P.O. Box
Winston-Salem, NC 27102
336-741-4500

Lobbyists:
Cassie Folk
David Powers

Ravitz, John
108 Corporate Park Drive
Suite 101
White Plains, NY 10604
914-948-2110

Clients:
Business Council of Westchester (The)

Lobbyists:
Marsha Gordon

Raustiala, Margaret
428 River Rd
Nissequogue, NY 11780
631-724-7767

Clients:
Alliance of Long Island Agencies

RBC Capital Markets (FKA RBC Dain Rausher)
677 Broadway
Suite 305
Albany, NY 12207
518-432-5071

Lobbyists:
Michael Baumrin
Thomas Berger
Peter Brodie
Thomas Cullinan
Daniel Hemowitz
Andrew Mendelson
John Puig

Real Estate Board of NY Inc
570 Lexington Ave
New York, NY 10022
212-532-3100
e-mail: jdoyle@rebny.com
Web site: www.rebny.com

Clients:
Real Estate Board of NY Inc

Lobbyists:
Marolyn Davenport
John Doyle
Shannon Fales
Brian Klimas
Michael Slattery
Steven Spinola
Carol Van Guilder

Political Parties, Lobbyists & PACs

Offices and agencies generally appear in alphabetical order, except when specific order is requested by listee.

Real Rent Reform Campaign
C/O Metropolitan Council on Housing
339 Lafayette Street
Suite 301
New York, NY 10012
917-669-2977

Lobbyists:
Michael McKee

Red Land Strategy, Inc.
50 Meritoria Drive
East Williston, NY 11596
516-567-0345

Clients:
TEI Group

Lobbyists:
Michael Balboni

Reenergy Holdings LLC
30 Century Hill Drive
Suite 101
Latham, NY 12110
518-810-0200

Lobbyists:
Sarah Boggess

Rehabilitation Assn Inc (NYS)
155 Washington Ave, Ste 410
Albany, NY 12210-2332
518-449-2976
e-mail: nysra@nyrehab.org
Web site: www.nyrehab.org

Clients:
Rehabilitation Assn Inc (NYS)

Lobbyists:
Patricia Dowse
Jeffrey Wise

Related Companies, LP (The)
60 Columbus Circle
New York, NY 10023
212-421-5333

Lobbyists:
Bruce A. Beal, Jr.
Jeff T. Blau
Jay Cross
Glenn Goldstein
Gregory Gushee
Jay Kriegel
Stephen M. Ross
Avi Kollenscher
Michael Samuelian
Dean Vanderwarker

Related Fund Management LLC
60 Columbus Circle
New York, NY 10023
212-801-3392

Lobbyists:
Justin Metz

Rensselaer Polytechnic Institute
110 8th Street
Troy, NY 12180
518-276-8432

Lobbyists:
Erin Crotty
Craig Dory
Shirley Jackson
Eddie Knowles
Russ Leslie
Allison Newman
Chris Nolin
Diane Piester
Mark Rea
Wolf Von Maltzahn
John Wen

Rent Stabilization Assn of NYC Inc
123 William St, 14th Fl
New York, NY 10038
212-214-9266

Clients:
Rent Stabilization Assn of NYC Inc

Lobbyists:
Jack Freund
Jacqueline Monterosso
Mitchell Posilkin
Frank P Ricci
Joseph Strasburg

Repas, Peter G
33 Elk St
Albany, NY 12207
518-462-1590
e-mail: apbs@wxxi.org

Clients:
Assn of Public Broadcasting Stations of NY

Retired Public Employees Association, Inc.
435 New Karner Road
Albany, NY 12205-3858
618-869-2542

Lobbyists:
Michael Fitzgerald

RG Group
One Penn Plaza
36th Floor
New York, NY 10119
212-786-7627

Clients:
Benjamin Partners, Inc.
Building Owners and Managers Association of Greater New York, Inc.
Charleston Equities LLC
Computer Aid, Inc.
Dell Public Sector, Inc.
Edgewater Industrial Park LLC
Hunter College
PEC Group of NY, Inc.
Technology Enterprise Corporation
Triangle Enterprise Development Company LLC

Lobbyists:
Catherine Giuliani
Alan Rosenberg

Richardson Management
295 Main Street
Suite 214
Buffalo, NY 14203
716-854-2400

Lobbyists:
Richard Winter

Riddell Group, LLC (The)
119 Washington Avenue, 2nd Floor
Albany, NY 12210
518-434-7400

Lobbyists:
Michael Houseknecht
Glenn Riddell

Riddett Associates, Inc. (FKA Riddett, Kenneth E. Associates Inc.)
PO Box 7141
Albany, NY 12224
518-225-9986

Lobbyists:
Kenneth Riddett

Riddle, Gary
7 Willway Avenue
Richmond, VA 23226
804-450-0965

Clients:
EISAI, Inc.

Ridge Policy Group LLC
1140 Connecticut Avenue NW
Suite 510
Washington, DC 20036
202-480-8093

Clients:
Transcore

Lobbyists:
Mark Holman

Right to Life Committee Inc (NYS)
41 State St. M-100
Albany, NY 12207
518-434-1293
e-mail: lhougens1@aol.com
Web site: www.nysrighttolife.org

Clients:
Right to Life Committee Inc (NYS)

Lobbyists:
Debra J. Cody
Lori Kehoe

Roarke, Robert R.
Wilson Elser, Moskowitz, Edelman and Dicker, LLP
150 East 42nd Street
New York, NY 10017
212-490-3000

Lobbyists:
Peter Lauricella
Theresa Marangas
Theresa Russo
Cynthia Shenker

Robinson & Cole LLP
666 Third Avenue
20th Floor
New York, NY 10017
212-451-2900

Lobbyists:
Andrew Roffe
Christine Rutigliano

Rochester Business Alliance, Inc.
150 State Street
Suite 400
Rochester, NY 14614-1308
585-256-4627

Lobbyists:
Colleen DiMartino
Brian Sampson
Chris West

Ronald Poppel
32 Regatta View Drive
Saratoga Springs, NY 12866
518-583-4986

Clients:
Bristol-Myers Squibb Company

Rooney, Timothy J.
C/O Yonkers Raceway
Yonkers & Central Aves.
Yonkers, NY 10704
914-968-4200

Lobbyists:
Robert J. Galterio
Wayne Smith

Rosenthal, Harvey
One Columbia Place
2nd Floor
Albany, NY 12207
518-436-0008

Clients:
Association of Psychiatric Rehabilitation Services

Royal Realty Corp.
One Bryant Park
New York, NY 10036
212-257-6600

Lobbyists:
Jordan Barowitz

Political Parties, Lobbyists & PACs

Offices and agencies generally appear in alphabetical order, except when specific order is requested by listee.

Rreef America LLC
535 Anton Blvd
Suite 200
Costa Mesa, CA 92626
415-262-2003

Lobbyists:
Terry Doyle
Laura Gaylord
Todd Henderson

Rubin, Jamie Lyn
5001 Angel Canyon Road
Kanab, UT 84741
435-644-2001

Clients:
Best Friends Animal Society

Rubin, Kate
860 Courtlandt Ave
Bronx, NY 11230
718-838-7869

Clients:
Bronx Defenders

Lobbyists:
Kamau Butcher
Emma Ketteringham
Molly Kovel
Justine Olderman
Seann Riley
J. McGregor Smyth
Alexandra St. Charles
Robin Steinberg
Joanna Zuckerman-Bernstein

Runes, Richard
3 Kirby Ln N
Rye, NY 10580
212-457-9679
e-mail: rrunes@amlaw.com

Clients:
American Lawyer Media

Russo, Michael
400 Stone Break Road Ext.
Malta, NY 12020
518-305-9023

Clients:
GlobalFoundries US, Inc.

Rutnik Law Firm (The)
80 State St, 9th Fl
Albany, NY 12207
518-436-9646

Clients:
DMJM & Harris Inc
Genentech Inc

Lobbyists:
Douglas P Rutnik

Ryan, Desmond
150 Motor Pkwy, Ste LL60
Hauppauge, NY 11772
631-951-2410

Clients:
Alliance of Long Island Agencies
Bethpage Federal Credit Union
Stop & Shop Supermarket Co (The)

Safe Horizon, Inc.
2 Lafayette Street
New York, NY 10007
212-577-7735

Lobbyists:
Nancy Arnow
Shonnie Ball
Pilar Bernabe
Christian W. Burgess
Cecilia Castelino
Lydia Colon-Fores
Marsha Genwright
Arthur Goodman
Bea Hanson
Alice Hawks
Jennifer Kob
Susan Loeb
Erika Miller
Lynn Neugebauer
J. Bukurije Pirane
Michael Polenberg
Myra Shapiro
Nancy Shea
Danny Stewart
Lac Tran
Michele Vigeant
Kathy Wickham
Michael Williams
Ariel Zwang

Sampson, Rick J
Restaurant Association (NYS)
409 New Karner Rd
Albany, NY 12205
518-452-4222
e-mail: ricks@nysra.org
Web site: www.nysra.org

Clients:
Restaurant Assn (NYS)

Lobbyists:
Melissa Fleischut
E Charles Hunt

Samuel A. Ramirez & Co., Inc.
61 Broadway
29th Floor
New York, NY 10006
212-248-0525

Lobbyists:
Amy Bartoletti
Ryan Donovan
Nicholas Fluehr
Robert Foran
Daniel Keating
Robert Pattison

Offices and agencies generally appear in alphabetical order, except when specific order is requested by listee.

Frederick Putnam
Samuel Ramirez
Theodore Sobel
Richard Tilghman
John Young

Sanctuary for Families
P.O. Box 1406
Wall Street Station
New York, NY 10268-1406
212-349-6009
Web site: www.sanctuaryforfamilies.org

Lobbyists:
Molly Bowen
Elizabeth Brownback
Yijen Scarlett Chang
Betty Chen
Elisandro De La Cruz
Julie Dinnerstein
Laurel W. Eisner
Helene Feldman
Jill Fernandez
Brett Figlewski
Carolien Hardenbol
Veronique Harvey
Colleen Hodgetts
Vivian Huelgo
Dorchen Leidholdt
Linda Lopez
Loretta McCarthy
Ted McCourtney
Sonia Monsoor
Krystle Montalvo
Avideh Moussavian
Lisa Mueller
Noreen Muhib
Romona Mukjerjee
Amanda Norcjko
Sophia Pazos
Allison Rose
Catherine Shurgrue Dos Santos
Beth Silverman-Yam
Andrew Sta. Ana
Betsy Tsai
Diana Urquhart
Willie Werwaiss
John Wyeht

Sanzillo, Francis J. & Associates
130 Washington Avenue
Albany, NY 12203
914-448-0199

Lobbyists:
Francis Sanzillo

Saratoga Harness Racing, Inc.
P.O. Box 356
342 Jefferson Street
Saratoga Springs, NY 12866
518-584-2110

Clients:
Gaming Association, Inc.

Lobbyists:
George Carlson
Rita Cox
Daniel Gerrity
James Hartman

SAS Institute, Inc.
100 SAS Campus Drive
Cary, NC 27513
919-531-5865

Lobbyists:
Arielle Bernstein
Tim Finnegan
Jeremy Racine

Scenic Hudson Inc
One Civic Center Plaza
Ste 200
Poughkeepsie, NY 12601-3157
845-473-4440
e-mail: wreiss@scenichudson.org
Web site: www.scenichudson.org

Clients:
Scenic Hudson Inc

Lobbyists:
John Anzevino
Andrew Bicking
James Burgess
Raymond Curran
Margery Groten
Charles Laing
Donna Lenhart
Seth Martel
Maryanne McGovern
Seth McKee
Althea Mullarkey
Ivy Reeves
Warren Reiss
Steven Rosenberg
Rita Shaheen
James Slaughter
Reed Sparling
Sacha Spector
Edward O Sullivan
Jason Taylor
Cari Watkins-Bates

Schillo, John
14954 Madison Street NE
Ham Lake, MN 55304
763-413-5113

Clients:
Lundbeck Pharmaceutical Services LLC

Schlein, Stanley Esq.
481 King Ave
Bronx, NY 10464
917-359-3186

Clients:
Bronx Museum
Daimler Chrysler Corporation
Easton Bell Sports
Exxon Mobil Corporation
Hall of Sciences (NY)
SAS Institute Inc
Women's Housing & Economic Development Corporation

Offices and agencies generally appear in alphabetical order, except when specific order is requested by listee.

Political Parties, Lobbyists & PACs

Schmidt, James A.
East River Realty Company, LLC
9 West 57th Street
New York, NY 10019
212-715-0293

Lobbyists:
James A. Schmidt

Schnell, William A & Associates Inc
51 E Main Street, 2nd Fl
Smithtown, NY 11787
631-724-6569
e-mail: wmasainc@earthlink.net

Clients:
Amusement & Music Owners Assn of NY
Federation of Organizations Inc
Long Island Gasoline Retailers Assn Inc
SDR Pharmaceuticals Inc
Securitas
Suffolk County Ambulance Chiefs Assoc
Suffolk County Deputy Sheriff's Police Benevolent Assn

Lobbyists:
William A Schnell

Schnur Associates, Inc.
25 West 45th Street
Suite 1405
New York, NY 10036
212-489-0600

Lobbyists:
Joel Schnur

Schomberg, Dora
P.O. Box 8832
Albany, NY 12208
518-478-9760

Clients:
Humane Society of the United States (The)

School Administrators Association of NYS
8 Airport Park Blvd
Latham, NY 12110
518-782-0600

Clients:
School Administrators Association of NYS

Lobbyists:
William Adam
Santo Barbarino
Paul Berkheimer
Roberto Calderin
Joyce Carr
Kevin Casey
Marystephanie Corsones
Paul Gasparini
Peter Griffin
Carrie Harvey-Zales
Shannon Karazuba
Lawrence King
Frederick Kirsch
Linda Klime
Elizabeth Mascitti-Miller
Frank McDermott
George Montone
Linda Mulvey
Don Nickson
Brian Nolan
Nancy Noonan
Tom O'Brien
Greg Paterniti
Maureen Patterson
Jennie Pennington
Deborah Price
Deborah Rider
Kevin Sheehan
Elisabeth Smith
Jeff Spiro
Jerry Tagliaferri
Robert Thomann
Richard Tomlinson
Bonnie Tryon
James Viola

School Boards Assn (NYS)
24 Century Hill Dr
Latham, NY 12110
518-783-0200
e-mail: nyssba@nyssba.org
Web site: www.nyssba.org

Lobbyists:
Francine Campbell
Michael Fox
Meghana Godambe
Timothy Kremer
David Little
Thomas Nespeca
Jay Worona

Schuh, Paul
35 George Karl Blvd
Suite 100
Amherst, NY 14221
716-632-1540

Clients:
UAW Region 9

Schuyler Center for Analysis & Advocacy
540 Broadway
Albany, NY 12207
518-463-1896

Lobbyists:
Kate Breslin
Dorothy Hill
Kari Siddiqui
Helen W. Smith
Bridget Walsh

Scotts Miracle-Gro Company
14111 Scottslawn Road
Marysville, OH 43041
937-644-7606

Lobbyists:
Ann Aquillo
Jeff Garascia
Richard Shank
Chris Wible

Offices and agencies generally appear in alphabetical order, except when specific order is requested by listee.

Securities Industry & Financial Markets Association
120 Broadway
35th Floor
New York, NY 10271
212-313-1233

Lobbyists:
Marin Gibson
Nancy Lancia

Seneca Nation of Indians
12837 Route 438
Irving, NY 14801
716-532-4900

Lobbyists:
Mike John
Robert Porter
Peter Colavito

Shanahan Group
4019 County Rte 21
Schodack Landing, NY 12156
518-732-3312
e-mail: tom@shanahangroup.com
Web site: www.shanahangroup.com

Clients:
Guide Dog Foundation for the Blind Inc
Irrigation Assn of New York
Long Island Water Conference
Rural Water Assn (NY)
Suffolk County Water Authority

Lobbyists:
Thomas Shanahan

Shank, Suzanne
C/O Siebert Brandford Shank & Co., LLC
100 Wall Street
18th Floor
New York, NY 10005
646-775-4841

Lobbyists:
John Carter
William Thompson Jr.

Shapiro, Brian
P.O. Box 1111
Woodstock, NY 12498
845-707-5350

Clients:
Humane Society of the United States (The)

Sheehan Green Carraway Golderman & Jacques LLP
54 State Street
Suite 1001
Albany, NY 12207
518-462-0110

Lobbyists:
Jacques Keith

Sheinkopf, Ltd
152 Madison Ave
Ste 1603
New York, NY 10016
212-725-2378

Clients:
Committee to Save St Brigid's

Lobbyists:
Hank Sheinkopf
Henry A Sheinkopf

Shelter Rock Strategies, LLC
300 Garden City Plaza
4th Floor
Garden City, NY 11530
516-294-4000

Lobbyists:
Henry Berger
Douglas Forand
Thomas Garry
Marc Lapidus
Steven Schlesinger
Nathan Smith

Sherin, James R.
C/O Retail Council of NYS
258 State Street
PO Box 1992
Albany, NY 12210-1992
518-465-3586

Lobbyists:
Milissa Googas
Edward Potrikus

Lobbyists:
Lawrence Curtis
Joseph Eddy
Michael Putziger
Gilbert Winn

Siconolfi, Patrick
377 Broadway
3rd Floor
New York, NY 10013
212-838-7442

Siena College
515 Loudon Road
Office of Government Relations
Loudonville, NY 12211-1462
518-783-2307

Lobbyists:
Alfredo Medina Jr.
Fr. Kevin Mullen, OFM

Simons & Wright LLC
60 East 42nd Street
Suite 1420
New York, NY 10165
646-370-3689

Clients:
Morgan B. Realty LLC

Political Parties, Lobbyists & PACs

Offices and agencies generally appear in alphabetical order, except when specific order is requested by listee.

Lobbyists:
Emily Simons

Skybridge Capital II LLC
527 Madison Avenue
16th Floor
New York, NY 10022
212-485-3100

Lobbyists:
Peter Carey

Slippen, Daniel
Central Park West & 79th Street
New York, NY 10024-5192
212-769-5033

Clients:
American Museum of Natural History

Lobbyists:
Ellen Futter
Lisa Gugenheim

Smith, Joseph
38 Westbrook Road
Newburgh, NY 12550
845-522-0801

Clients:
Arent Fox LLP
Choice Self Insurance Trust
FCS Administrators, Inc.
Gardere Wynne Sewell LLP
Niagara Business Trust

Smith, Robert
Farm Credit East, ACA
2668 State Rte 7, Ste 21
Cobleskill, NY 12043-9707
518-296-8188

Clients:
First Pioneer Farm Credit ACA

Smyth, A Advocacy
130 Washington Ave, Ste A
Albany, NY 12210
518-426-8354
e-mail: asmyth@capital.net

Lobbyists:
Andrea Smyth

Sobol, Peter
328 A Wanser Avenue
Inwood, NY 11096
516-371-3882

Lobbyists:
Peter Sobol

Society of CPA's
3 Park Avenue
18th Floor
New York, NY 10016
212-719-8300

Lobbyists:
Joanne Barry
Ernest Markezin
Bradley Pryba

Solar Energy Industries Association
600 14th Street NW
Suite 400
Washington, DC 20005
202-682-0556

Lobbyists:
Sean Gallagher

Solowan, Richard
GEICO
One Geico Plaza
Washington, DC 20076
301-986-3948
e-mail: rsolowan@geico.com

Clients:
Government Employees Insurance Co (GEICO)

Soloway, Ronald
155 Washington Ave
Albany, NY 12210
518-436-1091
e-mail: solowayr@ujafedny.org
Web site: www.ujafedny.org

Clients:
United Jewish Appeal Federation - Jewish Philanthropies NY

Lobbyists:
Anita Altman
Chantall Askins
Cara Berkowitz
Allison Grant
Edie Mesick
John Ruskay

Solus Alternative Asset Management LP
410 Park Ave
11th Floor
New York, NY 10022
212-284-4300

Lobbyists:
Janice Yu

Southern Tier Independence Center
135 East Frederick Street
Binghamton, NY 13904
607-724-2111

Lobbyists:
Thea Arnold
Danny Cullen
Robert Deemie
Ken Dibble
Maria Dibble
Darlene Dickinson
Jonathan Dollhopf
Kami Giglio
Sue Hoyt
Margret Hurlbert
Jody Kenyon

Charles Kramer
Susan Link
Jane Long
Cynthia Meredith
Joanne Novicky
Frank Pennisi
Jeff Rogers
Sue Ruff
Peg Schadt
Jennifer Watson

Starwood Capital LLC
591 West Putnam Avenue
Greenwich, CT 06830
203-422-7775

Lobbyists:
Jerome Silvey
Lanhee Yung

State & Broadway, Inc.
99 Washington Avenue
Suite 803
Albany, NY 12210
518-729-4555

Lobbyists:
Musa Moore
Perry M. Ochacher
Lawrence Scherer
Jacqueline Williams

State Advisers, LLC
146 State Street
Suite 101 M
Albany, NY 12207
516-776-1500

Lobbyists:
Keith D. Sernick

State University of New York at Potsdam
44 Pierrepont Avenue
Potsdam, NY 13676-2294
315-267-2190

Lobbyists:
William Fisher
Sherry Paradis
Galen Pletcher
John Schwaller
Vicki Templeton-Cornell
Elizabeth Tuttle

State University of New York at Stony Brook
Administration Building
Room 310
Stony Brook, NY 11794-0701
631-632-6302

Lobbyists:
Peter Baigent
Bridget Baio
Henry Bokuniewicz
Ruth Brandwein
Helen Carrano
Marie Chandick
Barbara Chernow
Lisa Clark
Ellen Cohen
David Conover
Virginia Cover
Paul Edelson
Diane Fabel
Suzanne Fields
Chris Filstrup
Richard Fine
James Fiore
Deborah Firestone
Patricia Gilbert
Ray Goldstein
Mary Graves
Karol Gray
Gail Habicht
Gary Halada
Vanessa Herman
Mary Hotaling
Eric Kaler
Evonne Kaplan
Susan Katz
Theresa Leonard
John Lutterbie
Monica Mahaffey
Robert McGrath
Jennifer McMahon
Mario Mignone
Mary Pearl
John Pomeroy
Joe Puccio
Joseph Scaduto
Wolf Schaefer
Mark Sedler
Fred Sganga
Shetal Shah
Yacov Shamash
Denise Snow
Jonathan Spier
Samuel Stanley
Steven Strongwater
Larry Swanson
Bruce Teifer
Carlos Vidal
Lawrence Weber

State University of NY, System Administration
State University Plaza
Albany, NY 12246
518-443-5355

Lobbyists:
Pedro Caban
James Campbell
Johanna Duncan-Poitier
Dennis Golladay
Stacey Hengsterman
David Lavallee
Carlos Medina
John O'Connor
Monica Rimai
Nicholas Rostow
Michael Trunzo
Philip Wood
Nancy Zimpher

Stendardi, Deborah M
30 Lomb Memorial Dr
Rochester, NY 14534-5604
585-475-5040
e-mail: dmsgrl@rit.edu

Offices and agencies generally appear in alphabetical order, except when specific order is requested by listee.

Clients:
Rochester Institute of Technology

Lobbyists:
William Destler
Cynthia Gray
Nabil Nasr

Strategic Services, Inc
170 E Post Rd, Ste 207B
White Plains, NY 10601
914-946-8400

Clients:
City of Mount Vernon
Westchester Jewish Community Services

Lobbyists:
Arnold Linhardt

Stroock & Stroock & Lavan LLP
180 Maiden Lane
New York, NY 10038-4982
212-806-5400
Web site: www.strook.com

Lobbyists:
Glenn Borin
Leonard Boxer
Robert M. Fettman
Joseph B. Giminaro
Joon Kim
Penny Levine
Martin Minkowitz
Ross F. Moskowitz
Hon. Stanley Parness
Susan Shaw
Richard Siegler
E. Gail Suchman
Eva Talel

Stryker, Patricia
International Brotherhood of Teamsters
C/O Local 237
216 W 14th St.
New York, NY 10011
212-924-2000

Clients:
Teamsters Local 237

Stuto, Diane D
111 Washington Ave, Ste 300
Albany, NY 12210
518-436-8417
Web site: www.licony.org

Clients:
Life Insurance Council of NY Inc

Lobbyists:
John Kisson
Jana Lee Pruitt
Timothy A. Walsh
Thomas E Workman

SUNY College of Environmental Science and Forestry (FKA Micheal Brower)
C/O Suny College of Environmental
Science & Forestry
1 Forestry Drive
Syracuse, NY 13210-2778
315-470-6681

Lobbyists:
Maureen Fellows
Cornelius Murphy

SUNY Fredonia
272 Central Avenue
Fredonia, NY 14063
716-673-3321

Lobbyists:
Dennis Hefner
Timothy Murphy

SUNY Upstate Medical University
750 East Adams Street
Syracuse, NY 13210
315-464-4832
Web site: www.upstate.edu

Lobbyists:
Steven Brady
Daniel Hurley
Phillip Schaengold
David Smith

Supportive Housing Network of New York, Inc.
247 West 37th Street
18th Floor
New York, NY 10018
646-619-9640

Lobbyists:
Nicole Branca
Ted Houghton
Hilary Morgan
Stephen Piasecki

Taxpayers for Economic Justice, Inc. (NY)
P.O. Box 4543
New York, NY 10136
888-472-1555

Lobbyists:
Steven Day
Raymond Desposito
Richard Giliotti
Linda Isaacson
Robert Schmidlin
Sal Turano
John Welling
Charles Wimer

Technology Enterprise Corporation (NYS)
500 Avery Lane
Suite A
Griffis Industrial Park
Rome, NY 13441
315-338-5818

Lobbyists:
Jana Behe
Michael Donovan
William Pirillo
Michael Walsh

Thomson Strategies, LLC
176-25 Union Turnpike
Suite 200
Fresh Meadows, NY 11366
718-487-3375

Lobbyists:
Terri Thomson

Time Warner Cable
120 East 23 Street
Att: Nina Facini (9th Floor)
New York, NY 10010
212-598-7223

Lobbyists:
Steve Arvan
Marion Boykin
Nickolas Darling
Thomas Doheny
Mark Dunford
John Fogarty
Sharon Hanson
John Keib
Brien Kelley
John Mucha
Chris Mueller
Harriet Novet
Brenda Parks
John Quigley
Terrence Rafferty
Whelan Rory
Howard Szarfarc
Peter Taubin
Jeff Unaitis
Roger Wells
David Whalen
Charles Williams III
Robin Wolfgang

Tishman Speyer Properties, L.P.
45 Rockefeller Plaza
New York, NY 10111
212-593-9480

Lobbyists:
George Hatzmann

TLM Associates LLC
233 Broadway, Suite 702
New York, NY 10007
646-467-8536

Lobbyists:
Jean Kim
Thomas McMahon
Ian Riley-Clendened

Tommasino, Nicholas
Deloitte & Touche LLP
1633 Broadway
New York, NY 10019
212-492-3746

Lobbyists:
Greg Durant
John Fogarty
Lawrence Kramer
Donal O'Callaghan
Kelly Saunders
Beth A. Schneider
Lisa Tracy Smith

Tourism Industry Coalition (TIC)
1 Computer Drive South
Albany, NY 12205
518-465-2300

Lobbyists:
Jan Marie Chesterton

Lobbyists:
Peter Goldwasser
Lindsey Lusher-Shute
Paul Steely White

Tranter Jr. G. Thomas
C/O Corning Incorporated
MP-BH-06
Corning, NY 14831
607-974-7818

Clients:
Corning Incorporated

Trial Lawyers Association (NYS) (FKA Feldman, Daniel)
C/O Trial Lawyers Association (NYS)
132 Nassau Street
New York, NY 10038
212-349-5890

Lobbyists:
Anna Adler
Joseph Awad
Richard Binko
David Golomb
Martin Edelman
Jeffrey Lichtman
Nicholas Papain
Lawrence Park
Tara Quinlan

Tribeca Film Institute
32 Avenue of the Americas
27 FL
New York, NY 10013
212-274-8080

Lobbyists:
Anna Ponder

Trustees of Columbia University in the City of NY (The)
535 West 116th St
302 Low Library
New York, NY 10027
212-854-3738

Clients:
Trustees of Columbia University in the City of NY (The)

Lobbyists:
Lee Bollinger
Alan Brinkley
Loftin Flowers
Ross Frommer
Lee Goldman
Lisa Hogarty
Maxine Griffith
Victoria Hamilton
Sandra Harris
David Hirsch
Lisa Hogarty
Joseph Ienuso
Howard Jacobson
Robert Kasdin
Dolores Kreisman
Ira Lamster
Jeffrey Lieberman
Victoria Mason-Ailey
Philip Pitruzzello
Jeffrey Sachs
Philip Silverman
Anne Sullivan
Marcelo Velez

Turner, Francine
Civil Service Employees PAC
143 Washington Ave
Albany, NY 12210
518-436-8622
e-mail: turner@cseainc.org

Clients:
Civil Service Employees Political Action Fund

Lobbyists:
Adam Acquario
John Belmont
Courtney Brunelle
Matthew D'Amico
Kelley Johnson
Bryan Miller
Ricky Noreault
Cody Peluso
Gretchen Penn
Robert Scholz
Joshua Terry
William Walsh

Tyson, Lisa
90 Pennsylvania Ave
Massapequa, NY 11758-4978
516-541-1006
e-mail: lisa@lipc.org
Web site: www.lipc.org

Clients:
Long Island Progressive Coalition

U.S. Green Building Council, New York Chapter
20 Broad Street
Suite 709
New York, NY 10005
212-514-9380

Lobbyists:
Richard Leigh
Jonah Cecil""
Russell Unger

UCB, Inc.
1950 Lake Park Drive
Smyrna, GA 30080
770-970-8949

Lobbyists:
Dale Aldrich

Ungar, Robert A Associates Inc
200 Garden City Plaza
Ste 201
Garden City, NY 11530
516-227-2400
e-mail: fireandems@aol.com

Clients:
Assn of Plumbing Heating Cooling Contractors Inc (NYS)
Building & Construction Trades Council (NYS)
Building & Construction Trades Council of Greater NY
Building Contractors' Assn, Inc
Building Trades Employers' Assn
Civil Svc Technical Guild, Local 375 DC-37, AFSCME AFL-CIO
Council of Administrators & Supervisors
Local 3, IBEW Communications Electricians
Local 246, SEIU
Nassau County PHCC
Plumbing Contractors Assn of Long Island Inc
Plumbing Foundation City of NY Inc
Purvis Systems Inc
Service Station Dealers of Greater NY, Inc
TBTA Maintenance Employees, Local 1931, DC-37, AFSCME
Uniformed EMT's & Paramedics, Local 2507-FDNY
Uniformed Fire Alarm Dispatchers Benevolent Assn-FDNY
Uniformed Firefighters Assn

Lobbyists:
Robert A Ungar

Uniformed Firefighters Association
204 E 23rd St.
New York, NY 10010
212-683-4832

Lobbyists:
Stephen Cassidy
James Slevin

United Healthcare Services, Inc.
UnitedHealth Group
284 State Street
Albany, NY 12210
518-432-0893

Clients:
United Healthcare Services, Inc

Lobbyists:
Jeffrey Alter
William Goldman
Carolyn Kerr
Carl Mattson
Judah Sommer

United Neighborhood Houses of NY
70 West 36th Street
5th Floor
New York, NY 10018-8007
212-967-0322

Lobbyists:
Clara Botstein
Gregory Brender
Anthony Ng
Susan Stamler
Carin Tinney
Nancy Wackstein

University at Albany (FKA Williams, Charlie)
C/O University at Albany
1400 Washington Avenue
UNH 302
Albany, NY 12222
518-956-8010
Web site: www.albany.edu

Lobbyists:
Stephen Beditz
Kristin Christodulu
Jose Cruz
Vincent Delio
James Diaz
Michael Fancher
Alain Kaloyeros
Brian Keough
Kim Clifford
George Phillip
Susan Phillips
Stephanie Wacholder

University of Rochester
601 Elmwood Avenue
Box 706
Rochester, NY 14642
585-273-5955

Lobbyists:
Nancy Bennett
Bradford Berk
Raffaella Borasi
Jonathan Burdick
Eric Caine
Rob Clark
Glenn Currier
Tony Dechario
Joshua Farrelman
Richard Fisher
Steven Goldstein
Michael Goonan
David Guzick
Amy Happ
Victoria Hines
Grant Holcomb
Allen Ibrisimovic
Katrina Korfmacher
Ralph Kuncl
Peter Lennie
Douglas Lowry
Theresa Mazzullo
Colleen McCarthy
Robert McCrory
Cyril Meyerowitz
Charles Murphy
Mark Noble
Ronald Paprocki
Kathy Parker
Kathy Parrinello
Douglas Phillips
Richard Pifer
Peter Robinson
Joel Seligman
Gaurav Sharma
Leonard Shute
Sue Stewart
Mary Tantillo
Mary Taubman
Barry Watkins

Upstate Consultants
78 Oakland Place
Suite 210
Buffalo, NY 14222
716-432-3602

Clients:
Botanical Medicines
Catholic Health System
Gateway-Longview Inc.

Lobbyists:
Gregory Sehr

Upstate Niagara Cooperative (FKA Upstate Farms Cooperative)
25 Anderson Rd
Buffalo, NY 14225
716-892-3156

Lobbyists:
Timothy Harner
Kimberly Pickard-Dudley
Thomas Rodak
William Young

Urban Justice Center
123 William Street
16th Floor
New York, NY 10012
646-602-5600

Lobbyists:
Sean Basinski
Madeline Garcia Bigelow
Molly Biklen
Jonathan Cohen
David Colodny
Jim Dike
Harvey Epstein
Shannon Ferguson
Susan Hazeldean
April Herms
Doug Lasdon
Bill Leinhard
Anya Mukarji-Connolly
Gerni Oster
Jennifer Parish
Thomas Renyak

Vantagepoint Management, Inc.
1001 Bayhill Drive
Suite 300
San Bruno, CA 94066
650-866-3100

Lobbyists:
J. Stephan Dolezalek
Stephen D. Gray
Robert F. Kennedy, Jr.

Political Parties, Lobbyists & PACs

Offices and agencies generally appear in alphabetical order, except when specific order is requested by listee.

Patricia M. Roboostoff
Alan E. Salzman

Venable LLP
1270 Avenue of the Americas
24th Floor
New York, NY 10020
212-307-5500

Clients:
USTA/National Tennis Center, Inc.

Lobbyists:
Gordon Davis
Susan Golden

Vera Institute of Justice, Inc.
233 Broadway
12th Floor
New York, NY 10279
212-334-1300
Web site: www.vera.org

Lobbyists:
Adrienne Austin
Jean Callahan
Siobhan Carney
Jintana Chiu
Roohi Choudhry
Reagan Daly
Evan Elkin
Elizabeth Elston
Jennifer Fratello
Megan Golden
Karen Goldstein
Alexandra Hezir
Michael Jacobsen
Krista Larson
Peggy Ann McGarry
Joan Meyer
Sara Mogulescu
James Parsons
Celine Quashie
Oren Root
Timothy Ross
Ann Salsich
Danielle Sered
Susan Shah
Alison Shames
Andrea Snelson
Stacy Strongarone
Neil Weiner
Daniel Wilhelm
Michael Woodruff

Verizon
140 West Street
Floor 30
New York, NY 10007
518-396-1086

Clients:
Verizon

Lobbyists:
Richard Bozsik
John Butler
Sam Caldwell
Keefe Clemons
Catherine Gasteyer
April Horton
Andres Irlando
June Jee
Kathleen Kittrick
Czykanne Kowal
David Lamendola
Patrick Lespinasse
Eileen Mannion
Maureen Rasp-Glose
Sandra Wilson
Richard Windram
Susanna Zwerling

Vertex Pharmaceuticals, Inc.
50 Northern Avenue
Boston, MA 02210
617-341-6100

Lobbyists:
Gina Black
Paul Pereira

Vidal Group, LLC (The)
90 South Swan Street
Suite 112
Albany, NY 12210
518-434-5856

Clients:
ALM Medica Inc
American College of Occupational Environmental Medicine
Circulo De La Hispanidad
Earthwatch LTD
Hispanic Counseling Center Inc
Hispanic Federation
Hispanic Information Telecommunications Network
Latino Commission on AIDS
Glenwood Management Corporation
Oasis Children's Service LLC
Rain Inc
Partnership for NYC
Sepracor

Lobbyists:
Mary Briwa
Glen Casey
Jennifer Muthig
Alfredo Vidal

Village Care of New York, Inc.
154 Christopher Street
New York, NY 10014
212-337-5601

Lobbyists:
Emma Devito
Matthew Lesieur

Vista Equity Partners III LLC
4 Embarcadero Center
20th Floor
San Francisco, CA 94111
415-765-6500

Lobbyists:
Brian Sheth
Robert Smith
Martin Taylor

John Warnken-Brill

Vornado Realty Trust
210 Route 4 East
Paramus, NJ 07652
201-587-1000

Lobbyists:
Kate Ascher
Michael Fascitelli
David Greenbaum
Barry Langer
Sandeep Mathrani
Myron Mauer
Steven Roth

Vose, Margie
500 Salem Street
Smithfield, RI 02917-0000
401-292-6515

Clients:
Fidelity Investments Institutional Services Company, Inc.

Lobbyists:
Marissa Hedge
Steve Johnson
Edward Schollmeyer

Wachtel & Masyr, LLP
110 East 59th Street
27th Floor
New York, NY 10022
212-909-9500
Web site: www.wmllp.com

Clients:
Ascent Real Estate Advisors
Blumenfeld Development Group
Botanical Garden (NY) (The)
Related Companies, LP (The)
Thor Properties, LLC (Acquisitions)

Lobbyists:
Ethan Goodman
Jerald Johnson
Raymond Levin
Jesse Masyr

Wal-Mart Stores, Inc.
702 SW 8th Street
MS 0350
Bentonville, AR 72716-0130
479-204-8119

Lobbyists:
Philip Serghini
Alexandra Serra

Walgreen Co.
104 Wilmot Rd
MS 1444
Deerfield, IL 60015
847-315-6829

Lobbyists:
Mike Altier

Walmart Free NYC
50 Broadway
29th Floor
New York, NY 10001
347-387-3549

Lobbyists:
Stephanie Yazgi

Walters Group (The)
95 Columbia Street
Albany, NY 12210
518-432-0488

Clients:
Accenture LLP
Annese and Associates, Inc.
Buckeye Partners, L.P.
CA, Inc.
Care One Services, Inc.
Computer Aid, Inc.
Light Tower Fiber LLC
Pitney Bowes, Inc.

Lobbyists:
Carrie Cody
Ruth Walters

Walton, Leigh
1 Elmcroft Road
Stamford, CT 06926-0700
203-351-6633

Lobbyists:
Alfie Charles

Weiss, Michael A.
15 Waldorf Court
Brooklyn, NY 11230
646-739-5391

Clients:
Marine Park Seaside Links LLC
Pennoni Engineering & Surveying of New York, PC

Wells Capital Management, Inc.
525 Market Street
10th Floor
San Francisco, CA 94105
414-577-7630

Lobbyists:
Meredith Ashwell
Rick Bisignano
Jeff Lang
Ann Larson
Frank Marckioni
Kathryn Schmidt

Wells Fargo and Company
301 South College Street
Charlotte, NC 28288
704-383-1554

Lobbyists:
Milton Aronowitz
Martin Bingham
Rick Bisignano
Jay Blanton

Todd Bleakney
Jennifer Bonita
Carrie Callahan
Felipe Comacho
Peter Cannava
John Caswell
Pam Clayton
Tom Clune
Sean Corrigan
Marie Day
Paul Digrado
Will Driver
Jennifer Ernest
Holger Ebert
Suanne Falvey
Nancy Feldman
Howard Forman
Scott Frail
Nick Gage
Elena Gallo
Dan George
Corbin Hankins
Rick Hartley
Angel Helm
Kevin Henson
Luke Hermann
Peter Hill
Rick Hollar
Jean Halloway
Craig Hrinkevich
Vanessa Hubbard
Steve Hudd
Glenn Johnson
Weldon Jones
Adam Joseph
Michael Karlosky
Bryan Kern
Robert Kinney
Jennifer Kirby
Vin Kurian
Ann Larson
Tommy Lawson
Tammy Leisen
Andrew Levenson
Robert Little
Monique Lopez
Zach Love
Robert Lubonski
Frank Marckioni
Matt Marone
Keziah McGuiness
Walker McQuage
John Menard
Richard Miller
Brian Mulligan
Mike Norman
William O'Conner
Shawn O'Sullivan
John Pedersen
Laurie Post
Bernardo Ramos
Larry Richardson
Casey Rogers
Patrick Russell
Mimi Sapp
Leela Scattum
Janelle Scheuer
Wayne Seaton
Phil Smith
Ronald Stack
Arthur Staub
Joseph Steniger
Karl Tourville
Michel Tram
Rick White
Janine Wilcox
Tim Wilk
Adam Woodard
John Wooten
Erin Young

West Firm PLLC (The)
677 Broadway
8th Floor
Albany, NY 12207-2990
518-641-0501

Clients:
American Natural Gas, LLC
Chesapeake Appalachia LLC
Deer & Elk Farmers Association
Independent Oil & Gas Association of NY

Lobbyists:
Amy Abbatti
Alita Giuda
Thomas S. West

West Harlem Environmental Action, Inc.
1854 Amsterdam Avenue
2nd Floor
New York, NY 10031
212-961-1000

Lobbyists:
Adrienne L. Hollis
Cecil Corbin-Mark
Aurash Khawarzad
Peggy Shepard
Kerene Tayloe

Westfield LLC
2049 Century Park East
41st Floor
Century City, CA 90067
310-478-4456

Lobbyists:
Peter Huddle
Michael McNaughton
Philip Poppinga

White and Williams LLP
7 Times Square
Suite 2900
New York, NY 10036-6524
212-244-9500

Clients:
American Insurance Association

Lobbyists:
John McCarrick
Maurice Pesso

Whiteman Osterman & Hanna LLP
One Commerce Plaza, 19th Fl
Albany, NY 12260
518-487-7741
Web site: www.woh.com

Clients:
American Express Co
AIA New York State Inc
Assn of Homes & Services for the Aging (NY)
Bristol-Myers Squibb Co
Central Boiler Inc
COFCCA Inc
Council of New York Cooperatives
Creosote Council III
Distilled Spirits Council of the US
Educational Testing Service
Empire State Petroleum Assn Inc
Gillen Brewer School (The)
Hertz Corporation (The)
Institute for Student Achievement
Johnson & Johnson
Long Island Life Sciences Initiative
MCI
Metropolitan Museum of Art (The)
NYS Coalition of 853 Schools Inc
NYS Funeral Directors Assn Inc
Physical Therapy Assn (NY)
Presbyterian Hospital (NY)
Preserve Associates LLC
Public Employer Risk Management Assn
Questar III
Quest Diagnostics Inc
Reinsurance Assn of America
Roundabout Theatre Co
SC Johnson & Son Inc
Society for Respiratory Care Inc (NYS)
Advantage Capital Partners
Syracuse University
Teachers Insurance & Annuity Assn/College Retirement Equities Fun
Thomson West
Haverstraw-Stony Point Central School District
Managed Funds Association
MBIA Insurance Corporation
Natural Resources Defense Council Inc
Sanofi Pasteur Inc
St Elizabeth Medical Center
Scotts Company (The)

Lobbyists:
William Y Crowell III
John Dunne
Philip Gitlen
Katherine Herlihy
Aggie Leahy
Richard E Leckerling
Brian J Lucey
Kevin Quinn
Daniel Ruzow
Michael Whiteman

Wiener, Judith R
2 Westchester Plaza
Elmsford, NY 10523
914-345-8737

Clients:
Lower Hudson Education Coalition

Wilder Balter Partners, Inc.
570 Taxter Road
6th Floor
Elmsford, NY 10523
914-610-3655
Web site: www.wbhomes.com

Lobbyists:
John Bainlardi
Robert Wilder

Wildlife Conservation Society
2300 Southern Blvd.
Bronx, NY 10460
718-220-7353

Lobbyists:
John Cavelli
Rosemary DeLuca
Nicole Robinson-Etienne
Janet Torres

Wilson Elser Moskowitz Edelman & Dicker
677 Broadway
Albany, NY 12207
518-449-8893
Web site: www.wemed.com

Clients:
1765 1st Associates LLC
250 E 57th Street, LLC
Albany Medical Ctr
Albert Lindley Lee Memorial Hospital
Alice Hyde Medical Center
American Insurance Assn
American International Group Inc (AIG)
Alliance of Resident Theatres (NY)
Assn of Professional Land Surveyors Inc (NYS)
Assn of Realtors Inc (NYS)
Athletic Trainers' Assn (NYS)
Assn of Independent Commercial Producers Inc
Asurion Corp & Subsidiaries (FKA Lock/Line LLC (DST Systems))
Ballet Theatre Foundation Inc/American Ballet Theatre
Bankers Assn (NY)
Barnes & Noble College Book Sellers (Dewey Square Group)
Brooklyn Adult Care Center
Brooklyn Hospital Center (The)
Canton-Potsdam Hospital
Carnegie Hall
Cathedral Church of St John the Devine (The)
Catholic Conference Policy Group Inc
College Board
Combined Coordinating Council Inc
Community Hospital Network of NY Eductl & Rsch Fund Inc
Community Service Society of NY
Consolidated Edison Co of NY Inc
Cortland Regional Medical Center (FKA Cortland Memorial Hospital)
Crouse Hospital
Center for Disability Services
CGI (FKA CGI Group)
Children's Institute
City of Syracuse Industrial Development Agency
Dell Inc
David B Kriser Dental Center of NY University
DeVry Incorporated
Deloitte & Touche, LLP
Education Management LLC
Elant, Inc
Elliott Management
Epilepsy Institute
Elizabethtown Community Hospital
Ernst & Young, LLP
Excelsior Racing Association (Powers & Company)
Family Planning Advocates
Forest City Ratner Companies
Glens Falls Hospital
Greater New York Automobile Dealers Assn

Offices and agencies generally appear in alphabetical order, except when specific order is requested by listee.

Political Parties, Lobbyists & PACs

Groton Community Health Care Center
HANYS Services, Inc; D/B/A HANYS Solutions, Inc
Harbar Motors, Ltd
Healthcare Assn of NYS
Hebrew Home for the Aged at Riverdale (The)
Hedgewood Home for Adults
Henry Schein Inc
Hertz Corporation (The)
Hospitality & Tourism Assn (NYS)
Hospitals Insurance Company Inc
Hudson Valley Economic Development Corp
Hotel Assn of NYC Inc
IMG Models
Intrepid Museum Foundation
JXQ Holding Company, Inc
Jewish Guild for the Blind (The)
KPMG, LLP
Law School Admissions Council
League of American Theatres & Producers Inc
Lesbian Gay Bisexual & Transgender Community Center (The)
Jewish Museum (The)
John T Mather Memorial Hospital
Long Island Health Network
Long Island University
MCIC Vermont Inc
Marshals Assn (NYC)
Merchants Protective Co, Inc (NY)
Medtronic Inc (FKA Medtronic Sofamor Danek)
Taconic IPA Inc
Metropolitan Parking Assn
Morgan Stanley (Multistate Associates)
Nassau-Suffolk Hospital Association
New Brookhaven Town House for Adults
Norwegian Cruise Line
Niagara Mohawk Holdings, Inc., & NMPC DBA National Grid
New York University-College of Nursing
Nassau County Firefighter's Museum & Education Center
Northern Metropolitan Hospital Assn
Northern Westchester Hospital
North Country Healthcare Providers Eductl & Rsch Fund Inc (North Country Healthcare Providers, LLC)
Peconic Bay Medical Center
Phelps Memorial Hospital Center
Planned Parenthood of NYC Inc
Pricewaterhouse Coopers, LLP
Queens Adult Care Center
Queens-Long Island Medical Group, P.C.
Real Estate Board of NY
Rochester Institute of Technology
Samaritan Medical Center
Sanctuary for Families
School Bus Contractor's Coalition, Inc. (NY)
Segway Inc. (Multistate Associates)
Society for Clinical Social Work Inc (NYS)
St Luke's Cornwall Hospital
St Margaret's Center
St Mary's Healthcare System for Children Inc
T-Mobile USA Inc
To Life
Tanglewood Manor
United Hospital Fund
University (NY)
University School of Medicine (NY) & Hospitals (NY)
Viahealth

Lobbyists:
Nicholas Antenucci
Alexander L Betke
Martin Bienstock
Douglas Clark
Donna Clyne
Laurie T Cohen
Elizabeth Colombo
Victoria M Contino
Kathleen Corkery
Diana Georgia
John N Herring
Jerry S Hoffman
Darrell E Jeffers
Gerald J Jennings
Arnold Kideckel
Andrew Marocco
Lisa M Marrello
Mary Ann Mclean
Stuart Miller
Samir Nejame
Anthony Piscitelli
Peter A Piscitelli
Fred Pomerantz
Jessica Reinhardt
Philip Rosenberg
Theresa Russo
Jill Sandhaas
Kenneth L Shapiro
Cynthia D Shenker
Lester Shulklapper
Mark Thomas
Michael Weisberg
Jacob Wilkinson

Wilson, Alex
27 Elk Street
Albany, NY 12207
518-434-9091

Clients:
Sheriffs' Association

Wisneski, Jessica
c/o Citizen Action of New York
94 Central Avenue
Albany, NY 12206
518-465-4600

Lobbyists:
Pam Bennett
Kathleen Campbell
Diana Cihak
Mary Clark
Bob Cohen
Shanna Goldman
Tanika Jones
Chynel Lee
Karen Scharff
Lea Webb

Wladis Law Firm
P.O. Box 245
Syracuse, NY 13214
315-445-1700
Web site: www.wladislawfirm.com

Lobbyists:
Ryan Moses
Joe Rossi
Matthew Tynan

Worker Justice Center of New York, Inc.
1187 Culver Road
Rochester, NY 14609-5448

Offices and agencies generally appear in alphabetical order, except when specific order is requested by listee.

585-325-3050

Lobbyists:
Milan Bhatt
Emma Kreyche
Lewis Papenfuse

Working Assets Funding Service, Inc.
101 Market Street
Suite 700
San Francisco, CA 94105
415-369-2000

Lobbyists:
Leah Adler

Working Families Organization
2 Nevins Street
3rd Floor
Brooklyn, NY 11217
718-222-3796

Lobbyists:
Joseph Berry
Mike Boland
Emmanuel Caicedo
Dan Cantor
Bryan Collinsworth

Wright Group NY, Inc. (The)
151 West 30th Street
11th Floor
New York, NY 10001
212-216-0684

Clients:
Amigos Del Museo Del Barrio, Inc.
ANHD, Inc.
Botanical Garden (The)
Brooklyn Community Services
Carnegie Hall Corporation (The)
Coalition of Behavioral Health Agencies, Inc.
Connect, Inc.
Cool Culture, Inc.
Crenulated Company LTD DBA New Settlement Apartmens (The)
Cultural Institutions Group
Goddard Riverside Community Center
Greenwich House, Inc.
Hudson Guild
Lawyers for the Public Interest
LEAP
Learning Leaders
Legal Services for the Working Poor
Legal Services NYC
Legal Services NYC
MFY Legal Services, Inc.
New York City Ballet, Inc. and the David H. Koch Theater at Lincoln Center
Northern Manhattan Improvement Corporation
Powerplay NYC, Inc.
Sauti Yetu Center for African Women
Services & Advocacy for Gay, Lesbian, Bisexual & Transgender Elders
St. Ann's Warehouse
Union Theological Seminary

Lobbyists:
Lashaun Lesley
Barbara Martinez
Ayana Partee
Patricia Pulvirenti
Antonio Quesada
Larisa Wick
John Wright

Yankosky, Mary Ellen
146 Trenton Street
Suite 1
Boston, MA 02128
617-997-1551

Clients:
Dental Hygienists Association of the State of New York, Inc.

Yavornitzki, Mark L.
GR Initiatives LLC
121 State Street
4th Floor
Albany, NY 12207
518-426-8178

Clients:
Association of Insurance & Financial Advisors, Inc.

Yeshiva University
500 West 18th Street
New York, NY 10033
212-960-5400

Lobbyists:
Gordon Earle
Michael Heller
Joshua Joseph
Andrew Lauer
Allison Liebman Rubin
Jeffrey Rosengarten

YMCA of Greater New York
5 West 63rd Street
6th Floor
New York, NY 10023
212-630-9600

Lobbyists:
Paul Custer
Sharon Greenberger
Sharon Levy
Joshua Wojehowski

YMCAs of NYS, Inc.
33 Elk Street
2nd Floor
Albany, NY 12207
518-462-8241

Lobbyists:
Kyle Stewart

Yockel, James
800 West Metro Park
Suite C
Rochester, NY 14623
585-341-2128

Clients:
Greater Rochester Association of Realtors, Inc.

York Group Associates
893 Myrtle Avenue
Suite 2B
Brooklyn, NY 11206
347-560-0139

Clients:
Bronx Community College
City University of New York
Greenetrack
Rocket Learning, Inc.

Yoswein New York Inc
111 Broadway
Suite 1504
New York, NY 10006
212-233-5700
Web site: www.yny.com

Clients:
40th Street Development LLC
Academy of Medicine (NY)
Bailey House Inc.
Brooklyn Chamber of Commerce
Brooklyn Philharmonic
Brooklyn Technical High School Alumni Assn
Business Council of NYS, Inc (The)
Ceruzzi Holdings
College Community Services, Inc (DBA Brooklyn Center for the Performing Arts)
Cypress Equities
Flushing Commons, LLC
Gateway Properties Phase II, LLC
Groundwork, Inc.
KeySpan Energy/National Grid
Maimonides Medical Center
Metropolitan Funeral Directors Assn
Mt Sinai Hospital of Queens
New 42nd Street/New Victory Theater
Outward Bound Center (NYC)
Pfizer Inc.
Sierra Club
St. Francis College
Standardbred Owners Assn of NY
SUNY Downstate Medical Center

Lobbyists:
Jeffrey Denman
Kai Feder
Jamie Van Bramer
Joni A. Yoswein

Young Jr. William N.
1881 Western Avenue
Suite 140
Albany, NY 12203
518-456-6767

Clients:
Association of Fire Districts of the State of New York, Inc.

Zalcman, Fred
16 Windaway Road
Bethel, CT 06801
203-743-5447

Clients:
SunEdison LLC

Zaleski, Terence M
437 Old Albany Post Rd
Garrison, NY 10524
845-788-5070
e-mail: tzaleski@sprynet.com

Clients:
Coalition of NYS Career Schools
Green Chimneys Children's Services Inc

ZGA LLC
27 Elk Street
Albany, NY 12207
518-426-0214

Clients:
Association of Agricultural Fairs
Northeast Ag and Feed Alliance
Syngenta Crop Protection LLC

Lobbyists:
Rick Zimmerman

Zuffa LLC
P.O. Box 26959
Las Vegas, NV 89126
702-588-5509

Lobbyists:
Lawrence Epstein
Lorenzo Fertitta
Michael Mersch
Mark Ratner
Dana White

Offices and agencies generally appear in alphabetical order, except when specific order is requested by listee.

POLITICAL ACTION COMMITTEES

1199/SEIU New York State Political Action Fund
330 West 42nd Street, 7th Floor, New York, NY 10036
212-603-1737
George K. Gresham, Treasurer

2013 Committee to Elect Gwen Goodwin
152 East 100th Street, Suite 5E, New York, NY 10029
Gwen Goodwin, Treasurer

A Different Approach
19 East 213th Street, Suite 4C, Bronx, NY 10467
718-600-5054
Joseph Smith, Treasurer

ACEC New York City PAC
8 West 38th Street, Suite 1101, New York, 10018
212-682-6336
Raymond Daddazio, Chairman
Hannah O'Grady

Advertising Development Political Action Committee
PO Box 2269, New York, NY 10163
917-363-2323
Marty Judge, Chairman/Treasurer

AECOM US FEDERAL PAC
201 Wilson Boulevard, Suite 700, Arlington, VA 22201
703-465-5872
Nancy Butler, Chairwoman

Akiel Taylor For Council
186 Lefferts Place, Brooklyn, NY 11238
917-620-5725
Joseph N. Taylor, Treasurer

Albert 2013
427 Bronx Park Avenue, Bronx, NY 10460
347-427-8822
Luis C. Torres, Treasurer

Alex For NYC
10 Bethune Street, Suite 3A, New York, NY 10014
305-992-6875
Ryan S. Reynolds, Treasurer

Alicia 4 Council 7
3333 Broadway, Suite D35A, New York, NY 10031
212-283-2019
Sandra Dawson, Treasurer

American Insurance Association New York City PAC
2101 L Street Northwest, Suite 400, Washington, DC 20037
202-828-7100
JS Zielezienski, Chairman

Andy King 2013
21 Riverdale Avenue, White Plains, NY 10607
646-644-9414
Katrina P. DeLa Cruz, Treasurer

AON Corporation Political Action Committee
200 East Randolph, Chicago, IL 60601
312-381-3352
Paul Hagy, Treasurer

Ari Kagan For City Council
330 Ocean Parkway, Suite C3, Brooklyn, NY 11218
347-556-4205
Alyona Badalova, Treasurer

Arroyo 2013
694 East 133rd Street, #2, Bronx, NY 10454
347-820-3723
Carmen M. Aquino, Treasurer

Asbestos Workers Local 12 Political Action Committee
25-19 43rd Avenue, Long Island City, NY 11101
718-784-3456
Nick Grgas, Chairman

AT&T PAC - New York
111 Washington Avenue, Albany, NY 12210
518-463-3092
Marissa J. Shorenstein, Chairwoman

ATU New York Cope Fund
5025 Wisconsin Avenue, Northwest, Washington, DC 20016
202-537-1645
Lawrence J. Hanley, Treasurer

Bank of America New York Political Action Committee
1100 North King Street, DE5-001-02-07, Wilmington, DE 19884
302-432-0956
Brian P. Grip, Chairman

Bendetto For Assembly
3280 Giegerich Place, Bronx, NY 10465
718-931-6675
Michael R. Bendetto, Chairman

Bill Thompson For Mayor
16 Court Street, 35th Floor, Brooklyn, NY 11241
718-855-2324
James F. Ross, Treasurer

Blishteyn For NYC
175-10 Jewel Avenue, Fresh Meadows, NY 11365
718-757-7389
Ross P. Weiner, Treasurer

Brab PAC, Inc.
850 Bronx River Road, Suite 105, Yonkers, NY 10708
914-966-2000
Michael Laub, Treasurer

Brad Lander 2013
256 13th Street, Brooklyn, NY 11215
917-822-4584
Margaret R. Barnette, Treasurer

Bricklayers & Allied Craftworkers Local 1 PAC
4 Court Square, Long Island City, NY 11108
718-392-0525
Jermiah Sullivan Jr., Chairman
Santo Lantzfamne, Treasurer

Bristol-Meyers Squibb Company Political Action Committee
345 Park Avenue, New York, NY 10154
609-252-5352
John E. Celentano, Chairman

Bryan Block 2013
120-43 219th Street, Cambria Heights, NY 11411
917-837-6102
Sanu K. Thomas, Treasurer

Building & Construction Trades Council PAC
71 West 23rd Street, Suite 501, New York, NY 10010
212-647-0700
Gary LaBarbera, Treasurer

Offices and agencies generally appear in alphabetical order, except when specific order is requested by listee.

Building Industry Association of NYC, Inc.
3130 Amboy Road, Staten Island, NY 10306
718-720-3070
Frank Naso, Chairman

Cablevision Systems New York PAC
1111 Stewart Avenue, Bethpage, NY 11714
516-803-2387
Thomas M. Rutledge, Chairman

Cabrera For City Council
2792 Sedgwick Avenue, 4A, Bronx, NY 10468
917-804-9298
Paul Susana, Treasurer

Captains Endowment Association
233 Broadway, Suite 1801, New York, NY 10279
212-791-8292
Roy T. Richter, Chairman

Carlo 2013
1275 81st Street, Brooklyn, NY 11228
917-622-4063
Camille Arezzo, Treasurer

Carlos For Council
215 Terrace Place, #3, Brooklyn, NY 11218
646-305-5224
Aimee Davis, Treasurer

Carolyn's PAC
24 East 93rd Street, Suite 1B, New York, NY 10128
212-987-5516
Carolyn B. Maloney, Chairwoman

Carrion 2013
1 Stuyvesant Oval, 11D, New York, NY 10009
917-952-1915
Loretta Class, Treasurer

Catholic Citizens Committee PAC
106 First Place, Brooklyn, NY 11231
917-685-5264
Martin Cottingham, Chairman

Central Brooklyn Independent Democrats
476 Tenth Street, Brooklyn, NY 11215
718-788-8698
Lucy Koteen, Chairwoman

CIR/SEIU Local 1957 Health Care Advocacy Fund
520 8th Avenue, Suite 1200, New York, NY 10018
212-356-8100
Eric Scherzer, Treasurer

CITIGROUP Inc. Political Action Committee - Federal/State
1101 Pennsylvania Avenue Northwest, #1000, Washington, DC 20004
202-879-6805
S. Colin Dowling, Chairman

Citizens For Sports & Arts, Inc.
58-12 Queens Boulevard, Suite 1, Woodside, NY 11377
718-786-7110
Lewis H. Hartman, Chairman

Civil Service Employees Political Action Fund
143 Washington Avenue, Albany, NY 12210
518-436-8622
Danny F. Donohue, Chairman

Cliff Stanton For Council
3861 Cannon Place, Bronx, NY 10463
917-699-5241
Joseph V. Kullhanek, Treasurer

Clifton Stanley Diaz For NYC Council
172-20 133rd Avenue, 2D, Jamaica, NY 11434
917-856-5454
David E. Diaz, Treasurer

Climate Action PAC
30 Broad Street, 30th Floor, New York, NY 10004
212-361-6350
Robert Hallman, Chairman

Cohen For Council
444 East 86th Street, 17H, New York, NY 10028
212-879-2971
Esther Fink-Sinovsky, Treasurer

Committee For Effective Leadership
63 Carriage Place, c/o William J. He, Edison, NJ 08820
732-744-1413
Lewis H. Goldstein, Chairman

Committee to Elect Abiodun Bello
PO Box 520843, Bronx, NY 10452
917-603-3553
Shakiru O. Kazeem, Treasurer

Committee to Elect Andy King
952 East 218th Street, PH, Bronx, NY 10469
718-515-5464
Winslow Luna, Treasurer

Committee to Elect Ariel Guerrero
411 East 118th Street, #35, New York, NY 10035
917-826-9661
Nicholas S. Burke, Treasurer

Committe to Elect Ceceilia Berkowitz for Mayor
143 East 30th Street, #402, New York, NY 10016
917-923-5760
Alex Castillo, Treasurer

Committee to Elect Charles A. Bilal 2010
121 03 Sutphin Boulevard, Jamaica, NY 11431
718-607-9119
Aziza N. Bilal, Treasurer

Committee to Elect Christopher Banks
669 Van Siclen Avenue, PH, Brooklyn, NY 11207
718-257-3050
Claudette Elliott, Treasurer

Committee to Elect Eric Adams
593 Vanderbilt Avenue, #305, Brooklyn, NY 11238
Eric Adams, Chairman

Committee to Elect Philip Marks For Mayor
1658 Ralph Avenue, 6C, Brooklyn, NY 11236
Philip A. Marks, Treasurer

Committee to Elect Robert E. Cornegy Jr.
653 Putnam Avenue, Brooklyn, NY 11221
917-586-7444
Michelle R. Cornegy, Treasurer

Committee to Elect Robert M. Waterman
207 Lewis Avenue, Brooklyn, NY 11221
Avis Jones, Treasurer

Committee to Elect Stephen S. Jones to City Council
107-52 139th Street, Jamaica, NY 11435
347-447-8148
Kenneth E. Nelson, Treasurer

Committee to Re-Elect Lawrence A. Warden
1103 East Gun Hill Road, Bronx, NY 10469
917-345-6860
Marcia E. McGann, Treasurer

Committee to Re-Elect Nydia M. Velazquez to Congress
315 Inspiration Lane, Gaithersburg, MD 20878
301-947-0278
Nydia M. Velazquez, Chairwoman

Committee to Re-Elect Mathieu Eugene
40 Argyle Road, C6, Brooklyn, NY 11218
347-725-6725
Delsie L. Lawson, Treasurer

Communications Workers of America Local 1180
6 Harrison Street, New York, NY 10013
212-226-6565
Arthur Cheliotes, Chairman

Community Campaign For Naaimat
10 Richman Plaza, 1K, Bronx, NY 10453
646-470-3436
Momodou S. Sawaneh, Treasurer

Community For Lynn Nunes
115-13 Jamaica Avenue, Richmond Hill, NY 11418
347-242-6600
George Parpas, Treasurer

Community Mental Health Political Action Committee, Inc.
52 Dublin Drive, Niskayuna, NY 12309
518-783-1417
Christopher Burke, Chairman

Comrie For NYC
115-03 Farmers Boulevard, St. Albans, NY 11412
718-772-3975
Tyrone A. Sellers, Treasurer

Conrad Tillard For Council
315 Flatbush Avenue, 521, Brooklyn, NY 11217
347-766-3628
Suedamay A. Monderson, Treasurer

Conservative Party Campaign Committee
32 Cunard Place, Staten Island, NY 10304
718-816-2237
Carmine Ragucci, Chairman

Consolidated Edison, Inc. Employees' Political Action Committee
4 Irving Place, New York, NY 10003
212-460-4202
Frances Resheske, Chairwoman

Correy For Council
777 Sixth Avenue, 6D, New York, NY 10001
917-750-5289
Mathew Bergman, Treasurer

Correction Captains Association - PAC
189 Montague Street, Suite 400, Brooklyn, NY 11201
718-243-0222
Patrick W. Ferraiuolo, Chairman

Correction Officers Benevolent Association
75 Broad Street, Suite 810, New York, NY 10004
212-274-8000
Norman Seabrook, Chairman

Council of School Supervisors and Administrators, Local 1 AFSA
16 Court Street, 4th Floor, Brooklyn, NY 11241
718-852-3000
Ernest Logan, Chairman

Cozen O'Connor Empire State PAC
1900 Market Street, Philadelphia, PA 19103
215-665-2000
Thomas A. Decker, Chairman

Craig Caruana 2013
7921 67 Drive, Middle Village, NY 11379
917-648-4787
Lawrence J. Caruana, Treasurer

Crowley For Congress
84-56 Grand Avenue, Elmhurst, NY 11373
718-639-7010
Joseph Crowley, Chairman

CWA District One PAC
80 Pine Street, 37th Floor, New York, NY 10005
212-344-2515
Christopher M. Shelton, Chairman

CWA SSF (NY)
80 Pine Street, 37th Floor, NY 10005
212-344-2515
Christopher M. Shelton, Chairman

Cynthia For Change
2375 Marion Avenue, 2C, Bronx, NY 10458
917-292-7015
Luana Malavolta, Treasurer

D & M P.A.C. LLC
605 Third Avenue, New York, NJ 10158
212-557-7200
Arthur Goldstein, Treasurer

David Kayode 2013
106-23 153rd Street, 1, Jamaica, NY 11433
Omolola Kayode, Treasurer

Davis 2013
459 Columbus Avenue, 365, New York, NY 10024
917-716-9236
Adam B. Karl, Treasurer

DC 37 Local 299
125 Barclay Street, New York, NY 10007
212-815-1299
Jackie Rowe-Adams, Chairwoman

DC 37 Political Action Committee
125 Barclay Street, New York, NY 10007
212-815-1550
Lillian Roberts, Chairwoman

Democracy For America - NYC
38 Eastwood Drive, Suite 300, South Burlington, VT 05403
802-651-3200
Arshad Hasan, Chairman

Political Parties, Lobbyists & PACs

Offices and agencies generally appear in alphabetical order, except when specific order is requested by listee.

Democrat, Republican, Independent Voter Education
25 Louisiana Avenue Northwest, Washington, DC 20001
202-624-6821
James P. Hoffa, Chairman

Detectives Endowment Association - COPE
26 Thomas Street, New York, NY 10007
212-587-1000
Michael J. Palladino, Chairman

Diallo For Council 2013
3396 3rd Avenue, Suite 1A, Bronx, NY 10456
347-754-8239
Adama I. Barry, Treasurer

District Council 1707, AFSCME
101 Avenue of the Americas, 4th Floor, New York, NY 10013
212-219-0022
Raglan George Jr., Chairman

District Council No. 9 Political Action Committee
45 West 14th Street, New York, NY 10011
212-255-2950
Joseph Ramaglia, Chairman

DLA Piper New York Political Action Committee
1251 Avenue of the Americas, 29th Floor, New York, NY 10020
202-799-4349
John A. Merrigan, Chairman

Doctors Council SEIU COPE
50 Broadway, 11th Floor, Suite 1101, New York, NY 10004
212-532-7690
Barry L. Liebowitz, M.D., Chairman

Dodge Landesman For State Committee
4 Lexington Avenue, New York, NY 10010
917-453-1523
Dodge Landesman, Treasurer

Dromm For NYC
35-24 78th Street, B28, Jackson Heights, NY 11372
718-457-2928
Andrew P. Ronan, Treasurer

Duane For New York
43-07 Westmoreland Street, Little Neck, NY 11363
212-949-6720
Margaret M. McConnell, Treasurer

Duane Morris LLP Government Committee - New York Fund
30 South 17th Street, Philadelphia, PA 19103
215-979-1450
Lewis F. Gould Jr., Chairman

Educational Justice Political Action Committee
76 East 51st Street, 2F, Brooklyn, NY 11203
718-813-6229
Shelly L. Barrow, Treasurer

Effective Leadership Committee, Inc.
165 West End Avenue, 14R, New York, NY 10023
212-799-3312
Raymond Hodell, Chairman

EFO Jeffrey P. Gardner
124 Highview Terrace, Hawthorne, NJ 07506
973-951-7081
Jeffrey P. Gardner, Chairman

EISPAC
3 Park Avenue, 28th Floor, c/o Robe, New York, NY 10016
212-689-7744
Paul Eisland, Chairman

Elaine Nunes 2010
95-16 123rd Street, Richmond Hill, NY 11419
646-430-9067
Jaime Nunes, Treasurer

Eleanor Roosevelt Legacy Committee
PO Box 20293, New York, NY 10010
646-430-9067
Judith Hope, Chairwoman

Elect Newsome 2013
955 Sheridan Avenue, 5B, Bronx, NY 10456
347-913-3694
Chivona R. Newsome, Treasurer

Elizabeth Crowley 2013
77-24 83rd Street, Glendale, NY 11385
347-891-3973
Moira McDermott, Treasurer

Emily's List NY
1120 Connecticut Avenue Northwest, Suite 1100, Washington, DC 20036
202-326-1400
Amy Dacey, Treasurer

Empire Dental Political Action Committee
20 Corporate Woods Boulevard, Suite 602, Albany, NY 12211
518-465-0044
Lawrence E. Volland, Treasurer

Entergy Corporation Political Action Committee - New York
440 Hamilton Avenue, White Plains, NY 10601
914-272-3558
Michael Balduzzi, Chairman

Eric Adams 2013
PO Box 250-294, Brooklyn, NY 11225
917-327-3804
Emrod Martin, Treasurer

Eric Ulrich 2013
101-17 84th Street, Ozone Park, NY 11416
917-951-7251
Ronald Kulick, Treasurer

Ernst & Young Committee For Good Government
5 Times Square, New York, NY 10036
212-773-7111
David G. Bonagura, Chairman

Espinal For City Council
52 Hale Avenue, Brooklyn, NY 11208
347-967-9896
Wilson Rodriguez, Treasurer

Evergreen For City Council
41-34 Frame Place, 5K, Flushing, NY 11355
718-888-7412
Justin Lieu, Treasurer

Farrell 2012
31 Bleecker Place, Albany, NY 12202
Herman D. Farrell, Jr., Chairman

Federal Express New York State Political Action Committee
942 South Shady Grove Road, 1st Floor, Memphis, TN 38120
901-818-7407
Gina F. Adams, Chairwoman

Flowers For NYC
226-16 139th Avenue, Laurelton, NY 11413
718-928-5511
Raymond Baynard Jr., Treasurer

Food Industry Political Action Committee - NYC
130 Washington Avenue, Albany, NY 12210
914-220-8347
Jay M. Peltz, Chairman

Frank's Friends
9306 Flatlands Avenue, Suite A, Brooklyn, NY 11236
Jaime Rivas-Williams, Treasurer

Freelancers Union Political Action Committee
20 Jay Street, Suite 700, Brooklyn, NY 11201
718-532-1515
Ann Boger, Chairwoman

Friends For Peter Koo
133-24A 41st Avenue, Flushing, NY 11355
718-961-2931
Xiao Yun M. Yu, Treasurer

Friends For Ryan Wright
3025 Kingsland Avenue, PH, Bronx, NY 10469
Daphne C. Lewis, Treasurer

Friends of Alfonso Quiroz
76-10 34th Avenue, 2P, Jackson Heights, NY 11372
212-460-1372
Matthew Baker, Treasurer

Friends of Angel Molina
411 East 139th Street, Bronx, NY 10454
718-930-9712
Angel D. Molina, Treasurer

Friends of Antonio Reynoso
359 South 2nd Street, 3D, Brooklyn, NY 11211
718-909-3888
Pedro Pena, Treasurer

Friends of Assembly Speaker Joe Roberts
PO Box 1326, Bellmawr, NJ 08099
609-575-8893
Joe Roberts, Chairman

Friends of Assemblyman Jeffrey Dinowitz
c/o Heidi Schwartz, 3050 Fairfiel, Bronx, NY 10463
718-549-1729
Jeffrey Dinowitz, Chairman

Friends of Audrey Pheffer
8800 Shore Front Parkway, 10E, Rockaway Beach, NY 11693
917-501-5489
Stacey G. Amato, Treasurer

Friends of Austin Shafran
14-23 209th Street, 2F, Bayside, NY 11360
917-838-2404
Jennifer B. Krinsky, Treasurer

Friends of Balboni
9 Legends Circle, Melville, NY 11747
631-242-0548
Michael A. Balboni, Chairman

Friends of Benjamin Kallos
535 East 88th Street, 5A, New York, NY 10128
212-600-4960
David Kogelman, Treasurer

Friends of Bill Suggs
929 Lincoln Place, Brooklyn, NY 11213
646-596-1527
Elizabeth N. Suggs, Treasurer

Friends of Bola Omotosho
146 Morton Place, Bronx, NY 10453
718-644-0108
Anthony K. Adjei, Treasurer

Friends of Breina Payne
121-02 Sutphin Boulevard, E103, Jamaica, NY 11434
347-894-1287
Nadja M. Taffe, Treasurer

Friends of Brodie Enoch 2013
247 West 145th Street, 6A, New York, NY 10039
347-476-9057
Donna L. Linzy, Treasurer

Friends of Carl E. Heastie
PO Box 840, Bronx, NY 10469
718-570-1881
Carl E. Heastie, Chairman

Friends of Catherine Nolan
6464 229th Street, Oakland Gardens, NY 11364
718-229-4201
Catherine T. Nolan, Chairwoman

Friends of Costa Constantinides
24-60 28th Street, Astoria, NY 11102
917-716-4540
Leah A. Carter, Treasurer

Friends of Cultural Institutions
540 Broadway, 7th Floor, Albany, NY 12207
518-426-8111
Richard J. Miller, Treasurer

Friends of Dara Adams
171 East 77th Street, 2B, New York, NY 10017
646-543-9166
Marilyn Feuer, Treasurer

Friends of David Kayode For Council
106-23 153rd Street, #1, Jamaica, Queens, NY 11433
917-747-0837
Alfred Oyewole, Treasurer

Friends of DeMeo
2023 73rd Street, Brooklyn, NY 11204
917-913-9111
Claudio DeMeo, Chairman

Friends of Donovan Richards 2013
1526 Central Avenue, Far Rockaway, NY 11691
718-471-1117
Carol Richards, Treasurer

Friends of Dorothy Phelan
35-53 82nd Street, 1C, Jackson Heights, NY 11372
718-424-2162
Dorothy A. Phelan, Chairwoman

Friends of Ed Hartzog
300 East 75th Street, 12J, New York, NY 10021
917-705-6126
Cabot J. Marks, Treasurer

Offices and agencies generally appear in alphabetical order, except when specific order is requested by listee.

Friends of Ede Fox
315 Saint Johns Place, 4E, Brooklyn, NY 11238
347-262-7977
Judith T. Pierce, Treasurer

Friends of Erick Salgado
2502 86th Street, 3rd Floor, Brooklyn, NY 11214
718-266-4778
Yury S. Rozel, Treasurer

Friends of F. Richard Hurley 2013
150 Crown Street, C4, Brooklyn, NY 11225
917-297-9429
Dwayne A. Nicholson, Treasurer

Friends of Felipe de Los Santos
2446 University Avenue, 4A, Bronx, NY 10468
718-825-7037
Carlos J. De La Cruz, Treasurer

Friends of Gale Brewer - 2013
29 West 95th Street, New York, NY 10025
917-881-3375
Adele Bartlett, Treasurer

Friends of Harpreet
79-19 257th Street, Floral Park, NY 11004
718-343-9146
Manjit King, Treasurer

Friends of I. Daneek Miller
1078 Clyde Road, Baldwin, NY 11510
516-369-8735
Mark A. Henry, Treasurer

Friends of Inez Barron
744 Bradford Street, 2nd Floor, Brooklyn, NY 11207
917-853-9615
Rosalyn C. McIntosh, Treasurer

Friends of James Vacca
PO Box 562, Bronx, NY 10461
646-269-8414
Jonathan D. Conte, Treasurer

Friends of Jean Similien
3420 Avenue H, 3C, Brooklyn, NY 11210
347-709-5326
Antoine C. Coq, Treasurer

Friends of Joe Lazar
1430 East 24th Street, Brooklyn, NY 11210
917-968-5250
Aaron Biderman, Treasurer

Friends of Joe Marthone
116-37 227th Street, Cambria Heights, NY 11411
347-722-1126
Henry Derenoncourt, Treasurer

Friends of Joel R. Rivera
209 East 165th Street, 1B, Bronx, NY 10456
646-345-4263
Dion J. Powell, Treasurer

Friens of John Calvelli
11 Island View Place, New Rochelle, NY 10801
914-636-4045
John F. Calvelli, Chairman

Friends of John Lisyanskiy
155 Bay 20th Street, 2-D, Brooklyn, NY 11214
718-996-4609
Bella Waldman, Treasurer

Friends of John Liu
PO Box 520631, Flushing, NY 11352
917-501-6781
Shiang Liu, Treasurer

Friends of Johnnie Goff
2952 Laconia Avenue, Bronx, NY 10469
917-797-1771
Deborah Wilkerson, Treasurer

Friends of Jonathan J. Judge
345 Webster Avenue, 2N, Brooklyn, NY 11230
718-853-1932
Victoria A. Judge, Treasurer

Friends of Joseph Nwachukwu
1416 East Gunhill Road, Bronx, NY 10469
917-705-2478
Henrietta U. Ilomudio, Treasurer

Friends of Joyce Johnson
733 Amsterdam Avenue, 28B, New York, NY 10025
646-244-8630
Manuel Casanova, Treasurer

Friends of JR
321 West 89th Street, 6, New York, NY 10024
646-337-7700
Darrell L. Paster, Treasurer

Friends of Julio Pabon
143 East 150th Street, Bronx, NY 10451
718-402-9310
Blanca Canino-Vigo, Treasurer

Friends of Kevin P. Coenen Jr. Inc.
417 East 60th Street, 21, New York, NY 10022
917-603-9330
Kevin P. Coenen Jr., Treasurer

Friends of Kimberly Council
102 Etna Street, Brooklyn, NY 11208
347-645-1877
Trevor A. Hyde Jr., Treasurer

Friends of Kirsten John Foy
215 East 23rd Street, Brooklyn, NY 11226
James Sanon, Treasurer

Friends of Larry Hirsch 2010
321 West 89th Street, 6, New York, NY 10024
646-337-7700
Larry Hirsch, Chairman

Friends of Luis Tejada
157-10 Riverside Drive, New York, NY 10032
646-399-6163
Aydee Martinez, Treasurer

Friends of Manny Caughman Committee
115-05 179th Street, Saint Albans, NY 11412
718-809-6354
Andrea C. Scarborough, Treasurer

Friends of Marie Adam-Ovide For Council 31
121-12 234th Street, Laurelton, NY 11422
718-723-0645
Robinson Ovide, Treasurer

Offices and agencies generally appear in alphabetical order, except when specific order is requested by listee.

Friends of Mark Thompson
77 West 55th Street, 12B, New York, NY 10019
212-616-5810
Joseph G. Hagelmann III, Treasurer

Friends of Mark Weprin 2013
80-15 233rd Street, Queens Village, NY 11427
718-898-8500
Jack M. Friedman, Treasurer

Friends of Mark Winston Griffith
1238 Dean Street, Brooklyn, NY 11216
917-837-1587
Sharon M. Griffith, Treasurer

Friends of Martha Taylor
175-14 Mayfield Road, Jamaica, NY 11432
718-300-7308
Robert P. Miraglia, Treasurer

Friends of Martha Taylor Butler
133-02 133rd Avenue, South Ozone Park, NY 11420
917-364-7097
Martha T. Butler, Treasurer

Friends of Martin For City Council
292 Martin Avenue, Staten Island, NY 10314
718-698-1776
Martin S. Krongold, Treasurer

Friends of Menegon
31 East 92nd Street, 2B, New York, NY 10128
Karl Seidenwurm, Treasurer

Friends of Michael A. Alvarez
6120 North Kirkwood, Chicago, IL 60646
847-791-4105
Michael A. Alvarez, Chairman

Friends of Michael Duncan 2013
130-05 235th Street, Rosedale, NY 11422
347-528-4479
Tahisha Salmon, Treasurer

Friends of Michael Simanowitz
137-31 71st Avenue, Flushing, NY 11367
646-235-5095
Simon Pelman, Treasurer

Friends of Mike Gianaris
17 Canterbury Road South, Harrison, NY 10528
917-322-9212
Michael N. Gianaris, Treasurer

Friends of Mike Treybich
2925 West 5th Street, 23B, Brooklyn, NY 11224
718-288-3625
Daniel Dugan, Treasurer

Friends of Nicole Paultre Bell
129-10 Liberty Avenue, Floor 2, Richmond Hill, NY 11419
347-355-2324
Laura A. Harper, Treasurer

Friends of Olanike Alabi
PO Box 380075, Brooklyn, NY 11238
718-398-0750
Olanike T. Alabi, Chairman

Friends of Osina
1092 Beach 12th Street, Far Rockaway, NY 11691
718-868-2720
Eli Shapiro, Treasurer

Friends of Paul Drucker
PO Box 393, Paoli, PA 19301
480-275-1876
Paul Drucker, Chairman

Friends of Pedro Alvarez
1411 Townsend Avenue, A3, Bronx, NY 10452
917-775-9865
Jerson R. Mezquita, Treasurer

Friends of Randy Credico
4712 Vernon Boulevard, Long Island City, NY 11101
212-924-6980
Melchior Leone, Treasurer

Friends of Richard del Rio
208 East Broadway, J604, New York, NY 10002
646-257-9062
Stephanie D. Curry, Treasurer

Friends of Ruben Wills
194-19 115th Drive, St. Albans, NY 11412
516-663-0630
Sharon Carnegie-Hall, Treasurer

Friends of Sean K. Henry 2013
659 Ashford Street, 2, Brooklyn, NY 11207
718-216-6188
Sean K. Henry, Treasurer

Friends of Selvena Brooks
PO Box 130379, Springfield Gardens, NY 11413
347-564-0730
Nyoka Dada, Treasurer

Friends of Seymour Lachman
1207 Avenue N, Brooklyn, NY 11230
718-887-6449
Seymour P. Lachman, Chairman

Friends of Steve Cohn
16 Court Street, Brooklyn, NY 11241
718-875-7057
Steven Cohn, Chairman

Friends of Theresa Scavo
2626 Homecrest Avenue, 7T, Brooklyn, NY 11235
347-668-4548
Anthony Scavo, Treasurer

Friends of Todd Dobrin
4216 Manhattan Avenue, Brooklyn, NY 11224
917-667-2139
Deena L. Venezia-Dobrin, Treasurer

Friends of Tommy Torres
401 Morgan Avenue, Brooklyn, NY 11211
718-812-0515
Samuel Rodriguez, Treasurer

Friends of Torres
PO Box 670192, Bronx, NY 10467
718-635-2827
Marjorie Velazquez, Treasurer

Friends of Yetta
350 Broadway, Suite 701, New York, NY 10013
718-852-3710
Leo Glickman, Treasurer

Garodnick 2013
132 East 43rd Street, #560, New York, NY 10017
212-210-9362
Andrew J. Ehrlich, Treasurer

Gay and Lesbian Victory Fund
1133 15th Street, Northwest, Suite 350, Washington, DC 20005
202-842-8679
Charles A. Wolfe, Chairman

Gentile For the Future
8901 Shore Road, 7E, Brooklyn, NY 11209
347-272-9734
Mary Brannan, Treasurer

Gibson For Assembly
190 West Burnside Avenue, 2D, Bronx, NY 10453
917-309-7854
Vanessa L. Gibson, Chairwoman

Gibson For City Council
21 Riverdale Avenue, White Plains, NY 10607
646-644-9414
Katrina De La Cruz, Treasurer

Gibson, Dunn & Crutcher LLP PAC
333 South Grand Avenue, Suite 5208, Los Angeles, CA 90071
213-229-7252
Kenneth M. Doran, Treasurer

Gonzalez 2013
349 Bleecker Street, 1, Brooklyn, NY 11237
347-743-8322
Julissa G. Santiago, Treasurer

Gotlieb For City Council
2930 West 5th Street, 12G, Brooklyn, NY 11224
718-996-5668
Ira Spodek, Treasurer

Gramercy Stuyvesant Independent Democrats
145 East 15th Street, 4U, New York, NY 10003
917-445-3370
Sam Albert, Chairman

Grassy Sprain PAC
51 Pondfield Road, Bronxville, NY 10708
914-961-6100
William E. Griffin, Chairman

Greenberg Traurig PA PAC
54 State Street, 6th Floor, Albany, NY 12207
518-689-1400
Mark F. Glaser, Chairman

Greenfield 2010
1011 East 3rd Avenue, Brooklyn, NY 11230
347-985-1135
Jeffrey Leb, Treasurer

Grodenchik For Queens 2013
125-28 Queens Boulevard, 504, Kew Gardens Hill, NY 11415
718-670-0720
Simon Pelman, Treasurer

Gronowicz For Mayor
2267 Haviland Avenue, 11, Bronx, NY 10462
347-920-1606
Carl L. Lundgren, Treasurer

Guerriero For Advocate
PO Box 20105, New York, NY 10014
347-709-5406
Ray Guerriero, Chairman

Hakeem Jeffries For Assembly
28 Sterling Street, Brooklyn, NY 11225
212-239-7323
Hakeem Jeffries, Chairman

Halloran 2013
166-06 24th Road, Whitestone, NY 11357
Chrissy Voskerichian, Treasurer

Harlem Charter School Parents PAC
PO Box 1930, New York, NY 10025
646-363-9047
Thomas A. Lopez-Pierre, Treasurer

HCA PAC
433 Delaware Avenue, Delmar, NY 12054
518-810-0664
Joanne Cunningham, Treasurer

HDR, Inc. Political Action Committee - NY
8404 Indian Hills Drive, Omaha, NE 68114
248-371-7268
Bryan Foxx, Treasurer

He Gin Lee Committee to Elect For Mayor
34-16 149th Street, 2, Flushing, NY 11354
718-461-2917
Nick Polyzogopouos, Treasurer

Healthcare Association of New York State PAC
1 Empire Drive, Rensselaer, NY 12144
518-431-7600
Daniel Sisto, Chairman

Helal A. Sheikh 2013
190 Forbell Street, 1, Brooklyn, NY 11208
917-415-5681
Hifzur Rahman, Treasurer

Helen Rosenthal For City Council
225 West 83rd Street, 4K, New York, NY 10024
917-923-1019
Patricia Craddick, Treasurer

HF Responsibility Fund
2 Park Avenue, New York, NY 10016
212-592-1400
George J. Wolf, Treasurer

Hill 2013
509 East 81st Street, 10, New York, NY 10028
917-596-2432
Marianne P. Peterson, Treasurer

Hoffnung 2013
646 West 227th Street, Bronx, NY 10463
917-687-6106
Jay Horowitz, Treasurer

Holland and Knight Committee For Responsible Government
31 West 52nd Street, New York, NY 10019
212-513-3562
Frank G. Sinatra, Chairman

Hotel Association of New York City, Inc.
320 Park Avenue, 22nd Floor, New York, NY 10022
212-754-6700
Joseph E. Spinnato, Chairman

Offices and agencies generally appear in alphabetical order, except when specific order is requested by listee.

Housing New York Political Action Committee
5 Hanover Square, Suite 1605, New York, NY 10004
212-838-7442
Andrew K. Hoffman, Chairman

Hoylman For Senate
80 Eighth Avenue, Suite 1802, New York, NY 10011
212-206-0033
Brad Hoylman, Chairman

HSBC North America Political Action Committee
1401 Eye Street Northwest, Suite 520, Washington, DC 20005
202-466-3561
Kevin Fromer, Chairman

Human Rights Campaign New York PAC
1640 Rhode Island Avenue, Northwest, Washington, DC 20036
202-628-4160
Susanne Salkind, Chairwoman

Humberto Soto For New York City Council 2013
268 Jefferson Street, 2B, Brooklyn, NY 11237
917-651-5595
Humberto Soto Jr., Treasurer

Hunts Point Produce Redevelopment PAC - Corporate Contribution Account
464 NYC Terminal Market, Bronx, NY 10474
718-589-4095
Jeffrey Haas, Chairman

Hunts Point Produce Redevelopment PAC - Personal Contribution Account
464 NYC Terminal Market, Bronx, NY 10474
718-589-4095
Jeffrey Haas, Chairman

IAFF FIREPAC New York Non-Federal
1750 New York Avenue, Washington, DC 20006
202-737-8484
Harold Schaitberger, Chairman

IBT Joint Council No. 16 PAC
265 West 14th Street, Suite 1201, New York, NY 10011
212-924-0002
George Miranda, Chairman

Ignizio 2013
265 Barbara Street, Staten Island, NY 10306
917-763-0951
Susan LaForgia, Treasurer

Igor 2013
2928 West 5th Street, 2R, Brooklyn, NY 11224
718-648-9186
Dan U. Levitt, Treasurer

Int'l Longshoremen's Ass'n, AFL-CIO Committee on Political Education
17 Battery Place, Suite 930, New York, NY 10004
212-425-1200
Richard P. Hughes Jr., Chairman

International Brotherhood of Electrical Workers Political Action Committee
900 Seventh Street N.W., Washington, DC 20001
202-728-6046
Edwin D. Hill, Chairman

International Union of Operating Engineers Local 14-14B Voluntary Political Action Committee
141-57 Northern Boulevard, Flushing, NY 11354
718-939-0600
Edwin L. Christian, Treasurer

International Union of Operating Engineers Local 15 A B C D
265 West 14th Street, Room 505, New York, NY 10011
212-929-5327
James T. Callahan, Chairman

International Union of Painters and Allied Trades Political Action Committee
7234 Parkway Drive, Hanover, MD 21706
410-564-5880
James Williams, Chairman

Ironworkers Local 46 PAC
1322 3rd Avenue, New York, NY 10021
347-461-6300
Terrence Moore, Treasurer

Ironworkers Political Action League
1750 New York Avenue, NW, Washington, DC 20006
202-383-4881
Joseph J. Hunt, Chairman

IUOE Local 15 Political Action Fund
44-40 11th Street, Long Island City, NY 11101
212-929-5327
Daniel J. Schneider, Chairman

Iwachiw 4 Mayor
48-35 41st Street, PH, Sunnyside, NY 11104
347-239-0965
Walter Iwachiw, Treasurer

Jacques Leandre For New York
232-06A Merrick Boulevard, Laurelton, NY 11413
347-613-2315
John M. Hogan, Treasurer

Jennings NYC
130-35 126th Street, South Ozone Park, NY 11420
718-529-5339
Donovan O. Folkes, Treasurer

Jesse Hamilton 2013
910 Lincoln Place, Brooklyn, NY 11213
917-553-7953
Denise F. Mann, Treasurer

Jim Owles Liberal Democratic Club
450 West 17th Street, 2405, New York, NY 10011
212-741-3677
Allen Roskoff, Chairman

Joan Flowers For the 27th District
173-35 113th Avenue, Addisleigh Park, NY 11433
917-723-5713
Leon P. Hart Esq., Treasurer

Joe Lhota For Mayor, Inc.
132 East 43rd Street, New York, NY 10017
212-681-0055
Vincent A. Lapadula, Treasurer

Joel Bauza For City Council
PO Box 709, Bronx, NY 10460
917-349-2596
Rafael E. Abreu, Treasurer

John Catsimatidis For Mayor 2013 Committee, Inc.
823 Eleventh Avenue, New York, NY 10019
Deborah A. Heinichen, Treasurer

John Quaglione For City Council
449 81st Street, Brooklyn, NY 11209
347-560-4555
Georgea C. Kontzamanis, Treasurer

Johnson 2013
3856 Bronx Boulevard, 7H, Bronx, NY 10467
347-762-8683
Geneva A. Johnson, Treasurer

Johnson NYC 2013
1426 Morris Avenue, Bronx, NY 10456
718-930-5030
Geoffrey Longmore, Treasurer

JPMorgan Chase & Co. PAC
10 South Dearborn, IL 1-0520, Chicago, IL 60603
312-732-5852
Peter L. Scher, Chairman

JuanPagan2013
1225 FDR Drive, 4B, New York, NY 10009
646-730-6037
Lillian Rivera, Treasurer

Judge Analisa Torres For Supreme Court 2011
321 West 89th Street, #6, New York, NY 10024
646-337-7700
Analisa Torres, Chairwoman

Julie Menin 2013
PO Box 1261, New York, NY 10013
646-415-2050
Michael Connolly, Treasurer

Julissa 2013
104-01 Roosevelt Avenue, Suite 1, Corona, NY 11368
800-829-7059
Guiyermo DeJesus, Treasurer

Jumaane 2013
PO Box 100323, Brooklyn, NY 11210
Joan M. Alexandre-Bakiriddin, Treasurer

Keeling Campaign 2013
3614 Johnson Avenue,
Charles K. LaSister, Treasurer

Kellner Campaign 2013
135 East 61st Street, 4C, New York, NY 10065
917-558-3198
Cory A. Evans, Treasurer

Ken 2013
54 West 76th Street, 4R, New York, NY 10023
703-593-0608
Andrew W. Kalish, Treasurer

Kesselly For Council
353 Beach 57th Street, 2F, Arverne, NY 11692
718-233-2590
Hanif Russell, Treasurer

Khari Edwards 2013
463 Lincoln Place, Box 121, Brooklyn, NY 11238
347-915-6362
Tyieast S. Lloyd, Treasurer

Kings County Conservative Party Campaign Committee
486 78th Street, Brooklyn, NY 11209
718-921-2158
Gerard Kassar, Chairman

Lancman 2013
76-21 172nd Street, Hillcrest, NY 11366
917-363-9004
Stephanie Goldstone, Treasurer

Landis For New York
400 Central Park West, 6B, New York, NY 10025
917-338-6415
Audrey J. Isaacs, Treasurer

Lantigua 2013
230 West 103rd Street, 6G, New York, NY 10025
914-384-5062
Julio C. Negron, Treasurer

Laurie Cumbo 2013
2146 Canarsie Road, Brooklyn, NY 11236
917-518-6610
Shante L. Cozier, Treasurer

Lee New York Political Action Committee
1413 K Street, NW, 3rd Floor, Washington, DC 20005
202-552-2400
Mike Buman, Chairman

Lesbian & Gay Democratic Club of Queens
PO Box 857, Jackson Heights, NY 11372
Bruce I. Friedman, Chairman

Letitia James 2013
371 Utica Avenue, Brooklyn, NY 11213
347-470-8813
Latrice M. Walker, Treasurer

Levin 2013
576 Morgan Avenue, 3L, Brooklyn, NY 11222
908-380-7626
William J. Harris, Treasurer

Levine 2013
900 West 190th Street, 4K, New York, NY 10040
646-382-8992
Janet A. McDowell, Treasurer

Liutenants Benevolent Association NY Police Department PAC
233 Broadway, Suite 850, New York, NY 10279
646-610-8682
Dennis Gannon, Chairman

Lisa G For NY
45 Grymes Hill Road, Staten Island, NY 10301
718-448-1600
Michael J. Kuharski, Treasurer

Local 1182 Political Action Fund
108-18 Queens Boulevard, 7th Floor, Forest Hills, NY 11375
718-793-7755
James S. Huntley, Chairman

Local 1407 AFSCME Political Committee
125 Barclay Street, New York, NY 10007
212-815-1933
Maf M. Uddin, Chairman

Local 147 Political Action Committee
4332 Katonah Avenue, Bronx, NY 10470
718-994-6664
Christopher Fitzsimmons, Chairman

Offices and agencies generally appear in alphabetical order, except when specific order is requested by listee.

Local 1500 Political Candidates and Education Fund
425 Merrick Avenue, Westbury, NY 11590
516-214-1300
Bruce W. Both, Chairman

Local 1814 ILA AFL-CIO Political Action and Education Fund
70 20th Street, Brooklyn, NY 11232
718-499-9600
Raul Vasquez Jr., Chairman

Local 2021 AFSCME Political Action Account
125 Barclay Street, 7th, New York, NY 10007
212-815-1977
Leonard Allen, Chairman

Local 23-25 Unite State & Local Campaign Committee
33 West 14th Street, New York, NY 10011
212-929-2600
Edgar Romney, Chairman

Local 30 IUOE PAC
16-16 Whitestone Expressway, Whitestone, NY 11357
718-847-8484
Michael Spillane, Treasurer

Local 32BJ SEIU NY/NJ American Dream Fund
101 Avenue of the Americas, New York, NY 10013
212-388-2171
Hector J. Figueroa, Chairman

Local 372 Political Action
125 Barclay Street, New York, NY 10007
212-815-1960
Veronica Montgomery-Costa, Chairwoman

Local 4 Action Fund
2917 Glennwood Road, Brooklyn, NY 11210
718-252-8777
Lewis Resnick, Chairman

Local 6 Committee on Political Education
709 8th Avenue, New York, NY 10036
212-957-8000
Peter Ward, Chairman

Local 891 IUOE Political Education Committee
63 Flushing Avenue, Building 292, Suite 401, Brooklyn, NY 11205
718-455-9731
Margaret McMahon, Chairwoman

Local 891 IUOE State Engineers Political Education Committee
63 Flushing Avenue, Building 292, Suite 401, Brooklyn, NY 11205
718-455-9731
Margaret McMahon, Chairwoman

Local 94-94A-94B IUOE Political Action Committee
331-337 West 44th Street, New York, NY 10036
212-245-7040
Kuba Brown, Chairman

Lotovsky For City Council 2013
1318 Gravesend Neck Road, Brooklyn, NY 11229
718-554-1741
Alina G. Krasovskaya, Treasurer

Lundgren For Council
290 West 234th Street, Bronx, NY 10463
718-510-4926
John H. Reynolds, Treasurer

Lynn Sanchez For City Council
1505 Walton Avenue, 3J, Bronx, NY 10452
646-696-4056
Ronnette Summers, Treasurer

Mailman For Council
037 East 44th Street, 1403, New York, NY 10017
718-598-0609
Jessica A. Mailman, Treasurer

Maisel For Council
1757 Coleman Street, Brooklyn, NY 11234
Reeves Eisen, Treasurer

Mancuso For Council
41 Challenger Drive, Staten Island, NY 10312
718-701-3416
Nick Popolo, Treasurer

Margaret Chin 2013
3 Hanover Square, 7H, New York, NY 10004
917-582-1845
Yee S. Shau, Treasurer

Mark Gjonaj 2012
970 Morris Park Avenue, Bronx, NY 10462
917-731-6850
Mark Gjonaj, Chairman

Mark Otto For City Council
474 West 150 Street, 3D, New York, NY 10031
856-981-3656
Cavol Forbes, Treasurer

Mark Treyger For Council
2733 Mill Avenue, Brooklyn, NY 11234
917-434-5684
Elina Gofman, Treasurer

Mark Weprin For New York PAC
5 Peter Cooper Road, ME c/o E.A.S., New York, NY 10010
212-475-7389
Mark Weprin, Chairman

Markowitz/Brooklyn
15 Waldorf Court, Brooklyn, NY 11230
718-434-8430
Marty Markowitz, Chairman

Marthone For City Council
179-18 135th Avenue, Jamaica Avenue, NY 11434
917-504-4687
Joseph R. Marthone, Treasurer

Mason Tenders District Council of Greater New York Political Action Committee
266 West 37th Street, 7th Floor, New York, NY 10018
212-452-9552
Robert Bonanza, Chairman

Mateo 2013
2817 Fulton Street, Brooklyn, NY 11207
Crystal J. Flores, Treasurer

Matteo For Council
256 Wardwell Avenue, Staten Island, NY 10314
917-975-5541
Angela M. Thornton, Treasurer

Maximus Inc. Political Action Committee
1891 Metro Center Drive, Reston, VA 20190
703-251-8500
David Casey, Chairman

Offices and agencies generally appear in alphabetical order, except when specific order is requested by listee.

Political Parties Lobbyists & PACs

McDonald 2013
52 Main Street, c/o Parker, Bedford Hills, NY 10507
914-242-2090
Craig R. Parker, Treasurer

McKenna Long & Aldridge LLP NY PAC
303 Peachtree Street, Suite 5300, Atlanta, GA 30308
404-527-8527
Eric Tanenblatt, Chairman

Mel 2013
10 West 87th Street, 3B, New York, NY 10024
Ken Coughlin, Treasurer

Melinda Katz 2013
220 East 23rd Street, Suite 809, New York, NY 10010
212-231-9753
Jennie Berger, Treasurer

Meloni NYCC
21-17 23rd Avenue, Astoria, NY 11105
718-626-9514
Angela A. Meloni, Treasurer

Mercedes For Council
105-18 Avenue L, Brooklyn, NY 11236
347-731-5091
Lystra Moore-Besson, Treasurer

METLIFE, Inc. Employees' Political Participation Fund A
1095 Avenue of the Americas, New York, NY 10036
212-578-4133
Heather Wingate, Chairwoman

METRET PAC Inc.
51 East 42nd Street, 17th Floor, New York, NY 10017
212-682-8383
Thomas R. Zapf, Chairman

Metropolitan Funeral Directors PAC
322 8th Avenue, New York, NY 10001
800-763-8332
Peter DeLuca, Treasurer

Michael 2013
666 East 233 Street, 1C, Bronx, NY 10466
718-231-8003
Michael Welch, Treasurer

Middle Village Republican Club
64-82 83rd Street, Middle Village, NY 11379
718-326-8616
Rosemarie Toomey, Treasurer

Mike Duvalle 4 City Council
127-16 Liberty Avenue, Richmond Hill, NY 11419
718-323-1100
Michael Duvalle, Treasurer

Minerva For City Council
1755 York Avenue, 17D, New York, NY 10128
917-657-8184
Brian T. Carney, Treasurer

Molinari Republican Club
1010 Forest Avenue, Staten Island, NY 10310
718-442-0900
Robert J. Scamardella, Treasurer

Moore 2013
PO Box 927, Bronx, NY 10451
347-989-2013
Lynette A. Taylor, Treasurer

Morris & McVeigh NYS PAC
19 Dove Street, Albany, NY 12210
518-426-8111
Richard Miller, Jr., Treasurer

Moustafa For NYC
34-23 Steinway Street, Astoria, NY 11101
718-679-7959
Foseph E. Botros, Treasurer

MPAC
137 Fifth Avenue, 3rd Floor, New York, NY 10010
212-681-1380
Heather Swift, Treasurer

N.S.A. Inc. Action Fund
30-50 Whitestone Expressway, Suite 301, Whitestone, NY 11354
718-747-2860
Nelson Eusebio, Chairman

Nachman Caller Community First
4309 13th Avenue, Brooklyn, NY 11219
718-513-2055
Pesach Osina, Treasurer

Nadler For Congress
PO Box 40, Village Station, NY 10014
212-352-0370
Jerrold L. Nadler, Chairman

NARAL/NY Multcandidate Political Action Committee
470 Park Avenue South, 7th Floor South, New York, NY 10016
212-343-0114
Lorna Brett Howard, Chairwoman

National Grid Voluntary New York State Political Action Committee
40 Sylvan Road, Waltham, MA 02451
781-907-1764
Marcy L. Reed, Chairwoman

Ndigo For City Council
PO Box 820, New York, NY 10027
212-726-2063
Lylburn K. Downing, Treasurer

Neighborhood Preservation Political Action Fund
123 William Street, 14th Floor, New York, NY 10038
212-214-9266
Sandra K. Paul, Treasurer

Neighbors For Kenneth Rice
1345 East 4th Street, 6F, Brooklyn, NY 11230
516-817-0716
Eileen Flaherty, Treasurer

Neil Grimaldi For New York City Mayor
2860 Buhre Avenue, New York, NY 10461
646-229-7974
John Tamburri, Chairman

New Visions Democratic Club
PO Box 55, Jackson Heights, NY 11372
Yonel Letellier, Chairman

New York Bankers Political Action Committee
99 Park Avenue, 4th Floor, New York, NY 10016
212-297-1635
James J. Landy, Chairman

Offices and agencies generally appear in alphabetical order, except when specific order is requested by listee.

New York Building Congress State PAC
44 West 28th Street, 12th Floor, New York, NY 10038
212-481-1911
Richard T. Anderson, Treasurer

New York Check P.A.C., Inc.
286 Madison Avenue, Suite 907, New York, NY 10017
212-268-1911
Henry F. Shyne, Treasurer

New York City Central Labor Council Political Committee
275 7th Avenue, 18th Floor, New York, NY 10001
212-604-9552
Jinella Hinds, Treasurer

New York City Justice Political Action Committee
132 Nassau Street, Room 200, New York, NY 10038
212-349-5890
Jeffrey A. Lichtman, Treasurer

New York City Partnership State PAC
One Battery Park Plaza, 5th Floor, New York, NY 10004
212-493-7400
Barry M. Gosin, Chairman

New York County Dental Society Political Action Committee
6 East 43rd Street, New York, NY 10017
212-573-8500
Elliot Davis, Chairman

New York Hotel & Motel Trades Council Committee
707 Eighth Avenue, New York, NY 10036
212-245-8100
Christopher K. Cusack, Chairman

New York Professional Nurses Union Political Action Committee
1104 Lexington Avenue, New York, NY 10075
212-988-5565
Maureen McCarthy, Chairwoman

New York State AFL-CIO COPE
100 South Swan Street, Albany, NY 12210
518-436-8516
Mario Cilento, Chairman

New York State Association of PBA's PAC
23 Reynolds Road, Glen Cove, NY 11542
Thomas Willidigg, Chairman

New York State Council of Machinists PAC Fund
652 4th Avenue, Brooklyn, NY 11232
718-422-0090
James Conigliaro, Chairman

New York State Higher Education - PAC
3210 Avenue H, 6C, Brooklyn, NY 11210
646-331-4612
Robert Ramos, Chairman

New York State Laborers' Political Action Committee
18 Corporate Woods Boulevard, Albany, NY 12211
518-449-1715
George S. Truicko, Chairman

New York State Nurses Association Political Action Committee
11 Cornell Road, Latham, NY 12110
518-782-9400
Linda O'Brien, Chairwoman

New Yorkers For Affordable Housing
15 Verbena Avenue, Suite 100, Floral Park, NY 11001
516-277-9317
Sol Arker, Treasurer

New Yorkers For De Blasio
65 Broadway, 803, New York, NY 10006
917-558-1390
Mark Peters, Treasurer

New Yorkers For Katz
219-12 74th Avenue, Bayside, NY 11364
718-465-7839
Melinda R. Katz, Chairwoman

New Yorkers For Putting Students First
345 7th Avenue, Suite 501, New York, NY 10001
212-257-4411
Enoch Woodhouse, Treasurer

New Yorkers For Robert Jackson
499 Fort Washington Avenue, 3A, New York, NY 10033
917-733-0439
Nan Beer, Treasurer

Nikki Lucas 2013
566 Essex Street, 2nd Floor, Brooklyn, NY 11208
347-457-8556
Aysha J. Gourdine, Treasurer

Nixon Peabody LLP PAC
1300 Clinton Square, Rochester, NY 14604
585-263-1000
Stephen J. Wallace, Chairman

Noah E. Gotbaum 2013
330 West 87th Street, New York, NY 10024
212-799-7291
Jeffrey D. Ravetz, Treasurer

NY CCR Nonpartisan PAC For Good Government
1 Coca-Cola Plaza NW, Atlanta, GA 30313
404-676-2121
William Hawkins, Chairman

NY Region 9A UAW PAC Council
111 South Road, Farmington, CT 06032
860-674-0143
Julie Kushner, Chairwoman

NYC District Council of Carpenters PAC
395 Hudson Street, 9th Floor, New York, NY 10014
212-366-3388
Stephen C. McInnis, Treasurer

NYC Greenfield
1011 East 3rd Street, Brooklyn, NY 11230
347-985-1135
Jeffrey Leb, Treasurer

NYS Democratic Senate Campaign Committee
1275 Scotch Church Road, Pattersonville, NY 12137
Jeffrey Klein, Chairman

NYSAFAH PAC
450 7th Avenue, Suite 2401, New York, NY 10123
646-473-1207
Frank J. Anelante, Jr., Treasurer

NYSRPA-PVF
90 South Swan Street, Suite 395, Albany, NY 12210
518-272-2654
Thomas H. King, Chairman

Oddo For Staten Island
131 Old Town Road, Staten Island, NY 10304
917-533-8241
Marie Carmody-LaFrancesca, Treasurer

Olanike Alabi 2013
PO Box 380075, Brooklyn, NY 10304
718-398-0750
Sharon J. Pierre, Treasurer

Organization of Staff Analysts PAC
220 East 23 Street, Suite 707, New York, NY 10010
212-686-1229
Robert J. Croghan, Chairman

Otano 2013
367 South 5th Street, 2B, Brooklyn, NY 11211
917-566-7542
Emily E. Gallagher, Treasurer

PAC L375 CSTG
125 Barclay Street, New York, NY 10013
212-815-1375
Claude Fort, Chairman

PAC of the Patrolmen's Benevolent Association of NYC
125 Broad Street, 11th Floor, New York, NY 10004
212-233-5531
Joseph A. Alejandro, Chairman

Palma 2013
1510 UnionPort Road, 11F, Bronx, NY 10462
347-733-5145
Ricky Pizarro, Treasurer

Pamela Johnson For NYC Council
3856 Bronx Boulevard, 7H, Bronx, NY 10467
347-762-8683
Geneva Johnson, Treasurer

Paul Graziano 2013
146-24 32nd Avenue, Flushing, NY 11354
718-358-2535
Stephen Garza, Treasurer

People For Albert Baldeo
106-11 Liberty Avenue, Ozone Park, NY 11417
718-323-8260
Mandrawattie Singh, Treasurer

People For Bing
132 East 43rd Street, New York, NY 10022
646-228-9111
Jonathan L. Bing, Chairman

People For Brodsky
2121 Saw Mill River Road, White Plains, NY 10607
914-720-5206
Richard L. Brodsky, Chairman

People For Carlton Berkley
4555 Carpenter Avenue, PH, New York, NY 10470
917-468-8461
Alexander Williams, Treasurer

People For Cheryl
585 West 214 Street, 4C, New York, NY 10034
646-314-3079
Cheryl A. Pahaham, Treasurer

People For Debra Cooper
290 West End Avenue, 9A, New York, NY 10024
212-362-7788
Darrell L. Paster, Treasurer

People For Diaz
840 Grand Concourse, 1A, Bronx, NY 10451
718-731-2009
Kalman Yeger, Treasurer

People For Jelani
83 Lefferts Place, Brooklyn, NY 11238
718-753-3302
Kuzaliwa Campbell, Treasurer

People For Jerome Rice
1505 Metropolitan Avenue, MG, Bronx, NY 10462
347-631-4489
Dawn Jeffrey, Treasurer

People For John C. Whitehead
903 Drew Street, 410, Brooklyn, NY 11208
718-216-2169
Leslie A. Murray, Treasurer

People For Lappin
333 East 55th Street, New York, NY 10022
718-541-3278
Andrew W. Wuertele, Treasurer

People For Leroy Gadsen
87-60 113th, 3C, Richmond Hills, NY 11418
917-297-7824
Candace Prince, Treasurer

People For Miguel Estrella
3716 10th Avenue, 13L, New York, NY 10034
347-664-7147
Aria Vargas, Treasurer

People For Pu-Folkes
78-27 37th Avenue, Suite 4, Jackson Heights, NY 11372
718-595-2045
Bryan R. Pu-Folkes, Chairman

People For Ydanis
475 Atlantic Avenue, 3rd Floor, Brooklyn, NY 11217
917-582-1405
Roberto A. Cruz, Treasurer

People For Yudelka Tapia
1941 Mulliner Avenue, Bronx, NY 10462
917-685-7810
Juan Mora, Treasurer

Peralta 2013
635 Hicksville Road, Far Rockaway, NY 11691
917-723-2097
Monique Renaud, Treasurer

Peralta For Senate
635 Hicksville Road, Far Rockaway, NY 11691
718-471-2475
Jose Peralta, Chairman

Peterson 2013
25-10 30th Road, Astoria, NY 11102
David Haywood, Treasurer

Pfizer Inc. PAC
235 East 42nd Street, New York, NY 10017
212-573-1265
Sally Susman, Chairman

Plumbers & Steamfitters Local No. 73 State & Local PAC Fund
705 East Seneca Street, PO Box 911, Oswego, NY 13126
315-343-4037
Patrick Carroll, Treasurer

Offices and agencies generally appear in alphabetical order, except when specific order is requested by listee.

Plumbers Local Union No. 1 NYC - Political Action Committee
158-29 George Meany Boulevard, Howard Beach, NY 11414
718-738-7500
John J. Murphy, Treasurer

Port Authority PBA of NY PAC
611 Palisade Avenue, Englewood Cliffs, NJ 07632
201-871-2100
Paul Nunziato, Chairman

Port Authority Police DEA NY PAC
Po Box 300406, JFK Station, Jamaica, NY 11430
201-216-6549
Patrick McNerney, Chairman

Powell 2013
134-35 166th Place, 4B, Jamaica, NY 11434
Dawn P. Martin, Treasurer

PSC PAC
61 Broadway, 15th Floor, New York, NY 10006
212-354-1252
Steven London, Chairman

Queens County Republican Committee
24-55 Francis Lewis Boulevard, Whitestone, NY 11357
718-690-3737
Phil Ragusa, Chairman

Quinn For New York
30 Vesey Street, 1st Floor, New York, NY 10007
917-438-7063
Kenneth T. Monteiro, Treasurer

Ralina Cardona 2013
286 Alexander Avenue, Bronx, NY 10454
Wilfred Renta, Treasurer

Rangel For Congress NY State
193 Lenox Avenue, Suite 1, New York, NY 10023
212-862-4990
James E. Capel, Chairman

Raquel Batista 2013
2104 Clinton Avenue, 2, Bronx, NY 10457
Katiuska M. Lopez, Treasurer

Re-Elect Eric Ulrich
101-17 84th Street, Ozone Park, NY 11416
917-951-7251
Ronald Kulick, Treasurer

Re-Elect Koslowitz 2013
6940 108th Street, c/o R. Croce, 3A, Forest Hills, NY 11375
718-268-3626
Ronnie Croce, Treasurer

Re-Elect Mealy
800 Hancock Street, 2A, Brooklyn, NY 11233
Marjorie Parker, Treasurer

Recchia For New York
172 Gravesend Neck Road, Brooklyn, NY 11223
718-336-3441
Marianna Wilen, Treasurer

Regina Powell 2013
675 Lincoln Avenue, 16F, Brooklyn, NY 11208
917-285-4894
Barrington Rodney, Treasurer

Reginald Boddie For Supreme Court
387 Halsey Street, Brooklyn, NY 11233
917-660-1487
Reginald A. Boddie, Chairman

Rego Hills Republican Club
85-32 65th Road, c/o Dolores Maddis, Rego Park, NY 11374
718-275-6005
Thomas Hoar, Chairman

Republican Majority For Choice NF PAC
2417 Jericho Turnpike, Suite 303, Garden City Park, NY 11040
516-316-6982
Kellie R. Ferguson, Chairman

Rescare Inc. Advocacy Fund
9901 Linn Station Road, Louisville, KY 40223
502-394-2335
Roger LaPoint, Chairman

Reshma For New York
240 West 23rd Street, 3C, New York, NY 10011
646-386-6398
Sumana Setty, Treasurer

Retail Wholesale and Department Store Union C.O.P.E.
30 East 29th Street, New York, NY 10016
212-684-5300
Stuart Appelbaum, Chairman

Rhonda F. Joseph 2013
910 Lenox Road, Brooklyn, NY 11203
917-751-7516
Basil A. Davidson, Treasurer

Rivera 2013
601 Pelham Parkway North, 501, Bronx, NY 10467
347-601-1551
Joel Rivera, Treasurer

Rivera 2013
1936 Haviland Avenue, Bronx, NY 10472
646-533-5228
Kenneth J. Thomas, Treasurer

Rosenthal For Assembly
321 West 89th Street, 6, New York, NY 10024
646-337-7700
Linda B. Rosenthal, Chairwoman

Rosie Mendez 2013
52 East 1st Street, c/o Kaplan, 2A, New York, NY 10003
646-229-6127
Lisa M. Kaplan, Treasurer

RPAC of New York
130 Washington Avenue, Albany, NY 12210
518-463-0300
Harding Mason, Chairman

RSA PAC City Account
123 Williams Street, 14th Floor, New York, NY 10038
212-214-9266
Frank P. Ricci, Treasurer

Ruben Wills 2013
194-19 115 Drive, St. Albans, NY 11412
516-663-0630
Sharon Carnegie-Hall, Treasurer

Offices and agencies generally appear in alphabetical order, except when specific order is requested by listee.

RWDSU Local 338 Political Action Committee
1505 Kellum Place, Mineola, NY 11501
516-294-1338
John R. Durso, Chairman

Sal 2013
957 78th Street, Brooklyn, NY 11228
917-992-1693
John H. O'Donnell, Treasurer

Sanders For Senate
1526 Central Avenue, 3rd Floor, Far Rockaway, NY 11691
718-471-7111
Donovan J. Richards, Treasurer

Sanitation Officers Association Volunteer Political Action COPE Account
8510 Bay 16th Street, 2nd Floor, Brooklyn, NY 11214
718-837-9832
Joseph Mannion, Chairman

Santiago NYC 2013
50 Manhattan Avenue, 4H, Brooklyn, NY 11206
Juan C. Pocasangre, Treasurer

Santos 2013
420 East 21st Street, Brooklyn, NY 11226
307-340-1074
Luke L. Frye, Treasurer

Sarah M. Gonzalez 2013
512 83rd Street, Brooklyn, NY 11209
307-340-1074
Sonia Rodriguez, Treasurer

Sasson For NYC
43-70 Kissena Boulevard, 14H, Flushing, NY 11355
718-461-9338
Amul Mehta, Treasurer

Saundra Thomas 2013
490 Stratford Road, Brooklyn, NY 11218
718-282-5595
Gary M. Singer, Treasurer

Savino For New York
481 8th Avenue, Suite 1202, New York, NY 10001
212-239-7323
Diane J. Savino, Chairwoman

SEIU Political Education and State Action Fund
1800 Massachusetts Avenue, N.W., Washington, DC 20036
202-730-7000
Mary Kay Henry, Chairwoman

Semper Fi NYS PAC Inc.
17 Christopher Street, New York, NY 10014
212-269-7308
Christopher Johnson, Chairman

Sergeants Benevolent Association
35 Worth Street, New York, NY 10013
212-226-2180
Robert Ganley, Chairman

Service Corporation International Political Association Committee
1929 Allen Parkway, Houston, TX 77019
713-525-9062
Caressa F. Hughes, Chairwoman

Sidique Wai For Public Advocate
770 Empire Boulevard, 2N, Brooklyn, NY 11213
201-526-1422
Fritzner L. Altidor, Treasurer

Sierra 2013
1581 Fulton Avenue, 1B, Bronx, NY 10457
201-526-1422
Jonathan Vizcaino, Treasurer

Silverstein 2013
211-40 18th Avenue, 3K, Bayside, NY 11360
718-644-0791
Gary Jacobowitz, Treasurer

Simcha NY
475 Atlantic Avenue, 3rd Floor, Brooklyn, NY 11217
718-852-3710
Simcha Felder, Chairman

Simmons-Oliver For City Council
4120 Hutchinson River Parkway East, 15A, Bronx, NY 10475
917-596-7251
Rafael Paulino, Treasurer

SMWIA Local 28 Political Action Committee
500 Greenwich Street, New York, NY 10013
212-941-7700
Frederick Buckheit, Treasurer

SMWIA Political Action League Local 137
21-42 44th Drive, Long Island City, NY 11101
718-937-4514
Paul Collins, Jr., Chairman

Soft Drink and Brewery Workers Political Action Committee
445 Northern Boulevard, Great Neck, NY 11021
516-303-1455
John O'Neill, Chairman

Sondra Peeden 2013
40 Memorial Highway, 33F, New Rochelle, NY 10801
914-355-4197
Katrina De La Cruz, Treasurer

South Asians United For a Better America PAC
333 East 30th Street, 2D, New York, NY 10016
571-228-6925
Prince Agarwal, Chairman

Squadron For New York
219 West 81st Street, 8D, New York, NY 10024
212-228-5222
Anne S. Squadron, Treasurer

SSL Political Action Committee
180 Maiden Lane, 34th Floor, New York, NY 10038
212-806-5851
Leonard S. Boxer, Chairman

Staten Island PAC
32 Cunard Place, Staten Island, NY 10304
718-816-2237
James P. Molinaro, Chairman

Steamfitters Local 638 PAC
32-32 48th Avenue, Long Island City, NY 11101
718-392-3420
John J. Torpey, Chairman

Stringer 2013
40 Worth Street, Suite 812, New York, NY 10013
212-349-2013
Peter Frank, Treasurer

STV Engineers Inc. Political Action Committee
205 West Welsh Drive, Douglassville, PA 19518
610-385-8294
Dominick M. Servedio, Chairman

Suffolk County Association of Municipal Employees, Inc - Political Action Committee
30 Orville Drive, Suite A, Bohemia, NY 11716
631-589-8400
Cheryl A. Felice, Chairwoman

Sullivan For NYC
138 71st Street, 9F, Brooklyn, NY 11209
516-522-4033
Maureen J. Daly, Treasurer

Sunny Hahn For City Council
137-60 45th Avenue, 4N, Flushing, NY 11355
718-888-9420
Stuart Garmise, Treasurer

Tamika For City Council 2013
342 East 119th Street, 5B, New York, NY 10035
516-782-9339
Monisha R. Mapp, Treasurer

Taxpayers For an Affordable New York Political Action Committee
570 Lexington Avenue, 2nd Floor, New York, NY 10022
212-616-5224
Steven Spinola, Chairman

Team Greenfield
1011 East 3rd Street, Brooklyn, NY 11230
347-985-1135
Jeffrey Leb, Treasurer

Teamsters Local 813 PAC
45-18 Court Square, Suite 600, Long Island City, NY 11101
718-937-7010
Anthony Marino, Chairman

Tempo 802
322 West 48th Street, New York, NY 10036
John O'Connor, Chairman

The Committee to Re-Elect Inez E. Dickens 2013
2153 Adam Calyton Powell Jr. Boulevard, New York, NY 10027
212-749-3615
Delores Richards, Treasurer

The Debi Rose Campaign Committee
1300 Richmond Avenue, 23A, Staten Island, NY 10314
646-675-7617
Emanuel Braxton, Treasurer

The General Contractors Association of New York PAC
60 East 42nd Street, New York, NY 10165
212-687-3131
Denise M. Richardson, Chairwoman

The High-Need Hospital PAC, Inc.
12 Stuyvesant Oval, 9A, New York, NY 10009
212-674-6122
Mark Pollack, Chairman

The N.Y. Public Library Guild, Local 1930
125 Barclay Street, Room 701PAC, New York, NJ 10007
212-815-1930
Valentin Colon, Chairman

The NYS Economic Growth PAC
60 Columbus Circle, New York, NY 10023
212-801-1162
Eugene Angelo, Treasurer

Theatrical Teamsters Local 817 PAC Fund
127 Cutter Mill Road, Great Neck, NY 11021
516-365-3470
Thomas I. O'Donnell, Chairman

Thomas Lopez-Pierre For City Council 2013
927 Columbus Avenue, 5S, New York, NY 10025
646-363-9047
Thomas Lopez-Pierre, Treasurer

Tile, Marble & Terrazzo BAC Union Local 7 PAC Fund
45-34 Court Square, Long Island City, NY 11101
718-786-7648
Thomas W. Lane, Chairman

Toll Bros., Inc. PAC
250 Gibraltar Road, Horsham, PA 19044
215-938-8000
Zvi Barzilay, Chairman

Tom Allon 2013
17 east 17th Street, 4th Floor, New York, NY 10003
347-960-2399
Charles Platkin, Treasurer

Tom Duane For Senate
80 8th Avenue, #1802, New York, NY 10011
646-265-7082
Thomas K. Duane, Chairman

Tony Avella For Queens
PO Box 570052, Whitestone, NY 11357
718-762-0235
Rocco F. D'Erasmo, Treasurer

Torodash For Truth
12325 82nd Avenue, 5T, Kew Gardens, NY 11415
646-318-1426
Meredith Helfenbein, Treasurer

TPU Local One IATSE NYC
20 West 46th Street, New York, NY 10036
212-333-2500
James J. Claffey, Jr., Chairman

Transport Workers Union Local 100
195 Montague Street, 3rd Floor, Brooklyn, NY 11201
212-873-6000
John Samuelsen, Chairman

Ullico Inc. Political Action Committee
1625 Eye Street, NW, Washington, DC 20006
Edward M. Smith, Chairman

Uniformed Fire Officers 527 Account
225 Broadway, Suite 401, New York, NY 10007
212-293-9300
Alexander Hagan, Chairman

Uniformed Firefighters Association State FIREPAC
204 East 23rd Street, New York, NY 10010
212-683-4832
James Slevin, Chairman

Offices and agencies generally appear in alphabetical order, except when specific order is requested by listee.

Unite Here Local 2 PAC
209 Golden Gate Avenue, San Francisco, CA 94102
415-864-8770
Michael Casey, Treasurer

Unite Here Local 26 Political Committee
33 Harrison Avenue, 4th Floor, Boston, MA 02111
617-426-1515
Brian Lang, Chairman

Unite Here Local 5 PAC Fund
1516 South King Street, Honolulu, HI 96826
808-941-2141
Godfrey T. Maeshiro, Chairman

Unite Here Local 54 PAC Committee
203-205 North Sovereign Avenue, Atlantic City, NJ 08401
609-344-5400
Charles R. McDevitt, Chairman

Unite Here Tip State and Local Fund
275 Seventh Avenue, 11th Floor, New York, NY 10001
212-265-7000
Donald Taylor, Chairman

United Federation of Teachers (UFT) on Political Education
52 Broadway, New York, NY 10004
212-598-7744
Paul Egan, Chairman

United Food & Commercial Workers Active Ballot Club
1775 K Street, NW, Washington, DC 20006
202-223-3111
Joseph T. Hansen, Chairman

United Neighbors for Neville Mitchell
888 East 233rd Street, Bronx, NY 10469
347-224-9880
Derrick L. Shippy, Treasurer

United Parcel Service Inc. Political Action Committee - New York
55 Glenlake Parkway, NE, Atlanta, GA 30328
404-828-6012
Teri P. McClure, Chairwoman

UWUA Local 1-2 Non Federal PAC
5 West 37th Street, New York, NY 10018
212-575-4400
Lucia Pagano, Treasurer

Vallone For New York
22-45 31st Street, Suite 6, Astoria, NY 11105
718-274-0007
Albana Haxhia, Treasurer

Van Bramer 2013
39-19 46th Street, Sunnyside, NY 11104
718-786-1324
Phillip L. Velez, Treasurer

Vargas 2013
105 West 104th Street, 3A, New York, NY 10025
646-330-5411
Ruben Vargas, Sr., Treasurer

Veras For Council 2013
141-60 84th Road, 5C, Briarwood, NY 11435
917-589-1459
Zlata Akilova, Treasurer

Verizon Communications Good Government Club PAC
140 West Street, Floor 30, New York, NY 10007
212-321-8110
James J. Gerace, Chairman

Victor Babb For N.Y.C. Council
106-03 Liberty Avenue, Ozone Park, NY 11417
917-324-8071
Henderson Kinch, Treasurer

Vince Morgan 2013
130 Lenox Avenue, 1003, New York, NY 10026
347-602-0908
RD Snyden, Treasurer

Vish Mahadeo 2010
130-10 109th Avenue, South Ozone Park, NY 11420
646-918-0334
Videsh A. Persaud, Treasurer

Vito Lopez For City Council
1704 Decatur Street, Ridgewood, NY 11385
347-744-8632
Andy J. Marte, Treasurer

Viverito 2013
211 East 111th Street, 2, New York, NY 10029
212-426-7552
Randolph Mark, Treasurer

Vote Vallone 2013
25-59 Francis Lewis Boulevard, Flushing, NY 11358
718-428-7285
Vito Tautonico, Treasurer

VoteBhusan2013
2793 Brighton 8th Street, Brooklyn, NY 11235
646-295-0629
Leonard H. Sturner, Treasurer

Weiner For Mayor
254 Park Avenue South, 12A, New York, NY 10010
212-777-7755
Nelson Braff, Treasurer

Wilson Elser Moskowitz Edelman & Dicker LLP, PAC
677 Broadway, Albany, NY 12207
518-449-8893
Cynthia D. Shenker, Chairwoman

Win With Winslow
162-10 South Road, Jamaica, NY 11433
347-423-4233
Shannell T. Harper, Treasurer

WM NY PAC
701 Pennsylvania Avenue, NW, Suite 590, Washington, DC 20004
202-639-1221
Barry Caldwell, Chairman

Women's Democratic Club of NYC
100 West 12th Street, 4M, New York, NY 10113
646-657-8040
Patricia S. Rudden, Chairwoman

Wright 2013
297 Hancock Street, Brooklyn, NY 11216
718-399-3807
Kimberly B. Berry, Treasurer

Zead Ramadan 2013
5900 Arlington Avenue, 22V, Bronx, NY 10471
212-882-1520
Rasul H. Miller, Treasurer

ZETEPAC
PO Box 75021, Washington, DC 20013
202-210-5431
Dan Backer, Chairman

Section 5:
BUSINESS

CHAMBERS OF COMMERCE and ECONOMIC & INDUSTRIAL DEVELOPMENT ORGANIZATIONS

Provides a combined listing of public and private organizations involved in regional economic development.

Adirondack Economic Development Corporation
67 Main St, Ste 300, PO Box 747, Saranac Lake, NY 12983-0747
518-891-5523 or 888-243-2332 Fax: 518-891-9820
e-mail: nwright@aedconline.com
Web site: www.aedconline.com

Adirondack Regional Chambers of Commerce
136 Glen Street, Ste 3, Glens Falls, NY 12801
518-798-1761 Fax: 518-792-4147
e-mail: paust@adirondackchamber.org
Web site: www.adirondackchamber.org
Peter Aust, President & CEO

Adirondacks Speculator Region Chamber of Commerce
PO Box 184, Rts 30 & 8, Speculator, NY 12164
518-548-4521 Fax: 518-548-4905
e-mail: info@speculatorchamber.com
Web site: www.speculatorchamber.com
Cathleen Connolly, President

African American Chamber of Commerce of Westchester & Rockland Counties
100 Stevens Ave, Ste 202, Mount Vernon, NY 10550
914-699-9050 Fax: 914-699-6279
e-mail: robinlisadouglas@cs.com
Web site: www.aaccnys.org
Robin L Douglas, Founder & CEO & President

Albany County Industrial Development Agency
112 State St, Room 825, Albany, NY 12207-2017
518-447-7040 Fax: 518-447-5589
e-mail: county_executive@albanycounty.com
Web site: www.albanycounty.com
Daniel McCoy, County Executive

Albany-Colonie Regional Chamber of Commerce
5 Computer Drive South, Albany, NY 12205-1631
518-431-1400 Fax: 518-431-1402
e-mail: info@acchamber.org
Web site: www.acchamber.org
Mark Egan, CEO

Alden Chamber of Commerce
13500 Broadway, PO Box 149, Alden, NY 14004
716-937-6177 Fax: 716-937-4106
e-mail: secretary@aldenny.org
Web site: www.aldenny.org
Christopher Gust, President

Alexandria Bay Chamber of Commerce
7 Market St, Alexandria Bay, NY 13607
315-482-9531 or 800-541-2110 Fax: 315-482-5434
e-mail: info@alexbay.org
Web site: www.visitalexbay.org
Susan Boyer, Executive Director

Allegany County Office of Development & Industrial Development Agency (IDA)
Crossroads Commerce Center, 6087 NYS Rte 19 North, Suite 100, Belmont, NY 14813
585-268-5500 or 800-836-1869 Fax: 585-268-7473
e-mail: tourism@alleganyco.com
Web site: www.discoveralleganycounty.com
John E Foels, Director of Development & IDA

American Indonesian Chamber of Commerce
317 Madison Ave, Suite 1619, New York, NY 10017
212-687-4505
Web site: www.aiccusa.org
Wayne Forrest, President

Amherst Chamber of Commerce
Centerpointe Corporate Park, 350 Essjay Road, Suite 200, Williamsville, NY 14221
716-632-6905 Fax: 716-632-0548
e-mail: cdipirro@amherst.org
Web site: www.amherst.org
Colleen C DiPirro, CEO & President

Amherst Industrial Development Agency (Town of)
4287 Main Street, Amherst, NY 14226
716-688-9000 Fax: 716-688-0205
e-mail: jallen@amherstida.com
Web site: www.amherstida.com
James Allen, Executive Director

Amsterdam Industrial Development Agency
City Hall, 61 Church St, Amsterdam, NY 12010
518-841-4305 Fax: 518-841-4300
e-mail: fvaliante@amsterdamida.com
Web site: www.amsterdamida.com
Frank Valiante, Executive Director

Arcade Area Chamber of Commerce
684 W. Main St., Arcade, NY 14009
585-492-2114 Fax: 585-492-5103
e-mail: aacc278@verizon.net
Web site: www.arcadechamber.org
Dorie Clinch, Executive Secretary

Babylon Industrial Development Agency
47 West Main St, Ste 3, Babylon, NY 11702
631-587-3679 Fax: 631-587-3675
e-mail: info@babylonida.org
Web site: www.babylonida.org
Robert Stricoff, CEO

Bainbridge Chamber of Commerce
PO Box 2, Bainbridge, NY 13733
607-967-8700
e-mail: bainbridge.chamber@yahoo.com
Web site: www.bainbridgeny.org
Barb Mulkins, President

Baldwin Chamber of Commerce
PO Box 804, Baldwin, NY 11510
516-223-8080
e-mail: info@baldwinchamber.com
Web site: baldwinchamber.com
Eric Mahlar, Co-President; Ralph Rose, Co-President

Baldwinsville Chamber of Commerce (Greater Baldwinsville)
27 Marble Street, Baldwinsville, NY 13027
315-638-0550 Fax: 315-720-1450
e-mail: baldwinsvillechamger@gmail.com
Web site: www.baldwinsvillechamber.com
Anthony Saraceni, President

Bath Area Chamber of Commerce (Greater Bath Area)
10 Pulteney Square W, Bath, NY 14810
607-776-7122 Fax: 607-776-7122
e-mail: email@bathnychamber.com
Web site: www.americantowns.com
Jim Maglione, Co-President
Ed Panian, Co-President

Chambers of Commerce

Offices and agencies generally appear in alphabetical order, except when specific order is requested by listee.

Bayshore Chamber of Commerce
77 East Main St, PO Box 5110, Bayshore, NY 11706
631-665-7003 Fax: 631-665-5204
e-mail: bayshorecofcbid@optonline.net
Web site: www.bayshorecommerce.com
Donna Periconi, President

Bellmores Chamber of Commerce
2700 Pettit Avenue, N Bellmore, NY 11710
516-679-1875 Fax: 516-409-0544
e-mail: info@bellmorechamber.com
Web site: www.bellmorechamber.com
Debbie Izzo, President

Bethlehem Chamber of Commerce
184 Greenwood Avenue, Delmar, NY 12054
518-439-0512 Fax: 518-475-0910
e-mail: info@bethlehemchamber.com
Web site: www.bethlehemchamber.com
Lorraine Schrameck, Co-President
Lisa Whitmore, Co-President

Bethlehem Industrial Development Agency (Town of)
445 Delaware Ave, Delmar, NY 12054
518-439-4955 Fax: 518-439-5808
e-mail: mmorelli@townofbethlehem.org
Web site: www.bethlehemida.com
Michael Morellia, Executive Director & CEO

Bethpage Chamber of Commerce
PO Box 636, Bethpage, NY 11714
516-433-0010
Dennis Brady, President/CEO

Binghamton Chamber of Commerce (Greater Binghamton)
49 Court Street, PO Box 995, Binghamton, NY 13902
607-772-8860 Fax: 607-722-4513
e-mail: chamber@greaterbinghamtonchamber.com
Web site: www.greaterbinghamtonchamber.com
Lou Santoni, President & CEO

Black Lake Chamber of Commerce
PO Box 12, Hammond, NY 13646
315-375-8640
e-mail: info@blacklake.com
Web site: www.blacklakeny.com
William Dashnshaw, President
Carole McCann, President

Blue Mountain Lake Association
PO Box 724, Indian Lake, NY 12842
518-642-5112 Fax: 518-648-5489
Web site: indian-lake.com
Christine Pouch, President

Bolton Landing Chamber of Commerce
4928 Lake Shore Drive, Bolton Landing, NY 12814-0368
518-644-3831 Fax: 518-644-5951
e-mail: mail@boltonchamber.com
Web site: www.boltonchamber.com
Dave Forshay, President

Boonville Area Chamber of Commerce
122 Main St, PO Box 163, Boonville, NY 13309
315-942-5112 Fax: 315-942-6823
e-mail: info@boonvillechamber.com
Web site: www.boonvillechamber.com
Melinda Wittwer, Executive Secretary

Brewster Chamber of Commerce
16 Mount Ebo Road S, Ste 12A, Brewster, NY 10509
845-279-2477 Fax: 845-278-8349
e-mail: info@brewsterchamber.com
Web site: www.brewsterchamber.com
Rose Z. Aglieco, Executive Director

Brockport Chamber of Commerce (Greater Brockport)
PO Box 119, Brockport, NY 14420
585-234-1512
Web site: brockportchamber.org
Marie Bell, President

Bronx Chamber of Commerce
Hutchinson Metro Center, 1200 Waters Place, Suite 106, Bronx, NY 10461
718-828-3900 Fax: 718-409-3748
e-mail: info@bronxchamber.org
Web site: www.bronxchamber.org
Lenny Caro, President

Bronxville Chamber of Commerce
81 Pondfield Rd, Suite 7, Bronxville, NY 10708
914-337-6040 Fax: 914-337-6040
e-mail: bronxvillechamber@verizon.net
Web site: www.bronxvillechamber.com
Susan Miele, Executive Director

Town of Brookhaven Industrial Development Agency
1 Independence Hill, Farmingville, NY 11738
631-451-6563 Fax: 631-451-6925
e-mail: lmulligan@brookhaven.org
Web site: www.brookhavenida.org
Lisa Mulligan, CEO

Brooklyn Chamber of Commerce
25 Elm Place, Suite 200, 2nd Floor, Brooklyn, NY 11201
718-875-1000 Fax: 718-222-0781
e-mail: info@brooklynchamber.com
Web site: www.ibrooklyn.com
Veronica Harris, Director/HR/Administration/Operations

Brooklyn Economic Development Corporation
2001 Oriental Blvd, Brooklyn, NY 11235
718-368-6790 Fax: 718-368-6788

Broome County Industrial Development Agency
60 Hawley Street, 5th Floor, Binghamton, NY 13901
607-584-9000 Fax: 607-584-9009
e-mail: info@theagency-ny.com
Web site: www.theagency-ny.com
Kevin McLaughlin, Executive Director

Buffalo Economic Renaissance Corporation
Office of Strategic Planning, City of Buffalo, 920 City Hall, Buffalo, NY 14202-3309
716-851-5035 Fax: 716-842-6942
e-mail: contact@berc.org
Web site: www.berc.org
Timothy E Wanamaker, Interim President

Buffalo Niagara Partnership
665 Main Street, Suite 200, Buffalo, NY 14203-1487
716-852-7100 Fax: 716-852-2761
e-mail: arudnick@thepartnership.org
Web site: www.thepartnership.org
Andrew J Rudnick, President & CEO

Business Council of Westchester, The
108 Corporate Park Drive, Suite 101, White Plains, NY 10604
914-948-2110 Fax: 914-948-0122
Web site: www.westchesterny.org
Dr Marsha Gordon, President/CEO

Canandaigua Area Chamber of Commerce
113 S Main St, Canandaigua, NY 14424
585-394-4400 Fax: 585-394-4546
e-mail: chamber@canandaiguachamber.com
Web site: www.canandaiguachamber.com
Alison Grems, President & CEO

Canastota Chamber of Commerce
222 S Peterboro St, PO Box 206, Canastota, NY 13032
315-697-3677
Web site: www.canastota.org
Rick Stevens, President

Canton Chamber of Commerce
PO Box 369, 60 Main Street, Canton, NY 13617
315-386-8255 Fax: 315-386-8255
e-mail: cantoncc@northnet.org
Web site: www.cantonnychamber.org
Sally Hill, Executive Director

Cape Vincent Chamber of Commerce
PO Box 482, 173 N James Street, Cape Vincent, NY 13618
315-654-2481 Fax: 315-654-4141
e-mail: thecape@tds.net
Web site: www.capevincent.org
501C (6) organization supported by over 200 mebers including businesses, organizations, and individuals.
Shelley Higgins, Executive Director

Capitalize Albany Corporation
21 Lodge St, Albany, NY 12207
518-434-2532 Fax: 518-434-9846
e-mail: info@capitalizealbany.com
Web site: www.capitalizealbany.com
Michael Yevoli, CEO

Carthage Area Chamber of Commerce
120 S. Mechanic Street, Carthage, NY 13619
315-493-3590 Fax: 315-493-3590
e-mail: carthagechamber@centralny.twcbc.com
Web site: www.carthageny.com
Lori Borland, Executive Director

Cattaraugus Empire Zone Corporation
120 N Union St, Olean, NY 14760
716-373-9260 Fax: 716-372-7912
e-mail: meme@oleanny.com
Web site: www.cattempirezone.org
James Snyder, President

Cayuga County Chamber of Commerce
2 State Street, Auburn, NY 13021
315-252-7291 Fax: 315-255-3077
e-mail: admin@cayugacountychamber.com
Web site: www.cayugacountychamber.com
Andrew Fish, Executive Director

Cazenovia Area Chamber of Commerce (Greater Cazenovia Area)
59 Albany St, Cazenovia, NY 13035
315-655-9243 or 888-218-6305 Fax: 315-655-9244
e-mail: info@cazenovia.com
Web site: www.cazenoviachamber.com
Gene Gissin, Chairman

Central Adirondack Association
PO Box 68, Old Forge, NY 13420
315-369-6983 or 877-653-3674 Fax: 315-369-2676
e-mail: lbarkauskas@visitmyadirondacks.com
Web site: www.visitmyadirondacks.com
Laurie Barkauskas, Events Coordinator

Central Catskills Chamber of Commerce
PO Box 605, Margaretville, NY 12455
845-586-3300 Fax: 845-586-3161
e-mail: chamber@centralcatskills.com
Web site: www.centralcatskills.com
John Tufillaro, President

Chamber of Commerce of the Tonawandas
15 Webster Street, North Tonawanda, NY 14120
716-692-5120 Fax: 716-692-1867
e-mail: chamber@the-tonawandas.com
Web site: www.thetonawandas.com
Joyce M Santiago, Executive Director

Chaumont-Three Mile Bay Chamber of Commerce
PO Box 24, Three Mile Bay, NY 13693
315-694-3404
e-mail: chaumontchamber@yahoo.com
Web site: www.chaumontchamber.com
Amanda Miller, President

Chautauqua County Chamber of Commerce
512 Falconer St, Jamestown, NY 14701
716-484-1101 Fax: 716-487-0785
e-mail: cccc@chautauquachamber.org
Web site: www.chautauquachamber.org
Todd Tranum, President/CEO

Chautauqua County Chamber of Commerce, Dunkirk Branch
10785 Bennett Road, Dunkirk, NY 14048
716-366-6200 Fax: 761-366-4276
e-mail: cccc@chautauquachamber.org
Web site: www.chautauquachamber.org

Chautauqua County Industrial Development Agency
200 Harrison St, Jamestown, NY 14701
716-661-8900 Fax: 716-664-4515
e-mail: ccida@ccida.com
Web site: www.ccida.com
William Daly, CEO

Cheektowaga Chamber of Commerce
AppleTree Business Park, 2875 Union Road, Ste 50, Cheektowaga, NY 14227
716-684-5838 Fax: 716-684-5571
e-mail: chamber@cheektowaga.org
Web site: www.cheektowaga.org
Debra S Liegl, President & CEO

Chemung County Chamber of Commerce
400 E Church St, Elmira, NY 14901-2803
607-734-5137 Fax: 607-734-4490
e-mail: info@chemungchamber.org
Web site: www.chemungchamber.org
Kevin D Keeley, President & CEO

Chemung County Industrial Development Agency
400 Church Street, Elmira, NY 14901
607-733-6513 Fax: 607-734-2698
e-mail: gminer@steg.com
Web site: www.steg.com
George Miner, President

Chenango County Chamber of Commerce
15 South Broad Street, Norwich, NY 13815
607-334-1400 or 877-243-6264 Fax: 607-336-6963
e-mail: info@chenangony.org
Web site: www.chenangony.org
Steve Craig, President/CEO

Chambers of Commerce

Offices and agencies generally appear in alphabetical order, except when specific order is requested by listee.

Clarence Chamber of Commerce
8899 Main Street, Suite 4, Clarence, NY 14031
716-631-3888 Fax: 716-631-3946
e-mail: info@clarence.org
Web site: www.clarencechamber.org
Judy Sirianni, President

Clarence Industrial Development Agency (Town of)
1 Town Place, Clarence, NY 14031
716-741-8930 Fax: 716-741-4715
Web site: www.clarence.ny.us
David Hartzell, Chairman

Clayton Chamber of Commerce
517 Riverside Dr, Clayton, NY 13624
315-686-3771 or 800-252-9806 Fax: 315-686-5564
e-mail: info@1000islands-clayton.com
Web site: www.1000islands-clayton.com
Tricia Bannister, Executive Director

Clifton Springs Area Chamber of Commerce
2 E Main St, PO Box 86, Clifton Springs, NY 14432
315-462-8200 Fax: 315-548-6429
e-mail: info@cliftonspringschamber.com
Web site: www.cliftonspringschamber.com
Jeff Criblear, President

Clinton Chamber of Commerce Inc
PO Box 142, Clinton, NY 13323
315-853-1735 Fax: 315-853-1735
e-mail: info@clintonnychamber.org
Web site: www.clintonnychamber.org
Ferris J Betrus, Executive Vice President

Clinton County, The Development Corporation
190 Banker Rd, Suite 500, Plattsburgh, NY 12901
518-563-3100 or 888-699-6757 Fax: 518-562-2232
e-mail: tdc@thedevelopcorp.com
Web site: www.thedevelopcorp.com
Paul Grasso, President/CEO

Clyde Chamber of Commerce
24 Park Street, PO Box 69, Clyde, NY 14433
315-923-4862 Fax: 315-923-9862
e-mail: info@clydeontheerie.com
Web site: www.co.wayne.ny.us
Rudolph A DeLisio, President

Clyde Industrial Development Corporation
PO Box 92, Clyde, NY 14433
315-923-7238 Fax: 315-923-9863
e-mail: info@clydeontheerie.com
Web site: www.clydeontheerie.com
Kenneth DiSanto, President

Cohoes Industrial Development Agency (City of)
97 Mohawk Street, Cohoes, NY 12047
518-233-2117 Fax: 518-233-2168
e-mail: mayor@ci.cohoes.ny.us
Web site: www.cohoesida.org
Adam Hotaling, Chairman

Colonie Chamber of Commerce
950 New Loudon Rd, Latham, NY 12110
518-785-6995 Fax: 518-785-7173
e-mail: info@coloniechamber.org
Web site: www.coloniechamber.org
Tom Nolte, President

Columbia County Chamber of Commerce
1 North Front Street, Hudson, NY 12534
518-828-4417 Fax: 518-822-9539
e-mail: mail@columbiachamber-ny.com
Web site: www.columbiachamber-ny.com
David B Colby, President

Columbia Hudson Partnership
4303 Rte 9, Hudson, NY 12534-2415
518-828-4718 Fax: 518-828-0901
e-mail: kenneth.flood@columbiacountyny.com
Web site: www.chpartnership.com
Kenneth J Flood, Executive Director

Coney Island Chamber of Commerce
1015 Surf Ave, Brooklyn, NY 11224
718-266-1234 Fax: 718-714-0379
Norman Kaufman, President

Cooperstown Chamber of Commerce
31 Chestnut St, Cooperstown, NY 13326
607-547-9983 Fax: 607-547-6006
e-mail: info1@cooperstownchamber.org
Web site: www.cooperstownchamber.org
Susan O'Handley, Executive Director

Copiague Chamber of Commerce
PO Box 8, Copiague, NY 11726
631-226-2956
e-mail: info@copiaguechamber.org
Web site: copiaguechamber.org
Sharon Fattoruso, Board President

Corinth Industrial Development Agency (Town of)
600 Palmer Ave, Corinth, NY 12822
518-654-9232 Fax: 518-654-7615
e-mail: rlucia@townofcorinthny.com
Web site: www.townofcorinthny.com
Richard B Lucia, Chairman

Corning Area Chamber of Commerce
1 West Market Street, Suite 202, Corning, NY 14830
607-936-4686 or 866-463-6264 Fax: 607-936-4685
e-mail: info@corningny.com
Web site: www.corningny.com
Denise Ackley, President

Cortland County Chamber of Commerce
37 Church St, Cortland, NY 13045
607-756-2814 Fax: 607-756-4698
e-mail: info@cortlareachamber.com
Web site: www.cortlandareachamber.com
Bob Haight, Executive Director
Bradley Totman, President
Debbie Thayer, Manager of Member Services

Coxsackie Area Chamber of Commerce
PO Box 251, Coxsackie, NY 12051
518-731-7300
e-mail: info@coxsackieregionalchamber.com
Web site: www.coxsackieareachamber.com
Bradley Totman, President

Cutchogue-New Suffolk Chamber of Commerce
PO Box 610, Cutchogue, NY 11935
631-734-2335 Fax: 631-734-5050
Richard Noncarrow, President

Offices and agencies generally appear in alphabetical order, except when specific order is requested by listee.

Dansville Chamber of Commerce
126 Main St, PO Box 105, Dansville, NY 14437
585-335-6290 or 800-949-0174 Fax: 585-335-6296
e-mail: dansvillechamber@hotmail.com
Web site: www.dansvilleny.net
William Bacon, President

Delaware County Chamber of Commerce
5 1/2 Main Street, Delhi, NY 13753
607-746-2281 Fax: 607-746-3571
e-mail: info@delawarecounty.org
Web site: www.delawarecounty.org
Mary Beth Silano, Executive Director

Delaware County Planning Department
PO Box 367, Delhi, NY 13753
607-746-2944 Fax: 607-746-8479
e-mail: pln@co.delaware.ny.us
Web site: www.delawarecountyplanning.com
Nicole Franzese, Director of Planning

Deposit Chamber of Commerce
PO Box 222, Deposit, NY 13754
Web site: www.depositchamber.com
Nick Barone, President

Development Authority of the North Country
317 Washington Street, Watertown, NY 13601
315-661-3200 or 800-662-1220 Fax: 315-785-2591
e-mail: info@danc.org
Web site: www.danc.org
James Wright, Executive Director

Dover-Wingdale Chamber of Commerce
PO Box 643, Dover Plains, NY 12522
845-877-9800
Melanie Ryder, President

Downtown-Lower Manhattan Association
120 Broadway, Rm 3340, New York, NY 10271
212-566-6700 Fax: 212-566-6707
e-mail: contactus@downtownny.com
Web site: downtownny.com
Elizabeth Berger, President

Dutchess County Economic Development Corporation
3 Neptune Rd, Poughkeepsie, NY 12601
845-463-5400 or 845-463-5407 Fax: 845-463-5401
e-mail: pbalga@dcedc.com
Web site: http://thinkdutchess.com
Pamela J Balga, Administrative Services Manager

East Aurora Chamber of Commerce (Greater East Aurora)
652 Main Street, East Aurora, NY 14052-1783
716-652-8444 Fax: 716-652-8384
e-mail: eanycc@verizon.net
Web site: www.eanycc.com
Gary D Grote, Executive Director

East Hampton Chamber of Commerce
42 Gingerbread Lane, East Hampton, NY 11937
631-324-0362 Fax: 631-329-1642
e-mail: info@easthamptonchamber.com
Web site: www.easthamptonchamber.com
Marina Van, Executive Director

East Islip Chamber of Commerce
PO Box 88, East Islip, NY 11730
631-859-5000
Web site: www.isliplife.com/eastislipchamber
Tony Fanni, President

East Meadow Chamber of Commerce
PO Box 77, East Meadow, NY 11554
516-794-3727 Fax: 516-794-3729
Web site: www.eastmeadowchamber.com
Dolloras Rome, President

East Northport Chamber of Commerce
24 Larkfield Road, East Northport, NY 11731
631-261-3573 Fax: 631-261-9885
e-mail: enptcc@aol.com
Web site: www.eastnorthport.com
Brian Valeri, President
Jill Bergman, Vice President

Eastchester-Tuckahoe Chamber of Commerce
65 Main Street, Suite 202, Tuckahoe, NY 10707
914-779-7344
e-mail: cetcoc@aol.com
Web site: www.eastchestertuckahoechamberofcommerce.com
Mariam Janusz, Executive Director

Ellenville/Wawarsing Chamber of Commerce
PO Box 227, 124 Canal St, Ellenville, NY 12428
845-647-4620
e-mail: info@ewcoc.com
Web site: ewcoc.com
Dr. Mark Craft, President

Ellicottville Chamber of Commerce
9 W Washington St, PO Box 456, Ellicottville, NY 14731
716-699-5046 or 800-349-9099 Fax: 716-699-5636
e-mail: info@ellicottvilleny.com
Web site: www.ellicottvilleny.com
Heather Snyder, Administrative Assistant

Erie County Industrial Development Agency
143 Genesee Street, Buffalo, NY 14203
716-858-8500 Fax: 716-858-6679
e-mail: info@ecidany.com
Web site: www.ecidany.com
Mark Poloncarz, County Executive

Erie County Planning & Economic Development
95 Franklin St, 10th Floor, Buffalo, NY 14202
716-858-6170 Fax: 716-858-7248
Web site: www.erie.gov
Kathy Konst, Commissioner

Erwin Industrial Development Agency (Town of)
Three Rivers Dev Corp Inc, 114 Pine St Suite 201, Corning, NY 14830
607-962-4693 Fax: 607-936-9132
e-mail: info@3riverscorp.com
Web site: www.threeriversdevelopment.com
Jack Benjamin, President

Essex County Industrial Development Agency
7566 Court Street, PO Box 217, Elizabethtown, NY 12932
518-873-9114 Fax: 518-873-2011
e-mail: info@essexcountyida.com
Web site: www.essexcountyida.com
Carol Calabrese; Jody Olcott, Co-Executive Directors

Evans-Brant Chamber of Commerce
70 North Main Street, Angola, NY 14006
716-549-3221 Fax: 716-549-3475
e-mail: chamber@ebccny.org
Web site: www.ebccny.org
Michelle Parker, President

Fair Haven Area Chamber of Commerce
PO Box 13, Fair Haven, NY 13064
315-947-6037
e-mail: fairhaveninfo@fairhavenny.com
Web site: www.fairhavenny.com
Dan Larson, President

Farmington Chamber of Commerce
1000 County Rd, #8, Farmington, NY 14425
585-398-2861 Fax: 315-986-4377
Web site: www.farmingtoncofc.com
Cal Cobb, President

Farmingville/Holtsville Chamber of Commerce
PO Box 66, Holtsville, NY 11742
631-926-8259
James V Marciante, President

Fayetteville Chamber of Commerce
PO Box 712, Fayetteville, NY 13066
315-637-5544
e-mail: fayettevillechamber@twcny.rr.com
Web site: www.fayettevillechamber.org

Findley Lake Area Chamber of Commerce
PO Box 211, Findley Lake, NY 14736
716-769-7609 or 888-769-7609 Fax: 716-769-7609
e-mail: chamber@findleylakeinfo.org
Web site: www.findleylakeinfo.org

Fort Brewerton/Greater Oneida Lake Chamber
PO Box 655, Brewerton, NY 13029
315-668-3408 Fax: 315-668-3408
e-mail: info@oneidalakechamber.com
Web site: www.oneidalakechamber.com
Don Deval, President

Fort Edward Chamber of Commerce
PO Box 267, Fort Edward, NY 12828
518-747-3000 Fax: 518-747-0622
Web site: www.fortedwardchamber.com
Larry Moffitt, President

Franklin County Industrial Development Agency
10 Elm Street, Suite 2, Malone, NY 12953
518-483-9472 Fax: 518-483-2900
e-mail: jtubbs@franklinida.org
Web site: www.franklinida.org
John Tubbs, CEO

Franklin Square Chamber of Commerce
PO Box 11, Franklin Square, NY 11010
516-775-0001 Fax: 516-292-0930
Web site: www.fschamberofcommerce.com
Joseph Ardito, President

Fredonia Chamber of Commerce
5 East Main St, Fredonia, NY 14063
716-679-1565 Fax: 716-672-5240
e-mail: fredcham@netsync.net
Web site: www.fredoniachamber.org
Mary Beth Fagan, Executive Director

French-American Chamber of Commerce
1350 Broadway, Suite 2101, New York, NY 10018
212-867-0123 Fax: 212-867-9050
e-mail: info@faccnyc.org
Web site: www.faccnyc.org
Martin Biscoff, Director

Fulton County Economic Development Corporation
55 East Main Street, Suite 110, Johnstown, NY 12095
518-773-8700 Fax: 518-773-8701
e-mail: fccrg.org
Web site: www.sites4u.org
Mike Reese, President/CEO

Fulton County Industrial Development Agency
One East Montgomery St, Johnstown, NY 12095
518-736-5660 Fax: 518-762-4597
Web site: ida.fultoncountyny.gov
James Mraz, Director

Fulton County Reg Chamber of Commerce & Ind
2 N Main St, Gloversville, NY 12078
518-725-0641 or 800-676-3858 Fax: 518-725-0643
e-mail: info@fultoncountyny.org
Web site: fultoncountyny.org
Mark Kilmer, President

Garden City Chamber of Commerce
230 Seventh Street, Garden City, NY 11530
516-746-7724 Fax: 516-746-7725
e-mail: gcchamber@verizon.net
Web site: www.gardencitychamber.org
Althea Robinson, Executive Director

Genesee County Chamber of Commerce
210 E Main St, Batavia, NY 14020
585-343-7440 Fax: 585-343-7487
e-mail: chamber@geneseeny.com
Web site: www.geneseeny.com
Lynn Freeman, President

Genesee County Economic Development Center
99 MedTech Drive, Suite 106, Batavia, NY 14020
585-343-4866 or 877-343-4866 Fax: 585-343-0848
e-mail: gcedc@gcedc.com
Web site: www.gcedc.com
Steven G Hyde, CEO

Geneva Area Chamber of Commerce
41 Lake Street, PO Box 587, Geneva, NY 14456
315-789-1776 or 877-543-6382 Fax: 315-789-3993
e-mail: info@genevany.com
Web site: www.genevany.com
Elizabeth Winter, President/CEO

Geneva Industrial Development Agency (City of)
47 Castle St, Geneva, NY 14456
315-828-6550 Fax: 315-789-0604
e-mail: vbassett@geneva.ny.us
Web site: www.geneva.ny.us
Valerie Bassett, Executive Director

Glen Cove Chamber of Commerce
19 Village Square, 2nd Floor, Glen Cove, NY 11542
516-676-6666 Fax: 516-676-5490
e-mail: info@glencovechamber.org
Web site: www.glencovechamber.org
Phyllis Gorham, Executive Director

Gore Mountain Region Chamber of Commerce
228 Main Street, PO Box 84, North Creek, NY 12853
518-251-2612 Fax: 518-251-5317
e-mail: info@gorechamber.com
Web site: www.gorechamber.com
Ed Milner, President

Goshen Chamber of Commerce
223 Main Street, PO Box 506, Goshen, NY 10924
845-294-7741 Fax: 845-294-7746
e-mail: info@goshennychamber.com
Web site: www.goshennychamber.com
Lynn A Cione, Executive Director

Gouverneur Chamber of Commerce
214 East Main St, Gouverneur, NY 13642
315-287-0331 Fax: 315-287-3694
e-mail: info@governcurchamber.net
Web site: www.gouverneurchamber.net
Donna Lawrence, Executive Director

Gowanda Area Chamber of Commerce
49 W Main Street, PO Box 45, Gowanda, NY 14070
716-532-2834 Fax: 716-532-2834
e-mail: gowandachamber@yahoo.com
Web site: gowandachamber.com
Mary Pankow, President

Grand Island Chamber of Commerce
2257 Grand Island Blvd, Grand Island, NY 14072
716-773-3651 Fax: 716-773-3316
e-mail: info@gichamber.org
Web site: www.gichamber.org
Eric Fiebelkorn, President

Granville Chamber of Commerce
One Main St, PO Box 13, Granville, NY 12832
518-642-2815 Fax: 518-642-2772
e-mail: info@granvillechamber.com
Web site: www.granvillechamber.com
Charles King, President

Great Neck Chamber of Commerce
Kiosk Information Center, 1 Middle Neck Road, PO Box 220432, Great Neck, NY 11022
516-487-2000 Fax: 516-829-5472
e-mail: greatneckinfo@gmail.com
Web site: www.greatneckchamber.org
Hooshang Nematzadeh, President

Greater Cicero Chamber of Commerce
5701 East Circle Drive, #302, Cicero, NY 13039
315-699-1358
e-mail: info@cicerochamber.com
Web site: www.cicerochamber.com
John Annable, President

Greater Jamaica Development Corporation
90-04 161st Street, Jamaica, NY 11432
718-291-0282 Fax: 718-658-1405
Web site: www.gjdc.org
Carlisle Towery, President

The Greater Mahopac-Carmel Chamber of Commerce
953 South Lake Blvd, PO Box 160, Mahopac, NY 10541-0160
845-628-5553 Fax: 845-628-5962
e-mail: info@mahopaccarmelchamber.com
Web site: www.mahopaccarmelonline.com
Laurie Lee Ford, Chairwoman

The Greater Manlius Chamber of Commerce
425 E Genesee Street, Fayetteville, NY 13066
315-637-4760 Fax: 315-637-4762
e-mail: greatermanlius@windstream.net
Web site: www.manliuschamber.com
Kim Kutzer, President

Greater Massena Chamber of Commerce
16 Church Street, Massena, NY 13662
315-769-3525 Fax: 315-769-5295
e-mail: info@massenachamber.com
Web site: www.massenachamber.com
Nathan Lashomb, Executive Director

Greater Mexico Chamber of Commerce
3236 Main Street, Mexico, NY 13114
315-963-1042
e-mail: secretary@mexico-cofc.org
Web site: www.mexicocofc.net
Adam Judware, President

Greater New York Chamber of Commerce
20 W 44th Street, 4th Floor, New York, NY 10036
212-686-1772 Fax: 212-686-7232
e-mail: info@ny-chamber.com
Web site: www.ny-chamber.com
Mark Jaffe, President & CEO

Greater Oneida Chamber of Commerce
136 Lenox Ave, Oneida, NY 13421
315-363-4300 Fax: 315-361-4558
e-mail: oneidachamber@cnymail.com
Web site: www.oneidachamberny.org
Rebecca Halstrom-O'Bierne, President
Tari Timmer, Executive Assistant

Greater Ossining Chamber of Commerce, The
2 Church Street, Suite 205, Ossining, NY 10562
914-941-0009 or 914-941-0812
e-mail: info@ossiningchamber.org
Web site: www.ossiningchamber.org
Kay Hawley, Administrator

Greater Port Jefferson Chamber of Commerce
118 W Broadway, Port Jefferson, NY 11777-1314
631-473-1414 Fax: 631-474-4540
e-mail: info@portjeffchamber.com
Web site: www.portjeffchamber.com
Suzanne Velazquez, President

Greece Chamber of Commerce
2402 West Ridge Rd, Suite 201, Rochester, NY 14626-3053
585-227-7272 Fax: 585-227-7275
e-mail: info@greecechamber.org
Web site: www.greecechamber.org
Jodie Perry, President

Green Island Industrial Development Agency (Village of)
20 Clinton St, Green Island, NY 12183
518-273-2201 Fax: 518-273-2235
Web site: www.villageofgreenisland.com
Local government, Industrial Development Agency
Kristen Swinton, Chief Executive Officer

Greene County Department of Planning & Economic Development
411 Main Street, Catskill, NY 12414
518-719-3290 Fax: 518-719-3789
e-mail: business@discovergreene.com
Web site: www.greenebusiness.com
Warren Hart, AICP Director

Greene County Tourism Promotion
700 Rte 23B, Leeds, NY 12451
518-943-3223 or 800-355-CATS Fax: 518-943-2296
e-mail: tourism@discovergreene.com
Web site: www.greenetourism.com
Warren Hart, Director

Offices and agencies generally appear in alphabetical order, except when specific order is requested by listee.

Greenport-Southold Chamber of Commerce
PO Box 1415, Southold, NY 11971
631-765-3161
e-mail: info@northforkchamber.org
Web site: www.greenportsoutholdchamber.org
Andy Binkowski, President

Greenvale Chamber of Commerce
PO Box 123, Greenvale, NY 11548
516-621-6545
Web site: www.greenvalechamber.com
Ken White, Board President

Greenwich Chamber of Commerce (Greater Greenwich)
6 Academy St, Greenwich, NY 12834
518-692-7979 Fax: 518-692-7979
e-mail: info@greenwichchamber.org
Web site: www.greenwichchamber.org
Kathy Nichols-Tomkins, Secretary

Greenwich Village-Chelsea Chamber of Commerce
129 West 27th Street, 6th Floor, New York, NY 10001
646-470-1773 Fax: 212-924-0714
e-mail: info@villagechamber.com
Web site: www.villagechelsea.com
Lauren Danziger, Executive Director

Greenwood Lake Chamber of Commerce
PO Box 36, Greenwood Lake, NY 10925
845-477-0112 Fax: 914-477-2798
Joyce Monti, Contact

Guilderland Chamber of Commerce
2050 Western Ave, Guilderland, NY 12084
518-456-6611 Fax: 518-456-6690
e-mail: kburbank@guilderlandchamber.com
Web site: www.guilderlandchamber.com
Kathy Burbank, Executive Director

Guilderland Industrial Development Agency (Town of)
Town Hall, PO Box 339, Guilderland, NY 12084
518-356-1980 Fax: 518-356-5514
Web site: www.townofguilderland.org
William N Young, Jr., Chairman

Hague on Lake George Chamber of Commerce
PO Box 615, Hague, NY 12836
518-543-6441 Fax: 518-585-9890
e-mail: haguechamberofcommerce@yahoo.com
Web site: www.visithague.com

Hamburg Chamber of Commerce
6122 S Park Ave, Hamburg, NY 14075
716-649-7917 or 877-322-6890 Fax: 716-649-6362
e-mail: mailhcc@hamburg-chamber.org
Web site: www.hamburg-chamber.org
Cindy Galley, Executive Director

Hamburg Industrial Development Agency
S6100 South Park Avenue, Hamburg, NY 14075
716-648-4145 Fax: 716-648-0151
Web site: www.hamburgida.com
Michael J Bartlett, Executive Director

Hammondsport Chamber of Commerce
47 Shethar Street, Hammondsport, NY 14840
607-569-2989
e-mail: info@hammondsport.org
Web site: www.hammondsport.org

Hampton Bays Chamber of Commerce
140 West Main St, Hampton Bays, NY 11946
631-728-2211
Web site: www.hamptonbayschamber.com
Stan Glinka, President

Hancock Area Chamber of Commerce
Box 525, Hancock, NY 13783-0525
607-637-4756 or 800-668-7624 Fax: 607-637-4756
e-mail: hancockchamber@hancock.net
Web site: www.hancockareachamber.com
Lori Ray, President

Harlem Chamber of Commerce (Greater Harlem)
200 A West 136th St, New York, NY 10030
212-862-7200 or 877-427-5364 Fax: 212-862-8745
e-mail: info@harlemdiscover.com
Web site: www.greaterharlemchamber.com
Lloyd Williams, President

Hastings-on-Hudson Chamber of Commerce
PO Box 405, Hastings-on-Hudson, NY 10706
914-478-0900 Fax: 914-478-1720
Web site: www.hohchamber.com
Joseph R LoCascio, Jr, President

Hempstead Industrial Development Agency (Town of)
350 Front St, Rm 234-A, Hempstead, NY 11550
516-489-5000 x4200 or 800-593-3870 Fax: 516-489-3179
e-mail: fparola@tohmail.org
Web site: www.tohida.org
Frederick Parola, Executive Director

Henderson Harbor Area Chamber of Commerce
PO Box 468, Henderson Harbor, NY 13651
315-938-5568 or 888-938-5568
e-mail: thechambertreasure@gmail.com
Web site: www.hendersonharborny.com

Herkimer County Chamber of Commerce
420 East German Street, Herkimer, NY 13350
315-866-7820 or 877-984-4636 Fax: 315-866-7833
e-mail: jscarano@herkimercountychamber.com
Web site: www.herkimercountychamber.com
John Scarano, Executive Director

Herkimer County Industrial Development Agency
320 N Prospect Street, PO Box 390, Herkimer, NY 13350
315-867-1373 Fax: 315-867-1515
e-mail: markfeane@herkimercounty.org
Web site: www.herkimercountyida.com
Mark Feane, Executive Director

Hicksville Chamber of Commerce
10 W Marie St, Hicksville, NY 11801
516-931-7170 Fax: 516-931-8546
Web site: www.hicksvillechamber.com
Lionel Chitty, President

Holbrook Chamber of Commerce, The
PO Box 565, Holbrook, NY 11741
631-471-2725 Fax: 631-343-4816
e-mail: info@holbrookchamber.com
Web site: www.4holbrook.com
Rick Ammirati, President

Offices and agencies generally appear in alphabetical order, except when specific order is requested by listee.

Hornell Area Chamber of Commerce/Hornell Industrial Development Agency (City of)
40 Main St, Hornell, NY 14843
607-324-0310 or 877-HORNELL Fax: 607-324-3776
e-mail: margie@hornellny.com
Web site: www.hornellny.com
James W Griffin, President & Executive Director

Hudson Valley Gateway Chamber of Commerce
One S Division St, Peekskill, NY 10566
914-737-3600 Fax: 914-737-0541
e-mail: info@hvgatewaychamber.com
Web site: www.hvgatewaychamber.com
Deborah Milone, Executive Director

Hunter Chamber of Commerce (Town of)
PO Box 177, Hunter, NY 12442
518-263-4900 Fax: 518-589-0117
e-mail: chamberinfo@hunterchamber.org
Web site: www.hunterchamber.org
Michael McCrary, President

Huntington Township Chamber of Commerce
164 Main St, Huntington, NY 11743
631-423-6100 Fax: 631-351-8276
e-mail: info@huntingtonchamber.com
Web site: www.huntingtonchamber.com
Ellen O' Brien, Executive Director

Hyde Park Chamber of Commerce
PO Box 17, Hyde Park, NY 12538
845-229-8612 Fax: 845-229-8638
e-mail: info@hydeparkchamber.org
Web site: www.hydeparkchamber.org
Dave Stewart, President

Indian Lake Chamber of Commerce
PO Box 724, Indian Lake, NY 12842
518-648-5112 or 800-328-5253 Fax: 518-648-5489
e-mail: info@indian-lake.com
Web site: www.indian-lake.com
Christine Pouch, President

Inlet Information Office
160 State Route 28 at Arrowhead Park, Inlet, NY 13360
315-357-5501 or 866-GOINLET Fax: 315-357-3570
e-mail: info@inletny.com
Web site: www.inletny.com
Adele Burnett, Director of Information & Tourism

Irvington-on-Hudson Chamber of Commerce
PO Box 161, Irvington, NY 10533
914-473-4819
e-mail: bettylaurenson@gmail.com
Web site: www.irvingtonnychamber.com
Eric Spino; Betty Laurenson, Presidents

Islip Chamber of Commerce
PO Box 112, Islip, NY 11751-0112
631-581-2720 Fax: 631-581-2720
e-mail: info@islipchamberofcommerce.com
Web site: www.islipchamberofcommerce.org
Jim Guariglia, President

Islip Economic Development Division & Industrial Development Agency (Town of)
40 Nassau Ave, Islip, NY 11751
631-224-5512 Fax: 631-224-5532
e-mail: ecodev@townofislip-ny.gov
Web site: www.islipida.com
Tom Croci, Supervisor

Islip Industrial Development Agency (Town of)
40 Nassau Ave, Islip, NY 11751
631-224-5512 Fax: 631-224-5532
e-mail: ecodev@townofislip-ny.gov
Web site: www.townofislip-ny.gov
Phil Nolan, Chairman

Jamaica Chamber of Commerce
157-11 Rockaway Boulevard, Jamaica, NY 11432
718-413-7182 Fax: 718-413-2325
Robert M Richards, President

Jeffersonville Area Chamber of Commerce, The
PO Box 463, Jeffersonville, NY 12748
845-482-3652
Web site: www.jeffersonvilleny.com

Japanese Chamber of Commerce
145 W 57th St, New York, NY 10019
212-246-8001 Fax: 212-246-8002
e-mail: info@jcciny.org
Web site: www.jcciny.org
Seiei Ono, President

Katonah Chamber of Commerce
PO Box 389, Katonah, NY 10536
914-232-2668
e-mail: info@katonahchamber.org
Web site: www.katonahchamber.org
Edris Scherer; Christopher Roberts, Presidents

Kenmore-Town of Tonawanda Chamber of Commerce
3411 Delaware Ave, Kenmore, NY 14217
716-874-1202 Fax: 716-874-3151
e-mail: info@ken-ton.org
Web site: www.ken-ton.org
Tracey M Lukasik, Executive Director

Kings Park Chamber of Commerce
3 Main St, PO Box 322, Kings Park, NY 11754
631-269-7678 Fax: 631-269-5575
e-mail: info@kingsparkli.com
Web site: www.kingsparkli.com
Dee Grasso, Executive Director

Lackawanna Area Chamber of Commerce
638 Ridge Rd, Lackawanna, NY 14218
716-823-8841 Fax: 716-823-8848
e-mail: info@lackawannachamber.com
Web site: www.lackawannachamber.com
Michael J Sobaszek, Executive Director

Lake George Regional Chamber of Commerce
PO Box 272, Lake George, NY 12845
518-668-5755 or 800-705-0059 Fax: 518-668-4286
e-mail: info@lakegeorgechamber.com
Web site: www.lakegeorgechamber.com
Janice Bartkowski-Fox, President

Lake Luzerne Chamber of Commerce
PO Box 222, Lake Luzerne, NY 12846-0222
518-696-3500 Fax: 518-696-6122
Web site: www.lakeluzernechamber.org
George Beagle, President

Lake Placid Chamber of Commerce
2608 Main Street, Lake Placid, NY 12946-1592
518-523-2445 or 800-447-5224 Fax: 518-523-2605
Web site: www.lakeplacid.com
James McKenna, CEO

Lancaster Area Chamber of Commerce
11 W Main Street, Suite 100, PO Box 284, Lancaster, NY 14086
716-681-9755 Fax: 716-684-3385
e-mail: info@laccny.org
Web site: www.laccny.org
Megan Burns-Moran, Executive Director

Lancaster Industrial Development Agency (Town of)
21 Central Avenue, Lancaster, NY 14086
716-683-1610 Fax: 716-683-0512
e-mail: lida@lancasterny.com
Web site: www.lancasterny.com
Dino J Fudoli, Chairman

Lewis County Chamber of Commerce
7576 South State Street, Lowville, NY 13367
315-376-2213 or 800-724-0242 Fax: 315-376-0326
e-mail: info@lewiscountychamber.org
Web site: www.lewiscountychamber.org
Anne Merrill, Executive Director

Lewis County Industrial Development Agency
7642 State St, PO Box 106, Lowville, NY 13367
315-376-3014
e-mail: lcida@lcida.org
Web site: www.lcida.org
Richard Porter, Executive Director

Lindenhurst Chamber of Commerce
101 Montauk Hwy, Lindenhurst, NY 11757
631-226-4641
Web site: lindenhurstchamber.org
Jo-Ann Boettcher, President

Liverpool Chamber of Commerce (Greater Liverpool)
314 Second St, Liverpool, NY 13088
315-457-3895 Fax: 315-234-3226
e-mail: chamber@liverpoolchamber.com
Web site: www.liverpoolchamber.com
Dennis Hebert, President

Livingston County Chamber of Commerce
4635 Millennium Dr, Geneseo, NY 14454-1134
585-243-2222 Fax: 585-243-4824
e-mail: llane@livingstoncountychamber.com
Web site: www.livingstoncountychamber.com
Laura Lane, President

Livingston County Economic Development Office & Industrial Development Agency
6 Court St, Room 306, Geneseo, NY 14454-1043
585-243-7124 Fax: 585-243-7126
e-mail: info@build-here.com
Web site: www.build-here.com
Julie Marshall, Executive Director

Lockport Industrial Development Agency (Town of)
6560 Dysinger Rd, Lockport, NY 14094
716-439-9535 Fax: 719-439-9715
e-mail: LES@elockport.com
Web site: www.lockporteconomicdevelopment.com
David Kinyon, Administrative Director

Locust Valley Chamber of Commerce
PO Box 178, Locust Valley, NY 11560
516-671-1310
Web site: www.locustvalleychamber.com
Len Margolis, President

Long Beach Chamber of Commerce
350 National Blvd, Long Beach, NY 11561-3312
516-432-6000 Fax: 516-432-0273
Web site: www.thelongbeachchamber.com
Michael J Kerr, President

Long Island Association
300 Broadhollow Road, Suite 110 W, Melville, NY 11747-4840
631-493-3000 Fax: 631-499-2194
e-mail: perlkamer@hotmail.com
Web site: www.liaonline.org
Pearl M Kamer, Chief Economist

Long Island Council of Dedicated Merchants Chamber of Commerce
PO Box 512, Miller Place, Long Island, NY 11764
631-821-1313
Web site: www.cdmlongisland.com
Dr Tom Ianniello, President

Long Island Development Corporation
400 Post Avenue, Suite 201A, Westbury, NY 11590
866-433-5432 Fax: 516-433-5046
e-mail: info@lidc.org
Web site: www.lidc.org
Roslyn D Goldmacher, President & CEO

Lynbrook Chamber of Commerce
PO Box 624, Lynbrook, NY 11563
516-599-5946
e-mail: info@lynbrookusa.com
Web site: www.lynbrookusa.com
Denise Rogers, President

Madison County Industrial Development Agency
3215 Seneca Turnpike, Canastota, NY 13032
315-697-9817 Fax: 315-697-8169
e-mail: direector@madisoncountyida.com
Web site: www.madisoncountyida.com
Kipp Hicks, Director

Malone Chamber of Commerce
497 East Main Street, Malone, NY 12953
518-483-3760 or 877-625-6631 Fax: 518-483-3172
Web site: www.visitmalone.com
Dene Savage, President

Mamaroneck Chamber of Commerce
430 Center Ave, Mamaroneck, NY 10543
914-698-4400
e-mail: chamber10543@optonline.net
Web site: www.mamaroneckchamberofcommerce.org
Rose Silvestro, President

Manhasset Chamber of Commerce
PO Box 754, Manhasset, NY 11030
516-627-8688
e-mail: limanhassetcc@aol.com
Web site: www.manhassetny.org
Les Forrai, President

Manhattan Chamber of Commerce Inc
1375 Broadway, Third Floor, New York, NY 10018
212-479-7772 Fax: 212-473-8074
e-mail: info@manhattancc.org
Web site: www.manhattancc.org
Nancy Ploeger, President

Offices and agencies generally appear in alphabetical order, except when specific order is requested by listee.

Marcy Chamber of Commerce
PO Box 429, Marcy, NY 13403
315-725-3294 Fax: 315-865-6144
e-mail: marcycofc@gmail.com
Web site: www.marcychamber.com
Lesley Grogan, Board President

Massapequa Chamber of Commerce
674 Broadway, Massapequa, NY 11758
516-541-1443 Fax: 516-541-8625
e-mail: masscoc@aol.com
Web site: www.massapequachamber.com
Patricia Orzano, President

Mastics/Shirley Chamber of Commerce
PO Box 4, Mastic, NY 11950
631-399-2228
e-mail: admin@masticshirleychamber.com
Web site: masticshirleychamber.com
Mark Smothergill, President

Mattituck Chamber of Commerce
PO Box 1056, Mattituck, NY 11952
631-298-5757
e-mail: info@mattituckchamber.org
Web site: www.mattituckchamber.org
Donielle Cardinale, President

Mayville/Chautauqua Chamber of Commerce
PO Box 22, Mayville, NY 14757
716-753-3113 Fax: 716-753-3113
e-mail: maychautcham@yahoo.com
Web site: www.chautaquachamber.org
Deborah Marsala, Coordinator

Mechanicville Area Chamber of Commerce
312 N 3rd Ave, Mechanicville, NY 12118
518-664-7791 Fax: 518-664-0826
Web site: www.mechancvilleareachamber.com
Barbara Corsale, President

Mechanicville/Stillwater Industrial Development Agency
City Hall, 36 North Main Street, Mechanicville, NY 12118
518-664-8331
Web site: www.mechanicville-stillwater-ida.org
Barbara Zecca Corsale, Chair

Merrick Chamber of Commerce
124 Merrick Ave, PO box 53, Merrick, NY 11566
516-771-1171 Fax: 516-868-6692
e-mail: merrickchamber@aol.com
Web site: www.merrickchamber.org
Randy Shotland, President

Mid-Hudson Pattern for Progress
Desmond Campus, 6 Albany Post Rd, Newburgh, NY 12550
845-565-4900 Fax: 845-565-4918
e-mail: jdrapkin@pfprogress.org
Web site: www.pattern-for-progress.org
Jonathan Drapkin, President

Miller Place/Mt Sinai/Sound Beach/Rocky Point Chamber of Commerce
5507-10 Nesconet Highway, #410, Mount Sinai, NY 11766
631-821-1313
Web site: www.northbrookhavenchamber.org
Dr Tom Ianniello, President

Mineola Chamber of Commerce
PO Box 62, Mineola, NY 11501
516-408-3554 Fax: 516-408-3554
Web site: www.mineolachamber.com
Ray Sikorski, President

Mohawk Valley Chamber of Commerce
Radisson Hotel, Suite 1, 200 Genessee St, Utica, NY 13502
315-724-3151 Fax: 315-724-3177
e-mail: info@mvchamber.org
Web site: www.mvchamber.org
Thomas Bashant, President

Mohawk Valley Economic Development District
26 W Main St, PO Box 69, Mohawk, NY 13407-0106
315-866-4671 Fax: 315-866-9862
e-mail: info@mvedd.org
Web site: www.mvedd.org
Regional Economic Development Activities
Stephen Smith, Director

Mohawk Valley Economic Development Growth Enterprises
584 Phoenix Drive, Rome, NY 13441-4105
315-338-0393 or 800-765-4990 Fax: 315-338-5694
e-mail: mrizzo@mvedge.org
Web site: www.mvedge.org
Laura Casamento, President

Monroe County Industrial Development Agency (COMIDA)
CityPlace, 50 W Main St, Suite 8100, Rochester, NY 14614
585-753-2000 Fax: 585-753-2002
Web site: www.growmonroe.org
Theresa Mazzullo, Chairman

Montauk Chamber of Commerce, The
742 Montauk Hwy, Montauk, NY 11954-5338
631-668-2428 Fax: 631-668-9363
e-mail: info@montaukchamber.com
Web site: www.montaukchamber.com

Montgomery County Chamber of Commerce/Montgomery County Partnership
1166 Riverfront Center, Amsterdam, NY 12010
518-842-8200 Fax: 518-684-0111
e-mail: chamber@montgomerycountyny.com
Web site: www.montgomerycountyny.com
Peter Capobianco, President

Moravia Chamber of Commerce
PO Box 647, Moravia, NY 13118
315-497-1431 Fax: 315-497-9319
Web site: www.moravia-lockeny.com
Dennis Bilow, President

Mount Kisco Chamber of Commerce
3 N Moger Ave, Mount Kisco, NY 10549
914-666-7525 Fax: 914-666-7663
e-mail: mtkiscochamber@aol.com
Web site: www.mtkiscochamber.com
Phil Bronzi, President

Mount Vernon Chamber of Commerce
65 Haven Ave, PO Box 351, Mount Vernon, NY 10550
914-667-7500 or 888-716-2460 Fax: 914-699-0139
e-mail: info@mtvernonchamber.org
Web site: www.mtvernonchamber.org
Frank T Fraley, President

Mount Vernon Industrial Development Agency (City of)
City Hall, Roosevelt Square, Mount Vernon, NY 10550
914-665-2300 Fax: 914-665-2496
Web site: www.cmvny.com
Yolanda Robinson, Chief of Staff

Nassau Council of Chambers
PO Box 365, Bellmore, NY 11710
516-248-1112 Fax: 516-663-6715
Web site: www.ncchambers.org
Julie Marchesella, President

Offices and agencies generally appear in alphabetical order, except when specific order is requested by listee.

Nassau County Industrial Development Agency
1550 Franklin Avenue, Suite 235, Mineola, NY 11501
516-571-1945 Fax: 516-571-1076
e-mail: cpereira@nassauida.com
Web site: www.nassauida.com
Colleen Pereira, Administrative Director

New City Chamber of Commerce
65 N Main St, New City, NY 10956
845-638-1395 Fax: 845-638-1395
e-mail: info@newcitychamber.com
Web site: www.newcitychamberofcommerce.org
Gary Oteri, President

New Hyde Park Chamber of Commerce
PO Box 247, New Hyde Park, NY 11040
888-400-0311
e-mail: info@nhpchamber.com
Web site: www.nhpchamber.com
Mark Laytin, President

New Paltz Regional Chamber of Commerce
257 Main St, New Paltz, NY 12561-1525
845-255-0243 Fax: 845-255-5189
e-mail: info@newpaltzchamber.org
Web site: www.newpaltzchamber.org
Michael Smith, President

New Rochelle, Chamber of Commerce, Inc
459 Main St, PO Box 140, New Rochelle, NY 10801-6412
914-632-5700 Fax: 914-632-0708
e-mail: info@newrochellechamber.org
Web site: www.newrochellechamber.org
Rosemary McLaughlin, President

New York Chamber of Commerce (Greater New York)
20 West 44th Street, 4th fl, New York, NY 10036
212-686-7220 Fax: 212-686-7232
e-mail: info@chamber.com
Web site: www.ny-chamber.com
Mark S Jaffe, President & CEO

New York City, Partnership for
One Battery Park Plaza, 5th Floor, New York, NY 10004
212-493-7400 Fax: 212-344-3344
e-mail: info@pfnyc.org
Web site: www.pfnyc.org
Kathryn S Wylde, President & CEO

New Yorktown Chamber of Commerce (The)
PO Box 632, Parkside Corner, Yorktown Heights, NY 10598
914-245-4599 Fax: 914-734-7111
e-mail: info@yorktownchamber.org
Web site: www.yorktownchamber.org
Nancy Stingone, Operations Director

Newark Chamber of Commerce
199 Van Buren St, Newark, NY 14513
315-331-2705 Fax: 315-331-2705
e-mail: supportnewarknychamber.com
Web site: www.newarknychamber.org
Tammra Schiller, President

Niagara County Center for Economic Development
6311 Inducon Corporate Dr, Ste 1, Sanborn, NY 14132-9099
716-278-8750 Fax: 716-278-8757
e-mail: info@niagaracountybusiness.com
Web site: www.nccedev.com
Samuel M Ferraro, Commissioner

Niagara Falls Chamber of Commerce
6311 Inducon Corporate Drive, Sanborn, NY 14132
716-285-9141 Fax: 716-285-0941
e-mail: dalteriobrennen@niagarachamber.org
Web site: niagarachamber.org
Deanna Alterio Brennen, President/CEO

Niagara USA Chamber of Commerce
6311 Inducon Corporate Dr, Sanborn, NY 14132
716-285-9141 Fax: 716-285-0941
e-mail: dalteriobrennen@niagarachamber.org
Web site: niagarachamber.org
Deanna Alterio Brennen, President

North Fork Chamber of Commerce
PO Box 1415, Southold, NY 11971
631-765-3161 Fax: 631-765-3161
e-mail: info@northforkchamber.org
Web site: www.northforkchamber.org
Andy Binkowski, President

North Greenbush IDA
2 Douglas Street, Wynantskill, NY 12198-7561
518-283-5313 Fax: 518-283-5345
e-mail: ashworth@townofng.com
Web site: www.townofng.com
James Flanigan, Chairman

Northport Chamber of Commerce
PO Box 33, Northport, NY 11768
631-754-3905
Web site: www.northportny.com

North Warren Chamber of Commerce
PO Box 490, 3 Dynamite Hill, Chestertown, NY 12817
518-494-2722 Fax: 518-494-2722
e-mail: info@northwarrenchamber.com
Web site: www.northwarren.com
Promoting local business Sponsors Tourist Information Center on route 8 in Chestertown.
Barbara Thomas, President

Nyack Chamber of Commerce
PO Box 677, Nyack, NY 10960
845-353-2221 Fax: 845-353-4204
Web site: www.nyackchamber.com
Carlo Pelligrini, President

Oceanside Chamber of Commerce
PO Box 1, Oceanside, NY 11572
516-763-9177 Fax: 516-766-4575
Web site: www.oceansidechamber.org
Gail Carlin, President

Ogdensburg Chamber of Commerce (Greater Ogdensburg)
1 Bridge Plaza, Ogdensburg, NY 13669
315-393-3620 Fax: 315-393-1380
e-mail: chamber@gisco.net
Web site: www.ogdensburgny.com
Sandra Porter, President

Olean Area Chamber of Commerce (Greater Olean)
120 N Union Street, Olean, NY 14760
716-372-4433 Fax: 716-372-7912
e-mail: info@oleanny.com
Web site: www.oleanny.com
Jim Stitt Jr, President

Offices and agencies generally appear in alphabetical order, except when specific order is requested by listee.

Oneida Industrial Development Agency (City of)
584 Phoenix Drive, Rome, NY 13441
315-338-0393 or 800-765-4990 Fax: 315-338-5694
e-mail: info@mvedge.org
Web site: www.oniedacountyida.org
David C Grow, Chairman

Onondaga County Industrial Development Agency
333 West Washington Street, Suite 130, Syracuse, NY 13202
315-435-3770 or 877-797-8222 Fax: 315-435-3669
e-mail: info@syracusecentral.com
Web site: www.syracusecentral.com
Marth Beth Primo, Director of Economic Development

Ontario Chamber of Commerce
PO Box 100, Ontario, NY 14519-0100
315-524-5886
e-mail: ontarionychamber.org
Web site: www.ontariotown.org
Donna Burolla, Chamber Board of Directors

Ontario County Industrial Development Agency & Economic Development
20 Ontario Street, Suite 106-B, Canandaigua, NY 14424
585-396-4460 Fax: 585-396-4594
e-mail: info@ontariocountydev.org
Web site: www.ontariocountydev.org
Michael J Manikowski, Executive Director

Orange County Chamber of Commerce Inc
30 Scott's Corners Drive, Montgomery, NY 12549
845-457-9700 Fax: 845-457-8799
e-mail: info@orangeny.com
Web site: www.orangeny.com
Dr John A D'Ambrosio, President

Orange County Partnership
40 Matthews St, Suite 108, Goshen, NY 10924
845-294-2323 Fax: 845-294-8023
e-mail: maureen@ocpartnership.org
Web site: www.ocpartnership.org
Scott Batulis, President & CEO

Orchard Park Chamber of Commerce
4211 N Buffalo St, Ste 14, Orchard Park, NY 14127-2401
716-662-3366 Fax: 716-662-5946
e-mail: opcc@orchardparkchamber.com
Web site: www.orchardparkchamber.com
Nancy L Conley, Executive Director

Orleans County Chamber of Commerce
102 N Main St, Albion, NY 14411
585-589-7727 Fax: 585-589-7326
e-mail: ckelly@orleanschamber.com
Web site: www.orleanschamber.com
Cindy Robinson, President

Orleans Economic Development Agency (OEDA)
121 N Main St, Albion, NY 14411
585-589-7060 Fax: 585-589-5258
e-mail: jwhipple@orleansdevelopment.org
Web site: www.orleansdevelopment.org
James Whipple, CEO & CFO

Oswego-Fulton Chamber of Commerce
44 East Bridge Street, Oswego, NY 13126
315-343-7681 Fax: 315-342-0831
e-mail: gofcc@oswegofultonchamber.com
Web site: www.oswegofultonchamber.com
Beth A Hilton, Executive Director

Oswego County, Operation/Oswego County Industrial Development Agency
44 West Bridge St, Oswego, NY 13126
315-343-1545 Fax: 315-343-1546
e-mail: ooc@oswegocounty.org
Web site: www.oswegocounty.org
L Michael Treadwell, Executive Director

Otsego County Chamber (The)
189 Main Street, Suite 201, Oneonta, NY 13820
607-432-4500 or 877-5-OTSEGO Fax: 607-432-4506
e-mail: info@otsegocountychamber.com
Web site: www.otsegocountychamber.com
Barbara Ann Heegan, Executive Director

Otsego County Economic Development Department & Industrial Development Agency
242 Main St, Oneonta, NY 13820
607-432-8871 Fax: 607-432-5117
e-mail: info@otsegoeconomicdevelopment.com
Web site: www.otsegoeconomicdevelopment.com
Joseph A Bernier, Chair

Oyster Bay Chamber of Commerce
PO Box 21, Oyster Bay, NY 11771
516-922-6464 Fax: 516-624-8082
e-mail: obenchamber@gmail.com
Web site: www.visitoysterbay.com
Dottie Simmons, President

Painted Post Area Board of Trade
304 South Hamilton Street, PO Box 128, Painted Post, NY 14870
607-937-6162
e-mail: info@paintedpostny.com
Web site: www.paintedpostny.com
Jean Wise-Wicks, President

Patchogue Chamber of Commerce (Greater Patchogue)
15 N Ocean Ave, Patchogue, NY 11772
631-207-1000 or 631-475-0121 Fax: 631-475-1599
e-mail: info@patchoguechamber.com
Web site: www.patchoguechamber.com
Gail Hoag, Executive Director

Patterson Chamber of Commerce
PO Box 316, Patterson, NY 12563
845-363-6304 Fax: 845-363-6304
e-mail: info@pcofc.org
Web site: www.pcofc.org
Debra Boccarossa, President

Peekskill Industrial Development Agency (City of)
840 Main Street, Room 31, Peekskill, NY 10566-2016
914-737-3400 Fax: 914-737-2688
Web site: www.cityofpeekskill.com
Brian Havranek, Executive Director

Perry Area Chamber of Commerce
102 N Center St, PO Box 35, Perry, NY 14530
585-237-5040
e-mail: joinus@perrychamber.com
Web site: www.perrychamber.com
Lorraine Sturm, Secretary

Chambers of Commerce

Offices and agencies generally appear in alphabetical order, except when specific order is requested by listee.

Phelps Chamber of Commerce
PO Box 1, Phelps, NY 14532
315-548-5481
e-mail: chamber@phelpsny.com
Web site: www.phelpsny.com

Plainview-Old Bethpage Chamber of Commerce
PO Box 577, Plainview, NY 11803
516-937-5646
e-mail: chamber@pobcoc.com
Web site: www.plainview-oldbethpage.org
Gary Epstein, President

Plattsburgh-North Country Chamber of Commerce
7061 Route 9, PO Box 310, Plattsburgh, NY 12901
518-563-1000 Fax: 516-563-1028
e-mail: chamber@northcountrychamber.com
Web site: www.northcountrychamber.com
Garry Douglas, CEO & President

Port Chester-Rye Brook Rye Town Chamber of Commerce
222 Grace Church Street, Port Chester, NY 10573
914-939-1900 Fax: 914-437-7779
e-mail: pcrbchamber@gmail.com
Web site: www.portchesterchamber.com
Ken Manning, Executive Director

Port Jefferson Chamber of Commerce
118 W Broadway, Port Jefferson, NY 11777
631-473-1414 Fax: 631-474-4540
e-mail: info@portjeffchamber.com
Web site: www.portjeffchamber.com
Suzanne Velazquez, President

South Bronx Overall Economic Development Corporation
555 Bergen Ave, Bronx, NY 10455
718-292-3113 Fax: 718-292-3115
e-mail: info@sobro.org
Web site: www.sobro.org
Phillip Morrow, President/CEO

Port Washington Chamber of Commerce
PO Box 121, Port Washington, NY 11050
516-883-6566 Fax: 516-883-6591
e-mail: pwcoc@optonline.net
Web site: pwguide.com
Bobbie Polay, Executive Director

Potsdam Chamber of Commerce
One Market Street, Potsdam, NY 13676
315-274-9000 Fax: 315-274-9222
e-mail: potsdam@slic.com
Web site: www.potsdamchamber.com
Marylee Ballou, Executive Director

Dutchess County Regional Chamber of Commerce
One Civic Center Plaza, Suite 400, Poughkeepsie, NY 12601
845-454-1700 Fax: 845-454-1702
e-mail: info@dcrcoc.org
Web site: www.dcrcoc.org
Charles S North, President & CEO

Pulaski-Eastern Shore Chamber of Commerce
3044 State Route 13, PO Box 34, Pulaski, NY 13142-0034
315-298-2213
Web site: www.pulaskinychamber.com
Nancy Farrell, President

Putnam County Economic Development Corporation
34 Gleneida Ave, Carmel, NY 10512
845-228-8066 Fax: 845-225-0311
e-mail: meghan.taylor@putnamcountyny.gov
Web site: www.putnamedc.org
Kevin Bailey, President

Queens Chamber of Commerce (Borough of)
75-20 Astoria Blvd, Suite 140, Jackson Heights, NY 11370
718-898-8500 Fax: 718-898-8599
e-mail: info@queenschamber.org
Web site: www.queenschamber.org
Carol Consiato, President

Red Hook Area Chamber of Commerce
PO Box 254, Red Hook, NY 12571-0254
845-758-0824 Fax: 845-758-0824
e-mail: info@redhookchamber.org
Web site: www.redhookchamber.org
Ray Amater, President

Rensselaer County Regional Chamber of Commerce
255 River St, Troy, NY 12180
518-274-7020 Fax: 518-272-7729
e-mail: info@renscochamber.com
Web site: www.renscochamber.com
Linda Hillman, President

Rhinebeck Area Chamber of Commerce
PO Box 42, 23F E Market Street, Rhinebeck, NY 12572
845-876-5904 Fax: 845-876-8624
e-mail: info@rhinebeckchamber.com
Web site: www.rhinebeckchamber.com
Colleen Cruishank, Executive Director

Richfield Springs Area Chamber of Commerce
PO Box 909, Richfield Springs, NY 13439-0909
315-858-7028
e-mail: elbudro@aol.com
Web site: www.richfieldspringschamber.org
E Lawrence Budro, Executive Director

Riverhead Chamber of Commerce
542 E Main St, Suite 2, Riverhead, NY 11901
631-727-7600 Fax: 631-727-7946
e-mail: info@riverheadchamber.com
Web site: www.riverheadchamber.com
Tracy Stark James, President
Mary Hughes, Executive Director

Rochester Business Alliance Inc
150 State St, Ste 400, Rochester, NY 14614-1308
585-244-1800 Fax: 585-263-3679
e-mail: sandyp@rballiance.com
Web site: www.rochesterbusinessalliance.com
Sandra Parker, President & CEO

Rochester Downtown Development Corporation
One HSBC Plaza, 100 Chestnut Street, Suite 1910, Rochester, NY 14604
585-546-6920 Fax: 585-546-4784
e-mail: rddc@rddc.org
Web site: www.rochesterdowntown.com
Heidi N Zimmer-Meyer, President

Rochester Economic Development Corporation
30 Church Street, Room 223B, Rochester, NY 14614
585-428-8801 Fax: 585-428-6042
e-mail: carballc@cityofrochester.gov
Web site: www.cityofrochester.gov
R Carlos Carballada, President

Offices and agencies generally appear in alphabetical order, except when specific order is requested by listee.

Rockaway Development & Revitalization Corporation
1920 Mott Ave, 2nd Fl, Far Rockaway, NY 11691
718-327-5300 Fax: 718-327-4990
e-mail: info@rdrc.org
Web site: www.rdrc.org
Kevin W Alexander, Executive Director

Rockaways, Chamber of Commerce, Inc
253 Beach 116th St, Rockaway Park, NY 11694
718-634-1300 Fax: 718-634-9623
e-mail: rockawaychamberofcommerce@gmail.com
Web site: www.rockawaychamberofcommerce.com

Rockland Chamber of Commerce
PO Box 2001, New City, NY 10956
914-634-4646 Fax: 914-353-5533
e-mail: martreal@aol.com
Martin Bernstein, President

Rockland Economic Development Corporation
2 Blue Hill Plaza, PO Box 1575, Pearl River, NY 10965-1575
845-735-7040 Fax: 845-735-5736
e-mail: stevenp@redc.org
Web site: www.redc.org
Michael DiTullo, President & CEO

Rockville Centre Chamber of Commerce
PO Box 226, Rockville Centre, NY 11571
516-766-0666 Fax: 516-706-1550
e-mail: info@rockvillecentrechamber.com
Web site: www.rvcchamber.com
Lawrence G Siegel, President

Rome Area Chamber of Commerce
139 West Dominick St, Rome, NY 13440-5809
315-337-1700 Fax: 315-337-1715
e-mail: info@romechamber.com
Web site: www.romechamber.com
William K Guglielmo, President

Rome Industrial Development Corporation
584 Phoenix Drive, Rome, NY 13441
315-338-0393 Fax: 315-338-5694
e-mail: mkaucher@mvedge.org
Web site: www.romeny.org
Mark Kaucher, Executive Director

Ronkonkoma Chamber of Commerce
PO Box 2546, Ronkonkoma, NY 11779
631-963-2796
e-mail: info@ronkonkomachamber.com
Web site: www.ronkonkomachamber.com
Denise Schwartz, President

Sackets Harbor Chamber of Commerce
PO Box 17, 301 W Main Street, Sackets Harbor, NY 13685
315-646-1700 Fax: 315-646-2160
e-mail: shvisit@gisco.net
Web site: www.visitsackets.com
Anita Prather Harvell, President

Sag Harbor Chamber of Commerce
PO Box 2810, Sag Harbor, NY 11963
631-725-0011 Fax: 631-919-1662
e-mail: info@sagharborchamber.com
Web site: www.sagharborchamber.com
Kelly Connaughton, President

Salamanca Area Chamber of Commerce
26 Main St, Salamanca, NY 14779
716-945-2034 Fax: 716-945-2034
e-mail: info@salmun.com
Web site: www.salamancachamber.org
Jayne L Fenton, President

Salamanca Industrial Development Agency
225 Wildwood Ave, Salamanca, NY 14779-1547
716-945-3230 Fax: 716-945-8289
e-mail: pwelch1@salmun.com
Web site: www.salmun.com
Patrick Welch, Office Manager

Saranac Lake Area Chamber of Commerce
193 River St, Saranac Lake, NY 12983
518-891-1990 or 800-347-1992 Fax: 518-891-7042
e-mail: info@saranaclake.com
Web site: www.saranaclake.com
Katy Van Anden, Executive Director

Saratoga County Chamber of Commerce
28 Clinton St, Saratoga Springs, NY 12866
518-584-3255 Fax: 518-587-0318
e-mail: info@saratoga.org
Web site: www.saratoga.org
Todd Shimkus, President

Saratoga County Industrial Development Agency
50 W High St, Ballston Spa, NY 12020
518-884-4705 Fax: 518-884-4780
e-mail: larrybeuton61@msn.com
Web site: www.saratogacountyida.org
Raymond F Callanan, Chairman

Saratoga Economic Development Corporation
28 Clinton St, Saratoga Springs, NY 12866
518-587-0945 Fax: 518-587-5855
Web site: www.saratogaedc.com
Dennis Brobston, President

Sayville Chamber of Commerce (Greater Sayville)
Bud Van Wyen Memorial BUilding, PO Box 235, Sayville, NY 11782-0235
631-567-5257 Fax: 631-218-0881
e-mail: info@sayvillechamber.com
Web site: www.greatersayvillechamber.com
Bill Etts, President

Scarsdale Chamber of Commerce
PO Box 635, Scarsdale, NY 10583
914-620-2426
Web site: www.scarsdalechamber.org
Lewis Arlt, President

Schenectady County Chamber of Commerce
306 State St, Schenectady, NY 12305-2302
518-372-5656 or 800-962-8007 Fax: 518-370-3217
e-mail: info@schenectadychamber.org
Web site: www.schenectadychamber.org
Charles P Steiner, President

Schenectady County Industrial Development Agency/Economic Development Corporation
Center City Plaza, Schenectady, NY 12305
518-377-1109 Fax: 518-382-2575
Web site: www.schenectadycounty.com
Jayme Lahut, President

Offices and agencies generally appear in alphabetical order, except when specific order is requested by listee.

Schoharie County Chamber of Commerce
143 Caverns Road, Howes Cave, NY 12092
518-296-8820 Fax: 518-296-8825
e-mail: info@schohariechamber.com
Web site: www.schohariechamber.com
Georgia Van Dyke, Interim Executive Director

Schoharie County Industrial Development Agency
349 Mineral Springs Rd, Cobleskill, NY 12043
518-234-7604 Fax: 518-234-4346
e-mail: rfscrpc@nycap.rr.com
Web site: www.growscny.com
Ronald Filmer, Director

Schroon Lake Area Chamber of Commerce
1075 US Rte 9, PO Box 726, Schroon Lake, NY 12870-0726
518-532-7675 or 888-SCHROON
e-mail: chamber@schroonlakeregion.com
Web site: www.schroonlakechamber.com
Mike Bush, President

Schuyler County Industrial Development Agency
2 N Franklin St, Ste 330, Watkins Glen, NY 14891
607-535-4341 Fax: 607-535-7221
e-mail: kelsey@scoped.biz
Web site: www.scoped.biz
J. Kelsey Jones, Executive Director

Schuyler County Partnership for Economic Development
2 N Franklin St, Ste 330, Watkins Glen, NY 14891
607-535-4341 Fax: 607-535-7221
e-mail: brian@scoped.biz
Web site: www.scoped.biz
Brian Williams, Economic & Community Development Specialist

Seaford Chamber of Commerce
2479 Jackson Avenue, PO Box 1634, Seaford, NY 11783
516-221-2888 Fax: 516-221-8683
e-mail: likoub@gmail.com
Web site: www.seafordchamberofcommerce.com
Kenneth Jacobsen, President

Seneca County Chamber of Commerce
2020 Rtes 5 & 20 West, Seneca Falls, NY 13148
315-568-2906 or 800-732-1848 Fax: 315-568-1730
e-mail: info@senecachamber.org
Web site: www.senecachamber.org
Jeff Shipley, Executive Director

Seneca County Industrial Development Agency
One Di Pronio Dr, Waterloo, NY 13165
315-539-1725 Fax: 315-539-4340
e-mail: raronson@co.seneca.ny.us
Web site: www.senecacountyida.org
Robert J Aronson, Executive Director

Sidney Chamber of Commerce
24 River St, PO Box 2295, Sidney, NY 13838
607-561-2642 Fax: 607-561-2644
e-mail: office@sidneychamber.org
Web site: www.sidneychamber.org
Kerri Green, President

Skaneateles Area Chamber of Commerce
22 Jordan St., PO Box 199, Skaneateles, NY 13152
315-685-0552 Fax: 315-685-0552
e-mail: info@skaneateles.com
Web site: www.skaneateles.com
Susan Dove, Executive Director

Sleepy Hollow Chamber of Commerce
1 Neperan Rd, Tarrytown, NY 10591-3660
914-631-1705 Fax: 914-366-4291
e-mail: info@sleepyhollowchamber.com
Web site: www.sleepyhollowchamber.com
John Sardy, Executive Director

Slovak American Chamber of Commerce
10 E 40th Street, New York, NY 10016
212-532-4920

Smithtown Chamber of Commerce
79 E Main Street, Suite E, PO Box 1216, Smithtown, NY 11787
631-979-8069 Fax: 631-979-2206
e-mail: info@smithtownchamber.com
Web site: www.smithtownchamber.com
Barbara Franco, Executive Director

South Jefferson Chamber of Commerce
PO Box 73, Adams, NY 13605
315-232-4215 or 888-476-5333 Fax: 315-232-3967
Web site: www.1000islands.com

Southampton Chamber of Commerce
76 Main St, Southampton, NY 11968
631-283-0402 Fax: 631-283-8707
e-mail: info@southamptonchamber.com
Web site: www.southamptonchamber.com
Micah Schlendorf, President

Southeastern New York, Council of Industry of
6 Albany Post Rd, Newburgh, NY 12550
845-565-1355 Fax: 845-565-1427
e-mail: hking@councilofindustry.org
Web site: www.councilofindustry.org
Robert Miniger, President

Southern Dutchess Chamber of Commerce (Greater Southern Dutchess)
Nussbickel Building, 2582 S Ave (Route 9D), Wappingers Falls, NY 12590
845-296-0001 Fax: 845-296-0006
e-mail: webmaster@gsdcc.org
Web site: www.gsdcc.org
Ann M Meagher, President/CEO

Southern Madison County Chamber of Commerce
10 Utica Street, 2nd Floor, PO Box 3, Hamilton, NY 13346
315-824-8213 or 315-824-0002 Fax: 315-824-0086
Web site: www.hamiltonny.com

Southern Saratoga County Chamber of Commerce
15 Park Avenue, Suite 7, Clifton Park, NY 12065
518-371-7748 Fax: 518-371-5025
e-mail: info@southernsaratoga.org
Web site: www.southernsaratoga.org
Southern Saratoga Countys premier local business advocate with over 1025 members.
Pete Bardunias, President & CEO
Loretta Rigney, Vice President

Southern Tier Economic Growth Inc
400 Church St, Elmira, NY 14901
607-733-6513 Fax: 607-734-2698
e-mail: info@steg.com
Web site: www.steg.com
George Miner, President

Southern Ulster County Chamber of Commerce
3553 Route 9W, PO Box 320, Highland, NY 12528
845-691-6070 Fax: 845-691-9194
e-mail: info@southernulsterchamber.org
Web site: www.southernulsterchamber.org
William Farrell, President

Springville Area Chamber of Commerce
23 N Buffalo St, PO Box 310, Springville, NY 14141-0310
716-592-4746 Fax: 716-592-4746
e-mail: info@springvillechamber.com
Web site: www.springvillechamber.com
Duane W Fischer, Executive Director

St James Chamber of Commerce
PO Box 286, St James, NY 11780
631-584-8510 Fax: 631-862-9839
e-mail: info@stjameschamber.org
Web site: www.stjameschamber.org
Ryan McKenna, President

St Lawrence County Chamber of Commerce
101 Main Street, Canton, NY 13617-1248
315-386-4000 or 877-228-7810 Fax: 315-379-0134
e-mail: pmck123@aol.com
Web site: www.northcountryguide.com
Patricia McKeown, Executive Director

St Lawrence County Industrial Development Agency
19 Commerce Lane, Suite 1, Canton, NY 13617-1496
315-379-9806 Fax: 315-386-2573
e-mail: info@slcida.com
Web site: www.slcida.com
Patrick Kelly, Chief Executive Officer

Staten Island Chamber of Commerce
130 Bay St, Staten Island, NY 10301
718-727-1900 Fax: 718-727-2295
e-mail: info@sichamber.com
Web site: www.sichamber.com
Linda M Baran, President & CEO

Staten Island Economic Development Corporation
900 South Ave, Ste 402, Staten Island, NY 10314
718-477-1400 Fax: 718-477-0681
e-mail: newsinfo@sicdc.net
Web site: www.siedc.org
Cesar J Claro, President & CEO

Steuben County Industrial Development Agency
7234 Rte 54, PO Box 393, Bath, NY 14810-0390
607-776-3316 Fax: 607-776-5039
e-mail: scida@steubencountyida.com
Web site: www.steubencountyida.com
James Johnson, Executive Director

Suffern Chamber of Commerce
PO Box 291, 71 Lafayette Avenue, Suffern, NY 10901
845-357-8424
e-mail: sufffernchamberofcommerce@yahoo.com
Web site: www.suffernchamberofcommerce.com

Sullivan County Chamber of Commerce
PO Box 405, Mongaup Valley, NY 12762
845-791-4200 Fax: 845-791-4220
e-mail: chamber@catskills.com
Web site: www.catskills.com
Terri Ward, President & CEO

Sullivan County Industrial Development Agency
1 Cablevision Ctr, Ferndale, NY 12734
845-295-2603 Fax: 845-295-2604
e-mail: scida@hvc.rr.com
Web site: www.sullivanida.com
Jennifer C S Brylinski, Executive Director & COO

Syracuse & Central NY, Metropolitan Development Association of
572 South Salina Street, Syracuse, NY 13202
315-422-8284 Fax: 315-471-4503
e-mail: ceo@centerstateceo.com
Web site: www.centerstateceo.com
Robert Simpson, President & CEO

Syracuse Chamber of Commerce (Greater Syracuse)
572 S Salina St, Syracuse, NY 13202-3320
315-470-1800 Fax: 315-471-8545
e-mail: ceo@centerstateceo.com
Web site: www.centerstateceo.com
Robert Simpson, President

Syracuse Economic Development
333 Washington Street, Suite 130, Syracuse, NY 13202
315-435-3770 Fax: 315-435-3669
e-mail: info@syracusecentral.com
Web site: www.syracusecentral.com
Mary Beth Primo, Director of Economic Development

Syracuse Industrial Development Agency
City Hall, 233 E Washington St, Syracuse, NY 13202
315-448-8100 Fax: 315-448-8036
e-mail: bwalsh@ci.syracuse.ny.us
Web site: www.syracuse.ny.us
William M Ryan, Chair

Three Rivers Development Foundation Inc
114 Pine St, Suite 201, Corning, NY 14830
607-962-4693 Fax: 607-936-9132
e-mail: info@3riverscorp.com
Web site: www.3riverscorp.com
Jack Benjamin, President

Ticonderoga Area Chamber of Commerce
94 Montcalm Street, Suite 1, Ticonderoga, NY 12883
518-585-6619 Fax: 518-585-9184
e-mail: chamberinfo@ticonderogany.com
Web site: www.ticonderogany.com
Pamela Nolan, Executive Director

Tioga County Chamber of Commerce
80 North Avenue, Owego, NY 13827
607-687-8255 Fax: 607-687-1435
e-mail: business@tiogachamber.com
Web site: www.tiogachamber.com
Douglas Barton, Director

Tioga County Industrial Development Agency
County Office Bldg, 56 Main Street, Owego, NY 13827
607-687-8259 Fax: 607-687-8282
e-mail: ida@developtioga.com
Web site: www.developtioga.com
Aaron Gowan, Chairman

Tompkins County Area Development
401 East State Street, Suite 402B, Ithaca, NY 14850
607-273-0005 Fax: 607-273-8964
e-mail: info@tcad.org
Web site: www.tcad.org
John Rudd, President

Tompkins County Chamber of Commerce
904 E Shore Drive, Ithaca, NY 14850
607-273-7080 Fax: 607-272-7617
e-mail: marilyn@tompkinschamber.org
Web site: www.tompkinschamber.org
Jean McPheeters, President

Offices and agencies generally appear in alphabetical order, except when specific order is requested by listee.

Tonawanda (Town Of) Development Corporation
169 Sheridan Parkside Dr, Tonawanda, NY 14150
716-871-8847 Fax: 716-871-8857
e-mail: ttdc@tonawanda.ny.us
Web site: www.tonawanda.com
James Hartz, Director

Tonawandas, Chamber of Commerce of the
15 Webster St, North Tonawanda, NY 14120
716-692-5120 Fax: 716-692-1867
e-mail: chamber@the-tonawandas.com
Web site: www.the-tonawandas.com
Joyce M Santiago, President

Tri-State Chamber of Commerce
PO Box 386, Lakeville, CT 06039-0386
860-435-0740
e-mail: info@tristatechamber.com
Web site: www.tristatechamber.com
Susan Dickinson, President
Cheryl Reynolds, President

Tupper Lake Chamber of Commerce
121 Park Street, PO Box 987, Tupper Lake, NY 12986
518-359-3328 Fax: 518-359-2434
e-mail: chamber@tupper-lake.com
Web site: www.tupper-lake.com
David Tomerlin, President

Ulster County Chamber of Commerce
214 Fair Street, Kingston, NY 12401
845-338-5100 Fax: 845-338-0968
e-mail: info@ulsterchamber.org
Web site: www.ulsterchamber.org
Ward Todd, President

Ulster County Development Corporation/Ulster County Industrial Development Agency
244 Fair Street, PO Box 4265, Kingston, NY 12402-4265
845-340-3556 Fax: 845-334-5373
e-mail: oed@co.ulster.ny.us
Web site: www.ulstercountyny.gov
Michael Horodyski, Chair

Union Local Development Corporation (Town of)
3111 E Main St, Endwell, NY 13760
607-786-2900 Fax: 607-786-2998
e-mail: economicdevelopment@townofunion.com
Web site: www.townofunion.com
Joseph M Moody, Director of Economic Development

Utica Industrial Development Agency (City of)
One Kennedy Plz, Utica, NY 13501
315-792-0195 Fax: 315-792-9819
e-mail: jspaeth@cityofutica.com
Web site: www.cityofutica.com
Jack N Spaeth, Executive Director

Valley Stream Chamber of Commerce
PO Box 1016, Valley Stream, NY 11580-1016
516-825-1741
e-mail: valleystreamcc@gmail.com
Web site: www.valleystreamchamber.org

Victor Chamber of Commerce
37 East Main Street, Victor, NY 14564
585-742-1476 Fax: 585-924-0523
e-mail: info@victorchamber.com
Web site: www.victorchamber.com
Mitch Donovan, President

Waddington Chamber of Commerce
PO Box 291, Waddington, NY 13694
315-388-4765 or 315-388-5576
e-mail: waddingtonchamber@gmail.com
Web site: www.waddingtonny.us/chamber
Alicia Murphy, President

Walton Chamber of Commerce
129 North Street, Walton, NY 13856-1217
607-865-6656
e-mail: waltonchamber@yahoo.com
Web site: www.waltonchamber.com
Maureen Wacha, President

Wantagh Chamber of Commerce
Pond Rd, PO Box 660, Wantagh, NY 11793
516-679-0100 or 516-781-6145
e-mail: denise@langweberlaw.com
Web site: www.wcc.li
Denise Langweber, President

Warren & Washington Industrial Development Agency
5 Warren St, Suite 210, Glens Falls, NY 12801
518-792-1312 Fax: 518-792-4147
e-mail: info@warren-washingtonida.com
Web site: www.warren-washingtonida.com
Harold Taylor, Chairman

Warren County Economic Development Corporation
234 Glen Street, Glens Falls, NY 12801
518-761-6007 Fax: 518-761-9053
e-mail: info@edcwc.org
Web site: www.edcwc.org
Leonard Fosbrook, President

Warrensburg Chamber of Commerce
3728 Main St, Warrensburg, NY 12885
518-623-2161 Fax: 518-623-2184
e-mail: info@warrensburgchamber.com
Web site: www.warrensburgchamber.com
Lynn Smith, President

Warsaw Chamber of Commerce (Greater Warsaw)
PO Box 221, Warsaw, NY 14569
585-786-3989 Fax: 585-786-3083
e-mail: info@warsawchamber.com
Web site: warsawchamber.com
Becky Ryan, President

Warwick Valley Chamber of Commerce
South St, Caboose, PO Box 202, Warwick, NY 10990
845-986-2720 Fax: 914-986-6982
e-mail: info@warwickcc.org
Web site: www.warwickcc.org
Michael Johndrow, Executive Director

Washington County Local Development Corporation
383 Broadway, Building A, Fort Edward, NY 12828
518-746-2292 Fax: 518-746-2293
e-mail: info@wcldc.org
Web site: www.wcldc.org
Tori J.E. Riley, President

Watertown Empire Zone
PO Box 3367, Saratoga Springs, NY 12866
315-782-1167 Fax: 518-899-9642
e-mail: michael@camoinassociates.com
Web site: www.watertownempirezone.com
R Michael N'dolo, Zone Coodinator

Watertown-North Country Chamber of Commerce (Greater Watertown)
1241 Coffeen St, Watertown, NY 13601
315-788-4400 Fax: 315-788-3369
e-mail: chamber@watertownny.com
Web site: www.watertownny.com
Lynn Pietroski, President & CEO

Watkins Glen Area Chamber of Commerce
214 N Franklin St, St Rte 14, Watkins Glen, NY 14891
607-535-4300 or 800-607-4552 Fax: 607-535-6243
e-mail: info@watkinsglenchamber.com
Web site: www.watkinsglenchamber.com
Rebekah LaMoreaux, President/CEO

Wayne County Industrial Development Agency & Economic Development
16 William St, Lyons, NY 14489
315-946-5917 or 888-219-2963 Fax: 315-946-5918
e-mail: wedcny@co.wayne.ny.us
Web site: www.wedcny.org
Peg Churchill, Executive Director

Webster Chamber of Commerce
1110 Crosspointe Lane, Ste C, Webster, NY 14580-3280
585-265-3960 Fax: 585-265-3702
e-mail: info@websterchamber.com
Web site: www.websterchamber.com
Barry Howard, President/CEO

Weedsport Area Chamber of Commerce
PO Box 973, Weedsport, NY 13166
315-834-2280
e-mail: weedsportchamber@yahoo.com
Web site: www.weedsportchamber.org
Penny Fay, President

Wellsville Area Chamber of Commerce
114 N Main St, Wellsville, NY 14895
585-593-5080 Fax: 585-593-5088
e-mail: info@wellsvilleareachamber.com
Web site: www.wellsvilleareachamber.com
Steven Havey, Executive Director

Westbury-Carle Place Chamber of Commerce
PO Box 474, Westbury, NY 11590
516-997-3966
e-mail: info@wcpchamber.com
Web site: www.wcpchamber.com
Frank Frisone, President

West Manhattan Chamber of Commerce
150 W 88 St, PO Box 1028, New York, NY 10024
212-787-1112 Fax: 212-787-1115
e-mail: mail@westmanhattanchamber.org
Web site: www.westmanhattanchamber.org
Andrew Albert, Executive Director

West Seneca Chamber of Commerce
950A Union Rd, Suite 5, West Seneca, NY 14224
716-674-4900 Fax: 716-674-5846
e-mail: director@westseneca.org
Web site: www.westseneca.org
Frank Calieri, Executive Director

Westchester County Association Inc (The)
1133 Westchester Avenue, Suite S-217, White Plains, NY 10604
914-948-6444 Fax: 914-948-6913
e-mail: info@westchester.org
Web site: www.westchester.org
William M Mooney, Jr, President & Chief Executive Officer

Westchester County Chamber of Commerce
108 Corporate Park Dr, Ste 101, White Plains, NY 10604
914-948-2110 Fax: 914-948-0122
e-mail: mpgordon@westchesterny.org
Web site: www.westchesterny.org
Dr Marsha Gordon, President & CEO

Westchester County Industrial Development Agency
Room 903, Michaelian Office Building, 148 Martine Avenue, White Plains, NY 10601
914-995-2963 Fax: 914-995-3044
e-mail: jcoleman@westchestergov.com
Web site: www.thinkingwestchester.com
Jim Coleman, Executive Director

Westfield/Barcelona Chamber of Commerce
27 East Main St, PO Box 125, Westfield, NY 14787-1319
716-326-4000 Fax: 716-326-2299
Tony Pisicoli, President

Westhampton Chamber of Commerce (Greater Westhampton)
PO Box 1228, 7 Glovers Lane, Westhampton Beach, NY 11978
631-288-3337 Fax: 631-288-3322
e-mail: info@whbcc.org
Web site: www.whbcc.org
Dwayne Wagner, President

Whiteface Mountain Regional Visitor's Bureau
PO Box 277, Wilmington, NY 12997
518-946-2255 or 888-Whiteface Fax: 518-946-2683
e-mail: info@whitefaceregion.com
Web site: www.whitefaceregion.com
Diane Buckley, Office Manager

Whitehall Area Chamber of Commerce
PO Box 97, Whitehall, NY 12887
518-499-4435
Web site: www.whitehall-chamber.org

Williamson Chamber of Commerce
PO Box 907, Williamson, NY 14589
315-589-2020 Fax: 315-589-9682
e-mail: williamsoncofc@aol.com
Web site: www.williamsonchamberofcommerceny.org
TBA, President

Willistons Chamber of Commerce
PO Box 207, Williston Park, NY 11596
516-739-1943 Fax: 516-294-1444
e-mail: info@chamberofthewillistons.org
Web site: www.chamberofthewillistons.org
Bobby Shannon, President

Woodstock Chamber of Commerce & Arts
PO Box 36, Woodstock, NY 12498
845-679-6234
e-mail: info@woodstockchamber.com
Web site: www.woodstockchamber.com
Nick Altomare, President

Wurtsboro Board of Trade
PO Box 907, Wurtsboro, NY 12790
845-888-4884
Web site: www.wurtsboro.org
James Arnott, President

Wyoming County Chamber of Commerce
6470 Route 20A, Suite 2, Perry, NY 14530-9798
585-237-0230 or 800-839-3919 Fax: 585-237-0231
e-mail: info@wycochamber.org
Web site: www.wycochamber.org
Laura Lane, President/CEO

Yates County Chamber of Commerce
2375 Rte 14A, Penn Yan, NY 14527
800-868-YATES Fax: 315-536-3791
e-mail: info@yatesny.com
Web site: www.yatesny.com
Michael Linehan, President/CEO

Finger Lakes Economic Development Center
One Keuka Business Park, Penn Yan, NY 14527
315-536-7328 Fax: 315-536-2389
e-mail: info@fingerlakesedc.com
Web site: www.fingerlakesedc.com
Steve Griffin, CEO

Yonkers Chamber of Commerce
55 Main Street, Yonkers, NY 10701
914-963-0332 Fax: 914-963-0451
e-mail: info@yonkerschamber.com
Web site: www.yonkerschamber.com
Kevin T Cacace, President

Yonkers Economic Development/Yonkers Industrial Development Agency (City of)
470 Nepperhan Ave, Suite 200, Yonkers, NY 10701
914-509-8651 Fax: 914-509-8651
e-mail: info@yonkersida.com
Web site: www.cityofyonkersida.com
Melvina Carter, President/CEO

Offices and agencies generally appear in alphabetical order, except when specific order is requested by listee.

Section 6:
NEWS MEDIA

NEWS MEDIA

This chapter identifies key journalists and editorial management for daily and weekly newspapers in New York State, major news services with reporters assigned to cover State government, radio stations with a news format and television stations with news staff.

NEWSPAPERS

Newspapers included in this chapter employ reporters who cover state and regional news. The newspapers are listed alphabetically by primary city served.

ALBANY

Legislative Gazette *Weekly Circulation: 13,222*

Legislative Gazette
Empire State Plaza, Concourse Level, PO Box 7329, Room 106, Albany, NY 12224
518-473-9739 Fax: 518-486-6609
e-mail: editor@legislativegazette.com
Web site: www.legislativegazette.com
Executive Publisher/Project Director . . . . Professor Alan S Chartock
Editor . . . . James Gormley
e-mail: editor@legislativegazette.com
Assistant General Manager / Circulation / Production Manager . . . Beth Rider
e-mail: ads@legislativegazette.com

American City Business Journals *Weekly Circulation: 4,000,000*

The Business Review
40 British American Blvd, Latham, NY 12210
518-640-6800 Fax: 518-640-6801
e-mail: albany@bizjournals.com
Web site: www.albany.bizjournals.com
Publisher . . . . Carolyn M Jones
e-mail: cmjones@bizjournals.com
Editor-in-Chief . . . . Michael Hendricks
e-mail: mhendricks@bizjournals.com
Managing Editor . . . . Robin E Cooper
e-mail: rcooper@bizjournals.com

Times Union *Weekday Circulation: 96,974*

Times Union
645 Albany Shaker Road, Albany, NY 12211
518-454-5694 Fax: 518-454-5628
e-mail: tubusiness@timesunion.com
Web site: www.timesunion.com
Publisher/CEO . . . . George R Hearst III
e-mail: rsmith@timesunion.com
VP/Editor. . . . . Rex Smith
e-mail: rsmith@timesunion.com
Associate Editor. . . . . Michael V Spain
e-mail: mspain@timesunion.com
Director of Circulation . . . . Mark Vinciguerra
e-mail: mvinciguerra@timesunion.com
Senior Editor/Features. . . . . Tracy Ormsbee
e-mail: tormsbee@timesunion.com
Senior News Editor . . . . Teresa Buckley
e-mail: tbuckley@timesunion.com
Senior News Editor/Information Services . . . . Tena Tyler
e-mail: ttyler@timesunion.com

AMSTERDAM

Recorder (The) *Weekly Circulation: 8,000*

Recorder (The)
One Venner Rd, Amsterdam, NY 12010
518-843-1100 or 800-453-6397 Fax: 518-843-6580
e-mail: news@recordernews.com
Web site: www.recordernews.com
Publisher . . . . Kevin McClary
e-mail: kevin@recordernews.com
Associate Publisher . . . . Geoff Dylong
e-mail: geoff@recordernews.com
Executive Editor . . . . Kevin Mattison
e-mail: kmattison@recordernews.com
Advertising/Marketing Director . . . . Brian Krohn
e-mail: briankrohn@recordernews.com
Editor . . . . Charlie Kraebel
e-mail: ckraebel@recordernews.com
Business Manager . . . . Bill Brzezicki
e-mail: bbrzezicki@recordernews.com

AUBURN

Citizen (The) *Circulation: Daily 11,770; Sunday 13,600*

Auburn Publishers Inc
25 Dill St, Auburn, NY 13201-3605
315-253-3700 Fax: 315-253-6031
e-mail: newsroom@tds.net
Web site: www.auburnpub.com
Publisher . . . . Michael Rifanburg
e-mail: michael.rifanburg@lee.net
Executive Editor . . . . Jeremy Boyer
e-mail: jeremy.boyer@lee.net
Managing Editor . . . . Michael Dowd
e-mail: michael.dowd@lee.net
Advertising Director . . . . Sarah Dunham
e-mail: sarah.dunham@lee.net
Circulation Directory. . . . . Todd Ackerman
e-mail: todd.ackerman@lee.net
Asst News Editor . . . . Chris Sciria
e-mail: chris.sciria@lee.net

BINGHAMTON

Press & Sun Bulletin *Weekday Circulation: 37,915*

Gannet Co Inc
33 Lewis Rd, Binghamton, NY 13905-1044
607-798-1234 Fax: 607-352-2645
e-mail: bgm-newsroom@gannett.com
Web site: www.pressconnects.com
Publisher. . . . . Sherman M Bodner
e-mail: sbodner@gannett.com
Executive Editor . . . . Calvin Stovall
e-mail: cstovall@binghamt.gannett.com
Assistant Managing Editor . . . . Al Vieira
e-mail: avieira@binghamt.gannett.com
Circulation Director . . . . Anthony Rapczynski
e-mail: arapczyn@binghamt.gannett.com
Advertising Director . . . . Jodie Riesbeck
e-mail: jriesbec@binghamt.gannett.com

BRONXVILLE-EASTCHESTER

Review *Weekly Circulation: 35,000*

Journal News (The)/Gannett Co Inc
5910 Firestone Drive, Syracuse, NY 13206
315-434-8889 Fax: 315-434-8883
e-mail: newsroom@cnylink.com
Web site: www.cnylink.com/about/review.php
Publisher....David Tyler
e-mail: dtyler@eaglenewsonline.com
Editor....Sarah Hall
e-mail: editor@eaglestarreview.com

BROOKLYN

Brooklyn Daily Eagle *Weekly Circulation: 13,000*

Brooklyn Daily Eagle
16 Court St, Ste 1208, Brooklyn, NY 11241
718-422-7400
e-mail: jdh@brooklyneagle.com
Web site: www.brooklyneagle.com
Publisher....J Dozier Hasty
e-mail: jdh@brooklyneagle.com

Canarsie Courier Publications, Inc. *Weekly Circulation: 10,000*

Canarsie Courier
1142 East 92nd Street, Brooklyn, NY 11236
718-257-0600 Fax: 718-272-0870
e-mail: canarsiec@aol.com
Web site: www.canarsiecourier.com
Associate Editor....Dara Mormile
e-mail: canarsiec@aol.com
Publisher....Donna M Marra
Managing Editor....Charles Rogers
Associate Editor....Neil Friedman
Business Manager....Catherine Rosa

New York Daily Challenge (The) *Weekday Circulation: 81,000*

New York Daily Challenge (The)
1195 Atlantic Ave, Brooklyn, NY 11216
718-636-9500 Fax: 718-857-9115
Publisher....Thomas H Watkins, Jr
e-mail: t.watkins@challenge-group.net
Managing Editor....Duwad Philip

BUFFALO

Buffalo Business First *Weekly Circulation: 10,000*

Buffalo Business First
465 Main Street, Buffalo, NY 14203-1793
716-854-5822 Fax: 716-854-7960
e-mail: buffalo@bizjournals.com
Web site: www.bizjournals.com/buffalo
Publisher....Jack Connors
Editor....Tim O'Shei
Advertising Director....Shelley Rohaurer
Circulation Marketing Director....Karen Schiffmacher

Buffalo News (The) *Weekday Circulation: 191,000*

Buffalo News (The)
1 News Plaza, Buffalo, NY 14240-0100
716-849-4444 Fax: 716-856-5150
e-mail: citydesk@buffnews.com
Web site: www.buffalonews.com
Editor....Mike Connelly
e-mail: editor@buffnews.com
Managing Editor....Brian Connolly
e-mail: bconnolly@buffnews.com
Deputy Managing Editor....Stan L Evans
e-mail: sevans@buffnews.com
Assistant Managing Editor....Margaret Kenny
e-mail: mkenny@buffnews.com
Editorial Page Editor....John Neville
e-mail: jneville@buffnews.com
City Editor....William Flynn
e-mail: wflynn@buffnews.com

CANANDAIGUA

Daily Messenger (The) *Weekly Circulation: 400,000*

Messenger Post Newspapers
73 Buffalo St, Canandaigua, NY 14424
585-394-0770 Fax: 585-394-1675
e-mail: messenger@mpnewspapers.com
Web site: www.mpnnow.com
Publisher....Richard Procida
General Manager/Advertising Director....Beth Kesel
e-mail: bkesel@messengerpostmedia.com
Regional Editor....Allison Cooper
e-mail: acooper@messengerpostmedia.com
Local Editor/Wayne County....Steve Buchiere
e-mail: sbuchiere@messengerpostmedia.com
Local Editor/Ontario County....Nora Hicks
e-mail: nhicks@messengerpostmedia.com

CATSKILL

Daily Mail (The) *Weekday Circulation: 3,524*

Hudson Valley Newspapers Inc
414 Main St, PO Box 484, Catskill, NY 12414
518-943-2100 Fax: 518-943-2063
e-mail: editorial@thedailymail.net
Web site: www.thedailymail.net
Publisher....Roger F Coleman
e-mail: rpignone@thedailymail.net
Managing Editor....Ray Pignone
e-mail: rpignone@thedailymail.net
Executive Editor....Theresa Hyland
e-mail: thyland@thedailymail.net
Advertising Director....Pamela Geskie
e-mail: pgeskie@registerstar.net

CORNING

Corning Leader (The) *Weekday Circulation: 13,585*

GateHouse Media
34 W Pulteney St, Corning, NY 14830
607-936-4651
Web site: www.the-leader.com
Publisher....Fred Benson
e-mail: fbenson@the-leader.com
News Editor....Stella Dupree
e-mail: sdupree@the-leader.com

Circulation Manager . . . . Elmer Kuehner
e-mail: ejkuehner@the-leader.com

CORTLAND

Cortland Standard Printing Co Inc *Weekday Circulation: 10,500*

Cortland Standard
110 Main St, Cortland, NY 13045
607-756-5665 Fax: 607-756-5665
e-mail: news@cortlandstandard.net
Web site: www.cortland.org/news
Publisher. . . . . Kevin R Howe
Managing/News Editor . . . . Kevin Conlon
Editorial Page Editor . . . . Skip Chapman

DUNKIRK-FREDONIA

Observer Today *Weekday Circulation: 11,648*

Observer (The)
10 E Second st, PO Box 391, Dunkirk, NY 14048-0391
716-366-3000 Fax: 716-366-3005
e-mail: editorial@observertoday.com
Web site: www.observertoday.com
Publisher. . . . . John D'Agostino
e-mail: jdagostino@observertoday.com
Managing Editor . . . . Greg Bacon
e-mail: gbacon@observertoday.com
News Editor . . . . Bill Hammond
e-mail: bhammond@observertoday.com
City Editor . . . . Gib Snyder
e-mail: gsnyder@observertoday.com

CHEMUNG

Star-Gazette *Weekday Circulation: 73,000*

Gannett Co Inc
201 Bladwin Street, Elmira, NY 14901
607-734-5151 Fax: 607-732-3786
e-mail: news@stargazette.com
Web site: www.stargazette.com
Publisher. . . . . Sherman M Bodner
e-mail: sbodner@gannett.com
Managing Editor & General Manager . . . . Lois Wilson
e-mail: lowilson@elmira.gannett.com
Circulation Director . . . . Anthony Rapczynski
e-mail: arapczyn@binghamt.gannett.com

GENEVA

Finger Lakes Times *Circulation: Sunday: 19,102; Daily: 16,185*

Finger Lakes Printing Co
218 Genesee St, Geneva, NY 14456
315-789-3333 or 800-388-6652 Fax: 315-789-4077
e-mail: fltimes@fltimes.com
Web site: www.fltimes.com
President/Publisher. . . . . William L McLean III
Executive Editor . . . . Michael J. Cutillo
Managing Editor . . . . Chuck Schading
e-mail: cschading@fltimes.com
News Editor . . . . Alan Brignall

GLENS FALLS

Post-Star (The) *Weekday Circulation: 29,000*

Lee Enterprises Inc
76 Lawrence St, Glens Falls, NY 12801
518-792-3131 ext3220 or 800-724-2543 Fax: 518-761-1255
e-mail: obits@poststar.com
Web site: www.poststar.com
Publisher . . . . Rick Emanuel
e-mail: emanuel@poststar.com
City Editor . . . . Bob Condon
e-mail: condon@poststar.com
News Editor . . . . Rhonda Triller
e-mail: rtriller@poststar.com
Sunday Editor. . . . . Todd Kehoe
e-mail: tkehoe@poststar.com
Online News Editor. . . . . Lindsey Hollenbaugh
e-mail: lhollenbaugh@poststar.com
Circulation Director. . . . . Michelle Giorgianni
e-mail: giorgianni@poststar.com
Editor . . . . Ken Tingley
e-mail: tingley@poststar.com
News Editor. . . . . Mary Serkalow
e-mail: serkalow@poststar.com
News Editor . . . . Paul Tackett
e-mail: tackett@poststar.com

GLOVERSVILLE-JOHNSTOWN

Leader-Herald (The) *Weekday Circulation: 11,500*

William B Collins Co
8 E Fulton St, PO Box 1280, Gloversville, NY 12078
518-725-8616 Fax: 518-725-7407
e-mail: news@leaderherald.com
Web site: www.leaderherald.com
Publisher . . . . Patricia Beck
e-mail: pbeck@leaderherald.com
Managing Editor. . . . . Tim Fonda
e-mail: tfonda@leaderherald.com
Sr. News Editor . . . . Rodney Minor
e-mail: rminor@leaderherald.com
Sunday Editor. . . . . Bill Ackerbauer
Circulation Manager . . . . Toni Mosconi

HERKIMER

Telegram (The) *Weekday Circulation: 6,000*

GateHouse Media Inc.
111 Green St, Herkimer, NY 13350
315-866-2220 Fax: 315-866-5913
e-mail: news@herkimertelegram.com
Web site: www.herkimertelegram.com
Publisher & Advertising Director . . . . Beth A Brewer
e-mail: beth@herkimertelegram.com
Features Editor . . . . Donna Thompson
Managing Editor . . . . Todd Dewan
e-mail: tdewan@littlefallstimes.com

HORNELL

Evening Tribune (The) *Weekday Circulation: 7,562*

GateHouse Media Inc.
85 Canisteo St, Hornell, NY 14843
607-324-1425 Fax: 607-324-2317
Web site: www.eveningtribune.com
Publisher . . . . Tom Connors
e-mail: tomconnors@eveningtribune.com
Marketing Director . . . . John Frungillo
e-mail: john@eveningtribune.com
Managing Editor . . . . Andrew Thompson
e-mail: andythompson@eveningtribune.com
Circulation . . . . Gary Shaver
e-mail: garyshaver@eveningtribune.com

HUDSON

Register-Star *Weekday Circulation: 6,100*

Johnson Newspaper Corporation
One Hudson City Centre, Hudson, NY 12534
518-828-1616 Fax: 518-828-3870
e-mail: editorial@registerstar.com
Web site: www.registerstar.com
Publisher . . . . Harold B Johnson II
e-mail: publisher@registerstar.com
Executive Editor . . . . Theresa Hyland
e-mail: thyland@registerstar.com
City Editor . . . . Mary Dempsey
e-mail: mdempsey@registerstar.com
Editor . . . . Lori Anander
Editor . . . . Karrie Allen

ITHACA

Ithaca Journal (The) *Weekday Circulation: 10,371*

Gannett Co Inc
123 W State St, Ithaca, NY 14850
607-272-2321 Fax: 607-272-4248
Web site: www.theithacajournal.com
Publisher . . . . Sherman M Bodner
e-mail: sbodner@gannett.com
Managing Editor/General Manager . . . . Bruce Estes
e-mail: bestes@ithaca.gannett.com
News Editor . . . . Steve Gattine
e-mail: sgattine@ithaca.gannett.com
Assistant Managing Editor . . . . Dave Bohrer
e-mail: dbohrer@ithacajournal.com

JAMESTOWN

Post-Journal, The *Weekday Circulation: 20,000*

Post-Journal, The
PO Box 3386, Jamestown, NY 14702-3386
716-487-1111 or 866-756-9600 Fax: 716-664-3119
e-mail: editorial@post-journal.com
Web site: www.post-journal.com
Publisher . . . . Michael Bird
e-mail: mbird@post-journal.com
Editor . . . . John Whittaker
e-mail: jwhittaker@post-journal.com
Editor . . . . Matt Spielman
e-mail: mspielman@post-journal.com
News/Wire Editor . . . . Mike Rukavina
e-mail: mrukavina@post-journal.com
Circulation Director . . . . Andrew Gee
e-mail: agee@post-journal.com

KINGSTON

Daily Freeman *Weekday Circulation: 20,391*

Journal Register Company
79 Hurley Ave, Kingston, NY 12401
845-331-5000 Fax: 845-331-3557
e-mail: jdewey@journalregister.com
Web site: www.dailyfreeman.com
Publisher . . . . Jan Dewey
e-mail: jdewey@journalregister.com
Managing Editor . . . . Tony Adamis
e-mail: tadamis@freemanonline.com
City Editor . . . . Jeremy Schiffres
e-mail: jschiffres@freemanonline.com
Regional Circualtion Director . . . . Jim Collier
e-mail: jcollier@journalregister.com

LITTLE FALLS

Times (The) *Weekday Circulation: 5,042*

GateHouse Media Inc.
347 S 2nd St, Little Falls, NY 13365
315-823-3680 Fax: 315-823-4086
e-mail: news@littlefallstimes.com
Web site: www.littlefallstimes.com
Publisher . . . . Beth Brewer
e-mail: bethtimes@twcny.rr.com
Production Manager . . . . Wayne Galt
News Editor . . . . Todd Dewan
e-mail: news@littlefallstimes.com

LOCKPORT

Journal-Register, The *Weekday Circulation: 3,500*

Greater Niagara Newspapers
170 East Ave, Medina, NY 14094
585-798-1400 Fax: 585-798-0290
e-mail: jr@gnnewspaper.com
Web site: www.journal-register.com
Publisher . . . . Diane Crowe
Managing Editor . . . . John Hopkins
e-mail: john.hopkins@journal-register.com
Circulation Manager . . . . Beth Podgers
e-mail: elizabeth.podgers@lockportjournal.com

Lockport Union-Sun & Journal *Weekday Circulation: 12,300*

Greater Niagara Newspapers
170 East Ave, Lockport, NY 14094
716-439-9222 Fax: 716-439-9249
Web site: www.lockportjournal.com
Publisher . . . . Diane Crowe
e-mail: diane.crowe@lockportjournal.com
Managing Editor . . . . John Hopkins
e-mail: john.hopkins@lockportjournal.com
Night/City Editor . . . . Scott Leffler
e-mail: scott.leffler@lockportjournal.com
Circulation Manager . . . . Elizabeth Podgers
e-mail: elizabeth.podgers@lockportjournal.com

LONG ISLAND

Newsday *Weekday Circulation: 470,316*

Newsday Inc
235 Pinelawn Rd, Melville, NY 11747-4250
631-843-2700 or 800-639-7329 Fax: 631-843-2953
e-mail: web@newsday.com
Web site: www.newsday.com
Publisher . . . . Fred Groser
e-mail: publisher@newsday.com
Editor-in-Chief. . . . . Theresa Mills
e-mail: editor@newsday.com
Editor . . . . Howard Schneider
Editor . . . . Ronald Roel
Editor . . . . Valerie Kellogg
Circulation Manager. . . . . Sandy Elder

Queens Gazette *Weekly Circulation: 160,000*

Queens Gazette
42-16 34th Avenue, Long Island City, NY 11101
718-361-6161 Fax: 718-784-7552
e-mail: qgazette@aol.com
Web site: www.qgazette.com
Publisher/Editor. . . . . Tony Barsamian
Associate Editor. . . . . Jason D. Antos
Contibuting Editor . . . . Linda Wilson

MALONE

Malone Telegram, The *Weekday Circulation: 6,000*

Johnson Newspaper Corporation
469 E Main St, Malone, NY 12953
518-483-2000 Fax: 518-483-8579
e-mail: news@mtelegram.com
Web site: www.mtelegram.com
Publisher . . . . Russell Webster
Editor . . . . Doug Buchanan
e-mail: dbuchanan@mtelegram.com
Managing Editor . . . . Connie Jenkins

MASSENA

Daily Courier-Observer *Weekday Circulation: 7,800*

Johnson Newspaper Corporation
1 Harrowgate Commons, PO Box 300, Massena, NY 13662
315-265-6000 Fax: 315-265-6001
e-mail: rmartin@ogd.com
Web site: www.mpcourier.com
Publisher . . . . Charles Kelly
e-mail: ckelly@ogd.com
Managing Editor . . . . Ryne Martin
e-mail: rmartin@ogd.com
Editor . . . . Bob Beckstead
e-mail: bbeckstead@ogd.com
District Circulation Manager . . . . Cris Pitts

MEDINA

Journal-Register, The *Weekday Circulation: 3,500*

Greater Niagara Newspapers
541-543 Main St, Medina, NY 14103
585-798-1400 Fax: 585-798-0290
e-mail: jr@gnnewspaper.com
Web site: www.journal-register.com
Publisher . . . . Diane Crowe
Managing Editor . . . . John Hopkins
Circulation Manager. . . . . Beth Podgers

MIDDLETOWN

Times Herald-Record *Weekday Circulation: 80,000*

Times Herald-Record
40 Mulberry St, POÆBox 2046, Middletown, NY 10940-6357
845-343-2181 or 800-620-1700 Fax: 845-343-2170
e-mail: readeradvocate@th-recordonline.com
Web site: www.recordonline.com
Executive Editor . . . . Derek Osenenko
e-mail: dosenenko@th-record.com
Senior Editor/Local News . . . . Adrianne Reilly
Editor/Local News . . . . Mike Carey
Editor/Night Publications . . . . Robert Berczuk
Editor/Community News . . . . Eric Stutz

NEW YORK CITY

AM Law Daily, The *Weekday Circulation: 16,000*

American Lawyer Media
120 Broadway, 5th Fl, New York, NY 10271
800-888-8300 Fax: 646-822-5146
Web site: www.alm.com
Editor-in-Chief . . . . Robin Sparkman
e-mail: rsparkman@alm.com
VP/Group Publisher . . . . Scott Pierce
e-mail: spierce@alm.com
Executive Editor. . . . . Emily Barker
Managing Editor . . . . Maryann Saltser
Editor/New Media . . . . Jonathan Hayter
. . . .
e-mail: news@joc.com
SVP/Strategy. . . . . Peter M Tirschwell
e-mail: ptirschwell@joc.com
Executive Editor . . . . Chris Brooks
e-mail: jbonney@joc.com
Publisher. . . . . Tony Stein
e-mail: tstein@joc.com
Managing Editor . . . . Barbara Wyker
e-mail: bwyker@joc.com
Senior Editor . . . . Joseph Bonney
e-mail: jbonney@joc.com

Wall Street Journal (The) *Daily Circulation: 2,000,000*

Dow Jones & Company
1211 Avenue of the Americas, New York, NY 10036
212-416-2000 or 800-568-7625 Fax: 212-416-2653
e-mail: nywireroom@dowjones.com
Web site: www.wsj.com
Publisher . . . . Lex Fenwick
Managing Editor. . . . . Gerard Baker
Managing Editor/Newswires. . . . . Neal Lipschutz
Editor-in-Chief/Dow Jones . . . . Gerard Baker
Managing Director/Dow Jones . . . . Kelly E. Leach

People's World *Weekly Circulation: 27,000*

Long View Publishing Co
235 W 23rd St, New York, NY 10011
212-924-2523 Fax: 212-229-1713
e-mail: ny@peoplesworld.org
Web site: www.peoplesworld.org
Co-editor. . . . . Teresa Albano
e-mail: talbano@peoplesworld.org
Managing Editor . . . . Dan Margolis
e-mail: dmargolis@peoplesworld.org

Offices and agencies generally appear in alphabetical order, except when specific order is requested by listee.

Labor Editor . . . . . John Wojcik
e-mail: jwojcik@peoplesworld.org

New York Post *Weekday Circulation: 686,207*

NYP Holdings Inc
1211 Ave of the Americas, New York, NY 10036-8790
212-930-8000 Fax: 212-930-8005
e-mail: letters@nypost.com
Web site: www.nypost.com
Publisher . . . . . Paul Carlucci
Managing Editor . . . . . Frank Zini
Editor . . . . . Debra Birnbaum
Editor . . . . . Muhammad Cohen

New York Daily News *Weekday Circulation: 688,584*

New York Daily News
4 New York Plaza, New York, NY 10004
212-210-2100 Fax: 212-643-7831
e-mail: news@edit.nydailynews.com
Web site: www.nydailynews.com
Publisher . . . . . Mortimer Zuckerman
e-mail: mzuckerman@edit.nydailynews.com
Editor-in-Chief . . . . . Kevin R. Coney
News Editor . . . . . John Oswald
Managing Editor . . . . . Robert Sapio
e-mail: rsapio@edit.nydailynews.com
Editor . . . . . Arthur Browne

The Independent News *Weekly Circulation: 50,000*

The Independent News
74 Montauk Highway, Suite 16, East Hampton, NY 11937
631-324-2500 Fax: 631-324-2544
e-mail: news@indyeastend.com
Web site: www.indyeastend.com
Editor-in-Chief . . . . . Rick Murphy
e-mail: rmurphy@indyeastend.com
Publisher . . . . . James J. Mackin
e-mail: jim@indyeastend.com
News Editor . . . . . Kitty Merrill
e-mail: kmerrill@indyeastend.com

New York Observer (The) *Weekday Circulation: 50,000*

The New York Observer
321 W. 44th St, 6th Floor, New York, NY 10036
212-755-2400 or 800-542-0420 Fax: 212-980-2087
e-mail: editorial@observer.com
Web site: www.observer.com
Publisher . . . . . Jared Kushner
Editor-in-Chief . . . . . Peter Feld
Editor . . . . . Elizabeth Spiers
City Editor . . . . . Terry Golway

The New York Times *Weekday Circulation: 1,121,057*

The New York Times
620 Eighth Avenue, New York, NY 10018
212-556-1234 Fax: 212-556-3815
e-mail: letters@nytimes.com
Web site: www.nytimes.com
Publisher . . . . . Arthur O. Sulzberger, Jr
e-mail: publisher@nytimes.com
Executive Editor . . . . . Jill Abramson
e-mail: abramson@nytimes.com
Editorial Page Editor . . . . . Andrew M. Rosenthal
e-mail: rosenthal@nytimes.com

The Putnam County News and Recorder *Weekly Circulation: 4,000*

The Putnam County News and Recorder
144 Main Street, Cold Spring, NY 10516
845-265-2468 Fax: 845-265-2144
e-mail: editor@pcnr.com
Web site: www.pcnr.com
Publisher . . . . . Elizabeth Ailes
Associate Publisher/Editor-in-Chief . . . . . Douglas Cunningham
e-mail: doug@pcner.com

Village Voice (The) *Weekly Circulation: 250,000*

Village Voice Media, Inc
36 Cooper Sq, New York, NY 10003
212-475-3333 Fax: 212-475-8944
e-mail: editor@villagevoice.com
Web site: www.villagevoice.com
Editor-in-Chief . . . . . Will Bourne
Deputy Editor . . . . . Jessica Lustig
Senior Associate Editor . . . . . Angela Ashman
Senior Associate Editor . . . . . Araceli Cruz

Wave Publishing Co. *Weekly Circulation: 12,300*

The Wave
88-08 Rockaway Beach Blvd, PO Box 930097, Rockaway Beach, NY 11693-0097
718-634-4000 Fax: 718-945-0913
e-mail: editor@rockawave.com
Web site: www.rockawave.com
Publisher . . . . . Susan B. Locke
e-mail: sbl@rockawave.com
General Manager . . . . . Sanford M. Bernstein
e-mail: smb@rockawave.com
Associate Editor . . . . . Dan Guarino
Contributing Editor . . . . . Miriam Rosenberg
e-mail: miriamsue18@aol.com

NIAGARA FALLS

Niagara Gazette *Weekday Circulation: 20,268*

Greater Niagara Newspapers
310 Niagara St, PO Box 549, Niagara Falls, NY 14302-0549
716-282-2311 Fax: 716-286-3895
e-mail: bevacquad@gnnewspaper.com
Web site: www.niagara-gazette.com
Publisher . . . . . Peter Mio
e-mail: peter.mio@niagara-gazette.com
Managing Editor . . . . . Matt Winterhalter
e-mail: matt.winterhalter@niagara-gazette.com
City Editor . . . . . Mark Scheer
e-mail: scheerm@gnnewspaper.com

NORWICH

Evening Sun *Weekday Circulation: 5,200*

Snyder Communications Corp
29 Lackawanna Ave, PO Box 151, Norwich, NY 13815
607-334-3276 Fax: 607-334-8273
e-mail: news@evesun.com
Web site: www.evesun.com
Publisher . . . . . Richard Snyder
e-mail: dsnyder@evesun.com
Managing Editor . . . . . Brian Golden
e-mail: bgolden@evesun.com
Circulation Manager . . . . . Lori Chmieliowiec
e-mail: lchmieliowiec@evesun.com

OGDENSBURG

The Journal *Weekday Circulation: 5,200*

St Lawrence County Newspapers
308 Isabella St, PO Box 409, Ogdensburg, NY 13669
315-393-1003 Fax: 315-393-5108
Web site: www.ogd.com
City Editor . . . . Elizabeth Lyons
e-mail: egraham@wdt.net
District Circulation Manager . . . . Michael Eldridge
e-mail: meldridge@ogd.com

OLEAN

Olean Times Herald *Weekday Circulation: 15,000*

Bradford Publications Inc
639 Norton Dr, Olean, NY 14760
716-372-3121 Fax: 716-373-6397
e-mail: news@oleantimesherald.com
Web site: www.oleantimesherald.com
Publisher/General Manager . . . . Bill Fitzpatrick
Managing Editor . . . . Jim Eckstrom
e-mail: jeckstrom@oleantimesherald.com
City Editor . . . . Brian Lothridge
e-mail: blothridge@oleantimesherald.com

ONEIDA

Oneida Daily Dispatch *Weekday Circulation: 6,818*

Journal Register Co
130 Broad Street, Oneida, NY 13421
315-363-5100 Fax: 315-363-9832
e-mail: newsroom@oneidadispatch.com
Web site: www.oneidadispatch.com
Publisher . . . . Jan Dewey
e-mail: jdewey@journalregister.com
News Editor . . . . Kurt W Wanfried
e-mail: kwanfried@oneidadispatch.com
General Manager . . . . Karen Alvord
e-mail: kalvord@journalregister.com
Circulation Manager . . . . Sabrina Sharkey
e-mail: ssharkey@oneidadispatch.com

ONEONTA

Daily Star (The) *Weekday Circulation: 21,000*

Ottaway Newspapers Inc
102 Chestnut St, Oneonta, NY 13820
607-432-1000 Fax: 607-432-5847
e-mail: webmaster@thedailystar.com
Web site: www.thedailystar.com
Publisher . . . . Mitchell D. Lynch
e-mail: mlynch@thedailystar.com
Editor . . . . Sam Pollak
e-mail: spollak@thedailystar.com
Editor . . . . Mark Boshnack
e-mail: mboshnack@thedailystar.com
News Editor . . . . Denise Richardson
e-mail: drichardson@thedailystar.com

OSWEGO-FULTON

Palladium-Times (The) *Weekday Circulation: 8,500*

The Palladium-Times
140 W First St, Oswego, NY 13126
315-343-3800 Fax: 315-343-0273
e-mail: editor@palltimes.com
Web site: www.pall-times.com
Publisher . . . . Jon Spaulding
e-mail: jspaulding@palltimes.com
Editor . . . . Sarah McCrobie
e-mail: smccrobie@palltimes.com
Advertising Manager . . . . Kate Percival
e-mail: kpercival@palltimes.com
Circulation . . . . Tom Van Schaack
e-mail: tvanschaack@palltimes.com

PLATTSBURGH

Press-Republican *Weekday Circulation: 20,210*

Press-Republican
PO Box 459, Plattsburgh, NY 12901
518-565-4131 Fax: 518-561-3362
e-mail: news@pressrepublican.com
Web site: www.pressrepublican.com
Publisher . . . . Robert W. Parks
Editor . . . . Lois M. Clermont
News Editor . . . . Suzanne Moore
Managing Editor . . . . Nathan Ovalle

POUGHKEEPSIE

Poughkeepsie Journal *Weekday Circulation: 40,202*

Gannett Co Inc
PO Box 1231, Poughkeepsie, NY 12602
845-437-4800 Fax: 845-437-4921
e-mail: newsroom@poughkee.gannett.com
Web site: www.poughkeepsiejournal.com
Publisher/President . . . . Barry Rothfeld
e-mail: brothfeld@gannett.com
Executive Editor . . . . Stuart Shinske
e-mail: sshinske@poughkeepsie.gannett.com
Local Editor . . . . Kevin Lenihan
e-mail: klenihan@poughkeepsie.gannett.com
Circulation Manager . . . . Bill Farrell
e-mail: farrellb@poughkeepsie.gannett.com
Editorial Page Editor . . . . John Penney
e-mail: jpenney@poughkeepsie.gannett.com

ROCHESTER

Daily Record (The) *Weekly Circulation: 4,500*

The Dolan Company
16 W Main St, Rochester, NY 14614
585-232-6920 Fax: 585-232-2740
Web site: www.nydailyrecord.com
Publisher . . . . Kevin Momot
e-mail: kevin.momot@nydailyrecord.com
Associate Editor . . . . Kristy O'Malley
e-mail: kristy.omalley@nydailyrecord.com
News Reporter . . . . Denise Champagne
e-mail: denise.champagne@nydailyrecord.com

Offices and agencies generally appear in alphabetical order, except when specific order is requested by listee.

Democrat and Chronicle *Weekday Circulation: 170,000*

Gannett Co Inc
55 Exchange Blvd, Rochester, NY 14614
585-232-7100 Fax: 585-258-2237
e-mail: webmaster@democratandchronicle.com
Web site: www.democratandchronicle.com
President/Publisher . . . . Michael Kane
e-mail: mgkane@democratandchronicle.com
Vice President/Editor . . . . Karen Magnuson
e-mail: kmagnuso@democratandchronicle.com
Local Editor . . . . Catherine Roberts
e-mail: cathyr@democratandchronicle.com
Editorial Page Editor . . . . James Lawrence
e-mail: jlawrenc@democratandchronicle.com

Suburban News & Hamlin Clarkson Herald *Weekly Circulation: 32,000*

Westside News Inc
1776 hilton-Parma Corners Road, PO Box 106, Spencerport, NY 14559
585-352-3411 Fax: 585-352-4811
e-mail: editor@westsidenewsny
Web site: www.westsidenewsny.com
Publisher . . . . Keith Ryan
Editor . . . . Evelyn Dow
e-mail: ediotr@westsidenewsny.com
Circulation Manager . . . . Don Griffin
e-mail: circulation@westsidenewsny.com

ROME

Daily Sentinel *Weekday Circulation: 16,500*

Rome Sentinel Co
333 W Dominick St, Rome, NY 13440-5701
315-337-4000 Fax: 315-337-4704
e-mail: sentinel@rny.com
Web site: www.romesentinel.com
Publisher . . . . Stephen Waters
e-mail: dswanson@rny.com
Managing Editor . . . . David C Swanson
Editor . . . . Thomas Merz
e-mail: editor@rny.com
News Editor . . . . Kathleen Twellman Haley
e-mail: editor@rny.com

SALAMANCA

Salamanca Press *Weekday Circulation: 2,200*

Bradford Publishing Co
36 River St, Salamanca, NY 14779
716-945-1644 Fax: 716-945-4285
e-mail: salpressnews@verizon.net
Web site: www.salamancapress.com
Managing Editor . . . . Rich Place
e-mail: salpressnews@verizon.net

SARANAC LAKE

Adirondack Daily Enterprise *Weekday Circulation: 5,000*

Adirondack Publishing Co Inc
54 Broadway, PO Box 318, Saranac Lake, NY 12983
518-891-2600 Fax: 518-891-2756
e-mail: adenews@adirondackdailyenterprise.com
Web site: www.adirondackdailyenterprise.com
Publisher . . . . Catherine Moore
e-mail: cmoore@adirondackdailyenterprise.com
Managing Editor . . . . Peter Crowley
e-mail: pcrowley@adirondackdailyenterprise.com
News Editor . . . . Brittany Proulx
e-mail: adenews@adirondackdailyenterprise.com
Circulation Manager . . . . Trinity Bushey
e-mail: circulation@adirondackdailyenterprise.com

SARATOGA SPRINGS

Saratogian (The) *Weekday Circulation: 10,000*

Journal Register Company
20 Lake Ave, Saratoga Springs, NY 12866
518-584-4242 Fax: 518-587-7750
e-mail: news@saratogian.com
Web site: www.saratogian.com
Publisher . . . . Michael F. O'Sullivan
e-mail: mosullivan@journalregister.com
Managing Editor . . . . Barbara A Lombardo
e-mail: blombardo@journalregister.com
Editor . . . . Donna Bell
e-mail: cnews@saratogian.com
Regional Circulation Director . . . . Jim Collier
e-mail: jcollier@journalregister.com

SCHENECTADY

Daily Gazette (The) *Weekday Circulation: 53,800*

Daily Gazette Co
2345 Maxon Road Extension, Schenectady, NY 12308
518-374-4141 Fax: 518-395-3089
e-mail: news@dailygazette.com
Web site: www.dailygazette.com
Publisher . . . . John E N Hume, III
City Editor . . . . Irv Dean
News Editor . . . . William Finelli
Online Editor . . . . Jeffrey Haff
Day City Editor . . . . Miles Reed
Circulation Supervisor . . . . Brian Zarelli

STATEN ISLAND

Staten Island Advance *Circulation: Monday, Tuesday, Wednesday, Friday: 59,000; Thursday: 67,000; Sunday: 77,000*

Advance Publications Inc
950 Fingerboard Rd, Staten Island, NY 10305
718-981-1234 Fax: 718-981-5679
e-mail: editor@siadvance.com
Web site: www.silive.com
Publisher . . . . Caroline Diamond Harrison
Circulation Manager . . . . Richard Salemo
e-mail: salemo@siadvance.com
Editor . . . . Brian J. Laline
e-mail: laline@siadvance.com
Managing Editor . . . . William A. Huus
e-mail: bhuus@siadvance.com
Editorial Page Editor . . . . Mark Hanley
e-mail: hanley@siadvance.com
City Editor . . . . Tom Checchi
e-mail: checchi@siadvance.com
News Editor . . . . Richard Ryan
e-mail: ryan@siadvance.com

SYRACUSE

Post-Standard (The) *Weekday Circulation: 115,000*

Syracuse Newspapers Inc
PO Box 4915, Syracuse, NY 13221
315-470-0011 Fax: 315-470-3081
e-mail: business@syracuse.com
Web site: www.syracusemediagroup.com
Vice President of Content . . . . Michael J Connor
e-mail: mconnor@syracuse.com
Director of Content. . . . . John Lammers
e-mail: jlammers@syracuse.com
Director of Publications . . . . Stan Linhorst
e-mail: slinhorst@syracuse.com
Managing Producer/Editor . . . . Steven M. Billmeyer
e-mail: sbillmeyer@syracuse.com

TONAWANDA

Tonawanda News *Weekday Circulation: 9,000*

Greater Niagara Newspapers
435 River Road, PO Box 668, North Tonawanda, NY 14120-6809
716-693-1000 Fax: 716-693-0124
e-mail: newsroom@tonawanda-news.com
Web site: www.tonawanda-news.com
Managing Editor. . . . . Eric DuVall
e-mail: duvalle@gnnewspaper.com
Circulation Director . . . . Ken Skryp
Advertising Director . . . . John Brundo
Publisher. . . . . Peter Mio

TROY

Record (The) *Weekday Circulation: 16,872*

Journal Register Co
501 Broadway, Troy, NY 12180
518-270-1200 Fax: 518-270-1202
e-mail: letters@troyrecord.com
Web site: www.troyrecord.com
Publisher. . . . . Michael F. O'Sullivan
e-mail: mosullivan@journalregister.com
Editor . . . . Lisa Robert Lewis
e-mail: llewis@troyrecord.com
City Editor. . . . . James V. Franco
e-mail: jfranco@troyrecord.com
Regional Circulation Director . . . . Jim Collier
e-mail: jcollier@journalregister.com

UTICA

Observer-Dispatch *Weekday Circulation: 45,956*

GateHouse Media
221 Oriskany Plz, Utica, NY 13501
315-792-5000 Fax: 315-792-5033
e-mail: news@uticaod.com
Web site: www.uticaod.com
President/Publisher . . . . Donna Donovan
e-mail: ddonovan@uticaod.com
Editor . . . . Kris Worrell
e-mail: kworrell@uticaod.com
Managing Editor . . . . Ron Johns
e-mail: rjohns1@uticaod.com
News Editor. . . . . Fran Perritano
e-mail: fperrita@utica.gannett.com

WATERTOWN

Watertown Daily Times *Weekday Circulation: 27,020*

Johnson Newspaper Corp
260 Washington St, Watertown, NY 13601
315-782-1000 Fax: 315-661-2523
e-mail: news@wdt.net
Web site: www.watertowndailytimes.com
Executive Editor . . . . Bert Gault
e-mail: bgault@wdt.net
Managing Editor . . . . Robert Gorman
e-mail: bgorman@wdt.net
Editorial Page Editor. . . . . Francis Pound
e-mail: fpound@wdt.net
Editor (Sunday) . . . . Mary Kaskan
e-mail: mkaskan@wdt.net

WELLSVILLE

Wellsville Daily Reporter/Spectator *Weekday Circulation: 4,400*

Gate House Media
159 N Main St, Wellsville, NY 14895
585-593-5300 Fax: 585-593-5303
e-mail: editor@wellsvilledaily.com
Web site: www.wellsvilledaily.com
Publisher . . . . Oak Duke
Editor . . . . John Anderson
Reporter . . . . Kathryn Ross
Sports. . . . . Heather Matta

NEWS SERVICES/MAGAZINES

ABC News (New York Bureau)
47 W 66th St, New York, NY 10023
212-456-7777 Fax: 212-456-2795
e-mail: nctavdr@abc.com
Web site: www.abcnews.go.com
President & Publisher . . . . Ellen Archer
Bureau Chief . . . . Amy Brenholts
Director/Domestic News . . . . Wendy Fisher

American Metal Market
225 Park Avenue South, 6th Floor, New York, NY 10003
212-213-6202 Fax: 212-213-6617
e-mail: helpdesk@amm.com
Web site: www.amm.com
President . . . . Raju Daswani
e-mail: rdaswani@amm.com
Editor. . . . . Jo Isenberg-O'Loughlin
e-mail: jisenberg@amm.com
Senior Vice President . . . . David Brooks
e-mail: dbrooks@amm.com
Deputy Managing Editor . . . . Josephine Mason
e-mail: jmason@amm.com
Chief Correspondent, Steel . . . . Scott Robertson
e-mail: srobertson@amm.com

Associated Press (New York/Metro)
450 West 33rd St, New York, NY 10001
212-621-1500 or 212-621-5447 Fax: 212-621-1679
e-mail: info@ap.org
Web site: www.ap.org
Bureau Chief. . . . . Howard Goldberg
e-mail: hgoldberg@ap.org
Executive Editor . . . . Kathleen Carroll
Editor/West Region . . . . Traci Carl
Editor/Asia Pacific . . . . Brian Carovillano
Editor/South Region. . . . . Lisa Pane

Offices and agencies generally appear in alphabetical order, except when specific order is requested by listee.

Editor/Central Region . . . . . David Scott

BNA (formerly Bureau of National Affairs)
PO Box 7169, Albany, NY 12224
518-399-8414 Fax: 518-399-8403
Web site: www.bna.com
NYS Correspondent . . . . . Gerald Silverman

Business Review
40 British American Blvd, Latham, NY 12110
518-640-6800 Fax: 518-640-6801
e-mail: albany@bizjournals.com
Web site: www.bizjournals.com/albany
Publisher . . . . . Carolyn Jones
e-mail: cjones@bizjournals.com
Managing Editor . . . . . Neil Springer
e-mail: nspringer@bizjournals.com

CBS News (New York)
51 West 52nd St, New York, NY 10019-6188
212-975-4321 Fax: 212-975-9387
Web site: www.cbsnews.com
Editor-in-Chief . . . . . Jeremy Murphy
Executive Editor . . . . . Jack Otter
Executive Story Editor . . . . . Victoria M. Gordon
Executive News Producer . . . . . Peter Wilgoren
News Planning Editor . . . . . Abby Lawing
News Planning Editor . . . . . Gretchen White
News Writer . . . . . Arlene Lebe
News Director . . . . . Jeff Hatthorn

Central New York Business Journal
231 Walton Street, Syracuse, NY 13202
315-472-3104 Fax: 315-472-3644
e-mail: info@cnybj.com
Web site: www.cnybj.com
Publisher . . . . . Norman Poltenson
e-mail: npoltenson@cnybj.com
Editor-in-Chief . . . . . Adam Rombel
e-mail: arombel@cnybj.com

City Journal (Manhattan Institute for Policy Research)
52 Vanderbilt Ave, 3rd Floor, New York, NY 10017
212-599-7000 Fax: 212-599-0371
e-mail: cj@city-journal.org
Web site: www.city-journal.org
Editor . . . . . Brian C Anderson
e-mail: banderson@city-journal.org
Managing Editor . . . . . Benjamin Plotinsky

Crain's New York Business
711 Third Ave, New York, NY 10017
212-210-0100 Fax: 212-210-0799
e-mail: ecordova@crainsnewyork.com
Web site: www.crainsnewyork.com
Publisher & Vice President . . . . . Jill Kaplan
e-mail: jkaplan@crainsnewyork.com
Editor . . . . . Glenn Coleman
e-mail: gcoleman@crainsnewyork.com
Managing Editor . . . . . Jeremy Smerd
e-mail: jsmerd@crainsnewyork.com
Deputy Managing Editor . . . . . Valerie Block
e-mail: vblock@crainsnewyork.com
Copy Chief . . . . . Stephen Noveck
e-mail: snoveck@crainsnewyork.com

Cuyler News Service
PO Box 7205, State Capitol, Albany, NY 12224
518-465-1745 Fax: 518-465-6849
e-mail: efmnews@aol.com
Owner . . . . . Elizabeth G Flood
Contact . . . . . Janet Sanders
Contact . . . . . Amy Despirito

Dow Jones Newswires (Dow Jones & Company)
1155 Ave of the Americas, 7th Fl, New York, NY 10036
201-938-5400 Fax: 201-938-5600
Web site: www.dowjonesnews.com
Editor-in-Chief . . . . . Gerard Baker
Managing Editor . . . . . Neal Lipschutz

Empire State Report (CINN Worldwide Inc)
PO Box 9001, Mount Vernon, NY 10553
914-966-3180 Fax: 914-966-3264
e-mail: empire@cinn.com
Web site: www.empirestatereport.com
Associate Publisher/Editor . . . . . Maria Chiulli
Head of Circulation . . . . . Jennifer Jehn

Gannett News Service
150 State St, 2nd Fl, Albany, NY 12207
518-436-9781 Fax: 518-436-0130
e-mail: gannett@albany.net
Web site: www.gannett.com
Bureau Chief . . . . . Joseph Spector
e-mail: spector@gannett.com
Correspondent . . . . . Jon Campbell
Correspondent . . . . . Cara Matthews
e-mail: clmatthe@gannett.com

Hudson Valley Business Journal
86 East Main Street, Wappingers Falls, NY 12590
845-298-6236 Fax: 845-298-6238
e-mail: debhvbj@gmail.com
Web site: www.hvbj.com
Publisher . . . . . Debbie Kwiatoski
e-mail: debhvbj@gmail.com

ITAR-TASS News Agency
780 Third Ave, 19th Fl, New York, NY 10017
212-245-4250 Fax: 212-245-4258
e-mail: info@itar-tass.com
Web site: www.itar-tass.com
Bureau Chief . . . . . Vladimir Kikilo

Legislative Correspondents Association
PO Box 7340, State Capitol, 3rd Fl, Albany, NY 12224
518-455-2388
Web site: www.lgapressroom.blogspot.com
Press Room Supervisor . . . . . Jean Gutbtodt
President . . . . . Brendan Scott

Long Island Business News
2150 Smithtown Avenue, Ronkonkoma, NY 11779
631-737-1700 Fax: 631-737-1890
e-mail: editor@libn.com
Web site: www.libn.com
Managing Editor . . . . . Andrea Jones
e-mail: andrea.jones@libn.com
Publisher . . . . . John Kominicki
e-mail: andrea.jones@libn.com

Mid-Hudson News Network
42 Marcy Lane, Middletown, NY 10941
845-537-1500 or 845-695-2923 Fax: 845-692-2921
e-mail: news@midhudsonnews.com
Web site: www.midhudsonnews.com
Managing Director/Publisher . . . . . Hank Gross

. . . . .
President/NBC News . . . . . Steve Capus
SVP/News Marketing and Communications . . . . . Lauren Kapp

NY Capitolwire
172 W State St, Trenton, NJ 08608
717-986-0225
e-mail: info@capitolwire.com
Web site: www.capitolwire.com
President/Publisher....Craig Leach

New York Magazine (New York Media, LLC)
75 Varick Street, 4th Floor, New York, NY 10013
212-508-0700 Fax: 212-221-9195
e-mail: nyletters@nymag.com
Web site: www.nymag.com
Editor-in-Chief....Adam Moss
e-mail: adam_moss@newyorkmag.com
Executive Editor....John Homans
e-mail: john_homans@newyorkmag.com
Managing Editor....Ann Clarke
e-mail: ann_clarke@newyorkmag.com
Publisher....Lawrence Burstein
e-mail: larry_burstein@newyorkmag.com
....Jared Hohlt

Newsweek/The Daily Beast
7 Hanover Sq, New York, NY 10004
212-445-4600 Fax: 212-445-4425
e-mail: editors@newsweek.com
Web site: www.newsweek.com
Publisher....Rhona Murphy
e-mail: rhona.murphy@newsweek.com
Editor/Newsweek International....Fareed Zakaria
Executive Editor....Justine A. Rosenthal
Editor-at-Large....Kyle Pope

Ottaway News Service (NYS only)
N State Capitol, 3rd Fl, Albany, NY 12224
518-463-1157 Fax: 518-463-7486
Legislative Correspondent....John Milgrim
e-mail: jmottaway@aol.com

Reuters (Thomson Reuters Markets LLC)
3 Times Square, New York, NY 10036
646-223-4000 Fax: 646-223-4001
Web site: www.reuters.com
Bureau Chief....Matthew Bigg
Editor-in-Chief....Stephen J. Adler
Chief White House Correspondent....Steve Holland
Correspondent....Scott Malone
Correspondent....Sam Nelson

Rochester Business Journal
45 E Avenue, Suite 500, Rochester, NY 14604
585-546-8303 Fax: 585-546-3398
e-mail: rbj@rbj.net
Web site: www.rbjdaily.com
Editor/Vice President....Paul Ericson
e-mail: pericson@rbj.net
Associate Editor....Smriti Jacob
e-mail: sjacob@rbj.net
Managing Editor....Michael Dickinson
e-mail: mdickinson@rbj.net
President/Publisher....Susan Holliday
e-mail: mdickinson@rbj.net

Scripps Howard News Service
1090 Vermont Ave NW, Ste 1000, Washington, DC 20005
202-408-1484 Fax: 202-408-2062
Web site: www.shns.com
Desk Editor....Carol Guensburg
Photo Editor....Sheila Person
e-mail: persons@shns.com
Content Editor....Carolyn Cerbin
National Correspendent....Thomas Hargrove

RADIO

Stations included in this chapter produce news and/or public affairs programming and are listed alphabetically by primary service area.

ALBANY

WAMC (90.3 FM)
WAMC, Northeast Public Radio, PO Box 66600, Albany, NY 12206
518-465-5233 or 800-323-9262 Fax: 518-432-6974
e-mail: mail@wamc.org
Web site: www.wamc.org
President & CEO....Alan Chartock
e-mail: alan@wamc.org
Associate News Director....Joe Donahue
e-mail: jcd@wamc.org
News Director....Ian Pickus
e-mail: ipick@wamc.org

BALDWINSVILLE

WSEN (92.1 FM)
8456 Smokey Hollow Road, PO Box 1050, Baldwinsville, NY 13027-1050
315-635-3971 Fax: 315-635-3490
e-mail: webmaster@wsenfm.com
Web site: www.wsenfm.com
General Manager....Judy Kelly
e-mail: jkelly@lmgiradio.com

BATH

WCIK (103.1 FM)
7634 Campbell Creek Rd, PO Box 506, Bath, NY 14810-0506
607-776-4151 Fax: 607-776-6929
e-mail: mail@fln.org
Web site: www.fln.org
President/General Manager....Rick Snavely
Program Director....John Owens
VP/CFO....Dick Snavely

BEACON

WSPK (104.7 FM)
715 Rte 52, PO Box 310, Beacon, NY 12508
845-838-6000 Fax: 845-838-2109
Web site: www.k104online.com
General Manager....Jason Finkelberg
e-mail: jfinkelberg@pamal.com
Promotions Director....Megan Denaut
e-mail: mdenaut@pamal.com
News Director....Allison Dunne
News Director....Brian Jones

BINGHAMTON

WINR (680 AM)
320 N Jensen Road, Vestal, NY 13850
607-584-5800 Fax: 607-584-5900
e-mail: www.680winr.com
General Manager....Tom Barney
News Director....Dave Lozzi

WNBF (1290 AM)
PO Box 414, Binghamton, NY 13902-0414
607-772-8400 Fax: 607-772-9806
Web site: www.wnbf.com
News Director....Bernie Fionte
Program Director....Roger Neal

Offices and agencies generally appear in alphabetical order, except when specific order is requested by listee.

Talk Show Host . . . . Tony Russell
e-mail: roger@wnbf.com

WSKG (89.3 FM), WSQX (91.5 FM)
PO Box 3000, Binghamton, NY 13902
607-729-0100 Fax: 607-729-7328
e-mail: wskg_mail@wskg.pbs.org
Web site: www.wskg.com
Program Director . . . . Ken Campbell
e-mail: ken_campbell@wskg.pb.org
Music Director . . . . Bill Snyder
President . . . . Brian Sickora

BRONX

WFUV (90.7 FM)
441 East Fordham Road, Fordham University, Bronx, NY 10458-5149
718-817-4550 Fax: 718-365-9815
e-mail: thefolks@wfuv.org
Web site: www.wfuv.org
General Manager . . . . Dr Ralph Jennings
News & Public Affairs Director . . . . George Bodarky
Program Director . . . . Chuck Singleton
e-mail: chucksingleton@wfuv.org

BUFFALO

WBEN (930 AM/FM)
800 Corporate Parkway, Suite 200, Buffalo, NY 14226
716-803-0930 or 716-843-0600 Fax: 716-832-3080
Web site: www.wben.com
Operations Manager . . . . Tim Wenger
Anchor/Reporter/Editor . . . . Dave Debo
Sales Director . . . . Tim Holly

WBLK (93.7 FM), WJYE (96.1 FM)
14 Lafayette Sq, Ste 1300, Buffalo, NY 14203
716-852-9393 or 800-828-2191 Fax: 716-852-9390
Web site: www.wjye.com; www.wblk.com
General Manager . . . . Jeff Silver
Production & Program Director . . . . Chris Reynolds
Production Director . . . . Frank Dawkins
Program Director (WJYE) . . . . Joe Chille

WDCX (99.5 FM)
625 Delaware Avenue, Suite 308, Buffalo, NY 14202
716-883-3010 Fax: 716-883-3606
e-mail: wcdxinfo@crawfordbroadcastin.com
Web site: www.wdcxfm.com
General Manager . . . . Nev Larson
Writer/Producer . . . . Keri Cardinale
Chief Engineer . . . . Brian Cunningham

WHTT (104.1 FM)
50 James Casey Drive, Buffalo, NY 14206
716-881-4555 Fax: 716-884-2931
Web site: www.whtt.com
Regional President . . . . Kevin LeGrett
e-mail: wedg@wedg.com
General Manager . . . . Chet Osadchey
Program Director . . . . Joe Siragusa
e-mail: joe.siragusa@citcomm.com

WNED (94.5 FM)
140 Lower Terr., PO Box 1263, Buffalo, NY 14240-1263
716-845-7000 Fax: 716-845-7043
Web site: www.wned.org
Program Director . . . . Al Wallack
News Director . . . . Jim Ranney
e-mail: jranney@wned.org

WYRK (106.5 FM), WBUF (92.9 FM)
14 Lafayette Sq., Suite 1200, Buffalo, NY 14203
716-852-9292 Fax: 716-852-9290
General Manager . . . . Jeff Silver
Program Director (WYRK) . . . . RW Smith
Program Director (WBUF) . . . . Joe Russo
Sales Manager (WYRK) . . . . Mark Plimpton
General Sales Manager (WBUF) . . . . Rose Vecchiarelli

CHAMPLAIN

WCHP (760 AM)
137 Rapids Road, PO Box 888, Champlain, NY 12919
518-298-2800 Fax: 518-298-2604
e-mail: wchp@wchp.com
Web site: www.wchp.com
General Manager . . . . Teri Billiter
e-mail: teri@wchp.com
Program Director . . . . Brandi Lloyd
e-mail: brandi@wchp.com
Operations Manager . . . . Tonya Billiter
e-mail: tonya@wchp.com

CORTLAND

WKRT (920 AM), WIII (99.9 or 100.3 FM)
277 Tompkins Street, Cortland, NY 13045
607-257-6400 Fax: 607-257-6497
e-mail: i100@wiii.com
Web site: www.i100rocks.com
General Manager . . . . Susan Johnston
Operations Manager . . . . Chris Allinger
e-mail: mark.vanness@citcomm.com
Director of Sales . . . . Margaret Tollner
e-mail: margaret.tollner@citcomm.com

ELMIRA

WPGI (100.9 FM), WWLZ (820 AM)
2205 College Avenue, Elmira, NY 14903-1201
607-732-4400 Fax: 607-732-7774
General Manager (WWLZ) . . . . Kevin White
Program Director (WWLZ) . . . . Scott Free
e-mail: scott.free@bybradio.com
Program Director (WWLZ) . . . . James Poteat
e-mail: vinny@bybradio.com

HORNELL

WKPQ (105.3 FM)
1484 Beech St, PO Box 726, Hornell, NY 14843-9404
607-654-0322 Fax: 877-575-1320
e-mail: news@hornellradio.com
Web site: www.wkpq.com
General Manager . . . . Kevin White
Station Manager . . . . Richard O Stevenson

HORSEHEADS

WMTT (94.7 FM)
734 Chemung Street, Horseheads, NY 14845
607-795-0795 Fax: 607-795-1095
e-mail: bob@themetrocks.com
Web site: www.themetrocks.com
General Manager . . . . George Hawras
Opertions Manager . . . . Steve Shimer
Station Manager . . . . Bob Smith

Offices and agencies generally appear in alphabetical order, except when specific order is requested by listee.

ITHACA

WHCU (870 AM)
1751 Hanshaw Road, Ithaca, NY 14850
607-257-6400 Fax: 607-257-6497
e-mail: info@whcu870.com
Web site: www.whcu870.com
General Manager . . . . Susan Johnston
e-mail: sjohnston@cyradiogroup.com
BPD/News Director/Program Director . . . . Geoff Dunn
e-mail: gdunn@cyradiogroup.com

JAMESTOWN

WKZA (106.9 FM)
106 West 3rd Street, Suite 106, Jamestown, NY 14701
716-487-1106 or 866-367-1069 Fax: 716-488-2169
e-mail: morningshow@1069kissfm.com
Web site: www.1069kissfm.com
Sales Manager . . . . Sherrie Brookmire
Program Director . . . . Steve Rockford

LATHAM

WROW (590 AM)
6 Johnson Road, Latham, NY 12110-5641
518-786-6600 Fax: 518-786-6695
e-mail: wrownews@albanybroadcasting.com
Web site: www.wrow.com
General Manager . . . . Dan Austin
e-mail: DAustin@albanybroadcasting.com
News Director . . . . Mike Carey
e-mail: mcarey@albanybroadcasting.com
Public Affairs Director . . . . Joe Condon
e-mail: jcondon@albanyradio.net
Program Director . . . . Scott Miller

WPYX (106.5 FM), WRVE (99.5 FM)
1203 Troy Schenectady Road, Latham, NY 12110
518-452-4800 Fax: 518-452-4813
e-mail: feedback@pyx106.com
Web site: www.pyx106.com
Operations Manager & Program Director (WPYX) . . . . John Cooper
e-mail: johncooper@clearchannel.com
VP/General Manager . . . . Kristen Delaney

NEW ROCHELLE

WVOX (1460 AM)
1 Broadcast Forum, New Rochelle, NY 10801-2094
914-636-1460 Fax: 914-636-2900
e-mail: don@wvox.com
Web site: www.wvox.com
Editorial Director/President/CEO . . . . William O'Shaughnessy
Operations Manager . . . . Don Stevens

NEW YORK CITY

WABC (770 AM)
2 Penn Plaza, 17th Floor, New York, NY 10121
212-613-3800 Fax: 212-613-3823
e-mail: info@wabc.com
Web site: www.wabcradio.com
Program Director/News Director . . . . Phil Boyce
e-mail: phil.boyce@abc.com
General Manager . . . . Mitch Dolan
Promotions Director . . . . Eric Lemieux
e-mail: ericlemieux@clearchannel.com
Promotions Director/Public Affairs . . . . Russ King
Music Director . . . . Eric Wellman
e-mail: ericwellman@clearchannel.com

WBBR (1130 AM) Bloomberg News
499 Park Avenue, New York, NY 10022-1240
212-318-2300 or 800-955-4003 Fax: 917-369-5000
e-mail: mwomack4@bloomberg.net
Web site: www.bloomberg.com/radio
Editor-in-Chief . . . . Matthew Winkler
Managing Editor . . . . Michael Clancy
Press Contact . . . . Amanda Cowie
e-mail: acowie@bloomberg.net

WCBS (880 AM)
345 Hudson Street, New York, NY 10014
212-975-4321 Fax: 212-975-4675
e-mail: wcbsamdesk@wcbs880.com
Web site: www.wcbs880.com
General Manager/VP . . . . Chad Brown
Director of News & Programming . . . . Tim Scheld
e-mail: tscheld@wcbs880.com

WINS (1010 AM)
345 Hudson Street, 10th Floor, New York, NY 10014
212-315-7000 Fax: 212-315-7015
e-mail: mevorach@wins.com
Web site: www.1010wins.com
News Director . . . . Ben Mevorach
e-mail: mevorach@wins.com
News Editor . . . . Ralph Saro
e-mail: saro@wins.com

WLTW (106.7 FM)
32 Avenue of the Americas, New York, NY 10013
212-377-7900 Fax: 212-603-4602
e-mail: info@wltw.com
Web site: www.1067litefm.com
Program Director . . . . Jim Ryan
Marketing Director . . . . Susan Bacich

WOR (710 AM)
32 Avenue of the Americas, New York, NY 10013
212-337-7900
e-mail: news@wor710.com
Web site: www.wor710.com
General Manager . . . . Jerry Crowley
News Director . . . . Joe Bartlett

OLEAN

WPIG (95.7 FM), WHDL (1450 AM)
3163 NYS Route 417, Olean, NY 14760-1853
716-372-0161 or 800-877-9749 Fax: 716-372-0164
e-mail: wpig.production@bybradio.com
Web site: www.wpig.com
General Manager . . . . John Morton
e-mail: john.morton@bybradio.com
Program Manager . . . . Mark Thompson
e-mail: mark.thompson@bybradio.com

PEEKSKILL

WHUD (100.7 FM)
715 Rte 52, Box 310, Beacon, NY 12508
845-838-6000 Fax: 845-838-2109
e-mail: newsroom@pamal.com
Web site: www.whud.com
General Manager . . . . Jason Finkelberg
e-mail: jfinkelberg@pamal.com
Program Director . . . . Steve Petrone
e-mail: spetrone@pamal.com

News Media

Offices and agencies generally appear in alphabetical order, except when specific order is requested by listee.

News Director . . . . Brian Jones
e-mail: newsroom@pamal.com

MIDDLETOWN

WRRV (92.7 FM)
2 Pendell Road, Poughkeepsie, NY 12601
845-471-1500 Fax: 845-454-1204
Web site: www.wrrv.com
Business Manager . . . . Kathy Butsko
e-mail: kathy.butsko@cumulus.com
Program Directory. . . . . Andrew Boris
e-mail: andrew.boris@cumulus.com

POUGHKEEPSIE

WPDH (101.5 FM)
2 Pendell Road, Poughkeepsie, NY 12601
845-471-1500 Fax: 845-454-1204
Web site: www.wpdh.com
Business Manager . . . . Kathy Butsko
e-mail: kathy.butsko@cumulus.com
Program Director. . . . . Andrew Boris
e-mail: andrew.boris@cumulus.com
Branch Manager . . . . Chuck Benfer
e-mail: chuck.benfer@cumulus.com
Promotions Manager. . . . . Anthony Verano
e-mail: anthony.verano@cumulus.com

ROCHESTER

WHAM (1180 AM)
1700 HSBC Plaza, 100 Chestnut Street, Rochester, NY 14604-2016
585-454-4884 Fax: 585-454-5081
e-mail: whamnews@wham1180.com
Web site: www.wham1180.com
Station Manager. . . . . Jeff Howlett
e-mail: jeffhowlett@wham1180.com
Promotions Director . . . . Brian Guck
e-mail: brianguck@clearchannel.com
News Director . . . . Randy Gorbman
e-mail: randygorbman@wham1180.com

SCHENECTADY

WGNA (107.7 FM)
1241 Kings Road, Suite 4200, Schenectady, NY 12303
518-881-1515 or 800-476-1077 Fax: 518-881-1516
e-mail: john.hirsch@regentcomm.com
Web site: www.wgna.com
Regional Vice President/General Manager. . . . . Robert Ausfeld
e-mail: robert.ausfeld@regentcomm.com
Operations Manager/Program Director . . . . Tom Jacobsen
e-mail: bbrindle@wgna.com
Station Manager . . . . John Hirsh
e-mail: johnhirsch@regentcomm.com
Music Director . . . . Bill Earley
e-mail: bearley@wgna.com

SYRACUSE

WNTQ (93.1 FM), WAQX (95.7 FM)
1064 James St, Syracuse, NY 13203
315-472-0200 Fax: 315-478-5625
Web site: www.93Q.com; www.95x.com
General Manager . . . . Dan Austin
Program Director (WNTQ). . . . . Janice Cole
Program Director (WAQX). . . . . Hunter Scott

WVOA (103.9 FM)
7095 Myers Road, East Syracuse, NY 13057-9748
315-656-2231 Fax: 315-656-2259
e-mail: programming@wvoaradio.com
Web site: www.wvoaradio.com
General Manager . . . . Sam Furco
Public Service Coordinator . . . . Susan Anderson
Music Director . . . . Allen Elson

WYYY (94.5 FM)
500 Plum St, Suite 100, Syracuse, NY 13204
315-472-9797 Fax: 315-472-1904
Web site: www.sybercuse.com
Program Director . . . . Kathy Rowe
Operations Manager. . . . . Rich Lauber
e-mail: richlauber@clearchannel.com

UTICA

WOUR (96.9 FM)
39 Kellogg Rd, New Hartford, NY 13413
315-797-0803 Fax: 315-738-1073
e-mail: ask@wour.com
Web site: www.wour.com
General Manager/Sales Manager . . . . Brian Delaney
e-mail: brianelany@clearchannel.com
Program Director . . . . Tom Starr
e-mail: tomstarr@clearchannel.com

WATERTOWN

WFRY (97.5 FM)
134 Mullin Street, Watertown, NY 13601
315-788-0790 Fax: 315-788-4379
e-mail: eliva.gaines@smgny.com
Web site: www.froggy97.com
General Manager. . . . . Don Wagner
Program Director. . . . . Matt Raisman

TELEVISION

Stations included in this chapter produce news and/or public affairs programming and are listed alphabetically by primary service area.

ALBANY

WMHT (17) Public Broadcasting-NY Capitol Region
4 Global View Road, Troy, NY 12180
518-880-3400 Fax: 518-880-3409
e-mail: email@wmht.org
Web site: www.wmht.org
Production Manager . . . . Dominick Figliomeni
e-mail: dfigliomeni@wmht.org
Producer/Director . . . . Joanne Durfee
e-mail: jdurfee@wmht.org
Senior Producer/Director . . . . Dave Povero
e-mail: dpovero@wmht.org
President/CEO . . . . Robert Altman
e-mail: raltman@wmht.org
Chief Technology Officer. . . . . Anthony Tassarotti
e-mail: atassarotti@wmht.org

WNYT (12)
715 N Pearl Street, PO Box 4035, Albany, NY 12204
518-486-4991 or 518-207-4700 Fax: 518-434-0659
e-mail: comments@wnyt.com
Web site: www.wnyt.com
General Manager . . . . Steve Baboulis
e-mail: sbaboulis@wnyt.com

Offices and agencies generally appear in alphabetical order, except when specific order is requested by listee.

Director Public Affairs/Programming .... Maryann Ryan
e-mail: maryan@wnyt.com
News Director .... Paul Lewis
General Sales Manager........................ Tony McManus
Engineering Director........................ Richard Klein

WRGB (6)
1400 Balltown Rd, Schenectady, NY 12309
518-346-6666 or 800-666-3355 Fax: 518-381-3736
e-mail: news@cbs6albany.com
Web site: www.cbs6albany.com
General Manager .... Bob Furlong
e-mail: bfurlong@wrgb.com
News Director/Station Manager .... Lisa Jackson
e-mail: ljackson@wrgb.com
Production Manager........................ Bill Brandt
Producer........................ Jessica Harrison

WTEN (10)
341 Northern Blvd, Albany, NY 12204
518-436-4822 or 800-888-9836 Fax: 518-462-6065
e-mail: news@news10.com
Web site: www.news10.com
Senior Producer .... Jeanne Beatty
e-mail: jeanne.beatty@wten.com
Programming Coordinator .... Chris Terwilliger
e-mail: cterwilliger@wten.com
President & General Manager........................ Rene LaSpina
e-mail: cterwilliger@wten.com

WXXA (23)
341 Northern Blvd, Albany, NY 12204
518-436-4822 Fax: 518-426-4792
e-mail: news@news10.com
Web site: www.news10.com
General Manager .... Ron Romines
News Director .... Matt Miller
President........................ Sheldon Galloway
Program Director .... Paul Pelliccia

WYPX DT-50
1 Charles Blvd, Guilderland, NY 12084
518-464-0143 or 800-646-7296 Fax: 518-464-0633
Web site: www.ionline.tv
Station Manager .... Renee Osterlitz
Public Service Director........................ Chris Iorio

BINGHAMTON

WBNG-TV (7)
560 Columbia Dr, Johnson City, NY 13790
607-729-8812 Fax: 607-797-6211
e-mail: wbng@wbngtv.com
Web site: www.wbng.com
News Director........................ Greg Catlin
e-mail: catlin@wbngtv.com
President/General Manager........................ Matt Rosenfeld
e-mail: chapman@wbngtv.com

WICZ (40)
4600 Vestal Pkwy E, Vestal, NY 13850
607-770-4040 Fax: 607-798-7950
e-mail: fox40@wicz.com
Web site: www.wicz.com
General Manager .... John Leet
e-mail: wicztv@aol.com
News Director........................ Suh Neubauer
e-mail: fox40suh@wicz.com
Program Director .... Vernon Rowlands
News Director .... Kent Garrett

WIVT (34)
203 Ingraham Hill Rd, Binghamton, NY 13903
607-771-3434 Fax: 607-723-1034
e-mail: newschannel34@newschannel34.com
Web site: www.newschannel34.com
News Director .... Jim Ehmke
Promotions Manager........................ Jim La Vasser

WSKG (46) Public Broadcasting
601 Gates Road, Vestal, NY 13850
607-729-0100 Fax: 607-729-7328
e-mail: mail@wskg.org
Web site: www.wskg.org
President/CEO/General Mgr .... Brian Sicora
Station Manager .... Juan Martinez
Operations Director/General Sales Mgr .... Nancy Christensen

BUFFALO

WGRZ (33)
259 Delaware Ave, Buffalo, NY 14202
716-849-2222 or 716-849-2200 Fax: 716-849-7602
e-mail: newsdesk@wgrz.com
Web site: www.wgrz.com
News Director .... Jeff Woodard
e-mail: ecrookge@wgrz.gannett.com
Assignment Editor .... Maria Sisti
General Manager/President........................ Jim Toellner
e-mail: james.toellner@wgrz.com

WIVB-TV (39)
2077 Elmwood Ave, Buffalo, NY 14207
716-874-4410 Fax: 716-879-4896
e-mail: newsroom@wivb.com
Web site: www.wivb.com
News Director........................ Joseph Schlaerth
Senior Producer .... Vic Baker
Producer........................ Mary Czopp
e-mail: mary.czopp@wivb.com
News Producer .... Lynne Donley
e-mail: lynne.donley@wivb.com
Executive Producer .... Jeff Sabato
e-mail: jeff.sabato@wivb.com
Producer........................ Andrew Tamutus

WKBW-TV (38)
7 Broadcast Plaza, Buffalo, NY 14202
716-845-6100 Fax: 716-842-1855
e-mail: news@wkbw.com
Web site: www.wkbw.com
News Director........................ Glen Horn
Station Manager........................ Michael Nurse
Senior Producer........................ Paula D'Amico

WNED (43) Western NY Public Broadcasting
Horizon's Plaza, 140 Lower Terr., PO Box 1263, Buffalo, NY 14202
716-845-7000 Fax: 716-845-7036
Web site: www.wned.org
Station Manager........................ Ron Santora
e-mail: rdaly@wned.org
VP TV Production .... David Rotterman
e-mail: drotterman@wned.org

WETM (18)
101 E Water Street, Box 1207, Elmira, NY 14901
607-733-5518 Fax: 607-734-1176
e-mail: info@wetmtv.com
Web site: www.wetmtv.com
General Manager........................ Randy Reid
News Director........................ Scott Nichols
e-mail: snichols@wetmtv.com

Offices and agencies generally appear in alphabetical order, except when specific order is requested by listee.

News Media

Chief Managing Editor ... Jeff Stone
e-mail: jstone@wetmtv.com

HORSEHEADS

WENY (36)
474 Old Ithaca Rd, Horseheads, NY 14845
607-739-3636 Fax: 607-739-1418
e-mail: info@weny.com
Web site: www.weny.com
Anchor ... Sarah Sheridan
Executive Producer ... Renata Stiehl
News Director ... Scott Cook
President & CEO ... Kevin Lilly

KINGSTON

WRNN (48)
800 Westchester Avenue, Suite S-640, Rye Brook, NY 10573
914-417-2700 Fax: 914-696-0279
e-mail: comments@rnntv.com
Web site: www.rnntv.com
General Manager ... Richard French
Executive Producer ... Don Dudley

LONG ISLAND

WLIW (21) Public Broadcasting
Box 21, Plainview, NY 11803
516-367-2100 Fax: 516-692-7629
e-mail: programming@wliw.org
Web site: www.wliw.org
General Manager ... Terrel Cass
e-mail: terrel_cass@wliw.pbs.org
Executive Producer ... Tom Casciato
President ... Neal Shapiro

MELVILLE

WLNY (47)
270 S Service Road, Suite 55, Melville, NY 11747
631-777-8855 Fax: 631-777-8180
e-mail: ny55news@aol.com
Web site: www.wlnytv.com
Sales VP ... Elliot Simmons
News Director ... Richard Rose

NEW YORK CITY

Bloomberg Television
499 Park Avenue, New York, NY 10022
212-318-2300 Fax: 917-617-5999
e-mail: mwomack@bloomberg.net
Web site: www.bloomberg.com/tv/
Editor-in-Chief ... Matthew Winkler
Managing Editor ... Michael Clancy
e-mail: mclancy@bloomberg.net
Press Contact ... Amanda Cowie
e-mail: acowie@bloomberg.net

Fox News Channel
1211 Ave of the Americas, 2nd Floor, New York, NY 10036
212-301-3000 or 888-369-4762 Fax: 212-301-8274
e-mail: newsmanager@foxnews.com
Web site: www.foxnews.com
SVP/News Operations ... Sharri Berg
EVP/Executive Editor ... John Moody
EVP/News ... Michael Clemente

New York 1 News (1)
75 Ninth Avenue, New York, NY 10011
212-691-6397 Fax: 212-379-3575
e-mail: ny1news@ny1.com
Web site: www.ny1.com
Albany Reporter ... Erin Billups
Geeral Assignment Reporter ... Roger Clark
Anchor ... Lewis Dodley
Politcal Reporter ... Bobby Cuza

WABC (7)
7 Lincoln Sq, New York, NY 10023
917-260-7697 Fax: 212-456-2290
e-mail: iwitness@wabc.com
Web site: www.7online.com
News Director ... Ken Plotnik
VP of Programming ... Art Moore
e-mail: art.moore@abc.com
Executive Producer ... Nancy Kennedy
...
e-mail: cbsnewyork@cbs.com
News Director ... David M. Friend
Executive Producer ... Byron Harmon
e-mail: bharmon@cbs.com

WNBC (4)
30 Rockefeller Plaza, New York, NY 10112
212-664-4444 Fax: 212-664-2994
e-mail: newstips@wnbc.com
Web site: www.wnbc.com
Executive Editor ... Richard Wolfe
VP/News & Product ... Gregory Gittrich
Editor ... Erica Tilles
Senior Editor ... John Baiata

WNYW (44)
205 E 67th St, New York, NY 10021
212-452-5555 Fax: 212-452-5750
Web site: www.myfoxny.com
Executive Producer ... Byron Harmon
News Writer ... Donielle Stanton

WPIX (11)
220 East 42nd St, 2nd Fl, New York, NY 10017
212-210-2411 Fax: 212-210-2591
e-mail: news@pix11.com
Web site: www.pix11.com
Executive Producer ... Monica Zack
Editor ... Brian Waizel
Editor ... Reynaldo Meno
Senior Editor ... Jennifer Tanaka

WWOR (UPN 9)
205 E 67th Street, New York, NY 10065-6050
212-852-7000 Fax: 212-852-7145
Web site: www.my9tv.com
President & Editor ... Edwin A. Finn, Jr.
Managing Editor ... Richard Rescigno
Senior Deputy Managing Editor ... Jonathan Krim

PLATTSBURGH

WPTZ (5) NBC
5 Television Dr, Plattsburgh, NY 12901
518-561-5555 Fax: 518-561-5940
e-mail: newstips@wptz.com
Web site: www.wptz.com
President/General Manager ... Paul Sands
News Director ... Kyle Grimes
Assignment Editor ... Matt Morin
e-mail: mmorin@herst.com

Offices and agencies generally appear in alphabetical order, except when specific order is requested by listee.

ROCHESTER

WHEC (10)
191 East Ave, Rochester, NY 14604
585-546-5670 Fax: 585-546-5688
e-mail: news1@whec.com
Web site: www.10nbc.com
News Director......................................Mike Goldrick
Producer..Carla Hanlon
e-mail: chanlon@whec.com
Executive Producer..................................Ray Sullivan
e-mail: news1@whec.com

WHAM (13)
4225 W Henrietta Road, Box 20555, Rochester, NY 14623
585-334-8700 Fax: 585-359-1570
e-mail: feedback@13wham.com
Web site: www.13wham.com
General Manager....................................Chuck Samuels
e-mail: csamuels@13wham.com
TV Community Affairs Director.......................Charlotte Clarke
News Director...Matt Malyn
General Manager....................................Kent Beckwith
e-mail: kbeckwith@13wham.com
Executive Producer....................................Brad Smith
e-mail: bsmith@13wham.com

WXXI (16) Public Broadcasting
280 State St, PO Box 30021, Rochester, NY 14603
585-325-7500 Fax: 585-258-0335
Web site: www.wxxi.org
Executive Producer/Assistant VP....................Todd Mccammon
e-mail: wxxi@wxxi.org
Vice President, Television............................Elissa Orlando
e-mail: emarra@wxxi.org
News Director..Peter Iglinksi
e-mail: newsroom@wxxi.org

SYRACUSE

WCNY (25)
415 W Fayette Street, PO Box 2400, Syracuse, NY 13220-2400
315-453-2424 Fax: 315-451-8824
Web site: www.wcny.org
Program Manager....................................Dale Wagner
President/CEO.......................................Robert Daino
e-mail: robert_daino@wcny.org
News/Public Affairs Director.........................Susan Arbetter

WSYR (17)
5904 Bridge St, Box 699, East Syracuse, NY 13057
315-446-9999 Fax: 315-446-9283
e-mail: newschannel9@9wsyr.com
Web site: www.9wsyr.com
News Director...Jim Tortora
VP/General Manager...........................Theresa Underwood

WSTM (24)
1030 James St, Syracuse, NY 13203
315-477-9400 Fax: 315-474-5082
Web site: www.wstm.com
Anchor...Matt Mulcahy
Chief Investigative Reporter..............................Jim Kenyon
e-mail: pphillip@wstm.com
Chief Engineer......................................Kevin Tubbs
e-mail: pphillip@wstm.com
News Director.......................................Peggy Phillip
e-mail: pphillip@wstm.com

WSYT (19)
1000 James St, Syracuse, NY 13203
315-472-6800 Fax: 315-471-8889
e-mail: info@wsyt68.com
Web site: www.wsyt68.com
Program Coordinator.................................Becky Walsh

WTVH (47)
980 James St, Syracuse, NY 13203
315-425-5555 Fax: 315-425-5513
e-mail: wtvh@wtvh.com
Web site: www.wtvh.com
Executive Producer.................................Megan Tennyson
e-mail: mtennyson@wtvh.com
General Manager/President...........................Matt Rosenfeld
News Director.......................................Frank Kracher

UTICA

WKTV (29)
5936 Smith Hill Rd, PO Box 2, Utica, NY 13503
315-733-0404 Fax: 315-793-3498
e-mail: newslink2@wktv.com
Web site: www.wktv.com
Program Director......................................Tom Coyne
e-mail: tcoyne@wktv.com
News Director......................................Steve McMurray
e-mail: smcmurray@wktv.com
Vice President/General Manager..........................Vic Vetters
e-mail: vvetter@wktv.com

WATERTOWN

WWNY (7)
120 Arcade St, Watertown, NY 13601
315-788-3800 Fax: 315-788-3787
e-mail: wwny@wwnytv.net
Web site: www.wwnytv.net
General Manager.....................................Cathy Pircsuk
e-mail: cpircsuk@wwnytv.net
News Director.......................................Scott Atkinson
e-mail: satkinsn@wwnytv.net
Producer/Assistant News Director.......................Anne Richter

WWTI (21)
Box 6250, 1222 Arsenal St, Watertown, NY 13601
315-785-8850 Fax: 315-785-0127
e-mail: news@myabc50.com
Web site: www.newswatch50.com
General Mgr/Sales Mgr...............................David J Males
News Director...John Moore
e-mail: johnmoore@clearchannel.com

Section 7:
EDUCATION

COLLEGES AND UNIVERSITIES

STATE UNIVERSITY OF NEW YORK

SUNY Board of Trustees

State University of New York
State University Plz
353 Broadway
Albany, NY 12246
518-320-1157 or 800-342-3811 Fax: 518-443-5131
e-mail: trustees@suny.edu
Web site: www.suny.edu

Chair:
H. Carl McCall 212-239-2362
Member:
Joseph Belluck 315-320-1157
Member:
Henrik Dullea 518-320-1157
Member:
Ronald Ehrenberg 518-320-1157
Member:
Angelo Fatta 518-320-1157
Member:
Tina Good 518-320-1256
Member:
Stephen Hunt 914-232-6259
Member:
Eunice A. Lewin 518-320-1157
Member:
Marshall Lichtman 518-320-1157
Member:
John Murad 518-320-1157
Member:
Kenneth O'Brien 518-443-5326
Member:
Kevin Rea 518-320-1157
Member:
Linda Sanford 914-766-3800
Member:
Richard Socarides 518-320-1157
Member:
Carl Spielvogel 212-641-6522
Member:
Cary Staller 518-320-1157
Member:
Gerri Warren-Merrick 212-694-4933

SUNY System Administration & Executive Council

State University Plz
353 Broadway
Albany, NY 12246
518-443-5555
Web site: www.suny.edu

Chancellor:
Nancy L. Zimpher 518-320-1355
e-mail: Nancy.Zimpher@suny.edu
Executive Vice Chancellor & Provost:
David K. Lavallee 518-320-1251
Senior Vice Chancellor for Community Colleges & the Education Pipeline:
Johanna Duncan-Poitier 518-320-1276
Senior Vice Chancellor & General Counsel, Secretary of the University:
William F. Howard
Vice Chancellor for Academic Programs and Planning & Vice Provost:
Elizabeth L. Bringsjord 518-320-1356
Vice Chancellor for Capital Facilities & General Manager/Construction Fund:
Robert Haelen 518-320-1502
Vice Chancellor for Financial Services & CFO:
Brian Hutzley 518-320-1497
Vice Chancellor for Global Affairs:
Mitch Leventhal 212-317-3546
Vice Chancellor for Human Resources:
Curtis L. Lloyd 518-320-1192
Vice Chancellor for Research & President of the Research Foundation:
Timothy Killeen
Associate Vice Chancellor for Health Affairs:
Lora Lefebvre 518-320-1193
Assistant Vice Chancellor for External Affairs:
Jennifer LoTurco 518-320-1805
Assistant Vice Chancellor for Government Relations:
Stacey Hengsterman 518-320-1148
Assistant Vice Chancellor for Strategic Planning & University Advancement:
Kaitlin Gambrill 212-364-5789
Associate Provost & Associate Vice Chancellor for Diversity, Equity & Inclusion:
Carlos Medina 518-320-1176
Director of Communications:
David Doyle 518-320-1311
President, Student Assembly:
Kevin Rea
President, University Faculty Senate:
Kenneth O'Brien
President, Faculty Council of Community Colleges:
Tina Good 518-320-1256

New York Network .... fax: 518-426-4198

Suite 146, South Concourse, Empire State Plaza, Albany, NY 12223
518-443-5333 Fax: 518-426-4198
e-mail: mscinfo@ogs.ny.gov
Web site: www.nyn.suny.edu

Executive Director:
Neil Satterly 518-443-5333/fax: 518-426-4198
Production Manager:
Sara Hill
Senior Producer:
Chris Conto 518-443-5333
Supervising Television Engineer:
Patrick Roche 518-443-5333

Rockefeller Institute of Government .... fax: 518-443-5788

411 State St, Albany, NY 12203-1003
518-443-5522 Fax: 518-443-5788
e-mail: info@rockinst.org
Web site: www.rockinst.org

Director:
Thomas Gais 518-443-5238
e-mail: gaist@rockinst.org
Deputy Director of Research:
Jason E. Lane 518-443-5825
e-mail: jlane@albany.edu
Deputy Director for Operations:
Robert E. Bullock
e-mail: rbullock@albany.edu
Senior Policy Analyst:
Lucy Dadayan 518-443-5828
e-mail: dadayanl@rockinst.org

SUNY Center for Student Recruitment .... fax: 518-320-1573

33 W 42nd St (across from Bryant Park), New York, NY 10036
212-364-5821 Fax: 518-320-1573
e-mail: csr@suny.edu
Web site: www.suny.edu/student/mrc.cfm

Director:
Beryl S. Jeffers

Offices and agencies generally appear in alphabetical order, except when specific order is requested by listee.

Associate Director for Financial Aid Services:
Julieta Schiffino
Assistant to the Director for Special Programs:
Gail Reilly
Admissions Recruitment Advisor:
Cynthia Marino
Admissions Recruitment Advisor:
Beverly Santos

Small Business Development Center
State University Plaza, Administration Office, 22 Corporate Woods Bldg, 3rd Fl, Albany, NY 12246
518-443-5398 or 800-732-7232
Web site: www.nyssbdc.org
State Director:
James L King 518-443-5398 x166/fax: 518-443-5275
e-mail: j.king@nyssbdc.org

State University Construction Fund
353 Broadway, Albany, NY 12246
518-320-3200
Web site: www.sucf.suny.edu
General Manager:
Robert Haelen 518-320-1502
Counsel:
William K Barczak 518-320-1746

UNIVERSITY CENTERS

Binghamton University, State University of New York
4400 Vestal Parkway East
PO Box 6000
Binghamton, NY 13902-6000
607-777-2000
e-mail: info@binghamton.edu
Web site: www.binghamton.edu

President:
Harvey G. Stenger 607-777-2131/fax: 607-777-2533

College of Agriculture & Life Sciences at Cornell University
177 Roberts Hall
Ithaca, NY 14853
607-255-2241 Fax: 607-255-3803
Web site: www.cals.cornell.edu

Dean:
Kathryn Boor 607-255-2241
e-mail: kjb4@cornell.edu

College of Human Ecology at Cornell University
170 Martha Van Rensselaer Hall
Ithaca, NY 14853-4401
607-255-5471 Fax: 607-255-2293
e-mail: humec_admissions@cornell.edu
Web site: www.human.cornell.edu

Dean:
Alan Mathios. 607-255-2138
e-mail: adm5@cornell.edu

College of Veterinary Medicine at Cornell University
Cornell University
Ithaca, NY 14853
607-253-3000 Fax: 607-253-3701
Web site: www.vet.cornell.edu

Dean:
Michael I Kotlikoff 607-253-3771

NYS College of Ceramics at Alfred University
2 Pine St
Alfred, NY 14802
607-871-2137 Fax: 607-871-2339
e-mail: mastin@alfred.edu
Web site: nyscc.alfred.edu

Provost:
Suzanne Buckley. 607-871-2137

SUNY Downstate Medical Center
450 Clarkson Ave
Brooklyn, NY 11203
718-270-1000 Fax: 718-270-7592
Web site: www.downstate.edu

President:
John C LaRosa 718-270-2611
e-mail: jclarosa@downstate.edu

SUNY State College of Optometry
33 West 42nd St
New York, NY 10036-8003
212-938-4000 or 212-938-4001
Web site: www.sunyopt.edu

President:
Dr David A Heath 212-938-5650
e-mail: dheath@sunyopt.edu

SUNY Upstate Medical University
750 E Adams St
Syracuse, NY 13210
315-464-5540 Fax: 315-464-4838
Web site: www.upstate.edu

President:
David R Smith. 315-464-5540
e-mail: smith@upstate.edu

School of Industrial & Labor Relations at Cornell University (ILR School)
309 Ives Hall
Ithaca, NY 14853
607-255-2762 Fax: 607-255-7774
e-mail: info@ilr.cornell.edu
Web site: www.ilr.cornell.edu

Dean:
Harry C Katz. 607-255-2185
e-mail: hck2@cornell.edu

State University of New York at Albany
1400 Washington Ave
Albany, NY 12222
518-442-3300
Web site: www.albany.edu

President:
George Philip 518-956-8010
e-mail: presmail@uamail.albany.edu

State University of New York College of Environmental Science & Forestry
One Forestry Dr
Syracuse, NY 13210
315-470-6500 or TDD: 315-470-6966 Fax: 315-470-6933
e-mail: esfinfo@esf.edu
Web site: www.esf.edu

President:
Cornelius B Murphy Jr 315-470-6681/fax: 315-470-6977
e-mail: cbmurphy@esf.edu

Stony Brook University, SUNY
118 Administration Bldg
Stony Brook, NY 11794
631-632-6000
Web site: www.sunysb.edu

President:
Samuel L Stanley. 631-632-6265/fax: 631-632-6621
e-mail: samuel.stanley@stonybrook.edu

University at Buffalo, State University of New York
12 Capen Hall
Buffalo, NY 14260
716-645-2000
Web site: www.buffalo.edu

President:
John B Simpson. 716-645-2901/fax: 716-645-3728
e-mail: simpson@buffalo.edu

UNIVERSITY COLLEGES

Buffalo State College
1300 Elmwood Ave
Buffalo, NY 14222-1095
716-878-4000 or TTD 716-878-3182 Fax: 716-878-3039
e-mail: webadmin@buffalostate.edu
Web site: www.buffalostate.edu

President:
Aaron Podolefsky 716-878-4101/fax: 716-878-6527
e-mail: president@buffalostate.edu

College at Brockport
350 New Campus Dr
Brockport, NY 14420
585-395-2211 or 585-395-2796 Fax: 585-395-2401
Web site: www.brockport.edu

President:
John R Halstead 585-395-2361
e-mail: halstead@brockport.edu

Purchase College, State University of New York
735 Anderson Hill Rd
Purchase, NY 10577
914-251-6000
Web site: www.purchase.edu

President:
Thomas J Schwarz. 914-251-6010/fax: 914-251-6014
e-mail: thomas.schwarz@purchase.edu

State University at Old Westbury
223 Store Hill Rd
PO Box 210
Old Westbury, NY 11568-0210
516-876-3000
Web site: www.oldwestbury.edu

President:
Calvin O Butts, III 516-876-3160/fax: 516-876-3347
e-mail: buttsc@oldwestbury.edu

State University at Potsdam
44 Pierrepont Ave
Potsdam, NY 13676
315-267-2000 or 877-768-7326
Web site: www.potsdam.edu

President:
John Schwaller 315-267-2100
e-mail: schwaljf@potsdam.edu

State University College at Cortland
Graham Ave
PO Box 2000
Cortland, NY 13045
607-753-2011 Fax: 607-753-5688
Web site: www.cortland.edu

President:
Erik J Bitterbaum. 607-753-2201/fax: 607-753-5993
e-mail: bitterbaume@cortland.edu

State University College at Geneseo
1 College Circle
Geneseo, NY 14454-1450
585-245-5000 Fax: 585-245-5005
e-mail: web@geneseo.edu
Web site: www.geneseo.edu

President:
Christopher Dahl. 585-245-5501
e-mail: cdahl@geneseo.edu

State University College at New Paltz
1 Hawk Drive
New Paltz, NY 12561
845-257-7869 or 877-696-7411 Fax: 845-257-3009
Web site: www.newpaltz.edu

Interim President:
Donald Christian 845-257-3288/fax: 845-257-3389
e-mail: poskanzer@newpaltz.edu

State University Empire State College
One Union Ave
Saratoga Springs, NY 12866
518-587-2100 Fax: 518-587-3033
Web site: www.esc.edu

President:
Alan Davis 518-587-2100 x2260/fax: 518-587-2886
e-mail: president@esc.edu

State University of New York, Fredonia
280 Central Ave
Fredonia, NY 14063-1136

Offices and agencies generally appear in alphabetical order, except when specific order is requested by listee.

Colleges, Universities & School Districts

716-673-3111 Fax: 716-673-3156
Web site: www.fredonia.edu

President:
Dennis L Hefner 716-673-3456
e-mail: dennis.hefner@fredonia.edu

State University of New York at Oneonta
108 Ravine Pkwy
Oneonta, NY 13820
607-436-3500
Web site: www.oneonta.edu

President:
Nancy Kleniewski 607-436-2500/fax: 607-436-3089
e-mail: klenien@oneonta.edu

State University of New York at Oswego
7060 Route 104
Oswego, NY 13126
315-312-2500 Fax: 315-312-2863
e-mail: proffice@oswego.edu
Web site: www.oswego.edu

President:
Deborah F Stanley 315-312-2211
e-mail: stanley@oswego.edu

State University of New York at Plattsburgh
101 Broad St
Plattsburgh, NY 12901
518-564-2000 Fax: 518-564-2094
Web site: www.plattsburgh.edu

President:
John Ettling 518-564-2010/fax: 518-564-3932
e-mail: president_office@plattsburgh.edu

COLLEGES OF TECHNOLOGY

Alfred State College of Technology
10 Upper College Dr
Alfred, NY 14802
607-587-4215 or 800-425-3733 Fax: 607-587-4299
Web site: www.alfredstate.edu

President:
John M Anderson 607-587-4010/fax: 607-587-4209
e-mail: presidentsoffice@alfredstate.edu

Farmingdale State College of Technology
2350 Broadhollow Rd
Farmingdale, NY 11735-1021
631-420-2000 Fax: 631-420-2633
e-mail: regoff@farmingdale.edu
Web site: www.farmingdale.edu

President:
W Hubert Keen 631-420-2239/fax: 631-420-2753
e-mail: keenhu@farmingdale.edu

Morrisville State College
Administration Bldg, South St
PO Box 901
Morrisville, NY 13408
315-684-6000 or 800-258-0111 Fax: 315-684-6116
Web site: www.morrisville.edu

President:
Raymond W Cross. 315-684-6044/fax: 315-684-6109
e-mail: crossrw@morrisville.edu

SUNY College of Agriculture & Technology at Cobleskill
State Route 7
Cobleskill, NY 12043
518-255-5700 or 800-295-8988 Fax: 518-255-6769
Web site: www.cobleskill.edu

President:
Donald Zingdale 518-255-5111

State University College of Technology at Canton
34 Cornell Drive
Canton, NY 13617
315-386-7011 or 800-388-7123 Fax: 315-386-7929
e-mail: admissions@canton.edu
Web site: www.canton.edu

President:
Joseph L Kennedy 315-386-7204/fax: 315-386-7934
e-mail: president@canton.edu

State University College of Technology at Delhi
2 Main St
Delhi, NY 13753
607-746-4550 or 800-963-3544 Fax: 607-746-4104
Web site: www.delhi.edu

President:
Candace S Vancko. 607-746-4090/fax: 607-746-4346
e-mail: vanckocs@delhi.org

State University Institute of Technology
Horatio St, Marcy Campus
100 Seymour Road
Utica, NY 13502
315-792-7500 Fax: 315-792-7837
Web site: www.sunyit.edu

Interim President:
Wolf Yeigh 315-792-7400/fax: 315-792-7407
e-mail: yeighw@sunyuit.edu

State University of New York Maritime College
6 Pennyfield Ave
Throgs Neck, NY 10465
718-409-7200 or 800-642-1874 Fax: 718-409-7465
Web site: www.sunymaritime.edu

President:
John W Craine Jr. 718-409-7271

COMMUNITY COLLEGES

Adirondack Community College
640 Bay Rd
Queensbury, NY 12804
518-743-2200 Fax: 518-745-1433
e-mail: info@sunyacc.edu
Web site: www.sunyacc.edu

President:
Ronald Heacock 518-743-2237/fax: 518-743-2262
e-mail: heacockr@sunyacc.edu

Offices and agencies generally appear in alphabetical order, except when specific order is requested by listee.

Broome Community College
PO Box 1017
Binghamton, NY 13902
607-778-5000 Fax: 607-778-5310
Web site: www.sunybroome.edu

Interim President:
Kevin E Drumm 607-778-5100
e-mail: oday-p@sunybroome.edu

Cayuga Community College
197 Franklin St
Auburn, NY 13021
315-255-1743 Fax: 315-255-2117
Web site: www.cayuga-cc.edu

President:
Daniel Paul Larson 315-255-1743 x2208
e-mail: daniel.larson@cayuga-cc.edu

Clinton Community College
136 Clinton Point Dr
Plattsburgh, NY 12901
518-562-4200 Fax: 518-562-4159
Web site: www.clinton.edu

Clinton Community College
518-562-4100

Columbia-Greene Community College
4400 Route 23
Hudson, NY 12534-0327
518-828-4181 Fax: 518-828-8543
e-mail: info@sunycgcc.edu
Web site: www.sunycgcc.edu

President:
James R Campion 518-828-4181x3325/fax: 518-822-2006
e-mail: campion@sunycgcc.edu

Corning Community College
1 Academic Dr
Corning, NY 14830
607-962-9222 or 800-358-7171 Fax: 607-962-9456
Web site: www.corning-cc.edu

President:
Floyd F Amann....................607-962-9232 x9232/fax: 607-962-9485
e-mail: amann@corning-cc.edu

Dutchess Community College
53 Pendell Rd
Poughkeepsie, NY 12601-1595
845-431-8000 Fax: 845-431-8984
e-mail: communityrelations@sunydutchess.edu
Web site: www.sunydutchess.edu

President:
D David Conklin....................845-431-8980
e-mail: conklin@sunydutchess.edu

Erie Community College
121 Ellicott St
Buffalo, NY 14203-2698
716-851-1322
e-mail: info@ecc.edu
Web site: www.ecc.edu

President:
Jack Quinn 716-851-1200
e-mail: jquinn@ecc.edu

Fashion Institute of Technology
7th Ave at 27th St
New York, NY 10001-5992
212-217-7999
e-mail: fitinfo@fitnyc.edu
Web site: www.fitnyc.edu

President:
Joyce F Brown....................212-217-4000/fax: 212-217-7639

Finger Lakes Community College
3325 Marvin Sands Drive
Canandaigua, NY 14424
585-394-3500 or 585-394-3522 Fax: 585-394-5017
e-mail: admissions@flcc.edu
Web site: www.fingerlakes.edu

President:
Dr. Barbara Risser 585-394-3500 x7201
e-mail: risserbg@flcc.edu

Fulton-Montgomery Community College
2805 State Hwy 67
Johnstown, NY 12095-3790
518-762-4651 Fax: 518-762-4334
e-mail: geninfo@fmcc.suny.edu
Web site: www.fmcc.suny.edu

President:
Dustin Swanger....................518-762-9651 x 8000

Genesee Community College
One College Rd
Batavia, NY 14020-9704
585-343-0055 Fax: 585-343-4541
Web site: www.genesee.edu

President:
Stuart Steiner 585-343-0055 x6201
e-mail: ssteiner@genesee.edu

Herkimer County Community College
100 Reservoir Rd
Herkimer, NY 13350-9987
315-866-0300 or 888-464-4222 Fax: 315-866-7253
Web site: www.herkimer.edu

President:
Ann Marie Murray 315-866-0300 x8261/fax: 315-866-5539
e-mail: president@herkimer.edu

Hudson Valley Community College
80 Vandenburgh Ave
Troy, NY 12180
518-629-4822 or 877-325-4822 Fax: 518-629-8070
e-mail: input@hvcc.edu
Web site: www.hvcc.edu

President:
Andrew Matonak 518-629-4530
e-mail: a.matonak@hvcc.edu

Jamestown Community College
525 Falconer St
PO Box 20
Jamestown, NY 14702-0020
716-338-1000 or 800-388-8557 Fax: 716-338-1466
Web site: www.sunyjcc.edu

President:
Gregory T DeCinque 716-665-5220 x2315
e-mail: gregdecinque@mail.sunyjcc.edu

Jefferson Community College
1220 Coffeen St
Watertown, NY 13601
315-786-2200 Fax: 315-786-0158
e-mail: webmaster@sunyjefferson.edu
Web site: www.sunyjefferson.edu

President:
Carole A McCoy 315-786-2230
e-mail: cmccoy@sunyjefferson.edu

Mohawk Valley Community College
1101 Sherman Dr
Utica, NY 13501-5394
315-792-5400 Fax: 315-792-5666
Web site: www.mvcc.edu

President:
Randall S Van Wagoner 315-792-5333/fax: 315-792-5678
e-mail: rvanwagoner@mvcc.edu

Monroe Community College
1000 E Henrietta Rd
Rochester, NY 14623-5780
585-292-2000 Fax: 585-292-3060
e-mail: collcommrelations@monroecc.edu
Web site: www.monroecc.edu

President:
Anne M Kress PhD 585-292-2100/fax: 585-292-3870
e-mail: akress@monroecc.edu

Nassau Community College
1 Education Dr
Garden City, NY 11530-6793
516-572-7501 Fax: 516-572-8118
e-mail: info@ncc.edu
Web site: www.ncc.edu

President:
Donald P Astrab 516-572-7205
e-mail: presidentsoffice@ncc.edu

Niagara County Community College
3111 Saunders Settlement Rd
Sanborn, NY 14132
716-614-6222 Fax: 716-614-6700
Web site: www.niagaracc.suny.edu

President:
James P Klyczek 716-614-5901
e-mail: klyczek@niagaracc.suny.edu

North Country Community College
23 Santanoni Ave
PO Box 89
Saranac Lake, NY 12983-0089
518-891-2915 or 888-879-6222 Fax: 518-891-6562
e-mail: helpdesk@nccc.edu
Web site: www.nccc.edu

President:
Carol Brown 518-891-2915 x201/fax: 518-891-5029
e-mail: president@nccc.edu

Onondaga Community College
4585 West Seneca Turnpike
Syracuse, NY 13215
315-498-2622 Fax: 315-469-4475
e-mail: occinfo@sunyocc.edu
Web site: www.sunyocc.edu

President:
Debbie L Sydow 315-498-2211
e-mail: sydowd@sunyocc.edu

Orange County Community College
115 South St
Middletown, NY 10940
845-344-6222 Fax: 845-343-1228
Web site: www.sunyorange.edu

President:
William Richards 845-341-4701
e-mail: president@sunyorange.edu

Rockland Community College
145 College Rd
Suffern, NY 10901
845-574-4000
Web site: www.sunyrockland.edu

President:
Cliff L Wood....................................845-574-4214
e-mail: cwood@sunyrockland.edu

Schenectady County Community College
78 Washington Ave
Schenectady, NY 12305
518-381-1200 Fax: 518-346-0379
Web site: www.sunysccc.edu

President:
Dr Quintin B Bullock 518-381-1304/fax: 518-346-8680
e-mail: bullocqb@sunysccc.edu

Suffolk County Community College
533 College Rd
Selden, NY 11784
631-451-4000 Fax: 631-451-4090
Web site: www3.sunysuffolk.edu

President:
Shaun L McKay 631-451-4736
e-mail: mckays@sunysuffolk.edu

Sullivan County Community College
112 College Rd
PO Box 4002
Loch Sheldrake, NY 12759

845-434-5750 or 800-577-5243 Fax: 845-434-4806
e-mail: sccc@sullivan.suny.edu
Web site: www.sullivan.suny.edu

President:
Mamie Howard Golladay 845-434-5750 x4261/fax: 845-434-9308
e-mail: mgollada@sullivan.suny.edu

Tompkins Cortland Community College
170 North St
PO Box 139
Dryden, NY 13053
607-844-8211 or 888-567-8211 Fax: 607-844-9665
Web site: www.tc3.edu

President:
Carl E Haynes. 607-844-8222 x4368/fax: 607-844-6545
e-mail: haynesc@tc3.edu

Ulster County Community College
491 Cottekill Rd
Stone Ridge, NY 12484
845-687-5000 or 800-724-0833 Fax: 845-687-5083
Web site: www.sunyulster.edu

President:
Donald C Katt 845-687-5050/fax: 845-687-5292
e-mail: kattd@sunyulster.edu

Westchester Community College
75 Grasslands Rd
Valhalla, NY 10595-1693
914-606-6600 Fax: 914-785-6565
e-mail: info@sunywcc.edu
Web site: www.sunywcc.edu

President:
Joseph N Hankin 914-606-6707/fax: 914-785-6780
e-mail: joseph.hankin@sunywcc.edu

EDUCATIONAL OPPORTUNITY CENTERS

Bronx Educational Opportunity Center
1666 Bathgate Ave
Bronx, NY 10457
718-530-7000 Fax: 718-530-7047
Web site: www.brx.eoc.suny.edu

Executive Director:
Stephen H Adolphus 718-530-7040

Brooklyn Educational Opportunity Center
111 Livingston St
Brooklyn, NY 11201
718-802-3300 Fax: 718-802-3381
e-mail: admissions@beoc.suny.edu
Web site: www.bkl.eoc.suny.edu

Executive Director/Dean:
Lois Blades-Rosado 718-246-2057
e-mail: rosadol@bklyn.eoc.cuny.edu

Buffalo Educational Opportunity Center
465 Washington St
Buffalo, NY 14203
716-849-6727 x500 Fax: 716-849-6738
e-mail: eoc465@buffalo.edu
Web site: www.bfl.eoc.suny.edu

Director:
Sherryl D Weems. 716-849-6727 x125
e-mail: weems@buffalo.edu

Capital District Educational Opportunity Center
145 Congress St
Troy, NY 12180
518-273-1900 Fax: 518-273-1919
e-mail: eocinfo@hvcc.edu
Web site: www.hvcc.edu/eoc/

Executive Director/VP:
Lucille A Marion 518-273-1900 x2212
e-mail: l.marion@hvcc.edu

Educational Opportunity Center of Westchester
26 S Broadway
Yonkers, NY 10701
914-606-7600 Fax: 914-606-7640
Web site: www.ynk.eoc.suny.edu

Director/Associate Dean:
Renee Guy. 914-606-7612
e-mail: renee.guy@sunywcc.edu

Long Island Educational Opportunity Center
269 Fulton Ave
Hempstead, NY 11550
516-489-8705
Web site: www.li.sunyeoc.org

Dean/Executive Director:
Veronica Henry. 631-420-2507
e-mail: henryv@farmingdale.edu

Manhattan Educational Opportunity Center
163 W 125th St
New York, NY 10027
212-961-4400 Fax: 212-961-4343
e-mail: info@meoc.suny.edu
Web site: www.man.eoc.suny.edu

Executive Director/Dean:
Rodney Alexander 212-961-4320
e-mail: rodney.alexander@man.eoc.suny.edu

North Bronx Career Counseling & Outreach Center
2901 White Plains Road
Bronx, NY 10467
718-547-1001 Fax: 718-547-1973
Web site: www.nbx.sunyeoc.org

Director:
Mitch Duren. 718-547-1001 x204
e-mail: mmduren@sunyeoc.org

Queens Educational Opportunity Center
SUNY
158-29 Archer Ave
Jamaica, NY 11433
718-725-3300 Fax: 718-658-5604
Web site: www.qns.eoc.suny.edu

Director:
Khayriyyah Ali 718-725-3403
e-mail: ali_29@eoc.suny.edu

Rochester Educational Opportunity Center
305 Andrews St
Rochester, NY 14604
585-232-2730 Fax: 585-546-7824
Web site: www.reoc.brockport.edu

Dean/Executive Director:
Melva L Brown 585-232-2730 x269/fax: 585-232-8154
e-mail: mebrown@brockport.edu

SUNY College & Career Counseling Center
120 Emmons St
Schenectady, NY 12304
518-370-2654 Fax: 518-370-2661

Director:
Lois M Tripp 518-370-2654
e-mail: sunyccc@nycap.rr.com

Syracuse Educational Opportunity Center
100 New St
Syracuse, NY 13202
315-472-0130 Fax: 315-472-1241
e-mail: wallam@morrisville.edu
Web site: www.syracuseeoc.com

Vice President:
Tim Penix 315-472-0130/fax: 315-472-1241

THE CITY UNIVERSITY OF NEW YORK

CUNY Board of Trustees
535 E 80th St
New York, NY 10021
212-794-5450 Fax: 212-794-5678
Web site: www.cuny.edu

Chair:
Benno C. Schmidt Jr. 212-794-5450
Vice Chair:
Philip Alfonso Berry 212-794-5450
Member:
Valerie Lancaster Beal 212-794-5450
Member:
Wellington Z. Chen. 212-794-5450
Member:
Rita DiMartino 212-794-5450
Member:
Freida Foster 212-794-5450
Member:
Judah Gribetz 212-794-5450
Member:
Joseph J. Lhota 212-794-5450
Member:
Hugo M. Morales 212-794-5450
Member:
Brian D. Obergfell 212-794-5450
Member:
Peter S. Pantaleo 212-794-5450
Member:
Kathleen M. Pesile 212-794-5450
Member:
Carol A. Robles-Roman 212-794-5450
Member:
Charles A. Shorter. 212-794-5450
Member:
Jeffrey A. Weisenfeld 212-794-5450
Member:
Kafui Kouakou 212-794-5450
Member:
Terrence F. Martell 212-794-5450

CUNY Central Administration
205 East 42nd Street
New York, NY 10017
646-664-9100
Web site: www.cuny.edu

Chancellor:
James B. Milliken 646-664-9100/fax: 646-664-3868
Executive Vice Chancellor & COO:
Allan H. Dobrin 646-664-2888
Executive Vice Chancellor & University Provost:
Vita C. Rabinowitz 646-664-8075
Senior Vice Chancellor, University Relations & Secretary of the Board:
Jay Hershenson 646-664-9001
Senior Vice Chancellor, Legal Affairs & General Counsel:
Frederick P. Schaffer 646-664-9210
Vice Chancellor, Budget & Finance:
Matthew Sapienza. 646-746-4275
Vice Chancellor for Student Affairs:
Frank D. Sanchez 646-664-8759
Vice Chancellor, Labor Relations:
Pamela S. Silverblatt. 646-664-2977
Vice Chancellor, Research:
Gillian Small. 646-664-8910
Vice Chancellor, Human Resources Management:
Gloriana Waters 646-664-3254
Vice Chancellor, Facilities Planning, Construction & Management:
Judith Bergtraum. 646-664-2605
Vice Chancellor & University CIO:
Brian Cohen 646-664-2365

City University Construction Fund . . . . . fax: 212-541-0175
555 W 57th St, 10th Fl, New York, NY 10019
212-541-0171 Fax: 212-541-0175

Acting Chairman:
Philip Berry. 212-541-0171
Member:
Wellington Z. Chen. 212-541-5315
Member:
Noel N. Hankin
Executive Director:
Iris Weinshall 212-794-5315
Counsel:
Frederick P. Schaffer 212-794-5506
Deputy Executive Director:
Howard Alschuler. 212-541-0999
Administrative Officer:
Denise Philips 212-541-0190
Special Assistant:
Nancy Nichols. 212-541-0442

Bernard M Baruch College
One Bernard Baruch Way
New York, NY 10010
646-312-1000 Fax: 646-312-1362
Web site: www.baruch.cuny.edu

President:
Mitchel Wallerstein. 646-312-3310/fax: 646-312-3311

Offices and agencies generally appear in alphabetical order, except when specific order is requested by listee.

Borough of Manhattan Community College
199 Chambers St
New York, NY 10007
212-220-8000 Fax: 212-220-1244
Web site: www.bmcc.cuny.edu

President:
Antonio Perez 212-220-1230 x1234
e-mail: aperez@bmcc.cuny.edu

Bronx Community College
2155 University Ave
Bronx, NY 10453
718-289-5100
e-mail: webmaster@bcc.cuny.edu
Web site: www.bcc.cuny.edu

Senior VP:
Carolyn Williams 718-289-5151

Brooklyn College
2900 Bedford Ave
Brooklyn, NY 11210
718-951-5000
Web site: www.brooklyn.cuny.edu

President:
Karen L Gould 718-951-5671/fax: 718-951-4872
e-mail: klgould@brooklyn.cuny.edu

City College of New York, The
160 Covent Ave
New York, NY 10031
212-650-7000
Web site: www1.ccny.cuny.edu

Interim President:
Lisa Staiano-Coico 212-650-7285
e-mail: president@ccny.cuny.edu

College of Staten Island
2800 Victory Blvd
Staten Island, NY 10314
718-982-2000
Web site: www.csi.cuny.edu

President:
Tomas Morales 718-982-2000 x2400
e-mail: president@csi.cuny.edu

Graduate Center
365 Fifth Ave
New York, NY 10016-4309
212-817-7000 or 877-428-6942
Web site: www.gc.cuny.edu

President:
William P Kelly 212-817-7100/fax: 212-817-1606
e-mail: pres@gc.cuny.edu

Graduate School of Journalism
219 W 40th St
New York, NY 10018
646-758-7800
Web site: www.journalism.cuny.edu

Dean:
Steve Shepard 646-758-7816/fax: 646-758-7809
e-mail: steve.shepard@journalism.cuny.edu

Hostos Community College
500 Grand Concourse
Bronx, NY 10451
718-518-4444 or 718-518-4100
Web site: www.hostos.cuny.edu

President:
Felix V Matos Rodriguez 718-518-4300
e-mail: president@hostos.cuny.edu

Hunter College
695 Park Ave
New York, NY 10021
212-772-4000
Web site: www.hunter.cuny.edu

President:
Jennifer J Raab 212-772-4242/fax: 212-772-4724
e-mail: jennifer.raab@hunter.cuny.edu

John Jay College of Criminal Justice
899 Tenth Ave
New York, NY 10019
212-237-8000 Fax: 212-237-8607
Web site: www.jjay.cuny.edu

President:
Jeremy Travis 212-237-8600
e-mail: jtravis@jjay.cuny.edu

Kingsborough Community College
2001 Oriental Blvd
Brooklyn, NY 11235-2398
718-265-5343
e-mail: info@kbcc.cuny.edu
Web site: www.kbcc.cuny.edu

President:
Regina S Peruggi 718-368-5100
e-mail: president@kingsborough.edu

LaGuardia Community College
31-10 Thomson Ave
Long Island City, NY 11101
718-482-7200
Web site: www.lagcc.cuny.edu

President:
Gail O Mellow 718-482-5050
e-mail: gmellow@lagcc.cuny.edu

Lehman College
250 Bedford Park Blvd West
Bronx, NY 10468
718-960-8000 or 877-534-6261
Web site: www.lehman.edu

President:
Ricardo R Fernandez 718-960-8111/fax: 718-584-1765
e-mail: president@lehman.cuny.edu

Medgar Evers College
1650 Bedford St
Brooklyn, NY 11225

718-270-4900
Web site: www.mec.cuny.edu

President:
William Pollard 718-270-5000/fax: 718-270-5126
e-mail: wlpollard@mec.cuny.edu

New York City College of Technology
300 Jay St
Brooklyn, NY 11201
718-260-5000
e-mail: connect@citytech.cuny.edu
Web site: www.citytech.cuny.edu

President:
Russell K Hotzler 718-260-5400
e-mail: rhotzler@citytech.cuny.edu

Queens College
65-30 Kissena Blvd
Flushing, NY 11367-1597
718-997-5000
Web site: www.qc.cuny.edu

President:
Felix V. Matos Rodriguez. 718-997-5550

Queensborough Community College
222-05 56th Ave
Bayside, NY 11364-1497
718-631-6262
Web site: www.qcc.cuny.edu

President:
Diane Call 718-631-6222/fax: 718-281-5588

School of Law at Queens College
2 Court Square
Long Island City, NY 11101-4356
718-340-4200 Fax: 718-340-4435
Web site: www.law.cuny.edu

Dean:
Michelle J. Anderson 718-340-4201
e-mail: anderson@law.cuny.edu

School of Professional Studies
101 West 31st St
New York, NY 10001
212-652-2869
Web site: sps.cuny.edu

Dean:
John Mogulescu 212-794-5429
e-mail: john.mogulescu@mail.cuny.edu

Sophie Davis School of Biomedical Education
160 Convent Ave
New York, NY 10031
212-650-7000 Fax: 212-650-6696
Web site: med.cuny.edu

Dean:
Eitan Friedman 212-650-5275/fax: 212-650-6696
e-mail: friedman@med.cuny.edu

York College
94-20 Guy R Brewer Blvd
Jamaica, NY 11451
718-262-2000
Web site: york.cuny.edu

President:
Marcia Keizs 718-262-2350/fax: 718-262-2352
e-mail: president@york.cuny.edu

INDEPENDENT COLLEGES & UNIVERSITIES

Adelphi University
1 South Ave
PO Box 701
Garden City, NY 11530
516-877-3050 or 800-233-5744 Fax: 516-877-3090
Web site: www.adelphi.edu

President:
Robert A Scott 516-877-3838/fax: 516-877-3845

Albany College of Pharmacy
106 New Scotland Ave
Albany, NY 12208-3492
518-694-7200 or 888-203-8010 Fax: 518-694-7202
e-mail: info@acphs.edu
Web site: www.acphs.edu

President:
James J Gozzo. 518-694-7255
e-mail: gozzoj@acphs.edu

Albany Law School
80 New Scotland Ave
Albany, NY 12208-3494
518-445-2311 Fax: 518-445-2315
e-mail: info@albanylaw.edu
Web site: www.albanylaw.edu

President/Dean:
Thomas F Guernsey. 518-445-2380/fax: 518-472-5865
e-mail: tguer@albanylaw.edu

Albany Medical College
43 New Scotland Ave
Albany, NY 12208
518-262-3125 Fax: 518-262-6515
e-mail: webmaster@mail.amc.edu
Web site: www.amc.edu

Dean:
Vincent P Verdile 518-262-6008
e-mail: verdilv@mail.amc.edu

Alfred University
1 Saxon Dr
Alfred, NY 14802-1205
800-541-9229 or 607-871-2175 Fax: 607-871-2339
Web site: www.alfred.edu

President:
Charles M Edmondson 607-871-2101
e-mail: edmondson@alfred.edu

Offices and agencies generally appear in alphabetical order, except when specific order is requested by listee.

American Academy McAllister Institute of Funeral Service
619 West 54th St, 2nd Fl
New York, NY 10019
212-757-1190 Fax: 212-765-5923
e-mail: info@funeraleducation.org
Web site: www.funeraleducation.org

President/CEO:
Meg Dunn 212-757-1190

American Academy of Dramatic Arts
120 Madison Ave
New York, NY 10016-7004
212-686-9244 or 800-463-8990
Web site: www.aada.org

Acting President:
Susan Zech 212-686-9244

Bank Street College of Education/Graduate School
610 West 112th St
New York, NY 10025-1898
212-875-4400 Fax: 212-875-4678
e-mail: collegepubs@bankstreet.edu
Web site: www.bankstreet.edu

President:
Elizabeth D Dickey 212-875-4595/fax: 212-875-4594
e-mail: presidentoffice@bankstreet.edu
Dean, Graduate School:
Virginia Roach 212-875-4466
e-mail: vroach@bankstreet.edu

Bard College
PO Box 5000
Annandale-on-Hudson, NY 12504-5000
845-758-6822 Fax: 845-758-5208
Web site: www.bard.edu

President:
Leon Botstein 845-758-7423
e-mail: president@bard.edu

Barnard College
3009 Broadway
New York, NY 10027
212-854-5262 Fax: 212-854-6220
Web site: www.barnard.edu

President:
Deborah L Spar....212-854-2021
e-mail: dspar@barnard.edu

Boricua College
3755 Broadway
New York, NY 10032
212-694-1000 Fax: 212-694-1015
e-mail: acruz@boricuacollege.edu
Web site: www.boricuacollege.edu

President:
Victor G Alicea....212-694-1000
e-mail: valicea@boricuacollege.edu

Bramson ORT College
69-30 Austin St
Forest Hills, NY 11375-4239
718-261-5800 Fax: 718-575-5118
Web site: www.bramsonort.org

Director:
Ephraim Buhks 718-261-5800 x102
e-mail: ebuhks@bramsonort.edu

Brooklyn Law School
250 Joralemon St
Brooklyn, NY 11201-3798
718-625-2200 Fax: 718-780-0393
Web site: www.brooklaw.edu

President:
Joan G Wexler....718-780-7900
e-mail: joan.wexler@brooklaw.edu

Canisius College
2001 Main St
Buffalo, NY 14208-1098
716-883-7000 Fax: 716-888-2525
Web site: www.canisius.edu

President:
John J Huxley 716-888-2100/fax: 716-888-3220

Cazenovia College
22 Sullivan St
Cazenovia, NY 13035
315-655-7000 or 800-654-3210 Fax: 315-655-4143
e-mail: admissions@cazenovia.edu
Web site: www.cazenovia.edu

President:
Mark John Tierno 315-655-7116
e-mail: mtierno@cazenovia.edu

Christ the King Seminary
711 Knox Rd
East Aurora, NY 14052-0607
716-652-8900 Fax: 716-652-8903
e-mail: cksacad@cks.edu
Web site: www.cks.edu

President/Rector:
Rev Peter J Drilling....716-652-8900
e-mail: pdrilling@cks.edu

Clarkson University
8 Clarkson Ave
Potsdam, NY 13699
315-268-6400 or 800-527-6577 Fax: 315-268-7993
Web site: www.clarkson.edu

President:
Anthony G Collins 315-268-6444
e-mail: collins@clarkson.edu

Cochran School of Nursing
St John's Riverside Hospital
967 N Broadway, Andrus Pavilion
Yonkers, NY 10701

914-964-4296 Fax: 914-964-4266
e-mail: admissions@cochranschoolofnursing.us
Web site: www.cochranschoolofnursing.us

Vice President & Dean:
Kathleen Dirschel 914-964-4280
e-mail: kdirschel@riversidehealth.org
Director, Administration:
David T George 914-964-4296
e-mail: dgeorge@riversidehealth.org

Colgate Rochester Crozer Divinity School
1100 S Goodman St
Rochester, NY 14620-2589
585-271-1320 Fax: 585-271-8013
Web site: www.crcds.edu

President:
Rev. Jack McKelvey 585-340-9680

Colgate University
13 Oak Dr
Hamilton, NY 13346
315-228-1000 Fax: 315-228-7798
Web site: www.colgate.edu

President:
Jeffrey Herbst 315-228-7444/fax: 315-228-6010
e-mail: jherbst@colgate.edu

College of Mount Saint Vincent
6301 Riverdale Ave
Riverdale, NY 10471-1093
800-665-2678 or 718-405-3267
Web site: www.mountsaintvincent.edu

President:
Charles L Flynn Jr. 718-405-3233
e-mail: president@mountsaintvincent.edu

College of New Rochelle (The)
Brooklyn Campus
29 Castle Pl
New Rochelle, NY 10805-2339
914-654-5000 or 800-211-7077 Fax: 914-654-5833
e-mail: info@cnr.edu
Web site: www.cnr.edu

President:
Stephen J Sweeny 914-654-5430
e-mail: ssweeny@cnr.edu

College of Saint Rose (The)
432 Western Ave
Albany, NY 12203-1490
800-637-8556
Web site: www.strose.edu

President:
R Mark Sullivan 518-454-5120
e-mail: sullivan@strose.edu

Columbia University
2960 Broadway
New York, NY 10027
212-854-1754 Fax: 212-854-9973
Web site: www.columbia.edu

President:
Lee C Bollinger 212-854-9970/fax: 212-854-9973
e-mail: officeofthepresident@columbia.edu

Concordia College
171 White Plains Rd
Bronxville, NY 10708
914-337-9300 Fax: 914-395-4500
Web site: www.concordia-ny.edu

President:
Viji D George 914-337-9300 x2111
e-mail: viji.george@concordia-ny.edu

Cooper Union for the Advancement of Science & Art
30 Cooper Sq, 8th floor
New York, NY 10003-7120
212-353-4100 Fax: 212-353-4327
e-mail: webmaster@cooper.edu
Web site: www.cooper.edu

President:
Jamshed Bhurucha 212-353-4195

Cornell University
300 Day Hall
Ithaca, NY 14853
607-254-4636 Fax: 607-254-5175
e-mail: info@cornell.edu
Web site: www.cornell.edu

President:
David J Skorton 607-255-5201/fax: 607-255-9924
e-mail: president@cornell.edu

Crouse Hospital School of Nursing
736 Irving Ave
Syracuse, NY 13210
315-470-7481 Fax: 315-470-7232
e-mail: crouseson@crouse.org
Web site: www.crouse.org/nursing

Director:
Ann Sedore 315-470-7932

Culinary Institute of America
1946 Campus Drive
Hyde Park, NY 12538-1499
845-452-9600 or 800-285-4627 Fax: 845-451-1068
e-mail: admissions@culinary.edu
Web site: www.ciachef.edu

President:
Tim Ryan. 845-451-1352

D'Youville College
320 Porter Ave
Buffalo, NY 14201
716-829-8000 or 800-777-3921 Fax: 716-881-7790
Web site: www.dyc.edu

President:
Sister Denise A Roche 716-829-7673
e-mail: roche@dyc.edu

Daemen College
4380 Main St
Amherst, NY 14226

Offices and agencies generally appear in alphabetical order, except when specific order is requested by listee.

716-839-3600 or 800-462-7652 Fax: 716-839-8516
Web site: www.daemen.edu

President:
Martin J Anisman 716-839-8210/fax: 716-839-8279
e-mail: manisman@daemen.edu

Davis College
400 Riverside Dr
Johnson City, NY 13790
607-729-1581 or 877-949-3248 Fax: 607-729-2962
e-mail: info@davisny.edu
Web site: www.davisny.edu

President:
Dino Pedrone 607-729-1581 x316/fax: 607-729-1581
e-mail: president@davisny.edu

Dominican College
470 Western Highway
Orangeburg, NY 10962
845-359-7800 Fax: 845-359-2313
Web site: www.dc.edu

President:
Sister Mary Eileen O'Brien. 845-848-7801/fax: 845-359-7988
e-mail: mary.eileen.obrien@dc.edu

Dorothea Hopfer School of Nursing at Mount Vernon Hospital
53 Valentine St
Mount Vernon, NY 10550
914-361-6221 Fax: 914-665-7047
e-mail: hopferadmissions@sshsw.org
Web site: www.hopfer.org

Dean of Nursing Education:
Joanna Scalabrini 914-361-6220
e-mail: hopfcr@sshsw.org

Dowling College
150 Idle Hour Blvd
Oakdale, NY 11769
800-369-5464 Fax: 631-589-6644
Web site: www.dowling.edu

President:
Jeremy Brown 631-244-3200

Ellis Hospital School of Nursing
1101 Nott St
Schenectady, NY 12308
518-243-4471 Fax: 518-243-4470
Web site: www.ehson.org

Director:
Marilyn Stapleton 518-243-4471
CEO:
Jim Connolly. 518-243-4000

Elmira College
One Park Pl
Elmira, NY 14901
607-735-1800 or 800-935-6472
e-mail: admissions@elmira.edu
Web site: www.elmira.edu

President:
Thomas K Meier 607-735-1790
e-mail: tmeier@elmira.edu

Excelsior College
7 Columbia Cir
Albany, NY 12203-5159
518-464-8500 or 888-647-2388 Fax: 518-464-8777
e-mail: info@excelsior.edu
Web site: www.excelsior.edu

President:
John F Ebersole. 518-464-8500

Fordham University
Rose Hill
441 East Fordham Rd
Bronx, NY 10458
718-817-1000
Web site: www.fordham.edu

President:
Joseph M McShane 718-817-3000/fax: 718-817-3005

General Theological Seminary of the Episcopal Church
175 Ninth Ave
Chelsea Sq
New York, NY 10011-4977
212-243-5150 Fax: 212-727-3907
Web site: www.gts.edu

Interim President/Dean:
Lang Lowrey 212-243-5150 x302

Hamilton College
198 College Hill Rd
Clinton, NY 13323
315-859-4421 or 800-843-2655 Fax: 315-859-4457
Web site: www.hamilton.edu

President:
Joan Hinde Stewart. 315-859-4104
e-mail: jstewart@hamilton.edu

Hartwick College
PO Box 4020
Oneonta, NY 13820-4020
800-427-8942 or 607-431-4000 Fax: 607-431-4102
Web site: www.hartwick.edu

President:
Dr Margaret L Drugovich. 607-431-4990
e-mail: prcsidcnt@hartwick.edu

Hebrew Union College - Jewish Institute of Religion
The Brookdale Center
One W 4th St
New York, NY 10012
212-674-5300 Fax: 212-388-1720
Web site: www.huc.edu

President:
David Ellenson 800-424-1336 x2201/fax: 212-979-0853
e-mail: presoff@huc.edu

Helene Fuld College of Nursing North General Hospital
24 East 120th St
New York, NY 10035

Colleges, Universities & School Districts

Offices and agencies generally appear in alphabetical order, except when specific order is requested by listee.

212-616-7200
Web site: www.helenefuld.edu

President:
Margaret Wines 212-423-2750

Hilbert College
5200 South Park Ave
Hamburg, NY 14075
716-649-7900 Fax: 716-649-0702
e-mail: info@hilbert.edu
Web site: www.hilbert.edu

President:
Cynthia Zane 716-649-7900 x200
e-mail: czane@hilbert.edu

Hobart & William Smith Colleges
300 Pulteney Street
Geneva, NY 14456
315-781-3000 or 800-852-2256
Web site: www.hws.edu

President:
Mark D Gearan 315-781-3309
e-mail: gearan@hws.edu

Hofstra University
100 Fulton Ave
Hempstead, NY 11550
800-463-7872 or 516-463-6600 Fax: 516-463-4867
Web site: www.hofstra.edu

President:
Stuart Rabinowitz 516-463-6800/fax: 516-463-6096
e-mail: president@hofstra.edu

Houghton College
1 Willard Avenue
Houghton, NY 14744-0128
800-777-2556 Fax: 585-567-9572
Web site: www.houghton.edu

President:
Shirley Mullen 585-567-9310
e-mail: cindy.lastoria@houghton.edu

Institute of Design & Construction
141 Willoughby St
Brooklyn, NY 11201
718-855-3661 Fax: 718-852-5889
e-mail: info@idc.edu
Web site: www.idc.edu

Executive Director:
Vincent C Battista 718-855-3661
e-mail: vcbattista@idc.edu

Iona College
715 North Ave
New Rochelle, NY 10801
914-633-2000 or 800-231-4662 Fax: 914-633-2018
Web site: www.iona.edu

President:
Joseph Nyre 914-633-2203

Ithaca College
953 Danby Rd
Ithaca, NY 14850
607-274-3011 Fax: 607-274-1900
e-mail: thurston@ithaca.edu
Web site: www.ithaca.edu

President:
Thomas R Rochon 607-274-3111/fax: 607-274-3064
e-mail: president@ithaca.edu

Jewish Theological Seminary
3080 Broadway
New York, NY 10027-4649
212-678-8000 Fax: 212-678-8947
Web site: www.jtsa.edu

Chancellor/President of Faculties:
Arnold Eisen 212-678-8072
e-mail: arreisen@jtsa.edu

Juilliard School (The)
60 Lincoln Center Plz
New York, NY 10023-6588
212-799-5000 Fax: 212-724-0263
Web site: www.juilliard.edu

President:
Joseph W Polisi 212-799-5000 X207
Dean & Provost:
Ara Guzalimian 212-799-5000 x204

Keuka College
141 Central Ave
Keuka Park, NY 14478
315-279-5000 or 800-335-3852 Fax: 315-279-5216
Web site: www.keuka.edu

President:
Joseph Burke 315-279-5201/fax: 315-279-5335
e-mail: president@keuka.edu

King's College (The)
56 Broadway
New York, NY 10004
888-969-7200 or 212-659-7200 Fax: 212-659-7210
Web site: www.tkc.edu

President:
Gregory Alan Thornbury 212-659-7200

Le Moyne College
1419 Salt Springs Rd
Syracuse, NY 13214-1301
315-445-4100 Fax: 315-445-4540
Web site: www.lemoyne.edu

President:
Dr. Fred Pestello 315-445-4120
e-mail: president@lemoyne.edu

Long Island College Hospital School of Nursing
340 Court St
Brooklyn, NY 11231
718-780-1953 Fax: 718-780-1936
Web site: www.futurenurselich.org

Dean:
Nancy Dimauro 718-780-1998

Long Island University
700 Northern Blvd
Brookville, NY 11548
516-299-2000 Fax: 516-299-2072
Web site: www.liu.edu

President:
David J Steinberg 516-299-2501/fax: 516-229-2590
e-mail: president@liu.edu

Manhattan College
4513 Manhattan College Pkwy
Riverdale, NY 10471
718-862-8000 or 800-622-9235
Web site: www.manhattan.edu

President:
Brother Brennan O'Donnell 718-862-7301/fax: 718-862-8030
e-mail: brennan.odonnell@manhattan.edu

Manhattan School of Music
120 Claremont Ave
New York, NY 10027
212-749-2802 Fax: 212-749-5471
Web site: www.msmnyc.edu

President:
Robert Sirota 212-749-2802 x4477
e-mail: officeofthepresident@msmnyc.edu

Manhattanville College
2900 Purchase St
Purchase, NY 10577
914-694-2200 Fax: 914-694-2386
Web site: www.manhattanville.edu

President:
Molly E Smith 914-323-5230/fax: 914-694-6234
e-mail: president@mville.edu

Maria College of Albany
700 New Scotland Ave
Albany, NY 12208
518-438-3111 Fax: 518-453-1366
Web site: www.mariacollege.edu

President:
Sister Laureen A Fitzgerald 518-438-3111 x213
e-mail: lfitz@mariacollege.edu

Marist College
3399 North Rd
Poughkeepsie, NY 12601
845-575-3000
e-mail: timmian.massie@marist.edu
Web site: www.marist.edu

President:
Dennis J Murray 845-575-3600
e-mail: dennis.murray@marist.edu

Marymount Manhattan College
221 East 71st St
New York, NY 10021
800-627-9668 or 212-517-0400 Fax: 212-517-0567
Web site: www.mmm.edu

President:
Judson R Shaver 212-517-0560
e-mail: jshaver@mmm.edu

Medaille College
18 Agassiz Cir
Buffalo, NY 14214
716-880-2000 or 800-292-1582
Web site: www.medaille.edu

President:
Richard Jurasek 716-880-2201
e-mail: richard.t.jurasek@medaille.edu

Memorial Hospital School of Nursing
600 Northern Blvd
Albany, NY 12204
518-471-3221 Fax: 518-447-3559
e-mail: dorseyp@nehealth.com
Web site: www.nehealth.com

Director:
Mary-Jane Araldi 518-471-3260
e-mail: martinm@nehealth.com

Mercy College
Main Campus
555 Broadway
Dobbs Ferry, NY 10522
877-637-2946 Fax: 914-674-7382
e-mail: admissions@mercy.edu
Web site: www.mercy.edu

President:
Kimberly Cline 914-674-7307/fax: 914-674-5978
e-mail: Kcline@mercy.edu

Metropolitan College of New York
431 Canal St
New York, NY 10013
212-343-1234 or 800-338-4465 Fax: 212-343-7399
Web site: www.metropolitan.edu

President:
Vinton Thompson 212-343-1234 x3301
e-mail: vthompson@metropolitan.edu

Mid-America Baptist Theological Seminary Northeast Branch
2810 Curry Rd
Schenectady, NY 12303
518-355-4000 or 800-209-3447 Fax: 518-355-8298
e-mail: mjohn@mabtsne.edu
Web site: www.mabts.edu

Director:
Shawn Buice 518-355-4000
e-mail: sbuice@mabtsne.edu

Molloy College
1000 Hempstead Ave
PO Box 5002
Rockville Centre, NY 11571-5002

516-678-5000 or 888-466-5569
Web site: www.molloy.edu

President:
Drew Bogner 516-678-5000 x6200/fax: 516-678-5321
e-mail: presidentdrew@molloy.edu

Mount Saint Mary College
330 Powell Ave
Newburgh, NY 12550
845-561-0800 Fax: 845-562-6762
Web site: www.msmc.edu

President:
Fr Kevin E Mackin OFM 845-569-3202
e-mail: mackin@msmc.edu

Mount Sinai School of Medicine of NYU
One Gustave L Levy Pl
New York, NY 10029-6574
212-241-6500
Web site: www.mssm.edu

President/CEO/Dean:
Kenneth L Davis 212-659-8888/fax: 212-659-9800
e-mail: kenneth.davis@mssm.edu

Nazareth College of Rochester
4245 East Ave
Rochester, NY 14618-7390
585-389-2525 Fax: 585-586-2452
Web site: www.naz.edu

President:
Daan Braveman 585-389-2004/fax: 585-389-2015
e-mail: dbravem7@naz.edu

New School University (The)
66 West 12th St
New York, NY 10011
212-229-5600 Fax: 212-229-5937
e-mail: kerreyb@newschool.edu
Web site: www.newschool.edu

President:
David VanZandt 212-229-5656
Dean:
Linda Dunne 212-229-5613
e-mail: dunnel@newschool.edu

New York Academy of Art Inc
111 Franklin St
New York, NY 10013
212-966-0300 Fax: 212-966-3217
e-mail: info@nyaa.edu
Web site: www.nyaa.edu

President:
David Kratz. 212-966-0300
Dean:
Peter Drake 212-966-0300

New York Chiropractic College
2360 Route 89
Seneca Falls, NY 13148
315-568-3000 or 800-234-6922 Fax: 315-568-3012
Web site: www.nycc.edu

President:
Frank J Nicchi. 315-568-3100
e-mail: fnicchi@nycc.edu

New York College of Health Professions
6801 Jericho Tpke
Suite 300
Syosset, NY 11791
516-364-0808 or 800-922-7337 Fax: 516-364-0989
e-mail: info@nycollege.edu
Web site: www.nycollege.edu

President:
Lisa E Pamintuan 516-364-0808
e-mail: pamintuan@nycollege.edu

New York College of Podiatric Medicine
53 East 124th St.
New York, NY 10035-1940
212-410-8000 Fax: 212-722-4918
e-mail: admissions@nycpm.edu
Web site: www.nycpm.edu

President/CEO:
Louis L Levine 212-410-8024/fax: 212-876-7670
e-mail: llevine@nycpm.edu

New York College of Traditional Chinese Medicine
155 First St.
Mineola, NY 11501
516-739-1545
Web site: www.nyctcm.edu

President:
Yemeng Chen 212-685-0888

New York Institute of Technology
Northern Blvd
PO Box 8000
Old Westbury, NY 11568-8000
516-686-1000 or 800-345-6948 Fax: 516-686-7613
e-mail: asknyit@nyit.edu
Web site: www.nyit.edu

President:
Edward Guiliano. 516-686-7650
e-mail: nyitop@nyit.edu

New York Law School
185 W Broadway
New York, NY 10013
212-431-2872 or 212-431-2100 Fax: 212-406-0103
e-mail: alevat@nyls.edu
Web site: www.nyls.edu

President/Dean:
Richard A Matasar. 212-431-2840/fax: 212-219-3752
e-mail: ddean@nyls.edu

New York Medical College
Administration Bldg
40 Sunshine Cottage Rd
Valhalla, NY 10595
914-594-4000
Web site: www.nymc.edu

President/CEO:
Karl P Adler, M.D. 914-594-4600

Offices and agencies generally appear in alphabetical order, except when specific order is requested by listee.

New York School of Interior Design
170 East 70th St
New York, NY 10021
212-472-1500 or 800-336-9743 Fax: 212-472-3800
e-mail: info@nysid.edu
Web site: www.nysid.edu

President:
Christopher Cyphers 212-472-1500 x401/fax: 212-472-1952

New York Theological Seminary
475 Riverside Dr, Ste 500
New York, NY 10115-0083
212-870-1211 Fax: 212-870-1236
e-mail: online@nyts.edu
Web site: www.nyts.edu

President:
Dale T Irvin. 212-870-1223
e-mail: dirvin@nyts.edu

New York University
70 Washington Square South
New York, NY 10012
212-998-1212
Web site: www.nyu.edu

President:
Andrew Hamilton 212-998-2345/fax: 212-995-4790
e-mail: andrew.hamilton@nyu.edu

Niagara University
Lewiston Rd
Niagara University, NY 14109
716-285-1212 or 800-778-3450 Fax: 716-286-8710
Web site: www.niagara.edu

President:
Rev Joseph L Levesque. 716-286-8350/fax: 716-286-8350
e-mail: jll@niagara.edu

Northeastern Seminary
2265 Westside Dr
Rochester, NY 14624
585-594-6802 or 800-777-4792 Fax: 585-594-6801
e-mail: seminary@roberts.edu
Web site: www.nes.edu

President:
John A Martin 585-594-6100
e-mail: martinj@roberts.edu

Nyack College
1 South Blvd
Nyack, NY 10960-3698
845-358-1710 Fax: 845-358-1751
e-mail: president@nyack.edu
Web site: www.nyack.edu

President:
Michael Scales 845-358-1710 x310

Pace University
1 Pace Plz
New York, NY 10038
212-346-1200 or 800-722-3338 Fax: 212-346-1933
Web site: www.pace.edu

President:
Stephen J Friedman 212-346-1097/fax: 212-346-1384
e-mail: sfriedman@pace.edu

Paul Smith's College
Routes 86 & 30
PO Box 265
Paul Smiths, NY 12970-0265
518-327-6227 or 800-421-2605 Fax: 518-327-6016
e-mail: kaaron@paulsmiths.edu
Web site: www.paulsmiths.edu

President/Acting Provost:
John W Mills 518-327-6223/fax: 518-327-6060
e-mail: millsj@paulsmiths.edu

Phillips Beth Israel School of Nursing
776 Ave of Americas
4th Fl
New York, NY 10001-6354
212-614-6110 Fax: 212-614-6109
Web site: www.futurenursebi.org

Dean:
Janet MacKin 212-614-6107
e-mail: jmackin@chpnet.org

Polytechnic University
Main Campus
6 MetroTech Ctr
Brooklyn, NY 11201-2999
718-260-3600 Fax: 718-260-3136
e-mail: inquiry@poly.edu
Web site: www.poly.edu

President:
Jerry MacArthur Hultin 718-260-3500/fax: 718-260-3755
e-mail: hultin@poly.edu

Pratt Institute
200 Willoughby Ave
Brooklyn, NY 11205
718-636-3600 Fax: 718-636-3785
e-mail: info@pratt.edu
Web site: www.pratt.edu

President:
Thomas F Schutte 718-636-3646
e-mail: tschutte@pratt.edu

Professional Business College
125 Canal St
New York, NY 10002
212-226-7300
Web site: www.pbcny.edu

President:
Leon Y Lee 212-226-7300

Rensselaer Polytechnic Institute
110 8th St
Troy, NY 12180
518-276-6000
Web site: www.rpi.edu

President:
Shirley Ann Jackson 518-276-6211/fax: 518-276-8702
e-mail: president@rpi.edu

Colleges, Universities & School Districts

Offices and agencies generally appear in alphabetical order, except when specific order is requested by listee.

Roberts Wesleyan College
2301 Westside Dr
Rochester, NY 14624-1997
585-594-6000 or 800-777-4792 Fax: 585-594-6371
e-mail: admissions@roberts.edu
Web site: www.roberts.edu

President:
John A Martin 585-594-6100/fax: 585-594-6780
e-mail: presidentsoffice@roberts.edu

Rochester Institute of Technology
One Lomb Memorial Dr
Rochester, NY 14623-5603
585-475-2411 Fax: 585-475-5700
Web site: www.rit.edu

President:
William W Destler 585-475-2394
e-mail: bill.destler@rit.edu

Rochester, University of
Wallis Hall
Administration
Rochester, NY 14627
585-275-2121 Fax: 585-275-0359
Web site: www.rochester.edu

President:
Joel Seligman. 585-275-8356/fax: 585-256-2473
e-mail: seligman@rochester.edu

Rockefeller University
1230 York Ave
New York, NY 10065
212-327-8000 Fax: 212-327-7974
e-mail: pubinfo@rockefeller.edu
Web site: www.rockefeller.edu

President:
Marc Tessier-Lavigne. 212-327-8000
e-mail: marc.tessier-lavigne@rockefeller.edu

Sage Colleges (The)
65 1st Street
Troy, NY 12180
518-244-2000 or 888-837-9724 Fax: 518-244-2470
Web site: www.sage.edu

President:
Susan Scrimshaw 518-244-2214
e-mail: scrims@sage.edu

Salvation Army School for Officer Training
201 Lafayette Ave
Suffern, NY 10901
845-368-7200 Fax: 845-357-6644
Web site: www.use.salvationarmy.org

Director of Business:
Major Ivan Rock 845-244-2214
e-mail: Ivan.Rock@use.salvationarmy.org

Samaritan Hospital School of Nursing
2215 Burdett Ave
Troy, NY 12180
518-271-3300 Fax: 518-271-3303
e-mail: dorseyp@nehealth.com
Web site: www.nehealth.com

Director:
Susan Birkhead 518-271-3285

Sarah Lawrence College
1 Mead Way
Bronxville, NY 10708-5999
914-337-0700 Fax: 914-395-2515
e-mail: slcadmit@slc.edu
Web site: www.slc.edu

President:
Karen Lawrence. 914-395-2201/fax: 914-395-2668
e-mail: president@sarahlawrence.edu
Dean:
Jerrilynne Dodds 914-395-2303
e-mail: jdodds@sarahlawrence.edu

Seminary of the Immaculate Conception
440 West Neck Rd
Huntington, NY 11743
631-423-0483 Fax: 631-423-2346
e-mail: info@icseminary.edu
Web site: www.icseminary.edu

Rector:
Rev Msgr Peter Vaccari 631-423-0483
e-mail: pvaccari@icseminary.edu

Siena College
515 Loudon Rd
Loudonville, NY 12211-1462
518-783-2300 or 888-287-4362 Fax: 518-783-4293
Web site: www.siena.edu

President:
Fr Kevin Mullen 518-783-2302
e-mail: kmullen@siena.edu

Skidmore College
815 N Broadway
Saratoga Springs, NY 12866-1632
518-580-5000 Fax: 518-580-5699
e-mail: info@skidmore.edu
Web site: www.skidmore.edu

President:
Philip A Glotzbach 518-580-5700/fax: 518-580-5699
e-mail: pglotzba@skidmore.edu

St Bernard's School of Theology & Ministry
120 French Rd
Rochester, NY 14618
585-271-3657 Fax: 585-271-2045
Web site: www.stbernards.edu

President:
Patricia A Schoelles. 585-271-3657 x298
e-mail: pschoelles@stbernards.edu

St Bonaventure University
3261 W State Rd
St Bonaventure, NY 14778-2284
716-375-2000 or 800-462-5050
Web site: www.sbu.edu

President:
Sister Margaret Carney 716-375-2222
e-mail: mcarney@sbu.edu

St Elizabeth College of Nursing
2215 Genesee St
Utica, NY 13501
315-798-8144 Fax: 315-798-8271
e-mail: conadmin@secon.edu
Web site: www.secon.edu

Interim President:
Marian Kovatchitch 315-798-8125
e-mail: mkovatch@secon.edu

St Francis College
180 Remsen St
Brooklyn Heights, NY 11201
718-489-5200 or 718-522-2300 Fax: 718-237-8964
Web site: www.stfranciscollege.edu

President:
Brendan J Dugan 718-489-5416
e-mail: bdugan@stfranciscollege.edu

St John Fisher College
3690 East Ave
Rochester, NY 14618
585-385-8000 Fax: 585-385-8289
Web site: www.sjfc.edu

President:
Donald E Bain 585-385-8010
e-mail: dbain@sjfc.edu

St John's University
Queens Campus
8000 Utopia Pkwy
Queens, NY 11439
718-990-2000 or 888-978-5646 Fax: 718-990-5723
e-mail: admhelp@stjohns.edu
Web site: www.stjohns.edu

President:
Conrado Gempesaw 718-990-2000

St Joseph's College
Main Campus
245 Clinton Ave
Brooklyn, NY 11205-3688
718-940-5300 Fax: 718-636-7242
Web site: www.sjcny.edu

President:
Elizabeth A Hill 718-940-5989/fax: 718-636-6102
e-mail: ehill@sjcny.edu

St Joseph's Seminary Institute of Religious Studies
201 Seminary Ave
Yonkers, NY 10704-1896
914-968-6200 Fax: 914-376-2019
e-mail: vocations@archny.org
Web site: www.ny-archdiocese.org/seminary

Dean:
Kevin P O'Reilly 914-968-6200

St Lawrence University
23 Romoda Dr
Canton, NY 13617
315-229-5011 or 800-285-1856 Fax: 315-229-7422
Web site: www.stlawu.edu

President:
William L Fox 315-229-5892
e-mail: wfox@stlawu.edu

St Thomas Aquinas College
125 Route 340
Sparkill, NY 10976-1050
845-398-4100
Web site: www.stac.edu

President/CEO:
Margaret M Fitzpatrick 845-398-4012/fax: 845-359-8136
e-mail: mfitzpat@stac.edu

St Vladimir's Orthodox Theological Seminary
575 Scarsdale Rd
Yonkers, NY 10707
914-961-8313 Fax: 914-961-4507
e-mail: info@svots.edu
Web site: www.svots.edu

Dean:
Very Rev John Behr 914-961-8313 X326
e-mail: jbehr@svots.edu

Sunbridge College
285 Hungry Hollow Rd
Chesnut Ridge, NY 10977
845-425-0055 Fax: 845-425-1413
e-mail: info@sunbridge.edu
Web site: www.sunbridge.edu

Executive Director:
Jessica H Ziegler 845-425-0055 x23
e-mail: jziegler@sunbridge.edu

Syracuse University
Skytop Office Building
Syracuse, NY 13244-1100
315-443-1870 Fax: 315-443-3503
Web site: www.syr.edu

Chancellor & President:
Nancy Cantor 315-443-2235
e-mail: ncantor@syr.edu

Teachers College, Columbia University
525 W 120th St
New York, NY 10027
212-678-3000
Web site: www.tc.columbia.edu

President:
Dr Susan H Fuhrman 212-678-3131/fax: 212-678-3205
e-mail: susanf@exchange.tc.columbia.edu

Touro College
500 Seventh Avenue
New York, NY 10018
212-463-0400 Fax: 212-627-9144
Web site: www.touro.edu

Colleges, Universities & School Districts

Offices and agencies generally appear in alphabetical order, except when specific order is requested by listee.

President:
Alan Kadish 212-463-0400

Trocaire College
360 Choate Ave
Buffalo, NY 14220-2094
716-826-1200 Fax: 716-828-6109
e-mail: info@trocaire.edu
Web site: www.trocaire.edu

President:
Paul B Hurley, Jr. 716-826-1200
e-mail: hurleyp@trocaire.edu

Unification Theological Seminary
30 Seminary Dr
Barrytown, NY 12507
845-752-3000 Fax: 845-752-3014
e-mail: registrar@uts.edu
Web site: www.uts.edu

President:
Richard Panzer. 212-563-6647 x110

Union College
807 Union St
Schenectady, NY 12308-3107
518-388-6000 Fax: 518-388-6006
Web site: www.union.edu

President-Elect:
Stephen C Ainlay 518-388-6101
e-mail: ainlays@union.edu
Dean:
Steve Leavitt 518-388-6116/fax: 518-388-6648
e-mail: leavitts@union.edu

Union Theological Seminary
3041 Broadway at 121st St
New York, NY 10027
212-662-7100 Fax: 212-280-1416
e-mail: contactus@uts.columbia.edu
Web site: www.utsnyc.edu

President:
Serene Jones 212-280-1403
e-mail: sjones@uts.columbia.edu

Utica College
1600 Burrstone Rd
Utica, NY 13502-5159
315-792-3006 Fax: 315-792-3003
Web site: www.utica.edu

President:
Todd S Hutton. 315-792-3222
e-mail: thutton@utica.edu

Vassar College
124 Raymond Ave
Poughkeepsie, NY 12604
845-437-7000 Fax: 845-437-7187
Web site: www.vassar.edu

President:
Catharine B Hill 845-437-7200

Vaughn College of Aeronautics & Technology
86-01 23rd Ave
Flushing, NY 11369
718-429-6600 or 866-682-8446 Fax: 718-779-2231
Web site: www.vaughn.edu

President:
John C Fitzpatrick 718-429-6600 x104/fax: 718-429-4020
e-mail: john.fitzpatrick@vaughn.edu

Villa Maria College of Buffalo
240 Pine Ridge Rd
Buffalo, NY 14225
716-896-0700 Fax: 716-961-1871
e-mail: admissions@villa.edu
Web site: www.villa.edu

President:
Sr Marcella Marie Garus. 716-961-1868
e-mail: smgarus@villa.edu

Wagner College
1 Campus Rd
Staten Island, NY 10301
718-390-3100 or 800-221-1010 Fax: 718-390-3105
Web site: www.wagner.edu

President:
Richard Guarasci 718-390-3131/fax: 718-390-3170
e-mail: guarasci@wagner.edu

Watson School of Biological Sciences at Cold Spring Harbor Laboratory
One Bungtown Rd
Cold Spring Harbor, NY 11724
516-367-8800 Fax: 516-367-6919
e-mail: gradschool@cshl.edu
Web site: www.cshl.edu/gradschool

President/CEO:
Bruce Stillman 516-367-6890

Webb Institute
298 Crescent Beach Rd
Glen Cove, NY 11542-1398
516-671-2213 or 866-708-9322 Fax: 516-674-9838
Web site: www.webb-institute.edu

President:
Admiral Robert Olsen 516-671-2213 x102
e-mail: rolsen@webb-institute.edu

Wells College
170 Main St
Aurora, NY 13026-0500
315-364-3266
Web site: www.wells.edu

President:
Lisa Marsh Ryerson. 315-364-3265/fax: 315-364-3335
e-mail: president@wells.edu

Yeshiva University
Wilf Campus
500 W 185th St
New York, NY 10033-3201

212-960-5400
e-mail: administration@yu.edu
Web site: www.yu.edu

President:
Richard M Joel 212-960-5300
e-mail: president@yu.edu

PROPRIETARY COLLEGES

ASA Institute of Business & Computer Technology
81 Willoughby St
Brooklyn, NY 11201
877-679-8772
Web site: www.asa.edu

President:
Alex Shchegol. 877-679-8772

Art Institute of New York City (The)
218-232 West 40th Street
New York, NY 10018
212-226-5500 or 800-654-2433 Fax: 212-818-1079
e-mail: ainycadm@aii.edu
Web site: www.artinstitutes.edu/new-york

President:
Jennifer Ramey

Berkeley College, New York City Campus
3 East 43rd St
New York, NY 10017
212-986-4343 or 800-446-5400 Fax: 212-697-3371
e-mail: info@berkeleycollege.edu
Web site: www.berkeleycollege.edu

President:
Darlo A Cortes. 973-278-5400 x1102
e-mail: president@berkeleycollege.edu

Berkeley College, Westchester Campus
99 Church St
White Plains, NY 10601
914-694-1122 Fax: 914-328-9469
e-mail: info@berkeleycollege.edu
Web site: www.berkeleycollege.edu

SVP, Administration:
Cynthia Rubino 914-694-1122

Briarcliffe College-Bethpage
1055 Stewart Ave
Bethpage, NY 11714
516-918-3600 or 88-348-4999 Fax: 516-470-6020
e-mail: info@bcl.edu
Web site: www.bcbeth.com

President:
George Santiago, Jr. 516-918-3603
e-mail: gsantiago@bcl.edu

Briarcliffe College-Patchogue
225 West Main St
Patchogue, NY 11772
631-654-5300
Web site: www.bcpat.com

President:
George Santiago, Jr. 631-654-5300

Bryant & Stratton College-Albany Campus
1259 Central Ave
Albany, NY 12205
518-437-1802
e-mail: rpferrell@bryantstratton.edu
Web site: www.bryantstratton.edu

Campus Director:
Michael Gutierrez 518-437-1802
e-mail: magutierrez@bryantstratton.edu

Bryant & Stratton College-Amherst Campus
3650 Millersport Highway
Getzville, NY 14068
716-625-6300
e-mail: amherst@brayntstratton.edu
Web site: www.bryantstratton.edu

Campus Director:
Michael Mariani 716-625-6300

Bryant & Stratton College-Buffalo Campus
465 Main St, Ste 400
Buffalo, NY 14203
716-884-9120
e-mail: buffalo@bryantstratton.edu
Web site: www.bryantstratton.edu

Campus Director:
Marvel Ross-Jones 716-884-9120

Bryant & Stratton College-Greece Campus
150 Bellwood Dr
Rochester, NY 14606
585-720-0660
e-mail: bjdinell@bryantstratton.edu
Web site: www.bryantstratton.edu

Campus Director:
Marc Ambrosi 585-720-0660

Bryant & Stratton College-Henrietta Campus
1225 Jefferson Rd
Rochester, NY 14623
585-292-5627
e-mail: djprofita@bryantstratton.edu
Web site: www.bryantstratton.edu

Director of Rochester Colleges:
Jeffrey Moore 585-292-5627

Bryant & Stratton College-Southtowns Campus
200 Red Tail
Orchard Park, NY 14127
716-677-9500
e-mail: southtowns@bryantstratton.edu
Web site: www.bryantstratton.edu

Campus Director:
Paul Bahr. 716-677-9500

Bryant & Stratton College-Syracuse Campus
953 James St
Syracuse, NY 13203-2502

315-472-6603
e-mail: syracusedt@bryantstratton.edu
Web site: www.bryantstratton.edu

Campus Director:
Michael Sattler 315-472-6603

Bryant & Stratton College-Syracuse North Campus
8687 Carling Rd
Liverpool, NY 13090
315-652-6500
e-mail: sninfo@bryantstratton.edu
Web site: www.bryantstratton.edu

Campus Director:
Susan Cumoletti 315-652-6500

Business Informatics Center
134 S Central Ave
Valley Stream, NY 11580
516-561-0050 Fax: 516-561-0074
e-mail: info@thecollegeforbusiness.com
Web site: www.thecollegeforbusiness.com

President:
Constance Brown 516-561-0050

Christie's Education Inc
11 W 42 St
8th Fl
New York, NY 10036
212-355-1501 Fax: 212-355-7370
e-mail: christieseducataion@christies.com
Web site: www.christieseducation.com

Director of Studies:
Veronique Chagnon-Burke 212-355-1501
e-mail: vchagnon-burke@christies.com

College of Westchester (The)
325 Central Park Ave
PO Box 710
White Plains, NY 10606
914-831-0200 or 800-660-7093 Fax: 914-948-5441
Web site: www.cw.edu

President:
Karen J Smith 914-831-0200

DeVry Institute of Technology, College of New York
180 Madison Av., Suite 900
New York, NY 10016
212-312-4301
Web site: www.ny.devry.edu

Director:
Newton Myvett 212-312-4301

Elmira Business Institute
Langdon Plaza
303 N Main St
Elmira, NY 14901-2731
607-733-7177 or 800-843-1812 Fax: 607-733-7178
e-mail: info@ebi-college.com
Web site: www.ebi-college.com

President:
Brad C Phillips 607-733-7177 x202

Elmira Business Institute-Vestal
Vestal Executive Pk
4100 Vestal Rd
Vestal, NY 13850
607-729-8915 or 866-703-7550 Fax: 607-729-8916
e-mail: info@ebi-college.com
Web site: www.ebi-college.com

Campus Director:
Bob Williams 607-729-8915 x202

Everest Institute
1630 Portland Ave
Rochester, NY 14621-3007
585-266-0430 or 888-741-4270 Fax: 585-266-8243
Web site: www.everest.edu

Five Towns College
305 N Service Rd
Dix Hills, NY 11746-5871
631-656-2110 Fax: 631-424-7008
e-mail: info@ftc.edu
Web site: www.ftc.edu

President:
Stanley G Cohen 631-424-7000/fax: 631-656-2172

Globe Institute of Technology
500 7th Ave
New York, NY 10018
212-349-4330 Fax: 212-227-5920
Web site: www.globe.edu

President:
Martin Oliner 212-349-4330
e-mail: moliner@globe.edu

ITT Technical Institute
13 Airline Dr
Albany, NY 12205
518-452-9300 or 800-489-1191 Fax: 518-452-9393
Web site: www.itt-tech.edu

Director:
Michael Mariani 518-452-9300
e-mail: mmariani@itt-tech.edu

Island Drafting & Technical Institute
128 Broadway, Route 110
Amityville, NY 11701-2704
631-691-8733 Fax: 631-691-8738
e-mail: info@idti.edu
Web site: www.idti.edu

President:
James G DiLiberto 631-691-8733
e-mail: dilibertoj@idti.edu

Jamestown Business College
7 Fairmount Ave
Jamestown, NY 14701
716-664-5100 Fax: 716-664-3144
Web site: www.jbcny.org

Offices and agencies generally appear in alphabetical order, except when specific order is requested by listee.

President:
David Conklin....716-664-5100
e-mail: davidconklin@jamestownbusinesscollege.edu

Laboratory Institute of Merchandising
12 E 53 St
New York, NY 10022
212-752-1530 or 800-677-1323 Fax: 212-750-3432
e-mail: info@limcollege.edu
Web site: www.limcollege.edu

President:
Elizabeth S Marcuse....212-752-1530
e-mail: execs@limcollege.edu

Long Island Business Institute-Commack
6500 Jericho Tpke
Commack, NY 11725
631-499-7100 Fax: 631-499-7114
e-mail: info@libi.edu
Web site: www.libi.edu

President:
Monica Foote....631-499-7100

Long Island Business Institute-Flushing
136-18 39 Ave
Flushing, NY 11354
718-939-5100 Fax: 718-939-9235
Web site: www.libi.edu

President:
Monica Foote....718-939-5100

Mandl School
254 W 54th St
New York, NY 10019
212-247-3434
Web site: www.mandlschool.com

Mildred Elley
855 Central Ave
Albany, NY 12206
518-786-0855 or 800-622-6327 Fax: 518-786-0898
e-mail: admissions@mildred-elley.edu
Web site: www.mildred-elley.edu

President:
Faith A Takes....518-786-0855 x1213/fax: 518-785-7560
e-mail: faith.takes@mildred-elley.edu

Monroe College-Bronx
2501 Jerome Ave
Bronx, NY 10468
718-933-6700 or 800-556-6676 Fax: 718-364-3552
Web site: www.monroecollege.edu

President:
Stephen J Jerome....718-933-6700 x8252

Monroe College-New Rochelle
434 Main St
New Rochelle, NY 10801
914-632-5400 Fax: 914-632-5462
Web site: www.monroecollege.edu

President:
Stephen J Jerome

New York Career Institute
11 Park Place
4th Fl
New York, NY 10007
212-962-0002 Fax: 212-385-7574
e-mail: info@nyci.com
Web site: www.nyci.com

CEO:
Ivan Londa....212-962-0002

Olean Business Institute
301 North Union St
Olean, NY 14760
716-372-7978 Fax: 716-372-2120
e-mail: admin@obi.edu
Web site: www.obi.edu

President:
Jennifer L Madison....716-372-7978

Pacific College of Oriental Medicine
110 William Street
19th Floor
New York, NY 10038
212-982-3456 or 800-729-3468 Fax: 212-982-6514
Web site: www.pacificcollege.edu

Dean & Research Director:
Belinda Anderson....212-982-3456
e-mail: banderson@pacificcollege.edu

Plaza College
118-33 Queens Blvd
Forest Hills, NY 11375
718-779-1430 Fax: 718-779-7423
e-mail: info@plazacollege.edu
Web site: www.plazacollege.edu

President:
Charles E Callahan....718-779-1430

School of Visual Arts
209 East 23rd St
New York, NY 10010
212-592-2000 or 888-220-5782 Fax: 212-725-3587
e-mail: admissions@sva.edu
Web site: www.schoolofvisualarts.edu

President:
David John Rhodes....212-592-2350

Swedish Institute
226 W 26th St
New York, NY 10001
212-924-5900 Fax: 212-924-7600
Web site: www.swedishinstitute.org

President:
William C Ehrhardt

Technical Career Institutes Inc
320 W 31st St
New York, NY 10001

212-594-4000 or 800-878-8246
e-mail: admissions@tcicollege.edu
Web site: www.tcicollege.edu

President:
James Melville 212-594-4000
e-mail: jmelville@tcicollege.edu

Tri-State College of Acupuncture
80th Ave, Ste 400
New York, NY 10011
212-242-2255 Fax: 212-242-2920
Web site: www.tsca.edu

CEO:
Mark D Seem 212-496-7514

US Merchant Marine Academy
300 Steamboat Road
Kings Point, NY 11024
516-773-5000 Fax: 516-773-5774
Web site: www.usmma.edu

Superintendent & Dean:
Phillip Greene, Jr.

US Military Academy at West Point
626 Swift Road
West Point, NY 10996
845-938-4041 or 800-367-2884 Fax: 845-938-2363
Web site: www.usma.edu

Superintendent:
LTG Franklin L Hagenbeck 845-938-2610

Utica School of Commerce
201 Bleecker St
Utica, NY 13501
315-733-2300 or 800-321-4872 Fax: 315-733-9281
Web site: www.uscny.edu

President:
Philip M Williams 315-733-2309 x2214
e-mail: pwilliams@uscny.edu

Wood Tobe-Coburn
8 E 40th St
New York, NY 10016
212-686-9040 or 800-394-9663 Fax: 212-686-9171
Web site: www.woodtobecoburn.edu

President:
Sandi Gruninger 212-686-9040
e-mail: sgruninger@woodtobecoburn.edu

PUBLIC SCHOOL DISTRICTS

SCHOOL DISTRICT ADMINISTRATORS

ALBANY

Albany City SD
Academy Park, Albany, NY 12207-1099
518-475-6010 Fax: 518-475-7295
e-mail: rcolucciello@albany.k12.ny.us
Web site: www.albanyschools.org
Raymond Colucciello, Superintendent

Berne-Knox-Westerlo CSD
1738 Helderberg Trl, Berne, NY 12023-2926
518-872-1293 Fax: 518-872-0341
e-mail: pdorward@bkwcsd.k12.ny.us
Web site: www.bkwcsd.k12.ny.us
Paul Dorward, Superintendent

Bethlehem CSD
90 Adams Place, Delmar, NY 12054
518-439-7098 Fax: 518-475-0352
e-mail: mtebbano@bcsd.neric.org
Web site: bcsd.k12.ny.us
Dr Michael D Tebbano, Superintendent

Cohoes City SD
7 Bevan Street, Cohoes, NY 12047-3299
518-237-0100 Fax: 518-237-2912
e-mail: rlibby@cohoes.org
Web site: www.cohoes.org
Robert K Libby, Superintendent

Green Island UFSD
171 Hudson Ave, Green Island, NY 12183-1293
518-273-1422 Fax: 518-270-0818
e-mail: mmugits@greenisland.org
Web site: www.greenisland.org
Michael Mugits, Superintendent

Guilderland CSD
6076 State Farm Rd, Guilderland, NY 12084-9533
518-456-6200 Fax: 518-456-1152
e-mail: wilesm@guilderlandschools.org
Web site: www.guilderlandschools.org
Marie Wiles, Superintendent

Menands UFSD
19 Wards Ln, Menands, NY 12204-2197
518-465-4561 Fax: 518-465-4572
e-mail: kmeany@nycap.rr.com
Web site: www.menandsschool.nycap.rr.com
Kathleen Meany, Interim Superintendent

North Colonie CSD
91 Fiddler's Ln, Latham, NY 12110-5349
518-785-8591 Fax: 518-785-8502
e-mail: dcorr@ncolonie.org
Web site: www.northcolonie.org
Joseph Corr, Superintendent

Ravena-Coeymans-Selkirk CSD
26 Thatcher St, Selkirk, NY 12158-0097
518-756-5200 Fax: 518-767-2644
e-mail: dteplesky@rcscsd.org
Web site: www.rcscsd.org
Daniel Teplesky, Superintendent

South Colonie CSD
102 Loralee Dr, Albany, NY 12205-2298
518-869-3576 Fax: 518-869-6481
Web site: www.southcolonieschools.org
Jonathan Buhner, Superintendent

Voorheesville CSD
432 New Salem Rd, Voorheesville, NY 12186-0498
518-765-3313 Fax: 518-765-2751
e-mail: tsnyder@vcsdk12.org
Web site: vcsd.neric.org
Teresa T Snyder, Superintendent

Watervliet City SD
1245 Hillside Dr, Watervliet, NY 12189
518-629-3200 Fax: 518-629-3265
e-mail: ppadalin@vliet.neric.org
Web site: www.watervlietcityschools.org
Paul Padalino, Superintendent

ALLEGANY

Alfred-Almond CSD
6795 Rt 21, Almond, NY 14804-9716
607-276-6500 Fax: 607-276-6304
e-mail: rcalkins@aacs.wnyric.org
Web site: www.aacs.org
Richard Calkins, Superintendent

Andover CSD
31-35 Elm St, PO Box G, Andover, NY 14806-0508
607-478-8491 x222 Fax: 607-478-8833
e-mail: wberg@andovercsd.org
Web site: www.andovercsd.org
William C Berg, Superintendent

Belfast CSD
1 King St, Belfast, NY 14711
585-365-9940
e-mail: jmay@belf.wnyric.org
Web site: www.belfast.wnyric.org
Judy May, Superintendent

Bolivar-Richburg CSD
100 School St, Bolivar, NY 14715
585-928-2561 Fax: 585-928-1368
e-mail: mcapawan@brcs.wnyric.org
Web site: www.brcs.wnyric.org
Marilyn Capawan, Superintendent

Canaseraga CSD
4-8 Main St, PO Box 230, Canaseraga, NY 14822-0230
607-545-6421 Fax: 607-545-6265
e-mail: mblum@ccsdny.org
Web site: www.ccsdny.org
Marie Blum, Superintendent

Cuba-Rushford CSD
5476 Rt 305, Cuba, NY 14727-1014
585-968-2650 x4426
e-mail: kshanley@crcs.wnyric.org
Web site: www.crcs.wnyric.org
Kevin Shanley, Superintendent

Fillmore CSD
104 W. Main St, Fillmore, NY 14735-0177
585-567-2251
e-mail: mcox@fillmore.wnyric.org
Web site: www.fillmorecsd.org
Martin D Cox, Superintendent

Offices and agencies generally appear in alphabetical order, except when specific order is requested by listee.

Friendship CSD
46 W Main St, Friendship, NY 14739-9702
716-973-3311 Fax: 716-973-2023
Web site: www.friendship.wnyric.org
Maureen Donahue, Superintendent

Genesee Valley CSD
1 Jaguar Dr, Belmont, NY 14813-9788
585-268-7900
Web site: www.genvalley.org
Ralph Wilson, Superintendent

Scio CSD
3968 Washington St, Scio, NY 14880-9507
716-593-5510 Fax: 716-593-3468
e-mail: tpreston@scio.wnyric.org
Web site: scio.schooltools.us
Tracie Preston, Superintendent

Wellsville CSD
126 W State St, Wellsville, NY 14895
585-596-2170 Fax: 585-596-2177
Web site: www.wellsville.wnyric.org
Kimberly Mueller, Superintendent

Whitesville CSD
692 Main St, Whitesville, NY 14897
607-356-3301 Fax: 607-356-3598
Web site: www.whitesville.wnyric.org
Douglas H Wyant, Superintendent

BROOME

Binghamton City SD
164 Hawley St, Binghamton, NY 13901-2126
607-762-8100 x318
e-mail: wozniakp@binghamtonschools.org
Web site: www.binghamtonschools.org
Peggy J Wozniak, Superintendent

Chenango Forks CSD
One Gordon Dr, Binghamton, NY 13901-5614
607-648-7543 Fax: 607-48-7560
e-mail: bundyr@cforks.org
Web site: www.cforks.org
Robert Bundy, Superintendent

Chenango Valley CSD
221 Chenango Bridge Road, Binghamton, NY 13901-1653
607-762-6800 Fax: 607-762-6890
e-mail: tdouglas@cvcsd.stier.org
Web site: www.cvcsd.stier.org
Dr Thomas Douglas, Superintendent

Deposit CSD
171 Second St, Deposit, NY 13754-1397
607-467-5380 Fax: 607-467-5535
e-mail: bhauber@deposit.stier.org
Web site: www.depositcsd.org
Bonnie Hauber, Superintendent

Harpursville CSD
54 Main St, Harpursville, NY 13787-0147
607-693-8101
Web site: www.hcs.stier.org
Kathleen M Wood, Superintendent

Johnson City CSD
666 Reynolds Rd, Johnson City, NY 13790-1398
607-763-1230 Fax: 607-729-2767
e-mail: mfrys@jcschools.stier.org
Web site: www.jcschools.com
Mary Kay Frys, Superintendent
Joseph F Stoner, Superintendent

Susquehanna Valley CSD
1040 Conklin Rd, Conklin, NY 13748-0200
607-775-0170
Web site: www.svsabers.org
Gerardo Tagliaferri, Acting Superintendent

Union-Endicott CSD
1100 E Main St, Endicott, NY 13760-5271
607-757-2103 Fax: 607-757-2809
Web site: www.uek12.org
Suzanne McLeod, Superintendent

Vestal CSD
201 Main St, Vestal, NY 13850-1599
607-757-2241
e-mail: mdlaroach@vcs.stier.org
Web site: www.vestal.stier.org
Mark LaRoach, Superintendent

Whitney Point CSD
10 Keibel Rd, Whitney Point, NY 13862-0249
607-692-8202 Fax: 607-692-4434
e-mail: mhibbard@wpcsd.org
Web site: www.wpcsd.org
Mary Hibbard, Superintendent

Windsor CSD
1191 NY Route 79, Windsor, NY 13865-4134
607-655-8216 Fax: 607-655-3553
e-mail: jandrews@windsor-csd.org
Web site: www.windsor-csd.org
Jason A Andrews, Superintendent

CATTARAUGUS

Allegany - Limestone CSD
3131 Five Mile Rd, Allegany, NY 14706-9627
716-375-6600 x2006
e-mail: dmunro@alli.wnyric.org
Web site: www.alli.wnyric.org
Diane M Munro, Superintendent

Cattaraugus-Little Valley CSD
207 Rock City St, Little Valley, NY 14755-1298
716-938-9155 x2210 Fax: 716-938-9367
Web site: www.cattlv.wnyric.org
Jon W Peterson, Superintendent

Ellicottville CSD
5873 Route 219, Ellicottville, NY 14731-9719
716-699-2368 Fax: 716-699-6017
e-mail: mward@eville.wnyric.org
Web site: www.ellicottvilecentral.com
Mark Ward, Superintendent

Franklinville CSD
31 N Main St, Franklinville, NY 14737-1096
716-676-8029 Fax: 716-676-3779
e-mail: mspasiano@frkl.wnyric.org
Web site: www.tbafcs.org/franklinville/
Michael Spasiano, Superintendent

Gowanda CSD
10674 Prospect St, Gowanda, NY 14070
716-532-3325 Fax: 716-995-2156
e-mail: crinaldi@gowcsd.org
Web site: www.gowcsd.org
Charles J Rinaldi, Superintendent

Hinsdale CSD
3701 Main St, Hinsdale, NY 14743-0278
716-557-2227 x401
e-mail: jmccarthy@hinsdale.wnyric.org
Judy McCarthy, Superintendent

Olean City SD
410 W Sullivan St, Olean, NY 14760-2596
716-375-8001
e-mail: ctaggerty@olean.wnyric.org
Web site: www.oleanschools.org
Colleen Taggerty, Superintendent

Yorkshire-Pioneer CSD
12125 County Line Rd, Yorkshire, NY 14173-0579
716-492-9300 Fax: 716-492-9360
e-mail: jbowen@pioneercsd.org
Jeffrey Bowen, Superintendent

Portville CSD
500 Elm Street, Portville, NY 14770-9791
716-933-6000 Fax: 716-933-7124
Web site: www.portville.wnyric.org
Thomas J Simon, Superintendent

Randolph Academy UFSD
336 Main Street ER, Randolph, NY 14772-9696
716-358-6866 Fax: 716-358-9076
Web site: www.randoplhacademy.org
Lori DeCarlo, Superintendent

Randolph CSD
18 Main St, Randolph, NY 14772-1188
716-358-7005 or 716-358-6161 Fax: 716-358-7072
e-mail: kmortiz@rand.wnyric.org
Web site: www.randolphcsd.org
Kimberly Moritz, Superintendent

Salamanca City SD
50 Iroquois Dr, Salamanca, NY 14779-1398
716-945-2403 Fax: 716-945-3964
e-mail: dhay@salamancany.org
Web site: www.salamancany.org
J Douglas Hay, Superintendent

West Valley CSD
5359 School St, West Valley, NY 14171
716-942-3293 Fax: 716-942-3440
e-mail: hbowen@wvalley.wnyric.org
Web site: www.wvalley.wnyric.org
Hillary W Bowen, Superintendent

CAYUGA

Auburn Enlarged City SD
78 Thornton Ave, Auburn, NY 13021-4698
315-255-8835
Joseph D Pabis, Superintendent

Cato-Meridian CSD
2851 NYS Rt 370, Cato, NY 13033-0100
315-626-3439 Fax: 315-626-2888
W Noel Patterson, Superintendent

Moravia CSD
68 S Main St, Moravia, NY 13118-1189
315-497-2670 Fax: 315-497-2260
Michelle Brantner, Superintendent

Port Byron CSD
30 Maple Ave, Port Byron, NY 13140-9647
315-776-5728 Fax: 315-776-4050
e-mail: nobrien@portbyron.cnyric.org
Web site: www.portbyron.cnyric.org
Neil F O'Brien, Superintendent

Southern Cayuga CSD
2384 State Rt 34B, Aurora, NY 13026-9771
315-364-7211 Fax: 315-364-7863
e-mail: worthmk@southerncayuga.org
Web site: www.southerncayuga.org
Mary Kay Worth, Superintendent

Union Springs CSD
239 Cayuga St, Union Springs, NY 13160
315-889-4101
e-mail: lrice@unionspringscsd.org
Web site: www.uscsd.info
Linda Rice, Superintendent

Weedsport CSD
2821 E Brutus St, Weedsport, NY 13166-9105
315-834-6637
Shaun A O'Connor, Superintendent

CHAUTAUQUA

Bemus Point CSD
3980 Dutch Hollow Rd, Bemus Point, NY 14712
716-386-2375
Web site: www.bemusptcsd.org
Albert D'Attilio, Superintendent

Brocton CSD
138 W Main St, Brocton, NY 14716
716-792-2121 Fax: 716-792-7944
e-mail: jhertlein@broc.wynric.org
Web site: www.broctoncsd.org
John Hertlein, Superintendent

Cassadaga Valley CSD
5935 Route 60, PO Box 540, Sinclairville, NY 14782-0540
716-962-5155
e-mail: JBrown@cvcs.wnyric.org
John Brown, Superintendent

Chautauqua Lake CSD
100 N Erie St, Mayville, NY 14757
716-753-5808 Fax: 716-753-5813
e-mail: bspitzer@clake.org
Web site: www.clake.org
Benjamin B Spitzer, Superintendent

Clymer CSD
8672 E Main St, Clymer, NY 14724-0580
716-355-4444
Web site: www.clymercsd.org
Scott D Smith, Superintendent

Dunkirk City SD
620 Marauder Dr, Dunkirk, NY 14048-1396
716-366-9300
Web site: www.dunkirkcsd.org
Gary Cerne, Superintendent

Offices and agencies generally appear in alphabetical order, except when specific order is requested by listee.

Falconer CSD
2 East Ave N, Falconer, NY 14733
716-665-6624 x4101 Fax: 716-665-9265
e-mail: spenhollow@falcon.wnyric.org
Web site: wwwfalconerschools.org
Stephen Penhollow, Superintendent

Forestville CSD
12 Water St, Forestville, NY 14062-9674
716-965-2742 Fax: 716-965-2265
e-mail: jconnor@forestville.wnyric.org
Web site: www.forestville.com
John O'Connor, Superintendent

Fredonia CSD
425 E Main St, Fredonia, NY 14063
716-679-1581
Web site: www.fredonia.wnyric.org
Paul Di Fonzo, Superintendent

Frewsburg CSD
26 Institute St, Frewsburg, NY 14738
716-569-9241
Web site: www.frewsburgcsd.org
Stephen Vanstrom, Superintendent

Jamestown City SD
197 Martin Road, Jamestown, NY 14701
716-483-4350
Web site: www.jamestownpublicschools.org
Daniel E Kathman, Superintendent

Panama CSD
41 North St, Panama, NY 14767-9775
716-782-2455 Fax: 716-782-4674
e-mail: blictus@mx.pancent.org
Web site: www.pancent.org
Bert Lictus, Superintendent

Pine Valley CSD (South Dayton)
7755 Rt 83, South Dayton, NY 14138
716-988-3293 Fax: 716-988-3864
Web site: www.pval.org
Peter Morgante, Superintendent

Ripley CSD
12 N State St, Ripley, NY 14775
716-736-6201 Fax: 716-736-6226
Web site: ripleycsd.wnyric.org
Karen Krause, Interim Superintendent

Sherman CSD
127 Park St, PO Box 950, Sherman, NY 14781-0950
716-761-6122 x1289 Fax: 716-761-6119
e-mail: tschmidt@sherman.wnyric.org
Web site: www.sherman.wnyric.org
Thomas Schmidt, Superintendent

Silver Creek CSD
1 Dickinson St, PO Box 270, Silver Creek, NY 14136
716-934-2603 Fax: 716-934-7983
Web site: www.silvercreek.wnyric.org
David O'Rourke, Superintendent

Southwestern CSD at Jamestown
600 Hunt Rd, Jamestown, NY 14701
716-484-1136
Web site: swcs.wnyric.org
Daniel A George, Superintendent

Westfield CSD
203 E Main St, Westfield, NY 14787
716-326-2151
Web site: www.wacs.wnyric.org
Mark Sissel, Superintendent

CHEMUNG

Elmira City SD
951 Hoffman St, Elmira, NY 14905-1715
607-735-3000 Fax: 607-735-3002
Web site: www.elmiracityschools.com
Joseph E Hochreiter, Superintendent

Elmira Heights CSD
2083 College Ave, Elmira Heights, NY 14903-1598
607-734-7114 Fax: 607-734-7134
e-mail: mbfiore@gstboces.org
Web site: www.heightsschools.com
Mary Beth Fiore, Superintendent

Horseheads CSD
One Raider Ln, Horseheads, NY 14845-2398
607-739-5601 x4200
e-mail: hcsdinfo@horseheadsdistrict.com
Web site: www.horseheadsdistrict.com
Ralph Marino, Superintendent

CHENANGO

Afton CSD
29 Academy St, PO Box 5, Afton, NY 13730-0005
607-639-8229
Web site: www.afton.stier.org
Elizabeth A Briggs, Superintendent

Bainbridge-Guilford CSD
18 Juliand St, Bainbridge, NY 13733
607-967-6321 Fax: 607-967-4231
Web site: www.bgcsd.org
Karl Brown, Superintendent

Greene CSD
40 S Canal St, Greene, NY 13778
607-656-4161
Web site: www.greenecsd.org
Jonathan R Rietz, Superintendent

Norwich City SD
89 Midland Drive, Norwich, NY 13815
607-334-1600 X5523 Fax: 607-336-8652
e-mail: gosulliv@norwich.stier.org
Web site: www.norwichcsd.org
Gerard M O'Sullivan, Superintendent

Georgetown-South Otselic CSD
125 County Rd 13A, South Otselic, NY 13155-0161
315-653-7591 Fax: 315-653-7500
Web site: www.ovcs.org
Richard Hughes, Superintendent

Oxford Academy & CSD
12 Fort Hill Park, PO Box 192, Oxford, NY 13830-0192
607-843-2025 x4041 Fax: 607-843-3241
Web site: www.oxac.org
Randall Squier, Superintendent

Offices and agencies generally appear in alphabetical order, except when specific order is requested by listee.

Sherburne-Earlville CSD
15 School St, Sherburne, NY 13460-0725
607-674-7300 Fax: 607-674-7386
Web site: www.secsd.org
Gayle H Hellert, Superintendent

Unadilla Valley CSD
4238 State Hwy 8, New Berlin, NY 13411
607-847-7500 Fax: 607-847-9194
Web site: www.uvstorm.org
Robert J Mackey, Superintendent

CLINTON

Ausable Valley CSD
1273 Rt 9N, Clintonville, NY 12924-4244
518-834-2845 Fax: 518-834-2843
e-mail: psavage@avcsk12.org
Web site: avcs.org
Paul D Savage, Superintendent

Beekmantown CSD
37 Eagle Way, West Chazy, NY 12992-2577
518-563-8250 x5501 Fax: 518-563-8132
e-mail: amo.scott@bcsdk12.org
Web site: www.bcsdk12.org
Scott A Amo, Superintendent

Chazy Central RSD
609 Miner Farm Rd, Chazy, NY 12921-0327
518-846-7135 Fax: 518-846-8322
e-mail: jfairchild@chazy.org
Web site: www.chazy.org
John Fairchild, Superintendent

Northeastern Clinton CSD
103 Route 276, Champlain, NY 12919
518-298-8242 Fax: 518-298-4293
Web site: www.nccscougars.org
Peter J Turner, Superintendent

Northern Adirondack CSD
5572 Rt 11, Ellenburg Depot, NY 12935-0164
518-594-7060
Web site: www.nacs1.org
Laura Marlow, Superintendent

Peru CSD
17 School St, PO Box 68, Peru, NY 12972-0068
518-643-6000
Web site: www.perucsd.org
A Paul Scott, Superintendent

Plattsburgh City SD
49 Broad St, Plattsburgh, NY 12901-3396
518-957-6002 Fax: 518-957-6026
e-mail: jshort@plattscsd.org
Web site: www.plattscsd.org
James Short, Superintendent

Saranac CSD
32 Emmons St, Dannemora, NY 12929
518-565-5600
e-mail: kcringle@saranac.org
Web site: www.saranac.org
Kenneth O Cringle, Superintendent

COLUMBIA

Berkshire UFSD
13640 Rt 22, Canaan, NY 12029-0370
518-781-3500 X3545
e-mail: jgaudette@berkshireufsd.k12.ny.us
James G Gaudette, Superintendent

Chatham CSD
50 Woodbridge Ave, Chatham, NY 12037-1397
518-392-2400
Web site: www.chathamcentralschools.com
Cheryl Nuciforo, Superintendent

Germantown CSD
123 Main St, Germantown, NY 12526
518-537-6280 Fax: 518-537-3284
Web site: germantowncsd.org
Patrick Gabriel, Superintendent

Hudson City SD
215 Harry Howard Ave, Hudson, NY 12534-4011
518-828-4360 x2101
Web site: www.hudsoncityschooldistrict.com
John F Howe, Superintendent

Ichabod Crane CSD
2910 Rt 9, Valatie, NY 12184-0137
518-758-7575 x3002 Fax: 518-758-7579
e-mail: lbordick@ichabodcrane.org
Web site: www.ichabodcrane.org
Lee Bordick, Superintendent

New Lebanon CSD
14665 Route 22, New Lebanon, NY 12125-2307
518-794-9016 Fax: 518-766-5574
e-mail: kmcgraw@newlebanoncsd.org
Web site: www.newlebanoncsd.org
Karen McGraw, Superintendent

Taconic Hills CSD
73 County Rt 11A, PO Box 482, Craryville, NY 12521
518-325-0313 Fax: 518-325-3557
e-mail: info@taconichills.k12.ny.us
Web site: www.taconichills.k12.ny.us
Mark A Sposato, Superintendent

CORTLAND

Cincinnatus CSD
2809 Cincinnatus Rd, Cincinnatus, NY 13040-9698
607-863-3200 Fax: 607-863-4109
e-mail: shubbard@cc.cnyric.orgic.org
Web site: www.cc.cnyric.org
Steven V Hubbard, Superintendent

Cortland Enlarged City SD
1 Valley View Dr, Cortland, NY 13045-3297
607-758-4100 Fax: 607-758-4128
e-mail: superintendent@cortlandschools.org
Web site: www.cortlandschools.org
Larry Spring, Superintendent

Homer CSD
Route 281, PO Box 500, Homer, NY 13077-0500
607-749-7241
Web site: www.homercentral.org
Nancy Ruscio, Superintendent

Marathon CSD
1 E Main St, PO Box 339, Marathon, NY 13803-0339
607-849-3251 Fax: 607-849-3305
e-mail: turecekt@marathon.cnyric.org
Web site: www.marathonschools.org
Timothy Turecek, Superintendent

McGraw CSD
W Academy St, PO Box 556, McGraw, NY 13101-0556
607-836-3636 Fax: 607-836-3635
e-mail: mcurcio@mcgrawschools.org
Web site: www.mcgrawschools.org
Mary Curcio, Superintendent

DELAWARE

Andes CSD
85 Delaware Ave, PO Box 248, Andes, NY 13731-0248
845-676-3167 Fax: 845-676-3181
e-mail: rchakar@andescentralschool.org
Web site: www.andescentralschool.org
Robert Chakar, Superintendent

Charlotte Valley CSD
15611 St Hwy 23, Davenport, NY 13750-0202
607-278-5511 Fax: 607-278-5900
e-mail: dupra.mark@charlottevalley.org
Mark R Dupra, Superintendent

Delhi CSD
2 Sheldon Dr, Delhi, NY 13753-1276
607-746-1300 Fax: 607-746-6028
Web site: www.delhischools.org
Roger W Adams, Superintendent

Downsville CSD
Maple St, Po Box J, Downsville, NY 13755
607-363-2101 Fax: 607-363-2105
Web site: www.dcseagles.org
James F Abrams, Superintendent

Franklin CSD
26 Institute St, Franklin, NY 13775-0888
607-829-3551 x309 Fax: 607-829-2101
Web site: www.franklincsd.org
Gordon Daniels, Superintendent

Hancock CSD
67 Education Ln, Hancock, NY 13783
607-637-1301
Web site: hancock.stier.org
Terrance Dougherty, Superintendent

Margaretville CSD
415 Main St, Margaretville, NY 12455-0319
845-586-2647 Fax: 845-586-2949
e-mail: talbanese@margaretvillecs.org
Web site: www.margaretvillecs.org
Anthony R Albanese, Superintendent

Roxbury CSD
53729 NYS Route 30, Roxbury, NY 12474-0207
607-326-4151 Fax: 607-326-4154
e-mail: tobrien@roxburycs.org
Thomas J O'Brien, Superintendent

Sidney CSD
95 W Main St, Sidney, NY 13838-1699
607-563-2135 Fax: 607-563-4275
Web site: www.sidneycsd.org
William Christensen, Superintendent

South Kortright CSD
58200 State Hwy 10, South Kortright, NY 13842-0113
607-538-9111 Fax: 607-538-9205
Web site: www.skcs.org
Patricia Norton-White, Superintendent

Stamford CSD
1 River St, Stamford, NY 12167-1098
607-652-7301 Fax: 607-652-3446
Web site: www.stamfordcs.org
Tonda Dunbar, Superintendent

Walton CSD
47-49 Stockton Ave, Walton, NY 13856
607-865-4116 Fax: 607-865-8568
Web site: www.waltoncsd.org
Thomas P Austin, Superintendent

DUTCHESS

Arlington CSD
696 Dutchess Tpke, Poughkeepsie, NY 12603
845-486-4460
Web site: www.arlingtonschools.org
Geoffrey Hicks, Superintendent

Beacon City SD
10 Education Dr, Beacon, NY 12508
845-838-6900 x2010
e-mail: aefsky.f@beaconcityk12.org
Web site: www.beaconcityk12.org
Fern Aefsky, Superintendent

Dover UFSD
2368 Rt 22, Dover Plains, NY 12522
845-832-4500 Fax: 845-832-4511
e-mail: mike.tierney@doverschools.org
Web site: www.doverschools.org
Michael Tierney, Superintendent

Hyde Park CSD
11 Boice Rd, PO Box 2033, Hyde Park, NY 12538-1632
845-229-4000 Fax: 845-229-4056
Web site: www.hydeparkschools.org
Greer Fischer, Superintendent

Millbrook CSD
PO Box AA-3323 Franklin, Millbrook, NY 12545
845-677-4200 x101
e-mail: lloyd.jaeger@millbrookcsd.org
Web site: www.millbrookcsd.org
Lloyd Jaeger, Superintendent

Pawling CSD
515 Route 22, Pawling, NY 12564
845-855-4600
Web site: www.pawlingschools.org
Joseph Sciortino, Superintendent

Pine Plains CSD
2829 Church St, Pine Plains, NY 12567-5504
518-398-7181 Fax: 518-398-6592
Web site: www.pineplainsschools.org
Linda Kaumeyer, Superintendent

Poughkeepsie City SD
11 College Ave, Poughkeepsie, NY 12603-3313
845-451-4950 Fax: 845-451-4954
e-mail: lwilson@poughkeepsieschools.org
Web site: www.poughkeepsieschools.org
Laval S Wilson, Superintendent

Red Hook CSD
7401 South Broadway, Red Hook, NY 12571-9446
845-758-2241 Fax: 845-758-4720
e-mail: pfinch@rhcsd.org
Web site: www.redhookcentralschools.org
Paul Finch, Superintendent

Rhinebeck CSD
North Park Rd, Rhinebeck, NY 12572
845-871-5520 Fax: 845-876-4276
e-mail: jphelan@rhinebeckcsd.org
Web site: www.rhinebeckcsd.org
Joseph L Phelan, Superintendent

Spackenkill UFSD
15 Croft Rd, Poughkeepsie, NY 12603-5028
845-463-7800 Fax: 845-463-7804
Web site: www.spackenkillschools.org
Lois Powell, Superintendent

Wappingers CSD
167 Meyers Corners Rd, Wappingers Falls, NY 12590-3296
845-298-5000
Web site: www.wappingersschools.org
James Parla, Superintendent
David Paciencia, Superintendent

ERIE

Akron CSD
47 Bloomingdale Ave, Akron, NY 14001-1197
716-542-5010 Fax: 716-542-5018
e-mail: rzymroz@akronschools.org
Web site: www.akronschools.org
Robin B Zymroz, Superintendent of Schools

Alden CSD
13190 Park St, Alden, NY 14004
716-937-9116
Web site: aldenschools.org
Lynn Marie Fusco, Superintendent

Amherst CSD
55 Kings Hwy, Amherst, NY 14226
716-362-3051 Fax: 716-836-2537
Web site: www.amherstschools.org
Laura Chabe, Superintendent

Buffalo SD
712 City Hall, Buffalo, NY 14202-3375
716-816-3500 Fax: 716-816-3600
Web site: www.buffaloschools.org
James A Williams, Superintendent

Cheektowaga CSD
3600 Union Rd, Cheektowaga, NY 14225-5170
716-686-3606 Fax: 716-681-5232
Web site: www.cheektowagaschools.org
Dennis Kane, Superintendent

Cheektowaga-Sloan UFSD
166 Halstead Ave, Sloan, NY 14212
716-891-6402
Web site: www.sloanschools.org
James P Mazgajewski, Superintendent

Clarence CSD
9625 Main St, Clarence, NY 14031-2083
716-407-9102
e-mail: tcoseo@clar.wnyric.org
Web site: www.clarenceschools.org
Thomas G Coseo, Superintendent

Cleveland Hill UFSD
105 Mapleview Rd, Cheektowaga, NY 14225-1599
716-836-7200
Web site: www.clevehill.wnyric.org
Sharon Huff, Superintendent

Depew UFSD
591 Terrace Blvd, Depew, NY 14043-4535
716-686-5105 Fax: 716-686-2269
e-mail: jrabey@depew.wnyric.org
Web site: www.depewschools.org
Jeffrey Rabey, Superintendent

East Aurora UFSD
430 Main St, East Aurora, NY 14052
716-687-2302
Web site: www.eaur.wnyric.org
Brian Russ, Superintendent

Eden CSD
3150 Schoolview Rd, Eden, NY 14057
716-992-3629
Web site: www.edencentral.org
Ronald Buggs, Superintendent

Evans-Brant CSD (Lake Shore)
959 Beach Rd, Angola, NY 14006
716-549-2300 or 716-926-2201 Fax: 716-549-6407
e-mail: jprzepasniak@lakeshore.wnyric.org
Web site: www.lakeshore.wnyric.org
James Przepasniak, Superintendent

Frontier CSD
5120 Orchard Ave, Hamburg, NY 14075-5657
716-926-1700 Fax: 716-926-1776
Web site: www.frontier.wnyric.org
James Bodziak, Superintendent

Grand Island CSD
1100 Ransom Rd, Grand Island, NY 14072-1460
716-773-8801
e-mail: robertchristmann@k12.ginet.org
Web site: www.k12.ginet.org
Robert W Christmann, Superintendent

Hamburg CSD
5305 Abbott Rd, Hamburg, NY 14075
716-646-3220 Fax: 716-646-3209
Web site: www.hamburgschools.org
Steven Achramovitch, Superintendent

Holland CSD
103 Canada St, Holland, NY 14080
716-537-8222
e-mail: djohnson@holland.wnyric.org
Web site: www.hlnd.wnyric.org
Dennis Johnson, Superintendent

Hopevale UFSD at Hamburg
3780 Howard Rd, Hamburg, NY 14075-2252
716-648-1930 Fax: 716-648-2361
Web site: www.hopevale.com
Cynthia Stachowski, Superintendent

Iroquois CSD
2111 Girdle Rd, Elma, NY 14059-0032
716-652-3000
Web site: www.iroquoiscds.org
Bruce Fraser, Superintendent

Offices and agencies generally appear in alphabetical order, except when specific order is requested by listee.

Kenmore-Tonawanda UFSD
1500 Colvin Blvd, Buffalo, NY 14223-1196
716-874-8400 Fax: 716-874-8624
Web site: www.kenton.k12.ny.us
Mark P Mondanaro, Superintendent

Lackawanna City SD
245 South Shore Blvd, Lackawanna, NY 14218
716-827-6767 Fax: 716-827-6710
Web site: www.lackawannaschools.org
Nicholas Korach, Superintendent

Lancaster CSD
177 Central Ave, Lancaster, NY 14086-1897
716-686-3200
Web site: www.lancasterschools.org
Edward Myszka, Interim Superintendent

Cheektowaga-Maryvale CSD
1050 Maryvale Dr, Cheektowaga, NY 14225-2386
716-631-0300 Fax: 716-635-4699
Web site: www.maryvale.wnyric.org
Deborah Ziolkowski, Superintendent

North Collins CSD
2045 School St, North Collins, NY 14111
716-337-0101
Web site: www.northcollins.com
Benjamin A Halsey, Superintendent

Orchard Park CSD
3330 Baker Rd, Orchard Park, NY 14127
716-209-6280 Fax: 716-209-6353
Web site: www.opschools.org
Matthew McGarrity, Superintendent

Springville-Griffith Inst CSD
307 Newman St, Springville, NY 14141
716-592-3200 or 716-592-3412
Web site: www.spingvillegi.org
Paul Hashem, Superintendent

Sweet Home CSD
1901 Sweet Home Rd, Amherst, NY 14228
716-250-1402 Fax: 716-250-1374
e-mail: aday@shs.k12.ny.us
Web site: www.sweethomeschools.com
Anthony Day, Superintendent

Tonawanda City SD
100 Hinds St, Tonawanda, NY 14150
716-694-7690
Web site: www.tonawandacsd.org
Whitney K Vantine, Superintendent

West Seneca CSD
1397 Orchard Park Rd, West Seneca, NY 14224-4098
716-677-3101
Web site: www.wscschools.org
Mark Crawford, Superintendent

Williamsville CSD
105 Casey Rd, PO Box 5000, East Amherst, NY 14051-5000
716-626-8005 Fax: 716-626-8089
Web site: www.williamsvillek12.org
Howard S Smith, Superintendent

ESSEX

Crown Point CSD
2758 Main St, Crown Point, NY 12928-0035
518-597-4200 Fax: 518-597-4121
Web site: www.cpcsteam.org
Shari L Brannock, Superintendent

Elizabethtown-Lewis CSD
7530 Court St, Elizabethtown, NY 12932-0158
518-873-6371 Fax: 518-873-9552
Web site: elcs.neric.org
Gail J Else, Superintendent

Keene CSD
33 Market St, PO Box 67, Keene Valley, NY 12943-0067
518-576-4555 Fax: 518-576-4599
e-mail: cfjkcs@yahoo.com
Web site: www.keenecentralschool.org
Cynthia Ford-Johnston, Superintendent

Lake Placid CSD
23 Cummings Rd, Lake Placid, NY 12946-1500
518-523-2475
Randy Richards, Superintendent

Minerva CSD
1466 County Rt 29, Olmstedville, NY 12857-0039
518-251-2000 Fax: 518-251-2395
e-mail: farrellt@minervasd.org
Web site: www.minervasd.org
Timothy Farrell, Superintendent

Moriah CSD
39 Viking Ln, Port Henry, NY 12974
518-546-3301 Fax: 518-546-7895
Web site: www.moriahk12.org
William Larrow, Superintendent

Newcomb CSD
5535 Rt 28 N, Newcomb, NY 12852-0418
518-582-3341 Fax: 518-582-2163
Web site: www.newcombcsd.org
Clark Hults, Superintendent

Schroon Lake CSD
1125 US Rt 9, PO Box 338, Schroon Lake, NY 12870-0338
518-532-7164 Fax: 518-532-0284
Web site: www.schroonschool.org
Gerald Blair, Superintendent

Ticonderoga CSD
5 Calkins Place, Ticonderoga, NY 12883
518-585-9158
Web site: www.ticonderogak12.org
John C McDonald Jr, Superintendent

Westport CSD
25 Sisco St, Westport, NY 12993
518-962-8244 Fax: 518-962-4571
Web site: www.westportcs.org
John W Gallagher, Superintendent

Willsboro CSD
29 School Lane, Willsboro, NY 12996-0180
518-963-4456 Fax: 518-963-7577
Web site: www.willsborocsd.org
Stephen Broadwell, Superintendent

Offices and agencies generally appear in alphabetical order, except when specific order is requested by listee.

FRANKLIN

Brushton-Moira CSD
758 County Rt 7, Brushton, NY 12916
518-529-7342 Fax: 518-529-6062
e-mail: district@bmcsd.org
Web site: www.bmcsd.org
Steven Grenville, Superintendent

Chateaugay CSD
42 River St, PO Box 904, Chateaugay, NY 12920-0904
518-497-6611 Fax: 518-497-3170
e-mail: dbreault@mail.fehb.org
Web site: www.chateaugay.org
Dale L Breault, Superintendent

Malone CSD
42 Huskie Ln, PO Box 847, Malone, NY 12953-1118
518-483-7800 Fax: 518-483-3071
Web site: www.malone.k12.ny.us
Wayne C Walbridge, Superintendent

Salmon River CSD
637 County Rt 1, Fort Covington, NY 12937-9722
518-358-6600 Fax: 518-358-3492
e-mail: jcollins@srk12.org
Web site: www.srk12.org
Jane A Collins, Superintendent

Saranac Lake CSD
79 Canaras Ave, Saranac Lake, NY 12983-1500
518-891-5460
Gerald A Goldman, Superintendent

St Regis Falls CSD
92 N Main St, PO Box 309, St Regis Falls, NY 12980-0309
518-856-9421
Web site: www.stregisfallscsd.org
Beverly Ouderkirk, Superintendent

Tupper Lake CSD
294 Hosley Ave, Tupper Lake, NY 12986-1899
518-359-3371 Fax: 518-359-7862
Seth McGowan, Superintendent

FULTON

Broadalbin-Perth CSD
20 Pine St, Broadalbin, NY 12025-9997
518-954-2500 Fax: 51-954-2509
Web site: www.bpcsd.org
Stephen M Tomlinson, Superintendent

Gloversville Enlarged SD
243 Lincoln St, PO Box 593, Gloversville, NY 12078
518-775-5700 Fax: 518-725-8793
Robert DeLilli, Superintendent

Greater Johnstown SD
1 Sir Bills Circle, Ste 101, Johnstown, NY 12095
518-762-4611 Fax: 518-726-6379
Web site: www.johnstownschools.org
Katherine A Sullivan, Superintendent

Mayfield CSD
27 School Street, Mayfield, NY 12117-0216
518-661-8207 Fax: 518-661-7666
e-mail: williamson.paul@mayfieldcsd.org
Web site: www.mayfieldk12.com
Paul G Williamson, Superintendent

Northville CSD
131 S Third St, PO Box 608, Northville, NY 12134-0608
518-863-7000 x4121
Web site: northvillecsd.k12.ny.us
Kathy Dougherty, Superintendent

Oppenheim-Ephratah CSD
6486 State Hwy 29, St Johnsville, NY 13452-9309
518-568-2014 Fax: 518-568-2941
e-mail: dmrussom@oecs.k12.ny.us
Web site: www.oecs.k12.ny.us
Dan M Russom, Superintendent

Wheelerville UFSD
PO Box 756, Caroga Lake, NY 12032
518-835-2171 Fax: 518-835-3551
Web site: www.wufselementary.k12.ny.us
David D Carr, Superintendent

GENESEE

Alexander CSD
3314 Buffalo St, Alexander, NY 14005-9769
585-591-1551 Fax: 585-591-2257
Web site: www.alexandercsd.org
Kathleen Maerten, Superintendent

Batavia City SD
39 Washington Ave, Batavia, NY 14020
585-343-2480 Fax: 585-344-8204
e-mail: mpuzio@bataviacsd.org
Web site: www.bataviacsd.org
Margaret L Puzio, Superintendent

Byron-Bergen CSD
6917 W Bergen Rd, Bergen, NY 14416
585-494-1220 Fax: 585-494-2613
Web site: www.bbschools.org
Scott G Martzloff, Superintendent

Elba CSD
57 S Main St, Elba, NY 14058
585-757-9967 x1034
Web site: www.elbacsd.org
Jerome Piwko Jr, Superintendent

Le Roy CSD
2-6 Trigon Park, Le Roy, NY 14482
585-768-8133
Web site: www.leroycsd.org
Kim Cox, Superintendent

Oakfield-Alabama CSD
7001 Lewiston Rd, Oakfield, NY 14125
585-948-5211 Fax: 585-948-9362
Web site: www.oacs.k12.ny.us
Christopher Todd, Superintendent

Pavilion CSD
7014 Big Tree Rd, Pavilion, NY 14525
585-584-3115
Web site: www.pavilioncsd.org
Kenneth J Ellison, Superintendent

Pembroke CSD
Rt 5 & 77, PO Box 308, Corfu, NY 14036
585-599-4525 Fax: 585-762-9993
Web site: www.pembroke.k12.ny.us
Gary T Mix Sr, Superintendent

Offices and agencies generally appear in alphabetical order, except when specific order is requested by listee.

Colleges, Universities & School Districts

GREENE

Cairo-Durham CSD
424 Main St, Cairo, NY 12413-0780
518-622-8534
e-mail: ssharkey@cairodurham.org
Web site: www.cairodurham.org
Sally Sharkey, Superintendent

Catskill CSD
343 W Main St, Catskill, NY 12414-1699
518-943-4696 Fax: 518-943-7116
Web site: www.catskillcsd.org
Kathleen Farrell, Superintendent

Coxsackie-Athens CSD
24 Sunset Blvd, Coxsackie, NY 12051-1132
518-731-1700 Fax: 518-731-1729
Web site: www.coxsackie-athens.org
Annemarie Barkman, Interim Superintendent

Greenville CSD
4976 Route 81, Greenville, NY 12083-0129
518-966-5070
Web site: www.greenville.k12.ny.us
Cheryl Dudley, Superintendent

Hunter-Tannersville CSD
6094 Main St, Tannersville, NY 12485-1018
518-589-5400 Fax: 518-589-5403
e-mail: psweeney@htcsd.org
Web site: www.htcsd.org
Patrick Darfler-Sweeney, Superintendent

Windham-Ashland-Jewett CSD
5411 State Route 23, PO Box 429, Windham, NY 12496-0429
518-734-3403 Fax: 518-734-6050
e-mail: jwiktorko@wajcs.org
John Wiktorko, Superintendent

HAMILTON

Indian Lake CSD
28 W Main St, Indian Lake, NY 12842-9716
518-648-5024 Fax: 518-648-6346
e-mail: brandm@ilcsd.org
Web site: www.ilcsd.org
Mark T Brand, Superintendent

Inlet Common School
3002 Rt 28, Old Forge, NY 13420
315-369-3222 Fax: 315-369-6216
e-mail: dgooley@tows.moric.org
Donald Gooley, Superintendent

Lake Pleasant CSD
120 Elm Lake Rd, PO Box 140, Speculator, NY 12164-0140
518-548-7571 Fax: 518-548-3230
Web site: www.lpschools.com
Ernest D Virgil, Superintendent

Long Lake CSD
20 School Lane, PO Box 217, Long Lake, NY 12847-0217
518-624-2221 Fax: 518-624-3896
Web site: www.longlakecsd.org
Mary Jo Dickerson, Acting Superintendent

Piseco Common SD
Rt 8, Piseco, NY 12139
518-548-7555 Fax: 518-548-5310
Peter J Hallock, Superintendent

Raquette Lake UFSD
PO Box 10, Raquette Lake, NY 13436-0010
315-354-4733
Peter J Hallock, Superintendent

Wells CSD
1571 Route 30, PO Box 300, Wells, NY 12190-0300
518-924-6000
Web site: www.wellscsd.com
John Zeis, Superintendent

HERKIMER

Dolgeville CSD
38 Slawson St, Dolgeville, NY 13329
315-429-3155 x3500 Fax: 315-429-8473
e-mail: creynolds@dolgeville.org
Web site: www.dolgeville.org
Christine Reynolds, Superintendent

Frankfort-Schuyler CSD
605 Palmer St, Frankfort, NY 13340
315-894-5083 Fax: 315-895-7011
e-mail: rreina@frankfort-schuyler.org
Web site: www.frankfort-schuyler.org
Robert Reina, Superintendent

Herkimer CSD
801 W German St, Herkimer, NY 13350-2199
315-866-2230
Web site: www.herkimercsd.org
Carol Zygo, Superintendent

Ilion CSD
1 Golden Bomber Dr, PO Box 480, Ilion, NY 13357-0480
315-894-9934 Fax: 315-894-2716
e-mail: ctangorra@ilioncsd.org
Web site: www.ilioncsd.org
Cosimo Tangorra, Superintendent

Little Falls City SD
15 Petrie St, Little Falls, NY 13365
315-823-1470
Web site: www.lfcsd.com
Louis J Patrei, Superintendent

Mohawk CSD
28 Grove St, Mohawk, NY 13407-1782
315-867-2904
e-mail: jcaputo@mohawkcsd.org
Joyce M Caputo, Superintendent

Mount Markham CSD
500 Fairground Rd, West Winfield, NY 13491-0500
315-822-2800
Web site: www.mmcsd.org
Casey Barduhn, Superintendent

Poland CSD
74 Cold Brook St, Poland, NY 13431
315-826-0203 Fax: 315-826-7516
Web site: www.polandcs.com
Laura Dutton, Superintendent

Town of Webb UFSD
3002 State Route 28, PO Box 38, Old Forge, NY 13420-0038
315-369-3222 Fax: 315-369-6216
Web site: www.towschool.org
Donald Gooley, Superintendent

Van Hornesville-Owen D Young CSD
2316 State Rt 80, PO Box 125, Van Hornesville, NY 13475-0125
315-858-0729 Fax: 315-858-2019
Web site: www.odyoungcsd.org
Virginia Keegan, Superintendent

West Canada Valley CSD
5447 State Rt 28, Newport, NY 13416-0360
315-845-6800 Fax: 315-845-8652
e-mail: jbanek@westcanada.org
Web site: www.westcanada.org
John Banek, Superintendent

JEFFERSON

Alexandria CSD
34 Bolton Ave, Alexandria Bay, NY 13607-1699
315-482-9971
Web site: www.alexandriacentral.org
Robert Wagoner, Superintendent

Belleville Henderson CSD
8372 County Rt 75, Belleville, NY 13611-0158
315-846-5826
e-mail: rmoore@bhpanthers.org
Web site: www.bhpanthers.org
Rick T Moore, Superintendent

Carthage CSD
25059 County Rt 197, Carthage, NY 13619-9527
315-493-5000
Web site: www.carthagecsd.org
Joseph Catanzaro, Superintendent

General Brown CSD
PO Box 500, Dexter, NY 13634
315-639-5100 Fax: 315-639-6916
e-mail: svigliotti@gblions.org
Web site: www.gblions.org
Stephan J Vigliotti Sr, Superintendent

Indian River CSD
32735-B County Rt 29, Philadelphia, NY 13673-0308
315-642-3441
Web site: www.ircsd.org
James Kettrick, Superintendent

La Fargeville CSD
20414 Sunrise Ave, PO Box 138, La Fargeville, NY 13656
315-658-2241 Fax: 315-658-4223
Web site: www.lafargevillecsd.org
Susan Whitney, Superintendent

Lyme CSD
11868 Academy St, PO Box 219, Chaumont, NY 13622-0219
315-649-2417 Fax: 315-649-2663
Web site: www.lymecsd.org
Karen M Donahue, Superintendent

Sackets Harbor Central School
215 S Broad St, Sackets Harbor, NY 13685
315-646-3575 Fax: 315-646-1038
e-mail: fhall@sacketspatriots.org
Web site: www.sacketspatriots.org
Frederick E Hall, Superintendent

South Jefferson CSD
PO Box 10, Adams, NY 13605
315-583-6104
e-mail: jmoese@spartanpride.org
Web site: www.spartanpride.org
Jamie A Moesel, Superintendent

Thousand Islands CSD
8483 County Rt 9, PO Box 1000, Clayton, NY 13624-1000
315-686-5594 Fax: 315-686-5511
Web site: www.1000islandschools.org
Joseph Menard, Superintendent

Watertown City SD
1351 Washington St, PO Box 586, Watertown, NY 13601
315-785-3700 Fax: 315-785-6855
e-mail: tfralick@watertowncsd.org
Web site: www.watertowncsd.org
Terry N Fralick, Superintendent

LEWIS

Beaver River CSD
9508 Artz Rd, Beaver Falls, NY 13305-0179
315-346-1211 Fax: 315-346-6775
Web site: www.brcsd.org
Leueen Smithing, Interim Superintendent

Copenhagen CSD
3020 Mechanic St, Copenhagen, NY 13626-0030
315-688-4411 Fax: 315-688-2001
Web site: www.ccsknights.org
Scott Connell, Superintendent

Harrisville CSD
14371 Pirate Lane, PO Box 200, Harrisville, NY 13648
315-543-2707
Web site: www.hcsk12.org
Rolf A Waters, Superintendent

Lowville Academy & CSD
7668 State St, Lowville, NY 13367
315-376-9000 Fax: 315-376-1933
Web site: www.lacs-ny.org
Kenneth J McAuliffe, Superintendent

South Lewis CSD
PO Box 10, Turin, NY 13473-0010
315-348-2500
Web site: www.southlewis.org
Douglas E Premo, Superintendent

LIVINGSTON

Avon CSD
191 Clinton St, Avon, NY 14414
585-226-2455 x1318 Fax: 585-226-8202
e-mail: bamey@avoncsd.org
Web site: www.avoncsd.org
Bruce Amey, Superintendent

Caledonia-Mumford CSD
99 North St, Caledonia, NY 14423
585-538-3400
e-mail: ddinolfo@cal-mum.org
Web site: www.cal-mum.org
David V Dinolfo, Superintendent

Dansville CSD
284 Main St, Dansville, NY 14437-9798
585-335-4000 Fax: 585-335-4002
Web site: www.dansvillecsd.org
Alioto Paul, Superintendent

Offices and agencies generally appear in alphabetical order, except when specific order is requested by listee.

Geneseo CSD
4050 Avon Rd, Geneseo, NY 14454
585-243-3450 Fax: 585-243-9481
e-mail: timhayes@geneseocsd.org
Web site: www.geneseocsd.org
Timothy Hayes, Superintendent

Dalton-Nunda CSD (Keshequa)
13 Mill St, Nunda, NY 14517
585-468-2541 x1105 Fax: 585-468-3814
e-mail: jallman@keshequa.org
Web site: www.keshequa.org
John Allman, Superintendent

Livonia CSD
6 Puppy Lane, PO Box E, Livonia, NY 14487
585-346-4000 Fax: 585-346-6145
e-mail: sbischoping@livoniacsd.org
Web site: www.livoniacsd.org
Scott Bischoping, Superintendent

Mt Morris CSD
30 Bonadonna Ave, Mount Morris, NY 14510
585-658-2568 Fax: 585-658-4814
Web site: www.mtmorriscsd.org
Ed Orman, Superintendent

York CSD
2578 Genesee St, PO Box 102, Retsof, NY 14539-0102
585-243-1730 x2223 Fax: 585-243-5269
Web site: www.yorkcsd.org
Daniel Murray, Superintendent

MADISON

Brookfield CSD
1910 Fairground Rd, Brookfield, NY 13314-0060
315-899-3323 x200
Web site: www.bcsbeavers.org
Steve Szatko, Interim Superintendent

Canastota CSD
120 Roberts St, Canastota, NY 13032-1198
315-697-2025
Web site: www.canastotacsd.org
Frederick J Bragan, Superintendent

Cazenovia CSD
31 Emory Ave, Cazenovia, NY 13035-1098
315-655-1317 Fax: 315-655-1375
e-mail: rdubik@caz.cnyric.org
Web site: www.caz.cnyric.org
Robert Dubik, Superintendent

Chittenango CSD
1732 Fyler Rd, Chittenango, NY 13037-9520
315-687-2840 Fax: 315-687-2841
Web site: www.chittenangoschools.org
Thomas E Marzeski, Superintendent

De Ruyter CSD
711 Railroad St, Deruyter, NY 13052-0000
315-852-3410 Fax: 315-852-9600
Web site: www.deruyter.k12.ny.us
Charles W Walters, Superintendent

Hamilton CSD
47 W Kendrick Ave, Hamilton, NY 13346-1299
315-824-6310
e-mail: dbowers@hamiltoncentral.org
Web site: hamiltoncentral.org
Diana Bowers, Superintendent

Madison CSD
7303 State Route 20, Madison, NY 13402
315-893-1878
e-mail: cdedominick@madisoncentralny.org
Web site: www.madisoncentralny.org
Cynthia DeDominick, Superintendent

Morrisville-Eaton CSD
PO Box 990, Morrisville, NY 13408-0990
315-684-9300 Fax: 315-684-9399
e-mail: mdrahos@m-ecs.org
Web site: www.m-ecs.org
Michael Drahos, Superintendent

Oneida City SD
565 Sayles St, Oneida, NY 13421-0327
315-363-2550
e-mail: rspadafora@oneidacsd.org
Web site: www.oneida.org
Ronald R Spadafora Jr, Superintendent

Stockbridge Valley CSD
6011 Williams Rd, Munnsville, NY 13409-0732
315-495-4400 Fax: 315-495-4492
e-mail: cchafee@stockbridgevalley.org
Web site: www.stockbridgevalley.org
Chuck Chafee, Superintendent

MONROE

Brighton CSD
2035 Monroe Ave, Rochester, NY 14618-2027
585-242-5080 Fax: 585-242-5212
Web site: www.bcsd.org
Kevin McGowan, Superintendent

Brockport CSD
40 Allen St, Brockport, NY 14420-2296
585-637-1810
Web site: www.brockport.k12.ny.us
Garry Stone, Superintendent

Churchville-Chili CSD
139 Fairbanks Rd, Churchville, NY 14428-9797
585-293-1800 Fax: 585-293-1013
Web site: www.cccsd.org
Pam Kissel, Superintendent

East Irondequoit CSD
600 Pardee Rd, Rochester, NY 14609
585-339-1210 Fax: 585-288-0713
Web site: www.eicsd.k12.ny.us
Susan K Allen, Superintendent

East Rochester UFSD
222 Woodbine Ave, East Rochester, NY 14445
585-248-6302 Fax: 585-586-3254
Web site: www.erschools.org
Ray Giamartino, Jr, Superintendent

Fairport CSD
38 W Church St, Fairport, NY 14450-2130
585-421-2004 Fax: 585-421-3421
e-mail: jon_hunter@fairport.monroe.edu
Web site: www.fairport.org
Jon Hunter, Superintendent

Gates-Chili CSD
3 Spartan Way, Rochester, NY 14624
585-247-5050 x1217
Web site: www.gateschili.org
Mark C Davey, Superintendent

Offices and agencies generally appear in alphabetical order, except when specific order is requested by listee.

Greece CSD
PO Box 300, N Greece, NY 14515-0300
585-966-2000 Fax: 585-581-8203
Web site: www.greece.k12.ny.us
John O'Rourke, Interim Superintendent

Hilton CSD
225 West Ave, Hilton, NY 14468-1283
585-392-1000 Fax: 585-392-1038
Web site: www.hilton.k12.ny.us
David Dimbleby, Superintendent

Honeoye Falls-Lima CSD
20 Church St, Honeoye Falls, NY 14472-1294
585-624-7010
e-mail: michelle_kavanaugh@hflcsd.org
Web site: www.hflcsd.org
Michelle Kavanaugh, Superintendent

Penfield CSD
PO Box 900, Penfield, NY 14526-0900
585-249-5700 Fax: 585-248-8412
Web site: penfield.edu
John D Carlevatti, Superintendent

Pittsford CSD
75 Barker Road, Pittsford, NY 14534
585-267-1000 Fax: 585-381-2105
e-mail: maryalice_price@pittsford.monroe.edu
Web site: www.pittsfordschools.com
Mary Alice Price, Superintendent

Rochester City SD
131 W Broad St, Rochester, NY 14614
585-262-8100
Web site: www.rcsdk12.org
Jean Claude Brizard, Superintendent

Rush-Henrietta CSD
2034 Lehigh Station Rd, Henrietta, NY 14467-9692
585-359-5012 Fax: 585-359-5045
e-mail: kgraham@rhnet.org
Web site: www.rhnet.org
Kenneth Graham, Superintendent

Spencerport CSD
71 Lyell Ave, Spencerport, NY 14559-1899
585-349-5000 Fax: 585-349-5011
e-mail: bseaburn@spencerportschools.org
Web site: www.spencerportschools.org
Bonnie Seaburn, Superintendent

Webster CSD
119 South Ave, Webster, NY 14580-3594
585-216-0001 Fax: 585-265-6561
Web site: www.websterschools.org
Adele Bovard, Superintendent

West Irondequoit CSD
321 List Ave, Rochester, NY 14617-3125
585-336-2983 Fax: 585-266-1556
e-mail: marykay_herman@westiron.monroe.edu
Web site: www.westirondequoit.org
Jeffrey B Crane, Superintendent

Wheatland-Chili CSD
13 Beckwith Ave, Scottsville, NY 14546
585-889-4500 Fax: 585-889-6284
Web site: www.wheatland.k12.ny.us
Thomas Gallagher, Superintendent

MONTGOMERY

Canajoharie CSD
136 Scholastic Way, Canajoharie, NY 13317
518-673-6302 Fax: 518-673-3177
e-mail: richard.rose@canjo.org
Web site: www.canajoharieschools.org
Richard Rose, Superintendent

Fonda-Fultonville CSD
112 Old Johnstown Rd, Fonda, NY 12068-1501
518-853-4415 Fax: 518-853-4461
e-mail: jhoffman@ffcsd.org
Web site: www.ffcsd.org
James Hoffman, Superintendent

Fort Plain CSD
25 High St, Fort Plain, NY 13339-1218
518-993-4000 Fax: 518-993-3393
e-mail: fpcsss@hotmail.com
Web site: www.fortplain.org
Douglas C Burton, Superintendent

Greater Amsterdam SD
11 Liberty St, Amsterdam, NY 12010
518-843-3180 Fax: 518-842-0012
e-mail: tperillo@gasd.org
Web site: gasd.org
Thomas F Perillo, Superintendent

St Johnsville CSD
44 Center St, St Johnsville, NY 13452
518-568-7024 Fax: 518-568-5407
Web site: www.sjcsd.org
Ralph Acquaro, Superintendent

NASSAU

Baldwin UFSD
960 Hastings St, Baldwin, NY 11510
516-377-9200 Fax: 516-377-9421
Web site: www.baldwin.k12.ny.us
James Mapes, Superintendent

Bellmore UFSD
580 Winthrop Ave, Bellmore, NY 11710-5099
516-679-2909 Fax: 516-679-3027
Web site: www.bellmore.k12.ny.us
Joseph S Famularo, Superintendent

Bellmore-Merrick Central HS District
1260 Meadowbrook Rd, North Merrick, NY 11566
516-992-1000
Web site: www.bellmore-merrick.k12.ny.us
Henry Kiernan, Superintendent

Bethpage UFSD
10 Cherry Ave, Bethpage, NY 11714
516-644-4001
e-mail: tclark@bethpage.ws
Web site: wwwbethpagecommunity.com/Schools
Terrence Clark, Superintendent

Carle Place UFSD
168 Cherry Ln, Carle Place, NY 11514
516-622-6575
Web site: www.cps.k12.ny.us
David Flatley, Superintendent

East Meadow UFSD
718 The Plain Road, Westbury, NY 11590
516-478-5776
Web site: www.eastmeadow.k12.ny.us
Louis R DeAngelo, Superintendent

East Rockaway UFSD
443 Ocean Ave, East Rockaway, NY 11518
516-887-8300
Web site: www.eastrockawayschools.org
Dr. Roseanne Melucci, Superintendent

East Williston UFSD
11 Bacon Rd, Old Westbury, NY 11568
516-333-3758 Fax: 516-333-1937
Web site: www.ewsdonline.org
Lorna R Lewis, Superintendent

Elmont UFSD
135 Elmont Rd, Elmont, NY 11003-1609
516-326-5500 Fax: 516-326-5574
Web site: www.elmontschools.org
Al Harper, Superintendent

Farmingdale UFSD
50 Van Cott Ave, Farmingdale, NY 11735
516-752-6510
Web site: www.farmingdaleschools.org
John Lorentz, Superintendent

Floral Park-Bellerose UFSD
One Poppy Pl, Floral Park, NY 11001
516-327-9300 Fax: 516-327-9304
Web site: www.floralpark.k12.ny.us
Lynn Pombonyo, Superintendent

Franklin Square UFSD
760 Washington St, Franklin Square, NY 11010
516-481-4100
e-mail: info@franklinsquare.k12.ny.us
Web site: franklinsquare.k12.ny.us
Patrick Manley, Superintendent

Freeport UFSD
235 N Ocean Ave, Freeport, NY 11520
516-867-5205 Fax: 516-623-4759
e-mail: kkuncham@freeportschools.org
Web site: www.freeportschools.org
Dr. Kishore Kunchan, Superintendent

Garden City UFSD
56 Cathedral Ave, PO Box 216, Garden City, NY 11530-0216
516-478-1000
Web site: www.gardencity.k12.ny.us
Robert Feirsen, Superintendent

Glen Cove City SD
150 Dosoris Ln, Glen Cove, NY 11542
516-801-7001
Web site: www.glencove.k12.ny.us
Joseph Laria, Superintendent

Great Neck UFSD
345 Lakeville Rd, Great Neck, NY 11020
516-441-4001 Fax: 516-773-6685
e-mail: tdolan@greatneck.k12.ny.us
Web site: www.greatneck.k12.ny.us
Dr Thomas P Dolan, Superintendent

Hempstead UFSD
185 Peninsula Blvd, Hempstead, NY 11550
516-292-7111 x1001
Web site: www.hempsteadschools.org
Patricia Watkins, Superintendent

Herricks UFSD
999 B Herricks Rd, New Hyde Park, NY 11040
516-305-8901
e-mail: jbierwirth@herricks.org
Web site: www.herricks.org
John E Bierwirth, Superintendent

Hewlett-Woodmere UFSD
1 Johnson Pl, Woodmere, NY 11598
516-374-8100 Fax: 516-374-8101
Web site: www.hewlett-woodmere.net
Joyce Bisso, Superintendent

Hicksville UFSD
200 Division Ave-Adm, Hicksville, NY 11801-4800
516-733-2110
Web site: www.hicksvillepublicschools.org
Maureen K Bright, Superintendent

Island Park UFSD
150 Trafalgar Blvd, Island Park, NY 11558
516-431-8100 Fax: 516-431-7550
Web site: www.ips.k12.ny.us
Rosmarie Bovino, Superintendent

Island Trees UFSD
74 Farmedge Rd, Levittown, NY 11756
516-520-2100
e-mail: cmurphy@islandtrees.org
Web site: www.islandtrees.org
Charles J Murphy, Superintendent

Jericho UFSD
99 Cedar Swamp Rd, Jericho, NY 11753
516-203-3600 x3201
e-mail: hgrishman@jerichoschools.org
Web site: www.bestschools.org
Henry L Grishman, Superintendent

Lawrence UFSD
195 Broadway, Lawrence, NY 11559
516-295-8000
Web site: www.lawrence.org
John T Fitzsimons, Superintendent

Levittown UFSD
150 Abbey Ln, Levittown, NY 11756
516-520-8300 Fax: 516-520-8314
Web site: www.levittownschools.com
Herman A Sirois, Superintendent

Locust Valley CSD
22 Horse Hollow Rd, Locust Valley, NY 11560
516-277-5001
e-mail: ahunderfund@lvcsd.k12.ny.us
Web site: www.lvcsd.k12.ny.us
Anna Hunderfund, Superintendent

Long Beach City SD
235 Lido Blvd, Long Beach, NY 11561-5093
516-897-2104
Web site: www.lbeach.org
Robert Greenberg, Superintendent

Lynbrook UFSD
111 Atlantic Ave, Lynbrook, NY 11563
516-887-0253
Web site: www.lynbrook.k12.ny.us
Santo Barbarino, Superintendent

Malverne UFSD
301 Wicks Ln, Malverne, NY 11565-2244
516-887-6400
Web site: www.malverne.k12.ny.us
James H Hunderfund, Superintendent

Manhasset UFSD
200 Memorial Pl, Manhasset, NY 11030
516-267-7705 Fax: 516-627-8158
e-mail: ccardillo@manhasset.k12.ny.us
Web site: www.manhasset.k12.ny.us
Charles S Cardillo, Superintendent

Massapequa UFSD
4925 Merrick Rd, Massapequa, NY 11758
516-308-5001
Web site: www.msd.k12.ny.us
Charles Sulc, Superintendent

Merrick UFSD
21 Babylon Rd, Merrick, NY 11566
516-992-7240
Web site: www.merrick-k6.org
Ranier W Melucci, Superintendent

Mineola UFSD
121 Jackson Ave, Mineola, NY 11501
516-237-2001 Fax: 516-237-2008
e-mail: mnagler@mineola.k12.ny.ua
Web site: www.mineola.k12.ny,us
Michael Nagler, Superintendent

New Hyde Park-Garden City Park UFSD
1950 Hillside Ave, New Hyde Park, NY 11040
516-352-6257 x221
e-mail: rkatulak@nhp-gcp.org
Web site: www.nhp-gcp.org
Robert Katulak, Superintendent

North Bellmore UFSD
2616 Martin Ave, Bellmore, NY 11710
516-992-3000 x4001
Web site: www.northbellmoreschools.org
Arnold Goldstein, Superintendent

North Merrick UFSD
1057 Merrick Ave, Merrick, NY 11566
516-292-3694 Fax: 516-292-3097
Web site: www.nmerrickschools.org
David S Feller, Superintendent

North Shore CSD
112 Franklin Ave, Sea Cliff, NY 11579
516-277-7800 or 516-277-7801
Web site: www.northshore.k12.ny.us
Edward K Melnick, Superintendent

Oceanside UFSD
145 Merle Ave, Oceanside, NY 11572-2206
516-678-1215
e-mail: hbrown@oceanside.k12.ny.us
Web site: www.oceanside.k12.ny.us
Herb R Brown, Superintendent

Oyster Bay-East Norwich CSD
1 McCouns Ln, Oyster Bay, NY 11771-3105
516-624-6505
e-mail: pharrington@obenschools.org
Web site: obenschools.org
Phyllis Harrington, Superintendent

Plainedge UFSD
241 Wyngate Dr, PO Box 1669, North Massapequa, NY 11758
516-992-7455 Fax: 516-992-7446
Web site: www.plainedgeschools.org
Christine P'Simer, Superintendent

Plainview-Old Bethpage CSD
106 Washington Ave, Plainview, NY 11803-3612
516-937-6301
Web site: www.pob.k12.ny.us
Gerald W Dempsey, Superintendent

Port Washington UFSD
100 Campus Dr, Port Washington, NY 11050
516-767-5005 Fax: 516-767-5007
e-mail: gng@portnet.k12.ny.us
Web site: www.portnet.k12.ny.us
Geoffrey N Gordon, Superintendent

Rockville Centre UFSD
128 Shepherd St, Rockville Centre, NY 11570-2298
516-255-8920
Web site: www.rvcschools.org
William H Johnson, Superintendent

Roosevelt UFSD
240 Denton Pl, Roosevelt, NY 11575-1539
516-345-7001 Fax: 516-379-0178
e-mail: rwharris@rooseveltufsd.com
Web site: www.rooseveltufsd.com

Roslyn UFSD
300 Harbor Hill Rd, Roslyn, NY 11576-1531
516-625-6303 Fax: 516-625-6336
e-mail: roslynsd@roslynschools.org
Web site: www.roslynschools.org
Daniel Brenner, Superintendent

Seaford UFSD
1600 Washington Ave, Seaford, NY 11783
516-592-4002
e-mail: bconboy@mail.seaford.k12.ny.us
Web site: www.seaford.k12.ny.us
Brian Conboy, Superintendent

Sewanhaka Central HS District
77 Landau Ave, Floral Park, NY 11001
516-488-9800 Fax: 516-488-9899
Web site: www.sewanhaka.k12.ny.us
Warren A Meierdiercks, Superintendent

Syosset CSD
99 Pell Ln, PO Box 9029, Syosset, NY 11791
516-364-5605
Web site: www.syosett.k12.ny.us
Carole G Hankin, Superintendent

Uniondale UFSD
933 Goodrich St, Uniondale, NY 11553-2499
516-560-8824 Fax: 516-292-2659
e-mail: wlloyd@uniondaleschools.org
Web site: district.uniondaleschools.org
William K Lloyd, Superintendent

Offices and agencies generally appear in alphabetical order, except when specific order is requested by listee.

Valley Stream 13 UFSD
585 N Corona Ave, Valley Stream, NY 11580
516-568-6100 Fax: 516-825-2537
e-mail: elison@valleystream13.com
Web site: www.valleystream13.com
Elizabeth Lison, Superintendent

Valley Stream 24 UFSD
75 Horton Ave, Valley Stream, NY 11581-1420
516-256-0153
Web site: www.valleystreamdistrict24.com
Edward M Fale, Superintendent

Valley Stream 30 UFSD
175 N Central Ave, Valley Stream, NY 11580-3801
516-285-9881
Web site: www.valleystream30.com
Elaine Kanas, Superintendent

Valley Stream Central HS District
One Kent Rd, Valley Stream, NY 11580-3398
516-872-5601 Fax: 516-872-5658
Web site: www.vschsd.org
Richard Marsh, Superintendent

Wantagh UFSD
3301 Beltagh Ave, Wantagh, NY 11793-3395
516-679-6300
e-mail: wantaghinfo@wantaghschools.org
Web site: www.wantaghschools.org
Lydia Begley, Superintendent

West Hempstead UFSD
252 Chestnut St, West Hempstead, NY 11552-2455
516-390-3107 Fax: 516-489-1776
Web site: www.whufsd.com
John J Hogan, Superintendent

Westbury UFSD
2 Hitchcock Ln, Old Westbury, NY 11568-1624
516-876-5016 Fax: 516-876-5187
e-mail: cclark-snead@westburyschools.org
Web site: www.westburyschools.org
Constance R Clark-Snead, Superintendent

NEW YORK CITY

NYC Chancellor's Office
52 Chambers St, New York, NY 10007
212-374-6000 Fax: 212-374-5763
Cathie Black, Chancellor

NYC Citywide Alternative HS District & Programs
9027 Sutphin Blvd, Jamaica, NY 11435
718-557-2681
Cami Anderson, Senior Superintendent

NYC Citywide Special Ed District 75
400 First Ave, New York, NY 10010
212-802-1500
Web site: schools.nycenet.edu/d75/
Gary Hecht, Superintendent

NYC Region 1
1 Fordham Plz, Rm 81, Bronx, NY 10458
718-741-7030
Yvonne Torres, Superintendent

NYC Region 2
1230 Zerega Ave, Bronx, NY 10462
718-828-2440
Timothy Behr, Superintendent

NYC Region 3
30-48 Linden Pl, Flushing, NY 11354
718-281-7575
Anita Saunder, Superintendent

NYC Region 4
28-11 Queens Plz N, Long Island City, NY 11101
718-391-8300
Madeline Chan, Superintendent

NYC Region 5
82-01 Rockaway Blvd, Queens, NY 11416
718-270-5800 or 718-922-4960
Kathleen M Cashin, Superintendent

NYC Region 6
5619 Flatlands Ave, Brooklyn, NY 11234
718-968-6100
Jean Claude Brizard, Superintendent

NYC Region 7
715 Ocean Terr, Building 1, Staten Island, NY 10301
718-556-8350
Margaret Schultz, Superintendent

NYC Region 8
131 Livingston St, Brooklyn, NY 11201
718-935-3900
Anita Scop, Superintendent

NYC Region 9
333 7th Ave & 28th St, Room 712, New York, NY 10001
212-356-7500
Luz Cortazzo, Superintendent

NYC Region 10
4360 Broadway, Rm 52, New York, NY 10033
917-521-3700
Gale Reeves, Superintendent

NIAGARA

Barker CSD
1628 Quaker Rd, Barker, NY 14012-0328
716-795-3832
Dr Roger J Klatt, Superintendent

Lewiston-Porter CSD
4061 Creek Rd, Youngstown, NY 14174-9799
716-286-7266
e-mail: rappoldd@lew-port.com
Web site: www.lew-port.com
R Christopher Roser, Superintendent

Lockport City SD
130 Beattie Ave, Lockport, NY 14094-5099
716-478-4835 Fax: 716-478-4863
e-mail: tacarbone@lockport.wnyric.org
Web site: www.lockportschools.wnyric.org
Terry Ann Carbone, Superintendent

Newfane CSD
6273 Charlotteville Rd, Newfane, NY 14108
716-778-6850 Fax: 716-778-6852
Web site: www.newfane.wnyric.org
Christine Tibbetts, Superintendent

Niagara Falls City SD
630-66th Street, Niagara Falls, NY 14304
716-286-4205 Fax: 716-286-4283
e-mail: cbianco@nfschools.net
Web site: www.nfschools.net
Cynthia A Bianco, Superintendent

Niagara-Wheatfield CSD
6700 Schultz St, Niagara Falls, NY 14304
716-215-3003 Fax: 716-215-3039
e-mail: jhoward@nwcsd.wnyric.org
Web site: www.nwcsd.k12.ny.us
Carl H Militello, Superintendent

North Tonawanda City SD
175 Humphrey St, North Tonawanda, NY 14120-4097
716-807-3500
Web site: www.ntschools.org
Gregory Woytila, Superintendent

Royalton-Hartland CSD
54 State St, Middleport, NY 14105-1199
716-735-3031 Fax: 716-735-3660
e-mail: macdonaldk@royhart.org
Web site: www.royhart.org
Kevin MacDonald, Superintendent

Starpoint CSD
4363 Mapleton Rd, Lockport, NY 14094
716-210-2342
e-mail: dwhelan@starpointcsd.org
Web site: www.starpointcsd.org
C Douglas Whelan, Superintendent

Wilson CSD
412 Lake St, Wilson, NY 14172
716-751-9341
Web site: www.wilson.wnyric.org
Michael Wendt, Superintendent

ONEIDA

Adirondack CSD
110 Ford St, Boonville, NY 13309-1200
315-942-9200 Fax: 315-942-5522
Web site: www.adirondackcsd.org
David Hubman, Superintendent

Camden CSD
51 Third St, Camden, NY 13316-1114
315-245-4075
Web site: www.camdenschools.org
Dr Jeffrey K Bryant, Superintendent

Clinton CSD
75 Chenango Ave, Clinton, NY 13323
315-557-2253 Fax: 315-853-8727
e-mail: mreilly@ccs.edu
Web site: www.ccs.edu
Matthew Reilly, Superintendent

Holland Patent CSD
9601 Main St, Holland Patent, NY 13354-4610
315-865-7221
Web site: www.hpschools.org
Kathleen M Davis, Superintendent

NY Mills UFSD
1 Marauder Blvd, New York Mills, NY 13417-1566
315-768-8127 Fax: 315-768-3521
Web site: www.newyorkmills.org
Kathy Houghton, Superintendent

New Hartford CSD
33 Oxford Rd, New Hartford, NY 13413
315-624-1218
Web site: www.newhartfordschools.org
Robert J Nole, Superintendent

Oriskany CSD
1313 Utica St, Oriskany, NY 13424-0539
315-768-2058 Fax: 315-768-2057
Web site: www.oriskanycsd.org
Gregory Kelahan, Superintendent

Remsen CSD
9733 Davis Dr, PO Box 406, Remsen, NY 13438
315-831-3797
Web site: www.remsencsd.org
Joanne Shelmidine, Superintendent

Rome City SD
409 Bell Rd, Rome, NY 13440
315-338-6500 Fax: 315-334-7409
Web site: www.romecsd.org
Jeffrey Simons, Superintendent

Sauquoit Valley CSD
2601 Oneida St, Sauquoit, NY 13456-1000
315-839-6311
Web site: www.svcsd.org
Ronald J Wheelock, Superintendent

Sherrill City SD
5275 State Route 31, PO Box 128, Verona, NY 13478-0128
315-829-2520 Fax: 315-829-4949
Web site: www.vvsschools.org
Norman Reed, Superintendent

Utica City SD
106 Memorial Parkway, Utica, NY 13501-3709
315-792-2222
Web site: www.uticaschools.org
James Willis, Superintendent

Vernon-Verona-Sherrill CSD
5275 State Rt 31, Verona, NY 13478-0128
315-829-2520 Fax: 315-829-4949
Web site: www.vvscentralschools.org
Norman Reed, Superintendent

Waterville CSD
381 Madison St, Waterville, NY 13480-1100
315-841-3900
e-mail: districtoffice@watervilleschools.org
Web site: www.watervilleschools.org
Gary Lonczak, Superintendent

Westmoreland CSD
5176 Rt 233, Westmoreland, NY 13490-0430
315-557-2601
e-mail: tkulak@westmorelandschool.org
Web site: www.westmorelandschool.org
Rocco Migliori, Superintendent

Whitesboro CSD
67 Whitesboro St, PO Box 304, Yorkville, NY 13495-0304
315-266-3303 Fax: 315-768-9723
Web site: www.wboro.org
Dave Langone, Superintendent

ONONDAGA

Baldwinsville CSD
29 E Oneida St, Baldwinsville, NY 13027-2480
315-638-6043 Fax: 315-638-6041
e-mail: jdangle@bville.org
Web site: www.bville.org
Jeanne M Dangle, Superintendent

East Syracuse-Minoa CSD
407 Fremont Rd, East Syracuse, NY 13057-2631
315-434-3012 Fax: 315-434-3020
e-mail: mvasiloff@esmschools.org
Web site: www.esmschools.org
Dr Donna J DeSiato, Superintendent

Fabius-Pompey CSD
1211 Mill St, Fabius, NY 13063-8719
315-683-5301 Fax: 315-683-5827
e-mail: tryan@fabius.cnyric.org
Web site: www.fabiuspompey.org
Timothy P Ryan, Superintendent

Fayetteville-Manlius CSD
8199 E Seneca Tpke, Manlius, NY 13104-2140
315-692-1200 Fax: 315-692-1227
e-mail: ckaiser@fmschools.org
Web site: www.fmschools.org
Corliss Kaiser, Superintendent

Jamesville-Dewitt CSD
6845 Edinger Dr, PO Box 606, Dewitt, NY 13214-0606
315-445-8304 Fax: 315-445-8477
e-mail: ckendrick@jd.cnyric.org
Web site: www.jamesvilledewitt.org
Alice Kendrick, Superintendent

Jordan-Elbridge CSD
9 N Chappell St, Jordan, NY 13080
315-689-8500 or 315-689-0084
e-mail: mdominick@jecsd.org
Web site: www.jecsd.org
Lawrence Zacher, Superintendent

LaFayette CSD
5955 Rt 20 W, Lafayette, NY 13084-9701
315-677-9728 Fax: 315-677-3372
e-mail: ptigh@lafcs.cnyric.org
Web site: www.lafayetteschools.org
Peter A Tigh, Superintendent

Liverpool CSD
195 Blackberry Rd, Liverpool, NY 13090
315-622-7125 Fax: 315-622-7115
e-mail: jan@liverpool.k12.ny.us
Web site: www.liverpool.k12.ny.us
Dr Richard N Johns, Superintendent

Lyncourt UFSD
2707-2709 Court St, Syracuse, NY 13208
315-455-7571 Fax: 315-455-7573
e-mail: msandore@lyncourt.cnyric.org
Web site: www.lyncourt.cnyric.org
Michael Schiedo, Superintendent

Marcellus CSD
2 Reed Pkwy, Marcellus, NY 13108-1199
315-673-0201 Fax: 315-673-0329
e-mail: ctice@mcs.cnyric.org
Web site: marcellusschools.org
Craig J Tice, Superintendent

North Syracuse CSD
5355 W Taft Rd, North Syracuse, NY 13212-2796
315-218-2151
e-mail: jmelvin@nscsd.org
Web site: www.nscsd.org
Jerome F Melvin, Superintendent

Onondaga CSD
4466 S Onondaga Rd, Nedrow, NY 13120-9715
315-552-5000
Web site: www.ocs.cnyric.org
Joseph Rotella, Superintendent

Skaneateles CSD
45 E Elizabeth St, Skaneateles, NY 13152
315-685-8361 Fax: 315-685-0347
Web site: www.skanschools.org
Philip D D'Angelo, Superintendent

Solvay UFSD
103 3rd St, Solvay, NY 13209-1532
315-468-1111 Fax: 315-468-2755
e-mail: manningj@solvay.cnyric.org
Web site: www.solvayschools.org
J Francis Manning, Superintendent

Syracuse City SD
725 Harrison St, Syracuse, NY 13210
315-435-4161 Fax: 315-435-4015
e-mail: dlowengard@scsd.us
Web site: www.syracusecityschools.com
Daniel G Lowengard, Superintendent

Tully CSD
20 State St, PO Box 628, Tully, NY 13159-0628
315-696-6204
e-mail: kraig@pobox.com
Web site: www.tullyschools.org
Kraig D Pritts, Superintendent

West Genesee CSD
300 Sanderson Dr, Camillus, NY 13031-1655
315-487-4562 Fax: 315-487-2999
e-mail: rrubeis@wgmail.cnyric.org
Web site: www.westgenesee.org
Dr Christopher R Brown, Superintendent

Westhill CSD
400 Walberta Rd, Syracuse, NY 13219-2214
315-426-3000 Fax: 315-488-6411
e-mail: sbocciolatt@westhillschools.org
Web site: www.westhillschools.org
Stephen A Bocciolatt, Superintendent

ONTARIO

Thomas Strining, Interim Superintendent

Canandaigua City SD
143 N Pearl St, Canandaigua, NY 14424-1496
585-396-3700
e-mail: rawd@canandaiguaschools.org
Web site: www.canandaiguaschools.org
Ronald Raw Jr, Superintendent

East Bloomfield CSD
1 Oakmont Avenue, East Bloomfield, NY 14443
585-657-6121
Web site: www.bloomfieldcsd.org
Michael J Midey, Superintendent

Offices and agencies generally appear in alphabetical order, except when specific order is requested by listee.

Geneva City SD
400 W North St, Geneva, NY 14456
315-781-0400 Fax: 315-781-4128
e-mail: ryoung@genevacsd.org
Web site: www.genevacsd.org
Robert C Young Jr, Superintendent

Gorham-Middlesex CSD (Marcus Whitman)
4100 Baldwin Road, Rushville, NY 14544
585-554-4848 X1805
Web site: www.mwcsd.org
Michael Chirco, Superintendent

Honeoye CSD
8523 Main St, Honeoye, NY 14471-0170
585-229-4125
Web site: www.honeoye.org
David C Bills, Superintendent

Manchester-Shortsville CSD
1506 Rt 21, Shortsville, NY 14548-9502
585-289-3964 Fax: 585-289-6660
e-mail: rleiby@redjacket.org
Web site: www.redjacket.org
Robert E Leiby, Superintendent

Marcus Whitman CSD
4100 Baldwin Rd, Rushville, NY 14544-9799
585-554-4848
e-mail: mchirco@mwcsd.org
Web site: www.mwcsd.org
Michael Chirco, Superintendent

Naples CSD
136 N Main St, Naples, NY 14512-9201
585-374-7901
e-mail: kward@naples.k12.ny.us
Web site: www.naples.k12.ny.us
Kimberle Ward, Superintendent

Phelps-Clifton Springs CSD
1490 Rt 488, Clifton Springs, NY 14432-9334
315-548-6420
Web site: www.midlakes.org
Michael J Ford, Superintendent

Victor CSD
953 High St, Victor, NY 14564-1167
585-924-3252 x1400 Fax: 585-742-7090
e-mail: santiago-marullod@victorschools.org
Web site: www.victorschools.org
Dawn A Santiago-Marullo, Superintendent

ORANGE

Chester UFSD
64 Hambletonian Ave, Chester, NY 10918
845-469-5052
Sean Michel, Superintendent

Cornwall CSD
24 Idlewild Ave, Cornwall on Hudson, NY 12520
845-534-8000 Fax: 845-534-4231
e-mail: trehm@cornwallschools.com
Web site: www.cornwallschools.com
Timothy J Rehm, Superintendent

Florida UFSD
51 N Main St, PO Box 7, Florida, NY 10921-0757
845-651-3095
e-mail: dburnside@floridaufsd.org
Web site: www.floridaufsd.org
Douglas Burnside, Superintendent

Goshen CSD
227 Main St, Goshen, NY 10924
845-615-6720 Fax: 845-615-6725
Web site: www.goshenschoolsny.org
Daniel T Connor, Superintendent of Schools

Greenwood Lake UFSD
PO Box 8, Greenwood Lake, NY 10925
845-782-8678
e-mail: rbrockel@gwlufsd.org
Web site: www.gwlufsd.org
Dr Richard J Brockel, Superintendent

Highland Falls CSD
PO Box 287, Highland Falls, NY 10928
845-446-9575 Fax: 845-446-3321
Web site: www.hffmcsd.org
Dr Debra Jackson, Superintendent

Kiryas Joel Village UFSD
48 Bakertown Rd- Ste 401, Monroe, NY 10950-0398
845-782-2300
Joel Petlin, Superintendent

Middletown City SD
223 Wisner Ave Ext, Middletown, NY 10940-3240
845-326-51158 Fax: 845-343-9938
e-mail: keastwood@ecsdm.org
Web site: middletowncityschools.org
Kenneth Eastwood, Superintendent

Minisink Valley CSD
Rt 6, PO Box 217, Slate Hill, NY 10973-0217
845-355-5110
Web site: www.minisink.com
John Latini, Superintendent

Monroe-Woodbury CSD
278 Rte 32, Educ Ctr, Central Valley, NY 10917-1001
845-460-6200 Fax: 845-460-6080
Web site: www.mw.k12.ny.us
Edward Mehrhof, Superintendent

Newburgh Enlarged City SD
124 Grand St, Newburgh, NY 12550-4600
845-563-3400 Fax: 845-563-3501
e-mail: rpizzo1@necsd.net
Web site: www.newburghschools.org
Ralph A Pizzo, Superintendent

Pine Bush CSD
156 State Rt 302, PO Box 700, Pine Bush, NY 12566-0700
845-744-2031
Web site: www.pinebushschools.org
Philip G Steinberg, Superintendent

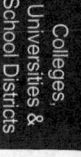

Port Jervis City SD
9 Thompson St, Port Jervis, NY 12771-3058
845-858-3100 Fax: 845-856-1885
e-mail: jxanthis@pjschools.org
Web site: www.pjschools.org
John P Xanthis, Superintendent

Tuxedo UFSD
Route 17, Box 2002, Tuxedo Park, NY 10987
845-351-2296 Fax: 845-351-5296
e-mail: clomascolo@tuxedoschooldistrict.com
Web site: www.tuxedoschooldistrict.com
Carol Lomascolo, Superintendent

Valley CSD (Montgomery)
944 State Rt 17k, Montgomery, NY 12549-2240
845-457-2400
Web site: www.vcsd.k12.ny.us
Richard M Hooley, Superintendent

Warwick Valley CSD
PO Box 595, Warwick, NY 10990-0595
845-987-3010
e-mail: fbryant@wvcsd.org
Web site: www.warwickvalleyschools.org
Dr Raymond W Bryant, Superintendent

Washingtonville CSD
52 W Main St, Washingtonville, NY 10992-1492
845-497-4000 Fax: 845-496-4031
Roberta Green, Superintendent

ORLEANS

Albion CSD
324 East Ave, Albion, NY 14411
585-589-2056
Web site: www.albionk12.org
Michael Bonnewell, Superintendent

Holley CSD
3800 N Main St, Holley, NY 14470-9330
585-638-6316
Web site: www.holleycsd.org
Robert C D'Angelo, Superintendent

Kendall CSD
1932 Kendall Rd, Kendall, NY 14476-0777
585-659-2741
e-mail: kcsd@kendallschools.org
Web site: www.kendallschools.org
Julie Christensen, Interim Superintendent

Lyndonville CSD
25 Housel Ave, Lyndonville, NY 14098-0540
585-765-2251 x3101
e-mail: bdeane-williams@lyndonville.wnyric.org
Web site: www.lyndonvillecsd.org
Barbara Deane-Williams, Superintendent

Medina CSD
One Mustang Dr, Medina, NY 14103-1845
585-798-2700
e-mail: rgalante@medinacsd.org
Web site: www.medinacsd.org
Neal S Miller, Superintendent

OSWEGO

Altmar-Parish-Williamstown CSD
639 County Rt 22, Parish, NY 13131
315-625-5251
e-mail: dhaab@apw.cnyric.org
Gerry D Hudson, Superintendent

Central Square CSD
642 S Main St, Central Square, NY 13036-3511
315-668-4220
e-mail: ccostello@cssd.org
Carolyn Costello, Superintendent

Fulton City SD
167 S Fourth St, Fulton, NY 13069-1859
315-593-5510
e-mail: blynch@fulton.cnyric.org
William R Lynch, Superintendent

Hannibal CSD
928 Cayuga St, Hannibal, NY 13074
315-564-7900
e-mail: mdifabio@hannibal.cnyric.org
Michael J DiFabio, Superintendent

Mexico CSD
40 Academy St, Mexico, NY 13114-3432
315-963-8400
Robert Pritchard, Superintendent

Oswego City SD
120 E 1st St, Oswego, NY 13126-2114
315-341-2001
e-mail: wcrist@oswego.org
Web site: www.oswego.org
William Crist, Superintendent

Phoenix CSD
116 Volney St, Phoenix, NY 13135-9778
315-695-1555
Web site: www.phoenixcsd.org
Judy Belfield, Superintendent

Pulaski CSD
2 Hinman Rd, Pulaski, NY 13142-2201
315-298-5188
e-mail: mmarshal@pacs.cnyric.org
Marshall Marshall, Superintendent

Sandy Creek CSD
124 Salisbury St, Sandy Creek, NY 13145-0248
315-387-3445
e-mail: samell@sccs.cnyric.org
Stewart R Amell, Superintendent

OTSEGO

Cherry Valley-Springfield CSD
597 County Hwy 54, Cherry Valley, NY 13320-0485
607-264-3265 Fax: 607-264-3458
e-mail: info@cvscs.org
Web site: www.cvscs.org
Robert Miller, Superintendent

Cooperstown CSD
39 Linden Ave, Cooperstown, NY 13326-1496
607-547-5364 Fax: 607-547-1000
Web site: www.cooperstowncs.org
Clifton Hebert, Superintendent

Edmeston CSD
11 North St, PO Box 5129, Edmeston, NY 13335-0529
607-965-8931 Fax: 607-965-8942
e-mail: drowley@edmeston.net
David Rowley, Superintendent

Gilbertsville-Mount Upton CSD
693 State Hwy 51, Gilbertsville, NY 13776
607-783-2207
e-mail: gmu@gmucsd.org
Web site: www.gmucsd.org
Glenn R Hamilton, Superintendent

Laurens CSD
PO Box 301, Laurens, NY 13796-0301
607-432-2050 Fax: 607-432-4388
e-mail: rwenck@laurenscs.org
Romona N Wenck, Superintendent

Milford CSD
42 W Main St, Milford, NY 13807-0237
607-286-3341 Fax: 607-286-7879
Peter N Livshin, Superintendent

Morris CSD
65 Main St, Morris, NY 13808-0040
607-263-6100 Fax: 607-263-2483
e-mail: mvigil@morriscs.org
Matthew Sheldon, Superintendent

Oneonta City SD
189 Main St, Ste 302, Oneonta, NY 13820-1142
607-433-8232 Fax: 607-433-3641
e-mail: mshea@oneontacsd.org
Web site: www.oneontacsd.org
Michael P Shea, Superintendent

Otego-Unadilla CSD
2641 State Hwy 7, Otego, NY 13825
607-988-5038 Fax: 607-988-1039
Web site: www.unatego.org
Charles Molloy, Superintendent

Richfield Springs CSD
93 Main St, PO Box 631, Richfield Springs, NY 13439-0631
315-858-0610
Web site: www.richfieldcsd.org
Robert Barraco, Superintendent

Schenevus CSD
159 Main St, Schenevus, NY 12155-0008
607-638-5530 Fax: 607-638-5600
e-mail: lbooknard@schenevuscs.org
Lynda Booknard, Superintendent

Unatego CSD
2641 State Hwy 7, Otego, NY 13825
607-988-5000 Fax: 607-988-1039
Web site: www.unatego.org
Charles Molloy, Superintendent

Worcester CSD
198 Main St, Worcester, NY 12197
607-397-8785 Fax: 607-397-9454
e-mail: seloverj@worcestercs.org
Gary M Kuch, Superintendent

PUTNAM

Brewster CSD
30 Farm-to-Market Rd, Brewster, NY 10509-9956
845-279-8000
e-mail: jsandbank@brewsterschools.org
Web site: www.brewsterschools.org
Jane Sandbank, Superintendent

Carmel CSD
81 South St, PO Box 296, Patterson, NY 12563-0296
845-878-2094 Fax: 845-878-4337
e-mail: info@ccsd.k12.ny.us
Web site: www.ccsd.k12.ny.us or www.carmelschools.com
James M Ryan, Superintendent

Garrison UFSD
1100 Rt 9 D, Garrison, NY 10524-0193
845-424-3689 Fax: 845-424-4733
e-mail: gcolucci@gufs.org
Web site: www.gufs.org
Gloria J Colucci, Superintendent

Haldane CSD
15 Craigside Dr, Cold Spring, NY 10516-1899
845-265-9254
Web site: www.haldaneschool.org
Mark Villanti, Superintendent

Mahopac CSD
179 East Lake Blvd, Mahopac, NY 10541-1666
845-628-3415 ext 326 Fax: 845-628-5502
Web site: www.mahopac.k12.ny.us
Thomas J Manko, Superintendent

Putnam Valley CSD
146 Peekskill Hollow Rd, Putnam Valley, NY 10579-3238
845-528-8143 Fax: 845-528-0274
e-mail: bfuchs@pvcsd.org
Web site: www.pvcsd.org
Barbara Fuchs, Superintendent

RENSSELAER

Averill Park CSD
146 Gettle Rd, Averill Park, NY 12018-9798
518-674-7055 Fax: 518-674-3802
e-mail: mocciaj@averillpark.k12.ny.us
Web site: www.averillpark.k12.ny.us
Josephine Moccia, Superintendent

Berlin CSD
53 School St, PO Box 259, Berlin, NY 12022-0259
518-658-2690 Fax: 518-658-3822
e-mail: tdiamond@berlincentral.org
Web site: www.berlincentral.org
Brian Howard, Acting Superintendent

Brunswick CSD (Brittonkill)
3992 NY Rt 2, Troy, NY 12180-9034
518-279-4600 x602 Fax: 518-279-1918
e-mail: dburnham@brittonkill.k12.ny.us
Louis C McIntosh, Superintendent

East Greenbush CSD
29 Englewood Ave, East Greenbush, NY 12061
518-207-2500
Web site: www.egcsd.org
Dr Angela M Guptill, Superintendent

Hoosic Valley CSD
2 Pleasant Ave, Schaghticoke, NY 12154
518-753-4450
Web site: www.hoosickvalley.k12.ny.us
Douglas Kelley, Superintendent

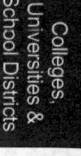

Hoosick Falls CSD
21187 NY Rt 22, PO Box 192, Hoosick Falls, NY 12090-0192
518-686-7012 Fax: 518-686-9060
Kenneth A Facin, Superintendent

Lansingburgh CSD
576 Fifth Ave, Troy, NY 12182-3295
518-233-6850
George Goodwin, Superintendent

North Greenbush Common SD (Williams)
476 N Greenbush Rd, Rensselaer, NY 12144
518-283-6748
Mary Ann Taylor, Superintendent

Rensselaer City SD
25 Van Rensselaer Dr, Rensselaer, NY 12144-2694
518-465-7509
Web site: www.rcsd.k12.ny.us
Sally Ann Shields, Superintendent

Schodack CSD
1216 Maple Hill Rd, Castleton, NY 12033-1699
518-732-2297 Fax: 518-732-7710
Web site: www.schodack.k12.ny.us
Robert Horan, Superintendent

Troy City Enlarged SD
2920 5th Ave, Troy, NY 12180
518-328-5052
Fadhilika Atiba-Weza, Superintendent

Wynantskill UFSD
East Ave, PO Box 345, Wynantskill, NY 12198-0345
518-283-4679 Fax: 518-283-3799
e-mail: chamill@wynantskillufsd.org
Web site: www.wynantskillufsd.org
Christine Hamill, Superintendent

ROCKLAND

Clarkstown CSD
62 Old Middletown Rd, New City, NY 10956
845-639-6419 Fax: 845-639-6488
e-mail: mkeller@ccsd.edu
Web site: www.ccsd.edu
Margaret Keller-Cogan, Superintendent

East Ramapo CSD (Spring Valley)
105 S Madison Ave, Spring Valley, NY 10977
845-577-6011
e-mail: mschwartz@ercsd.k12.ny.us
Web site: www.eram.k12.ny.us
Ira E Oustatcher, Superintendent

Haverstraw-Stony Point CSD
65 Chapel Street, Garnerville, NY 10923
845-942-3002
Web site: www.nrcsd.org
Ileana Eckert

Nanuet UFSD
101 Church St, Nanuet, NY 10954-3000
845-627-9890
e-mail: mmcneil@nufsd.lhric.org
Web site: nanunet.lhric.org
Mark S McNeill, Superintendent

North Rockland CSD
65 Chapel St, Garnerville, NY 10923
845-942-3000 Fax: 845-942-3047
e-mail: ieckert@nrcsd.org
Web site: www.nrcsd.org
Ileana Eckert, Superintendent

Nyack UFSD
13A Dickinson Ave, Nyack, NY 10960-2914
845-353-7015 Fax: 845-353-7019
Web site: www.nyackschools.org
Jason Friedman, Acting Superintendent

Pearl River UFSD
275 E Central Ave, Pearl River, NY 10965-2799
845-620-3900 Fax: 845-620-3927
e-mail: auriemmaf@pearlriver.org
Web site: www.pearlriver.k12.ny.us
Frank V Auriemma, Superintendent

Ramapo CSD (Suffern)
45 Mountain Ave, Hillburn, NY 10931-0935
845-357-7783 Fax: 845-357-5707
e-mail: rmacnaughton@ramapocentral.org
Web site: www.ramapocentral.org
Robert B MacNaughton, Superintendent

South Orangetown CSD
160 Van Wyck Rd, Blauvelt, NY 10913-1299
845-680-1050
Web site: www.socsd.org
Kenneth Mitchell, Superintendent

SARATOGA

Ballston Spa CSD
70 Malta Ave, Ballston Spa, NY 12020-1599
518-884-7195 Fax: 518-885-3201
e-mail: jdragone@bscsd.org
Web site: www.bscsd.org
Joseph P Dragone, Superintendent

Burnt Hills-Ballston Lake CSD
50 Cypress Dr, Glenville, NY 12302
518-399-9141 x5002
e-mail: jschultz@bhbl.org
Web site: www.bhbl.org
James Schultz, Superintendent

Corinth CSD
105 Oak St, Corinth, NY 12822-1295
518-654-2601 Fax: 518-654-6266
Web site: www.corinthcsd.org
Daniel Starr, Superintendent

Edinburg Common SD
4 Johnson Rd, Edinburg, NY 12134-5390
518-863-8412
Randy W Teetz, Superintendent

Galway CSD
5317 Sacandaga Rd, Galway, NY 12074-0130
518-882-1033 Fax: 518-882-5250
Web site: www.galwaycsd.org
Kimberly Labelle, Superintendent

Mechanicville City SD
25 Kniskern Ave, Mechanicville, NY 12118-1995
518-664-5727
Web site: www.mechanicville.org
Michael J McCarthy, Superintendent

Saratoga Springs City SD
3 Blue Streak Blvd, Saratoga Springs, NY 12866-5967
518-583-4709
Web site: www.saratogaschools.org
Janice M White, Superintendent

Offices and agencies generally appear in alphabetical order, except when specific order is requested by listee.

Schuylerville CSD
14 Spring St, Schuylerville, NY 12871-1098
518-695-3255 Fax: 518-695-6491
e-mail: administration@scuylerville.org
Web site: www.schuylervilleschools.org
Ryan C Sherman, Superintendent

Shenendehowa CSD
5 Chelsea Pl, Clifton Park, NY 12065-3240
518-881-0600
e-mail: robioliv@shenet.org
Web site: www.shenet.org
L Oliver Robinson, Superintendent

South Glens Falls CSD
6 Bluebird Rd, South Glens Falls, NY 12803-5704
518-793-9617
Web site: www.sgfallssd.org
Gregory J Aidala, Superintendent

Stillwater CSD
1068 N Hudson Ave, Stillwater, NY 12170-0490
518-373-6100
e-mail: smaziejka@scsd.org
Web site: www.scsd.org
Stanley Maziejka, Superintendent

Waterford-Halfmoon UFSD
125 Middletown Rd, Waterford, NY 12188-1590
518-237-0800 Fax: 518-237-7335
e-mail: tlange@whufsd.org
Web site: www.whufsd.org
Timothy Lange, Superintendent

SCHENECTADY

Duanesburg CSD
133 School Dr, Delanson, NY 12053-0129
518-895-2279 Fax: 518-895-2626
Web site: duanesburg.org
Christine Crowley, Superintendent

Mohonasen CSD
2072 Curry Rd, Schenectady, NY 12303-4400
518-356-8200 Fax: 518-356-8247
e-mail: kspring@mohonasen.org
Web site: www.mohonasen.org
Kathleen A Spring, Superintendent

Niskayuna CSD
1239 Van Antwerp Rd, Schenectady, NY 12309-5317
518-377-4666 x206 Fax: 518-377-4074
e-mail: baughman.k@nisk.k12.ny.us
Web site: www.niskayunaschools.org
Kevin S Baughman, Superintendent

Rotterdam-Mohonasen CSD
2072 Curry Road, Schenectady, NY 12303
518-356-8200
e-mail: kspring@mohonasen.org
Web site: www.mohonasen.org
Kathleen A Spring

Schalmont CSD
4 Sabre Dr, Schenectady, NY 12306-1981
518-355-9200 Fax: 518-355-9203
e-mail: vkelsey@sabrenet.net
Web site: www.schalmont.org
Valerie Kelsey, Superintendent

Schenectady City SD
108 Education Dr, Schenectady, NY 12303-3442
518-370-8100 Fax: 518-370-8173
Web site: www.schenectady.k12.ny.us
John Yagielski, Superintendent

Scotia-Glenville CSD
900 Preddice Pkwy, Scotia, NY 12302-1049
518-382-1215 Fax: 518-386-4336
e-mail: sshwartz@sgcsd.net
Web site: www.sgcsd.neric.org
Susan M Swartz, Superintendent

SCHOHARIE

Cobleskill-Richmondville CSD
155 Washington Ave, Cobleskill, NY 12043-1099
518-234-4032 Fax: 518-234-7721
e-mail: macanl@crcs.k12.ny.us
Web site: www.crcs.k12.ny.us
Lynn Macan, Superintendent

Gilboa-Conesville CSD
132 Wyckoff Rd, Gilboa, NY 12076-9703
607-588-7541 Fax: 607-588-6820
Web site: www.gilboa-conesville.k12.ny.us
Ruth Reeve, Superintendent

Jefferson CSD
1332 St Rt 10, Jefferson, NY 12093-0039
607-652-7821 Fax: 607-652-7806
e-mail: c.mummenthey@jeffersoncs.org
Web site: www.jeffersoncs.org
Carl J Mummenthey, Superintendent

Middleburgh CSD
168 Main St, Middleburgh, NY 12122
518-827-5567 Fax: 518-827-6632
e-mail: michele.weaver@middleburghcsd.org
Web site: www.middleburghcsd.org
Michele R Weaver, Superintendent

Schoharie CSD
136 Academy Drive, PO Box 430, Schoharie, NY 12157-0430
518-295-6679 Fax: 518-295-8178
e-mail: bsherman@schoharie.k12.ny.us
Web site: www.schoharieschools.org
Brian Sherman, Superintendent

Sharon Springs CSD
514 State Rt 20, PO Box 218, Sharon Springs, NY 13459-0218
518-284-2266 Fax: 518-284-9033
e-mail: pgreen@sharonsprings.org
Web site: www.sharonsprings.org
Patterson Green, Superintendent

SCHUYLER

Odessa-Montour CSD
300 College Ave, PO Box 430, Odessa, NY 14869-0430
607-594-3341 Fax: 607-594-3976
e-mail: jframe@gstboces.org
Web site: www.omschools.org
James R Frame, Superintendent

Watkins Glen CSD
303 12th St, Watkins Glen, NY 14891-1699
607-535-3219
e-mail: tphillips@watkinsglenschools.com
Web site: www.watkinsglenschools.com
Tom Phillips, Superintendent

Offices and agencies generally appear in alphabetical order, except when specific order is requested by listee.

SENECA

Romulus CSD
5705 Rt 96, Romulus, NY 14541-9551
866-810-0345 x399
e-mail: mmidey@rcs.k12.ny.us
Web site: www.rcs.k12.ny.us
Michael J Hoose, Superintendent

Seneca Falls CSD
98 Clinton St, Seneca Falls, NY 13148-1090
315-568-5500 Fax: 315-568-0535
e-mail: gmacaluso@sfcs.k12.ny.us
Web site: www.sfcs.k12.ny.us
Robert McKeveny, Superintendent

South Seneca CSD
7263 Main St, Ovid, NY 14521-9586
607-869-9636
e-mail: jnusser@southseneca.k12.ny.us
Web site: www.southseneca.com
Janie L Nusser, Superintendent

Waterloo CSD
109 Washington St, Waterloo, NY 13165
315-539-1500
Web site: www.waterloocsd.org
Terry MacNabb, Superintendent

ST. LAWRENCE

Brasher Falls CSD
1039 State Hwy 11C, Brasher Falls, NY 13613-0307
315-389-5131 Fax: 315-389-5245
e-mail: sputnam@bfcsd.org
Web site: www.bfcsd.org
Stephen Putman, Superintendent

Canton CSD
99 State St, Canton, NY 13617-1099
315-386-8561
Web site: www.ccsdk12.org
William A Gregory, Superintendent

Clifton-Fine CSD
11 Hall Ave, PO Box 75, Star Lake, NY 13690-0075
315-848-3335 x190
Web site: www.cfeagles.org
Denise Dzikowski, Superintendent

Colton-Pierrepont CSD
4921 State Hwy 56, Colton, NY 13625-0005
315-262-2100 Fax: 315-262-2644
e-mail: bregg@cpcs.us
Web site: www.cpcs.k12.ny.us
Martin Bregg, Superintendent

Edwards-Knox CSD
2512 County Hwy 24, PO Box 630, Russell, NY 13684-0630
315-562-8130 Fax: 315-562-2477
Web site: www.ekcsk12.org
Suzanne Kelly, Superintendent

Gouverneur CSD
133 E Barney St, Gouverneur, NY 13642-1100
315-287-4870
e-mail: clarose@gcs.neric.org
Christine J Larose, Superintendent

Hammond CSD
51 S Main St, PO Box 185, Hammond, NY 13646-0185
315-324-5931 x811
Web site: hammond.sllboces.org
Douglas McQueer, Superintendent

Hermon-Dekalb CSD
709 E DeKalb Rd, DeKalb Junction, NY 13630-0213
315-347-3442 Fax: 315-347-3817
e-mail: aadams@mum.neric.org
Web site: www.hdcsk12.org
Ann M Adams, Superintendent

Heuvelton CSD
87 Washington St, PO Box 375, Heuvelton, NY 13654-0375
315-344-2414 Fax: 315-344-2349
e-mail: stodd@heuvelton.k12.ny.us
Web site: www.heuvelton.schoolfusion.us
Susan E Todd, Superintendent

Lisbon CSD
6866 County Rt 10, PO Box 39, Lisbon, NY 13668
315-393-4951 Fax: 315-393-7666
e-mail: woodse@lisbon.k12.ny.us
Web site: lisboncs.schoolwires.com
Erin E Woods, Superintendent

Madrid-Waddington CSD
2582 State Hwy 345, Madrid, NY 13660-0067
315-322-5746
e-mail: lroy@mwcsk12.org
Web site: www.mwcsk12.org
Lynn Roy, Superintendent

Massena CSD
84 Nightengale Ave, Massena, NY 13662-1999
315-764-3700 x3005 Fax: 315-764-3701
e-mail: dhuntley@mcs.k12.ny.us
Web site: www.mcs.k12.ny.us
Roger B Clough, Superintendent

Morristown CSD
408 Gouverneur St, Morristown, NY 13664-0217
315-375-8814
Web site: mcsd.schoolfusion.us
David J Glover, Superintendent

Norwood-Norfolk CSD
PO Box 194, 7852 State Hwy 56, Norwood, NY 13668-0194
315-353-9951
Web site: www.nncsk12.org
Elizabeth Kirnie, Superintendent

Ogdensburg City SD
1100 State St, Ogdensburg, NY 13669-3398
315-393-0900 Fax: 315-393-2767
Web site: www.ogdensburg12.org
Timothy M Vernsey, Superintendent

Parishville-Hopkinton CSD
12 County Rt 47, Parishville, NY 13672-0187
315-265-4642 Fax: 315-268-1309
Web site: phcs.neric.org
Darin P Saiff, Superintendent

Potsdam CSD
29 Leroy St, Potsdam, NY 13676-1787
315-265-2000 Fax: 315-265-2048
e-mail: pbrady@potsdam.k12.ny.us
Web site: www.potsdam.k12.ny.us
Patrick Brady, Superintendent

Offices and agencies generally appear in alphabetical order, except when specific order is requested by listee.

STEUBEN

Addison CSD
7787 State Rt 417, Addison, NY 14801
607-359-2244 Fax: 607-359-2246
e-mail: bstiker@addison.wnyric.org
Betsey A Stiker, Superintendent

Arkport CSD
35 East Ave, PO Box 70, Arkport, NY 14807-0070
607-295-7471 Fax: 607-295-7473
Web site: www.acs.stev.net
Glenn Niles, Superintendent

Avoca CSD
17-29 Oliver St, Avoca, NY 14809-0517
607-566-2221 Fax: 607-566-2398
e-mail: ryochem@avocacsd.org
Richard Yochem, Superintendent

Bath CSD
25 Ellas Ave, Bath, NY 14810-1107
607-776-3301 Fax: 607-776-5021
Web site: www.bathcsd.org
Patrick Kelley, Superintendent

Bradford CSD
2820 Rt 226, Bradford, NY 14815-9602
607-583-4616 Fax: 607-583-4013
e-mail: wfield@bradfordcsd.org
Wendy S Field, Superintendent

Campbell-Savona CSD
8455 County Rt 125, Campbell, NY 14821-9518
607-527-9800 Fax: 607-527-8363
e-mail: khagen@cscsd.org
Web site: www.cscsd.org
Kathy Hagenbuch, Superintendent

Canisteo-Greenwood CSD
84 Greenwood St, Canisteo, NY 14823-1299
607-698-4225 Fax: 607-698-2833
e-mail: jmatteson@cgcsd.org
Web site: www.cgcsd.org
Jeffrey A Matteson, Superintendent

Corning-Painted Post Area SD
165 Charles St, Painted Post, NY 14870-1199
607-936-3704 Fax: 607-654-2735
Michael Ginalski, Superintendent

Hammondsport CSD
PO Box 368, Hammondsport, NY 14840-0368
607-569-5200 Fax: 607-569-5212
e-mail: kbower@hport.wnyric.org
Kyle C Bower, Superintendent

Hornell City SD
25 Pearl St, Hornell, NY 14843-1504
607-324-1302 Fax: 607-324-4060
e-mail: george.kiley@hornellcsd.org
Web site: www.hornellcityschools.com
George Kiley, Superintendent

Jasper-Troupsburg CSD
3769 N Main St, Jasper, NY 14855
607-792-3675 Fax: 607-792-3749
e-mail: chadgroff@jt.wnyric.org
Chad C Groff, Superintendent

Prattsburgh CSD
1 Academy St, Prattsburgh, NY 14873-0249
607-522-3795 Fax: 607-522-6221
e-mail: jrumsey@pratts.wnyric.org
Joseph L Rumsey, Superintendent

Wayland-Cohocton CSD
2350 Rt 63, Wayland, NY 14572
585-728-2211
e-mail: mwetherbee@wccsk12.org
Web site: www.wccsk12.org
Michael J Wetherbee, Superintendent

SUFFOLK

Amagansett UFSD
320 Main St, PO Box 7062, Amagansett, NY 11930-7062
631-267-3572 Fax: 631-267-7504
Web site: www.amagansettschool.org
Eleanor Tritt, Superintendent

Amityville UFSD
150 Park Ave, Amityville, NY 11701-3195
631-598-6520 Fax: 631-598-6516
e-mail: jwilliams@amityvilleufsd.org
Web site: www.amityville.k12.ny.us
John R Williams, Superintendent

Babylon UFSD
50 Railroad Ave, Babylon, NY 11702-2221
631-893-7925
Web site: www.babylon.k12.ny.us
Ellen Best-Laimit, Superintendent

Bay Shore UFSD
75 W Perkal St, Bayshore, NY 11706-6696
631-968-1117 Fax: 631-968-1129
Web site: www.bayshore.k12.ny.us
Evelyn B Holman, Superintendent

Bayport-Blue Point UFSD
189 Academy St, Bayport, NY 11705
631-472-7860 Fax: 631-472-7873
Web site: www.bbpschools.org
Anthony J Annunziato, Superintendent

Brentwood UFSD
52 Third Ave, Brentwood, NY 11717-6198
631-434-2325 Fax: 631-434-6575
Web site: www.brentwood.k12.ny.us
Joseph Bond, Superintendent

Bridgehampton UFSD
2685 Montauk Hwy, PO Box 3021, Bridgehampton, NY 11932-3021
631-537-0271 Fax: 631-537-1030
Web site: www.bridgehampton.k12.ny.us
Lois Favre, Superintendent

Brookhaven-Comsewogue UFSD
290 Norwood Ave, Port Jefferson, NY 11776-2999
631-474-8105 Fax: 631-474-8399
Joseph Rella, Superintendent

Center Moriches UFSD
529 Main Street, Center Moriches, NY 11934
631-878-0052 Fax: 631-878-4326
Web site: www.centermoriches.k12.ny.us
Russell Stewart

Offices and agencies generally appear in alphabetical order, except when specific order is requested by listee.

Central Islip UFSD
50 Wheeler Road, Central Islip, NY 11722-9027
631-348-5112 Fax: 631-348-0366
Web site: www.centralislip.k12.ny.us
Craig Carr, Superintendent

Cold Spring Harbor CSD
75 Goose Hill Rd, Cold Spring Harbor, NY 11724-9813
631-367-5931
Web site: www.csh.k12.ny.us
Judith A Wilansky, Superintendent

Commack UFSD
480 Clay Pitts Rd, East Northport, NY 11731-3828
631-912-2010
e-mail: djames@commack.k12.ny.us
Web site: www.commack.k12.ny.us
Donald James, Superintendent

Connetquot CSD
780 Ocean Ave, Bohemia, NY 11716
631-244-2215 Fax: 631-589-0683
Web site: www.connetquot.k12.ny.us
Alan B Groveman, Superintendent

Copiague UFSD
2650 Great Neck Rd, Copiague, NY 11726-1699
631-842-4015 x501
Web site: www.copiague.k12.ny.us
Charles A Leunig, Superintendent

Deer Park UFSD
1881 Deer Park Ave, Deer Park, NY 11729-4326
631-274-4010
Web site: www.deerparkschools.org
Eva J Demyen, Superintendent

East Hampton UFSD
4 Long Ln, East Hampton, NY 11937
631-329-4100 Fax: 631-329-0109
Web site: www.easthampton.k12.ny.us
Raymond D Gualtieri, Superintendent

East Islip UFSD
1 Craig B Gariepy Ave, Islip Terrace, NY 11752
631-224-2000 Fax: 631-581-1617
e-mail: wchu@eischools.org
Web site: www.eischools.org
Wendell Chu, Superintendent

East Moriches UFSD
9 Adelaide Ave, East Moriches, NY 11940-1320
631-878-0162 Fax: 631-878-0186
e-mail: crusso@emo.ny.k12us.com
Web site: www.eastmoriches.k12.ny.us
Charles Russo, Superintendent

East Quogue UFSD
6 Central Ave, East Quogue, NY 11942
631-653-5210 Fax: 631-653-8644
Web site: www.eastquogue.k12.ny.us
Les Black, Acting Superintendent

Eastport-South Manor CSD
149 Dayton Ave, Manorville, NY 11949
631-874-6720 Fax: 631-878-6308
e-mail: nocero@esmonline.org
Web site: www.esmonline.org
Mark A Nocero, Superintendent

Elwood UFSD
100 Kenneth Ave, Greenlawn, NY 11740-2900
631-266-5402
e-mail: superintendent@elwood.k12.ny.us
Web site: www.elwood.k12.ny.us
Peter C Scordo, Superintendent

Fire Island UFSD
Surf Rd, PO Box 428, Ocean Beach, NY 11770-0428
631-583-5626 Fax: 631-583-5167
e-mail: wchu@fi.k12.ny.us
Web site: www.fi.k12.ny.us
Loretta Ferraro, Superintendent

Fishers Island UFSD
PO Drawer A, Fishers Island, NY 06390
631-788-7444 Fax: 631-788-5532
Web site: www.fischool.com
Charles Meyers, Superintendent

Greenport UFSD
720 Front St, Greenport, NY 11944
631-477-1950 Fax: 631-477-2164
Web site: www.greenport.k12.ny.us
Micahel Comanda, Superintendent

Half Hollow Hills CSD
525 Half Hollow Rd, Dix Hills, NY 11746-5899
631-592-3008
e-mail: superintendent@hhh.k12.ny.us
Web site: www.halfhollowhills.k12.ny.us
Sheldon Karnilow, Superintendent

Hampton Bays UFSD
86 E Argonne Rd, Hampton Bays, NY 11946
631-723-2100 Fax: 631-723-2109
Web site: www.hbschools.us
Lars Clemensen, Superintendent

Harborfields CSD
2 Oldfield Rd, Greenlawn, NY 11740
631-754-5320 x321
e-mail: carasitif@harborfieldscsd.net
Web site: www.harborfieldscsd.net
Frank J Carasiti, Superintendent

Hauppauge UFSD
495 Hoffman Ln, PO Box 6006, Hauppauge, NY 11788
631-761-8208 Fax: 631-265-3649
Web site: www.hauppauge.k12.ny.us
Patricia Sullivan-Kriss, Superintendent

Huntington UFSD
50 Tower St, Huntington Station, NY 11746
631-673-2038
e-mail: jfinello@hufsd.edu
Web site: www.hufsd.edu
John J Finello, Superintendent

Islip UFSD
215 Main St, Islip, NY 11751-3435
631-650-8200 Fax: 631-650-8218
Web site: www.islipufsd.org
Susan Schnebel, Superintendent

Kings Park CSD
101 Church St, Kings Park, NY 11754-1769
631-269-3310
Web site: www.kpcsd.k12.ny.us
Susan Agruso, Superintendent

Offices and agencies generally appear in alphabetical order, except when specific order is requested by listee.

Lindenhurst UFSD
350 Daniel St, Lindenhurst, NY 11757-0621
631-867-3001
Web site: www.lindenhurstschools.org
Richard Nathan, Superintendent

Little Flower UFSD
2460 N Wading River Rd, Wading River, NY 11792
631-929-4300 Fax: 631-929-0303
Web site: www.littleflowerufsd.org
George Grigg, Superintendent

Longwood CSD
35 Yaphank-Mid Isl Rd, Middle Island, NY 11953-2369
631-345-2172 Fax: 631-345-2166
Web site: www.longwood.k12.ny.us
Allan Gerstenlauer, Superintendent

Mattituck-Cutchogue UFSD
385 Depot Ln, PO Box 1438, Cutchogue, NY 11935
631-298-4242 Fax: 631-298-8520
Web site: www.mufsd.com
James McKenna, Superintendent

Middle Country CSD
Eight 43rd St, Centereach, NY 11720-2325
631-285-8005
Web site: www.middlecountry.k12.ny.us
Roberta Gerold, Superintendent

Miller Place UFSD
275 Route 25A, Miller Place, NY 11764-2036
631-474-2700 Fax: 631-331-8832
Web site: www.millerplace.k12.ny.us
Susan Hodun, Superintendent

Montauk UFSD
50 S Dorset Rd, Montauk, NY 11954
631-668-2474 Fax: 631-668-1107
Web site: www.montaukschool.org
J Philip Perna, Superintendent

Mt Sinai UFSD
148 N Country Rd, Mount Sinai, NY 11766-0397
631-870-2554 Fax: 631-473-0905
e-mail: mts@mtsinai.k12.ny.us
Web site: www.mtsinai.k12.ny.us
Dr Anthony J Bonasera, Superintendent

New Suffolk Common SD
7605 New Suffolk Rd, PO Box 111, New Suffolk, NY 11956-0111
631-734-6940 Fax: 631-734-6940
e-mail: superintendent@newsuffolkschool.com
Web site: www.newsuffolkschool.com
Robert Feger, Superintendent

North Babylon UFSD
5 Jardine Pl, North Babylon, NY 11703-4203
631-321-3226
Web site: www.northbabylonschools.net
Patricia Godek, Superintendent

Northport-East Northport UFSD
158 Laurel Ave, Northport, NY 11768-3455
631-262-6604
e-mail: mmcdermott@northport.k12.ny.us
Web site: www.northport.k12.ny.us
Marylou McDermott, Superintendent

Oysterponds UFSD
23405 Main Rd, PO Box 98, Orient, NY 11957
631-323-2410 Fax: 631-323-3713
Web site: www.oysterponds.org
Joan Frisicano, Superintendent

Patchogue-Medford UFSD
241 S Ocean Ave, Patchogue, NY 11772-3787
631-687-6380
e-mail: mmostow@pmschools.org
Web site: www.pmschools.org
Michael Mostow, Superintendent

Port Jefferson UFSD
550 Scraggy Hill Rd, Port Jefferson, NY 11777-1969
631-476-4404
Web site: www.portjeff.k12.ny.us
Max Riley, Superintendent

Quogue UFSD
10 Edgewood Rd, PO Box 957, Quogue, NY 11959-0957
631-653-4285 Fax: 631-653-4864
e-mail: super@quogueschool.com
Web site: www.quogue.k12.ny.us
Richard J Benson, Superintendent

Remsenburg-Speonk UFSD
11 Mill Rd, PO Box 900, Remsenburg, NY 11960-0900
631-325-0203 Fax: 631-325-8439
Web site: www.rsufsd.org
Ronald Masera, Superintendent

Riverhead CSD
700 Osborne Ave, Riverhead, NY 11901
631-369-6717 Fax: 631-369-6718
Web site: www.riverhead.net
Nancy Carney, Superintendent

Rocky Point UFSD
170 Rt 25A, Rocky Point, NY 11778-8401
631-744-1600
Web site: www.rockypointschools.org
Michael Ring, Superintendent

Sachem CSD
245 Union Ave, Holbrook, NY 11741
631-471-1300 Fax: 631-471-1341
Web site: www.sachem.edu
James Nolan, Superintendent

Sag Harbor UFSD
200 Jermain Ave, Sag Harbor, NY 11963-3549
631-725-5300 Fax: 631-725-5330
e-mail: jgratto@sagharborschools.org
Web site: www.sagharborschools.org

Sagaponack Common SD
Main St, PO Box 1500, Sagaponack, NY 11962-1500
631-537-0651 Fax: 631-537-2342
Lee Ellwood, Superintendent

Sayville UFSD
99 Greeley Ave, Sayville, NY 11782
631-244-6510 Fax: 631-244-6504
Web site: www.sayville.k12.ny.us
Walter F Schartner, Superintendent

Shelter Island UFSD
33 North Ferry Rd, PO Box 2015, Shelter Island, NY 11964-2015
631-749-0302 Fax: 631-749-1262
Web site: www.shelterisland.k12.ny.us
Robert Parry, Superintendent

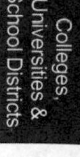

Offices and agencies generally appear in alphabetical order, except when specific order is requested by listee.

Shoreham-Wading River CSD
250B Rt 25A, Shoreham, NY 11786
631-821-8105 Fax: 631-929-3001
Web site: www.swrcsd.org
Harriet Copel, Superintendent

Smithtown CSD
26 New York Ave, Smithtown, NY 11787-3435
631-382-2005 Fax: 631-382-2010
Web site: www.smithtown.k12.ny.us
Edward Ehmann, Superintendent

South Country CSD
189 Dunton Ave, East Patchogue, NY 11772
631-730-1510 Fax: 631-286-6394
Web site: www.southcountry.org
Joseph Cipp Jr, Superintendent

South Huntington UFSD
60 Weston St, Huntington Station, NY 11746-4098
631-812-3070 Fax: 631-425-5362
e-mail: tshea@shufsd.org
Web site: www.shuntington.k12.ny.us
Thomas C Shea, Superintendent

Southampton UFSD
70 Leland Ln, Southampton, NY 11968
631-591-4510 Fax: 631-287-2870
Web site: www.southhampton.k12.ny.us
Richard Boyes, Superintendent

Southold UFSD
420 Oaklawn Ave, PO Box 470, Southold, NY 11971-0470
631-765-5400 Fax: 631-765-5086
Web site: www.southoldufsd.net
David A Gamberg, Superintendent

Springs UFSD
48 School St, East Hampton, NY 11937
631-324-0144 Fax: 631-324-0269
Web site: www.springs.k12.ny.us
Michael Hartner, Superintendent

Three Village CSD
100 Suffolk Ave, Stony Brook, NY 11790
631-730-4010 Fax: 631-474-7784
e-mail: nlederer@3villagecsd.org
Web site: www.threevillagecsd.org
Neil Lederer, Superintendent

Tuckahoe Common SD
468 Magee St, Southampton, NY 11968-3216
631-283-3550 Fax: 631-283-3469
Web site: www.tuckahoe.k12.ny.us
Chris Dyer, Superintendent

Wainscott Common SD
PO Box 79, Wainscott, NY 11975-0079
631-537-1080 Fax: 631-537-6977
Stuart Rachlin, Superintendent

West Babylon UFSD
10 Farmingdale Rd, West Babylon, NY 11704-6289
631-321-3142 Fax: 631-661-5166
Web site: www.wbschools.org
Anthony Cacciola, Superintendent

West Islip UFSD
100 Sherman Ave, West Islip, NY 11795-3237
631-893-3200 Fax: 631-893-3217
Web site: www.wi.k12.ny.us
Richard Simon, Superintendent

Westhampton Beach UFSD
340 Mill Rd, Westhampton Beach, NY 11978
631-288-3800 Fax: 631-288-8351
Web site: www.westhamptonbeach.k12.ny.us
Lynn Schwartz, Superintendent

William Floyd UFSD
240 Mastic Beach Rd, Mastic Beach, NY 11951
631-874-1201 Fax: 631-281-3047
Web site: www.wfsd.k12.ny.us
Paul Casciano, Superintendent

Wyandanch UFSD
1445 MLK Jr Blvd, Wyandanch, NY 11798-3997
631-870-0400 Fax: 631-491-3032
Web site: www.wyandanch.k12.ny.us
Pless Dickerson, Superintendent

SULLIVAN

Eldred CSD
600 Rt 55, Eldred, NY 12732-0249
845-456-1100 Fax: 845-557-3672
e-mail: dufourr@eldred.k12.ny.us
Web site: www.eldredschools.org
Robert Dufour, Superintendent

Fallsburg CSD
115 Brickman Rd, PO Box 124, Fallsburg, NY 12733-0124
845-434-5884 x1215
e-mail: ikatz@fallsburgcsd.net
Web site: www.fallsburg.net
Ivan J Katz, Interim Superintendent

Liberty CSD
115 Buckley St, Liberty, NY 12754-1600
845-292-6990 Fax: 845-292-1164
e-mail: vanyomic@libertyk12.org
Web site: www.libertyk12.org
Michael B Vanyo, Superintendent

Livingston Manor CSD
19 School St, Livingston Manor, NY 12758-0947
845-439-4400 Fax: 845-439-4717
Web site: lmcs.k12.ny.us
Deborah Fox, Superintendent

Monticello CSD
237 Forestburgh Rd, Monticello, NY 12701
845-794-7700 Fax: 845-794-7710
Web site: www.monticelloschools.org
Edward Rhine, Acting Superintendent

Roscoe CSD
6 Academy St, Roscoe, NY 12776-0429
607-498-4126
Web site: roscoe.k12.ny.us
John P Evans, Superintendent

Sullivan West CSD
33 Schoolhouse Rd, Jeffersonville, NY 12748
845-482-4610 x3000
Web site: www.swcsd.org
Kenneth H Hilton, Superintendent

Tri-Valley CSD
34 Moore Hill Rd, Grahamsville, NY 12740-5609
845-985-2296 x5101
Web site: tvcs.k12.ny.us
Thomas W Palmer, Superintendent

TIOGA

Candor CSD
1 Academy St, PO Box 145, Candor, NY 13743-0145
607-659-5010
e-mail: jkisloski@candor.org
Web site: www.candor.org
Jeffrey J Kisloski, Superintendent

Newark Valley CSD
79 Whig St, Newark Valley, NY 13811-0547
607-642-3221
Web site: www.nvcs.stier.org
Ryan Dougherty, Superintendent

Owego-Apalachin CSD
36 Talcott St, Owego, NY 13827-9965
607-687-6224
e-mail: russellw@oacsd.org
Web site: www.oacsd.org
Bill Russell, Superintendent

Spencer-Van Etten CSD
16 Dartts Crossroad, PO Box 307, Spencer, NY 14883
607-589-7100 Fax: 607-589-3010
Web site: www.svecsd.org
Joseph Morgan, Superintendent

Tioga CSD
27 Fifth Ave, Tioga Center, NY 13845-0241
607-687-8001
Web site: www.tiogacentral.org
Scot Taylor, Superintendent

Waverly CSD
15 Frederick St, Waverly, NY 14892-1294
607-565-2841 Fax: 607-565-4997
e-mail: mmcmahon@gstboces.org
Web site: www.waverlyschools.com
Michael W McMahon, Superintendent

TOMPKINS

Dryden CSD
118 Freeville Road, PO Box 88, Dryden, NY 13053
607-844-8694 x601
Web site: www.dryden.k12.ny.us
Sandra R Sherwood, Superintendent

George Junior Republic UFSD
24 McDonald Rd, Freeville, NY 13068-9699
607-844-6343
Web site: www.georgejuniorrepublic.com
J Brad Herman, Superintendent

Groton CSD
400 Peru Rd, Groton, NY 13073-1297
607-898-5301 Fax: 607-898-4647
e-mail: jabrams@groton.cnyric.org
Web site: www.grotoncs.org
James Abrams, Superintendent

Ithaca City SD
400 Lake St, Ithaca, NY 14851-0549
607-274-2101
Web site: www.icsd.k12.ny.us
Luvelle Brown, Superintendent

Lansing CSD
284 Ridge Rd, Lansing, NY 14882
607-533-4294 Fax: 607-533-3602
e-mail: stephen.grimm@lcsd.k12.ny.us
Web site: www.lcsd.k12.ny.us
Stephen L Grimm, Superintendent

Newfield CSD
247 Main St, Newfield, NY 14867-9313
607-564-9955
Web site: www.newfieldschools.org
Cheryl Thomas, Superintendent

Trumansburg CSD
100 Whig St, Trumansburg, NY 14886-9179
607-387-7551 x421
Web site: www.tburg.k12.ny.us
Paula Hurley, Superintendent

ULSTER

Ellenville CSD
28 Maple Ave, Ellenville, NY 12428
845-647-0100 Fax: 845-647-0105
Web site: www.ecs.k12.ny.us
Lisa A Wiles, Superintendent

Highland CSD
320 Pancake Hollow Rd, Highland, NY 12528-2317
845-691-1012 Fax: 845-691-3904
Web site: www.highland-k12.org
Deborah A Haab, Superintendent

Kingston City SD
61 Crown St, Kingston, NY 12401-3833
845-339-3000
Web site: www.kingstoncityschools.org
Gerard M Gretzinger, Superintendent

Marlboro CSD
1510 Route 9W, Suite 201, Marlboro, NY 12542
845-236-5804 Fax: 848-236-5817
Web site: marlboroschools.org
Raymond Castellani, Superintendent

New Paltz CSD
196 Main St, New Paltz, NY 12561-1200
845-256-4020 Fax: 845-256-4025
Web site: www.newpaltz.k12.ny.us
Maria Rice, Superintendent

Onteora CSD
PO Box 300, Boiceville, NY 12412-0300
845-657-6383 Fax: 845-657-9687
e-mail: pmcgill@onteora.k12.ny.us
Web site: onteora.k12.ny.us
Phyllis Spiegel McGill, Superintendent

Rondout Valley CSD
122 Kyserike Rd, PO Box 9, Accord, NY 12404-0009
845-687-2400 Fax: 845-687-9577
Web site: www.rondout.k12.ny.us
Rosario Agostaro, Superintendent

Saugerties CSD
Call Box A, Saugerties, NY 12477
845-247-6500 Fax: 845-246-8364
Seth Turner, Superintendent

Colleges, Universities & School Districts

Offices and agencies generally appear in alphabetical order, except when specific order is requested by listee.

Wallkill CSD
19 Main St, Wallkill, NY 12589
845-895-7101
Web site: www.wallkillcsd.k12.ny.us
William J Hecht, Superintendent

West Park UFSD
2112 Rt 9W, West Park, NY 12493-0010
845-384-6710
Joyce Mucci, Superintendent

WARREN

Bolton CSD
26 Horicon Ave, Bolton Landing, NY 12814-0120
518-644-2400
e-mail: info@boltoncsd.org
Web site: www.boltoncsd.org
Raymond Ciccarelli Jr, Superintendent

Glens Falls City SD
15 Quade St, Glens Falls, NY 12801-2725
518-792-1212
e-mail: tmcgowan@gfsd.org
Web site: www.gfsd.org
Thomas F McGowan, Superintendent

Glens Falls Common SD
120 Lawrence St, Glens Falls, NY 12801-3758
518-792-3231 Fax: 518-792-2557
Ella W Collins, Superintendent

Hadley-Luzerne CSD
273 Lake Ave, Lake Luzerne, NY 12846
518-696-2112 x134
Web site: www.hlcsd.org
Irwin H Sussman, Superintendent

Johnsburg CSD
165 Main St, North Creek, NY 12853-0380
518-251-2921 Fax: 518-251-2562
Web site: www.johnsburgcsd.org
Michael Markwica, Superintendent

Lake George CSD
381 Canada St, Lake George, NY 12845-1197
518-668-5456 Fax: 518-668-2285
Web site: www.lkgeorge.org
Patrick Dee, Superintendent

North Warren CSD
6110 State Rt 8, Chestertown, NY 12817
518-494-3015
Web site: www.northwarren.k12.ny.us
Joseph R Murphy, Superintendent

Queensbury UFSD
429 Aviation Rd, Queensbury, NY 12804-2914
518-824-5602 Fax: 518-793-4476
Web site: www.queensburyschool.org
Douglas W Huntley, Superintendent

Warrensburg CSD
103 Schroon River Rd, Warrensburg, NY 12885-4803
518-623-2861
e-mail: lawsont@wcsd.org
Web site: www.wcsd.org
Timothy D Lawson, Superintendent

WASHINGTON

Argyle CSD
5023 State Rt 40, Argyle, NY 12809-0067
518-638-8243 Fax: 518-638-6373
e-mail: jehring_j@argylecsd.org
Web site: www.argylecsd.org
Jan Jehring, Superintendent

Cambridge CSD
58 S Park St, Cambridge, NY 12816
518-677-8527 Fax: 518-677-3889
Web site: www.cambridgecsd.org
Vincent Canini, Superintendent

Fort Ann CSD
One Catherine St, Fort Ann, NY 12827-5039
518-639-5594 Fax: 518-639-8911
e-mail: mvanburen@fortannschool.org
Web site: www.fortannschool.org
Maureen VanBuren, Superintendent

Fort Edward UFSD
220 Broadway, Fort Edward, NY 12828-1598
518-747-4594 x100
Web site: www.fortedward.org
Jeffery Ziegler, Superintendent

Granville CSD
58 Quaker St, Granville, NY 12832-1596
518-642-1051 Fax: 518-642-2491
Web site: www.granvillecsd.org
Mark Bessen, Superintendent

Greenwich CSD
10 Gray Ave, Greenwich, NY 12834-1107
518-692-9542
Web site: www.greenwichcsd.org
Matthias Donnelly, Superintendent

Hartford CSD
4704 State Rt 149, Hartford, NY 12838-0079
518-632-5931
Web site: www.hartfordcsd.org
Thomas W Abraham, Administrator

Hudson Falls CSD
1153 Burgoyne Ave, Hudson Falls, NY 12839-0710
518-747-2121
e-mail: mdoody@hfcsd.org
Web site: www.hfcsd.org
Mark E Doody, Superintendent

Putnam CSD
126 County Rt 2, PO Box 91, Putnam Station, NY 12861
518-547-8266 Fax: 518-547-9567
e-mail: matthew.boucher@putnamcsd.org
Web site: putnamcsd.org
Matthew Boucher, Superintendent

Salem CSD
41 E Broadway, Salem, NY 12865-0517
518-854-7855
Web site: www.salemcsdnyk-12.org
Kerri Erin Piemme, Superintendent

Whitehall CSD
87 Buckley Rd, Whitehall, NY 12887-3633
518-499-1772
e-mail: jwatson@railroaders.net
Web site: www.railroaders.net
James Watson, Superintendent

WAYNE

Clyde-Savannah CSD
215 Glasgow St, Clyde, NY 14433-1222
315-902-3000
Web site: www.clydesavannah.org
Theresa Pulos, Superintendent

Gananda CSD
1500 Dayspring Ridge, Walworth, NY 14568
315-986-3521
Web site: www.gananda.org
Shawn Van Scoy, Superintendent

Lyons CSD
10 Clyde Rd, Lyons, NY 14489-9371
315-946-2200
e-mail: ramundson@lyonscsd.org
Web site: www.lyonscsd.org
Richard Amundson, Superintendent

Marion CSD
4034 Warner Rd, Marion, NY 14505-0999
315-926-4228
Web site: www.marioncs.org
Kathryn A Wegman, Superintendent

Newark CSD
100 E Miller St, Newark, NY 14513-1599
315-332-3217
e-mail: hhann@newark.k12.ny.us
Web site: www.newark.k12.ny.us
Henry Hann, Acting Superintendent

North Rose-Wolcott CSD
11669 Salter-Colvin Rd, Wolcott, NY 14590-9398
315-594-3141 Fax: 315-594-2352
Web site: www.nrwcs.org
John C Walker, Superintendent

Palmyra-Macedon CSD
151 Hyde Pkwy, Palmyra, NY 14522-1297
315-597-3401
Web site: www.palmac.k12.ny.us
Robert Ike, Superintendent

Red Creek CSD
6815 Church St, PO Box 190, Red Creek, NY 13143-0190
315-754-2010 Fax: 315-754-8169
e-mail: dsholes@rccsd.org
Web site: www.rccsd.org
David G Sholes, Superintendent

Sodus CSD
PO Box 220, Sodus, NY 14551-0220
315-483-5201 Fax: 315-483-4755
e-mail: ssalvaggio@soduscsd.org
Web site: www.soduscsd.org
Susan Kay Salvaggio, Superintendent

Wayne CSD
6076 Ontario Ctr Rd, Ontario Center, NY 14520-0155
315-524-1001
Web site: www.wayne.k12.ny.us
Renee Garrett, Superintendent

Williamson CSD
PO Box 900, Williamson, NY 14589-0900
315-589-9661
e-mail: mehresman@williamsoncentral.org
Web site: www.williamsoncentral.org
Maria Ehresman, Superintendent

WESTCHESTER

Abbott UFSD
100 N Broadway, Irvington, NY 10533-1254
914-591-7428
Web site: www.abbottufsd.org
Harold A Coles, Superintendent

Ardsley UFSD
500 Farm Rd, Ardsley, NY 10502-1410
914-693-6300
Web site: www.ardsleyschools.k12.ny.us
Lauren Allan, Superintendent

Bedford CSD
Fox Lane Campus, PO Box 180, Mt. Kisco, NY 10549
914-241-6010
Web site: www.bedford.k12.ny.us
Jere Hochman, Superintendent

Blind Brook-Rye UFSD
390 North Ridge St, Rye Brook, NY 10573-1105
914-937-3600
Web site: www.blindbrook.org
William J Stark, Superintendent

Briarcliff Manor UFSD
45 Ingham Rd, Briarcliff Manor, NY 10510-2221
914-941-8880 x303
Web site: www.briarcliffschools.org
Jerry Cicchelli, Superintendent

Bronxville UFSD
177 Pondfield Rd, Bronxville, NY 10708-4829
914-395-0500
e-mail: quattrod@bronxville.k12.ny.us
Web site: www.bronxville.lhric.org
David Quattrone, Superintendent

Byram Hills CSD
10 Tripp Ln, Armonk, NY 10504-2512
914-273-4082
e-mail: jtaylor@byramhills.org
Web site: www.byramhills.org
Jacquelyn Taylor, Superintendent

Chappaqua CSD
66 Roaring Brook Rd, Chappaqua, NY 10514-1703
914-238-7200 Fax: 914-238-7231
Web site: www.chappaqua.k12.ny.us/ccsd/
John Chambers, Superintendent

Croton-Harmon UFSD
10 Gerstein St, Croton-on-Hudson, NY 10520-2303
914-271-4793 or 914-271-4713 Fax: 914-271-8685
e-mail: efuhrman@croton-harmonschools.org
Web site: www.croton-harmonschools.org
Edward R Fuhrman Jr, Superintendent

Dobbs Ferry UFSD
505 Broadway, Dobbs Ferry, NY 10522-1118
914-693-1506 Fax: 914-693-1787
e-mail: kapland@dfsd.org
Web site: www.dfsd.org
Debra Kaplan, Superintendent

Eastchester UFSD
580 White Plains Rd, Eastchester, NY 10709
914-793-6130 Fax: 914-793-9006
Web site: www.eastchester.k12.ny.us
Marilyn Terranova, Superintendent

Edgemont UFSD
300 White Oak Ln, Scarsdale, NY 10583-1725
914-472-7768 Fax: 914-472-6846
Web site: www.edgemont.org
Nancy L Taddiken, Superintendent

Elmsford UFSD
98 South Goodwin Ave, Elmsford, NY 10523
914-592-6632
Web site: www.elmsd.org
Barbara Peters, Superintendent

Greenburgh 7 CSD
475 W Hartsdale Ave, Hartsdale, NY 10530-1398
914-761-6000 x3103
Web site: www.greenburgh.k12.ny.us
Ronald L Smalls, Superintendent

Greenburgh Eleven UFSD
Children's Vlg Campus-W, PO Box 501, Dobbs Ferry, NY 10522-0501
914-693-8500
Sandra G Mallah, Superintendent

Greenburgh-Graham UFSD
One S Broadway, Hastings-on-Hudson, NY 10706-3809
914-478-1106
Amy J Goodman, Superintendent

Greenburgh-North Castle UFSD
71 S Broadway, Dobbs Ferry, NY 10522-2834
914-693-4309
Edward Placke, Superintendent

Harrison CSD
50 Union Ave, Harrison, NY 10528-2032
914-630-3021
Web site: www.harrisoncsd.org
Louis N Wool, Superintendent

Hastings-On-Hudson UFSD
27 Farragut Ave, Hastings-on-Hudson, NY 10706-2395
914-478-6200
Web site: www.hastings.k12.ny.us
Timothy P Connors, Acting Superintendent

Hawthorne-Cedar Knolls UFSD
226 Linda Ave, Hawthorne, NY 10532-2099
914-749-2903 Fax: 914-749-2904
Web site: www.hcks.org
Mark K Silverstein, Superintendent

Hendrick Hudson CSD
61 Trolley Rd, Montrose, NY 10548-1199
914-257-5100 Fax: 914-257-5101
e-mail: dmccann@henhudschools.org
Web site: www.henhudschools.org
Daniel McCann, Superintendent

Irvington UFSD
6 Dows Ln, Irvington, NY 10533-1328
914-591-8501
e-mail: kmatusiak@irvingtonschools.k12.ny.us
Web site: www.irvingtonschools.org
Kathleen Matusiak, Superintendent

Katonah-Lewisboro UFSD
PO Box 387, Katonah, NY 10536
914-763-7003 Fax: 914-763-7033
Web site: www.klschools.org
Michael Jumper, Superintendent

Lakeland CSD
1086 Main St, Shrub Oak, NY 10588-1507
914-245-1700
Web site: www.lakelandschools.org
George Stone, Superintendent

Mamaroneck UFSD
1000 W Boston Post Rd, Mamaroneck, NY 10543-3399
914-220-3005
Web site: www.mamkschools.org
Robert Shaps, Superintendent

Mt Pleasant CSD
Westlake Drive, Thornwood, NY 10594
914-769-5500 Fax: 914-769-3733
e-mail: sguiney@mtplcsd.org
Web site: www.mtplcsd.org
Susan Guiney, Acting Superintendent

Mt Pleasant-Blythedale UFSD
95 Bradhurst Ave, Valhalla, NY 10595-1697
914-347-1800 Fax: 914-592-5484
e-mail: ebergman@mpbschools.org
Web site: www.mpbschools.org
Ellen Bergman, Superintendent

Mt Pleasant-Cottage UFSD
1075 Broadway, Pleasantville, NY 10570-0008
914-769-0456 Fax: 914-769-7853
e-mail: nfreimark@mail.mpcsny.org
Web site: www.mpcsny.org
Norman Freimark, Superintendent

Mt Vernon City SD
165 N Columbus Ave, Mount Vernon, NY 10553-1199
914-665-5000
Web site: mtvernoncsd.org
Welton L Sawyer, Superintendent

New Rochelle City SD
515 North Ave, New Rochelle, NY 10801-3416
914-576-4200 Fax: 914-632-4144
e-mail: rorganisciak@nred.org
Web site: www.nred.org
Richard Organisciak, Superintendent

North Salem CSD
230 June Rd, North Salem, NY 10560-1211
914-669-5414
Web site: www.northsalemschools.org
Kenneth Freeston, Superintendent

Ossining UFSD
190 Croton Ave, Ossining, NY 10562
914-941-7700 Fax: 914-941-2794
Web site: www.ossiningufsd.org
Phyllis Glassman, Superintendent

Peekskill City SD
1031 Elm St, Peekskill, NY 10566-3499
914-737-3300 Fax: 914-737-3912
Web site: www.peekskillcsd.org
Lorenzo Licopoli, Superintendent

Pelham UFSD
18 Franklin Pl, Pelham, NY 10803
914-738-3434
Web site: www.pelhamschools.org
Dennis Lauro, Superintendent

Pleasantville UFSD
60 Romer Ave, Pleasantville, NY 10570-3157
914-741-1400 Fax: 914-741-1499
Web site: www.pleasantvilleschools.com
Mary Fox-Alter, Superintendent

Pocantico Hills CSD
599 Bedford Rd, Sleepy Hollow, NY 10591-1215
914-631-2440 Fax: 914-631-3280
e-mail: vdouglas@pocanticohills.org
Web site: www.pocanticohills.org
Valencia Douglas, Superintendent

Port Chester SD
113 Bowman Ave, Port Chester, NY 10573-2851
914-934-7901 Fax: 914-934-0727
Web site: www.portchesterschools.org
Thomas Elliott, Superintendent

Rye City SD
411 Theodore Fremd Ave, South Lobby, Rye, NY 10580-3899
914-967-6100 Fax: 914-967-6957
e-mail: shinee@ryeschools.org
Web site: www.ryeschools.org
Edward J Shine, Superintendent

Rye Neck UFSD
310 Hornidge Rd, Mamaroneck, NY 10543-3898
914-777-5200
e-mail: pmustich@ryeneck.k12.ny.us
Web site: www.ryeneck.k12.ny.us
Peter J Mustich, Superintendent

Scarsdale UFSD
2 Brewster Rd, Scarsdale, NY 10583-3049
914-721-2410
e-mail: mmcgill@scarsdaleschools.k12.ny.us
Web site: www.scarsdaleschools.k12.ny.us
Michael V McGill, Superintendent

Somers CSD
334 Route 202, PO Box 620, Somers, NY 10589
914-277-2400
Web site: www.somers.k12.ny.us
Raymond Blanch, Superintendent

Tarrytown UFSD
200 N Broadway, Sleepy Hollow, NY 10591-2696
914-332-6241 Fax: 914-332-4690
e-mail: hwsmith@tufsd.org
Web site: www.tufsd.org
Howard W Smith, Superintendent

Tuckahoe UFSD
29 Elm St, Tuckahoe, NY 10707
914-337-6600
Web site: www.tuckahoeschools.org
Michael Yazurlo, Superintendent

Valhalla UFSD
316 Columbus Ave, Valhalla, NY 10595-1300
914-683-5040 Fax: 914-683-5075
Web site: valhalla.k12.ny.us
Brenda Myers, Superintendent

White Plains City SD
5 Homeside Ln, White Plains, NY 10605-4299
914-422-2019 or 914-422-2029 Fax: 914-422-2024
Web site: www.wpcsd.k12.ny.us
Dr Christopher P Clouet, Superintendent

Yonkers City SD
1 Larkin Center, Yonkers, NY 10701
914-376-8100
Web site: www.yonkerspublicschools.org
Bernard P Pierorazio, Superintendent

Yorktown CSD
2725 Crompond Rd, Yorktown Heights, NY 10598
914-243-8001
e-mail: rnapolitano@yorktown.org
Web site: www.yorktowncsd.org
Ralph Napolitano, Superintendent

WYOMING

Attica CSD
3338 E Main St, Attica, NY 14011
585-591-2173
Web site: www.atticacs.k12.ny.us
Bryce L Thompson, Superintendent

Letchworth CSD
5550 School Rd, Gainesville, NY 14066
585-493-5450
Web site: www.letchworth.k12.ny.us
Joseph W Backer, Superintendent

Perry CSD
33 Watkins Ave, Perry, NY 14530
585-237-0270 x1000 Fax: 585-237-6172
e-mail: dwhite@perry.k12.ny.us
Web site: www.perry.k12.ny.us
William Stavisky, Superintendent

Warsaw CSD
153 W Buffalo St, Warsaw, NY 14569
585-786-8000 Fax: 585-786-8008
Web site: www.warsaw.k12.ny.us
Valerie K Burke, Superintendent

Wyoming CSD
Route 19, PO Box 244, Wyoming, NY 14591-0244
585-495-6222 Fax: 585-495-6341
Web site: www.wyoming.k12.ny.us
Sandra B Duckworth, Superintendent

YATES

Dundee CSD
55 Water St, Dundee, NY 14837-1099
607-243-5533 Fax: 607-243-7912
Web site: www.dundeecs.org
Kathy Ring, Superintendent

Penn Yan CSD
One School Dr, Penn Yan, NY 14527-1099
315-536-3371
Web site: www.pycsd.org
Thomas A Cox, Acting Superintendent

BOCES DISTRICT SUPERINTENDENTS

Broome-Delaware-Tioga BOCES
435 Glenwood Rd, Binghamton, NY 13905-1699
607-766-3802 Fax: 607-763-3691
e-mail: abuyck@btboces.org
Web site: www.btboces.org
Allen D Buyck

Capital Region (Albany-Schoharie-Schenectady) BOCES
900 Watervliet-Shaker Rd, Albany, NY 12205-2106
518-862-4901 Fax: 518-862-4903
Web site: www.capregboces.org
Charles Dedrick, District Superintendent

Cattaraugus-Allegany-Erie-Wyoming BOCES
Olean Center, 1825 Windfall Rd, Olean, NY 14760-9303
716-376-8246 or 716-376-8200 Fax: 716-376-8452
Web site: www.caboces.org
Tim Cox

Cayuga-Onondaga BOCES
1879 West Genesee Street Road, Auburn, NY 13021-9430
315-253-0361 Fax: 315-252-6493
e-mail: bspeck@cayboces.org
Web site: www.cayboces.org
William S Speck

Champlain Valley Educational Svcs (Clinton-Essex-Warren-Washington)
1585 Military Tpk, PO Box 455, Plattsburgh, NY 12901-0455
518-536-7340
Web site: www.cves.org
Craig L King

Delaware-Chenango-Madison-Otsego BOCES
6678 County Rd #32, Norwich, NY 13815-3554
607-335-1233 Fax: 607-334-9848
Web site: www.dcmoboces.com
Bill Tammaro

Dutchess BOCES
5 Boces Rd, Poughkeepsie, NY 12601-6599
845-486-4800 Fax: 845-486-4981
e-mail: john.pennoyer@dcboces.org
Web site: www.dcboces.org
John C Pennoyer

Eastern Suffolk BOCES
James Hines Administration Ctr, 201 Sunrise Hwy, Patchogue, NY 11772-1868
631-687-3006 Fax: 631-289-2529
e-mail: ezero@esboces.org
Web site: www.esboces.org
Edward J Zero

Erie 1 BOCES
355 Harlem Rd, West Seneca, NY 14224-1892
716-821-7001 Fax: 716-821-7452
Web site: www.e1b.org
Donald A Ogilvie, District Superintendent

Erie 2-Chautauqua-Cattaraugus BOCES
8685 Erie Rd, Angola, NY 14006-9620
716-549-4454 or 800-228-1184 Fax: 716-549-5181
Web site: e2ccb.org
Robert S Guiffreda

Franklin-Essex-Hamilton BOCES
23 Huskie Lane, PO Box 28, Malone, NY 12953-0028
518-483-6420 Fax: 518-483-2178
Web site: www.fehb.org
Stephen T Shafer

Genesee-Livingston-Steuben-Wyoming BOCES
80 Munson St, LeRoy, NY 14482-8933
585-658-7903 Fax: 585-344-7903
Web site: www.gvboces.org
Michael A Glover

Greater Southern Tier BOCES (Schuyler-Chemung-Tioga-Allegany-Steuben)
9579 Vocational Dr, Painted Post, NY 14870
607-654-2283 or 607-962-3175 Fax: 607-962-1579
Web site: www.gstboces.org
Horst Graefe

Hamilton-Fulton-Montgomery BOCES
2755 St Hwy 67, Johnstown, NY 12095
518-736-4300 Fax: 518-736-4301
Web site: www.hfmboces.org
Patrick Michel

Herkimer-Fulton-Hamilton-Otsego BOCES
352 Gros Blvd, Herkimer, NY 13350-1499
315-867-2000 Fax: 315-867-2024
e-mail: ssimpson@herkimer-boces.org
Web site: www.herkimer-boces.org
Sandra A Simpson

Jefferson-Lewis-Hamilton-Herkimer-Oneida BOCES
20104 State Rte 3, Watertown, NY 13601-5560
315-779-7010 Fax: 315-779-7009
e-mail: jboak@mail.boces.com
Web site: www.boces.com
Jack J Boak Jr

Madison-Oneida BOCES
4937 Spring Rd, PO Box 168, Verona, NY 13478-0168
315-361-5510 Fax: 315-361-5595
e-mail: districtsuperintendent@moboces.org
Web site: www.moboces.org
Jacklin G Starks

Monroe 1 BOCES
41 O'Connor Rd, Fairport, NY 14450-1390
585-388-2200 Fax: 585-383-6404
Web site: www.monroe.edu
Frederick A Wille

Monroe 2-Orleans BOCES
3599 Big Ridge Rd, Spencerport, NY 14559-1799
585-352-2400 Fax: 585-352-2442
Web site: www.monroe2boces.org
Jo Anne Antonacci

Nassau BOCES
71 Clinton Rd, PO Box 9195, Garden City, NY 11530-9196
516-396-2500 or 516-396-2200 Fax: 516-997-8742
Web site: www.nassauboces.org
James D Mapes

Oneida-Herkimer-Madison BOCES
PO Box 70, 4747 Middle Settlement Rd, New Hartford, NY 13413-0070
315-793-8561 Fax: 315-793-8541
e-mail: tdorr@oneida-boces.org
Web site: www.oneida-boces.org
Thomas Dorr

Onondaga-Cortland-Madison BOCES
6820 Thompson Rd, PO Box 4754, Syracuse, NY 13221-4754
315-433-2602 Fax: 315-437-4816
e-mail: jcohen@ocmboces.org
Web site: ocmboces.org
Jessica F Cohen

Orange-Ulster BOCES
53 Gibson Rd, Goshen, NY 10924-9777
845-291-0100 Fax: 845-291-0118
e-mail: jpennoyer@ouboces.org
Web site: www.ouboces.org
John Pennoyer

Orleans-Niagara BOCES
4232 Shelby Basin Rd, Medina, NY 14103-9515
585-344-7903 Fax: 585-798-1317
Web site: www.onboces.org
Clark J Godshall

Oswego BOCES
179 County Rte 64, Mexico, NY 13114-4498
315-963-4222 Fax: 315-963-7131
Web site: www.oswegoboces.org
Joseph P Camerino

Otsego Northern Catskills BOCES (Otsego-Delaware-Schoharie-Greene)
1914 County Route 35, PO Box 57, Milford, NY 13807
607-286-7715 Fax: 607-652-1215
Web site: www.oncboces.org
Nicholas Savin, District Superintendent

Putnam-Northern Westchester BOCES
200 Boces Dr, Yorktown Heights, NY 10598-4399
914-245-2700 or 914-248-2302 Fax: 914-248-2308
e-mail: jlanglois@pnwboces.org
Web site: www.pnwboces.org
James T Langlois

Rensselaer-Columbia-Greene (Questar III) BOCES
10 Empire State Blvd, 2nd Fl, Castleton, NY 12033-2692
518-477-8771 Fax: 518-477-9833
Web site: www.questar.org
Charles Dedrick

Rockland BOCES
65 Parrott Rd, West Nyack, NY 10994-0607
845-627-4700 or 845-627-4702 Fax: 845-624-1764
e-mail: mmarsico@rboces.org
Web site: www.rocklandboces.org
Dr. Mary Jean Marsico, Superintendent

Southern Westchester BOCES
17 Berkeley Dr, Rye Brook, NY 10573-1422
914-937-3820 x535 Fax: 914-937-7850
Web site: www.swboces.org
James T Langlois, Superintendent

St Lawrence-Lewis BOCES
139 State Street Rd, PO Box 231, Canton, NY 13617
315-386-4504 Fax: 315-386-3395
e-mail: tburns@sllboces.org
Web site: www.sllboces.org
Thomas R Burns

Sullivan BOCES
6 Wierk Ave, Liberty, NY 12754-2151
845-295-4000 Fax: 845-292-8694
e-mail: lthomas@scboces.org
Web site: www.scboces.org
Lawrence Thomas

Tompkins-Seneca-Tioga BOCES
555 Warren Rd, Ithaca, NY 14850-1833
607-257-1551 x201 Fax: 607-257-2825
e-mail: eodonnell@mail.tstboces.org
Web site: www.tstboces.org
Ellen O'Donnell

Ulster BOCES
175 Rte 32 North, New Paltz, NY 12561-1034
845-255-1400 or 845-255-3040 Fax: 845-255-7942
e-mail: lthomas@scboces.org
Web site: www.ulsterboces.org
Lawrence Thomas

Washington-Saratoga-Warren-Hamilton-Essex BOCES
1153 Burgoyne Ave, Ste 2, Fort Edward, NY 12828-1134
518-746-3310 or 518-581-3310 Fax: 518-746-3319
e-mail: jdexter@wswheboces.org
Web site: www.wswheboces.org
James P Dexter

Wayne-Finger Lakes BOCES
131 Drumlin Ct, Newark, NY 14513-1863
315-332-7284 Fax: 315-332-7425
e-mail: cmurray@wflboces.org
Web site: www.wflboces.org
Joseph J Marinelli, District Superintendent

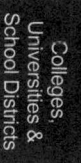

Western Suffolk BOCES
507 Deer Park Rd, PO Box 8007, Huntington Station, NY 11746-9007
631-549-4900 x222 Fax: 631-623-4996
e-mail: centraladmin@wsboces.org
Web site: www.wsboces.org
Thomas Rogers, Interim Superintendent

Section 8: BIOGRAPHIES

Executive Branch 605
NY State Senate 606
NY State Assembly 618
US Senate: New York Delegation 644
US House of Representatives: New York Delegation 645

BIOGRAPHIES

EXECUTIVE BRANCH

ANDREW M CUOMO (D)

Andrew M Cuomo was elected New York's 56th governor in 2010, and was re-elected on November 4, 2014. As governor, Cuomo has presided over passage of the state's first ever property tax cap, signed the marriage equality law that legalized gay marriage, and banned hydraulic fracturing, also called fracking, in New York. Prior to his election as governor, Cuomo served four years as New York's Attorney General, bringing national reform to the student loan industry, uncovering health insurance fraud, and making the Internet safer for children. His investigations ended decades of government corruption in New York's pension system. In 1997, President Clinton appointed Cuomo as Secretary of Housing and Urban Development (HUD). Under Cuomo's leadership, HUD earned the 'Innovations in American Government Award' from Harvard University's Kennedy's School of Government and the Ford Foundation three times. While in office, he brought over 2,000 anti-discrimination cases across the country. Cuomo established Housing Enterprise for Less Privileged (HELP) in 1986, which became the nation's largest private provider of transitional and low-income housing. Based on his pioneering work, he was appointed in 1991 by New York City Mayor David Dinkins to lead the New York City Commission on the Homeless. Cuomo worked as an assistant district attorney in Manhattan and at a NYC law firm after graduating from Fordham University in 1979 and Albany Law School in 1982. He is the son of former New York Gov. Mario Cuomo, and has three daughters, twins Mariah and Cara, and Michaela.

LT. GOV. KATHLEEN C HOCHUL, (D)

Kathleen C. Hochul was elected New York's 77th Lieutenant Governor on November 4, 2014, and inaugurated January 1, 2015. She previously served as a Group Vice President for Strategic Relationships at M&T Bank, and was a liaison for community issues and key economic development projects. She served two years in Congress, from 2011 to 2013, elected from New York's 26th Congressional District. Prior to that time, she was the Erie County Clerk from 2007 to 2011. Her public service also includes 14 years as a Hamburg Town Councilmember. An attorney by training, she was in private practice early in her career, working for a large Washington D.C. firm as well as a major corporation. She then served as legal counsel and legislative assistant to Congressmen John LaFalce (D-NY) and NY Sen. Daniel Patrick Moynihan. With her mother and aunt, she established a transitional home for victims of domestic violence called Kathleen Mary House, and also co-founded the Village Action Coalition to help local business compete with big box stores. She and her husband, Bill, are parents to a daughter and son.

THOMAS P DINAPOLI (D)

New York State Comptroller Thomas P DiNapoli became New York State's 54th Comptroller in 2007. DiNapoli has instilled reforms to make government more effective, efficient and ethical, and has pushed for increased transparency and accountability. As trustee of New York State's $176.8 billion pension fund, DiNapoli has imposed controls including new reporting requirements on investments, fees and other information; barring investment firms contributing to his campaign from doing business with the state pension; and creating opportunities for minority and women fund managers. He has completed a five-year school accountability project that audited all 733 school districts, and launched a fiscal monitoring system to rate communities on their fiscal condition and sending an early warning to those in trouble. Prior to becoming State Comptroller, DiNapoli represented northwestern Nassau County in the New York State Assembly for nearly 20 years. At age 18, he was elected to the Mineola Board of Education He is a lifelong resident of Nassau County, and graduated from Hofstra University and holds a master's degree in management and urban policy from The New School University.

ERIC T SCHNEIDERMAN (D)

Eric T Schneiderman was elected the 65th Attorney General of New York State on November 2, 2010. A key priority is ensuring one set of rules applies to all, regardless of wealth or power. He used funds recovered from drug traffickers to pay for bulletproof vests for local police officers when federal funding was cut. He created the Homeownership Protection Program, which has served 24,000 homeowners at risk of foreclosure. He was active in securing a $13 billion settlement with JP Morgan Chase for their role in the housing crisis. In addition, Attorney General Schneiderman created the Community Overdose Prevention program, a $5 million plan to equip law enforcement agencies with naloxone, which can immediately stop a heroin overdose. Before becoming Attorney General, Schneiderman served in the New York State Senate as a reformer, which included chairing the committee to expel a corrupt senator for the first time in modern history. Prior to that time he was an attorney in private practice. He is a graduate of Amherst College and Harvard Law School, and the father of one.

NEW YORK STATE SENATE

JOSEPH P ADDABBO JR (D)
15th - Part of Queens County

159-53 102nd Street, Howard Beach, NY 11414
718-738-1111/addabbo@nysenate.gov

66-85 73rd Place, Middle Village, NY 11379
718-497-1630

88-08 Rockaway Beach Blvd. Room 311, Rockaway Beachn, NY 11693
718-318-0194

188 State Street Room 613, Legislative Office Building, Albany, NY 12247
518-455-2322

Joseph Addabbo Jr. was most recently elected to the New York Senate in 2014, having first been elected in 2008. He carries on the tradition of public service of his father, Congressman Joseph P. Addabbo, Sr. Addabbo's district includes all or part of the following communities: Broad Channel, Elmhurst, Forest Hills, Glendale, Hamilton Beach, Kew Gardens, Kew Gardens Hills, Maspeth, Middle Village, Ozone Park, Rego Park, Richmond Hill, Ridgewood, South Ozone Park, Woodhaven, Woodside, and the Rockaways. Addabbo, a lifelong resident of Queens, is the ranking member of the standing committee on racing, gaming and wagering, as well as veterans, homeland security and military affairs. He also sits on the following standing committees: aging; civil service; environmental conservation; and labor. He sat on the Senate Bipartisan Task Force on Hurricane Sandy, which impacted his district, to help the community recover from the devastating storm. In addition to his legislative duties, Addabbo sponsors and organizes events for his constituency ranging from job fairs to health screenings. He formerly chaired the Senate Elections Committee and worked to pass ethics reform and to force large companies to disclose their information about money they spend to influence elections. In addition, Addabbo opposes hydraulic fracking. Addabbo practiced law for 10 years at Addabbo and Greenberg. In 2001, he was elected to the New York City Council and served for eight years and secured millions of dollars in funding for improvements in infrastructure, school technology, and senior and youth services. Joseph Addabbo graduated from St. John's University and Touro Law School. He is married with two daughters.

FRED AKSHAR (R)
52 - Binghamton and the Southern Tier

44 Hawley Street, Room 1607, Binghamton, NY 13901
607-773-8771/akshar@nysenate.gov

Legislative Office Building, Room 805, Albany, NY 12247
518-455-2677

Fred Akshar was sworn into office as a New York State Senator for the 52nd District on November 3, 2015. As a State Senator, Fred's priorities are strengthening the Southern Tier economy by helping small businesses succeed and create jobs, battling drug addiction and making our communities safer, as well as fighting for a fair shake from Albany. Fred serves as Chair of the Elections Committee in the Senate. He also serves on the Banks, Cities, Codes, Consumer Protection, Crime Victims, Crime and Corrections and Labor Committees and as a member of the Senate Rural Resources Commission. Fred lives in Colesville with his partner Kate.

GEORGE AMEDORE (R)
46 - Montgomery, Ulster, Greene

20 Park Street Room 121, Fonda, NY 12068
518-853-3401/Amedore@nysenate.gov

721 Broadway, Suite 100, Kingston, NY 12407
845-331-3810

George Amedore was elected to the New York State Senate in 2014. He chairs the Committee on Alcoholism and Drug Abuse and the Heroin Task Force. In addition, he sits on the following standing committees: banks; consumer protection; elections; judiciary; social services; and veterans, homeland security and military affairs. Sen. Amedore previously served in the New York State Assembly, where he worked to create a property tax cap and also aided communities impacted by the floods that followed Tropical Storms Irene and Lee. His family business is Amedore Homes, which has built more than 3,500 homes around the Capital Region. He is the married father of three.

TONY AVELLA (D)
11th - Part of Queens County

38-50 Bell Boulevard Suite C, Bayside, NY 11361
718-357-3094/avella@nysenate.gov

Room 902, LOB, Albany, NY 12247
518-455-2210

Tony Avella was first elected to the New York State Senate in 2010. In 2014, he joined the Independent Democratic Conference, five Democratic senators working toward efficiency and bipartisanship in the Senate. He chairs the Ethics Committee and vice-chairs the environmental conservation committee. He sits on the following committees: banks; cultural affairs, tourism, parks and recreation; education; housing, construction and community development; insurance; judiciary; and transportation. The former chair of the Social Services Committee, Avella now chairs the Senate Task Force on the Delivery of Social Services to New York City, aimed at improving access to social services programs. In 2015, he spearheaded legislation to bring transparency to the budgetary process at the Queens Public Library, as well as changes to its leadership and organization. Avella is also a noted opponent of hydraulic fracking, and is fighting against increased airplane noise in Queens and the city.

Prior to being elected to the Senate, Avella served as an aide to New York City Council Member Peter Vallone, Sr., to Mayors Koch and Dinkins and as Chief of Staff to the late State Senator Leonard Stavisky and to State Senator Toby Stavisky. In 2001, he was elected to Council, where he served as Chair of the Zoning and Franchises Committee. He was also the founder and Chair of the first Italian-American Caucus of the City Council. Avella graduated from Hunter College. He is married and resides in Whitestone, Queens.

JOHN J BONACIC (R-C-IP)
42nd - Sullivan County, Parts of Delaware, Orange and Ulster counties

201 Dolson Avenue, Suite F, Middletown, NY 10940
845-344-3311/bonacic@nysenate.gov

111 Main Street, Delhi, NY 13753
607-746-6675

John Bonacic was first elected to the New York State Senate in 1998 and was most recently re-elected in 2014. He chairs the Senate Judiciary Committee, as well as the Racing, Gaming and Wagering Committee. In addition he serves on the following standing committees: alcoholism and drug abuse; banks; children and families; cultural affairs, tourism, parks and recreation; finance; housing, construction and community development, and rules. Prior to his election to the Senate, he served seventeen years as an Orange County Legislator, including as Chairman. In addition, he served as Assistant District Attorney for Orange County. In 1990, Bonacic was elected to the New York State Assembly, where he served until his election to the Senate. His Senate legislative achievements include sponsoring the Women's Health and Wellness Act, which grants women equality in healthcare services covered by insurance. He also has negotiated agreements that kept two rural hospitals in his district open, and negotiated the re-opening of Tri-Town Regional Hospital. He also led the effort to affiliate Catskill Regional Medical Center with the Orange Regional Medical Center, and created a public-private partnership to improve the Catskill Regional Medical Center's emergency room services. In a prior role as chairman of the Senate Committee on Housing, Construction, and Community Development he sponsored legislation that allowed for the creation of thousands of new housing opportunities. Bonacic holds an undergraduate degree from Iona College and a JD from Fordham Law School. He and his wife have two children and three grandchildren.

PHILIP M. BOYLE (R)
4th - Part of Suffolk County

69 W Main Street Suite B, Bay Shore, NY 11706
631-665-2311
/pboyle@nysenate.gov

Philip Boyle was elected to the New York State Senate in 2012. He is chairman of the Commerce, Economic Development and Small Business Committee. In addition, he is a member of the following standing committees: codes; consumer protection; housing, construction and community development; local government; and racing, gaming and wagering. Prior to his election to the Senate, Boyle served in the New York State Assembly from 1994-2002, and again starting in 2006. He also served many years as a senior congressional aide in Washington, D.C. to the late U.S. Rep. Frank Horton as legislative director, then as campaign manager and chief of staff to former U.S. Rep. Frank Lazio. He is a founding partner in the law firm of Steinberg & Boyle LLC, and is now an attorney with the law firm of Cronin, Cronin, Harris and O'Brien, PC. He is active in his community, including as a volunteer firefighter for the Great River Fire Department. He holds a B.A. from the University of North Carolina/Chapel Hill, a JD from Albany Law School, and a MPA from the Rockefeller College of Public Affairs and Policy at the University of Albany. He is married and the stepfather to two.

NEIL D BRESLIN (D-IP-WF)
44th - Parts of Albany and Rensselaer counties

172 State Street, Room 414, Capitol, Albany, NY 12247
518-455-2225/breslin@nysenate.gov

Neil Breslin was first elected to the New York State Senate in 1996. He sits on the following standing committees: banks; education; finance; higher education; insurance; judiciary; and rules. Breslin has been an associate or partner in law firms, and currently is of counsel to the firm of Hiscock & Barclay. He is an active member of the New York State Bar Association, as well as the National Conference of Insurance Legislators (NCOIL), where he is President of the Executive Committee and former chair of the State/Federal Relations Committee. His civic involvement includes serving for many years on the board of Arbor House, a women's residence facility, including seven years as its president. In addition, he has been the attorney for St Anne's Institute in Albany. The Albany native graduated from Fordham University with a BS degree in Political Science. He received his JD from the University of Toledo in Toledo, Ohio. His is married with three children.

DAVID CARLUCCI (D-WF)
38th - Parts of Rockland and Westchester counties

95 South Middletown Road, Nanuet, NY 10954
845-623-3627/carlucci@nysenate.gov

David Carlucci was first elected to the New York State Senate 2010. He is the Independent Democratic Conference Whip, and chairs the Senate Committee on Social Services. In addition, he sits on the following committees: alcoholism and drug abuse; energy and telecommunications; infrastructure and capital investment; insurance; investigations and government operations; mental health and developmental disabilities; racing, gaming and wagering; rules, transportation; and veterans, homeland security and military affairs. He formerly co-chaired the Administrative Regulations Review Commission. He formerly chaired the Senate Mental Health and Developmental Disabilities Committee, where he worked to restore key funding to provide services and assistance to this population. Prior to being elected to the Senate, Carlucci served three terms as Town Clerk of Clarkstown in Rockland County where he digitized hundreds of thousands of records and created a mobile office that took town clerk services to residents. He graduated from Rockland Community College and holds a B.S. from Cornell University. He is a married father of one and resides in Clarkstown.

LEROY COMRIE (D)
14th- Southeast Queens

205-20 Jamaica Avenue 2nd Floor, Hollis, NY 11423
718-454-0162/ Comrie@nysenate.gov

Leroy Comrie was elected to the New York State Assembly in 2014 to represent a Queens district that includes portions of Jamaica, Cambria Heights, Queens Village, Hollis, St. Albans, Laurelton, Jamaica Estates, Briarwood, and Kew Gardens. He is Ranking Minority Member of the Consumer Protection Committee and the Elections Committee. He also sits on the following committees: civil service and pensions; judiciary; racing, gaming & wagering; veterans, homeland security & military affairs.

Prior to his election, he was Deputy Majority Leader of the New York City Council and Chairman of the Queens Delegation, where his legislative achievements include increasing tax and property exemptions for seniors and instituting the city's first foreclosure prevention program. He was also President of his local Community School Board. The South Queens native attended the University of Bridgeport and is the married father of two.

THOMAS D CROCI (R)
3rd - Part of Suffolk County

250 Veterans Memorial Highway NYS Office Building, Room 2a-1
Hauppauge, NY 11788
631-361-3356
/croci@nysenate.gov

Tom Croci was elected to the New York State Senate in 2014. He chairs the Committee on Veterans, Homeland Security and Military Affairs, and sits on the following committees: alcoholism and drug abuse; civil service and pensions; energy and telecommunications; higher education; and infrastructure and capital investment. The former Islip Town Supervisor is himself a veteran, having received a commission from the Navy Officer Candidate School in Pensacola, Fla., and having spent more than eight years on active duty. He rose to the rank of Commander and served active duty tours in the Arabian Gulf, Afghanistan, and in the Office of Naval Intelligence. He ended his active duty as Senior Duty Office in the White House Situation Room, National Security Council, Executive Office of the President where he supported the President and National Security Advisor. He then was appointed by President Bush to serve on the Homeland Security Council Staff and the Obama Administration requested that he stay on the Presidential Transition Team. He went back to active duty to Afghanistan with a Navy SEAL team. In 2013 he was mobilized again to active duty. He returned home to Long Island in 2014. He and his family support local charitable causes and the Senator is President of the Tom & Jo-Ann Croci Foundation - named in memory of his parents - to provide educational scholarships and grants to support youth. Sen. Croci holds a BS from James Madison University, and graduated from the The New York Law School.

JOHN A DEFRANCISCO (R)
50th - Most of Onondaga County

333 East Washington St, 800 State Office Bldg, Syracuse, NY 13202
315-428-7632/jdefranc@senate.state.ny.us

416 Capitol; Albany, NY 12247
518-455-3511

John A DeFrancisco was elected to the New York State Senate in 1992 and is the Chairman of the Senate Finance Committee, a position that gives him a key role in reviewing the governor's budget proposals and developing Senate budget priorities. He formerly chaired the Senate Judiciary Committee, of which he remains a member. He is also a member of the following standing committees: banks; cities; codes; crime victims, crime and correction; and labor. His long Senate career includes advocating for constituents in areas such as limiting the use of eminent domain, and creating a residential property tax exemption for Syracuse in an effort to alleviate the problem of vacant homes in the city. In 2014, his "Vince's Law" legislation, named for a constituent killed by a drunk driver with multiple prior DWI-related convictions, became law. It strengthened the law by allowing stronger penalties for people with multiple DWI convictions. He also backed legislation to provide for the Amber Alert System in New York. An attorney by profession, DeFrancisco worked in a New York City law firm, an Assistant District Attorney in Onondaga County and a Judge Advocate in the U.S. Air Force before going into private practice for good. He was an adjunct professor of law from 1978-1990 at Syracuse University College of Law and currently is of counsel to the DeFrancisco & Falgitano Law Firm. Prior to his election to the Senate, he served eleven years on the Syracuse Common Council. He holds a B.S. from Syracuse University's College of Engineering and a J.D. from Duke University. He is married with three children and eight grandchildren.

RUBÉN DÍAZ, SR (D)
32nd - Part of Bronx County

900 Rogers Place, Bronx, NY 10459
718-991-3161/diaz@nysenate.gov

188 State Street Room 606, LOB, Albany, NY 12247
518-455-2511

Reverend Rubén Díaz was elected to the New York State Senate in 2002 in the South Bronx, including the communities of Castle Hill, Longwood, Melrose, Morrisania, Parkchester, West Farms and Concourse Village. He sits on the following standing committees: aging; banks; finance, investigations and government operations; judiciary; and transportation. As State Senator, Reverend Díaz continues to work hard to improve economic opportunities, housing, health care, and education for the people of the Bronx. Prior to his election, he served on the New York City Council. Born in Bayamón, Puerto Rico, he served in the US Army before moving to New York City in 1965. In 1978, he became an ordained Minister of the Church of God. In 1977, Díaz founded, and until 2001 served as the Executive Director for, the Christian Community Benevolent Association Inc. He is also founder and pastor of the Christian Community Neighborhood Church. Díaz holds a B.A. from Herbert H. Lehman College, and a theological degree from Damascus Bible Institute. He is married with three children; one of his children is Bronx Borough President Rubén Díaz, Jr. He also has six grandchildren.

MARTIN M DILAN (D)
18th - Part of Kings County

786 Knickerbocker Ave, Brooklyn, NY 11207
718-573-1726/dilan@senate.state.ny.us

188 State Street Room 711B, LOB, Albany, NY 12247
518-455-2177

Martin M Dilan was first elected to the New York State Senate in 2002. His North Brooklyn district includes the communities of Bushwick, Williamsburg, Greenpoint, Cypress Hills, City-Line, East New York, Bedford-Stuyvesant, and Brownsville. Senator Dilan is the Assistant Minority Leader for Policy and Administration in the Senate's Democratic Conference. He sits on the following standing committees: civil service and pensions; elections; energy and telecommunications; finance; infrastructure and capital investment; judiciary; labor; rules; and transportation. He is the former Assistant Minority Leader of Conference Operations, Chairman of the Minority Conference, and Senior Assistant Majority Leader. His legislative achievements include fighting to form a non-partisan redistricting process as part of his membership on the Legislative Task Force on Demographic Research and Reapportionment, which he formerly co-chaired.

Prior to his election to the Senate, Dilan was a member of the New York City Council for ten years. He also served as a member of Community School Board #32 for fourteen years, seven as the Chair. He served as a Legislative Assistant for the US House of Representatives, as a Democratic District Leader, and as a Democratic State Committeeman. He attended a special baccalaureate degree program at Brooklyn College, and married with three children and two grandchildren. His son, Erik, is a state Assemblyman.

ADRIANO ESPAILLAT (D-WF)
31st - Part of New York County

5030 Broadway Suites 701 and 702, New York, NY 10034
212-544-0173/espailla@nysenate.gov

Room 513 LOB, Albany, NY 12247
518-455-2041

Andriano Espaillat was elected to the Senate in November 2010, where he represents a district that stretches from Manhattan's Upper West Side through Washington Heights and includes Riverdale, Marble Hill, and Hamilton Heights. He serves on the following committees: codes; environmental conservation; finance; higher education; housing, construction, and community development; insurance; judiciary; and rules. He is the top-ranking Democrat on the Senate Housing Committee, formerly chaired the Veterans Affairs Committee and the Small Businesses Committee, and chairs the Senate Puerto Rican/Latino Caucus. In addition, he is a member of Gov. Cuomo's Minority and Women-Owned Business Enterprise Team. Espaillat's legislative accomplishments include enacting legislation supporting over 40,000 livery drivers by extending protections from violent crimes and inclusion of the drivers in the Workers' Compensation benefits program. He also endorsed legislation allowing 35,000 daycare providers to organize and collectively bargain.

The Dominican Republic-born Espillat became the first Dominican-American elected to a state legislature when he was elected to the New York State Assembly in 1996. He formerly worked as the Director of Project Right Start, a Robert Woods Johnson Foundation-funded program to educate the parents of pre-school children to combat substance abuse, and as Director of the Washington Heights Victims Services Community Office. He also was a Manhattan Court Services Coordinator for the NYC Criminal Justice Agency, a subcontractor to the city. He holds a B.S. from Queens College and has completed post graduate courses in public administration at NYU and the Rutgers University Leadership for Urban Executives Institute. He is the married father of two.

HUGH T FARLEY (R-C-I)
49th - St. Lawrence, Hamilton, Clinton County, Fulton Counties, Saratoga County

199 Milton Avenue Suite 4, Ballston Spa, NY 12020
518-885-1829/farley@nysenate.gov

33-41 East Main Street City Hall, Johnstown, NY 12095
518-762-3733

188 State Street Room 711, LOB, Albany, NY 12247
518-455-2181

Senator Farley was elected to the New York State Senate in 1976 and is Vice President Pro Tempore. He is vice-chair of the Senate Committee on Banks and a member of the following committees: education; ethics; health; finance; rules; and social services. He has previously held a number of leadership positions, including Majority Whip, and has chaired the Aging, Banks, and Environmental Conservation committees. He has also been the Senate Chair of the General Government/Local Assistance budget conference committee, and Chair of the Senate Majority Program Development Committee. He also served as Chair of the Senate Subcommittee on Libraries, thereby sponsoring nearly every piece of significant library legislation from 1978 through 2008. He has backed legislation that defends personal privacy rights, and developed the Schenectady Metroplex law to help the renewal of industrial cities through public and private cooperation. He was a faculty member in the School of Business of the University of Albany and was named a professor emeritus of business law in 2000. First elected to public office in 1970, Senator Farley originally served as a Councilman and, later, Majority Leader in the Town of Niskayuna. He served in the U.S. Army in Germany. He graduated from Mohawk Valley Community College, holds a B.S. from the University of Albany; and holds a J.D. from the American University School of Law. He is married and the father of three.

SIMCHA FELDER (D)
17th - Parts of Brooklyn

1412 Avenue J, Suite. 2E, Brooklyn, NY 11230
718-253-2015

Simcha Felder was first elected to the New York State Senate in 2012. His Brooklyn district includes the neighborhoods of Midwood, Flatbush, Borough Park, Kensington, Sunset Park, Madison and Bensonhurst. He chairs the Children and Families Committee, as well as the Taskforce on the Delivery of Social Services for New York City. In addition, he is a member of the following committees: aging; commerce, economic development and small business; health; infrastructure and capital investment; and mental health and developmental disabilities. His legislative achievements include legislation that allows parents of special education children to more easily receive funding for their child's schooling. Professionally, he is a CPA and has been a professor of management at Touro College and CUNY's Brooklyn College. He was Deputy Comptroller for Budget, Accounting, Administration and Information Technology in the New York City Comptroller's Office. He also has worked for the New York State Assembly and as a tax auditor for the New York City Dept. of Finance. He also held previous elective office as a member of the New York City Council, where he chaired two committees. Felder holds an MBA from Baruch College. He and his family live close to the home where Felder was raised.

JOHN J FLANAGAN (R-C-I)
2nd - Part of Suffolk County

260 Middle Country Rd, Suite. 102, Smithtown, NY 11787
631-361-2154/flanagan@nysenate.gov

John J Flanagan was first elected to the New York State Senate in 2002 to a district that includes the town of Smithtown and portions of the towns of Brookhaven and Huntington. On May 11, 2015, he was elected Temporary President and Majority Leader of the Senate. He chaired the Committee on Education, and also serves on the following committees: codes; corporations, authorities and commissions; energy and telecommunications; finance; higher education; insurance; judiciary; rules; and veterans, homeland security and military affairs. In his role on the education committee, he has supported the Safe Schools Against Violence in Education Act, and worked to permanently extend the Child Safety Zone law that gives otherwise ineligible children access to bus service. He recently was instrumental in securing nearly a billion dollars in additional aid for New York school districts. He also sponsored a bill, signed into law in 2012, that ensures that mammography reports tell women their breast density so they may pursue other screening options. He served in the New York State Assembly for 16 years prior to his election to the senate, and was Deputy Minority Whip for one year. The Hamilton-raised Flanagan holds a B.A. from the College of William and Mary and a J.D. from the Touro Law School. He and his wife are parents to three. Flanagan is the son of the late New York State Assemblyman John Flanagan.

RICH FUNKE (R)
55th District - Monroe County, Ontario County

230 Packett's Landing, Fairport, NY 14450
585-223-2800
/Funke@nysenate.gov.

Rich Funke was first elected to the New York State Senate in 2014. He is Chair of the Committee on Elections, and also sits on the following committees: aging; cities; commerce, economic development and small business; consumer protection; environmental conservation; and higher education. He is a well-known broadcaster in the area, having retired in 2012 after a 44-year career that included many years at NEWS10 NBC where he went from the sports desk to the anchor chair. The Batavia native started out in local radio and then went to Miami, Fl., before returning to Rochester. He also has done play by play for the Rochester Knighthawks and Amerks, as well as local college and high school football and basketball games. His civic work includes co-hosting the annual telethon for Golisano Children's Hospital at Strong, serving on the boards of Cancer Action and Ronald McDonald House, and hosting a monthly radio show for Camp Good Days and Special Times. He holds a bachelor's degree in business from Adelphi University and has been married to his wife, Patricia, for 43 years.

PATRICK M GALLIVAN (R-C-IP)
59th - Wyoming, Livingston and Ontario Counties and Part of Erie County

2721 Transit Rd, Suite 116, Elma, NY 14059
716-656-8544
gallivan@nysenate.gov

143 North Main Street Room 103, Warsaw, NY 14569
585-786-2187

Livingston County Government Center, 6 Court Street, Rm 304, Geneseo, NY 14454
585-243-6929

900 Jefferson Rd., Ste 202, Henrietta, NY 14623
585-272-1032

Patrick M Gallivan was elected to the New York State Senate in 2010. He chairs the Crime Victims, Crime and Correction Committee, and also sits on the following committees: agriculture; codes; commerce, economic development and small business; elections; finance; higher education; housing, construction, and community development; infrastructure and capital investment; labor; and transportation. During his first term in the Senate, Gallivan drafted and introduced more than 20 bills that were signed into law by Governor Andrew Cuomo. His legislative achievements include a piece of Medicaid reform legislation to eliminate Medicaid's mandate burden on local governments. Prior to representing the citizens of Western New York in the Senate, Sen. Gallivan was twice-elected Sheriff of Erie County, Upstate New York's most populous county. Prior to that, he spent 15 years in the New York State Police, rising to the rank of captain. He is a former member of the New York State Executive Committee on Counter-terrorism, as well as a member of the

New York State Board of Parole. He founded and operates a professional investigation and security firm. He holds an undergraduate degree from Canisius College and a Master's degree in criminal justice from SUNY-Albany. He is the married father of two.

MICHAEL GIANARIS (D-WF)
12th - Part of Queens County

21-77 31st Street, Astoria, NY 11105
718-728-0960/gianaris@nysenate.gov

Michael Gianaris was elected to the State Senate in 2010 is Deputy Minority Leader. He sits on Ethics Committee and the Rules Committee. Prior to being elected to the Senate, he served for ten years in the New York State Assembly. He backed same-sex marriage throughout his public service career, and advocates against dysfunction in state government. His legislative achievements also include authorship of the Clean Energy Law. Prior to seeking elective office, he was an aide to Congressman Thomas Manton, Gov. Mario Cuomo's Queens County Regional Representative, and Counsel to the Speaker of the Assembly. He has also litigated cases in private practice. He holds an undergraduate degree from Fordham University and a J.D. from Harvard Law School.

MARTIN J GOLDEN (R-C-I)
22nd - Part of Kings County

7408 5th Avenue, 1st Floor, Brooklyn, NY 11209
718-238-6044/golden@nysenate.gov

3604 Quentin Rd., Brooklyn, NY 11234

Martin J Golden was first elected to New York State Senate in November 2002. He represents a Brooklyn district that includes the neighborhoods of Bay Ridge, Dyker Heights, Bensonhurst, Marine Park, Gerritsen Beach, Gravesend and parts of Sheepshead Bay, Borough Park and Midwood. He chairs the Civil Service and Pensions Committee, and is also a member of the following committees: aging; banks; codes; finance; health; insurance; investigations and government operations; and veterans, homeland security and military affairs. He is Chairman of the Republican Conference Steering Committee. He has held numerous leadership positions in the past, including service as the former Assistant Majority Whip and Chairman of the Republican Conference Steering Committee. His legislative output includes authorship over more than 222 laws with a focus on public safety, tax cuts, economic development, and issues of interest to senior citizens. As the former Chairman of the Senate Aging Committee, he was credited by nationally recognized advocacy groups for championing the rights of senior citizens through the Assisted Living Law of 2004. Under his leadership, a number of significant bills affecting older Americans were enacted, including a new elder law, the Senior Bill of Rights; Long Term Care Reform; internet posting of retail prescription drug prices; and a single EPIC/Medicare prescription drug card. Prior to his election, he served on the New York City Council. He is a former New York City police officer who retired after suffering a serious on-the-job injury. He is a graduate of St. John's University and is the married father of two.

JOSEPH A GRIFFO (R-C-I)
47th - Oneida, Lewis, and St. Lawrence counties

207 Genesee St, Room 408, Utica, NY 13501
315-793-9072/griffo@nysenate.gov

Joseph A. Griffo was elected to the New York State Senate in 2006. He is Chairman of the Energy and Telecommunications Committee. He also sits on the following committees: codes; commerce, economic development and small business; crime victims, crime and correction; cultural affairs, tourism, parks and recreation; finance; higher education; racing, gaming and wagering; and veterans, homeland security and military affairs. Prior to his election, Griffo held a number of public service positions including Oneida County executive for over three years. In that position, he played a key role in boosting the local economy by over 600 jobs by taking the principal role in efforts to protect U.S. Dept. of Defense-related jobs at the nearby Griffiss Air Force Base. He also served on the Board of Directors of the New York State Association of Counties. Griffo also served for 11 years as Mayor of his hometown of Rome, NY, an Oneida County legislator, director of community relations for the City of Rome, and as an administrative assistant to the Rome mayor. He holds a B.A. in Political Science from the State University of New York at Brockport. He is married and lives in Rome.

JESSE HAMILTON (D)
20 - Part of Kings County

1669 Bedford Avenue, 2nd Floor & Mezzanine, Brooklyn, NY 11225
718-284-4700/Hamilton@nysenate.gov

Jesse Hamilton was first elected to the New York State Senate in 2014. He sits on the following committees: agriculture; banks; codes; commerce, economic development and small business; education; energy and telecommunications; and mental health and developmental disabilities. Prior to his election he served as President of Community School Board 17 in Crown Heights and as District Leader of the 43rd Assembly District. He was Vice President of Community Board 8. He also spent 28 years conducting small claims hearings in the New York City Dept. of Finance. He holds an undergraduate degree from Ithaca College, an MBA from Long Island University and a JD from Seton Hall University. He is the married father of two children.

KEMP HANNON (R-C-IP)
6th - Part of Nassau County

595 Stewart Ave. Suite 540, Garden City, NY 11530
516-739-1700/hannon@nysenate.gov

Kemp Hannon was first elected to the New York State Senate in November 1989. He is Chairman of the Health Committee, and also sits on the following committees: finance; judiciary; labor; mental health and developmental disabilities; and rules. His interest and advocacy on behalf of health care been a hallmark of his legislative career. He was deeply involved with the reauthorization of the Health Care Reform Act and the development of New York's Assisted Living Program. During his Senate tenure, he also has served as Chairman of the Committee for Housing and Community Development, Assistant Majority Whip, as well as Chair of the National Conference of State Legislators' Health Committee. Hannon was a New York State Assemblyman for 12 years until his election to the Senate. An attorney by profession, Hannon holds a BA from Boston College and a JD from Fordham Law School. He is the married father of two.

RUTH HASSELL-THOMPSON (D-WF)
36th - Parts of Bronx and Westchester Counties

959 E. 233rd St, Bronx, NY 10466
718-547-8854/hasselt@senate.state.ny.us

First elected to the New York State Senate in 2000, Hassell-Thompson sits on the following committees: alcoholism and drug abuse; commerce, economic development and small business; crime victims, crime and correction; finance; health; judiciary; and rules. Her previous elective office was to the Mount Vernon City Council in 1993, where she served as both Council President and Acting Mayor. Prior to her election, Hassell-Thompson was the Executive Director of the Westchester Minority Contractors Association (WMCA). In this position, she became well versed in economic development issues that affect women and people of color. Among her many achievements was her ability to spearhead bank loans for financing minority and women-owned business activities. She also was CEO of Whart Development Company, Inc., a real estate development company. In addition, Hassell-Thompson is a retired nurse and counselor at Mount Vernon Hospital for 35 years, specializing in pediatrics and helping women with substance abuse issues. She has served as President and CEO of The Gathering, a volunteer-staffed women's center in Mount Vernon that provides counseling and support services. She graduated from Bronx Community College and holds two honorary doctorates. She is the widowed mother of two children and two grandchildren.

BRAD HOYLMAN (D)
27th - Part of New York County

322 Eighth Avenue, Suite 1700, New York, NY 10001
212-633-8052/hoylman@nysenate.gov

Brad Hoylman was elected to the New York State Senate in 2012. His Manhattan district includes Clinton/Hell's Kitchen, Chelsea, Greenwich Village, and parts of the Upper West Side, Midtown/East Midtown, the East Village, and the Lower East Side. He sits on the following committees: aging; cultural affairs, tourism, parks and recreation; environmental conservation; investigations and government operations; judiciary; and local government. Prior to being elected to the Senate, Hoylman was a three-term chair of Manhattan Community Board 2. In addition, he was a trustee of the Community Service Society, a board member of the Empire State Pride Agenda, Tenants & Neighborhoods, Class Size Matters and Citizen Action. He also served as general counsel of the Partnership for New York City, a non-profit business and civic organization. Hoylman holds an undergraduate degree from West Virginia University, a master's in politics from Oxford University, and a J.D. from Harvard Law School. He and his husband are parents to one.

TODD KAMINSKY (D)
9th - South Shore Long Island

55 Front Street, Rockville Centre, NY 11570-4040
516-766-8383/Kaminsky@nysenate.gov

Legislative Office Building, Room 311, Albany, NY 12247
518-455-3401

Todd Kaminsky represents New York's 20th Assembly District, including Long Beach, Atlantic Beach, East Atlantic Beach, Point Lookout, Lido Beach, Oceanside, Island Park, Lawrence, Cedarhurst, Hewlett, Woodmere, Inwood and portions of East Rockaway. Governor Cuomo announced his veto of the Port Ambrose terminal alongside Kaminsky on November 12, 2015. Todd also led on the issue of access to diplomas for special needs students, convening a forum of state officials where residents were allowed to ask questions and discussion options for alternatives to the former Regents diploma.

Todd received numerous awards for his work at the Eastern District, including the True American Hero Award from the Federal Drug Agents Foundation. As a community advocate, Todd has worked vigorously in support of the South Shore. He organized free legal clinics for those affected by Hurricane Sandy, and helped bring tens-of-thousands of dollars in relief funds to local residents. For his efforts, Todd was awarded the Community Service Award from the United States Attorney's Office for the Eastern District of New York and the Long Beach Martin Luther King Center's Sandy Relief Service Award.

Todd was born and raised in Lido Beach, New York. He graduated from Long Beach High School and attended the University of Michigan, where he graduated summa cum laude. He received his law degree from New York University's School of Law, where he graduated magna cum laude. Todd and his wife, Ellen, live in Long Beach with their son, Rafe.

TIMOTHY M KENNEDY (D-IP-WF)
63rd - Part of Erie County

2239 South Park Ave, Buffalo, NY 14220
716-826-2683/kennedy@nysenate.gov

Timothy M. Kennedy was elected to the New York State Senate in 2010, to a district comprised Cheektowaga, Lackawanna and most of the city of Buffalo. He is the Assistant Democratic Whip and sits on the following committees: banks; commerce, economic development and small business; cultural affairs, tourism, parks and recreation; energy and telecommunications; finance; infrastructure and capital investment; insurance; and transportation. His legislative achievements include sponsoring legislation to develop a green workforce for emerging clean technology industries. He also played a significant role in helping to strengthen state law against texting while driving. His prior public service includes service on the Erie County Legislature, Second District, where he chaired the Economic Development Committed and sat on the Board of Directors of the Erie County Industrial Development Agency. He spearheaded a push to include Buffalo Public School No. 84 in the school districts renovation program. As a result, children with the most severe disabilities in Erie County continue to receive good care and education. The licensed occupational therapist has worked with geriatric and pediatric populations. He holds both a bachelor's and a master's degree in occupational therapy from D'Youville College. He is the married father of three.

JEFFREY D KLEIN (D)
34th - Parts of Bronx and Westchester Counties

1250 Waters Place, Suite 1202, Bronx, New York 10461
718-822-2049/jdklein@senate.state.ny.us

Jeffrey Klein was first elected to the New York State Senate in 2004. He is the Senate Coalition Leader and Independent Democrat Conference Leader, a conference he co-founded in 2011. His previous leadership positions include Senate President Pro Tempore for two years, and Deputy Majority Leader for two years. He also formerly chaired the Senate Committee on Alcohol and Substance Abuse. Klein's legislative achievements include being the prime sponsor of the New York SAFE Act, major legislation that gave New York the nation's toughest gun laws. He has also worked to expand access to key programs and services such as fully-funded universal pre-kindergarten and increased eligibility for major senior support programs. Prior to his election to the Senate, Klein sat in the New York State Assembly for ten years. He holds a B.A. from Queens College, an M.P.A. from Columbia University, and a J.D. from the City of New York Law School and has lived in the northeast Bronx his entire life.

LIZ KRUEGER (D)
28th - Part of New York County, including the Upper East Side

1850 Second Ave, New York, NY 10128
212-490-9535/lkrueger@senate.state.ny.us

First elected to the New York State Senate in a Special Election in February 2002, Sen. Krueger is currently the Ranking Member of Senate Finance Committee. She is also a member of the following committees: codes; elections; higher education; housing, construction, and community development; mental health and developmental disabilities; and rules. She is also a founding co-chair of the New York State Bipartisan Legislative Pro-Choice Caucus and has been highly active in the area of women's health. She helped to lead the successful fight to pass the Women's Health and Wellness Act. Senator Krueger's legislative initiatives also efforts to expand and protect affordable housing, opposing hydofracking, and expanding access to food stamps and safety net assistance for those in need. She has chaired the New York City Food Stamp Task Force and has sat on the board of the City-Wide Task Force on Housing Court. She also served as Co-facilitator of the New York City Welfare Reform Network. Prior to being elected to the Senate, Krueger was Associate Director of the Community Food Resource Center for 15 years. She also was the founding Director of the New York City Food Bank. She holds a B.A. from Northwestern University and a Master's degree from the University of Chicago's Harris Graduate School of Public Policy. She and her husband live on Manhattan's East Side.

ANDREW J LANZA (R)
24th - Part of Richmond County

3845 Richmond Ave, Suite 2A, Staten Island, NY 10312
718-984-4073/lanza@senate.state.ny.us

Senator Lanza was elected to the New York State Senate in November 2006. He chairs the Cities Committee, and is Vice Chair of the Codes Committee. He also sits on the following committees: civil service and pensions; education; ethics; finance; insurance; and judiciary. His legislative achievements include authoring legislation to create an online database to allow doctors and pharmacists to report and track controlled narcotics in real time, an effort to combat prescription drug abuse. He also backed efforts to force New York City to restore bus service to Staten Island's 7th and 8th graders. In addition, Sen. Lanza passed legislation that created the 13th Judicial District in the State of New York, comprised solely of Richmond County, allowing Staten Island to have its own judicial district. Prior to being elected to the Senate, Lanza sat on the New York City Council and also served as a prosecutor. He holds a B.S. from St. John's University and a JD from Fordham University Law School. He and his wife have three children and reside in Great Kills.

WILLIAM J LARKIN, JR (R-C)
39th - Parts of Orange, Ulster and Rockland Counties

1093 Little Britain Road, New Windsor, NY 12553
845-567-1270/larkin@senate.state.ny.us

Senator Larkin was first elected to the New York State Senate in 1990 to a district that includes, in Orange County, the city of Newburgh and the Towns of Blooming Grove, Chester, Cornwall, Crawford, Highlands, Monroe, Montgomery, New Windsor, Newburgh, and Woodbury, and in Ulster County, the city of Kingston and the Towns of Plattekill and Marlborough, and Haverstraw and Stony Point in Rockland County. Sen. Larkin is Assistant Majority Leader for House Operations, and also serves on the new Senate Task Force on Workforce Development. He also serves on the following committees: corporations, authorities and commissions; finance; health; insurance; rules; transportation; and veterans, homeland security and military affairs.

Senator Larkin was Majority Whip from 2011 to 2015, and has served in other leadership positions during his Senate tenure. His legislative achievements include authoring a new law to change the operations and procedures of local Industrial Development Agencies (IDAs). The law increased the public accountability of IDAs while giving IDAs more flexibility to create jobs. As chair of the veterans' committee, he sponsored changes in veteran's benefits that increased the financial protections for families of U.S. servicemen fighting in the Persian Gulf War, as well as conflicts in Lebanon, Panama and Grenada. In addition, he is recognized for his expertise relating to the insurance industry; he is past president of the National Conference of Insurance Legislators (NCOIL). Senator Larkin is a veteran of 23 years of active military duty including combat assignments during World War II and the Korean War. He retired from the United States Army in 1967 with the rank of Lieutenant Colonel. Following his military service, Senator Larkin served as an Executive Assistant in the New York State Senate and as Supervisor of the Town of New Windsor in Orange County. The Troy native graduated from LaSalle Institute. He and his wife, between them, have eight children and 17 grandchildren.

GEORGE S. LATIMER (D)
37th - Part of Westchester County

222 Grace Church St., Port Chester, NY 10572
914-934-5256/latimer@nysenate.gov

George S. Latimer was first elected to the New York State Senate in 2012, and represents Bedford, Bronxville, Eastchester, Harrison, Larchmont, Mamaronck, New Rochelle, Port Chester, Rye, Rye Brook, Tuckahoe, White Plains, and Yonkers. He sits on the following committees: banks; consumer protection; education; environmental conservation; insurance; local government; and racing, gaming and wagering. Latimer previously served in the New York State Assembly, where he authored more than 20 new laws, and on the Westchester County Board of Legislators, including as Chairman and Minority Leader. During his chairmanship, the board oversaw the creation of smoke free workplace laws and the creation of a Human Rights Commission, among other accomplishments. Latimer also served on the Rye City Council for four years. He is a marketing executive by profession with project experience at major corporations. He holds a BA from Fordham University and an MPA from New York University's Wagner School. He is the married father of one.

KENNETH P LAVALLE (R)
1st - Part of Suffolk County

29 North Country Road, Suite 203, Mt. Sinai, NY 11766
631-473-1461/lavalle@nysenate.gov

Kenneth P LaValle was first elected to the New York State Senate in 1976. He is Chairman of the Senate Majority Conference, Chair of the Senate Committee on Higher Education. In addition, he sits on the following committees: aging; education; environmental conservation; finance; insurance; judiciary; rules; and social services. In his many years chairing the higher education committee, LaValle has helped shape higher education policy in New York State. In 2007, the governor appointed Senator LaValle to the New York State Commission on Higher Education that was charged with identifying ways of improving the quality of higher education. LaValle also served on the National Council of State Legislatures' Blue Ribbon Commission on Higher Education that sought to create awareness among state legislatures of their role in providing accessible and affordable public higher education. He has also been active in the healthcare arena, including work to establish a burn unit at Stony Brook University Medical Center. An attorney by profession, LaValle holds an undergraduate degree from Adelphi College, an education degree from SUNY New Paltz, and a J.D. from Touro College Jacob D. Fuchsberg Law Center. He has also completed graduate student in government and international relations at NYU. He is married and the father of two and grandfather to four.

ELIZABETH "BETTY" LITTLE (R-C-I)
45th - Clinton, Essex, Franklin, Warren and parts of St. Lawrence and Washington counties.

Betty Little was first elected to the New York State Senate in 2002. She serves as Deputy Majority Whip, and formerly served as Assistant Majority Whip. She chairs the Committee on Cultural Affairs, Tourism, Parks and Recreation, and also sits on the following committees: crime victims, crime and correction; education; energy and telecommunications; environmental conservation; finance; health; and rules. Her legislative achievements include creating the Adirondack Community Housing Trust and passing the Timber Theft Law. Prior to being elected to the Senate, she served in the New York State Assembly for seven years. She also served as an At-Large Supervisor to the Warren County Board of Supervisors for the Town of Queensbury. She holds a degree from the College of Saint Rose, and is the mother of six and grandmother of 14.

CARL LOUIS MARCELLINO (R)
5th - Parts of Nassau and Suffolk Counties

250 Townsend Square, Oyster Bay, NY 11771
516-922-1811/marcelli@senate.state.ny.us

Senator Carl Louis Marcellino was elected to the New York Senate in 1995. He is the Vice Chairman of the Senate Majority Conference, and also chairs the Committee on Infrastructure and Capital Investment, as well as the Committee on Investigations and Government Operations. In addition, Sen. Marcellino also serves on the Senate committees on banks; cultural affairs, tourism, parks and recreation; education; environmental conservation; finance; labor; and rules. He is Vice-Chair of the Transportation Committee. His legislative achievements include authorship of more than 100 environmental laws during his 1995 to 2008 chairmanship of the Senate Environmental Conservation Committee. Among them was his primary sponsorship of the Brownfield/Superfund Reform Law, the Pesticide Notification Law, and the first law in the county to phase out the groundwater contaminate MTBE from gasoline. He also focuses on health and safety issues, including efforts such as banning the use of handheld cell phones while driving in New York. In addition, he was the prime sponsor of the "Stephanie's Law" which made it a felony to engage in video voyeurism, the Unpaid Wages Prohibition Act, the disability registry that provides vital information to aid in rescues and evacuations, and the permanent COLA bill, granting retirees from state service annual cost-of-living adjustments. He is Chairman of the Oyster Bay Western Waterfront Committee and Chairman of the Council of State Governments. Prior to being elected to the Senate, Sen. Marcellino was a science teacher and administrator in the New York City School System, as well as the elected Oyster Bay Town Clerk. The Brooklyn-born Marcellino holds a B.S. and a M.S. from New York University and a Professional Diploma in Administration and Supervision from St. John's University. He and his wife are parents of two.

KATHLEEN A MARCHIONE (R-C)
43rd - Columbia County and Parts of Rensselaer, Saratoga and Washington Counties

2 Halfmoon Town Plaza, Halfmoon, NY 12065/marchione@nysenate.gov

560 Warren St., 2nd Floor, Hudson, NY 12534
518-828-5947

Kathleen A. Marchione was first elected to the New York State Senate in 2012. She chairs the Local Government Committee, and also sits on the following committees: aging; banks; consumer protection; cultural affairs, tourism, parks and recreation; elections; labor; and racing, gaming and wagering. Prior to her election to the Senate, Marchione was the Saratoga County Clerk for many years. She previously served as the Halfmoon Town Clerk and as a Halfmoon Town Supervisor. She is the former President of the New York State Association of County Clerks, former Chairwoman of the Capital District Regional District Planning Commission, and, for a decade, the chair of the New York State Regional Records Advisory Committee. She also sat on the New York State Local Government Records Committee. She has been deeply involved in her regional Republican clubs, and she has received numerous awards including the highest distinction that a record management professional can receive, the Wheeler B. Melius Award from the New York Association of Local Government Records Officers. She is the married mother of two, stepmother of one, and grandmother to four.

JACK M MARTINS (R)
7th - Part of Nassau County

252 Mineola Blvd., Mineola, NY 11501
516-746-5924/martins@nysenate.gov

Jack M. Martins was first elected to the New York State Senate in 2010. He chairs the Labor Committee, and sits on the following committees: banks; civil service and pensions; corporations, authorities and commissions; finance; health; insurance; social services; and transportation. His legislative achievements include working to cut middle class income tax rates and repealing the MTA Payroll Tax on counties, towns, villages, and libraries. He also authored the law that created the state's Homeless Veterans Assistance Fund, as well as the law to create the statewide Financial Restructuring Board for local governments, on which he serves. Prior to his election to the Senate, Martins served as Mayor of the Village of Mineola. He holds an undergraduate degree from American University and a J.D. from St. John's University School of Law. He and his wife and four children live in his hometown of Mineola.

VELMANETTE MONTGOMERY (D)
25th - Part of Kings County

30 3rd Ave, Brooklyn, NY 11217
718-643-6140/montgome@senate.state.ny.us

Velmanette Montgomery was first elected to the New York State Senate in 1984. She is Ranking Democrat on the Committee on Children and Families, and also serves on the following committees: agriculture; children and families; crime victims, crime and correction; education; finance; health; rules; social services; and finance. She previously served as Assistant Majority Whip. She advocates on behalf of school-based health care for delivery of comprehensive primary and mental health services to school children. She backed a measure that prevents the NYS Office of Children and Families from posting the home address or personal information of day care providers on the Internet. She is also the sponsor of the 2012 law that supports agriculture by requiring the state's Procurement Council to include a member of a non-profit organization that represents farming communities. Professionally, she has been a teacher, and she is former President of Community School Board 13 and co-founder of the Day Care Forum of New York City. She holds a BA and MS from NYU; she also attended the University of Accra in Ghana.

TERRENCE P MURPHY (R)
40 (Putnam, Dutchess, and Westchester counties)

Putnam County Office Bldg., 3rd Floor, 40 Gleneida Avenue, Carmel, NY 10512
845-225-3025

691 E. Main St, 1st Floor, Shrub Oak, NY 10588
914-962-2624
/murphy@nysenate.gov

Terrence Murphy was elected to the New York State Senate in 2014. He sits on the following committees: banks; ethics; health; investigations and government operations; labor; local government; and mental health and developmental disabilities. A chiropractor by training, he opened the Yorktown Health and Wellness Center in 1999, and opened Murphy's Irish Restaurant in Yorktown in 2006, along with his mother and siblings. The lifelong Hudson Valley resident was elected to the Yorktown Town Board in 2009, where his achievements included back-to-back tax cuts and $250 million in economic development. He is the married father of three.

MICHAEL F NOZZOLIO (R-IP-C)
54th - Seneca and Wayne Counties, Parts of Cayuga, Monroe, Ontario, and Tompkins Counties

119 Fall Street, Seneca Falls, NY 13148
1-888-568-9816/nozzolio@nysenate.gov

Michael F Nozzolio was first elected to the New York State Senate in 1992. He is Majority Whip and Chair of the Codes Committee. In the latter position, he guides the committee as it considers issues and legislation relating to New York's criminal and civil justice system. In addition, Sen. Nozzolio sits on the following committees: crime victims, crime and correction; elections; finance; housing, construction, and community development; investigations and government operations; judiciary; racing, gaming and wagering; rules; and transportation. Prior to his election to the New York State Senate, Nozzolio served for 10 years in the New York State Assembly, where he served as Deputy Minority Leader. He also served in the U.S. Naval Reserve as a JAG officer, and is a Commander in the New York Naval Militia. The Seneca Falls born-and-raised Nozzolio holds a bachelor's degree in labor relations and a Master's degree in public administration and agricultural economics from Cornell University. He holds a JD from Syracuse University College of Law. He and his wife reside in Seneca Falls.

THOMAS F O'MARA (R-C)
58th - Chemung, Schuyler, Steuben and Yates counties, and part of Tompkins County including the city and town of Ithaca, and the towns of Enfield, Newfield and Ulysses

333 East Water Street, 3rd Floor, Suite 301, Elmira, NY 14901
607-735-9671/omara@nysenate.gov

105 East Steuben Street, Bath, NY 14810
607-776-3201

Thomas F O'Mara was elected to the New York State Senate on November 2, 2010. He is Chair of the Environmental Conservation Committee, and also sits on the following committees: agriculture; banks; codes; energy and telecommunications; finance; insurance; investigations and government operations; judiciary; and transportation. He also is one of five senators sitting on the joint bipartisan Legislative Commission on the Development of Rural Resources. He has been a strong advocate of revitalizing Upstate New York's manufacturing sector. Prior to his election to the Senate, O'Mara sat in the New York State Assembly for three terms, where he rose to the rank of Assistant Minority Leader Pro Tempore. He is a former Chemung County District Attorney, Chemung County Attorney, and an Assistant District Attorney in both Manhattan and Chemung County. He remains active in his community, including as counsel to the Chemung County Industrial Development Agency. He holds a B.A. from the Catholic University of America and a J.D. from Syracuse University College of Law. He is married with three children and resides in Big Flats.

ROBERT ORTT (R)
62nd - Niagara, Orleans and Monroe Counties

175 Walnut Street, Suite 6, Lockport, NY 14094
716-434-0680/Ortt@nysenate.gov

Robert Ortt was first elected to the New York State Senate in 2014. He chairs the Committee on Mental Health and Developmental Disabilities, and also sits on the following committees: cities; civil service and pensions; corporations, authorities and commissions; environmental conservation; higher education; local government; and veterans, homeland security and military affairs. He is the former Mayor of North Tonawanda, where he served for four years and developed executive expertise. He was the City Treasurer and Clerk Treasurer from 2007-2010. He enlisted in the NY Army National Guard following the 9/11 attacks, and served in Afghanistan as the Executive Officer/Unit Movement Officer for an infantry company. His awards included the Bronze Star. He is a former independent personal financial analyst and lives in North Tonawanda with his wife.

MARC PANEPINTO (D)
60th - Erie County

65 Court Street, Rm. 213 (Mahoney State Office Building), Buffalo, NY 14202
(716) 854-8705/Panepinto@nysenate.gov

Marc Panepinto was elected to the New York State Senate in 2014 from a Western New York district that includes parts of the City of Buffalo, the City of Tonawanda, and the Towns of Grand Island, Tonawanda, Hamburg, Orchard Park, Evans, and Brant. He is Ranking Member on the Committee on Local Government and the Agriculture Committee. He also sits on the following committees: codes; health; housing, construction and community development; insurance; local government; transportation; veterans, homeland security and military affairs. He opposes the Gap Elimination Adjustment (GEA) and advocates to reform the education systems testing culture. He also backs the Jobs Protection Act, and increased funding for Erie County infrastructure. The Town of Tonawanda native graduated from the University of Buffalo, and went on to study Labor and Industrial Relations at the University of Illinois and become a union organizer. He received a law degree from the University of Buffalo and is principal in the law firm of Dolce Panepinto P.C. He is the married father of three.

KEVIN S PARKER (D-WF)
21st - Part of Kings County

55 Hansen Place Shirley A. Chisholm SOB, Suite 605, Brooklyn, NY 11217
718-629-6401/parker@senate.state.ny.us

Kevin S Parker was first elected to the New York State Senate in 2002. He represents an ethnically diverse district that includes Flatbush, East Flatbush, Midwood, Ditmas Park, Kensington, Windsor Terrace and Park Slope. The Brooklyn-born Parker is currently a member of the following committees: alcoholism and drug abuse; banks; cultural affairs, tourism, parks and recreation; energy and telecommunications; finance; higher education; insurance; and rules. He is former Majority Whip and a member of the New American Task Force. He is also Parliamentarian of the NY State Association of Black and Puerto Rican Legislators, Inc. Sen Parker was Special Assistant to former New York State Comptroller H. Carl McCall and managed intergovernmental relations in New York City, and also was liaison between the Comptroller and city, state and federal elected officials. He also was a New York City Urban Fellow and also served as a Special Assistant to former Manhattan Borough President Ruth Messinger; Legislative Aide to former New York City Councilmember Una Clarke and Special Assistant to Assemblyman Nick Perry. He has worked as a project manager with the New York State Urban Development Corporation, and on government affairs issues within the chairman's office of UBS PaineWebber. Parker previously served as 2nd vice-chairman and chair of Community Board 17's Education Committee. He has been a professor of African-American studies and political science at Baruch College-CUNY, SUNY Old Westbury, John Jay College, and Brooklyn College. Parker earned a B.S. from Penn State and an M.S. from the New School for Social Research Graduate School of Management and Urban Study. He is pursuing a doctorate in political science from CUNY's Graduate School and University Center.

JOSE PERALTA (D-WF)
13th - Part of Queens County

32-37 Junction Boulevard, East Elmhurst, NY 11369
718-205-3881/jperalta@nysenate.gov

Jose Peralta was first elected to the senate in a 2010 special election to a district that includes Corona, East Elmhurst, Elmhurst, Jackson Heights and parts of Woodside and Astoria. He is the Minority Whip, and also serves on the following committees: cities, consumer protection; crime victims, crime and correction; finance; higher education; and labor. Prior to his election to the senate, Peralta served in the New York State Assembly from 2002-2010. His legislative goals include efforts to bring economic development to Willets Point and neighboring communities, as well as a drive to rejuvenate Roosevelt Avenue. He holds a BA from Queens College and is the married father of two.

BILL PERKINS (D-WF)
30th - Part of New York County

163 West 125th Street, Harlem State Office Bldg., Suite 912, New York, NY 10027
212-222-7315/perkins@senate.state.ny.us

Bill Perkins was first elected to the New York State Senate in 2006 and represents a district that encompasses Harlem, the Upper West Side, and Washington Heights. He is the Senate's Deputy Minority Whip. He sits on the following committees: codes; corporations, authorities and commissions; crime victims, crime and correction; finance; judiciary; labor; rules; and transportation. A life-long resident of Harlem, Sen. Perkins started his political career as a community activist. Prior to his election to the Senate, he spent eight years on the New York City Council where he served as the Deputy Majority Leader. In this position, he was prime sponsor of the Childhood Lead Paint Poisoning Prevention Act of 2004. He holds a B.A. in political science from Brown University, and is the married father of four.

ROXANNE PERSAUD (D)
19th - Southeast Brooklyn

181 State Street, 504 Legislative Office Building, Albany, NY 12247
518-455-2788/persaud@nysenate.gov

1222 East 96th Street, Brooklyn, NY 11236
718-649-7653

Roxanne Jacqueline Persaud was elected to the State Senate in November 2015 after serving in the State Assembly.

Roxanne spent many years as a Higher Education Administrator prior to being elected to the State Legislature. In addition, she is a longtime advocate for the community. She served as President of the 69th Precinct Community Council in Canarsie, a member of Community Board 18 and Commissioner on the New York City Districting Commission. She also is a graduate of the NYPD Citizens Police Academy as well as, the New York City Office of Emergency Management-Community Emergency Response Team. Additionally, she was a member of Community Action Board of the New York City Department of Youth and Community Development and Chairperson of the Neighborhood Advisory Board - District 18. She also serves on organizations highlighting domestic violence and cancer awareness among others.

Roxanne was born in Guyana, South America and migrated to the United States with her parents and siblings. She is a graduate of Pace University from which she holds a Bachelor of Science and Master of Science in Education Administration. In the Senate, Roxanne's legislative priorities for the District will include safer communities, affordable housing, funding for schools and libraries, supportive services for youth and senior and quality healthcare. Roxanne lives in the Canarsie section of the 19th Senatorial District.

MICHAEL RANZENHOFER (R-C-IP)
61st - Genesee County and Parts of Erie and Monroe Counties

8203 Main Street, Suite 4, Williamsville, NY 14221
716-631-8695/ranz@senate.state.ny.us

Michael Ranzenhofer was first elected to the New York Senate in 2008. His district includes the towns of Amherst, Clarence and Newstead, and the villages of Akron and Williamsville in Erie County, the towns of Chili and Riga, the village of Churchville, and part of the city of Rochester in Monroe County, and all of Genesee County. He chairs the Corporations, Authorities and Commissions Committee, and also sits on the following committees: agriculture; education; finance; judiciary; racing, gaming and wagering; and transportation. His legislative achievements include working with non-profit organizations and the New York State Bar Association to pass legislation to overall the state's not-for-profit laws. Prior to his election, he served in the Erie County Legislature and was both Majority and Minority Leader. A lawyer by profession, Ranzenhofer is a partner at Friedman & Ranzenhofer, P.C. He holds a BA from SUNY-Albany and a JD from SUNY at Buffalo Law School. He and his wife have two children.

PATTY RITCHIE (R-C-IP)
48th - Oswego, Jefferson and St. Lawrence Counties

Dulles State Office Building, Room 418, Watertown, NY 13601
315-782-3418/ritchie@nysenate.gov

46 East Bridge St., 1st floor, Oswego, NY 13126
315-342-2057

330 Ford St. (basement of City Hall), Ogdensburg, NY 13669
315-393-3024

Patty Ritchie was elected to the State Senate in 2010. She is Deputy Majority Leader for Senate and Assembly Relations, as well as Chair of the Agriculture Committee. She also sits on the following committees: alcoholism and drug abuse; civil service and pensions; crime victims, crime and correction; cultural affairs, tourism, parks and recreation; energy and telecommunications; finance; higher education; local government; and transportation. Her legislative achievements include working to strengthen family farms, including authoring a new 2% cap on farmland assessments, and proposing the Young Farmers NY program to provide incentives to help new farmers. Prior to her election to the Senate, Sen. Ritchie served as St. Lawrence County Clerk for over a decade. As County Clerk, she made the County Clerk's Office more accessible and user-friendly for residents of her sprawling county; and established four local DMV offices that eliminated long lines, improved efficiency, and increased revenue for the county. She graduated from Mater Dei College and SUNY Potsdam, and lives in Oswegatchie with her husband. They have three children and three grandchildren.

GUSTAVO RIVERA (D-WF)
33rd - Part of Bronx County

2432 Grand Concourse, Suite 506, Bronx, NY 10458
718-933-2034/grivera@nysenate.gov

In 2010, Gustavo Rivera was elected to the New York State Senate. His district, from Northwest Bronx to parts of the East Bronx, includes Kingsbridge Heights, East Tremont, Crotona Park, Fordham, Belmont, Van Nest, Claremont, High Bridge, and Morris Park. He is the Ranking Minority Member on the Health Committee, and also sits on the following committees: crime victims, crime and correction; ethics; finance; higher education; labor; and mental health and developmental disabilities. Rivera had early success in the Senate: he introduced legislation that proposed making it mandatory for public officials to disclose all sources of income they receive apart from their government salary. This provision was included in Gov. Andrew Cuomo's ethics package that was signed into law. In addition, Rivera introduced and passed legislation that will allow charitable organizations throughout the state to post bail bonds for individuals who cannot afford to do so themselves. He is an adjunct professor at Pace University, and a former community organizer for candidates running for state senate and the NYC mayor's seats. SEIU hired Rivera to manage their activities on behalf of presidential candidate Barack Obama in a number of key states in 2008. He has also been Director of Community Outreach for U.S. Sen. Kirsten Gillibrand. The Santurce, Puerto Rico-born Rivera graduated from the University of Puerto Rico. He came to New York to attend a doctoral program at the CUNY's Graduate Center.

JOSEPH E ROBACH (R-C-IP)
56th - Part of Monroe County

2300 W. Ridge Road, Rochester, NY 14626
585-225-3650/robach@nysenate.gov

Joseph Robach was first elected to the New York State Senate in 2002. His district includes the Towns of Greece, Brighton, Parma, Clarkson, Gates, Hamlin, and parts of the City of Rochester. He chairs the Transportation Committee and sits on the following committees: commerce, economic development and small business; consumer protection; education; finance; higher education; infrastructure and capital investment, and labor. In addition, he chairs the Majority Steering Committee. Before his election to the Senate, Robach served as an Assemblyman for 11 years filling the seat vacated by the passing of his father, Roger Robach. He is also a member of the Finger Lakes Regional Economic Development Council. Sen. Robach holds both B.S. and M.P.A. degrees from the State University of New York College at Brockport. He is also a graduate of Aquinas Institute. He is the married father of three.

JAMES SANDERS, JR. (D)
10th - Parts of Queens County

142-01 Rockaway Blvd., South Ozone Park, NY 11436
718-523-3069/sanders@nysenate.gov

1931 Mott Avenue, Suite 305, Far Rockaway, NY 11691
718-327-7017

James Sanders Jr. was elected to represent the New York State Senate in 2012 to a district that includes South Jamaica, Rochdale Village, Rosedale, Richmond Hill, South Ozone Park, Springfield Gardens and most of the Rockaways. He is the ranking Democrat on the Civil Services & Pensions Committee, and also sits on the following committees: banks; commerce, economic development and small business; cultural affairs, tourism, parks and recreation; insurance; labor, racing, gaming and wagering; and veterans, homeland security and military affairs. He has advocated on behalf of higher wages for working people, including helping to lead the fight for higher pay for airport food servers employed by the Port Authority of New York and New Jersey.

Prior to being elected to the senate, Sen. Sanders was a member of the New York City Council for 12 years. He also sat on Queens School Board District 27 for a decade, including seven years as president, having been the first African-American who ascended to that post. He also served in the United States Marine Corps for three years, and holds an undergraduate degree from Brooklyn College. Sen. Sanders lives in Queens and is the married father of two.

DIANE J SAVINO (D-IP-WF)
23rd District - Parts of Kings and Richmond Counties

36 Richmond Terrace, Suite 112, Staten Island, New York 10301
718-727-9406/savino@senate.state.ny.us

2872 West 15th Street, Brooklyn, NY 11224
718-333-0311

Diane J Savino was first elected to the New York State Senate in 2004 to represent a district that encompasses the North and East Shore of Staten Island and portions of Southern Brooklyn, including Borough Park, Brighton Beach, Dyker Heights, Gravesend, Coney Island, Bensonhurst, and Sunset Park. She is Chairman of the Banks Committee, as well as a member of the following committees: children and families; civil service and pensions; consumer protection; elections; finance; health; higher education; and judiciary. Sen. Savino is co-founder of the Independent Democratic Conference and its liaison to the executive branch. Her many legislative successes include the nation's first Domestic Workers' Bill of Rights that expands basic worker protection rights to domestic workers; the Prompt Pay Bill that ensures prompt payment to construction contractors and their employees, and the Wage Theft Prevention Act that assesses preventative and punitive measures to employers who steal income from their employees.

Professionally, she worked as a caseworker for the New York City's Child Welfare Administration, and she has been active in her local labor union, where she rose through the ranks. She holds a BA from St. John's University and also graduated from Cornell School of Industrial and Labor Relations.

SUE SERINO (R)
41st - Dutchess County

117 Town Park Lane, Putnam Valley, NY 10579
518-455-2945/Serino@nysenate.gov

4254 Albany Post Road, Hyde Park, NY 12538
845-229-0106

Susan J. Serino was elected to the New York State Senate in 2014 and chairs the Aging Committee. In addition, she sits on the following committees: children and families; cultural affairs, tourism, parks and recreation; education; higher education; judiciary; mental health and development disabilities.

Her previous public service was as a member of the Hyde Park Town Board for a year, and then the Dutchess County Legislature where she advocated on behalf of holding the line on taxes and fees. She operates a Hyde Park-based real estate business. She is mother to one.

JOSE M SERRANO (D-WF)
29th - Parts of Bronx and New York Counties

1916 Park Ave., Suite 202, New York, NY 10037
212-828-5829/serrano@senate.state.ny.us

Senator Jose M Serrano was first elected to the New York State Senate in 2004 and represents the 29th Senate District which includes neighborhoods in the South and West Bronx, East Harlem, Upper Yorkville, Roosevelt Island, Central Park, and the Upper West Side. He is Chair of the Senate Democratic Conference and serves as the Ranking Member of the Committee on Cultural Affairs, Tourism, Parks and Recreation. He also sits on the following committees: aging, agriculture; children and families; consumer protection; environmental conservation; mental health and developmental disorders; and veterans, homeland security, and military affairs. His legislative achievements include Senate passage of bills that: require the Department of Environmental Conservation to publish a list of areas in the state that are most adversely affected by existing environmental hazards; to incentivize affordable development on vacant properties in Northern Manhattan; and to mandate the New York State Dept. of Health to conduct an intensive study on the high rates of asthma in the Bronx. Prior to his election to the Senate, Serrano was a member of Community Board 4 in the Bronx, Chairman of the Board for the Institute for Urban Family health, and, in 2001, he was elected to the New York City Council, where he chaired the Committee on Cultural Affairs. Serrano holds a BA from Manhattan College and lives with his wife and two children in the South Bronx.

JAMES L SEWARD (R-C-IP)
51st - Clinton, Cortland, Delaware, Herkimer, Otsego Ulster, and Schoharie counties

41 S Main Street, Oneonta, NY 13820
607-432-5524/seward@nysenate.gov

235 N. Prospect St., Herkimer, NY 13350
315-866-1632

4030 West Rd., Cortland, NY 13045
607-758-9005

James L Seward was first elected to the New York State Senate in 1986. He chairs the Majority Program Development Committee, as well as the Senate's Insurance Committee, and has held numerous leadership positions during his Senate tenure. He also sits on the following committees: agriculture; education; finance; health; higher education; mental health and developmental disabilities; and rules. In his role on the insurance committee, Seward's legislative successes include passage of legislation in 2002 that extends group health insurance offered by chambers of commerce to sole proprietors of businesses, and in 2008 Sen. Seward secured legislative approval of a bill to provide short-term health insurance policies to young adults and college students. In addition, he has advocated on behalf of education, jobs, and business growth. Seward is a former Milford town justice, and remains active in his community, including in such posts as trustee of Glimmerglass Opera. He holds a B.A. from Hartwick College, and also studied at the Nelson Rockefeller Institute of SUNY Albany. He is the married father of two.

DANIEL L SQUADRON (D-WF)
26th - Parts of Kings and New York Counties

250 Broadway, Suite 2011, New York, NY 10007
212-298-5565/squadron@nysenate.gov

209 Joralemon Street, Suite 310 Brooklyn, NY 11201
718-875-1517

Elected to the New York State Senate in 2008, Daniel Squadron's district includes the Brooklyn neighborhoods of Greenpoint, Williamsburg, Vinegar Hill, DUMBO, Fulton Ferry, Brooklyn Heights, Downtown Brooklyn, Boerum Hill, Cobble Hill, Carroll Gardens, and Columbia Waterfront, and the Manhattan neighborhoods of Tribeca, Battery Park City, the Lower East Side, Chinatown, the Financial District, Little Italy, SoHo, and the East Village. He sits on the following committees: cities; codes; corporations, authorities and commissions; finance; investigations and government operations; social services; and transportation. Among his legislative achievements is passage into law of his bill to allow more than $1 billion in federal funds for New York City public housing over 15 years, as well as backing a bill to create benefit corporations, which are a new type of business that can pursue both profit and social good. Prior to his election to the Senate, Squadron was a top aide to U.S. Sen. Chuck Shumer. Squadron holds an undergraduate degree from Yale University and resides in Carroll Gardens with his wife and two children.

TOBY ANN STAVISKY (D)
16th - Part of Queens County

142-29 37th Ave Suite 1, Flushing, NY 11354
718-445-0004/stavisky@nysenate.gov

Toby Ann Stavisky was first elected to the Senate in 1999 and is the first woman from Queens County elected to the State Senate and the first woman to chair the Senate Committee on Higher Education. Currently, Stavisky is the Ranking Minority Member of the Higher Education Committee, and also sits on the following committees: education; finance; health; judiciary; and transportation. She is Leader for Conference Operations and previously served as Assistant Minority Whip. Prior to entering public life, Stavisky worked in the actuarial department of a major insurance company and taught social studies in the New York City high schools, and served as district manager in Northeast Queens for the U.S. Census. She holds an undergraduate degree from Syracuse University, and two M.A. degrees: one from Hunter College, and one from Queens College.

ANDREA STEWART-COUSINS (D-IP-WF)
35th - Part of Westchester County

28 Wells Ave, Bldg 3, Yonkers, NY 10701
914-423-4031/scousins@senate.state.ny.us

Andrea Stewart-Cousins was first elected to the New York State Senate in 2006 and her district includes Greenburgh, and parts of White Plains, New Rochelle, Yonkers and Scarsdale. She is the Leader of the Senate Democratic Conference, becoming the state's first female leader of a legislative conference. Stewart-Cousins also sits on the Rules Committee. Her legislative achievements include sponsoring and passing the Government Reorganization and Citizen Empowerment Act, which empowers communities to consolidate local governments, which reduces overlap of municipal services and saves taxpayer dollars. She also sponsored and passed Jimmy Nolan's law in 2009, which extends the time by which 9/11 responders can file compensation claims for injuries sustained from the World Trade Center rescue, recovery or cleanup operations. Finally, she sponsored and passed the Child Health Plus and School Meal Enrollment Coordination Law, the 2010 law that allows families to use their proof of eligibility for Free or Reduced Price School Meal Programs as proof of income to enroll their child in Medicaid and Child Health Plus. Stewart-Cousins previously served as Westchester County Legislator, and was the first African American Director of Community Affairs for the City of Yonkers. She holds a BS from Pace University, earned her teaching credentials from Lehman College, and holds a MPA from Pace University. She is the widowed mother of three and grandmother of two.

DAVID J VALESKY (D-IP)
53rd - Madison County and Parts of Oneida County and Onondaga County including the city of Syracuse

333 East Washington St, 805 State Office Building, Syracuse, NY 13202
315-478-8745/valesky@nysenate.gov

Senator David J Valesky was elected to the New York State Senate in 2004. He is the Deputy Independent Democratic Conference Leader for Legislative Operations and also is Vice Chair of the Health Committee. In addition, he sits on the following committees: aging; agriculture; commerce, economic development and small business; education; finance; higher education; local government, and transportation. Valesky has sponsored several laws that promote investment in communities and make it easier for businesses to locate and stay in New York State. Prior to his election, Valesky served as an aide to former State Assembly Majority Leader Michael Bragman. He then became Vice President of Communications at WCNY, the public television and radio station of Central New York, a post he occupied from 1995 to 2004. There, he hosted the midday talk show HOUR CNY. The Oneida native holds an undergraduate degree from SUNY Potsdam and a Master's degree from the University of Connecticut. He is the married father of three.

MICHAEL VENDITTO (R-C-I)
8th - Nassau County and part of Suffolk County

5550 Merrick Road, Suite 205, Massapequa, NY 11758
516-882-0630/Venditto@nysenate.gov

Michael Venditto was elected to the New York State Senate in 2014 from a district that includes the Towns of Hempstead and Oyster Bay, and the Town of Babylon. He chairs the Consumer Protection Committee and also is a member of the following committees: crime victims, crime and correction; insurance; judiciary; and labor. He's an advocate for strong schools, and responds to citizens' concerns about issues that threaten community.The lifelong resident of the South Shore was a Nassau County Legislator who is concerned about the middle class and champions small businesses. He holds a B.A. from Hofstra University and a J.D. from St. John's University School of Law. He and his wife are parents to one.

CATHARINE M YOUNG (R-C-IP)
57th - Allegany, Cattaraugus, Chautauqua County

Westgate Plaza, 700 West State Street, Olean, NY 14760
716-372-4901/cyoung@senate.state.ny.us

2-6 East 2nd Street Fenton Building, Suite 302, Jamestown, NY 14701
716-664-4603

Catharine Young was first elected to the New York Senate in 2005. She is Assistant Senate Majority Whip, chairs the Legislative Commission on Rural Resources, and chairs the Housing, Construction, and Community Development Committee. She also sits on the following committees: agriculture; children and families; environmental conservation; finance; health; insurance; rules and transportation. She also founded the Legislative Wine and Grape Caucus to boost the industry-sponsored legislation that formed the New York State Council on Food Policy. She previously served in the New York State Assembly, where she helped pass Penny's Law, which ensures that violent killers are not released prematurely. She also served on the Cattaraugus County Legislature including a leadership post as Majority Whip, and was a member of the Cattaraugus County Board of Health. She graduated from St. Bonaventure University and is a major in the Civil Air Patrol. She is the married mother of three.

NEW YORK STATE ASSEMBLY

PETER J ABBATE, JR (D)
49th - Part of Kings County

6605 Fort Hamilton Parkway, Brooklyn, NY 11219
718-236-1764/abbatep@assembly.state.ny.us

Peter Abbate was first elected to the New York State Assembly in 1986. His district includes Dyker Heights, Bath Beach, Bensonhurst, and Borough Park in Brooklyn. He is chair of the Governmental Employees Committee, a position he first assumed in 2002. He is also a member of the following committees: aging; banks; consumer affairs and protection; and labor. In addition, he chairs the Subcommittee on Safety in the Workplace. Abbate is also treasurer of the New York Conference of Italian American State Legislators. Abbate has sponsored legislation creating a wide range of laws, including laws to stop unscrupulous prize award schemes by providing for mandatory disclosure, requiring that school bus lights be illuminated while students are being transported, and allowing civil servants union representation during investigation reviews. In addition, he is responsible for a number of laws relating to real taxes, including one to allow a property tax exemption for improvements made to comply with the Americans with Disabilities Act. Rep. Abbate worked as a legislative assistant to then-Assemblyman Stephen J. Solarz; when Solarz was elected to Congress Abbate became his district representative. Abbate has received numerous awards from a range of community groups, including Man of the Year by the Federation of Italian American Organizations of Brooklyn and the Council of Neighborhood Organizations. The lifelong resident of Bensonhurst earned an undergraduate degree in political science from St. John's University.

THOMAS J ABINANTI (D)
92nd - Parts of Westchester and New York Counties

303 South Broadway, Suite 229, Tarrytown, NY 10591
914-631-1605/abinantit@assembly.state.ny.us

Thomas J. Abinanti was first elected to the New York State Assembly in 2010. His District includes the Towns of Greenburgh and Mount Pleasant. He is Chair of the Libraries and Education Technology Committee, and is a member of the following committees: codes; corporations, authorities and commissions, election law, environmental conservation, and health. Prior to his election to the Assembly, Abinanti spent ten terms in the Westchester County Legislature where he served three times as Majority Leader. He was instrumental in establishing the Westchester Medical Center as an independent public benefit corporation. In addition, Abinanti sat on the Greenburgh Town Council for two terms. Prior to his election, he worked as legislative counsel to Congresswoman Nita Lowey and as staff counsel to the New York State Assembly. He also served as prosecuting attorney for the Villages of Ardsley and Dobbs Ferry, and has taught at Pace Law School and Mercy College of Dobbs Ferry. Abinanti received his undergraduate degree from Fordham College and his JD from New York University School of Law. He is married and has two children.

CARMEN E ARROYO (D)
84th - Part of Bronx County

384 E 149th St, Suite 301, Bronx, NY 10455
718-292-2901/arroyoc@assembly.state.ny.us

In a special election in February 1994, Carmen E. Arroyo became the first and only Puerto Rican/Hispanic woman elected to the New York State Assembly. She is chair of the Majority Program. In addition, she is a member of the following standing committees: aging, alcoholism & drug abuse; children and families; and education.

Assemblywoman Arroyo was born, raised, and educated in Corozal, Puerto Rico. She came to the mainland U.S. in 1964 and worked in a factory in New York, and sent for her seven children in 1965. Her experience during this time, which included receiving public assistance for nine months, led her to found the South Bronx Action Group, where she served as executive director and advocated on behalf of tenant needs such as employment, health, adult education and welfare. She also served as a member and President of Community School Board 7 for 20 years, and was the state's first Puerto Rican housing developer in the state, and has served on a number of boards. She also writes poetry. She earned an associate's degree from Eugenio Maria de Hostos Community College, and an undergraduate degree from the College of New Rochelle. In addition to her seven children, she has 13 grandchildren.

JEFFRION L AUBRY (D-L)
35th - Part of Queens County

98-09 Northern Blvd, Corona, NY 11368
718-457-3615/aubryj@assembly.state.ny.us

Jeffrion Aubry was first elected to the New York State Assembly in 1992. Assemblyman Aubry is the New York State Speaker Pro Tempore, and is a member of the following committees: ways and means, rules, social services and governmental employees. He also chairs the Board of Justice Center, a national organization which provides technical assistance to states to develop data-driven consensus-supported criminal justice policies to reduce crime and decrease the cost of incarceration nationwide. Assemblyman Aubry is a member of the Council of State Governments and is a "Toll Fellow," a distinguished association of state legislators from across the country. His legislative achievements include backing a 2009 measure that that significantly reformed the Rockefeller Drug Laws in New York State by returning discretion to judges to sentence drug-addicted offenders to treatment as an alternative to prison. He also led the fight to ensure that prisoners suffering from serious mental illness receive needed treatment, and are not confined under inhumane conditions through the enactment of the Special Housing Unit Exclusion Law. Professionally, Assemblyman Aubrey has been the Director of Economic Development for the Borough President's Office of Queens, Executive Director of Elmcor Youth and Adult Activities, and Director of the North Shore Fair Housing Center. He has received numerous awards and holds an undergraduate degree from the College of Santa Fe. He is the married father of five.

WILLIAM A BARCLAY (R)
120th - Parts of Onondaga, Oswego and Jefferson Counties, the cities of Oswego and Fulton

200 N Second St, Fulton, NY 13069
315-598-5185/ barclaw@assembly.state.ny.us

William A Barclay was first elected to the New York State Assembly in 2002. He State Assembly Deputy Minority Leader. He is Ranking Minority Member of the Assembly Insurance Committee, and also sits on the following committees: energy; judiciary; rules; and ways and means. He is a partner in the Syracuse law firm of Hiscock and Barclay, specializing in business law, and he serves as a board member of Pathfinder Bank and Countryway Insurance Company. Assemblyman Barclay served as a clerk for Judge Roger Miner of the US Court of Appeals, Second Circuit, in Albany and New York City. His civic activity has included membership on the boards of directors for the Friends of the Rosamond Gifford Zoo at Burnet Park, the Everson Museum of Art, and Northern Oswego County Health Services. He is a graduate of St. Lawrence University and Syracuse University College of Law. Assemblyman Barclay represents the eighth generation of his family to live n Pulaski, Oswego County, where he resides with his wife and two sons.

DIDI BARRETT (D-WP)
106th - Parts of Columbia and Dutchess Counties

12 Raymond Ave. Suite 105, Poughkeepsie, NY 12603
845-454-2408
/BarrettD@assembly.state.ny.us

751 Warren St., Hudson, NY 12534
518-828-1961

Didi Barrett was elected to the New York State Assembly on March 20, 2012. She serves on the following committees: aging; veterans' affairs; agriculture; mental health; economic development, job creation, commerce and industry; and tourism, parks, arts and sports development. In addition, Barrett is a member of the Task Force on Legislative Women's Caucus. Barrett has long been active among not-for-profit organizations throughout the Hudson Valley. She helped create and serves on the board of the North East Dutchess Fund (NED) of the Berkshire Taconic Community Foundation, an initiative that focuses on improving life in several towns in northeastern Dutchess County. Additionally, she helped pioneer NED Corps alongside the Dutchess Community Action Partnership and serves on its affiliated Latino Roundtable, working to provide social services to this region's communities that are more rural. She is a member of the board of Spout Creek Farm, an educational farm, and led the creation of the Dutchess Girls Collaborative to support young women and girls. She is the founding chair of Girls Incorporated of NYC, a former board member of NARAL Pro-Choice New York, and a trustee emeritus of the American Folk Art Museum. Barrett holds an undergraduate degree in speech communications from UCLA and a MA in Folk Art Studies from NYU. She and her husband have two children.

CHARLES BARRON (D)
60 - Part of Kings County

669 Vermont St., Brooklyn, NY 11207
718-257-5824/barronc@assembly.state.ny.us

Charles Barron was elected to the New York State Assembly in 2014. He sits on the following committees: aging; alcoholism and drug abuse; economic development, job creation, commerce and industry; energy; small business; and social services. He previously served on the New York City Council for 13 years, where he chaired the Committee on Higher Education and secured funding for parks, schools, and funding for the Black Male Initiative for City University of New York. A community activist for more than 45 years, Assemblyman Barron is a founding member of Operation POWER (People Organizing and Working for Empowerment and Respect), the founding chairperson of the National Black United Front's Harlem Chapter, Chief of Staff to the Chair of the National Black United Front, and Secretary General of African Peoples Christian Organization, operated by Re. Dr. Herbert Daughtry, Chair of the NBUF. Assemblyman Barron holds an associate's degree from New York Technical College and a B.A. from Hunter College. He is the married father to two children.

MICHAEL R BENEDETTO (D)
82nd - Part of Bronx County

177 Dreiser Loop, Rm 12, Bronx, NY 10475
718-320-2220

3602 E. Tremont Ave, Suite 201, Bronx, NY 10465
718-892-2235/benedettom@assembly.state.ny.us

Michael R Benedetto was first elected to the New York State Assembly in 2004. He chairs the Committee on Cities, and also sits on the following committees: agriculture; education; governmental operations; labor; and ways and means. The Bronx native spent 35 years teaching elementary and secondary school students. In 1974, he joined the New York City public school system as a teacher of mentally and physically challenged students; in 1977 he was assigned to PS 160, the Walt Disney School, and in 1988 became coordinator of the special education unit. He is currently an adjunct instructor at Mercy College. While with the NYC schools, Assemblyman Benedetto ran the first "very special" Olympics for multiply handicapped children. In addition, he established the Throggs Neck Community Players Community Theater and served as member of Community Planning Board #10. Assemblyman Benedetto also started the Bronx Times Reporter, which became the largest community paper in the Bronx. He has received numerous awards. He holds an undergraduate degree in history and education from Iona College, and also earned a MA in social studies and education.

RODNEYSE BICHOTTE (D)
42 - Part of King's County

1414 Cortelyou Road, Brooklyn, NY 11226
718-940-0428/bichotter@assembly.state.ny.us

Rodneyse Bichotte was elected to the New York State Assembly in 2014. She sits on the following committees: banks; economic development, job creation, commerce and industry; housing; mental health; small business; and social services. She was elected District Leader in 2010, and in that position has sponsored events in Flatbush such as a Voter's Forum; a mayoral debate; and annual senior luncheons. Professionally, she has been a public school teacher, an engineer, and a finance manager. Of Haitian descent, she has traveled the world, including for work. She is also active in her community, including as a Community Board 17 member and Scholarship Chair of Chicago Urban League Metroboard Scholarship. She holds an MBA from Northwestern University's Kellogg School of Management, an MS in Electrical Engineering from Illinois Institute of Technology, a BS in Electrical Engineering from SUNY Buffalo, a BS in Mathematics in Secondary Education, and a BT in Electrical Engineering, both from Buffalo State College. She was born and raised in Brooklyn.

MICHAEL BLAKE (D)
79 - Part of Bronx County

780 Concourse Village West, Ground Fl. Professional, Bronx, NY 10451
718-538-3829/BlakeM@assembly.state.ny.us

Michael Blake was elected to the New York State Assembly in 2014 and sits on the following committees: banks; correction; election law; housing; and veterans' affairs. His district includes parts of Concourse Village, Morrisania, Melrose, Claremont and East Tremont. He is the Founding Principal of Atlas Strategy Group, which focuses on political and economic empowerment for communities of color. He also served as Director of Public Policy & External Affairs for Green For All, and a Senior Advisor for Operation Hope. Assemblyman Blake joined the Obama Campaign's "Yes We Can" political training program in 2006, and went on to successfully co-organize three state house campaigns. He worked in the Obama campaign in Iowa, and went on to work for the Presidential Inaugural Committee, and then joined the White House staff where he created the White House Urban Entrepreneurship Summit Series. He also worked for President Obama's 2012 re-election campaign. He is a graduate of the Medill School of Journalism at Northwestern University.

KEN BLANKENBUSH (R)
117th - Lewis County, Parts of St. Lawrence, Jefferson and Oswego Counties

40 Franklin St., Suite 2, Carthage, NY 13619
315-493-3909/blankenbushk@assembly.state.ny.us

Ken Blankenbush was first elected to the New York State Assembly in 2010. His district includes Lewis County and parts of Oneida, Saint Lawrence, and Jefferson counties. He sits on the following committees: agriculture; corporations, authorities and commissions; insurance; and tourism, parks, arts and sports development. The longtime Black River resident is a U.S. Air Force veteran of the Vietnam War who was stationed at Plattsburg Air Force Base upon his return. He worked at Metropolitan Life Insurance Company prior to launching BEL Associates, his Watertown-based insurance and financial services business.
Blankenbush's public service includes eight years as a councilman in LeRay, and two terms as chair of the Jefferson County Board of Legislators. His memberships include the Association of the United States Army, the Greater Watertown Chamber, Watertown Elks, Black River

American Legion, and National Assoc. of Insurance and Financial Advisers. He holds a B.S. from SUNY Plattsburg, and also finished two years at Monroe Community College. He is married with two children and six grandchildren.

KARL A BRABENEC (R)
98 - Orange and Rockland counties

123 Rt. 94 South, Suite 2, Warwick, NY 10990,
845-544-7551/brabeneck@assembly.state.ny.us

Karl Brabenec was elected to the New York State Assembly in 2014 from a district that includes the City of Port Jervis and the towns of Deerpark, Greenville, Minisink, Warwick, Monroe, Tuxedo, and portions of Ramapo. He sits on the following committees: aging; cities; election law; labor; and local governments. His priorities include alleviating residents' tax burden, and cutting red tape to create jobs and business growth. Prior to his election, he was Deerpark Town Supervisor, an assistant to the former Orange County Executive, a member of the Deerpark Town Council, and the Deerpark Zoning Board. He holds an undergraduate degree from Mount Saint Mary College and an MPA from the John Jay College of Criminal Justice. He is the married father of two.

EDWARD C BRAUNSTEIN (D)
26th - Part of Queens County

213-33 39th Ave, Suite 238, Bayside, NY 11361
718-357-3588/braunsteine@assembly.state.ny.us

Assemblyman Edward C. Braunstein was elected to the New York State Assembly in November, 2010. His Northeast Queens district that includes the neighborhoods of Auburndale, Bay Terrace, Bayside, Bayside Hills, Broadway-Flushing, Douglaston, Floral Park, Glen Oaks, Little Neck, New Hyde Park, North Shore Towers, Oakland Gardens, and Whitestone. Assemblyman Braunstein chairs the Subcommittee on Trust and Estates, and is a member of the following committees: Aging; Cities; Health; Insurance, Judiciary, Small Business, and Transportation. His legislative achievements include leading the effort to ban so-called "bath salts," and also protecting New Yorkers from fraudulent attorneys by making it a felony to practice law without a license. Assemblyman Braunstein's professional background includes serving as a legislative assistant in Assembly Speaker Sheldon Silver's New York City office. He also served on Community Board 11. He holds a BS in Finance from the University at Albany, a law degree from New York Law School, and lives in Whitestone with his wife.

JAMES F BRENNAN (D-WF)
44th - Part of Kings County

416 Seventh Ave, Brooklyn, NY 11215
718-788-7221

1414 Cortelyou Road, Brooklyn, NY 11226
718-940-0641/brennanj@assembly.state.ny.us

James Brennan was first elected to the New York State Assembly in 1984, and his Brooklyn district includes sections of Park Slope, Flatbush, Kensington, Midwood, and Windsor Terrace. Assemblyman Brennan chairs the Committee on Corporations, Authorities and Commissions and is a member of the committees on Codes; Education; and Real Property Taxation. His legislative successes including funding 5,000 units of housing and allowing half-fare on the MTA system for people with mental illness; exposing - via a report called Delaying Necessities, Denying Needs - the shortcomings and delays of the New York State Dept. of Health's program to provide durable medical equipment to people with disabilities; and creating a $300 million urban revitalization fund known as Restoring New York Communities. He holds an undergraduate degree from Yale University and a JD from Brooklyn Law School.

ANTHONY J BRINDISI (D)
119th - Part of Oneida County

207 Genessee St, Rm 401, Utica, NY 13501
315-732-1055/brindisia@assembly.state.ny.us

Anthony J. Brindisi was elected to the New York State Assembly in a special election in 2011. His Mohawk Valley district includes the cities of Utica and Rome and the towns of Floyd, Frankfort, Marcy, and Whitestown. He is chair of the Subcommittee on Volunteer Emergency Services, and sits on the following committees: aging; economic development, job creation, commerce and industry; energy; higher education; transportation; and veterans' affairs. Among the initiatives Assemblyman Brindisi has backed are efforts to create a Career and Technical Education diploma pathway for high school students, as well as bipartisan efforts to revitalize the economy in the Mohawk Valley. He has been instrumental in helping to secure millions of dollars, including $108 million for the Nano Utica project on the SUNY Polytechnic Institute campus in Marcy, and millions for cyber-security and unmanned aerial vehicle research and development at Griffiss Business and Technology Park in Rome.

Assemblyman Brindisi is a former Utica School Board member, and a partner in the law firm of Bridisi, Murad, Brindisi, Pearlman, Julian & Pertz. He graduated from Siena College and Albany Law School, and is married with two children.

HARRY B BRONSON (D)
138th - Part of Monroe County

840 University Ave, Rochester, NY 14607
585-244-5255/bronsonh@assembly.state.ny.us

Harry Bronson was first elected to the New York State Assembly in 2010. His district includes parts of the City of Rochester and the towns and villages of Chili and Henrietta. He sits on the following committees: agriculture; economic development, job creation, commerce and industry; labor; local governments; transportation. In addition, he chairs the Commission on Skills Development and Career Education. He is a former law partner at Blitman and King. He currently co-owns Equal=Grounds, a coffeehouse noted as a neighborhood meeting place in the Southwedge part of the 138th Assembly District. His public service resume includes service as Assistant Minority Leader and Minority Leader of the Monroe County Legislature. He holds an undergraduate degree in public justice from SUNY Oswego and a JD from the University of Buffalo.

DAVID BUCHWALD (D)
93rd - Parts of Westchester County

125-131 East Main St., Suite 204, Mount Kisco, NY 10549
914-244-4450/BuckwaldD@assembly.state.ny.us

David Buchwald was elected to the New York State Assembly in 2012, and sits on the following committees: consumer affairs and protection; corporations, authorities and commissions; election law; governmental operations, judiciary; and local governments. His legislative advocacy includes efforts to increase state aid to local school districts. In addition, he is lead sponsor of a bill to strip public officials of their state pensions if they commit a felony involving a violation of the public trust. He is a former member of the White Plains Common Council, where he authored legislation to strengthen the city's code of ethics, improve sidewalk snow removal, combat illegal dumping, and allow council members to have unpaid interns. He also chaired the White Plains Traffic Commission. Buchwald also served as a Westchester representative to the Metro-North Railroad Commuter Council, a position he was appointed to by then-Gov. David Patterson. Buchwald went on to chair the MNRCC. His resume also includes three years in the Manhattan offices of economics research firm NERA, and he worked for the law firm of Paul Weiss, Rifkind, Wharton & Garrison, representing business and pro bono clients on tax cases. Buckwald is a former board member of the White Plains Historical Society and the White Plains Downtown Residents Association. The Larchmont native holds a BS in physics from Yale University and a JD from Harvard Law School. In addition, he holds a Master's of Public Policy from the John F. Kennedy School of Government.

MARC W BUTLER (R-C-I)
118th - Fulton and Herkimer counties and parts of Otsego County

33-41 East Main St, Johnstown, NY 12095
518-762-6486

235 North Prospect St, Herkimer, NY 13350
315-866-1632/butlerm@assembly.state.ny.us

Marc W. Butler was first elected to the New York State Assembly in 1995. He is the Ranking Minority Member on the Economic Development, Job Creation, Commerce and Industry Committee, and also sits on the following committees: agriculture; environmental conservation; higher education, insurance, and rules. As a freshman legislator in Albany, he joined with several other legislators in developing the legislation that ultimately resulted in the STAR Tax Exemption Program. Prior to his election to the Assembly, his political career included service as a Newport Village Trustee and Deputy Mayor and two terms in the Herkimer County Legislature, where he was elected Majority Leader in 1993.He is a former reporter for the Utica Observer-Dispatch and also worked as a corporate communications specialist for Utica National Insurance. He holds a bachelor's degree in English from SUNY Potsdam and is married with two children.

KEVIN A CAHILL (D)
103rd - Parts of Dutchess and Ulster Counties

Gov Clinton Bldg, Suite G-4, 1 Albany Ave, Kingston, NY 12401
845-338-9610/ cahillk@assembly.state.ny.us

Kevin Cahill was first elected to the New York State Assembly in from 1993 to 1995, and was re-elected in 1998. He chairs the Committee on Insurance, and also sits on the following committees: economic development, job creation, commerce and industry; ethics and guidance; health; higher education; and ways and means. He has backed legislation to place a moratorium on fracking. He formerly chaired the Committee on Energy, which allowed him to focus on issues surrounding energy efficiency. Legislation was passed to take proceeds from RGGI, the carbon emission cap and trade program, and direct the funding toward communities and small businesses to create a workforce aimed at improving building energy efficiency. He also helped to increase investments in energy efficiency and renewable power, green the state's facilities and vehicle fleet, and make New York's net-metering law one of the most expansive in the country. In addition, he has backed education, helping to secure $100 million to modernize the campuses of Ulster County Community College and SUNY New Paltz. He formerly served as minority leader of the Ulster County Legislature, and has worked as an attorney and director of a Medicare health plan. He has an undergraduate degree from SUNY New Paltz, a law degree from Albany Law School, is father to two daughters, and is a lifelong resident of Kingston.

ALICE CANCEL (D)
65th - Lower East Side of Manhattan

250 Broadway Room 2212, New York, NY 10007
212-312-1420/CancelA@nyassembly.gov

Born in Puerto Rico, Alice Cancel's family moved to the South Bronx and then to the lower east side in the 1970s.

Prior to her election to the New York State Assembly, Alice worked for 26 years as the area's district leader. She also worked in the state senate and in the New York City comptroller's office. She has long been recognized as a lower east side activist. She has served in many capacities – as board member, chair, president, volunteer, founder, and community leader in numerous organizations in her community.

Alice has been a liaison between offices dealing with many issues ranging from potholes to noise proliferation. She has been an advocate for individuals in private and public housing, assisted homeless families and children, and worked with domestic violence victims to assist with legal representation, counseling, and providing for emergency food and clothing. Alice lives on the lower East Side with her husband and three sons.

RON CASTORINA, JR (R)
62nd - South Shore Staten Island

101 Tyrellan Avenue Suite 200, Staten Island, NY 10309
718-967-5194/castorinar@nyassembly.gov

Ron Castorina, Jr. was elected to the New York State Assembly in a special election on April 19, 2016. He has a strong passion for public service. He served as Commissioner of the Board of Elections on Staten Island from 2013 to 2015 and reformed the voting process. He promises to fight for conservative values and traditions. Ron graduated from St. Francis College and SUNY Buffalo School of Law. He lives in Richmond Valley and has a law practice in Eltingville.

JOHN D CERETTO (R-I)
145th - Part of Niagara County and Erie County

800 Main Street, Suite 2C, Niagara Falls, NY 14301
716-282-6062/cerettoj@assembly.state.ny.us

John D. Ceretto was first elected to the New York State Assembly in 2010. His district includes the city of Niagara Falls and the towns of Cambria, Niagara, Lewiston and Wheatfield, as well as portions of the City of North Tonawanda and the town of Grand Island in Erie County. He is Ranking Minority Member on the Tourism, Parks, Arts and Sports Development Committee, and a member of the following committees: cities; education; energy; and labor. His legislative achievements include backing bi-partisan measures such as the property tax cap. Assemblyman Ceretto's elected public service career began in 1995 when he became a councilman on the Lewiston Town Board, a post he held for ten years. In 2005, Ceretto was elected Niagara County Legislator in the 12th District. In addition, he was vice chairman of the Niagara County Economic Development Committee and chaired the Niagara County Refuse Department. Ceretto is active in his local community of Lewiston, and is married with four children. He holds bachelors and master's degrees in education and administration from Niagara University.

WILLIAM COLTON (D-WF)
47th - Part of Kings County

155 Kings Highway, Brooklyn, NY 11223
718-236-1598/coltonw@assembly.state.ny.us

William Colton was elected to the New York State Assembly in November 1996 to a district that includes the neighborhoods of Bensonhurst, Gravesend, Bath Beach, Dyker Heights, and Midwood. He is the Assembly's Majority Whip and sits on the following committees: correction; environmental conservation; government employees; labor; rules; and ways and means. Prior to running for the Assembly, Colton was co-founder and organizer of the Bensonhurst Tenants Council, and also was the attorney in a successful lawsuit to halt the opening of the Southwest Brooklyn Incinerator. In the Assembly, he also was appointed Chair of the Legislative Commission on Solid Waste Management, and currently serves as Chair of the Majority Conference. Colton has remained active in his community, including sitting on the Board of Trustees of the Verrazano Lodge of the Order of the Sons of Italy and the Board of Directors of the Cardinal Stritch Knights Corporation of the Cardinal Stritch Knights of Columbus Council. He has received numerous awards for teaching and for community service. He is a former school teacher, is married with two stepchildren, and holds an undergraduate degree in urban education from St. John's University, an M.S. in Urban Education from Brooklyn College, and a J.D. from St. John's School of Law.

VIVIAN E COOK (D)
32nd - Part of Queens County

142-15 Rockaway Blvd, Jamaica, NY 11436
718-322-3975/cookv@assembly.state.ny.us

Vivian Cook was elected to the New York State Assembly in 1990. She sits on the following standing committees: codes; corporations, authorities and commissions; housing; insurance; rules; and ways and means. Her previous leadership posts include former service as the Assembly's former Majority Whip. She also chaired the Task Force on Food, Farm and Nutrition Policy. The Rock Hill, South Carolina native has served as District Leader of Queens County for more than 25 years. She founded the Rockaway Boulevard Local Development Corporation. She has supported community housing programs that provide residents with affordable homes, as well as projects to improve senior services and recreational facilities. She is the recipient of many awards for her community and civic service. She is a graduate of the DeFrans Business Institute.

JANE L CORWIN (R-C-I)
144th - Parts of Erie, Niagara, and Orleans counties

8180 Main St, Clarence, NY 14221
716-839-4691/CorwinJ@assembly.state.ny.us

Jane Corwin was elected to the New York State Assembly in 2008, and currently serves as Minority Leader Pro Tempore. She is the Ranking Minority member of the Corporations, Authorities and Commissions Committee, and also serves on the following standing committees: education; environmental conservation; mental health; ways and means. She is a strong backer of small businesses in Western New York, and led efforts to call for an overhaul of the New York State Thruway Authority's fiscal management while successfully opposing a 45 percent toll increase. Professionally, Corwin was Director of Research at Henry Ansbacher, Inc. on Wall Street, and Vice President at the Talking Book in Western New York. In addition to her Assembly duties, she is a full-time mother and active in her community where she is president and founder of the Philip M. and Jane Lewis Corwin Foundation, which funds educational, medical and religious charities to benefit children. She holds an undergraduate degree from the State University of New York at Albany and a Master's in business administration from Pace University. Corwin lives in Clarence with her husband and three children.

MARCOS A CRESPO (D-WF)
85th - Part of Bronx County

1163 Manor Avenue, Bronx, NY 10472
718-893-0202/crespom@assembly.state.ny.us

Marcos A. Crespo was first elected to the New York State Assembly in 2009 and is Chair of the Peurto Rican/Hispanic Task Force. He also sits on the following standing committees: alcoholism and drug abuse; cities; energy; environmental conservation; insurance; and transportation. In his role as Chairman of the Assembly Task Force on New Americans, he worked to address major issues for New York's 4.3 million immigrants, as well as to highlight their major economic contributions. In addition to fighting on behalf of his constituency, Crespo has backed such proposals as a new law to create an emergency energy backup system for critical state health and safety infrastructure during a natural disaster. Crespo was born in Puerto Rico and moved with his family to New York as a young age. He also lived in Lima, Peru during his early years, and returned to Puerto Rico where he finished high school. After that, he returned to New York City. He holds a BA from John Jay College of Criminal justice and is the married father of two.

CLIFFORD W CROUCH (R)
122nd - Parts of Broome, Chenango, Delaware and Otsego Counties

1 Kattelville Rd, Suite 1, Binghamton, NY 13901
607-648-6080/crouchc@assembly.state.ny.us

Clifford Crouch was first elected to the New York State Assembly in 1995. He chairs the Minority Conference, and sits on the following standing committees: agriculture; economic development, job creation, commerce and industry; labor, rules, and ways and means. He advocates on behalf of budget reform and mandate relief, as well as education funding, common core reform, and responsible teacher evaluation. Prior to serving in the Assembly, Crouch was a Town Councilman for the Town of Bainbridge from 1982 to 1986, and then a town Supervisor until he was elected to the Assembly. He also served from 1993 until 1995 as Chairman of the Board of Supervisors in Chenango County. His efforts on behalf of his community include leading the siting of the Chenango County landfill and the implementation of the county recycling program in his position as chair of the Chenango County Solid Waste Committee. He has been a member of the Bainbridge Local Development Corporation, the Board of Directors of the Broome Cooperative Fire Insurance Company, and other civic and community organizations. Crouch holds an AAS in Dairy Science from Cornell University and owned and operated a 180-head dairy farm on 350 acres from 1967 to 1989. He and his wife live in Bainbridge and have three children and seven grandchildren.

BRIAN F. CURRAN (R)
21st - Part of Nassau County

108 Merrick Road, Lynbrook, NY 11563
516-561-8216/curranb@assembly.state.ny.us

Brian Curran was elected to the New York State Assembly in 2010 to a Long Island district that includes Lynbrook, Rockville Centre, and parts of the towns of South Hempstead, West Hemmpstead, Baldwin, Oceanside, East Rockaway, Malverne, Franklin Square, Freeport, and Hewlett.He is Ranking Minority Member on the Ethics and Guidance Committee, and also serves on the following standing committees: banks; insurance; labor; and veterans' affairs. At the time he was elected to the Assembly, Curran was Lynbrook's mayor. Curran's professional resume includes service as a legislative counsel to the Assembly. He was also the Nassau Deputy County Attorney in the Litigation Bureau and Municipal Contracts and the Assistant Village Prosecutor of Lynbrook. He is currently a partner in the private law firm of Nicolini, Paradise, Ferretti, and Sabella. He graduated from Wilkes University and holds a JD from CUNY Law School. Curran is involved in a number of community organizations in his hometown, where he lives with his wife and four children.

MICHAEL J CUSICK (D)
63rd - Part of Richmond County

1911 Richmond Ave, Staten Island, NY 10314
718-370-1384/cusickm@assembly.state.ny.us

Michael Cusick was first elected to the New York State Assembly in 2002. He currently chairs the Election Law Committee. Cusick is also a member of the following standing committees in the Assembly: governmental employees; higher education; mental health; transportation; veterans' affairs; and ways and means. Prior to launching his own elective bid, Cusick was Director of Constituent Services for U.S. Sen. Charles E. Schumer, and managed the day-to-day operations for Schumer's New York City office. Prior to that, he was chief of staff to former Staten Island Assemblyman Eric N. Vitaliano and Special Assistant to former President of the City Council Andrew J Stein. Among his legislative achievements since taking office are authoring a law to set a building moratorium that paved the way for the Mid-Island Blue Belt and requiring notice to neighborhood landowners of an application to build on wetland areas. He also created "Total Fitness Challenge" in 2008 to boost youth reading and exercising during summer break. Cusick has sat on the boards of the Staten Island Board of Directors of the Catholic Youth Organization and the Boy Scouts of America. He received his undergraduate degree from Villanova University and is married and lives in his native Staten Island.

STEVEN H CYMBROWITZ (D)
45th - Part of Kings County

1800 Sheepshead Bay Rd, Brooklyn, NY 11235
718-743-4078/cymbros@assembly.state.ny.us

Steven Cymbrowitz was first elected to the New York State Assembly in November 2000. He represents the 45th Assembly District in Brooklyn that includes parts of Sheepshead Bay, Midwood, Manhattan Beach, Gravesend, and Brighton Beach. Cymbrowitz is Chair of the Committee on Aging, and also sits on the following committees: codes; environmental conservation; health; and insurance. His was among the districts hard-hit by Hurricane Sandy and has actively worked to help his constituents through the recovery. He also has worked to open the Lena Cymbrowitz Pavilion of the Maimonides Cancer Center in tribute to his late wife, Assemblywoman Lena Cymbrowitz. Before his election to the Assembly, he served as Executive Director of the North Brooklyn Development Corporation, Director of Housing and Community Development for the Metropolitan New York Coordinating Council on Jewish Poverty, Assistant Commissioner of the Division of Homeless Housing Development for the New York City Department of Housing Preservation and Development (HPD), Assistant Commissioner of the Division of Housing Production and Finance for HPD, and Deputy Commissioner of Development at HPD. He also served as the New York City Housing Authority's Director of Intergovernmental Relations. He holds a bachelor's degree from C.W. Post College, a master's degree in social work from Adelphi University and a law degree from Brooklyn Law School.

MARITZA DAVILA (D)
53rd - Parts of Kings County

249 Wilson Avenue, Brooklyn, NY 11237
718-443-1205/DavilaM@assembly.state.ny.us

Maritza Davila was elected to the New York State assembly on November 5, 2013. She is Chair of the Subcommittee on Retention of Homeownership and Stabilization of Affordable Housing, and also sits on the following committees: housing; alcoholism and drug abuse; children and families; correction; economic development, job creation, commerce and industry; and social services. Prior to her election, she served as President of the Community School Board of Education of District 32, and also as the Director of a state-wide program to raise awareness for the dangers of lead-based paint. In addition, she advocates for women's rights; as a founding member of the North Brooklyn Coalition Against Domestic Violence she served on its Board for two years. Assemblywoman Davila founded the Northern Brooklyn Residents Association to advocate on behalf of affordable housing and community development. Originally a native of Catano, Puerto Rico, she moved to Bushwick, Brooklyn as a young girl and has lived there ever since. She holds an AA in Political Science from Long Island University and is mother to three children.

MICHAEL G DENDEKKER (D-WF)
34th - Part of Queens County

75-35 31st Avenue Suite 206B (2nd Floor), East Elmhurst, NY 11370/DenDekkerM@assembly.state.ny.us

Michael DenDekker was elected to the New York State Assembly in 2008 and his district, where he has lived his whole life, includes Jackson Heights, East Elmhurst and Woodside. He is Chair of the Committee on Veterans' Affairs, and a member of the following committees: aging; alcoholism and drug abuse; governmental employees; labor; and transportation. His legislative efforts include establishing a voluntary state database for video camera surveillance. He was also instrumental in bringing the retired space shuttle Enterprise to New York City as part of the Intrepid Sea, Air & Space Museum. Professionally, DenDekker has worked as facilities manager for the New York City Council, responsible for day-to-day operations for city council offices, as well as assisting with city hall operations. Previously, he was Supervisor in the New York City Department of Sanitation. He was a member of the Bureau of Public Information and Community Affairs and, after 9/11, served as a public information officer in the Joint Information Center of the Mayor's Office of Emergency Management. DenDekker is also a member of the Screen Actors Guild, with movie and TV credits. His community involvement has included serving on Community Board #3, and as Deputy Chief for the Jackson Heights-Elmhurst Volunteer Ambulance Corp. He majored in Automotive Technology at SUNY Farmington, and lives in Jackson Heights with his wife. They have four children and two grandchildren.

ERIC M DILAN (D)
54 - Part of King's County

366 Cornelia St, Brooklyn, NY 11237
718-386-4576/DilanE@assembly.state.ny.us

Erik Dilan was elected to the New York State Assembly in 2014 from a district that includes parts of Bedford Stuyvesant, Bushwick, Cypress-Hills, and East New York. He sits on the following committees: cities; consumer affairs and protection; corporations, authorities and commissions; governmental operations; housing; and insurance. Prior to his election, Assemblyman Dilan served 12 years on the New York City Council, where his leadership posts included chairing the housing and building committee; the Brooklyn Delegation, and as a member of the budget negotiating team. The lifelong resident of North Brooklyn holds an A.S. degree in business administration from St. John's University and lives with his wife and two children in Cypress-Hills.

JEFFREY DINOWITZ (D-L-WF)
81st - Part of Bronx County

3107 Kingsbridge Ave, Bronx, NY 10463
718-796-5345/dinowij@assembly.state.ny.us

Jeffrey Dinowitz was first elected to the New York State Assembly in 1994. The district includes Riverdale, Kingsbridge, Van Cortlandt Village, Norwood, Woodlawn, and Wakefield. Dinowitz chairs the Committee on Consumer Affairs and Protection and serves on the following standing committees: election law; health; rules; and judiciary. Dinowitz previously chaired the Committee on Aging, the Committee on Alcoholism and Drug Abuse, and the Legislative Commission on Government Administration, as well as others. His legislative interests focus on senior issues, education reform, housing, the environment, and increased education aid for New York City. Assemblyman Dinowitz's professional resume prior to holding elective office includes a decade spent as an Administrative Law Judge for the State of New York for 10 years. In addition, he has served in numerous community organizations, including Vice President of the Riverdale Community Council, member of Bronx Area Policy Board #7, and member of the Boards of Directors for the Bronx High School of Science Foundation and for the Bronx Council for Environmental Quality. His extensive community activity also includes service on the Executive Committee of the Riverdale-Hudson Chapter of B'nai B'rith. In addition, he has been a member of District Council 37 and the Public Employees Federation. The Bronx native is married with two children. He earned a BA from Herbert Lehman College of City University of New York and a JD from Brooklyn Law School.

DAVID DIPIETRO (R)
147th - Parts of Erie County and Wyoming County

411 Main Street, East Aurora, NY 14052
716-655-0951/DiPietroD@assembly.state.ny.us

David DiPietro was elected to serve the constituents of the 147th Assembly District on November 6, 2012. His district includes the southern portion of Erie County and all of Wyoming County. He sits on the following committees: alcoholism and drug abuse; economic development, job creation, commerce and industry; labor; small business; and transportation. He previously served as Trustee and Mayor of the Village of East Aurora and was recognized at the State of the County of Erie conference as the leader in New York State in mergers and consolidations of government departments and services. As Mayor of East Aurora, DiPietro cut taxes for three consecutive years, and reduced the overall size of the government. His private sector experience includes positions at M&T Bank in Buffalo, Trust Division, and computer and accounting consultant to small businesses in Western New York. He received his B.S. degree in Business Administration from Wittenberg University. He is married and has three children.

JANET L DUPREY (R-I)
115th - Clinton and Franklin Counties and Part of St. Lawrence County

202 U.S. Oval, Plattsburg, NY 12903
518-562-1986/DupreyJ@assembly.state.ny.us

Janet L Duprey was first elected to the New York State Assembly in November 2006 to represent her district that includes all of Clinton and Franklin counties, as well as four towns in St. Lawrence County. She is Ranking Minority member on the Governmental Operations Committee, and also sits on the following committees: correction; higher education; rules; and ways and means. In addition, she is Vice Chairman of the Minority Program Committee. Prior to being elected to the Assembly, Duprey was Clinton County Treasurer from 1986-2006. She the first woman elected to the Clinton County Legislature, where she served for ten years, including two as chair. The Assemblywoman has been active for many years in her community and has received numerous honors. She has served on the boards of directors of the Champlain Valley Physicians Hospital Medical Center, the Clinton-Northern Essex Chapter American Red Cross and others. Assemblywoman Duprey is married with two children and four grandchildren

STEVEN C ENGLEBRIGHT (D)
4th - Part of Suffolk County

149 Main Street, E Setauket, NY 11733
631-751-3094/engles@assembly.state.ny.us

Steve Englebright was elected to the New York State Assembly in 1992. His north shore, Long Island district includes Port Jefferson Station and sections of Coram, Centereach, Selden and Lake Grove as well as the historic maritime communities that developed around the harbors of Stony Brook, Setauket, Port Jefferson and Mt. Sinai. Englebright chairs the Assembly's Committee on Environmental Conservation, and sits on the following standing committees: education, energy, higher education, and rules. Trained as a geologist and biologist, his scientific background informs his legislative approach, such as his successful advocacy on behalf of a state ban on the sale of baby bottles and other childcare products containing BPA, bisphenol-A which disrupts estrogen. He also has pushed successfully for the NYS Pine Barrens Protection Act., authored New York's solar and wind net-metering laws in the 1990s and successfully pushed in 2008 for the expansion of solar net-metering to include all utility customer classes. He has advocated on behalf of advancing the NY-SUNY2020 Challenge Grant Program in an effort to expand research and economic development, as well as increase access to education at Stony Brook. Assemblyman Englebright's previous elective office includes service in the Suffolk County Legislature from 1983-1992. The Georgia-born Englebright holds a B.S. from the University of Tennessee, and a M.S. in Paleontology/Sedimentology from SUNY Stony Brook. The father of two children lives in Setauket.

PATRICIA FAHY (D)
109th - City of Albany and Towns of Bethlehem, Guilderland and New Scotland

LOB 452, Albany, NY 12248
518-455-4178/FahyP@assembly.state.ny.us

Patricia Fahy was first elected to the New York State Assembly in 2012. She chairs the Subcommittee on Oversight of the Department of Environmental Conservation. She also sits on the following standing committees: banks; children and families; environmental conservation; higher education; and tourism, parks, arts and sports development. Prior to running for the Assembly, Fahy served as President of the Albany City School Board for one of her four years on the board. Professionally, Fahy boasts an extensive background in labor-related, legislative issues. She was Associate Commissioner of Intergovernmental Affairs and Federal Policy at the NYS Department of Labor for five years. She co-chaired the Disconnected Youth Work Group of Gov. Paterson's Children's Cabinet. Prior to moving to Albany in 1997, she was Executive Director of the Chicago Workforce Board. Prior to that time, she worked as both a legislative assistant and a legislative analyst on Capitol Hill in Washington, DC, then went on to become the Associate Director for Employment and Training in the U.S. Dept. of Labor Congressional Affairs Office. The Chicago-area native has been active within her community, including service on the Boys and Girls Club of Albany's board of directors since 2005. She earned a B.S. from Northern Illinois University and a Masters of Public Administration from the University of Illinois at Chicago. She is married to RPI professor Dr. B. Wayne Bequette. The couple has two children.

HERMAN D FARRELL, JR (D)
71st - Part of New York City

2541-55 Adam Clayton Powell Jr. Blvd, New York, NY 10039
212-234-1430/farrelh@assembly.state.ny.us

751 W 183rd St, New York, NY 10033
212-568-2828/farrelh@assembly.state.ny.us

Herman Farrell was first elected to the New York State Assembly in 1974. He represents the district that encompasses West Harlem, Washington Heights and Inwood. He has chaired the powerful Ways and Means Committee since 1994. In addition, he is a member of the Rules Committee. He formerly chaired the Banks Committee from 1979-1994 and has held other leadership positions. Farrell has been highly active in Democratic politics, serving in numerous capacities, and also has been honored by numerous organizations. For nearly two decades he served as the leader of the New York County Democratic Committee, finally stepping down in 2009. Within the Assembly, Farrell is known for his banking legislation, notably the passage of the Omnibus Consumer Protection and Banking Legislation Act with consumer protections in the auto leasing industry; the establishment of a toll-free number at the New York State Banking Department to enable consumers to receive free information on credit card interest rates, fees and grace periods; and a requirement that banks provide low-cost lifeline checking accounts. In addition, the bill prohibits discrimination based on residency in the opening of bank accounts, and requires banks to make annual reports of the number and amount of small business and small farm loans. His other legislative achievements include the Neighborhood Preservation Companies Act that enables the state to fund community groups to provide tenant advocacy and fight housing abandonment in their neighborhoods. Prior to his election, he served as Assistant Director of the Mayor's Office in Washington Heights, and also served as a Confidential Aide to a state Supreme Court Justice. Farrell grew up 20 blocks from where he now resides, in Washington Heights. He has three children and two grandchildren and has been recognized by numerous organizations.

GARY D FINCH (R-I)
126th - Parts of Cayuga, Chenango, Cortland and Onandaga Counties

69 South Street, Auburn, NY 13021
315-255-3045/ finchg@assembly.state.ny.us

Gary Finch was first elected to the New York State Assembly in 1999 to represent a large Upstate New York district and currently serves as Assistant Minority Leader. He sits on the following committees: agriculture; banks; correction; insurance; and rules. He previously served as ranking minority member of the Assembly's Corrections Committee and continues to advocate on behalf of correction officers, their families and correction issues. Professionally, Finch for 35 years has been owner and COO of Brew-Finch Funeral Homes, Inc., operating in northern, central, and southern New York. He was first elected to public office in 1979 as a Village of Aurora Trustee, and in 1982, he was elected mayor, a post he held for eight years. His extensive community service includes chairing the Board of Trustees at his alma mater, Cayuga Community College. He also has served as Cayuga County United Way's president and campaign chair and as a member of its executive and finance committees. He is a past member of Leadership Cayuga's Curriculum Program; former chair of the membership committee for the Cayuga County Chamber of Commerce; and a charter member, past president, and big brother for Big Brothers and Big Sisters. He and his wife are parents to two children, and live in Springport.

MICHAEL J FITZPATRICK (R)
8th - Part of Suffolk County

50 Rte 111, Suite 202, Smithtown, NY 11787
631-724-2929/fitzpatrickm@assembly.state.ny.us

Michael J. Fitzpatrick was elected to the New York State Assembly representing the 7th Assembly District in November 2002. His district includes the town of Smithtown and parts of Islip and Brookhaven townships. He is the Ranking Minority Member of the Housing Committee, and also sits on the following committees: higher education; labor; and ways and means. Professionally, Fitzpatrick is an investment associate in with Morgan Stanley in the firm's Port Jefferson branch office. Prior to his election to the Assembly, Fitzpatrick was an elected member of the Smithtown Town Council for 15 years, from 1988 through 2003. Fitzpatrick is secretary of the New York State American-Irish Legislators Society, and active in his local community. Born in Jamaica, Queens and raised in Hauppauge, Fitzpatrick received his B.A. in business administration from St. Michael's College in Vermont. He and his wife live in St. James, in Smithtown, and are parents to two children.

CHRISTOPHER S FRIEND (R)
124th - Tioga County and parts of Broome and Chemung Counties.

476 Maple Street, PO Box 441, Big Flats, NY 14814
607-562-3602/friendc@assembly.state.ny.us

Christopher Friend was elected to the New York State Assembly in 2011. His district includes all of Tioga County; the Town of Maine in Broome County; the city of Elmira; the towns of Ashland, Baldwin, Big Flats, Chemung, Elmira, Horseheads, Southport, and the villages of Elmira Heights, Horseheads, and Wellsburg in Chemung County. He is the Ranking Minority Member on the Committee on Children and Families and the Committee on Local Governments, and also sits on the following committees: aging; corporations, authorities and commissions; and housing. A chemist by traning, he has published more than 20 scientific papers and symposiums. Friend's public service began with work on advisory boards and commissions for the Town of Big Flats starting in 2004. He moved on to the Chemung County Legislature, to which he was elected in 2004. Assemblyman Friend holds a B.S. in chemistry from the University of New Hampshire, as well as a Master's and Ph.D. in chemistry from the State University of New York at Buffalo. He and his wife live in Big Flats with their four children.

SANDRA R GALEF (D)
95th - Parts of Westchester County

2 Church Street, Ossining, NY 10562
914-941-1111/galefs@assembly.state.ny.us

Sandy Galef was first elected to the Assembly in 1992. Her district covers the Towns of Cortlandt, Ossining, Kent, Philipstown, and the City of Peekskill. She chairs the Real Property Tax Committee and also serves on the following committees: corporations, authorities, and commissions; election law; government operations, and health. She has held previous leadership positions, including chair of the Libraries and Education Technology Committee. Her recent legislative successes include Assembly passage of legislation to end sexual harassment in smaller businesses and work environments. Before her election to the Assembly, Galef sat on the Westchester County Legislature for 13 years, including eight as the Board of Legislator's minority leader. Galef also serves on the Assembly Majority Steering Committee and the Hudson Valley Greenway Communities Council. Galef is a former teacher in the Scarsdale school system and has been deeply active in Westchester community affairs for many years. Nationally, she chaired the National Association of Counties' Labor and Employee Benefits Steering Committee, and received an Eastern Leadership Academy fellowship from the University of Pennsylvania Fels Institute Of Government. Galef has sat on the boards of directors of numerous health or educational organizations in the Westchester region, and has received numerous awards. She also hosts two TV shows, called "Dear Sandy" and "Speakout with Sandy Galef."She holds a B.S. from Purdue University and an M.Ed from the University of Virginia. Galef, a widow, resides in Ossining and has two children.

DAVID F GANTT (D)
137th - Part of Monroe County

74 University Ave, Rochester, NY 14605
585-454-3670/ganttd@assembly.state.ny.us

David F. Gantt was first elected to the Assembly in 1982. His district includes the northeastern and southwestern sections of the City of Rochester and the suburban town of Gates. He chairs the Committee on Transportation, and is a member of the following committees: economic development, job creation, commerce and industry; local governments; rules; and ways and means. Among his many legislative achievements, he has advocated on behalf of affordable housing development, health care and services for the young and elderly; maintaining transportation infrastructure safety; laws extending and expanding the 65 mph speed limit; and numerous laws to ensure voters equal access to their local polling places. His professional experience includes serving as the administrator of the Anthony L. Jordan Health Center; a working member of the Lithographers and Photoengravers International Union Local 230, and as a youth counselor to the City of Rochester. Prior to joining the Assembly, Gantt served nine years in the Monroe County Legislature, where he was Assistant Majority leader among other leadership positions. He became Monroe County's first elected African-American to hold a statewide office. Gantt attended Roberts Wesleyan College and the Rochester Institute of Technology.

ANDREW R. GARBARINO (R-C-I)
7th - Parts of Suffolk County

859 Montauk Hwy, Suite 1, Bayport, NY 11705
631-589-0348/GarbarinoA@assembly.state.ny.us

Andrew Garbarino was first elected to the New York State Assembly in 2012. His district includes much of the South Shore and Fire Island. He is a member of the following committees: banks; environmental conservation; health; higher education; and racing and wagering. His legislative achievements include the recent passage of legislation he co-sponsored to establish greater protections for women who become sex trafficking victims. Professionally, Garbarino is an attorney and works in his family's Sayville law firm. He is active in his local community, and serves as counsel to the Captain Merrill H. Masin and Graham D. Masin Foundation, which annually awards over $25,000 in local scholarships to high school students. The Sayville native holds a B.A. from the George Washington University in Washington, D.C. and a law degree from Hofstra University School of Law.

JOSEPH M GIGLIO (R-C-I)
148th - Cattaraugus County, Allegany County and parts of Steuben County

700 West State St, Olean, NY 14760
716-373-7103/GiglioJ@assembly.state.ny.us

Joseph Giglio was first elected to the Assembly in 2005.His district includes all of Cattaraugus and Allegany counties, as well as the towns of Greenwood, Jasper, Troupsburg and West Union in Steuben County. The district also includes parts of three Seneca Nation of Indians reservations. He chairs the Assembly Minority Conference's Steering Committee and is Ranking Minority Member of the Corrections Committee. His other committee memberships are as follows: aging; children and families; codes; ethics and guidance. Within the Assembly, Giglio co-chaired the Minority Statewide Forum on Workforce Issues in the Correctional System. Giglio is a former State Deputy Inspector General, focused on investigating criminal and corruption in state agencies and those who do business with the state within the Western New York area. He also previously worked as a special assistant in the State Attorney General's office, and he also worked for both the Cattaraugus and Erie County sheriff's departments. His many awards include one from the New York State Farm Bureau as a member of their "circle of friends" for his perfect voting record in support of agricultural issues. He holds a bachelor's degree from the State University of New York at Buffalo. He is married, the father of four, and lives in Gowanda.

MARK GJONAJ (D)
80th - Part of Bronx County

1126 Pelham Parkway South, Bronx, NY 10461
718-409-0109/GjonajM@assembly.state.ny.us

Mark Gjonaj was elected to represent New York's 80th Assembly District in 2012. His district encompasses the neighborhoods of Allerton, Bedford Park, Morris Park, Mosholu Parkway, Norwood, Pelham Gardens, Pelham Parkway, and Van Nest in the Bronx. Gjonaj has devoted significant efforts to community activities and organizations, including the Illyria Clinic at Jacobi Medical Center, Einstein College of Medicine Community Advisory Council, and Westchester School for Special Children. Previously he served as Commissioner of the NYC Taxi and Limousine Commission, a volunteer board that regulates the taxi, livery and black car industry.. He has served as president of M.P. Realty Group Corporation, and holds a bachelor's degree from St. John's University. He and his wife have two sons.

DEBORAH J GLICK (D)
66th - Part of New York County

853 Broadway, Suite 1518, New York, NY 10003
212-674-5153/glickd@assembly.state.ny.us

Deborah Glick was first elected to the Assembly in 1990, and is the first openly lesbian or gay member of the New York State Legislature. She chairs the Higher Education Committee, and also sits on the following committees: environmental conservation; governmental operations; rules; and ways and means. Prior to being elected to the Assembly, Glick owned and managed a small TriBeCa printing business, and later became Deputy Director of General Services for the City Department of Housing, Preservation and Development. Her legislative achievements include passage of the Sexual Orientation Non-Discrimination Act (SONDA), which was signed into law in 2002, as well as the Women's Health and Wellness Act, which became law in 2003. She saw her Hospital Visitation Bill, which gives domestic partners the same rights as spouses and next-of-kin when the loved one is in a hospital or nursing facility, became law in 2004. She also backed the Loft Law, which brings former commercial buildings up to residential code and protects current tenants, many of them artists, from eviction. She graduated from the City University of New York's Queens College and holds an MBA from Fordham University.

PHILLIP GOLDFEDER (R)
23rd - Part of Queens County

95-16 Rockaway Beach Blvd., Rockaway Beach, NY 11693
718-945-9550
/goldfederp@assembly.state.ny.us.

162-38 Crossbay Blvd., Howard Beach, NY 11414
718-641-8755

Phillip Goldfeder was elected to the New York State Assembly in September 2011. His district includes Ozone Park, Lindenwood, Howard Beach, Hamilton Beach, Broad Channel and the Rockaways in Southwest Queens. Sandy. He is Chair of the Subcommittee on Autism Retention, and sits on the following committees: aging; corporations, authorities and commissions; governmental employees; insurance; mental health; racing and wagering. His career in public service began as a community liaison for the New York City Council. He also worked in the Mayor's Office as the representative to the borough of Queens, and for Senator Charles E. Schumer, where he worked as Director of Intergovernmental Affairs. His district was severely impacted by Superstorm Sandy and Assemblyman Goldfeder has been instrumental in helping his constituents recover. The Far Rockaway native graduated from CUNY Brooklyn College, and he lives in his hometown with his wife and two children.

ANDREW W. "ANDY" GOODELL (R-C-I)
150th - Chatauqua County

Fenton Bldg, 2 E. 2nd St, Suite 320, Jamestown, NY 14701
716-664-7773/goodella@assembly.state.ny.us

Andy Goodell was elected to the New York State Assembly in 2010. He sits on the following committees: governmental operations; health; judiciary; and social services. He is managing partner at the law firm of Goodell & Rankin. Goodell's public service includes eight years as County Executive for Chautauqua County. As County Executive, he cut the tax rate six years in a row. In the community, he is founding member and former officer of the Chautauqua Leadership Network, past president of the Jamestown Rotary, treasurer for Bemus Bay Pops, and former co-chair of the United Way Professional Division. Goodell has earned numerous awards, including the Ed Crawford Award, the highest honor bestowed by the New York State Association of Counties. He holds an undergraduate degree from Williams College and his law degree from Cornell Law School, where he was a member of the Cornell Law Review. He is married with three daughters, a stepson, and several grandchildren.

RICHARD N GOTTFRIED (D-WF)
75th - Part of New York County

242 W 27th Street, New York, NY 10001
212-807-7900/GottfriedR@assembly.state.ny.us

Richard N. Gottfried was first elected to the New York State Assembly in 1971 and represents a district that includes Chelsea, Hell's Kitchen, Murray Hill, Midtown and part of the Lincoln Center area in Manhattan. He has chaired the Assembly Committee on Health since 1987. In addition, Gottfried sits on the higher education and rules committees. He is the former Deputy Majority Leader and Assistant Majority Leader, and has chaired major committees. Gottfried's achievements in his long tenure helming the health committee are numerous; he was a major architect of New York's landmark managed care reforms. His legislative achievements include the passage of the Prenatal Care Assistance Program for low-income women; the Child Health Plus Program that allows low- and moderate-income parents to get free or low-cost health insurance for their children; Family Health Plus that provides free health coverage for low-income adults; and the Health Care Proxy Law. He has advocated on behalf of patient autonomy, especially in end-of-life care, and reproductive freedom. Gottfried introduced the first same-sex marriage bill in the Assembly in 2003, and was a co-sponsor of the bill that became law in 2011. He also sponsors the Gender Non-Discrimination Act (GENDA), to prohibit discrimination based on gender identity (transgender); a bill to prohibit NY-licensed health professionals from cooperating in the torture or improper treatment of prisoners; and the bill to legalize the use of medical marijuana. He is a fellow of the New York Academy of Medicine, holds an undergraduate degree from Cornell University and a JD from Columbia Law School. He lives in Manhattan with his wife. They have one child and a grandchild.

AL GRAF (R)
5th - Part of Suffolk County

991 Main Street, Suite 202, Holbrook, NY 11741
631-585-0310
/grafa@assembly.state.ny.us

Al Graf was elected to the New York State Assembly in 2010. His district includes parts of the towns of Brookhaven and Islip, including Holbrook, Lake Ronkonkoma, Ronkonkoma, Holtsville, Centereach, as well as parts of Farmingville, Islandia, North Patchogue and Stony Brook. He sits on the following committees: codes; education; housing; and judiciary. Graf has worked on behalf of bringing lower cost hydropower to Long Island during his Assembly tenure. Professionally, Graf is a practicing attorney who began his career by enlisting in the U.S. Navy. He rose to the rank of Operations Specialist Third Class Petty Officer, then joined the New York City Police Department and worked his way up to a plainclothes unit prior to retiring due to an on-the-job injury. His public service has included two terms as a Town of Brighton Supervisor, and he remains active in his community. Graf earned an undergraduate degree in elementary education from SUNY Plattsburg and a JD from Touro Law School. He and his wife live in Holbrook and have three children.

AILEEN M GUNTHER (D-I-WF)
100th - Sullivan and Orange counties

Middletown City Hall, 3rd Floor, 16 James Street, Middletown, NY 10940
845-342-9304

18 Anawana Lake Road, Monticello, NY 12701
845-794-5807 GuntheA@assembly.state.ny.us

Aileen Gunther was first elected to the Assembly in 2003 to fill the vacancy created by the untimely death of her husband, Assemblyman Jake Gunther. She chairs the Mental Health Committee and also sits on the following committees: agriculture; environmental conservation; health, racing and wagering; and real property taxation. Gunther is a registered nurse and worked many years at Catskill Regional Medical Center, where she rose to Director of Performance Improvement and Risk Management. Among the legislation she has introduced are measures to enact the New York state nursing shortage correction act; establish the nurse loan repayment program; and create a rural home health flexibility program. She holds a nursing degree from Orange County Community College. Gunther.

PAMELA HARRIS (D)
46th - Coney Island

2823 West 12th Street, Suite 1F, Brooklyn, NY 11224
718-266-0267/harrisp@nyassembly.gov

Pamela was elected in the 2015 Special Election to fill an open seat in the 46th Assembly District. The district includes Bay Ridge, Beach Haven, Brightwater Towers, Brighton Beach, Coney Island, Dyker Heights, Luna Park, Sea Gate, Trump Village and Warbasse communities. Pamela founded the Coney Island Generation Gap, a non-profit organization aiming to educate and empower youth to get them off the streets and away from crime. Prior to her work with local children, Pamela served as a correction officer. Pamela attended John Jay College of Criminal Justice, where she obtained an Associate's degree in General Studies. She also holds a Bachelor's degree in Health and Human services from St. Joseph's College, as well as a Master's degree in Human Development and Family Studies from Capella University. Pamela Harris is a lifelong resident of Coney Island, where she and her husband, Leon, currently reside.

STEPHEN HAWLEY (R-I-C)
139th - Genesee County, parts of Monroe and Orleans counties

121 N Main Street, Suite 100, Albion, NY 14411
585-589-5780/hawleys@assembly.state.ny.us

Stephen Hawley was elected to the New York State Assembly during a special election in 2006. His district includes all of Genesee County; the Towns of Clarkson, Hamlin, Sweden and Riga in Monroe County; and all of Orleans County except the town of Shelby. He is Assistant Minority Leader, Minority Whip, and formerly served as Deputy Minority Whip. He is a member of the following committees: agriculture; insurance; veterans' affairs; and ways and means. Professionally, Hawley owned and operated Hawley Farms, and now owns The Insurance Center in his hometown of Batavia. In addition, Hawley sells residential and commercial property in the region. He also served in the Ohio Army National Guard, and the U.S. Army Reserves. Hawley has been highly involved in his community, and his involvement includes former service on the Genesee County Legislature, the Board of Directors of the Genesee Community College Foundation, as president of the Genessee County Empire Zone Development Board, Cornell Cooperative Extension of Genesee County, and many other local organizations. During his Assembly tenure, Hawley has helped develop substantial legislation that prevents registered level two or three sex offenders from working in amusement parks and requires that certain sex offenders' addresses be reported to the Division of Criminal Justice Services. He authored several pieces of legislation that would assist the agricultural industry including exempting owners of farms and the owners of multiple dwellings from the Scaffold Law. He holds a B.S. in education from the University of Toledo and is father to two sons.

CARL E HEASTIE (D)
83rd - Part of Bronx County

1446 E Gun Hill Road, Bronx, NY 10469
718-654-6539/Speaker@assembly.state.ny.us

Carl E Heastie was first elected to the New York State Assembly in 2000 and, in February 2015, was elected to the position of Speaker of the Assembly. He is the first African America to hold the post. His first budget as Speaker makes a $1.8 billion investment in education; addresses homelessness; and gives working families resources to achieve financial independence. He retains a seat on the Rules Committee., which he chairs. His legislative achievements prior to ascending to the Speaker position include being a principal negotiator to secure a minimum wage increase that took effect January 1, 2014. He has also advocated on behalf of increases in unemployment insurance benefits. Professionally, Heastie was a budget analyst in the New York City comptroller's office prior to his election to the Assembly. He holds a BS in applied mathematics and

Biographies

statistics from SUNY Stony Brook, and an MBA from Bernard M. Baruch College.

ANDREW HEVESI (D)
28th - Parts of Queens County

70-50 Austin St, Suite 110, Forest Hills, NY 11375
718-263-5595/hevesia@assembly.state.ny.us

Andrew Hevesi was first elected to the New York State Assembly in May 2005. His district includes Forest Hills, Rego Park, Ridgewood, Richmond Hill, Middle Village, Glendale, and Kew Gardens. He chairs the Committee on Social Services, and also sits on the following standing committees: energy; health; insurance; and labor. In his role on the social services committee, he has started initiatives that seek to assist individuals on the verge of homelessness to remain sheltered in their communities. His legislative achievements also include laws to enhance renewable energy generation in New York State. He is the former Chairman of the Assembly's Oversight, Analysis, and Investigations Committee. Professionally, Hevesi was Director of Community Affairs for the New York City Public Advocate, as well as Chief of Staff to former Assemblyman Jeff Klein, who is now a state senator. He also worked for the Queens County District Attorney's office. He holds a bachelor's degree in political science from Queens College and is married with one child.

DOV HIKIND (D)
48th - Part of Kings County

1310 48th St, Brooklyn, NY 11219
718-853-9616/hikindd@assembly.state.ny.us

Dov Hikind was first elected to the New York State Assembly in 1982. His district includes Borough Park, Dyker Heights, and sections of Flatbush in Brooklyn. In the Assembly, he serves as Assistant Majority Leader. Assemblyman Hikind formerly chaired the Subcommittee on Human Rights. He is a strong proponent of Israel, and provided funds for closed-circuit cameras in nine subway stations on the N, D, and F lines following terrorism concerns. The son of Holocaust survivors, he has traveled widely to fight anti-Semitism. He has been married for over three decades and is father to three children.

EARLENE HOOPER (D-L)
18th - Part of Nassau County

33 Front St, Suite 104, Hempstead, NY 11550
516-489-6610

Earlene Hooper was elected to the New York State Assembly in 1988. She serves as Deputy Speaker, the first woman to hold the office and therefore the highest-ranking female in the New York State legislature. She is a member of the following committees: education; rules; and ways and means. Her legislative priorities include increased funding for local school districts and strengthening economic development. Professionally, Hooper is a social worker who has worked as an administrator in the New York State Department of Social Services, Division of Children and Family Services. She is an adjunct professor at Adelphi University's Graduate School of Social Work. She is widely active in her community. As legislative chair of the Nassau County Chapter of Jack and Jill of America, she established the DEALS project (Developing and Expanding Adult Life Skills). She is an active member of the NAACP, the Central Nassau Chapter of the Negro Business and Professional Women's Association and Delta Sigma Theta Sorority. She holds a BA in English from Norfolk State College and a MSW from Adelphi University. She also holds a Doctor of Humane Letters from Five Towns College. She is married.

PAMELA HUNTER (D)
128th - East Side of Syracuse and Surrounding Towns
711 East Genesee Street, 2nd Floor, Syracuse, NY 13210
315-449-9536/HunterP@nyassembly.gov

Pamela Hunter is a native of Upstate New York and a U.S. Army Veteran, currently representing the south and east sides of Syracuse as well as the surrounding towns of Salina, Dewitt and Onondaga.

Prior to her election to the New York State Assembly, she served on the Syracuse Common Council, most recently as chair of the Public Safety Committee. She sat on the board of the Syracuse Industrial Development Agency, working to create jobs and grow the economy. She has a long history of leadership in local nonprofit organizations, including Epilepsy-Pralid, Inc., the Syracuse Community Health Center, Home Aides of CNY, Catholic Charities and AccessCNY. Pamela lives in Syracuse with her husband and son.

ALICIA HYNDMAN (D)
29th - Part of Queens

232-06A Merrick Blvd, Springfield Gardens, NY 11413
718-732-5412/HyndmanA@nyassembly.gov

Alicia L. Hyndman was elected to the New York State Assembly on November 10, 2015 in the 29th AD, encompassing the neighborhoods of Laurelton, Rosedale, St. Albans, Addisleigh Park, Hollis, Springfield Gardens and Jamaica. The daughter of Caribbean immigrants, Assemblywoman Hyndman emigrated to the U.S. from London, England as a young child. Assemblywoman Hyndman served on the NYC Department of Education's Community District Education Council 29 (CEC 29) for ten years, the last four years as President. As a longtime community education advocate, Assemblywoman Hyndman plans to focus on bringing resources and information back into the community to support youth and senior services, alleviate flooding, grow small businesses, and provide access to living wage jobs and entrepreneurial opportunities. Assemblywoman Hyndman holds a Bachelor of Arts Degree from the State University of New York at New Paltz, and a Master's Degree in Public Administration from Framingham State College, Mass. She resides in Rosedale, Queens with her daughters Nia and Nyla.

ELLEN JAFFEE (D)
97th - Part of Rockland County

1 Blue Hill Plaza, Suite 1116, PO Box 1549, Pearl River, NY 10965
845-624-4601/JaffeeE@assembly.state.ny.us

Ellen Jaffee was first elected to the New York State Assembly in November 2006. Her district includes Orangetown, the Ramapo Villages of Spring Valley, Suffern, Airmont, Chestnut Ridge, Hillburn, parts of Montebello, New Square, and areas in unincorporated Ramapo including sections of Monsey. She chairs the Committee on Oversight, Analysis and Investigation, and is a member of the following committees: children and families; economic development, job creation, commerce and industry; environmental conservation; health; higher education; and mental health. Her legislative achievements include the Breast Density Inform Law that helps to increase early detection standards in breast cancer screenings; banning smoking outside on hospital and residential health care facility grounds; and prohibiting over-the-counter sales of medicines that contain DXM to people under 18 without a prescription. Prior to her election to the Assembly, Jaffee served as Rockland County Legislator and a trustee for the Village of Suffern. She has received numerous awards. The Brooklyn native has lived in Rockland County since 1978, and holds a B.A. from Brooklyn College and an M.S. in Special Education from Fordham University. She and her husband are parents to two children and grandparents to three.

KIMBERLY JEAN-PIERRE (D)
11 - Suffolk County

640 West Montauk Highway, Lindenhurst, NY 11757-5538
631-957-2087/jeanpierrek@assembly.state.ny.us

Kimberly Jean-Pierre was first elected to the New York State Assembly in 2014. She sits on the following committees: banks; economic development, job creation, commerce and industry; local governments; mental health; and transportation. Prior to her election she served as Vice President of Properties for the Town of Babylon's Industrial Development Agency. Prior to that, she was a legislative aide to Congressman Steve Israel - as Community Outreach Coordinator - and to Suffolk County legislator DuWayne Gregory. She holds an undergraduate degree from Brooklyn College and an MS in Public Policy.

MARK JOHNS (R)
135th - Part of Monroe County

268 Fairport Village Landing, Fairport, NY 14450
585-223-9130/johnsm@assembly.state.ny.us

Mark Johns was elected to the New York State Assembly in 2010 to a district that includes the Monroe County communities of Webster, Penfield, Fairport/Perinton and East Rochester, and currently sits on the following committees: aging; alcoholism and drug abuse; governmental employees; governmental operations; and housing. He backs lower taxes, including the property tax cap. Professionally, he worked for the Monroe County Department of Public Education for more than 30 years. His public service includes membership on the Webster Conservation Board. In addition, he served two years on Webster's Town Board. He serves as Government Liaison to the Fairport-Perinton Chemical Advisory Prevention Committee, and volunteers for the Eastside and Bay View YMCA branches in Penfield. An Eagle Scout by age 14, he holds a bachelor's degree from St. John Fisher College.

LATOYA JOYNER (D)
77th - Bronx County

910 Grand Concourse, Suite 1JK, Bronx, NY 10451
718-538-2000/joynerl@assembly.state.ny.us

Latoya Joyner was first elected to the New York State Assembly in 2014 from a Bronx district that includes Claremont, Concourse, Highbridge, Mount Eden and Morris Heights. She sits on the following committees: aging; consumer affairs and protection; housing; insurance; and social services. Prior to her election, she was a member of Community Board 4 and the Neighborhood Advisory Board. She interned with Assemblywoman Aurelia Green, then became a community liaison in her district office. She holds an undergraduate degree from SUNY Stoney Brook, as well as a J.D. from the University at Buffalo Law School.

STEVE KATZ (R-C-I)
94th - Parts of Dutchess, Putnam, and Westchester Counties

947 S. Lake Blvd., Ste 1C, Mahopac, NY 10541
845-628-3781/katzs@assembly.state.ny.us

Steve Katz was first elected to the New York State Assembly in 2010. He sits on the following committees: aging; alcoholism and drug abuse; economic development, job creation, commerce and industry; housing; and mental health. He has advocated against the Common Core curriculum in the legislature. Assemblyman Katz, a veterinarian, spearheaded construction of a million-dollar veterinary hospital in the Bronx. He holds a B.S. in animal science from Cornell University; his studies included field research in French Guiana and Galapagos for the World Wildlife Fund. He earned his Doctor of Veterinary Medicine from the University of Pennsylvania. He is married with four children.

BRIAN P KAVANAGH (D)
74th - Part of New York County

237 1st Avenue (14th Street), Room 407, New York, NY 10003
212-979-9696/KavanaughB@assembly.state.ny.us

Brian P Kavanaugh was first elected to the New York State Assembly in November 2006; his district includes the Lower East Side, Stuyvesant Town, Peter Cooper Village, Union Square, Gramercy, East Midtown Plaza, Waterside Plaza, Kips Bay, Murray Hill, and Tudor City.. He chairs the Commission on Government Administration and sits on the following committees: cities; corporations, authorities and commissions; election law; environmental conservation; housing; and labor. He also chairs American State Legislators for Gun Violence Prevention among other leadership posts. His legislative successes include legislation to increase New York's commitment to energy efficiency, green energy and alternative to fossil fuels, and ensure equality in civil service laws. Professionally, Kavanagh in an attorney and has served as a Chief of Staff ,and as an aide to three New York City Mayors. Assemblyman Kavanagh has introduced well over 200 bills in the Assembly. He holds an undergraduate degree from Princeton University and a JD from New York University Law School.

MICHAEL P KEARNS (D)
142nd - Erie County

1074 Union Rd., West Seneca, NY 14224
716-608-6099/kearnsm@assembly.state.ny.us

Michael P. Kearns was first elected to the New York Assembly in a special election in March 2012. He sits on the following committees: banks; cities; housing; oversight, analysis and investigation. His public service career began in 2005 when he was elected to the South District Common Council Member for the City of Buffalo. His legislation includes sponsoring a Volunteer Tax Credit Bill to incentivize volunteering. Professionally, he worked as a sanitation worker for the City of Buffalo after college, and then worked for the Law Offices of Hiscock & Barclay while studying to become a paralegal. Then he went on to Kearns & Associations, where he worked his way up from fundraising consultant to vice president. The Buffalo native holds degrees from Erie Community College and Canisius College. He is married and has one child.

RONALD T KIM (D)
40 - Part of Queens County

136-20 38th Ave., Suite 10A, Flushing, NY 11354
718-939-0195/KimR@assembly.state.ny.us

Ron Kim was first elected to the New York State Senate in 2012. He sits on the following committees: children and families; corporations, authorities and commissions; education; governmental operations; housing; social services. Prior to his election, he most recently worked for The Parkside Group, which he joined after serving as a Regional Director for Government and Community Affairs in the administrations of Governors Eliot Spitzer and David A. Paterson. His other public service positions have included: working for then-Councilmember John C. Liu; as an aide to then-Assemblyman Mark Weprin; and working for the New York City Dept. of Buildings and the Dept. of Small Business Services. He became a National Urban Fellow, where he advised the Chief Education Office of the Chicago Public Schools while earning and Masters in Public Administration from Baruch College. He also holds a B.A. from Hamilton College. Assemblyman Kim lives in Flushing with his wife.

BRIAN M KOLB (R-C-I)
131st - Ontario County and Parts of Seneca County

607 W Washington St, Ste 2, Geneva, NY 14456
315-781-2030/ kolbb@assembly.state.ny.us

Brian Kolb was elected to the Assembly in 2000. He has served as Minority Leader since 2009, and serves on the Committee on Rules. He advocates on behalf of improved education, reduced taxes, sound health care, economic development, and reforming state government. Kolb - a business consultant, entrepreneur, COO, and notary public - formerly served as president of Refractron Technologies, and he co-founded the North American Filter Corporation. He also served as an adjunct professor in adult and graduate education at Roberts Wesleyan College. Within his community, with which he has been deeply involved, he chaired the Finger Lakes Community College Foundation and served on a variety of regional boards. His public service background includes service as Supervisor for the Town of Richmond, and as a member of the Ontario County Board of Supervisors and the New York State Public Authorities Control Board. He is also a member of numerous organizations. He both a B.S. and an M.S. from Roberts Wesleyan College. The Canadaigua resident is married with three children and one grandchild.

KIERAN MICHAEL LALOR (R)
105th - Parts of Dutchess County

North Hopewell Plaza, Ste 1, 1075 Rt. 82, Hopewell Junction, NY 12533
845-221-2202
lalork@assembly.state.ny.us

Kieran Michael Lalor was first elected to the Assembly in 2012 to a district that includes Beekman, Dover, East Fishkill, Fishkill, LaGrange, Pawling, Union Vale, Wappinger and Washington. He serves on the following committees: banks; governmental operations; real property taxation; small business and veterans' affairs. Professionally, he is the founder of KML Strategies, LLC, a business development and research services consulting firm working with companies that make safety products for military and law enforcement. He served as an infantryman in the Marine Corps Reserve and his unit was twice activated, including in Nasiriya, Iraq. He also helped rescue Gulf Coast residents impacted by Hurricane Katrina. Lalor is involved in numerous local and veteran's organizations. He holds a B.A. from Providence College and a J.D. from Pace Law School. The Fishkill resident is married and has four children.

CHARLES D LAVINE (D)
13th - Part of Nassau County

1 School Street, Suite 303-B, Glen Cove, NY 11542
516-676-0050/lavinec@assembly.state.ny.us

Charles D Lavine was elected to the New York State Assembly in 2004.

He chairs the Committee on Ethics and Guidance, and is a member of the following committees: codes; health; higher education; insurance; and judiciary. He also co- chairs the New York State Ethical Commission. He has sponsored legislation to increase penalties for those who use high-capacity magazines, as well as legislation to help halt illegal gun trafficking into New York. He is President of the New York Chapter of the National Association of Jewish Legislators. Prior to being elected to the Assembly, Lavine was appointed to the Glen Cove Planning Board. He later was appointed to a vacancy on the Glen Cove City Council and was subsequently elected.

Professionally, Lavine worked as an attorney in the Legal Aid Society of the City of New York, as well as his own private practice in Queens County and lower Manhattan. However, he has been a full-time legislator since becoming an Assembly member.

He holds a B.A. in English Literature from the University of Wisconsin and a J.D. from New York Law School. He and his wife have two children.

PETER A LAWRENCE (R-C-IP)
134 - Parts of Monroe County

2496 West Ridge Rd., Rochester, NY 14626
585-225-4190/lawrencep@assembly.state.ny.us

Peter Lawrence was first elected to the New York State Assembly in 2014 from a district that includes the towns of Greece, Ogden and Parma in western Monroe County. He serves on the following committees: ethics and guidance; higher education; oversight, analysis and investigation; racing and wagering; and small business. Prior to his election, Assemblyman Lawrence served nearly 29 years with the New York State Police, rising to the rank of Staff Inspector assigned to the International Affairs Division Headquarters. He retired in 2002 to become U.S. Marshal for the Western District of New York, appointed by President George W. Bush. He served in that post until 2010. His civic involvement includes serving as a board member of New York Law Enforcement, Inc., and founding an ALS golf tournament that has raised over $1.75 million to benefit patients who are receiving treatment at the University of Rochester Medical Center.

JOSEPH R LENTOL (D)
50th - Part of Kings County

619 Lorimer Street, Brooklyn, NY 11211
718-383-7474/ lentolj@assembly.state.ny.us

Joseph R. Lentol was first elected to the New York State Assembly in 1972. Both his father and grandfather served in the New York State Legislature as well. He chairs the Committee on Codes and also sits on the following committees: election law; rules; ways and means. In the past, he has been Chair of the Committee on Governmental Employees, which oversees the State's pension and employee benefits. In that capacity, Lentol presided over the state's divestiture of its pension fund's investments in South Africa. He also former Chair of the Committee on Governmental Operations. He co-sponsored the NY SAFE Act, the landmark gun control legislation passed and signed into law in 2013. Lentol, an attorney and lifelong resident of New York City, formerly served as Assistant District Attorney in Kings County. He holds a B.A. from the University of Dayton and a J.D. from Baltimore University School of Law.

BARBARA LIFTON (D-WF)
125th - Tompkins County and Part of Cortland County

106 E Court St, Ithaca, NY 14850
607-277-8030/liftonb@assembly.state.ny.us

Barbara Lifton was first elected to the New York State Assembly in 2002 and serves on the following standing committees: agriculture; education; election law; environmental conservation, higher education and rural resources. She has advocated on behalf of education and issues of importance to women. Prior to her election to the Assembly, she served as Chief of Staff to Assemblyman Marty Luster. She also was a public school teacher at Genesee Central School and in Ithaca schools for many years. Her civic and professional activities include membership on the steering committee of the Tompkins County Nuclear Weapons Freeze Campaign. In addition, she co-founded the Coalition for Community Unity and served two years on the Cornell/Community Waste Management Committee. She holds a B.A. and an M.A. in English from SUNY Genesee. She resides in Ithaca and has two children and two grandchildren.

GUILLERMO LINARES (D)
72 - New York County

210 Sherman Ave, Ste A&C, New York, NY 10034
212-544-2278/linaresg@assembly.state.ny.us

Guillermo Linares was elected to the New York State Assembly in 2014 from a district that includes Washington Heights, Inwood and Marble Hill in Northern Manhattan, having previously served in the chamber from 2011-2012. He sits on the following committees: aging; banks; cities; housing; and mental health. He previously served as Commissioner of the Mayor's Office of Immigrant Affairs from 2004-2009, on the New York City Council where he was Co-President of the council's Black and Latino Legislative Caucus, and Chair of the White House Initiative for Educational Excellence for Hispanic Americans. He also sat on the board of the National Council of La Raza. At the time Assemblyman Linares was elected to the City Council, in 1991, he was the first Dominican-born person to be elected to public office in the United States. He immigrated to the Bronx in 1966, drove a taxi, and pursued his education. He was instrumental in founding the CUNY Dominican Students Institute and the Center for Latin American and Latino Studies at the CUNY Graduate Center. He has been deeply involved in the community for decades as he seeks to improve public education and champion immigrant issues. He holds a BA and an MS from City College and a Professional Diploma in Administration and Supervision from Fordham University. In addition, he holds a Doctorate in Education - recently achieved - from Teachers College, Columbia University. He is the married father of two and grandparent to three.

PETER D LOPEZ (R)

102nd - Schoharie and Green counties, and parts of Delaware, Otsego, Columbia, Albany and Ulster counties.

45 Five Mile Woods Rd., Ste. 3, Catskill, NY 12414
518-943-1371

113 Park Place, Ste. 6, Schoharie, NY 12157
518-295-7250/lopezp@assembly.state.ny.us

Peter D. Lopez was first elected to the New York State Assembly in 2006. He is a member of the following committees: agriculture; alcoholism and drug abuse; corporations, authorities and commissions; education; and environmental conservation. His extensive background in public service includes serving as Schoharie County Clerk. Prior to his election to the Assembly, he spent 21 years on the staff of the New York State Legislature, where his duties included service as Associate Director of the Senate Agriculture Committee, Assistant Director of the Legislative Commission on Rural Resources, and District Office Director for Assembly Minority Leader John J. Faso. He was also Executive Assistant to Senator John J. Bonacic. In his community, he has also been village trustee, town Councilman, and a member of the Schoharie County Board of Supervisors. His extensive volunteer service ranges from Red Cross water safety instructor to founding member of a local Habitat for Humanity chapter. He graduated from the State University College at Cobleskill and holds a Master of Public Administration degree from the University at Albany. He and his wife have four children.

DONNA LUPARDO (D)

123rd - Part of Broome County

State Office Building, 17th Fl; 44 Hawley St, Binghamton, NY 13901
607-723-9047/lupardod@assembly.state.ny.us

Donna A Lupardo was elected to the New York State Assembly in 2004 to represent a district that includes the City of Binghamton and the Towns of Vestal and Union. She chairs the Committee on Children and Families and also sits on the following committees: economic development, job creation, commerce and industry; environmental conservation; higher education; and transportation. Her legislative achievements include backing the State Green Building Construction Act, tenant notification of environmental testing results, and authorship of the Contract Disclosure Act, which reformed the way state resources are allocated. Prior to being elected to the Assembly, she was an adjunct lecturer at SUNY Binghamton. She served on the Broome County Legislature from 1999 to 2000. She holds an undergraduate degree from Wagner College and a Master's degree in philosophy from SUNY Binghamton. She is married.

CHAD A LUPINACCI (R-C-I-WP)

10th - Part of Suffolk County

630 New York Avenue, Suite D, Huntington Station, NY 11746
631-271-8025/LupinacciC@assembly.state.ny.us

Chad A. Lupinacci was elected to the New York State Assembly in 2012 to a district that includes parts of the towns of Huntington and Babylon. He sits on the following committees: election law; higher education; judiciary; tourism, parks, arts and sports development; and transportation. His prior public service includes serving three terms as a Trustee for the South Huntington Union Free District, home of his high school alma mater, Walt Whitman High School. He is an attorney specializing in real estate and estate planning, and an adjunct professor of political science at St. Joseph's College and Hofstra University. He holds a BA, a JD, and a MBA, all from Hofstra University.

WILLIAM MAGEE (D)

121st - Madison County, Parts of Oneida and Otsego Counties

214 Farrier Ave, Oneida, NY 13421
315-361-4125, 607-432-1484/ mageew@assembly.state.ny.us

William Magee was elected to the New York State Assembly in 1990. He chairs the Committee on Agriculture, a post he has held since 1999. He is also a member of the following committees: aging; banks; higher education; and local governments. Prior to being elected to the Assembly, Magee served 19 years on the Madison County Board of Supervisors. In addition, he worked for the New York State Fair as manager of agriculture and livestock, equestrian events manager, and coordinator of special projects. He is also an auctioneer. As a member of the Assembly, Magee has supported numerous proposals to reduce state taxes, energy costs and bureaucracy. Assemblyman Magee's legislative achievements include the Agricultural Land Tax Cap, Farmland Viability Act, Farm to School Program, and authorship of laws that helped to bring back farm breweries and cideries - spurring new markets for apple growers and helping to revitalize the hops industry. He is a member of a variety of community organizations, and holds a bachelor's degree from Cornell University. He is married.

WILLIAM B MAGNARELLI (D)

129th - Parts of the City of Syracuse plus Geddes and Van Buren

Room 840, 333 East Washington St. Syracuse, NY 13202
315-428-9651/ magnarw@assembly.state.ny.us

William Magnarelli was first elected to the New York State Assembly in 1998. He is Chair of the Local Governments Committee. In addition, he sits on the following committees: economic development, job creation, commerce and industry; education; oversight, analysis and investigation; and rules. Prior to being elected to the Assembly, Magnarelli was Majority Leader of the Syracuse Common Council. By profession, he is a practicing attorney, and was a member of the U.S. Army Reserves where he rose to the rank of Captain. He backed the statewide Amber Plan law, and supported Family Health Plus that provides health care coverage to one million uninsured New Yorkers. In addition, he has secured funding for a variety of Central New York resources, such as $37 million for the Syracuse Center of Excellence, to boost the region's economic development. His community involvement includes serving on the board of the Arthritis Foundation and as president of Our Lady of Pompeii Church Parish Council. He attended Syracuse University and Syracuse University College of Law, where he received his law degree. He is married and the father of three children.

NICOLE MALLIOTAKIS (R-C)
64th - Parts of Richmond and Kings Counties

7408 Fifth Avenue, Brooklyn, NY 11209
718-987-0197

11 Maplewood Place, Staten Island, NY 10306
718-987-0197/malliotakisn@assembly.state.ny.us

Nicole Malliotakis was first elected to the New York State Assembly in 2010. She sits on the following committees: banks; corporations, authorities and commissions; governmental employees; transportation; and ways and means. Her public service background includes stints as a liaison for the late Sen. John Marchi and former Gov. George Pataki. More recently, she was public affairs manager for Consolidated Edison. In the Assembly, she has been active on behalf of those impacted by Hurricane Sandy. She also has backed efforts to restore and expand transit service in Brooklyn and Staten Island. She earned an undergraduate degree from Seton Hall University in South Orange, NJ, and an MBA from Wagner College on Staten Island.

MARGARET M MARKEY (D)
30th - Part of Queens County

55-19 69th St, Maspeth, NY 11378
718-651-3185/ markeym@assembly.state.ny.us

Margaret Markey was first elected to the New York State Assembly in 1998. Her district is comprised of the Queens neighborhoods of Maspeth, Woodside and parts of Long Island City, Middle Village, Astoria and Sunnyside. She chairs the Tourism, Parks, Arts, and Sports Committee. In addition, she sits on the following committees: governmental operations; labor; racing and wagering; and ways and means. Her legislative goals include growing the state's tourism industry, which generates more than $50 billion each year.Prior to joining the Assembly, she was Director of Marketing and Tourism for the Borough of Queens; and Assistant Director of Economic Development, Office of Queens Borough President Claire Shulman. She has long been active in her community and served as a member of Community Boards 2 and 5 and is the founder of Maspeth Town Hall, Inc., a community center that serves over 1000 families. She graduated from Berkeley Business School. The Queens-born Markey is the married mother of three children.

SHELLEY MAYER (D-WP-I)
90th - Part of Nassau County

35 E Grassy Sprain Rd, 406B, Yonkers, NY 10710
914-779-8805/MayerS@assembly.state.ny.us

Shelley Mayer was first elected to the New York State Assembly in 2012 to represent her hometown district comprised of Yonkers. She chairs the Subcommittee on Students with Special Needs, and sits on the following committees: children and families; cities; education; health; labor; and social services. Mayer brings a strong professional background to her elected position. Prior to joining the Assembly, she was a Senior Counsel at the National State Attorney General Program at Columbia Law School focusing on health care and labor law rights. Prior to that, she was Vice President of Government and Community Affairs at Continuum Health Partners, one of New York City's largest teaching hospital systems. From 1982 to 1994, she was an Assistant Attorney General in the office of New York Attorney General Bob Abrams. Mayer served in the Civil Rights Bureau, as Chief of the Westchester Regional Office, as the legislative liaison for the Attorney General and finally as a senior advisor to the Attorney General. She remains active in her community, and has served as a member of the Yonkers NAACP, Yonkers YWCA, Westchester Women's Bar Association, and Westchester Women's Agenda. She also served on the boards of the Jewish Council of Yonkers/ Westchester Community Partners and the Board of the Yonkers Public Library. She holds an undergraduate degree from UCLA and a JD from SUNY Buffalo School of Law. Mayer is the married mother of three.

JOHN T MCDONALD III (D)
108th - Parts of Albany, Renssalaer and Saratoga Counties

LOB 417, Albany, NY 12248
518-455-4474/McDonaldJ@assembly.state.ny.us

John T. McDonald III was elected to the New York State Assembly in 2012 to a district that includes sections of Albany, Troy and the communities of Green Island, North Greenbush, Rensselaer, Waterford and Watervliet. He chairs the Subcommittee on Effective Treatment, and sits on the following committees: aging; alcoholism and drug abuse; cities; insurance; mental health; and real property taxation. He is President of his family-owned Marra's Pharmacy in his hometown of Cohoes. Prior to being elected to the Assembly, McDonald spent 13 years as Mayor of Cohoes. In this role, he focused on economic development and revitalization or developments in key areas. As a result, 2,000 new residential units arrived in the city, downtown revitalization is underway, and improvements to the Cohoes Falls have helped to make it a regional attraction. McDonald was also actively involved in the New York State Conference of Mayors, including serving as president of the state-wide organization. He also has been actively involved on numerous boards, including chairing the Capital District Transportation Committee, and the Cohoes Industrial Development Agency, as well as sitting on boards such as the State Comptroller's Local Advisory Team. He holds a BS in pharmacy science from Albany College of Pharmacy, as well as a Doctorate of Humanity, and is the married father of three.

DAVID G MCDONOUGH (R)
14th - Part of Nassau County

404 Bedford Ave, Bellmore, NY 11710
516-409-2070/mcdonoughd@assembly.state.ny.us

David McDonough was first elected to the New York State Assembly in 2002, and sits on the following committees: consumer affairs and protection; education; health; transportation; and veterans' affairs. McDonough is past president of the Nassau County Council of Chambers of Commerce, a member of the Committee for the Merrick Downtown Revitalization Project, and four-term President for the Merrick Chamber of Commerce. In this role, his achievements included growing the membership ranks by 35 percent. In addition, he is a founding member and former board member of the Bellmore-Merrick Community Wellness Council and a member and past president of the Kiwanis Club of Merrick. In addition, McDonough served in both the U.S. Coast Guard and the U.S. Air Force. He holds a B.A. in economics from Columbia University, and is a graduate of the American Academy of Dramatic Arts. The Merrick resident is married with three children and four grandchildren.

TOM MCKEVITT (R)
17th - Part of Nassau County

1975 Hempstead Trnpke, Ste. 202, East Meadow, NY 11554
516-228-4960/mckevit@assembly.state.ny.us

Tom McKevitt was elected to the New York State Assembly in a special election in 2006. He is Assistant Minority Leader Pro Tempore, which means he holds the third ranking position in the Minority Conference and is responsible for assisting in the management of all floor activity and debates. He also serves on the following standing committees: codes; consumer affairs and protection; election law; and local governments. Prior to joining the Assembly, McKevitt worked in the offices of state Senator Kemp Hannon and U.S. Senator Alfonse D'Amato. He also was the Deputy Town Attorney for the Town of Hempstead, and he has been an attorney in private law firms in Nassau County, where he has lived all his life. He remains active in professional and civic organizations, including as past chair of the Nassau County Bar Association's Municipal Law Committee. He is a member of the East Meadow Chamber of Commerce and the East Meadow Kiwanis Club. He holds both an undergraduate degree and a JD from Hofstra University. The East Meadow resident is married and the father of two.

STEVEN F MCLAUGHLIN (R-C)
107th - Parts of Columbia, Washington, and Rensselaer Counties

258 Hoosick St., Ste 109, Troy, NY 12180
518-272-6149/ mclaughlins@assembly.state.ny.us

Steve McLaughlin was elected to the New York State Assembly in 2010 to his Upstate district in the Capital Region. He is a member of the following committees: children and families; economic development, job creation, commerce and industry; education; and social services. As an Assemblyman, his focus is on putting New Yorkers back to work, reducing spending and cleaning up corruption in Albany. In addition, he backs substantive ethics reform, including requiring the full disclosure of officials' outside income and imposing term limits on the legislative leadership. He received his commercial and instrument airplane ratings from Florida Institute of Technology, and earned his bachelor's degree from USNY and an MBA from the University of Phoenix. He has flown for both corporate and commercial airlines, and was a mortgage loan officer for Citizens Bank. Currently, he is works for Monolith Solar. He and his wife have two children.

MICHAEL G MILLER (D)
38th - Part of Queens County

83-91 Woodhaven Blvd, Woodhaven, NY 11421
718-805-0950/millermg@assembly.state.ny.us

Michael G. Miller was elected in September 2009 to a Queens County district that includes the neighborhoods of Woodhaven, Ridgewood, Richmond Hill, Ozone Park and Glendale. He is Chair of the Committee on House Operations, and also sits on the following committees: aging; banks; education; labor; racing and wagering; and veterans' affairs. Assemblyman Miller's achievements include authoring a law that requires level two sex offenders to register their employment address. He also has backed the $9 minimum wage increase, as well as a freight locomotive engine upgrade to reduce air pollution. Prior to his election, Miller sat on Community Board 5 and advocated for affordable housing, expansion of services for seniors and additional after-school programs. He was Capital Campaign Director for the Greater Ridgewood Youth Council, and he founded the Forest Park Aktion Club, which supports adults with mental disabilities. Professionally, Miller managed the New York office of Tiger Federal Credit Union. He attended both Queens College and the University of Georgia CUNA Management School.

MICHAEL A MONTESANO (R-I-C)
15th - Part of Nassau County

111 Levittown Parkway, Hicksville NY 11801
516-937-3571/montesanom@assembly.state.ny.us

Michael Montesano was elected to the New York State Assembly in 2010. He sits on the following committees: codes; corporations, authorities and commissions; ethics and guidance; judiciary; and oversight, analysis and investigation. Prior to his election, he was a police officer and detective for the NYPD for a decade and served as an EMT supervisor and investigator for the NYC Emergency Medical Service. In 1990 he started his own private practice law firm and served as Acting Village Justice in Roslyn Harbor. He also was a Village Prosecutor for Roslyn Harbor and adjunct professor at the New York Institute of Technology. He has served as a President, Vice-President and Trustee of the North Shore School District Board of Education. He holds an associate degree from Nassau County Community College, a bachelor's degree in Criminal Justice from St. John's University, and law degree from CUNY Law School at Queens College. He is married, resides in Glen Head, and has two children and two stepchildren.

JOSEPH D MORELLE (D)
136th - Cities of Irondequoit, Brighton, and Rochester

1945 E Ridge Rd, Rochester, NY 14622
585-467-0410/morellej@assembly.state.ny.us

Joseph Morelle was elected to the Assembly in 1990. He became the Assembly's Majority Leader in 2013, which makes him responsible for the day-to-day operations in the Assembly chamber, including running the floor during debates. He also sits on the Committee on Rules, and formerly chaired the Committee on Insurance. His legislative achievements include working with state and local leaders to bring 250 new, well-paying jobs to the Rochester region. He also sponsored New York's autism health insurance law, which requires carriers to cover the cost of autism screening and treatment. He has served on the Finger Lakes Regional Economic Development Council. Prior to his election to the Assembly, he served in the Monroe County Legislature. Morelle lives in Irondequoit, the Rochester suburb where he grew up, and holds a bachelor's degree in political science from SUNY Geneseo. He and his wife have three children.

WALTER T. MOSLEY (D)
57th - Part of Queens County

55 Hanson Place, Brooklyn, NY 11217
718-596-0100/MosleyW@assembly.state.ny.us

Walter T. Mosley was elected to the New York State Assembly in 2012 to a Brooklyn district that includes Clinton Hill, Fort Greene, Prospect Heights, and parts of Crown Heights, and Bed-Stuy. He chairs the subcommittee on regulated mortgage lenders, and sits on the following committees: banks; codes; correction; education; and housing. His first vote was on behalf of the NY Safe Act, the landmark gun control act signed into law in 2013. He also has introduced the Retail Anti-Profiling Act calling for more transparency regarding NYPD personnel in private businesses, and legislation to prohibit smoking on all State University of New York campuses. Prior to his election, Mosley was special advisor and external relations specialist for the New York State Senate Minority Conference and Director of Contract Compliance and Government & Community Relations for Spectrum Personal Communications. He holds a bachelor's degree from Pennsylvania State University at University Park, and a law degree from Howard University. He and his wife have two children.

FRANCISCO P MOYA (D-WF)
39th - Part of Queens County

82-11 37th Avenue, Ste 607, Jackson Heights, NY 11372
718-458-5367

Francisco P. Moya was elected to the New York State Assembly in 2010, which made the lifelong resident of Corona the first Ecuadorian-American elected to public office in the United States. He chairs the Commission on Science and Technology and the Subcommittee on Workplace Safety. In addition, he sits on the following committees: corporations, authorities and commissions; energy; housing; insurance; labor; and ways and means. Prior to his election, he worked for the Queens Health Network at Elmhurst Hospital, and served as Secretary to the Senate for former Senate Minority Leader David A. Patterson. After the 2008 beating death of Ecuadorian immigrant Jose Sucuzhanay, Moya acted as spokesperson for the family, and helped to organize community rallies and vigils. Long active in his community, he helped to start the after-school sports program at St. Leo's school. He holds an undergraduate degree from St. John's University and was selected a National Urban Fellow to get his master's degree in public administration.

DEAN MURRAY (R)
3 - Part of Suffolk County

1735 N. Ocean Ave., Ste. A, Medford, NY 11763
631-207-0073/murrayd@assembly.state.ny.us

Dean Murray was elected to the New York State Assembly in 2014 from a Suffolk County district that includes Medford and Mastic Beach. He previously represented the district from 2010-2013. He currently sits on the following committees: aging; education; small business; tourism, parks, arts and sports development; and transportation. He advocates on behalf of reduced property taxes and bi-partisan solutions to high taxes. He owns D & S Advertising Inc., a Long-Island based advertising agency that publishes publications such as the Long Island Job Finder and the Long Island Fugitive Finder. He previously worked in regional sales for TCI Cable, and prior to that was a radio and television news reporter in New York, Delaware, Maryland and Pennsylvania, where he covered the state capital for more than 100 radio stations. He is involved in his local community, graduated from the Broadcast Institute of Maryland, and is the married father of one.

BILL NOJAY (R)
133rd - Livingston County and Parts of Monroe and Steuben Counties

3011 Rochester Road, Ste 3, Lakeville, NY 14480
585-346-0002/NojayW@assembly.state.ny.us

Bill Nojay was elected to his upstate district in the New York State Assembly in 2012 and sits on the following committees: consumer affairs and protection; election law; mental health; and transportation. Nojay is an attorney by profession, and hosts a daily radio show on stations in Upstate New York. He is a small business owner. He is focused on improving the Upstate economy via cutting state spending and regulations, as well as reducing property taxes. Prior to his election to the Assembly, Nojay served as President of the International Business Council of the Greater Rochester Chamber of Commerce and Commissioner of the Rochester Genesee Regional Transportation Authority, including service as chairman. He chaired the Regional Trails Initiative Steering Committee for the Rochester Region. He was COO of Detroit's transportation system under Detroit Mayor David Bing. The Rochester native has been deeply involved in his community, formerly serving as director and treasurer of the Al Sigl Center for the Developmentally Disabled; Chairman of the Monroe County Sports Commission and Chairman of the U.S. Army's Community Advisory Board in the Rochester region. He has served as an election monitor for the International Republican Institute in Ukraine and Afghanistan and supported other democracy movements around the globe. He holds a JD from Columbia University, as well as an MBA, also from Columbia. He also received a certificate in international and comparative law from the Parker School of Columbia University and was a research fellow at Tribhuvan University in Kathmandu, Nepal when he lived there as a Thomas J. Watson Fellow. He and his wife live in Pittsford and are parents to three children.

CATHERINE T NOLAN (D)
37th - Part of Queens County

41-02 Queens Blvd, Ste 2B, Sunnyside, NY 11104
718-784-3194

61-08 Linden Street, Ridgewood, NY 11385
718-456-9492/nolanc@assembly.state.ny.us

Catherine Nolan was elected to the New York State Assembly in 1984 and represents a district that includes the neighborhoods of Sunnyside, Ridgewood, Long Island City, Queensbridge, Ravenswood, Astoria, Woodside, Maspeth, Dutch Kills and Blissville. She has chaired the Assembly's Committee on Education since 2006 and in that capacity has spearheaded efforts to achieve class size reduction, universal pre-K, middle school initiatives, and improve high school graduation rates. She also sits on the following committees: corporations, authorities and commissions; rules; veterans' affairs; and ways and means. She has previously chaired the Committee on Banks, the Committee on Labor, the Real Property Taxation Committee, and the Assembly's Commission on State-Federal Relations. She also represented the Assembly on the MTA Capital Program Review Board. She also serves on the Assembly Majority Steering Committee. She holds a B.A. from NYU and resides in Ridgewood with her husband and son.

DANIEL J O'DONNELL (D)
69th - Part of New York County

245 W 104th Street, New York, NY 10025
212-866-3970/odonnelld@assembly.state.ny.us

Daniel J O'Donnell was first elected to the New York State Assembly in 2002 and represents a district that includes Manhattan Valley, Morningside Heights, and parts of the Upper West Side. He chairs the Committee on Correction, as well as the Subcommittee on Criminal Procedure. In addition, he sits on the following committees: codes; education; environmental conservation; and tourism, parks, arts and sports development. O'Donnell is the first openly gay man elected to the New York State Assembly. During his tenure in the Assembly, he has been the prime sponsor of major legislation including the Marriage Equality Act, a bill O'Donnell led to passage in the Assembly five times; it was finally signed into law in June 2011. He also backed the Dignity for All Students Act, which requires public schools in New York to combat bias-based bullying and harassment. Prior to joining the Assembly, O'Donnell was a public defender in the Brooklyn office of the Legal Aid Society; he then opened his own public interest law firm. He earned a B.A from George Washington University and his J.D. from CUNY Law School. Born in Queens and raised in Commack, O'Donnell lives with his husband in Morningside Heights.

ROBERT C OAKS (R-C)
130th - Wayne County, Parts of Cayuga, and Oswego Counties

10 Leach Rd, Lyons, NY 14489
315-946-5166/oaksr@assembly.state.ny.us

Robert C. Oaks was first elected to the New York State Assembly in 1992; his district includes Wayne County, the towns of Aurelius, Brutus, Cato, Conquest, Ira, Mentz, Montezuma, Sennett, Sterling and Victory in Cayuga County, and the towns of Hannibal, Minetto, and Oswego in Oswego County. He sits on the Rules Committee and the powerful Ways and Means Committee, where he is the Ranking Minority Member. He previously served as the Deputy Minority Leader. Prior to his election to the Assembly, he was elected to three terms as Wayne County Clerk. Professionally, Oaks served as Assistant Director of the Continuing Education for the Greece Central School District, and Director of the Wayne County Youth Bureau. Oakes remains deeply involved with his community, including serving on the boards of directors for the Seneca Waterways Council, the Boy Scouts of America, and the Wayne County Community Endowment Advisory Board. He holds an undergraduate degree from Colgate University and a master's degree in recreational administration from the University of Montana. He and his wife reside in Macedon and are parents to two children.

FÉLIX ORTIZ (D)
51st - Part of Kings County

404 55th St, Brooklyn, NY 11220
718-492-6334/ortizf@assembly.state.ny.us

Félix Ortiz was elected to the New York State Assembly in 1994. He is Assistant Speaker of the New York State Assembly. He is a member of the following committees: correction; labor; rules; ways and means. His legislative achievements include backing a $2 billion bond act to repair the state's aging infrastructure, as well as a fight to create the state's first Child Obesity Education Program. He formerly chaired the Puerto Rican/Hispanic Task Force, as well as the cities; mental health, alcohol and substance abuse, and veterans' affairs committees. Assemblyman Ortiz was born and raised in La Playa De Salinas, Puerto Rico, and became the first member of his family to move to the U.S. mainland in 1980. He served in the U.S. Army for two years. Ortiz is also Vice President of the Parliamentary Confederation of the Americas; Executive Board member of the National Conference of State Legislatures, and also co-founded and served as President of the National Hispanic Caucus of State Legislatures, among other organizations. He holds a BS from Boricua College, and a Master's in Public Administration from New York University. He is married and father to three.

STEVEN OTIS (D)
91st - Part of Westchester County

222 Grace Church Street Suite 305, Port Chester, NY 10573
914-939-7167/OtisS@assembly.state.ny.us

Steven Otis was first elected in 2012 to the New York State Assembly to represent a district that includes the Sound Shore communities of Larchmont, Mamaroneck, New Rochelle, Port Chester, Rye and Rye Brook. He chairs the Commission on Solid Waste Management, and sits on the following committees: agriculture; corporations, authorities and commissions; environmental conservation; libraries and education technology; local governments; and tourism, parks, arts and sports development. Otis is the former Mayor of Rye, a post he held for 12 years, the longest in the city's history. He also served for many years as counsel and chief of staff to Sen. Suzi Oppenheimer from 1985 until his election to the Assembly. Prior to that, he was a Senate Fellow and legislative director to State Senator Jeremy S. Weinstein. He has been deeply involved in his community's civic life - particularly focusing on environment and water-related issues - for many years, including serving as chair of the City of Rye Conservation Commission, and Vice Chair of the Long Island Sound Watershed Intermunicipal Council. He graduated from Hobart & William Smith Colleges and holds a Master's degree in public administration from New York University and a JD from Hofstra University School of Law. He is married and lives with his wife in Rye.

PHILIP A PALMESANO (R-C-I)
132nd - Schuyler and Yates Counties, Parts of Steuben, Chemung, and Seneca Counties

105 E. Steuben St, Bath, NY 14810
607-776-9691/palmesanop@assembly.state.ny.us

Assemblyman Phil Palmesano was first elected to the Assembly in 2010. His district includes most of Steuben County, Schuyler and Yates counties, and the following towns in Chemung and Seneca counties: Catlin, Erin, Van Etten, Veteran, Covert, Lodi, Ovid and Romulus. He is Ranking Minority Member on the Energy Committee, and sits on the following Assembly committees: corporations, authorities and commissions; energy; libraries and education technology; real property taxation; and tourism, parks, arts and sports development.

His public service background includes stints as a legislative aide to former State Assemblyman Donald Davidsen; former State Assemblyman Jim Bacalles, and district director to former Congressman Randy Kuhl, Jr. In addition, Assemblyman Palmesano was the district director for New York State Senator George Winner, and represented the city of Corning in the Steuben County Legislature. He is active in community organizations such as the marketing committee of Catholic Charities of Steuben County. He holds a B.A. in political science from St. Bonaventure University, and resides in Corning with his wife and two children.

ANTHONY H PALUMBO (R-C)
2nd - Parts of Suffolk County
400 W. Main St., Suite 201, Riverhead, NY 11901
631-727-0204/palumboa@assembly.state.ny.us

Anthony H. Palumbo was elected to serve the residents of the 2nd Assembly District in a Special Election held on November 5, 2013. His district includes the North Fork of Long Island in Suffolk County. His legislative achievemets include sponsoring a tax-cut bill that would save the average Suffolk County resident over $2,500 per year. Prior to his election to the Assembly, he served as an assistant district attorney for the Suffolk County District Attorney's Office, where he prosecuted hundreds of cases on misdemeanor and felony levels. He served as Trial Supervisor to the five Eastern Suffolk Towns and he has also been in private practice. His community involvement includes serving as the Vice President of the Cutchogue-New Suffolk Library Board of Trustees. Palumbo received a degree in Government and Law from Lafayette College in Easton, Pennsylvania, and graduated from St. John's Law School in Jamaica, New York. He currently resides in New Suffolk with his wife Tracy and their two children.

AMY R PAULIN (D)
88th - Part of Westchester County
700 White Plains Rd, Ste 252, Scarsdale, NY 10583
914-723-1115/paulina@assembly.state.ny.us

Assemblywoman Amy Paulin was elected to the New York State Assembly in November 2000 and represents a district that includes Bronxville, Pelham, Pelham Manor, Scarsdale, Tuckahoe, Eastchester, and parts of New Rochelle and White Plains. She currently chairs the Assembly's Energy Committee, also serves on the following committees: education; health; and higher education. Her work in the energy committee is focused on encouraging renewable energy and ensuring a reliable electricity grid. Prior to joining the Assembly, she served as Executive Director of My Sisters' Place and as a member of the Scarsdale Village Board. She also was Founder and Chairwoman of the Westchester Women's Agenda.. She is the recipient of numerous awards. The Brooklyn-born Paulin graduated from SUNY-Albany, holds a Master's degree from SUNY-Albany and has completed doctoral coursework in Criminal Justice from the same school. She and her husband reside in Scarsdale and have three children.

CRYSTAL D PEOPLES-STOKES (D)
141st - Part of Erie County
792 E Delavan Ave, Buffalo, NY 14215
716-897-9714/peoplec@assembly.state.ny.us

Crystal Davis Peoples-Stokes was first elected to the New York State Assembly in 2002. She is Chair of the Committee on Governmental Operations. In addition, she sits on the following standing committees: alcoholism and drug abuse; environmental conservation; health; higher education; and insurance. She has been actively involved in making sure that minority and women-owned businesses have a fair chance at obtaining state contracts, including being appointed by Gov. Cuomo to sit on the Minority and Women Owned Business Enterprise Teach Task Force. She also has backed major funding for a number of Western New York projects such as funds for a new home for the Community Health Center of Buffalo and the city's Educational Opportunity Center's new facility. She holds an undergraduate degree from Buffalo State College, as well as a M.S. in student personnel training from the same school. She is married and lives in Buffalo, her hometown.

N NICK PERRY (D)
58th - Part of Kings County

903 Utica Avenue, Brooklyn, NY 11203
718-385-3336/ perryn@assembly.state.ny.us

N Nick Perry was elected to the New York State Assembly in 1992 to represent his Brooklyn district. He is the Assistant Speaker Pro Tempore also sits on the following committees: banks; codes; labor; transportation; and ways and means. He also is the Chairman of the New York State Association of Black and Puerto Rican Legislators and the Regional Chairman (for NY and PA) of the National Black Caucus of State Legislators. Perry, who emigrated from his native Jamaica, volunteered for the U.S. Army, where he served two years' active duty and four years' reserve. He has long been active in local public service, serving on his local Community Board as chair. He also served on the Brooklyn Borough Board. In the Assembly, Perry achieved two recent, significant victories with the Cyber Crime Youth Rescue Act and the Taxpayer Refund Choice Act. He holds a B.A. in political science from Brooklyn College and an M.A. in public policy and administration from the same school. He is the married father to two.

VICTOR M PICHARDO (D)
86th - Parts of New York County

2175C Jerome Ave., Bronx, NY 10453
718-933-6909/pichardov@assembly.state.ny.us

Victor M. Pichardo was elected to the represent New York Assembly District 86 during a special election held on November 5, 2013. His district includes University Heights and areas of West Bronx. He formerly served as Staff Assistant to Senator Chuck Schumer, and was promoted to Community Outreach Coordinator/Latino Liaison. He has also held the position of Associate Director of Public Relations at Mercy College, and the Director of Community Affairs for State Senator Gustavo Rivera in the Bronx. He holds a degree in Communications with double minors in English and Sociology from the University of Buffalo.

J. GARY PRETLOW (D)
89th - Part of Westchester County

6 Gramatan Ave, Mt Vernon, NY 10550
914-667-0127/pretlowj@assembly.state.ny.us

J Gary Pretlow was elected to the New York State Assembly in 1992 to represent a district that includes Mount Vernon and Yonkers. He chairs the Committee on Racing and Wagering, and also sits on the following standing committees: codes; insurance; rules; and ways and means. Assemblyman Pretlow is responsible for Cynthia's Law, a provision of which makes reckless assault of a child a class D felony. In addition, he has worked to stabilize the finances of the New York City Off Track Betting Corporation; he backs a state takeover. Professionally, he is financial planner with Moncur-Pretlow and Co. His previous public service includes the Mount Vernon City Council, where he chaired the Finance and Planning Committee, and the Capital Projects Board. He remains active in his local community and has received numerous awards. He holds a B.B.A. from Baruch College, and is the married father to one child.

DAN QUART (R)
73rd - Part of New York County

360 E 57th St, Mezzanine, New York, NY 10022
212-605-0937/quartd@assembly.state.ny.us

Assemblyman Dan Quart was elected in November 2011 to represent a district that encompasses the Upper East Side, Midtown East, Turtle Bay and Sutton Place. He is Chair of the Subcommittee on Museums & Cultural Institutions, and sits on the following standing committees: alcoholism and drug abuse; consumer affairs and protection; corporations, authorities and commissions; insurance; judiciary; and tourism, parks, arts and sports development. His previous public office was on Community Board 8, where he co-chaired the Transportation Committee and chaired the 2nd Avenue Subway Task Force. An attorney, Quart has been heavily involved in doing pro bono work for many years. He has served as a volunteer for the Housing Division of the Legal Aid Society, providing free representation for low-income tenants in eviction proceedings, since 2002. In 2003, New York State Chief Judge Judith Kaye awarded him the Pro Bono Publico Award as one of New York City's top pro bono attorneys. He also has been the pro bono attorney for the tenants in the Eastwood Housing complex on Roosevelt Island; and for the Disabled Veterans Consortium, representing a disabled veteran who was denied benefits. Beginning in 2009, Dan has partnered with Eviction Intervention Services to organize and lead a pro bono clinic representing tenants on the East Side who fall just above the monetary threshold for free legal services, but cannot afford an attorney of their own. He holds an undergraduate degree from SUNY Binghamton and a JD from St. John's Law School. He is the married father of one.

EDWARD P RA (R)
19th - Part of Nassau County

825 East Gate Blvd, Suite 207, Garden City, NY 11530
516-535-4095
rae@assembly.state.ny.us

Ed Ra was elected to the New York State Assembly in 2010 to a district on his native Long Island that includes parts of the Towns of Hempstead, North Hempstead, and Oyster Bay. He Ranking Minority member on the Education Committee and also sits on the following committees: codes; education; health; higher education; and transportation. He is also Vice-Chairman of the Minority Steering Committee. Ra has served as the Deputy Town Attorney for the Town of Hempstead and as a legal aide in the Office of the New York State Attorney General. He holds an undergraduate degree from Loyola College of Maryland, and a J.D. from St. John's University School of Law. Ra also holds an LL.M in Intellectual Property Law from Benjamin N. Cardozo School of Law. He and his wife live in Garden City South.

ANDREW P RAIA (R-I-C-WF)
12th - Part of Suffolk County

75 Woodbine Ave, Northport, NY 11768
631-261-4151/ raiaa@assembly.state.ny.us

Andrew P Raia was first elected to the New York State Assembly in 2002. He has been Deputy Minority Whip since 2014, and also serves as the Ranking Minority member on the Health Committee. He also sits on the following committees: banks; environmental conservation; health; housing; and rules. He is the former Ranking Minority Member of the Committee on Banks where he co-sponsored the Home Equity Theft Prevention Act. He also focuses on health care policy, senior issues, and efforts to rein in unfunded mandates that he believes stifle economic growth on Long Island and otherwise impose burdens on schools and governments there. Prior to being elected to the Assembly, Raia spent 12 years on the staffs of legislative offices in the State Assembly, State Senate, and the Suffolk County Legislature. He continues to be active within his community, including serving as a director of the Huntington Boys and Girls Club, the Huntington Freedom Day Care Center, and the Huntington Station Enrichment Center. Raia holds a bachelor's degree in political science from SUNY-New Paltz.

PHILIP R RAMOS (D-WF)
6th - Part of Suffolk County

1010 Suffolk Ave, Brentwood, NY 11717
631-435-3214/ ramosp@assembly.state.ny.us

Phil Ramos was first elected to the New York State Assembly in 2002 to a district that includes portions of the hamlets of Brentwood, Central Islip, Bay Shore, North Bay Shore, and Islandia. He is Deputy Majority Leader, and sits on the following standing committees: aging; economic development, job creation, commerce and industry; education; and local governments. Assemblyman Ramos is retired detective who rose through the ranks of the Suffolk County Police Department. During his two decades in law enforcement, Assemblyman Ramos worked undercover in the Narcotics Unit for eight years, then went on to become a detective. He joined with other Latino police officers to found the Suffolk County Police Hispanic Society to address Latino issues in the community, and he also helped organize the Long Island Latino Elected Officials Association. He began his working career as a therapy aide and Emergency Medical Technician. He is father to two.

DIANA C RICHARDSON (D-WF-G)
43 - Part of Kings County

1216 Union Street. Brooklyn, NY 11225
718-771-3105/richardsond@assembly.state.ny.us

Diana C. Richardson was first elected to the New York State Assembly in a special election on May 5, 2015 from a district that includes Crown Heights, Lefferts Gardens, Wingate and East Flatbush. She sits on the following committees: banks; corporations, authorities and commissions; economic development, job creation, commerce and industry; mental health; and small business. She was Director of Constituent Affairs for NYS Senator Kevin Parker, and has been Executive Member of Brooklyn's Community Board 9. She holds an undergraduate degree from CUNY Medgar Evers, and a Master's of Public Administration from CUNY Baruch College. She is mother of one.

JOSÉ RIVERA (D)
78th - Part of Bronx County

One Fordham Plaza, Ste 1008, 10th Fl, Bronx, NY 10458
718-933-2204/riveraj@assembly.state.ny.us

José Rivera was first elected to the New York State Assembly in 1982, where he served for five years. He then left office and was re-elected in 2000. He is Assistant Majority Whip, and a member of the following committees: aging; agriculture; insurance; and small business. He formerly chaired the Task Force on Food, Farm and Nutrition Policy. During his previous stint in the Assembly, he served as Treasurer, Vice Chair and Chairman of the Black and Puerto Rican Caucus. As the Chair of this committee, he was instrumental in establishing the Martin Luther King holiday in the state of New York. Rivera also has served on the New York City Council.

ANNETTE M ROBINSON (D)
56th - Part of Kings County

1360 Fulton Street, Rm 417, Brooklyn, NY 11216
718-399-7630/ RobinsonA@assembly.state.ny.us

Annette M Robinson was first elected to the New York State Assembly in 2002. She chairs the Committee on Banks, and also is a member of the following committees: aging; children and families; housing; oversight, analysis and investigation; real property taxation; and small business. She has long been involved in public service, having been elected to the first of three terms to the District 16 Community School Board in 1977, and then elected to the New York City Council in 1991. She is a District leader/State Committeewoman in the 56th A.D., has served as coordinator and liaison for former New York City Comptroller Harrison J. Goldin, and has been District Director for U.S. Congressman Major R. Owens. She earned both her bachelor's and Master's degrees from New Hampshire College. Now a widow, she and her husband William were married more than 50 years. She is the mother to six, and is also a grandmother and great-grandmother.

ROBERT J RODRIGUEZ (D)
68th - Part of New York County

55 E 115th St, New York, NY 10029
212-828-3953/rodriguezrj@assembly.state.us

Robert J. Rodriguez was elected to the New York State Assembly in 2010. He chairs the subcommittee on infrastructure, and is a member of the following standing committees: banks; corporations, authorities and commissions; housing; labor; mental health; and ways and means. His professional experience includes work as vice president of a minority-owned public finance firm. He served on Community Board 11, including as chair. In addition, he sat on the board of directors of the Upper Manhattan Empowerment Zone. Other community service includes sitting on the boards of the Terrence Cardinal Cooke Community Advisory Board, Catholic Charities Community Services of New York, and SCANNY, a youth and family services organization. Professionally, he was vice president of a minority-owned public finance firm prior to being elected to the Assembly. The East Harlem native holds an undergraduate degree from Yale University and an MBA from New York University.

LINDA B ROSENTHAL (D)
67th - Part of New York County

230 West 72nd St, Ste 2F, New York, NY 10023
212-873-6368/RosentL@assembly.state.ny.us

Linda B Rosenthal was first elected to the New York State Assembly in 2006. Her district includes the Upper West Side and parts of Clinton/Hell's Kitchen in Manhattan. She chairs the Committee on Alcoholism and Drug Abuse, and sits the following standing committees: agriculture; education; energy; health; housing; tourism, parks, arts and sports development. Among her legislative achievements is passage more than 40 laws, including laws that extend orders of protection to companion animals; allowing same sex couples to adopt non-biological children together in New York State, and banning the sale of electronic cigarettes to minors.. Prior to joining the legislature, Rosenthal served as Manhattan District Director and Director of Special Projects to Congressman Jerrold Nadler. She holds a B.A. from the University of Rochester, and is a lifelong resident of the Upper West Side.

NILY ROZIC (D)
25th - Part of Queens County

159-16 Union Turnpike, Flushing, NY 11366
718-820-0214/RozicN@assembly.state.ny.us

Nily Rozic was first elected to the New York State Assembly in 2012 to a district that includes northeast Queens neighborhoods including Flushing, Queensboro Hill, Hillcrest, Fresh Meadows, Oakland Gardens, Bayside and Douglaston. She chairs the Subcommittee on Emerging Workforce, and sits on the following committees: children and families; corporations, authorities and commissions; correction; environmental conservation; and labor. She is the former Chief of Staff to Assemblyman Brian Kavanaugh. Within her community, she served on Community Board 8. The Fresh Meadows resident, who was born in Jerusalem and raised in Queens, holds an undergraduate degree from New York University.

ADDIE J RUSSELL (D)
116th - Parts of Oswego, Jefferson and Saint Lawrence counties

Dulles State Office Bldg, Ste 210, 317 Washington Street, Watertown, NY 13601
315-786-0284

3 Remington Ave., Suite 1, Canton, NY 13617
315-386-2037/ RussellA@assembly.state.ny.us

Addie Jenne Russell was elected to the New York State Assembly in 2008 from a district that follows the shore of the St. Lawrence River from the northeast corner of Lake Ontario to the manufacturing town of Massena and borders Fort Drum and the Black River to the east. She chairs the Task Force on Food, Farm & Nutrition Policy and the Subcommittee on Women Veterans. She is also a member of the following standing committees: agriculture; corporations, authorities and commissions; economic development, job creation, commerce and industry; energy; local governments; and veterans' affairs. Prior to her election, she was an attorney at the law firm of Conboy, McKay, Bachman & Kendal, LLP. In addition, she served on the Jefferson County Board of Legislators from 2006-2009. She has been highly active in the community, serving as past President of the Jefferson County Branch of the American Association of University Women, on the Board of Directors of the Volunteer Transportation Center; and serving on Jefferson County's Community Services Board. She holds a B.A. from the University at Albany and a J.D. with a Certificate in Family Law and Social Policy from Syracuse University College of Law. The seventh generation of her family to live in the North Country, she and her husband reside in Theresa with their two children.

SEAN RYAN (D)
149th - Part of Erie County

936 Delaware Ave, Buffalo NY 14209
716-885-9630/RyanS@assembly.state.ny.us

Sean Ryan was first elected to the New York State Assembly in 2011. He chairs the Commission on State-Local Relations, and sits on the following standing committees: banks; energy; education; environmental conservation; local governments; and veterans' affairs. Prior to his election, Ryan worked with People United for Sustainable Housing, Inc. to create a non-profit development entity called the Buffalo Neighborhood Stabilization Company, Inc. (BNSC). He served as the Executive Director and General Counsel of BNSC, which secured more than $3 million in funding for construction projects to turn vacant houses into affordable housing. He has also worked for Neighborhood Legal Services, as well as sitting on the boards of directors and providing legal representation to non-profits including Buffalo Niagara River Keeper, Autistic Services Inc., and the City of Buffalo's Living Wage Commission. He received his undergraduate degree from SUNY College at Fredonia and his J.D. from Brooklyn Law School. He is married with two children and resides in Buffalo.

JOSEPH S SALADINO (R)
9th - Part of Nassau County

512 Park Blvd., Massapequa Park, NY 11762
516-541-4598/saladij@assembly.state.ny.us

Assemblyman Joseph Saladino was elected in a special election held in 2004. He is Chairman of the Minority Conference's Program Committee, and sits on the following standing committees: environmental conservation; governmental employees; labor; libraries and education technology; and ways and means. His legislative achievements include helping to sponsor and pass the current civil confinement law and fought for a newer and stronger Megan's Law. Prior to joining the Assembly, he had a career as a news anchor and reporter with Long Island's largest television and radio stations, was the Director of Operations for the Town of Oyster Bay and served as Executive Assistant for the Town of Hempstead. He has been a member of the area Kiwanis Club for many years, where he has served as President, as well as numerous other community organizations. He attended Tulane University in New Orleans, LA and holds a master's degree from the New York Institute of Technology.

ANGELO SANTABARBARA (D-WP-I)
111th - Montgomery, Schenectady and Albany counties

2550 Riverfront Center, Amsterdam, NY 12010
518-843-0227/SantabarbaraA@assembly.state.ny.us

433 State Street, Schenectady, NY 12305
518-381-2941

Angelo Santabarbara was first elected to the New York State Assembly in 2012. He chairs the Subcommittee on Agriculture Economic Development and Farmland Protection, and also sits on the following committees: agriculture; energy; governmental employees; racing and wagering; small business; veterans' affairs. Professionally, he is an engineer. He was previously elected to the Schenectady County Legislature where he chaired the transportation committee. In addition, he sits on the Board of Directors for the Autism Society of the Greater Capital Region. He started a cheese-making company and donates all profits to local children's charities. Santabarbara, a lifelong resident of Schenectady County, served in the US Army Reserves and is commander of AMVETS Post 35. He holds a bachelor's degree from SUNY Albany and lives in Rotterdam with his wife and two children.

MICHELLE SCHIMEL (D)
16th - Part of Nassau County

45 N Station Plaza, Suite 203, Great Neck, NY 11021
516-482-6966/scmimelm@assembly.state.ny.us

Michelle Schimel was first elected to the New York State Assembly in 2007 to represent her Long Island district. She is Majority Conference Chair, and sits on the following committees: environmental conservation; governmental operations; local governments; transportation; and veterans' affairs. The full-time legislator is focused on preventing gun violence and protecting the environment. She has served on the board of New Yorkers Against Gun Violence for 20 years, co-chairs State Legislators Against Illegal Guns, and is a member of American State Legislators for Gun Violence. She helped to assemble -after the Newtown massacre - a broad coalition to create an eight-point plan against gun violence, many of which were part of the NY SAFE Act, considered one of the country's toughest gun-safety acts. Prior to her election to the Assembly, she served eight years as North Hempstead Town Clerk. She also is the former vice president of a Manhattan-based fashion accessories company, and she also worked as a physical therapist at North Shore University Hospital. She holds an undergraduate degree from the University of Pennsylvania. She is mother to two children.

ROBIN L SCHIMMINGER (D-I-C)
140th - Parts of Erie and Niagara Counties

3514 Delaware Ave, Kenmore, NY 14217
716-873-2540/ schimmr@assembly.state.ny.us

Robin Schimminger was elected to the New York State Assembly in 1976. He is chair of the Economic Development, Job Creation, Commerce and Industry committee. In addition, he sits on the following committees: codes; health; and ways and means. During his long tenure in the Assembly he has been the first Chair of the Committee on Small Business; chaired the Committee on Economic Development, Job Creation, Commerce and Industry, and also served on the joint Legislative Commission on Government Administration. His numerous legislative accomplishments - nearly 400 laws - include his Omnibus Procurement Act, which maximizes the opportunity for in-state firms to do business with New York State. Prior to his election to the Assembly, he was twice elected to the Erie County Legislature, in 1973 and 1975 where he chaired the Public Health Committee. He has served on the boards of numerous civic organizations. He is a co-founder of the Buffalo Dortmund Sister City Committee. Schimminger holds a B.A. from Canisius College, and also studied at the William Butler Yeats International School of Literature and the University College, Dublin. He holds a J.D. from NYU School of Law. He is married and lives in Kenmore.

REBECCA A SEAWRIGHT (D)
76th - Part of New York County

1365 First Ave., New York, NY 10021
212-288-4607/SeawrightR@assembly.state.ny.us

Rebecca Seawright was elected to the New York State Assembly in 2014 from a district that includes Manhattan's Upper East Side, Yorkville, and Roosevelt Island. She sits on the following committees: banks; consumer affairs and protection; corporations, authorities and commissions; judiciary; and tourism, parks, arts and sports development. She is former Assistant District Attorney in the Brooklyn DA's office and legal counselor to small business owners and entrepreneurs. She is also a former member of Community Planning Board 8. In addition, she is Chair of the Board of Visitors of CUNY School of Law, and Chair of the Board of Directors for the Feminist Press. Originally from Texas, Assemblywoman Seawright was state director of the National Women's Political Caucus, and Chief of Staff for Texas legislator Bob Melton. She also worked in Washington, DC for former U.S. Sen. Lloyd Bensten, and Congressmen Charles Stenholm and the late Marvin Leath. An Upper East Side resident for more than 20 years, she holds a law degree from CUNY Law School. She is the married mother of one.

LUIS R SEPÚLVEDA (D-WF)

87th - Part of Bronx County

1973 Westchester Avenue, Bronx, NY 10462
718-931-2620/SepulvedaL@assembly.state.ny.us

Luis R. Sepulveda was first elected to the New York State Assembly in 2012. He chairs the Subcommittee on Transitional Services, and sits on the following committees: aging; agriculture; banks; correction; and housing. His legislative efforts include protecting privacy, including legislation to restrain the use of drones, and developing a workforce education bill to help unemployed workers transition to new fields. An attorney by training, he has a community law practice in the Bronx's Parkchester area. He has been appointed counsel to several New York State Senators and to the New York State Senate Majority Counsel's office. Previously, he ran a pro bono project to provide free legal assistance to Bronx residents. He and State Sen. Ruben Diaz co-founded the Parkchester Public Initiative, the Castle Hill Community Public Safety Project, and the West Farms/Lambert House Public Safety Office. He holds a B.A. from Hofstra University and a J.D., also from Hofstra. He entered his law program after a fellowship with the Council on Legal Educational Opportunities. He is married with two children.

MICHAEL SIMANOWITZ (D)

27th - Part of Queens County

159-06 71st Ave, Flushing, NY 11365
718-969-1508/simanowitzm@assembly.state.ny.us

Michael Simanowitz was elected to the New York State Assembly in 2011 to a district that includes College Point, Forest Hills, Kew Gardens Hills, Electchester, Pomonok, Briarwood, Kew Gardens, and Richmond Hill. He chairs the Commission on Toxic Substances and Hazardous Wastes, and sits on the following committees: aging; agriculture; consumer affairs and protection; economic development, job creation, commerce and industry; higher education; and small business. His legislative successes include passing legislation that requires children under 18 to receive written parental consent prior to obtaining a body piercing. Prior to his election, he served as the Chief of Staff to Assemblywoman Nettie Mayersohn for over 15 years until her retirement. Professionally, Simanowitz also was a Planner and Community Liaison at New York City Housing Preservation and Development where he worked on several major developments in Brooklyn including the completion of MetroTech Center and Atlantic Terminal. During his tenure with Mayersohn, Assemblyman Simanowitz worked closely with the Assemblywoman Mayersohn and the New York State Department of Health to develop development of a pilot program establishing stroke centers in Queens and Brooklyn. The success of the program prompted an expansion to 110 hospitals across New York State. He holds a B.A. from Queens College and lives in Electchester Housing Cooperative with his wife and four children.

JO ANNE SIMON

52nd - Part of Kings County

341 Smith Street, Brooklyn, NY 11231
718-246-4889/simonj@assembly.state.ny.us

Jo Anne Simon was elected to the New York State Assembly in 2014 and sits on the following committees: consumer affairs and protection; higher education; judiciary; labor, and transportation. She established a disability civil rights firm following positions such as teaching in Hofstra University School of Law's clinical program, and is a nationally-recognized expert in her field. She is also an adjust Assistant Professor of Law at Fordham University. She is highly active in area Democratic, civic and community affairs, including as President of the Boerum Hill Association, and has founded or co-founded organizations such as Council of Brooklyn Neighborhoods, the Downtown Brooklyn Traffic Calming Task Force, and the Association on Higher Education and Disability, of which she is general counsel. She also chaired the Gowanus Community Stakeholder Group and Gowanus Expressway Community Coalition. She holds a B.A. in Communication Sciences from Iona College, a Master's Degree in Education of the Deaf from Gallaudet University; and a law degree from Fordham University School of Law. A Brooklyn resident since 1981, the Yonkers native lives in Boerum Hill, Brooklyn, with her husband.

ARAVELLA SIMOTAS (D-WC)

36th - Part of Queens County

31-19 Newtown Avenue, Suite 401, Astoria, NY 11102
718-545-3889/simotasa@assembly.state.ny.us

Aravella Simotas was elected to the New York State Assembly in 2010, becoming the first woman elected to office in her district. She chairs the Task Force on Women's Issues and sits on the following standing committees: banks; corporations, authorities and commissions; consumer affairs and protection; and energy. Her legislative efforts have been aimed at promoting a revitalized New York economy, protecting neglected consumers, and strengthening the criminal justice system. Prior to her election to the New York State Assembly, Assemblywoman Simotas worked a as a district representative for New York City Council Speaker Peter F. Vallone, Sr. and Councilmember Peter F. Vallone, Jr. In addition, she worked for the New York State Department of Environmental Conservation during law school and collaborated with her predecessor, New York State Senator Michael Gianaris, in a battle to curb construction of additional power plants in western Queens. Professionally, she is an attorney who worked with the firm of Bickel & Brower and contributed her time to providing legal representation to those who could not afford it. She formerly served on the Queens Community Planning Board 1, as well as the boards of United Community Civic Association and the Hellenic Times Scholarship Fund. She holds a B.A. from Fordham University and a J.D. from Fordham Law School. She and her husband live in Astoria.

FRANK SKARTADOS (D)

104th - Dutchess and Orange counties

154 North Plank Road, Ste 2, Newburgh, NY 12550
845-562-0888/skartadosf@assembly.state.ny.us

Frank Skartados first served in the New York State Assembly from 2008-2010 then was elected again in a March 2012 special election. He sits on the following standing committees: agriculture; economic development, job creation, commerce and industry; local governments; small business; tourism, parks, arts and sports development; and transportation. Professionally, Skartados was a teacher and department chair at the New York Military Academy, and then focused on buying and renovating properties in downtown Poughkeepsie. He is founder and president of the Academy Street Business Association. In addition, he owns a small farm in Milton, NY. Assemblyman Skartados holds a bachelor's degree from SUNY New Paltz and a Master's degree in international studies from the

State University of California at Sacramento. He was born in Greece and moved to the U.S. with his mother when he was 14.

JAMES SKOUFIS (D-I-WF)
99th - Orange and Rockland Counties

11 Main Street, Chester, NY 10918
845-469-6929/SkoufisJ@assembly.state.ny.us

James Skoufis was first elected to the New York State Assembly in 2012. He chairs the Subcommittee on Catastrophic Natural Disasters, and sits on the following standing committees: agriculture; local governments; insurance; labor; and transportation; and veterans' affairs. His legislative priorities include raising the minimum wage to $9 and creating tax penalties for corporations that ship jobs overseas. Prior to his election to the Assembly, Skoufis sat on the Woodbury Town Council, where he led the local relief effort for those impacted by Hurricane Irene. He also worked as a project manager for Amerigard Alarm and Security Corporation. He holds a B.A. from the George Washington University and an M.A. from Columbia University.

MICHAELLE C SOLAGES (D)
22nd - Parts of Nassau County

1690 Central Court, Valley Streanm BT 11580
516-599-2972/SolagesM@assembly.state.ny.us

Michaelle Solages was first elected to the New York State Assembly in 2012. Her Long Island district includes North Valley Stream, Valley Stream, South Floral Park, Floral Park, Bellarose Terrace, North Woodmere, Elmont, Stewart Manor, and parts of Franklin Square. She chairs the Subcommittee on Product Safety, and sits on the following standing committees: consumer affairs and protection; governmental employees; libraries and education technology; racing and wagering; and social services. Professionally, she has worked in libraries as a supervisor of access services at her alma mater, Hofstra University, from which she holds a bachelor's degree. She and her husband live in Elmont.

DAN STEC (R-C-I)
114th - Essex and Warren Counties, Parts of Saratoga and Washington Counties

140 Glen St., Glens Falls, NY 12801
518-792-4546/StecD@assembly.state.ny.us
7559 Court St., Rm. 203, PO Box 217, Elizabethtown, NY 12932
518-873-3803

Dan Stec was elected to the New York State Assembly in 2012. He is Ranking Minority member on the Committee on Environmental Conservation, and also sits on the following committees: banks; local governments; social services; and tourism, parks, arts and sports development. Assemblyman Stec has been outspoken on behalf of pension forfeiture for corrupt legislators. Prior to his election, Stec was Queensbury Town Supervisor - where he returned nearly $10 million to local taxpayers in rebates - and Chairman of the Warren County Board of Supervisors. He also sat on the Queensbury town council and zoning board. The Navy veteran served for eight years as a nuclear engineer aboard the USS Truxtun and was stationed in the Persian Gulf during Operation Desert Storm. He holds a BS from Clarkson University and an MBA from the University of Rhode Island. The married father of one lives in his hometown of Queensbury.

PHIL STECK (D)
110th - Parts of Schenectady and Albany Counties

1609 Union St., Schenectady, NY 12309
518-377-0902/SteckP@assembly.state.ny.us

Phil Steck was first elected to the New York State Assembly in 2012. He chairs the Subcommittee on Insurer Investments and Market Practices and also sits on the following committees: children and families; health; insurance; judiciary; and transportation. In the legislature, among the issues he backs are single-payer health insurance and raising revenue through the stock transfer tax to pay for rebuilding the infrastructure of Upstate New York. Prior to his election to the Assembly, Steck served on the Albany County Legislature for four terms. An attorney by profession, he is a civil rights and employment law specialist in the firm of Cooper, Erving and Savage LLP. He also spent two years as Assistant District Attorney in Rensselaer and New York counties. He holds an undergraduate degree from Harvard University and a JD from the University of Pennsylvania Law School. The married father of two lives in Loudonville.

AL STIRPE (D)
127th - Part of Onondaga County

7293 Buckley Rd., Ste. 201, N. Syracuse, NY 13212
315-452-1115/StirpeA@assembly.state.ny.us

Al Stirpe was elected to the New York State Assembly in 2012. He previously served in the Assembly from 2007-2010. He chairs the Subcommittee on Export Trade, and sits on the following standing committees: agriculture; alcoholism and drug abuse; economic development, job creation, commerce and industry; higher education; tourism, parks, arts and sports development. Prior to his most recent election, Stirpe served as Executive Director of Synapse Sustainability Trust, an environmental non-profit that Stirpe's leadership. Professionally, he worked for General Electric, then spun off a GE operation to form CID Technologies and became its CFO until the company was sold. Stirpe then formed a new venture, Qube Software Inc., and took it from startup to multi-million dollar business. He has received awards including the first SUNY Empire State College Excellence in Environmental Sustainability Awards. He holds an undergraduate degree from the University of Notre Dame and is the married father of one and stepfather to two.

JAMES N TEDISCO (R-I-C)
112th - Parts of Schenectady and Saratoga Counties

636 Plank Rd, Ste 101, Clifton Park, NY 12065
518-370-2812/tediscj@assembly.state.ny.us

James Tedisco was first elected to the Assembly in 1982 and served as Minority Leader from 2005 to 2009. He currently sits on the following committees: banks; economic development, job creation, commerce and industry; racing and wagering; and rules. Tedisco's legislative successes include ensuring the passage of Buster's Law to make animal cruelty - often a bridge crime - a felony; legislation to make the state go digital with communications - thereby reducing paper waste - and authoring the property tax cap bill, the Property Taxpayers Protection Act. Assemblyman Tedisco worked in education from 1973 to 1982 as a guidance counselor, varsity basketball coach and athletic director, special education teacher, and resource room instructor. He went on to become a Schenectady City Councilman. He is active in his community, and holds a B.A. from Union College and an MA in special education from the College of Saint Rose. He is the married father to a son.

CLAUDIA TENNEY (R-C-I)
101st - Parts of Oneida, Herkimer, Otsego, Delaware, Ulster, Sullivan and Orange counties

4747 Middle Settlement Road, Po Box 627, New Hartford, NY 13413
315-736-3879
/tenneyc@assembly.state.ny.us

Claudia Tenney was elected to the New York State Assembly in 2010. She sits on the following committees: banks; codes; education; social services; and veteran's affairs. Prior to her election, she served as legal counsel and chief of staff to former District 115 Assemblyman David Townsend. She is also co-owner and legal counsel for her family's printing and manufacturing business, Mid-York Press. She served as publisher and corporate counsel to Tenney Media Group that she established, which published free community newspapers founded by her parents and grandparents. She also has been a radio and television host in the area. In addition, she has worked for the Consulate General of Yugoslavia and was a partner in the firm of Groben, Gilroy, Oster, and Saunders. Her community service includes stints on boards such as the Mohawk Valley Community College Foundation Board. Her father was is the late Hon. John R. Tenney, Justice of the Supreme Court of New York in the Fifth Judicial District for more than 30 years. She holds an undergraduate degree from Colgate University and a J.D. from the Taft College of law at the University of Cincinnati and is mother to one.

FRED W THIELE, JR (D-I-WF)
1st - Part of Suffolk County

2302 Main Street, Box 3062, Bridgehampton, NY 11932
631-537-2583/thielef@assembly.state.ny.us

Fred Thiele was elected to the New York State Assembly in 1995 and represents a district at the end of Long Island.. He chairs the Committee on Small Business, and sits on the following committees: education; election law; environmental conservation; oversight, analysis and investigation; transportation; and ways and means. His legislative successes include drafting and sponsoring legislation that created the Peconic Bay Community Preservation Fund Act which authorized the five towns in the region to establish dedicated funds, financed by a 2% real estate transfer tax, for land acquisition for open space, farmland, and historic preservation, as well as recreational purposes. This program was overwhelmingly approved in a public referendum in 1998 and has generated more than $150 million for land preservation efforts and has resulted in the preservation of thousands of acres of sensitive lands. He also has backed efforts to create Peconic County from Long Island's five easternmost towns, and has supported efforts to ensure fiscal responsibility at all levels of government. Prior to joining the Assembly, Theile was counsel to Assemblyman John Behan, then Southampton Town Attorney. In 1987 he served in the Suffolk County Legislature, and in 1991 he went on to become Southampton Town Supervisor. Thiele has been widely involved in legislative issues during his long tenure in the Assembly. For instance, he drafted and was a prime sponsor of legislation, which created the Peconic Bay Community Preservation Fund Act, Theile holds a B.A. from Long Island University, Southampton College, and a J.D. from Albany Law School. He is father to three and has lived in Sag Harbor for his entire life.

MATTHEW TITONE (D)
61st - Part of Richmond County

853 Forest Avenue, Staten Island, NY 10310
718-442-9932/ TitoneM@assembly.state.ny.us

Matthew Titone was first elected to the New York State Assembly during a special election in 2007. He chairs the Office of State-Federal Relations, and sits on the following standing committees: education; environmental conservation; health; judiciary; social services; and tourism, parks, arts and sports development. An attorney by profession, Titone has worked as a senior trial associate and managed the labor law litigation department for the Wall Street firm of Morgan, Melhuish, Monahan, Arvidson, Abrutyn & Lisowski. He left the firm in 1998 to open his own practice. He has provided pro bono services for many years. He serves on the Board of Directors of Community Health Action of Staten Island - formerly known as the Staten Island AIDS Task Force - and has also served on the Board of Trustees for Legal Services of New York. He also sits on the Board of Trustees for the Snug Harbor Cultural Center. He is the son of the Hon. Vito J. Titone and holds a law degree from St. John's University School of Law.

MICHELE R TITUS (D)
31st - Part of Queens County

131-17 Rockaway Blvd, South Ozone Park, NY 11420
718-322-4958

19-31 Mott Avenue, Far Rockaway, NY 11691
718-327-1845/titusm@state.ny.us

Michele Titus was elected to the New York State Assembly in 2002. She represents the communities of South Ozone Park, Springfield Gardens, Rosedale, Far Rockaway and Laurelton. Titus chairs the Committee on Labor, as well as the Legislative Women's Caucus. She also sits on the following standing committees: children and families; codes; education; ethics and guidance; and judiciary. Her legislative achievements include policy that would mandate after-school programs in every public school, expand early childhood education, and lower senior prescription costs. Prior to her election, Titus served as Chief of Staff to State Sen. Ada L. Smith, and then was Executive Director for the New York State Black and Puerto Rican Legislative Caucus. She also has been an attorney for the New York City Board of Education, the New York State Attorney General's Frauds Bureau, and the Integrity Bureau of the Queens County District Attorney's Office. She holds a B.A. from SUNY-Binghamton and a J.D. from Albany Law School. She lives in Queens with her husband and two children.

LATRICE MONIQUE WALKER (D)
55 - Part of Kings County

400 Rockaway Avenue, Brooklyn, NY 11212
718-498-8681/WalkerL@assembly.state.ny.us

Latrice Walker was elected to the New York State Assembly in 2014. She sits on the following committees: correction; economic development, job creation, commerce and industry; election law; energy; and housing. She previously served as Counsel to U.S. Rep. Yvette D. Clarke. She supports affordable housing while preserving and advocating on behalf of residents of the New York City Housing Authority. She is a founding member of the Ocean Hill-Brownsville Coalition of Young Professionals. She holds an undergraduate degree from SUNY Purchase College and a J.D. from Pace University, and is mother to one.

RAYMOND WALTER (R)
146th - Part of Erie County

5555 Main St, Williamsville, NY 14221
716-634-1895/ walterr@assembly.state.ny.us

Raymond Walter was elected to the New York State Assembly in 2011. His district includes the Towns of Amherst and Pendleton, and the Village of Williamsville. He sits on the following committees: economic development, job creation, commerce and industry; health; housing; insurance; and ways and means. An attorney by profession, Walter has worked for the law firm of Magavern Magavern Grimm LLP since 2007. While still in law school, he clerked for the US Attorney's Office and the Erie County District Attorney's Office. Assemblyman Walter also has a prior public service record; he was appointed and later elected to the Erie County Legislature. He remains active in his community, including sitting on the board for the Amherst Senior Citizens Foundation. He holds a B.A. from the University of New York College, Geneseo, and a J.D. from the SUNY School of Law, Buffalo. He lives in East Amherst with his wife and two children.

HELENE E WEINSTEIN (D)
41st - Part of Kings County

3520 Nostrand Ave, Brooklyn, NY 11229
718-648-4700/ weinsth@assembly.state.ny.us

Helene Weinstein was first elected to the New York State Assembly in 1980. Her district includes the Sheepshead Bay, Midwood, Flatlands, Canarsie, and East Flatbush communities in Brooklyn. She chairs the Committee on Judiciary - the first woman in the state to hold the position - and also sits on the following standing committees: aging; codes; rules; and ways and means. She has sponsored major reforms in the state's jury system and is the leading proponent of ensuring civil legal services for low-income New Yorkers. She is also a leading advocate for women, having chaired the Task Force on Women's Issues, and sponsored the Family Court Fair Access law of 2008, a reform measure that expanded access to civil orders of protection to domestic violence victims in dating and intimate relationships. Other major state laws she has sponsored include a law declaring surrogate parenting contracts void and against public policy and a rape shield extension law to protect crime victims. She has held a number of significant posts and has received numerous awards. Her civic involvement includes sitting on the board of the Center for Women in Government. She holds a B.A. from American University and a J.D. from New England School of Law.

DAVID I WEPRIN (D)
24th - Part of Queens County

185-06 Union Turnpike, Fresh Meadows, NY11366
718-454-3027/weprind@assembly.state.ny.us

111-12 Atlantic Avenue, #5, Richmond Hill, NY 11419
718-805-2384

David Weprin was elected to the New York State Assembly in 2010 and now represents the same district his father, the late Assembly Speaker Saul Weprin, represented for 23 years. His brother Mark Weprin spent more than 15 years in the same seat. Weprin chairs the Task Force for People With Disabilities and sits on the following committees: banks; cities; codes; election law; judiciary; and ways and means. Professionally, Weprin spent many years in the financial services industry. From 1983 to 1987, he was Deputy Superintendent of Banks and Secretary of the Banking Board for New York State, an appointment made by former Gov. Mario Cuomo. As Deputy Superintendent, he advised the Banking Department on the formulation of banking standards, and exercised power to approve or disapprove the issuance of bank charters and licenses and the establishment of branch banks. His elected public service began when he was elected to the New York City Council in 2001. He holds a BA from SUNY-Albany and a JD from Hofstra University. He and his wife are parents to five children.

JAIME R. WILLIAMS (D)
59th - Part of Brooklyn

5318 Avenue N, 1st Floor, Brooklyn, NY 11234
718-252-2124/williamsja@assembly.state.ny.us

Jaime Williams was elected to serve the 59th Assembly District on April 19, 2016; encompassing the neighborhoods of Canarsie, Georgetown, Mill Basin, Marine Park and Gerritsen Beach. Originally from Trinidad and Tobago, she came to the United States in 1999, settling in New York City.

She obtained her GED when she first came to the U.S. and then attended Kingsborough Community College. She has a Bachelor's Degree in Social Work from York College and a Master's Degree in Social Work from Fordham University and is certified as an alcohol and substance abuse counselor. In 2007, she founded Empowerment = Courage to Heal Inc., an organization devoted to raising awareness against domestic violence. Assemblywoman Williams is a member of the Canarsie Lions Club, and the 69th Precinct Community Council.

CARRIE WOERNER (D)
113 - Saratoga and Washington counties.

112 Spring Street, Suite 109; Saratoga Springs, NY 12866;
518-584-5493/woernerc@assembly.state.ny.us

Carrie Woerner was elected to the New York State Assembly in 2014. She sits on the following committees: agriculture; local governments; racing and watering; small business; and tourism, parks, arts and sports development. She is Vice President and General Manager of MeetMax Conference Software, a division of The Wall Street Transcript, and established the software division in Saratoga Springs in 2008. She has also worked for Dell/Perot systems and IMB. She is the former Executive Director of the Saratoga Springs Preservation Foundation, where she expanded the organization, published a walking tour guide, and secured $130 in state funding to restore historic buildings in the Beekman Street Arts District. She also founded the Historic Saratoga Race Track Preservation Coalition. She served as a Round Lake Village Trustee for three terms, and is a member of the Town of Malta Planning Board. She holds a bachelor's degree from Carnegie Mellon University and a master's degree from Santa Clara University.

ANGELA M WOZNIAK (R)
143 - Erie County

2562 Walden Avenue, Suite 102, Cheektowaga, NY 14225
716-686-0080/wozniaka@assembly.state.ny.us

Angela M. Wozniak was first elected to the New York State Assembly in 2014 from a district that includes the Towns of Cheektowaga and Lancaster and the Village of Depew. She sits on the following committees: aging; children and families; cities; labor; and local governments. Prior to her election, she sat on the Town Council for the Town of Cheektowaga starting in 2011, where she advocated on behalf of tax and ethics reform, as well as term limits and school board consolidation. She operates The Angela Wozniak Insurance Agency. She holds a degree in business management from D'Youville College. She and her husband are parents to one.

KEITH L T WRIGHT (D)
70th - Part of New York County

163 W 125th St, Ste 911, Adam Clayton Powell Jr Bldg, New York, NY 10027
212-866-5809/wrightk@assembly.state.ny.us

Keith Wright was first elected to the Assembly in 1992. He currently chairs the Committee on Housing. He served as Assistant Majority Whip from 1998-2012, and is also the former chair of the Committee on Labor. He also sits on the following committees: codes; correction; rules; and ways and means. He has held previous committee chairmanships, including the election law, social services, and labor committees. In his current capacity, he has authored numerous pieces of legislation to strengthen the rights of tenants against unscrupulous landlords. Prior to his election to the Assembly, the lifelong Harlem resident held positions in the New York City Human Resources Administration, the Manhattan Borough President's Office, and the New York City Transit Authority. Wright holds a MA from Tufts University, and a JD from Rutgers University. He is the married father of two children and the son of the late New York Supreme Court Justice Bruce Wright.

KENNETH ZEBROWSKI (D)
96th - Rockland County

67 North Main St, New City, NY 10956
845-634-9791/zebrowskik@assembly.state.ny.us

Ken Zebrowski was first elected to the New York State Assembly on May 1, 2007 during a special election held to fill the seat of his late father, Assemblyman Kenneth P Zebrowski. He currently chairs the Commission on Administrative Regulations Review, and he sits on the following standing committees: codes; environmental conservation; ethics and guidance; governmental employees; judiciary; and labor. His legislative efforts have been aimed at recuing unfunded mandates, cutting government waste, fostering business and job growth, keeping seniors' prescription costs down, and protecting youth athletes from concussions. Prior to his election, Zebrowski served in the Rockland County Legislature. He founded the law firm of Zebrowski & Zebrowski with his father, and is currently of counsel to the New City law firm of Braunfotel & Frendel, LLC. He holds a B.A. from SUNY-Albany and a JD from Seton Hall University School of Law.

US SENATE: NEW YORK DELEGATION

KIRSTEN E GILLIBRAND (D)

478 Russell Senate Office Building, Washington, DC 20510
202-224-4451/fax: 202-228-0282/www.gillibrand.senate.gov

780 Third Avenue, Suite 2601, New York, NY 10017
212-688-6262/fax: 866-824-6340

P.O. Box 893, Mahopac, NY 10541
845-875-4585/fax: 845-875-9099

Kenneth B. Keating Federal Building, 100 State Street, Room 4195, Rochester, NY 14614
585-263-6250/fax: 585-263-6247

James M. Hanley Federal Building, 100 S. Clinton Street, Room 1470, PO Box 7378, Syracuse, NY 13261
315-448-0470/fax: 315-448-0476

155 Pinelawn Road, Suite 250 North, Melville, NY 11747
631-249-2825/fax: 631-249-2847

P.O. Box 273, Lowville, NY 13367
315-376-6118/fax: 315-376-6118

Leo W. O'Brien Federal Building, 11A Clinton Square, Room 821, Albany, NY 12207
518-431-0120/fax: 518-431-0128

Larkin at Exchange, 726 Exchange Street, Suite 511, Buffalo, NY, 14210
716-854-9725/fax: 716-854-9731

Kirsten E. Gillibrand was sworn in as United States Senator from New York in January 2009, filling the seat that opened up when former Secretary of State, Hillary Rodham Clinton, first took the diplomatic post. Gillibrand was subsequently re-elected in 2012. In the Senate, Gillibrand has focused on transparency, even posting her personal tax returns online, and worked to repeal "Don't Ask Don't Tell," the policy that bans gays from serving openly in the military. She sits on the Agriculture, Nutrition and Forestry Committee - New York's first senator to do so in almost 40 years - and also sits on the Senate Armed Services Committee, the Committee on Environment and Public Works, and the Special Committee on Aging. Her legislative agenda puts middle class and working families first, and her FAMILY Act would create a national paid leave program for all workers. Prior to her service in the Senate, Gillibrand served in the United States House of Representatives, representing New York's 20th Congressional District, after being elected to the post in 2006. An attorney by profession, she served as Special Counsel to then-U.S. Secretary of Housing and Urban Development, current New York Gov. Andrew Cuomo. She received her undergraduate degree from Dartmouth College, and earned her law degree from the UCLA School of Law and clerked in the Second Circuit Court of Appeals. The Upstate native is married with two children and lives in Brunswick.

CHARLES E SCHUMER (D)

322 Hart Senate Office Bldg, Washington, DC 20510
202-224-6542/http:// schumer.senate.gov

780 3rd Ave, Ste 2301, New York, NY 10017
212-486-4430

Leo O'Brien Bldg, Rm 420, Albany, NY 12207
518-431-4070

15 Henry St, Rm 100 A-F, Binghamton, NY 13901
607-772-6792

130 S Elmwood Ave, #660, Buffalo, NY 14202
716-846-4111

One Park Place, Ste 100, Peekskill, NY 10566
914-734-1532

145 Pine Lawn Road, #300, Melville, NY 11747
631-753-0978

100 State St, Rm 3040, Rochester, NY 14614
585-263-5866

100 S. Clinton St, Rm 841, Syracuse, NY 13261
315-423-5471

In 1998, Charles E. Schumer was elected to the U.S. Senate; he became New York's senior senator when Senator Daniel Patrick Moynihan retired in 2000. Senator Schumer is the Ranking Member of the Senate Rules Committee, which oversees federal elections, voting rights, campaign finance, and the operation of the Senate complex. In addition, Senator Schumer sits on the following committees: banking, housing and urban affairs; finance; judiciary; and the Joint Committee on the Library. Senator Schumer also sits on the Joint Committee on the Library, Joint Committee on Printing, and the U.S. Senate Caucus on International Narcotics Control. Senator Schumer continues the tradition he began in his first term: visiting each of New York's 62 counties each year. His achievements have included bringing affordable air service to Upstate New York and the Hudson Valley and securing over $20 billion in aid to New York City following the attacks on September 11, 2001. He authored legislation that eliminated barriers that delay low-cost generic medications from entering the marketplace. In the Senate, he is the Chairman of the Democratic Policy and Communications Center. Prior to serving in the Senate, the Brooklyn-born Schumer was elected to the U.S. House of Representatives where he served from 1980-1998 and represented Brooklyn and Queens. He also served six years in the New York State Assembly. He holds both a BA and a JD from Harvard University, and is the married father of two children.

US HOUSE OF REPRESENTATIVES: NEW YORK DELEGATION

YVETTE D CLARKE (D)
9th - Part of Kings County

2351 Rayburn House Office Building, Washington, DC 20515
202-225-6231/clarke.house.gov

123 Linden Boulevard, 4th Floor, Brooklyn, NY 11226
718-287-1142

Yvette D Clarke was first elected to the US House of Representatives in 2006. She represents the 9th Congressional District which includes the communities of Brownsville, Crown Heights, East Flatbush, Flatbush, Gerritsen Beach, Madison, Midwood, Ocean Hill, Park Slope and Flatlands, Prospect Heights, Prospect-Lefferts Gardens, Sheepshead Bay, and Windsor Terrace. She sits on the following committees: energy and commerce - including three of its subcommittees - and the Ethics Committee. In Congress, Clarke has secured funding for major Brooklyn institutions including the Brooklyn Botanic Garden and the Brooklyn Public Library. Prior to being elected to Congress, she served three terms in the New York City Council and chaired the Contracts Committee and co-chaired the New York City Women's Caucus. Professionally, her positions included Director of Business Development for the Bronx Empowerment Zone. The Brooklyn native is a graduate of Oberlin College.

CHRIS COLLINS (R)
27th - Parts of Erie, Niagara, Orleans, Genesee, Wyoming, Monroe, Livingston and Ontario Counties

1117 Longworth House Office Building, Washington, DC 20515
202-225-5265/chriscollins.house.gov

128 Main St., Geneseo, NY 14454
585-519-4002

2813 Wehrle Dr., Ste 13, Williamsville, NY 14221
716-634-2324

Chris Collins was first elected to the U.S. House of Representatives in 2012 and represents a large Western New York/Finger Lakes district. He sits on the Energy and Commerce Committee and three of its subcommittees. Prior to his election to Congress, Collins was elected Erie County Executive at a time the county was in dire fiscal shape and operated under a state-imposed control board. In four years, the county's saw its debt reduced by more than $120 million, a cash surplus created of more than $100 million, the infrastructure and recreational facilities were reopened; the county workforce was reduced by 22 %, and the control board was gone within 18 months. He began his career with Westinghouse Electric. He holds a BS in mechanical engineering from NC State and an MBA in Finance from the University of Alabama - Birmingham. He is the married father of three, and grandfather of three.

JOSEPH CROWLEY (D)
14th - Parts of Bronx and Queens Counties

1436 Longworth House Office Building, Washington, DC 20515
202-225-3965/Crowley.house.gov

82-11 37th Avenue, Ste 402, Queens, NY 11372
718-779-1400

2800 Bruckner Blvd, Ste 201, Bronx, NY 10465
718-931-1400

Joseph Crowley was first elected to the US House of Representatives in November 1998.. He sits on the powerful Ways and Means Committee, as well as two of its subcommittees, and is the Vice Chair of the Democratic Caucus. In Congress, Rep. Crowley has focused on building strong communities, creating jobs, protecting senior benefits, and increasing educational opportunities for working families. Rep. Crowley, who lost a cousin who was a first responder on 9/11, authored the 9/11 Heroes Medal of Valor Act, passed unanimously in the House and Senate, which calls for a special Public Safety Office Medal of Valor, honored rescue workers who died while responding to the terrorist attacks. Congressman Crowley also has advocated for New York City's Homeland Security requirements, and led the creation of the Urban Area Security Initiative that targets homeland security funding to at-risk urban centers. Prior to his election to Congress, Crowley ran a successful small business and sat in the New York State Assembly for 12 years. He holds an undergraduate degree from Queens College. He is the married father of three.

DANIEL DONOVAN, JR (R)
11th - Richmond County

1725 Longworth HOB, Washington, DC 20515
(202) 225-3371/https://Donovan.house.gov

Daniel M. Donovan Jr. was elected to the U.S. House of Representatives on May 5, 2015, and was sworn in to office one week later. Prior to his election, he was District Attorney for Richmond County for 12 years, and, prior to that, he was Deputy Borough President for Staten Island. He began his professional career an assistant to longtime New York District Attorney Robert M. Morgenthau in Manhattan for a number of years after he graduated from law school. Then, Rep. Donovan became Chief of Staff to then-Richmond County Borough President Guy V. Molinari prior to being appointed Deputy Borough President. He is active in professional circles, having been elected President of the New York State District Attorney's Association, as well as the New York State Director for the National District Attorneys Association. He holds a B.A. from St. John's University and a J.D. from Fordham University School of Law.

ELIOT L ENGEL (D)
16th - Parts of Bronx and Westchester Counties

2162 Rayburn House Office Bldg, Washington, DC 20515
202-225-2464/engle.house.gov

3655 Johnson Ave, Bronx, NY 10463
718-796-9700

177 Dreiser Loop, Room 3, Bronx, NY 10475
718-320-2314

6 Gramatan Ave, Ste 205, Mt Vernon, NY 10550
914-699-4100

Eliot Engel was first elected to the US House of Representatives in 1988. He is the Ranking Member of the House Foreign Affairs Committee. In addition, he serves on the Energy and Commerce Committee including the Subcommittee on Health, and the Subcommittee on Energy and Power. He founded and co-chairs the House Oil and National Security Caucus, focused on clean and energy-efficient alternatives to oil, and he serves on the Commission on Human Rights. He created the Dependence Reduction through Innovation in Vehicles and Energy (DRIVE) Act to help reduce American dependence on imported oil, and saw many of its provisions signed into law as part of the energy bill signed in 2007. In addition, he authored the ALS Registry Act to establish a national registry for the collection and storage of data on people suffering from ALS. Prior to his election to Congress, Engel was a teacher and guidance counselor in the New York City public school system and then served twelve years in the New York State Assembly (1977-1988). He holds an undergraduate degree from Hunter College and a Master's degree from Herman H. Lehman College of the City University of New York. He also holds a JD from New York Law School. He and his wife have three children.

CHRIS GIBSON (R)
19th - Delaware, Columbia, Greene, Otsego, Rensselaer, Sullivan, Schoharie, Ulster, and Dutchess Counties

1708 Longworth House Office Bldg, Washington, DC 20515
202-225-5614/http://gibson.house.gov/

721 Broadway, Kingston, NY 12401
845-514-2322

2 Hudson St, PO Box 775, Kinderhook, NY 12106
518-610-8133

92 Sullivan Avenue, PO Box 578, Ferndale, NY 12754
845-747-9261

111 Main Street, Delhi, NY 13753
607-746-9537

25 Chestnut Street; Cooperstown, NY 13326
(607) 282-4002

92 Sullivan Avenue, PO Box 578, Ferndale, NY 12754
(845) 747-9261

4328 Albany Post Road, Hyde Park, NY 12538
845-698-0132

Chris Gibson was elected to the US House of Representatives in 2010. He sits on the House Armed Services Committee (Subcommittees on Readiness and Emerging Threats and Capabilities), the House Agriculture Committee and the House Small Business Committee. Prior to being elected to Congress, Gibson served in the U.S. Army for 24 years, rising to the rank of Colonel. He was deployed seven times, including four combat tours to Iraq, and separate deployments to Kosovo, and the Southwestern U.S. for a counter-drug operation. Most recently, he was deployed to Haiti where he commanded the 82nd Airborne Division's 2nd Brigade Combat Team during the opening month of a humanitarian relief operation. Other key assignments included tours teaching American Politics at the United States Military Academy at West Point, serving as a Congressional Fellow with US Representative Jerry Lewis (R-CA), the Chairman of the Defense Appropriations Subcommittee, and completing a Hoover National Security Affairs Fellowship at Stanford University. He holds an undergraduate degree from Siena College, an MPA and a PhD from Cornell University. In addition, he is the author of Securing the State, a 2008 book on national security decision-making. He and his wife are parents to three.

RICHARD HANNA (R)
22nd - Broome, Chenango, Cortland, Herkimer, Madison, Oneida, Ontario, Otsego, and Tioga Counties

319 Cannon House Office Bldg, Washington, DC 20515
202-225-3665/http://hanna.house.gov/

258 Genesee St, Utica, NY 13502
315-724-9740

49 Court St., Ste. 230, Binghamton, NY 13901
607-723-0212

Congressman Richard Hanna was elected to the US House of Representatives in 2010. He sits on the Transportation and Infrastructure Committee, as well as the Committee on Small Business. He is also a member of a number of subcommittees, including the Subcommittee on Railroads, Pipelines, and Hazardous Material, the Subcommittee on Highways and Transit, and the Subcommittee on Aviation. Prior to his election, he was president of Hanna Construction, which has grown from the small company Hanna founded to one that employed more than 450 people and handled multi-million dollar commercial and municipal projects in Upstate New York. Hanna is a licensed pilot with high performance and seaplane certifications. He has been deeply involved in his community, including ten years of service on the board of The Community Foundation of Herkimer and Oneida Counties, Inc., including two years as the board chairperson. He graduated from Reed College in Portland, Oregon, and is the married father of two.

Hanna holds an undergraduate degree from Reed College and is the married father of two.

BRIAN M. HIGGINS (D)
27th - Parts of Niagara and Erie Counties

2459 Rayburn House Office Bldg, Washington, DC 20515
202-225-3306

726 Exchange St., Ste. 601, Buffalo, NY 14210
716-852-3501

640 Park Place, Niagara Falls, NY 14301
716-282-1274

Brian Higgins was first elected to the US House of Representatives in 2004. His district includes most or all of the cities of Buffalo, Lackawanna, Niagara Falls, North Tonawanda and Tonawanda, as well as a number of towns and villages in the area. He serves on the Committee on Homeland Security - where he is Ranking Member of the Subcommittee on Counterterrorism and Intelligence - and the Committee on Foreign Affairs. He formerly sat on the powerful Ways and Means Committee but stepped down due to a realignment of seats. He will re-join the committee when a seat opens up. In Congress, Higgins was instrumental in securing at $279 million settlement from the New York Power Authority that is earmarked for development along Buffalo's inner and outer harbor fronts. Prior to his election, Higgins sat on the New York State Assembly for four years, and prior to that he was a member of the Buffalo Common Council. He was an instructor at Buffalo State College, where he earned an undergraduate degree. He also holds a MA in public policy and administration from Harvard University's Kennedy School. He and his wife have two children.

STEVE ISRAEL (D)
3rd - Parts of Nassau, Suffolk, and Queens Counties

2457 Rayburn House Office Bldg, Washington, DC 20515
202-225-3335/http://www.house.gov/israel

534 Broad Hollow Road, Ste 302, Melville, NY 11747
631-777-7391/Suffolk
516-505-1448/Nassau/718-875-1675/Queens

Steve Israel was first elected to the US House of Representatives in November 2000. His district includes northeast Queens and the townships of, North Hempstead, Oyster Bay, Huntington and Smithtown. He sits on the Appropriations Committee and two of its subcommittees: defense; and interior, environment, and related agencies. He is the sixth ranking member of the House Democratic Leadership, serving as Chair of Policy & Communications where he focuses on middle-class economic security and opportunity. He served as the Chairman of the Democratic Congressional Campaign Committee from 2011-2015. Among his achievements is funding the U.S.-Israel Energy Cooperation Act and the Advanced Research Projects Agency for Energy; launching an initiative to require full ingredient labeling on household cleaning products; and an advocate of tax code revisions to reflect regional variations in cost-of-living. Prior to his election to Congress, Israel was an elected member of the Huntington Town Board and Congressional aide. He holds an undergraduate degree from George Washington University and an AA from Nassau Community College. He and his wife have two children.

HAKEEM JEFFRIES (D)
8th - Parts of Kings County and Southwest Queens

1607 Longworth HOB, Washington, DC 20515
202-225-5936/Jeffries.house.gov

56 Hanson Place, Ste 603, Brooklyn, NY 11217
718-237-2211

445 Neptune Ave, First Floor, Brooklyn, NY 11224
718-373-0033

Hakeem Jeffries was first elected to the U.S. House of Representatives in 2012 and sits on the Education and the Workforce Committee and the Judiciary Committee, a two subcommittees of each Senate committee. In addition, he is Congressional Black Caucus Whip, and a member of the Democratic Caucus Steering and Policy Committee. He opposes turning Social Security and Medicare cuts and backed measures to help those impacted by Superstorm Sandy. Prior to his election to Congress, Jeffries spent six years in the New York State Assembly. His legislative successes there included a 2010 law that prohibits the New York Police Department from keeping electronic data on people stopped, questioned and frisked - but not charged - during an encounter with police.. An attorney by profession, Jeffries clerked for Hon. Harold Baer Jr. of the U.S. District Court for the Southern District of New York, and then entered private practice, including as counsel in the litigation departments for Viacom Inc. and CBS. He holds a BA from SUNY-Binghamton, a master's in public policy from Georgetown University, and a JD from New York University Law School. He is married with two children.

JOHN KATKO (R)
24th - Onondaga, Cayuga, Wayne and Oswego counties

1123 Longworth House Office Building, Washington, DC 20515, (202) 225-3701/https://katko.house.gov

71 Genesee St., Auburn, NY 13021, (315) 253-4068

7376 State Route 31, Lyons, NY 14489

13 W. Oneida St., 2nd Floor, Oswego, NY 13126

440 South Warren St., 7th Floor Suite 711, Syracuse, NY 13202, (315) 423-5657

John Katko was elected to the US House of Representatives in 2014. He sits on the Homeland Security Committee and two of its subcommittees, including the Subcommittee on Transportation Security of which is he chair. In addition, he sits on the Transportation and Infrastructure Committee and three of its subcommittees. Professionally, he served as Assistant District Attorney. He began his professional career in Washington, DC, where he worked in private practice, then joined the US Securities and Exchange Commission as a Senior Trial Attorney. He went on to become an Assistant U.S. Attorney at the U.S. Dept. of Justice for 20 years, practicing in Virginia, Texas, and Puerto Rico early in his career as a federal prosecutor with the Dept. of Justice's Criminal Division, Narcotics & Dangerous Drug Section. He went on to move back to his upstate New York roots with his family, and prosecuted organized crime in the Northern District of New York for 15 years. He has lectured at Syracuse University College of Law and at Cornell Law School, and has led attorney trainings for criminal investigations and prosecutions around the world. He holds an undergraduate degree from Niagara University and a J.D. from Syracuse University College of Law. He remains active in his community, and he and his wife are parents to three children.

PETER T KING (R)
2nd - Parts of Nassau and Suffolk counties

339 Cannon House Office Bldg, Washington, DC 20515
202-225-7896/peteking.house,gov

1003 Park Blvd, Massapequa Park, NY 11762
516-541-4225

Peter King was first elected to the US House of Representatives in 1992. His Long Island district includes the Townships of Hempstead, Oyster Bay, Baylon, Islip, and much of Fire Island National Seashore. He sits on the Homeland Security Committee, which he previously chaired, as well as its subcommittee on counterterrorism and intelligence, which he chairs. He also serves on the Financial Services Committee and the Permanent Select Committee on Intelligence. King successfully fought to secure $60.4 million emergency funding for Hurricane Sandy victims. He began his political career in November 1977 by winning election to the Hempstead Town Council. Subsequently, he was elected to three terms as Comptroller of Nassau County. Prior to entering public service, he was a practicing attorney. He holds an undergraduate degree from St. Francis College in Brooklyn and a JD from the University of Notre Dame Law School. He and his wife have two children and two grandchildren.

NITA M LOWEY (D)
17th - Parts of Rockland and Westchester Counties

2365 Rayburn House Office Bldg, Washington, DC 20515
202-225-6506/http://lowey.house.gov

222 Mamaroneck Ave, Ste 310, White Plains, NY 10605
914-428-1707

67 North Main St., Ste 101, New City, NY 10956
845-639-3485

Nita Lowey was first elected to the US House of Representatives in 1988. She is the Ranking Democrat on the powerful House Appropriations Committee, the first woman to lead either party on the committee. She is also Ranking Democrat on the State and Foreign Operations Subcommittee. . During her long tenure in Congress, Lowey has had numerous successes, from helping to secure $20 billion recovery money after the 9/11 terrorist attacks to helping to obtain $68 million in federal funding to develop local bioterrorism response plans and equip first responders. She has defended the National Endowment for the Arts, and authored the first-ever bill to mandate clear and concise food allergen labeling. On the Appropriations Committee, she advocates on behalf of increased federal funding for biomedical research into diseases such as cancer, diabetes and Alzheimer's at the National Institute of Health. She is the former Chair of the Congressional Women's Caucus. Prior to her election to Congress, she was the State of New York's Assistant Secretary of State. She holds an undergraduate degree from Mount Holyoke College, and is the married mother of three children and eight grandchildren.

CAROLYN B MALONEY (D)
12th = Manhattan, Queens, Brooklyn

Carolyn B. Maloney was first elected to the US House of Representatives in 1992. She sits on the House Financial Services Committee and the House Oversight and Government Reform Committee. In addition, she is Vice Chair of the House Democrats' Steering and Policy Committee, and former Chair of the Joint Economic Committee. Her legislative achievements include the Credit Cardholders' Bill of Rights, signed by President Obama in 2009. She co-founded the House 9/11 Commission Caucus, working to write and pass legislation to implement the 9/11 Commission's recommendations for improved intelligence gathering, as well as the James Zadroga 9/11 Health Care and Compensation Act, signed in 2011, to provide health care and compensation for 9/11 first responders. She has also helped pass legislation to target the 'demand' side of sex trafficking and increased funding for law enforcement to process DNA rape kids, among other strong efforts on behalf of women and women's health. She began her professional career as a community affairs coordinator for the New York City board of education welfare education program, and went on to work for the New York State Assembly and Senate, and sit on the New York City Council. She holds an undergraduate degree from Greensboro College.

SEAN P MALONEY (D)
18th - Orange, Rockland, Putnam, Dutchess and Westchester Counties

1529 Longworth House Office Building, Washington, DC 20515
202-225-5441/seanmaloney.house.gov

123 Grand St., 2nd Floor, Newburgh, NY 12550
845-561-12550

Sean Maloney was first elected to the U.S. House of Representatives in 2012 from his Hudson Valley district. He serves on the House Agriculture Committee, the Transportation and Infrastructure Committee and three of its subcommittees. Prior to his election he was a senior advisor to President Bill Clinton, a post he left to build a high-tech startup. He also has been a senior staff member to two Democratic governors from New York. He holds both a BA and a JD from the University of Virginia and is the married father of three.

GREGORY W MEEKS (D)
5th - Part of Queens County

2324 Rayburn House Office Bldg, Washington, DC 20515
202-225-3461/ http://meeks.house.gov/

153-01 Jamaica Avenue, 2nd Floor, Jamaica, NY 11432
718-725-6000

67-12, Far Rockaway, Rockaway Beach Blvd., Arverne, NY 11692
347-230-4032

Gregory W Meeks was first elected to the US House of Representatives in 1998. He is a senior member of the House Financial Services Committee and serves on two of its committees. He also serves on the House Foreign Affairs Committee where he is Ranking Member of the Subcommittee on Europe and Eurasia and Emerging Threats, and also sits on the Subcommittee on the Western Hemisphere. He works to promote policies that strengthen the United States's economic and national security and build relationships with other nations in an increasingly globalized world, and co-chairs the Brazil Caucus and Columbia Caucus in the House of Representatives, as well as the Organization of American States Caucus. He holds undergraduate degrees from Adelphi University and a JD from Howard University Law School. He is the married father of three.

GRACE MENG (D)
6th - Part of Queens County

1317 Longworth HOB, Washington, DC 20515
202-225-2601
meng.house.gov

40-13 159th Street, Flushing, NY 11358
718-358-MENG

118-35 Queens Boulevard, 17th Floor, Forest Hills, NY 11375
718-358-MENG

Grace Meng was first elected to the U.S. House of Representatives in 2012, New York's first Asian American member of Congress. She sits on two standing legislative committees, the House Foreign Affairs Committee and the House Small Business Committee and two of its subcommittees, Agriculture, Energy and Trade, and Contracting and Workforce, where she is the Ranking Member. In the former committee's subcommittee structure, she sits on the Subcommittee on Asia and the Pacific, and the Subcommittee on The Middle East and North Africa. She also founded and co-chairs the bipartisan Kids' Safety Caucus. Prior to her election to Congress, Meng served in the New York State Assembly. Prior to entering elective office, she was a public interest attorney. She holds an undergraduate degree from the University of Michigan and a JD from Yeshiva University's Benjamin Cardozo School of Law. She is the married mother of two.

JERROLD L NADLER (D)
10th - Parts of New York and Kings Counties

2109 Rayburn House Office Bldg, Washington, DC 20515
202-225-5635/ http://nadler.house.gov

445 6605 Fort Hamilton Pkwy, Brooklyn, NY 11219
718-373-3198

201 Varick St, Ste 669, New York, NY 10014
212-367-7350

Jerrold "Jerry" Nadler was first elected to the U.S. House of Representatives in 1992. His district includes much of the West Side of Manhattan, the Financial District as well as a diverse group of Brooklyn neighborhoods. He is a member of the powerful Judiciary Committee, and also the Transportation and Infrastructure Committee. He sits on two subcommittees of the each standing committee, and has been either Chair or Ranking Member of the Judiciary Subcommittee on the Constitution and Civil Justice. He is also the Ranking Democrat on the Subcommittee on Courts, Intellectual Property and the Internet. He is an Assistant Democrat Whip. Nadler's district includes Ground Zero, the site where the World Trade Center towers collapsed during the 9/11 terrorist attacks. After the attacks, he was instrumental in securing $20 billion in federal funds to rebuild Lower Manhattan. He has also been instrumental in addressing the health and environmental impacts of the collapse on first responders and area residents, workers and students. He also has advocated on behalf of increased funding for New York's mass transit system. Prior to becoming a Congressman, Nadler was a member of the New York State Assembly for 16 years. He also was a member of Community Planning Board 7 in Manhattan. He graduated from Columbia University and holds a JD from Fordham University Law School. He is the married father of one.

CHARLES B RANGEL (D)
13th - Part of New York and Bronx counties

2354 Rayburn House Office Bldg, Washington, DC 20515
202-225-4365/ http://rangel.house.gov/

163 W 125th St, Ste 737, New York, NY 10027
212-663-3900

Charles Rangel was first elected to the U.S. House of Representatives in 1970. His district includes Central and East Harlem, Manhattanville, Morningside Heights, Hamilton Heights, Washington Heights, Inwood, Marble Hill and the Bronx neighborhoods of Kingsbridge, Norwood, Bedford Park, Fordham, and University Heights. He is currently senior member of the powerful Ways and Means Committee, a committee he formerly chaired starting in 2007. At that time, he was the first African American to chair the committee. In addition, he is a founding member of the Congressional Black Caucus. Rep. Rangel's Congressional achievements are many over the years, and examples include authoring the Empowerment Zone program that provides $3.5 billion for urban and rural development; expanding the earned income tax credit; spearheading a program that generates investment in low- and moderate-income housing construction and rehabilitation; and numerous programs investing in the arts, healthcare facilities, and community programs. He also led efforts to award a Congressional Gold Medal on behalf of the Tuskegee Airmen. He served in the US Army from 1948 to 1952 in Korea, earned a BS from New York University School of Commerce in 1957 and a JD from St John's University School of Law. He served as assistant US Attorney in the Southern District of New York, and later served as General Counsel to the National Advisory Commission on Selective Service. In 1967, he was elected to the New York State Assembly. He is the married father of two.

TOM REED III (R)
23rd - Allegany, Cattaraugus, Chatauqua, Chemung, Ontario, Schuyler, Seneca, Steuben, Tioga, Tompkins, and Yates Counties

2437 Rayburn House Office Building, Washington, DC 20515
202-225-3161/http://reed.house.gov/

89 W. Market Street, Corning, NY 14830
607-654-7566

One Bluebird Square, Olean, NY 14760
716-379-8434

433 Exchange St., Geneva, NY 14456
315-759-5229

2 East 2nd St, Suite 300, Jamestown, NY 14701
716-379-8434

401 E. State St. Suite 304-1, Ithacan, NY 14850
607-222-2027

Congressman Tom Reed was elected to the U.S. House of Representatives in 2010. Since 2011, he has sat on the powerful Committee on Ways and Means and three of its subcommittees: Human Resources; Select Revenue Measures; and Social Security. He also co-chairs the House Manufacturing Caucus and the Congressional Natural Gas Caucus, and is Vice Chair of the Congressional Diabetes Caucus. An attorney by profession, he opened a private practice as well as other real estate and mortgage brokerage businesses. He served one term as Mayor of Corning. He graduated from Alfred University and holds a JD from the Ohio Northern University College of Law. He is the married father of two.

KATHLEEN M RICE (D)
4th - Nassau County

1508 Longworth H.O.B., Washington, DC 20515
(202) 225-5516/https://kathleenrice.house.gov

300 Garden City Plaza Suite 200, Garden City, NY 11530
(516) 739-3008

Kathleen M. Rice was elected to the U.S. House of Representatives in 2014. She serves on the Homeland Security Committee and is Ranking Member on the Subcommittee on Transportation Security, one of the Committee's three subcommittees on which she sits. She also sits on the Veterans' Affairs Committee and two of its subcommittees. Prior to being elected to Congress, she was Nassau County District Attorney from 2006-2014, becoming Long Island's first DA and focusing on combatting drunk driving. Her professional life began as an Assistant District Attorney in Brooklyn, and she also served as Assistant U.S. Attorney in Philadelphia. She holds a J.D. from Touro Law Center and a B.A. from Catholic University.

JOSÉ E SERRANO (D)
15th - Part of Bronx County

2227 Rayburn House Office Bldg, Washington, DC 20515
202-225-4361/Serrano.house.gov

1231 Lafayette Ave, 4th Fl, Bronx, NY 10474
718-620-0084

José E Serrano was first elected to the U.S. House of Representatives in 1990. His Bronx district includes the neighborhoods of Mott Haven, Hunts Point, Melrose, High Bridge, Morrisania, East Tremont, Tremont, Morris Heights, University Heights, Belmont, Fordham, Bedford Park, West Farms, the Longwood Avenue Historic District, and parts of Soundview. He sits on the House Appropriations Committee and three of its subcommittees; he is Ranking Member of the Subcommittee on Financial Services and General Government. He is Senior Whip for the Majority Whip operation, and an active member of the Congressional Hispanic Caucus, which he formerly chaired. As an appropriator, Serrano has secured millions of dollars in federal funding for his Bronx district; perhaps the most significant project has been the environmental restoration of the Bronx River. He also proposed the bill, signed into law as part of a larger bill, which grants posthumous citizenship to non-citizens who died because of the 9/11 attack and who had already initiated the process to become US citizens. He served in the New York State Assembly from 1975-1990 1990, and also served on the New York City Board of Education. He served in the US Army Medical Corps. The Mayaguez, Puerto Rico-born Serrano holds an undergraduate degree from Lehman College of CUNY and is married with five children.

LOUISE MCINTOSH SLAUGHTER (D)
25th - Monroe County

2469 Rayburn House Office Bldg, Washington, DC 20515
202-225-3615/ louise.house.gov

3120 Federal Bldg, 100 State St, Rochester, NY 14614
585-232-4850

Louise McIntosh Slaughter was first elected to the U.S. House of Representatives in 1986, the first woman to represent western New York, and serves as the Ranking Member of the Rules Committee, which she formerly chaired - also the first woman to do so. As chair of this committee, she helped shepherd legislation such as the Affordable Care Act. Her legislative achievements also include establishing the Office of Research on Women's Health at NIH, as well as allocating the first $500 million in federal funding at NIH. She co-authored the Violence Against Women Act in 1994. She opposes free trade agreements, believing those have caused Rochester business serious harm and led to widespread hardship in local communities. She successfully passed the STOCK Act, which outlawed insider trading by members of Congress and their staffs. She served in the Monroe County Legislature from 1976 to 1979 and in the New York State Assembly from 1982 to 1986. She attended the University of Kentucky, where she received a BS degree in Microbiology and a Master of Science degree in Public Health; she is the only microbiologist in Congress. She was married for 57 years to the late Robert Bruce Slaughter, Jr.; they are parents to three children and grandparents to seven.

ELISE STEFANIK (R)
21 - Jefferson, Lewis, St. Lawrence, Franklin, Hamilton, Herkimer, Fulton, Saratoga, Washington, Warren, Essex, Clinton and Franklin counties

512 Cannon House Office Building, Washington, DC 20515, (202) 225-4611/https://stefanik.house.gov

136 Glen Street, Glens Falls, NY 12801
518-743-0964

23 Durkee Street Suite C, Plattsburgh, NY 12901
518-561-2324

120 Washington St. Suite 200, Watertown, NY 13601
(315) 782-3150

Elise Stefanik was first elected to the U.S. House of Representatives in 2014; at the time of her swearing she was the youngest Congresswoman in history. She serves on the Armed Services Committee and three of its subcommittees, and on the Education and the Workforce Committee, and two of its subcommittees. She also served as the Freshman Representative to the Policy Committee.

She served on President George W. Bush's Domestic Police Council staff and in the Chief of Staff's office. She has served in a number of positions such as Vice President of Debate Prep for candidate Paul Ryan, and Director of Communications for the Foreign Policy Initiative which launched Defending Defense, a coalition of think tanks warning of the dangers of the sequester. Prior to being elected to Congress, she worked for Premium Plywood Products, Inc., her family business. She graduated from Harvard University.

PAUL TONKO (D)
20th - Albany, Montgomery, Rensselaer, Saratoga and Schenectady Counties

2463 Rayburn House Office Building, Washington, DC 20515
202-225-5076/ tonko.house.gov

61 Columbia St, 4th Fl, Albany, NY 12210
518-465-0700

105 Jay Street, Rm 15, Schenectady, NY 12305
518-374-4547

61 Church St, Room 309, Amsterdam, NY 12010
518-843-3400

Paul Tonko was elected to his first term in the U.S. House of Representatives in 2008. His district includes the communities of Albany, Schenectady, Troy, Saratoga Springs, and Amsterdam. He sits on the Energy and Commerce Committee and three of its subcommittees including the Subcommittee on Environment and the Economy of which he is Ranking Member. He also sits on the Science, Space and Technology Committee and one of its subcommittees. Among his recent legislation is a proposal to ask the Energy Dept. to carry out a research, development, and technology demonstration program to improve the efficiency of gas turbines used in power generation systems and to identify the technologies that will lead to gas turbine combined cycle efficiency of 65 percent or simple cycle efficiency of 50 percent. He holds a BA in mechanical and industrial engineering from Clarkson University.

NYDIA M VELAZQUEZ (D)
7th - Parts of New York, Queens and Kings Counties

2302 Rayburn House Office Bldg, Washington, DC 20515
202-225-2361/velazquez.house.gov

266 Broadway, Ste 201, Brooklyn, NY 11211
718-599-3658

500 Pearl Street, Ste 973, New York, NY 10007
212-619-2606

16 Court Street, Ste 1006, Brooklyn, NY 11241
718-222-5819

Nydia Velazquez was first elected to the U.S. House of Representatives in 1992. She is the Ranking Member of the House Small Business Committee and a senior member of the Financial Services Committee; she sits on two of the latter committee's subcommittees. The Yabucoa, Puerto Rico-born Velazquez was the first Puerto Rican woman elected to the U.S. House of Representatives, the first Hispanic woman to serve as Ranking Member of a full House Committee, and the first Latina to chair a full Congressional committee, the latter achievement coming in 2006 when she chaired the House Small Business Committee. She is a former teacher of Puerto Rican Studies at CUNY's Hunter College, former Special Assistant to Congressman Edolphus Towns, and the New York City Council's first Latina member. She also was the Director of the Department of Puerto Rican Community Affairs in the U.S. She holds a degree from the University of Puerto Rico in Rio Piedras, and a master's degree from NYU. She is married.

LEE M. ZELDIN (R)
1st - Suffolk County

1517 Longworth House Office Building, Washington, DC 20515
(202) 225-3826/https://zeldin.house.gove

31 Oak Street Suite 20, Patchogue, NY 11772, (631) 289-1097

Lee Zeldin was first elected to the U.S. House of Representatives in 2014 from a district at the east end of Long Island. He sits on the Foreign Affairs Committee and three of its subcommittees; the Transportation and Infrastructure Committee and three of its subcommittees; the Veterans' Affairs Committee, and two of its subcommittees; and the Transportation & Infrastructure Committee. He served in the New York State Senate from 2010-2014, where he chaired the Consumer Protection Committee. His legislative achievements included securing funding for the PFC Joseph Dwyer Program, a state-wide program that helps veterans cope with post-traumatic stress disorder, or PTSD, and traumatic brain injury (TBI). He also wrote the law to protect fallen veterans and their families from protests and military burials. Rep. Zeldin spent four years on active duty in the US Army, including a 2006 deployment to Iraq. He is a major in the US Army Reserves, an attorney by profession, and holds a BA from SUNY-Albany and a JD from Albany Law School. He is the married father of two.

APPENDICES

CASH DISBURSEMENTS BY FUNCTION
ALL GOVERNMENTAL FUNDS
(thousands of dollars)

	FY 2016 Results	FY 2017 Enacted	FY 2018 Projected	FY 2019 Projected	FY 2020 Projected
ECONOMIC DEVELOPMENT AND GOVERNMENT OVERSIGHT					
Agriculture and Markets, Department of	103,855	96,983	91,561	98,061	98,197
Alcoholic Beverage Control, Division of	17,277	12,836	12,683	12,683	12,744
Economic Development Capital	6,614	23,000	29,276	24,250	23,000
Economic Development, Department of	92,494	99,197	91,552	102,428	88,278
Empire State Development Corporation	738,836	1,614,289	1,681,999	1,423,028	1,283,928
Energy Research and Development Authority	15,191	23,450	23,000	14,724	13,000
Financial Services, Department of	361,476	350,490	359,586	362,129	365,668
Olympic Regional Development Authority	10,611	10,386	2,886	2,886	2,886
Power Authority, New York	0	2,500	2,500	1,244	0
Public Service Department	71,087	74,968	76,233	77,632	77,632
Regional Economic Development Program	2,787	1,500	512	356	355
Strategic Investment Program	1,427	6,000	6,000	7,371	7,000
Functional Total	1,421,655	2,315,599	2,377,788	2,126,792	1,972,688
PARKS AND THE ENVIRONMENT					
Adirondack Park Agency	4,350	4,682	4,682	4,682	4,682
Environmental Conservation, Department of	878,293	991,032	1,131,493	1,144,424	1,093,785
Hudson River Park Trust	3,452	0	0	0	0
Parks, Recreation and Historic Preservation, Office of	344,507	328,567	322,168	318,443	318,443
Functional Total	1,230,602	1,324,281	1,458,343	1,467,549	1,416,910
TRANSPORTATION					
Metropolitan Transportation Authority	0	512,171	643,685	250,000	350,000
Motor Vehicles, Department of	292,446	301,333	302,493	305,100	305,441
Thruway Authority, New York State	17,948	0	0	0	0
Transportation, Department of	9,124,697	9,547,990	9,639,208	9,753,978	9,915,494
Functional Total	9,435,091	10,361,494	10,585,386	10,309,078	10,570,935
HEALTH					
Aging, Office for the	229,479	252,479	248,653	235,580	240,891
Health, Department of	55,632,709	57,450,431	60,211,431	62,246,515	64,102,136
Medical Assistance	48,094,607	48,960,356	51,254,852	53,117,328	54,961,917
Essential Plan	1,539,298	2,460,805	2,534,705	2,609,498	2,682,684
Medicaid Administration	1,666,498	1,626,185	1,616,059	1,574,988	1,571,479
Public Health	4,332,306	4,403,085	4,805,815	4,944,701	4,886,056
Medicaid Inspector General, Office of the	51,999	51,204	51,204	51,204	51,204
Functional Total	55,914,187	57,754,114	60,511,288	62,533,299	64,394,231
SOCIAL WELFARE					
Children and Family Services, Office of	3,015,520	3,076,943	3,046,592	3,070,120	3,092,287
OCFS	2,926,598	2,986,670	2,954,592	2,977,939	2,998,218
OCFS - Other	88,922	90,273	92,000	92,181	94,069
Housing and Community Renewal, Division of	217,494	310,489	485,925	706,422	736,272
Human Rights, Division of	14,639	14,226	14,289	14,343	14,343
Labor, Department of	546,390	577,958	569,612	569,612	569,612
National and Community Service	15,100	14,909	16,029	16,335	16,335
Nonprofit Infrastructure Capital Investment Program	0	13,000	30,000	27,000	20,000
Temporary and Disability Assistance, Office of	5,289,204	5,093,085	5,114,014	5,134,985	5,144,785
Welfare Assistance	3,985,752	3,784,769	3,806,699	3,818,699	3,820,699
All Other	1,303,452	1,308,316	1,307,315	1,316,286	1,324,086
Functional Total	9,098,347	9,100,610	9,276,461	9,538,817	9,593,634
MENTAL HYGIENE					
Alcoholism and Substance Abuse Services, Office of	594,596	623,833	652,641	669,631	691,636
OASAS	507,773	541,444	569,476	585,535	606,480
OASAS - Other	86,823	82,389	83,165	84,096	85,156
Developmental Disabilities Planning Council	3,386	4,200	4,200	4,200	4,200
Justice Center	40,205	42,671	43,325	44,226	44,921
Mental Health, Office of	3,359,196	3,379,610	3,519,094	3,715,234	3,817,067
OMH	1,560,431	1,683,475	1,787,515	1,929,699	1,984,639
OMH - Other	1,798,765	1,696,135	1,731,579	1,785,535	1,832,428

CASH DISBURSEMENTS BY FUNCTION
ALL GOVERNMENTAL FUNDS
(thousands of dollars)

	FY 2016 Results	FY 2017 Enacted	FY 2018 Projected	FY 2019 Projected	FY 2020 Projected
Mental Hygiene, Department of	219	0	0	0	0
People with Developmental Disabilities, Office for	3,223,358	3,070,514	3,500,494	3,740,881	3,942,562
OPWDD	370,536	451,304	505,356	554,274	609,319
OPWDD - Other	2,852,822	2,619,210	2,995,138	3,186,607	3,333,243
Functional Total	7,220,960	7,120,828	7,719,754	8,174,172	8,500,386
PUBLIC PROTECTION/CRIMINAL JUSTICE					
Correction, Commission of	2,297	2,651	2,651	2,651	2,651
Correctional Services, Department of	2,982,445	2,944,414	2,961,650	2,946,406	2,956,561
Criminal Justice Services, Division of	224,078	240,778	230,643	230,643	230,643
Disaster Assistance	(51,789)	0	0	0	0
Homeland Security and Emergency Services, Division of	1,974,600	1,717,876	1,081,529	808,143	781,664
Indigent Legal Services, Office of	60,116	86,695	105,295	105,295	105,295
Judicial Conduct, Commission on	5,567	5,584	5,584	5,643	5,708
Judicial Nomination, Commission on	20	30	30	30	30
Judicial Screening Committees, New York State	14	38	38	38	38
Military and Naval Affairs, Division of	102,534	104,972	104,781	105,252	91,252
State Police, Division of	733,485	782,241	795,014	785,213	775,133
Statewide Financial System	30,070	30,137	30,143	30,143	30,143
Victim Services, Office of	64,276	66,230	76,090	76,090	76,090
Functional Total	6,127,713	5,981,646	5,393,448	5,095,547	5,055,208
HIGHER EDUCATION					
City University of New York	1,565,917	1,582,601	1,616,576	1,659,427	1,687,020
Higher Education - Miscellaneous	259	390	390	390	390
Higher Education Facilities Capital Matching Grants Program	136	20,000	25,000	22,000	13,000
Higher Education Services Corporation, New York State	1,084,054	1,126,926	1,161,881	1,182,477	1,193,979
State University of New York	8,042,846	7,939,225	8,003,502	8,071,607	8,160,523
Functional Total	10,693,212	10,669,142	10,807,349	10,935,901	11,054,912
EDUCATION					
Arts, Council on the	42,178	46,213	45,953	45,953	45,953
Education, Department of	32,811,466	34,311,622	35,822,041	37,243,633	38,559,783
School Aid	25,501,461	27,450,245	29,121,439	30,465,647	31,722,716
STAR Property Tax Relief	3,334,700	3,227,844	2,976,792	2,921,232	2,869,171
Special Education Categorical Programs	2,201,098	2,258,850	2,369,590	2,495,380	2,630,228
All Other	1,774,207	1,374,683	1,354,220	1,361,374	1,337,668
Functional Total	32,853,644	34,357,835	35,867,994	37,289,586	38,605,736
GENERAL GOVERNMENT					
Budget, Division of the	24,227	31,022	30,596	30,596	30,596
Civil Service, Department of	13,424	13,381	13,381	13,507	13,617
Deferred Compensation Board	524	866	866	866	873
Elections, State Board of	12,447	14,982	14,982	8,587	8,697
Employee Relations, Office of	2,247	2,581	2,581	2,601	2,621
Gaming Commission, New York State	251,588	267,907	289,803	314,803	314,803
General Services, Office of	268,221	302,887	286,767	301,397	270,397
Inspector General, Office of the	7,061	7,367	7,367	7,427	7,487
Labor Management Committees	24,882	25,300	25,300	25,300	25,306
Prevention of Domestic Violence, Office for	2,056	2,381	2,481	2,481	2,581
Public Employment Relations Board	3,433	3,572	3,573	3,604	3,634
Public Integrity, Commission on	4,332	5,531	5,531	5,576	5,630
State, Department of	128,351	136,155	126,397	126,653	127,008
Tax Appeals, Division of	3,035	3,040	3,040	3,040	3,040
Taxation and Finance, Department of	354,936	352,264	353,066	353,241	353,066
Technology, Office for	602,366	604,824	622,121	607,636	606,936
Veterans' Affairs, Division of	13,612	17,161	15,546	15,631	15,631
Welfare Inspector General, Office of	569	672	672	686	701
Workers' Compensation Board	194,970	201,679	213,633	215,416	217,219
Functional Total	1,912,281	1,993,572	2,017,703	2,039,048	2,009,843
ELECTED OFFICIALS					
Audit and Control, Department of	174,200	185,836	182,409	181,070	181,253
Executive Chamber	13,704	13,578	13,578	13,578	13,578
Judiciary	2,764,517	2,850,600	2,926,553	2,961,553	2,961,553
Law, Department of	225,402	233,535	236,334	238,104	240,705
Legislature	215,580	218,795	218,795	218,795	218,795

CASH DISBURSEMENTS BY FUNCTION
ALL GOVERNMENTAL FUNDS
(thousands of dollars)

	FY 2016 Results	FY 2017 Enacted	FY 2018 Projected	FY 2019 Projected	FY 2020 Projected
Lieutenant Governor, Office of the	499	614	614	614	614
Functional Total	3,393,902	3,502,958	3,578,283	3,613,714	3,616,498
LOCAL GOVERNMENT ASSISTANCE					
Aid and Incentives for Municipalities	728,288	714,756	762,710	763,347	763,347
Efficiency Incentive Grants Program	1,289	0	0	0	0
Miscellaneous Financial Assistance	11,846	9,646	0	0	0
Municipalities with VLT Facilities	29,331	29,331	29,331	29,331	29,331
Small Government Assistance	217	218	218	218	218
Functional Total	770,971	753,951	792,259	792,896	792,896
ALL OTHER CATEGORIES					
General State Charges	4,681,599	4,738,965	5,077,501	5,276,235	5,663,396
Long-Term Debt Service	5,635,102	5,242,440	6,305,861	6,820,767	7,281,488
Miscellaneous	(406,371)	(259,066)	(25,796)	(273,035)	(266,292)
Special Infrastructure Account	725,592	1,148,615	1,197,241	1,077,610	810,750
Functional Total	10,635,922	10,870,954	12,554,807	12,901,577	13,489,342
TOTAL ALL GOVERNMENTAL FUNDS SPENDING	150,708,487	156,106,984	162,940,863	166,817,976	171,073,219

GSC: Agency disbursements include grants to local governments, state operations and general state charges, which is a departure from prior Financial plan publications. In prior reports, general state charges were excluded from agency spending totals.

Note: *This information is excerpted from the New York State FY 2017 Enacted Budget Financial Plan. All Governmental Funds combines activity in the four governmental fund types: General Fund; Special Revenue Funds; Capital Projects Funds; and Debt Service Funds.*

Name Index

Aaron, Merik A., 55
Aaron, Stewart D, 217
Aarons, Sharon A. M., 45
Aarons, Sharon, 48
Abate, Catherine, 257
Abbate, Jr, Peter J, 28, 35, 36, 38, 40, 242, 618
Abbate, Jr., Peter, 35
Abbate, Richard D., 373
Abbatti, Amy, 474
Abbitt, Viola I, 251
Abbott, Mark, 438
Abdallah, Jill, 30
Abdelaal, Hany, 444
Abdelazim, Tarik, 342
Abdus-Salaam, Sheila, 45
Abercrombie, Neil, 318
Abernethy, David, 410
Abernethy, Samuel F., 92
Abesamis-Mendoza, Noilyn, 382
Abinanti, Thomas J, 618
Abinanti, Thomas, 28, 36, 37, 38, 39, 40, 124
Abraham, Thomas W, 596
Abram, Brian C, 131
Abrams, Barry, 357
Abrams, James F, 572
Abrams, James, 595
Abrams, Karl G, 330
Abrams, Kristin, 451
Abrams, Laura A, 330
Abramson, Jill, 528
Abreu, Rafael E., 487
Abril, Victoria, 179
Acampora, Patricia L, 11
Accetta, Joseph, 60
Achille, Anthony, 397
Achramovitch, Steven, 573
Ackerbauer, Bill, 525
Ackerman, Andra, 62
Ackerman, Gary L, 311, 319, 320
Ackerman, Gary, 319, 320
Ackerman, Todd, 523
Ackerson, Anne, 279
Ackley, Denise, 504
Acosta, Rolando T, 45
Acquario, Adam, 470
Acquario, Stephen J, 238
Acquario, Stephen J., 171
Acquario, Stephen, 383
Acquaro, Ralph, 579
Adabbo, Joseph, 23
Adair, Jeffrey R, 331
Adair, Scott, 106, 288
Adam, William, 464
Adamis, Tony, 526
Adams, Ann M, 590
Adams, Christopher, 180, 223
Adams, Eric R, 53
Adams, Eric, 480
Adams, Gina F., 482
Adams, Kendra, 292
Adams, Mary, 58, 447
Adams, Rachel A., 46
Adams, Rachel Amy, 49
Adams, Roger W, 572
Adams, Thomas A., 47
Adams, Thomas, 210
Adams-Keane, Helen, 378
Adams-Sarthou, Anna, 384
Addabbo Jr, Joseph P, 16, 20, 22, 24, 26, 606
Addabbo Jr., Joseph, 21, 25
Addabbo, Jr, Joseph P, 295
Addabbo, Jr, Joseph, 275
Addabbo, Jr., Joseph, 266
Addepalli, Rajendra, 12, 141
Addison, Sharon, 367
Aderholt, Robert B, 317
Aderholt, Robert, 73
Adjei, Anthony K., 483
Adler, Anna, 469
Adler, Harold, 49
Adler, Leah, 477
Adler, Lester B, 47
Adler, M.D., Karl P, 558
Adler, Sol, 377
Adler, Stephen J., 533
Adolf, Jay, 439
Adolf, Maureen E., 457
Adolphus, Stephen H, 549
Aefsky, Fern, 572
Affronti, Francis A, 47
Agans, Barbara, 65
Agard, Michele D, 98, 210
Agarwal, Prince, 494
Agata, Seth H, 11, 241
Agata, Seth, 103, 137, 164
Agate, Augustus C, 48
Agin, Susan, 397
Agins, Bruce D, 174
Aglieco, Rose Z., 502
Agostaro, Rosario, 595
Agostino, Aprilanne, 45
Agostino, Tom, 202, 221
Agrawal, Rajendra, 177
Agruso, Susan, 592
Aguilar, Karina, 179
Ahl, Caroline, 5, 234, 240
Ahlers, Kate, 356
Ahmad, Iftikhar, 358
Ahmad, Zainab, 115, 213
Aidala, Gregory J, 589
Aiello, Greg, 280
Aiello, Kathleen, 56
Aiken, Doris, 118
Aiken, Robert, 235, 246, 264
Aikens, Patricia, 217
Ailes, Elizabeth, 528
Aimer, Alicia, 458
Aina, Eileen, 134
Aini, Cheryl, 177
Ainlay, Stephen C, 562
Aitken, David, 406
Ajemian, Peter, 18
Akaka, Daniel K, 315
Akaka, Daniel, 316
Akilova, Zlata, 496
Akin, W Todd, 318
Akshar, Fred, 606
Akshar, II, Frederick J, 16, 20, 21, 22, 24, 137
Alabi, Olanike T., 485
Alagno, Louis, 351
Alazraki, Marcia, 439
Alba, Gil, 116
Alba-Foster, Joanne, 71
Albanese, Anthony J, 81
Albanese, Anthony R, 572
Albano, Teresa, 527
Albee, Amy, 267
Albert, Andrew, 519
Albert, Patricia, 201, 219
Albert, Sam, 486
Albert, Thomas, 414
Alberti, Peter P, 333
Albrecht, Greg, 70
Albrecht, Kathy, 30
Albro, George, 383
Albunio, Catherine, 343
Alch, Bruce, 141
Alden, Amie, 331
Aldous, Ken, 148, 176
Aldrich, Dale, 470
Alegre, Nathalie, 429
Alejandro, Joseph A., 492
Alessandrino, Daniel M., 46
Alessandro, Francis M, 49
Alexander, Catherine, 299
Alexander, Emily, 447
Alexander, Kevin W, 515
Alexander, Lamar, 125, 143, 180, 224, 255, 312, 314, 315
Alexander, Lanny R, 357
Alexander, Louis, 8, 147
Alexander, Paul, 21, 22
Alexander, Rodney, 549
Alexander, Valerie, 61
Alexandre-Bakiriddin, Joan M., 488
Alfieri, Joseph, 455
Alfieri, Victor J., 47

Appendices: Financial Plan, Indexes & Maps

Name Index

Alford, Gary R, 64
Alger, Mark R, 337
Alger, Robin L, 131
Ali, Khayriyyah, 550
Ali, Shaazad, 358
Alicea, Victor G, 553
Aliotta, Thomas P., 48
Allan, Jon W, 87, 97, 150
Allan, Lauren, 597
Allaud, Aimee, 434
Allegretti, Daniel, 413
Allen, Amy, 445
Allen, Bradley, 8, 161
Allen, Bruce, 49
Allen, Dennis, 104, 273
Allen, Gail, 379
Allen, Gregory, 9, 175, 200, 219
Allen, James, 3, 69, 76, 78, 83, 108, 119, 130, 140, 147, 160, 173, 187, 194, 200, 206, 219, 227, 234, 240, 245, 250, 263, 270, 283, 293, 303, 382, 501
Allen, Jim, 283
Allen, John, 24, 229
Allen, Karrie, 526
Allen, Leonard, 489
Allen, Leslie, 136
Allen, Lofthouse, 372
Allen, Lora A., 134
Allen, Maureen, 30
Allen, Susan K, 578
Allen, Wayne D, 326
Allen, William A, 133
Allessandrino, Daniel M., 54
Alleva, Frank, 24
Allibone, Peter, 292
Allinger, Chris, 534
Allinson, Bradford J., 459
Allison, William, 423
Allman, John, 578
Aloi, Anthony F, 56
Aloise, Michael B, 48
Alonso, Esti, 175
Alpert, David A, 372
Alpert, Paul L., 49
Alquist, Mark H, 136
Alquist, Mark H., 374
Alschuler, Howard, 550
Alschuler, John, 426
Alston, Timothy J, 13, 265
Alt, Carol, 48
Alter, Jeffrey, 470
Altidor, Fritzner L., 494
Altier, Mike, 473
Altieri, Carol, 443, 444
Altieri, Stephen, 350
Altman, Anita, 466
Altman, Michael, 428
Altman, Robert, 536
Altman, Vivian, 428
Altmire, Jason, 322
Altomare, Nick, 519
Alund, Chris, 220
Alvarado, Efrain L., 49
Alvarellos, Omar, 431
Alvarez, Michael A., 485
Alvaro, Michael, 404
Alvord, Karen, 529
Alworth, Tom, 149, 271
Alzate, Luis, 384
Aman, Dan, 342
Amann, Floyd F, 547
Amarosa, Ellen, 144
Amater, Ray, 514
Amati, Patricia, 101, 113
Amato, Gail, 386
Amato, Michael J, 332
Amato, Stacey G., 483
Amberg-Blyskal, Patricia, 296
Ambro, Richard, 47
Ambrose, Paul, 175
Ambrosi, Marc, 563
Ambrosio, Michael A, 50
Amedore Jr, George A, 20
Amedore Jr, George, 20, 21, 22, 24, 25, 26
Amedore, George, 606
Amedore, Jr, George A, 21
Amedore, Jr, George, 17
Amell, Stewart R, 586
Amell, Thomas L., 82, 171
Amer, Fatma, 352
Ames, Margery E, 232
Ames, William F, 52
Amey, Bruce, 577
Amico, Virginia O, 331
Amler, Robert W., 185
Ammerman, Steven, 413
Ammirati, Rick, 508
Amo, Scott A, 571
Amodeo, John, 207
Amodeo, Thomas P, 62
Amodio, Tom, 350
Amoia-Kowalczyk, Sandra, 109
Amoroso, Edward, 143
Amoroso, Esq., Gregory J., 333
Amoroso, Gregory J., 65
Ampry-Samuel, Alicha, 34
Amthor, Arnold, 351
Amundson, Richard, 597
Anagnost, Stephen, 451
Anagnostopoulos, Photeine, 353
Anander, Lori, 526
Anarella, Joseph, 175
Anatharam, P V, 357
Anaya, Antonio, 399
Ancowitz, Richard, 40
Anderson, Adrian H, 328
Anderson, Belinda, 565
Anderson, Brian C, 532
Anderson, Cami, 582
Anderson, Chris, 383
Anderson, Colleen, 133
Anderson, Ellen, 175
Anderson, James, 352
Anderson, Jamie, 131
Anderson, Jeff, 385
Anderson, John M, 546
Anderson, John, 531
Anderson, Kristin, 32
Anderson, Michelle J., 552
Anderson, Michelle, 397
Anderson, Nora S., 55
Anderson, Richard T., 93, 192, 491
Anderson, Susan, 536
Andino, Nelson, 440
Andino, Thomas, 361
Andito, Lloyd, 421
Andrade, Karyn, 175
Andreozzi, Holly, 384
Andres, Jr., Richard L., 360
Andrews, Carl, 394
Andrews, Daniel, 335, 359
Andrews, Faye, 341
Andrews, Jason A, 568
Andrews, Kyle R, 332
Andrews, Robert, 318
Andrews, Ross P, 66
Andreychek, Melissa, 412
Andrias, Richard T, 45
Andruili, Anthony, 133
Anelante, Jr., Frank J., 491
Angell, Thomas, 328
Angelo, Eugene, 495
Anger, Tamara, 420
Anglin, Laura L., 126
Angus, William, 29
Anisman, Martin J, 555
Anjam, Saima, 412
Ann Shields, Sally, 588
Annable, John, 507
Annucci, Anthony J, 11, 112
Annucci, Anthony, 6, 108
Annunziata, Albert A, 247
Annunziata, Anthony M, 96, 285
Annunziata, Mark L., 55
Annunziato, Anthony J, 591
Ansty, Martha F., 154
Antenucci, Nicholas, 476
Anthony, Patricia, 346
Antonacci, Jo Anne, 600
Antonacci, Robert E, 333
Antonelli, Debra, 62
Antonelli, John J, 353
Antonucci, Carol, 360
Antos, Jason D., 527
Antos, Susan, 410
Anzalone, Anna, 47
Anzevino, John, 463
Aoyama-Martin, Jane, 453
Apolito, Nancy, 77
Apotheker, Charles A, 58
Appel, Janet F, 266
Appel, Larry, 162, 236
Appelbaum, Stuart, 493

Apple, Douglas, 355
Apple, Sr., Craig D., 325
Apse, Colin, 449
Aquillo, Ann, 464
Aquino, Carmen M., 479
Araldi, Mary-Jane, 557
Aram, Janet, 434
Aramanda, James, 80
Araujo, Jose M, 133
Arbetter, Susan, 539
Archambault, William, 346
Archer, Ellen, 531
Arcuri, Michael A, 322, 323
Ardito, Joseph, 506
Ardito, Lori, 358
Arena, David, 247
Ares, Gabrielle, 251
Arezzo, Camille, 480
Argento, Victoria M, 55
Arisohn, Barbara, 121
Ark, John J., 47
Arker, Sol, 491
Arlt, Lewis, 515
Armbuster, William, 414
Armitage, John, 113
Armour-Garb, Allison, 270
Armstrong, Adrian N, 64
Armstrong, John, 416
Armstrong, Karen, 385
Armstrong, Regina B, 239, 269
Arnold, Dawn, 284
Arnold, Judith, 175
Arnold, Phyllis, 390
Arnold, Thea, 466
Arnone, Kym, 385
Arnott, James, 519
Arnow, Nancy, 462
Aronowitz, Milton, 473
Aronson, Robert J, 516
Aronson, Sam, 389
Aronson, Stephen D, 62
Aronson, Stephen D., 56
Aronstein, Lois, 255
Arpey, Michelle, 120
Arriaga, Frederick, 49
Arroyo, Carmen E, 28, 37, 618
Arroyo, Carmen, 27, 35, 36
Arsenault, Walter M, 107, 222, 288, 310
Artus, Dale, 110
Artus, Michelle, 109
Arvan, Steve, 469
Arzt, George, 382
Asante, Katrina, 19
Ascher, Kate, 473
Asciutto, Georgia M., 126
Ash, Sylvia, 46
Asher, W. Gerard, 47
Ashman, Angela, 528
Ashton, Judith, 260
Ashwell, Meredith, 473
Asiedu, Kojo, 409
Asiello, John P, 45
Askey, John C, 341
Askins, Chantall, 466
Assini Jr, Charles J, 424
Assini, Mark W, 346
Astacio, Leticia D, 65
Astorino, Robert P., 339
Astrab, Donald P, 548
Astrab, Donald, 447
Atchie, Michael, 396
Athens, Virginia, 58
Atias, David, 395
Atiba-Weza, Fadhilika, 588
Atkins, Kim, 183, 198
Atkins, Phil, 76
Atkins, Richard, 134
Atkins, Rodney, 454
Atkins, Tamara, 435
Atkinson, Cheryl, 120, 174, 227
Atkinson, Scott, 539
Auberger, John T, 346
Aubrey, Jeffrion L., 27
Aubry, Jeffrion L, 28, 38, 41, 42, 618
Aubry, Jeffrion, 42
Auffredov, Martin D., 338
Aulisi, Richard T, 46
Aumand, Matthew, 37
Auriemma, Frank V, 588
Ausfeld, Robert, 536
Auslander, Douglas, 396
Aust, Peter, 501
Auster, Adam, 307
Auster, Esq., Morris, 443
Austin, Adrienne, 472
Austin, Dan, 535, 536
Austin, James, 141
Austin, Jeffrey, 392
Austin, Leonard B., 45
Austin, Thomas P, 572
Avaltroni, Robert, 402
Avanessians, Natasha, 388
Avella, Michael, 442
Avella, Tony, 16, 17, 20, 22, 23, 24, 26, 178, 254, 606
Avery, Amanda A, 96, 285
Avery, Eileen, 451
Avery, Susan, 49
Aviles, Alan D, 354
Aviles, Victor, 203
Avner, Judith I, 231
Avrick, Stuart J., 371
Awad Jr, George C, 338
Awad, Joseph, 469
Awner, Maxine, 443
Axelson, Cliff, 458
Aydinian, Philip, 135
Ayotte, Darren, 108
Ayotte, Kelly, 143
Ayres, Bill, 262
Ayres, David J, 55
Azia, Jane, 78, 84, 112, 188, 207
Baa-Danso, Nancy, 175, 293
Babb, Valerie, 395
Babbitt, Deborah, 163
Babcock, Louis C, 134
Babette, Gary, 433
Baboulis, Steve, 536
Babu, S V, 84, 122
Baca, Joe, 317
Bacceilieri, Chief Joseph, 210
Bachant, Raymond, 388
Bacharach, Samuel B, 225
Bacheller, John M, 12
Bacheller, John M., 235, 245, 264
Bacher, Jessica, 453
Bachus, Spencer, 319
Bacich, Susan, 535
Backer, Dan, 497
Backer, Joseph W, 599
Backstrom, Brian D, 399
Backus, Michael C., 334
Backus, Michael, 375
Bacon, Bernie, 106, 288
Bacon, Greg, 525
Bacon, Jennie H, 135
Bacon, William, 505
Badain, David, 416
Badalova, Alyona, 479
Badalucco, Matthew, 443
Badger, Mary Ann, 53
Badillo, Gilbert, 49
Baehrel, Bambi, 413
Baerman, Lawrence K., 212
Baggiano, Frank, 51
Bagnoli, Eileen, 455
Bahr, Paul, 563
Bahren, Susan, 134
Baiata, John, 538
Baigent, Peter, 467
Bailey, Georgi Ann, 90, 190
Bailey, Jonathan, 36
Bailey, Kevin, 514
Bailey, Megan, 453
Bailie, Roger, 220
Bailly, Rose Mary, 104, 211, 309
Baily-Schiffman, Loren, 49
Bain, Donald E, 561
Baines, Michelle, 451
Bainlardi, John, 475
Baio, Bridget, 467
Baird, Brian, 322
Baird, Maureen, 114
Baisley, Jr, Paul J, 47
Baker, Aaron, 31
Baker, Brooks, 337
Baker, Donald, 388
Baker, Erin, 34
Baker, Francine, 64
Baker, Gerard, 146, 527, 532
Baker, Irene, 446
Baker, James, 347
Baker, Judith, 373

Baker, Matthew, 483
Baker, Paul, 73, 75
Baker, Sherry L, 62
Baker, Vic, 537
Balaban, Maura, 308
Balassie, Kate, 306
Balbick, Robert J, 62
Balboni, Michael A., 483
Balboni, Michael A.L., 420
Balboni, Michael, 444, 460
Baldauf, Gary A, 177, 207
Baldock, Melissa, 446
Balduzzi, Michael, 482
Baldwin, James N, 120
Bale, Bonnie, 432
Balga, Pamela J, 505
Balkin, Ruth C, 45
Balko, Al, 444
Ball Chinian, Alane, 272
Ball, Chaunda, 414
Ball, Lawrence E, 63
Ball, Maureen, 63
Ball, Richard A, 86, 96
Ball, Richard, 4, 69, 250, 413
Ball, Shonnie, 462
Ball, Todd, 423
Ballantyne, Christian, 8, 148
Ballantyne, Suzy, 449
Ballard, Yvonne, 294
Ballmann, Frank, 103, 124
Ballou, Marylee, 514
Balmas, Anna Mae, 136
Balsamini, Dean, 397
Banach, Michael, 432
Banek, John, 577
Baneky, Willaim, 407
Banes, Kevin, 408
Banker, Eileen, 31
Banks III, John H., 143
Banks, John, 401
Banks, Steven, 216
Bannister, Christine, 235, 246, 264
Bannister, Doris, 340
Bannister, Tracey A, 47
Bannister, Tricia, 504
Bannon, Nancy M., 46
Bannon, Nancy, 49
Banville, John, 20
Baran, Linda M, 517
Baran, Marie, 224
Barash, Mark D., 154
Barbara, Leslie, 405
Barbarino, Santo, 464, 581
Barbarotta, Ann Marie, 228
Barbatis, Peter, 397
Barbato, Ben R., 49
Barbato, Robert, 5, 7, 83, 160, 234, 235, 263
Barber, Carmen, 25
Barber, James, 72
Barber, Jerry, 162, 236
Barber, John R., 348
Barber, Mary, 412
Barber, Robert, 443
Barbera-Dalli, Janine A., 61
Barbot, Heriberto, 10, 283, 359
Barclay, William A, 28, 39, 40, 43, 618
Barclay, William, 28, 38, 41, 202
Barczak, William K, 544
Barduhn, Casey, 576
Bardunias, Pete, 516
Barefoot, Sara A, 59
Bargnesi, James F, 53
Barkan, Lou-Ellen, 379
Barkauskas, Laurie, 503
Barker, Emily, 527
Barker, Jr, Lawrence L, 225
Barkley, Mike, 73
Barkman, Annemarie, 576
Barletta, Lou, 190
Barmore, Heather, 379
Barnard, Robert, 106, 288
Barnes, Joseph L, 298
Barnes, Philip, 376
Barnes, Richard E, 260
Barnes, Richard E., 128
Barnett, Gary, 413
Barnette, Margaret R., 479
Barney, Julie, 42
Barney, Tom, 533
Barney, Tracy, 432
Baron, Eve, 446
Baron, Judith L, 98, 151
Baron, Rob, 415
Baron, Robert, 270
Barone, II, Nathaniel L., 326
Barone, John A, 48
Barone, Nick, 505
Baroody, Walter, 295, 296
Barowitz, Jordan, 408, 461
Barr, John F., 274, 287
Barra, Robert, 366
Barrack, Pamela, 328
Barraco, Robert, 587
Barral, Roland, 266
Barrasso, John, 169, 197, 277, 290, 314, 315, 316, 458
Barrella, Nicholas, 393
Barresi, James S., 153
Barrett, Daniel G., 60
Barrett, Didi, 29, 35, 37, 41, 42, 618
Barrett, Larry, 167
Barrett, Laura, 171
Barrett, Michael V, 385
Barrett, Patricia C., 432
Barrett, Philip, 344
Barrett, RA, E Bruce, 100, 123
Barrington, Martin J, 90
Barrio, Ana, 353
Barrios-Paoli, Lilliam, 352
Barron, Charles, 29, 35, 37, 38, 41, 42, 619
Barron, James, 5, 251
Barrow, Shelly L., 482
Barry, Adama I., 482
Barry, Angela M., 425
Barry, Esq., Nancy J., 60
Barry, Joanne S., 93
Barry, Joanne, 466
Barry, Justin, 49
Barry, Maria, 384
Barry, Mary Anne, 12, 162, 236
Barry, Peter, 456
Barry, Timothy, 451
Barry, William, 373
Barsamian, Tony, 527
Bartell, Thomas, 423
Barth, Richard, 352
Bartikofsky, Gary, 83, 263
Bartkowski-Fox, Janice, 509
Bartlett, Adele, 484
Bartlett, Catherine M., 47
Bartlett, Henry, 231
Bartlett, III, George R, 58
Bartlett, Jay, 396
Bartlett, Joe, 535
Bartlett, Michael J, 508
Bartlett, Ricky, 110
Bartlett, Roscoe G, 318
Bartley, A. Kirke, 49
Bartoletti, Amy, 462
Bartoletti, Barbara, 434
Barton, Douglas, 517
Barton, Joe, 318
Barton, Lynn, 367
Barton, Pamela, 346
Bartone, Helen A, 332
Barton-Richardson, Valerie, 392
Bartow, John, 156
Bartstone, Lewis, 49
Barzilay, Zvi, 495
Bashant, Thomas, 511
Bashein, Benjamin, 400
Basile, Carm, 96, 285
Basinski, Sean, 471
Basli, Andrea, 134
Basloe, Marsha, 257, 408
Bass, Michael, 176
Bassanese, Lynn A., 275
Bass-Cors, Sandy, 398
Bassett, Valerie, 506
Bastedo, George, 339
Batch, Mary, 9
Batchelder, Myra, 447
Bates, Bruce, 345
Bates, Justyn, 120
Batista, Aneiry, 17
Batista, Hector, 95, 256, 272
Batista, Julio, 457
Batt, John F., 56
Battaglia, Jack, 46
Battalia, Christina, 350
Battista, John, 354
Battista, Vincent C, 556

Battiste, Philip, 110
Battle, Aiesha, 6, 83, 140, 303
Batulis, Scott, 513
Baucus, Max, 267, 290, 312, 314, 324
Bauer, Chris, 34
Bauer, Elizabeth, 352
Bauer, Randall, 458
Baughman, Kevin S, 589
Baum, Hilary, 77
Bauman, Caroline, 275
Baumer, Bennett, 426
Baumgartner, Alice, 40
Baumrin, Michael, 459
Baur, Gene, 74
Bautz, Doug, 264
Bavaro, Laura, 449
Baxter, Brendan, 388
Baxter, Todd, 346
Bayer, Wayne, 396
Bayh, Evan, 313
Baynard Jr., Raymond, 483
Baynes, A.J., 17
Baynes, Johnny Lee, 49
Baynes, Peter A, 238, 268
Baynes, Peter, 400
Bazan Pazik, Wendi, 398
Bazan, Julie, 409
Bazydlo, Charles T, 351
Beach, Pamela, 362
Beagle, George, 509
Beal, Jr, Bruce A, 248
Beal, Jr., Bruce A., 460
Beal, Robert E, 95
Beal, Robert E., 150
Beams, Mary Ellen, 350
Bean, Harold, 409
Bean, Toni A, 61
Beard, Martha, 430
Bearden, Roger, 10, 229
Beardsley, Fred, 334
Beasley, Brian, 345
Beato, Carlos, 455
Beattie, Eric, 455
Beattie, Sandra, 5, 83, 160, 234, 263
Beatty, Jeanne, 537
Beaudoin, Heather, 386, 401
Beaver, Sarah, 40
Bebon, Mike, 389
Becerra, Xavier, 255
Bechtel, Doug, 155
Beck, Matt, 252
Beck, Patricia, 525
Beck, Thomas C, 362
Becker, Bruce, 291
Becker, John M, 331
Becker, Margaret A, 254
Becker, Margaret N., 162
Beckman, John, 128
Beckstead, Bob, 527
Beckstrom, Brad, 446
Beckwith, Kent, 539
Becoat, W. Charles, 179
Beditz, Stephen, 471
Bednar, Mary E, 50
Bee, Peter A, 386
Beeman, William, 404
Been, Vicki, 100, 189
Beer, Nan, 491
Beers, Andrew, 11, 149, 271
Beganskas, Michael, 61
Begley, Alice, 347
Begley, Lydia, 582
Begun, Martin, 440
Beha, Alyson, 386
Behan, Mark, 386
Behar, Stephen M., 59
Behe, Jana, 469
Behler, Jeff T., 88
Behnke, Charlene, 384
Behr, Timothy, 582
Behr, Very Rev John, 561
Beier, David, 388
Beilein, Thomas A, 101, 113
Beilman, Patricia, 429
Beirne, John P, 357
Belfield, Judy, 586
Belfort, Robert, 439
Bell, Chuck, 402
Bell, Donna, 530
Bell, Fredric, 381
Bell, James, 15
Bell, Karyn, 439
Bell, Marie, 502
Bell, Mayra, 356
Bell, Richard A, 202
Bell, Richard, 328
Bellamy, Karen, 108
Bellantoni, Orazio, 47
Bellardini, Mark, 374
Bellini, Elma A., 47
Bellis, Darlene, 345
Bellitto, Joseph A, 349
Bellnier, Joseph, 6, 108
Bellone, Steve, 96, 150
Bellone, Steven, 337
Belloni, Francis L., 185
Belluck, Joseph W, 103, 211
Belluck, Joseph, 543
Belmont, John, 470
Belmont, Ron, 347
Beloten, Robert E, 14, 202, 221
Belt, Seth, 135
Beltramo, Wade, 400
Ben-Amotz, Pico, 9, 177, 220, 253
Bence, Patricia, 374
Bencik, Jeffrey W., 361
Bender, Bruce, 386
Bender, Dennis F, 58
Bender, Jeffrey, 6, 111, 206, 235
Bendetto, Michael R., 479
Benedetto, Michael R, 29, 619
Benedetto, Michael, 35, 36, 37, 39, 40, 42, 87, 237
Benedict, Timothy, 363
Benefield, Tyrone S., 254
Benfanti, William, 390
Benfer, Chuck, 536
Benigno, Samuel, 384
Benincasa, Charles A, 363
Benitez, Jaime, 202, 221
Benitez, Peter J., 50
Benjamin, Jack, 505, 517
Benjamin, Lori, 135
Benjamin, Neil, 390
Bennardo, Raymond, 17
Bennet, Michael F., 267
Bennet, Michael, 155
Bennet-Rodriguez, Linda, 410
Bennett Jr, Donald G, 278
Bennett, Bob, 316
Bennett, Debby, 448
Bennett, Douglas A., 430
Bennett, Heather, 386
Bennett, Joel H, 292
Bennett, John, 393
Bennett, Joy, 117
Bennett, Nancy, 471
Bennett, Pam, 476
Bennett, Robert F, 324
Bennett, Robert, 312, 324
Bennett, Stacy D., 47
Bennett, Theodore A, 326
Bennett, Wayne, 364
Bennett-Pagan, Sandra, 179
Bennison, Pat, 284
Bennison, Patrick, 284
Benoit, Jim, 264
Benoit, Mark, 418
Benson, Christina, 59
Benson, Deborah, 5, 252, 303
Benson, Donna L, 333
Benson, Eugene L., 337
Benson, Fred, 524
Benson, Richard J, 593
Bentsen Jr., Kenneth E, 82
Berardi, Jr, Eugene J, 277
Berchtold, Scott, 277
Berck, Gregory, 37, 39
Berczuk, Robert, 527
Berezny, Peter, 108
Berg, Ann Marie, 339
Berg, James, 226, 248
Berg, Joel, 259, 398
Berg, Sharri, 538
Berg, William C, 567
Berger, David, 366
Berger, Elizabeth, 379, 505
Berger, Henry, 465
Berger, Jennie, 490
Berger, Kim, 356
Berger, Mary K, 16
Berger, Theodore S, 280

Appendices: Financial Plan, Indexes & Maps

Berger, Thomas, 459
Berger, Tina, 95, 150, 306
Bergeron, Peg, 297
Bergin, Robert, 363
Bergman, Ellen, 598
Bergman, Jill, 505
Bergman, Mathew, 481
Bergmann, Sven, 379
Bergstraesser, Edward, 384
Bergtraum, Judith, 97, 123, 550
Berk, Bradford, 471
Berkheimer, Paul, 464
Berkley, Denise, 398
Berkley, Richard, 145
Berkman, Jeffrey D, 333
Berkman, Tom, 8, 147
Berkowitz, Cara, 466
Berkowitz, Meryl J, 55
Berkowitz, Nancy, 192
Berlin, Elizabeth, 7, 120, 174, 227, 252, 270
Berlin, Gordon, 127, 225
Berlin, Michael, 421
Berliner, David, 416
Berliner, Robert M., 47
Berlinski, Kenneth L, 34
Berman, Doug, 422
Berman, Greg, 215
Berman, Herb, 397
Berman, Howard L, 319
Bermingham, Patrick, 345
Bermudez, Miguel, 345
Bermudez, Zultan, 198
Bernabe, Pilar, 462
Bernacchio, Paul, 184, 299
Bernard, Adrienne, 416
Bernard, Len, 345
Bernardi, Natalie, 24
Bernardo, Terry L, 338
Bernbach, Justin, 98, 286
Berne, Robert, 427
Berner, Kristi L., 13, 195, 253, 305
Bernhardt, Annette, 448
Bernice Johnson, Eddie, 143
Bernier, Joseph A, 513
Bernier, Kathleen, 427
Bernier, Lucy P, 64
Berninghausen, Mark, 74
Berns, Linda, 454
Bernstein, Arielle, 463
Bernstein, Kevin M., 197
Bernstein, Martin, 515
Bernstein, Marvin, 209, 230
Bernstein, Sanford M., 528
Bernstein, Steve, 430
Bernstein, William, 439
Bernstein, Zachary, 416
Berry, Daniel, 241
Berry, Deborah, 57
Berry, Jeffrey G, 56
Berry, Jennifer, 279, 435
Berry, Jill, 355
Berry, John, 451
Berry, Joseph, 477
Berry, Kevin J., 196, 222
Berry, Kimberly B., 496
Berry, Philip Alfonso, 550
Berry, Philip, 550
Bershadker, Matthew, 73, 116
Bertino Beaser, Lisa, 212
Bertoni, Fabio, 217
Berwanger, A, 339
Bessen, Mark, 596
Bessette, Ken, 204
Best, Jennifer, 38, 39, 40, 41
Best, Miriam, 50
Best-Laimit, Ellen, 591
Besunder, Harvey, 216
Betancourt, Bonny, 403
Bethencourt, Ramon, 350
Betke, Alexander L, 476
Betro, James W, 65
Betrus, Ferris J, 504
Betts, Julie D, 340
Betty Laurenson, Eric Spino, 509
Betz, Peter, 329
Beville, Judith A, 347
Bewlay, Shoshanah, 5, 140, 160
Beyer, William D, 60
Bhagwati, Anu, 417
Bhandarkar, Kalpana, 439
Bharara, Preet, 115, 213
Bhatt, Milan, 477
Bhurucha, Jamshed, 554
Bianchi, Eileen, 61
Bianchi, Richard D, 107, 274
Bianco, Cynthia A, 583
Biasotti, Michael C, 351
Biberman, Nancy, 193
Bichotte, Rodneyse, 29, 35, 37, 39, 41, 42, 619
Bick, Jonathan, 175
Bickford, Peggy, 134
Bicking, Andrew, 463
Bidell, Mary, 283
Biderman, Aaron, 484
Biehl, Marisa, 449
Bielak, Gerard, 457
Bielecki, Emil, 366
Bielecki, Robert J, 367
Bielefeldt, Ralph, 175
Bienstock, Martin, 476
Bierbaum, Deborah, 384
Bierman, Laura Ladd, 138, 170
Bierman, Laura, 434
Bierwirth, John E, 580
Bigelow, Madeline Garcia, 471
Bigelsen, Jayne, 214
Bigg, Matthew, 533
Biggerstaff, Robert, 127
Biggert, Judy, 319
Bigham, Timothy, 413
Bigness, Katie, 76
Biklen, Doug, 455
Biklen, Molly, 471
Bilal, Aziza N., 480
Bilbray, Brian, 321
Bilich, John, 357
Bilirakis, Gus, 320
Billings, Angela, 295
Billings, John, 185
Billings, Lucy, 46
Billiter, Teri, 534
Billiter, Tonya, 534
Billmeyer, Steven M., 531
Bills, David C, 585
Billups, Erin, 538
Bilow, Dennis, 511
Bing, Jonathan L., 186, 492
Bingaman, Jeff, 314
Bingham, Martin, 473
Binko, Richard, 469
Binkowski, Andy, 508, 512
Bird, Michael, 526
Birkhead, Susan, 560
Birkholz, Carol, 371, 372
Birmingham, Micaela, 446
Birnbaum, Arthur, 49
Birnbaum, Debra, 528
Birnbaum, Ronni D, 49
Birtwistle, John, 251
Bischoff, Theresa, 437
Bischoping, Scott, 578
Biscoff, Martin, 506
Bishop, Lloyd, 420
Bishop, Rob, 143, 154, 276, 321
Bishop, Robert, 455
Bishop, Tim, 318
Bishop, Timothy H, 224, 290, 311, 318, 322, 323
Bisignano, Rick, 473
Bisso, Joyce, 580
Bissonette, Matthew, 396
Bitterbaum, Erik J, 545
Bivona, Andrew P, 56
Bizarro MD, Thomas, 175, 293
Bjorkander, John, 371
Bjorneby, Eric, 61
Black, Cathie, 582
Black, Christopher, 379
Black, Gina, 472
Black, John, 425
Black, Les, 592
Black, William, 327
Blackerby, Joel, 115
Blades-Rosado, Lois, 549
Blair, Craig, 344
Blair, Gerald, 574
Blair, Jason, 457
Blake, Cheryl, 57
Blake, Michael, 29, 35, 37, 38, 39, 42, 619
Blanch, Raymond, 599
Blanchard, John, 417
Blanchard, Thomas, 395

Blanchard, Timothy, 125
Blanchfield, Mark W., 65
Blankenberger, L J, 79
Blankenbush, Ken, 37, 40, 42, 619
Blankenbush, Kenneth, 29, 35, 70
Blankfein, Lloyd C, 80
Blanton, Jay, 473
Blatt, Karen, 26, 43, 137
Blau, Jeff T., 460
Blausten, Frederica, 231
Blazer, Ted, 104, 273
Blazosky, Kelly, 275
Bleakney, Todd, 474
Bledi, Rachel L, 130
Bledi, Rachel, 375
Bleiwas, Ken, 12, 236
Blennon, Timothy, 10, 283
Bliewas, Ken, 162
Bligh, Matthew, 202, 221
Bligh, Tom, 296
Bliss, Elizabeth, 398
Bloch Rodwin, Lisa, 53
Block, Andrew, 342
Block, Valerie, 532
Blodgett, Edgar T, 329
Blog, M.D., Debra, 174
Bloise, Denise, 437
Bloom, William, 385, 443
Bloomberg, Michael R, 352
Blowers, Carol, 413
Blue, James A, 296
Blum, Marie, 567
Blum, Michael, 298
Blume, Jr., Paul, 457
Blume, Lawerence, 80, 91
Blumenfeld, Joel L., 50
Blumenthal, David, 182
Bluth, Arlene P, 49
Bluth, Arlene, 46
Bluth, Randall G, 98, 163, 307
Blythe, Michael, 351
Blythe, Richard R, 325
Boak Jr, Jack J, 600
Boatswain, Pearl L, 358
Boccard, Thomas J, 348
Boccarossa, Debra, 513
Boccio, Frank J, 53
Bocciolatt, Stephen A, 584
Bochenski, Melissa, 3
Bochiechio, Beth, 35
Bocko, Mark, 84, 122
Bodarky, George, 534
Boddie, Reginald A., 49, 493
Boden, Jolene, 429
Bodine, Karen, 134
Bodner, Sherman M, 523, 525, 526
Bodziak, James, 573
Boecher, Lynne, 374
Boening, Pamela Walsh, 345
Boerner, Emily, 458
Boettcher, Jo-Ann, 510
Bogacz, Gerard J, 101, 287
Bogacz, Stephen J, 50
Bogan, Vanessa E, 66
Bogardus, Brent, 132, 375
Bogdan III, Edward A, 387
Bogdanowicz, Jan, 105, 152
Boger, Ann, 483
Boggess, Sarah, 460
Bogner, Drew, 558
Bogucz, Edward, 455
Bohley, Michele B., 184
Bohrer, Dave, 526
Bokuniewicz, Henry, 467
Boland, David, 234, 240
Boland, Eileen, 32
Boland, Kathleen, 207
Boland, Mike, 477
Boldesser, Amy, 447
Boling-Barton, Crystal, 414
Boll, Maureen, 108
Boller, M William, 47
Bolling, Suzanne, 120
Bollinger, Lee C, 554
Bollinger, Lee, 470
Bolter, Paul, 181
Bolton, Christina M., 388
Boltz, John J, 388
Bombard, James, 294
Bombardier, Christopher, 438
Bombardiere, Ralph, 291
Bonacci, Lisa, 83, 263
Bonacic, J. Scott, 440
Bonacic, John J, 17, 20, 23, 25, 211, 266, 275, 606
Bonacic, John J., 20, 24
Bonacic, John, 25
Bonacic, Melissa, 333
Bonacquist, Mark, 6, 111
Bonagura, David G., 482
Bonamici, Suzanne, 155
Bonan, Michele, 380
Bonancic, John J, 15, 24
Bonanza, Robert, 489
Bonasera, Dr Anthony J, 593
Bond, Christopher S, 314, 316
Bond, Christopher, 313
Bond, Jay, 381
Bond, Joseph, 591
Bone, Tequila, 412
Bonesteel, Sara, 458
Boniello, III, Ralph A, 47
Bonilla, Mark A, 347
Bonita, Jennifer, 474
Bonn, Fred, 274
Bonn, Ruth, 434
Bonneau, Peggy, 173
Bonner, Jo, 322
Bonnewell, Michael, 586
Bonney, Joseph, 527
Bono, Vincent, 330
Booker, Cory, 155
Booknard, Lynda, 587
Bookstaver, David, 210, 305
Boone, Jasaun, 409
Boone, Jerry, 13, 86, 265
Boone, William, 397
Boonshoft, Kay, 429
Boor, Kathryn, 544
Booth, Antonia, 365
Booth, Carol, 98, 141, 151, 307
Booth, Ellie, 403
Booth, Wayne C, 360
Boozang, Patricia, 439
Boozman, John, 323
Borakove, Ellen, 357
Borasi, Raffaella, 471
Borchert, Dawn L, 281
Bordallo, Madelaine Z, 321
Borden, Michael, 185, 456
Bordick, Lee, 571
Borelli, Anthony, 409
Borenstein, Susan, 201, 220
Borgeest, Dawn, 394
Borges, Michael J, 435
Borges, Michael J., 127
Borgognoni, Charles, 395
Borin, Glenn, 468
Boris, Andrew, 536
Borland, Lori, 503
Borrelli, Kelley M, 136
Borrello, Vito J, 257
Borsody, Robert P., 186
Bortman, Marci, 449
Bortoloni, Augusto, 201, 219
Borys, Michael, 419
Bosch, Joseph, 428
Boshart, Don, 380
Boshnack, Mark, 529
Bosse, Diane F, 101, 211
Bostic, Yolanda, 42
Boswell, Leonard L, 317
Bosworth, David A, 256
Bosworth, Lynelle, 421
Both, Bruce W., 489
Botros, Foseph E., 490
Botstein, Clara, 471
Botstein, Leon, 553
Bott, Marian, 434
Botta, Chris, 280
Bouchard, Jeff, 157
Boucher, Matthew, 596
Boucher, Rick, 318
Bourgeois, Karen, 401
Bourne, Frances, 448
Bourne, Will, 528
Bourque, Debra, 111, 235
Bourscheidt, Randall, 277
Bouska, Aaron, 389
Boustany, Jr, Charles W, 323
Bouteiller, William, 140
Boutelle, Brandon E, 329
Bovard, Adele, 579

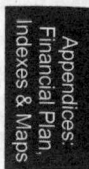

Bovino, Rosmarie, 580
Bowen, Hillary W, 569
Bowen, Jeffrey, 569
Bowen, Mike, 384
Bowen, Molly, 463
Bower, George, 333
Bower, Kyle C, 591
Bower, Laurie A, 57
Bowerman, Shawn J, 332
Bowers, Diana, 578
Bowers, Richard, 378
Bowers, Robert, 451
Bowles, Bernie, 254
Bowles, Jonathan, 191, 225
Bowman, Adam, 457
Bowser, Andre, 154
Boxer, Barbara, 137, 155, 169, 290, 314, 315, 316
Boxer, Leonard S., 494
Boxer, Leonard, 468
Boxley, Michael, 390
Boyce Martinez, Debra, 444
Boyce, Marion M., 336
Boyce, Phil, 535
Boyd, David, 381
Boyd, Mark, 33
Boyd, Regina, 22
Boyer, Jeremy, 523
Boyer, Susan, 501
Boyes, Richard, 594
Boykin, Carl J, 112
Boykin, Marion, 469
Boylan, Denis, 418
Boylan, Jeremy, 327, 328
Boyle, Philip M, 607
Boyle, Philip M., 17
Boyle, Philip, 21, 23, 24, 25, 87, 237, 246, 288
Boyle, Valerie, 54
Boylet, Denis J., 50
Bozsik, Richard, 472
Bozzolo, Ellis W., 53
Braack, Craig R, 325
Brabenec, Karl A, 620
Brabenec, Karl, 29, 35, 36, 38, 40, 195, 202, 222, 242
Brabham, Lola, 5, 194, 234, 240
Bracken, John P, 214
Bradbury, Donna, 228
Braddick, Theresa, 357
Bradford, Col. Dennis, 110
Bradley, James, 367
Bradley, Vincent, 4, 83, 104, 263
Bradstreet, Peter C, 59
Bradt, Mark, 108
Bradwell, Paula, 174, 251
Brady, Dennis, 502
Brady, Kevin, 180, 323, 324
Brady, Patrick, 590
Brady, Robert A, 320
Brady, Scott, 173, 250
Brady, Steven, 468
Brady, Thomas C., 326
Braff, Nelson, 496
Bragan, Frederick J, 578
Bragg, Jr, Alvin L, 10, 112, 149, 177, 188, 195, 207, 221, 245, 263
Bramson, Noam, 351
Branca, Nicole, 468
Brancaccio, Barbara, 355
Brancatella, Sarah, 383
Branch, Tyesha, 392
Branchini, Frank, 410
Brand, Mark T, 576
Brand, Martin, 148
Brandau, Susan, 251
Brandfield, Julie, 434
Brandi, Scott, 281
Brandon, Ann, 434
Brands, James V, 47
Brandt, Bill, 537
Brandt, Marc N, 232
Brandveen, Antonio I, 48
Brandveen, Antonio, 47
Brandwein, Ruth, 467
Brandwene, Merle, 251
Brannan, Mary, 486
Brannock, Shari L, 574
Bransten, Eileen, 46
Brantner, Michelle, 569
Braslow, Stephen L, 59
Brathwaite Nelson, Valerie, 45, 48
Braudy, Erica, 454
Braunstein, Edward C, 620
Braunstein, Edward C., 29
Braunstein, Edward, 35, 36, 39, 40, 43
Brauth, Sorelle, 12, 141
Braveman, Daan, 558
Braveman, Deanne, 444
Braverman, Robert, 299
Braxton, Emanuel, 495
Brazill, Caitlyn, 392
Breakell, Douglas J, 15
Breakell, Douglas, 16, 17
Breault, Dale L, 575
Breault, Robert, 153
Brecher, Charles, 237, 268
Brechko, Robert, 136
Brede, Tom, 106, 288, 309
Bredhoff, Nancy, 158, 186
Breen, Cathleen, 458
Breen, Paula M, 176
Breen, Peg, 192, 248
Bregg, Martin, 590
Brehm, Robert A, 7, 130
Breig, Thomas, 264
Brender, Gregory, 471
Brenholts, Amy, 531
Brennan, James F, 29, 36, 37, 41, 87, 165, 288, 620
Brennan, James F., 36
Brennan, John E, 342
Brennan, John J., 54
Brennan, Leslie, 147
Brennan, Patricia, 357
Brennan, Thomas A, 349
Brennan, Thomas, 103, 124
Brennan, Timothy, 448
Brennecke, Marcus, 412
Brennen, Deanna Alterio, 512
Brenner, Daniel, 581
Brenon, Joan M, 366
Bresch, Debora, 432
Brescia, Ray, 169
Breslin, Dennis, 110
Breslin, Ellen, 306
Breslin, Kate, 128, 199, 233, 464
Breslin, Neil D, 17, 20, 22, 23, 24, 25, 202, 607
Breslin, Neil D., 16
Breslin, Thomas A., 46
Bresnan, Chris, 35
Bressman, Susan B, 186
Bretschneider, Stuart, 239, 244
Brett Howard, Lorna, 490
Brew, James, 389
Brewer, Aida M, 13
Brewer, Aida, 86, 265
Brewer, Beth A, 525
Brewer, Beth, 526
Brewer, Jean N, 356
Brezinski, John L, 330
Briand, Elizabeth H, 256
Briccetti, Heather C., 91, 94, 155
Briccetti, Heather, 391
Brick, Errol, 458
Brickman, Ellen, 451
Bridenstine, Jim, 155
Bridson, Marjorie M, 136
Brier, Stephen, 397
Briffault, Richard, 138, 238
Briganti-Hughes, Mary, 48
Briggs, Daniel, 337
Briggs, Elizabeth A, 570
Briggs, Vernon, 225
Bright, Joan H, 352
Bright, Maureen K, 580
Brignall, Alan, 525
Brimhall, Carianne, 58
Brindisi, Anthony J , 620
Brindisi, Anthony J, 29
Brindisi, Anthony, 35, 37, 39, 42
Bringsjord, Elizabeth L., 543
Brinkley, Alan, 470
Brinn, Ronald, 195
Brisky, Michael M, 130
Brisky, Michael, 30
Bristol, Beth, 162, 236
Brittain, MD, David C., 176
Briwa, Mary, 472
Brizard, Jean Claude, 579, 582
Brizzolara, Thomas, 401
Broadwell, Stephen, 574

Broberg, Christian, 412
Brobston, Dennis, 515
Brochstein, Phyllis, 434
Brock, Kyle, 415
Brockel, Dr Richard J, 585
Brockett, Steven, 64
Brockman, Edward J, 340
Brockway, Erin, 132
Brodick, James, 417
Brodie, Peter, 459
Brodoe, Katharine, 454
Brodsky, Richard L., 492
Brodt, John, 386
Brody, Willa, 457
Bronfenbrenner, Kate, 243
Brongo, Richard J, 343
Bronson, Harry B, 620
Bronson, Harry, 29, 35, 37, 40, 42, 43, 124, 222
Bronstein, Richard W, 248
Bronston, David, 455
Bronzi, Phil, 511
Brook-Krasny, Alec, 38
Brookmire, Sherrie, 535
Brooks, Chris, 527
Brooks, David, 531
Brooks, Jevonni, 31
Brooks, Julie, 60
Brooks, Katharine, 84, 112, 177, 201, 208, 245
Brooks, Kermit, 389
Brooks, Maggie, 331
Brooks, Nancy, 349
Brooks, Tracey M., 413
Brooks, Wayne, 371
Brosen, Donald, 356
Brosnahan Sullivan, Mary, 399
Broughton, Barbara, 130
Broussea, Esq., Cara J, 104, 164, 211
Brower, Ellen, 54
Brower, Michael, 446
Brower, Peter, 363
Brown Phillips, Wilma, 13, 253
Brown, Abbie, 412
Brown, Arthur, 448
Brown, Brenda, 6, 270
Brown, Byron W, 342
Brown, Carol, 127, 548
Brown, Chad, 535
Brown, Charles N, 366
Brown, Charley, 374
Brown, Conchetta M, 58
Brown, Constance, 564
Brown, Corrine, 323
Brown, Craig Stephen, 52
Brown, Dan, 401
Brown, David J, 349
Brown, Deborah A., 223
Brown, Deborah, 420
Brown, Dennis M, 337
Brown, Dr Christopher R, 584
Brown, Frank, 280
Brown, Gary S, 208
Brown, George, 351
Brown, Gordon, 376
Brown, Herb R, 581
Brown, Jason, 9, 84, 112, 161, 177, 188, 201, 208, 245, 264
Brown, Jay, 81
Brown, Jeffrey S., 47
Brown, Jeremy, 555
Brown, John, 569
Brown, Joseph, 284
Brown, Joyce F, 547
Brown, Jr, Henry E, 321, 323
Brown, Karl, 570
Brown, Kristin, 410
Brown, Kuba, 489
Brown, LaRay, 354
Brown, Leighann, 161
Brown, Luvelle, 595
Brown, Lynne, 427
Brown, Margaret, 448
Brown, Maria C, 360
Brown, Matt, 212
Brown, Matthew, 65
Brown, Meg, 21
Brown, Melva L, 550
Brown, Michael, 452
Brown, Mickey J, 88, 152
Brown, Milton, 113
Brown, Myra, 32
Brown, Patrick, 390
Brown, Paul C, 322
Brown, Richard A, 335
Brown, Richard, 46
Brown, Sherrod, 80, 190, 203, 313
Brown, T. Andrew, 119
Brown, Terry, 451
Brown, Thomas Henry, 131
Brown, Thomas Paul, 51
Brown, Tricia, 446
Brownback, Elizabeth, 463
Brownback, Sam, 312, 314, 324
Browne, Arthur, 528
Browne, David, 345
Browne, Paul J, 357
Brownell, Karyn, 384
Brownell, Michael, 396
Brownell, Stan, 335
Brown-Jackson, Debora, 228
Brown-Johnson, Debora, 121
Brown-Johnson, Deborah, 228
Brownstein, Mark, 412
Bruce, Anthony M., 115, 213
Bruce, Dennis, 58
Bruce, Raymond L., 49
Bruce, Thomas R, 215
Bruening, Glen T., 48
Brundo, John, 531
Brune, Matt, 355
Brunelle, Courtney, 470
Brunetti, John J, 48
Bruno, Robert A., 47
Bryan, Bernard, 445
Bryan, Kathleen A, 215
Bryant, Dirk, 449
Bryant, Dr Jeffrey K, 583
Bryant, Dr Raymond W, 586
Bryant, Staff Sgt. Vito, 125
Brylinski, Jennifer C S, 517
Brynien, Kenneth D, 243
Brynien, Kenneth, 404
Brzezicki, Bill, 523
Buanno, Marie, 132
Bucaria, Stephen A, 47
Bucci, Anthony, 72, 166, 167
Bucci, Joseph, 14, 163, 253
Buccowich, Mark P., 153
Buchanan, Doug, 527
Buchanan, Thomas, 46
Buchanan, Vern, 322
Buchiere, Steve, 524
Buchko, Gerard J., 430
Buchter, Richard Lance, 48
Buchwald, David, 29, 36, 37, 38, 39, 40
Buck III, Lyman A., 432
Buck"", Howard P., 297
Buckheit, Frederick, 494
Bucki, Carl L., 212
Buckley, Diane, 519
Buckley, Kelly, 51
Buckley, Lurlene, 444
Buckley, Suzanne, 544
Buckley, Teresa, 523
Buckley, Timothy J, 63
Bucklin, Patricia K., 432
Buckman, Michael R, 113
Buckwald, David, 620
Budd, Marlene, 59
Budelmann, Jon E, 326
Buder, Andrew, 38
Budro, E Lawrence, 514
Budzik, Valerie, 353
Buerkle, Ann Marie, 311
Buery, Richard, 396
Buffardi, Harry C, 364
Bugbee, Larry A, 134
Buggs, Cheree A., 49
Buggs, Ronald, 573
Bugliosi, Edward F., 153
Buhks, Ephraim, 553
Buhner, Jonathan, 567
Buholtz, Eileen E, 203, 215
Buhrmaster, James, 336
Buhrmaster, Jim, 376
Buice, Shawn, 557
Buley, Jeffrey, 390
Bull, Pierce, 448
Bullard, John K., 152
Bullerdick, Ryan, 458
Bulley, Karen L., 347
Bullock, Dr Quintin B, 548

Bullock, Robert E., 543
Bulman, Robert, 393
Buman, Mike, 488
Bumgarner, Jennifer S, 334
Bundy, Robert, 568
Buniak, Kenneth R, 111
Bunning, Jim, 313, 314
Bunyi, Milo, 362
Buonfiglio, Michelle L., 430
Burbank, Kathy, 508
Burch, David, 425
Burckard, Nicole, 451
Burden, Amanda M, 352
Burdi, Michael, 113
Burdick, Jonathan, 471
Burdick, Robert, 394
Burgdorf, Robert, 450
Burgess, Christian W., 462
Burgess, James, 463
Burgess, Kathleen H, 11, 140
Burgess, Marry, 384
Burgess, Michael, 380
Burgos, Jemine, 391
Burgos, Tonio, 391, 451
Burin, John J, 345
Burke, Alison, 420
Burke, Christopher, 481
Burke, COL Mark F, 298
Burke, Edward, 359
Burke, James M., 50
Burke, Joseph, 556
Burke, Kerryanne, 38
Burke, Kevin A., 58
Burke, Kevin, 401
Burke, Michael S., 155
Burke, Nicholas S., 480
Burke, Robert E, 233
Burke, Steven J., 372
Burke, Terence, 450
Burke, Thomas, 6, 194, 227, 252
Burke, Valerie K, 599
Burleski, Timothy, 220
Burleson, Kevin, 130
Burman, Diane X, 11
Burman, Diane, 15
Burner, Nancy, 98, 210
Burnett, Adele, 509
Burney, David J, 353
Burns, Brian D, 57
Burns, Brian O, 52
Burns, Christopher J, 47
Burns, Ed, 264
Burns, Edmund, 10
Burns, Elizabeth A, 62
Burns, John P, 330
Burns, Karyn, 92, 440
Burns, Lee, 176
Burns, Thomas R, 601
Burns, Timothy P, 102, 151
Burnside, Douglas, 585
Burns-Moran, Megan, 510
Burolla, Donna, 513
Burr, Richard, 169, 297, 313, 314, 315, 316
Burrell, Wayne, 430
Burris, Mary Ellen, 94
Burriss, Lindsay, 132
Burstein, Dan, 78
Burstein, Lawrence, 533
Burtes, Maria, 276
Burton Jr, Joseph, 361
Burton, Dan, 320
Burton, Douglas C, 579
Burton, Nancy, 241
Buscaglia, Russell P, 48
Buscaglia, Russell, 47
Busch, Kathryn J., 384
Busche, Mark E, 361
Bush Jr., Harold, 374
Bush, Cornelia W., 333
Bush, Kevin, 284
Bush, Mike, 516
Bush, Pamela, 97, 150
Bush, Steven C, 80
Bushey, Trinity, 530
Butcher, Barbara, 357
Butcher, Kamau, 462
Butler, Denis J., 48
Butler, John, 366, 472
Butler, Marc W, 29, 39, 40, 621
Butler, Marc, 28, 35, 37, 38, 41
Butler, Martha T., 485
Butler, Nancy, 479
Butler-Sahai, Tara, 31
Butsko, Kathy, 536
Button, Linda H, 102, 124, 164, 178
Button, Stephen D., 337
Butts, III, Calvin O, 545
Buyck, Allen D, 599
Buyer, Deborah, 358
Buyer, Steve, 323
Bykowski, Michael, 105, 287
Byrd, Arthur, 410
Byrd, Robert C, 312
Byrne, Deirdre, 396
Byrne, Eileen, 66
Byrne, Jeffrey, 104, 273
Byrne, Kevin, 391
Byrne, Sean M, 234
Byrne, Sean M., 4, 173, 227, 250
Byrne, Sean, 173
Byrnes, David, 364
Bystryn, Marcia, 138, 157, 434
Caban, Pedro, 467
Cabusora, Haidee, 417
Cacace, Kevin T, 520
Cacace, Susan, 60
Caccese, Albert, 384
Cacciola, Anthony, 594
Caceres, Hillary, 379
Cadigan, Michael, 454
Cadrette, Mark, 148
Cadrette, Patricia, 192
Cady, Cindy L, 135
Cafarell, Frances E, 45
Cafasso, George, 50
Caforio, Giovanni, 181
Caggana, Michele, 176
Caggiano-Siino, Kathleen, 227
Cahill, Christopher E, 46
Cahill, Diane, 420
Cahill, James, 93, 225, 391
Cahill, John, 190
Cahill, Kevin A, 29, 37, 39, 42, 621
Cahill, Kevin, 39, 161, 202, 245
Cahill, Sean, 418
Caicedo, Emmanuel, 477
Cain, Daniel, 405
Caine, Claudia, 437
Caine, Eric, 471
Cairns, Stephen, 457
Cairo, Jr., Joseph G, 273
Cairo, Jr., Joseph G., 100
Calabrese, Alexander, 50
Calabrese, Carl, 441
Calabrese, Joseph, 55
Calamari, Andrew, 89
Calarco, Deborah, 131
Calarco, Jacqueline, 360
Calarco, Rob, 337
Caldara, Lu, 298
Calderin, Roberto, 464
Calderone, Joseph, 99, 286
Calderone, Philip F, 341
Caldwell, Alfred B, 297
Caldwell, Barry, 496
Caldwell, Freddie, 256
Caldwell, Mike, 153
Caldwell, Randall B, 56
Caldwell, Sam, 472
Cales, Roy, 448
Calicchia, Christy, 10, 103, 264, 272, 304
Calieri, Frank, 519
Calkins, Christopher, 451
Calkins, Richard, 567
Call, Diane, 397, 552
Call, Dona, 111
Call, Peter, 75
Callahan II, James J, 332
Callahan, Brian, 101, 113
Callahan, Carrie, 474
Callahan, Charles E, 565
Callahan, Charles, 430
Callahan, James T., 487
Callahan, Jean, 472
Callan, Andrea, 454
Callanan, Raymond F, 515
Callard, David, 333
Callen, William, 386
Callery, Kate, 410
Calman, Neil S., 183
Calogero, Caitlin, 29
Calpin, James, 443
Calvelli, John F., 159, 484

Calvin, III, Dr. Mathis A., 252
Calvin, Jim, 93
Calvo, Joseph, 204
Calvo-Torres, Betty, 62
Camarda, Alex, 404
Cambridge, Michael, 148, 175
Camerino, Joseph P, 601
Cameron, Laura A, 259
Cameron, Michelle, 25
Camp, Dave, 267, 323
Campagiorni, Anthony, 395
Campanella, Ottavio, 62
Campanie, S John, 331
Campbell, Aurelie, 268
Campbell, Christopher, 451
Campbell, Francine, 464
Campbell, Gregory, 131
Campbell, James, 467
Campbell, Jon, 532
Campbell, Julie A, 52
Campbell, Karen A., 190
Campbell, Kathleen, 476
Campbell, Ken, 534
Campbell, Kim, 401
Campbell, Kuzaliwa, 492
Campbell, Randall, 445
Campbell, Scott, 427
Campbell, Valerie, 433
Campbell, William J, 131
Campion, James R, 547
Camuglia, Michelle, 241
Cancel, Alice, 29, 36, 39, 42, 621
Cancellieri, Anthony, 453
Candreva, Elizabeth, 210
Canellos, Peter C, 269
Canepa, Judith K., 399
Cangemi, Agostino, 448
Cangilos-Ruiz, Margaret, 212
Canini, Vincent, 596
Canino-Vigo, Blanca, 484
Canizio, BettyAnn, 133
Cannava, Peter, 474
Cannerelli, Gary, 451
Cannizzo, Jeffrey, 76
Cannon, David, 99, 285, 307
Canovas, Joseph, 200, 219, 449
Canter, Louis, 163
Cantone, Scott, 386
Cantor, Dan, 477
Cantor, David, 354
Cantor, Nancy, 455, 561
Cantore, Anthony, 244
Cantwell, Maria, 143, 155, 314
Canty, Tim, 96, 188, 306
Canzanelli, Linda, 276
Capalino, James F, 392
Capawan, Marilyn, 567
Cape, John, 458
Capeci, Susan M, 60
Capel, James E., 493
Capel, Rodney, 3
Capella, Joseph, 49
Capers, Robert L., 115, 213
Capetanakis, Charles, 405
Capetola, Julianne, 47
Capezzuti, Debbie, 34
Capito, Shelley Moore, 319
Capobianco, Peter, 511
Capone, Donald P, 232
Capone, Michelle, 86, 97, 188
Caporale, Patricia, 368
Cappocia, Donald, 95, 272
Capra, Michael, 110
Capron, Lori, 432
Capus, Steve, 532
Caputo, Elizabeth, 428
Caputo, Joyce M, 576
Caputo, Natasha, 275
Caputo, Susan, 444
Caraley, Demetrios James, 169
Carasiti, Frank J, 592
Carballada, R Carlos, 514
Carbone, Angelo, 78, 200
Carbone, Anthony A., 64
Carbone, Larry, 401
Carbone, Perry, 115, 213
Carbone, Terry Ann, 582
Card, Tiffany, 31
Carden, Tim, 458
Cardieri, Joseph, 356
Cardillo, Al, 426
Cardillo, Charles S, 581
Cardillo, Dominic, 187
Cardillo, John, 104, 124, 242, 309
Cardin, Ben, 90
Cardin, Benjamin L, 314, 316
Cardinale, Concetta (Tina), 65
Cardinale, Donielle, 511
Cardinale, Frank, 374
Cardinale, Keri, 534
Cardona, Blanca, 187
Cardona, David, 52
Cardona, Reinaldo, 447
Cardone, Carolann N., 134
Cardone, Joseph V, 333
Cardoza, Dennis A, 317
Cardozo, Michael A, 356
Carethers, Paula R, 100, 189
Carey, Christopher J., 335
Carey, Corinne, 454
Carey, Dorothy, 9, 200, 219
Carey, Gregory, 419
Carey, Jeffrey, 443
Carey, Mary, 15
Carey, Michael, 394, 417
Carey, Mike, 527, 535
Carey, Peter, 466
Carey, Sheila M, 6, 194, 227, 252
Carey, Thom, 187
Carey, Tobe, 282
Cargill-Cramer, Holly, 75
Caridi, Joseph J, 247
Carillo, Catherine, 201, 219
Carino, Lillie, 377
Carl, Traci, 531
Carlberg, Roy, 409
Carlevatti, John D, 579
Carlin, Gail, 512
Carlin, Jr, William J, 334
Carlos Smith, Rhonda, 395
Carlson, Eric, 411
Carlson, George, 463
Carlucci, David , 607
Carlucci, David, 16, 17, 20, 22, 24, 25, 26, 178, 254
Carlucci, Paul, 528
Carmody-LaFrancesca, Marie, 491
Carnegie-Hall, Sharon, 485, 493
Carnevale, Carmella, 394
Carney Jr, Alfonso L, 102, 124, 164, 178
Carney, Brian T., 490
Carney, Christopher P, 320
Carney, Greg, 427
Carney, Mary G, 53
Carney, Michael, 134
Carney, Nancy, 593
Carney, Patrick M, 62
Carney, Robert M, 336
Carney, Siobhan, 472
Carney, Sister Margaret, 561
Carney, Tom, 384
Carni, Edward D., 45
Carnright, D Holley, 338
Caro, Lenny, 502
Caros, Leonard C, 371
Carovillano, Brian, 531
Carpenter III, Philip M., 428
Carpenter, Bill, 106, 288
Carpenter, Catherine, 300
Carpenter, Cheryl W, 289
Carpenter, Natalie, 459
Carper, Thomas R, 314, 315
Carper, Thomas R., 137, 169, 242, 267
Carpinelli, Michael, 331
Carpinello, Amy, 309
Carr, Aaron, 29
Carr, Craig, 592
Carr, David D, 575
Carr, Eleanor, 256
Carr, James, 425
Carr, Joyce, 464
Carr, M. Audrey, 434
Carr, Mary Alice, 447
Carr, Michael, 449
Carr, Peter, 385
Carrano, Helen, 467
Carraway, Natalie A, 77
Carreker-Voigt, Suzanne, 77
Carriero, James, 432
Carro, Gregory, 48, 50
Carroll, Darlene, 341
Carroll, David, 450
Carroll, Kathleen, 531

Carroll, Leo, 346
Carroll, Patrick J, 351
Carroll, Patrick, 492
Carroll, Thomas J, 48
Carroll, Thomas, 416
Carron, Dr. Andrew, 145
Carruthers, Richard D., 50
Carson, Andre, 190
Carson, Ann, 406
Carson, Deidre, 421
Carswell, Lois, 278
Cartagena, Juan, 198
Carter, Brenda, 43, 124, 222
Carter, Janet, 417
Carter, Jerald S, 55
Carter, John, 465
Carter, Kevin M, 53
Carter, Leah A., 483
Carter, Melvina, 520
Carter, Michael, 255
Carter, William A, 61
Cartier, Karen, 404
Cartwright PhD, Alexander N., 84, 122
Cartwright, Echo, 448
Caruana, Anthony F, 365
Caruana, Lawrence J., 481
Caruso, Frank, 47
Caruso, Mark J, 65, 336
Caruso, Vito C, 46
Caruso, Vito, 209
Carvelli, Anthony R, 333
Carver, James, 383
Carvill, Al, 348
Carvin, Joseph, 364
Carzo, Joe, 86, 265
Casals, Gonzalo, 416
Casamento, Laura, 511
Casanova, Manuel, 484
Casciano, Paul, 594
Casciato, Tom, 538
Case, Kenneth, 53
Case, Kevin, 157, 433
Case, Laurie L, 52
Case, Leann, 347
Casella, Gary L, 208
Casey, David, 489
Casey, Glen, 394, 472
Casey, Jr, Robert P, 315
Casey, Kevin S., 128
Casey, Kevin, 464
Casey, Mary Beth, 136
Casey, Michael, 496
Casey, Tracey S., 72, 167
Cashin, Kathleen M, 119, 582
Cashwell, John, 422
Caslen, Jr., Lt. Gen. Robert L., 125
Cass, Stephen W, 51
Cass, Terrel, 538
Cassano, Salvatore J, 354
Cassella, Daniel, 384
Cassella, Rochelle A, 261
Cassidy, Daniel, 295
Cassidy, Joseph R., 59
Cassidy, Linda, 11, 113, 253
Cassidy, Stephen, 470
Castelino, Cecilia, 462
Castellani, Raymond, 595
Castelli, Brian, 457
Castelli, Joe, 450
Castellucci Jr, Donald, 361
Castiglione, Mark, 8, 9, 149, 271, 304
Castillion, Kimberly, 223
Castillo, Alex, 480
Castillon, Kim, 180
Castine, Susan R, 131
Castle, Michael N, 318
Castorina, Jr, Ron, 29
Castorina, Jr, Ronald, 133
Castorina, Ron, 621
Castoro, William J, 346
Castro, Melchor E, 65
Caswell, John, 474
Catalano, D. Chase, 455
Catalano, Michael, 347
Cataldo, John, 50
Cataldo, Robert, 19
Catalfamo, David, 393
Catanzaro, Joseph, 577
Catapano-Fox, Tracy, 47
Catena, Felix J, 55
Cates-Williams, Sharon, 7, 120
Cathcart, Kevin M., 198
Catlin, Greg, 537
Catman, Kelly J., 240
Cattalani, Mark, 228, 229
Caudill-Mirillo, Ashley, 167, 196
Cavaliere, Michael, 403
Cavanagh, Robert, 456
Cavanaugh, James, 411
Cavelli, John, 475
Caviglia, Marco, 131
Cawley, Joseph, 51
Cawley, Richard, 451
Cawley, Timothy P., 145
Cea, Christine D, 119
Cecala, Suzanne, 11, 113, 253, 305
Cechnicki, Brian, 120
Cecil"", Jonah, 470
Cecile, James H, 66
Cecile, Julie A., 56
Cecula III, John F, 332
Cekovic, Mickey, 455
Celentano, John E., 479
Cenci, Cathleen, 103, 211
Centeno, Lourdes, 9, 304
Centi, Rosemary, 347
Centra, John V, 45
Cerbin, Carolyn, 533
Ceresia Jr, George B, 46
Ceresia, Andrew G., 57
Ceresney, Andrew, 89
Ceretto, John D, 29, 621
Ceretto, John, 38, 40, 42, 275
Cerio, Jr., Donald F., 47
Cerminaro, Michael T., 366
Cerne, Gary, 569
Cernik, Christopher, 421
Cerrachio, Ronald M, 58
Cerreto, Anthony, 362
Cerro-Reehil, Patricia, 158
Cesa, Edward T., 153
Cestaro, Glenn, 344
Cestero, Rafael E., 191
Cestero, Rafael, 400
Cetrino, Maureen, 17
Cetrino, Thomas, 396
Chabe, Laura, 573
Chabot, Steve, 90
Chachere, Matthew, 450
Chacon, Michael, 451
Chafee, Chuck, 578
Chaffetz, Jason, 137, 168, 321
Chaffetz, Nancy G., 352
Chaffin, Ron, 444
Chagnon-Burke, Veronique, 564
Chakar, Robert, 572
Chalfy, Amy, 429
Chamberlain, Elizabeth, 166
Chambers, Cheryl E, 45
Chambers, John, 597
Chambliss, Saxby, 312
Champagne, Denise, 529
Champagne, Derek P, 53, 329
Champagne, Katherine, 187
Chan, Claudia, 397
Chan, Daniel, 86, 265
Chan, Madeline, 582
Chan, Margaret A., 49
Chan, Margaret, 46
Chandick, Marie, 467
Chaney, Frank, 390
Chang, Yijen Scarlett, 463
Chapman, Sandra, 330, 359
Chapman, Skip, 525
Chappelle Golston, Robin, 430
Chappelle, Rita, 88
Chappius, Paul, 109
Charland, Liz, 95, 285
Charles, Alfie, 473
Charles, Sophine, 399
Charlson, John, 391
Charney, Darius, 395
Charpentier, Elaine, 451
Chartock, Alan, 533
Chartock, Professor Alan S, 523
Chartoff, Beth, 422
Chase Granshaw, Alison, 448
Chase, Roberta, 398
Chase, Vicki, 27, 306
Chassis, Sarah, 448
Chaszczewski, Edward, 13, 86, 265
Chauvette, Derek, 432
Chauvin, Caroline, 19, 20

Chauvin, Robert J., 46
Chavez Romano, Virginia, 112
Chavez, John, 223
Chavez, Roberto, 195
Checchi, Tom, 530
Cheliotes, Arthur, 481
Chella, John, 360
Chellis, Brett B, 326
Chen, Betty, 463
Chen, Holly, 416
Chen, Wellington Z., 550
Chen, Yemeng, 558
Cheng, Bernard, 59
Cherian, Kuruvilla, 365
Chernow, Barbara, 467
Cherry, William E, 336
Cherubin, David, 13, 283, 284
Chesterton, Jan Marie, 469
Chiaverini, Linda A, 218
Chichester, Laurie, 444
Chick, Fred, 264
Chilimuri, Dr. Sridhar, 181
Chille, Joe, 534
Chimes, Deborah A., 47
Chin Brandt, Dorothy K., 49
Chin, Judith, 119
Chin, Ken, 168
Chin, Rockwell J, 194
Ching, Jennifer, 434
Chirco, Michael, 585
Chirco, Michele, 416
Chirillo, Michael, 99, 286
Chirlin, John, 102, 124, 164, 178, 308
Chitty, Lionel, 508
Chiu, Jintana, 472
Chiulli, Maria, 532
Chlad, Kevin, 378
Chmieliowiec, Lori, 528
Cho, James R., 115, 213
Cho, Julianne, 352
Choi, Steven, 199
Choi, Victoria, 41
Cholakis, Catherine, 57
Chorost, Sherry, 423
Choudhry, Roohi, 472
Christakis, Christa R., 181, 380
Christakis, Christa, 423
Christensen, Francis P, 12, 113
Christensen, Julie, 586
Christensen, Nancy, 537
Christensen, William, 572
Christian Bullock, Claudette, 111, 252
Christian, Bryan P., 168
Christian, Donald, 545
Christian, Edwin L., 487
Christiansen, Kyle R., 387
Christie, Karen, 330
Christie, Louis Patrick, 132
Christman, Bryon, 113
Christman, Robert L, 325
Christman, Robert, 372
Christmann, Robert W, 573
Christodulu, Kristin, 471
Christopher Roberts, Edris Scherer, 509
Christopher, Linda, 47
Chu, Wendell, 592
Chua, Mildred, 99, 285
Chu-Fong, Alexander F, 13, 265
Chuhta, Pat, 362
Chun, Danny K., 50
Chun, Elsie, 176
Chung, Jonathan, 356
Church, Judson, 411
Church, PhD, Sarah, 231, 233
Church, Philip R, 334
Church, Sanford A, 334
Churchill, Peg, 519
Chwalinski, Gerald, 342
Chytilo, Jan, 380
Ciacco, Christopher, 55
Ciampoli, John, 22, 332
Cicale, Robert L, 61
Cicale, Robert L., 348
Ciccarelli Jr, Raymond, 596
Cicchelli, Jerry, 597
Ciccone, Kathleen, 423
Cichetti, Wayne, 362
Cifone, Eileen, 448
Cihak, Diana, 476
Cilento, Mario, 449, 491
Cinquanti, Michael, 402
Cione, Lynn A, 507
Ciotti, John J, 332
Cipolla, Vin, 446
Cipollino, Michael, 59
Cipp Jr, Joseph, 594
Cipriani, Michelle, 430
Cipriano, Antoinette, 65
Cirillo, Frank J, 354
Cirolia, Donna, 399
Cisek, Ed, 379
Cisneros, Robert, 410
Citron, Jeff, 405
Cittadino, Peter, 380
Ciuffo, Anthony, 180
Ciulla Jr, John H, 64, 335
Claffey, Jr., James J., 495
Claire, Judith S, 51
Clancy, Margaret L, 48
Clancy, Michael, 360, 535, 538
Clancy, Patricia F., 443
Clapp, Christopher, 449
Clapp, Douglas, 342
Clare, Samantha, 417
Clarey, Don, 456
Clark Tetamore, Marcea, 331
Clark, Bernadette T., 46
Clark, Christine M., 45, 46
Clark, Douglas, 476
Clark, Gerald, 10, 283
Clark, Hillary, 380
Clark, Kathleen, 334
Clark, Lisa, 467
Clark, Mary, 476
Clark, Michael, 260
Clark, Rob, 471
Clark, Robert, 289
Clark, Roger, 538
Clark, Steven B, 48
Clark, Terrence, 579
Clark, Terry, 330
Clark, Vincent, 397
Clark, Warren G, 47
Clark, Yvette D, 320, 322
Clarke, Ann, 533
Clarke, Barry, 56
Clarke, Charlotte, 539
Clarke, Donald L, 144
Clarke, Esquire, Barry, 46
Clarke, Yvette D, 311, 320, 645
Clarke, Yvette, 89, 90, 142, 154, 180, 224, 318
Clarkin, Sarah, 449
Clark-Snead, Constance R, 582
Clarkson, John, 342
Clarkson, Thomas W., 159
Claro, Cesar J, 517
Class, Loretta, 480
Claudio, Steven, 113
Clavasquin, Jasmin, 33
Clay, William Lacy, 321
Clayton, Pam, 474
Cleare, Cordell, 19
Cleary, Kevin J., 398
Cleary, Susan, 161, 271
Cleaver, Emanuel, 190
Clemensen, Lars, 592
Clemente, Michael, 538
Clemons, Keefe, 472
Clermont, Katrice, 440
Clermont, Lois M., 529
Clifford, David, 365
Clifford, Kim, 471
Clinch, Dorie, 501
Cline, Kimberly, 557
Clingan, Thomas G, 325
Clinton, Eileen, 423
Clinton, Hillary Rodham, 315
Clouet, Dr Christopher P, 599
Clough, Roger B, 590
Clune, Tom, 474
Clyne Jr., James W., 183
Clyne, Donna, 476
Clyne, Elizabeth, 414
Clyne, Matthew J., 372
Clyne, Matthew, 130
Coats, Daniel, 90
Cobb, Benjamin, 54, 66
Cobb, Cal, 506
Cobb, Jr, James H, 292
Coble, Howard, 321
Coburn, John, 315
Coburn, Tom, 242, 267, 315, 316

Cocchiola, Carol A, 62
Coccoma, Ellen, 334
Coccoma, Michael V., 46, 209
Cochran, Alexander, 3, 160, 303
Cochran, John, 4, 250
Cochran, Lisa, 105, 152, 309
Cochran, Thad, 73, 143, 312
Cocks, Janice A, 351
Coco, Frank, 121, 252
Cocola, Thomas, 359
Coddington, David E, 63
Cody, Carrie, 473
Cody, Debra J., 461
Cody, James, 296
Coenen Jr., Kevin P., 484
Coffey, Kevin, 392
Coffey, Peter V, 215
Coffman, Richard, 428
Cofsky, Martin, 4, 200
Cohalan, Pierce F, 61
Cohen, Adam S., 114
Cohen, Amy, 419
Cohen, Bob, 476
Cohen, Brian, 550
Cohen, Daniel, 396
Cohen, David P., 49
Cohen, David, 357
Cohen, Dennis S, 54
Cohen, Devin P., 49
Cohen, Ellen, 467
Cohen, H Rodgin, 82
Cohen, Hannah, 49
Cohen, Ira J, 337
Cohen, Jeffrey A., 45
Cohen, Jeffrey, 409
Cohen, Jessica F, 600
Cohen, Jonathan, 471
Cohen, Joshua, 415
Cohen, Laurie T, 476
Cohen, Linda J, 260
Cohen, Michael E., 342
Cohen, Muhammad, 528
Cohen, Stanley G, 564
Cohen, Steve, 320
Cohen, Steven, 156, 170
Cohn, Barbara, 5, 140, 160
Cohn, Steven, 485
Coin, Ellen M., 46, 50
Coker, Spencer, 443
Colaiacovo, Emilio, 47
Colangelo, John, 47
Colarusso, Janis, 361
Colarusso, Thomas, 71
Colavita, Anthony S, 345
Colavito, Peter, 465
Colby, David B, 504
Colby, Gerard, 226
Cole, Clifford, 448
Cole, David V., 337
Cole, Janice, 536
Cole, Lauri, 232, 403
Cole, Robert, 87, 107, 165
Cole, Stephen J, 87, 97, 150
Cole, Steven, 94, 205
Coleman, Dorothy, 182
Coleman, Glenn, 532
Coleman, Isobel, 168
Coleman, Jeff, 344
Coleman, Jim, 519
Coleman, Johanna M, 349
Coleman, Joseph, 29
Coleman, Karen A., 220, 253
Coleman, Karen, 9, 220, 253
Coleman, Marcia, 30
Coleman, Norm, 312
Coleman, Peggy, 275
Coleman, Roger F, 524
Coles, Harold A, 597
Coletti, Edmund, 175, 293
Colety, Douglas A, 136
Colety, Douglas, 376
Colica, Leonard T., 430
Colimon, Claude, 255
Collado, Carmen, 435
Coller, Jeremy, 400
Collie, Craig E, 261
Collier, Jim, 526, 530, 531
Colling, Brenden, 458
Collini, Robert J, 48
Collini, Robert J., 48
Collins, Anthony G, 398, 553
Collins, Barbara, 32
Collins, Bill, 27
Collins, Catherine, 119
Collins, Chris, 89, 142, 154, 180, 645
Collins, Christopher, 358
Collins, Ella W, 596
Collins, Francis T, 48
Collins, Jane A, 575
Collins, John B., 47
Collins, John F., 186
Collins, John P., 50
Collins, John, 278
Collins, Jr., Paul, 494
Collins, Lloyd, 294
Collins, Mary, 131
Collins, Michael P, 96, 285
Collins, Robert, 381
Collins, Ronna J, 63
Collins, Scott, 72, 89, 142, 189
Collins, Sr., Daniel, 166
Collins, Susan M, 312
Collins, Susan M., 180
Collins, Susan, 255, 315
Collinsworth, Bryan, 477
Collorafi, Joseph, 296
Colman, Rebecca, 251
Colodny, David, 471
Colombo, Elizabeth, 476
Colon, Linda, 179, 196, 255
Colon, Mark, 187
Colon, Noel, 4, 83
Colon, Valentin, 495
Colon-Fores, Lydia, 462
Colonna, Donna, 118
Colton, Howard E, 345
Colton, Michael, 445
Colton, William, 27, 29, 37, 38, 40, 41, 42, 621
Colucci, Gloria J, 587
Colucciello, Raymond, 567
Colvin, John, 109
Comacho, Felipe, 474
Comanda, Micahel, 592
Comar, Sheila, 139, 372, 374
Combs, Dan, 406
Comenzo, Susan, 241
Comins, Dan, 251
Commerford, Robin J., 432
Commesso, Stephen, 451
Como, Joseph, 48, 58
Complaints, Consumer, 141
Compliance Call Center, Campaign Finance/, 130
Compo, Sarah, 19
Compton, Linda M, 336
Comrie, Leroy G, 352
Comrie, Leroy, 17, 20, 21, 22, 24, 25, 26, 87, 137, 165, 178, 607
Comstock, Clyde, 424
Conacchio, Barbara, 133
Conaway, K Michael, 317
Conaway, K. Michael, 73, 154, 180
Conboy, Brian, 581
Conboy, James E, 332
Conde, Nancy, 19
Condon, Bob, 525
Condon, Joe, 535
Condon, William J., 47
Cone, Jason, 182
Coney, Kevin R., 528
Coneys, Patricia, 86, 265
Congdon, Thomas, 11
Congel, Robert, 406
Conigliaro, James, 491
Conklin, D David, 547
Conklin, David, 565
Conklin, John W, 7, 130, 136, 304
Conklin, Susan L, 329
Conley, Nancy L, 513
Conley, Richard, 400
Conlin, Kelli, 447
Conlon, Kevin, 525
Connaughton, Kelly, 515
Conneely, John P, 79
Connell, Jim, 296
Connell, Scott, 577
Connelly, Maureen, 400, 401
Connelly, Mike, 524
Conner, Caitlin, 440
Conners, II, Michael F, 325
Connerton, Rita, 51
Connolly, Brian, 524

Connolly, Cathleen, 501
Connolly, Francesca E., 45
Connolly, Francesca, 47
Connolly, Gerald, 137
Connolly, Jim, 555
Connolly, Kenneth, 22
Connolly, Melissa, 426
Connolly, Michael, 488
Connolly, Thomas E, 136
Connolly, Tom, 17, 388
Connolly, William, 109
Connor, Daniel T, 585
Connor, Gary R, 187
Connor, Jr., John, 63
Connor, Margaret M., 98, 286
Connor, Michael J, 531
Connors, Daniel, 339
Connors, Gerard, 233
Connors, Jack, 524
Connors, Jr, John P, 215
Connors, Nancy, 432
Connors, Stacy, 415
Connors, Timothy P, 598
Connors, Tom, 526
Conole, Patrick, 426
Conover, Dave, 157
Conover, David, 467
Conovitz, Jennifer, 396
Conrad, Kent, 312, 313, 315
Conrad, Lowell, 375
Conroe, Douglas E, 105, 152
Conroy, Michael, 225
Conroy, Robert, 374
Consiato, Carol, 514
Conslato, Carol, 459
Constantine, Christine, 208
Constantino, Louis A., 430
Constantino, Susan, 126, 182, 231, 256, 404
Constantinople III, Anthony, 402
Constantinople Jr., Anthony, 402
Constantinople, Francis, 402
Conte, Jonathan D., 484
Conti, Alexis, 35
Conti, Richard, 30
Contino, Victoria M, 476
Conto, Chris, 543
Conviser, Daniel, 50
Conway, Deborah, 276
Conway, Eugene J, 344
Conway, Jr, Robert G, 10, 293
Conway, Jr., Gerard L., 145
Conyers, Jr, John, 320
Conyers, Jr., John, 116, 214
Coogan, Mary Ann, 343
Cook, Christopher J, 15
Cook, Janean, 59
Cook, Jason, 340
Cook, Jennifer, 28
Cook, Rev. Peter M., 199
Cook, Scott, 538
Cook, Thomas D., 371
Cook, Valli, 397
Cook, Vivian E, 27, 29, 36, 37, 39, 41, 42, 622
Cooke, Daniel, 409
Cooke, Mary, 346
Cooke, William, 397
Cookfair, III, John R., 138
Coomb, Richard, 376
Coombe, Elizabeth C., 115, 213
Coon, Don, 375
Coonan, Thomas, 141
Cooney, Gail, 388
Cooper, Allison, 524
Cooper, Barbara J, 76
Cooper, Benjamin, 396
Cooper, Gary, 328
Cooper, John, 535
Cooper, Linda, 272
Cooper, Marianne, 454
Cooper, Matthew F., 49
Cooper, Matthew, 46
Cooper, Omoye, 220
Cooper, Robin E, 523
Cooper, Steve, 283
Cooper, Teria, 25
Cooper, Wendy E, 203
Cooperman, Arthur J, 48
Coopersmith, Kenneth, 87, 107, 165, 310
Copanas, John P, 365
Copel, Harriet, 594
Copertino, Carl, 61
Copperman, Joel, 116
Coppola, Thomas, 346
Copps, Anne Reynolds, 216, 259
Coq, Antoine C., 484
Corbat, Michael L, 80
Corbett, Jane, 355
Corbin-Mark, Cecil, 474
Corcoran, Eugene J., 212
Corcoran, Kevin, 346
Corcoran, Kimberly, 360
Corcoran, Thomas, 108
Cordiello, Michael, 384
Cordo, John, 402
Corera, Michael, 399
Corker, Bob, 90, 313, 315
Corker, Joyce, 29
Corkery, Kathleen, 476
Corl, Jim, 343
Corlett, John, 290
Cornegy, Michelle R., 480
Cornell, Harriet D, 335
Cornell-Bechelli, Jackie, 179, 196
Cornick, Dennis, 418
Cornish, Angelia M, 135
Cornyn, John, 316
Corpus, Ben, 397
Corr, Joseph, 567
Corrado, Marie, 246, 284
Corrigan, Michael T, 102, 124, 164, 178
Corrigan, Sean, 474
Corrigan, Teresa K., 55
Corsale, Barbara, 511
Corsi, Angie, 175
Corsi, Louis G, 342
Corso, Michael, 11, 141
Corsones, Marystephanie, 464
Cort, Rebecca, 120
Cortazzo, Luz, 582
Cortes, Carlos, 359
Cortes, Darlo A, 563
Cortese, Philip V, 55
Cortez, Diana, 180, 223
Corum, Danny, 19
Corwin, Jane L, 29, 37, 41, 622
Corwin, Jane, 28, 36, 38, 43, 87, 165, 288
Corwin, MD, Steven J., 185
Cosenza, Albert, 99, 286
Cosenza, Bernard, 9, 161
Coseo, Thomas G, 573
Cosgrove, Theresa, 455
Cosilmon, Tracy M, 343
Coss, Vicki L, 267
Cossaboom, J V, 389
Costa, Jim, 154, 321
Costa, Sarah, 199
Costello, Carolyn, 586
Costello, III, Bartley J, 425
Costello, Jerry F, 322
Costello, John, 379
Costello, Laura P, 133
Costello, Mark, 388
Costello, Susan A, 251
Cote, Jamie, 169
Cote, Tom, 232
Cotler, Bruce, 145
Cotrona, Christopher, 394
Cottingham, Martin, 480
Cotton, Ashley, 416
Cotton, Rick, 3
Cottrell, Barbara, 57
Cottrell, James E, 119
Coughlan, Jim, 328
Coughlin, Christina, 121
Coughlin, Ken, 490
Coulter, John, 99, 286
Coven, Phyllis, 167, 196
Cover, Virginia, 467
Coverick, Thomas, 432
Covucci, Chris, 31
Cowan, VADM Mike, 181
Cowie, Amanda, 535, 538
Cox, Edward F, 374
Cox, Graham, 384
Cox, John, 105, 287
Cox, Kathleen, 260
Cox, Kelly, 132
Cox, Kim, 575
Cox, Linda, 389
Cox, Martin D, 567
Cox, Rita, 463
Cox, Thomas A, 599

Cox, Tim, 600
Coyle, Ellen M, 187
Coyle, Ian M, 331
Coyne, Tom, 539
Cozier, Shante L., 488
Cozzens, Jr., Robert B, 47
Craddick, Patricia, 486
Craft, Dr. Mark, 505
Craft, Rebecca, 401
Craig, Carla E., 212
Craig, MPH, Susan A, 4, 173, 227, 250, 303
Craig, Steve, 503
Craine Jr, John W, 546
Cramer, Joan M, 297
Crandall, Curtis W, 325
Crandall, Dona, 339
Crandall, John H, 330
Crandall, John H., 54
Crane, Constance, 404
Crane, II, James B., 144, 170
Crane, James B, 404
Crane, Jeanne, 373
Crane, Jeffrey B, 579
Crane, Thomas R, 87, 97, 150
Crapo, Mike, 312, 313, 314
Craw, Marc, 428
Crawford, Douglas, 451
Crawford, Kevin, 204, 239
Crawford, Marcy, 130
Crawford, Mark, 574
Crawford, Ralph H., 153
Crawford, Rick, 154
Crawford, RJ, 181
Creahan, Emmett J, 209, 230
Crean, Diane, 289
Crecca, Andrew A., 47
Cree, Elizabeth W, 136
Creedon, Paul, 396
Creedon, Richard, 205
Crehan, Vincent, 384
Cremo, John, 112, 201, 208, 221, 264
Crescenzi, Alfred, 153, 167
Crescenzo, Bob, 225
Crespo, Marcos A, 26, 43, 137, 622
Crespo, Marcos, 29, 36, 38, 39, 42, 43, 195, 222, 254
Criblear, Jeff, 504
Crimi Jr, Charles F, 65
Crimi, Eugene, 65
Cringle, Kenneth O, 571
Criniti, James G, 432
Crisafulli, Joseph, 283
Crist, William, 586
Critchlow, Paul, 443
Croce, Ronnie, 493
Croci, Thomas D, 17, 607
Croci, Thomas, 20, 21, 22, 23, 24, 26, 165, 295
Croci, Tom, 348, 509
Crocker, Alison, 112, 188, 201, 208, 245
Crockett, Lester, 398
Croft, Catherine, 134
Croghan, Robert J., 492
Cronin Esq, Elizabeth, 6, 111, 252
Cronin, John, 453
Cropp, Michael, 427
Cross, Jay, 460
Cross, Jeannie, 444
Cross, Raymond W, 546
Crossdale, Corinda, 4, 250
Crossley, Dennis J, 277
Crossman, Gordan, 329
Crotty, Erin, 155, 460
Crotty, Jane, 382
Crotty, John A, 102, 272
Crouch, Clifford W, 28, 29, 37, 40, 41, 43, 622
Crouch, Clifford, 35
Crouse, Peter R, 405
Crouse, PhD, David T., 85, 122
Crow, Kimberly, 65
Crowe, Diane, 526, 527
Crowe, Michael, 337
Crowell III, William Y, 475
Crowell III, William Y., 144
Crowell, Ann C., 46
Crowell, Anthony W, 356
Crowell, Dan, 334
Crowley, Christine, 589
Crowley, Jerry, 535
Crowley, Joseph, 180, 255, 267, 311, 319, 320, 323, 373, 481, 645
Crowley, Peter, 530
Crowley, Sean, 405
Crowley, Terri, 425
Crowley, William, 4, 83, 104, 263, 303, 309
Cruishank, Colleen, 514
Crummey, Caron, 425
Cruz, Adria, 396
Cruz, Araceli, 528
Cruz, Jose, 471
Cruz, Raul, 49
Cruz, Roberto A., 492
Cruz, Ted, 143
Cruz, Veronica, 150, 163, 236
Cruzado, Jose, 54
Cruz-Carnall, Linda, 88
Crystal, Robert, 118
Cucchiaro, J., 355
Cudahy, Cathy, 440
Cudahy, Kathy, 401
Cuellar, Henry, 320
Cuevas, Michael R, 346
Cuffy, Gordon J, 333
Cuffy, Gordon, 104, 273, 287
Culbertson, James A, 331
Cullen, Danny, 466
Cullen, John M., 339
Culley, Anna, 48
Cullinan, Dennis, 300
Cullinan, Thomas, 459
Cullinane, Shawn, 349
Cully, Malcolm, 109
Cultrara, James, 385
Cummings, Christine, 401
Cummings, Elijah E, 322
Cummings, Elijah, 137, 168, 242
Cummings, Kelly, 16, 306
Cummings, Michelle, 438
Cummings, Patrick, 383
Cummings, Rick, 144
Cummins, Seth, 99, 286
Cumoletti, Steven F, 12
Cumoletti, Susan, 564
Cunningham, Brian, 534
Cunningham, Col Patrick, 299
Cunningham, Dany, 392
Cunningham, Douglas, 528
Cunningham, Erin, 35
Cunningham, Glenn, 201, 219
Cunningham, Joanne, 183, 426, 486
Cunningham, John H, 344
Cunningham, Matthew, 417
Cunningham, Peter, 384
Cunningham, Robert, 110
Cunningham, Sherri, 202, 221
Cuomo, Andrew M, 3, 69, 78, 83, 97, 108, 119, 130, 140, 147, 150, 160, 173, 187, 194, 200, 206, 219, 227, 234, 240, 245, 250, 263, 270, 283, 293, 605
Curcio, Anthony, 448
Curcio, Mary, 572
Curr, John, 454
Currado, Melissa, 403
Curran, Brian F, 622
Curran, Brian, 29, 36, 38, 40, 42, 165
Curran, James, 21, 22
Curran, John M, 45
Curran, Mary B, 58
Curran, Paul, 451
Curran, Raymond, 463
Curren, Kathryn F, 42
Currie, Jim, 182
Currier, Glenn, 471
Curro, PE, Stephen D, 102, 124, 164, 178
Curry, Christopher J., 426
Curry, Stephanie D., 485
Curti, MIchael V., 367
Curtin, Robert, 161
Curtis, Harry, 384
Curtis, Jeffrey J, 136
Curtis, Kathleen, 398
Curtis, Lawrence, 465
Curtis, Victoria A, 134
Cusack, Christopher K., 491
Cusack, Clare, 385
Cusack, Michael, 102, 124, 164, 178
Cushman, James G., 64
Cushman, John, 365
Cusick, Michael J, 29, 38, 39, 41, 42, 622
Cusick, Michael, 37, 42, 43, 137
Custer, Paul, 477
Custodio, M.D., Marcelito, 381

Cuthbert, Jason, 346
Cutillo, Michael J., 525
Cutler, Kimberley, 402
Cutolo, Frank (Chuck), 447
Cutting Jr, Ernest R, 327
Cutting, Richard C, 329
Cuza, Bobby, 538
Cymbrowitz, Steven H, 30, 39, 623
Cymbrowitz, Steven, 36, 38, 39, 178, 195, 253
Cymbrowiz, Steven, 35
Cypher, Robert S., 65
Cyphers, Christopher, 559
Cyr, Judi, 384
Cyrulnik, Myriam, 50
Czaczkes, Michael, 417
Czajka, John, 6, 111, 206, 235
Czajka, Paul, 327
Czarny, Dustin M., 134
Czopp, Mary, 537
Czygier, Jr, John M, 59
D'Agati, John, 7, 121
D'Agati, Rebecca, 28
D'Agostino, Dominic A., 336
D'Agostino, John, 525
D'Amato, Alfonse M, 453
D'Amato, Armand, 453
D'Amato, Christopher P, 453
D'Amato, Paul, 148
D'Ambrosio, Dr John A, 513
D'Ambroso, PhD, Paul S, 279
D'Amico, Gloria, 335
D'Amico, Joseph A, 12, 113
D'Amico, Matthew, 470
D'Amico, Paula, 537
D'Amico, Robert, 187
D'Ancona, Luigi, 190
D'Angelo, Frank G, 216
D'Angelo, Philip D, 584
D'Angelo, Robert C, 586
D'Antonio, Nicolas J, 341
D'Aquila, Maureen, 47
D'Attilio, Albert, 569
D'Auguste, James E., 49
D'Aurizio, Mary Joyce, 348
D'Emic, Matthew J, 48
D'Emic, Matthew J., 46
D'Erasmo, Rocco F., 495
D'Silva DDS, Mary, 110
D'Ulisse, Gabriel, 458
DaBella, Paula, 62
Dabiri, Gloria, 46
Dacey, Amy, 482
Dada, Nyoka, 485
Dadayan, Lucy, 543
Daddario, Richard A, 357
Daddazio, Raymond, 479
Dadey, Dick, 170, 238
Dadey, Tom, 375
Dagen, Paula, 445
Daglian, Lisa, 101, 287
Dagostino, Judith, 336
Dahill, Kevin, 423, 450
Dahl, Brian P, 326
Dahl, Christopher, 545
Dahl, Patricia, 183
Dahlkemper, Kathy, 322
Daily, Don, 457
Daimwood, Diana, 233
Daines, Amy J, 136
Daino, Robert, 539
Dale, Thomas V., 332
Daley, Martin, 453
Dalmata, Cory, 63
Daly, Jennifer, 420
Daly, Maureen J., 495
Daly, Reagan, 472
Daly, Thomas P., 430
Daly, Thomas R, 66
Daly, William, 503
Daly-Browne, Sharon, 392
Dambakly, Thomas, 392
Damchieco, Tracy, 54
Dame, Ginger, 241
Dames, Cynthia, 439
Damiani, Lisa, 176
Damico, Edward J., 448
Damrath, Joseph E, 63
Danaher, Philip, 335
Dane, Edmund M., 55
Danegger, Anna, 420
Dangle, Jeanne M, 584
Daniels, Anita, 228, 229
Daniels, Brian S, 5, 251
Daniels, Gordon, 572
Daniels, Julie, 120
Daniels, Robert, 120, 271
Danner, Rosalind P., 93
Danovitz, Burt, 261
Dantz, Robert, 96, 273
Danziger, Lauren, 508
Danziger, Mitchell, 49
Danzinger, Peter, 452
Darche, Samantha, 34
Darcy, James M., 61
Darden, James, 184
Darden, Lawrence, 64
Dardia, Michael, 357
Darfler-Sweeney, Patrick, 576
Darin, John, 447
Darling, Bruce, 395
Darling, Nickolas, 469
Darman, Jeremy, 400
Darman, Laura, 439
Darrell, Andrew, 412
Darwell, Wendy, 423
Darwin, David L, 333
Dasgupta, Anisha, 112
Dashnshaw, William, 502
Daswani, Raju, 531
Dattilio, Daniel J, 276
Dauman, Philippe, 146
Davenport, Marolyn, 459
Davey, Mark C, 578
David, Alphonso, 3, 69, 78, 83, 108, 119, 130, 140, 147, 160, 173, 187, 194, 200, 206, 219, 227, 234, 240, 245, 250, 263, 270, 283, 293
David, Courtney, 426
David, Joshua, 416
David, Kristy, 432
David, Sara, 450
Davidoff, Sid, 405
Davidson, Basil A., 493
Davidson, Robert L, 255
Davidson, Robert, 255
Davidson, Sheila, 428
Davie, Duncan S, 19
Davies, Mark, 353
Davies, Robert, 147
Davies-Griffin, Sara, 135
Davila, Maritza, 30, 35, 36, 37, 39, 42, 623
Davis, Aimee, 480
Davis, Alan, 545
Davis, Amanda, 421
Davis, Carrie, 435
Davis, Chester, 183
Davis, Darryl, 445
Davis, Darwin M, 260
Davis, Derrick, 17
Davis, Diana L, 62
Davis, Doreen, 373
Davis, Elliot, 491
Davis, Ernest D., 351
Davis, Gordon, 472
Davis, Heather, 398
Davis, Ivy L., 137, 196
Davis, Janna, 34
Davis, Jerome, 356
Davis, Karen A, 130
Davis, Karen, 6, 111, 206, 235
Davis, Kathleen M, 583
Davis, Kenneth L, 558
Davis, Laura, 434
Davis, MD, Kenneth L., 184
Davis, Michelle S., 179
Davis, Patricia, 394
Davis, Perry, 94
Davis, R. Leland, 451
Davis, Robert, 64, 390
Davis, Rodney, 154
Davis, Sandra T., 430
Davis, Susan A, 318
Davis, Virginia, 11, 271
Davis, Wade A, 105, 287, 309
Davis, Wade, 72, 167
Davitian, Harry, 144
Davoli, Michael, 380
Dawkins, Frank, 534
Dawson, Donald, 121
Dawson, Joseph J., 50
Dawson, Lori, 434
Dawson, Sandra, 479

Dawson, Tandra L., 50
Dawson, Tandra, 46, 50
Day, Anthony, 574
Day, Eric, 327
Day, Julia, 195
Day, Luke, 342
Day, Lynne, 52
Day, Marie, 474
Day, Steven, 468
De Blasio, Bill, 357
De Bow, W. Brooks, 48
De Felice, Arianna, 380
De La Cruz, Carlos J., 484
De La Cruz, Elisandro, 463
De La Cruz, Katrina, 486, 494
De Leon Bhargava, Elizabeth, 3, 219
De Milly, Michele, 418
De Rome, Paul, 412
De Santis, Gene, 439
Deal, Nathan, 319
DeAmelia, Victor, 194
Dean, Adam, 111, 206
Dean, Irv, 530
Deane, Ciara Imelda, 415
Deane-Williams, Barbara, 586
Deangelis, Benjamin, 458
DeAngelo, Louis R, 580
Dear, Noach, 46, 49
Dearing, John, 441
Dears, Elizabeth, 183
DeBarr, Michael, 202, 221
DeBenedetto, Karen, 66
Debesu, Saba, 434
DeBlasi, Ann, 153
Deblasio, Danna, 438
Debo, Dave, 534
Debow, Andrea, 404, 410
DeCamp III, William, 418
DeCarlo, Lori, 569
DeCataldo, Robert T, 48
DeCerce, Jessica, 20
Dechario, Tony, 471
DeCicco, Louis F., 371
DeCinque, Gregory T, 548
Decker, Darryl, 240
Decker, Lori S, 59
Decker, Rita S, 58
Decker, Thomas A., 481
DeCostanzo, Donna, 448
DeDominick, Cynthia, 578
Dedrick, Charles, 600, 601
Dee, Patrick, 596
Deemie, Robert, 466
Deetz, Valerie, 176
DeFazio, Peter A, 323
DeFazio, Peter A., 155, 190
Defedericis, Dan, 456
Defenders PLLC, Lewis, 331
DeFrancisco, Joe, 331
DeFrancisco, John A, 15, 17, 25, 608
DeGenova, Deborah W., 364
Degnan, John J, 105, 287
DeGraaff, Bill, 289
Degree, Nancy, 119, 251
DeGregorio, Georgia, 434
DeGroat, Stephen F., 335
Dehkan, Aziz, 157
DeJesus, Guiyermo, 488
DeJoseph, Brian F, 46
DeJoseph, Brian F., 45
Dejung, Trilby, 410
Del Cogliano, David, 70
Del Giorno, Jon, 455
Del Giorno, Sheila, 133
Del Guercio, Michelle, 417
Del Guidice, Vincent M, 48
Del Senno, Nina, 101, 287
DeLa Cruz, Katrina P., 479
Delahunt, Bill, 320
Delair, Samantha, 395
Delaney, Brian, 536
Delaney, Kerry, 10, 229
Delaney, Kristen, 535
Delano, Alexandra, 199
Delano, Stephen, 451
DeLaurentis, Ambassador Jeffrey, 297
DeLauro, Rosa, 317
DeLaus, Daniel, 106, 288
Delbello, Alfred, 406
DelBene, Suzan, 154
Delehanty, Sean, 31
DeLessio, John P., 372
Delgado, Ryan, 404, 449
DeLilli, Robert, 575
Delio, Vincent, 471
DeLisio, Rudolph A, 504
DeLisle, Dennis, 103, 164, 265
Dell, Lisa, 350
Dellamere, Diana, 421
Dellapina, Mario, 397
Delligatti, Angelo A., 55
DeLorenzo, James P., 252
DeLorenzo, James, 228
Delorenzo, Robert, 451
Delory, Diane, 291
Delruelle, Antoinette, 434
DelTorto, Elizabeth A, 344
DeLuca, Peter, 490
DeLuca, Rosemary, 475
DelVecchio, David, 365
DeMarco, Allen, 11
DeMarco, John L, 55
DeMarco, Robert, 292
DeMarco, Vincent F, 337
DeMarest, Carolyn, 46
Demarest, Cynthia, 127
Demarest, David R, 46
Demars, John, 108
DeMartin, Andrew, 360
DeMartino, Joe, 355
DeMasi, Mary, 5, 252
Demauro Busketta, Carol, 133
DeMay, Karen R, 333
Dember, Andrew, 115
DeMeglio, Louis, 351
DeMeo, Claudio, 483
Demeo, Frank, 440
DeMichele, Paul, 308
DeMichiel, Robert, 396
Demilia, Regina, 394
DeMint, Jim, 313, 315
Demo, Nicole, 132
Dempsey Scialdo, Deborah, 29
Dempsey, Gerald W, 581
Dempsey, Mary, 526
Demyen, Eva J, 592
Denaut, Megan, 533
DenDekker, Michael G, 30, 35, 38, 42
Dendekker, Michael G, 623
DenDekker, Michael, 35, 40, 42, 295
Denerstein, Mylan, 354
Denison, Lauren, 41
Denman, Jeffrey, 478
Denn, James, 12, 140, 305
Dennison, Thomas, 455
Denniston, Dave, 74
Denson, Pam, 457
Dent, Charles W., 137, 169
Dent, Charlie, 320
Dent, Marc, 451
Dent, Valerie P., 9, 194
Denz, Daniel, 367
DePass, Michelle J., 184
DePass, Michelle, 192
DePerno, Sandra J, 332
Depew, Dan, 366
DePhillips, Guy P., 50
DePippo, Thomas, 355
DeProspo, William L, 375
Derbyshire, Keith, 176
Derbyshire, Vicky, 176
Derbyshire, Victoria, 148
Derenda, Daniel, 342
Derenoncourt, Henry, 484
DeRiso, Frank C, 226
DeRooy, Judy, 346
DeRosa, Georgio, 388
DeRosa, Melissa, 3, 69, 78, 83, 108, 119, 130, 140, 147, 160, 173, 187, 194, 200, 206, 219, 227, 234, 240, 245, 250, 263, 270, 283, 293
DeRosa, Nicholas, 56
Desai, Kavan, 409
DeSantis, Emily, 8, 147, 148, 304
DeSanto, Helene, 10
Desany, Christopher G, 96, 285, 306
Desch, Carol Ann, 120
Desdunes, Marthe, 34
DeShong, Jelanie, 3
DeSiato, Dr Donna J, 584
Designee, Republican Leader, 315
DeSio, John, 359
Deska, Christine, 414

Desmond, Anthony F, 336
Desmond, Sarah, 426
Despirito, Amy, 532
Desposito, Raymond, 468
DesRosiers, Jill, 3, 160, 250
Dessables, Mary Jane, 399
Dessen, Eric, 401
DeStefano, Joseph M, 350
DeStefano, Joseph P, 101, 236
DeStefano, Vito M., 47
Destito, RoAnn, 8, 161, 245, 271
Destler, William W, 560
Destler, William, 468
DeThomasis, Lena, 35
DeTraglia, Esq., Erica, 53
Deutsch, Ron, 170
Deval, Don, 506
DeVille, Jackie, 230
Devine, Debra, 42
Devine, Eugene P., 45
Devine, Jim, 27
Devine, Lawrence M, 296
Devine, Sharon, 187
Devita, Joseph, 457
Devito, Emma, 472
Devlin Jr, Richard, 334
Devlin, Diane Y, 47
Devoe, Kristin, 7, 160, 235, 304
DeWald, PE, Brian, 246, 284
Dewan, Todd, 525, 526
DeWeese, Chuck, 283
Dewey, Jan, 526, 529
DeWitt, Stephen M, 136
DeWolf, John, 426
Dexter, James P, 601
Deyoe, PE, Erik, 161
DeYoung, Gary, 275
Deyss, Christine, 261
Di Fonzo, Paul, 570
Di Mezza, Traci, 63
Di Sibio, Carmine, 388
Diab, Mohamed, 410
DiAgostino, Carol, 353
Diagostino, Jennifer, 399
Diamond, Arthur M, 47
Diamond, Charles E, 50, 51
Diamond, Marilyn G., 49
Diamond, Seth, 355
Diamonstein-Spielvogel, Dr Barbaralee, 6, 270
Diana, Edward A, 333
DiAngelo, Jacqueline, 60
Diaz Jr, Ruben, 325
Diaz Jr, Rueben, 359
Diaz Jr., Francisco, 391, 451
Diaz Sr, Ruben, 17, 20, 23, 24, 26, 178, 195, 254
Diaz, Alex, 446
Diaz, Antonio, 49
Diaz, David E., 480
Diaz, Edward L., 297
Diaz, James, 471
Diaz, Jessica, 356
Diaz, Luis M., 325
Diaz, Raymond, 98, 286
Díaz, Sr, Rubén, 608
Diaz-Balart, Lincoln, 321
Diaz-Balart, Mario, 323
Dibble, Ann, 434
Dibble, Ken, 466
Dibble, Maria, 466
Dibella, James, 375
Dibella, Robert M., 47
DiBenedetto, James, 409
Dibenedetto, Patricia, 379
Dibernardo, Blaise S., 440
DiBernardo, Blaise, 383
Dibiase, Jon, 418
DiBlasi, Willie, 419
DiCarlo, Ambassador Rosemary A., 297
DiCarlo, Anthony, 334
DiCarlo, Joseph, 347
DiCaro, David R, 346
Dichiara, Joseph, 409
DiChristopher, Mary Ann, 4, 173, 227, 250
Dickens, Ron, 111
Dickerson, Mary Jo, 576
Dickerson, Pless, 594
Dickerson, Thomas A, 45
Dickert, Catherine, 147
Dickey, Elizabeth D, 553
Dickinson, Christina, 442
Dickinson, Darlene, 466
Dickinson, Michael, 533
Dickinson, Randall L, 289
Dickinson, Susan, 518
Dicks, Norman D, 317
Dickson, Lori Lee, 361
Dickson, William, 228
Dickson-McMahon, Martha, 343
DiDomenico, Catherine M., 48
Diebel, Beth, 46
Diebold, William, 383
Dieterich, Scott, 99, 286
Dietrich, David, 187
Dietrich, Martin A, 81
DiFabio, Michael J, 586
Difiore, Janet, 339
DiFiore, Janet, 45
DiGangi, Thomas, 420
DiGiacomo, Michael, 115, 213
DiGiovanni, Jr., Robert A., 158
Digirolamo, Karla, 192
Digman, John R, 111
Digrado, Paul, 474
Dike, Jim, 471
Dikranis, Frank, 64
Dilan, Eric M, 623
Dilan, Erik M, 30
Dilan, Erik, 36, 37, 39
Dilan, ErikM, 39
Dilan, Martin M, 16, 17, 608
Dilan, Martin Malave, 22, 23, 24, 25, 237, 288
Dilemani, Jake, 454
DiLiberto, James G, 564
Dill, Col. J.J., 295
Dill, Jean, 62
Dillon, James, 47, 421
Dillon, Mark C, 45
Dilorenzo, Jay, 457
DiMaria, Paul, 360
DiMartino, Colleen, 461
DiMartino, Rita, 550
Dimauro, Nancy, 557
Dimbleby, David, 579
Dimeo, Jessica, 381
DiMezza, Richard, 251
DiMillo, Thomas M, 63
Dimitrov, Danielle, 397
Dimon, Jamie, 81
Din, April L, 59
Dinallo, Eric R., 406
DiNapoli, Thomas P, 3, 12, 162, 235, 241, 605
DiNapoli, Thomas, 149
Ding, George, 121
Dings, Michael, 388
Dini, Lou, 383
Dinkin, Casey, 388
Dinnerstein, Julie, 463
Dinolfo, Cheryl, 331
Dinolfo, David V, 577
Dinolfo, Gwynne, 167, 196
Dinolfo, Vincent M, 55
DiNoto, Darryl, 134
Dinowitz, Jeffrey, 30, 36, 38, 39, 40, 41, 87, 165, 178, 372, 483, 623
DiPalo, Dotty, 136
DiPasquale, David, 133
DiPietro, David, 30, 35, 37, 40, 41, 42, 87, 624
DiPirro, Colleen C, 501
Dircks, Ken, 377
Director
Dirschel, Kathleen, 554
DiSalvo, Frank, 156
DiSanto, Kenneth, 504
Diskin, Michael G, 329
Disman, Beatrice M, 254
Dissek, Philip C, 224
Ditman, Lenn, 6, 270, 303
Ditton, Andrew, 396
Dittus, Ashley, 136
DiTullio, Sheila, 53
DiTullo, Michael, 515
Diubaldo, Robert, 377
Dixon, Angela, 12, 162, 236
Dixon, Maija C, 65
Doan, Sue, 294
Doar, Robert, 355
Dobrin, Allan H., 550
Dobrin, Allan, 397

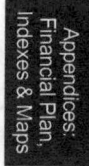

Appendices: Financial Plan, Indexes & Maps

Dodd, Christopher J, 313, 315
Dodds, Jerrilynne, 560
Dodge, Ryan, 357
Dodley, Lewis, 538
Doern, James E, 65
Doersam, Paul M, 254
Dogal, MA, Richard, 298
Doheny, Thomas, 469
Doherty, John J, 358
Doherty, Kevin, 173
Doherty, Linda, 345
Doherty, Marian C., 49
Doherty, Mary Anne, 66
Doherty, Thomas, 443
Doick, Robin, 409
Dolan, Dr Thomas P, 580
Dolan, Farrell, 115
Dolan, Katie, 449
Dolan, Laura, 418
Dolan, Maureen, 397
Dolan, Mitch, 535
Dolce, Sandra, 109
Dolci, Joel A., 92
Dolezalek, J. Stephan, 471
Doll, Josephine, 60
Dollard, Mary K., 49
Dollhopf, Jonathan, 466
Dollinger, Richard, 47
Dominelli, Joseph S, 243
Donaghy, John, 368
Donaher, Tim, 331
Donahue, Joe, 533
Donahue, Karen M, 577
Donahue, Maureen, 568
Donald, Cheryl, 179
Donaldson, David B., 338
Donalty, Barry M, 56
Donar, Lt. Col. Mark T., 295
Dong, Helen, 39
Donley, Lynne, 537
Donnaruma, Mary Ann, 439
Donnellan, Alfred, 406
Donnellan, Gerald, 335
Donnellan, James F, 204
Donnellan, Jr, John J, 296
Donnelly, David, 412
Donnelly, Dennis, 210
Donnelly, Matthias, 596
Donnelly, Patrick F, 337
Donnelly, Susanne, 361
Donner, Kathy, 19
Donofrio, Gail A., 55
Donohue, Danny F., 480
Donohue, Danny, 225, 243, 398
Donohue, Gavin J., 144
Donovan Jr, Daniel M, 335
Donovan Jr., Daniel F., 371
Donovan, Dan, 169
Donovan, Daniel, 90, 197
Donovan, David, 144, 389
Donovan, Dawn T, 345
Donovan, Donna, 531
Donovan, Jr, Daniel, 645
Donovan, Kathleen A, 130
Donovan, Kelly, 10, 112, 161, 177, 207
Donovan, Maureen, 446
Donovan, Michael, 266, 469
Donovan, Mitch, 518
Donovan, Ryan, 462
Doochin, Jonathan, 146
Doody, Mark E, 596
Dooha, Susan, 197, 256
Doolan, Sean M, 425
Dooley, Kevin P, 51
Doorley, Sandra, 331
Dopico, Jorge, 208
Doran, Craig J., 47, 210
Doran, III, Arthur J, 66
Doran, Kenneth M., 486
Doran, Kimberly, 284
Dorgan, Byron L, 313, 316
Dorgan, Byron, 312
Dority, Pamela, 121
Dorkey III, Charles E., 442
Dorlon, Daniel, 403
Dorman, Daniel, 142
Dorman, Jan, 184
Dormin, John, 9, 220, 253
Dorn, Alan, 244
Dorr, Thomas, 600
Dorsey, Stephen M, 335
Dorward, Paul, 567
Dory, Craig, 460
Doss, Matthew, 87, 97, 150
Dougher, Brendan, 457
Dougher, Darleen, 363
Dougherty, Donna, 429
Dougherty, Joseph, 425
Dougherty, Kathy, 575
Dougherty, Maureen L, 338
Dougherty, Ryan, 595
Dougherty, Stephen J, 66
Dougherty, Terrance, 572
Doughtie, Lynne, 238
Douglas, Dena E., 49
Douglas, Dr Thomas, 568
Douglas, Garry, 514
Douglas, Jewel A, 103
Douglas, Jewel A., 265
Douglas, Laura G, 48
Douglas, Laura G., 49
Douglas, Leonie, 362
Douglas, Lucille, 407
Douglas, Randall T, 328
Douglas, Robin L, 501
Douglas, Valencia, 599
Dove, Susan, 516
Dow, Debra, 58
Dow, Evelyn, 530
Dowd, Kevin M, 47
Dowd, Michael, 523
Dowd, Patrick, 386
Dowling, S. Colin, 480
Downey, Caroline, 9, 194
Downey, James, 64
Downey, Matt, 103, 124
Downey, Sandy, 108
Downing, Lylburn K., 490
Downs, Jennifer, 18
Downs, Roger, 159
Downs, Timothy M., 128
Dowse, Patricia, 460
Doyle, Daniel, 47
Doyle, David, 543
Doyle, III, Vincent E., 170
Doyle, John, 459
Doyle, Michael R., 456
Doyle, Pat, 187
Doyle, Shona, 132
Doyle, Terry, 462
Drabicki, Judy, 148
Drader, James, 376
Drag, Walter F, 62
Drager, Laura E., 46, 50
Dragone, Jackie, 437
Dragone, Joseph P, 588
Drahos, Michael, 578
Drake, Daniel A, 208
Drake, Michael, 4, 83, 263
Drake, Peter, 558
Drapkin, Jonathan, 92, 191, 511
Draves, Edward, 388
Draxler, Donna, 326
Dreier, David, 321
Dreslin, MS, RN, Sally, 8, 148, 174
Dreslin, Sally, 434
Dreyer, Liz, 278
Drilling, Rev Peter J, 553
Drinane, Monica, 50
Driscoll Hopkins, Esq., Kathryn, 47
Driscoll, Justin E, 101, 141
Driscoll, Justin, 390
Driscoll, Matthew J, 13, 246, 283
Driscoll, Paul, 365
Driscoll, Sharon A, 331
Driscoll, Timothy S., 47
Driscoll, William, 454
Driver, Will, 474
Droesch, Edward, 419
Dropkin, Robin, 453
Dros, Kathy, 392
Drucker, Paul, 485
Drucker, Richard, 96, 295, 306
Drugovich, Dr Margaret L, 555
Drumm, Kevin E, 547
Drumm, Robert, 132
Drury, Timothy, 47
Dry, Verna, 51, 64
Dua, Stephanie, 353
Duane, Gregory J, 362
Duane, Thomas K., 495
Dube, Arthur, 223
Dubensky, Joyce S., 199

Dubik, Robert, 578
DuBois, Carl E, 333
DuBois, Robert, 234, 240
Dubois, Robert, 5
Dubuque, Lewis, 92, 391
Duchesne, Tammy, 276
Duchessi, Jamie M, 133
Duckham, Nicole, 33
Duckworth, Sandra B, 599
Dudden, Marcia, 234, 240
Dudley, Cheryl, 576
Dudley, David, 453
Dudley, Don, 538
Dudley, William C, 79
Dudup, Gary, 454
Dudziak, John M, 349
Duff, Ricky, 451
Dufficy, Timothy J., 49
Duffiey, Timothy, 48
Duffy, Colleen, 45
Duffy, Monica A., 208
Duffy, Patricia, 457
Duffy, Terrence A., 93
Dufour, Robert, 594
Dugan, Brendan J, 561
Dugan, Daniel, 485
Dugan, Deborah, 283
Dugan, Theresa E, 132
Duggan, Aine, 415
Duggan, Charles S., 91
Duke, Oak, 531
Dulchin, Benjamin, 191, 381
Dullea, Henrik, 543
Dumas, Frances, 340
Dumka, Catherine A, 134
Dumm, Thomas, 451
Dumser, James, 351
Dunbar, Tonda, 572
Duncan, Jr, John J, 323
Duncan, Liza, 120
Duncan, Mackenzie, 383
Duncan-Poitier, Johanna, 467, 543
Duncombe, Raynor B, 336
Dunford, Jan, 436
Dunford, Mark, 469
Dunham Jr., Wolcott B., 406
Dunham, Sarah, 523
Dunham, Stephanie, 230
Dunham, Thomas, 15
Dunhan, Rose, 423
Dunkel, Jill, 174
Dunkelberger, Ed, 457
Dunlea, Mark, 427
Dunn, Catherine, 458
Dunn, Christopher, 454
Dunn, Geoff, 535
Dunn, Karen, 241
Dunn, Kevin, 127
Dunn, Meg, 553
Dunne, Allison, 533
Dunne, Charles, 115, 213
Dunne, James, 245
Dunne, John, 475
Dunne, Linda, 558
Dunne, Richard T., 61
Dunning, David, 343
Dunoyer, Theo, 384
Dunwell, Frances, 148
Dupra, Mark R, 572
Dupree, Stella, 524
Duprey, Janet L, 30, 37, 38, 624
Duprey, Janet, 28, 39, 41, 43, 165
Durant, Greg, 469
Durant, Michael P., 93, 226, 268, 448
Durbin, Richard J, 316
Durbin, Richard, 312
Duren, Mitch, 549
Durfee, Joanne, 536
Durniak, Andrew, 421
Durso, John R., 494
Durso, John, 447
Duryea, Christopher, 404
Dussing, Thomas, 451
Dutko, Christina, 130
Dutton, Laura, 576
Dutton, Melinda, 439
DuVall, Eric, 531
Duvalle, Michael, 490
Duve, Nicole M, 337
Dvorin, Jeffrey, 112, 149, 177, 188, 201, 208, 264
Dwyer, Jay, 451
Dwyer, Mary, 298
Dwyer, Michael L, 56
Dwyer, Susan M, 326
Dyckman, Joann, 344
Dyer, Chris, 594
Dyer, Jill, 329
Dyer, Mary R, 131
Dygert, Jeff, 341
Dyjak, Anne, 457
Dylong, Geoff, 523
Dyster, Paul, 360
Dzikowski, Denise, 590
Dzurinko, Ted, 363
Eades, Jeffrey, 432
Eagan, Mark, 379
Eagan, Mike, 280
Eagan, Susan, 62
Eannace, Ralph J, 66
Earisman, Peggy, 434
Earle, Gordon, 477
Earle, Steven, 120
Earley, Bill, 536
Earley, David, 389
Earnshaw, Amanda, 432
Eastman, Karen E, 106
Easton, William, 379
Eastwood, Kenneth, 585
Eaton, Craig, 375
Ebanks, Jacqueline M., 139
Ebersole, John F, 555
Ebert, Holger, 474
Ebert, Jhone, 7, 120
Ecker Jr, Edward V, 345
Ecker, Gerry, 284
Ecker, Lawrence H., 47
Eckert, Ileana, 588
Eckle, Sarah, 397
Eckler, Steven, 451
Eckstein, Katherine, 396
Eckstrom, Jim, 529
Ecroyd, Gilda Ventresca, 427
Eddington, Patricia, 342
Eddy, Joseph, 465
Edelman, Martin, 469
Edelson, Paul, 467
Eder, Tim A, 87, 97, 150
Edert, James P, 255
Edert, James P., 179
Edick, Cindy, 331
Edick, Sharon, 343
Edmead, Carol R, 46
Edmondson, Charles M, 552
Edmunds Jr, David L, 83, 263
Edsall, Allison A, 350
Edwards, Brian, 451
Edwards, Camille, 451
Edwards, Chet, 317
Edwards, Genine D., 49
Edwards, Gregory J, 326
Edwards, Janet E, 33
Edwards, Joan, 174
Edwards, John S, 361
Edwards, Kaida, 392
Edwards, Sherry, 220
Edwards, William, 64
Effler, Steven W., 159
Effman, Norman P, 339
Efman, Martin I., 47
Efron, William H., 88
Egan Jr., John C, 45
Egan, Mark, 501
Egan, Paul, 496
Egan, Theresa L, 10, 283
Egan, Tracy, 104, 273, 309
Egers, Dan, 421
Egger, Mary, 133
Eggert, Diane, 74
Eggert, Lawrence, 349
Eggleston, Alan P, 80
Egitto, Joseph, 53
Egri, Marianne, 100, 123
Ehlers, Vernon J, 322
Ehmann, Edward, 594
Ehmke, Jim, 537
Ehrenberg, David, 95, 295
Ehrenberg, Ronald, 543
Ehresman, Maria, 597
Ehrhardt, William C, 565
Ehrlich, Andrew J., 486
Ehrlich, Carolyn, 413
Ehrlich, Clifford, 279

Ehrlich, Paul, 18
Eichelberger, Clayton, 385
Eichelberger, S Earl, 385
Eicheldinger, Joseph, 432
Eichenbaum-Pikser, Gina, 181
Eidlin, Mark, 443
Eigendorff, Donald W, 247
Einbinder, Robin, 448
Eisel, Sr, James E, 328
Eisen, Arnold, 556
Eisen, Reeves, 489
Eisenberg, Arthur, 454
Eisenpress, Sherri L., 58
Eisgruber, Judith, 190
Eisland, Evan, 99, 285
Eisland, June, 409
Eisland, Paul, 482
Eisman, Julianne S, 55
Eisner, Laurel W., 463
Elan-Mangano, Cindy, 348
Elcock, Soroya, 422
Elder, Lance W, 258
Elder, Lance W., 117
Elder, Sandy, 527
Eldon, Ethan C, 291
Eldon, Ethan, 159
Eldridge, Araina, 54
Eldridge, Michael, 529
Elek, Steven, 457
Elena-Gonzalez, Maria, 352
Elfner, Douglas, 140
Elia, MaryEllen, 7, 119, 174, 227, 252, 270
Elie, Joyce, 33
Elijah, Soffiyah, 117
Eliuk, Stacey, 199
Elkin, Evan, 472
Elkins, Carolyn, 135
Elkordy, Mohamed, 385
Ellenbogen, Amy, 417
Ellenson, David, 555
Elliman, Christopher J., 158
Elliot, David, 48
Elliott, Claudette, 480
Elliott, D Stephen, 278
Elliott, Deborah, 451
Elliott, Jack, 65
Elliott, Raymond, 46
Elliott, Robert, 86
Elliott, Thomas, 599
Elliott-Davis, Gigi, 32
Ellis, Anthony G, 12, 113
Ellis, Bradley, 455
Ellis, John, 46
Ellis, Nacole, 131
Ellis, Pierson, 19, 22
Ellis, Robert, 251
Ellison, Kenneth J, 575
Ellman, Barbara K., 443
Ellman, Christopher, 452
Ellsworth, Lisa, 201, 219
Ellwood, Lee, 593
Elmendorf II, Michael J, 90
Elmendorf II, Michael, 404
Elmendorf, Michael, 382
Elmer, Alicia, 458
Elmore, Chris, 419
Else, Gail J, 574
Elsner, Timmie E., 49
Elson, Allen, 536
Elston, Elizabeth, 472
Elton, Wally, 453
Emad, Jeff, 173, 227, 250
Emanuel, Rick, 525
Emanuel, Staci, 397
Emanuele, Joe, 375
Emberger, Charles, 362
Emerson, Elizabeth H, 47
Emerson, Jo Ann, 317
Emmer, Cindy, 131
Empire, Jamie, 63
Emrick, John, 18
Enck, Judith A., 154
Enderlin, E., 355
Endries, Laurie, 200, 219
Enea, Kim, 330
Eng, Phillip, 13, 246, 283
Eng, Randall T., 45, 209
Engel, Andrew M., 61
Engel, Eliot L, 311, 318, 319, 320, 645
Engel, Eliot L., 89, 142, 143, 154, 180, 197
Engel, Eliot, 320
Engelman, James T., 266
Engelmann, Carol, 132
Englander, Franklin, 83, 263
Englebright, Steve, 41
Englebright, Steven C, 30, 37, 39, 624
Englebright, Steven C., 38
Englebright, Steven, 38, 152
English, Janice, 357
English, Mark, 373
English, Tom, 428
Engman, Herb, 348
Engoron, Arthur F., 46, 49
Ensign, John, 313, 315
Enzi, Michael B, 315
Enzi, Michael B., 180, 267
Eppel, William, 455
Eppelmann, Christine, 38
Eppler, Klaus, 94, 218
Eppolito, Anthony P, 64
Epstein, Gary, 514
Epstein, Harvey, 471
Epstein, Lawrence, 478
Epstein, Mark, 291
Epstein, Ron, 13, 283, 284
Epting, Rahna, 412
Erdman, Joe, 25
Erhard, Michael, 392
Erickson, Anne, 215, 258, 410
Ericson, Paul, 533
Erlbaum, William M, 48
Ernest, Jennifer, 474
Erodes, Nancy, 430
Ertel, David, 385
Erwin, Darren, 72, 167
Eschler, William E, 329
Escobales, Elaine, 258
Escudier, Stephen, 412
Eshoo, Anna G, 324
Esner, Sandra, 444
Espaillat, Adriano, 17, 21, 23, 24, 25, 189, 237, 246, 608
Esposito, Adrienne, 397
Esposito, Jacqueline, 427
Esposito, James, 354
Esposito, Joseph J., 49
Estepa, Sandra, 255
Estes, Bruce, 526
Estey, Cynthia, 71
Estrich, Donna, 342
Estroff, Rachel A., 32
Esty, Scott, 30
Etringer, Lindsey, 414
Ettinger, Ilana, 416
Ettling, John, 546
Etts, Bill, 515
Eubank, Matthew, 207
Eubanks, Mary Lynn, 422
Eudicone, Gregory, 441
Eusebio, Nelson, 490
Evans, Andrew, 172
Evans, Cory A., 488
Evans, Donna, 98, 286
Evans, Dwight, 18, 22
Evans, Ellen, 12, 162, 236
Evans, Heather, 425
Evans, James, 451
Evans, Jeff, 251
Evans, John P, 594
Evans, Judy, 270
Evans, Melanie, 379
Evans, Patricia E., 327
Evans, Peter, 339
Evans, Saralee, 49
Evans, Stan L, 524
Evans, William E, 327
Eve Jr, Arthur O, 132
Evenbeck, Scott, 397
Evensen, James, 141
Everett, David F., 60
Evers, John T., 325
Every, Jackie, 364
Ewashko, John, 435
Eygabroad Garretson, Rita, 410
Fabel, Diane, 467
Fabella, Victoria, 338
Faber, Jill, 208
Faber, Stephen, 455
Fabrizio, Ralph A., 50
Facciola, Susan, 432
Facin, Kenneth A, 587
Factor, Mallory, 81
Fafinski, Theodore, 333

Fagan, Dennis A, 336
Fagan, Mary Beth, 506
Fagan, Michael, 356
Faherty, Peter, 24
Fahey, Catherine, 30
Fahey, Eugene M, 45
Fahey, James, 409
Fahey, Joseph E, 56
Fahs, Marianne, 259
Fahy, Maureen, 6, 252
Fahy, Patricia, 30, 35, 36, 38, 39, 42, 624
Faiella, Matt, 454
Fairben, Erin, 228
Fairchild, John, 571
Fairgrieve, Scott, 61
Faison-Miller, Nikki, 419
Faist, Thomas W, 413
Faith, Thomas, 185
Falbo, Bruce, 188
Falco, III, Louis, 335
Fale, Edward M, 582
Faleomavaega, Eni F H, 320
Fales, Shannon, 459
Falk, Mark D., 223
Falk, Michael, 113
Falkena, Ronda, 72, 142, 189
Fallin, Governor Mary, 98, 141, 151
Fallin, Mary, 322
Fallon, Michael, 425
Falls, Wendy, 334
Falvey, Scott P., 340
Falvey, Suanne, 474
Falvey, W Patrick, 60
Falvey, W. Patrick, 58
Famularo, Joseph S, 579
Fancher, Michael, 85, 122, 471
Fandrich, Mark H, 51
Fanikos, Paul, 386
Fanni, Tony, 505
Fanshawe, Frank, 447
Faragon, William F., 181
Farber, Christopher P, 330
Farber, Felice, 291
Farber, Thomas A., 50
Farber, William G, 330
Farbstein, Lisa, 167, 289
Fare, Edwin, 366
Farenthold, Blake, 242
Farfaglia, Dick, 377
Fariello, R.A., Thomas, 352
Farina, Carmen, 100, 123
Farkas, Sara Sheldon, 56
Farley, Barbara, 113
Farley, Bob, 26
Farley, Craig, 294
Farley, Hugh T, 15, 17, 20, 22, 23, 25, 26, 608
Farley, Robert, 20, 24
Farley, Thomas, 354
Farman, Gayle, 423
Farmer, Robin, 65
Farnetti, Joseph, 59
Faron, Barbara, 231
Farquhar, Kelly A., 332
Farr, Sam, 73
Farrell Jr, John P, 330
Farrell, Bill, 529
Farrell, Dennis M, 238, 268
Farrell, Dennis, 445
Farrell, Diana, 133
Farrell, Edward C, 378
Farrell, James R, 337
Farrell, Jerry, 298
Farrell, Jr, Herman D, 27, 30, 41, 42, 165, 237, 265, 624
Farrell, Jr., Herman D., 482
Farrell, Kathleen, 576
Farrell, Leah, 395
Farrell, Michael J, 357
Farrell, Nancy, 514
Farrell, Patrick, 341
Farrell, Susan M., 430
Farrell, Tim, 229
Farrell, Timothy, 574
Farrell, William, 516
Farrelman, Joshua, 471
Farrugia, David J, 332
Fasano, Anthony, 94
Fasano, Phil, 80
Fascitelli, Michael, 473
Faso, John, 439
Fasser, Deborah, 402
Fatato, Joel, 427
Fatta, Angelo, 543
Fattoruso, Sharon, 504
Faughnan, Eugene D., 47
Fauss, Rachel, 404
Faux, Meghan, 434
Favilla, Michael, 19
Favre, Lois, 591
Favreau, William, 327
Favro, David N, 327
Fawcett Jr., Roscoe K., 375
Fay, Penny, 519
Fazio, Alfred, 448
Fazio, Marcia, 229
Fazzary, Joseph G, 336
Fazzary, Joseph, 135
Feagles, Jeffrey, 367
Feane, Mark, 508
Feasel, Justin, 331
Featherstone, Wendy, 109
Featherstonhaugh, James, 414, 417
Febraio, Kathy, 186
Fecko, Christine M, 98, 210
Feder, Harry, 428
Feder, Kai, 478
Federman, John, 425
Federoff, George, 15
Fedorchak, James M, 328
Fedorko, Michael A, 105, 288
Feeney, Brian, 276
Feeney, Michael, 230
Feger, Robert, 593
Fehrenbach, William, 443
Feinberg, Wayne, 248
Feiner, Paul J, 347
Feingold, Russell D, 315, 316
Feinman, Carol, 49
Feinman, Paul G., 45, 49
Feinman, Thomas, 47
Feinstein, Dianne, 143, 169, 312, 316
Feirsen, Robert, 580
Feld, Dennis, 209
Feld, Peter, 528
Felder, Simcha, 17, 20, 21, 23, 24, 25, 26, 87, 237, 494, 609
Feldman, Barbara, 443
Feldman, Cheryl, 434
Feldman, D.M.D., Mark J., 184
Feldman, Eli, 444
Feldman, Helene, 463
Feldman, Ira, 174
Feldman, Jessica, 386
Feldman, Nancy, 474
Feldstein, S Peter, 54
Felice, Cheryl A., 495
Feliciano, Elba, 357
Feller, David S, 581
Fellows, Anne, 447
Fellows, Maureen, 468
Fellows, Sharon, 326
Felser, Jacqueline A., 367
Felt, Kevin, 337
Felter, Laurie, 173, 227, 250
Femia, Robert J., 181
Fennell, Timothy J, 214
Fenno, Nathan R, 292
Fenton, Jayne L, 515
Fenwick, Jason, 432
Fenwick, Lex, 527
Ferdinand, Joann, 50
Ferguson, Bruce W, 278
Ferguson, Dorothy H, 247
Ferguson, Kellie R., 493
Ferguson, Marcus, 391
Ferguson, Shannon, 471
Ferguson, Tony L., 153
Ferguson, Wayne V, 101, 287, 308
Fernandes, Paul, 391
Fernandez, David, 379
Fernandez, Hermes, 388
Fernandez, Jill, 463
Fernandez, Joanne, 411
Fernandez, Ricardo R, 551
Fernandez, Ricardo R., 397
Fernbach, Karen P., 222
Fernley, Kyle, 184
Feroleto, Paula L., 47, 210
Ferradino, Stephen A, 46
Ferraiole, Susan, 125
Ferraiuolo, Patrick W., 481
Ferrante, Mark, 357

Ferrara, Anthony J., 50
Ferrara, Michael, 360
Ferrara, Richard J, 97, 98, 150, 307
Ferrara, Robert J, 151
Ferrara, Stephen, 185
Ferrarese, Thomas F, 133
Ferraro, Loretta, 592
Ferraro, Rocco A, 96, 188
Ferraro, Samuel M, 512
Ferreira, James H., 48
Ferrell, Donna, 296
Ferrell, Tricia M., 61
Ferrer, Fernando, 443
Ferri, Nannette, 108
Ferster, Leah, 429
Fertel, Greg, 432
Fertitta, George, 275
Fertitta, Lorenzo, 478
Fesen, Michael, 450
Fesko, Julia, 174
Fettman, Robert M., 468
Fetyko, Lynnore, 247
Feuer, Marilyn, 483
Feuerstadt, Jan, 446
Fiacco, William T., 372
Fiala, Stephen J, 335
Fibig, Andreas, 92
Ficalora, Joseph R., 81, 192
Fiebelkorn, Eric, 507
Field, Bradley J, 98, 141, 151
Field, Wendy S, 591
Fields, Leroy, 109
Fields, Suzanne, 467
Fierro, Scott N, 327
Figlewski, Brett, 463
Figliola, Anthony, 410
Figliomeni, Dominick, 536
Figueroa, Elizabeth, 389
Figueroa, Hector J., 489
Filburn, Susan, 161
Filiault, Ann, 457
Filippelli, John, 154
Filjones, Denise, 51
Filler, Allan, 415
Filmer, Ronald, 516
Filner, Bob, 323
Filstrup, Chris, 467
Fina, Perry, 261
Finan, Joe, 276
Finch, Doug, 28, 375
Finch, Gary D, 30, 625
Finch, Gary, 28, 35, 36, 37, 40, 41
Finch, Pamela, 411
Finch, Paul, 573
Fine, Douglas, 100, 151
Fine, Liz, 7
Fine, Richard, 467
Finegan, Michael, 296
Finelli, William, 530
Finello, John J, 592
Fingar, Greg, 375
Finger, Bernard, 296
Fink, Bob, 399
Fink, Christopher, 443
Fink, Jill, 377
Fink, Shea, 352
Finke, Dan, 410
Finkel, Beth, 414
Finkel, Richard S, 360
Finkelberg, Jason, 533, 535
Finkelstein, Arthur J., 137
Finkelstein, Barbara D, 216
Finkelstein, Marc, 49
Finkelstein, Ruth, 377
Finkle, Florence L, 177
Finkle, Mark M, 97, 150
Fink-Sinovsky, Esther, 480
Finn, Josephine, 119
Finn, Jr., Edwin A., 538
Finnegan, Candace K, 202, 222
Finnegan, Jack, 351
Finnegan, Kevin, 435
Finnegan, Martin, 365
Finnegan, Rachel M, 53
Finnegan, Tim, 463
Fionte, Bernie, 533
Fiordaliso, Joseph, 451
Fiore, James, 467
Fiore, Mary Beth, 570
Fiore-Lehman, Marilyn, 349
Fiorella, Anthony J., 49
Fiorella, Joseph A, 62
Fiori, Anthony, 439
Fiorini, Gerald J, 332
Firestone, Deborah, 467
Firetog, Neil Jon, 50
Firkins, Kathryn J, 346
Fischer, David, 29
Fischer, Duane W, 517
Fischer, Greer, 572
Fischer, Rhonda E., 61
Fischman, Martin, 103, 164, 265
Fisenne, P.E., Robert R., 345
Fish, Andrew, 503
Fish, Diana, 378
Fish, Keith, 98, 151
Fish, MD, Douglas, 175
Fishberg, Gerard, 225, 238
Fisher Jr., Daniel, 415
Fisher, Arnold, 247
Fisher, Curtis, 157
Fisher, Donald A, 248
Fisher, Fern A, 48
Fisher, Fern A., 49, 209
Fisher, Fern, 46
Fisher, Frank R, 336
Fisher, Harrison, 121, 174, 228
Fisher, Joel, 446
Fisher, Kenneth R, 47
Fisher, Kenneth, 403
Fisher, Lisa M., 46
Fisher, Nancy, 33
Fisher, Neil, 27
Fisher, Pamela, 49
Fisher, Richard, 471
Fisher, Stephen, 451
Fisher, Sue Ann, 376
Fisher, Wendy, 531
Fisher, William, 467
Fishman, Gary, 112, 207
Fishman, Richard D, 86, 162
Fisler, Carol, 417
Fitch, H Taylor, 340
Fitzgerald, Brandan, 3, 78, 83
Fitzgerald, Daniel P., 50
Fitzgerald, Gary, 183
Fitzgerald, Meg, 21
Fitzgerald, Michael, 460
Fitzgerald, Molly, 47
FitzGerald, Peter D, 215
Fitzgerald, Rosalie, 55
Fitzgerald, Sean, 187
Fitzgerald, Sister Laureen A, 557
Fitzpatrick, Bill, 529
Fitzpatrick, Carolyn D, 330
Fitzpatrick, Diane L, 48
Fitzpatrick, John C, 562
Fitzpatrick, Joshua, 18
Fitzpatrick, Margaret M, 561
Fitzpatrick, Michael J, 30, 39, 189, 237, 246, 625
Fitzpatrick, Michael, 28, 40, 43
Fitzpatrick, Thomas M., 49
Fitzpatrick, William J, 333
Fitzsimmons, Christopher, 488
Fitzsimmons, Robert J, 327
Fitzsimmons, Robert, 347
Fitzsimons, John T, 580
Flack, Jeff, 156
Flagg, Harith, 256
Flaherty, Eileen, 490
Flahive, Robert E, 433
Flake, Jeff, 321
Flanagan, Colleen A, 62
Flanagan, James P, 61
Flanagan, John J, 15, 17, 25, 165, 609
Flanagan, Neil, 409
Flanigan, James, 512
Flanigan, Kevin B., 11, 241
Flannelly, Eileen M, 358
Flateau, John, 133
Flatley, David, 579
Flatley, Martin, 365
Fleet, John, 299
Fleischer, Mark, 176
Fleischman, Maralyne P, 187
Fleischut, Melissa Autilio, 93
Fleischut, Melissa, 462
Fleming, David, 414
Fleming, George, 451
Fleming, James P., 396
Fleming, John, 143
Fleming, Mary Pat, 115, 213

Fletcher, Bonnie, 437
Fleuranges, Paul, 100, 286, 307
Fliegel, Seymour, 126
Flint, Margaret M, 218
Flint, Margaret M., 118
Flint, Steve, 147
Flood, Ed, 32
Flood, Elizabeth G, 532
Flood, Kenneth J, 504
Flores, Crystal J., 489
Flores, John Rafael, 381
Flowers, Denise, 187
Flowers, Loftin, 470
Floyd, William, 419
Fluehr, Nicholas, 462
Flug, Jacqueline, 4, 83, 104, 263
Flug, Phyllis Orlikoff, 48
Flumignan, Jeffrey, 290
Flung, Arthur, 397
Flynn Jr, Charles L, 554
Flynn, Deanne, 362
Flynn, John J, 365
Flynn, Michael, 329
Flynn, Shaun, 451
Flynn, Susan, 400
Flynn, William, 524
Flynn, Winona B., 340
Foehser, II, Charles, 335
Foels, John E, 501
Fogarty, Andrew, 185, 423
Fogarty, John, 469
Fogel, Usher, 434
Foglia, Linda, 6, 108, 303
Folchetti, Gregory, 343
Folcomer, David, 432
Foley, David, 326
Foley, Elizabeth, 402
Folk, Cassie, 459
Folk, Tiffany, 135
Folkes, Donovan O., 487
Folmer, John, 375
Foltan, Robert S, 97, 150
Folts, James, 120
Fonda, Tim, 525
Fonda, Vernon, 108, 110
Font, Jose, 154
Fontana, Richard A., 342
Fontanella, Patricia, 127
Fontas, George, 392
Foo, Steven, 352
Foote, Howard, 94
Foote, Monica, 565
Foote, Ned D, 300
Foran, Robert E, 286
Foran, Robert E., 98, 286
Foran, Robert, 462
Forand, Douglas, 465
Forbes, Cavol, 489
Forbes, Gordon, 455
Forbes, J Randy, 318
Ford, Carl F, 284
Ford, Daniel L, 344
Ford, Henry, 372
Ford, Michael J, 585
Ford, Phyllis, 190
Ford, William G, 47
Forde, Judith, 118
Ford-Johnston, Cynthia, 574
Forero, Jaime, 190
Forezzi Sr, Robert, 341
Forinca, Dorothy, 445
Forkas, Lisa, 37
Forman, Howard, 474
Forman, Peter M., 52
Formosa, John, 289
Forrai, Les, 510
Forrest, Linda A, 131
Forrest, Steven W, 62
Forrest, Todd, 389
Forrest, Wayne, 501
Forrestel, II, E Peter, 80
Forsgren, Peter, 384
Forshay, Dave, 502
Forst, Nicholas, 35, 38, 40
Forst, Robin, 95, 272, 306
Forster, Nick J., 373
Fort, Claude, 492
Forte, Michael, 357
Fortenberry, Jeff, 317
Fortino, Jessica, 91
Fosbrook, Leonard, 518
Foster, David L, 63
Foster, Freida, 202, 222, 550
Foster, Helen Diane, 9, 194
Foster, Mary F, 362
Foster, Tara, 434
Foulkes, Thomas, 411
Fountaine, Eduardo, 223
Fowler, Craig, 384
Fowler, Frank L, 365
Fox Jr., Hugh, 372
Fox, Charles, 386
Fox, Deborah, 594
Fox, James, 451
Fox, Michael J., 366
Fox, Michael, 464
Fox, William L, 561
Fox-Alter, Mary, 599
Foxx, Bryan, 486
Foy, Veronica J, 296
Foye, Patrick, 105, 287
Frado, Rosemary, 452
Frail, Scott, 474
Fraley, Frank T, 511
Fraley-Corrado, Rebecca, 100, 123
Fralick, Terry N, 577
Frame, James R, 589
Franchini, Annette, 120
Franchini, Deborah, 10, 229
Francis, Brennan, 450
Francis, Paul, 3, 173, 227, 250
Francisco, Holly, 35
Franck, John, 364
Franco, Barbara, 516
Franco, James V., 531
Franco, Melissa, 9, 194
Francois, Shaun D., 127
Franczyk, T P, 53
Franey, Bart, 448
Franger, Katie, 378
Frank, Barney, 319
Frank, David, 121
Frank, Eileen A, 200, 219
Frank, Kenneth, 342
Frank, Kristin, 37, 39, 40
Frank, Larry, 109
Frank, Linda, 326
Frank, Peter, 495
Frank, Robin, 423
Frank, Teresa, 235, 246, 264
Frankel, David M, 354
Franklin, Andrew, 418
Franklin, Carol A, 131
Franklin, Kevin, 344
Franklin, Robert, 331
Franko, Eileen, 9, 177, 220, 253
Franks, Trent, 320
Franzese, Nicole, 505
Fraser, Bruce, 573
Fraser, Charles, 356, 358
Fraser, David W, 350
Fraser, Lori, 177, 200
Fraser, Michael, 28, 306
Fraser, Ronald, 82
Fratello, Jennifer, 472
Frateschi, Timothy A., 364
Fraunfelder, Grant, 445
Frazee, Evelyn, 47
Frazer, Jr, Leroy, 217, 243
Frazier, Diane E, 387
Fredericks, Albert, 433
Fredericks, K L, 89
Frederique, Kassandra, 408
Frediani, Jeffrey, 402
Fredman, Rachel, 429
Fredrich, Dolores, 426
Free, Scott, 534
Freebern, Joseph, 229
Freed, Kathryn E., 46, 49
Freedman, Brenda, 53
Freedman, Spencer, 112, 161, 305
Freehill, Robert H, 47
Freehill, Robert H., 56
Freeman, Debra, 212
Freeman, Jennifer, 12, 162, 236, 305
Freeman, Linda, 432
Freeman, Lynn, 506
Freeman, Robert J, 163, 236
Freeman, Spencer, 9
Freeman, Timothy, 94
Freeman, William, 396
Freemantle, Lester, 186
Freese, Jeffrey, 432

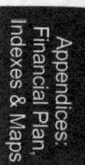

Appendices: Financial Plan, Indexes & Maps

Freeston, Kenneth, 598
Freimark, Norman, 598
Frelinhuysen, Rodney P, 317
French, Douglas E, 133
French, Elizabeth, 430
French, Richard, 7, 538
Frentzel, Pattie, 346
Fresher, Allison, 384
Fresina, Samuel, 442
Freund, Jack, 460
Freundlich, Alex, 458
Freundlich, David, 59
Frey, Thomas, 248, 268
Fried, Gloria, 361
Fried, Linda, 182, 198
Friedfel, David, 325
Friedland, Edward, 212
Friedlander, Ezra, 416
Friedlander, Mark, 48
Friedman, Adam, 193
Friedman, Bruce I., 488
Friedman, Carol, 447
Friedman, Daniel A, 297
Friedman, David, 45
Friedman, Don, 410
Friedman, Eitan, 552
Friedman, Eric, 352
Friedman, Gary, 72, 166, 167
Friedman, Jack M., 485
Friedman, Jack, 459
Friedman, Jason, 588
Friedman, Lawrence, 329
Friedman, Lucy N., 126
Friedman, Lucy, 378
Friedman, Marcy S., 46, 49
Friedman, Michael B., 443
Friedman, Neil, 524
Friedman, Stephen J, 559
Friedman, Stephen, 453
Friedman, Will, 139, 171
Friedrich, Gary, 456
Friend, Christopher S, 625
Friend, Christopher, 30, 35, 36, 37, 39, 40, 189, 237
Friend, David M., 538
Frier, Irma, 402
Friesen, Julie, 354
Friia, JoAnn, 66
Frisch, Richard, 416
Frisicano, Joan, 593
Friske, William, 231
Frisone, Frank, 519
Fritz, William, 397
Froehlich, Daniel, 428
Froehlich, Richard, 100, 189
Fromberg, Allan J, 358
Fromer, Kevin, 426, 487
Frommer, Ross, 470
Fronczak, Jennifer, 134
Fronk, Laura, 135
Frost, Jack, 170, 182
Frost, Jerome K, 335
Frost, Laura, 173
Frost-Amusa, Teneka, 163
Fruci, William, 135
Frungillo, John, 526
Fry P.E., L.S., Shawn, 327
Frye, Luke L., 494
Frye, Mary B, 234, 240
Frys, Mary Kay, 568
Fuchs, Barbara, 587
Fucilli, Michael J, 98, 286
Fudoli, Dino J, 349, 510
Fuentes, Rachel, 30
Fuhrman Jr, Edward R, 597
Fuhrman, Dr Susan H, 561
Fuhrman, Susan H., 129
Fuller, Paul, 188
Fullington, Kevin, 424
Fulton, Christine, 366
Fung, Margaret, 197, 214, 259
Funke, Rich, 17, 20, 21, 22, 23, 275, 609
Furco, Sam, 536
Furfure, Marianne, 59
Furillo, Jill, 185
Furlong, Bob, 537
Furman, James H., 153
Furnare, Laurie, 55
Furnish, Mark, 176
Furniss, Robert E, 388
Furno, Frank J, 333
Fusco Jr, Joseph R, 363
Fusco, Christine, 349
Fusco, John A., 48
Fusco, Lynn Marie, 573
Fusco, Vince, 408
Futter, Ellen V, 277
Futter, Ellen V., 155
Futter, Ellen, 466
Fyvie, Noreen, 252
Gabay, Donald D, 204
Gable, Walter, 336
Gabler, Laura, 51
Gabler, William J, 64, 65
Gabor, William G, 331
Gabriel, Patrick, 571
Gabriel, Tara, 173, 227, 250
Gaddy, Edward J., 372
Gaddy, Robert, 412
Gaebler, Melissa L, 132
Gaetano, Edward, 85, 123
Gaffney, Edward J., 66
Gaffney, Mike, 27
Gagan, Kevin T, 12, 103, 113, 137, 164, 308
Gage, Nick, 474
Gagliano, James L., 429
Gahan, Christina, 423
Gais, Thomas L, 260
Gais, Thomas L., 127, 171
Gais, Thomas, 543
Gaiss, Ralph, 94
Gala, Kanti, 409
Gala, Neil, 409
Galante, Thomas W, 356
Galarza, Maria, 381
Galasso, John M., 55
Galasso, John Michael, 47
Galef, Sandra R, 30, 37, 39, 41, 246, 265, 625
Galef, Sandra R., 38
Galeon, Lydia, 444
Gall, Erin P., 46
Gallagher III, Gerard A., 156
Gallagher, Bridget, 429
Gallagher, Dr John, 327
Gallagher, Ed, 404
Gallagher, Emily E., 492
Gallagher, James, 429
Gallagher, Jennifer, 351
Gallagher, John W, 574
Gallagher, John, 55, 244
Gallagher, Kathleen M, 385
Gallagher, Mark, 415
Gallagher, Michael D, 278
Gallagher, Sean, 466
Gallagher, Thomas, 579
Gallaher, Patricia, 55
Gallay, Paul, 158
Gallegly, Elton, 320
Gallent, Judith, 390
Galley, Cindy, 508
Gallino, Anthony J, 101, 236
Gallivan, Patrick M, 15, 114, 609
Gallivan, Patrick M., 17, 21
Gallivan, Patrick, 20, 21, 22, 23, 24, 25, 195
Gallmann, Paul W, 325
Gallo, Carmine, 289
Gallo, Diane, 444
Gallo, Elena, 474
Gallo, Evan, 29
Gallo, Martha J, 95, 272
Gallo, Shayne R, 349
Gallo, Stacey, 63
Gallo-Kotcher, Sharon, 99, 285
Galloway, Andrew, 448
Galloway, Sheldon, 537
Galt, Wayne, 526
Galterio, Robert J., 461
Galvez, Kathleen, 397
Galvin, Kimberly, 7, 130
Galvin, Nanette, 54
Gamberg, David A, 594
Gamboli, Michael J, 347
Gambrill, Kaitlin, 543
Gammerman, Ira, 46
Gammon, Larry, 409
Gandhi, Kirti, 291
Gangel-Jacob, Phyllis, 46
Gangsei, Paul, 439
Ganley, Robert, 451, 494
Gannon, Dennis, 488
Gannon, John C, 65

Gannon, Karen S, 132
Gannon, Maureen, 168
Gans, Jason, 385
Gans, Richard, 99, 286
Gantt, David F, 30, 37, 40, 41, 42, 237, 288, 625
Garafola, Robert L, 357
Garascia, Jeff, 464
Garavelli, Nancy, 53
Garba, Joseph N., 356
Garbarino, Andrew R, 30, 625
Garbarino, Andrew, 36, 38, 39, 41, 265, 275
Garber, Don, 438
Garceau, Annemarie, 161
Garceau, Kelly, 184
Garcia, Ana, 377
Garcia, Carlos, 396
Garcia, CDR Vince D., 295
Garcia, Eric, 146
Garcia, Karla, 381
Garcia, Kathryn, 354
Garcia, Marisa, 66
Garcia, Michael J, 45
Garcia, Norma, 402
Garcia, Roberto, 445
Gardell, Jr., John P., 430
Gardella, Ronald G., 213
Gardella, Sheila, 104, 124, 242
Gardiner, David, 202, 221
Gardiner, Warren, 357
Gardner, Charles, 368
Gardner, Colleen, 9, 200, 219
Gardner, Jeffrey P., 482
Gardner, Kathy Sinnott, 334
Gardner, Kevin, 334
Gardner, Lisa R, 62
Gardner, Michael S., 430
Gardner, Ronald D, 73
Gardner, Stephen, 448
Gargano, Donna, 413
Garguilo, Jerry, 47
Garibaldi, Mike, 432
Garipoli, Rosemarie, 435
Garlick Lorenzetti, Cindy, 336
Garmise, Stuart, 495
Garnett, William E., 50
Garofano, Todd, 275
Garretson, Sara, 85, 123
Garrett, Kent, 537
Garrett, Renee, 597
Garrett, Scott, 203, 319
Garrett, Thomas O, 366
Garrison, Judith A., 328
Garrison, Judith, 131
Garrison, Kathy, 398
Garry, Elizabeth A., 45
Garry, Thomas, 465
Garson, Robin S., 49
Gartenman, Eric, 361
Garus, Sr Marcella Marie, 562
Garvey, John E., 333
Garvey, Margaret, 47
Garza, Stephen, 492
Gaspard, Patrick, 377
Gasparini, Paul, 464
Gast, George W., 105, 287
Gast, Tracy, 114
Gasteyer, Catherine, 472
Gates, Gregory A., 47
Gates, Moses, 381
Gatling, Patricia L, 355
Gattine, Steve, 526
Gatto, Anthony, 383
Gatto, Tom, 40
Gaudette, James G, 571
Gaul, John, 286
Gault, Bert, 531
Gauthier, Paul, 283
Gauthier, Robert, 341
Gaven, Patricia, 294
Gavin Jr., Robert A., 212
Gavin, Christina, 161
Gavin, Darrell L., 48
Gay, Janice W., 182
Gaylor, Roseanne, 229
Gaylord, Laura, 462
Gaynes, Elizabeth A., 118
Gaynor, Michael G, 208
Gazzillo, Ralph T, 59
Gearan, Mark D, 556
Geary, Pat, 228
Geary, Patricia J., 252
Gebreselassie, Tsedeye, 448
Gecsedi, Renee, 451
Geddis, Carol, 126
Geduldig, Karen, 12, 141, 305
Gee, Andrew, 526
Gee, Kay, 180, 223
Gee, Stanley, 283
Geer, Nancy P., 192
Gehrer, Teresa, 103, 124
Geiger, Bruce W, 417
Geisinger, Ethel Z, 238
Geist, David, 416
Geist, Gerry, 383
Gelfand, Maya, 382
Gell, Richard, 451
Gellineau, Sidney, 286
Gellineau, Signey, 100
Gelman, Audrey, 359
Gemerek, Sean, 423
Gempesaw, Conrado, 561
Gendell, Stephanie, 397
Generoso, James, 64
Genier, Barbara, 348
Genna, Vito, 212
Gennario, Charles, 363
Gent, Geena, 380
Gentile, Debra B., 430
Genwright, Marsha, 462
George Jr., Raglan, 482
George, Dan, 474
George, Daniel A, 570
George, David T, 554
George, Thomas, 105, 287
George, Viji D, 554
Georgia, Diana P., 440
Georgia, Diana, 410, 476
Georgiana, Anthony, 71
Gerace, James J., 496
Gerace, Joseph A, 326
Geraci, Jr., Frank P., 212
Geraghty, Kevin B., 338
Gerald, Lenora, 50
Gerardi, Tina, 451
Gerber, Tomi, 411
Gerbing, Kathleen, 110
Gerentine, Richard A., 101, 287
Gerhardt, Joan, 386
Germain, Robert M, 344
German, Anthony P., 10, 293
German, Major Gen Anthony P, 10, 293
German, Scott D, 329
Germinaro, Frank, 347
Gerold, Roberta, 593
Gerrity, Daniel, 463
Gerrity, Sam, 438
Gerstein, Michael, 49
Gerstenlauer, Allan, 593
Gerstl, Carol, 409
Gerstle, Donna, 397
Gerstman, Bradley, 420
Gerstman, Sharon Stern, 217
Gerstner, James, 367
Gersztoff, Stephen, 306
Gerwitz, Colleen, 141
Gerwitz, Richard, 396
Gerych, Betty, 59
Geskie, Pamela, 524
Gesmer, Ellen Frances, 49
Gesmer, Ellen, 45, 46
Gesten, MD, FACP, Foster, 175
Getlin, Josh, 359
Geto, Ethan, 170, 418
Getty Jr, Charles, 330
Gewanter, Barrie, 454
Ghartey Ogundimu, Lisa, 251
Ghenoiu, Lisa, 63
Giacchetta, Timothy, 116
Giacomo, William J, 47
Giamartino, Jr, Ray, 578
Giambra, Joel, 453
Giammalvo, Gregory J, 361
Gianaris, Michael N, 17
Gianaris, Michael N., 485
Gianaris, Michael, 16, 23, 25, 165, 610
Gianelli, Sharon, 47
Giannoulis, Harry, 454
Gibbon, Robert, 24, 25
Gibbons, Peter, 451
Gibbs, Bob, 155
Gibbs, Doon, 142, 389
Gibbs, Kenneth, 409

Giblin, Vincent, 455
Gibney, Brian, 284
Gibson, Chris, 90, 297, 311, 646
Gibson, Don, 427
Gibson, Marin, 465
Gibson, Peter, 430
Gibson, Robert W., 430
Gibson, Vanessa L., 486
Giddens, Maurien, 49
Gidlund, Leonora, 358
Gielisse, Victor A.L., 278
Gierlinger, Loren, 30
Gifford, Gladys, 434
Gifford, Neil, 449
Gifford, Patricia G, 76
Giffords, Gabrielle, 322
Gigante, Robert J., 57
Gigliello, Teresa, 100, 189
Giglio, Joe, 30, 36, 114, 195
Giglio, Joseph M, 626
Giglio, Joseph, 28, 35, 36, 37
Giglio, Jospeh, 38
Giglio, Kami, 466
Gigliotti, Anthony J, 208
Gigliotti, Louis P., 56
Gilbane, III, William, 418
Gilberg, Neil, 202, 221
Gilbert, Hugh A, 46
Gilbert, Joseph M., 337
Gilbert, Michael, 277
Gilbert, Patricia, 467
Gilbert, Paula, 192
Gilbride, Mickey, 383
Giles, Bennie F, 351
Giliberto, James, 15, 306
Giliotti, Richard, 468
Gilkey, Jamie, 31
Gill Jr, Gerald, 349
Gill, Bradley, 144
Gill, Kathleen, 351
Gillespie, William, 410
Gilliam, Frederick C, 96, 285
Gillian, David C., 104, 124, 242
Gillibrand, Kirsten E, 311, 644
Gillibrand, Kirsten, 155, 290
Gillibrand, Kisrten, 314
Gilligan, Kevin, 361
Gilligo, Alaina, 359
Gillingham, Wes, 452
Gillis, Carol, 76
Gillis, Conor, 24, 25
Gillson, James, 443
Gilman, Paul, 403
Gilmartin, Maryanne, 416
Gilmartin, Thomas, 429
Gilmore, James, 95, 150
Gilmore, Keith, 229
Gilpatric, James, 46
Gilson, Shannon, 142
Gilstrap, John, 7, 84, 97, 188
Giltner, Phil, 69
Giminaro, Joseph B., 468
Ginalski, Michael, 591
Gines, Col. Eluyn, 295
Ginn, Kathleen, 454
Ginnetti, James, 410
Ginsberg, Dr. Joshua R., 156
Ginsberg, Lev, 391
Ginsberg, Mara, 425
Giorgianni, Joseph J, 246
Giorgianni, Michelle, 525
Girardi, Joseph, 61
Giraud, Marie E, 354
Giris, Janet, 406
Girourard, Diane, 37
Giroux, Joseph W, 327
Giruzzi, F Christopher, 66
Gische, Judith J., 45
Giske, Emily, 388
Gissin, Gene, 503
Gitlen, Philip, 475
Gittrich, Gregory, 538
Giuda, Alita, 474
Giuliani, Catherine, 461
Giulietti, Joseph, 99, 286
Givens, Debra L, 62
Givner, Jennifer, 5, 104, 119, 251, 274, 287, 309
Gjonaj, Mark, 30, 35, 40, 41, 42, 489, 626
Glanowski, Teresa, 427
Glaser, Mark F, 106, 165, 211
Glaser, Mark F., 486
Glaser, Mark, 421
Glassberg, Fred, 289
Glassman, Linda L, 13
Glassman, Phyllis, 598
Glasso, Louise, 363
Glatz, Jeffrey M, 332
Glave, Judith, 99, 285, 307
Gleason, Kevin, 148, 174
Gleim, Patrice M, 63
Glick, Deborah J, 30, 38, 39, 41, 42, 124, 626
Glick, Deborah, 39
Glickman, Leo, 485
Glied, Sherry, 170
Glinka, Stan, 508
Gliss, Robert, 290
Gloak, Geoffrey, 13, 86, 265, 305
Glock, Shelly, 176
Glotzbach, Philip A, 560
Glover, David J, 590
Glover, Michael A, 600
Glownia, Joseph R, 47
Gmach, David, 401
Gnacik, Carole, 141
Gober, Hershel, 299
Godambe, Meghana, 464
Godek, Patricia, 593
Godfrey, Peter, 346
Godshall, Clark J, 601
Goehler, Edward, 327
Goertz, Keith, 148
Goetz, William, 452
Goff, Andrew C., 432
Goff, MD, Donald C., 229
Gofman, Elina, 489
Goggi, Peter, 77
Gohmert, Louie, 321
Goidel, Dee Dee, 414
Goitein, Eliza, 389
Gold, Jeffrey, 423
Gold, Josh, 426
Gold, Marlene A, 353
Gold, Steve, 34
Goldberg, Alison, 392
Goldberg, Arlene D., 50
Goldberg, Beth, 88
Goldberg, Edward Jay, 92
Goldberg, Howard, 531
Goldberg, Joel M., 50
Goldberg, Sandra, 328
Golden, Brian, 528
Golden, Jay, 190
Golden, Martin J, 15, 20, 21, 23, 24, 26, 165, 242, 610
Golden, Martin J., 17
Golden, Martin, 20, 21
Golden, Megan, 472
Golden, Susan, 472
Goldfarb, Michael, 231
Goldfeder, Philip, 37, 38, 39, 41
Goldfeder, Phillip, 30, 35, 626
Goldhaber, Mark, 136
Goldhill, Nancy, 434
Goldmacher, Roslyn D, 510
Goldman, Douglas, 38, 39, 40
Goldman, Fatima, 258
Goldman, Gerald A, 575
Goldman, Howard, 419
Goldman, Jason, 409
Goldman, Jasper, 446
Goldman, Lee, 470
Goldman, Shanna, 476
Goldman, William, 470
Goldmann, Eileen, 397
Goldrick, Mike, 539
Goldsborough, Judith, 450
Goldson, Neville, 175, 293
Goldstein, Arnold, 581
Goldstein, Arthur, 405, 481
Goldstein, Carla, 261
Goldstein, Eric, 448
Goldstein, Evan, 408
Goldstein, Glenn, 460
Goldstein, Ira, 358
Goldstein, Karen, 472
Goldstein, Katie, 192
Goldstein, Laura W., 167
Goldstein, Lewis H., 480
Goldstein, Matthew, 397
Goldstein, Ray, 467
Goldstein, Steven, 471

Goldstein, Wendy, 437
Goldstein, William, 99, 285
Goldstock, Ronald, 107, 222, 288
Goldstone, Stephanie, 488
Goldwasser, Peter, 469
Golia, James J, 48
Golladay, Dennis, 467
Golladay, Mamie Howard, 549
Golomb, David, 469
Golovner, David, 395
Golub, Jerel, 419
Golub, Joel, 354
Golub, Neil, 419
Golumb, Tal, 416
Golway, Terry, 528
Gomez, Todd, 384
Goncalves, Joseph, 204
Gonor, Brian, 428
Gonsalves, Maggi, 120
Gonyea, Paul, 109
Gonzales, Rayana, 119, 251
Gonzales, Silvia, 427
Gonzalez, Adrian, 19
Gonzalez, Cheryl, 49
Gonzalez, Dennis, 255
Gonzalez, Doris, 49
Gonzalez, Dr. Mark, 125
Gonzalez, Jose R., 80, 191
Gonzalez, Lizbeth, 49
Gonzalez, Luis A., 209
Gonzalez, Priscilla, 450
Gonzalez, Ralph, 233
Gonzalez, Yvonne, 48
Gonzalez-Sanchez, Arlene, 4, 173, 227, 250
Good, Tina, 543
Goodbee, Arndreia M, 31
Goodell, Andrew W. "Andy", 626
Goodell, Andrew, 30, 36, 39, 40, 41, 254
Goodlatte, Bob, 116, 214, 317
Goodman, Amy J, 598
Goodman, Andrew, 355
Goodman, Arthur, 462
Goodman, Ethan, 473
Goodman, Norman, 46, 55, 332
Goodrich, William, 99, 286
Goodsell, David, 61
Goodstein, Jeffrey A., 47
Goodwin, Dianna, 37
Goodwin, George, 588
Goodwin, Gwen, 479
Goodwin, Jeff, 410
Goodwin, Jeffrey, 204
Goodwin, Lisa, 361
Googas, Milissa, 465
Gooley, Donald, 576
Goonan, Michael, 471
Gorbman, Randy, 536
Gordon, Alfred, 448
Gordon, Anne M, 338
Gordon, Bart, 322
Gordon, Dr Marsha, 502, 519
Gordon, Geoffrey N, 581
Gordon, Karen E, 257
Gordon, Kathryn, 380
Gordon, Kenneth W., 342
Gordon, Louis, 384
Gordon, Marsha, 459
Gordon, Victoria M., 532
Goren, Lela, 413
Gorenstein, Judie, 434
Gorga, Jr, Peter L, 267
Gorham, Phyllis, 506
Gorich, MD, George, 175, 293
Gorka, Chris, 162, 236
Gorman, George, 271
Gorman, James, 81
Gorman, Robert, 531
Gormley, James, 523
Gorny, Wolfgang, 412
Gorrell, Jr., J. Warren, 144
Gorton, Matthew, 446
Gorton, William, 284
Gosdeck, Thomas J, 424
Gosin, Barry M., 491
Goss, Bill, 299
Gotbaum, Betsy, 332
Gotcsik, Frances, 453
Gotla, Ricardo, 434
Gotsch, Maria, 454
Gottfried, Richard N, 30, 39, 41, 178, 626
Gottlieb, Stephen S., 49
Gouer, Kevin, 276
Gould Jr., Lewis F., 482
Gould, David S, 326
Gould, Karen L, 551
Gould, Karen, 397
Gould, Ross, 412
Gourdine, Aysha J., 491
Governo, Tom, 266
Gowan, Aaron, 517
Goyal, Ambuj, 454
Gozzo, James J, 552
Graber, Dr. Nathan, 148, 174
Graber, Robert M, 328
Graber, Vincent, 425
Grabowski, Janice F, 134
Grace, Michael, 368
Grad, Patricia, 428
Gradess, Jonathan E, 217
Gradess, Jonathan E., 117
Gradess, Jonathan, 406
Grady, William V, 328
Graefe, Horst, 600
Graf, Al, 36, 37, 39, 40, 114, 211, 627
Graf, Alfred C, 30
Graham, Bernard J., 49
Graham, BG William H., 152
Graham, Chris, 442
Graham, Emma, 6
Graham, Harold, 108
Graham, James, 432
Graham, Jeffrey E, 367
Graham, Kenneth, 579
Graham, Lindsey O, 313, 315, 316
Graham, Lindsey, 169
Graham, Richard, 331
Graham, Scott, 437
Graham, Wanda, 8, 79, 103, 187, 189
Graham, Yvonne, 174
Graham-Hunt, Stacy, 101, 287, 308
Grainger, Katherine, 447
Grance, Sandra, 380
Grande, Mike, 364
Granet, Russell, 435
Granger, Kay, 317
Granger, Noel, 252
Grannis, Pete, 12, 149, 162, 236, 241
Grannum, Sandra J, 207
Grant Flynn, Patricia, 61
Grant, Allison, 466
Grant, Betty Jean, 328
Grantham, Deb, 156
Grassley, Chuck, 116, 169, 214, 314
Grasso, Dee, 509
Grasso, Jennifer, 38, 42
Grasso, Michael, 376
Grasso, Paul, 504
Grasso, Vito F., 184
Grattidge, Alan, 335
Gratton, Patrick M, 327
Graubard, Sidney S, 326
Graves, Leon, 404
Graves, Mary, 467
Graves, Sam, 224, 322
Gray, Cynthia, 468
Gray, Diane, 81
Gray, Karol, 467
Gray, Oliver, 407
Gray, Roger, 251
Gray, Stephen D., 471
Grays, Marguerite A, 48
Grayson, Alan, 143
Graziano, Ellen, 130
Graziano, Jr, John A, 393
Graziano, Michael, 109
Graziano, Peter J, 266
Graziano, RS, Leah, 179, 254
Greco, Anna Lisa, 405
Greco, Marguerite, 365
Greco, Michael, 116, 214
Greco, Rudolph E., 49
Greco, Rudolph, 48
Green, Alice P, 215
Green, Allyson, 281
Green, Darcy L., 440
Green, David C, 134
Green, Deborah, 351
Green, Desmond A., 49
Green, Dr. Alice P., 117
Green, Gene, 180
Green, George A, 351
Green, John, 379
Green, Kerri, 516

Green, Michael C, 6, 111, 206, 234
Green, Norman P, 131
Green, Norman, 373
Green, Patterson, 589
Green, Robert A., 208
Green, Roberta, 586
Green, Stanley, 49
Green, Thomas, 396
Greenbaum, David, 473
Greenberg, Elayne E, 215
Greenberg, Ellen R., 55
Greenberg, Ethan, 50
Greenberg, Henry M., 170
Greenberg, Henry, 102, 211, 308
Greenberg, Julie, 431
Greenberg, Richard, 364
Greenberg, Robert, 580
Greenberger, Sharon, 477
Greenblatt, Jonathan, 197
Greene, Aurelia, 325, 359
Greene, Carolyn, 354
Greene, Courtney Canfield, 134
Greene, Jeanique, 5, 83, 234, 240
Greene, Jr., Phillip, 566
Greene, Leonard M, 259
Greene, Mark, 451
Greene, Nathanael, 448
Greene, Norman L., 106, 164, 211
Greene, Shirley, 266
Greene, Virginia, 69
Greenleaf, Ronald K., 372
Greenspun, Jonathan, 443
Greenwald, Barbara, 452
Greenwald, J. Patrick, 392
Greenwood, Donald A, 46
Greer, Jacqueline, 347
Gregg, Judd, 312, 313
Gregor, Alex D, 365
Gregory, Andrew, 402
Gregory, DuWayne, 337
Gregory, William A, 590
Greilsheimer, James, 433
Grela, Joan, 19
Grella, Philip M, 48
Greller, Matthew, 451
Grems, Alison, 503
Grenci, Tod, 96, 273
Grenville, Steven, 575
Gresham, George K., 479
Gresham, George, 224, 377
Gretzinger, Gerard M, 595
Greve Milton, Karen, 212
Grevelding, Peter, 451
Grewatz, Vincent E., 153
Grey, Valerie, 423
Grgas, Nick, 479
Gribbon, Francis X, 354
Gribbon, Margaret, 57
Gribetz, Judah, 550
Gribetz, Sidney, 50
Grieco, Scott, 451
Grier, Bernell, 449
Grier, Mark, 458
Griffen, Sara, 8, 149, 271
Griffin, Don, 530
Griffin, James P., 50
Griffin, James W, 509
Griffin, John, 422
Griffin, Kerry, 439
Griffin, Love, 63
Griffin, Mary, 396
Griffin, Patrick, 110
Griffin, Peter, 464
Griffin, Steve, 520
Griffin, Thomas, 109
Griffin, William E., 486
Griffith, James R, 56
Griffith, James, 326
Griffith, Maxine, 470
Griffith, Michael F, 60
Griffith, Sharon M., 485
Griffith, Tom, 388
Griffo, Joseph A, 18, 21, 22, 23, 142, 610
Griffo, Joseph A., 22
Griffo, Joseph, 15, 22, 25
Grigg, George, 593
Griggs Pauly, Leah, 439
Grijalva, Raul M, 321
Grijalva, Raul M., 143, 276
Grijalva, Raul, 154
Grillo, Al, 401
Grillo, Lorraine, 100, 123
Grills, George, 84, 122
Grim, David, 89
Grima, Lydia, 48
Grimaldi, Christopher, 434, 438
Grimaldi, Rose, 134
Grimes, Kyle, 538
Grimm, Michael, 311
Grimm, Peter, 335
Grimm, Stephen L, 595
Grimmelmann, Erik, 93, 145
Grimmett, Gail, 406
Grip, Brian P., 479
Grip, Brian, 384
Grippo, Vincent, 357
Grisanti, Mark J., 47
Grisham, Michelle Lujan, 154
Grishman, Henry L, 580
Grobe, Sharon L, 29
Grobe, Sharon, 37
Groden, Shaun S, 329
Grodenchik, Barry, 334, 359, 454
Groenwegen, Nancy, 12, 149, 162, 236
Groff, Chad C, 591
Grogan, Lesley, 511
Grogan, Mary T., 54
Groll, Heather, 8, 161, 245, 271, 304
Gromack, Alexander J, 343
Groser, Fred, 527
Gross, Hank, 532
Gross, Leslie, 360
Gross, Marjorie, 4, 177, 200
Gross, Michael A., 50
Grossman, Beverly, 400
Grossman, Jennifer, 452
Grossman, Robert, 427
Grossman, Scott M., 430
Grossman, Victor, 47, 373
Grote, Gary D, 505
Grote, Mae Watson, 417
Groten, Margery, 463
Groth, Donald J, 96, 273, 306
Grothe, Wayne, 449
Grout, Douglas E, 95, 150
Grove, Brian, 396
Groveman, Alan B, 592
Groves, Connie, 35
Grow, David C, 513
Gruber, Ken, 432
Gruebel, Liana, 49
Gruen, Vanessa, 446
Gruninger, Sandi, 566
Gsell, Jay, 329
Gualtieri, Raymond D, 592
Guarasci, Richard, 562
Guard, Josephine, 63
Guariglia, Jim, 509
Guarinello, William R, 258
Guarino, Dan, 528
Guarino, Maragret, 384
Guarnaccia, Rita, 59
Guastaferro, Lynette, 129
Guastella, Maria R, 133
Gubbay, Josephe, 50
Guck, Brian, 536
Guensburg, Carol, 533
Guererri, Laurie, 296
Guerin, Doreen, 100, 273
Guerling, Mark, 384
Guernsey, Thomas F, 552
Guernsey, Thomas, 378
Guerra, III, Joseph M., 115, 213
Guerrero, Antoine, 453
Guerriero, Ray, 486
Guevara, Richard, 266
Gugenheim, Lisa, 466
Gugerty, David J, 133
Guglielmo, William K, 515
Guido, Phillip, 454
Guiffreda, Robert S, 600
Guiliano, Edward, 558
Guinare, Matthew, 161
Guiney, John, 71, 89, 152
Guiney, Susan, 598
Gulino, John, 373
Gulino, Mary, 243
Gulnick, Jr., Burt, 338
Gump, Dan, 69
Gumson, Robert, 121
Gunn Barrett, Leah, 449
Gunther, Aileen M, 30, 38, 39, 41, 627
Gunther, Aileen, 35, 40, 41, 195, 230

Gupta, Ashok, 448
Gupta, D K, 291
Gupta, Sumil, 397
Guptill, Dr Angela M, 587
Gurien, Alan, 447
Gurnett, Donna S., 126
Gurnett, Kate, 112
Gurney, Gardner, 10, 264
Gurtman, Steven, 457
Gushee, Gregory, 460
Gust, Christopher, 501
Gustafsson, Hanna, 416
Gutbtodt, Jean, 532
Guthrie, Brett, 318
Guthrie, Bronwyn, 454
Gutierrez, Luis V, 319
Gutierrez, Michael, 563
Gutman, Henry, 95, 295
Gutmann, Linda, 300
Gutzler, Barbara, 366
Guy, David H., 51
Guy, Renee, 549
Guzalimian, Ara, 556
Guzick, David, 471
Guzman, Raymond, 46
Guzman, Wilma, 48
Gwinner, Donald E., 372
Haab, Deborah A, 595
Haas, James, 107, 274, 310
Haas, Jeffrey, 487
Haas, Matthew, 283
Haas, Raizy, 413
Habbe, Stephen, 380
Haber, G Jeffrey, 237, 268
Haber, Selin, 289
Habicht, Gail, 467
Hackel, Arlene, 210
Hackeling, C Stephen, 61
Hackett, Edward J., 432
Hackett, Fran, 280
Hadley, Paul H, 331
Hadsell, Margaret, 366
Haelen, Esq., Joanne B., 46
Haelen, Robert M, 106, 124
Haelen, Robert, 543, 544
Haendiges, Deborah A, 47
Haff, Jeffrey, 530
Hafner, Jr, Walter W, 57
Hagan, Alexander, 495
Hagelin, Theodore, 455
Hagelmann III, Joseph G., 485
Hageman-Clark, Jill, 344
Hagemann, Harold, 271
Hagemann, III, Robert F, 330
Hagenbeck, LTG Franklin L, 566
Hagenbuch, Kathy, 591
Hage-Perez, Cheryl, 294
Haggerty, Bart, 133
Haggett, William, 109
Haggler, Shlomo S., 49
Hagler, Shlomo S., 46
Hagy, Paul, 479
Hahn, Arlene H., 49
Hahn, Christopher, 391
Hahn, Kara, 337
Haight, Bob, 504
Haight, David, 73, 155, 380
Haight, Erik, 131
Haignere, Lois, 434
Haines, Jennifer, 341
Haines, Justin, 434
Hakanson, Elizabeth S., 119
Hakim, Veronique, 100, 286
Halada, Gary, 467
Halbritter, Ray, 166
Hale, Geoffrey, 410
Hale, Krenda, 130
Halevy, Richard, 368
Halftown, Clint, 166
Hall Jr, John S, 60
Hall Sr, Wayne J, 347
Hall, Babette M., 132
Hall, Courtenay W, 58
Hall, Cyndy, 373
Hall, Dr Matthew M, 84, 122
Hall, Frederick E, 577
Hall, Goeffrey T, 336
Hall, Jim, 272
Hall, John J, 322, 323
Hall, John, 323
Hall, L. Priscilla, 45
Hall, Myrna, 358
Hall, PhD, Donna, 228
Hall, Ralph M, 322
Hall, Sarah, 524
Hall, Steven, 396
Hall, Trevor, 75
Hall, Warren, 168
Hall, William R., 360
Hallacy, John, 443
Hallenbeck, Bruce, 161
Hallenbeck, Dan, 414
Hallenbeck, David, 109
Halliburton, Philip, 401
Halliday, Scott, 388
Hallman, Robert, 480
Hallock, Kevin, 126, 198
Hallock, Peter J, 576
Hallock, Renee, 251
Halloran, Jean, 73, 402
Halloway, Jean, 474
Halpert, Arlene, 423
Halpin, Patrick, 422
Halprin, Sheldon J., 49
Halsey, Benjamin A, 574
Halstead, John R, 545
Halstead, Kathleen L., 57
Halstrom-O'Bierne, Rebecca, 507
Halter, Cheryl, 25
Halton-Pope, Leah, 38
Halvorsen, Adam, 396
Hamell, Donna, 60
Hamill, Christine, 588
Hamilton, Andrew, 559
Hamilton, Edward J, 10, 84, 122
Hamilton, Glenn R, 587
Hamilton, James, 364
Hamilton, Jesse, 18, 20, 21, 22, 24, 25, 79, 196, 230, 610
Hamilton, Norma W, 76
Hamilton, Stephen, 12, 162, 236
Hamilton, Tracy M, 208
Hamilton, Victoria, 470
Hamilton, William, 413
Hamilton-Thompson, Tracy, 6, 270
Hamlin, Dave C., 375
Hamlin, Frank H, 80
Hamlin, George W, 80
Hamm, Carol, 210
Hammar, Claudia, 184
Hammer, David, 445
Hammill, Terrence, 106, 288
Hammond, Bill, 525
Hammond, Gail, 8, 161
Hammond, Gregory, 168
Hammond, Robert, 416
Han, Peter, 168
Hanauer, William R, 361
Hancox, Steve, 162, 236
Handrik, Jessica, 435
Handy, Edna Wells, 352
Hanes, Stephen, 423
Haney, Lori, 295
Hanify, Elizabeth, 391
Hanin, Laurie, 182
Hankin, Carole G, 581
Hankin, Joseph N, 549
Hankin, Noel N., 550
Hankins, Corbin, 474
Hanley, James F, 356
Hanley, Lawrence J., 479
Hanley, Mark, 530
Hanley, Mike, 410
Hanlon, Carla, 539
Hanlon, Christine, 398
Hanlon, Nadine P, 333
Hanlon, Pat, 280
Hanly, Eric, 384
Hann, Henry, 597
Hanna, Kevin, 384
Hanna, Richard L., 155, 190, 224, 290
Hanna, Richard, 90, 311, 646
Hannaford, Wendell, 170
Hannah, Craig D, 62
Hannan, Kirby T, 422
Hannigan, Anthony, 256
Hanno, Douglas P, 330
Hannon, Kemp, 15, 18, 23, 24, 25, 178, 610
Hanrahan, Anmari, 435
Hanrahan, Mary, 457
Hansbury, Brian, 66
Hansen, Joseph T., 496
Hansen, Jr, Stanley S, 121

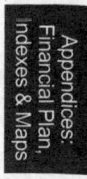

Hansen, Kelly, 400
Hansen, Kristen, 238
Hansen, Michael, 402
Hanson, Bea, 462
Hanson, Georgana, 413
Hanson, Jr., Robert E., 454
Hanson, Sharon, 469
Hanson, Steve, 4, 174, 251
Hanson, William A., 372
Hanuszczak, Michael, 56
Happ, Amy, 471
Harblin, Matthew, 384
Harckham, Peter, 339
Hard, Judith A, 48
Hardenbol, Carolien, 463
Harder, David E, 325
Hardiman, Ann M, 232
Hardiman, Ann, 383
Hardiman, Thomas O, 135
Hardin, Russell, 139
Hardin, Ursula, 282
Harding, Paul B, 103, 211
Harding, Robert, 421
Harding-Keefe, Claire, 392
Hardy, John, 414
Hardy, Kimberly D, 355
Hardy, Michael, 274
Hargrave, Pamela A, 335
Hargrove, Thomas, 533
Hariton, David P, 268
Harkavy, Stephen, 209
Harkin, Tom, 224, 255, 312
Harloff, Jeffrey R, 333
Harman, Jane, 320
Harmon, Byron, 538
Harnedy, Thomas, 153
Harner, Timothy, 471
Harper, Al, 580
Harper, Laura A., 485
Harper, Mary, 355
Harper, Shannell T., 496
Harrigan, Sheila, 260, 459
Harriman, Kimberly, 11, 140
Harrington, Dawn, 15
Harrington, Phyllis, 581
Harrington, William K., 214
Harrington, William S., 50
Harris Kluger, Judy, 209
Harris, Caroline, 419
Harris, Darlene D, 135
Harris, Darlene D., 61
Harris, David, 73, 167, 197
Harris, Gerald, 353
Harris, John, 390
Harris, Lisa, 21, 25
Harris, Merry, 342
Harris, Michael, 161
Harris, Pamela, 35, 36, 39, 40, 42, 627
Harris, Patricia E, 352
Harris, Sandra, 470
Harris, Stacy Ann, 392
Harris, Steven, 402, 422
Harris, Veronica, 502
Harris, William J., 488
Harris, William R, 297
Harrison Jr, David W, 327
Harrison, Caroline Diamond, 530
Harrison, Jessica, 537
Harrison, Richard, 105, 152
Harrison-Ross M.D., Phyllis, 101
Harrison-Ross, Phyllis, 101, 113
Harris-Shrachan, Vaunda L., 50
Hart Esq., Leon P., 487
Hart, Dr. John P., 120, 270
Hart, Duane A, 48
Hart, Jim, 119
Hart, Joseph K., 91
Hart, Julianne, 381
Hart, Laurie, 202, 221
Hart, Michelle, 451
Hart, Warren, 507
Harter, Kathy L, 131
Harting, Ronald, 451
Hartley, Rick, 474
Hartline, Jeffrey, 73
Hartman, James, 463
Hartman, Lewis H., 480
Hartman, Melanie, 62
Hartman, Paul, 396, 449
Hartmayer, C Douglas, 105, 287, 309
Hartner, Michael, 594
Hartnett, Steve, 235, 246, 264
Hartnett, Thomas, 444
Hartsfield, Yvette E., 367
Hartunian, Richard S., 115, 213
Hartz, James, 518
Hartzell, David, 504
Hartzell, Jr., David C., 343
Harvey, Christina, 207
Harvey, Rose, 11, 149, 271
Harvey, Veronique, 463
Harvey-Zales, Carrie, 464
Harwell, Stephen, 423
Hasan, Arshad, 481
Hasanoeddin, Evelyn, 50
Hasbrouck, Jr, Emerson C, 95, 150
Haseley, Laurence, 349
Hashem, Paul, 574
Haslett Rudiano, Diane, 133
Hass, Steven, 458
Hassberg, Linda, 410
Hassell-Thompson, Ruth, 16, 18, 21, 22, 23, 24, 25, 114, 195, 212, 610
Hassett, Col John J, 298
Hassett, Eva, 198
Hasso, David J, 149
Hasson, Arthur, 161
Hastings, Alcee L, 321
Hastings, Doc, 276, 321
Hastings, Terry, 420
Hasty, J Dozier, 524
Hatch, Orrin G, 314, 316
Hatch, Orrin G., 90, 203, 267
Hatfield, Jerome, 167, 180
Hatfield, Michael, 384
Hatthorn, Jeff, 532
Hatzmann, George, 469
Hauber, Bonnie, 568
Hauer, Jerome M, 102, 164, 237, 308
Hauryski, Colleen A, 135
Hauryski, Joseph J, 337
Hausler, Michael P., 51
Haven, Russ, 458
Haverly, Ferd, 231
Havey, Steven, 519
Havranek, Beatrice, 338
Havranek, Brian, 362, 513
Hawkins, David, 448
Hawkins, Dennis R, 215
Hawkins, Dennis, 423
Hawkins, Laura Jean, 408
Hawkins, Nancy, 374
Hawkins, William, 491
Hawks, Alice, 462
Hawley, Kay, 507
Hawley, Stephen, 28, 31, 35, 40, 42, 43, 295, 627
Hawley, Wayne G, 353
Hawras, George, 534
Hawthorne, David H, 62
Hawver, Chris, 449
Haxhia, Albana, 496
Hay, Cliff, 374
Hay, Clifford C, 135
Hay, J Douglas, 569
Hayden, James T, 52
Hayes, Anthony, 417
Hayes, Connie C, 340
Hayes, John, 409
Hayes, Kevin G, 339
Hayes, Michael, 350
Hayes, Robert, 182
Hayes, Roger S., 50
Hayes, Stephen, 394
Hayes, Timothy, 578
Hayford, Esq., Stephen, 441
Haynes, Carl E, 549
Haynes, Eileen, 98, 151
Haynie, J. Michael, 455
Hays, James, 215, 257
Hayssen, Robert W, 336
Hayter, Jonathan, 527
Haywood, David, 492
Hayworth, Nan, 311
Hazeldean, Susan, 471
Heacock, Ronald, 546
Healy, Joseph, 413
Healy, Maureen, 49
Healy, Mike, 375
Healy, Richard, 339
Heaphy, Jane, 127
Heard, Susan M, 334
Hearn, Rose Gill, 356

Hearst III, George R, 523
Heary, Cherl, 131, 375
Heastie, Carl E, 27, 31, 627
Heastie, Carl E., 483
Heastie, Carl, 41, 165
Heath, Dr David A, 544
Heath, Helena, 61
Heath, J. Lynn, 10, 228
Hebert, Clifton, 586
Hebert, Dennis, 510
Hebert, William, 112
Hecht, Gary, 582
Hecht, William J, 596
Heckathorne, James, 451
Hecken, Phil, 18
Hecker, Elissa D, 278
Heckman, Howard, 47
Hecox, Scott, 251
Hedge, James, 384
Hedge, Marissa, 473
Heegan, Barbara Ann, 513
Hefner, Dennis L, 546
Hefner, Dennis, 468
Hegarty, James, 442
Heggen, Mark, 344
Heggie, Dianne, 399
Heider, Steven H, 344
Heider, Travis, 380
Heigel, Frederick, 423
Heimann, Farris H, 339
Heimroth, Heath, 17
Hein, Michael P, 338
Heinichen, Deborah A., 488
Heinrich, William, 141
Heintz, Paul B., 54
Heitler, Sherry Klein, 46
Heitner, Carl, 201, 219
Held, Amy, 112, 177, 207
Held, Diane, 380
Held, Jacqueline, 83, 263
Helfenbein, Meredith, 495
Helfrich, Todd G, 91
Helgerson, Jason A, 8
Helgerson, Jason A., 175
Helis, RADM James A., 290
Helis, Rear Admiral James A., 125
Heller, Anne, 355
Heller, Danielle, 380
Heller, Dean, 203
Heller, Karen, 420
Heller, Michael, 477
Hellert, Gayle H, 571
Hellwig, Spencer P, 335
Helm, Angel, 474
Helmer, Maureen O., 425
Helmerson, Karen, 270
Hemowitz, Daniel, 459
Hemsworth, Robert, 96, 273
Henderson, Mark, 342
Henderson, Scott, 403
Henderson, Sue, 397
Henderson, Todd, 462
Henderson, William, 291
Hendrick, Richard, 95, 285, 306
Hendricks, Carly J, 131
Hendricks, Michael, 523
Hendricks-Atkins, Julie, 418
Hendrickson, Allan, 375
Hendry III, James M, 65
Hengsterman, Stacey, 467, 543
Henk, Dianne, 229, 304
Henley, Cara, 423
Henley, Nicholas, 423
Henn, Robert, 267
Henne, Sandra, 279
Hennessey, Mark, 176
Hennessey, Sean, 373
Hennessy, Peter, 247
Henning, Gary, 381
Henning, Marjorie, 357
Henrici, Michael, 134
Henry, Alexis, 397
Henry, Jennifer A., 61
Henry, Mark A., 484
Henry, Mark, 384
Henry, Patricia E., 50
Henry, Sean K., 485
Henry, Veronica, 549
Hensarling, Jeb, 79, 190, 203, 319
Henson, Kevin, 474
Herbeck, Richard F, 360
Herbst, Jeffrey, 554
Herbst, Marc, 436
Herchel, Dennis, 441
Herd, Gregory J, 101, 287
Herger, Wally, 323
Herlica, Debra, 290
Herlihy, Katherine, 475
Herlitz, Grant, 426
Herman, Bruce, 220, 253, 293
Herman, Christina, 60
Herman, Dale, 367
Herman, Frank, 113
Herman, J Brad, 595
Herman, Mitchell, 399
Herman, Vanessa, 467
Hermann, Luke, 474
Herms, April, 471
Hernandez, David J, 175, 293
Hernandez, Gilda, 202, 221
Hernandez, Ismaela, 345
Hernandez, Michael, 42
Hernick, Joanne I, 175, 293
Herrera, Jose R., 432
Herrick, John, 376
Herrick, Richard J., 185
Herrick, Richard, 423
Herrick, Stephen W, 50
Herring, John N, 476
Herrington, Kenneth H, 335
Herrion, John, 194
Herron, Kristen, 270
Hershenson, Jay, 397, 550
Hershey, Jill, 398
Herskowitz, Orin, 91
Hertlein, John, 569
Hertman, Robert, 366
Hertz, Michael, 451
Herzog, Betsy, 355
Herzog, Thomas, 110
Heslin, Martin, 401
Hess, John B., 144
Hess, Scott D, 334
Hester, Samuel D, 46
Hetherington, Bryan, 410
Heuber, Antoinette, 402
Heuer, Gary, 255
Heuer, Steven, 427
Hevesi, Andrew, 31, 38, 39, 40, 41, 254, 628
Heyman, Neil J., 185
Heyman, Neil, 418
Heyward, Leon W, 358
Hezir, Alexandra, 472
Hibbard, Jay, 407
Hibbard, Mary, 568
Hickey, Brian, 125
Hickey, Chris, 403
Hickey, Michael J., 91
Hickey-Martin, Monica, 177
Hickman Jr, John L, 344
Hicks, Geoffrey, 572
Hicks, Kipp, 510
Hicks, Lisa U, 217
Hicks, Nora, 524
Hickson Jr., Lenel, 71, 88
Hider, Kathleen, 296
Hiffa, Frederick T, 453
Higby, David, 449
Higgins, Brian M, 646
Higgins, Brian, 89, 168, 169, 197, 311, 323, 394
Higgins, Christopher, 22, 24
Higgins, Jennifer, 394
Higgins, John J, 247
Higgins, Marilyn, 455
Higgins, Mark D, 202, 221
Higgins, Sharon, 88, 196
Higgins, Shelley, 503
High, Raymond, 396
Hikind, Dov, 27, 31, 628
Hilado, Sony, 403
Hild, Amy M, 135
Hilderbrant, Chris, 395
Hildreth, Anne, 139, 171
Hilenski, Karen, 458
Hill, Catharine B, 562
Hill, Dorothy, 464
Hill, Edwin D., 487
Hill, Elizabeth A, 561
Hill, Elizabeth, 432
Hill, J. Tomlinson, 386
Hill, Jeffrey L, 74, 424

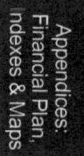

Hill, Peter, 474
Hill, Sally, 503
Hill, Sara, 543
Hill, Sidney, 166
Hille, Anne, 415
Hiller, Amanda, 13, 86, 265
Hiller, Edward, 200, 219
Hillman, Hilary, 131
Hillman, Linda, 514
Hilmey, Rose, 166
Hiltbrand, Robert, 271
Hilton, Beth A, 513
Hilton, Kenneth H, 594
Himes, Christine L, 261
Hinchey, Maurice D, 311, 317, 321, 324
Hinckley, Robert R, 393
Hinds, Jinella, 491
Hinds-Radix, Sylvia C., 45
Hine, Christian, 451
Hines Kramer, Amy, 384
Hines, Evan, 356
Hines, Kelly, 449
Hines, Mary, 8, 240
Hines, Victoria, 471
Hiney, Barbara, 444
Hinkemeyer, Arlene, 434
Hinkson, Susan M, 358
Hinojosa, Rub,n, 318
Hinrichs, C. Randall, 47
Hinrichs, C.ÆRandall, 210
Hirsch Riback, Melanie, 29
Hirsch, David, 470
Hirsch, Larry, 484
Hirsch, Michelle, 202, 221
Hirschstein, Cary, 426
Hirsh, John, 536
Historical Society, Lewis County, 331
Hitchcock, Kent, 445
Hite, Robert, 11, 241
Hitt, Dan, 246, 284
Ho, Wayne H, 257
Ho, Wayne, 382
Hoag, Bonnie, 156
Hoag, Gail, 513
Hoagland, Wayne, 451
Hoar, Thomas, 493
Hoare, Frank, 414
Hobbs, Gary C, 63
Hoberman, Brian, 358
Hobson, Mike, 450
Hobson, Tracy, 256
Hochbrueckner, George, 418
Hochman, Jere, 3, 119, 597
Hochreiter, Joseph E, 570
Hochul, Jr., William J., 115, 213
Hochul, Kathleen C, 3, 160, 605
Hockens, Nick, 421
Hodell, Raymond, 482
Hodes, Nancy L, 426
Hodges, Elizabeth, 379
Hodges, Mary C, 59
Hodgetts, Colleen, 463
Hodgkins, Christie, 392
Hodin-Baier, Ali, 352
Hodun, Susan, 593
Hoekstra, Peter, 324
Hofer, Andrew P, 80
Hoffa, James P., 482
Hoffer, Mark D, 354
Hoffman, Andrew K., 487
Hoffman, Diana, 71
Hoffman, Douglas E., 46, 50
Hoffman, Douglas, 50
Hoffman, James, 339, 579
Hoffman, Jennifer, 396
Hoffman, Jeremy, 409
Hoffman, Jerry S, 476
Hoffman, Linda, 259
Hoffman, Maria, 30
Hoffman, Peter, 35
Hoffman, Richard, 59
Hoffman, Robert W, 65
Hoffmeister, Mark, 458
Hoffnung, Ari, 353
Hogan, Carla, 421
Hogan, John J, 582
Hogan, John M., 487
Hogan, Joseph, 382
Hogan, Kate, 118
Hogan, Kathleen B, 338
Hogan, Shawn D., 374
Hogan, William F., 4, 173, 227, 250
Hoganbruen, Matt, 384
Hogarty, Lisa, 470
Hoglund, Robert, 401
Hohauser, William, 61
Hohlt, Barbara, 449
Hohlt, Jared, 533
Holahan, Paul, 363
Holbrook, Elizabeth, 56
Holcomb, Betty, 395
Holcomb, Grant, 471
Holcomb, Julie Conley, 348
Holden, Maria, 120
Holden, Ross J, 100, 123
Holden, Tim, 317
Holdener, Richard E, 345
Holder, Annika, 357
Holder, David, 275, 395
Holdorf, Armin, 200, 219
Holland, Karen, 379
Holland, Steve, 533
Hollar, Rick, 474
Hollenbaugh, Lindsey, 525
Hollenbeck, Lee A, 132
Holliday, Susan, 533
Holliday, Terrance, 358
Hollie, Ronald D, 48
Hollis, Adrienne L., 474
Hollis, Richard, 130
Hollister, William, 448
Hollmen, Linda, 110
Holloway, Cas, 352
Holloway, Lew, 309
Holly, Tim, 534
Hollyer, A Rene, 216
Holman, Evelyn B, 591
Holman, Kathryn, 393
Holman, Marcia, 233
Holman, Mark, 461
Holmes Norton, Eleanor, 323
Holmes, Angela, 342
Holmes, Steve, 199, 233
Holtby, Tammey, 73
Holtz, Mary F, 343
Holtzclaw, Derek, 251
Holtzer, Russell, 397
Holzer, Edith, 399
Hom, Vincent, 190
Homans, John, 533
Hong, Chung-Wha, 427
Honorof, Alan L, 48
Hood, Jr., Jay, 335
Hood, Kelley S, 133
Hooker, Patrick, 3, 69
Hooks, William J, 103, 164, 211, 309
Hooley, Richard M, 586
Hooper, Earlene, 27, 31, 37, 41, 42, 628
Hoose, Matthew J., 333
Hoose, Michael J, 590
Hooton, Angela, 447
Hoover, Barbara, 450
Hoover, Darby, 448
Hoover, Tom, 101, 163, 164, 273, 308
Hope, Judith, 482
Hopkins, John, 526, 527
Hopkins, Kathryn D, 55
Hopkins, Theodore L, 325
Horan, Allison, 30
Horan, Hon James F, 243
Horan, James, 176
Horan, Robert, 588
Horn, Glen, 537
Horn, Mary, 100, 189
Horner, Blair, 158, 171, 380, 458
Horodnicaenu, Michael, 292
Horodniceanu, Dr Michael, 99, 285
Horodyski, Michael, 518
Horohoe, William, 248
Horowitz, Evelyn, 353
Horowitz, Jay, 486
Horr, III, Robert G, 106, 288, 310
Horsman, Elizabeth, 115, 213
Horstmyer, Ryan V., 440
Horton, April, 472
Horton, Gary, 329
Horwitz, Daniel J, 103, 137, 164
Hotaling, Adam, 504
Hotaling, Mary, 467
Hotzler, Russell K, 552
Houghton, Kathy, 583
Houghton, Ted, 468
Hourihan, Maureen, 64

House, Cecil, 355
Houseknecht, Michael, 461
Houseman, Wayne F, 333
Houser, Donald, 407
Houston, Jarvis, 18
Houts, Jonah, 413
Howard, Barry, 519
Howard, Brian, 587
Howard, Gary W, 338
Howard, John D., 428
Howard, Lalena, 447
Howard, Laura, 130
Howard, Marilyn, 413
Howard, Matt, 104, 274, 287
Howard, Matthew, 27
Howard, Shevonn, 377
Howard, Stephen, 385
Howard, Timothy B, 328
Howard, Wayne, 325
Howard, William F., 543
Howard-Cooper, Ellen, 355
Howe, Barbara, 53
Howe, Bill, 283
Howe, Jim, 449
Howe, John F, 571
Howe, John, 327
Howe, Kevin R, 525
Howe, Robert C, 131
Howell, Mary, 327
Howey, Katrina, 433
Howlett, Jeff, 536
Hoye, Polly A, 33
Hoylman, Brad, 18, 20, 22, 23, 24, 25, 152, 165, 487, 611
Hoyos, Inez, 49
Hoyt, Sue, 466
Hoyt, William, 96, 285
Hrinkevich, Craig, 474
Hripcsak, George, 84, 122
Hsiang, William, 72
Huang, Albert, 448
Huang, Margaret, 197
Hubbard, Laurie, 52
Hubbard, Steven V, 571
Hubbard, Vanessa, 474
Huberman, Anne, 434
Hubert, James W, 60
Hubman, David, 583
Hudak, Patricia A, 332
Hudd, Steve, 474
Hudder, John, 27
Huddle, Peter, 474
Hudson, Donald, 114
Hudson, Dr Lee, 355
Hudson, Gerry D, 586
Hudson, James C, 59
Hudson, Michael E, 48
Huelgo, Vivian, 463
Huelle, James M, 10, 294
Huether, Gregory J, 208
Huff, Carol E., 46
Huff, Sharon, 573
Huffman, Jared, 143
Hughes Jr., Richard P., 487
Hughes, Caressa F., 494
Hughes, Catherine K, 327
Hughes, Charles, 210
Hughes, Everett, 359
Hughes, Gary, 336
Hughes, James, 383
Hughes, Mary, 514
Hughes, Richard, 570
Hughes, Robert C, 348
Hughes, Robert J., 443
Hughes, Scott, 382
Hull, Linda, 202, 221
Hulse, Lisa, 52
Hults, Clark, 574
Hume, Dr. Robert J., 170
Hume, III, John E N, 530
Hunderfund, Anna, 580
Hunderfund, James H, 581
Hunsinger, Pamela, 363
Hunt, Beth, 330
Hunt, E Charles, 462
Hunt, James J., 114
Hunt, John M., 50
Hunt, Joseph J., 487
Hunt, Matthew, 432
Hunt, Richard V, 54
Hunt, Stephen, 543
Hunter, Alexander W, 18
Hunter, Alexander, 46
Hunter, Caroline C., 137
Hunter, Danielle, 448
Hunter, Jon, 578
Hunter, Judith M, 337
Hunter, Judith, 373
Hunter, Pamela, 31, 42, 628
Huntley, Alan, 153
Huntley, Douglas W, 596
Huntley, James S., 488
Hurd, Raymond, 179
Hurlbert, Margret, 466
Hurley, Daniel, 468
Hurley, John J., 392
Hurley, Jr, Paul B, 562
Hurley, Mark, 381
Hurley, Paula, 595
Hurray, Carol, 344
Hurst, Steve, 377
Hurt, Michael, 108
Hussey, John F, 58
Hussman, MD, Donna, 175, 293
Husted, Stacey B, 336
Hutchins, Julie, 330
Hutchinson, Jamie, 214
Hutchison, Kay Bailey, 312, 313
Hutter, Dr. Adam, 153, 167
Hutton, Carol R, 361
Hutton, Carol R., 361
Hutton, MPH, Brad, 8, 175
Hutton, Todd S, 562
Hutzley, Brian, 543
Huus, William A., 530
Huxley, John J, 553
Hvisdak, Andrew, 163
Hwang, Jeffrey, 81
Hyde Jr., Trevor A., 484
Hyde, Steven G, 506
Hyland, Theresa, 524, 526
Hyman, Shari, 95, 272
Hyndman, Alicia, 31, 35, 37, 41, 42, 628
Hynes, Charles J, 330
Hynes, Ken, 299
Iachetta, Stephen A, 95, 285
Iacovetta, Nicholas, 50
Ianello, Stephen, 401
Iannacci, Angela G, 47
Iannarelli, Rocco, 101, 141
Iannicco, Cosmo, 448
Ianniello, Dr Tom, 510, 511
Iannuzzi, Richard, 243, 379
Ibrisimovic, Allen, 471
Idoni, Timothy C, 339
Ienuso, Joseph, 470
Iglesias, Ariel, 154
Iglinksi, Peter, 539
Ignaszak, Kevin, 451
Ihde, Erin, 422
Ike, Robert, 597
Iliou, John, 59
Ilomudio, Henrietta U., 484
Imbro, Joseph, 415
Imperati, Doris, 406
Indelicato, Charlene M, 106, 189, 274
Indelicato, Jr., Joseph J., 104, 124, 242
Infante, Rolando, 401
Information, , 161
Information, General, 15
Inga, Nick, 401
Ingargiola, Susan, 439
Ingerson, Marianne B., 134
Ingleman, Ann, 434
Inglis, Bob, 322
Ingraham-Roberts, Bridgett, 420
Ingram, John G, 48
Ingrassia, Louisa, 366
Inhofe, James M, 314
Inhofe, James M., 155, 297
Inlaw, Evan, 66
Inouye, Daniel K, 312
Inouye, Daniel, 312
Inserra, Michael, 351
Intschert, Cindy, 330
Inwald, Jacob, 434
Iorio, Chris, 537
Irani, Rian, 458
Ireland, Kim, 448
Ireland, Kimberly, 385
Irick, Darryl, 99
Irick, Daryl, 285
Irizarry, Dora L., 212

Irlando, Andres, 472
Irvin, Dale T, 559
Irving, Mark, 401
Irwin, Bradley, 76
Irwin, David, 414
Irwin, Julie, 294
Isaacs, Audrey J., 488
Isaacs, Daniel, 375
Isaacson, Linda, 468
Isaksen, Suzanne, 351
Isakson, Johnny, 137, 169, 314, 315, 316
Iselin, Harold, 421
Isenberg, Andrew B, 47
Isenberg-O'Loughlin, Jo, 531
Ishida, Dr. Maria, 69
Israel, Steve, 73, 142, 311, 317, 646
Issa, Darrell E, 321
Issa, Darrell E., 242
Itite, Patricia A., 194, 234, 240
Ivanhoe, Robert, 421
Ivanoff, Nick, 290
Iverson, Rachel, 174
Ives, Kirk, 18
Iwachiw, Walter, 487
Iwama, Kenichi, 397
Iwanowicz, Peter, 156
Izeman, Mark, 448
Izzo, Debbie, 502
Jack, Kevin, 220
Jackman Brown, Pam, 48
Jackman-Brown, Pam, 49
Jackson, Doretha L., 210
Jackson, Dr Debra, 585
Jackson, Jane, 450
Jackson, Kara, 449
Jackson, Lillie, 296
Jackson, Lisa, 537
Jackson, Melissa C., 50
Jackson, Ronald, 375
Jackson, Shirley Ann, 559
Jackson, Shirley, 460
Jackson, Terri, 389
Jackson, Wayne P, 27
Jackson-Chase, Courtenaye, 353
Jackstadt, Christian, 161
Jacob, Andrew, 105, 152
Jacob, Smriti, 533
Jacobie, John, 294
Jacobowitz, Gary, 494
Jacobs, Christopher L, 328
Jacobs, Dorine, 51
Jacobs, Jay S., 373
Jacobs, Qa'id, 395
Jacobs, Robert, 388
Jacobsen, Catherine, 6, 108, 110
Jacobsen, Kenneth, 516
Jacobsen, Michael, 472
Jacobsen, Patty, 136
Jacobsen, Tom, 536
Jacobson, Howard, 470
Jacobson, Jonathan G, 373
Jacobson, Laura Lee, 46
Jacobson, Michael, 218
Jacobson, Richard, 20, 21, 24
Jacobs-Roraback, Clarissa, 120
Jacome, Helen, 17
Jaeger, Lloyd, 572
Jaeger, Marjory, 341
Jaeger, Steven M, 55
Jaffe, Barbara, 46, 49
Jaffe, Mark S, 512
Jaffe, Mark, 507
Jaffe, Rachel, 426
Jaffee, Ellen, 31, 36, 37, 38, 39, 41, 165, 628
Jagenberg, Christian, 81
Jagow, Wayne F, 332
Jakway, Beverly A., 372
James, Debra A., 46, 49
James, Donald, 592
James, Douglas C., 355
James, Francine, 200
James, Guy, 325
James, Jr., Seymour W., 117, 199, 432
James, Nathaniel, 297
James, T. Mark, 413
Jamieson, Linda S, 47
Jamison, Jeffrey, 341
Jamison, Marilyn, 448
Janeski, Katherine, 358
Janeway, William C., 155
Jang, Michael, 443
Jankowski, Janet M., 326
Jankowski, Michael, 339
Jannsen, Joseph, 449
Janowitz, Norman, 47
Jansen, LTC Karl D., 152
Janusz, Mariam, 505
Jaquish, Donald, 329
Jardine, Anne S, 177, 207
Jarose, Thomas A, 7, 130
Jasewicz, Edmund C., 373
Jasinski, Ann, 121
Jaskier, Krista, 76
Jasmin, Noramie, 365
Jay"", Frank, 326
Jayaram, Lena, 397
Jaycox, M Indica, 336
Jayson, Larry, 191
Jazzo, Frank, 347
Jean, Alexandra, 458
Jean-Pierre, Kimberly, 31, 36, 37, 40, 41, 42, 629
Jee, June, 472
Jeffers, Beryl S., 543
Jeffers, Darrell E, 476
Jefferson, Gail, 82
Jefferson, Nicole, 384
Jeffords, H Susan, 243
Jeffrey, Dawn, 492
Jeffrey, Randal, 434
Jeffries, Hakeem S., 125, 196
Jeffries, Hakeem, 116, 214, 267, 486, 646
Jehn, Jennifer, 532
Jehring, Jan, 596
Jellinek, Igal, 403
Jenison, Tom, 376
Jenkins, Alison, 412
Jenkins, Connie, 527
Jenkins, Kenneth W, 339
Jenkins, Nathaniel, 36
Jennings, Dr Ralph, 534
Jennings, Gerald D, 341
Jennings, Gerald J, 476
Jennings, Jim, 281
Jennings, John, 423
Jensen Bergan, Jennifer, 58
Jensen, Beverly, 166
Jensen, Donald, 413
Jensen, Jennifer, 73
Jeppe, Ptahra, 34
Jerome, Stephen J, 565
Jesep, Paul, 11, 84, 122
Jeune, Jessica, 20
Jicha, Jean, 65
Jilnicki, John, 345
Jimenez, Catherine, 391
Jimenez, Dave, 396
Jimenez, Lorena, 396
Jimenez-Salta, Dawn M., 49
Jiminez, Angela, 11, 113
Jimino, Kathleen M, 335
Jody Olcott, Carol Calabrese, 505
Joel, Richard M, 563
Joerg, Claude A, 332
Johannesen, Jeremy, 127, 279
Johansen, Eric, 362
Johanson Berg, Liv, 434
Johanson, Kristen, 396
John, Dennis B, 326
John, Mike, 465
John, Sr, Maurice A, 166
Johndrow, Michael, 518
Johns, Dr Richard N, 584
Johns, F. Joe, 98, 151
Johns, Mark, 31, 35, 38, 39, 114, 178, 230, 253, 629
Johns, Ron, 531
Johnsen, Peter D., 430
Johnson II, Harold B, 526
Johnson, Adrienne, 33
Johnson, Audrey M, 362
Johnson, Casey, 62
Johnson, Celeste M, 176
Johnson, Chad, 78, 84, 207, 245, 263
Johnson, Christopher, 100, 286, 494
Johnson, Craig H, 360
Johnson, Debbie, 447
Johnson, Dennis, 396, 573
Johnson, Diana A., 54
Johnson, Eddie Bernice, 154, 323
Johnson, Emily, 355
Johnson, Geneva A., 488

Johnson, Geneva, 492
Johnson, Glenn, 474
Johnson, Hank, 321
Johnson, Howard, 397
Johnson, James V, 334
Johnson, James, 517
Johnson, Jeanine, 35
Johnson, Jerald, 473
Johnson, Jessica, 427
Johnson, Judith, 119
Johnson, Kelley, 470
Johnson, Kenneth, 71, 89, 152
Johnson, Kevin, 204
Johnson, Linda E, 356
Johnson, Lise, 52
Johnson, Lucy, 157
Johnson, Marc, 202, 221
Johnson, Michael R, 343
Johnson, Neal J, 281
Johnson, Nichelle A, 64
Johnson, Paul, 412
Johnson, PhD, Candace S, 176
Johnson, Philip, 43
Johnson, Reginald, 65
Johnson, Robert T, 325
Johnson, Ron, 137, 169
Johnson, Rosemary, 121, 228
Johnson, Sam, 255, 323
Johnson, Samuel, 388
Johnson, Scott, 364
Johnson, Steve, 473
Johnson, Susan, 218
Johnson, Teresa D, 65
Johnson, Tim, 312, 313, 420
Johnson, Tyler, 434
Johnson, William H, 581
Johnson-Kelly, Laura, 348
Johnson-Lee, Barbara, 62
Johnston, Brian, 447
Johnston, Christine, 430
Johnston, Laurie, 53
Johnston, Stella, 65
Johnston, Susan, 534, 535
Jonas, Rose I, 224
Jones, Amy, 423
Jones, Andrea, 532
Jones, Angela, 454
Jones, Ann L, 133
Jones, Avis, 480
Jones, Brian, 533, 536
Jones, Carolyn M, 523
Jones, Carolyn, 532
Jones, Claudia, 60
Jones, D. Billy, 329
Jones, David R., 191
Jones, E Thomas, 341
Jones, Eric, 374
Jones, J. Kelsey, 516
Jones, Kenneth, 451
Jones, Loretta C., 157
Jones, Michael, 83, 263
Jones, Robert Kevin, 402
Jones, Serene, 562
Jones, Tanika, 476
Jones, Tim, 400
Jones, Tom, 353
Jones, Weldon, 474
Jones, Wells B, 258
Jonsson, Conni, 412
Jordan, Daphne, 25
Jordan, Jim, 321
Jordan, Karen, 52
Jordan, Marilyn, 449
Joseph, Adam, 474
Joseph, Arthur S., 223, 242
Joseph, Heidi, 80
Joseph, Ingrid, 49
Joseph, Jahmila, 394
Joseph, Joshua, 477
Joseph, Lisa, 403
Joseph, Steven, 289
Joseph, Tim, 271
Josephson, Edward, 434
Joslin IV, Charles, 406
Joyce, Charles P., 374
Joyce, Linda A., 251
Joyce, Sister Maureen, 261
Joyner, Latoya, 31, 35, 36, 39, 40, 42, 629
Joynes, Clarice, 358
Judge, Marty, 479
Judge, Victoria A., 484
Judware, Adam, 507
Juliano, Matt F., 429
Jumper, Michael, 598
Jun, Michelle, 402
Jun, Susan, 443
Juneja, Robert, 428
Jung, Heather, 391
Jurado-Nieves, Ellie, 422
Jurasek, Richard, 557
Juriaco, Annette, 446
Juron, Donald, 120
Jurysta, Steve, 168
Juteau, Linda A, 216
K. O, Cao, 256
Kachalsky, Lowell, 451
Kacica, Marilyn, 174
Kaczmar, Swiatoslav, 451
Kadish, Alan, 562
Kaggen, Dr Lois, 281
Kahn, Alfred E, 291
Kahn, Barbara, 59
Kahn, Marcy L, 45
Kahn, Marcy L., 50
Kaiman, Jon, 360
Kaiser, BG Richard G., 152
Kaiser, Corliss, 584
Kajunju, Amini, 125
Kaler, Eric, 467
Kaler, Patrick, 274
Kalikow, Peter S, 247
Kalin, Robert, 426
Kalish, Andrew W., 488
Kalish, Robert, 49
Kalish, William, 49
Kalka, Marie F., 326
Kalkines, George, 439
Kallop, A George, 204
Kalmus, Jane, 359
Kalogrichs, Stefan, 399
Kaloyeros, Alain, 471
Kalyvas, Andreas, 139, 199
Kambolis, Nick, 410
Kamer, Pearl M, 510
Kamins, Barry, 49, 209
Kaminski, Darrell F, 284
Kaminsky, Karen, 427
Kaminsky, Todd, 18, 20, 21, 23, 25, 26, 189, 237, 611
Kamp, Dave, 255
Kampnich, Trina L, 132
Kamya PhD, Moses M, 8
Kanaley, Edward, 212
Kanas, Elaine, 582
Kanauer, Kathy, 362
Kane, Dennis, 573
Kane, James, 411
Kane, Kathleen G, 247
Kane, Michael D, 107, 274
Kane, Michael, 27, 306, 530
Kane, Robert J., 430
Kane, Terrence, 386
Kang, Joo-Hyun, 450
Kang, Yun Joo, 453
Kanjorski, Paul E, 319
Kantor, Craig M., 430
Kantor, Jon, 398
Kantor, Paul, 238
Kaplan, David J., 49
Kaplan, Deborah A., 49
Kaplan, Deborah, 46
Kaplan, Debra, 597
Kaplan, Evonne, 467
Kaplan, Jill, 532
Kaplan, Lisa M., 493
Kaplan, Sabina, 109
Kapnick, Barbara R, 45
Kapnick, Barbara R., 46
Kapp, Lauren, 532
Kaptur, Marcy, 142
Kapur, Aseem, 401
Karalunas, Deborah H, 46
Karaszewski, Joseph J., 115, 213
Karazuba, Shannon, 464
Karin, Daniel B, 363
Karl, Adam B., 481
Karlosky, Michael, 474
Karmel, Philip, 390
Karnilow, Sheldon, 592
Karnovsky, David, 352
Karopkin, Martin G, 357
Karp, Jordan S, 134
Karp, Vicki, 357

Appendices: Financial Plan, Indexes & Maps

Karp, Warren, 421
Karpati, Adam, 354
Kasdin, Robert, 470
Kashyap, Saraiya, 377
Kasirer, Sara, 431
Kaskan, Mary, 531
Kaskan, Michael E, 330
Kass, Daniel, 355
Kassar, Gerard, 17, 371, 488
Kassel, Lara, 395
Kast, Lawrence, 426
Kaszluga, Catherine, 128
Kathman, Daniel E, 570
Katko, John, 155, 169, 190, 647
Katt, Donald C, 549
Katulak, Robert, 581
Katz, Angela, 30
Katz, Anita S, 135
Katz, Anne, 49
Katz, Harry C, 544
Katz, Ivan J, 594
Katz, Melinda R., 491
Katz, Michael, 49
Katz, Robert, 458
Katz, Steve, 31, 35, 37, 39, 40, 629
Katz, Steven, 35, 195, 230
Katz, Susan, 467
Katzman, Sarah, 59
Kaucher, Mark, 515
Kaufer, Lisa, 359
Kauffman, Richard L, 102, 141, 151
Kauffman, Richard, 3, 69, 140, 147
Kaufman, Nancy K., 198
Kaufman, Norman, 504
Kaumeyer, Linda, 572
Kava, Janine, 6, 111, 206, 235, 303
Kavanagh, Brian P, 31, 38, 39, 40, 629
Kavanagh, Brian P., 36, 37, 38, 242
Kavanagh, Brian, 26, 43
Kavanagh, Laura, 378
Kavanagh, Liam, 357
Kavanaugh, Brian, 165
Kavanaugh, Michelle, 579
Kay Henry, Mary, 494
Kay, Jonathan, 223
Kaye, Seth, 391
Kayode, Omolola, 481
Kayser, Jeffrey, 451
Kayser, Kraig H, 77
Kazeem, Shakiru O., 480
Kazi, Cyrus, 197
Kaznowski, Christopher, 31
Keane, John, 443
Keane, Joseph, 99, 285
Keane, Kevin J, 62
Kearney, John, 409
Kearns, Deborah, 51
Kearns, Michael P, 31, 629
Kearns, Michael, 35, 36, 39, 41
Kearse, Diana M, 208
Keating, Brad, 74
Keating, Daniel, 462
Keating, William, 197
Keays, Tracey, 458
Keef, Tim, 342
Keefe, Dan, 11, 271, 305
Keefe, Kirsten, 410
Keefe, Thomas K, 61
Keegan, Tara, 31
Keegan, Virginia, 577
Keeler, PJ, 327
Keeley, Kevin D, 503
Keen, W Hubert, 546
Keenan-Thomas, Tara, 454
Keene, Gerald, 59
Kehn, Jill, 66
Kehoe, Dennis M, 60
Kehoe, Lori, 138, 461
Kehoe, Peter R, 243
Kehoe, Peter R., 118
Kehoe, Todd, 525
Keib, John, 469
Keihm, Robert, 284
Keith, Jacques, 465
Keizs, Marcia, 397, 552
Kelahan, Gregory, 583
Kelleher, Terence, 424
Keller, Joseph, 326
Keller, Steven, 141
Keller-Cogan, Margaret, 588
Kelley, Barbara J, 325
Kelley, Brien, 469
Kelley, Chris Ann, 61
Kelley, Douglas, 587
Kelley, Nancy, 449
Kelley, Patrick, 591
Kellner, Douglas A, 7, 130
Kellogg, Amy, 423
Kellogg, MaryKaye, 397
Kellogg, Valerie, 527
Kelly, Brian, 284
Kelly, Charles, 109, 527
Kelly, Daniel, 445
Kelly, John, 59, 454
Kelly, Judy, 533
Kelly, Meagan, 449
Kelly, Michael, 383
Kelly, Patrick, 448, 517
Kelly, Paul, 96, 295
Kelly, Peter, 57
Kelly, Philip, 163
Kelly, Raymond W, 357
Kelly, Sean Patrick, 117
Kelly, Suzanne, 590
Kelly, Thomas, 418
Kelly, William A, 47
Kelly, William P, 551
Kelly, William, 397
Kelsey, Lorraine, 225
Kelsey, Valerie, 589
Kelso, Maria, 375
Kelson, Michelle, 360
Kemp, Tim, 430
Kempf, Brian, 149, 271
Kempner, Peter, 434
Kenan, Bruce, 406
Kendall, Bradford, 328
Kendall, Christopher J., 371
Kendrick, Alice, 584
Kennard, John, 99, 286
Kenneally, Diane, 284
Kenneally, Mike, 383
Kenneally, William, 419
Kennedy Jr, John M, 337
Kennedy, Andrew, 3
Kennedy, Diane, 145, 449
Kennedy, Edward M, 313, 315
Kennedy, Joseph L, 546
Kennedy, Jr., Robert F., 471
Kennedy, Judy, 360
Kennedy, Nancy, 538
Kennedy, Patricia E, 233, 261, 262
Kennedy, Robert T., 345
Kennedy, Tanya, 46, 49
Kennedy, Timothy M, 20, 611
Kennedy, Timothy, 16, 18, 21, 22, 23, 24, 25, 87, 237, 246, 288
Kennedy-Sadler, Jacqueline, 413
Kenney, Joan M., 49
Kenney, Karen R., 241
Kenny, Brianna, 154
Kenny, Cathy, 445
Kenny, Joan, 46
Kenny, Judith E, 163
Kenny, Margaret, 524
Kent, Fred, 193
Kent, Robert, 4, 173, 250
Kent, Robin M., 55
Kent, Susan, 396
Kent, William J, 47
Kentoffio, Paul, 241
Kenyon, Jim, 539
Kenyon, Jody, 466
Kenyon, Lori, 75
Keogh, Karen P., 430
Keogh, Michael, 388
Keough, Brian, 471
Kepich, Daniel J, 71
Keren, Gail, 78, 177, 200
Kergaravat, Anthony, 39
Kern, Bryan, 474
Kern, Cynthia, 46
Kerr, Carolyn, 390, 470
Kerr, James T., 254
Kerr, Karen, 61
Kerr, Kristen, 127
Kerr, Michael J, 510
Kerrigan, Kevin, 48
Kerry, John F, 315
Kerry, John, 313
Kerry, Natasha, 403
Kersavage, Lisa, 446
Kershko, Paulette M, 60

Kertesz-Lee, Dawn H., 345
Kerwin, Jr., Donald M., 197
Kerwin, Kevin M., 432
Kesel, Beth, 524
Keshner, Cheryl, 410
Kesner, Marcie, 433
Ketcher, MBA/HCM, Martha, 255
Ketchum, Cheryl J, 339
Ketterer, Krista, 306
Ketteringham, Emma, 462
Kettner, Susan I, 64
Kettrick, James, 577
Ketzer, Bill, 432
Keville, Debra, 271
Kevins, Linda J, 61
Keyser, Robert, 451
Khawarzad, Aurash, 474
Kideckel, Arnold, 476
Kiedaisch, Debra, 56
Kiedrowski, Scott P, 360
Kiedrowski, Scott, 19
Kiefer, Kristin, 79
Kieff, Kevin, 272
Kiernan, Henry, 579
Kiernan, John B, 405
Kiernan, Peter J, 104, 211
Kiesel, Diane R., 50
Kietzman, Paul, 419
Kiggins-Walsh, Helen M, 134
Kijne, Hugo, 397
Kikilo, Vladimir, 532
Kilcullen, Brian, 364
Kildee, Dale E, 318
Kilduff, Edward, 354
Kiley, George, 591
Kiley, Thomas M., 145
Killeen, Timothy, 543
Kilmer, Mark, 506
Kim, Byron, 352
Kim, David, 381
Kim, Jean, 469
Kim, Joon H., 115, 213
Kim, Joon, 468
Kim, Kevin, 4, 83, 104, 263
Kim, PJ, 198
Kim, Ron, 31, 37, 39, 42
Kim, Ronald T, 629
Kimball, Wilson, 367
Kimble, Cynthia, 278
Kimmel, Jonathan L, 358
Kincaid, Kyle, 384
Kinch, Henderson, 496
Kindberg, Maria, 326
Kinder, Heather, 181
King, Bernard T, 224
King, Charles, 191, 446, 507
King, Craig L, 600
King, Daniel R., 54
King, Derick, 383
King, Edgar A, 12, 235, 264
King, Edgar A., 245
King, James L, 544
King, James, 163
King, Jaz-Michael, 428
King, Joanne, 357
King, Kathy J., 49
King, Kevin, 69, 250
King, Lawrence, 464
King, Manjit, 484
King, Margaret, 364
King, Pete, 311
King, Peter T, 319, 320, 647
King, Peter T., 79, 168, 169, 190, 203
King, Peter, 319
King, Russ, 535
King, Sandra, 376
King, Steve, 321
King, Thomas H., 491
King-Festa, Marilyn, 352
Kingston, Jack, 317
Kinirons, Kimberly, 208
Kink, Michael, 258
Kinley, Daniel, 379
Kinner, Steve, 457
Kinney, Cassie, 65
Kinney, David L, 360
Kinney, Richard, 101, 113
Kinney, Robert, 474
Kinstlick, Riva F., 457
Kinyon, David, 510
Kipp, Alcxander, 353
Kirby, Jeff, 76
Kirby, Jennifer, 474
Kirincich, Zelko N., 106, 288, 309
Kirk, Timothy, 115
Kirnie, Elizabeth, 590
Kirsch, Anne, 99, 286
Kirsch, Frederick, 464
Kirschner, Chief Jay, 11
Kirschner, Jay, 149, 271
Kirschner, Philip W., 63
Kirven, Louis C, 368
Kisloski, Jeffrey J, 595
Kissel, Pam, 578
Kisselstein, Bonnie, 350
Kissinger, Mark, 175
Kisson, John, 468
Kist, Greg, 153
Kistela, Stanley, 345
Kitchner, Roseanne, 283
Kitson, Anita, 267
Kittrick, Kathleen, 472
Kitzes, Orin R, 48
Kiyonaga, Nancy B., 234
Kiyonaya, Nancy B., 240
Kladis, Emily, 136
Klahn, Jacqueline, 71
Klainberg, Joshua, 434
Klass, Perri, 139, 226
Klatt, Dr Roger J, 582
Kleiman, Joel, 333
Klein, Carol S, 56
Klein, Corey E, 64
Klein, Corey, 350
Klein, George, 87, 107, 165
Klein, Jefffrey, 435
Klein, Jeffrey D, 18, 611
Klein, Jeffrey D., 16
Klein, Jeffrey, 491
Klein, Matthew, 426
Klein, Michael A, 46, 218
Klein, Michael L, 363
Klein, Michael, 442, 451
Klein, Monte, 11, 241
Klein, Randall, 444
Klein, Richard, 537
Klein, Stuart, 357
Kleinbaum, Ben, 392
Kleinberg, Gary, 444
Klein-Heitler, Sherry, 209
Kleinman, Andrew Y., 443
Kleinmann, Teri, 35
Kleist, Gary, 367
Klemens, Gregory, 397
Kleniewski, Nancy, 546
Klett, Andrea, 338
Kliever, Launa, 448
Klim, Barbara K, 344
Klimas, Brian, 459
Klime, Linda, 464
Kline, Gregory J, 10, 283
Kline, Jerald R., 49
Kline, John, 125, 196, 224, 318
Kline, Julian, 388
Klippel, Andrew, 120
Klobuchar, Amy, 313, 314
Kloch Sr, Richard C, 47
Kloch, Richard C, 48
Kloppel, Michael, 372
Klos, Jessica, 408
Klotz, Mark, 147
Kluewer, Susan T., 61
Klug, Ronald, 78, 200, 303
Kluger, Barry L, 100, 286, 307
Klyczek, James P, 548
Knab, Sheryl, 129
Knapp, III, Robert P., 171
Knapp, Ronald, 362
Knickerbocker, Lawrence J, 62
Knight, Celeste, 16
Knighton, Ethel, 410
Knipel, Lawrence, 46, 209
Knirk, Maria, 4, 69
Knobel, Gary F., 47
Knoblauch, Valerie, 275
Knoll, Adrienne, 30
Knopf, Stephen, 48
Knowles, Eddie, 460
Knowling, Michael, 458
Kob, Jennifer, 462
Koch III, Art, 300
Koch, John, 71, 88
Kocher, Williamk F, 56

Kochian, Leon V., 71
Koeleveld, Celeste, 78
Koelmel, John R., 101, 141
Koenig, Thomas, 187
Koenigsmann MD, Carl, 108, 110
Koenigsmann, Carl, 6
Koessel, Michael, 396
Koetzle, Christopher A, 346
Kogelman, David, 483
Kohl, Herb, 312, 316
Kohl, Lynn M, 54
Kohler, Kris, 442
Kohm, Robert C, 48
Kohomban, PhD, Jeremy, 231, 257
Kohout, Joan S., 55
Kokkoris, Steve, 284
Kolb, Brian M, 28, 31, 41, 165, 629
Kolceski, Michael, 451
Kollenscher, Avi, 460
Komanoff, Charles, 144, 291
Kominicki, John, 532
Konheim, Carolyn, 291
Konigsberg, Jan, 430
Konopelski, Cyril, 412
Konopko, Deborah, 255, 445
Konst, Kathy, 505
Kontzamanis, Georgea C., 488
Kontzamanis, Georgea, 133
Konviser, Jill, 50
Koonce, Michael, 177
Kopka, Lynn, 366
Kopko, Kim, 182
Kopley, Mary K, 387
Korach, Nicholas, 574
Koral, Alan M, 226
Korfmacher, Katrina, 471
Korkhov, Alexander, 355
Korn, Bradley, 432
Korn, Douglas, 428
Kornreich, Shirley, 46
Korotkin, Paul, 110
Kortright, Kevin C, 339
Kosakoski, James, 383
Koshgarian, Phd, Bryon, 297
Kosinski, Peter S, 7, 130
Koski, Andrew, 426
Kosmider, Bethany A., 373
Kosovych, Anna, 58
Kossover, Andrew, 338
Kostik, Carol, 353
Kostmayer, Peter, 397
Koteen, Lucy, 480
Kotier, Lynn R., 49
Kotkin, Roberta, 385
Kotlikoff, Michael I, 544
Kotlow, Ellen, 434
Kotowski, John, 397
Kouakou, Kafui, 550
Koury, Walter C, 333
Kovatchitch, Marian, 561
Kovel, Molly, 462
Kowal, Czykanne, 472
Kowal, Frederick E., 129
Kowalski, Ken, 222
Kowalski, Nikki, 112
Koweek, Richard, 52
Kozakiewicz, Robert, 363
Kracher, Frank, 539
Kraebel, Charlie, 523
Krafchin, Alan, 256
Krajewski, Kenneth A., 90
Krajick, Ruby J., 212
Krakowski, Molly, 429
Kramer, Adam, 34
Kramer, Barry D., 46
Kramer, Charles, 467
Kramer, Lawrence, 469
Kramer, Lisa, 424
Kramer, Robin, 433
Kranov, Shane, 432
Krantz, Joseph L, 361
Krasovskaya, Alina G., 489
Kratt, Dwayne, 407
Kratz, David, 558
Kratz, Stacy, 414
Kraus, Sabrina B., 49
Kraus, William A, 13, 294
Krause, Karen, 570
Krause, Mary A., 333
Krauss, Sarah L., 49
Krauss, Sarah, 358
Krauza, Kathleen, 51
Krebbeks, Joyce A, 136
Krege, Michele, 30
Kreisler, Nancy, 52
Kreisman, Dolores, 470
Kremer, Arthur Jerry, 410
Kremer, Timothy G., 128
Kremer, Timothy, 464
Krenning, Amanda, 413
Krens, Thomas, 281
Krepp, John M., 289
Kress PhD, Anne M, 548
Kresser, Michele, 361
Kretser, Rachel L, 61
Kretzler, Laurene R, 27
Kreyche, Emma, 477
Kriegel, Jay, 460
Krieger, Erika, 163
Krieger, Vivien, 403
Kriesberg, Robin, 389
Krim, Jonathan, 538
Krinsky, Barry, 396
Krinsky, Jennifer B., 483
Krishnaswany, Pavita, 434
Kriss, Mark C, 291
Kriss, Mark, 433
Krogmann, David B., 46
Krohn, Brian, 523
Krokoff, Steven, 341
Krokondelas, Peter, 431
Kroll, Steven, 423
Kron, Barry, 50
Kronau, Maureen, 411
Kronenberg, Marc B, 31
Krongold, Martin S., 485
Kronstadt, Denise, 423
Krooks, Bernard A, 259
Krooks, Harold S, 216
Krueger, Beth, 182
Krueger, Liz, 16, 18, 21, 22, 23, 24, 25, 165, 237, 265, 611
Krug, Kelly, 31
Krupke, Bruce W, 77
Krupp, Fred, 156
Krupski, Christine, 296
Krusen, Mike, 375
Kruzansky, Charles J., 459
Krzeminski, Joseph, 362
Kubik, Jennine, 33
Kuch, Gary M, 587
Kucinich, Dennis J, 321
Kuehner, Elmer, 525
Kuharski, Michael J., 488
Kuhn, Polly, 434
Kuhns, Michael, 100, 151
Kui, Christopher, 256
Kulick, Robert D., 180
Kulick, Robert, 223
Kulick, Ronald, 482, 493
Kulkin, Peter M, 64
Kullas, Joel, 49
Kullhanek, Joseph V., 480
Kumro, Richard, 400
Kunakowsky, Victor, 432
Kunchan, Dr. Kishore, 580
Kuncl, Ralph, 471
Kunkel Jr, Kenneth J, 331
Kunkel, Ken, 375
Kunken, Dr. Gilbert, 179
Kunz, David F., 170
Kunz, David, 203
Kunzwiler, Michael, 334, 373
Kupferman, Richard, 58
Kurabi, Chloe, 278
Kurian, Vin, 474
Kus, Christopher A, 174
Kushner, Jared, 528
Kushner, Julie, 491
Kushner, Susan, 50
Kusnierz, Todd, 20
Kutzer, Kim, 507
Kuvshinoff, MD, Boris, 176
Kuzdale, John M, 62
Kwatra, Neal, 436
Kwiatoski, Debbie, 532
Kyl, Jon, 315, 316
Kyles, James, 451
Kyriacou, Mike, 99, 285
L. Berlin, Scott, 428
La Vasser, Jim, 537
Labarbera, Gary, 391
LaBarbera, Gary, 479

LaBarge, Martha A, 53
LaBarren, Sandra, 415
Labbe, Normand, 177, 221
LaBelle, Jr, Francis, 281
Labelle, Kimberly, 588
LaBelle, Thomas, 243
LaBoda, Esq., Katherine D, 104, 164
LaBoda, Katherine D, 211, 309
Laboy-Diaz, C., 355
Labriola, Steven L, 361
LaBuda, Frank J, 59
LaBuda, Kathleen, 337
Labuda, Melissa, 445
Lacertosa, Rocco, 144
Lacewell, Linda, 3
Lacey, Clinton, 357
Lacey, Kate, 373
Lacey, Katie, 131
Lachanski, William, 227
Lachman, Seymour P., 485
Lackman, Abe, 378
Lackman, Abraham M., 433
LaClair, Darwin, 109
LaClair, Vanessa E., 92
LaColla, Robert, 345
Lacroix, Robert, 448
Ladopoulos, Niko, 25
Ladov, Mark, 389
Lafave, Meredith, 399
LaFave, Michelle, 132
LaFayette, Reginald A, 136
LaFayette, Reginald A., 374
Laffey, Philip, 409
Laffin Sr, Timothy, 110
LaFleur, Robert C., 159
LaForgia, Susan, 487
LaFountain, Nicole, 120, 270
LaFountain, Tony, 362
Lagapa, Debra, 32
Lagatta, James, 427
Lahr, Eric, 148
Lahtinen, John A, 45
Lahut, Jayme, 515
Lai, Lydia C., 49
Laing, Charles, 463
Lake-Maynard, Karen, 333
Laline, Brian J., 530
LaLonde, Carole L, 330
Lalor, Keiran Michael, 36
Lalor, Kieran Michael, 31, 39, 41, 42, 246, 265
Lalor, Kieran, 630
LaLota, Nick, 135
Lam, Alice, 439
Lam, Felix, 355
Lam, Linda, 388
LaMacchia, Samuel J, 105, 287
LaMancuso, John L, 63
Lamanna, Esq., Paul, 61
LaMarco, Raymond, 283
Lamb, Thomas, 66
Lambert, Herbert, 100, 286
Lambert, John F, 52, 57
Lambert, Linda A., 181
Lamborn, Doug, 143, 321, 323
Lambright, W. Henry, 159
Lamendola, David, 146, 472
Lammers, John, 531
Lamont, Seth, 398
LaMoreaux, Rebekah, 519
Lamoreaux, William, 410
Lamorte, Nicholas, 398
Lamot, William, 9, 194
Lampert, Scott J., 179
Lampl, John, 290
Lamster, Ira, 470
Lanahan, Kevin, 145, 401
Lancaster Beal, Valerie, 550
Lancaster, Brooks, 381
Lance, Avalon, 184
Lance, Donald, 261
Lance, Jack, 122
Lance, John, 188
Lancette, Colleen, 296
Lanchanski, William, 251
Lancia, Nancy, 465
Landa, Marjorie, 356
Landau, Eric, 457
Landau, Lisa, 177, 207
Lander, Devin, 127
Landes, Robin, 392
Landesman, Dodge, 482
Landicino, Carl J., 46
Landin, Teri, 241
Landis, Jennifer, 449
Landon, Douglas E, 332
Landor, Nancy, 423
Landrieu, Mary L, 315, 316
Landrieu, Mary L., 224
Landry, Joe, 360
Landy, James J., 490
Lane, Cheryl D, 330
Lane, Eric, 117, 157, 191
Lane, Howard G, 48
Lane, Jason E., 543
Lane, Jeffrey, 382
Lane, Laura, 510, 519
Lane, Robin, 255
Lane, Thomas W., 495
Laney, Carolyn, 389
Lang, Brian, 496
Lang, Jeff, 473
Lang, Jonathan, 399
Lang, Wilda, 36
Langan, John J, 135
Langan, Thomas R, 65
Lange, Timothy, 589
Langer, Barry, 473
Langfelder, Richard, 437
Langford, George, 455
Langhorne, Earnest, 187
Langley, Jr, James R, 327
Langlois, James T, 601
Langmead, Ben, 445
Langone, Dave, 583
Langweber, Denise, 518
Langworthy, Nickolas, 375
Lannon, Venetia, 3, 147
Lansden, John S., 49
Lansing, Kenneth W, 338
Lant, Steven, 395
Lantzfamne, Santo, 479
Lanza, Andrew J, 18, 23, 24, 25, 165, 612
Lanza, Andrew, 15, 21, 22, 23, 26, 43
Lanzetta, Mary Ann, 392
Lapadula, Vincent A., 487
Lapatine, Justin, 419
LaPerche, James, 367
Lapham, Douglas, 420
Lapidus, Marc, 465
Lapinski, Anne, 147
LaPlace, Lisa, 455
LaPoint, Roger, 493
LaPorte, Evelyn J., 49
LaPosta, Dore, 154
Laquidara, Carmelo, 65
Lara, David, 5, 83, 160, 234, 263
Larabee, Susan R., 50
Large, James, 447
Largeteau, Sheryl, 336
Laria, Joseph, 580
Larkin Jr, William J, 15, 18, 23, 24, 25, 26
Larkin, Elizabeth P, 327
Larkin, Jr, William J, 612
Larkin, Jr., William L., 21
Larkin, Margaret, 8, 161
LaRoach, Mark, 568
LaRock, Michelle, 13, 294
LaRosa, John C, 544
Larose, Christine J, 590
Larose, Nicole, 380
Larow, John, 418
Larrabee, Paul, 402
Larrow, William, 574
Larsen, Elizabeth, 433
Larson, Ann, 473, 474
Larson, Dan, 506
Larson, Frederick A, 63
Larson, Krista, 472
Larson, Nev, 534
Lasak, Gregory L, 48
Lasala, Richard, 443
LaSalle, Hector D, 45
LaSalle, Hector D., 47
Lasdon, Doug, 471
Lashbrook, Brett, 438
Lashford, Sarah, 414
Lashomb, Nathan, 507
Lasicki, Antonia M., 190, 383
Lasicki, Antonia, 231
LaSister, Charles K., 488
Lasker, Councilman Shirley, 343
Lasko, Kathy, 60

Lasky, Elizabeth M, 393
Lasky, James A, 387
Lasky, Roy E, 393
LaSpaluto, Eileen, 127
LaSpina, Rene, 537
Lassen, Craig, 426
Latella, John B., 50
Latham, Joseph W, 59
Latham, Michael, 70
Latham, Tom, 317
Lathrop, John, 346
Latimer, George S, 612
Latimer, George S., 18
Latimer, George, 20, 21, 22, 23, 24, 25, 125
Latin, Richard, 49
Latini, John, 585
Latterman, Carol, 168
Lattin, C W, 334
Latwin, Joseph L., 65
Lau, Fai Lin, 379
Lau, Laurie L., 49
Laub, Michael, 479
Lauber, Rich, 536
Laudato, Paul, 11, 149, 271
Lauer, Andrew, 477
Laufer, David, 416
Lauri, Marjorie V., 430
Lauria, Mark W., 128
Lauricella, Peter, 461
Lauricella, Richard, 409
Laurie, Kim, 29
Laurito, James, 395
Lauro, Dennis, 598
Lautenberg, Frank R, 314
Lauterbach, Nicole, 33
Lautneberg, Frank R, 314
LaValle, John Jay, 376
LaValle, Kenneth P, 15, 18, 20, 23, 24, 25, 125, 612
LaValle, Kenneth P., 22
Lavallee, David K., 543
Lavallee, David, 467
LaValley, Thomas, 109
Lavare, Maureen, 121
Lavender, Philip, 440
LaVenia, Peter, 374
LaVigne PhD, Marnie, 84, 122
Lavigne, Jan M, 52
Lavigne, Mark, 383
Lavin, Patricia, 396
Lavine, Aaron O., 348
Lavine, Charles D, 26, 31, 36, 39, 40, 630
Lavine, Charles D., 43
Lavine, Charles, 38, 165
LaViolette, Mark, 336
Lavis, Angela L., 430
Law, Kevin, 86, 265
Lawing, Abby, 532
Lawitts, Steven, 354
Lawitz, Alan, 251
Lawliss, Timothy J, 52
Lawlor, Carol, 347
Lawlor, John, 443
Lawrence, C Bruce, 214
Lawrence, Donna, 507
Lawrence, James, 101, 114, 530
Lawrence, Karen, 560
Lawrence, Peter A, 630
Lawrence, Peter, 31, 38, 39, 41, 165
Lawson, Delsie L., 481
Lawson, Jane, 58
Lawson, Robert, 9, 200, 219, 304
Lawson, Timothy D, 596
Lawson, Tommy, 474
Layman, Lin, 136
Laytin, Mark, 512
Layton, Jr, Daniel M, 224
Lazar, Joseph, 259
Lazarou, Robert W, 161, 245
Lazarski, Andrea J, 102, 164, 273, 308
Le Coney, Patricia, 108
Le, Linh, 174, 176
Leach, Craig, 533
Leach, David J., 152, 153
Leach, Kelly E., 527
Leahy Scott, Catharine, 161
Leahy Scott, Catherine, 9, 14, 112, 163, 253
Leahy, Aggie, 475
Leahy, Patrick J, 312, 316
Leahy, Patrick, 116, 169, 214, 312
Leak, Barbara A, 66
Leamer, Robert, 444
Leary, Clare, 451
Lease, Peter, 388
Leath, Susan E, 342
Leavitt, Steve, 562
Leb, Jeffrey, 486, 491, 495
LeBarron, Debora, 423
Lebe, Arlene, 532
Lebedeff, Diana A., 49
Leberstein, Sarah, 448
LeBlanc Jr, Norman, 63
Lebous, Ferris D, 47
LeBoutillier, John, 447
Lebovitz, Gerald, 49
Lebowitz, Jeffrey D., 48
Lebron, Roberto, 207
Lebwhol, Dennis, 49
Leccese, Joseph M., 158
Leckerling, Richard E, 475
Leclerc, Paul, 458
LeConey, Patricia, 109
LeCount, Richard, 338
Lederbach, David, 454
Lederer, Neil, 594
LeDet, Kellie, 88
Lee Ford, Laurie, 507
Lee, Allison, 405
Lee, Anastasiya, 379
Lee, Brian S., 139
Lee, Brian, 417
Lee, Cara, 449
Lee, Christopher, 319
Lee, Chynel, 476
Lee, Damon, 458
Lee, David, 457
Lee, Don, 375
Lee, Elizabeth, 382
Lee, Emily, 439
Lee, Eric, 426
Lee, Jennifer, 424
Lee, Joann, 168
Lee, Judith, 11, 140
Lee, Leon Y, 559
Lee, Margaret, 255
Lee, Milly, 458
Lee, Portia, 102, 124, 164, 178
Lee, Richard, 96, 246, 283, 285, 306
Lee, Robert, 354
Lee, Sharon, 379
Lee, Sheila Jackson, 116
Lee, Sheila Jackson-, 320
Lee, Thomas F, 6, 194, 227, 252, 303
Lee, Thomas K, 104, 124, 242
Lee, Todd, 445
Lee, Ulysses, 422
Lee, William, 109
Leege, William, 114
Lee-Glauser, Gina, 455
Lees, Ilene, 5, 234, 240
Leet, John, 537
Lefebvre, Kim F., 212
Lefebvre, Lora, 543
Leff, Gene, 8, 147
Leffler, Mike, 396
Leffler, Scott, 526
Lefkowich, Shmuel, 444
Lefkowitz, Jerome, 201, 220
Lefkowitz, Joan B, 47
Lefkowitz, Stephen, 416
Legaspi, Mark, 409
Legere, Kristin, 414
LeGrett, Kevin, 534
Lehenbauer, Lori L, 134
Lehman, Greg, 133
Lehman, Maria, 104, 273, 274, 287
Lehner, Peter, 448
Lehrer, Andrew, 49
Lehtinen, Ileana Ros-, 319
Leiby, Robert E, 585
Leicht, Holly M., 189
Leicht, Holly, 386
Leidholdt, Dorchen, 463
Leigh, Richard, 470
Leinhard, Bill, 471
Leins, Richard A, 361
Leinung, Dan, 23
Leinung, Mark, 121, 228
Leis III, H. Patrick, 47
Leisen, Tammy, 474
Leitz, Thomas, 329
Lejava, Jeffrey, 453
Leland, Richard, 416

Leman, Matthew P., 396
Lemieux, Eric, 535
Lempke, John, 109
Lemson, Stephen, 80
Lence, George, 449
Lendler, Ernest, 138
Lenhart, Donna, 463
Lenihan, Kevin, 529
Lenihan, Leonard, 131
Lennie, Peter, 471
Lentivech, Douglas, 7, 121, 174, 227, 252
Lentol, Joseph R, 31, 36, 38, 41, 43, 114, 211, 630
Lentz, Philip, 310
Leo, Chris, 8
Leo, Christopher, 396
Leo, John J., 47
Leo, John, 401
Leonard, Alexander B., 430
Leonard, Don, 376
Leonard, Sandy, 350
Leonard, Theresa, 467
Leonard, William, 284
Leone, Julius, 326
Leone, Melchior, 485
Leone, Thomas G, 51
Leppert, Richard, 292
Lerner, Georgia, 118
Lerner, Joel, 179, 255
Lerner, Robert G., 185
Lerner, Susan, 138, 170
Lerose, Douglas J., 61
LeRoy, Rose, 120
Lesieur, Matthew, 472
Leskc, Diane, 399
Lesley, Lashaun, 477
Leslie, Robert P, 98, 151
Leslie, Russ, 460
Lesnick, Chuck, 367
Lespinasse, Patrick, 472
Lesser, Peter, 278
Lesser, William, 74
Lester, Harriet, 289
Letellier, Yonel, 490
Lettre, Edward J., 372
Leung, Edward, 270
Leung, Susan, 18
Leung, Vanessa, 382
Leunig, Charles A, 592
Leveille, Nancy, 423
Leven, Nancy L, 133
Levenberg, Dana, 30
Levenson, Andrew, 474
Levenson, Scott, 378
Leventhal, John M, 45
Leventhal, Mitch, 543
Leveret, Ulysses B., 49
Levernois, Cindy, 424
Levesque, Rev Joseph L, 559
Levien, Vincent, 406
Levin, A Thomas, 216
Levin, Carl, 297, 313, 315
Levin, Gary, 399
Levin, Jerry, 261
Levin, Kate D, 353
Levin, Raymond, 473
Levin, Rich, 279
Levin, Sander M, 323
Levin, Sander, 180, 267
Levine, Andrew T, 91
Levine, Danielle, 176
Levine, James R, 102, 151
Levine, Jed, 379
Levine, Katherine A., 49
Levine, Lawrence, 448
Levine, Louis L, 558
Levine, Mark, 103, 211
Levine, Matthew L., 78
Levine, Meredith, 79, 103
Levine, Michele Mark, 359
Levine, Penny, 468
Levine, Rachel, 355
Levine, Randi, 378
Levine, Randy, 281
Levine, Shaun Marie, 138
Levitt, Dan U., 487
Levy, Adam, 334
Levy, Chad M., 430
Levy, Harlan, 221
Levy, Jennifer, 434
Levy, Joel M, 233, 262
Levy, Norman, 435
Levy, Reynold, 435
Levy, Sharon, 477
Levy, Shirley, 353
Lew, David, 142
Lewin, Donna, 109
Lewin, Eunice A., 543
Lewis, Daniel, 48
Lewis, Daphne C., 483
Lewis, Donald D., 106, 189, 274
Lewis, Jeffrey, 3, 261
Lewis, Jerry, 317
Lewis, John, 323
Lewis, Lorna R, 580
Lewis, Paul, 209, 537
Lewis, Robert M., 54
Lewis, William R, 64
Lewyckyj, John D, 161
Ley, Rhonda P., 222
Lhota, Joseph J., 550
Li, Kam Chi, 449
Li, Margaret E, 336
Libby, Robert K, 567
Liberman, Joseph I, 313
Libert, Jack L, 47
Licata, James D, 335
Lichtman, Jeffrey A., 491
Lichtman, Jeffrey, 469
Lichtman, Marshall, 543
Licopoli, Lorenzo, 598
Lictus, Bert, 570
Lieb, Judith S., 50
Lieberman, Donna, 199, 454
Lieberman, Ellen, 215
Lieberman, Geoff, 399
Lieberman, Jeffrey, 470
Lieberman, Joseph I, 315
Lieberman, MD, Jeffrey A, 229
Liebermann, Mark, 367
Lieblong, Robert, 99, 286
Liebman Rubin, Allison, 477
Liebman, Glen, 232
Liebman, Glenn, 443
Liebowitz, M.D., Barry L., 482
Liebschutz, Elizabeth, 141
Liegl, Debra S, 503
Lienhard, Bill, 218
Lieu, Justin, 482
Liff, Mark, 443
Liff, Robert, 438
Lifton, Barbara S, 31, 38, 39
Lifton, Barbara, 27, 35, 37, 38, 70, 630
Lilac, Dean, 66
Lillo, Patrick J, 432
Lilly, Kevin, 538
Lim, Arnold, 50
Lim, Deborah, 270
Lim, Jr., Howard, 371
LiMandri, Robert D, 352, 357
Limberger, Ron, 176
Limiti, Donna, 229, 230
Limpert, Theodore H., 66
Lin, Keli, 419
Linares, Guillermo, 31, 35, 36, 39, 40, 630
Lincoln, Blanche L, 312, 315
Lindenbaum, Samuel H, 433
Linder, John, 323
Lindley, Stephen K., 45
Lindner, Edward, 103, 211
Lindsay, Ian, 445
Lindsley, Laura, 366
Linehan, Michael, 520
Ling, Elisabeth, 409
Ling-Cohan, Doris, 46
Linhardt, Arnold, 468
Linhorst, Stan, 531
Link, Susan, 467
Linker, Wayne A, 280
Linn, Jennifer, 412
Linnertz, Paul, 365
Linville, Robert W., 327
Linzy, Donna L., 483
Lipfert, Angela, 279
Lipinski, Daniel, 322
Lippman, Jonathan, 209
Lipschutz, Neal, 527, 532
Lipsky, David, 225
Lipton, Bill, 139
Lipton, Frank R, 355
Lipton, Jody, 357
Lira, Michael, 109
Lisa Miller, Carolyn, 353

Lisberg, Adam, 99, 286, 307
Lison, Elizabeth, 582
Liss, David, 457
Little, David A., 126
Little, David, 464
Little, Elizabeth O'C, 15, 18, 22, 23
Little, Elizabeth O'C., 22, 23, 25, 189, 237, 246
Little, Elizabeth, 612
Little, James C, 226, 292
Little, Joyce, 444
Little, Robert, 474
Little, Sondra, 284
Litwin, Leonard, 247
Litz, Franz, 453
Liu, John C, 353
Liu, Shiang, 484
Liu, Ya-Ting, 438
Liverani, Lynette, 32
Liverzani, Michael, 350
Livingstone, David, 396
Livolsi, Bartley, 396
Livshin, Peter N, 587
Lizardo, Maria, 450
Lloyd, Brandi, 534
Lloyd, Curtis L., 543
Lloyd, Tracy, 425
Lloyd, Tyieast S., 488
Lloyd, Vallencia, 175
Lloyd, William K, 581
Lo Presti, Frank, 99, 286
Lobban, Loren, 202, 221
Lobdell, Robert, 161, 245
Lobianco, Roberto, 458
LoBiondo, Frank, 322
Lobis, Joan B., 46
Lobosco, Anna, 6, 194, 227, 252
LoCascio, Jr, Joseph R, 508
LoCicero, John, 436
Locke, Susan B., 528
Lockhart, Paula K, 111, 206
Lockwood, Roberta Byron, 275
Loconte, Richard A., 78
LoCurto, Christine, 96, 285
Loder, Earl, 343
Loeb, Susan, 462
Loehr, Gerald, 47
Loeser, Jessica, 378
Loeser, Stu, 352
Loewenguth, Mary C., 212
Lofgren, Zoe, 321, 322
Lofrumento, Anthony, 119, 304
Logan, Ernest, 126, 414, 481
Logan, Janine, 424, 450
Logue, Alexandra, 397
Logue, Christopher, 70
Loguercio, Caren, 59
Logus, Maria, 209
Lomascolo, Carol, 586
Lombardi Jr., Tarky, 418
Lombardi, Sal, 346
Lombardo, Barbara A, 530
Lombardo, Lisa, 34, 41
Lomonaco, Sr. Paulette, 419
Lonczak, Gary, 583
Londa, Ivan, 565
London, Steven, 493
Long, Gregory, 74, 389
Long, Jane, 467
Long, Michael R., 371
Long, Richard B, 106, 164, 211, 310
Long, Thomas M., 372
Longhany, Lorie J, 132
Longhany, Lorie, 373
Longhi, William, 401
Longmore, Geoffrey, 488
Longworth, George, 339
Lonial, Sayar, 427
Loomis, Edward, 153
Loomis, Robert, 12, 162, 236, 241
Loper, William, 298
Lopez Torres, Margarita, 54
Lopez, Dennis, 384
Lopez, Edgardo, 251
Lopez, Gene R., 50
Lopez, Katiuska M., 493
Lopez, Linda, 463
Lopez, Monique, 474
Lopez, Norma I, 352
Lopez, Peter D, 31, 631
Lopez, Peter D., 38
Lopez, Peter, 28, 35, 37, 70
Lopez-Pierre, Thomas A., 486
Lopez-Pierre, Thomas, 495
Lopez-Summa, Gina, 48
Lopinski, John, 105, 287
Loprest, Amy M, 352
Loprest, Amy M., 138, 359
Lopresto, Charles, 49
Lorentz, John, 580
Lorenzo, Albert, 48
Lorey, Scott, 378
Lorey, Thomas J, 329
Lorigo, Ralph C., 371
Lorman, Lisa W, 61
LoSasso, Bill, 74, 156
Loshbaugh, Chad, 78, 83, 263
Loske, Robin, 332
Lothridge, Brian, 529
LoTurco, Jennifer, 543
Lotz, Christina L, 336
Loughren, Thomas, 101, 113
Louloudes, Virginia P, 277
Lounsbury, Lee, 399
LoVallo, Sharon, 53
Love, Zach, 474
Lovejoy, Cassandra, 454
Lovelett, Steven S, 163
Lovell, Jeffrey, 393
Lovell, Magaly, 122
Lovinger, Cynthia, 433
Lovric, Miro, 115, 213
Lovullo, Brendon, 136
Lowengard, Daniel G, 584
Lowenstein, Daniel, 457
Lowenthal, Alan, 143
Lower, Conrad W, 202, 221
Lowey, Nita M, 311, 317, 647
Lowey, Nita M., 267
Lowey, Nita, 73
Lowrey, Charles F., 458
Lowrey, Lang, 555
Lowrie, Stuart, 449
Lowry, Barbara, 450
Lowry, David, 120
Lowry, Douglas, 471
Lowry, Marcia Robinson, 257
Loyola, Guido A, 65
Lozito, Gaetan B, 61
Lozzi, Dave, 533
Lubell, Lewis, 47
Lubonski, Robert, 474
Lubow, Fran L., 50
Lubrant, John, 360
Lucas, Dave, 383
Lucas, Frank D, 316
Lucey, Brian J, 475
Luchsinger, David, 276
Lucia, Janene, 75
Lucia, Richard B, 504
Luciani, Robert, 458
Luciano, Mark, 34
Luckey, Jeff, 325
Ludington, Spencer, 57
LuDuc, Charles, 39
Ludwig, Bruce, 372
Ludwig, Joseph, 348
Luetkemeyer, Blaine, 190, 322
Luft, Martha L, 59
Lugar, Richard G, 315
Lugaro, Jose, 435
Lugo, Eric, 397
Luisi-Potts, Billie, 280
Lujan, Ben Ray, 138
Lukas, Susan, 300
Lukasik, Tracey M, 509
Lukens, Daniel, 256
Luker, John, 69
Luly, Christine, 121
Lum, May, 228
Lumbra, Casey, 13, 294
Luna, Winslow, 480
Lundgren, Carl L., 486
Lundgren, Dan, 320
Lundin, Jon, 104, 273, 309
Lunney, J Robert, 299
Lupardo, Donna A, 31
Lupardo, Donna, 36, 37, 38, 39, 42, 178, 254, 631
Lupe, George, 163
Lupinacci, Chad A, 32, 631
Lupinacci, Chad, 38, 39, 40, 42, 124
Lupkin, Stanley N., 117

Lurie, Alvin D, 268
Luryi, Serge, 84, 122
Lusher-Shute, Lindsey, 469
Lussier, Nancy, 147
Lustig, Jessica, 528
Luthin, Catherine, 437
Lutterbie, John, 467
Lyman, James, 118
Lyman, Richard, 349
Lynch, John J, 4, 250
Lynch, John, 294
Lynch, Jr., William, 437
Lynch, Kenneth, 8, 147, 148
Lynch, Kevin G., 144
Lynch, Marge, 389
Lynch, Melissa, 458
Lynch, Michael C., 45
Lynch, Mitchell D., 529
Lynch, Patricia, 438
Lynch, Patrick J., 118
Lynch, Patrick, 243
Lynch, Peter, 50
Lynch, Rebecca, 386
Lynch, Stephen F, 321
Lynch, Stephen F., 242
Lynch, Stephen J., 48
Lynch, Steve, 326
Lynch, William R, 586
Lynch, William, 437
Lynch-Landy, Virginia, 426
Lyng, Nancy, 110
Lynn, Suzanne M, 359
Lyon, Barbara, 444
Lyons, Elizabeth, 529
Lyons, John, 384
Lyons, Patrick, 379
Lyons, Sarah D., 374
Lysyczyn, Gina, 86, 265
Lytle, James, 439
M. Lowey, Nita, 142
Mabee, Mike, 456
Macan, Lynn, 589
MacArthur Hultin, Jerry, 559
Macarthur, Dwight, 451
MacAvoy, Harry, 28
MacClelland, June, 231
MacDonald, Kevin, 583
MacDougall, Ian, 360
Maceko, Emma, 22
MacEnroe, Paul, 85, 123
MacEntee, Daniel, 18
Macielak, Paul F, 423
Maciol, Rob M., 333
Mack, Connie, 320
Mack, Martin J, 10, 207
Mackay, Daniel, 457
MacKenzie, Carol, 47
MacKenzie, Duncan R, 248
Mackenzie, Kate, 397
Mackenzie, Leslie, 171
MacKenzie, Maureen, 347
MacKenzie, Tracy, 52
Mackey, Robert J, 571
Mackey, Rosemary, 437
Mackin OFM, Fr Kevin E, 558
Mackin, James J., 528
MacKin, Janet, 559
Mackle, Jon, 222
Macklin, Ron, 448
MacKrell, Patrick J., 93
MacMillan, Kelly, 393
MacMurray, Worth, 457
MacNabb, Terry, 590
MacNaughton, Robert B, 588
MacNeal, K., 355
MacPeek, Robert, 349
MacPherson, Maria, 176
MacRae, Patrick F, 46
Madden, Joan A., 46
Madden, Kim, 378
Madden, Terrence, 451
Madeiros, Pamela, 421
Madhavan, Jaya, 49
Madia, Cali, 34
Madigan, Charlotte E, 361
Madigan, Michele, 364
Madison, Elizabeth, 447
Madison, Jennifer L, 565
Madlon, Doug M, 349
Madoff, Eric, 9, 200, 219
Maerten, Kathleen, 575
Maeshiro, Godfrey T., 496
Maffei, Dan, 297, 319, 320
Maffei, Michael, 78, 200
Magaliff, Gail, 258
Magdon-Ismail, Zainab, 381
Magee, Elsa, 103, 124
Magee, Karen E., 128
Magee, William, 32, 35, 39, 40, 70, 631
Maggio, Barbara, 161, 271
Maggiore, John, 3, 119, 160, 270
Magguilli, Michael C, 344
Magierski, Alice, 343
Maglione, Jim, 501
Magnarelli, William B, 32, 37, 40, 41, 189, 237, 631
Magnarelli, William, 41
Magnuson, Karen, 530
Mago, Patrice, 37
Maguire, Raymond, 345
Maguire, Sheila, 226, 261
Maha, Gary T, 329
Mahaffey, Monica, 467
Mahan, Paula A, 344
Mahanna, Brian, 84, 140, 149, 177, 188, 195, 201, 207, 221
Mahar, Jack, 335
Mahar, Michael, 156
Maher, Charlene, 410
Maher, Daniel F, 203
Maher, Nicole, 449
Mahon, Cathie, 81
Mahon, Roy S, 47
Mahoney, Elizabeth, 176
Mahoney, Joanne M, 104, 273, 287, 333
Mahoney, Paul J, 207
Mahoney, Ruth, 81
Maiano, Niurqui, 380
Maier, Brian, 443
Maier, Christopher T, 66
Maier, Philip, 353
Mailander, Edward, 410
Maillard, James, 299
Mailman, Jessica A., 489
Main, Jr, Robert G, 53
Mainiero, Crystal, 382
Mais, Andrew, 5, 303
Maisano, James, 339
Majerus, Kenneth J, 356
Makarowski, Jeremiah, 458
Maker, Ruhi, 410
Malagna, Christian, 37
Malatras, James, 3, 206, 234, 250
Malave, Jr., Ernesto, 397
Malave-Gonzalez, Nelinda, 49, 51
Malavolta, Luana, 481
Males, David J, 539
Maleski, Susan, 58
Malik, Bilal, 31
Malina, Joel, 126
Malinoski, Mark, 147
Malinoski, Michael, 102, 151
Malinovitz, Ayala, 99, 285
Malinowski, Katie, 105, 152, 309
Malito, Robert J., 420
Malito, Stephen A, 405
Malkin, Arthur, 438, 439
Mallah, Sandra G, 598
Mallalieu, Julia, 36, 40
Malliotakis, Nicole , 632
Malliotakis, Nicole, 32, 36, 37, 38, 42, 43, 242
Mallison, Victor, 18
Mallow, Betsy, 79, 103
Mallow, Rich, 117
Malmquist, Rebecca A, 51
Malone, Cheryl, 403
Malone, Dr. Beverly, 184
Malone, Joy, 63
Malone, Lawrence, 403
Malone, Scott, 533
Malone, Sonya, 57
Maloney Jr, John C, 215
Maloney, Carolyn B, 242, 311, 319, 321, 324
Maloney, Carolyn B., 79, 137, 168, 190, 203, 480
Maloney, Carolyn D, 321
Maloney, Carolyn, 90
Maloney, Darlene, 12, 235, 245, 264
Maloney, Sean P, 648
Maloney, Sean Patrick, 155, 190, 290
Maloney, Suzanne, 156

Malony, Carolyn B, 647
Maloy, Danielle, 122
Maltese, Joseph J, 45
Maltese, Joseph J., 46, 48
Malyn, Matt, 539
Mami-Moore, Kathleen, 29
Mammas, Carmela, 89
Mammen, David, 238
Mamousette, Eliel, 161
Manchin, Joe, 276
Mancini, John, 400
Mancini, Michael, 411
Mancini, Nicole, 384
Mancino, Anthony, 61
Mancuso, Tom, 248
Mandelbaum, David, 457
Mandelker, Lawrence A, 431
Mandell, Lawrence, 261
Maneely, Linda S., 132
Maney, Gerard E, 50
Maney, James, 232
Maney, Nancy, 13, 253
Mangan, Robert J, 346
Mangano, Edward P, 332
Mangano, Jr, Guy J, 48
Mangieri, Vincent, 291
Mangione, Jay, 92
Mango, James, 277
Mangold, Nancy M, 210
Mangold, Nancy M., 47
Maniglia, Andrew, 418
Manikowski, Michael J, 513
Manion, Nonie, 13, 86, 265
Mankiewicz, David, 395
Manko, Thomas J, 587
Manley, Patrick, 580
Mann, Denise F., 487
Mann, Joanne, 60
Mann, Melissa, 309
Mann, Roanne L., 212
Mann, Tim, 454
Mannarino, Anthony, 413
Manning III, Daniel, 329
Manning, David, 142
Manning, Donald, 429
Manning, J Francis, 584
Manning, Ken, 514
Manning, Peter, 395
Mannion, Eileen, 472
Mannion, Joseph, 494
Mannion, Patrick A., 400
Mannix Jr., Martin, 373
Mannix, Mark, 99, 286, 307
Mannix, W. Thomas, 309
Manoff, Mark, 388
Mansfield, Melissa, 424
Mantello, Sylvio, 14, 202, 221
Manurekar, Sunita, 447
Manzanet-Daniels, Sallie, 45
Manzella, Betty, 135
Manzi, Patricia, 449
Manzullo, Donald A, 320
Mapes, James D, 600
Mapes, James, 579
Mapp, Monisha R., 495
Mar, Nelson, 434
Maragos, George, 332
Marangas, Theresa, 461
Marano, Anthony, 47
Marber, Randy S., 47
Marcelle, Thomas, 62, 325
Marcellino, Carl L, 15, 18, 20, 22, 23, 24, 25, 125, 612
Marcellino, Carl L., 22
Marcellino, Carl, 23
Marcellus, John, 135
March, Jennifer, 197, 257, 397
March, Sandra, 409
Marchan, Juan, 50
Marchese, Leonard J., 365
Marchesella, Julie, 511
Marchi, Edmond, 182
Marchione, Kathleen A, 613
Marchione, Kathleen A., 18, 20
Marchione, Kathleen, 20, 22, 23, 25, 26, 189, 237
Marchione, Richard, 246, 284
Marciante, James V, 506
Marckioni, Frank, 473, 474
Marco, Diane M., 364
Marcus, Jed S., 440
Marcus, Martin, 48
Marcus, Patricia, 217
Marcuse, Elizabeth S, 565
Marcy, Joan, 31
Mareane, Joe, 338
Marengo, Ana, 354
Margeson, John E, 325
Margolis, Bernard, 120, 304
Margolis, Dan, 527
Margolis, Len, 510
Margulis, Ira H., 49
Margulis, Reed, 157
Mariani, Michael, 563, 564
Marie, Shaun, 371
Marilla, Robin, 27, 306
Marin, Alan C, 48
Marin, Laurie, 49
Marinacci, Leo, 296
Marinelli, Joseph J, 601
Marinich, Jerry F, 325
Marino, Anthony, 495
Marino, Cynthia, 544
Marino, Ralph, 570
Marino, Rebecca, 393
Marino, Richard, 220, 253
Marino, Ronald, 396
Marion, Dick, 145
Marion, Lucille A, 549
Marion, Lucille, 427
Mark Moore, Stephen, 457
Mark, Carol B., 430
Mark, Randolph, 496
Markee, Patrick, 399
Markert, Maureen, 451
Markey, Ed, 324
Markey, Edward J, 318
Markey, Edward J., 276
Markey, Margaret M, 32, 40, 41, 632
Markey, Margaret, 41, 42, 43, 275
Markezin, Ernest, 466
Markov, Peter, 330
Markowicz, Shai, 396
Markowitz, Marty, 330, 359, 489
Marks, Cabot J., 483
Marks, Lawrence K, 209
Marks, Lawrence, 46, 50
Marks, Philip A., 480
Markus, Marvin, 419
Markwica, Michael, 596
Marlow, Laura, 571
Marlowe, Francis, 350
Marmurstein, Mark, 291
Marocco, Andrew, 405, 476
Maron, Edward A., 47
Marone, Matt, 474
Marotta, Victoria, 341
Maroun, Paul A, 329
Marquette, James, 339
Marra, Donna M, 524
Marra, JanŠt, 335
Marraccini, Anthony, 347
Marrano, Frederic J, 63
Marrazzo, Jr., Orlando, 49
Marrello, Lisa M, 476
Marrin, Mary Margaret, 379
Marrone, Paul, 32
Marrus, Alan D., 50
Marsala, Deborah, 511
Marsh, Kerry D., 440
Marsh, Norman L., 326
Marsh, Richard, 582
Marsh, Susan, 326
Marshall, Dale W, 360
Marshall, Frederick J, 47
Marshall, Glenn, 351
Marshall, Helen M, 334, 359
Marshall, Julie, 510
Marshall, Marshall, 586
Marshall, Timothy D., 337
Marsico, Dr. Mary Jean, 601
Marsico, Ron, 105, 287, 309
Marsili, Denise, 59
Marte, Andy J., 496
Martel, Seth, 463
Martell, Terrence F., 550
Martens, Joseph J, 147
Martens, Joseph, 150, 452
Marthone, Joseph R., 489
Martin, Christine, 51
Martin, Daniel J, 10, 264
Martin, Daniel, 48
Martin, Dawn P., 493

Martin, Emrod, 482
Martin, James, 331
Martin, Jay, 17
Martin, Joanne, 42
Martin, John A, 559, 560
Martin, Kirk, 338
Martin, La Tia W, 48
Martin, Larry, 46
Martin, Lekeya, 37
Martin, Marissa, 382
Martin, Rebecca, 115
Martin, Robert A, 10, 294
Martin, Ryne, 527
Martin, Sarah, 120
Martin, Shawn P, 367
Martin, Virginia, 131
Martin, Will, 234, 240
Martindale, Suzanne, 402
Martinelli, Michael A, 66
Martinez LMSW, Johanna, 258
Martinez, Aydee, 484
Martinez, Barbara, 477
Martinez, Felix, 353
Martinez, Gina N, 9, 194
Martinez, Guillermo, 43, 195, 222, 254
Martinez, Herminio, 31
Martinez, Juan A., 440
Martinez, Juan, 537
Martinez, Luis, 448
Martinez, Mel, 313
Martinez, Miriam, 201, 219
Martinez, Sonia, 437
Martinez, Yvette, 414
Martinkovic, Richard A, 337
Martino, Deborah, 364
Martino, Jeffrey, 89, 212
Martino, Laura, 32
Martino, Ruben A., 50
Martino, Rubin, 49
Martino, Terry, 95, 150, 272
Martins, Jack M, 613
Martins, Jack, 18, 20, 21, 22, 23, 24, 25, 195, 202, 222, 242
Martinson, Kelley, 447
Martoche, Amy C, 62
Marton, Elana, 5, 252
Marton, Gary, 49
Martorana, Vincent J., 61
Martos, Randi, 30
Martucci, Kathleen, 175, 293
Martucci, Victor, 441
Martuscello III, Daniel F., 6, 108
Martuscello, Daniel, 109
Martuscello, William, 332
Martusewicz, Kim H, 54
Martz, Robert D, 284
Martzloff, Scott G, 575
Marutollo, Joseph Anthony, 115, 213
Marvel, Misha, 388
Marvin, Seth L., 50
Marx, Dr. Anthony W., 356
Marx, Paul I., 47
Marzeski, Thomas E, 578
Marzziotti, Robert, 388
Mascialino, John, 409, 421
Mascitti-Miller, Elizabeth, 464
Masera, Ronald, 593
Mashariki, Job, 298
Masi, Nicholas, 413
Masiello, Anthony, 441
Maskin, Daniel, 260
Masley, Andrea, 49
Mason, Harding, 493
Mason, Josephine, 531
Mason-Ailey, Victoria, 470
Massa, Eric JJ, 317, 320
Massarini, Roberta, 131
Massaro, Dominic R., 48
Massell, Martin J, 61
Massetti, John, 201, 220
Massimino, Elisa, 198
Masters, Kathleen, 392
Masterson, Gavin, 99, 285
Masterson, Kathleen, 270
Mastro, Bill, 410
Mastro, William F., 45
Mastromarino, John A, 332
Mastropietro, Joseph, 247
Masucci, Rosanna, 89
Masyr, Jesse, 473
Mataraso, Matthew, 455
Matarazzo, John R, 281
Matarazzo, Lou, 383
Matarazzo, Louis, 440
Matasar, Richard A, 558
Mateja, Kelly, 4, 250
Mathas, Theodore, 428
Mathews, Kelly, 403
Mathiesen, Christian, 364
Mathios, Alan, 544
Mathrani, Sandeep, 473
Matias, Beni, 277
Mativi, Lisa, 454
Matiychenko, Irina, 434
Matonak, Andrew, 427, 547
Matos Rodriguez, Felix V, 551
Matos-Rodgriguez, Felix, 397
Matott, Harold, 121
Matta, Heather, 531
Matter, Scott, 441
Mattera, Gloria, 374
Mattera-Russell, Pat, 354
Matteson, Jeffrey A, 591
Matthews, Brian C, 161
Matthews, Brian, 162, 236
Matthews, Cara, 532
Matthews, Gail, 115, 213
Matthews, James F, 61
Matthews, Joan, 154
Mattice, Barbara, 284
Mattie, John, 457
Mattimore, Gerald, 409
Mattison, Kevin, 523
Mattox, Cheryl, 175
Mattson, Carl, 470
Matundan, Jillian, 441
Maturo, Deborah L, 333
Matusiak, Kathleen, 598
Matyi, Ashton, 407
Matyszczyk, Terry, 59
Matz, Elliot S., 95, 295
Mauer, Jennifer, 76
Mauer, Myron, 473
Maupin, Patricia, 366
Maurer, Eric, 54
Maurer, Kirk, 230
Mauro, Frank, 268
Mauro, Thomas, 362
Maxwell, Daniel, 251
Maxwell, Greg, 364
Maxwell, James M., 372
Maxwell, Marcia, 419
May, Judy, 567
May, MD, John, 76
Mayberger, Robert D, 45
Maybury, Joan A, 351
Mayer, Amy, 440
Mayer, Carol, 429
Mayer, Cheryl, 339
Mayer, Frank C., 388
Mayer, Frank, 168
Mayer, Peter H., 47
Mayer, Shelley, 36, 37, 39, 40, 42, 632
Mayer, Shelly, 32
Mayers, Vaughn, 19
Mayersohn, Lee A., 48
Mayeux, Richard, 183
Maynard, Douglas B., 357
Mayo, Kathleen, 383
Mazeau, Adrienne, 174
Mazgajewski, James P, 573
Maziejka, Stanley, 589
Mazur, Thomas J., 328
Mazzaferro, John J, 363
Mazzarelli, Angela M, 45
Mazzola, Lawrence, 153
Mazzullo, Theresa, 471, 511
Mazzulo, Donald S, 423
Mbuyi, Dennis, 121
McAdams, Kevin, 419
McAlary, John J, 101, 211, 308
McAllister, James, 60
McAllister, Patrick, 337
McAllister, Ryan, 21, 24
McAndrew-Plate, Hillary, 435
McArdle, Barry, 110
McAuley, Kathleen, 161
McAuliffe, Jr, J Gerard, 329
McAuliffe, Kenneth J, 577
McAuliffe, Kevin R., 425
McAusland, Linda L, 105, 287
McBrayer, Kara, 131
McBride, Robert, 453

McCabe, Catherine, 154
McCabe, Patricia, 16
McCaffey, Kevin, 349
McCaffrey, Gregory J., 331
McCaffrey, Kevin, 337
McCahey, Stephen J., 89, 212
McCain, John, 313
McCall, H. Carl, 543
McCall, Michael, 320
Mccammon, Todd, 539
McCann, Ann, 338
McCann, Carole, 502
McCann, Daniel, 598
McCann, Dean, 354
McCann, Hugh P, 105, 287
McCann, Jeffery, 346
McCann, Joseph D, 63
McCann, Michael, 457
McCann, William, 130
McCardle, Jonathan, 414
McCarran, Cynthia, 141
McCarrick, John, 474
McCarron, Greg, 158
McCarthy, Bill, 388
McCarthy, Carolyn, 224, 311, 318, 319
McCarthy, Casey, 132
McCarthy, Christopher, 48
McCarthy, Colleen, 471
McCarthy, Dan, 70
McCarthy, Elizabeth, 105, 287
McCarthy, Gary, 364
McCarthy, III, Edward W., 55
McCarthy, James, 46
McCarthy, John, 388
McCarthy, Judy, 569
McCarthy, Justin, 431
McCarthy, Katherine, 381
McCarthy, Laura, 384
McCarthy, Loretta, 463
McCarthy, Maryann, 445
McCarthy, Mathew Kelly, 62
McCarthy, Maureen, 491
McCarthy, Michael J, 588
McCarthy, Patrick, 438
McCarthy, Pete, 276
McCarthy, Peter, 428
McCarthy, William E, 45
McCarthy, William F, 56
McCartney, Brian P, 187
McCartney, Jim, 456
McCartney, John G, 289
McCartney, Timothy, 99, 286
McCarty, Kathleen, 27
McCaskill, Claire, 180
McCaul, Michael, 168
McClanahan, Kevin, 49
McClary, Kevin, 523
McClure, Christopher W., 351
McClure, Teri P., 496
McClure, Walt, 206
McClure, Walter J, 308
McClure, Walter, 101, 114, 308
McCluskey, Linda, 60
McClusky, James P., 46
McCollum, Cynthia, 443
McConnell, Margaret M., 482
McConnell, Shawn, 453
McConney, Norman, 437
McCord, Richard J, 63
McCormack, James P, 55
McCormack, James, 47
McCormack, Kathy, 162, 236
McCormack, Michael, 375
McCormick, Bruce, 109
McCormick, Debra A, 341
McCormick, Jen, 4, 69, 250
McCormick, Jim, 75
McCormick, John, 386
McCormick, Mary, 144, 238
McCormick, Maureen, 435
McCormick, Michael J, 130
McCormick, Robert, 430
McCormick, Zvia, 199
McCourtney, Ted, 463
McCoy, Alyssa, 42
McCoy, Carole A, 548
McCoy, Daniel P., 325
McCoy, Daniel, 501
McCoy, Shirley, 430
McCrary, Michael, 509
McCrobie, Sarah, 529
McCrory, Robert, 471
McCue, Casey, 70
McCulley, James, 393
McCullom, Ellen, 79
McCullough, Bonnie, 417
McCullough, Daniel, 50
McCullough, Randy, 417
McCullough, Sterling, 377
McCurnin, Richmond, 187
McCutcheon, Burleigh, 98, 163
McCutcheon, Steve, 40
McDade III, Herbert H, 214
McDade, John M., 289
McDermott, Dennis K, 54
McDermott, Frank, 464
McDermott, Jim, 180, 323
McDermott, Maggie, 33
McDermott, Marylou, 593
McDermott, Moira, 482
McDermott, Richard, 445
McDevitt, Charles R., 496
McDonald III, John T, 32, 632
McDonald III, John, 35, 36, 40, 41
McDonald Jr, John C, 574
McDonald, Audra, 174
McDonald, Keith, 341
McDonald, Kevin, 449
McDonald, Mary Pat, 22
McDonald, Robert J, 48
McDonald, Tom, 384
McDonnell, Brian, 242
McDonnell, Jean A, 13, 265, 305
McDonnell, John J, 244
McDonnell, Nancy K., 430
McDonough, Daniel, 424
McDonough, David G, 32, 39, 42, 237, 288, 632
McDonough, David, 28, 36, 37, 42
McDonough, Edward G, 134
McDonough, James, 61
McDonough, Kathleen, 176
McDowell, Janet A., 488
McElroy, Edward J, 224
McElwain, Steve, 86, 97, 188
McElyea, Gary, 399
McEneny, Rachel, 14, 202, 221, 305
Mcentire, Michelle, 451
McEvoy, Robert J, 361
McFadden, James P, 338
McFadden, Tim, 426
McGahay, Allison, 132
McGahay, William, 371, 393
McGann, Marcia E., 481
McGarrity, Matthew, 574
McGarry, Peggy Ann, 472
McGaugh, James, 417
McGee, Kathleen, 78, 84, 140, 207, 263
McGiffert, Elizabeth, 402
McGill, Edward, 424
McGill, Michael V, 599
McGill, Patrick R, 52
McGill, Phyllis Spiegel, 595
McGinty, Anthony, 60
McGlew, Patrick, 449
McGlinn, Mike, 459
McGlynn, James, 455
McGovern Jr, Thomas, 367
McGovern, Carol, 334
McGovern, James F, 321
McGovern, Jim, 154, 180
McGovern, Margaret, 426
McGovern, Maryanne, 463
McGovern, Michael, 57
McGowan, Kevin, 578
McGowan, Peter, 140
McGowan, R Moke, 275
McGowan, Seth, 575
McGowan, Susan, 99, 286, 307
McGowan, Thomas F, 596
McGown, Michael, 347
McGrath, Ann Marie, 108
McGrath, George, 441
McGrath, John, 409
McGrath, Joseph, 163
McGrath, Kevin, 455
McGrath, Patrick J, 46
McGrath, Robert, 467
McGrath, Sharon, 294
McGrath, Siobhan, 393
McGrattan, Steve, 69
McGraw, Karen, 571
McGreevy, James, 380

McGrogan, Donna, 348
McGuiness, Keziah, 474
McGuire, Jason J., 371
McGuire, Jr., William L., 50
McGuire, Michael, 59
McGuirl, Kate, 364
McHenry Esq, Barnabas, 9
McHenry, Barnabas, 149, 271
McHenry, Patrick T., 190, 203
McHenry, Patrick, 321
McHugh, John M, 317, 321
McHugh, Joseph, 448
McHugh, Patrick J., 440
McInerney, MD, Joan, 296
McInerney, William A, 366
McInnes, John P, 8, 176
McInnis, Stephen C., 491
McIntosh, Louis C, 587
McIntosh, Rosalyn C., 484
McIntyre, Brian, 280
McIntyre, Carlene V, 105, 287
McIntyre, James, 445
McIntyre, Mike, 317
McKane, Laura, 366
McKay, Osbourne A, 108
McKay, Sandra P, 136
McKay, Shaun L, 548
McKeage, Louis G., 93
McKee, Michael, 460
McKee, Seth, 463
McKeever, Keith, 95, 150, 272, 306
McKeighan, Kelly S, 60
McKelvey, Lynn, 56
McKelvey, Rev. Jack, 554
McKenna, James, 274, 509, 593
McKenna, Ryan, 517
McKenzie, Wayne, 357
McKeon, Douglas E, 48
McKeon, Douglas E., 48, 210
McKeon, Howard P (Buck), 318
McKeon, Michael F, 62
McKeon, Michael, 443
McKeown, Patricia, 517
McKeown, Sadie, 400
McKeveny, Robert, 590
McKevitt, Tom, 28, 32, 36, 38, 40, 632
McKie, Karen, 54
McKillop, John P, 217, 243
McKinstry, JoAnn, 338
McKnight, Colin, 192
McKnight, Donald, 10, 293
McKoy, A Richard, 34
McKoy, Jeffrey, 108, 110
McLarty, Michael, 415
McLaughlin, Andrew, 358
McLaughlin, Carolyn, 341
McLaughlin, Edward, 50
McLaughlin, Elizabeth J, 136
McLaughlin, John, 203
McLaughlin, Kevin, 502
McLaughlin, Martin, 401, 438, 440
McLaughlin, Rosemary, 512
McLaughlin, Steve, 32
McLaughlin, Steven F, 633
McLaughlin, Steven, 36, 37, 38, 42
McLaughlin, Stevenr, 178, 254
McLean III, William L, 525
Mclean, Mary Ann, 476
McLean, Ronald D., 433
McLees, Andrew M., 266
McLeod, James A, 62
McLeod, Robert, 424
McLeod, Suzanne, 568
McLetchie, Antony A.L., 128
McMahon II, J. Ryan, 333
McMahon, Brian T, 409
McMahon, Brian T., 93
McMahon, Daniel, 368
McMahon, Edmund J, 91
McMahon, James, 428
McMahon, Jennifer, 467
McMahon, John, 401
McMahon, Judith N., 48, 210
McMahon, Kathy A, 258
McMahon, Margaret, 489
McMahon, Michael E, 319, 320, 322, 323
McMahon, Michael W, 595
McMahon, Michael, 424
McMahon, Rory A., 66
McMahon, Ruth, 430
McMahon, Thomas, 469
McManmon, James, 106, 274
McManus, John, 207
McManus, Michael, 244
McManus, Tony, 537
McMaster, Robert, 396
McMath-Turner, Lavita, 397
McMullen, Joseph, 398
McMurray, Steve, 539
McNally Jr, Richard J, 46, 335
McNally, Charles, 190
McNally, David, 414
McNally, Peter, 414, 436
McNally, Regina, 204
McNamara, Scott D, 333
McNamara, Thomas J, 48
McNaughton, Michael, 474
McNeil, Lureen, 173
McNeil, Patrick, 373
McNeil, Susan, 375
McNeill, Mark S, 588
McNerney, Patrick, 493
McNulty, David, 116, 213, 214
McNulty, Michael, 425, 436
McPheeters, Jean, 517
McPherson, Pat, 366
McPherson, Sybil, 407
McQuade, Jack, 266
McQuade, John, 114
McQuage, Walker, 474
McQuair, Ida, 32
McQueer, Douglas, 590
McRedmond, Barbara, 20, 26, 43, 87, 152
McShane, Eric S, 245
McShane, Eric S., 161
McShane, Joseph M, 555
McShane, Joseph M., 126
McShane, Owen, 283
McSweeney, Mary M, 234, 240
McTamaney, Mary, 360
McVinney, Richard W., 64
Meacham, Joseph D, 343
Meacham, Lisa, 63
Mead, Nan Eileen, 119
Mead, Robert, 371
Meade, Michael, 207
Meadows Shuford, Maxine, 120
Meadows, Mark, 137
Meagher, Ann M, 516
Meagher, Terese, 106, 124
Mealey, Karen L, 52
Meany, Kathleen, 567
Meara, Brian R, 442
Meara, Brian, 442
Mears, Doug, 457
Mechanic, Jonathan, 416
Meckler, Lawrence M., 343
Medbury, Scot, 155, 277
Meddaugh, Mark M, 59
Medina Jr., Alfredo, 465
Medina, Carlos, 467, 543
Meeder, Curt N, 51
Meegan, Sheila, 367
Meehan, Avice, 183
Meehan, Robert, 339
Meek Gallagher, Craig, 148
Meeks, Gregory W, 311, 319, 320, 648
Meeks, Gregory W., 79, 89, 190, 197, 203
Meeks, Simone-Marie, 377
Meeks, Stephanie K., 192
Mehiel, Dennis, 95, 272
Mehrhof, Edward, 585
Mehrota, Apurva, 397
Mehta, Amul, 494
Meier, Donna, 75
Meier, Henry, 433
Meier, Raymond, 388
Meier, Thomas G., 367
Meier, Thomas K, 555
Meierdiercks, Warren A, 581
Meister, Adam, 426
Meister, Cliff, 201, 219
Meixell, David, 451
Melchionni, Ellen, 204, 428
Mele, Amy, 344
Melecio, Jacqueline, 260
Melendez, Michael, 179, 254
Melendez, Suzanne J., 50
Melendez, Thalia, 120
Melfi, Joyce, 373
Melfi, Lindsey, 378
Melish, Tara J., 199
Melkonian, Michael, 57

Appendices: Financial Plan, Indexes & Maps

Mella, Rita, 49
Meller, Carol, 434
Mellin, William J, 81
Mellin, William, 433
Mellow, Gail O, 551
Mellow, Gail, 397
Melnick, Edward K, 581
Melnitsky, Sheldon, 187
Meloni, Angela A., 490
Melson, Nick, 29
Melucci, Dr. Roseanne, 580
Melucci, Ranier W, 581
Melville, James, 566
Melville, John P, 7, 160, 235
Melvin, Jerome F, 584
Menapace, John, 100, 273
Menard, John, 474
Menard, Joseph, 577
Menchini, Gino, 448
Mendelson, Andrew, 459
Mendelson, Richard, 223
Mendelson, Sarah, 168
Mendez, Manuel J., 49
Mendez, Manuel, 46
Mendoza, Kenny, 42
Menendez, Robert, 313, 315
Meng, Grace, 89, 90, 197, 224, 648
Meng, Socheaita, 454
Menges, Patricia, 167, 196
Menkin, Cori, 432
Mennin, Felicia A., 353
Meno, Reynaldo, 538
Mensch, Rebecca S, 62
Menschel, Ronay, 438
Menz, Ronald, 73, 167
Merchant, Rahul N., 355
Mercure, Thomas, 209
Meredith, Cynthia, 467
Meredith, Suzanne, 366
Merino, Robert, 64
Merkley, Jeff, 73
Merklinger, John M, 363
Merola, Frank, 335
Merrell, Bill C, 247
Merrell, Charles C., 46
Merrick, Greg, 348
Merrick, James C, 331
Merrigan, John A., 482
Merrill, Anne, 510
Merrill, Kitty, 528
Merrill, Thomas, 355
Merriman, Edward, 107, 274
Merriman, James D., 395
Mersch, Michael, 478
Merz, Thomas, 530
Mesick, Edie, 466
Messing, Dean, 328
Messner, Kurt, 72, 178
Metcalf, James M, 64
Metz, Justin, 460
Metzdorff, Howard, 210
Metzger, Nancy C, 343
Metzger, Rabbi Aaron, 70
Metzko, Lori, 52
Metzler, Marie, 132
Mevorach, Ben, 535
Meyer, Alan J., 50
Meyer, Chris, 402
Meyer, Deborah, 455
Meyer, Esq., Gregory, 19
Meyer, Joan, 472
Meyer, Lisa Marie, 64
Meyer, Louise R., 430
Meyer, Richard D, 53
Meyerhoffer, Mark, 438
Meyerowitz, Cyril, 471
Meyers, Charles, 592
Meyers, Melanie, 416
Meyers, Michael, 199
Mezquita, Jerson R., 485
Mica, John L, 322
Miccoli, Vinny, 229
Michaels, Glen, 208
Michaels, Lance, 378
Michalek, John A, 47
Michalenko, Edward M, 344
Michalski, John L., 47
Michaud, Michael H., 297
Michaud, Mike, 323
Michel, Michael, 133
Michel, Patrick, 600
Michel, Sean, 585
Michelini, Adam, 60
Michels, Shari, 49
Middlebrook, Brian, 428
Midey Jr, Nicholas V, 48
Midey, Michael J, 584
Midey, Paul, 20, 23
Miele, Angela, 446
Miele, Susan, 502
Migaleddi, Mark F., 295
Migliori, Rocco, 583
Mignano, Stephen J, 48
Mignone, Mario, 467
Miguel Araiza, Francisco, 397
Mihaltses, George D., 356
Mikk, Katherine, 443
Mikula, Edward, 349
Mikulsi, Barbara, 312
Mikulski, Barbara A., 73, 143, 267
Mikulski, Barbara, 312, 315
Milani, Fred T., 419
Milano, Frank P., 48
Milbrath, Kim, 438
Milch, Ronald, 444
Miles, Donald A., 49
Miles, Evelyn, 70
Miles, George R, 192
Miletich, Radmila, 407
Miletti, John D, 379
Milgrim, John, 533
Miliano, Michael, 9, 219
Milin, Maria, 49
Militello, Carl H, 583
Miljoner, Irv, 223
Milkosky, David, 388
Millea, Matthew, 3
Miller II, Richard H, 51
Miller, Alan Gifford, 416
Miller, Amanda, 503
Miller, Anita, 98, 286
Miller, Arthur, 419
Miller, Brad, 322
Miller, Bryan, 470
Miller, Christopher, 352
Miller, Daniel, 131
Miller, Deborah Long, 240
Miller, Eileen, 16
Miller, Elizabeth, 167, 196
Miller, Erika, 462
Miller, Gary, 319
Miller, George, 224, 318
Miller, Ira, 384
Miller, Janet, 392
Miller, Jeff, 139, 297, 318, 324
Miller, Johanna, 454
Miller, Jonathan J, 329
Miller, Jr., Richard, 490
Miller, Kathy E, 75
Miller, Lindsey, 383
Miller, Lorellei, 329
Miller, M. Julie, 372
Miller, Maggie, 3, 5, 140, 160
Miller, Marci, 434
Miller, Matt, 537
Miller, Melvin, 453
Miller, Michael G, 633
Miller, Michael S., 198
Miller, Michael, 27, 32, 35, 37, 40, 41, 42
Miller, Michele, 132
Miller, Mitchell W, 432
Miller, Neal S, 586
Miller, Paul, 384
Miller, Paula, 58
Miller, Rasul H., 497
Miller, Rebecca, 60
Miller, Richard J., 483
Miller, Richard, 474
Miller, Robert J, 45
Miller, Robert, 586
Miller, Ron, 179
Miller, Sam, 354
Miller, Sandra, 401
Miller, Sarah, 428
Miller, Scott A., 63
Miller, Scott, 535
Miller, Stephen T, 65
Miller, Stuart, 476
Miller, Susan, 362
Miller, Tech Sgt. Eric, 295
Miller, Thomas J., 56
Miller, Virginia A, 111
Miller, Virginia, 6, 252

Miller, Wesley Preston, 295
Miller, William, 50
Miller-Foster, Christina, 424
Milliken, James B., 550
Million, Katie, 104, 273
Millock, Peter, 450
Mills, Cheryl, 296
Mills, G Foster, 356
Mills, Heather, 409
Mills, James, 367
Mills, John J, 328
Mills, John W, 559
Mills, Steve, 454
Mills, Theresa, 527
Mills, Thomas E, 328
Milner, Ed, 506
Milone, Deborah, 509
Milot, Michelle, 38
Minahan, Timothy, 430
Minardo, Philip G., 48
Minarik, Hon Renee Forgensi, 217
Minarik, Renee Forgensi, 48
Minaya, Julio, 397
Mincher, Rachael L, 244
Mincher, Rachael L., 118
Miner, George, 503, 516
Miner, Glenn R, 113
Miner, Julie, 427
Miner, Stephanie A, 365
Miner, Thomas A, 325
Mingione, Emanuel J, 288
Miniger, Robert, 516
Minissale, Theodore T, 187
Minkel, Kimberley A, 105, 287
Minkowitz, Martin, 468
Minnick, Thomas, 391
Minor, Rodney, 525
Minter-Brooks, Sheryl, 229, 230
Mintz, Jonathan, 353
Mio, Peter, 528, 531
Mirabal, Manuel, 451
Mirabito, Jerome A, 62
Miraglia, Robert P., 485
Miranda Jr, Luis A, 445
Miranda, David P., 144
Miranda, George, 487
Miras, Floyd, 290
Miringoff, Lee M., 138
Mirras, Michael J, 336
Mirto, Joseph, 410
Misa, Elizabeth, 175
Misewich, Jim, 389
Misiaszek, Michael J, 64
Misztal, Richard, 73
Mitchell, Erin, 414
Mitchell, Harry E, 323
Mitchell, Kathy, 402
Mitchell, Kenneth C., 282
Mitchell, Kenneth, 588
Mitchell, Linda M, 373
Mitchell, Maria K, 380
Mitchell, MD, Margaret, 175, 293
Mitchell, Richard C, 334
Mitchell, Stuart J., 77, 192
Mitchell, Susan T, 266
Mitchell, Tammy, 141
Mitchell, Teresa, 281
Mitchell, Terry A, 53
Mitchell, William, 266
Mithen-Demasi, Lori, 383
Mitola, Michele, 416
Mitrano, III, Salvatore, 363
Mittenthal, Matt, 10, 78, 84, 112, 140, 149, 177, 188, 195, 201, 207, 221, 304
Mitterway, Kathleen, 360
Mix Sr, Gary T, 575
Mizbani, Reza, 4, 250, 303
Mizel, Marianne O, 60
Mizener, Kathy, 432
Mizer, Benjamin C, 89
Moccia, Josephine, 587
Mochrie, Doreen, 454
Mock, Janice F, 53
Modafferi, Tony, 144
Modica, Paul J., 365
Modica, Salvatore J., 50
Moehle, William W, 342
Moeller, Henry, 365
Moesel, Jamie A, 577
Moffett, Tara Lynn, 198
Moffitt, Larry, 506
Mogulescu, John, 397, 552
Mogulescu, Sara, 472
Mogulescu, William I., 50
Mohaghan, Luke, 401
Mohan, George, 432
Mohr, Ralph M, 132
Mohun, Michael, 60
Mok, Martin, 412
Mole, Tina, 328
Molea, Richard, 48
Molia, Denise F., 59
Molina Rojas, Suzanna, 45
Molina, Ada, 49
Molina, Angel D., 483
Molinaro, James P, 335, 359
Molinaro, James P., 494
Molinaro, Marcus J., 328
Molinaro, Peter, 453
Molke, Richard, 445
Moll, Steven, 428
Mollen, Gerald F, 325
Mollenkopf, John, 138
Mollohan, Alan B, 317
Mollot, Richard J., 436
Molloy, Charles, 587
Molloy, Paul, 277
Molluso, Christopher, 17
Molnar, Janice, 119, 251
Momot, Kevin, 529
Momplaisir-Ellis, Marjorie, 392
Monaco, Eugene J, 233
Monahan, Mary Lou A, 131
Mondanaro, Mark P, 574
Mondello, Joseph, 375
Monderson, Suedamay A., 481
Mondo, Suzanne M., 50
Mondrick, Lynne, 64
Mone, Lawrence J., 92, 170
Money, Dorothy, 34
Mongiardo, Eve, 428
Mongillo, Paul, 72, 166, 167
Mongold, Edward D, 365
Monjeau, Julianna, 352
Monroe, Cynthia, 327
Monroe, James E, 203
Monson, Charles W, 4, 173, 227, 251
Monsoor, Sonia, 463
Montalbano, Vincent, 445
Montalbo, Marjoel, 356
Montalvo, Krystle, 463
Montano, Alfonso J., 289
Montbach, Joan, 426
Monte, Linda, 153
Monteiro, Kenneth T., 493
Monteiro, Paul, 89
Montellione, Robert, 457
Monterosso, Jacqueline, 460
Montesano, Michael A, 633
Montesano, Michael, 28, 32, 36, 37, 38, 40, 41, 211
Montgomery, Velmanette, 16, 18, 20, 22, 23, 25, 178, 254, 613
Montgomery-Costa, Veronica, 243, 489
Monti, Joyce, 508
Montminy, Renee, 30
Montone, George, 464
Montour, Mark A., 47
Moody, John, 538
Moody, Joseph M, 518
Moody-Czub, Jackie, 4, 69
Moon, ACCS Mark, 289
Moon, Felipe, 335
Mooney, Jr, William M, 519
Mooney, Stephen, 451
Moonves, Leslie, 143
Mooradian, Susan, 432
Moore, Art, 538
Moore, Bonnie, 343
Moore, Catherine, 530
Moore, Dennis, 319
Moore, Gary D, 331
Moore, Jeffrey, 563
Moore, John S., 50
Moore, John, 539
Moore, Kenneth, 427
Moore, Linda D., 372
Moore, Michael J., 210
Moore, Michele M, 260
Moore, Musa, 396, 404, 467
Moore, Patrick C, 80
Moore, Rick T, 577
Moore, Robert J, 412

Moore, Robert J., 412
Moore, Robert, 458
Moore, Ryan, 393
Moore, Suzanne, 529
Moore, Tasha, 194
Moore, Terrence, 487
Moore, Tishima, 458
Moore, Vickie, 358
Moore-Besson, Lystra, 490
Moquin, Nanci, 342
Mora, Frank M., 65
Mora, Juan, 492
Morabito, Rocky, 362
Morales, Hugo M., 550
Morales, Ricardo E., 353
Morales, Tomas, 551
Moran, Jerry, 73, 317
Moran, Karin, 447
Moran, Leslie S, 423
Moran, Thomas, 47, 54
Moranda, Susan, 380
Morcom-Kenney, Elizabeth, 120
Moreau, Karen, 145
Moree, Maggie, 378
Morehouse, William C, 366
Morell, Jeannine, 241
Morelle, Joseph D, 32, 41, 373, 633
Morelle, Joseph, 27
Morellia, Michael, 502
Moreno, Joseph, 296
Moreschi, Nikki J, 63
Morgan Jr., Paul V., 57
Morgan MD, Charles W, 4
Morgan, Barry, 297
Morgan, Dorothy, 134
Morgan, Edward, 375
Morgan, Frank, 400
Morgan, Hilary, 468
Morgan, Joseph, 595
Morgan, Kevin, 128
Morgan, MD, Charles W, 173, 227, 250
Morgan, Stephen D, 292
Morgan, Stephen, 414
Morgan, Steven, 333
Morgante, Peter, 570
Morgante, Samuel, 418
Mori, Brenda, 337
Moriarity III, Jeremiah J, 48
Moriarty, III, Jeremy J., 47
Moriarty, Michael, 4, 78, 200
Morik, Helen, 457
Morillo, H., 355
Morin, Matt, 538
Moritz, Kimberly, 569
Moritz, Tom, 448
Mormile, Dara, 524
Morris, Carolyn, 328
Morris, Cecelia G., 212
Morris, Cecily L., 58
Morris, Cheryl V, 110
Morris, David A., 61
Morris, David J, 331
Morris, Dennis J., 58
Morris, Jackson, 448, 453
Morris, Karen, 423
Morris, Michael, 455
Morris, Phyllis, 13, 195, 253
Morris, Shawn, 78, 140, 177, 207
Morris, Virginia E, 132
Morrisey, Marcilyn, 56
Morrison, Caroline, 65
Morrison, Christina A, 134
Morrison, Mark, 432
Morrison, Trevor W., 217
Morrison, Valerie, 5, 240
Morrissey, Eric, 453
Morrissey, Joe, 6, 69, 111, 206, 235
Morrissey, Joseph, 10, 283, 304
Morrisson, Valerie, 234
Morrone, Thomas L, 375
Morrow, Phillip, 514
Morse, Alan R., 183
Morse, Deanna L., 54
Morse, Lorraine, 112, 305
Morse, Ralph, 451
Morse, Shawn M., 325
Morse, Thomas R, 65
Morton, John, 535
Morton, Karen, 447
Morton, Margaret, 353
Moschetti, Peter, 102, 272
Mosconi, Toni, 525
Moseley, Roberta, 13, 265
Moser, Ezra, 419
Moser, Kathy, 8, 147, 449
Moser, Kimberly, 49
Moser, Leanne, 331
Moses, C Warren, 257
Moses, Richard, 417
Moses, Ryan, 393, 476
Moses, Stanley, 191
Mosesian, Ken, 186
Mosher, Michael L., 143
Moskowitz, Karla, 45
Moskowitz, Ross F., 468
Mosley, Walter T, 32
Mosley, Walter, 35, 36, 37, 39
Mosley, Water T, 633
Moson, Robert, 64
Mosquera, Manuel, 250
Moss, Adam, 533
Moss, Christopher J, 327
Moss, Michael, 432
Moss, Mitchell L., 192, 239
Moss, Ron, 255
Moss, Ronald, 179
Moss, Violet, 454, 457
Mostajo, Maria, 308
Mostert, Eric, 13, 86, 265
Mostow, Michael, 593
Motl, David, 267
Motley, Duane, 441
Mott, Richard, 46
Mott, Samuel, 382
Moulin, Edward, 445
Moulton, Peter H., 46
Moulton, Peter K., 49
Moulton, Peter, 46
Mount, Chester, 210
Moussavian, Avideh, 463
Moy, Jeanette, 84, 112, 161, 206
Moya, Francisco P, 633
Moya, Francisco, 32, 37, 38, 39, 40, 43
Moynihan, Brian T, 80
Mraz, James, 506
Mucci, John, 401
Mucci, Joyce, 596
Mucha, John, 469
Mudie, Rebecca, 36, 39, 42
Muehl, John M, 334
Mueller, Chris, 469
Mueller, Kimberly, 568
Mueller, Lisa, 463
Mueller, Robin, 22
Muendell, Edward J., 430
Mugdan, Walter, 154
Muggeridge, John, 415
Mugica, Yerina, 448
Mugits, Michael, 567
Muhib, Noreen, 463
Muirhead, Lucy, 138
Mujanovic, Elvir, 444
Mujica, Robert F, 5, 83, 160, 234, 263
Mujica, Robert, 16, 23
Mukarji-Connolly, Anya, 471
Mukjerjee, Romona, 463
Mulcahy, Matt, 539
Mulford, Ruth, 434
Mulgrew, Michael, 129
Mulham, Charles, 114, 266
Mulholland, Nancy, 140, 160, 283
Mulieri, Richard, 99, 285
Mulkins, Barb, 501
Mullaney, Dr Roxanne C, 72
Mullarkey, Althea, 463
Mullarkey, Janet, 254
Mullen, Cassandra, 50
Mullen, Fr Kevin, 560
Mullen, Gloria, 445
Mullen, Joseph, 9, 200, 219
Mullen, Michael F, 48
Mullen, OFM, Fr. Kevin, 465
Mullen, Shirley, 556
Muller, Kate, 102, 141, 151, 308
Muller, Robert J, 46
Muller, William J, 332
Muller, William J., 115, 213
Mullgrav, Jeanne B, 359
Mulligan, Brian, 474
Mulligan, Jeff, 358
Mulligan, Lisa, 502
Mulligan, Michelle, 206
Mulligan, Seth, 395

Mullings, Pauline, 50
Mullins, Betsy, 139
Mulqueen, Cliff, 355
Mulrow, William, 3, 69, 78, 83, 108, 119, 130, 140, 147, 160, 173, 187, 194, 200, 206, 219, 227, 234, 240, 245, 250, 263, 270, 283, 293
Mulroy, Martha E, 56
Multer, Susan, 434
Mulvay, Robert C, 45
Mulverhill, Kevin, 329
Mulvey, Erin, 114
Mulvey, Linda, 464
Mulvey, Robert C., 47
Mulvey, Robert, 209
Mummenthey, Carl J, 589
Mumpton, F James, 96, 273, 306
Mundinger, Elizabeth, 439
Mundy, Marina, 49
Mungeer, Thomas, 456
Munger, Arthur R., 371
Munger, Teresa, 134
Muniz, Felix, 22, 23
Munn, Norma P, 279
Munn, Norma, 382
Munnelly, Ken, 14, 202, 221
Munnelly, Kenneth, 221
Munro, Diane M, 568
Munro, James, 458
Munroe, Kaitesi, 41
Munzinger, Kate, 19
Murad, David A., 46
Murad, John, 543
Mural, Catherine, 413
Muratore, Joseph, 429
Muratori, Jill, 385
Murkowski, Lisa, 143, 155, 276, 314
Murphy III, James A, 58
Murphy Jr, Cornelius B, 545
Murphy McGraw, Denise, 424
Murphy, Alicia, 518
Murphy, Charles J, 580
Murphy, Charles, 471
Murphy, Chris, 145
Murphy, Col Patricia M, 297
Murphy, Cornelius, 468
Murphy, Daniel C, 281
Murphy, Ed, 373
Murphy, Ellen, 266
Murphy, Elysia, 397
Murphy, III, James A, 335
Murphy, J Emmett, 47
Murphy, James P, 46
Murphy, James T., 458
Murphy, Jeff, 339
Murphy, Jeremy, 532
Murphy, Jerome, 47
Murphy, John J., 493
Murphy, John, 381, 396, 404
Murphy, Joseph R, 596
Murphy, Karen, 47
Murphy, Martin P., 50
Murphy, Matthew J, 56
Murphy, Michael, 55, 107, 222, 288, 349, 421
Murphy, Nicole, 63
Murphy, Peter, 399, 416
Murphy, Rhona, 533
Murphy, Rich, 26, 43
Murphy, Rick, 528
Murphy, Roberta, 451
Murphy, Scott, 318
Murphy, Steve, 414
Murphy, Terence P., 61
Murphy, Terrance, 24
Murphy, Terrence P, 613
Murphy, Terrence, 18, 20, 23, 24, 25, 26, 43
Murphy, Thomas C., 415
Murphy, Thomas J, 456
Murphy, Timothy, 468
Murphy, William, 121
Murran, Pam, 135
Murray, Ann Marie, 547
Murray, Brian, 72, 189
Murray, Daniel, 578
Murray, Dean, 32, 35, 37, 41, 42, 634
Murray, Dennis J, 557
Murray, Derek, 444
Murray, Francis X, 363
Murray, Gregory, 210, 305
Murray, Kate, 347
Murray, Kevin, 162, 236, 241
Murray, Leslie A., 492
Murray, Meg, 283
Murray, Olga H., 348
Murray, Patty, 125, 180, 267, 313, 315
Murray, Rita, 449
Murray, William P., 85, 123
Murray, William, 76
Mursko, Frank, 458
Murtagh, Karen L., 118
Murtagh, Wanda D, 329
Murtha, John P, 317
Muscarella, Joseph, 447
Musich, Thomas, 34
Musolino, Mario, 9, 201, 220, 253, 293
Mustich, Peter J, 599
Musumeci, MaryAnn, 296
Muterspaw, Alice, 224, 256
Muthig, Jennifer, 472
Muyskens, James, 397
Muzio, David, 289
Mycek, William J, 61
Mychajliw, Stefan I., 328
Myers, Brenda, 599
Myers, Cheryl, 37
Myers, Douglas I., 95, 284, 306
Myers, Kelly, 364
Myers, Kevin, 458
Myers, PhD, Robert, 228
Myrick, Sue, 324
Myrick, Svante, 348
Myrie, S., 355
Myrie, Sharon A., 434
Myszka, Edward, 574
Myvett, Newton, 564
N'dolo, R Michael, 518
Naccarato, Susan, 121, 174, 228
Nachmias, Stuart, 401
Nacinovich, Anne, 434
Nadeau, Katherine, 412
Nadeau, Robert, 267
Nadelstern, Eric, 353
Nadler, Jerrold L, 648
Nadler, Jerrold L., 490
Nadler, Jerrold, 116, 155, 190, 214, 290, 311, 320, 321, 322, 323
Nadol, Michael, 458
Nagel, William, 447
Nagengast, Mary Ellen, 86, 265
Naggs, Amy, 40
Nagler, Michael, 581
Nahman, Robert, 48
Napier, William W., 331
Napolitano, Diana, 455
Napolitano, Grace F, 321
Napolitano, Grace F., 155
Napolitano, Ralph, 599
Naramore, David, 427
Nasca PhD, Philip C, 175
Nasca, Samuel, 244, 292
Nash, Loreen, 55
Naso, Frank, 480
Nasr, Nabil, 468
Nasr, Sami, 451
Nastke, Jason, 131
Natale, Marci, 8, 148, 176, 304
Natanus, Burt, 399
Nathan, Larry, 184
Nathan, Richard P, 268
Nathan, Richard, 593
Nathanson, Bruce, 429
Nation, Courtney, 163
Natoli, James, 429, 456
Natoli, Joseph, 419
Natrella, Maureen L., 371
Nattanmai, Mahesh, 5, 140, 160
Naumchik, John, 350
Navarra Bradley, Kathryn, 427
Navone, Sperry, 33
Nazarko, Michael J., 148, 174
Nazon, Deborah E., 108
Neagle, Brian, 341
Neal, Connie, 398
Neal, Mark, 355
Neal, Richard E, 323
Neal, Roger, 533
Neals, Linda, 346
Neary, Kevin, 336
Nebush Jr, Frank J, 333
Necroto, Louis A., 365
Negri, Jacqueline, 383, 399
Negron, Julio C., 488

Appendices: Financial Plan, Indexes & Maps

Negus, Lisa, 86, 265
Neidhardt, Kurt, 388
Neidl, Michael, 449
Neimeier, Robert, 451
Neira, Maria, 379
Neives, Ines, 5, 119, 251
Nejame, Samir, 476
Nellegar, James, 10, 229
Nelligan, Matt, 17
Nelson, Ben, 312, 313
Nelson, Bill, 90, 143, 155, 255, 313, 314
Nelson, Claude, 40
Nelson, Deanna, 208
Nelson, James, 350
Nelson, Judith, 422
Nelson, Kenneth E., 481
Nelson, Lori A., 430
Nelson, Patty, 110
Nelson, Paul, 443
Nelson, Randy, 388
Nelson, Sam, 533
Nelson, Sheila, 423
Nelson, Steve, 428
Nelson, William K, 58
Nematzadeh, Hooshang, 507
Nemeth, Frank, 424
NeMoyer, Patrick H., 45
Nenno, Michael L, 51
Nervo, Frank, 49
Nesbitt Jr, Charles H, 333
Nesbitt Perez, Susan, 381
Nesbitt, Bonnie, 381
Nesbitt, Charles H, 13, 265
Nesbitt, John B, 60
Nesbitt, Ronald, 367
Nesich, Jeffrey, 11, 112
Nespeca, Thomas, 464
Nessel, Jennifer, 395
Nesser, Joseph G., 55
Netherland, Julie, 408
Neubauer, Suh, 537
Neuburger, Jeffrey D, 214
Neugebauer, Lynn, 462
Neugebauer, Randy, 317
Neumann, Cirel, 17
Neustadt, David, 177
Neville, Elizabeth A, 365
Neville, John, 524
Neville, Michael D, 209, 230
Nevins, Michael James, 430
New, Lois, 147
Newcomb, Lisa, 182, 411
Newell, Donald, 232, 259
Newell, Jeremy, 398
Newman, Allison, 128, 460
Newman, Barbara F., 50
Newman, Clare, 96, 295
Newman, Edward A., 167, 196
Newman, Glenn, 358
Newman, Michelle, 39
Newmark, Steven, 357
Newmark, William, 371
Newsome, Chivona R., 482
Newsome, Moses, 397
Newton, Juanita B, 48
Newton, Karen, 34
Newtown, Jamie Dirk, 451
Neznek, Joyce M, 176
Ng, Anthony, 471
Ng, Eliza, 410
Ng, Sylvia, 409, 456
Nicalozzo, Frank, 298
Nicchi, Frank J, 558
Nicholas, Cristyne, 449
Nicholas, Holly, 451
Nichols, Brian C, 345
Nichols, Dan, 163
Nichols, George, 429
Nichols, Jennifer, 458
Nichols, Jonathan D, 52
Nichols, Karen A, 57
Nichols, Nancy, 550
Nichols, Robert, 77
Nichols, Scott, 537
Nichols, Thomas A, 135
Nichols, Timothy D., 183
Nicholson, Dwayne A., 484
Nicholson, Judith, 429
Nicholson, Kristin, 57
Nicholson, Leah, 161, 245
Nicholson, Mary C, 28
Nichols-Tomkins, Kathy, 508
Nickerson, Shawn P, 64, 360
Nickson, Amy, 8, 175
Nickson, Don, 464
Nicolai, Francis A., 47
Nicolato, Jerome, 110
Nicoletta, Gavin S, 141
Nicoletti Jr, Joseph, 367
Nicotra, Mark A, 364
Niedermaier, Kevin, 331
Nielsen, Signe, 352
Nieves, Maria, 415
Nigro, Joanne, 110
Nigro, Joseph, 143
Niles, Glenn, 591
Niles, John F., 65
Nilsson, Kelly, 69
Niou, Yuh-Line, 31
Nissen, Janice, 141
Nixon, Andrew, 274
Noble, Mark, 471
Noble, Timothy G., 430
Nocerino, Frank A, 237
Nocerino, Joseph, 409
Nocero, Mark A, 592
Noel, Cecile, 355
Nogid, Jeff, 350
Nojay, Bill, 32, 36, 37, 41, 42, 137, 634
Nolan, Brian, 464
Nolan, Catherine T, 32, 41, 42, 43, 124, 634
Nolan, Catherine T., 37, 483
Nolan, Catherine, 37
Nolan, David, 363
Nolan, James, 593
Nolan, Jr., Thomas D, 46
Nolan, Pamela, 517
Nolan, Phil, 509
Nolan, Philip C., 106, 274
Nolan, William S., 199
Nole, Robert J, 583
Nolette, Albert, 339
Nolin, Chris, 460
Nolin, Christopher, 381
Noll, Patricia J, 56
Nolon, Jennie, 453
Nolon, John, 453
Nolte, Tom, 504
Noncarrow, Richard, 504
Noonan, Nancy, 464
Noonan, Robert C, 53
Noonan, Rosemarie, 191, 238
Nooyi, Indra K., 94
Noppe-Brandon, Scott, 435
Norden, Larry, 389
Noreault, Ricky, 470
Norejko, Amanda, 463
Norgrove, Jessica, 37
Norman, Laura, 136
Norman, Mike, 474
Normile, James, 241
Norris, Michael, 375
North, Charles S, 514
Northrup Jr, Richard D, 52
Northrup, Jr, Richard D, 328
Northrup, Michael J, 134
Norton, Dean, 413
Norton, John, 228
Norton-White, Patricia, 572
Nortz, Ann M, 132
Nortz, Ann, 399
Norwood, Wade S, 119
Notkin, David, 443
Noto, Paul, 364
Nottke, Barbara, 360
Novakovic, Andrew, 74
Novakowski, Lauren, 381
Noveck, Stephen, 532
Novet, Harriet, 469
Novicky, Joanne, 467
Novik, Richard, 389
Novo, Karen, 105, 287
Novoa, Minerva, 402
Nowacki, Craig, 404
Nowak, Henry, 47
Nowak, Kathy, 241
Nowakowski, Patrick A, 99, 286
Nowosielski, Audra, 42
Nowyj, Mary, 361
Noyes, Pamela, 289
Nozzolio, Michael F, 15, 18, 24, 25, 26, 43, 114, 137, 613
Nozzolio, Michael F., 21, 211

Nozzolio, Michael, 22
Nuciforo, Cheryl, 571
Nudelman, Jodi, 179, 255
Nugent Lussier, Georgeanna, 96, 285
Nugent-Panepinto, Catherine, 47
Nulty, Kevin A, 361
Nunes, Devin, 169
Nunes, Jaime, 482
Nunez, Patricia M., 50
Nunziato, Paul, 383, 493
Nurse, Michael, 537
Nussbaum, David, 444
Nusser, Janie L, 590
Nye III, Glenn C, 322
Nyre, Joseph, 556
O' Brien, Ellen, 509
O'Brien, Allyce, 445
O'Brien, Christopher, 457
O'Brien, Frank, 457
O'Brien, Glenn, 458
O'Brien, Holly, 223
O'Brien, Kenneth, 543
O'Brien, Kerri, 4, 83, 104, 263
O'Brien, Linda, 491
O'Brien, Lynette, 230
O'Brien, Mark, 218
O'Brien, Michael T, 326
O'Brien, Neil F, 569
O'Brien, Patricia, 331
O'Brien, Sean, 200, 219
O'Brien, Sherrill A, 135
O'Brien, Sister Mary Eileen, 555
O'Brien, Ted, 208
O'Brien, Thomas J, 572
O'Brien, Timothy, 11, 113
O'Brien, Tom, 464
O'Brien, William J, 61
O'Brien, William, 457
O'Callaghan, Donal, 469
O'Connell, Dan, 8, 174
O'Connell, Estelle, 248
O'Connell, Jessica, 138
O'Connell, Maureen, 332
O'Connell, Peter, 422
O'Conner, William, 474
O'Connor, Daniel, 389
O'Connor, James, 443
O'Connor, Janice, 251
O'Connor, John, 467, 495, 570
O'Connor, Karen, 57
O'Connor, Kathleen, 442
O'Connor, Matthew, 425
O'Connor, Michael, 458
O'Connor, Michele, 426
O'Connor, Robert, 419
O'Connor, Shaun A, 569
O'Connor, Terrence, 49
O'Dell, Sharon, 328
O'Dell, Twila, 337
O'Donnell PE, John A, 95, 284
O'Donnell, Brother Brennan, 557
O'Donnell, Colin F., 61
O'Donnell, Daniel J, 32, 37, 38, 42, 634
O'Donnell, Daniel J., 36
O'Donnell, Daniel, 37, 114, 195
O'Donnell, Ellen, 601
O'Donnell, John F, 47
O'Donnell, John H., 494
O'Donnell, John, 388
O'Donnell, Katy A., 430
O'Donnell, Patricia A., 430
O'Donnell, Patricia, 344
O'Donnell, Thomas I., 495
O'Donoghue, Mary, 49, 50
O'Donoghue, Peter, 48
O'Donovan, James, 248
O'Flynn, Patrick M, 331
O'Geen, Donald G, 339
O'Gorman, James, 110
O'Grady, Hannah, 479
O'Hagan Wolfe, Catherine, 212
O'Handley, Susan, 504
O'Hare, John, 91
O'Hearn, Annemarie, 446
O'Hearn, Timothy M, 336
O'Keefe, Dr. James, 357
O'Keefe, Kathy, 229
O'Leary, Brian, 449
O'Leary, Dennis, 268
O'Leary, Peter, 342
O'Loughlin, Michael, 438
O'Malley, Christopher, 98, 210, 307
O'Malley, Elizabeth, 255
O'Malley, Kristy, 529
O'Malley, Ute, 353
O'Mara, Terence P, 12, 113
O'Mara, Thomas F, 19, 614
O'Mara, Thomas, 20, 21, 22, 23, 24, 25, 152
O'Meara, Dianne, 343
O'Meara, Elizabeth, 109
O'Neil, Michael, 374
O'Neil, Peter, 206
O'Neill Levy, Kelly, 46
O'Neill, James R, 282
O'Neill, James R., 128
O'Neill, John, 494
O'Neill, Kelly, 49
O'Neill, Nicholas, 32
O'Neill, Thomas J, 65
O'Reilly, Kevin P, 561
O'Reilly, William, 95, 284
O'Rourke, David, 570
O'Rourke, Jeanne, 135
O'Rourke, John, 579
O'Rourke, Jonathan, 241
O'Shaughnessy, William, 535
O'Shea, Ann E., 49
O'Shea, Daniel, 122
O'Shea, Jeremiah, 446
O'Shea, Judith F, 47
O'Shei, Tim, 524
O'Sullivan, Gerard M, 570
O'Sullivan, Jennifer, 10, 304
O'Sullivan, Michael F., 530, 531
O'Sullivan, Patrick J, 54
O'Sullivan, Shawn, 474
O'Sullivan, Timothy, 98, 210, 307
Oakes, Gregory S., 334
Oakes, Victoria A, 82
Oakley, David, 439
Oaks, Bob, 42, 165, 237, 265
Oaks, Robert C, 32, 41, 634
Oaks, Robert, 28
Oates, Joseph, 401
Obenauer, Cheryl Lidell, 59
Obergfell, Brian D., 550
Oberman, Nathan, 363
Oberstar, James L, 322
Obey, David R, 317
Obus, Michael J., 50
Obus, Michael, 46, 209
Ochacher, Perry M., 467
Ochrym, Ron, 95, 272, 306
Ockner, Barry, 230
Oddo, James S, 352
Odell, Mary Ellen, 334
Odell, Zack, 449
Odorisi, J. Scott, 47
Ofer, Udi, 454
Offensend, David, 356
Offutt, Perry J., 445
Ofshtein, Eleanora, 49
Ogger, Sara, 403
Ogilvie, Donald A, 600
Oglesby, Debra, 69
Ognibene, Michael, 357
Ohrenstein, Manfred, 452
Oing, Jeffrey K., 46
Okotieuro, Gbubemi, 397
Okpeseyi, Osarhiemen, 444
Olch, Norman A, 217
Oldenburg, James, 334
Olderman, Justine, 462
Oldhoff, Glenn, 372
Oleck, Renee, 72
Oleske, Michael, 429
Oliker, David, 447
Olin, Veronica, 135
Oliner, Martin, 564
Oliver, Eugene, 50
Oliver, Katherine, 354
Oliver, Russell, 220, 293
Olivo, Jennifer, 451
Olmstcd, Austin W., 372
Olsen, Admiral Robert, 562
Olsen, Carl, 161
Olsen, Greg, 4, 250
Olsen, John, 414
Olshansky, Emily M., 50
Olson, Daniel, 376
Olson, James, 349
Olson, Pete, 322

Olson, Richard, 69, 70
Olson, Sandra M, 14, 202, 222
Olson, Sarah, 276
Olver, John W, 317
Onalfo, V James, 357
Ono, Seiei, 509
Onofry, Robert A, 56
Onofry, Robert A., 47
Ooms, Eric, 413
Oplustil, Joanne, 392
Oppenheimer, Joshua, 421
Opperman, Cyril, 106, 189, 274
Opperman, Pamela, 385
Orengo, Jose, 429
Orewyler, Tom, 117
Organisciak, Richard, 598
Oriola, Deb, 175
Orlando, Elissa, 539
Orlando, Frank, 5, 78, 200
Orlow, Jodi, 49
Orman, Ed, 578
Orman, Jim H, 326
Ormsbee, Michele, 58
Ormsbee, Tracy, 523
Oros, Joseph, 386
Orozco, Fidelia, 454
Orriols, Mirza, 189
Ortiz, Felix W, 32, 37, 40, 41
Ortiz, Felix, 27, 43
Ortiz, Félix, 634
Ortiz, Jason, 299
Ortiz, Jorge, 87, 107, 165
Ortiz, Linda, 89
Ortiz, Solomon P, 318
Ortt, Robert G, 19, 21, 23, 24, 25, 26, 196, 230, 360
Ortt, Robert, 614
Orzano, Patricia, 511
Osadchey, Chet, 534
Osborne, Mary, 113
Osborne, William, 375
Osenenko, Derek, 527
Osina, Pesach, 490
Osinaga, MD, Alda, 175
Osnes, Eric, 99, 286
Ossorio, Sonia, 139, 198
Ost, Barbara, 110
Osten, Wayne, 457
Oster, Gerni, 471
Osterhout, Thomas, 161
Osterlitz, Renee, 537
Ostertag, Robert L, 218
Ostraszewski Anderson, Donna, 278
Ostroff, Richard L, 453
Ostrowski, Stephanie, 174
Oswald, John, 528
Oteri, Gary, 512
Otero, Maria, 94
Othmer, Jr., Richard T., 334
Otis, Pamela, 149, 272
Otis, Steven, 32, 35, 37, 38, 40, 42, 635
Otsubo, Emiko, 354
Ott, Lisa, 450
Otte, Kathleen, 179, 254
Ottenschot, Barbara, 367
Otter, Jack, 532
Ottley, Lisa S., 49
Ottney Mahar, Jessica, 449
Ouderkirk, Beverly, 575
Ourderkirk, Beverly, 119
Ourlicht, David E, 200, 219
Oustatcher, Ira E, 588
Ovalle, Nathan, 529
Overton, Fred, 345
Overton, Tom, 74
Ovesey, Michele, 355
Ovide, Robinson, 484
Owens II, Col. Thomas J., 295
Owens, Bill, 267, 311
Owens, Donna D, 360
Owens, Greg, 251
Owens, John M, 55
Owens, John, 47, 533
Owens, Kelli, 413
Owens, Lester J., 430
Owens, Thomas, 95, 285, 348
Owsiany, Carol, 9, 220
Oyewole, Alfred, 483
Ozimek, Kathryn, 181
P'Simer, Christine, 581
Pabis, Joseph D, 569
Pablo, Robert, 207
Pace, Ronald, 179, 255
Pacholczak, Walter, 382, 404
Paciencia, David, 573
Pacilio, Mark, 33
Packer, Mary Jeanne, 73, 75
Padalino, Paul, 567
Padden, Linda, 64
Padilla, Jose A., 49
Padro, Eduardo, 50
Paduano, Lynette, 451
Pae, Sandy, 419
Pagan, Mary, 455
Pagano, Anthony, 368
Pagano, Lucia, 496
Pagano, Neil J., 362
Pagdanganan, Belinda, 448
Page, Jerome F, 98, 286
Page, JoAnne, 117
Page, Mark, 357
Page, Penny, 214, 256
Pagliaccio, Elliot, 162, 236
Pagones, James D, 52
Pagones, James D., 47
Pagones, Timothy G, 62
Pahaham, Cheryl A., 492
Pajaron, Gertrudes, 381
Palazola, Jeannie L, 136
Palermo, Catherine J., 66
Palladino, Harry R, 105, 287
Palladino, Lou, 445
Palladino, Michael J., 482
Palladino, Michael, 383
Palladino, Peter A, 53
Pallone, Frank, 89, 142, 154, 180
Pallone, Jr, Frank J, 319
Pallotta, Andrew, 379
Palmer, Daniel, 328
Palmer, Dixon, 456
Palmer, Douglas C., 212
Palmer, Geoff, 69
Palmer, Laura, 414
Palmer, Linda D, 326
Palmer, Mike, 363
Palmer, Thomas W, 594
Palmero, Christina, 141
Palmesano, Philip A, 635
Palmesano, Philip, 28, 33, 37, 38, 40, 41, 42, 142
Palmieri, Daniel, 47
Palmieri, Michael J, 255
Palmieri, Robert, 366
Palmisano, Danielle, 429
Palmisano, David A., 220
Palombo, Anthony J, 365
Paloski, Janet, 173, 251
Paltrowitz, Ronald, 439
Palumbo, Anthony H, 33
Palumbo, Anthony H., 635
Palumbo, Anthony, 36, 38, 40, 42, 87, 165, 178
Palumbo, Daniel R, 64
Pamintuan, Lisa E, 558
Pancella, Anthony, 106, 274
Panday, Ambika, 417
Pandya, Alpa, 449
Pane, Lisa, 531
Panek, Ronald, 451
Panepento, Susan, 353
Panepinto, Barbara I., 48, 49
Panepinto, Marc, 19, 20, 24, 70, 614
Panian, Ed, 501
Pankok, Lindsay, 417
Pankow, Mary, 507
Pannucci, Cynthia, 277
Pantaleo, Peter S., 550
Panwar, Shivendra S, 85, 123
Panzer, Richard, 562
Paolicelli, Thomas G, 359
Paolilli, Eric, 348
Paolini, Roger, 281
Papa, Richard, 234, 240
Papa, Terri, 5, 140, 160
Papagiannis, Johnny, 412
Papain, Nicholas, 469
Papale, Andy, 161, 245
Paparatto, Michael, 61
Papenfuse, Lewis, 477
Paprocki, Bernard J, 88
Paprocki, Ellen O, 202, 222
Paprocki, Ronald, 471
Paradis, Sherry, 467

Paradiso, Anthony W, 61
Paradiso, Anthony W., 61
Parameswar, Ramesh, 445
Parauda, Martina A, 296
Parchment, Deborah, 228
Parden, Kelly, 385
Pardes, MD, Herbert, 457
Pardes, Sondra K., 47
Pardo, Theresa, 169
Pardo, Tracy, 48
Paredes, Jacqueline, 379
Parent, Thomas G, 105, 152, 309
Parga, Anthony L, 47
Paris, Anthony J, 46
Paris, Donald, 350
Parish, Jennifer, 471
Parisi, Gerard, 33
Parisi, Patrick, 99, 285
Park, Debra, 392
Park, Lawrence, 217, 469
Park, Lee, 10
Park, Mike, 327
Parker, A. Charles, 158
Parker, Craig R., 490
Parker, Elkin, 72
Parker, Kathy, 471
Parker, Kevin S, 19, 23, 24, 25, 614
Parker, Kevin S., 16, 20
Parker, Kevin, 20, 22, 142
Parker, Marjorie, 493
Parker, Michelle, 505
Parker, Richard, 272
Parker, Sandra, 514
Parker, Terrence M., 51
Parkes, Joseph P, 352
Parkes, Joseph P., 359
Parkinson, Carol, 279
Parks, Brenda, 469
Parks, Kenneth H., 371
Parks, Robert W., 529
Parla, James, 573
Parment, Doris, 131
Parmer Jr., Raymond R., 166
Parness, Hon. Stanley, 468
Parola, Frederick, 508
Parpas, George, 481
Parrella, Nicholas, 15
Parrinello, Kathy, 471
Parrington, Debbi, 234, 240
Parrish, Mark, 451
Parrott, Colonel Leon F., 152
Parry, Robert, 593
Parslow, Jaime, 132
Parsons, Amanda, 354
Parsons, Debra, 348
Parsons, James, 472
Parsons, Patrick, 148, 176
Parsons, Randy, 449
Partee, Ayana, 477
Partello, Patricia, 112, 207
Partnow, Mark I, 46
Pascal, Woody, 188
Pascale, Judith A, 337
Pascarella, Randy M., 372
Pasceri, Maria, 447
Pasceri, Richelle J., 349
Paskoff, Alan, 99, 286
Pasquini, Julie, 111, 206
Passero, Nicholas J., 371
Passuite, Thomas J, 349
Pastel, Robert S, 454
Paster, Darrell L., 484, 492
Pastoressa, Joseph C., 47
Patel, Bindi, 443
Patel, Faiza, 389
Patel, Mehul J., 84, 97, 188
Patel, Mehul, 7
Paterniti, Greg, 464
Paterson, Peter B, 383
Patience, Francis W, 15
Patino, Manny, 430
Patrei, Louis J, 576
Patricof, Rochelle, 354
Patterson, Dianne, 204, 413
Patterson, Gary, 74
Patterson, John, 376
Patterson, L. Eric, 167
Patterson, Maureen, 464
Patterson, Mitchell, 395
Patterson, Richard, 423
Patterson, W Noel, 569
Patti, Douglas, 339
Patti, Philip J, 48
Pattison, Robert, 462
Paul Larson, Daniel, 547
Paul, Alioto, 577
Paul, Andrew, 100, 286
Paul, Barry S, 337
Paul, Patricia, 441
Paul, Ron, 319
Paul, Sandra K., 490
Paulin, Amy R, 33, 37, 39, 635
Paulin, Amy, 38, 142
Paulino, Alejandra, 21
Paulino, Jose, 456
Paulino, Rafael, 494
Paulsen, David J, 330
Paulsen, James G., 222
Pautz, Jennifer, 427
Pavlakos, Yianna, 355
Pavlides, Aris, 409
Pawelczak, Ronald, 47
Pawelko, Ronora, 413
Payne, Donald M, 319
Payne, Donald M., 169
Payne, Jennifer, 440
Payne, Kibbie F., 49
Paynter, Steven W., 48
Pazos, Sophia, 463
Peake, Catherine E, 31
Pearce, Robert, 365
Pearl, Jane, 50
Pearl, Mary, 467
Pearl, Rick, 267
Pearlman, Jeffery, 20
Pearlman, Jeffrey, 3, 303, 421
Pearsall, Charles, 342
Pease, Denise L., 168, 246
Pebbles, Victoria, 87, 97, 150
Pechenik, Stephen A, 335
Pecheone, Kristine K, 56
Pecheone, Steven R, 66
Pechtel, Antonella, 377
Peck Kelleher, Deborah, 24
Peck, Brian, 29
Peck, Donald, 336
Peck, George R, 55
Peck, George, 47
Peckham, Mark, 149, 271
Pecora, Geryl, 294
Pedersen, John, 474
Pedo, Susan, 448
Pedro, Richard M, 297
Pedrone, Dino, 555
Peebles, David E., 212
Pegg, Jennifer A., 430
Peirez, Susan, 270
Pelella, William C, 62
Pelersi, Helen, 86, 265
Pellegri-Buono, Michelle, 35, 37
Pellegrino, Rick, 346
Pellegrino, Robin M., 185
Pellegrino, Robin, 452
Pelliccia, Paul, 537
Pelligrini, Carlo, 512
Pelman, Simon, 485, 486
Peltonen, Matti, 5, 78, 200
Peltz, Adam, 412
Peltz, Jay M., 483
Peltz, Jay, 415
Peluso, Cody, 470
Pemberton, Tina, 346
Pena, Pedro, 483
Pendergast, David, 331
Pendergast, Kathy, 15
Penhollow, Stephen, 570
Penix, Tim, 550
Penn, George, 404
Penn, Gretchen, 470
Pennacchia, Robert, 176
Pennel, Joshua, 33
Penney, John, 529
Pennington, Jennie, 464
Pennisi, Frank, 467
Pennisi, Joseph, 16
Pennoyer, John C, 600
Pennoyer, John, 600
Penrose, Pauline, 342
Pentkowski, Ann, 427
Penziul, Kelly J, 135
Peoples-Stokes, Crystal D, 33, 35, 38, 39, 635
Peoples-Stokes, Crystal, 38, 165

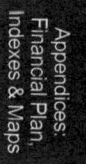

Appendices: Financial Plan, Indexes & Maps

Pepe, Ross, 292
Peppenelli, Jenna, 427
Pepper, Joshua, 10, 228
Peradotto, Erin M, 45
Perales, Cesar A, 218
Peralta, Jose R, 24, 196, 202, 222, 242
Peralta, Jose, 16, 19, 21, 22, 23, 492, 614
Percival, Kate, 529
Perdue, David, 155
Pereira, Colleen, 512
Pereira, Paul, 472
Perera, Suresh, 391
Peres, Kenneth, 441
Peretti, Tina, 351
Perez, Ada, 109
Perez, Antonio, 397, 551
Perez, Bianca, 133
Perez, CDR Rick, 289
Perez, Lilliam, 207
Perez, Myrna, 389
Perez, Nelson, 401
Perez, Patricia, 347
Perez, Robert E., 167
Perez, Robert, 177, 220, 266
Perez-Almeida, Liseth, 359
Periconi, Donna, 502
Perillo, Thomas F, 579
Perine, Jerilyn, 191
Perkal, Richard L., 428
Perkins, Bill, 16, 19, 21, 22, 24, 25, 87, 165, 288, 614
Perkins, Edward, 383
Perkins, Pamela Green, 133
Perkins, Pamela, 354
Perks, Debra, 341
Perkus, Paul C, 358
Perle, Ellen, 203
Perlman, Georgene, 264
Perlman, Lee, 420
Perlmutter, Barbara S, 204
Perlmutter, Margery, 390
Perna, J Philip, 593
Perrin, Fred, 413
Perrin, Richard, 238
Perrine, Lt. Col. Christopher, 295
Perritano, Fran, 531
Perry Hellerstein, Lisa, 400
Perry, Christopher, 266
Perry, Ed, 454
Perry, Jeffrey, 417
Perry, Jodie, 507
Perry, N Nick, 27, 33, 36, 40, 41, 42, 43
Perry, N Nickolas, 635
Perry, N. Nick, 35
Perry, Scott, 169
Perry, Suzanne, 434
Perry-Coon, Timothy, 176
Persaud, Jagarnauth, 71
Persaud, Nadera, 418
Persaud, Roxanne, 19, 20, 21, 22, 23, 25
Persaud, Videsh A., 496
Persaud, Videsh, 30
Persaus, Roxanne, 615
Persell, Patricia, 5, 252
Persky, Ira, 397
Person, Sheila, 533
Persons, Eric, 129, 455
Persons, Melinda, 379
Perticone, John, 130
Peruggi, Regina S, 551
Peruggi, Regina, 397
Pesce, Michael L, 46
Peschel, Laura, 350
Pesile, Kathleen M., 550
Pesso, Maurice, 474
Pestello, Dr. Fred, 556
Pester, Marc, 458
Peters, Angela, 132
Peters, Barbara, 598
Peters, Gary, 143
Peters, Karen K, 45
Peters, Karen K., 209
Peters, Mark, 491
Peters, Morris, 5, 83, 160, 234, 263, 303
Peters, Thomas J., 144
Peters, Thomas, 411
Petersen, Matthew S., 137
Peterson, Collin C, 316
Peterson, Collin C., 73, 154, 180
Peterson, Donald L, 297
Peterson, Gregory P, 7, 130
Peterson, Jon W, 568
Peterson, Jr, Victor L, 247
Peterson, Marianne P., 486
Petlin, Joel, 585
Petracca, Lester, 95, 272
Petraglia, David, 385
Petragnani, Amy, 8, 240
Petri, Thomas E, 322
Petro, Melissa, 459
Petroccione, Emilio, 400
Petrocelli, Joseph, 99, 286
Petrone, Frank P, 348
Petrone, Steve, 535
Petroski, Judith, 122
Pettigrew, John, 448
Pettit Rieman, Lori, 326
Pettit, Stacy, 50
Peverly, Francis, 401
Pezzolesi, Tim, 69
Pfau, Ann, 46, 50
Pfeifer, Maxwell S, 214
Pfeiffer, Alice Randel, 159
Pfeiffer, Debbie, 106, 274
Pfeiffer, Justin, 176
Pfendler, Lori, 54
Pferr, Laurie, 4, 250
Pfieffer, Debbie, 310
Pfister, Helen, 439
Pfisterer, Kurt, 251
Pham, Bich Ha, 259
Phaneuf, Joseph E., 158
Phelan Jr., Edward F., 168
Phelan, Dorothy A., 483
Phelan, Joseph L, 573
Philip, Duwad, 524
Philip, George, 544
Philips, Denise, 550
Phillip, George, 471
Phillip, Peggy, 539
Phillips, Brad C, 564
Phillips, Doug, 457
Phillips, Douglas, 471
Phillips, Francis D, 333
Phillips, Henry, 406
Phillips, Jr, Howard T, 347
Phillips, Karen, 272
Phillips, Sr, Thomas G, 85, 123
Phillips, Susan, 471
Phillips, Tanya L, 226
Phillips, Tom, 589
Phillips, Tweeps, 388
Phillips, Wendy, 251
Phillips, Wilma Brown, 195
Phinney, Debbie, 385
Phister, Nicole, 458
Phoenix, Andrea, 61
Piasecki, Stephen, 468
Piazza, Jeffrey, 51
Piccone, Colleen, 167
Picente Jr, Anthony J, 332
Picerno, Michael G, 295, 296
Pichardo, Sonia, 284
Pichardo, Victor M, 636
Pichardo, Victor, 33, 36, 39, 41, 42
Pickard-Dudley, Kimberly, 471
Pickering, Gerald, 367
Pickering, Laurel, 185
Pickett, Geraldine, 49
Pickholz, Ruth, 50
Pickreign, Joseph, 373
Pickus, Ian, 533
Piemme, Kerri Erin, 596
Pierce, Judith T., 484
Pierce, Paige, 231, 413
Pierce, Rhonda, 339
Pierce, Scott, 527
Pierce, Steven M., 432
Pierce-Smith, Tracey, 16
Pierorazio, Bernard P, 599
Pierpont, Ruth, 11, 149, 271
Pierre, Jude, 392
Pierre, Sharon J., 492
Pierre-Louis, Rose, 359
Piesman, Marissa, 78
Piester, Diane, 460
Piester, Ronald E, 163, 236
Pietanza, Kathleen, 135
Pietroski, Lynn, 519
Pietrusza, Patricia, 17
Pietruszka, Michael F, 53
Pifer, Richard, 471
Pignataro, Maria, 399

Pignone, Ray, 524
Pigott, Eugene F, 45
Pike, Susan, 254
Pilch, Patrick, 457
Pile, Bryan, 202, 221
Pillmeier, Michael R, 333
Pina, Judith, 121
Pinckney, Michael J., 49
Pincus, Judith, 356
Pineda-Kirwan, Diccia, 48
Pineiro, Rafael, 357
Pines, Spero, 51
Pingelski, Annemarie, 161
Pinon, Adriana, 455
Pinsky, Angela, 90, 191
Pinsky, Seth W, 353
Pinson, Stephanie L, 92
Piperato, Paul, 335
Pipia, Robert E., 61
Pirane, J. Bukurije, 462
Pirani, Sylvia, 175
Pircsuk, Cathy, 539
Pirillo, William, 469
Pirro Bailey, Michele, 56
Pirro, Nicholas, 450
Pisani, Salvatore, 290
Pisciotta, Alice, 397
Pisciotta, Frank, 406
Piscitelli, Anthony, 476
Piscitelli, Peter A, 476
Piscitelli, Skip, 21, 22
Pisco, Jay T., 339
Pisicoli, Tony, 519
Pitcheralle, Sam, 335
Pitman, Carol, 451
Pitruzzello, Philip, 470
Pitta, Jacquelyn, 125
Pitta, Vincent, 455
Pitta, Vito, 455
Pitts, Arthur G, 47
Pitts, Cris, 527
Pitts, Joseph, 180
Piwko Jr, Jerome, 575
Pizarro, Ricky, 492
Pizzo, Ralph A, 585
Pizzola, Lorrie, 187
Place, Rich, 530
Placke, Edward, 598
Plant, William, 383
Plastiras, James C, 8, 148, 176, 304
Platkin, Charles, 495
Platkin, Richard, 48
Plattner, Robert D, 13, 86, 265
Platts, Todd (Russell), 318
Pleskach, Bart R, 54
Pletcher, Galen, 467
Plewa, Art, 346
Plimpton, Mark, 534
Pliscofsky, Megan, 391
Pliss, Alla, 429
Ploeger, Nancy, 439, 510
Ploetz, Ronald D, 51
Plotinsky, Benjamin, 532
Plotnik, Ken, 538
Plummer, Daniel, 456
Plummer, Joseph D, 330
Plummer, Viola, 29
Plummer, Wilbert L, 114
Plunkett, Kevin J., 339
Plunkett, Matthew J., 441
Plunkett, Timothy, 442
Pocasangre, Juan C., 494
Podber, Sarah, 434
Podbielski, Gregory G., 450
Podell, Tamar, 435
Podgers, Beth, 526, 527
Podgers, Elizabeth, 526
Podolefsky, Aaron, 545
Podziba, Kenneth J, 358
Poe, Ted, 197
Poehlman, Lauren, 341
Pohlid, Dorothy, 17
Pohlman, Ray, 398
Pokalsky, Kenneth, 391
Poklemba, John J, 102
Poklemba, John, 272
Polan, Steve, 439
Polanco, Francisco, 39
Poland, Gregory, 241
Polaro, Jennifer, 32
Polay, Bobbie, 514
Polayes, Faye, 426
Polenberg, Michael, 462
Poleto, David, 453
Poleto, Molly, 424
Polf, PhD, William A, 457
Polisi, Joseph W, 556
Poliski, Ellen, 176
Polite, Dionne, 414
Politi, Robert T, 328
Polito, William P, 47
Polivy, Steven, 378
Polk, Jill S, 58
Pollack, Jessica, 21
Pollack, Mark, 495
Pollack, Martha, 429
Pollak, Daniel, 371
Pollak, Sam, 529
Pollard, William, 397, 552
Polletta, Leonard, 201, 220
Pollock, John J., 216
Polmateer, Allan, 329
Poloncarz, Mark C, 328
Poloncarz, Mark, 505
Polshek, James Stewart, 352
Polsinelli, Federico, 161
Poltak, Ronald F, 100, 151
Poltenson, Norman, 532
Polyzogopouos, Nick, 486
Pombonyo, Lynn, 580
Pomerantz, Fred, 476
Pomerantz, Rachel, 125
Pomeroy, John, 467
Ponder, Anna, 282, 469
Poole, Loretta, 173, 227
Poole, Sheila, 5, 119, 251
Pope, Alan J, 366
Pope, Kyle, 533
Popeo, Gerald J, 66
Popolo, Nick, 489
Popowski, Deborah, 395
Poppinga, Philip, 474
Poray, Bill, 362
Porcelain, D. Kim, 99, 286
Porpiglia, Michael, 380
Porsch, Barry, 336
Porta, Barbara A, 56
Porter Campbell, Kay-Ann, 210
Porter, Cathy, 353
Porter, David, 98, 141, 151
Porter, Richard, 510
Porter, Robert, 465
Porter, Sandra, 512
Portin, Mark, 63
Posilkin, Mitchell, 460
Posner, Joan, 52
Post, Jennifer, 13, 283, 305
Post, Laurie, 474
Postel, John J, 103, 211
Postiglione, Andrew, 22
Postupack, Nina, 338
Poteat, James, 534
Potera, Jannette, 283
Potosek, Joshua, 337
Potrikus, Edward, 465
Potrikus, Ted, 94
Potter, James, 342
Potter, Jeff, 104, 273
Potuto Kimble, Tina, 212
Pouch, Christine, 502, 509
Poulopoulos, Michael, 171
Pound, Francis, 531
Poupore, Rhonda, 58
Pourakis, George, 179
Poust, Dennis, 385
Poust-Lopez, Linda, 49
Povero, Dave, 536
Powell, Bob, 299
Powell, David, 194
Powell, Dion J., 484
Powell, Lisa, 458
Powell, Lois, 573
Power Tharp, Lorraine, 218, 239
Power, Padraig, 104, 273
Power, Samantha, 168
Powers, David, 459
Powers, Ed, 385
Powers, Evelyn R, 98, 151, 307
Powers, James P, 433
Powers, Jason A, 456
Powers, Kate M, 207
Powers, Keith, 402
Powers, Mark L, 58

Powers, Mary, 411
Powers, Matthew, 456
Powers, Michael B., 117
Powers, Paul B., 410
Powers, Peter, 456
Powers, Rosemary, 3, 160, 206
Powers, William, 108, 456
Poy, Irving, 359
Pozon, Sheila, 433
Prack, Albert, 110
Prager, Erica L, 61
Prather Harvell, Anita, 515
Pratt, Jennifer, 381
Pratt, Terri, 6, 108
Pratt, Terry, 439
Preddice, Lisa, 457
Prehoda, Debbie, 338
Premo, Douglas E, 577
Prendergast, Thomas F., 98, 99, 100, 286
Prendergest, Marc, 161
Preska, Loretta A., 212
Press, Eric P, 66
Presser, Stewart, 420
Pressman, David, 168
Pressman, Michael, 430
Preston, Brett A, 63
Preston, Debra A., 325
Preston, Jane, 421
Preston, Lisa, 55
Preston, Tracie, 568
Pretlow, James Gary, 33, 36, 40, 41, 43, 265, 275, 636
Previte, David, 23
Price, David E, 317
Price, Deborah, 464
Price, Gabrielle, 328
Price, Lee A, 327
Price, Mary Alice, 579
Price, Mike, 389
Price, Randolph, 401
Price, Richard L, 48
Price, Sandy, 373
Price, Tom, 318
Prickett, Connie, 449
Pridgen, JaHarr, 62
Primavera, John, 153
Primavera, Kelly K, 134
Primeau, Michael J, 8
Primeau, Michael, 175
Primeau, Zach, 22
Primo, Esq., David, 56
Primo, Marth Beth, 513
Primo, Mary Beth, 517
Prince, Candace, 492
Principato, Brendan, 439
Pring, Emily, 444
Priputen-Madrian, Nancy, 96, 273
Pritchard, Robert, 586
Pritts, Kraig D, 584
Pritzker, Stan, 46
Privett, LCSW, David, 229
Probst, Marian, 74
Probst, Nancy, 20
Prochera, Lee, 5, 251
Procida, Richard, 524
Protos, Grace, 223
Proud, Jessica, 449
Proulx, Brittany, 530
Proulx, Geoff, 445
Proulx, Paul, 403
Proulx, Travis, 412
Provenzano, Vincent, 383
Provoncha, Joseph A, 329
Provost, Ricky, 329
Prudenti, A. Gail, 47, 209
Pruitt, Jana Lee, 468
Prus, Eric I, 46
Prusinski, Ann, 135
Pryba, Bradley, 466
Pryor, Mark L, 315
Pryor, Mark, 313
Pryor, Vikki, 204
Przepasniak, James, 573
Pucci, Carl, 423
Puccio, Joe, 467
Pucillo, Emilio, 255
Puckett, Robert R., 145
Puerzer, Thomas O., 213
Pu-Folkes, Bryan R., 492
Puglisi, Linda D, 344
Puglisi, Linda, 344
Puig, John, 459
Puleo, Vincent, 364
Puliese, Christopher J., 432
Pullar, Judith, 418
Pulling, Kyle, 428
Pullo, Vincent, 355
Pulos, Theresa, 597
Pulvirenti, Patricia, 477
Punch, James P, 57
Purcell, James, 399
Purcell, Jennifer, 400
Purcell, Jim, 257
Purcell, John, 394
Purcell, Kevin, 411
Purdue, Marsha, 330
Purdy, Sarah, 340
Purificacion, Leslie J., 48, 49
Purser, Edward, 327
Putman, Stephen, 590
Putnam, Frederick, 463
Putney, Jonathan S., 336
Putterman, Harriet, 448
Putziger, Michael, 465
Puzio, Margaret L, 575
Puzon, Ike, 299
Pycior, Anna, 31
Pyle, Jennifer, 382
Pyle, Nicholas, 459
Pyronneau, Patrick, 392
Quackenbush, Marjorie, 367
Quackenbush, Molly, 276
Quackenbush, Susan, 267
Quail, Brian M, 130
Quail, Brian, 374
Quain, Jeff, 36
Quall, Robert, 296
Qualls, Bridgette, 296
Quarantello, Russell G, 105, 287
Quart, Dan, 33, 35, 36, 37, 40, 42, 636
Quashie, Celine, 472
Quattrone, David, 597
Quay, Gloria, 289
Quay, Mary, 13, 294
Queally, Doyle, 422
Quebral, Roderick, 208
Quenneville, Gary, 432
Quent, Jim, 438
Quesada, Antonio, 477
Quesada, Jose, 434
Quigley, John, 469
Quigley, Judith M, 338
Quigley, Matthew, 422
Quigley, Mike, 169
Quiles, Joy, 14, 163, 253
Quill, Michael, 341
Quiniones, Gil C, 101, 141
Quinlan, Robert F, 47
Quinlan, Tara, 469
Quinn, Catherine, 65
Quinn, Christine C, 352
Quinn, David P, 11, 241
Quinn, Doreen, 54
Quinn, Jack, 428, 547
Quinn, James F., 59
Quinn, Jr., James F., 372
Quinn, Kevin, 475
Quinones, Mary, 437
Quinones, Thomas, 66
Quinonez, Judith Garcia, 354
Quintanilla, F., 397
Quirk, Carol, 341
Quirk, William J, 50
Ra, Edward P, 636
Ra, Edward, 28, 33, 36, 37, 39, 42, 124
Raab, Jennifer J, 551
Raab, Jennifer J., 397
Rabey, Jeffrey, 573
Rabii, Robin R, 241
Rabinowitz, Stuart, 426, 556
Rabinowitz, Vita C., 550
Rabsatt, Calvin, 110
Raccuia, Joseph, 415
Race, Patricia, 174
Racette, Steve, 109
Rachlin, Stuart, 594
Rachmiel, William, 5, 200
Racine, Jeremy, 463
Racko, Thomas, 201, 219
Radanovich, George, 318
Raddant, Andrew L., 153
Radensky, Laura, 429
Radow, Beth, 434

Raezer, Joyce, 299
Rafalsky, Thomas, 93
Raffaele, Thomas, 48
Rafferty, Emily K, 79
Rafferty, Terrence, 469
Ragbir, Tara, 444
Ragucci, Carmine, 481
Ragusa, Phil, 493
Ragusa, Philip, 375
Rahall II, Nick J., 290
Rahall, II, Nick J, 321
Rahman, Hifzur, 486
Rahrle, David J, 350
Raia, Andrew P, 33, 39, 636
Raia, Andrew, 28, 36, 38, 39, 41, 178
Raia, Jo-Ann, 348
Raichel, Daniel, 449
Rainey, Charles, 298
Raisman, Matt, 536
Raisner, Jack A., 159
Rakower, Eileen A., 49
Ralph Rose, Eric Mahlar, Co-President, 501
Ramaglia, Joseph, 101, 287, 482
Ramey, Jennifer, 563
Ramirez Sr, Roberto, 445
Ramirez, Camilo, 395
Ramirez, Edith, 92
Ramirez, Leticia, 49
Ramirez, Samuel, 463
Ramirez-Romero, Doris, 110
Ramos, Bernardo, 474
Ramos, Kim, 445
Ramos, Norma, 3, 130, 187, 194
Ramos, Phil, 27, 35, 43
Ramos, Philip R, 33, 37, 40, 636
Ramos, Robert, 491
Ramos, Theresa, 168
Ramsey, Taylor Owen, 125
Ramsey, Virginia, 157, 183
Ranalli, Daniel J, 13, 265
Ranalli, Michael, 346
Rand, Benjamin, 85, 123
Rand, Matthew, 12, 235, 245, 264
Randall, Douglas A, 55
Randazzo, Ben, 29
Ranellone, Dan, 21, 25
Rangan, Urvashi, 402
Rangel, Charles B, 311, 323, 324, 648
Rangel, Charles B., 180, 255, 267
Rangel, Nic, 26
Ranney, Jim, 534
Ranzenhofer, Michael H, 19, 22, 24, 25
Ranzenhofer, Michael N., 23
Ranzenhofer, Michael, 15, 20, 21, 25, 87, 165, 288, 615
Rao, Rajiv, 5, 140, 160
Rapczynski, Anthony, 523, 525
Raphael, Ava S, 56
Rapoport, Frank, 442
Rascoe, Roger, 376
Rashford, Eardell J., 49
Raske, Kenneth E., 183
Raske, Kenneth, 420
Raskin, John, 417
Rasmussen, Erik F, 71
Rasmussen, Raun, 434
Rasmussen, Rebecca, 42
Raspberry, Tiffany, 454
Rasp-Glose, Maureen, 472
Ratanski, Robert, 50
Ratcliffe, Carolyn, 417
Ratcliffe, John, 169
Rathbun, Raymond, 339
Ratner, Bruce, 416
Ratner, Mark, 478
Rattmann, Thomas, 400
Rattner, Howard, 351
Raufer, Susan, 167, 196
Ravel, Ann M., 137
Ravetz, Jeffrey D., 491
Ravin, Richard L, 216
Ravin, Richard L., 92
Raw Jr, Ronald, 584
Rawlins, Virginia, 35
Ray, Lori, 508
Rayball, Michael, 344
Raynoff, Rachaele, 352
Raynor, Bruce, 226
Rea, Kevin, 543
Rea, Mark, 460
Rea, Michelle K., 144
Reap, Joshua, 434
Reape, Rebecca, 443
Reardon, Eileen, 181
Reardon, Roberta, 9, 177, 201, 220, 252, 293
Rebholz, Nick, 429
Rebisz, Donna L., 94
Rebolini, William B, 47
Rechler, Scott H, 105, 287
Recktenwald, Monica, 114
Record, EdD, RN, CNE, Victoria, 183
Record, Mary, 280
Reda, Louis J., 345
Reda, Vincent, 376
Redmond, Suzanne, 30
Redmond, Timothy, 344
Redon, Leonard E., 363
Redvers, Chris, 430
Redzeposki, Lucy, 447
Reed, Frederick G, 56
Reed, Jack, 313
Reed, Karen, 134
Reed, Marcy L., 490
Reed, Marcy, 448
Reed, Miles, 530
Reed, Norman, 583
Reed, Robert R., 49
Reed, Ronald, 201, 219
Reed, Tom, 180, 255, 267, 311, 649
Reeder, Mark, 141
Reese, Mike, 506
Reeve, Ruth, 589
Reeves, Brian, 76
Reeves, Gale, 582
Reeves, Ivy, 463
Refki, Dina, 171
Regan, Frances, 266
Regan, George, 282
Regan, Judy, 141
Reginer, Michael, 395
Rehm, Robert J., 430
Rehm, Timothy J, 585
Reicher, Andrew, 193
Reid, Delano, 114, 266
Reid, Felicia, 35, 39
Reid, Lisa P, 26, 43
Reid, Lisa P., 165
Reid, Lisa, 438
Reid, Martin T, 335
Reid, Randy, 537
Reidenbach, Dennis R., 276
Reidy, John, 207
Reidy, Jr., Robert J., 128
Reidy, William, 457
Reilich, Bill, 374
Reilich, William, 375
Reilly, Adrianne, 527
Reilly, David, 47
Reilly, Edward T, 90
Reilly, Eileen, 392
Reilly, Gail, 544
Reilly, Janet L, 16
Reilly, Jeff, 240
Reilly, John, 341
Reilly, Jr., Richard F, 57
Reilly, Jr., Vincent J, 46
Reilly, Matthew, 583
Reilly, Patricia, 388
Rein, Briget, 409
Rein, Carol, 443
Rein, Richard, 385
Reina, Robert, 576
Reinemann, Peter H., 429
Reinfurt, Edward, 10, 84, 122
Reinfurt, Susan B, 66
Reinhardt, Jessica, 401, 476
Reinhardt, John, 349
Reinhart, Kenneth, 401
Reinhold, Mann, 389
Reininga, Daniel, 81
Reiss, Dale Anne, 247
Reiss, Warren, 463
Reith, Christina B, 120
Reith, John, 176
Reitz, James F, 57
Reitz, Jeanette, 50
Rella, Joseph, 591
Relyea, Michael, 380
Remolete Hayashi, Reyna, 411
Remus, Laurel, 304
Renaud, Monique, 492
Rendino, Michael A, 133

Renfro, Sally, 352
Renta, Wilfred, 493
Renwick, Dianne T, 45
Renyak, Thomas, 471
Renzi, Alex R., 47
Renzi, Eugene R, 66
Repas, Peter, 143
Rescigno, Richard, 538
Resheske, Frances, 401, 481
Resnick, Caryn, 352
Resnick, Lewis, 489
Resnick, Richard A., 115, 213
Ress, Connie, 355
Ressos, Maria, 49
Rest, George, 451
Restaino, Danielle, 64
Restrepo, Humberto, 430
Retkin, Randye, 434
Rettig, Dave, 284
Reuss, Mark, 283
Reverri, Erin, 131
Reville, Michael W, 217
Revoir, Frank B., 52
Reyes, Ana Garcia, 397
Reyes, Luis O, 119
Reyes, Melanie, 427
Reyes, Nardo, 374
Reyes, Silvestre, 324
Reyes-Finch, Jasmin, 64
Reynolds, Andrew, 399
Reynolds, Cheryl, 518
Reynolds, Chris, 534
Reynolds, Christine, 576
Reynolds, James, 143
Reynolds, John H., 489
Reynolds, Levy, 435
Reynolds, Ryan S., 479
Reynolds, Thomas, 450
Reynolds, Wayne, 328
Reynolds, William P., 9, 161
Reynolds, William, 304
Rhea, John B, 355
Rhine, Edward, 594
Rhinevault, Carey, 348
Rhodes, David John, 565
Rhodes, John B, 102, 141, 151
Riazi, A., 355
Ribustello, Anthony J, 133
Riccaldo, Billy, 398
Ricci, Carol, 359
Ricci, Deborah, 60
Ricci, Frank P, 460
Ricci, Frank P., 493
Riccio, Anthony, 402
Rice, Ambassador Susan E., 297
Rice, Kathleen M, 332, 649
Rice, Kathleen M., 168, 169
Rice, Linda, 569
Rice, Maria, 595
Rice, Paula, 380
Rice, Stephen, 427
Rich Jr, Richard W, 52
Rich, David, 420
Rich, Howard, 139
Rich, Richard W, 52
Rich, Robert, 458
Rich, Tracy, 422
Richard, Rachelle, 367
Richard, Ryan, 13
Richards, Carol, 483
Richards, Delores, 495
Richards, Donovan J., 494
Richards, Jerome J, 58
Richards, Randy, 574
Richards, Robert M, 509
Richards, Thomas S, 363
Richards, William, 548
Richardson, Adam, 23, 24
Richardson, Clark V., 50
Richardson, Denise M., 92, 495
Richardson, Denise, 413, 529
Richardson, Dennis, 424
Richardson, Diana C, 33
Richardson, Diana, 36, 37, 41
Richardson, Diane, 41
Richardson, Larry, 474
Richardson-Mendelson, Edwina G., 50
Richardson-Mendelson, Edwina, 209
Richarson, Diana C, 637
Richart, Meejin, 395
Richberg, Jason, 337
Richey, John F, 58
Richey, Patrick, 392
Richmond, Cedric L., 169
Richroath, Marybeth S., 50
Richter, Anne, 539
Richter, John, 443
Richter, Marc, 401
Richter, Ronald E., 356
Richter, Rosalyn H, 45
Richter, Roy T., 480
Ricigliano, Francis, 47, 61
Ricketts, Rhonda, 78, 200
Riddell, Glenn, 461
Riddett, Kenneth, 461
Rider, Beth, 523
Rider, Deborah, 464
Rider, Renee, 121
Ridler, Susan M., 430
Riedman, John, 374
Riegle, Christian, 278
Rienas, Ron, 96, 285, 306
Rienzi, Leonard P., 48, 50
Riesbeck, Jodie, 523
Rietz, Jonathan R, 570
Riexinger, Patricia, 147
Rifanburg, Michael, 523
Rifkin, Richard, 432
Rigby Riehle, Brenda A, 325
Rigby, Gregory S., 371
Riggi, Denise, 58
Rigney, Loretta, 516
Riley, Allen, 331
Riley, Amanda, 58
Riley, Max, 593
Riley, Seann, 462
Riley, Timothy J, 55
Riley, Tori J.E., 518
Riley-Clendened, Ian, 469
Rimai, Monica, 467
Rinaldi, Charles J, 569
Rinaldi, Thomas, 101, 236
Ring, Kathy, 599
Ring, Michael, 593
Ring, Timothy, 418
Ringel, Josh, 30
Riordan, John, 248
Rios, Jaime Antonio, 48
Risch, James E, 314, 315
Risch, James E., 224
Risser, Dr. Barbara, 547
Ritche, Patricia, 70
Ritchie, Patricia, 15, 19, 20, 21, 22, 23, 25, 26, 43, 70, 87, 152
Ritchie, Patty, 615
Ritholtz, Martin E, 48
Ritter, Elizabeth, 110
Rittler, Joe, 331
Rittner, Don, 364
Ritton, Kevin N., 334
Rivadeneyra, Michael, 389
Rivara, Karen, 75
Rivas-Williams, Jaime, 483
Rivera, Albert, 99, 285
Rivera, Alice, 437
Rivera, Augie, 397
Rivera, Francois A, 46
Rivera, Gustavo, 16, 23, 615
Rivera, J Gustavo, 19, 22, 23, 24, 25
Rivera, J. Gustavo, 23, 178
Rivera, Jenny, 45
Rivera, Joel, 493
Rivera, José , 637
Rivera, Jose, 27, 33, 35, 40, 41
Rivera, Joshua, 397
Rivera, Jr., Reinaldo, 213
Rivera, Lillian, 488
Rivera, Lisa, 434
Rivera, Pablo, 410
Rivera, PE, Jose, 246, 284
Rivera, Peter M., 200, 219
Rivera, Reinaldo E, 45
Rivera, Richard, 50, 350
Rivers, Bernie, 456
Rivers, Brenda, 251
Rivers, N., 355
Rivet, Clayton, 40
Rivett, Lauren, 18
Roa, Raveen, 457
Roach, Karen, 424
Roach, Thomas M, 367
Roach, Virginia, 553

Robach, Joseph E, 19, 21, 22, 23, 25, 237, 615
Robach, Joseph, 15, 24, 25, 288
Robarge, Tricia, 60
Robb, Judith, 342
Robbins, Donald, 425
Robbins, Tammy S, 55
Roberson, Lucy, 69
Robert Lewis, Lisa, 531
Roberti, Hannah, 31
Roberti, Scott, 417
Roberts, Alex, 111, 206
Roberts, Andrew, 13, 294
Roberts, Catherine, 530
Roberts, Cathy, 411
Roberts, Gayle P., 50
Roberts, Greg, 229
Roberts, Joe, 483
Roberts, Lillian, 481
Roberts, Mary Ann, 361
Roberts, MaryAnn, 361
Roberts, Michael, 284
Roberts, Pat, 73, 155, 180, 312, 315
Roberts, Phillip T., 222
Roberts, Samuel D, 13, 195, 253
Robertson, Martha, 338
Robertson, Michael, 345
Robertson, Scott, 531
Robichaud, Kathleen L, 65
Robillard, Deborah L, 62
Robillard, Robin, 66
Robinson, Alphonso, 430
Robinson, Althea, 506
Robinson, Annette M, 39, 41, 637
Robinson, Annette M., 36
Robinson, Annette, 33, 35, 79
Robinson, Anthony P, 347
Robinson, Brett, 356
Robinson, Christine, 113
Robinson, Cindy, 513
Robinson, Cynthia, 50
Robinson, Derrick, 61
Robinson, Dominic, 395
Robinson, Ellen, 210, 305
Robinson, Hon Van B, 365
Robinson, Jeff, 412
Robinson, L Oliver, 589
Robinson, Nicholas A., 158
Robinson, Peter, 471
Robinson, Sally, 434
Robinson, Yolanda, 511
Robinson-Etienne, Nicole, 475
Robles-Roman, Carol A, 352
Robles-Roman, Carol A., 550
Roboostoff, Patricia M., 472
Roche, Esq., Philip J., 337
Roche, Patrick, 543
Roche, Sister Denise A, 554
Roche, Tim, 251
Rochon, Thomas R, 556
Rock, David, 110
Rock, Krista, 13, 253
Rock, Major Ivan, 560
Rock, Ron, 390
Rockefeller IV, John D, 290
Rockefeller, IV, John D, 313, 314
Rockford, Steve, 535
Rockoff, Elaine, 429
Rodak, Thomas, 471
Rodenhausen, Patricia M, 223
Rodgers, Cathy McMorris, 321
Rodney, Barrington, 493
Rodney, Gary D, 100, 189
Rodrigues, J Miguel, 350
Rodriguez Lopez, Lillian, 258, 399
Rodriguez, Al, 359
Rodriguez, Diego, 114
Rodriguez, Felix V. Matos, 552
Rodriguez, Isamar, 28
Rodriguez, Julia I., 49
Rodriguez, Lenny, 435
Rodriguez, Marysol, 407, 454
Rodriguez, Ramon, 173
Rodriguez, Rick, 392
Rodriguez, Robert J, 33, 637
Rodriguez, Robert, 36, 37, 39, 40, 41, 43
Rodriguez, Rolon Alithia, 436
Rodriguez, Samuel, 485
Rodriguez, Sonia, 494
Rodriguez, Susan, 417
Rodriguez, Teresita, 381
Rodriguez, Wilson, 482
Rodriguez-Rolon, Alithia, 414
Rodriguez-Samuelson, Deborah, 258
Roe, Phil, 323
Roel, Ronald, 527
Roest, Anne, 111, 206, 235
Roffe, Andrew, 461
Rog, Stewart, 406
Rogers, Casey, 474
Rogers, Cathleen E, 132
Rogers, Charles, 524
Rogers, Denise, 510
Rogers, Durin B, 62
Rogers, Erin, 33
Rogers, Gerard, 135
Rogers, Harold, 73, 142, 267, 317
Rogers, James T, 415
Rogers, James, 296
Rogers, Jeff, 467
Rogers, Jr, Joseph P, 268
Rogers, Mark J, 65
Rogers, Mark, 320
Rogers, Mike, 324
Rogers, Robert, 212
Rogers, Thomas, 136, 601
Rogriguez, Jose, 49
Rohaurer, Shelley, 524
Rohr, Aileen, 348
Rohrabacher, Dana, 320
Roker, Alice, 368
Roland, John, 351
Roland, Steven, 451
Roldan, Eva, 385
Rolison, Robert, 328
Roll, Kenneth, 61
Rollins, Holly, 132
Romaine, Edward P., 96, 150, 342
Romaine, Stephen S, 82
Roman, David J, 64
Roman, Scott, 327
Roman, Sheri S, 45
Romanik, Peg, 154
Romano, Ronald P, 260
Romano, Vince, 364
Romanowski, Thomas, 163
Rombel, Adam, 532
Rome, Dolloras, 505
Romeo, Michael, 458
Rometty, Virginia M., 92
Romines, Ron, 537
Romney, Edgar, 489
Romney, Roxanne, 451
Ronan, Andrew P., 482
Ronda, Linda, 241
Rondo, Jannette, 11, 84, 122, 305
Ronk, Jr., Kenneth J., 338
Roohan, J Thomas, 249
Roohan, Patrick, 175
Rooney, Frank, 69
Rooney, James T, 57
Rooney, John, 451
Rooney, Kevin M., 145
Rooney, Stephen J, 48
Rooney, Stephen J., 48
Rooney, Timothy, 282
Rooney, Tom, 169
Roosa, Bryan, 417
Roosevelt, V. Theodore, 419
Root, Oren, 472
Rory, Whelan, 469
Rosa, Alexandra, 359
Rosa, Betty A, 119
Rosa, Catherine, 524
Rosa, Chris, 397
Rosa, Gary A, 52
Rosa, Maria G., 47
Rosado, Lourdes, 112, 188, 195, 207, 221, 245
Rosado, Maria, 223
Rosado, Rossana, 3, 12, 85, 149, 162, 236
Rosales, Leo, 9, 177, 201, 220, 253, 304
Rosamilia, Lou, 366
Rosario, Stephen, 90
Rosato, Joanna, 247
Rose, Allison, 463
Rose, David, 436
Rose, Esq., Wesley A., 336
Rose, James, 127
Rose, Kate, 445
Rose, Mark, 63
Rose, Ray, 140, 160
Rose, Rebecca, 63

Rose, Richard, 538, 579
Rose, Susan, 440
Rose-Craig, Veronica, 121
Rosen, Benjamin, 10, 229, 304
Rosen, Corinne, 415
Rosen, Michael E, 415, 454
Rosen, Michael, 74, 92
Rosenbaum, Marty, 36
Rosenbaum, Matthew A, 47
Rosenberg, Alan, 461
Rosenberg, Joseph, 355
Rosenberg, Karen B., 46
Rosenberg, Martin B., 146
Rosenberg, Miriam, 528
Rosenberg, Philip, 218, 476
Rosenberg, Saul, 298
Rosenberg, Steven, 463
Rosenberger, Sara, 424
Rosenberry, Douglas, 251
Rosenblatt, Lois M, 335
Rosenblatt, Michael, 188
Rosenblum, Jay, 223
Rosenblum, Lisa, 143
Rosenburg, Joseph, 394
Rosenburg, Nathan, 449
Rosenfeld, Kenneth, 450
Rosenfeld, Matt, 537, 539
Rosenfeld, Michel, 197
Rosenfeld, Paul, 413
Rosengarten, Jeffrey, 477
Rosengarten, Roger N, 48
Rosenstein, Brad, 88
Rosenstein, Neal, 458
Rosenstock, Jeff, 397
Rosenthal, Andrew M., 528
Rosenthal, Carol, 416
Rosenthal, Doug, 40
Rosenthal, Harvey, 232
Rosenthal, Jean, 283
Rosenthal, Justine A., 533
Rosenthal, Kate, 66
Rosenthal, Linda B, 33, 39, 637
Rosenthal, Linda B., 493
Rosenthal, Linda, 35, 37, 38, 42, 114, 178, 230, 253
Rosenzweig, Claire, 90
Roser, R Christopher, 582
Roskoff, Allen, 487
Rosmarin, Ari, 454
Ross, Donald, 439
Ross, James F., 479
Ross, Kathryn, 531
Ross, Kimberly, 136
Ross, Laura Weigley, 210
Ross, Mark, 171
Ross, Neil E., 50
Ross, Robert A, 233
Ross, Sheila, 372, 375
Ross, Stephen M., 460
Ross, Terri L, 325
Ross, Thomas H, 243
Ross, Thomas H., 118
Ross, Timothy, 472
Ross, Tom, 276
Ross, William L, 332
Rossetti, Vincent, 39
Rossi, Joe, 476
Rossi, John, 341
Rossi, Mary Ann, 6, 111, 206, 235
Ross-Jones, Marvel, 563
Rossland, John, 414
Rostow, Nicholas, 467
Rotella, Joseph, 584
Roth, Allen, 371
Roth, Christopher, 342
Roth, Kenneth, 198
Roth, Steven, 473
Rothenberg, Karen, 46
Rothermel, Barbara, 457
Rothermel, Richard A, 334
Rothfeld, Barry, 529
Rothschild, Leslie, 29
Rothwell Davis, Mary, 98, 210
Rotruck, Scott, 396
Rotterman, David, 537
Roulin CPA, Brian, 268
Roulin, Brian L, 363
Roundpoint, Betty, 166
Routhier, Giselle, 399
Rouzer, David, 154
Rowan, Sylvia M, 330
Rowan, Sylvia, 375
Rowe, C. Mitchell, 336
Rowe, David, 392
Rowe, Donn, 403
Rowe, Kathy, 536
Rowe-Adams, Jackie, 481
Rowland, Lee, 389
Rowlands, Vernon, 537
Rowley, David, 586
Rowley, John C, 59
Rowse, Glenwood, 121
Roy, Lynn, 590
Royce, Edward R, 320
Royce, Edward R., 89, 196
Rozdzielski, Debra, 168
Rozel, Yury S., 484
Rozic, Nily, 33, 36, 37, 38, 40, 637
Rozzi, Cheryl, 331
Rubendall, Robert L., 159
Ruberto, Carmine, 220, 253
Rubin PhD, Clinton T, 85, 122
Rubin, Alan, 403
Rubin, James S, 8, 79, 103, 187
Rubinger, Michael, 191
Rubino, Cynthia, 563
Rubio, Marco, 155
Rubscha, Lynne, 132
Ruchelsman, Leon, 46
Rudd, John, 517
Rudden, Patricia S., 496
Ruderman, Hon Terry Jane, 215
Ruderman, Terry J, 48
Rudnick, Andrew J, 502
Rudolph, Kyle, 336
Ruff, Edwin, 14, 202, 221
Ruff, Sue, 467
Ruggiero, Joseph, 101, 287
Ruggiero, Steve, 247
Ruggles, Catharine, 58
Ruggles, Kristin, 402
Ruglis, Lucas M., 430
Ruhlmann, Dandrea L., 55
Ruiz, Norma, 48
Rukavina, Mike, 526
Ruller, Thomas, 120
Rumsey, Joseph L, 591
Rumsey, Phillip R, 47
Runge, MAJ Jared E., 152
Runion, Kenneth, 347
Rupert, Clarke, 97, 150, 307
Rupp, MaryLou, 337
Ruppersberger, C A Dutch, 324
Rupright, Rachel, 388
Ruscio, Nancy, 571
Rush, Bobby L, 318
Rush, Bobby L., 143
Rush, David, 445
Rush, James, 177, 220
Rushdoony, Jonathan, 79
Rusinek, Melissa, 402
Ruskay, John S, 249
Ruskay, John, 466
Ruslander, Betsy R, 208
Russ, Brian, 573
Russell Jr, Robert T, 62
Russell, Addie J, 33, 37, 40, 42, 637
Russell, Addie J., 37
Russell, Addie, 35, 38, 43, 70
Russell, Bill, 595
Russell, Bonnie, 128
Russell, Hanif, 488
Russell, Mark, 367
Russell, Patrick E, 330
Russell, Patrick, 474
Russell, Peter, 228
Russell, Robin, 56
Russell, Scott A, 365
Russell, Tony, 534
Russell, Whitney, 163
Russi, Eugenio, 113
Russianoff, Gene, 292, 458
Russo, Charles, 592
Russo, J. Michael, 207
Russo, Joe, 534
Russo, Salvatore J, 354
Russo, Stephen, 63
Russo, Theresa, 461, 476
Russom, Dan M, 575
Rustin, John, 375
Ruth, Lawrence, 153, 167
Rutherford, Thad, 34
Rutigliano, Christine, 461

Rutledge, Thomas M., 480
Rutnik, Douglas P, 462
Rutter, Hillary, 181
Ruzow, Daniel A., 159
Ruzow, Daniel, 475
Ryan, Becky, 518
Ryan, Colleen, 374
Ryan, Gary, 457
Ryan, James M, 587
Ryan, James, 443
Ryan, Jim, 535
Ryan, Keith, 530
Ryan, Kelly, 425
Ryan, Kevin K., 52
Ryan, Kevin R, 335
Ryan, Lorraine, 420
Ryan, Margaret, 117
Ryan, Martha, 380
Ryan, Maryann, 537
Ryan, Matt, 429
Ryan, Matthew T, 342
Ryan, Maura K, 239
Ryan, Michael J, 133
Ryan, Michael, 176
Ryan, Paul, 267, 318
Ryan, Peter J., 209
Ryan, Richard, 530
Ryan, Rick, 5, 13, 251, 253
Ryan, Sean, 33, 36, 37, 38, 40, 42, 638
Ryan, Tim, 554
Ryan, Timothy P, 584
Ryan, William M, 517
Ryan-Lynch, Blaine, 234, 240
Ryba, Christine, 46
Rybczynski, Catherine A, 347
Ryder, Melanie, 505
Ryerson, Lisa Marsh, 562
Rymph, John A., 338
Saarinen, Jussi, 412
Sabatino, Theresa, 341
Sabato, Jeff, 537
Sabel, Janet, 9, 84, 112, 161, 177, 188, 201, 208, 245, 264
Sabella, Rachel, 378
Sabo, Michael A, 296
Sabo, Michael A., 296
Sacco, Elizabeth, 421
Sacco, Helene, 50
Sacco, Jennifer, 35, 42
Saccocio, John, 425
Sachs, Darcy, 451
Sachs, Jeffrey, 470
Sack, PE, Robert, 246, 284
Sacket, James L, 336
Sackett, Robert A, 48
Sackman, Bobbie, 403
Saddlemire, Sandra, 135
Sadik-Khan, Janette, 358
Sadocha, Susan, 89
Sady, Joan, 338
Safer-Espinoza, Laura, 49
Safrey, Ed, 267
Saiff, Darin P, 590
Sais, Michael, 17
Saitta, Wayne P, 46
Saladino, Joseph S, 33, 638
Saladino, Joseph S., 38
Saladino, Joseph, 28, 38, 40, 43, 124
Saleh, John, 266
Salemo, Richard, 530
Salerno, Gregory J., 210
Salerno, Louis, 161, 245
Sales, Angela, 397
Sales, Fred, 383
Salina, Charles, 116, 214
Salinitro, Barbara, 50
Salisbury, John A, 350
Salkin, Andrew, 358
Salkin, Patricia, 378
Salkind, Susanne, 487
Salkowe, Jerry, 424
Sall, Brandon R., 60
Salman, Barry, 48
Salmon, Tahisha, 485
Salo, Terry, 6, 111, 206
Salotti, Mary Q, 134
Salsich, Ann, 472
Saltarelli, Mark, 66
Salter, Raya, 412
Saltonstall, David, 359
Saltser, Maryann, 527
Salvaggio, Susan Kay, 597
Salvin, Daniel, 37
Salzman, Alan E., 472
Samach, Ariel, 455
Samaniuk, John, 13, 283, 284
Same, Beth, 280
Same, Carl J, 135
Same, Ruth V, 135
Sammons, Ann, 111
Samoyedny, Deborah, 54
Sample, Barry C, 102, 272
Sampson, Barbara A., 357
Sampson, Barbara, 357
Sampson, Brian, 90, 461
Sampson, Christian G, 363
Sampson, Frederick D R, 48
Sampson, J. David, 47
Sampson, Rick J, 281
Sams, Lisa, 22
Samson, Anne, 161
Samuel, Peter, 276
Samuelian, Michael, 460
Samuels, Chuck, 539
Samuels, Debrarose, 49
Samuels, Paul N, 216
Samuels, Paul N., 117
Samuelsen, John, 495
Samuelson, Scott B, 337
San Filippo, Andrew, 162
Sanabria, Diana, 56
Sanchala, Sarah, 30
Sanchez, Frank D., 550
Sanchez, Frank, 397
Sanchez, Linda T., 137, 169
Sanchez, Loretta, 320
Sanchez, Willie, 41
Sanchis, Frank, 446
Sandbank, Jane, 587
Sander, Lucia, 66
Sanders Jr, James, 22, 24
Sanders, Bernard, 297, 314
Sanders, Bernie, 180
Sanders, James, 19
Sanders, Janet, 532
Sanders, Jr., James, 20, 21, 24, 25, 26, 165, 242, 616
Sanders, Steven, 404, 429, 439, 457
Sanderson, Melinda, 392
Sandhaas, Jill, 476
Sandlin, Stephanie Herseth, 323
Sandner, Rick, 403
Sandow, Dawn, 133, 354
Sands, Paul, 538
Sandy, Stephen R, 299
SanFilippo, Andrew, 236
Sanfilippo, Kelly, 52
Sanford, Linda, 454, 543
Sanghvi, Ami, 454
Sanit, Gordon, 406
Sano, Joseph, 452
Sanon, James, 484
Sant, Dennis J, 334
Santabarbara, Angelo, 33, 35, 38, 41, 42, 638
Santamarina, Sue, 69
Santana, Sandy, 197
Santella, Frank, 168
Santelli, Charles, 379
Santeramo, Michael, 133
Santiago, Elizabeth, 380
Santiago, Guillermo, 440
Santiago, Joyce M, 503, 518
Santiago, Jr., George, 563
Santiago, Julissa G., 486
Santiago, Karen, 100, 189
Santiago-Marullo, Dawn A, 585
Santilli, Loretta, 174
Santino, Joseph, 355
Santoni, Lou, 274, 502
Santora, Ron, 537
Santorelli, Joseph A., 47
Santoro, Anthony, 339
Santoro, Joseph, 385
Santos, Beverly, 544
Santos, Daryl, 85, 123
Santos, Stanley, 390
Santulli, Thomas J, 327
Sanzillo, Francis, 463
Saperia, Phillip A, 231
Sapienza, Matt, 397
Sapienza, Matthew, 550
Sapio, Robert, 528

Appendices: Financial Plan, Indexes & Maps

Sapir, Zev, 223
Sapolin, Matthew P, 353
Saporito, Carol, 75
Sapp, Mimi, 474
Saraceni, Anthony, 501
Sardy, John, 516
Sargis, Gregory, 449
Sarlin Wright, Kay, 7, 84, 97, 147, 188, 271, 304, 307
Saro, Ralph, 535
Sarratori, Frank C., 455
Sarson, Matthew B., 430
Saskena, Rahul, 454
Sassower, Doris L, 215
Satish, Sandeep, 396
Satterly, Neil, 543
Sattler, Michael, 564
Sauer, Doug, 257
Sauer, William, 403
Sauerbrey, Martha, 338
Saul Rich, Jennifer, 374
Saunder, Anita, 582
Saunders, Ann, 367
Saunders, Jeff, 399
Saunders, Kelly, 469
Saunders, Verna, 49
Sauter, Thomas R, 86, 97, 188
Savage, Dene, 510
Savage, Gerard, 18
Savage, Paul D, 571
Savage, Peter, 379
Savage, Susan, 12, 235, 245, 264
Savanyu, Esq, Jean M, 103, 211
Savell, Roger, 388
Savin, Nicholas, 601
Savinetti, Louis G, 133
Savino, Diane J, 19, 20, 21, 22, 24, 79, 616
Savino, Diane J., 16, 494
Savino, Diane, 20, 21, 23, 24
Savino, Jay, 375
Savona, Keri, 60
Savransky, Ariel, 397
Sawaneh, Momodou S., 481
Sawicki, P David, 4, 173, 227, 250
Sawyer, Erin, 69
Sawyer, Paul, 88, 196
Sawyer, Welton L, 598
Saxe, David B, 45
Saxe, Phyllis, 49
Sayegh, Gabriel, 408
Sayre, Gregg C., 11
Sayres, Edwin, 432
Scaduto, Joseph, 467
Scagnelli, John M, 98, 151
Scagnelli, Peter, 360
Scalabrini, Joanna, 555
Scalcione, Vincent, 168
Scalera, Patricia, 158
Scales, Michael, 559
Scalia, Joann, 18
Scalzo, Lynda, 240, 304
Scamardella, Robert J., 490
Scamardella, Robert, 376
Scanlan, Richard E, 423
Scanlon, Sr, Kevin E, 217, 243
Scannapieco, Jr, Anthony G, 134
Scarano, John, 508
Scarborough, Andrea C., 484
Scarchilli, John, 455
Scarcia, Susan, 178
Scardino, Michael, 47, 59
Scarpechi, Helen J, 136
Scarpulla, Saliann, 49
Scatena, Casey, 65
Scattum, Leela, 474
Scaturro, Angelo F., 330
Scavo, Anthony, 485
Scearce, Dena, 443
Scemama, Isabelle, 384
Schaaf, Eric, 154
Schachner, Elliot M., 115, 213
Schachner, Larry S., 49
Schachner, Larry, 48
Schachter, Robert, 448
Schack, Arthur M, 46
Schading, Chuck, 525
Schadt, Peg, 467
Schaefer, Kevin, 104, 124, 242
Schaefer, Martha, 10, 228
Schaefer, Nathan, 399
Schaefer, Wolf, 467
Schaefering, Lynn, 32
Schaeffer, Dana, 448
Schaeffer, Raymond, 99, 286
Schaengold, Phillip, 468
Schaewe, Catherine C., 48
Schafer, Christa M, 328
Schaffer, Carolyn, 374
Schaffer, Frederick P., 550
Schaffer, Frederick, 97, 123, 306, 397
Schaffer, Rich, 341
Schaffer, Richard H., 374
Schaffer, W. John, 366
Schaffer-Cohen, Phyllis, 418
Schafran, Brooke, 392
Schafroth, Jessica, 439
Schaitberger, Harold, 487
Schakowsky, Jan, 324
Schaming, Mark A, 120
Schaming, Mark, 270
Schantz, Lawrence, 241
Scharff, Karen, 138, 476
Schartner, Walter F, 593
Schatz, Jane, 358
Schau, Sandra, 444
Schechter, Barbara, 358
Schechter, Stephen, 397
Scheckowitz, Bruce E., 49
Schecter, Jennifer, 49, 50
Schedler, Matthew, 392
Scheer, Mark, 528
Scheibel, Michael, 449
Scheidelman, Scott, 451
Scheifer, Charles, 161
Scheinkman, Alan, 210
Scheld, Tim, 535
Schell, Catherine A, 52
Schenck, Dr. Marcus, 80
Schenk, Kevin, 343
Schepp, Sandra A., 333
Scher, Anne, 279
Scher, Peter L., 488
Scherer, John, 344
Scherer, Lawrence, 467
Schermerhorn, Paula, 131
Schermeyer, Hon Sundy A, 365
Scherzer, Eric, 480
Schettino, John P, 61
Scheuer, Janelle, 474
Scheuerman, William E, 244
Schick, Robert, 147
Schick, Stephan G., 46
Schiedo, Michael, 584
Schiera, Roger J, 135
Schifeling, Iris, 427
Schiff, Adam, 169
Schiff, Michael A, 337
Schiffer, Richard A., 185
Schiffino, Julieta, 544
Schiffmacher, Karen, 524
Schiffman, Mark, 99, 286
Schiffres, Jeremy, 526
Schillaci, Theresa, 141
Schiller, Tammra, 512
Schimel, Michelle, 27, 33, 38, 39, 40, 42, 638
Schimmerling, Tom, 373
Schimminger, Robin L, 34, 37, 39, 43, 87, 237, 246, 288, 638
Schimminger, Robin L., 36
Schiraldi, Peter, 384
Schlaerth, Joseph, 537
Schleifer, Leonard S., 186
Schlein, Stanley, 409
Schlendorf, Micah, 516
Schlesinger, Herbert J, 232
Schlesinger, Steven, 465
Schlick, James E, 136
Schlientz, Hubert, 451
Schlueter, Thomas, 224
Schmeling, Mary, 363
Schmiddlapp, Carol, 450
Schmidlin, Robert, 468
Schmidt Jr., Benno C., 550
Schmidt, David, 46
Schmidt, James A., 464
Schmidt, Jean, 317
Schmidt, Kathryn, 473
Schmidt, Thomas, 570
Schmitt, Kenneth, 343
Schmitt, Peter J, 332
Schnabel, Martin, 100, 286
Schnakenberg, David, 446

Schnebel, Susan, 592
Schneider, Beth A., 406, 469
Schneider, Daniel J., 487
Schneider, Deanna, 21
Schneider, Erasmus, 148, 176
Schneider, Gary, 415
Schneider, Howard, 527
Schneider, Jean T., 49
Schneider, Joe, 148
Schneider, Rob, 402
Schneider, William J., 367
Schneiderman, Eric T, 3, 9, 78, 84, 112, 140, 149, 161, 177, 188, 195, 201, 206, 221, 245, 263, 605
Schnell, William A, 464
Schneyer, Edward C, 337
Schnirman, Jack, 350
Schnur, Joel, 464
Schock, Aaron, 322
Schoelle, Jr, Robert L, 345
Schoelles, Patricia A, 560
Schoen, Neal, 10, 283
Schoenfeld, Jay, 410
Schoenfeld, Marc, 446
Schoenwetter, Sara, 401
Schollmeyer, Edward, 473
Scholz, Robert, 470
Schonfeld, Diane, 334
Schonfeld, Ivan, 390
Schoolman, Maureen, 43, 87, 124
Schoonover, Laura, 133
Schopp, Steven E., 128
Schopp, Steven, 281
Schor, Jeff, 430
Schorr, Allegra, 182
Schrader, Dennis, 440
Schrader, Kurt, 322
Schrader, Richard, 449
Schrameck, Lorraine, 502
Schramm, Linda, 122
Schraver, David M., 432
Schreiber, Lawrence, 182, 203
Schreiber, Michelle D., 49
Schreyer, Paul, 420
Schrialdi, Vincent N, 357
Schrier, Katherine D., 201, 220
Schriro, Dora B, 353
Schroeder, Mark JF, 342
Schroeter, Helga, 434
Schubel, David C, 333
Schuh, Philip, 443
Schuler, George, 449
Schulkin, Alan, 133, 404
Schulman, Martin J, 48
Schulte, Jerry, 105, 152
Schultz, Brian M, 96, 285
Schultz, Daniel P., 125
Schultz, James, 588
Schultz, Margaret, 582
Schultz, Naomi, 36
Schulz, Dana, 421
Schulz, Garth, 443
Schuman, Adam, 79, 103
Schumann, Bethany, 373
Schumer, Charles E , 644
Schumer, Charles E, 80, 311, 316, 324
Schumer, Charles E., 169, 190, 214
Schumer, Charles, 116
Schuppenhauer, John A, 62
Schupper, Yehuda, 34
Schussheim, Michael, 363
Schuster, Bill, 323
Schuster, Lauren, 33
Schuster, Robert, 296
Schutte, Thomas F, 559
Schwab, Kevin, 395
Schwabrow, Adam, 332
Schwadron, Carolyn, 426
Schwaller, John, 467, 545
Schwark, Linda M, 57
Schwartz, Amy, 411
Schwartz, Andrew, 358
Schwartz, Barry, 49
Schwartz, Brian, 386
Schwartz, David, 420
Schwartz, Denise, 515
Schwartz, JoAnne, 122
Schwartz, Kevin, 445
Schwartz, Lynn, 594
Schwartz, Mark, 223
Schwartz, William, 36
Schwarz, Michael, 406
Schwarz, Thomas J, 545
Schweikert, David, 224
Schweitzer, Dan, 428
Schweitzer, Melvin, 48
Schwerzmann, Peter A, 54
Sciarrino, Jr., Matthew, 50
Scime, Michael, 180
Sciortino, Franklin J, 88
Sciortino, Joseph, 359, 572
Sciortino, Sandra, 47
Sciotti, Nicholas A, 336
Sciria, Chris, 523
Scirocco, Anthony, 364
Sclafani, Tony, 308
Sclater, Alison, 434
Scleicher, Sandra, 173
Scop, Anita, 582
Scopelianos, Margaret, 385
Scordo, Peter C, 592
Scott, A Paul, 571
Scott, Ann, 10, 283
Scott, Brendan, 532
Scott, David, 317, 532
Scott, Hugh B., 212
Scott, Hunter, 536
Scott, Melinda, 11, 149, 271
Scott, Michael, 141
Scott, Robert A, 552
Scott, Robert C, 321
Scott, Robert C., 125, 196
Scott, Sherry M, 365
Scotti, Steven, 401
Scott-McFadden, Marricka, 133
Scova, Patricia June, 351
Scozzafava, Dierdre, 12, 149, 162, 163, 236
Screnci, Diane, 142
Scriber, William, 106, 288
Scrimshaw, Susan, 560
Scruggs, Jeffrey, 419
Scuccimarra, Thomas H, 48
Scudder, Henry J., 45
Scudder, Henry, 209
Scully, Mona, 174
Scully, Peter A, 96, 150, 306
Seabrook, Norman, 481
Seaburn, Bonnie, 579
Seager, Kimberly M., 57
Sealy, Annie C, 348
Searles, Jack, 326
Sears, Jaclyn, 413
Searson, Gloria, 417
Seaton, Wayne, 474
Seavers, Dean, 448
Seawright, Rebecca A, 638
Seawright, Rebecca, 34, 36, 37, 40, 42
Sebastian, Chris, 443
Sebesta, Paul, 360
Sebesta, Rebecca, 163
Sechrist, Roderic, 13, 246, 283, 284
Seckerson, Tina, 339
Secor, Dawn, 388
Seddio, Frank, 373
Sederer, MD, Lloyd I, 10, 228
Sedita III, Frank A, 328
Sedler, Mark, 467
Sedore, Ann, 554
Seebald, Kelly, 175
Seeley, Gregory R, 330
Seem, Mark D, 566
Seery, Sheila C, 381
Segal, Elizabeth, 384
Segal, Jay, 421
Segarra, Joseph, 401
Segarra, Ninfa, 391, 451
Segermeister, David, 168, 247
Seggos, Basil, 8, 87, 97, 100, 105, 151, 152
Seguin, Rachael, 112
Sehgal, Mona, 352
Sehr, Gregory, 471
Seiden, Adam, 64
Seiden, Daniel L, 62
Seidenwurm, Karl, 485
Seidman, A. Alan, 91
Seiff, Eric A, 98, 210
Seilback, Michael, 181
Seiler, Judy, 157
Seiter Jr, Norman W, 46
Selby, Doug, 341
Seligman, Joel, 471, 560
Seligson, Nancy, 350
Sellers, Corlis L, 223

Sellers, Tyrone A., 481
Selver, Paul D, 433
Semansky, Joseph A, 223
Seme, Elizabeth, 75
Semmel, Col. Greg A., 295
Semmeles, John, 399
Sendall, Jim, 85, 123
Senez, Karen, 111
Senft, Anthony, 61
Senior, Marsha, 455
Sennett, John, 141
Sensenbrenner, Jr, F James, 321
Sensenbrenner, Jr, James F, 324
Sensenbrenner, Jr., Jim, 116
Senterman, Jeff, 156
Senti Jr, Frederick, 101, 236
Senulis, Joseph, 296
Sepulveda, Luis R, 34
Sepúlveda, Luis R, 639
Sepulveda, Luis, 35, 36, 37, 39, 41
Serafino, L.D., 51
Sered, Danielle, 472
Sereti, Rosemary, 266
Serghini, Philip, 473
Serino, Sue, 19, 20, 22, 23, 24, 25, 178, 195, 254, 616
Serio, Gregory, 453
Serkalow, Mary, 525
Sernick, Keith D., 467
Serra, Alexandra, 473
Serrano, José E, 649
Serrano, Jose E, 73, 267, 311, 317
Serrano, Jose E., 142
Serrano, Jose M, 19
Serrano, Jose M., 16, 21
Serrano, Jose, 20, 22, 25, 26, 275, 317
Serrano, Jose, M, 616
Servedio, Dominick M., 495
Servis, Keith W, 175
Servoss, Stephanie A., 212
Seserman, Michael, 184
Sessions, Jeff, 169, 267, 313, 316
Sessions, Pete, 321
Sesto, Patricia, 98, 151
Setty, Sumana, 493
Seward, James L, 15, 19, 20, 22, 23, 24, 25, 202, 616
Seward, James, 25
Seward, Karen, 427
Sewell, Alexa, 193, 400
Sewell, Brad, 449
Sewell, Valerie, 220, 293
Sexton, John, 427
Sexton, Michael, 176
Seymour, Jude, 132
Sganga, Fred, 467
Sgroi, Robert, 348
Sgroi, Sandra L., 45
Shaakir, Zakiyah, 379
Shacknai, Daniel, 354
Shafer, Stephen T, 600
Shafit, Matthew, 355
Shah, Sanjiv, 385
Shah, Shetal, 467
Shah, Susan, 472
Shaheen, Jeanne, 90, 315
Shaheen, John, 451
Shaheen, Rita, 463
Shahen, Michael, 344
Shainberg, Andrew, 458
Shallman, John E, 254
Shamash, Yacov, 467
Shames, Alison, 472
Shamoun, Simon, 133
Shanahan, Thomas, 465
Shank, Richard, 464
Shanley, Kevin, 567
Shannon, Bobby, 519
Shannon, Kimberly, 37
Shapiro, Brian, 75, 259
Shapiro, Daniel, 12, 85, 149, 162, 236
Shapiro, Eli, 485
Shapiro, Jack, 298
Shapiro, Kenneth L, 476
Shapiro, Myra, 462
Shapiro, Neal, 146, 538
Shapiro-Shellaby, Micaela, 399
Shaps, Robert, 598
Sharkey, Sabrina, 529
Sharkey, Sally, 576
Sharma, Gaurav, 471
Sharp, Kay, 434
Sharp, Susan D, 9, 200, 219
Sharp, William, 12, 86, 149, 162, 236
Shau, Yee S., 489
Shaver, Gary, 526
Shaver, Judson R, 557
Shaver, Wendy D., 133
Shaw, Christina, 168
Shaw, Elliott, 400
Shaw, John D., 185
Shaw, Marc, 397
Shaw, Margaret L, 216
Shaw, Melanie, 383
Shaw, Noah C, 102, 141, 151
Shaw, Susan, 468
Shaw, Wendy, 174
Shazor, Marilyn G., 289
Shchegol, Alex, 563
Shea, Brian, 7, 160, 235
Shea, Carol A, 65
Shea, Michael P, 587
Shea, Nancy, 462
Shea, Sheila E, 209, 230
Shea, Thomas C, 594
Sheahan, Michael, 109
Shearer, Jessica, 377
Shearer, Robert, 445
Shearer, Sarah, 35, 39, 41
Sheares, Robin K., 49
Sheehan, James G, 207, 263
Sheehan, James, 355
Sheehan, Jeremiah, 439
Sheehan, Joseph W, 64
Sheehan, Kathy, 341
Sheehan, Kevin, 464
Sheehan, Tim, 110
Shehadi, John, 344
Sheifer, Charles, 245
Sheinkman, Alan B, 47
Sheinkopf, Hank, 139, 465
Sheinkopf, Henry A, 465
Sheinkopf, Henry, 435
Shelby, Richard C, 313
Shelby, Richard C., 267
Shelby, Richard, 80, 190, 312
Sheldon, Matthew, 587
Shelmidine, Joanne, 583
Shelton, Christopher M., 481
Shelton, Christopher, 225
Shelton, Tracy, 458
Shemesh, Ron, 418
Shenker, Cynthia D, 476
Shenker, Cynthia D., 496
Shenker, Cynthia, 461
Shenker, Joseph, 82
Shepard, Peggy, 474
Shepard, Stephen, 397
Shepard, Steve, 551
Shephard, Ann, 75
Shepherd, Connie L, 132
Sheppard, Daniel B, 8, 175
Sheppard, David, 7, 160, 235
Sheppard, James, 363
Sheppard, Matt, 396
Sheppard, Patrick, 122
Sher, Barry N., 139
Sher, Denise, 47
Sherburne, Abbott, 455
Sheridan, Robert, 69
Sheridan, Sarah, 538
Sheridan, Timothy, 393
Sherlock, Jerry, 279
Sherman, Brad, 320
Sherman, Brian, 589
Sherman, Howard H., 48
Sherman, John, 419
Sherman, Kenneth, 46, 49
Sherman, Ryan C, 589
Sherman, Steven I., 185
Sherman, Stuart C, 176
Sherwin, Dawn, 147
Sherwin, Galen, 454
Sherwin, Peter J.W., 171
Sherwood, O. Peter, 48
Sherwood, Sandra R, 595
Sheth, Brian, 472
Sheth, Manisha, 10, 78, 84, 112, 140, 188, 207, 263
Shields, Beverly J, 328
Shields, Col. Raymond L., 10
Shields, Maureen, 397
Shields, R. Stratford, 445

Shifflett, Joseph, 53
Shimer, Steve, 534
Shimkus, John, 154
Shimkus, Todd, 515
Shine, Edward J, 599
Shinn, Robin R., 125
Shinske, Stuart, 529
Shipley, Jeff, 516
Shipley, John, 108
Shipley, Robert, 336
Shipp, Crystal, 451
Shippy, Derrick L., 496
Shirreffs, Donna F., 168
Shkane, Joan E., 56
Shoaf, Victoria, 204
Shoemaker, James E., 207
Shoemaker, Sylvia, 134
Shoer, Howard, 385
Sholes, David G, 597
Shorenstein, Marissa J., 479
Shorenstein, Marissa, 384
Shorenstein, Stuart, 404
Short, David, 366
Short, James, 571
Shorter, Charles A., 550
Shotland, Randy, 511
Shover, Emily, 32
Shrager, Steven, 173, 227
Shudofsky, Sara L., 115, 213
Shuffler, Matthew, 29
Shufro, Joel, 226
Shuler, Heath, 322
Shulklapper, Lester, 476
Shulman, Barry, 96, 285
Shulman, Martin, 46
Shulman, Sabrina, 447
Shultes, Richard, 135
Shure, Kathleen, 420
Shurgrue Dos Santos, Catherine, 463
Shuster, Bill, 155, 190, 290
Shute, Leonard, 471
Shyne, Henry F., 491
Sibbison, Virginia Hayes, 262
Sica, Robert J., 115
Siciliano, Bradley, 100, 273
Siciliano, Margaret A, 62
Sickora, Brian, 534
Siconolfi, Patrick J., 191
Sicora, Brian, 537
Siddiqui, Kari, 464
Siddiqui, Norain, 380
Siebert, Richard, 132, 375
Sieg, Andy M, 81
Siegal, Bernice D., 48
Siegel, Alfred, 417
Siegel, Lawrence G, 515
Siegel, Norman I, 48
Siegel, Norman I., 46
Siegler, Richard, 468
Siglin, Robert D, 131
Siglow, John, 404
Signor, John F, 96, 273
Sikora, Peter, 441
Sikorski, Ray, 511
Sikowitz, Marcia, 49
Sikula, Michael, 70
Silano, Mary Beth, 505
Silber, Debra, 46, 49
Silber, Yeruchim, 444
Siller, Michael, 356
Siller, Scott H., 61
Siller, Sidney, 298
Sillerman, Michael T, 433
Silsby, Sue, 409
Silvaggio, Mary Ann, 267
Silvan, Jon, 419
Silver, George J., 49
Silver, George, 46
Silver, Janet, 425
Silver, Jeff, 534
Silver, Sandy, 121
Silverblatt, Pamela S., 550
Silverblatt, Pamela, 397
Silverman, David J, 269
Silverman, Gerald, 532
Silverman, Henry, 100, 273
Silverman, Isabelle, 412
Silverman, Philip, 470
Silverman-Yam, Beth, 463
Silverstein, Larry A, 249
Silverstein, Mark K, 598
Silvestri, Carlo, 358
Silvestro, Rose, 510
Silvey, Jerome, 467
Simanowitz, Michael, 34, 35, 36, 37, 39, 41, 639
Simas, Michael, 454
Simberg, Marianne, 373
Simberkoff, Michael S, 296
Simeone, John, 430
Simmons, Dottie, 513
Simmons, Elliot, 538
Simmons, Randy, 149
Simon, Avalyn, 171
Simon, Earl, 397
Simon, Jo Ann, 639
Simon, Jo Anne, 34, 36, 39, 40, 42
Simon, Randy, 271
Simon, Richard, 290, 594
Simon, Thomas J, 569
Simone, Matthew, 418
Simons, Emily, 466
Simons, Hon Richard D, 216
Simons, Hon Richard D., 171
Simons, Jeffrey, 583
Simons, Randy, 305
Simotas, Aravella, 27, 34, 36, 37, 38, 40, 43, 195, 222, 254, 639
Simpson, Elizabeth, 56
Simpson, John B, 545
Simpson, Michael K, 317
Simpson, Mike, 142
Simpson, Robert, 517
Simpson, Sandra A, 600
Simpson, Shawndaya L., 49
Simpson, Wendy, 136
Simpsons, Robert, 395
Simson, Jay J, 90
Sinacori, Steven, 378
Sinatra, Frank G., 486
Sinclair, Kristin, 23
Sinclair, Steven, 105, 152
Sinding, Christian, 412
Sinding-Daly, Katherine, 449
Sinel, Shawn, 409
Singer, Conrad D., 55
Singer, Debbi D, 51
Singer, Gary M., 494
Singer, Leonard, 403
Singh, Anil C., 49
Singh, Mandrawattie, 492
Singh, Susan, 419
Singleton, Chuck, 534
Singleton, Valerie, 207
Sinnott, Richard, 400
Sinton, Jennifer, 434
Sio, Benjamin, 395
Sion, Robin, 132
Siperstein, Alan, 289
Sira, Louise K, 53
Sira, Louise K., 329
Siracuse, Kraig, 453
Sirago, Tanja, 217, 239
Siragusa, Joe, 534
Sirianni, Judy, 504
Sirois, Herman A, 580
Sirota, Robert, 557
Sise, Joseph, 46
Sise, Richard E, 48, 209
Siskind, PhD, Alan B, 232
Sison, Michele J., 168
Sissel, Mark, 570
Sisti, Maria, 537
Sisto, Daniel, 383, 424, 456, 486
Siwek, Donna M, 47
Sizer, Sean, 294
Skaggs, Adam, 389
Skartados, Frank, 26, 34, 35, 37, 40, 41, 42, 43, 70, 87, 152, 639
Skelton, Ike, 317
Skidmore, Susan J., 345
Skidmore, Susan, 373
Skoda, Edward F., 53
Skoog-Harvey, Jen, 29
Skorton, David J, 554
Skorton, David J., 459
Skoufis, James, 34, 35, 40, 42
Skoufis,James, 640
Skowfoe, Jr., Philip, 336
Skretta, Angela, 424
Skrill, Leonard, 187
Skryp, Ken, 531
Skrzeckowski, Jim, 229

Skype, Judy, 28, 31
Slade, David, 412
Slade, Frank, 234, 240
Slade, William, 401
Slagen, Jennifer, 26
Slane, Emil, 10, 229
Slaten, Reginald, 255
Slater, Matthew, 18
Slattery, Michael, 459
Slattery, Timothy, 450
Slaughter, James, 463
Slaughter, Louise M, 311
Slaughter, Louise McIntosh, 321, 649
Slawson, Michael J, 335
Sledge, Joe, 296
Slemp, Teresa, 52
Slep, Keith, 325
Slevin, James, 470, 495
Slevin, Kate, 292
Slingerland, Molly, 379
Sloan, Stephen R, 203
Sloane, David, 418
Sloane, Sandra, 140
Sloat, Jr, Major Ellwood A, 113
Slobod, Elaine, 47
Slocum, Christine H, 32
Sloma, Rich, 120
Slone-Goldstein, Tara, 126
Sluszka, Joseph, 294
Slutsky, Lorie A, 260
Slutzky, Orville A, 279
Small, Esq., Charles A., 46, 54
Small, Gilian, 397
Small, Gillian, 550
Small, Rachel, 3, 160, 240, 283
Small, William, 64
Smalls, Ronald L, 598
Smart, Colin, 401
Smayda, Beth N., 367
Smelkinson, Ira, 445
Smerd, Jeremy, 532
Smikle Jr, Basil, 372
Smiljic, Goran, 366
Smith Boivin, Elizabeth, 181
Smith, Adam, 297, 318, 412
Smith, Adrian, 322
Smith, Alan, 187
Smith, Alex, 350
Smith, Amy L., 115, 213
Smith, Barbara, 60, 162, 236
Smith, Blair, 70, 72
Smith, Bob, 534
Smith, Brad, 539
Smith, Brandon, 109
Smith, Brian, 168, 397
Smith, Carol, 404
Smith, Christopher H, 319
Smith, Christopher, 424
Smith, Constance O, 367
Smith, Corwin, 437
Smith, Dana, 328
Smith, David R, 544
Smith, David, 468
Smith, Donald Blaine, 334
Smith, Dr. David, 69
Smith, Edward M., 495
Smith, Elisabeth, 464
Smith, Georgeann, 267
Smith, Gerald R, 326
Smith, Gordon, 316
Smith, Gregory, 79, 88
Smith, Guy, 329
Smith, Helen W., 464
Smith, Hilary, 449
Smith, Howard S, 574
Smith, Howard W, 599
Smith, James E, 362
Smith, James, 402
Smith, Jeanne, 57
Smith, Jennifer L., 78
Smith, JoAnn M, 258
Smith, Joann, 439
Smith, Joseph, 110, 479
Smith, Karen J, 564
Smith, Karen, 49
Smith, Kevin, 7, 121, 228, 252, 451
Smith, Kimberleigh, 422
Smith, Lamar S, 320
Smith, Lamar, 143, 154
Smith, Linda, 31
Smith, Lisa Tracy, 406, 469
Smith, Logan, 38, 40, 41, 42
Smith, Lori, 36, 37, 42
Smith, Luther, 437
Smith, Lynn, 518
Smith, Marc, 349
Smith, Mark, 449
Smith, Mary C, 349
Smith, Mary H, 47
Smith, Mary L., 179
Smith, Michael P, 81
Smith, Michael P., 385
Smith, Michael, 512
Smith, Mike, 98, 141, 151
Smith, Molly E, 557
Smith, Nancy E, 45
Smith, Nathan, 465
Smith, Patricia M, 355
Smith, Phil, 474
Smith, Phillip H., 241
Smith, Rex, 523
Smith, Richard, 163
Smith, Rick, 411
Smith, Robert, 472
Smith, Rusty, 376
Smith, RW, 534
Smith, Scott D, 569
Smith, Sheila, 326
Smith, Stephen, 511
Smith, Stuart, 356
Smith, Tawana, 432
Smith, Terrance J, 133
Smith, Thomas, 456
Smith, Wallace, 277, 290
Smith, Wayne, 461
Smithing, Leueen, 577
Smoot, J. Patricia Wilson, 116
Smord, Kristy, 381
Smothergill, Mark, 511
Smyth, Andrea, 399, 459, 466
Smyth, J. McGregor, 462
Smyth, McGregor, 192, 199
Snavely, Dick, 533
Snavely, Rick, 533
Snell Jr, Joseph F, 343
Snellings, Harry, 349
Snelson, Andrea, 472
Snow, Denise, 467
Snowe, Olympia J, 314, 316
Snyden, RD, 496
Snyder, Abby, 148
Snyder, Arthur R, 338
Snyder, Bill, 534
Snyder, Connie, 111
Snyder, Gib, 525
Snyder, Heather, 505
Snyder, Jackie, 6, 270, 352
Snyder, James J, 326
Snyder, James, 503
Snyder, Jared, 8, 147
Snyder, John, 295
Snyder, Michael J, 271
Snyder, Patricia Di Benedetto, 280
Snyder, Paula, 375
Snyder, Phyllis, 260
Snyder, Richard, 528
Snyder, Scott, 342
Snyder, Teresa T, 567
Snyder, Todd R, 102, 272
Snyder, Vic, 318
Snyder, Warren, 89
Soares, P David, 325
Sobaszek, Michael J, 509
Sobel, Peter, 375
Sobel, Theodore, 463
Sobol, Peter, 466
Socarides, Richard, 543
Sochet, Charni, 8, 187, 189, 304, 309
Sokloski, Lee, 418
Sokolow, Alan V, 238, 268
Solages, Michaelle C, 34, 640
Solages, Michaelle, 36, 38, 40, 41, 42
Solarz, Ron, 233
Sold, Joanne, 28
Soldevere, Joe, 353
Sollazzo, Lucille, 451
Soller, Chris, 276
Soller, K. Christopher, 153
Sollis, Mary Lou, 386
Solomon, Amy, 442
Solomon, Charles H., 50
Solomon, Charles, 49
Solomon, Mark J, 216

Solomon, Martin M, 46
Solomon, Stephen, 427
Solomonow, Seth, 358
Somers, Bob, 69
Sommer, Dan, 417
Sommer, Jeffrey, 103, 164, 265, 308
Sommer, Judah, 470
Son, Shin, 259
Sonberg, Michael R., 50
Song, Chia-Chia, 458
Sonn, Paul, 448
Sonnenberg, Stacy, 419
Sonnenblick, Arthur I, 249
Soodsma, Norma, 7
Soos-Kobylski, Paula, 403
Sopak, Sandra K, 326
Sorbero, Joseph, 15
Sordi, Michael C, 365
Sorensen, Jon, 102, 151, 308
Sorenson, Alan J., 337
Sorial, Phoebe S, 107
Sorrell, Karen, 362
Sosa, Enrique, 438
Sosa-Lintner, Gloria, 50
Sotak, Rose, 366
Soto Jr., Humberto, 487
Soto, Eric, 401
Soto, Faviola, 48
Soucia, Thomas G, 329
Souder, Mark, 320
Soule, Norman, 278
Southard-Kreiger, Rebecca, 41
Souza, Richard, 373
Spacher, Kevin, 362
Spacone, PhD, Celia, 228
Spadafora Jr, Ronald R, 578
Spaeth, Jack N, 518
Spain, John, 142
Spain, Michael V, 523
Spano, Andrew J, 7, 130
Spano, John J., 411
Spano, Mike, 367
Spano, Vincent E., 367
Spar, Deborah L, 553
Sparacio, John J, 100, 273
Sparkman, Robin, 527
Sparks, Tracy, 132
Sparling, Reed, 463
Sparrow, Paul M., 125
Spasiano, Michael, 568
Spatafora, Frances, 32
Spatz, Donald, 179
Spatz, Sherrill, 210
Spaulding, Jon, 529
Spears, Alan L, 65
Spears, Brenda S., 49
Speck, William S, 600
Specter, Arlen, 312, 314, 316
Specter, P.E., L.S, Marvin M, 217
Spector, Joseph, 532
Spector, Sacha, 463
Speenburgh, Wayne, 329
Speer, Lisa, 449
Speight, Bruce, 280
Speiller, Lenny, 353
Spencer, Gary, 45, 210
Spencer, James, 455
Spencer-El, Erica, 309
Spenziero, Nancy, 283
Spergel, Robert H., 55
Spero, Donald, 99, 285
Spero, James C., 166
Speyer, Jerry I, 249
Spicer, Joe, 426
Spiegel, Stuart, 451
Spielman, Matt, 526
Spielvogel, Carl, 543
Spier, Jonathan, 467
Spiers, Elizabeth, 528
Spies, F Christian, 58
Spigelmyer, David, 396
Spike, Ronald G, 340
Spilde, LCSWR, ACSW, Duane, 232
Spillane, Michael, 489
Spilman, Joan, 190
Spina Jr., Thomas, 115, 213
Spina, Eric, 455
Spingle, Serena, 49
Spinnato, Joseph E, 279
Spinnato, Joseph E., 486
Spinner, Jeffrey Arlen, 59
Spinney, Richard B, 328
Spinola, Steven, 248, 459, 495
Spiro, Jeff, 464
Spitzberg, Samuel, 13, 294, 305
Spitzer, Benjamin B, 569
Spivak, Lewis, 254
Spodek, Ellen, 46
Spodek, Ira, 486
Spofford, Ann, 343
Sponsler, Michael, 455
Sposato, Mark A, 571
Spota, Thomas J, 337
Sprague, Kristy, 329
Spratt, Jr, John M, 318
Spring, Kathleen A, 589
Spring, Larry, 571
Springer, Gail L, 366
Springer, Neil, 532
Sproat, Christine A, 47
Sproat, James, 8, 161, 245
Squadron, Anne S., 494
Squadron, Daniel L, 23, 25, 26, 617
Squadron, Daniel L., 21, 211
Squadron, Daniel, 16, 19, 20, 24, 87, 114, 237
Squeri, Christopher, 281
Squier, Randall, 570
Squires, David, 338
Squires, William, 72
Srinivasan, Meenakshi, 358
Srolovic, Lemuel, 149, 207
St George, Norman, 61
St Hilaire, Karen, 337
St John, Keith, 16, 23
St Lawrence, Christopher P, 363
St Paul Joseph, Christene, 175, 293
St. Charles, Alexandra, 462
St. Cyr, Julie, 427
St. Germain, Maribeth, 86, 162
Sta. Ana, Andrew, 463
Stabenow, Debbie, 73, 155, 180, 203, 312, 314
Stachowski, Cynthia, 573
Stack, Eileen, 13, 253
Stack, Richard M., 371
Stack, Ronald, 474
Stackhouse, Charles, 158
Stackrow, David M, 96, 285
Staehr, Ed, 74
Stafford, George, 150, 162, 236
Stahlberg, Jan, 412
Staiano-Coico, Lisa, 551
Staller, Cary, 543
Stallings, Ericka, 381
Stallman, Michael D., 49
Stallman, Michael, 46
Stallone, David, 109
Stamler, Susan, 471
Stamm, Kari L, 136
Stamm, Monica, 103, 137, 164
Stamm-Philipps, Esq., Angela, 56
Stampas, Triada, 415
Stanceu, Timothy C., 212
Standard, Kenneth G, 217
Standard, Kenneth G., 198
Stander, Thomas A, 47
Standish-Kuon, Terri, 381
Stankowski, Gary, 447
Stanley, Deborah F, 546
Stanley, John, 49
Stanley, Lisa, 364
Stanley, Samuel L, 545
Stanley, Samuel, 467
Stanton, Donielle, 538
Stapleton, Marilyn, 555
Starace, James A, 106, 288
Stark James, Tracy, 514
Stark, Fortney Pete, 323
Stark, Shirley, 9, 200, 219
Stark, William J, 597
Starks, Jacklin G, 600
Starr, Daniel, 588
Starr, Tom, 536
Starr, Tracy, 15
State, David J, 105, 287
Staton, Betty, 435
Statz, David, 391
Staub, Arthur, 474
Stauder, Paul, 403
Stauffer, Kent T, 221
Stauffer, Kent T., 188, 201, 208
Stauffer, Sanford, 405

Stavisky, Evan, 454
Stavisky, Toby A, 617
Stavisky, Toby Ann, 16, 19, 22, 23, 24, 26, 125
Stavisky, William, 599
Stay, Tom, 341
Steadman, Marty, 408
Stearns, Cliff, 318
Stec, Dan, 34, 36, 38, 40, 42, 152, 363, 640
Steck, Phil, 34, 36, 39, 40, 42, 640
Steed, Dietra, 427
Steel, Alan, 100, 273
Steel, Robert K., 352
Steele, Jennifer, 64
Steele, Norman, 220
Steely White, Paul, 292, 469
Steenstra, Chris, 92
Steers, Christopher, 362
Stefanik, Elise, 125, 196, 649
Stefanko, Jeffrey, 8, 147
Steffens, Georgette, 95, 285
Stefko, Dr. Joseph, 169
Stegemann, Robert, 148
Steigerwald, Barbara Lee, 453
Stein, Dale, 70
Stein, Daniel, 115, 213
Stein, Elizabeth, 412
Stein, Irene W., 374
Stein, Leslie E, 45
Stein, Tony, 527
Stein, William, 347
Steinbach, Maria C, 234, 240
Steinberg, David J, 557
Steinberg, James B., 128, 172
Steinberg, Joel, 429
Steinberg, Kathy, 138
Steinberg, Philip G, 585
Steinberg, Robin, 462
Steiner, Charles P, 515
Steiner, Stuart, 547
Steinhauer, Alan, 451
Steinman, Leonard, 47
Steklof, Amy, 362
Stelling, Joe, 458
Stelling, Joseph, 458
Stempel, Jr, Vincent F, 218
Stenberg, Jack S, 336
Stenger, Harvey G., 544
Stenger, Harvey, 386
Steniger, Joseph, 474
Stephany, Mark, 228
Stephen, Larry R., 50
Stephens, David, 443
Stephenson, Edward, 351
Stephenson, Greg, 401
Sterling, Carla, 380
Sterling, Joan, 380
Stern, Andrew, 447
Stern, Robert, 35, 43, 165, 237
Stern, Sandra, 106, 164, 211
Stettner, Andrew, 448
Stevason, Anne P, 201, 220
Stevens, Bryant, 7, 160, 235
Stevens, Carol D, 329
Stevens, Don, 535
Stevens, Ellen, 120
Stevens, Jane Greengold, 434
Stevens, Lyn, 174
Stevens, Rick, 503
Stevenson, Richard O, 534
Stevenson, Vans, 446
Stewart, Andy, 361
Stewart, Cathy L., 374
Stewart, Christopher, 89, 142, 189
Stewart, Damon, 407, 454
Stewart, Danny, 462
Stewart, Dave, 509
Stewart, Deb, 71
Stewart, Delores, 179
Stewart, Geoffrey, 458
Stewart, Joan Hinde, 555
Stewart, Kyle, 477
Stewart, Regina, 280
Stewart, Russell, 591
Stewart, Sue, 471
Stewart-Cousins, Andrea, 16, 20, 25, 165, 617
Stich, Stephen, 69
Stickles, Tara, 350
Stiebeling, Adam B., 334
Stiegel, James, 426
Stiehl, Renata, 538
Stigberg, Eric, 277
Stiglmeier, Gary F, 61
Stiker, Betsey A, 591
Stiller, Brian G., 296
Stillman, Bruce, 562
Stillman, Charles A., 116
Stillman, Waddell, 279
Stingone, Nancy, 512
Stirpe, Al, 27, 34, 35, 37, 39, 42
Stitt Jr, Jim, 512
Stix, Joseph D, 224, 242
Stock, Eric J, 78, 84, 112, 207
Stockton, Todd, 411
Stockwell, Geoff, 422
Stockwell, Shannon, 209
Stoiano-Coico, Lisa, 397
Stokes, Gerry, 389
Stokinger, Carol Ann, 50
Stoklosa, Jennifer, 427
Stoller, Jack, 49
Stoller, Kenneth, 381
Stolper, Giselle, 232, 443
Stolz, Robert M., 50
Stone, Christopher, 199
Stone, Deborah, 59
Stone, Garry, 578
Stone, George, 598
Stone, Jeff, 538
Stone, Jeffrey, 432
Stoneman-Bell, Sierra, 449
Stoner, Joseph F, 568
Stoner, Will, 414
Storne, Karen, 451
Stout, Brenda L., 432
Stout, Doris, 12, 140
Stovall, Calvin, 523
Strada, Frank, 114
Strahle, Tom, 389
Straniere, Philip S., 49
Strasburg, Joseph, 193, 460
Strathearn, Mary Lou, 53
Stratton, Brian U., 104
Stratton, Martha, 115
Straub, Christopher, 444
Strauss, Bonnie, 186
Strauss, Sidney F, 48
Strickland, Carter, 354
Stricoff, Robert, 501
Strine, Michael, 79
Stringer, Scott M, 332, 359
Strining, Thomas, 584
Stripe, Al, 640
Strobel, Mary, 66
Strobridge, Col Steve, 299
Strome III, Charles B, 351
Strongarone, Stacy, 472
Strongwater, Steven, 467
Struck, Richard, 401
Strutton, Rebecca, 429
Struzzi, Diane, 356
Stuart, Mark, 95, 272
Stuart, Shirlie, 343
Stuart, William, 345
Stucchi, Victor, 103, 124
Stuchin, Hillary, 380
Stuhlman, Joseph, 284
Stulberg, Gita J., 246
Stumpp, Margaret S., 459
Stupak, Bart, 319
Stupp, Hon. Herbert W., 259
Sturcken, Charles G, 354
Sturim, Howard E, 47
Sturm, Lorraine, 513
Sturner, Leonard H., 496
Stuto, Peter F, 95, 285
Stutz, Eric, 527
Suarez, Captain Estrella, 106, 189, 274
Suarez, Darren, 391
Suarez, Julie, 413
Suben, Mark, 327
Suchman, E. Gail, 468
Suddaby, Glenn T., 212
Sugarman, Risa, 7, 111, 130
Suggs, Aaron, 38, 42
Suggs, Elizabeth N., 483
Suh, Rhea, 157
Suhr, Eric, 121
Suhre, Elizabeth, 229
Sula, Jeffrey, 444
Sulc, Charles, 581
Sullivan Jr., Jermiah, 479

Sullivan MD, Ann Marie T, 10, 228
Sullivan, Anne, 470
Sullivan, Bernard, 358
Sullivan, David P, 55
Sullivan, David P., 61
Sullivan, Dennis, 243
Sullivan, Edward O, 463
Sullivan, Evan, 25
Sullivan, James P, 46
Sullivan, Joan, 145
Sullivan, Johanna, 11, 253
Sullivan, Katherine A, 575
Sullivan, Maria, 429
Sullivan, Mark A, 248, 269
Sullivan, Mary Brosnahan, 257
Sullivan, Mary, 398
Sullivan, Ned, 159
Sullivan, Neil, 409
Sullivan, Patrick, 433
Sullivan, R Mark, 554
Sullivan, Ray, 539
Sullivan, Susan, 100, 151
Sullivan, Veronica, 449
Sullivan-Kriss, Patricia, 592
Sulyma, Stephanie, 175, 293
Sulzberger, Jr, Arthur O., 528
Sumer, Zeynep, 420
Summers, Ronnette, 489
Sumner, Elisa, 373
Sun, Dr. Jian, 85, 123
Sunshine, Jeffrey, 46
Sunshine, Nancy T, 330
Suozzi, Ralph V, 346
Superville, Charmaine, 358
Suprenant, Melinda, 136
Surplus, Lisa, 190
Susana, Paul, 480
Susman, Sally, 492
Suss, Stuart, 397
Susser, Kim, 434
Sussman, Irwin H, 596
Sutherland, Glenn, 82
Sutnick, Gary, 392
Svizzero, Anna E, 136
Svizzero, Anne E, 7
Svoboda, Stephen, 277
Swain, Elizabeth H., 182
Swain, Elizabeth, 400
Swan, Michael R., 338
Swanger, Dustin, 547
Swanson, David C, 530
Swanson, Josephine, 257
Swanson, Larry, 467
Swartz, Caroline, 133
Swartz, Michael, 296
Swartz, Susan M, 589
Sweder, Kevin, 455
Sweeney, Gerard J, 335
Sweeney, Peter Paul, 49
Sweeney, Peter, 46
Sweeny Jr, John W, 45
Sweeny, Jack, 222
Sweeny, Stephen J, 554
Sweet, Justin, 344
Sweet, Kim, 125
Sweet, Paul, 385
Sweet, Timothy, 455
Sweetland, Raymond, 458
Sweeton, Michael, 367
Sweitzer, Donald, 422
Swenson, Guy, 451
Swidler, Barry, 9, 200, 219
Swidorski, Teresa, 39
Swiecki, Craig, 40
Swift, Carol, 408
Swift, Heather, 490
Swink, Phillip, 389
Swinton, Kristen, 507
Sydow, Debbie L, 548
Sylvan, David J, 432
Symonds, Steve, 455
Sypniewski, Matthew J, 58
Sywulski, Robin, 264
Syzdek, Stephen, 4, 250
Szablewski, Joan, 346
Szafron, Brent, 290
Szarfarc, Howard, 469
Szatko, Steve, 578
Szczur, Margaret O, 53
Szlos, Olivier, 437
Szubielski, Jola, 4, 69, 250, 303
Szydlo, Michael, 36
Taber, Terry, 91
Tackett, Paul, 525
Taddeo, Ann Marie, 47
Taddiken, Nancy L, 598
Tadio, Meghan, 32
Tafelski, Judy M, 346
Taffe, Nadja M., 483
Taft, Dave, 276
Taggart, John, 418
Taggerty, Colleen, 569
Tagliaferri, Gerardo, 568
Tagliaferri, Jerry, 464
Tagliaferro, Letizia, 13, 86, 265
Taglienti, Perry, 284
Tailleur, Charles M., 53
Tait, Jeffrey A, 47
Takes, Faith A, 565
Talar, Judith, 36
Talavera, Sheila, 11, 241
Talbot, William, 401
Talel, Eva, 468
Tallarino, Frank, 364
Tallman, Sandra J., 86, 162
Tallmer, Megan, 50
Tallon, Jr, James R, 119
Tallon, Jr., James R., 186
Talluto, Marc, 11
Tambini, Steve, 97, 150
Tamburlin, Mary Jo, 332
Tamburri, John, 490
Tamkus, Mark, 294
Tammaro, Bill, 600
Tamutus, Andrew, 537
Tan, Eva, 436
Tanaka, Jennifer, 538
Tanea, Kathy, 367
Tanenbaum, Susie, 359
Tanenblatt, Eric, 490
Taneredi, Todd, 362
Tang, Angelica O, 223
Tangjerd, Megan, 430
Tangney, Michael, 350
Tangorra, Cosimo, 576
Tanner, Holly C, 327
Tanner, John S, 323
Tansil, Anton, 458
Tanski, Ronald J., 145
Tantillo, Mary, 471
Tantillo, R Michael, 333
Tanzi, Angelo, 384
Tao, Leonard, 142
Taormina, JoAnne, 360
Tapiat, Fernando, 49
Tarantelli, Mary M, 52
Tarantino Jr, Andrew G, 59
Tarantino, Daniel, 176
Tarantino, Lousie, 411
Taranto, Vincent, 346
Taratus, Caley, 402
Tario, LeRoy, 266
Tarnoff, Gary R, 433
Tarnowski, Christine, 13, 294
Tassarotti, Anthony, 536
Tassone, Frank, 26, 43, 137
Tator, Aisha, 379
Tatum, III, William P., 328
Tauber, Lacey, 446
Taubin, Peter, 469
Taubman, Adam, 433
Taubman, Mary, 471
Tauscher, Ellen O, 318
Tautel, Laurie, 34
Tautonico, Vito, 496
Tavares, Arelis, 437
Tave, Stephen, 126
Tavella PhD, Christopher, 229
Tavella, PhD, Christopher, 229
Tawil, Jacob, 350
Tayloe, Kerene, 474
Taylor, Carolyn D, 331
Taylor, Curtis, 306
Taylor, Deirdre, 5, 194, 234, 240
Taylor, Donald, 496
Taylor, Elizabeth, 49
Taylor, Gene, 318
Taylor, Harold, 518
Taylor, Jacquelyn, 597
Taylor, Janice A, 48
Taylor, Jason, 463
Taylor, Jill, 176
Taylor, Joseph N., 479

Appendices: Financial Plan, Indexes & Maps

Taylor, Lynette A., 490
Taylor, Martin, 472
Taylor, Mary Ann, 588
Taylor, Mattie W, 103, 164, 265
Taylor, PhD, Jill, 8, 148
Taylor, Rona, 29
Taylor, Ronald C, 349
Taylor, Samantha, 395
Taylor, Scot, 595
Taylor, Thomas E, 347
Taylor, William R., 179
Tazzi, Louis, 358
TBA, , 519
Tear, Timothy, 449
Tebbano, Dr Michael D, 567
Tedesco, John, 366
Tedford, Jeffrey, 108
Tedisco, James N, 34, 640
Tedisco, James, 28, 36, 37, 41
Teetz, Randy W, 588
Teifer, Bruce, 467
Tekin, John, 158
Telega, Stanley, 246
Telisky, John, 403
Tellado, Marta, 91
Teltsch, John, 454
Tembeckjian, Robert H, 103, 211, 309
Temperine, Brian, 289
Temperine, Carolyn, 289
Templeman, Leslie, 121
Templeton-Cornell, Vicki, 467
Ten Eyck, Laurie, 380
Tendy, Thomas, 99, 286, 307
Tennen, Steven, 277
Tenney, C. Thomas, 389
Tenney, Claudia, 34, 35, 36, 37, 42, 79, 640
Tennyson, Megan, 539
Teplesky, Daniel, 567
Teresi, Joseph C, 46
Teresi, Samuel, 349
Tergis, Alexander, 351
Ternes, Marie, 405
Terracciano, Stephen A., 153
Terraferma, Carrie, 419
Terranova, Marilyn, 597
Territo, Mark, 344
Terry, Charise L., 354
Terry, Joshua, 470
Terry, M. Margaret, 99, 285
Terry, Travis, 392
Terwilliger, Chris, 537
Terwilliger, Marguerite, 138
Terwilliger, Paulette, 348
Tesoriero, James, 174
Tesseyman, Matthew, 396
Tessier-Lavigne, Marc, 560
Testani, Jim, 373
Testani, Nancy, 410
Tester, Jon, 169, 197
Testone, Glennda, 198, 259, 435
Tetrault, Paul, 447
Tewksbury, Joseph, 108
Thames, Miguel C., 458
Thaniel, Ron, 3, 283
Thayer, Debbie, 504
Thayer, John W., 332
Thayer, Steven P, 348
Theobald, Edmond J, 350
Theobalds, Kenneth R, 9, 200, 219
Theobalds, Kenneth, 411
Theodore-Greene, Leticia, 9, 194
Therriault, Mary, 424
Thiel, NancyLynn, 21
Thiele, Jr, Fred W, 34, 37, 38, 641
Thiele, Jr, Fred, 41, 87
Thiele, Jr., Fred W, 42, 43
Thiele, Jr., Fred W., 41
Tholl, Debbi M., 430
Thomann, Robert, 464
Thomas, Allan, 260
Thomas, Anthony, 395
Thomas, Barbara, 434, 445, 512
Thomas, Cheryl, 595
Thomas, Delores, 46
Thomas, Denise, 72, 178
Thomas, Donald, 389
Thomas, Gail, 109
Thomas, George, 156
Thomas, Helen, 76
Thomas, James M., 371
Thomas, Joyce A., 178, 254
Thomas, Kenneth J., 493
Thomas, Lawrence, 601
Thomas, Lloyd, 412
Thomas, Mark, 272, 476
Thomas, Rolland, 375
Thomas, Sanu K., 479
Thomas-Oravsky, Esq., Alison, 55
Thompson Jr, John E, 222
Thompson Jr., John E., 196
Thompson Jr., William, 465
Thompson, Andrew, 526
Thompson, Bennie G, 320
Thompson, Bennie G., 168
Thompson, Bryce L, 599
Thompson, Dean, 411
Thompson, Donna, 525
Thompson, Ed, 208
Thompson, Erwin, 412
Thompson, Glenn, 154
Thompson, Harriet, 49
Thompson, Jim, 138
Thompson, Jr, Kenneth, 48
Thompson, Kris, 306
Thompson, Louis R., 436
Thompson, Mark, 392, 535
Thompson, Michael K, 238, 291
Thompson, Michael, 47, 53
Thompson, Mike, 324
Thompson, Philip, 145
Thompson, Shawn, 12, 149, 162, 236, 241
Thompson, Vinton, 557
Thomson, Jonathan, 69
Thomson, Pamela T., 430
Thomson, Tamara B., 115, 213
Thomson, Terri, 469
Thony, Nick, 30
Thornberry, Mack, 324
Thornbury, Gregory Alan, 556
Thorne, Chuck, 364
Thorne, Lisa, 251
Thorne-Begland, Michael, 379
Thornton, Angela M., 489
Thornton, Melissa, 435
Thornton, Michael B., 212
Thorpe, Christopher, 278
Thouin, Thomas, 455
Throne-Holst, Anna E, 97, 150
Throne-Holst, Anna, 365
Thrope, Jeffrey, 415, 439
Thune, John, 90, 143, 155, 290, 312, 313, 314
Thurnau, Carl, 121
Thurston, David B, 62
Tiahrt, Todd, 317
Tibbetts, Christine, 582
Tiberi, Pat, 90, 180, 323
Tiberio, Melissa, 383
Tice, Craig J, 584
Tichansky, Peter J, 91
Ticknor, Jennifer, 207
Tidona, George T, 200
Tidona, George, 219
Tierney, James, 8, 147
Tierney, John F, 321
Tierney, Michael, 572
Tierney, Robert B, 356
Tierno, Mark John, 553
Tigh, Peter A, 584
Tilghman, Richard, 463
Tilles, Erica, 538
Tilles, Roger B, 119
Timbs, Rick, 395
Timmer, Tari, 507
Tinari, Marion Rose, 61
Tingley, Ken, 525
Tingling, Milton A., 46
Tinker, PhD, Nathan P., 93
Tinney, Carin, 471
Tinti, Egidio F., 349
Tintori Wells, Leanne, 270
Tirschwell, Peter M, 527
Tisenchek, Catherine J, 64
Titone, Alfred, 88
Titone, Matthew, 34, 37, 38, 39, 40, 42, 43, 165, 237, 641
Tittler, Andrew, 154
Titus, Michele R, 34, 36, 40, 641
Titus, Michele R., 36, 38
Titus, Michele, 37, 40, 195, 202, 222, 242
Tkazyik, John C, 362
To, Kim, 382
Toal, Gloria S, 253

Tobias, Lauren, 8, 174
Tobias, Louie, 23
Tobin, Barbara, 113
Tobin, Michael J, 429
Todd, Christopher, 575
Todd, Donald E., 57
Todd, Reuel A, 334
Todd, Susan E, 590
Todd, Ward, 518
Todorovich Messick, Petra, 448
Toellner, Jim, 537
Tokasz, Paul, 438
Tolbert, Bruce E, 47
Tolkoff, Andrew, 121
Toll, Sandi, 3, 83, 108, 130, 206, 240, 245, 270
Tollisen, Brian S., 163
Tollner, Margaret, 534
Tolokonsky, Theresa, 380
Tolve, Harriet, 399
Tom, Peter, 45
Tomassone, Joseph, 119
Tome, Daniel, 458
Tomerlin, David, 518
Tomlin, John, 16
Tomlinson, Guy P, 55
Tomlinson, Kevin, 286
Tomlinson, Richard, 464
Tomlinson, Stephen M, 575
Tompkins, Dennis, 7, 119, 252, 303
Tomson, Daniel, 396
Tonacle, Luke, 449
Tonello, Matteo, 91
Tonko, Paul D, 312, 322
Tonko, Paul, 89, 142, 143, 154, 180, 224, 318, 650
Toole, Elisabeth A, 63
Toole, Laurence O, 335
Toombs, Bernadette M, 135
Toomey, Mark, 424
Toomey, Patrick J., 203
Toomey, Rosemarie, 490
Toporek, Jill, 419
Torella, Carolyn, 381
Torforice, Deborah, 49
Torkin, Jeff, 413
Tormey III, James C, 46
Tormey, James C, 209
Torpey, John J., 494
Torres, Analisa, 49, 50, 488
Torres, Angela, 409
Torres, Catherine, 445
Torres, Janet, 475
Torres, Luis A, 221
Torres, Luis C., 479
Torres, Robert E, 48
Torres, Robert, 48, 210
Torres, Yvonne, 582
Torreto, Corey, 458
Torrey, Matthew G., 371
Torsiglieri, William, 409
Tortora, III, Ralph, 177, 207
Tortora, Jim, 539
Tortorici, Peter A, 326
Tosh, Michael, 457
Totman, Bradley, 504
Tourville, Karl, 474
Toussaint, Wavny, 49
Toutebon, Ouida Foster, 127
Towers, Brian, 330
Towery, Carlisle, 507
Towns, Darryl C., 189
Towns, Edolphus, 312, 321
Townsend, James, 95, 150, 272
Townsend, Maj. Stephen J., 295
Townsend, Sharon S., 47
Toye, Bill, 406
Trachte, Paul D, 64
Trachtenberg, Robert I, 85, 123
Tracy, Robert, 427
Tracy, Terrence X, 11, 113
Traill, Saskia, 378
Traister, Matthew, 451
Tram, Michel, 474
Tramontano, Christine, 439
Tramontano, Frank, 454
Tran, Lac, 462
Tranum, Todd, 503
Traschen, Ida, 283
Trautwein, Richard, 7
Trautwein, Robert, 120, 174, 227, 270
Travers, Eugene, 419
Travis, Jeremy, 116, 397, 551
Traylor, James, 6, 194, 227, 252
Traylor, John, 12, 162, 236, 241
Treadwell, L Michael, 513
Treanor, Elin, 409
Treasure, David, 99, 286
Tress, Tracy, 439
Treuber, Robert, 248, 433
Trezise, James, 77, 281
Tricozzi, Lisa, 53
Triller, Rhonda, 525
Trimble, Melanie, 454
Tringali, Joseph, 401
Tripi, Deanne, 53
Tripi, Florence, 398
Tripp, Jim, 412
Tripp, Lois M, 550
Tritt, Eleanor, 591
Trivisonno, Michael, 361
Troia, Charles, 48
Trolio, Peter, 241
Trombley, Dallas, 39
Trombley, Samuel J, 327
Trommer, Scott, 458
Tropea, Frank L., 59
Tropea, Tom, 401
Trouche, Wanda, 111, 206, 235
Troupe, Dawne, 168
Troutman, Shirley, 45
Troy, Matthew, 435
Truax, Julie, 449
True, Sally T., 186
Truicko, George S., 491
Trujillo, Anthony, 166
Trunzo, Michael, 467
Tryniski, Mark, 80
Tryon, Bonnie, 464
Tsai, Betsy, 463
Tsamardinos, Jane, 400
Tsang, Marjorie, 162
Tse, Joey, 455
Tsimis, Evlyn, 449
Tubbs, John, 506
Tubbs, Kevin, 539
Tubian, Daron, 385
Tuchman, Michelle, 405
Tucker, F Michael, 85, 123
Tucker, Maryann, 86, 265
Tucker, Michael W, 349
Tucker, Susan, 403
Tuell, Jason, 88
Tuell, Ph.D., Jason, 71, 152
Tuey, John, 349
Tufillaro, John, 503
Tuggle, Reginald, 447
Tuitt, Alison Y, 48
Tully Abdo, Susan, 378
Tully Jr, James H, 13, 265
Tully, Catherine, 430
Turano, Sal, 468
Turbow, Daniel, 50
Turck, Gary, 86, 97, 188
Turco, Thomas F, 136
Turecek, Timothy, 572
Turkin, Jane, 177, 207
Turner, Christopher, 457
Turner, Matthew J, 66
Turner, Michael, 318
Turner, Nicholas, 118
Turner, Pamela, 228
Turner, Peter J, 571
Turner, Seth, 595
Turner, Yehuda, 88, 196
Turney, Carol, 135
Turoski, John, 18
Turpin, Carm, 70
Turpin, Carmela, 141
Turral, Lateef, 19
Turso, Vito A, 358
Tuttle, Carrie, 86, 97, 188
Tuttle, Elizabeth, 467
Twellman Haley, Kathleen, 530
Twitmyer, Julie, 416
Twomey, John, 225
Twomey, Michael T., 411
Ty, Sabrina M, 102, 151
Tyksinski, Patrick M, 351
Tyler, David, 524
Tyler, Karen B, 8, 161, 245, 271
Tyler, Kelly, 102, 141, 151
Tyler, Tena, 523

Tynan, Matthew, 476
Tyner-Doyle, Paula, 121
Tyrrell, Joseph, 391
Tyszko, Mary Ann, 455
Udall, Mark, 276, 314
Uddin, Maf M., 488
Ukeiley, Stephen L., 61
Ulatowski, Damian M, 344
Ulberg, John, 175
Ulfelder, Bill, 158, 449
Ulrich, Leilani, 95, 150, 272
Umane, Frederic M, 133
Umane, Frederic M., 354
Unaitis, Jeff, 469
Underer, Sarah, 455
Underwood, Barbara D, 10, 84, 112, 207
Underwood, Theresa, 539
Ungar, Robert A, 470
Unger, David, 110
Unger, Russell, 470
Unowsky, Cara, 429
Unterricht, Sam L., 443
Updegrove, Richard, 332
Uplinger, Karen M, 66
Upton, Fred, 89, 142, 154, 180, 318
Urbinder, Seth, 17
Urlass, Steve, 289
Urquhart, Diana, 463
Urtz, Cindy, 331
Usher, Brad, 18
Ustin, Mark, 439
Utz, David, 419
Uviller, Rena, 46
Uviller, Renak, 50
Vacant, , 5, 7, 8, 11, 12, 13, 14, 16, 26, 27, 28, 33, 36, 43, 60, 63, 70, 71, 72, 78, 83, 86, 87, 88, 91, 100, 102, 103, 108, 111, 112, 113, 120, 121, 123, 124, 125, 130, 140, 148, 149, 151, 160, 161, 162, 165, 173, 174, 175, 176, 177, 179, 187, 189, 194, 200, 201, 202, 206, 207, 210, 211, 220, 221, 223, 227, 234, 235, 236, 237, 240, 241, 242, 247, 250, 251, 252, 253, 254, 263, 264, 266, 270, 271, 283, 284, 289, 293, 294, 303, 305, 306, 307, 308, 312, 325, 334, 338, 339, 340, 348, 353, 354, 356, 358, 361, 363, 372
Vacca, Carolyn, 331
Vaccari, Rev Msgr Peter, 560
Vagelatos, John, 115, 213
Vainisi, Bill, 408
Valdes, Gil, 429
Valdez, Eddy, 48, 51
Vale, Andrew, 114
Valenchis, Kevin, 229
Valente, Daniel J, 243
Valente, Daniel, 403
Valente, Edmond, 408
Valenti, Aurora R, 338
Valentine, Chief John, 365
Valentine, Ronald C, 339
Valentine, Todd, 7, 130
Valeri, Brian, 505
Valesky, David J, 20, 21, 23, 25, 617
Valesky, David J., 16
Valesky, David, 20, 22, 23, 25
Valiante, Frank, 501
Valle, Glenn, 113
Valle, Lisa A., 430
Valletta, Robert, 457
Valley, Nancy, 170
Vallone Sr., Peter, 402
Vallone, Paul, 402
Vallone, Perry, 402
Valone, Gloria, 329
Vamuateas, Adrianna, 223
Van Alstyne, David, 111
Van Anden, Katy, 515
Van Blarcum, PJ, 338
Van Bramer, Jamie, 478
Van Buren, Diane L, 6, 108
Van De Loo, Kathleen A, 90, 291
Van Dyke, Georgia, 516
Van Epps, Barbara, 400
Van Epps, Tammy, 117
Van Guilder, Carol, 459
Van Hollen, Chris, 267
Van Horn, John, 227
Van Kerkhove, Barbara, 411
Van Loon, Jerry, 277
Van Nest, Elizabeth, 381
Van Ooyen, Marcel, 74, 126, 157, 191
Van Patten, Carlene, 148, 176
Van Praagh, Ian R, 105, 287
Van Ross, Clement, 334
Van Schaack, Tom, 529
Van Scoy, Shawn, 597
Van Varick, David, 133
Van Voorhis, Steve, 76
Van Voorst, Mark, 232
Van Wagoner, Randall S, 548
Van, Marina, 505
VanAmburgh, Judy, 33
Vanblarcom, Dave, 409
VanBuren, Maureen, 596
Vancavage, Robert E, 384
Vancavage, Robert, 93, 292
Vance, Jr., Cyrus, 332
Vancko, Candace S, 546
Vandawalker, Robert, 330
Vandemark, Louise, 134
Vandenwalker, Ian, 389
Vanderhoef, C Scott, 335
VanDermark, Brenda, 54
Vandermark, David, 345
Vanderpoel, Mark, 70
Vanderwarker, Amber, 403
Vanderwarker, Dean, 460
VanDyke, Dr Marilyn, 363
Vanecek, William, 105, 287
Vaneo, Clyde, 19
Vanluven, David, 412
Vanselow, Jodie, 153
Vanslyke, William, 424
Vanstrom, Stephen, 570
Vantine, Whitney K, 574
Vanyo, Michael B, 594
VanZandt, David, 558
Varano, Catherine, 230
Vargas, Aria, 492
Vargas, Sr., Ruben, 496
Varghese, Sunil R., 167, 196
Varin, Byron A, 329
Varma, Jay, 354
Varoli, David, 353
Varshney, Pramod, 85, 122
Vartigan, Lee, 294
Vasquez Jr., Raul, 489
Vasquez, Erik, 33
Vasquez, Jessica, 257
Vasti, Donald, 49
Vatter, Michael, 360
Vaughan, David B, 46
Vaughan, Peter B, 258
Vaughn, Nicholas, 379
Vavrina, Christopher, 430
Vazquez, Angel, 32
Vazquez, Carmen, 398
Vazquez, Valerie, 354
Vazquez-Doles, Maria S., 47
Vazzana, James A, 55
Vecchiarelli, Rose, 534
Vecchio, Patrick R, 364
Vega, Enrique, 437
Velasquez, Carmen R., 49
Velazquez, Marjorie, 485
Velazquez, Miguel A, 106, 288
Velazquez, Nydia M, 312, 319, 650
Velazquez, Nydia M., 79, 190, 203, 481
Velazquez, Nydia, 90, 224, 322
Velazquez, Suzanne, 507, 514
Velez, Carlos, 355
Velez, Laura, 5, 119, 251
Velez, Marcelo, 470
Velez, Phillip L., 496
Velez, Ricardo, 5, 200
Vella-Marrone, Frances, 371
Venditti, Jaime, 428
Venditto, John, 361
Venditto, Michael, 20, 21, 22, 23, 24, 87, 165, 178, 617
Venezia, Valerie, 403
Venezia-Dobrin, Deena L., 485
Vennard, Michele, 274
Venter, Anton, 175
Ventosa, John A., 144
Ventre, Jeannie, 364
Ventrice, Angela, 30
Ventura, Victoria, 33
Verano, Anthony, 536
Verdile, Vincent P, 552
Vernsey, Timothy M, 590
Versaci, Vincent W., 58

Veruto, Esq., Michael C., 56
Vescio, Kathryn, 383
Vespia, Hope B, 364
Vetter, Donald F., 55
Vetters, Vic, 539
Vevle, Mark, 279
Victor, Paul, 292
Vidal, Alfredo, 472
Vidal, Carlos, 467
Vieira, Al, 523
Vientos, Victor, 448
Vietri, Joseph, 153
Vigdor, Justin L., 106, 164, 211
Vigeant, Michele, 462
Vigil, Marcos, 12, 86, 162
Vigliotti Sr, Stephan J, 577
Vignier, Marline, 179
Vijaykumar, Kumar, 163
Vilar, Manny, 456
Villacci, Irene, 15
Villagomez, Michelle, 432
Villani, Miriam E., 159
Villanti, Mark, 587
Villarrubia, Nelson, 159
Villegas, George, 48
Villella, Louis J., 49
Villena, Daniel, 411
Villenas, Christian, 378
Vimo, Jacqueline, 427
Vinciguerra, Mark, 523
Vineyard, Ryan, 38
Viola, James, 464
Violante, Mark A, 64
Violante, Michael J, 332
Virgil, Ernest D, 576
Virtanen, John W., 124, 242
Virts, Barry, 339
Virtuoso, Dennis F, 332
Visclosky, Peter J, 317
Visconsi, Charles, 445
Viscosi, Michael C, 63
Viscovich, William A., 49
Visnauskas, RuthAnne, 79, 103
Vitale, David, 147
Vitale, Robin, 381
Vitek, Lorene, 360
Vitello, Diane, 64
Vitiello, Michael, 356
Vitiello, Neil, 365
Vito, DC, 417
Vitter, David, 90, 290, 313, 314
Vives, Nairobi, 38
Vizcaino, Jonathan, 494
Vladeck, Judith, 226
Vogel, John, 79
Vogel, Pamela J, 338
Voggel, Gerhard O, 432
Voinovich, George V, 312, 315
Volforte, Michael N, 7, 240
Volland, Lawrence E., 482
Vollick, Rick, 105, 152
Von Maltzahn, Wolf, 460
Vona, John L, 135
Vosburgh, Frederick, 430
Voskerichian, Chrissy, 486
Vossler, Mary, 365
Vottis, Theresa, 284
Voutour, James R, 332
Voutsinas, Helen, 61
Vullo, Maria T, 4, 78, 177, 200
Waaler, Edgar, 120
Wacha, Maureen, 518
Wacholder, Stephanie, 471
Wachtler, Lauren J, 217
Wackstein, Nancy, 261, 471
Wade, Carolyn E., 49
Wade, Thomas W., 373
Wafer, Shelby, 424
Waffner, Troy, 70, 86, 96, 306
Wagar Sabo, Shelley, 423
Wagner, Carl, 458
Wagner, Catherine, 177, 207
Wagner, Colleen, 63
Wagner, Dale, 539
Wagner, David, 398
Wagner, Don, 536
Wagner, Dwayne, 519
Wagner, Elise, 433
Wagner, Harold J., 372
Wagner, John, 413
Wagner, Linda, 184, 383
Wagner, Mary, 444
Wagner, Paul, 334
Wagner, Sue Ellen, 424
Wagoner, James, 71
Wagoner, Robert, 577
Wahlig, William, 85, 123
Wait, Jeffrey D., 65
Waithe, Deighton S., 49
Waizel, Brian, 538
Waizer, PhD, Jonas, 231
Walbridge, Wayne C, 575
Walcott, Dennis M, 352, 353
Walden, Greg, 319
Waldman, Bella, 484
Waldman, Martha, 177, 220
Waldman, Michael, 389
Waldron, WIlliam H., 329
Waldstreicher, Jeff, 71, 88
Walfrand, Jim, 72, 142, 189
Walker, Deanna, 400
Walker, Edgar G., 49
Walker, Emily, 386
Walker, John C, 597
Walker, Latrice M., 488
Walker, Latrice Monique, 641
Walker, Latrice, 34, 37, 38, 39
Walker, Maureen, 351
Walker, Sam, 47
Walker, Timothy, 47
Wall, Duane D, 82
Wallace, Barbara, 174
Wallace, Edward, 386, 421
Wallace, Harry, 166
Wallace, Jr, James W, 330
Wallace, Jr., William E., 225
Wallace, Richard M, 63
Wallace, Stephen J., 491
Wallach, Rebecca, 438
Wallack, Al, 534
Wallender, Michael, 403
Wallerstein, Mitchel, 550
Wallerstein, Mitchell, 398
Wallin, Warren, 103, 124
Wallinder, Marcus, 412
Wallwin, Amanda, 33
Walorski, Jackie, 154, 180
Walp, Rebecca, 52
Walpert, J., 355
Walsh Hood, Martha, 56
Walsh, Anne, 148, 176
Walsh, Becky, 539
Walsh, Bridget, 464
Walsh, Daniel, 247
Walsh, Ed, 5, 194, 234, 240, 303
Walsh, Elizabeth Marie, 57
Walsh, II, Thomas E, 58
Walsh, James E, 55
Walsh, James, 38, 439
Walsh, Jr., Edward M., 372
Walsh, Julia, 416
Walsh, Kevin E, 333
Walsh, LTC Bill, 289
Walsh, Margaret T, 50
Walsh, Maureen, 355
Walsh, Michael, 469
Walsh, Mike, 145
Walsh, Robert W, 358
Walsh, Thomas F, 425
Walsh, Timothy A., 468
Walsh, William, 458, 470
Walter, Christopher, 417
Walter, Dale, 374
Walter, M. Todd, 157
Walter, Mark J., 254
Walter, Raymond, 34, 37, 39, 40, 43, 87, 237, 246, 288, 641
Walter, Sean M, 97, 150
Walter, Sean, 363
Walters, Charles W, 578
Walters, Joan P., 289
Walters, Ruth, 448, 473
Walters, S. Anthony, 210
Walters, Steven J, 347
Walther, Steven T., 137
Waltman, Susan, 420
Walton, Frances, 106, 189, 274
Waltz, Edward, 186
Walz, Timothy J., 154
Wambua, Mathew M, 355
Wamp, Zach, 317
Wanamaker, Beth, 87, 97, 150, 307
Wanamaker, Timothy E, 502

Wanfried, Kurt W, 529
Wang, Ying, 175
Waples, Karla, 441
Wappett, John P M, 338
Warager, Col David, 10
Warager, David, 294, 304
Warchal, Jason, 380
Ward, Andrew, 457
Ward, Ellie, 380
Ward, John T, 51
Ward, Kimberle, 585
Ward, Laura A., 50
Ward, Mark, 568
Ward, Peter, 489
Ward, Robert, 12, 162, 235
Ward, Terri, 517
Wardally, Kevin, 437
Warden, Therese, 434
Wareham, Wanda, 410
Warhit, Barry, 60
Warneck, Douglas, 451
Warner, Deborah, 395
Warner, Richard A, 346
Warnick, Mike, 398
Warnick, Thomas A, 339
Warnken-Brill, John, 473
Warnock, Gordon, 383, 456
Warren Dickerson, Annette, 395
Warren, Anne Marie, 432
Warren, Barbara, 156
Warren, Kenneth J, 97, 150
Warren, Lovely A, 363
Warren, Vincent, 197, 395
Warren, William P, 58
Warren-Merrick, Gerri, 543
Warrier, Sujata, 11, 253
Wasch, Ken, 94
Washington, Blake G, 42
Washington, Jennifer, 4, 250
Washington, Shelda, 109
Wasik, Joseph, 223
Wasley, Cheryl, 283
Wason, Jr, Jay, 205
Wasserman Schultz, Debbie, 317
Wasserman, Ed, 454
Wassermann, Edward H, 440
Wassermann, Edward, 410
Wassner, Ed, 399
Waterhouse, Erin T, 453
Waters, Gloriana, 550
Waters, Maxine, 79, 190, 203, 319
Waters, Rolf A, 577
Waters, Stephen, 530
Watkins, Barry, 279, 471
Watkins, Christopher, 191
Watkins, Edward, 194
Watkins, Jr, Thomas H, 524
Watkins, Patricia, 580
Watkins-Bates, Cari, 463
Watras, John J., 345
Watroba, Chelsey, 23
Watson Coleman, Bonnie, 169
Watson, David, 403
Watson, Denise M., 52
Watson, Diane E, 321
Watson, Greg, 187
Watson, James, 596
Watson, Jennifer, 467
Watson, John, 6, 111, 252
Watson, Joy M., 61
Watson, Matthew, 11, 84, 122
Watson, Tony, 410
Watson, William J, 63
Watt, Melvin L, 319
Watters, Linda, 429
Waxman, Henry A, 318
Wayne, Patricia, 348
Weamer, Michael, 184
Weaver, Allen, 458
Weaver, Michele R, 589
Webb, Erika, 62
Webb, Jim, 315
Webb, Lea, 476
Webb, Marcel, 96, 273
Webb, Rick, 377
Webber, Troy K., 45
Weber, Lawrence, 467
Weber, Randy, 143
Weber, Wendi, 153, 276
Webster, Lawrence, 77
Webster, Russell, 527
Weed, Harry, 363
Weems, Sherryl D, 549
Wegener, Thomas, 202, 221
Wegman, Kathryn A, 597
Wehle, Patrick, 356
Weiden, Philip, 436
Weidenfeld, Hal, 446
Weidman, Mary C, 327
Weik, Alexis, 348
Weill, Charles B, 246
Weimersheimer, Betti, 258
Weinberg, Hugh, 359
Weinberg, Patti, 428
Weinberg, Richard M., 50
Weine, Ken, 356
Weiner, Anthony D, 312, 318, 320
Weiner, Audrey, 184, 429
Weiner, Barbara, 411
Weiner, Neil, 472
Weiner, Pamela, 448
Weiner, Ross P., 479
Weingarten, Mark, 406
Weingartner, Jason, 139, 374
Weinraub, David, 390
Weinreb, David, 426
Weinshall, Iris, 398, 550
Weinstein Esq, Ellen S, 56
Weinstein, Barry A, 341
Weinstein, David A., 48
Weinstein, Helene E, 34, 41, 43, 211, 641
Weinstein, Helene E., 40
Weinstein, Helene, 35, 36
Weinstein, Jeremy S, 48
Weinstein, Jeremy S., 47
Weinstein, Jeremy, 210
Weinstein, Mark, 121
Weinstein, Robin, 386
Weinstein, Stewart H., 50
Weinstock, Frances, 392
Weinstock, Rivka, 352
Weintraub, Ellen L., 137
Weintraub, Henry, 176
Weir, William, 385
Weirauch, Toni, 266
Weisberg, Michael, 476
Weisberg, William, 396
Weisenfeld, Jeffrey A., 550
Weiser, Wendy, 389
Weisfield, Daniel, 29
Weiskopf, Lynn, 284
Weisman, MD, Jay, 254
Weiss, Allan B, 48
Weiss, Daniel, 372
Weiss, Howard, 405
Weiss, Jerry A., 436
Weiss, Jerry, 425
Weiss, MS, Lisa W., 296
Weiss, Richard, 445
Weissman, Steven A., 49
Weite, Lisa, 57
Weitz, Daniel M, 210
Welch, Jr, George J, 62
Welch, Katherine, 416
Welch, Laura, 455
Welch, Michael, 490
Welch, Patrick, 515
Weld, Tim, 457
Weldon, Mark, 455
Weldy, Troy, 449
Welling, John, 468
Wellman, Eric, 535
Wells, Darcy, 12, 305
Wells, Earl, 408
Wells, Fonza, 455
Wells, Jordan, 444
Wells, Kameron, 400
Wells, Kevin M, 337
Wells, Richard, 118, 244, 456
Wells, Roger, 469
Wellspeak, John P, 27
Welsh, Edward, 402
Weltman, Eric, 415
Welz, Edward A, 101, 141
Wemple, Stephen, 401
Wen, John, 85, 122, 460
Wenck, Romona N, 587
Wenderlich, Stephen, 110
Wendt, Michael, 583
Wendt, Peter, 49
Wenger, Tim, 534
Wentlent, Christopher, 413
Weprin, David I, 27, 34, 642

Weprin, David, 36, 38, 40, 43
Weprin, Mark, 489
Werwaiss, Willie, 463
Wescott, Andrew, 72, 167
Wescott, Drew, 266
Wessell, Eric, 384
West, Chris, 461
West, Jennifer, 362
West, Judi, 195
West, Michael, 336
West, Mike, 403
West, Thomas S., 474
Westfall-Owens, Michele, 53
Westhuis, Todd B, 284
Westle, Thomas, 409
Westmoreland, Lynn A., 190
Westmoreland, Lynn, 322
Weston, Michelle, 46
Westphal, Fredrick, 326
Wetherbee, Michael J, 591
Wetmore, Weeden A, 327
Wexler, Joan G, 214, 553
Wexler, Robert, 320
Wexler, Scott, 91, 278, 453
Whalen, David, 469
Whalen, Dennis, 183, 424
Whalen, Gerald J., 45
Whalen, Joseph A, 258
Whalen, Mark R, 325
Whalen, Maureen, 79
Wheaton, Colleen, 398
Whedon, Ralph, 451
Wheeler, Douglas A., 429
Wheeler, Rob, 259
Wheeler, Robert, 435
Wheeler, William, 98
Wheelock, Ronald J, 583
Whelan, C Douglas, 583
Whelan, Theresa, 59
Whelan, Thomas F, 47
Whelpley, Dennis, 106, 288
Whipple, James, 513
Whitaker, G Warren, 215, 268
White, Alan, 395, 449
White, Carol, 398
White, Chris, 3
White, Dana, 478
White, Daniel, 418
White, David, 299
White, Douglas, 354
White, Gretchen, 532
White, Janice M, 588
White, John F., 458
White, Joyce, 230
White, Ken, 508
White, Kevin, 534
White, Megan, 6, 270
White, Michael, 349
White, Phyllis, 158
White, Renee A., 50
White, Rick, 474
White, Robert E., 371
White, Valerie, 174
White, Veronica M., 357
White, William R, 107, 274
White, William R., 372
White, William, 401
Whitecomb, Mark, 272
Whitehead, Merle, 248
Whitehead, Sheldon, 316
Whitehouse, Sheldon, 169, 314
Whiteman, Michael, 475
Whitfield Jr, Garnell W, 343
Whitfield, Brian, 454
Whitfield, Ed, 143
Whitfield, Jr., Garnell W., 343
Whitmore, Lisa, 502
Whitney, Mark C., 132
Whitney, Rick, 325
Whitney, Susan, 577
Whittaker, John, 526
Whitton, William, 346
Whitworth, Suzanne, 406
Whyland, Michael, 27
Whyman, Gary, 336
Whynot, Kathleen, 32
Wible, Chris, 464
Wice, Jeffrey, 32
Wick, David, 98, 151, 307
Wick, Edmund V, 36, 39, 41
Wick, Larisa, 402, 477
Wickens, Lisa, 453
Wicker, Roger F, 313, 315
Wickes, Roger A, 339
Wickham Jr, J Thomas, 23
Wickham, Gregory, 405
Wickham, Kathy, 462
Wickham, Lindsay, 413
Wickham, Melanie, 74
Wickham, Tom, 23
Wickman, Marilyn, 294
Widelo, Christopher, 414
Wiederhorn, Jo, 126, 181, 382
Wiernak, Roberta, 434
Wigger, Scott, 456
Wiggins, Robert B, 54
Wigzell, Barbara, 187
Wiktorko, John, 576
Wilansky, Judith A, 592
Wilber, Jay L, 325
Wilbert, Elizabeth, 346
Wilcox, Anna M., 371
Wilcox, Arthur, 420
Wilcox, Janine, 474
Wilcox, Lawrence N, 327
Wilcox, Peter, 389
Wilder, Robert, 475
Wilen, Marianna, 493
Wiles, Lisa A, 595
Wiles, Marie, 567
Wiley, Linda, 52
Wiley, Maxwell T, 48
Wiley, Maxwell, 50
Wilgoren, Peter, 532
Wilhelm, Daniel, 472
Wilhelm, Diane M, 363
Wilhelm, Terry J, 329
Wilhelm, Terry J., 53
Wilk, Tim, 474
Wilkerson, Deborah, 484
Wilkins, Cathy, 381
Wilkinson, Gwen, 338
Wilkinson, Jacob, 476
Wilkinson, Steve, 374
Wilkinson, Tony, 449
Wilkinson, William J, 345
Wille, Frederick A, 600
Willens, Kevin, 419
Williams II, Richard T, 362
Williams III, Charles, 469
Williams Jr, Paul T, 102, 124, 164, 178
Williams, Alexander, 492
Williams, Angela J, 345
Williams, An-Tuan, 395
Williams, Barbara S., 213
Williams, Barika, 381
Williams, Betty J., 49
Williams, Bob, 564
Williams, Bradley, 457
Williams, Brian, 516
Williams, Carly, 349
Williams, Carolyn, 551
Williams, Cathy, 52
Williams, Christina, 43, 195, 222, 254
Williams, David H, 366
Williams, David, 245
Williams, Dominick, 357
Williams, Donald, 60
Williams, E. Loren, 64
Williams, Henri, 173, 250
Williams, Irene, 64
Williams, Jack, 284
Williams, Jacqueline, 49, 467
Williams, Jacquelyn, 377
Williams, Jaime R, 34
Williams, Jaime, 36, 38, 42, 642
Williams, James A, 573
Williams, James, 208, 487
Williams, Jeanne M, 136
Williams, Jeffrey, 413
Williams, Jennifer, 132
Williams, Joe, 409
Williams, John R, 591
Williams, Katherine, 255
Williams, Kelly, 389
Williams, Kimberly, 443
Williams, Lloyd, 508
Williams, Luke, 93
Williams, Mark S, 326
Williams, Michael J., 50
Williams, Michael, 462
Williams, MSGT Jason, 289
Williams, Patricia Anne, 50

Williams, Philip M, 566
Williams, Robert, 10, 102, 264, 272
Williams, Samuel G, 202, 222
Williams, Wanda, 242, 407
Williamson, Anahita, 154
Williamson, Jan, 229
Williamson, Paul G, 575
Willidigg, Thomas, 491
Willis, James, 583
Willis, Nicole, 413
Wilmers, Robert G, 81
Wilner, MD, Phillip, 457
Wilpon, Fred, 281
Wilson, Bill, 389
Wilson, David, 451
Wilson, James, 412
Wilson, Joe, 318
Wilson, John H., 49
Wilson, Joseph, 266, 341
Wilson, Kevin, 209, 230
Wilson, Laval S, 572
Wilson, Lewis L, 135
Wilson, Lewis, 376
Wilson, Linda, 527
Wilson, Lois, 525
Wilson, Maureen D, 248
Wilson, Michael P, 105, 152
Wilson, Michele, 385
Wilson, Ralph, 568
Wilson, Ross, 354
Wilson, Sandra, 472
Wilson, Susan, 57
Wilson-Hew, Elmina, 175, 293
Wilt, Samantha, 449
Wilton, Michael, 417
Wilutis, Karen M, 61
Wimer, Charles, 468
Winans, Bob, 284
Winchell, Andrew, 17
Windram, Richard, 472
Wines, Margaret, 556
Wingate, Heather, 490
Wingender, Karen, 247
Winkler, Matthew, 535, 538
Winn, Gilbert, 465
Winn, Thomas, 343
Winslow, Carol B., 61
Winslow, F Dana, 47
Winslow, Joanne, 47
Winsten, Richard D, 444
Winston, Linda, 293
Winter, Don, 439
Winter, Elizabeth, 506
Winter, Ethan, 433
Winter, Nancy A, 296
Winter, Neil, 401
Winter, Richard, 461
Winterhalter, Matt, 528
Winters, Fred, 382
Winyland, Michael, 305
Winzinger, Robert, 300
Wirth, William, 267
Wise, Carly, 434
Wise, JD, Jeff, 233, 260
Wise, Jeffrey, 460
Wise, Peter, 406
Wise, William, 157
Wisely, Kevin, 333
Wiseman, Cherylann, 451
Wise-Wicks, Jean, 513
Wisniewski, Vanessa, 439
Witherow, Matthew D., 65
Witherspoon, Karen, 398
Witkowski, John J, 81
Witt, Jr, Richard, 444
Witt, Richard, 261
Witte, Linda, 326
Wittenberg, Carol, 225
Wittman, Rob, 318
Wittner, Bonnie G., 50
Wittner, Therese, 451
Wittwer, Melinda, 502
Wochele, Chuck, 290
Woelzl, Susan, 280
Woerner, Carrie, 34, 35, 40, 41, 42, 642
Woersching, Joanne, 184
Wohl, Honora, 135
Woiwode, Nathan, 449
Wojcik, John, 528
Wojehowski, Joshua, 477
Wojtaszek, Henry, 107, 274
Wojtaszek, Paul B., 47
Wojtaszek-Gariano, Kathleen, 56
Wojtowicz, Jim, 362
Wolanin Young, Gail, 351
Wolf, David, 86, 97, 188
Wolf, Frank R, 317
Wolf, George J., 486
Wolf, Mark, 107, 274
Wolf, Stacy, 432
Wolfe, Charles A., 486
Wolfe, Dorothy A, 356
Wolfe, Richard, 538
Wolff, Raymond, 266
Wolff, Scott, 34
Wolfgang, Penny, 47
Wolfgang, Robin, 469
Wolfson, Howard, 352
Wolham, John, 235, 246, 264
Wolken, Randall, 440
Wolman, Derek, 405
Woloz, Michael, 400, 401, 440
Wone, Carey, 49
Wong, Calvin, 378
Wong, Douglas S., 50
Wong, Jackie, 427
Wong, Kam, 81
Wong, Martin, 156
Wong, Tanya, 435
Wong, Veronica, 445
Wood, Charles D., 47
Wood, Cliff L, 548
Wood, David J, 332
Wood, Jeff, 115
Wood, Jodi L., 53
Wood, Jonathan, 338
Wood, Jr, Robert H, 398
Wood, Kathleen M, 568
Wood, Lee F., 457
Wood, Michael, 6, 111, 206, 235
Wood, Mick, 409
Wood, Philip, 467
Wood, Thomas F, 344
Woodard, Adam, 474
Woodard, Jeff, 537
Woodard, Michele M, 47
Woodard, Tracy, 450
Woodford, R C, 327
Woodhouse, Enoch, 491
Wooding, Martha, 444
Woodruff, Michael, 472
Woodruff, Sheryl, 421
Woods, Curtis J, 351
Woods, Erin E, 590
Woods, Lori Currier, 56
Woods, MaryBeth, 14, 201, 221
Woodward, John J, 336
Woodward, Nala, 341
Woodworth, Robert, 435
Wool, Louis N, 598
Woolsey, Lynn C, 318
Wooten, John, 474
Wooten, Paul, 46
Worden, Michael, 141
Work, C Victor, 136
Work, Mary MacMaster, 60
Workman, Thomas E, 204, 468
Worona, Jay, 464
Worrell, Kris, 531
Worth, Mary Kay, 569
Woytila, Gregory, 583
Wozniak, Angela M, 35, 36, 40, 178, 195, 253, 642
Wozniak, Peggy J, 568
Wray, Diane, 62
Wray, Ken, 192
Wrege, Paul F, 72
Wright, Bill, 333
Wright, Bob, 111
Wright, Deborah, 383, 451
Wright, G Stephen, 254
Wright, Geoffrey D.S., 46
Wright, Gwen, 11, 113, 253
Wright, James, 86, 97, 188, 307, 505
Wright, John, 477
Wright, Keith L T, 35, 41, 43, 642
Wright, Keith L. T., 37
Wright, Keith L., 36
Wright, Keith L.T., 39, 189, 237, 246, 373
Wright, Schawannah, 277
Wright, Tamara, 342, 411
Wright, Thomas K., 94, 193
Wrobel, Miriam, 396

Wrona, Christine, 51
Wu, David, 322
Wu, Johnny, 385
Wu, Mitchell, 382
Wu, Steven, 112
Wuertele, Andrew W., 492
Wvjcik, James, 339
Wyant, Douglas H, 568
Wyden, Ron, 90, 203, 276, 314
Wyeht, John, 463
Wyker, Barbara, 527
Wylde, Kathryn S, 512
Wylde, Kathryn S., 94
Wylde, Kathryn, 454
Wylie, Andrew J, 327
Wyner, Scott, 4, 69
Wynn, Elisabeth, 420
Wynnyk, Bohdan, 220
Wyzykowski, James, 175, 293
Xanthis, John P, 585
Yacknin, Ellen, 65
Yaggi, Marc, 159
Yagielski, John, 589
Yalin Tao, Elizabeth J., 49
Yan, Jimmy, 359
Yanche, Michelle, 419
Yannello, Heather, 190
Yarger, Tricia, 396
Yasgur, Sam, 337
Yassky, David, 358
Yatauro, Diane, 332
Yates, William, 396
Yavornitzki, Mark L, 204
Yazgi, Stephanie, 473
Yazurlo, Michael, 599
Yearwood, Alvin M., 50
Yeary, Lon M., 153
Yedin, Jonathan, 378
Yee, Yue, 220
Yeger, Kalman, 492
Yeh, Bervan, 419
Yeigh, Wolf, 546
Yelich, Bruce, 108
Yeomans, Gayle A, 204
Yessman Jr, William E, 336
Yeung, Miriam, 232
Yevoli, Michael, 503
Yochem, Richard, 591
Yolles, James, 386
York, John M, 331
York, Lois B., 46
Yoswein, Joni A., 478
Young Jr, Robert C, 585
Young, Bruce E, 98, 151
Young, C W Bill, 317
Young, Carl, 260
Young, Catharine M, 15, 20, 23, 24, 25, 165, 237, 265, 617
Young, Catharine, 20
Young, Chauniqua, 395
Young, Debra J, 57
Young, Erin, 474
Young, Gregory, 176
Young, John, 463
Young, Jr, Lester W, 119
Young, Jr., William N, 508
Young, Kelly, 413
Young, Kevin G, 46
Young, Lindsay, 238, 268
Young, Mark H, 51
Young, Matthew A., 388
Young, Oliver C., 171
Young, Rachael, 110
Young, Richard, 104, 124, 242
Young, Sonny, 280
Young, Stephen, 71
Young, Theodore H, 374
Young, William N, 101, 237, 308
Young, William, 471
Younkins, Ron, 209
Yu, Derick, 353
Yu, Janice, 466
Yu, Xiao Yun M., 483
Yudelson, Michael B, 347
Yuille Williams, Antonia, 356
Yung, Lanhee, 467
Zaccone, John, 359
Zacher, Lawrence, 584
Zack, David, 343
Zack, Monica, 538
Zaeske, Mark, 80
Zagame, John, 453
Zagor, David J, 352
Zahn, Steven, 148
Zahnleuter, Richard J, 8, 176
Zakaria, Fareed, 533
Zalduondo-Henriquez, Paulette, 398
Zaleski, Terence M, 257
Zaleski, Terence M., 126
Zamani, Nahal, 395
Zambelli, Barbara G, 60
Zane, Cynthia, 556
Zannoni, Joanne, 117, 398
Zapf, Thomas R., 490
Zapson, Michael, 405
Zarcone, Michael, 418
Zarcone, Peter, 442
Zarecki, Jane S., 330
Zarelli, Brian, 530
Zaron, Barbara, 243, 452
Zarrella, Dominick, 112, 207
Zarutskie, Andrew J, 360
Zaslow, Jennifer, 356
Zaso, Suzanne, 342
Zayas, Joseph A., 50
Zayas, Joseph, 47, 210
Zayas, Robert, 127
Zebrowski Stavisky, Kristen, 373
Zebrowski, Kenneth, 26, 35, 36, 38, 40, 43, 642
Zebrowski, Kristen, 134
Zecca Corsale, Barbara, 511
Zech, Susan, 553
Zeigler, Neldra M, 357
Zeis, John, 576
Zeitz, Steve, 298
Zelamsky, David, 392
Zelazny, Donald, 148
Zeldin, Lee M, 650
Zeldin, Lee M., 90, 197
Zellner, Jeremy, 373
Zemsky, Howard, 7, 84, 97, 105, 147, 188, 271, 287
Zenzen, Sheryl, 109, 110
Zeosky, Gerald M, 113
Zero, Edward J, 600
Zeytoonjian, Fred, 382
Zezula, Tiffany, 453
Zhong, Gan-Yuan, 71
Zhou, Mei, 121, 174, 228
Zhou, Sam, 284
Zhuang, Susan, 29
Zibelman, Audrey, 11, 140
Ziegler, Jeffery, 596
Ziegler, Jessica H, 561
Ziegler, Laurence, 267
Zieglmeier, Elizabeth, 407
Zielezienski, JS, 479
Zielinski, Phillip, 417
Zikuski, Joseph, 342
Zimardo, Robert, 419
Zimmer, Michael E, 361
Zimmerman, Hope, 47
Zimmerman, Rick, 478
Zimmer-Meyer, Heidi N, 514
Zimpher, Nancy L., 543
Zimpher, Nancy, 467
Zingdale, Donald, 546
Zini, Frank, 528
Zins, Rosemary, 398
Ziolkowski, Deborah, 574
Zipser, Howard, 378
Zitek, Craig, 363
Zogby, Jonathan, 94, 139
Zolberg, Vera, 280
Zollo, John B., 365
Zordon, Robert D., 372
Zuber, Paul, 405
Zuber-Wilson, Patricia, 4, 173, 250
Zuchlewski, Pearl, 216, 225
Zucker, Howard, 238
Zucker, Marian, 8, 189
Zucker, MD, JD, Howard, 8, 148, 174
Zuckerman, David S., 60
Zuckerman, Mortimer, 528
Zuckerman-Bernstein, Joanna, 462
Zugibe, Thomas P, 335
Zumbo, Marilyn, 428
Zumbolo, Anthony, 11, 241, 305
Zupan, Jeffrey M, 292
Zurack, Marlene, 354
Zurlo, John H, 327
Zurlo, Michael E, 327

Zutes, Sandra F., 362
Zwack, Henry F., 57
Zwang, Ariel, 462
Zweben, Andrew, 349
Zweibel, Ronald A., 46
Zweibel, Ronald, 50
Zwerling, Susanna, 472
Zwickel, Victoria, 439
Zwicker, Lori, 240
Zwiebel, Dovid, 126
Zygo, Carol, 576
Zymanek, James J, 341
Zymroz, Robin B, 573

Organization Index

Includes the names of the top three levels in all New York State executive departments and agencies; public corporations; authorities; commissions; all organizations listed in the Private Sector sources segment of each policy chapter; lobbyist organizations; political action committees; chambers of commerce; newspapers; news services; radio and television stations; SUNY and CUNY locations; and private colleges.

10th Judicial District, 47
11 East 68th Street LLC, 382
114 Kenmare Associates, LLC, 405
117th Street Equities LLC, 416
1199 SEIU & GNYHA Healthcare Education Project, 402
1199 SEIU Greater New York Worker Participation Fund, 444
1199 SEIU United Healthcare Workers East, 224, 387, 402
1199 SEIU United Healthcare Workers East (FKA 1199/SEIU New York's Health & Human Service Union), 377
1199/SEIU & GNYHA Healthcare Education Project, 377
1199/SEIU New York State Political Action Fund, 479
1199/SEIU New York's Health & Human Services Union, 444
11th Judicial District, 47
125 MEC Center LLC, 394
12th Judicial District, 48
133 Greenwich Street Associates LLC, 401
13th Avenue Supermarket LLC, 420
13th Judicial District, 48
145 Americas Condominium, 431
176 Woodward Owner LLC, 407
1765 1st Associates LLC, 475
195 Broadway LLC, 394
1st Department, 45
1st Judicial District, 46
2013 Committee to Elect Gwen Goodwin, 479
212 LaFayette Associates, LLC, 405
219-25 LLC, 420
249 W 28th Street Properties, LLC, 377
250 E 57th Street, LLC, 475
250 East 57th Street, LLC, 392
28 New York Masters of Foxhounds, 417
2nd Department, 45
2nd Judicial District, 46
328-36 West 53rd Street Redevelopment Company, LP, 392
341-363 West 50th Street, LLC, 392
345 E 62nd Street Associate, 453
3530 WPR LLC, 392
369th Veterans Association Inc, 297
380 Development LLC, 401, 452
384 Bridge Street LLC, 431
39 West 23rd Street, LLC, 392
390 Tower Associates LLC, 390
390 Tower LLC, 431
3M Company, 456
3rd Department, 45
3rd Judicial District, 46
40th Street Development LLC, 478
414-24 West 48th Street Redevelopment Company, LP, 392
4201 Schools Association, 402, 424
444 Realty Company, LLC, 392
47th Street Business Improvement District, 382
4th Department, 45
4th Judicial District, 46
50 Varick LLC, 431
525 West 52nd Street Development LLC, 432
580 Park Avenue, Inc., 401
5th Judicial District, 46
62 Wooster LLC, 419
6th Judicial District, 46
7-Eleven, Inc., 428
7th Judicial District, 47
83-30 Austin Street LLC, 439
88 Greenwich Owner LLC, 437
8th Judicial District, 47
92nd Street Young Men's and Young Women's Hebrew Association, 377
99 Solutions LLC, 377
9th Judicial District, 47
A Different Approach, 479
A&W Architects and Engineers, 290
A. Servidone, Inc., 405
A.M Property Holding Corp., 382
AAA New York State, Inc., 402, 414
AAA Northway, 277
AAA Western and Central NY, 277
AAFE Managment Co, 453
AARP, 255, 414
ABBVIE, Inc., 405
ABC Inc, 442
ABC News (New York Bureau), 531
ACEC New York City PAC, 479
ACS Home Care LLC, 411
ADT Security Services Inc., 456
AECOM Environmental Services, 155
AECOM US FEDERAL PAC, 479
AFL-CIO, 420, 449
AFSCME District Council 37, 242
AFSCME Local 2021, 453
AHRC New York City, 231, 437
AHRC-NYC, 431
AIA New York State Inc, 475
AIA New York State, Inc. (FKNA Rodriguez, Barbara J.), 378
AIDS Healthcare Foundation, 387
AIDS Service Center of NYC, 438
AIM Services Inc, 231
AIRBNB, Inc., 387
AJ Consulting Services LLC, 378
ALCOA, Inc., 438
ALM Medica Inc, 472
ALS Association of Greater New York (The), 442
ALSTOM Transportation Inc, 290
AM Law Daily, The, 527
AMAC, Association for Metroarea Autistic Children, 231
AMDEC Foundation, 380
AMDEC Foundation, Inc., 387
AMDEC Foundation, Inc. (FKA AMDEC Policy Group, Inc.), 380
AMGEN, 381
AMSUS-The Society of Federal Health Professionals, 181
AMTRAK, 448
AMV Unitel LLC, 432
ANHD, Inc., 381, 477
AOL, LLC, 424
AON Corporation Political Action Committee, 479
APAX Partners, LP, 381
APICHA Community Health Center, 381
ARE-East River Science Park LLC, 404
ASA Institute of Business & Computer Technology, 563
ASPIRA of New York Inc, 125
AT&T, 443
AT&T Corporation, 143
AT&T Inc. and Its Affiliates (FKA Roos, David), 384
AT&T PAC - New York, 479
AT&T Services, Inc., 420
AT&T, Inc., 424
ATCO Properties & Management, Inc., 431
ATM Industry Association, 440
ATU NY State Legislative Conference Board, 384, 423
ATU New York Cope Fund, 479
AU Foundation, Inc., 420
AXA Equitable Life Insurance Company, 389

AXA Real Estate Investment Managers US, 384
Abax Incorporated, 382
Abbott Laboratories, 405
Abbott UFSD, 597
Abilities Inc, Abilities!, 224
Abilities Inc, at Abilities!, 256
Absolut Management Facilities, Inc., 408
Academic Dental Centers (NYS), 424
Academy of Medicine (NY), 392, 438, 478
Academy of Medicine (NY) (The), 377
Academy of Political Science, 169
Acadia 161st Street, LLC, 392
Acadia Insurance Company, 385
Accela, Inc., 390
Accenture LLP, 377, 473
Accenture, LTD., 390
Ace Group - North America, 377
Ace Group- North America, 420
Acquard, Milissa, 377
Action for a Better Community Inc, 256
Actors Fund of America (The), 444
Adams, Daniel J, 377
Adams, John, 377
Addiction Treatment Providers Association, 443
Addison CSD, 591
Adelante of Suffolk County, Inc, 428
Adelphi NY Statewide Breast Cancer Hotline & Support Program, 181
Adelphi University, 405, 552
Adirondack CSD, 583
Adirondack Community College, 546
Adirondack Council Inc (The), 155, 377, 378
Adirondack Daily Enterprise, 530
Adirondack Economic Development Corporation, 501
Adirondack Lakes Center for the Arts, 277
Adirondack Park Agency, 95, 150, 272, 306
Adirondack Pine Hill NY Trailways, 452
Adirondack Publishing Co Inc, 530
Adirondack Regional Chambers of Commerce, 501
Adirondack/Pine Hill/NY Trailways, 277
Adirondacks Speculator Region Chamber of Commerce, 501
Administrative Regulations Review, Legislative Commission on, 26, 43
Adolf, Jay, 378
Adult Day Health Care Council (ADHCC), 415
Advance Group Inc (The), 378
Advance Publications Inc, 530
Advanced Biohealing a Shire Company, 443
Advantage Capital Partners, 475
Advertising Development Political Action Committee, 479
Advocacy Association, Inc., 403
Advocates for Adult Day Services, 393
Advocates for Children of New York Inc, 125
Advocates for Children of New York, Inc. (FKA Sweet, Kim), 378
Aeon Nexus Corporation, 390
Aetna, 378, 398
Aetna Inc, 453
Aetna, Inc., 433
Africa-America Institute (The), 125
African American Chamber of Commerce of Westchester & Rockland Counties, 501
After-School Corporation (The), 378
After-School Corporation (The) (FKA Ford, Barry), 378
Afton CSD, 570
Age 680 Madison LLC, 382
Aging, 20, 35
Committee Staff, 20, 35
Key Assembly Staff Assignments, 35
Membership, 20, 35
Majority, 20, 35
Minority, 20, 35
Aging, Office for the, 3, 250, 303
Aging Projects, 250
Federal Relations, 250
Aging, Special Committee on, 316
Agricultural Affiliates, 73
Agriculture, 20, 35, 316
Committee Staff, 20, 35
Key Assembly Staff Assignments, 35
Key Senate Staff Assignments, 20
Membership, 20, 35
Majority, 20, 35
Minority, 20, 35
Subcommittees, 317
Conservation, Credit, Energy, and Research, 317
Department Operations, Oversight, Nutrition, & Forestry, 317
General Farm Commodities & Risk Management, 317
Horticulture and Organic Agriculture, 317
Livestock, Dairy, and Poultry, 317
Specialty Crops, Rural Development and Foreign Agriculture, 317
Agriculture & Markets Department, 4, 69, 250, 303
Agricultural Development Division, 69, 250
Agricultural Districts, 69
Animal Industry, 69
Brooklyn, 69
Buffalo, 69
Counsel's Office, 69
Fiscal Management, 69
Food Laboratory, 69
Food Safety & Inspection, 69
Field Operations, 69
Hauppauge, 70
Human Resources, 70
Information Systems, 70
Kosher Law Enforcement, 70
Milk Control & Dairy Services, 70
New York City Office, 70
Plant Industry, 70
Rochester, 70
Soil & Water Conservation Committee, 70
State Fair, 70
Statistics, 70
Syracuse, 70
Weights & Measures, 70
Agriculture & NYS Horse Breeding Development Fund, 95, 272, 306
Agriculture, Nutrition & Forestry, 312
Subcommittees, 312
Domestic and Foreign Marketing, Inspection and Plant & Animal Health, 312
Energy, Science and Technology, 312
Nutrition & Food Assistance, Sustainable & Organic Agriculture & Gen Legis, 312
Production, Income Protection and Price Support, 312
Rural Revitalization, Conservation, Forestry and Credit, 312
Agudath Israel of America, 126
Ahern, Barbara J, 378
Air Force Association (AFA), 297
Air Force Sergeants Association (AFSA), Division 1, 297
Air Force Women Officers Associated (AFWOA), 297
Air-Conditioning, Heating and Refridgeration Institute, 403
Akerman Senterfitt LLP (FKA Stadtmauer Bailkin LLP), 378
Akiel Taylor For Council, 479
Akron CSD, 573
Akwesasne Convenience Store Association, 405
Albany, 61
Civil Court, 61
Criminal Court, 61
Traffic Court, 61
Albany City SD, 567
Albany College of Pharmacy, 552
Albany County, 50, 325
County Court, 50
Family, 50
Supreme Court & Surrogate, 51
Albany County Airport Authority, 95, 284, 306
Albany County Industrial Development Agency, 501
Albany County Rural Housing Alliance Inc, 190
Albany Housing Coalition Inc, 297
Albany Information Technology Group, LLC, 404
Albany Law School, 552
Albany Law School of Union University, 378

Albany Law School, Government Law Center, 169
Albany Medical College, 552
Albany Medical Ctr, 475
Albany Port District Commission, 95, 285, 306, 437
Albany, City of, 341
Albany-Colonie Regional Chamber of Commerce, 379, 501
Albee Development, LLC, 392
Albert 2013, 479
Albert Einstein College of Medicine, 424
Albert Einstein College of Medicine - Division of Substance Abuse, 231
Albert Lindley Lee Memorial Hospital, 475
Albion CSD, 586
Alcoholism & Drug Abuse, 20, 35
Committee Staff, 35
Key Assembly Staff Assignments, 35
Membership, 20, 35
Majority, 20, 35
Minority, 20, 35
Alcoholism & Substance Abuse Services, Office of, 4, 173, 227, 250, 303
Bureau of Housing
Bureau of Housing, 173
Bureau of Management Services, 173
Bureau of Prevention Services, 173
Information Technology Services, 173
Bureau of Public Information & Communications, 173, 250
Bureau of Research, Epidemiology & Practice Improvement
Bureau of Research, Epidemiology & Practice Improvement, 173
Fiscal Administration Division, 173, 227, 250
Bureau of Budget Management, 173
Bureau of Capital Management, 173
Bureau of Financial Management, 173
Bureau of Health Care Financing & 3rd Party Reimbursement, 173
Office of Counsel & Internal Controls, 173
Office of Governmental Affairs & Grants Mgmt, 173
Office of Medical Director, 173
Office of NYC Operations, Affirmative Action & Bureau of Recovery, 173
Office of Statewide Field Operations, 173
Outcome Management & System Information Division, 173, 227, 250
Bureau of Data Analysis, Data Quality & Evaluation, 173
Bureau of State/Local Planning, 173
Prevention, Housing & Management Services Division, 173, 250
Prevention, Housing, Technology & Management Services Division, 227
Quality Assurance & Performance Improvement Division, 173, 227, 251
Bureau of Certification & Systems Management, 173
Bureau of Standards Compliance, 174
Bureau of Talent Management & Credentializing, 174
Treatment & Practice Innovation Division, 174, 251
Bureau of Addiction Treatment Centers, 174
Alden CSD, 573
Alden Chamber of Commerce, 501
Alex For NYC, 479
Alexander CSD, 575
Alexandria Bay Chamber of Commerce, 501
Alexandria CSD, 577
Alfred State College of Technology, 546
Alfred University, 387, 552
Alfred-Almond CSD, 567
Algin Management Co., LLC, 418
Alice Hyde Medical Center, 475
Alicia 4 Council 7, 479
All Shows LLC, 405
All Stars Project, Inc., The, 392
Allegany - Limestone CSD, 568
Allegany County, 51, 325
Supreme, County, Family & Surrogate's Courts, 51
Allegany County Office of Development & Industrial Development Agency (IDA), 501
Allegue, Raul R, 379
Allergan USA, Inc., 440
Allergan, Inc, 423
Allergan, Inc., 428
Alliance for Children with Special Needs-School Age (NYS), 420
Alliance for Clean Energy New York, Inc., 438
Alliance for Donation, Inc. (New York) (FKA Stark, Lynette), 379
Alliance for Downtown New York, Inc., 379, 437
Alliance for Fine Wine Wholesalers, Ltd (NY), 423
Alliance for Positive Health, 181
Alliance for Quality Education, 379
Alliance for Quality Education (FKA Easton, Regina N), 379
Alliance for the Arts, 277
Alliance of Automobile Manufacturers, 424
Alliance of Boys & Girls Clubs, Inc. (NYS), 424
Alliance of Long Island Agencies, 459, 462
Alliance of New York State YMCAs, Inc., 387
Alliance of Resident Theatres (NY), 475
Alliance of Resident Theatres/New York, 436
Alliance of Resident Theatres/New York (ART/New York), 277
Alliant Insurance Services, 405
Alliantgroup, 437
Allinger, Stephen (FKA Nelson, Debra), 379
Allocco, Carol, 379
Allstate Insurance Company, 408, 420
Alston & Bird LLP, 214
Altman, Frederick M, 379
Altman, Robert S., 379
Altmar-Parish-Williamstown CSD, 586
Altria Client Services, 90
Altria Client Services Inc. and its Affiliates, 379, 401, 406
Altria Client Services, Inc., 388, 414, 416
Altria Corporate Services Inc (ALCS), 442
Alvin D Lurie PC, 268
Alzheimer's Association, New York City Chapter, 379, 438
Alzheimer's Association, Northeastern NY, 181
Alzheimer's Disease Resource Center, 417
Amagansett UFSD, 591
Amanus Consulting Group, 380
Ambrose Employer Group, LLC, 385
Amdursky Pelky Fennell & Wallen, 214
Ameican Farmland Trust, 380
Amerada Hess Corporation, 452
American Academy McAllister Institute of Funeral Service, 553
American Academy of Dramatic Arts, 553
American Academy of Pediatrics District II (NYS), 380
American Airlines, 391
American Beverage Association, 380
American Cancer Society Cancer Action Network, 380
American Cancer Society, Inc., 380, 431
American Cancer Society-Capital NY Region, 181
American Chemistry Council, 90, 437
American Chemistry Council, Inc., 428
American City Business Journals, 523
American Cleaning Institute, 424
American Coatings Association, Inc., 398
American College of Nurse-Midwives, NYC Chapter, 181
American College of Occupational Environmental Medicine, 472
American College of Occupational and Environmental Medicine, 394
American College of Physicians Services, Inc. (NY), 433
American College of Physicians, New York Chapter, 181
American Congress of Obstetricians & Gynecologists, Inc., 380
American Congress of Obstetricians & Gynecologists, Inc. District II, 380
American Congress of Obstetricians & Gynecologists/NYS, 181
American Council of Engineering Companies of NY (ACEC New York), 90

Appendices: Financial Plan, Indexes & Maps

American Council of Engineering Companies of NY (FKA Association of Consulting Engineers (NYS)), 387
American Council of Engineering Companies of New York, 403
American Council of Life Insurers, 432, 439
American Diabetes Association, 380
American Express Co, 475
American Express Company, 80
American Fair Credit Council, 420
American Farmland Trust, 380
American Farmland Trust, New York Office, 73, 155
American Federation of State, County and Municipal Employees (AFSCME), 242
American Federation of Teachers, 224
American Forest & Paper Association (Multistate Associates Incorporated), 425
American Heart Assn/American Stroke Assn, 381
American Heart Association Founders Affiliate, 181
American Higher Education Development Corporation, 126
American Indonesian Chamber of Commerce, 501
American Institute of Architects (AIA) New York State Inc, 90, 190
American Institute of Architects - New York Chapter, 381, 392
American Institute of Architects New York Chapter, 381
American Insurance Assn, 381, 475
American Insurance Association, 474
American Insurance Association New York City PAC, 479
American International Group Inc, 80, 203
American International Group Inc (AIG), 475
American International Group, Inc., 390, 413
American Jewish Committee, 197
American Lawyer Media, 435, 462, 527
American Lawyer Media Co, 442
American Legion, Department of New York, 297
American Liver Foundation, Greater NY Chapter, 181
American Lung Association of NYS Inc, 181
American Lung Association of New York, 438
American Management Association International, 90
American Massage Therapy Assoc. - NY Chapter, 393
American Metal Market, 531
American Military Retirees Association Inc, 297
American Museum of Natural History, 155, 277, 466
American Museum of the Moving Image Inc, 453
American Natural Gas, LLC, 474
American Petroleum Institute, 406, 445
American Racing and Entertainment, LLC, 377
American Red Cross in Greater NY, 389
American Red Cross in NYS, 256
American Safety Council, 425
American Safety Institute, Inc., 393
American Society for the Prevention of Cruelty to Animals (ASPCA), 73, 116, 432
American Solar Partners, 387
American Traffic Solutions, 437
American Youth Hostels, Inc., 392
Americans United for Life, 425
America's Health Insurance Plans, 385
America's Natural Gas Alliance, Inc., 410
Amerigroup New York LLC, 408
Amerigroup New York LLC/Amerigroup Community Care (FKA Care Plus Health Plan), 440
Amerigroup New York, LLC (DBA Amerigroup Community Care), 402
Amherst CSD, 573
Amherst Chamber of Commerce, 501
Amherst Industrial Development Agency (Town of), 501
Amherst, Town of, 341
AmidaCare, 438
Amigos Del Museo Del Barrio, Inc., 477
Amityville UFSD, 591
Ammann & Whitney Consulting Engineers, 290
Amnesty International USA, 197
Amsterdam, 61
Civil & Criminal Courts, 62
Amsterdam Industrial Development Agency, 501
Amsterdam Nursing Home Corp., 387
Amusement & Music Owners Assn of NY, 464
Andes CSD, 572
Andover CSD, 567
Andy King 2013, 479
Anglin, Laura L., 381
Anheuser-Busch Companies, Inc., 387
Annese and Associates, Inc., 473
Anson, Joseph L., 381
Antalek & Moore Insurance Agency, 80
Anti-Defamation League, 197
Aon Service Corporation, 203
Apple Association, Inc. (NY), 381
Apple Bank for Savings, 80
Apple Inc., 382
Apple Valley Waste Conversions, 387
Applied Materials, 390
Applied Projects Company, Inc., 401
Appraisal Education Network School & Merrell Institute, 247
Appropriations, 312, 317
Subcommittees, 312, 317
Agriculture, Rural Development, FDA & Related Agencies, 317
Agriculture, Rural Development, FDA, and Related Agencies, 312
Commerce, Justice, Science and Related Agencies, 312, 317
Defense, 312, 317
Energy and Water Development, 312, 317
Financial Services and General Government, 312, 317
Homeland Security, 312, 317
Interior, Environment and Related Agencies, 312, 317
Labor, Health & Human Services, Education and Related Agencies, 317
Labor, Health and Human Services, Education and Related Agencies, 312
Legislative Branch, 312, 317
Military Construction, Veterans Affairs and Related Agencies, 312, 317
State, Foreign Operations and Related Programs, 312, 317
Transportation, Housing and Urban Development, and Related Agencies, 313, 317
Aquest South Park LLC, 387
Arc Inc (NYS), 419
Arcade Area Chamber of Commerce, 501
Arcadis U.S., Inc., 431, 440
Arcadis-US, 393
Archdiocese of New York, 416
Ardsley UFSD, 597
Are-East Rive Science Park, LLC, 429
Area Property Partners, 431
Arent Fox LLP, 466
Argonaut Holdings LLC, 420
Argyle CSD, 596
Ari Kagan For City Council, 479
Ariel Investments LLC, 427
Arise, Inc., 424
Arista Networks, 394
Arista Power, Inc., 430
Arker Diversified Companies, 420
Arkport CSD, 591
Arlington CSD, 572
Armed Services, 313, 317
Subcommittees, 313, 318
Air and Land Forces, 318
Airland, 313
Emerging Threats & Capabilities, 313
Military Personnel, 318
Oversight and Investigations, 318
Personnel, 313
Readiness, 318
Readiness & Management Support, 313
SeaPower, 313
Seapower and Expeditionary Forces, 318
Strategic Forces, 313, 318

Terrorism, Unconventional Threats and Capabilities, 318
Armory Foundation (The), 406
Army Aviation Association of America (AAAA), 297
Army Aviation Association of America (AAAA), Empire Chapter, 298
Arnot-Ogden Medical Center, 390
Arroyo 2013, 479
Art & Science Collaborations Inc, 277
Art Institute of New York City (The), 563
Arthur J Finkelstein & Associates Inc, 137
Arts Coalition (NYC), 382
ArtsConnection Inc (The), 277
Arvai, Joni, 382
Arzt, George Communications Inc, 382
Asbestos Workers Local 12 Political Action Committee, 479
Ascension Health, 438
Ascent Real Estate Advisors, 473
Asciutto, Georgia M, 382
Asian & Pacific Islander Coalition on HIV/AIDS, Inc., 381
Asian American Coalition for Children and Families, 382
Asian American Coalition for Children and Families, Inc., 382
Asian American Federation, 256
Asian American Legal Defense and Education Fund, 197, 214
Asian Americans for Equality, 256
Assembly, 305
Assembly Legislative Commissions, 237
State Federal Relations, Task Force on, 237
Assembly Standing Committees, 70, 79, 87, 114, 124, 137, 142, 152, 165, 178, 189, 195, 202, 211, 222, 230, 237, 242, 246, 253, 265, 275, 288, 295
Aging, 178, 195, 253
Agriculture, 70
Alcoholism & Drug Abuse, 114, 178, 230, 253
Banks, 79
Children & Families, 178, 254
Cities, 87, 237
Codes, 114, 211
Consumer Affairs & Protection, 87, 165, 178
Corporations, Authorities & Commissions, 87, 165, 288
Correction, 114, 195
Economic Development, Job Creation, Commerce & Industry, 87, 237, 246, 288
Education, 124
Election Law, 137
Energy, 142
Environmental Conservation, 152
Ethics & Guidance, 165
Governmental Employees, 242
Governmental Operations, 165
Health, 178
Higher Education, 124
Housing, 189, 237, 246
Insurance, 202
Judiciary, 211
Labor, 195, 202, 222, 242
Libraries & Education Technology, 124
Local Government, 189, 237
Mental Health, 195, 230
Oversight, Analysis & Investigation, 165
Racing & Wagering, 265, 275
Real Property Taxation, 246, 265
Rules, 165
Small Business, 87
Social Services, 254
Tourism, Parks, Arts & Sports Development, 275
Transportation, 237, 288
Veterans Affairs, 295
Ways & Means, 165, 237, 265
Assembly Task Force, 70
Food, Farm & Nutrition, Task Force on, 70
Assembly Task Forces, 87, 124, 195, 222, 254
Puerto Rican/Hispanic Task Force, 195, 222, 254
Skills Development & Career Education, Legislative Commission on, 124, 222
University-Industry Cooperation, Legislative Task Force on, 124
University-Industry Cooperation, Task Force on, 87
Women's Issues, Task Force on, 195, 222, 254
Assembly Task Forces & Caucus, 165
State-Federal Relations Task Force, 165
Assembly of the Association of Surgical Technologists, 438
Assistant Deputy Warden - Deputy Warden's Association, 414
Assisted Living Federation of America (ALFA), 425
Assn for Community Living, 382, 383
Assn for Neurologically Impaired Brain Injured Children Inc, 453
Assn for the Advancement of Blind & Retarded Inc, 453
Assn of Alcoholism & Substance Abuse Providers Inc (NY), 402
Assn of Community & Residential Agencies (NYS), 383
Assn of Convenience Stores (NY), 391
Assn of Counties & Its Affiliated Organizations (NYS), 383
Assn of Electrical Workers (NYS), 404
Assn of Homes & Services for the Aging (NY), 475
Assn of Independent Commercial Producers Inc, 475
Assn of Independent Schools (NYS), 440
Assn of Laser Hair Removal Specialists, Inc (NYS), 450
Assn of PBAS, Inc (NYS), 383
Assn of Plumbing Heating Cooling Contractors Inc (NYS), 470
Assn of Professional Land Surveyors Inc (NYS), 475
Assn of Public Broadcasting Stations of NY, 439, 460
Assn of Realtors Inc (NYS), 475
Assn of Service Stations & Repair Shops, Inc. (NYS), 388
Assn of Town Superintendents of Highways Inc (NYS), 452
Assn of Wholesale Marketers & Distributors (NYS), 431
Associated Builders & Contractors, Construction Training Center of NYS, 224
Associated Builders & Contractors, Empire State Chapter, 90
Associated Builders and Contractors, Inc., 434
Associated Dog Clubs of New York State, Inc., 417
Associated General Contractors of America, NYS Chapter, 90
Associated General Contractors of New York State, LLC, 382
Associated Licensed Detectives of NYS, Inc, 379
Associated Licensed Detectives of New York State, 116
Associated Medical Schools of NY, 425
Associated Medical Schools of New York, 126, 181, 382
Associated Musicians of Greater New York, Local 802 AFM, AFL-CIO, 277
Associated New York State State Food Processors Inc, 73
Associated Press (New York/Metro), 531
Associated Risk Managers of New York Inc, 203
Association Development Group Inc, 90
Association for Addiction Professionals of New York, 231
Association for Community Living, 190, 231
Association for Eating Disorders - Capital Region, 231
Association for Neighborhood & Housing Development, 191
Association for Pupil Transportation (New York), 439
Association for Superintendents of School Buildings & Grounds (NYS), 425
Association for a Better New York, 90, 191
Association of Agricultural Fairs, 478
Association of Alcoholism & Substance Abuse Providers, Inc. (NY), 390
Association of Ambulatory Surgery Centers, 408

Appendices: Financial Plan, Indexes & Maps

Association of Car Wash Owners, Inc., 386
Association of Cemeteries (NYS), 414
Association of Central Service Professionals, 438
Association of Chiefs of Police, 383
Association of County Health Officials (New York State), 383
Association of Financial Guarantee Insurers, 394
Association of Fire Districts of the State of NY Inc, 237
Association of Fire Districts of the State of New York, Inc., 478
Association of Government Accountants, NY Capital Chapter, 169
Association of Health Care Providers, Inc., 430
Association of Independent Video & Filmmakers (AIVF), (The), 277
Association of Insurance & Financial Advisors, Inc., 477
Association of Legal Aid Attorneys UAW 2325, 437
Association of Legal Aid Attorneys UAW 2325 (AFL-CIO), 383
Association of Licensed Midwives, 420
Association of Marraige and Family Therapy, Inc., 424
Association of Military Surgeons of the US (AMSUS), NY Chapter, 298
Association of New York State Youth Bureaus, 383
Association of Nurse Anesthetists, Inc. (NYS), 387
Association of PBAS, Inc., 440
Association of Plumbing, Heating & Cooling Contractors, Inc. (NYS), 393
Association of Proprietary Colleges, 126, 402, 425, 429
Association of Psychiatric Rehabilitation Services, 461
Association of Public Broadcasting Stations of NY Inc, 143
Association of Realtors, 403
Association of Realtors (New York State) (FKA-Mackenzie, Duncan), 383
Association of Safety Group Managers, 423
Association of School Psychologists, 420
Association of Towns of the State of NY, 383
Association of Towns of the State of New York, 237, 268
Association of Water & Sewer Excavators, Inc, 405
Association of Wholesale Marketers and Distributors (NYS), 420
Association of the Bar of the City of New York, 214
Association of the US Army (AUSA), 298
Association on Independent Living, 383
Association on Independent Living (NY), 383
Association on Independent Living, Inc. (NY), 398
Assurant Solutions, 442
Astellas, 390
Astellas Pharma, 384
Astellas Pharma US, Inc., 384
Astoria Bank, 80
Astoria Generating Company LP, 431
Astrazeneca Pharmaceuticals, 387
Asurion Corp & Subsidiaries (FKA Lock/Line LLC (DST Systems)), 475
Athletic Trainers' Assn (NYS), 475
Athletic Trainers' Association New York State, 442
Atlantic Auto Mall, 405
Atlantic Development Co, 445
Atlantic Realty Development Corporation, 418
Atlantic States Marine Fisheries Commission, 95, 150, 306
Atlantic Yards Development Company, 431
Atomic Learning Inc, 440
Attica CSD, 599
Attorney Grievance Committee, 208
1st Judicial Dept, Judicial Dist 1, 12, 208
2nd Judicial Dept, Judicial Dist 2, 9, 10, 11, 13, 208
Judicial Dist 10, 208
Judicial Dist 2, 11, 13, 208
Judicial Dist 9, 208
3rd Judicial Dept, Judicial Dist 3, 4, 6, 208
4th Judicial Dept, Dist 5, 7, 8, 208
Judicial Dist 5, 208
Judicial Dist 7, 208
Judicial Dist 8, 208
Auburn, 62
Civil & Criminal Courts, 62
Auburn Enlarged City SD, 569
Auburn Publishers Inc, 523
Auburn, City of, 341
Audubon New York, 155, 384
Audubon Society of NYS Inc (The) / Audubon International, 155
Ausable Valley CSD, 571
Auto Collision Technician's Association, Inc., 421
AutoDesk, Inc., 443
Automobile Club of New York, 277, 290
Automobile Club of New York, Inc., 402
Automobile Dealers Assn (NYS), 384
Automobile Dealers Association (NYS), 388
Automobile Insurance Plan (NY), 385
Automotive Recyclers Association, 393
Automotive Technology & Energy Group of Western NY, 290
Auxilia, 440, 456
Avalonbay Communities, Inc., 406
Avaya, 394
Averill Park CSD, 587
Aviation Management Association (NY) (Association of Counties (NY)), 417
Avis Budget Car Rental LLC, 437
Avis Budget Group, Inc., 446
Avoca CSD, 591
Avon CSD, 577
Axis Group, Inc., 392
Axton Owner, LLC, 392
Azimuth Development Group, LLC, 378
BALCONY-Business and Labor Coalition of New York, 384
BCMUSA, 431
BMC, 394
BMM Testlabs, 387
BNA (formerly Bureau of National Affairs), 532
BP America Inc, 393
BSDM Inc., 392
Babylon Industrial Development Agency, 501
Babylon UFSD, 591
Babylon, Town of, 341
Bailey House Inc., 478
Bainbridge Chamber of Commerce, 501
Bainbridge-Guilford CSD, 570
Baker & Hostetler LLP, 384
Baker Victory Services, 387
Baldwin Chamber of Commerce, 501
Baldwin UFSD, 579
Baldwinsville CSD, 584
Baldwinsville Chamber of Commerce (Greater Baldwinsville), 501
Ballard Spahr LLP New York, 116
Ballet Theatre Foundation Inc/American Ballet Theatre, 475
Ballston Spa CSD, 588
Balmar Parc LLC, 401
Bank Street College of Education, 454
Bank Street College of Education/Graduate School, 553
Bank of Akron, 80
Bank of America Corporation and Subsidiaries, 384, 441
Bank of America New York Political Action Committee, 479
Bankers Assn (NY), 475
Bankers Association, Inc., 385
Banking, Housing & Urban Affairs, 313
Subcommittees, 313
Economic Policy, 313
Financial Institutions, 313
Housing, Transportation and Community Development, 313
Securities, Insurance and Investment, 313
Security and International Trade and Finance, 313
Banks, 20, 35
Committee Staff, 20, 35
Key Assembly Staff Assignments, 35

Key Senate Staff Assignments, 20
Membership, 20, 35
Majority, 20, 35
Minority, 20, 36
Banks, Steven, 385
Bar Association, 421
Bar Association (NYS), 432
Barclays Capital Inc., 385
Barclays Capital, Inc., 421
Bard College, 425, 553
Barker CSD, 582
Barlette, Richard, 385
Barnard College, 553
Barnes & Noble College Book Sellers (Dewey Square Group), 475
Barnes, Richard E, 385
Barrett Associates, 385
Barrier Free Living Family of Companies, 438
Bartimole, John E (FKA Western NY Healthcare Association) (FKA Larowe, Mary), 385
Batavia, 62
Civil & Criminal Courts, 62
Batavia City SD, 575
Bath Area Chamber of Commerce (Greater Bath Area), 501
Bath CSD, 591
Battery Park City Authority (Hugh L Carey), 95, 272, 306
Battery and Energy Storage Technology Consortium, Inc., 393
Bausch & Lomb Inc, 181
Bay Shore UFSD, 591
Bayer Healthcare, 439
Bayer Healthcare LLC, 381
Bayonne Energy Center LLC, 401
Bayport-Blue Point UFSD, 591
Bayrock Sapir Organization LLC, 401
Bayshore Chamber of Commerce, 502
Bayview Asset Management, 385
Beacon, 62
Civil & Criminal Courts, 62
Beacon City SD, 572
BearingPoint, 456
BearingPoint Inc., 456
Beaudoin & Company (FKA Beaudoin, Heather), 385
Beauty Schools Association, 409
Beaver River CSD, 577
Bedford CSD, 597
Bee Ready Fishbein Hatter & Donovan, LLP (FKA Bee, Peter A), 386
Beech-Nut Nutrition Corporation, 408
Beekmantown CSD, 571
Beer Wholesalers Association, Inc. (NYS), 402
Beha, Alyson, 386
Behan Communications, Inc., 386
Belfast CSD, 567
Bellefaire JCB, 442
Belleville Henderson CSD, 577
Bellevue Women's Medical Center, Inc, 450
Bellmore UFSD, 579
Bellmore-Merrick Central HS District, 579
Bellmores Chamber of Commerce, 502
Bemus Point CSD, 569
Ben Barnes Group LP, 391
Benchmark Senior Living, 425
Bender Cantone Consulting, 386
Bendetto For Assembly, 479
Benjamin Partners, Inc., 460
Bennett Firm, Inc (The), 386
Berkeley College, New York City Campus, 563
Berkeley College, Westchester Campus, 563
Berkshire Farm Center & Services for Youth, 116, 256
Berkshire UFSD, 571
Berlin CSD, 587
Bernard M Baruch College, 550
Berne-Knox-Westerlo CSD, 567
Best Friends Animal Society, 462
Beth Israel Medical Center, 392, 456
Beth Israel Medical Ctr, 432
Bethlehem CSD, 567
Bethlehem Chamber of Commerce, 502
Bethlehem Industrial Development Agency (Town of), 502
Bethlehem, Town of, 341
Bethpage Chamber of Commerce, 502
Bethpage Federal Credit Union, 462
Bethpage UFSD, 579
Better Business Bureau of Metropolitan New York, 90
Beverage Works NY, Inc. (The), 391
Big Brothers Big Sisters of NYC, 256, 431
Bikepath Country, 411
Bill Thompson For Mayor, 479
Billig, Jacob, 386
Binghamton, 62
Civil & Criminal Courts, 62
Binghamton Chamber of Commerce (Greater Binghamton), 502
Binghamton City SD, 568
Binghamton University, 386
Binghamton University, State University of New York, 544
Binghamton, City of, 342
Biotechnology Assn Inc (NY), 423
Birchez Associates, LLC, 405
Birds Eye Foods Inc, 73
Bizzi & Partners Development LLC, 401
Black Car Assistance Corporation, 442
Black Car Operators' Injury Compensation Fund (NY), 442
Black Lake Chamber of Commerce, 502
Black Veterans for Social Justice Inc, 298
Blackstone Alternative Asset Management L.P, 386
Blind Brook-Rye UFSD, 597
Blinded Veterans Association New York Inc, 298
Blishteyn For NYC, 479
Blitman & King LLP, 224
Blood Center (NY), 382
Bloom Energy Corporation, 386
Bloomberg Television, 538
Blue Mountain Lake Association, 502
Bluestone Gas Corporation of New York, Inc., 387
Bluestone Organization (The), 436
Blumenfeld Development Group, 473
Board of Regents, 119
Boces Educational Consortium (The), 425
Boehringer Ingelgheim Pharmaceuticals, Inc., 425
Boehringer Ingelheim Pharmaceuticals, Inc., 386
Bogdan Lasky & Frazier, LLC, 386
Bolivar-Richburg CSD, 567
Bolton CSD, 596
Bolton Landing Chamber of Commerce, 502
Bolton St. Johns, Inc., 387
Boltz, John J Consulting, 388
Bombardier Transit Corporation, 388, 442
Bombardier Transit Corporation & Affiliates (FKA Bombardier Transit Corporation), 388
Bombardiere, Ralph, 388
Bonagura, David, 388
Bond Schoeneck & King PLLC, 197
Bond, Schoeneck & King, PLLC, 388
Bookman, Esq., Robert S, 388
Boonville Area Chamber of Commerce, 502
Bopp, Linda, 388
Boricua College, 553
Borough of Manhattan Community College, 551
Botanical Garden (NY) (The), 388, 473
Botanical Garden (The), 477
Botanical Garden (The) (NY), 388
Botanical Medicines, 471
Bottlers Association (NYS), 414
Bottlers Association (New York State), 389
Boucher, Paul, 389
Bowling Proprietors Association, 410
Boyd Gaming, 438
Boylan Brown, 214
Brab PAC, Inc., 479
Bracken Margolin Besunder LLP, 214
Brad Lander 2013, 479
Bradford CSD, 591
Bradford Publications Inc, 529
Bradford Publishing Co, 530
Brain Injury Association of NYS (BIANYS), 181, 231
Brain Trauma Foundation, 439
Bramson ORT College, 553
Branford Communications, 137
Brasher Falls CSD, 590
Brennan Center for Justice, 440

Brennan Center for Justice at New York, 389
Brentwood UFSD, 591
Brescia, Richard, 389
Brewers Association, Inc (NYS), 377
Brewster CSD, 587
Brewster Chamber of Commerce, 502
Briand, Elizabeth H (FKA Striar, Gary), 389
Briarcliff Manor UFSD, 597
Briarcliffe College-Bethpage, 563
Briarcliffe College-Patchogue, 563
Brickfield, Burchette, Ritts & Stone, P.C., 389
Bricklayers & Allied Craftworkers Local 1 PAC, 479
Bridgehampton UFSD, 591
Brighter Choice Foundation, 389
Brighter Choice Foundation (The), 433
Brighton CSD, 578
Brighton, Town of, 342
Bristol-Meyers Squibb Company, 382
Bristol-Meyers Squibb Company Political Action Committee, 479
Bristol-Myers Squibb Co, 181, 475
Bristol-Myers Squibb Company, 431, 461
British Airways PLC, 290
Broadalbin-Perth CSD, 575
Broadcasters Assn (NYS), 456
Broadcasters Association, Inc., 389
Broadway 4D Theater NY, LLC, 391
Broadway Trio, 382
Broadway Trio LLC, 432
Brockport CSD, 578
Brockport Chamber of Commerce (Greater Brockport), 502
Brocton CSD, 569
Bronx Chamber of Commerce, 502
Bronx Community College, 478, 551
Bronx County, 51
COUNTY & FAMILY COURTS: See New York City Courts, 51
Supreme & Surrogate's Courts, 51
Bronx County (NYC Borough of the Bronx), 325
Bronx Defenders, 462
Bronx Educational Opportunity Center, 549
Bronx Museum, 463
Bronx River Alliance, Inc., 389
Bronx-Lebanon Hospital Center, 181
Bronxville Chamber of Commerce, 502
Bronxville UFSD, 597
Brookdale University Hospital and Medical Center, 415
Brookfield CSD, 578
Brookfield Financial Properties, Inc., 431
Brookfield Properties Corporation, 247
Brookhaven Memorial Hospital Medical Center, 442
Brookhaven Science Associates, LLC, 389
Brookhaven, Town of, 342
Brookhaven-Comsewogue UFSD, 591
Brooklyn Adult Care Center, 475
Brooklyn Bar Association Volunteer Lawyers Project, 420
Brooklyn Botanic Garden, 155, 277, 438
Brooklyn Botanic Garden Corporation, 431
Brooklyn Chamber of Commerce, 478, 502
Brooklyn Children's Museum, 408
Brooklyn College, 551
Brooklyn Community Services, 477
Brooklyn Daily Eagle, 524
Brooklyn Economic Development Corporation, 502
Brooklyn Educational Opportunity Center, 549
Brooklyn Hospital Center (The), 475
Brooklyn Housing & Family Services Inc, 191
Brooklyn Information & Culture, 439
Brooklyn Law School, 214, 553
Brooklyn Museum, 389
Brooklyn Museum of Art, 277
Brooklyn Navy Yard Cogeneration Partners L.P., 401
Brooklyn Navy Yard Development Corporation, 95, 294, 306
Brooklyn Philharmonic, 478
Brooklyn Public Library, 444, 453
Brooklyn Technical High School Alumni Assn, 478
Brooks, Helen M, 390
Broome Community College, 547
Broome County, 51, 325
County, Family, 51
Surrogate & Supreme Court, 51
Broome County Industrial Development Agency, 502
Broome-Delaware-Tioga BOCES, 599
Brotherhood/Sister Sol, 438
Brown & Kelly, LLP, 90
Brown & Weinraub, PLLC, 390
Brown Brothers Harriman & Co, 80
Brown, Arthur M., 390
Browne, Brian, 390
Brunswick CSD (Brittonkill), 587
Brushton-Moira CSD, 575
Bryan Block 2013, 479
Bryan Cave, LLP, 390
Bryant & Stratton College-Albany Campus, 563
Bryant & Stratton College-Amherst Campus, 563
Bryant & Stratton College-Buffalo Campus, 563
Bryant & Stratton College-Greece Campus, 563
Bryant & Stratton College-Henrietta Campus, 563
Bryant & Stratton College-Southtowns Campus, 563
Bryant & Stratton College-Syracuse Campus, 563
Bryant & Stratton College-Syracuse North Campus, 564
Buckeye Partners, L.P, 385
Buckeye Partners, L.P., 473
Budget, 313, 318
Budget, Division of the, 5, 83, 160, 234, 263, 303
Buffalo, 62
Civil & Criminal Courts, 62
Buffalo & Fort Erie Public Bridge Authority (Peace Bridge Authority), 96, 285, 306
Buffalo & Pittsburgh Railroad Inc, 423
Buffalo Bills, 277
Buffalo Business First, 524
Buffalo City Cemetary, Inc., 440
Buffalo Economic Renaissance Corporation, 502
Buffalo Educational Opportunity Center, 549
Buffalo News (The), 524
Buffalo Niagara Medical Campus, Inc., 437
Buffalo Niagara Partnership, 502
Buffalo Police Benevolent Association, Inc., 408
Buffalo SD, 573
Buffalo Sabres, 277
Buffalo State College, 390, 437, 545
Buffalo Trotting Association Inc, 277
Buffalo Zoo, 440
Buffalo, City of, 342
Builders Association (NYS), 391
Builders Exchange, Inc., 424
Building & Construction Trades Council (NYS), 390, 391, 470
Building & Construction Trades Council PAC, 479
Building & Construction Trades Council of Greater NY, 391, 470
Building & Construction Trades Council of Greater New York, 385
Building & Realty Institute, 247
Building Congress (NY) (The), 414
Building Contractors Association, 91
Building Contractors' Assn, Inc, 470
Building Industry Assn of NY Inc, 379
Building Industry Association of NYC Inc, 91
Building Industry Association of NYC, Inc., 480
Building Owners and Managers Association of Greater New York, Inc., 460
Building Trades Employers Association, 401
Building Trades Employers' Assn, 470
Bureau Veritas North America Inc., 456
Burgos, Tonio & Associates, 391
Burnt Hills-Ballston Lake CSD, 588
Bus Association of NYS Inc, 442
Business Council for International Understanding, 91
Business Council of NYS, Inc (The), 478
Business Council of NYS, Inc., 391
Business Council of NYS, Inc. (The), 391

Business Council of New York State Inc, 91, 155
Business Council of Westchester (The), 459
Business Council of Westchester, The, 502
Business Informatics Center, 564
Business Outreach Center Network Inc, 453
Business Outreach Center Network, Inc., 407, 438
Business Review, 532
Bynum, Thompson, Ryer, 138
Byram Hills CSD, 597
Byrne, Elizabeth, 391
Byrne, Kevin, 391
Byron-Bergen CSD, 575
CA, Inc., 473
CAMBA (FKA Church Avenue Merchants Block Association, Inc.), 390
CAMBA, Inc., 418
CASA - Advocates for Children of NYS, 214, 256
CATS VLT, LLC (Canadian American Transportation Systems), 452
CBS Corporation, 143, 442
CBS News (New York), 532
CBS Outdoor, 442
CBS Outdoor, Inc. (FKA Viacom Outdoor, Inc.), 392
CCS Oncology, 440
CDS Monarch, 430
CEMUSA, Inc., 431
CGI (FKA CGI Group), 475
CHIP-Community Housing Improvement Program, Inc, 401
CIDNY - Queens, 197, 256
CIO & Office of Information Technology Services (ITS), 5, 140, 160, 303
Administration, 140
CIR/SEIU Local 1957 Health Care Advocacy Fund, 480
CITIGROUP Inc. Political Action Committee - Federal/State, 480
CNA, 398, 421
COFCCA Inc, 399, 475
COFCCA, Inc., 425
COMCAST, 404
CP Rail System, 290
CPR, The International Institute for Conflict Prevention & Resolution, 215
CPS Fee Company LLC, 382
CRP/Extell Riverside LP, 382
CSC Holdings Inc, 437
CSC Holdings LLC, 431
CSC Holdings, Inc, 455
CSC Holdings, Inc. FKA Cablevision Systems Corporation, 405
CSC Holdings, LLC (Cablevision), 377
CUNY Board of Trustees, 550
CUNY Central Administration, 550
City University Construction Fund, 550
CUNY Graduate School, Center for Urban Research, 138
CUNY Hunter College, Urban Affairs & Planning Department, 191
CUNY John Jay College of Criminal Justice, 116
CUNY New York City College of Technology, Hospitality Mgmt, 277
CVS Caremark Corporation, 402
CVS Pharmacy, Inc., 398, 414
CWA District One PAC, 481
CWA Local 1182, 443
CWA SSF (NY), 481
CWM Chemical Services LLC, 156
Cable Telecommunications Assn of NY, Inc (The), 404
Cable Telecommunications Association of NY, 445
Cable Telecommunications Association of NY, Inc. (The), 405
Cable Telecommunications Association of New York, Inc, 143
Cablevision, 437
Cablevision (CSC Holdings, Inc.), 386, 422
Cablevision Systems Corporation, 143
Cablevision Systems New York PAC, 480
Cabrera For City Council, 480
Caesars Entertainment Operating Company, Inc., 387, 391
Cairo-Durham CSD, 576
Caithness Long Island II LLC, 410
Caithness Long Island II, LLC, 436
Caledonia-Mumford CSD, 577
Calgon Carbon Corporation, 377
Callen-Lorde Coomunity Health Center, 439
Calvin, James S, 391
Cam-Held Enterprise, Inc. DBA Just Kids, 420
Camba, Inc. (FKA Church Avenue Merchants Block Association, Inc.), 391
Cambridge CSD, 596
Cambridge Petroleum Corporation, 394
Camden CSD, 583
Camelot Global Services Limited, 402
Camillus, Town of, 343
Camp Directors, 438
Camp Dresser McKee & Smith, 387
Camp Venture Inc, 256
Campbell-Savona CSD, 591
Campground Owners of New York, 278
Campground Owners of New York, Inc., 422
Canadian American Transportation Systems, LLC, 453
Canadian National Railway, 440
Canajoharie CSD, 579
Canandaigua, 62
Civil & Criminal Courts, 62
Canandaigua Area Chamber of Commerce, 503
Canandaigua City SD, 584
Canandaigua National Bank & Trust Co, 80
Canarsie Courier, 524
Canarsie Courier Publications, Inc., 524
Canaseraga CSD, 567
Canastota CSD, 578
Canastota Chamber of Commerce, 503
Candor CSD, 595
Canisius College, 392, 553
Canisteo-Greenwood CSD, 591
Canton CSD, 590
Canton Chamber of Commerce, 503
Canton-Potsdam Hospital, 475
Cantore, Anthony S., 392
Capalino, James F & Associates Inc, 392
Cape Vincent Chamber of Commerce, 503
Capital District Educational Opportunity Center, 549
Capital District Physicians' Health Plan Inc, 393
Capital District Physician's Health Plan, 425
Capital District Regional Off-Track Betting Corporation, 96, 272, 306, 430
Capital District Regional Planning Commission, 96, 188, 306
Capital District Transportation Authority, 96, 285, 306
Capital One Bank, 80
Capital One Financial Corporation, 385
Capital Public Affairs, 393
Capital Region (Albany-Schoharie-Schenectady) BOCES, 600
Capital Region Building Owners and Managers Association, 393
Capital Region Center for Arts in Education, 456
Capital Region Council for Young Children with Special Needs, 421
Capital Region Norml NY, 435
Capitalize Albany Corporation, 503
Capitol Consultants Inc (NY), 393
Capitol Group, LLC, 393
Capitol Hill Management Services Inc, 393
Capitol Public Strategies, LLC (FKA McCulley & Associates, Inc.), 393
Capitol Strategies Group, LLC, 393
Cappelli Enterprises, Inc., 406
Captains Endowment Assn, NYC Police Department, 441
Captains Endowment Association, 480
Capvest Partners LLP, 394
Carahsoft Technology Corporation, 393
Caramoor, 437
Carco Group Inc, 454
Cardozo School of Law, 197
Cardtronics LP, 440
Care One Services, Inc., 473
Care One Services, Inc. (National Strategies, LLC), 385
Care for the Homeless, 387
Carey Group LLC, 394
Carl Andrews & Associates, Inc., 394
Carle Place UFSD, 579
Carlo 2013, 480

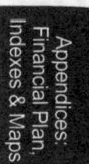

Carlos For Council, 480
Carmel CSD, 587
Carmel Car and Limousine Service, 401
Carmel, Town of, 343
Carnegie Hall, 475
Carnegie Hall Corporation (The), 477
Carnevale Consulting, LLC, 394
Carolyn's PAC, 480
Carpet and Rug Institute (The), 405
Carpino, Peter, 394
Carrion 2013, 480
Carson, Martin, 394
Carthage Area Chamber of Commerce, 503
Carthage CSD, 577
Cary Institute of Ecosystem Studies, 156
Casey Strategic Relations, 394
Casey, Teresa M., 394
Casey, William R., 394
Cassadaga Valley CSD, 569
Castagna Realty, 405
Catapult Learning, 401
Caterpillar, Inc., 425
Cathedral Church of St John the Devine (The), 475
Cathedral of the Immaculate Conception Restoration Committee, 437
Catholic Charities of Onondaga County, 256
Catholic Citizens Committee PAC, 480
Catholic Community Relations Council of New York, Inc., 394
Catholic Conference (NYS), 385
Catholic Conference Policy Group Inc, 475
Catholic Conference Policy Group, Inc., 386, 437
Catholic Family Center, 452
Catholic Health Services of Long Island, 390
Catholic Health System, 437, 471
Catholic School Administrators Association of NYS, 126
Catholic War Veterans of the United States of America, 298
Cato-Meridian CSD, 569
Catskill CSD, 576
Catskill Center for Conservation & Development, The, 156
Catskill Center for Conservation and Development, Inc., 395
Catskill Off-Track Betting Corporation, 96, 273, 306, 409, 418
Catskill Regional Off-Track Betting Corporation, 390
Cattaraugus County, 51, 326
Supreme & Family Court, 51
Supreme, County & Surrogate's Courts, 51
Cattaraugus Empire Zone Corporation, 503
Cattaraugus-Allegany-Erie-Wyoming BOCES, 600
Cattaraugus-Little Valley CSD, 568
Cayuga Community College, 547
Cayuga County, 51, 326
Family Court, 51
Cayuga County Chamber of Commerce, 503
Cayuga Nation of New York, 166
Cayuga-Onondaga BOCES, 600
Cazenovia Area Chamber of Commerce (Greater Cazenovia Area), 503
Cazenovia CSD, 578
Cazenovia College, 553
Cement League, 407
Cemetery Employer Assn of Greater NY, 452
Cendant Car Rental Group Inc, 453
Center Against Domestic Violence, 418
Center Moriches UFSD, 591
Center for Alternative Sentencing & Employment Services (CASES), 116
Center for Anti-Violence Education Inc, 256
Center for Charter School Excellence (NYC), 395
Center for Children's Initiatives, Inc., 395
Center for Constitutional Rights, 197, 395
Center for Constitutional Rights (501C3 Organization With 501H Election), 395
Center for Court Innovation, 215
Center for Disability Rights, Inc., 395
Center for Disability Services, 256, 475
Center for Discovery, 390
Center for Economic Growth Inc, 91
Center for Educational Innovation - Public Education Association, 126
Center for Educational Innovation - Public Education Association (CEI-PEA), 405
Center for Environmental Information Inc, 156
Center for Family & Youth (The), 256
Center for Governmental Research Inc (CGR), 169
Center for Hearing and Communication, 182
Center for Independence of the Disabled in NY (CIDNY), 197, 256
Center for Judicial Accountability Inc (CJA), 215
Center for Law & Justice, 117, 215
Center for Liver Transplantation, 395
Center for Migration Studies of New York Inc, 197
Center for Policy Research, 261
Center for Technology in Government, University at Albany, SUNY, 169
Center for Urban Community Services, 256
Center for an Urban Future, 191, 225
Centerlight Health Systems, 413, 443
Centers for Specialty Care Group, 425
Centerstate Corporation for Economic Opportunity, 395
Central Adirondack Association, 503
Central Boiler Inc, 475
Central Brooklyn Independent Democrats, 480
Central Catskills Chamber of Commerce, 503
Central Hudson Gas & Electric Corporation, 143
Central Hudson Gas & Electric Corporation (FKA Glusko, John), 395
Central Islip UFSD, 592
Central Labor Council (NYC), 395, 453
Central Life Sciences (Fleishman-Hillard, Inc.), 405
Central Mutual Fire Insurance Co. (NY), 385
Central NY Railroad, 452
Central New York Business Journal, 532
Central New York Regional Market Authority, 86, 96, 306
Central New York Regional Transportation Authority, 96, 285, 306
Central New York School Boards Association, 395
Central Park Boathouse LLC, 456
Central Pine Barrens Joint Planning & Policy Commission, 96, 150, 306
Central Square CSD, 586
Central United Talmudical Academy, 392
Century Foundation (The), 138
Cephalon Inc, 452
Cerebral Palsy Associations of New York State, 126, 182, 231, 256
Certification Board for Nutrition Specialists, 421
Ceruzzi Holdings, 478
Cetrino, Thomas, 395
Chadwick, Cindy, 396
Chamber Alliance of New York State, 393
Chamber Players International, 415
Chamber of Commerce of the Tonawandas, 503
Champion Learning Center LLC, 437
Champlain Valley Educational Svcs (Clinton-Essex-Warren-Washington), 600
Changaris, Steve, 396
Chappaqua CSD, 597
Charles T. Sitrin Network of Homes & Services, Inc., 390
Charleston Equities LLC, 460
Charlotte Valley CSD, 572
Charlton Soho LLC, 432
Charter School Association, 433
Chase Paymentech Solutions, LLC, 396
Chateaugay CSD, 575
Chatham CSD, 571
Chaumont-Three Mile Bay Chamber of Commerce, 503
Chautauqua County, 51, 326
Family Court, 51
Supreme & County Courts, 51
Surrogate Court, 51
Chautauqua County Chamber of Commerce, 503
Chautauqua County Chamber of Commerce, Dunkirk Branch, 503
Chautauqua County Industrial Development Agency, 503

Chautauqua Lake CSD, 569
Chazy Central RSD, 571
Cheektowaga CSD, 573
Cheektowaga Chamber of Commerce, 503
Cheektowaga, Town of, 343
Cheektowaga-Maryvale CSD, 574
Cheektowaga-Sloan UFSD, 573
Chemical Alliance (NYS), 413
Chemung County, 52, 326
Family Court, 52
Supreme & County Courts, 52
Surrogate Court, 52
Chemung County Chamber of Commerce, 503
Chemung County Industrial Development Agency, 503
Chenango County, 52, 327
Supreme, County, Family & Surrogate's Courts, 52
Chenango County Chamber of Commerce, 503
Chenango Forks CSD, 568
Chenango Valley CSD, 568
Cherry Valley-Springfield CSD, 586
Chesapeake Appalachia LLC, 474
Chesapeake Appalachia, LLC, 396
Chester UFSD, 585
Chesterton, Jan Marie, 396
Chetrit Group (The), 401
Chief Executives Network for Manufacturing, 440
Child Center of New York, 407
Child Resource Center, Inc., 421
Children & Families, 20, 36
Committee Staff, 36
Key Assembly Staff Assignments, 36
Membership, 20, 36
Majority, 20, 36
Minority, 20, 36
Children & Family Services, Office of, 5, 119, 251, 303
Administration, Division of, 251
Financial Management, Office of, 251
Adoption Services, 251
Adult Protective Services, 251
Bureau of Policy, Research & Planning
Bureau of Interagency Coordination & Case Resolution, 252
Bureau of Policy, Research & Planning, 252
Child Welfare and Community Services, Division of (CWCS), 251
Commission for the Blind & Visually Handicapped (CBVH), 251
Communications, Office of, 251
Community Partnerships, Office of, 251
Council on Children & Families, 5, 303
Council on Children & Families (CCF), 252
Facility Management, Office of, 251
Information Technology, Division of, 251
Juvenile Justice & Opportunities for Youth, Division of (DJJOY), 251
Legal Affairs, Division of, 251
Native American Services, 251, 252
Regional Operations, 119
Special Investigations Unit, 251
Special Populations, Office of
Child Care Services, Division of (DCCS), 251
Prevention, Permanency & Program Support, Office of, 251
Special Populations, Office of, 251
State Central Registry, 251
Strategic Planning & Policy Development, Office of, 251
Youth Development, Office of, 252
Children's Aid Society (The), 257, 396, 425
Children's Day Treatment Coalition, 421
Children's Health Fund, 378
Children's Health Fund (The), 396
Children's Hospital of Philadelphia, 443
Children's Institute, 409, 475
Children's Rights Inc, 197, 257
Children's Village (The), 231, 257
Chili, Town of, 343
Chin, Francis Y., 396
Chinese-American Planning Council, Inc., 428
Chiropractic Assn Inc (NYS), 423
Chittenango CSD, 578
Choice Self Insurance Trust, 466
Christ the King Seminary, 553
Christie's, 421
Christie's Education Inc, 564
Christmas Tree Farmers Association of New York Inc, 73
Chrsitian Science Committee on Publication for NY, 422
Chubb & Son (Division of Federal Insurance Co), 454
Chubb & Son, a Division of Federal Insurance Company, 452
Church Avenue Merchants Block Association Inc, 453
Churchville-Chili CSD, 578
Cicero, Town of, 343
Cigar Association of America, Inc., 402
Cigna Companies, 425
Cincinnatus CSD, 571
Circle Entertainment, Inc., 392
Circulo De La Hispanidad, 472
Citi Group Global Markets, Inc., 396
CitiBank, N.A., 415
CitiGroup Management Corp., 396
Cities, 20, 36
Committee Staff, 20, 36
Key Assembly Staff Assignments, 36
Key Senate Staff Assignments, 21
Membership, 21, 36
Majority, 21, 36
Minority, 21, 36
Citigroup Inc, 80
Citizen (The), 523
Citizen Action of New York, 138
Citizen Schools, Inc., 401
Citizens Budget Commission, 237, 268
Citizens Campaign for the Environment, 397
Citizens Committee for Children of NY, Inc., 438
Citizens Committee for New York City, 397
Citizens For Sports & Arts, Inc., 480
Citizens Housing & Planning Council of New York, 191
Citizens Union of the City of New York, 170, 238, 404
Citizens' Committee for Children of New York Inc, 197, 257, 397
Citizens' Environmental Coalition, 156
City College of New York, The, 551
City Harvest, 397
City Journal (Manhattan Institute for Policy Research), 532
City Meals-On-Wheels, 431
City University Construction Fund, 97, 123, 306
City University of New York, 478
City University of New York (CUNY), 397
City Works Foundation, (The), 444
City of Buffalo, 437
City of Lackawanna, 387
City of Mount Vernon, 468
City of Syracuse Industrial Development Agency, 475
City of Yonkers, 437
Civil Court, NYC, 48
Bronx County, 48
Housing Court Judges, 49
Kings County, 48
New York County, 49
Queens County, 49
Richmond County, 49
Civil Liberties Union (NY), 454
Civil Service & Pensions, 21
Committee Staff, 21
Key Senate Staff Assignments, 21
Membership, 21
Majority, 21
Minority, 21
Civil Service Department, 5, 194, 234, 240, 303
Civil Service Commission, 5, 234, 240
Classification & Compensation Division, 194
Divisions, 234, 240
Classification & Compensation Division, 234, 240
Commission Operations & Municipal Assistance Division, 234, 240
Employee Benefits Division, 234, 240
Employee Health Services Division, 234, 240

Information Resource Management, 234, 240
Staffing Services Division, 234, 240
Testing Services Division, 234, 240
Civil Service Employees Assn of NY (CSEA), Local 1000, AFSCME, AFL-CIO, 243
Civil Service Employees Assn, Inc, 398
Civil Service Employees Political Action Fund, 470, 480
Civil Service Employees Union (CSEA), Local 1000, AFSCME, AFL-CIO, 225
Civil Svc Technical Guild, Local 375 DC-37, AFSCME AFL-CIO, 470
Clarence Building Materials and Supplies/Ray-Gar Construction, 441
Clarence CSD, 573
Clarence Chamber of Commerce, 504
Clarence Industrial Development Agency (Town of), 504
Clarence, Town of, 343
Clarity Imaging Technologies, Inc., 393
Clark Patterson Lee, 387
Clarkson University, 398, 553
Clarkson University (FKA Wood Jr., Robert H.), 398
Clarkstown CSD, 588
Clarkstown, Town of, 343
Clay, Town of, 344
Clayton Chamber of Commerce, 504
Clean and Healthy New York, Inc., 398
Clear Channel Outdoor, 401
Clearing House Association, LLC (The), 390
Clearing House Payments Company L.L.C., 398
Cleary, Kevin Government Relations, LLC, 398
Cleveland Hill UFSD, 573
Client:, 419
Cliff Stanton For Council, 480
Clifton Park, Town of, 344
Clifton Springs Area Chamber of Commerce, 504
Clifton Stanley Diaz For NYC Council, 480
Clifton-Fine CSD, 590
Climate Action PAC, 480
Clinical Laboratory Assn Inc (NYS), 423
Clinton CSD, 583
Clinton Chamber of Commerce Inc, 504
Clinton Community College, 547
Clinton County, 52, 327
Supreme, County, Family & Surrogate's Courts, 52
Clinton County, The Development Corporation, 504
Clorox Company (The), 393
Clyde Chamber of Commerce, 504
Clyde Industrial Development Corporation, 504
Clyde-Savannah CSD, 597
Clymer CSD, 569
Coach Farm Enterprises, Inc., 392
Coach USA Northeast, Inc., 401
Coalition Against Domestic Violence (NYS), 398
Coalition Against Domestic Violence, NYS, 117, 257
Coalition Against Hunger (NYC), 398
Coalition Against Sexual Assault (NYS), 117, 398
Coalition for Asian American Children & Families, 257
Coalition for Auto Repair Equality (CARE), 398
Coalition for Children With Special Needs, 421
Coalition for Children's Mental Health Services (NYS), 399
Coalition for Economic Justice, 399
Coalition for Education Reform & Accountability, 399
Coalition for Medically Fragile Children, 439
Coalition for Mold Reform (State Farm Insurance Cos), 454
Coalition for Opportunity in Education, Inc., 407, 433
Coalition for Quality Assisted Living, Inc., 421
Coalition for the Homeless, 257, 399, 438, 445
Coalition for the Homeless, Inc., 437
Coalition for the Last Store on Main Street, 399
Coalition of 853 Schools, Inc., 425
Coalition of Animal Care Societies (The), 257
Coalition of Behavioral Health Agencies, Inc (The), 231
Coalition of Behavioral Health Agencies, Inc., 438, 477
Coalition of Community Development Financial Institutions, 421
Coalition of Fathers & Families NY, 182, 257
Coalition of Fathers & Families NY, PAC, 170, 215
Coalition of Ignition Interlock Manufacturers, 421
Coalition of Institutionalized Aged and Disabled (FKA Lieberman, Geoff), 399
Coalition of Living Museums, 278
Coalition of NYS Career Schools, 478
Coalition of Neighborhood Centers, 412
Coalition of New York State Alzheimer's Association Chapters, 438
Coalition of New York State Career Schools (The), 126
Coalition of Prepaid Health Svcs Plans (NYS), 439
Coalition of Special Acts School Districts, 425
Coalition of Specialty Care Physicians, 386
Coalition of Voluntary Safety Net Hospitals (NYS), 439
Coastal Communications Services Inc, 453
Coastal Distribution, LLC, 404
Cobb Jr, James H, 399
Cobleskill-Richmondville CSD, 589
Coca-Cola Refershments USA, Inc., 399
Coca-Cola Refreshments USA, Inc., 399, 437
Cochran School of Nursing, 553
Codes, 21, 36
Committee Staff, 21, 36
Key Assembly Staff Assignments, 36
Key Senate Staff Assignments, 21
Membership, 21, 36
Majority, 21, 36
Minority, 21, 36
Coffin, Brian M., 399
Cohen For Council, 480
Cohoes, 62
Civil, Criminal & Traffic Courts, 62
Cohoes City SD, 567
Cohoes Industrial Development Agency (City of), 504
Cold Spring Harbor CSD, 592
Cold Spring Harbor Fish Hatchery & Aquarium, 278
Cold Spring Harbor Laboratory, 423
Colgate Rochester Crozer Divinity School, 554
Colgate University, 388, 554
Colgate University, Department of Geology, 156
Colgate-Palmolive Company, 384
Collectors Association, Inc. (NYS), 388
College Board, 475
College Board (The), 401
College Community Services, Inc (DBA Brooklyn Center for the Performing Arts), 478
College at Brockport, 545
College of Agriculture & Life Sciences at Cornell University, 544
College of Human Ecology at Cornell University, 544
College of Mount Saint Vincent, 554
College of New Rochelle (The), 554
College of Saint Rose (The), 554
College of Staten Island, 551
College of Veterinary Medicine at Cornell University, 544
College of Westchester (The), 564
Coller Capital Limited and it's Affiliate Coller Capital, Inc., 400
Coller Capital, Inc., 400
Colonie Chamber of Commerce, 504
Colonie, Town of, 344
Colony Liquor & Wine Distributors, LLC, 456
Colt Refining and Recycling, 393

Colton-Pierrepont CSD, 590
Columbia County, 52, 327
Supreme, County, Family & Surrogate's Courts, 52
Columbia County Chamber of Commerce, 504
Columbia Development Companies, 437
Columbia Hudson Partnership, 504
Columbia Law School, Legislative Drafting Research Fund, 138, 238
Columbia University, 554
Columbia University, Exec Graduate Pgm in Public Policy & Administration, 170
Columbia University, MPA in Environmental Science & Policy, 156
Columbia University, Mailman School of Public Health, 182, 198
Columbia University, School of the Arts, 278
Columbia University, Technology Ventures, 91
Columbia-Greene Community College, 547
Columbian Mutual Life Insurance Comapny, 406
Columbian Mutual Life Insurance Company, 400
Columbus Square Management LLC, 432
Colwell Colwell & Petroccione, LLP (FKA Colwell Ferrentino & Petroccione, LLP), 400
Combined Coordinating Council Inc, 475
Commack UFSD, 592
Commerce, Economic Development & Small Business, 21
Committee Staff, 21
Key Senate Staff Assignments, 21
Membership, 21
Majority, 21
Minority, 21
Commerce, Science & Transportation, 313
Subcommittees, 313
Aviation Operations, Safety & Security, 313
Communications, Technology, & the Internet, 313
Consumer Protection, Product Safety, & Insurance, 313
Oceans, Atmosphere, Fisheries and Coast Guard, 314
Science and Space, 314
Surface Transportation & Merchant Marine Infrastructure, Safety & Security, 314
Commission on Economic Opportunity for the Greater Capital Region, 257
Commission on Independent Colleges & Universities, 126
Commission on Independent Colleges & Universities (CICU), 381, 402
Commissioned Officers Assn of the US Public Health Svc Inc (COA), 182, 298
Committe to Elect Ceceilia Berkowitz for Mayor, 480
Committee For Effective Leadership, 480
Committee for Hispanic Children & Families, 453
Committee for Occupational Safety & Health (NY), 444
Committee for Taxi Safety, 387
Committee for Workers' Compensation Reform, 444
Committee of Methadone Program Administrators Inc of NYS (COMPA), 182, 231
Committee to Elect Abiodun Bello, 480
Committee to Elect Andy King, 480
Committee to Elect Ariel Guerrero, 480
Committee to Elect Charles A. Bilal 2010, 480
Committee to Elect Christopher Banks, 480
Committee to Elect Eric Adams, 480
Committee to Elect Philip Marks For Mayor, 480
Committee to Elect Robert E. Cornegy Jr., 480
Committee to Elect Robert M. Waterman, 480
Committee to Elect Stephen S. Jones to City Council, 481
Committee to Re-Elect Lawrence A. Warden, 481
Committee to Re-Elect Mathieu Eugene, 481
Committee to Re-Elect Nydia M. Velazquez to Congress, 481
Committee to Save St Brigid's, 465
Commodity Futures Trading Commission, 70, 87
Eastern Region, 70, 88
Common Cause/NY, 138, 170
Commonwealth Fund, 182
Communication Workers of America Local 1180, 378, 453
Communication Workers of America, Local 1182, 453
Communications Workers of America Local 1180, 481
Communications Workers of America, District 1, 225, 441
Communities United for Police Reform, 450
Community & Economic Development, 77
Community & Regional Development Institute (CaRDI), 73
Community Bancorp, Inc., 405
Community Bank (NY), 453
Community Bank N.A., 80
Community Bankers Assn of NY State, Accounting & Taxation Cmte, 268
Community Bankers Assn of NY State, Mortgages & Real Estate Cmte, 248
Community Campaign For Naaimat, 481
Community Financial Services Association of America, 453
Community First Party, 416
Community For Lynn Nunes, 481
Community Health Care Assoc of NYS, 439
Community Health Care Association of NYS, 182
Community Health Care Association of New York State, 390, 400
Community Health Project, Inc., 387
Community Healthcare Network, 182, 257
Community Hospital Network of NY Eductl & Rsch Fund Inc, 475
Community Housing Improvement Program (CHIP), 191
Community Housing Improvement Program, Inc. (CHIP), 400
Community Mental Health Political Action Committee, Inc., 481
Community Preservation Corporation (The), 191, 400, 436
Community Research Initiative on AIDS, Inc., 400
Community Service Society, 433
Community Service Society of NY, 475
Community Service Society of New York, 191
Community Works, 408
CompPharma LLC, 402
Compliance Technologies Corporation, Inc., 421
Comprehensive Health Management, Inc. (FKA Wellcare Health Plans, Inc.), 400
Computer Aid, Inc., 390, 460, 473
Computer Associates, 456
Computer Sciences Corporation, 425
Computers for Youth, 392
Comrie For NYC, 481
Concentra Health Services, Inc., 424
Concepts of Independent Choices, 439
Concerned Home Care Providers, 453
Concerned Physicians for Long Island College Hospital, Inc., 382
Concordia College, 554
Condon, Joseph M., 400
Coney Island Chamber of Commerce, 504
Coney Island Holdings LLC, 405
Conference Board (The), 91
Conference of Big 5 School Districts, 126, 382
Conference of Local Mental Hygiene Directors (NYS), 400
Conference of Mayors & Municipal Officials (NYS), 400
Congregation of Yeshiva Machzikei Hadas, 438
Connect, Inc., 477
ConnectEdu, Inc., 437
Connelly Communications, Inc., 400
Connelly McLaughlin & Woloz, 401
Connetquot CSD, 592
Connors & Connors, PC, 215
Connors & Corcoran LLP, 215

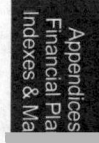

Connors & Corcoran PLLC, 203
Connors LLP, 170
Conpor Conference of Private Organizations (NYS), 422
Conrad Tillard For Council, 481
Conservation Service Group, 444
Conservative Party Campaign Committee, 481
Conservative Party of NYS, 138
Consolidated Edison Co of NY Inc, 475
Consolidated Edison Company of NY, Inc., 425
Consolidated Edison Company of New York, Inc., 401, 405
Consolidated Edison Energy, 143
Consolidated Edison, Inc. Employees' Political Action Committee, 481
Consortium for Worker Education, 401, 402
Consortium for Workers Education, 444
Constantinople & Vallone Consulting LLC (FKA Constantinople Consulting), 401
Constellation Energy, 143
Construction Contractors Association of the Hudson Valley Inc, 91
Construction Industry Cncl of Westchester & Hudson Valley Inc, 454
Construction Industry Council of Westchester & Hudson Valley, Inc., 414
Consumer Affairs & Protection, 36
Committee Staff, 36
Key Assembly Staff Assignments, 36
Membership, 36
Majority, 36
Minority, 36
Consumer Data Industry Association, 424
Consumer Directed Personal Assistance Association of NYS, 398
Consumer Electronics Association, 425
Consumer Healthcare Products Assn, 393
Consumer Power Advocates, 437
Consumer Product Safety Commission, 88
Eastern Regional Center, 88
Consumer Protection, 21
Committee Staff, 21
Key Senate Staff Assignments, 21
Membership, 21
Majority, 21
Minority, 21
Consumer Protection, Division of, 6, 83, 140, 303
Consumers Union, 73, 91
Consumers Union of US, Inc., 402
Contemporary Services Corporation, 425
Conti of New York LLC, 456
Continuing Care Leadership Coalition, 387
Convention Centers & Visitors Bureaus, 274
Albany County Convention & Visitors Bureau, 274
Buffalo Niagara Convention & Visitors Bureau, 274
Chautauqua County Visitors Bureau, 274
Greater Binghamton New York Convention and Visitors Bureau, 274
Greater Rochester Visitors Association, 274
Ithaca/Tompkins County Convention & Visitors Bureau, 274
Lake Placid/Essex County Convention & Visitors Bureau, 274
Long Island Convention & Visitors Bureau & Sports Commission, 274
NYC & Company/Convention & Visitors Bureau, 275
Oneida County Convention & Visitors Bureau, 275
Ontario County/Finger Lakes Visitors Connection, 275
Saratoga Convention & Tourism Bureau, 275
Steuben County Conference & Visitors Bureau, 275
Sullivan County Visitors Association, 275
Syracuse Convention & Vistors Bureau, 275
Tourism Bureau of the Thousand Islands Region, 275
Westchester County Tourism & Film, 275
Cookfair Media Inc, 138
Cool Culture, Inc., 477
Cooper Union for Advancement of Science and Art (The), 431
Cooper Union for the Advancement of Science & Art, 554
Cooper and 6th Property LLC, 382
Cooperstown CSD, 586
Cooperstown Chamber of Commerce, 504
Copenhagen CSD, 577
Copiague Chamber of Commerce, 504
Copiague UFSD, 592
Coppola, John, 402
Cordo & Company, LLC, 402
Corinth CSD, 588
Corinth Industrial Development Agency (Town of), 504
Corizon Health, Inc., 387
Corlett, John A (FKA Marta Genovese), 402
Cornell Cooperative Extension, Agriculture & Food Systems Program, 74
Cornell Cooperative Extension, College of Human Ecology, Nutrition, Food Safety & Security, 182
Cornell Cooperative Extension, College of Human Ecology, Nutrition, Health, 257
Cornell Cooperative Extension, Community & Economic Vitality Program, 191
Cornell Cooperative Extension, Environment & Natural Resources Initiative, 156
Cornell Cooperative Extension, Pesticide Management Education Program, 73
Cornell Law School, Legal Information Institute, 215
Cornell University, 126, 416, 431, 554
Cornell University Atkinson Center for a Sustainable Future, 156
Cornell University, Department of Applied Economics & Management, 74
Cornell University, Economics Department, 80, 91
Cornell University, FarmNet Program, 74
Cornell University, Institute on Conflict Resolution, 225
Cornell University, PRO-DAIRY Program, 74
Cornell University, Rural Schools Association of NYS, 126
Cornell University, Sch of Industr & Labor Relations Institute for Workplace Studies, 225
Cornell University, School of Industrial & Labor Relations, 126, 198, 225, 243
Corning, 62
Civil & Criminal Courts, 62
Corning Area Chamber of Commerce, 504
Corning Community College, 547
Corning Incorporated, 469
Corning Leader (The), 524
Corning Place Consulting, LLC, 402
Corning-Painted Post Area SD, 591
Cornwall CSD, 585
Corporation for National & Community Service, 254
New York Program Office, 254
Corporation for Supportive Housing, 439
Corporations, Authorities & Commissions, 21, 36
Committee Staff, 21, 37
Key Assembly Staff Assignments, 37
Key Senate Staff Assignments, 21
Membership, 21, 37
Majority, 21, 37
Minority, 21, 37
Correct Captain's Association, Dept. of Corrections, City of New York, 414
Correction, 37
Committee Staff, 37
Key Assembly Staff Assignments, 37
Membership, 37
Majority, 37
Minority, 37
Correction Captains Association - PAC, 481
Correction Officers & Police Benevolent Assn Inc, 453
Correction Officers Benevolent Association, 481
Correction Officers' Benevolent Association, City of New York, Inc., 430
Correctional Association of New York, 117
Correctional Officers & Police Benevolent Association, Inc. (NYS) (FKA Leo, Christopher), 403
Correctional Officers and Police Benevolent Association, Inc. (NYS), 387

Corrections & Community Supervision Department, 6, 108, 303
Adirondack Correctional Facility, 108
Administrative Services, 108
Budget & Finance Division, 108
Diversity Management, 108
Human Resources Management Division, 108
Inmate Grievance, 108
Internal Controls, 108
Training Academy, 108
Albion Correctional Facility, 108
Altona Correctional Facility, 108
Attica Correctional Facility, 108
Auburn Correctional Facility, 108
Bare Hill Correctional Facility, 108
Bayview Correctional Facility, 108
Beacon Correctional Facility, 108
Bedford Hills Correctional Facility, 109
Butler Correctional Facility, 109
Cape Vincent Correctional Facility, 109
Cayuga Correctional Facility, 109
Chateaugay Correctional Facility, 109
Clinton Correctional Facility, 109
Collins Correctional Facility, 109
Correctional Facility Operations, 108
Correctional Industries Division, 108
Facilities, 108
Security Staffing Unit, 110
Special Operations, 110
Coxsackie Correctional Facility, 109
Downstate Correctional Facility, 109
Eastern NY Correctional Facility, 109
Edgecombe Correctional Facility, 109
Elmira Correctional Facility, 109
Fishkill Correctional Facility, 109
Five Points Correctional Facility, 109
Franklin Correctional Facility, 109
Gouverneur Correctional Facility, 109
Gowanda Correctional Facility, 109
Great Meadow Correctional Facility, 109
Green Haven Correctional Facility, 109
Greene Correctional Facility, 109
Groveland Correctional Facility, 109
Hale Creek ASACTC, 109
Health Services Division, 110
Correctional Health Services, 110
Dental Services, 110
Mental Health, 110
Hudson Correctional Facility, 109
Lakeview Shock Incarceration Correctional Facility, 109
Lincoln Correctional Facility, 109
Livingston Correctional Facility, 109
Marcy Correctional Facility, 109
Mid-State Correctional Facility, 109
Mohawk Correctional Facility, 109
Monterey Shock Incarceration Correctional Facility, 109
Moriah Shock Incarceration Correctional Facility, 109
Mt McGregor Correctional Facility, 109
Ogdensburg Correctional Facility, 109
Orleans Correctional Facility, 109
Otisville Correctional Facility, 109
Population Management, 110
Management Information Services, 110
Program Planning, Research & Evaluation, 110
Program Services, 110
Education, 110
Guidance & Counseling, 110
Library Services, 110
Ministerial, Family & Volunteer Services, 110
Substance Abuse Treatment Services, 110
Queensboro Correctional Facility, 110
Riverview Correctional Facility, 110
Rochester Correctional Facility, 110
Shawangunk Correctional Facility, 110
Sing Sing Correctional Facility, 110
Southport Correctional Facility, 110
Sullivan Correctional Facility, 110
Support Operations, 108
Taconic Correctional Facility, 110
Ulster Correctional Facility, 110
Upstate Correctional Facility, 110
Wallkill Correctional Facility, 110
Washington Correctional Facility, 110
Watertown Correctional Facility, 110
Wende Correctional Facility, 110
Willard Drug Treatment Center, 110
Woodbourne Correctional Facility, 110
Wyoming Correctional Facility, 110
Correy For Council, 481
Cortland, 62
Civil & Criminal Courts, 62
Cortland County, 52, 327
Supreme, County, Family & Surrogate's Courts, 52
Cortland County Chamber of Commerce, 504
Cortland Enlarged City SD, 571
Cortland Regional Medical Center (FKA Cortland Memorial Hospital), 475
Cortland Standard, 525
Cortland Standard Printing Co Inc, 525
Cortlandt, Town of, 344
Couch White, LLP, 403
Council Management Inc, 453
Council for Community Behavioral Healthcare, 403
Council for Unity, 444
Council for the Humanities, 403
Council for the Humanities (NY), 402
Council of Administrators & Supervisors, 470
Council of Community Services of NYS Inc, 257
Council of Family & Child Caring Agencies, 257
Council of Industry of Southeastern NY, 439
Council of Insurance Brokers of Greater NY, Inc, 413
Council of New York Cooperatives, 475
Council of Nonprofits, Inc., 403
Council of Professional Geologists NYS, 422
Council of School Supervisors & Administrators, 126, 405, 436
Council of School Supervisors and Administrators, Local 1 AFSA, 481
Council of Senior Centers & Services of NYC, Inc., 403
Council of Senior Centers and Services, 393
Council of Senior Ctrs & Services of NYC Inc, 436
Council of Sheet Metal Workers Int'l Assn (NYS), 404
Council of State Governments, Eastern Conference, 170, 238, 268
Council of the City of New York (The), 403
Council on the Arts, 6, 270, 303
Administrative Services, 270
Fiscal Management, 270
Information Technology, 270
Program Staff, 270
Architecture & Design/Facilities/Museum, 270
Arts Education/Literature, 270
Dance/Theatre/Individual Artists, 270
Electronic Media & Film/Visual Arts, 270
Folk Arts/Music, 270
Special Arts Services/Regional Economic Development, 270
Council on the Environment of NYC, Environmental Education, 126
County Highway Superintendents Assn (NYS) (Association of Counties (NYS)), 417
County Medical Society (New York), 403
County Medical Society New York (FKA Malone, Cheryl), 403
County Nursing Facilities of New York Inc, 182
County of Niagara, 441
County of Suffolk Department of Economic Development and Planning, 386
Court Appointed Special Advocates, 438
Court Clerks Assn (NYS), 435
Court Officers Assn (NYS), 442
Court Officers Benevolent Association of Nassau County, Inc., 428
Court Reporters Association, Inc. (NYS), 405
Court of Appeals, 45
Associate Judges, 45
Court of Claims, 48, 215
Courtroom Television Network, 452
Covanta Energy Corp, 436, 453
Covanta Energy Corporation, 403
Covenant House NY, 445

Coventry, 385
Coxsackie Area Chamber of Commerce, 504
Coxsackie-Athens CSD, 576
Cozen O'Connor (FKA Wolfblock LLP), 403
Cozen O'Connor Empire State PAC, 481
Craig Caruana 2013, 481
Crain's New York Business, 532
Crane & Parente, PLLC, 143, 170
Creative Coalition (The), 452
Creative Mobile Technology, 401
Credit Union Association, 433
Credit Union Association of New York, 421
Creditors Bar Association, 405
Crenulated Company LTD DBA New Settlement Apartmens (The), 477
Creosote Council III, 475
Crime Victims, Crime & Correction, 21
Committee Staff, 22
Key Senate Staff Assignments, 22
Membership, 22
Majority, 22
Minority, 22
Criminal Court, NYC, 49
Bronx County, 49
Kings County, 49
New York County, 49
Queens County, 49
Richmond County, 49
Criminal Justice Services, Division of, 6, 111, 206, 234, 303
Administration Office, 111
Administrative Services, 111
Human Resources Management, 111
State Finance & Budget, 111
Advisory Groups, 111
Juvenile Justice Advisory Group, 111
NYS Motor Vehicle & Insurance Fraud Prevention Board, 111
Commission on Forensic Science, 111, 206
Office of Forensic Services, 111, 206
Funding & Program Development Office
Funding & Program Development Office, 206, 235
Highway Safety & Technology Unit
Highway Safety & Technology Unit, 206
Human Resources Management
Human Resources Management, 206, 235
State Finance & Budget, 206, 235
Legal Services, 111, 206, 235
Missing & Exploited Children Clearinghouse, 111
Office of Criminal Justice Operations, 111, 206, 235
Office of Operations, 111
Office of Forensic Services, 235
Office of Justice Information Services, 111
Information Technology Development Group, 111
Information Technology Services Group, 111
Office of Sex Offender Management, 111
Office of Justice Information Systems, 206, 235
Information Technology Development Group, 206
Information Technology Services Group, 206
Office of Sex Offender Registry, 206
Office of Justice Research & Performance, 206
Office of Justice Statistics & Performance, 111
Office of Public Safety, 111, 206, 235
Law Enforcement Accreditation Council, 111
Law Enforcement Accreditation Program, 206, 235
Missing Persons Clearinghouse, 206
Municipal Police Training Council, 111
Police & Peace Officer Registry & Training, 206
Security Guard Program, 206
State Committee for Coordination of Police Services for Elderly (TRIAD), 111
Statewide Law Enforcement Telecommunications Committee, 111
Office of Strategic Planning, 111
Funding & Program Assistance Office, 111
Justice Systems Analysis Unit, 111
Operation IMPACT Coordinator, 111, 206
Crisis Program (The), 404, 452
Croplife America, 378
Crosier, Barbara V, 404
Cross Harbor Railroad (NY), 452
Crossbow Coalition,Inc., 393
Crossroads Ventures, LLC, 382
Croton-Harmon UFSD, 597
Crouse Hospital, 475
Crouse Hospital School of Nursing, 554
Crowley For Congress, 481
Crown Point CSD, 574
Crystal Window & Door Systems, Ltd, 453
Cuba-Rushford CSD, 567
Cubic Transportation Systems, Inc., 431
Culinary Institute of America, 278, 554
Cullen & Dykman LLP, 225, 238
Cultural Affairs, Tourism, Parks & Recreation, 22
Committee Staff, 22
Key Senate Staff Assignments, 22
Membership, 22
Majority, 22
Minority, 22
Cultural Institutions Group, 477
Cumberland Packing Corporation, 452
Curran, Brian F, 404
Custom Crews, Inc., 393
Cutchogue-New Suffolk Chamber of Commerce, 504
Cuyler News Service, 532
Cynthia For Change, 481
Cypress Equities, 478
D & M P.A.C. LLC, 481
D H Ferguson, Attorney, PLLC, 247
D&D Power, Inc., 405
DC 37 Local 299, 481
DC 37 Political Action Committee, 481
DCI Group AZ, LLC (FKA DCI Group, LLC), 405
DDC Advocacy, 406
DKI Engineering & Consulting USA, PC, Corporate World Headquarters, 291
DLA Piper New York Political Action Committee, 482
DMJM & Harris Inc, 462
DTZ/Cushman & Wakefield, 247
Dack Consulting Services, Inc., 405
Dadey, Dick (FKA Citizens Union of the City of New York), 404
Daemen College, 554
Dagnello, Vito, 404
Daiichi Sankyo, Inc., 404, 421
Daily Courier-Observer, 527
Daily Freeman, 526
Daily Gazette (The), 530
Daily Gazette Co, 530
Daily Mail (The), 524
Daily Messenger (The), 524
Daily Record (The), 529
Daily Sentinel, 530
Daily Star (The), 529
Daimler Chrysler Corporation, 463
Dairy Farmers of America Northeast, 74
Dairylea Cooperative, Inc., 404
Dale Carnegie & Associates Inc, 91
Dalton-Nunda CSD (Keshequa), 578
Dan Klores Communications, Inc. DBA DKC Government Affairs, 405
Danaher Controls Inc, 453
Dansville CSD, 577
Dansville Chamber of Commerce, 505
Darden Restaurants, Inc., 387
Darien Lake Theme Park Resort, 278
Dart Container Corporation, 443
Darwak, Stephanie, 405
Data Industries, 456
David B Kriser Dental Center of NY University, 475
David Kayode 2013, 481
Davidoff, Hutcher & Citron LLP, 405
Davis 2013, 481
Davis College, 555
Davis Polk & Wardwell, 91
Davita Inc., 417

Daw Systems, Inc., 393
Day Pitney LLP, 215, 268
Daytop Village, Inc., 391
De Ruyter CSD, 578
DeGraff, Foy & Kunz, LLP, 170
DeGraff, Foy, & Kunz, LLP, 203
DePaul, 390
DeVry Incorporated, 475
DeVry Institute of Technology, College of New York, 564
DeWitt, Town of, 344
Debevoise & Plimpton LLP, 117, 215, 406
Deepwater Wind,LLC, 391
Deer & Elk Farmers Association, 474
Deer Park UFSD, 592
Defenders Association, 438
Defenders Association (NYS), 438
Defenders Justice Fund, NYS, 406
Defoyd, Katherine, 406
Delaware County, 52, 328
Supreme, County, Family & Surrogate's Courts, 52
Delaware County Chamber of Commerce, 505
Delaware County Planning Department, 505
Delaware Engineering, 455, 456
Delaware North Companies Gaming & Entertainment Inc, 442
Delaware North Companies, Inc, 404
Delaware River Basin Commission, 97, 150, 307
Delaware-Chenango-Madison-Otsego BOCES, 600
Delbello Donnellan Weingarten Wise & Wiederkehr LLP, 437
Delbello Donnellan Weingarten Wise & Wiederkehr, LLP, 406
Delhi CSD, 572
Dell Inc, 475
Dell Public Sector, Inc., 460
Deloitte & Touche LLP, 406
Deloitte & Touche, LLP, 475
Deloitte Consulting, 406
Delta Air Lines, Inc., 405, 406, 431
Delta Dental of Pennsylvania, 398
Delta Sonic, 441
Democracy For America - NYC, 481
Democrat and Chronicle, 530
Democrat, Republican, Independent Voter Education, 482
Democratic Congressional Campaign Committee, 138
Demographic Research & Reapportionment, Legislative Task Force on, 26, 43
DentaQuest LLC, 425
Dental Association, 433
Dental Hygienists Association of the State of New York, Inc., 477
Dental Hygienists' Association of the State of New York Inc, 182
Depew UFSD, 573
Deposit CSD, 568
Deposit Chamber of Commerce, 505
Desales Media Group, Inc., 406
Destiny USA, 437
Destiny USA Management Company, LLC, 406
Detectives Endowment Assn, Police Dept of NYC, 441
Detectives Endowment Association - COPE, 482
Deutsch, Ronald, 406
Deutsche Bank, 80
Deutsche Bank Trust Company, 406
Development Authority of the North Country, 86, 97, 188, 307, 505
Development Counsellors International, 91
Developmental Disabilities Planning Council, 6, 194, 227, 252, 303
Developmental Disability Alliance of Western New York, 407
Devon Capital LLP, 437
Devry Incorporated, 442
Diageo, 407
Diageo, PLC, 407
Dial 7 Car and Limousine Service, Inc., 401
Diallo For Council 2013, 482
Dietetic Association, 425
Dig Safely New York, Inc., 393
Dimaio, Mark, 407
Dionondehowa Wildlife Sanctuary & School - Not For Profit, 156
Diorio, L Todd, 407
DirecTv, 407
Direct Buy Holdings and it's Affiliates, 421
Direct Marketers and Publishers, 438
Direct Marketing Association, 455
Disabled American Veterans, Department of New York, 298
Distilled Spirits Council of the US, 475
Distilled Spirits Council of the US (FKA Wojnar, David E.), 407
Distinctive Public Affairs, LLC, 407
District Council 1707, AFSCME, 482
District Council 37, AFSCME, 407
District Council 37, AFSCME, AFL-CIO, 243
District Council No. 9 Political Action Committee, 482
Ditmas Park Rehab Care Center, 390
Dobbs Ferry UFSD, 597
Doctors Council, 400
Doctors Council SEIU COPE, 482
Doctors Without Borders USA, 182
Dodge Landesman For State Committee, 482
Dolgeville CSD, 576
Dominican College, 410, 555
Dominican Village, 425
Dominion Resources, 407
Dominion Voting Systems Inc., 390
Donohue, Gavin J, 407
Dorothea Hopfer School of Nursing at Mount Vernon Hospital, 555
Douglaston Development LLC, 392
Dover UFSD, 572
Dover-Wingdale Chamber of Commerce, 505
Dow Jones & Company, 527
Dow Jones Newswires (Dow Jones & Company), 532
Dowling College, 555
Downsville CSD, 572
Downtown Brooklyn Partnership (The), 437
Downtown Brooklyn Partnership, Inc., 377
Downtown-Lower Manhattan Association, 505
Dr Pepper Snapple Group, 428
Drexel Hamilton, 393
Drexelius, Jr., John R., 407
Dreyfus Corporation (The), 452
Driscoll Group, Inc., 407
DriversEd.com, 405
Dromm For NYC, 482
Drug Policy Alliance, 407, 438
Drum Major Institute for Public Policy - Not For Profit, 198
Drum Route 11, 437
Dryden CSD, 595
Dryfoos Group, 408
Duane For New York, 482
Duane Morris LLP, 408
Duane Morris LLP Government Committee - New York Fund, 482
Duanesburg CSD, 589
Duca, Anthony, 408
Duffy, Margaret, 408
Duke Energy Corporation, 452
Dundee CSD, 599
Dunkin' Brands, Inc., 437
Dunkirk, 62
Civil & Criminal Courts, 62
Dunkirk City SD, 569
Dunne, John, 408
Dupee & Monroe, PC, 203
Durrani, Waqas, 408
Durst Development LLC, 408
Durst Organization (The), 416
Durst Organization, Inc. (The), 408
Dutchess BOCES, 600
Dutchess Community College, 547
Dutchess County, 52, 328
Family Court, 53
Supreme, County & Surrogate's Courts, 53
Dutchess County Economic Development Corporation, 505
Dutchess County Regional Chamber of Commerce, 514
D'Ambrosio, John A, 404
D'Onofrio, Paul, 404
D'Youville College, 554
E-3 Communications, 408

Appendices: Financial Plan, Indexes & Maps

E.I. Du Pont De Nemours and Company, 413
EAC Inc, 435, 442
ECG Engineering P.C., 411
EFO Jeffrey P. Gardner, 482
EISAI, Inc., 408, 461
EISPAC, 482
ELAD US Holding, Inc., 431
EMD Serono, Inc., 410
EMILY's List, 138
ENDO Pharmaceuticals, Inc., 387
ENT and Allergy Associates, LLP, 418
EPIC-Every Person Influences Children Inc, 257
EPL/Environmental Advocates, 412
EQT Partner AS, 412
EQT Partners AB, 412
EQT Partners Asia Limited, 412
EQT Partners GMBH, 412
EQT Partners UK Advisors LLP, 412
EQT Partners, Inc., 412
EVCI Career Colleges Holding Corp, 91
EXG 430W37 LLC, 382
Early Care & Learning Council, 257
Early Care and Learning Council, 408
Earthwatch LTD, 472
East Aurora Chamber of Commerce (Greater East Aurora), 505
East Aurora UFSD, 573
East Bloomfield CSD, 584
East Fishkill, Town of, 344
East Greenbush CSD, 587
East Hampton Chamber of Commerce, 505
East Hampton UFSD, 592
East Hampton, Town of, 345
East Irondequoit CSD, 578
East Islip Chamber of Commerce, 505
East Islip UFSD, 592
East Meadow Chamber of Commerce, 505
East Meadow UFSD, 580
East Moriches UFSD, 592
East Northport Chamber of Commerce, 505
East Quogue UFSD, 592
East Ramapo CSD (Spring Valley), 588
East Rochester UFSD, 578
East Rockaway UFSD, 580
East Side Rezoning Alliance, 439
East Syracuse-Minoa CSD, 584
East Williston UFSD, 580
Eastchester UFSD, 597
Eastchester, Town of, 345
Eastchester-Tuckahoe Chamber of Commerce, 505
Easter Seals New York, 408
Eastern Contractors Association Inc, 91
Eastern Paramedics, Inc., 437
Eastern Region Helicopter Council, 431
Eastern Suffolk BOCES, 600
Eastman Kodak Company, 91, 421
Easton Bell Sports, 463
Eastport-South Manor CSD, 592
Easy Choice Health Plan of New York, 405
Ebay, Inc., 385
Eber, Lester, 409
Ecology & Environment Inc, 156
Economic Committee, Joint, 324
Economic Development Council, 437
Economic Development Council Inc (NYS), 409
Economic Development, Job Creation, Commerce & Industry, 37
Committee Staff, 37
Key Assembly Staff Assignments, 37
Membership, 37
Majority, 37
Minority, 37
Eden CSD, 573
Edgemont UFSD, 598
Edgestone Group LLC, 407
Edgewater Industrial Park LLC, 460
Edinburg Common SD, 588
Edison Spring Street Company LLC, 409
Edmeston CSD, 586
Education, 22, 37
Committee Staff, 22, 37
Key Assembly Staff Assignments, 37
Key Senate Staff Assignments, 22
Membership, 22, 37
Majority, 22, 37
Minority, 22, 37
Education & Assistance Corp Inc, 258
Education & Assistance Corporation Inc, 117
Education & Labor, 318
Subcommittees, 318
Early Childhood, Elementary and Secondary Education, 318
Health, Employment, Labor and Pensions, 318
Healthy Families and Communities, 318
Higher Education, Lifelong Learning, and Competitiveness, 318
Workforce Protections, 318
Education & Research Network, Inc., 425
Education & Work Consortium (The), 440
Education Department, 7, 119, 174, 227, 252, 270, 303
Albany District Office, 121
Bronx District Office, 121
Brooklyn District Office, 121
Buffalo District Office, 121
Child Nutrition Program Administration, 121
College & University Evaluation, 121
Cultural Education Office, 120, 270
Educational Television & Public Broadcasting, 120
Research and Collections, 120, 270
State Archives, 120
State Library, 120
State Museum Office, 120, 270
Educational Management Services, 121
Facilities & Planning, 121
Garden City District Office, 121
Grants Management, 121
Hauppauge District Office, 121
Malone District Office, 121
Manhattan District Office, 122
Mid-Hudson District Office, 122
Office of Adult Career & Continuing Education Services (ACCES), 121, 228, 252
Fiscal & Administrative Services, 121, 228
Quality Assurance - Statewide Special Education, 228
State School for the Blind at Batavia, 228, 252
Vocational Rehabilitation Administration, 121
Vocational Rehabilitation Operations, 228, 252
Office of Higher Education, 121
Office of K-16 Initiatives & Access Programs, 121
Office of Teaching Initiatives, 121
Office of P-12 Education Policy, 120
P-12 School Services, 120
Office of Performance Improvement & Management Services/CFO, 120
Information Technology Services, 120
Office of the Professions, 121, 174, 227, 252
Office of Professional Responsibility, 121, 174, 228
Professional Education Program Review, 121, 174, 228
Professional Licensing Services, 121, 174, 228
Special Education, 252
Professional Examinations, 121
Queens District Office, 122
Research & Information Systems, 121
Rochester District Office, 122
Southern Tier District Office, 122
State Library, 304
Syracuse District Office, 122
Teacher Certification, Teacher Policy & School Personnel Review, 121
Utica District Office, 122
White Plains District Office, 122
Education Management LLC, 475
Education Reform Now Advocacy, Inc., 409
Education Reform Now, Inc., 409
Educational Assistance Corporation, 453
Educational Houseing Servies, Inc., 410
Educational Housing Services, 456
Educational Housing Services (Regional Programs Inc), 442
Educational Housing Services, Inc., 437
Educational Justice Political Action Committee, 482
Educational Opportunity Center of Westchester, 549
Educational Testing Service, 475

Edward K. Flynn, 409
Edwards-Knox CSD, 590
Edwin Gould Services for Children & Families, 418
Effective Leadership Committee, Inc., 482
Egan, Paul (FKA Reiskin, Marvin), 409
Egg (The), Center for the Performing Arts, 278
Eisland Strategies LLC, 409
El Paso Corporation, 439
Elaine Nunes 2010, 482
Elant, Inc, 475
Elayne E Greenberg, MS, Esq, 215
Elba CSD, 575
Eldred CSD, 594
Eleanor Roosevelt Legacy Committee, 482
Elect Newsome 2013, 482
Election Computer Services Inc, 138
Election Law, 37
Committee Staff, 37
Key Assembly Staff Assignments, 37
Membership, 38
Majority, 38
Minority, 38
Elections, 22
Committee Staff, 22
Key Senate Staff Assignments, 22
Membership, 22
Majority, 22
Minority, 22
Elections, State Board of, 7, 130, 304
Administrative Services, 130
Bronx, 133
Campaign Finance, 130
Counsel/Enforcement, 130
County Boards of Elections, 130
Albany, 130
Allegany, 130
Broome, 130
Cattaraugus, 130
Cayuga, 130
Chautauqua, 131
Chemung, 131
Chenango, 131
Clinton, 131
Columbia, 131
Cortland, 131
Delaware, 131
Dutchess, 131
Erie, 131
Essex, 132
Franklin, 132
Fulton, 132
Genesee, 132
Greene, 132
Hamilton, 132
Herkimer, 132
Jefferson, 132
Lewis, 132
Livingston, 133
Madison, 133
Monroe, 133
Montgomery, 133
Nassau, 133
New York City, 133
Niagara, 133
Oneida, 134
Onondaga, 134
Ontario, 134
Orange, 134
Orleans, 134
Oswego, 134
Otsego, 134
Putnam, 134
Rensselaer, 134
Rockland, 134
Saint Lawrence, 135
Saratoga, 135
Schenectady, 135
Schoharie, 135
Schuyler, 135
Seneca, 135
Steuben, 135
Suffolk, 135
Sullivan, 135
Tioga, 135
Tompkins, 136
Ulster, 136
Warren, 136
Washington, 136
Wayne, 136
Westchester, 136
Wyoming, 136
Yates, 136
Election Operations, 136
General Information, 136
Information Technology Unit, 136
Kings, 133
New York, 133
Queens, 133
Richmond, 133
Electric & Gas Corp (NYS), 396
Electric & Gas Corporation (NYS), 452
Elevator Industry Work Preservation Fund, 387
Elisa Seeger, 402
Elissa D Hecker, Esq, 278
Elizabeth Crowley 2013, 482
Elizabeth Pierce Olmsted Medical Center for the Visually Impaired, 377
Elizabeth Seton Pediatric Center, 425
Elizabethtown Community Hospital, 475
Elizabethtown-Lewis CSD, 574
Elk Street Group LLC, 409
Ellenville CSD, 595
Ellenville/Wawarsing Chamber of Commerce, 505
Ellicottville CSD, 568
Ellicottville Chamber of Commerce, 505
Elliott Management, 438, 475
Ellis Hospital School of Nursing, 555
Elmhurst Dairy, Inc., 401
Elmira, 62
Civil & Criminal Courts, 62
Elmira Business Institute, 564
Elmira Business Institute-Vestal, 564
Elmira City SD, 570
Elmira College, 555
Elmira Heights CSD, 570
Elmira, City of, 345
Elmont UFSD, 580
Elmsford UFSD, 598
Elwood UFSD, 592
EmblemHealth Services Company, LLC, 391
Emblemhealth Services Company, LLC, 410
Emeritus Senior Living, 425
Emily's List NY, 482
Empire Advocates LLC, 410
Empire Blue Cross & Blue Shield, 182, 203
Empire Center for New York State Policy, 91
Empire City Labs, 410
Empire Consultants, 410
Empire Dental Political Action Committee, 482
Empire Education Corporation, 387
Empire Generating Co. LLC, 410
Empire Generating Co., LLC, 390
Empire Government Strategies, 410
Empire Justice Center, 215, 258, 410
Empire Justice Center (FKA Greater Upstate Law Project), 410
Empire Merchants North, LLC, 414
Empire Merchants, LLC, 414
Empire Office, Inc., 401
Empire Racing Associates, 404
Empire Resorts Inc, 442
Empire Resorts, Inc., 405, 415
Empire State Assn of Adult Homes & Assist Living Facilities, 442
Empire State Association of Assisted Living, 182, 402, 425
Empire State Association of Assisted Living (FKA Empire State Association of Adult Homes & Assisted), 411
Empire State College, State University of NY, 411
Empire State Development Corporation, 7, 83, 97, 147, 188, 271, 304, 307
Empire State Forest Products Association, 156, 411
Empire State Honey Producers Association, 74
Empire State Marine Trades Association, 393
Empire State Marine Trades Association (Capitol Group, LLC), 417
Empire State Passengers Association, 291, 437
Empire State Petroleum Assn Inc, 475
Empire State Petroleum Association Inc, 144

Empire State Petroleum Association, Inc., 400, 411, 423
Empire State Potato Growers Inc, 74
Empire State Pride Agenda, Inc., 387
Empire State Regional Council of Carpenters, 225
Empire State Report (CINN Worldwide Inc), 532
Empire State Restaurant & Tavern Assn, 452
Empire State Restaurant & Tavern Association Inc, 91, 278
Empire State Society of Association Executives Inc, 92
Empire State Subcontractors Assn, 450
Empire State Towing & Recovery Association, 422
Empire State Water Well Drillers Association, 421
Empire Strategic Planning, Inc., 411
Employee Relations, Governor's Office of, 7, 240, 304
Labor/Management Committees, 240
Family Benefits Committee, 240
NYS/CSEA Discipline Unit, 241
NYS/CSEA Partnership for Education & Training, 241
NYS/SSU Joint Labor-Management Committee, 241
NYS/UUP Labor-Management Committee, 241
Statewide Employee Assistance Programs, 241
Employer Alliance for Affordable Health Care, 411
Energy, 38
Committee Staff, 38
Key Assembly Staff Assignments, 38
Membership, 38
Majority, 38
Minority, 38
Energy & Commerce, 318
Subcommittees, 318
Commerce, Trade & Consumer Protection, 318
Communications, Technology & the Internet, 318
Energy & the Environment, 318
Health, 319
Oversight & Investigations, 319
Energy & Natural Resources, 314
Subcommittees, 314
Energy, 314
National Parks, 314
Public Lands & Forests, 314
Water & Power, 314
Energy & Telecommunications, 22
Committee Staff, 22
Key Senate Staff Assignments, 22
Membership, 22
Majority, 22
Minority, 22
Energy Coalition New York, 144
Energy East Corporation, 453
Energy Independence & Global Warming, House Select Committee on, 324
Englert, Coffey, McHugh & Fantauzzi LLP, 215
Entek Power Services, 144
Entergy Corporation Political Action Committee - New York, 482
Entergy Nuclear Northeast, 144
Entergy Nuclear Operations Inc, 453
Entergy Nuclear Operations, Inc, 411
Entergy Nuclear Operations, Inc., 390, 414
Enterprise Holdings, 411
Enterprise Holdings, Inc., 421
Entertainment Software Association, 278, 387, 411
Environment & Public Works, 314
Subcommittees, 314
Children's Health, 314
Clean Air and Nuclear Safety, 314
Green Jobs and the New Economy, 314
Oversight, 314
Superfund, Toxics and Environmental Health, 314
Transportation & Infrastructure, 314
Water & Wildlife, 314
Environmental Advocates of NY, 411
Environmental Advocates of New York, 156
Environmental Business Association of NYS Inc, 156
Environmental Conservation, 22, 38
Committee Staff, 22, 38
Key Assembly Staff Assignments, 38
Key Senate Staff Assignments, 23
Membership, 23, 38
Majority, 23, 38
Minority, 23, 38
Environmental Conservation Department, 8, 147, 304
Air Resources, Climate Change & Energy Office, 147
Air Resources Division, 147
Climate Change Office, 147
General Counsel's Office, 147
Hearings & Mediation Services Office, 147
Information Services Division
Information Services Division, 147
Management & Budget Division, 147
Office of Employee Relations, 148
Operations Division, 147
Public Affairs & Education Division, 148
Natural Resources Office, 147
Fish, Wildlife & Marine Resources Division, 147
Lands & Forests Division, 147
Office of Remediation & Materials Management, 147
Environmental Remediation Division, 147
Materials Management Division, 147
Mineral Resources Division, 147
Public Information, 148
Public Protection Office, 148
Forest Protection & Fire Management Division, 148
Law Enforcement Division, 148
Regional Offices, 148
Region 1, 148
Region 2, 148
Region 3, 148
Region 4, 148
Region 5, 148
Region 6, 148
Region 7, 148
Region 8, 148
Region 9, 148
Special Programs, 148
Great Lakes Program, 148
Hudson River Estuary Program, 148
Water Resources Office, 147
Water Division, 147
Environmental Defense Fund, 156, 412
Envisage Information Systems, LLC, 393
Epilepsy Coalition of New York State Inc, 182
Epilepsy Foundation of Northeastern New York, Inc., 393
Epilepsy Institute, 475
Eponymous Associates, 427
Eponymous Associates LLC (FKA Steiner Studios), 452
Epstein Becker & Green, PC, 198
Equal Employment Opportunity Commission, 196, 222
New York District, 196, 222
Buffalo Local, 196, 222
Equality Charter School, 392
Equinox, Inc., 425
Equitable Life Assurance Society of the US, 203
Equity One, Inc., 394
Eric Adams 2013, 482
Eric Mower & Associates, 92
Eric Ulrich 2013, 482
Erie 1 BOCES, 600
Erie 2-Chautauqua-Cattaraugus BOCES, 600
Erie Basin Marine Associates (Kelly & Roth), 436
Erie Community College, 547
Erie County, 53, 328
Family Court, 53
Supreme & County Court, 53
Surrogate's Court, 53
Erie County Industrial Development Agency, 505
Erie County Planning & Economic Development, 505
Ernst & Young, 247

Ernst & Young Committee For Good Government, 482
Ernst & Young LLP, 388
Ernst & Young, LLP, 475
Erwin Industrial Development Agency (Town of), 505
Espinal For City Council, 482
Essex County, 53, 328
Supreme, County, Family & Surrogate's Courts, 53
Essex County Industrial Development Agency, 505
Estate of Marilyn Monroe LLC, 414
Estee Lauder Companies, Inc., 425
Ethan C Eldon Associates Inc, 291
Ethics, 23
Key Senate Staff Assignments, 23
Membership, 23
Majority, 23
Minority, 23
Ethics & Guidance, 38
Membership, 38
Majority, 38
Minority, 38
Ethics Committee, Legislative, 26, 43
Ethics, Select Committee on, 316
Evans-Brant CSD (Lake Shore), 573
Evans-Brant Chamber of Commerce, 505
Evening Sun, 528
Evening Tribune (The), 526
Everest Institute, 564
Evergreen For City Council, 482
Every Voice, 412
Everyone Reading, Inc., 407
Excellus BCBS, 182
Excellus Health Plan Inc, 203
Excellus Health Plan, Inc., 425
Excelsior Advocates, LLC, 412
Excelsior College, 555
Excelsior Racing Association (Powers & Company), 475
Excess Line Assn of NY, 438
Excess Line Association of NY, 406
Excess Line Association of New York, 203
Exelon Generation Company LLC, 413
Exhibition Alliance Inc (The), 278
ExpandED Schools, 126
Experience Hendrix LLC, 414
Explore Information Services, LLC, 421
Export Import Bank of the United States, 79, 88
Northeast Regional Office, 79, 88
Express Scripts Holding Co., 413
Express Scripts, Inc., 387
Extell 57th Tower LLC, 382
Extell Development Company, 382, 413
Extell GT LLC, 382
Extended Home Care, 390
Exxon Mobil Corporation, 144, 409, 426, 441, 463
Eye-Bank for Sight Restoration Inc (The), 183
Eyemed Vision Care LLC, 440
FC Yonkers Associates LLC, 406, 418
FCC Construction, Inc., 431
FCS Administrators, Inc., 466
FJC Security Services, Inc., 443
FMC Corporation, 413
FMR LLC, 415
Fabius-Pompey CSD, 584
Facebook, Inc., 424
Fahs Construction Group (Fahs-Rolston Paving Corp), 452
Fair Committee, 441
Fair Haven Area Chamber of Commerce, 506
Fairmont Capital LLC, 405
Fairport CSD, 578
Faist Government Affairs Group, LLC, 413
Falconer CSD, 570
Fallsburg CSD, 594
Families Together in NYS Inc, 231
Families Together in NYS, Inc., 413
Family Court, NYC, 50
Bronx County, 50
Kings County, 50
New York County, 50
Queens County, 50
Richmond County, 50
Family Planning Advocates, 475
Family Planning Advocates of New York State, 183, 198, 258, 413
Family Residences & Essential Enterprises, 420
Farber, Felice, 413
Fareri Associates, 406
Farm Bureau, Inc. (NY), 413
Farm Credit East, 455
Farm Sanctuary, 74
Farmedic Training Program, 74
Farmers Insurance Group, 413
Farmers' Market Federation of NY, 74
Farmer's Museum (The), 278
Farmingdale State College, 405
Farmingdale State College of Technology, 546
Farmingdale UFSD, 580
Farmington Chamber of Commerce, 506
Farmingville/Holtsville Chamber of Commerce, 506
Farrell 2012, 482
Fashion Institute of Technology, 387, 436, 547
Fashion Jewelry Trade Association, 413
Fassler, Michael S, 413
Faucher, Jennifer, 414
Fayetteville Chamber of Commerce, 506
Fayetteville-Manlius CSD, 584
Featherstonhaugh, Wiley & Clyne, LLP, 414
FedEx Corporation, 390
Federal Communications Commission, 142
Office of Media Relations, 142
Federal Deposit Insurance Corporation, 79
Division of Depositor and Consumer Protection, 79
Federal Election Commission, 137
Federal Express New York State Political Action Committee, 482
Federal Home Loan Bank of New York, 80, 191
Federal Labor Relations Authority, 222
Boston Regional Office, 222
Federal Maritime Commission, 288
New York Area Office, 288
Federal Mediation & Conciliation Service, 222
Northeastern Region, 222
Federal Reserve System, 79
Federal Reserve Bank of New York, 79
Federal Trade Commission, 88, 92
Northeast Regional Office, 88
Federation Employment & Guidance Service (FEGS) Inc, 231, 258
Federation of Mental Health Services, Inc., 425
Federation of Mental Health Services, Inc. (The), 414
Federation of Organizations Inc, 231, 464
Federation of Protestant Welfare Agencies, 438
Federation of Protestant Welfare Agencies Inc, 258, 439
Federation of School Administrators, 425
Federation of School Administrators (NYS) (FKA Gibbons, Brian), 414
Feld Entertainment, 414, 428
Feld Entertainment, Inc, 414
Feld Entertainment, Inc., 402
Ferramosca, Joseph, 414
Ferris, William E, 414
Fidelity Capital Markets, a Division of National Financial Services, 391
Fidelity Investments, 405
Fidelity Investments Institutional Services Company, Inc., 473
Fifth Avenue Arcade, Inc., 387
Fig LLC, 402
Figli Di San Gennaro, Inc., 405
Figure Skating in Harlem, Inc., 387
Filipino American Human Services Inc (FAHSI), 198, 258
Fillmore CSD, 567
Film/Video Arts, 278
Finance, 23, 314
Committee Staff, 23
Key Senate Staff Assignments, 23
Membership, 23
Majority, 23
Minority, 23
Subcommittees, 314
Energy, Natural Resources and Infrastructure, 314

Health Care, 314
International Trade, and Global Competitiveness, 314
Social Security, Pensions, and Family Policy, 315
Taxation, IRS Oversight and Long-Term Growth, 315
Financial Service Centers of New York, 414
Financial Service Centers of New York, Inc., 388
Financial Services, 319
Subcommittees, 319
Capital Markets, Insurance & Government Sponsored Enterprises, 319
Domestic Monetary Policy & Technology, 319
Financial Institutions & Consumer Credit, 319
Housing & Community Opportunity, 319
International Monetary Policy & Trade, 319
Oversight & Investigations, 319
Financial Services Department, 4, 78, 177, 200, 303
Banking Division, 78, 200
Capital Markets Division, 78, 200
Financial Frauds & Consumer Protection Division, 78, 200
Health Bureau, 177
Insurance Division, 78, 200
Life Bureau, 177
Real Estate Finance Division, 78
Financial Services Forum, 80
Financial Services Institute, Inc., 387
Finch Paper LLC, 386, 414
Findley Lake Area Chamber of Commerce, 506
Finger Lakes Community College, 547
Finger Lakes Economic Development Center, 520
Finger Lakes Health Systems Agency, 390
Finger Lakes Horsemen's Benv & Protective Assn Inc, 423
Finger Lakes Printing Co, 525
Finger Lakes Racing Association, 278, 442
Finger Lakes Times, 525
Finger Lakes Tourism Alliance, 278
Fire Island Association, Inc., 442
Fire Island UFSD, 592
Fireman's Fund Insurance Co, 454
Firemen's Association of the State of NY, 422
First (NY), 445
First Alert, 387
First Data Corporation & Subsidiaries, 378
First Data Corporation & its Subsidiaries (Barbara J. Ahern), 388
First Equity Abstract Corporation, 420
First Lincoln Holdings LLC, 425
First Pioneer Farm Credit ACA, 466
FirstService Williams, 247
Fiscal Policy Institute, 170, 268
Fisher Brothers, 247
Fisher Development Strategies, 415
Fishers Island UFSD, 592
Fishkill, Town of, 345
FitzGerald Morris et al, 215
Fitzgerald, Gary J, 415
Fitzgerald, Kevin, 415
Fitzpatrick, Christine M, 415
Five Towns College, 564
Flair Beverage Corp., 420
Flaum Management Company, Inc., 430
Fleet Reserve Association (FRA), 298
Fleet Reserve Association (FRA), NE Region (NJ, NY, PA), 298
FlexCare, 452
Floral Park-Bellerose UFSD, 580
Florida Compass Group/Premier Pawn & Jewelry in New York, 420
Florida UFSD, 585
Flowers For NYC, 483
Fluor Enterprises, Inc., 437
Flushing Commons, 436
Flushing Commons LLC, 453
Flushing Commons, LLC, 478
Flushing Council on Culture & the Arts Inc, 453
Focus Media Group, Inc., 415
Focused Technologies Imaging Services LLC, 387
Foley & Lardner LLP, 415
Fonda-Fultonville CSD, 579
Food & Water Watch, 415
Food Bank for New York City, 415
Food Industry Alliance of NYS, 445
Food Industry Alliance of NYS Inc, 415
Food Industry Alliance of New York State Inc, 74, 92
Food Industry Political Action Committee - NYC, 483
Food and Water Watch, 438
Food, Farm & Nutrition, Task Force on, 43
For the Benefit of Red Hook 100 LLC, Red Hook 212 LLC, and Red Hook 300 LLC, 431
Ford Gum & Machine Company, Inc., 437
Fordham University, 126, 555
Fordham University, Department of Political Science, 170, 238
Fordham University, Graduate School of Social Service, 258
Foreign Affairs, 319
Subcommittees, 319
Africa & Global Health, 319
Asia, the Pacific and the Global Environment, 320
Europe, 320
International Organizations, Human Rights and Oversight, 320
Middle East and South Asia, 320
Terrorism, Nonproliferation and Trade, 320
Western Hemisphere, 320
Foreign Relations, 315
Subcommittees, 315
African Affairs, 315
East Asian & Pacific Affairs, 315
European Affairs, 315
International Development, Foreign Assist, Economic Affairs & Environment, 315
International Ops & Orgs, Human Rights, Democracy & Global Women's Issues, 315
Near Eastern and South and Central Asian Affairs, 315
Western Hemisphere, Peace Corps & Narcotics Affairs, 315
Forest City Ratner Companies, 415, 436, 444, 475
Forest City Residential Group, Inc., 406
Forest Lawn Cemetery/Cremation Group (The), 414
Forestcitydaly Housing, 435
Forestdale, Inc., 401
Forests Lots LLC, 421
Forestville CSD, 570
Fort Ann CSD, 596
Fort Brewerton/Greater Oneida Lake Chamber, 506
Fort Edward Chamber of Commerce, 506
Fort Edward UFSD, 596
Fort Plain CSD, 579
Fortune Society (The), 117
Forum Strategies & Communications, 416
Foundation for Opportunity in Education (The), 416
Foundling, 425
Foundling Hospital, 431
Fountain House, 398
Fox News Channel, 538
Frack Action Fund, Inc., 416
Fractured Atlas, 444
Frankfort-Schuyler CSD, 576
Franklin CSD, 572
Franklin County, 53, 329
Supreme, County, Family & Surrogate's Courts, 53
Franklin County Industrial Development Agency, 506
Franklin Square Chamber of Commerce, 506
Franklin Square UFSD, 580
Franklin-Essex-Hamilton BOCES, 600
Franklinville CSD, 568
Frank's Friends, 483
Fredonia CSD, 570
Fredonia Chamber of Commerce, 506
Free Community Papers of New York, 425
Freelancers Union Political Action Committee, 483

Freeport UFSD, 580
Freeport, Village of, 345
Freeze Frame LLC, 392
French-American Chamber of Commerce, 506
Fresenius Medical Care North America, 425
Fresh Direct, LLC, 453
Frewsburg CSD, 570
Fried Frank Harris Shriver & Jacobson, LLP, 416
Friedlander Group (The), 416
Friedman & Moses, 429
Friedman, John P, 416
Friends & Relatives of Institutionalized Aged Inc (FRIA), 258
Friends For Peter Koo, 483
Friends For Ryan Wright, 483
Friends of Alfonso Quiroz, 483
Friends of Angel Molina, 483
Friends of Antonio Reynoso, 483
Friends of Assembly Speaker Joe Roberts, 483
Friends of Assemblyman Jeffrey Dinowitz, 483
Friends of Audrey Pheffer, 483
Friends of Austin Shafran, 483
Friends of Balboni, 483
Friends of Benjamin Kallos, 483
Friends of Bill Suggs, 483
Friends of Bola Omotosho, 483
Friends of Breina Payne, 483
Friends of Brodie Enoch 2013, 483
Friends of Carl E. Heastie, 483
Friends of Catherine Nolan, 483
Friends of Costa Constantinides, 483
Friends of Cultural Institutions, 483
Friends of Dara Adams, 483
Friends of David Kayode For Council, 483
Friends of DeMeo, 483
Friends of Democracy New York, 414
Friends of Donovan Richards 2013, 483
Friends of Dorothy Phelan, 483
Friends of Ed Hartzog, 483
Friends of Ede Fox, 484
Friends of Erick Salgado, 484
Friends of F. Richard Hurley 2013, 484
Friends of Felipe de Los Santos, 484
Friends of Gale Brewer - 2013, 484
Friends of Harpreet, 484
Friends of I. Daneek Miller, 484
Friends of Inez Barron, 484
Friends of JR, 484
Friends of James Vacca, 484
Friends of Jean Similien, 484
Friends of Joe Lazar, 484
Friends of Joe Marthone, 484
Friends of Joel R. Rivera, 484
Friends of John Lisyanskiy, 484
Friends of John Liu, 484
Friends of Johnnie Goff, 484
Friends of Jonathan J. Judge, 484
Friends of Joseph Nwachukwu, 484
Friends of Joyce Johnson, 484
Friends of Julio Pabon, 484
Friends of Kevin P. Coenen Jr. Inc., 484
Friends of Kimberly Council, 484
Friends of Kirsten John Foy, 484
Friends of Larry Hirsch 2010, 484
Friends of Luis Tejada, 484
Friends of Manny Caughman Committee, 484
Friends of Marie Adam-Ovide For Council 31, 484
Friends of Mark Thompson, 485
Friends of Mark Weprin 2013, 485
Friends of Mark Winston Griffith, 485
Friends of Martha Taylor, 485
Friends of Martha Taylor Butler, 485
Friends of Martin For City Council, 485
Friends of Menegon, 485
Friends of Michael A. Alvarez, 485
Friends of Michael Duncan 2013, 485
Friends of Michael Simanowitz, 485
Friends of Mike Gianaris, 485
Friends of Mike Treybich, 485
Friends of NY Racing Inc, 444
Friends of Nicole Paultre Bell, 485
Friends of Olanike Alabi, 485
Friends of Osina, 485
Friends of Paul Drucker, 485
Friends of Pedro Alvarez, 485
Friends of Randy Credico, 485
Friends of Richard del Rio, 485
Friends of Ruben Wills, 485
Friends of Sean K. Henry 2013, 485
Friends of Selvena Brooks, 485
Friends of Seymour Lachman, 485
Friends of Steve Cohn, 485
Friends of Theresa Scavo, 485
Friends of Todd Dobrin, 485
Friends of Tommy Torres, 485
Friends of Torres, 485
Friends of Yetta, 485
Friends of the High Line, 405
Friends of the High Line, Inc., 416
Friendship CSD, 568
Friens of John Calvelli, 484
Frontier CSD, 573
Frontier Communications, 444
Frontier Healthcare Management Services, Inc., 405, 406
Frontier, A Citizens Communications Co, 144
Frost, Robert D., 416
Fulton, 62
Civil & Criminal Courts, 62
Fulton City SD, 586
Fulton County, 53, 329
Supreme, County, Family & Surrogate's Courts, 53
Fulton County Economic Development Corporation, 506
Fulton County Industrial Development Agency, 506
Fulton County Reg Chamber of Commerce & Ind, 506
Fulton-Montgomery Community College, 547
Fund for Animals (The), 74
Fund for Modern Courts, 423
Fund for Modern Courts (The), 215
Fund for the City of New York, 238
Fund for the City of New York (FKA Employment & Training Coalition (NYC)), 416
Fund for the City of New York, Center for Internet Innovation, 144
Funeral Directors Association, Inc. (NYS), 417
GCOM, 394
GE Transportation Systems Global Signaling LLC, 431
GKC Industries, Inc., 421
GSO Capital Partners LP, 422
GT Forge, Inc. DBA GET Taxi, 431
GTech Corporation, 414
Gaia Plant Based Medicine, 437
Gallo, Richard J., 417
Galway CSD, 588
Gaming Association, 417, 437
Gaming Association, Inc., 405, 414, 463
Gananda CSD, 597
Gandhi Engineering Inc, 291
Gannet Co Inc, 523
Gannett Co Inc, 525, 526, 529, 530
Gannett Fleming Engineers & Architects PC, 436
Gannett News Service, 532
Gansevoort Market, Inc., 392
Gansevoort Street Properties, LLC, 401
Gar Associates, Inc., 437
Garden City Chamber of Commerce, 506
Garden City UFSD, 580
Garden City, Village of, 345
Garden Gate Greenhouse, 74
Gardere Wynne Sewell LLP, 466
Garfinkel, Neil, 417
Garment Industry Development Corporation, 444
Garodnick 2013, 486
Garrison UFSD, 587
Gartner Inc., 393
Gate House Media, 531
GateHouse Media, 524, 531
GateHouse Media Inc., 525, 526
Gates, Town of, 346
Gates-Chili CSD, 578
Gateway College AS, 405
Gateway Properties Phase II, LLC, 478
Gateway-Longview Inc., 471
Gaucho LLC, 454
Gay & Lesbian Anti-Violence Project (NYC), 387

Gay Men's Health Crisis Inc, 417
Gay Men's Health Crisis, Inc., 438
Gay and Lesbian Victory Fund, 486
Geiger, Bruce W & Associates, 417
Genentech Inc, 462
General Brown CSD, 577
General Contractors Association of NY, 92, 291
General Contractors Association of NY, Inc., 413
General Contractors Association of NY, Inc. (The), 414
General Electric Company, 417, 431, 455
General Electric Company (FKA Farrell, Pamela), 417
General Motors Corporation, 412, 417
General Motors LLC, 434, 437
General Services, Office of, 8, 160, 245, 271, 304
Administration, 161
Support Services, 161
Design & Construction, 161
Empire State's Convention & Cultural Events Office, 271
Information Technology & Procurement Services, 161
Information Resource Management, 161
Procurement Services Group, 161
Real Estate Planning & Development Group, 161, 245
Real Property Management Group, 161, 245
Empire State's Convention & Cultural Events Office, 161
General Theological Seminary of the Episcopal Church, 555
Generation 21 NY, Inc., 382
Generic Pharmaceutical Association, 183
Genesee & Wyoming Railroad Company, 423
Genesee Community College, 547
Genesee County, 53, 329
Supreme, County, Family & Surrogate's Courts, 53
Genesee County Chamber of Commerce, 506
Genesee County Economic Development Center, 506
Genesee Transportation Council, 238
Genesee Valley CSD, 568
Genesee-Livingston-Steuben-Wyoming BOCES, 600
Geneseo CSD, 578
Genessee County Economic Development Center, 430
Geneva, 63
Civil & Criminal Courts, 63
Geneva Area Chamber of Commerce, 506
Geneva City SD, 585
Geneva Industrial Development Agency (City of), 506
Geneva Worldwide, Inc., 421
Genon Bowline, LLC, 391
Genovese, John, 417
Gentile For the Future, 486
Genting NY, 386
Genting New York LLC, 402, 419, 437
Genworth Financial, 418, 455
George J. Hochbrueckner & Associates, Inc., 418
George Junior Republic UFSD, 595
Georgetown-South Otselic CSD, 570
Gerard Avenue LLC, 390
Gergela III, Joseph, 418
Germantown CSD, 571
Gershon & Company, 423
Gertrude H Sergievsky Center (The), 183
Gertrude Stein Repertory Theatre (The), 278
Getnick, Livingston, Atkinson, Gigliotti & Priore LLP, 216
Geto & De Milly Inc, 418
Geto & de Milly Inc, 170
Gibson For Assembly, 486
Gibson For City Council, 486
Gibson, Dunn & Crutcher LLP PAC, 486
Gilbane Building Company, 382, 418, 442
Gilbert Tweed Associates Inc, 92
Gilberti Stinziano Heintz & Smith, PC (FKA) Devorsetz Stinziano Gilberti Heintz & Smith, PC, 418
Gilbertsville-Mount Upton CSD, 587
Gilboa-Conesville CSD, 589
Gillen Brewer School (The), 475
Girvin & Ferlazzo, PC, 198
GlaxoSmithKline, PLC, 423, 436
Glazer, Robert, 418
Glen Cove, 63
Civil & Criminal Courts, 63
Glen Cove Chamber of Commerce, 506
Glen Cove City SD, 580
Glen Cove, City of, 346
Glens Falls, 63
Civil & Criminal Courts, 63
Glens Falls City SD, 596
Glens Falls Common SD, 596
Glens Falls Hospital, 475
Glenville, Town of, 346
Glenwood Management Corp, 394, 435
Glenwood Management Corporation, 247, 411, 442, 456, 472
Glenwood POH LLC, 382
Glenwood Poh, 418
Glenwood Poh LLC, 418
Glimmerglass Coalition, 439
Global Aerospace, Inc. and United States Aviation Underwriters, Inc, 431
Global Gardens Program, New York Botanical Garden (The), 74
Global Strategy Group, 419
GlobalFoundries US, Inc., 462
Globe Institute of Technology, 564
Gloria Wise Boys & Girls Club Inc, 453
Gloversville, 63
Civil & Criminal Courts, 63
Gloversville Enlarged SD, 575
Goddard Riverside Community Center, 477
Goens, Darin, 419
Gold Star Wives of America Inc, 298
Golden Tree Asset Management LP, 419
Golden, Ben, 419
Goldman Harris LLC (FKA Law Offices of Howard Goldman, LLC), 419
Goldman Sachs & Co, 80
Goldman Sachs & Co., 419
Goldman Sachs Group, Inc. (The) & Its Subsidiaries & Affiliates, 414
Golub Corporation (The), 419
Golub, David, 419
Gonzalez 2013, 486
Gonzalez Saggio & Harlan LLP, 387
Good Shepherd Services, 419, 428
Goode, Christian, 419
Goodman & Zuchlewski LLP, 216
Google, Inc., 387, 419
Gordian Group, Inc. (The), 420, 442
Gore Mountain Region Chamber of Commerce, 506
Gorham-Middlesex CSD (Marcus Whitman), 585
Goshen CSD, 585
Goshen Chamber of Commerce, 507
Gotham Government Relations, 420
Gotlieb For City Council, 486
Gould, David (FKA Tallon Jr., James R.), 420
Gouverneur CSD, 590
Gouverneur Chamber of Commerce, 507
Government Administration, Legislative Commission on, 26, 43
Government Employees Insurance Co (GEICO), 466
Government Employees Insurance Company (GEICO), 390
Governmental Employees, 38
Committee Staff, 38
Key Assembly Staff Assignments, 38
Membership, 38
Majority, 38
Minority, 38
Governmental Insight LTD, 420
Governmental Operations, 38
Committee Staff, 38
Key Assembly Staff Assignments, 38
Membership, 39
Majority, 39
Minority, 39
Governor's Office, 3, 69, 78, 83, 108, 119, 130, 140, 147, 160, 173, 187, 194, 200, 206, 219, 227, 234, 240, 245, 250, 263, 270, 283, 293, 303
Communications, 3

Counsel, 3
New York City Office, 3, 160, 234
Office of the Secretary, 3
Washington Office of the Governor, 3, 160, 303
Gowanda Area Chamber of Commerce, 507
Gowanda CSD, 569
Gowanus Village 1 Inc, 454
Graduate Center, 551
Graduate School of Journalism, 551
Grahel Associates LLC, 411
Gramercy Stuyvesant Independent Democrats, 486
Grand Island CSD, 573
Grand Island Chamber of Commerce, 507
Grand Island, Town of, 346
Grant Thornton LLP, 420
Granville CSD, 596
Granville Chamber of Commerce, 507
Grassy Sprain PAC, 486
Gray Media, 420
Great Escape Theme Park LLC (The), 278
Great Lakes Commission, 86, 97, 150, 307
Great Neck Chamber of Commerce, 507
Great Neck UFSD, 580
Greater Amsterdam SD, 579
Greater Cicero Chamber of Commerce, 507
Greater Jamaica Development Corporation, 382, 507
Greater Johnstown SD, 575
Greater Massena Chamber of Commerce, 507
Greater Mexico Chamber of Commerce, 507
Greater NY Health Care Facilities Assn, 452
Greater NY Health Care Facilities Assoc, 440
Greater NY Hospital Association, Subsidiaries & Affiliate (FKA Greater NY Hospital Association), 420
Greater New York Automobile Dealers Assn, 475
Greater New York Chamber of Commerce, 507
Greater New York Health Care Facilities Association, 420, 421
Greater New York Hospital Association, 183, 387, 391, 437
Greater Niagara Newspapers, 526, 527, 528, 531
Greater Oneida Chamber of Commerce, 507
Greater Ossining Chamber of Commerce, The, 507
Greater Port Jefferson Chamber of Commerce, 507
Greater Rochester Association of Realtors Inc, 247
Greater Rochester Association of Realtors, Inc., 477
Greater Southern Tier BOCES (Schuyler-Chemung-Tioga-Allegany-Steuben), 600
Greater Syracuse Association of Realtors Inc, 247
Greece CSD, 579
Greece Chamber of Commerce, 507
Greece, Town of, 346
Green Chimneys Children's Services Inc, 478
Green Chimneys School-Green Chimneys Children's Services Inc, 258
Green Island Industrial Development Agency (Village of), 507
Green Island UFSD, 567
Green-Wood Cemetary (The), 414
GreenThumb, 74, 156
Greenberg Traurig PA PAC, 486
Greenberg Traurig, LLP, 170, 420
Greenburgh 7 CSD, 598
Greenburgh Eleven UFSD, 598
Greenburgh, Town of, 346
Greenburgh-Graham UFSD, 598
Greenburgh-North Castle UFSD, 598
Greene CSD, 570
Greene County, 53, 329
Supreme, County, Family & Surrogate's Courts, 54
Greene County Coalition for Economic Equality, LLC, 455
Greene County Department of Planning & Economic Development, 507
Greene County Soil & Water Conservation District, 156
Greene County Tourism Promotion, 507
Greene International Golf Assn, 440
Greenetrack, 478
Greenfield 2010, 486
Greenmarket/Council on the Environment of NYC, 74
Greenmarket/Grow NYC, 157
Greenpoint Industrial Center, Inc., 403
Greenpoint Landing Associates LLC, 416
Greenport UFSD, 592
Greenport-Southold Chamber of Commerce, 508
Greenvale Chamber of Commerce, 508
Greenville CSD, 576
Greenwich CSD, 596
Greenwich Chamber of Commerce (Greater Greenwich), 508
Greenwich House, Inc., 477
Greenwich Village Society for Historic Preservation, 421
Greenwich Village-Chelsea Chamber of Commerce, 508
Greenwood Lake Chamber of Commerce, 508
Greenwood Lake UFSD, 585
Greller, Matthew, 421
Griffin Associates, LLC, 421
Griffiss Local Development Corporation, 388
Grocery Manufacturers Assn (FKA Grocery Manufacturers of America), 393
Grodenchik For Queens 2013, 486
Gronowicz For Mayor, 486
Groton CSD, 595
Groton Community Health Care Center, 476
Groundwork, Inc., 478
Group Health Inc, 183, 204
Group Health Incorporated, 439
Grow NYC, 191
Gtech Corporation, 422
Guardian Life Insurance Co of America, 413
Guardian Life Insurance Company, 422
Guardian Life Insurance Company of America (The), 422, 442
Guerriero For Advocate, 486
Guide Dog Foundation for the Blind Inc, 258, 465
Guilderland CSD, 567
Guilderland Chamber of Commerce, 508
Guilderland Industrial Development Agency (Town of), 508
Guilderland, Town of, 347
H J Kalikow & Co LLC, 247
H&M LLC, 401
H.O. Penn Caterpillar, 425
H.W. Lochner, Inc., 421
HANYS Services, Inc
D/B/A HANYS Solutions, Inc, 476
HCA PAC, 486
HDR, Inc. Political Action Committee - NY, 486
HF Responsibility Fund, 486
HFZ Highline LLC, 392
HNTB Corporation, 442
HR&A Advisors, Inc., 426
HSBC - North America Holdings, Inc., 426
HSBC North America, 425
HSBC North America Political Action Committee, 487
HSBC USA Inc, 80
Habitat for Humanity of New York State, 422
Hackensack University Medical Center, 422
Hadley-Luzerne CSD, 596
Hager, Susan, 422
Hague on Lake George Chamber of Commerce, 508
Hailo Network USA, Inc., 387
Hakeem Jeffries For Assembly, 486
Haldane CSD, 587
Half Hollow Hills CSD, 592
Hall of Science (NY), 423
Hall of Sciences (NY), 463
Halloran 2013, 486
Halmar International LLC, 402
Halogenated Solvents Industry Alliance, Inc., 413
Halpin Public Affairs, 422
Hamburg CSD, 573
Hamburg Chamber of Commerce, 508

Hamburg Industrial Development Agency, 508
Hamburg, Town of, 347
Hamilton CSD, 578
Hamilton College, 555
Hamilton County, 54, 330
County, Family & Surrogate's Courts, 54
Hamilton-Fulton-Montgomery BOCES, 600
Hamister Group, Inc., 441
Hammond CSD, 590
Hammondsport CSD, 591
Hammondsport Chamber of Commerce, 508
Hampton Bays Chamber of Commerce, 508
Hampton Bays UFSD, 592
Hancock Area Chamber of Commerce, 508
Hancock CSD, 572
Hands Across Long Island Inc, 428
Hannaford Supermarkets, 422
Hannan and O'Connell, Inc., 422
Hannesson, Paul (FKA McCormick, Lynde) (FKA Gaylord, Joan), 422
Hannibal CSD, 586
Harbar Motors, Ltd, 476
Harborfields CSD, 592
Harlem Chamber of Commerce (Greater Harlem), 508
Harlem Charter School Parents PAC, 486
Harlem Children Society, 437
Harlem United: Community AIDS Center, Inc., 422
Harpursville CSD, 568
Harris Beach LLP, 216
Harris Poll (The), 138
Harris, Steven W., LLC, 422
Harrison CSD, 598
Harrison, Town/Village of, 347
Harrisville CSD, 577
Harter Secrest & Emery, LLP, 423
Hartford CSD, 596
Hartford Financial Services Group, Inc., 421
Hartford Financial Services Group, Inc. (The Hartford), 423
Hartford Financial Services Group, Inc. (The), 423
Hartland Asset Management, 387, 390
Hartman & Winnicki, PC, 92, 216
Hartwick College, 555
Harvestworks, 279
Harvey B Besunder PC, 216
Hastings-On-Hudson UFSD, 598
Hastings-on-Hudson Chamber of Commerce, 508
Hauppauge UFSD, 592
Haverstraw, Town of, 347
Haverstraw-Stony Point CSD, 588
Haverstraw-Stony Point Central School District, 475
Hawayek, Jonathan F, 423
Hawk Creek Wildlife Center Inc, 157
Hawkins Delafield & Wood LLP, 238, 268
Hawkins, Dennis (FKA Jockers, Ken), 423
Hawthorne-Cedar Knolls UFSD, 598
He Gin Lee Committee to Elect For Mayor, 486
Health, 23, 39
Committee Staff, 23, 39
Key Assembly Staff Assignments, 39
Key Senate Staff Assignments, 23
Membership, 23, 39
Majority, 23, 39
Minority, 23, 39
Health & Hospitals Corp (NYC), 439
Health Care Subrogation Group, 453
Health Department, 8, 148, 174, 293, 304
AIDS Institute, 174
Center for Community Health, 174
Chronic Disease Prevention & Adult Health Division, 174
Epidemiology Division, 174
Family Health Division, 174
Information Technology & Project Management, 174
Minority Health, 174
Nutrition Division, 174
Center for Environmental Health, 148, 174
Division of Environmental Health Assessment, 148, 174
Division of Environmental Health Investigation, 148, 175
Division of Environmental Health Protection, 148, 175
Division of Administration, 174
Division of Council Operations, 175
Division of External Affairs, 175
Division of Governmental Affairs, 175
Executive Offices, 175
Office of Governmental & External Affairs, 175
Office of Health Insurance Programs, 175
Office of Public Health, 175
Office of Quality & Patient Safety, 175
School of Public Health, SUNY at Albany, 175
Health Facilities Management, 175, 293
Helen Hayes Hospital, 175, 293
New York State Veterans' Home at Batavia, 175, 293
New York State Veterans' Home at Montrose, 175, 293
New York State Veterans' Home at Oxford, 175, 293
New York State Veterans' Home at St Albans, 175, 293
Health Research Inc, 175
Human Resources Management Group, 176
Operations Management Group, 176
Legal Affairs, 176
Task Force On Life & The Law, 176
Office of Information Technology Services (ITS) Health Cluster, 176
Office of Primary Care & Health Systems Management, 175
Office of the Commissioner, 174
Public Affairs, 148, 176
Regional Offices, 176
Central New York Regional Office, 176
Metropolitan Area/Regional Office, 176
Western Regional Office, 176
Roswell Park Cancer Institute Corporation, 176
Wadsworth Center, 148, 176
Environmental Health Sciences, 148, 176
Genetics, 176
Herbert W Dickerman Library, 176
Infectious Disease, 176
Laboratory Quality Certification, 176
Translational Medicine, 177
Health Facilities Association, 423
Health Plan Assn Inc (NY), 423
Health Plan Association, 421
Health Transportation Network, 441
Health, Education, Labor, & Pensions, 315
Subcommittees, 315
Children and Families, 315
Employment & Workplace Safety, 315
Retirement and Aging, 315
HealthFirst, 425
HealthPass, 442
Healthcare Assn of NYS, 476
Healthcare Association of New York State, 183, 423
Healthcare Association of New York State PAC, 486
Healthcare Chaplaincy, The, 392
Healthcare Education Project, 445
Healthcare Professionals Insurance Company, 446
Healthcare Tort Reform Coalition (NY), 424
Healthplex Inc, 445
Healthplex, Inc., 421
Healthport Technologies, LLC, 421
Healthy Schools Network, Inc., 430
Hearing Healthcare Alliance of NY Inc (HHCANY), 378
HeartShare Human Services of New York, Roman Catholic Diocese of Brooklyn, 258
Hebrew Home at Riverdale Foundation, 432
Hebrew Home for the Aged at Riverdale (The), 476
Hebrew Union College - Jewish Institute of Religion, 555
Hedgewood Home for Adults, 476
Helal A. Sheikh 2013, 486
Helen Keller Services for the Blind, 258, 405
Helen Rosenthal For City Council, 486
Helene Fuld College of Nursing North General Hospital, 555

Hempstead Industrial Development Agency (Town of), 508
Hempstead UFSD, 580
Hempstead, Town of, 347
Hempstead, Village of, 347
Henderson Global Investors (North America) Inc., 424
Henderson Harbor Area Chamber of Commerce, 508
Hendrick Hudson CSD, 598
Henningson Durham & Richardson Architecture and Engineering P.C., 437
Henningson, Durham, & Richardson Architecture and Engineering, PC, 382
Henrietta, Town of, 347
Henry Schein Inc, 476
Herkimer CSD, 576
Herkimer County, 54, 330
Family Court, 54
Supreme, County & Surrogate's Courts, 54
Herkimer County Chamber of Commerce, 508
Herkimer County Community College, 547
Herkimer County Industrial Development Agency, 508
Herkimer-Fulton-Hamilton-Otsego BOCES, 600
Hermon-Dekalb CSD, 590
Herrick, Feinstein LLP, 424
Herricks UFSD, 580
Hertz Corporation (The), 475, 476
Heslin Rothenberg Farley & Mesiti PC, 144
Hess Corporation, 144, 456
Heuvelton CSD, 590
Hewlett Packard Company, 431
Hewlett-Packard Company, 439
Hewlett-Woodmere UFSD, 580
Heyman, Neil, 424
Hicksville Chamber of Commerce, 508
Hicksville UFSD, 580
Higgins Roberts Beyerl & Coan, PC, 424
Higher Education, 23, 39
Committee Staff, 23, 39
Key Assembly Staff Assignments, 39
Key Senate Staff Assignments, 23
Membership, 23, 39
Majority, 23, 39
Minority, 23, 39
Higher Education Initiative, 433
Higher Education Initiative (New York State), 404
Highland CSD, 595
Highland Falls CSD, 585
Hilbert College, 556
Hill & Gosdeck, 424
Hill 2013, 486
Hill, Gosdeck & McGraw LLC, 74
Hillside Family of Agencies, 424, 425
Hilton CSD, 579
Hinman Straub Advisors, LLC, 424
Hinsdale CSD, 569
Hiscock & Barclay, LLP, 425
Hispanic Counseling Center Inc, 472
Hispanic Federation, 258, 472
Hispanic Information Telecommunications Network, 472
Hispanic Outreach Services, 258
Historic Hudson Valley, 279
Historical Society, 431
Historical Society (NY), 445
Hitachi Data Systems Corporation, 393
Hobart & William Smith Colleges, 556
Hodes & Landy, 425
Hodgson Russ LLP, 456
Hoffnung 2013, 486
Hofstra University, 425, 426, 556
Hofstra University, School of Law, 117, 157, 191
Hogan Lovells US LLP, 144
Holbrook Chamber of Commerce, The, 508
Holland CSD, 573
Holland Patent CSD, 583
Holland and Knight Committee For Responsible Government, 486
Holley CSD, 586
Holloway, Jr, Floyd, 426
Hollyer Brady et al, 216
Home Care Assn of NYS Inc, 426
Home Care Association of NYS, 405
Home Care Association of New York State Inc, 183
Homeland Security, 320
Subcommittees, 320
Border, Maritime and Global Counterterrorism, 320
Emergency Communications, Preparedness and Response, 320
Emerging Threats, Cybersecurity and Science and Technology, 320
Intelligence, Information Sharing and Terrorism Risk Assessment, 320
Management, Investigations and Oversight, 320
Transportation Security and Infrastructure Protection, 320
Homeland Security & Emergency Services, Division of, 7, 160, 235, 304
Homeland Security & Governmental Affairs, 315
Subcommittees, 315
Disaster Recovery, 315
Federal Financial Mgt, Govt Info, Federal Svcs, & International Security, 315
Oversight of Government Management,Federal Workforce & District of Columbia, 315
Permanent Subcommittee on Investigations, 315
State, Local, and Private Sector Preparedness and Integration, 315
Homeless Services United, 438
Homeless Services United (FKA Council on Homeless Policies & Services), 426
Homer CSD, 571
Homeward Bound Adirondacks, 405
Honda North America, Inc., 421
Honeoye CSD, 585
Honeoye Falls-Lima CSD, 579
Honeywell International, Inc., 426, 437
Hoosic Valley CSD, 587
Hoosick Falls CSD, 587
Hope Network, 390
Hopevale UFSD at Hamburg, 573
Hornell, 63
Civil & Criminal Courts, 63
Hornell Area Chamber of Commerce/Hornell Industrial Development Agency (City of), 509
Hornell City SD, 591
Horseheads CSD, 570
Horton, Dan J, 426
Hospice & Palliative Care Association of NYS Inc, 183, 258
Hospice and Palliative Care Association of NYS, 442
Hospital Medical Center of Queens (NY), 453
Hospital for Special Surgery, 436
Hospitality & Tourism Assn (NYS), 476
Hospitality & Tourism NYS, 396
Hospitality Alliance, Inc., 388
Hospitals Insurance Company Inc, 476
Hospitals Insurance Company, Inc., 390
Host Hotels and Resorts L.P., 431
Hostos Community College, 551
Hotel & Motel Trades Council, AFL-CIO, 426
Hotel Assn of NYC Inc, 476
Hotel Association of New York City Inc, 279
Hotel Association of New York City, Inc., 486
Hotel and Motel Trades Council AFL-CIO (NY), 378
Houghton College, 556
Houghton Mifflin Harcourt Publishing Company, 403
House Administration, 320
House of Representatives Standing Committees, 73, 79, 89, 116, 125, 137, 142, 154, 168, 180, 190, 196, 203, 214, 224, 242, 255, 267, 276, 290, 297
Agriculture, 73, 154, 180
Subcommittee, 180
Subcommittees, 154
Agriculture, Rural Development, FDA & Related Agencies, 73
Appropriations, 73, 142, 267
Subcommittee, 73, 142
Armed Services, 297
Biotechnology, Horticulture & Research, 154

Budget, 267
Capital Markets & Government Sponsored Enterprises, 203
Conservation & Forestry, 154
Contracting and Workforce, 224
Counterterrorism & Intelligence, 169
Crime, Terrorism, Homeland Security & Investigations, 116
Cybersecurity, Infrastructure Protection, and Security Technologies, 169
Economic Development, Public Buildings & Emergency Management, 190
Education & Labor, 224
Education & the Workforce, 125, 196
Emergency Preparedness, Response and Communications, 169
Emerging Threats, 169
Energy, 143
Energy & Commerce, 89, 142, 154, 180
Subcommittee, 143, 180
Subcommittees, 154
Energy & Mineral Resources, 143
Energy & Power, 143
Energy & Water Development, 142
Environment, 155
Environment & the Economy, 154
Ethics, 137, 169
Federal Workforce, Postal Service and the District of Columbia, 242
Financial Services, 79, 190, 203
Subcommittee, 190, 203
Foreign Affairs, 89, 196
Subcommittee, 197
General Farm Commodities & Risk Management, 154
Government Operations, 137
Health, 180
Homeland Security, 168
Subcommittees, 169
Housing & Insurance, 190
Intelligence, Permanent Select Committee on, 169
Subcommittee, 169
Judiciary, 116, 214
Subcommittee, 116
Livestock & Foreign Agriculture, 154
Natural Resources, 143, 154, 276
Subcommittee, 276
Subcommittees, 143
Nutrition, 154, 180
Oversight & Government Reform, 137, 168
Subcommittee, 137
Oversight & Management Efficiency, 169
Oversight and Government Reform, 242
Subcommittee, 242
Public Lands & Environmental Regulations, 276
Science, Space & Technology, 143, 154
Subcommittee, 143, 155
Small Business, 90, 224
Subcommittees, 224
Social Security, 255
Terrorism, Nonproliferation and Trade, 197
Transportation & Infrastructure, 155, 190, 290
Subcommittee, 155, 190
Transportation Security, 169
Veterans' Affairs, 297
Water Resources & Environment, 155
Water, Power & Oceans, 143
Ways & Means, 180, 255, 267
Subcommittee, 180, 255
Housing, 39
Committee Staff, 39
Key Assembly Staff Assignments, 39
Membership, 39
Majority, 39
Minority, 39
Housing & Community Renewal, 8
Housing & Community Renewal, Division of, 187, 304
Administration, 187
Housing Information Systems, 187
Office of Training & Professional Development, 187
Support Services/Processing Services Unit, 187
Community Development, 187
Community Service Bureau/Technical Assistance Unit, 187
Energy Rehabilitation Services, 187
Environmental Analysis Unit, 187
Housing Trust Fund Program, 187
Regional Offices, 187
Fair Housing & Equal Opportunity, 187
Finger Lakes, Western NY, Southern Tier, 187
Housing Operations, 187
Housing Management Bureau, 187
Manufactured Homes, 187
Legal Affairs, 187
General Law, 187
Mobile Home Unit, 187
New York City, Long Island, Hudson Valley, 187
Policy & Intergovernmental Relations, 187
Rent Administration, 188
Luxury Decontrol/Overcharge, 188
Property Management, 188
Rent Control/ETPA, 188
Rent Information Services, 188
Subsidy Services, 187
Housing Action Council Inc - Not For Profit, 191, 238
Housing Association, Inc., 421
Housing Conservation Coordinators, 426
Housing New York Political Action Committee, 487
Housing Works Inc, 191, 258
Housing, Construction & Community Development, 23
Committee Staff, 23
Key Senate Staff Assignments, 24
Membership, 24
Majority, 24
Minority, 24
Howard Hughes Corporation (The), 426
Hoylman For Senate, 487
Hubbell Galvanizing, 452
Hudson, 63
City Court, 63
Hudson Alliance for Children with Special Needs, 421
Hudson Center for Health Equity & Quality, 425
Hudson City SD, 571
Hudson Eagle LLC, 427
Hudson Eagle, LLC, 392
Hudson Falls CSD, 596
Hudson Guild, 477
Hudson Headwaters Health Network, 390
Hudson River Cruises, 279
Hudson River Environmental Society, Inc, 157
Hudson River Pilots' Association, 430
Hudson River Sloop Clearwater Inc, 157
Hudson River Valley Greenway, 8, 148, 271, 304
Greenway Conservancy for the Hudson River Valley, 8, 149, 271
Hudson River Valley Greenway Communities Council, 9, 149, 271
Hudson River-Black River Regulating District, 97, 150, 307
Hudson Valley Building & Construction Trades Council, 407
Hudson Valley Business Journal, 532
Hudson Valley Community College, 427, 547
Hudson Valley Economic Development Corp, 476
Hudson Valley Fois Gras (HVFG, LLC), 405
Hudson Valley Gateway Chamber of Commerce, 509
Hudson Valley Newspapers Inc, 524
Hudson Valley Pattern for Progress, 191
Human Rights Campaign New York PAC, 487
Human Rights First, 198
Human Rights Watch, 198
Human Rights, State Division of, 9, 194, 304
Regional Offices, 194
Albany, 194
Binghamton, 194
Brooklyn, 194
Buffalo, 194
Housing Investigations Unit, 194
Manhattan (Upper), 194
Nassau County, 194
Peekskill, 195

Rochester, 195
Suffolk County, 195
Syracuse, 195
Human Services Council, 438
Humane Society of the United States (The), 433, 464, 465
Humane Society of the United States, New York State, 75, 259
Humberto Soto For New York City Council 2013, 487
Hunger Action Network of NYS, 427
Hunger Action Network of NYS (HANNYS), 259
Hunter Chamber of Commerce (Town of), 509
Hunter College, 401, 460, 551
Hunter College, Brookdale Center for Healthy Aging and Longevity, 259
Hunter Mountain Ski Bowl, 279, 455
Hunter-Tannersville CSD, 576
Huntington Township Chamber of Commerce, 509
Huntington UFSD, 592
Huntington, Town of, 347
Hunts Point Cooperative Market, Inc., 421
Hunts Point Produce Redevelopment PAC - Corporate Contribution Account, 487
Hunts Point Produce Redevelopment PAC - Personal Contribution Account, 487
Hunts Point Terminal Produce Cooperative Association, Inc., 405
Hurley, Alicia D. (FKA Haberman, Michael), 427
Hutton & Solomon, LLP, 427
Hyde Park CSD, 572
Hyde Park Chamber of Commerce, 509
Hyde Park, Town of, 348
Hynes, Daniel, 427
IAAC, Inc., 385
IAFF FIREPAC New York Non-Federal, 487
IBM Corporation, 92, 443
IBT Joint Council No. 16 PAC, 487
ICONPLANS LLC, 403
IDT Energy, 405
IMG Models, 476
IMS Health, 421
INFORM Inc, 157, 183
ING America Insurance Holdings, 391
IRX Therapeutics Inc, 81
ISJ Commercial Corp., 392
ITAR-TASS News Agency, 532
ITT Technical Institute, 564
IUOE Local 15 Political Action Fund, 487
IUOE Local 17, 387
Ianno, Dominick, 427
Ichabod Crane CSD, 571
Ignizio 2013, 487
Igor 2013, 487
Ilion CSD, 576
Illinois Tool Works Inc, 377
Immigration Coalition, Inc (NY), 427
Immigration Coalition, Inc., 387
Independent Bankers Association of NYS, 81
Independent Bankers Association of New York State, 427
Independent Care System (ICS), 439
Independent Health Association, Inc., 393, 427
Independent Insurance Agents & Brokers of NY, 385
Independent Oil & Gas Association of NY, 425, 474
Independent Oil & Gas Association of New York, 144
Independent Oil and Gas Association of NY, 402
Independent Power Producers of NY Inc, 144
Independent System Operator, Inc., 405
Independent System Operator, Inc. (New York), 385
Indian Affairs, Committee on, 316
Indian Lake CSD, 576
Indian Lake Chamber of Commerce, 509
Indian River CSD, 577
Industco Holdings, LLC, 416, 421
Industrial Technology Assistance Corp, 437
Industries for the Blind of NYS, Inc., 400
Industry AD HOC Committee on Pilotage, 430
Industry City Associates, LLC, 392
Infrastructure & Capital Investment, 24
Committee Staff, 24
Membership, 24
Majority, 24
Minority, 24
Injured Workers Alliance, 420
Inlet Common School, 576
Inlet Information Office, 509
Innocence Project (The), 410
Inside Broadway, 408
Insight Associates, 441
Inspector General (NYS), Office of the, 9, 112, 161, 304
Insperity Services, L.P., 425
Institute for Community Living, Inc., 398
Institute for Family Health (The), 183
Institute for International Bankers, 442
Institute for Puerto Rican/Hispanic Elderly, 444
Institute for Socio-Economic Studies, 259
Institute for Special Education, 425
Institute for Student Achievement, 475
Institute of Design & Construction, 556
Institute of International Bankers, 428
Institute of Public Administration/NYU Wagner, 170, 238
Institutional Life Markets Association, Inc, 404
Insurance, 24, 39
Committee Staff, 24, 39
Key Assembly Staff Assignments, 39
Key Senate Staff Assignments, 24
Membership, 24, 39
Majority, 24, 39
Minority, 24, 40
Insurance Association, Inc. (NY), 428
Insurance Brokers' Association of the State of New York, 204, 454
Insurance Fund (NYS), 9, 200, 219, 304
Administration, 200, 219
Claims & Medical Operations, 200, 219
Confidential Investigations, 200, 219
Field Services, 200, 219
Information Technology Service, 200, 219
Insurance Fund Board of Commissioners, 9, 200, 219
Investments, 201, 219
NYSIF District Offices, 201, 219
Albany, 201, 219
Binghamton, 201, 219
Buffalo, 201, 219
Nassau County, Long Island, 201, 219
Rochester, 201, 219
Suffolk County, Long Island, 201, 219
Syracuse, 201, 219
White Plains, 201, 219
Premium Audit, 201, 219
Underwriting, 201, 220
Insurance Premium Finance Assn Inc, 442
Integrated Medical Professionals PLLC, 437
Intelligence, House Permanent Select Committee on, 324
Subcommittees, 324
Intelligence Community Management, 324
Oversight and Investigations, 324
Technical and Tactical Intelligence, 324
Terrorism/HUMIT, Analysis and Counterintelligence, 324
Intelligence, Select Committee on, 316
InterAgency Council of Mental Retardatn & Developmental Disabilities, 232
Interest on Lawyer Account (IOLA) Fund of the State of NY, 98, 210, 307
Intergraph Corporation, 443
Interior Designers for Legislation in New York, 437
International American University College of Medicine, 421
International Bottled Water Association, 425
International Brotherhood of Electrical Workers Political Action Committee, 487
International Brotherhood of Teamsters Port Division, 385
International Business Machine Corporation, 424
International Code Council, Inc., 401
International Council of Shopping Centers, 387
International Flavors & Fragrances Inc, 92

International Game Technology, 387
International Imaging Technology Council (I-ITC), 452
International Institute of Buffalo, NY, Inc, 198
International Longshoremen's Association, AFL-CIO, 440
International Paper, 424
International Union of Operating Engineers Local 14-14B Voluntary Political Action Committee, 487
International Union of Operating Engineers Local 15 A B C D, 487
International Union of Painters and Allied Trades Political Action Committee, 487
Interstate Environmental Commission, 98, 151, 307
Interstate Oil & Gas Compact Commission, 98, 141, 151, 307
Intrepid Museum Foundation, 476
Intuit, Inc., 388
Int'l Brotherhood of Teamsters, AFL-CIO (Local 237), 444
Int'l Longshoremen's Ass'n, AFL-CIO Committee on Political Education, 487
Inventiv Health, Inc., 428
Investigations & Government Operations, 24
Committee Staff, 24
Key Senate Staff Assignments, 24
Membership, 24
Majority, 24
Minority, 24
Inwood House, 392
Iona College, 556
Irondequoit, Town of, 348
Ironworkers Local 46 PAC, 487
Ironworkers Political Action League, 487
Iroquois CSD, 573
Iroquois Healthcare Alliance, 183, 415
Iroquois Pipeline Operating Company, 425
Irrigation Assn of New York, 465
Irving Place Capital Management L.P., 428
Irvington UFSD, 598
Irvington-on-Hudson Chamber of Commerce, 509
Island Drafting & Technical Institute, 564
Island Harvest LTD, 425
Island Park UFSD, 580
Island Peer Review Organization, Inc., 428
Island Peer Review Organization, Inc. (IPRO), 387
Island Public Affairs, 428
Island Tennis LP D/B/A Sportime, 418
Island Trees UFSD, 580
Islip Chamber of Commerce, 509
Islip Economic Development Division & Industrial Development Agency (Town of), 509
Islip Industrial Development Agency (Town of), 509
Islip UFSD, 592
Islip, Town of, 348
Ithaca, 63
Civil & Criminal Courts, 63
Ithaca City SD, 595
Ithaca College, 556
Ithaca Journal (The), 526
Ithaca, City of, 348
Ithaca, Town of, 348
Iwachiw 4 Mayor, 487
J J Higgins Properties Inc, 247
J Strategies, Inc., 427
J.H. Reid, General Contractor, 401
J.P. Morgan Securities Inc., 428
JAMS, 216, 225
JBI International, 436
JC Penney Corporation, Inc., 401
JEM Associates NY, Inc., 428
JGN Associates LLC, 429
JJMH Consulting, 429
JLO Consultant, Inc., 429
JMA, 437
JMED Holding LLC, 407
JP Morgan Chase & Co., 405
JPAY, Inc., 387
JPMorgan Chase & Co, 81
JPMorgan Chase & Co. PAC, 488
JPMorgan Chase Bank, National Association, 430
JXQ Holding Company, Inc, 476
Jacobs Engineering, 291
Jacques Leandre For New York, 487
Jamaica Chamber of Commerce, 509
Jamaica Ctr for Arts & Learning Inc, 453
Jamaica Hospital Medical Center, 415, 452
Jamestown, 63
Civil & Criminal Courts, 63
Jamestown Business College, 564
Jamestown City SD, 570
Jamestown Community College, 548
Jamestown Premier Chelsea Market, L.P., 416
Jamestown Premier Chelsea Market, LP, 392
Jamestown, City of, 349
Jamesville-Dewitt CSD, 584
Janney Montgomery Scott LLC, 428
Japanese American Social Services Inc, 259
Japanese Chamber of Commerce, 509
Jasper-Troupsburg CSD, 591
Jefferies LLC, 409
Jefferson CSD, 589
Jefferson Community College, 548
Jefferson County, 54, 330
County, Family & Surrogate's Courts, 54
Supreme Court, 54
Jefferson-Lewis-Hamilton-Herkimer-Oneida BOCES, 600
Jeffersonville Area Chamber of Commerce, The, 509
Jenkins, Joanne E, 428
Jennings NYC, 487
Jennison Associates LLC, 429
Jericho UFSD, 580
Jerome, Stephen, 429
Jesse Hamilton 2013, 487
Jets (NY), 454
Jets LLC (NY), 442
Jewish Association for Services for the Aged (FKA Saiger, Molly), 429
Jewish Board of Family & Children's Services, 232
Jewish Board of Family & Children's Services Inc, 435
Jewish Community Relations Council of NY Inc, 198
Jewish Education Project (The), 126
Jewish Guild for the Blind (The), 446, 476
Jewish Home & Hospital Lifecare System, 418
Jewish Home Lifecare, 421
Jewish Home and Hospital for Aged (The), 429
Jewish Home of Rochester (The), 425
Jewish Museum (The), 279, 476
Jewish Senior Life, 390
Jewish Theological Seminary, 556
Jewish War Veterans of the USA, 298
Jewish War Veterans of the USA, State of NY, 298
Jim Owles Liberal Democratic Club, 487
Joan Flowers For the 27th District, 487
Jobs with Justice (NY), 429
Jockey Club (The), 429
Joe Lhota For Mayor, Inc., 487
Joel Bauza For City Council, 487
John Catsimatidis For Mayor 2013 Committee, Inc., 488
John Hancock Life Insurance, 429
John Jay College of Criminal Justice, 551
John Mezzalingua Associates D/B/A PPC, 437
John Quaglione For City Council, 488
John T Mather Memorial Hospital, 476
John W. Danforth Company, 441
Johnsburg CSD, 596
Johnson & Johnson, 475
Johnson & Johnson Health Care Systems, Inc., 429
Johnson & Johnson Services, 379
Johnson 2013, 488
Johnson City CSD, 568
Johnson NYC 2013, 488
Johnson Newspaper Corp, 531
Johnson Newspaper Corporation, 526, 527
Johnson, Russ, 430
Johnston, Christine, 430
Johnstown, 63
Civil & Criminal Courts, 63
Johnstown Fire Fighters Association Local 779, 425
Joint Commission on Public Ethics (JCOPE), 103, 136, 164, 308

Joint Council #16, International Brotherhood of Teamsters, 385
Joint Industry Board of the Electrical Industry, 430
Joint Senate & House Standing Committees, 90, 267
Economic Committee, Joint, 90
Joint Committee on Taxation, 267
Jones Lang Lasalle, 391
Jones, Jeff, 430
Jordan-Elbridge CSD, 584
Journal News (The)/Gannett Co Inc, 524
Journal Register Co, 529, 531
Journal Register Company, 526, 530
Journal-Register, The, 526, 527
JuanPagan2013, 488
Judge Analisa Torres For Supreme Court 2011, 488
Judge Rotenberg Center, 404, 438
Judiciary, 24, 40, 316, 320
Committee Staff, 24, 40
Key Assembly Staff Assignments, 40
Membership, 24, 40
Majority, 24, 40
Minority, 24, 40
Subcommittees, 316, 320
Administrative Oversight & the Courts, 316
Antitrust, Competition Policy & Consumer Rights, 316
Commercial & Administrative Law, 320
Constitution, Civil Rights and Civil Liberties, 321
Constitution, The, 316
Courts & Competition Policy, 321
Crime & Drugs, 316
Crime, Terrorism and Homeland Security, 321
Immigration, Citizenship, Refugees, Border Security and International Law, 321
Immigration, Refugees and Border Security, 316
Juilliard School (The), 556
Jujamcyn Theaters LLC, 432
Julie Menin 2013, 488
Julissa 2013, 488
Jumaane 2013, 488
Junior Tennis League (NY), 408
Junior Tennis League, Inc., 401
Just Energy New York Corporation (FKA Energy Savings), 414
Just Kids Diagnostic and Treatment Center, 421
Just Kids Early Childhood Learning Center, 421
Justice, Lawrence P., 430
Justin McCarthy Consulting Services, Inc., 430
KCI Technologies Inc., 457
KM Associates of NY, Inc., 431
KPMG LLP, 170, 238
KPMG, LLP, 390, 476
Kalanz, Edward, 431
Kaleida Health, 387, 441
Kantor Davidoff Mandelker Twomey Gallanty & Kesten, PC, 431
Kaplan Higher Education, 421
Kaplan, Alden B., 431
Kasirer Consulting, 431
Katonah Chamber of Commerce, 509
Katonah-Lewisboro UFSD, 598
Katz, Arthur H, 431
Kaye Scholer LLP, 225
Kaysen, Mary, 431
Keeling Campaign 2013, 488
Keene CSD, 574
Kehoe, Clare, 431
Kellner Campaign 2013, 488
Ken 2013, 488
Kendall CSD, 586
Kenmore-Tonawanda UFSD, 574
Kenmore-Town of Tonawanda Chamber of Commerce, 509
Kennedy, Ronald F., 432
Kesselly For Council, 488
Ketzer, Bill, 432
Keuka College, 556
KeyBank, 81
KeySpan Energy/National Grid, 478
Keycorp & Subsidiaries, 387, 432
Khari Edwards 2013, 488
Kiernan-Pagani, Kathleen, 432
King Street Capital Management, L.P., 394
King, Barbara, 432
Kings County, 54
COUNTY & FAMILY COURTS: See New York City Courts, 54
Supreme Court, 54
Surrogate's Court, 54
Kings County (NYC Borough of Brooklyn), 330
Kings County Conservative Party Campaign Committee, 488
Kings Park CSD, 592
Kings Park Chamber of Commerce, 509
Kingsborough Community College, 551
Kingsbrook Jewish Medical Center, 387
Kingston, 63
City Court, 63
Kingston Avenue Development LLC, 436
Kingston City SD, 595
Kingston, City of, 349
King's College (The), 556
Kiryas Joel Village UFSD, 585
Kissling Interests (The), 441
Knic Partners LLC, 392
Knickerbocker Plaza Associates, 436
Koch Companies Public Sector, LLC and it's Affiliates, 442
Kohl Partners, 414
Komanoff Energy Associates, 144, 291
Konheim & Ketcham Inc, 291
Korean Community Services of Metropolitan NY, 259
Korean War Veterans, 298
Kraft Foods Global, Inc,, 388
Kramer Levin Naftalis & Frankel, LLP, 432
Kramer, Jason, 433
Kraus & Zuchlewski LLP, 225
Kriss Kriss & Brignola, LLP, 433
Kriss, Kriss, Brignola & Persing, LLP, 291
Kudlow & Company LLC, 81
Kulanu, 437
Kwan, Patrick, 433
L & M Development Partners, Inc., 377
LB Furniture Industries LLC, 440
LCI LLC, 434
LCO Buildings LLC, 437
LEAP, 477
LI CSP-MSA Association, 438
LJM Rad, LLC, 435
LM Legacy Group LLC, 418
LS Power Associates LLC, 453
LV Apartments LP, 390
La Fargeville CSD, 577
LaFayette CSD, 584
LaGuardia Community College, 429, 551
LaSalle School, 402
Labor, 24, 40
Committee Staff, 24, 40
Key Assembly Staff Assignments, 40
Key Senate Staff Assignments, 24
Membership, 24, 40
Majority, 24, 40
Minority, 24, 40
Labor Department, 9, 177, 201, 220, 252, 293, 304
Administration & Public Affairs, 220
Asbestos Control Bureau, 177, 220
Central/Mohawk Valley, 220
Counsel's Office, 220
Employability Development/Apprentice Training, 220
Employment Relations Board, 201, 220
Federal Programs, 220, 253, 293
Employment Services Division, 220, 253, 293
Unemployment Insurance Division, 220, 253
Workforce Development & Training Division, 220, 253
Finger Lakes Region, 220
Greater Capital District, 220
Hazard Abatement Board, 201, 220
Hudson Valley, 220
Industrial Board of Appeals, 201, 220
Industry Inspection Unit, 177, 220
Labor Planning & Technology, 220
Labor Standards Division
Labor Standards Division, 253
Safety & Health Division, 253

Long Island Region, 220
New York City, 220
On-Site Consultation Unit, 177
On-site Consultation Unit, 220
Public Employees Safety & Health (PESH) Unit, 177, 221
Research & Statistics Division, 220
Southern Tier, 220
Special Investigations, 220
State Workforce Investment Board, 201
Unemployment Insurance Appeal Board, 201, 220
Veterans Services, 220, 253, 293
Employer Services, 220, 293
Regional Offices, 220
Western Region, 220
Worker Protection, 177, 220, 253
Labor Standards Division, 220
Public Work Bureau, 220
Safety & Health Division, 177, 220
Laboratory Institute of Merchandising, 565
Laborers Int'l Union of North America AFL-CIO, Local 17, 407
Laborers PAC (NYS), 456
Laborers' Political Action Committee (NYS), 444
Lackawanna, 63
Civil & Criminal Courts, 63
Lackawanna Area Chamber of Commerce, 509
Lackawanna City SD, 574
Lackawanna School District, 387
Lackman, Abraham M., 433
Lake George CSD, 596
Lake George Park Commission, 98, 151, 307
Lake George Regional Chamber of Commerce, 509
Lake Luzerne Chamber of Commerce, 509
Lake Placid CSD, 574
Lake Placid Chamber of Commerce, 509
Lake Pleasant CSD, 576
Lake Shore Savings, 81
Lakeland CSD, 598
Lambda Legal, 198
Lambert, Linda A, 433
Lancaster Area Chamber of Commerce, 510
Lancaster CSD, 574
Lancaster Industrial Development Agency (Town of), 510
Lancaster, Town of, 349
Lancer Insurance Co/Lancer Compliance Services, 225
Lancman 2013, 488
Land Title Association, Inc., 433
Land Trust Alliance Northeast Program, 157, 430, 433
Landauer Realty Group Inc, 247
Landis For New York, 488
Lands End Associates, LP, 392
Langan Engineering & Environmental Services, Inc., 392
Langdon, David, 433
Lanotte, Michael A., 433
Lansing CSD, 595
Lansingburgh CSD, 588
Lantigua 2013, 488
Lasky, Roy, 433
Latino Commission on AIDS, 472
LatinoJustice PRLDEF, 198
Laurens CSD, 587
Laurie Cumbo 2013, 488
Law Department, 9, 78, 84, 112, 140, 149, 161, 177, 188, 195, 201, 206, 221, 245, 263, 304
Administration, 206
Budget & Fiscal Management, 206
Human Resources Management, 207
Legal Recruitment, 207
Appeals & Opinions, 112
Law Library, 112
Appeals & Opinions Division, 207
Law Library, 207
Criminal Justice, 112, 177, 207
Criminal Enforcement & Financial Crimes Bureau, 112, 207
Guns, Gangs & Drugs Initiative, 112
Medicaid Fraud Control Unit, 112, 177, 207
Economic Justice, 78, 84, 112, 140, 188, 207, 263
Antitrust Bureau, 78, 84, 112, 207
Consumer Frauds & Protection Bureau, 78, 188, 207
Consumer Frauds Bureau, 84, 112
Internet Bureau, 78, 84, 140, 207, 263
Investor Protection Bureau, 78, 84, 207, 263
Real Estate Finance Bureau, 78
Intergovernmental Relations, 207
Investigations, 112, 207
Office of the Attorney General, 207
Regional Offices Division, 207
Binghamton, 207
Brooklyn, 207
Buffalo, 207
Harlem, 207
Nassau, 207
Plattsburgh, 208
Poughkeepsie, 208
Rochester, 208
Suffolk, 208
Syracuse, 208
Utica, 208
Watertown, 208
Westchester, 208
Social Justice, 112, 149, 177, 188, 195, 207, 221, 245, 263
Charities Bureau, 207, 263
Civil Rights Bureau, 112, 188, 195, 207, 221, 245
Environmental Protection Bureau, 149, 207
Healthcare Bureau, 177, 207
Investor Protection Bureau, 245
State Counsel, 84, 112, 177, 188, 201, 208, 221, 245, 264
Civil Recoveries Bureau, 112, 201, 208, 221, 264
Claims Bureau, 84, 112, 177, 201, 208, 245
Litigation Bureau, 112, 177, 188, 201, 208, 264
Real Property Bureau, 112, 188, 201, 208, 245
Law Enforcement Officers Union, Distr Cncl 82 (NYS), 456
Law Guardian Program, 208
3rd Judicial Dept, 208
4th Judicial Dept, 208
Law Office of Anne Reynolds Copps, 216, 259
Law Office of Usher Fogel, 433
Law Offices of Frank G. D'Angelo & Associates, 216
Law Offices of Stanley N Lupkin, 117
Law School Admission Council, 410
Law School Admissions Council, 476
Lawley Insurance, 408
Lawrence UFSD, 580
Lawyers for the Public Interest, 477
Lawyers' Fund for Client Protection, 98, 210, 307
Le Moyne College, 425, 556
Le Roy CSD, 575
LeRay, Town of, 349
Leader House Associates, LP, 392
Leader-Herald (The), 525
LeadingAge New York, 183, 425
League of American Theatres & Producers Inc, 476
League of Conservation Voters, 434
League of Women Voters of New York State, 138, 170, 238, 434
Learning Leaders, 127, 477
Learning Through an Expanded Arts Program, 438
Lee Enterprises Inc, 525
Lee New York Political Action Committee, 488
Lefebvre, Steve, 434
Legal Action Center, 117, 216
Legal Aid Society, 117, 216
Legal Aid Society (The), 385, 437
Legal Assistance Group, 431, 438
Legal Assistance Group (NY), 434
Legal Information for Families Today (LIFT), 434
Legal Services NYC, 434, 477
Legal Services for the Elderly, Disabled or Disadvantaged of Western New York, Inc., 450
Legal Services for the Working Poor, 477
Legal Services of the Hudson Valley, 216

Legislative Bill Drafting Commission, 98, 163, 307
Legislative Retrieval System, 98, 163
Legislative Correspondents Association, 532
Legislative Gazette, 523
Legislative Library, 306
Lehman College, 551
Lehrer, Sander, 435
Lend Lease (US) Construction LMB, Inc., 382
Lend Lease Construction LMB, Inc., 431
Lenox Terrace Development Associates, 432
Lesbian & Gay Community Services Center, Inc., 387
Lesbian & Gay Democratic Club of Queens, 488
Lesbian Gay Bisexual & Transgender Community Center (The), 476
Lesbian and Gay Community Services Center, Inc., 435
Lesbian, Gay, Bisexual & Transgender Community Center - Not For Profit, 198
Lesbian, Gay, Bisexual & Transgender Community Ctr - Not For Profit, 232, 259
Letchworth CSD, 599
Letitia James 2013, 488
Lettire Construction Corp., 386
Levene, Gouldin & Thompson LLP, 216
Levin 2013, 488
Levin, Brenda, 435
Levin, David, 435
Levine 2013, 488
Levine, Paul, 435
Levittown UFSD, 580
Levy Ratner P.C., 435
Levy, Norman P.C., 435
Lewis County, 54, 330
Supreme, County, Family & Surrogate's Courts, 54
Lewis County Chamber of Commerce, 510
Lewis County Industrial Development Agency, 510
Lewiston-Porter CSD, 582
Lexington School for the Deaf/Center for the Deaf, Inc., 421
Lexmark International, Inc., 393, 424
Liberty CSD, 594
Liberty Mutual Group, 421
Liberty Natural Gas LLC, 421
Libraries & Education Technology, 40
Committee Staff, 40
Key Assembly Staff Assignments, 40
Membership, 40
Majority, 40
Minority, 40
Libraries, Select Committee on, 26
Library Assn (NY), 435
Library Association (NY), 404
Library Trustees Association of NYS, 127
Library, Joint Committee on the, 324
Lieberman, Mark L, 435
Lieutenant Governor's Office, 3, 160, 303
Life Insurance Co (NY), 428
Life Insurance Council of NY Inc, 468
Life Insurance Council of New York, Inc, 204
Life Insurance Council of New York, Inc., 421, 425
Lifealike, LTD, 387
Lifeline Center for Child Development (The), 407
Lifespan of Greater Rochester, Inc., 437
Lifespire, 232
Lifetouch National School Studios, Inc., 425
Lift, 404
Light Tower Fiber LLC, 473
Lighthouse Guild, 183
Lightstone Bronx Venture LLC, 418
Lightstone Group LLC, 437
Lightstone Real Estate Partners LLC, 418
Lilac Capital LLC, 453
Lilly USA, 427
Lilly USA LLC, 435
Lincoln Center for the Performing Arts, 456
Lincoln Center for the Performing Arts Inc, 279, 442
Lincoln Center for the Performing Arts, Inc., 431, 435
Lindenhurst Chamber of Commerce, 510
Lindenhurst UFSD, 593
Lindenhurst, Village of, 349
Linium LLC, 405
Liquid Asphalt Distributors Assoc Inc of NY, 452
Lisa G For NY, 488
Lisbon CSD, 590
Literacy New York, Inc., 402, 425
Literacy, Inc., 408
Little Falls, 63
Civil & Criminal Courts, 63
Little Falls City SD, 576
Little Flower Children & Family Services, 259
Little Flower UFSD, 593
Littman Krooks LLP, 216, 259
Lieutenants Benevolent Association NY Police Department PAC, 488
Liverpool CSD, 584
Liverpool Chamber of Commerce (Greater Liverpool), 510
Living Essentials, LLC, 390
Living Independently Inc, 439
Livingston County, 54, 331
Supreme, County, Family & Surrogate's Courts, 54
Livingston County Chamber of Commerce, 510
Livingston County Economic Development Office & Industrial Development Agency, 510
Livingston Manor CSD, 594
Livonia CSD, 578
LoCicero & Tan Inc, 436
Local 1180, CWA, AFL-CIO, 444
Local 1182 Political Action Fund, 488
Local 1407 AFSCME Political Committee, 488
Local 147 Political Action Committee, 488
Local 1500 Political Candidates and Education Fund, 489
Local 1814 ILA AFL-CIO Political Action and Education Fund, 489
Local 2021 AFSCME Political Action Account, 489
Local 23-25 Unite State & Local Campaign Committee, 489
Local 246, SEIU, 470
Local 3, IBEW Communications Electricians, 470
Local 30 IUOE PAC, 489
Local 32BJ SEIU NY/NJ American Dream Fund, 489
Local 338 RWDSU, 387
Local 372 Political Action, 489
Local 4 Action Fund, 489
Local 6 Committee on Political Education, 489
Local 6, Hotel & Club Employees & Bartenders Union, AFL-CIO, 436
Local 802, American Federation of Musicians of Greater NY, 444
Local 802, American Federation of Musicians of Greater New York, 418
Local 891 IUOE Political Education Committee, 489
Local 891 IUOE State Engineers Political Education Committee, 489
Local 94-94A-94B IUOE Political Action Committee, 489
Local Control for Local Progress, Inc., 405
Local Government, 25
Committee Staff, 25
Key Senate Staff Assignments, 25
Membership, 25
Majority, 25
Minority, 25
Local Governments, 40
Committee Staff, 40
Key Assembly Staff Assignments, 40
Membership, 40
Majority, 40
Minority, 40
Local Initiatives Support Corporation, 191
Lockport, 63
Civil & Criminal Courts, 63
Lockport City SD, 582
Lockport Industrial Development Agency (Town of), 510
Lockport Union-Sun & Journal, 526
Lockport, City of, 349
Lockport, Town of, 349
Lockwood, Kessler & Bartlett Inc, 435

Locust Valley CSD, 580
Locust Valley Chamber of Commerce, 510
Logan, Ernest, 436
Logic Technology, Inc., 421
Long Beach, 64
Civil & Criminal Courts, 64
Long Beach Chamber of Commerce, 510
Long Beach City SD, 580
Long Beach, City of, 350
Long Island Association, 510
Long Island Board of Realtors (FKA Kaplan, Randy L.), 436
Long Island Business Institute-Commack, 565
Long Island Business Institute-Flushing, 565
Long Island Business News, 532
Long Island Coalition for Children with Special Needs, 421
Long Island College Hospital (The), 456
Long Island College Hospital School of Nursing, 556
Long Island Contractors Association, 414
Long Island Contractors Association, Inc., 436
Long Island Council of Dedicated Merchants Chamber of Commerce, 510
Long Island Development Corporation, 510
Long Island Educational Opportunity Center, 549
Long Island Farm Bureau, 75, 418
Long Island Federation of Labor, AFL-CIO, 387
Long Island Forum for Technology, 393
Long Island Gasoline Retailers Assn Inc, 464
Long Island Gasoline Retailers Association (William A. Schnell & Associates, Inc.), 417
Long Island Health Network, 476
Long Island Life Sciences Initiative, 475
Long Island Nursery & Landscape Association Inc, 75
Long Island Power Authority, 442
Long Island Progressive Coalition, 470
Long Island Rail Road Commuter's Council, 291
Long Island University, 476, 557
Long Island Water Conference, 465
Long Lake CSD, 576
Long Term Care Community Coalition (FKA Nursing Home Community Coalition), 436
Long View Publishing Co, 527
Longwood CSD, 593
Looks Great Services, Inc., 405, 431
Lorillard, Inc., 394
Losquadro, Steven E., 436
Lotovsky For City Council 2013, 489
Louloudes, Virginia, 436
Lower East Side District Management Association, Inc., 392
Lower Eastside Service Center, Inc., 438
Lower Hudson Education Coalition, 475
Lower Manhattan Cultural Council, 279
Lowville Academy & CSD, 577
Lowville Academy and Central School, 388
Lucid Solutions Group Inc., 456
Lundbeck Pharmaceutical Services LLC, 463
Lundgren For Council, 489
Luria, Robert S, 436
Luther Forest Technology Campus Economic Development, 380
Lutheran Augustana Center for Extended Care and Rehabilitation, 436
Lutheran Medical Center, 437
Luthin Associates, Inc, 437
Lutz, Jr., Alexander, 437
Lyme CSD, 577
Lynbrook Chamber of Commerce, 510
Lynbrook UFSD, 581
Lynch, Bill Associates, LLC, 437
Lynch, Patricia Associates, 437
Lyncourt UFSD, 584
Lyndonville CSD, 586
Lynn Sanchez For City Council, 489
Lyons CSD, 597
Lysander, Town of, 350
M + R Strategic Services (FKA M & R Strategic Services), 438
M&T Bank Corporation, 81
MBIA Insurance Corporation, 81, 238, 475
MC Asset Management Americas, LTD., 441
MC Financial Services LTD., 441
MCI, 475
MCIC Vermont Inc, 476
MDRC, 127, 225
METLIFE, Inc. Employees' Political Participation Fund A, 490
METRET PAC Inc., 490
MFY Legal Services, 444
MFY Legal Services, Inc., 477
MGM Resorts International, 421
MGM Resorts International Operations, Inc., 431
MJ Peterson Corporation, 247
MLOTTO, Inc., 387
MP Liberty Development, LLC, 382
MPAC, 490
MPE Hotel I Tenant (Downtown NY) LLC, 392
MS Hospital, 390
MSG Holdings L.P., 432, 437
MSG Holdings, L.P., 446
MTA (Metropolitan Transportation Authority), 98, 286, 307
MTA Bridges & Tunnels, 99, 285, 307
MTA Bus Company, 99, 285, 307
MTA Capital Construction, 285, 307
MTA Capital Construction Program, 99
MTA Long Island Rail Road, 99, 286, 307
MTA Metro-North Railroad, 99, 286, 307
MTA New York City Transit, 99, 286, 307
MTA Office of the Inspector General, 100, 286, 307
MTM Associates, LLC, 390, 392
MVP Health Insurance Co. and Its Affiliates (FKA MVP Service Corporation), 447
Macerich, 431
Macy's Inc, 92
Macy's Retail Holdings, Inc. (FKA Macys East a Division of Macy's Retail Holdings, Inc.), 378
Madden, Susan (FKA Benson, Kathleen), 438
Madison CSD, 578
Madison County, 54, 331
Supreme, County, Family & Surrogate's Courts, 54
Madison County Industrial Development Agency, 510
Madison Equities LLC, 392
Madison Realty Capital Advisors LLC (FKA Madison Realty Capital), 377
Madison Square Garden, 405
Madison Square Garden Corp, 279
Madison Square Garden L.P., 431
Madison Square Garden LP, 453
Madison-Oneida BOCES, 600
Madrid-Waddington CSD, 590
Magellan Health Services, Inc., 398
Magna Entertainment Corp, 453
Maher Jr., Daniel F., 438
Mahopac CSD, 587
Maid of the Mist Corporation, 437
Mailman For Council, 489
Maimonides Medical Center, 478
Maisel For Council, 489
Major League Baseball, 279
Major League Soccer, 385, 405, 426
Major League Soccer LLC, 416, 419
Major League Soccer, L.L.C., 387
Major League Soccer, LLC, 438
Make the Road New York, 438
Malkin & Ross, 438
Mallory Factor Inc, 81
Malone CSD, 575
Malone Chamber of Commerce, 510
Malone Telegram, The, 527
Malverne UFSD, 581
Mamaroneck Chamber of Commerce, 510
Mamaroneck UFSD, 598
Mamaroneck, Town of, 350
Managed Funds Association, 475
Manatt, Phelps & Phillips, LLP, 439
Manchester-Shortsville CSD, 585
Mancuso Business Development Group, 248
Mancuso For Council, 489
Mandl School, 565
Manhasset Chamber of Commerce, 510
Manhasset UFSD, 581
Manhattan Chamber of Commerce Inc, 510
Manhattan Chamber of Commerce, Inc., 439
Manhattan College, 557

Manhattan Educational Opportunity Center, 549
Manhattan Institute for Policy Research, 92, 170
Manhattan Institute, Center for Civic Innovation, 238, 268
Manhattan School of Music, 392, 557
Manhattan Theatre Club, 453
Manhattan by Sail Inc., 392
Manhattan-Bronx Minority Business Enterprise Center, 225
Manhattanville College, 557
Maniscalco, John D, 439
Manlius, Town of, 350
Mannella, Peter F., 439
Manufacturers Assn of Central NY Inc, 439
Manufacturers Association of Central New York, 92
Marathon CSD, 572
Marcellus CSD, 584
March of Dimes Birth Defects Foundation, 259
March of Dimes Birth Defects Foundation New York Chapter, 440
Marcus Attorneys, 440
Marcus Whitman CSD, 585
Marcy Chamber of Commerce, 511
Margaret Chin 2013, 489
Margaretville CSD, 572
Maria College of Albany, 557
Marine Corps League, 298
Marine Corps League (MCL), 298
Marine Corps League (MCL), Department of NY, 298
Marine Park Seaside Links LLC, 473
Marion CSD, 597
Marion S Whelan School of Practical Nursing, 183
Marist College, 557
Marist Institute for Public Opinion, 138
Maritato, Anna Maria, 440
Maritime Association, 437
Mark Gjonaj 2012, 489
Mark Otto For City Council, 489
Mark Treyger For Council, 489
Mark Weprin For New York PAC, 489
Markee, Lionel, 440
Markowitz/Brooklyn, 489
Marlboro CSD, 595
Marsh & McLennan Companies, 204
Marsh USA Inc, 452
Marsh, Wassermann & McHugh, LLC, 440
Marshall E. Bloomfield, 409
Marshals Assn (NYC), 476
Marthone For City Council, 489
Martin Begun D/B/A Martin S. Begun Consulting, 440
Martin J. McLaughlin Communications, Inc., 440
Marymount Manhattan College, 557
Masiello, Martucci, Calabrese and Associates (FKA Government Action Professionals, Inc.), 440
Mason Tenders District Council Greater NY & Long Island PAC, 442
Mason Tenders District Council of Greater New York Political Action Committee, 489
Massachusetts Mutual Life Insurance Company, 441
Massapequa Chamber of Commerce, 511
Massapequa UFSD, 581
Massena CSD, 590
Master Plumbers Council of the City of New York, Inc., 405
Master, Robert, 441
Mastics/Shirley Chamber of Commerce, 511
Matarazzo, Louis, 441
Mateo 2013, 489
Maternity & Early Childhood Foundation, Inc., 393
Mathews, Dan, 441
Matt Brewing Co (The), 377
Matt Brewing Company (The), 388
Matteo For Council, 489
Mattituck Chamber of Commerce, 511
Mattituck-Cutchogue UFSD, 593
Matusic, Karen, 441
Maximus, 421
Maximus Inc. Political Action Committee, 489
Mayfield CSD, 575
Mayville/Chautauqua Chamber of Commerce, 511
McCormack, Jr., R. Christopher, 441
McCormick Farms Inc, 75
McDonald 2013, 490
McDonnell, Brian, 441
McGrath Matter Associates, 441
McGrath Matter Associates, Inc., 401
McGraw CSD, 572
McGraw-Hill Education, 425
McGuire, Jason J., 441
McGuire, Michael J, 441
McKenna Long & Aldridge LLP NY PAC, 490
McKenna Long & Aldridge, LLP, 442
McKissack Group, Inc. (The), 414
McKissack and McKissack, 437
McLane Company, Inc., 387
McLean, Mary Ann, 442
McMahon & Grow, 171, 216
McMahon, Kathy A., 442
McManus, Michael T., 442
Meara Avella Dickinson, 442
Meara, Brian R, Public Relations Inc, 442
Mechanical Technology Incorporated, 144
Mechanicville, 64
Civil & Criminal Courts, 64
Mechanicville Area Chamber of Commerce, 511
Mechanicville City SD, 588
Mechanicville/Stillwater Industrial Development Agency, 511
MedBox, 394
Medaille College, 557
Medgar Evers College, 551
Media Metrica Ltd., 392
Medical Answering Services, 437
Medical Answering Services, LLC, 387
Medical College (NY), 425
Medical Liability Mutual Insurance Company, 433
Medical Society of the State of NY, Governmental Affairs Division, 183
Medical Society of the State of New York, 442
Medical Society of the State of New York, Div of Socio-Medical Economics, 204
Medical Staff Leadership Council, 410
Medimmune, Inc., 459
Medina CSD, 586
Medstat, 440
Medtronic Inc (FKA Medtronic Sofamor Danek), 476
Medtronic, Inc., 387
Medtronic, Inc. (FKA Dena Scearce), 443
Mega Contracting Group LLC, 401
Mehigan Bellone & Associates, Inc., 387
Mel 2013, 490
Melinda Katz 2013, 490
Meloni NYCC, 490
Memorial Hospital School of Nursing, 557
Memorial Sloan-Kettering Cancer Center, 183, 439, 443
Menaker & Herrmann LLP, 92
Menands UFSD, 567
Menorah Campus, Inc., 437
Mensch Capital Partners, Inc., 441
Mental Health, 40
Committee Staff, 40
Key Assembly Staff Assignments, 41
Membership, 41
Majority, 41
Minority, 41
Mental Health & Developmental Disabilities, 25
Committee Staff, 25
Key Senate Staff Assignments, 25
Membership, 25
Majority, 25
Minority, 25
Mental Health Association in NYS, 443
Mental Health Association of NYC Inc, 232, 443
Mental Health Association of NYS Inc, 232
Mental Health Association of New York, 443
Mental Health Counselors Association (NY), 425
Mental Health, Office of, 10, 228, 304

Center for Human Resource Management, 228
Center for Information Technology, 228
Division of Adult Services, 228
Division of Forensic Services, 228
Division of Integrated Community Services for Children & Families, 228
Facilities, 228
Bronx Psychiatric Center, 228
Brooklyn Children's Center, 228
Buffalo Psychiatric Center, 228
Capital District Psychiatric Center, 228
Central New York Psychiatric Center, 228
Creedmoor Psychiatric Center, 228
Elmira Psychiatric Center, 228
Greater Binghamton Health Center, 228
Hutchings Psychiatric Center, 228
Kingsboro Psychiatric Center, 228
Kirby Forensic Psychiatric Center, 229
Manhattan Psychiatric Center, 229
Mid-Hudson Forensic Psychiatric Center, 229
Mohawk Valley Psychiatric Center, 229
NYC Children's Center-Bronx Campus, 228
Nathan S Kline Institute for Psychiatric Research, 229
New York Psychiatric Institute, 229
Pilgrim Psychiatric Center, 229
Queens Children's Psychiatric Center, 229
Rochester Psychiatric Center, 229
Rockland Children's Psychiatric Center, 229
Rockland Psychiatric Center, 229
Sagamore Children's Psychiatric Center, 229
South Beach Psychiatric Center, 229
St Lawrence Psychiatric Center, 229
Western New York Children's Psychiatric Center, 229
Office of Consumer Affairs, 229
Office of Financial Management, 229
Office of Public Affairs, 229
Office of Quality Management, 229
Mental Hygiene Legal Service, 209, 230
1st Judicial Dept, 209, 230
2nd Judicial Dept, 209, 230
3rd Judicial Dept, 209, 230
4th Judicial Dept, 209, 230
Mentoring Partnership Coalition, 387
Mercedes For Council, 490
Merchants Protective Co, Inc (NY), 476
Merck Sharp & Dohme Corp. (Affiliates: Schering Corp and Merck Schering-Plough Pharmaceuticals), 443
Mercury Public Affairs LLC, 443
Mercy College, 378, 557
Merrick Chamber of Commerce, 511
Merrick UFSD, 581
Merrill Lynch & Co Inc, 81
Merrill Lynch & Company, Inc., 443
Merscorp, Inc., 390
Messenger & Courier Association, 411
Messenger Post Newspapers, 524
Messinger Woods Wildlife Care & Education Center Inc, 157
MetLife, 204
Metlife, 387
Metro Storage NY LLC, 419
Metro Storage NY, LLC, 392
Metro-North Railroad Commuter Council, 291
Metro/Colvin Realty Inc, 248
Metro/Horohoe-Leimbach, 248
Metropolitan Arts & Antiques Pavillion, LTD., 392
Metropolitan College of NY, 440
Metropolitan College of New York, 425, 557
Metropolitan Funeral Directors Assn, 478
Metropolitan Funeral Directors PAC, 490
Metropolitan Jewish Health System (FKA Cross, Jeannie H.), 444
Metropolitan Life Insurance Co, 453
Metropolitan Life Insurance Company, 414, 417
Metropolitan Museum of Art (The), 279, 387, 475
Metropolitan Package Store Association, 405
Metropolitan Parking Assn, 476
Metropolitan Parking Association, Inc., 401
Metropolitan Realty Group LLC, 431
Metropolitan Retail Assn, LLC (NY), 431
Metropolitan Taxi Board of Trade, 401
Metropolitan Transportation Authority, 421
Mexico CSD, 586
Meyer Suozzi English & Klein, PC, 216, 444
Michael 2013, 490
Michael Balboni, Esq., 444
Michael T Kelly, Esq, 117
Microsoft Corporation, 421
Mid-America Baptist Theological Seminary Northeast Branch, 557
Mid-Hudson Catskill Rural & Migrant Ministry Inc, 444
Mid-Hudson News Network, 532
Mid-Hudson Pattern for Progress, 92, 511
Middle Country CSD, 593
Middle Village Republican Club, 490
Middleburgh CSD, 589
Middletown, 64
Civil & Criminal Courts, 64
Middletown City SD, 585
Middletown, City of, 350
Midland Credit Management, Inc., 387
Midori and Friends, 408
Midtown Surgery Center, LLC, 387
Midtown Trackage Ventures LLC, 392, 432
Mike Duvalle 4 City Council, 490
Mikhail Strut, MD., 441
Mildred Elley, 565
Milford CSD, 587
Military & Naval Affairs, Division of, 10, 293, 304
Military Chaplains Association of the USA (MCA), 299
Military Officers Association of America, 299
Military Officers Association of America (MOAA), NYS Council, 299
Military Order of the Purple Heart, 299
Military Order of the Purple Heart (MOPH), 299
Millbrook CSD, 572
Millenium Laboratories, 422
Millenium Partners, 436
Millennium Pharmaceuticals, Inc., 421
Miller Place UFSD, 593
Miller Place/Mt Sinai/Sound Beach/Rocky Point Chamber of Commerce, 511
Miller, Craig J., 444
MillerCoors LLC, 424
Millercoors, LLC, 388
Millman, Claude, 444
Milroy, James, 444
Mineola Chamber of Commerce, 511
Mineola UFSD, 581
Minerva CSD, 574
Minerva For City Council, 490
Minisink Valley CSD, 585
Mirram Group, LLC (The), 445
Mirrer, Louise, 445
Mission Society (NYC), 431
Modutank Inc, 157
Mohawk Ambulance Service, 437
Mohawk CSD, 576
Mohawk Valley Chamber of Commerce, 511
Mohawk Valley Community College, 548
Mohawk Valley Economic Development District, 511
Mohawk Valley Economic Development Growth Enterprises, 511
Mohonasen CSD, 589
Molinari Republican Club, 490
Molloy College, 557
Momentive Performance Materials (Plummer & Associates, LLC), 421
Momentive Performance Materials USA Inc., 455
Momentive Performance Materials USA, Inc., 421
Monroe 1 BOCES, 600
Monroe 2-Orleans BOCES, 600
Monroe College, 445
Monroe College-Bronx, 565
Monroe College-New Rochelle, 565
Monroe Community College, 548
Monroe County, 55, 331, 393
Supreme, County, Family & Surrogate's Courts, 55
Monroe County Industrial Development Agency (COMIDA), 511

Monroe County Water Authority, 430
Monroe, Town of, 350
Monroe-Woodbury CSD, 585
Monsanto Company, 424
Montalbano Initiatives Inc, 445
Montauk Chamber of Commerce, The, 511
Montauk UFSD, 593
Montclare & Wachtler, 217
Montefiore Health System, Albert Einstein College of Medicine, OB/GYN & Women's Health, 184
Montefiore Medical Center, 445
Montefiore Medical Ctr, 439
Montford Point Marine Association, 299
Montgomery County, 55, 331
Supreme, County, Family & Surrogate's Courts, 55
Montgomery County Chamber of Commerce/Montgomery County Partnership, 511
Montgomery, Town of, 350
Monticello CSD, 594
Monticello Gaming & Raceway, 279
Monticello Raceway Management Inc, 404
Monument Builders Assn (NYS), 452
Moody's Investors Service, Public Finance Group, 238, 268
Moon Capital Management LP, 445
Mooney, William, 445
Moore 2013, 490
Moravia CSD, 569
Moravia Chamber of Commerce, 511
Moreau, Karen, 445
Morgan B. Realty LLC, 465
Morgan Construction Enterprises, Inc., 393
Morgan Stanley, 81
Morgan Stanley & Co. Incorporated, 445
Morgan Stanley (Multistate Associates), 476
Moriah CSD, 574
Morphotrust USA, Inc., 387
Morris & McVeigh NYS PAC, 490
Morris CSD, 587
Morris Heights Health Center, 445
Morris, Mark, 446
Morristown CSD, 590
Morrisville State College, 546
Morrisville-Eaton CSD, 578
Morse, Alan, 446
Mortgage Insurance Companies of America, 408
Morton Grove Pharmaceuticals, 440
Mosaic Federal Affairs LLC, 446
Mothers Against Drunk Driving (MADD) of NYS, 117
Motion Picture Association of America, Inc., 387, 431, 446
Motor Truck Association, 437
Motor Vehicles Department, 10, 283, 304
Administration, Office for, 283
Governor's Traffic Safety Committee, 283
Legal Affairs, Office for, 283
Operations & Customer Service, Office for, 283
Safety, Consumer Protection & Clean Air, Office for, 283
Motorola Inc., 456
Motorola, Inc., 446
Mount Kisco Chamber of Commerce, 511
Mount Markham CSD, 576
Mount Pleasant, Town of, 351
Mount Saint Mary College, 558
Mount Sanai Hospital (The), 406
Mount Sinai Health System, 184
Mount Sinai Hospital, 431
Mount Sinai Medical Center, 444, 446
Mount Sinai School of Medicine of NYU, 558
Mount St Mary's Hospital & Health Center, 452
Mount Vernon, 64
Civil & Criminal Courts, 64
Mount Vernon Chamber of Commerce, 511
Mount Vernon Industrial Development Agency (City of), 511
Mount Vernon, City of, 351
Moustafa For NYC, 490
Movement Group, LLC, 446
Movers & Warehousemens Association Inc (NYS), 423
Mt Morris CSD, 578
Mt Pleasant CSD, 598
Mt Pleasant-Blythedale UFSD, 598
Mt Pleasant-Cottage UFSD, 598
Mt Sinai Hospital of Queens, 478
Mt Sinai UFSD, 593
Mt Vernon City SD, 598
Mueller, Tricia, 446
Muhs, Robert E., 446
Mulholland & Knapp, LLP, 171
Mulvihill ICS Inc, 453
Municipal Art Society, 446
Municipal Credit Union, 81
Municipal Electric Utilities Association, 144, 423
Murray, Claire, 446
Museum Association of New York, 127, 279
Museum of Modern Art (The), 401
Mutualink Inc., 455
Mutualink, Inc., 429
My-T Acres Inc, 75
MyWireless.org, 447
N.S.A. Inc. Action Fund, 490
NADAP, 447
NAIFA - New York State, 204
NAMI-NYS, 232
NANOS Research, 387
NARAL Pro-Choice, New York, 447
NARAL/NY Multcandidate Political Action Committee, 490
NBC Universal, 431, 442
NBCUniversal, 449
NBT Bancorp Inc., 81
NOFA-NY Certified Organic LLC, 75
NP Associates, LLC, 450
NTT Data, Inc., 390, 421
NY Airport Service, 291
NY Association of Training & Employment Professionals (NYATEP), 225
NY CCR Nonpartisan PAC For Good Government, 491
NY Capitolwire, 533
NY Coalition of 100 Black Women - Not For Profit, 171
NY Commercial Association of Realtors, 248
NY Council on Problem Gambling, 232
NY Counseling Association Inc, 232, 259
NY County Lawyers' Association, 217
NY Farms!, 75
NY Film Academy, 279
NY Foundation for Senior Citizens Inc, 259
NY Health Information Management Association Inc, 184
NY Housing Association Inc, 191
NY League of Conservation Voters/NY Conservation Education Fund, 138, 157
NY Life Insurance Co, 204
NY Mills UFSD, 583
NY Oil Heating Association, 144
NY Physical Therapy Association, 184
NY Press Association, 144
NY Propane Gas Association, 144
NY Property Insurance Underwriting Association, 204
NY Region 9A UAW PAC Council, 491
NY Sea Grant, 157
NY Society of Association Executives Inc (NYSAE), 92
NY State Association of Town Superintendents of Highways Inc, 238, 291
NY State Historical Association/Fenimore Art Museum, 279
NY State Society of Physician Assistants, 184
NY StateWatch Inc, 171
NYC & Company, 442, 454
NYC 2012, 442
NYC Arts Coalition, 279
NYC Board of Education Employees, Local 372/AFSCME, AFL-CIO, 127, 243
NYC Campaign Finance Board, 138
NYC Chancellor's Office, 582
NYC Citywide Alternative HS District & Programs, 582
NYC Citywide Special Ed District 75, 582
NYC Coalition Against Hunger, 259
NYC Community Garden Coalition, 157
NYC District Council of Carpenters PAC, 491
NYC Greenfield, 491
NYC Region 1, 582
NYC Region 10, 582

NYC Region 2, 582
NYC Region 3, 582
NYC Region 4, 582
NYC Region 5, 582
NYC Region 6, 582
NYC Region 7, 582
NYC Region 8, 582
NYC Region 9, 582
NYMAGIC Inc, 204
NYP Holdings Inc, 528
NYS Academy of Family Physicians, 184
NYS Agricultural Society, 75
NYS Alliance for Arts Education, 127, 279
NYS Arborists, 75
NYS Arts, 279
NYS Association for Food Protection, 75
NYS Association for Health, Physical Education, Recreation & Dance, 127
NYS Association for Solid Waste Management, 157
NYS Association for the Education of Young Children, 127
NYS Association of Area Agencies on Aging, 259
NYS Association of Chiefs of Police Inc, 117, 243
NYS Association of Community & Residential Agencies, 232
NYS Association of Counties, 171, 238
NYS Association of County Health Officials, 184
NYS Association of Criminal Defense Lawyers, 217
NYS Association of Electrical Contractors, 92
NYS Association of Fire Chiefs, 243
NYS Association of Health Care Providers, 184
NYS Association of Nurse Anesthetists (NYSANA), 184
NYS Association of Realtors, 248
NYS Association of School Business Officials, 127
NYS Association of Service Stations & Repair Shops, 291
NYS Association of Small City School Districts, 127
NYS Association of Veterinary Technicians Inc, 75
NYS Bar Assn, Alternative Dispute Resolution Cmte, 215
NYS Bar Assn, Antitrust Law Section, 92
NYS Bar Assn, Attorneys in Public Service Cmte, 243
NYS Bar Assn, Business Law Section, 92
NYS Bar Assn, Children & the Law Committee, 259
NYS Bar Assn, Civil Practice Law & Rules Committee, 217
NYS Bar Assn, Cmte on Diversity & Leadership Development, 217
NYS Bar Assn, Cmte on the Jury System, 215
NYS Bar Assn, Commercial & Federal Litigation Section, 217
NYS Bar Assn, Court Operations Cmte, 216
NYS Bar Assn, Court Structure & Judicial Selection Cmte, 171, 216
NYS Bar Assn, Courts of Appellate Jurisdiction Cmte, 217
NYS Bar Assn, Criminal Justice Section, 117
NYS Bar Assn, Cyberspace Law Cmte, 214
NYS Bar Assn, Disability Rights Cmte, 198
NYS Bar Assn, Diversity & Leadership Development Cmte, 218
NYS Bar Assn, Diversity and Inclusion Cmte, 198
NYS Bar Assn, Elder Law Section, 216
NYS Bar Assn, Electronic Communications Task Force, 144
NYS Bar Assn, Entertainment, Arts & Sports Law Section, 278
NYS Bar Assn, Environmental Law Section, 159
NYS Bar Assn, Family Law Section, 218
NYS Bar Assn, Federal Constitution & Legislation Cmte, 171, 215
NYS Bar Assn, Fiduciary Appointments Cmte, 216
NYS Bar Assn, General Practice Section, 216
NYS Bar Assn, Health Law Section, 186, 218
NYS Bar Assn, Intellectual Property Law Section, 92, 216
NYS Bar Assn, International Law & Practice Section, 214
NYS Bar Assn, Judicial Campaign Conduct Cmte, 218
NYS Bar Assn, Judicial Campaign Monitoring Cmte, 218
NYS Bar Assn, Judicial Section, 215
NYS Bar Assn, Labor & Employment Law Section, 216, 225
NYS Bar Assn, Law Youth & Citizenship Committee, 171
NYS Bar Assn, Lawyer Referral Service Cmte, 214
NYS Bar Assn, Legal Aid Cmte/Funding for Civil Legal Svcs Cmte, 216
NYS Bar Assn, Legislative Policy Cmte, 170
NYS Bar Assn, Mass Disaster Response Committee, 171
NYS Bar Assn, Media Law Committee, 144, 217
NYS Bar Assn, Multi-jurisdictional Practice Cmte, 94, 218
NYS Bar Assn, Municipal Law Section, 217
NYS Bar Assn, Pension Simplification Cmte, 268
NYS Bar Assn, President's Cmte on Access to Justice, 214
NYS Bar Assn, Procedures for Judicial Discipline Cmte, 216
NYS Bar Assn, Public Trust & Confidence in the Legal System, 117, 215
NYS Bar Assn, Public Utility Law Committee, 145, 217
NYS Bar Assn, Real Property Law Section, 247
NYS Bar Assn, Real Property Section, 216
NYS Bar Assn, Resolutions Committee, 216
NYS Bar Assn, Review Judicial Nominations Cmte, 215
NYS Bar Assn, Review the Code of Judicial Conduct Cmte, 214
NYS Bar Assn, Task Force to Review Terrorism Legislation Cmte, 170
NYS Bar Assn, Tax Section, 268
NYS Bar Assn, Tort System Cmte, 214
NYS Bar Assn, Torts, Insurance & Compensation Law Section, 215
NYS Bar Assn, Trial Lawyers Section, 215
NYS Bar Assn, Trusts & Estates Law Section, 215, 268
NYS Bar Assn, Unlawful Practice of Law Cmte, 216
NYS Bar Association, 77
NYS Berry Growers Association, 75
NYS Broadcasters Association, 144
NYS Builders Association Inc, 92
NYS Building & Construction Trades Council, 93, 225
NYS Cheese Manufacturers Association, Department of Food Science, 75
NYS Clinical Laboratory Association Inc, 93
NYS Coalition of 853 Schools Inc, 475
NYS College of Ceramics at Alfred University, 544
NYS Conference of Local Mental Hygiene Directors, 232
NYS Conference of Mayors & Municipal Officials, 238, 268
NYS Corps Collaboration, 259
NYS Correctional Officers & Police Benevolent Association Inc, 117, 243
NYS Council for Community Behavioral Healthcare, 232
NYS Council of Health-System Pharmacists, 439
NYS Council of Probation Administrators, 117, 217
NYS County Hwy Super Assn / NY Aviation Mgt Assn / NY Public Transit Assn, 291
NYS Court Clerks Association, 217, 243
NYS Defenders Association, 117, 217
NYS Democratic Senate Campaign Committee, 491
NYS Dental Association, 184
NYS Deputies Association Inc, 118, 243
NYS Dispute Resolution Association, 217
NYS Economic Development Council, 93

NYS Federation of Physicians & Dentists, 184
NYS Forum Inc, 145
NYS Funeral Directors Assn Inc, 475
NYS Grange, 75
NYS Grievance Committee, 171
NYS Head Start Association, 127
NYS Health Department, 243
NYS Horticultural Society, 75
NYS Industries for the Disabled (NYSID) Inc, 225, 260
NYS Land Title Association, 248
NYS Law Enforcement Officers Union, Council 82, AFSCME, AFL-CIO, 118, 243
NYS Magistrates Association, 217, 239
NYS Nursery/Landscape Association, 75
NYS Office for People with Developmental Disabilities, 10, 229, 230, 304
Developmental Disabilities Services Offices - State Operations, 229
Bernard Fineson Developmental Disabilities Services O, 229
Brooklyn Developmental Disabilities Services Office, 229
Broome Developmental Disabilities Services Office, 229
Capital District Developmental Disabilities Services, 229
Central New York Developmental Disabilities Services, 230
Finger Lakes Developmental Disabilities Services Office, 230
Hudson Valley Developmental Disabilities Services Offic, 230
Long Island Developmental Disabilities Services Office, 230
Metro New York Developmental Disabilities Services Off, 230
Staten Island Developmental Disabilities Services Offic, 230
Sunmount Developmental Disabilities Services Office, 230
Taconic Developmental Disabilities Services Office, 230
Western New York Developmental Disabilities Services, 230
Information Support Services, 229
New York City Regional Office, 229
NYS Optometric Association Inc, 184
NYS Outdoor Guides Association, 280
NYS Parole Officers Association, 243
NYS Passenger Vessel Association, 280
NYS Psychological Association, 232
NYS Public Health Association, 184
NYS Public High School Athletic Association, 127
NYS Reading Association, 127
NYS Right to Life Committee, 138
NYS Sheriffs' Association, 118, 243
NYS Society of Certified Public Accountants, 93
NYS Society of Real Estate Appraisers, 248
NYS Supreme Court, 171, 217
NYS Technology Enterprise Corporation (NYSTEC), 145
NYS Theatre Institute, 280
NYS Trade Adjustment Assistance Center, 93
NYS Turfgrass Association, 75, 280
NYS Vegetable Growers Association Inc, 76
NYS Water Resources Institute of Cornell University, 157
NYS Weights & Measures Association, 76
NYSAFAH PAC, 491
NYSARC Inc, 232
NYSARC, Inc., 421
NYSCOP, Inc., 402
NYSHA Inc., 416
NYSPIA Political Committee, Inc., 451
NYSRPA-PVF, 491
NYSTAR - Division of Science, Technology & Innovation, 10, 84, 122, 305
Centers for Advanced Technology, 84, 122
Center for Advanced Ceramic Technology at Alfred University, 84, 122
Center for Advanced Information Management, 84, 122
Center for Advanced Materials Processing at Clarkson Univ, 84, 122
Center for Advanced Medical Biotechnology, 85, 122
Center for Advanced Tech in Biomedical & Bioengineering, 84, 122
Center for Advanced Technology in Life Science Enterprise, 84, 122
Center for Advanced Technology in Photonics Applications, 85, 122
Center for Automation Technologies & Systems at Rensselaer, 85, 122
Center for Computer Applications & Software Engineering, 85, 122
Center for Emerging & Innovative Sciences, 84, 122
Center in Nanomaterials and Nanoelectronics, 85, 122
Ctr for Advanced Tech in Telecommunications at Polytech Univ, 85, 122
Future Energy Systems CAT at Rensselaer Polytechnic Inst, 85, 123
Integrated Electronics Engineering Center at Binghamton, 85, 123
Sensor CAT-Diagnostic Tools & Sensor Systems, 84, 122
Regional Technology Development Centers, 85, 123
Alliance for Manufacturing & Technology, 85, 123
Center for Economic Growth, 85, 123
Central New York Technology Development Organization, 85, 123
Council for Interntl Trade, Tech, Education & Communication, 85, 123
High Technology of Rochester, 85, 123
Hudson Valley Technology Development Center, 85, 123
INSYTE Consulting (Western NY Technology Development Ctr), 85, 123
Industrial & Technology Assistance Corp, 85, 123
Long Island Forum for Technology, 85, 123
Mohawk Valley Applied Technology Corp, 85, 123
NYU Child Study Center, 453
NYU Hospitals Center, 440
NYU Langone Medical Center, 390
NYU School of Medicine, 436, 440, 442
Nachman Caller Community First, 490
Nadler For Congress, 490
Naftali Group (The), 431
Nagel Law Office, PLLC, 447
Nanuet UFSD, 588
Naples CSD, 585
Naral Pro-Choice NY, 438
Naral Pro-Choice New York, 438
Nasca, Samuel J, 447
Nassau BOCES, 600
Nassau Community College, 415, 447, 548
Nassau Council of Chambers, 511
Nassau County, 55, 61, 332
1st, 2nd & 4th District Courts, 61
3rd District Court, 61
County & Surrogate's Courts, 55
Family Court, 55
Supreme Court, 55
Nassau County Firefighters Museum & Education Ctr, 415
Nassau County Firefighter's Museum & Education Center, 476
Nassau County Industrial Development Agency, 512
Nassau County PHCC, 470
Nassau County Village Officials Assn, 405
Nassau Health Care Corporation, 415
Nassau Regional Off-Track Betting Corporation, 100, 273, 307, 435, 442
Nassau-Suffolk Hospital Association, 476
Nassau-Suffolk Hospital Council, Inc., 423
NationWide Mutual Insurance Company, 425
National Academy of Elder Law Attorneys New York Chapter, 421
National Academy of Forensic Engineers, 217
National Academy of Recording Arts & Sciences, 421

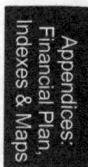

National Amputation Foundation Inc, 184, 299
National Archives & Records Administration, 125, 275
Franklin D Roosevelt Presidential Library & Museum, 125, 275
National Assn of Chain Drug Stores, 447
National Assn of Health Underwriters, 413
National Assn of Social Workers (NYS Chapter), 447
National Assn of Social Workers (NYS Chapter) (FKA Paupini, Sara), 447
National Association of Black Accountants, NY Chapter, 93
National Association of Mutual Insurance Companies (NAMIC), 447
National Association of Professional Employer Organizations, 393
National Association of Social Workers - New York City Chapter, 448
National Association of Social Workers, NYS Chapter, 260
National Association of Theatre Owners of NYS, 387
National Association of Theatre Owners, Inc., 421
National Basketball Association, 280
National Coalition of Pharmaceutical Distributors, 422
National Coffee Association, 76
National Conference of Commissioners in Uniform State Laws, 421
National Council of Jewish Women, 198, 260
National Council to Prevent Delinquency Inc, 454
National Credit Union Administration, 79
Albany Region, 79
National Economic Research Associates, 145, 291
National Employment Law Project, 448
National Employment Lawyers Association, 438
National Federation of Community Development Credit Unions, 81
National Federation of Independent Business, 93, 226, 268, 448
National Football League, 280
National Foundation for Human Potential Inc, 428
National Fuel Gas Company, 145, 408, 448
National Fuel Gas Distribution, 217
National Grape Cooperative-Welch Foods Inc, 76
National Grid, 145, 437, 448
National Grid USA, 391
National Grid Voluntary New York State Political Action Committee, 490
National Guard Association of the US (NGAUS), 299
National Health Care Associates, Inc., 425
National Hockey League, 280
National Insurance Crime Bureau, 405
National Labor Relations Board, 222
Albany Resident Office
Albany Resident Office, 222
Region 2 - New York City Metro Area, 222
Region 29 - Brooklyn Area, 222
Region 3 - Buffalo Area, 222
National League for Nursing (NLN), 184
National Marfan Foundation, 184
National Media Services, Inc., 392
National Military Family Association (NMFA), 299
National Multiple Sclerosis Society, NY MS Coalition Action Netwo, 439
National Multiple Sclerosis Society, New York City Chapter, 448
National Organization for Women, NYS, 139, 198
National Popular Vote, Inc., 402
National Pork Producers Council, 425
National Potato Board, 75
National Railroad Passenger Corporation, 448
National Rifle Association of America, 419
National Safety Commission Inc, 440
National Shooting Sports Foundation, Inc., 393
National Solid Wastes Management Association, 396
National Strategies, Inc., 448
National Transportation Safety Board, 288
Aviation Division, Northeast Regional Office, 288
Office of Administrative Law Judges, 289
National Trust for Historic Preservation, 192
National Urban League Inc (The), 260
National Wildlife Federation - Northeast Regional Center, 157
National Women's Hall of Fame, 280
National Writers Union, 226
National Youth Recovery Foundation, 387
Natural Resources, 321
Office of Indian Affairs, 321
Subcommittees, 321
Energy & Mineral Resources, 321
Insular Affairs, Oceans & Wildlife, 321
National Parks, Forests and Public Lands, 321
Water & Power, 321
Natural Resources Defense Council, 157, 430
Natural Resources Defense Council (FKA Goldstein, Eric), 448
Natural Resources Defense Council Inc, 475
Nature Conservancy (The), 158
Nature Conservancy (The) (FKA Janeway, William C.), 449
Nat'l Assn of Energy Service Companies, 418
Naval Enlisted Reserve Association (NERA), 299
Naval Reserve Association (NRA), 299
Navicore Solutions, 81
Navy League of the US (NLUS), 299
Navy League of the US (NLUS), New York Council, 299
Nazareth College of Rochester, 558
Ndigo For City Council, 490
Nederlander Organization, Inc., 432
Neidl, Michael, 449
Neighborhood Family Services Coalition, 449
Neighborhood Preservation Coalition of NYS Inc, 192
Neighborhood Preservation Political Action Fund, 490
Neighbors For Kenneth Rice, 490
Neil Grimaldi For New York City Mayor, 490
Nelson A Rockefeller Inst of Govt, Federalism Research Grp, 260
Nelson A Rockefeller Inst of Govt, Higher Education Program, 127
Nelson A Rockefeller Inst of Govt, Urban & Metro Studies, 192
Nelson A Rockefeller Institute of Government, 171, 268
Nestle Waters North America Holdings Inc, 405
Nestle Waters North America Holdings, Inc., 438
Nestle Waters North America Inc., 404
New 42nd Street/New Victory Theater, 478
New Amsterdam Public Market Association, Inc., 392
New Brookhaven Town House for Adults, 476
New City Chamber of Commerce, 512
New England Interstate Water Pollution Control Commission, 100, 151, 307
New England Steamship Agents Inc, 291
New Era Veterans, Inc, 299
New Hartford CSD, 583
New Hartford, Town of, 351
New Hyde Park Chamber of Commerce, 512
New Hyde Park-Garden City Park UFSD, 581
New Jewish Home (The), 184
New Lebanon CSD, 571
New Paltz CSD, 595
New Paltz Regional Chamber of Commerce, 512
New Partners for Community Revitalization, Inc., 430
New Planet Energy LLC, 431
New Rochelle, 64
Civil & Criminal Courts, 64
New Rochelle City SD, 598
New Rochelle, Chamber of Commerce, Inc, 512

New Rochelle, City of, 351
New School (The), 382, 387
New School University (The), 558
New School University, Department of Sociology, 280
New School University, Milano School of International Affairs, Management & Urban Policy, 184, 192
New School for Social Research, Department of Politics, 139, 199
New School for Social Research, Zolberg Institute on Migration & Mobility, 199
New Square Community Planning and Development Corporation, 428
New Suffolk Common SD, 593
New Visions Democratic Club, 490
New Visions for Public Schools, 445
New Visions for Public Schools, Inc., 431
New Windsor, Town of, 351
New York & Atlantic Railway (NYA), 292
New York 1 News (1), 538
New York AIDS Coalition, 184
New York Academy of Art Inc, 280, 558
New York Agriculture in the Classroom, 76
New York Alliance of Library Systems, 405
New York Apple Association Inc, 76
New York Aquarium, 280
New York Artists Equity Association Inc, 280
New York Association for New Americans, Inc (NYANA), 259
New York Association of Convenience Stores, 93
New York Association of Homes & Services for the Aging, 260
New York Association of Psychiatric Rehabilitation Services (NYAPRS), 232
New York Bankers Association, 81
New York Bankers Political Action Committee, 490
New York Beef Industry Council Inc, 76
New York Biotechnology Association (The), 93
New York Botanical Garden (The), 436
New York Building Congress, 93, 192
New York Building Congress State PAC, 491
New York Business Development Corporation, 93
New York Career Institute, 565
New York Cares Inc, 453
New York Center for Agricultural Medicine & Health, Bassett Healthcare, 76
New York Chamber of Commerce (Greater New York), 512
New York Check P.A.C., Inc., 491
New York Chiropractic College, 558
New York City, 351
Aging, Dept for the, NYC, 352
Buildings, Department of, NYC, 352
Campaign Finance Board, NYC, 352
City Council, NYC, 352
City Planning, Department of, NYC, 352
Citywide Administrative Services, Department of, NYC, 352
Civil Service Commission, NYC, 352
Collective Bargaining, Office of, NYC, 353
Comptroller, NYC, 353
Conflicts of Interest Board, NYC, 353
Consumer Affairs, Department of, NYC, 353
Correction, Board of, NYC, 353
Correction, Department of, NYC, 353
Cultural Affairs, Department of, NYC, 353
Design & Construction, Dept of, NYC, 353
Disabilities, Mayor's Office, for People with, 353
Economic Development Corp, NYC, 353
Education, Dept of, NYC, 353
Elections, Board of, NYC, 354
Environmental Protection, Department of, NYC, 354
Equal Employment Practices Commission, NYC, 354
Film, Theatre & Broadcasting, Mayor's Office of, NYC, 354
Finance, Department of, NYC, 354
Fire Department, NYC, 354
Health & Hospitals Corporation, NYC, 354
Health & Mental Hygiene, Dept of, NYC, 354
Homeless Services, Department of, NYC, 355
Housing Authority, NYC, 355
Housing Preservation & Development, Dept of, NYC, 355
Human Resources Administration, Dept of, NYC, 355
Human Rights Commission on, NYC, 355
Information Technology & Telecommunications, Dept of, NYC, 355
Investigation, Department of, NYC, 356
Juvenile Justice, Department of, NYC, 356
Labor Relations, Office of, NYC, 356
Landmarks Preservation Commission, NYC, 356
Law, Department of, NYC, 356
Legislative Affairs Office, NYC Mayor's City, 356
Legislative Affairs Office, NYC Mayor's State, 356
Library, Brooklyn Public, 356
Library, New York Public, 356
Library, Queens Borough Public, 356
Loft Board, NYC, 357
Management & Budget, Office of, NYC, 357
Medical Examiner, Office of Chief, NYC, 357
Parks & Recreation, Department of, NYC, 357
Police Department, NYC, 357
Probation, Department of, NYC, 357
Public Advocate, Office of the, 357
Public Design Commission, NYC, 352
Records & Information Services, Dept of, NYC, 358
Rent Guidelines Board, NYC, 358
Sanitation, Department of, NYC, 358
Small Business Services, Department of, NYC, 358
Sports Commission, NYC, 358
Standards & Appeals, Board of, NYC, 358
Tax Commission, NYC, 358
Taxi & Limousine Commission, NYC, 358
Transportation, Department of, NYC, 358
Veterans' Affairs, Mayor's Office of, NYC, 358
Voter Assistance Commission (VAC), NYC, 358
Water Finance Authority, Municipal, NYC, 359
Youth & Community Development, Department of, NYC, 359
New York City Ballet, Inc. and the David H. Koch Theater at Lincoln Center, 477
New York City Boroughs, 359
Bronx (Bronx County), 359
Brooklyn (Kings County), 359
Manhattan (New York County), 359
Queens (Queens County), 359
Staten Island (Richmond County), 359
New York City Central Labor Council Political Committee, 491
New York City College of Technology, 552
New York City Housing Development Corporation, 100, 189, 308
New York City Residential Mortgage Insurance Corporation, 100, 189
New York City Justice Political Action Committee, 491
New York City Opera, 280
New York City Partnership State PAC, 491
New York City School Construction Authority, 100, 123, 308
New York City, Partnership for, 512
New York Civil Liberties Union, 199
New York Civil Rights Coalition, 199
New York College of Health Professions, 558
New York College of Podiatric Medicine, 558
New York College of Traditional Chinese Medicine, 558
New York Committee for Occupational Safety & Health, 226
New York Community Bank, 81, 192, 248
New York Community College Trustees (NYCCT), 127

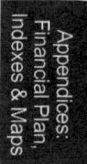

New York Community Colleges Association of Presidents, 127
New York Community Trust (The), 260
New York Convention Center Operating Corporation, 100, 273, 308
New York Corn & Soybean Growers Association, 76
New York Cosmos LLC, 405
New York County, 55
COUNTY & FAMILY COURTS: See New York City Courts, 55
SUPREME COURT, Civil Term, 55
SUPREME COURT, Criminal Term, 56
Surrogate's Court, 56
New York County (NYC Borough of Manhattan), 332
New York County Dental Society Political Action Committee, 491
New York Credit Union Association, 81
New York Daily Challenge (The), 524
New York Daily News, 528
New York English Schools Association (NYESA), 402
New York Farm Bureau, 76
New York Forest Owners Association Inc, 158
New York Foundation for the Arts, 280
New York Giants, 280
New York Hall of Science, 280
New York Health Care Alliance, 185
New York Health Plan Association, 185
New York Holstein Association, 76
New York Hotel & Motel Trades Council Committee, 491
New York Immigration Coalition (The), 199
New York Independent System Operator - Not For Profit, 145
New York Institute of Energy and Water, 405
New York Institute of Technology, 558
New York Insurance Association Inc, 204
New York Islanders, 280
New York Jets, 280
New York Landmarks Conservancy, 192, 248
New York Law School, 558
New York Lawyers for the Public Interest, 192, 199
New York Library Association (The), 127
New York Long-Term Care Brokers Ltd, 204
New York Magazine (New York Media, LLC), 533
New York Marine Trades Association, 281
New York Medical College, 185, 558
New York Medical College, Department of Medicine, 185
New York Medical College, School of Health Sciences and Practice, 185
New York Medical Staff Leadership Council, 442
New York Mercantile Exchange Inc, 93
New York Metropolitan Transportation Council, 101, 286, 308
New York Mets, 281
New York Municipal Insurance Reciprocal (NYMIR), 204, 239
New York News Publishers Association, 145
New York Observer (The), 528
New York Organization of Nurse Executives, 447
New York Pork Producers Coop, 76
New York Post, 528
New York Power Authority, 101, 141, 308
New York Presbyterian Hospital, 185
New York Presbyterian Hospital, Department of Psychiatry, 232
New York Press Photographers Association, 145
New York Professional Nurses Union Political Action Committee, 491
New York Public Interest Research Group, 158, 171
New York Public Interest Research Group Straphangers Campaign, 292
New York Public Welfare Association, 260
New York Racing Association, 281
New York Regional Office
New York Regional Office, 166
New York Republican State Committee, 139
New York Roadway Improvement Coalition (NYRIC), 292
New York School of Interior Design, 559
New York Schools Insurance Reciprocal (NYSIR), 204
New York Seed Improvement Project, Cornell University, Plant Breeding Department, 76
New York Shipping Association Inc, 292
New York Society for the Deaf, 260
New York State AFL-CIO COPE, 491
New York State Air Force Association, 299
New York State Assessors' Association, 248, 268
New York State Assn of Fire Districts, 101, 236, 308
New York State Association of Agricultural Fairs Inc, 76
New York State Association of Ambulatory Surgery Centers, 185
New York State Association of Family Service Agencies Inc, 260
New York State Association of Independent Schools, 128
New York State Association of PBA's PAC, 491
New York State Athletic Commission, 101, 164, 273, 308
New York State Auto Dealers Association, 93, 292
New York State Board of Law Examiners, 101, 211, 308
New York State Bridge Authority, 101, 287, 308
New York State Catholic Conference, 128, 260
New York State Citizens' Coalition for Children Inc, 260
New York State Commission of Correction, 101, 113, 308
New York State Commission on Judicial Nomination, 102, 211, 308
New York State Commission on the Restoration of the Capitol, 102, 164, 273, 308
New York State Community Action Association, 192, 260
New York State Congress of Parents & Teachers Inc, 128
New York State Conservation Council, 158
New York State Conservative Party, 371
County Chairs, 371
Albany, 371
Bronx, 371
Broome, 371
Cattaraugus, 371
Cayuga, 371
Chautauqua, 371
Chemung, 371
Columbia, 371
Delaware, 371
Dutchess, 371
Erie, 371
Essex, 371
Franklin, 371
Fulton, 371
Genesee, 371
Greene, 371
Herkimer, 371
Jefferson, 371
Kings, 371
Livingston, 371
Madison, 371
Monroe, 371
Montgomery, 371
Nassau, 371
New York, 371
Niagara, 372
Oneida, 372
Onondaga, 372
Ontario, 372
Orange, 372
Orleans, 372
Oswego, 372
Otsego, 372
Putnam, 372
Queens, 372
Rensselaer, 372
Richmond, 372
Rockland, 372
Saratoga, 372
Schenectady, 372
Schoharie, 372

Schuyler, 372
Seneca, 372
St Lawrence, 372
Steuben, 372
Suffolk, 372
Sullivan, 372
Tioga, 372
Ulster, 372
Warren, 372
Washington, 372
Wayne, 372
Westchester, 372
Statewide Party Officials, 371
New York State Council of Churches, 199
New York State Council of Machinists PAC Fund, 491
New York State Council of School Superintendents, 128
New York State Court of Claims, 217
New York State Democratic Committee, 139, 372
County Chairs, 372
Albany, 372
Allegany, 372
Bronx, 372
Broome, 373
Cattaraugus, 373
Cayuga, 373
Chautauqua, 373
Chemung, 373
Chenango, 373
Clinton, 373
Columbia, 373
Cortland, 373
Delaware, 373
Dutchess, 373
Erie, 373
Essex, 373
Franklin, 373
Fulton, 373
Genesee, 373
Greene, 373
Hamilton, 373
Herkimer, 373
Jefferson, 373
Kings, 373
Lewis, 373
Livingston, 373
Madison, 373
Monroe, 373
Montgomery, 373
Nassau, 373
New York, 373
Niagara, 373
Oneida, 373
Onondaga, 373
Ontario, 373
Orange, 373
Orleans, 373
Oswego, 373
Otsego, 373
Putnam, 373
Queens, 373
Rensselaer, 373
Richmond, 373
Rockland, 373
Saratoga, 374
Schenectady, 374
Schoharie, 374
Schuyler, 374
Seneca, 374
St Lawrence, 374
Steuben, 374
Suffolk, 374
Sullivan, 374
Tioga, 374
Tompkins, 374
Ulster, 374
Warren, 374
Washington, 374
Wayne, 374
Westchester, 374
Wyoming, 374
Yates, 374
Statewide Party Officials, 372
New York State Directory, 171
New York State Disaster Preparedness Commission, 102, 164, 237, 308
New York State Dormitory Authority, 102, 123, 164, 177, 308
New York State Electric & Gas Corporation (NYSEG), 145
New York State Energy Research & Development Authority, 102, 141, 151, 308
New York State Environmental Facilities Corp, 102, 151, 308
New York State Financial Control Board, 103, 164, 265, 308
New York State Gaming Commission, 10, 102, 264, 272, 304
Regional Offices, 264
Central/Finger Lakes Regions, 264
Eastern Region, 264
Gaming Commission, 264
Hudson Valley Region, 264
Long Island Region, 264
New York City Region, 264
Western Region, 264
Rochester Office, 264
Syracuse Office, 264
New York State Government Finance Officers Association Inc, 239, 268
New York State Green Party, 374
Statewide Party Officials, 374
New York State Health Facilities Association Inc, 185
New York State Higher Education - PAC, 491
New York State Higher Education Initiative, 424
New York State Higher Education Services Corp (NYSHESC), 103, 124, 308
New York State Homes & Community Renewal, 78, 103
New York State Hospitality & Tourism Association, 281
New York State Independence Party, 374
County Chairs, 374
Bronx, 374
Kings, 374
Manhattan, 374
Queens, 374
Richmond, 374
New York State Judicial Conduct Commission, 103, 211, 308
New York State Laborers' Political Action Committee, 491
New York State Law Enforcement Council, 118, 217, 243
New York State Law Reporting Bureau, 103, 164, 211, 309
New York State Law Revision Commission, 104, 211, 309
New York State Liquor Authority, 104, 309
New York State Liquor Authority (Division of Alcoholic Beverage Control), 4, 83, 263, 303
Administration, 83, 263
Licensing & Enforcement, 83, 263
Albany (Zone II), 83, 263
Buffalo (Zone III), 83, 263
New York City (Zone I), 83, 263
New York State Maple Producers Association Inc, 76
New York State Motor Truck Association, 292
New York State Nurses Association, 185, 226
New York State Nurses Association Political Action Committee, 491
New York State Olympic Regional Development Authority, 104, 273, 309
New York State Ophthalmological Society, 185
New York State Osteopathic Medical Society, 185
New York State Petroleum Council, 145
New York State Podiatric Medical Association, 185
New York State Public Employees Federation (PEF), 243
New York State Radiological Society Inc, 185
New York State Rehabilitation Association, 233, 260
New York State Republican Party, 374
County Officials, 375
Albany, 375
Allegany, 375
Bronx, 375
Broome, 375

Cattaraugus, 375
Cayuga, 375
Chautauqua, 375
Chemung, 375
Chenango, 375
Clinton, 375
Columbia, 375
Cortland, 375
Delaware, 375
Dutchess, 375
Erie, 375
Essex, 375
Franklin, 375
Fulton, 375
Genesee, 375
Greene, 375
Hamilton, 375
Herkimer, 375
Jefferson, 375
Kings, 375
Lewis, 375
Livingston, 375
Madison, 375
Monroe, 375
Montgomery, 375
Nassau, 375
New York, 375
Niagara, 375
Oneida, 375
Onondaga, 375
Ontario, 375
Orange, 375
Orleans, 375
Oswego, 375
Otsego, 375
Putnam, 375
Queens, 375
Rensselaer, 375
Richmond, 376
Rockland, 376
Saratoga, 376
Schenectady, 376
Schoharie, 376
Schuyler, 376
Seneca, 376
St Lawrence, 376
Steuben, 376
Suffolk, 376
Sullivan, 376
Tioga, 376
Tompkins, 376
Ulster, 376
Warren, 376
Washington, 376
Wayne, 376
Westchester, 376
Wyoming, 376
Yates, 376
Statewide Party Officials, 374
New York State Restaurant Association, 93, 281
New York State Right to Life Party, 376
New York State Rural Advocates, 192
New York State Rural Housing Coalition Inc, 192
New York State School Boards Association, 128
New York State School Music Association (NYSSMA), 128, 281
New York State Snowmobile Association, 281
New York State Society of Certified Public Accountants, 268
New York State Society of Enrolled Agents, 269
New York State Supreme Court Officers Association, 217, 243
New York State Teachers' Retirement System, 104, 124, 242, 309
New York State Telecommunications Association Inc, 145
New York State Theatre Education Association, 281
New York State Thoroughbred Breeding & Development Fund Corporation, 104, 273, 309
New York State Thruway Authority, 104, 273, 287, 309
New York State Canal Corporation, 104, 274, 287
New York State Transportation Engineering Alliance (NYSTEA), 292
New York State Travel & Vacation Association, 281
New York State Trial Lawyers, 217
New York State Tug Hill Commission, 104, 151, 309
New York State United Teachers/AFT, AFL-CIO, 243
New York State United Teachers/AFT, NEA, AFL-CIO, 128
New York State Veterinary Medical Society, 76
New York State Woodsmen's Field Days Inc, 158
New York State Working Families Party, 376
New York Stock Exchange, 81
New York Technology Council, 93, 145
New York Theological Seminary, 559
New York Thoroughbred Breeders Inc, 76
New York University, 128, 559
New York University School of Law, 217
New York University School of Medicine Bellevue Hospital Center, Department of Emergency Medicine, 181
New York University Stern School of Business, Berkley Center for Entrepreneurship & Innovation, 93
New York University, Departmentt of Politics, 139
New York University, Graduate School of Journalism, 139, 226
New York University, Robert F Wagner Graduate School of Public Service, 185
New York University, Tisch School of the Arts, 281
New York University, Wagner Graduate School, 192, 239
New York University-College of Nursing, 476
New York Urban League, 260
New York Water Environment Association Inc (NYWEA), 158
New York Wine & Grape Foundation, 77, 281
New York Wired for Education LLC, 139
New York Yankees, 281
New York Yankees Partnership, 386
New York, Susquehanna & Western Railway Corporation, The, 292
New Yorker, 217
New Yorkers Against Gun Violence, 449
New Yorkers For Affordable Housing, 491
New Yorkers For De Blasio, 491
New Yorkers For Katz, 491
New Yorkers For Putting Students First, 491
New Yorkers For Robert Jackson, 491
New Yorkers for Constitutional Freedoms, 441
New Yorkers for Fair Automobile Insurance Reform, Inc., 438
New Yorkers for Fiscal Fairness, 406
New Yorkers for Parks, 386
New Yorkers for Real Recycling Reform (Food Industry Alliance of NYS Inc), 415
New Yorktown Chamber of Commerce (The), 512
Newark CSD, 597
Newark Chamber of Commerce, 512
Newark Valley CSD, 595
Newburgh, 64
Civil & Criminal Courts, 64
Newburgh Enlarged City SD, 585
Newburgh, City of, 359
Newburgh, Town of, 360
Newcomb CSD, 574
Newfane CSD, 582
Newfield CSD, 595
News Corporation, 421
Newsday, 527
Newsday Inc, 527
Newspaper Publishers Assn (NY), 449
Newspaper Publishers Association, 424
Newsweek/The Daily Beast, 533
Next Wave Inc, 185
Nextel Operations Inc, 454
Niagara Business Trust, 466
Niagara County, 56, 332
County, Family & Surrogate's Courts, 56
County, Supreme & Family Courts, 56

Niagara County Center for Economic Development, 512
Niagara County Community College, 548
Niagara Falls, 64
Civil & Criminal Courts, 64
Niagara Falls Bridge Commission, 105, 287, 309
Niagara Falls Chamber of Commerce, 512
Niagara Falls City SD, 583
Niagara Falls, City of, 360
Niagara Frontier Transportation Authority, 105, 287, 309
Niagara Frontier Transpotation Authority, 441
Niagara Gazette, 528
Niagara Mohawk Holdings, Inc., & NMPC DBA National Grid, 476
Niagara USA Chamber of Commerce, 512
Niagara University, 128, 437, 559
Niagara-Wheatfield CSD, 583
Nicholas & Lence Communications LLC, 449
Nicholas Noyes Memorial Hospital, 390
Nicolson, Karen, 450
Nightingale-Bamford School, 401
Nikki Lucas 2013, 491
Niskayuna CSD, 589
Niskayuna, Town of, 360
Nissan North America, Inc., 424, 450
Nixon Peabody LLP PAC, 491
Nixon Peabody, LLP, 450
Noah E. Gotbaum 2013, 491
Noble Environmental Power LLC, 437
Noco Energy Corporation, 408
Nolan & Heller, LLP, 450
Nonprofit Coordinating Committee of New York, 260
Nontraditional Employment for Women, 431
Norddeutsche Landesbank Girozentrale, 81
Norfolk Southern Corporation, 410, 450
Norman A Olch, Esq, 217
Norstar Development USA, LP, 441
North Babylon UFSD, 593
North Bellmore UFSD, 581
North Bronx Career Counseling & Outreach Center, 549
North Collins CSD, 574
North Colonie CSD, 567
North Country Community College, 548
North Country Healthcare Providers Eductl & Rsch Fund Inc (North Country Healthcare Providers, LLC), 476
North Country Savings Bank, 82
North Country Vietnam Veterans Association, Post 1, 299
North Fork Bank, 268
North Fork Chamber of Commerce, 512
North Greenbush Common SD (Williams), 588
North Greenbush IDA, 512
North Hempstead, Town of, 360
North Merrick UFSD, 581
North Rockland CSD, 588
North Rose-Wolcott CSD, 597
North Salem CSD, 598
North Shore Animal League America, 261
North Shore Board of Education, 421
North Shore CSD, 581
North Shore Land Alliance, 450
North Star Fund, 450
North Syracuse CSD, 584
North Tonawanda, 64
Civil & Criminal Courts, 64
North Tonawanda City SD, 583
North Tonawanda, City of, 360
North Warren CSD, 596
North Warren Chamber of Commerce, 512
Northeast Ag and Feed Alliance, 478
Northeast Business Group on Health Inc, 185
Northeast Dairy Foods Association Inc, 77
Northeast Equipment Dealers Association Inc, 94
Northeast Gas Association, 145
Northeast Government Consulting LLC, 450
Northeast Kidney Foundation, 405
Northeast Organic Farming Association of New York, 77
Northeast Regional Council of Carpenters NY Political Education Committee, 446
Northeastern Clinton CSD, 571
Northeastern Forest Fire Protection Commission, 105, 152, 309
Northeastern Loggers' Association, 158
Northeastern Seminary, 559
Northern Adirondack CSD, 571
Northern Manhattan Improvement Corporation, 450, 477
Northern Metropolitan Hospital Assn, 450, 476
Northern Metropolitan Hospital Association, 423
Northern Westchester Hospital, 476
Northport Chamber of Commerce, 512
Northport-East Northport UFSD, 593
Northside Center for Child Development, Inc., 431
Northville CSD, 575
Norwegian Cruise Line, 476
Norwich, 64
Civil & Criminal Courts, 64
Norwich City SD, 570
Norwood-Norfolk CSD, 590
Nostradamus Advertising, 139
Novartis Pharmaceuticals Corporation, 390, 450
Novell, 393
Nuclear Regulatory Commission, 142
REGION I (includes New York State), 142
Nucor Steel Aubrun, Inc., 404
Nucor Steel Auburn, Inc., 389
Nurse Practitioner Association NYS, 421
Nurse Practitioner Association NYS (The), 185
Nurses Association, 438
Nurses Association (NYS), 450
Nutrition Association, 414
Nutrition Consortium of NYS, Inc., 388
Nyack Chamber of Commerce, 512
Nyack College, 559
Nyack UFSD, 588
Nyprocoa, Inc., 451
O-At-Ka Milk Products Cooperative, Inc., 423
ODA Primary Health Care Center, 390
OHEL Children's Home & Family Services, 443
OTG Management, 442
Oakfield-Alabama CSD, 575
Oasis Children's Service LLC, 472
Observer (The), 525
Observer Today, 525
Observer-Dispatch, 531
Oceanside Chamber of Commerce, 512
Oceanside UFSD, 581
Oddo For Staten Island, 491
Odessa-Montour CSD, 589
Office of Chief, Army Reserves, 300
Office of David J Silverman, 269
Ogdensburg, 64
Civil & Criminal Courts, 64
Ogdensburg Bridge & Port Authority, 105, 287, 309
Ogdensburg Chamber of Commerce (Greater Ogdensburg), 512
Ogdensburg City SD, 590
Ohio River Valley Water Sanitation Commission, 105, 152, 309
Ohrenstein & Brown, LLP, 452
Oil Heat Institute of Long Island, 145
Oil Heating Assn (NY), 401
Oil Heating Assoc, 439
Olanike Alabi 2013, 492
Old Westbury College Foundation, Inc., 420
Olean, 64
Civil & Criminal Courts, 64
Olean Area Chamber of Commerce (Greater Olean), 512
Olean Business Institute, 565
Olean City SD, 569
Olean Times Herald, 529
Oliveira Contracting, Inc., 394
Omni Childhood Center, 404, 429
One York Street Condominium, 401
Oneida, 64
Civil & Criminal Courts, 64
Oneida City SD, 578
Oneida County, 56, 332
Supreme, County & Family Courts, 56
Surrogate's Court, 56
Oneida Daily Dispatch, 529
Oneida Indian Nation, 166

Oneida Industrial Development Agency (City of), 513
Oneida Tribe of Wisconsin (Power Plant Entertainment NY), 456
Oneida-Herkimer-Madison BOCES, 600
Oneonta, 64
Civil & Criminal Courts, 64
Oneonta City SD, 587
Onexim Basketball, LLC, 386
Onondaga CSD, 584
Onondaga Community College, 548
Onondaga County, 56, 333
Supreme, County, Family & Surrogate's Courts, 56
Onondaga County Industrial Development Agency, 513
Onondaga Nation, 166
Onondaga, Town of, 361
Onondaga-Cortland-Madison BOCES, 600
Ontario Chamber of Commerce, 513
Ontario County, 56, 333
Supreme, County, Family & Surrogate's Courts, 56
Ontario County Industrial Development Agency & Economic Development, 513
Onteora CSD, 595
Open Society Foundations, 199
Open Space Institute, 158, 438, 452
Open View Consulting, 387
Ophthalmological Society, 425
Ophthalmological Society (NYS), 452
Oppenheim-Ephratah CSD, 575
Oracle America, Inc., 387, 390
Orange & Rockland Utilities Inc, 145
Orange County, 56, 333
Supreme, County & Family Courts, 56
Surrogate's Court, 57
Orange County Chamber of Commerce (The), 404
Orange County Chamber of Commerce Inc, 513
Orange County Community College, 548
Orange County Partnership, 513
Orange Regional Medical Center, 452
Orange-Ulster BOCES, 600
Orangetown, Town of, 361
Orchard Park CSD, 574
Orchard Park Chamber of Commerce, 513
Orchard Park, Town of, 361
Org of NYS Mgmt/Confidential Employees, Inc, 452
Organization of NYS Management Confidential Employees, 243
Organization of NYS Management/Confidential Employees Inc, 452
Organization of NYS Management/Confidential Employees, Inc., 425
Organization of Staff Analysts PAC, 492
Oriskany CSD, 583
Orleans County, 57, 333
Supreme, County, Family & Surrogate's Courts, 57
Orleans County Chamber of Commerce, 513
Orleans Economic Development Agency (OEDA), 513
Orleans-Niagara BOCES, 601
Osborne Association, 118, 226, 410
Ossining UFSD, 598
Ossining, Town of, 361
Ossining, Village of, 361
Osteopathic Medical Society, 452
Ostertag O'Leary & Barrett, 218
Ostroff, Hiffa & Associates Inc, 452
Oswego, 64
Civil & Criminal Courts, 65
Oswego BOCES, 601
Oswego City SD, 586
Oswego County, 57, 334
Family Court, 57
Supreme, County & Surrogate's Courts, 57
Oswego County, Operation/Oswego County Industrial Development Agency, 513
Oswego-Fulton Chamber of Commerce, 513
Otano 2013, 492
Otego-Unadilla CSD, 587
Otsego County, 57, 334
Family Court, 57
Supreme, County, & Surrogate's Courts, 57
Otsego County Chamber (The), 513
Otsego County Economic Development Department & Industrial Development Agency, 513
Otsego Northern Catskills BOCES (Otsego-Delaware-Schoharie-Greene), 601
Otsuka America Pharmaceutical, Inc., 407
Ottaway News Service (NYS only), 533
Ottaway Newspapers Inc, 529
Outdoor Advertising Council of NY, Inc., 393
Outlook Group, Inc., 422
Outreach & Extension, 182
Outward Bound Center (NYC), 478
Ovation LLC, 420
Oversight and Government Reform, 321
Subcommittees, 321
Domestic Policy, 321
Federal Workforce, Postal Service and the District of Columbia, 321
Government Management, Organization and Procurement, 321
Information Policy, Census and National Archives, 321
National Security and Foreign Affairs, 321
Oversight, Analysis & Investigation, 41
Membership, 41
Majority, 41
Minority, 41
Owego, Town of, 361
Owego-Apalachin CSD, 595
Oxford Academy & CSD, 570
Oxford Nursing Home, Inc., 405
Oyster Bay Chamber of Commerce, 513
Oyster Bay, Town of, 361
Oyster Bay-East Norwich CSD, 581
Oysterponds UFSD, 593
Oz Systems, 402
O'Brien & Gere Limited, 451
O'Connell and Aronowitz, 451
O'Connell, Maurice J., 452
O'Connor Capital Partners, 405
O'Connor Davies Munns & Dobbins LLP, 411
O'Malley, Michael, 452
P.S. 1 Contemporary Art Center, 453
PAC L375 CSTG, 492
PAC of the Patrolmen's Benevolent Association of NYC, 492
PCV St Owner LP, 382
PEC Group of NY, Inc., 460
PFM Asset Management, LLC, 455
PMSI, 404, 410
PSC PAC, 493
PSCH Inc., 456
PSCH, Inc., 405
Pace University, 453, 559
Pace University, School of Law Center for Environmental Legal Studies, 158
Pace University, School of Law, John Jay Legal Services Inc, 118, 218
Pacific College of Oriental Medicine, 565
Pacifica Ventures, LLC, 390
Paco Realty, LLC, 431
Painted Post Area Board of Trade, 513
Palladia Inc (Formerly Project Return Foundation Inc), 405
Palladian Health, 441
Palladium-Times (The), 529
Palliatech, Inc., 413
Palma 2013, 492
Palmyra-Macedon CSD, 597
Pamela Johnson For NYC Council, 492
Panama CSD, 570
Paraco Gas, 411
Parent Child HOme Program, Inc., 438
Parishville-Hopkinton CSD, 590
Park Avenue Armory, 401
Park Outdoor Advertising of NY, Inc., 414
Park Resident Homeowners' Association Inc, 192
Park Strategies, LLC, 453
Parker Jewish Inst for Health Care & Rehab, 442
Parker Jewish Institute for Health Care & Rehabilitation, 425
Parks & Trails New York, 453
Parks, Recreation & Historic Preservation, NYS Office of, 11, 149, 271, 305
Concession Management, 271

Environmental Management, 272
Environmental Management, 149
Field Services
Field Services, 149
Historic Sites Bureau, 149
Historic Preservation, 271
Field Services, 271
Historic Sites Bureau, 271
Marine & Recreational Vehicles, 149, 271
Regional Offices, 271
Central Region, 271
Finger Lakes Region, 271
Long Island Region, 271
Palisades Region, 272
Saratoga/Capital District Region, 272
Thousand Islands Region, 272
Regional Offices-Downstate District, 272
New York City Region, 272
Taconic Region, 272
Regional Offices-Western District, 272
Allegany Region, 272
Genesee Region, 272
Niagara Region & Western District Office, 272
Parkside Group, LLC, 453
Parodneck Foundation (The), 192
Parole Board, The, 11, 112, 305
Administrative Services, 112
Clemency Unit, 113
Executive Office, 112
Information Services, 113
Office of Counsel, 113
Parole Operations Unit, 113
Policy Analysis, 113
Victim Impact Unit, 113
Parsons Brinckerhoff, 292
Parsons Brinckerhoff, Inc., 390
Partners Health Plan, Inc., 421
Partnership for NYC, 472
Partnership for NYC (FKA Mele, Don), 454
Partnership for New York City, 94
Partnership of Upstate Legal Services, 410
Passero Associates, 430
Pastel & Rosen, LLP, 454
Patchogue Chamber of Commerce (Greater Patchogue), 513
Patchogue-Medford UFSD, 593
Path2Parenthood, 186
PathStone Corporation, 77, 192, 261
Patrick F. Adams, P.C., 410
Patrolmen's Benevolent Association, 118, 243, 454
Patterson Chamber of Commerce, 513
Paul Graziano 2013, 492
Paul Smith's College, 559
Pavilion CSD, 575
Pawling CSD, 572
Pearl River UFSD, 588
Peconic Bay Medical Center, 476
Peekskill, 65
Civil & Criminal Courts, 65
Peekskill City SD, 598
Peekskill Industrial Development Agency (City of), 513
Peekskill, City of, 361
Pelham UFSD, 598
Pembroke CSD, 575
Penfield CSD, 579
Penfield, Town of, 362
Penn Credit Corporation, 456
Penn Yan CSD, 599
Pennoni Engineering & Surveying of New York, PC, 473
Penzim Produce Corp, 405
People For Albert Baldeo, 492
People For Bing, 492
People For Brodsky, 492
People For Carlton Berkley, 492
People For Cheryl, 492
People For Debra Cooper, 492
People For Diaz, 492
People For Jelani, 492
People For Jerome Rice, 492
People For John C. Whitehead, 492
People For Lappin, 492
People For Leroy Gadsen, 492
People For Miguel Estrella, 492
People For Pu-Folkes, 492
People For Ydanis, 492
People For Yudelka Tapia, 492
People with Disabilities Task Force, 43
People, Inc., 387
People's World, 527
Pepe, Ross J, 454
Pepsi Co, 94
Peralta 2013, 492
Peralta For Senate, 492
Perinton, Town of, 362
Perry Area Chamber of Commerce, 513
Perry CSD, 599
Perry Capital LLC, 454
Perry Davis Associates, 94
Perry, Edmund F., 454
Perry, Robert, 454
Pershing Square Capital Management L.P., 455
Persons, Eric, 455
Peru CSD, 571
Pest Management Coalition, 422
Peterson 2013, 492
Pfizer Inc, 440
Pfizer Inc., 420, 478
Pfizer Inc. PAC, 492
Pfizer, Inc., 387, 391, 410, 427, 430
Pharmaceutical Research and Manufacturers of America, 427, 437
Pharmacists Society, 438
Pharmacists Society of the State of NY, 393
Pharmacists Society of the State of New York, 186
Phelps Chamber of Commerce, 514
Phelps Dodge Refining Corporation (Subsidiary of Freeport-McMoran Corporation), 387
Phelps Memorial Hospital Center, 476
Phelps-Clifton Springs CSD, 585
Phillips 66 Company, 421
Phillips Beth Israel School of Nursing, 559
Phillips Lytle, 455
Phillips Lytle LLP, 441
Phillips Nizer, LLP, 455
Phoenix CSD, 586
Physical Therapy Assn (NY), 475
Physicians Reciprocal Insurers, 393
Physicians' Reciprocal Insurers, 442
Physician's Reciprocal Insurers, 378
Pine Bush CSD, 585
Pine Plains CSD, 572
Pine Valley CSD (South Dayton), 570
Pinelawn Cemetery, 417
Pioneer Savings Bank, 82, 171, 455
Pipe Trades Association, 387
Piseco Common SD, 576
Pitney Bowes, Inc., 385, 473
Pitta, Bishop, Del Giorno & Giblin, LLC, 455
Pittsford CSD, 579
Pittsford, Town of, 362
Plainedge UFSD, 581
Plainview-Old Bethpage CSD, 581
Plainview-Old Bethpage Chamber of Commerce, 514
Planned Parenthood of NYC Inc, 476
Planned Parenthood of NYC, Inc, 261
Plattsburgh, 65
Civil & Criminal Courts, 65
Plattsburgh City SD, 571
Plattsburgh-North Country Chamber of Commerce, 514
Plaza College, 453, 565
Pleasantville UFSD, 599
Plug Power Inc, 145
Plumbers & Steamfitters Local No. 73 State & Local PAC Fund, 492
Plumbers Local Union No. 1 NYC - Political Action Committee, 493
Plumbing Contractors Assn of Long Island Inc, 470
Plumbing Foundation City of NY Inc, 470
Plumbing Foundation City of New York, Inc., 410, 431
Plummer & Wigger, LLC (FKA Griffin, Plummer & Associates), 455
Plyndirio LLC, 405
Pocantico Hills CSD, 599
Podiatric Medical Association, 421
Podiatric Medical Association (NYS), 456
Poland CSD, 576
Police Benevolent Assn of the NYS Troopers Inc, 456
Police Benevolent Association of New York State, 402, 425, 438, 456

Police Conference of NY Inc (PCNY), 118, 244
Police Conference of NY, Inc., 456
Polytechnic University, 559
Polytechnic University of New York University, 437
Pomeroy Appraisal Associates Inc, 248
Port Authority PBA of NY PAC, 493
Port Authority Police DEA NY PAC, 493
Port Authority of New York & New Jersey, 105, 287, 309
Port Byron CSD, 569
Port Chester SD, 599
Port Chester, Village of, 362
Port Chester-Rye Brook Rye Town Chamber of Commerce, 514
Port Jefferson Chamber of Commerce, 514
Port Jefferson UFSD, 593
Port Jervis, 65
Civil & Criminal Courts, 65
Port Jervis City SD, 585
Port Washington Chamber of Commerce, 514
Port Washington UFSD, 581
Port of Oswego Authority, 106, 288, 309
Ports America Inc., 456
Portville CSD, 569
Post-Journal, The, 526
Post-Standard (The), 531
Post-Star (The), 525
Postgrad Center for Mental Health, Child, Adolescent & Family-Couples, 233
Postgraduate Center for Mental Health, 233
Potsdam CSD, 590
Potsdam Chamber of Commerce, 514
Poughkeepsie, 65
Civil & Criminal Courts, 65
Poughkeepsie City SD, 572
Poughkeepsie Journal, 529
Poughkeepsie, City of, 362
Poughkeepsie, Town of, 362
Powell 2013, 493
Powerplay NYC, Inc., 477
Powers & Company, 456
Powers Global Strategies, LLC, 456
Pratt Center for Community Development, 193
Pratt Center for Community Direct Marketing Association, 438
Pratt Holdings USA (FKA Visy Paper (NY)), 387
Pratt Institute, 428, 452, 559
Pratt Institute for Community & Environment Development, 454
Prattsburgh CSD, 591
Praxiis Business Advisors, 456
Premier Exhibitions, Inc., 423
Premier Kids Care, Inc., 443
Premier Magnesia LLC, 401
Premier Senior Living LLC, 186
Premium Finance Association, 390
Presbyterian Hospital (NY), 457, 475
Preservation League of NYS (FKA DiLorenzo, Jay), 457
Preserve Associates LLC, 475
Press & Sun Bulletin, 523
Press-Republican, 529
Prestige Properties and Development Co., 401
Prevent Child Abuse New York, 261
Prevention of Domestic Violence, Office for the, 11, 113, 253, 305
PriceWaterhouseCoopers LLP, 457
Pricewaterhouse Coopers, LLP, 476
PricewaterhouseCoopers LLP, 171
Primary Care Development Corporation, 439, 457
Prime LLC, 437
Primerica Life Insurance Company, 421
Printing Industries Alliance, 94
Printing, Joint Committee on, 324
Prismatic Development Corporation, 401
Prisoners' Legal Services of New York, 118, 218
Pro Bono Net, 218
Pro Tech Monitoring Inc., 456
ProLiteracy Worldwide, 128, 261
Procter & Gamble, 385
Proctors Theater, 424
Production Alliance (NY), 444
Professional Agencies for Children's Therapy Services, 457
Professional Business College, 559
Professional Fire Fighters Association Inc (NYS), 244
Professional Fire Fighters Association, Inc., 402, 425, 442
Professional Insurance Agents of New York, 405
Professional Insurance Agents of New York State, 204
Professional Insurance Wholesalers Assoc of NYS Inc, 454
Professional Staff Congress (The), 379
Progressive Insurance Companies, 454
Project Renewal, 431
Project Samaritan AIDS Services Inc, 439
Project for Public Spaces, 193
Promontory Interfinancial Network LLC, 457
Propane Gas Association (NY), 389
Property Casualty Insurers Association of America (PCI), 402
Property Casualty Insurers Association of America (PCI) (FKA O'Brien, Frank), 457
Property Insurance Underwriting Association, 385
Proskauer Rose LLP, 94, 158, 171, 218
Prospect Park Alliance, 457
Protecting America.org, 445
Proton Management LLC, 394
Proton Management, LLC, 390
Providers Alliance, 387
Prudential Financial, Inc., 421
Prudential Financial, Inc. (Formerly Michael F. McCann), 457
Prudential Insurance Company of America (The) (Formerly John J. Kalamarides), 458
Prudential Investment Management, Inc. (Formerly Bernard B. Winograd), 458
Psychiatric Association, Inc. (NYS), 417
Psychotherapy & Counseling Center (New York), 390
Public Adjusters Association, 393
Public Agenda, 139, 171
Public Consulting Group, 425
Public Employee Conference (NYS), 441
Public Employees Federation, 396, 414
Public Employer Risk Management Assn, 475
Public Employment Relations Board, 11, 241, 305
Administration Section, 241
Conciliation Office, 241
District Offices, 241
Buffalo, 241
New York City, 241
Employment Practices & Representation Section, 241
Legal Section, 241
Public Financial Management, Inc., 458
Public Health Solutions, 425
Public Interest Research Group (NY), 458
Public Interest Research Group Fund, Inc. (New York), 458
Public Library (NY), Astor, Lenox & Tilden Foundations, 452
Public Library, Astor, Lenox & Tilden Foundations (NY), 458
Public Library, Astor, Lenox & Tilden Foundations (NY) (The), 458
Public Markets Partners/Baum Forum, 77
Public Policy Institute of NYS Inc, 94
Public Service Commission, 11, 140, 305
Accounting & Finance Office, 140
Consumer Policy Office, 140
Consumer Services Office, 140
Electric, Gas & Water Office, 141
Energy Efficiency & the Environment, 141
Hearings & Alternative Dispute Resolution Office, 141
Industry & Governmental Relations Office, 141
Office of Administration, 141
Office of Telecommunications, 141
Regulatory Economics Office, 141
Public Utility Law Project of New York Inc, 145
Public Welfare Assn (NY), 458
Public/Private Ventures, 226, 261
Puerto Rican Legal Defense & Education Fund Inc (PRLDEF), 218
Puerto Rican/Hispanic Task Force, 43

Pujolas, Elizabeth, 459
Pulaski CSD, 586
Pulaski-Eastern Shore Chamber of Commerce, 514
Pullium, Daniel, 459
Purchase College, State University of New York, 545
Purdue Pharma L.P., 459
Purvis Systems Inc, 470
Putnam CSD, 596
Putnam County, 57, 334
Supreme, County & Family Courts, 57
Surrogate's Court, 57
Putnam County Economic Development Corporation, 514
Putnam Valley CSD, 587
Putnam-Northern Westchester BOCES, 601
Putting New Yorkers to Work, 377
Pyle & Associates, Inc., 459
Pyramid Management Group LLC, 437
QSAC, 408
QSAC, Inc., 401
Quadlogic Controls Corporation, 402
Quantitative Management Associates LLC, 459
Queens & Bronx Building Assn, 379
Queens Adult Care Center, 476
Queens Borough Public Library, 405
Queens Centers for Progress Inc, 453
Queens Chamber of Commerce, 453, 459
Queens Chamber of Commerce (Borough of), 514
Queens Child Guidance Center Inc, 453
Queens College, 552
Queens College (Research Foundation of the City University of New York), 407
Queens College Foundation-Research of CUNY, 454
Queens County, 57
COUNTY & FAMILY COURTS: See New York City Courts, 57
Supreme & Surrogate's Courts, 57
Queens County (NYC Borough of Queens), 334
Queens County Republican Committee, 493
Queens Economic Development Corp, 453
Queens Economic Development Corporation, 407
Queens Educational Opportunity Center, 549
Queens Gazette, 527
Queens Theatre in the Park, 453
Queens-Long Island Medical Group, P.C., 476
Queensborough Comm College Auxiliary Enterprise Assn Inc, 453
Queensborough Community College, 552
Queensbury UFSD, 596
Queensbury, Town of, 362
Quest Diagnostics Inc, 475
Quest Public Sector, Inc., 394
Questar III, 475
Quinn For New York, 493
Quogue UFSD, 593
R W Bronstein Corporation, 248
RAI Services Company, 387, 422, 428, 441
RAI Services Company (FKA Reynolds American, Inc.), 459
RBC Capital Markets (FKA RBC Dain Rausher), 459
RCN Telecom Services, Inc., 405
RG Group, 460
RJM/EM 4 E 94th Street, LLC, 382
RPAC of New York, 493
RSA PAC City Account, 493
RWDSU Local 338 Political Action Committee, 494
Racing & Wagering, 41
Committee Staff, 41
Key Assembly Staff Assignments, 41
Membership, 41
Majority, 41
Minority, 41
Racing Association, Inc., 459
Racing and Gaming Services Inc, 456
Racing, Gaming & Wagering, 25
Committee Staff, 25
Membership, 25
Majority, 25
Minority, 25
Radar Associates, Inc., 421
Radiac Environmental Services, 158
Radon Testing Corp of America Inc, 158, 186
Railroads of New York, 455
Rain Inc, 472
Rainbow Media Holdings LLC, 431
Ralina Cardona 2013, 493
Ralph Lauren Center for Cancer Care & Prevention, 439
Ramapo CSD (Suffern), 588
Ramapo Organized for Sustainability and a Safe Aquifer, 410
Ramapo, Town of, 363
Randolph Academy UFSD, 569
Randolph CSD, 569
Rangel For Congress NY State, 493
Raquel Batista 2013, 493
Raquette Lake UFSD, 576
Rational Services Limited, 403
Raustiala, Margaret, 459
Ravena-Coeymans-Selkirk CSD, 567
Ravitz, John, 459
Raytheon Company, 444
Re-Elect Eric Ulrich, 493
Re-Elect Koslowitz 2013, 493
Re-Elect Mealy, 493
Reach Out and Read of Greater New York, 428
Real Estate Board of NY, 476
Real Estate Board of NY Inc, 459
Real Estate Board of NY, Inc., 417
Real Estate Board of New York, 377
Real Estate Board of New York Inc, 248
Real Estate Tax Review Bar Association, 390
Real Property Tax Services, Office of, 12, 235, 245, 264, 305
Albany (Northern Region)
Albany (Northern Region), 235, 264
Batavia (Western Region), 235, 264
Long Island Satellite Office, 235, 264
Ray Brook Satellite Office, 235, 264
South, 235, 264
Syracuse (Central Region), 235, 264
Real Property Taxation, 41
Committee Staff, 41
Key Assembly Staff Assignments, 41
Membership, 41
Majority, 41
Minority, 41
Real Rent Reform Campaign, 460
Realty Advisory Board on Labor Relations, 226, 248
Realty USA, 248
Recchia For New York, 493
Reckitt Benckiser Pharmaceuticals, Inc., 398
Reckitt Benckiser, Inc., 410
Record (The), 531
Recorder (The), 523
Recording Industry Association of America, Inc., 387
Rector, Church-Wardens and Vestrymen of Trinity Church in the City of New York (The), 416
Red Apple Group, 420
Red Barn Properties, 248
Red Creek CSD, 597
Red Hook Area Chamber of Commerce, 514
Red Hook CSD, 573
Red Land Strategy, Inc., 460
Redvision Systems, Inc., 405
Reed Elsevier, Inc., 405, 421
Reenergy Holdings LLC, 410, 460
Refuah Health Center, 390
Regeneron Pharmaceuticals Inc, 186
Regina Powell 2013, 493
Reginald Boddie For Supreme Court, 493
Regional Community Service Programs, 438
Regional Farm & Food Project, 77
Regional Plan Association, 94, 193, 292
Register-Star, 526
Rego Hills Republican Club, 493
Rehabilitation Assn Inc (NYS), 460
Rehabilitation Association, 438
Reinsurance Assn of America, 475
Related Companies L.P., 437
Related Companies LP, 248
Related Companies, L.P (The), 416
Related Companies, LP (The), 460, 473
Related Fund Management LLC, 460
Reliant Resources Inc, 442
Remove Intoxicated Drivers (RID-USA Inc), 118

Remsen CSD, 583
Remsenburg-Speonk UFSD, 593
Rensselaer, 65
Civil & Criminal Courts, 65
Rensselaer City SD, 588
Rensselaer County, 57, 335
Family Court, 57
Supreme, County & Surrogate's Courts, 57
Rensselaer County Regional Chamber of Commerce, 514
Rensselaer Polytechnic Inst, Ecological Economics, Values & Policy Program, 158
Rensselaer Polytechnic Institute, 128, 460, 559
Rensselaer-Columbia-Greene (Questar III) BOCES, 601
Rent A Center (Stateside Associates), 393
Rent Stabilization Assn of NYC Inc, 193, 460
Repas, Peter G, 460
Republican Majority For Choice NF PAC, 493
Rescare Inc. Advocacy Fund, 493
Rescare, Inc., 425, 431
Research Foundation for Mental Hygiene Inc, 233
Research Foundation of SUNY, 128
Research, Information & Policy Development
Albany (Northern Region)
Albany (Northern Region), 245
Batavia (Western Region), 246
Long Island Satellite Office, 246
Newburgh (South), 246
Ray Brook Satellite Office, 246
Syracuse (Central Region), 246
Research, Information & Policy Development, 245
Reserve Officers Association (ROA), 300
Reshma For New York, 493
Resource Center for Independent Living (RCIL), 199, 261
Resources for Artists with Disabilities Inc, 281
Responsible Industry for a Sound Environment (RISE), 378
Restaurant Assn (NYS), 462
Restoration Project, 431
Retail Council of New York State, 94
Retail Wholesale Department Store Union, 444
Retail Wholesale and Department Store Union C.O.P.E., 493
Retail, Wholesale and Department Store Union (RWDSU), 387
Retailers Alliance (The), 442
Retired Public Employees Association, 244
Retired Public Employees Association, Inc., 392, 460
Reuters (Thomson Reuters Markets LLC), 533
Review, 524
Rhinebeck Area Chamber of Commerce, 514
Rhinebeck CSD, 573
Rhonda F. Joseph 2013, 493
Richardson Management, 461
Richfield Springs Area Chamber of Commerce, 514
Richfield Springs CSD, 587
Richmond County, 57
COUNTY & FAMILY COURTS: See New York City Courts, 57
Supreme & Surrogate's Courts, 57
Richmond County (NYC Borough of Staten Island), 335
Richmond University Medical Center, 390
Riddell Group, LLC (The), 461
Riddett Associates, Inc. (FKA Riddett, Kenneth E. Associates Inc.), 461
Riddle, Gary, 461
Ridge Policy Group LLC, 461
Right to Life Committee Inc (NYS), 461
Ripley CSD, 570
Rite Aid Corporation, 393
Rivera 2013, 493
Riverhead CSD, 593
Riverhead Chamber of Commerce, 514
Riverhead Foundation for Marine Research & Preservation (The), 158
Riverhead, Town of, 363
Riverkeeper Inc, 158
Riverside South Planning Corp, 452
Riverview Redevelopment Company LP, 392
Rivington House- The Nicholas A. Rango Health Care Facility, 392
Road Runners Foundation (NY), 406
Roadway Imporvement Coalition (NY), 414
Roarke, Robert R., 461
Robert Schalkenbach Foundation, 248, 269
Roberts Wesleyan College, 423, 560
Robinson & Cole LLP, 461
Rochester, 65
Civil Court, 65
Criminal Court, 65
Rochester & Southern Railroad Inc, 423
Rochester Business Alliance Inc, 514
Rochester Business Alliance, Inc., 461
Rochester Business Journal, 533
Rochester City SD, 579
Rochester Downtown Development Corporation, 514
Rochester Economic Development Corporation, 514
Rochester Educational Opportunity Center, 550
Rochester Gas & Electric Corp, 396, 452
Rochester Gas & Electric Corporation, 145
Rochester Gas and Electric Corporation, 145
Rochester Genesee Regional Transportation Authority, 412, 437
Rochester Institute of Technology, 468, 476, 560
Rochester Interfaith Jail Ministry Inc, 118
Rochester Malls, LLC, 390
Rochester School for the Deaf, 128
Rochester Technology & Manufacturing Association, Inc., 423
Rochester, City of, 363
Rochester, University of, 560
Rochester-Genesee Regional Transportation Authority-RTS, 106, 288, 309
Rockaway Development & Revitalization Corp, 453
Rockaway Development & Revitalization Corporation, 515
Rockaways, Chamber of Commerce, Inc, 515
Rockefeller University, 560
Rocket Learning, Inc., 478
Rocking the Boat, Inc., 387
Rockland BOCES, 601
Rockland Chamber of Commerce, 515
Rockland Community College, 548
Rockland County, 58, 335
Supreme, County, Family & Surrogate's Courts, 58
Rockland Economic Development Corporation, 515
Rockville Centre Chamber of Commerce, 515
Rockville Centre UFSD, 581
Rockville Centre, Village of, 363
Rocky Point UFSD, 593
Roman Catholic Diocese of Albany, Catholic Charities, 261
Rome, 65
Civil & Criminal Courts, 65
Rome Area Chamber of Commerce, 515
Rome City SD, 583
Rome Industrial Development Corporation, 515
Rome Sentinel Co, 530
Rome, City of, 363
Romulus CSD, 590
Ronald Poppel, 461
Rondout Valley CSD, 595
Ronkonkoma Chamber of Commerce, 515
Roohan Realty, 249
Rooney, Timothy J., 461
Roosevelt Island Operating Corporation (RIOC), 106, 189, 274, 309
Roosevelt UFSD, 581
Roscoe CSD, 594
Rose Group Park Ave. LLC, 410
Rosenthal For Assembly, 493
Rosenthal, Harvey, 461
Rosie Mendez 2013, 493
Roslyn UFSD, 581
Roswell Park Cancer Institute, 390

Rotterdam, Town of, 364
Rotterdam-Mohonasen CSD, 589
Roundabout Theatre Co, 475
Roundabout Theatre Company, 404
Roxbury CSD, 572
Royal Realty Corp., 461
Royalton-Hartland CSD, 583
Rreef America LLC, 462
Rubber Manufacturers Association, 423
Ruben Wills 2013, 493
Rubin, Jamie Lyn, 462
Rubin, Kate, 462
Rudin Management Company, Inc., 416
Rules, 25, 41, 321
Membership, 25, 41
Majority, 25, 41
Minority, 25, 41
Subcommittees, 321
Legislative & Budget Process, 321
Rules & Organization of the House, 321
Rules & Administration, 316
Runes, Richard, 462
Rural & Migrant Ministry Inc, 261
Rural Electric Cooperative Association, Inc. (NYS), 417
Rural Resources, Legislative Commission on, 26, 43
Rural Water Assn (NY), 465
Rural Water Association, 158
Rush-Henrietta CSD, 579
Russo, Michael, 462
Rutnik Law Firm (The), 462
Ryan, Desmond, 462
Rye, 65
Civil & Criminal Courts, 65
Rye City SD, 599
Rye Neck UFSD, 599
Rye, Town of, 364
S.L. Green Realty Corporation, 419
S.W. Anderson Sales Corporation, 407
SAS Institute Inc, 463
SAS Institute, Inc., 463
SBLI USA Mutual Life Insurance Company Inc, 204
SC Johnson & Son Inc, 475
SCA Tissue North America LLC, 424
SCS Engineers PC, 158
SDR Pharmaceuticals Inc, 464
SDS Great Jones LLC, 431
SEIU Local 200 United, 404, 444
SEIU Political Education and State Action Fund, 494
SEIU, Local 300, 444
SHFL Entertainment, Inc., 437
SJP TS JV, LLC, 382
SL Green Realty Company, 416, 431
SL Green Realty Corp, 436
SMWIA Local 28 Political Action Committee, 494
SMWIA Political Action League Local 137, 494
SSL Political Action Committee, 494
SSP Companies, 440
STV Engineers Inc. Political Action Committee, 495
SUNY Board of Trustees, 543
SUNY Buffalo Human Rights Center, 199
SUNY College & Career Counseling Center, 550
SUNY College of Agriculture & Technology at Cobleskill, 546
SUNY College of Environmental Science and Forestry (FKA Micheal Brower), 468
SUNY Downstate Medical Center, 478, 544
SUNY Fredonia, 468
SUNY Geneseo, 444
SUNY State College of Optometry, 544
SUNY System Administration & Executive Council, 543
New York Network, 543
Rockefeller Institute of Government, 543
SUNY Center for Student Recruitment, 543
Small Business Development Center, 544
State University Construction Fund, 544
SUNY Upstate Medical University, 468, 544
SUNY at Albany, Center for Women in Government & Civil Society, 171
SUNY at Albany, Nelson A Rockefeller College, 139
SUNY at Albany, Professional Development Program, NE States Addiction, 233
SUNY at Albany, Rockefeller College, 171
SUNY at Albany, School of Public Health, Center for Public Health Preparedness, 186
SUNY at Cortland, Center for Environmental & Outdoor Education, 159
SUNY at New Paltz, College of Liberal Arts & Sciences, 139, 171
SUNY at New Paltz, Department of History, 171
Sacandaga Protection Company, 387
Sachem CSD, 593
Sackets Harbor Central School, 577
Sackets Harbor Chamber of Commerce, 515
Safe Horizon, Inc., 431, 438, 462
Safe Space, 392
Safelite Group, Inc., 442
Sag Harbor Chamber of Commerce, 515
Sag Harbor UFSD, 593
Sagaponack Common SD, 593
Sage Colleges (The), 560
Sahn Ward Coschignano, PLLC, 159
Saint Joseph's Medical Center, 411
Sal 2013, 494
Salamanca, 65
Civil & Criminal Courts, 65
Salamanca Area Chamber of Commerce, 515
Salamanca City SD, 569
Salamanca Industrial Development Agency, 515
Salamanca Press, 530
Salem CSD, 596
Salesforce.com, Inc., 394
Salient Corporation, 456
Salina, Town of, 364
Sallie Mae, Inc., 443
Salmar Properties LLC, 394
Salmon River CSD, 575
Salvation Army School for Officer Training, 560
Salvation Army, Empire State Division, 261
Samaritan Hospital School of Nursing, 560
Samaritan Medical Center, 476
Samaritan Village Inc, 233, 439
Sampson, Rick J, 462
Samuel A. Ramirez & Co., Inc., 462
Sanctuary for Families, 463, 476
Sanders For Senate, 494
Sandy Creek CSD, 586
Sanitary District No 6, 435
Sanitation Officers Association Volunteer Political Action COPE Account, 494
Sanitation Officer's Association, 440
Sanofi Pasteur Inc, 475
Santiago NYC 2013, 494
Santos 2013, 494
Sanzillo, Francis J. & Associates, 463
Sarah Lawrence College, 560
Sarah M. Gonzalez 2013, 494
Saranac CSD, 571
Saranac Lake Area Chamber of Commerce, 515
Saranac Lake CSD, 575
Saratoga County, 58, 335
Family Court, 58
Supreme, County & Surrogate's Courts, 58
Saratoga County Chamber of Commerce, 515
Saratoga County Industrial Development Agency, 515
Saratoga Economic Development Corporation, 515
Saratoga Gaming & Raceway, 281
Saratoga Harness Racing, Inc., 463
Saratoga Hospital, 387
Saratoga Springs, 65
Civil & Criminal Courts, 65
Saratoga Springs City SD, 588
Saratoga Springs, City of, 364
Saratogian (The), 530
Sasson For NYC, 494
Saugerties CSD, 595
Saugerties, Town of, 364
Saundra Thomas 2013, 494
Sauquoit Valley CSD, 583
Sauti Yetu Center for African Women, 477
Savino For New York, 494
Sayville Chamber of Commerce (Greater Sayville), 515
Sayville UFSD, 593

Scarsdale Chamber of Commerce, 515
Scarsdale UFSD, 599
Scenic Hudson, 159
Scenic Hudson Inc, 463
Schalmont CSD, 589
Schenectady, 65
Civil Court, 65
Criminal Court, 65
Schenectady City SD, 589
Schenectady County, 58, 335
Family Court, 58
Supreme, County & Surrogate's Courts, 58
Schenectady County Chamber of Commerce, 515
Schenectady County Community College, 548
Schenectady County Industrial Development Agency/Economic Development Corporation, 515
Schenectady Metroplex Development Authority, 455
Schenectady, City of, 364
Schenevus CSD, 587
Schillo, John, 463
Schlather, Geldenhuys, Stumbar & Salk, 216
Schlein, Stanley Esq., 463
Schmidt, James A., 464
Schnell, William A & Associates Inc, 464
Schnur Associates, Inc., 464
Schodack CSD, 588
Schoharie CSD, 589
Schoharie County, 58, 336
Supreme, County, Family & Surrogate's Courts, 58
Schoharie County Chamber of Commerce, 516
Schoharie County Industrial Development Agency, 516
Schomberg, Dora, 464
School Administrators Association of NYS, 128, 464
School Administrators Association of New York State, 408
School Boards Assn (NYS), 464
School Boards Association (NYS), 404
School Bus Contractor's Coalition, Inc. (NY), 476
School Nutrition Association, 439
School for Language and Communication Development, 420
School of Industrial & Labor Relations at Cornell University (ILR School), 544
School of Law at Queens College, 552
School of Professional Studies, 552
School of Visual Arts, 565
Schroon Lake Area Chamber of Commerce, 516
Schroon Lake CSD, 574
Schuh, Paul, 464
Schuyler Center for Analysis & Advocacy, 464
Schuyler Center for Analysis & Advocacy (SCAA), 128, 199, 233
Schuyler County, 58, 336
Supreme, County, Family & Surrogate's Courts, 58
Schuyler County Industrial Development Agency, 516
Schuyler County Partnership for Economic Development, 516
Schuylerville CSD, 589
Science & Technology, 322
Subcommittees, 322
Energy & Environment, 322
Investigations and Oversights, 322
Research and Science Education, 322
Space and Aeronautics, 322
Technology and Innovation, 322
Science & Technology, Legislative Commission on, 43
Science Application International Corp., 456
Science, Technology, Incubation & Entrepreneurship, Select Committee on, 26
Scio CSD, 568
Scotia-Glenville CSD, 589
Scotts Company (The), 475
Scotts Miracle-Gro Company, 464
Screen Actors Guild (National & Hollywood Offices), 444
Scripps Howard News Service, 533
Sea Crest Construction Corp., 456
Seaford Chamber of Commerce, 516
Seaford UFSD, 581
Seaway Trail Inc, 281
Second Stage Theatre, 392
Securitas, 464
Securities Industry & Financial Markets Association, 465
Securities Industry & Financial Markets Association (SIFMA), 82, 214
Segway Inc. (Multistate Associates), 476
Selective Staffing Solutions, 387
Self Advocacy Association of NYS, 199, 233
Selfhelp Community Services, Inc., 425
Seminary of the Immaculate Conception, 560
Semper Fi NYS PAC Inc., 494
Senate, 306
Senate Standing Committees, 70, 73, 79, 80, 87, 90, 114, 116, 125, 137, 142, 143, 152, 155, 165, 169, 178, 180, 189, 190, 195, 197, 202, 203, 211, 214, 222, 224, 230, 237, 242, 246, 254, 255, 265, 267, 275, 276, 288, 290, 295, 297
Aging, 178, 195, 254
Aging, Special Committee on, 180, 255
Agriculture, 70
Agriculture, Nutrition & Forestry, 73, 155, 180
Subcommittee, 155
Agriculture, Rural Development, FDA & Related Agencies, 73
Appropriations, 73, 143, 267
Subcommittee, 73, 143
Armed Services, 297
Aviation Operations, Safety & Security, 143
Banking, Housing & Urban Affairs, 80, 190
Banks, 79
Budget, 267
Children & Families, 178, 254
Cities, 87, 237
Civil Service & Pensions, 165, 242
Codes, 114, 211
Commerce, Economic Development & Small Business, 87, 237, 246, 288
Commerce, Science & Transportation, 90, 143, 155, 290
Subcommittee, 143, 155
Conservation, Forestry & Natural Resources, 155
Consumer Protection, 87, 165, 178
Corporations, Authorities & Commissions, 87, 165, 288
Crime & Terrorism, 169
Crime Victims, Crime & Correction, 114, 195
Cultural Affairs, Tourism, Parks & Recreation, 275
Education, 125
Elections, 137
Energy & Natural Resources, 143, 155, 276
Subcommittees, 276
Energy & Telecommunications, 142
Energy & Water Development, 143
Environment & Public Works, 155, 290
Subcommittee, 290
Environmental Conservation, 152
Ethics, 165
Ethics, Select Committee on, 137, 169
Finance, 90, 165, 203, 237, 265, 267
Subcommittee, 267
Subcommittees, 203
Foreign Relations, 90
Health, 178
Health Care, 203
Health, Education, Labor & Pensions, 125, 180, 224, 255
Subcommittees, 180
Higher Education, 125
Homeland Security & Governmental Affairs, 137, 169, 242, 267
Housing Construction & Community Development, 246
Housing, Construction & Community Development, 189, 237
Immigration and The National Interest, 169
Indian Affairs, Committee on, 169, 197

Insurance, 202
Intelligence, Select Committee on, 169
Investigations & Government Operations, 165
Judiciary, 116, 169, 211, 214
Subcommittees, 169
Labor, 195, 202, 222, 242
Local Government, 189, 237
Mental Health & Developmental Disabilities, 196, 230
National Parks, 276
Oceans, Atmosphere, Fisheries and Coast Guard, 155
Primary Health & Retirement Security, 180
Public Lands, Forests & Mining, 276
Racing, Gaming & Wagering, 266, 275
Rules, 165
Small Business & Entrepreneurship, 90, 224
Social Security, Pensions and Family Policy, 203
Social Services, 178, 254
Space, Science & Competitiveness, 143
Taxation & IRS Oversight, 267
Transportation, 237, 288
Transportation & Infrastructure, 290
Veterans, Homeland Security & Military Affairs, 295
Veterans' Affairs, 297
Senate/Assembly Legislative Commissions, 70, 87, 137, 152, 165, 242
Demographic Research & Reapportionment, Legislative Task Force on, 137
Ethics Committee, Legislative, 165
Government Administration, Legislative Commission on, 165, 242
Rural Resources, Legislative Commission on, 70, 87, 152
Seneca County, 58, 336
Supreme, County, Family & Surrogate's Courts, 58
Seneca County Chamber of Commerce, 516
Seneca County IDA, 430
Seneca County Industrial Development Agency, 516
Seneca Falls CSD, 590
Seneca Flight Operations, 292
Seneca Foods Corporation, 77
Seneca Nation of Indians, 166, 425, 465
Senior Care Pharmacy Alliance, 421
Senior Whole Health, 421
Sephardic Bikur Holim, 439
Sepracor, 472
Sequoia Community Initiatives (Consumer Info & Dispute Resolution), 436
Sergeants Benevolent Association, 387, 494
Service Corporation International Political Association Committee, 494
Service Employees International Union, Local 300, 453
Service Station Dealers of Greater NY, Inc, 470
Servicemaster Company (The), 421
Services & Advocacy for Gay, Lesbian, Bisexual & Transgender Elders, 477
Services for the UnderServed (SUS), 118
Settlement Housing Fund Inc, 193
Sewanhaka Central HS District, 581
Shaker Museum (The), 456
Shanahan Group, 465
Shank, Suzanne, 465
Shapiro, Brian, 465
Share Our Strength, Inc., 387
Shareing & Careing Inc, 408
Sharon Springs CSD, 589
Shawanga Lodge, LLC, 387
Shea's Buffalo Theatre, 441
Sheehan Green Carraway Golderman & Jacques LLP, 465
Sheinkopf Communications, 139
Sheinkopf, Ltd, 465
Shell Energy North America, 387
Shelter Island UFSD, 593
Shelter Rock Strategies, LLC, 465
Shema Kolainu-Hear Our Voices, 416
Shenendehowa CSD, 589
Shephardic Heritage Museum, 437
Sherburne-Earlville CSD, 571
Sheriff Officers Assn, 453
Sheriffs' Association, 476
Sherin, James R., 465
Sherman CSD, 570
Sherrill, 65
Civil & Criminal Courts, 65
Sherrill City SD, 583
Shikibo LTD., 402
Shinnecock Indian Nation, 166
Shinnecock Nation Gaming Authority, 442, 443
Shipping Association, Inc (NY), 399
Shipping Association, Inc., 391
Shoreham-Wading River CSD, 594
Short Term Rental and Hospitality Association, 402
Shubert Organization, Inc. (The), 432
Sibley Redevelopment Limited Partnership, 390
Siconolfi, Patrick, 465
Sidique Wai For Public Advocate, 494
Sidney CSD, 572
Sidney Chamber of Commerce, 516
Siemens Enterprise Communications, Inc., 402
Siemens Industry, Inc., 387
Siena College, 456, 465, 560
Sierra 2013, 494
Sierra Club, 478
Sierra Club, Atlantic Chapter, 159
Silver Creek CSD, 570
Silvercup Studios, 442
Silverite Construction, 431
Silverstein 2013, 494
Silverstein Properties Inc, 249
Simcha NY, 494
Simmons-Boardman Publishing Corp, 292
Simmons-Oliver For City Council, 494
Simon Weisenthal Ctr Museum of Tolerance, 442
Simon Wiesenthal Center, Museum of Tolerance NY, 199
Simons & Wright LLC, 465
Sithe Global, 146
Ska Marin, 382
Skaneateles Area Chamber of Commerce, 516
Skaneateles CSD, 584
Ski Areas of NY, Inc., 388
Ski Areas of New York Inc, 281
Skidmore College, 560
Skills Development & Career Education, Legislative Commission on, 43
Skybridge Capital II LLC, 466
Sleepy Hollow Chamber of Commerce, 516
Slippen, Daniel, 466
Slovak American Chamber of Commerce, 516
Small Business, 41, 322
Committee Staff, 41
Key Assembly Staff Assignments, 41
Membership, 41
Majority, 41
Minority, 41
Subcommittees, 322
Contracting and Technology, 322
Finance and Tax, 322
Investigations and Oversight, 322
Regulations and Health Care, 322
Rural and Urban Entrepreneurship, 322
Small Business & Entrepreneurship, 316
Small Business Administration, 88
Buffalo, 88
New Jersey, 88
New York City, 88
Region II New York, 88
District Offices, 88
New York Small Business Development Center, 88
Syracuse, 88
Small Customer Marketer Coalition, 400, 434
Smith, Joseph, 466
Smith, Robert, 466
Smithsonian Institution, 275
Cooper-Hewitt National Design Museum, 275
National Museum of the American Indian-George Gustav Heye Center, 275
Smithtown CSD, 594
Smithtown Chamber of Commerce, 516

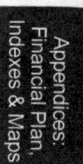

Smithtown, Town of, 364
Smyth, A Advocacy, 466
Snowmobile Association (NYS), 393
Snowmobile Association (NYS) (Capitol Group, LLC), 417
Snowplow LLC, 392
Snug Harbor Cultural Center, 436
Snyder Communications Corp, 528
Sobol, Peter, 466
Social Security Administration, 254
Region 2-New York, 254
Office of Hearings & Appeals, 254
Office of Quality Assurance, 254
Office of the General Counsel, 254
Program Operations Center, 254
Public Affairs, 254
Social Services, 25, 41
Committee Staff, 25, 42
Key Assembly Staff Assignments, 42
Key Senate Staff Assignments, 25
Membership, 25, 42
Majority, 25, 42
Minority, 25, 42
Society for Clinical Social Work Inc (NYS), 476
Society for Respiratory Care Inc (NYS), 475
Society of Anesthesiologists, Inc (NYS), 424
Society of CPA's, 466
Society of Clinical Social Work, Inc. (NYS), 442
Society of New York Office Based Surgery Facilities, 387
Society of Opticians, Inc. (NYS), 393
Society of Oral and Maxillofacial Surgeons (NYS), 393
Society of Orthopaedic Surgeons (NYS), 386
Society of Physician Assistants (NYS), 414
Society of Professional Engineers, Inc., 433
Sodus CSD, 597
Soft Drink and Brewery Workers Political Action Committee, 494
Software & Information Industry Association, 94
Solar Energy Industries Association, 390, 466
Soligent Distribution LLC - East Coast Distribution Center, 146
Solomon R Guggenheim Foundation, 281
Solomon R. Guggenheim Museum, 392
Solow Management Company, 442
Solow Management Corp., 402
Solowan, Richard, 466
Soloway, Ronald, 466
Solus Alternative Asset Management LP, 466
Solvay UFSD, 584
Somers CSD, 599
Sondra Peeden 2013, 494
Sonnenblick-Goldman Company, 249
Sony Pictures Entertainment, 425
Sophie Davis School of Biomedical Education, 552
Sorrento Lactalis, Inc., 437
Sotheby's, 421
Source Corp., 443
South Asians United For a Better America PAC, 494
South Bronx Overall Economic Development Corporation, 514
South Buffalo Railway Company, 423
South Colonie CSD, 567
South Country CSD, 594
South Glens Falls CSD, 589
South Huntington UFSD, 594
South Jefferson CSD, 577
South Jefferson Chamber of Commerce, 516
South Kortright CSD, 572
South Lewis CSD, 577
South Orangetown CSD, 588
South Queens Boys & Girls Club Inc, 453
South Seneca CSD, 590
South Street Seaport L.P., 432
South Street Seaport Limited Partnership, 431
Southampton Chamber of Commerce, 516
Southampton Hospital, 390
Southampton UFSD, 594
Southampton, Town of, 365
Southeastern New York, Council of Industry of, 516
Southern Cayuga CSD, 569
Southern Dutchess Chamber of Commerce (Greater Southern Dutchess), 516
Southern Madison County Chamber of Commerce, 516
Southern NY Assn, 424
Southern Saratoga County Chamber of Commerce, 516
Southern Tier Acquisition, LLC, 442
Southern Tier Economic Growth Inc, 516
Southern Tier Independence Center, 466
Southern Ulster County Chamber of Commerce, 516
Southern Westchester BOCES, 601
Southern Wine & Spirits of America, Inc., 405, 409
Southold UFSD, 594
Southold, Town of, 365
Southwestern CSD at Jamestown, 570
Southworth-Milton, 425
Spackenkill UFSD, 573
Spanish Broadcasting System Network Inc, 146
Spec Cmte on Collateral Consequence of Criminal Proceedings, 171
Special Committee on Animals & the Law, 77
Special Olympics New York, Inc, 281
Specialty Wine Retailers Association, 411
Spectra Environmental Group Inc, 159
Spencer-Van Etten CSD, 595
Spencerport CSD, 579
Sports & Arts in School Foundation, 408
Sports & Arts in Schools Foundation, 128, 282, 431
Sports and Arts in Schools Foundation, 402
Spring Valley, Village of, 365
Springbrook, 233
Springbrook NY, Inc, 261
Springs UFSD, 594
Springville Area Chamber of Commerce, 517
Springville-Griffith Inst CSD, 574
Sprint Nextel Corporation, 387
Squadron For New York, 494
St Bernard's School of Theology & Ministry, 560
St Bonaventure University, 560
St Elizabeth College of Nursing, 561
St Elizabeth Medical Center, 475
St Francis College, 561
St James Chamber of Commerce, 517
St John Fisher College, 561
St Johnsville CSD, 579
St John's University, 390, 561
St John's University, School of Law, 159
St John's University-Peter J Tobin College of Business, School of Risk Mgmt, 204
St Joseph's College, 561
St Joseph's Rehabilitation Center Inc, 233
St Joseph's Seminary Institute of Religious Studies, 561
St Lawrence County, 58, 336
Supreme, County, Family & Surrogate's Courts, 58
St Lawrence County Chamber of Commerce, 517
St Lawrence County Industrial Development Agency, 517
St Lawrence County Newspapers, 529
St Lawrence University, 561
St Lawrence-Lewis BOCES, 601
St Luke's Cornwall Hospital, 476
St Luke's-Roosevelt Hospital Centers, 456
St Luke's-Roosevelt Hospital Ctrs, 432
St Margaret's Center, 476
St Mary's Healthcare System for Children Inc, 476
St Raymond Community Outreach, 439
St Regis Falls CSD, 575
St Regis Mohawk Tribe, 166
St Thomas Aquinas College, 561
St Vladimir's Orthodox Theological Seminary, 561
St. Anns of Greater Rochester, Inc., 425
St. Ann's Warehouse, 477
St. Barnabas Hospital, 382
St. Francis College, 478
St. John Fruit Belt Development Corporation, 441
St. Johns Riverside Hospital, 443
St. Joseph's College, 432

St. Mary's Healthcare System For Children, Inc., 387
St. Michael's Cemetary, 402
St. Regis Mohawk Tribe, 387
Staffing Assn (NY), 405
Stahl York Avenue LLC, 431
Stamford CSD, 572
Standardbred Owners Assn of NY, 478
Standards of Official Conduct, 322
Star-Gazette, 525
Starpoint CSD, 583
Starwood Capital LLC, 467
State & Broadway, Inc., 467
State Advisers, LLC, 467
State Comptroller, Office of the, 12, 149, 162, 235, 241, 305
Executive Office, 149, 162, 236, 241
Human Resources & Administration, 162, 236
Inspector General, 162, 236
Intergovernmental Affairs, 162, 236
Legal Services, 162, 236
Local Government & School Accountability, 162
Oil Spill Fund Office, 149
Operations, 162, 236, 241
Payroll & Revenue Services Division, 241
Pension Investment & Cash Management, 162
Retirement, 162, 236
Retirement Services, 241
Accounting Bureau, 241
Actuarial Bureau, 241
Benefit Calculations & Disbursements, 241
Disability Processing/Hearing Administration, 241
Member & Employee Services, 241
Retirement Communications, 241
State Government Accountability, 162, 236
Local Government and School Accountability, 236
State Department, 12, 85, 149, 162, 236, 305
Administrative Rules Division
Administrative Rules Division, 162
Cemeteries Division, 162
Corporations, State Records & UCC Division, 162
Licensing Services Division, 86, 162
Administrative Rules Division, 86
Cemeteries Division, 86
Corporations, State Records & UCC Division, 86
Local Government & Community Services, 149, 162, 236
Coastal Resources & Waterfront Revitalization Division, 150, 162, 236
Code Enforcement & Administration Division, 163, 236
Community Services Division, 150, 163, 236
Local Government Services Division, 163, 236
Open Government Committee, 163, 236
Operations, 163
Administrative Support Services, 163
Affirmative Action, 163
Fiscal Management, 163
Human Resources Management, 163
Information Technology Management, 163
Internal Audit, 163
Region 1 - Buffalo Office, 163
Region 10 - Northern New York Office, 163
Region 12/13 - Long Island Office, 163
Region 2 - Peekskill Office, 163
Region 4 - Kingston Office, 163
Region 5 - Syracuse Office, 163
Region 6 - Utica Office, 163
Region 7/8 - Western New York Office, 163
Region 9 - Capital District Office, 163
Regional Offices
Regional Offices, 163
Regional Services, 163
State Athletic Commission, 163
State Employees Federal Credit Union, 244
State Farm Insurance Companies, 408, 426
State Osteopathic Medical Society (NY), 405
State Police, Division of, 12, 113, 305
Administration, 113
Forensic Investigation Center, 113
Public Information, 113
Employee Relations, 113
Human Resources, 113
State Police Academy, 113
Field Command, 113
Internal Affairs, 113
State University College at Cortland, 545
State University College at Geneseo, 545
State University College at New Paltz, 545
State University College of Technology at Canton, 546
State University College of Technology at Delhi, 546
State University Construction Fund, 106, 124, 309
State University Empire State College, 545
State University Institute of Technology, 546
State University at Old Westbury, 545
State University at Potsdam, 545
State University of NY, System Administration, 467
State University of New York College of Environmental Science & Forestry, 545
State University of New York Maritime College, 546
State University of New York at Albany, 544
State University of New York at Oneonta, 546
State University of New York at Oswego, 546
State University of New York at Plattsburgh, 546
State University of New York at Potsdam, 467
State University of New York at Stony Brook, 425, 467
State University of New York, Fredonia, 545
State of New York Mortgage Agency (SONYMA), 189, 309
State of New York Municipal Bond Bank Agency (MBBA), 310
State-Federal Relations, Legislative Task Force on, 43
Staten Island Advance, 530
Staten Island Chamber of Commerce, 517
Staten Island Economic Development Corporation, 517
Staten Island PAC, 494
Staten Island Zoo, 282
Statewide Black & Puerto Rican/Latino Substance Abuse Task Force, 233
Stealth Communications Services LLC, 455
Steamfitters Local 638 PAC, 387, 494
Steinway Child and Family Services, 431
Stendardi, Deborah M, 467
Steuben County, 59, 337
Supreme, County, Family & Surrogate's Courts, 59
Steuben County Industrial Development Agency, 517
Stiles Properties, LLC, 392
Stillwater CSD, 589
Stockbridge Valley CSD, 578
Stonehenge Capital Corporation, 425
Stoneriver Pharmacy Solutions, Inc., 410
Stoneriver Pharmacy Solutions, Inc. (FKA Third Party Solutions), 404
Stony Brook Drinking Driver Program LLC, 118
Stony Brook Foundation, 433
Stony Brook Foundation, Inc., 438
Stony Brook University Hospital, 390
Stony Brook University, SUNY, 545
Stop & Shop Supermarket Co (The), 462
Stop DWI Coordinators Association, 421
StoryCorps, 387
Strategic 34th Street LLC, 432
Strategic Services, Inc, 468
Strike Force Protective Services, Inc., 410
Stringer 2013, 495
Strive, 453
Stroock & Stroock & Lavan LLP, 204, 468
Structural Biology Center (NY), 439
Structured Employment Economic Development Corp, 439

Structured Employment and Economic Development Corporation, 382
Stryker, Patricia, 468
Stuto, Diane D, 468
Stuyvesant Town-Peter Cooper Village Tenants Association, 429
Suburban Hospital Alliance of New York State, 423
Suburban News & Hamlin Clarkson Herald, 530
Subway Surface Supervisors Assn, 453
Success Academy Charter Schools, 438
Suffern Chamber of Commerce, 517
Suffolk County, 59, 61, 337
1ST DISTRICT COURT, Civil Term, 61
1ST DISTRICT COURT, Criminal Term, 61
2nd District Court, 61
3rd District Court, 61
4th District Court, 61
5th District Court, 61
6th District Court, 61
County Court, 59
Family Court, 59
Supreme Court, 59
Surrogate's Court, 59
Suffolk County Ambulance Chiefs Assoc, 464
Suffolk County Association of Municipal Employees, Inc - Political Action Committee, 495
Suffolk County Community College, 548
Suffolk County Correction Officers Assn, 444
Suffolk County Court Employees, 442
Suffolk County Deputy Sheriff's Police Benevolent Assn, 464
Suffolk County Water Authority, 465
Suffolk Regional Off-Track Betting Corporation, 106, 274, 310, 442
Suit-Kote Corp, 452
Sullivan & Cromwell, 82
Sullivan & Cromwell LLP, 268
Sullivan BOCES, 601
Sullivan County, 59, 337
Supreme & County Court, 59
Surrogate's & Family Courts, 59
Sullivan County Chamber of Commerce, 517
Sullivan County Community College, 548
Sullivan County Industrial Development Agency, 517
Sullivan For NYC, 495
Sullivan West CSD, 594
SunEdison LLC, 478
Sunbridge College, 561
Sunny Hahn For City Council, 495
Sunnyside Community Services, Inc., 392
Sunrun, Inc., 390
Sunshine Development School, Inc., 404
Superfund Coalition, Inc. (NYS), 425
Supershuttle NY Inc, 453
Support Services Alliance Inc, 94, 205
Support Services Alliance, Inc., 425
Supportive Housing Network of New York, Inc., 468
Supreme Court, 218
Supreme Court Justices Association of the City of New York, 425
Surf Manor Home for Adults, 438
Suse and Peter Lowenstein, 438
Susquehanna & Western Railway Corp (NY), 444
Susquehanna Valley CSD, 568
Sustainable Management LLC, 159
Swedish Institute, 565
Sweet Home CSD, 574
Syngenta Crop Protection LLC, 478
Syosset CSD, 581
Syracuse, 66
Civil & Criminal Courts, 66
Syracuse & Central NY, Metropolitan Development Association of, 517
Syracuse Chamber of Commerce (Greater Syracuse), 517
Syracuse City SD, 584
Syracuse Economic Development, 517
Syracuse Educational Opportunity Center, 550
Syracuse Industrial Development Agency, 517
Syracuse Newspapers Inc, 531
Syracuse University, 455, 475, 561
Syracuse University Press, 159
Syracuse University, Maxwell School of Citizenship & Public Affairs, 128, 159, 172, 239, 244, 261
Syracuse University, Office of Government & Community Relations, 129
Syracuse, City of, 365
Sysco Food Services of Albany, LLC, 387
Systech International, 393
Systra Consulting Inc, 292
T&T Scrap LLC, 431
T-Mobile USA Inc, 476
TA Ahern Contractors Corp., 402
TBTA Maintenance Employees, Local 1931, DC-37, AFSCME, 470
TD Bank N.A., 82
TD Bank US Holding Company, 402
TD Bank, N.A., 394
TDC Development & Construction Corp, 436
TEI Group, 460
TF Cornerstone, Inc., 416
TKGG LLC, 436
TLM Associates LLC, 469
TPU Local One IATSE NYC, 495
TRC, 456
TVG Network, 445
TWC Administration LLC, 393, 405
Taconic Hills CSD, 571
Taconic IPA Inc, 476
Takeda Pharmaceuticals America, 439
Talisman Energy USA, Inc., 442
Talon Air, Inc., 420
Tamika For City Council 2013, 495
Tanenbaum Center for Interreligious Understanding, 199
Tanglewood Manor, 476
Tappan Zee Constructors, LLC, 438
Tarrytown UFSD, 599
Taubman Company (The), 438
Tax Appeals, Division of, 12, 264, 305
Administrative Law Judges & Officers, 13, 265
Tax Appeals Tribunal, 13, 265
Taxation & Finance Department, 13, 86, 265, 305
Office of Budget & Management Analysis, 86, 265
Planning & Management Analysis Bureau, 86, 265
Office of Criminal Enforcement, 86, 265
Audit Division, 86, 265
Collections & Civil Enforcement, 86, 265
Office of Information Technology Services, 86, 265
Office of Processing & Taxpayer Services, 86, 265
Office of Processing & Taxpayer Services (OPTS), 86, 265
Human Resources Management, 86, 265
Operations Support Bureau, 86, 265
Office of State Treasury, 86, 265
Office of Tax Policy Analysis, 86, 265
Taxation, Joint Committee on, 324
Taxicab Service Assn, 405
Taxpayers For an Affordable New York Political Action Committee, 495
Taxpayers for Economic Justice, Inc. (NY), 468
Tea Association of the USA Inc, 77
Teachers College, Columbia University, 129, 561
Teachers Insurance & Annuity Assn/College Retirement Equities Fun, 475
Teacher's College, Columbia University, 403
Teaching Matters Inc, 129
Team Greenfield, 495
Teamsters Local 237, 445, 468
Teamsters Local 813 PAC, 495
Tech Valley School Foundation, 425
Technet, 438
Technical Career Institutes Inc, 565
Technology Enterprise Corporation, 460
Technology Enterprise Corporation (NYS), 468
Tecmar, LTD, 387
Tectonic Engineering & Surveying Consultants P.C., 425
Telebeam Telecommunications Corp, 453

Telecommunications Assn Inc (NYS), 423
Telegram (The), 525
Tempo 802, 495
Temporary & Disability Assistance, Office of, 13, 195, 253, 305
Budget, Finance & Data Management, 253
Center for Child Well-Being, 253
Center for Employment & Economic Supports, 195, 253
Disability Determinations Division, 253
Information Technology Services, 253
Legal Affairs Division, 253
Operations & Program Support, 195, 253
Public Information, 253
Tenants & Neighbors, 192
Teva Pharmaceuticals USA, Inc., 421
The Bachmann-Strauss Dystonia & Parkinson Foundation Inc, 186
The Business Review, 523
The Clearing House Association, LLC, 80
The Committee to Re-Elect Inez E. Dickens 2013, 495
The Debi Rose Campaign Committee, 495
The Dolan Company, 529
The General Contractors Association of New York PAC, 495
The Greater Mahopac-Carmel Chamber of Commerce, 507
The Greater Manlius Chamber of Commerce, 507
The High-Need Hospital PAC, Inc., 495
The Independent News, 528
The Journal, 529
The Legal Aid Society, 199
The N.Y. Public Library Guild, Local 1930, 495
The NYS Economic Growth PAC, 495
The New York Observer, 528
The New York State Society of Professional Engineers Inc (NYSSPE), 94
The New York Times, 528
The Palladium-Times, 529
The Putnam County News and Recorder, 528
The Wave, 528
Theatrical Teamsters Local 817 PAC Fund, 495
Thelen Reid Brown Raysman & Steiner, 214
Therapeutic Communities Association of NY, Inc., 439
Thomas Lopez-Pierre For City Council 2013, 495
Thomson Strategies, LLC, 469
Thomson West, 475
Thor 280 Richards Street LLC, 437
Thor Properties, LLC (Acquisitions), 473
Thoroughbred Horsemens Association, Inc. (NY), 414
Thousand Islands Bridge Authority, 106, 288, 310
Thousand Islands CSD, 577
Three Rivers Development Foundation Inc, 517
Three Village CSD, 594
Thrivent Financial for Lutherans, 421
TicketNetwork, Inc., 459
Ticonderoga Area Chamber of Commerce, 517
Ticonderoga CSD, 574
Tier Technologies, 440
Tile, Marble & Terrazzo BAC Union Local 7 PAC Fund, 495
Time Warner Cable, 394, 469
Time Warner, Inc., 387
Times (The), 526
Times Herald-Record, 527
Times Union, 523
Tioga CSD, 595
Tioga County, 59, 338
Supreme County, Family & Surrogate's Courts, 59
Tioga County Chamber of Commerce, 517
Tioga County Industrial Development Agency, 517
Tishman Speyer Properties, 249
Tishman Speyer Properties, L.P., 469
To Life, 425, 476
Tobacconist Association of NYS, 393
Toll Bros., Inc. PAC, 495
Toll Brothers, Inc., 401
Tom Allon 2013, 495
Tom Duane For Senate, 495
Tommasino, Nicholas, 469
Tompkins Cortland Community College, 549
Tompkins County, 59, 338
Supreme, County, Family & Surrogate's Courts, 59
Tompkins County Area Development, 517
Tompkins County Chamber of Commerce, 517
Tompkins Financial Corporation, 82
Tompkins-Seneca-Tioga BOCES, 601
Tomra, 421
Tonawanda, 66
Civil & Criminal Courts, 66
Tonawanda (Town Of) Development Corporation, 518
Tonawanda City SD, 574
Tonawanda News, 531
Tonawanda, Town of, 365
Tonawandas, Chamber of Commerce of the, 518
Tony Avella For Queens, 495
Torodash For Truth, 495
Total Recall Corporation, 421
Tourism Industry Coalition (TIC), 469
Tourism, Parks, Arts & Sports Development, 42
Committee Staff, 42
Key Assembly Staff Assignments, 42
Membership, 42
Majority, 42
Minority, 42
Touro College, 405, 561
Towers at Spring Creek, 436
Town Clerks Assn Inc (NYS), 440
Town Hall Foundation, Inc., 405
Town of Brookhaven Industrial Development Agency, 502
Town of Hempstead, 435
Town of Huntington, 421
Town of Riverhead, 418
Town of Webb UFSD, 576
Toy Industry Association, Inc., 387
Toyota Motor North America, Inc., 425
Toys, 421
Tracfone Wireless, Inc., 402, 414
Trading Cove NY, LLC, 386
Trading Cove New York, LLC, 390
Traffipax Inc, 444
Transcore, 461
Transit Alliance, 442
Transmission Developers, Inc., 405
Transport Workers Union Local 100, 495
Transport Workers Union of America, AFL-CIO, 226, 292
Transport Workers Union, Local 100, 445
Transportation, 25, 42
Committee Staff, 25, 42
Key Assembly Staff Assignments, 42
Key Senate Staff Assignments, 25
Membership, 25, 42
Majority, 25, 42
Minority, 25, 42
Transportation & Infrastructure, 322
Subcommittees, 322
Aviation, 322
Coast Guard & Maritime Transportation, 322
Economic Development, Public Buildings & Emergency Management, 323
Highway and Transit, 323
Railroads, Pipelines and Hazardous Materials, 323
Water Resources & Environment, 323
Transportation Alternatives, 292
Transportation Alternatives, Inc., 387
Transportation Department, 13, 246, 283, 305
Administrative Services Division, 283
Audit & Civil Rights Division, 284
Engineering Division, 246, 283
Information Technology Division, 284
Legal Affairs Division, 284
Office of Regional Affairs, 284
Regional Offices, 284
Operations & Asset Management Division, 284
Policy & Planning Division, 284
Region 1, 284
Region 10, 284
Region 11, 284

Region 2, 284
Region 3, 284
Region 4, 284
Region 5, 284
Region 6, 284
Region 7, 284
Region 8, 284
Region 9, 284
Transpro Consulting LLC, 438
Tranter Jr. G. Thomas, 469
Travelers Indemnity Company (The), 379, 385
Treated Wood Council, Inc., 425
Trees New York, 159
Tri-State Chamber of Commerce, 518
Tri-State College of Acupuncture, 566
Tri-State Transportation Campaign, 292
Tri-Valley CSD, 594
Triad Group LLC, 420
Trial Lawyers Association, 405, 454
Trial Lawyers Association (NYS) (FKA Feldman, Daniel), 469
Triangle Enterprise Development Company LLC, 460
Triangle Equities, 394
Tribeca Film Institute, 282, 469
Trinet, 438
Trinity School, 392
TripAdvisor Media Group, 402
Trocaire College, 562
Trooper Foundation-State of New York Inc, 118, 244
Troy, 66
Civil & Criminal Court, 66
Troy City Enlarged SD, 588
Troy, City of, 365
True, Walsh & Sokoni, LLP, 186
Trumansburg CSD, 595
Trust for Public Land, 445
Trustco Bank, 456
Trustees of Columbia University in the City of NY (The), 387, 437, 469
Try-It Distributing Company, 441
Tuckahoe Common SD, 594
Tuckahoe UFSD, 599
Tully CSD, 584
Tupper Lake CSD, 575
Tupper Lake Chamber of Commerce, 518
Turner, Francine, 470
Tuxedo UFSD, 586
Twin America, 443
Two Bridges Associates, LP, 392
Tyson, Lisa, 470
U.S Communities, 410
U.S. Green Building Council, New York Chapter, 470
UAW Region 9, 464
UBS Securities, 445
UCB, Inc., 425, 470
UHY Advisors, 94
UJA-Federation of New York, 249
UNISYS Corporation, 414
UNITE HERE, 226
US BioLogic, 425
US Commerce Department, 71, 88, 152, 196
Census Bureau, 88
New York Region, 88
Economic Development Administration, 88
Philadelphia Region (includes New York), 88
Minority Business Development Agency, 88, 196
New York Business Center, 88, 196
New York Region, 88, 196
South Bronx Business Center, 88, 196
Williamsburg Business Center, 88, 196
National Oceanic & Atmospheric Administration, 71, 88, 152
National Marine Fisheries Svc, Greater Atlantic Regional Office, 152
National Weather Service, 89
National Weather Service, Eastern Region, 71, 88, 152
US Commercial Service - International Trade Administration, 89
Buffalo US Export Assistance Center, 89
Harlem US Export Assistance Center, 89
Long Island US Export Assistance Center, 89
New York US Export Assistance Center, 89
US Commission on Civil Rights, 137, 196
EASTERN REGION (includes New York State), 137, 196
US Defense Department, 125, 152, 295
AIR FORCE-National Media Outreach, 295
Air National Guard, 295
Francis S Gabreski Airport, 106th Rescue Wing, 295
Hancock Field, 174th Fighter Wing, 295
Army, 295
Fort Drum, 295
Fort Hamilton, 295
Watervliet Arsenal, 295
Army Corps of Engineers, 152
Great Lakes & Ohio River Division (Western NYS), 152
North Atlantic Division, 152
Buffalo District Office, 152
Marine Corps, 295
1st Marine Corps District, 295
Public Affairs Office, 295
Navy, 295
Saratoga Springs Naval Support Unit, 295
Program Directorate, 153
Regional Business Directorate, 153
US Military Academy, 125
US Department of Agriculture, 71, 89, 142, 153, 178, 189, 246
Agricultural Marketing Service, 71
Dairy Programs, 71
Specialty Crops Program, 71
USDA-AMS Poultry Grading Branch, 71
Agricultural Research Service, 71
Northeast Area, 71
Animal & Plant Health Inspection Service, 71
Plant Protection Quarantine (PPQ) Programs-Eastern Region, 71
Veterinary Services, 72
Avoca Work Unit, 71
Buffalo Work Station, 71
Canandaigua Work Station, 71
Champlain Work Station, 71
Cornell Cooperative Extension Service, 72
Ellicottville Work Station, 71
Farm Service Agency, New York State Office, 72
Finger Lakes National Forest, 153
Food & Nutrition Service, 72, 178
New York City Field Office, 72, 178
Northeast Regional Office, 72, 178
Food Safety & Inspection Service, 72, 178
Field Operations-Philadelphia District Office (includes New York), 178
Forest Service-Northeastern Area State & Private Forestry, 153
Forest Service-Northern Research Station, 153
Forest Service-Region 9, 153
Green Mountain & Finger Lakes, 153
Gastonia Region-New York Office, 71
Geneva NY Research Units, 71
Ithaca NY Research Units, 71
JFK International Airport Inspection Station, 71
NY Animal Import Center, 72
National Agricultural Statistics Service-NY Field Office, 72
Natural Resources Conservation Service, 153
New York Area Office, 72
New York State Office, 71
Northeast Marketing Area, 71
Office of the Inspector General, Northeast Region, 72
Oneida Work Station, 71
Plant Genetic Resources & Grape Genetic Research Units, 71
Robert W Holley Center for Agriculture & Health, 71
Rural Development, 72, 89, 142, 189, 246
Eastern New York Office, 142
New York State Office, 89, 142, 189, 246
New York State Regional Office, 72

Western New York Office, 142
SC Inspection Division-Bronx Office, 71
SC Inspection Division-Jamaica Office, 71
USDA/GIPSA, Packers & Stockyards Programs Eastern Regional Office, 72
Westhampton Beach Work Station, 72
US Department of Energy, 142
External Affairs & Stakeholder Relations, 142
Federal Energy Regulatory Commission, 142
New York Regional Office, 142
Office of External Affairs, 142
Laboratories, 142
Brookhaven National Laboratory, 142
Knolls Atomic Power Laboratory-KAPL Inc, 142
Office of the Director, 142
US Department of Health & Human Services, 178, 196, 254
Administration for Children & Families, 178, 254
Administration on Aging, 179, 254
Centers for Disease Control & Prevention, 179, 254
Agency for Toxic Substances & Disease Registry-EPA Region 2, 179, 254
New York Quarantine Station, 179, 254
Centers for Medicare & Medicaid Services, 179, 254
Medicaid and Children's Health (DMCH), 254
Medicaid and Children's Health Operations, 179
Medicare Financial Management & Fee for Service Operations, 179
Medicare Financial Management (DMFM), 254
Medicare Operations Division (DMO), 255
Medicare Quality Improvement and Survey & Certification Operations, 179
Food & Drug Administration, 179, 255
Northeast Region, 179, 255
Health Resources & Svcs Admin Office of Performance Review, 255
Health Resources & Svcs Admin-Region 2, 179
Indian Health Services-Area Office, 179, 255
New York District Office, 179, 255
Northeast Regional Laboratory, 179, 255
Office of Assistant Secretary for Preparedness & Response, 179
National Disaster Medical System, 179
Office of Secretary's Regional Representative-Region 2-NY, 179, 196, 255
Office for Civil Rights, 179, 196, 255
Office of General Counsel, 179, 255
Office of Inspector General, 179, 255
Office of Public Health & Science, 255
Office of the Assistant Secretary for Health (ASH), 179
US Department of Homeland Security (DHS), 72, 153, 166, 179, 196, 266, 289
Albany Field Office, 167
Albany Sub Office, 196, 266
Albany, Port of, 72, 167, 266
Alexandria Bay, 72
Alexandria Bay, Port of, 167
Binghamton Airport, 72
Binghamton, Port of, 167
Buffalo Office, 166
Buffalo, Port of, 72, 166, 167, 266
Bureau of Immigration & Customs Enforcement (ICE), 166, 266
New York District Office, 166, 266
Champlain, Port of, 72, 166, 167, 266
Customs & Border Protection (CBP), 72, 166, 266
Agricultural Inspections (AI), 72
Agriculture Inspections (AI), 166
Buffalo Field Office, 166, 266
New York Field Office, 167, 266
Federal Emergency Management Agency (FEMA), 167, 179
New York Regional Office, 167, 179
Federal Protective Service (The), 167
Field Counsel - New York, 167, 266
JFK International Airport Area Office, 72, 166
Laboratory Division, 167, 266
Long Island Field Office, 167, 196
Massena, Port of, 72, 167
National Urban Security Technology Laboratory, 153, 167
Administration, 153, 167
Systems Division, 153, 167
Testbeds Division, 153, 167
New York Asylum Office, 167, 196
Newark Asylum Office-Including NYS not served by New York City, 167, 196
Ogdensburg, Port of, 72, 167, 266
Plum Island Animal Disease Center, 167
Queens Field Office, 168
Rochester, Port of, 72, 167
Rome, Port of, 167
Syracuse, Port of, 73, 167
Transportation Security Administration (TSA), 167, 289
Trout River, Port of, 73, 167
US Citizenship & Immigration Services (USCIS), 167, 196
Buffalo District Office, 167, 196
CIS Asylum Offices, 167, 196
New York City District Office, 167, 196
US Department of Veterans Affairs, 295
Albany VA Medical Center, 296
Batavia VA Medical Center, 296
Bath VA Medical Center, 296
Brooklyn Campus of the NY Harbor Healthcare System, 296
Buffalo VA Medical Center, 296
Canandaigua VA Medical Center, 296
Castle Point Campus of the VA Hudson Vly Healthcare System, 296
James J. Peters VA Medical Center, 296
Montrose Campus of the VA Hudson Valley Healthcare System, 296
National Cemetery Administration, 295
Bath National Cemetery, 295
Calverton National Cemetery, 295
Cypress Hills National Cemetery, 295
Gerald B.H. Solomon Saratoga National Cemetery, 295
Long Island National Cemetery, 295
Woodlawn National Cemetery, 296
New York Campus of the NY Harbor Healthcare System, 296
Northport VA Medical Center, 296
Syracuse VA Medical Center & Clinics, 296
VA Regional Office of Public Affairs, Field Operations Svc, 296
Veterans Benefits Administration, 296
Buffalo Regional Office, 296
New York City Regional Office, 296
Veterans Health Admin Integrated Svc Network (VISN), 296
VA Healthcare Network Upstate New York (VISN2), 296
VA NY/NJ Veterans Healthcare Network (VISN3), 296
US Department of the Interior, 153, 276
Bureau of Land Management, 153
Eastern States Office (includes New York State), 153
Coram Sub-District Office, 153
Fish & Wildlife Service, 153
Northeast Region (includes New York State), 153
Fish & Wildlife Service-Northeast Region, 276
Geological Survey, 153
Water Resources Division - New York State District Office, 153
Ithaca Sub-District Office, 153
Jamaica Bay Unit, 276
National Park Service-Northeast Region, 153, 276
Fire Island National Seashore, 153, 276
Fort Stanwix National Monument, 276
Gateway National Recreation Area, 276
Manhattan Sites, 276
Martin Van Buren National Historic Site, 276
Roosevelt-Vanderbilt National Historic Sites, 276

Appendices: Financial Plan, Indexes & Maps

Sagamore Hill National Historic Site, 276
Saratoga National Historical Park, 276
Statue of Liberty National Monument & Ellis Island, 276
Theodore Roosevelt Inaugural National Historic Site, 276
Women's Rights National Historical Park, 276
Office of the Secretary, Environmental Policy & Compliance, 153
Northeast Region (includes New York State), 153
Office of the Solicitor, 154
Northeast Region (includes New York State), 154
Sandy Hook Unit, 276
Staten Island Unit, 276
US Digital Gaming, Inc., 438
US Education Department, 125
Region 2 - NY, NJ, PR, Vi, 125
Civil Rights, 125
Federal Student Aid, 125
Office of Inspector General, 125
Office of Management, 125
US Environmental Protection Agency, 154
Region 2 - New York, 154
Caribbean Environmental Protection Division (CEPD), 154
Clean Air & Sustainability Division (CASD), 154
Clean Water Division (CWD), 154
Division of Enforcement & Compliance Assistance (DECA), 154
Division of Environmental Science & Assessment (DESA), 154
Emergency & Remedial Response Division (ERRD), 154
Policy & Management, Office of, 154
Public Affairs Division (PAD), 154
Regional Counsel, Office of (ORC), 154
US Federal Courts, 212
US Bankruptcy Court - New York, 212
Eastern District, 212
Northern District, 212
Southern District, 212
Western District, 212
US Court of Appeals for the Second Circuit, 212
US Court of International Trade, 212
US DISTRICT COURT - NEW YORK (part of the Second Circuit), 212
Eastern District, 212
Northern District, 212
Southern District, 212
Western District, 212
US Tax Court, 212
US General Services Administration, 168, 246
Region 2-New York, 168, 246
Administration, 246
Federal Acquisition Service, 168
Federal Supply Service, 246
Federal Technology Service, 247
Inspector General's Office, 168, 247
Public Buildings Service, 168, 247
US Government Printing Office, 168
Region 2-I (New York), 168
Printing Procurement Office, 168
US Housing & Urban Development Department, 189
Albany Area Office & Financial Operations Center, 190
Buffalo Area Office, 190
New York State Office, 189
Administration, 190
Community Planning & Development, 190
Fair Housing & Equal Opportunity Office, 190
Field Offices, 190
General Counsel, 190
Housing, 190
Inspector General, 190
Public Housing, 190
US Justice Department, 89, 114, 212, 266
Albany, 115, 213
Antitrust Division-New York Field Office, 89
Antitrust Division-New York Field Office, 212
Binghamton, 115, 116, 213
Brooklyn, 115, 213
Buffalo, 115, 116, 213, 214
Bureau of Alcohol, Tobacco, Firearms & Explosives, 114, 266
New York Field Division, 114, 266
Central Islip, 115, 213
Civil Division - Commercial Litigation Branch, 212
Civil Division-Commercial Litigation Branch, 89
Community Relations Service, 89
Community Relations Service - Northeast & Caribbean Region, 213
Community Relations Service-Northeast & Caribbean Region, 89
Drug Enforcement Administration - New York Task Force, 114
Federal Bureau of Investigation - New York Field Offices, 114
Albany, 114
Buffalo, 114
New York City, 114
Federal Bureau of Prisons, 114
Brooklyn Metropolitan Detention Center, 114
CCM New York, 114
Federal Correctional Institution at Otisville, 114
Metropolitan Correctional Center, 114
Ray Brook Federal Correctional Institution, 114
New York City, 115, 213
OFFICE OF INSPECTOR GENERAL (including New York State), 213
Audit Division, 213
Investigations Division, 213
Plattsburgh, 115, 213
Rochester, 115, 116, 213, 214
Secret Service - New York Field Offices, 114
Albany, 114
Buffalo, 114
JFK/LGA, 114
Melville, 115
New York City, 115
Rochester, 115
Syracuse, 115
White Plains, 115
Syracuse, 115, 116, 213
US Attorney's Office - New York, 115, 213
Eastern District, 115, 213
Northern District, 115, 213
Southern District, 115, 213
Western District, 115, 213
US Marshals' Service - New York, 115, 213
Eastern District, 115, 213
Northern District, 115, 213
Southern District, 116, 214
Western District, 116, 214
US Parole Commission, 116
US Trustee - Bankruptcy, Region 2, 214
Utica, 116, 213
White Plains, 115, 213
US Labor Department, 180, 223, 296
Albany, 297
Albany District Office, 223
Brooklyn, 297
Buffalo District Office, 223
Bureau of Labor Statistics (BLS), 223
Employee Benefits Security Administration (EBSA), 223
Employment & Training Administration (ETA), 223
Employment Standards Administration, 223
Federal Contract Compliance Programs Office (OFCCP), 223
Labor-Management Standards Office (OLMS), 223
Wage-Hour Division (WHD)-Northeast Regional Office, 223
Workers' Compensation Programs (OWCP), 223
Field Offices, 297
New York State Field Offices, 297
Inspector General, 223
Inspector General's Office for Audit (OIG-A), 223
Long Island District Office, 223

New York City District Office, 223
New York District Office, 223
Occupational Safety & Health Administration (OSHA), 223
Albany Area Office, 223
Buffalo Area Office, 223
Manhattan Area Office, 223
Queens Area Office, 223
Syracuse Area Office, 223
Tarrytown Area Office, 223
Occupational Safety & Health Adminstration (OSHA), 180
Albany Area Office, 180
Buffalo Area Office, 180
Long Island Area Office, 180
Manhattan Area Office, 180
Syracuse Area Office, 180
Tarrytown Area Office, 180
Office of Asst Secretary for Administration & Mgmt (OASAM), 223
Office of the Solicitor, 223
Region 2 - New York Office of Secretary's Representative, 223
Jobs Corps (JC), 223
Office of Public Affairs (OPA) (serving New York State), 223
Region 2 New York - Women's Bureau (WB), 223
US Merchant Marine Academy, 566
US Merit Systems Protection Board, 223, 242
New York Field Office, 223, 242
US Military Academy at West Point, 566
US Office of Personnel Management, 224, 242
PHILADELPHIA SERVICE CENTER (serving New York), 224, 242
US Postal Service, 168
NORTHEAST AREA (Includes part of New York State), 168
US Railroad Retirement Board, 224
New York District Offices, 224
Albany, 224
Buffalo, 224
New York, 224
Westbury, 224
US Securities & Exchange Commission, 89
New York Regional Office, 89
US State Department, 168, 297
Bureau of Educational & Cultural Affairs-NY Pgm Branch, 168
US Mission to the United Nations, 168, 297
US Term Limits Foundation, 139
US Transportation Department, 125, 289
Air Force Regional Representatives, 289
Army Regional Representatives, 289
Federal Aviation Administration-Eastern Region, 289
Accounting Division, 289
Aerospace Medicine Division, 289
Air Traffic Division, 289
Airports Division, 289
Aviation Information & Services Division, 289
Engineering Services, 289
Flight Standards Division, 289
Human Resource Management Division, 289
Logistics Division, 289
Military Liaison Officers to the Federal Aviation Admin (NYS), 289
Runway Safety Manager, 289
Federal Highway Administration-New York Division, 289
Federal Motor Carrier Safety Admin-New York Division, 289
Federal Railroad Administration-Field Offices, 289
Hazardous Material, 289
Highway-Rail Grade Crossing, 289
Federal Transit Administration, Region II-New York, 289
Maritime Administration, 290
Great Lakes Region (includes part of New York State), 290
North Atlantic Region, 290
US Merchant Marine Academy, 290
National Highway Traffic Safety Administration, Reg II-NY, 290
Navy Regional Representatives, 289
Office of Inspector General, Region II-New York, 290
Saint Lawrence Seaway Development Corporation, 290
US Merchant Marine Academy, 125
US Treasury Department, 79, 266
Albany Territory, 267
Andover Campus Service Center, 267
Area 1 Director's Office, 267
Brookhaven Campus Service Center, 267
Brooklyn Office, 267
Buffalo Territory, 267
Comptroller of the Currency, 79
Northeastern District Office, 79
Internal Revenue Service, 266
Appeals Unit - Office of Directors, 266
Criminal Investigation Unit - New York Field Office, 266
Large & Mid-Size Business Division (LMSB), 266
Management Information Technology Services - Northeast Area, 266
Office of Chief Counsel, 266
Small Business & Self-Employed Division (SBSE), 266
Tax Exempt & Government Entities Div (TEGE)-Northeast Area, 266
Taxpayer Advocate Service (TAS), 267
Wage & Investmnt Div-Stakehldr Partnership Ed & Comm (SPEC), 267
Manhattan Office, 267
New York SBSE Compliance Services, 266
New York Territory, 267
Office of Chief Counsel LMSB Area 1, 266
Office of Director, Area 1 (New York State & New England), 267
SBSE-Compliance Area 2/New York, 266
SBSE-Taxpayer Education & Communication (TEC), 266
TEGE Area Counsel's Office, 267
US Mint, 79, 267
Upstate New York Office, 267
Western New York State Office, 267
USA Track & Field, Adirondack Association Inc, 282
USA Training Company, Inc., 424
USPLabs LLC, 410
UST Public Affairs Inc, 440, 452
USTA/National Tennis Center, Inc., 472
UWUA Local 1-2 Non Federal PAC, 496
Ullico Inc. Political Action Committee, 495
Ulster BOCES, 601
Ulster County, 60, 338
Family Court, 60
Supreme & County Courts, 60
Surrogate's Court, 60
Ulster County Chamber of Commerce, 518
Ulster County Community College, 549
Ulster County Development Corporation/Ulster County Industrial Development Agency, 518
Ulster Savings Bank, 82
Unadilla Valley CSD, 571
Unatego CSD, 587
Underground Development Foundation, 392
Underground Utilities, Inc., 431
Ungar, Robert A Associates Inc, 470
Unification Theological Seminary, 562
Unified Court System, 209, 305
10th Judicial District (Judicial Department 2), 210
11th Judicial District (Judicial Department 2), 210
12th Judicial District (Judicial Department 1), 210
1st Judicial Department, 209
1st Judicial District (Judicial Department 1), 209
2nd Judicial Department, 209
2nd Judicial District (Judicial Department 2), 209
3rd Judicial Department, 209
3rd Judicial District (Judicial Department 3), 209
4th Judicial Department, 209
4th Judicial District (Judicial Department 3), 209
5th Judicial District (Judicial Department 4), 209
6th Judicial District (Judicial Department 3), 209

7th Judicial District (Judicial Department 4), 210
8th Judicial District (Judicial Department 4), 210
9th Judicial District (Judicial Department 2), 210
Administrative Board of the Courts, 209
Appellate Division, 209
Court of Appeals, 209
Administrative Services Office, 210
Civil Court, 209
Court Administration, 209
Administrative Judge to the Court of Claims (NYS), 209
Administrative Judges to the Courts in New York City, 209
Administrative Judges to the Courts outside New York City, 209
Counsel's Office, 210
Management Support, 210
Court Operations, 210
Criminal Court, 209
Family Court, 209
Financial Management & Audit Services, 210
Public Affairs Office, 210
Workforce Diversity, 210
Uniform State Laws Commission, 106, 164, 211, 310
Uniformed EMT's & Paramedics, Local 2507-FDNY, 470
Uniformed Fire Alarm Dispatchers Benevolent Assn-FDNY, 470
Uniformed Fire Officers 527 Account, 495
Uniformed Fire Officers Assn (NYC), 442
Uniformed Fire Officers Association, 244
Uniformed Fire Officers Association (NYC), 408
Uniformed Firefighters Assn, 470
Uniformed Firefighters Association, 470
Uniformed Firefighters Association State FIREPAC, 495
Union College, 421, 562
Union Community Health Center, 391
Union Local Development Corporation (Town of), 518
Union Springs CSD, 569
Union Theological Seminary, 477, 562
Union of Police Associations, 420
Union, Town of, 366
Union-Endicott CSD, 568
Uniondale UFSD, 581
Unique Comp, Inc., 390
Unite Here, 444
Unite Here Local 2 PAC, 496
Unite Here Local 26 Political Committee, 496
Unite Here Local 5 PAC Fund, 496
Unite Here Local 54 PAC Committee, 496
Unite Here Tip State and Local Fund, 496
United Ambulette Coalition, 443
United American Land LLC, 431
United Cerebral Palsy Associations of NYS, 404
United Correction Officers Coalition, 404
United Dairy Cooperative Services Inc, 77
United Federation of Teachers, 129, 409
United Federation of Teachers (UFT) on Political Education, 496
United Food & Commercial Workers Active Ballot Club, 496
United Food & Commercial Workers Dist Cncl of NY & Northern NJ, 453
United Food & Commercial Workers Local 1, 226
United Health Services, 452
United Healthcare Services, Inc, 470
United Healthcare Services, Inc., 390, 414, 470
United Hebrew of New Rochelle, 405
United Hospital Fund, 420, 476
United Hospital Fund of New York, 186
United Jewish Appeal Federation - Jewish Philanthropies NY, 466
United Jewish Appeal-Federation of Jewish Philanthropies of NY, 261
United NY Ambulance Network, 404
United Nations Development Corporation, 87, 106, 165, 310, 435
United Neighborhood Houses - Not For Profit, 261
United Neighborhood Houses of NY, 470
United Neighbors for Neville Mitchell, 496
United New York Ambulance Network, 410
United New York Ambulance Network (UNYAN), 186
United Parcel Service, 456
United Parcel Service Inc. Political Action Committee - New York, 496
United Services Automobile Assn (USAA), 416
United Services Automobile Association (USAA), 385
United Spinal Association, 300
United Teachers (NYS), 379
United Transportation Union, 244, 292, 447
United University Professions, 129, 244
United Water New York, Inc., 391
United Way of Central New York, 261
United Way of Greater Rochester, 394
United Way of NYS, 422
United Way of New York City, 261, 439
Unity Mutual Life Insurance Co, 205
Universal Dynamix LLC, 456
University (NY), 427, 476
University (New York), 377, 390
University School of Medicine (NY) & Hospitals (NY), 476
University at Albany (FKA Williams, Charlie), 471
University at Buffalo, Research Institute on Addictions, 233
University at Buffalo, State University of New York, 545
University of Rochester, 471
University of Rochester School of Medicine, 159
University-Industry Cooperation, Task Force on, 43
Univision Communications, Inc., 391
Unkechaug Nation, 166
Unshackle Upstate, 425
Unshackle Upstate (Rochester Business Alliance), 402
Upstate Consultants, 471
Upstate Freshwater Institute, 159
Upstate Homes for Children & Adults Inc, 262
Upstate New York Transplant Services, 387
Upstate Niagara Cooperative (FKA Upstate Farms Cooperative), 471
Upstate Niagara Cooperative Inc, 77
Upstate Niagara Cooperative Inc (FKA Upstate Farms Cooperative Inc), 423
Urban Health Plan Inc, 445
Urban Homesteading Assistance Board, 193
Urban Justice Center, 471
Urban Muse LLC, 392
Urban Space Holdings, Inc., 392
Urban Strategic Partners, LLC, 377
Urbanomics, 239, 269
Urbitran Group, 292
Utica, 66
Civil & Criminal Courts, 66
Utica City SD, 583
Utica College, 562
Utica Industrial Development Agency (City of), 518
Utica Mutual Insurance Co, 205
Utica School of Commerce, 566
Utica, City of, 366
Utility Workers Union, Local 1-2, AFL-CIO, 444
Utility Workers of America Local 1-2, 420
VNA of Albany, Inc., 390
VSweeps, 422
Valeray Real Estate Co. Inc., 456
Valhalla UFSD, 599
Valley CSD (Montgomery), 586
Valley National Bank, 82
Valley Stream 13 UFSD, 582
Valley Stream 24 UFSD, 582
Valley Stream 30 UFSD, 582
Valley Stream Central HS District, 582
Valley Stream Chamber of Commerce, 518
Valley Stream, Village of, 366
Vallone For New York, 496
Van Bramer 2013, 496
Van Hornesville-Owen D Young CSD, 577
Van Wagner Communications LLC, 443
Vanguard Car Rental USA Inc, 442
Vantagepoint Management, Inc., 471
Vargas 2013, 496

Varsity Bus Co. Inc., 456
Vassar College, 562
Vaughn College of Aeronautics & Technology, 562
Vector Group, Ltd, 453
Vedder Price PC, 226
Velodrome of New York City, Inc., 401
Venable LLP, 472
Vera Institute of Justice, 118, 218
Vera Institute of Justice, Inc., 472
Veras For Council 2013, 496
Verax Biomedical Incorporated, 421
Verde Electric Corporation, 405
Verifone, Inc., 421
Verizon, 442, 456, 472
Verizon Communications, 146
Verizon Communications Good Government Club PAC, 496
Verizon Corporate Resources Group LLC (FKA Verizon NY), 391
Verizon NY, 425, 440
Verizon New York, Inc., 387
Verizon Services Group, 456
Verizon Wireless, 439
Vernon Downs/Gaming-Racing-Entertainment, 282
Vernon-Verona-Sherrill CSD, 583
Vertex Pharmaceuticals, Inc., 472
Vestal CSD, 568
Vestal, Town of, 366
Veterans of Foreign Wars, 300
Veterans of Foreign Wars (VFW), 300
Veterans, Homeland Security & Military Affairs, 26
Committee Staff, 26
Key Senate Staff Assignments, 26
Membership, 26
Majority, 26
Minority, 26
Veterans' Affairs, 42, 316, 323
Committee Staff, 42
Key Assembly Staff Assignments, 42
Membership, 42
Majority, 42
Minority, 42
Subcommittees, 323
Disability Assistance & Memorial Affairs, 323
Economic Opportunity, 323
Health, 323
Oversight & Investigations, 323
Veterans' Affairs, Division of, 13, 294, 305
Bureau of Veterans Education, 294
Counseling & Claims Service, 294
Eastern Region, 294
Western Region, 294
Veterans' Service Organizations, 294
Albany Housing Coalition Inc, 294
COPIN HOUSE (Homeless Veterans), 294
Continuum of Care for Homeless Veterans in New York City, 294
30th Street Shelter, 294
Project TORCH, Veterans Health Care Center, 294
Hicksville Counseling Center, Veterans' Resource Center, 294
Saratoga Cnty Rural Preservation Co (Homeless Veterans), 294
Suffolk County United Veterans Halfway House Project Inc, 294
Veterans House (The), 294
Veterans Outreach Center Inc, 294
Veterans Services Center of the Southern Tier, 294
Veterans' Coalition of the Hudson Valley, 294
Veterans' Widows International Network Inc (VWIN), 300
Veterinary Medical Society, 424
Viacom Inc, 146
Viahealth, 476
Victim Services, Office of, 6, 110, 252, 303
Victor Babb For N.Y.C. Council, 496
Victor CSD, 585
Victor Chamber of Commerce, 518
Vidal Group, LLC (The), 472
Vietnam Veterans of America, NYS Council, 300
Vietnam Veterans of America, New York State Council, 440
Villa Maria College of Buffalo, 562
Village Care of NY Inc, 436
Village Care of New York, Inc., 472
Village Voice (The), 528
Village Voice Media, Inc, 528
Village of Kiryas Joel, 439
Vince Morgan 2013, 496
Vincent F Stempel, Jr Esq, 218
Vinyl Institute (The), 408
Virtu Financial LLC, 386
Visa, Inc., 439
Viscardi Center, The, 402
Vish Mahadeo 2010, 496
Vision Quest Lighting, 418
Vision Rehabilitation Assn (NYVRA) (NY), 405
Visiting Nurse Service of NY, 402, 439
Vista Developers Corp, 411
Vista Equity Partners III LLC, 472
Vito Lopez For City Council, 496
Viverito 2013, 496
Vladeck, Waldman, Elias & Engelhard PC, 226
Volunteers of Legal Service, Inc, 218
Voorheesville CSD, 567
Vornado Realty L.P., 387, 438
Vornado Realty Trust, 473
Vose, Margie, 473
Vote Vallone 2013, 496
VoteBhusan2013, 496
WABC (7), 538
WABC (770 AM), 535
WAMC (90.3 FM), 533
WB Stellar IP Owner LLC, 401
WBBR (1130 AM) Bloomberg News, 535
WBEN (930 AM/FM), 534
WBLK (93.7 FM), WJYE (96.1 FM), 534
WBNG-TV (7), 537
WCBS (880 AM), 535
WCHP (760 AM), 534
WCIK (103.1 FM), 533
WCNY (25), 539
WDCX (99.5 FM), 534
WENY (36), 538
WETM (18), 537
WFRY (97.5 FM), 536
WFUV (90.7 FM), 534
WGNA (107.7 FM), 536
WGRZ (33), 537
WHAM (1180 AM), 536
WHAM (13), 539
WHCU (870 AM), 535
WHEC (10), 539
WHTT (104.1 FM), 534
WHUD (100.7 FM), 535
WICZ (40), 537
WINR (680 AM), 533
WINS (1010 AM), 535
WIVB-TV (39), 537
WIVT (34), 537
WKBW-TV (38), 537
WKPQ (105.3 FM), 534
WKRT (920 AM), WIII (99.9 or 100.3 FM), 534
WKTV (29), 539
WKZA (106.9 FM), 535
WLIW (21) Public Broadcasting, 538
WLNY (47), 538
WLTW (106.7 FM), 535
WM NY PAC, 496
WMHT (17) Public Broadcasting-NY Capitol Region, 536
WMTT (94.7 FM), 534
WNBC (4), 538
WNBF (1290 AM), 533
WNED (43) Western NY Public Broadcasting, 537
WNED (94.5 FM), 534
WNET, 428
WNET New York Public Media, 146
WNET.org, 405
WNTQ (93.1 FM), WAQX (95.7 FM), 536
WNYT (12), 536
WNYW (44), 538
WOR (710 AM), 535
WOUR (96.9 FM), 536
WPDH (101.5 FM), 536
WPGI (100.9 FM), WWLZ (820 AM), 534
WPIG (95.7 FM), WHDL (1450 AM), 535
WPIX (11), 538
WPTZ (5) NBC, 538

WPYX (106.5 FM), WRVE (99.5 FM), 535
WRGB (6), 537
WRNN (48), 538
WROW (590 AM), 535
WRRV (92.7 FM), 536
WSEN (92.1 FM), 533
WSKG (46) Public Broadcasting, 537
WSKG (89.3 FM), WSQX (91.5 FM), 534
WSPK (104.7 FM), 533
WSTM (24), 539
WSYR (17), 539
WSYT (19), 539
WTEN (10), 537
WTVH (47), 539
WVOA (103.9 FM), 536
WVOX (1460 AM), 535
WW Acquisitions and Development LLC, 392
WWNY (7), 539
WWOR (UPN 9), 538
WWTI (21), 539
WXXA (23), 537
WXXI (16) Public Broadcasting, 539
WYPX DT-50, 537
WYRK (106.5 FM), WBUF (92.9 FM), 534
WYYY (94.5 FM), 536
Wachtel & Masyr, LLP, 473
Wachtell, Lipton, Rosen & Katz, 269
Waddington Chamber of Commerce, 518
Wagner College, 562
Wainscott Common SD, 594
Wal-Mart Stores, Inc., 473
Walgreen Co., 402, 424, 473
Wall Street Journal (The), 146, 527
Wallkill CSD, 596
Wallkill, Town of, 366
Walmart Free NYC, 473
Walt Disney Company (The), 438
Walter Kidde Portable Equipment, Inc., 421
Walters Group (The), 473
Walton CSD, 572
Walton Chamber of Commerce, 518
Walton, Leigh, 473
Wantagh Chamber of Commerce, 518
Wantagh UFSD, 582
Wappinger, Town of, 366
Wappingers CSD, 573
Warren & Washington Industrial Development Agency, 518
Warren County, 60, 338
Supreme, County, Family & Surrogate's Courts, 60
Warren County Economic Development Corporation, 518
Warrensburg CSD, 596
Warrensburg Chamber of Commerce, 518
Warsaw CSD, 599
Warsaw Chamber of Commerce (Greater Warsaw), 518
Warwick Valley CSD, 586
Warwick Valley Chamber of Commerce, 518
Warwick, Town of, 367
Washington Cemetery, 452
Washington County, 60, 338
Supreme, County, Family & Surrogate's Courts, 60
Washington County Local Development Corporation, 518
Washington-Saratoga-Warren-Hamilton-Essex BOCES, 601
Washingtonville CSD, 586
Waste Management, 393
Waste Management of New York LLC, 402
Waterford-Halfmoon UFSD, 589
Waterfront Commission of New York Harbor, 107, 222, 288, 310
Waterkeeper Alliance, 159
Waterloo CSD, 590
Watertown, 66
Civil & Criminal Courts, 66
Watertown City SD, 577
Watertown Daily Times, 531
Watertown Empire Zone, 518
Watertown, City of, 367
Watertown-North Country Chamber of Commerce (Greater Watertown), 519
Waterview at Greenpoint LLC, 421
Waterville CSD, 583
Watervliet, 66
Civil & Criminal Courts, 66
Watervliet City SD, 567
Watkins Glen Area Chamber of Commerce, 519
Watkins Glen CSD, 589
Watson School of Biological Sciences at Cold Spring Harbor Laboratory, 562
Wave Publishing Co., 528
Waverly CSD, 595
Wayland-Cohocton CSD, 591
Wayne CSD, 597
Wayne County, 60, 339
Supreme, County, Family & Surrogate's Courts, 60
Wayne County Industrial Development Agency & Economic Development, 519
Wayne-Finger Lakes BOCES, 601
Ways & Means, 42, 323
Committee Staff, 42
Key Assembly Staff Assignments, 42
Membership, 42
Majority, 42
Minority, 43
Subcommittees, 323
Health, 323
Income Security and Family Support, 323
Oversight, 323
Select Revenue Measures, 323
Social Security, 323
Trade, 323
We Move, 186
Webb Institute, 562
Webster CSD, 579
Webster Chamber of Commerce, 519
Webster, Town of, 367
Weedsport Area Chamber of Commerce, 519
Weedsport CSD, 569
Wegmans Food Markets Inc, 94
Wegmans Food Markets Inc., 456
Weiner For Mayor, 496
Weiss, Michael A., 473
Welfare Inspector General, Office of NYS, 13, 163, 253, 305
Welfare Research Inc, 262
Wellcare of NY, 421
Wellpoint, Inc., 425
Wells CSD, 576
Wells Capital Management, Inc., 473
Wells College, 562
Wells Fargo and Company, 473
Wellsville Area Chamber of Commerce, 519
Wellsville CSD, 568
Wellsville Daily Reporter/Spectator, 531
Wendel LLC, 441
West Babylon UFSD, 594
West Canada Valley CSD, 577
West Firm PLLC (The), 474
West Genesee CSD, 584
West Harlem Environmental Action, Inc., 474
West Hempstead UFSD, 582
West Irondequoit CSD, 579
West Islip UFSD, 594
West Manhattan Chamber of Commerce, 519
West Park UFSD, 596
West Seneca CSD, 574
West Seneca Chamber of Commerce, 519
West Seneca, Town of, 367
West Valley CSD, 569
WestField, LLC, 387
Westbury UFSD, 582
Westbury-Carle Place Chamber of Commerce, 519
Westchester Community College, 549
Westchester County, 60, 339
Supreme, County & Family Courts, 60
Surrogate's Court, 60
Westchester County Association Inc (The), 519
Westchester County Chamber of Commerce, 519
Westchester County Correction Superior Officers Association, 411
Westchester County Industrial Development Agency, 519
Westchester County PBA, 418
Westchester Jewish Community Services, 468
Western Central Coalition for Children with Special Needs, 421
Western NY Energy LLC, 452

Western New York Library Resources Council, 129
Western Regional Off-Track Betting Corp, 107, 274, 310
Western Regional Off-Track Betting Corp., 438
Western Suffolk BOCES, 601
Western Union, 387, 440
Westfield CSD, 570
Westfield LLC, 474
Westfield/Barcelona Chamber of Commerce, 519
Westhampton Beach UFSD, 594
Westhampton Chamber of Commerce (Greater Westhampton), 519
Westhill CSD, 584
Westmoreland CSD, 583
Westmoreland Consulting, LLC, 390
Westport CSD, 574
Westside News Inc, 530
Wheatland-Chili CSD, 579
Wheelerville UFSD, 575
White & Case LLP, 82
White Birch, LLC (FKA Camarda Realty Investments), 411
White Plains, 66
Civil & Criminal Courts, 66
White Plains City SD, 599
White Plains, City of, 367
White and Williams LLP, 474
Whiteface Mountain Regional Visitor's Bureau, 519
Whitehall Area Chamber of Commerce, 519
Whitehall CSD, 596
Whiteman Osterman & Hanna LLP, 159, 199, 218, 239, 474
Whitesboro CSD, 583
Whitesville CSD, 568
Whitney Capital LLC, 390
Whitney M. Young Jr. Health Services, 439
Whitney Point CSD, 568
Wholeness of Life Center, Inc., 392
Wholesale Beer Distributors Association (NYS), 387
Wiener, Judith R, 475
Wilder Balter Partners, Inc., 406, 475
Wildlife Conservation Society, 159, 475
William B Collins Co, 525
William F. Ryan Health Center, 390
William Floyd UFSD, 594
William Gottlieb Management Co. LLC, 401
Williams Companies (The), 391
Williams Companies, Inc., 410
Williamson CSD, 597
Williamson Chamber of Commerce, 519
Williamsville CSD, 574
Willistons Chamber of Commerce, 519
Willow Mixed Media Inc, 282
Willsboro CSD, 574
Wilmorite Holdings, LP, 442
Wilson CSD, 583
Wilson Elser Moskowitz Edelman & Dicker, 186, 218, 475
Wilson Elser Moskowitz Edelman & Dicker LLP, PAC, 496
Wilson, Alex, 476
Win With Winslow, 496
Windham-Ashland-Jewett CSD, 576
Window Covering Manufacturers Association, 387
Windsor CSD, 568
Windstream Corporation, 394
Wine & Grape Foundation (NY), 413
Wine Institute, 387
Wing of the Civil Air Patrol, 425
Winn Companies, 427
Winthrop University Hospital, 186
Wisneski, Jessica, 476
Wladis Law Firm, 476
Women Marines Association, 300
Women's Bar Association of the State of New York, 218
Women's Business Center of New York State, 94
Women's Campaign Fund, 139
Women's City Club of New York, 139
Women's Democratic Club of NYC, 496
Women's Housing & Economic Development Corporation, 387, 463
Women's Housing & Economic Development Corporation (WHEDCO), 193
Women's Issues, Task Force on, 43
Women's Prison Association & Home Inc, 118
Women's Refugee Commission, 199
Women's Venture Fund Inc, 94
Wood Tobe-Coburn, 566
Woodlawn Cemetery (The), 414
Woodstock Chamber of Commerce & Arts, 519
Worcester CSD, 587
Worker Justice Center of New York, Inc., 476
Workers' Compensation Alliance, 444
Workers' Compensation Board, 14, 201, 221, 305
Administration, 202, 221
Albany, 202, 221
Binghamton, 202, 221
Brooklyn, 202, 221
Buffalo, 202, 221
Information Management Systems, 202, 221
Long Island, 202, 221
Manhattan, 202, 221
Operations, 202, 221
District Offices, 202, 221
Peekskill, 202, 221
Queens, 202, 221
Rochester, 202, 221
Syracuse, 202, 221
Workers' Compensation Board of Commissioners, 202, 221
Working Assets Funding Service, Inc., 477
Working Families Organization, 477
Working Families Party, 139
Working Today, 444
World Hunger Year Inc, 262
World Trade Center Properties, 445
Wright 2013, 496
Wright Group NY, Inc. (The), 477
Wurtsboro Board of Trade, 519
Wyandanch UFSD, 594
Wynantskill UFSD, 588
Wyoming CSD, 599
Wyoming County, 60, 339
Supreme, County, Family & Surrogate's Courts, 60
Wyoming County Chamber of Commerce, 519
X-Ray Optical Systems, Inc., 425
XChange Telecom Corp., 416
YAI/National Institute for People with Disabilities, 233, 262
YMCA of Greater New York, 477
YMCAs of NYS, Inc., 477
YYY 35th Street LLC, 402
Yaddo, 414
Yahoo! Inc., 390
Yankees Partnership (NY), 442, 456
Yankosky, Mary Ellen, 477
Yates County, 60, 340
Supreme, County, Family & Surrogate's Courts, 61
Yates County Chamber of Commerce, 520
Yavornitzki, Mark L., 477
Yeled V'Yalda Early Childhood Center, 439
Yeshiva University, 438, 477, 562
Yeshiva University, A Einstein Clg of Med, Div of Subs Abuse, 233
Yockel, James, 477
Yonkers, 66
Civil & Criminal Courts, 66
Yonkers Chamber of Commerce, 520
Yonkers City SD, 599
Yonkers Contracting Co Inc, 436
Yonkers Economic Development/Yonkers Industrial Development Agency (City of), 520
Yonkers Raceway, 282, 393
Yonkers, City of, 367
York CSD, 578
York College, 552
York Group Associates, 478
Yorkshire Towers, 402
Yorkshire-Pioneer CSD, 569
Yorktown CSD, 599
Yorktown, Town of, 368
Yoswein New York Inc, 478
Young Adult Institute, Inc., 390, 405
Young Jr. William N., 478

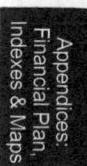

Young Men's Christian Association and Women's Community Center of Rome, New York, Inc., 418
Young Women's Leadership Network, 392
Yum! Brands, Inc., 388
ZETEPAC, 497
ZGA LLC, 478
Zachy's Wine & Liquor Store, Inc., 411
Zalcman, Fred, 478
Zaleski, Terence M, 478
Zead Ramadan 2013, 497
Zelle Hoffmann Voelbel & Mason LLP, 404
Zogby Analytics, 94, 139
Zuffa LLC, 390, 478
Zurich, 42

Geographic Index

Includes the names of the top three levels in all New York State executive departments and agencies; public corporations; authorities; commissions; all organizations listed in the Private Sector sources segment of each policy chapter; lobbyist organizations; political action committees; chambers of commerce; newspapers; news services; radio and television stations; SUNY and CUNY locations; and private colleges.

Alabama

Montgomery
US Department of Agriculture
Agricultural Marketing Service, 71

Arizona

Phoenix
DCI Group AZ, LLC (FKA DCI Group, LLC), 405

Arkansas

Bentonville
Wal-Mart Stores, Inc., 473

California

Century City
Westfield LLC, 474

Costa Mesa
Rreef America LLC, 462

Los Angeles
Gibson, Dunn & Crutcher LLP PAC, 486

Mill Valley
Apple Inc., 382

San Bruno
Vantagepoint Management, Inc., 471

San Francisco
Consumers Union of US, Inc., 402
Unite Here Local 2 PAC, 496
Vista Equity Partners III LLC, 472
Wells Capital Management, Inc., 473
Working Assets Funding Service, Inc., 477

San Rafael
Google, Inc., 419
Grant Thornton LLP, 420
Horton, Dan J, 426
Inventiv Health, Inc., 428
Matusic, Karen, 441

Colorado

Aurora
Veterans' Widows International Network Inc (VWIN), 300

Connecticut

Bethel
Zalcman, Fred, 478

Fairfield
Kudlow & Company LLC, 81

Farmington
NY Region 9A UAW PAC Council, 491

Greenwich
Starwood Capital LLC, 467

Hartford
Aetna, 378
Allegue, Raul R, 379
Empire Generating Co. LLC, 410
Henderson Global Investors (North America) Inc., 424
Prudential Insurance Company of America (The) (Form, 458
US Treasury Department
Area 1 Director's Office, 267

Lakeville
Tri-State Chamber of Commerce, 518

Monroe
Army Aviation Association of America (AAAA), 297

Norwalk
Diageo, 407

Simsbury
Hartford Financial Services Group, Inc. (The), 423

South Windsor
Pullium, Daniel, 459

Stamford
Purdue Pharma L.P., 459
Walton, Leigh, 473

West Hartford
Arvai, Joni, 382
Gray Media, 420

Windsor
Byrne, Elizabeth, 391
US Postal Service
NORTHEAST AREA (Includes part of New York State), 168

Delaware

Hockessin
Dimaio, Mark, 407

Wilmington
Bank of America New York Political Action Committee, 479

District of Columbia

Washington
AMGEN, 381
ATU New York Cope Fund, 479
Accenture LLP, 377
Aging, Special Committee on, 316
Agriculture, 316
Agriculture, Nutrition & Forestry, 312
Altria Client Services Inc. and its Affiliates, 379
American Beverage Association, 380
American Federation of Teachers, 224
American Insurance Association New York City PAC, 479
Appropriations, 312, 317
Armed Services, 313, 317
Baker & Hostetler LLP, 384
Banking, Housing & Urban Affairs, 313
Brickfield, Burchette, Ritts & Stone, P.C., 389
Budget, 313, 318
Bynum, Thompson, Ryer, 138
CITIGROUP Inc. Political Action Committee - Federal/State, 480
CitiGroup Management Corp., 396
Clearing House Payments Company L.L.C., 398
Commerce, Science & Transportation, 313

Appendices: Financial Plan, Indexes & Maps

Listings appear in alphabetical order by state, then city.

Commodity Futures Trading Commission, 70
Daiichi Sankyo, Inc., 404
Democrat, Republican, Independent Voter Education, 482
Democratic Congressional Campaign Committee, 138
Distilled Spirits Council of the US (FKA Wojnar, David E.), 407
EMD Serono, Inc., 410
EMILY's List, 138
Education & Labor, 318
Emily's List NY, 482
Energy & Commerce, 318
Energy & Natural Resources, 314
Energy Independence & Global Warming, House Select Committee on, 324
Entertainment Software Association, 411
Environment & Public Works, 314
Ethics, Select Committee on, 316
Every Voice, 412
Express Scripts Holding Co., 413
Federal Communications Commission
Office of Media Relations, 142
Federal Election Commission, 137
Finance, 314
Financial Services, 319
Financial Services Forum, 80
Foreign Affairs, 319
Foreign Relations, 315
Gay and Lesbian Victory Fund, 486
General Electric Company (FKA Farrell, Pamela), 417
General Motors Corporation, 417
Generic Pharmaceutical Association, 183
Genworth Financial, 418
Governor's Office
Washington Office of the Governor, 3, 160
HSBC North America Political Action Committee, 487
Health, Education, Labor, & Pensions, 315
Homeland Security, 320
Homeland Security & Governmental Affairs, 315
Honeywell International, Inc., 426
House Administration, 320
Human Rights Campaign New York PAC, 487
IAFF FIREPAC New York Non-Federal, 487
Indian Affairs, Committee on, 316
Intelligence, Select Committee on, 316
International Brotherhood of Electrical Wor, 487
Ironworkers Political Action League, 487
Jewish War Veterans of the USA, 298
Judiciary, 316, 320
Kiernan-Pagani, Kathleen, 432
Lee New York Political Action Committee, 488
Lilly USA LLC, 435
Motion Picture Association of America, Inc., 446
MyWireless.org, 447
National Guard Association of the US (NGAUS), 299
National Railroad Passenger Corporation, 448
National Transportation Safety Board
Office of Administrative Law Judges, 289
National Trust for Historic Preservation, 192
Natural Resources, 321
Oversight and Government Reform, 321
Perry, Edmund F., 454
Pyle & Associates, Inc., 459
Reserve Officers Association (ROA), 300
Ridge Policy Group LLC, 461
Rules, 321
Rules & Administration, 316
SEIU Political Education and State Action Fund, 494
Science & Technology, 322
Scripps Howard News Service, 533
Small Business, 322
Small Business & Entrepreneurship, 316
Software & Information Industry Association, 94
Solar Energy Industries Association, 466
Solowan, Richard, 466
Standards of Official Conduct, 322
Taxation, Joint Committee on, 324
Transportation & Infrastructure, 322
US Commerce Department, 71
National Oceanic & Atmospheric Administration, 71
US Commission on Civil Rights
EASTERN REGION (includes New York State), 137, 196
US Department of Agriculture, 71
US Department of Energy
Office of External Affairs, 142
US Department of Health & Human Services
National Disaster Medical System, 179
US Department of the Interior
Eastern States Office (includes New York State), 153
US Justice Department
Civil Division-Commercial Litigation Branch, 89
Community Relations Service, 89
US Parole Commission, 116
US Term Limits Foundation, 139
Ullico Inc. Political Action Committee, 495
United Food & Commercial Workers Active Ballot Club, 496
Veterans of Foreign Wars (VFW), 300
Veterans' Affairs, 316, 323
WM NY PAC, 496
Ways & Means, 323
Women's Campaign Fund, 139
ZETEPAC, 497

Florida

Coral Gables

Bayview Asset Management, 385

Poinciana

McLean, Mary Ann, 442

Tampa

Comprehensive Health Management, Inc. (FKA Wellcare Health Plans, In, 400

Georgia

Atlanta

Coca-Cola Refreshments USA, Inc., 399
McKenna Long & Aldridge LLP NY PAC, 490
NY CCR Nonpartisan PAC For Good Government, 491
US Department of Agriculture
USDA/GIPSA, Packers & Stockyards Programs Eastern Regional Office, 72
United Parcel Service Inc. Political Action Committee - New York, 496

Smyrna

UCB, Inc., 470

Hawaii

Honolulu

Unite Here Local 5 PAC Fund, 496

Illinois

Chicago

AON Corporation Political Action Committee, 479
CNA, 398
Friends of Michael A. Alvarez, 485
Hynes, Daniel, 427
JPMorgan Chase & Co. PAC, 488
US Transportation Department
Great Lakes Region (includes part of New York State), 290

Deerfield

Walgreen Co., 473

Northbrook

Astellas Pharma US, Inc., 384

Schaumburg

Motorola, Inc., 446

Listings appear in alphabetical order by state, then city.

Indiana

Indianapolis
National Association of Mutual Insurance Companies (NAMIC), 447

Kentucky

Louisville
Rescare Inc. Advocacy Fund, 493

Maine

China Village
Northeastern Forest Fire Protection Commission, 105, 152

Maryland

Bethesda
AMSUS-The Society of Federal Health Professionals, 181

Gaithersburg
Committee to Re-Elect Nydia M. Velazquez to Congress, 481

Hanover
International Union of Painters and Allied Trades Poli, 487

Landover
Commissioned Officers Assn of the US Public Health Svc Inc (COA), 182, 298

National Harbor
DDC Advocacy, 406

Rockville
US Department of Health & Human Services
Indian Health Services-Area Office, 179

Massachusetts

Andover
US Treasury Department
Andover Campus Service Center, 267

Auburn
Changaris, Steve, 396

Beverly Farms
Kaysen, Mary, 431

Boston
Byrne, Kevin, 391
FMR LLC, 415
Federal Labor Relations Authority
Boston Regional Office, 222
Ianno, Dominick, 427
John Hancock Life Insurance, 429
Pujolas, Elizabeth, 459
US Department of Agriculture
Northeast Regional Office, 72, 178
US Department of the Interior
Northeast Region (includes New York State), 153
US Labor Department
Employment & Training Administration (ETA), 223
Office of Public Affairs (OPA) (serving New York State), 223
Unite Here Local 26 Political Committee, 496
Vertex Pharmaceuticals, Inc., 472
Yankosky, Mary Ellen, 477

Burlington
US Transportation Department
Military Liaison Officers to the Federal Aviation Admin (NYS), 289

Chelmsford
NYS Association of Nurse Anesthetists (NYSANA), 184

Concord
National Grape Cooperative-Welch Foods Inc, 76

Dorchester
Women Marines Association, 300

Framingham
American Diabetes Association, 380

Gloucester
US Commerce Department
National Marine Fisheries Svc, Greater Atlantic Regional Office, 152

Hadley
US Department of the Interior
Fish & Wildlife Service-Northeast Region, 276
Northeast Region (includes New York State), 153

Lowell
New England Interstate Water Pollution Control Commission, 100, 151

Needham
Northeast Gas Association, 145

Newton
US Department of the Interior
Northeast Region (includes New York State), 154

Springfield
Massachusetts Mutual Life Insurance Company, 441

Still River
National Assn of Chain Drug Stores, 447

Waltham
National Grid Voluntary New York State Political Action Committee, 490

Michigan

Ann Arbor
Great Lakes Commission, 86, 97, 150

Minnesota

Ham Lake
Schillo, John, 463

Minneapolis
Medtronic, Inc. (FKA Dena Scearce), 443

Nebraska

Omaha
HDR, Inc. Political Action Committee - NY, 486

Nevada

Las Vegas
Caesars Entertainment Operating Company, Inc., 391
Zuffa LLC, 478

New Hampshire

Dover
Air Force Sergeants Association (AFSA), Division 1, 297

New Jersey

Allenhurst
Luthin Associates, Inc, 437

Atlantic City
Unite Here Local 54 PAC Committee, 496

Bedminster
AT&T Corporation, 143

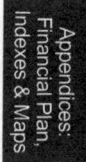

Listings appear in alphabetical order by state, then city.

Bellmawr
Friends of Assembly Speaker Joe Roberts, 483

Cranbury
Soligent Distribution LLC - East Coast Distribution Center, 146

East Hanover
Novartis Pharmaceuticals Corporation, 450

East Rutherford
New York Giants, 280

Edison
Cobb Jr, James H, 399
Committee For Effective Leadership, 480
Mueller, Tricia, 446
US Environmental Protection Agency
Division of Environmental Science & Assessment (DESA), 154

Englewood Cliffs
Port Authority PBA of NY PAC, 493

Florham Park
Friedman, John P, 416

Hackensack
Hackensack University Medical Center, 422

Hawthorne
EFO Jeffrey P. Gardner, 482

Iselin
New York Shipping Association Inc, 292

Lawrenceville
Gilbane Building Company, 418

Lyndhurst
US Department of Homeland Security (DHS)
Newark Asylum Office-Including NYS not served by New York City, 167, 196

Manalapan
Navicore Solutions, 81

Maplewood
Defoyd, Katherine, 406

Medford
Duca, Anthony, 408

Millburn
Greller, Matthew, 421

Morristown
Covanta Energy Corporation, 403

New York
D & M P.A.C. LLC, 481
The N.Y. Public Library Guild, Local 1930, 495

Newark
249 W 28th Street Properties, LLC, 377
Edison Spring Street Company LLC, 409
Federal Mediation & Conciliation Service
Northeastern Region, 222
Prudential Financial, Inc. (Formerly Michael F. McCann), 457
Prudential Investment Management, Inc. (Formerly Bernard B. Winograd, 458
Quantitative Management Associates LLC, 459
Small Business Administration
New Jersey, 88

Paramus
Hartman & Winnicki, PC, 92, 216
NYS Bar Assn, Intellectual Property Law Section, 92, 216
Vornado Realty Trust, 473

Parsippany
Birds Eye Foods Inc, 73
National Transportation Safety Board
Aviation Division, Northeast Regional Office, 288

Princeton
American Higher Education Development Corporation, 126
Bloom Energy Corporation, 386

Trenton
NY Capitolwire, 533

Warren
O'Malley, Michael, 452

Wayne
Enterprise Holdings, 411
Valley National Bank, 82

West Trenton
Delaware River Basin Commission, 97, 150

New York, 481

Accord
Rondout Valley CSD, 595

Adams
South Jefferson CSD, 577
South Jefferson Chamber of Commerce, 516

Addisleigh Park
Joan Flowers For the 27th District, 487

Addison
Addison CSD, 591

Afton
Afton CSD, 570

Akron
Akron CSD, 573
Bank of Akron, 80
New York State Travel & Vacation Association, 281

Akwesasne
St Regis Mohawk Tribe, 166

Albany
3rd Department, 45
AFSCME District Council 37, 242
AIA New York State, Inc. (FKNA Rodriguez, Barbara J.), 378
AT&T Inc. and Its Affiliates (FKA Roos, David), 384
AT&T PAC - New York, 479
Aging, Office for the, 3, 250
Agriculture & Markets Department, 4, 69, 250
Soil & Water Conservation Committee, 70
Ahern, Barbara J, 378
Albany
Civil Court, 61
Criminal Court, 61
Traffic Court, 61
Albany City SD, 567
Albany College of Pharmacy, 552
Albany County, 325
County Court, 50
Family, 50
Supreme Court & Surrogate, 51
Albany County Airport Authority, 95, 284
Albany County Industrial Development Agency, 501
Albany Housing Coalition Inc, 297
Albany Law School, 552
Albany Law School of Union University, 378
Albany Law School, Government Law Center, 169
Albany Medical College, 552
Albany Port District Commission, 95, 285
Albany, City of, 341
Albany-Colonie Regional Chamber of Commerce, 379, 501
Alcoholism & Substance Abuse Services, Office of, 4, 173, 227, 250
Alliance for Positive Health, 181
Alliance for Quality Education (FKA Easton, Regina N), 379
Altman, Frederick M, 379
Altria Client Services, 90
Alzheimer's Association, Northeastern NY, 181
American Cancer Society Cancer Action Network, 380
American Chemistry Council, 90
American College of Physicians, New York Chapter, 181
American Congress of Obstetricians & Gynecologists, Inc. District II, 380
American Congress of Obstetricians & Gynecologists/NYS, 181

Listings appear in alphabetical order by state, then city.

American Council of Engineering Companies of NY (ACEC New York), 90
American Federation of State, County and Municipal Employees (AFSCME), 242
American Heart Assn/American Stroke Assn, 381
American Institute of Architects (AIA) New York State Inc, 90, 190
American Insurance Assn, 381
American Legion, Department of New York, 297
American Lung Association of NYS Inc, 181
American Red Cross in NYS, 256
Anglin, Laura L., 381
Asciutto, Georgia M, 382
Assn of Community & Residential Agencies (NYS), 383
Assn of Counties & Its Affiliated Organizations (NYS), 383
Assn of PBAS, Inc (NYS), 383
Associated General Contractors of America, NYS Chapter, 90
Associated General Contractors of New York State, LLC, 382
Associated Licensed Detectives of New York State, 116
Associated Risk Managers of New York Inc, 203
Association Development Group Inc, 90
Association for Addiction Professionals of New York, 231
Association of County Health Officials (New York State), 383
Association of Government Accountants, NY Capital Chapter, 169
Association of New York State Youth Bureaus, 383
Association of Proprietary Colleges, 126
Association of Public Broadcasting Stations of NY Inc, 143
Association of Realtors (New York State) (FKA-Mackenzie, Duncan), 383
Association of Towns of the State of NY, 383
Association of Towns of the State of New York, 237, 268
Association on Independent Living, 383
Attorney Grievance Committee
3rd Judicial Dept, Judicial Dist 3, 4, 6, 208
Audubon New York, 384
Automobile Dealers Assn (NYS), 384
BNA (formerly Bureau of National Affairs), 532
Barnes, Richard E, 385
Barrett Associates, 385
Bennett Firm, Inc (The), 386
Board of Regents, 119
Bogdan Lasky & Frazier, LLC, 386
Bolton St. Johns, Inc., 387
Bombardiere, Ralph, 388
Bond, Schoeneck & King, PLLC, 388
Bopp, Linda, 388
Bottlers Association (New York State), 389
Brain Injury Association of NYS (BIANYS), 181, 231
Briand, Elizabeth H (FKA Striar, Gary), 389
Brighter Choice Foundation, 389
Broadcasters Association, Inc., 389
Brown & Weinraub, PLLC, 390
Bryant & Stratton College-Albany Campus, 563
Budget, Division of the, 5, 83, 160, 234, 263
Builders Association (NYS), 391
Building & Construction Trades Council (NYS), 391
Business Council of NYS, Inc., 391
Business Council of New York State Inc, 91, 155
CASA - Advocates for Children of NYS, 214, 256
CIO & Office of Information Technology Services (ITS), 5, 140, 160
Cable Telecommunications Association of New York, Inc, 143
Calvin, James S, 391
Capital District Physicians' Health Plan Inc, 393
Capital District Regional Planning Commission, 96, 188
Capital District Transportation Authority, 96, 285
Capital Public Affairs, 393
Capital Region (Albany-Schoharie-Schenectady) BOCES, 600
Capitalize Albany Corporation, 503
Capitol Consultants Inc (NY), 393
Capitol Group, LLC, 393
Capitol Hill Management Services Inc, 393
Capitol Public Strategies, LLC (FKA McCulley & Associates, Inc.), 393
Capitol Strategies Group, LLC, 393
Capvest Partners LLP, 394
Carl Andrews & Associates, Inc., 394
Casey, Teresa M., 394
Center for Disability Services, 256
Center for Economic Growth Inc, 91
Center for Family & Youth (The), 256
Center for Law & Justice, 117, 215
Center for Technology in Government, University at Albany, SUNY, 169
Cetrino, Thomas, 395
Chesterton, Jan Marie, 396
Children & Family Services, Office of
Information Technology, Division of, 251
Citizen Action of New York, 138
Citizens' Environmental Coalition, 156
City University of New York (CUNY), 397
Civil Service Department, 5, 194, 234, 240
Civil Service Employees Assn of NY (CSEA), Local 1000, AFSCME, AFL-, 243
Civil Service Employees Assn, Inc, 398
Civil Service Employees Political Action Fund, 480
Civil Service Employees Union (CSEA), Local 1000, AFSCME, AFL-CIO, 225
Clean and Healthy New York, Inc., 398
Cleary, Kevin Government Relations, LLC, 398
Coalition Against Domestic Violence (NYS), 398
Coalition Against Domestic Violence, NYS, 117, 257
Coalition Against Sexual Assault (NYS), 117, 398
Coalition for Children's Mental Health Services (NYS), 399
Coalition for the Homeless, 399
Coalition for the Last Store on Main Street, 399
Coffin, Brian M., 399
College of Saint Rose (The), 554
Colwell Colwell & Petroccione, LLP (FKA Colwell Ferr, 400
Commission on Independent Colleges & Universities, 126
Committee of Methadone Program Administrators Inc of NYS (COMPA), 182, 231
Conference of Big 5 School Districts, 126
Conference of Local Mental Hygiene Directors (NYS), 400
Conference of Mayors & Municipal Officials (NYS), 400
Connelly Communications, Inc., 400
Connelly McLaughlin & Woloz, 401
Consumer Protection, Division of, 6, 83, 140
Convention Centers & Visitors Bureaus
Albany County Convention & Visitors Bureau, 274
Coppola, John, 402
Cordo & Company, LLC, 402
Corning Place Consulting, LLC, 402
Correctional Officers & Police B, 403
Corrections & Community Supervision Department, 6, 108
Correctional Industries Division, 108
Training Academy, 108
Couch White, LLP, 403
Council for Community Behavioral Healthcare, 403
Council of Community Services of NYS Inc, 257
Council of Nonprofits, Inc., 403
Council of the City of New York (The), 403
County Nursing Facilities of New York Inc, 182
Court of Appeals, 45
Court of Claims, 48

Listings appear in alphabetical order by state, then city.

Crane & Parente, PLLC, 143, 170
Criminal Justice Services, Division of, 6, 111, 206, 234
Crisis Program (The), 404
Crosier, Barbara V, 404
Curran, Brian F, 404
Cuyler News Service, 532
Dan Klores Communications, Inc. DBA DKC Government Affairs, 405
Davidoff, Hutcher & Citron LLP, 405
DeGraff, Foy & Kunz, LLP, 170
DeGraff, Foy, & Kunz, LLP, 203
Defenders Justice Fund, NYS, 406
Deloitte Consulting, 406
Dental Hygienists' Association of the State of New York Inc, 182
Deutsch, Ronald, 406
Developmental Disabilities Planning Council, 6, 194, 227, 252
DirecTv, 407
Donohue, Gavin J, 407
Duane Morris LLP, 408
D'Onofrio, Paul, 404
EPL/Environmental Advocates, 412
EQT Partner AS, 412
EQT Partners AB, 412
EQT Partners Asia Limited, 412
EQT Partners GMBH, 412
EQT Partners UK Advisors LLP, 412
Early Care & Learning Council, 257
Early Care and Learning Council, 408
Eastern Contractors Association Inc, 91
Economic Development Council Inc (NYS), 409
Education Department, 7, 119, 174, 227, 252, 270
Albany District Office, 121
Cultural Education Office, 120, 270
Office of Adult Career & Continuing Education Services (ACCES), 121, 228, 252
Office of Higher Education, 121
Office of P-12 Education Policy, 120
Office of the Professions, 121, 174, 227, 252
State Library, 120
Egg (The), Center for the Performing Arts, 278
Elections, State Board of, 7, 130
Albany, 130
Elk Street Group LLC, 409
Empire Advocates LLC, 410
Empire Center for New York State Policy, 91
Empire Dental Political Action Committee, 482
Empire Justice Center, 215, 258
Empire State Development Corporation, 7, 83, 97, 147, 188, 271
Empire State Petroleum Association, Inc., 411
Empire State Regional Council of Carpenters, 225
Empire State Restaurant & Tavern Association Inc, 91, 278
Empire Strategic Planning, Inc., 411
Employee Relations, Governor's Office of, 7, 240
Family Benefits Committee, 240
NYS/CSEA Discipline Unit, 241
NYS/CSEA Partnership for Education & Training, 241
NYS/SSU Joint Labor-Management Committee, 241
NYS/UUP Labor-Management Committee, 241
Statewide Employee Assistance Programs, 241
Employer Alliance for Affordable Health Care, 411
Energy Coalition New York, 144
Environmental Advocates of NY, 411
Environmental Advocates of New York, 156
Environmental Business Association of NYS Inc, 156
Environmental Conservation Department, 8, 147
Excelsior Advocates, LLC, 412
Excelsior College, 555
Faist Government Affairs Group, LLC, 413
Families Together in NYS Inc, 231
Families Together in NYS, Inc., 413
Family Planning Advocates of New York State, 183, 198, 258, 413
Farm Bureau, Inc. (NY), 413
Farrell 2012, 482
Featherstonhaugh, Wiley & Clyne, LLP, 414
Ferris, William E, 414
Food Industry Alliance of NYS Inc, 415
Food Industry Alliance of New York State Inc, 74, 92
Food Industry Political Action Committee - NYC, 483
Friends of Cultural Institutions, 483
Funeral Directors Association, Inc. (NYS), 417
Gallo, Richard J., 417
Gaming Association, 417
Gannett News Service, 532
Geiger, Bruce W & Associates, 417
General Services, Office of, 8, 160, 245, 271
Girvin & Ferlazzo, PC, 198
Governor's Office, 3, 69, 78, 83, 108, 119, 130, 140, 147, 160, 173, 187, 194, 200, 206, 219, 227, 234, 240, 245, 250, 263, 270, 283, 293
Greenberg Traurig PA PAC, 486
Greenberg Traurig, LLP, 170, 420
Griffin Associates, LLC, 421
Hager, Susan, 422
Hannan and O'Connell, Inc., 422
Harris, Steven W., LLC, 422
Health Department, 8, 148, 174, 293
Health Facilities Association, 423
Health Plan Assn Inc (NY), 423
Heslin Rothenberg Farley & Mesiti PC, 144
Hill & Gosdeck, 424
Hill, Gosdeck & McGraw LLC, 74
Hinman Straub Advisors, LLC, 424
Hispanic Outreach Services, 258
Hodes & Landy, 425
Home Care Assn of NYS Inc, 426
Home Care Association of New York State Inc, 183
Homeland Security & Emergency Services, Division of, 7, 160, 235
Hospice & Palliative Care Association of NYS Inc, 183, 258
Housing & Community Renewal, 8
Housing & Community Renewal, Division of, 187
Hudson River Valley Greenway, 8, 148, 271
Hudson River-Black River Regulating District, 97, 150
Human Rights, State Division of
Albany, 194
Hunger Action Network of NYS, 427
Hunger Action Network of NYS (HANNYS), 259
ITT Technical Institute, 564
Independent Bankers Association of NYS, 81
Independent Bankers Association of New York State, 427
Independent Power Producers of NY Inc, 144
Inspector General (NYS), Office of the, 9, 112, 161
Insurance Association, Inc. (NY), 428
Insurance Brokers' Association of the State of New York, 204
Insurance Fund (NYS), 9, 200, 219
Albany, 201, 219
JEM Associates NY, Inc., 428
JJMH Consulting, 429
Jenkins, Joanne E, 428
Jerome, Stephen, 429
Johnston, Christine, 430
Joint Commission on Public Ethics (JCOPE), 103, 136, 164
Jones, Jeff, 430
Justice, Lawrence P., 430
Justin McCarthy Consulting Services, Inc., 430
KPMG LLP, 170
Kennedy, Ronald F., 432
Kramer, Jason, 433
Kriss Kriss & Brignola, LLP, 433
Kriss, Kriss, Brignola & Persing, LLP, 291
LCI LLC, 434
LJM Rad, LLC, 435
Labor Department, 9, 177, 201, 220, 252, 293

Listings appear in alphabetical order by state, then city.

Greater Capital District, 220
Lambert, Linda A, 433
Langdon, David, 433
Lanotte, Michael A., 433
Lasky, Roy, 433
Law Department, 9, 78, 84, 112, 140, 149, 161, 177, 188, 195, 201, 206, 221, 245, 263
Administration, 206
Law Guardian Program
3rd Judicial Dept, 208
Law Office of Anne Reynolds Copps, 216, 259
Lawyers' Fund for Client Protection, 98, 210
League of Women Voters of New York State, 138, 170, 238, 434
Legislative Bill Drafting Commission, 98, 163
Legislative Retrieval System, 98, 163
Legislative Correspondents Association, 532
Legislative Gazette, 523
Library Trustees Association of NYS, 127
Lieutenant Governor's Office, 3, 160
Long Island Nursery & Landscape Association Inc, 75
Lynch, Patricia Associates, 437
Malkin & Ross, 438
Manatt, Phelps & Phillips, LLP, 439
Mannella, Peter F., 439
Maria College of Albany, 557
Maritato, Anna Maria, 440
Markee, Lionel, 440
Marsh, Wassermann & McHugh, LLC, 440
Martin J. McLaughlin Communications, Inc., 440
McCormack, Jr., R. Christopher, 441
McDonnell, Brian, 441
McKenna Long & Aldridge, LLP, 442
McMahon, Kathy A., 442
McManus, Michael T., 442
Meara Avella Dickinson, 442
Mechanical Technology Incorporated, 144
Medical Society of the State of NY, Governmental Affairs Division, 183
Medical Society of the State of New York, 442
Memorial Hospital School of Nursing, 557
Mental Health Association in NYS, 443
Mental Health Association of NYS Inc, 232
Mental Health, Office of, 10, 228
Capital District Psychiatric Center, 228
Mental Hygiene Legal Service
3rd Judicial Dept, 209, 230
Meyer Suozzi English & Klein, PC, 444
Mildred Elley, 565
Montefiore Medical Center, 445
Moreau, Karen, 445
Morris & McVeigh NYS PAC, 490
Morris, Mark, 446
Motor Vehicles Department, 10, 283
NAIFA - New York State, 204
NAMI-NYS, 232
NY Association of Training & Employment Professionals (NYATEP), 225
NY Commercial Association of Realtors, 248
NY Council on Problem Gambling, 232
NY Counseling Association Inc, 232, 259
NY Health Information Management Association Inc, 184
NY State Association of Town Superintendents of Highways Inc, 238, 291
NY StateWatch Inc, 171
NYS Academy of Family Physicians, 184
NYS Alliance for Arts Education, 127, 279
NYS Arborists, 75
NYS Association for the Education of Young Children, 127
NYS Association of Area Agencies on Aging, 259
NYS Association of Community & Residential Agencies, 232
NYS Association of Counties, 171, 238
NYS Association of County Health Officials, 184
NYS Association of Health Care Providers, 184
NYS Association of Realtors, 248
NYS Association of School Business Officials, 127
NYS Association of Service Stations & Repair Shops, 291
NYS Bar Assn, Attorneys in Public Service Cmte, 243
NYS Bar Assn, Children & the Law Committee, 259
NYS Bar Assn, Cmte on Diversity & Leadership Development, 217
NYS Bar Assn, Disability Rights Cmte, 198
NYS Bar Assn, Diversity & Leadership Development Cmte, 218
NYS Bar Assn, Electronic Communications Task Force, 144
NYS Bar Assn, Health Law Section, 186, 218
NYS Bar Assn, Legislative Policy Cmte, 170
NYS Bar Assn, Real Property Section, 216
NYS Bar Association, 77
NYS Broadcasters Association, 144
NYS Builders Association Inc, 92
NYS Building & Construction Trades Council, 93, 225
NYS Conference of Local Mental Hygiene Directors, 232
NYS Conference of Mayors & Municipal Officials, 238, 268
NYS Correctional Officers & Police Benevolent Association Inc, 117, 243
NYS Council for Community Behavioral Healthcare, 232
NYS Council of Probation Administrators, 117, 217
NYS County Hwy Super Assn / NY Aviation Mgt Assn / NY Public, 291
NYS Defenders Association, 117, 217
NYS Dental Association, 184
NYS Economic Development Council, 93
NYS Forum Inc, 145
NYS Head Start Association, 127
NYS Health Department, 243
NYS Industries for the Disabled (NYSID) Inc, 225, 260
NYS Law Enforcement Officers Union, Council 82, AFSCME, AFL-CIO, 118, 243
NYS Nursery/Landscape Association, 75
NYS Office for People with Developmental Disabilities, 10, 229
NYS Optometric Association Inc, 184
NYS Parole Officers Association, 243
NYS Psychological Association, 232
NYS Public Health Association, 184
NYS Reading Association, 127
NYS Right to Life Committee, 138
NYS Sheriffs' Association, 118, 243
NYS Society of Real Estate Appraisers, 248
NYS Technology Enterprise Corporation (NYSTEC), 145
NYSPIA Political Committee, Inc., 451
NYSRPA-PVF, 491
NYSTAR - Division of Science, Technology & Innovation, 10, 84, 122
Center for Economic Growth, 85, 123
Center in Nanomaterials and Nanoelectronics, 85, 122
Nasca, Samuel J, 447
National Assn of Social Workers (NYS Chapter) (FKA Paupini, Sara), 447
National Association of Social Workers, NYS Chapter, 260
National Credit Union Administration
Albany Region, 79
National Federation of Independent Business, 93, 226, 268, 448
National Grid, 448
National Labor Relations Board
Albany Resident Office, 222
National Strategies, Inc., 448
Nature Conservancy (The), 158
Nature Conservancy (The) (FKA Janeway, William C.), 449
Neidl, Michael, 449
Neighborhood Preservation Coalition of NYS Inc, 192
Nelson A Rockefeller Inst of Govt, Federalism Research Grp, 260
Nelson A Rockefeller Inst of Govt, Higher Education Program, 127
Nelson A Rockefeller Inst of Govt, Urban & Metro Studies, 192

Listings appear in alphabetical order by state, then city.

Nelson A Rockefeller Institute of Government, 171, 268
New York Association of Convenience Stores, 93
New York Association of Homes & Services for the Aging, 260
New York Association of Psychiatric Rehabilitation Services (NYAPRS), 232
New York Business Development Corporation, 93
New York City
Legislative Affairs Office, NYC Mayor's State, 356
New York Community College Trustees (NYCCT), 127
New York Credit Union Association, 81
New York Farm Bureau, 76
New York Health Plan Association, 185
New York Insurance Association Inc, 204
New York Municipal Insurance Reciprocal (NYMIR), 204, 239
New York News Publishers Association, 145
New York Public Welfare Association, 260
New York Republican State Committee, 139
New York State AFL-CIO COPE, 491
New York State Association of Independent Schools, 128
New York State Auto Dealers Association, 93, 292
New York State Board of Law Examiners, 101, 211
New York State Catholic Conference, 128, 260
New York State Commission of Correction, 101, 113
New York State Commission on Judicial Nomination, 102, 211
New York State Commission on the Restoration of the Capitol, 102, 164, 273
New York State Congress of Parents & Teachers Inc, 128
New York State Council of Churches, 199
New York State Council of School Superintendents, 128
New York State Disaster Preparedness Commission, 102, 164, 237
New York State Dormitory Authority, 102, 123, 164, 177
New York State Energy Research & Development Authority, 102, 141, 151
New York State Environmental Facilities Corp, 102, 151
New York State Government Finance Officers Association Inc, 239, 268
New York State Health Facilities Association Inc, 185
New York State Higher Education Services Corp (NYSHESC), 103, 124
New York State Homes & Community Renewal, 79, 103
New York State Hospitality & Tourism Association, 281
New York State Judicial Conduct Commission, 103, 211
New York State Laborers' Political Action Committee, 491
New York State Law Reporting Bureau, 103, 164, 211
New York State Law Revision Commission, 104, 211
New York State Liquor Authority, 104
New York State Liquor Authority (Division of Alcoholic Beverage, 83, 263
New York State Liquor Authority (Division of Alcoholic Beverage Control), 4
Albany (Zone II), 83, 263
New York State Motor Truck Association, 292
New York State Petroleum Council, 145
New York State Public Employees Federation (PEF), 243
New York State Rehabilitation Association, 233, 260
New York State Republican Party, 374
New York State Restaurant Association, 93, 281
New York State Right to Life Party, 376
New York State Rural Housing Coalition Inc, 192
New York State Teachers' Retirement System, 104, 124, 242
New York State Telecommunications Association Inc, 145
New York State Thruway Authority, 104, 273, 287
New York State Transportation Engineering Alliance (NYSTEA), 292
New York State Veterinary Medical Society, 76
New York Wired for Education LLC, 139
Newspaper Publishers Assn (NY), 449
Next Wave Inc, 185
Nixon Peabody, LLP, 450
Nolan & Heller, LLP, 450
Organization of NYS Management Confidential Employees, 243
Organization of NYS Management/Confidential Employees Inc, 452
Ostroff, Hiffa & Associates Inc, 452
Ottaway News Service (NYS only), 533
O'Connell and Aronowitz, 451
Parks & Trails New York, 453
Parks, Recreation & Historic Preservation, NYS Office of, 11, 149, 271
Parole Board, The, 11, 112
Clemency Unit, 113
Pastel & Rosen, LLP, 454
Pharmacists Society of the State of New York, 186
Pitta, Bishop, Del Giorno & Giblin, LLC, 455
Plummer & Wigger, LLC (FKA Griffin, Plummer & Associates), 455
Police Benevolent Assn of the NYS Troopers Inc, 456
Police Benevolent Association of New York State, 456
Police Conference of NY Inc (PCNY), 118, 244
Police Conference of NY, Inc., 456
Powers & Company, 456
Preservation League of NYS (FKA DiLorenzo, Jay), 457
Prevent Child Abuse New York, 261
Prevention of Domestic Violence, Office for the, 11, 113, 253
PriceWaterhouseCoopers LLP, 457
Prisoners' Legal Services of New York, 118
Professional Agencies for Children's Therapy Services, 457
Professional Fire Fighters Association Inc (NYS), 244
Property Casualty Insurers Association of America (PCI), 457
Public Employment Relations Board, 11, 241
Public Policy Institute of NYS Inc, 94
Public Service Commission, 11, 140
Public Utility Law Project of New York Inc, 145
Public Welfare Assn (NY), 458
RBC Capital Markets (FKA RBC Dain Rausher), 459
RPAC of New York, 493
Real Property Tax Services, Office of, 12, 235, 245, 264
Albany (Northern Region), 235, 264
Rehabilitation Assn Inc (NYS), 460
Repas, Peter G, 460
Research Foundation of SUNY, 128
Research, Information & Policy Development
Albany (Northern Region), 245
Retail Council of New York State, 94
Retired Public Employees Association, 244
Retired Public Employees Association, Inc., 460
Riddell Group, LLC (The), 461
Riddett Associates, Inc. (FKA Riddett, Kenneth E. Associates Inc.), 461
Right to Life Committee Inc (NYS), 461
Roman Catholic Diocese of Albany, Catholic Charities, 261
Rosenthal, Harvey, 461
Rutnik Law Firm (The), 462
SUNY Board of Trustees, 543
SUNY System Administration & Executive Council, 543
New York Network, 543
Rockefeller Institute of Government, 543
Small Business Development Center, 544

Listings appear in alphabetical order by state, then city.

State University Construction Fund, 544
SUNY at Albany, Center for Women in Government & Civil Society, 171
SUNY at Albany, Nelson A Rockefeller College, 139
SUNY at Albany, Professional Development Program, NE States Addiction, 233
SUNY at Albany, Rockefeller College, 171
Sampson, Rick J, 462
Sanzillo, Francis J. & Associates, 463
Schomberg, Dora, 464
Schuyler Center for Analysis & Advocacy, 464
Schuyler Center for Analysis & Advocacy (SCAA), 128, 199, 233
Sheehan Green Carraway Golderman & Jacques LLP, 465
Sherin, James R., 465
Sierra Club, Atlantic Chapter, 159
Small Business Administration
New York Small Business Development Center, 88
Smyth, A Advocacy, 466
Soloway, Ronald, 466
South Colonie CSD, 567
Special Committee on Animals & the Law, 77
State & Broadway, Inc., 467
State Advisers, LLC, 467
State Comptroller, Office of the, 12, 149, 162, 235, 241
State Department, 12, 85, 149, 162, 236
Region 9 - Capital District Office, 163
State Employees Federal Credit Union, 244
State Police, Division of, 12, 113
State University Construction Fund, 106, 124
State University of NY, System Administration, 467
State University of New York at Albany, 544
Stuto, Diane D, 468
Tax Appeals, Division of, 12, 264
Taxation & Finance Department, 13, 86, 265
Temporary & Disability Assistance, Office of, 13, 195, 253
The Bachmann-Strauss Dystonia & Parkinson Foundation Inc, 186
The New York State Society of Professional Engineers Inc (NYSSPE), 94
Times Union, 523
Tourism Industry Coalition (TIC), 469
Transportation Department, 13, 246, 283
Region 1, 284
Turner, Francine, 470
UHY Advisors, 94
US Commerce Department
National Weather Service, 89
US Department of Agriculture
Gastonia Region-New York Office, 71
National Agricultural Statistics Service-NY Field Office, 72
New York Area Office, 72
New York State Office, 71
Northeast Marketing Area, 71
US Department of Homeland Security (DHS)
Albany Sub Office, 266
Albany, Port of, 72, 167, 266
US Department of Veterans Affairs
Albany VA Medical Center, 296
VA Healthcare Network Upstate New York (VISN2), 296
US Federal Courts
Northern District, 212
US Housing & Urban Development Department
Albany Area Office & Financial Operations Center, 190
US Justice Department
Albany, 114, 115, 213
US Labor Department
Albany, 297
Albany Area Office, 180, 223
Albany District Office, 223
US Railroad Retirement Board
Albany, 224
US Transportation Department
Federal Highway Administration-New York Division, 289
Federal Motor Carrier Safety Admin-New York Division, 289
US Treasury Department
Albany Territory, 267
Upstate New York Office, 267
Unified Court System, 209
3rd Judicial Department, 209
Administrative Judge to the Court of Claims (NYS), 209
Financial Management & Audit Services, 210
United Healthcare Services, Inc., 470
United New York Ambulance Network (UNYAN), 186
United Transportation Union, 244, 292
United University Professions, 244
University at Albany (FKA Williams, Charlie), 471
Veterans of Foreign Wars, 300
Veterans' Affairs, Division of, 13, 294
Veterans' Service Organizations
Albany Housing Coalition Inc, 294
Veterans House (The), 294
Victim Services, Office of, 6, 110, 252
Vidal Group, LLC (The), 472
WAMC (90.3 FM), 533
WNYT (12), 536
WTEN (10), 537
WXXA (23), 537
Walters Group (The), 473
Welfare Inspector General, Office of NYS, 13, 163
Welfare Research Inc, 262
West Firm PLLC (The), 474
Whiteman Osterman & Hanna LLP, 159, 199, 218, 239, 474
Wilson Elser Moskowitz Edelman & Dicker, 186, 218, 475
Wilson Elser Moskowitz Edelman & Dicker LLP, PAC, 496
Wilson, Alex, 476
Wisneski, Jessica, 476
Workers' Compensation Board
Albany, 202, 221
YMCAs of NYS, Inc., 477
Yavornitzki, Mark L., 477
Young Jr. William N., 478
ZGA LLC, 478

Albertson
Abilities Inc, Abilities!, 224
Abilities Inc, at Abilities!, 256

Albion
Albion CSD, 586
Corrections & Community Supervision Department
Albion Correctional Facility, 108
Orleans Correctional Facility, 109
Elections, State Board of
Orleans, 134
Orleans County, 333
Supreme, County, Family & Surrogate's Courts, 57
Orleans County Chamber of Commerce, 513
Orleans Economic Development Agency (OEDA), 513

Alden
Alden CSD, 573
Alden Chamber of Commerce, 501
Corrections & Community Supervision Department
Wende Correctional Facility, 110

Alexander
Alexander CSD, 575

Alexandria Bay
Alexandria Bay Chamber of Commerce, 501
Alexandria CSD, 577
Convention Centers & Visitors Bureaus
Tourism Bureau of the Thousand Islands Region, 275
Parks, Recreation & Historic Preservation, NYS Office of
Thousand Islands Region, 272
Thousand Islands Bridge Authority, 106, 288
US Department of Homeland Security (DHS)
Alexandria Bay, 72
Alexandria Bay, Port of, 167

Alfred
Alfred State College of Technology, 546
Alfred University, 552

Listings appear in alphabetical order by state, then city.

NYS College of Ceramics at Alfred University, 544
NYSTAR - Division of Science, Technology & Innovation
Center for Advanced Ceramic Technology at Alfred University, 84, 122

Allegany
Allegany - Limestone CSD, 568

Almond
Alfred-Almond CSD, 567

Altona
Corrections & Community Supervision Department
Altona Correctional Facility, 108

Amagansett
Amagansett UFSD, 591

Amenia
New York State Directory, 171

Amherst
Amherst CSD, 573
Amherst Industrial Development Agency (Town of), 501
Daemen College, 554
MJ Peterson Corporation, 247
Printing Industries Alliance, 94
Schuh, Paul, 464
Sweet Home CSD, 574

Amityville
Amityville UFSD, 591
Island Drafting & Technical Institute, 564
New York Marine Trades Association, 281

Amsterdam
Amsterdam
Civil & Criminal Courts, 62
Amsterdam Industrial Development Agency, 501
Greater Amsterdam SD, 579
Montgomery County Chamber of Commerce/Montgomery County Partnership, 511
Recorder (The), 523

Andes
Andes CSD, 572

Andover
Andover CSD, 567

Angola
Erie 2-Chautauqua-Cattaraugus BOCES, 600
Evans-Brant CSD (Lake Shore), 573
Evans-Brant Chamber of Commerce, 505

Annandale-on-Hudson
Bard College, 553

Apalachin
Owego, Town of, 361

Arcade
Arcade Area Chamber of Commerce, 501

Ardsley
Ardsley UFSD, 597

Argyle
Argyle CSD, 596

Arkport
Arkport CSD, 591

Arkville
Catskill Center for Conservation & Development, The, 156
Catskill Center for Conservation and Development, Inc., 395

Armonk
Building & Realty Institute, 247
Byram Hills CSD, 597
IBM Corporation, 92
MBIA Insurance Corporation, 238

Arverne
Kesselly For Council, 488

Astoria
Dryfoos Group, 408
Friends of Costa Constantinides, 483
Meloni NYCC, 490
Moustafa For NYC, 490
Peterson 2013, 492
Vallone For New York, 496

Attica
Attica CSD, 599
Corrections & Community Supervision Department
Attica Correctional Facility, 108
Wyoming Correctional Facility, 110

Auburn
Auburn
Civil & Criminal Courts, 62
Auburn Enlarged City SD, 569
Auburn Publishers Inc, 523
Auburn, City of, 341
Cayuga Community College, 547
Cayuga County, 326
Family Court, 51
Cayuga County Chamber of Commerce, 503
Cayuga-Onondaga BOCES, 600
Citizen (The), 523
Corrections & Community Supervision Department
Auburn Correctional Facility, 108
Elections, State Board of
Cayuga, 130

Aurora
Southern Cayuga CSD, 569

Wells College, 562

Averill Park
Averill Park CSD, 587

Avoca
Avoca CSD, 591
US Department of Agriculture
Avoca Work Unit, 71

Avon
Avon CSD, 577
Environmental Conservation Department
Region 8, 148

Babylon
Babylon Industrial Development Agency, 501
Babylon UFSD, 591
Halpin Public Affairs, 422

Bainbridge
Bainbridge Chamber of Commerce, 501
Bainbridge-Guilford CSD, 570

Baldwin
Baldwin Chamber of Commerce, 501
Baldwin UFSD, 579
Friends of I. Daneek Miller, 484
Gold Star Wives of America Inc, 298

Baldwinsville
Baldwinsville CSD, 584
Baldwinsville Chamber of Commerce (Greater Baldwinsville), 501
Johnson, Russ, 430
Lysander, Town of, 350
WSEN (92.1 FM), 533

Ballston Lake
Adams, Daniel J, 377

Ballston Spa
Ballston Spa CSD, 588
Elections, State Board of
Saratoga, 135
Saratoga County, 335
Family Court, 58
Supreme, County & Surrogate's Courts, 58
Saratoga County Industrial Development Agency, 515
US Transportation Department
Highway-Rail Grade Crossing, 289
Veterans' Service Organizations
Saratoga Cnty Rural Preservation Co (Homeless Veterans), 294

Barker
Barker CSD, 582

Barrytown
Unification Theological Seminary, 562

Listings appear in alphabetical order by state, then city.

Batavia
Batavia
Civil & Criminal Courts, 62
Batavia City SD, 575
Education Department
State School for the Blind at Batavia, 228, 252
Elections, State Board of
Genesee, 132
Genesee Community College, 547
Genesee County, 329
Supreme, County, Family & Surrogate's Courts, 53
Genesee County Chamber of Commerce, 506
Genesee County Economic Development Center, 506
Health Department
New York State Veterans' Home at Batavia, 175, 293
Mancuso Business Development Group, 248
My-T Acres Inc, 75
NYS Vegetable Growers Association Inc, 76
Real Property Tax Services, Office of
Batavia (Western Region), 235, 264
Research, Information & Policy Development
Batavia (Western Region), 246
US Department of Veterans Affairs
Batavia VA Medical Center, 296
Western Regional Off-Track Betting Corp, 107, 274

Bath
Bath Area Chamber of Commerce (Greater Bath Area), 501
Bath CSD, 591
Elections, State Board of
Steuben, 135
Steuben County, 337
Supreme, County, Family & Surrogate's Courts, 59
Steuben County Industrial Development Agency, 517
US Department of Veterans Affairs
Bath National Cemetery, 295
Bath VA Medical Center, 296
WCIK (103.1 FM), 533

Bay Shore
NYSTAR - Division of Science, Technology & Innovation
Long Island Forum for Technology, 85

Bayport
Bayport-Blue Point UFSD, 591

Bayshore
Bay Shore UFSD, 591
Bayshore Chamber of Commerce, 502

Bayside
Friends of Austin Shafran, 483
New Yorkers For Katz, 491
Queensborough Community College, 552
Silverstein 2013, 494

Beacon
Antalek & Moore Insurance Agency, 80
Beacon
Civil & Criminal Courts, 62
Beacon City SD, 572
Corrections & Community Supervision Department
Beacon Correctional Facility, 108
Fishkill Correctional Facility, 109
Hudson River Sloop Clearwater Inc, 157
WHUD (100.7 FM), 535
WSPK (104.7 FM), 533

Bear Mountain
Parks, Recreation & Historic Preservation, NYS Office of
Palisades Region, 272

Beaver Dams
Corrections & Community Supervision Department
Monterey Shock Incarceration Correctional Facility, 109

Beaver Falls
Beaver River CSD, 577

Bedford Hills
Corrections & Community Supervision Department
Bedford Hills Correctional Facility, 109
Taconic Correctional Facility, 110
McDonald 2013, 490

Belfast
Belfast CSD, 567

Bellerose
Mental Health, Office of
Queens Children's Psychiatric Center, 229

Belleville
Belleville Henderson CSD, 577

Bellmore
Bellmore UFSD, 579
Nassau Council of Chambers, 511
North Bellmore UFSD, 581

Belmont
Allegany County, 325
Supreme, County, Family & Surrogate's Courts, 51
Allegany County Office of Development & Industrial Devel, 501
Elections, State Board of
Allegany, 130
Genesee Valley CSD, 568

Bemus Point
Bemus Point CSD, 569

Bergen
Byron-Bergen CSD, 575

Berlin
Berlin CSD, 587

Berne
Berne-Knox-Westerlo CSD, 567

Bethpage
Bethpage Chamber of Commerce, 502
Bethpage UFSD, 579
Briarcliffe College-Bethpage, 563
Cablevision Systems Corporation, 143
Cablevision Systems New York PAC, 480
NYSTAR - Division of Science, Technology & Innovation
Long Island Forum for Technology, 123
US Department of Homeland Security (DHS)
New York Asylum Office, 167, 196

Binghamton
Binghamton
Civil & Criminal Courts, 62
Binghamton Chamber of Commerce (Greater Binghamton), 502
Binghamton City SD, 568
Binghamton University, 386
Binghamton University, State University of New York, 544
Binghamton, City of, 342
Broome Community College, 547
Broome County, 325
County, Family, 51
Surrogate & Supreme Court, 51
Broome County Industrial Development Agency, 502
Broome-Delaware-Tioga BOCES, 599
Chadwick, Cindy, 396
Chenango Forks CSD, 568
Chenango Valley CSD, 568
Columbian Mutual Life Insurance Company, 400
Convention Centers & Visitors Bureaus
Greater Binghamton New York Convention and Visitors Bureau, 274
Education Department
Southern Tier District Office, 122
Elections, State Board of
Broome, 130
Gannet Co Inc, 523
Human Rights, State Division of
Binghamton, 194
Law Department
Binghamton, 207
Levene, Gouldin & Thompson LLP, 216
Mental Health, Office of
Greater Binghamton Health Center, 228
NOFA-NY Certified Organic LLC, 75

Appendices: Financial Plan, Indexes & Maps

Listings appear in alphabetical order by state, then city.

NYS Office for People with Developmental Disabilities
Broome Developmental Disabilities Services Office, 229
NYS Trade Adjustment Assistance Center, 93
NYSTAR - Division of Science, Technology & Innovation
Alliance for Manufacturing & Technology, 85, 123
Integrated Electronics Engineering Center at Binghamton, 85, 123
New York State Electric & Gas Corporation (NYSEG), 145
Press & Sun Bulletin, 523
Rochester Gas and Electric Corporation, 145
Southern Tier Independence Center, 466
Transportation Department
Region 9, 284
US Justice Department
Binghamton, 115, 116, 213
Uniform State Laws Commission, 106, 164, 211
Veterans' Service Organizations
Veterans Services Center of the Southern Tier, 294
WIVT (34), 537
WNBF (1290 AM), 533
WSKG (89.3 FM), WSQX (91.5 FM), 534
Workers' Compensation Board
Binghamton, 202, 221

Blauvelt
South Orangetown CSD, 588

Bliss
McCormick Farms Inc, 75
National Potato Board, 75

Blue Mountain Lake
Adirondack Lakes Center for the Arts, 277
New York State Rural Advocates, 192

Bohemia
Appraisal Education Network School & Merrell Institute, 247
Connetquot CSD, 592
Suffolk County Association of Municipal, 495
US Commerce Department
National Weather Service, Eastern Region, 71, 88, 152

Boiceville
Onteora CSD, 595

Bolivar
Bolivar-Richburg CSD, 567

Bolton Landing
Bolton CSD, 596
Bolton Landing Chamber of Commerce, 502

Boonville
Adirondack CSD, 583
Boonville Area Chamber of Commerce, 502
New York State Woodsmen's Field Days Inc, 158

Boston
US Labor Department
Jobs Corps (JC), 223

Bradford
Bradford CSD, 591

Brasher Falls
Brasher Falls CSD, 590
Empire State Honey Producers Association, 74

Brentwood
Brentwood UFSD, 591

Brewerton
Fort Brewerton/Greater Oneida Lake Chamber, 506

Brewster
Brewster CSD, 587
Brewster Chamber of Commerce, 502
Green Chimneys School-Green Chimneys Children's Services Inc, 258

Briarcliff Manor
Briarcliff Manor UFSD, 597

Briarwood
Samaritan Village Inc, 233
Veras For Council 2013, 496

Bridgehampton
Bridgehampton UFSD, 591

Brightwaters
NYS Passenger Vessel Association, 280

Broadalbin
Broadalbin-Perth CSD, 575

Brockport
Brockport CSD, 578
Brockport Chamber of Commerce (Greater Brockport), 502
College at Brockport, 545

Brocton
Brocton CSD, 569
Corrections & Community Supervision Department
Lakeview Shock Incarceration Correctional Facility, 109

Bronx
A Different Approach, 479
Albert 2013, 479
Albert Einstein College of Medicine - Division of Substance Abuse, 231
Arroyo 2013, 479
Bendetto For Assembly, 479
Botanical Garden (The) (NY), 388
Bronx Chamber of Commerce, 502
Bronx Community College, 551
Bronx County
Supreme & Surrogate's Courts, 51
Bronx County (NYC Borough of the Bronx), 325
Bronx Educational Opportunity Center, 549
Bronx River Alliance, Inc., 389
Bronx-Lebanon Hospital Center, 181
Cabrera For City Council, 480
Civil Court, NYC
Bronx County, 48
Cliff Stanton For Council, 480
Committee to Elect Abiodun Bello, 480
Committee to Elect Andy King, 480
Committee to Re-Elect Lawrence A. Warden, 481
Community Campaign For Naaimat, 481
Criminal Court, NYC
Bronx County, 49
Cynthia For Change, 481
Diallo For Council 2013, 482
Distinctive Public Affairs, LLC, 407
Education Department
Bronx District Office, 121
Eisland Strategies LLC, 409
Elect Newsome 2013, 482
Elections, State Board of
Bronx, 133
Family Court, NYC
Bronx County, 50
Fassler, Michael S, 413
Fordham University, 126, 555
Fordham University, Department of Political Science, 170, 238
Friends For Ryan Wright, 483
Friends of Angel Molina, 483
Friends of Assemblyman Jeffrey Dinowitz, 483
Friends of Bola Omotosho, 483
Friends of Carl E. Heastie, 483
Friends of Felipe de Los Santos, 484
Friends of James Vacca, 484
Friends of Joel R. Rivera, 484
Friends of Johnnie Goff, 484
Friends of Joseph Nwachukwu, 484
Friends of Julio Pabon, 484
Friends of Pedro Alvarez, 485
Friends of Torres, 485
Gibson For Assembly, 486
Global Gardens Program, New York Botanical Garden (The), 74
Gronowicz For Mayor, 486
Hoffnung 2013, 486
Hostos Community College, 551
Human Rights, State Division of, 9, 194
Housing Investigations Unit, 194
Hunts Point Produce Redevelopment PAC - Corporate Contribution Accou, 487

Listings appear in alphabetical order by state, then city.

Hunts Point Produce Redevelopment PAC - Personal Contribution Account, 487
Joel Bauza For City Council, 487
Johnson 2013, 488
Johnson NYC 2013, 488
Lehman College, 551
Local 147 Political Action Committee, 488
Lundgren For Council, 489
Lynn Sanchez For City Council, 489
Mark Gjonaj 2012, 489
Mental Health, Office of
Bronx Psychiatric Center, 228
NYC Children's Center-Bronx Campus, 228
Michael 2013, 490
Monroe College-Bronx, 565
Montefiore Health System, Albert Ein, 184
Moore 2013, 490
NYC Region 1, 582
NYC Region 2, 582
New Era Veterans, Inc, 299
New York City Boroughs
Bronx (Bronx County), 359
New York Yankees, 281
North Bronx Career Counseling & Outreach Center, 549
Osborne Association, 118, 226
Palma 2013, 492
Pamela Johnson For NYC Council, 492
People For Diaz, 492
People For Jerome Rice, 492
People For Yudelka Tapia, 492
Public Markets Partners/Baum Forum, 77
Ralina Cardona 2013, 493
Raquel Batista 2013, 493
Rivera 2013, 493
Rubin, Kate, 462
Schlein, Stanley Esq., 463
Sierra 2013, 494
Simmons-Oliver For City Council, 494
South Bronx Overall Economic Development Corporation, 514
US Commerce Department
South Bronx Business Center, 88, 196
US Department of Agriculture
SC Inspection Division-Bronx Office, 71
US Department of Veterans Affairs
James J. Peters VA Medical Center, 296
VA NY/NJ Veterans Healthcare Network (VISN3), 296
Unified Court System
12th Judicial District (Judicial Department 1), 210
United Neighbors for Neville Mitchell, 496
WFUV (90.7 FM), 534
Wildlife Conservation Society, 159, 475
Women's Housing & Economic Development Corporation (WHEDCO), 193
Yeshiva University, A Einstein Clg of Med, Div of Subs Abuse, 233
Zead Ramadan 2013, 497

Bronxville

Bronxville Chamber of Commerce, 502
Bronxville UFSD, 597
Concordia College, 554
Grassy Sprain PAC, 486
Sarah Lawrence College, 560

Brookfield

Brookfield CSD, 578

Brooklyn

2nd Department, 45
99 Solutions LLC, 377
ASA Institute of Business & Computer Technology, 563
Agriculture & Markets Department
Brooklyn, 69
New York City Office, 70
Akiel Taylor For Council, 479
American College of Nurse-Midwives, NYC Chapter, 181
Ari Kagan For City Council, 479
Attorney Grievance Committee
Judicial Dist 2, 11, 13, 208
Bill Thompson For Mayor, 479
Black Veterans for Social Justice Inc, 298
Brad Lander 2013, 479
Brooklyn Botanic Garden, 155, 277
Brooklyn Chamber of Commerce, 502
Brooklyn College, 551
Brooklyn Daily Eagle, 524
Brooklyn Economic Development Corporation, 502
Brooklyn Educational Opportunity Center, 549
Brooklyn Housing & Family Services Inc, 191
Brooklyn Law School, 214, 553
Brooklyn Museum, 389
Brooklyn Museum of Art, 277
Brooklyn Navy Yard Development Corporation, 95, 294
CUNY New York City College of Technology, Hospitality Mgmt, 277
Camba, Inc. (FKA Church Avenue Merchants Block Association, Inc.), 391
Canarsie Courier, 524
Canarsie Courier Publications, Inc., 524
Carlo 2013, 480
Carlos For Council, 480
Catholic Citizens Committee PAC, 480
Center for Alternative Sentencing & Employment Services (CASES), 116
Center for Anti-Violence Education Inc, 256
Central Brooklyn Independent Democrats, 480
Civil Court, NYC
Kings County, 48
Coalition of Living Museums, 278
Committee to Elect Christopher Banks, 480
Committee to Elect Eric Adams, 480
Committee to Elect Philip Marks For Mayor, 480
Committee to Elect Robert E. Cornegy Jr., 480
Committee to Elect Robert M. Waterman, 480
Committee to Re-Elect Mathieu Eugene, 481
Coney Island Chamber of Commerce, 504
Conrad Tillard For Council, 481
Correction Captains Association - PAC, 481
Council of School Supervisors and Administrators, Local 1 AFSA, 481
Criminal Court, NYC
Kings County, 49
Desales Media Group, Inc., 406
Education Department
Brooklyn District Office, 121
Educational Justice Political Action Committee, 482
Elections, State Board of
Kings, 133
Eric Adams 2013, 482
Espinal For City Council, 482
Family Court, NYC
Kings County, 50
Faucher, Jennifer, 414
Ferramosca, Joseph, 414
Food & Water Watch, 415
Forest City Ratner Companies, 415
Frack Action Fund, Inc., 416
Frank's Friends, 483
Freelancers Union Political Action Committee, 483
Friends of Antonio Reynoso, 483
Friends of Bill Suggs, 483
Friends of DeMeo, 483
Friends of Ede Fox, 484
Friends of Erick Salgado, 484
Friends of F. Richard Hurley 2013, 484
Friends of Inez Barron, 484
Friends of Jean Similien, 484
Friends of Joe Lazar, 484
Friends of John Lisyanskiy, 484
Friends of Jonathan J. Judge, 484
Friends of Kimberly Council, 484
Friends of Kirsten John Foy, 484
Friends of Mark Winston Griffith, 485
Friends of Mike Treybich, 485
Friends of Olanike Alabi, 485
Friends of Sean K. Henry 2013, 485
Friends of Seymour Lachman, 485
Friends of Steve Cohn, 485
Friends of Theresa Scavo, 485
Friends of Todd Dobrin, 485
Friends of Tommy Torres, 485
Gentile For the Future, 486
Gonzalez 2013, 486
Gotlieb For City Council, 486
Greenfield 2010, 486
Hakeem Jeffries For Assembly, 486

Listings appear in alphabetical order by state, then city.

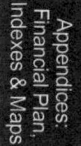

HeartShare Human Services of New York, Roman Catholic Dioce, 258
Helal A. Sheikh 2013, 486
Helen Keller Services for the Blind, 258
Housing Works Inc, 191, 258
Human Rights, State Division of
Brooklyn, 194
Humberto Soto For New York City Council 2013, 487
INFORM Inc, 183
Igor 2013, 487
Institute of Design & Construction, 556
Jesse Hamilton 2013, 487
John Quaglione For City Council, 488
Jumaane 2013, 488
Katz, Arthur H, 431
Kehoe, Clare, 431
Khari Edwards 2013, 488
Kings County
Supreme Court, 54
Surrogate's Court, 54
Kings County (NYC Borough of Brooklyn), 330
Kings County Conservative Party Campaign Committee, 488
Kingsborough Community College, 551
Konheim & Ketcham Inc, 291
Laurie Cumbo 2013, 488
Law Department
Brooklyn, 207
Legal Information for Families Today (LIFT), 434
Letitia James 2013, 488
Levin 2013, 488
Little Flower Children & Family Services, 259
Local 1814 ILA AFL-CIO Political Action and Education Fund, 489
Local 4 Action Fund, 489
Local 891 IUOE Political Education Committee, 489
Local 891 IUOE State Engineers Political Education Committee, 489
Logan, Ernest, 436
Long Island College Hospital School of Nursing, 556
Lotovsky For City Council 2013, 489
Lutheran Augustana Center for Extended Care and Rehabilitation, 436
Lutheran Medical Center, 437
Maisel For Council, 489
Marcus Attorneys, 440
Mark Treyger For Council, 489
Markowitz/Brooklyn, 489
Mateo 2013, 489
Medgar Evers College, 551
Mental Health, Office of
Brooklyn Children's Center, 228
Kingsboro Psychiatric Center, 228
Mercedes For Council, 490
Metropolitan Jewish Health System (FKA Cross, Jeannie H.), 444
NY Airport Service, 291
NYC Greenfield, 491
NYC Region 6, 582
NYC Region 8, 582
NYS Bar Assn, Mass Disaster Response Committee, 171
NYS Clinical Laboratory Association Inc, 93
NYS Grievance Committee, 171
NYS Office for People with Developmental Disabilities
Brooklyn Developmental Disabilities Services Office, 229
NYSTAR - Division of Science, Technology & Innovation
Ctr for Advanced Tech in Telecommunications at Polytech Univ, 85, 122
Nachman Caller Community First, 490
National Labor Relations Board
Region 29 - Brooklyn Area, 222
Neighbors For Kenneth Rice, 490
New York Aquarium, 280
New York City
Fire Department, NYC, 354
Library, Brooklyn Public, 356
New York City Boroughs
Brooklyn (Kings County), 359
New York City College of Technology, 552
New York Daily Challenge (The), 524
New York State Conservative Party, 371
New York State Council of Machinists PAC Fund, 491
New York State Higher Education - PAC, 491
New York State Working Families Party, 376
Nikki Lucas 2013, 491
Olanike Alabi 2013, 492
Otano 2013, 492
People For Jelani, 492
People For John C. Whitehead, 492
People For Ydanis, 492
Polytechnic University, 559
Pratt Center for Community Development, 193
Pratt Institute, 559
Prospect Park Alliance, 457
Public Employment Relations Board
New York City, 241
Radiac Environmental Services, 158
Re-Elect Mealy, 493
Recchia For New York, 493
Regina Powell 2013, 493
Reginald Boddie For Supreme Court, 493
Rhonda F. Joseph 2013, 493
SUNY Downstate Medical Center, 544
Sal 2013, 494
Sanitation Officers Association Volunteer Political Action COPE, 494
Santiago NYC 2013, 494
Santos 2013, 494
Sarah M. Gonzalez 2013, 494
Saundra Thomas 2013, 494
Sidique Wai For Public Advocate, 494
Simcha NY, 494
St Joseph's College, 561
Statewide Black & Puerto Rican/Latino Substance Abuse Task Force, 233
Sullivan For NYC, 495
Team Greenfield, 495
Transport Workers Union Local 100, 495
US Commerce Department
Williamsburg Business Center, 88, 196
US Defense Department
North Atlantic Division, 152
US Department of Veterans Affairs
Brooklyn Campus of the NY Harbor Healthcare System, 296
Cypress Hills National Cemetery, 295
US Federal Courts
Eastern District, 212
US DISTRICT COURT - NEW YORK (part of the Second Circuit), 212
US Justice Department
Brooklyn, 115, 213
Brooklyn Metropolitan Detention Center, 114
CCM New York, 114
Eastern District, 115, 213
New York City, 115
US Labor Department
Brooklyn, 297
US Treasury Department
Brooklyn Office, 267
SBSE-Taxpayer Education & Communication (TEC), 266
Tax Exempt & Government Entities Div (TEGE)-Northeast Area, 266
Unified Court System
2nd Judicial Department, 209
2nd Judicial District (Judicial Department 2), 209
Veterans' Affairs, Division of
Eastern Region, 294
Veterans' Service Organizations
Project TORCH, Veterans Health Care Center, 294
Victim Services, Office of, 6, 111, 252
VoteBhusan2013, 496
Weiss, Michael A., 473
Welfare Inspector General, Office of NYS, 253
Workers' Compensation Board
Brooklyn, 202, 221
Working Families Organization, 477
Working Families Party, 139
Wright 2013, 496
York Group Associates, 478

Brooklyn Heights

St Francis College, 561

Listings appear in alphabetical order by state, then city.

Brookville
Long Island University, 557

Brushton
Brushton-Moira CSD, 575

Buffalo
AAA Western and Central NY, 277
Acquard, Milissa, 377
Agriculture & Markets Department
Buffalo, 69
Attorney Grievance Committee
Judicial Dist 8, 208
Brown & Kelly, LLP, 90
Bryant & Stratton College-Buffalo Campus, 563
Buffalo
Civil & Criminal Courts, 62
Buffalo & Fort Erie Public Bridge Authority (Peace Bridge Authority), 96, 285
Buffalo Business First, 524
Buffalo Economic Renaissance Corporation, 502
Buffalo Educational Opportunity Center, 549
Buffalo News (The), 524
Buffalo Niagara Partnership, 502
Buffalo SD, 573
Buffalo Sabres, 277
Buffalo State College, 390, 545
Buffalo, City of, 342
Canisius College, 392, 553
Coalition for Economic Justice, 399
Connors LLP, 170
Convention Centers & Visitors Bureaus
Buffalo Niagara Convention & Visitors Bureau, 274
Drexelius, Jr., John R., 407
D'Youville College, 554
E-3 Communications, 408
EPIC-Every Person Influences Children Inc, 257
Education Department
Buffalo District Office, 121
Elections, State Board of
Erie, 131
Empire State Development Corporation, 7, 84, 97, 147, 188, 271
Environmental Conservation Department
Great Lakes Program, 148
Region 9, 148
Equal Employment Opportunity Commission
Buffalo Local, 196, 222
Erie Community College, 547
Erie County, 328
Family Court, 53
Supreme & County Court, 53
Surrogate's Court, 53
Erie County Industrial Development Agency, 505
Erie County Planning & Economic Development, 505
Health Department
Roswell Park Cancer Institute Corporation, 176
Western Regional Office, 176
Housing & Community Renewal, Division of
Finger Lakes, Western NY, Southern Tier, 187
Human Rights, State Division of
Buffalo, 194
Independent Health Association, Inc., 427
Insurance Fund (NYS)
Buffalo, 201, 219
International Institute of Buffalo, NY, Inc, 198
Kenmore-Tonawanda UFSD, 574
Labor Department
Western Region, 220
Law Department
Buffalo, 207
M&T Bank Corporation, 81
Masiello, Martucci, Calabrese a, 440
Medaille College, 557
Mental Health, Office of
Buffalo Psychiatric Center, 228
Michael T Kelly, Esq, 117
NYS Bar Assn, Civil Practice Law & Rules Committee, 217
NYS Bar Assn, Criminal Justice Section, 117
NYS Bar Assn, Law Youth & Citizenship Committee, 171
NYS Bar Assn, Public Utility Law Committee, 217
NYS Bar Assn, Task Force to Review Terrorism Legislation Cmte, 170
NYS Supreme Court, 171, 217
NYSTAR - Division of Science, Technology & Innovation
Center for Advanced Tech in Biomedical & Bioengineering, 84, 122
INSYTE Consulting (Western NY Technology Development Ctr), 85, 123
National Fuel Gas Distribution, 217
National Labor Relations Board
Region 3 - Buffalo Area, 222
New York State Dormitory Authority, 102, 124, 164, 178
New York State Gaming Commission
Western Region, 264
New York State Green Party, 374
New York State Liquor Authority (Division of Alcoholic Beverage Control), 4
Buffalo (Zone III), 83, 263
New York State Theatre Education Association, 281
Niagara Frontier Transportation Authority, 105, 287
Nicolson, Karen, 450
PricewaterhouseCoopers LLP, 171
Public Employment Relations Board
Buffalo, 241
R W Bronstein Corporation, 248
Richardson Management, 461
SUNY Buffalo Human Rights Center, 199
Small Business Administration
Buffalo, 88
State Department
Region 1 - Buffalo Office, 163
Transportation Department
Region 5, 284
Trocaire College, 562
US Commerce Department
Buffalo US Export Assistance Center, 89
US Defense Department
Buffalo District Office, 152
US Department of Agriculture
Buffalo Work Station, 71
US Department of Homeland Security (DHS)
Buffalo District Office, 167, 196
Buffalo Field Office, 166, 266
Buffalo, Port of, 72, 166, 167, 266
US Department of Veterans Affairs
Buffalo Regional Office, 296
Buffalo VA Medical Center, 296
US Department of the Interior
Theodore Roosevelt Inaugural National Historic Site, 276
US Federal Courts
Western District, 212
US Housing & Urban Development Department
Buffalo Area Office, 190
US Justice Department
Buffalo, 114, 115, 116, 213, 214
US Labor Department
Buffalo Area Office, 180, 223
Buffalo District Office, 223
US Railroad Retirement Board
Buffalo, 224
US Treasury Department
Western New York State Office, 267
Unified Court System
8th Judicial District (Judicial Department 4), 210
University at Buffalo, Research Institute on Addictions, 233
University at Buffalo, State University of New York, 545
Upstate Consultants, 471
Upstate Niagara Cooperative (FKA Upstate Farms Cooperative), 471
Upstate Niagara Cooperative Inc, 77
Veterans' Affairs, Division of
Western Region, 294
Villa Maria College of Buffalo, 562
WBEN (930 AM/FM), 534
WBLK (93.7 FM), WJYE (96.1 FM), 534
WDCX (99.5 FM), 534
WGRZ (33), 537
WHTT (104.1 FM), 534
WIVB-TV (39), 537
WKBW-TV (38), 537

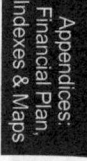

Listings appear in alphabetical order by state, then city.

WNED (43) Western NY Public Broadcasting, 537
WNED (94.5 FM), 534
WYRK (106.5 FM), WBUF (92.9 FM), 534
Workers' Compensation Board
Buffalo, 202, 221

Cairo
Cairo-Durham CSD, 576
Greene County Soil & Water Conservation District, 156

Caledonia
Caledonia-Mumford CSD, 577

Calverton
Gergela III, Joseph, 418
Long Island Farm Bureau, 75
US Department of Veterans Affairs
Calverton National Cemetery, 295

Cambria Heights
Bryan Block 2013, 479
Friends of Joe Marthone, 484

Cambridge
Cambridge CSD, 596

Camden
Camden CSD, 583

Camillus
West Genesee CSD, 584

Campbell
Campbell-Savona CSD, 591

Canaan
Berkshire Farm Center & Services for Youth, 116, 256
Berkshire UFSD, 571

Canajoharie
Canajoharie CSD, 579

Canandaigua
Canandaigua
Civil & Criminal Courts, 62
Canandaigua Area Chamber of Commerce, 503
Canandaigua City SD, 584
Canandaigua National Bank & Trust Co, 80
Convention Centers & Visitors Bureaus
Ontario County/Finger Lakes Visitors Connection, 275
Daily Messenger (The), 524
Elections, State Board of
Ontario, 134
Finger Lakes Community College, 547
Messenger Post Newspapers, 524
New York Wine & Grape Foundation, 77, 281
Ontario County, 333
Supreme, County, Family & Surrogate's Courts, 56
Ontario County Industrial Development Agency & Economic Development, 513
US Department of Agriculture
Canandaigua Work Station, 71
US Department of Veterans Affairs
Canandaigua VA Medical Center, 296

Canaseraga
Canaseraga CSD, 567

Canastota
Canastota CSD, 578
Canastota Chamber of Commerce, 503
Madison County Industrial Development Agency, 510

Candor
Candor CSD, 595
NY Farms!, 75

Canisteo
Canisteo-Greenwood CSD, 591

Canton
Canton CSD, 590
Canton Chamber of Commerce, 503
Elections, State Board of
Saint Lawrence, 135
North Country Savings Bank, 82
St Lawrence County, 336
Supreme, County, Family & Surrogate's Courts, 58
St Lawrence County Chamber of Commerce, 517
St Lawrence County Industrial Development Agency, 517
St Lawrence University, 561
St Lawrence-Lewis BOCES, 601
State University College of Technology at Canton, 546

Cape Vincent
Cape Vincent Chamber of Commerce, 503
Corrections & Community Supervision Department
Cape Vincent Correctional Facility, 109

Carle Place
Carle Place UFSD, 579

Carmel
Elections, State Board of
Putnam, 134
Putnam County, 334
Supreme, County & Family Courts, 57
Surrogate's Court, 57
Putnam County Economic Development Corporation, 514

Caroga Lake
Wheelerville UFSD, 575

Carthage
Carthage Area Chamber of Commerce, 503
Carthage CSD, 577

Castile
Parks, Recreation & Historic Preservation, NYS Office of
Genesee Region, 272

Castle Point
US Department of Veterans Affairs
Castle Point Campus of the VA Hudson Vly Healthcare System, 296

Castleton
Rensselaer-Columbia-Greene (Questar III) BOCES, 601
Schodack CSD, 588

Cato
Cato-Meridian CSD, 569

Catskill
Catskill CSD, 576
Daily Mail (The), 524
Elections, State Board of
Greene, 132
Greene County, 329
Supreme, County, Family & Surrogate's Courts, 54
Greene County Department of Planning & Economic Development, 507
Hudson Valley Newspapers Inc, 524

Cazenovia
Cazenovia Area Chamber of Commerce (Greater Cazenovia Area), 503
Cazenovia CSD, 578
Cazenovia College, 553

Cedarhurst
Law Office of Usher Fogel, 433

Center Moriches
Center Moriches UFSD, 591

Centereach
Middle Country CSD, 593

Central Islip
Central Islip UFSD, 592
Suffolk County
1ST DISTRICT COURT, Criminal Term, 61
Family Court, 59
US Justice Department
Central Islip, 115, 213

Central Square
Central Square CSD, 586

Central Valley
Monroe-Woodbury CSD, 585

Champlain
Northeastern Clinton CSD, 571
US Department of Agriculture

Listings appear in alphabetical order by state, then city.

Champlain Work Station, 71
US Department of Homeland Security (DHS)
Champlain, Port of, 72, 166, 167, 266
WCHP (760 AM), 534

Chappaqua
Chappaqua CSD, 597

Chateaugay
Chateaugay CSD, 575
Corrections & Community Supervision Department
Chateaugay Correctional Facility, 109

Chatham
Chatham CSD, 571

Chaumont
Lyme CSD, 577

Chautauqua
Convention Centers & Visitors Bureaus
Chautauqua County Visitors Bureau, 274

Chazy
Chazy Central RSD, 571

Cheektowaga
Automotive Technology & Energy Group of Western NY, 290
Cheektowaga CSD, 573
Cheektowaga Chamber of Commerce, 503
Cheektowaga, Town of, 343
Cheektowaga-Maryvale CSD, 574
Cleveland Hill UFSD, 573
US Treasury Department
Buffalo Territory, 267
Western New York Library Resources Council, 129

Cherry Valley
Cherry Valley-Springfield CSD, 586

Chesnut Ridge
Sunbridge College, 561

Chester
Chester UFSD, 585

Chestertown
North Warren CSD, 596
North Warren Chamber of Commerce, 512

Chittenango
Chittenango CSD, 578

Churchville
Churchville-Chili CSD, 578

Cicero
Cicero, Town of, 343
Greater Cicero Chamber of Commerce, 507

Cincinnatus
Cincinnatus CSD, 571

Clarence
Clarence CSD, 573
Clarence Chamber of Commerce, 504
Clarence Industrial Development Agency (Town of), 504
Clarence, Town of, 343

Claverack
Rural Water Association, 158

Clay
Clay, Town of, 344

Clayton
Clayton Chamber of Commerce, 504
Thousand Islands CSD, 577

Clifton Park
Amanus Consulting Group, 380
Army Aviation Association of America (AAAA), Empire Chapter, 298
Assn for Community Living, 382
Association for Community Living, 190, 231
Boltz, John J Consulting, 388
CP Rail System, 290
Clifton Park, Town of, 344
Coalition for Education Reform & Accountability, 399
Coalition of Fathers & Families NY, 257
Coalition of Fathers & Families NY, PAC, 215
DKI Engineering & Consulting USA, PC, Corporate World Headquarters, 291
Em, 411
Empire State Association of Assisted Living, 182
Empire State Petroleum Association Inc, 144
Fitzgerald, Gary J, 415
Iroquois Healthcare Alliance, 183
NY Propane Gas Association, 144
New York Long-Term Care Brokers Ltd, 204
Nurse Practitioner Association NYS (The), 185
Shenendehowa CSD, 589
Southern Saratoga County Chamber of Commerce, 516

Clifton Springs
Clifton Springs Area Chamber of Commerce, 504
Phelps-Clifton Springs CSD, 585

Clinton
Clinton CSD, 583
Clinton Chamber of Commerce Inc, 504
Hamilton College, 555

Clintonville
Ausable Valley CSD, 571

Clyde
Clyde Chamber of Commerce, 504
Clyde Industrial Development Corporation, 504
Clyde-Savannah CSD, 597

Clymer
Clymer CSD, 569

Cobleskill
Cobleskill-Richmondville CSD, 589
SUNY College of Agriculture & Technology at Cobleskill, 546
Schoharie County Industrial Development Agency, 516
Smith, Robert, 466

Cohoes
Cohoes
Civil, Criminal & Traffic Courts, 62
Cohoes City SD, 567
Cohoes Industrial Development Agency (City of), 504
NY Press Association, 144

Cold Spring
Haldane CSD, 587
The Putnam County News and Recorder, 528

Cold Spring Harbor
Cold Spring Harbor CSD, 592
Cold Spring Harbor Fish Hatchery & Aquarium, 278
Watson School of Biological Sciences at Cold Spring Harbor, 562

Collins
Corrections & Community Supervision Department
Collins Correctional Facility, 109

Colton
Colton-Pierrepont CSD, 590

Commack
Long Island Business Institute-Commack, 565
NYS Office for People with Developmental Disabilities
Long Island Developmental Disabilities Services Office, 230

Comstock
Corrections & Community Supervision Department
Great Meadow Correctional Facility, 109
Washington Correctional Facility, 110

Conesus
State Department
Region 7/8 - Western New York Office, 163

Congers
Office of Chief, Army Reserves, 300

Listings appear in alphabetical order by state, then city.

Conklin
Susquehanna Valley CSD, 568

Constable
US Department of Homeland Security (DHS)
Trout River, Port of, 73, 167

Cooperstown
Cooperstown CSD, 586
Cooperstown Chamber of Commerce, 504
Elections, State Board of
Otsego, 134
Farmer's Museum (The), 278
NY State Historical Association/Fenimore Art Museum, 279
New York Center for Agricultural Medicine & Health, Bassett He, 76
New York, Susquehanna & Western Railway Corporation, The, 292
Otsego County, 334
Family Court, 57
Supreme, County, & Surrogate's Courts, 57

Copenhagen
Copenhagen CSD, 577

Copiague
Copiague Chamber of Commerce, 504
Copiague UFSD, 592

Coram
US Department of the Interior
Coram Sub-District Office, 153

Corfu
Pembroke CSD, 575

Corinth
Corinth CSD, 588
Corinth Industrial Development Agency (Town of), 504

Corning
Convention Centers & Visitors Bureaus
Steuben County Conference & Visitors Bureau, 275
Corning
Civil & Criminal Courts, 62
Corning Area Chamber of Commerce, 504
Corning Community College, 547
Corning Leader (The), 524
Erwin Industrial Development Agency (Town of), 505
GateHouse Media, 524
Three Rivers Development Foundation Inc, 517
Tranter Jr. G. Thomas, 469

Cornwall on Hudson
Cornwall CSD, 585

Corona
Julissa 2013, 488

Cortland
Cortland
Civil & Criminal Courts, 62
Cortland County, 327
Supreme, County, Family & Surrogate's Courts, 52
Cortland County Chamber of Commerce, 504
Cortland Enlarged City SD, 571
Cortland Standard, 525
Cortland Standard Printing Co Inc, 525
Elections, State Board of
Cortland, 131
Farmedic Training Program, 74
NYS Grange, 75
SUNY at Cortland, Center for Environmental & Outdoor Education, 159
State University College at Cortland, 545
US Department of Agriculture
Western New York Office, 142
WKRT (920 AM), WIII (99.9 or 100.3 FM), 534

Cortlandt Manor
Cortlandt, Town of, 344

Coxsackie
Corrections & Community Supervision Department
Greene Correctional Facility, 109
Coxsackie Area Chamber of Commerce, 504
Coxsackie-Athens CSD, 576

Craryville
Taconic Hills CSD, 571

Croton-on-Hudson
Croton-Harmon UFSD, 597

Crown Point
Crown Point CSD, 574

Cuba
Cuba-Rushford CSD, 567

Cutchogue
Cutchogue-New Suffolk Chamber of Commerce, 504
Mattituck-Cutchogue UFSD, 593

Dannemora
Corrections & Community Supervision Department
Clinton Correctional Facility, 109
Saranac CSD, 571

Dansville
Dansville CSD, 577
Dansville Chamber of Commerce, 505

Darien Center
Darien Lake Theme Park Resort, 278

Davenport
Charlotte Valley CSD, 572

DeKalb Junction
Hermon-Dekalb CSD, 590

Deer Park
Deer Park UFSD, 592

Delanson
Duanesburg CSD, 589

Delhi
Delaware County, 328
Supreme, County, Family & Surrogate's Courts, 52
Delaware County Chamber of Commerce, 505
Delaware County Planning Department, 505
Delhi CSD, 572
Elections, State Board of
Delaware, 131
State University College of Technology at Delhi, 546

Delmar
Bethlehem CSD, 567
Bethlehem Chamber of Commerce, 502
Bethlehem Industrial Development Agency (Town of), 502
Bethlehem, Town of, 341
Golden, Ben, 419
HCA PAC, 486
NYS Magistrates Association, 217, 239
NYSARC Inc, 232
New York State Ophthalmological Society, 185
Ophthalmological Society (NYS), 452

Depew
Depew UFSD, 573
New York Pork Producers Coop, 76

Deposit
Deposit CSD, 568
Deposit Chamber of Commerce, 505

Deruyter
De Ruyter CSD, 578

Dewitt
Jamesville-Dewitt CSD, 584

Dexter
General Brown CSD, 577

Dix Hills
Five Towns College, 564
Half Hollow Hills CSD, 592
Mental Health, Office of
Sagamore Children's Psychiatric Center, 229

Dobbs Ferry
Children's Village (The), 231, 257

Listings appear in alphabetical order by state, then city.

Dobbs Ferry UFSD, 597
Greenburgh Eleven UFSD, 598
Greenburgh-North Castle UFSD, 598
Mercy College, 557

Dolgeville
Dolgeville CSD, 576

Dover Plains
Dover UFSD, 572
Dover-Wingdale Chamber of Commerce, 505

Downsville
Downsville CSD, 572

Dryden
Dryden CSD, 595
Tompkins Cortland Community College, 549

Dundee
Dundee CSD, 599

Dunkirk
Chautauqua County Chamber of Commerce, Dunkirk Branch, 503
Dunkirk
Civil & Criminal Courts, 62
Dunkirk City SD, 569
Lake Shore Savings, 81
Observer (The), 525
Observer Today, 525

East Amherst
Williamsville CSD, 574

East Aurora
Christ the King Seminary, 553
East Aurora Chamber of Commerce (Greater East Aurora), 505
East Aurora UFSD, 573
Hawayek, Jonathan F, 423
Hawk Creek Wildlife Center Inc, 157

East Bloomfield
East Bloomfield CSD, 584

East Elmhurst
US Department of Homeland Security (DHS)
Transportation Security Administration (TSA), 167

East Greenbush
East Greenbush CSD, 587
Luria, Robert S, 436

East Hampton
East Hampton Chamber of Commerce, 505
East Hampton UFSD, 592
East Hampton, Town of, 345
Springs UFSD, 594
The Independent News, 528

East Islip
East Islip Chamber of Commerce, 505

East Meadow
East Meadow Chamber of Commerce, 505

East Moriches
East Moriches UFSD, 592

East Northport
Commack UFSD, 592
East Northport Chamber of Commerce, 505

East Patchogue
South Country CSD, 594

East Quogue
East Quogue UFSD, 592

East Rochester
East Rochester UFSD, 578

East Rockaway
East Rockaway UFSD, 580

East Schodack
NYS Association of Fire Chiefs, 243

East Setauket
Entek Power Services, 144

East Syracuse
Associated Builders & Contractors, Construction Training Cen, 224
Central New York School Boards Association, 395
DeWitt, Town of, 344
East Syracuse-Minoa CSD, 584
Lefebvre, Steve, 434
Municipal Electric Utilities Association, 144
O'Brien & Gere Limited, 451
WSYR (17), 539
WVOA (103.9 FM), 536

East Williston
Michael Balboni, Esq., 444
Red Land Strategy, Inc., 460

Eastchester
Eastchester UFSD, 597
Eastchester, Town of, 345

Eden
Eden CSD, 573

Edinburg
Edinburg Common SD, 588

Edmeston
Edmeston CSD, 586

Elba
Elba CSD, 575

Eldred
Eldred CSD, 594

Elizabethtown
Adirondack Council Inc (The), 155, 377
Elections, State Board of
Essex, 132
Elizabethtown-Lewis CSD, 574
Essex County, 328
Supreme, County, Family & Surrogate's Courts, 53
Essex County Industrial Development Agency, 505

Ellenburg Depot
Northern Adirondack CSD, 571

Ellenville
Ellenville CSD, 595
Ellenville/Wawarsing Chamber of Commerce, 505

Ellicottville
Ellicottville CSD, 568
Ellicottville Chamber of Commerce, 505
US Department of Agriculture
Ellicottville Work Station, 71

Elma
Iroquois CSD, 573

Elmhurst
Crowley For Congress, 481

Elmira
Chemung County, 326
Family Court, 52
Supreme & County Courts, 52
Surrogate Court, 52
Chemung County Chamber of Commerce, 503
Chemung County Industrial Development Agency, 503
Corrections & Community Supervision Department
Elmira Correctional Facility, 109
Elections, State Board of
Chemung, 131
Elmira
Civil & Criminal Courts, 62
Elmira Business Institute, 564
Elmira City SD, 570
Elmira College, 555
Elmira, City of, 345
Gannett Co Inc, 525
Mental Health, Office of
Elmira Psychiatric Center, 228
Southern Tier Economic Growth Inc, 516
Star-Gazette, 525
US Department of Veterans Affairs
Woodlawn National Cemetery, 296
WETM (18), 537
WPGI (100.9 FM), WWLZ (820 AM), 534

Elmira Heights
Elmira Heights CSD, 570

Listings appear in alphabetical order by state, then city.

Elmont
Elmont UFSD, 580

Elmsford
Elmsford UFSD, 598
Radon Testing Corp of America Inc, 158, 186
Wiener, Judith R, 475
Wilder Balter Partners, Inc., 475

Endicott
Habitat for Humanity of New York State, 422
Insurance Fund (NYS)
Binghamton, 201, 219
Labor Department
Southern Tier, 220
Union-Endicott CSD, 568

Endwell
Union Local Development Corporation (Town of), 518
Union, Town of, 366

Evans Mill
LeRay, Town of, 349

Fabius
Fabius-Pompey CSD, 584

Fair Haven
Fair Haven Area Chamber of Commerce, 506

Fairport
Fairport CSD, 578
Monroe 1 BOCES, 600
Perinton, Town of, 362

Falconer
Falconer CSD, 570

Fallsburg
Corrections & Community Supervision Department
Sullivan Correctional Facility, 110
Fallsburg CSD, 594

Far Rockaway
Friends of Donovan Richards 2013, 483
Friends of Osina, 485
Peralta 2013, 492
Peralta For Senate, 492
Rockaway Development & Revitalization Corporation, 515
Sanders For Senate, 494

Farmingdale
Citizens Campaign for the Environment, 397
Farmingdale State College of Technology, 546
Farmingdale UFSD, 580
US Department of Veterans Affairs
Long Island National Cemetery, 295

Farmington
Farmington Chamber of Commerce, 506
Finger Lakes Racing Association, 278
Northeast Organic Farming Association of New York, 77

Farmingville
Brookhaven, Town of, 342
Town of Brookhaven Industrial Development Agency, 502

Fayetteville
Farmers' Market Federation of NY, 74
Fayetteville Chamber of Commerce, 506
Manlius, Town of, 350
The Greater Manlius Chamber of Commerce, 507

Ferndale
Convention Centers & Visitors Bureaus
Sullivan County Visitors Association, 275
Sullivan County Industrial Development Agency, 517

Fillmore
Fillmore CSD, 567

Findley Lake
Findley Lake Area Chamber of Commerce, 506

Fishers
Apple Association, Inc. (NY), 381
New York Apple Association Inc, 76

Fishers Island
Fishers Island UFSD, 592

Fishkill
Corrections & Community Supervision Department
Downstate Correctional Facility, 109
Fishkill, Town of, 345
New York State Gaming Commission
Hudson Valley Region, 264

Floral Park
Floral Park-Bellerose UFSD, 580
Friends of Harpreet, 484
New Yorkers For Affordable Housing, 491
Sewanhaka Central HS District, 581

Florida
Florida UFSD, 585

Flushing
CIDNY - Queens, 256
Evergreen For City Council, 482
Friends For Peter Koo, 483
Friends of John Liu, 484
Friends of Michael Simanowitz, 485
He Gin Lee Committee to Elect For Mayor, 486
International Union o, 487
Joint Industry Board of the Electrical Industry, 430
Long Island Business Institute-Flushing, 565
NYC Region 3, 582
New York City
Environmental Protection, Department of, NYC, 354
New York Mets, 281
Paul Graziano 2013, 492
Queens College, 552
Sasson For NYC, 494
Sunny Hahn For City Council, 495
Vaughn College of Aeronautics & Technology, 562
Vote Vallone 2013, 496

Fonda
Elections, State Board of
Montgomery, 133
Fonda-Fultonville CSD, 579
Montgomery County, 331
Supreme, County, Family & Surrogate's Courts, 55

Forest Hills
Bramson ORT College, 553
Elections, State Board of
Queens, 133
Local 1182 Political Action Fund, 488
Plaza College, 565
Re-Elect Koslowitz 2013, 493

Forestville
Forestville CSD, 570

Fort Ann
Fort Ann CSD, 596

Fort Covington
Salmon River CSD, 575

Fort Drum
US Defense Department
Fort Drum, 295

Fort Edward
Elections, State Board of
Washington, 136
Fort Edward Chamber of Commerce, 506
Fort Edward UFSD, 596
Washington County, 338
Supreme, County, Family & Surrogate's Courts, 60
Washington County Local Development Corporation, 518
Washington-Saratoga-Warren-Hamilton-Essex BOCES, 601

Fort Plain
Fort Plain CSD, 579

Frankfort
Frankfort-Schuyler CSD, 576

Listings appear in alphabetical order by state, then city.

Franklin
Franklin CSD, 572

Franklin Square
Franklin Square Chamber of Commerce, 506
Franklin Square UFSD, 580

Franklinville
Franklinville CSD, 568

Fredonia
Fredonia CSD, 570
Fredonia Chamber of Commerce, 506
SUNY Fredonia, 468
State University of New York, Fredonia, 545

Freeport
Freeport UFSD, 580
Freeport, Village of, 345

Freeville
George Junior Republic UFSD, 595

Fresh Meadows
Blishteyn For NYC, 479
Thomson Strategies, LLC, 469

Frewsburg
Frewsburg CSD, 570

Friendship
Friendship CSD, 568

Fulton
Fulton
Civil & Criminal Courts, 62
Fulton City SD, 586

Gainesville
Letchworth CSD, 599

Galway
Galway CSD, 588

Garden City
Adelphi NY Statewide Breast Cancer Hotline & Support Program, 181
Adelphi University, 552
American Academy of Pediatrics District II (NYS), 380
Automobile Club of New York, 277, 290
Corlett, John A (FKA Marta Genovese), 402
Cullen & Dykman LLP, 225, 238
Education Department
Garden City District Office, 121
Garden City Chamber of Commerce, 506
Garden City UFSD, 580
Garden City, Village of, 345
Gotham Government Relations, 420
Law Offices of Frank G. D'Angelo & Associates, 216
Meyer Suozzi English & Klein, PC, 216
NYS Bar Assn, Family Law Section, 218
NYS Bar Assn, General Practice Section, 216
NYS Bar Assn, Resolutions Committee, 216
Nassau BOCES, 600
Nassau Community College, 447, 548
New York State Gaming Commission
Long Island Region, 264
New York State Radiological Society Inc, 185
Ohrenstein & Brown, LLP, 452
Shelter Rock Strategies, LLC, 465
US Defense Department
1st Marine Corps District, 295
Ungar, Robert A Associates Inc, 470
Vincent F Stempel, Jr Esq, 218

Garden City Park
Republican Majority For Choice NF PAC, 493

Garnerville
Haverstraw, Town of, 347
Haverstraw-Stony Point CSD, 588
North Rockland CSD, 588

Garrison
Coalition of Animal Care Societies (The), 257
Coalition of New York State Career Schools (The), 126
Garrison UFSD, 587
Zaleski, Terence M, 478

Gates
Gates, Town of, 346

Geneseo
Elections, State Board of
Livingston, 133
Geneseo CSD, 578
Livingston County, 331
Supreme, County, Family & Surrogate's Courts, 54
Livingston County Chamber of Commerce, 510
Livingston County Economic Development Office & Indu, 510
Milroy, James, 444
State University College at Geneseo, 545

Geneva
Finger Lakes Printing Co, 525
Finger Lakes Times, 525
Geneva
Civil & Criminal Courts, 63
Geneva Area Chamber of Commerce, 506
Geneva City SD, 585
Geneva Industrial Development Agency (City of), 506
Hobart & William Smith Colleges, 556
Marion S Whelan School of Practical Nursing, 183
NYS Horticultural Society, 75
US Department of Agriculture
Plant Genetic Resources & Grape Genetic Research Units, 71

Germantown
Germantown CSD, 571

Getzville
Bryant & Stratton College-Amherst Campus, 563

Gilbertsville
Gilbertsville-Mount Upton CSD, 587

Gilboa
Gilboa-Conesville CSD, 589

Glen Cove
Glen Cove
Civil & Criminal Courts, 63
Glen Cove Chamber of Commerce, 506
Glen Cove City SD, 580
Glen Cove, City of, 346
New York State Association of PBA's PAC, 491
Webb Institute, 562

Glendale
Elizabeth Crowley 2013, 482
New York & Atlantic Railway (NYA), 292

Glenford
Willow Mixed Media Inc, 282

Glenmont
Ketzer, Bill, 432
NYS Association of Veterinary Technicians Inc, 75
Professional Insurance Agents of New York State, 204

Glens Falls
Adirondack Regional Chambers of Commerce, 501
Behan Communications, Inc., 386
Finch Paper LLC, 414
FitzGerald Morris et al, 215
Glens Falls
Civil & Criminal Courts, 63
Glens Falls City SD, 596
Glens Falls Common SD, 596
Lee Enterprises Inc, 525
NYS Bar Assn, Cmte on the Jury System, 215
Post-Star (The), 525
Warren & Washington Industrial Development Agency, 518
Warren County Economic Development Corporation, 518

Glenville
Burnt Hills-Ballston Lake CSD, 588
Glenville, Town of, 346

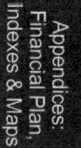

Appendices: Financial Plan, Indexes & Maps

Listings appear in alphabetical order by state, then city.

Gloversville
Fulton County Reg Chamber of Commerce & Ind, 506
Gloversville
Civil & Criminal Courts, 63
Gloversville Enlarged SD, 575
Leader-Herald (The), 525
Miller, Craig J., 444
William B Collins Co, 525

Goshen
Dupee & Monroe, PC, 203
Elections, State Board of
Orange, 134
Focus Media Group, Inc., 415
Goshen CSD, 585
Goshen Chamber of Commerce, 507
Orange County, 333
Supreme, County & Family Courts, 56
Surrogate's Court, 57
Orange County Partnership, 513
Orange-Ulster BOCES, 600

Gouverneur
Corrections & Community Supervision Department
Gouverneur Correctional Facility, 109
Gouverneur CSD, 590
Gouverneur Chamber of Commerce, 507

Gowanda
Corrections & Community Supervision Department
Gowanda Correctional Facility, 109
Gowanda Area Chamber of Commerce, 507
Gowanda CSD, 569

Grahamsville
Tri-Valley CSD, 594

Grand Island
Grand Island CSD, 573
Grand Island Chamber of Commerce, 507
Grand Island, Town of, 346

Granville
Granville CSD, 596
Granville Chamber of Commerce, 507

Great Neck
Elayne E Greenberg, MS, Esq, 215
Great Neck Chamber of Commerce, 507
Great Neck UFSD, 580
Law Offices of Stanley N Lupkin, 117
NYS Bar Assn, Alternative Dispute Resolution Cmte, 215
Nassau County
3rd District Court, 61
Soft Drink and Brewery Workers Political Action Committee, 494
Theatrical Teamsters Local 817 PAC Fund, 495

Greece
Greece, Town of, 346

Green Island
Green Island Industrial Development Agency (Village of), 507
Green Island UFSD, 567

Greenburgh
Greenburgh, Town of, 346

Greene
Greene CSD, 570

Greenlawn
Elwood UFSD, 592
Harborfields CSD, 592

Greenport
Greenport UFSD, 592
US Department of Homeland Security (DHS)
Plum Island Animal Disease Center, 167

Greenvale
Greenvale Chamber of Commerce, 508

Greenville
Greenville CSD, 576

Greenwich
Greenwich CSD, 596
Greenwich Chamber of Commerce (Greater Greenwich), 508

Greenwood Lake
Greenwood Lake Chamber of Commerce, 508
Greenwood Lake UFSD, 585

Groton
Groton CSD, 595

Guilderland
Guilderland CSD, 567
Guilderland Chamber of Commerce, 508
Guilderland Industrial Development Agency (Town of), 508
Guilderland, Town of, 347
Library Assn (NY), 435
New York Library Association (The), 127
New York State Community Action Association, 192, 260
WYPX DT-50, 537

Hague
Hague on Lake George Chamber of Commerce, 508

Hamburg
Buffalo Trotting Association Inc, 277
Frontier CSD, 573
Hamburg CSD, 573
Hamburg Chamber of Commerce, 508
Hamburg Industrial Development Agency, 508
Hamburg, Town of, 347
Hilbert College, 556
Hopevale UFSD at Hamburg, 573
Independent Oil & Gas Association of New York, 144

Hamilton
Colgate University, 554
Colgate University, Department of Geology, 156
Exhibition Alliance Inc (The), 278
Hamilton CSD, 578
Southern Madison County Chamber of Commerce, 516

Hammond
Black Lake Chamber of Commerce, 502
Hammond CSD, 590

Hammondsport
Hammondsport CSD, 591
Hammondsport Chamber of Commerce, 508

Hampton Bays
Hampton Bays Chamber of Commerce, 508
Hampton Bays UFSD, 592

Hancock
Hancock Area Chamber of Commerce, 508
Hancock CSD, 572

Hannibal
Hannibal CSD, 586

Happauge
Agriculture & Markets Department
Hauppauge, 70

Harpursville
Harpursville CSD, 568

Harrison
Friends of Mike Gianaris, 485
Harrison CSD, 598
Harrison, Town/Village of, 347

Harrisville
Harrisville CSD, 577

Hartford
Hartford CSD, 596

Hartsdale
Greenburgh 7 CSD, 598

Hastings-on-Hudson
Greenburgh-Graham UFSD, 598
Hastings-On-Hudson UFSD, 598
Hastings-on-Hudson Chamber of Commerce, 508

Hauppauge
Attorney Grievance Committee
Judicial Dist 10, 208

Listings appear in alphabetical order by state, then city.

Convention Centers & Visitors Bureaus
Long Island Convention & Visitors Bureau & Sports Commission, 274
Durrani, Waqas, 408
Education Department
Hauppauge District Office, 121
Hauppauge UFSD, 592
Human Rights, State Division of
Suffolk County, 195
Law Department
Suffolk, 208
Long Island Contractors Association, Inc., 436
Northern Metropolitan Hospital Assn, 450
Oil Heat Institute of Long Island, 145
Real Property Tax Services, Office of
Long Island Satellite Office, 235, 264
Research, Information & Policy Development
Long Island Satellite Office, 246
Ryan, Desmond, 462
State Department
Region 12/13 - Long Island Office, 163
Suffolk County
4th District Court, 61
Suffolk Regional Off-Track Betting Corporation, 106, 274
Transportation Department
Region 10, 284
Workers' Compensation Board
Long Island, 202, 221

Hawthorne
Hawthorne-Cedar Knolls UFSD, 598
National Academy of Forensic Engineers, 217

Hector
US Department of Agriculture
Finger Lakes National Forest, 153

Hempstead
Education & Assistance Corp Inc, 258
Education & Assistance Corporation Inc, 117
Hempstead Industrial Development Agency (Town of), 508
Hempstead UFSD, 580
Hempstead, Town of, 347
Hempstead, Village of, 347
Hofstra University, 426, 556
Hofstra University, School of Law, 117, 157, 191
Human Rights, State Division of
Nassau County, 194
Long Island Educational Opportunity Center, 549
Nassau County
1st, 2nd & 4th District Courts, 61
New York Jets, 280

Henderson Harbor
Henderson Harbor Area Chamber of Commerce, 508

Henrietta
Henrietta, Town of, 347
Rush-Henrietta CSD, 579

Herkimer
Elections, State Board of
Herkimer, 132
GateHouse Media Inc., 525
Herkimer CSD, 576
Herkimer County, 330
Family Court, 54
Supreme, County & Surrogate's Courts, 54
Herkimer County Chamber of Commerce, 508
Herkimer County Community College, 547
Herkimer County Industrial Development Agency, 508
Herkimer-Fulton-Hamilton-Otsego BOCES, 600
Telegram (The), 525

Heuvelton
Heuvelton CSD, 590

Hicksville
Hicksville Chamber of Commerce, 508
Hicksville UFSD, 580
Labor Department
Long Island Region, 220
Veterans' Service Organizations
Hicksville Counseling Center, Veterans' Resource Center, 294

Highland
Highland CSD, 595
New York State Bridge Authority, 101, 287
Southern Ulster County Chamber of Commerce, 516

Highland Falls
Highland Falls CSD, 585

Hillburn
Ramapo CSD (Suffern), 588

Hillcrest
Lancman 2013, 488

Hilton
Hilton CSD, 579

Hinsdale
Hinsdale CSD, 569

Holbrook
Holbrook Chamber of Commerce, The, 508
Sachem CSD, 593

Holland
Holland CSD, 573

Holland Patent
Holland Patent CSD, 583

Holley
Holley CSD, 586

Holtsville
Farmingville/Holtsville Chamber of Commerce, 506
Stony Brook Drinking Driver Program LLC, 118
US Department of Homeland Security (DHS)
Long Island Field Office, 167, 196
US Treasury Department
Brookhaven Campus Service Center, 267

Homer
Homer CSD, 571

Honeoye
Honeoye CSD, 585

Honeoye Falls
Honeoye Falls-Lima CSD, 579

Hoosick Falls
Hoosick Falls CSD, 587

Hopewell Junction
East Fishkill, Town of, 344

Hornell
ALSTOM Transportation Inc, 290
Evening Tribune (The), 526
GateHouse Media Inc., 526
Hornell
Civil & Criminal Courts, 63
Hornell Area Chamber of Commerce/Hornell Indus, 509
Hornell City SD, 591
Transportation Department
Region 6, 284
WKPQ (105.3 FM), 534

Horseheads
Horseheads CSD, 570
WENY (36), 538
WMTT (94.7 FM), 534

Houghton
Houghton College, 556

Howard Beach
Plumbers Local Union No. 1 NYC - Political Action Committee, 493

Howes Cave
Schoharie County Chamber of Commerce, 516

Hudson
Columbia County, 327
Supreme, County, Family & Surrogate's Courts, 52

Appendices: Financial Plan, Indexes & Maps

Listings appear in alphabetical order by state, then city.

Columbia County Chamber of Commerce, 504
Columbia Hudson Partnership, 504
Columbia-Greene Community College, 547
Corrections & Community Supervision Department
Hudson Correctional Facility, 109
Elections, State Board of
Columbia, 131
Hudson
City Court, 63
Hudson City SD, 571
Johnson Newspaper Corporation, 526
Register-Star, 526

Hudson Falls
Hudson Falls CSD, 596

Hunter
Hunter Chamber of Commerce (Town of), 509
Hunter Mountain Ski Bowl, 279

Huntington
Huntington Township Chamber of Commerce, 509
Huntington, Town of, 347
Seminary of the Immaculate Conception, 560

Huntington Station
Huntington UFSD, 592
Mothers Against Drunk Driving (MADD) of NYS, 117
South Huntington UFSD, 594
Suffolk County
3rd District Court, 61
Western Suffolk BOCES, 601

Hurley
Adirondack/Pine Hill/NY Trailways, 277

Hyde Park
Culinary Institute of America, 278, 554
Hyde Park CSD, 572
Hyde Park Chamber of Commerce, 509
Hyde Park, Town of, 348
National Archives & Records Administration
Franklin D Roosevelt Presidential Library & Museum, 125, 275
US Department of the Interior
Roosevelt-Vanderbilt National Historic Sites, 276

Ilion
Ilion CSD, 576
New York State Conservation Council, 158

Indian Lake
Blue Mountain Lake Association, 502
Hamilton County
County, Family & Surrogate's Courts, 54
Indian Lake CSD, 576
Indian Lake Chamber of Commerce, 509

Inlet
Inlet Information Office, 509

Inwood
Sobol, Peter, 466

Irving
Seneca Nation of Indians, 166, 465

Irvington
Abbott UFSD, 597
Arthur J Finkelstein & Associates Inc, 137
Elissa D Hecker, Esq, 278
Irvington UFSD, 598
Irvington-on-Hudson Chamber of Commerce, 509
NYS Bar Assn, Entertainment, Arts & Sports Law Section, 278

Island Park
Island Park UFSD, 580

Islandia
Bracken Margolin Besunder LLP, 214
Harvey B Besunder PC, 216
NYS Bar Assn, Fiduciary Appointments Cmte, 216
NYS Bar Assn, Tort System Cmte, 214

Islip
Islip Chamber of Commerce, 509
Islip Economic Development Division & Industrial Devel, 509
Islip Industrial Development Agency (Town of), 509
Islip UFSD, 592
Islip, Town of, 348

Islip Terrace
East Islip UFSD, 592

Ithaca
College of Agriculture & Life Sciences at Cornell University, 544
College of Human Ecology at Cornell University, 544
College of Veterinary Medicine at Cornell University, 544
Community & Regional Development Institute (CaRDI), 73
Convention Centers & Visitors Bureaus
Ithaca/Tompkins County Convention & Visitors Bureau, 274
Cornell Cooperative Extension, College of Hum, 182
Cornell Cooperative Extension, College of Human Ecology, Nu, 257
Cornell Cooperative Extension, Community & Economic Vitality Program, 191
Cornell Cooperative Extension, Environment & Natural Resource, 156
Cornell Cooperative Extension, Pesticide Management Education Program, 73
Cornell Law School, Legal Information Institute, 215
Cornell University, 126, 554
Cornell University Atkinson Center for a Sustainable Future, 156
Cornell University, Department of Applied Economics & Management, 74
Cornell University, Economics Department, 80, 91
Cornell University, FarmNet Program, 74
Cornell University, Institute on Conflict Resolution, 225
Cornell University, PRO-DAIRY Program, 74
Cornell University, Rural Schools Association of NYS, 126
Cornell University, School of Industrial & Labor Relations, 126, 198, 225, 243
Elections, State Board of
Tompkins, 136
Gannett Co Inc, 526
Ithaca
Civil & Criminal Courts, 63
Ithaca City SD, 595
Ithaca College, 556
Ithaca Journal (The), 526
Ithaca, City of, 348
Ithaca, Town of, 348
NYS Association for Food Protection, 75
NYS Bar Assn, Unlawful Practice of Law Cmte, 216
NYS Cheese Manufacturers Association, Department of Food Science, 75
NYS Water Resources Institute of Cornell University, 157
NYSTAR - Division of Science, Technology & Innovation
Center for Advanced Technology in Life Science Enterprise, 84, 122
National Economic Research Associates, 291
New York Agriculture in the Classroom, 76
New York Holstein Association, 76
New York Seed Improvement Project, Cornell Univ, 76
New York State Citizens' Coalition for Children Inc, 260
Outreach & Extension, 182
Prisoners' Legal Services of New York, 218
Schlather, Geldenhuys, Stumbar & Salk, 216
School of Industrial & Labor Relations at Cornell University (, 544
Tompkins County, 338
Supreme, County, Family & Surrogate's Courts, 59
Tompkins County Area Development, 517
Tompkins County Chamber of Commerce, 517
Tompkins Financial Corporation, 82
Tompkins-Seneca-Tioga BOCES, 601
True, Walsh & Sokoni, LLP, 186
US Department of Agriculture

Listings appear in alphabetical order by state, then city.

Cornell Cooperative Extension Service, 72
Robert W Holley Center for Agriculture & Health, 71
US Department of the Interior
Ithaca Sub-District Office, 153
Unified Court System
6th Judicial District (Judicial Department 3), 209
WHCU (870 AM), 535

Jackson Heights
British Airways PLC, 290
Dromm For NYC, 482
Friends of Alfonso Quiroz, 483
Friends of Dorothy Phelan, 483
Lesbian & Gay Democratic Club of Queens, 488
New Visions Democratic Club, 490
People For Pu-Folkes, 492
Queens Chamber of Commerce, 459
Queens Chamber of Commerce (Borough of), 514
United Spinal Association, 300

Jamaica
Civil Court, NYC
Queens County, 49
Clifton Stanley Diaz For NYC Council, 480
Committee to Elect Charles A. Bilal 2010, 480
Committee to Elect Stephen S. Jones to City Council, 481
David Kayode 2013, 481
Family Court, NYC
Queens County, 50
Federal Maritime Commission
New York Area Office, 288
Filipino American Human Services Inc (FAHSI), 198, 258
Friends of Breina Payne, 483
Friends of Martha Taylor, 485
Goode, Christian, 419
Greater Jamaica Development Corporation, 507
Health Department
New York State Veterans' Home at St Albans, 175, 293
Jamaica Chamber of Commerce, 509
MTA Long Island Rail Road, 99, 286
NYC Citywide Alternative HS District & Programs, 582
New York City
Library, Queens Borough Public, 356
New York Racing Association, 281
Port Authority Police DEA NY PAC, 493
Powell 2013, 493
Queens County
Supreme & Surrogate's Courts, 57
Queens Educational Opportunity Center, 549
US Department of Agriculture
JFK International Airport Inspection Station, 71
SC Inspection Division-Jamaica Office, 71
US Department of Health & Human Services
New York Quarantine Station, 179, 254
Northeast Region, 179, 255
Northeast Regional Laboratory, 179
US Department of Homeland Security (DHS)
JFK International Airport Area Office, 72, 166
US Transportation Department
Federal Aviation Administration-Eastern Region, 289
Hazardous Material, 289
Unified Court System
11th Judicial District (Judicial Department 2), 210
Win With Winslow, 496
Workers' Compensation Board
Queens, 202, 221
York College, 552

Jamaica Avenue
Marthone For City Council, 489

Jamaica, Queens
Friends of David Kayode For Council, 483

Jamestown
Chautauqua County Chamber of Commerce, 503
Chautauqua County Industrial Development Agency, 503
Jamestown
Civil & Criminal Courts, 63
Jamestown Business College, 564
Jamestown City SD, 570
Jamestown Community College, 548
Jamestown, City of, 349
Post-Journal, The, 526
Southwestern CSD at Jamestown, 570
WKZA (106.9 FM), 535

Jamesville
Parks, Recreation & Historic Preservation, NYS Office of
Central Region, 271

Jasper
Jasper-Troupsburg CSD, 591

Jefferson
Jefferson CSD, 589

Jeffersonville
Jeffersonville Area Chamber of Commerce, The, 509
Sullivan West CSD, 594

Jericho
Jericho UFSD, 580

Johnson City
Davis College, 555
Johnson City CSD, 568
US Department of Homeland Security (DHS)
Binghamton Airport, 72
Binghamton, Port of, 167
WBNG-TV (7), 537

Johnstown
Corrections & Community Supervision Department
Hale Creek ASACTC, 109
Elections, State Board of
Fulton, 132
Fulton County, 329
Supreme, County, Family & Surrogate's Courts, 53
Fulton County Economic Development Corporation, 506
Fulton County Industrial Development Agency, 506
Fulton-Montgomery Community College, 547
Greater Johnstown SD, 575
Hamilton-Fulton-Montgomery BOCES, 600
Johnstown
Civil & Criminal Courts, 63

Jordan
Jordan-Elbridge CSD, 584

Katonah
Katonah Chamber of Commerce, 509
Katonah-Lewisboro UFSD, 598

Keene Valley
Keene CSD, 574

Kendall
Kendall CSD, 586

Kenmore
Kenmore-Town of Tonawanda Chamber of Commerce, 509
Metro/Colvin Realty Inc, 248
Metro/Horohoe-Leimbach, 248
Tonawanda, Town of, 365

Keuka Park
Keuka College, 556

Kew Gardens
CIDNY - Queens, 197
Criminal Court, NYC
Queens County, 49
New York City Boroughs
Queens (Queens County), 359
Queens County (NYC Borough of Queens), 334
Torodash For Truth, 495

Kew Gardens Hill
Grodenchik For Queens 2013, 486

Kinderhook
US Department of the Interior

Listings appear in alphabetical order by state, then city.

Martin Van Buren National Historic Site, 276

Kings Park
Island Public Affairs, 428
Kings Park CSD, 592
Kings Park Chamber of Commerce, 509

Kings Point
US Merchant Marine Academy, 566
US Transportation Department
US Merchant Marine Academy, 125, 290

Kingston
Daily Freeman, 526
Elections, State Board of
Ulster, 136
Hudson River Cruises, 279
Journal Register Company, 526
Kingston
City Court, 63
Kingston City SD, 595
Kingston, City of, 349
State Department
Region 4 - Kingston Office, 163
Ulster County, 338
Family Court, 60
Supreme & County Courts, 60
Surrogate's Court, 60
Ulster County Chamber of Commerce, 518
Ulster County Development Corporation/Ulste, 518
Ulster Savings Bank, 82

Kirkville
J Strategies, Inc., 427

La Fargeville
La Fargeville CSD, 577

Lackawanna
Lackawanna
Civil & Criminal Courts, 63
Lackawanna Area Chamber of Commerce, 509
Lackawanna City SD, 574

Lafayette
LaFayette CSD, 584

Lake George
Elections, State Board of
Warren, 136
Great Escape Theme Park LLC (The), 278
Lake George CSD, 596
Lake George Park Commission, 98, 151
Lake George Regional Chamber of Commerce, 509
State Department
Region 10 - Northern New York Office, 163
Warren County, 338
Supreme, County, Family & Surrogate's Courts, 60

Lake Luzerne
Hadley-Luzerne CSD, 596
Lake Luzerne Chamber of Commerce, 509

Lake Placid
Convention Centers & Visitors Bureaus
Lake Placid/Essex County Convention & Visitors Bureau, 274
Lake Placid CSD, 574
Lake Placid Chamber of Commerce, 509
NYS Outdoor Guides Association, 280
New York State Olympic Regional Development Authority, 104, 273

Lake Pleasant
Elections, State Board of
Hamilton, 132
Hamilton County, 330

Lake Success
Astoria Bank, 80
Island Peer Review Organization, Inc., 428

Lancaster
Ecology & Environment Inc, 156
Lancaster Area Chamber of Commerce, 510
Lancaster CSD, 574
Lancaster Industrial Development Agency (Town of), 510
Lancaster, Town of, 349

Lansing
Lansing CSD, 595

Larchmont
Alvin D Lurie PC, 268
NYS Bar Assn, Pension Simplification Cmte, 268

Latham
Allinger, Stephen (FKA Nelson, Debra), 379
American Cancer Society, Inc., 380
American Cancer Society-Capital NY Region, 181
American City Business Journals, 523
Business Review, 532
Colonie Chamber of Commerce, 504
Fiscal Policy Institute, 170, 268
Fitzpatrick, Christine M, 415
Foundation for Opportunity in Education (The), 416
LeadingAge New York, 183
Military & Naval Affairs, Division of, 10, 293
NY Housing Association Inc, 191
NY Physical Therapy Association, 184
NYS Association of Electrical Contractors, 92
NYS Corps Collaboration, 259
NYS Public High School Athletic Association, 127
NYS Turfgrass Association, 75, 280
New York State Nurses Association, 226
New York State Nurses Association Political Action Committee, 491
New York State School Boards Association, 128
New York State United Teachers/AFT, AFL-CIO, 243
New York State United Teachers/AFT, NEA, AFL-CIO, 128
North Colonie CSD, 567
Nurses Association (NYS), 450
Plug Power Inc, 145
Reenergy Holdings LLC, 460
School Administrators Association of NYS, 128, 464
School Boards Assn (NYS), 464
Spectra Environmental Group Inc, 159
TD Bank N.A., 82
The Business Review, 523
Trooper Foundation-State of New York Inc, 118, 244
US Department of Homeland Security (DHS)
Albany Field Office, 167
Albany Sub Office, 196
United University Professions, 129
WPYX (106.5 FM), WRVE (99.5 FM), 535
WROW (590 AM), 535

Laurel
George J. Hochbrueckner & Associates, Inc., 418

Laurelton
Flowers For NYC, 483
Friends of Marie Adam-Ovide For Council 31, 484
Jacques Leandre For New York, 487

Laurens
Laurens CSD, 587

Lawrence
Governmental Insight LTD, 420
Lawrence UFSD, 580

Le Roy
Le Roy CSD, 575

LeRoy
Genesee-Livingston-Steuben-Wyoming BOCES, 600

Leeds
Greene County Tourism Promotion, 507

Levittown
Island Trees UFSD, 580
Levittown UFSD, 580

Lewiston
Niagara Falls Bridge Commission, 105, 287

Liberty
Liberty CSD, 594

Listings appear in alphabetical order by state, then city.

Sullivan BOCES, 601

Lima
New York Forest Owners Association Inc, 158

Lindenhurst
Babylon, Town of, 341
Lindenhurst Chamber of Commerce, 510
Lindenhurst UFSD, 593
Lindenhurst, Village of, 349
Suffolk County
2nd District Court, 61

Linwood
NYS Agricultural Society, 75

Lisbon
Lisbon CSD, 590

Little Falls
GateHouse Media Inc., 526
Little Falls
Civil & Criminal Courts, 63
Little Falls City SD, 576
NYS Association for Health, Physical Education, Recreation & Dance, 127
Times (The), 526

Little Neck
Duane For New York, 482
US Labor Department
Queens Area Office, 223

Little Valley
Cattaraugus County, 326
Supreme, County & Surrogate's Courts, 51
Cattaraugus-Little Valley CSD, 568
Elections, State Board of
Cattaraugus, 130

Liverpool
Bryant & Stratton College-Syracuse North Campus, 564
Insurance Fund (NYS)
Syracuse, 201, 219
Liverpool CSD, 584
Liverpool Chamber of Commerce (Greater Liverpool), 510
NYSTAR - Division of Science, Technology & Innovation
Central New York Technology Development Organization, 85, 123
Northeast Equipment Dealers Association Inc, 94
Salina, Town of, 364

Livingston Manor
Livingston Manor CSD, 594

Livonia
Livonia CSD, 578

Loch Sheldrake
Sullivan County Community College, 548

Lockport
Elections, State Board of
Niagara, 133
Greater Niagara Newspapers, 526
Lockport
Civil & Criminal Courts, 63
Lockport City SD, 582
Lockport Industrial Development Agency (Town of), 510
Lockport Union-Sun & Journal, 526
Lockport, City of, 349
Lockport, Town of, 349
Niagara County, 332
County, Family & Surrogate's Courts, 56
Starpoint CSD, 583

Locust Valley
Locust Valley CSD, 580
Locust Valley Chamber of Commerce, 510

London
Coller Capital Limited and it's Affiliate Coller Capital, Inc., 400

Long Beach
Lancer Insurance Co/Lancer Compliance Services, 225
Long Beach
Civil & Criminal Courts, 64
Long Beach Chamber of Commerce, 510
Long Beach City SD, 580
Long Beach, City of, 350

Long Island
Long Island Council of Dedicated Merchants Chamber of Commerce, 510

Long Island City
Asbestos Workers Local 12 Political Action Committee, 479
Bricklayers & Allied Craftworkers Local 1 PAC, 479
Corrections & Community Supervision Department
Queensboro Correctional Facility, 110
Education Department
Queens District Office, 122
Environmental Conservation Department
Region 2, 148
Fortune Society (The), 117
Friends of Randy Credico, 485
IUOE Local 15 Political Action Fund, 487
LaGuardia Community College, 551
MetLife, 204
Modutank Inc, 157
NYC Region 4, 582
New York City
Design & Construction, Dept of, NYC, 353
New York City School Construction Authority, 100, 123
P.S. 1 Contemporary Art Center, 453
Queens Gazette, 527
SMWIA Political Action League Local 137, 494
School of Law at Queens College, 552
Steamfitters Local 638 PAC, 494
Teamsters Local 813 PAC, 495
Tile, Marble & Terrazzo BAC Union Local 7 PAC Fund, 495
Transportation Department
Region 11, 284

Long Lake
Long Lake CSD, 576
New York State Snowmobile Association, 281

Loudonville
Brescia, Richard, 389
Siena College, 465, 560

Lowville
Elections, State Board of
Lewis, 132
Lewis County, 330
Supreme, County, Family & Surrogate's Courts, 54
Lewis County Chamber of Commerce, 510
Lewis County Industrial Development Agency, 510
Lowville Academy & CSD, 577
NYS Weights & Measures Association, 76

Lynbrook
Disabled American Veterans, Department of New York, 298
Lynbrook Chamber of Commerce, 510
Lynbrook UFSD, 581

Lyndonville
Lyndonville CSD, 586

Lyons
Elections, State Board of
Wayne, 136
Lyons CSD, 597
Wayne County, 339
Supreme, County, Family & Surrogate's Courts, 60
Wayne County Industrial Development Agency & Economic Development, 519

Madison
Madison CSD, 578

Madrid
Madrid-Waddington CSD, 590

Mahopac
Carmel, Town of, 343
JLO Consultant, Inc., 429
Mahopac CSD, 587
The Greater Mahopac-Carmel Chamber of Commerce, 507

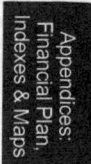

Appendices: Financial Plan, Indexes & Maps

Listings appear in alphabetical order by state, then city.

Malone
Corrections & Community Supervision Department
Bare Hill Correctional Facility, 108
Franklin Correctional Facility, 109
Upstate Correctional Facility, 110
Education Department
Malone District Office, 121
Elections, State Board of
Franklin, 132
Franklin County, 329
Supreme, County, Family & Surrogate's Courts, 53
Franklin County Industrial Development Agency, 506
Franklin-Essex-Hamilton BOCES, 600
Johnson Newspaper Corporation, 527
Malone CSD, 575
Malone Chamber of Commerce, 510
Malone Telegram, The, 527

Malta
Russo, Michael, 462

Malverne
Association of Military Surgeons of the US (AMSUS), NY Chapter, 298
Malverne UFSD, 581
National Amputation Foundation Inc, 184, 299

Mamaroneck
Mamaroneck Chamber of Commerce, 510
Mamaroneck UFSD, 598
Mamaroneck, Town of, 350
Rye Neck UFSD, 599

Manhasset
Manhasset Chamber of Commerce, 510
Manhasset UFSD, 581
North Hempstead, Town of, 360

Manlius
Fayetteville-Manlius CSD, 584

Manorville
Eastport-South Manor CSD, 592

Marathon
Marathon CSD, 572

Marcellus
Marcellus CSD, 584

Marcy
Corrections & Community Supervision Department
Marcy Correctional Facility, 109
Mid-State Correctional Facility, 109
Marcy Chamber of Commerce, 511
Mental Health, Office of
Central New York Psychiatric Center, 228

Margaretville
Central Catskills Chamber of Commerce, 503
Margaretville CSD, 572

Marion
Marion CSD, 597
Seneca Foods Corporation, 77

Marlboro
Hudson River Environmental Society, Inc, 157
Marlboro CSD, 595

Massapequa
Massapequa Chamber of Commerce, 511
Massapequa UFSD, 581
New York State Assn of Fire Districts, 101, 236
Tyson, Lisa, 470

Massena
Daily Courier-Observer, 527
Greater Massena Chamber of Commerce, 507
Johnson Newspaper Corporation, 527
Massena CSD, 590
US Transportation Department
Saint Lawrence Seaway Development Corporation, 290

Mastic
Mastics/Shirley Chamber of Commerce, 511
Unkechaug Nation, 166

Mastic Beach
William Floyd UFSD, 594

Mattituck
Mattituck Chamber of Commerce, 511
NYS Arts, 279

Mayfield
Mayfield CSD, 575

Mayville
Chautauqua County, 326
Family Court, 51
Supreme & County Courts, 51
Surrogate Court, 51
Chautauqua Lake CSD, 569
Elections, State Board of
Chautauqua, 131
Mayville/Chautauqua Chamber of Commerce, 511

McGraw
McGraw CSD, 572

Mechanicville
Mechanicville
Civil & Criminal Courts, 64
Mechanicville Area Chamber of Commerce, 511
Mechanicville City SD, 588
Mechanicville/Stillwater Industrial Development Agency, 511

Medina
Greater Niagara Newspapers, 526, 527
Journal-Register, The, 526, 527
Medina CSD, 586
Orleans-Niagara BOCES, 601

Melville
Capital One Bank, 80
Community Bankers Assn of NY State, Accounting & Taxation Cmte, 268
Friends of Balboni, 483
Insurance Fund (NYS)
Nassau County, Long Island, 201, 219
Suffolk County, Long Island, 201, 219
Long Island Association, 510
Newsday, 527
Newsday Inc, 527
North Fork Bank, 268
US Justice Department
Melville, 115
WLNY (47), 538

Menands
Allocco, Carol, 379
Brooks, Helen M, 390
Corrections & Community Supervision Department
Support Operations, 108
Health Department
Health Research Inc, 175
Menands UFSD, 567
Research Foundation for Mental Hygiene Inc, 233

Merrick
Merrick Chamber of Commerce, 511
Merrick UFSD, 581
New York State Air Force Association, 299
North Merrick UFSD, 581

Mexico
Greater Mexico Chamber of Commerce, 507
Mexico CSD, 586
Oswego BOCES, 601

Middle Falls
Carson, Martin, 394

Middle Island
Longwood CSD, 593

Middle Village
Craig Caruana 2013, 481
Middle Village Republican Club, 490

Middleburgh
Middleburgh CSD, 589

Middleport
Royalton-Hartland CSD, 583

Listings appear in alphabetical order by state, then city.

Middletown
Frontier, A Citizens Communications Co, 144
Mid-Hudson News Network, 532
Middletown
Civil & Criminal Courts, 64
Middletown City SD, 585
Middletown, City of, 350
New York State Assessors' Association, 248, 268
Orange County Community College, 548
Orange Regional Medical Center, 452
Times Herald-Record, 527
US Department of Agriculture
Eastern New York Office, 142
Wallkill, Town of, 366

Milford
Milford CSD, 587
Otsego Northern Catskills BOCES (Otsego-Delaware-Schoharie-Greene), 601

Millbrook
Cary Institute of Ecosystem Studies, 156
Millbrook CSD, 572

Miller Place
Miller Place UFSD, 593

Mineola
Bee Ready Fishbein Hatter & Donovan, LLP (FKA Bee, Peter A), 386
Elections, State Board of
Nassau, 133
Law Department
Nassau, 207
Mental Hygiene Legal Service
2nd Judicial Dept, 209, 230
Mineola Chamber of Commerce, 511
Mineola UFSD, 581
Nassau County, 332
County & Surrogate's Courts, 55
Supreme Court, 55
Nassau County Industrial Development Agency, 512
Nassau Regional Off-Track Betting Corporation, 100, 273
New York College of Traditional Chinese Medicine, 558
RWDSU Local 338 Political Action Committee, 494
Winthrop University Hospital, 186

Mineville
Corrections & Community Supervision Department
Moriah Shock Incarceration Correctional Facility, 109

Model City
CWM Chemical Services LLC, 156

Mohawk
Mohawk CSD, 576
Mohawk Valley Economic Development District, 511

Mongaup Valley
Sullivan County Chamber of Commerce, 517

Monroe
Kiryas Joel Village UFSD, 585
Monroe, Town of, 350

Montauk
Montauk Chamber of Commerce, The, 511
Montauk UFSD, 593

Montgomery
D'Ambrosio, John A, 404
Montgomery, Town of, 350
Orange County Chamber of Commerce Inc, 513
Valley CSD (Montgomery), 586

Monticello
Elections, State Board of
Sullivan, 135
Monticello CSD, 594
Monticello Gaming & Raceway, 279
Sullivan County, 337
Supreme & County Court, 59
Surrogate's & Family Courts, 59

Montrose
Health Department
New York State Veterans' Home at Montrose, 175, 293
Hendrick Hudson CSD, 598
US Department of Veterans Affairs
Montrose Campus of the VA Hudson Valley Healthcare System, 296

Moravia
Corrections & Community Supervision Department
Cayuga Correctional Facility, 109
Moravia CSD, 569
Moravia Chamber of Commerce, 511

Morris
Morris CSD, 587

Morristown
Morristown CSD, 590

Morrisville
Morrisville State College, 546
Morrisville-Eaton CSD, 578

Mount Kisco
Mount Kisco Chamber of Commerce, 511

Mount Morris
Mt Morris CSD, 578

Mount Sinai
Miller Place/Mt Sinai/Sound Beach/Rocky Point Chamber of Commerce, 511
Mt Sinai UFSD, 593

Mount Vernon
African American Chamber of Commerce of Westchester & Rockl, 501
Dorothea Hopfer School of Nursing at Mount Vernon Hospital, 555
Empire State Report (CINN Worldwide Inc), 532
Mount Vernon
Civil & Criminal Courts, 64
Mount Vernon Chamber of Commerce, 511
Mount Vernon Industrial Development Agency (City of), 511
Mount Vernon, City of, 351
Mt Vernon City SD, 598

Mt. Kisco
Bedford CSD, 597

Munnsville
Stockbridge Valley CSD, 578

N Bellmore
Bellmores Chamber of Commerce, 502

N Greece
Greece CSD, 579

Nanuet
Camp Venture Inc, 256
Nanuet UFSD, 588

Napanoch
Corrections & Community Supervision Department
Eastern NY Correctional Facility, 109
Ulster Correctional Facility, 110

Naples
Naples CSD, 585

Nassau
JGN Associates LLC, 429

Nedrow
Onondaga CSD, 584
Onondaga Nation, 166

New Baltimore
Levin, David, 435

New Berlin
Unadilla Valley CSD, 571

New City
Clarkstown CSD, 588
Clarkstown, Town of, 343
Elections, State Board of
Rockland, 134
New City Chamber of Commerce, 512
Rockland Chamber of Commerce, 515

Rockland County, 335
Supreme, County, Family & Surrogate's Courts, 58

New Hampton
Mental Health, Office of
Mid-Hudson Forensic Psychiatric Center, 229

New Hartford
New Hartford CSD, 583
New Hartford, Town of, 351
Oneida-Herkimer-Madison BOCES, 600
WOUR (96.9 FM), 536

New Hyde Park
Glenwood Management Corporation, 247
Herricks UFSD, 580
New Hyde Park Chamber of Commerce, 512
New Hyde Park-Garden City Park UFSD, 581

New Lebanon
New Lebanon CSD, 571

New Paltz
Environmental Conservation Department
Hudson River Estuary Program, 148
Region 3, 148
New Paltz CSD, 595
New Paltz Regional Chamber of Commerce, 512
SUNY at New Paltz, College of Liberal Arts & Sciences, 139, 171
SUNY at New Paltz, Department of History, 171
State University College at New Paltz, 545
Ulster BOCES, 601

New Rochelle
College of New Rochelle (The), 554
Friens of John Calvelli, 484
Iona College, 556
Monroe College-New Rochelle, 565
New Rochelle
Civil & Criminal Courts, 64
New Rochelle City SD, 598
New Rochelle, Chamber of Commerce, Inc, 512
New Rochelle, City of, 351
Sondra Peeden 2013, 494
WVOX (1460 AM), 535

New Suffolk
New Suffolk Common SD, 593

New Windsor
New Windsor, Town of, 351

New York
1199 SEIU Unit, 377
1199 SEIU United Healthcare Workers East, 224
1199/SEIU & GNYHA Healthcare Education Project, 377
1199/SEIU New York State Political Action Fund, 479
1st Department, 45
2013 Committee to Elect Gwen Goodwin, 479
369th Veterans Association Inc, 297
92nd Street Young Men's and Young Women's Hebrew Association, 377
A&W Architects and Engineers, 290
AARP, 255
ABC News (New York Bureau), 531
AECOM Environmental Services, 155
AHRC New York City, 231
AM Law Daily, The, 527
AMAC, Association for Metroarea Autistic Children, 231
AMDEC Foundation, Inc. (FKA AMDEC Policy Group, Inc.), 380
ANHD, Inc., 381
APAX Partners, LP, 381
APICHA Community Health Center, 381
ASPIRA of New York Inc, 125
AXA Real Estate Investment Managers US, 384
Academy of Medicine (NY) (The), 377
Academy of Political Science, 169
Adolf, Jay, 378
Advance Group Inc (The), 378
Advertising Development Political Action Committee, 479
Advocates for Children of New York Inc, 125
Advocates for Children of New York, Inc. (FKA Sweet, Kim), 378
Africa-America Institute (The), 125
After-School Corporation (The) (FKA Ford, Barry), 378
Agudath Israel of America, 126
Akerman Senterfitt LLP (FKA Stadtmauer Bailkin LLP), 378
Alcoholism & Substance Abuse Services, Office of, 4, 173, 227, 250
Alex For NYC, 479
Alicia 4 Council 7, 479
Alliance for Downtown New York, Inc., 379
Alliance for the Arts, 277
Alliance of Resident Theatres/New York (ART/New York), 277
Alston & Bird LLP, 214
Altman, Robert S., 379
Alzheimer's Association, New York City Chapter, 379
American Academy McAllister Institute of Funeral Service, 553
American Academy of Dramatic Arts, 553
American Express Company, 80
American Heart Association Founders Affiliate, 181
American Indonesian Chamber of Commerce, 501
American Institute of Architects New York Chapter, 381
American International Group Inc, 80, 203
American Jewish Committee, 197
American Lawyer Media, 527
American Liver Foundation, Greater NY Chapter, 181
American Management Association International, 90
American Metal Market, 531
American Museum of Natural History, 155, 277
American Society for the Prevention of Cruelty to Animals (ASPCA), 73, 116
Ammann & Whitney Consulting Engineers, 290
Amnesty International USA, 197
Anti-Defamation League, 197
Aon Service Corporation, 203
Apple Bank for Savings, 80
Art & Science Collaborations Inc, 277
Art Institute of New York City (The), 563
Arts Coalition (NYC), 382
ArtsConnection Inc (The), 277
Arzt, George Communications Inc, 382
Asian American Coalition for Children and Families, Inc., 382
Asian American Federation, 256
Asian American Legal Defense and Education Fund, 197, 214
Asian Americans for Equality, 256
Associated Medical Schools of New York, 126, 181, 382
Associated Musicians of Greater New York, Local 802 AFM, AFL-CIO, 277
Associated Press (New York/Metro), 531
Association for Neighborhood & Housing Development, 191
Association for a Better New York, 90, 191
Association of Independent Video & Filmmakers (AIVF), (The), 277
Association of Legal Aid Attorneys UAW 2325 (AFL-CIO), 383
Association of the Bar of the City of New York, 214
Attorney Grievance Committee
1st Judicial Dept, Judicial Dist 1, 12, 208
BALCONY-Business and Labor Coalition of New York, 384
Ballard Spahr LLP New York, 116
Bank Street College of Education/Graduate School, 553
Bank of America Corporation and Subsidiaries, 384
Bankers Association, Inc., 385
Banks, Steven, 385
Barclays Capital Inc., 385
Barnard College, 553

Listings appear in alphabetical order by state, then city.

Battery Park City Authority (Hugh L Carey), 95, 272
Beaudoin & Company (FKA Beaudoin, Heather), 385
Beha, Alyson, 386
Bender Cantone Consulting, 386
Berkeley College, New York City Campus, 563
Bernard M Baruch College, 550
Better Business Bureau of Metropolitan New York, 90
Big Brothers Big Sisters of NYC, 256
Blackstone Alternative Asset Management L.P, 386
Blinded Veterans Association New York Inc, 298
Bloomberg Television, 538
Bonagura, David, 388
Bookman, Esq., Robert S, 388
Boricua College, 553
Borough of Manhattan Community College, 551
Boucher, Paul, 389
Branford Communications, 137
Brennan Center for Justice at New York, 389
Bristol-Meyers Squibb Company Political Action Committee, 479
Bristol-Myers Squibb Co, 181
Brookfield Properties Corporation, 247
Brown Brothers Harriman & Co, 80
Browne, Brian, 390
Bryan Cave, LLP, 390
Building & Construction Trades Council PAC, 479
Building & Construction Trades Council of Greater NY, 391
Building Contractors Association, 91
Burgos, Tonio & Associates, 391
Business Council for International Understanding, 91
CBS Corporation, 143
CBS News (New York), 532
CIR/SEIU Local 1957 Health Care Advocacy Fund, 480
COFCCA Inc, 399
CPR, The International Institute for Conflict Prevention & Resoluti, 215
CUNY Board of Trustees, 550
CUNY Central Administration, 550
City University Construction Fund, 550
CUNY Graduate School, Center for Urban Research, 138
CUNY Hunter College, Urban Affairs & Planning Department, 191
CUNY John Jay College of Criminal Justice, 116
CWA District One PAC, 481
Capalino, James F & Associates Inc, 392
Captains Endowment Association, 480
Cardozo School of Law, 197
Carey Group LLC, 394
Carolyn's PAC, 480
Carrion 2013, 480
Casey, William R., 394
Catholic Community Relations Council of New York, Inc., 394
Catholic War Veterans of the United States of America, 298
Center for Charter School Excellence (NYC), 395
Center for Children's Initiatives, Inc., 395
Center for Constitutional Rights, 197
Center for Constitutional Rights (501C3 Organization With 501H, 395
Center for Court Innovation, 215
Center for Educational Innovation - Public Education Association, 126
Center for Hearing and Communication, 182
Center for Independence of the Disabled in NY (CIDNY), 197, 256
Center for Migration Studies of New York Inc, 197
Center for Urban Community Services, 256
Center for an Urban Future, 191, 225
Central Labor Council (NYC), 395
Century Foundation (The), 138
Cerebral Palsy Associations of New York State, 126, 182, 231, 256
Children's Aid Society (The), 257, 396
Children's Health Fund (The), 396
Children's Rights Inc, 197, 257
Chin, Francis Y., 396
Christie's Education Inc, 564
Citigroup Inc, 80
Citizens Budget Commission, 237, 268
Citizens Committee for New York City, 397
Citizens Housing & Planning Council of New York, 191
Citizens Union of the City of New York, 170, 238
Citizens' Committee for Children of New York Inc, 197, 257, 397
City College of New York, The, 551
City Harvest, 397
City Journal (Manhattan Institute for Policy Research), 532
City University Construction Fund, 97, 123
Civil Court, NYC
New York County, 49
Climate Action PAC, 480
Coalition Against Hunger (NYC), 398
Coalition for Asian American Children & Families, 257
Coalition for the Homeless, 257
Coalition of Behavioral Health Agencies, Inc (The), 231
Coalition of Institutionalized Aged and Disabled (FKA Lieberman,, 399
Cohen For Council, 480
Columbia Law School, Legislative Drafting Research Fund, 138, 238
Columbia University, 554
Columbia University, Exec Graduate Pgm in Public Policy & Adm, 170
Columbia University, MPA in Environmental Science & Policy, 156
Columbia University, Mailman School of Public Health, 182, 198
Columbia University, School of the Arts, 278
Columbia University, Technology Ventures, 91
Committe to Elect Ceceilia Berkowitz for Mayor, 480
Committee to Elect Ariel Guerrero, 480
Commodity Futures Trading Commission
Eastern Region, 70, 88
Common Cause/NY, 138, 170
Commonwealth Fund, 182
Communications Workers of America Local 1180, 481
Communications Workers of America, District 1, 225
Community Health Care Association of NYS, 182
Community Health Care Association of New York State, 400
Community Healthcare Network, 182, 257
Community Housing Improvement Program (CHIP), 191
Community Preservation Corporation (The), 191, 400
Community Research Initiative on AIDS, Inc., 400
Community Service Society of New York, 191
Condon, Joseph M., 400
Conference Board (The), 91
Consolidated Edison Company of New York, Inc., 401
Consolidated Edison Energy, 143
Consolidated Edison, Inc. Employees' Political Action Committee, 481
Consortium for Worker Education, 401
Constantinople & Vallone Consulting LLC (FKA Constantinople Cons, 401
Constellation Energy, 143
Consumer Product Safety Commission
Eastern Regional Center, 88
Convention Centers & Visitors Bureaus
NYC & Company/Convention & Visitors Bureau, 275
Cooper Union for the Advancement of Science & Art, 554
Cornell Cooperative Extension, Agriculture & Food Systems Program, 74
Cornell University, Sch of Industr &, 225
Correction Officers Benevolent Association, 481
Correctional Association of New York, 117
Corrections & Community Supervision Department
Bayview Correctional Facility, 108
Edgecombe Correctional Facility, 109

Lincoln Correctional Facility, 109
Correy For Council, 481
Council for the Humanities, 403
Council of Family & Child Caring Agencies, 257
Council of School Supervisors & Administrators, 126
Council of Senior Centers & Services of NYC, Inc., 403
Council of State Governments, Eastern Conference, 170, 238, 268
Council on the Arts, 6, 270
Council on the Environment of NYC, Environmental Education, 126
County Medical Society New York (FKA Malone, Cheryl), 403
Cozen O'Connor (FKA Wolfblock LLP), 403
Crain's New York Business, 532
Criminal Court, NYC
New York County, 49
DC 37 Local 299, 481
DC 37 Political Action Committee, 481
DLA Piper New York Political Action Committee, 482
DTZ/Cushman & Wakefield, 247
Dadey, Dick (FKA Citizens Union of the City of New York), 404
Dale Carnegie & Associates Inc, 91
Davis 2013, 481
Davis Polk & Wardwell, 91
Day Pitney LLP, 215, 268
DeVry Institute of Technology, College of New York, 564
Debevoise & Plimpton LLP, 117, 215, 406
Deloitte & Touche LLP, 406
Delta Air Lines, Inc., 406
Detectives Endowment Association - COPE, 482
Deutsche Bank, 80
Deutsche Bank Trust Company, 406
Development Counsellors International, 91
District Council 1707, AFSCME, 482
District Council 37, AFSCME, 407
District Council 37, AFSCME, AFL-CIO, 243
District Council No. 9 Political Action Committee, 482
Doctors Council SEIU COPE, 482
Doctors Without Borders USA, 182
Dodge Landesman For State Committee, 482
Dow Jones & Company, 527
Dow Jones Newswires (Dow Jones & Company), 532
Downtown-Lower Manhattan Association, 505
Drug Policy Alliance, 407
Drum Major Institute for Public Policy - Not For Profit, 198
Duffy, Margaret, 408
Dunne, John, 408
Durst Development LLC, 408
Durst Organization, Inc. (The), 408
EISPAC, 482
EQT Partners, Inc., 412
Easter Seals New York, 408
Education Department
Manhattan District Office, 122
Professional Examinations, 121
Education Reform Now Advocacy, Inc., 409
Education Reform Now, Inc., 409
Edward K. Flynn, 409
Effective Leadership Committee, Inc., 482
Egan, Paul (FKA Reiskin, Marvin), 409
Eleanor Roosevelt Legacy Committee, 482
Elections, State Board of
New York, 133
New York City, 133
Emblemhealth Services Company, LLC, 410
Empire Blue Cross & Blue Shield, 182, 203
Empire Consultants, 410
Empire State Development Corporation, 7, 83, 97, 147, 188, 271
Entertainment Software Association, 278
Environmental Defense Fund, 156, 412
Epstein Becker & Green, PC, 198
Equal Employment Opportunity Commission
New York District, 196, 222
Equitable Life Assurance Society of the US, 203
Ernst & Young, 247
Ernst & Young Committee For Good Government, 482
Ethan C Eldon Associates Inc, 291
Excess Line Association of New York, 203
ExpandED Schools, 126
Export Import Bank of the United States
Northeast Regional Office, 79, 88
Extell Development Company, 413
Eye-Bank for Sight Restoration Inc (The), 183
Family Court, NYC
New York County, 50
Farber, Felice, 413
Fashion Institute of Technology, 547
Federal Deposit Insurance Corporation
Division of Depositor and Consumer Protection, 79
Federal Home Loan Bank of New York, 80, 191
Federal Reserve System
Federal Reserve Bank of New York, 79
Federal Trade Commission, 92
Northeast Regional Office, 88
Federation Employment & Guidance Service (FEGS) Inc, 231, 258
Federation of Mental Health Services, Inc. (The), 414
Federation of Protestant Welfare Agencies Inc, 258
Federation of School Administrators (NYS) (FKA Gibbons, Brian), 414
Film/Video Arts, 278
Financial Services Department, 4, 78, 177, 200
FirstService Williams, 247
Fisher Brothers, 247
Foley & Lardner LLP, 415
Food Bank for New York City, 415
Fordham University, Graduate School of Social Service, 258
Forum Strategies & Communications, 416
Fox News Channel, 538
French-American Chamber of Commerce, 506
Fried Frank Harris Shriver & Jacobson, LLP, 416
Friedlander Group (The), 416
Friends & Relatives of Institutionalized Aged Inc (FRIA), 258
Friends of Benjamin Kallos, 483
Friends of Brodie Enoch 2013, 483
Friends of Dara Adams, 483
Friends of Ed Hartzog, 483
Friends of Gale Brewer - 2013, 484
Friends of JR, 484
Friends of Joyce Johnson, 484
Friends of Kevin P. Coenen Jr. Inc., 484
Friends of Larry Hirsch 2010, 484
Friends of Luis Tejada, 484
Friends of Mark Thompson, 485
Friends of Menegon, 485
Friends of Richard del Rio, 485
Friends of Yetta, 485
Friends of the High Line, Inc., 416
Frost, Robert D., 416
Fund for Animals (The), 74
Fund for Modern Courts (The), 215
Fund for the City of New York, 238
Fund for the City of New York (FKA Employment & Training Coa, 416
Fund for the City of New York, Center for Internet Innovation, 144
GSO Capital Partners LP, 422
Gandhi Engineering Inc, 291
Garfinkel, Neil, 417
Garodnick 2013, 486
Gay Men's Health Crisis Inc, 417
General Contractors Association of NY, 92, 291
General Theological Seminary of the Episcopal Church, 555
Genovese, John, 417
Gertrude H Sergievsky Center (The), 183
Gertrude Stein Repertory Theatre (The), 278
Geto & De Milly Inc, 418
Geto & de Milly Inc, 170
Gilbert Tweed Associates Inc, 92
Glenwood Poh, 418
Global Strategy Group, 419
Globe Institute of Technology, 564
Golden Tree Asset Management LP, 419

Goldman Harris LLC (FKA Law Offices of Howard Goldman, LLC), 419
Goldman Sachs & Co, 80
Goldman Sachs & Co., 419
Good Shepherd Services, 419
Goodman & Zuchlewski LLP, 216
Gould, David (FKA Tallon Jr., James R.), 420
Governor's Office
New York City Office, 3, 160, 234
Graduate Center, 551
Graduate School of Journalism, 551
Gramercy Stuyvesant Independent Democrats, 486
Greater NY Hospi, 420
Greater New York Chamber of Commerce, 507
Greater New York Health Care Facilities Association, 420
Greater New York Hospital Association, 183
GreenThumb, 74, 156
Greenmarket/Council on the Environment of NYC, 74
Greenmarket/Grow NYC, 157
Greenwich Village Society for Historic Preservation, 421
Greenwich Village-Chelsea Chamber of Commerce, 508
Group Health Inc, 183, 204
Grow NYC, 191
Guardian Life Insurance Company, 422
Guerriero For Advocate, 486
H J Kalikow & Co LLC, 247
HF Responsibility Fund, 486
HR&A Advisors, Inc., 426
HSBC - North America Holdings, Inc., 426
HSBC USA Inc, 80
Hannesson, Paul (FKA McCormick, Lynde) (FKA Gaylord, Joan), 422
Harlem Chamber of Commerce (Greater Harlem), 508
Harlem Charter School Parents PAC, 486
Harlem United: Community AIDS Center, Inc., 422
Harvestworks, 279
Hawkins Delafield & Wood LLP, 238, 268
Hawkins, Dennis (FKA Jockers, Ken), 423
Health Department
Metropolitan Area/Regional Office, 176
Task Force On Life & The Law, 176
Healthcare Tort Reform Coalition (NY), 424
Hebrew Union College - Jewish Institute of Religion, 555
Helen Rosenthal For City Council, 486
Helene Fuld College of Nursing North General Hospital, 555
Herrick, Feinstein LLP, 424
Hess Corporation, 144
Heyman, Neil, 424
Hill 2013, 486
Hispanic Federation, 258
Hogan Lovells US LLP, 144
Holland and Knight Committee For Responsible Government, 486
Hollyer Brady et al, 216
Homeland Security & Emergency Services, Division of, 7, 160, 235
Homeless Services United (FKA Council on Homeless Policies & Servi, 426
Hotel & Motel Trades Council, AFL-CIO, 426
Hotel Association of New York City Inc, 279
Hotel Association of New York City, Inc., 486
Housing & Community Renewal, 8
Housing & Community Renewal, Division of, 187
New York City, Long Island, Hudson Valley, 187
Housing Conservation Coordinators, 426
Housing New York Political Action Committee, 487
Hoylman For Senate, 487
Hudson Eagle LLC, 427
Human Rights First, 198
Human Rights Watch, 198
Human Rights, State Division of
Manhattan (Upper), 194
Humane Society of the United States, New York State, 75, 259
Hunter College, 551
Hunter College, Brookdale Center for Healthy Aging and Longevity, 259
Hurley, Alicia D. (FKA Haberman, Michael), 427
Hutton & Solomon, LLP, 427
IBT Joint Council No. 16 PAC, 487
INFORM Inc, 157
IRX Therapeutics Inc, 81
ITAR-TASS News Agency, 532
Immigration Coalition, Inc (NY), 427
Inspector General (NYS), Office of the, 9, 112
Institute for Family Health (The), 183
Institute of International Bankers, 428
Institute of Public Administration/NYU Wagner, 170, 238
Insurance Fund (NYS), 9, 200, 219
InterAgency Council of Mental Retardatn & Developmental Disabilities, 232
Interest on Lawyer Account (IOLA) Fund of the State of NY, 98, 210
International Flavors & Fragrances Inc, 92
International Union of Operating Engineers Local 15 A B C D, 487
Int'l Longshoremen's Ass'n, AFL-CIO Committee on Political Education, 487
Ironworkers Local 46 PAC, 487
Irving Place Capital Management L.P., 428
J.P. Morgan Securities Inc., 428
JAMS, 216, 225
JPMorgan Chase & Co, 81
JPMorgan Chase Bank, National Association, 430
Jacobs Engineering, 291
Janney Montgomery Scott LLC, 428
Japanese American Social Services Inc, 259
Japanese Chamber of Commerce, 509
Jennison Associates LLC, 429
Jewish Association for Services for the Aged (FKA Saiger, Molly), 429
Jewish Board of Family & Children's Services, 232
Jewish Community Relations Council of NY Inc, 198
Jewish Education Project (The), 126
Jewish Home and Hospital for Aged (The), 429
Jewish Museum (The), 279
Jewish Theological Seminary, 556
Jewish War Veterans of the USA, State of NY, 298
Jim Owles Liberal Democratic Club, 487
Jobs with Justice (NY), 429
Jockey Club (The), 429
Joe Lhota For Mayor, Inc., 487
John Catsimatidis For Mayor 2013 Committee, Inc., 488
John Jay College of Criminal Justice, 551
JuanPagan2013, 488
Judge Analisa Torres For Supreme Court 2011, 488
Juilliard School (The), 556
Julie Menin 2013, 488
KPMG LLP, 238
Kantor Davidoff Mandelker Twomey Gallanty & Kesten, PC, 431
Kaplan, Alden B., 431
Kasirer Consulting, 431
Kaye Scholer LLP, 225
Kellner Campaign 2013, 488
Ken 2013, 488
King, Barbara, 432
King's College (The), 556
Komanoff Energy Associates, 144, 291
Korean Community Services of Metropolitan NY, 259
Kramer Levin Naftalis & Frankel, LLP, 432
Kraus & Zuchlewski LLP, 225
Kwan, Patrick, 433
Labor Department
New York City, 220
Laboratory Institute of Merchandising, 565
Lackman, Abraham M., 433
Lambda Legal, 198
Land Title Association, Inc., 433
Landauer Realty Group Inc, 247
Landis For New York, 488
Lantigua 2013, 488
LatinoJustice PRLDEF, 198
Law Department, 9, 78, 84, 112, 140, 149, 161, 177, 188, 195, 201, 206, 221, 245, 263

Harlem, 207
Medicaid Fraud Control Unit, 112, 207
League of Conservation Voters, 434
Learning Leaders, 127
Legal Action Center, 117, 216
Legal Aid Society, 117, 216
Legal Assistance Group (NY), 434
Legal Services NYC, 434
Lehrer, Sander, 435
Lesbian and Gay Community Services Center, Inc., 435
Lesbian, Gay, Bisexual & Transgender Community Center - Not For P, 198
Lesbian, Gay, Bisexual & Transgender Community Ctr - Not For Profit, 232, 259
Levin, Brenda, 435
Levine 2013, 488
Levine, Paul, 435
Levy Ratner P.C., 435
Levy, Norman P.C., 435
Lieutenant Governor's Office, 3, 160
Life Insurance Council of New York, Inc, 204
Lifespire, 232
Lighthouse Guild, 183
Lincoln Center for the Performing Arts Inc, 279
Lincoln Center for the Performing Arts, Inc., 435
Littman Krooks LLP, 259
Liutenants Benevolent Association NY Police Department PAC, 488
LoCicero & Tan Inc, 436
Local 1407 AFSCME Political Committee, 488
Local 2021 AFSCME Political Action Account, 489
Local 23-25 Unite State & Local Campaign Committee, 489
Local 32BJ SEIU NY/NJ American Dream Fund, 489
Local 372 Political Action, 489
Local 6 Committee on Political Education, 489
Local 6, Hotel & Club Employees & Bartenders Union, AFL-CIO, 436
Local 94-94A-94B IUOE Political Action Committee, 489
Local Initiatives Support Corporation, 191
Long Island Rail Road Commuter's Council, 291
Long Term Care Community Coalition (FKA Nursing Home Communi, 436
Long View Publishing Co, 527
Louloudes, Virginia, 436
Lower Manhattan Cultural Council, 279
Lutz, Jr., Alexander, 437
Lynch, Bill Associates, LLC, 437
M + R Strategic Services (FKA M & R Strategic Services), 438
MC Asset Management Americas, LTD., 441
MDRC, 127, 225
METLIFE, Inc. Employees' Political Participation Fund A, 490
METRET PAC Inc., 490
MPAC, 490
MSG Holdings, L.P., 446
MTA (Metropolitan Transportation Authority), 98, 286
MTA Bridges & Tunnels, 99, 285
MTA Bus Company, 99, 285
MTA Capital Construction, 285
MTA Capital Construction Program, 99
MTA Metro-North Railroad, 99, 286
MTA New York City Transit, 99, 286
MTA Office of the Inspector General, 100, 286
Macy's Inc, 92
Madden, Susan (FKA Benson, Kathleen), 438
Madison Square Garden Corp, 279
Maher Jr., Daniel F., 438
Mailman For Council, 489
Major League Baseball, 279
Major League Soccer, LLC, 438
Mallory Factor Inc, 81
Mandl School, 565
Manhattan Chamber of Commerce Inc, 510
Manhattan Chamber of Commerce, Inc., 439
Manhattan Educational Opportunity Center, 549
Manhattan Institute for Policy Research, 92, 170
Manhattan Institute, Center for Civic Innovation, 238, 268
Manhattan School of Music, 557
Manhattan-Bronx Minority Business Enterprise Center, 225
Maniscalco, John D, 439
March of Dimes Birth Defects Foundation New York Chapter, 440
Margaret Chin 2013, 489
Mark Otto For City Council, 489
Mark Weprin For New York PAC, 489
Marsh & McLennan Companies, 204
Martin Begun D/B/A Martin S. Begun Consulting, 440
Marymount Manhattan College, 557
Mason Tenders District Council of Greater New York, 489
Master, Robert, 441
Mathews, Dan, 441
McGrath Matter Associates, 441
McGuire, Michael J, 441
Meara, Brian R, Public Relations Inc, 442
Mel 2013, 490
Melinda Katz 2013, 490
Memorial Sloan-Kettering Cancer Center, 183, 443
Menaker & Herrmann LLP, 92
Mental Health Association of NYC Inc, 232
Mental Health Association of New York, 443
Mental Health, Office of
New York Psychiatric Institute, 229
Mental Hygiene Legal Service
1st Judicial Dept, 209, 230
Mercury Public Affairs LLC, 443
Merrill Lynch & Co Inc, 81
Merrill Lynch & Company, Inc., 443
Metro-North Railroad Commuter Council, 291
Metropolitan College of New York, 557
Metropolitan Funeral Directors PAC, 490
Metropolitan Museum of Art (The), 279
Millman, Claude, 444
Minerva For City Council, 490
Mirram Group, LLC (The), 445
Mirrer, Louise, 445
Montalbano Initiatives Inc, 445
Montclare & Wachtler, 217
Montford Point Marine Association, 299
Moody's Investors Service, Public Finance Group, 238, 268
Moon Capital Management LP, 445
Morgan Stanley, 81
Morgan Stanley & Co. Incorporated, 445
Morse, Alan, 446
Mount Sinai Health System, 184
Mount Sinai Medical Center, 446
Mount Sinai School of Medicine of NYU, 558
Movement Group, LLC, 446
Mulholland & Knapp, LLP, 171
Municipal Art Society, 446
Municipal Credit Union, 81
NADAP, 447
NARAL Pro-Choice, New York, 447
NARAL/NY Multcandidate Political Action Committee, 490
NBCUniversal, 449
NY Coalition of 100 Black Women - Not For Profit, 171
NY County Lawyers' Association, 217
NY Film Academy, 279
NY Foundation for Senior Citizens Inc, 259
NY League of Conservation Voters/NY Conservation Education Fund, 138, 157
NY Life Insurance Co, 204
NY Oil Heating Association, 144
NY Property Insurance Underwriting Association, 204
NY Society of Association Executives Inc (NYSAE), 92
NYC Arts Coalition, 279
NYC Board of Education Employees, Local 372/AFSCME, AFL-CIO, 127, 243
NYC Campaign Finance Board, 138
NYC Chancellor's Office, 582
NYC Citywide Special Ed District 75, 582
NYC Coalition Against Hunger, 259

NYC Community Garden Coalition, 157
NYC District Council of Carpenters PAC, 491
NYC Region 10, 582
NYC Region 9, 582
NYMAGIC Inc, 204
NYP Holdings Inc, 528
NYS Association of Criminal Defense Lawyers, 217
NYS Bar Assn, Antitrust Law Section, 92
NYS Bar Assn, Business Law Section, 92
NYS Bar Assn, Commercial & Federal Litigation Section, 217
NYS Bar Assn, Courts of Appellate Jurisdiction Cmte, 217
NYS Bar Assn, Cyberspace Law Cmte, 214
NYS Bar Assn, Diversity and Inclusion Cmte, 198
NYS Bar Assn, Federal Constitution & Legislation Cmte, 171, 215
NYS Bar Assn, International Law & Practice Section, 214
NYS Bar Assn, Labor & Employment Law Section, 216, 225
NYS Bar Assn, Media Law Committee, 144, 217
NYS Bar Assn, Multi-jurisdictional Practice Cmte, 94, 218
NYS Bar Assn, Procedures for Judicial Discipline Cmte, 216
NYS Bar Assn, Public Trust & Confidence in the Legal System, 117, 215
NYS Bar Assn, Review the Code of Judicial Conduct Cmte, 214
NYS Bar Assn, Tax Section, 268
NYS Bar Assn, Trusts & Estates Law Section, 215, 268
NYS Court Clerks Association, 217, 243
NYS Federation of Physicians & Dentists, 184
NYS Land Title Association, 248
NYS Office for People with Developmental Disabilities
Metro New York Developmental Disabilities Services Office, 230
New York City Regional Office, 229
NYS Society of Certified Public Accountants, 93
NYSAFAH PAC, 491
NYSTAR - Division of Science, Technology & Innovation
Center for Advanced Information Management, 84, 122
Center for Advanced Technology in Photonics Applications, 85, 122
Industrial & Technology Assistance Corp, 85, 123
Nagel Law Office, PLLC, 447
National Association of Black Accountants, NY Chapter, 93
National Association of Social Workers - New York City Chapter, 448
National Basketball Association, 280
National Coffee Association, 76
National Council of Jewish Women, 198, 260
National Economic Research Associates, 145
National Employment Law Project, 448
National Federation of Community Development Credit Unions, 81
National Football League, 280
National Hockey League, 280
National Labor Relations Board
Region 2 - New York City Metro Area, 222
National League for Nursing (NLN), 184
National Multiple Sclerosis Society, New York City Chapter, 448
National Organization for Women, NYS, 139, 198
National Urban League Inc (The), 260
National Writers Union, 226
Natural Resources Defense Council, 157
Natural Resources Defense Council (FKA Goldstein, Eric), 448
Navy League of the US (NLUS), New York Council, 299
Ndigo For City Council, 490
Neighborhood Family Services Coalition, 449
Neighborhood Preservation Political Action Fund, 490
Neil Grimaldi For New York City Mayor, 490
New Jewish Home (The), 184
New School University (The), 558
New School University, Department of Sociology, 280
New School University, Milano, 184, 192
New School for Social Research, Department of Politics, 139, 199
New School for Social Research, Zolberg Institute on Migrat, 199
New York 1 News (1), 538
New York AIDS Coalition, 184
New York Academy of Art Inc, 280, 558
New York Artists Equity Association Inc, 280
New York Association for New Americans, Inc (NYANA), 259
New York Bankers Association, 81
New York Bankers Political Action Committee, 490
New York Biotechnology Association (The), 93
New York Building Congress, 93, 192
New York Building Congress State PAC, 491
New York Career Institute, 565
New York Chamber of Commerce (Greater New York), 512
New York Check P.A.C., Inc., 491
New York City, 351
Aging, Dept for the, NYC, 352
Buildings, Department of, NYC, 352
Campaign Finance Board, NYC, 352
City Council, NYC, 352
City Planning, Department of, NYC, 352
Citywide Administrative Services, Department of, NYC, 352
Civil Service Commission, NYC, 352
Collective Bargaining, Office of, NYC, 353
Comptroller, NYC, 353
Conflicts of Interest Board, NYC, 353
Consumer Affairs, Department of, NYC, 353
Correction, Board of, NYC, 353
Correction, Department of, NYC, 353
Cultural Affairs, Department of, NYC, 353
Disabilities, Mayor's Office, for People with, 353
Economic Development Corp, NYC, 353
Education, Dept of, NYC, 353
Elections, Board of, NYC, 354
Equal Employment Practices Commission, NYC, 354
Film, Theatre & Broadcasting, Mayor's Office of, NYC, 354
Finance, Department of, NYC, 354
Health & Hospitals Corporation, NYC, 354
Health & Mental Hygiene, Dept of, NYC, 354
Homeless Services, Department of, NYC, 355
Housing Authority, NYC, 355
Housing Preservation & Development, Dept of, NYC, 355
Human Resources Administration, Dept of, NYC, 355
Human Rights Commission on, NYC, 355
Information Technology & Telecommunications, Dept of, NYC, 355
Investigation, Department of, NYC, 356
Juvenile Justice, Department of, NYC, 356
Labor Relations, Office of, NYC, 356
Landmarks Preservation Commission, NYC, 356
Law, Department of, NYC, 356
Legislative Affairs Office, NYC Mayor's City, 356
Library, New York Public, 356
Loft Board, NYC, 357
Management & Budget, Office of, NYC, 357
Medical Examiner, Office of Chief, NYC, 357
Parks & Recreation, Department of, NYC, 357
Police Department, NYC, 357
Probation, Department of, NYC, 357
Public Advocate, Office of the, 357

Appendices: Financial Plan, Indexes & Maps

Listings appear in alphabetical order by state, then city.

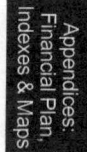

Public Design Commission, NYC, 352
Records & Information Services, Dept of, NYC, 358
Rent Guidelines Board, NYC, 358
Sanitation, Department of, NYC, 358
Small Business Services, Department of, NYC, 358
Sports Commission, NYC, 358
Standards & Appeals, Board of, NYC, 358
Tax Commission, NYC, 358
Taxi & Limousine Commission, NYC, 358
Transportation, Department of, NYC, 358
Veterans' Affairs, Mayor's Office of, NYC, 358
Voter Assistance Commission (VAC), NYC, 358
Water Finance Authority, Municipal, NYC, 359
Youth & Community Development, Department of, NYC, 359
New York City Boroughs
Manhattan (New York County), 359
New York City Central Labor Council Political Committee, 491
New York City Housing Development Corporation, 100, 189
New York City Justice Political Action Committee, 491
New York City Opera, 280
New York City Partnership State PAC, 491
New York City, Partnership for, 512
New York Civil Liberties Union, 199
New York Civil Rights Coalition, 199
New York College of Podiatric Medicine, 558
New York Committee for Occupational Safety & Health, 226
New York Community Trust (The), 260
New York Convention Center Operating Corporation, 100, 273
New York County
SUPREME COURT, Civil Term, 55
SUPREME COURT, Criminal Term, 56
Surrogate's Court, 56
New York County (NYC Borough of Manhattan), 332
New York County Dental Society Political Action Committee, 491
New York Daily News, 528
New York Foundation for the Arts, 280
New York Health Care Alliance, 185
New York Hotel & Motel Trades Council Committee, 491
New York Immigration Coalition (The), 199
New York Landmarks Conservancy, 192, 248
New York Law School, 558
New York Lawyers for the Public Interest, 192, 199
New York Magazine (New York Media, LLC), 533
New York Mercantile Exchange Inc, 93
New York Metropolitan Transportation Council, 101, 286
New York Observer (The), 528
New York Post, 528
New York Presbyterian Hospital, 185
New York Presbyterian Hospital, Department of Psychiatry, 232
New York Press Photographers Association, 145
New York Professional Nurses Union Political Action Committee, 491
New York Public Interest Research Group, 158, 171
New York Public Interest Research Group Straphangers Campaign, 292
New York Regional Office
New York Regional Office, 166
New York School of Interior Design, 559
New York Society for the Deaf, 260
New York State Athletic Commission, 101, 164, 273
New York State Democratic Committee, 139, 372
New York State Dormitory Authority, 102, 124, 164, 178
New York State Financial Control Board, 103, 164, 265
New York State Gaming Commission
New York City Region, 264
New York State Homes & Community Renewal, 78, 103
New York State Independence Party, 374
New York State Judicial Conduct Commission, 103, 211
New York State Law Enforcement Council, 118, 217, 243
New York State Liquor Authority (Division of Alcoholic Beverag, 4
New York State Liquor Authority (Division of Alcoholic Beverage Control), 83, 263
New York City (Zone I), 83, 263
New York State Nurses Association, 185
New York State Osteopathic Medical Society, 185
New York State Podiatric Medical Association, 185
New York State Society of Certified Public Accountants, 268
New York State Society of Enrolled Agents, 269
New York State Supreme Court Officers Association, 217, 243
New York State Trial Lawyers, 217
New York Stock Exchange, 81
New York Technology Council, 93, 145
New York Theological Seminary, 559
New York Un, 181
New York Universi, 93
New York University, 128, 559
New York University School of Law, 217
New York University, Departmentt of Politics, 139
New York University, Graduate School of Journalism, 139, 226
New York University, Robert F Wagner Graduate School of Public Se, 185
New York University, Tisch School of the Arts, 281
New York University, Wagner Graduate School, 192, 239
New York Urban League, 260
New Yorker, 217
New Yorkers Against Gun Violence, 449
New Yorkers For De Blasio, 491
New Yorkers For Putting Students First, 491
New Yorkers For Robert Jackson, 491
Newsweek/The Daily Beast, 533
Nicholas & Lence Communications LLC, 449
Noah E. Gotbaum 2013, 491
Nonprofit Coordinating Committee of New York, 260
Norddeutsche Landesbank Girozentrale, 81
Norman A Olch, Esq, 217
North Star Fund, 450
Northeast Business Group on Health Inc, 185
Northern Manhattan Improvement Corporation, 450
Nostradamus Advertising, 139
Nyprocoa, Inc., 451
Office of David J Silverman, 269
Open Society Foundations, 199
Open Space Institute, 158, 452
Organization of Staff Analysts PAC, 492
Osteopathic Medical Society, 452
PAC L375 CSTG, 492
PAC of the Patrolmen's Benevolent Association of NYC, 492
PSC PAC, 493
Pace University, 453, 559
Pacific College of Oriental Medicine, 565
Park Strategies, LLC, 453
Parks, Recreation & Historic Preservation, NYS Office of
New York City Region, 272
Parkside Group, LLC, 453
Parodneck Foundation (The), 192
Parsons Brinckerhoff, 292
Partnership for NYC (FKA Mele, Don), 454
Partnership for New York City, 94
Path2Parenthood, 186
Patrolmen's Benevolent Association, 118, 243, 454
People For Bing, 492
People For Carlton Berkley, 492
People For Cheryl, 492
People For Debra Cooper, 492
People For Lappin, 492
People For Miguel Estrella, 492
People's World, 527
Perry Capital LLC, 454

Listings appear in alphabetical order by state, then city.

Perry Davis Associates, 94
Perry, Robert, 454
Pershing Square Capital Management L.P., 455
Pfizer Inc. PAC, 492
Phillips Beth Israel School of Nursing, 559
Phillips Lytle, 455
Phillips Nizer, LLP, 455
Planned Parenthood of NYC, Inc, 261
Podiatric Medical Association (NYS), 456
Port Authority of New York & New Jersey, 105, 287
Postgrad Center for Mental Health, Child, Adolescent & Family-Coupl, 233
Postgraduate Center for Mental Health, 233
Powers Global Strategies, LLC, 456
Premier Senior Living LLC, 186
Presbyterian Hospital (NY), 457
Prevention of Domestic Violence, Office for the, 11, 113
Primary Care Development Corporation, 457
Pro Bono Net, 218
Professional Business College, 559
Project for Public Spaces, 193
Proskauer Rose LLP, 94, 158, 171, 218
Public Agenda, 139, 171
Public Financial Management, Inc., 458
Public Interest Research Group (NY), 458
Public Interest Research Group Fund, Inc. (New York), 458
Public Library, Astor, Lenox & Tilden Foundations (NY) (The), 458
Public/Private Ventures, 226, 261
Puerto Rican Legal Defense & Education Fund Inc (PRLDEF), 218
Quinn For New York, 493
RG Group, 460
RSA PAC City Account, 493
Racing Association, Inc., 459
Rangel For Congress NY State, 493
Real Estate Board of NY Inc, 459
Real Estate Board of New York Inc, 248
Real Rent Reform Campaign, 460
Realty Advisory Board on Labor Relations, 226, 248
Regional Plan Association, 94, 193, 292
Related Companies LP, 248
Related Companies, LP (The), 460
Related Fund Management LLC, 460
Rent Stabilization Assn of NYC Inc, 193, 460
Reshma For New York, 493
Resources for Artists with Disabilities Inc, 281
Retail Wholesale and Department Store Union C.O.P.E., 493
Reuters (Thomson Reuters Markets LLC), 533
Roarke, Robert R., 461
Robert Schalkenbach Foundation, 248, 269
Robinson & Cole LLP, 461
Rockefeller University, 560
Rosenthal For Assembly, 493
Rosie Mendez 2013, 493
Royal Realty Corp., 461
SBLI USA Mutual Life Insurance Company Inc, 204
SMWIA Local 28 Political Action Committee, 494
SSL Political Action Committee, 494
SUNY State College of Optometry, 544
SUNY System Administration & Executive Council
SUNY Center for Student Recruitment, 543
Safe Horizon, Inc., 462
Samuel A. Ramirez & Co., Inc., 462
Sanctuary for Families, 463
Savino For New York, 494
Schmidt, James A., 464
Schnur Associates, Inc., 464
School of Professional Studies, 552
School of Visual Arts, 565
Securities Industry & Financial Markets Association, 465
Securities Industry & Financial Markets Association (SIFMA), 82, 214
Semper Fi NYS PAC Inc., 494
Sergeants Benevolent Association, 494
Services for the UnderServed (SUS), 118
Settlement Housing Fund Inc, 193
Shank, Suzanne, 465
Sheinkopf Communications, 139
Sheinkopf, Ltd, 465
Siconolfi, Patrick, 465
Silverstein Properties Inc, 249
Simmons-Boardman Publishing Corp, 292
Simon Wiesenthal Center, Museum of Tolerance NY, 199
Simons & Wright LLC, 465
Sithe Global, 146
Skybridge Capital II LLC, 466
Slippen, Daniel, 466
Slovak American Chamber of Commerce, 516
Small Business Administration
New York City, 88
Region II New York, 88
Smithsonian Institution
Cooper-Hewitt National Design Museum, 275
National Museum of the American Indian-George Gustav Heye Center, 275
Social Security Administration
Region 2-New York, 254
Society of CPA's, 466
Solomon R Guggenheim Foundation, 281
Solus Alternative Asset Management LP, 466
Sonnenblick-Goldman Company, 249
Sophie Davis School of Biomedical Education, 552
South Asians United For a Better America PAC, 494
Spanish Broadcasting System Network Inc, 146
Spec Cmte on Collateral Consequence of Criminal Proceedings, 171
Squadron For New York, 494
State Comptroller, Office of the, 12, 149, 162, 235, 241
State Department, 12, 85, 149, 162, 236
State Athletic Commission, 163
State of New York Mortgage Agency (SONYMA), 189
Stringer 2013, 495
Stroock & Stroock & Lavan LLP, 204, 468
Stryker, Patricia, 468
Sullivan & Cromwell, 82
Sullivan & Cromwell LLP, 268
Supportive Housing Network of New York, Inc., 468
Sustainable Management LLC, 159
Swedish Institute, 565
Systra Consulting Inc, 292
TLM Associates LLC, 469
TPU Local One IATSE NYC, 495
Tamika For City Council 2013, 495
Tanenbaum Center for Interreligious Understanding, 199
Taxpayers For an Affordable New York Political Action Committee, 495
Taxpayers for Economic Justice, Inc. (NY), 468
Tea Association of the USA Inc, 77
Teachers College, Columbia University, 129, 561
Teaching Matters Inc, 129
Technical Career Institutes Inc, 565
Tempo 802, 495
Tenants & Neighbors, 192
The Clearing House Association, LLC, 80
The Committee to Re-Elect Inez E. Dickens 2013, 495
The General Contractors Association of New York PAC, 495
The High-Need Hospital PAC, Inc., 495
The Legal Aid Society, 199
The NYS Economic Growth PAC, 495
The New York Observer, 528
The New York Times, 528
Thelen Reid Brown Raysman & Steiner, 214
Thomas Lopez-Pierre For City Council 2013, 495
Time Warner Cable, 469
Tishman Speyer Properties, 249
Tishman Speyer Properties, L.P., 469
Tom Allon 2013, 495
Tom Duane For Senate, 495
Tommasino, Nicholas, 469
Touro College, 561

Listings appear in alphabetical order by state, then city.

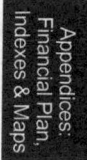

Transport Workers Union of America, AFL-CIO, 226, 292
Transportation Alternatives, 292
Trees New York, 159
Tri-State College of Acupuncture, 566
Tri-State Transportation Campaign, 292
Trial Lawyers Association (NYS) (FKA Feldman, Daniel), 469
Tribeca Film Institute, 282, 469
Trustees of Columbia University in the City of NY (The), 469
U.S. Green Building Council, New York Chapter, 470
UJA-Federation of New York, 249
UNITE HERE, 226
US Commerce Department
Harlem US Export Assistance Center, 89
New York Business Center, 88, 196
New York Region, 88, 196
New York US Export Assistance Center, 89
US Defense Department
AIR FORCE-National Media Outreach, 295
Fort Hamilton, 295
Public Affairs Office, 295
US Department of Agriculture
New York City Field Office, 72, 178
Office of the Inspector General, Northeast Region, 72
US Department of Energy
New York Regional Office, 142
US Department of Health & Human Services
Administration for Children & Families, 178, 254
Administration on Aging, 179, 254
Agency for Toxic Substances & Disease Registry-EPA Region 2, 179, 254
Centers for Medicare & Medicaid Services, 179, 254
Health Resources & Svcs Admin Office of Performance Review, 255
Health Resources & Svcs Admin-Region 2, 179
Office for Civil Rights, 179, 196, 255
Office of General Counsel, 179, 255
Office of Public Health & Science, 255
Office of Secretary's Regional Representative-Region 2-NY, 179, 196, 255
Office of the Assistant Secretary for Health (ASH), 179
US Department of Homeland Security (DHS)
Federal Protective Service (The), 167
National Urban Security Technology Laboratory, 153, 167
New York City District Office, 167, 196
New York District Office, 166, 266
New York Field Office, 167, 266
New York Regional Office, 167, 179
Queens Field Office, 168
Transportation Security Administration (TSA), 289
US Department of Veterans Affairs
New York Campus of the NY Harbor Healthcare System, 296
New York City Regional Office, 296
VA Regional Office of Public Affairs, Field Operations Svc, 296
US Department of the Interior
Manhattan Sites, 276
Statue of Liberty National Monument & Ellis Island, 276
US Education Department
Region 2 - NY, NJ, PR, Vi, 125
US Environmental Protection Agency
Region 2 - New York, 154
US Federal Courts
Southern District, 212
US Court of Appeals for the Second Circuit, 212
US Court of International Trade, 212
US General Services Administration
Region 2-New York, 168, 246
US Government Printing Office
Printing Procurement Office, 168
US Housing & Urban Development Department
New York State Office, 189
US Justice Department
Antitrust Division-New York Field Office, 89
Antitrust Division-New York Field Office, 212
Civil Division - Commercial Litigation Branch, 212
Community Relations Service - Northeast & Caribbean Region, 213
Community Relations Service-Northeast & Caribbean Region, 89
Drug Enforcement Administration - New York Task Force, 114
Investigations Division, 213
Metropolitan Correctional Center, 114
New York City, 114, 213
New York Field Division, 114, 266
Southern District, 115, 116, 214
US Trustee - Bankruptcy, Region 2, 214
US Labor Department
Bureau of Labor Statistics (BLS), 223
Employee Benefits Security Administration (EBSA), 223
Federal Contract Compliance Programs Office (OFCCP), 223
Inspector General's Office for Audit (OIG-A), 223
Manhattan Area Office, 180, 223
New York City District Office, 223
New York District Office, 223
Occupational Safety & Health Administration (OSHA), 223
Occupational Safety & Health Adminstration (OSHA), 180
Office of Asst Secretary for Administration & Mgmt (OASAM), 223
Office of the Solicitor, 223
Region 2 - New York Office of Secretary's Representative, 223
Region 2 New York - Women's Bureau (WB), 223
Workers' Compensation Programs (OWCP), 223
US Merit Systems Protection Board
New York Field Office, 223, 242
US Railroad Retirement Board
New York, 224
US Securities & Exchange Commission
New York Regional Office, 89
US State Department
Bureau of Educational & Cultural Affairs-NY Pgm Branch, 168
US Mission to the United Nations, 168, 297
US Transportation Department
Federal Transit Administration, Region II-New York, 289
North Atlantic Region, 290
Office of Inspector General, Region II-New York, 290
US Treasury Department
Appeals Unit - Office of Directors, 266
Large & Mid-Size Business Division (LMSB), 266
Management Information Technology Services - Northeast Area, 266
Manhattan Office, 267
New York SBSE Compliance Services, 266
New York Territory, 267
Northeastern District Office, 79
Office of Chief Counsel, 266
Office of Chief Counsel LMSB Area 1, 266
Office of Director, Area 1 (New York State & New England), 267
SBSE-Compliance Area 2/New York, 266
UWUA Local 1-2 Non Federal PAC, 496
Unified Court System, 209
1st Judicial Department, 209
Civil Court, 209
Court of Appeals, 209
Criminal Court, 209
Family Court, 209
Uniformed Fire Officers 527 Account, 495
Uniformed Fire Officers Association, 244
Uniformed Firefighters Association, 470
Uniformed Firefighters Association State FIREPAC, 495
Union Theological Seminary, 562
Unite Here Tip State and Local Fund, 496
United Federation of Teachers, 129
United Federation of Teachers (UFT) on Political Education, 496
United Hospital Fund of New York, 186

Listings appear in alphabetical order by state, then city.

United Jewish Appeal-Federation of Jewish Philanthropies of NY, 261
United Nations Development Corporation, 87, 106, 165
United Neighborhood Houses - Not For Profit, 261
United Neighborhood Houses of NY, 470
United Way of New York City, 261
Urban Homesteading Assistance Board, 193
Urban Justice Center, 471
Urbanomics, 239, 269
Urbitran Group, 292
Vargas 2013, 496
Vedder Price PC, 226
Venable LLP, 472
Vera Institute of Justice, 118, 218
Vera Institute of Justice, Inc., 472
Verizon, 472
Verizon Communications, 146
Verizon Communications Good Government Club PAC, 496
Veterans' Service Organizations
30th Street Shelter, 294
Viacom Inc, 146
Village Care of New York, Inc., 472
Village Voice (The), 528
Village Voice Media, Inc, 528
Vince Morgan 2013, 496
Viverito 2013, 496
Vladeck, Waldman, Elias & Engelhard PC, 226
Volunteers of Legal Service, Inc, 218
WABC (7), 538
WABC (770 AM), 535
WBBR (1130 AM) Bloomberg News, 535
WCBS (880 AM), 535
WINS (1010 AM), 535
WLTW (106.7 FM), 535
WNBC (4), 538
WNET New York Public Media, 146
WNYW (44), 538
WOR (710 AM), 535
WPIX (11), 538
WWOR (UPN 9), 538
Wachtel & Masyr, LLP, 473
Wachtell, Lipton, Rosen & Katz, 269
Wall Street Journal (The), 146, 527
Walmart Free NYC, 473
Waterfront Commission of New York Harbor, 107, 222, 288
Waterkeeper Alliance, 159
We Move, 186
Weiner For Mayor, 496
West Harlem Environmental Action, Inc., 474
West Manhattan Chamber of Commerce, 519
White & Case LLP, 82
White and Williams LLP, 474
Women's Bar Association of the State of New York, 218
Women's City Club of New York, 139
Women's Democratic Club of NYC, 496
Women's Prison Association & Home Inc, 118
Women's Refugee Commission, 199
Women's Venture Fund Inc, 94
Wood Tobe-Coburn, 566
Workers' Compensation Board
Manhattan, 202, 221
World Hunger Year Inc, 262
Wright Group NY, Inc. (The), 477
YAI/National Institute for People with Disabilities, 233, 262
YMCA of Greater New York, 477
Yeshiva University, 477, 562
Yoswein New York Inc, 478

New York Mills
NY Mills UFSD, 583

Newark
Newark CSD, 597
Newark Chamber of Commerce, 512
Wayne-Finger Lakes BOCES, 601

Newark Valley
Newark Valley CSD, 595

Newburgh
Construction Contractors Association of the Hudson Valley Inc, 91
Diorio, L Todd, 407
Hudson Valley Pattern for Progress, 191
Mid-Hudson Pattern for Progress, 92, 511
Mount Saint Mary College, 558
NYSTAR - Division of Science, Technology & Innovation
Hudson Valley Technology Development Center, 85, 123
Newburgh
Civil & Criminal Courts, 64
Newburgh Enlarged City SD, 585
Newburgh, City of, 359
Newburgh, Town of, 360
Research, Information & Policy Development
Newburgh (South), 246
Smith, Joseph, 466
Southeastern New York, Council of Industry of, 516

Newcomb
Newcomb CSD, 574

Newfane
Newfane CSD, 582

Newfield
Newfield CSD, 595

Newport
West Canada Valley CSD, 577

Newtonville
Colonie, Town of, 344

Niagara Falls
Greater Niagara Newspapers, 528
Niagara County
County, Supreme & Family Courts, 56
Niagara Falls
Civil & Criminal Courts, 64
Niagara Falls City SD, 583
Niagara Falls, City of, 360
Niagara Gazette, 528
Niagara-Wheatfield CSD, 583
Parks, Recreation & Historic Preservation, NYS Office of
Niagara Region & Western District Office, 272
Veterans' Service Organizations
COPIN HOUSE (Homeless Veterans), 294

Niagara University
Niagara University, 128, 559

Niskayuna
Community Mental Health Political Action Committee, Inc., 481
Higgins Roberts Beyerl & Coan, PC, 424
New England Steampship Agents Inc, 291
Niskayuna, Town of, 360
Northeast Government Consulting LLC, 450
US Department of Energy
Knolls Atomic Power Laboratory- KAPL Inc, 142

Nissequogue
Raustiala, Margaret, 459

North Babylon
North Babylon UFSD, 593

North Collins
North Collins CSD, 574

North Creek
Gore Mountain Region Chamber of Commerce, 506
Johnsburg CSD, 596

North Massapequa
Association of Fire Districts of the State of NY Inc, 237
Plainedge UFSD, 581

North Merrick
Bellmore-Merrick Central HS District, 579

North Salem
North Salem CSD, 598

North Syracuse
Greater Syracuse Association of Realtors Inc, 247
North Syracuse CSD, 584
Northeast Dairy Foods Association Inc, 77
US Department of Homeland Security (DHS)
Syracuse, Port of, 73

Listings appear in alphabetical order by state, then city.

Appendices: Financial Plan, Indexes & Maps

US Labor Department
Syracuse Area Office, 180, 223

North Tonawanda
Chamber of Commerce of the Tonawandas, 503
Greater Niagara Newspapers, 531
North Tonawanda
Civil & Criminal Courts, 64
North Tonawanda City SD, 583
North Tonawanda, City of, 360
Tonawanda News, 531
Tonawandas, Chamber of Commerce of the, 518

Northport
Northport Chamber of Commerce, 512
Northport-East Northport UFSD, 593
US Department of Veterans Affairs
Northport VA Medical Center, 296

Northville
Northville CSD, 575

Norwich
Chenango County, 327
Supreme, County, Family & Surrogate's Courts, 52
Chenango County Chamber of Commerce, 503
Delaware-Chenango-Madison-Otsego BOCES, 600
Elections, State Board of
Chenango, 131
Evening Sun, 528
NBT Bancorp Inc., 81
Norwich
Civil & Criminal Courts, 64
Norwich City SD, 570
Snyder Communications Corp, 528

Norwood
Norwood-Norfolk CSD, 590

Nunda
Dalton-Nunda CSD (Keshequa), 578

Nyack
Nyack Chamber of Commerce, 512
Nyack College, 559
Nyack UFSD, 588

Oakdale
Dowling College, 555

Oakfield
Oakfield-Alabama CSD, 575

Oakland Gardens
Friends of Catherine Nolan, 483

Ocean Beach
Fire Island UFSD, 592

Oceanside
Oceanside Chamber of Commerce, 512
Oceanside UFSD, 581

Odessa
Odessa-Montour CSD, 589

Ogdensburg
Corrections & Community Supervision Department
Ogdensburg Correctional Facility, 109
Riverview Correctional Facility, 110
Mental Health, Office of
St Lawrence Psychiatric Center, 229
Ogdensburg
Civil & Criminal Courts, 64
Ogdensburg Bridge & Port Authority, 105, 287
Ogdensburg Chamber of Commerce (Greater Ogdensburg), 512
Ogdensburg City SD, 590
St Lawrence County Newspapers, 529
The Journal, 529
US Department of Homeland Security (DHS)
Ogdensburg, Port of, 72, 167, 266

Old Forge
Central Adirondack Association, 503
Inlet Common School, 576
Northeastern Loggers' Association, 158
Town of Webb UFSD, 576

Old Westbury
East Williston UFSD, 580
New York Institute of Technology, 558
North Shore Land Alliance, 450
State University at Old Westbury, 545
US Commerce Department
Long Island US Export Assistance Center, 89
Westbury UFSD, 582

Olean
Bradford Publications Inc, 529
Cattaraugus County
Supreme & Family Court, 51
Cattaraugus Empire Zone Corporation, 503
Cattaraugus-Allegany-Erie-Wyoming BOCES, 600
Olean
Civil & Criminal Courts, 64
Olean Area Chamber of Commerce (Greater Olean), 512
Olean Business Institute, 565
Olean City SD, 569
Olean Times Herald, 529
WPIG (95.7 FM), WHDL (1450 AM), 535

Olmstedville
Minerva CSD, 574

Oneida
Greater Oneida Chamber of Commerce, 507
Journal Register Co, 529
Oneida
Civil & Criminal Courts, 64
Oneida City SD, 578
Oneida Daily Dispatch, 529
Oneida Indian Nation, 166
Support Services Alliance Inc, 94
US Department of Agriculture
Oneida Work Station, 71

Oneonta
Daily Star (The), 529
Hartwick College, 555
Oneonta
Civil & Criminal Courts, 64
Oneonta City SD, 587
Otsego County Chamber (The), 513
Otsego County Economic Development Department & Indu, 513
Ottaway Newspapers Inc, 529
Springbrook, 233
Springbrook NY, Inc, 261
State University of New York at Oneonta, 546
Upstate Homes for Children & Adults Inc, 262

Ontario
Ontario Chamber of Commerce, 513
Park Resident Homeowners' Association Inc, 192

Ontario Center
Wayne CSD, 597

Orangeburg
Dominican College, 555
KeyBank, 81
Mental Health, Office of
Nathan S Kline Institute for Psychiatric Research, 229
Rockland Children's Psychiatric Center, 229
Rockland Psychiatric Center, 229
Orangetown, Town of, 361

Orchard Park
Bryant & Stratton College-Southtowns Campus, 563
Buffalo Bills, 277
Messinger Woods Wildlife Care & Education Center Inc, 157
Orchard Park CSD, 574
Orchard Park Chamber of Commerce, 513
Orchard Park, Town of, 361
Realty USA, 248

Orient
Oysterponds UFSD, 593

Listings appear in alphabetical order by state, then city.

Oriskany
Oriskany CSD, 583
United Food & Commercial Workers Local 1, 226

Ossining
Corrections & Community Supervision Department
Sing Sing Correctional Facility, 110
Greater Ossining Chamber of Commerce, The, 507
Ossining UFSD, 598
Ossining, Town of, 361
Ossining, Village of, 361
Riverkeeper Inc, 158

Oswego
Amdursky Pelky Fennell & Wallen, 214
Elections, State Board of
Oswego, 134
NYS Bar Assn, Lawyer Referral Service Cmte, 214
Oswego
Civil & Criminal Courts, 65
Oswego City SD, 586
Oswego County, 334
Family Court, 57
Supreme, County & Surrogate's Courts, 57
Oswego County, Operation/Oswego County Industrial Development Agency, 513
Oswego-Fulton Chamber of Commerce, 513
Palladium-Times (The), 529
Plumbers & Steamfitters Local No. 73 State & Local PAC Fund, 492
Port of Oswego Authority, 106, 288
State University of New York at Oswego, 546
The Palladium-Times, 529

Otego
Otego-Unadilla CSD, 587
Unatego CSD, 587

Otisville
Corrections & Community Supervision Department
Otisville Correctional Facility, 109
US Justice Department
Federal Correctional Institution at Otisville, 114

Ovid
South Seneca CSD, 590

Owego
Elections, State Board of
Tioga, 135
Owego-Apalachin CSD, 595
Tioga County, 338
Supreme County, Family & Surrogate's Courts, 59
Tioga County Chamber of Commerce, 517
Tioga County Industrial Development Agency, 517

Oxford
Health Department
New York State Veterans' Home at Oxford, 175, 293
Oxford Academy & CSD, 570

Oyster Bay
Oyster Bay Chamber of Commerce, 513
Oyster Bay, Town of, 361
Oyster Bay-East Norwich CSD, 581
US Department of the Interior
Sagamore Hill National Historic Site, 276

Ozone Park
Eric Ulrich 2013, 482
People For Albert Baldeo, 492
Re-Elect Eric Ulrich, 493
Victor Babb For N.Y.C. Council, 496

Painted Post
Corning-Painted Post Area SD, 591
Greater Southern Tier BOCES (Schuyler-Chemung-Tioga-Allegany-St, 600
Painted Post Area Board of Trade, 513

Palmyra
Palmyra-Macedon CSD, 597

Panama
Panama CSD, 570

Parish
Altmar-Parish-Williamstown CSD, 586

Parishville
Parishville-Hopkinton CSD, 590

Parsippany
Muhs, Robert E., 446

Patchogue
Briarcliffe College-Patchogue, 563
Eastern Suffolk BOCES, 600
Patchogue Chamber of Commerce (Greater Patchogue), 513
Patchogue-Medford UFSD, 593
Suffolk County
6th District Court, 61
US Department of the Interior
Fire Island National Seashore, 153, 276
Veterans' Service Organizations
Suffolk County United Veterans Halfway House Project Inc, 294

Patterson
Carmel CSD, 587
Patterson Chamber of Commerce, 513

Pattersonville
NYS Democratic Senate Campaign Committee, 491

Paul Smiths
Paul Smith's College, 559

Pavilion
Pavilion CSD, 575

Pawling
Pawling CSD, 572

Pearl River
Orange & Rockland Utilities Inc, 145
Pearl River UFSD, 588
Rockland Economic Development Corporation, 515

Peekskill
Hudson Valley Gateway Chamber of Commerce, 509
Human Rights, State Division of
Peekskill, 195
Peekskill
Civil & Criminal Courts, 65
Peekskill City SD, 598
Peekskill Industrial Development Agency (City of), 513
Peekskill, City of, 361
State Department
Region 2 - Peekskill Office, 163
Workers' Compensation Board
Peekskill, 202, 221

Pelham
Pelham UFSD, 598

Penfield
Penfield CSD, 579
Penfield, Town of, 362

Penn Yan
Elections, State Board of
Yates, 136
Finger Lakes Economic Development Center, 520
Finger Lakes Tourism Alliance, 278
Penn Yan CSD, 599
Seneca Flight Operations, 292
Yates County, 340
Supreme, County, Family & Surrogate's Courts, 61
Yates County Chamber of Commerce, 520

Perry
Perry Area Chamber of Commerce, 513
Perry CSD, 599
Wyoming County Chamber of Commerce, 519

Perrysburg
Garden Gate Greenhouse, 74

Peru
Peru CSD, 571

Phelps
Phelps Chamber of Commerce, 514

Appendices: Financial Plan, Indexes & Maps

Listings appear in alphabetical order by state, then city.

Philadelphia
Indian River CSD, 577

Phoenix
Phoenix CSD, 586

Pine Bush
Pine Bush CSD, 585

Pine City
Corrections & Community Supervision Department
Southport Correctional Facility, 110

Pine Plains
Election Computer Services Inc, 138
Pine Plains CSD, 572

Piseco
Piseco Common SD, 576

Pittsford
Campground Owners of New York, 278
D H Ferguson, Attorney, PLLC, 247
Harris Beach LLP, 216
J J Higgins Properties Inc, 247
NYS Bar Assn, Real Property Law Section, 247
Pittsford CSD, 579
Pittsford, Town of, 362
Red Barn Properties, 248

Plainview
New York Islanders, 280
Plainview-Old Bethpage CSD, 581
Plainview-Old Bethpage Chamber of Commerce, 514
WLIW (21) Public Broadcasting, 538

Plattsburgh
American Military Retirees Association Inc, 297
Bombardier Transit Corporation & Affiliates, 388
Champlain Valley Educational Svcs (Clinton-Essex-Warren-Washington), 600
Clinton Community College, 547
Clinton County, 327
Supreme, County, Family & Surrogate's Courts, 52
Clinton County, The Development Corporation, 504
Elections, State Board of
Clinton, 131
Law Department
Plattsburgh, 208
North Country Vietnam Veterans Association, Post 1, 299
Plattsburgh
Civil & Criminal Courts, 65
Plattsburgh City SD, 571
Plattsburgh-North Country Chamber of Commerce, 514
Press-Republican, 529
State University of New York at Plattsburgh, 546
US Justice Department
Plattsburgh, 115, 213
WPTZ (5) NBC, 538

Pleasantville
Mt Pleasant-Cottage UFSD, 598
Pleasantville UFSD, 599

Poland
Poland CSD, 576

Pomona
Catskill Off-Track Betting Corporation, 96, 273

Port Byron
Port Byron CSD, 569

Port Chester
Port Chester SD, 599
Port Chester, Village of, 362
Port Chester-Rye Brook Rye Town Chamber of Commerce, 514
Rye, Town of, 364

Port Henry
Moriah CSD, 574

Port Jefferson
Brookhaven-Comsewogue UFSD, 591
Greater Port Jefferson Chamber of Commerce, 507
Port Jefferson Chamber of Commerce, 514
Port Jefferson UFSD, 593

Port Jervis
Port Jervis
Civil & Criminal Courts, 65
Port Jervis City SD, 585

Port Washington
National Marfan Foundation, 184
North Shore Animal League America, 261
Port Washington Chamber of Commerce, 514
Port Washington UFSD, 581

Portville
Portville CSD, 569

Potsdam
Clarkson University, 553
Clarkson University (FKA Wood Jr., Robert H.), 398
NYSTAR - Division of Science, Technology & Innovation
Center for Advanced Materials Processing at Clarkson Univ, 84, 122
Council for Interntl Trade, Tech, Education & Communication, 85, 123
Potsdam CSD, 590
Potsdam Chamber of Commerce, 514
State University at Potsdam, 545
State University of New York at Potsdam, 467

Poughkeepsie
Agriculture & Markets Department
Weights & Measures, 70
Arlington CSD, 572
Central Hudson Gas & Electric Corporation, 143
Central Hudson Gas & Electric Corporation (FKA Glusko, John), 395
Dutchess BOCES, 600
Dutchess Community College, 547
Dutchess County, 328
Family Court, 53
Supreme, County & Surrogate's Courts, 53
Dutchess County Economic Development Corporation, 505
Dutchess County Regional Chamber of Commerce, 514
Education Department
Mid-Hudson District Office, 122
Elections, State Board of
Dutchess, 131
Gannett Co Inc, 529
Law Department
Poughkeepsie, 208
Marist College, 557
Marist Institute for Public Opinion, 138
Mid-Hudson Catskill Rural & Migrant Ministry Inc, 444
NYS Bar Assn, Judicial Campaign Monitoring Cmte, 218
New York State Association of Family Service Agencies Inc, 260
Ostertag O'Leary & Barrett, 218
Poughkeepsie
Civil & Criminal Courts, 65
Poughkeepsie City SD, 572
Poughkeepsie Journal, 529
Poughkeepsie, City of, 362
Poughkeepsie, Town of, 362
Rural & Migrant Ministry Inc, 261
Scenic Hudson, 159
Scenic Hudson Inc, 463
Spackenkill UFSD, 573
Transportation Department
Region 8, 284
Vassar College, 562
Veterans' Service Organizations
Veterans' Coalition of the Hudson Valley, 294
WPDH (101.5 FM), 536
WRRV (92.7 FM), 536

Prattsburgh
Prattsburgh CSD, 591

Pulaski
Pulaski CSD, 586

Listings appear in alphabetical order by state, then city.

Pulaski-Eastern Shore Chamber of Commerce, 514

Purchase
MBIA Insurance Corporation, 81
Manhattanville College, 557
Pepsi Co, 94
Purchase College, State University of New York, 545

Putnam Station
Putnam CSD, 596

Putnam Valley
Putnam Valley CSD, 587

Queens
NYC Region 5, 582
New York Hall of Science, 280
St John's University, 561
St John's University, School of Law, 159
St John's University-Peter J Tobin College of Business, S, 204
US Department of Health & Human Services
Northeast Regional Laboratory, 255

Queens Village
Friends of Mark Weprin 2013, 485
Mental Health, Office of
Creedmoor Psychiatric Center, 228

Queens Vlg
NYS Office for People with Developmental Disabilities
Bernard Fineson Developmental Disabilities Services Office, 229

Queensbury
Adirondack Community College, 546
Queensbury UFSD, 596
Queensbury, Town of, 362
Vietnam Veterans of America, NYS Council, 300

Quogue
Quogue UFSD, 593

Randolph
Randolph Academy UFSD, 569
Randolph CSD, 569

Raquette Lake
Raquette Lake UFSD, 576

Ray Brook
Adirondack Park Agency, 95, 150, 272
Corrections & Community Supervision Department
Adirondack Correctional Facility, 108
Environmental Conservation Department
Region 5, 148
Real Property Tax Services, Office of
Ray Brook Satellite Office, 235, 264
Research, Information & Policy Development
Ray Brook Satellite Office, 246
US Justice Department
Ray Brook Federal Correctional Institution, 114

Red Creek
Corrections & Community Supervision Department
Butler Correctional Facility, 109
Red Creek CSD, 597

Red Hook
Red Hook Area Chamber of Commerce, 514
Red Hook CSD, 573

Rego Park
Rego Hills Republican Club, 493

Remsen
Remsen CSD, 583

Remsenburg
Remsenburg-Speonk UFSD, 593

Rensselaer
Barlette, Richard, 385
Children & Family Services, Office of, 5, 119, 251
Council on Children & Families, 5
Council on Children & Families (CCF), 252
Youth Development, Office of, 252
Corporation for National & Community Service
New York Program Office, 254
Empire State Forest Products Association, 156, 411
Health Department
School of Public Health, SUNY at Albany, 175
Healthcare Association of New York State, 183
Healthcare Association of New York State PAC, 486
Murray, Claire, 446
New York Independent System Operator - Not For Profit, 145
North Greenbush Common SD (Williams), 588
Rensselaer
Civil & Criminal Courts, 65
Rensselaer City SD, 588
SUNY at Albany, School of Public Health, Center, 186

Rensselear
Healthcare Association of New York State, 423

Retsof
York CSD, 578

Rexford
Anson, Joseph L., 381

Rhinebeck
Rhinebeck Area Chamber of Commerce, 514
Rhinebeck CSD, 573

Rhinecliff
CSC Holdings, LLC (Cablevision), 377
Downtown Brooklyn Partnership, Inc., 377
L & M Development Partners, Inc., 377
Madison Realty Capital Advisors LLC (FKA Madison Realty Capital), 377
Putting New Yorkers to Work, 377
Real Estate Board of New York, 377
University (New York), 377
Urban Strategic Partners, LLC, 377

Richfield Springs
Richfield Springs Area Chamber of Commerce, 514
Richfield Springs CSD, 587

Richmond Hill
Community For Lynn Nunes, 481
Elaine Nunes 2010, 482
Friends of Nicole Paultre Bell, 485
Mike Duvalle 4 City Council, 490

Richmond Hills
People For Leroy Gadsen, 492

Ridgewood
Vito Lopez For City Council, 496

Ripley
Ripley CSD, 570

Riverdale
College of Mount Saint Vincent, 554
Manhattan College, 557

Riverhead
Riverhead CSD, 593
Riverhead Chamber of Commerce, 514
Riverhead Foundation for Marine Research & Preservation (The), 158
Riverhead, Town of, 363
Suffolk County
County Court, 59
Supreme Court, 59
Surrogate's Court, 59

Rochester
4th Department, 45
Action for a Better Community Inc, 256
Agriculture & Markets Department
Rochester, 70
Associated New York State State Food Processors Inc, 73
Attorney Grievance Committee
Judicial Dist 7, 208
Bausch & Lomb Inc, 181
Boylan Brown, 214
Brighton CSD, 578
Brighton, Town of, 342

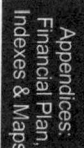

Appendices: Financial Plan, Indexes & Maps

Listings appear in alphabetical order by state, then city.

Bryant & Stratton College-Greece Campus, 563
Bryant & Stratton College-Henrietta Campus, 563
Carpino, Peter, 394
Center for Disability Rights, Inc., 395
Center for Environmental Information Inc, 156
Center for Governmental Research Inc (CGR), 169
Chili, Town of, 343
Colgate Rochester Crozer Divinity School, 554
Community & Economic Development, 77
Connors & Corcoran LLP, 215
Connors & Corcoran PLLC, 203
Convention Centers & Visitors Bureaus
Greater Rochester Visitors Association, 274
Corrections & Community Supervision Department
Rochester Correctional Facility, 110
Daily Record (The), 529
Democrat and Chronicle, 530
East Irondequoit CSD, 578
Eastman Kodak Company, 91
Eber, Lester, 409
Education Department
Rochester District Office, 122
Elections, State Board of
Monroe, 133
Empire Justice Center (FKA Greater Upstate Law Project), 410
Everest Institute, 564
Excellus BCBS, 182
Excellus Health Plan Inc, 203
Gannett Co Inc, 530
Gates-Chili CSD, 578
Genesee Transportation Council, 238
Greater Rochester Association of Realtors Inc, 247
Greece Chamber of Commerce, 507
Harris Poll (The), 138
Harter Secrest & Emery, LLP, 423
Hillside Family of Agencies, 424
Human Rights, State Division of
Rochester, 195
Insurance Fund (NYS)
Rochester, 201, 219
Irondequoit, Town of, 348
Korean War Veterans, 298
Labor Department
Finger Lakes Region, 220
Law Department
Rochester, 208
Law Guardian Program
4th Judicial Dept, 208
Mental Health, Office of
Rochester Psychiatric Center, 229
Mental Hygiene Legal Service
4th Judicial Dept, 209, 230
Monroe Community College, 548
Monroe County, 331
Supreme, County, Family & Surrogate's Courts, 55
Monroe County Industrial Development Agency (COMIDA), 511
NYS Bar Assn, Municipal Law Section, 217
NYS Bar Assn, President's Cmte on Access to Justice, 214
NYS Bar Assn, Torts, Insurance & Compensation Law Section, 215
NYS Deputies Association Inc, 118, 243
NYS Office for People with Developmental Disabilities
Finger Lakes Developmental Disabilities Services Office, 230
NYSTAR - Division of Science, Technology & Innovation
Center for Emerging & Innovative Sciences, 84, 122
Nazareth College of Rochester, 558
New York State Court of Claims, 217
New York State Gaming Commission
Rochester Office, 264
Nixon Peabody LLP PAC, 491
Northeastern Seminary, 559
PathStone Corporation, 77, 192, 261
Roberts Wesleyan College, 560
Rochester
Civil Court, 65
Criminal Court, 65
Rochester Business Alliance Inc, 514
Rochester Business Alliance, Inc., 461
Rochester Business Journal, 533
Rochester City SD, 579
Rochester Downtown Development Corporation, 514
Rochester Economic Development Corporation, 514
Rochester Educational Opportunity Center, 550
Rochester Gas & Electric Corporation, 145
Rochester Institute of Technology, 560
Rochester Interfaith Jail Ministry Inc, 118
Rochester School for the Deaf, 128
Rochester, City of, 363
Rochester, University of, 560
Rochester-Genesee Regional Transportation Authority-RTS, 106, 288
St Bernard's School of Theology & Ministry, 560
St John Fisher College, 561
Stendardi, Deborah M, 467
The Dolan Company, 529
Transportation Department
Region 4, 284
US Department of Homeland Security (DHS)
Rochester, Port of, 72, 167
US Justice Department
Rochester, 115, 116, 213, 214
Unified Court System
4th Judicial Department, 209
7th Judicial District (Judicial Department 4), 210
University of Rochester, 471
University of Rochester School of Medicine, 159
Veterans' Service Organizations
Veterans Outreach Center Inc, 294
WHAM (1180 AM), 536
WHAM (13), 539
WHEC (10), 539
WXXI (16) Public Broadcasting, 539
Wegmans Food Markets Inc, 94
West Irondequoit CSD, 579
Worker Justice Center of New York, Inc., 476
Workers' Compensation Board
Rochester, 202, 221
Yockel, James, 477

Rock Tavern

US Department of Agriculture
NY Animal Import Center, 72

Rockaway Beach

Friends of Audrey Pheffer, 483
The Wave, 528
Wave Publishing Co., 528

Rockaway Park

Rockaways, Chamber of Commerce, Inc, 515

Rockhill

Billig, Jacob, 386

Rockville Centre

Matarazzo, Louis, 441
Molloy College, 557
Rockville Centre Chamber of Commerce, 515
Rockville Centre UFSD, 581
Rockville Centre, Village of, 363

Rocky Point

Losquadro, Steven E., 436
Rocky Point UFSD, 593

Rome

Corrections & Community Supervision Department
Mohawk Correctional Facility, 109
Daily Sentinel, 530
McMahon & Grow, 171, 216
Mohawk Valley Economic Development Growth Enterprises, 511
NYS Bar Assn, Court Structure & Judicial Selection Cmte, 171, 216
NYS Office for People with Developmental Disabilities
Central New York Developmental Disabilities Services Office, 230

Listings appear in alphabetical order by state, then city.

Oneida Industrial Development Agency (City of), 513

Rome

Civil & Criminal Courts, 65

Rome Area Chamber of Commerce, 515

Rome City SD, 583

Rome Industrial Development Corporation, 515

Rome Sentinel Co, 530

Rome, City of, 363

Technology Enterprise Corporation (NYS), 468

US Department of Homeland Security (DHS)

Rome, Port of, 167

US Department of the Interior

Fort Stanwix National Monument, 276

Romulus

Corrections & Community Supervision Department

Five Points Correctional Facility, 109

Romulus CSD, 590

Ronkonkoma

Long Island Business News, 532

Ronkonkoma Chamber of Commerce, 515

Suffolk County

1ST DISTRICT COURT, Civil Term, 61

5th District Court, 61

Roosevelt

Roosevelt UFSD, 581

Roosevelt Island

Roosevelt Island Operating Corporation (RIOC), 106, 189, 274

Rooseveltown

US Department of Homeland Security (DHS)

Massena, Port of, 72, 167

Roscoe

Roscoe CSD, 594

Rosedale

Friends of Michael Duncan 2013, 485

Roslyn

Roslyn UFSD, 581

Rotterdam

Rotterdam, Town of, 364

Roxbury

Roxbury CSD, 572

Rushville

Gorham-Middlesex CSD (Marcus Whitman), 585

Marcus Whitman CSD, 585

Russell

Edwards-Knox CSD, 590

Rye

Runes, Richard, 462

Rye

Civil & Criminal Courts, 65

Rye City SD, 599

Rye Brook

Blind Brook-Rye UFSD, 597

Southern Westchester BOCES, 601

WRNN (48), 538

Sackets Harbor

Sackets Harbor Central School, 577

Sackets Harbor Chamber of Commerce, 515

Seaway Trail Inc, 281

Sag Harbor

Sag Harbor Chamber of Commerce, 515

Sag Harbor UFSD, 593

Sagaponack

Sagaponack Common SD, 593

Saint Albans

Friends of Manny Caughman Committee, 484

Salamanca

Bradford Publishing Co, 530

Parks, Recreation & Historic Preservation, NYS Office of

Allegany Region, 272

Salamanca

Civil & Criminal Courts, 65

Salamanca Area Chamber of Commerce, 515

Salamanca City SD, 569

Salamanca Industrial Development Agency, 515

Salamanca Press, 530

Salem

Christmas Tree Farmers Association of New York Inc, 73

Salem CSD, 596

Sanborn

Agricultural Affiliates, 73

NYS Berry Growers Association, 75

Niagara County Center for Economic Development, 512

Niagara County Community College, 548

Niagara Falls Chamber of Commerce, 512

Niagara USA Chamber of Commerce, 512

Sandy Creek

Sandy Creek CSD, 586

Saranac Lake

Adirondack Daily Enterprise, 530

Adirondack Economic Development Corporation, 501

Adirondack Publishing Co Inc, 530

North Country Community College, 548

Saranac Lake Area Chamber of Commerce, 515

Saranac Lake CSD, 575

St Joseph's Rehabilitation Center Inc, 233

Saratoga Springs

AIM Services Inc, 231

American Farmland Trust, 380

American Farmland Trust, New York Office, 73, 155

Association for Eating Disorders - Capital Region, 231

Convention Centers & Visitors Bureaus

Saratoga Convention & Tourism Bureau, 275

Empire State College, State University of NY, 411

Farmers Insurance Group, 413

Journal Register Company, 530

Land Trust Alliance Northeast Program, 157, 433

New York Thoroughbred Breeders Inc, 76

Parks, Recreation & Historic Preservation, NYS Office of

Saratoga/Capital District Region, 272

Regional Farm & Food Project, 77

Ronald Poppel, 461

Roohan Realty, 249

Saratoga County Chamber of Commerce, 515

Saratoga Economic Development Corporation, 515

Saratoga Gaming & Raceway, 281

Saratoga Harness Racing, Inc., 463

Saratoga Springs

Civil & Criminal Courts, 65

Saratoga Springs City SD, 588

Saratoga Springs, City of, 364

Saratogian (The), 530

Skidmore College, 560

State University Empire State College, 545

US Defense Department

Saratoga Springs Naval Support Unit, 295

Watertown Empire Zone, 518

Saugerties

Saugerties CSD, 595

Saugerties, Town of, 364

Sauquoit

Sauquoit Valley CSD, 583

Sayville

Sayville Chamber of Commerce (Greater Sayville), 515

Sayville UFSD, 593

Scarsdale

Edgemont UFSD, 598

Scarsdale Chamber of Commerce, 515

Scarsdale UFSD, 599

Appendices: Financial Plan, Indexes & Maps

Listings appear in alphabetical order by state, then city.

Schaghticoke
Hoosic Valley CSD, 587
New York State Association of Agricultural Fairs Inc, 76

Schenectady
AAA Northway, 277
ATU NY State Legislative Conference Board, 384
Agriculture & NYS Horse Breeding Development Fund, 95, 272
Association of Chiefs of Police, 383
Cantore, Anthony S., 392
Capital District Regional Off-Track Betting Corporation, 96, 272
Conservative Party of NYS, 138
Daily Gazette (The), 530
Daily Gazette Co, 530
Elections, State Board of
Schenectady, 135
Ellis Hospital School of Nursing, 555
Englert, Coffey, McHugh & Fantauzzi LLP, 215
Environmental Conservation Department
Region 4, 148
Golub, David, 419
Mid-America Baptist Theological Seminary Northeast Branch, 557
Mohonasen CSD, 589
NYS Association of Chiefs of Police Inc, 117, 243
NYS Bar Assn, Review Judicial Nominations Cmte, 215
NYS Office for People with Developmental Disabilities
Capital District Developmental Disabilities Services Office, 229
Information Support Services, 229
New York State Conservative Party, 371
New York State Gaming Commission, 10, 102, 264, 272
Eastern Region, 264
New York State Thoroughbred Breeding & Development Fund Corporation, 104, 273
Niskayuna CSD, 589
Remove Intoxicated Drivers (RID-USA Inc), 118
Rotterdam-Mohonasen CSD, 589
SUNY College & Career Counseling Center, 550
Schalmont CSD, 589
Schenectady
Civil Court, 65
Criminal Court, 65
Schenectady City SD, 589
Schenectady County, 335
Family Court, 58
Supreme, County & Surrogate's Courts, 58
Schenectady County Chamber of Commerce, 515
Schenectady County Community College, 548
Schenectady County Industrial Developmen, 515
Schenectady, City of, 364
Self Advocacy Association of NYS, 199, 233
Special Olympics New York, Inc, 281
Unified Court System
4th Judicial District (Judicial Department 3), 209
Union College, 562
WGNA (107.7 FM), 536
WRGB (6), 537
Workers' Compensation Board, 14, 201, 221

Schenevus
Schenevus CSD, 587

Schnectady
MVP Health Insurance Co. and Its Affiliates (FKA MVP Servi, 447

Schodack Landing
Shanahan Group, 465

Schoharie
Elections, State Board of
Schoharie, 135
Schoharie CSD, 589
Schoharie County, 336
Supreme, County, Family & Surrogate's Courts, 58
Support Services Alliance Inc, 205

Schroon Lake
Schroon Lake Area Chamber of Commerce, 516
Schroon Lake CSD, 574

Schuylerville
Schuylerville CSD, 589
US Department of Veterans Affairs
Gerald B.H. Solomon Saratoga National Cemetery, 295

Scio
Scio CSD, 568

Scotia
Scotia-Glenville CSD, 589

Scottsville
Wheatland-Chili CSD, 579

Sea Cliff
North Shore CSD, 581

Seaford
Seaford Chamber of Commerce, 516
Seaford UFSD, 581

Selden
Suffolk County Community College, 548

Selkirk
O'Connell, Maurice J., 452
Ravena-Coeymans-Selkirk CSD, 567

Seneca Falls
Cayuga Nation of New York, 166
National Women's Hall of Fame, 280
New York Chiropractic College, 558
Seneca County Chamber of Commerce, 516
Seneca Falls CSD, 590
US Department of the Interior
Women's Rights National Historical Park, 276
United Dairy Cooperative Services Inc, 77

Sharon Springs
Sharon Springs CSD, 589

Shelter Island
Shelter Island UFSD, 593

Sherburne
Sherburne-Earlville CSD, 571

Sherman
Sherman CSD, 570

Sherrill
Sherrill
Civil & Criminal Courts, 65

Shoreham
Shoreham-Wading River CSD, 594

Shortsville
Manchester-Shortsville CSD, 585

Shrub Oak
Lakeland CSD, 598

Shushan
Dionondehowa Wildlife Sanctuary & School - Not For Profit, 156

Sidney
Sidney CSD, 572
Sidney Chamber of Commerce, 516

Silver Creek
Silver Creek CSD, 570

Silver Springs
New York Corn & Soybean Growers Association, 76

Sinclairville
Cassadaga Valley CSD, 569

Skaneateles
Skaneateles Area Chamber of Commerce, 516
Skaneateles CSD, 584

Slate Hill
Minisink Valley CSD, 585

Listings appear in alphabetical order by state, then city.

Sleepy Hollow
Pocantico Hills CSD, 599
Tarrytown UFSD, 599

Slingerlands
NYS Association of Small City School Districts, 127

Sloan
Cheektowaga-Sloan UFSD, 573

Smithtown
Guide Dog Foundation for the Blind Inc, 258
Schnell, William A & Associates Inc, 464
Smithtown CSD, 594
Smithtown Chamber of Commerce, 516
Smithtown, Town of, 364
Suffolk County, 337

Sodus
Sodus CSD, 597

Solvay
Solvay UFSD, 584

Somers
Somers CSD, 599

Sonyea
Corrections & Community Supervision Department
Groveland Correctional Facility, 109
Livingston Correctional Facility, 109

South Dayton
Pine Valley CSD (South Dayton), 570

South Glens Falls
South Glens Falls CSD, 589

South Kortright
South Kortright CSD, 572

South Otselic
Georgetown-South Otselic CSD, 570

South Ozone Park
Friends of Martha Taylor Butler, 485
Jennings NYC, 487
Vish Mahadeo 2010, 496

Southampton
Shinnecock Indian Nation, 166
Southampton Chamber of Commerce, 516
Southampton UFSD, 594
Southampton, Town of, 365
Tuckahoe Common SD, 594

Southold
Greenport-Southold Chamber of Commerce, 508
North Fork Chamber of Commerce, 512
Southold UFSD, 594
Southold, Town of, 365

Sparkill
St Thomas Aquinas College, 561

Speculator
Adirondacks Speculator Region Chamber of Commerce, 501
Brown, Arthur M., 390
Lake Pleasant CSD, 576

Spencer
Spencer-Van Etten CSD, 595

Spencerport
McGuire, Jason J., 441
Monroe 2-Orleans BOCES, 600
Spencerport CSD, 579
Suburban News & Hamlin Clarkson Herald, 530
Westside News Inc, 530

Spring Valley
East Ramapo CSD (Spring Valley), 588
Spring Valley, Village of, 365

Springfield Gardens
Friends of Selvena Brooks, 485
US Justice Department
JFK/LGA, 114

Springville
Springville Area Chamber of Commerce, 517
Springville-Griffith Inst CSD, 574

St Bonaventure
St Bonaventure University, 560

St James
St James Chamber of Commerce, 517

St Johnsville
Oppenheim-Ephratah CSD, 575
St Johnsville CSD, 579

St Regis Falls
St Regis Falls CSD, 575

St. Albans
Comrie For NYC, 481
Friends of Ruben Wills, 485
Ruben Wills 2013, 493

St. James
Dagnello, Vito, 404

St. Johnsville
NYS Association for Solid Waste Management, 157

Staatsburg
Parks, Recreation & Historic Preservation, NYS Office of
Taconic Region, 272

Stamford
Stamford CSD, 572

Stanley
Empire State Potato Growers Inc, 74

Star Lake
Clifton-Fine CSD, 590

Staten Island
Advance Publications Inc, 530
Building Industry Association of NYC Inc, 91
Building Industry Association of NYC, Inc., 480
Civil Court, NYC
Richmond County, 49
College of Staten Island, 551
Connors & Connors, PC, 215
Conservative Party Campaign Committee, 481
Criminal Court, NYC
Richmond County, 49
Elections, State Board of
Richmond, 133
Family Court, NYC
Richmond County, 50
Friends of Martin For City Council, 485
Ignizio 2013, 487
Interstate Environmental Commission, 98, 151
Kalanz, Edward, 431
Lisa G For NY, 488
Mancuso For Council, 489
Marine Corps League (MCL), Department of NY, 298
Matteo For Council, 489
Mental Health, Office of
South Beach Psychiatric Center, 229
Molinari Republican Club, 490
NYC Region 7, 582
NYS Bar Assn, Trial Lawyers Section, 215
NYS Office for People with Developmental Disabilities
Institute for Basic Research in Developmental Disabilities, 230
Staten Island Developmental Disabilities Services Office, 230
New York City Boroughs
Staten Island (Richmond County), 359
Oddo For Staten Island, 491
Richmond County
Supreme & Surrogate's Courts, 57
Richmond County (NYC Borough of Staten Island), 335
Staten Island Advance, 530
Staten Island Chamber of Commerce, 517
Staten Island Economic Development Corporation, 517
Staten Island PAC, 494
Staten Island Zoo, 282
The Debi Rose Campaign Committee, 495
US Department of the Interior
Gateway National Recreation Area, 276
Wagner College, 562

Listings appear in alphabetical order by state, then city.

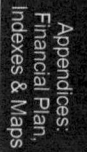

Stillwater
Coalition of Fathers & Families NY, 182
Coalition of Fathers & Families NY, PAC, 170
Darwak, Stephanie, 405
Stillwater CSD, 589
US Department of the Interior
Saratoga National Historical Park, 276

Stone Ridge
Ulster County Community College, 549

Stony Brook
Environmental Conservation Department
Region 1, 148
NY Sea Grant, 157
NYSTAR - Division of Science, Technology & Innovation
Center for Advanced Medical Biotechnology, 85, 122
Sensor CAT-Diagnostic Tools & Sensor Systems, 84, 122
State University of New York at Stony Brook, 467
Stony Brook University, SUNY, 545
Three Village CSD, 594

Stormville
Corrections & Community Supervision Department
Green Haven Correctional Facility, 109

Suffern
Ramapo, Town of, 363
Rockland Community College, 548
SCS Engineers PC, 158
Salvation Army School for Officer Training, 560
Suffern Chamber of Commerce, 517

Sunnyside
Driscoll Group, Inc., 407
Iwachiw 4 Mayor, 487
Van Bramer 2013, 496

Syosset
New York College of Health Professions, 558
Syosset CSD, 581

Syracuse
Agriculture & Markets Department
State Fair, 70
Syracuse, 70
Associated Builders & Contractors, Empire State Chapter, 90
Attorney Grievance Committee
Judicial Dist 5, 208
Blitman & King LLP, 224
Bond Schoeneck & King PLLC, 197
Bryant & Stratton College-Syracuse Campus, 563
Camillus, Town of, 343
Catholic Charities of Onondaga County, 256
Center for Policy Research, 261
Centerstate Corporation for Economic Opportunity, 395
Central New York Business Journal, 532
Central New York Regional Market Authority, 86, 96
Central New York Regional Transportation Authority, 96, 285
Community Bank N.A., 80
Convention Centers & Visitors Bureaus
Syracuse Convention & Vistors Bureau, 275
Cookfair Media Inc, 138
Crouse Hospital School of Nursing, 554
Dairy Farmers of America Northeast, 74
Dairylea Cooperative, Inc., 404
Destiny USA Management Company, LLC, 406
Education Department
Syracuse District Office, 122
Elections, State Board of
Onondaga, 134
Empire State Passengers Association, 291
Environmental Conservation Department
Region 7, 148
Eric Mower & Associates, 92
Gilberti Stinziano Heint, 418
Health Department
Central New York Regional Office, 176
Hiscock & Barclay, LLP, 425
Human Rights, State Division of
Syracuse, 195
Journal News (The)/Gannett Co Inc, 524
Law Department
Syracuse, 208
Le Moyne College, 556
Lyncourt UFSD, 584
Manufacturers Assn of Central NY Inc, 439
Manufacturers Association of Central New York, 92
Mental Health, Office of
Hutchings Psychiatric Center, 228
Military Order of the Purple Heart, 299
Mosaic Federal Affairs LLC, 446
NP Associates, LLC, 450
NYS Bar Assn, Judicial Campaign Conduct Cmte, 218
NYSTAR - Division of Science, Technology & Innovation
Center for Computer Applications & Software Engineering, 85, 122
National Grid, 145
New York Community Colleges Association of Presidents, 127
New York State Gaming Commission
Syracuse Office, 264
New York State Maple Producers Association Inc, 76
New York Water Environment Association Inc (NYWEA), 158
Onondaga Community College, 548
Onondaga County, 333
Supreme, County, Family & Surrogate's Courts, 56
Onondaga County Industrial Development Agency, 513
Onondaga, Town of, 361
Onondaga-Cortland-Madison BOCES, 600
Persons, Eric, 455
Pomeroy Appraisal Associates Inc, 248
Post-Standard (The), 531
ProLiteracy Worldwide, 128, 261
Real Property Tax Services, Office of
Syracuse (Central Region), 235, 264
Research, Information & Policy Development
Syracuse (Central Region), 246
Review, 524
SUNY College of Environmental Science and Forestry (FKA Micheal, 468
SUNY Upstate Medical University, 468, 544
Salvation Army, Empire State Division, 261
Small Business Administration
Syracuse, 88
State Department
Region 5 - Syracuse Office, 163
State University of New York College of Environmental Science, 545
Supreme Court, 218
Syracuse
Civil & Criminal Courts, 66
Syracuse & Central NY, Metropolitan Development Association of, 517
Syracuse Chamber of Commerce (Greater Syracuse), 517
Syracuse City SD, 584
Syracuse Economic Development, 517
Syracuse Educational Opportunity Center, 550
Syracuse Industrial Development Agency, 517
Syracuse Newspapers Inc, 531
Syracuse University, 561
Syracuse University Press, 159
Syracuse University, Maxwell School of Citizenship & Public Affairs, 128, 159, 172, 239, 244, 261
Syracuse University, Office of Government & Community Relations, 129
Syracuse, City of, 365
Transportation Department
Region 3, 284
US Defense Department
Hancock Field, 174th Fighter Wing, 295
US Department of Agriculture
Farm Service Agency, New York State Office, 72
Natural Resources Conservation Service, 153
New York State Office, 89, 142, 189, 246
New York State Regional Office, 72

Listings appear in alphabetical order by state, then city.

US Department of Homeland Security (DHS)
Syracuse, Port of, 167
US Department of Veterans Affairs
Syracuse VA Medical Center & Clinics, 296
US Federal Courts
Northern District, 212
US Justice Department
Syracuse, 115, 116, 213
Unified Court System
5th Judicial District (Judicial Department 4), 209
United Way of Central New York, 261
Unity Mutual Life Insurance Co, 205
Upstate Freshwater Institute, 159
WCNY (25), 539
WNTQ (93.1 FM), WAQX (95.7 FM), 536
WSTM (24), 539
WSYT (19), 539
WTVH (47), 539
WYYY (94.5 FM), 536
Westhill CSD, 584
Wladis Law Firm, 476
Workers' Compensation Board
Syracuse, 202, 221

Tannersville
Hunter-Tannersville CSD, 576

Tarrytown
Glazer, Robert, 418
Historic Hudson Valley, 279
Housing Action Council Inc - Not For Profit, 191, 238
New York Roadway Improvement Coalition (NYRIC), 292
Pepe, Ross J, 454
Regeneron Pharmaceuticals Inc, 186
Sleepy Hollow Chamber of Commerce, 516
US Labor Department
Tarrytown Area Office, 180, 223

Thiells
NYS Office for People with Developmental Disabilities
Hudson Valley Developmental Disabilities Services Office, 230

Thornwood
Mt Pleasant CSD, 598

Three Mile Bay
Chaumont-Three Mile Bay Chamber of Commerce, 503

Throgs Neck
State University of New York Maritime College, 546

Ticonderoga
Ticonderoga Area Chamber of Commerce, 517
Ticonderoga CSD, 574

Tioga Center
Tioga CSD, 595

Tonawanda
Bartimole, John E (FKA Western NY Healthcare Associat, 385
Tonawanda
Civil & Criminal Courts, 66
Tonawanda (Town Of) Development Corporation, 518
Tonawanda City SD, 574

Troy
Alliance for Donation, Inc. (New York) (FKA Stark, Lynette), 379
Audubon New York, 155
Audubon Society of NYS Inc (The) / Audubon International, 155
Brunswick CSD (Brittonkill), 587
Capital District Educational Opportunity Center, 549
Catholic School Administrators Association of NYS, 126
Center for Liver Transplantation, 395
Commission on Economic Opportunity for the Greater Capital Region, 257
Elections, State Board of
Rensselaer, 134
Empire State Society of Association Executives Inc, 92
Health Department
Center for Environmental Health, 148
Hudson Valley Community College, 427, 547
Journal Register Co, 531
Lansingburgh CSD, 588
Museum Association of New York, 127, 279
NYS Dispute Resolution Association, 217
NYS Theatre Institute, 280
NYSTAR - Division of Science, Technology & Innovation
Center for Automation Technologies & Systems at Rensselaer, 85, 122
Future Energy Systems CAT at Rensselaer Polytechnic Inst, 85, 123
Pioneer Savings Bank, 82, 171, 455
Record (The), 531
Rensselaer County, 335
Family Court, 57
Supreme, County & Surrogate's Courts, 57
Rensselaer County Regional Chamber of Commerce, 514
Rensselaer Polytechnic Inst, Ecological Economics, Values & P, 158
Rensselaer Polytechnic Institute, 128, 460, 559
Sage Colleges (The), 560
Samaritan Hospital School of Nursing, 560
Troy
Civil & Criminal Court, 66
Troy City Enlarged SD, 588
Troy, City of, 365
US Department of the Interior
Water Resources Division - New York State District Office, 153
USA Track & Field, Adirondack Association Inc, 282
Unified Court System
3rd Judicial District (Judicial Department 3), 209
WMHT (17) Public Broadcasting-NY Capitol Region, 536

Trumansburg
Parks, Recreation & Historic Preservation, NYS Office of
Finger Lakes Region, 271
Trumansburg CSD, 595

Tuckahoe
Eastchester-Tuckahoe Chamber of Commerce, 505
Tuckahoe UFSD, 599

Tully
Tully CSD, 584

Tupper Lake
NYS Office for People with Developmental Disabilities
Sunmount Developmental Disabilities Services Office, 230
Ski Areas of New York Inc, 281
Tupper Lake CSD, 575
Tupper Lake Chamber of Commerce, 518

Turin
South Lewis CSD, 577

Tuxedo Park
Tuxedo UFSD, 586

Union Springs
Union Springs CSD, 569

Uniondale
Empire Government Strategies, 410
NYS Bar Assn, Environmental Law Section, 159
New York Schools Insurance Reciprocal (NYSIR), 204
Sahn Ward Coschignano, PLLC, 159
Uniondale UFSD, 581

Upton
Brookhaven Science Associates, LLC, 389
US Department of Energy
External Affairs & Stakeholder Relations, 142
Office of the Director, 142

Utica
Convention Centers & Visitors Bureaus

Oneida County Convention & Visitors Bureau, 275
Education Department
Utica District Office, 122
Elections, State Board of
Oneida, 134
GateHouse Media, 531
Getnick, Livingston, Atkinson, Gigliotti & Priore LLP, 216
Labor Department
Central/Mohawk Valley, 220
Law Department
Utica, 208
Mental Health, Office of
Mohawk Valley Psychiatric Center, 229
Mohawk Valley Chamber of Commerce, 511
Mohawk Valley Community College, 548
NYS Bar Assn, Court Operations Cmte, 216
NYSTAR - Division of Science, Technology & Innovation
Mohawk Valley Applied Technology Corp, 85, 123
Observer-Dispatch, 531
Oneida County, 332
Supreme, County & Family Courts, 56
Surrogate's Court, 56
Resource Center for Independent Living (RCIL), 199, 261
St Elizabeth College of Nursing, 561
State Department
Region 6 - Utica Office, 163
State University Institute of Technology, 546
Transportation Department
Region 2, 284
US Justice Department
Utica, 116, 213
Utica
Civil & Criminal Courts, 66
Utica City SD, 583
Utica College, 562
Utica Industrial Development Agency (City of), 518
Utica Mutual Insurance Co, 205
Utica School of Commerce, 566
Utica, City of, 366
WKTV (29), 539
Women's Business Center of New York State, 94
Zogby Analytics, 94, 139

Valatie
Ichabod Crane CSD, 571

Valhalla
Mount Pleasant, Town of, 351
Mt Pleasant-Blythedale UFSD, 598
New York Medical College, 185, 558
New York Medical College, Department of Medicine, 185
New York Medical College, School of Health Sciences and Practice, 185
Valhalla UFSD, 599
Westchester Community College, 549

Valley Stream
Business Informatics Center, 564
Valley Stream 13 UFSD, 582
Valley Stream 24 UFSD, 582
Valley Stream 30 UFSD, 582
Valley Stream Central HS District, 582
Valley Stream Chamber of Commerce, 518
Valley Stream, Village of, 366

Van Hornesville
Van Hornesville-Owen D Young CSD, 577

Vernon Downs
Vernon Downs/Gaming-Racing-Entertainment, 282

Verona
Madison-Oneida BOCES, 600
Sherrill City SD, 583
Vernon-Verona-Sherrill CSD, 583

Vestal
Elmira Business Institute-Vestal, 564
Vestal CSD, 568
Vestal, Town of, 366
WICZ (40), 537
WINR (680 AM), 533
WSKG (46) Public Broadcasting, 537

Victor
Victor CSD, 585
Victor Chamber of Commerce, 518

Village Station
Nadler For Congress, 490

Voorheesville
AJ Consulting Services LLC, 378
Albany County Rural Housing Alliance Inc, 190
Voorheesville CSD, 567

Waddington
Waddington Chamber of Commerce, 518

Wading River
Little Flower UFSD, 593

Wainscott
Wainscott Common SD, 594

Wallkill
Corrections & Community Supervision Department
Shawangunk Correctional Facility, 110
Wallkill Correctional Facility, 110
Wallkill CSD, 596

Walton
Walton CSD, 572
Walton Chamber of Commerce, 518

Walworth
Gananda CSD, 597

Wampsville
Elections, State Board of
Madison, 133
Madison County, 331
Supreme, County, Family & Surrogate's Courts, 54

Wantagh
Wantagh Chamber of Commerce, 518
Wantagh UFSD, 582

Wappinger Falls
Wappinger, Town of, 366

Wappingers Falls
Hudson Valley Business Journal, 532
Southern Dutchess Chamber of Commerce (Greater Southern Dutchess), 516
Wappingers CSD, 573

Wards Island
Mental Health, Office of
Kirby Forensic Psychiatric Center, 229
Manhattan Psychiatric Center, 229

Warrensburg
Warrensburg CSD, 596
Warrensburg Chamber of Commerce, 518

Warsaw
Elections, State Board of
Wyoming, 136
Warsaw CSD, 599
Warsaw Chamber of Commerce (Greater Warsaw), 518
Wyoming County, 339
Supreme, County, Family & Surrogate's Courts, 60

Warwick
Warwick Valley CSD, 586
Warwick Valley Chamber of Commerce, 518
Warwick, Town of, 367

Washingtonville
Washingtonville CSD, 586

Wassaic
NYS Office for People with Developmental Disabilities
Taconic Developmental Disabilities Services Office, 230

Waterford
Parks, Recreation & Historic Preservation, NYS Office of
Field Services, 149, 271
Historic Sites Bureau, 149, 271
Waterford-Halfmoon UFSD, 589

Listings appear in alphabetical order by state, then city.

Waterloo
Elections, State Board of
Seneca, 135
Seneca County, 336
Supreme, County, Family & Surrogate's Courts, 58
Seneca County Industrial Development Agency, 516
Waterloo CSD, 590

Watertown
Corrections & Community Supervision Department
Watertown Correctional Facility, 110
Development Authority of the North Country, 86, 97, 188, 505
Elections, State Board of
Jefferson, 132
Environmental Conservation Department
Region 6, 148
Jefferson Community College, 548
Jefferson County, 330
County, Family & Surrogate's Courts, 54
Supreme Court, 54
Jefferson-Lewis-Hamilton-Herkimer-Oneida BOCES, 600
Johnson Newspaper Corp, 531
Law Department
Watertown, 208
New York State Tug Hill Commission, 104, 151
Transportation Department
Region 7, 284
WFRY (97.5 FM), 536
WWNY (7), 539
WWTI (21), 539
Watertown
Civil & Criminal Courts, 66
Watertown City SD, 577
Watertown Daily Times, 531
Watertown, City of, 367
Watertown-North Country Chamber of Commerce (Greater Watertown), 519

Waterville
Waterville CSD, 583

Watervliet
US Defense Department
Watervliet Arsenal, 295
Watervliet
Civil & Criminal Courts, 66
Watervliet City SD, 567

Watkins Glen
Elections, State Board of
Schuyler, 135
Farm Sanctuary, 74
Schuyler County, 336
Supreme, County, Family & Surrogate's Courts, 58
Schuyler County Industrial Development Agency, 516
Schuyler County Partnership for Economic Development, 516
Watkins Glen Area Chamber of Commerce, 519
Watkins Glen CSD, 589

Waverly
Waverly CSD, 595

Wayland
Wayland-Cohocton CSD, 591

Webster
Webster CSD, 579
Webster Chamber of Commerce, 519
Webster, Town of, 367

Weedsport
Weedsport Area Chamber of Commerce, 519
Weedsport CSD, 569

Wells
Wells CSD, 576

Wellsville
Gate House Media, 531
Wellsville Area Chamber of Commerce, 519
Wellsville CSD, 568
Wellsville Daily Reporter/Spectator, 531

West Babylon
Federation of Organizations Inc, 231
Long Island Board of Realtors (FKA Kaplan, Randy L.), 436
Parks, Recreation & Historic Preservation, NYS Office of
Long Island Region, 271
West Babylon UFSD, 594

West Brentwood
Mental Health, Office of
Pilgrim Psychiatric Center, 229

West Chazy
Beekmantown CSD, 571

West Coxsackie
Corrections & Community Supervision Department
Coxsackie Correctional Facility, 109

West Haverstraw
Health Department
Helen Hayes Hospital, 175, 293

West Hempstead
West Hempstead UFSD, 582

West Henrietta
NYSTAR - Division of Science, Technology & Innovation
High Technology of Rochester, 85, 123

West Islip
West Islip UFSD, 594

West Nyack
Epilepsy Coalition of New York State Inc, 182
Rockland BOCES, 601

West Park
West Park UFSD, 596

West Point
US Defense Department
US Military Academy, 125
US Military Academy at West Point, 566
US Treasury Department
US Mint, 267

West Seneca
Erie 1 BOCES, 600
Mental Health, Office of
Western New York Children's Psychiatric Center, 229
NYS Office for People with Developmental Disabilities
Western New York Developmental Disabilities Services Office, 230
New York State Association of Ambulatory Surgery Centers, 185
Praxiis Business Advisors, 456
West Seneca CSD, 574
West Seneca Chamber of Commerce, 519
West Seneca, Town of, 367

West Valley
West Valley CSD, 569

West Winfield
Mount Markham CSD, 576

Westbury
Community Bankers Assn of NY State, Mortgages & Real Estate Cmte, 248
East Meadow UFSD, 580
Exxon Mobil Corporation, 144
Fisher Development Strategies, 415
Lieberman, Mark L, 435
Local 1500 Political Candidates and Education Fund, 489
Long Island Development Corporation, 510
Medical Society of the State of New York, Div of Socio-Medica, 204
Nassau County
Family Court, 55
New York Community Bank, 81, 192, 248
New York State School Music Association (NYSSMA), 128, 281
US Labor Department
Long Island Area Office, 180
Long Island District Office, 223
US Railroad Retirement Board
Westbury, 224
US Treasury Department

Listings appear in alphabetical order by state, then city.

Appendices: Financial Plan, Indexes & Maps

TEGE Area Counsel's Office, 267
Westbury-Carle Place Chamber of Commerce, 519

Westfield
Westfield CSD, 570
Westfield/Barcelona Chamber of Commerce, 519

Westhampton Beach
Central Pine Barrens Joint Planning & Policy Commission, 96, 150
US Defense Department
Francis S Gabreski Airport, 106th Rescue Wing, 295
US Department of Agriculture
Westhampton Beach Work Station, 72
Westhampton Beach UFSD, 594
Westhampton Chamber of Commerce (Greater Westhampton), 519

Westmoreland
New York Beef Industry Council Inc, 76
Westmoreland CSD, 583

Westport
Westport CSD, 574

White Plains
Andy King 2013, 479
Attorney Grievance Committee
Judicial Dist 9, 208
Berkeley College, Westchester Campus, 563
Business Council of Westchester, The, 502
Center for Judicial Accountability Inc (CJA), 215
College of Westchester (The), 564
Convention Centers & Visitors Bureaus
Westchester County Tourism & Film, 275
Court of Claims, 215
Delbello Donnellan Weingarten Wise & Wiederkehr, LLP, 406
Education Department
White Plains District Office, 122
Elections, State Board of
Westchester, 136
Entergy Corporation Political Action Committee - New York, 482
Entergy Nuclear Northeast, 144
Entergy Nuclear Operations, Inc, 411
Gibson For City Council, 486
Institute for Socio-Economic Studies, 259
Insurance Fund (NYS)
White Plains, 201, 219
Labor Department
Hudson Valley, 220
Law Department
Westchester, 208
Legal Services of the Hudson Valley, 216
Littman Krooks LLP, 216
March of Dimes Birth Defects Foundation, 259
Marine Corps League, 298
Mooney, William, 445
NYS Bar Assn, Elder Law Section, 216
NYS Bar Assn, Judicial Section, 215
NYS Bar Assn, Legal Aid Cmte/Funding for Civil Legal Svcs Cmte, 216
New York Power Authority, 101, 141
Pace University, School of Law Center for Environmental Legal S, 158
Pace University, School of Law, John Jay Legal Services Inc, 118, 218
People For Brodsky, 492
Ravitz, John, 459
Real Property Tax Services, Office of
South, 235, 264
Strategic Services, Inc, 468
US Federal Courts
Southern District, 212
US Justice Department
White Plains, 115, 213
US Transportation Department
National Highway Traffic Safety Administration, Reg II-NY, 290
Unified Court System
9th Judicial District (Judicial Department 2), 210
Westchester County, 339
Supreme, County & Family Courts, 60
Surrogate's Court, 60
Westchester County Association Inc (The), 519
Westchester County Chamber of Commerce, 519
Westchester County Industrial Development Agency, 519
White Plains
Civil & Criminal Courts, 66
White Plains City SD, 599
White Plains, City of, 367

Whitehall
Whitehall Area Chamber of Commerce, 519
Whitehall CSD, 596

Whitestone
Halloran 2013, 486
Local 30 IUOE PAC, 489
N.S.A. Inc. Action Fund, 490
Queens County Republican Committee, 493
Tony Avella For Queens, 495

Whitesville
Whitesville CSD, 568

Whitney Point
Whitney Point CSD, 568

Willard
Corrections & Community Supervision Department
Willard Drug Treatment Center, 110

Williamson
Williamson CSD, 597
Williamson Chamber of Commerce, 519

Williamsville
Amherst Chamber of Commerce, 501
Amherst, Town of, 341
Military Officers Association of America (MOAA), NYS Council, 299
NYS Bar Assn, Public Utility Law Committee, 145
National Fuel Gas Company, 145, 448
US Department of Homeland Security (DHS)
Buffalo Office, 166

Williston Park
Willistons Chamber of Commerce, 519

Willsboro
Willsboro CSD, 574

Wilmington
Whiteface Mountain Regional Visitor's Bureau, 519

Wilson
Wilson CSD, 583

Wilton
Corrections & Community Supervision Department
Mt McGregor Correctional Facility, 109

Windham
Windham-Ashland-Jewett CSD, 576

Windsor
Windsor CSD, 568

Wolcott
North Rose-Wolcott CSD, 597

Woodbourne
Corrections & Community Supervision Department
Woodbourne Correctional Facility, 110

Woodmere
Hewlett-Woodmere UFSD, 580

Woodside
Citizens For Sports & Arts, Inc., 480
Sports & Arts in Schools Foundation, 128, 282

Woodstock
Shapiro, Brian, 465
Woodstock Chamber of Commerce & Arts, 519

Worcester
Worcester CSD, 587

Wurtsboro
Wurtsboro Board of Trade, 519

Wyandanch
Wyandanch UFSD, 594

Wynantskill
Carnevale Consulting, LLC, 394
North Greenbush IDA, 512
Wynantskill UFSD, 588

Wyoming
Wyoming CSD, 599

Yaphank
Elections, State Board of
Suffolk, 135

Yonkers
Brab PAC, Inc., 479
Cochran School of Nursing, 553
Consumers Union, 73, 91
EVCI Career Colleges Holding Corp, 91
Educational Opportunity Center of Westchester, 549
Rooney, Timothy J., 461
St Joseph's Seminary Institute of Religious Studies, 561
St Vladimir's Orthodox Theological Seminary, 561
Yonkers
Civil & Criminal Courts, 66
Yonkers Chamber of Commerce, 520
Yonkers City SD, 599
Yonkers Economic Development/Yonkers Industrial Develo, 520
Yonkers Raceway, 282
Yonkers, City of, 367

Yorkshire
Yorkshire-Pioneer CSD, 569

Yorktown Heights
New Yorktown Chamber of Commerce (The), 512
Putnam-Northern Westchester BOCES, 601
Yorktown CSD, 599
Yorktown, Town of, 368

Yorkville
Whitesboro CSD, 583

Youngstown
Lewiston-Porter CSD, 582

North Carolina

Cary
SAS Institute, Inc., 463

Charlotte
Wells Fargo and Company, 473

Raleigh
Boehringer Ingelheim Pharmaceuticals, Inc., 386

US Department of Agriculture
Plant Protection Quarantine (PPQ) Programs-Eastern Region, 71

Winston-Salem
RAI Services Company (FKA Reynolds American, Inc.), 459

Ohio

Cincinnati
Ohio River Valley Water Sanitation Commission, 105, 152
US Defense Department
Great Lakes & Ohio River Division (Western NYS), 152

Cleveland
Keycorp & Subsidiaries, 432

Marysville
Scotts Miracle-Gro Company, 464

Oklahoma

Oklahoma City
Chesapeake Appalachia, LLC, 396
Interstate Oil & Gas Compact Commission, 98, 141, 151

Pennsylvania

Chadds Ford
Holloway, Jr, Floyd, 426

Churchville
Johnson & Johnson Health Care Systems, Inc., 429

Douglassville
STV Engineers Inc. Political Action Committee, 495

Harrisburg
Norfolk Southern Corporation, 450

Horsham
Toll Bros., Inc. PAC, 495

Kennett Square
Exelon Generation Company LLC, 413

King of Prussia
Nuclear Regulatory Commission
REGION I (includes New York State), 142

Newtown Square
US Department of Agriculture
Forest Service-Northeastern Area State & Private Forestry, 153
Forest Service-Northern Research Station, 153

North Wales
Merck Sha, 443

Paoli
Friends of Paul Drucker, 485

Philadelphia
Ace Group - North America, 377
Cozen O'Connor Empire State PAC, 481
Duane Morris LLP Government Committee - New York Fund, 482
Fleet Reserve Association (FRA), NE Region (NJ, NY, PA), 298
NY State Society of Physician Assistants, 184
PFM Asset Management, LLC, 455
US Commerce Department
Philadelphia Region (includes New York), 88
US Department of Agriculture
Field Operations-Philadelphia District Office (includes New York), 178
US Department of the Interior
National Park Service-Northeast Region, 153, 276
US Justice Department
Audit Division, 213
US Labor Department
Wage-Hour Division (WHD)-Northeast Regional Office, 223
US Office of Personnel Management
PHILADELPHIA SERVICE CENTER (serving New York), 224, 242

Pittsburgh
Adams, John, 377

Rhode Island

Providence
Gtech Corporation, 422

Smithfield
Vose, Margie, 473

South Carolina

Greenville
Gordian Group, Inc. (The), 420

Tennessee

Franklin
Nissan North America, Inc., 450

Listings appear in alphabetical order by state, then city.

Memphis
Federal Express New York State Political Action Committee, 482

Nashville
US Department of Health & Human Services
Indian Health Services-Area Office, 255

Texas

Dallas
Chase Paymentech Solutions, LLC, 396
Howard Hughes Corporation (The), 426

Houston
Service Corporation International Political Association Committee, 494

San Antonio
Air Force Women Officers Associated (AFWOA), 297

Utah

Kanab
Rubin, Jamie Lyn, 462

Vermont

Montpelier
National Wildlife Federation - Northeast Regional Center, 157

Rutland
US Department of Agriculture
Green Mountain & Finger Lakes, 153

South Burlington
Democracy For America - NYC, 481

Virginia

Alexandria
Coalition for Auto Repair Equality (CARE), 398
Fleet Reserve Association (FRA), 298
Military Officers Association of America, 299
National Military Family Association (NMFA), 299
Naval Reserve Association (NRA), 299

Arlington
AECOM US FEDERAL PAC, 479
Air Force Association (AFA), 297
Association of the US Army (AUSA), 298
Atlantic States Marine Fisheries Commission, 95, 150
Military Chaplains Association of the USA (MCA), 299
Navy League of the US (NLUS), 299
Promontory Interfinancial Network LLC, 457

Fairfax
Goens, Darin, 419

Falls Church
Naval Enlisted Reserve Association (NERA), 299

Merrifield
Marine Corps League (MCL), 298

Reston
Fitzgerald, Kevin, 415
Maximus Inc. Political Action Committee, 489

Richmond
Dominion Resources, 407
Riddle, Gary, 461

Springfield
Military Order of the Purple Heart (MOPH), 299

Vienna
Feld Entertainment, 414

Listings appear in alphabetical order by state, then city.

Demographic and Reference Maps

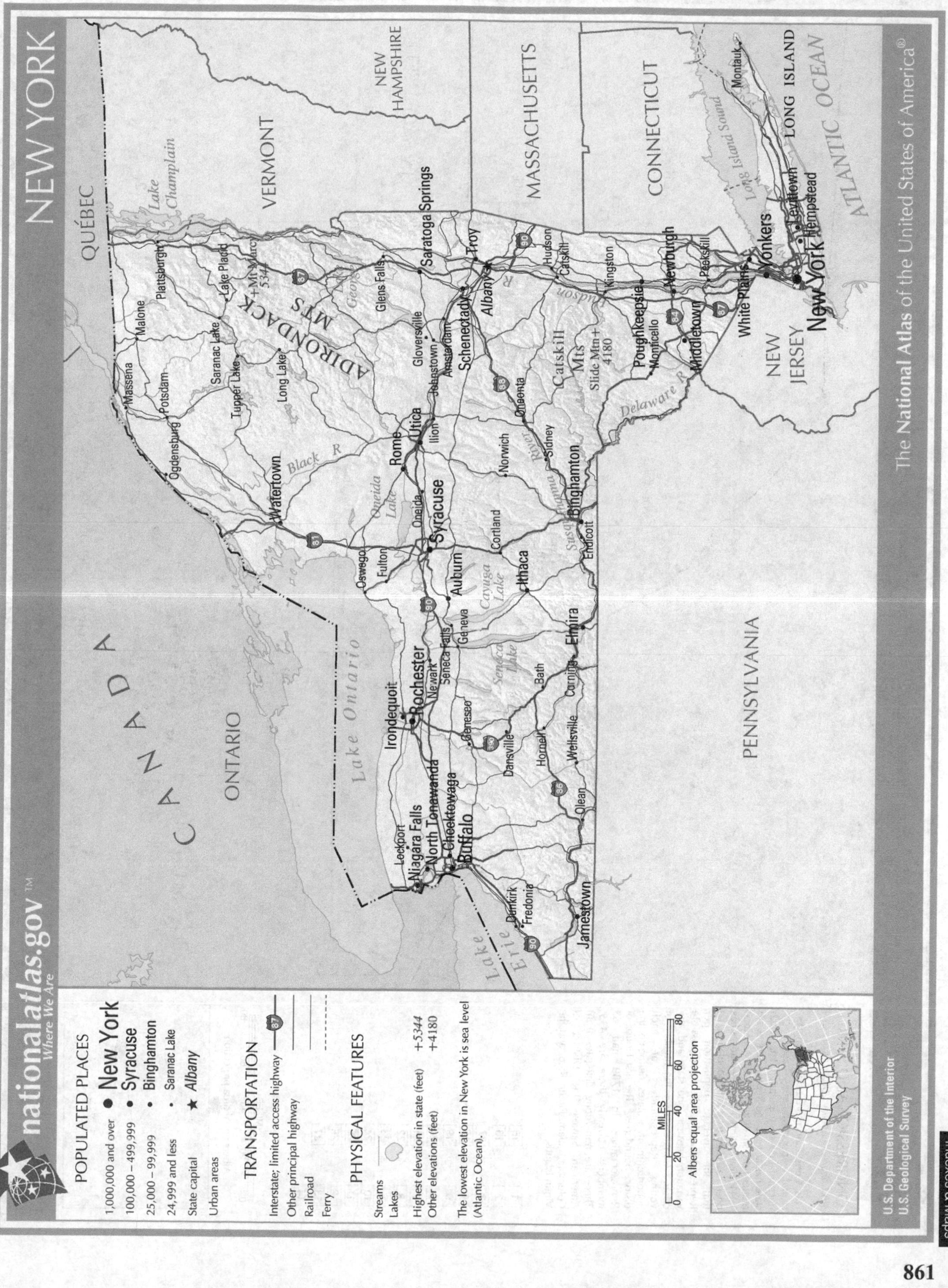
NEW YORK
nationalatlas.gov™
Where We Are
POPULATED PLACES
1,000,000 and over
New York
100,000 – 499,999
Syracuse
25,000 – 99,999
Binghamton
24,999 and less
Saranac Lake
State capital
Albany
Urban areas
TRANSPORTATION
Interstate; limited access highway
Other principal highway
Railroad
Ferry
PHYSICAL FEATURES
Streams
Lakes
Highest elevation in state (feet) +5344
Other elevations (feet) +4180
The lowest elevation in New York is sea level (Atlantic Ocean).
MILES
0 20 40 60 80
Albers equal area projection
U.S. Department of the Interior
U.S. Geological Survey
The National Atlas of the United States of America®
CANADA
ONTARIO
QUÉBEC
VERMONT
NEW HAMPSHIRE
MASSACHUSETTS
CONNECTICUT
NEW JERSEY
PENNSYLVANIA
LONG ISLAND
ATLANTIC OCEAN
Lake Ontario
Lake Erie
Lake Champlain
Long Island Sound
ADIRONDACK MTS
Catskill Mts
Mt Marcy 5344
Slide Mtn 4180
Oneida Lake
Cayuga Lake
Seneca Lake
Lake George
Black R
Hudson R
Delaware R
Susquehanna River
New York
Yonkers
Buffalo
Rochester
Syracuse
Albany
Binghamton
Utica
Schenectady
Troy
Niagara Falls
Irondequoit
Cheektowaga
North Tonawanda
Lockport
Jamestown
Dunkirk
Fredonia
Olean
Wellsville
Hornell
Dansville
Geneseo
Bath
Corning
Elmira
Ithaca
Cortland
Auburn
Geneva
Seneca Falls
Newark
Oswego
Fulton
Oneida
Rome
Watertown
Ogdensburg
Potsdam
Massena
Malone
Plattsburgh
Saranac Lake
Lake Placid
Tupper Lake
Long Lake
Glens Falls
Saratoga Springs
Gloversville
Johnstown
Amsterdam
Ilion
Norwich
Oneonta
Sidney
Endicott
Hudson
Catskill
Kingston
Poughkeepsie
Monticello
Middletown
Newburgh
Peekskill
White Plains
Levittown
Hempstead
Montauk

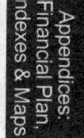

nationalatlas.gov™
Where We Are

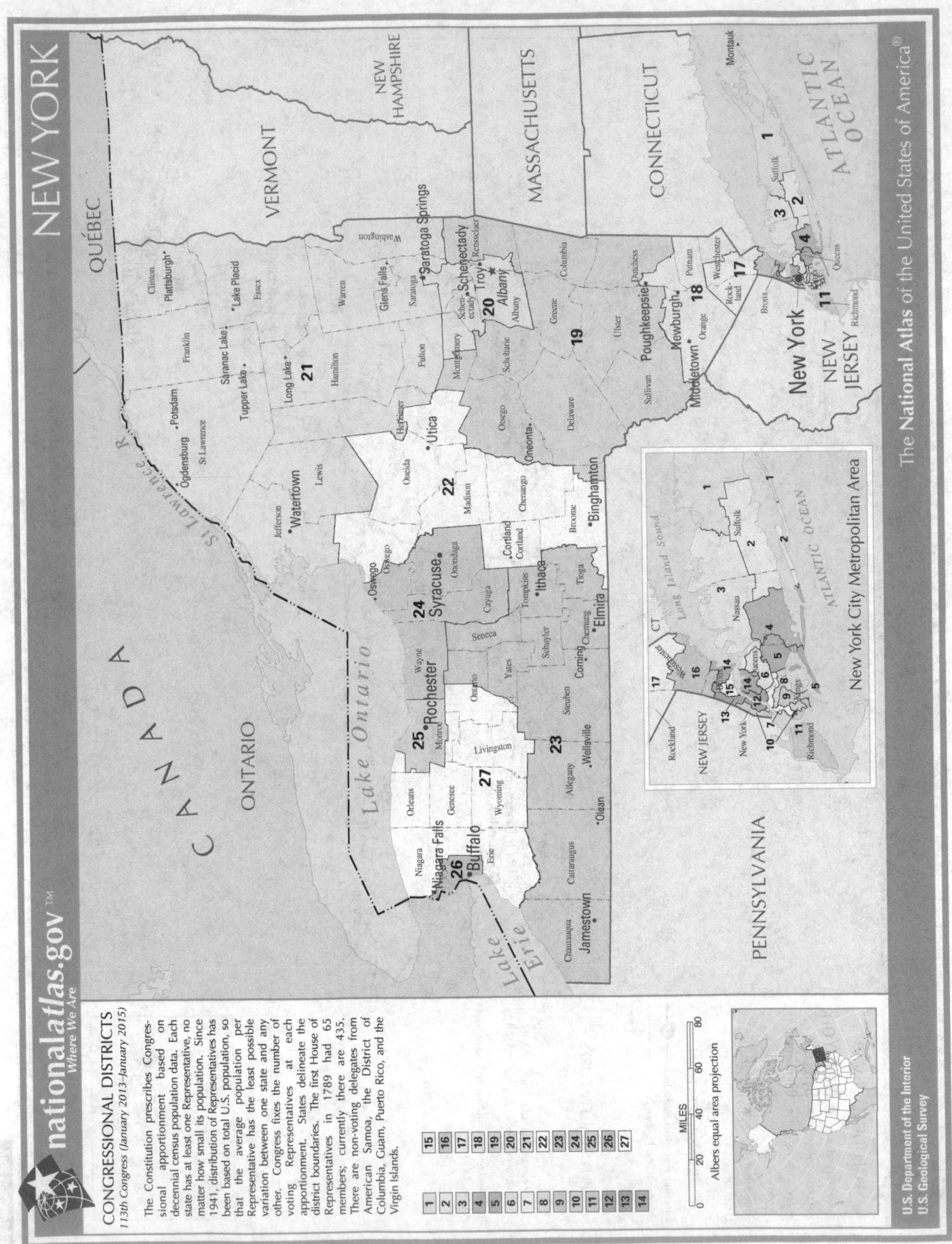

NEW YORK

CONGRESSIONAL DISTRICTS

113th Congress (January 2013–January 2015)

The Constitution prescribes Congressional apportionment based on decennial census population data. Each state has at least one Representative, no matter how small its population. Since 1941, distribution of Representatives has been based on total U.S. population, so that the average population per Representative has the least possible variation between one state and any other. Congress fixes the number of voting Representatives at each apportionment. States delineate the district boundaries. The first House of Representatives in 1789 had 65 members; currently there are 435. There are non-voting delegates from American Samoa, the District of Columbia, Guam, Puerto Rico, and the Virgin Islands.

1	15
2	16
3	17
4	18
5	19
6	20
7	21
8	22
9	23
10	24
11	25
12	26
13	27
14	

MILES
0 20 40 60 80

Albers equal area projection

U.S. Department of the Interior
U.S. Geological Survey

The **National Atlas** of the United States of America®

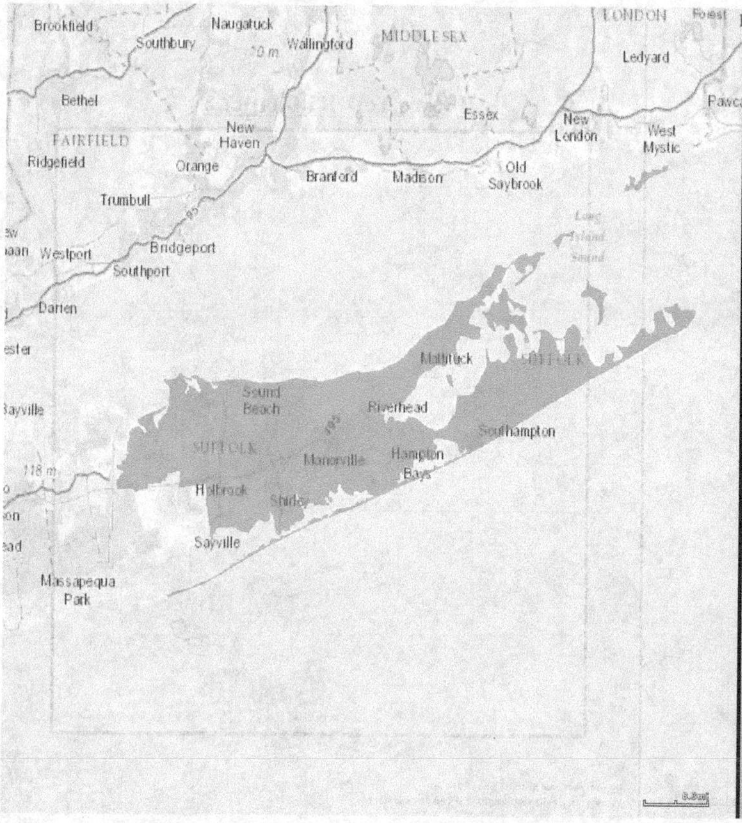

New York US District 1

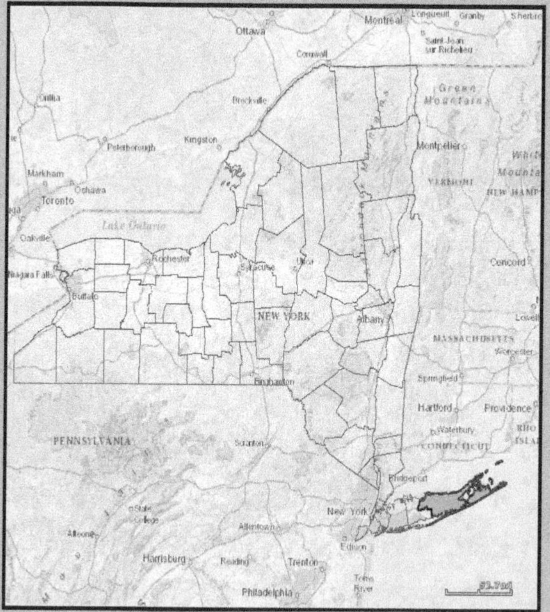

US Congressional districts since 2013
Source: http://nationalatlas.gov, 1 Million Scale project.

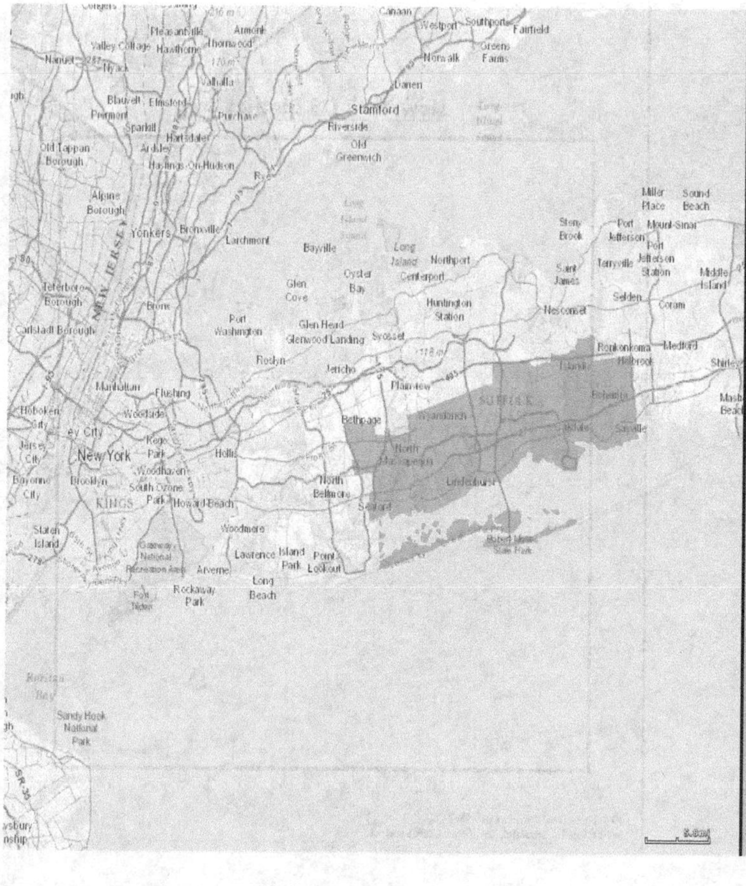

New York US District 2

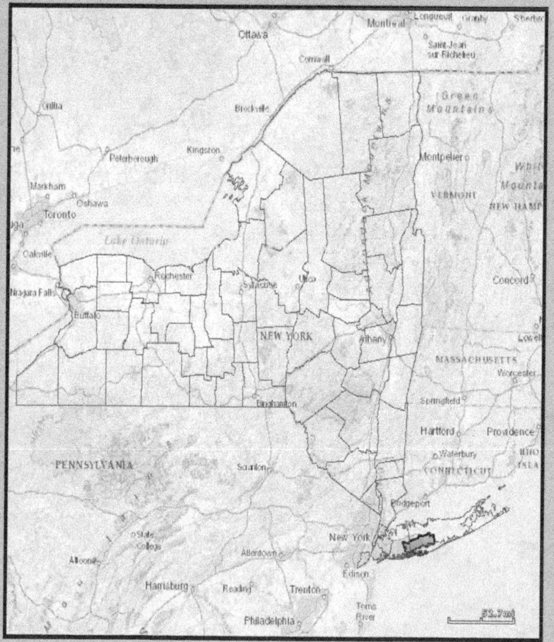

US Congressional districts since 2013
Source: http://nationalatlas.gov, 1 Million Scale project.

Appendices: Financial Plan, Indexes & Maps

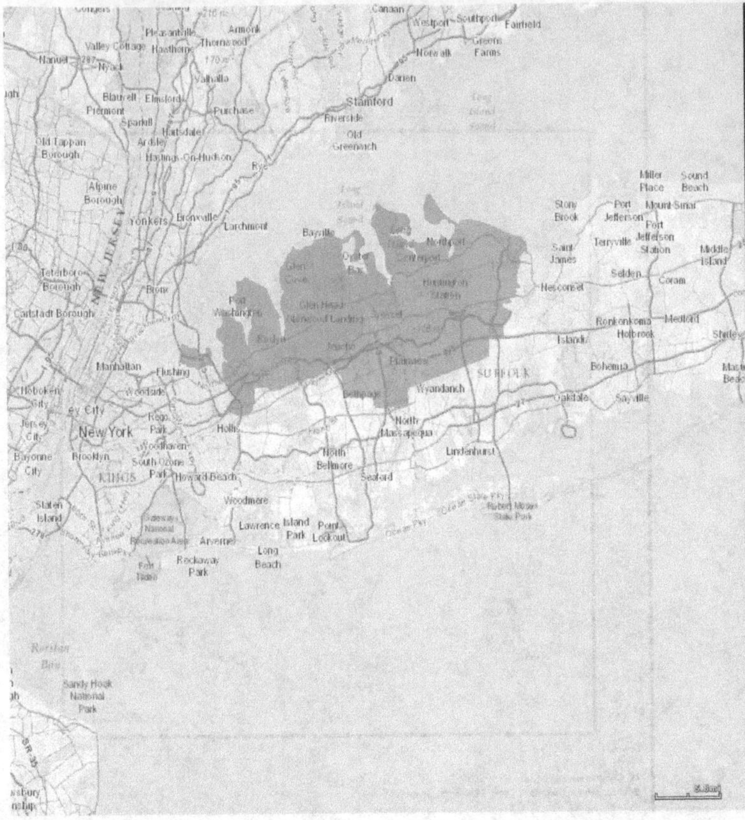

New York US District 3

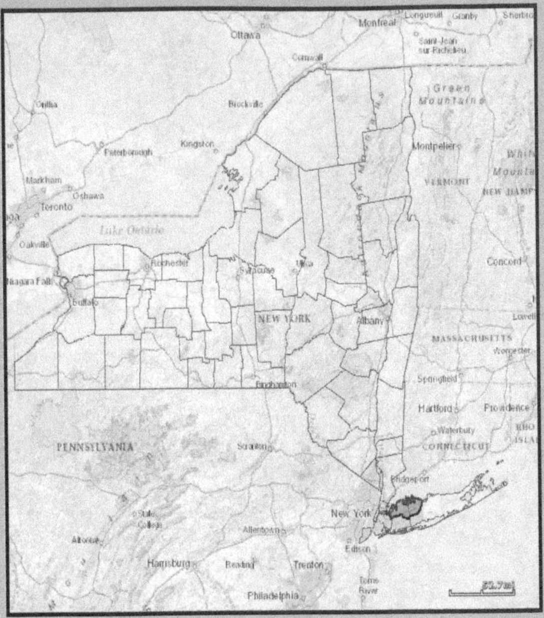

US Congressional districts since 2013
Source: http://nationalatlas.gov, 1 Million Scale project.

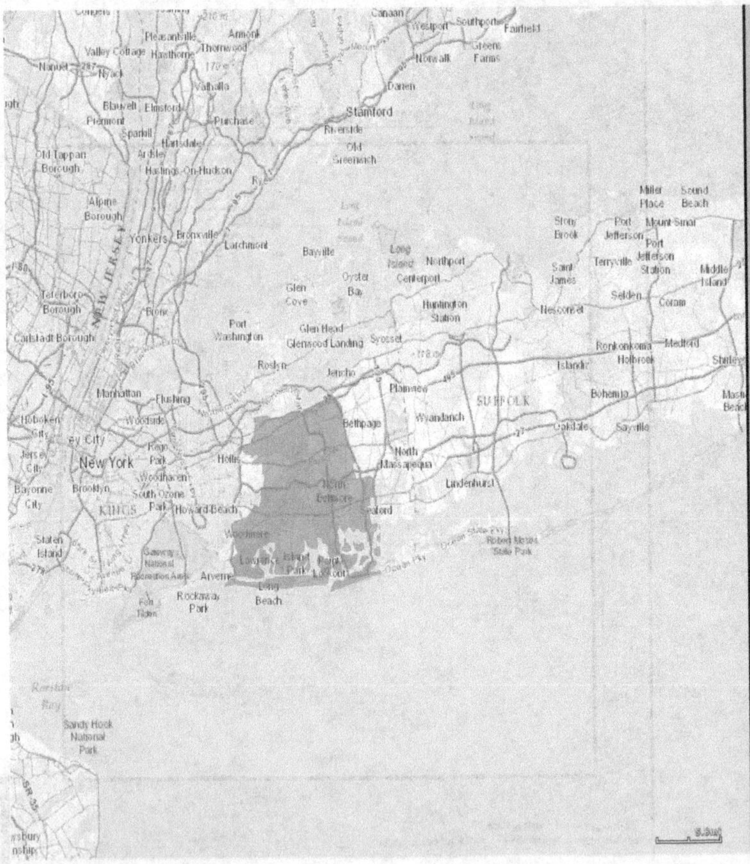

New York US District 4

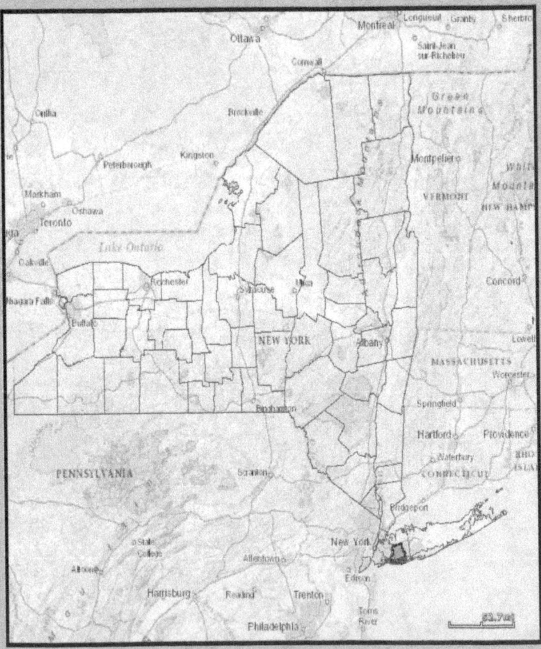

US Congressional districts since 2013
Source: http://nationalatlas.gov, 1 Million Scale project.

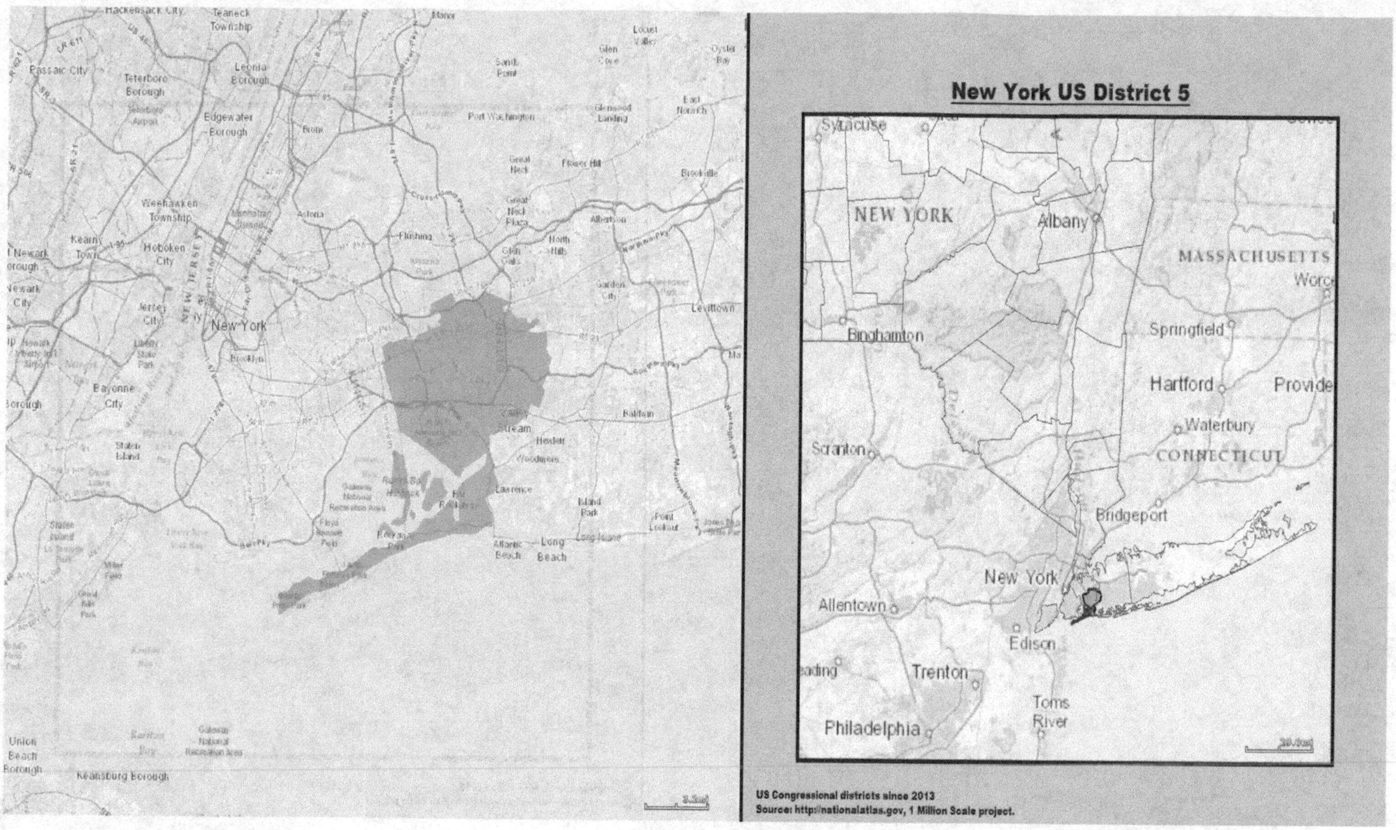
New York US District 5
Syracuse
NEW YORK
Albany
MASSACHUSETTS
Binghamton
Springfield
Hartford
Waterbury
CONNECTICUT
Scranton
Bridgeport
New York
Allentown
Edison
Trenton
Toms River
Philadelphia
US Congressional districts since 2013
Source: http//nationalatlas.gov, 1 Million Scale project.

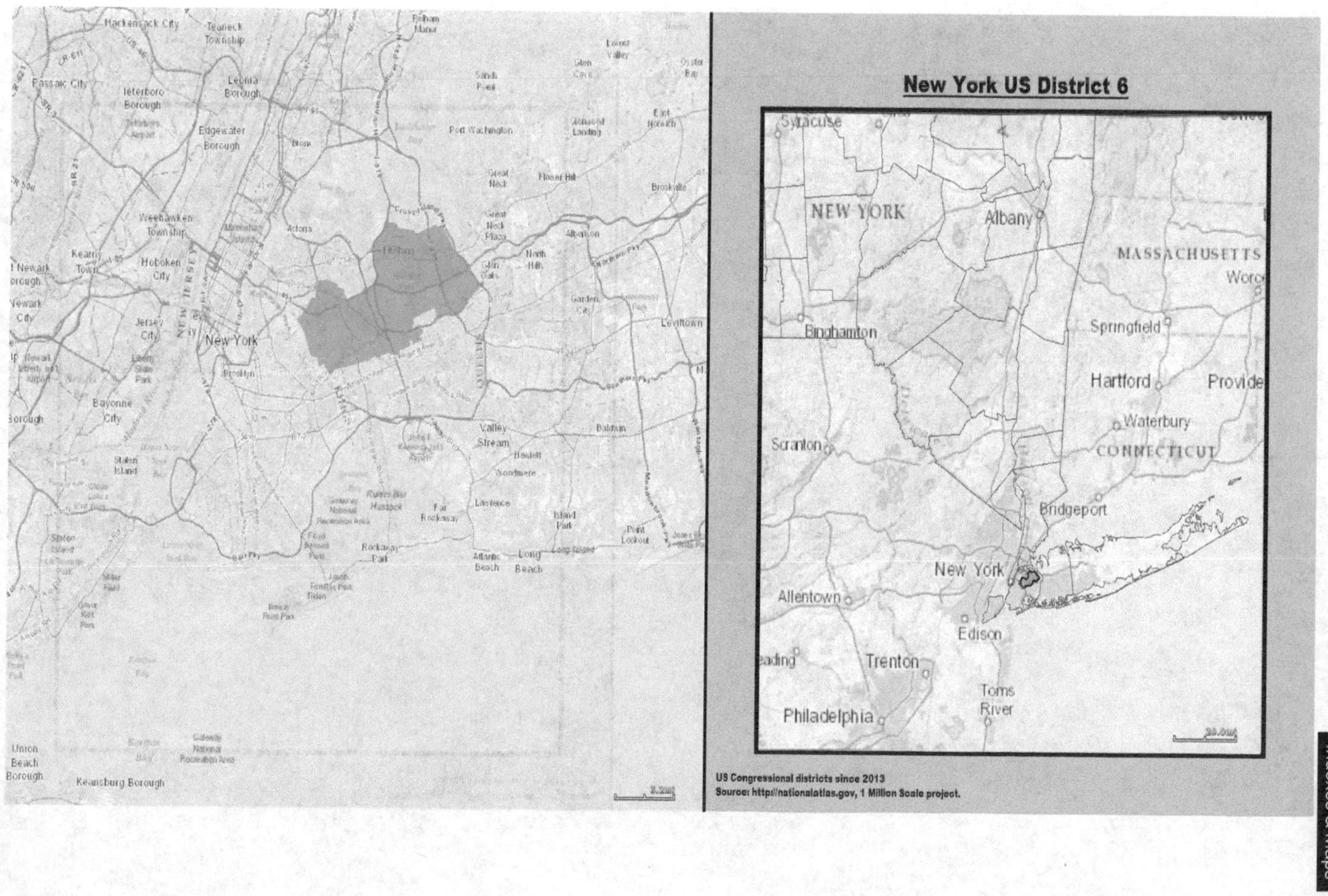
New York US District 6
Syracuse
NEW YORK
Albany
MASSACHUSETTS
Binghamton
Springfield
Hartford
Waterbury
CONNECTICUT
Scranton
Bridgeport
New York
Allentown
Edison
Trenton
Toms River
Philadelphia
US Congressional districts since 2013
Source: http//nationalatlas.gov, 1 Million Scale project.

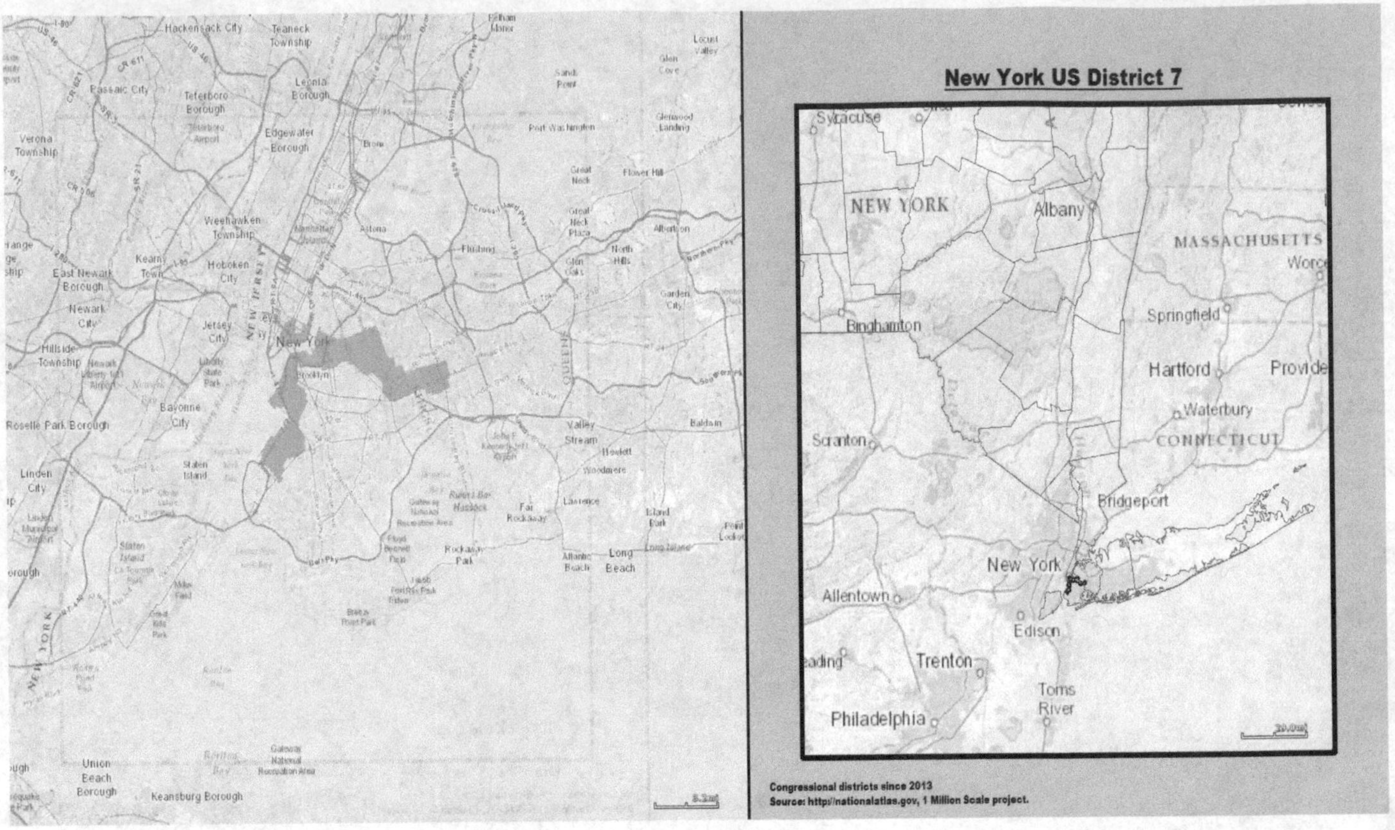
New York US District 7
Syracuse
NEW YORK
Albany
MASSACHUSETTS
Binghamton
Springfield
Hartford
Waterbury
CONNECTICUT
Scranton
Bridgeport
New York
Allentown
Edison
Trenton
Toms River
Philadelphia
Congressional districts since 2013
Source: http://nationalatlas.gov, 1 Million Scale project.
Hackensack City
Teaneck Township
Passaic City
Teterboro Borough
Verona Township
Edgewater Borough
Weehawken Township
East Newark Borough
Hoboken City
Newark City
Jersey City
Hillside Township
Bayonne City
Roselle Park Borough
Linden City
Staten Island
Valley Stream
Long Beach
Rockaway Park
Union Beach Borough
Keansburg Borough

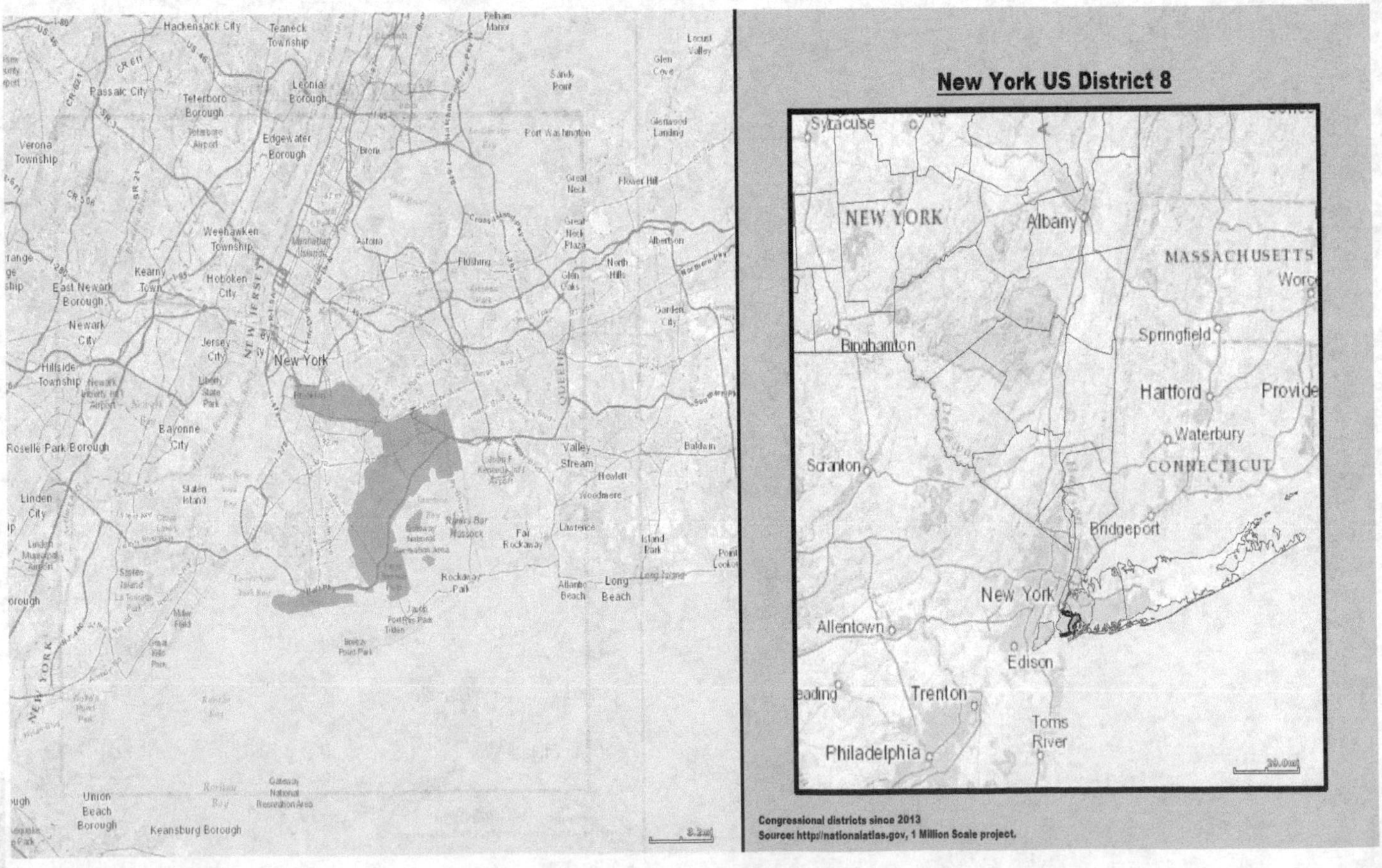
New York US District 8
Syracuse
NEW YORK
Albany
MASSACHUSETTS
Binghamton
Springfield
Hartford
Waterbury
CONNECTICUT
Scranton
Bridgeport
New York
Allentown
Edison
Trenton
Toms River
Philadelphia
Congressional districts since 2013
Source: http://nationalatlas.gov, 1 Million Scale project.
Hackensack City
Teaneck Township
Passaic City
Teterboro Borough
Verona Township
Edgewater Borough
Weehawken Township
East Newark Borough
Hoboken City
Newark City
Jersey City
Hillside Township
Bayonne City
Roselle Park Borough
Linden City
Staten Island
Valley Stream
Long Beach
Rockaway Park
Union Beach Borough
Keansburg Borough

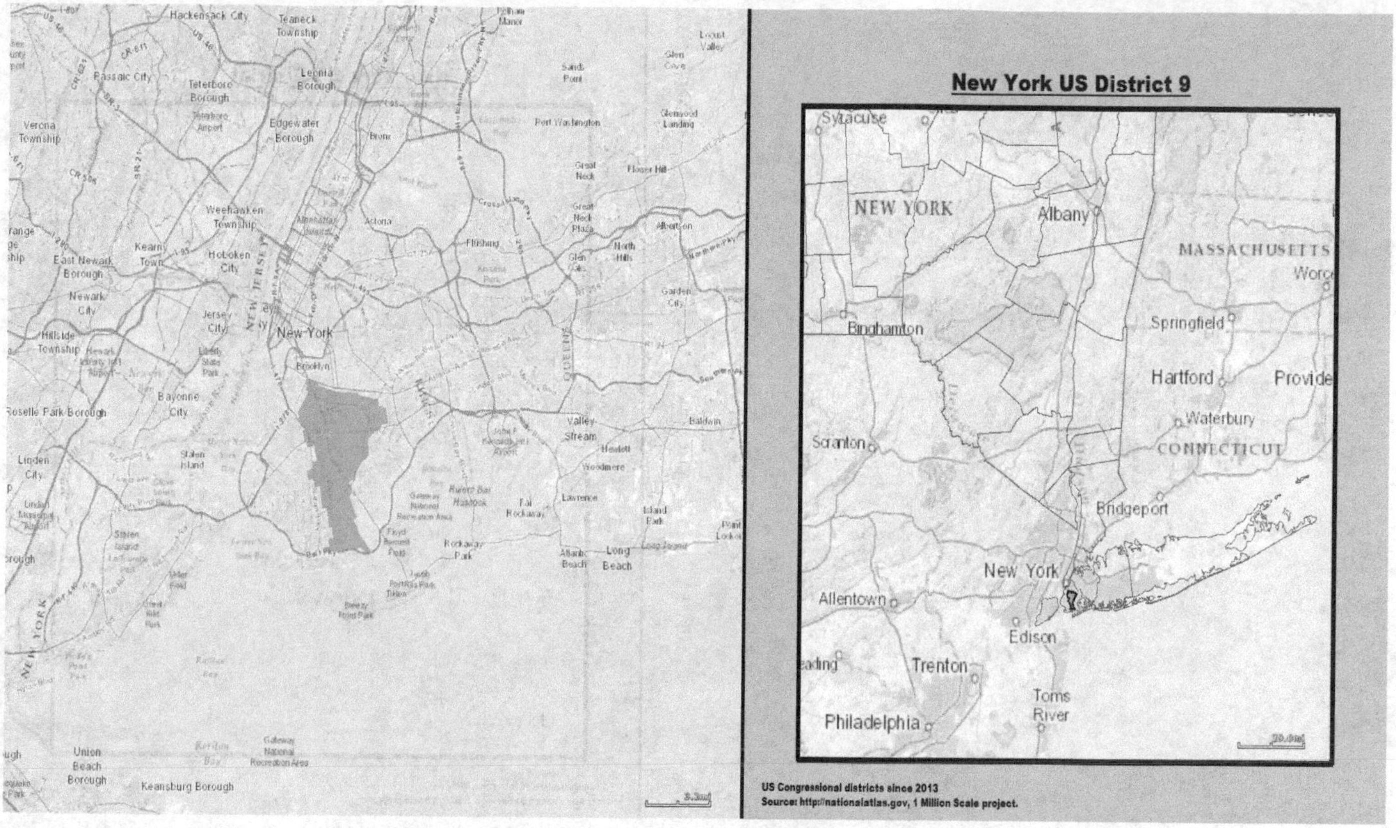
New York US District 9
Syracuse
NEW YORK
Albany
MASSACHUSETTS
Binghamton
Springfield
Hartford
Waterbury
CONNECTICUT
Scranton
Bridgeport
New York
Allentown
Edison
Trenton
Toms River
Philadelphia
Hackensack City
Teaneck Township
Passaic City
Teterboro Borough
Leonia Borough
Edgewater Borough
Verona Township
Weehawken Township
Kearny Town
Hoboken City
East Newark Borough
Newark City
Jersey City
Hillside Township
Bayonne City
Roselle Park Borough
Linden City
Staten Island
Astoria
Flushing
Valley Stream
Baldwin
Long Beach
Rockaway Park
Union Beach Borough
Keansburg Borough
US Congressional districts since 2013
Source: http://nationalatlas.gov, 1 Million Scale project.

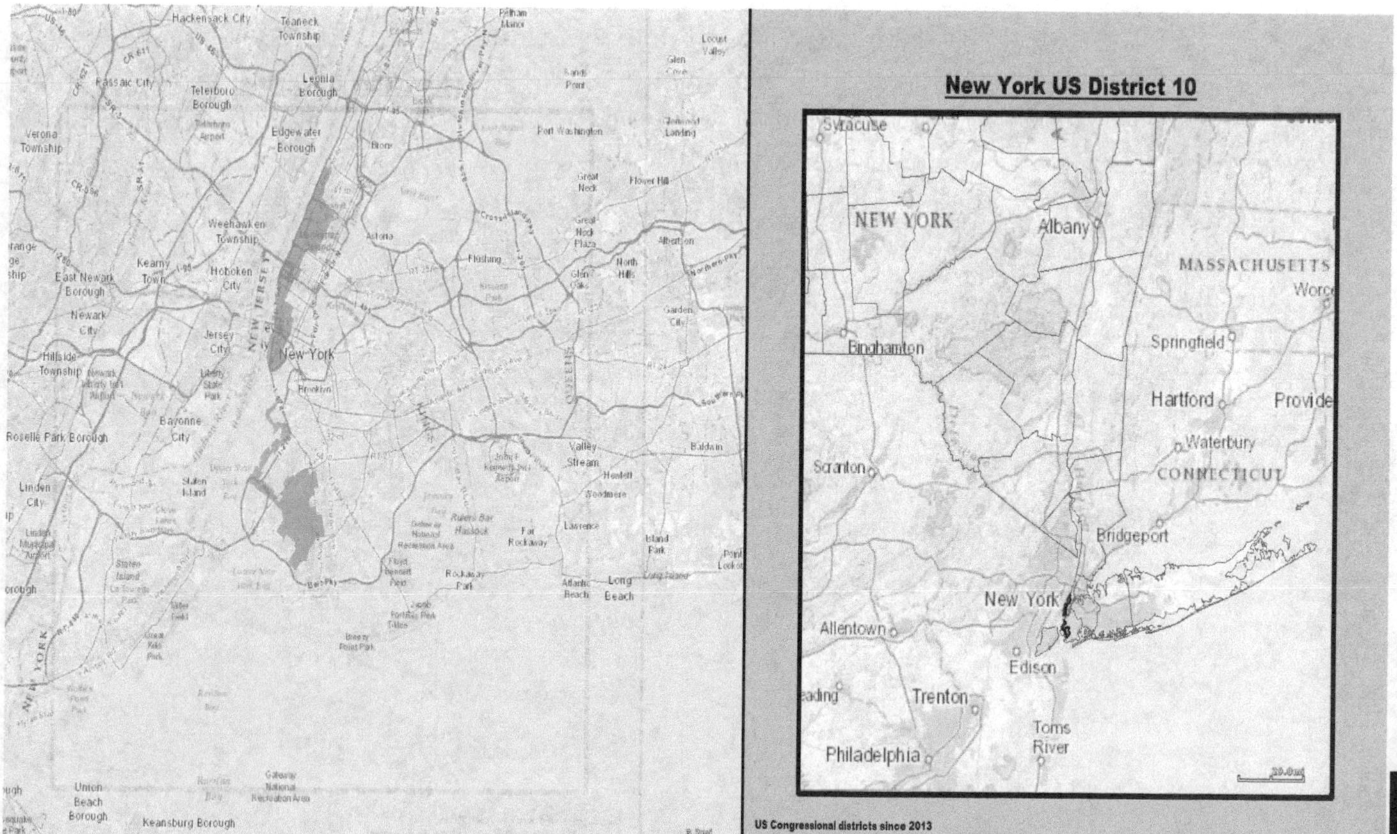
New York US District 10
Syracuse
NEW YORK
Albany
MASSACHUSETTS
Binghamton
Springfield
Hartford
Waterbury
CONNECTICUT
Scranton
Bridgeport
New York
Allentown
Edison
Trenton
Toms River
Philadelphia
Hackensack City
Teaneck Township
Passaic City
Teterboro Borough
Leonia Borough
Edgewater Borough
Verona Township
Weehawken Township
Kearny Town
Hoboken City
East Newark Borough
Newark City
Jersey City
Hillside Township
Bayonne City
Roselle Park Borough
Linden City
Staten Island
Astoria
Flushing
Valley Stream
Baldwin
Long Beach
Rockaway Park
Union Beach Borough
Keansburg Borough
US Congressional districts since 2013
Source: http://nationalatlas.gov, 1 Million Scale project.

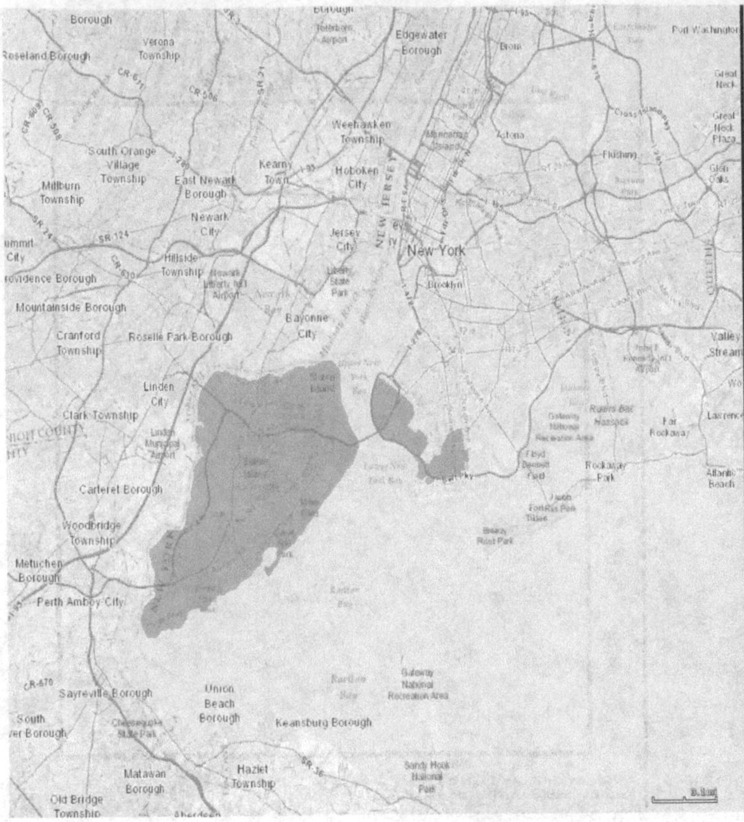

New York US District 11

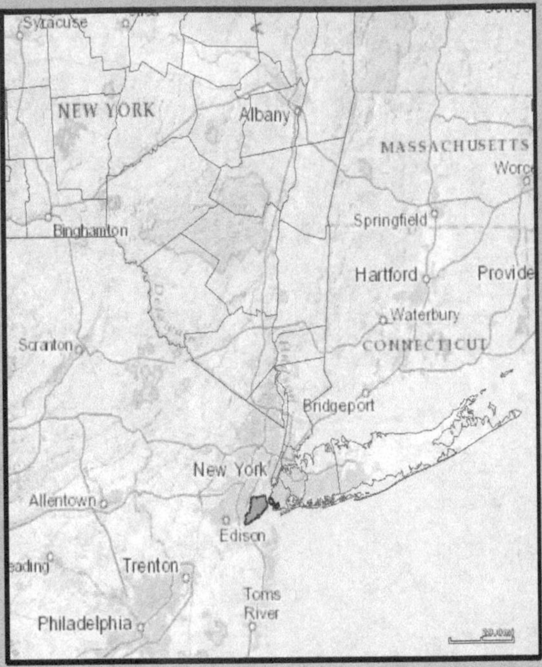

US Congressional districts since 2013
Source: http://nationalatlas.gov, 1 Million Scale project.

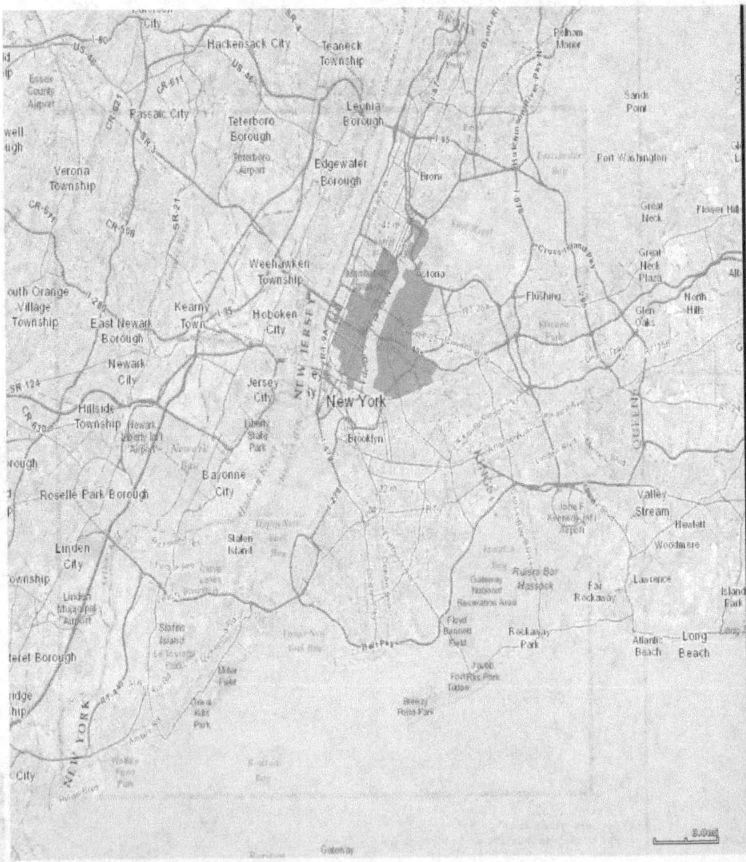

New York US District 12

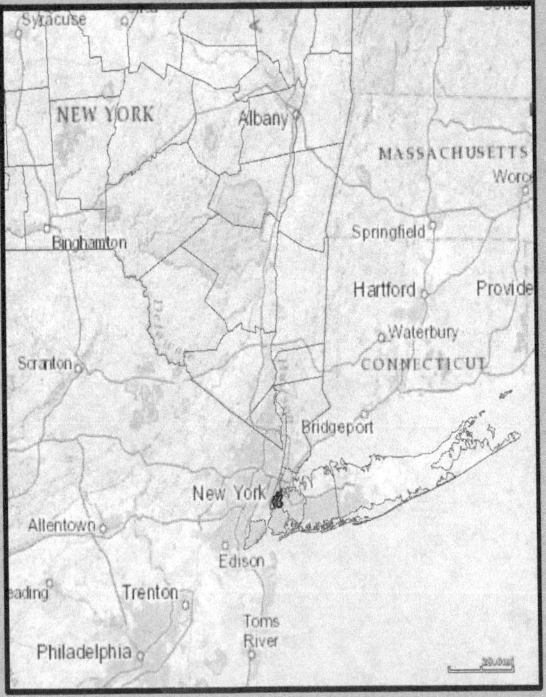

US Congressional districts since 2013
Source: http://nationalatlas.gov, 1 Million Scale project.

New York US District 13

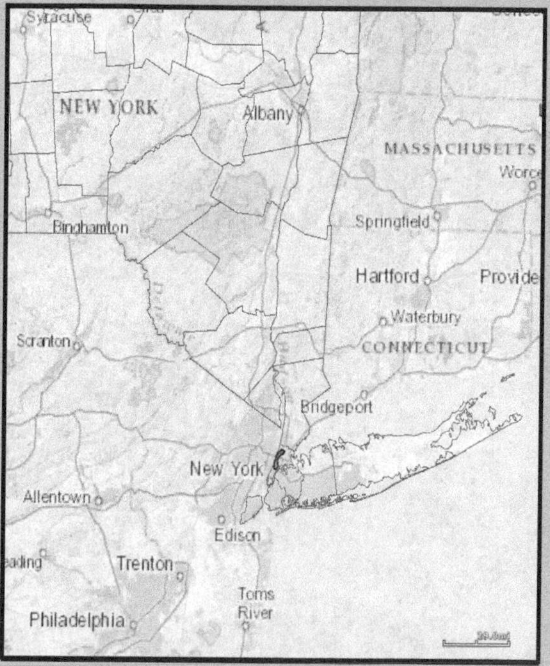

US Congressional districts since 2013
Source: http://nationalatlas.gov, 1 Million Scale project.

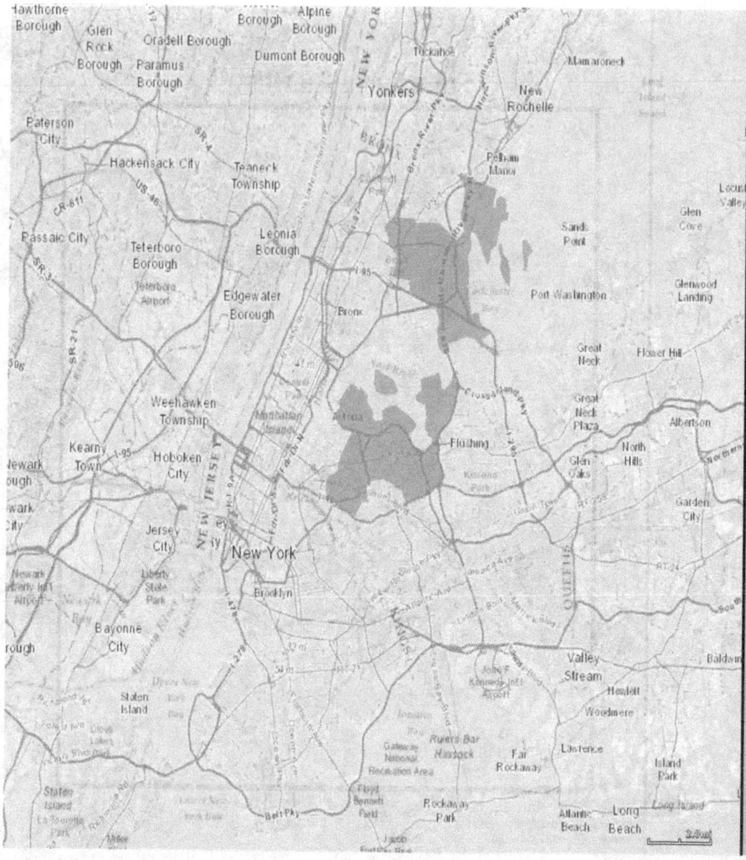

New York US District 14

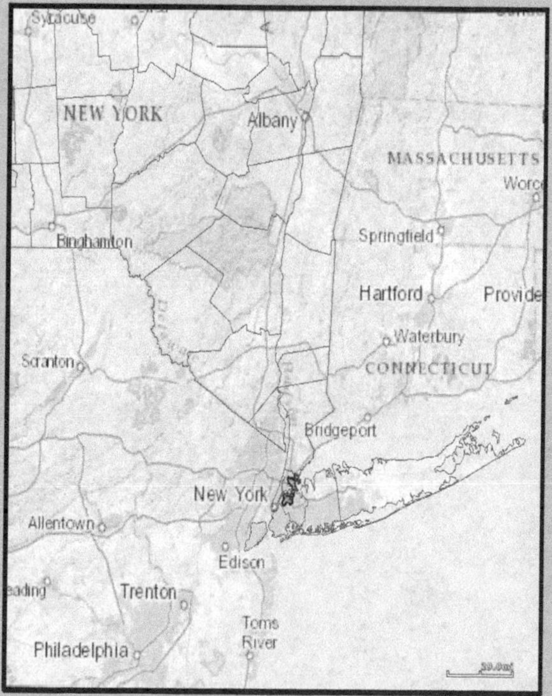

US Congressional districts since 2013
Source: http://nationalatlas.gov, 1 Million Scale project.

Appendices: Financial Plan, Indexes & Maps

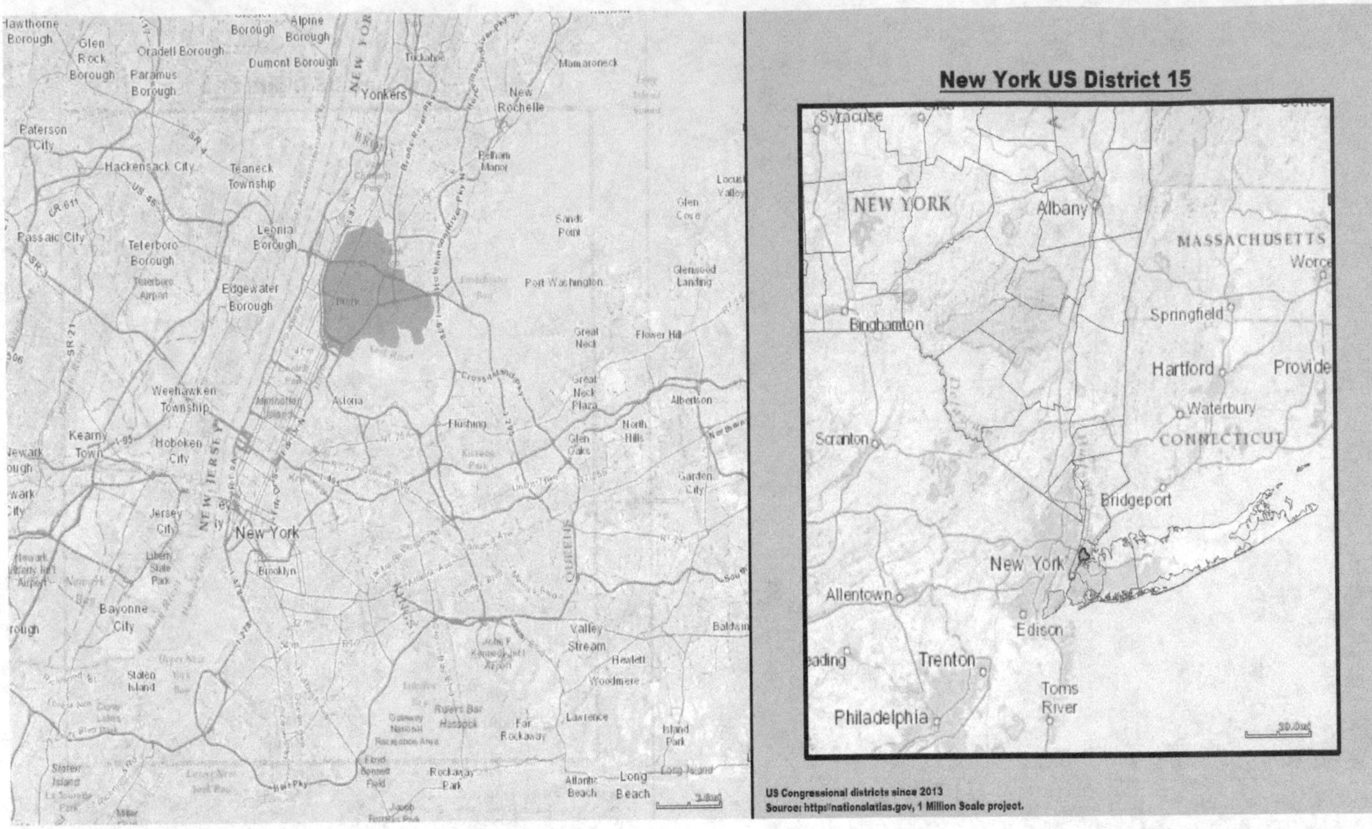
New York US District 15
Syracuse
NEW YORK
Albany
MASSACHUSETTS
Binghamton
Springfield
Hartford
Waterbury
CONNECTICUT
Scranton
Bridgeport
New York
Allentown
Edison
Trenton
Toms River
Philadelphia
US Congressional districts since 2013
Source: http://nationalatlas.gov, 1 Million Scale project.
Yonkers
New Rochelle
Paterson City
Hackensack City
Teaneck Township
Passaic City
Teterboro Borough
Edgewater Borough
Weehawken Township
Hoboken City
Jersey City
Astoria
Flushing
Port Washington
Brooklyn
Bayonne City
Valley Stream
Long Beach

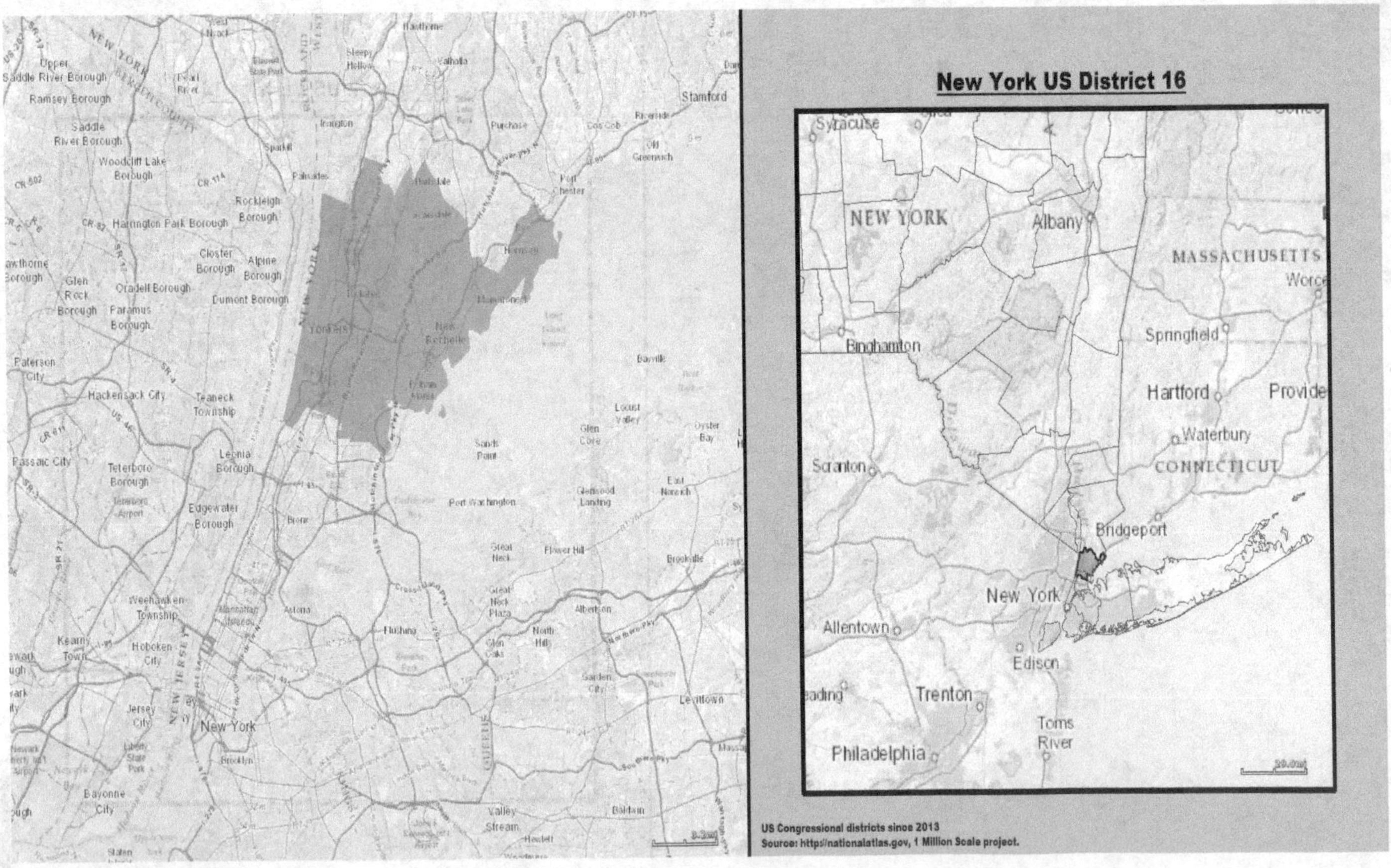
New York US District 16
Syracuse
NEW YORK
Albany
MASSACHUSETTS
Binghamton
Springfield
Hartford
Waterbury
CONNECTICUT
Scranton
Bridgeport
New York
Allentown
Edison
Trenton
Toms River
Philadelphia
US Congressional districts since 2013
Source: http://nationalatlas.gov, 1 Million Scale project.
Stamford
Upper Saddle River Borough
Ramsey Borough
Harrington Park Borough
Closter Borough
Alpine Borough
Dumont Borough
Paterson City
Hackensack City
Teaneck Township
Passaic City
Teterboro Borough
Edgewater Borough
Weehawken Township
Hoboken City
Jersey City
New York
Astoria
Flushing
Port Washington
Levittown
Bayonne City
Valley Stream

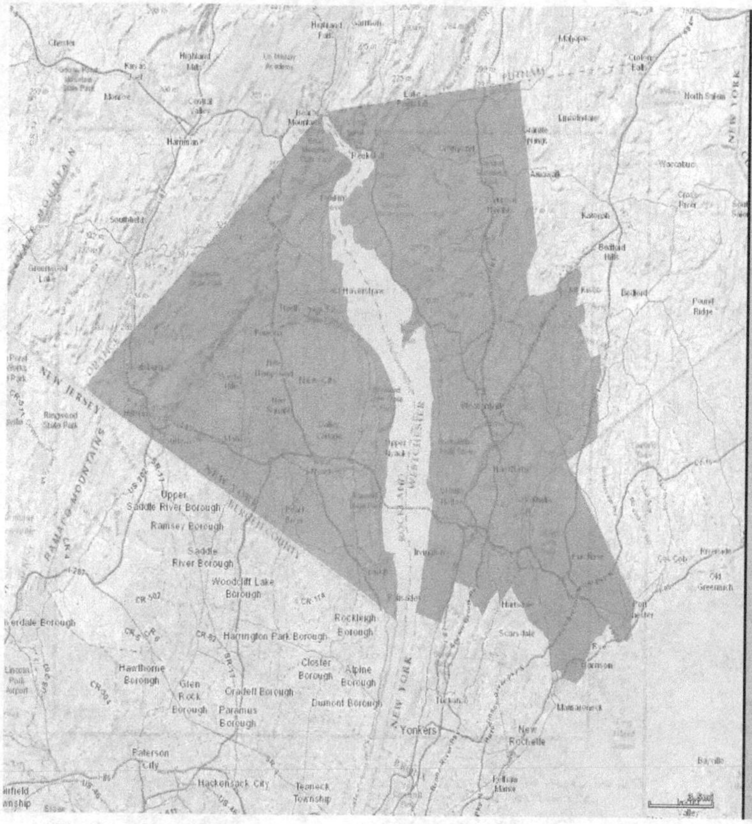

New York US District 17

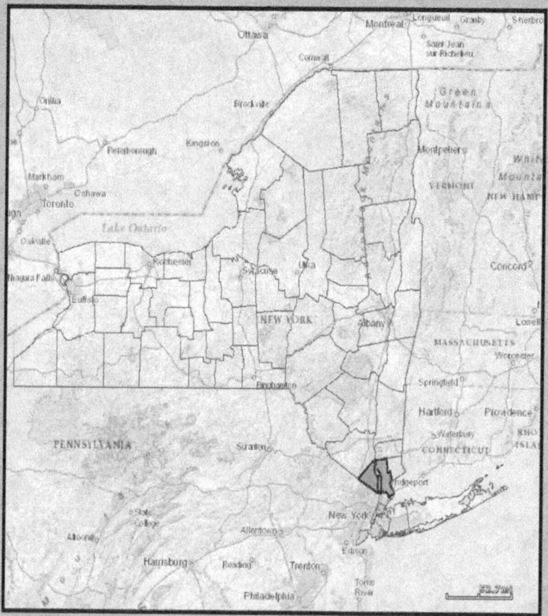

US Congressional districts since 2013
Source: http//nationalatlas.gov, 1 Million Scale project.

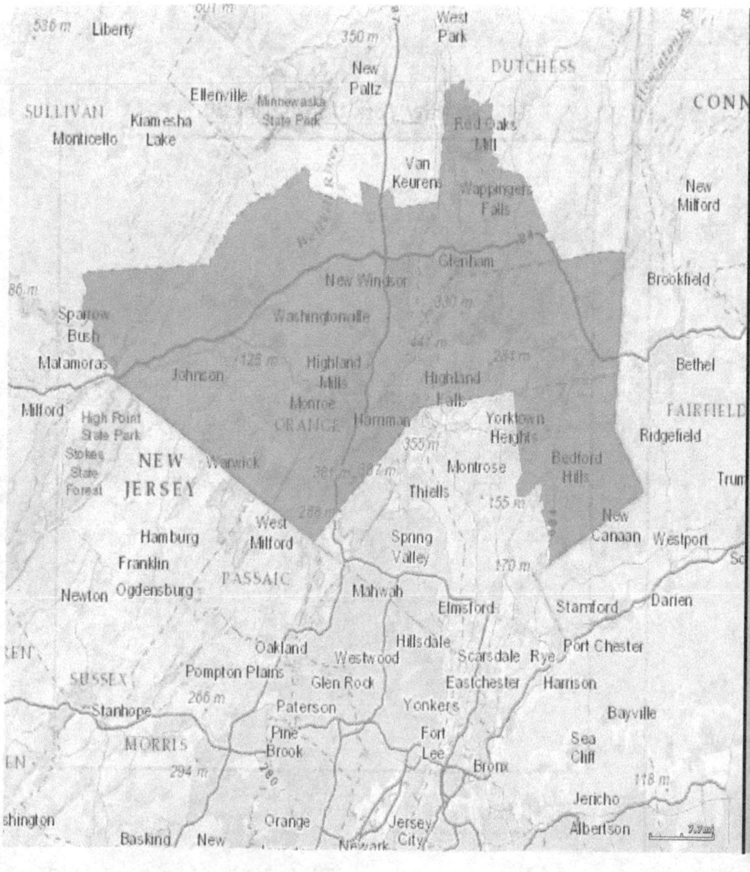

New York US District 18

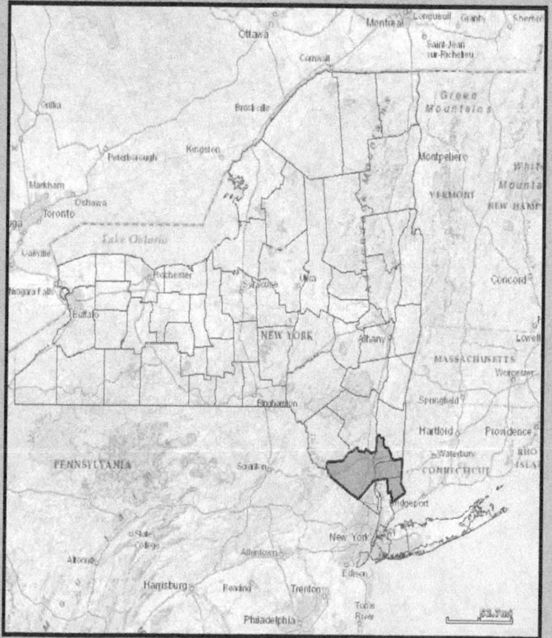

US Congressional districts since 2013
Source: http//nationalatlas.gov, 1 Million Scale project.

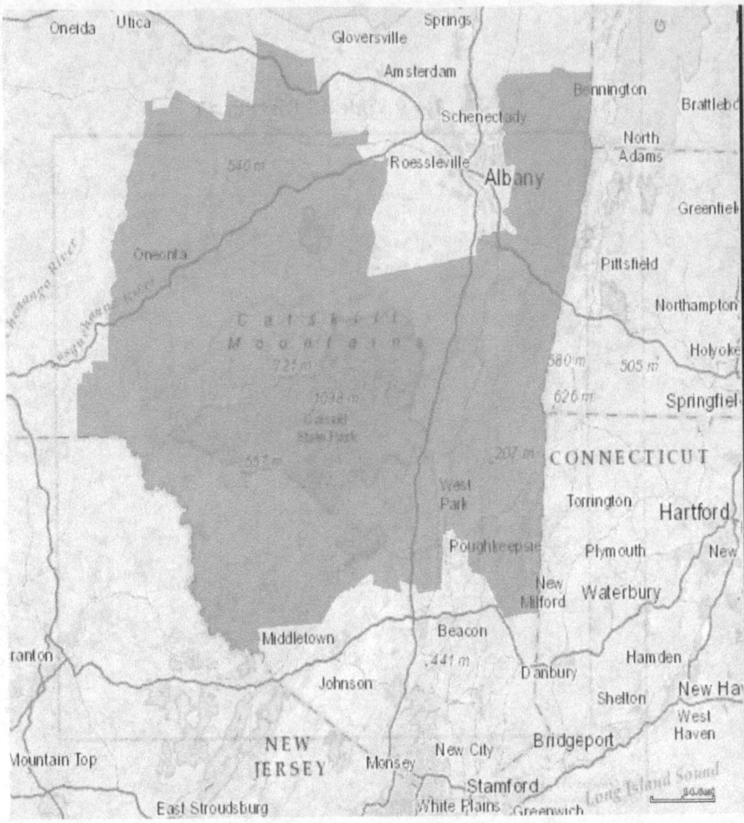

New York US District 19

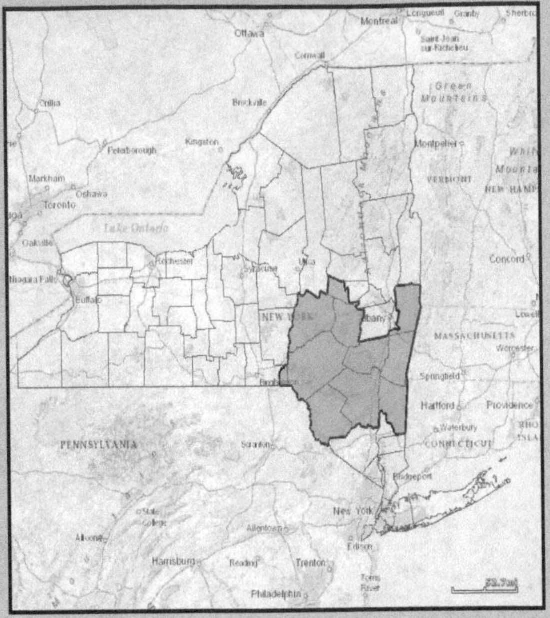

US Congressional districts since 2013
Source: http://nationalatlas.gov, 1 Million Scale project.

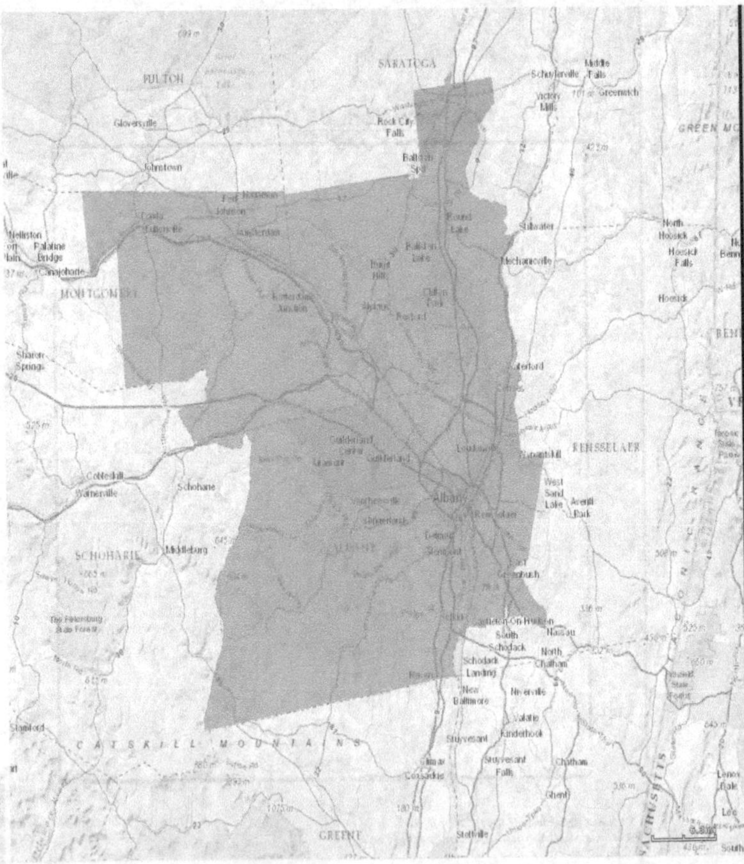

New York US District 20

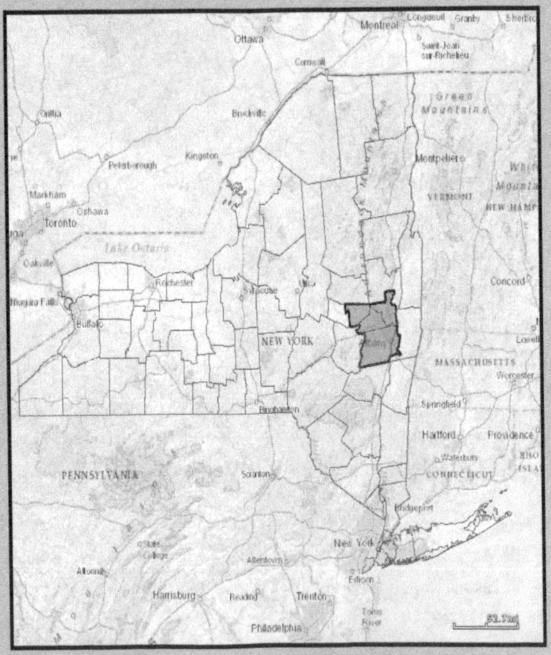

US Congressional districts since 2013
Source: http://nationalatlas.gov, 1 Million Scale project.

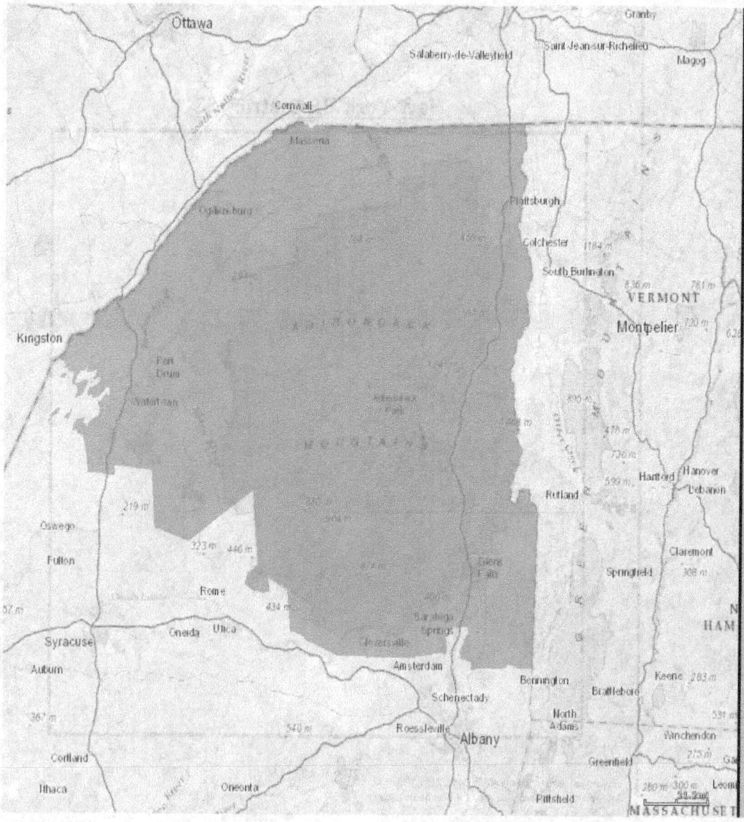

New York US District 21

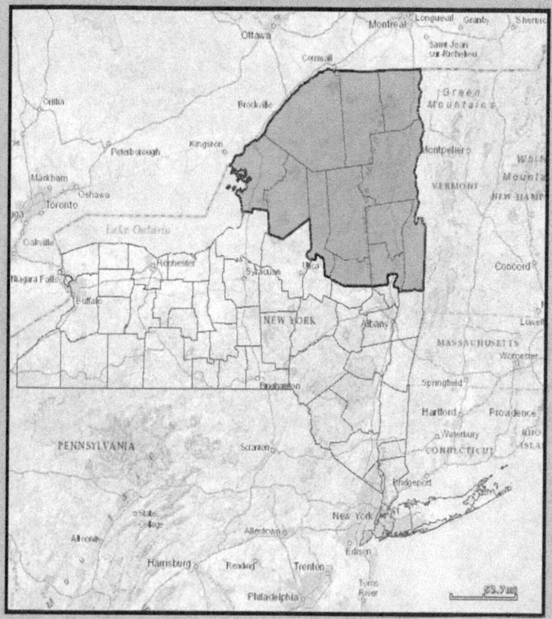

US Congressional districts since 2013
Source: http://nationalatlas.gov, 1 Million Scale project.

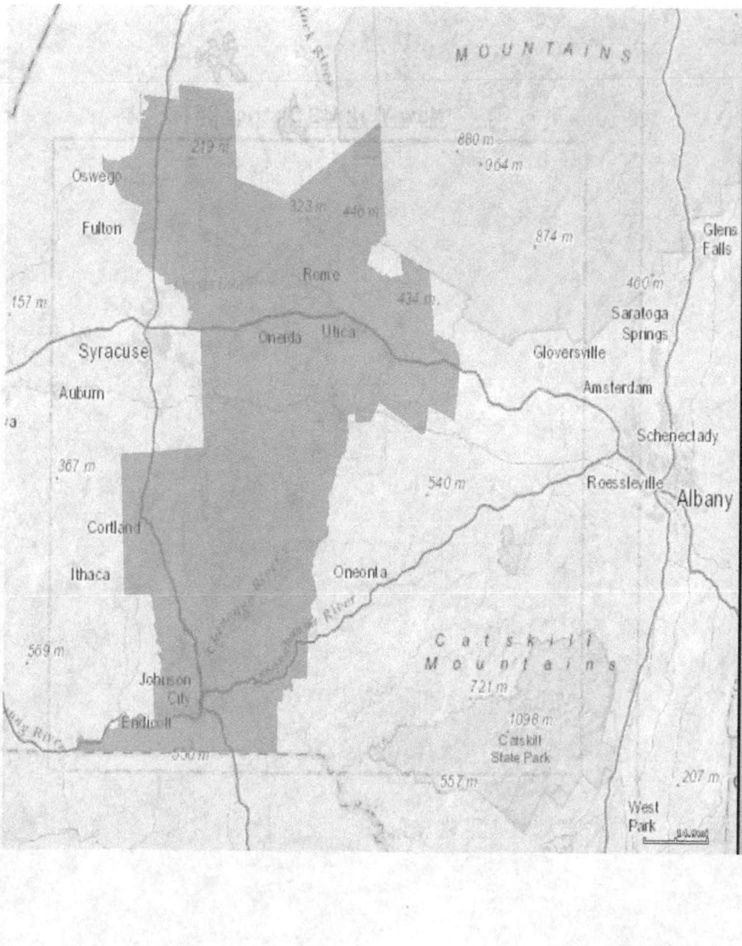

New York US District 22

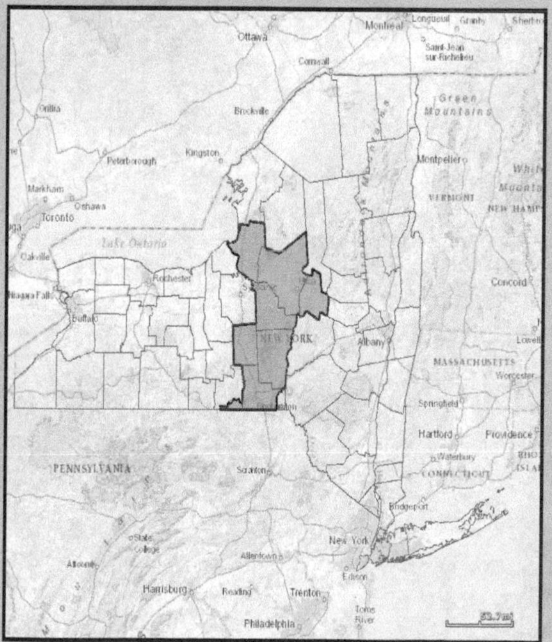

US Congressional districts since 2013
Source: http://nationalatlas.gov, 1 Million Scale project.

Appendices: Financial Plan, Indexes & Maps

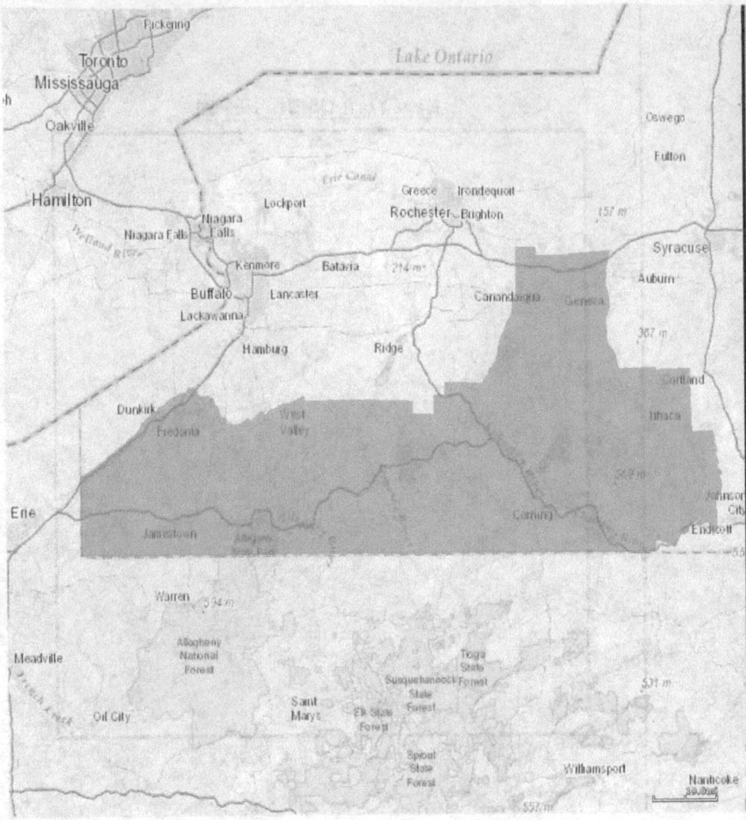

New York US District 23

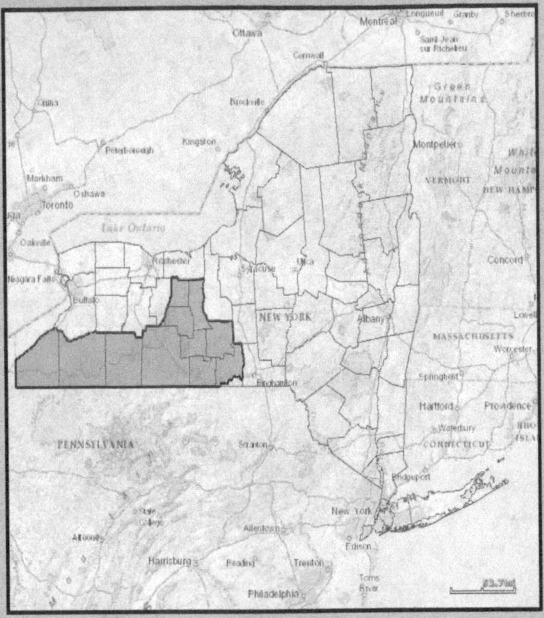

US Congressional districts since 2013
Source: http://nationalatlas.gov, 1 Million Scale project.

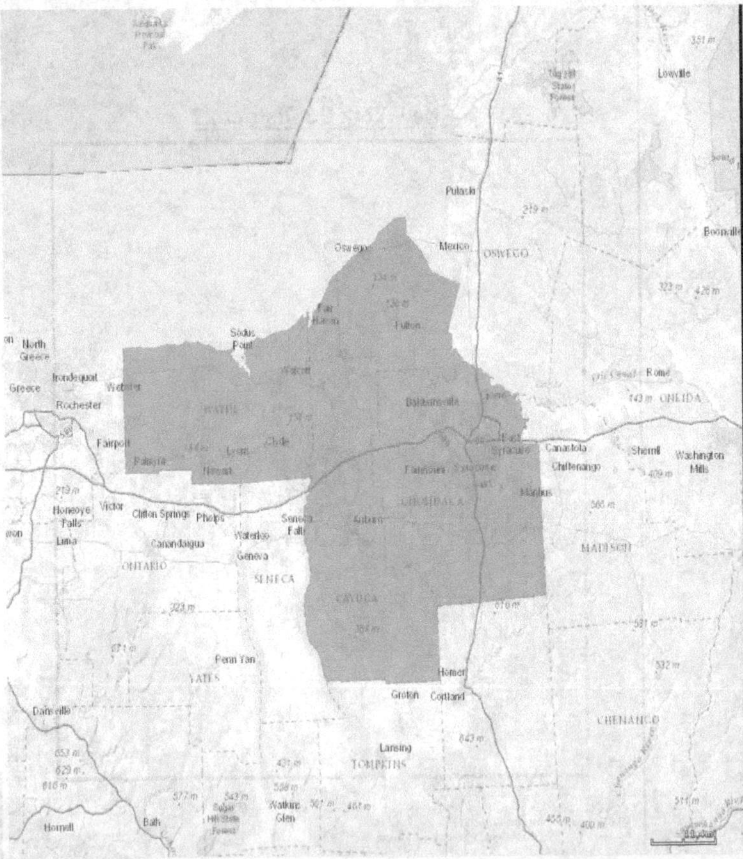

New York US District 24

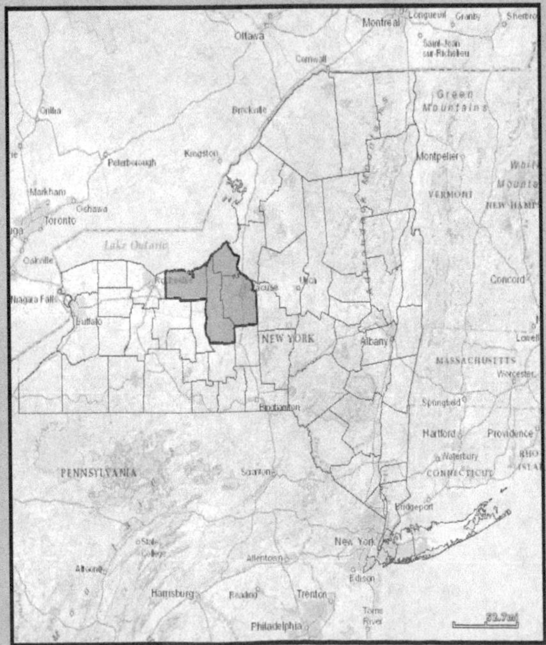

US Congressional districts since 2013
Source: http://nationalatlas.gov, 1 Million Scale project.

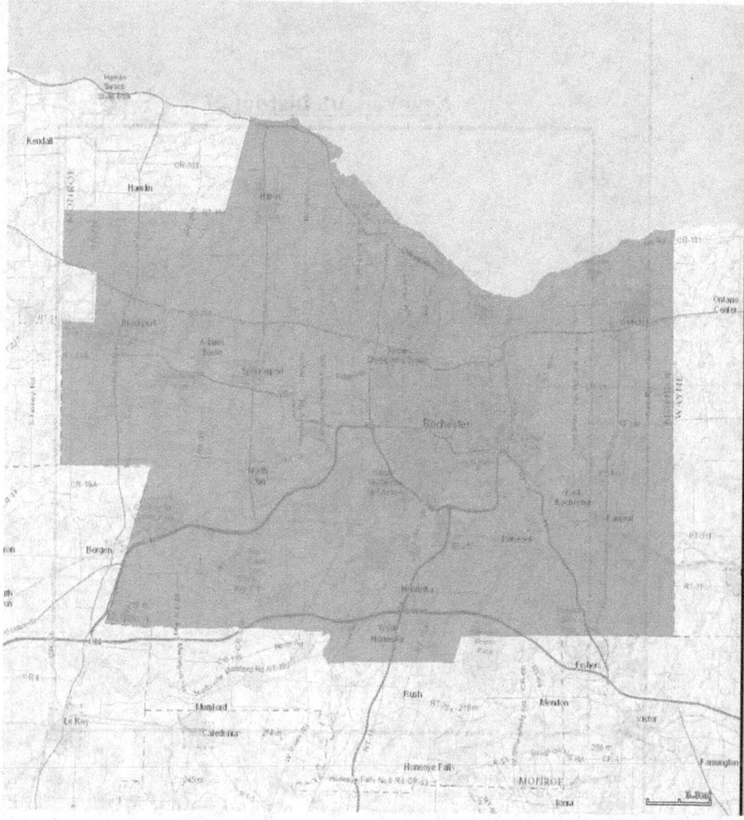

New York US District 25

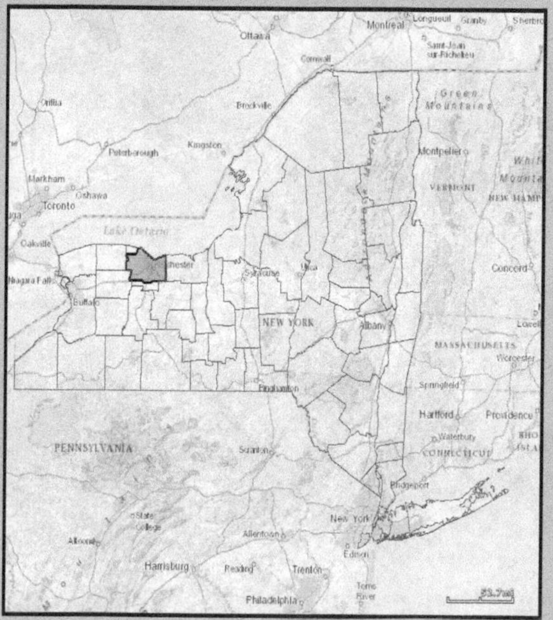

US Congressional districts since 2013
Source: http://nationalatlas.gov, 1 Million Scale project.

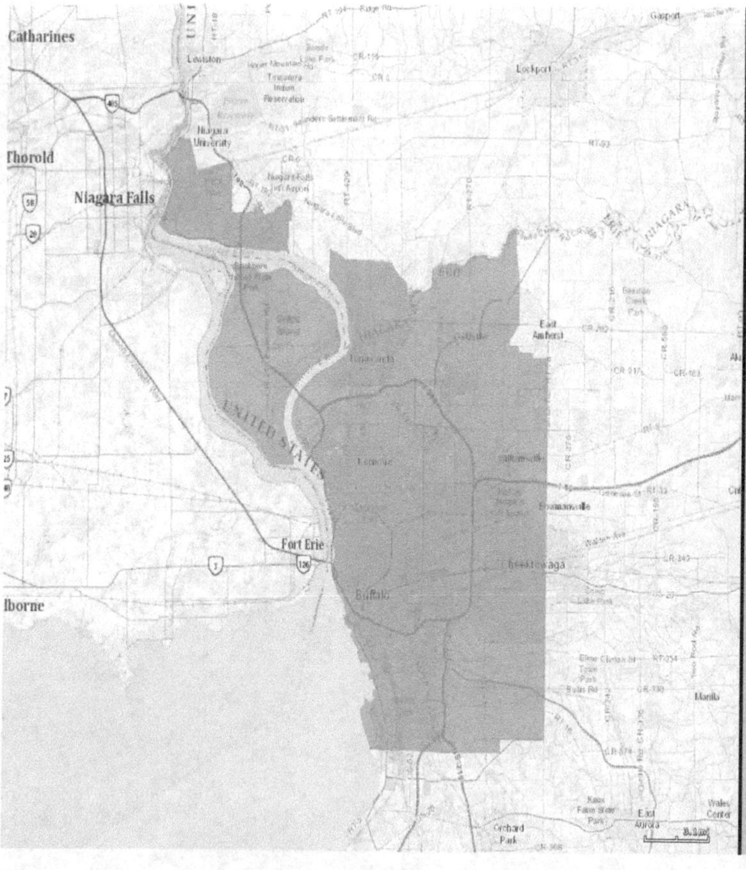

New York US District 26

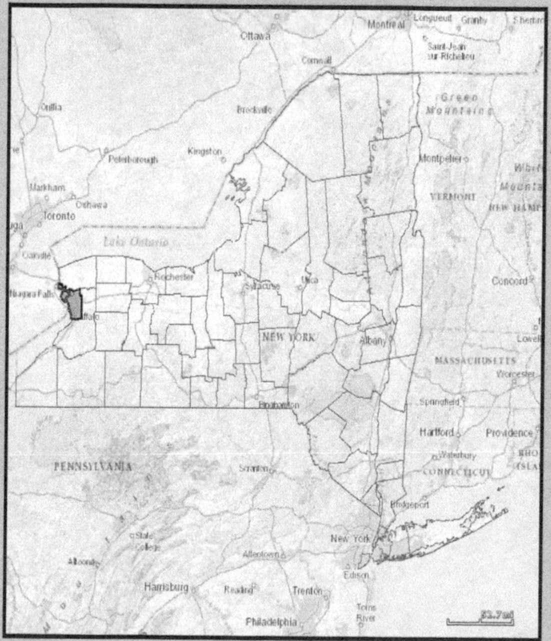

US Congressional districts since 2013
Source: http://nationalatlas.gov, 1 Million Scale project.

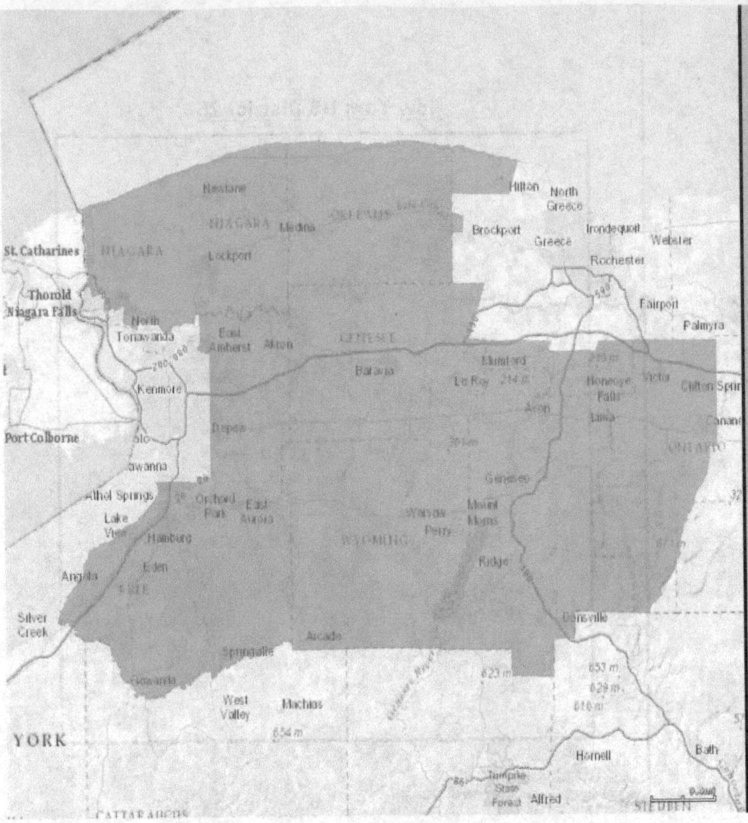

New York US District 27

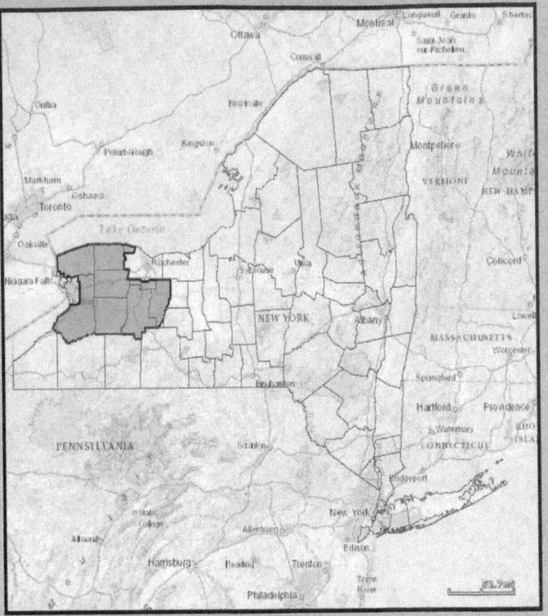

US Congressional districts since 2013
Source: https://nationalatlas.gov, 1 Million Scale project.

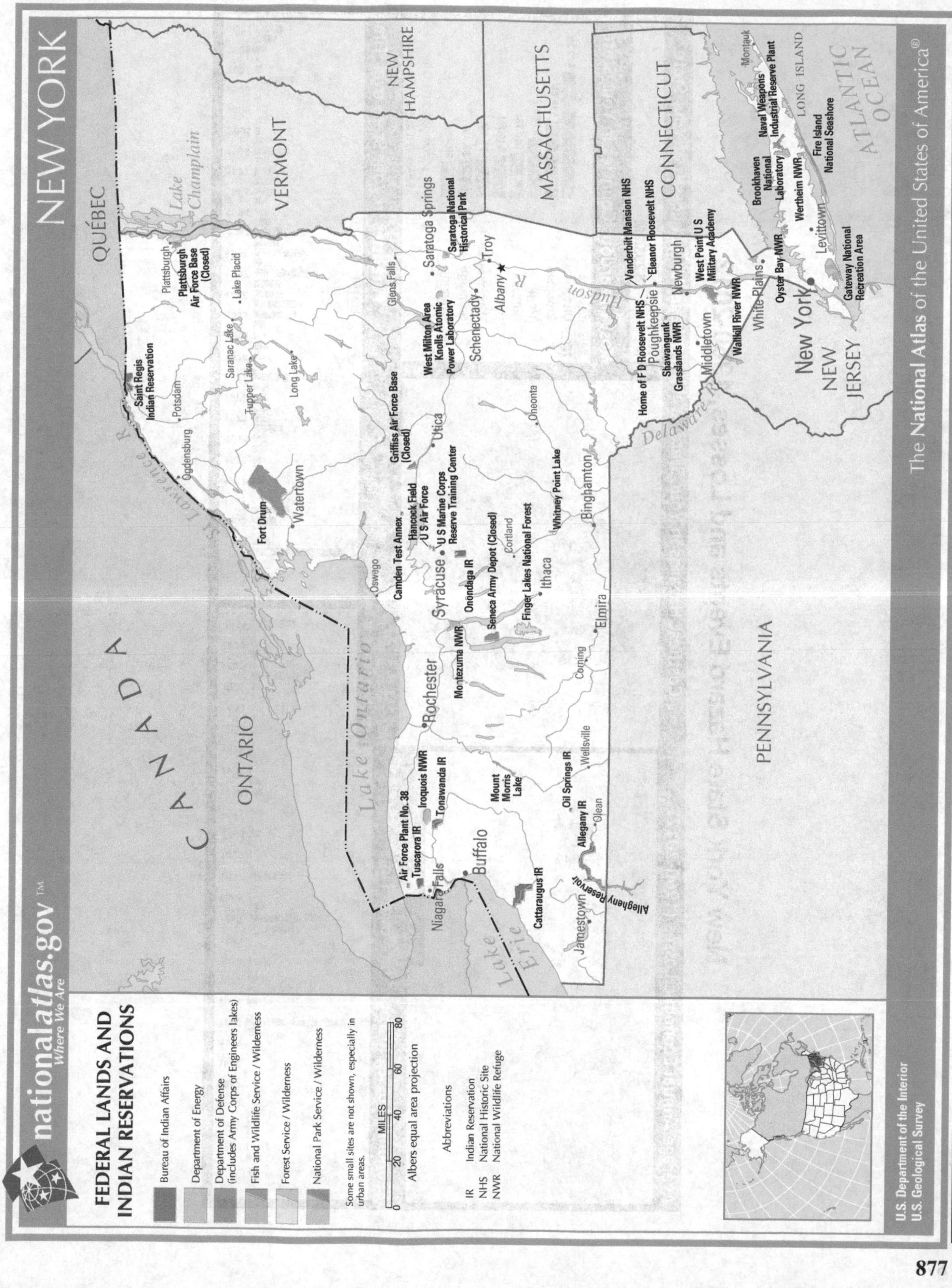
nationalatlas.gov™
Where We Are
NEW YORK
FEDERAL LANDS AND INDIAN RESERVATIONS
Bureau of Indian Affairs
Department of Energy
Department of Defense (includes Army Corps of Engineers lakes)
Fish and Wildlife Service / Wilderness
Forest Service / Wilderness
National Park Service / Wilderness
Some small sites are not shown, especially in urban areas.
MILES
0 20 40 60 80
Albers equal area projection
Abbreviations
IR Indian Reservation
NHS National Historic Site
NWR National Wildlife Refuge
U.S. Department of the Interior
U.S. Geological Survey
The National Atlas of the United States of America®
CANADA
ONTARIO
QUÉBEC
VERMONT
NEW HAMPSHIRE
MASSACHUSETTS
CONNECTICUT
PENNSYLVANIA
NEW JERSEY
ATLANTIC OCEAN
LONG ISLAND
Lake Ontario
Lake Erie
Lake Champlain
St Lawrence R
Hudson R
Delaware R
Allegheny Reservoir
Saint Regis Indian Reservation
Plattsburgh Air Force Base (Closed)
Fort Drum
Griffiss Air Force Base (Closed)
Camden Test Annex
Hancock Field U S Air Force
U S Marine Corps Reserve Training Center
Onondaga IR
Seneca Army Depot (Closed)
Finger Lakes National Forest
Montezuma NWR
Whitney Point Lake
Air Force Plant No. 38
Tuscarora IR
Iroquois NWR
Tonawanda IR
Mount Morris Lake
Oil Springs IR
Allegany IR
Cattaraugus IR
West Milton Area Knolls Atomic Power Laboratory
Saratoga National Historical Park
Home of F D Roosevelt NHS
Vanderbilt Mansion NHS
Eleanor Roosevelt NHS
Shawangunk Grasslands NWR
West Point U S Military Academy
Wallkill River NWR
Oyster Bay NWR
Gateway National Recreation Area
Brookhaven National Laboratory
Naval Weapons Industrial Reserve Plant
Wertheim NWR
Fire Island National Seashore
Plattsburgh
Lake Placid
Saranac Lake
Tupper Lake
Long Lake
Potsdam
Ogdensburg
Watertown
Oswego
Syracuse
Utica
Rochester
Buffalo
Niagara Falls
Jamestown
Olean
Wellsville
Corning
Elmira
Ithaca
Cortland
Binghamton
Oneonta
Schenectady
Albany
Troy
Saratoga Springs
Glens Falls
Poughkeepsie
Newburgh
Middletown
White Plains
New York
Levittown
Montauk

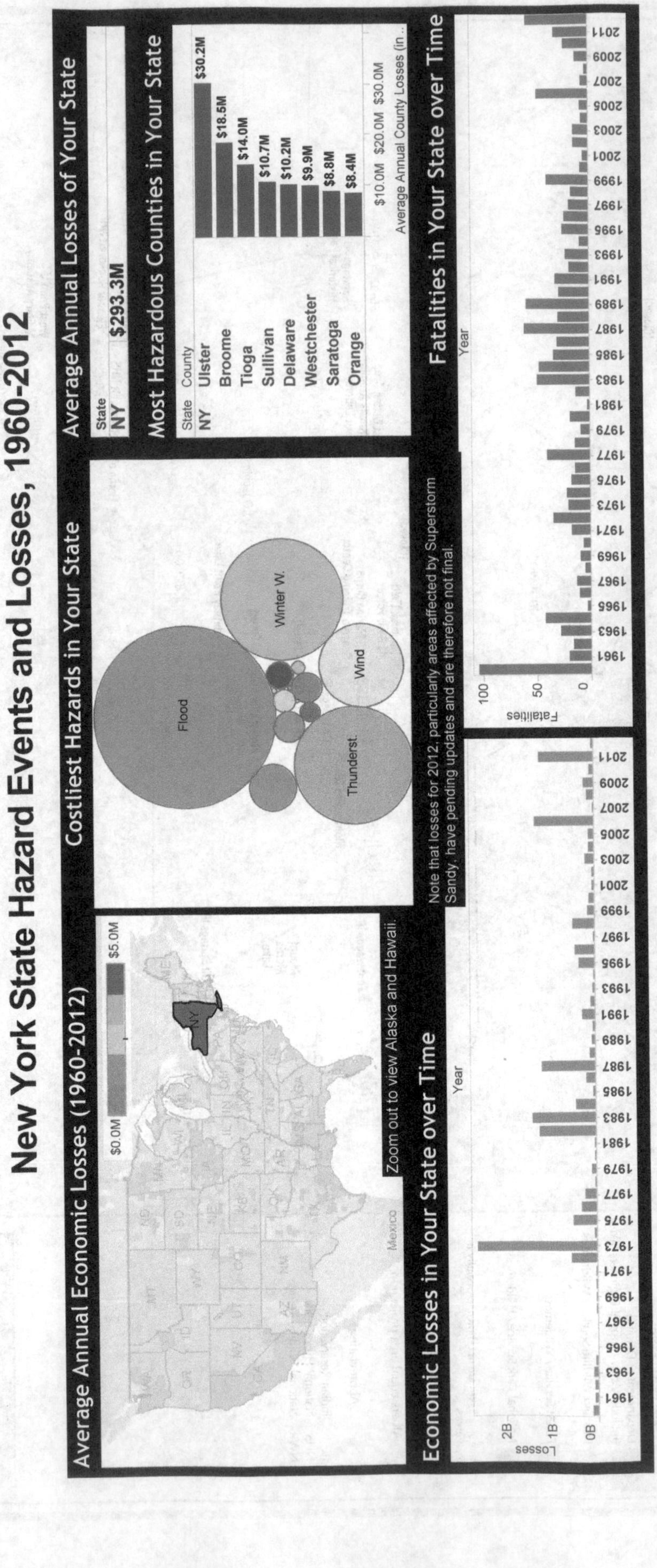
New York State Hazard Events and Losses, 1960-2012
Average Annual Economic Losses (1960-2012)
$0.0M
$5.0M
Zoom out to view Alaska and Hawaii.
Costliest Hazards in Your State
Flood
Winter W.
Wind
Thunderst.
Note that losses for 2012, particularly areas affected by Superstorm Sandy, have pending updates and are therefore not final.
Average Annual Losses of Your State
State
NY
$293.3M
Most Hazardous Counties in Your State
State
County
NY
Ulster $30.2M
Broome $18.5M
Tioga $14.0M
Sullivan $10.7M
Delaware $10.2M
Westchester $9.9M
Saratoga $8.8M
Orange $8.4M
$10.0M $20.0M $30.0M
Average Annual County Losses (in ...
Economic Losses in Your State over Time
Losses
2B
1B
0B
Year
Fatalities in Your State over Time
Fatalities
100
50
0
Year

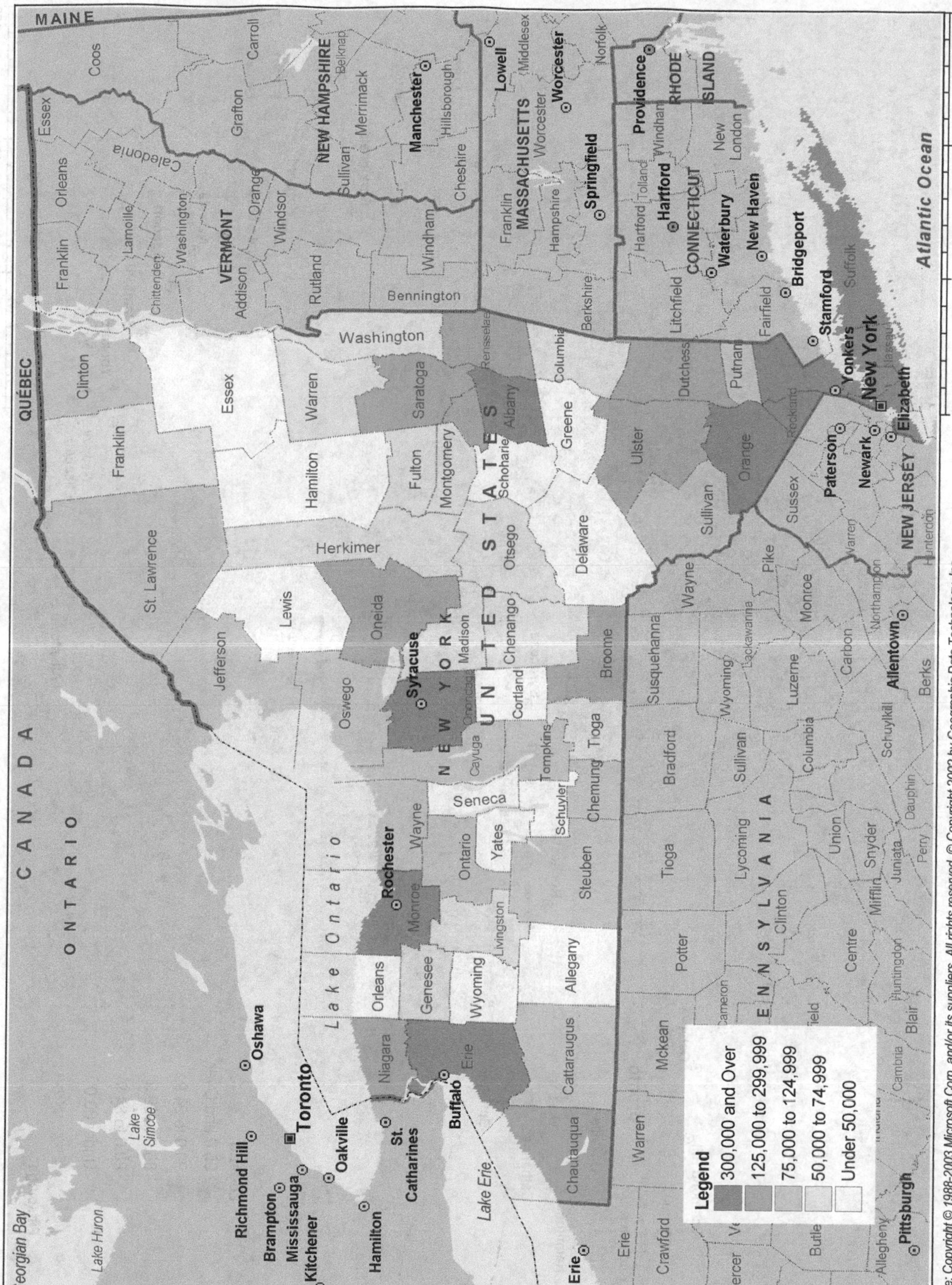
Population
Legend
300,000 and Over
125,000 to 299,999
75,000 to 124,999
50,000 to 74,999
Under 50,000
CANADA
ONTARIO
QUÉBEC
UNITED STATES
NEW YORK
PENNSYLVANIA
VERMONT
NEW HAMPSHIRE
MASSACHUSETTS
CONNECTICUT
RHODE ISLAND
NEW JERSEY
MAINE
Lake Ontario
Lake Erie
Lake Huron
Georgian Bay
Lake Simcoe
Atlantic Ocean
Toronto
Buffalo
Rochester
Syracuse
New York
Hartford
Springfield
Worcester
Providence
0 mi
50
100
150

Percent White

Note: Copyright © 1988-2003 Microsoft Corp. and/or its suppliers. All rights reserved. © Copyright 2002 by Geographic Data Technology, Inc. All rights reserved. © 2002 Navigation Technologies. All rights reserved.

Percent Black

Note: Copyright © 1988-2003 Microsoft Corp. and/or its suppliers. All rights reserved. © Copyright 2002 by Geographic Data Technology, Inc. All rights reserved. © 2002 Navigation Technologies. All rights reserved.

Percent Asian

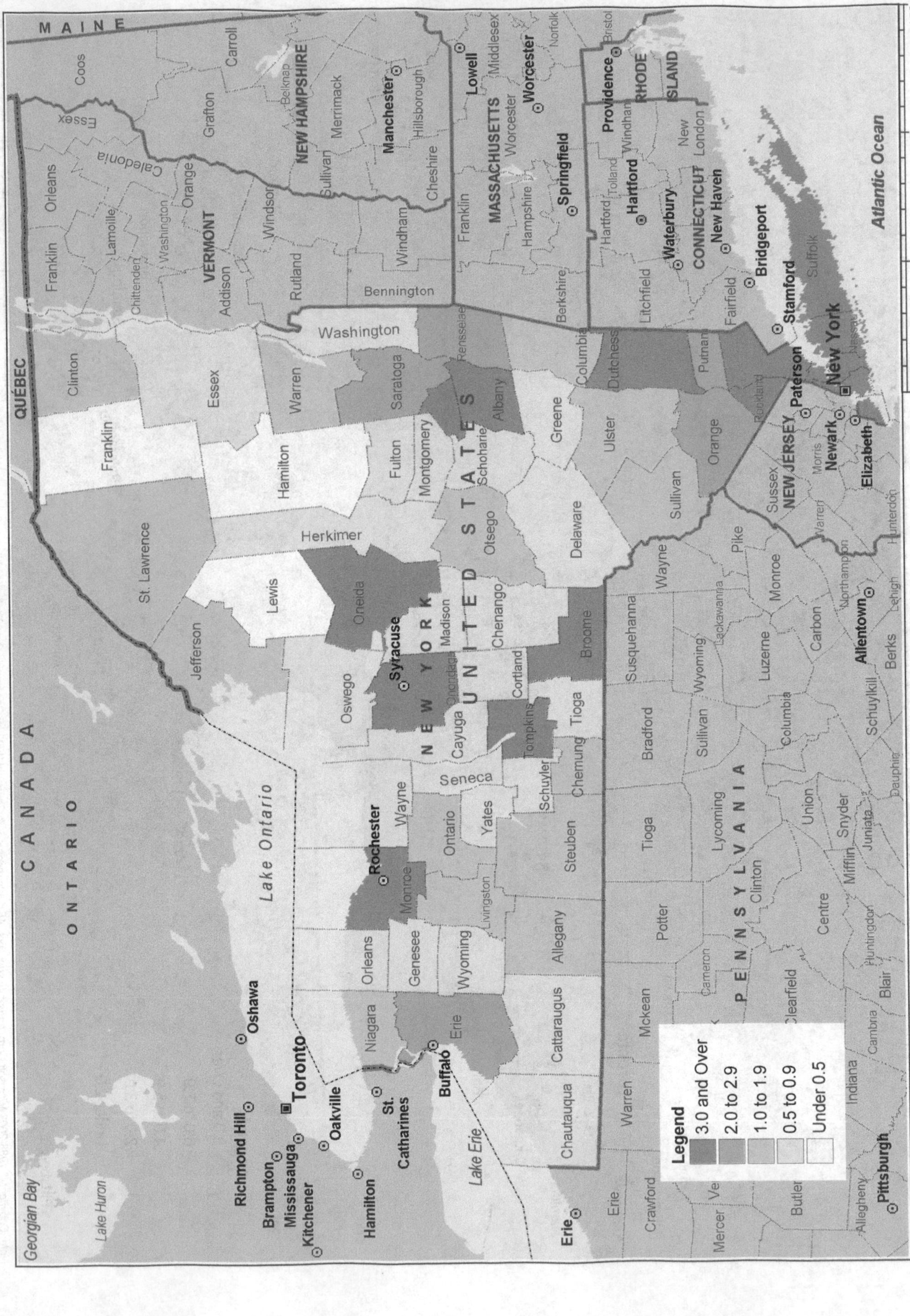

Percent Hispanic

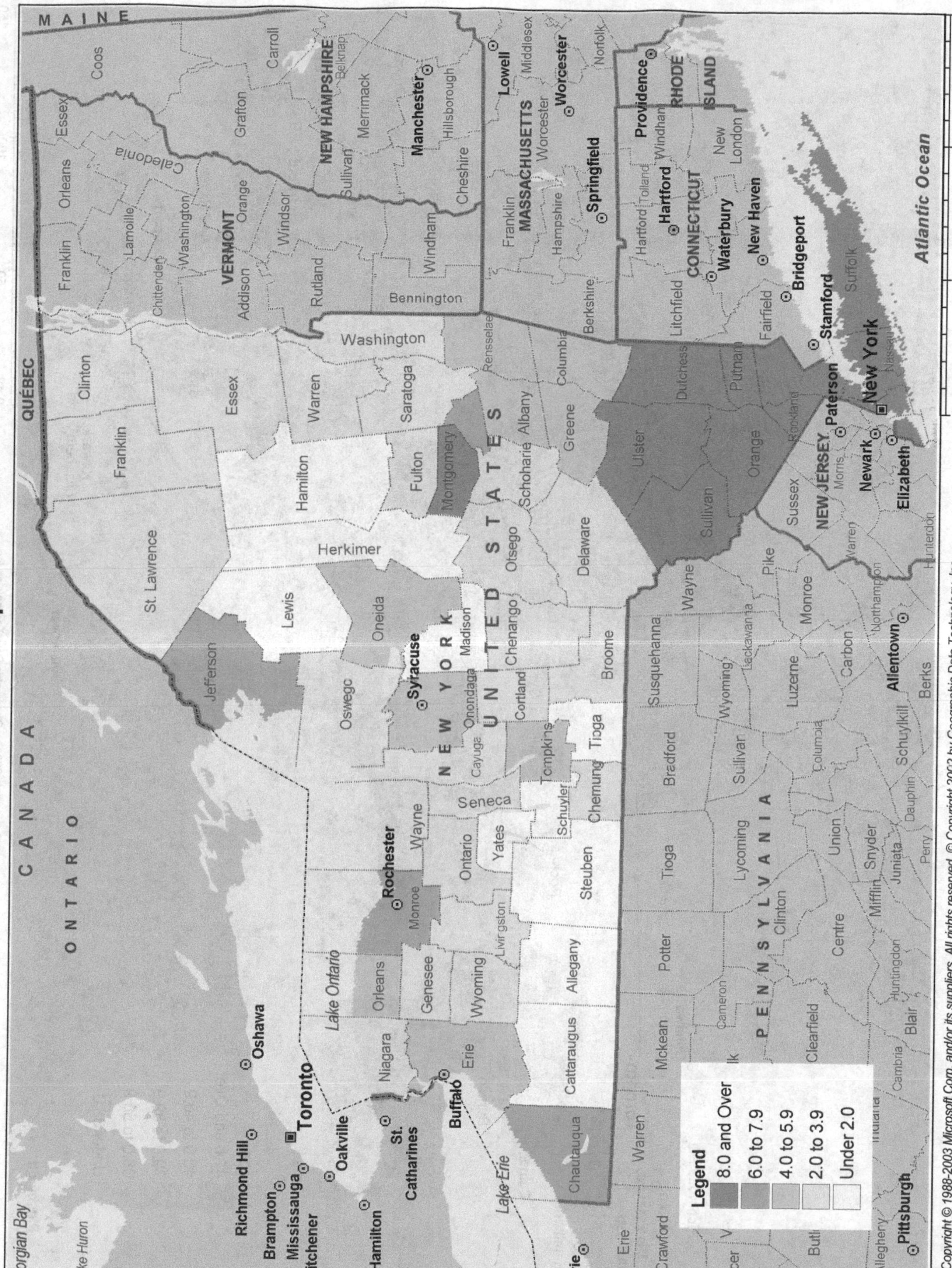

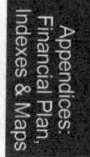

Median Age

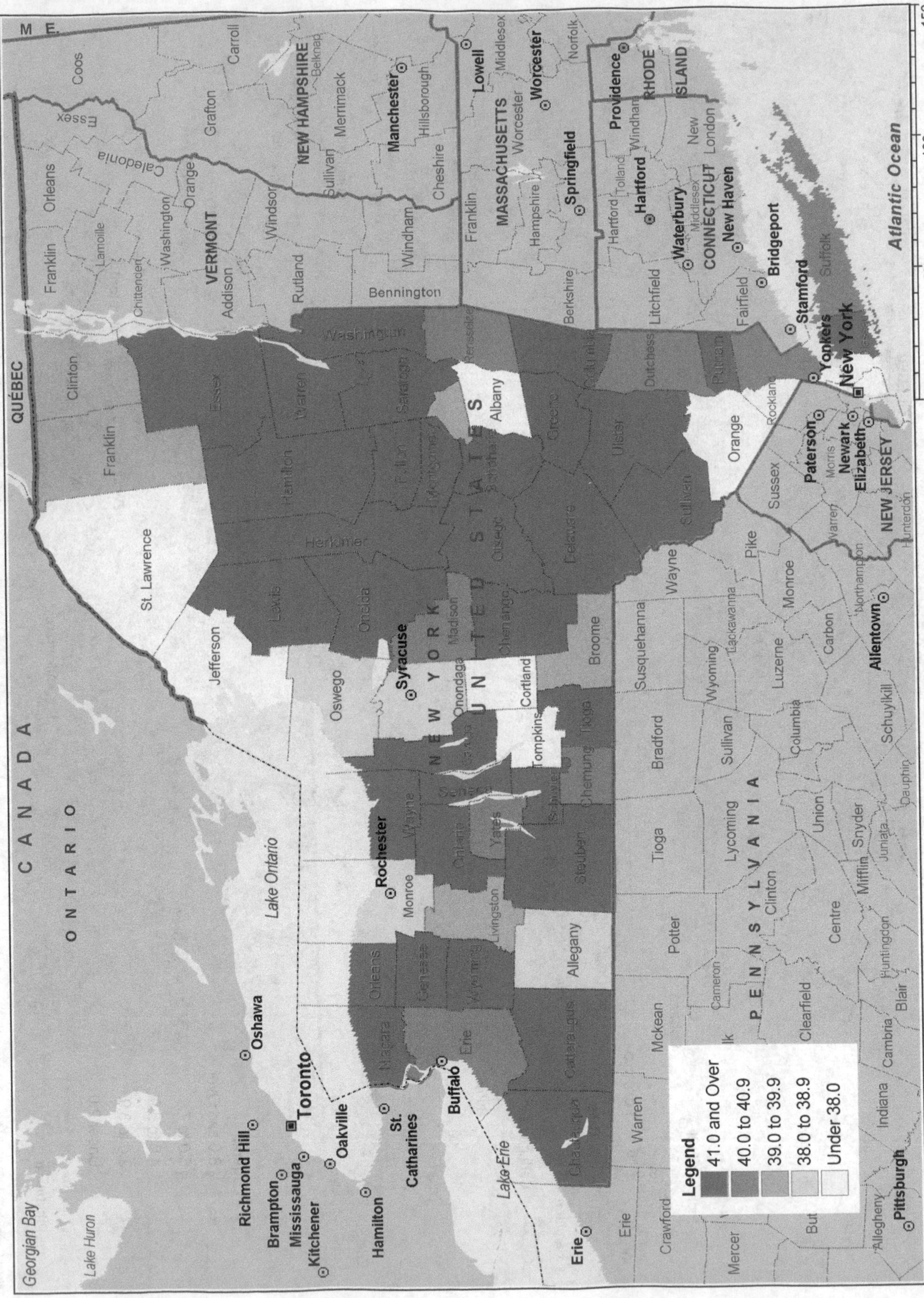
Legend
41.0 and Over
40.0 to 40.9
39.0 to 39.9
38.0 to 38.9
Under 38.0
CANADA
ONTARIO
QUÉBEC
NEW YORK
UNITED STATES
PENNSYLVANIA
NEW JERSEY
VERMONT
NEW HAMPSHIRE
MASSACHUSETTS
CONNECTICUT
RHODE ISLAND
Lake Ontario
Lake Erie
Lake Huron
Georgian Bay
Atlantic Ocean
Toronto
Buffalo
Rochester
Syracuse
Albany
New York
Yonkers
Paterson
Newark
Elizabeth
Stamford
Bridgeport
New Haven
Waterbury
Hartford
Springfield
Worcester
Providence
Lowell
Manchester
Allentown
Pittsburgh
Erie
Hamilton
St. Catharines
Oakville
Mississauga
Brampton
Kitchener
Richmond Hill
Oshawa
0 mi
50
100
150

Median Household Income

Note: Copyright © 1988-2003 Microsoft Corp. and/or its suppliers. All rights reserved. © Copyright 2002 by Geographic Data Technology, Inc. All rights reserved. © 2002 Navigation Technologies. All rights reserved.

Median Home Value
Legend
200,000 and Over
175,000 to 199,999
150,000 to 174,999
125,000 to 149,999
100,000 to 124,999
Under 100,000
CANADA
ONTARIO
QUÉBEC
UNITED STATES
NEW YORK
PENNSYLVANIA
VERMONT
NEW HAMPSHIRE
MASSACHUSETTS
CONNECTICUT
RHODE ISLAND
NEW JERSEY
Lake Ontario
Lake Erie
Lake Huron
Georgian Bay
Atlantic Ocean
Toronto
Buffalo
Rochester
Syracuse
New York
Yonkers
Stamford
Bridgeport
New Haven
Waterbury
Hartford
Springfield
Worcester
Providence
Lowell
Manchester
Newark
Paterson
Elizabeth
Allentown
Pittsburgh
Erie
Hamilton
Oakville
Mississauga
Brampton
Kitchener
Richmond Hill
Oshawa
St. Catharines
0 mi
50
100
150

High School Graduates*

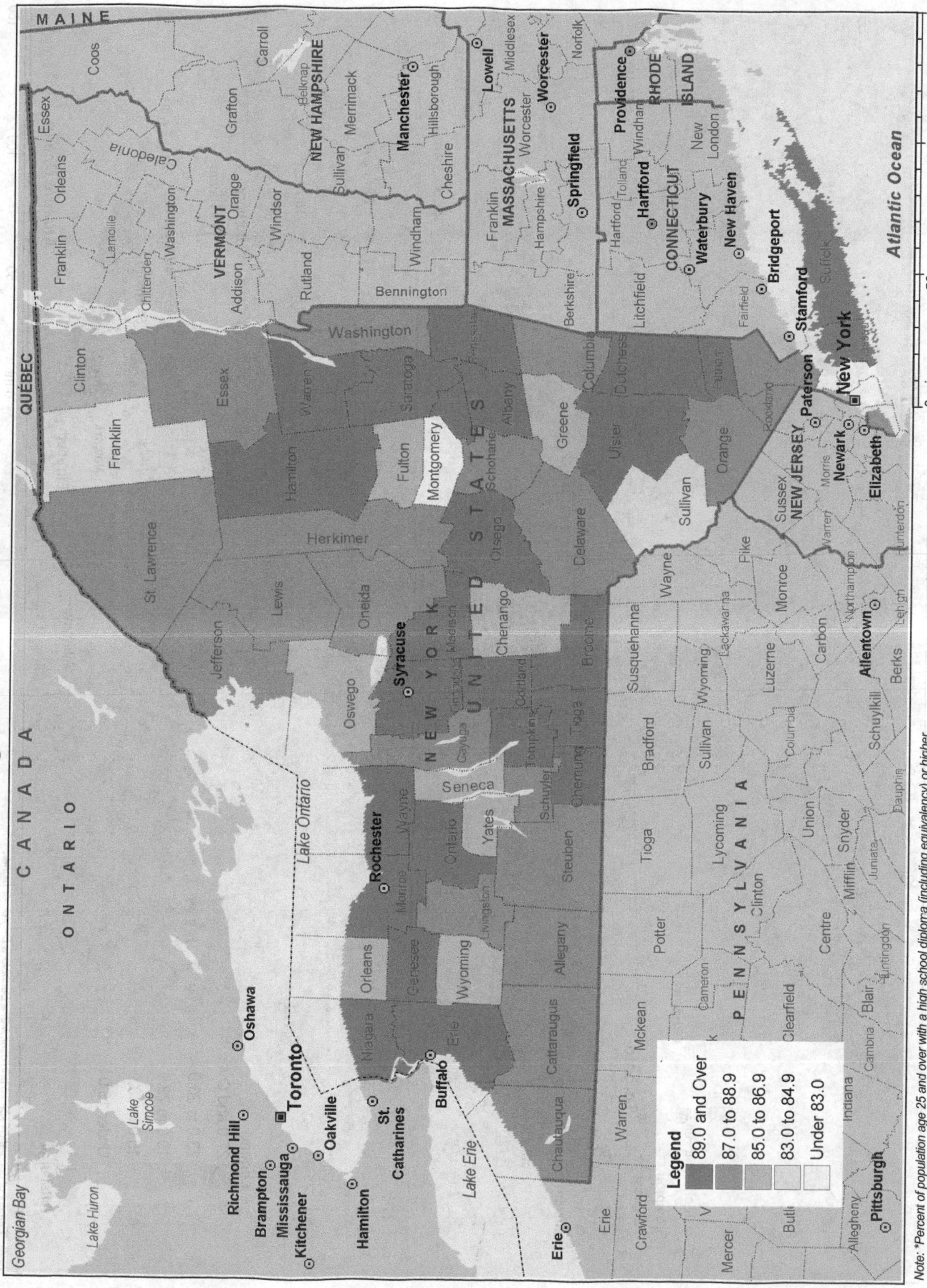

Note: *Percent of population age 25 and over with a high school diploma (including equivalency) or higher.

College Graduates*

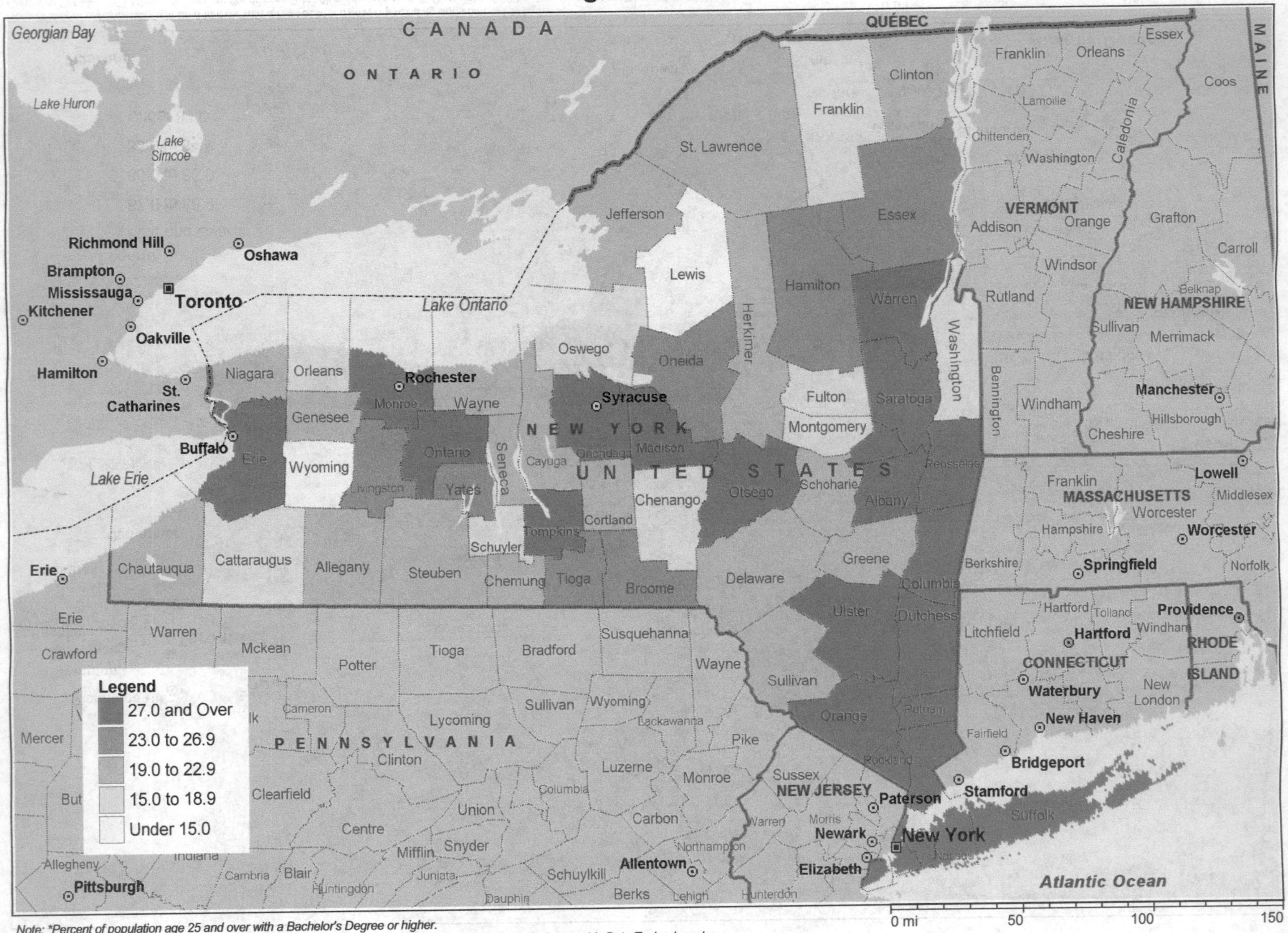

Note: *Percent of population age 25 and over with a Bachelor's Degree or higher.

Percent of Population Who Voted for Barack Obama in 2012

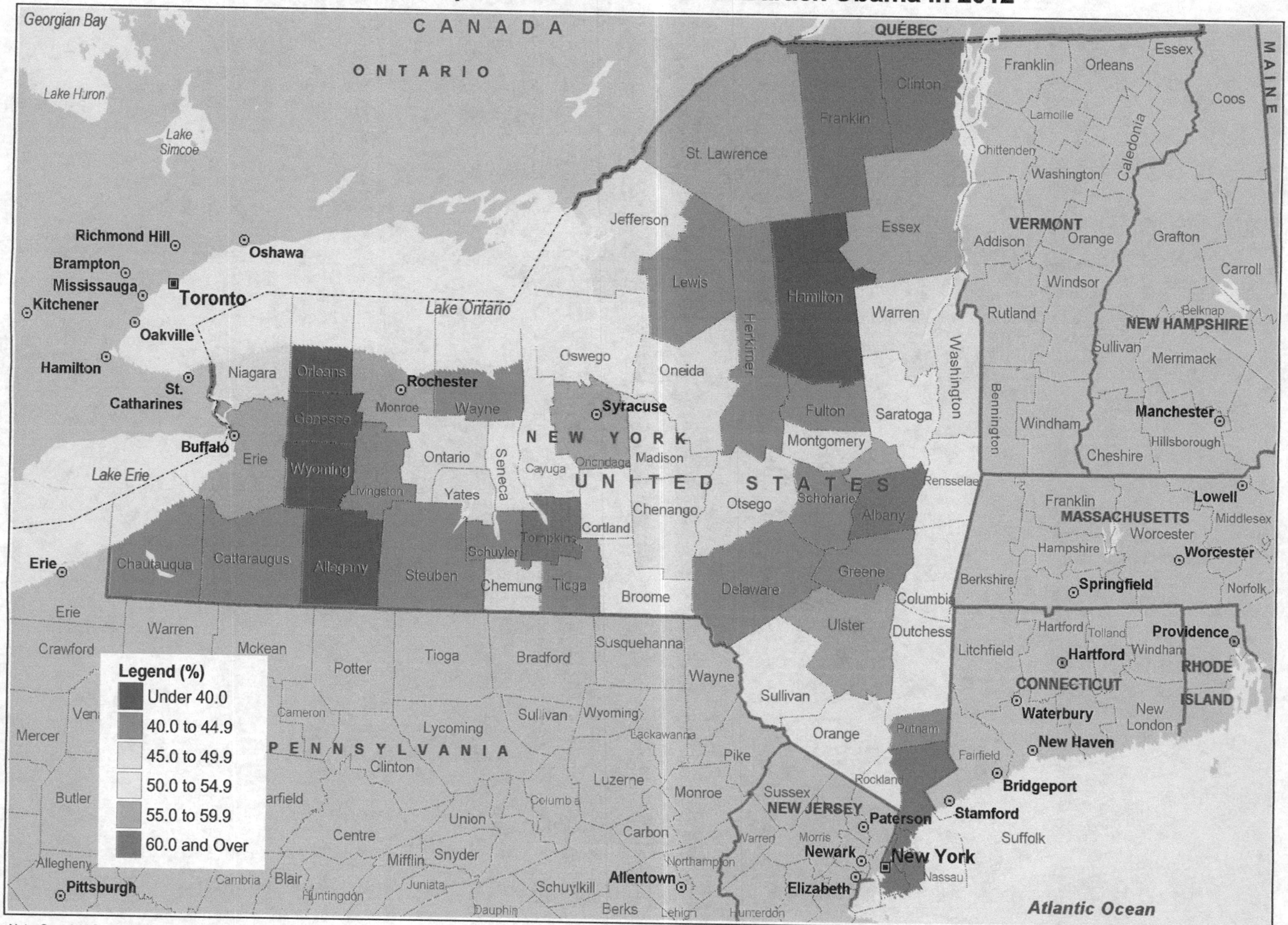

2016 Title List

Visit www.GreyHouse.com for Product Information, Table of Contents, and Sample Pages.

General Reference
An African Biographical Dictionary
America's College Museums
American Environmental Leaders: From Colonial Times to the Present
Encyclopedia of African-American Writing
Encyclopedia of Constitutional Amendments
Encyclopedia of Gun Control & Gun Rights
An Encyclopedia of Human Rights in the United States
Encyclopedia of Invasions & Conquests
Encyclopedia of Prisoners of War & Internment
Encyclopedia of Religion & Law in America
Encyclopedia of Rural America
Encyclopedia of the Continental Congress
Encyclopedia of the United States Cabinet, 1789-2010
Encyclopedia of War Journalism
Encyclopedia of Warrior Peoples & Fighting Groups
The Environmental Debate: A Documentary History
The Evolution Wars: A Guide to the Debates
From Suffrage to the Senate: America's Political Women
Global Terror & Political Risk Assessment
Nations of the World
Political Corruption in America
Privacy Rights in the Digital Era
The Religious Right: A Reference Handbook
Speakers of the House of Representatives, 1789-2009
This is Who We Were: 1880-1900
This is Who We Were: A Companion to the 1940 Census
This is Who We Were: In the 1910s
This is Who We Were: In the 1920s
This is Who We Were: In the 1940s
This is Who We Were: In the 1950s
This is Who We Were: In the 1960s
This is Who We Were: In the 1970s
U.S. Land & Natural Resource Policy
The Value of a Dollar 1600-1865: Colonial Era to the Civil War
The Value of a Dollar: 1860-2014
Working Americans 1770-1869 Vol. IX: Revolutionary War to the Civil War
Working Americans 1880-1999 Vol. I: The Working Class
Working Americans 1880-1999 Vol. II: The Middle Class
Working Americans 1880-1999 Vol. III: The Upper Class
Working Americans 1880-1999 Vol. IV: Their Children
Working Americans 1880-2015 Vol. V: Americans At War
Working Americans 1880-2005 Vol. VI: Women at Work
Working Americans 1880-2006 Vol. VII: Social Movements
Working Americans 1880-2007 Vol. VIII: Immigrants
Working Americans 1880-2009 Vol. X: Sports & Recreation
Working Americans 1880-2010 Vol. XI: Inventors & Entrepreneurs
Working Americans 1880-2011 Vol. XII: Our History through Music
Working Americans 1880-2012 Vol. XIII: Education & Educators
World Cultural Leaders of the 20th & 21st Centuries

Education Information
Charter School Movement
Comparative Guide to American Elementary & Secondary Schools
Complete Learning Disabilities Directory
Educators Resource Directory
Special Education: A Reference Book for Policy and Curriculum Development

Health Information
Comparative Guide to American Hospitals
Complete Directory for Pediatric Disorders
Complete Directory for People with Chronic Illness
Complete Directory for People with Disabilities
Complete Mental Health Directory
Diabetes in America: Analysis of an Epidemic
Directory of Drug & Alcohol Residential Rehab Facilities
Directory of Health Care Group Purchasing Organizations
Directory of Hospital Personnel
HMO/PPO Directory
Medical Device Register
Older Americans Information Directory

Business Information
Complete Television, Radio & Cable Industry Directory
Directory of Business Information Resources
Directory of Mail Order Catalogs
Directory of Venture Capital & Private Equity Firms
Environmental Resource Handbook
Food & Beverage Market Place
Grey House Homeland Security Directory
Grey House Performing Arts Directory
Grey House Safety & Security Directory
Grey House Transportation Security Directory
Hudson's Washington News Media Contacts Directory
New York State Directory
Rauch Market Research Guides
Sports Market Place Directory

Statistics & Demographics
American Tally
America's Top-Rated Cities
America's Top-Rated Smaller Cities
America's Top-Rated Small Towns & Cities
Ancestry & Ethnicity in America
The Asian Databook
Comparative Guide to American Suburbs
The Hispanic Databook
Profiles of America
"Profiles of" Series - State Handbooks
Weather America

Financial Ratings Series
TheStreet Ratings' Guide to Bond & Money Market Mutual Funds
TheStreet Ratings' Guide to Common Stocks
TheStreet Ratings' Guide to Exchange-Traded Funds
TheStreet Ratings' Guide to Stock Mutual Funds
TheStreet Ratings' Ultimate Guided Tour of Stock Investing
Weiss Ratings' Consumer Guides
Weiss Ratings' Guide to Banks
Weiss Ratings' Guide to Credit Unions
Weiss Ratings' Guide to Health Insurers
Weiss Ratings' Guide to Life & Annuity Insurers
Weiss Ratings' Guide to Property & Casualty Insurers

Bowker's Books In Print® Titles
American Book Publishing Record® Annual
American Book Publishing Record® Monthly
Books In Print®
Books In Print® Supplement
Books Out Loud™
Bowker's Complete Video Directory™
Children's Books In Print®
El-Hi Textbooks & Serials In Print®
Forthcoming Books®
Large Print Books & Serials™
Law Books & Serials In Print™
Medical & Health Care Books In Print™
Publishers, Distributors & Wholesalers of the US™
Subject Guide to Books In Print®
Subject Guide to Children's Books In Print®

Canadian General Reference
Associations Canada
Canadian Almanac & Directory
Canadian Environmental Resource Guide
Canadian Parliamentary Guide
Canadian Venture Capital & Private Equity Firms
Financial Post Directory of Directors
Financial Services Canada
Governments Canada
Health Guide Canada
The History of Canada
Libraries Canada
Major Canadian Cities

SALEM PRESS

2016 Title List

Visit **www.SalemPress.com** for Product Information, Table of Contents, and Sample Pages.

Science, Careers & Mathematics

Ancient Creatures
Applied Science
Applied Science: Engineering & Mathematics
Applied Science: Science & Medicine
Applied Science: Technology
Biomes and Ecosystems
Careers in Building Construction
Careers in Business
Careers in Chemistry
Careers in Communications & Media
Careers in Environment & Conservation
Careers in Healthcare
Careers in Hospitality & Tourism
Careers in Human Services
Careers in Law, Criminal Justice & Emergency Services
Careers in Manufacturing
Careers in Physics
Careers in Sales, Insurance & Real Estate
Careers in Science & Engineering
Careers in Technology Services & Repair
Computer Technology Innovators
Contemporary Biographies in Business
Contemporary Biographies in Chemistry
Contemporary Biographies in Communications & Media
Contemporary Biographies in Environment & Conservation
Contemporary Biographies in Healthcare
Contemporary Biographies in Hospitality & Tourism
Contemporary Biographies in Law & Criminal Justice
Contemporary Biographies in Physics
Earth Science
Earth Science: Earth Materials & Resources
Earth Science: Earth's Surface and History
Earth Science: Physics & Chemistry of the Earth
Earth Science: Weather, Water & Atmosphere
Encyclopedia of Energy
Encyclopedia of Environmental Issues
Encyclopedia of Environmental Issues: Atmosphere and Air Pollution
Encyclopedia of Environmental Issues: Ecology and Ecosystems
Encyclopedia of Environmental Issues: Energy and Energy Use
Encyclopedia of Environmental Issues: Policy and Activism
Encyclopedia of Environmental Issues: Preservation/Wilderness Issues
Encyclopedia of Environmental Issues: Water and Water Pollution
Encyclopedia of Global Resources
Encyclopedia of Global Warming
Encyclopedia of Mathematics & Society
Encyclopedia of Mathematics & Society: Engineering, Tech, Medicine
Encyclopedia of Mathematics & Society: Great Mathematicians
Encyclopedia of Mathematics & Society: Math & Social Sciences
Encyclopedia of Mathematics & Society: Math Development/Concepts
Encyclopedia of Mathematics & Society: Math in Culture & Society
Encyclopedia of Mathematics & Society: Space, Science, Environment
Encyclopedia of the Ancient World
Forensic Science
Geography Basics
Internet Innovators
Inventions and Inventors
Magill's Encyclopedia of Science: Animal Life
Magill's Encyclopedia of Science: Plant life
Notable Natural Disasters
Principles of Astronomy
Principles of Chemistry
Principles of Physics
Science and Scientists
Solar System
Solar System: Great Astronomers
Solar System: Study of the Universe
Solar System: The Inner Planets
Solar System: The Moon and Other Small Bodies
Solar System: The Outer Planets
Solar System: The Sun and Other Stars
World Geography

Literature

American Ethnic Writers
Classics of Science Fiction & Fantasy Literature
Critical Insights: Authors
Critical Insights: Film
Critical Insights: Literary Collection Bundles
Critical Insights: Themes
Critical Insights: Works
Critical Survey of Drama
Critical Survey of Graphic Novels: Heroes & Super Heroes
Critical Survey of Graphic Novels: History, Theme & Technique
Critical Survey of Graphic Novels: Independents/Underground Classics
Critical Survey of Graphic Novels: Manga
Critical Survey of Long Fiction
Critical Survey of Mystery & Detective Fiction
Critical Survey of Mythology and Folklore: Heroes and Heroines
Critical Survey of Mythology and Folklore: Love, Sexuality & Desire
Critical Survey of Mythology and Folklore: World Mythology
Critical Survey of Poetry
Critical Survey of Poetry: American Poets
Critical Survey of Poetry: British, Irish & Commonwealth Poets
Critical Survey of Poetry: Cumulative Index
Critical Survey of Poetry: European Poets
Critical Survey of Poetry: Topical Essays
Critical Survey of Poetry: World Poets
Critical Survey of Shakespeare's Plays
Critical Survey of Shakespeare's Sonnets
Critical Survey of Short Fiction
Critical Survey of Short Fiction: American Writers
Critical Survey of Short Fiction: British, Irish, Commonwealth Writers
Critical Survey of Short Fiction: Cumulative Index
Critical Survey of Short Fiction: European Writers
Critical Survey of Short Fiction: Topical Essays
Critical Survey of Short Fiction: World Writers
Critical Survey of Young Adult Literature
Cyclopedia of Literary Characters
Cyclopedia of Literary Places
Holocaust Literature
Introduction to Literary Context: American Poetry of the 20th Century
Introduction to Literary Context: American Post-Modernist Novels
Introduction to Literary Context: American Short Fiction
Introduction to Literary Context: English Literature
Introduction to Literary Context: Plays
Introduction to Literary Context: World Literature
Magill's Literary Annual 2015
Magill's Survey of American Literature
Magill's Survey of World Literature
Masterplots
Masterplots II: African American Literature
Masterplots II: American Fiction Series
Masterplots II: British & Commonwealth Fiction Series
Masterplots II: Christian Literature
Masterplots II: Drama Series
Masterplots II: Juvenile & Young Adult Literature, Supplement
Masterplots II: Nonfiction Series
Masterplots II: Poetry Series
Masterplots II: Short Story Series
Masterplots II: Women's Literature Series
Notable African American Writers
Notable American Novelists
Notable Playwrights
Notable Poets
Recommended Reading: 600 Classics Reviewed
Short Story Writers

SALEM PRESS

SALEM PRESS

2016 Title List

Visit **www.SalemPress.com** for Product Information, Table of Contents, and Sample Pages.

History and Social Science

The 2000s in America
50 States
African American History
Agriculture in History
American First Ladies
American Heroes
American Indian Culture
American Indian History
American Indian Tribes
American Presidents
American Villains
America's Historic Sites
Ancient Greece
The Bill of Rights
The Civil Rights Movement
The Cold War
Countries, Peoples & Cultures
Countries, Peoples & Cultures: Central & South America
Countries, Peoples & Cultures: Central, South & Southeast Asia
Countries, Peoples & Cultures: East & South Africa
Countries, Peoples & Cultures: East Asia & the Pacific
Countries, Peoples & Cultures: Eastern Europe
Countries, Peoples & Cultures: Middle East & North Africa
Countries, Peoples & Cultures: North America & the Caribbean
Countries, Peoples & Cultures: West & Central Africa
Countries, Peoples & Cultures: Western Europe
Defining Documents: American Revolution
Defining Documents: Civil Rights
Defining Documents: Civil War
Defining Documents: Emergence of Modern America
Defining Documents: Exploration & Colonial America
Defining Documents: Manifest Destiny
Defining Documents: Postwar 1940s
Defining Documents: Reconstruction
Defining Documents: 1920s
Defining Documents: 1930s
Defining Documents: 1950s
Defining Documents: 1960s
Defining Documents: 1970s
Defining Documents: American West
Defining Documents: Ancient World
Defining Documents: Middle Ages
Defining Documents: Vietnam War
Defining Documents: World War I
Defining Documents: World War II
The Eighties in America
Encyclopedia of American Immigration
Encyclopedia of Flight
Encyclopedia of the Ancient World
Fashion Innovators
The Fifties in America
The Forties in America
Great Athletes
Great Athletes: Baseball
Great Athletes: Basketball
Great Athletes: Boxing & Soccer
Great Athletes: Cumulative Index
Great Athletes: Football
Great Athletes: Golf & Tennis
Great Athletes: Olympics
Great Athletes: Racing & Individual Sports
Great Events from History: 17th Century
Great Events from History: 18th Century
Great Events from History: 19th Century
Great Events from History: 20th Century (1901-1940)
Great Events from History: 20th Century (1941-1970)
Great Events from History: 20th Century (1971-2000)
Great Events from History: Ancient World
Great Events from History: Cumulative Indexes
Great Events from History: Gay, Lesbian, Bisexual, Transgender Events
Great Events from History: Middle Ages
Great Events from History: Modern Scandals
Great Events from History: Renaissance & Early Modern Era
Great Lives from History: 17th Century
Great Lives from History: 18th Century
Great Lives from History: 19th Century
Great Lives from History: 20th Century
Great Lives from History: African Americans
Great Lives from History: American Women
Great Lives from History: Ancient World
Great Lives from History: Asian & Pacific Islander Americans
Great Lives from History: Cumulative Indexes
Great Lives from History: Incredibly Wealthy
Great Lives from History: Inventors & Inventions
Great Lives from History: Jewish Americans
Great Lives from History: Latinos
Great Lives from History: Middle Ages
Great Lives from History: Notorious Lives
Great Lives from History: Renaissance & Early Modern Era
Great Lives from History: Scientists & Science
Historical Encyclopedia of American Business
Issues in U.S. Immigration
Magill's Guide to Military History
Milestone Documents in African American History
Milestone Documents in American History
Milestone Documents in World History
Milestone Documents of American Leaders
Milestone Documents of World Religions
Music Innovators
Musicians & Composers 20th Century
The Nineties in America
The Seventies in America
The Sixties in America
Survey of American Industry and Careers
The Thirties in America
The Twenties in America
United States at War
U.S.A. in Space
U.S. Court Cases
U.S. Government Leaders
U.S. Laws, Acts, and Treaties
U.S. Legal System
U.S. Supreme Court
Weapons and Warfare
World Conflicts: Asia and the Middle East
World Political Yearbook

Health

Addictions & Substance Abuse
Adolescent Health & Wellness
Cancer
Complementary & Alternative Medicine
Genetics & Inherited Conditions
Health Issues
Infectious Diseases & Conditions
Magill's Medical Guide
Psychology & Behavioral Health
Psychology Basics

HW WILSON

HW WILSON

2016 Title List

Visit **www.HWWilsonInPrint.com** for Product Information, Table of Contents and Sample Pages

Current Biography

Current Biography Cumulative Index 1946-2013
Current Biography Monthly Magazine
Current Biography Yearbook: 2003
Current Biography Yearbook: 2004
Current Biography Yearbook: 2005
Current Biography Yearbook: 2006
Current Biography Yearbook: 2007
Current Biography Yearbook: 2008
Current Biography Yearbook: 2009
Current Biography Yearbook: 2010
Current Biography Yearbook: 2011
Current Biography Yearbook: 2012
Current Biography Yearbook: 2013
Current Biography Yearbook: 2014
Current Biography Yearbook: 2015

Core Collections

Children's Core Collection
Fiction Core Collection
Graphic Novels Core Collection
Middle & Junior High School Core
Public Library Core Collection: Nonfiction
Senior High Core Collection
Young Adult Fiction Core Collection

The Reference Shelf

Aging in America
American Military Presence Overseas
The Arab Spring
The Brain
The Business of Food
Campaign Trends & Election Law
Conspiracy Theories
The Digital Age
Dinosaurs
Embracing New Paradigms in Education
Faith & Science
Families: Traditional and New Structures
The Future of U.S. Economic Relations: Mexico, Cuba, and Venezuela
Global Climate Change
Graphic Novels and Comic Books
Immigration
Immigration in the U.S.
Internet Safety
Marijuana Reform
The News and its Future
The Paranormal
Politics of the Ocean
Racial Tension in a "Postracial" Age
Reality Television
Representative American Speeches: 2008-2009
Representative American Speeches: 2009-2010
Representative American Speeches: 2010-2011
Representative American Speeches: 2011-2012
Representative American Speeches: 2012-2013
Representative American Speeches: 2013-2014
Representative American Speeches: 2014-2015
Representative American Speeches: 2015-2016
Rethinking Work
Revisiting Gender
Robotics
Russia
Social Networking
Social Services for the Poor
Space Exploration & Development
Sports in America
The Supreme Court
The Transformation of American Cities
U.S. Infrastructure
U.S. National Debate Topic: Surveillance
U.S. National Debate Topic: The Ocean
U.S. National Debate Topic: Transportation Infrastructure
Whistleblowers

Readers' Guide

Abridged Readers' Guide to Periodical Literature
Readers' Guide to Periodical Literature

Indexes

Index to Legal Periodicals & Books
Short Story Index
Book Review Digest

Sears List

Sears List of Subject Headings
Sears: Lista de Encabezamientos de Materia

Facts About Series

Facts About American Immigration
Facts About China
Facts About the 20th Century
Facts About the Presidents
Facts About the World's Languages

Nobel Prize Winners

Nobel Prize Winners: 1901-1986
Nobel Prize Winners: 1987-1991
Nobel Prize Winners: 1992-1996
Nobel Prize Winners: 1997-2001

World Authors

World Authors: 1995-2000
World Authors: 2000-2005

Famous First Facts

Famous First Facts
Famous First Facts About American Politics
Famous First Facts About Sports
Famous First Facts About the Environment
Famous First Facts: International Edition

American Book of Days

The American Book of Days
The International Book of Days

Junior Authors & Illustrators

Eleventh Book of Junior Authors & Illustrations

Monographs

The Barnhart Dictionary of Etymology
Celebrate the World
Guide to the Ancient World
Indexing from A to Z
The Poetry Break
Radical Change: Books for Youth in a Digital Age

Wilson Chronology

Wilson Chronology of Asia and the Pacific
Wilson Chronology of Human Rights
Wilson Chronology of Ideas
Wilson Chronology of the Arts
Wilson Chronology of the World's Religions
Wilson Chronology of Women's Achievements

Grey House Publishing | Salem Press | H.W. Wilson | 4919 Route, 22 PO Box 56, Amenia NY 12501-0056